International Dictionary of Films and Filmmakers- 2

DIRECTORS

International Dictionary of Films and Filmmakers

Volume 1
FILMS

Volume 2
DIRECTORS

Volume 3
ACTORS and ACTRESSES

Volume 4
WRITERS and PRODUCTION ARTISTS

International Dictionary of Films and Filmmakers- 2

DIRECTORS

THIRD EDITION

EDITOR

LAURIE COLLIER HILLSTROM

PICTURE EDITOR

CLAIRE LOFTING

ST. JAMES PRESS

AN IMPRINT OF GALE

Detroit • New York • Toronto • London

Laurie Collier Hillstrom, *Editor*

ST. JAMES PRESS STAFF

Nicolet V. Elert, *Project Coordinator*
Laura Standley Berger, Peg Bessette, Joann Cerrito, David Collins, Miranda H. Ferrara,
Janice Jorgensen, Margaret Mazurkiewicz, Michael J. Tyrkus, *Contributing Editors*
Peter M. Gareffa, *Managing Editor, St. James Press*

Mary Beth Trimper, *Production Director*
Shanna Heilveil, *Production Assistant*

Cynthia Baldwin, *Art Director*
C. J. Jonik, *Desktop Publisher*
Pamela A. Hayes, *Photography Coordinator*
Randy Bassett, *Image Database Supervisor*
Mikal Ansari, Robert Duncan, *Imaging Specialists*

Victoria B. Cariappa, *Research Manager*
Jennifer Lund, *Research Specialist*
Julia C. Daniel, *Research Associate*

∞™ The paper used in this publication meets the minimum requirements of American National Standard for Information Sciences—Permanence Paper for Printed Library Materials, ANSI Z39.48-1984.

This book is printed on recycled paper that meets Environmental Protection Agency Standards.

International dictionary of films and filmmakers. — 3rd ed.
p. cm.
Includes bibliographical references and indexes.
Contents: v. 1. Films / editors, Nicolet V. Elert, Aruna Vasudeyan — v. 2. Directors / editor, Laurie Collier Hillstrom — v. 3. Actors and actresses / editor, Amy Unterburger — v. 4. Writers and production artists / editor, Grace Jeromski.
ISBN 1-55862-300-0 (v. 1 : alk. paper). — ISBN 1-55862-301-9 (v. 2 : alk. paper). — ISBN 1-55862-302-7 (v. 3 : alk. paper). — ISBN 1-55862-303-5 (v. 4 : alk. paper)
1. Motion pictures—Plots, themes, etc. 2. Motion picture producers and directors—Biography—Dictionaries. 3. Motion picture actors and actresses—Biography—Dictionaries.
PN1997.8.I58 1996
791.43'03—dc20
96-31536
CIP

Printed in the United States of America

St. James Press is an imprint of Gale

Cover photograph—Henry Hathaway courtesy Kobal Collection

10 9 8 7 6 5 4 3 2 1

P75847

CONTENTS

EDITOR'S NOTE

This is a revised edition of the second volume of the *International Dictionary of Films and Filmmakers.* The book comprises more than 500 entries, each consisting of a brief biography, a complete filmography, a selected bibliography of works on and by the entrant, and an expository essay by a specialist in the field. Most of the entries from the previous edition have been retained here, although all have been thoroughly updated. There are, however, some 65 entrants new to this edition. For the new edition, the format has been adapted and expanded for greater clarity. Since film is primarily a visual medium, the majority of entries are illustrated, either by a portrait or by a representative still from the entrant's *oeuvre.*

The selection of entrants is once again based on the recommendations of the advisers listed on page xiii. It was not thought necessary to propose criteria for selection: the book is intended to represent the wide range of interests within North American, British, and West European film scholarship and criticism. The eclecticism in both the list of entrants and the critical stances of the different writers emphasizes the multifarious notions of the cinema, and indeed of the director's role within it. On the vexing question of authorship in the cinema, it is to be hoped that this volume is properly seen in the context of a series which also focuses on the contribution to the cinema of actors and actresses (Volume 3), along with screenwriters, cinematographers, editors, animators, composers, and other production artists (Volume 4), as well as the individual films themselves (Volume 1).

Thanks are due to the following: Nicolet Elert at St. James Press, for her tireless work in coordinating the series; Kevin Hillstrom at Northern Lights Writers Group, for his invaluable assistance in copyediting the entries for this volume; and all the advisers and contributors, for their gracious participation.

A NOTE ON THE ENTRIES

Non-English language film titles are given in the original language or a transliteration of it. Alternate release titles in the original language(s) are found within parentheses, followed by release titles in English (American then British if there is a difference) and translations. The date of a film is understood to refer to its year of release unless stated otherwise.

In the list of films in each entry, information within parentheses following each film modifies, if necessary, then adds to the subject's principal function(s). The most common abbreviations used are:

pr	producer
d	director
sc	scenarist or scriptwriter
ph	cinematographer or director of photography
ed	editor
assoc	associate
asst	assistant
ro	role

"Co-" preceding a function indicates collaboration with one or more persons. Other abbreviations that may be used to clarify the nature of an individual film are "doc"—documentary; and "ep"—episode. A name in parentheses following a film title is that of the director. A film title in boldface type indicates that complete coverage of that film may be found in the *International Dictionary of Films and Filmmakers, Volume 1: Films.*

PICTURE ACKNOWLEDGEMENTS

We are grateful to the following for supplying photographs, and granting permission to reproduce them in this volume.

Adventure Pictures (Sally Potter)

Allied Artists (courtesy Kobal Collection) (Don Siegel)

American Zoetrope/Warner Bros. (courtesy Kobal Collection) (George Lucas)

Arrow Film Distributors Ltd. (Agnieszka Holland)

Artificial Eye Film Company Ltd. (Bertrand Blier, Hou Hsiao-Hsien, Jim Jarmusch, Aki Kaurismaki, Nanni Moretti)

Artificial Eye - Mayfair Films (Alex Cox, Jonathan Demme, John Duigan)

British Film Institute, Department of Stills, Posters and Designs

Buena Vista UK International (Ang Lee)

C. Callas (Paul Schrader)

Cannon (courtesy Kobal Collection) (Andrei Mikhalkov-Konchalovsky)

Castle Rock/Detour (courtesy Kobal Collection) (Richard Linklater)

Cinemateca do Cuba (Santiago Alvarez, Sara Gómez, Humberto Solas)

Cinemateca do Museu de Arte Moderna, Rio de Janeiro (Humberto Mauro)

ciné-tamaris (Jacques Demy)

Cinepromotion, Berlin (Margarethe Von Trotta)

Columbia Pictures Industries Inc. (Budd Boetticher, Peter Bogdanovich, Richard Brooks, John Cassavetes, Ján Kadár, Elia Kazan, Fritz Lang, Anatole Litvak, Sidney Lumet, Anthony Mann, Sam Peckinpah, Bob Rafelson, Alan Rudolph, Claude Sautet, Franklin J. Schaffner, Steven Spielberg, Charles Vidor)

Contemporary Films Limited (Věra Chytilová, Victor Erice, Werner Herzog, Satyajit Ray, Alain Resnais)

El Deseo-Lauren (courtesy Kobal Collection) (Pedro Almodóvar)

Stephane Fefer (courtesy Kobal Collection) (Wim Wenders)

Film Polski (Jerzy Kawalerowicz, Andrzej Munk)

Les Films du Carrosse - photo Raymond Cauchetier (François Truffaut)

Les Films du Losange (Jacques Rivette, Eric Rohmer)

Hulton Deutsch Collection (Edward Dmytryk, Allan Dwan, Jerry Lewis, Walter Ruttmann, Mack Sennett, George Stevens, King Vidor, Erich Von Stroheim, Harry Watt, James Whale)

IGA Projects (Chen Kaige, Tian Zhuangzhuang, Edward Yang)

IRS Media (courtesy Kobal Collection) (Penelope Spheeris)

ITC Entertainment Group (courtesy Kobal Collection) (John Dahl)

J&M Entertainment Limited (Errol Morris)

Kindai Eiga Kyokai Co, Ltd. (Kaneto Shindo)

The Kobal Collection (Allison Anders, Luc Besson, Kenneth Branagh, Luis Buñuel, Tim Burton, Jame Campion, George Cukor, Blake Edwards, Abel Ferrara, Bill Forsyth, Terry Gilliam, Henry Hathaway, Monte Hellman, Alexander Kluge, Sergio Leone, Rouben Mamoulian, Michael Mann, Lewis Milestone, Alan J. Pakula, Alan Parker, Arthur Penn, Wolfgang Petersen, Sydney Pollack, Robert Redford, Rob Reiner, Ken Russell, Barbet Schroeder, Joel Schumacher, Ettore Scola, Steven Soderbergh, Oliver Stone, Paolo & Vittorio Taviani, Paul Verhoeven, Peter Watkins, Peter Weir, Orson Welles, John Woo)

Ladd Company/Warner Bros. (courtesy Kobal Collection) (Lawrence Kasdan, Philip Kaufman)

Andy Lane (Constantin Costa-Gavras, Terence Davies, Stephen Frears, Derek Jarman, Neil Jordan)

Live Entertainment (courtesy Kobal Collection) (Quentin Tarantino)

Lumiere Pictures Limited (Charles Crichton, Basil Dearden, Robert Hamer, Ken Loach)

Magyar Filmunio (Márta Mészáros)

Roger Mayne (Lindsay Anderson)

MGM (courtesy Kobal Collection) (John Ford)

Mercure Distribution (Arturo Ripstein)

Orion (courtesy Kobal Collection) (Woody Allen, Kevin Costner, Jodie Foster)

Paramount (courtesy Kobal Collection) (Gregory La Cava, Barry Levinson, Albert Lewin, Robert Zemeckis)

Per Holst Films A/S - photo Rolf Konow (Bille August)

PolyGram Filmed Entertainment (Joel Coen, David Lynch)

The Rank Organisation plc (David Cronenberg, Michael Powell and Emeric Pressburger, Robert Stevenson)

The Samuel Goldwyn Company (Henry King)

Sandrew Film AB (Jörn Donner, Mai Zetterling)

Osvald Schorm (Evald Schorm)

Seda Spettacoli/International Classics - Twentieth Century Fox (courtesy Kobal Collection) (Dario Argento)

Shochiku Co., Ltd. (Heinosuke Gosho, Masaki Kobayashi)

South Australian Film Corporation (Bruce Beresford)

AB Svensk Filmindustri (Gustaf Molander)

AB Svensk Filmindustri-Filmteknik (courtesy Kobal Collection) (Lasse Hallstrom)

Svensk Filminstitutet (Mauritz Stiller, Jan Troell)

Twentieth Century Fox (courtesy Kobal Collection) (John Boorman, Fred Zinnemann)

United Artists (courtesy Kobal Collection) (Billy Wilder, Robert Wise)

Universal (courtesy Kobal Collection) (Edgar Ulmer)

Wade Williams Distribution (Edward D. Wood, Jr.)

Warner Bros. (courtesy Kobal Collection) (Michael Curtiz, Clint Eastwood, Roland Joffé, Terrence Malick)

Yanco/Tao/Recorded Picture Company (courtesy Kobal Collection) (Bernardo Bertolucci)

Zenith/British Screen/Film Four International (courtesy Kobal Collection) (Mike Newell)

Zoetrope/United Artists (courtesy Kobal Collection) (Francis Ford Coppola)

ADVISERS

Dudley Andrew
Jeanine Basinger
Jack C. Ellis
Ben Gibson
Rajko Grlic
Ib Monty
Julian Petley
Christopher Pickard
Paul Shields
Leonardo Garcia Tsao
Aruna Vasudev
Robin Wood

CONTRIBUTORS

Charles Affron
Mirella Jona Affron
Dudley Andrew
Roy Armes
José Arroyo
Erik Barnouw
Jeanine Basinger
John Baxter
Audie Bock
DeWitt Bodeen
David Bordwell
Ronald Bowers
Stephen E. Bowles
Geoff Brown
Robert Burgoyne
Julianne Burton
Fred Camper
Michel Ciment
Elizabeth Cline
Tom Conley
Samantha Cook
Kevin J. Costa
R. F. Cousins
Tony D'Arpino
Charles Derry
Wheeler Winston Dixon
Susan M. Doll
Robert Dunbar
Raymond Durgnat
Rob Edelman
Robert Edmonds
Jack C. Ellis
Gretchen Elsner-Sommer
Patricia Erens
Mark W. Estrin
Quentin Falk
Greg S. Faller
Rodney Farnsworth
Howard Feinstein
Susan Felleman
Leslie Felperin
Lilie Ferrari
Theresa FitzGerald
Manuel Dos Santos Fonseca
Alexa Foreman
Saul Frampton
Anita Gabrosek
Frances Gateward
John Gillett
Verina Glaessner
Douglas Gomery
Joseph A. Gomez
Patricia King Hanson
Stephen L. Hanson
Ann Harris
Louise Heck-Rabi
Kevin Hillstrom
Kyoko Hirano
Judy Hoffman
Deborah H. Holdstein
Guo-Juin Hong
Vivian Huang
Peter Hutchings
Stuart M. Kaminsky
Joel Kanoff
Dave Kehr
Philip Kemp
Satti Khanna
Katherine Singer Kovács
Audrey E. Kupferberg
Joseph Lanza
James L. Limbacher
Richard Lippe
Kimball Lockhart
Janet E. Lorenz
Ed Lowry
G. C. Macnab
Elaine Mancini
Roger Manvell
Gina Marchetti
Gerald Mast
John McCarty
Vacláv Merhaut
Russell Merritt

Lloyd Michaels
Joseph Milicia
Norman Miller
Ib Monty
James E. Morrison
John Mraz
William T. Murphy
Ray Narducy
Dennis Nastav
Kim Newman
Bill Nichols
Clea H. Notar
Linda J. Obalil
Daniel O'Brien
John O'Kane
Liam O'Leary
Vladimír Opěla
R. Barton Palmer
Robert J. Pardi
Richard Peña
Julian Petley
Duncan J. Petrie
Gene D. Phillips
Zuzana Mirjam Pick
Dana B. Polan
Richard Porton
Lauren Rabinovitz
Maria Racheva
Herbert Reynolds
E. Rubinstein
Marie Saeli
Curtis Schade
Lillian Schiff
H. Wayne Schuth
Michael Selig
David Shipman
Ulrike Sieglohr
Charles L. P. Silet
Scott Simmon
P. Adams Sitney
Josef Skvorecký
Anthony Slide
Edward S. Small
Eric Smoodin
Cecile Starr
Karel Tabery
Richard Taylor
J. P. Telotte
Nicholas Thomas
John C. Tibbetts
Doug Tomlinson
Andrew Tudor
Blažena Urgošíková
Ravi Vasudevan
Dorothee Verdaasdonk
Ginette Vincendeau
Mark Walker
James M. Welsh
Dennis West
M. B. White
Colin Williams
Bill Wine
Rob Winning
Jessica R. Wolff
Robin Wood

International Dictionary of Films and Filmmakers- 2

DIRECTORS

LIST OF ENTRANTS

Chantal Akerman
Robert Aldrich
Woody Allen
Pedro Almodóvar
Robert Altman
Santiago Alvarez
Allison Anders
Lindsay Anderson
Theodoros Angelopoulos
Kenneth Anger
Michelangelo Antonioni
Gregg Araki
Dario Argento
Gillian Armstrong
Dorothy Arzner
Hal Ashby
Anthony Asquith
Alexandre Astruc
Bille August
Claude Autant-Lara

Hector Babenco
Lloyd Bacon
Bruce Baillie
Juan Antonio Bardem
Boris Barnet
Evgeni Bauer
Jacques Becker
Marco Bellocchio
Maria Luisa Bemberg
Shyam Benegal
Robert Benton
Bruce Beresford
Ingmar Bergman
Busby Berkeley
Bernardo Bertolucci
Luc Besson
Fernando Birri
J. Stuart Blackton
Alessandro Blasetti
Bertrand Blier
August Blom
Budd Boetticher
Peter Bogdanovich
John Boorman
Frank Borzage
Roy and John Boulting
Stan Brakhage
Kenneth Branagh
Robert Bresson
Mel Brooks
Richard Brooks
Clarence Brown
Tod Browning
Luis Buñuel
Charles Burnett
Tim Burton

Michael Cacoyannis
Jane Campion
Frank Capra
Marcel Carné
John Carpenter
John Cassavetes
Renato Castellani
Alberto Cavalcanti
Claude Chabrol
Youssef Chahine
Charles Chaplin
Chen Kaige
Benjamin Christensen
Věra Chytilová
Michael Cimino
René Clair
Shirley Clarke
Jack Clayton
René Clement
Henri-Georges Clouzot
Jean Cocteau
Joel Coen
Luigi Comencini
Bruce Conner
Francis Ford Coppola
Roger Corman
Constantin Costa-Gavras
Kevin Costner
Alex Cox
Wes Craven
Charles Crichton
John Cromwell
David Cronenberg
James Cruze
George Cukor
Michael Curtiz

John Dahl
Jules Dassin
Delmer Daves
Terence Davies
Emile De Antonio
Basil Dearden
Fernando De Fuentes
Jean Delannoy
Louis Delluc
André Delvaux
Cecil B. De Mille
Jonathan Demme
Jacques Demy
Brian De Palma
Maya Deren
Giuseppe De Santis
Vittorio De Sica
Thorold Dickinson
Carlos Diegues
William Dieterle
Edward Dmytryk
Stanley Donen
Jörn Donner
Mark Donskoi
Alexander Dovzhenko
Carl Theodor Dreyer
John Duigan
Germaine Dulac
E. A. Dupont
Marguerite Duras
Guru Dutt
Julien Duvivier
Allan Dwan

Clint Eastwood
Blake Edwards
Sergei Eisenstein
Ed Emshwiller
Jean Epstein
Victor Erice

Zoltán Fábri
Rainer Werner Fassbinder
Paul Fejös
Federico Fellini
Emilio Fernández
Abel Ferrara
Marco Ferreri
Louis Feuillade
Jacques Feyder
Terence Fisher
Robert Flaherty
Richard Fleischer
Victor Fleming
Robert Florey
John Ford
Milos Forman
Bill Forsyth
Bob Fosse
Jodie Foster
Hollis Frampton
Georges Franju
John Frankenheimer
Stephen Frears
Martin Frič
William Friedkin
Samuel Fuller

István Gaál
Urban Gad
Abel Gance
Luis García Berlanga
Tay Garnett
Sergei Gerasimov
Pietro Germi
Terry Gilliam
Jean-Luc Godard
Sara Gómez
Claude Goretta
Heinosuke Gosho
Edmund Goulding
Peter Greenaway
Jean Grémillon
John Grierson
D. W. Griffith
Ruy Guerra
Sacha Guitry
Yilmaz Güney
Tomás Gutiérrez Alea
Alice Guy
Patricio Guzmán

Bert Haanstra
Lasse Hallstrom
Robert Hamer
Susumi Hani
Hal Hartley
Henry Hathaway
Howard Hawks
Todd Haynes
Josef Heifitz
Monte Hellman
Astrid and Bjarne Henning-Jensen
Cecil Hepworth
Werner Herzog
George Roy Hill
Walter Hill
Alfred Hitchcock
Holger-Madsen
Agnieszka Holland
Med Hondo
Hou Hsiao-Hsien
William K. Howard
John Huston

Kon Ichikawa
Tadashi Imai
Shohei Imamura
Rex Ingram
Otar Ioseliani
Juzo Itami
Joris Ivens
James Ivory

Peter Jackson
Miklós Jancsó
Derek Jarman
Jim Jarmusch
Humphrey Jennings
Norman Jewison
Jaromil Jireš
Roland Joffé
Neil Jordan
Claude Jutra

Karel Kachyňa
Ján Kadár
Raj Kapoor
Lawrence Kasdan
Philip Kaufman
Aki Kaurismaki
Helmut Käutner
Jerzy Kawalerowicz
Elia Kazan
Buster Keaton
Krzysztof Kieślowski
Henry King
King Hu
Keisuke Kinoshita
Teinosuke Kinugasa
Alexander Kluge
Masaki Kobayashi
Barbara Kopple
Alexander Korda
Grigori Kozintsev
Stanley Kramer
Stanley Kubrick
Lev Kuleshov
Akira Kurosawa
Emir Kusturica

Gregory La Cava
Fritz Lang
Alberto Lattuada
Frank Launder and Sidney Gilliat
Richard Leacock
David Lean
Patrice Leconte
Paul Leduc
Ang Lee
Spike Lee
Jean-Pierre Lefebvre
Mike Leigh
Claude Lelouch
Paul Leni
Sergio Leone
Mervyn Leroy
Richard Lester
Barry Levinson
Albert Lewin
Jerry Lewis
Joseph H. Lewis
Marcel L'Herbier
Richard Linklater
Miguel Littin
Anatole Litvak
Ken Loach
Pare Lorentz
Joseph Losey
Ernst Lubitsch
George Lucas
Sidney Lumet
Louis Lumière
David Lynch

Alexander Mackendrick
Dušan Makavejev
Terrence Malick
Louis Malle
Rouben Mamoulian
Joseph L. Mankiewicz
Anthony Mann
Michael Mann
Chris Marker
Gregory Markopoulos
Penny Marshall
Humberto Mauro
Albert and David Paul Maysles
Paul Mazursky
Leo McCarey
Mehboob Khan
Jonas Mekas
Georges Méliès
Jean-Pierre Melville
Jiři Menzel
Márta Mészáros
Oscar Micheaux
Nikita Mikhalkov
Andrei Mikhalkov-Konchalovsky
Lewis Milestone
Claude Miller
George Miller
Vincente Minnelli
Kenji Mizoguchi
Gustaf Molander
Nanni Moretti
Errol Morris
Robert Mulligan
Andrzej Munk
F. W. Murnau

Mikio Naruse
Marshall Neilan
Jan Nemec
Mike Newell
Fred Niblo
Mike Nichols

Manoel de Oliveira
Ermanno Olmi
Marcel Ophuls
Max Ophüls
Nagisa Oshima
Yasujiro Ozu

G. W. Pabst
Marcel Pagnol
Alan J. Pakula
Sergei Paradzhanov

Alan Parker
Pier Paolo Pasolini
Giovanni Pastrone
George Pearson
Sam Peckinpah
Arthur Penn
Nelson Pereira dos Santos
Lester James Peries
Pierre Perrault
Wolfgang Petersen
Elio Petri
Aleksandar Petrovic
Dadasaheb Phalke
Maurice Pialat
Lupu Pick
Roman Polanski
Sydney Pollack
Abraham Polonsky
Gillo Pontecorvo
Edwin S. Porter
Sally Potter
Michael Powell and Emeric Pressburger
Otto Preminger
Yakov Protazanov
Vsevolod Pudovkin

Bob Rafelson
Yvonne Rainer
Nicholas Ray
Satyajit Ray
Robert Redford
Carol Reed
Rob Reiner
Karel Reisz
Jean Renoir
Alain Resnais
Tony Richardson
Hans Richter
Leni Riefenstahl
Arturo Ripstein
Dino Risi
Martin Ritt
Jacques Rivette
Glauber Rocha
Robert Rodriguez
Nicolas Roeg
Eric Rohmer
George A. Romero
Jørgen Roos
Francesco Rosi
Roberto Rossellini
Robert Rossen
Paul Rotha
Jean Rouch
Bimal Roy
Alan Rudolph
Raul Ruiz
Ken Russell
Walter Ruttmann

Helma Sanders-Brahms
Jorge Sanjinés
Carlos Saura
Claude Sautet
Victor Saville
John Sayles
Franklin J. Schaffner
Fred Schepisi
John Schlesinger
Volker Schlöndorff
Ernest B. Schoedsack
Evald Schorm
Paul Schrader
Barbet Schroeder
Werner Schroeter
Joel Schumacher
Ettore Scola
Martin Scorsese
Ridley Scott
Ousmane Sembene
Mrinal Sen
Mack Sennett
Jim Sheridan
Kaneto Shindo
Masahiro Shinoda
Esther Shub
Don Siegel
Joan Micklin Silver
Robert Siodmak
Douglas Sirk
Alf Sjöberg
Victor Sjöström
Jerzy Skolimowski
Michael Snow
Steven Soderbergh
Fernando E. Solanas and Octavio Getino
Humberto Solas
Penelope Spheeris
Steven Spielberg
John M. Stahl
Wolfgang Staudte
George Stevens
Robert Stevenson
Mauritz Stiller
Oliver Stone
Henri Storck
Jean-Marie Straub and Danièle Huillet
John Sturges
Preston Sturges
Arne Sucksdorff
Hans-Jurgen Syberberg
István Szabó

Alain Tanner
Quentin Tarantino
Andrei Tarkovsky
Frank Tashlin
Jacques Tati
Bertrand Tavernier
Paolo and Vittorio Taviani
Tian Zhuangzhuang
Guiseppe Tornatore
Leopoldo Torre Nilsson
Jacques Tourneur
Maurice Tourneur
Jan Troell
François Truffaut

Edgar Ulmer

Roger Vadim
Stan Vanderbeek
W. S. Van Dyke
Willard Van Dyke
Gus Van Sant
Agnès Varda
Sergei and Georgi Vasiliev
Paul Verhoeven
Dziga Vertov
Charles Vidor
King Vidor
Jean Vigo
Luchino Visconti
Josef Von Sternberg
Erich Von Stroheim
Margarethe Von Trotta

Andrzej Wajda
Raoul Walsh
Charles Walters
Vincent Ward
Andy Warhol
John Waters
Peter Watkins
Harry Watt
Lois Weber
Peter Weir
Jiři Weiss
Orson Welles
William Wellman
Wim Wenders
James Whale
Robert Wiene
Billy Wilder
Robert Wise
Frederick Wiseman
John Woo
Edward D. Wood, Jr.
Sam Wood
Basil Wright
William Wyler

Xie Jin

Edward Yang
Kozabura Yoshimura

Krzysztof Zanussi
Franco Zeffirelli
Robert Zemeckis
Mai Zetterling
Fred Zinnemann

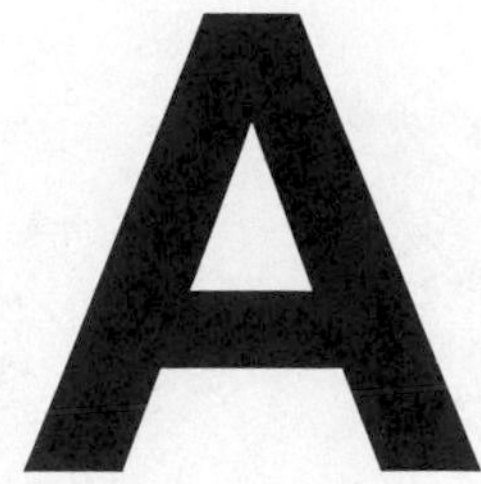

AKERMAN, Chantal

Nationality: Belgian. **Born:** Brussels, June 1950. **Education:** INSAS film school, Brussels, 1967-68; studied at Université Internationale du Théâtre, Paris, 1968-69. **Career:** *Saute ma vie* entered in Oberhausen festival, 1971; lived in New York, 1972; returned to France, 1973.

Films as Director:

1968 *Saute ma vie*
1971 *L'Enfant aimé*
1972 *Hotel Monterey*; *La Chambre*
1973 *Le 15/18* (co-d); *Hanging Out Yonkers* (unfinished)
1974 *Je tu il elle*
1975 ***Jeanne Dielman, 23 Quai du Commerce, 1080 Bruxelles***
1977 *News from Home*
1978 *Les Rendez-vous d'Anna*
1980 *Dis-moi*
1982 *Toute une nuit* (*All Night Long*)
1983 *Les Années 80* (*The Golden Eighties*) (co-sc); *Un Jour pina a demandé*
1984 *L'Homme à la valise*; *J'ai faim, j'ai froid* (episode in *Paris vu par ... 20 ans après*); *Family Business*; *New York, New York Bis*
1987 *Seven Women, Seven Sins* (co-d)
1988 *Un jour Pina m'a demande*
1989 *Histoires d'Amérique: Food, Family and Philosophy/American Stories*
1991 *Nuit et jour*
1992 *Contre l'oubli*
1993 *D'est* (+ sc); *Moving In* (*Le Déménagement*)
1994 *Portrait of a Young Girl at the End of the 1960s in Brussels* (+ sc)

Publications

By AKERMAN: book—

Les Rendez-vous d'Anna, Paris, 1978.

By AKERMAN: articles—

Interview with C. Alemann and H. Hurst, in *Frauen und Film* (Berlin), March 1976.

Interview with Danièle Dubroux, and others, in *Cahiers du Cinéma* (Paris), July 1977.

Interview with P. Carcassone and L. Cugny, in *Cinématographe* (Paris), November 1978.

Interview in *Stills* (London), December 1984/January 1985.

Interview in *Inter/View* (New York), February 1985.

Interview in *Cinéma* (Paris), 25 June 1986.

Interview in *Nouvel Observateur* (Paris), 28 September 1989.

Interview in *Filmihullu,* no. 4, 1991.

On AKERMAN: articles—

Bertolina, G., "Chantal Akerman: il cinema puro," in *Filmcritica* (Rome), March 1976.

Creveling, C., "Women Working," in *Camera Obscura* (Berkeley), Fall 1976.

Mairesse, E., "A propos des films de Chantal Akerman: Un temps atmosphere," in *Cahiers du Cinéma* (Paris), October 1977.

Bergstrom, Janet, in *Camera Obscura* (Berkeley), Fall 1978.

Martin, Angela, "Chantal Akerman's Films," in *Feminist Review,* no. 3, 1979.

Seni, N., in *Frauen und Film* (Berlin), September 1979.

Perlmutter, Ruth, "Visible Narrative, Visible Woman," in *Millenium* (New York), Spring 1980.

Delavaud, G., "Les chemins de Chantal Akerman," in *Cahiers du Cinéma* (Paris), April 1981.

Philippon, A., "Fragments bruxellois/Nuit torride," in *Cahiers du Cinéma* (Paris), November 1982.

Dossier on Akerman, in *Versus* (Nijmegen), no. 1, 1985.

Barrowclough, S., "Chantal Akerman: Adventures in perception," in *Monthly Film Bulletin* (London), April 1984.

Squire, C., "Toute une heure," in *Screen* (London), November/December 1984.

Castiel, E., in *24 Images* (Montreal), nos. 34/35, 1987.

Paskin, Sylvia, "Waiting for the next shot," in *Monthly Film Bulletin* (London), March 1990.

Bahg, P. von, "Keskusteluvuorossa: Chantal Akerman," in *Filmihullu,* no. 4, 1991.

Williams, B., "Splintered Perspectives: Counterpoint and Subjectivity in the Modernist Film Narrative," in *Film Criticism,* no. 2, 1991.

Roberti, B., "Tradire l'immagine," *Filmcritica,* September/October 1991.

Klerk, N. de, "Chantal Akerman," in *Skrien,* June/July 1992.

McRobbie, A., "Passionate Uncertainty," in *Sight & Sound,* September 1992.

Chang, Chris, "Ruined," in *Film Comment,* November/December 1993.

* * *

At the age of fifteen Chantal Akerman saw Godard's *Pierrot le fou* and realized that filmmaking could be experimental and personal. She dropped in and out of film school and has since created short and feature films for viewers who appreciate the opportunity her works provide to think about sounds and images. Her films are often shot in real time, and in space that is part of the characters' identity.

During a self-administered apprenticeship in New York (1972-73) shooting short films on very low budgets, Akerman notes that she learned much from the work of innovators Michael Snow and Stan Brakhage. She was encouraged to explore organic techniques for her personal subject matter. In her deliberately paced films there are long takes, scenes shot with stationary camera, and a play of light in relation to subjects and their space. (In *Jeanne Dielman, 23 Quai du*

Chantal Akerman

Commerce, 1080 Bruxelles, as Jeanne rides up or down in the elevator, diagonals of light from each floor cut across her face in a regular rhythm.) Her films feature vistas down long corridors, acting with characters' backs to the camera, and scenes concluded with several seconds of darkness. In Akerman films there are hotels and journeys, little conversation. Windows are opened and sounds let in, doors opened and closed; we hear a doorbell, a radio, voices on the telephone answering machine, footsteps, city noises. Each frame is carefully composed, each gesture the precise result of Akerman's directions. A frequent collaborator is her sensitive cameraperson, Babette Mangolte, who has worked with Akerman on such works as *Jeanne Dielman, 23 Quai du Commerce, 1080 Bruxelles, News from Home,* and *Toute une nuit.* Mangolte has also worked with avant guardists Yvonne Rainer, Marcel Hanoun, and Michael Snow.

Plotting is minimal or non-existent in Akerman films. Old welfare clients come and go amid the impressive architecture of a once splendid hotel on New York's Upper West Side in *Hotel Monterey.* New York City plays its busy, noisy self for the camera as Akerman's voice on the sound track reads concerned letters from her mother in Belgium in *News from Home.* A young filmmaker travels to Germany to appear at a screening of her latest film, meets people who distress her, and her mother who delights her, and returns home in *Les Rendez-vous d'Anna.* Jeanne Dielman, super-efficient housewife, earns money as a prostitute to support herself and her son. Her routine breaks down by chance, and she murders one of her customers.

The films (some of which are semi-autobiographical) are not dramatic in the conventional sense, nor are they glamorized or eroticized; the excitement is inside the characters. In a film which Akerman has called a love letter to her mother, Jeanne Dielman is seen facing the steady camera as members of a cooking class might see her, and she prepares a meatloaf—in real time. Later she gives herself a thorough scrubbing in the bathtub; only her head and the motion of her arms are visible. Her straightening and arranging and smoothing are seen as a child would see and remember them.

In *Toute une nuit* Akerman displays her precision and control as she stages the separate, audience-involving adventures of a huge cast of all ages that wanders out into Brussels byways on a hot, stormy night. In this film, reminiscent of Wim Wenders and his wanderers and Marguerite Duras's inventive sound tracks, choreography, and sense of place, Akerman continues to explore her medium using no conventional plot, few spoken words, many sounds, people who leave the frame to a lingering camera, and appealing images. A little girl asks a man to dance with her, and he does. The filmmaker's feeling for the child and the child's independence can't be mistaken.

Akerman's *Moving In,* meanwhile, centers on a monologue delivered by a man who has just moved into a modern apartment. A film of "memory and loss," according to *Film Comment,* he has left behind "a melancholy space of relations, relations dominated by his former neighbors, a trio of female 'social science students.'"

—Lillian Schiff

ALDRICH, Robert

Nationality: American. **Born:** Cranston, Rhode Island, 9 August 1918. **Education:** Moses Brown School, Providence, and University of Virginia, graduated (law and economics) 1941. **Family:** Married Harriet Foster, 1941 (divorced 1965); children: Adell, William, Alida, and Kelly; married fashion model Sibylle Siegfried, 1966. **Career:** Worked for RKO studios, 1941-1944; under contract to Enterprise studios, 1945-1948; TV director, from 1952; founded "Associates and Aldrich Company," 1955; signed contract for Columbia Pictures, then fired after refusing to "soften" script of *The Garment Jungle*; after five year period working abroad, returned to Hollywood, 1962; after *The Dirty Dozen,* established Aldrich Studios, 1967, but forced to sell, 1973; elected president of the Directors Guild, 1975; "Aldrich Company" reorganised, 1976. **Awards:** Silver Prize, Venice Festival, for *The Big Knife,* 1955; Silver Bear Award for Best Direction, Berlin Festival, for *Autumn Leaves,* 1956; Italian Critics Award, Venice Festival, for *Attack!,* 1956. **Died:** In Los Angeles, of kidney failure, 5 December 1983.

Films as Director:

1953 *The Big Leaguer*
1954 *World for Ransom* (+ co-pr); *Apache*; *Vera Cruz*
1955 ***Kiss Me Deadly*** (+ pr); *The Big Knife* (+ pr)
1956 *Autumn Leaves*; *Attack!* (+ pr)
1957 *The Garment Jungle* (un-credited)
1959 *The Angry Hills*; *Ten Seconds to Hell* (+ co-sc)
1961 *The Last Sunset*
1962 *Sodoma e Gomorra* (*Sodom and Gomorrah*); *Whatever Happened to Baby Jane?* (+ pr)
1963 *Four for Texas* (+ co-pr, co-sc)
1964 *Hush ... Hush, Sweet Charlotte* (+ pr)
1966 *Flight of the Phoenix* (+ pr)
1967 *The Dirty Dozen*
1968 *The Legend of Lylah Clare* (+ pr); *The Killing of Sister George* (+ pr)
1969 *Too Late the Hero* (+ pr, co-sc)
1971 *The Grissom Gang* (+ pr)
1972 *Ulzana's Raid*
1973 *Emperor of the North* (*The Emperor of the North Pole*)
1974 *The Longest Yard* (*The Mean Machine*)
1975 *Hustle* (+ co-pr)
1977 *Twilight's Last Gleaming*; *The Choirboys*
1979 *The Frisco Kid*
1981 *All the Marbles* (*California Dolls*)

Other Films:

1945 ***The Southerner*** (Renoir) (1st asst-d)
1946 *The Story of G.I. Joe* (Wellman) (1st asst-d); *Pardon My Past* (Fenton) (1st asst-d); *The Strange Love of Martha Ivers* (Milestone) (1st asst-d)
1947 *The Private Affairs of Bel Ami* (Lewin) (1st asst-d); *Body and Soul* (Rossen) (1st asst-d)
1948 *Arch of Triumph* (Milestone) (1st asst-d); *So This Is New York* (Fleischer) (1st asst-d); *No Minor Vices* (Milestone) (1st asst-d)
1949 *Force of Evil* (Polonsky) (1st asst-d); *The Red Pony* (Milestone) (1st asst-d); *A Kiss for Corliss* (Wallace) (1st asst-d)
1950 *The White Tower* (Tetzlaff) (1st asst-d); *Teresa* (Zinnemann) (pre-production work)
1951 *The Prowler* (Losey) (1st asst-d); *M* (Losey) (1st asst-d); *Of Men and Music* (Reis) (1st asst-d); *New Mexico* (Reis) (1st asst-d)
1952 *Abbott and Costello Meet Captain Kidd* (Lamont) (1st asst-d); ***Limelight*** (Chaplin) (1st asst-d); *The Trio: Rubinstein, Heifetz and Piatigorsky* (*Million Dollar Trio*) (Dassin) (1st asst-d); *The Steel Trap* (Stone) (pr supervision)
1957 *The Ride Back* (pr)
1969 *Whatever Happened to Aunt Alice?* (pr)

Publications

By ALDRICH: articles—

Interview with George Fenin, in *Film Culture* (New York), July/August 1956.
Interviews with François Truffaut, in *Cahiers du Cinéma* (Paris), November 1956 and April 1958.
"High Price of Independence," in *Films and Filming* (London), June 1958.
"Learning from My Mistakes," in *Films and Filming* (London), June 1960.
"Hollywood ... Still an Empty Tomb," in *Cinema* (Beverly Hills), May/June 1963.
"What Ever Happened to American Movies?," in *Sight and Sound* (London), Winter 1963/64.
Interview with Joel Greenburg, in *Sight and Sound* (London), Winter 1968/69.
"Why I Bought My Own Studio," in *Action* (Los Angeles), January/February 1969.
"Impressions of Russia," in *Action* (Los Angeles), July/August 1971.
"Dialogue," with Bernardo Bertolucci, in *Action* (Los Angeles), March/April 1974.
"Up to Date with Robert Aldrich," interview with Harry Ringel, in *Sight and Sound* (London), Summer 1974.
"Aldrich Interview," with Pierre Sauvage, in *Movie* (London), Winter 1976/77.
"Dialogue on Film: Robert Aldrich," in *American Film* (Washington, D.C.), November 1978.

On ALDRICH: books—

Micha, Rene, *Robert Aldrich,* Brussels, 1957.
Higham, Charles, *The Celluloid Muse: Hollywood Directors Speak,* London, 1969.
Silver, Alain, and Elizabeth Ward, *Robert Aldrich: A Guide to References and Resources,* Boston, 1979.
Salizzato, Claver, *Robert Aldrich,* Florence, 1983.
Piton, Jean-Pierre, *Robert Aldrich,* Paris, 1985.
Arnold, Edwin T., and Eugene L. Miller, *The Films and Career of Robert Aldrich,* Knoxville, Tennessee, 1986.
Maheo, Michel, *Robert Aldrich,* Paris, 1987.

On ALDRICH: articles—

Rivette, Jacques, "On Revolution," in *Cahiers du Cinéma* (Paris), no. 54, 1955.
Jarvie, Ian, "Hysteria and Authoritarianism in the Films of Robert Aldrich," in *Film Culture* (New York), Summer 1961.
Cameron, Ian, and Mark Shivas, "Interview and Filmography," in *Movie* (London), April 1963.
Bitsch, Charles, and Bertrand Tavernier, "La Fonction de Producer," and Claude Chabrol, "Directed By:," in *Cahiers du Cinéma* (Paris), December/January 1964/65.
Silke, James, editor, "Robert Aldrich," in *Dialogue on Film* (Washington, D.C.), no. 2, 1972.
Silver, Alain, "Mr. Film Noir Stays at the Table," in *Film Comment* (New York), Spring 1972.

Robert Aldrich

Beaupre, Lee, "Bob Aldrich: Candid Maverick," in *Variety* (New York), 27 June 1973.

Ringel, Harry, "Robert Aldrich: The Director as Phoenix," in *Take One* (Montreal), September 1974.

Silver, Alain, "*Kiss Me Deadly*: Evidence of a Style," in *Film Comment* (New York), March/April 1975.

Combs, Richard, "Worlds Apart: Aldrich Since *The Dirty Dozen,*" in *Sight and Sound* (London), Spring 1976.

Duval, B., "Aldrich le rebelle," in *Image et Son* (Paris), May 1976.

Legrand, Gerard, "Robert Aldrich et l'incompletude du nihilism," in *Positif* (Paris), June 1976.

Gazano, R., and M. Cusso, "L'Homme d'Aldrich," in *Cinéma* (Paris), June 1980.

McCarthy, T., obituary of Aldrich in *Variety* (New York), 7 December 1983.

"Aldrich Section" of *Cinéma* (Paris), February 1984.

"Robert Aldrich," in *Film Dope* (London), March 1985, and March 1988.

Lang, Robert, "Looking for the 'Great Whatzit': *Kiss Me Deadly* and Film Noir," in *Cinema Journal* (Champaign, Illinois), Spring 1988.

* * *

Despite a commercially respectable career both within the studio system and as an independent producer-director, Robert Aldrich remains an ill-appreciated, if not entirely bothersome presence for most American critics. Andrew Sarris did praise Aldrich in 1968 as "one of the most strikingly personal directors of the past two decades"; yet, for the most part, it has remained to the French and the English to attempt to unravel the defiant quirkiness of Aldrich's career. Only the otherworldly *Kiss Me Deadly,* which Paul Schrader unequivocably dubbed "the masterpiece of film noir," has received anything like the attention it deserves on this side of the Atlantic; yet the film is quite indicative of the bitter ironies, bizarre stylistics, and scathing nihilism characteristic of most of Aldrich's work.

In bringing Mickey Spillane's neo-fascist hero Mike Hammer to the screen, *Kiss Me Deadly* plays havoc with the conventions of the hardboiled detective, turning the existential avenger into a narcissistic materialist who exploits those around him for the benefit of his plush lifestyle. In an outrageous alteration of the novel's plot, Hammer becomes a modern neanderthal whose individualism is revealed as insanity when it causes him to botch a case involving a box of pure nuclear energy and thus the fate of the world. The result is a final shot of a mushroom cloud rising from a California beachhouse, consuming both Hammer and the bad guys. Only at this extreme and this distance in time has Aldrich's acute sense of irony impressed itself upon a liberal critical establishment whose repugnance to the surfaces of his films has usually served as an excuse for ignoring their savage, multilayered critiques of Hollywood genres and American ideology.

The extremity of Aldrich's reinterpretations of the Western in *Ulzana's Raid,* of the war movie in *Attack!,* of the cop film in *The Choirboys,* and of the women's melodrama in *Autumn Leaves* betrays a cynicism so bitter that it could only arise from a liberal sensibility utterly disillusioned by an age in which morality has become a cruel joke. In fact, the shattering of illusions is central to Aldrich's work, and it is a powerfully self-destructive process, given the sweetness of the illusions and the anger of his iconoclasm. In *Whatever Happened to Baby Jane?,* a gothic horror film whose terms are explicitly the hideous realities hidden beneath the sugarcoating of the entertainment industry, Aldrich virtually defines the genre of camp, offering derisive laughter as the only alternative to an unbearably absurd cosmos. This sense of black comedy (which Aldrich shares with, and developed at the same time as, Hollywood contemporary Stanley Kubrick) has frequently been responsible for the volatile relationship his films have had with popular audiences. Given the context of a life-and-death prison football game in *The Longest Yard,* Aldrich was able to enlist the audience in the hero's bitter laughter in the face of a triumphant totalitarian authority. But when he adopted the same black humor toward the scandalous chicanery of the marginally psychotic cops in *The Choirboys,* he angered almost everybody, not the least of whom was the novel's author, Joseph Wambaugh.

Turned in an introspective direction, Aldrich's acid sensibility resulted in an intensely discomforting, stylistically alienated version of Clifford Odets's Hollywood-hating *The Big Knife* and the madly ambitious *The Legend of Lylah Clare,* an *8-1/2* cum *Vertigo* far too complex by any Hollywood standard. When turned outward toward the world at large, that same sensibility was responsible for a downbeat, disheartening masterpiece like the much-maligned *Hustle,* a film which succeeds better than almost any other in summing up the moral displacement and emotional anguish of the whole decade of the 1970s.

At his most skillful, Aldrich could juggle ideologically volatile issues so well that his most popular film, *The Dirty Dozen,* made during the politically turbulent period of the Vietnam War, played equally well to hawks and doves. Its story of death row prisoners exploited by the military bureaucracy into participation in a suicide raid, where they are to attack a chateau, slaughtering both German officers and civilians, seemed explicitly antiwar in its equation of heroism and criminality and its critique of the body-count mentality of a morally corrupt system. Yet, *The Dirty Dozen* still managed to emerge as a gung-ho war movie in the best Hollywood tradition. The multiple contradictions of the film's stance are nowhere clearer than in its climactic scene, where Aldrich has black athlete Jim Brown re-create one of his famous touchdown runs in order to set off an underground holocaust explicitly parallelled to Auschwitz.

In a far less popular film, the revisionist western *Ulzana's Raid,* Aldrich does confront the horrors of Vietnam with a nearly intolerable accuracy via the properly bloody metaphor of a cavalry company using West Point tactics to fight a band of Apache guerilla warriors. The film relentlessly refuses to diminish the brutality of the red man; even as it demonstrates the poverty of the white man's Christian idealism. The result is perhaps the first western ever to cast America's doctrine of Manifest Destiny in explicitly colonial terms.

More than any other mainstream director, Aldrich insisted on presenting the radical contradictions of American ideology. If we adopt a stance not nearly as cynical as his own in most of his films, we might observe that his capacity to do so has frequently resulted in sizable profits. Yet it is also important to remember that, while Stanley Kubrick (whose 1950s films bear striking stylistic and thematic similarities to those of Aldrich) found it necessary to retreat to England, reducing his output to two or three films a decade, Aldrich chose to fight it out in Hollywood, where his capacity for money-making allowed him the space to vent his own personal anger at the compromises we all must make.

—Ed Lowry

ALEA, Tomás Gutiérrez *See* **GUTIÉRREZ ALEA, Tomás**

ALLEN, Woody

Nationality: American. **Born:** Allen Stewart Konigsberg in Brooklyn, New York, 1 December 1935. **Education:** Attended Midwood High School, Brooklyn; New York University, 1953; City College (now City College of the City University of New York), 1953. **Family:** Married 1) Harlene Rosen, 1954 (divorced); 2) Louise Lasser, 1966 (divorced); one son, Satchel, by actress Mia Farrow, with whom Allen maintained a thirteen-year relationship, 1979-92; legally adopted two of Farrow's thirteen adopted children (one son, Moses; one daughter, Dylan), 1991. **Career:** Began writing jokes for columnists and television celebrities while still in high school; joined staff of National Broadcasting Company, 1952, writing for such television comedy stars as Sid Caesar, Herb Shriner, Buddy Hackett, Art Carney, Carol Channing, and Jack Paar; also wrote for *The Tonight Show* and *The Garry Moore Show;* began performing as stand-up comedian on television and in nightclubs, 1961; hired by producer Charles Feldman to write *What's New, Pussycat?,* 1964; production of his play *Don't Drink the Water* opened on Broadway, 1966; wrote and starred in Broadway run of *Play it Again, Sam,* 1969-70 (filmed 1972); began collaboration with writer Marshall Brickman, 1976; wrote play *The Floating Light Bulb,* produced at Lincoln Center, New York, 1981. **Awards:** Sylvania Award, 1957, for script of *The Sid Caesar Show*; Academy Awards (Oscars) from the Academy of Motion Picture Arts and Sciences for Best Director and Best Original Screenplay (co-recipient), New York Film Critics Circle Award, and National Society of Film Critics Award, all 1977, all for *Annie Hall*; British Academy Award and New York Film Critics Award, 1979, for *Manhattan*; Academy Award for Best Original Screenplay, New York Film Critics Award, and Los Angeles Film Critics Award, all 1986, all for *Hannah and Her Sisters.* **Agent**: Rollins and Joffe, 130 W. 57th Street, New York, NY 10009, U.S.A. **Address:** 930 Fifth Avenue, New York, NY 10021, U.S.A.

Films as Director, Scriptwriter, and Actor:

1969 *Take the Money and Run*
1971 *Bananas* (co-sc)
1972 *Everything You Always Wanted to Know about Sex but Were Afraid to Ask*
1973 *Sleeper*
1975 *Love and Death*
1977 ***Annie Hall*** (co-sc)

1978 *Interiors* (d, sc only)
1979 ***Manhattan*** (co-sc)
1980 *Stardust Memories*
1982 *A Midsummer Night's Sex Comedy*
1983 ***Zelig***
1984 *Broadway Danny Rose*
1985 *The Purple Rose of Cairo* (d, sc only)
1986 *Hannah and Her Sisters*
1987 *Radio Days* (role as narrator)
1988 *September* (d, sc only); *Another Woman* (d, sc only)
1989 *Crimes and Misdemeanors*; "Oedipus Wrecks" episode in *New York Stories*
1990 *Alice* (d, sc only)
1992 *Shadows and Fog*; *Husbands and Wives*
1993 *Manhattan Murder Mystery*
1994 *Bullets over Broadway* (d, co-sc only); *Don't Drink the Water* (for TV)
1995 *Mighty Aphrodite*

Other Films:

1965 *What's New, Pussycat?* (sc, role)
1966 *What's Up, Tiger Lily?* (co-sc, assoc pr, role as host/narrator); *Don't Drink the Water* (play basis)
1967 *Casino Royale* (Huston and others) (role)
1972 *Play It Again, Sam* (Ross) (sc, role)
1976 *The Front* (Ritt) (role)
1987 *King Lear* (Godard) (role)
1991 *Scenes from a Mall* (Mazursky) (role)

Publications

By ALLEN: books—

Don't Drink the Water (play), 1967.
Play It Again, Sam (play), 1969.
Getting Even, New York, 1971.
Death: A Comedy in One Act and *God: A Comedy in One Act* (plays), 1975.
Without Feathers, New York, 1975.
Side Effects, New York, 1980.
The Floating Lightbulb (play), New York, 1982.
Four Films of Woody Allen (*Annie Hall, Interiors, Manhattan, Stardust Memories*), New York, 1982.
Hannah and Her Sisters, New York, 1987.
Three Films of Woody Allen (*Zelig, Broadway Danny Rose, The Purple Rose of Cairo*), New York, 1987.
The Complete Prose of Woody Allen (contains *Getting Even, Without Feathers,* and *Side Effects*), New York, 1992.
The Illustrated Woody Allen Reader, edited by Linda Sunshine, New York, 1993.
Woody Allen on Woody Allen: In Conversation with Stig Bjorkman, London, 1994.

By ALLEN: articles—

"Woody Allen Interview," with Robert Mundy and Stephen Mamber, in *Cinema* (Beverly Hills), Winter 1972/73.
"The Art of Comedy: Woody Allen and *Sleeper,*" interview with J. Trotsky, in *Filmmakers Newsletter* (Ward Hill, Massachusetts), Summer 1974.
"A Conversation with the Real Woody Allen (or Someone Just Like Him)," with K. Kelley, in *Rolling Stone* (New York), 1 July 1976.
"Woody Allen Is Feeling Better," interview with B. Drew, in *American Film* (Washington, D.C.), May 1977.
"Comedy Directors: Interviews with Woody Allen," with M. Karman, in *Millimeter* (New York), October 1977.
"Scenes from a Mind," interview with I. Halberstadt, in *Take One* (Montreal), November 1978.
"Vous avez dit Woody?," interview with Robert Benayoun, in *Positif* (Paris), May 1984.
"The Kobal Tapes: Woody Allen," interview with John Kobal, in *Films and Filming* (London), December 1985.
"Fears of a Clown," an interview with Tom Shales, and "Killing Joke," an interview with Roger Ebert, in *Time Out* (London), 1 November 1989.
Interview with Silvio Bizio, in *Empire* (London), August 1990.
"The Heart Wants What it Wants," an interview with Walter Isaacson, in *Time,* 31 August 1992.
"Unhappily Ever After," an interview with J. Adler and others, in *Newsweek,* 31 August 1992.
Interview with S. Bjorkman, in *Cahiers du Cinema,* vol. 87, 1992.
Interview with A. DeCurtis, in *Rolling Stone,* 16 September 1993.
"Rationality and the Fear of Death," in *The Metaphysics of Death,* edited by John Martin Fischer, 1993.
Interview with Studs Terkel, in *Four Decades with Studs Terkel,* audiocassette collection of interviews with various figures (recorded between 1955 and 1989), HighBridge Company, 1993.
"Woody Allen in Exile" (also cited as "'So, You're the Great Woody Allen?' A Man on the Street Asked Him," an interview with Bill Zehme, in *Esquire,* October 1994.

By ALLEN: television interviews—

Interview with Morley Safer, broadcast on the *60 Minutes* television program, Columbia Broadcasting System, 13 December 1987.
Interview with Steve Croft, broadcast on the *60 Minutes* television program, Columbia Broadcasting System, 22 November 1992.
Interview with Melvyn Bragg, broadcast on *The South Bank Show,* London, 16 January 1994.
"Woody!," an interview with Bob Costas, broadcast in two segments on the *Dateline NBC* television program, National Broadcasting Company, 29 and 30 November 1994.

On ALLEN: books—

Lax, Eric, *On Being Funny: Woody Allen and Comedy,* New York, 1975.
Yacowar, Maurice, *Loser Take All: The Comic Art of Woody Allen,* Oxford, 1979; expanded edition, 1991.
Jacobs, Diane, *... But We Need the Eggs: The Magic of Woody Allen,* New York, 1982.
Brode, Douglas, *Woody Allen: His Films and Career,* London, 1985.
Benayoun, Robert, *Woody Allen: Beyond Words,* London, 1987; as *The Films of Woody Allen,* New York, 1987.
Bendazzi, Giannalberto, *The Films of Woody Allen,* Florence, 1987.
de Navacelle, Thierry, *Woody Allen on Location,* London, 1987.
Pogel, Nancy, *Woody Allen,* Boston 1987.
Sinyard, Neil, *The Films of Woody Allen,* London, 1987.
Altman, Mark A., *Woody Allen Encyclopedia: Almost Everything You Wanted to Know about the Woodster but Were Afraid to Ask,* Pioneer Books, 1990.
McCann, Graham, *Woody Allen: New Yorker,* New York, 1990.
Hirsch, Foster, *Love, Sex, Death, and the Meaning of Life: The Films of Woody Allen,* revised and updated, Limelight, 1991.
Lax, Eric, *Woody Allen: A Biography,* London, 1991.
Weimann, Frank, *Everything You Always Wanted to Know about Woody Allen,* New York, 1991.
Wernblad, Annette, *Brooklyn Is Not Expanding: Woody Allen's Comic Universe,* Rutherford, New Jersey, 1992.

Carroll, Tim, *Woody and His Women,* London, 1993.
Girgus, Sam B., *The Films of Woody Allen,* Cambridge, 1993.
Groteke, Kristi, *Woody and Mia: The Nanny's Tale,* London, 1994.
Spignesi, Stephen, *The Woody Allen Companion,* London, 1994.
Blake, Richard A., *Woody Allen: Profane and Sacred,* Metuchen, New Jersey, 1995.
Hamill, Brian, *Woody Allen at Work: The Photographs of Brian Hamill,* New York, 1995.

On ALLEN: articles—

"Woody, Woody Everywhere," in *Time* (New York), 14 April 1967.
"Woody Allen Issue," of *Cinema* (Beverly Hills), Winter 1972/73.
Wasserman, Harry, "Woody Allen: Stumbling Through the Looking Glass," in *Velvet Light Trap* (Madison), Winter 1972/73.
Maltin, Leonard, "Take Woody Allen—Please!," in *Film Comment* (New York), March-April 1974.
Remond, A., "*Annie Hall,*" in *Avant-Scène du Cinéma* (Paris), 15 December 1977.
Yacowar, Maurice, "Forms of Coherence in the Woody Allen Comedies," in *Wide Angle* (Athens, Ohio), no. 2, 1979.
Canby, Vincent, "Film View: Notes on Woody Allen and American Comedy," in *New York Times,* 13 May 1979.
Dempsey, M., "The Autobiography of Woody Allen," in *Film Comment* (New York), May/June 1979.
Teitelbaum, D., "Producing Woody: An Interview with Charles H. Joffe," in *Cinema Papers* (Melbourne), April/May 1980.
Combs, Richard, "Chameleon Days: Reflections on Non-Being," in *Monthly Film Bulletin* (London), November 1983.
Lahr, John, in *Automatic Vaudeville: Essays on Star Turns,* New York, 1984.
Liebman, R.L., "Rabbis or Rakes, Schlemiels or Supermen? Jewish Identity in Charles Chaplin, Jerry Lewis and Woody Allen," in *Literature/Film Quarterly* (Salisbury, Maryland), July 1984.
Caryn James, "Auteur! Auteur! The Creative Mind of Woody Allen," in *New York Times Magazine,* 19 January 1986.
"Woody Allen Section," of *Film Comment* (New York), May-June 1986.
Combs, Richard, "A Trajectory Built for Two," in *Monthly Film Bulletin* (London), July 1986.
Morris, Christopher, "Woody Allen's Comic Irony," in *Literature/Film Quarterly* (Salisbury, Maryland), vol. 15, no. 3, 1987.
Yacowar, Maurice, "Beyond Parody: Woody Allen in the Eighties," in *Post Script* (Jacksonville, Florida), Winter 1987.
Dunne, Michael, "*Stardust Memories, The Purple Rose of Cairo,* and the Tradition of Metafiction," in *Film Criticism* (Meadville, Pennsylvania), Fall 1987.
Preussner, Arnold W., "Woody Allen's *The Purple Rose of Cairo* and the Genres of Comedy," and Paul Salmon and Helen Bragg, "Woody Allen's Economy of Means: An Introduction to *Hannah and Her Sisters,*" in *Literature/Film Quarterly* (Salisbury, Maryland), vol. 16, no. 1, 1988.
"Woody Allen," in *Film Dope* (London), March 1988.
Downing, Crystal, "Broadway Roses: Woody Allen's Romantic Inheritance," and Ronald D. LeBlanc, "*Love and Death* and Food: Woody Allen's Comic Use of Gastronomy," in *Literature/Film Quarterly* (Salisbury, Maryland), vol. 17, no. 1, 1989.
Girlanda, E., and A. Tella, "Allen: Manhattan Transfer," in *Castoto Cinema,* July/August 1990.
Comuzio, E., "*Alice,*" in *Cinema Forum,* vol. 31, 1991.
Green, D., "The Comedian's Dilemma: Woody Allen's 'Serious' Comedy," in *Literature/Film Quarterly,* vol. 19, no. 2, 1991.
Tutt, R., "Truth, Beauty, and Travesty: Woody Allen's Well-Wrought Run," in *Literature/Film Quarterly,* vol. 19, no. 2, 1991.
Welsh, J., "Allen Stewart Konigsberg Becomes Woody Allen: A Comic Transformation," in *Literature/Film Quarterly,* vol. 19, no. 2, 1991.
Quart, L., "Woody Allen's New York," in *Cineaste,* vol. 19, no. 2, 1992.
Mitchell, Sean, "The Clown Who Would Be Chekhov," in *The Guardian* (U.K.), 23 March 1992.
Rockwell, John, "Woody Allen: France's Monsieur Right," in *New York Times,* 5 April 1992.
Corliss, Richard, "Scenes from a Breakup," in *Time,* 31 August 1992.
Cagle, Jess, "Love and Fog," in *Entertainment Weekly,* 18 September 1992.
Hoban, Phoebe, "Everything You Always Wanted to Know about Woody and Mia but Were Afraid to Ask," in *New York,* 21 September 1992.
Johnstone, Iain, "Moving Pictures Drawn from Life," in *The Sunday Times* (London), 25 October 1992.
Romney, J. "*Husbands and Wives,*" in *Sight and Sound,* November 1992.
Perez-Pena, R., "Woody Allen Tells of Affair as Custody Battle Begins," in *New York Times,* 20 March 1993.
Marks, P., "Allen Loses to Farrow in Bitter Custody Battle," in *New York Times,* 8 June 1993.
Baumgarten, Murray, "Film and the Flattening of American Jewish Fiction: Bernard Malamud, Woody Allen, and Spike Lee in the City," in *Contemporary Literature,* Fall 1993.
Desser, David, "Woody Allen: The Schlemiel as Modern Philosopher," in *American-Jewish Filmmakers: Traditions and Trends,* University of Illinois Press, 1993.
Troncale, J. C., "Illusion and Reality in Woody Allen's Double Film of *The Purple Rose of Cairo,*" in *Proceedings of the Conference on Film and American Culture,* edited by Joel Schwartz, College of William and Mary, 1994.
Romney, Jonathan, "Shelter from the Storm," in *Sight and Sound,* February 1994.
Davis, Robert, "A Stand-Up Guy Sits Down: Woody Allen's Prose," in *Short Story,* Fall 1994.
McGrath, Douglas, "If You Knew Woody Like I Knew Woody," in *New York,* 17 October 1994.

On ALLEN: film—

Woody Allen: An American Comedy (Harold Mantell), 1978.

* * *

Woody Allen's roots in American popular culture are broad and laced with a variety of European literary and filmic influences, some of them paid explicit homage within his films (Ingmar Bergman and Dostoevsky, for example), others more subtly woven into the fabric of his work from a wide range of earlier comic traditions. Allen's genuinely original voice in the cinema recalls writer-directors like Buster Keaton, Charlie Chaplin, and Preston Sturges, who dissect their portions of the American landscape primarily through comedy. In his creative virtuosity Allen also resembles Orson Welles, whose visual and verbal wit, though contained in seemingly non-comic genres, in fact exposes the American character to satirical scrutiny.

Allen generally appears in his own films, resembling the great silent-screen clowns who created, then developed, an ongoing screen presence. However, Allen's film persona depends upon *heard* dialogue and especially thrives as an updated, urbanly hip, explicitly Jewish amalgam of personality traits and delivery methods associated with comic artists who reached their pinnacle in radio and film in the 1930s and 1940s. The key figures Allen plays in his own films puncture the dangerous absurdities of their universe and guard themselves against them by maintaining a cynical, even misogynistic verbal offense in the manner of Groucho Marx and W. C. Fields, but alternating it with incessant displays of self-deprecation, in the manner of the cowardly, unhandsome persona established by Bob Hope in, for example, his *Road* series.

Allen's early films emerge logically from the sharp, pointedly exaggerated jokes and sketches he wrote for others, then delivered himself as a stand-up comic in clubs and on television. Like the early films of Buster Keaton, most of these early films depend upon explicit parody of recognizable film genres. Even the films of this pre-*Annie Hall* period which do not formally rely upon a particular film genre incorporate references to various films and directors as commentary on the specific targets of social, political, or literary satire: political turbulence of the 1960s via television news coverage in *Bananas*; the pursuit by intellectuals of large religious and philosophical questions via the methods of Tolstoy and Dostoevsky in *Love and Death*; American sexual repression via the self-discovery guarantees offered by sex manuals in *Everything You Always Wanted to Know about Sex*.

All these issues will reappear in Allen's later, increasingly mature work—and they will persist in revealing an anomaly: Allen's comedy is cerebral in nature, dependent even in its occasional sophomoric moments upon an educated audience that responds to his brand of self-reflexive, literary, political, and sexual humor. But Allen distrusts and satirizes formal education and institutionalized discourse, which in his films lead repeatedly to humorless intellectual preening. "Those who can't do, teach, and those who can't teach, teach gym," declares Alvy Singer in *Annie Hall*. No character in that film is treated with greater disdain than the Columbia professor who smugly pontificates on Fellini while standing in line waiting to see *The Sorrow and the Pity*; Allen inflicts swift, cinematically appropriate justice. Yale, a university professor of English, bears the brunt of *Manhattan*'s moral condemnation as a self-rationalizing cheat who is far "too easy" on himself.

In *Annie Hall*, his Oscar-winning breakthrough film, Allen the writer (with Marshall Brickman) recapitulates and expands emerging Allen topics but removes them from the highly exaggerated apparatus of his earlier parodies. Alvy Singer (Allen) and Annie Hall (Diane Keaton in her most important of several roles in Allen's films) enact an urban-neurotic variation on the mismatched lovers of screwball comedy, now oriented away from farce and toward character analysis set against a realistic New York City *mise-en-scène*.

Annie Hall makes indelible the Woody Allen onscreen persona—a figure somehow involved in show business or the arts and obsessive about women, his parents, his childhood, his values, his terror of illness and death; perpetually and hilariously taking the mental temperature of himself and everyone around him. Part whiner, part *nebbish*, part hypochondriac, this figure is also brilliantly astute and consciously funny, miraculously irresistible to women—for a while—particularly (as in *Annie Hall* and *Manhattan*) when he can serve as their teacher. This developing figure in Allen's work is both comic victim and witty victimizer, a moral voice in an amoral age who repeatedly discovers that the only true gods in a Godless universe are cultural and artistic—movies, music, art, architecture—a perception pleasurably reinforced visually and aurally throughout his best films. With rare exception—*Hannah* is a notable one—this figure at the film's fadeout appears destined to remain alone, by implication enabling him to continue to function as a sardonically detached observer of human imperfection, including his own. In *Annie Hall*, this characterization, despite its suffusion in *angst*, remains purely comic but Allen becomes progressively darker—and harder on himself—as variants of this figure emerge in the later films.

Comedy, even comedy that aims for a laughter of recognition based on credibility of character and situation, depends heavily upon exaggeration. In *Zelig*, the tallest of Woody Allen's cinematic tall tales, the film's central figure is a human chameleon who satisfies his overwhelming desire for conformity by physically transforming himself into the people he meets. Zelig's bizarre behavior is made even more visually believable by stunning shots that appear to place the character of Leonard Zelig (Allen) alongside famous historical figures within actual newsreel footage of the 1920s and 1930s.

Shot in Panavision and velvety black-and-white, and featuring a Gershwin score dominated by "Rhapsody in Blue," *Manhattan* reiterates key concerns of *Annie Hall* but enlarges the circle of participants in a sexual *la ronde* that increases Allen's ambivalence toward the moral terrain occupied by his characters—especially by Ike Davis (Allen), a forty-two-year-old man justifying a relationship with a seventeen-year-old girl. By film's end she has become an eighteen-year-old woman who has outgrown him, just as Annie Hall outgrew Alvy Singer. The film (like *Hannah and Her Sisters* later) is, above all, a celebration of New York City, which Ike, like Allen, "idolize[s] all out of proportion."

In the Pirandellian *Purple Rose of Cairo*, the fourth Allen film to star Mia Farrow, a character in a black-and-white film within the color film leaps literally out of the frame into the heroine's local movie theatre. Here film itself—in this case the movies of the 1930s—both distorts reality (by setting dangerously high, incongruous expectations) and makes it more bearable (by permitting Cecilia, Allen's heroine, to escape from her dismal Depression existence). Like *Manhattan* before it, and *Hannah and Her Sisters* and *Radio Days* after it, *Purple Rose of Cairo* examines the healing power of popular art.

Arguably Allen's finest film to date, *Hannah and Her Sisters* shifts his own figure further away from the center of the story than he has ever been before, treating him as one of nine prominent characters in the action. Allen's screenplay weaves an ingenious tapestry around three sisters, their parents, assorted mates, lovers, and friends (including Allen as Hannah's ex-husband Mickey Sachs). A Chekhovian exploration of the upper-middle-class world of a group of New Yorkers a decade after *Annie Hall*, Hannah is deliberately episodic in structure, its sequences separated by Brechtian title cards that suggest thematic elements of each succeeding segment. Yet it is an extraordinarily seamless film, unified by the family at its center; three Thanksgiving dinner scenes at key intervals; an exquisite color celebration of an idyllic New York City; and music by Cole Porter, Rodgers and Hart, and Puccini (among others) that italicizes the genuinely romantic nature of the film's tone. The most optimistic of Allen's major films, *Hannah* restores its inhabitants to a world of pure comedy, their futures epitomized by the fate of Mickey Sachs. For once, the Allen figure is a man who will live happily ever after, a man formerly sterile, now apparently fertile, as is comedy's magical way.

Crimes and Misdemeanors further marginalizes—and significantly darkens—the figure Woody Allen invites audiences to confuse with his offscreen self. The self-reflexive plight of filmmaker Cliff Stern (Allen) alternates with the central dilemma confronted by ophthalmologist Judah Rosenthal, a medical pillar of society who bears primary, if indirect, responsibility for the murder of his mistress. Religious and philosophical issues present in Allen's films since *Love and Death* achieve a new and serious resonance, particularly through the additional presence of a faith-retaining rabbi gradually (in one of numerous Oedipal references in Allen's work) losing his sight, and a Holocaust survivor-philosopher who preaches the gospel of endurance—then commits suicide by (as his note prosaically puts it) "going out the window." In its pessimism diametrically opposed to the joyous *Hannah and Her Sisters, Crimes and Misdemeanors* posits a universe utterly devoid of poetic justice. The picture's genuinely comic sequences, usually involving Cliff and his fatuous producer brother-in-law ("Comedy is tragedy plus time!") do not contradict the fact that it is Allen's most somber major film, a family comedy-melodrama that in its final sequence crosses the brink to the level of domestic tragedy. Here, the Allen figure is not only alone, as he has been in the past, but alone and *in despair*.

In entirely contrasting visual ways, *Alice* and *Shadows and Fog* exhibit immediately recognizable Allen concerns in highly original fashion. A glossy, airy, gently satiric modern fairy tale, *Alice* implicitly functions as Allen's most open love letter to Mia Farrow. Her idealized title character searches for meaning in a Yuppified New York

Woody Allen (right) with Sven Nykvist on the set of *Another Woman*

City. Eventually, she finds it by leaving her husband, meeting Mother Theresa, and, especially, by discovering that her two children offer her the only genuine vehicle for romance in this romantic comedy *manque.* The film's final shot displays a glowing Alice joyfully pushing them on playground swings as two former women friends, in voice-over dialogue, bemoan her self-selected maidless and nannyless condition, one which the film clearly intends us to embrace.

In *Shadows and Fog,* Allen employs a specific film genre more directly than at any time since the 1970s. His homage to German Expressionism, *Shadows and Fog* is shot in black and white in a manner deliberately reminiscent of the films of Pabst, Lang, and Murnau. That visual style and the placement at the film's center of a distinctly Kafkaesque hero (played by Allen) combine to make *Shadows and Fog* Allen's most explicitly "European," most wryly metaphysical film since *Interiors* fourteen years earlier. Not surprisingly, *Shadows and Fog* was greeted by critics much more favorably in Europe than in the United States.

As Chekhov's forgiving spirit energizes the comic tone of *Hannah and Her Sisters,* so the playwright August Strindberg's hostility controls the dark marital terrain of *Husbands and Wives.* Strindbergian gender battles frequently appear in earlier Allen films, but they are more typically rescued back from the precipice into a healing world of comedy. Allen's partial attempt to attribute comic closure to *Husbands and Wives* pleases but inadequately convinces. While the film (which might have been more accurately titled *Husbands, Wives, and Lovers*) is often extremely funny, its portrait of two deteriorating marriages is as corrosive as anything in the Allen canon. *Husbands and Wives* contains other elements long present in Allen's films: multiple story-lines, a deliberately episodic structure covering a period of about a year (as in *Hannah* and *Crimes and Misdemeanors*), and the involvement of a central character, Gabe Roth (played by Allen), with a woman young enough to be his daughter. Unlike Ike Davis's relationship with Tracy in *Manhattan,* however, this one is consummated—and concluded—with only a kiss.

Despite the presence of familiar material, *Husbands and Wives* shows Allen continuing to break new ground, particularly in the film's visual virtuosity. The frequent use of a hand-held camera reinforces the neurotic, darting, unpredictable behavior of key characters. Moving beyond his use of title cards to provide Brechtian distancing in *Hannah and Her Sisters,* Allen here employs a documentary technique to punctuate the main action of the film. The central characters and a minor one (the ex-husband of Judy Roth, the woman played by Mia Farrow) are individually interviewed by an off-screen male voice, which appears to function simultaneously as documentary recorder of their woeful tales *and* as therapist to their psyches. These sequences are inserted periodically throughout the film, as the interviewees speak directly to the camera—and therefore to *us,* thus forcing the audience to participate in the filmmaker-interviewer's role as therapist.

Husbands and Wives deserves a place alongside *Hannah and Her Sisters* and *Crimes and Misdemeanors* to represent Allen's most textured and mature work to date. But the film's visual and thematic pleasures have been obscured by audience desires to see in *Husbands and Wives* the spectacle of art imitating life with a vengeance; and, in fact, *Husbands and Wives* does contain uncanny links to the Allen-Farrow breakup even though the film was completed before their relationship came to a dramatic and highly visible end.

The type of ethical dilemma which occupies such a central place in the Allen canon (and which usually finds its most articulate definition in the mouths of characters played by Allen himself) appeared to have tumbled out of an Allen movie and onto worldwide front pages. ("Life doesn't imitate art; it imitates bad television," says Allen's Gabe Roth in *Husbands and Wives*.) In 1992, shortly before the release of *Husbands and Wives,* Allen's romantic relationship with Soon-Yi Previn, Mia Farrow's twenty-one-year-old adopted daughter, was discovered by her mother, who made the fact public. Furious and ugly charges and countercharges ensued and led to Allen's loss of custody of his three children a year later. Legal challenges continue as of 1996.

Allen has made four films since *Husbands and Wives* was released, all of them reverting to the explicit world of comedy: *Don't Drink the Water,* adapted from his early Broadway play and first shown in America on network television; *Manhattan Murder Mystery,* a comedy-mystery in the manner of *The Thin Man* films and the *Mr. and Mrs. North* radio and television series (with Diane Keaton replacing Mia Farrow, who was originally scheduled to play Allen's wife); *Bullets over Broadway,* in which John Cusack plays a younger Allen stand-in, a playwright grappling with his first Broadway production; and *Mighty Aphrodite,* which again tempts audiences to see elements of Allen's life reflected in the central plot issue of child adoption. But with its parodies of Greek tragedy and its broadly satiric array of characters, *Mighty Aphrodite* rarely strays from its identification as genuine Allen *comedy.* These 1990s films reveal yet again why so many actors want to work with Allen: Dianne Wiest won her second supporting actress Oscar for her role in an Allen film for *Bullets over Broadway* (her first was for *Hannah*); and Mira Sorvino won the same award for *Mighty Aphrodite* the following year.

Allen's primary response to the tarnish on his personal reputation has been to keep making films. He has always denied that his film persona is related to his own, although it is often justifiably difficult for us to believe that. "Is it over? Can I go now?" asks Gabe Roth of the off-screen interviewer in the final shot of *Husbands and Wives.* Divorced from his wife, Gabe is now alone, but he *chooses* be to alone. Gabe may not be happy—rarely is any character played by Woody Allen ever actually *happy*—but, unlike Clifford Stern at the end of *Crimes and Misdemeanors,* Gabe is decidedly *not* in despair. As the comic spirit of Allen's recent films suggests, that fact would appear to bode extremely well for Allen's future work and, especially, for those who love his films.

—Mark W. Estrin

ALMODÓVAR, Pedro

Nationality: Spanish. **Born:** Calzada de Clatrava, La Mancha, Spain, 1951 (some sources say 1947). **Career:** Moved to Madrid and worked for National Telephone Company, 1967; wrote comic strips and articles for underground magazines; joined independent theatre group *Los Goliardos* and started making Super-8 films with them, 1974; first feature, *Pepi,* released 1980; also a rock musician, has written music for his own films. **Awards:** Glauber Rocha Award for Best Director, Rio Film Festival, and Los Angeles Film Critics Association "New Generation" Award, 1987, for *Law of Desire;* National Society of Film Critics Award, special citation for originality, 1988; Venice International Film Festival best screenplay award, National Board of Review of Motion Pictures best foreign film, New York Film Critics Circle best foreign film, and Felix Award for best young film, all 1988, and Academy Award nomination for best foreign film, Orson Welles Award for best foreign-language film, both 1989, all for *Women on the Verge of a Nervous Breakdown.* **Agent:** El Deseo SA, 117 Velázquez, Madrid, Spain.

Films as Director:

1974 *Dos putas, o, Historia de amor que termina en boda* (*Two Whores, or, A Love Story Which Ends in Marriage*) (Super-8); *La caida de Sodoma* (*The Fall of Sodom*) (Super-8)
1975 *Homenaje* (*Homage*) (Super-8)
1976 *La estrella* (*The Stars*) (Super-8)
1977 *Sexo va: Sexo vienne* (*Sex Comes and Goes*) (Super-8); *Complementos* (shorts)
1978 *Folle, folle, folleme, Tim* (*Fuck Me, Fuck Me, Fuck Me, Tim*) (Super-8, full-length); *Salome* (16mm)
1980 *Pepi, Luci, Bom y otras chicas de montón* (*Pepi, Luci, Bom and Lots of Other Girls*) (+ sc)
1982 *Laberinto de pasiones* (*Labyrinth of Passions*) (+ sc, role)
1983 *Entre tinieblas* (*Into the Dark*; *The Sisters of Darkness*)(+ sc, song)
1984 *Qué me hecho yo para merecer esto?* (*What Have I Done to Deserve This?*) (+ sc)
1986 *Matador* (+ sc); *La ley del deseo* (*Law of Desire*) (+ sc, score, song)
1987 ***Mujeres al borde de un ataque de nervios*** (*Women on the Verge of a Nervous Breakdown*) (+ sc)
1990 *Atame!* (*Tie Me Up, Tie Me Down!*) (+ sc)
1991 *Tacomes lejanos* (*High Heels*) (+ sc, song)
1993 *Kika* (+ sc)
1995 *Le flor de mi secreto* (*The Flower of My Secret*) (+ sc)

Publications

By ALMODÓVAR: books—

El sueno de la razon (short stories), Madrid, 1980.
Fuego en las entranas (*Fire Deep Inside*) (novel), Madrid, 1982.
Patty Diphusa y otros textos (*Patty Diphusa and Other Writings*), Barcelona, 1991.

By ALMODÓVAR: articles—

Interview in *Contracampo* (Madrid), September 1981.
Interview with J. C. Rentero, in *Casablanca* (Madrid), May 1984.
"Pleasure and the New Spanish Mentality," an interview with Marsha Kinder, in *Film Quarterly* (Berkeley), Fall 1987.
Interview in *Time Out* (London), 2 November 1988.
Interview in *Film Comment* (New York), November/December 1988.
Interview in *Films and Filming* (London), June 1989.
Interview in *Inter/View* (New York), January 1990.
Interview in *City Limits* (London), 5 July 1990.
Interview with J. Schnabel, in *Interview* (New York), January 1992.
"Perche il melodrama," an interview with E. Imparato, in *Cineforum* (Bergamo, Italy), April 1992.
Interview with F. Strauss, in *Cahiers du Cinéma* (Paris), May 1992.
Regular column (as "Patty Diphusa") in *La Luna* (Madrid)

By ALMODÓVAR: books—

Bouza Vidal, Nuria, *El cine de Pedro Almodóvar* (*The Films of Pedro Almodóvar*), Madrid, 1988.

Films as Director:

1954 *The Builders* (medium length publicity film)
1955 *The Delinquents* (+ pr, sc)
1957 *The James Dean Story* (co-d, + co-pr, co-ed)
1964 *The Party* (short); *Nightmare in Chicago* (*Once Upon a Savage Night*) (for TV)
1965 *Pot au Feu* (short); *The Katherine Reed Story* (short)
1967 *Countdown* (moon-landing sequence uncred by William Conrad)
1969 *That Cold Day in the Park*
1970 ***M*A*S*H***; *Brewster McCloud* (+ pr)
1971 *McCabe and Mrs. Miller* (+ co-sc)
1972 *Images* (+ pr,sc)
1973 *The Long Goodbye*
1974 *Thieves Like Us* (+ co-sc); *California Split* (+ co-pr)
1975 ***Nashville*** (+ co-pr, co-songwriter: "The Day I Looked Jesus in the Eye")
1976 *Buffalo Bill and the Indians, or Sitting Bull's History Lesson* (+ pr, co-sc)
1977 *Three Women* (+pr, sc)
1978 *A Wedding* (+ pr, co-sc)
1979 *Quintet* (+ pr, co-sc); *A Perfect Couple* (+ pr, co-sc)
1979 *Health* (+ pr, sc)
1980 *Popeye*
1981 *The Easter Egg Hunt*
1982 *Come Back to the Five and Dime, Jimmy Dean, Jimmy Dean*; *Two by South* ("Rattlesnake in a Cooler" and "Precious Blood") (for TV) (+pr)
1983 *Streamers* (+ pr); *O.C. and Stiggs* (+ pr) (released 1987)
1984 *Secret Honor* (*Secret Honor: The Political Testament of Richard M. Nixon*; *Secret Honor: A Political Myth*) (+ pr)
1985 *The Laundromat* (for TV)
1986 *Fool for Love*
1987 "Les Boreades" in *Aria*; *Beyond Therapy* (+ co-sc); *The Room* (for TV); *The Dumb Waiter* (for TV)
1988 *Tanner '88*; *The Caine Mutiny Court-Martial* (+ pr)
1990 *Vincent and Theo*
1992 ***The Player***
1993 ***Short Cuts***
1994 *The Real McTeague* (for TV, opera)
1995 *Ready to Wear* (*Pret a Porter*)

Other Films:

1948 *Bodyguard* (co-story)
1951 *Corn's-A-Poppin'* (co-sc)
1976 *Welcome to L.A.* (Rudolph) (pr)
1977 *The Late Show* (Benton) (pr)
1978 *Remember My Name* (Rudolph) (pr)
1979 *Rich Kids* (Young) (pr)

Publications

By ALTMAN: book—

Buffalo Bill and the Indians, or Sitting Bull's History Lesson, with Alan Rudolph, New York, 1976.
Short Cuts: The Screenplay, Santa Barbara, CA, 1993.
Robert Altman's Pret a Porter, New York, 1994.

By ALTMAN: articles—

Interview with S. Rosenthal, in *Focus on Film* (London), Spring 1972.
Interview with Russell Auwerter, in *Directors in Action,* edited by Bob Thomas, New York, 1973.
Interview with Michel Ciment and Bertrand Tavernier, in *Positif* (Paris), February 1973.
"Robert Altman Speaking," interview with J. Dawson, in *Film Comment* (New York), March/April 1974.
"An Altman Sampler," interview with B.J. Demby, in *Filmmakers Newsletter* (Ward Hill, Massachusetts), October 1974.
Robert Altman Seminar, in *Dialogue on Film* (Beverly Hills), February 1975.
"The Artist and the Multitude Are Natural Enemies," interview with F.A. Macklin, in *Film Heritage* (Dayton, Ohio), Winter 1976/77.
Interview with Jean-André Fieschi, in *Cinématographe* (Paris), June 1977.
Interview with Jonathan Rosenbaum and Charles Michener, in *Film Comment* (New York), September/October 1978.
Interview and article by J.-P. Le Pavec and others, in *Cinéma* (Paris), November 1978.
"Jumping Off the Cliff," in *Monthly Film Bulletin* (London), December 1978.
Interview with Michel Ciment and M. Henry, in *Positif* (Paris), March 1979.
"Robert Altman: Backgammon and Spinach," interview with Tom Milne and Richard Combs, in *Sight and Sound* (London), Summer 1981.
"Peripheral Vision," interview with A. Stuart, in *Films* (London), July 1981.
Interview with Leo Braudy and Robert Phillip Kolker, in *Post Script* (Jacksonville, Florida), Fall 1981 and Winter 1982.
"'A Foolish Optimist': Interview with Robert Altman," by H. Kloman, Lloyd Michaels, and Virginia Wright Wexman, in *Film Criticism* (Meadville, Pennsylvania), Spring 1983.
Interview with Michel Ciment, in *Positif* (Paris), June 1984.
Stills (London), November 1984.
Interview with Richard Combs, in *Monthly Film Bulletin* (London), January 1985.
"On the Road with Robert Altman," an interview with Nick Roddick, in *Cinema Papers* (Melbourne), September 1986.
Interview with Steven Aronson, in *Architectural Digest,* March 1990.
"Mrs. Miller's Tale," an interview with Sheila Johnston, in the *Independent* (London), 6 April 1990.
"How the Western Was Lost," an interview with Derek Malcolm, in the *Guardian* (London), 11 April 1990.
Interview with Richard Combs in *Monthly Film Bulletin* (London), July 1990.
"Robert Altman: The Rolling Stone Interview," interview with David Breskin, in *Rolling Stone,* 16 April 1992.
Interview with Graham Fuller, *Interview,* May 1992.
Interview with Jean-Pierre Coursodon and M. Henry, "Hollywood n'est qu'une metaphore," in *Positif,* June 1992.
"Death and Hollywood," interview with P. Keogh, in *Sight and Sound,* June 1992.
Interview with Janice M. Richolson and others, "The Player," in *Cineaste,* No. 2/3, 1992.
Interview with David Breskin, *InnerViews: Filmmakers in Conversation,* Boston: Faber and Faber, 1992.
"Reimagining Raymond Carver on Film: A Talk with Robert Altman and Tess Gallagher," interview with R. Stewart, in *New York Times,* 12 September 1993.

On ALTMAN: film—

"Robert Altman," for *South Bank Show,* London Weekend Television, April 1990.

On ALTMAN: books—

Hardin, Nancy, editor, *On Making a Movie: Brewster McCloud,* New York, 1971.

Feineman, Neil, *Persistence of Vision: The Films of Robert Altman,* New York, 1976.
Tewkesbury, Joan, *Nashville,* New York, 1976.
Kass, Judith M., *Robert Altman: American Innovator,* New York, 1978.
Terry, Bridget, *The Popeye Story,* New York, 1980.
Kolker, Robert Phillip, *A Cinema of Loneliness: Penn, Kubrick, Coppola, Scorsese, Altman,* Oxford, 1980, revised edition, 1988.
Bourget, Jean-Loup, *Robert Altman,* Paris, 1981.
Karp, Alan, *The Films of Robert Altman,* Metuchen, New Jersey, 1981.
Fink, Guido, *I film Di Robert Altman,* Rome, 1982.
Kagan, Norman, *American Skeptic: Robert Altman's Genre-Commentary Films,* Ann Arbor, Michigan, 1982.
Micciche, Lino, *L'incubo americano: Il cinema di Robert Altman,* Venice, 1984.
Wexman, Virginia Wright, and Gretchen Bisplinghoff, *Robert Altman: A Guide to References and Resources,* Boston, 1984.
Plecki, Gerard, *Robert Altman,* Boston, 1985.
Weis, Elisabeth, and John Belton, editors, *Film Sound: Theory and Practice,* New York, 1985.
Wood, Robin, *Hollywood from Vietnam to Reagan,* New York, 1986.
McGilligan, Patrick, *Robert Altman: Jumping off the Cliff—A Biography,* New York, 1988.
Keyssar, Helene, *Robert Altman's America,* New York, 1991.
Bourget, Jean-Loup, *Robert Altman,* Paris, 1994.
O'Brien, Daniel, *Robert Altman: Hollywood Survivor,* New York, 1995.

On ALTMAN: articles—

Cutts, John, "*MASH, McCloud,* and *McCabe,*" in *Films and Filming* (London), November 1971.
Dawson, J., "Altman's Images," in *Sight and Sound* (London), Spring 1972.
Engle, Gary, "*McCabe and Mrs. Miller*: Robert Altman's Anti-Western," in *Journal of Popular Film* (Bowling Green, Ohio), Fall 1972.
Baker, C.A., "The Theme of Structure in the Films of Robert Altman," in *Journal of Popular Film* (Bowling Green), Summer 1973.
Brackett, Leigh, "From *The Big Sleep* to the *The Long Goodbye* and More or Less How We Got There," in *Take One* (Montreal), January 1974.
Stewart, Garrett, "*The Long Goodbye* from *Chinatown,*" in *Film Quarterly* (Berkeley), Winter 1974/75.
Rosenbaum, Jonathan, "Improvisations and Interactions in Altmanville," in *Sight and Sound* (London), Spring 1975.
Oliver, Bill, "*The Long Goodbye* and *Chinatown*: Debunking the Private Eye Tradition," in *Literature/Film Quarterly* (Salisbury, Maryland), Summer 1975.
"Altman Issue" of *Film Heritage* (Dayton, Ohio), Fall 1975.
Wood, Robin, "Smart-ass and Cutie-pie: Notes Toward an Evaluation of Altman," in *Movie,* Fall 1975.
Benayoun, Robert, "Altman, U.S.A.," in *Positif* (Paris), December 1975.
Byrne, Connie and William O. Lopez, "*Nashville* (An Interview Documentary)," in *Film Quarterly* (Berkeley), Winter 1975/76.
Self, Robert, "Invention and Death: The Commodities of Media in Robert Altman's *Nashville,*" in *Journal of Popular Film* (Bowling Green, Ohio), no. 5, 1976.
Levine, R., "R. Altman & Co.," in *Film Comment* (New York), January/February 1977.
Canby, Vincent, "Film View: Altman—A Daring Filmmaker Falters," in *The New York Times,* 18 February 1979.
"Playing the Game, or Robert Altman and the Indians," in *Sight and Sound* (London), Summer 1979.
Bonnet, J.-C., and others, "Dossier: Robert Altman," in *Cinématographe* (Paris), January 1980.
Yacowar, Maurice, "Actors as Conventions in the Films of Robert Altman," in *Cinema Journal* (Evanston), Fall 1980.
Eyman, S., "Against Altman," in *Focus on Film* (London), October 1980.
Altman, D., "Building Sand Castles," in *Cinema Papers* (Melbourne), July/August 1981.
Self, Robert, "The Art Cinema and Robert Altman," in *Velvet Light Trap* (Madison, Wisconsin), no. 19, 1982.
Durgnat, Raymond, "Popeye Pops Up," in *Films* (London), April and May 1982.
Self, Robert, "The Perfect Couple: 'Two are Halves of One,' in the Films of Robert Altman," in *Wide Angle* (Athens, Georgia), vol. 5, no. 4, 1983.
Edgerton, G., "Capra and Altman: Mythmaker and Mythologist," in *Literature/Film Quarterly* (Salisbury, Maryland), January 1983.
Jaehne, K., and P. Audferheide, "Secret honor," in *Cineaste* (New York), vol. 14, no. 2, 1985.
Farber, Stephen, "Five Horsemen After the Apocalypse," in *Film Comment* (New York), July/August 1985.
Self, Robert, "Robert Altman and the Theory of Authorship," in *Cinema Journal* (Champaign, Illinois), Fall 1985.
"Altman Section" of *Positif* (Paris), January 1986.
White, A., "Play Time," in *Film Comment* (New York), January-February 1986.
Self, Robert, and Leland Poague, "Dialogue," in *Cinema Journal* (Champaign, Illinois), Spring 1986.
Combs, Richard, "A trajectory built for two," in *Monthly Film Bulletin* (London), July 1986.
"Robert Altman," in *Film Dope* (London), March 1988.
Wolcott, James, "Jack Tanner, For Real," in *Vanity Fair,* July 1988.
Film Comment (New York), September/October 1989.
"Altman at Calvin," in *Sight and Sound* (London), no. 2, 1990.
McGilligan, Patrick, "Altman in Kansas City," in *Sight and Sound,* no. 2, 1990.
Combs, R., "The World is a Bad Painting," in *Monthly Film Bulletin,* July 1990.
Giddins, Gary, "Altman's Back," in *Village Voice,* 6 November 1990.
Fisher, W., "Vincent and Theo and Bob," in *Millimeter,* September 1990.
Sanjek, David, "The Case for Robert Altman," in *Literature/Film Quarterly,* no. 1, 1991.
Walker, Beverly, "Altman '91," in *Film Comment,* January/February 1991.
Andersen, Kurt, "A Player Once Again," in *Time,* April 20, 1992.
Ansen, David, and others, "Hollywood is Talking: The Player," in *Newsweek,* 2 March 1992.
Kasindorf, Jeanine, "Home Movies," in *New York,* 16 March 1992.
Kroll, Jack, "Robert Altman Gives Something Back," in *Esquire,* May 1992.
Myers, E., "Mining McTeague's Gold," in *New York Times,* 25 October 1992.
Pond, Steve, "Flushing the Locusts," in *Premiere,* May 1992.
Schiff, Stephen, "Auteur! Auteur!" in *Vanity Fair,* April 1992.
Smith, Gavin and Jameson, Richard T., "The Movie You Saw is the Movie We're Going to Make," in *Film Comment,* May/June 1992.
Rico, Diana, "S*M*A*S*H," in *Gentleman's Quarterly,* May 1992.
Wilmington, Michael, "Robert Altman and the Player—Laughing and Killing: Death and Hollywood," in *Sight and Sound,* June 1992.
Hoberman, J., "Rerunning for President," in *Village Voice,* 14 July 1992.
Weinraub, B., "Robert Altman, Very Much a Player Again," in *New York Times,* 29 July 1993.
Henry, B., Gavin Smith, and F. Anthony Macklin, "Back/Roads to Short Cuts: Faultlines of a Daydream Nation," in *Film Comment,* September/October 1993.
Sugg, Richard, "The Role of the Writer in the Player," in *Literature/Film Quarterly,* no. 1, 1994.
Murphy, Kathleen, "A Lion's Gate: The Cinema According to Robert Altman," in *Film Comment,* 1994.

Romney, Jonathan, "In the Time of Earthquakes," in *Sight and Sound,* March 1994.
Wollen, Peter, "Strike a Pose," in *Sight and Sound,* March 1995.

* * *

The American 1970s may have been dominated by a "New Wave" of younger, auteurist-inspired filmmakers including George Lucas, Peter Bogdanovich, Steven Spielberg, Martin Scorsese, and Francis Ford Coppola, all contemporaries as well as sometime colleagues. It is, however, an outsider to this group, the older Robert Altman, perhaps that decade's most consistent chronicler of human behavior, who could be characterized as the artistic rebel most committed to an unswerving personal vision. If the generation of whiz kids tends to admire the American cinema as well as its structures of production, Altman tends to regard the American cinema critically and to view the production establishment more as an adversary to be cunningly exploited on the way to an almost European ambiguity.

Although Altman has worked consistently within American genres, his work can instructively be seen as anti-genre: *McCabe and Mrs. Miller* is a kind of anti-western, exposing the myth of the heroic westerner (as described by Robert Warshow and executed by John Wayne and John Ford) and replacing it with an almost Marxist view of the Westerner as financier, spreading capitalism and corruption with opportunism and good cheer. *The Long Goodbye* sets itself in opposition to certain aspects of the hard-boiled detective genre, as Elliott Gould's Philip Marlowe reflects a moral stance decidedly more ambiguous than that of Raymond Chandler's conventional lonely moralist. Similarly, *Countdown* can be seen in relationship to the science-fiction film; *Thieves Like Us* (based on *They Live by Night*) in relationship to the bandit-gangster film; *That Cold Day in the Park* in relationship to the psychological horror film inaugurated by Alfred Hitchcock's *Psycho*; and *California Split* in relationship to that generic phenomenon so common to the 1970s, the "buddy film." Even *Nashville,* Altman's complex bicentennial musical released in 1975, can be seen in relationship to a generic tradition with roots in *Grand Hotel* and branches in *Earthquake,* for it is a kind of disaster film about the American dream.

Aside from his generic preoccupations, Altman seems especially interested in people. His films characteristically contain perceptive observations, telling exchanges, and moments of crystal clear revelation of human folly. Altman's comments are made most persuasively

Robert Altman

in relationship to a grand social organization: that of the upper classes and *nouveaux riches* in *A Wedding*; health faddists and, metaphorically, the American political process, in *Health*; and so forth. Certainly, Altman's films offer a continuous critique of American society: people are constantly using and exploiting others, though often with the tacit permission of those being exploited. One thinks of the country-western singers' exploitation by the politician's p.r. man in *Nashville,* for instance, or the spinster in *That Cold Day in the Park.* Violence is often the climax of an Altman film—almost as if the tensions among the characters must ultimately explode. Notable examples include the fiery deaths and subsequent "surprise ending" in *A Wedding,* or the climactic assassination in *Nashville.*

Another recurring interest for Altman in his preoccupation with the psychopathology of women: one thinks of the subtly encroaching madness of Sandy Dennis's sexually repressed spinster in *That Cold Day in the Park,* an underrated, early Altman film; the disturbing instability of Ronee Blakley in *Nashville*; the relationships among the unbalanced subjects of *Three Women,* based on one of Altman's own dreams; and the real/surreal visions of Susannah York in the virtual horror film, *Images.* Because almost all of Altman's characters tend to be hypocritical, psychotic, weak, or morally flawed in some way, with very few coming to a happy end, Altman has often been attacked for a kind of trendy cynicism. The director's cynicism, however, seems a result of his genuine attempt to avoid the conventional mythmaking of the American cinema. Altman imbues as many of his characters as possible with that sloppy imperfection associated with human beings as they are, with life as it is lived.

Performers enjoy working with Altman in part because he provides them with the freedom to develop their characters and often alter the script through improvisation and collaboration. Like Bergman, Altman has worked often with a stock company of performers who appear in one role after another, among them Elliott Gould, Sally Kellerman, Rene Auberjonois, Keith Carradine, Shelley Duvall, Michael Murphy, Bert Remsen, and Henry Gibson.

Altman's distinctive style transforms whatever subject he approaches. He often takes advantage of widescreen compositions in which the frame is filled with a number of subjects and details that compete for the spectator's attention. Working with cinematographer Vilmos Zsigmond, he has achieved films that are visually distinguished and tend toward the atmospheric. Especially notable are the use of the zoom lens in the smoky cinematography of *McCabe and Mrs. Miller*; the reds, whites, and blues of *Nashville*; the constantly mobile camera, specially mounted, of *The Long Goodbye,* which so effortlessly reflects the hazy moral center of the world the film presents; and the pastel prettiness of *A Wedding,* particularly the first appearance of that icon of the American cinema, Lillian Gish, whose subsequent filmic death propels the narrative.

Altman's use of multi-track sound is also incredibly complex: sounds are layered upon one another, often emanating from different speakers in such a way that the audience member must also decide what to listen for. Indeed, watching and listening to an Altman film inevitably requires an active participant: events unroll with a Bazinian ambiguity. Altman's Korean War comedy *M*A*S*H* was the director's first public success with this kind of soundtrack. One of his more extreme uses of this technique can be found in *McCabe and Mrs. Miller,* generally thought to be among the director's finest achievements.

Nashville, Altman's most universally acclaimed work, provides a panoramic view of the American experience and society as it follows the interrelated experiences of twenty-four characters in the country-western music capital. In its almost three-hour length, *Nashville* accumulates a power of the whole even greater than the vivid individual parts which themselves resonate in the memory: the incredibly controlled debut performance of Lily Tomlin and the sensitive performances of at least a dozen others; the lesson on sexual politics Altman delivers when he photographs several women listening to a song by Keith Carradine; the vulnerability of Ronee Blakley, who suffers a painful breakdown in front of her surprisingly fickle fans; the expressions on the faces of the men who watch Gwen Welles's painfully humiliating striptease; and the final cathartic song of Barbara Harris, as Altman suddenly reveals the conventional "Star is Born" myth in his apparent anti-musical, like a magician stunning us with an unexpected trick.

Overall, Altman's career itself has been rather weird. His output since *M*A*S*H* has been prodigious indeed, especially in light of the fact that a great number of his films have been financial and/or critical failures. In fact, several of his films, among them *A Perfect Couple* and *Quintet* (with Paul Newman) barely got a national release; and *Health* (which starred Glenda Jackson, Carol Burnett, James Garner, and Lauren Bacall) languished on the shelf for years before achieving even a limited release in New York City. The most amazing thing about Altman's *Popeye,* which was relatively successful with critics and the public (though not the blockbuster that Hollywood had counted on), was that Altman managed to secure the assignment at all. The film that emerged was one of the most cynical and ultimately disturbing of children's films, in line with Altman's consistent vision of human beings and social organization.

Altman's career in the 1980s veered sharply away from mainstream film, dominated instead by a number of film adaptations of theatre pieces, including *Come Back to the Five & Dime, Jimmy Dean, Jimmy Dean*; *Streamers*; *The Laundromat*; *Secret Honor*; *Beyond Therapy*; and *Fool for Love.* Although many of these works are fascinating and contain incredibly modulated performances and surprisingly evocative cinematography (particularly *Jimmy Dean*), these films have not been particularly influential or financially successful. But they allowed Altman to continue to make notable films in a Spielberg-dominated era that was otherwise largely hostile to his provocative filmmaking.

Vincent and Theo, one of the few Altman films in this period which did not start out as a play, received much positive notice. Altman's decision to preface his film with documentary footage of a present-day auction in which millions of dollars are offered for a single Van Gogh painting was particularly stunning in a Brechtian way. He then begins his narrative story of Van Gogh's lifetime financial failure, trying to remain true to his painter's vision. Certainly, it is the parallels between Van Gogh and Altman which incite the director's interest. *Tanner '88,* a mock documentary about the 1988 American presidential campaign which many critics consider among Altman's master works, was even more amazing. It was a cult hit which marked Altman's return to the kind of satire with which he had already excelled. Unfortunately, its distribution on cable TV prevented this work from reaching a wide audience.

The most stunning development in Altman's career is the total critical and financial comeback he made with 1992's *The Player,* a film that appeared long after most Hollywood executives had written him off. The most insightful and scathing satire about Hollywood and filmmaking today, *The Player* hilariously skewered one target after another (the pitch, the Hollywood restaurant, the Hollywood party, the dispensable writer), in the process winning the New York Film Critics Circle awards for Best Film and Best Director. Contributing to the film's popular success were the dozens of stars who took cameos as themselves in order to support Altman, whom they have always admired.

The success of *The Player* allowed Robert Altman to go forward with his most ambitious project since *Nashville,* another panoramic narrative featuring dozens of characters, this time set in contemporary Los Angeles and based on a group of interlocking stories by Raymond Carver. The result, *Short Cuts,* seems unquestionably a masterpiece, one of those rare contemporary American films which truly attempts to examine American values (or what passes for them) and dissect life as it is being lived today. The film is memorable in many respects, from its opening images of helicopters sweeping over Los Angeles to spray for the Med-fly infestation to its depictions of phone sex, urban violence, and earthquake; from its depiction of Angelenos struggling to connect with each other to their debilitating failures; from its overwhelmingly rich soundtrack and striking cinematography to its complex narrative structure and brilliant performances. *Short Cuts* is a key Altman film which will undoubtedly come to be regarded as a masterpiece of the American cinema as well.

In 1994 Altman took on the fashion industry in *Ready to Wear (Pret a Porter).* Critics and the public were much less kind in their regard for this panoramic satire, but the film was nevertheless witty and controlled, more subtle and light-hearted than had been anticipated. The film's finale—whereby a group of models parade naked—marked the witty and appropriate conclusion of Altman's satire on the political and ideological implications of fashion and its capacity to demean our values.

As a postscript on Altman, one should add that he, more than any other director, should never be counted out as an important force in American film culture. If his work is sometimes uneven, the fact that he continues to work on projects which are political, ideological, and personal—refusing to compromise his own artistic vision—is a sign that he remains, even in his seventies, the United States' single most ambitious *auteur.* His own future agenda includes two films based on the two plays comprising Tony Kushner's award-winning panorama *Angels in America,* widely praised as the most important American piece of theatre since Arthur Miller's *Death of a Salesman.* Although Altman might seem to be the perfect director, in a culminating masterpiece, to deal with AIDS, racism, homophobia, McCarthyism, Ethel Rosenberg, Mormon fundamentalism, the fall of Communism, the nature of capitalism, and God's culpability for problems in contemporary America, Altman's peripatetic popularity with Hollywood backers suggests that realization of these interlocking projects is by no means a sure thing, no matter how eagerly anticipated the results.

—Charles Derry

ALVAREZ, Santiago

Nationality: Cuban. **Born:** Havana, 1919. **Education:** University of Havana; Columbia University, New York. **Career:** After revolution, served as vice-president of newly formed Instituto Cubano del Arte e Industria Cinematograficas (ICAIC), 1959; director of the Latin American ICAIC newsreel, from 1960.

Films as Director:

1960 *Un año de libertad* (co-d)
1961 *Escambray*; *Muerte al invasor* (co-d)
1962 *Forjadores de la paz*; *Cumplimos*; *Crisis en el Caribe*
1963 *Ciclon*; *El Barbaro del Ritmo*; *Fidel en la URSS*
1964 *Via libre a la zafra del '64*; *Primeros Juegos Deportivos Militares*
1965 *Solidaridad Cuba y Vietnam*; *Cuba dos de enero*; *Pedales sobra Cuba*; *Now*; *Segunda Declaracion de la Habana*; *La escalada del chantaje*
1966 *Abril de Giron*; *Cerro Pelado*; *Año Siete*; *Ocho años de Revolucion*
1967 *La guerra olvidados* (*Laos, the Forgotten War*); *Hasta la victoria siempre* (*Till Victory Always*); *Golpeando en la selva*; *Hanoi, martes 13*
1968 *Amarrando el Cordon*; *L.B.J.*
1969 *Despegue a la 18.00*; *79 Primaveras* (*79 Springtimes of Ho Chi Minh*)
1970 *Once por cero*; *Piedra sobre piedra*; *El sueño del Pongo*; *Yanapanacuna*
1971 *Quemando tradiciones*; *Como, por qué y para qué asesina a un general?*; *La estampida*; *El pájaro del faro*
1972 *De America soy hijo ... y a ella me debo*
1973 *Y el cielo fue tomado por asalto*; *El tigre salto y mato ... pero morira ... morira* (*The Tiger Leaped and Killed, But He Will Die, He Will Die*)
1974 *60 Minutos con el primer mundial de boxeo amateur*; *Rescate*; *Los cuatro puentes*
1975 *Abril de Vietnam en el año del gato*; *El primer delegado*
1976 *El Tiempo es el viento*; *El sol no se puede tapar con un dedo*; *Luanda ya no es de San Pablo*; *Morir por la patria es vivir*; *Maputo*; *Meridiano Novo*; *Los Dragones de Ha-Long*
1977 *Mi Hermano Fidel*; *El Octubre de todos*
1978 *Sobre el problema fronterizo entre Kampuchea y Vietnam*; *... y la noche se hizo arcoiris*
1979 *El Gran salto al vacio*; *Tengo fe en ti*; *La cumbre que nos une*; *El desafio*
1980 *Celia, imagen del pueblo*; *Marcha del pueblo combatiente*; *El mayo de las tres banderas*; *Un Amazonus de pueblo embravecido*; *Lo que el viento se llevó*; *La guerra necessaria*
1981 *La importancia universal del hueco*; *Tiempo libre a la roca*; *Comenzo a retumbar el Momtombo*; *26 es también 19*; *Mazazo macizo*; *Contrapunto*
1982 *Nova sinfonia*; *A galope sobre la historia*; *Operación abril del Caribe*
1983 *Los refugiados de la Cueva del Muertro* (+ sc); *Biografía de un carnaval*; *Las campanas tambien pueden doblar mañana*
1984 *Gracias Santiago*; *Dos rostros y una sola imagen*; *El soñador del Kremlin*; *Por primera vez elecciones libres*
1985 *Taller de la vida*; *La soledad de los dioses*; *Reencuentro*
1986 *Las antípodas de la victoria*; *Aires de renovación en el meridiano 37*; *Memorias de un reencuentro*

Publications

By ALVAREZ: book—

Santiago Alvarez: Cronista del tercer mundo, edited by Edmundo Aray, Caracas, 1983.

By ALVAREZ: articles—

"Santiago Alvarez habla de su cine," in *Hablemos de Cine* (Lima), July/August 1970.
Interview in *Cineaste* (New York), vol. 6, no. 4, 1975.
"El Periodismo cinematografico," in *Cine Cubano* (Havana), no. 94, 1979.
"Cinema and Revolution: Talking with Santiago Alvarez," in *Issues: A Monthly Review of International Affairs* (London), May 1980.
Interview with M. Pereira, in *Cine Cubano* (Havana), no. 104, 1983.
Interview with C. Galiano and R. Chavez, in *Cine Cubano* (Havana), no. 107, 1984.
"Now," in *Cine Cubano* (Havana), no. 110, 1984.
"Hablar de estas fotos: Conversación con Santiago Alvarez," in *Revolución y Cultura* (Havana), November 1986.

On ALVAREZ: books—

Nelson, L., *Cuba: The Measure of a Revolution,* Minneapolis, 1972.

Santiago Alvarez

Myerson, Michael, *Memories of Underdevelopment: The Revolutionary Films of Cuba,* New York, 1973.
Chanan, Michael, editor, *Santiago Alvarez,* London, 1982.
Waugh, Thomas, editor, *"Show Us Life": Toward a History and Aesthetics of the Committed Documentary,* Metuchen, New Jersey, 1984.
Chanan, Michael, *The Cuban Image: Cinema and Cultural Politics in Cuba,* London, 1985.

On ALVAREZ: articles—

Sutherland, Elizabeth, "Cinema of Revolution—90 Miles from Home," in *Film Quarterly* (Berkeley), Winter 1961/62.
Douglas, M.E., "The Cuban Cinema," in *Take One* (Montreal), July/August 1968.
Adler, Renata, in *New York Times,* 10, 11, and 12 February 1969.
Engel, Andi, "Solidarity and Violence," in *Sight and Sound* (London), Autumn 1969.
Rubenstein, Lenny, "*79 Springtimes of Ho Chi Minh,*" in *Cineaste* (New York), Winter 1970/71.
Sauvage, P., "Cine Cubano," in *Film Comment* (New York), Spring 1972.
Chávez, R., "El internaciolalismo en el obra de Santiago Alvarez," in *Cine Cubano* (Havana), March 1978.
Burton, Julianne, "Introduction to Revolutionary Cuban Cinema," in *Jump Cut* (Chicago), December 1978.
Hood, Stuart, "Murder on the Way: Santiago Alvarez Season at NFT," in *New Statesman* (London), April 1980.
Mraz, John, "Santiago Alvarez: From Dramatic Form to Direct Cinema," in *Documentary Strategies: Society/Ideology/History in Latin American Documentary, 1950-1985,* Pittsburgh, 1990.

* * *

Predominantly associated with the educational or the exotic in the United States, the documentary film occupies a very different place in the cinema of revolutionary Cuba. Between 90 and 95 percent of the films produced under the revolution have been documentaries, and the man most responsible for the international stature of Cuban documentary cinema is Santiago Alvarez.

As the director of the weekly "Latin American Newsreel" produced by the Cuban Film Institute (ICAIC), Alvarez has directed an enormous number of newsreels as well as many other short and feature-length documentaries. Never having formally studied cinema, he became a filmmaker by "handling millions of feet of film." Alvarez feels himself to be a journalist, but believes that cinematic journalism should have a permanence beyond simple reportage. To achieve such transcendency, Alvarez's newsreels are typically monothematic and integrated, with the result that they appear more like individual documentary films than the sort of generalized news reporting normally associated with newsreels.

The dominant characteristic of Alvarez's style is the extraordinarily rhythmic blend of visual and audio forms. Alvarez utilizes everything at hand to convey his message: live and historical documentary footage, still photos, bits from TV programs and fiction films, animation, and an incredible range of audio accompaniment. Believing that "50 percent of the value of a film is in the soundtrack," Alvarez mixes rock, classical, and tropical music, sound effects, participant narration—even silence—into the furious pace of his visual images. For Alvarez, cinema has its own language, different from that of television or of radio, and the essence of this language is montage.

Alvarez's documentaries focus on both national and international themes. For example, *Ciclon* is an early newsreel on the effects of hurricane Flora in Cuba. Although it lacks the elaborate visual montage for which Alvarez later became famous, the film shows great skill in the use of sound. There is no verbal narration, and the track is limited to the source sound of trucks and helicopters, and the organ music which eerily punctuates the scenes of caring for the wounded and burying the dead.

Now, a short dealing with racism in the U.S. and edited to the rhythm of Lena Horne's song, shows the master at his best in working with still photographs. Particularly effective is a sequence in which Alvarez cuts between the chained hands of arrested blacks and the linked hands of protestors to suggest a dynamic of collective struggle in which people are seen not only as products of their circumstances, but as historical actors capable of changing their circumstances. Here, Alvarez fuses ideology and art by making graphic the third of Marx's "Theses on Feuerbach." Alvarez's tribute to Che Guevara, *Hasta la victoria siempre,* deals with much the same concept. He begins with a series of beautifully shot stills of poverty in the Altiplano. Then, following footage of Che speaking in the Sierra Maestra of Cuba, he dissolves a still of Che into a still of a Gulf Oil Company camp in Bolivia. Through this technique he links the earlier struggle in Cuba with the later guerrilla war in the Andes.

One of the finest examples of Alvarez's work is *79 Springtimes,* a beautifully controlled montage on Ho Chi Minh's life and death. He opens the short by ironically mixing elapsed-time photography of flowers opening with slow-motion footage of bombs falling from U.S. planes. He goes on to cut between scenes of U.S. atrocities in Vietnam and protest marches in the U.S., visually depicting the position that the real enemy is not the people of the U.S., but the ruling class and its mercenaries. In the final sequence, Alvarez uses what seems to be every available visual effect—torn and burned strips of film, film frames, bits of paper—to create an incredible animated montage. The soundtrack underscores the visual dynamic with music and poems by Ho Chi Minh and Jose Martí.

Alvarez continues to be thought of as one of the foremost documentary filmmakers in Latin America, although some consider his earlier short films to be superior to the later and longer works. This may result from the fact that in the earlier films the line between heroes (Che, Ho Chi Minh) and villains (U.S. imperialism and racism) was more clearly drawn, while the later works reflect the international compromises with the Soviet Union and reformist Latin American governments that have been required of the Cuban revolution. Nonetheless, Alvarez persists in his indefatigable quest for an "audacious and constantly renewed optic."

—John Mraz

ANDERS, Allison

Nationality: American. **Born:** Kentucky, 1955. **Education:** High-school dropout; attended junior college and graduated from the University of Southern California at Los Angeles, School of Theater, Film and Television. **Family:** Became unwed mother at age nineteen; two daughters. **Career:** Became acquainted with Wim Wenders, early 1980s; kept a journal while on the set of Wenders's *Paris, Texas,* 1983; waitressed and lived on and off welfare while attempting to start her career, mid-1980s; co-directed first feature, *Border Radio,* 1988; earned international acclaim for second feature, *Gas Food Lodging,* 1992. **Awards:** Nicholl Fellowship, Academy of Motion Picture Arts and Sciences; Samuel Goldwyn Award, for screenplay *Lost Highway;* Best New Director, New York Film Critics Circle, for *Gas Food Lodging,* 1992. **Address:** Cineville, Inc., Skywalker Studios, 1861 S. Bundy Drive, Los Angeles, CA 90025, U.S.A.

Films as Director/Screenwriter:

1988 *Border Radio* (co-d, co-sc)
1992 *Gas Food Lodging*
1993 *Mi Vida Loca (My Crazy Life)*
1995 *Four Rooms* (one segment of four-part film)

Publications

By ANDERS: articles—

"*Gas Food Lodging,*" interview by D. E. Williams in *Film Threat* (Beverly Hills, California), October 1992.
"Girl Gangs Get Their Colors," interview by Sheila Benson in *Interview* (New York), June 1994.

On ANDERS: articles—

Benenson, L. H., "A Director's Life Fuels Her Film," in *New York Times,* 26 July 1992.
Connelly, C., "Allison Anders," in *Premiere* (New York), August 1992.
Dargis, M., "Giving Direction," in *Village Voice* (New York), 18 August 1992.
Kort, M., "Filmmaker Allison Anders: Her Crazy Life," in *MS* (New York), May/June 1994.
McDonagh, Maitland, "Sad Girls," in *Film Comment* (New York), September/October 1994.

* * *

Allison Anders's most consequential film to date is *Gas Food Lodging,* a sharply observed character study which is most effective as a refreshingly realistic look at the travails of motherhood without fatherhood. Set within a family whose members are all women, it is a story of motherly love and concern, daughterly yearnings for freedom and independence, the realities of romantic love, and the characters' vulnerabilities and cravings for compassion and understanding.

Anders tells the story of Nora Evans (Brooke Adams), a truck stop waitress in the dusty town of Laramie, New Mexico. Nora is attempting to rear her two teenaged daughters, whose father "walked off" when they were very young. The eldest, seventeen-year-old Trudi (Ione Skye), is as rebellious and promiscuous as she is pretty. She has accumulated one too many unexcused absences from school; among her peers, she has earned a reputation for being "easy." Nora and Trudi constantly squabble, most particularly upon Trudi's arrival home at ungodly hours after hot-and-heavy dates with men who promise her the love and affection she covets. Nora is distressed because she does not want Trudi to be victimized by suitors who will make commitments they have no intention of keeping.

Trudi's kid sister, Shade (Fairuza Balk), is a sweetly innocent romantic who has not yet discovered the pitfalls of sexuality. Her concept of love has been gained from watching corny Spanish-language movies at the local theater. Shade longs for the traditional nuclear

Allison Anders

family, and is intent upon instigating a relationship between her mom and a man—just about any male who might make an appropriate mate for Nora and stepdad for her and Trudi. Will such a situation ever be possible? Or will there always be roadblocks that will prevent Shade's dream from becoming real (or, more to the point, from reflecting the outcomes of the movies to which she is addicted)?

The latter is certain to be the case, because Anders's characters exist within a world that is more reflective of reality. Unlike more traditional celluloid portraits of women on their own, none of the characters ends up being saved by a man. There are no handsome hunks on white horses to whisk them away from the drudgery of their lives. *Gas Food Lodging* is the polar opposite of a Hollywood assembly-line product like *Pretty Woman,* a Cinderella story whose spunky, squeaky-clean heroine just so happens to be a Hollywood Boulevard whore. She may love old movies just as passionately as Shade, do dental floss rather than crack, and be played by Julia Roberts; her savior may be a profiteer, but he is cute, doesn't drink, says no to drugs, and is transformed by love into a constructive citizen. *Pretty Woman* is a sugary entertainment package which, in its own perverse way, serves as a recruiting poster for a career as a hooker. It is also the type of film which, one safely assumes, would disgust Allison Anders.

Furthermore, in *Gas Food Lodging* Anders depicts characters you rarely see in Hollywood films: blue-collar workers who live ordinary lives and struggle for survival in unglamorous environments. Nora's plight as a single mother may be common in today's society, but it is one that rarely is acknowledged with any thought or depth in mainstream movies. Yet the lives of such characters are rich in dramatic possibility. At the core of *Gas Food Lodging* is an intelligent, nonsensationalistic story featuring women's points-of-view regarding men, sex, love, and dreams. Additionally, the film is highly autobiographical. While trying to jump-start her career, Anders herself worked as a waitress—and she is the single mother of two daughters (born in 1974 and 1977). However, the filmmaker has claimed that she modelled the character of Nora Evans after her own mother.

The films Anders made before and after *Gas Food Lodging* have been much less spectacular. *Border Radio,* set amid the Los Angeles punk scene, was barely noticed. *Mi Vida Loca (My Crazy Life)* is a well-intentioned chronicle of the plights of Latina girl gang members in East Los Angeles. Unlike most "teen-gang" movies, which focus on the personalities of males—with their female counterparts either decorations or prizes to be won in rumbles—*Mi Vida Loca* offers portraits of adolescent girls. Their evocative nicknames—Sad Girl, Mousie, Whisper—tell you all you need to know about them. And here, too, Anders is mostly interested in the manner in which the characters share camaraderie and form identities apart from the men. Unfortunately, the result is dramatically vague, a series of pasted-together episodes that do not add up to a cohesive whole.

Anders's attempt at a full-bodied portrayal of Latino girls in *Mi Vida Loca* may be linked to a secondary plot line in *Gas Food Lodging.* At one point, Trudi callously dismisses a young Mexican-American busboy as a wetback; later on, a friend of Shade whispers that the same character is a "cholo," a gangster and dope dealer who robs pizza deliverymen and steals car radios to support his illegitimate children. The lad, of course, proves to be something else altogether, an entirely sympathetic character.

Anders's segment in *Four Rooms,* a four-part feature co-directed with Alexandre Rockwell, Robert Rodriguez, and Quentin Tarantino, is equally run-of-the-mill. Titled *Strange Brew,* it is the senseless story of a coven of witches who go about trying to raise their goddess from the dead.

Anders's career is at a crossroads. Will she be able to come up with a commendable follow-up to *Gas Food Lodging,* or will history prove her a one-shot artist, a footnote among women filmmakers?

—Rob Edelman

ANDERSON, Lindsay

Nationality: British. **Born:** Lindsay Gordon Anderson in Bangalore, South India, 17 April 1923. **Education:** Attended Cheltenham College and Wadham College, Oxford. **Military Service:** Member of Army Intelligence Corps during World War II. **Career:** Editor, *Sequence* magazine, 1947-52; helped organize first Free Cinema program, National Film Theatre, 1956; directed first feature, *This Sporting Life,* 1963; associate artistic director, Royal Court Theatre, 1971-75; also directed TV plays and commercials. **Awards:** Oscar for Best Short Subject, for *Thursday's Children,* 1955; Palme d'Or, Cannes Festival, for *If...,* 1969. **Died:** Of a heart attack while vacationing in the Dordagne region of France, 30 August 1994.

Films as Director:

1948 *Meet the Pioneers* (+ sc, co-ed, narration)
1949 *Idlers That Work* (+ sc, narration)
1952 *Three Installations* (+ sc, narration); *Trunk Conveyor* (+ sc, narration); *Wakefield Express* (+ sc)
1953 *Thursday's Children* (co-d, + co-sc); *O Dreamland* (+ sc)
1955 *Green and Pleasant Land* (+ sc); *Henry* (+ sc, role); *The Children Upstairs* (+ sc); *A Hundred Thousand Children* (+ sc); *£20 a Ton* (+ sc); *Energy First* (+ sc); *Foot and Mouth* (+ sc, narration)
1957 *Every Day Except Christmas* (+ sc)
1963 *This Sporting Life*
1967 *The White Bus*; *Raz, dwa, trzy* (*The Singing Lesson*) (+ sc)
1969 *If...* (+ pr)
1972 *O Lucky Man!* (+ co-pr)
1974 *In Celebration*
1982 *Britannia Hospital*
1985 *Wish You Were There* (*Foreign Skies*)
1986 *The Whales of August*
1988 *Glory! Glory!*
1993 *Is That All There Is?* (+ sc, role)

Other Films:

1949 *Out of Season* (Brendon) (narrator)
1952 *The Pleasure Garden* (Broughton) (pr, role)
1956 *Together* (Mazzetti) (supervising ed)
1958 *March to Aldermaston* (supervising ed)
1960 *Let My People Go* (Krish) (sponsor)
1962 *The Story of Private Pooley* (Alsen) (English-language version of *Der Schwur des Soldaten Pooley*) (narrator)
1965 *The Threatening Sky* (Ivens) (English-language version of *Le Ciel, la terre*) (narrator)
1966 *Mucednici lásky* (*Martyrs of Love*) (Nemec) (role)
1967 *About "The White Bus"* (Fletcher) (role as himself)
1968 *Abel Gance—The Charm of Dynamite* (Brownlow) (for TV) (narrator); *Inadmissable Evidence* (Page) (role)
1969 *The Parachute* (Page) (for TV) (role)
1970 *Hetty King—Performer* (Robinson) (narrator)
1971 *A Mirror from India* (Sarabhai) (narrator)
1981 *Chariots of Fire* (Hudson) (role as schoolmaster)
1991 *Prisoner of Honor* (for TV) (role as war minister)
1992 *Blame It on the Bellboy* (role as Mr. Marshall)
1994 *Lucky Man* (role as himself)

Publications

By ANDERSON: books—

Making a Film: The Story of "Secret People," London, 1952.

If...: A Film by Lindsay Anderson, with David Sherwin, New York, 1969.
O Lucky Man!, with David Sherwin, New York, 1973.

By ANDERSON: articles—

"Angles of Approach," in *Sequence* (London), Winter 1947.
"The Need for Competence," in *Sequence* (London), Spring 1948.
"What Goes On," in *Sequence* (London), Summer 1948.
"Creative Elements," in *Sequence* (London), Autumn 1948.
"British Cinema: The Descending Spiral," in *Sequence* (London), Spring 1949.
"The Film Front," in *Sequence* (London), Summer 1949.
"Films of Alfred Hitchcock," in *Sequence* (London), Autumn 1949.
"Notes at Cannes," in *Sequence* (London), New Year issue 1950.
"The Director's Cinema?," in *Sequence* (London), Autumn 1950.
"Retrospective Review: *Wagonmaster* and *Two Flags West,*" in *Sight and Sound* (London), December 1950.
"Goldwyn at Claridges," in *Sequence* (London), New Year issue 1951.
"John Ford," in *Films in Review* (New York), February 1951.
"Minnelli, Kelly and *An American in Paris,*" in *Sequence* (London), New Year issue 1952.
"As the Critics Like It: Some Personal Choices," in *Sight and Sound* (London), October/December 1952.
"Only Connect: Some Aspects of the Work of Humphrey Jennings," in *Sight and Sound* (London), April/June 1953; reprinted in *The Documentary Tradition,* edited by Lewis Jacobs, New York, 1974.
"Encounter with Prévert," in *Sight and Sound* (London), July/September 1953.
"French Critical Writing," in *Sight and Sound* (London), October/December 1954.
"Stand Up! Stand Up!," in *Sight and Sound* (London), Autumn 1956.
"Notes from Sherwood," in *Sight and Sound* (London), Winter 1956.
"Ten Feet Tall," in *Sight and Sound* (London), Summer 1957.
"The Critical Issue: A Discussion Between Paul Rotha, Basil Wright, Lindsay Anderson, Penelope Houston," in *Sight and Sound* (London), Autumn 1957.
"Two Inches Off the Ground," in *Sight and Sound* (London), Winter 1957.
"Get Out and Push!," in *Declaration,* edited by Tom Maschler, London, 1958.
"Sport, Life and Art," in *Films and Filming* (London), February 1963.
"An Interview with Lindsay Anderson," with Peter Cowie, in *Film Quarterly* (Berkeley), Summer 1964.
"The Film Maker and the Audience," in *Film Makers on Film Making,* edited by Harry Geduld, Bloomington, Indiana, 1967.
Interview, in *Documentary Explorations: 15 Interviews with Filmmakers,* by G. Roy Levin, New York, 1971.
"Stripping the Veils Away," an interview with David Robinson, in the *Times* (London), 21 April 1973.
"From Theater to Film ... Lindsay Anderson," an interview with M. Carducci, in *Millimeter* (New York), January 1975.
"Revolution Is the Opium of the Intellectuals," an interview with E. Rampell, in *Cineaste* (New York), vol. 12, no. 4, 1983.
"Lindsay Anderson, Unfashionable Humanist, in Conversation," an interview with Gerald Pratley, in *Cinema Canada* (Montreal), June 1985.
Interview in *American Cinematographer* (Los Angeles), October 1987.
Interview with John Russell Taylor, in *Films and Filming* (London), March 1988.
Interview with S. Stewart and L. Friedman, in *Film Criticism,* vol. 16, no. 1, 1991/92.

On ANDERSON: books—

Manvell, Roger, *New Cinema in Britain,* New York, 1969.
Sussex, Elizabeth, *Lindsay Anderson,* New York, 1969.
Barsam, Richard, *Nonfiction Film,* New York, 1973.
Silet, Charles L. P., *Lindsay Anderson: A Guide to References and Resources,* Boston, 1979.
Graham, Allison, *Lindsay Anderson,* Boston, 1981.

On ANDERSON: articles—

Berger, John, "Look at Britain!," in *Sight and Sound* (London), Summer 1957.
Milne, Tom, "*This Sporting Life,*" in *Sight and Sound* (London), Summer 1962.
Robinson, David, "Anderson Shooting *If...,*" in *Sight and Sound* (London), Summer 1968.
Gladwell, David, "Editing Anderson's *If...,*" in *Screen* (London), January/February 1969.
Lovell, Alan, and Jim Hillier, "Free Cinema," in *Studies in Documentary,* New York, 1972.
Lovell, Alan, "The Unknown Cinema of Britain," in *Cinema Journal* (Evanston), Spring 1972.
Wilson, D., "*O Lucky Man!,*" in *Sight and Sound* (London), Summer 1973.
Taylor, John, "Lindsay Anderson," in *Directors and Directions,* London, 1975.
Lovell, Alan, "Brecht in Britain—Lindsay Anderson," in *Screen* (London), Winter 1975.
Durgnat, Raymond, "Britannia Waives the Rules," in *Film Comment* (New York), July/August 1976.
Lefèvre, Raymond, "Lindsay Anderson, ou la fidelité au Free Cinema," in *Image et Son* (Paris), October 1982.
Schickel, Richard, "Ford Galaxy," in *Film Comment* (New York), March-April 1984.
Houston, Penelope, "Parker, Attenborough, Anderson," in *Sight and Sound* (London), Summer 1986.
McCarthy, Todd, "Lindsay Anderson," in *Variety,* 5 September 1994.
Kenny, Glenn, "The Magnificient Anderson," in *Entertainment Weekly,* 16 September 1994.
Cox, Jay, "Lindsay Anderson, 1923-1994: In Celebration," in *Film Comment,* November/December 1994.

* * *

In a 1958 essay entitled "Get Out and Push," Lindsay Anderson expressed his approach to working in the cinema. The way Anderson, the individual, approached working in the cinema paralleled the world view he put forth in feature films: the individual must examine the basis of the system within which he finds himself, "the motives that sustain it and the interests that it serves." It is the responsibility of the individual to actively seek a new self-definition beyond the confines of the established system; the individual cannot look for change to come from or through any outside authority—political, social, or spiritual. This theme is consistently present in Anderson's feature films.

In *This Sporting Life,* Anderson approaches the repression of a traditionally structured society through the personal, subjective story of Frank Machin and Margaret Hammond. The setting of *This Sporting Life,* an industrial northern city, is an environment divided into economic classes, a division which serves to emphasize the central problem of the film—the division within Frank Machin. Machin finds himself limited to the realm of the physical, and constantly attempts to connect with others on an emotional level. Despite his attempts, he is only seen in terms of his physical qualities; he is valued only when he is participating in the physical act of playing rugby.

Frank Machin is aware of his limitations but does not know how to change; he lacks direction. He tries to make others responsible for his

Lindsay Anderson © Roger Mayne

happiness: Margaret Hammond, the rugby team, and even the elites of society who populate the world of Mr. and Mrs. Weaver, owners of the rugby team. Machin constantly attempts to break into the established system, seemingly unaware that it is this same system which controls and restrains him.

Mick Travis, the protagonist of Anderson's second feature film, *If...*, struggles instead to break out of the established system. Mick takes on the responsibility of action, and although his revolution is not complete, he does not remain trapped like Frank. The environment in *If...*, the English public school system, is a metaphor for the "separation of intellect from imagination," according to Elizabeth Sussex. The environment of College House does not allow for the creative development of the individual. It encourages separation and fragmentation of the self.

Film technique in *If...* also serves to reveal the narrative theme of the division of the self. The chapter headings physically divide the film into rigidly ordered sections, reflecting the separation of intellect and imagination encouraged by the nature of the tradition of College House. These chapter headings, along with the alternation between black and white and color film, function as distancing devices, making the viewer more aware of the medium.

A narrative technique Anderson used to illustrate the process that leads to Mick's eventual break from the system is the establishment of verbal language as an essential part of the structure of College House. When Mick expresses his disdain for College House through words, they are simply absorbed by the system. There is no change in Mick's situation until he initiates action by bayoneting the college chaplain. After this point, Mick no longer recites revolutionary rhetoric; in fact, he rarely speaks. He is no longer existing within the structure of College House. Totally free of the system, Mick launches into the destruction of the established order. Mick is no longer acted upon but is the creator of action; in this respect, he triumphs where Frank Machin fails.

In *O Lucky Man!*, the thematic sequel to *If...*, the medium of film itself becomes one of the narrative themes, and self-reflexive film techniques serve to reveal not only the narrative theme of self-definition, but also the process of filmmaking. The titles used in *O Lucky Man!* announce the different sections of the film but do not impose order; on the contrary, their abrupt appearance and brevity tend to interrupt the order of the narrative. It is as if the medium of film itself breaks through to remind the viewer of its existence. Indeed the medium, specifically the energy the medium generates, is one of the themes of *O Lucky Man!* The process of creation in the medium far exceeds anything Mick accomplishes in the narrative until the two meet in the final sequence.

Mick Travis, the character, confronts Lindsay Anderson, the director, at an audition for the film *O Lucky Man!* Mick obediently projects the different emotions Anderson demands of him until he is asked to smile. It is at this point that Mick finally takes action and rejects a direct order: "What is there to smile about?" he asks. Mick is looking outside himself for motivation, as he has done throughout the film, before he will take action. Anderson, exasperated, strikes Mick with a script. After receiving the blow, Mick is able to smile. He soon finds that he is one of the actors in the film; he too is capable of creating action.

Britannia Hospital, the final work in the series begun by *If...*, presents a much darker vision than Anderson's previous films. As in *If...*, the physical environment of the film—the hospital—is a metaphor for a static, repressive system. Unlike *If...*, this film contains little hope for change or progress, not for the individual and certainly not within the system itself. Mick Travis appears in this film as an investigative reporter who has achieved success by selling "something the people want," a reference to his former position in *O Lucky Man!* and a description of his motives as a news reporter. He is attempting to expose the questionable experiments of Britannia Hospital staff member Dr. Millar, the same unethical researcher from *O Lucky Man!* Although Mick puts up a fight, the system finally overwhelms him in this film.

Glory! Glory!, a Home Box Office production, is somewhat of a synthesis of Anderson's previous work in both theme and technique. The institution that stands as metaphor in this case is one peculiar to the United States, a television evangelism empire—The Church of the Companions of Christ. Like the school in *If...*, this institution has a verbal language essential to its structure, the use of which sanctions just about any action. Throughout the film people have "revelations" or "visions" in which God makes key decisions for them, removing all personal responsibility. Any action is justifiable—deception, fraud, blackmail—as long as it is done in "a holy cause" or "for the church."

The film techniques Anderson uses in *Glory! Glory!* are related to his earlier works. The medium is present throughout the narrative in the form of chapter headings and blackouts between chapters. Music is important to the narrative, as it is in *O Lucky Man!*, but in the later film it is integrated into the narrative structure rather than used as a distancing device.

The theme of personal responsibility for self-definition is clearly seen in the character of Ruth. She struggles throughout the film with the idea of who she wants to be and with the identities others want to impose on her. She reaches a key point in her personal progression when she admits that she has always needed some kind of crutch—sex, drugs, God. Not long after realizing that she has been looking outside herself for an identity, Ruth reveals that she finally understands God. In essence, she has created her own god, her own mythology. Ruth remains within the system, but for the first time actually believes in what she is "selling" because she has defined for herself the "authority" and the basis for the system.

Anderson's other features, *In Celebration* and *The Whales of August,* contain more subjective narratives but still explore the theme of the individual's responsibility for self-definition. In his last film, *Is That All There Is?*, an autobiographical documentary made for the BBC, Anderson presents himself as such an individual: an independent artist who actively sought a self-definition beyond the confines of the established system.

—Marie Saeli

ANGELOPOULOS, Theodoros

Nationality: (Surname also spelled "Anghelopoulos") Greek. **Born:** Athens, 27 April 1935. **Education:** Studied in Athens, 1953-59, Sorbonne, Paris, 1961-64, and at IDHEC, Paris, 1962-63. **Military Service:** 1959-60. **Career:** Film critic for left-wing journal *Dimoktatiki Allaghi* until its suppression in 1967 coup; worked as lawyer until 1969; began association with cinematographer Giorgios Arvanitis on *Reconstruction,* 1970; taught at Stavrakou Film School in 1970s. **Awards:** Georges Sadoul Award, 1971; FIPRESCI Award, 1973, for *Days of '36*; FIPRESCI Grand Prix, Golden Age Award, B.F.I. Best Film, Interfilm Award, for *The Travelling Players*; Golden Hugo Award, for *The Hunters*; Golden Lion Award, Venice, 1980; Chevalier des Arts et des Lettres.

Films as Director and Scriptwriter:

1968 *Ekpombi* (*The Broadcast*; *L'Emission*)
1970 *Anaparastassi* (*Reconstruction*; *Reconstitution*) (+ ro)
1972 *Mères tou 36* (*Days of '36*; *Jours de 36*)

1975 ***O Thiasos*** *(The Travelling Players; Le Voyage des comédiens)*
1977 *I Kynighi (The Hunters)* (+ co-pr)
1980 *O Megalexandros (Alexander the Great)* (+ pr)
1982 *Athens* (doc)
1984 *Taxidi sta Kithira (Voyage to Cythera)*
1986 *O Melissokomos (The Beekeeper)*
1988 *Topio stia Omichli (Landscape in the Mist)*
1991 *The Suspended Step of the Stork* (+pr)
1995 *Ulysses' Gaze* (+pr)

Other Films:

1968 *Kieron* (role)

Publications

By ANGELOPOULOS: articles—

"Mes films sont des appels à la discussion ...," interview with N. Ghali, in *Cinéma* (Paris), September/October 1975.
"*Le Voyage des comédiens*," interview with J.-P. Brossard and others, in *Image et Son* (Paris), November 1975.
Interview with Michel Ciment, in *Positif* (Paris), June 1977.
Interview with D. Rabourdin, in *Cinéma* (Paris), August/September 1977.
"Les Chasseurs," interview with O. Barrot and M. Demopoulos, in *Ecran* (Paris), November 1977.
"Animating Dead Space and Dead Time," interview and article with T. Mitchell, in *Sight and Sound* (London), Winter 1980-81.
Interviews with Michel Ciment, in *Positif* (Paris), February 1985, May 1987, and May 1991.
Interview with G. Merat, in *Revue du Cinéma* (Paris), November 1988.
Interview with H. Petrakis, in *Positif* (Paris), December 1991.
Interview with E. Castiel, in *Sequences*, January 1992.
"National Culture and Individual Vision," interview with A. Horton and D. Georgakas, in *Cineaste*, vol. 19, no. 2/3, 1992.
Interview with C. Siniscalchi, in *Rivista del Cinematografo*, March 1993.
Interview with A. Faber, in *Filmvilag*, vol. 36, no. 1, 1993.

On ANGELOPOULOS: books—

Schuster, Mel, *The Contemporary Greek Cinema*, Metuchen, New Jersey, 1979.
Orati, Daniela, *Thodoros Anghelopoulos*, Venice, 1982.
Estève, Michel, *Theo Angelopoulos*, Paris, 1985.
Ciment, Michel, and Hélène Tiarchent, *Theo Angelopoulos*, Paris, 1989.
Kolovos, Nikos, *Theo Angelopoulos*, Athens, 1990.
O'Grady, Gerald, editor, *Theo Angelopoulos* (MOMA Exhibition Catalogue), New York, 1990.

On ANGELOPOULOS: articles—

Cineforum (Bergamo), September 1975.
Positif (Paris), October 1975.
Avant-Scène du Cinéma (Paris), December 1975.
Giacci, V., in *Cineforum* (Bergamo), September 1976.
Horton, Andrew, "Theodoros Angelopoulos and the New Greek Cinema," in *Film Criticism* (Meadville, Pennsylvania), Fall 1981.
Dossier on Angelopoulos, in *Cinéma* (Paris), November 1982.
"Angelopoulos Section" of *Revue du Cinéma/Image et Son* (Paris), January 1985.
Amengual, Barthélémy, "Une esthetique 'théatrale' de la realité: sur Theo Angelopoulos," in *Positif* (Paris), February 1985.
"Angelopoulos Issue" of *Revue Belge du Cinéma* (Brussels), Spring 1985.
Sight and Sound (London), Winter 1988 and Autumn 1989.
Brown, Georgia, in *Village Voice* (New York), 20 February 1990.
Holden, S., "A Search for a Fictive Father," in *New York Times*, 14 September 1990.
Rollet, S., "Theo Angelopoulos ou le cinema comme theatre du temps," in *Positif* (Paris), December 1991.
"Der Fundamentalismus kennt nur Grenzen," in *Filmbulletin*, vol. 33, no. 5/6, 1991.
Bolzoni, F., "Contro l'effimero," in *Rivista del Cinematografo*, March 1993.

* * *

Theodoros Angelopoulos's considerable achievements in cinema during the 1970s and 1980s have made him not only the most important Greek filmmaker to date, but one of the truly creative and original artists of his time. In 1970 he convinced producer George Papalios to finance his first film, *Anaparastassi*. The story follows the pattern of a crime tale à la James Cain. A Greek peasant is killed by his wife and her lover on his return from Germany, where he had gone to find work. A judge tries to reconstruct the circumstances of the murder, but finds himself unable to communicate with the accused, who belong to a totally different culture. To shoot this Pirandellian story of misunderstanding, Angelopoulos adopted an austere style featuring long camera movements that show a bleak and desolate Greek landscape far removed from the tourist leaflets. Reminiscent of Visconti's *Ossessione*, this is a film noir that opens the way to more daring aesthetic ventures.

Angelopoulos's trilogy of *Days of 36, The Travelling Players*, and *The Hunters* can be seen as an exploration of contemporary Greek history. If his style shows some influences—particularly Jancsó's one reel-one take methodology and Antonioni's slow, meditative mood—Angelopoulos has nevertheless created an authentic epic cinema akin to Brecht's theatre in which aesthetic emotion is counterbalanced by a reflexive approach that questions the surfaces of reality. The audience is not allowed to identify with a central character, nor to follow a dramatic development, nor given a reassuring morality. The director boldly goes from the present to the past within the same shot, and in *The Hunters* broadens his investigation by including the fantasies of his characters. The sweep of a movie like *Travelling Players*, which includes songs and dances, is breathtaking. Its tale of an actors group circulating through Greece from 1939 to 1952 performing a pastoral play is transformed into a four-hour earth odyssey.

Angelopoulos's masterpiece was preceded by the haunting *Days of 36*. This political thriller about a murder in a prison proved a prelude to events of national importance. It is the director's most radical use of off-screen space and off-screen sound, of the dialectic between the seen and the unseen. With its closed doors, whispering voices in corridors, and silhouettes running to and fro, it evokes the mystery that surrounds the exercise of power.

Angelopoulos's fifth film, *Alexander the Great*, breaks new ground: it deals with myth and develops the exploration of the popular unconscious already present in *Travelling Players* and *The Hunters*. At the turn of the twentieth century, a bandit is seen as the reincarnation of the Macedonian king. He kidnaps some English residents in Greece and leads them to the mountains. The kidnapper tries to blackmail the British government but ends up killing his hostages. Angelopoulos opposes several groups: the foreigners, the outlaws, some Italian anarchists who have taken refuge in Greece, and village people who try to establish a utopian community. The director's indictment of hero-worship and his portrayal of diverse forms of political failure reveal a

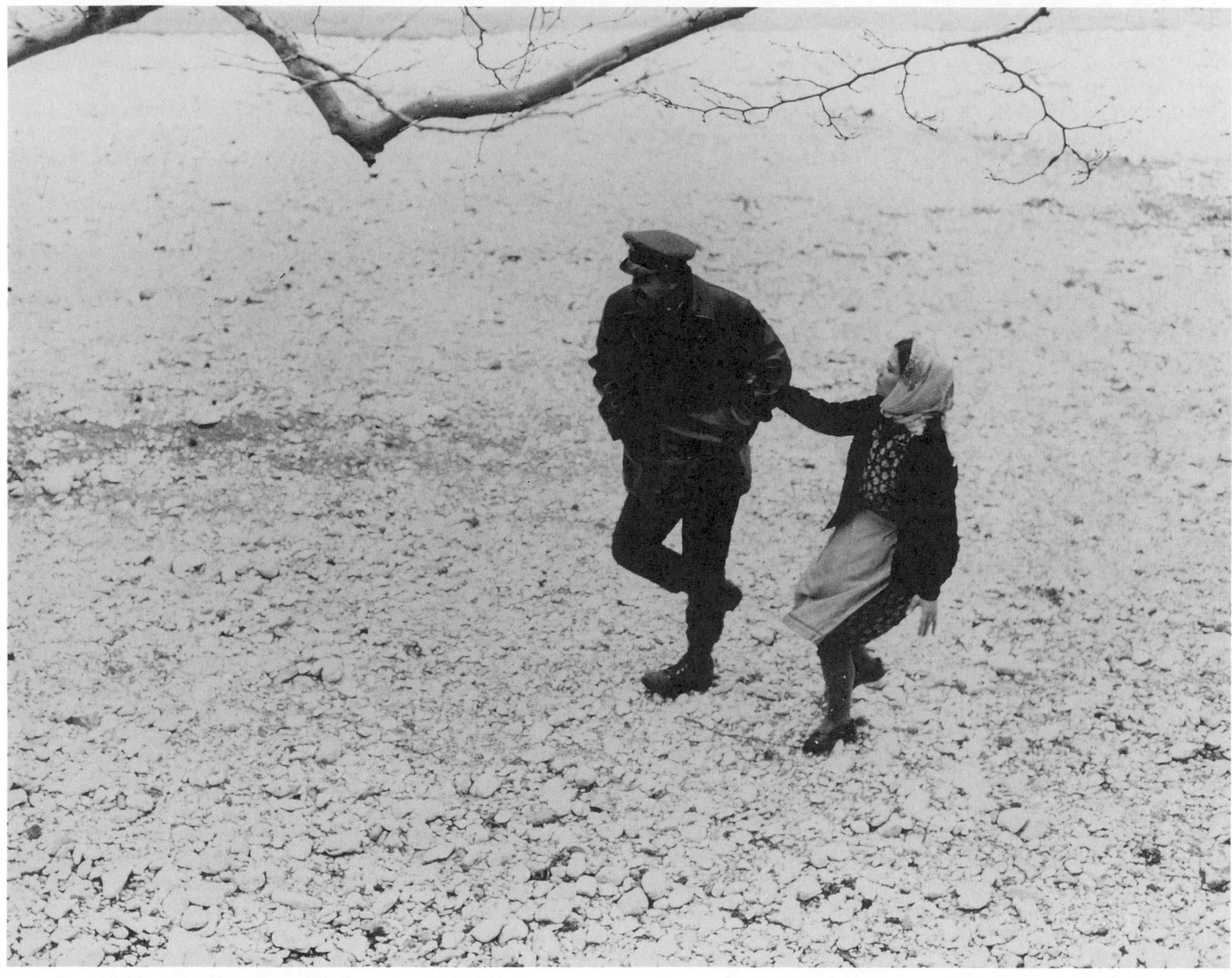

Theodoros Angelopoulos: ***Anaparastassi***

growing pessimism in his works. But his style is as masterful as ever, reaching a kind of austere grandeur reminiscent of Byzantine mosaics. Few have blended political investigation with a search for new forms of expression with such satisfying results.

—Michel Ciment

ANGER, Kenneth

Nationality: American. **Born:** Santa Monica, California, 1930. **Career:** Played changeling in Max Reinhardt's film *A Midsummer Night's Dream,* 1934; studied tap-dancing in class including Shirley Temple, 1935; completed first film, 1941; after moving to Europe, first edition of *Hollywood Babylon* published in France, 1959; returned to U.S., 1962; following destruction of his film *Lucifer Rising,* placed an ad in *Variety* "In Memoriam Kenneth Anger 1947-1967," and returned to Europe, 1967; completed second version of *Lucifer Rising,* 1974 (released 1980). **Address:** c/o American Federation of Arts Film Program, 41 E. 65th St., New York, NY 10021, U.S.A.

Films (Conception, Direction, Photography, and Editing):

1941 *Who Has Been Rocking My Dream Boat*
1941/42 *Tinsel Tree*
1942 *Prisoner of Mars*
1943 *The Nest*
1944 *Escape Episode*
1945 *Drastic Demise*
1946 *Escape Episode* (sound version)
1947 *Fireworks** (+ role as The Dreamer)
1948 *Puce Women* (unfinished)
1949 *Puce Moment**; *The Love That Whirls* (unfinished)
1950 *La Lune des Lapins** (*Rabbit's Moon*) (conception, d, and ed only, + prod. design)
1951/52 *Maldoror* (unfinished)
1953 *Eaux d'artifice** (+ costume design); *Le Jeune Homme et la mort*
1954 *Inauguration of the Pleasure Dome** (+ role as Hecate)

1955 *Thelema Abbey* (conception, d, and ed only)
1962/63 ***Scorpio Rising****
1965 *Kustom Kar Kommandos**
1969 *Invocation of My Demon Brother**
1971 *Rabbit's Moon*
1974 *Lucifer Rising**
1980 *Lucifer Rising** (second version) (+ role as Magus)
1989 *Mouse Heaven*

Note: * indicates films contained and distributed in Anger's definitive portfolio "The Magick Lantern Cycle."

Other Films:

1985 *He Stands in a Desert Counting the Seconds of His Life* (role as himself)
1992 *Hollywood Babylon* (for TV) (advisor)
1993 *Jonas in the Desert* (role as himself)

Publications

By ANGER: books—

Hollywood Babylon, Phoenix, Arizona, 1965; reprinted San Francisco, 1975.
Magick Lantern Cycle: A Special Presentation in Celebration of the Equinox Spring 1966, New York, 1966.
Hollywood Babylon II, New York, 1984.

By ANGER: articles—

Interview in *Spider Magazine,* v. 1, no. 13, 1965.
Interview in *Film Culture* (New York), Spring 1966.
Article in *Filmmakers on Filmmaking,* edited by Harry Geduld, Bloomington, Indiana, 1967.
Interview with Bruce Martin and Joe Medjuck, in *Take One* (Montreal), August 1967.
Interview with Lenny Lipton, in *Filmmakers Newsletter* (Ward Hill, Massachusetts), November 1967.
Correspondence between Kenneth Anger and Paul Johnston, in *Film Culture* (New York), nos. 70-71, 1983.
Interview with J. English, in *On Film* (Los Angeles), Summer 1983.
Interview in *City Limits* (London), 7 February 1986.

On ANGER: books—

Battcock, Gregory, editor, *The New American Cinema,* New York, 1967.
Youngblood, Gene, *Expanded Cinema,* New York, 1970.
Sitney, P. Adams, *Visionary Film,* New York, 1974.
Hanhardt, John, and others, *A History of the American Avant-Garde Cinema,* New York, 1976
Haller, Robert A., *Kenneth Anger,* St. Paul, Minnesota, 1980.
Burchfield, John, *Kenneth Anger: The Shape of His Achievements,* New York, n.d.
O'Pray, Michael, and Jayne Pilling, *Into the Pleasure Dome: The Films of Kenneth Anger,* London, 1990.

On ANGER: articles—

"Filmography of Kenneth Anger," in *Film Culture* (New York), no. 31, 1963/64.
Kelman, Kenneth, "Thanatos in Chrome," and P. Adams Sitney, "Imagism in Four Avant-Garde Films," in *Film Culture* (New York), Winter 1963/64.
Micha, Rene, "Le Nouveau Cinéma," in *Les Temps modernes* (Paris), no. 214, 1964.
Kelman, Kenneth, "Appendix to Thanatos in Chrome," in *Film Culture* (New York), Spring 1964.
Alexander, Thomas, "San Francisco's Hipster Cinema," in *Film Culture* (New York), no. 44, 1967.
Cornwall, Regina, "On Kenneth Anger," in *December* (New York), no. 1, 1968.
Rayns, Tony, "*Lucifer*: A Kenneth Anger Kompendium," in *Cinema* (Cambridge), October 1969.
Sitney, P. Adams, "The Avant-Garde: Kenneth Anger and George Landow," in *Afterimage* (Rochester, New York), no. 2, 1970.
Mekas, Jonas, Richard Whitehall, and P. Adams Sitney, "Three Notes on *Invocation of My Demon Brother,*" in *Film Culture* (New York), Winter/Spring 1970.
Magny, Joel, "Collectif jeune cinéma: 3e nuit blanche," in *Cinéma* (Paris), April 1972.
"Anger at Work," in *Cinema Rising,* April 1972.
Rowe, C., "Illuminating Lucifer," in *Film Quarterly* (Berkeley), Summer 1974.
Saslow, James, "Kenneth Anger: Holding a Magick Lantern Up to the Future," in *Advocate,* 23 July 1981.
Hardy, Robin, "Kenneth Anger: Master in Hell," and Michael Wade, "Kenneth Anger: Personal Traditions and Satanic Pride," in *Body Politic,* April 1982.
Hoberman, J., "Sympathy for the Devil," in *American Film* (Washington, D.C.), March 1981.
Wees, W. C., "Before *Lucifer*: Preternatural Light in the Films of Kenneth Anger," in *Cine-Tracts* (Montreal), Summer-Fall 1982.
Rayns, Tony, "The Elusive Lucifer," in *Monthly Film Bulletin* (London), September 1982.
"Kenneth Anger," in *Film Dope* (London), March 1988.

* * *

One of the key figures of the postwar American avant-garde, Kenneth Anger represents a fiercely original talent, relatively free of the independent circles and movements which his own work managed to anticipate in almost every case. Creator of an *oeuvre* and a persona defined by their dialectical relationship to dominant representational, ideological, industrial, sexual, and aesthetic practices, Anger embodies the "radical otherness" of the avant-garde filmmaker, casting himself not only outside the mainstream, but as its negative image. While other experimentalists were exploring "ways of seeing" through cinematic abstraction, Anger remained committed to a search for meanings, even as his films pursued a variety of aesthetic paths. Anger's meanings emerge from his subversive reworkings of sources already charged with significance: the iconography of American popular culture (movie stars, comic strips, car clubs); the conventional rhetoric of narrative forms (from the *commedia dell'arte* to the lyrics of rock songs); the imagery of classic cinema (Cocteau, Eisenstein, DeMille); and the symbolism of various mythologies (Egyptian, Greek, astrological, alchemical), centered by the cosmology of master "magickian" Aleister Crowley.

Anger gained international prominence and notoriety at the age of seventeen with his film *Fireworks,* in which he appeared as the protagonist of a homoerotic fantasy in the oneiric tradition of Cocteau and Maya Deren, shot through with the romantic sadism of the American film noir. Three years later, he made *Rabbit's Moon,* a delicately humorous, Méliès-like fantasy involving a Pierrot character and a magic lantern, shot in Cocteau's own studio in Paris. Another three years found Anger in Italy, where he choreographed an elaborately baroque game of hide-and-seek through Tivoli's water gardens in *Eaux d'artifice.* Focusing at intervals on the visual patterns of water flowing from the fountains, this film experiments with the textures of an

Kenneth Anger with the star of *Mouse Heaven*

abstract filmic image a full two years before Brakhage's *Wonder Ring*. Yet, characteristically, the multiple superimpositions of Anger's colorful mass/masquerade *Inauguration of the Pleasure Dome* have less to do with abstraction than with an effort to achieve a magical condensation of mythological imagery. *Scorpio Rising,* however, remains Anger's most influential and original work. A tour-de-force collage of pop imagery, it is a paean to the American motorcyclist, a revelation of the violent, homoerotic undercurrent of American culture, and a celebration of the forces of chaos in the universe.

Anger spent most of the mid- to late-1960s on two abortive projects. His *Kustom Kar Kommandos* was cut short by the death of the young man playing its protagonist, although one sensual sequence, involving the dusting of a custom hot rod with a powder puff, has survived. Far more ambitious, however, was a master opus entitled *Lucifer Rising,* a project cut tragically short when, at a 1967 San Francisco screening of the work-in-progress, the single print of the film was stolen by one of the film's actors, Manson cultist Bobby Beausoleil, and was supposedly buried somewhere in Death Valley, never to be recovered. This event was followed by Anger's self-imposed retirement, interrupted in 1969 by the appearance of an eleven-minute structural black mass constructed largely of *Lucifer's* outtakes, backed by a maddeningly monotonous soundtrack by Mick Jagger, and entitled *Invocation of My Demon Brother.*

By 1974, however, Anger had completed another version of *Lucifer Rising,* a dense meditative work shot mostly in Egypt, imbued with Crowleian mysticism and most memorable for the thoroughly uncanny image of a pinkish flying saucer hovering above the pyramids. The far more complete version finally released by Anger in 1980 marks a quantum leap in terms of *Lucifer Rising's* complexity, and remains the *chef-d'oeuvre* of Anger's career.

—Ed Lowry

ANTONIONI, Michelangelo

Nationality: Italian. **Born:** Ferrara, Italy, 29 September 1912. **Education:** Studied at University of Bologna, 1931-35, and at Centro Sperimentale di Cinematografica, Rome, 1940-41. **Career:** Journalist and bank teller, 1935-39; moved to Rome, 1939; film critic for *Cinema* (Rome) and others, 1940-49; assistant director on *I due Foscari* (Fulchignoni), 1942; wrote screenplays for Rossellini, Fellini, and others, 1942-52; directed first film, *Gente del Po,* 1943 (released 1947). **Awards:** Special Jury Prize, Cannes Festival, for *L'avventura,* 1960, and *L'eclisse,* 1962; FIPRESCI Award from Venice Festival, for *Il deserto Rosso,* 1964; Best Director Award, National Society of Film Critics, for *Blow-Up,* 1966; Palme d'Or, Cannes Festival, for *Blow-Up,* 1967. **Address:** Via Vicenzo Tiberio 18, Rome, Italy.

Films as Director:

1950 *Cronaca di un amore* (*Story of a Love Affair*) (+ co-sc)
1952 *I Vinti* (*I nostri figli*; *The Vanquished*) (+ co-sc)
1953 *La signora senza camelie* (*Camille without Camelias*) (+ co-sc); "Tentato suicidio" episode of *L'Amore in città* (+ sc)
1955 *Le amiche* (*The Girlfriends*) (+ co-sc)
1957 *Il grido* (*The Outcry*) (+ co-sc)
1959 ***L'avventura*** (+ co-sc)
1960 ***La notte*** (*The Night*) (+ co-sc)
1962 ***L'eclisse*** (*The Eclipse*) (+ co-sc)
1964 ***Deserto rosso*** (*Red Desert*) (+ co-sc)
1965 "Prefizione" episode of *Tre Volti* (+ sc)
1966 ***Blow-Up*** (+ co-sc)
1970 *Zabriskie Point* (+ co-sc)
1972 *Chung Kuo* (*La cina*) (+ sc)
1975 ***Professione: Reporter*** (*The Passenger*) (+ co-sc)
1979 *Il mistero di Oberwald* (*The Oberwald Mystery*) (+ sc)
1982 *Identificazione di una donna* (+ sc)
1989 *Kumbha Mela*; *Roma '90*
1992 *Noto—Mandorli—Vulcano—Stromboli—Carnevale*
1995 *Beyond the Clouds* (+ sc)

Short Films as Director and Scriptwriter:

1947 *Gente del Po*
1948 *N.U.* (Nettezza urbana); *Roma—Montevideo*; *Oltre l'oblio*
1949 *L'amorosa menzogna*; *Bomarzo*; *Superstizione*; *Ragazze in bianco*
1950 *Sette canne e un vestito*; *La villa dei mostri*; *La funivia del Faloria*; *Uomini in piú*

Other Films:

1984 *Chambre 666* (role as himself)
1995 *Making a Film for Me Is Living* (role as himself)

Publications

By ANTONIONI: books—

La Nuit: La Notte, with Tonino Guerra and E. Flaiano, Paris, 1961.
L'eclisse, with Tonino Guerra and E. Bartolini, Capelli, 1962.
Screenplays by Michelangelo Antonioni, New York, 1963.
Michelangelo Antonioni, Rome, 1964.
Blow-Up, with Tonino Guerra, Turin, 1968; New York, 1971.
L'Avventura, with E. Bartolini, New York, 1969; New Brunswick, New Jersey, 1989.
Il Primo Antonioni (screenplays or working scripts for early Antonioni documentaries and films), edited by Carlo di Carlo, Bologna, 1973.
Il mistero di Oberwald, Turin, 1980.
That Bowling Alley on the Tiber: Tales of a Director, Oxford, 1986.

By ANTONIONI: articles—

"Brevario del cinema," in *Cinema* (Rome), nos. 11, 16, 20, 37, 41, 1949.
"Le allegre ragazze del '24," in *Cinema Nuovo* (Turin), 1956.
"There Must Be a Reason for Every Film," in *Films and Filming* (London), April 1959.
Interview with M. Manceaux and Richard Roud, in *Sight and Sound* (London), Winter 1960/61.
Interview with André Labarthe, in *New York Film Bulletin,* no. 8, 1961.
"Reflections on a Film Career," in *Film Culture* (New York), no. 22-23, 1961.
"Eroticism—The Disease of Our Age," in *Films and Filming* (London), January 1961.
"La malattia dei sentimenti," in *Bianco e Nero* (Rome), February-March 1961.
"Making a Film Is My Way of Life," in *Film Culture* (New York), Spring 1962.
"The Event and the Image," in *Sight and Sound* (London), Winter 1963/64.
"What Directors Are Saying," in *Action* (Los Angeles), September/October 1969.
"Conversazione con Michelangelo Antonioni," in *Filmcritica* (Rome), March 1975.
"Antonioni after China: Art versus Science," interview with Gideon Bachmann, in *Film Quarterly* (Berkeley), Summer 1975.
"Antonioni Speaks ... and Listens," interview with R. Epstein, in *Film Comment* (New York), July/August 1975.
"Antonioni and the Two-Headed Monster," interview with J. F. Lane, in *Sight and Sound* (London), Winter 1979/80.
Antonioni, Michelangelo, "Il 'big bang' della nascita di un film," in *Cinema Nuovo* (Bari), December 1981.
Interview with Gideon Bachman, in *Film Quarterly* (Berkeley), Summer 1983.
Interview with F. Tomasulo, in *On Film* (Los Angeles), Fall 1984.
"Michelangelo critico cinematografico (1935-1949)," edited by Aldo Tassone, in *Bianco e Nero* (Rome), July-September 1985.
"Quel big-bang con cui esplose lo spazio," in *Cinema Nuovo* (Bari), January/February 1987.

On ANTONIONI: books—

Carpi, Fabio, *Michelangelo Antonioni,* Parma, 1958.
Cowie, Peter, *Antonioni, Bergman, Resnais,* New York, 1963.
Leprohon, Pierre, *Michelangelo Antonioni: An Introduction,* New York, 1963.
Taylor, John Russell, *Cinema Eye, Cinema Ear,* New York, 1964.
Strick, Philip, *Antonioni,* London, 1965.
Sarris, Andrew, *Interviews with Film Directors,* New York, 1967.
Cameron, Ian, and Robin Wood, *Antonioni,* New York, 1969.
Huss, Roy, editor, *Focus on 'Blow-Up',* Englewood Cliffs, New Jersey, 1971.
Samuels, Charles Thomas, *Encountering Directors,* New York, 1972.
Rifkin, Ned, *Antonioni's Visual Language,* Ann Arbor, Michigan, 1982.
Barthes, Roland, and others, *Michelangelo Antonioni,* Munich, 1984.
Biarese, Cesare, and Aldo Tassone, *I film di Michelangelo Antonioni,* Rome, 1985.
Chatman, Seymour, *Antonioni; or, The Surface of the World,* Berkeley, 1985.
Dervin, Daniel, *Through a Freudian Lens deeply: A Psychoanalysis of Cinema,* Hillsdale, New Jersey, 1985.
Mancini, Michele, and Giuseppe Perrella, *Michelangelo: Architecture in Vision,* Rome, 1986.
Perry, Ted, and René Prieto, *Michelangelo Antonioni: A Guide to References and Resources,* Boston, 1986.
Rohdie, Sam, *Antonioni,* London, 1990.
Michelangelo Antonioni, Rainer Werner Fassbinder, Margarethe von Trotta, Zurich, 1991.
Predal, Rene, *Michelangelo Antonioni, ou, La vigilance du desir,* Paris, 1991.
Arrowsmith, William, *Antonioni: The Poet of Images,* New York, 1995.

On ANTONIONI articles—

Bollero, Marcello, "Il documentario: Michelangelo Antonioni," in *Sequenze* (Italy), December 1949.
Cavallaro, Giambattista, "Michelangelo Antonioni, simbolo di una generazione," in *Bianco e Nero* (Rome), September 1957.
Renzi, Renzo, "Cronache del l'angoscia in Michelangelo Antonioni," in *Cinema Nuovo* (Turin), May/June 1959.
Roud, Richard, "Michelangelo Antonioni: Five Films," in *Sight and Sound* (London), Winter 1960/61.
Kauffmann, Stanley, "Arrival of an Artist," in the *New Republic* (New York), 10 April 1961.
Pepper, C. F., "Rebirth in Italy: Three Great Movie Directors," in *Newsweek* (New York), 10 July 1961.
Special Issue of *Film Quarterly* (Berkeley), Fall 1962.
"Antonioni issue" of *Seventh Art* (New York), Spring 1963.
Barthelme, Donald, "L'lapse," in the *New Yorker,* 2 March 1963.
Gerard, L. N., "Antonioni," in *Films in Review* (New York), April 1963.
"Michelangelo Antonioni: l'homme et l'objet," in *Etudes Cinématographiques* (Paris), no. 36-37, 1964.
Houston, Penelope, "Keeping up with the Antonionis," in *Sight and Sound* (London), Autumn 1964.
Garis, R., "Watching Antonioni," in *Commentary* (New York), April 1967.
Kinder, Marsha, "Antonioni in Transit," in *Sight and Sound* (London), Summer 1967.
Simon, J., and others, "Antonioni: What's the Point," in *Film Heritage* (Dayton, Ohio), Spring 1970.
Gow, Gordon, "Antonioni Men," in *Films and Filming* (London), June 1970.
Hernacki, T., "Michelangelo Antonioni and the Imagery of Disintegration," in *Film Heritage* (Dayton, Ohio), Fall 1970.
Lane, J. F., "Antonioni Discovers China," in *Sight and Sound* (London), Spring 1973.
Strick, Philip, "Antonioni Report," in *Sight and Sound* (London), Winter 1973/74.
Renzi, Renzo, "Antonioni nelle vesti del drago bianco," in *Cinema Nuovo* (Turin), May/June 1974.
Bachmann, Gideon, "Antonioni Down Under," in *Sight and Sound* (London), no. 4, 1976.
Burke, F., "The Natural Enmity of Words and Moving Images: Language, *La notte,* and the Death of the Light," in *Literature/Film Quarterly* (Salisbury, Maryland), no. 1, 1979.
Barthes, Roland, "Lettre à Antonioni," in *Cahiers du Cinéma* (Paris), May 1980.

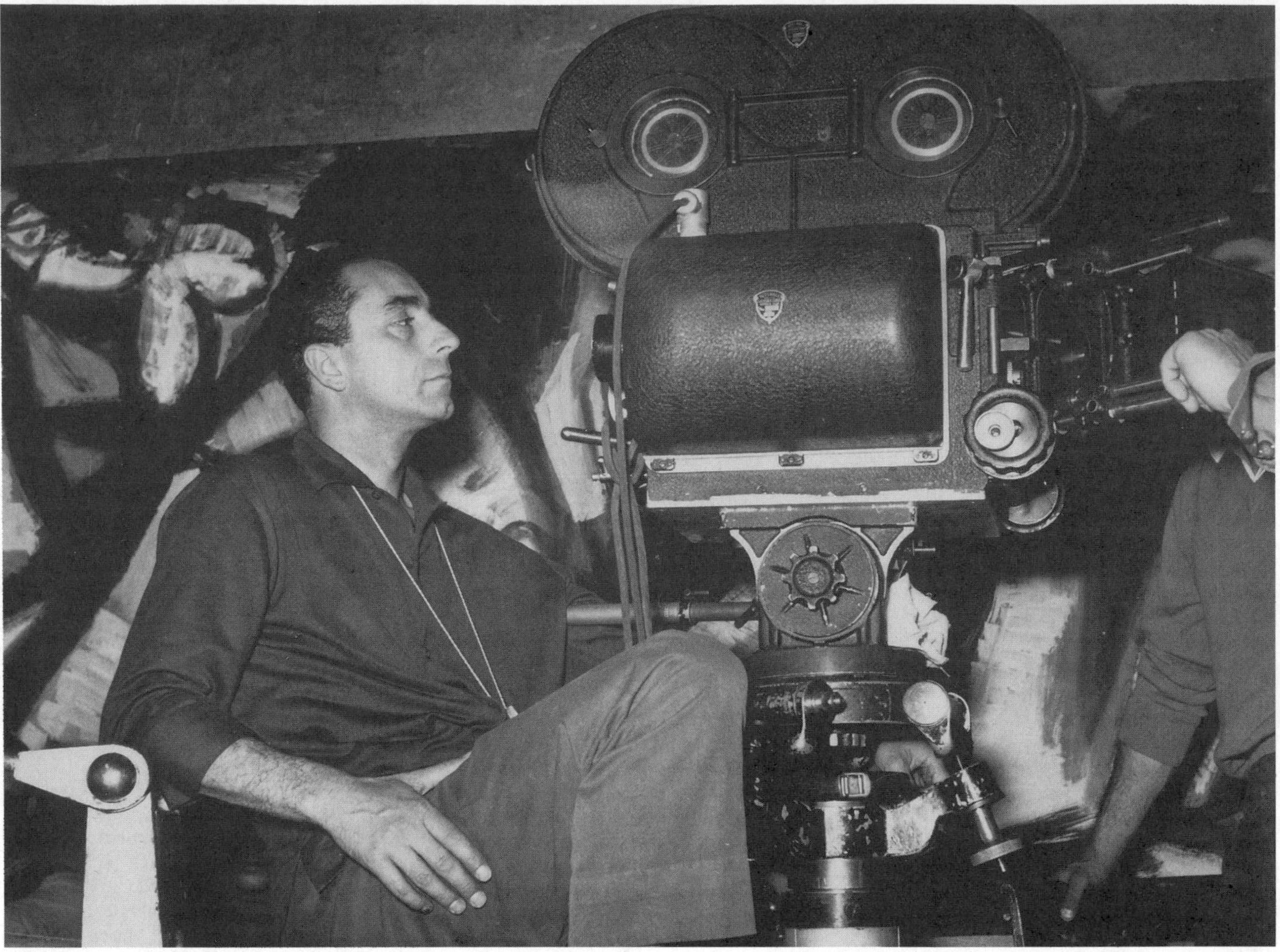

Michelangelo Antonioni

Special Issue of *Camera/Stylo* (Paris), November 1982.

"Antonioni Section" of *Cahiers du Cinéma* (Paris), December 1982.

"Antonioni Section" of *Positif* (Paris), January 1983.

Ranvaud, Don, "Chronicle of a Career: Michelangelo Antonioni in Context," in *Monthly Film Bulletin* (London), March 1983.

Aristarco, G., "Notes on Michelangelo Antonioni," and A. Graham, "The Phantom Self," in *Film Criticism* (Meadville, Pennsylvania), Fall 1984.

Casetti, Francesco, "Antonioni and Hitchcock: Two Strategies of Narrative Investment," *SubStance* (Madison, Wisconsin), vol. 15, no. 3, 1986.

"Michelangelo Antonioni," in *Film Dope* (London), March 1988.

Lev, Peter, "*Blow Up*, Swinging London, and the Film Generation," in *Literature/Film Quarterly* (Salisbury, Maryland), vol. 17, no. 2, 1989.

* * *

Antonioni's cinema is one of non-identification and displacement. In almost all of his films shots can be found whose striking emphasis on visual structure works in opposition to the spectator's desire to identify, as in classical Hollywood cinema, with either a protagonist's existential situation or with anything like a seamless narrative continuity—the "impression of reality" so often evoked in conjunction with the effect of fiction films on the spectator.

Since his first feature, *Cronaca di un amore,* Antonioni's introduction of utterly autonomous, graphically stunning shots into the film's narrative flow has gradually expanded to the point where, in *Professione: Reporter,* but even more emphatically in *Il mistero di Oberwald* and *Identificazione di una donna,* the unsettling effect of these discrete moments in the narrative continuity of the earlier work has taken over entirely. If these graphically autonomous shots of Antonioni's films of the fifties and sixties functioned as striking "figures" which unsettled the "ground" of narrative continuity, his latest films undo altogether this opposition between form and content, technique and substance, in order to spread the strangeness of the previously isolated figure across the entirety of the film which will thus emphatically establish itself as a "text."

That which might at first seem to mark a simple inversion of this opposition—where narrative substance would take a back seat to formal technique—instead works to question, in a broad manner, the ways in which films establish themselves as fictions. Antonioni's cinema strains the traditional conventions defining fiction films to the breaking point where, beginning at least as early as *Professione: Reporter,* those aspects always presumed to define what is "given" or "specific" or "proper" to film (which are commonly grouped together under the general heading of "technique") find themselves explicitly incorporated into the overall fabric of the film's narration; technique finds itself drawn into that which it supposedly presents neutrally, namely, the film's fictional universe. One might name this strategy the fictionalization of technique.

Such a strategy, however, is anything but self-reflexive, nor does it bcar upon the thematics of Antonioni's films. In even those films where the protagonist has something to do with producing images, narratives, or other works of art (the filmmaker of *La signora senza camelie,* the architect of *L'avventura,* the novelist of *La notte,* the photographer of *Blow-up,* the television reporter of *Professione: Reporter,* the poet of *Il mistero di Oberwald,* and the film director of *Identificazione di una donna*), their professions remain important only on the level of the film's drama, never in terms of its technique. It is as though the image of the artist were trapped in a world where self-reflection is impossible. Indeed, one common strand linking the thematics of all of Antonioni's films—the impossibility for men to communicate with women—might be seen to illustrate, on the level of drama, the kind of communicational impasse to be found on the level of "technique" in his cinema. Though his films are far from "experimental" in the sense of the work of Hollis Frampton, Michael Snow, or Andy Warhol, Antonioni's fictional narratives always feel flattened or, to borrow a term from Roland Barthes, they seem curiously *mat,* as if the spectator's ability to gain immediate access to the fiction were being impeded by something.

Antonioni's films, then, are not simply "about" the cinema, but rather, in attempting to make films which always side-step the commonplace or the conventional (modes responsible for spectatorial identification and the "impression of reality"), they call into question what is taken to be a "language" of cinema by constructing a kind of textual idiolect which defies comparison with any other film, even Antonioni's other films. This may at least in part account for the formidable strangeness and difficulty of Antonioni's work, not just for general audiences but for mainstream critics as well. One constantly has the impression that the complexity of his films requires years in the cellar of critical speculation before it is ready to be understood; a film that is initially described as sour and flat ends up ten years later, as in the case of *L'avventura,* being proclaimed one of the ten best films of all time ("International Critics Poll," *Sight and Sound*). To judge from the reception in the United States of his most recent work, it appears that we are still at least ten years behind Antonioni.

As Antonioni has himself stressed repeatedly, the dramatic or the narrative aspect of his films—telling a story in the manner of literary narrative—comes to be of less and less importance; frequently, this is manifested by an absurd and complete absence of dramatic plausibility (*Zabriskie Point, Professione: Reporter, Il mistero di Oberwald*). The nonverbal logic of what remain narrative films depends, Antonioni says, upon neither a conceptual nor emotional organization: "Some people believe I make films with my head; a few others think they come from the heart; for my part, I feel as though I make them with my stomach."

—Kimball Lockhart

ARAKI, Gregg

Nationality: American. **Education:** Attended college in Santa Barbara, California. **Career:** Made first feature film, *Three Bewildered People in the Night,* for $5,000 in 1987. **Address:** Lives in Los Angeles.

Films as Director:

1987 *Three Bewildered People in the Night*
1989 *Long Weekend (o' Despair)*
1992 *The Living End*
1993 *Totally F* * *ed Up*
1995 *The Doom Generation*

Publications

By ARAKI: articles—

"Absorbing Alternative," an interview with Chris Chang, in *Film Comment,* September/October 1994.

On ARAKI: articles—

Ansen, David, "*The Living End,*" in *Newsweek,* 31 August 1992.
Ehrenstein, David, "Gay Film's Bad Boy," in *Advocate,* 8 September 1992.
Minkowitz, Donna, "A Milieu of Misogyny," in *Advocate,* 3 November 1992.
Maslin, Janet, "*Totally F* * *ed Up,*" in *New York Times,* 14 October 1993.
Yutani, Kimberly, "Gregg Araki and the Queer New Wave," in *Amerasia Journal,* Winter 1994.
Corliss, Richard, "*The Doom Generation,*" in *Time,* 6 November 1995.

* * *

Of the heterogeneous group of young gay filmmakers currently lumped together under the term "New Queer Cinema," Gregg Araki is arguably the most challenging and audacious. The very titles of the three films that have received a limited theatrical release and secured him a reputation (*The Living End, Totally F* * *ed Up, The Doom Generation*) suggest the impulses that drive his work: anger, desperation, a sense of imminent apocalypse, a passionate and reckless romanticism. A possible motto for his work might be the famous line "Freedom's just another word for nothing left to lose." The films have been labeled "nihilistic." To anyone truly alive to the realities of contemporary life (not only *gay* life), they might equally be found inspirational. Nihilism means a belief in nothing; it should never be confused with pessimism. Araki's passionate commitment to his characters ("totally f* * *ed up" as their lives may be) is anything but nihilistic.

Araki's aesthetic allegiances are clear already in *The Living End:* its subtitle, "An Irresponsible Movie," refers (if somewhat esoterically) to Hawks's *Bringing Up Baby,* but the most obvious influence is Godard—the early, anarchic Godard of *Breathless,* who also lost no opportunity (as both critic and filmmaker) to express his commitment to the more subversive of the Hollywood genres. The film also introduces the themes ("radical" in every sense of the word) that propel Araki's work: gay life in the age of AIDS, human life at the end of western civilization. The question, What can one still find to live for in a world in which there really is "nothing left to lose"?, generates the extraordinary fury, intensity, and desperate humor of this film and its successors.

Just as *The Living End* can be seen as a loose remake of (or gay variant on) *Breathless,* so *Totally F* * *ed Up* (the asterisks are Araki's, not imposed by censorship) relates structurally to *Masculin, Féminin.* But Araki's characters are no longer "the children of Marx and Coca-Cola": they inhabit the desolate landscape of America in the 1990s, where Marx is not available, consumerism has overwhelmed the culture, concepts no longer apply, and the only fragile hope lies in the precarious and elusive possibility of an ever-more-vulnerable human contact.

The Doom Generation (subtitled "A Heterosexual Movie," it could only have been made by a gay director) is Araki's most fully achieved statement to date. Because he does not make overt *political* statements, one should not assume that his films have no political meaning. Apocalypse is expressed in *The Doom Generation* not only in the running gag of every storekeeper charging $6.66, or in the "Welcome to Hell" of the opening. It is there in the fleeting landscapes through which the characters pass: the clouds of smoke, the graveyard of wrecked cars—the destructiveness and detritus of Capitalism. Araki himself has drawn a comparison (favorable, and quite rightly) between his film and *Kids.* Larry Clark's kids are mainly treated as passive objects for his gaze, the gaze expressing simultaneous desire and repugnance. Araki identifies with *his* kids up to the hilt, without ever glamorizing or idealizing them. He knows and they know that they are living near the endpoint of the decline of western civilization, that they have no viable future and nowhere to go (his next film is entitled *Nowhere*), but he loves them, believes in their impulses, and allows them authentically to find each other, while Clark's kids just meanly manipulate.

Araki himself has insisted that the film is not nihilistic. Nihilism is what Capitalism has brought us to, and a stand against it is becoming increasingly problematic, but Araki (the true rebel, unlike, say, Lynch and Tarantino, whose alleged "audacities" merely reinforce contemporary alienation) is exempt from it. *The Doom Generation* actually achieves, immediately before the climactic bloodbath, the realization of a utopian sexuality: the three characters, having progressively cast off all the bourgeois constraints and inhibitions (including, importantly, squeamishness about bodily functions), have by the end of the film not only all fallen in love with each other but are able to accept the fact, without jealousy or possessiveness. The essentially obsolete patriarchal notion that fidelity can or should be judged in terms of sex finally disintegrates.

The culminating bloodbath (the most terrifying I have ever seen, perhaps deriving from, but outdoing, the murder at the end of *Looking for Mr. Goodbar*), whatever the narrative motivation, seems precipitated by the image of the three having sex together, two males, one female, each loving the other two: the image of the not-to-be-tolerated. The bloodbath itself juxtaposes two images of "America." As a prelude to the castration and murder of Jordan/James Duval (one of the sweetest and most touching characters in modern cinema), the gang of healthy all-American boys displays the American flag and plays "Stars and Stripes Forever" on a ghetto-blaster; these are presented as mere empty signifiers, long ago drained of all substance, relics of an always dubious patriotism that has lost whatever meaning it once had, reduced to a pretext for malicious violence, the mindless crushing out of any sign of new life, of the possible future toward which the film has moved. Against this is set Araki's America, exemplified in the essential purity of his three transgressive characters: Xavier Red, Jordan White, Amy Blue—a possible future the past is committed to stamping out, an America that might have been.

—Robin Wood

ARGENTO, Dario

Nationality: Italian. **Born:** Rome, Italy, 7 September 1940. **Family:** Married the actress Daria Nicolodi (separated). **Career:** Film critic for *Paesa Cera,* mid-1960s; screenwriting debut, *Cemetery without Crosses,* 1967; co-directed the feature *Probability Zero,* 1968; solo directorial debut with *The Bird with the Crystal Plumage,* 1970; produced the series *Door into Darkness* for Italian television, 1978. **Address:** G. Davoti 16, Rome, Italy.

Films as Director and Screenwriter:

1968 *Zero Probability* (co-d)
1970 *The Bird with the Crystal Plumage*
1971 *The Cat o' Nine Tails*; *Four Flies on Grey Velvet*
1973 *Five Days in Milan* (co-sc)
1976 *Deep Red* (co-sc); *Suspiria* (co-sc)
1980 *Inferno*
1982 *Tenebrae*
1985 *Phenomena* (co-sc)
1988 *Opera* (co-sc, pr)
1990 *Two Evil Eyes* (co-d, co-pr, co-sc)
1994 *Trauma* (co-sc, ed)

Other Films:

1967 *Cemetery without Crosses* (co-sc)
1968 *Once Upon a Time in the West* (co-sc); *Today Me ... Tomorrow You* (co-sc); *One Night at Dinner* (co-sc); *Sex Revolution* (sc)
1969 *Commandos* (sc); *Legion of the Damned* (co-sc, dialogue supervisor); *Seasons of Love* (co-sc)
1970 *Five Man Army* (co-sc)
1979 *Dawn of the Dead* (co-pr)
1986 *Demons* (pr, co-sc)
1987 *Demons 2* (pr, co-sc)
1989 *The Church* (pr, co-sc, story)
1990 *The Sect* (pr, sc, story)
1992 *Innocent Blood* (role)

Publications

By ARGENTO: articles—

"Argento," *Cinefantastique,* 1983.
"Pour une esthetique de la cruaute," *Visions,* 1985.
"Demons," *Cinefantastique,* 1986.
"Dario Argento on Edgar Allan Poe," *Cinefantastique,* 1990.
"*Trauma,* una storia d'amore," *Segno,* 1993.

On ARGENTO: books—

Balestrini, Nanni, *Profondo Thrilling,* Milan, 1975.
Domenico, Milan, *Enciclopedia illustrata del cinema horror e di frantascienza,* Rome, 1982.
McCarty, John, *Splatter Movies: Breaking the Last Taboo of the Screen,* New York, 1984.
Petrignani, Sandra, *Fantasia & Fantastico,* Brescia, Italy, 1985.
Giovanni, Fabio, *Dario Argento: il brivido, il sangue, il thrilling,* Bari, Italy, 1986.
Pugliese, Roberto, *Dario Argento,* Firenze, Italy, 1987.
Cozzi, Luigi, *Dario Argento,* Rome, 1991.
McCarty, John, *Movie Psychos and Madmen,* Secaucus, New Jersey, 1993.
McDonagh, Maitland, *Broken Mirrors/Broken Minds: The Dark Dreams of Dario Argento,* Secaucus, New Jersey, 1994.
McCarty, John, *The Fearmakers,* New York, 1994.

On ARGENTO: articles—

Cozzi, L., "Argento: Some Personal Reflections on the Director," *Photon,* 1974.
Menello, R., "Dark Universe: The World of Dario Argento," *Photon,* 1974.

Dario Argento: *Suspiria*

Soren, D., "More Flies on Grey Velvet: A Further Look at the Cinema of Dario Argento," *Photon,* 1977.
Rausa, G., "La musica della paura nel cinema di Argento," *Segno,* 1985.
Fischer, D. K., "Dario Argento: Current King of Italian Horror," *Midnight Marquee,* 1988.
Jones, A., "Dario Argento's World of Horror," *Cinefantastique,* 1988.
McDonagh, Maitland, "The Elegant Brutality of Dario Argento," *Film Comment,* 1993.
Williams, D. E., "Argento's Enigma," *Film Threat,* 1993.

* * *

The son of Italian film producer Salvatore Argento, Dario Argento began his career as a film critic. He soon became assistant to Mario Bava, the Italian shockmaster best known for such horror classics as *Black Sunday.* By the late 1960s, Argento was sharing screenwriting credits with Italian cinema greats Bernardo Bertolucci and Sergio Leone as co-writer of the ultimate spaghetti western: *Once Upon a Time in the West.*

Argento's directorial debut, *The Bird with the Crystal Plumage,* was the first in his string of "giallo," or "yellow," shockers. (The term stems from the color of the book jackets that identified lurid novels of this type in Italian popular fiction.) In the film, American writer Tony Musante sees a woman attacked by a knife-wielding crazy in a Rome art gallery. He alerts the police and is rewarded by becoming the killer's next target, so he must solve the mystery himself to avert his death. The film was a huge commercial success, although critical reaction to it—and to Argento's subsequent work—remains divided. On the basis of Argento's fondness for creeping camera work, garish lighting, and convoluted plots, some critics accuse him of celebrating style over substance. Others rationalize his excesses as attempts to "choreograph nightmares." He has been unfairly dismissed as a no-talent hack, as well as overpraised as "the Italian Hitchcock." Reaction to him has never been lukewarm.

The success of *The Bird with the Crystal Plumage* inspired Argento to continue making films in the same kinetically charged vein. But he was not alone. Other Italian directors, inspired by his success, jumped on the bandwagon. Soon there were numerous imitations of the Argento style on the market. In their attempts to identify with the success of Argento's film, his imitators often went to absurd lengths, generating such titles as *Scorpion with Two Tails, Don't Torture a Duckling,* and *Black Belly of the Tarantula.*

Argento launched his second "giallo," *The Cat o' Nine Tails,* immediately. The film opens with a bungled break-in—at a genetics lab—and quickly escalates to homicidal madness, the pace enlivened by several murder scenes staged at warp speed. *Four Flies on Grey Velvet,* which followed a year later, maintained the formula. Featuring a throbbing musical score by legendary composer Ennio Morricone, the film is based on the premise that a killer's image is imprinted on the retinas of his victims. Quite bloody and gruesome in its original form, *Four Flies on Grey Velvet* was heavily trimmed by Paramount for American release—a problem that has plagued the director throughout his career.

Argento dabbled in the supernatural with his next film by combining psychics with psychos. In its original, uncut version, *Deep Red* easily lived up to its title. In the film a renowned psychic lecturing in Rome senses the presence of a killer in the auditorium and soon becomes the killer's victim. The murder is witnessed by David Hemmings, who, like all Argento protagonists, rushes in to personally solve the crime. *Deep Red* arrived as the era of increasingly graphic horror on the screen had begun to flower. The film is awash in scenes of meticulously staged carnage. In addition to introducing a supernatural element into his work for the first time, Argento made another substantial change—the film's music score was supplied by a group called Goblin instead of Ennio Morricone. Both the supernatural *and* the music of Goblin became staples of Argento's films in the years to come.

Dario Argento plunged into the world of the supernatural for his next two films, beginning with *Suspiria*—the first installment in a projected trilogy about witches at work in the modern world. An avowed admirer of the works of Edgar Allan Poe and Roger Corman's ornate shockers based on Poe, *Suspiria* revealed the influence of both sources in its ghastly red/blue/black color schemes and its pyrotechnical holocaust of an ending. The film hit with one shock after another, culminating in an incredible scene involving a rainstorm of maggots.

Argento took time out from his proposed supernatural trilogy to team up with George A. Romero, the American director of the classic *Night of the Living Dead.* The result: the 1979 film *Dawn of the Dead.* In 1980, Argento returned to his proposed trilogy about witches with *Inferno.* The film contains some of the most frightening imagery in the Argento canon. Though *Suspiria* and *Inferno* provide terrifying first and second chapters in Argento's proposed witch trilogy, and were quite successful at the box office, he has yet to deliver the final installment.

The year 1982 saw the release of *Tenebrae.* The title refers to a novel being written by the film's lead character and to the "darkness in man's soul," a recurring Argento theme. Murders commence when writer Anthony Franciosa travels to Rome to promote this novel. Victims are slashed to ribbons and pages of the book are crammed into their mouths. While the killers in *Tenebrae* were busy carving victims, the U.S. distributor was busy butchering the film itself. Instead of pages from a book, an emasculated version of Argento's original film was shoved down viewers' throats. Argento's next film, *Phenomena,* released in the United States as *Creepers,* suffered a similar fate. The American version of the film was so heavily censored that the story was all but impossible to follow.

Argento has been known to get behind the careers of up-and-coming filmmakers whose talents he admires. He did so with Lamberto Bava, the son of the great stylist Mario Bava, who had given Argento his own start in the business. In 1986, Argento produced Lamberto Bava's *Demons,* which starred another Argento apprentice, Michele Soavi. Soavi later filmed a tribute to his mentor titled *Dario Argento's World of Horror.* Argento produced *The Church* for Soavi in 1989, and both wrote and produced *The Sect* for Soavi in 1990.

In 1988, Dario Argento made the word "opera" synonymous with visceral horror in *Opera,* released uncut in the United States as *Terror at the Opera.* The film boasts some of the most relentlessly suspenseful sequences of Argento's career, as well as a grim backstage atmosphere and some dizzying camerawork capable of inducing vertigo. Argento's devotion to Edgar Allan Poe found expression again when he reteamed with George Romero to create *Two Evil Eyes,* an anthology film comprised of two well-known Poe tales: "The Facts in the Case of M. Valdemar" and "The Black Cat." Romero directed the "Valdemar" segment, while Argento filmed "The Black Cat," incorporating elements from many other Poe stories into his screenplay. Argento's most recent film is the appropriately titled *Trauma,* which he also edited.

—John McCarty

ARMSTRONG, Gillian

Nationality: Australian. **Born:** Melbourne, 18 December 1950. **Education:** Swinburne College, studied filmmaking at Melbourne and Australian Film and Television School, Sydney. **Family:** Married, one daughter. **Career:** Worked as production assistant, editor, art director, and assistant designer, and directed several short films; directed first feature, *My Brilliant Career,* 1979; directed first American film, *Mrs. Soffel,* 1984; returned to Australia to direct *High Tide,* 1987; has since made films both in Australia and the United States; also director of documentaries and commercials. **Awards:** Best Short Fiction Film, Sydney Festival, for *The Singer and the Dancer,* 1976; British Critics' Award and Best Film and Best Director, Australian Film Institute Awards, for *My Brilliant Career,* 1979. **Agent:** Judy Scott-Fox, William Morris Agency, 151 El Camino Drive, Beverly Hills, CA 90212.

Films as Director:

1970 *Old Man and Dog* (short)
1971 *Roof Needs Mowing* (short)
1973 *Gretel*; *Satdee Night*; *One Hundred a Day* (shorts)
1975 *Smokes and Lollies* (doc)
1976 *The Singer and the Dancer* (+ pr, sc)
1979 ***My Brilliant Career***
1980 *Fourteen's Good, Eighteen's Better* (doc) (+ pr); *Touch Wood* (doc)
1982 *Starstruck*
1983 *Having a Go* (doc)
1984 *Mrs. Soffel*
1986 *Hard to Handle: Bob Dylan with Tom Petty and the Heartbreakers*
1987 *High Tide*
1988 *Bingo, Bridesmaids and Braces* (+ pr)
1991 *Fires Within*
1992 *The Last Days of Chez Nous*
1994 *Little Women*

Publications

By ARMSTRONG: articles—

Interviews in *Cinema Papers* (Melbourne), January 1974, March-April 1979, October 1992.
Films in Review (New York), June-July 1983.
Interview in *Encore* (Manly, New South Wales), 31 January 1985.
"Gillian Armstrong Returns to Eden," an interview with A. Grieve, in *Cinema Papers* (Melbourne), May 1987.

Interview in *Encore* (Manly, New South Wales), 29 September 1988.

On ARMSTRONG: books—

Tulloch, John, *Australian Cinema: Industry, Narrative, and Meaning,* Sydney and London, 1982.
McFarlane, Brian, *Words and Images: Australian Novels into Films,* Richmond, Victoria, 1983.
Mathews, Sue, *35mm Dreams: Conversations with Five Australian Directors,* Ringwood, Victoria, 1984.
Hall, Sandra, *Critical Business: The New Australian Cinema in Review,* Adelaide, 1985.
Moran, Albert, and Tom O'Regan, editors, *An Australian Film Reader,* Sydney, 1985.
McFarlane, Brian, *Australian Cinema 1970-85,* London, 1987.
Acker, Ally, *Reel Women: Pioneers of the Cinema, 1896 to the Present,* New York, 1991.

On ARMSTRONG: articles—

"Profile," in *Time Out* (London), 24 January 1980.
Rickey, C., "Where the Girls Are," in *American Film* (Washington, D.C.), January-February 1985.
Enker, D., "Coming in from the Cold," in *Cinema Papers* (Melbourne), July 1985.
Grieve, A., "Gillian Armstrong returns to Eden," in *Cinema Papers* (Melbourne), May 1987.
Forsberg, M., "Partnership swells *High Tide,*" in *The New York Times,* 6 March 1988.
Harker, P., "Gillian Armstrong and three times three," in *Cinema Papers* (Melbourne), November, 1988.
N. Graham, "Directors' pet projects," in *Premiere* (New York), December 1988.
Mordue, Mark, "Homeward Bound: a profile of Gillian Armstrong," in *Sight and Sound* (London), Autumn 1989.
Urban, A.L. "The Last Days of Chez Nous," in *Cinema Papers* (Melbourne), May 1991.
Haskell, Molly, "Wildflowers," in *Film Comment* (New York), March/April 1993.
Dargis, M., "Her brilliant career," in *Village Voice* (New York), 2 March 1993.
Dougherty, M., "Look homeward, Aussie," in *Premiere* (New York), May 1993.

* * *

While women directors in film industries around the world are still seen as anomalous (if mainstream) or marginalized as avant garde, the Antipodes have been home to an impressive cadre of female filmmakers who negotiate and transcend such notions.

Before the promising debuts of Ann Turner (*Celia*) and Jane Campion (*Sweetie*), Gillian Armstrong blazed a trail with *My Brilliant Career,* launching a brilliant career of her own as an international director. Like Turner and Campion, Armstrong makes films that resist easy categorization as either "women's films" or Australian ones. Her films mix and intermingle genres in ways which undermine and illuminate afresh, if not openly subvert, filmic conventions—as much as the films of her male compatriots, like Peter Weir, Bruce Beresford, or Paul Cox. Formally, however, the pleasures of her films are traditional ones, such as sensitive and delicate cinematography (often by Russell Boyd), fluid editing, an evocative feel for setting and costume, and most importantly, a commitment to solid character development and acting. All in all, her work reminds one of the best of classical Hollywood cinema, and the question of whether her aim is parody or homage is often left pleasingly ambiguous.

Although Armstrong has often spoken in interviews about her discomfort at being confined to the category of woman filmmaker of women's films, and has articulated her desire to reach an audience of both genders and all nationalities, her work continually addresses sexual politics and family tensions. Escape from and struggle with traditional sex roles and the pitfalls and triumphs therein are themes frequently addressed in her films—from *One Hundred a Day,* her final-year project at the Australian Film and Television School, through *My Brilliant Career,* her first and best-known feature, to *High Tide.* Even one of her earliest films at Swinburne College, the short *Roof Needs Mowing,* obliquely tackled this theme, using a typical student filmmaker's pastiche of advertising and surrealism. Like most maturing filmmakers with an eye on wider distribution, Armstrong dropped the "sur" from surrealism in her later work, so that by *One Hundred a Day*—an adaptation of an Alan Marshall story about a shoe-factory employee getting a back-street abortion in the 1930s—she developed a more naturalistic handling of material, while her use of soundtrack and fast editing remained highly stylized and effective.

Made on a tiny budget and heavily subsidized by the Australian Film Commission, the award-winning *The Singer and the Dancer* was a precocious study of the toll men take on women's lives that marked the onset of Armstrong's mature style. On the strength of this and *One Hundred a Day,* producer Margaret Fink offered Armstrong the direction of *My Brilliant Career.* Daunted at first by the scale of the project and a lack of confidence in her own abilities, she accepted because she "thought it could be bungled by a lot of men."

While *The Singer and the Dancer* had been chastised by feminist critics for its downbeat ending, in which the heroine returns to her philandering lover after a half-hearted escape attempt, *My Brilliant Career* was widely celebrated for its feminist fairy-tale story as well as its employment of women crew members. Adapted from Miles Franklin's semi-autobiographical novel, *My Brilliant Career,* with its turn-of-the-century setting in the Australian outback, works like *Jane Eyre* in reverse (she does not marry him), while retaining the romantic allure of such a story and all the glossy production values of a period setting that Australian cinema had been known for up until then. Distinguished by an astonishing central performance by the then-unknown Judy Davis (fresh from playing Juliet to Mel Gibson's Romeo on the drama-school stage), the film managed to present a positive model of feminine independence without belying the time in which it was set. Like Armstrong's later *Mrs. Soffel, My Brilliant Career* potently evokes smothered sensuality and conveys sexual tension by small, telling details, as in the boating scene.

Sadly, few of Armstrong's later films have been awarded commensurate critical praise or been as widely successful, possibly because of her refusal to conform to expectations and churn out more upbeat costume dramas. Her next feature, *Starstruck,* although it too features a spunky, ambitious heroine, was a rock musical set in the present and displaying a veritable rattle bag of influences—including Judy Garland-Mickey Rooney "lets-put-on-a-show" films, Richard Lester editing techniques, new wave pop videos, and even Sternberg's *Blond Venus,* when the heroine sheds her kangaroo suit to sing her "torch song" à la Marlene Dietrich. Despite a witty script and fine bit characters, the music is somewhat monotonous, and the film was only mildly successful.

Armstrong's first film to be financed and filmed in America was *Mrs. Soffel.* Based on a true story and set at the turn of the century, it delineated the tragic story of the eponymous warden's wife who falls in love with a convict, helps him escape, and finally runs off with him. The bleak, monochrome cinematography is powerfully atmospheric but was not to all reviewers' tastes, especially in America. For Armstrong, the restricted palette was quite deliberate, so that the penultimate images of blood on snow would be all the more striking and effective. A sadly under-rated film, it features some unexpectedly fine performances from Diane Keaton in the title role, Mel Gibson as

Gillian Armstrong

her paramour (a fair impersonation of young Henry Fonda), and the young Matthew Modine as his kid brother. At its best, it recalls, if not *McCabe and Mrs. Miller,* then at least *Bonnie and Clyde.*

High Tide returns to Australia for its setting in a coastal caravan park, and comes up trumps as an unabashedly sentimental weepie, and none the worse for it. It features three generations of women: Lilli (Judy Davis again), backup singer to an Elvis impersonator and drifter; Ally (Claudia Karvan), the pubescent daughter she left behind; and mother-in-law Bet (Jan Adele), who vies with Lilli for Ally's affections. In terms of camera work, it is Armstrong's most restless film, utilizing nervous zip pans, fast tracking, and boomshots, and then resting for quiet, intense close-ups on surfboards, legs being shaved, and shower nozzles, all highly motivated by the characters' perspectives. Like *Mrs. Soffel, High Tide* uses colors symbolically to contrast the gentle tones of the seaside's natural landscape with the garish buildings of the town called Eden.

Armstrong wears her feminist credentials lightly, never on her sleeve. Nevertheless, her fiction films—like her documentaries, which have followed three women from the ages of fourteen to twenty-five—can be seen as charting over the years the trajectory of the women's movement: *My Brilliant Career* in the 1970s celebrated women's independence, as Sybylla rejects the roles of wife and mother; *Mrs. Soffel* in the mid-1980s reopens negotiations with men (with tragic results); and finally *High Tide* returns to the rejected motherhood role, with all its attendant joys and anxieties.

Fires Within is a well-meaning but insipid tale of a Cuban political prisoner and his encounter with his family in Miami. A fiasco, Armstrong lost control of the project during post-production. The filmmaker bounced back strongly, however, with two impressive films centering on the relationships between female siblings.

The Last Days of Chez Nous, which Armstrong directed back in Australia, is a thoughtful, well-acted drama focusing on the emotional plight of a pair of sisters. One (Lisa Harrow) is a bossy, forty-something writer, and the other (Kerry Fox) has just emerged from an unhappy love affair. The scenario centers on events that take place after the latter becomes romantically involved with the former's husband (Bruno Ganz). The film's major strength is the depth and richness of its female characters. Its theme, consistent with Armstrong's best previous work, is the utter necessity of women's self-sufficiency.

Little Women, based on Louisa May Alcott's venerable 1868 novel of four devoted sisters coming of age in Concord, Massachusetts, during the Civil War, was Armstrong's first successful American-made film. It may be linked to *My Brilliant Career* as a story of feminine independence set in a previous era. Alcott's book had been filmed a number of times before: a silent version, made in 1918; most enjoyably by George Cukor, with Katharine Hepburn, in 1933; far less successfully, with a young Elizabeth Taylor (among others), in 1949; and in a made-for-TV movie in 1978. Armstrong's version is every bit as fine as the Cukor-Hepburn classic. Her cast is just about perfect, with Wynona Ryder deservedly earning an Academy Award nomination as the headstrong Jo March. Ryder is ably supported by Trini Alvarado, Claire Danes, Samantha Mathis, and Kirsten Dunst, and Susan Sarandon offers her usual solid performance as Marmee, the March girls' mother. If the film has one fault, it is the contemporary-sounding feminist rhetoric that Marmee spouts: the dialogue is completely out of sync with the spirit and reality of the times. But this is just a quibble. This new *Little Women* is a fine film, at once literate and extremely enjoyable.

—Leslie Felperin, updated by Rob Edelman

ARZNER, Dorothy

Nationality: American. **Born:** San Francisco, 3 January 1900. **Education:** Studied medicine at University of Southern California. **Military Service:** Ambulance driver in World War I, 1917-18. **Career:** Typist for William C. De Mille, at Famous Players-Lasky (Paramount), 1919; editor for "Realart," a subsidiary of Paramount, 1922; wrote and edited *Old Ironsides* (Cruze), 1925; directed Paramount's first sound film, *Wild Party,* 1929; retired from directing, 1943. **Awards:** Honored at First International Festival of Women's Films, New York, 1972, and by Director's Guild of America, 1975. **Died:** 1 October 1979.

Films as Director:

1927 *Fashions for Women*; *Get Your Man*; *10 Modern Commandments*
1928 *Manhattan Cocktail*
1929 *The Wild Party*
1930 *Sarah and Son*; "The Gallows Song—Nichavo" sequence in *Paramount on Parade*; *Anybody's Woman*; *Behind the Makeup* (co-d); *Charming Sinners* (co-d, uncredited)
1931 *Honor among Lovers*; *Working Girls*
1932 *Merrily We Go to Hell*
1933 *Christopher Strong*
1934 *Nana (Lady of the Boulevard)*
1936 *Craig's Wife*
1937 *The Bride Wore Red*; *The Last of Mrs. Cheyney* (co-d, uncredited)
1940 ***Dance, Girl, Dance***
1943 *First Comes Courage*

Other Films:

1922 *Blood and Sand* (ed)
1923 *The Covered Wagon* (ed)
1924 *Inez from Hollywood* (ed, sc); *The Bread of the Border* (sc); *The No-Gun Man* (sc)
1925 *Red Kimono* (sc); *When Husbands Flirt* (sc)
1926 *Old Ironsides* (ed, sc)

Publications

By ARZNER: article—

Interview with Gerald Peary, in *Cinema* (Beverly Hills), no. 34, 1974.

On ARZNER: books—

Brownlow, Kevin, *The Parade's Gone By,* New York, 1968.
Johnston, Claire, *Notes on Women's Cinema,* London, 1973.
Pratt, George, *Spellbound in Darkness: A History of Silent Film,* Greenwich, Connecticut, 1973.
Rosen, Marjorie, *Popcorn Venus: Women, Movies, and the American Dream,* New York, 1973.
Haskell, Molly, *From Reverence to Rape: The Treatment of Women in the Movies,* New York, 1974.
Smith, Sharon, *Women Who Make Movies,* New York, 1975.
Johnston, Claire, editor, *The Work of Dorothy Arzner: Towards a Feminist Cinema,* London, 1975.
Slide, Anthony, *Early Women Directors,* South Brunswick, New Jersey, 1977.
Heck-Rabi, Louise, *Women Filmmakers: A Critical Reception,* Metuchen, New Jersey, 1984.
Penley, Constance, editor, *Feminism and Film Theory,* London, 1988.

On ARZNER: articles—

"Hollywood Notes," in *Close-Up* (London), April 1928.
Cruikshank, H., "Sketch," in *Motion Picture Classic* (Brooklyn), September 1929.
Potamkin, H. A., "The Woman as Film Director," in *American Cinematographer* (Los Angeles), January 1932.
St. John, Adela Rogers, "Get Me Dorothy Arzner," in *Silver Screen* (New York), December 1933.
"They Stand Out from the Crowd," in *Literary Digest* (New York), 3 November 1934.
Feldman, J. and H., "Women Directors," in *Films in Review* (New York), November 1950.
Pyros, J., "Notes on Women Directors," in *Take One* (Montreal), November/December 1970.
Henshaw, Richard, "Women Directors," in *Film Comment* (New York), November 1972.
Parker, F., "Approaching the Art of Arzner," in *Action* (Los Angeles), July/August 1973.
Slide, Anthony, "Forgotten Early Women Directors," in *Films in Review,* March 1974.
Castle, W., "Tribute to Dorothy Arzner," in *Action* (Los Angeles), March/April 1975.
Kaplan, E. Ann, "Aspects of British Feminist Film Theory," in *Jump Cut* (Berkeley), no. 12-13, 1976.
Johnston, Claire, in *Jump Cut* (Berkeley), 30 December 1976.
Bergstrom, J., "Rereading the Work of Claire Johnston," in *Camera Obscura* (Berkeley), Summer 1979.
Obituary, in *New York Times,* 12 October 1979.
Houston, Beverle, "Missing in Action: Notes on Dorothy Arzner," in *Wide Angle* (Athens, Georgia), vol. 6, no. 3, 1984.
Forster, A., "*Dance, Girl, Dance,*" in *Skrien* (Amsterdam), September-October 1984.

* * *

Dorothy Arzner's career as a commercial Hollywood director covered little more than a decade, but she had prepared for it by extensive editing and script writing work. Ill health forced her to abandon a career that might eventually have led to the recognition she deserved from her contemporaries. One of only a handful of women operating within the structure of Hollywood's post-silent boom, Arzner has been the subject of feminist critical attention, with film retrospectives of her work both in the United States and United Kingdom in the 1970s, when her work was "rediscovered."

Most feminists would recognize that the mere re-insertion of women into a dominant version of film history is a dubious activity, even

Dorothy Arzner

while asserting that women's contributions to cinema have been excluded from most historical accounts. Recognition of the work of a "popular" director like Arzner and an evaluation of her contribution to Hollywood cinema must be set against an awareness of her place in the dominant patriarchal ideology of classic Hollywood cinema. Arzner's work is particularly interesting in that it was produced *within* the Hollywood system with all its inherent constraints (time, budget, traditional content requirements of particular genres, etc.).

While Arzner directed "women's pictures"—classic Hollywood fare—she differed from other directors of the genre in that, in place of a narrative seen simply from a female point of view, she actually succeeded in challenging the orthodoxy of Hollywood from within, offering perspectives that questioned the dominant order.

The films often depict women seeking independence through career—a burlesque queen and an aspiring ballerina (*Dance, Girl, Dance*), a world champion aviatrix (*Christopher Strong*). Alternatively, the escape route can be through exit from accepted female positions in the hierarchy—a rich daughter "escaping" into marriage with a poverty-stricken drunk (*Merrily We Go to Hell*). Even excess can be a way of asserting independence, as with the obsessive housekeeper rejecting family relationships in favor of a passion for domesticity and the home (*Craig's Wife*).

The films frequently play with notions of female stereotyping (most notably in *Dance, Girl, Dance,* with its two central female types of Nice Girl and Vamp). Arzner's "nice girls" are likely to have desires which conflict with male desires, while narrative requirements will demand that they still please the male. While these tensions are not always resolved, Arzner's strategies in underlining these opposing desires are almost gleeful at times.

In addition, Arzner's films offer contradictions which disturb the spectator's accepted relationship with what is on screen—most notably in *Dance, Girl, Dance,* when dancer Judy O'Brien turns on her Burlesque (male) audience and berates them for their voyeurism. This scene has been the focus for much debate about the role of the spectator in relation to the woman as spectacle (notably in the work of Laura Mulvey).

Although the conventions of plot and development are present in Arzner's films, Claire Johnston sees these elements as subverted by a "women's discourse": the films may offer us the kinds of narrative closure we expect from the classic Hollywood text—the "happy" or the "tragic" ending—but Arzner's insistence on this female discourse gives the films an exciting and unsettling quality. In Arzner's work, she argues, it is the male universe which invites scrutiny and which is "rendered strange."

Dorothy Arzner's position inside the studio system has made her a unique subject for debate. As the women's movement set about reassessing the role of women in history, so feminist film theorists began not only to re-examine the role of women as a creative force in cinema, but also to consider the implications behind the notion of women as spectacle. The work of Dorothy Arzner has proved a rich area for investigation into both these questions.

—Lilie Ferrari

ASHBY, Hal

Nationality: American. **Born:** Ogden, Utah, 1932. **Education:** Attended Utah State University. **Career:** Mimeographer in Universal script department, Los Angeles, 1950-51; worked at Republic studios, becoming assistant editor, 1950s; became full editor, 1963; directed first feature, *The Landlord,* 1970. **Awards:** Oscar for Best Editing, for *In the Heat of the Night,* 1967. **Died:** In Los Angeles, 27 December 1988.

Films as Director:

1970 *The Landlord*
1971 *Harold and Maude*
1973 *The Last Detail*
1975 *Shampoo*
1976 *Bound for Glory*
1978 *Coming Home*
1979 *Being There* (+ ed)
1981 *Second Hand Hearts* (+ ed)
1982 *Lookin' to Get Out* (+ co-ed); *Let's Spend the Night Together*
1983 *Time is On Our Side* (+ ed)
1984 *The Slugger's Wife*
1985 *Eight Million Ways to Die*

Other Films:

1958 *The Big Country* (Wyler) (asst ed); *The Diary of Anne Frank* (Stevens) (asst ed)
1961 *The Young Doctors* (Karlson) (asst ed)
1962 *The Children's Hour* (*The Loudest Whisper*) (Wyler) (asst ed)
1964 *The Best Man* (Schaffner) (asst ed)
1965 *The Greatest Story Ever Told* (Stevens) (asst ed); *The Loved One* (co-ed); *The Cincinnati Kid* (Jewison) (ed); *The Russians Are Coming, the Russians Are Coming* (Jewison) (ed)
1967 *In the Heat of the Night* (Jewison) (ed)
1968 *The Thomas Crown Affair* (Jewison) (assoc pr, supervising ed)
1969 *Gaily, Gaily* (Jewison) (assoc pr)

Publications

By ASHBY: articles—

"Breaking Out of the Cutting Room," in *Action* (Los Angeles), September/October 1970.
Interview with L. Salvato and D. Schaefer, in *Millimeter* (New York), October 1976.
"David Carradine and Hal Ashby on *Bound for Glory*," interview with C. Amata, in *Focus on Film* (London), no. 27, 1977.
"Positive Thinking: Hal Ashby," interview with R. Appelbaum, in *Films and Filming* (London), July 1978.
"Dialogue on Film: Hal Ashby," in *American Film* (Washington, D.C.), May 1980.

On ASHBY: book—

Tuska, Jon, editor, *Close-Up: The Contemporary Director,* Metuchen, New Jersey, 1981.

On ASHBY: articles—

Jörgensen, U., "Hal Ashby—en auteur?" in *Kosmorama* (Copenhagen), September 1974.
Harmetz, A., "Gambling on a Film About the Great Depression," in *New York Times,* 5 December 1976.
Jacobs, Diane, "Hal Ashby," in *Hollywood Renaissance* (New York), 1977.
Pollock, Dale, "Whatever Happened to Hal Ashby?" in *Los Angeles Times,* 17 October 1982.

"Hal Ashby," in *Film Dope* (London), March 1988.
Obituary in *Ciné Revue* (Paris), 5 January 1989.
Obituary in *Screen International* (London), 7 January 1989.

* * *

Hal Ashby has a reputation for showing a light touch as a director; he stated that he preferred to let the actors develop their characters. During the filming of *Coming Home,* for example, he threw out a script when actor Jon Voight envisioned one of the major characters differently than the screenwriter. The people in his films generally face choices in situations that reflect major social concerns. In *The Landlord* characters have to make decisions involving the issue of race; in *Shampoo* they must decide which side they are on in a complex political and sexual skirmish set in the turbulent summer of 1968; and in *Coming Home,* the effects of the Vietnam War force characters involved directly with the war as well as those at home to deal with unexpected changes in their lives. The solutions to decisions faced by Ashby's characters are never facile. In *Harold and Maude,* Harold gains some degree of maturity but loses the love of his life, Maude; the military police of *The Last Detail* give a prisoner a way to face life, but also deliver him to prison; while George in *Shampoo* realizes how empty his life is and appears to want to change it, but at the same time he has lost what chances he had for happiness.

Ashby's experience as an editor is evident; he employed a wide variety of editing effects in his films. His use of both dissolves and rapid cutting to show the passage of time in *The Last Detail* serves as an example of his background. His predilection for varying editing techniques could explain in part an aspect of his filmmaking that Ashby himself admitted: he did not rely on a distinctive style, but rather attempted to adapt his style to the type and subject of each film.

Though he has been called a "maverick director," Ashby's career garnered him a good deal of respect from the critics, and his films have done well at the box office. *Shampoo, Coming Home,* and *Being There* represent his major financial successes, while the reputation of *Harold and Maude* was made in a slightly different manner. After an initial panning and a short general release, the film caught on in the Midwest, running in several theaters for over a year. The film has since become a cult favorite and has received positive critical response.

—Ray Narducy

ASQUITH, Anthony

Nationality: British. **Born:** London, 9 November 1902; commonly known by childhood name "Puffin"; son of the Liberal Prime Minister H. H. Asquith. **Education:** Winchester, and at Balliol College, Oxford 1921-25. **Career:** Founding member of London Film Society, 1925; visited Hollywood as guest of Douglas Fairbanks and Mary Pickford, 1926; joined British Instructional Films, 1926; directed (sometimes uncredited or credited as co-director) first feature, *Shooting Stars,* from his own screenplay, 1927; signed to Gainsborough Films, 1932; president of Association of Cinematographic Technicians, 1937-68; began association with writer Terence Rattigan, 1939; produced *Carmen* for Covent Garden, 1953; directed ballets for television, mid-1950s. **Awards:** Fellow, British Film Institute, Commander of the Order of Al Merito della Republica, Italy. **Died:** In London, 21 February 1968.

Films as Director:

1927 *Shooting Stars* (+ sc)
1928 *Underground* (+ sc); *The Runaway Princess* (*Princess Priscilla's Fortnight*) (+ sc)
1929 *A Cottage on Dartmoor* (*Escape from Dartmoor*) (+ sc)
1931 *Tell England* (*Battle of Gallipoli*) (co-d, co-sc); *Dance, Pretty Lady* (+ sc, adapt)
1933 *The Lucky Number*
1934 *Unfinished Symphony* (co-d for English version only)
1935 *Moscow Nights* (*I Stand Condemned*) (+ co-sc)
1938 *Pygmalion* (co-d, co-sc)
1939 *French without Tears*
1940 *Freedom Radio* (*The Voice in the Night*); *Quiet Wedding*; *Channel Incident* (doc) (+ pr)
1941 *Rush Hour* (doc); *Cottage to Let* (*Bombsight Stolen*)
1942 *Uncensored*
1943 *We Dive at Dawn*; *The Demi-Paradise* (*Adventure for Two*); *Welcome to Britain* (doc)
1944 *Fanny by Gaslight* (*Man of Evil*); *Two Fathers* (doc)
1945 *The Way to the Stars* (*Johnny in the Clouds*)
1947 *While the Sun Shines*
1948 *The Winslow Boy*
1950 *The Woman in Question* (*Five Angles on Murder*); *The Browning Version*
1951 *The Importance of Being Earnest* (+ sc)
1952 *The Net* (*Project M7*); *The Final Test*
1954 *The Young Lovers* (*Chance Meeting*)
1955 *On Such a Night*
1956 *Carrington VC* (*Court Martial*)
1958 *Orders to Kill*; *The Doctor's Dilemma*
1959 *Libel!*
1960 *The Millionairess*; *Zero*
1961 *Two Living, One Dead*
1962 *Guns of Darkness*
1963 *The VIPs*; *An Evening with the Royal Ballet* (doc) (co-d)
1964 *The Yellow Rolls-Royce*

Other Films:

1927 *Boadicea* (Hill) (asst-d)
1932 *Marry Me* (Thiele) (sc)
1933 *Letting in the Sunshine* (Lane) (sc)

Publications

By ASQUITH: articles—

"Anthony Asquith and His Art," in *Film Weekly* (London), 26 November 1928.
"Anthony Asquith's Defence," in *Film Weekly* (London), 7 November 1931.
"The Secrets of Screen Success," in *Picturegoer* (London), 20 May 1933.
"The Director and the Actor," in *Picturegoer* (London), 9 November 1935.
"Wanted—A Genius," in *Sight and Sound* (London), Spring 1938.
"Ten Years of Technique," in *Film Weekly* (London), 22 October 1938.
"I Decide to Be a Film Director," in *Listener* (London), 11 June 1942.
"The Tenth Muse Climbs Parnassus," in *Penguin Film Review* (London), no. 1, 1946.
"A Style in Film Direction," in *Cine-Technician* (London), July-August 1951.

"The Directorial Touch," in *Cine-Technician* (London), September-October 1951.

"Days with Chaplin: Hollywood Memories of the 1920s," in *Cine Technician* (London), November/December 1952.

"The Importance of Being Faithful," in *Theatre Arts* (London), April 1953.

"Note on Americanization," in *Film* (London), September/October 1955.

"The Play's the Thing," in *Films and Filming* (London), February 1959.

On ASQUITH: books—

Noble, Peter, *Anthony Asquith,* London, 1951.

Elvin, George, and others, editors, *Anthony Asquith: A Tribute,* London, 1968.

Durgnat, Raymond, *A Mirror for England,* London, 1970.

Minney, R. J., *"Puffin" Asquith: A Biography of the Hon. Anthony Asquith, Aesthete, Aristocrat, Prime Minister's Son and Film Maker,* London, 1973; as *The Films of Anthony Asquith,* New York, 1976.

Armes, Roy, *A Critical History of the British Cinema,* London, 1978.

Association of Cinematograph, Television and Allied Technicians, *ACTION! Fifty Years in the Life of a Union,* London, 1983.

Richards, Jeffrey, and Tony Aldgate, *Britain Can Take It: The British Cinema and the Second World War,* London, 1983.

On ASQUITH: articles—

Benedict, William, "Limelight on Anthony Asquith," in *Picturegoer* (London), 21 March 1942.

Woodhouse, Bruce, "Asquith the Enthusiastic," in *Picturegoer* (London), 14 August 1948.

Massie, Paul, "What Asquith Did for Me," in *Films and Filming* (London), February 1958.

Cowie, Peter, "This England," in *Films and Filming* (London), October 1963.

de Grunwald, Anatole, "The Champagne Set," in *Films and Filming* (London), February 1965.

Balcon, Michael, "Anthony Asquith, 1902-1968," in *Sight and Sound* (London), April 1968.

Kalish, Robert, "Filmed Theatre: The Importance of Being Asquith," in *Thousand Eyes Magazine* (New York), November 1975.

"Anthony Asquith," in *Film Dope* (London), March 1988.

* * *

Anthony Asquith was a competent, occasionally brilliant director whose career in the British film industry spanned an unbroken period of over forty years. Yet while several of his peers and contemporaries have been lauded and rediscovered as a byproduct of the critical rehabilitation of the British cinema undertaken over the last fifteen or so years, Asquith's place in the pantheon of great British filmmakers is far from established. Perhaps this is because, with the anglophobia endemic in the history of British film criticism (despite the contribution to world cinema of Chaplin, Grierson, Hitchcock, Lean, and Powell, among others), the *auteurs* of British cinema tend to be seen as working outside a mainstream which, though dismissed, is never clearly defined. Asquith "fails" as an *auteur* because, despite attempts to categorize him as a director of "mere" literary adaptations, his *oeuvre* contains a wide range of generic styles and influences, making an authorial, individuated presence difficult to detect. Yet in this very "failure" he may be said to represent, to a greater degree than any other director, the diverse and often contradictory nature of British cinema's mainstream.

Given his privileged background as the Oxford-educated son of the Prime Minister, his membership in the London Film Society of the 1920s, and his early eagerness to incorporate techniques from German, Swedish, Soviet, and French cinema into his own films, Asquith might have fitted more easily into the stereotype of the documentary filmmaker. Yet, although invited to join the Empire Marketing Board by John Grierson in the early 1930s, he chose to remain in the far-from-respectable popular field. His background had enabled him to visit Hollywood in 1926 and stay as a guest at Pickfair while observing Lubitsch and Chaplin at work, but on his return he began in a humble role with Harry Bruce Woolfe's British Instructional Films. Within a year he was allowed to develop his own original script, and with the veteran director A. V. Bramble nominally in charge, *Shooting Stars* was made. With its cinematic wit, its audacious self-reflexivity, and its stylistic bravura, the film is clearly Asquith's.

Yet his career—despite the promise of *Shooting Stars* and films such as *A Cottage on Dartmoor,* compared at the time to Hitchcock not only for its lower-middle-class murder milieu—floundered somewhat in the early 1930s. The presence of a soundtrack suddenly made Asquith's characters seem unappealingly fey in contrast to the apparently classless stars of the American cinema. Despite being contracted to Alexander Korda and Michael Balcon, the two foremost producers of the period, Asquith (like the British cinema as a whole) made little of note during the mid-1930s.

The turning point came with *Pygmalion,* where, ironically, the very issues of class and accent, so problematic for Asquith's career and for the British cinema, are central to the film. *Pygmalion* was especially popular in America, and the inventiveness and fluidity with which Shaw's wordy (though Oscar-winning) screenplay is treated by Asquith and his editor, David Lean, make this—far from being a "stagey" adaptation—a film which bears comparison with the masterpieces of the French cinema of the time, whose roots were often similarly theatrical. From this success Asquith went on, during the war, to a run of films which perhaps represent the peak of his filmmaking career.

The Way to the Stars is perhaps his finest film. An evocation of the lives of British and American airmen on a wartime air base, the film—with its opening shots of a deserted base and its notable absence of any gung-ho jerry-bashing—struck a deep chord with audiences in 1945. In its understated, reserved tone, however, it seems a long way from the less "serious" Gainsborough melodrama *Fanny by Gaslight,* made the year before; a film nevertheless richly enjoyable. The narrative tension aboard the stranded submarine in *We Dive at Dawn* parallels the struggle between the documentary mode employed and Asquith's more dramatic concerns, while the film itself features, like so many of the director's, an outstanding acting performance, here by the brooding Eric Portman. The pictures of Englishness—towards which Asquith's direction displays a curious ambivalence—in the documentary *A Welcome to Britain* (aimed at American servicemen), and in the intriguingly bizarre *The Demi-Paradise* (uniquely, a pro-Soviet film), together with the polished comedy of *Quiet Wedding* and the spy thriller-comedy of *A Cottage to Let* (in which the apparently redoubtable John Mills plays a Nazi spy), complete a body of work which, in its generic diversity as much as its concentration of purpose, might stand for many of the achievements of the British cinema as a whole during the Second World War.

Equally important in Asquith's contribution to British film culture—the environment in which films are made, seen, and discussed—was his work in helping to establish, then lead, the unionization of the British film industry. As president of the Association of Cine-Technicians from its beginnings in the late 1930s to his death, he played a key role, especially during the Second World War, in fighting for continuity of film production in Britain, gaining powerful enemies in the process. His motivation, unlike that of many of his colleagues in the ACTT, did not spring from a radical political position so much as from an indefatigable commitment to the British cinema. This, together with his appreciation of his fellow technicians' role in the

Anthony Asquith

filmmaking process, was reflected also in his theoretical discussions of cinema which, in the 1930s especially, appeared in the popular film magazines of the day. That he wrote for *Picturegoer* and not its highbrow equivalents typified his belief in an intelligent but ultimately popular British cinema.

In the immediate postwar years, when the British cinema underwent a genuine revival, Asquith, despite his earlier successes, did not play such a prominent role. His collaborations with the playwright Terence Rattigan (characterized by Raymond Durgnat as "Rattigasquith") were, with their upper-middle-class world view, representative of a certain form of "quality" cinema. Though dismissed subsequently as stuffy and irredeemably bourgeois, the films occasionally transcend the class-bound world they inhabit: *The Browning Version,* for instance, rather than being a repressed film, may be seen now as a moving and beautifully pointed study of repression.

Although Asquith regularly directed films throughout the 1950s, to generally favorable reviews, most have been overlooked. Several from this period, made before the better-known but embarrassingly banal star-studded efforts of the early 1960s, are worth reassessing. In *Orders to Kill,* Asquith uses music, always a notable element in his work, to chilling effect: the murder scene should be compulsory viewing for those who dismiss him as a "cozy" or "safe" director. *Libel,* in which Dirk Bogarde portrays three apparently identical characters—one a nobleman, one a charlatan, and one a shambling wreck—perhaps offers a comment on the director's own personal struggles. Where the earlier *Fanny by Gaslight,* in the context of a jolly costume romp, worked through the all-important questions of class and respectability (questions from which this honorable son of the Prime Minister, despite regulation on-set attire of a boiler suit, never managed to escape), *Libel,* thanks to Bogarde's performance, transcends the realms of the courtroom drama to offer a fascinating study of lost identity—a problem shared by the British cinema and Asquith (exacerbated in his case by a struggle against alcoholism).

Yet by the end of the decade, the new generation who came out of Oxford to take the world of cinema by storm saw in Asquith's work much of what they perceived to be wrong with British cinema, and turned their cameras towards the rugged working classes. The angry young men were cruelly dismissive of their predecessor, a blow from which his reputation has yet to recover, despite the ironic similarities between "Puffin" Asquith and, for instance, the ever-irascible Lindsay Anderson. For his directing, his union activities, but above all for his attempts, while working in the mainstream, to transcend the binary oppositions endemic in British cinema—documentary/melodrama, union/management, popular/avant-garde, upper class/working class, literary/cinematic—Asquith should now be seen as one of the key figures in its reconstructed history.

—Nicholas Thomas

ASTRUC, Alexandre

Nationality: French. **Born:** Paris, 13 July 1923. **Education:** Saint-Germain-en-Laye, and at Polytechnique. **Family:** Married Elyette Helies, 1983. **Career:** Literary and film critic, since 1945; published novel *Les Vacances,* 1945; assistant to Marcel Achard and Marc Allegret, 1946-47; made two short films, 1948-49; began series of six feature-length films with *Mauvaises rencontres,* 1955; TV reporter for Radio Luxembourg, 1969-72. **Awards:** Chevalier de la Légion d'honneur; Officier de l'Ordre du Mérite; Officier des Arts et des Lettres. **Address:** 168 rue de Grenelle, 75007 Paris, France.

Films as Director:

1948 *Aller et retour* (*Aller-retour*) (+ sc)
1949 *Ulysse ou Les Mauvaises rencontres* (+ sc)
1953 *Le Rideau cramoisi* (*The Crimson Curtain*) (+ sc)
1955 *Les Mauvaises rencontres* (+ co-sc)
1958 *Une Vie* (*End of Desire*) (+ co-sc)
1960 *La Proie pour l'ombre* (+ co-sc)
1962 *L'Education sentimentale* (+ sc)
1963 *Le Puits et le pendule* (*The Pit and the Pendulum*) (for TV) (+ sc)
1965 *Evariste Galois* (+ sc)
1966 *La Longue Marche* (+ co-sc)
1968 *Flammes sur l'Adriatique* (+ co-sc)
1976 *Sartre par lui-même* (co-d)

Other Films:

1948 *Jean de la Lune* (Achard) (co-sc)
1949 *La P ... respecteuse* (Pagliero) (co-sc); *La Valse de Paris* (Achard) (role)
1950 *L'Affaire Manet* (Aurel) (commentary)
1954 *Le Vicomte de Bragelonne* (Cerchio) (co-sc)
1964 *Bassae* (Pollet) (sc)
1974 *La Jeune Fille assassinee* (role as Publisher)
1993 *Francois Truffaut: Stolen Portraits* (role as himself)

Publications

By ASTRUC: books—

Les Vacances, 1945.
La Tête la première, Ciel de Cendres, 1975.
Le Serpent Jaune, 1976.
Sartre, Paris, 1977.
Quand la chouette s'envole, 1978.
Le Permissionnaire, 1982.
Le Roman de Descartes, 1989.
De la caméra au stylo, 1992.
L'autre versant de la colline, Paris, 1993.

By ASTRUC: articles—

"Le Feu et la glace," in *Cahiers du Cinéma* (Paris), December 1952; as "Fire and Ice," in *Cahiers du Cinéma in English* (New York), January 1966.
Interview in *Film Français* (Paris), 6 March 1987.
"'L'aurore' sur un drap," in *Cahiers du Cinéma* (Paris), May 1991.

On ASTRUC: articles—

Eisner, Lotte, "Venice Film Festival," in *Film Culture* (New York), vol. 2, no. 1, 1956.
Weber, Eugene, "An Escapist Realism," in *Film Quarterly* (Berkeley), Winter 1959.
"Sur une émission de télévision," in *Cahiers du Cinéma* (Paris), February/March 1974.
Beylie, Claude, "Quatre de la forfanterie," in *Ecran* (Paris), October 1975.
"Alexandre Astruc," in *Film Dope* (London), March 1988.
Moullet, L., "Splendeurs et vanites du lyrisme," in *Cahiers du Cinéma,* October 1992.

* * *

Alexandre Astruc was the embodiment of the revolutionary hopes of a renewed cinema after the war. True, Clément, Bresson, and Melville were already making films in a new way, but making them in the age-old industry. Astruc represented a new, arrogant sensibility. He had grown up on the ideas of Sartre and was one of the youthful literati surrounding the philosopher in the St. Germain-des-Prés cafes. There he talked of a new French culture being born, one that demanded new representations in fiction and film.

His personal aspirations were great and grew even greater when his novel *Les Vacances* was published by the prestigious N.R.F., almost winning an important prize. While writing essays on art and culture for *Combat* and *L'Ecran français* he became convinced that the cinema must replace the novel.

But first the cinema must become more like the novel. In his crucial essay "Le Caméra stylo," written the same year as Sartre's "Situation of the Writer in 1948," he called for an end to institutional cinema and for a new style that would be both personal and malleable. He wanted cinema to be able to treat diverse ideas and a range of expressions. He, like Sartre, wanted to become ethical.

This was the first loud clarion cry of the New Wave and it provoked attention in its own day. Astruc found himself linked with Bazin, Cocteau, Marker, and Tacchella against the Stalinists at *L'Ecran français,* led by Louis Daquin. Banding together to form "Objectif 48," these men created a new atmosphere for cinema, attracting the young Truffaut and Godard to their screenings.

Everyone looked to Astruc to begin turning out short films, but his 16mm efforts ran aground. Soon he began writing scripts for acceptable standard directors like Marc Allégret. Finally in 1952 he was able to make *Le Rideau cramoisi* in his own way. It was a remarkable way: this nineteenth-century mystery tale was reduced to a set of unforgettable images and a soundtrack that contained no dialogue whatsoever. Pushing the voice-over discoveries of Bresson and Melville to the limit, Astruc's narrational device places the film somewhere between dream and memory. This coincides perfectly with the haunting night photography and Anouk Aimée's inscrutably romantic performance.

There followed more adaptations, not because Astruc had joined the industry's penchant for such quality material, but because he always believed in the overriding import of style, seeing plots as pretexts only. The color photography in *Une Vie,* for example, explores the painterly concerns of the impressionists. But since the plot comes from a Maupassant tale written in the same era, the result is unpretentious.

In his older age Astruc has renounced this obsession with style. The themes that possess him now, crises in marriage and love, can actually be seen in all his earlier work as well. Now he can explore these issues in television, the medium that seems perfectly suited to his early ideas. Only now his ideas have changed and so has his following. Alexandre Astruc must always be mentioned in any chronicle of modern French cinema, but his career can only be thought of as disappointing.

—Dudley Andrew

AUGUST, Bille

Nationality: Danish. **Born:** Copenhagen, 9 November 1948. **Education:** Studied advertising photography; earned diploma as a director of photography from Danish Film School, 1971. **Family:** Married Pernilla Ostergren, star of *Den Goda Viljan,* 1991. **Career:** Selected by filmmaker Jorn Donner as cinematographer on *Homeward in the Night,* 1976; directed his first feature, *Honningmane,* 1978; also directed dramas for Danish television, as well as episode of *The Young Indiana Jones Chronicles* for American television. **Awards:** Outstanding Film of the Year, London Festival, for *Zappa,* 1983; Special Jury Prize, Young Peoples' Cinema Festival at Lyon, and Best Danish Film Award, for *Tro, hab og kaerlighed,* 1984; Culture Award, Danish Trades Union Congress, 1984; Oscar, Best Foreign Film, and Palme d'or, Cannes Festival, for *Pelle erobreren,* 1987; Palme d'or, Cannes Festival, for *Den goda viljan,* 1992. **Agent:** Tom Chasin, The Chasin-Becsey Agency, 190 N. Canon Drive., Suite 201, Beverly Hills, CA 90210-5319, U.S.A.

Films as Director:

1978 *Honningmane* (*Honeymoon in My Life*) (+ sc); *Kim G.*
1983 *Zappa* (+ co-sc)
1984 *Tro, hab og kaerlighed* (*Twist and Shout*) (+ co-sc); *Busters verden* (*The World of Buster*) (for television)
1987 *Pelle erobreren* (*Pelle the Conqueror*) (+ co-sc)
1992 *Den goda viljan* (*The Best Intentions*)
1994 *House of the Spirits* (+ sc)

Films as Cinematographer:

1977 *Hemåt i Natten* (*Homeward in the Night*) (Lindstrom); *Miesta ei voi raiskata* (*Men Can't Be Raped*) (Donner)
1980 *Karleken* (*Love*) (Kallifatides)
1982 *The Grass Is Singing* (Raeburn)

Publications

By AUGUST: articles—

Interview in *Cinema* (Paris), April/May 1986.
Interview with Y. Alion, in *La Revue du Cinema* (Paris), November 1988.
Interview in *Positif* (Paris), November 1988.
"Film: Bille's Feast," an interview with J. Jensen, in *Village Voice* (New York), 7 June 1988.

On AUGUST: articles—

Brovik, I., article in *Chaplin* (Stockholm), vol. 30, 1988.
Flamm, Matthew, article in *New York Post,* 30 December 1988.

Bille August: Pelle Hvengegaard in *Pelle erobreren*

Lohr, Steve, "For Bergman, a New Twist on an Old Love," in *New York Times,* 6 September 1989.
"Bille August to Helm Script by Bergman," in *Variety* (New York), 13 September 1989.
Bjorkman, Stig, article in *Chaplin* (Stockholm), vol. 33, 1991/1992.
Maslin, Janet, "Swedish Film Takes Top Honor at Cannes," in *New York Times,* 19 May 1992.
Alderman, Bruce, "Intentions Bests Cannes Field," in *Variety* (New York), 25 May 1992.
Gritten, David, article in *Los Angeles Times,* 12 July 1992.
Jones, Andy, article in *Newsday* (Melville, New York), 16 July 1992.
Camhi, Leslie, "He Said, She Said," in *Village Voice* (New York), 28 July 1992.
Moerk, Christian, "Reluctant August Shuns Hollywood," in *Variety* (New York), 3 August 1992.
Cowie, Peter, "Directors of the Year," *International Film Guide* (London, Hollywood), 1994.

* * *

Since the retirement of Ingmar Bergman from film directing in the mid-1980s, Bille August has become Scandinavia's premiere international filmmaker.

August's debut feature, *In My Life,* the story of a seemingly bright and optimistic middle-class Copenhagen couple and how their hopes steadily disintegrate, heralded the appearance of an important young talent. His follow-up features, *Zappa* and *Twist and Shout,* are keenly observed tales of teen angst in the 1960s. For international audiences, they served as reminders that adolescent dilemmas and concerns cut across cultures and language barriers. August's next project was *The World of Buster,* an amusing made-for-TV kiddie film which ultimately is a minor credit on his filmography.

In *Zappa* and *Twist and Shout,* August examines the distinction between characters from separate social classes. This also is the case in the feature he made after *The World of Buster.* This work, the career-defining *Pelle the Conqueror,* is a wonderful, universal film about desire and disappointment, dignity and dreams. Along with Gabriel Axel's *Babette's Feast,* it was the first Scandinavian film since the heyday of Bergman to earn a high international profile.

Set at the turn of the twentieth century, it is the story of Lasse (Max von Sydow), a humble old widower who has emigrated with his son Pelle from poverty-stricken Sweden to the relative prosperity of Denmark. Lasse and Pelle are in search of a better life. Instead, they find themselves practically indentured servants on the aptly named Stone Farm, a harsh and dreary estate owned by a penny-pinching philanderer and his frustrated, faded beauty of a wife.

Pelle the Conqueror is a subtle film, the kind in which the characters' quick glances reveal volumes about what they are thinking and feeling but never, ever could articulate. Its multi-faceted narrative presents a landscape of villains and victims, a world in which any hint of true love is stifled, and an environment in which the well-heeled but repressed upper classes use and abuse their power by brutalizing the lower classes.

As the seasons turn and the plot unfolds, Pelle begins to transcend the mysteries and fears of childhood. It becomes clear to the boy that if he is ever to get beyond the stifling existence of Stone Farm, he will have to part with his loving, well-meaning, but weak father and set forth into the world. Indeed, the force that holds the film together is the relationship between Pelle and Lasse. There is a poignant, life-sustaining bond between the boy, whose experiences here clearly will shape the course of his future, and his father.

August never overplays the story's melodramatics. His direction is sure-handed as he weaves the tale, allowing the viewer to come to know Lasse, Pelle, and the other characters. As much as anything else, *Pelle the Conqueror* is a film about physical presences, such as the great ship that brings Lasse and Pelle to their new land, the rural landscape of Stone Farm, and the everyday details of farm labor. The images, stunningly captured by cinematographer Jorgen Persson, are as beautiful as they are loaded with drama and emotion.

Unlike dozens of filmmakers from across the world who have impressed with films not nearly as striking as *Pelle the Conqueror,* August has refused to go Hollywood. Instead, he has staunchly criticized films whose prime aesthetic motivations are car crashes and special effects, and has chosen to remain in his homeland and direct films which are motivated more by character and plot development.

Upon the success of *Pelle the Conqueror,* August was the logical choice to be selected by Bergman to direct the latter's autobiographical script, *The Best Intentions,* a follow-up to *Fanny and Alexander. The Best Intentions* is the story of the courtship and marriage of Bergman's parents; the end result is a film of which the master could be proud. The third film in the trilogy, *Sunday's Children,* was directed by Bergman's son, Daniel.

After *Pelle the Conqueror,* August had attempted to film *The House of the Spirits,* based on Isabel Allende's best-selling novel, but could not obtain adequate funding. He eventually got the film made on an estimated $27-million budget. The film was his first major foray into international filmmaking, but it also proved to be his first major failure. The *House of the Spirits* charts forty-five momentous years in the lives of the South American Trueba family. August directed a notable cast that included Meryl Streep, Jeremy Irons, Glenn Close, Winona Ryder, Vanessa Redgrave, Armin Mueller-Stahl, and Antonio Banderas. Unfortunately, the result was wholly unsuccessful, with many of the actors miscast and seeming out of place in the setting.

—Rob Edelman

AUTANT-LARA, Claude

Nationality: French. **Born:** Luzarches (Seine-et-Oize), 5 August 1903. **Education:** Lycée Janson-de-Sailly, Paris, at Ecole nationale supérieure des arts décoratifs, at Ecole des Beaux Arts, and at Mill Hill School, London. **Family:** Married Ghislain Auboin (deceased). **Career:** Art director on L'Herbier's *Le Carnaval des vérités,* 1925; made several avant-garde films, and worked as assistant to René Clair, 1923-25; made French versions of American films in Hollywood, 1930-32; returned to France and directed first feature, 1933; president of Syndicat des techniciens du cinéma, 1948-55; president of Fédération nationale du spectacle, 1957-63. **Awards:** Grand prix du Cinema français, 1954; Prix Europa, Rome, 1974; Chevalier de la Légion d'honneur; Commandeur des Arts et des Lettres. **Address:** 66 rue Lepic, 75018 Paris, France.

Films as Director:

1923 *Faits divers*
1926 *Construire un feu*; *Vittel*
1930 *Buster se marie* (d of French version of American film *Parlor, Bedroom and Bath* [Sedgwick])
1931 *Le Plumbier amoureux* (d of French version of American film *The Passionate Plumber* [Sedgwick]); *Le Fils du Rajah* (d of French version of American film *Son of India* [Feyder]); *La Pente* (d of French version of American film); *Pur Sang* (d of French version of American film)
1932 *L'Athlète incomplet* (d of French version of American film); *Le Gendarme est sans pitié*; *Un Client sérieux*; *Monsieur le Duc*; *La Peur des coups*; *Invite Monsieur à dîner*
1933 *Ciboulette* (+ co-sc, co-costume des)

1936 *My Partner Mr. Davis* (*The Mysterious Mr. Davis*) (+ co-sc)
1937 *L'Affaire du courrier de Lyon* (*The Courier of Lyon*) (co-d)
1938 *Le Ruisseau* (co-d)
1939 *Fric-Frac* (co-d)
1942 *Le Mariage de Chiffon*; *Lettres d'amour*
1943 *Douce* (*Love Story*)
1944 *Sylvie et le fantôme* (*Sylvie and the Phantom*)
1947 ***Le Diable au corps*** (*Devil in the Flesh*)
1949 *Occupe-toi d'Amélie* (*Oh Amelia!*)
1951 *L'Auberge rouge* (*The Red Inn*) (+ co-sc)
1952 "L'Orgueil" ("Pride") episode of *Les 7 Péchés capitaux* (*The Seven Deadly Sins*) (+ co-sc)
1953 *Le Bon Dieu sans confession* (+ co-sc); *Le Blé en herbe* (*The Game of Love*) (+ co-sc)
1954 *Le Rouge et le noir*
1956 *Marguerite de la nuit*; *La Traversée de Paris* (*Four Bags Full*)
1958 *En Cas de malheur* (*Love Is My Profession*); *Le Joueur*
1959 *La Jument verte* (*The Green Mare*) (+ pr)
1960 *Les Régates de San Francisco*; *Le Bois des amants*
1961 *Tu ne tueras point* (*Non uccidere*; *Thou Shalt Not Kill*) (+ co-pr); *Le Comte de Monte Cristo* (*The Story of the Count of Monte Cristo*)
1962 *Vive Henri IV ... Vive l'amour!*
1963 *Le Meurtrier* (*Enough Rope*)
1964 *Le Magot de Joséfa* (+ co-sc); "La Fourmi" episode of *Humour noir*
1965 *Le Journal d'une femme en blanc* (*A Woman in White*)
1966 *Le Nouveau Journal d'une femme en blanc* (*Une Femme en blanc se révolte*)
1967 "Aujourd'hui" ("Paris Today") episode of *Le Plus Vieux Métier du monde* (*The Oldest Profession*); *Le Franciscain de Bourges*
1969 *Les Patates* (+ co-sc)
1971 *Le Rouge et le blanc*
1973 *Lucien Leuwen* (for TV)
1977 *Gloria* (+ co-sc)

Other Films:

1919 *Le Carnaval des vérités* (L'Herbier) (art d, costume des); *L'Ex-voto* (L'Herbier) (art d, costume des)
1920 *L'Homme du large* (L'Herbier) (art d, costume des)
1921 *Villa Destin* (L'Herbier) (art d, costume des); *Eldorado* (L'Herbier) (co-art d, costume des)
1922 *Don Juan et Faust* (L'Herbier) (art d, costume des)
1923 *L'Inhumaine* (L'Herbier) (co-art d, costume des); *Le Marchand de plaisir* (Catelain) (co-art d, costume des); *Nana* (Renoir) (co-art d, co-costume des)
1927 *Le Diable au coeur* (L'Herbier) (art d, costume des)

Publications

By AUTANT-LARA: books—

La Rage dans le couer: Chronique cinématographique du 20ème siècle, Paris, 1984.
Hollywood Cake-walk (1930-1932): Chronique cinématographique du 20ème siècle, Paris, 1985.

By AUTANT-LARA: articles—

"Styles du cinéma français," in *La Livre d'or du Cinéma Français 1947-48,* edited by René Jeanne and Charles Ford, Paris, 1948.
Numerous polemical articles on the state of French cinema and studios, and attacking government policies, in *La Technicien du Film* (Paris), *Les Lettres Françaises* (Paris), and other French periodicals, early to mid-1950s.
"*La Traversée de Paris* est un film insolité," interview with Martine Monod, in *Les Lettres Françaises* (Paris), 4 October 1956.
"Les Etrennes du cinéma françaises," in *Les Lettres Françaises* (Paris), 3 January 1957.
"Attention, notre métier n'est pas un métier d'hurluberlus," in *La Technicien du Film* (Paris), May 1958.
"La Parole est à Claude Autant-Lara," interview with Marcel Oms, in *Cahiers de la Cinématheque* (Paris), Summer 1973.
Interview with J. C. Bonnet and others, in *Cinématographe* (Paris), April 1978.
"Lausanne (Autant-Lara)," in *Positif* (Paris), December 1981.
Interview in *Cahiers du Cinéma* (Paris), Summer 1983.
Interview in *Film Français* (Paris), 6 March 1987.

On AUTANT-LARA: books—

Buache, Freddy, *Claude Autant-Lara,* Lausanne, 1982.
L'Institut Lumière présente Claude Autant-Lara en 33 films, Lyons, 1983.

On AUTANT-LARA: articles—

de la Roche, Catherine, "The Fighter," in *Films and Filming* (London), January 1955.
Durgnat, Raymond, "The Rebel with Kid Gloves," in *Films and Filming* (London), October and November 1960.
Biofilmography in *Film Dope* (London), no. 2, 1973.
Special issue of *Cahiers de la Cinématheque* (Paris), Spring 1973.
"*L'Auberge rouge* Dossier," in *Cinéma* (Paris), July-August 1982.
Carbonnier, A., and Joel Magny, in *Cinéma* (Paris), September 1982.
"Claude Autant-Lara," in *Film Dope* (London), March 1988.
Joffre, Laurent, "La tache brune: De l'affaire du Carmel aux propos d'Autant-Lara," in *Nouvel Observateur* (Paris), 14 September 1989.
Bergan, Ronald, "Out of Sight, Out of Mind," in *Guardian* (London), 28 September 1989.

* * *

Claude Autant-Lara is best known for his post-World War II films in the French "tradition of quality." His earliest work in the industry was more closely related to the avant-garde movements of the 1920s than to the mainstream commercial cinema with which he was later identified. He began as a set designer in the 1920s, serving as art director for several of Marcel L'Herbier's films, including *L'Inhumaine,* and for Jean Renoir's *Nana*; he also assisted René Clair on a number of his early shorts. After directing several films, he worked on an early wide-screen experiment, *Construire un feu,* using the Hypergonar system designed by Henri Chretien. On the basis of his work in this format, he was brought to Hollywood and ended up directing French-language versions of American films for several years. He returned to France and directed his first feature of note, *Ciboulette,* in 1933.

During the war Autant-Lara exercised greater control in his choice of projects and started working with scenarists Jean Aurenche and Pierre Bost, who would continue to be among his most consistent collaborators. He also started assembling a basic crew that worked with him through the 1960s: composer René Cloerec, designer Max Douy, editor Madeleine Gug, and cameraman Jacques Natteau. Autant-Lara rapidly established his reputation as a studio director in the tradition of quality. For many, the names Aurenche, Bost, and Autant-Lara are synonymous with this movement. Their films are characterized by an emphasis on scripting and dialogue, a high proportion of literary

Claude Autant-Lara

adaptations, a solemn "academic" visual style, and general theatricality (due largely to the emphasis on dialogue and its careful delivery to create a cinematic world determined by psychological realism). They frequently attack or ridicule social groups and institutions.

Autant-Lara's first major postwar film, *Le Diable au corps,* was adapted from a novel by Raymond Radiguet. Set during World War I, it tells the story of an adolescent's affair with a young married woman whose husband is away at war. While the film was considered scandalous by many for its valorization of adultery and tacit condemnation of war, it was also seen to express the cynical mood of postwar youth. Autant-Lara's films seem to revel in irreverent depictions of established authority and institutions. *L'Auberge rouge* is a black comedy involving murderous innkeepers, a group of insipid travellers (representing a cross-section of classes), and a monk trapped by the vows of confession.

Throughout the 1950s Autant-Lara was extremely active. His successes of the period include *Le Rouge et le noir,* adapted from Stendhal; *La Traversée de Paris,* a comedy about black-market trading in occupied France; and *En cas de malheur,* a melodrama involving a middle-aged lawyer, his young client, and her student lover. At the same time Autant-Lara was an active spokesman for the French film industry. As head of several film trade unions and other groups promoting French film, he criticized (often harshly) the Centre National du cinéma française (CNC) for its inadequate support of the industry; the American film industry for its stultifying presence in the French market; and government censorship policies for limiting freedom of expression.

Autant-Lara's prominence was effectively eclipsed with the emergence of the French New Wave, although he continued directing films. In the 1950s he, along with Aurenche and Bost, had been subject to frequent critical attacks, most notably by François Truffaut. In the wake of the success of the new generation of directors, Autant-Lara's work is often seen as no more than the "stale" French cinema of the 1950s which was successfully displaced by the more vital films of the New Wave. Yet in spite of, indeed owing to, their "armchair" criticism of authority, bleak representation of human nature, and slow-paced academic style, they possess a peculiarly appealing, insolent sensibility.

—M. B. White

BABENCO, Hector

Nationality: Argentinian. **Born:** Buenos Aires, 7 February 1946. **Career:** Travelled to Europe, 1963; worked as Bible salesman and as extra for Cinecitta, Rome; moved to São Paolo, Brazil, 1971; made first feature, *Rei da noite,* 1976; made first English-language film, *Kiss of the Spider Woman,* 1983.

Films as Director:

1975 *Rei da noite* (*King of the Night*)
1978 *Lúcio Flávio*
1981 ***Pixote*** (+ sc)
1985 *Kiss of the Spider Woman*
1988 *Ironweed*; *The Second Killing of the Dog*
1990 *My Foolish Heart*
1991 *At Play in the Fields of the Lord* (+ co-sc)

Other Films:

1987 *Besame mucho* (pr)

Publications

By BABENCO: articles—

"Individual Solutions," an interview with G. Csicsery, in *Film Quarterly* (Los Angeles), Fall 1982.
Interview with B. Kawin, in *Film Quarterly* (Los Angeles), February 1986.
"Dialogue on Film: Hector Babenco," in *American Film* (Washington, D.C.), April 1986.
"Hector Babenco: Bear-Faced Brilliance," an interview with D. Nicholson, in *Films and Filming* (London), May 1988.
Interview in *Time Out* (London), 18 May 1988.
"Manchmal gehen Armut und Ehre Hand in Hand," an interview in *Film und Fernsehen,* vol 18, no. 7, 1990.
"Babenco and Zaentz," an interview with P. Mertens, in *Film en Televisie + Video,* April 1992.
Interview with N. Okrent, in *Cineaste,* vol. 19, no. 1, 1992.

On BABENCO: articles—

Yakir, Dan, "Braziliant," in *Film Comment* (New York), May/June 1984.
Stone, J., "On the Edge," in *American Film* (Washington, D.C.), October 1984.
Chaillet, Jean Paul, "Hector Babenco: Le franc-tireur," in *Première* (Paris), June 1985.
Zajc, M., "Hector Babenco," in *Ekran,* vol. 16, no. 3, 1991.
McDonough, M., "*At Play in the Fields of the Lord,*" in *Film Journal,* December 1991.
Niogret, H., "En liberte dans les champs du Seigneur," in *Positif,* May 1992.

* * *

Hector Babenco, an Argentinean who has so far filmed only in Brazil and the United States, is one of the current cinema's most consistent miners of marginality. If his burrowing has not always hit gold, it has resulted in a relatively small number of films that, as a body of work, represent a penetrating and richly variegated portrait of marginality in the Americas. His debut film's very title, *King of the Night,* is telling. In the film, a bourgeois man's hypocritical and cowardly rejection of a prostitute's love is the catalyst for a descent into promiscuity, alcoholism, murder, and jail. The film ends with him drunk, alone, and out on the street. Night conjures up crime, sex, deviance, and dreams, and a materialist but poetic rendering of its conjurations is the fabric of Babenco's *oeuvre.*

Outsiders are at the center of Babenco's work. The eponymous hero of *Lúcio Flávio* is a bandit; the gang of delinquents in *Pixote* are escapees from juvenile prison who make a living selling drugs, stealing, pimping, and killing; the two cellmates in *Kiss of the Spiderwoman* are a political prisoner and a homosexual; and lastly, the romantic lovers in *Ironweed* are a pair of Bowery bums.

Babenco's outsiders differ from those of many other directors in that their alienation is not merely internal. As *Pixote* clearly exemplifies, it has its origins outside the psyche and is the result of social, political, and/or economic exclusion. Even in *Ironweed,* though Francis (Jack Nicholson) decides to leave his family when he drops his baby, that fatal accident is the culmination of a powerlessness brought to an increasingly unbearable pitch by low wages, strike-breaking, and unemployment. On the rare occasion that Babenco's characters choose to opt out of society (Frank, Valentin in *Kiss*) their decision is also rooted in the social. More often, they are kicked out (Molina in *Kiss*) or prevented from entering it (the children in *Pixote*).

Marginalization, however, does have psychological repercussions, and Babenco does not ignore them. By the standards of middle-class morality, his characters are warped. They lie, steal, and sometimes even kill. And they perceive these acts as bordering on the banal. The extraordinary power of *Pixote* is due partly to its graphic depiction of the facility with which children can perform the most grisly actions, incorporate them into their quotidian, yet still retain a childish innocence.

The social and psychological alienation experienced by Babenco's characters is not, as is often the case in American films, accompanied by emotional retardation. On the contrary, love, desire, want, or need are articulately expressed through either word or gesture then spontaneously gratified or denied. In Babenco's films only the bourgeois (Valentin in *Kiss,* for example) are scared of, or stingy with, their emotions. The rest are free with their feelings. However, the expression of emotion is not an end in itself for Babenco: his characters can be changed by it (some, like Molina, for the better, others, like the King of the Night, for the worse). Love can keep one going. But it is

Hector Babenco directing William Hurt in *Kiss of the Spider Woman*

often unreliable and impermanent and, more importantly, it doesn't get one a meal, better living conditions, or out of jail. Life has made Babenco's characters hard. They are cynical about institutions and experience has taught that justice exists only for others. Yet in each other they continue to hope and trust; to each other they often become family.

Babenco's characters can escape the material world only in fantasy. Sometimes the dream sequence is really a nightmare, as when Lúcio Flávio dreams first of his girlfriend's murder and then, near the end of the film, of his own. Sometimes the fantasies are only verbalized: in *Pixote,* the children *tell* each other their hopes of being rich, owning a car, and living on the beach. Yet the dream sequence we are shown is Pixote's nightmare of running nude through the night attempting to escape a flashing car. Fantasy, of course, is the very heart of *Kiss*—it is what makes Molina and Valentin's life bearable.

Babenco makes no great distinction between the real and the imaginary. Dreams inform life, are part of life. In some instances, the films' movement from external to internal world is motivated (Pixote sniffs glue, Molina begins to weave his story). But Babenco has the facility of shifting from the real to the imaginary with a cut. Indeed his talent for transporting the viewer in and out of people's heads is Tolstoyan. In *Ironweed,* for example, Francis's past, the ghosts that haunt him, and Helen's fantasy of herself as a singer share equal billing with their external reality. The film changes point-of-view without heavy symbolism or visible strain.

In spite of the dream or fantasy elements, Babenco's films are various attempts at representations of realism. *Lúcio Flávio* was based on a life of a real outlaw who collaborated with the police. *Pixote* began as a documentary and was turned into a fiction film only when the authorities refused Babenco permission to shoot in the juvenile detention centers. Both *Lúcio* and *Pixote* were marketed as *exposés.* Babenco himself is on camera in front of a slum at the beginning of *Pixote* introducing the film and simultaneously testifying to the authenticity of the problem that is about to be dramatized. The Brazilian films were received as realist; at home, audience and author share in the cultural negotiations of such definitions. In North America and Western Europe, on-location shootings, non-professional actors, and themes of poverty and deprivation are commonly accepted as the signifiers that best communicate Latin America.

It is Babenco's American films, however, which reveal the extent to which a text is understood in light of its context. The cultural specificity of the notion of realism is made manifest in *Kiss of the Spiderwoman,* Babenco's first American film. The film tries to make a distinction between the artifices of the black-and-white fantasy movie-within-the-movie and the supposedly stark steely hued realism of the protagonists' life in jail, but it doesn't quite succeed. Realism is ning, while his collage editing and soundtrack again create an bility leading to "nothingness." *Castro Street,* which depicts an strialized area, is extraordinary for its combination of diverse ographic representations—black and white, color, positive and ative—in editing and superimposition. *Quick Billy* contains the- c and stylistic elements of most of Baillie's previous films; its ifs include autobiography, "portrait"-like representation of people events, and an underlying theme, made explicit in the film's final ion, of Western man's aggressiveness toward his surroundings.

—Fred Camper

ARDEM, Juan Antonio

tionality: Spanish. **Born:** Juan Antonio Bardem-Munoz in Madrid, uly 1922. **Education:** Instituto de Investigaciones Cinematograficas, 47-48. **Career:** Worked for Spanish Ministry of Agriculture, as- gned to Cinema section, 1946; wrote for film periodicals, and on ripts with Luis Berlanga, from 1947; began film magazine *Objectivo,* 53 (banned by government, 1955); arrested for political reasons, 56 and later; produced through Uninci company, 1958-61; head of panish directors' guild, 1970's; directed Bulgarian/U.S.S.R./East Ger- an production of *The Warning,* 1981.

ilms as Director:

949 *Paseo sobre una guerra antigua* (co-d, co-sc) (silent short incorporated by Luis Escobar into feature *La honradez de la cerradura)*
1950 *Barajas, aeropuerto internacional* (short) (+ sc)
1951 *Esa pareja feliz* (*That Happy Pair*) (co-d, co-sc)
1954 *Cómicos* (*Comedians*) (+ sc); *Felices Pascuas* (+ co-sc)
1955 ***Muerte de un ciclista*** (*Death of a Cyclist*; *Age of Infidelity*) (+ sc)
1956 *Calle Mayor* (*Grand Rue*; *The Lovemaker*) (+ sc)
1957 La muerte de Pio Baroja (unreleased) (+ sc); *La venganza* (*The Vengeance*) (+ sc)
1959 *Sonatas* (+ pr, sc)
1960 *A las cinco de la tarde* (+ pr, co-sc)
1962 *Los inocentes* (+ co-sc)
1963 *Nunca pasa nada* (+ co-sc)
1965 *Los pianos mécanicos* (*Les Pianos méchaniques*; *The Uninhibited*) (+ sc)
1969 *El ultimo dia de la guerra* (*The Last Day of the War*) (+ co-sc)
1971 *Varietes* (+ sc)
1973 Four versions of *The Mysterious Island*: 1. *La isla misteriosa* (for Spanish and Latin American distribution), 2. *L'isola misteriosa e il Capitano Nemo* (for Italian distribution, incorporates material directed by Henri Colpi), 3. *L'ile mystérieuse* and *The Mysterious Island* (French, English and international version, co-d with Colpi), 4. six-hour TV version for international distribution; *La corrupción de Chris Miller* (*The Corruption of Chris Miller*) (+ role); *Behind the Shutters*
1976 *El podor del deseo*; *Foul Play*
1977 *The Dog*; *El puente*
1979 *7 Dias de enero* (*Seven Days in January*) (+ sc)
1982 *The Warning*
1987 *Lorca, la Muerte de un Poeta* (+ sc)

Other Films:

1952 *Bienvenido, Mr. Marshall!* (*Welcome, Mr. Marshall!*) (Berlanga) (co-sc)
1953 *Novio a la vista* (Berlanga) (co-sc)
1954 *El torero* (Wheeler) (Spanish version of *Châteaux en Espagne*) (co-dialogue)
1955 *Playa prohibida* (*El esconocido*) (Soler) (sc)
1956 *El amór de Don Juan* (*Don Juan*) (Berry) (co-sc); *Carte a Sara* (Manzanos and Bercovici) (sc)
1958 *L'uomo dai calzoni corti* (*Tal vez mañana*) (Pellegrini) (pr)
1961 ***Viridiana*** (Buñuel) (pr)

Publications

By BARDEM: articles—

"Spanish Highway," in *Films and Filming* (London), June 1957.
Film Makers on Filmmaking, edited by Harry Geduld, Bloomington, Indiana, 1967.
"Cara a cara ... Bardem-Berlanga," in *Cinema 2002* (Madrid), July/ August 1980.
Interview with P. Farinas, in *Cine Cubano* (Havana), no. 103, 1983.

On BARDEM: books—

Oms, Marcel, *J.A. Bardem,* Lyons (Premier Plan no. 21).
Scwartz, Ronald, *Spanish Film Directors: 21 Profiles,* Metuchen, New Jersey, 1986.
Hopewell, John, *Out of the Past: Spanish Cinema After Franco,* London, 1987.
Higginbotham, Virginia, *Spanish Film Under Franco,* Austin, Texas, 1988.

On BARDEM: articles—

"The Arrest," in *Sight and Sound* (London), Spring 1956.
Aranda, J.F., "Bardem: Une Méthode de travail," in *Cinéma* (Paris), no. 33, 1959.
Durand, Philippe, "Juan Antonio Bardem, homme d'Espagne," in *Image et Son* (Paris), October 1959.
Carril, M. Martinex, "Despues de 27 años, Bardem se revitaliza," in *Cinemateca Revista* (Andes), July 1980.
Biofilmography, in *Cahiers de la Cinémathèque* (Perpignan), Winter 1984.

* * *

A pioneer figure in Spanish film, Juan Antonio Bardem is also one of Spain's most consistently political filmmakers. In his early movies *Esa pareja feliz* and *Bienvenido Mr. Marshall,* co-directed with Luis Garcia Berlanga, he broke with prevailing Francoist film traditions that emphasized militarism, folklore, literary adaptations and costume dramas. Bardem and Berlanga chose instead to present scenes of contemporary Spanish life and used humor to describe and criticize aspects of Spanish society. With *Bienvenido Mr. Marshall* the two directors were recognized as leading filmmakers and, along with others of their generation, they set out to revitalize the Spanish film industry and to rescue Spanish films from mediocrity. At a meeting held in Salamanca in 1955, they drafted a statement of principles in which Bardem wrote: "After 60 years, Spanish cinema is politically futile, socially false, intellectually worthless, aesthetically valueless and industrially paralytic." Bardem went on to note that Spanish cinema "had turned its back on reality ... (and was) totally removed from Spanish realistic traditions [as found] in paintings and novels."

the style that most successfully hides its artifices from its audience. The sets, the social setting, and the acting of William Hurt and Raul Julia (as Molina and Valentin respectively) seemed forced. Likewise one could argue that *Ironweed* is too dreamy and too verbose for a big-budget American star vehicle, however Bowery the setting. In transplanting his style to a different context, Babenco's work seems transformed. Aesthetic strategies such as on-location shooting, the combination of professional and non-professional actors, relatively lengthy shots, and dream sequences had made his Brazilian films seem the height of gritty realism. Similar strategies make his American films seem slow and self-consciously poetic.

Babenco's work makes great raw material for investigations of the limits of cross-cultural communication. But the reason why one returns to see his films again is because Babenco makes us understand and identify with his derelicts. That identification creates a complicity with the characters' actions and is therefore the catalyst for an existential dilemma that most of us would not normally face. The audience is confronted with the possibility that given certain options, they too might choose to sell their bodies, steal, or kill, and that this might not necessarily make them evil. Babenco's greatest gift is how in all of his films he extracts and highlights a moral dimension from the conventionally immoral.

—José Arroyo

BACON, Lloyd

Nationality: American. **Born:** San Jose, California, 16 January 1890. **Education:** Attended California public schools and Santa Clara College. **Military service:** Served in photo department, U.S. Navy, 1917. **Family:** Married Margaret Balach. **Career:** Member of David Belasco's Los Angeles stock company, 1911; stage actor in Lloyd Hamilton comedies, 1913; worked in Chaplin comedies, 1916; actor at Mutual, 1918, and at Triangle, 1919; director for Mack Sennett and Lloyd Hamilton, 1921; moved to Warner Bros. and directed first feature, *Broken Hearts of Hollywood,* 1926; moved to 20th Century-Fox, 1944; finished career with two films at Universal and two at RKO, 1953-54. **Died:** In Burbank, California, 15 November 1955.

Films as Director:

1926 *Broken Hearts of Hollywood*; *Private Izzy Murphy*
1927 *Finger Prints*; *White Flannels*; *The Heart of Maryland*; *A Sailor's Sweetheart*; *Brass Knuckles*
1928 *Pay as You Enter*; *The Lion and the Mouse*; *Women They Talk About*; *The Singing Fool*
1929 *Stark Mad*; *No Defense*; *Honky Tonk*; *Say It with Songs*; *So Long Letty*
1930 *The Other Tomorrow*; *She Couldn't Say No*; *A Notorious Affair*; *Moby Dick*; *The Office Wife*
1931 *Sit Tight*; *Kept Husbands*; *Fifty Million Frenchmen*; *Gold Dust Gertie*; *Honor of the Family*
1932 *Manhattan Parade*; *Fireman Save My Child*; *Alias the Doctor*; *The Famous Ferguson Case*; *Miss Pinkerton*; *Crooner*; *You Said a Mouthful*
1933 ***42nd Street***; *Picture Snatcher*; *Mary Stevens M.D.*; *Footlight Parade*; *Son of a Sailor*
1934 *Wonder Bar*; *A Very Honorable Guy*; *He Was Her Man*; *Here Comes the Navy*; *Six-Day Bike Rider*
1935 *Devil Dogs of the Air*; *In Caliente*; *Broadway Gondolier*; *The Irish in Us*; *Frisco Kid*
1936 *Sons o' Guns*; *Cain and Mabel*; *Gold Diggers of 1937*
1937 *Marked Woman*; *Ever Since Eve*; *San Quentin*; *Submarine D-1*
1938 *A Slight Case of Murder*; *Cowboy from Brooklyn*; *Rocket Busters*; *Boy Meets Girl*
1939 *Wings of the Navy*; *The Oklahoma Kid*; *Indianapolis Speedway*; *Espionage Agent*
1940 *A Child Is Born*; *Invisible Stripes*; *Three Cheers for the Irish*; *Brother Orchid*; *Knute Rockne—All American*
1941 *Honeymoon for Three*; *Footsteps in the Dark*; *Affectionately Yours*; *Navy Blues*
1942 *Larceny, Inc.*; *Wings for the Eagle*; *Silver Queen*
1943 *Action in the North Atlantic*
1944 *Sunday Dinner for a Soldier*
1945 *Captain Eddie*
1946 *Home Sweet Homicide*; *Wake Up and Dream*
1947 *I Wonder Who's Kissing Her Now*
1948 *You Were Meant For Me*; *Give My Regards to Broadway*; *Don't Trust Your Husband* (*An Innocent Affair*)
1949 *Mother Is a Freshman*; *It Happens Every Spring*; *Miss Grant Takes Richmond*
1950 *Kill the Umpire*; *The Good Humor Man*; *The Fuller Brush Girl*
1951 *Call Me Mister*; *The Frogmen*; *Golden Girl*
1953 *The I Don't Care Girl*; *The Great Sioux Uprising*; *Walking My Baby Back Home*
1954 *The French Line*; *She Couldn't Say No*

Other Films:

1915 *The Champion* (Chaplin) (role); *In the Park* (Chaplin) (role); *The Jitney Elopement* (Chaplin) (role); *The Bank* (Chaplin) (role); *The Tramp* (Chaplin) (role)
1916 *The Floorwalker* (Chaplin) (role); *The Vagabond* (Chaplin) (role); *Behind the Screen* (Chaplin) (role); *The Rink* (Chaplin) (role); *The Fireman* (Chaplin) (role)
1919/20 Roles for Mutual and Triangle studios

Publications

On BACON: books—

Meyer, William, *Warner Brothers Directors*, New York, 1978.
Fuments, Rocco, editor, *42nd Street*, Madison, Wisconsin, 1980.
Feuer, Jane, *The Hollywood Musical*, London, 1982.
Roddick, Nick, *A New Deal in Entertainment: Warner Brothers in the 1930's*, London, 1983.
Altman, Rick, *The American Film Musical*, Bloomington, Indiana, and London, 1989.

On BACON: articles—

"Lloyd Bacon ... Warner Brothers' Ace," in *Cue* (New York), 6 April 1935.
Parsons, Louella, "Cosmopolitan's Citation for the Best Direction of the Month," in *Cosmopolitan* (New York), May 1949.

* * *

Lloyd Bacon is probably best known for his director's credit on such classic Warner Bros. films as *42nd Street, Footlight Parade, Knute Rockne—All American,* and *Action in the North Atlantic.* Still, other film personalities are better remembered for these films: choreographer Busby Berkeley for the musicals, and actors Pat O'Brien, Ronald Reagan, and Humphrey Bogart for the 1940s films. Today Bacon is lost in the literature about Warner Bros.

Lloyd Bacon directing Monte Blue in *No Defense*

In his day, however, Lloyd Bacon was recognized as a consummate Hollywood professional. One cannot help standing in some awe of Bacon's directorial output in the era from the coming of sound to the Second World War. During those fourteen years he directed an average of five films per annum for Warner Bros. (Seven were released in 1932 alone.) Bacon's *42nd Street* and *Wonder Bar* were among the industry's top-grossing films of the decade. For a time Bacon was considered to be the top musicals specialist at Warner Bros. The corporation paid him accordingly, some $200,000 per year, making him one of its highest paid contract directors of the 1930s.

Bacon's status declined during the 1940s. His craftsmanship remained solid, for he knew the classical Hollywood system of production as well as anyone on the Warner lot. But Bacon never seemed to find his special niche. Instead, he skipped from one genre to another. He seemed to evolve into the Warner Bros. handyman director. His greatest success during this period came with war films. For example, *Wings of the Navy* had a million dollar budget and helped kick off the studio's string of successful World War II films. Bacon's best-remembered film of the 1940s is probably *Action in the North Atlantic*, a tribute to the U.S. Merchant Marine. This movie was Bacon's last film at Warner Bros.

In 1944 Bacon moved to Twentieth Century-Fox to work for his former boss, Darryl F. Zanuck. There he re-established himself in musicals as well as films of comedy and family romance, but still seemed unable to locate a long-term specialty. He finished at Fox with an early 1950s series of Lucille Ball comedies, and ended his directorial career in somewhat ignominious fashion, helping Howard Hughes create a 3-D Jane Russell spectacle, *The French Line*.

Bacon's most significant contribution to film history probably came during his early days at Warner Bros. as that studio pioneered new sound technology in the late 1920s. Bacon presided over several significant transitional films, none more important than *The Singing Fool*. Although *The Jazz Singer* usually gets credit as the first (and most important) transitional talkie, *The Singing Fool* should receive far more credit because for more than a decade, this film stood as the highest grossing feature in Hollywood annals. As its director, Bacon was honored by the trade publication *Film Daily* as one of the top ten directors of the 1928-29 season. As a consequence of his involvement on this and other films, Bacon established his reputation as a director who helped thrust Hollywood into an era of movies with sound.

—Douglas Gomery

BAILLIE, Bruce

Nationality: American. **Born:** Aberdeen, South Dakota, 24 September 1931. **Education:** University of Minnesota, B.A., 1955; attended University of California at Berkeley, 1956-58; attended London School of Film Technique, 1959. **Military Service:** Served in the U.S. Navy during Korean War, 1951-53. **Career:** Worked under Will Hindle for "PM West," CBS, and for Marvin Becker Films, San Francisco, and began first film, *On Sundays*, 1960; founded Canyon Cinema Film Cooperative, San Francisco, 1960; taught film at Rice University, Houston, 1969-70, Bard College, New York, 1974-77, and Evergreen State College, Olympia, Washington, 1981-82; founder, with Bonnie Jones, Olympia Zen-Kai, 1982; touring lecturer, 1963—. **Awards:** Rockefeller Foundation Fellowship, 1966; Creative Arts Award for Filmmaking, Brandeis University, 1971; honorary M.F.A., San Francisco Art Institute, 1971; National Endowment for the Arts Fellowship, 1971, 1981; CAPS, NY, 1981; Maya Deren Award, Vermont Institute, 1981, American Film Institute, 1991; San Francisco International Film Festival Golden Gate Award; Ann Arbor Grand Prize; Moholy Nagy Award; Guggenheim Fellowship; American Film Institute Fellowship. **Address:** 669 W. Kodiak Ave., Camano Island, WA 98292, U.S.A.

Films as Director:

1960/61 *On Sundays*
1961 *David Lynn's Sculpture* (unfinished); *Mr Hayashi*; *The Gymnasts*
1962 *Friend Fleeing* (unfinished); *Everyman*; *News No. 3*; *Have You Thought of Talking to the Director?*; *Here I Am*
1962/63 *A Hurrah for Soldiers*
1963 *To Parsifal*
1964 *Mass for the Dakota Sioux*; *The Brookfield Recreation Center*
1964/65 *Quixote* (revised 1967)
1965 *Yellow Horse*
1966 *Tung*; *Castro Street*; *All My Life*; *Still Life*; *Termination*; *Port Chicago Vigil*; *Show Leader*
1967 *Valentin de las Sierras*
1970 *Quick Billy*
1971-present *Roslyn Romance* (multi-part film)
1978 *Roslyn Romance (Is It Really True?): Intro. I and II*
1981-present *The Cardinal's Visit* (final section of *Roslyn Romance*)
1987-present *Dr. Bish Remedies II*
1990 *The P-38 Pilot*; *The Bus Driver's Tale*; *Dr. Bish Remedies I*
1995 *Commute*; *Kindergarten*

Publications

By BAILLIE: articles—

Frequent poems and letters, in *Canyon Cinema News* (San Francisco)
"Letters: San Francisco Film Scene," in *Film Culture* (New York), Summer 1963.
Interview with Richard Whitehall, in *Film Culture* (New York), Summer 1969.
Interview in *Film Culture* (New York), Spring 1971.
"Bruce Baillie," in *Film Comment* (New York), Spring 1971.
"Dr. Bish," in *Downtown Review*, Fall/Winter 1979/80, Spring 1980, Fall 1980.

On BAILLIE: books—

Hanhardt, John, and others, *A History of the American Avant-Garde Cinema*, New York, 1976.
Callenbach, Ernest, *Bruce Baillie*, St. Paul, Minnesot
MacDonald, Scott, *A Critical Cinema*, Vol. 2, Berke
1992.

On BAILLIE: articles—

Callenbach, Ernest, "Bruce Baillie," in *Film Quarterly* (
1964.
Polt, Harriet, "The Films of Bruce Baillie," in *Film C*
York), Fall 1964.
Kent, Thomas, "San Francisco's Hipster Cinema," in *Film*
York), Spring 1967.
"Baillie Issue" of *Harbinger* (Houston), July 1967.
"Baillie Section" of *Film Culture* (New York), no. 67-6
Nygren, Scott, "*Quick Billy*" (Ph.D. thesis) (Buffalo, New
Connor, Kathleen, "Brigid Rose and Dr. Bish: A Celtic Jour
thesis) (British Columbia), 1988.
Connor, Kathleen, "*Quick Billy* and W.B. Yeats' *The W*
Oisin" (Ph.D. thesis) (Athens, Ohio), 1994.

* * *

The career of Bruce Baillie has two central aspects, wh
features of the whole American avant-garde film moveme
films are generally intensely poetic, lyrical evocations of
places in which the subject matter is transformed by the
methods used to photograph it. Second, many of his film
strong social awareness, describing attitudes critical towards
ated from, mainstream American society. In many cases, B
these concerns within single films.

Stylistically, Baillie's films are characterized by images o
evanescent beauty. An object will appear with spectacular cl
to dissolve away an instant later. Light itself often becomes
shining across the frame or reflected from objects, suggesti
of poetry in the subject matter that lies beyond easy inter
Baillie combines images with other images, and images with
dense, collage-like structures. Thus, many of his films cut fr
between scenes, or superimpose objects on each other. On
stantly aware of a restlessness, an instability, which seems
from his images' appearance and flow. It is significant, too, th
of Baillie's films contain, or are structured as, journeys.

The effect of Baillie's films is to make the viewer feel th
moment of the viewing, any single image he is looking at is
illusion that will soon vanish. The sensuousness of the light and
only heighten one's awareness of their unreality. It is as if the
void, a nothingness, that lies behind all things. It is not irreleva
this regard that Baillie has evidenced strong interest, over the yea
Eastern religious thought.

Some degree of social comment is present in most of Baillie's fi
but in widely varying degrees. *Mr. Hayashi* places the poetic and
social in a very precise balance. The imagery consists of evocati
sun-drenched images forming a short, haiku-like portrait of a man.
the soundtrack, we hear the man speak of his life, and his difficulty
finding work. *Mass* and *Quixote* indict American society as overl
aggressive, toward its citizens, toward Native Americans, and towar
nature; as impersonal and dehumanizing; as lacking physical or moral
roots. For *Quixote*, Baillie uses an extremely dense, collage-like form,
in which images and fragments of images are intercut with and superimposed on others, with a similarly complex soundtrack. At times, the film's multiple themes seem to blur into each other, as if the filmmaker is acknowledging that he is as "lost" as the society he is depicting.

Castro Street, *Tung*, and *Valentin de las Sierras* are, by contrast, apparently simpler portraits of people and places. By keeping his camera very close to things, Baillie renders their details ever more

Juan Antonio Bardem

Bardem and other filmmakers who attended the meeting at Salamanca also deplored the lack of general film culture in Spain, noting that it was not possible to see 95% of movies made abroad. Bardem felt that it was important for Spaniards to keep abreast of worldwide trends in filmmaking and especially to become familiar with Italian neo-realism. This was the single most important influence in the development of his own cinematic style. Both in his movies and in his writings he remained faithful to the tenets of neo-realism. In order to foster a film culture in Spain, Bardem founded Objetivo, a cinema journal that was eventually banned by the government. During its brief existence, Objetivo nevertheless became a rallying point for Spanish cineastes, raised the level of film criticism in Spain and informed readers about prohibited films. Several years later, in yet another effort to ensure the autonomy and integrity of Spanish film, Bardem joined with Berlanga, Carlos Saura, and other directors and founded a production company, UNINCI, which operated until 1962, when it was closed down for co-producing Luis Buñuel's *Viridiana.*

Because of these endeavors as well as his political outspokenness, Bardem was arrested seven times during the Franco years. He nevertheless persisted in his efforts to make political films in Spain. In spite of his lack of favor at home, he won many prizes at film festivals around the world and directed co-productions in Italy, France, Argentina, and Bulgaria.

Bardem is most closely associated with films that chronicle the negative effects of Francoism on the psyche of Spaniards of different classes, regions and social milieus. In several films he dramatizes the alienation fostered by Francoism by focusing on a single individual who often bears Bardem's own given name—Juan. This Spanish everyman feels frustrated and stifled in a closed society. He attempts to find outlets through hobbies, intrigues, and even through radio contests, but all means prove unsatisfactory. In the course of his efforts, Juan is led to reevaluate himself and the world around him in order to find new options. The films depict the choices that each Juan makes, becoming increasingly critical of individuals who act selfishly, cowardly, or who refuse to take a stand. These general themes continue in the movies Bardem has made since the death of Franco.

—Katherine Singer Kovács

BARNET, Boris

Nationality: Russian. **Born:** Moscow, 1902, grandson of an English settler. **Education:** Studied at School of Art and Architecture, Moscow. **Military Service:** Joined Red Army, 1919, later PT instructor for Army. **Career:** Professional boxer; joined Lev Kuleshov's "Eccentric Workshop," 1924; directed first film, 1926. **Awards:** Retrospectives at La Rochelle Festival, 1982, and Locarno Festival, 1985. **Died:** By suicide, 8 January 1965.

Films as Director:

1926 *Miss Mend* (serial) (co-d, co-sc, role)
1927 *Devushka s korobkoi* (*The Girl with the Hat Box*); *Moskva v oktyabre* (*Moscow in October*) (+ role)
1928 *Dom na Trubnoi* (*House on Trubnaya*)
1929 *Zhivye dela* (*Living Things*) (short) (+ co-sc)
1930 *Proizvodstvo muzykal'nykh instrumentov* (*The Manufacture of Musical Instruments*) (short)
1931 *Ledolom* (*The Thaw*)
1933 *Okraina* (*Outskirts*; *Patriots*) (+ co-sc)
1935 *U samogo sinego morya* (*By the Deep Blue Sea*)
1939 *Noch' v sentyabre* (*One September Night*) (+ role)
1940 *Staryi nayezdnik* (*The Old Jockey*) (released 1959)
1941 "Muzhestvo" ("Courage") episode of *Boyevoy kinosbornik no. 3* (*Fighting Film Album no. 3*)
1942 "Bestsennaya golova" ("A Priceless Head") episode of *Boyevoy kinosbornik no. 10* (*Fighting Film Album no. 10*)
1943 *Novgorodtsy* (*Men of Novgorod*) (not released)
1945 *Odnazhdy noch'yu* (*Once One Night*) (+ role)
1947 *Podvig razvedchika* (*The Exploits of an Intelligence Agent*) (+ role)
1948 *Stranitsy zhizni* (*Pages from a Life*) (co-d)
1950 *Schedroe leto* (*A Bounteous Summer*)
1952 *Kontsert masterov ukrainskogo iskusstva* (*Masters of Ukrainian Art in Concert*) (+ sc)
1955 *Lyana* (+ co-sc)
1957 *Poet* (*The Poet*); *Borets i kloun* (*The Wrestler and the Clown*) (co-d)
1959 *Annushka*
1961 *Alyonka*
1963 *Polustanok* (*The Whistle-Stop*) (+ co-sc)

Films as Actor Only:

1924 ***Neobychainiye priklucheniya Mistera Vesta v stranye Bolshevikov*** (*The Adventures of Mr. West in the Land of the Bolsheviks*) (Kuleshov)
1925 *Shakhmatnaya goryachka* (*Chess fever*) (Pudovkin) (short); *Na vernom sledu* (*On the Right Track*) (A. Dmitriyev)
1926 *Protsess o trekh millionakh* (*The Three Millions Trial*) (Protazanov)
1928 ***Potomok Chingis-khana*** (*The Heir to Genghis Khan*; *Storm Over Asia*) (Pudovkin)
1929 *Zhivoi trup* (*The Living Corpse*) (Otsep)
1936 *Lyubov' i nenavist'* (*Love and Hate*) (A. Endelstein)
1946 *Sinegoriya* (*The Blue Mountains*) (Garin and Lokshina)

Publications

On BARNET: books—

Kushnirov, M., *Zhizn' i fil'my Boris Barneta* [The Life and Films of Boris Barnet], Moscow, 1977.
Albera, F., and R. Cosandey, editors, *Boris Barnet: Ecrits, Documents, Etudes, Filmographie*, Locarno, 1985.

On BARNET: articles—

Obituary in *Kino* (Warsaw), no. 2, 1965.
Obituary in *Cinéma* (Paris), no. 96, 1965.
"Boris Barnet," in *Film Culture* (New York), Fall 1965.
Kuzmina, "A Tribute to Boris Barnet," in *Film Comment* (New York), Fall 1968.
"Boris Barnet," in *Film Dope* (London), March 1973.
Gillett, John, in *National Film Theatre Booklet* (London), July 1980.
Gillett, John, in *Sight and Sound* (London), Autumn 1980.
Cahiers du Cinéma (Paris), November 1982.
Revue du Cinéma (Paris), October 1983.
Jeune Cinéma (Paris), November 1984.
Cahiers du Cinéma (Paris), October 1985.
Eisenschitz, B., "A Fickle Man, or Portrait of Boris Barnet as a Soviet Director," in *Inside the Film Factory: New Approaches to Russian and Soviet Cinema*, edited by Richard Taylor and Ian Christie, London and New York, 1991.

* * *

Boris Barnet: *Okraina*

Boris Barnet's career as a director has been much underrated in the West, yet it spanned almost forty years of Soviet filmmaking. After a brief period as a PT instructor in the Red Army and then as a professional boxer, he joined Kuleshov's workshop as an actor and handyman. In 1924 Barnet played the part of Cowboy Jeddy, a grotesque caricature of an American, in Kuleshov's eccentric comedy *The Extraordinary Adventures of Mr. West in the Land of the Bolsheviks.* He frequently appeared later in his own films, often in cameo roles.

Like Kuleshov, Barnet went to work for the Mezhrabpom-Rus studio, where experimentation was combined with the production of films that were commercially successful. Barnet collaborated with Fyodor Otsep on the serial thriller *Miss Mend* and then made his first two feature films, *The Girl with the Hatbox* and *The House on Trubnaya.* Both films involved actors from the Kuleshov workshop and both were light-hearted comedies, satirising the excesses of the New Economic Policy and the social and economic tensions associated with it. The first centred on a lost lottery ticket and the second on the arrival of a country girl in Moscow, but Barnet managed very gently to broaden their frame of reference. His deft touch on these two films marked him out by the end of the 1920s as a director of originality and distinction.

The advent of sound seems to have caused Barnet fewer problems than it did other directors: he made two sound shorts about musical instruments in 1930, neither of which has been preserved. His first sound feature film, *Okraina,* was produced in 1933. This was a remarkably powerful, and in some ways almost Chekhovian, portrayal of life in a provincial Russian town during the First World War and the start of the Revolution. The lives of the characters are almost imperceptibly intertwined with the historical events unfolding far away. The relationship between individuals and events was, however, portrayed in too subtle a fashion for many of Barnet's contemporaries and, like so many other Soviet filmmakers of the time, he was attacked for ideological obscurantism. Hence it was that Barnet later remarked that he was not merely a "film director" but a "Soviet film director."

The reception for Barnet's next film, *By the Deep Blue Sea,* was even more hostile. On one level the film was a light-hearted love intrigue set on a collective farm on the banks of the Caspian Sea. On another level, however, it can be read as an allegorical tale of the eternal struggle between dream and reality, with the collective farm itself as a latter-day utopia, emphasised by the somewhat ironic title—a dangerous comparison in 1936 in the Soviet Union. Given the atmosphere of the time, it is perhaps not altogether surprising that Barnet's next film, *One September Night,* was devoted to a more conventional account of the birth of the Stakhanovite movement. In this film the secret police were portrayed as heroes, defending the Soviet Union against sabotage. But *The Old Jockey,* made the year after, fell afoul of the authorities and was not released until 1959.

The Second World War dominated Barnet's output for the next few years and his efforts were rewarded with the Stalin Prize in 1948. He returned to his true métier, comedy, in 1950, with his first colour film, *A Bounteous Summer,* made in the Ukraine. Another film, *Lyana,* was made in Moldavia five years later. Barnet's last completed film, *The Whistle-Stop,* was also a comedy, but other films that he made during the last decade of his life are more properly characterised as dramas. But to say that is to underestimate Barnet, because his films cannot be easily pigeon-holed.

Barnet's career in Soviet cinema spanned four decades. He belonged to the generation of lesser known filmmakers who in fact constituted the backbone of that cinema, while taking a back seat in the theoretical polemics that attracted international curiosity and focused attention on the avant-garde. His films displayed a mastery of visual technique and a disciplined economy of style. He was a mainstream director but a subversive artist, whose work, tinged with warmth, humour, and humanity, constantly attracted Soviet audiences. He took his own life in 1965.

—Richard Taylor

BAUER, Evgeni

Nationality: Russian. **Born:** Evgeni Frantsevich Bauer, 1865. **Education:** The Moscow College of Painting, Sculpture, and Architecture. **Family:** Son of a zither player; married Lina Anvharova, a dancer and later actress in his films. **Career:** Worked as a magazine caricaturist, newspaper satirist, theatre impresario, and set designer; started directing films in 1913, working for Pathé, Drankov, and Taldykin; joined Khanzhonkov's company, becoming one of the main shareholders, late 1913. **Died:** Of pneumonia, 9 June 1917.

Films as Director:

1913 *Sumerki Zhenskoi Dushi* (*The Twilight of a Woman's Soul*) (+ art dir)

1914 *Ditya Bol'shogo Goroda* (*Child of the Big City*; *Devushka s Ulitsy*; *The Girl from the Street*) (+ art dir); *Ee Geroiski Podvig* (*Her Heroic Feat*); *Lyulya Bek*; *Slava Nam—Smert' Vagram* (*Glory to Us, Death to the Enemy*); *Tol'ko Raz v Godu* (*Only Once a Year*; *Doroga v ad*; *The Road to Hell*); *Kholodnye Dushi* (*Cold Showers*; *Frigid Souls*)

1915 *Grezy* (*Daydreams*; *Obmanutye Mechty*; *Deceived Dreams*); *Deti Veka* (*Children of the Age*); *Zhemchuzhnoe Ozherel'e* (*The Pearl Necklace*); *Leon Drey* (*Pokoritel' Zhenskikh Serdets*; *The Lady-Killer*) (+ art dir); *Pervaya Lyubov'* (*First Love*); *Schast'e Vechnoi Nochi* (*The Happiness of Eternal Night*); *Tysyacha Vtoraya Khitrost* (*The Thousand and Second Ruse*); *Yuri Nagornyi* (*Obol'stitel*; *The Seducer*)

1916 *Zhizn' za Zhizn'* (*A Life for a Life*; *Za Kazhduyu slezu po Kable Krovi*; *A Tear for Every Drop of Blood*; *Sestry-Sopernitsy*; *The Rival Sisters*) (+ sc); *Nelly Raintseva*; *PriklyuchenieLiny v Sochi* (*Lina's Adventure in Sochi*)

1917 *Umirayushchii Lebed'* (*The Dying Swan*); *Za Schast'em* (*For Luck*); *Korol' Parizha* (*The King of Paris*) (+ co-sc); *Lina Pod Ekspertizoi ili Buinyi Pokoinik* (*Lina Under Examination*; *The Turbulent Corpse*); *Nabat* (*The Alarm*) (+ sc); *Revolyutsioner* (*The Revolutionary*)

Note: These are the only films that remain from the 82 with which he has been credited.

Publications

On BAUER: book—

Tsivian, Yuri, and others, *Silent Witnesses: Russian Films 1908-1919,* (in English and Italian), London and Pordenone, 1989.

On BAUER: articles—

Revue Internationale d'Histoire du Cinéma (Paris), no. 1, 1975.
Robinson, David, "Evgeni Bauer and the Cinema of Nikolai II," in *Sight and Sound* (London), Winter 1989-90.

* * *

When, in 1989, the Russians released a hoard of movies of the Czarist era, few of which had been seen in the West, we discovered a new "great" director. Evgeni Bauer was found to tower over all his contemporaries, including Victor Sjöström; for while Bauer's films could be as emotionally complex as those of Sjöström, he was a marvel at something which did not motivate the Swedish master—the mechanics of cinema. Bauer understood the language of the cinema better than any of his contemporaries, and in that silent era, he exploited silence as no one else did until Keaton. The Hollywood of Keaton's time, ten years later, was still only groping towards some of Bauer's techniques—the traveling or roving camera, the sudden or unexpected close-up, the zoom-in (if used in a primitive way), angle-shots from above, the masked screen, the use of movement and editing (e.g., in a frenzied dance) to build to a climax, the split screen, vivid composition. Visually then, his films are exciting, and furthermore he uses locations tellingly to enhance his dramatic material, as we may expect from a former art director. These elements, when added to natural playing and generally above-average stories—which invariably include a biting, if implicit, commentary on bourgeois society—make up a body of work unparalleled in early cinema. And who else at this time could take his narrative from A to D, without plodding through B and C?

Bauer entered the cinema as set designer for Drankov, but when in that capacity he moved over to Khanzhonov, he was given an entirely free hand, directing as well for him—and Bauer's first film as such, *Twilight of a Woman's Soul* (1913), still survives. Like most Russian filmmakers of this period, Bauer gave audiences the doom and gloom they craved, often with a last-reel suicide—but he did it with a sophistication matched only by Yakov Protazanov. For instance, in *Child of the Big City* a working-girl is wooed by a rich man, attracted to women outside his own class; after marriage he bores her and she seduces a valet before deciding to use her husband's friends to become a courtesan, because she does not wish to give up a life of luxury. He, ruined, seeks her out, only to find her no less contemptuous than she was when their marriage ended.

In *Silent Witnesses* the title characters are the servants of Moscow's sybaritic high society, but they have an independent life of their own, caring and principled. When one young maid has a mind to the advantages of being a rich man's lady and, after a half-hearted refusal, acquiesces, she finds her position too insecure to protest against his continuing infidelities. In all of Bauer's films drunken parties and sexual license are the prerogatives of the rich, who are also vindictive, cruel, and without moral values—but they are also dangerously attractive. In *Children of the Age* a loving young wife allows an aged roué to seduce her and remains with him even after he has reduced her husband to penury by having him sacked. Her options are open, and furthermore she remains sympathetic, though the peasant audiences of Czarist Russia might well have thought that this brutally unequal society ought to be destroyed forthwith. It would be an overstatement to describe Bauer as subversive, but the society he depicts is wholly unadmirable, mortally sick.

There is abnormal psychology—perhaps specifically of the Russian variety—at the heart of both *Daydreams* and *After Death.* In the first a man becomes a recluse after his wife's death, only to become obsessed by an actress who resembles her; and she, while perhaps still loving him, fatally mocks his passion for his dead wife. In the second a man, inconsolable after the death of his mother, drives to suicide the actress who has aspired to be the new woman in his life, then kills himself after reading her diaries to discover her motives. *Happiness of Eternal Night* marks a firm return to Bauer's central theme, the rottenness of society, but the plot is a silly thing about a wealthy blind girl who marries a rake, persuaded by his brother who, because of his love for her, had trained to be an eye-surgeon in order to cure her.

Because Bauer was his leading director, Khanzonkov offered him a choice of subjects when he decided to make a super-production to rival Yermoliev's *Queen of Spades.* Bauer chose a now-forgotten French novel, which emerged as *A Life for a Life,* a complex melange of high-society gambols, infidelity, and debts. Since all the characters are well-off and one of them, a wealthy widow, does an exemplary job in running a factory, the film (unlike any of Bauer's others still extant) lacks any immediate revolutionary portents. *Yuri Nagorni* was designed to tell its story without inter-titles, thus pushing us willy-nilly into an incomprehensible plot about an adulterous wife who makes a play for a libidinous opera-singer, the eponymous Yuri: she leaves him at the end of the first half to die in a fire, but the second part, in flashback, contains all that we need to know.

Bauer was fascinated by the underside of life, the past and dreams, and both feature in a return to the subject of death, in *The Dying Swan,* in which an artist fantasizes about a ballerina as she expires. *To Happiness* holds to this theme as a widow encourages her longtime admirer to court her adolescent daughter, whose fatal illness is halted when she conceives a passion for him. This was Bauer's last completed film, and the dialectic is less "true" than the first of his movies, but he atones for the deficiencies of the plot by setting it lovingly in the shimmering Crimean sun, with distant vistas of the sea. It also shows, rarely for its time, two mature people genuinely in love with each other.

Evgeni Bauer: *Deti Veka*

Bauer died in the Crimea, after sustaining an accident while scouting locations for his next film, *The King of Paris* (1917), completed after the February revolution by Olga Rakhmanova, who had acted in several of his pictures. The inter-titles have not survived, so the plot is not easy to follow, but it is only clear, in this tale of intrigue and blackmail, that the two leading characters are homosexual. The sequence in which the older man takes home a young stranger, having impulsively paid his gambling debts, is quite extraordinary, as the two of them look guiltily about them.

Bauer's films, with their predatory, managing women and their weak, hedonistic men, suggest a homosexual sensitivity, but he is too modern in outlook to be categorized. With Sjöström, he is the only director of the teens of the twentieth century whose work can still be watched with satisfaction and enjoyment. Sjöström's studies of rural life in the last century are valuable, but Bauer's portraits of Czarist Russia in its last days are even more so, because he was actually there. We have to wait for Lamprecht's *Berlin* and Ozu's *Tokyo* before we have any other filmed record of a contemporary society; and Ozu is far less pungent, perhaps because, unlike Bauer and Lamprecht, he did not see that as his aim. Bauer made over eighty films, of which only one third have survived. Sjöström made forty-five films in Sweden, of which only thirteen were known to be extant—but two turned up in the 1980s. May we dare hope that there are still some Bauers to come to light?

—David Shipman

BECKER, Jacques

Nationality: French. **Born:** Paris, 15 September 1906. **Education:** Lycée Condorcet, and Schola Cantorum, Paris. **Family:** Married actress Françoise Fabian, a son, Jean, and daughter. **Career:** Became assistant to Jean Renoir, 1932; made first short film, *Le Commissaire ...*, 1935; German prisoner of war, 1941-42; directed first feature, *Le Dernier Atout,* 1942; son and assistant Jean Becker completed *Le Trou* following his death. **Died:** 1960.

Films as Director:

1935 *Le Commissaire est bon enfant, le gendarme est sans pitie* (co-d, co-sc with Pierre Prevert); *Tête de turc* (*Une Tête qui rapporte*) (+ co-sc)
1938 short documentary on Communist Party Congress at Arles
1939 *L'Or du Cristobal* (co-d, uncredited)
1942 *Le Dernier Atout* (+ co-pr, co-sc)
1943 *Goupi Mains rouges* (*It Happened at the Inn*) (+ co-sc)
1945 *Falbalas* (*Paris Frills*) (+ co-sc)
1947 *Antoine et Antoinette* (+ co-sc)
1949 *Rendez-vous de Juillet* (+ co-sc)
1951 *Édouard et Caroline* (+ co-sc)
1952 ***Casque d'Or*** (+ co-sc)
1953 *Rue de l'Estrapade*
1954 *Touchez pas au Grisbi* (*Grisbi*) (+ co-sc); *Ali Baba et les quarante voleurs* (*Ali Baba*) (+ co-sc)
1956 *Les Aventures d'Arsène Lupin* (*The Adventures of Arsène Lupin*) (+ co-sc)
1957 *Montparnasse 19* (*Modigliani of Montparnasse*) (+ co-sc)
1960 *Le Trou* (*The Night Watch, The Hole*) (+ co-d, co-sc)

Other Films:

1929 *Le Bled* (Renoir) (role); *Le Rendez-vous de Cannes* (Petrossian—documentary) (appearance)
1932 ***Boudu sauvé des eaux*** (Renoir) (asst, role); *La Nuit du carrefour* (Renoir) (asst)
1933 *Chotard & Compagnie* (Renoir) (asst)
1934 *Madame Bovary* (uncredited, asst)
1935 ***Le Crime de Monsieur Lange*** (Renoir) (asst); *Toni* (Renoir) (asst)
1936 *Les Bas-Fonds* (Renoir) (asst, role); ***Une Partie de campagne*** (Renoir) (asst, role); *La Vie est à nous* (Renoir) (asst, role)
1938 ***La Grande Illusion*** (Renoir) (asst, role); *La Marseillaise* (Renoir) (asst); ***La Bête humaine*** (Renoir) (asst)
1939 ***Le Règle du jeu*** (Renoir) (asst); *L'Héritier des Montdésir* (Valentin) (asst)

Publications

On BECKER: book—

Armes, Roy, *French Cinema Since 1946: Vol. I—The Great Tradition,* New York, 1970.

On BECKER: articles—

De la Roche, Catherine, "The Stylist," in *Films and Filming* (London), March 1955.
Lisbona, Joseph, "Microscope Director," in *Films and Filming* (London), December 1956.
Baxter, Brian, "Jacques Becker and Montparnasse 19," in *Film* (London), September/October 1958.
"Becker," in *Sight and Sound* (London), Spring 1960.
Guillermo, Gilberto Perez, "Jacques Becker: Two Films," in *Sight and Sound* (London), Summer 1969.
Lederlé, J. L., "Un Couple sans histoire," in *Cinématographe* (Paris), May 1977.
Aubert, F., "Françoise Fabian parle de Becker," and Rene Predal, "Jacques Becker," in *Cinéma* (Paris), 11 December 1985.
Chevrie, Marc, "Un Pur Cinéaste," in *Cahiers du Cinéma* (Paris), December 1985.

On BECKER: film—

Viallet, Pierre, and Marcel L'Herbier, *Portraits filmés ... Jacques Becker*, 1954.

* * *

Next to Jean Grémillon, Jacques Becker is surely the most neglected of France's great directors. Known in France for *Goupi Mains rouges* and *Antoine et Antoinette,* his only film to reach an international critical audience was *Casque d'Or.* But from 1942 to 1959 Becker fashioned thirteen films, none of which could be called a failure and each of which merits respect and attention.

Tied to Jean Renoir through a youthful friendship (their families were both close to the Cézannes), Becker began assisting Renoir in 1932. For eight years he helped put together some of the greatest films ever made, allowing the generous genius of Renoir to roam, unconcerned over the details he had already prearranged. Becker gave Renoir the kind of grounding and order which kept his films from flying into thin air. His fastidiousness and precision made him the perfect assistant. Many of his friends, however, doubted that such a sensibility could ever command the energy needed to finish a film.

Nevertheless, film direction was Becker's ambition from the beginning of his career. It was he who developed the idea for *Le Crime de M. Lang,* and when the producer insisted that Renoir take over, it cost them their friendship for a time. Soon Becker was directing a cheap

Jacques Becker with Claire Maffei on the set of *Antoine et Antoinette*

anarchist subject, *Le Commissaire est bon enfant,* with the Octobre groupe company of actors. He wasn't to be held back.

Like so many others, Becker was given his chance with the Occupation. A producer handed Becker the reins of a detective comedy, *Le Dernier Atout,* which he brought in under budget and to a good box office response. This opened his career, permitting him to film the unforgettable *Goupi.* Georges Sadoul claims that after the war an American firm bought up the film and had it destroyed so that it wouldn't compete with American products as *Open City* had done. Whether this is true or not, the film remains impressive in the clarity of its partly cynical, partly mysterious tone. In addition, the work shows Becker to be a brilliant director of actors.

The sureness of touch in each of Becker's films derives from a precision some link to craftsmanship; but Becker was striving for far more than competence, veneer, or "quality." He was first and always interested in rhythm. A musician, he was obsessed with jazz and ragtime. No other standard director spent so much time collaborating with his editor (Marguerite Renoir).

Goupi is only the first of a host of Becker films whose subjects are difficult to define. Becker seems to have gone out of his way to set himself problems. Many of his films are about groups of characters, most notably his final work, *Le Trou.* Others feature widely diverse settings: *Antoine et Antoinette* captures the working class quarters of Paris; *Rendez-vous de Juillet* must be the first film anywhere to explicitly bring out the youth culture of postwar Europe; *Falbalas* evokes the world of high fashion as only someone raised in such a world could know it; and, of course, *Casque d'Or* makes the turn-of-the century Parisian underworld come to life with a kind of grim romanticism.

Becker stated that his fastidious attention to milieu was the only way he could approach his characters. Bazin goes further, claiming that only through the exactitude of social particularity could the universality of his characters and their situations come to life. For Bazin, *Edouard et Caroline* is, if not his greatest film, at least his most revealing one. This brilliant farce in the style of Marivaux is virtually plotless. Becker was able, via the minuteness of his *découpage* and the sympathy he had for his actors, to build a serious moral comedy from literally nothing. *Edouard et Caroline,* along with *Le Trou,* shows him working at his best, working without plots and without the luxury of breadth. Both films take place in prison cells, *Le Trou* in an actual prison, *Edouard et Caroline* in the dingy apartment they share and the more menacing jail of her uncle's mansion.

Becker has been called "the mechanic" of cinema, for he took a delight in its workings and he went about his own job with such order and method. This separates him further from such "quality" directors as Autant-Lara, Cayatte, and Delannoy, whose themes may seem grander. Becker was interested in what the cinema could do just as he was interested in what men and women do. Never searching for the extraordinary, he would go to endless lengths to bring out not some abstract rhythm in the lives of people (as René Clair did) but the true style and rhythm of their sensibilities.

In 1956 Max Ophuls bequeathed to Becker his project on the life of Modigliani. While the resultant film, *Montparnasse 19,* is one of his least successful, its style is illustrative. Within weeks after Becker assumed control of the project, both the scriptwriter (Henri Jeanson) and the set designer (Annenkov) left in outrage, for Becker refused to let them show off with words and drapery. His was always a reduced idea of cinema, even when, as in *Falbalas*, his subject was fashion. Nor did he ever choose name actors, except perhaps Gérard Philipe as Modigliani. He had a sureness of taste, backed up by scrupulous reflection. Becker viewed filmmaking as an endless series of choices, each of which could founder the project.

Truffaut once claimed that Becker had his own pace of living; he would linger over meals, but race his car. He would spend hours of film over minor incidents in the lives of his characters, while whipping through the core of the intrigue that brought those characters together. Perhaps this is why *Le Trou* is a fitting finale to his career. For here the intrigue is given in advance and in a sense is without interest: five men struggling to escape from jail. For two and a half hours we observe the minutiae of their efforts and the silent camaraderie that develops among them. This is, for Becker, the state of life on earth: despite the ingenuity we bring to our struggle for freedom, we are doomed to failure; but in the effort we come upon another value, greater even than liberty, an awareness that our struggle is shared and of the friendship and respect that shared effort confers. If *Casque d'Or* is destined to remain his most popular and most acclaimed film (it was his personal favorite), it will not betray these sentiments, for the character of Manda gives up not only liberty, but also life with Marie-Casque d'Or, in order to be true to his friend. The stunning scene at the guillotine which ends that film evokes a set of emotions as contradictory as life itself. Jacques Becker was uniquely able to express such contradictions.

—Dudley Andrew

BELLOCCHIO, Marco

Nationality: Italian. **Born:** Piacenza, 9 November 1939. **Education:** Educated in Milan, at Centro Sperimentale di Cinematografica, Rome, and at Slade School of Fine Arts, London (on scholarship), 1959-63. **Career:** Directed first feature, *I pugni in tasca,* 1965; joined cooperative dedicated to militant cinema, 1968; co-directed 5-part series for TV, *La macchina cinema,* 1977-78.

Films as Director:

1965 ***I pugni in tasca*** (*Fists in the Pocket*) (+ sc)
1967 *La Cina è vicina* (*China is Near*) (+ co-sc)
1969 "Discutiamo discutiamo" episode of *Amore e rabbia* (*Vangelo '70*) (+ co-sc, role)
1971 *Nel nome del padre* (*In the Name of the Father*) (+ sc)
1972 *Sbatti il mostro in prima pagina* (*Strike the Monster on Page One*) (co-d uncredited, co-sc)
1974 *Nessuno o tutti—Matti da slegare* (co-d, co-sc)
1976 *Marcia trionfale* (+ co-sc)
1977 *Il gabbiano* (+ co-sc)
1979 *Salto nel vuoto* (+ sc)
1980 *Leap into the Void* (+ sc)
1981 *Vacanze in Valtrebbia*
1982 *Gli occhi, la bocca* (*The Eyes, the Mouth*)
1983 *Enrico IV* (*Henry IV*)
1986 *Devil in the Flesh*
1987 *La visionè del sabba* (*The Visions of Sabbath*)
1988 *La sorciere*
1991 *La condanna* (+sc)
1994 *Sogno della Farfalla*

Other films:

1958 *La colpa e la pena, Abbasso lo zio* (as student at Centro Sperimentale); *Ginepro fatto uomo* (diploma film at Centro Sperimentale)

Publications

By BELLOCCHIO: books—

La Cina è vicina, Bologna, 1967; as *China is Near,* New York, 1969.
I pugni in tasca, Milan, 1967.

By BELLOCCHIO: articles—

Interview in *Film Society Review* (New York), January 1972.
"La Place de la politique," an interview with G. Fofi, in *Positif* (Paris), April 1972.
Interview with N. Zalaffi, in *Sight and Sound* (London), Autumn 1973.
"Marco Bellocchio on Victory March," interview with R. Schar, in *Cinema Papers* (Melbourne), September/October 1976.
"Marco Bellocchio—l'alibi du grand public n'est qu'une justification hypocrite," interview with D. Rabourdin, in *Cinéma* (Paris), March 1977.
Interview with Dan Yakir, in *Film Comment* (New York), March-April 1983.
Interview with J.C. Bonnet, in *Cinématographe* (Paris), June 1986.
Interview in *Filmcritica* (Florence), April-May 1988.

On BELLOCCHIO: books—

Wlaschin, Ken, *Italian Cinema Since the War,* Cranbury, New Jersey, 1971.
Leprohon, Pierre, *The Italian Cinema,* New York, 1972.
Tassone, Aldo, *Le Cinema italien parle,* Paris, 1982.
Michalczyk, John J., *The Italian Political Filmmakers,* Cranbury, New Jersey, 1986.

On BELLOCCHIO: articles—

Tessier, Max, "Au nom du père et de la politique," in *Ecran* (Paris), February 1973.
Comuzio, E., "Marco Bellocchio au miroir de Tchekhov," in *Jeune Cinéma* (Paris), April/May 1979.
Croyden, Margaret, "A Fresh Cinematic Voice from Italy," in *New York Times,* 11 December 1983.
Martin, Marcel, "Les yeux, la bouche" in *Revue du Cinéma/Image et Son* (Paris), November 1984, + filmo.
Stefanutto-Rosa, S., "Il diavola nel subconscio dello psicoanalista selvaggio," in *Cinema Nuovo* (Bari), March-April 1986.

* * *

One of the healthiest aspects of the ever-more impressive cinematic output of the 1960's was the greater respect accorded to different, even opposing, approaches to political filmmaking. Thus, a Godard or a Straub could comfortably accept being called a political filmmaker while their work analyzed the process of creating meaning in cinema. One of Italy's most gifted directors to have emerged since the

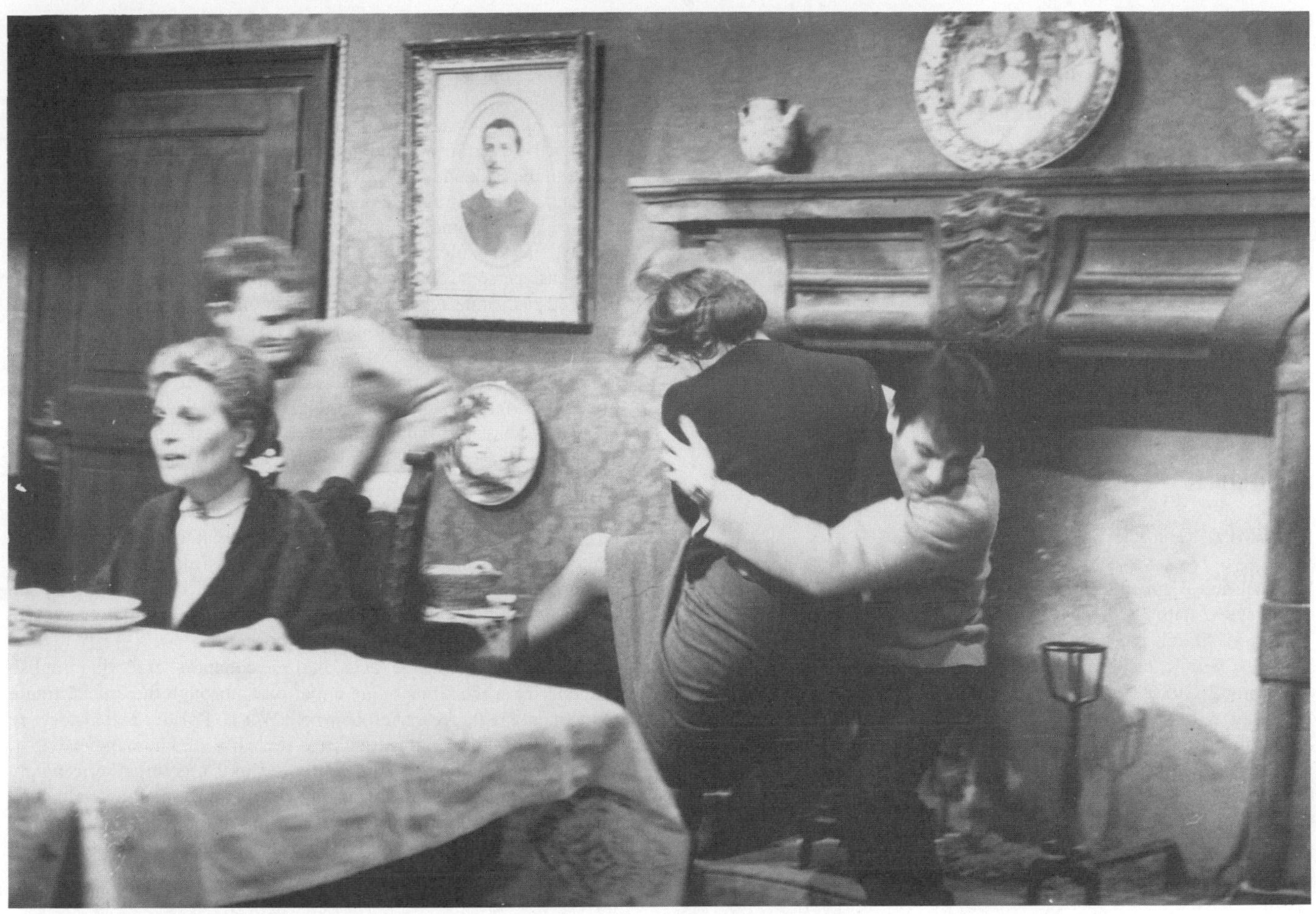

Marco Bellocchio: *I pugni in tasca*

war, Marco Bellocchio chose to delve into his own roots and scrutinize those primary agents of socialization—the classroom, the church, and most crucially for him, the family. Besides serving to reproduce selected values and ideas about the world, these structures are depicted by Bellocchio to be perfect, if microcosmic, reflections of society at large.

Bellocchio's films are black comedies centered around the threat of impending chaos. Typically, Bellocchio's protagonists are outsiders who, after learning the rules by which social structures remain intact, set about circumventing or ignoring them. Through their actions they expose the fragility of the social order by exposing the fragility of all presumed truths. The judge in *Leap into the Void,* for example, devises a bizarre plot to have his sister killed in order to avoid suffering the embarrassment of sending her to a mental institution.

The nuclear family, as an incarnation of the social order, represents a system of clearly understood, if unexpressed, power relationships within a fixed hierarchy. These power relationships are expressed in familial terms: Bellocchio's women, for example, are usually defined as mothers or sisters. Even the radical political beliefs that some of his characters profess must be judged with regard to their application in the family sphere: shocked to discover that his sister is no longer a virgin, Vittorio in *China Is Near* admits, "You can be a Marxist-Leninist but still insist that your sister doesn't screw around."

Along with his countryman Bernardo Bertolucci, Bellocchio is a primary example of the first European generation of film-school-educated directors. Often, these directors—perhaps under the influence of *la politique des auteurs*—tended to exhibit an extreme self-conciousness in their films. While watching a Bellocchio film, one is struck at how little or nothing is left open to interpretation—everything seems achingly precise and intentional. Yet what saves his films from seeming airless or hopelessly "arty" is that they're often outrageously funny. The havoc his characters wreak on all those around them is ironically counterpointed to the controlled precision of the direction. There is a kind of mordant delight in discovering just how far Bellocchio's characters will go in carrying out their eerie intrigues. The sense of shrewd critical intelligence orchestrating comic pandemonium into lucid political analyses is one of the most pleasurable aspects of his cinema.

—Richard Peña

BEMBERG, Maria Luisa

Nationality: Argentinian. **Born:** Buenos Aires, 1925. **Family:** Divorced, four children. **Career:** Established Argentina's Teatro del Globo theater company, 1950s; wrote her first screenplay, *Cronica de una Senora (Chronicle of a Woman),* 1971; moved to New York and attended the Strasberg Institute, late 1970s; returned to Argentina and directed her first feature, *Momentos,* 1981.

Films as Director and Scriptwriter:

1981 *Momentos* (*Moments*)
1982 *Señora de Nadie* (*Nobody's Woman*)
1984 *Camila*
1987 *Miss Mary*
1990 *Yo, la peor de todas* (*I, the Worst of Them All*)
1993 *De eso no se habla* (*I Don't Want to Talk About It*) (co-sc)

Films as Scriptwriter Only:

1971 *Cronica de una Señora* (*Chronicle of a Woman*)
1972 *El Mundo de la Mujer* (short)
1975 *Triangulo de Cuatro* (Ayala)
1978 *Juguetes* (short)

Publications

By BEMBERG: articles—

"Maria Luisa Bemberg: El rescate de la mujer en el cine Argentino," an interview with J.C. Huayhuaca and others, in *Hablemos de Cine* (Lima), March 1984.

Interview with K. Jaehne and G. Crowdus, in *Cineaste* (New York), vol. 14, no. 3, 1986.

Interview with Sheila Whitaker, in *Monthly Film Bulletin* (London), October 1987.

On BEMBERG: book—

King, John, and Nissa Torrents, *The Garden of Forking Paths: Argentine Cinema,* London, 1988.

On BEMBERG: articles—

Maeckley, Monika, "Machismo Takes a Knock," in *Guardian* (London), 10 December 1982.

Rich, B. Ruby, "After the revolutions: the second coming of Latin American cinema," in *Village Voice* (New York), 10 February 1987.

Jackson, L. and Jaehne, K., "Eavesdropping in female voices," in *Cineaste* (New York), no. 1/2, 1987-1988.

* * *

Maria Luisa Bemberg entered the filmmaking world only after leading an "asphyxiating and uneventful" life (her own words). Born into one of the wealthiest families in Buenos Aires, she entered the film industry at age forty-six after her children had grown and she had obtained a divorce. Despite her belated entry into the profession, Bemberg is now one of the most subversive and popular Argentinian directors. In addition, she has been acclaimed in Europe and the States.

Bemberg's first (semi-autobiographical) screenplay, *Cronica de una Señora,* gained acclaim as a contemporary domestic drama, focusing on a regressive political system as it affected the female protagonist. Wishing to exert more control over her screenplays, but with no formal training, she spent three months as an actress at the Lee Strasberg Institute in New York and returned to Argentina to direct. In 1982 she caused a stir with *Senora de Nadie,* which featured a friendship between a gay man and a separated woman, challenging in one swoop the sacred notions of marriage, family, and the Church. Released on the day that Argentina invaded the Malvinas (Falklands), the film's impact was overshadowed somewhat by political events, but the crumbling state of the military regime (which had exerted so much censorship and control over the country's film industry that by the late 1970s only twelve films were being produced per year) ultimately helped the film succeed. Hugely popular with female audiences, it made a powerful and overtly feminist intervention into a culture crippled by its own repression and machismo.

After the overthrow of the military regime, and the humiliation of defeat in the Falklands War, Bemberg still saw much to come to terms with and much to struggle against in her national identity. She felt that her role as a filmmaker, and as a woman in a fiercely patriarchal society, was to explore political oppression as a backdrop and context for intense personal conflict. Her films dwell anxiously on Argentina's troubled past, and suggest that only by coming to terms with it can the nation—and the individual—put it to rest.

In 1984 Bemberg directed *Camila,* the first Argentinian film ever to break into the American market. Recipient of an Oscar nomination for best foreign language film, it is all the more remarkable in that many other directors who wanted to film this true story of illicit love between a priest and a young woman in 1847 had previously been prevented from doing so by the government. By casting the Priest as a beautiful object of desire and Camila (historically portrayed as the innocent victim) as the temptress, Bemberg created a passionate melodrama in which she consciously moved away from her earlier, hard-bitten domestic dramas into a more emotional, lyrical sphere. The historical basis of *Camila* offers a mythical arena in which to explore her very real contemporary political concerns.

Miss Mary continues to focus on these concerns, exploring English influence over the Argentinian upper class through the crucial figure of the nanny in the years before World War II. Politics and history are expressed through family structures, sexuality, and human behaviour. Female characters, even the repressed and unsympathetic nanny (played by Julie Christie), are portrayed with understanding—although Miss Mary is a reactionary agent of oppression, the film works to explore *why* she is so—in an attempt to study the forces that could create both she and the sick family for which she works.

Bemberg's strong sense of the melancholy is an integral part of her work, causing an uneasy tension in all her films: while all her works indict the reactionary political system, they are also impregnated with a tragic sensibility that presents events as somehow out of the protagonists' control. The bleak endings (in which transgressors are punished and traditional structures remain apparently intact) of Bemberg's films might seem pessimistic. But the very expression of transgression in the films—along with the tentative exploration of the disruptions that inevitably threaten an apparently monolithic system—by an individual who could so easily be a victim of that system (female, bourgeois, divorced), is not merely laudable, but remarkable.

Camila and *Miss Mary* remain exceptional films, the former a passionate and profound examination of a doomed romance and the latter a sumptuous, evocative account of a repressed woman. If both films are not overtly autobiographical, they do deal in very personal ways with Bemberg's own identity as a woman existing in a male-dominated society. A third, most impressive, feature from Bemberg is *I, The Worst of Them All,* set in Mexico during the seventeenth century. Her heroine is a nun possessed of a deep thirst for knowledge who becomes a writer. She also is destined to becomes the antagonist of her country's misogynist archbishop. Bemberg followed that up with *I Don't Want to Talk About It,* a fitfully interesting drama about two women—one a dwarf and the other her physically appealing but obnoxiously controlling mother—who become involved with an aging but still-suave bachelor (impeccably played by Marcello Mastroianni).

The unfortunate aspect of Bemberg's career is that it began so late in her life, thus robbing her of time to write and direct other films. Still, she has been able to transcend the repressive political forces at work in her country and the constraints placed upon her because of her sex. Moreover, her films show her ability to discerningly philosophize about these aspects of existence in her country.

—Samantha Cook, updated by Rob Edelman

BENEGAL, Shyam

Nationality: Indian. **Born:** Alwal, near Hyderabad, 14 December 1934. **Education:** Osmania University. **Career:** Advertising copywriter and director (over 620 advertising shorts) for Lintas Agency, Bombay, 1960-66; received Bhabha fellowship and worked in U.S.; returned to India and became independent producer, 1970; directed first feature in Hindi, *Ankur,* 1974; director of the Indian National Film Development Corporation, 1980s; made TV mini-series *The Discovery of India,* 1989.

Films as Director:

1967 *A Child of the Streets* (doc short)
1968 *Close to Nature* (doc short); *Indian Youth—An Exploration* (doc short); *Sinhasta or The Path to Immortality* (doc short)
1969 *Poovanam* (*The Flower Path*) (doc short)
1970 *Horoscope for a Child* (doc short)
1971 *Pulsating Giant* (doc short); *Steel: A Whole New Way of Life* (doc short); *Raga and the Emotions* (doc short)
1972 *Tala and Rhythm* (doc short); *The Shruti and Graces of Indian Music* (doc short); *The Raag Yaman Kalyan* (doc short); *Notes on a Green Revolution* (doc short); *Power to the People* (doc short); *Foundations of Progress* (doc short)
1974 *Ankur* (*The Seedling*) (+ sc)
1974/5 *Learning Modules for Rural Children* (doc)
1975 *Nishant* (*Night's End*); *Charandas Chor* (*Charandas the Thief*)
1975 *A Quiet Revolution* (doc)
1976 *Manthan* (*The Churning*); *Tomorrow Begins Today*; *Industrial Research* (short); *Epilepsy* (short)
1977 ***Bhumika*** (*The Role*) (+ co-sc); *Kondura/Anugrahan* (Telugu version) (*The Boon*) (+ co-sc); *New Horizons in Steel* (doc)*Junoon* (*The Obsession*)
1980 *Hari Hondal Bargadar* (*Share Cropper*) (+ sc)
1981 *Kalyug* (*The Machine Age*)
1982 *Arohan* (*Ascending Scale*)
1983 *Mandi* (*The Market Place*)
1985 *Jawaharlal Nehru* (doc); *Satyajit Ray* (doc); *Trikaal* (*Past, Present, and Future*) (+sc)
1986 *Susman* (*The Essence*) (+ p)
1993 *Suraj Ka Satvan Ghoda*

Publications

By BENEGAL: book—

The Churning, with Vijay Tendulkar, Calcutta, 1984.

By BENEGAL: articles—

Interview with Behroze Gandhy, in *Framework* (Norwich), no. 12, 1980.
Interview with F. El Guedj, in *Cinématographe* (Paris), September-October 1983.
Interview in *Screen International* (London), 13 December 1986.

On BENEGAL: books—

da Cunha, Uma, editor, *Film India: The New Generation 1960-1980,* New Delhi, 1981.
Willemen, Paul, and Behroze Gandhy, *Indian Cinema,* London, 1982.
Pfleiderer, Beatrix, and Lothar Lutze, *The Hindi Film: Agent and Re-Agent of Cultural Change,* New Delhi, 1985.
Ramachandran, T.M., *70 Years of Indian Cinema (1913-1983),* Bombay, 1985.
Armes, Roy, *Third World Filmmaking and the West,* Berkeley, 1987.

On BENEGAL: articles—

"Shyam Benegal," article and interview in *Cinéma* (Paris), September/October 1975.
Dharker, Anil, "Shyam Benegal," in *International Film Guide 1979,* London, 1978.
Posthumus, P., and T. Custers, "Film in India: interview—achtergrondon—Shyam Benegal," in *Skrien* (Amsterdam), Winter 1980/81.
Tesson, C., "La Route des Indes," in *Cahiers du Cinéma* (Paris), September 1983.
Gillett, John, "Style and Passion: The Films of Shyam Benegal," in *National Film Theatre Programme* (London), May 1988.
Saran, S., "The Question of Influences," in *Cinema in India,* No. 12, 1991.
Denis, F., "Of Truth and Invention," in *Cinema in India,* No. 9, 1992.

* * *

The career of Shyam Benegal, which began with his first feature in 1974, has some similarity in terms of both approach and tenacity to that of Satyajit Ray twenty years earlier. Among shared aspects one may note a background in the film society movement, a strong western influence, commercial work in an advertising agency, and direction of children's film (in Benegal's case the feature length *Charandas the Thief,* made in 1975 for the Children's Film Society). But Benegal was forty by the time he made his first feature and had already directed a large number of sponsored documentaries and commercials. Moreover, virtually all of his films have been in Hindi, the language of the commercial "all-India" movie, not in a regional dialect.

Benegal's personal style is already apparent and fully formed in the loose trilogy of studies of rural oppression made between 1974 and 1976: *The Seedling, Night's End* and *The Churning,* the latter financed collectively—at two rupees apiece—by the farmers of Gujarat state. In each case the interaction of the rural populace and often well-meaning outsiders ends disastrously, but the note of revolt is very muted. Though Benegal's social commitment is unquestionable, he does not offer any clear way out for his characters. In *The Seedling,* the seduction and abandoning of a servant girl is followed by the savage beating of her deaf-mute husband, but the only answer is the stone thrown at the landlord's house by a small boy in the film's final sequence. This is the "seedling," but Benegal offers no indication as to how it can be nurtured. In *Night's End,* a schoolmaster's efforts lead to violence when his wife is kidnapped by a landlord's family who are accustomed to exploiting and brutalizing peasants at will. But the final peasant revolt stirred up by the middle class hero gets totally and blindly out of hand, and one knows that it will be put down—no doubt savagely—by the authorities and that passivity will resume. *The Churning* is more optimistic, but even here the advocates of change are eventually defeated, though their efforts may some day bear fruit. Typical of Benegal's approach is the way in which women—so often a personification of new values in third world films—are depicted as

Shyam Benegal: ***Arohan***

passive suffering figures. Benegal's style is always solidly realistic, with stress on a carefully worked out narrative line and well-drawn characters. The pace is generally slow and measured but enlivened by excellent observation and fine choice of significant detail.

In the late 1970s, Benegal retained this somewhat austere style with a total professionalism but without ever slipping into the extravagance or melodrama of the conventional Hindi film. *The Role,* one of his richest films, tells of a more dynamic woman, a film star who tries desperately to live her own life but is cruelly exploited by men throughout her life. The film, essentially a problem picture of a kind familiar in the West, has a muted, open ending and is enlivened by vigorously recreated extracts from the films in which the actress is purported to star. Subsequently, Benegal continued the widening of his chosen area of subject matter. *The Boon,* a film shot in two language versions and known as *Kondura* in Hindi and *Anugrahan* in Telegu, is a study of the tragic effect of a young man's belief that he has been granted supernatural powers. *The Obsession* is a tale of interracial love set at the time of the Indian Mutiny, and *The Machine Age* is a story of bitter rivalry between industrialists—an archetypal conflict based on an ancient Hindi epic. But *Ascending Scale,* which depicts a peasant family destroyed as it is pitted against the reactionary forces of rural India, shows Benegal's fidelity to the themes with which he had begun his career. Working aside from the dominant Hindi traditions, the director offers a striking example of integrity and commitment to an unrelenting vision.

—Roy Armes

BENTON, Robert

Nationality: American. **Born:** Robert Douglas Benton in Waxahachie, Texas, 29 September 1932. **Education:** University of Texas, and at Columbia University, New York City. **Military Service:** Served in U.S. Army, 1954-56. **Family:** Married Sally Rendigs, 1964, one son. **Career:** Art Director of *Esquire* magazine, New York, 1957-61 (consulting editor, 1962-); began screenwriting partnership with David Newman, on *Bonnie and Clyde,* 1967; directed first feature, *Bad Company,* 1972. **Awards:** National Society of Film Critics Award, New York Film Critics Award, Writers Guild of America Award and Oscar nomination, Best Screenplay, for *Bonnie and Clyde,* 1967; Oscar nomination, Best Screenplay, for *The Late Show,* 1977; Oscars and Los Angeles Film Critics Association Awards for Best Screenplay and Best Director, Golden Globe Award for Best Screenplay, Writers Guild of America Award and Best Director, National Society of Film Critics and Directors Guild of America, for *Kramer vs Kramer,* 1979; Oscar for Best Screenplay, for *Places in the Heart,* 1984; Oscar nomination for Best Screenplay, for *Nobody's Fool,* 1994. **Address:** c/o Sam Cohn, International Creative Management, 40 W. 57th Street, New York, NY 10019, U.S.A.

Films as Director and Co-Scriptwriter:

1972 *Bad Company*
1977 *The Late Show* (sc)

1979 *Kramer vs. Kramer*
1982 *Still of the Night*
1984 *Places in the Heart* (*The Texas Project*)
1987 *Nadine*
1991 *Billy Bathgate*
1994 *Nobody's Fool*

Films as Scriptwriter Only (with David Newman except as indicated):

1967 ***Bonnie and Clyde*** (Penn)
1970 *There Was a Crooked Man* (J. Mankiewicz)
1972 *What's Up Doc?* (Bogdanovich) (co-sc with Newman and Buck Henry)
1978 *Superman* (Donner) (co-sc with David Newman, Mario Puzo, and Leslie Newman)

Other Films:

1988 *The House on Carroll Street* (Yates) (co-exec pr)

Publications

By BENTON: books—

The In and Out Book, with Harvey Schmidt, New York, 1959.
Little Brother, No More, New York, 1960.
The Worry Book, with Harvey Schmidt, New York, 1962.
Extremism: A Non-Book, with David Newman, New York, 1964.
Don't Ever Wish for a Seven Foot Bear, with Sally Rendigs, New York, 1972.

By BENTON: articles—

Interviews in *Film Comment* (New York), March/April 1973, January/February 1977, and July/August 1978.
Interview in *American Film* (Washington, D.C.), July/August 1979.
Interview in *Image et Son* (Paris), April 1980.
Interview with Leslie Bennetts, in *New York Times,* 7 October 1984.
Interview in *Time Out* (London), 28 February 1985.
Interview with Sheila Johnston, in *Stills* (London), March 1985.
Interview with P. Calum and A. Skytte in *Kosmorama* (Copenhagen), May 1985.
Interview with P. Freeman, in *American Screenwriter,* vol. 4, no. 4, 1987.
Interview with L. Vincenzi in *Millimeter* (Cleveland), August 1987.

On BENTON: articles—

"Robert Benton," in *Film Dope* (London), August 1973.
Sight and Sound (London), Autumn 1973.
Millimeter (New York), October 1976.
Collins, G., "Robert Benton Goes Back to Texas for a Little Fun," in *New York Times,* 2 August 1987.
Sarris, Andrew, "A Low-Rent Romance," in *Village Voice* (New York), 11 August 1987.
Almendros, Nestor, "Benton, Texas," in *American Cinematographer* (Los Angeles), September 1987.
Talty, S., "Inside *Billy Bathgate,*" in *American Film* (Los Angeles), July 1991.
Weinraub, Bernard, "With Kevin's Gate and Billygate, Filmdom's Love of Gossip Blooms," in *New York Times,* 17 September 1991.
James, Caryn, "Film View: A Hole in the Heart of *Billy Bathgate,*" in *New York Times,* 3 November 1991.
Krohn, B., "Histoires de gangsters, historie d'Amerique," in *Cahiers du Cinema* (Paris), February 1992.
Campbell, V. and Margulies, E., "Shrink to Fit," in *Movieline* (Los Angeles), October 1992.

* * *

There were many ways to make it as a bigtime Hollywood director in the 1970s. Robert Benton's experience provides a common mode: a successful screenwriter turned director. Benton teamed with another aspiring author, David Newman, to pen the script of Arthur Penn's wildly successful, highly influential *Bonnie and Clyde* (1967), a film that showed Hollywood how to meld comedy, melodrama, and social commentary. The story of how Benton and Newman came to write *Bonnie and Clyde* is the stuff of Hollywood legend. In 1964 they were working for *Esquire* magazine, developing the magazine's annual college issue. As they were crafting the magazine's infamous Dubious Achievement Awards, they became caught up with the art cinema of Ingmar Bergman, Federico Fellini, and Akira Kurosawa. They decided to attempt an American version of Jean-Luc Godard's *Breathless* through the story of two desperados of the 1930s, Bonnie Parker and Clyde Barrow.

Benton and Newman wrote a seventy-page treatment in which they tried to make their film feel like an Hitchcock thriller, but with the comic violent tone of François Truffaut's *Shoot the Piano Player.* First they sent the "Bonnie and Clyde" script to Truffaut, who passed on it, as did Jean-Luc Godard. Warren Beatty rescued the project, agreed to produce it, and Arthur Penn became the director. Here were the first members of the film generation of the 1960s making what in some ways came to represent the most influential film of the decade, for it captured the restlessness of an age as well as the era's ethical ambiguity. *Bonnie and Clyde* at once demonstrated that Hollywood films could successfully incorporate the stylistic flourishes of the French New Wave into Classic Hollywood genre material.

The *Bonnie and Clyde* script won numerous awards, and the duo went on to co-script *There Was a Crooked Man* (1970), *What's Up Doc?* (1972), and *Superman* (1978). The latter two proved Benton and Newman were able to make movies that made money. *What's Up Doc?* finished in the top ten earners for 1971; *Superman* generated more than 100 million dollars worldwide. But Benton aspired to be his own director, and he worked single-mindedly at that goal during the 1970s.

Success came with *Kramer vs. Kramer* (1979), Benton's third directorial effort. Based on his screenplay, *Kramer vs. Kramer* won the Oscar for Best Picture, Best Actor (Dustin Hoffman), Best Screenplay, Best Director, and Best Supporting Actress (Meryl Streep), a sweep rarely accomplished in Hollywood history. More importantly for Benton's future, *Kramer vs. Kramer* finished atop the domestic box-office rankings for the year. Robert Benton had reached his goal; he was as hot a property as there was in Hollywood as the 1980s opened.

But thereafter Benton's filmmaking successes were limited. Benton did reach another peak in 1984 with *Places in the Heart.* The film, which featured Benton's award-winning screenplay, was one man's affectionate look at life in his hometown of Waxahachie, Texas, during the hard days of the great depression. On the other hand, Benton's *Nadine* (1987) was also set in Texas, but this comedy failed to capture either the fancy of the critics or the public.

As Benton moved into the 1990s, many saw Benton as the principle case of the power of the screenwriter as auteur. Perhaps this is so, but continuing success at the top—a Hollywood prerequisite if one wants to control one's movies—seemed to have sucked the life from Benton's story-telling ability. Some speculated that Benton, who had crafted fine stories of outsiders from Bonnie Parker to the aging detective of *The Late Show,* had difficulty functioning as a member of the Hollywood establishment.

Benton's most recent films have been set in the environs of upstate New York. *Billy Bathgate,* based on the E.L. Doctorow novel about a young man's involvement with mobster Dutch Schultz, has much going for it, beginning with a talented cast (headed by Dustin Hoffman and Nicole Kidman) and superlative production design. But the shoot was troubled, resulting in acrimony between Benton and Hoffman and a curiously emotionless and eminently forgettable film, despite the presence of the always watchable Hoffman (cast as Schultz—a character altogether different from his Ted Kramer character).

Nobody's Fool, based on a novel by Richard Russo, is far more successful. The characters are less flamboyant than those found in *Billy Bathgate*; as an evocation of time and place, and a portrait of small-town American life, the film is closer in spirit to *Places in the Heart.* Paul Newman is nothing short of superb as Donald "Sully" Sullivan, an aging, out-of-work construction worker. Long-estranged from his family, the film follows events when he is forced to deal with his son and grandson. Also central to the story are Sullivan's relationships with various townsfolk, including his landlady (Jessica Tandy), who once was his eighth-grade teacher, his sometime employer (Bruce Willis), and the latter's neglected wife (Melanie Griffith). *Nobody's Fool* works best as a film of moods and feelings; ultimately, it is a knowing, entertaining blend of poignancy and humor. As in his earlier films, Benton draws fine performances from his cast. While one would expect exceptional acting from Newman and Tandy, the filmmaker elicits solid work from Griffith and Willis, who rarely have been better on screen.

—Douglas Gomery, updated by Rob Edelman

BERESFORD, Bruce

Nationality: Australian. **Born:** 1940. **Education:** Sydney University. **Family:** Married, three children. **Career:** Worked in advertising and for ABC TV, late 1950s; moved to London, 1961, and taught at girl's school, Willesden; film editor, East Nigerian Film Unit, 1964-66; head of British Film Institute Production Board, 1966-70: produced eighty-six films, notably short documentaries; moved to Australia, 1971; directed first feature, *The Adventures of Barry MacKenzie,* 1972; moved to United States, 1981. **Awards:** Best Director, Australian Film Awards, for *Don's Party,* 1976, and *Breaker Morant,* 1980; Best Director, American Film Institute Awards, for *Don's Party,* 1977; Best Director, Canadian Film Awards, for *Black Robe,* 1991. **Agent:** William Morris Agency, Beverly Hills, CA.

Films as Director:

1972 *The Adventures of Barry MacKenzie* (+ sc)
1974 *Barry MacKenzie Holds His Own* (+ co-sc, p)
1975 *Don's Party*
1977 *The Getting of Wisdom*
1978 *Money Movers* (+ sc)
1980 *Breaker Morant* (+ sc)
1981 *The Club*
1982 *Puberty Blues*
1983 *Tender Mercies*
1985 *King David*; *Fringe Dwellers* (+ sc)
1986 *Crimes of the Heart*
1987 *Aria* (directed one episode)
1989 *Driving Miss Daisy*
1990 *Her Alibi*
1991 *Mister Johnson* (+ co-sc)
1992 *Black Robe*
1993 *Rich in Love*
1994 *A Good Man in Africa*; *A Silent Fall*

Publications

By BERESFORD: articles—

"An Aussie in Hollywood," an interview with G. Crowdus and U. Gupta, in *Cineaste* (New York), vol. 12, no. 4, 1983.
Interview in *Screen International* (London), 21 May 1983.
"The Paramount *King David,*" an interview with Brent Lewis, in *Films* (London), December 1984/January 1985.
"Tender Crimes," an interview with Margy Rochlin, in *American Film* (Washington, D.C.), January/February 1987.

On BERESFORD: books—

Reade, Eric, *History and Heartburn: The Saga of Australian Film, 1896-1978,* Sydney, 1979.
Stratton, David, *The Last New Wave: The Australian Film Reader,* Sydney, 1980.
Tulloch, John, *Australian Cinema: Industry, Narrative, and Meaning,* Sydney and London, 1982.
White, David, *Australian Movies to the World: The International Success of Australian Films Since 1970,* Sydney, 1984.
Bruce Beresford: An Annotated Bibliography, Melbourne, 1985.
Hall, Sandra, *Critical Business: The New Australian Cinema in Review,* Adelaide, 1985.
Moran, Albert, and Tom O'Regan, editors, *An Australian Film Reader,* Sydney, 1985.
Radcliff-Umstead, Douglas, ed., *National Traditions in Motion Pictures,* Kent, Ohio, 1985.
Lewis, Glen, *Australian Movies and the American Dream,* New York, 1987.
McFarlane, Brian, *Australian Cinema 1970-85,* London, 1987.
Bennett, Bruce, ed., *A Sense of Exile,* Nedlands, Australia, 1988.
Dermony, Susan, and Elizabeth Jacka, *The Screening of Australia: Anatomy of a National Cinema,* Vol. II, Sydney, 1988.
Bertrand, Ira, ed., *Cinema of Australia: A Documentary History,* New South Wales, 1989.
Radcliff-Umstead, Douglas, ed., *Motion Pictures and Society,* Kent, Ohio, 1990.
Rattigan, Neil, *Images of Australia: 100 Films of the New Australian Cinema,* Dallas, 1991.
McFarlane, Brian, and Geoff Mayer, *New Australian Cinema: Sources and Parallels in American and British Film,* Cambridge, England, 1992.
Radcliff-Umstead, Douglas, ed., *Varieties of Filmic Expression,* Kent, Ohio, 1992.
Murray, Scott, *Australian Cinema,* St. Leonards, Australia, 1994.

On BERESFORD: articles—

Connelly, Keith, "The Films of Bruce Beresford," in *Cinema Papers* (Melbourne), August/September 1980.
Robinson, David, "Bruce Beresford's New Australian Cinema," in the *Times* (London), 23 October 1980.
Heung, Marina, "Breaker Morant and the Melodramatic Treatment of History," in *Film Criticism,* Winter 1984.
Quartermain, Peter, "Two Australian Films: Images and Contexts for *The Term of His Natural Life* (1927) and *Don's Party,*" in *Commonwealth Essays and Studies* (Dijon, France), Spring 1984.
Lewis, Brent, "A Deft Talent," in *Films* (London), February 1985.
"Bruce Beresford is Home," in *Encore* (Manly, New South Wales), 7 November 1985.
Bryant, Hallman B., "*Breaker Morant* in Fact, Fiction, and Film," *Literature/Film Quarterly,* 1987.

Rochlin, Margy, "Tender Crimes," *American Film*, January/February 1987.

Davidson, Jim, "Locating Crocodile Dundee," *Meanjin* (Victoria, Australia), March 1987.

Pym, John, "*Mister Johnson*," in *Sight and Sound* (London), Spring 1990.

Vann, Helene, and Jane Caputi, "Driving Miss Daisy: A New Song of the South," *Journal of Popular Film and Television*, Summer 1990.

Freebury, Jane, "*Black Robe*: Ideological Cloak and Dagger?" in *Australian Canadian Studies* (Wollongong, Australia), 1992.

Mortimer, Lorraine, "The Soldier, the Shearer and the Mad Man: Horizons of Community in Some Australian Films," *Literature/Film Quarterly*, 1993.

* * *

Bruce Beresford's career has been described as both interesting and uneven. Since his debut as a maker of feature films in 1972 with the broad comedy *The Adventures of Barry MacKenzie*, Beresford has made a wide variety of movies. But there is unity in this variety. If his Australian films, such as *The Getting of Wisdom* and *Breaker Morant*, seem more hard-edged and political than *Tender Mercies*, *Crimes of the Heart*, or *Driving Miss Daisy*, his latest American films nevertheless carry a social comment, if conveyed ever so quietly.

Beresford showed an interest in making films from an early age but moved to England when he saw little chance of being able to direct in Australia. After holding a number of jobs abroad, including a stint working for the British Film Institute, he returned home when government subsidies offered the possibilities for an expanded local production schedule. His first film, *The Adventures of Barry MacKenzie*, was deliberately commercial and pitched at a popular level since he felt that Australian films needed to prove their marketability at that time. The success of this film and his next "ocker" epic, *Barry MacKenzie Holds His Own*, gave him the leverage within the industry to be able to explore a different kind of work.

The more serious social comment of *Don's Party*, a film set against the failure of the Labor Party in the national elections of 1969, offered a clear-eyed look at Australian society of the 1960s and pursued in a more serious way the contradictions in the Australian character. *Don's Party* is a small movie based on David Williamson's play, and it was filmed largely within the confines of a suburban house. Its intense probing of character and the film's at-times claustrophobic atmosphere surfaced in the director's later, better-known films.

Beresford next turned to a project he had wanted to do for some time, *The Getting of Wisdom*, based on the autobiographical novel by H. H. Richardson. The story traces the adventures of a young woman who arrives from the outback to receive a proper education at a city girl's school. The film is a period piece but provides a devastating look at the overly genteel pretensions of class-bound, nineteenth-century Australian society. Not yet secure in its own identity, the film noted that the society still copied the Victorian social arrangements of the motherland. A stunningly beautiful film, *The Getting of Wisdom* established Beresford as a maker of serious and thoughtful films in the European art film tradition.

After shooting a caper film, *The Money Movers*, Beresford made *Breaker Morant*, which returned to Australia's past and explored the country's colonial relationship with Great Britain against the background of the Boer War. The film confirmed Beresford's international reputation and opened the way for him to make films outside the rather limited resources of the Australian cinema. *Breaker Morant* contains a savage look at British attitudes towards its former colony and examines the exploitation and condescension such attitudes produce. Although the film's leading character was played by an Englishman, the movie was also a showcase for Australian acting talent.

With *The Club* and *Puberty Blues*, Beresford returned to contemporary Australia. *The Club*, adapted from another of Bruce Williamson's plays, is a satire on the inner workings of an Australian football club, including its financial woes, moral tensions, and labor disputes. *Puberty Blues* deals with a pair of would-be "surfer-girls" growing up along the southern beachside suburbs of Sydney. The film deftly explores the macho world of Australian surfers while offering up an unflattering picture of how young women in this world are exploited and abused.

In part because of his growing international reputation, Beresford moved to the United States to direct his next film, *Tender Mercies*, from a Horton Foote script about a down and out country singer who finds love and solace with a small town Texan widow and her son. At first glance the story seems an unusual subject for Beresford to film, but *Tender Mercies* contains much of the same social commentary and the visual beauty of his earlier films. The acting is notable, as is the evocation of locale, which is not unlike the arid spaces of the Australian outback. It is a quiet, small film, the kind of movie Beresford was used to making, and it set the pattern for the other successful American films that followed. Only when venturing into the mega-epic with *King David* did the Beresford touch falter.

Returning to Australia, Beresford made *The Fringe Dwellers*, a movie about a family of aborigines and their attempts to integrate themselves into white Australian society. Their failure to do so causes a split between the generations and a dissolution of the family itself. Long a touchy subject in Australia, Beresford handled the integration issue with sensitivity, tracing the sad divisions between the races. *King David* came next. Although fraught with high expectations, the film was a critical and box-office disaster. He recouped whatever damage the fiasco might have done to his career by turning to *Crimes of the Heart*, an adaptation of Beth Henley's play about three eccentric sisters who have come together as a result of a family crisis. Once again, the director captured the ambience of small-town Southern society with gentleness and affection. The three sisters, all played by major Hollywood stars who worked remarkably well together under Beresford's direction, come off as a loving but eccentric by-product of regional gentility and repression. Underlying the film is a steady and unblinking look at the place of women in this traditional society.

It is noteworthy that Beresford's next film rated a large spread in the financial section of the *New York Times*. *Driving Miss Daisy* cleaned up at the box-office as well as at the Oscars, and made Beresford's name a known quantity among general film audiences around the world. A quiet film about the relationship between a black man and his elderly Jewish female employer in the South, the work features tour de force acting performances from both of the principal stars, Morgan Freeman and Jessica Tandy. For the most part the film does not deal with racial or social problems, but prejudice hovers around the edges of the world of the film and subtly affects its tone. It is another of Beresford's small films, a work of intense concentration that focuses on a microcosm of the modern world and which, in its unfolding, explores broad human as well as social issues.

Beresford's films of the 1990s have met with mixed critical and financial success. *Mister Johnson*, based on a Joyce Cary novel, follows the adventures of an English engineer in West Africa during the 1920s. The engineer, who has been hired to build a road through the native bush, is accompanied by Mr. Johnson, his wily local assistant. Like many of his other films, it is a tragic story about the clash between societies in a colonial setting. *Black Robe* is a larger-scale historical film set in the Canadian wilderness. In 1734 a French Jesuit priest accompanies a tribe of Algonquins to his mission among the Hurons. The priest's spirituality is challenged by the hardships he faces in the wilderness and with the North American Indians. It is a grim film with bleak, scenic locations that create a thoughtful and stark background for its message of cultural friction.

The same creative team that filmed *Driving Miss Daisy* reunited to film Josephine Humphreys' novel about a Southern family whose conventional lives are disrupted when the mother unexpectedly, and

Bruce Beresford: *Breaker Morant*

without explanation, leaves her husband and children. *Rich in Love* deals with the various members of the family but focuses on the coming-of-age of the youngest daughter, who has taken over the mother's duties. Both the acting and the screen adaptation were critically praised. In *A Good Man in Africa,* starring Sean Connery, the director returned to Africa, where the locals and the British were still at odds. The film was rather badly reviewed and several of the critics found the portrayal of both sides stereotypical and dated. *Silent Fall* is a suspense film about a psychiatrist who solves a double murder witnessed by the victims' nine-year-old son. It was released right on the heels of *A Good Man in Africa* and might have helped to save Beresford's current reputation, but it was so infrequently and so negatively reviewed that it only multiplied his troubles.

Although in many ways Bruce Beresford has become a Hollywood director, one who likes large filming budgets and the options that such budgets afford, his films remain really quite consistent. Preferring ensemble acting to star vehicles, smaller films to epics (even though *Breaker Morant* was favorably compared to a David Lean epic by the critics, the film is still basically an intimate courtroom drama) and always infusing his films with an insistent social critique, especially on the question of racism, Beresford has fashioned a remarkably consistent career for all of its seeming diversity.

—Charles L. P. Silet

BERGMAN, Ingmar

Nationality: Swedish. **Born:** Ernst Ingmar Bergman in Uppsala, Sweden, 14 July 1918. **Education:** Palmgrens School, Stockholm, and Stockholm University, 1938-40. **Family:** Married 1) Else Fisher, 1943 (divorced 1945), one daughter; 2) Ellen Lundström, 1945 (divorced 1950), two sons, two daughters; 3) Gun Grut, 1951, one son; 4) Käbi Laretei, 1959 (separated 1965), one son; 5) Ingrid von Rosen, 1971. Also one daughter by actress Liv Ullmann. **Career:** Joined Svensk Filmindustri as scriptwriter, 1943; director of Helsingborg City Theatre, 1944; directed first film, *Kris,* 1946; began association with producer Lorens Marmstedt, and with Gothenburg Civic Theatre, 1946; began association with cinematographer Gunnar Fischer, 1948; director, Municipal Theatre, Malmo, 1952-58; began associations with Bibi Andersson and Max von Sydow, 1955; began association with cinematographer Sven Nykvist, 1959; became artistic advisor at Svensk Filmindustri, 1961; head of Royal Dramatic Theatre, Stockholm, 1963-66; settled on island of Faro, 1966; established Cinematograph production company, 1968; moved to Munich, following arrest on alleged tax offences and subsequent breakdown, 1976; formed Personafilm production company, 1977; director at Munich Residenzteater, 1977-82; returned to Sweden, 1978; announced retirement from filmmaking, following *Fanny and Alexander,* 1982; directed *These Blessed Two* for Swedish television, 1985; concentrated on directing for the theater, 1985; Film Society of Lincoln Center presented a retrospective of almost all of Bergman's films as director, 1995; Brooklyn Academy of Music honored Bergman with a four-month-long Bergman Festival, 1995; The Museum of Television & Radio honored Bergman with a retrospective titled "Ingmar Bergman In Close-Up: The Television Work," 1995. **Awards:** Golden Bear, Berlin Festival, for *Wild Strawberries,* 1958; Gold Plaque, Swedish Film Academy, 1958; Oscars for Best Foreign Language Film, *The Virgin Spring* (1961), *Through a Glass Darkly* (1962), and *Fanny and Alexander* (1983); Oscar nominations, Best Director, for *Cries and Whispers* (1973), *Face to Face* (1976), and *Fanny and Alexander* (1983); Oscar nominations, Best Screenplay, for *Wild Strawberries* (1958), *Through a Glass Darkly* (1962), *Cries and Whispers* (1973), *Face to Face* (1976), and *Fanny and Alexander* (1983); co-winner of International Critics Prize, Venice Film Festival, for *Fanny and Alexander*; Erasmus Prize (shared with Charles Chaplin), Netherlands, 1965; Irving G. Thalberg Memorial Award, 1970; Order of the Yugoslav Flag, 1971; Luigi Pirandello International Theatre Prize, 1971; honorary doctorate of philosophy, Stockholm University, 1975; Gold Medal of Swedish Academy, 1977; European Film Award, 1988; Le Prix Sonning, 1989; Praemium Imperiale Prize, 1991.

Films as Director:

1946 *Kris* (*Crisis*) (+ sc); *Det regnar på vår kärlek* (*It Rains on Our Love*; *The Man with an Umbrella*) (+ co-sc)
1947 *Skepp till Indialand* (*A Ship Bound for India*; *The Land of Desire*) (+ sc)
1948 *Musik i mörker* (*Music in Darkness*; *Night Is My Future*); *Hamnstad* (*Port of Call*) (+ co-sc)
1949 *Fängelse* (*Prison*; *The Devil's Wanton*) (+ sc); *Törst* (*Thirst*; *Three Strange Loves*)
1950 *Till glädje* (*To Joy*) (+ sc); *Sånt händer inte här* (*High Tension*; *This Doesn't Happen Here*)
1951 *Sommarlek* (*Summer Interlude*; *Illicit Interlude*) (+ co-sc)
1952 *Kvinnors väntan* (*Secrets of Women*; *Waiting Women*) (+ sc)
1953 *Sommaren med Monika* (*Monika*; *Summer with Monika*) (+ co-sc); ***Gycklarnas afton*** (*The Naked Night*; *Sawdust and Tinsel*) (+ sc)
1954 *En lektion i kärlek* (*A Lesson in Love*) (+ sc)
1955 *Kvinnodröm* (*Dreams*; *Journey into Autumn*) (+ sc); ***Sommarnattens leende*** (*Smiles of a Summer Night*) (+ sc)
1957 ***Det sjunde inseglet*** (*The Seventh Seal*) (+ sc); ***Smultronstället*** (*Wild Strawberries*) (+ sc)
1958 *Nära livet* (*Brink of Life*; *So Close to Life*) (+ co-sc); *Ansiktet* (*The Magician*; *The Face*) (+ sc)
1960 *Jungfrukällen* (*The Virgin Spring*); *Djävulens öga* (*The Devil's Eye*) (+ sc)
1961 *Såsom i en spegel* (*Through a Glass Darkly*) (+ sc)
1963 *Nattvardsgästerna* (*Winter Light*) (+ sc); ***Tystnaden*** (*The Silence*) (+ sc)
1964 *För att inte tala om alla dessa kvinnor* (*All These Women*; *Now About These Women*) (+ co-sc under pseudonym "Buntel Eriksson")
1966 ***Persona*** (+ sc)
1967 "Daniel" episode of *Stimulantia* (+ sc, ph)
1968 *Vargtimmen* (*Hour of the Wolf*) (+ sc); *Skammen* (*Shame*; *The Shame*) (+ sc)
1969 *Riten* (*The Ritual*; *The Rite*) (+ sc); *En passion* (*The Passion of Anna*; *A Passion*) (+ sc); *Fårö-dokument* (*The Fårö Document*) (+ sc)
1971 *Beröringen* (*The Touch*) (+ sc)
1973 ***Viskningar och rop*** (*Cries and Whispers*) (+ sc); *Scener ur ett äktenskap* (*Scenes from a Marriage*) (+ sc, + narration, voice of the photographer) in six episodes: "Oskuld och panik (Innocence and Panic)"; "Kunsten att sopa unter mattan (The Art of Papering Over Cracks)"; "Paula"; "Tåredalen (The Vale of Tears)"; "Analfabeterna (The Illiterates)"; "Mitt i natten i ett mörkt hus någonstans i världen (In the Middle of the Night in a Dark House Somewhere in the World)" (shown theatrically in shortened version of 168 minutes)
1977 *Das Schlangenei* (*The Serpent's Egg*; *Ormens ägg*) (+ sc)
1978 *Herbstsonate* (*Autumn Sonata*; *Höstsonaten*) (+ sc)
1979 *Fårö-dokument 1979* (*Fårö 1979*) (+ sc, narration)
1980 *Aus dem Leben der Marionetten* (*From the Life of the Marionettes*) (+ sc)
1982 ***Fanny och Alexander*** (*Fanny and Alexander*) (+ sc)
1983 *Efter Repetitioner* (*After the Rehearsal*) (+ sc)
1985 *Karin's Face* (short)

Other Films:

1944 *Hets* (*Torment*; *Frenzy*) (Sjöberg) (sc)
1947 *Kvinna utan ansikte* (*Woman Without a Face*) (Molander) (sc)
1948 *Eva* (Molander) (co-sc)
1950 *Medan staden sover* (*While the City Sleeps*) (Kjellgren) (synopsis)
1951 *Frånskild* (*Divorced*) (Molander) (sc)
1956 *Sista paret ut* (*Last Couple Out*) (Sjöberg) (sc)
1961 *Lustgården* (*The Pleasure Garden*) (Kjellin) (co-sc under pseudonym "Buntel Eriksson")
1974 *Kallelsen* (*The Vocation*) (Nykvist) (pr)
1975 *Trollflöjten* (*The Magic Flute*) (for TV) (+ sc)
1976 *Ansikte mot ansikte* (*Face to Face*) (+ co-pr, sc) (for TV, originally broadcast in serial form); *Paradistorg* (*Summer Paradise*) (Lindblom) (pr)
1977 *A Look at Liv* (Kaplan) (role as interviewee)
1986 *Dokument: Fanny och Alexander* (Carlsson) (subject)
1992 *Den Goda Viljan* (*The Best Intentions*) (sc); *Sondagsbarn* (*Sunday's Children*) (sc)

Publications

By BERGMAN: books—

Four Screenplays of Ingmar Bergman, New York, 1960.
The Virgin Spring, New York, 1960.
A Film Trilogy (Through a Glass Darkly, Winter Light, and *The Silence),* New York, 1967.
Persona and Shame, New York, 1972.
Bergman on Bergman, edited by Stig Björkman and others, New York, 1973.
Scenes from a Marriage, New York, 1974.
Face to Face, New York, 1976.
Four Stories by Ingmar Bergman, New York, 1977.
The Serpent's Egg, New York, 1978.
Autumn Sonata, New York, 1979.
From the Life of the Marionettes, New York, 1980.
Fanny and Alexander, New York, 1982; London, 1989.
Talking with Ingmar Bergman, edited by G. William Jones, Dallas, Texas, 1983.
The Marriage Scenarios: Scenes From a Marriage; Face to Face; Autumn Sonata, New York, 1983.
The Seventh Seal, New York, 1984.
Laterna Magica, Stockholm, 1987; as *The Magic Lantern: An Autobiography,* London, 1988.

Bilder, Stockholm, 1988; published as *Images: My Life in Film,* New York, 1993.
Den goda viljan, Stockholm, 1991; published as *The Best Intentions,* New York, 1993.
Sondagsbarn, Stockholm, 1993; published as *Sunday's Children,* New York, 1994.

By BERGMAN: articles—

"Self-Analysis of a Film-Maker," in *Films and Filming* (London), September 1956.
"Dreams and Shadows," in *Films and Filming* (London), October 1956.
Interview with Jean Béranger, in *Cahiers du Cinéma* (Paris), October 1958.
"Each Film is My Last," in *Films and Filming* (London), July 1959.
"Bergman on Victor Sjöstrom," in *Sight and Sound* (London), Spring 1960.
"The Snakeskin," in *Sight and Sound* (London), August 1965.
"Schizophrenic Interview with a Nervous Film Director," by 'Ernest Riffe' (pseudonym), in *Film in Sweden* (Stockholm), no. 3, 1968, and in *Take One* (Montreal), January/February 1969.
"Moment of Agony," interview with Lars-Olof Löthwall, in *Films and Filming* (London), February 1969.
"Conversations avec Ingmar Bergman," with Jan Aghed, in *Positif* (Paris), November 1970.
Interview with William Wolf, in *New York,* 27 October 1980.
"The Making of *Fanny and Alexander,*" interview in *Films and Filming* (London), February 1983.
Interview with Peter Cowie, in *Monthly Film Bulletin* (London), April 1983.
"Goodbye to all that: Ingmar Bergman's farewell to film," an interview with F. van der Linden and B.J. Bertina, in *Cinema Canada* (Montreal), February 1984.
Bergman, Ingmar, *Kak suzdavalas,* Chaplin (Stockholm), vol. 30, no. 2/3, 1988.
Interview with S. Bjorkman and O. Assayas, in *Cahiers du Cinema* (Paris), October 1990.

On BERGMAN: books—

Béranger, Jean, *Ingmar Bergman et ses films,* Paris, 1959.
Donner, Jörn, *The Personal Vision of Ingmar Bergman,* Bloomington, Indiana, 1964.
Maisetti, Massimo, *La Crisi spiritulai dell'uomo moderno nei film di Ingmar Bergman,* Varese, 1964.
Nelson, David, *Ingmar Bergman: The Search for God,* Boston, 1964.
Steene, Birgitta, *Ingmar Bergman,* New York, 1968.
Gibson, Arthur, *The Silence of God: Creative Response to the Films of Ingmar Bergman,* New York, 1969.
Wood, Robin, *Ingmar Bergman,* New York, 1969.
Sjögren, Henrik, *Regi: Ingmar Bergman,* Stockholm, 1970.
Young, Vernon, *Cinema Borealis: Ingmar Bergman and the Swedish Ethos,* New York, 1971.
Simon, John, *Ingmar Bergman Directs,* New York, 1972.
Kaminsky, Stuart, editor, *Ingmar Bergman: Essays in Criticism,* New York, 1975.
Bergom-Larsson, Maria, *Ingmar Bergman and Society,* San Diego, 1978.
Kawin, Bruce, *Mindscreen: Bergman, Godard and the First-Person Film,* Princeton, 1978.
Sjöman, Vilgot, *L. 136. Diary with Ingmar Bergman,* Ann Arbor, Michigan, 1978.
Manvell, Roger, *Ingmar Bergman: An Appreciation,* New York, 1980.
Mosley, Philip, *Ingmar Bergman: The Cinema as Mistress,* Boston, 1981.
Petric, Vlada, editor, *Film and Dreams: An Approach to Ingmar Bergman,* South Salem, New York, 1981.
Cowie, Peter, *Ingmar Bergman: A Critical Biography,* New York, 1982.
Livingston, Paisley, *Ingmar Bergman and the Ritual of Art,* Ithaca, New York, 1982.
Marker, Lise-Lone, *Ingmar Bergman: Four Decades in the Theater,* New York, 1982.
Steene, Birgitta, *A Reference Guide to Ingmar Bergman,* Boston, 1982.
Lefèvre, Raymond, *Ingmar Bergman,* Paris, 1983.
Dervin, Daniel, *Through a Freudian Lens Deeply: A Psychoanalysis of Cinema,* Hillsdale, New Jersey, 1985.
Gado, Frank, *The Passion of Ingmar Bergman,* Durham, North Carolina, 1986.
Ketcham, Charles B., *The Influence of Existentialism on Ingmar Bergman: An Analysis of the Theological Ideas Shaping a Filmmaker's Art,* Lewiston, New York, 1986.
Steene, Birgitta, *Ingmar Bergman: A Guide to References and Resources,* Boston, 1987.
Lauder, Robert E., *God, Death, Art and Love: The Philosophical Vision of Ingmar Bergman,* Mahwah, New Jersey, 1989.
Marty, Joseph, *Ingmar Bergman, une poetique du desir,* Paris, 1991.
Cowie, Peter, *Ingmar Bergman: A Critical Biography,* New York, 1992.
Marker, Lise-Lone, *Ingmar Bergman: A Life in the Theater,* New York, 1992.
Bragg, Melvin, *The Seventh Seal,* London, 1993.
Cohen, Hubert I., *Ingmar Bergman: The Art of Confession,* Boston, 1993.
Gibson, Arthur, *The Rite of Redemption in the Films of Ingmar Bergman,* Lewiston, Maine, 1993.
Tornqvist, Egil, *Filmdiktaren Ingmar Bergman,* Stockholm, 1993.
Long, Robert Emmet, *Ingmar Bergman: Film and Stage,* New York, 1994.

On BERGMAN: articles—

Ulrichsen, Erik, "Ingmar Bergman and the Devil," in *Sight and Sound* (London), Summer 1958.
Godard, Jean-Luc, "Bergmanorama," in *Cahiers du Cinéma* (Paris), July 1958.
Archer, Eugene, "The Rack of Life," in *Film Quarterly* (Berkeley), Summer 1959.
Alpert, Hollis, "Bergman as Writer," in *Saturday Review* (New York), 27 August 1960.
Alpert, Hollis, "Style Is the Director," in *Saturday Review* (New York), 23 December 1961.
Nykvist, Sven, "Photographing the Films of Ingmar Bergman," in *American Cinematographer* (Los Angeles), October 1962.
Persson, Göran, "Bergmans trilogi," in *Chaplin* (Stockholm), no. 40, 1964.
Fleisher, Frederic, "Ants in a Snakeskin," in *Sight and Sound* (London), Autumn 1965.
Lefèvre, Raymond, "Ingmar Bergman," in *Image et Son* (Paris), March 1969.
"Director of the Year," *International Film Guide* (London, New York), 1973.
Sammern-Frankenegg, Fritz, "Learning 'A Few Words in the Foreign Language': Ingmar Bergman's 'Secret Message' in the Imagery of Hand and Face," in *Scandinavian Studies,* Summer 1977.
Sorel, Edith, "Ingmar Bergman: I Confect Dreams and Anguish," in *New York Times,* 22 January 1978.
Kinder, Marsha, "*From the Life of the Marionettes* to *The Devil's Wanton,*" in *Film Quarterly* (Berkeley), Spring 1981.
Lundell, T., and A. Mulac, "Husbands and Wives in Bergman films: A close analysis based on empirical data," in *Journal of University Film Association* (Carbondale, Illinois), Winter 1981.

Nave, B., and H. Welsh, "Retour de Bergman: Au ciné-club et au stage de Boulouris," in *Jeune Cinéma* (Paris), April-May 1982.

Cowie, Peter, "Bergman at Home," in *Sight and Sound* (London), Summer 1982.

Corliss, Richard, and W. Wolf, "God, Sex, and Ingmar Bergman," in *Film Comment* (New York), May-June 1983.

McLean, T., "Knocking on Heaven's door," in *American Film* (Washington, D.C.), June 1983.

Boyd, D., "*Persona* and the cinema of representation," in *Film Quarterly* (Los Angeles), Winter 1983-84.

Tornqvist, E., "August StrindBERGman Ingmar," in *Skrien* (Amsterdam), Winter 1983-84.

Koskinen, M., "The typically Swedish in Ingmar Bergman," in 25th Anniversary issue of *Chaplin* (Stockholm), 1984.

Ingemanson, B., "The screenplays of Ingmar Bergman: Personification and olfactory detail," and J.F. Maxfield, "Bergman's *Shame*: A dream of punishment," in *Literature/Film Quarterly* (Salisbury, Maryland), January 1984.

"Dialogue on Film: Sven Nykvist," in *American Film* (Washington, D.C.), March 1984.

"Ingmar Bergman Section" of *Positif* (Paris), March 1985.

Barr, Alan P., "The Unraveling of Character in Bergman's *Persona,*" in *Literature/Film Quarterly* (Salisbury, Maryland), vol. 15, no. 2, 1987.

O'Connor, John J., "Museum tribute to Ingmar Bergman, in *New York Times,* 18 February 1987.

Chaplin (Stockholm), no. 30, vol 2/3, 1988.

American Film (Washington, D.C.), October 1988.

Corliss, Richard, "The Glass Eye," in *Film Comment* (New York), November-December 1988.

Tobin, Yann, article in *Positif* (Paris), December 1988.

Lohr, S., "For Bergman, a New Twist on an Old Love," in *New York Times,* 6 September 1989.

"Bille August to Helm Script by Bergman," in *Variety* (New York), 13 September 1989.

Nystedt, H., article in *Chaplin* (Stockholm), vol. 32, no. 1, 1990.

Oliver, Roger W., "Bergman's Trilogy: Tradition and Innovation," in *Performing Arts Journal* (New York), January 1992.

Bonneville, L. "Les meilleures intentions. Par Ingmar Bergman," in *Sequences,* January 1993.

Kauffmann, Stanley, "The Abduction From the Theater: Mozart Opera on Film," in *Yale Review* (New Haven), January 1993.

Lahr, John, "Ingmar's Woman," in *New Yorker* (New York), 17 May 1993.

James, C. "Scenes Froma Chilly Marriage," in *New York Times,* May 23, 1993.

"New York Institutions Honor Ingmar Bergman," in *New York Times,* 13 December 1994.

Riding, Alan, "Face to Face With a Life of Creation: at 76, the Eminent Director Ingmar Bergman Seems Even to Have His Demons Under Control," in *New York Times,* 30 April 1995.

Murphy, Kathleen, "A Clean, Well-lighted Place: Ingmar Bergman's Dollhouse," in *Film Comment* (New York), May-June 1995.

James, Caryn, "Sweden's Poet of Film and Stagecraft," in *New York Times,* 5 May 1995

Jefferson, Margo, "Bergman Conquers, Not Once But Twice," in *New York Times,* 18 June 1995.

On BERGMAN: film—

Greenblatt, Nat, producer, *The Directors,* 1963 (appearance).

Donner, Jörn, director, *Tre scener med Ingmar Bergman (Three Scenes with Ingmar Bergman)* (for Finnish TV), 1975.

Donner, Jörn, director, *The Bergman File,* 1978.

* * *

Ingmar Bergman's unique international status as a filmmaker would seem assured on many grounds. His reputation can be traced to such diverse factors as his prolific output of largely notable work (40 features from 1946-82); the profoundly personal nature of his best films since the 1950s; the innovative nature of his technique combined with its essential simplicity, even when employing surrealistic and dreamlike treatments (as, for example, in *Wild Strawberries* and *Persona*); his creative sensitivity in relation to his players; and his extraordinary capacity to evoke distinguished acting from his regular interpreters, notably Gunnar Björnstrand, Max von Sydow, Bibi Andersson, Ingrid Thulin, and Liv Ullmann.

After an initial period of derivative, melodramatic filmmaking largely concerned with bitter man-woman relationships ("I just grabbed helplessly at any form that might save me, because I hadn't any of my own," he confesses in *Bergman on Bergman*), Bergman reached an initial maturity of style in *Summer Interlude* and *Summer with Monika,* romantic studies of adolescent love and subsequent disillusionment. In *The Naked Night* he used a derelict travelling circus—its proprietor paired with a faithless young mistress and its clown with a faithless middle-aged wife—as a symbol of human suffering through misplaced love and to portray the ultimate loneliness of the human condition, a theme common to much of his work. Not that Bergman's films are all gloom and disillusionment. He has a recurrent, if veiled, sense of humour. His comedies, such as *A Lesson in Love* and *Smiles of a Summer Night,* are ironically effective ("You're a gynecologist who knows nothing about women," says a man's mistress in *A Lesson in Love*), and even in *Wild Strawberries* the aged professor's relations with his housekeeper offer comic relief. Bergman's later comedies, the Shavian *The Devil's Eye* and *Now About All These Women,* are both sharp and fantastic.

"To me, religious problems are continuously alive ... not ... on the emotional level, but on an intellectual one," wrote Bergman at the time of *Wild Strawberries. The Seventh Seal, The Virgin Spring, Through a Glass Darkly, Winter Light,* and *The Silence* lead progressively to the rejection of religious belief, leaving only the conviction that human life is haunted by "a virulent, active evil." The crusading knight of *The Seventh Seal* who cannot face death once his faith is lost survives only to witness the cruelty of religious persecution. In Bergman's view, faith belongs to the simple-minded and innocent. *The Virgin Spring* exposes the violence of vengeance in a period of primitive Christianity.

Bergman no longer likes these films, considering them "bogus"; nevertheless, they are excellently made in his highly professional style. Disillusionment with Lutheran denial of love is deep in *Winter Light.* "In *Winter Light* I swept my house clean," Bergman has said. Other Bergman films reflect his views on religion as well: the mad girl in *Through a Glass Darkly* perceives God as a spider, while the ailing sister in *The Silence* faces death with a loneliness that passes all understanding as a result of the frigid silence of God in the face of her sufferings. In *The Face,* however, Bergman takes sardonic delight in letting the rationalistic miracle-man suspect in the end that his bogus miracles are in fact genuine.

With *Wild Strawberries,* Bergman turned increasingly to psychological dilemmas and ethical issues in human and social relations once religion has proved a failure. Above all else, the films suggest, love, understanding, and common humanity seem lacking. The aged medical professor in *Wild Strawberries* comes through a succession of dreams to realize the truth about his cold and loveless nature. In *Persona,* the most psychologically puzzling, controversial, yet significant of all Bergman's films—with its Brechtian alienation technique and surreal treatment of dual personality—the self-imposed silence of the actress stems from her failure to love her husband and son, though she responds with horror to the self-destructive violence of the world around her. This latter theme is carried still further in *The Shame,* in which an egocentric musician attempts non-involvement in his country's war only to collapse into irrational acts of violence himself through sheer panic. *The Shame* and *Hour of the Wolf* are concerned with artists who

Ingmar Bergman

are too self-centered to care about the larger issues of the society in which they live.

"It wasn't until *A Passion* that I really got to grips with the man-woman relationship," says Bergman. *A Passion* deals with "the dark, destructive forces" in human nature which sexual urges can inspire. Bergman's later films reflect, he claims, his "ceaseless fascination with the whole race of women," adding that "the film ... should communicate psychic states." The love and understanding needed by women is too often denied them, suggests Bergman. Witness the case of the various women about to give birth in *Brink of Life* and the fearful, haunted, loveless family relationships in *Cries and Whispers.* The latter, with *The Shame* and *The Serpent's Egg,* is surely among the most terrifying of Bergman's films, though photographed in exquisite color by Sven Nykvist, his principal cinematographer.

Man-woman relationships are successively and uncompromisingly examined in a series of Bergman films. *The Touch* shows a married woman driven out of her emotional depth in an extra-marital affair; *Face to Face,* one of Bergman's most moving films, concerns the nervous breakdown of a cold-natured woman analyst and the hallucinations she suffers; and a film made as a series for television (but reissued more effectively in a shortened, re-edited form for the cinema, *Scenes from A Marriage*) concerns the troubled, long-term love of a professional couple who are divorced but unable to endure separation. Supreme performances were given by Bibi Andersson in *Persona* and *The Touch,* and by Liv Ullmann in *Cries and Whispers, Scenes from a Marriage* and *Face to Face.*

Bergman's later films, made in Sweden or during his period of self-imposed exile, are more miscellaneous. *The Magic Flute* is one of the best, most delightful of opera-films. *The Serpent's Egg* is a savage study in the sadistic origins of Nazism, while *Autumn Sonata* explores the case of a mother who cannot love. Bergman declared his filmmaking at an end with his brilliant, German-made misanthropic study of a fatal marriage, *From the Life of the Marionettes,* and the semi-autobiographical television series *Fanny and Alexander.* Swedish-produced, the latter work was released in a re-edited version for the cinema. Set in 1907, *Fanny and Alexander* is the gentle, poetic story of two years in the lives of characters who are meant to be Bergman's maternal grandparents.

After *Fanny and Alexander,* Bergman directed *After the Rehearsal,* a small-scale drama which reflected his growing preoccupation with working in the theater. It features three characters: an aging, womanizing stage director mounting a version of Strindberg's *The Dream Play*; the attractive, determined young actress who is his leading lady; and his former lover, once a great star but now an alcoholic has-been, who accepts a humiliating bit role in the production.

After the Rehearsal was not Bergman's cinematic swan song. He went on to author two scripts which are autobiographical outgrowths of *Fanny and Alexander. The Best Intentions,* directed by Bille August, is a compassionate chronicle of ten years in the tempestuous courtship and early marriage of Bergman's parents. His father starts out as an impoverished theology student who is unyielding in his views. His mother is spirited but pampered, the product of an upper-class upbringing. The film also is of note for the casting of Max von Sydow as the filmmaker's maternal grandfather. The actor's presence is most fitting, given the roots of the scenario and his working relationship with Bergman, which dates back to the 1950s.

The Best Intentions was followed by *Sunday's Children,* directed by Bergman's son Daniel. The film is a deeply personal story of a ten-year-old boy named Pu, who is supposed to represent the young Ingmar Bergman. Pu is growing up in the Swedish countryside during the 1920s. The scenario focuses on his relationship to his minister father and other family members; also depicted is the adult Pu's unsettling connection to his elderly dad.

—Roger Manvell, updated by Rob Edelman

BERKELEY, Busby

Nationality: American. **Born:** Busby Berkeley William Enos in Los Angeles, 29 November 1895. **Education:** Mohegan Military Academy, Peekshill, New York, 1907-14. **Military Service:** Organized marching drills and touring stage shows for U.S. and French armies, and served as aerial observer in U.S. Air Corps, 1917-19. **Family:** Married six times. **Career:** Actor, stage manager, and choreographer, 1919-27; director of *A Night in Venice* on Broadway, 1928; director of dance numbers in *Whoopee* for Samuel Goldwyn, 1930; worked for Warner Bros., 1933-39; hired as dance advisor and director by MGM, 1939; returned to Warner Bros., 1943; released from Warner Bros. contract, returned to Broadway, 1944; directed last film, *Take Me Out to the Ball Game,* 1949. **Died:** 14 March 1976.

Films as Director:

1933 *She Had to Say Yes* (co-d, ch)
1935 *Gold Diggers of 1935* (+ ch); *Bright Lights* (+ ch); *I Live for Love* (+ ch)
1936 *Stage Struck* (+ ch)
1937 *The Go-Getter* (+ ch); *Hollywood Hotel* (+ ch)
1938 *Men Are Such Fools* (+ ch); *Garden of the Moon* (+ ch); *Comet Over Broadway* (+ ch)
1939 *They Made Me a Criminal* (+ ch); *Babes in Arms* (+ ch); *Fast and Furious* (+ ch)
1940 *Strike Up the Band* (+ ch); *Forty Little Mothers* (+ ch)
1941 *Blonde Inspiration* (+ ch); *Babes on Broadway* (+ ch)
1942 *For Me and My Gal* (+ ch)
1943 *The Gang's All Here* (+ ch)
1946 *Cinderella Jones* (+ ch)
1949 *Take Me Out to the Ball Game* (+ ch)

Other Films:

1930 *Whoopee* (ch)
1931 *Palmy Days* (ch); *Flying High* (ch)
1932 *Night World* (ch); *Bird of Paradise* (ch); *The Kid from Spain* (ch)
1933 ***42nd Street*** (ch); *Gold Diggers of 1933* (ch); *Footlight Parade* (ch); *Roman Scandals* (ch)
1934 *Wonder Bar* (ch); *Fashions of 1934* (ch); *Dames* (ch)
1935 *Go Into Your Dance* (ch); *In Caliente* (ch); *Stars Over Broadway* (ch)
1937 *Gold Diggers of 1937* (ch); *The Singing Marine* (ch); *Varsity Show* (ch)
1938 *Gold Diggers in Paris* (ch)
1939 *Broadway Serenade* (ch)
1941 *Ziegfield Girl* (ch); *Lady Be Good* (ch); *Born to Sing* (ch)
1943 *Girl Crazy* (ch)
1950 *Two Weeks with Love* (ch)
1951 *Call Me Mister* (ch); *Two Tickets to Broadway* (ch)
1952 *Million Dollar Mermaid* (ch)
1953 *Small Town Girl* (ch); *Easy to Love* (ch)
1954 *Rose Marie* (ch)
1962 *Jumbo* (ch)
1970 *The Phynx* (role in cameo appearance)

Publications

By BERKELEY: book—

The Busby Berkeley Book, with Tony Thomas and Jim Terry, New York, 1973.

By BERKELEY: articles—

Interview with John Gruen, in *Close-Up* (New York), 1968.
Interview with P. Brion and R. Gilson, in *Contracampo* (Madrid), September 1981.

On BERKELEY: books—

Dunn, Bob, *The Making of "No, No, Nanette,"* New York, 1972.
Pike, Bob, and Dave Martin, *The Genius of Busby Berkeley,* Reseda, California, 1973.
Meyer, William, *Warner Brothers Directors,* New York, 1978.
Hirschhorn, Clive, *The Warner Bros. Story,* New York, 1979.
Delamater, Jerome, *Dance in the Hollywood Musical,* Ann Arbor, Michigan, 1981.
Feuer, Jane, *The Hollywood Musical,* London, 1982.
Morsiani, Alberto, *Il Grande Busby: Il Cinema di Busby Berkeley,* Modena, 1983.
Roddick, Nick, *A New Deal in Entertainment: Warner Brothers in the 1930's,* London, 1983.
Altman, Rick, *The American Film Musical,* Bloomington, Indiana, and London, 1989.

On BERKELEY: articles—

Sarris, Andrew, "Likable but Elusive," in *Film Culture* (New York), Spring 1963.
Comolli, Jean-Louis, "Dancing Images," and Patrick Brion and René Gilson, "A Style of Spectacle," in *Cahiers du Cinema in English* (New York), no. 2, 1966.
Jenkinson, Philip, "The Great Busby," in *Film* (London), Spring 1966.
Thomas, John, "The Machineries of Joy," in *Film Society Review* (New York), February 1967.
Bevis, D.L., "A Berkeley Evening," in *Films in Review* (New York), June/July 1967.
Roman, R.C., "Busby Berkeley," in *Dance* (New York), February 1968.
Sidney, George, "The Three Ages of the Musical," in *Films and Filming* (London), June 1968.
"What Directors are Saying," in *Action* (Los Angeles), May/June 1970.
Gorton, D., "Busby and Ruby," in *Newsweek* (New York), 3 August 1970.
Knight, Arthur, "Busby Berkeley," in *Action* (Los Angeles), May/June 1974.
Roth, M., "Some Warners Musicals and the Spirit of the New Deal," in *Velvet Light Trap* (Madison), Winter 1977.
Tessier, Max, "Busby Berkeley 1895-1976," in *Avant-Scène du Cinéma* (Paris), 15 April 1978.
Delamater, Jerome, "Busby Berkeley: an American Surrealist," in *Wide Angle* (Athens, Ohio), vol. 1, no. 1, 1979.
Telotte, J.P., "A Gold Digger Aesthetic: The Depression Musical and its Audience," in *Post Script* (Jacksonville, Florida), Fall 1981.
Durgnat, Raymond, "Busby Berkeley: Filmed Theatre and Pure Theatre," in *Films* (London), January 1982.

* * *

No American film director explored the possibilities of the mobile camera more fully or ingeniously than Busby Berkeley. He was the Méliès of the musical, the corollary of Vertov in the exploration of the possibilities of cinematic movement. His influence has since been felt in a wide array of filmmaking sectors, from movie musicals to television commercials.

Certain aspects of Berkeley's personal history are obvious in their importance to a discussion of his cinematic work, most specifically his World War I service and his work in the theatre. Born to a theatrical family, Berkeley learned early of the demands of the theatrical profession: when his father died, his mother refused to take the night off, instilling in Busby the work ethic of "the show must go on." Throughout most of his career, Gertrude Berkeley and her ethic reigned, no wife successfully displacing her as spiritual guide and confidante until after her death in 1948. Even then, Berkeley drove himself at the expense of his many marriages.

Berkeley's World War I service was significant for the images he created in his musical sequences. He designed parade drills for both the French and U.S. armies, and his later service as an aerial observer with the Air Corps formed the basis of an aesthetic which incorporated images of order and symmetry often seen from the peculiar vantage of an overhead position. In addition, that training developed his approach to economical direction. Berkeley often used storyboarding to effect his editing-in-the-camera approach, and provided instruction to chorus girls on a blackboard, which he used to illustrate the formations they were to achieve.

Returning from war, Berkeley found work as a stage actor. His first role was directed by John Cromwell, with Gertrude serving as his dramatic coach. He soon graduated to direction and choreography, and in 1929 he became the first man on Broadway to direct a musical for which he also staged the dance numbers, setting a precedent for such talents as Jerome Robbins, Gower Champion, Bob Fosse, and Tommy Tune. When Samuel Goldwyn invited him to Hollywood in 1930 as a dance director, however, that Broadway division of labor remained in effect. Berkeley had to wait until *Gold Diggers of 1935* before being allowed to do both jobs on the same film.

From 1933 through 1939 Berkeley worked for Warner Bros., where he created a series of dance numbers which individually and collectively represent much of the best Hollywood product of the period. An examination of his work in this period in relation to the Production Code and the developing conventions of the musical genre illustrates his unique contribution to cinema.

Boy/girl romance and the success story were standard narrative ingredients of 1930s musicals, and Berkeley's work contributed significantly to the formulation of these conventions. Where he was unique was in his visualization of the onstage as opposed to the backstage segments of these dramas. Relying on his war service, he began to fashion onstage spectacles which had been impossible to perform on the Broadway stage. In his films he was able to explode any notion of the limitations of a proscenium and the relationship of the theatre spectator to it: the fixed perspective of that audience was abandoned for one which lacked defined spatial or temporal coordinates. His camera was regularly mounted on a crane (or on the monorail he invented) and swooped over and around or toward and away from performers in a style of choreography for camera which was more elaborate than that mapped out for the dancers. Amusingly, he generally reversed this procedure in his direction of non-musical scenes; he typically made the backstage dramas appear confined within a stage space and bound to the traditions of theatrical staging and dialogue.

As Berkeley created the illusion of theatre in his musical numbers, so too he created the illusion of dance. Having never studied dance, he rarely relied on trained dancers. Instead, he preferred to create movement through cinematic rather than choreographic means. Occasionally, when he included sophisticated dance routines, such as in the Lullaby of Broadway number from *Gold Diggers of 1935,* he highlighted the dancers' virtuosity in a series of shots which preserved the integrity of their movement without infringing on the stylistic nuances of his camerawork.

The virtuosity of Berkeley's camera movement remains important not only for a discussion of aesthetics, but also for understanding the meaning he brought to the depiction of sexual fantasy and spectacle in a period of Hollywood history when the Production Code Administration was keeping close watch over screen morality. Throughout the 1930s, Berkeley's camera caressed as if involved in foreplay, penetrated space as if seeking sexual gratification, and soared in an ap-

Busby Berkeley

proximation of sexual ecstasy. Whether tracking through the legs of a line of chorus girls in *42nd Street,* swooping over an undulating vagina-shaped construction of pianos in *Gold Diggers of 1935,* or caressing gigantic bananas manipulated by scantily clad chorines in *The Gang's All Here,* his sexual innuendos were titillating in both their obviousness and seeming naiveté. Berkeley's ability to inject such visual excitement meant that he was often called upon to rescue a troubled picture by adding one or more extravagantly staged musical numbers.

After leaving Warner Bros. in 1939, Berkeley returned to MGM where, although generally less innovative, his work set precedents for the genre: he directed the first Judy Garland/Mickey Rooney musical, the first Garland/Gene Kelly film, and with his last effort as a director, introduced the team of Gene Kelly and Stanley Donen. Undoubtedly the master director of American musicals in the first decade of sound film and a huge influence on many of the musical talents of succeeding decades, Berkeley worked only occasionally through the 1950s, staging musical numbers for various studios. The last of these was the 1962 MGM film *Jumbo.*

With the nostalgia craze of the late 1960s, Berkeley's aesthetic was resurrected. In 1971 he triumphantly returned to the Broadway stage, where he directed a revival of the 1920s hit *No, No, Nanette,* starring his leading lady of the 1930s, Ruby Keeler, herself in retirement for thirty years. That moment was surely the fulfillment of all the success stories he had directed over his long career.

—Doug Tomlinson

BERLANGA, Luis García *See* **GARCÍA BERLANGA, Luis**

BERTOLUCCI, Bernardo

Nationality: Italian. **Born:** Parma, Italy, 16 March 1940. **Education:** Attended University of Rome, 1960-62. **Family:** Married Clare Peptoe, 1978. **Career:** Assistant director on *Accattone* (Pasolini), 1961; directed first feature, *La commare secca,* 1962; joined Italian Communist Party (PCI), late 1960s. **Awards:** Special Award, Cannes Festival, for *Prima della revoluzione,* 1964; Best Director Award, National Society of Film Critics, for *Il conformista,* 1971; Oscars for Best Director and Best Screenplay, and Directors Guild of America Award for Outstanding Feature Film Achievement, for *The Last Emperor,* 1987. **Address:** via della Lungara 3, Rome 00165, Italy.

Films as Director:

1962 *La commare secca* (*The Grim Reaper*) (+ sc)
1964 *Prima della rivoluzione* (*Before the Revolution*) (+ co-sc)
1965/66 *La vie del Petrolio* (+ sc); *Il canale* (+ sc)
1966/67 *Ballata de un milliardo* (+ co-sc)
1967 "Il fico infruttuoso" episode of *Amore e rabbia* (*Vangelo '70; Love and Anger*) (+ sc)
1968 *Partner* (+ co-sc)
1969 *La strategia del ragno* (*The Spider's Stratagem*) (+ co-sc)
1970 ***Il conformista*** (*The Conformist*) (+ sc)
1971 *La saluta e malato o I poveri muorioro prima* (*La Sante est malade ou Les Pauvres meurent les premiers*) (+ sc); *L'inchiesa* (+ co-sc)
1972 ***Last Tango in Paris*** (*Le Dernier Tango à Paris; Ultimo tango a Parigi*) (+ co-sc)
1976 ***1900 (Novecento)*** (presented in two parts in Italy: *Novecento atto I* and *Novecento atto II*) (+ co-sc)
1979 *La luna* (+ co-sc)
1981 *La tragedia di un uomo ridicolo* (*La Tragedie d'un homme ridicule; The Tragedy of a Ridiculous Man*) (+ sc)
1987 ***The Last Emperor*** (+co-sc)
1990 *The Sheltering Sky* (+co-sc)
1994 *Little Buddha*

Other Films:

1961 ***Accattone*** (Pasolini) (asst-d)
1967 ***C'era una volta il West*** (*Once Upon a Time in the West*) (Leone) (co-sc)

Publications

By BERTOLUCCI: books—

In cerca del mistero, Milan, 1962.
Bertolucci by Bertolucci, interviewed by Don Ranvaud and Enzo Ungari, London, 1987.

By BERTOLUCCI: articles—

Interview with Jacques Bontemps and Louis Marcorelles, in *Cahiers du Cinéma* (Paris), March 1965.
"A Conversation with Bernardo Bertolucci," with John Bragin, in *Film Quarterly* (Berkeley), Fall 1966.
"Versus Godard," in *Cahiers du Cinéma* (Paris), January 1967; also in *Cahiers du Cinéma in English* (New York), May 1967.
"Prima della rivoluzione," in *Avant-Scène du Cinéma* (Paris), June 1968.
"Bertolucci on *The Conformist,*" with Marilyn Goldin, in *Sight and Sound* (London), Spring 1971.
Interview with Amos Vogel, in *Film Comment* (New York), Fall 1971.
"A Conversation with Bernardo Bertolucci," by Joan Mellen, in *Cinéaste* (New York), vol. 5, no.4, 1973.
"Every Sexual Relationship Is Condemned: Interview," with Gideon Bachmann, in *Film Quarterly* (Berkeley), Spring 1973.
"Dialogue: Bertolucci and Aldrich," in *Action* (Los Angeles), March/April 1974.
"Dialogue on Film," in *American Film* (Washington, D.C.), April 1974.
"Films Are Animal Events," interview with Gideon Bachmann, in *Film Quarterly* (Berkeley), Autumn 1975.
"Propos de Bernardo Bertolucci," interview with Guy Braucourt, in *Ecran* (Paris), October 1976.
Interview with D. Buckley and others, in *Cineaste* (New York), Winter 1976/77.
Interview with D. O'Grady, in *Cinema Papers* (Melbourne), July 1977.
"History Lessons," interview with D. Young, in *Film Comment* (New York), November/December 1977.
Interview with Gordon Gow, in *Films and Filming* (London), June 1978.
"Bertolucci on *La Luna,*" an interview with Richard Roud, in *Sight and Sound* (London), no.4, 1979.
"Bernardo Bertolucci on *Luna,*" an interview with M. Sclauzero, in *Interview* (New York), October 1979.
Interview with Michel Ciment and Gerard Legrand, in *Positif* (Paris), November 1979.
"*Luna* and the Critics," interview with G. Crowdus and D. Georgakas, in *Cineaste* (New York), Winter 1979/80.

"Dialogue on Film: Bernardo Bertolucci," in *American Film* (Washington, D.C.), January/February 1980.
Interview with M. Magill, in *Films in Review* (New York), April 1982.
Interview with G. Graziani, in *Filmcritica* (Florence), February/March 1983.
"After the Revolution? A Conversation with Bernardo Bertolucci," by D. Lavin, in *Literature/Film Quarterly* (Salisbury, Maryland), January 1984.
Interview about Pasolini, in *Cinema e Cinema* (Rome), May/August 1985.
Interview with A. Philippon and S. Toubiana, in *Cahiers du Cinéma* (Paris), November 1987.
Article in *Film Comment* (New York), November/December 1987.
Interview in *Films in Review* (New York), March 1988.
"Radical Sheik," an interview with Harlan Kennedy, in *American Film* (Washington D.C.) December, 1990.
"Love and Sand," an interview with R. Gerber, in *Interview,* January 1991.
"Bernardo Bertolucci: Intravenous Cinema," an interview with Chris Wagstaff, in *Sight and Sound* (London), vol. 4, no. 4, 1994.

On BERTOLUCCI: books—

Leprohon, Pierre, *Le Cinéma italien,* Paris, 1966.
Gelmis, Joseph, *The Film Director as Superstar,* Garden City, New York, 1970.
Mellen, Joan, *Women and Sexuality in the New Film,* New York, 1973.
Casetti, F., *Bertolucci,* Florence, 1975.
Ungari, Enzo, *Bertolucci,* Milan, 1982.
Kolker, Robert Phillip, *Bernardo Bertolucci,* London, 1985.
Kline, T. Jefferson, *Bertolucci's Dream Loom: A Psychoanalytical Study of the Cinema,* Amherst, Massachusetts, 1987.
Negri, Livio, and Fabien S. Gerard, eds., *The Sheltering Sky: A Film by Bernardo Bertolucci Based on the Novel by Paul Bowles,* London, 1990.
Burgoyne, Robert, *Bertolucci's 1900: A Narrative and Historical Analysis,* Detroit, 1991.
Loshitzky, Yosefa, *The Radical Faces of Godard and Bertolucci,* Detroit, 1995.

On BERTOLUCCI: articles—

Kael, Pauline, "Starburst by a Gifted Twenty-Two-Year-Old," in *Life* (New York), 13 August 1965.
Beck, Julian, "Tourner avec Bertolucci," in *Cahiers du Cinéma* (Paris), October 1967.
Tailleur, Roger, "Les Vacances rouges," in *Positif* (Paris), May 1968.
Purdon, N., "Bernardo Bertolucci," in *Cinema* (London), no. 8, 1971.
Kreitzman, R., "Bernardo Bertolucci, an Italian Young Master," in *Film* (London), Spring 1971.
Roud, Richard, "Fathers and Sons," in *Sight and Sound* (London), Spring 1971.
"*Le Dernier Tango à Paris,*" in *Avant-Scène du Cinéma* (Paris), February 1973.
Kinder, Marsha, and Beverle Houston, "Bertolucci and the Dance of Danger," in *Sight and Sound* (London), Autumn 1973.
Lopez, D., "The Father Figure in *The Conformist* and in *Last Tango in Paris,*" in *Film Heritage* (New York), Summer 1976.
Aitken, W., "Bertolucci's Gay Images," in *Jump Cut* (Berkeley), November 1977.
Schwartzman, P., "Embarrass Me More!," in *Film Comment* (New York), November/December 1979.
Horton, A., "History as Myth and Myth as History in Bertolucci's *1900,*" in *Film and History* (Newark, New Jersey), February 1980.
"*La Luna* Issue" of *Avant-Scène du Cinéma* (Paris), 15 November 1980.
Magny, Joel, "Biofilmographie commentée de Bernardo Bertolucci," in *Cinéma* (Paris), October 1981.
Gentry, R., "Bertolucci Directs Tragedy of a Ridiculous Man," in *Millimeter* (New York), December 1981.
Ranvaud, Don, "After the Revolution," in *American Film* (Washington, D.C.), October 1986.
"*Last Emperor* Section" of *Cinéma* (Paris), 25 November 1987.
Article in *Film Comment* (New York), July/August 1989.
Burgoyne, Robert, "The Somatization of History in Bertolucci's *1900,*" in *Film Quarterly* (Berkeley), Fall 1986.
Burgoyne, Robert, "Temporality as Historical Argument in Bertolucci's *1900,*" in *Cinema Journal* (Austin), vol. 28, no. 3, 1989.
Burgoyne, Robert, "*The Last Emperor:* The Stages of History," in *SubStance* (Madison, Wisconsin) no. 59, 1989.
Bundtzen, L. K., "Bertolucci's Erotic Politics and the Auteur Theory: From *Last Tango in Paris* to *The Last Emperor,*" in *Western Humanities Review,* vol. 44, no. 2, 1990.
Loshitzky, Yosefa, "'Memory of My Own Memory': Processes of Private and Collective Remembering in Bertolucci's *The Spider's Stratagem* and *The Conformist,*" in *History and Memory,* vol. 3, no. 2, 1991.
Thomson, David, "Gone Away," in *Film Comment,* May/June 1991.
Loshitzky, Yosefa, and Raya Meyouhas, "'Ecstacy of Difference': Bertolucci's *The Last Emperor,*" in *Cinema Journal* Austin), vol. 31, no. 2, 1992.
McAuliff, Jody, "The Church of the Desert: Reflections on *The Sheltering Sky,*" in *South Atlantic Quarterly,* vol. 91, no. 2, 1992.
Loshitzky, Yosefa, "The Tourist/Traveler Gaze: Bertolucci and Bowles' *The Sheltering Sky,*" in *East-West Film Journal* (Honolulu), vol. 7, no. 2, 1993.
Buck, Joan Juliet, "The Last Romantic," in *Vogue,* March 1994.
Robert Horton, "Nonconformist: Bernardo Bertolucci's *Little Buddha,*" in *Film Comment,* July/August 1994.

* * *

At the age of twenty-one, Bernardo Bertolucci established himself as a major artist in two distinct art forms, winning a prestigious award in poetry and receiving high critical acclaim for his initial film, *La commare secca.* This combination of talents is evident in all of his films, which have a lyric but exceptionally concrete style. His father, Attilio Bertolucci, was famous in his own right as a critic, professor, and poet, and in 1961 introduced Bernardo to Pier Paolo Pasolini, an esteemed literary figure. This friendship led both writers, ironically, away from poetry and into the cinema. Serving as the assistant director on Pasolini's inaugural film, *Accattone,* Bertolucci was very quickly entrusted with the full direction of Pasolini's next project, *La commare secca,* based on a story by the writer.

La commare secca is an auspicious debut; as both screenwriter and director, Bertolucci found at once the high visual style and narrative complexity which distinguish his later films. The sex murder of a prostitute is its central narrative event; as the probable witnesses and suspects are brought in for questioning, a series of lives are unraveled, with each sad story winding toward the city park where the murder occurred. Formally, the film is an ambitious amalgam of a film noir atmosphere and narrative style with a neorealist concentration on behavioral detail and realistic settings.

In *Before the Revolution,* Bertolucci first presents the theme which will become foremost in his work: the conflict between freedom and conformity. Fabrizio, the leading character, is obliged to decide between radical political commitment and an alluring marriage into the bourgeoisie. In this reworking of Stendhal's *The Charterhouse of Parma,* Bertolucci expressly delineates the connection between politics and sexuality. The film also establishes the Freudian theme of the totemic father, which will recur throughout Bertolucci's work, here emblematized in the figure of Fabrizio's communist mentor, whom Fabrizio must renounce as a precondition to his entry into moneyed society.

Bertolucci diverged from the style of his first two critically successful films with *The Partner,* a complex, experimental work based on Dostoevski's *The Double.* Heavily influenced by the films of Godard and the events of May 1968, it eschews narrative exposition, developing instead a critique of literary consumerism, academic pacifism, and the student left, through a series of polemical debates between a bookish student and his radical double. For the most part *The Partner* is an anomalous film, which conveys very little of the heightened lyricism of his major works.

With *The Spider's Stratagem,* originally made for television in 1969, and *The Conformist,* Bertolucci combines an experimental narrative technique with lavish visual design, achieving in *The Conformist* an unprecedented commercial and critical triumph. Sexuality is here explicitly posited as the motor of political allegiance, as Marcello, the lead character in *The Conformist,* becomes a Fascist in order to suppress his growing recognition of his homosexuality. The character performs an outlandishly deviant act—killing his former professor, now a member of the Resistance, in order to declare his own conventionality and membership in the Fascist order. Conformity and rebellion are thus folded together, not only in the psyche of Marcello, but in the culture as a whole, as Bertolucci examines the interpenetrating structures, the twin pathologies, of family and politics. Bertolucci here unveils the full range of stylistic features—the elaborate tracking shots, the opulent color photography (realized by the virtuoso cinematographer Vittorio Storara), the odd, surrealistic visual incongruities—that give his work such a distinctive surface. It is here, also, that Bertolucci connects most directly with the general evolution of the postwar Italian cinema. Beginning with Visconti, and continuing with Antonioni and Bellocchio, an increasing emphasis is placed on the psychology of transgression, a motif which links politics and the libido. The inner life of the alienated protagonist becomes the lens displaying the spectrum of social forces, as the politics of the state are viewed in the mimetic behavior of disturbed individuals.

Last Tango in Paris depicts the last week in the life of Paul, played by Marlon Brando, as a man who is both geographically and spiritually in exile. His orbit crosses that of "the girl," played by Maria Schneider. The raw sexual encounters which ensue serve as a kind of purgation for the Brando character, who retaliates against the hypocrisy of cultural institutions such as family, church, and state through the medium of Jeanne's body. Sex is used as a weapon and symbolic cure, as the libidinal rage of the character is focused on the entire apparatus of social constraints. The outsized human passion Bertolucci depicts, chiefly through the threatening figure of Marlon Brando, seems to literalize the filmmaker's comment that "films are animal events." In addition to the players, the music by Gatto Barbieri and the cinematography of Vittorio Storaro contribute to the febrile intensity of the work.

The world acclaim brought by *Last Tango* assured Bertolucci of the financial resources to complete the long-planned Marxian epic, *1900.* Setting the film in the rural areas of Parma, a few miles from his childhood home, Bertolucci set out to compose a paean to a way of life that was passing—the "culture of the land" of the peasant farmers, seen as a native and pure form of communism. The film depicts the cruel historical awakening of the farmers of the region, part of an entire class that has been regularly brutalized, first by aristocratic landowners, and then by the Fascist regime. Bertolucci localizes this conflict in the twin destinies of two characters born on the same day in *1900*—Olmo, who becomes a peasant leader, and Alfredo, the scion of the feudal estate in which the film takes place.

The controversial work was released in a six-hour form in Europe, and shortened to three hours for American release. Bertolucci had complete control of the cutting of the film, and considers the shorter version a more finished work. The epic sweep remains, as do the contradictions—for the film amalgamates the most divergent elements: a Marxian epic, it is furnished with an international star cast; a portrait of the indigenous peasantry, its principle language is English. Intentionally fashioned for wide commercial appeal, it nonetheless broaches untried subject matter. The film keeps these elements in suspension, never dissolving these differences into an ideological portrait of life "after the revolution." The film's ending seems instead to return to the customary balance and tension between historical forces and class interests.

In *Luna,* Bertolucci turns to a much more intimate subject: the relation between mother and son. The work has a diminutive scale but a passionate focus, a quality crystallized in the opera scenes in which the mother, Caterina, performs. The reconciliation of mother, son, and father occurs during a rehearsal in which the mother reveals, through song, the identity of father and son. This cathartic and bravura scene plays in high relief the characteristic patterns of Bertolucci's cinema, in which the family drama is played against the backdrop of a ritualized art form, opera in this case, dance in *Last Tango,* and theater (the *Macbeth* scene in *Before the Revolution*).

With *Tragedy of a Ridiculous Man,* Bertolucci continues his inquiry into the relations between politics and family life, here framing the ambivalent bond between father and son with the correlative conflict between capitalism and political terror.

Bertolucci returned to the wide canvas of the historical film with *The Last Emperor* in 1987. Frustrated by his inability to acquire financing for a film of the Dashiell Hammett story *Red Harvest,* and unhappy with the state of filmmaking in Italy, the director turned to the autobiography of Pu Yi, China's last emperor, and had the privilege not only of filming in China but also of filming in the Forbidden City in Beijing, the first time such access had been allowed.

The story of Pu Yi illustrates a striking change in the political focus of Bertolucci's filmmaking. The relationship between individual psychology and the political and historical forces that mold it remains, as before, the central subject of the film, linking it to works such as *Before the Revolution, The Conformist,* and *1900.* But the resolution of the film seems to take place outside the political and historical context. The transformation of Pu Yi, in Bertolucci's words, from "a dragon to a butterfly," occurs only in the context of individual friendship. In depicting the rise and fall of imperialism, republicanism, and fascism, and ending the film with a portrayal of the harsh excesses of the Cultural Revolution, Bertolucci depicts a sequence of destructive political "solutions" that somehow clear the way for the journey of the main character from "darkness to light."

Following *The Last Emperor,* Bertolucci continued his exploration of non-Western cultures with *The Sheltering Sky* and *Little Buddha,* opening his work to existential and philosophical themes that would almost seem to defy dramatic expression. In *The Sheltering Sky,* Bertolucci fashions a disturbing portrait of a consciousness in search of its own annihilation. Drawn from the Paul Bowles novel of the same title, the film, in its first half, focuses on the pathos of a couple who adore each other but cannot be happy, on the difficulty of romantic love. The work centers on the willful isolation and self-loathing of the character Porter, who has traveled to Morocco in 1947 with his wife Kit and a friend, Tunner, in order to escape the bitter sense of his own emptiness and artistic impotence. Like the character Paul in *Last Tango in Paris,* Porter is a dangerous and mesmerizing character whose self-absorption creates a kind of vortex which draws others down with him. As the two main characters, Port and Kit, push deeper into the Sahara, the physical hardships they encounter seem more and more like rites of purgation, as if only the heat and dirt of the desert could wear down the various masks and poses that they continually display to each other. Port dies a horrifying death from typhus, revealing the depths of his love for Kit only as the curtain descends. Kit, cast adrift deep in Morocco, hitches up with a caravan of Tuareg nomads and allows the remains of her Western identity to dissolve; she becomes

Bernardo Bertolucci directing *The Last Emperor*

the lover of the leader of the caravan, her Western clothes are buried in the desert, and she enters his harem disguised as a boy, dressed in the indigo robes, turban, and sword of a Tuareg tribesman. In a sense, Kit becomes possessed by Porter's spirit, his taste for uncharted experience, without, however, assuming his arrogance or corrosive unhappiness. Kit's story, which Bertolucci poetically links with the phases of the moon and nocturnal shades of blue, becomes dream-like, a carnal utopia of full and expressive passion in which she submerges her identity and becomes whole, albeit temporarily.

The Sheltering Sky has much in common with Bertolucci's earlier films, particularly *Last Tango in Paris;* as Bertolucci says in an interview, "Isn't the empty flat of *Last Tango* a kind of desert and isn't the desert an empty flat?" By filming in North Africa, however, Bertolucci allows the landscape to provide a kind of silent commentary on the doomed protagonists, whose profound unhappiness is made more piercing by the almost cosmic scale of the environment. The film abounds in visual ideas, finding in the mountain overlooks, wind-blown expanses, and fly-infested outposts a kind of encompassing dimension comparable to the role played by history in other Bertolucci films. Here, cinematographer Vittorio Storaro composes scenes around the division of color temperatures associated with the two main characters, red and blue, in ways that accentuate their irreconcilability. Exceptional acting by John Malkovich and Debra Winger gives *The Sheltering Sky* a sense of emotional truth that stays with the spectator, like the tattoos on fingers and feet that Kit receives in the deepest Sahara.

Little Buddha, released in 1994, completes what Bertolucci has called his Eastern trilogy. Although it shares the exoticism and the chromatic richness of *The Last Emperor* and *The Sheltering Sky, Little Buddha* is a sharp departure from its predecessors. It is, Bertolucci has said, a story without dramatic conflicts, a story in which the dualism and division that animates his other films is resolved into a kind of harmonious unity. Weaving together the ancient tale of Siddartha and his quest for enlightenment with a contemporary story of an eight-year-old American boy who may be the reincarnation of a famous Buddhist master, the film aims for a simplicity of tone and address that could be understood and appreciated by children: indeed, Bertolucci has called *Little Buddha* a film for children, arguing that when it comes to Buddhism, everyone in the Western world is a child.

Little Buddha features a striking visual style, marked by heightened color abstraction. Vittorio Storaro, Bertolucci's cinematographer for all his films except one, has said in an interview that *Little Buddha* represents the culmination of his exploration into light, and that it may be a film that is "impossible to go beyond." The painterly style of *Little Buddha* is keyed not only to the contrast between the blue tonality of Seattle and the red and gold of the Siddartha story, but also to the four elements and the movement of the celestial spheres. When Siddartha achieves enlightenment under the banyan tree after staving off temptation and fear, harmony and balance are signified by the simultaneous appearance of the sun and the moon in the sky, and by the balanced color temperature of the sequence. In his career-long work with Bertolucci, Storaro has progressed from an exploration of light and shadow, to an exploration of the contrast of colors within light, to an exploration of the harmony within the spectrum.

The fascinating sequences of Siddartha's journey to enlightenment have a distinctly magical, storybook quality, a tone that is achieved partly by filming these scenes in 65 millimeter. The precision and detail that sets these sequences apart gives them the quality of an illuminated manuscript, or of a dazzling storybook of hand-colored pages. Also important here is the acting of Keanu Reeves, who embodies the part of a beautiful youth determined to find the true value of life. The slightly unformed, open innocence of Reeve's Siddartha is perfectly attuned to the enchanted vision of this benevolent film, which discovers in a tale of reincarnation a kind of dispensation from the drama of political and sexual conflict that had defined Bertolucci's filmmaking to this point.

—Robert Burgoyne

BESSON, Luc

Nationality: French. **Born:** Paris, 18 March 1959. **Career:** Worked as assistant director on films in Paris and Hollywood, as well as first assistant director for several advertising films; directed first feature, 1983.

Films as Director:

1983 *Le Dernier Combat* (+ pr, sc)
1985 *Subway* (+ pr, sc)
1987 *Kamikaze* (co-d with Didier Grousset, + pr)
1988 *Le Grand bleu* (*The Big Blue*) (+ sc, lyrics, camera op, submarine crew)
1990 *La Femme Nikita* (*Nikita*) (+ sc, song)
1991 *Atalantis* (+ cin)
1995 *The Professional*

Other Films:

1985 *Le Grabd Carnaval* (2nd unit d)
1986 *Taxi Boy* (tech advisor)

Publications

On BESSON: articles—

Chevallier, J., "*Le Denier Combat,*" in *Revue du Cinema* (France).
"L'Age du Capitaine," in *Cahiers du Cinema* (Paris), June 1985.
Ferguson, K. "Tarzan Goes Underground," in *Photoplay,* September 1985.
Bodtker, H., "Splatter—'videovold' i naerbilber," in *Film & Kino* (Oslo), no. 3, 1985.
Chion, M., "Silka Kot Riba v Zvocnem Akvariju," in *Ekran* (Yugoslavia), no. 3/4, 1988.
Tangen, J. "'Det Store Bia': en dyp Film fra Besson?," in *Z Filmtidsskrift* (Oslo), no. 27, 1989.
Bassan, R., "Trois Neobaroques Francais," in *Revue du Cinema* (France), May 1989.
Strauss, F. "La Planete Besson," in *Cahiers du Cinema* (Paris), no. 409, 1988.
Caron, A., "Pour quelques Besson de plus!," in *Sequences* (Montreal), September 1990.
Kelleher, E., "French Box Office Hit *Nikita* Bows Stateside via Goldwyn," in *Film Journal* (New York), March 1991.
Murray, S., "European Notes," in *Cinema Papers* (Victoria, Australia), August 1990.
Graye, J., and J. Noel, "*Nikita,*" in *Grand Angle* (Belgium), April 1990.
Lubelski, T., "Besson," in *Kino* (Warsaw), August 1991.
Ostria, V., "Besson Manque d'Air," in *Cahiers du Cinema* (Paris), October 1991.
Jousse, T., "L'Ecran Aquarium," in *Cahiers du Cinema* (Paris), October 1991.
Lefebvre, P., "*Atalantis,*" in *Grand Angle* (Belgium), September/October 1991.
James, C., "Film View: Word from *Nikita*: Hold the Subtitles," in *New York Times,* May 5, 1991.
Pezzotta, A., "*Atalantis,*" in *Segnocinema* (Italy), May/June 1992.

* * *

Most noted for their stunning visuals, Luc Besson's film works often invite scrutiny of the blurred line between the artistic and the commercial. Furthermore, with their imbalanced successes in European and American markets, Besson's films are situated in a position where issues of spectatorship are once again engaging beyond box-office reports.

Making his directorial debut with *Le Dernier Combat,* Besson's beautifully executed black-and-white cinematography earned him a chance to make his first major feature, *Subway,* a film described by Michael Wilmington as "Steven Spielberg gone existentialist." Shot mostly at Beverly Center Cineplex, *Subway* creates an underground world of the Paris Metro, both eerie in its fluorescent darkness and charming in the interweaving of fast-paced editing and charismatic characters. A seemingly complex narrative of three separate strands is treated with a simple-mindedness that makes it almost comic-book-like. It is at its best a skillful show of light and shadows, and at worst a flashy skeleton of a film that befits its inhabitants.

The Big Blue, Besson's third film, was, as John Wakesman notes, "a huge commercial success at home but a failure in the international marketplace." A story about the lifetime friendship and rivalry between two free-divers, plus breathtaking cinematography and an American journalist (played by Rosanna Arquette), *The Big Blue* entangles too many elements at once to make sense. Jacques' mysterious bond with the ocean, as emphasized time and again by his ties with dolphins—it is not a coincidence that his production company in France is called Les Films du Dolphin—never goes beyond a pretentious justification for the showy underwater photography. The American journalist Joanna's fascination with Jacques, on the other hand, also never once sparks any romantic fulfillment. It is Jacques' peculiar friend, Enzo (played by Jean Reno, who later stars in *The Professional*), who anchors the film with his stocky rotundness and almost laughable yet respectable stubbornness. Jean proved to be not enough of a draw for audiences, outside of France, at least.

Produced by Samuel Goldwyn Company, *La Femme Nikita* returns to cityscapes and paints a bizarre picture of a female hitperson, working for the French equivalent of the CIA. Ultra-violence adorned with a triangular romance and spy-thriller suspense, *Nikita* seems to be the most interesting of Besson's films; or, at least, its complexity stems neither from the semi-hallucinatory ambiance in *Subway* nor the pretentious mythicism in *The Big Blue,* but rather from an uncanny interest and concern that develop in the viewer about Nikita, "so interesting a wanderer between stages of moral consciousness that violence becomes one of the film's essentials," proclaims Stanley

Luc Besson on the set of *La Femme Nikita*

Kauffmann. A genuine interest in his character's psychology as revealed in *Nikita* provides the emotional depth that was lacking in his previous works.

Besson's most recent film, *The Professional,* continues his psychological study of marginalized, on-the-edge people: this time, a hit*man,* Leon, played by Jean Reno. Leon is the "Cleaner," New York's top hitman. He is never emotional; or better yet, as a professional, he never allows himself to be emotional. Through some inopportune circumstances he meets the twelve-year-old Mathilda (played convincingly by Natalie Portman). In her attempt to be trained as a hitperson in order to avenge her parents' murder, the process of Mathilda's makeover is in fact a vehicle for exploring the relationship between this odd couple. Walking the thin line between the innocent affection of a man and a child bonding (as in *Paper Moon*) and a portrayal redolent of a pedophile liaison, Besson's incisive direction turns the film from a cliched story into an almost lyrical character study.

One would certainly welcome the maturing of a director like Luc Besson, whose natural knack for cinematographic beauty is now enriched with some psychological depth. Going beyond the flashiness, Besson has shown in his more recent films a high potential for artistry, one that goes into the visuality of the imagistic world and actually strives for meanings. But questions still remain: what is it that we seek in cinema (a medium that is first and foremost visual) other than the visuals?

—Guo-Juin Hong

BIRRI, Fernando

Nationality: Argentinian. **Born:** In Santa Fe, 13 March 1925. **Education:** Universidad Nacional del Litoral, Santa Fe, Argentina, 1942-47, and at Centro Sperimentale de Cinematografia, Rome, 1950-52. **Career:** Assistant to Vittorio De Sica on *Il tetto,* 1954; returned to Argentina to found Instituto de Cinematografia, later La Escuela Documental de Santa Fe, 1956; left Argentina for political reasons, 1963; moved to Italy, 1964; attended 1st International Festival of the New Latin American Cinema, Havana, 1979; taught at Universidad Nacional Autonoma de Mexico, 1980, and at Film School of Universidad de Los Andes, Merida, Venezuela, 1980-83. Director of International School of Cinema and TV of San Antonio de Los Banos, 1983- . **Awards:** Grand Prize, SODRE Festival, Montevideo, for *Tire Die,* 1960; Golden Lion, Venice Festival, for *Los Inundados,* 1962; honored at Festivals in Benalmadena, Spain, 1979, and Pesaro, Italy, 1981.

Films as Director:

1951 *Selinunte* (short); *Alfabeto notturno* (short)
1952 *Immagini Populari Siciliane Sacre*; *Immagini Populari Siciliane Profane*
1959 *La primera fundacion de Buenos Aires* (animation)
1960 ***Tire die*** (*Toss Me a Dime*) (co-sc, co-d, co-ph); *Buenos dias, Buenos Aires* (short)

1961 *Los inundados (Flooded Out)*
1962 *Che, Buenos Aires* (comprising two previous films); *La pampa gringa* (doc)
1966 *Castagnino, diario romano* (short)
1979 *Org* (co-d)
1983 *Rafael Alberti, un retrato del poeta por Fernando Birri*
1984 *Rte.: Nicaragua (carta al mundo)* (short film)
1985 *Mi hijo, el Chei: Un retrato de familia de Don Ernesto Guevara*
1988 *Un senor muy viejo con unas alas enormes* (+ a, sc)

Other Films:

1955 *Gli sbanditi* (Maselli) (role)
1982 *La Rose des vents* (P. Guzman) (role)

Publications

By BIRRI: book—

La Escuela Documental de Santa Fe, Santa Fe, Argentina, 1964.

By BIRRI: articles—

"Cine y subdesarrollo," in *Cine Cubano* (Havana), May/July 1967.
"Revolución en la revolución del nuevo cine latinoamericano," in *Cine Cubano* (Havana), August/December 1968.
"Fernando Birri y las raices del huevo cine latinoamericano," an interview with Francisco Lombardi, in *Hablemos de Cine* (Lima), March 1984.
"For a nationalist, realist, critical and popular cinema," in *Screen* (London), May-August 1985.

On BIRRI: books—

Mahieu, Jose Agustin, *Breve historia del cine argentino,* Buenos Aires, 1966.
Micciche, Lino, editor, *Fernando Birri e la Escuela Documental de Santa Fe,* Pesaro, Italy, 1981.
Burton, Julianne, *The New Latin American Cinema: An Annotated Bibliography of Sources in English, Spanish, and Portuguese,* New York, 1983.
Burton, Julianne, editor, *Cinema and Social Change in Latin America: Conversations with Filmmakers,* Austin, Texas, 1986.
King, John, and Nissa Torrents, *The Garden of Forking Paths: Argentine Cinema,* London, 1986.

On BIRRI: articles—

Pussi, Dolly, "Breve historia del documental en la Argentina," in *Cine Cubano* (Havana), October 1973.
Burton, Julianne, "The Camera as Gun: Two Decades of Film Culture and Resistance in Latin America," in *Latin American Perspectives,* Austin, Texas, 1978.
"Fernando Birri Section" of *Cine Cubano* (Havana), no. 100, 1981.
Mahieu, A., "Revision critica del cine argentino," in *Cine Cubano* (Havana), no. 107, 1984.
Martinez Carril, M., "Fernando Birri, un mito, una obra," in *Cinemateca Revista* (Montevideo), February 1986.

* * *

Fernando Birri is a key figure in the history of the New Latin American Cinema because he was more interested in creating filmmakers than in creating films; because he offered a sustained and systematic counter-example to existing industrial modes of filmmaking and to the ideological assumptions that limited both the process and the product; because he developed a concrete theoretical-practical approach and founded the first school of documentary filmmaking in Latin America in order to teach that methodology; and, finally, because his students fanned out across the continent putting his ideas into practice.

Born in the provincial capital of Santa Fe, Birri was a poet and puppeteer before turning to the cinema in search of a broad popular audience. Unable to break into the tightly controlled national film industry, Birri travelled to Italy to study at Rome's Centro Sperimentale de Cinematografia during the early 1950's, when the neo-realist movement was still at its height. Profoundly influenced by the ideology, aesthetics, and methodology of this first anti-industrial, anti-Hollywood model for a national cinema, Birri returned to Argentina in 1956 hoping to found a national film school. Rejecting the closed commercialism of the Buenos Aires-based film industry, one of the three largest in Latin America at the time, Birri returned to Santa Fe.

Birri recalls: "Fresh from Europe, what I had in mind was a film school modeled on the Centro Sperimentale, a fictional film school which would train actors, directors, cinematographers, set designers, etc. But when I confronted the actual conditions in Argentina and in Santa Fe, I realized that my plan was premature. What was needed was something else: a school which would not only provide apprenticeship in filmmaking, but also in sociology, and even in Argentine history, geography and politics, because the most essential quest is the quest for national identity, in order to recover and rediscover what had been alienated, distorted and destroyed by centuries of cultural penetration. This search for a national identity is what led me to pose the problem in strictly *documentary* terms, because I believe that the first step for any national cinema is to document its own reality."

La Escuela Documental de Santa Fe grew out of the Instituto de Cinematografia, which was in turn an outgrowth of a 4-day seminar on filmmaking led by Birri. Birri's goal was to lay the foundations for a regional film industry that would be "national, realist, and popular": national by addressing the most pressing problems of national life; realist (documentary) in approach in contrast to the highly artificial style and milieux of the "official" film industry; popular by focusing on and appealling to the less privileged classes. In keeping with his determination to integrate theory and practice, Birri emphasized process over product, viewing each film project as the opportunity for practical apprenticeship on the part of the largest possible number of students. He was the first of the Latin American filmmakers to posit technical imperfection as a positive attribute, preferring *un sentido imperfecto a una perfeccion sin sentido* (an imperfect/sincere meaning to a meaningless perfection).

Birri's best-known films are the 33-minute documentary *Tire die (Toss Me a Dime)* and *Los inundados (Flooded Out),* a picaresque feature in the neorealist style about the adventures of a squatter family displaced by seasonal floods. Both played to huge and enthusiastic audiences at their local premieres but could not achieve broad national exhibition even after winning important prizes in international festivals.

An inhospitable political climate compelled Birri to leave Argentina in 1963. Subsequent months in São Paulo catalyzed an important documentary movement there, but Birri himself returned to Italy and relative obscurity until the late 1970s. His presence at the First International Festival of the New Latin American Cinema in Havana in 1979 signaled renewed activity and recognition. Since then, Birri has taught at Mexico's national university and at the University of Los Andes in Venezuela. The Benalmadena and Pesaro Festivals (Spain, 1979, and Italy, 1981) organized special programs honoring his work.

—Julianne Burton

BLACKTON, J. Stuart

Nationality: American. **Born:** James Stuart Blackton in Sheffield, England, 5 January 1875. **Education:** City College, New York. **Family:** Married four times. **Career:** Moved to United States, 1885; as journalist-illustrator for *New York World,* met Edison, who, using his Kinematograph camera, made *Blackton, the Evening World Cartoonist,* 1895; formed Vitagraph Company with Albert E. Smith and William T. Rock, 1897; president of Vitagraph, 1900-15; formed Vitagraph stock of actors, 1905; built glass-enclosed studios in Flatbush, Brooklyn, 1905-06; made series of animated films, pioneering single-frame animation techniques, 1906-10; organized and became president of Motion Picture Board of Trade (later Association of Motion Picture Producers and Distributors of America), also publisher and editor, *Motion Picture Magazine,* 1915; independent producer, from 1917; directed in England, and experimented with color film, early 1920s; Vitagraph sold to Warner Bros. for $1,000,000; retired from filmmaking, 1925; bankrupt, 1931; went on relief, directed federal work relief movie project, 1935; director of production for Anglo-American Film Company, late 1930s. **Died:** In Hollywood following auto accident, 13 August 1941.

Films as Director (Partial listing as no director's credit given on Vitagraph's early films):

1898 *Burglar on the Roof* (+ role)
1899 *A Visit to the Spiritualist*
1900 *Happy Hooligan* series (+ role); *The Enchanted Drawing*
1905 *Monsieur Beaucaire* (+ role); *The Automobile Thieves* (+ role); *Raffles, the Amateur Cracksman*
1906 *Humorous Phases of Funny Faces*; *100 to 1 Shot*
1907 *The Haunted Hotel*
1909 *The Magic Fountain Pen*; *Princess Nicotine*
1909/10 *The Life of Moses*
1917 *The Message of the Mouse*; "Country Life" series; *The Judgment House* (+ sc, pr)
1918 *World for Sale* (+ pr); *Missing* (+ pr, co-sc); *The Common Cause* (+ pr); *Safe for Democracy* (+ pr)

J. Stuart Blackton (holding script) directing *The Gypsy Cavalier*

1919 *The Moonshine Trail* (+ pr, co-sc); *My Husband's Other Wife* (+ pr); *A House Divided* (+ pr); *Dawn* (+ pr)
1920 *Respectable By Proxy* (+ pr); *The Blood Barrier* (+ pr); *Passers-By* (+ pr); *The House of the Tolling Bell* (+ pr); *Forbidden Valley* (+ pr)
1922 *The Glorious Adventure* (+ pr); *The Gypsy Cavalier* (+ pr)
1923 *The Virgin Queen* (+ pr); *On the Banks of the Wabash* (+ pr)
1924 *Let Not Man Put Asunder* (+ pr); *Between Friends* (+ pr); *Behold This Woman* (+ pr); *The Clean Heart* (+ pr); *The Beloved Brute* (+ pr)
1925 *The Redeeming Sin* (+ pr); *Tides of Passion* (+ pr); *The Happy Warrior* (+ pr)
1926 *Bride of the Storm* (+ pr); *The Gilded Highway* (+ pr); *Hell-Bent for Heaven* (+ pr); *The Passionate Quest* (+ pr)
1933 *The Film Parade* (*March of the Movies*; *Cavalcade of the Movies*) (+ pr) (compilation film with some footage "recreated" by Blackton)

Publications

By BLACKTON: book—

Marine Studies, n.p., n.d.

By BLACKTON: articles—

Interview, in *The Moving Picture World,* 19 December 1908.
Introduction to *The Photodrama* by Henry Phillips, 1914.
"Awake America!," in *The Theatre* (New York), September 1915.
"The Battle Cry of Peace," in *Motion Picture* (New York), September 1915/January 1916.
"Yesterdays of Vitagraph," in *Photoplay* (New York), July 1919.
"The Movies Are Growing Up," in *Motion Picture* (New York), February 1925.

On BLACKTON: books—

Orman, Felix, *The Pioneer of the Photoplay,* pamphlet n.d. (ca. 1921).
Slide, Anthony, *The Big V: A History of the Vitagraph Company,* 1976.
Trimble, Marian Blackton, *J. Stuart Blackton: A Personal Biography,* Metuchen, New Jersey, 1984.

On BLACKTON: articles—

Haskins, H., article in *Motion Picture Classic* (Brooklyn), September 1918.
Sketch in *Current Biography,* New York, 1941.
Obituary in the *New York Times,* 14 August 1941.
Slide, Anthony, "Films on 8 & 16," in *Films in Review* (New York), February 1978.
Desmond, Kevin, "Props from Spools: The story of J. Stuart Blackton," in *Eyepiece* (London), Christmas 1986.

* * *

J. Stuart Blackton was both a pioneering producer/director and a pioneering animator. The American film industry may well be said to have its origins in the founding by Blackton and Albert E. Smith of the Vitagraph Company, and most historians agree that film animation originates with Blackton's 1907 production of *The Haunted Hotel.*

The Haunted Hotel combined animation, live action, and special effects and had its origins in the fantasies of Georges Méliès. In France the film certainly influenced the work of Emile Cohl. Of course, Blackton had experimented with a form of animation long before *The Haunted Hotel.* In the undated *Cohen and Coon,* Blackton writes those two words on a blackboard and proceeds to translate each word into the appropriate stereotype, while with *Humorous Phases of Funny Faces,* Blackton again created comic faces on blackboards.

As a pioneering producer, J. Stuart Blackton was required to serve as producer and director, as well as occasional cameraman and actor, on the films released by Vitagraph through 1909. With his recreation of *The Battle of Manila Bay,* Blackton introduced a form of special effects to the cinema. The same film demonstrated the patriotic and propaganda value of the motion picture, which Blackton was later to exploit to its fullest with *The Battle Cry of Peace,* which he co-directed and conceived of in partnership with Theodore Roosevelt. The latter film was intended to provide a message of preparedness for the people of the United States at a time when many were advocating U.S. noninvolvement in the First World War.

Albert E. Smith was the business head of Vitagraph, as well as the company's first cameraman, while Blackton took responsibility for the production end of the company. With an artistic genius such as Blackton at the production helm, the company saw an influx of considerable creativity and ingenuity. Thanks to Blackton, the films of the Vitagraph Company through the mid-teens were and are considered some of the best produced in the United States.

However, Blackton failed to keep abreast of changes in the industry, as indicated by the poor quality and equally poor reception of the independent features he directed after leaving Vitagraph in 1917. Yet he remained an innovator, as evidenced by *The Glorious Adventure,* shot in Prizma Color in England, an impressive if dull attempt at historical spectacle. Blackton continued to direct through 1926, but his films received little attention, and those that have survived appear unimpressive.

A social climber who amassed and lost great sums of money during his career, Blackton was also a fun-loving filmmaker, and nowhere is this more evident than in his last fling. *The Film Parade* (also known as *The March of the Movies*) was a highly personal history of the cinema that Blackton made in association with his former director, William P.S. Earle, in the early 1930s. Blackton blithely recreated his own early films and even donned blackface to impersonate Al Jolson in *The Jazz Singer. The Film Parade* is no masterpiece, but it is a fitting tribute to a major, and much underrated, figure in American film history.

—Anthony Slide

BLASETTI, Alessandro

Nationality: Italian. **Born:** Rome, 3 July 1900. **Education:** Doctor of Law. **Career:** Gave up law practice, 1924; founded *Il mondo dello schermo (Screen World),* 1926; joined Alessandro, Barbaro, and others in filmmaking cooperative Augustus; founded *Cinematografo* and *Lo spettacolo d'Italia,* 1928; directed and produced first film, *Sole,* 1929; director of first Italian film school at music academy S. Cecile, Rome. **Died:** In Rome, 2 February 1987.

Films as Director:

1929 *Sole* (+ ed, co-sc, pr)
1930 *Nerone* (+ co-sc, co-ed)
1931 *Resurrectio* (+ co-sc, co-ed); *Terra madre* (+ co-sc, co-ed)
1932 *Palio* (+ co-sc, co-ed); *La tavola dei poveri* (+ co-sc, co-ed)
1933 *Il caso Haller* (+ co-sc, co-ed)
1934 *1860* (*Gesuzza la sposa Garibaldina*) (+ co-sc, co-ed); *L'impiegata di papa* (+ co-sc, co-ed); *Vecchia guardia* (+ co-sc, co-ed)

Alessandro Blasetti

1935 *Aldebaran* (+ co-sc, role)
1937 *La contessa di Parma* (+ co-sc, co-ed)
1938 *Ettore Fieramosca* (+ co-sc, co-ed); *Caccia alla volpe* (+ co-sc, co-ed)
1939 *Retroscena* (+ co-sc, co-ed)
1940 *Un'avventura di Salvator Rosa* (+ co-sc, co-ed); *Napoli e le terre d'oltremare* (unfinished) (+ co-sc, co-ed)
1941 *La corona di ferro* (*The Iron Crown*) (+ co-sc); *La cena delle beffe* (+ co-sc)
1942 *Quattro passi fra le nuvole* (*Four Steps in the Clouds*) (+ co-sc, role)
1943 *Nessuno torna indietro* (+ co-sc)
1946 *Un giorno nella vita* (+ co-sc); *La gemma orientale di Papi* (+ co-sc); *Il Duomo di Milano* (+ co-sc); *Castel Sant'Angelo* (+ co-sc)
1948 *Fabiola* (+ co-sc)
1950 *Prima comunione* (*Father's Dilemma*) (+ co-sc); *Ippodromi all'Alba* (+ co-sc)
1952 *Altri tempi* (*Times Gone By*) (+ co-sc); *La fiammata* (+ co-sc)
1953 *Tempi nostri* (*Anatomy of Love*) (+ co-sc)
1954 *Peccato che sia una canaglia* (*Too Bad She's Bad*) (+ co-sc)
1955 *La fortuna di essere donna* (*Lucky to Be a Woman*) (+ co-sc)
1957 *Amore e chiacchiere* (+ co-sc)
1959 *Europa di notte* (*European Nights*)
1961 *Io amo, tu ami* (*I Love—You Love*) (+ co-sc)
1963 "La lepre e la tartaruga" episode of *Le quattro verita* (+ co-sc)
1964 *Liolà*
1966 *Io, io, io ... e gli altri* (+ co-sc)
1967 *La ragazza del bersagliere* (+ co-sc)
1969 *Simon Bolivar* (+ co-sc)
1982 *Venezia, una Mostra per il cinema* (documentary) (+ co-sc)

Publications

By BLASETTI: books—

Come nasce un film, Rome, 1932.
Scritti sul cinema, edited by Adriano Apra, Venice, 1982.
Il cinema che ho vissuto, Bari, 1982.
Sole, with Alberto Boero and Aldo Vergano, Rome, 1985.

By BLASETTI: articles—

"Alessandro Blasetti/ogni volta da capo," interview in *Bianco e nero* (Rome), September/December 1975.
"La storia dei miei stivali de Sole per tufta la mia vita," in *Cinema Nuovo* (Bari), May-June 1978.
"Andai a Mosca per incontrare Nikolaj Ekk," in *Cinema Nuovo* (Bari), August 1980.
"Quel folle amore dinanzi allo specchio," in *Cinema Nuovo* (Bari), December 1980.
"Sur le seuil de ma vie," in *Positif* (Paris), March 1981.
Interview and article with F. Cuel and B. Villien, in *Cinématographe* (Paris), November 1981.

On BLASETTI: books—

Gori, Gianfranco, *Alessandro Blasetti,* Florence, 1984.
Salizzato, Claver, and Vito Zagarrio, editors, *La corona di ferro: Un modo di produzione italiano,* Rome, 1985.

On BLASETTI: articles—

"The Big Screen," in *Sight and Sound* (London), Spring 1955.
Jeancolas, J.P., "Ni chemises noires, ni telephones blancs: cinema italien 1923-1943 (Pesaro)," and P. Mereghetti, "Blasetti, le fascisme et la virilité ... ," in *Positif* (Paris), October 1976.
"Blasetti Issue" of *Bianco e Nero* (Rome), April-June 1985.
Stuart, J., obituary, in *Variety* (New York), 4 February 1987.
Obituary in *Film Français* (Paris), 13 February 1987.

* * *

After a period as both lawyer and film critic, Alessandro Blasetti collaborated with several other young film enthusiasts in forming a filmmaking co-operative called Augustus. His first film as director, *Sole,* exists only as a fragment, but it contains powerful imagery clearly influenced by the Soviet school of the 1920s. His first really important work was *La Tavola dei poveri,* a remarkable precursor of later "neo-realism" in that its plot (a group of aristocrats banding together to feed the poor) bears a close resemblance to De Sica's *Miracle in Milan.* Blasetti's treatment had much formal ingenuity, as he used a very mobile camera style somewhat akin to Max Ophüls' work at this time. Another film in a "neo-realist" vein was *1860,* which concerned Garibaldi's conquest of Sicily. This was contrasted with the controversial *Vecchia Guardia* which, although seemingly siding with the Blackshirts, told its family story with a good deal of genuine warmth and observation.

After this, Blasetti embarked on a series of lavish costume dramas which established him as a technically fluent dramatic director: *La Contessa di Parma, Ettore Fieramosca,* and particularly *Un'avventura di Salvator Rosa* and *La Corona di ferro.* In these films, Blasetti created a kind of swashbuckling historical/fantasy world with elaborate settings and costumes, well-staged action scenes, and a sense of romance not without its tongue-in-cheek elements. His dashing heroes and hapless heroines belong to a long tradition of romantic adventurers (both European and American) which can be traced right up to Indiana Jones and his companions.

Alongside these spectaculars, Blasetti made several more intimate local comedies featuring working-class characters and the trappings of "neo-realism." Two of the best of these were *Four Steps in the Clouds* and *Prima Comunione,* which received much wider world distribution than his more substantial dramas and historical films.

If Mario Camerini was the leading director of comedies and light social dramas in the Italian film world in the 1930s and 1940s, Blasetti must be regarded as the leading exponent of period pieces and more politically motivated dramas. It is curious that after their many successes in this period, the post-war work of both directors saw a serious falling-off. Blasetti made a few more rather empty spectacles like *Fabiola* and a series of raucous comedies and episode films (in colour and 'Scope) which often starred Sophia Loren. Despite some lively moments, these efforts were distressingly similar to the commercial fodder being turned out by many other directors. His career virtually ended with the large-scale, South American epic *Simon Bolivar,* which was hardly shown anywhere. Of his several acting appearances, the most notable was his portrayal of a Cinecittá film director in Visconti's *Bellissima* with Anna Magnani.

All in all, Blasetti's was a curiously uneven and ambiguous career that included not only a flirtation with Fascism in the 1930s, but also a subsequent period when he turned his back on the contemporary scene in favour of period escapism. He will probably be best remembered for these vigorous, sometimes outrageous, historical romps, which still give much pleasure today.

—John Gillett

BLIER, Bertrand

Nationality: French. **Born:** Paris, 14 March 1939. **Career:** Assistant director on films of Lautner, Christian-Jaque, Delannoy, and others, 1960-63; directed first feature, *Hitler? Connais pas!*, 1963. **Awards:** Oscar for Best Foreign Language Film, for *Preparez vos mouchoirs,* 1978; Cesar for the screenplay of *Buffet froid,* 1979; Special Jury Prize, Cannes Film Festival, for *Trop belle pour toi (Too Beautiful for You),* 1989.

Films as Director:

1963 *Hitler? Connais pas!* (+ sc)
1966 *La Grimace* (+ sc)
1967 *Si j'etais un espion* (*Breakdown*; *If I Were a Spy*) (+ co-sc)
1973 *Les Valseuses* (*Going Places*) (+ sc)
1975 *Calmos* (*Femmes Fatales*) (+ co-sc)
1977 *Preparez vos mouchoirs* (*Get Out Your Handkerchiefs*) (+ sc)
1979 *Buffet froid* (+ sc)
1981 *Beau-père* (+ sc)
1982 *La Femme de mon pote* (*My Best Friend's Girl*) (+ co-sc)
1984 *Notre Histoire* (*Our Story*) (+ sc)
1986 *Tenue de soirée* (*Menage*) (+sc)
1989 *Trop belle pour toi* (*Too Beautiful for You*) (+sc)
1991 *Merci la vie* (*Thanks, Life*) (+ sc, pr)
1993 *Un deux trois soleil* (*One Two Three Sun*) (+ sc)

Other Films:

1970 *Laisse aller, c'est une valse* (Lautner) (sc)
1992 *Patrick Dewaere* (role as himself)

Publications

By BLIER: books—

Les Valseuses, Paris, 1972.
Beau-père, Paris, 1980.

By BLIER: articles—

"*Les Valseuses* de Bertrand Blier: le nuvité du cinéma français," interview with R. Gay, in *Cinéma Québec* (Montreal), vol. 3, no. 8, 1974.
Interview with B. Villien and P. Carcassonne, in *Cinématographe* (Paris), January 1980.
"*Beau-père*: Entretien avec Bertrand Blier," with C. de Béchade and H. Descrues, in *Image et Son* (Paris), September 1981.
"A la recherche de l'histoire," an interview with Marc Chevrie and D. Dubroux, in *Cahiers du Cinéma* (Paris), May 1985.
Interview with Sheila Johnston, in *Stills* (London), May 1985.
Interview with P. Le Guay, in *Cinématographe* (Paris), May 1986.
"Manhandler," interview with Dan Yakir, in *Film Comment* (New York), September/October 1986.
Interview with Serge Toubiana, in *Cahiers du Cinema* (Paris), May 1988.
Interview in *La Revue du Cinema* (Paris), July-August 1988.
Interview in *Première* (Paris), May 1989.
Interview with Serge Toubiana and T. Jousse, in *Cahiers du Cinema* (Paris), May 1989.
Interview with F. Aude and J.P. Jeancolas, in *Positif* (Paris), June 1989.
Interview in *Time Out* (London), 14 February 1990.
Interview with Serge Toubiana, in *Cahiers du Cinema* (Paris), March 1991.
Blier, Bertrand, "Boule blanche," *Cahiers du Cinema* (Paris), May 1991 (supplement).

On BLIER: articles—

Buckley, T., "The Truth About Making a Movie in Singapore," in *New York Times,* 2 February 1979.
Alion, Yves, "*Buffet froid* Issue" of *Avant-Scène du Cinéma* (Paris), 15 March 1980.
"Blier Section," in *Cinéma* (Paris), July-August 1981.
Rickey, C., "Lolita Française," in *American Film* (Washington, D.C.), October 1981.
Toubiana, Serge, and Pierre Bonitzer, "Le cauchemar d'Antoine. Les mots et les choses," in *Cahiers du Cinéma* (Paris), April 1986.
Blier Section of *Revue du Cinéma* (Paris), June 1986.
Chutnow, P., "Blier Puts a Fresh Wrinkle in the Old Triangle," in *New York Times,* 17 September 1989.
Toubiana, S., "Entretien avec Bertrand Blier," in *Cahiers du Cinema* (Paris), March 1991.
Jousse, T., article in *Cahiers du Cinema* (Paris), April 1991.

* * *

Bertrand Blier directs erotic buddy movies featuring men who are exasperated by the opposite sex, who perceive of themselves as macho but are incapable of satisfying the women in their lives. In actuality, his heroes are terrified of feminism, of the "new woman" who demands her right to experience and enjoy orgasm. But Blier's females are in no way villainesses. They are just elusive—and so alienated that they can only find fulfillment from oddballs or young boys.

Going Places (Les Valseuses, which in French is slang for testicles), based on Blier's best-selling novel, was a box office smash in France. Gérard Depardieu and Patrick Dewaere both achieved stardom as a couple of outsiders, adult juvenile delinquents, whose sexual and sadistic adventures are chronicled as they travel across France. They are both unable to bring to orgasm a young beautician (played by Miou-Miou) they pick up and take on as a sexual partner. They then attempt to please an older woman (Jeanne Moreau), who has just spent ten years in prison. After a night together, she commits suicide by shooting herself in the vagina. Eventually, Miou-Miou is sexually satisfied by a crazy, physically unattractive ex-con.

In *Femmes Fatales* middle-aged Jean-Pierre Marielle and Jean Rochefort, one a gynaecologist and the other a pimp, decide to abandon wives and mistresses for the countryside, but end up pursued by an army of women intent on enslaving them as studs. Again, men cannot escape women's sexual demands: here, the latter come after the former with tanks and guns. And in *Get Out Your Handkerchiefs,* driving instructor Depardieu is so anxious to please bored, depressed wife Carol Laure that he finds her a lover. Both the husband and the stranger, a playground instructor (Dewaere), feel that she will be happy if she can only have a child. She in her own way does this, finding a substitute for them in a precocious young boy barely into his teens. *Handkerchiefs* is a prelude of sorts to *Beau-Père,* which features only one male lead (as does the later *Trop Belle Pour Toi,* in which Depardieu is at the centre of a love triangle). Here, a struggling pianist, played by Dewaere, is seduced by the refreshingly self-confident 14-year-old daughter of his recently deceased lover. The teenager's feelings are deep and pure, while the "adult" is immature, too self-conscious and self-absorbed to accept her.

In Blier's films, men do not understand women. "Maybe one day I'll do *Camille,*" the filmmaker says. "But I won't do *An Unmarried Woman,* because I don't feel I have the right to do it. I don't know what goes on in a woman's head. I believe I know what certain men think, but not women." As a result, the sexual barriers between the

Bertrand Blier directing Carole Bouquet and Gérard Depardieu in *Trop belle pour toi*

sexes seem irrevocable in Blier's movies. His men are more at ease talking among themselves about women than with actually being with wives or lovers; their relationships with each other are for them more meaningful than their contacts with the opposite sex. There are alternatives to women, such as turning to homosexual relationships (the characters in *Going Places* sleep with each other when they are lonely or celibate).

Another Blier film, *Buffet Froid,* is also about male bonding: Depardieu, as a psychopathic killer, becomes involved with a mass murderer (Jean Carmet) and a homicidal cop (the director's father, the distinguished character actor Bernard Blier). However, *Buffet Froid* is mostly a study of alienation in urban society, and the acceptance of random, irrational violence. It is thematically more closely related to Jules Feiffer's *Little Murders* than *Going Places* or *Get Out Your Handkerchiefs.*

Quality-wise, Blier's most recent films have added little luster to his career. However, the film maker seems to have tired of making films about men. Beginning with *Trop belle pour toi (Too Beautiful for You),* the most accessible of his latter-career works, his primary characters have been women. *Trop belle pour toi* does feature a clever take on extramarital relationships. Blier regular Gerard Depardieu plays a car dealer whose wife is beautiful and intelligent; nonetheless, he cheats on her with his otherwise ordinary, chubby temporary receptionist. Despite this intriguing premise and recognition with a Cannes Film Festival Special Jury Prize, the film lacks the spark and outrageousness of his earlier work.

The director's other features include *Merci la vie (Thanks, Life),* a feminist take on *Going Places* that sparked controversy upon its opening in France. It is a road movie which chronicles the sexual exploits of two young women, one sluttish and the other naive. *Un deux trois soliel (One Two Three Sun)* focuses on the plight of a young girl, growing up in a public housing project in Marseilles, who adores her alcoholic father and is mortified by her mother's affectations.

Bertrand Blier best explains what he attempts to communicate in his films: "The relations between men and women are constantly evolving and it's interesting to show people leading the lifestyle of tomorrow."

—Rob Edelman

BLOM, August

Nationality: Danish. **Born:** 26 December 1869. **Family:** Married 1) Agnete von Prangen, 1908; 2) Johanne Fritz-Petersen. **Career:** Actor at Folketeatret, Copenhagen, from 1893; actor at Nordisk Films Kompagni, 1908; director for Nordisk Films Kompagni, 1910-24; manager of Copenhagen cinema, 1934-47. **Died:** 10 January 1947.

Films as Director:

1910 *Livets Storme* (*Storms of Life*); *Robinson Crusoe*; *Den hvide Slavehandel I* (*The White Slave*); *Spinonen fra Tokio* (*The Red Light*); *Den skaebnesvangre Opfindelse* (*Dr. Jekyll and Mr. Hyde*); *Jagten paa Gentlemanrøveren*; *Singaree*; *Hamlet*; *Spøgelset i Gravkaelderen* (*The Ghost of the Variety*); *Den dø des Halsbaand* (*The Necklace of the Dead*)

1911 *Den hvide Slavehandel II* (*In the Hands of Impostors*); *Den farlige Alder* (*The Price of Beauty*); *Ved Faengslets Port* (*Temptations of a Great City*); *Vildledt Elskov* (*The Bank Book*); *Potifars Hustru* (*The Victim of a Character*); *Politimesteren* (*Convicts No. 10 and No. 13*); *Den blaa Natviol* (*The Daughter of the Fortune Teller*); *Damernes Blad* (*The Ladies' Journal*); *Balletdanserinden* (*The Ballet Dancer*); *Jernbanens Datter* (*The Daughter of the Railway*); *Den naadige Frøken* (*Lady Mary's Love*); *En Lektion* (*Aviatikeren og Journalistens Hustru*; *The Aviator and the Journalist's Wife*); *Ekspeditricen* (*Ungdom og Letsind*; *In the Prime of Life*); *Desdemona*; *En Opfinders Skaebne* (*The Aeroplane Inventor*); *Fader og Søn* (*Onkel og Nevø*; *A Poisonous Love*); *Dødsdrømmen* (*A Dream of Death*); *Min første Monocle* (*Herr Storms første Monocle*; *His First Monocle*); *Fru Potifar* (*Den skaebnesvangre Løgn*; *A Fatal Lie*); *Kaerlighedens Styrke* (*The Power of Love*); *Mormonens Offer* (*The Victims of the Mormon*); *Haevnet* (*Det bødes der for*; *Vengeance*); *Det mørke Punkt* (*Mamie Rose*; *Annie Bell*); *Eventyr paa Fodrejsen* (*Den udbrudte Slave*; *The Two Convicts*); *Ungdommens Ret* (*The Right of Youth*); *Tropisk Kaerlighed* (*Love in the Tropics*); *Vampyrdanserinden* (*The Vampire Dancer*); *Det gamle Købmandshus* (*Midsommer*; *Midsummer-Time*); *Dødens Brud Gadeoriginalen* (*A Bride of Death*)

1912 *Brillantstjernen* (*For Her Sister's Sake*); *Guvernørens Datter* (*The Governor's Daughter*); *Kaerlighed gør blind* (*Love Is Blind*); *Dyrekøbt Venskab* (*Dearly Purchased Friendship*); *Den sorte Kansler* (*The Black Chancellor*); *Hjertets Guld* (*Et Hjerte af Guld*; *Faithful Unto Death*); *Direktørens Datter* (*Caught in His Own Trap*); *Det første Honorar* (*Hans første Honorar*; *His First Patient*); *Elskovs Magt* (*Gøgleren*; *Man's Great Adversary*); *Historien om en Moder* (*En Moders Kaerlighed*; *The Life of a Mother*); *De tre Kammerater* (*The Three Comrades*); *Operabranden* (*Bedstemoders Vuggevise*) *The Song Which Grandmother Sang*; *Den første Kaerlighed* (*Her First Love Affair*); *Hjerternes Kamp* (*A High Stake*); *Hans vanskeligste Rolle* (*His Most Difficult Part*); *Den tredie Magt* (*The Secret Treaty*); *Fodselsdagsgaven* (*Gaven*; *The Birthday Gift*); *En Hofintrige* (*A Court Intrigue*); *Den sande Kaerlighed* (*Flugten gennem Skyerne*; *The Fugitives*); *Hvem var Forbryderen?* (*Samvittighedsnag*; *At the Eleventh Hour*); *Alt paa ét Kort* (*Guldmønten*; *Gold from the Gutter*)

1913 *Pressens Magt* (*Et Bankrun*; *A Harvest of Tears*); *Troløs* (*Gøglerblod, Artists*); *Højt Spil* (*Et forfejlet Spring*; *A Dash for Liberty*); *Naar Fruen gaar paa Eventyr* (*Pompadourtasken*; *The Lost Bag*); *Bristet Lykke* (*A Paradise Lost*); *Fem Kopier* (*Five Copies*); *Atlantis*; *En farlig Forbryder* (*Knivstikkeren*; *A Modern Jack the Ripper*); *Af Elskovs Naade* (*Acquitted*); *Elskovsleg* (*Love's Devotee*); *Vasens Hemmelighed* (*Den kinesiske Vase*; *The Chinese Vase*)

1914 *Sønnen* (*Her Son*); *Den store Middag* (*The Guestless Dinner Party*); *Tugthusfange No. 97* (*En Gaest fra en anden Verden*; *The Outcast's Return*); *Faedrenes Synd* (*Nemesis*); *Aegteskab og Pigesjov* (*Mr. King paa Eventyr*; *A Surprise Packet*); *Aeventyrersken* (*Exiled*); *En ensom Kvinde* (*Hvem er han?*; *The Doctor's Legacy*); *Revolutionsbryllup* (*A Revolution Marriage*); *Et Laereaar* (*The Reformation*); *Den lille Chauffør* (*The Little Chauffeur*); *Den største Kaerlighed* (*En Moders Kaerlighed*; *"Escaped the Law, But ..."*); *Pro Patria*; *Kaerligheds-Vaeddemaalet* (*The Wager*)

1915 *Du skal elske din Naeste* (*For de Andre*; *The Samaritan*); *Giftpilen* (*The Poisonous Arrow*); *Hjertestorme*; *Kaerligheds Laengsel* (*Den Pukkelryggede*; *The Cripple Girl*); *Lotteriseddel No. 22152* (*Den blinde Skaebne*; *Blind Fate*); *Rovedderkoppen* (*Den røde Enke*); *Syndens Datter* (*Den, der sejrer*; *Nobody's Daughter*); *Syndig Kaerlighed* (*Eremitten*; *The Hermit*); *Truet Lykke* (*Et Skud i Mørket*; *The Evil Genius*); *Verdens Undergang* (*Flammesvaerdet*; *The Flaming Sword*); *For sit Lands Aere* (*Hendes Aere*; *For His Country's Honor*)

1916 *Den mystiske Selskabsdame* (*The Mysterious Companion*); *Gillekop*

1918 *Grevindens Aere* (*Kniplinger*; *Lace*); *Maharadjaens Yndlingshustru II* (*The Favorite Wife of the Maharaja II*; *A Daughter of Brahma*); *Via Crucis*

1919 *Prometheus I-II* (*Bonds of Hate*)

1920 *Hans gode Genius* (*Mod Stjernerne*; *His Guardian Angel*); *Praesten i Vejlby* (*The Vicar of Vejlby*; *The Land of Fate*)

1924 *Det store Hjerte* (*Lights from Circus Life*; *Side Lights of the Sawdust Ring*); *Den store Magt*

1925 *Hendes Naade*; *Dragonen*

Other Films:

1909 *Droske 519* (*Cab No. 519*) (role); *En Kvinde af Folket* (*A Woman of the People*) (role): *Dr. Nicola I* (*Den skjulte Skat*) (role); *Dr. Nicola* (*Hvorledes Dr. Nicola erhvervede den kinesiske Stok*; *How Dr. Nicola Procured the Chinese Cane*) (role); *Barnet* (*A Child's Love*) (role); *Madame Sans Gène* (role); *Faderen* (*A Father's Grief*) (role); *Museumsmysteriet* (*The Mystery of the Museum*) (role); *Dr. Nicola III* (*Dr. Nicola in Tibet*) (role); *Et Budskab til Napoleon paa Elba* (*A Message to Napoleon*) (role); *Revolutionsbryllup* (*A Wedding during the French Revolution*) (role)

1910 *Sølvdaasen med Juvelerne* (*The Jewel Case*) (role); *Tyven* (*A Society Sinner*) (role); *To Tjenestepiger* (*The Rival Servants*) (role); *Kean* (role); *Medbejlerens Haevn* (*Caught in His Own Net*) (role); *Forraederen* (*A Traitor to His Country*) (role)

* * *

When August Blom came to Nordisk Films Kompagni in 1909 it was the major film production company in Denmark, having been founded in 1906 by Ole Olsen. Nordisk dominated the so-called "belle époque" (from 1910 to 1914) in Danish filmmaking, and August Blom was the leading force in this period. In 1911 Blom became head of production at Nordisk, maintaining his position as a director at the same time. In charge of scripts and actors, Blom launched the career of Valdemar Psilander, who showed a natural talent for understated and realistic film acting. The actor became an immensely popular star in Denmark and Europe until his premature death in 1917. In 1911 Blom directed sixteen of Psilander's seventeen films.

In 1910 Blom made *Ved Faengslets Port* (released 1911) which, with Urban Gad's *Afgrunden*, introduced the erotic melodrama, a genre refined by Blom in the following years. *Ved Faengslets Port* is typical of the kind of films which made Nordisk famous all over the world. The story is about a young aristocrat who is in the grip of a moneylender and at the same time loves the moneylender's daughter. Although Blom tried to introduce contemporary themes in his films, the

August Blom: ***Atlantis***

stories were always the weak part of his and most other Danish films in this period. The compensation for the banal magazine stories was found in the way Blom told these stories. His films are often about contrasts, social and sexual. The films are passionate and reveal the many faces of love with great imagination. As a former actor Blom put great weight on acting, and he had a fine feeling for the direction of actresses. His portraits of women are quite often subtle and daring.

Blom put immense care into the making of his films. The sets were used in a dramatic way, playing an important role in the story as a means of characterizing the people. His narrative technique made use of cross-cutting and, assisted by his favourite cameraman, Johan Ankerstjerne, he was an innovator in lighting. One of his stylistic devices, used to great and surprising effect, was the use of mirrors as a means of expanding the dramatic content of a scene.

Blom must be considered as one of the important pioneers in the early silent film. It was quite natural that Blom was commissioned to direct the greatest and most ambitious film of the period, a film which introduced a literary era in the Danish film. This was *Atlantis,* based on Gerhart Hauptmann's novel of 1912. This ambitious attempt to transpose a modern novel with a complicated plot and interesting characters to film benefited from the director's steady hand. Blom's direction of the film is astonishingly mature, confident, and imaginative, and in many ways *Atlantis* is ahead of its time. Johan Ankerstjerne's camerawork, for instance, points forward to the expressionist-inspired German films. Another fine film by Blom was *Verdens Undergang.*

Blom made seventy-eight of his approximately one hundred films in the years 1910-14, but he was a company man, and he stayed with Nordisk in the years of decline. He left filming in 1924. During the golden age of the Danish cinema, however, Blom was the great stylist, a gifted and civilized director.

—Ib Monty

BOETTICHER, Budd

Nationality: American. **Born:** Oscar Boetticher, Jr., in Chicago, 29 July 1916. **Education:** Ohio State University. **Career:** Football star at Ohio State, early 1930s; after recuperating from football injury in Mexico, became professional matador, 1940; technical advisor on Mamoulian's *Blood and Sand,* 1940; messenger boy at Hal Roach studios, 1941-1943; assistant to William Seiter, George Stevens, and Charles Vidor, 1943-44; military service, made propaganda films, 1946-47; made cycle of Westerns for Ranown production company, 1956-

60; left Hollywood to make documentary on matador Carlos Arruza, 1960; after many setbacks, returned to Hollywood, 1967.

Films as Director:

(as Oscar Boetticher)

1944 *One Mysterious Night*; *The Missing Juror*; *Youth on Trial*
1945 *A Guy, a Gal and a Pal*; *Escape on the Fog*
1946 *The Fleet That Came to Stay* (and other propaganda films)
1948 *Assigned to Danger*; *Behind Locked Doors*
1949 *Black Midnight*; *Wolf Hunters*
1950 *Killer Shark*

(as Budd Boetticher)

1951 *The Bullfighter and the Lady* (+ co-story); *The Sword of D'Artagnan*; *The Cimarron Kid*
1952 *Bronco Buster*; *Red Ball Express*; *Horizons West*
1953 *City Beneath the Sea*; *Seminole*; *The Man from the Alamo*; *Wings of the Hawk*; *East of Sumatra*
1955 *The Magnificent Matador* (+ story); *The Killer is Loose*
1956 *Seven Men from Now*
1957 *The Tall T*; *Decision at Sundown*
1958 *Buchanan Rides Alone*
1959 *Ride Lonesome* (+ pr); *Westbound*
1960 *Comanche Station*; *The Rise and Fall of Legs Diamond*
1971 *Arruza* (+ pr, co-sc; production completed 1968); *A Time for Dying* (+ sc; production completed 1969)
1985 *My Kingdom for...* (+ sc)

Other Films:

1970 *Two Mules for Sister Sara* (Siegel) (sc)

Publications

By BOETTICHER: book—

When in Disgrace, New York, 1971.

By BOETTICHER: articles—

Interview with Bertrand Tavernier, in *Cahiers du Cinéma* (Paris), July 1964.
Interviews with Michel Ciment and others, in *Positif* (Paris), November 1969.
Interview, in *The Director's Event* by Eric Sherman and Martin Rubin, New York, 1970.
Interview with O. Assayas and B. Krohn, in *Cahiers du Cinéma* (Paris), April 1982.
"The Bullfighter and the Director," in *American Film* (Washington, D.C.), October 1985.

On BOETTICHER: books—

Kitses, Jim, *Horizons West,* Bloomington, Indiana, 1969.
Kitses, Jim, editor, *Budd Boetticher: The Western,* London, 1969.
Buscombe, Ed, editor, *BFI Companion to the Western,* London, 1988.
Budd Boetticher, Madrid (La Filmoteca Espanola), n.d.

On BOETTICHER: articles—

"The Director and the Public: a Symposium," in *Film Culture* (New York), March/April 1955.
"Un Western exemplaire," in *Qu'est-ce que le cinéma* by André Bazin, Paris, 1961.
Sarris, Andrew, "Esoterica," in *Film Culture* (New York), Spring 1963.
Schmidt, Eckhart, "B.B. wie Budd Boetticher," in *Film* (Germany), October/November 1964.
Russell, Lee, "Budd Boetticher," in *New Left Review,* July/August 1965.
Coonradt, P., "Boetticher Returns," in *Cinema* (Los Angeles), December 1968.
Wicking, Christopher, "Budd Boetticher," in *Screen* (London), July/October 1969.
Sequin, Louis, "Deu Westerns d'Oscar 'Budd' Boetticher," in Positif (Paris), November 1969.
Schrader, Paul, "Budd Boetticher: A Case Study in Criticism," in *Cinema* (Los Angeles), Fall 1970.
Millar, Gavin, "Boetticher's Westerns," in *Listener* (London), 6 October 1983.
Hollywood Reporter, 2 July 1984.
Krohn, B., "Le retour de Budd Boetticher," in *Cahiers du Cinéma* (Paris), November 1987.

* * *

Budd Boetticher will be remembered as a director of Westerns, although his bullfight films have their fervent admirers, as does his *Scarface*-variant, *The Rise and Fall of Legs Diamond.* Since Boetticher's Westerns are so variable in quality, it is tempting to overcredit Burt Kennedy, the scriptwriter for all of the finest. But Kennedy's own efforts as director (*Return of the Seven, Hannie Caulder, The War Wagon,* etc.) are tediously paced dramas or failed comedies. Clearly the Boetticher/Kennedy team clicked to make Westerns significantly superior to what either could create on their own. Indeed, *The Tall T, Seven Men from Now,* and (on a slightly lower level) *Ride Lonesome* look now like the finest work in the genre during the 1950s, less pretentious and more tightly controlled than even those of Anthony Mann or John Ford.

Jim Kitses's still-essential *Horizons West* rightly locates Boetticher's significant Westerns in the "Ranown" cycle (a production company name taken from producer Harry Joe Brown and his partner Randolph Scott). But the non-Kennedy entries in the cycle have, despite Scott's key presence, only passing interest. One might have attributed the black comedy in the series to Kennedy without the burlesque *Buchanan Rides Alone,* which wanders into an episodic narrative opposite to the taut, unified action of the others; *Decision at Sundown* is notable only for its remarkably bitter finale and a morally pointless showdown, as if it were a cynic's answer to *High Noon.*

The Tall T's narrative is typical of the best Boetticher/Kennedy: it moves from a humanizing comedy so rare in the genre into a harsh and convincing savagery. Boetticher's villains are relentlessly cruel, yet morally shaded. In *The Tall T,* he toys with the redeemable qualities of Richard Boone, while deftly characterizing the other two (Henry Silva asks, "I've never shot me a woman, have I Frank?"). Equally memorable are Lee Marvin (in *Seven Men from Now*) and Lee Van Cleef (*Ride Lonesome*).

Randolph Scott is the third essential collaborator in the cycle. He is generally presented by Boetticher as a loner not by principle or habit but by an obscure terror in his past (often a wife murdered). Thus, he's not an asexual cowpoke so much as one who, temporarily at least, is beyond fears and yearnings. There's a Pinteresque sexual confrontation in *Seven Men from Now* among Scott, a pioneer couple, and an insinuating Lee Marvin when the four are confined in a wagon. And, indeed, the typical Boetticher landscape—smooth, rounded, and yet impassible boulders—match Scott's deceptively complex character as much as the majestic Monument Valley towers match Wayne in Ford's Westerns, or the harsh cliffs match James Stewart in Mann's.

Budd Boetticher: Maureen O'Sullivan, Randolph Scott, and Richard Boone in *The Tall T*

Clearly the Westerns of the sixties and seventies owe more to Boetticher than Ford. Even such very minor works as *Horizons West, The Wings of the Hawk,* and *The Man from the Alamo* have the tensions of Spaghetti Westerns (without the iciness), as well as the Peckinpah fantasy of American expertise combining with Mexican peasant vitality. If Peckinpah and Leone are the masters of the post-"classic" Western, then it's worth noting how *The Wings of the Hawk* anticipates *The Wild Bunch,* and how *Once Upon a Time in the West* opens like *Seven Men from Now* and closes like *Ride Lonesome.* Boetticher's films are the final great achievement of the traditional Western, before the explosion of the genre.

—Scott Simmon

BOGDANOVICH, Peter

Nationality: American. **Born:** Kingston, New York, 30 July 1939. **Education:** Collegiate School, New York; studied acting at Stella Adler's Theatre Studio. **Family:** Married 1) Polly Platt, 1962 (divorced 1970), two daughters; 2) Louise Stratten (Hoogstraten), 1988, sister of murdered former lover Dorothy Stratten.. **Career:** Actor in American and New York Shakespeare Festivals, 1956-58; first play as producer, *The Big Knife,* off-Broadway, 1959; film critic for *Esquire, New York Times,* and *Cahiers du Cinéma,* among others, from 1961; moved to Hollywood, 1964; 2nd unit director on *The Wild Angels* (Corman), 1966; directed first film, *Targets* (produced by Corman), 1968; Paramount formed and financed The Directors Company, independent unit partnership of Bogdanovich, Francis Ford Coppola, and William Friedkin, 1973; formed Copa de Oro production company, 1975; owner, Crescent Moon Productions, Inc., from 1986. **Awards:** New York Film Critics Award and British Academy Award for Best Screenplay, for *The Last Picture Show,* 1971; Writer's Guild of America Award for Best Screenplay, for *What's Up, Doc?,* 1972; Critics Prize, Venice Festival, for *Saint Jack,* 1979. **Address:** c/o William Peiffer, 2040 Avenue of the Stars, Century City, CA 90067, U.S.A.

Films as Director:

1967 *Targets* (+ co-sc, pr, ed, role as Sammy Michaels)
1971 *Directed by John Ford* (+ sc); ***The Last Picture Show*** (+ co-sc)

1972 *What's Up, Doc?* (+ pr, co-sc)
1973 *Paper Moon* (+ pr)
1974 *Daisy Miller* (+ pr)
1975 *At Long Last Love* (+ pr, sc, co-songwriter: "Poor Young Millionaire")
1976 *Nickelodeon* (+ co-sc)
1979 *Saint Jack* (+ co-sc, role as Eddie Schuman)
1983 *They All Laughed* (+ sc)
1984 *Mask*
1987 *Illegally Yours*
1990 *Texasville*
1992 *Noises Off* (+ exec pr)
1993 *The Thing Called Love*

Other Films:

1966 *The Wild Angels* (Corman) (co-sc, 2nd unit d, all uncredited, + bit role, voice); *Voyage to the Planet of the Prehistoric Women* (*Gill-Women of Venus*) (from Russian science fiction film by Pavel Klushantsev, *Planeta Burg* [*Cosmonauts on Venus*; *Storm Clouds of Venus*], dubbed and re-edited for American Int'l Pictures) (supervising ed, d of add'l scenes under pseudonym Derek Thomas and/or Peter Stewart)
1967 *The Trip* (Corman) (role)
1969 *Lion's Love* (Varda) (guest star role)
1970 *The Other Side of the Wind* (Welles, unreleased) (role as Higgam)
1973 *F for Fake* (Welles) (voice-over)
1975 *Diaries, Notes & Sketches* volume 1, reels 1-6: *Lost Lost Lost* (Jonas Mekas) (appearance in reel 3); *The Gentleman Tramp* (Patterson) ("special thanks" credit for supervising scenes shot at Charles Chaplin's home in Switzerland)
1978 *Opening Night* (Cassavetes) (guest star role)

Publications

By BOGDANOVICH: books—

The Cinema of Orson Welles, New York, 1961.
The Cinema of Howard Hawks, New York, 1962.
The Cinema of Alfred Hitchcock, New York, 1963.
Fritz Lang in America, New York, 1967; revised edition, 1981.
John Ford, Berkeley, California, 1968; revised edition, 1978.
Alan Dwan: The Last Pioneer, New York, 1971; revised edition, 1981.
Pieces of Time, New York, 1973; revised, as *Pieces of Time: Peter Bogdanovich on the Movies 1961-85,* New York, 1985.
The Killing of the Unicorn: Dorothy Stratten (1960-1980), New York, 1984.
This Is Orson Welles, New York, 1992.

By BOGDANOVICH: articles—

"Bogie in Excelsis," in *Esquire* (New York), September 1964.
"Go-Go and Hurry: It's Later Than You Think," in *Esquire* (New York), February 1965.
"Th' Respawnsibility of Bein' J ... Jimmy Stewart. Gosh!," in *Esquire* (New York), July 1966.
"Godard in Hollywood," in *Take One* (Montreal), June 1968.
"*Targets,*" in *Sight and Sound* (London), Winter 1969/70.
"Inter/View with Peter Bogdanovich," with G. O'Brien and R. Feiden, in *Inter/View* (New York), March 1972.
"Without a Dinosaur," interview with Gordon Gow, in *Films and Filming* (London), June 1972.
"Peter Bogdanovich on *Paper Moon,*" interview with D. Lyons and others, in *Interview* (New York), July 1973.
"Cybill and Peter," interview with Andy Warhol and others, in *Inter/View* (New York), June 1974.
"Polly Platt: Sets the Style," interview with M. McAndrew, in *Cinema* (Beverly Hills), no. 35, 1976.
"Dialogue on Film: Peter Bogdanovich," in *American Film* (Washington, D.C.), December/January 1978/79.
Interview with O. Assayas and B. Krohn, in *Cahiers du Cinéma* (Paris), April 1982.
Interview with Thomas J. Harris, in *Literature/Film Quarterly* (Salisbury, Maryland), vol. 16, no. 4, 1988.

On BOGDANOVICH: books—

Sherman, Eric, and Martin Rubin, *The Director's Event,* New York, 1970.
Giacci, V., *Bogdanovich,* Florence, 1975.
Tuska, Jon, editor, *Close-Up: The Contemporary Director,* Metuchen, New Jersey, 1981.
Harris, Thomas J., *Bogdanovich's Picture Shows,* Metuchen, New Jersey, 1990.
Yule, Andrew, *Picture Shows: The Life and Films of Peter Bogdanovich,* New York, 1992.

On BOGDANOVICH: articles—

Houston, Penelope, "Hitchcockery," in *Sight and Sound* (London), Autumn 1968.
Patterson, R., "*Directed by John Ford*: Producing a Compilation Documentary," in *American Cinematographer* (Los Angeles), November 1971.
Rainer, P., "Bogged Down: A Twitch in the Auteur Niche," in *Film Critic* (New York), September/October 1972.
Kasindorf, Martin, "Peter Bogdanovich," in *Action* (Los Angeles), July/August 1973.
Starr, Cecile, "Peter Bogdanovich Remembered and Assessed," in *Filmmakers Newsletter* (Ward Hill, Massachusetts), September 1973.
Dawson, Jan, "The Continental Divide," in *Sight and Sound* (London), Winter 1973/74.
Fieschi, J., "Dossier Hollywood '79: Peter Bogdanovich," in *Cinématographe* (Paris), March 1979.
Buckley, T., "How Bogdanovich Learned to Think Small Again," in *New York Times,* 20 April 1979.
Le Fanu, Mark, "Peter Bogdanovich," in *Films and Filming* (London), August 1984.
de Waal, F., "In Memoriam Peter Bogdanovich," in *Skoop* (Amsterdam), May 1985.
"Dialogue on Film: Peter Bogdanovich," in *American Film* (Washington, D.C.), June 1986.
Harrison, B. G., "Peter Bogdanovich Comes Back from the Dead," in *Esquire,* August 1990.
"Peter Bogdanovich," in *CinemAction!* (Toronto), January 1992.
Schwager, J., "The Trick of It," in *Boxoffice,* January 1992.
McKibbins, A., "Bogdanovich Looks at the Past through the Present," in *Filmnews,* vol. 22, no. 3, 1992.
White, A., "Directed by Peter Bogdanovich," in *Film Comment,* March/April 1993.

* * *

Of all trades ancillary to the cinema, few offer worse preparation for a directing career than criticism. Bogdanovich's background as Hollywood historian and profiler of its legendary figures inevitably invited comparisons between his movies and those of directors like Ford, Hawks, and Dwan, whom he had deified. That he should have occasionally created films which deserve such comparison argues for his skill and resilience.

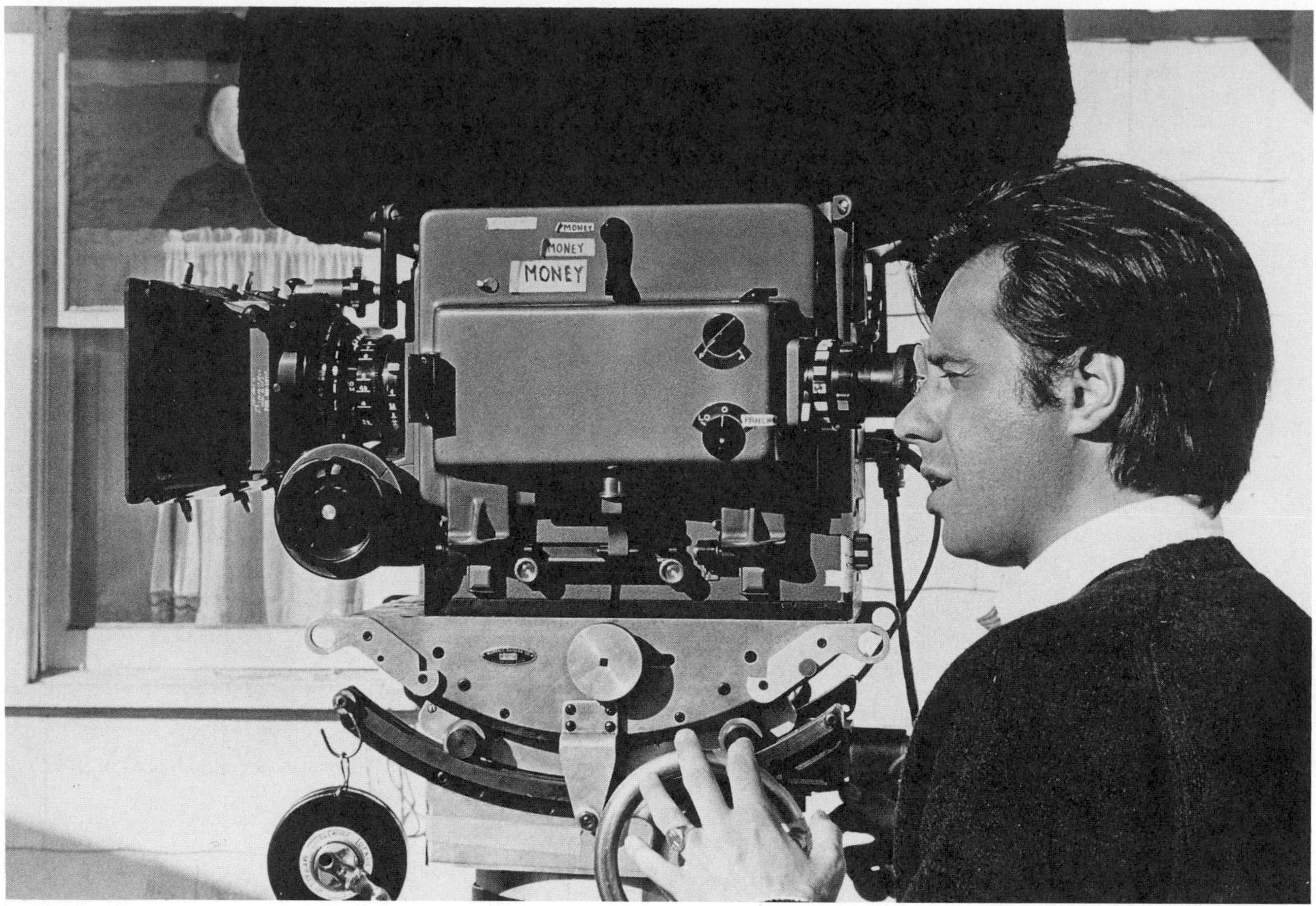

Peter Bogdanovich

He first attracted attention with *Targets,* a flashy exercise with an ailing Karloff playing straight man to Bogdanovich's film-buff director and a psychotic sniper menacing the audience at a drive-in cinema. The documentary *Directed by John Ford* likewise exploited Hollywood history, but with uncertain scholarship and even less certain taste. Yet in his first major fiction feature, based on Larry McMurtry's rural nocturne *The Last Picture Show,* Bogdanovich created a precise and moving chronicle of small-town values eroded by selfishness and disloyalty. He also showed a flair for casting in his choice of underrated veterans and fresh newcomers. Ben Johnson, Cloris Leachman, and Ellen Burstyn earned new respect, while Timothy Bottoms, Jeff Bridges, and Cybill Shepherd received boosts to nascent careers—though Shepherd, via her relationship with the director, was to prove a troublesome protegée.

What's Up, Doc? and *Paper Moon* are among the shapeliest comedies of the 1970s, trading on nostalgia but undercutting it with sly character-playing and dead-pan wit. Ryan and Tatum O'Neal achieve a stylish ensemble performance in the latter as 1930s con-man and unwanted orphan auxiliary; in the former, O'Neal makes a creditable attempt at playing Cary Grant to Barbra Streisand's Hepburn, backed up by a typically rich character cast—notably Austin Pendleton, Kenneth Mars, and the ululating Madeline Kahn.

Daisy Miller, a period vehicle for Shepherd more redolent of Henry King than Henry James, inaugurated Bogdanovich's decline. An attempt at a 1930s Cole Porter musical, *At Long Last Love* likewise flopped, as did *Nickelodeon,* an unexpectedly leaden tribute to pioneer moviemaking. He returned to form with a low-budget adaptation of Paul Theroux's *Saint Jack,* dignified by Ben Gazzara's performance as the ironic man of honor coping with Occidental venality and Asian corruption. And the Manhattan comedy *They All Laughed,* though widely disliked, showed a truer synthesis of screwball humour and sentimentality than other equivalent films, and marked a return by Bogdanovich to the spirit of the classical directors he admires.

Bogdanovich worked little in the 1980s, apparently traumatised by the murder of his lover Dorothy Stratten shortly after her acting debut in *They All Laughed.* At decade's end, in a twin return to his roots that offered some hope for his future, he married Stratten's sister and directed *Texasville,* a *Last Picture Show* sequel with many of the original cast.

Texasville, like most sequels, fails because what made the original interesting and valuable cannot be repeated. Like Bogdanovich himself, then at the beginning of his career, the characters in *The Last Picture Show* were embarked, with tragi-comic results, on the painful journey into adulthood; the loss of childhood certainties was mirrored by the film's detailed mise-en-scène, a small Texas town that loses its heart and soul when a benevolent patriarch dies suddenly. Grown up, they are no longer connected by the irresistible force of adolescence, and Bogdanovich's film—though based on novelist Larry McMurtry's often poignant continuation—wanders in search of a plot, boring the spectator with childish antics meant to signify the onset of a collective life crisis. The story goes on, but without much interest or direction.

Much the same might be said of his career in the 1990s, which has continued but not prospered. *The Thing Called Love* tries to recapture

Bogdanovich's earlier success with coming-of-age stories (not only *The Last Picture Show* but also *Paper Moon*). However, this overly predictable and slow-moving saga of young adults trying to make it big in the highly competitive world of country music deservedly failed to find much of an audience. *Noises Off,* based on Michael Frayn's hugely successful play, has moments that recall Bogdanovich's earlier success with fast-paced farce (the delightful *What's Up, Doc?*), but lacks a firm sense of directorial control; a fine cast—including Michael Caine and Carol Burnett—never becomes an effective ensemble, and the film's only virtues derive from Frayn's play, whose commercial productions are far superior to this screen version.

—John Baxter, updated by R. Barton Palmer

BOORMAN, John

Nationality: British. **Born:** Shepperton, Middlesex, 18 January 1933. **Education:** Salesian College. **Military Service:** Sergeant in British Army, 1951-53. **Family:** Married Christel Kruse, 1957, one son (actor Charley Boorman), three daughters. **Career:** Film critic for BBC Radio and for *Manchester Guardian,* 1950-54; film editor, Independent Television News, 1955-58; head of documentaries, BBC Television, 1960-64; directed first feature, *Catch Us If You Can,* 1965; moved to United States to make *Point Blank,* 1967; chairor, National Film Studios of Ireland, 1975-85; governor, British Film institute, from 1985; founder and co-editor of *Projections,* published annually in London since 1992. **Awards:** Best Director Award, Cannes Festival, for *Leo the Last,* 1970; Chevalier de l'Ordre des Arts et Lettres, 1985; New York Film Critics Circle Awards for Best Director and Best Screenplay, for *Hope and Glory,* 1987. **Agent:** Edgar Gross, International Business Management, 1801 Century Park E., Suite 1132, Los Angeles, CA 90067, U.S.A. **Address:** The Glebe, Annamoe, County Wicklow, Ireland.

Films as Director:

1965 *Catch Us If You Can* (*Having a Wild Weekend*)
1967 *Point Blank*
1968 *Hell in the Pacific*
1970 *Leo the Last* (+ sc)
1972 ***Deliverance*** (+ pr)
1973 *Zardoz* (+ sc, pr)
1977 *Exorcist II: The Heretic* (+ pr)
1981 *Excalibur* (+ pr, co-sc)
1985 *The Emerald Forest* (+ pr)
1987 *Hope and Glory* (+ pr, sc)
1990 *Where the Heart Is* (+ sc, pr)
1991 *I Dreamt I Woke Up* (+ role)
1995 *Two Nudes Bathing* (+ sc, pr); *Beyond Rangoon* (+ pr)

Other Films:

1976 *Target of an Assassin* (*The Long Shot*) (role)
1982 *Dream One* (pr)

Publications

By BOORMAN: books—

Zardoz, London, 1983.
Money Into Light: The Emerald Forest: A Diary, London, 1985.
Hope and Glory, London, 1987.

By BOORMAN: articles—

"Playboy in a Monastery," interview with Gordon Gow, in *Films and Filming* (London), February 1972.
"Conversation with John Boorman," with L. Strawn, in *Action* (Los Angeles), November/December 1972.
"*Zardoz,*" interview with Philip Strick, in *Sight and Sound* (London), Spring 1974.
Interviews with Michel Ciment, in *Positif* (Paris), March 1974 and February 1978.
"Director John Boorman Talks About His Work," in *American Cinematographer* (Los Angeles), March 1975.
Interview with J.-P. Le Pavec and D. Rabourdin, in *Cinéma* (Paris), March 1978.
"The Sorcerer: John Boorman Interviewed," by D. Yakir, in *Film Comment* (New York), May/June 1981.
"The Technology of Style," interview with J. Verniere, in *Filmmakers Monthly* (Ward Hill, Massachusetts), June 1981.
"The World of King Arthur according to John Boorman," an interview with H. Kennedy, in *American Film* (Washington, D.C.), March 1981.
"Jungle John," an interview with G. Fuller, in *Stills* (London), November 1985.
"John Boorman en quête de mythologie," an interview with C. Blanchet, in *Cinéma* (Paris), 19 February 1986.
"Christopher Isherwood: Stranger in Paradise," in *American Film* (Washington, D.C.), October 1986.
Interview in *Positif* (Paris), November 1987.
"Worshipping at the Shrine: Los Angeles in the Season of the Oscars," in *Sight and Sound* (London), Summer 1988.
"Gardening and Parking," in *Sight and Sound* (London), Autumn 1988.
"Bohemian Rhapsody," an interview with Brian Case, in *Time Out* (London), 1 August 1990.
Interview with Michel Ciment, in *Positif* (Paris), no. 355, 1990.
Interview with Michel Ciment, in *Positif* (Paris), no. 411, 1995.
Interview with Gavin Smith, in *Film Comment* (New York), vol. 31, no. 4, 1995.

On BOORMAN: books—

Piccardi, Adriano, *John Boorman,* Florence, 1982.
Holdstock, Robert, *John Boorman's "The Emerald Forest,"* New York, 1985.
Ciment, Michel, *John Boorman,* Paris, 1985; London, 1986.

On BOORMAN: articles—

Farber, Stephen, "The Writer in American Films," in *Film Quarterly* (Berkeley), Summer 1968.
Brown, John, "Islands of the Mind," in *Sight and Sound* (London), Winter 1969/70.
McGillivray, D., "John Boorman," in *Focus on Film* (London), Autumn 1972.
Dempsy, M., "*Deliverance*/Boorman: Dickey in the Woods," in *Cinema* (Beverly Hills), Spring 1973.
Legrand, Gérard, "Hommage à Boorman," in *Positif* (Paris), March 1974.
Stair, Bill, "En travaillant avec Boorman," in *Positif* (Paris), March 1974.
McCarthy, T., "The Exorcism of *The Heretic,*" in *Film Comment* (New York), September/October 1977.
"*Exorcist II* Issue" of *Avant-Scène du Cinéma* (Paris), 1 February 1978.
Sineux, M., "Un Héraut de notre temps," in *Positif* (Paris), October 1981.
"John Boorman Section" of *Positif* (Paris), July-August 1985.
Comiskey, R., "Man, myth, and magic," in *Cinema Papers* (Melbourne), November 1985.
Camy, G., "John Boorman, l'enchanteur moraliste," in *Jeune Cinéma* (Paris), November-December 1985.

John Boorman (left) with Sean Connery on the set of *Zardoz*

"John Boorman Section" of *Positif* (Paris), November 1987.

Stanbrook, A., "Is God in Show Business Too?" in *Sight and Sound* (London), no. 4, 1990.

Williams, L. R., "Blood Brothers," in *Sight and Sound* (London), no. 9, 1994.

* * *

"Film making is the process of turning money into light and then back into money again." John Boorman's neat epigram will probably haunt him for the rest of his filmmaking days, not simply because it is so tidy a formulation, but because the tensions it articulates have played such a prominent part in his own career.

Boorman has always been much concerned with the look of his films. In both *Deliverance* and *Point Blank* (shot, incidentally, in exquisite 'scope) he went to unusual lengths to control colour tones; *Zardoz* and *Exorcist II: The Heretic* are remarkable for their pictorial inventiveness; the images of the Irish countryside in *Excalibur* and of the Brazilian rain forest in *The Emerald Forest* are carefully imbued with a luminous, almost magical quality; and the extraordinary street of housing built for *Hope and Glory* (one of the largest sets constructed in Britain since the heyday of the studio system) speaks volumes for Boorman's commitment to a cinema of distinctively visual qualities.

Boorman has certainly proven himself able to turn money into light. Turning it back into money, however, has not always proved so easy, and the commercial weakness of *Zardoz* and the near total box-office disaster of *Exorcist II* were no help to him in trying to develop his ambitious projects of the 1980s. After all, an Irish-based adaptation of Malory's *Morte d'Arthur* (*Excalibur*), a "green" allegory scheduled for location filming in South America (*Emerald Forest*), and an autobiographical evocation of his wartime childhood (*Hope and Glory*) are hardly the most obviously marketable ideas, even from a thoroughly bankable director. Yet sell them he did, and if *The Emerald Forest* doesn't come off as well as either *Excalibur* or *Hope and Glory,* two out of three is no mean record for an independent-minded filmmaker with a taste for startling visuals and unusual stories.

Boorman's is a high-risk approach. When it goes wrong, it goes wrong with a vengeance, and both *Exorcist II* and *The Emerald Forest* sacrifice narrative conviction in the cause of pictorial splendour and some risible metaphysics. But when his approach goes right, the results are sufficient to justify his reputation as one of the most courageous and imaginative filmmakers still working in the commercial mainstream.

At its best (in *Point Blank, Deliverance, Excalibur,* and *Hope and Glory*) Boorman's cinema is rich and subtle, his fascination with images matched by taut story-telling and a nice sense of the opacity of people's motives, his characters constantly made aware of the complex and unanticipated consequences of their actions. In many of his films, strong-willed individualists find themselves embroiled in a clash between established order and disorder, a context within which they appear as representative figures caught up in near mythical confrontations. In *Hell in the Pacific,* for instance, Lee Marvin and Toshiro Mifune play two enemy soldiers stranded on an island. As they continue to conduct the war their roles become emblematic, and they play out the tensions between conditioned aggression and common humanity.

In *Point Blank,* perhaps Boorman's most elegantly realised film, the force for disorder is Walker (Lee Marvin), a man obsessed by what he considers to be his just desserts. Double-crossed in a robbery, he wants only his share of the spoils, a goal he pursues step by step up the hierarchy of a criminal syndicate. The film leaves us little choice but to identify with Walker who is, like Sean Connery in *Zardoz,* an absolute individualist, a man who cannot be restrained by the hierarchical order on which he impinges so forcefully.

Yet *Point Blank* somehow transcends the conventional morality of assertive individualism. Walker is ruthless and violent, certainly, but it is his symbolic force to which we respond. The movie creates a paradox in which this unlovely figure comes to represent a more human spirit than that embodied in the syndicate's bureaucratic order. As ever, Boorman provides no easy solutions. After much death and violence it emerges that Walker, too, has been manipulated. Sharing his perspective as we do, we are left with a pervasive sense of impotence in the face of larger impersonal forces.

Deliverance, too, shows us order and certainty revealed as precarious fabrications. It concerns four men on a canoe trip through the wilderness who are forced to recognise that their ideas about morality and their belief in the social niceties are ineffectual constructs in the face of adverse and unintelligible circumstances. After killing a man who had buggered one of their party at gunpoint, they find that the action leads them down a path of lies and death. "There's no end to it," one character observes, close to despair.

Excalibur, perhaps inevitably given its source in Arthurian myth, tells of the imposition of order onto chaos and of the terrible price to be paid when that order is not firmly based. Human frailty destroys Camelot when Arthur finds Guinevere and Lancelot asleep together in the forest; in another of Boorman's inspired cinematic images, Arthur plunges the sword Excalibur into the ground between them. The despairing Guinevere is left curled naked around the sword while the land falls into pestilence and war.

In these three films Boorman ensures that we appreciate how difficult it is to make judgments of good and evil, how tangled the threads of motivation can be. But he does so not only as a pessimistic observer of human failings; he also has hope. There is a lovely scene in *Hope and Glory,* his most romantic of films, when young Bill (Boorman himself, for the film is autobiographical) has the "googly" explained to him by his father. When he realises what it involves (bowling a cricket ball so that it turns one way but with a bowling action which suggests that it will turn in the opposite direction) he is both horrified and fascinated. "That's like telling fibs," he says, a child's term for lying which is as accurate to the period as it is precise in its childish evocation of acceptable untruth. In Bill's (and Boorman's) world, people are forever telling fibs; like the googly, things are not always what they seem. But, also like the googly, that complexity can be a matter as much for celebration as for concern.

—Andrew Tudor

BORZAGE, Frank

Nationality: American. **Born:** Salt Lake City, Utah, 23 April 1893. **Family:** Married 1) Rena Rogers (divorced 1945); 2) Edna Marie Stillwell, 1945 (divorced 1949); 3) Juanita Borzage. **Career:** Joined theatrical touring company as prop boy, 1906; moved to California, 1912; actor in many Ince Westerns and Mutual Comedies, 1913-15; began directing for Universal, 1916; signed to MGM, 1935-42; joined Republic Pictures as producer-director, 1945. **Awards:** Oscars for Best Director, for *Seventh Heaven,* 1927/28, and *Bad Girls,* 1931/32. **Died:** Of cancer in Los Angeles, 19 June 1962.

Films as Director:

1916 *That Gal of Burke's* (+ role); *Mammy's Rose* (co-d, role); *Life's Harmony* (co-d, role); *The Silken Spider* (+ role); *The Code of Honor* (+ role); *Nell Dale's Men Folks* (+ role); *The Forgotten Prayer* (+ role); *The Courtin' of Calliope Clew* (+ role); *Nugget Jim's Pardner* (+ role); *The Demon of Fear* (+ role); *Land o' Lizards* (*Silent Shelby*) (+ role); *Immediate Lee* (*Hair Trigger Casey*) (+ role); *Enchantment* (+ sc, role); *The Pride and the Man* (+ sc, role); *Dollars of Dross* (+ sc)
1917 *Wee Lady Betty* (co-d, role); *Flying Colors*; *Until They Get Me*
1918 *The Atom* (+ role); *The Gun Woman* (+ role); *Shoes That Danced*; *Innocent's Progress*; *An Honest Man*; *Society for Sale*; *Who Is to Blame?*; *The Ghost Flower*; *The Curse of Iku* (+ role)
1919 *Toton*; *Prudence of Broadway*; *Whom the Gods Destroy*; *Ashes of Desire*
1920 *Humoresque*
1921 *The Duke of Chimney Butte*; *Get-Rich-Quick Wallingford*
1922 *Back Pay*; *Billy Jim*; *The Good Provider*; *Hair Trigger Casey* (re-ed version); *Silent Shelby* (reissue of *Land o'Lizards*); *The Valley of Silent Men*; *The Pride of Palomar*
1923 *The Nth Commandment*; *Children of the Dust*; *Age of Desire*
1924 *Secrets*
1925 *The Lady*; *Daddy's Gone A-Hunting*; *Lazybones*; *Wages for Wives*; *The Circle*
1926 *The First Year*; *The Dixie Merchant*; *Early to Wed*; *Marriage License?*
1927 *Seventh Heaven*
1928 *Street Angel*
1929 *The River*; *Lucky Star*; *They Had to See Paris*
1930 *Son o' My Heart*; *Liliom*
1931 *Doctors' Wives*; *Young as You Feel*; *Bad Girl*
1932 *After Tomorrow*; *Young America*; *A Farewell to Arms*
1933 *Secrets* (remake of 1924 film); *Man's Castle*
1934 *No Greater Glory*; *Little Man What Now?* (+ pr); *Flirtation Walk* (+ pr)
1935 *Living on Velvet*; *Stranded*; *Shipmates Forever*
1936 *Desire*; *Hearts Divided*
1937 *Green Light*; *History Is Made at Night*; *Big City*
1938 *Mannequin*; *Three Comrades*; *The Shining Hour*
1939 *Disputed Passage* (+ co-pr)
1940 *Strange Cargo*; *The Mortal Storm* (+ co-pr)
1941 *Flight Command*; *Smilin' Through*
1942 *The Vanishing Virginian*; *Seven Sweethearts*
1943 *Stage Door Canteen*; *His Butler's Sister* (+ co-pr)
1944 *Till We Meet Again* (+ pr)
1945 *The Spanish Main*
1946 *I've Always Loved You* (+ pr); *Magnificent Doll*
1947 *That's My Man* (+ pr)
1948 *Moonrise*
1958 *China Doll* (+ pr)
1959 *The Big Fisherman*

Publications

By BORZAGE: articles—

Article in *Motion Picture Directing: The Facts and Theories of the Newest Art,* by Peter Milne, New York, 1922.
Interview with V. Tully, in *Vanity Fair* (New York), February 1927.

"What's Wrong with the Movies?," in *Motion Picture* (New York), September 1933.

On BORZAGE: books—

Kyrou, Ado, *Amour, éroticisme et cinéma,* Paris, 1957.
Belton, John, *The Hollywood Professionals vol.3,* New York, 1974.
Lamster, Frederick, *Souls Made Great through Love and Adversity: The Film Work of Frank Borzage,* Metuchen, New Jersey, 1981.
Belton, John, *Cinema Stylists,* Metuchen, New Jersey, 1983.

On BORZAGE: articles—

Agel, Henri, "Frank Borzage," in *New York Film Bulletin,* no. 12-14, 1961.
Obituary in *New York Times,* 20 June 1962.
Sarris, Andrew, "Second Line," in *Film Culture* (New York), Spring 1963.
Belton, John, "Souls Made Great By Love and Adversity: Frank Borzage," in *Monogram* (London), no. 4, 1972.
Beylie, Claude, "Sur cinq films de Frank Borzage," in *Ecran* (Paris), September 1976.
Camper, Fred, "Disputed Passage," in *Cinema* (London), v. 9, no. 10.
Toulet, E., and Michel Ciment, "Avignon 1986: Panoramique du cinéma 1915-1920. Ford et Borzage," in *Positif* (Paris), September 1987.

* * *

Frank Borzage had a rare gift of taking characters, even those who were children of violence, and fashioning a treatment of them abundant with lyrical romanticism and tenderness, even a spirituality that reformed them and their story.

Borzage arrived in Hollywood in 1913, and Thomas H. Ince gave him his first small roles as a film actor, gradually promoting him to lead roles and providing him with his first opportunities to direct. He usually played the romantic lead in Westerns and romantic melodramas with such Triangle players as Sessue Hayakawa (*The Typhoon* and *Wrath of the Gods,* both 1914) and Olive Thomas (*Toton,* 1919). The first really important feature he directed was *Humoresque,* written by Frances Marion from a Fannie Hurst story. It had all the elements which were later to stamp a picture as a Borzage film—hope, love, and faith in oneself and others in a world that was poverty-stricken and could be cruel. It won *Photoplay Magazine*'s award as Best Picture of the year.

Borzage insisted that "real art is simple, but simplicity requires the greatest art," adding that "naturalness is the primary requisite of good acting. I like my players to perform as though there were no camera on the set."

Borzage did exceedingly well at Paramount's Cosmopolitan and at First National, where he directed two Norma Talmadge favorites, *Secrets* and *The Lady.* He then moved over to Fox, where, with the 1927 release of *Seventh Heaven,* he established himself as one of the best in the business. He directed two others with Janet Gaynor and Charles Farrell, *Street Angel* and *Lucky Star.* His *The River* of 1928, starring Farrell, is a virtual cinematic poem. In 1929 Borzage directed his first all-talking feature, *They Had to See Paris,* which starred Will Rogers, Fox's number one box-office star.

The year 1933 was probably Borzage's finest as a director, for he made three films which still rate as superb examples of the romantic cinema: *A Farewell to Arms,* from the Hemingway novel, with Gary Cooper and Helen Hayes; Mary Pickford's final and very best film, a re-make of the silent-era *Secrets,* which had originally starred Norma Talmadge; and *Man's Castle,* with Spencer Tracy and Loretta Young, a very moving romance.

There was a lasting tenderness about Borzage's treatment of a love story, and during the days of the Depression and the rise of Fascism, his pictures were ennobling melodramas about the power of love to create a heaven on earth. Penelope Gilliatt has remarked that Borzage "had a tenderness rare in melodrama and absolute pitch about period. He understood adversity." Outside of Griffith, there has never been another director in the business who could so effectively triumph over sentimentality, using true sentiment with an honest touch.

Borzage made four films with Margaret Sullavan that clearly indicated that she was the quintessential heroine for Borzage films: *Little Man, What Now?,* a study of love in the midst of deprivation and the growing terror in Germany; *Three Comrades,* in which Sullavan played an ill-fated tubercular wife; *The Shining Hour,* which featured her as a self-sacrificing woman; and *The Mortal Storm,* a moving film of the imminent battle with the Nazi forces.

Borzage also directed three other films during this time of stress that were extraordinary departures for him: *Desire,* a sleek romance in the Lubitsch tradition, starring Marlene Dietrich and Gary Cooper; *Mannequin,* co-starring Joan Crawford with Spencer Tracy, one of their best; and a drama that combined romance with effective disaster, *History Is Made at Night,* with Jean Arthur and Charles Boyer as lovers trapped in a Titanic-like explosion of violence. While in the case of *Desire* Ernst Lubitsch was producer, the picture features touches that are just as indicative of Borzage as they are of Lubitsch, for both were masters of cinematic subtlety. In the post-war period, it began to be clear that Borzage's career was on the wane. His best picture during this era was *Moonrise.*

—DeWitt Bodeen

BOULTING, Roy and John

Nationality: British. **Born:** Twins, in Bray, Berkshire, 21 November 1913. **Education:** McGill University, Toronto. **Career:** John entered film industry as office boy, worked as salesman, publicity writer, and editor, mid-1930's; introduced by John, Roy began as assistant director; they founded Charter Films, 1937; John served in Film Unit of Royal Air Force, Roy in British Army Film Unit, 1940-45; obtained leave at same time to make *Thunder Rock,* 1942; began series of comedies with *Seagulls Over Sorrento,* 1954; both joined board of British Lion Film Corp. **Died:** John died in Sunningdale, Berkshire, 17 June 1985.

Films with Roy as Director, John as Producer (though functions overlap):

1938 *The Landlady*; *Ripe Earth*; *Seeing Stars*; *Consider Your Verdict*
1939 *Trunk Crime*
1940 *Inquest*; *Pastor Hall*
1941 *Dawn Guard*
1942 *Thunder Rock*; *They Serve Abroad*
1943 *Desert Victory*
1944 *Tunisian Victory* (co-d)
1945 *Burma Victory*; *Journey Together* (John as d, Roy pr)
1947 *Fame Is the Spur*; *Brighton Rock* (*Young Scarface*) (John d and Roy pr)
1948 *The Guinea Pig* (*The Outsider*) (+ co-sc)
1950 *Seven Days to Noon* (John d and Roy pr)
1951 *Singlehanded* (*Sailor of the King*); *High Treason* (+ co-sc); *The Magic Box* (John d and Roy pr)
1954 *Seagulls Over Sorrento* (*Crest of the Wave*) (Roy and John co-d and co-pr, sc)

1955 *Josephine and Men*
1956 *Run for the Sun* (+ co-sc); *Private's Progress* (John d and Roy pr, co-sc)
1957 *Brothers in Law* (+ co-sc); *Happy Is the Bride* (+ co-sc); *Lucky Jim* (John d and Roy pr)
1959 *Carlton-Browne of the F.O.* (*Man in a Cocked Hat*) (co-d, co-sc); *I'm All Right Jack* (John d and Roy pr, co-sc)
1960 *A French Mistress* (+ co-sc); *Suspect* (*The Risk*) (Roy and John co-d and co-pr)
1963 *Heavens Above!* (John d and Roy pr, co-sc)
1965 *Rotten to the Core* (John d and Roy pr)
1966 *The Family Way* (+ co-adaptation)
1968 *Twisted Nerve* (+ co-sc)
1970 *There's a Girl in My Soup*
1974 *Soft Beds and Hard Battles* (*Undercovers Hero*) (+ co-sc)
1979 *The Number*
1979 *The Last Word*

Publications

By the BOULTINGS: articles—

"Bewitched, Bothered and Bewildered," in *Kine Weekly* (London), 9 November 1950.
"What Makes the British Laugh?," an interview with John, in *Films and Filming* (London), February 1959.
Interviews with John in *Today's Cinema* (London), 21 April and 5 December 1969.
"Who Dictates the Price of a Film," by John in *Today's Cinema* (London), 1 December 1970.
"Getting it Together," by Roy, in *Films and Filming* (London), February 1974.
Interview with Roy in *Photoplay Film Monthly* (London), March 1974.
"Flour Power," by both in *The Month in Yorkshire,* March 1981.
Letter signed by both in the *Times* (London), 10 April 1981.

On the BOULTINGS: books—

Durgnat, Raymond, *A Mirror for England,* London, 1970.
Hill, John, *Sex, Class, and Realism: British Cinema 1956-63,* London, 1986.
Murphy, Robert, *Realism and Tinsel,* London, 1989.

On the BOULTINGS: articles—

Watts, S., "The Boulting Twins," in *Films in Review* (New York), February 1960.
Sheed, W., "Pitfalls of Pratfalls: Boulting Brothers Comedies," in *Commonweal* (New York), 5 July 1963.
Film and TV Technician (London), March 1964.
Lewin, David, "Why the Boultings Can Be Bastards," in *Today's Cinema* (London), 24 November 1970.
Norman, Barry, "The Boultings: Fun at 60" in the *Times* (London), 26 January 1974.
"The Boulting Brothers," in *Film Dope* (London), March 1974.
Millar, Gavin, in *Listener* (London), 17 March 1983.
"John Boulting," in *St. James Press Annual Obituary 1985,* London, 1985.
McCarthy, T., obituary of John Boulting, in *Variety* (New York), 26 June 1985.
Tribute to John in *Screen International* (London), 29 June 1985.
"A Celebration for the Life of John Boulting," in *National Film Theatre Booklet* (London), September/October 1985.
TV Times (London), 16 November 1985.

* * *

The Boultings' *auteurial* films (interspersed by potboilers, usually comic) outline a "pilgrim's progress," or regress, from a moral earnestness and puritan conscience to a sort of hilarious gloom about the State of England.

Their first feature, *Pastor Hall,* was inspired by Martin Niemoller, the Nazi-defying German clergyman, via a play by ex-Expressionist Ernst Toller. With commentary by Eleanor Roosevelt added, it created a furor in isolationist America. *Thunder Rock,* adapted Robert Ardrey's pro-interventionist dream-play, is still remarkable for its didactic strategies—more persuasive than Brecht's—and its self-reflexivity à la Pirandello. After these calls to conscience came their war documentaries. *Desert Victory,* a compilation of newsreel footage and its famous "gunflash montage" of British artillery bombarding by night, won 10,000 bookings in U.S. theatres; its realism redirected U.S. propaganda strategies. *Tunisian Victory* was delayed by U.S. services' haggling over duly proportionate representation and by Churchill's wish to sit beside the moviola deciding the exact re-editing of its last shots.

The Boultings' next phase reflects the hopes, strains, and glooms of Austerity and the "Welfare Revolution." *Fame Is the Spur,* an adaptation of Howard Spring's best-seller, was inspired by Ramsay MacDonald's evolution from Socialist firebrand to the Labour Party's "Colonel Blimp." *The Guinea Pig* depicted a working-class scholarship boy's tribulations in an upper-crust school. The Boultings then switched their moral target from left-idealism becoming sluggish to left-idealism becoming fanatical. In *Seven Days To Noon* an atomic scientist vows to destroy London unless Britain unilaterally disarms. In *High Treason* a motley array of ultra-leftists sabotage British power-stations prior to invasion "from the East." Conversely, the noble hero of *Pastor Hall* finds his "antithesis"—The Boy—in *Brighton Rock,* from Grahame Greene's gangster novel. The Boy is petty, vile and doomed less through social environment than through *natural* evil and/or *spiritual* deprivation. *Vis-a-vis* atomic scientist and gangster alike, the Boultings' spokespersons for ordinary humanity are blowsy aging blondes, no better than they ought to be, as if to emblemise lowered expectations of human nature.

The Magic Box, a tribute to British film pioneer Friese-Greene, was the British film industry's "official" contribution to the Festival of Britain, and, like *Single-Handed,* a (dullish) tribute to old-fashioned British pluck. The mid-1950s' deepening anxieties about declining efficiency and social morality provoked the Boultings to satirical comedies; their sarcasms began where Ealing's left off. Typically, an earnest innocent (often Ian Carmichael) struggles against general moral grubbiness before giving up and joining it. The humour oscillates between tolerant and fraught, puritan and populist, realistic and farcical. *Private's Progress* targeted the army, *Brothers-in-Law* the law, and *Carleton-Brown of the F.O* the government. *Lucky Jim* (targeting Oxbridge) is a stodgy version of the Kingsley Amis novel, but *I'm All Right Jack* (industrial relations) is arguably *the* crucial movie about post-war Britain, Peter Sellers infusing with warmth and pathos a bloody-minded shop-steward. *Heaven's Above* (about the Anglican Church), from an idea by the Socialist-turned-Anglican Malcolm Muggeridge, intriguingly mixes *Carry On* buffoonery with Evelyn Waugh-type satire.

The Boultings' bouts of *Carry On*-type ribaldry aren't moral copout, but a deliberate moral position, an affectionate enjoyment of humanity despite its moral mediocrity and without the guilt of stereotypical puritanism. This mellowness keys their last serious films. In *The Family Way,* a working-class newly-wed's various troubles make him temporarily impotent; and his trusting father never realises that his best friend was the boy's real father. *The Twisted Nerve,* about a mongoloid's brother given to homicide, offended the mental health lobby, but sought to brood seriously on human nature, irreducible evil, and the everyday.

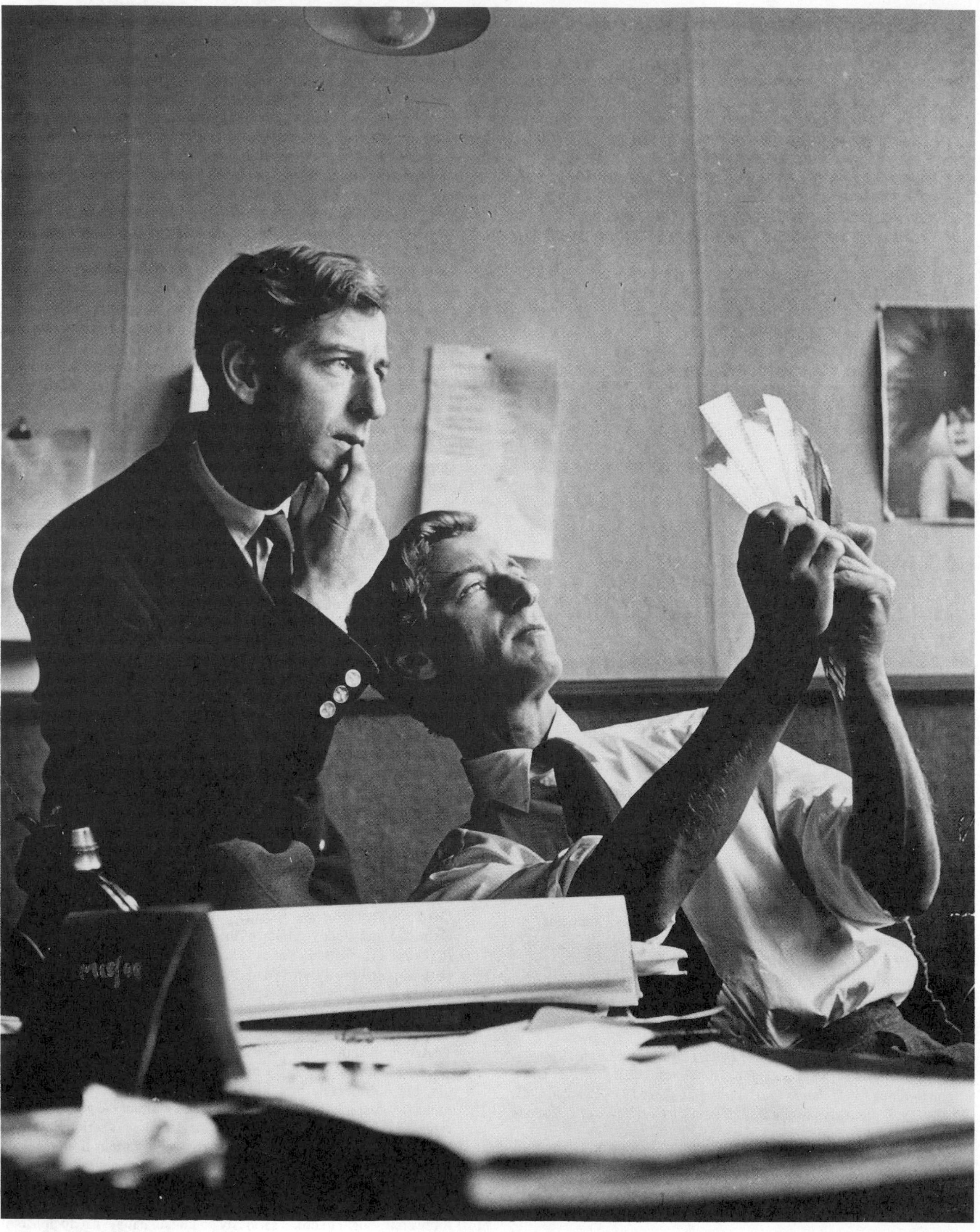

John and Roy Boulting

The overt discussion of moral fibre, choice, and consequence in *Thunder Rock* is the key to the Boultings' films. Contemplating the characters from outside, they ask moral questions rather than giving psychological data from the inside; and they stress the erosion of idealism, by puzzlement, weariness, or its paradoxical conflicts with decency. *Brighton Rock* focuses less on Pinky's mind, or the criminal *milieu,* than on the moral tropisms of the more hesitant characters. Such emphasis on "moral intuition" is central to the British character, and the Boultings' steady popularity evinces a profound, not a glib, affinity with audiences. The switch from very earnest to very satirical forms is another facet of their moralism.

Wherever possible, the Boultings operated as a semi-independent unit, often called Charter Films. On becoming Directors of British Lion in 1963, they were crucial in its renaissance, albeit embroiled in the controversial decisions preceding its dissolution.

—Raymond Durgnat

BRAKHAGE, Stan

Nationality: American. **Born:** Kansas City, Missouri, 14 January 1933. **Education:** Dartmouth College, 1951; attended Institute of Fine Arts, San Francisco, 1953. **Family:** Married 1) Jane Collum, 1957 (divorced, 1987), five children; 2) Marilyn Jull, 1989, one child. **Career:** Performed as boy soprano on live radio and recordings, 1937-46; dropped out of college, ran small theatre in Central City, Colorado, began making films, 1952; studies with Edgar Varese, New York, 1954; shot film for Joseph Cornell, 1955; worked for Raymond Rohauer in Los Angeles, 1956; made TV commercials and industrial films, 1956-64; moved to Denver, 1957; began lecturing on film, from 1960; completed major works *The Art of Vision* and *Dog Star Man,* 1964; lectured in film history and aesthetics, Colorado University, 1969; taught at School of the Art Institute, Chicago, from 1970; began working in super-8mm, 1976; teacher at Colorado, from 1981. **Awards:** James Ryan Morris Award, 1979; Telluride Film Festival Medallion, 1981; Maya Deren Award for Independent Film and Video Artists, 1986; MacDowell Medal, 1989. **Agent:** Film-Makers' Cooperative, 175 Lexington Ave., New York, NY 10016, U.S.A. **Address:** c/o Film Studies, Hunter 102, Campus Box 316, University of Colorado, Boulder, CO 80309, U.S.A.

Films as Director:

1952 *Interim*
1953 *Unglassed Windows Cast a Terrible Reflection*; *The Boy and the Sea*
1954 *Desistfilm*; *The Extraordinary Child*; *The Way to Shadow Garden*
1955 *In Between*; *Reflections on Black*; *The Wonder Ring* (with Joseph Cornell); "Tower House" (photographed for Joseph Cornell under working titles "Bolts of Melody" and "Portrait of Julie," finally became Cornell's *Centuries of June*); *Untitled Film of Geoffrey Holder's Wedding* (collaboration with Larry Jordan)
1956 *Zone Moment*; *Flesh of Morning*; *Nightcats*
1957 *Daybreak and Whiteye*; *Loving*; *Martin Missil Quarterly Reports* (commercial work)
1958 *Anticipation of the Night*; "Opening" for *G.E. Television Theatre* (commercial work)
1959 *Wedlock House: An Intercourse*; *Window Water Baby Moving*; *Cat's Cradle*; *Sirius Remembered*; *Untitled Film on Pittsburgh* (commercial work)
1960 *The Dead*
1961 *Thigh Line Lyre Triangular*; *Films by Stan Brakhage: An Avant-Garde Home Movie*; *The Colorado Legend and the Ballad of the Colorado Ute* (commercial work)
1962 *Blue Moses*; *Silent Sound Sense Stars Subotnick and Sender*; *Mr. Tomkins Inside Himself* (commercial work)
1963/5 Film on Mt. Rushmore, photographed for Charles Nauman's Part II film on Korczak Ziolkowski; film on Chief Sitting Bull
1963 *Oh Life—A Woe Story—The A Test News*; "Meat Jewel" (incorporated into *Dog Star Man: Part II*); *Mothlight*
1964 *Dog Star Man* (in prelude and four parts dated as follows: Prelude, 1962; Part I, 1963; Part II, 1964; Part III, 1964; Part IV, 1964)
1965 *The Art of Vision* (derived from *Dog Star Man*); *Three Films* (includes *Blue White*; *Blood's Tone*; *Vein*); *Fire of Waters*; *Pasht*; *Two: Creeley/McClure* (also incorporated in *Fifteen Song Traits*); *Black Vision*
1968 *Lovemaking*; *The Horseman, The Woman and The Moth*
1969 *Songs* (dated as follows: *Songs 1* to *8,* 1964; *Songs 9* to *14,* 1965; *15 Song Traits,* 1965; *Songs 16* to *22,* 1965; *23rd Psalm Branch: Part I,* 1966, and *Part II* and *Coda,* 1967; *Songs 24* and *25,* 1967; *Song 26,* 1968; *My Mountain Song 27,* 1968; *Song 27 (Part II) Rivers,* 1969; *Songs 28* and *29,* 1969; *American 30's Song,* 1969; *Window Suite of Children's Songs,* 1969)
1970 *Scenes from under Childhood* (dated as follows: *Section No. 1,* 1967; *Section No. 2,* 1969; *Section No. 3,* 1969; *Section No. 4,* 1970); *The Weir-Falcon Saga*; *The Machine of Eden*; *The Animals of Eden and After*
1971 *The Pittsburgh Documents* (*Eyes*; *Deus Ex*; *The Act of Seeing with One's Own Eyes*; *Foxfire Childwatch*; *Angels' Door*; *Western History*; *The Trip to Door*; *The Peaceable Kingdom*
1972 *Eye Myth* (begun in 1968 as sketch for *The Horseman, The Woman and The Moth*) (16mm version); *Sexual Meditations* (titled and dated as follows: *Sexual Meditation No. 1: Motel,* 1970; *Sexual Meditation: Room with View,* 1971; *Sexual Meditation: Faun's Room Yale,* 1972; *Sexual Meditation: Office Suite,* 1972; *Sexual Meditation: Open Field,* 1972; *Sexual Meditation: Hotel,* 1972); *The Process*; *The Riddle of Lumen*; *The Shores of Phos: A Fable*; *The Presence*; *The Wold Shadow*
1973 *Gift*; *Sincerity*; *The Women*
1974 *Skein*; *Aquarien*; *Hymn to Her*; *Star Garden*; *Flight*; *Dominion*; *he was born, he suffered, he died*; *Clancy*; *The Text of Light*; *The Stars Are Beautiful*; *Sol*
1975 *Sincerity II*; *Short Films: 1975* (divided into Parts I-X)
1976 *Gadflies*; *Sketches*; *Airs*; *Window*; *Trio*; *Desert*; *Rembrandt, Etc. and Jane*; *Short Films: 1976*; *Tragoedia*; *Highs*; *The Dream, NYC, The Return, The Flower*; *Absence*
1977 *Soldiers and Other Cosmic Objects*; *The Governor*; *The Domain of the Moment*
1978 *Sincerity III*; *Nightmare Series*; *Duplicity*; *Duplicity II*; *Purity and After*; *Centre*; *Bird*; *Thot Fal'n*; *Burial Path*; *Sluice*
1979 *Creation*
1980 *Sincerity IV*; *Sincerity V*; *Duplicity III*; *Salome*; *Other*; *Made Manifest*; *Aftermath*; *Murder Psalm*
1981 *Eye Myth* (original 35mm version); *Roman Numeral Series* (dated and titled as follows: *I* and *II,* 1979; *III, IV, V, VI, VII,* 1980; *VIII* and *IX,* 1981); *Nodes*; *RR*; *The Garden of Earthly Delights*; *Hell Spit Flexion*
1982 *Arabics* (dated and titled as follows: *1, 2* and *3,* 1980; *4, 5, 6, 7, 8, 9, 0 + 10, 11, 12, 13,* 1981; *14, 15, 16, 17, 18, 19,* 1982); *Unconscious London Strata*
1984 *Egyptian Series*; *Tortured Dust*

1986 *Jane*; *Caswallan Trilogy* (*The Aerodyne*; *Dance Shadows by Danielle Helander*; *Fireloop*); *The Loop*; *Nightmusic*; *Confession*
1987 *FaustFilm: An Opera*; *Loud Visual Noises*; *The Dante Quartet*; *Kindering*
1988 *Faust's Other: An Idyll*; *Faust 3: Candida Albacore*; *Matins*; *I ... Dreaming*; *Marilyn's Window*; *Rage Net*
1989 *Faust 4*; *Visions in Meditation No. 1*; *Babylon Series*
1990 *Babylon Series No. 2*; *City Streaming*; *The Thatch of Night*; *Glaze of Cathexis*; *Visions in Meditation No. 2*; *Passage Through: A Ritual*; *Vision of the Fire Tree*
1991 *Delicacies of Molten Horror Synapse*; *Christ Mass Sex Dance*; *Agnus Dei Kinder Synapse*; *A Child's Garden and the Serious Sea*
1992 *Crack Gloss Eulogy*; *Interpolations I-V*; *For Marilyn*; *Boulder Blues and Pearls and*
1993 *Blossom Gift Favor*; *Autumnal*; *The Harrowing*; *Tryst Haunt*; *Three Homerics*; *Stellar*; *Study in Color and Black and White*; *Ephemeral Solidity*
1994 *Elementary Phrases* (in collaboration with Phil Solomon); *Black Ice*; *First Hymn to the Night-Novalis*; *Naughts*; *Chartres Series*; *Paranoia Corridor*; *In Consideration of Pompeii*; *The Mammals of Victoria*; *I Take These Truths*; *We Hold These*
1994/95 *Trilogy* (comprises *I Take These Truths*; *We Hold These*; both 1994, and *I....*; 1995)
1995 *Cannot Exist*; *Cannot Not Exist*; *Earthen Aerie*; *Spring Cycle*; *I....*

Note: Beginning 1978, many films first issued in 8mm or Super-8mm reissued in 16mm.

Other Films:

1969 *Nuptiae* (Broughton) (ph)

Publications

By BRAKHAGE: books—

Metaphors on Vision, New York, 1963.
A Motion Picture Giving and Taking Book, West Newbury, Massachusetts, 1971.
The Brakhage Lectures, Chicago, 1972.
Stan Brakhage, Ed Emshwiller, edited by Rochelle Reed, Washington, D.C., 1973.
Seen, San Francisco, 1975.
Film Biographies, Berkeley, California, 1977.
Brakhage Scrapbook: Collected Writings 1964-1980, edited by Robert A. Haller, New York, 1982.
I ... Sleeping (Being a Dream Journal and Parenthetical Explication), New York, 1989.
Film at Wit's End—Eight Avant-Garde Filmmakers, New York, 1989.

By BRAKHAGE: articles—

"The Silent Sound Sense," in *Film Culture* (New York), Summer 1960.
"Province-and-Providential Letters," in *Film Culture* (New York), Spring 1962.
"Excerpts from Letters," in *Film Culture* (New York), Summer 1962.
"Sound and Cinema" (exchange of letters with James Tenney and Gregory Markopoulos), in *Film Culture* (New York), no. 29, 1963.
"Metaphors on Vision," in *Film Culture* (New York), no. 30, 1963.
Interview with P. Adams Sitney, in *Film Culture* (New York), Fall 1963.
"Letter to Gregory Markopoulos," in *Film Culture* (New York), Winter 1963/64.
"Letter from Brakhage: On Splicing," in *Film Culture* (New York), Winter 1964/65.
"Letter to Yves Kovacs," in *Yale Literary Magazine* (New Haven), March 1965.
"Stan Brakhage Letters," in *Film Culture* (New York), Spring 1966.
"A Moving Picture Giving and Taking Book," in *Film Culture* (New York), Summer 1966.
"On Dance and Film," in *Dance Perspectives,* Summer 1967.
"Letter to Jonas Mekas, September 1967," in *Filmmakers Newsletter* (Ward Hill, Massachusetts), December 1967.
"Transcription of Some Remarks...," in *Take One* (Montreal), September/October 1970.
"In Defense of the Amateur Filmmaker," in *Filmmakers Newsletter* (Ward Hill, Massachusetts), Summer 1971.
"Stan and Jane Brakhage Talking," with Hollis Frampton, in *Artforum* (New York), January 1973.
"On Filming Light," with Forrest Williams, in *The Structurist* (Saskatoon), no. 13/14, 1973-74.
Various writings, in *Film Culture* (New York), nos. 67-69, 1979.
"The Swiftly Perceived Blur," in *Rolling Stock* (Boulder, Colorado), Summer 1980.
"Stan Brakhage's Last Interview," by Marilynne Mason, in *Northern Lights: Studies in Creativity,* edited by Stanley Scott, Presque Isle, Maine, 1983.
"Brakhage at the Ninth Telluride," in *Rolling Stock,* no. 4, 1983.
"Brakhage Pans Telluride Gold," in *Rolling Stock,* no. 6, 1983.
"Telluride Zinc," in *Rolling Stock,* no. 8, 1984.
"Telluride Takes," in *Rolling Stock,* no. 11, 1986.
"Brakhage Observes Telluride the Thirteenth," in *Rolling Stock,* no. 12, 1986.
"Stan Brakhage at the Millennium, November 4, 1977," in *Millennium Film Journal,* Fall/Winter 1986/87.
"James Tenney," in *Perspectives on New Music,* vol. 25, 1987.
"Some Words on the North," in *American Book Review,* May/June 1988.
"Time ... on dit," series of seventeen articles in *Musicworks: The Canadian Journal of Sound Exploration,* vols. 45, 47-50, 52-63, Winter 1990-Fall 1995.
"Stan Brakhage Reviews the Fifteenth Telluride Film Festival," in *Rolling Stock* (Boulder, Colorado), Winter 1989.
"Gertrude Stein: Meditative Literature and Film," in *Millennium Film Journal,* Summer 1991.
"Screen Test," an interview with Jerry White, in *Emergency House,* Spring 1992.
"Manifesto," in *Cinematheque,* Spring 1993.
"All That Is Is Light: Brakhage at Sixty," an interview with Suranjan Ganguly, in *Sight and Sound,* October 1993.
"Stan Brakhage—The Sixtieth Birthday Interview," by Suranjan Ganguly, in *Film Culture,* Summer 1994.
"Stan Brakhage on Marie Menken," in *Film Culture,* Summer 1994.

On BRAKHAGE: books—

Clark, Dan, *Brakhage,* New York, 1966.
Richie, Donald, *Stan Brakhage—A Retrospective,* New York, 1970.
Mekas, Jonas, *Movie Journal, The Rise of a New American Cinema, 1959-1971,* New York, 1972.
Camper, Fred, *Stan Brakhage,* Los Angeles, 1976.
Hanhardt, John, and others, *A History of the American Avant-Garde Cinema,* New York, 1976.
Nesthus, Marie, *Stan Brakhage,* Minneapolis/St. Paul, 1979.
Sitney, P. Adams, *Visionary Film,* New York, 1979.
Camper, Fred, *By Brakhage: Three Decades of Personal Cinema* (catalogue), New York, 1981.

Barrett, Gerald R., and Wendy Brabner, *Stan Brakhage: A Guide to References and Resources,* Boston, 1983.
McBride, Joseph, editor, *Filmmakers on Filmmakers 2,* Los Angeles, 1983.
Keller, Marjorie, *The Untutored Eye: Childhood in the Films of Cocteau, Cornell and Brakhage,* Cranbury, New Jersey, 1986.
Elder, R. Bruce, *The Body in Film,* Toronto, Ontario, 1989.
James, David, E., *Allegories of Cinema: American Film in the Sixties,* Princeton, New Jersey, 1989.
Mellencamp, Patricia, *Indiscretions: Avant-Garde Film Video and Feminism,* Bloomington, Indiana, 1990.
Sitney, P. Adams, *Modernist Montage: The Obscurity of Vision in Cinema and Literature,* New York, 1990.
Wees, William, *Light Moving in Time: Studies in the Visual Aesthetics of Avant-Garde Film,* Berkeley, 1992.
MacDonald, Scott, *Film: Motion Studies,* London, 1993.
Bordwell, David, and Kristin Thompson, *Film Art: An Introduction,* New York, 1993.
Peterson, James, *Dreams of Chaos, Visions of Order: Understanding the American Avant-Garde Cinema,* Detroit, 1994.

On BRAKHAGE: articles—

Tyler, Parker, "Stan Brakhage," in *Film Culture* (New York), no. 18, 1958.
"Brakhage Issue" of *Filmwise,* no. 1, 1961.
Callenbach, Ernest, "Films of Stan Brakhage," in *Film Quarterly* (Berkeley), Spring 1961.
Sitney, P. Adams, "*Anticipation of the Night* and *Prelude,*" in *Film Culture* (New York), no. 26, 1962.
Brakhage, Jane, "The Birth Film," in *Film Culture* (New York), Winter 1963/64.
Hill, Jerome, "Brakhage and Rilke," in *Film Culture* (New York), no. 37, 1965.
Hill, Jerome, and Guy Davenport, "Two Essays on Brakhage and His Songs," in *Film Culture* (New York), Spring 1966.
Kroll, K. "Up from the Underground," in *Newsweek* (New York), 13 February 1967.
Camper, Fred, "*The Art of Vision,* a Film by Stan Brakhage," and "*23rd Psalm Branch (Song XXIII),* a Film by Stan Brakhage," in *Film Culture* (New York), Autumn 1967.
Camper, Fred, "*My Mtn. Song 27,*" in *Film Culture* (New York), Summer 1969.
Creeley, Robert, "Mehr Light...," in *Film Culture* (New York), Summer 1969.
Sitney, P. Adams, "Avant Garde Film," in *Afterimage* (Rochester), Autumn 1970.
Hill, Jerome, "Brakhage's Eyes," in *Film Culture* (New York), Spring 1971.
Camper, Fred, "*Sexual Meditation No.1: Motel,* a Film by Stan Brakhage," and P. Adams Sitney, "The Idea of Morphology," in *Film Culture* (New York), Spring 1972.
"Brakhage Issue" of *Artforum* (New York), January 1973.
Levoff, Daniel, "Brakhage's *The Act of Seeing with One's Own Eyes,*" in *Film Culture* (New York), Spring 1973.
Barr, William, "Brakhage: Artistic Development in Two Childbirth Films," in *Film Quarterly* (Berkeley), Spring 1976.
Kelman, Ken, "Animal Cinema," in *Film Culture* (New York), nos. 63-64, 1977.
Nesthus, Marie, "The Influence of Olivier Messiaen on the Visual Art of Stan Brakhage in *Scenes from under Childhood,* Part I," in *Film Culture* (New York), nos. 63-64, 1977.
Sitney, P. Adams, "Autobiography in Avant-Garde Film," in *Millenium* (New York), Winter 1977/78.
Cohen, Phoebe, "Brakhage's *Sincerity III,*" in *Millenium Film Journal* (New York), nos. 4-5, 1979.
Jenkins, Bruce, and Noel Carroll, "*Text of Light,*" in *Film Culture* (New York), nos. 67-69, 1979.
Sharrett, Christopher, "Brakhage's Dreamscape," in *Millenium Film Journal* (New York), Spring 1980.
Cohen, Phoebe, "Brakhage's *I, II, III,*" in *Millenium Film Journal* (New York), nos. 7-9, 1980/81.
Hoberman, J., "Duplicitously Ours: Brakhage in New York," in *Village Voice* (New York), 8 April 1981.
James, D., "The Filmmaker as Romantic Poet: Brakhage and Olson," in *Film Quarterly* (Los Angeles), Spring 1982.
Sharrett, Christopher, "Brakhage's Scrapbook," in *Millenium* (New York), Fall/Winter 1984/85.
"Brakhage Sections" of *Monthly Film Bulletin* (London), February and March 1986.
Sharrett, Christopher, "Brakhage's dreamscape," in *Millenium* (New York), Spring 1986.
Wees, William C., "Words and Images in Stan Brakhage's 23rd Psalm Branch," in *Cinema Journal* (Champaigne, Illinois), Winter 1988.
Camper, Fred, "Stan Brakhage's New Vision," in *Chicago Reader,* 27 January 1989.
Dargis, M., "The Old Garde Advances," in *Village Voice,* 12 March 1991.
Grimes, W., "A Film Maker in the Avant Garde for Forty Years," in *New York Times,* 6 February 1993.
Hoberman, J., "A Blast from the Past: Stan Brakhage's *A Child's Garden and the Serious Sea,*" in *The Village Voice,* 9 February 1993.
Camper, Fred, "A Musical Way of Seeing," in *Chicago Reader,* 16 April 1993.
Arthur, Paul, "Qualities of Light: Stan Brakhage and the Continuing Pursuit of Vision," in *Film Comment,* September/October 1995.
Annett, William, "Fire on the Mountain," in *Independent Film and Video Monthly,* July 1995.
Elder, Bruce, "On Brakhage," in *Stan Brakhage: A Retrospective 1977-1995,* Museum of Modern Art, New York, 1995.

* * *

Stan Brakhage was the last and youngest of the great generation of American avant-garde filmmakers who came to cinema during and soon after the Second World War. Between 1952 and 1995 he has made approximately 250 films, some shorter than a minute long and one more than four hours. Naturally, in this immense *oeuvre* the short films predominate; the majority fall between ten and forty minutes. Until 1964 he completed one or two films a year; the four of 1959 were an exception and signals of a major breakthrough in his art; since then the norm has been closer to five annually. Even Andy Warhol's astonishing fecundity dwarfs in comparison when we consider that his work was largely finished when he photographed a film—for he never edited and rarely even had to assemble or order reels—and that his most intense productivity was limited to a five-year period (1963-1968).

The sheer enormity of Brakhage's filmography encourages some sort of division into periods to facilitate discussion. The first six years—from *Interim* (1952) to *Anticipation of the Night* (1958), his first major work—can be considered Brakhage's apprenticeship to his art. These initial works were predominately psychodramas: often fantasies of suicide motored by sexual frustration and adolescent despair. He employed a version of the bodily camera movement Marie Menken perfected before he ever knew her work; but it was a commission from Joseph Cornell to film New York's Third Avenue E1 before it was torn down that inspired his recognition of the rhythmic and structural potential of vehicular motion (*The Wonder Ring,* 1955).

His marriage to Jane Collom at the end of 1957 coincided with a surge of invention and increased authority from the four films of 1959 (*Wedlock House: An Intercourse, Window Water Baby Moving, Cat's Cradle,* and *Sirius Remembered*)—in which he explored the

Stan Brakhage: *Mothlight*

possibilities of the cinematic crisis-lyric, which he had largely invented himself—to *Dog Star Man* (1961-64) and its four-and-one-half-hour exfoliation, *The Art of Vision* (1965). He abandoned what he had called "drama," a complex term that included the use of actors and staged fantasies, to concentrate on sights he encountered in his routine daily life. Eros and death (but no longer suicide) continued to be his central themes, along with a new preoccupation with childbirth—he filmed the arrival of the three children Jane bore during that period. Animal life (and death) too became the focus of several films, inspired by Jane, a passionate naturalist. During this time of fervor and enthusiasm he completed and published his most important theoretical volume, *Metaphors on Vision* (1964).

Brakhage, the most Emersonian of American filmmakers, struggled to make a virtue of his self-trust and of his dire economic poverty in the next phase of his career (1964-1970). When the theft of his 16mm equipment, from a car in New York City, curtailed the flood of highly original short lyrical films in 1964, he turned to inexpensive 8mm filmmaking and a series of thirty *Songs* (1964-69), until his elaborate editing and printing drove him yet again into serious debt. One solution to these costs was painting on film: *The Horseman, the Woman, and the Moth* (1968). By the end of the 1960s his severe poverty was slightly eased by minuscule production grants and exhausting lecture tours. To the abiding subjects of birth, sex, death, and animals he added a vigorous exploration of cinematic portraiture and an increasing attention to landscapes.

He was living with his wife and now five children in a very small cabin, purchased by his in-laws, high in the Colorado Rockies, when he initiated a large-scale autobiography in 16mm, of which the four-part *Scenes from under Childhood* and the three-part *The Weir-Falcon Saga* were completed by 1970. His project, tentatively called *The Book of the Film,* was to have been, he half-humorously predicted, a twenty-four-hour-long film. Initially he conceived the autobiography as generalized and emblematic: his observations of his young children would provide the visual materials for an allegory of the growth of his mind, as well as stimulate his buried memories.

In the first half of the 1970s oppositional pressures drove his work in two apparently opposite directions: his films became more reflective and subtle on the one hand, and more anxious to make contact with the world. Similarly, in his writings he attempted to reimagine the lives and reevaluate the achievements of the great filmmakers of the past, justifying his liberal elaboration of facts with the analogy of Gertrude Stein's biographical fantasias.

With the help of the Carnegie Institute in Pittsburgh he made three films he thought of as "documentaries," very personal views of a day in a police patrol car, another in a hospital operating theatre, and the most startling, a day at the morgue (*eyes, deux ex, The Act of Seeing with One's Own Eyes,* 1971). A series of *Sexual Meditations* (1970-72) pictured his erotic fantasies when he slept in motels on lecture tours; in making these too he had indirect institutional help: students in the colleges he visited willingly served a nude models. During the same years he made his first personal autobiography: *Sincerity* (reel one, 1973) uses childhood photographs, the environs of Dartmouth College (which he attended for a semester before quitting to make films), and filmed snippets of the making of his first film. He also created a number of "tone poems" which embodied his emerging theory of "moving visual thinking," the cinematic mimesis of elusive cognitive acts.

The harsh irony of this period, from 1970 to 1974, culminating in the completion of his long abstract film, *The Text of Light*—wholly composed of luscious splays of light passing through a crystal ashtray, it was the paradigm of his inward turn at the time—was that institutional support transformed but did not alleviate substantially his marginal economy. He was asked by the Art Institute of Chicago to give courses every spring semester: they paid his travel expenses and a rather high salary for the eight trips—every other week—he made from Colorado. But it added up to less than a poorly paid full-time teaching position. A sputtering trickle of grants and the distribution of his films through the filmmakers cooperatives in New York and San Francisco helped sustain his impressive productivity only with dramatically increasing debts to film laboratories.

The autobiographical series *Sincerity I-V* (1973-1980) and *Duplicity I-III* (1978-1980) dominate his work of the late 1970s. Brakhage had insisted on the aesthetic purity and visual intensification of silence since 1956, experimenting with sound tracks merely four times until a change of stance in the late 1980s. In an extreme and problematic extension of his confidence in the truth of vision, by making *The Governor* (1977), an hour-long silent scrutiny of Colorado Governor Richard Lamm at work and at home, he tried to apply the experience of his Pittsburgh films to "a study of light and power" as an optical examination of politics, personally observed.

Most of his energetic output of films in the 1980s refracted the prolonged crisis culminating in the end of the marriage in which he had been so invested as an artist and polemicist. The key documents representing aspects of that agony would be *Tortured Dust* (1984), a four-part film of sexual tensions surrounding life at home with his two teenage sons; *Confession* (1986), depicting a love affair near the end of his marriage (1987); and the *Faust* series (1987-1989), four autonomous sound films reinterpreting the legend that obsessed Brakhage throughout his career. He had begun the 1980s with two related series of silent "abstract" films—modulations of color and light without identifiable imagery—*The Roman Numeral Series* (1979-1981), nine films "which explore the possibilities of making equivalents of 'moving visual thinking,' that pre-language, pre-'picture' realm of the mind which provides the physical *grounds* for image making (imagination), thus the very substance of the birth of imagery"; and *The Arabic Numeral Series* (1980-1982), nineteen "abstract" films "formed by the intrinsic grammar of the most inner (perhaps pre-natal) structure of thought itself."

The most recent phase of Brakhage's filmmaking spans from 1989, the year he married Marilyn Jull and published *Film at Wit's End,* until 1995. In this 1989 book, his most lucid and coherent since *Metaphors on Vision,* Brakhage offered his analysis of the sensibilities of eight of his contemporaries in the avant-garde cinema. The filmmaker's often repeated tendency to elaborate on an isolated experiment or an idea from an earlier moment of his career, producing much later an extended series of films, makes demarcation of periods frustratingly unclear. Such is the unexpected production of eleven films with sound tracks out of the total of thirty films he made between 1987 and 1992. Although seven of his first twelve films (1952-1957) had sound tracks, only four (*Blue Moses* [1962], *Fire of Waters* [1965], *Scenes from under Childhood: Section No. 1* [1967], and *The Stars Are Beautiful* [1974]) of the some 200 films of the intervening years were not silent. Similarly, painting on film has been one of Brakhage's privileged strategies since 1961, but it did not assume a dominant place in his filmography until the 1980s. Not only does he call upon earlier options from his filmmaking for further exploration, but he measures and questions his development and its modes of consistency by returning to previously fecund themes, locations, and image associations. So the periods tentatively outlined here are traced within a palimpsest of filmic revisions.

—P. Adams Sitney

BRANAGH, Kenneth

Nationality: British. **Born:** Belfast, Northern Ireland, 10 December 1960; family moved to Reading, England, 1969. **Education:** Meadway Comprehensive School, Reading; Royal Academy of Dramatic Art, London, graduated 1982. **Family:** Married actress Emma Thompson, 1989 (separated). **Career:** Actor on the West End stage and on television, beginning 1982; early stage successes included *Another Country,* 1982, and *Francis* (as St. Francis of Assisi), 1984, both plays written by Julian Mitchell; joined the Royal Shakespeare Company, 1983, and at twenty-three became the youngest actor ever to play the title role in Shakespeare's *Henry V*; also appeared in the RSC's *Hamlet* (as Laertes) and *Love's Labour's Lost* (as the King of Navarre), playing the three roles in repertory in Stratford and London, 1984-85; wrote and directed play *Tell Me Honestly,* 1985; left RSC to produce and direct *Romeo and Juliet,* 1986 (in which he also starred); with actor David Parfitt, created the Renaissance Theatre Company, 1987; Renaissance productions in which Branagh played a prominent role included: *Public Enemy* (also written by Branagh); *Twelfth Night* (directed by Branagh; also televised), 1987; *Hamlet* (as Hamlet, directed by Derek Jacobi); *As You Like It* (as Touchstone, directed by Geraldine McEwan); *Much Ado about Nothing* (as Benedick, directed by Judi Dench), 1988; John Osborne's *Look Back in Anger* (as Jimmy Porter, also televised); *King Lear* (as Edgar, also directed); *A Midsummer Night's Dream* (as Peter Quince, also directed), 1989; *Uncle Vanya* (co-directed); and *Coriolanus* (title role), 1992. Returned to the Royal Shakespeare Company to star in *Hamlet* in London and Stratford, 1992-93; television work includes roles in *The Boy in the Bush,* the *Billy Trilogy,* adaptations of Virginia Woolf's *To the Lighthouse,* Ibsen's *Ghosts,* and O'Neill's *Strange Interlude, Fortunes of War* (mini-series), *The Lady's Not for Burning* and *Shadow of a Gunman,* 1982-1995; also narrated television documentary series, *Cinema Europe: The Other Hollywood,* 1995; acted in first film, *High Season,* 1987; formed film production company, Renaissance Films PLC, October 1988; directed first film, *Henry V,* 1989; acted in star-studded Renaissance Theatre Company radio broadcasts (available on CD and cassette) commissioned by the BBC to commemorate Shakespeare's birthday, 1992-94; other radio work includes *Diaries of Samuel Pepys* and Mary Shelley's *Frankenstein.* **Awards:** Bancroft Gold Medal, Royal Academy of Dramatic Art, 1982; Most Promising Newcomer Award, Society of West End Theatres, 1982, for *Another Country*; Best New Director from New York Film Critics Circle, *Evening Standard* Best Film of the Year, Best Film and Technical Achievement Award from British Film Institute, Best Director Award from British Academy of Film and Television Artists (BAFTA), and Best Director Award from

National Board of Review, all 1989-90, all for *Henry V*; Honorary D. Litt., Queen's University, Belfast, 1990. **Agent:** Rick Nicita, Creative Artists Agency, 9830 Wilshire Blvd., Beverly Hills, CA 90212, U.S.A. **Address:** Shepperton Studios, Studio Road, Shepperton, Middlesex, TW17 OQD England.

Films as Director and Actor:

1989 *Henry V* (+ adapt)
1991 *Dead Again*
1992 *Peter's Friends* (+ pr); *Swan Song* (d only)
1993 *Much Ado about Nothing* (+ adapt, co-pr)
1994 *Mary Shelley's Frankenstein* (+ co-pr)
1995 *In the Bleak Midwinter* (*A Midwinter's Tale*) (d only, + sc)
1996 *Hamlet* (+ adapt)

Other Films:

1987 *High Season* (ro); *A Month in the Country* (ro)
1993 *Swing Kids* (ro)
1994 *Gielgud: Scenes from Nine Decades* (doc for British TV) (narrator)
1995 *Othello* (ro, pr); *Anne Frank Remembered* (narrator); *Cinema Europe: The Other Hollywood* (doc series for British TV) (narrator)

Publications

By BRANAGH: books—

Public Enemy (play), 1988.
Beginning (autobiography), Norton, 1989.
Henry V (screen adaptation with introduction), Chatto & Windus, 1989.
Much Ado about Nothing (screen adaptation, introduction, and notes on the making of the film), Norton, 1993.
The Making of Mary Shelley's Frankenstein, 1994.
In the Bleak Midwinter (screenplay with introduction), Nick Hern Books, 1995.

By BRANAGH: articles and interviews—

"Formidable Force," an interview with Michael Billington, in *Interview*, October 1989.
Interview with Joan Lunden, broadcast on *Good Morning, America*, American Broadcasting Company, 23 August 1991 (program number 1355).
"*Hamlet* Takes to the Air," an interview with Heather Neill, in *Times Educational Supplement*, 24 April 1992.
Interview with Charles Gibson, broadcast on *Good Morning, America*, American Broadcasting Company, 21 December 1992 (program number 1701).
"Once More, onto the Screen," an interview with Peter Barnes, in *Los Angeles Times*, 2 May 1993.
"Kenneth Branagh and Emma Thompson Discuss Collaboration *Much Ado about Nothing*," an interview broadcast on *Showbiz Today*, CNN, 11 May 1993 (program number 293).
Interview with Iain Johnstone, in *Times* (London), 15 August 1993.
"Branagh Talks about *Mary Shelley's Frankenstein*," an interview with Charlie Rose, broadcast on the Public Broadcasting System, 26 October 1994 (program number 1234).
"It's a Monster!," an interview with Graham Fuller, in *Interview*, November 1994.
"Branagh Discusses His Life and Career," an interview with Charlie Rose, broadcast on the Public Broadcasting System, 30 December 1994 (program number 1281).
Interview with John Naughton, in *Premiere* (U.K. edition), December 1995.

On BRANAGH: book—

Shuttleworth, Ian, *Ken & Em: A Biography of Kenneth Branagh and Emma Thompson*, St. Martin's, 1995.

On BRANAGH: articles—

Whitebrook, Peter, "Branagh's Bugbear," in *Plays and Players*, March 1985.
Renton, Alex, "Renaissance Man," in *Plays and Players*, July 1987.
Forbes, Jill, review of *Henry V*, in *Sight and Sound*, Autumn 1989.
Nightingale, Benedict, "Henry V Returns as a Monarch for This Era," in *New York Times*, 5 November 1989.
Champlin, Charles, "The Wellesian Success of Citizen Branagh," in *Los Angeles Times*, 9 November 1989.
Fuller, Graham, "Journals: Two Kings—Kenneth," in *Film Comment*, November/December 1989.
Kliman, Bernice, "Branagh's *Henry V*: Allusion and Illusion," in *Shakespeare on Film Newsletter*, December 1989.
Willson, Robert F., Jr., "*Henry V*: Branagh's and Olivier's Choruses," in *Shakespeare on Film Newsletter*, April 1990.
Breight, Curtis, "Branagh and the Prince, or a 'Royal Fellowship of Death,'" in *Critical Quarterly*, Winter 1991.
Donaldson, Peter, "Taking on Shakespeare: Kenneth Branagh's *Henry V*," in *Shakespeare Quarterly*, Spring 1991.
Willson, Robert F., Jr., "War and Reflection on War: The Olivier and Branagh Films of *Henry V*," in *Shakespeare Bulletin*, Summer 1991.
Weber, Bruce, "From Shakespeare to Hollywood," in *New York Times*, 18 August 1991.
Booe, Martin, "Ken Again," in *Premiere*, September 1991.
Rafferty, Terrence, "Showoffs," in *New Yorker*, 9 September 1991.
Feeney, F. X., "Vaulting Ambition," in *American Film*, September/October 1991.
Deats, Sara Munson, "Rabbits and Ducks: Olivier, Branagh, and *Henry V*," in *Literature/Film Quarterly*, vol. 20, no. 4, 1992.
Pursell, Michael, "Playing the Game: Branagh's *Henry V*," in *Literature/Film Quarterly*, vol. 20, no. 4, 1992.
Tatspaugh, Patricia, "Theatrical Influences on Kenneth Branagh's Film: *Henry V*," in *Literature/Film Quarterly*, vol. 20, no. 4, 1992.
Smith, Dinitia, "Much Ado about Branagh," in *New York*, 24 May 1993.
Barton, Anne, "Shakespeare in the Sun," in *New York Review of Books*, 27 May 1993.
Sharman, Leslie F., review of *Much Ado about Nothing*, in *Sight and Sound*, September 1993.
Light, Allison, "The Importance of Being Ordinary," in *Sight and Sound*, September 1993.
Ryan, Richard, "Much Ado about Branagh," in *Commentary*, October 1993.
Lane, Robert, "When Blood Is Their Argument: Class, Character, and Historymaking in Shakespeare's and Branagh's *Henry V*," in *ELH*, Spring 1994.
Landy, Marcia, and Lucy Fisher, "Dead Again or Alive Again: Postmodern or Postmortem?," in *Cinema Journal*, Summer 1994.
Shaw, William P., "Textual Ambiguities and Cinematic Certainties in *Henry V*," in *Literature/Film Quarterly*, vol. 22, no. 2, 1994.
Parker, Daniel, Mark Kermode, and Pat Kirkham, "Making *Frankenstein* and the Monster," in *Sight and Sound*, November 1994.
Thomson, David, "Really a Part of Me," in *Film Comment*, January/February 1995.

Gritten, David, "Kenneth Branagh on the Rebound," in *Los Angeles Times,* 3 June 1995.

* * *

It is impossible to consider Kenneth Branagh's meteoric rise as a film director and actor without taking into account the career in the British theatre which shaped it—and to which Branagh still periodically returns. Classically trained at the Royal Academy of Dramatic Art in London, where he was awarded the prestigious Bancroft Gold Medal as outstanding student of the year, Branagh completed his course of study in 1982, then moved rapidly into a series of attention-getting roles on the West End and on television. His early association with Shakespeare's plays began with an invitation to join the Royal Shakespeare Company at the age of twenty-three, and he became the youngest actor ever to perform the title role in an RSC production of *Henry V.* Important parts in other Shakespeare productions in that 1984-85 season contributed to Branagh's emergence as a stage director soon thereafter.

He left the RSC to direct an independent production of *Romeo and Juliet* (in which he also starred) and, primarily, to form (with actor David Parfitt) his own production group, which became a reality in 1987 as the Renaissance Theatre Company. Renaissance acquired a high profile in rapid time, with Branagh and other major British actors directing a variety of productions in which they also appeared, in London and on national and international tours. *Hamlet* (with Branagh in the title role, directed by Derek Jacobi)—which, like *Henry V,* would become a play with which Branagh would be permanently linked—and *Twelfth Night* (directed by Branagh and later remounted for television) were among Renaissance's most successful late-1980s productions. The company's success enabled Branagh to make his first film, now financed through the production company he called Renaissance Films PLC.

Most actors who turn to film directing do so in mid-career, ordinarily after they have obtained considerable experience in front of the camera. Even Laurence Olivier, whose professional path Branagh's career so frequently appears to emulate, did not direct his first film until he was in his late thirties, and by then, after twenty-two screen appearances, he was a major star. In 1989, when Branagh directed his first film at the age of twenty-nine, his scant movie experience included just two feature films. By that time, however, he had achieved remarkable success as an actor, director, and producer on the British stage and in a variety of important television roles. And, as it happened, he had already written several plays of his own, one of them (*Tell Me Honestly*) produced by the RSC, another (*Public Enemy*) produced to launch the first Renaissance season. In this unusual, multitalented respect, Branagh's formative years most resemble the early career of Orson Welles—who made *Citizen Kane,* his first film, when he was twenty-six, after establishing a formidable theatre and radio presence in the late 1930s. Welles had the Mercury Theatre as his special training ground; Branagh had the Renaissance.

It is surely no accident, however, that the first film Branagh directed (and adapted and starred in) was the same first film which Laurence Olivier directed (and adapted and starred in): *Henry V,* the final history play in Shakespeare's tetralogy on kingship, which begins with *Richard II* and also includes *King Henry IV,* Parts One and Two. The comparisons and contrasts between the two films are genuinely striking, reflective of the periods in which they were made and of the imposing talents of the men who made them.

Olivier, responding to Winston Churchill's plea for a film to rally Britain in the final days of World War II, creates a ringingly, unambiguously heroic Henry for the ages, an idealized monarch who leads England to victory against France with commanding force tempered by humanity. Olivier's *Henry V* ensures that English history is represented as comedy. The excision of lines spoken by the Chorus in the play's final scene makes the romantic pairing of Henry and Katherine appear deceptively permanent, thereby assuring the wartime spectator of a stable English future in fact contradicted by Shakespeare's text and by English history. This interpretation is visually reinforced: Olivier's *Henry V* is artfully shot to highlight a deliberate sense of artificial *cinema* space; a Disneyesque mise-en-scene, with its heightened technicolored landscapes, illustrates a fairy-tale universe in which battles are won with little serious injury.

Olivier's and Branagh's versions of *Henry V* have virtually identical running times (136 and 138 minutes, respectively). Like Olivier's version, Branagh's attempts to create a reflexive illusion of theatre itself in the film's opening section, though Branagh alters and reduces Olivier's reconstruction of Shakespeare's Globe Theatre to insinuations of a movie sound stage. Like Olivier's version, Branagh's includes explicit references to Henry's earlier relationship with Falstaff in the two *Henry IV* plays. And, like Olivier's actors, Branagh's dazzling cast (many of them associated with Renaissance) includes some of the finest Shakespearean verse speakers available.

In virtually every other respect, Branagh's film diverges from Olivier's. His *Henry V* represents history as tragedy. Significant passages omitted by Olivier, because they reflect flaws in Henry's character or guilt at his father's usurpation of the crown from Richard II, are restored by Branagh. Although he properly retains the heroic elements required by such set speeches as the Saint Crispian's Day call to arms, his portrayal of the king emphasizes the dark and complex elements within Henry's character. Unlike Olivier's version, Branagh's film includes the conspiracy against Henry. This portion of the film is dimly lit, heavily shadowed. Henry behaves in Machiavellian fashion and appears unsympathetic in his own conspiratorial behavior. In text restored to the Harfleur sequence, Henry looks and sounds downright pathological. War scenes feature death marches; soldiers die in mud and muck. Quick cuts, slow-motion photography, extended tracking shots, and unusual framing perspectives are employed to heighten the inescapable anti-war ideology vital to Branagh's approach. A few more liberties are taken with the text than in Olivier's version, including the placement of the king at the hanging of Bardolph. The inclusion of liturgical music in Patrick Doyle's wonderfully evocative score contributes movingly to the film's power. Most notable of all, perhaps, Branagh restores the lines Olivier cut from the Chorus's speech which conclude the play on such a dark note. Henry V may, indeed, have created the world's "best garden," but the peaceful idyll he achieved was short-lived once his infant son inherited the throne: "Henry the Sixth, in infant bands crowned King/Of France and England, did this King succeed,/Whose state so many had the managing/That they lost France, and made his England bleed."

By any measure, Branagh's *Henry V* is a stunning film. That it succeeded so powerfully in duplicating, perhaps surpassing, Olivier's achievement is all the more striking in the context of its director's youthful audacity. Branagh's other Shakespeare films include the superb *Much Ado about Nothing, Hamlet* (scheduled for release in late 1996 or early 1997), and *Othello* (with Branagh cast as a vividly slimy Iago), which Branagh unfortunately did not direct. *Othello* is visually tame, the Shakespeare text excessively cut.

But *Much Ado about Nothing* proved that Branagh's success with *Henry V* was no fluke. Co-starring Emma Thompson as Beatrice opposite Branagh's Benedick, *Much Ado* certified his nimble approach in making Shakespeare accessible and *entertaining,* while preserving much of the original poetry and literacy. Branagh's screen adaptations of *Much Ado* and *Hamlet* also confirm what had become strikingly evident in his leadership of the Renaissance Theatre Company: He is a keenly savvy—some might say cynically savvy—marketer of his projects. By casting such actors as Keanu Reeves, Denzel Washington, and Robert Sean Leonard alongside Branagh, Thompson, and other British actors in *Much Ado,* and by casting Robin Williams, Jack Lemmon, Gerard Depardieu, and Billy Crystal alongside Branagh, Derek

Kenneth Branagh directing *Mary Shelley's Frankenstein*

Jacobi, John Gielgud, and Julie Christie in *Hamlet,* Branagh strengthens his films' potential international markets, particularly in the United States. Such patterns of casting do not always work, but they do help to attract financing and have influenced recent attempts by others to adapt Shakespeare to the screen.

Although the text of *Much Ado about Nothing* has been severely pruned by Branagh, like his *Henry V,* it emerges on screen as a highly intelligent, *clearly told* story. Filmed on location in Tuscany, *Much Ado* is visually enchanting, as vibrantly bright and sensually warm as *Henry V* is consciously dark and (until the wooing scene) cold. Like so much of his film work, Branagh's reading of *Much Ado* derives a great deal from his performance (also opposite Emma Thompson) in Renaissance's stage production of the play, directed by Judi Dench in 1988. Branagh has written of the potentially filmic images that haunted him during performances of that production in his introduction to the published screenplay: "One night during Balthasar's song 'Sigh No More, Ladies,' the title sequence of this film played over and over in my mind; heat, haze and dust, grapes and horseflesh, and a nod to *The Magnificent Seven.* The men's sexy arrival, the atmosphere of rural Messina, the vigour and sensuality of the women, possessed me in the weeks, months, and years that followed."

"Emotional volatility," Branagh writes in this essay, was the key to the Beatrice-Benedick relationship. But, most especially—in *Much Ado* as in virtually all Renaissance stage and screen productions—the rehearsal process depended on a genuine desire to eliminate "artificial Shakespeare voices" in favor of acting "naturalness" which would retain the poetry while conveying the "realistic, conversational tone" present in much of the play's original dialogue. The witty battle of the sexes, so often the essence of comedy, is splendidly articulated here in the Branagh-Thompson dueling lovers. Like *Henry V, Much Ado* proves in both visual and aural terms that, even when Branagh cuts Shakespeare's text perhaps more than he should, he knows *exactly* how and why he is doing it.

Among Branagh's non-Shakespearean films, *Dead Again* deserves special mention. A film in which Branagh and Emma Thompson both play dual roles, it reveals Branagh's knowledge of other films, filmmakers, and genres—and his considerable versatility as both actor and director. *Dead Again* employs numerous conventions of film noir, including the periodic insertion of a 1940s plot-line, shot in black and white, into the film's main story, which is photographed in color. Numerous references to specific films (including *Citizen Kane, Psycho, Vertigo,* and noir detective pictures) periodically appear. (*Dead Again* even makes droll reference to one of its featured actor's early television successes: Derek Jacobi's *I, Claudius* series.) The film's detective hero, Mike Church, displays Branagh in James Cagney mode. The screenplay and performances are extremely witty, by turns frightening the spectator into total identification or saturating him with over-the-top red herrings that become self-reflexively and genuinely funny. Robin Williams's uncredited appearance as a psychiatrist is among the film's cleverest surprises.

Peter's Friends and *In the Bleak Midwinter* are modest entertainments, partially autobiographical, it would appear, particularly *In the*

Bleak Midwinter (released in the United States as *A Midwinter's Tale*). Here, Branagh affectionately satirizes a group of actors attempting to mount a production of *Hamlet,* and the film appeals especially to admirers of British theatre. It should be noted, particularly in anticipation of Branagh's *Hamlet* movie, that he returned to the RSC to play the title role in a magnificent, sold-out production of that play (directed by Adrian Noble) during the 1992-93 season. In numerous ways, *Hamlet* is likely to be the Shakespeare play with which Branagh (who also directed the all-star BBC radio version) remains most closely identified.

Mary Shelley's Frankenstein is as "big" a Branagh film as *Peter's Friends* and *In the Bleak Midwinter* are small ones. Produced by Francis Ford Coppola and costing forty-four million dollars, the film stars Branagh (who also directed) as Victor Frankenstein and Robert De Niro as the tormented creature. It contains numerous imaginative pleasures, but its overblown representation of an implicitly overblown story brought general critical wrath upon Branagh's head at the time of its release. It has became a rare example of a Branagh film that (to date) is a commercial failure.

The careers of Kenneth Branagh and Emma Thompson, as frequent co-stars and a prominent acting couple, have attracted considerable publicity, especially since their marriage in 1989 and separation in 1995. (Their relationship has invited frequent comparison to the one between Laurence Olivier and Vivien Leigh, who eventually divorced.) Each has always made films without the other; and Thompson has won Oscars for Best Actress in *Howards End* and for Best Screenplay Adaptation for Jane Austen's *Sense and Sensibility.* Nevertheless, some of the most magical moments in Branagh's films feature the two of them together (*Henry V, Peter's Friends, Dead Again, Much Ado about Nothing*).

—Mark W. Estrin

BRESSON, Robert

Nationality: French. **Born:** Bromont-Lamothe (Puy-de-Dome), France, 25 September 1907. **Education:** Lycée Lakanal à Sceaux, Paris. **Family:** Married 1) Leidia van der Zee, 1926 (deceased); 2) Myline van der Mersch. **Career:** Attempted career as painter, to 1933; directed first film, *Affaires publiques,* 1934; German prisoner of war, 1940-41; directed first major film, *Les Anges du péché,* 1943; elected President d'honneur de la Societé des realisateurs de films, 1968. **Awards:** International Prize, Venice Film Festival, for *Journal d'un curé campagne,* 1951; Best Director Award, Cannes Festival, for *Un Condamné a mort s'est échappé,* 1957; Special Jury Prize, Cannes Festival, for *Procès de Jeanne d'Arc,* 1962; Ours d'Argent, Berlin, for *Le Diable probablement,* 1977; Grand Prix national des Arts et des Lettres (Cinéma), France, 1978; Grand Prize, Cannes Festival, for *L'Argent,* 1984; National Order of Merit, Commandeur of Arts and Letters of the Légion d'honneur; Lion d'Or, Venice, 1989; Felix Européen, Berlin, 1993. **Address:** 49 Quai de Bourbon, 75004 Paris, France.

Films as Director:

1934 *Affaires publiques* (+ sc)
1943 *Les Anges du péché* (*Angels of the Streets*) (+ sc)
1945 ***Les Dames du Bois de Boulogne*** (*The Ladies of the Bois de Boulogne*) (+ sc)
1950 ***Journal d'un curé de campagne*** (*Diary of a Country Priest*) (+ sc)
1956 ***Un Condamné a mort s'est échappé*** (*Le Vent souffle où il veut; A Condemned Man Escapes*) (+ sc)
1959 ***Pickpocket*** (+ sc)
1962 *Procès de Jeanne d'Arc* (*The Trial of Joan of Arc*) (+ sc)
1966 *Au hasard Balthazar* (*Balthazar*) (+ sc)
1967 *Mouchette* (+ sc)
1969 *Une Femme douce* (+ sc)
1971 *Quatre Nuits d'un rêveur* (*Four Nights of a Dreamer*) (+ sc)
1974 *Lancelot du Luc* (*Le Graal; Lancelot of the Lake*) (+ sc)
1977 *Le Diable probablement* (+ sc)
1983 *L'Argent* (+ sc)

Other Films:

1933 *C'était un musicien* (Zelnick and Gleize) (dialogue)
1936 *Les Jumeaux de Brighton* (Heymann) (co-sc); *Courrier Sud* (Billon) (co-adaptation)

Publications

By BRESSON: book—

Notes sur le cinématographe, Paris, 1975; as *Notes on the Cinematography,* New York, 1977, and London, 1978.

By BRESSON: articles—

"Bresson on Location: Interview," with Jean Douchet, in *Sequence* (London), no. 13, 1951.
Interview with Ian Cameron, in *Movie* (London), February 1963.
Interview with Jean-Luc Godard and M. Delahaye, in *Cahiers du Cinema in English* (New York), February 1967.
"Four Nights of a Dreamer," interview with Carlos Clarens, in *Sight and Sound* (London), Winter 1971/72.
"*Quatre Nuits d'un rêveur,*" interview with Claude Beylie, in *Ecran* (Paris), April 1972.
"*Lancelot du Lac,*" in *Avant-Scène du Cinéma* (Paris), February 1975.
Interview, in *Sight and Sound* (London), Winter 1976/77.
Interview with J. Fieschi, in *Cinématographe* (Paris), July/August 1977.
"Robert Bresson, Possibly," interview with Paul Schrader, in *Film Comment* (New York), September/October 1977.
"The Poetry of Precision," interview with Michel Ciment, in *American Film* (Washington, D.C.), October 1983.
"Bresson et lumiere," interview with David Thompson, in *Time Out* (London), 2 September 1987.

On BRESSON: books—

Sarris, Andrew, editor, *The Film,* Indianapolis, Indiana, 1968.
The Films of Robert Bresson, by five reviewers, New York, 1969.
Armes, Roy, *French Cinema Since 1946, Vol. 1,* New York, 1970.
Cameron, Ian, *The Films of Robert Bresson,* London, 1970.
Bazin, André, and others, *La Politique des auteurs: Entretiens avec Jean Renoir etc,* Paris, 1972; revised edition, 1989.
Schrader, Paul, *Transcendental Style on Film: Ozu, Bresson, Dreyer,* Los Angeles, 1972.
Sloan, Jane, *Robert Bresson: A Guide to References and Resources,* Boston, 1983.
Esteve, Michel, *La Passion du cinématographe,* Paris, 1985.
Hanlon, Lindley, *Fragments: Bresson's Film Style,* Cranbury, New Jersey, 1986.
Semolve Robert Bresson, Flemmarion, 1993.

On BRESSON: articles—

Lambert, Gavin, "Notes on Robert Bresson," in *Sight and Sound* (London), Summer 1953.
Monod, Roland, "Working with Bresson," in *Sight and Sound* (London), Summer 1957.
Gow, Gordon, "The Quest for Realism," in *Films and Filming* (London), December 1957.
Baxter, Brian, "Robert Bresson," in *Film* (London), September/October 1958.
Roud, Richard, "The Early Work of Robert Bresson," in *Film Culture* (New York), no. 20, 1959.
Ford, Charles, "Robert Bresson," in *Films in Review* (New York), February 1959.
Green, Marjorie, "Robert Bresson," in *Film Quarterly* (Berkeley), Spring 1960.
Roud, Richard, "French Outsider with the Inside Look," in *Films and Filming* (London), April 1960.
Sontag, Susan, "Spiritual Style in the Films of Robert Bresson," in *Seventh Art* (New York), Summer 1964.
Sarris, Andrew, "Robert Bresson," in *Interviews with Film Directors*, New York, 1967.
Skoller, S. Donald, "Praxis as a Cinematic Principle in the Films of Robert Bresson," in *Cinema Journal* (Evanston, Illinois), Fall 1969.
Rhode, Eric, "Dostoevsky and Bresson," in *Sight and Sound* (London), Spring 1970.
Zeman, Marvin, "The Suicide of Robert Bresson," in *Cinema* (Los Angeles), Spring 1971.
Prokosch, M., "Bresson's Stylistics Revisited," in *Film Quarterly* (Berkeley), vol. 15, no. 1, 1972.
Samuels, Charles, "Robert Bresson," in *Encountering Directors*, New York, 1972.
Polhemus, H.M., "Matter and Spirit in the Films of Robert Bresson," in *Film Heritage* (Dayton, Ohio), Spring 1974.
Westerbeck, Jr., Colin, "Robert Bresson's Austere Vision," in *Artforum* (New York), November 1976.
Nogueira, R., "Burel and Bresson," in *Sight and Sound* (London), Winter 1976/77.
Dempsey, M., "Despair Abounding: The Recent Films of Robert Bresson," in *Film Quarterly* (Los Angeles), Fall 1980.
Hourigan, J., "On Two Deaths and Three Births: The Cinematography of Robert Bresson," in *Stills* (London), Autumn 1981.
Latille Dactec, M., "Bresson, Dostoievski," in *Cinématographe* (Paris), December 1981.
Dossier on Robert Bresson, in *Cinéma* (Paris), June 1983.
Bergala, Alain, and others, "*L'Argent* de Robert Bresson," in *Cahiers du Cinéma* (Paris), June-July 1983.
"Bresson Issue," of *Camera/Stylo* (Paris), January 1985.
Affron, Mirella Jona, "Bresson and Pascal: Rhetorical Affinities," in *Quarterly Review of Film Studies* (New York), Spring 1985.
Milne, Tom, in *Sight and Sound* (London), Summer 1987.
Adair, "Lost and Found: Beby Re-inaugurates," in *Sight and Sound* (London), Autumn 1987.
Baxter, Brian, "Robert Bresson," in *Films and Filming* (London), September 1987.

On BRESSON: films—

Weyergans, Francois, *Robert Bresson*, 1965.
Kotulla, Theodor, *Zum Beispiel Bresson*, 1967.

* * *

Robert Bresson began and quickly gave up a career as a painter, turning to cinema in 1934. The short film he made that year, *Affaires publiques*, is never shown. His next work, *Les Anges du péché*, was his first feature film, followed by *Les Dames du Bois du Boulogne* and *Journal d'un curé de campagne*, which firmly established his reputation as one of the world's most rigorous and demanding filmmakers. In the next fifteen years he made only four films: *Un Condamné à mort s'est échappé, Pickpocket, Procès de Jeanne d'Arc*, and *Au hasard Balthazar*, each a work of masterful originality and unlike the others. Since then he has made films with more frequency and somewhat less intensity. In 1975 Gallimard published his gnomic *Notes sur le cinématographe*.

As a whole Bresson's oeuvre constitutes a crucial investigation of the nature of cinematic narration. All three films of the 1950s are variations on the notion of a written diary transposed to a voice-over commentary on the visualized action. More indirectly, *Procès de Jeanne d'Arc* proposes yet another variant through the medium of the written transcript of the trial; *Une Femme douce* is told through the voice of the husband as he keeps a vigil for his suicidal wife; and in *Quatre nuits d'un rêveur* both of the principal characters narrate their previous histories to each other. In all of these instances Bresson allows the tension between the continuity of written and spoken language and the fragmentation of shots in a film to become an important thematic concern. His narrators tell themselves (and us) stories in order to find meaning in what has happened to them. The elusiveness of that meaning is reflected in the elliptical style of Bresson's editing.

For the most part, Bresson employs only amateur actors. He avoids histrionics and seldom permits his "models" (as he calls them, drawing a metaphor from painting) to give a traditional performance. The emotional tensions of the films derive from the elaborate interchange of glances, subtle camera movements, offscreen sounds, carefully placed bits of baroque and classical music, and rhythmical editing.

The Bressonian hero is often defined by what he or she sees. We come to understand the sexual tensions of Ambricourt from a few shots seen from the country priest's perspective; the fierce desire to escape helps the condemned man to see the most ordinary objects as tools for his purpose; the risk the pickpocket initially takes to prove his moral superiority to himself leads him to see thefts where we might only notice people jostling one another: the film initiates its viewers into his privileged perspective. Only at the end does he realize that this obsessive mode of seeing has blinded him to a love which he ecstatically embraces.

Conversely, Mouchette kills herself suddenly when she sees the death of a hare (with which she identified herself); the heroine of *Une Femme douce* kills herself because she can see no value in things, while her pawnbroker husband sees nothing but the monetary worth of everything he handles. The most elaborate form this concentration on seeing takes in Bresson's cinema is the structure of *Au hasard Balthazar*, where the range of human vices is seen through the eyes of a donkey as he passes through a series of owners.

The intricate shot-countershot of Bresson's films reinforces his emphasis on seeing, as does his careful use of camera movement. Often he reframes within a shot to bring together two different objects of attention. The cumulative effect of this meticulous and often obsessive concentration on details is the sense of a transcendent and fateful presence guiding the actions of characters who come to see only at the end, if at all, the pattern and goal of their lives.

Only in *Un Condamné, Pickpocket*, and *Quatre Nuits* does the protagonist survive the end of the film. A dominant theme of his cinema is dying with grace. In *Mouchette, Une Femme douce*, and *Le Diable probablement* the protagonists commit suicide. In *Les Anges* and *L'Argent* they give themselves up as murderers. Clearly Bresson, who is the most prominent of Catholic filmmakers, does not reflect the Church's condemnation of suicide. Death, as he represents it, comes as the acceptance of one's fate. The three suicides emphasize the enigma of human will; they seem insufficiently motivated, but are pure acts of accepting death.

—P. Adams Sitney

Robert Bresson directing *Procès de Jeanne d'Arc*

BROOKS, Mel

Nationality: American. **Born:** Melvin Kaminsky in Brooklyn, New York, 28 June 1926. **Education:** Attended Virginia Military Institute, 1944. **Family:** Married 1) Florence Baum (divorced), two sons, one daughter; 2) actress Anne Bancroft, one son. **Military Service:** Combat engineer, U.S. Army, 1944-46. **Career:** Jazz drummer, stand-up comedian, and social director at Grossinger's resort; writer for Sid Caesar's "Your Show of Shows," 1954-57; conceived, wrote, and narrated cartoon short *The Critic,* 1963; co-creator (with Buck Henry) of *Get Smart* TV show, 1965; directed first feature, *The Producers,* 1968; founder, Brooksfilms, 1981. **Awards:** Academy Award for Best Short Subject, for *The Critic,* 1964; Academy Award for Best Story and Screenplay, and Writers Guild Award for Best Written Screenplay, for *The Producers,* 1968; Academy Award nomination, Best Song, for *Blazing Saddles,* 1974; Academy Award nomination, Best Screenplay, for *Young Frankenstein,* 1975; American Comedy Awards Lifetime Achievement Award, 1987. **Address:** Brooksfilms, Ltd., Culver Studios, 9336 W. Washington Blvd., Culver City, CA 90212, U.S.A.

Films as Director:

1963 *The Critic* (cartoon) (+ sc, narration)
1968 *The Producers* (+ sc, voice)
1970 *The Twelve Chairs* (+ co-sc, role)
1974 *Blazing Saddles* (+ co-sc, mus, role); *Young Frankenstein* (+ co-sc)
1976 *Silent Movie* (+ co-sc, role)
1977 *High Anxiety* (+ pr, co-sc, mus, role)
1981 *The History of the World, Part I* (+ pr, co-sc, mus, role)
1983 *To Be or Not to Be* (+ pr, co-sc, role)
1987 *Spaceballs* (+ pr, co-sc, role)
1991 *Life Stinks!* (+ co-sc, role)
1993 *Robin Hood: Men in Tights* (+ co-sc, role)

Films as Executive Producer:

1980 *The Elephant Man* (Lynch)
1985 *The Doctor and the Devils* (Francis)
1986 *The Fly* (Cronenberg); *Solarbabies* (Johnson)
1987 *84 Charing Cross Road* (Jones)
1992 *The Vagrant* (Walas)

Other Films:

1979 *The Muppet Movie* (Frawley) (role)
1991 *Look Who's Talking, Too!* (Heckerling) (voice, role)
1994 *Il silenzio dei prosciutti* (*The Silence of the Hams*) (Greggio) (role)

Publications

By BROOKS: books—

Silent Movie, New York, 1976.
The History of the World, Part I, New York, 1981.

By BROOKS: articles—

"Confessions of an Auteur," in *Action* (Los Angeles), November/December 1971.
Interview with James Atlas, in *Film Comment* (New York), March/April 1975.
"Fond Salutes and Naked Hate," interview with Gordon Gow, in *Films and Filming* (London), July 1975.
Interview with A. Remond, in *Ecran* (Paris), November 1976.
"Comedy Directors: Interview with Mel Brooks," with R. Rivlin, in *Millimeter* (New York), October and December 1977.
Interview with Alan Yentob, in *Listener* (London), 8 October 1981.
Interview in *Time Out* (London), 16 February 1984.
Interview in *Screen International,* 3 March 1984.
Interview in *Hollywood Reporter,* 27 October 1986.
"The Playboy Interview," interview with L. Stegel in *Playboy* (Chicago), January 1989.
"Mel Brooks: Of Woody, the Great Caesar, Flop Sweat and Cigar Smoke," *People Weekly* (New York), Summer 1989 (special issue).

On BROOKS: books—

Adler, Bill and Jeffrey Fineman, *Mel Brooks: The Irreverent Funnyman,* Chicago, 1976.
Bendazzi, G., *Mel Brooks: l'ultima follia di Hollywood,* Milan, 1977.
Holtzman, William, *Seesaw: A Dual Biography of Anne Bancroft and Mel Brooks,* New York, 1979.
Allen, Steve, *Funny People,* New York, 1981.
Yacowar, Maurice, *Method in Madness: The Comic Art of Mel Brooks,* New York, 1981.
Smurthwaite, Nick, and Paul Gelder, *Mel Brooks and the Spoof Movie,* London, 1982.
Squire, Jason, E., *The Movie Business Book,* Englewood Cliffs, New Jersey, 1983.

On BROOKS: articles—

"Two Thousand Year Old Man," in *Newsweek* (New York), 4 October 1965.
Diehl, D., "Mel Brooks," in *Action* (Los Angeles), January/February 1975.
Lees, G., "The Mel Brooks Memos," in *American Film* (Washington, D.C.), October 1977.
Carcassonne, P., "Dossier: Hollywood 79: Mel Brooks," in *Cinématographe* (Paris), March 1979.
Karoubi, N., "Mel Brooks Follies," in *Cinéma* (Paris), February 1982.
"Mel Brooks," in *Dictionary of Literary Biography, vol. 26: American Screenwriters,* Detroit, 1984.
Erens, Patricia, "You Could Die Laughing: Jewish Humor and Film," in *East-West Film Journal* (Honolulu), no. 1, 1987.
Carter, E.G., "The Cosmos According to Mel Brooks," in *Vogue* (New York), June 1987.
Dougherty, M., "May the Farce Be with Him: *Spaceballs* Rockets Mel Brooks Back into the Lunatic Orbit," in *People Weekly* (New York), 20 July 1987.
Frank, A., "Mel's Crazy Movie World," in *Photoplay Movies & Video* (London), January 1988.
Goldstein, T., "A History of Mel Brooks: Part I," in *Video* (New York), March 1988.
Stauth, C., "Mel and Me," in *American Film* (Los Angeles), April 1990.

* * *

Mel Brooks's central concern (with *High Anxiety* and *To Be or Not to Be* as possible exceptions) is the pragmatic, absurd union of two males, starting with the more experienced member trying to take advantage of the other, and ending in a strong friendship and paternal relationship. The dominant member of the duo, confident but ill-fated, is Zero Mostel in *The Producers,* Frank Langella in *The Twelve Chairs,* and Gene Wilder in *Blazing Saddles* and *Young Frankenstein.*

The second member of the duo, usually physically weak and openly neurotic, represents the victim who wins, who learns from his experience and finds friendship to sustain him. These "Jewish weakling" characters include Wilder in *The Producers,* Ron Moody, and Cleavon Little. Though this character, as in the case of Little, need not literally be Jewish, he displays the stereotypical characteristics.

Women in Brooks's films are grotesque figures, sex objects ridiculed and rejected. They are either very old or sexually gross and simple. The love of a friend is obviously worth more than such an object. The secondary male characters, befitting the intentional infantilism of the films, are men-babies given to crying easily. They are set up as examples of what the weak protagonist might become without the paternal care of his reluctant friend. In particular, Brooks sees people who hide behind costumes—cowboy suits, Nazi uniforms, clerical garb, homosexual affectations—as silly children to be made fun of.

The plots of Brooks's films deal with the experienced and inexperienced men searching for a way to triumph in society. They seek a generic solution or are pushed into one. Yet there is no escape into generic fantasy in the Brooks films, since the films take place totally within the fantasy. There is no regard, as in Woody Allen's films, for the pathetic nature of the protagonist in reality. In fact, the Brooks films reverse the Allen films' endings as the protagonists move into a comic fantasy of friendship. (A further contrast with Allen is in the nature of the jokes and gags. Allen's humor is basically adult embarrassment; Brooks's is infantile taboo-breaking.)

In *The Producers* the partners try to manipulate show business and wind up in jail, planning another scheme because they enjoy it. In *The Twelve Chairs* they try to cheat the government; at the end Langella and Moody continue working together though they no longer have the quest for the chairs in common. In *Blazing Saddles* Little and Wilder try to take a town; it ends with the actors supposedly playing themselves, getting into a studio car and going off together as pals into the sunset. In these films it is two men alone against a corrupt and childish society. Though their schemes fall apart—or are literally exploded as in *The Producers* and *The Twelve Chairs*—they still have each other.

Young Frankenstein departs from the pattern with each of the partners, monster and doctor, sexually committed to women. While the basic pattern of male buddies continued when Brooks began to act in his own films, he also winds up with the woman when he is the hero star (*High Anxiety, Silent Movie, The History of the World, To Be or Not to Be*). It is interesting that Brooks always tries to distance himself from the homosexual implications of his central theme by including scenes in which overtly homosexual characters are ridiculed. It is particularly striking that these characters are, in *The Producers, Blazing Saddles,* and *The Twelve Chairs,* stage or film directors.

Brooks's late-career films have been collectively disappointing. Upon its release, *Spaceballs* already was embarrassingly dated. It is meant to be a spoof of *Star Wars,* yet it came to movie screens a decade after the sci-fi epic. Comic timing used to be Brooks's strong point, yet the story has no momentum and the film's funniest line—"May the Schwartz be with you"—is repeated so often that the joke quickly becomes stale.

The bad-taste scenes in Brooks's earlier films, most memorably *Blazing Saddles* and *Young Frankenstein,* used to be considered provocative. Now that young filmmakers and television writers have stretched comedy to the extreme limits, Brooks has lost his ability to astound and appall the audience. His most recent feature, *Robin Hood: Men in Tights,* a parody of Errol Flynn-style swashbuckling adventures, is sorely lacking in laughs. The sole exception: Dom DeLuise's hilarious (but all too brief) *Godfather* spoof.

Life Stinks! is the most serious of all of Brooks's films. Rather than being a string of quick gags, it offers a slower-paced, more conventional narrative. As with *To Be Or Not To Be* (which is set in Poland at the beginning of World War II), he treats a sobering theme in a comic manner as he comments on the plight of the homeless. But while *To Be Or Not to Be* is as deeply moving as it is funny, *Life Stinks!* stinks. It is episodic and all too often flat, with its satire much too broad and all too rarely funny.

—Stuart M. Kaminsky, updated by Audrey E. Kupferberg

BROOKS, Richard

Nationality: American. **Born:** Philadelphia, 8 May 1912. **Education:** Temple University, Philadelphia. **Family:** Married actress Jean Simmons, 1961. **Military Service:** Served in U.S. Marine Corps., 1943-45. **Career:** Sports reporter for *Atlantic City Press Union,* then *World Telegram,* 1934-36; worked for radio station WNEW, then for NBC, 1936; director for Mild Pond Theatre, New York, 1940; wrote daily radio program from Hollywood, also collaborated on film scripts, 1941; after working with producer Mark Hellinger, signed for MGM, 1946; directed first feature, *Crisis,* 1950; became independent producer, 1965; formed production co., Crime Inc. Pictures, with actor Robert Culp, 1987. **Awards:** Oscar for Best Screenplay, and Writers Guild Award for Best-Written Drama, for *Elmer Gantry,* 1960; Laurel Award for Achievement, Writers Guild, 1966.

Films as Director:

1950 *Crisis* (+ sc)
1951 *The Light Touch* (+ sc)
1952 *Deadline USA* (+ sc)
1953 *Battle Circus* (+ sc); *Take the High Ground*
1954 *The Flame and the Flesh*; *The Last Time I Saw Paris* (+ co-sc)
1955 *The Blackboard Jungle* (+ sc)
1956 *The Last Hunt* (+ sc); *The Catered Affair*
1957 *Something of Value* (+ sc)
1958 *The Brothers Karamazov* (+ co-sc); *Cat on a Hot Tin Roof* (+ co-sc)
1960 *Elmer Gantry* (+ sc)
1961 *Sweet Bird of Youth* (+ sc)
1965 *Lord Jim* (+ sc)
1966 *The Professionals* (+ sc)
1967 *In Cold Blood* (+ sc)
1969 *The Happy Ending* (+ sc)
1971 *Dollars* (+ co-sc)
1975 *Bite the Bullet* (+ sc)
1977 *Looking for Mr. Goodbar* (+ sc)
1982 *Wrong is Right* (*The Man with the Deadly Lens*)
1985 *Fever Pitch*

Other Films:

1942 *Sin Town* (Enright) (co-sc); *Men of Texas* (co-sc)
1943 *The White Savage* (Lubin) (co-sc); *Cobra Woman* (Siodmak) (co-sc); *My Best Gal* (Anthony Mann) (co-sc); *Don Winslow of the Coast Guard* (co-sc)
1946 *Swell Guy* (Tuttle) (co-sc); ***The Killers*** (Siodmak) (co-sc)
1947 *Brute Force* (Dassin) (co-sc)
1948 *To the Victor* (Daves) (co-sc); *Key Largo* (Huston) (co-sc); ***The Naked City*** (Dassin) (co-sc)
1949 *Storm Warning* (Heisler) (co-sc); *Any Number Can Play* (John Sturges) (co-sc)
1950 *Mystery Street* (John Sturges) (co-sc)

Richard Brooks

Publications

By BROOKS: books—

The Brick Foxhole, New York, 1946.
The Boiling Point, New York, 1948.
The Producer, New York, 1951.

By BROOKS: articles—

"A Novel Isn't a Movie," in *Films in Review* (New York), February 1952.
"Two Story Conferences," with King Vidor, in *Sight and Sound* (London), October/December 1952.
"On Filming Karamazov," in *Films in Review* (New York), February 1958.
"Dostoievsky, Love and American Cinema," in *Films in Review* (New York), April 1958.
Interview with Charles Bitsch, in *Cahiers du Cinéma* (Paris), February 1959.
"Richard Brooks and *Lord Jim,*" interview with Paul Joyce, in *Film* (London), Winter 1964.
"*Lord Jim* Interview," in *Cinema* (Beverly Hills), March/April 1965.
"In Cold Blood," interview in *Cahiers du Cinema in English* (New York), no.5, 1966.
"Richard Brooks Directs *Looking for Mr. Goodbar,*" interview with J. Mariani, in *Millimeter* (New York), July/August 1977.
"Richard Brooks Seminar" in *American Film* (Washington, D.C.), October 1977.
Interview with J. Hurley, in *Films in Review* (New York), May 1982.
Interview with D. Rabourdin, in *Cinéma* (Paris), April 1983.

On BROOKS: book—

Brion, Patrick, *Richard Brooks,* Paris, 1986.

On BROOKS: articles—

"Personality of the Month," in *Films in Review* (New York), May 1956.
"Brooks Section" of *Positif* (Paris), July 1956.
Johnson, A., "Richard Brooks," in *Sight and Sound* (London), Autumn 1960.
Godard, Jean-Luc, "Note sur Richard Brooks," in *Cahiers du Cinéma* (Paris), December 1963.
"Brooks Section" of *Movie* (London), Spring 1965.
"Brooks Section" of *Image et Son* (Paris), May 1972.
Thomas, B., "The Secret Scripts of Richard Brooks," in *Action* (Los Angeles), September/October 1975.
Le Pavec, J.-P., and others, "Dossier auteur Richard Brooks," in *Cinéma* (Paris), December 1980.
Interim, L., "Le message de Richard Brooks," in *Cahiers du Cinéma* (Paris), November 1981.
Sinyard, Neil, "Directors of the decade: Richard Brooks," in *Films and Filming* (London), August 1983.
Holtsmark, E. B., "The Katabasis Theme in Modern Cinema," *Bucknell Review,* Spring 1991.

* * *

Richard Brooks had his literary education in the hard school of radio and the program picture, where "licking the story" and "getting out the pages" marked progress to an acceptable screenplay. He won critical acceptance with his bottom-drawer novel, *The Brick Foxhole,* later filmed (and traduced) as *Crossfire.* Projects of an increasing sophistication followed until he reached his goal of writing and directing serious, "significant" films, only to find the cinema moving toward a self-regarding personal style he was ill-fitted to pursue.

What won Brooks his commercial success and will continue to sustain his reputation, where films like *The Brothers Karamazov, Lord Jim, In Cold Blood* and *Looking For Mr. Goodbar* may not, are his films of action, for which he displayed a notable skill in his program days, and on which he capitalized in a series of polished and thoughtful westerns. *The Last Hunt, Bite the Bullet* and particularly *The Professionals* all deal effectively with arresting by-ways of the frontier experience. Brooks is interested in the interface between old and new ways, old and new men; the buffalo hunters of *The Last Hunt* represent the conflicting forces of ruthless slaughter and environmental protection, and the long-distance horse racers of *Bite the Bullet* present rival motives. The least overtly significant of them all, *The Professionals,* is also the most entertaining, a stylish and character-rich variation on *The Magnificent Seven* that repays frequent re-viewing.

Brooks's literary adaptations are sustained by their bravura performances. He coaxed high passion from Elizabeth Taylor in *Cat on a Hot Tin Roof,* and banked down the same fires in Burt Lancaster to make *Elmer Gantry* one of his best works. But in "licking" essentially unfilmable books like *Lord Jim, The Brothers Karamazov* and *In Cold Blood,* he remained doggedly faithful to the respective texts and drew mixed response. It may be that *The Blackboard Jungle,* once heralded for its social realism but subsequently considered second-rate, will be the production for which he is best remembered.

—John Baxter

BROWN, Clarence

Nationality: American. **Born:** Clinton, Massachusetts, 10 May 1890. **Education:** Studied engineering at University of Tennessee, 1910. **Military Service:** Served as aviator during World War I, 1918. **Family:** Married 1) actress Mona Maris; 2) actress Alice Joyce; 3) former secretary Marian Ruth Spies. **Career:** Worked for Moline Automobile Co. and Stephen Duryea Co., then founded Brown Motor Car Company, Birmingham, Alabama, 1911-12; became assistant to Maurice Tourneur, 1915; joined MGM, 1925; helped found Clarence Brown Theatre for the Performing Arts, University of Tennessee, Knoxville, 1971. **Died:** 17 August 1987.

Films as Director:

1920 *The Great Redeemer* (co-d with Maurice Tourneur); *The Last of the Mohicans* (co-d with Maurice Tourneur)
1921 *The Foolish Matrons* (co-d with Maurice Tourneur)
1922 *The Light in the Dark*
1923 *Don't Marry for Money*; *The Acquittal*
1924 *The Signal Tower*; *Butterfly*; *Smouldering Fires*
1925 *The Goose Woman*; *The Eagle*
1926 *Kiki*
1927 *The Flesh and the Devil*
1928 *A Woman of Affairs*
1929 *The Trail of '98*; *Wonder of Women*; *Navy Blues*
1930 *Anna Christie*; *Romance*
1931 *Inspiration*; *A Free Soul*; *Possessed*
1932 *Emma*; *Letty Lynton*; *The Son-Daughter*
1933 *Looking Forward*; *Night Flight*
1934 *Sadie McKee*; *Chained*
1935 *Anna Karenina*; *Ah Wilderness*

Clarence Brown

1936 *Wife Versus Secretary*; *The Gorgeous Hussy*
1937 *Conquest*
1938 *Of Human Hearts*
1939 *Idiot's Delight*; *The Rains Came*
1940 *Edison the Man*
1941 *Come Live with Me*; *They Met in Bombay*
1943 *The Human Comedy*
1944 *The White Cliffs of Dover*; *National Velvet*
1946 *The Yearling*
1947 *Song of Love* (+ pr)
1949 *Intruder in the Dust* (+ pr)
1950 *To Please a Lady* (+ pr)
1951 *Angels in the Outfield* (+ pr); episode of *It's a Big Country* (+ pr)
1952 *When in Rome* (+ pr); *Plymouth Adventure* (+ pr)

Other Films:

1949 *The Secret Garden* (Ardrey) (pr)
1953 *Never Let Me Go* (Daves) (pr)

Publications

By BROWN: articles—

"Bringing Saroyan to the Screen," in *Lion's Roar* (Hollywood), April 1943.
"The Producer Must Be Boss," in *Films in Review* (New York), February 1951.

On BROWN: books—

Brownlow, Kevin, *The Parade's Gone*, London and New York, 1968.
Estrin, Allen, *Capra, Cukor, Brown*, New York, 1980.

On BROWN: articles—

Manners, D., sketch in *Motion Picture Classic* (Brooklyn), April 1928.
Tully, J., "Estimate," in *Vanity Fair* (New York), April 1928.
Brion, P., "Clarence Brown: un grand cinéaste intimiste," in *Cinéma* (Paris), February 1979.
Cebe, G., and others, "Redecouvrir Clarence Brown," in *Ecran* (Paris), 15 June 1979.
Viviani, C., "Inspiration et romance chez Clarence Brown," in *Positif* (Paris), March 1980.
Hollywood Reporter, 19 and 21 August 1987.
McCarthy, T., obituary, in *Variety* (New York), 26 August 1987.
Obituary in *Revue du Cinéma* (Paris), November 1987.

* * *

It was in 1915 that Clarence Brown saw a movie being filmed at Fort Lee, New Jersey. He was so fascinated by what he saw that he sold the car company he had founded and apprenticed himself to Maurice Tourneur, who was about to direct Clara Kimball Young in a film version of *Trilby*. Twenty-five years old when he began his apprenticeship, Brown spent the next five years as assistant to Tourneur, whom he freely acknowledged as his god. "I owe it all to him," Brown once said. "Before he got into filmmaking, he was a painter. He used the screen like a canvas. Everything I know about lighting and composition and arrangement I learned from him."

During the making of *The Last of the Mohicans*, Tourneur was injured, and Clarence Brown finished the picture for him; they share the directorial credit. Tourneur and Brown collaborated once again when they co-directed another feature, *The Foolish Matrons*. Tourneur then told him that he was ready to direct a feature on his own.

Brown signed with Universal, then under the management of Carl Laemmle, where he found that he was happiest working with female stars like Pauline Frederick and Laura La Plante in *Smouldering Fires* and Louise Dresser in *The Goose Woman*. Joseph Schenck admired his work, and signed him to direct two films for him at United Artists—*The Eagle*, one of the few really good pictures that Rudolph Valentino made, and *Kiki*, which starred Schenck's wife, Norma Talmadge.

Brown signed then with MGM, where he remained for the rest of his career until 1952, save for only one loan-out to 20th-Century-Fox for *The Rains Came*, a picture he wanted to make. Louis B. Mayer always held him in high regard; in fact, he is the only director at MGM with whom Mayer did not at some time or another quarrel.

An important element of Brown's success was that MGM had a veritable galaxy of female stars, and it was the woman star with whom Brown felt most compatible. His range as a director at MGM was enviable; he was never pigeonholed. He moved from his first picture there, *Flesh and the Devil*, which made Garbo an important star, to an American epic like his last picture, *Plymouth Adventure*. In between he directed, among others, seven films for Garbo, five for Crawford, and two for Shearer. In spite of that record, he will probably be known best for his cinematic treatments of adventures in Americana like *Ah, Wilderness*, *Of Human Hearts*, *The Human Comedy*, *The Yearling*, and *Intruder in the Dust*.

—DeWitt Bodeen

BROWNING, Tod

Nationality: American. **Born:** Charles Albert Browning in Louisville, Kentucky, 12 July 1880. **Education:** Attended school in Churchill Downs. **Family:** Married Alice Houghton (actress Alice Wilson), 1918. **Career:** Ran away from home to join a carnival, 1898; worked carnival circuit, then Vaudeville and Burlesque shows; joined Biograph film studio as comedic actor, 1913; directed first film, *The Lucky Transfer*, 1915; joined Universal Studios, began association with Lon Chaney, 1919; signed by MGM, 1925. **Awards:** Honorary Life Membership, Directors Guild of America. **Died:** 6 October 1962.

Films as Director:

1915 *The Lucky Transfer*; *The Slave Girl*; *The Highbinders*; *The Living Death*; *The Burned Hand*; *The Woman from Warren's*; *Little Marie*; *The Story of a Story*; *The Spell of the Poppy*; *The Electric Alarm*
1916 *Puppets*; *Everybody's Doing It*; *The Deadly Glass of Beer* (*The Fatal Glass of Beer*)
1917 *Jim Bludso* (co-d, co-sc); *Peggy, The Will o' th' Wisp*; *The Jury of Fate*; *A Love Sublime* (co-d); *Hands Up!* (co-d)
1918 *The Eyes of Mystery*; *The Legion of Death*; *Revenge*; *Which Woman*; *The Deciding Kiss*; *The Brazen Beauty*; *Set Free* (+ sc)
1919 *The Wicked Darling*; *The Exquisite Thief*; *The Unpainted Woman*; *A Petal on the Current*; *Bonnie, Bonnie Lassie* (+ sc)
1920 *The Virgin of Stamboul* (+ sc)
1921 *Outside the Law* (+ co-sc); *No Woman Knows* (+ co-sc)
1922 *The Wise Kid*; *Under Two Flags* (+ co-sc); *Man Under Cover*

Tod Browning

1923 *Drifting* (+ co-sc); *White Tiger* (+ co-sc); *Day of Faith*
1924 *The Dangerous Flirt*; *Silk Stocking Girl* (*Silk Stocking Sal*)
1925 *The Unholy Three* (+ co-sc); *The Mystic* (+ co-sc); *Dollar Down*
1926 *The Black Bird* (+ co-sc); *The Road to Mandalay* (+ co-sc)
1927 *London After Midnight* (+ co-sc); *The Show*; *The Unknown* (+ co-sc)
1928 *The Big City* (+ co-sc); *West of Zanzibar*
1929 *Where East is East* (+ co-sc); *The Thirteenth Chair*
1930 *Outside the Law* (+ co-sc)
1931 ***Dracula*** (+ co-sc); *The Iron Man*
1932 ***Freaks***
1933 *Fast Workers*
1935 *Mark of the Vampire* (+ sc)
1936 *The Devil-Doll* (+ co-sc)
1939 *Miracles for Sale*

Other Films:

1913 *Scenting a Terrible Crime* (role); *A Fallen Hero* (role)
1914 *A Race for a Bride* (role); *The Man in the Couch* (role); *An Exciting Courtship* (role); *The Last Drink of Whiskey* (role); *Hubby to the Rescue* (role); *The Deceivers* (role); *The White Slave Catchers* (role); *Wrong All Around* (role); *Leave It to Smiley* (role); *The Wild Girl* (role); *Ethel's Teacher* (role); *A Physical Culture Romance* (role); *The Mascot* (role); *Foiled Again* (role); *The Million Dollar Bride* (role); *Dizzy Joe's Career* (role); *Casey's Vendetta* (role); *Out Again—In Again* (role); *A Corner in Hats* (role); *The Housebreakers* (role); *The Record Breakers* (role)
1914/15 Mr. Hadley in "Bill" series through no. 17; *Ethel Gets Consent* (role)
1915 *The Queen of the Band* (Myers) (story); *Cupid and the Pest* (role); *Music Hath Its Charms* (role); *A Costly Exchange* (role)
1916 *Sunshine Dad* (Dillon) (co-story); *The Mystery of the Leaping Fish* (Emerson) (story); *Atta Boy's Last Race* (Seligmann) (sc); ***Intolerance*** (Griffith) (role, asst d for crowd scenes)
1919 *The Pointing Finger* (Kull) (supervisor)
1921 *Society Secrets* (McCarey) (supervisor)
1928 *Old Age Handicap* (Mattison) (story under pseudonym Tod Underwood)
1946 *Inside Job* (Yarborough) (story)

Publications

By BROWNING: articles—

"A Maker of Mystery," interview with Joan Dickey, in *Motion Picture Classic* (Brooklyn), March 1928.

On BROWNING: articles—

Geltzer, George, "Tod Browning," in *Films in Review* (New York), October 1953.
Romer, Jean-Claude, "Tod Browning," in *Bizarre* (Paris), no. 3, 1962.
Obituary in *New York Times*, 10 October 1962.
Guy, Rory, "The Browning Version," in *Cinema* (Beverly Hills), June/July 1963.
Savada, Eli, "Tod Browning," in *Photon* (New York), no. 23, 1973.
Rosenthal, Stuart, "Tod Browning," in *The Hollywood Professionals* (London), vol. 4, 1975.
"*Freaks* Issue" of *Avant-Scène du Cinéma* (Paris), July/September 1975.
Garsault, A., "Tod Browning: à la recherche de la réalité," in *Positif* (Paris), July/August 1978.
Hoberman, James, "Tod Browning's Side Show," in the *Village Voice* (New York), 17 September 1979.

* * *

Although his namesake was the poet Robert Browning, Tod Browning became recognized as a major Hollywood cult director whose work bore some resemblance to the sensibilities of a much different writer: Edgar Allen Poe. However, unlike Poe, Tod Browning was, by all accounts, a quiet and gentle man who could nonetheless rise to sarcasm and sardonic remarks when necessary to bring out the best from his players or to ward off interference from the front office.

Browning came to Hollywood as an actor after working circus and vaudeville circuits. Browning tapped into this background in supplying elements of many of his films, notably *The Unholy Three, The Show,* and *Freaks.* He worked in the film industry as an actor until D.W. Griffith (for whom Browning had worked on *Intolerance* as both a performer and assistant director) gave him the chance to direct at the Fine Arts Company. Browning directed a few films for Metro, but came to fame at Universal with a series of features starring Priscilla Dean. Although *The Virgin of Stamboul* was admired by critics, it was his next film, *Outside the Law,* which has more historical significance, marking the first time that Browning directed Lon Chaney. (Browning remade the feature as a talkie.)

These Universal productions were little more than pretentious romantic melodramas, but they paved the way for a series of classic MGM horror films starring Lon Chaney, from *The Unholy Three* in 1925 through *Where East Is East* in 1929. These films were notable for the range of Chaney's performances—a little old lady, a cripple, an armless circus performer, a gangster, and so on—and for displaying Browning's penchant for the macabre. All were stylish productions, well directed, but all left the viewer with a sense of disappointment, of unfulfilled climaxes. Aside from directing, Tod Browning also wrote most of his films. He once explained that the plots of these works were secondary to the characterizations, a viewpoint that perhaps explains the dismal, unexciting endings to many of his features.

Tod Browning made an easy transition to sound films, although surprisingly he did not direct the 1930 remake of *The Unholy Three.* Instead, he directed the atmospheric *Dracula,* a skillful blend of comedy and horror that made a legend of the actor Bela Lugosi. A year later, Browning directed another classic horror talkie, *Freaks,* a realistic and at times offensive melodrama about the physically deformed members of a circus troupe. The film includes the marriage of midget Harry Earles to a trapeze artiste (Olga Baclanova).

Browning ended his career with *The Mark of the Vampire,* a remake of the Chaney feature *London After Midnight; The Devil Doll,* in which Lionel Barrymore appears as an old lady, a similar disguise to that adopted by Chaney in *The Unholy Three*; and *Miracles for Sale,* a mystery drama involving professional magicians. Tod Browning will, of course, be best remembered for his horror films, but it should also be recalled that during the first half of his directorial career he stuck almost exclusively to romantic melodramas.

—Anthony Slide

BUÑUEL, Luis

Nationality: Spanish. **Born:** Calanda, province of Teruel, Spain, 22 February 1900. **Education:** Jesuit schools in Zaragosa, 1906-15,

Residencia de Estudiantes, Madrid, 1917-20, and University of Madrid, graduated 1924. **Family:** Married Jeanne Rucar, 1933, two sons. **Career:** Assistant to Jean Epstein in Paris, 1925; joined Surrealist group, and directed first film, *Un Chien andalou,* 1929; worked for Paramount in Paris, 1933; Executive Producer for Filmofono, Madrid, 1935; served Republican government in Spain, 1936-39; worked at Museum of Modern Art, New York, 1939-42; produced Spanish versions of Warners films, Hollywood, 1944; moved to Mexico, 1946; returned to Spain to make *Viridiana,* 1961 (film suppressed). **Awards:** Best Director Award and International Critics Prize, Cannes Festival, for *Los olvidados,* 1951; Gold Medal, Cannes Festival, for *Nazarin,* 1959, and *Viridiana,* 1961; Golden Lion, Venice Festival, for *Belle de jour,* 1967. **Died:** In Mexico City, 29 July 1983.

Films as Director:

1929 ***Un Chien andalou*** (*Andalusian Dog*)(+ pr, co-sc, ed, role as Man with razor)
1930 ***L'Age d'or*** (+ co-sc, ed, mu)
1932 *Las Hurdes—Tierra sin pan* (*Land without Bread*) (+ sc, ed)
1935 *Don Quintin el amargao* (Marquina) (co-d uncredited, + pr, co-sc); *La hija de Juan Simón* (Sáenz de Heredia) (co-d uncredited, + pr, co-sc)
1936 *Centinela alerta!* (Grémillon) (co-d uncredited, + pr, co-sc)
1940 *El Vaticano de Pio XII* (*The History of the Vatican*) (short, special issue of *March of Time* series)
1947 *Gran Casino* (*Tampico*)
1949 *El gran calavera*
1950 ***Los olvidados*** (*The Forgotten*; *The Young and the Damned*) (+ co-sc); *Susana* (*Demonio y carne*) (+ co-sc)
1951 *La hija del engaño* (*Don Quintín el amargao*); *Cuando los hijos nos juzgan* (*Una mujer sin amor*); *Subida al cielo* (+ sc)
1952 *El Bruto* (+ co-sc); *Las aventuras de Robinson Crusoe* (*Adventures of Robinson Crusoe*) (+ co-sc); *El* (+ co-sc)
1953 *Abismos de pasión* (*Cumbres borrascoses*) (+ co-sc); *La ilusión viaja en tranvía* (+ co-sc)
1954 *El rio y la muerte* (+ co-sc)
1955 *Ensayo de un crimen* (*La Vida Criminal de Archibaldo de La Cruz*; *The Criminal Life of Archibaldo de la Cruz*) (+ co-sc); *Cela s'appelle l'Aurore* (+ co-sc)
1956 *La Mort en ce jardin* (*La muerte en este jardin*) (+ co-sc)
1958 *Nazarín* (+ co-sc)
1959 *La Fièvre monte à El Pao* (*Los Ambiciosos*) (+ co-sc)
1960 *The Young One* (*La Joven*; *La Jeune Fille*) (+ co-sc)
1961 ***Viridiana*** (+ co-sc, story)
1962 *El ángel exterminador* (*The Exterminating Angel*) (+ co-sc, story)
1963 *Le Journal d'une femme de chambre* (+ co-sc)
1965 *Simon del desierto* (+ co-sc)
1966 ***Belle de jour*** (+ co-sc)
1969 *La Voie lactée* (*The Milky Way*; *La via lattea*) (+ co-sc, mu)
1970 *Tristana* (+ co-sc)
1972 ***Le Charme discret de la bourgeoisie*** (*The Discreet Charm of the Bourgeoisie*) (+ co-sc)
1974 *Le Fantôme de la liberté* (*The Phantom of Liberty*) (+ sc, sound effects)
1977 *Cet obscur objet du desir* (*That Obsure Object of Desire*) (+ co-sc)

Other Films:

1926 *Mauprat* (Epstein) (asst d, role as monk)
1927 *La Sirène des tropiques* (Etiévant and Nalpas) (asst d)
1928 *La Chute de la maison Usher* (Epstein) (asst d)
1936 *Quién me quiere a mi?* (Sáenz de Heredia) (pr, co-sc, ed)
1937 *Espagne 1937/España leal en armas!* (compilation, ed)
1940 *Triumph of Will* (supervising ed, commentary, edited compilation of Riefenstahl's *Triumph des Willens* and Hans Bertram's *Feuertaufe*)
1950 *Si usted no puede, yo sí* (Soler) (co-story)
1964 *Llanto por un bandido* (*Lament for a Bandit*) (Saura) (role as the executioner; tech advisor on arms and munitions); *En este pueblo no hay ladrones* (Isaac) (role)
1972 *Le Moine* (Kyrou) (co-sc)
1973 *La Chute d'un corps* (Polac) (role)

Publications

By BUÑUEL: books—

Viridiana, Paris, 1962; Mexico City, 1963.
El ángel exterminador, Barcelona, 1964.
L'Age d'or and Une Chien andalou, London, 1968.
Three Screenplays: Viridiana, The Exterminating Angel, Simon of the Desert, New York, 1969.
Belle de Jour, London, 1971.
Tristana, London, 1971.
The Exterminating Angel/Nazarín/Los Olvidados, London, 1972.
My Last Breath, New York, 1983.

By BUÑUEL: articles—

Interview with Jacques Doniol-Valcroze and André Bazin, in *Cahiers du Cinéma* (Paris), June 1954.
Interview with Daniel Aubry and Jean Lacor, in *Film Quarterly* (Berkeley, California), Winter 1958.
"Poésie et cinéma," in *Cinéma* (Paris), June 1959.
"Luis Buñuel—A Statement," in *Film Culture* (New York), Summer 1960.
"The Cinema: An Instrument of Poetry," in *New York Film Bulletin,* February 1961.
Interview with Kenji Kanesaka, in *Film Culture* (New York), Spring 1962.
"Illisible, fils de flûte: synopsis d'un scénario non réalisé," with Jean Larrea, in *Positif* (Paris), March 1963.
"Luis Buñuel: voix off," an interview with Manuel Michel, in *Cinéma* (Paris), March 1965.
"Buñuel contre son mythe," an interview with Manuel Michel, in *Cinéma* (Paris), April 1966.
"Luis Buñuel," in *Interviews with Film Directors,* edited by Andrew Sarris, New York, 1967.
Interview with J. Cobos and G. S. de Erice, in *Cahiers du Cinéma* (Paris), June 1967.
"Buñuel Scenes," an interview with Carlos Fuentes, in *Movietone News* (Seattle), February 1975.
"Aragón, Madrid, Paris ... Entrevista con Luis Buñuel," with J. de la Colina and T. Pérez, in *Contracampo* (Madrid), October/November 1980.
Interview with Aldo Tassone, in *Chaplin* (Stockholm), vol. 24, no. 3, 1982.
"Dali intervista Buñuel," in *Cinema Nuovo* (Bari), December 1983.

On BUÑUEL: books—

Kyrou, Ado, *Luis Buñuel,* Paris, 1962.
Estève, Michel, editor, *Luis Buñuel,* Paris, 1962/63.
Durgnat, Raymond, *Luis Buñuel,* Berkeley, California, 1968.
Luis Buñuel: Biografia Critica, Madrid, 1969.
Buache, Freddy, *Luis Buñuel,* Lausanne, 1970; published as *The Cinema of Luis Buñuel,* London, 1973.
Matthews, J.H., *Surrealism and Film,* Ann Arbor, Michigan, 1971.

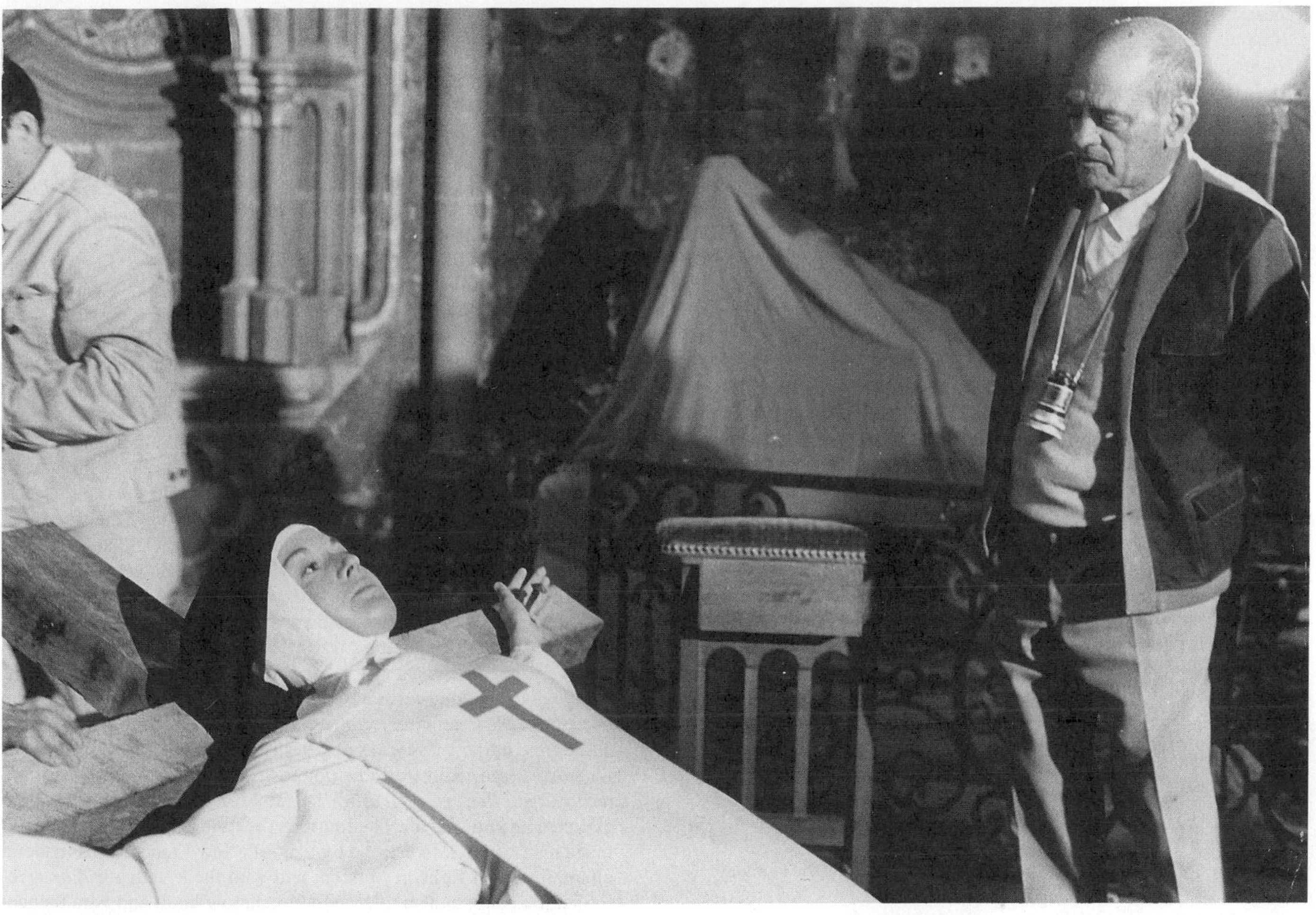

Luis Buñuel

Alcalá, Manuel, *Buñuel (Cine e ideologia),* Madrid, 1973.
Aranda, José Francisco, *Luis Buñuel: A Critical Biography,* New York, 1975.
Cesarman, Fernando, *El ojo de Buñuel,* Barcelona, 1976.
Drouzy, M., *Luis Buñuel, architecte du rêve,* Paris, 1978.
Mellen, Joan, editor, *The World of Luis Buñuel,* New York, 1978.
Cameron, Ian, *Luis Buñuel,* Berkeley, California, 1979.
Higginbotham, Virginia, *Luis Buñuel,* Boston, 1979.
Bazin, André, *The Cinema of Cruelty: From Buñuel to Hitchcock,* New York, 1982.
Cesarman, Fernando, *L'Oeil de Buñuel,* Paris, 1982.
Edwards, Gwynne, *The Discreet Art of Luis Buñuel: A Reading of His Films,* London, 1982.
Rees, Margaret A., *Luis Buñuel: A Symposium,* Leeds, 1983.
Lefèvre, Raymond, *Luis Buñuel,* Paris, 1984.
Vidal, Agustin Sanchez, *Luis Buñuel: Obra Cinematografica,* Madrid, 1984.
Aub, Max, *Conversaciones con Buñuel: Seguidas de 45 Entrevistas con Familiares, Amigos y Colaboradores del Cineasta Aragones,* Madrid, 1985.
Bertelli, Pino, *Buñuel: L'Arma dello Scandalo: L'Anarchia nel Cinema di Luis Buñuel,* Turin, 1985.
Oms, Marcel, *Luis Buñuel,* Paris, 1985.
De la Colina, José, and Tomas Perez Turrent, *Luis Buñuel: Prohibido Asomarse al Interior,* Mexico, 1986.
Sandro, Paul, *Diversions of Pleasure: Luis Buñuel and the Crises of Desire,* Columbus, Ohio, 1987.

On BUÑUEL: articles—

Demeure, Jacques, "Luis Buñuel: poète de la cruaute," in *Positif* (Paris), no. 10, 1954.
Richardson, Tony, "The Films of Luis Buñuel," in *Sight and Sound* (London), January/March 1954.
Robles, Emmanuel, "A Mexico avec Luis Buñuel," in *Cahiers du Cinéma* (Paris), October 1956.
Riera, Emilio, "The Eternal Rebellion of Luis Buñuel," in *Film Culture* (New York), Summer 1960.
Bazin, André, "Los Olvidados," in *Qu'est ce que le cinéma* (Paris) vol. 3, 1961.
Aranda, José Francisco, "Surrealist and Spanish Giant," in *Films and Filming* (London), October 1961.
Aranda, José Francisco, "Back from the Wilderness," in *Films and Filming* (London), November 1961.
"Buñuel Issue" of *Positif* (Paris), November 1961.
Prouse, Derek, "Interviewing Buñuel," in *Sight and Sound* (London), Summer 1962.
Almendros, Nestor, "Luis Buñuel: Cinéaste hispanique," in *Objectif* (Paris), July 1963.
Lovell, Alan, "Luis Buñuel," in *Anarchist Cinema,* London, 1964.
Hammond, Robert, "Luis Alcoriza and the Films of Luis Buñuel," in *Film Heritage* (Dayton, Ohio), Autumn 1965.
Milne, Tom, "The Mexican Buñuel," in *Sight and Sound* (London), Winter 1965/66.

Kanesaka, Kenji, "A Visit to Luis Buñuel," in *Film Culture* (New York), Summer 1966.
Harcourt, Peter, "Luis Buñuel: Spaniard and Surrealist," in *Film Quarterly* (Berkeley), Spring 1967.
Torres, Augusto, "Luis Buñuel/Glauber Rocha: échos d'une conversation," in *Cinéma* (Paris), February 1968.
"Buñuel Issue" of *Jeune Cinéma* (Paris), April 1969.
Pechter, William, "Buñuel," in *24 Times a Second,* New York, 1971.
"Buñuel Issue" of *Image et Son* (Paris), May 1971.
"Buñuel Issue" of *Cine Cubano,* no. 78/80, 1973.
Lyon, E.H., "Luis Buñuel: The Process of Dissociation in Three Films," in *Cinema Journal* (Evanston, Illinois), Fall 1973.
Fuentes, Carlos, "Spain, Catholicism, Surrealism and Anarchism: The Discreet Charm of Luis Buñuel," in *New York Times Magazine*, 11 March 1973.
Murray, S., "Erotic Moments in the Films of Luis Buñuel," in *Cinema Papers* (Melbourne), July 1974.
"*Le Fantôme de la liberté* Issue" of *Avant-Scène du Cinéma* (Paris), October 1974.
George, G.L., "The Discreet Charm of Luis Buñuel," in *Action* (Los Angeles), November/December 1974.
Mortimore, R., "Buñuel, Sáenz de Heredia and Filmófono," in *Sight and Sound* (London), Summer 1975.
Conrad, Randall, "The Minister of the Interior is on the Telephone: The Early Films of Luis Buñuel," in *Cineaste* (New York), no. 7, 1976.
Conrad, Randall, "A Magnificent and Dangerous Weapon: The Politics of Luis Buñuel's Later Films," in *Cineaste* (New York), no. 8, 1976.
Yutkevich, S., "Ein Realist—streng und mitleidlos," in *Film und Fernsehen* (Berlin), February 1980.
Wood, M., "The Discreet Charm of Luis Buñuel," in *American Film* (Washington, D.C.), September 1982.
Perez, G., "The Thread of the disconcerting," in *Sight and Sound* (London), Winter 1982-83.
Rubinstein, E., "Visit to a Familiar Planet: Buñuel among the Hurdanos," in *Cinema Journal* (Chicago), Summer 1983.
McCarthy, T., obituary in *Variety* (New York), 3 August 1983.
Millar, Gavin, "Buñuel—the careful entomologist," in *Listener* (London), 11 August 1983.
Mayersberg, P., "The happy ending of Luis Buñuel," in *Sight and Sound* (London), Autumn 1983.
"Buñuel Section" of *Cinématographe* (Paris), September-October 1983.
Yakir, Dan, and others, "Luis Buñuel, 1900-1983," in *Film Comment* (New York), September-October 1983.
"Buñuel Section" of *Positif* (Paris), October 1983.
Greenbaum, R., obituary in *Films in Review* (New York), October 1983.
"Buñuel Issue" of *Avant-Scène du Cinéma* (Paris), November 1983.
"Buñuel Issue," of *Bianco e Nero* (Rome), July-September 1984.
"Luis Buñuel," in *Film Dope* (London), March 1985.
Carrière, Jean-Claude, "Les aventures du sujet," in *Cahiers du Cinéma* (Paris), May 1985.
"*Cet objet obscur de desir* Issue" of *Avant-Scène du Cinéma* (Paris), November 1985.
Poplein, Michael, "Wuthering Heights and Its 'Spirit'," in *Literature/Film Quarterly* (Salisbury, Maryland), vol. 15, no. 2, 1987.
Taves, B., "Whose hand? Correcting a Buñuel Myth," in *Sight and Sound* (London), Summer 1987.

On BUÑUEL: films—

Bazin, Jeanine, and André Labarthe, *Cinéastes de notre temps,* for television, 1967.
Labarthe, André, *Luis Buñuel,* with interview with Georges Sadoul, Paris, 1967.

* * *

For all the critical attention (and furious critical controversy) his work occasioned over half a century, Luis Buñuel resisted our best taxonomical efforts. To begin with, while no artist of this century strikes one as more quintessentially Spanish than Buñuel, how can one apply the term "Spanish filmmaker" to a man whose *oeuvre* is far more nearly identified with France and Mexico than with the land of his birth? By the same token, can one speak of any film as "typical" of the man who made both *L'Age d'or* and *Nazarín,* both *Los olvidados* and *Belle de jour,* both *Land Without Bread* and *Le Charme discret de la bourgeoisie?* Nonetheless, from *Un Chien andalou* to *Cet obscur objet du désir,* a Buñuel film is always (albeit, as in many of the Mexican pieces of the 1940s and 1950s, only sporadically), a Buñuel film.

Perhaps the easiest way to deal with Buñuel's career is to suggest that certain avatars of Luis Buñuel may be identified at different (if sometimes slightly overlapping) historical periods. The first Luis Buñuel is the surrealist: the man who slit eyeballs (*Un Chien andalou*), the man to whom blasphemy was less a matter of specific utterances and gestures than a controlling style out of which might emerge new modes of feeling and of expression (*L'Age d'or*), the man who documentarized the unimaginable (*Land Without Bread*) and finally, the man who demonstrated more clearly than any other that surrealist perspectives demanded cinematographic realism. The second Luis Buñuel (and the saddest, and much the least identifiable, now as then) is the all-but-anonymous journeyman film professional: the collaborator, often unbilled and almost always unremarked, on Spanish films which to this day remain unknown to any but the most dogged researchers; the archivist and adapter and functionary in New York and Hollywood; the long-term absentee from the world's attention. The third is the Mexican director, the man who achieved a few works that at the time attracted varying degrees of notice outside the sphere of Latin American commercial distribution (*Los olvidados, Él, Archibaldo de la Cruz, Robinson Crusoe*) but also of others that at the time attracted no notice at all. The fourth is the Luis Buñuel who gradually made his way back to Europe by way of a few French films made in alternation with films in Mexico; and who then, with *Viridiana,* returned to appall, and so to reclaim, his native land; and who thenceforth, and no matter where or under what conditions he operated, persuasively reasserted himself as a figure of unmistakable moment in world cinema. The last Luis Buñuel, following his emergence in the mid-1960s, was the past master, at once awesome and beloved, as serene in his command of his medium as he was cheerfully intrepid in his pursuit of whatever of value might be mined from the depths of the previously unexplored.

Each of the Buñuels of the preceding catalogue, except for the obscure and essentially uncreative second one, is manifest, or at least implicit, in the others. Even in his Mexican work, which included some otherwise less than exalted assignments (and Buñuel himself, unlike certain of his more indiscriminate adulators, was perfectly willing to acknowledge that much of his Mexican work was shoddy or aborted or simply dull), the scion of surrealism showed his hand. There are several astonishing dream sequences, of course: the vision of slabs of raw meat hanging from the racks of a Mexico City streetcar (*La ilusión viaja en tranvía*), the incongruous verticality of the skeletal skyscrapers rising from the Mexico City slums (*Los olvidados*), and the necrophiliac ragings at the end of the Buñuel version of *Wuthering Heights* (*Abismos de pasión*). At the same time, it was in his Mexican studio movies, with their often absurdly brief shooting schedules, that Buñuel developed the unobtrusive but sovereign sway over narrative continuity and visual construction that so exhilarates admirers of such later works as *Le Journal d'une femme de chambre* or *Cet obscur objet du désir.* (According to Francisco Aranda, Alfred Hitchcock in 1972 called Buñuel "the best director in the world.")

Similarly, one may recognize in *Tristana* that same merciless anatomy of a specific social milieu, and in *The Exterminating Angel* that same theme of inexplicable entrapment, that one first encountered in *Land Without Bread.* In *El rio y la muerte* a man, all of him save his head imprisoned in an iron lung, submits to a round of face-slapping. We recognize in the image (and in the gasp of laughter it provokes) something of the merciless attack on our pieties of Buñuel's early surrealist works and something of the more offhand wicked humor of, say, *Le Charme discret.* When such a recognition is reached, we know that the variety of styles and accents in which Buñuel addressed us over the years is almost irrelevant. The political and social (or anti-social) canons of early surrealism could not contain him, nor could the foolish melodramatic conventions of some of his Mexican films stifle his humor, nor could the elegant actors and luxurious color cinematography of some of the later French films finally seduce him. Against all odds, his vision sufficed to transcend any and all stylistic diversions.

"Vision," perhaps the most exhausted word in the critical vocabulary, struggles back to life when applied to Buñuel and his camera. In the consistent clarity of its perception, in its refusal to distinguish between something called "reality" and something called "hallucination," Buñuel's camera always acts in the service of a fundamental surrealist principle, one of the few principles of any kind that Buñuel was never tempted to call into question. Whether focused on the tragic earthly destiny of an inept would-be saint (*Nazarín*) or on the bizarre obsessions of an inept would-be sinner (the uncle in *Viridiana,* among a good many others), Buñuel's camera is the instrument of the most rigorous denotation, invoking nothing beyond that which it so plainly and patiently registers. The uncertainties and ambivalences we may feel as we watch a Buñuel film arise not from the camera's capacity to mediate but from the camera's capacity to record: our responses are inherent in the subjects Buñuel selects, in those extremes of human experiences that we recognize as his special domain.

—E. Rubinstein

BURNETT, Charles

Nationality: American. **Born:** Vicksburg, Mississippi, 1944. **Education:** Studied electronics at Los Angeles Community College, and theater, film, writing, arts, and languages at the University of Southern California, Los Angeles. **Career:** Directed first feature film, *Killer of Sheep,* 1977. **Awards:** Guggenheim Foundation Fellowship, 1981;

Charles Burnett (left) directing *My Brother's Wedding*

Critics Prize, Berlin Festival, and First Prize, U.S. Festival, 1981, for *Killer of Sheep;* National Endowment for the Arts grant, MacArthur Foundation Fellowship, and Rockefeller Foundation Fellowship, 1988; Best Director and Best Screenplay, Independent Spirit Awards, Independent Feature Project/West, Best Film, Los Angeles Film Critics Association, and Best Film, National Society of Film Critics, 1990, for *To Sleep with Anger.* **Agent:** Triad Artists, Los Angeles.

Films as Director:

1969 *Several Friends* (short)
1973 *The House* (short)
1977 *Killer of Sheep* (+ sc, pr, ph, ed)
1983 *My Brother's Wedding* (+ sc, pr, ph)
1989 *Guests of Hotel Astoria* (+ ph)
1990 *To Sleep with Anger* (+ sc)
1994 *The Glass Shield* (+ sc)
1995 *When It Rains* (short)

Other Films:

1983 *Bless Their Little Hearts* (Woodbury) (sc, ph)
1985 *The Crocodile Conspiracy* (ph)
1987 *I Fresh* (sc)

Publications

By BURNETT: articles—

"Charles Burnett," interview by S. Sharp in *Black Film Review* (Washington, D.C.), no. 1, 1990.
"Entretien avec Charles Burnett," interview by M. Cientat and M. Ciment in *Positif* (Paris), November 1990.
"They've Gotta Have Us," interview by K. G. Bates in *New York Times,* 14 July 1991.
Burnett, Charles, and Charles Lane, "Charles Burnett and Charles Lane," in *American Film* (Los Angeles), August 1991.

On BURNETT: articles—

Reynaud, B., "Charles Burnett," in *Cahiers du Cinema* (Paris), June 1990.
Kennedy, L., "The Black Familiar," in *Village Voice* (New York), 16 October 1990.
Amiel, V., "To Sleep, to Dream," in *Positif* (Paris), November 1990.
"In from the Wilderness," in *Time* (New York), 17 June 1991.

* * *

Prior to the release of *To Sleep with Anger* in 1990, Charles Burnett had for two decades been writing and directing low-budget, little-known, but critically praised films that examined life and relationships among contemporary African Americans. *Killer of Sheep,* his first feature, is a searing depiction of ghetto life; *My Brother's Wedding* knowingly examines the relationship between two siblings on vastly different life tracks; *Bless Their Little Hearts* (directed by Billy Woodbury, but scripted and photographed by Burnett) is a poignant portrait of a black family. But how many had even heard of these films, let alone seen them? Thanks to the emergence in the 1980s of the prolific Spike Lee as a potent box office (as well as critical) force, however, a generation of African-American moviemakers have had their films not only produced but more widely distributed.

Such was the case with *To Sleep with Anger,* released theatrically by the Samuel Goldwyn Company. The film, like Burnett's earlier work, is an evocative, character-driven drama about relationships between family members and the fabric of domestic life among contemporary African Americans. It is the story of Harry Mention (Danny Glover), a meddlesome trickster who arrives in Los Angeles at the doorstep of his old friend Gideon (Paul Butler). The film details the manner in which Harry abuses the hospitality of Gideon, and his effect on Gideon's family. First there is the older generation: Gideon and his wife Suzie (Mary Alice), who cling to the traditions of their Deep South roots. Gideon has attempted to pass on his folklore, and his sense of values, to his two sons. One, Junior (Carl Lumbly), accepts this. But the other, Babe Brother (Richard Brooks), is on the economic fast track—and in conflict with his family.

While set within an African-American milieu, *To Sleep with Anger* transcends the ethnic identities of its characters; it also deals in a generic way with the cultural differences between parents and children, the manner in which individuals learn (or don't learn) from experience, and the need to push aside those who only know how to cause violence and strife. As such, it becomes a film that deals with universal issues.

The Glass Shield is a departure for Burnett in that his scenario is not set within an African-American universe. Instead, he places his characters in a hostile white world. *The Glass Shield* is a thinking person's cop film. Burnett's hero is a young black officer fresh out of the police academy, JJ Johnson (Michael Boatman), who becomes the first African American assigned to a corruption-laden, all-white sheriff's station in Los Angeles. Johnson is treated roughly by the station's commanding officer and some of the veteran cops. Superficially, it seems as if he is being dealt with in such a manner solely because he is an inexperienced rookie, in need of toughening and educating to the ways of the streets. But the racial lines clearly are drawn when one of his senior officers tells him, "You're one of us. You're not a brother." Johnson, who always has wanted to be a cop, desires only to do well and fit in. And so he stands by idly as black citizens are casually stopped and harassed by his fellow officers. Even more telling, with distressing regularity, blacks seem to have died under mysterious circumstances while in custody within the confines of the precinct.

As the film progresses, Burnett creates the feeling that a bomb is about to explode. And it does, when Johnson becomes involved in the arrest of a black man, framed on a murder charge, and readily agrees to lie in court to protect a fellow officer. Burnett's ultimate point is that in contemporary America it is impossible for a black man to cast aside his racial identity as he seeks his own personal destiny. First and foremost, he is an African American, existing within a society in which all of the power is in the hands of a white male elite. But African Americans are not the sole powerless entity in *The Glass Shield.* Johnson befriends his station's first female officer (Lori Petty), who must deal with sexism within the confines of her precinct house as much as on the streets. Together, this pair becomes united in a struggle against a white male-dominated system in which everyday corruption and hypocrisy are the rule.

Burnett's themes—African-American identity within the family unit and, subsequently, African-American identity within the community at large—are provocative and meaningful. It seems certain that he will never direct a film that is anything short of insightful in its content.

—Rob Edelman

BURTON, Tim

Nationality: American. **Born:** Burbank, California, 1958. **Education:** California Institute of Arts, B.A., 1981. **Family:** Married Lena Gieseke, 1989. **Career:** Cartoonist since grade school in Burbank;

Tim Burton directing Johnny Depp and Sarah Jessica Parker in *Ed Wood*

animator, Walt Disney Studios, Hollywood, California, 1981-85; director and producer of feature films, 1985—. **Awards:** Chicago Film Festival Award, 1982, for *Vincent;* Director of the Year, National Association of Theatre Owners. **Agent:** Creative Artists Agency, 9830 Wilshire Blvd., Beverly Hills, California, 90212.

Films as Director:

1982 *Vincent* (animated short); *Frankenweenie* (live-action short)
1985 *Pee-Wee's Big Adventure*
1988 *Beetlejuice*
1989 *Batman*
1990 *Edward Scissorhands* (+ co-sc, pr)
1992 *Batman Returns* (+ co-pr)
1994 *Ed Wood* (+ co-pr)
1995 *Vincent and Me*

Other Films:

1992 *Singles* (role)
1993 *Tim Burton's The Nightmare before Christmas* (sc, co-pr)
1994 *Cabin Boy* (co-pr)
1995 *Batman Forever* (exec pr)

Publications

By BURTON: books—

Tim Burton's The Nightmare before Christmas (children's book), 1993.

By BURTON: articles—

Interviews, in *Los Angeles Times,* 12 August 1990; 7 December 1990; 12 March 1992; 14 June 1992.
Interview, in *Washington Post,* 16 December 1990.
Interviews, in *Chicago Tribune,* 14 June 1992; 28 June 1992.
Interview, in *Vogue,* July 1992.
"Punching Holes in Reality," an interview with Gavin Smith, in *Film Comment,* November/December 1994.

On BURTON: articles—

Corliss, Richard, "A Sweet and Scary Treat: *The Nightmare before Christmas,*" in *Time,* 11 October 1993.
Thompson, Caroline, "On Tim Burton," in *New Yorker,* 21 March 1994.
Maio, Kathi, "Sick Puppy Auteur?," in *The Magazine of Fantasy and Science Fiction,* May 1994.

* * *

Although in the last resort I find his work more distinctive than distinguished, Tim Burton compels interest and attention by the way in which he has established within the Hollywood mainstream a cinema that is, to say the least, highly eccentric, idiosyncratic, and personal.

Burton's cinema is centered firmly on the figure of what I shall call (for want of a better term, and knowing that this one is now "politically incorrect") the freak. I define this as a person existing quite outside the bounds of the conventional notion of normality, usually (but not exclusively, as I include Burton's *Ed Wood* in this) because of some extreme physical peculiarity. Every one of the films, without exception, is built around at least one freak. One must then subdivide them into two categories: the "positive" freaks, who at least mean well, and the "negative" freaks, who are openly malignant. In the former category, in order of appearance: Pee-Wee Herman (*Pee-Wee's Big Adventure*), Edward Scissorhands, Catwoman (*Batman Returns*), Jack (*The Nightmare before Christmas*), Ed Wood; in the latter, the Joker (*Batman*) and the Penguin (*Batman Returns*). Beetlejuice (or "Betelgeuse") belongs ambiguously to both categories, though predominantly to the latter; to which one might also add, without stretching things too far, Riddler and Two-Face from *Batman Forever*—watered-down Burton, produced by him but written and directed by others, still owing a great deal to his influence. If one leaves aside *Pee-Wee's Big Adventure* and *The Nightmare before Christmas* (which Burton conceived and produced but did not direct), this gives us an alternative but exactly parallel division: three films with Michael Keaton, two with Johnny Depp (who might well have played Jack in *The Nightmare before Christmas* had Burton opted to make it as a live-action film).

Of the malignant freaks, Danny de Vito's Penguin is at once the most grotesque (to the verge of unwatchability) and the only one with an excuse for his malignancy: unlike the others he was *born* a freak, cast out and presumed to die by his parents, surviving by chance. The Joker and (if one permits the inclusion) Two-Face are physical freaks because of disfigurement, but this has merely intensified a malignancy already there. They are colorful and vivid, but not especially interesting: they merely embody a somewhat simplistic notion of evil, the worked-up energy of the over-the-top performances a means of concealing the essential emptiness at the conceptual level.

The benign freaks are more interesting. They are invariably associated with creativity: Pee-Wee, Edward Scissorhands, and Ed Wood are all artists, of a kind every bit as idiosyncratic as their creator's. This is set, obviously, against the determined destructiveness of the malignant freaks, who include in this respect Beetlejuice: the film's sympathetic characters (notably Winona Ryder) may find him necessary at times, but his dominant characteristic is a delight in destruction for its own sake. What gives the positive freaks (especially those played by Johnny Depp) an extra dimension is their extreme fragileness and vulnerability (the negative freaks always regard themselves, however misguidedly, as invincible).

Credit must be given to Burton's originality and inventiveness: he is an authentic artist in the sense that he is so clearly personally involved in and committed to his peculiar vision and its realization in film. What equally demands to be questioned is the degree of real intelligence underlying these qualities. The inventiveness is all on the surface, in the art direction, makeup, special effects. The conceptual level of the films does not bear very close scrutiny. The problem is there already, and in a magnified form, in *Beetlejuice:* the proliferation of invention is too grotesque and ugly to be funny, too wild, arbitrary, and unselfcritical to reward any serious analysis. The two *Batman* movies are distinguished by the remarkably dark vision (in a film one might expect to be "family entertainment") of contemporary urban/industrial civilization. But Michael Keaton's Batman, while unusually and mercifully restrained, fails to make any strong impression, and one is thrown back on the freaks who, with one notable exception, quickly outstay their welcome. The exception is Michelle Pfeiffer's Catwoman (in *Batman Returns*), and that is due primarily to one of the great screen presences of our time. Burton's overall project (in his work as a whole) seems to be to set his freaks (both positive and negative) against "normality" in order to show that normality, today, is every bit as weird: a laudable enough project, most evident in *Edward Scissorhands.* But the depiction of normality in that film (here, small-town suburbia) amounts to no more than amiable, simple-minded parody (despite the charm of Dianne Wiest's Avon Lady, but her role dwindles as the film proceeds). For all the grotesquerie of his monsters, Burton's cinema is ultimately too soft-centered, lacking in rigor and real *thinking.*

Ed Wood, however, may be taken as evidence that Burton is beginning to transcend the limitations of his previous work: it is far and away his most satisfying film to date. Here is surely one of cinema's most touching celebrations of the sheer joy of creativity with the irony, of course, that it is manifested in an "artist" of no talent whatever. Johnny Depp, in what is surely, with Pfeiffer's Catwoman, one of the two most complex and fully realized incarnations in Burton's work, magically conveys his character's absolute belief in the value of his own creations and his own personal joy and excitement in creating them, never realizing that they will indeed go down in film history as topping everyone's list of the worst films ever made. Yet his Ed Wood never strikes us as merely stupid: simply as a man completely caught up in his own delight in creative activity—always longing for recognition, but never self-serving or mercenary. This self-delusion, at once marvelous and pathetic, goes hand in hand with his growing compassion for and commitment to the decrepit and drug-addicted Bela Lugosi (Martin Landau, in a performance that, for once, fully deserved its Oscar), and his equally delusory conviction that Lugosi is still a great star. One's expectations of Burton's future work mount considerably after this film.

—Robin Wood

CACOYANNIS, Michael

Nationality: Greek. **Born:** Limassol, Cyprus, 11 June 1927. **Education:** Greek Gymnasium; Gray's Inn Law School, London, called to the Bar, 1948; Central School of Speech and Drama, London; Stage Directing course, Old Vic School, London. **Career:** Radio Producer for BBC and actor in London, early 1950's; returned to Greece and directed first film, *Windfall in Athens,* 1953; later directed stage productions in London and on Broadway. Lives in Greece. **Awards:** Grand Jury Prize, Cannes Film Festival, 1962, for *Electra.*

Films as Director:

1953 *Windfall in Athens*
1955 *Stella*
1957 *A Girl in Black*
1958 *The Final Lie* (*A Matter of Dignity*)
1959 *Our Last Spring*
1960 *The Wastrel*
1962 *Electra*
1964 ***Zorba the Greek***
1967 *The Day the Fish Came Out*
1971 *The Trojan Women* (*Women of Troy*)
1975 *Atilla 74* (doc)
1977 *Iphigenia*
1987 *Sweet Country*
1991 *Up, Down and Sideways*

Publications

By CACOYANNIS: articles—

Interview with Pierre Billard, in *Cinéma* (Paris), February 1957.
Interview in *Films and Filming* (London), January 1960.
Films and Filming (London), June 1963.
Interview in *Screen International* (London), 13 May 1978.
Interview with James Potts, in *Educational Broadcasting International,* September 1978.
Interview with M. McDonald, in *Bucknell Review,* Spring 1991.

On CACOYANNIS: book—

Schuster, Mel, *The Contemporary Greek Cinema,* Metuchen, New Jersey, 1979.

On CACOYANNIS: articles—

Stanbrook, Alan, "Rebel with a Cause," in *Film* (London), no. 24, 1960.
Bianco e Nero (Rome), December 1963.
"Michael Cacoyannis," in *Film Dope* (London), November 1974.
"Michael Cacoyannis," in *International Film Guide 1976,* edited by Peter Cowie, London, 1976.
National Film Theatre Booklet (London), April 1978.
Rivista del Cinematografo, May 1981.

* * *

A man between two worlds—this is how the life and work of Michael Cacoyannis could be characterized. The first world is one which draws on classical drama, his background in the modern theatre, and modern European cinema. The second world incorporates a mixture of the cultural knowledge acquired during his training in England with an inborn sense of the Greek tradition. This is the background from which Cacoyannis creates an original cinematographic depiction of contemporary life.

At the beginning of his career, Cacoyannis's inspiration came from the film classics as much as from his theatrical background; for his debut, *Kyriakatiko ksypnéma,* it is René Clair who appears to be his spiritual tutor. Cacoyannis's creative path then led from comedy to drama, to an analysis of the fragile nature of human relations. His stories, of Stella the singer, of the "girl in black" on the island of Hydros, or the story of the lost hopes of a broken family, are attempts to interpret contemporary Greek reality in a very raw way. The films capture the archaic rigidity of social relations and the feelings of loneliness. The random tragic moments in which city intellectuals as well as ordinary village people find themselves are milestones along their path to happiness. City streets, forgotten villages on lonely islands, and scorched foothills provide a suitably poignant backdrop for the fates of Cacoyannis's characters. It is said—with good reason—that early Cacoyannis films carry the spiritual heritage of Italian neo-realism.

These efforts culminated, through directly drawing upon literature, in the creation of a full-blooded renaissance figure, Alexis Zorba in *Zorba the Greek*—a portait of a man who lives (and loves) life to the full. The friendship of this "Man of Nature" with a young writer as shown in a confrontation of dramatically realistic (but also poetic) scenes, is the victory of the human spirit over convention. Also here in "sotto voce" is the pathos of sights and thoughts, a ghost-like echo of ancient Greek tragedy.

This element of contemporary drama is expanded to incorporate classic Greek traditions. Using locations in Greece under a blazing sun, Cacoyannis reworks not only the story of Elektra, but from mythology picks the story of the Trojans in *The Trojan Women,* while in the grand scenery of olive groves he sets Euripides talking about the Princess in *Iphigenia.* Cacoyannis does all this in order to address, for a contemporary audience, the eternal question of crime and punishment, to show that evil among people ultimately produces only more evil. For him the ancient myths encapsulate eternal conflicts of the human soul. Thus is Michael Cacoyannis a poet of the modern Greek cinema.

—Vacláv Merhaut

Michael Cacoyannis (left) on the set of *Our Last Spring*

CAMPION, Jane

Nationality: New Zealander. **Born:** Wellington, 30 April 1954. **Education:** Victoria University, Wellington, B.A. in structural arts; Chelsea School of Arts, London, diploma in fine arts (completed at Sydney College of the Arts); Australian Film and Television School, diploma in direction. **Family:** Parents are opera/theater director Richard Campion and actress/writer Edith Campion; married television producer/director Colin Englert. **Career:** Became interested in filmmaking and began making short films, late 1970s; short film, *Tissues,* led to her acceptance into the Australian Film and Television School, 1981; took job with Australia's Women's Film Unit, 1984; directed an episode of the television drama *Dancing Daze,* 1986; short films *Peel, Passionless Moments,* and *Girls Own Story* released theatrically in the United States, 1989-90; **Awards:** Diploma of Merit, Melbourne Festival, and Palme d'Or, Best Short Film, Cannes Film Festival, for *Peel,* 1983-86; Unique Artist Merit, Melbourne Festival, Best Experimental Film, Australian Film Institute, and Most Popular Short Film, Sydney Festival, for *Passionless Moments,* 1984-85; Rouben Mamoulian Award, Best Overall Short Film, Unique Artist Merit, Melbourne Festival, Best Direction and Screenplay, Australian Film Institute Awards, and First Prize, Cinestud Amsterdam Festival, for *Girls Own Story,* 1984-85; X. L. Elders Award and Best Short Fiction, Melbourne Festival, for *After Hours,* 1985; Golden Plaque, Chicago Festival, and Best Director and Best TV Film, Australian Film Institute, for *2 Friends,* 1987; Georges Sadoul Prize, Best Foreign Film, Best Film, and Best Director, Australian Critics Awards, New Generation Award, Los Angeles Film Critics Association, and Best Foreign Film, Independent Spirit Award, for *Sweetie,* 1989-90; Byron Kennedy Award, Special Jury Prize, Annual Elvira Notari Award, Si Presci Award, O.C.I.C. Award, Best Film for Young People, Cinema & Ragazzi, Otto Debelius Prize, Berlin Festival, Critics Award, Toronto Festival, and Best Foreign Film, Independent Spirit Award, for *An Angel at My Table,* 1990; Academy Award, Best Screenplay, Academy Award nomination, Best Director, Best Director, and Screenplay, New York Film Critics Circle, Best Director and Screenplay, Los Angeles Film Critics Association, Best Director and Screenplay, Australian Film Institute Awards, Best Director and Screenplay, Australian Film Critics, Best Director, Guild of Regional Film Writers, and Best Screenplay, Chicago Film Critics, for *The Piano,* 1993. **Address:** Hilary Linstead & Associates, Level 18, Plaza II, 500 Oxford Street, Bondi Junction, NSW 2022, Australia.

Films as Director:

1982 *Peel* (short) (+ sc)
1984 *Mishaps of Seduction and Conquest* (video short) (+ sc); *Passionless Moments* (short) (co-d, co-sc); *Girls Own Story* (short) (+ sc); *After Hours* (short) (+ sc)
1985 *2 Friends* (for Australian TV)
1989 *Sweetie* (co-sc)
1990 *An Angel at My Table* (for Australian TV; edited version released theatrically)
1993 ***The Piano*** (+ sc)
1996 *Portrait of a Lady*

Publications

By CAMPION: books—

The Piano, New York, 1993.
The Piano: The Novel, with Kate Pullinger, New York, 1994.

By CAMPION: articles—

Interview with Carla Hall, in *Washington Post,* 4 March 1990.
Interview with Donna Yuzwalk, in *Guardian* (London), 2 May 1990.
Interview with Maitland McDonagh, in *New York Times,* 19 May 1991.
Interview with Elizabeth Drucker, in *American Film* (Los Angeles), July 1991.
Interview with Katharine Dieckmann, in *Interview* (New York), January 1992.
"Jane Campion's Lunatic Women," with Mary Cantwell, in *New York Times Magazine,* 19 September 1993.
"Merchant of the Ivories," with Anne Thompson, in *Entertainment Weekly* (New York), 19 November 1993.

On CAMPION: articles—

Ansen, David, and Charles Fleming, "Passion for *Piano,*" in *Newsweek* (New York), 31 May 1993.
Travers, Peter, "Sex and *The Piano,*" in *Rolling Stone* (New York), 9 December 1993.
Article, in *New York Times,* 10 March 1994.

* * *

Whatever their quality, all of Jane Campion's feature films have remained consistent in theme. They depict the lives of girls and women who are in one way or another separate from the mainstream, because of physical appearance (if not outright physical disability) or personality quirk, and she spotlights the manner in which they relate to and function within their respective societies.

Campion began directing features after making several highly acclaimed, award-winning short films which were extensively screened on the international film festival circuit. Her first two features are alike in that they focus on the relationships between two young women, and how they are affected by the adults who control their world. Her debut, *2 Friends,* was made for Australian television in 1985 and did not have its American theatrical premiere until 1996. It is a depiction of the connection between a pair of adolescents, focusing on the changes in their friendship and how they are influenced by adult authority figures. The narrative is told in reverse time: at the outset, the girls are a bit older, and their developing personalities have separated them; as the film continues, they become younger and closer.

Sweetie, Campion's initial theatrical feature, is a pitch-black comedy about a young woman who is overweight, overemotional, and even downright crazy, with the scenario charting the manner in which she relates to her parents and her skinny, shy, easily manipulated sister. The film was controversial in that critics and viewers either raved about it or were turned off by its quirky nature. While not without inspired moments, both *Sweetie* and *2 Friends* lack the assurance of Campion's future work.

The filmmaker's unequivocal breakthrough as a world-class talent came in 1990 with *An Angel at My Table.* The theatrical version of the film is 158 minutes long and is taken from a three-part mini-series made for New Zealand television. *An Angel at My Table* did not benefit from the media hype surrounding *The Piano,* Campion's 1993 international art house hit, but it is as equally fine a work. It is an uncommonly literate portrait of Janet Frame, a plump, repressed child who was destined to become one of New Zealand's most renowned writers. Prior to her fame, however, she was falsely diagnosed as a schizophrenic, passed eight years in a mental hospital, and received over 200 electric shock treatments.

Campion evocatively depicts the different stages of Frame's life; the filmmaker elicits a dynamic performance from Kerry Fox as the

Jane Campion

adult Janet and, in visual terms, she perfectly captures the essence of the writer's inner being. At the same time, Campion bitingly satirizes the manner in which society patronizes those who sincerely dedicate their lives to the creation of art. She depicts pseudo-artists who would not know a poem from a Harlequin Romance, and publishers who think that for Frame to truly be a success she must have a best-seller and ride around in a Rolls Royce.

If *An Angel at My Table* spotlights the evolution of a woman as an intellectual being, Campion's next work, *The Piano,* depicts a woman's development on a sexual and erotic level. *The Piano,* like *The Crying Game* before it and *Pulp Fiction* later on, became the cinematic cause celebre of its year. It is a deceptively simple story, beautifully told, of Ada (Holly Hunter, in an Academy Award-winning performance), a Scottish widow and mute who arrives with her nine-year-old daughter (Anna Paquin, who also won an Oscar) in remote New Zealand during the 1850s. Ada is to be the bride in an arranged marriage with a stern, hesitant farmer (Sam Neill). But she becomes sexually and romantically involved with Baines (Harvey Keitel), her illiterate, vulnerable neighbor to whom she gives piano lessons: an arrangement described by Campion as an "erotic pact."

Campion succeeds in creating a story about the development of love, from the initial eroticism between the two characters to something deeper and more romantic. Ada has a symbolic relationship with the piano, which is both her refuge and way of self-expression. *The Piano* is an intensely haunting tale of exploding passion and deep, raw emotion, and it put its maker at the forefront of contemporary, world-class cinema. Campion's most recent project, due for release in 1996, is *Portrait of a Lady,* based on a Henry James novel.

—Rob Edelman

CAPRA, Frank

Nationality: American. **Born:** Bisaquino, Sicily, 18 May 1897; emigrated with family to Los Angeles, 1903. **Education:** Manual Arts High School, Los Angeles; studied chemical engineering at California Institute of Technology, Pasadena, graduated 1918. **Family:** Married 1) Helen Howell, 1924 (divorced 1938); 2) Lucille Reyburn, 1932, two sons, one daughter, Ballistics teacher, U.S. Army, 1918-19. **Career:** Lab assistant for Walter Bell, 1922-23; prop man, editor for Bob Eddy, writer for Hal Roach and Mack Sennett, 1923-25; hired by Columbia Pictures, 1928; began to work with Robert Riskin, 1931; elected President of Academy, 1935; elected President of Screen Directors' Guild, 1938; formed Frank Capra Productions with writer Robert Riskin, 1939; Major in Signal Corps, 1942-45; formed Liberty Films with Sam Briskin, William Wyler, and George Stevens, 1945 (sold to Paramount, 1948). **Awards:** Oscar for Best Director, for *It Happened One Night,* 1934, for *Mr. Deeds Goes to Town,* 1936, and

You Can't Take It With You, 1938; Distinguished Service Medal, U.S. Armed Forces, 1945; D.W. Griffith Award, Directors Guild of America, 1958; Honorary Doctorates, Temple University, Philadelphia, 1971, and Carthage College, Wisconsin, 1972. **Address:** P.O. Box 980, La Quinta, CA 92253, U.S.A.

Films as Director:

1922 *Fultah Fisher's Boarding House*
1926 *The Strong Man* (+ co-sc)
1927 *Long Pants*; *For the Love of Mike*
1928 *That Certain Thing*; *So This Is Love*; *The Matinee Idol*; *The Way of the Strong*; *Say It With Sables* (+ co-story); *Submarine*; *The Power of the Press*; *The Swim Princess*; *The Burglar* (*Smith's Burglar*)
1929 *The Younger Generation*; *The Donovan Affair*; *Flight* (+ dialogue)
1930 *Ladies of Leisure*; *Rain or Shine*
1931 *Dirigible*; *The Miracle Woman*; *Platinum Blonde*
1932 *Forbidden* (+ sc); *American Madness*
1933 *The Bitter Tea of General Yen* (+ pr); *Lady for a Day*
1934 ***It Happened One Night***; *Broadway Bill*
1936 *Mr. Deeds Goes to Town* (+ pr)
1937 *Lost Horizon* (+ pr)
1938 *You Can't Take It With You* (+ pr)
1939 ***Mr. Smith Goes to Washington*** (+ pr)
1941 *Meet John Doe* (+ pr)
1942 ***Why We Fight* (Part 1): *Prelude to War*** (+ pr)
1943 ***Why We Fight* (Part 2): *The Nazis Strike*** (co-d, pr); ***Why We Fight* (Part 3): *Divide and Conquer*** (co-d, pr)
1944 ***Why We Fight* (Part 6): *The Battle of China*** (co-d, pr); *Tunisian Victory* (co-d, pr); ***Arsenic and Old Lace*** (+ pr) (filmed in 1942)
1945 *Know Your Enemy: Japan* (co-d, pr); *Two Down, One to Go* (+ pr)
1946 ***It's a Wonderful Life*** (+ pr, co-sc)
1948 *State of the Union* (+ pr)
1950 *Riding High* (+ pr)
1951 *Here Comes the Groom* (+ pr)
1956 *Our Mr. Sun* (+ pr, sc) (Bell System Science Series Numbers 1 to 4)
1957 *Hemo the Magnificent* (+ pr, sc); *The Strange Case of the Cosmic Rays* (+ pr, co-sc)
1958 *The Unchained Goddess* (+ pr, co-sc)
1959 *A Hole in the Head* (+ pr)
1961 *Pocketful of Miracles* (+ pr)

Other Films:

1924 (as co-sc with Arthur Ripley on films featuring Harry Longdon): *Picking Peaches*; *Smile Please*; *Shanghaied Lovers*; *Flickering Youth*; *The Cat's Meow*; *His New Mama*; *The First Hundred Years*; *The Luck o' the Foolish*; *The Hansom Cabman*; *All Night Long*; *Feet of Mud*
1925 (as co-sc with Arthur Ripley on films featuring Harry Langdon): *The Sea Squawk*; *Boobs in the Woods*; *His Marriage Wow*; *Plain Clothes*; *Remember When?*; *Horace Greeley, Jr.*; *The White Wing's Bride*; *Lucky Stars*; *There He Goes*; *Saturday Afternoon*
1926 (as co-sc with Arthur Ripley on films featuring Harry Langdon): *Fiddlesticks*; *The Soldier Man*; *Tramp, Tramp, Tramp*
1943 ***Why We Fight* (Part 4): *The Battle of Britain*** (pr)
1944 *The Negro Soldier* (pr); ***Why We Fight* (Part 5): *The Battle of Russia*** (pr); *Know Your Ally: Britain* (pr)
1945 ***Why We Fight* (Part 7): *War Comes to America*** (pr); *Know Your Enemy: Germany* (pr)
1950 *Westward the Women* (story)

Publications

By CAPRA: books—

The Name Above the Title, New York, 1971.
It's a Wonderful Life, with Frances Goodrich and Albert Hackett, New York, 1986.

By CAPRA: articles—

"The Gag Man," in *Breaking Into Movies,* edited by Charles Jones, New York, 1927.
"Sacred Cows to the Slaughter," in *Stage* (New York), 13 July 1936.
"We Should All Be Actors," in *Silver Screen* (New York), September 1946.
"Do I Make You Laugh?," in *Films and Filming* (London), September 1962.
"Capra Today," with James Childs, in *Film Comment* (New York), vol.8, no.4, 1972.
"Mr. Capra Goes to College," with Arthur Bressan and Michael Moran, in *Interview* (New York), June 1972.
"Why We (Should Not) Fight," interview with G. Bailey, in *Take One* (Montreal), September 1975.
"'Trends Change Because Trends Stink'—An Outspoken Talk with Legendary Producer/Director Frank Capra," with Nancy Anderson, in *Photoplay* (New York), November 1975.
Interview with J. Mariani, in *Focus on Film* (London), no.27, 1977.
"Dialogue on Film," in *American Film* (Washington, D.C.), October 1978.
Interview with H.A. Hargreave, in *Literature/Film Quarterly* (Salisbury, Maryland), vol. 9, no. 3, 1981.

On CAPRA: books—

Griffith, Richard, *Frank Capra,* London, 1951.
Silke, James, *Frank Capra: One Man—One Film,* Washington, D.C., 1971.
Bergman, Andrew, *We're in the Money: Depression America and Its Films,* New York, 1972.
Willis, Donald, *The Films of Frank Capra,* Metuchen, New Jersey, 1974.
Glatzer, Richard, and John Raeburn, editors, *Frank Capra: The Man and His Films,* Ann Arbor, 1975.
Poague, Leland, *The Cinema of Frank Capra: An Approach to Film Comedy,* South Brunswick, New Jersey, 1975.
Bohn, Thomas, *An Historical and Descriptive Analysis of the 'Why We Fight' Series,* New York, 1977.
Maland, Charles, *American Visions: The Films of Chaplin, Ford, Capra and Welles, 1936-1941,* New York, 1977.
Scherle, Victor, and William Levy, *The Films of Frank Capra,* Secaucus, New Jersey, 1977.
Bohnenkamp, Dennis, and Sam Grogg, editors, *Frank Capra Study Guide,* Washington, D.C., 1979.
Maland, Charles, *Frank Capra,* Boston, 1980.
Giannetti, Louis, *Masters of the American Cinema,* Englewood Cliffs, New Jersey, 1981.
Zagarrio, Vito, *Frank Capra,* Florence 1985.
Carney, Raymond, *American Vision: The Films of Frank Capra,* Cambridge, 1986.
Lazere, Donald, editor, *American Media and Mass Culture: Left Perspectives,* Berkeley, 1987.

Wolfe, Charles, *Frank Capra: A Guide to References and Resources,* Boston, 1987.
McBride, Joseph, *Frank Capra: The Catastrophe of Success,* New York, 1992.

On CAPRA: articles—

"How Frank Capra Makes a Hit Picture," in *Life* (New York), 19 September 1938.
Hellman, Geoffrey, "Thinker in Hollywood," in *New Yorker,* 5 February 1940.
Ferguson, Otis, "Democracy at the Box Office," in *New Republic* (New York), 24 March 1941.
Salemson, Harold, "Mr. Capra's Short Cuts to Utopia," in *Penguin Film Review* no.7, London, 1948.
Deming, Barbara, "Non-Heroic Heroes," in *Films in Review* (New York), April 1951.
"Capra Issue" of *Positif* (Paris), December 1971.
Richards, Jeffrey, "Frank Capra: The Classic Populist," in *Visions of Yesterday,* London, 1973.
Nelson, J., "Mr. Smith Goes to Washington: Capra, Populism and Comic-Strip Art," in *Journal of Popular Film* (Bowling Green, Ohio), Summer 1974.
Badder, D.J., "Frank Capra," in *Film Dope* (London), November 1974 and October 1975.
"Capra Issue" of *Film Comment* (New York), vol.8, no.4, 1972.
Sklar, Robert, "The Making of Cultural Myths: Walt Disney and Frank Capra," in *Movie-Made America,* New York, 1975.
"Lost and Found: The Films of Frank Capra," in *Film* (London), June 1975.
Rose, B., "It's a Wonderful Life: The Stand of the Capra Hero," in *Journal of Popular Film* (Bowling Green, Ohio), v.6, no.2, 1977.
Quart, Leonard, "Frank Capra and the Popular Front," in *Cineaste* (New York), Summer 1977.
Gehring, Wes, "McCarey vs. Capra: A Guide to American Film Comedy of the '30s," in *Journal of Popular Film and Television* (Bowling Green, Ohio), vol.7, no.1, 1978.
Dickstein, M., "It's a Wonderful Life, But...," in *American Film* (Washington, D.C.), May 1980.
Jameson, R.T., "Stanwyck and Capra," in *Film Comment* (New York), March/April 1981.
"Capra Issue" of *Film Criticism* (Edinboro, Pennsylvania), Winter 1981.
Basinger, Jeanine, "America's love affair with Frank Capra," in *American Film* (Washington, D.C.), March 1982.
Edgerton, G., "Capra and Altman: Mythmaker and mythologist," in *Literature/Film Quarterly* (Salisbury, Maryland), January 1983.
Dossier on Capra, in *Positif* (Paris), July-August 1987.
American Film (Washington, D.C.), December 1987.
Gottlieb, Sidney, "From Heroine to Brat: Frank Capra's Adaptation of "Night Bus" (*It Happened One Night*)," in *Literature/Film Quarterly* (Salisbury, Maryland), vol. 16, no. 2, 1988.

* * *

The critical stock of Frank Capra has fluctuated perhaps more wildly than that of any other major director. During his peak years, the 1930's, he was adored by the press, by the industry and, of course, by audiences. In 1934 *It Happened One Night* won nearly all the Oscars, and through the rest of the decade a film of Frank Capra was either the winner or the strong contender for that honor. Long before the formulation of the *auteur* theory, the Capra signature on a film was recognized. But after World War II his career went into serious decline. His first post-war film, *It's a Wonderful Life,* was not received with the enthusiasm he thought it deserved (although it has gone on to become one of his most-revered films). Of his last five films, two are remakes of material he treated in the thirties. Many contemporary critics are repelled by what they deem indigestible "Capracorn" and have even less tolerance for an ideology characterized as dangerously simplistic in its populism, its patriotism, its celebration of all-American values.

Indeed, many of Capra's most famous films can be read as excessively sentimental and politically naive. These readings, however, tend to neglect the bases for Capra's success—his skill as a director of actors, the complexity of his staging configurations, his narrative economy and energy, and most of all, his understanding of the importance of the spoken word in sound film. Capra captured the American voice in cinematic space. The words often serve the cause of apple pie, mom, the little man and other greeting card clichés (indeed, the hero of *Mr. Deeds Goes to Town* writes verse for greeting cards). But often in the sound of the voice we hear uncertainties about those very clichés.

Capra's career began in the pre-talkie era, when he directed silent comic Harry Langdon in two successful films. His action films of the early thirties are not characteristic of his later work, yet already, in the films he made with Barbara Stanwyck, his individual gift can be discerned. The narrative pretext of *The Miracle Woman* is the urgency of Stanwyck's voice, its ability to move an audience, to persuade listeners of its sincerity. Capra exploited the raw energy of Stanwyck in this and other roles, where her qualities of fervor and near-hysterical conviction are just as essential to her persona as her hard-as-nails implacability would be in the forties. Stanwyck's voice is theatricalized, spatialized in her revivalist circus-tent in *The Miracle Woman* and on the hero's suicide tower in *Meet John Doe,* where her feverish pleadings are the only possible tenor for the film's unresolved ambiguities about society and the individual.

John Doe is portrayed by Gary Cooper, another American voice with particular resonance in the films of Capra. A star who seems to have invented the "strong, silent" type, Cooper first plays Mr. Deeds, whose platitudinous doggerel comes from a simple, do-gooder heart, but who enacts a crisis of communication in his long silence at the film's climax, a sanity hearing. When Mr. Deeds finally speaks it is a sign that the community (if not sanity) is restored—the usual resolution of a Capra film. As John Doe, Cooper is given words to voice by reporter Stanwyck, and he delivers them with such conviction that the whole nation listens. The vocal/dramatic center of the film is located in a rain-drenched ball park filled with John Doe's "people." The hero's effort to speak the truth, to reveal his own imposture and expose the fascistic intentions of his sponsor, is stymied when the lines of communication are literally cut between microphone and loudspeaker. The Capra narrative so often hinges on the protagonist's ability to speak and be heard, on the drama of sound and audition.

The bank run in *American Madness* is initiated by a montage of telephone voices and images, of mouths spreading a rumor. The panic is quelled by the speech of the bank president (Walter Huston), a situation repeated in more modest physical surroundings in *It's a Wonderful Life.* The most extended speech in the films of Capra occurs in *Mr. Smith Goes to Washington.* The whole film is a test of the hero's voice, and it culminates in a filibuster, a speech that, by definition, cannot be interrupted. The climax of *State of the Union* involves a different kind of audience and audition. There, the hero confesses his political dishonesty and his love for his wife on television.

The visual contexts, both simple and complex, never detract from the sound of Capra's films. They enhance it. The director's most elaborately designed film, *The Bitter Tea of General Yen* (recalling the style of Josef von Sternberg in its chiaroscuro lighting and its exoticism) expresses the opposition of cultural values in its visual elements, to be sure, but also in the voices of Stanwyck and Nils Asther, a Swedish actor who impersonates a Chinese war lord. Less unusual but not less significant harmonies are sounded in *It Happened One Night,* where a society girl (Claudette Colbert) learns "real" American speech

Frank Capra

from a fast-talking reporter (Clark Gable). The love scenes in *Mr. Deeds* are for Gary Cooper and Jean Arthur, another quintessential Capra heroine, whose vocal personality is at least as memorable as her physical one. In James Stewart Capra finds his most disquieting voice, ranging in *Mr. Smith* from ingenuousness to hysterical desperation and in *It's a Wonderful Life* to an even higher pitch of hysteria when the hero loses his identity.

The sounds and sights of Capra's films bear the authority of a director whose autobiography is called *The Name above the Title.* With that authority comes an unsettling belief in authorial power, the power dramatized in his major films, the persuasiveness exercised in political and social contexts. That persuasion reflects back on the director's own power to engage the viewer in his fiction, to call upon a degree of belief in the fiction—even when we reject the meaning of the fable.

—Charles Affron

CARNÉ, Marcel

Nationality: French. **Born:** Batignolles, Paris, 18 August 1909. **Career:** Worked as insurance clerk, mid-1920's; assistant to cameraman Georges Périnal on *Les Nouveaux Messieurs,* 1928; worked as film critic, and made short film, 1929; assistant to René Clair on *Sous les toits de Paris,* 1930; editor-in-chief, *Hebdo-Films* journal, and member, "October" group, early 1930's; assistant to Jacques Feyder, 1933-35; directed first feature, *Jenny,* 1936. **Awards:** Special Mention, Venice Festival, for *Quai des brumes,* 1938.

Films as Director:

1929 *Nogent, Eldorado du dimanche*
1936 *Jenny*
1937 *Dr le de drame* (*Bizarre Bizarre*)
1938 ***Quai des brumes*** (*Port of Shadows*); *Hotel du Nord*
1939 ***Le Jour se lève*** (*Daybreak*); *École communale* (abandoned due to war)
1942 *Les Visiteurs du soir* (*The Devil's Envoys*)
1945 ***Les Enfants du paradis*** (*Children of Paradise*)
1946 *Les Portes de la nuit* (*Gates of the Night*)
1947 *La Fleur de l'âge* (not completed)
1949 *La Marie du port* (+ co-sc)
1951 *Juliette ou la Clé des songes* (+ co-sc)
1953 *Thérèse Raquin* (*The Adulteress*) (+ co-sc)
1954 *L'Air de Paris* (+ co-sc)
1956 *Le Pays d'où je viens* (+ co-sc)
1958 *Les Tricheurs* (*The Cheaters*)
1960 *Terrain vague* (+ co-sc)
1962 *Du mouron pour les petits oiseaux* (+ co-sc)
1965 *Trois Chambres à Manhattan* (+ co-sc)
1967 *Les Jeunes Loups* (*The Young Wolves*)
1971 *Les Assassins de l'ordre* (+ co-sc)
1974 *La Merveilleuse Visite* (+ co-sc)
1976 *La Bible* (feature doc for TV and theatrical release)

Publications

By CARNÉ: book—

Les Enfants du Paradis, with Jacques Prevert, London, 1988.

By CARNÉ: articles—

Interview, with F. Cuel and others, in *Cinématographe* (Paris), May 1978.
"Comment est ne *Le Quai des brumes,*" in *Avant-Scène du Cinéma* (Paris), 15 October 1979.
"Marcel Carné sous la coupole," in *Avant-Scène du Cinéma* (Paris), 1 July 1980.
Interview in *Avant-Scène du Cinéma* (Paris), October 1988.

On CARNÉ: books—

Béranger, Jean-Louis, *Marcel Carné,* Paris, 1945.
Landrey, Bernard, *Marcel Carné, sa vie, ses films,* Paris.
Quéval, Jean, *Marcel Carné,* Paris, 1952.
Prévert, Jacques, *Children of Paradise,* New York, 1968.
Armes, Roy, *French Film Since 1946: The Great Tradition,* New York, 1970.
Prévert, Jacques, *Le Jour se lève,* New York, 1970.
Perez, Michel, *Les films de Carné,* Paris, 1986.
Turk, Edward Baron, *Child of Paradise: Marcel Carné and the Golden Age of Cinema,* Cambridge, Massachusetts, 1989.

On CARNÉ: articles—

Manvell, Roger, "Marcel Carné," in *Sight and Sound* (London), Spring 1946.
Lodge, J.F., "The Cinema of Marcel Carné," in *Sequence* (London), December 1946.
Lambert, Gavin, "Marcel Carné," in *Sequence* (London), Spring 1948.
Michel, J., "Carné ou la Clé des songes," in *Cinéma* (Paris), no.12, 1956.
Sadoul, Georges, "Les Films de Marcel Carné, expression de notre époque," in *Les Lettres Françaises* (Paris), 1 March 1956.
Stanbrook, Alan, "The Carné Bubble," in *Film* (London), November/December 1959.
"Carné Issue" of *Cahiers de la Cinémathèque* (Perpignan), Winter 1972.
Turk, Edward Baron, "The Birth of Children of Paradise," in *American Film* (Washington, D.C.), July/August 1979.
"*Le Quai des brumes* Issue" of *Avant-Scène du Cinéma* (Paris), 15 October 1979.
Gillett, John, "Salute to a French Master," in *Radio Times* (London), 2 March 1985.
Virmaux, A., and O. Virmaux, "La malediction: Le film inachève de Carné et Prevert," in *Cinématographe* (Paris), October 1986.
Thoraval, Yves, "Marcel Carné: Un Parisian à Toulouse," in *Cinéma* (Paris), 14 January 1987.
Kolker, Robert Phillip, "Carné's *Les Portes de la nuit* and the Sleep of French Cinema," in *Post Script* (Jacksonville, Florida), Fall 1987.

* * *

At a time when film schools were non-existent and training in filmmaking was acquired through assistantship, no one could have been better prepared for a brilliant career than Marcel Carné. He worked as assistant to René Clair on the first important French sound film, *Sous les toits de Paris,* and to Jacques Feyder on the latter's three great films of 1934-35. Though he had also made a successful personal documentary, *Nogent, Eldorado du dimanche,* and a number of publicity shorts, it was only thanks to the support of Feyder and his wife, the actress Françoise Rosay, that Carné was able to make his debut as a feature filmmaker with *Jenny* in 1936. If this was a routine melodrama, Carné was able in the next three years to establish himself as one of Europe's leading film directors.

Marcel Carné

During the period up to the outbreak of war in 1939 Carné established what was to be a ten-year collaboration with the poet and screenwriter Jacques Prévert, and gradually built up a team of collaborators—including the designer Alexandre Trauner and composer Maurice Jaubert—which was unsurpassed at this period. In quick succession Carné made the comedy *Drole de drame,* which owes more to Prévert's taste for systematic absurdity and surreal gags than to the director's professionalism, and a trio of fatalistic romantic melodramas, *Quai des brumes, Hotel du nord* and *Le Jour se lève.*

These are perfect examples of the mode of French filmmaking that had been established by Jacques Feyder: a concern with visual style and a studio-created realism, a reliance on detailed scripts with structure and dialogue separately elaborated, and a foregrounding of star performers to whom all elements of decor and photography are subordinate. Though the forces shaping a character's destiny may be outside his or her control, the story focuses on social behavior and the script offers set-piece scenes and confrontations and witty or trenchant dialogue that enables the stars to display their particular talents to the full.

The various advocates of either Prévert or Carné have sought to make exclusive claims as to which brought poetry to the nebulous and ill-defined "poetic realism" that these films are said to exemplify. In retrospect, however, these arguments seem over-personalized, since the pair seem remarkably well-matched. The actual differences seem less in artistic approach than in attitude to production. From the first, Carné, heir to a particular mode of quality filmmaking, was concerned with an industry, a technique, a career. Prévert, by contrast, though he is a perfect example of the archetypal 1930s screenwriter, able to create striking star roles and write dazzling and memorable dialogue, is not limited to this role and has a quite separate identity as surrealist, humorist and poet.

The pair share a certain fantastic conception of realism, with film seen as a studio construct in which fidelity to life is balanced by attention to a certain poetic atmosphere. Carné's coldly formal command of technique is matched by Prévert's sense of the logic of a tightly woven narrative. If it is Prévert's imagination that allows him to conceive both the *amour fou* that unites the lovers and the grotesque villains who threaten it, it is Carné's masterly direction of actors that turns Jean Gabin and Michèle Morgan into the 1930s ideal couple and draws such memorable performances from Michel Simon, Jules Berry and Arletty.

The collaboration of Prévert and Carné was sustained during the very different circumstances of the German Occupation, when they together made two films that rank among the most significant of the period. Since films in the mode of 1930s poetic realism were now banned, it is hardly surprising that Carné and Prévert should have found the need to adopt a radically new style. Remaining within the concept of the studio-made film, but leaving behind the contemporary urban gloom of *Le Jour se lève,* they opted for a style of elaborate and theatrical period spectacle. The medieval fable of *Les Visiteurs du soir* was an enormous contemporary success but it has not worn well. Working with very limited resources the filmmakers—assisted clandestinely by Trauner and the composer Joseph Kosma—succeeded in making an obvious prestige film, a work in which Frenchmen could take pride at a dark moment of history. But despite the presence of such players as Arletty and Jules Berry, the overall effect is ponderous and stilted.

Carné's masterpiece is *Les Enfants du paradis,* shot during the war years but released only after the Liberation. Running for over three hours and comprising two parts, each of which is of full feature length, *Les Enfants du paradis* is one of the most ambitious films ever undertaken in France. Set in the twin worlds of theatre and crime in nineteenth century Paris, this all-star film is both a theatrical spectacle in its own right and a reflection on the nature of spectacle. The script is one of Prévert's richest, abounding in wit and aphorism, and Carné's handling of individual actors and crowd scenes is masterly. The sustained vitality and dynamism of the work as it moves seemingly effortlessly from farce to tragedy, from delicate love scenes to outrageous buffoonery, is exemplary, and its impact is undimmed by the years.

Marcel Carné was still only thirty-six and at the height of his fame when the war ended. Younger than most of those who now came to the fore, he had already made masterly films in two quite different contexts and it seemed inevitable that he would continue to be a dominant force in French cinema despite the changed circumstances of the postwar era. But in fact the first post-war Carné-Prévert film, *Les Portes de la nuit,* was an expensive flop. When a subsequent film, *La Fleur de l'âge,* was abandoned shortly after production had begun, one of the most fruitful partnerships in French cinema came to an end. Carné directed a dozen more films, from *La Marie du port* in 1950 to *La Merveilleuse Visite* in 1973, but he was no longer a major force in French filmmaking.

Marcel Carné was an unfashionable figure long before his directing career came to an end. Scorned by a new generation of filmmakers, Carné grew more and more out of touch with contemporary developments, despite an eagerness to explore new subjects and use young performers. His failure is a measure of the gulf that separates 1950s and 1960s conceptions of cinema from the studio era of the war and immediate prewar years. He was, however, the epitome of this French studio style, its unquestioned master, even if—unlike Renoir—he was unable to transcend its limitations. While future critics are unlikely to find much to salvage from the latter part of his career, films like *Drole de drame* and *Quai des brumes, Le Jour se lève* and *Les Enfants du paradis,* remain rich and complex monuments to a decade of filmmaking that will reward fresh and unbiased critical attention.

—Roy Armes

CARPENTER, John

Nationality: American. **Born:** Carthage, New York, 16 January 1948. **Education:** Studied filmmaking at University of Southern California, graduated 1972. **Family:** Married actress Adrienne Barbeau, 1979 (later divorced). **Career:** Made first feature, *Dark Star,* 1974. **Awards:** Oscar for Best Short Subject, for *The Resurrection of Bronco Billy,* 1970.

Films as Director:

1970 *The Resurrection of Bronco Billy* (short) (+ ed, mus)
1974 *Dark Star* (+ pr, co-sc)
1977 *Assault on Precinct 13* (+ sc, mus)
1978 *Someone's Watching Me!* (+ sc); *Halloween* (+ co-sc)
1979 *Elvis* (for TV)
1980 *The Fog* (+ sc, mus)
1981 *Escape from New York* (+ co-sc, co-pr)
1982 *The Thing*
1983 *Christine*
1984 *Starman*
1986 *Big Trouble in Little China*
1987 *Prince of Darkness*; *Armed and Dangerous*
1988 *They Live* (+ co-mus)
1991 *Memoirs of an Invisible Man*
1995 *In the Mouth of Madness* (+ co-sc); *Village of the Damned* (+ co-sc)

Other Films:

1962-70 (short films, as director): *Revenge of the Colossal Beasts*; *Gorgon versus Godzilla*; *Terror from Space*; *Sorcerer from Outer Space*; *Warrior and the Demon*; *Gorgon, the Space Monster*
1978 *The Eyes of Laura Mars* (Kershner) (sc)
1981 *Halloween II* (Rosenthal) (pr, co-sc)
1983 *Halloween III: Season of the Witch* (Wallace) (mus)
1984 *The Philadelphia Experiment* (Raffill) (sc)
1986 *Black Moon Rising* (Cokliss) (co-sc)
1993 *Body Bags* (role)
1994 *The Silence of the Hams* (Greggio) (role)

Publications

By CARPENTER: articles—

"The Man in the Cyrogenic Freezer," an interview with Tom Milne and Richard Combs, in *Sight and Sound* (London), Spring 1978.

"Trick and Treat," an interview with T. McCarthy, in *Film Comment* (New York), January/February 1980.
"New Fright Master: John Carpenter," an interview with J. Wells, in *Films in Review* (New York), April 1980.
Interview in *Starburst* (London), nos. 36 and 37, 1981.
Interview in *Cahiers du Cinéma* (Paris), September 1982.
Interview in *Films* (London), May 1985.
Interview in *American Cinematographer* (Los Angeles), September 1988.
"Cheap Thrills and Dark Glasses," an interview with Sheila Johnston, in *The Independent* (London), 22 June 1989.

On CARPENTER: books—

Meyers, Richard, *For One Week Only: The World of Exploitation Films,* Piscataway, New Jersey, 1983.
McCarty, John, *Splatter Movies: Breaking the Last Taboo of the Screen,* New York, 1984.
Newman, Kim, *Nightmare Movies: A Critical History of the Horror Movie from 1968,* London, 1988.
McCarty, John, *Movie Psychos and Madmen,* Secaucus, New Jersey, 1993.
McCarty, John, *The Fearmakers,* New York, 1994.

On CARPENTER: articles—

Appelbaum, R., "From Cult Homage to Creative Control," in *Films and Filming* (London), June 1979.
Scanlon, P., "*The Fog*: A Spook Ride on Film," in *Rolling Stone* (New York), 28 June 1979.
Stevenson, James, "Profiles: People Start Running," in *New Yorker,* 28 January 1980.
Ross, P., "John Carpenter: Les rhythmes de l'angoisse," in *Revue du Cinéma* (Paris), February 1984.
"John Carpenter," in *Casablanca* (Madrid), November 1984.

* * *

While his career has been neither as erratic as Wes Craven's nor as disaster-littered as that of Tobe Hooper, John Carpenter currently stands as an out-of-time B specialist. His later directorial output has not exactly failed to live up to the promise of his earliest films, but nor has it been able to match their perfect achievements.

Carpenter's first three movies are marvelously economical, deftly exciting, genuinely distinctive, and slyly amusing, and cover a wide range of generic bases. *Dark Star,* which he made as a student in collaboration with Dan O'Bannon, is one of the miracles of the 1970s, an intelligent and approachable science fiction film made in the wake of *2001* but fresh and lively, with a satiric bite carried over from the *written* sf of the 1950s—its surfing punchline is an apt borrowing from Ray Bradbury—and a near-absurdist sense of humour. Its storyline concerns the crew of the spaceship Dark Star and its plunge into isolation-fueled insanity as their twenty-year mission to demolish useless planets with sentient bombs drags on and on. It is a film that repays many repeat viewings. *Assault on Precinct 13,* an urban Western rooted in *Rio Bravo* and *Night of the Living Dead,* is at once a lean, generic, action machine (its plot centers around a nightmarish street gang as it besieges and lays waste to an isolated police station) and a witty transposition of the certainties of a Hawksian ensemble piece into the racially and sexually tense 1970s. In these films, Carpenter demonstrated that suspense and humour could be combined. He also showed that he was a skilled handler of unfamiliar actors, concentrating unusually on nuances of character in forms where spectacle and effects often take precedence. Finally, he established himself as a talented composer of driving, minimalist, synthesizer-oriented musical themes.

Halloween is every bit as good as the first few films, but seems less fresh because it has been so influential. Itself a psycho suspense horror movie in the vein of *The Spiral Staircase* or *Black Christmas* (and Carpenter's lady-stalking 1978 TV movie *Someone's Watching Me*), *Halloween* single-handedly revived the drive-in horror movie in the late 1970s, inspiring such nasty pieces of work as *Friday the 13th* and literally hundreds of blatant imitations. It also inspired a series of sequels, including the intriguing Nigel Kneale-scripted box office failure *Halloween III: Season of the Witch,* the Carpenter-produced *Halloween II,* and a couple of *Halloween* films with which he was not involved in any capacity.

The original *Halloween,* which featured Jamie Lee Curtis pursued by an unkillable, masked madman and Donald Pleasence as a hammy shrink on the killer's trail, establishes its own world of horror, as enclosed and unreal as the Transylvanian backlots of the Universal or Hammer series. Carpenter utilizes a mythic American small town teenage milieu, where Halloween is a magical evocation of terror and delight, and where babysitting, trick-or-treating and blind-dating hold possibilities of joy and/or terror. With its absolute mastery of the hand-through-the-window shock moment, cunning use of the Panavision shape, and a shivery theme tune, *Halloween* is a slender but masterly confection, and it should not be blamed for the floodgates it opened.

However, Carpenter has seemed in his subsequent career to be unlearning many of the skills his first films exhibited. Although there are pleasures to be found in most of his works, he has never quite recaptured the confidence and streamlined form of the early pictures. *The Fog,* a maritime ghost story, and *Escape From New York,* a science fiction action picture, are enjoyable, entertaining movies that straggle through illogical plots, but nevertheless find performers—particularly Carpenter's then-wife Adrienne Barbeau, but also regulars Kurt Russell, Donald Pleasence, Tom Atkins, Nancy Loomis, and Chuck Cyphers—doing nice little things with characters, and individual suspense sequences in these films at times override the general messiness of the stories. The same feel can be found in films made by others from scripts he wrote in this period, such as Stewart Raffill's *The Philadelphia Experiment* and Harley Cokliss' *Black Moon Rising,* not to mention the 1990 TV Western *El Diabolo.* Stepping up into the studio big leagues, Carpenter was then given a chance to remake Hawks' and Nyby's *The Thing From Another World* (1950). He came through with *The Thing,* a controversially downbeat but genuinely effective movie in which an Arctic base is undermined by the presence of a shape-changing alien. The film is buoyed by the edgy, paranoid performances of a well-chosen cast of flabby, unreliable types and frequently punctuated by incredible bursts of special effects activity. *The Thing* handles its set-pieces—severed heads sprouting spiderlegs, a stomach opening up into a toothy mouth, a dog exploding into tentacular gloopiness—remarkably well, but Carpenter is also in control of the funny, tense, questioning passages in between.

Nevertheless, the commercial failure of *The Thing,* which arrived on Earth just as the box office was embracing *E.T.,* a film that rendered evil aliens temporarily unfashionable, appears to have sufficiently disconcerted Carpenter to force him into a succession of blighted big studio movies. *Christine* is the regulation Stephen King adaptation, loud and watchable but essentially empty and ordinary. *Starman* is an uncomfortable and impersonal hybrid of *It Happened One Night* and *The Man Who Fell to Earth.* Finally, *Big Trouble in Little China* is a wacky kung fu-monster-comedy-musical-action-adventure-horror-fantasy that features Kurt Russell's funniest Carpenter hero role (he had first joined up with the director for the TV *Elvis* in 1978) and some weird and wayward sequences, but it never quite catches the magic of the Hong Kong films upon which it is obviously based.

Subsequently, Carpenter deserted the big studios and handled a pair of smaller projects in an attempt to get back to the basics of his best work. The first of these, *Prince of Darkness,* is a labyrinthine and diffuse horror movie with a nuclear physics subplot, while *They Live* is a funny and pointed update of *Invasion of the Body Snatchers* in which the aliens have invaded earth to exploit it economically. These two films display traces of Carpenter's old flair, even if they both open a great deal better than they close; *They Live,* in particular, is as interesting and offbeat a movie as *The Fog* or *Escape From New York.* But neither film arrested the general drift of Carpenter's career. By this time, while he had not yet settled into the rut that Tobe Hooper has dug for himself, he had also not achieved the generic apotheosis of a George Romero or a David Cronenberg, either.

In the early 1990s, Carpenter harkened back to another of his favorite films of yesteryear, James Whale's *The Invisible Man.* Carpenter's variation on the theme, *Memoirs of an Invisible Man,* was based on a novel by H. F. Saint. The film presented huge challenges for Carpenter and his FX team in terms of making star Chevy Chase's escapades in invisibility absolutely convincing. Fanciful, funny, and a technical knockout, *Memoirs of an Invisible Man* was nonetheless not the kind of film that his fans wanted to see from cinema's "titan of trick or treat."

Carpenter's fans wanted Carpenter to return to his traditional landscape of chills and thrills. He did so with a vengeance, creating the most terrifying film he'd made since the halcyon days of *Halloween* and *The Thing*: the Lovecraftian titled *In the Mouth of Madness.* Now determined to stay the course in the cinema of fear and fright, Carpenter turned again to remaking another classic of his youth, *Village of the Damned,* originally a 1960 shocker about menacing, otherworldly children.

John Carpenter once called his movie *Halloween* the film equivalent of a haunted house exhibit at an old country fair. The scares are carefully calculated, coming at you at just the right moments between lulls to ensure a thrilling ride. Without apology, he notes that the film sums up the escapist entertainment that his movies are all about. After all, he says, it is the kind of entertainment he enjoys most himself.

—Kim Newman, updated by John McCarty

CASSAVETES, John

Nationality: American. **Born:** New York City, 9 December 1929. **Education:** Mohawk College, Colgate University, and New York Academy of Dramatic Arts, graduated 1950. **Family:** Married actress Gena Rowlands, 1958, two sons, one daughter. **Career:** Title character in TV series *Johnny Staccato,* 1959-60; directed first film, *Shadows,* 1960; hired by Paramount, then by Stanley Kramer, 1961; worked as independent filmmaker, from 1964. **Awards:** Critics Award, Venice Festival, for *Shadows,* 1960; Best Screenplay, National Society of Film Critics, and five awards from Venice Festival, for *Faces,* 1968; Golden Lion, Venice Festival, for *Gloria,* 1980; Golden Bear, Berlin Festival, for *Love Streams,* 1984; Los Angeles Film Critics Career Achievement Award, 1986. **Died:** Of cirrhosis of the liver, in Los Angeles, 3 February 1989.

Films as Director:

1960 *Shadows* (+ sc)
1961 *Too Late Blues* (+ sc, pr)
1962 *A Child is Waiting*
1968 ***Faces*** (+ sc)
1970 *Husbands* (+ sc, role as Gus)
1971 *Minnie and Moskowitz* (+ sc, role as Husband)
1974 *A Woman Under the Influence* (+ sc)
1976 *The Killing of a Chinese Bookie* (+ sc)
1977/78 *Opening Night* (+ sc)
1980 *Gloria*
1984 *Love Streams*
1986 *Big Trouble*

Other Films:

1951 *Fourteen Hours* (Hathaway) (role as extra)
1953 *Taxi* (Ratoff) (role)
1955 *The Night Holds Terror* (Stone) (role)
1956 *Crime in the Streets* (Siegel) (role)
1957 *Edge of the City* (Ritt) (role)
1958 *Saddle the Wind* (Parrish) (role); *Virgin Island* (P. Jackson) (role)
1962 *The Webster Boy* (Chaffey) (role)
1964 *The Killers* (Siegel) (role as Johnny North)
1967 *The Dirty Dozen* (Aldrich) (role as Victor Franko); *Devil's Angels* (Haller) (role)
1968 ***Rosemary's Baby*** (Polanski) (role as Rosemary's husband); *Gli Intoccabili* (*Machine Gun McCain*) (Montaldo) (role)
1969 *Roma coma Chicago* (*Bandits in Rome*) (De Martino) (role); *If It's Tuesday, This Must Be Belgium* (M. Stuart) (cameo role)
1976 *Two-Minute Warning* (Pearce) (role); *Mikey and Nicky* (May) (role)
1978 *The Fury* (De Palma) (role)
1982 *The Tempest* (Mazursky) (role)

Publications

By CASSAVETES: books—

Faces, New York, 1970.
John Cassavetes, Peter Falk, edited by Bruce Henstell, Washington, D.C., 1972.

By CASSAVETES: articles—

"What's Wrong with Hollywood," in *Film Culture* (New York), April 1959.
" ... and the Pursuit of Happiness," in *Films and Filming* (London), February 1961.
"Incoming Tide: Interview," in *Cinema* (Beverly Hills), no. 1, 1962.
"Faces: Interview," in *Cinema* (Beverly Hills), Spring 1968.
"Masks and Faces: Interview," with David Austen, in *Films and Filming* (London), September 1968.
"The Faces of the Husbands," in *New Yorker,* 15 March 1969.
Interview with Jonas Mekas, in *Village Voice* (New York), 23 December 1971.
Interview with L. Gross, in *Millimeter* (New York), April 1975.
"*Shadows* Issue" of *Avant-Scène du Cinéma* (Paris), 1 December 1977.
"Cassavetes on Cassavetes," in *Monthly Film Bulletin* (London), June 1978.
"Le Bal des vauriens. Entretien avec John Cassavetes," with Y. Lardeau and L. Marcorelles, in *Cahiers du Cinéma* (Paris), June 1978.
"Crucial Culture," interview with R. Appelbaum, in *Films* (London), January 1981.
"Retracting the stream of love," an interview with Richard Combs, in *Monthly Film Bulletin* (London), April 1984.
Interview with Brian Case, in *Stills* (London), June-July 1984.
Interview in *Film Comment* (New York), July-August 1988.

John Cassavetes (left) with Peter Falk and Ben Gazzara in *Husbands*

On CASSAVETES: books—

Loeb, Anthony, editor, *Filmmakers in Conversation,* Chicago, 1982.
Alexander, Georg, and others, *John Cassavetes,* Munich, 1983.
Carney, Raymond, *American Dreaming: The Films of John Cassavetes and the American Experience,* Berkeley, 1985.
Gavron, Laurence, and Denis Lenoir, *John Cassavetes,* Paris, 1986.

On CASSAVETES: articles—

Taylor, John Russell, "Cassavetes in London," in *Sight and Sound* (London), Autumn 1960.
Mekas, Jonas, "Cassavetes, the Improvisation," in *Film Culture* (New York), Spring 1962.
Sarris, Andrew, "Oddities and One-Shots," in *Film Culture* (New York), Spring 1963.
Guerin, A., "After Faces, a Film to Keep the Man-Child Alive," in *Life* (New York), 9 May 1969.
"Robert Aldrich on John Cassavetes," in *Dialogue on Film* (Washington, D.C.), no. 2, 1972.
Benoit, C., and A. Tournes, "Femmes et maris dans l'oeuvre de Cassavetes," in *Jeune Cinéma* (Paris), September/October 1976.
Simsolo, Noel, "Notes sur le cinéma de John Cassavetes," in *Cahiers du Cinéma* (Paris), May 1978.
Courant, G., and J. Farren, "John Cassavetes," in *Cinéma* (Paris), October 1979.
Stevenson, J., "John Cassavetes: Film's Bad Boy," in *American Film* (Washington, D.C.), January/February 1980.
Landy, M., and S. Shostack, "The Cinema of John Cassavetes," in *Ciné-Tracts* (Montreal), Winter 1980.
Prades, J., "La méthode de Cassavetes," in *Cinématographe* (Paris), April 1982.
"John Cassavetes Section" in *Positif* (Paris), January 1985.
Obituary in *Variety* (New York), 8 February 1989.
Obituary in *Time Out* (London), 15 February 1989.

* * *

As perhaps the most influential of the independently produced feature films of its era (1958-1967), *Shadows* came to be seen as a virtual breakthrough for American alternative cinema. The film and its fledgling writer-director had put a group of young, independent filmmakers on the movie map, together with their more intellectual, less technically polished, decidedly less commercial, low-budget alternatives to Hollywood features.

Begun as an improvisational exercise in the method-acting workshop that actor Cassavetes was teaching, and partly financed by his earnings from the *Johnny Staccato* television series, *Shadows* was a loosely plotted, heavily improvised work of cinema verité immediacy which explored human relationships and racial identity against the background of the beat atmosphere of the late 1950s, given coherence by the jazz score of Charles Mingus.

The origins and style of *Shadows* were to characterize John Cassavetes's work throughout his directorial career, once he got the studio-financed production bug out of his system—and his system out of theirs.

The five prizes garnered by *Shadows,* including the prestigious Critics Award at the 1960 Venice Film Festival, led to Cassavetes's unhappy and resentful experience directing two studio-molded productions (*Too Late Blues, A Child is Waiting*), both of which failed critically and commercially. Thereafter, he returned to independent filmmaking, although he continued to act in mainstream movies such as *The Dirty Dozen, Rosemary's Baby,* and *Two Minute Warning.* He continued directing feature films, however, in his characteristic, controversial style.

That style centers around a freedom afforded his actors to share in the creative process. Cassavetes's scripts serve as sketchy blueprints for the performers' introspective explorations and emotional embellishments. Consequently, camera movements, at the command of the actors' intuitive behavior, are of necessity spontaneous.

The amalgam of improvisational acting, hand-held camera work, grainy stock, loose editing, and threadbare plot give his films a texture of recreated rather than heightened reality, often imbuing them with a feeling of astonishing psychodramatic intensity as characters confront each other and lay bare their souls. Detractors, however, see Cassavetes as too dedicated to the performers' art and too trusting of the actor's self-discipline. They charge that the result is too often a mild form of aesthetic anarchy.

At worst Cassavetes's films are admittedly formless and self-indulgent. Scenes are stretched excruciatingly far beyond their climactic moments, lines are delivered falteringly, dialogue is repetitious. But, paradoxically, these same blemishes seem to make possible the several lucid, provocative, and moving moments of transcendent human revelation that a Cassavetes film almost inevitably delivers.

As his career progressed, Cassavetes changed his thematic concerns, upgraded his technical production values, and, not surprisingly, attracted a wider audience—but without overhauling his actor-as-auteur approach.

Faces represented Cassavetes's return to his favored semi-documentary style, complete with the seemingly obligatory excesses and gaffes. But the film also contained moments of truth and exemplary acting. Not only did this highly charged drama about the disintegration of a middle-class marriage in affluent Southern California find favor with the critical and filmmaking communities, it broke through as one of the first independent films to find a sizable audience among the general moviegoing public.

In *Husbands,* Cassavetes continued his exploration of marital manners, morals, and sexual identity by focusing on a trio of middle-class husbands—played by Cassavetes, Ben Gazzara, and Peter Falk—who confront their own mortality when a friend dies. Director Cassavetes's doubled-edged trademark—brilliant moments of intense acting amid the banal debris of over-indulgence—had never been in bolder relief.

Minnie and Moskowitz was Cassavetes's demonstration of a lighter touch, an amusing and touching interlude prior to his most ambitious and commercially successful film. The film starred Gena Rowlands (Cassavetes's wife) and Seymour Cassel as a pair of dissimilar but similarly lonely people ensnared in a manic romance. Cassavetes again examined miscommunication in *Minnie and Moskowitz,* but in a much more playful vein.

A Woman Under the Influence was by far Cassavetes's most polished, accessible, gripping, and technically proficient film. For this effort, Cassavetes departed from his accustomed style of working by writing a fully detailed script during pre-production. Starring Gena Rowlands in a magnificent performance as a lower-middle class housewife coming apart at the seams, and the reliable Peter Falk as the hardhat husband who is ill-equipped to deal with his wife's mental breakdown, *Woman* offered a more palatable balance of Cassavetes's strengths and weaknesses. The over-long scenes and overindulgent acting jags are there, but in lesser doses, while the privileged moments and bursts of virtuoso screen acting seem more abundant than usual.

Financed by Falk and Cassavetes, the film's crew and cast (including many family members) worked on deferred salaries. Promoted via a tour undertaken by the nucleus of the virtual repertory company (Cassavetes, Rowland, Falk) and booked without a major distributor, *Woman* collected generally ecstatic reviews, Academy Award nominations for Cassavetes and Rowlands, and impressive box office returns.

Cassavetes's next two films (*The Killing of a Chinese Bookie, Opening Night*) feature a return to his earlier structure (or lack thereof)—inaccessible, interminable, and insufferable for all but diehard buffs. However, *Gloria,* which showcased Rowlands as a former gangster's moll, while uneven in tone and erratic in pace, represented a concession by Cassavetes to filmgoers seeking heightened cinematic energy and narrative momentum.

"People who are making films today are too concerned with mechanics—technical things instead of feeling," Cassavetes told an interviewer in 1980. "Execution is about eight percent to me. The technical quality of a film doesn't have much to do with whether it's a good film."

—Bill Wine

CASTELLANI, Renato

Nationality: Italian. **Born:** Finale Ligure (Savona), 4 September 1913. **Education:** Educated in Argentina to 1925, then in Geneva; studied architecture in Milan. **Career:** Journalist, then scriptwriter for Camerini, Genina, Soldati, and Blasetti in 1930s; assistant to Blasetti, 1940; directed first film, *Un Colpo di pistola,* 1941. **Awards:** Best Film, Venice Festival, for *Sotto il sole di Roma,* 1948; Best Film, Cannes Festival, for *Due Soldi di speranza,* 1952; Golden Lion, Venice Festival, for *Giulietta e Romeo,* 1954. **Died:** 28 December 1985.

Films as Director:

1941 *Un Colpo di pistola* (+ co-sc)
1942 *Zaza* (+ sc)
1943 *La Donna del Montagna* (+ sc)
1946 *Mio Figlio Professore* (*Professor My Son*) (+ co-sc)
1948 *Sotto il sole di Roma* (*Under the Sun of Rome*) (+ sc)
1949 *E'primavera* (*It's Forever Springtime*) (+ co-sc)
1952 *Due Soldi di speranza* (*Two Cents Worth of Hope*) (+ sc)
1954 *Giulietta e Romeo* (*Romeo and Juliet*) (+ sc)
1957 *I sogni nel cassetto* (+ sc)
1959 *Nella città l'inferno* (*And the Wild, Wild Women*) (+ co-sc)
1961 *Il Brigante* (+ sc)
1962 *Mare Matto* (+ co-sc)
1964 "La Vedova" episode of *Tre notti di amore* (*Three Nights of Love*) (+ co-sc): "Una Donna d'Afari" episode of *Controsesso* (+ co-sc)
1967 *Questi fantasmi* (*Ghosts Italian Style*) (+ co-sc)
1969 *Una breve stagione* (+ co-sc)
1972 *Leonardo da Vinci* (condensed from five-part TV series) (+ co-sc)

Other Films:

1938 *L'oròlogio a Cucu* (Mastrocinque) (co-sc); *Batticuore* (Camerini) (co-sc); *Castelli in aria* (Camerini) (co-sc)
1939 *Grandi magazzini* (Camerini) (co-sc, asst d); *Il documento* (Camerini) (co-sc); *Un'avventura di Salvator Rosa* (Blasetti) (co-sc, asst d); *Due milioni per un sorriso* (Borghesio and Soldati) (co-sc)
1940 *Centomila dollari* (Camerini) (asst d); *Una romantica avventura* (Camerini) (co-sc); *La corona di ferro* (Blasetti) (co-sc, asst d)
1941 *La cena della beffe* (Blasetti) (co-sc)
1942 *Malombra* (Soldati) (co-sc)
1944 *Quartieri alti* (Soldati) (co-sc)
1945 *Malia* (Amato) (co-sc); *Notte di tempesta* (Franciolini) (sc)
1958 *Resurrezione (Auferstehung)* (Hansen) (co-sc)
1962 *Venere imperiale* (Delannoy) (idea only—begun by Castellani in 1958, discontinued due to dispute with producers and star Gina Lollobrigida)
1964 *Matrimonio all'italiana* (de Sica) (co-sc)

Publications

By CASTELLANI: article—

"Putting Gloss on Prison," in *Films and Filming* (London), April 1959.

On CASTELLANI: books—

Armes, Roy, *Patterns of Realism: A Study of Italian Neo-Realist Cinema,* New York, 1971.
Leprohon, Pierre, *The Italian Cinema,* New York, 1972.
Atti del Convegno della X mostra internazionale del nuovo cinema, Venice, 1975.
Verdone, Mario, *Cinema neo-realista da Rossellini a Pasolini,* Palermo, 1977.
Gili, Jean A., *Le Cinéma italien II,* Paris, 1982.
Trasatti, Sergio, *Renato Castellani,* Florence, 1984.

On CASTELLANI: articles—

Frosali, S., "Renato Castellani: Regista 'inattuale'?" in *Bianco e Nero* (Rome), January-March 1984.
Obituary in *Variety* (New York), 1 January 1986.
Pintus, Pietro, "Renato Castellani viaggiatore instancabile," in *Bianco e Nero* (Rome), April-June 1986.

* * *

Poggioli, Lattuada, Chiarini, Soldati—the "calligraphers"—were the directors, novelists, and critics with which Castellani was associated at the beginning of his film career (1940-1948). The "calligraphers" were interested in form above all, strongly attached to the narrative tradition of the nineteenth century, committed to an essentially bourgeois cinema, refined, cultivated, intellectual. Their aesthetic was articulated in theory and in practice, and resistant, even antithetical, to the demands of the new realism voiced by De Santis and others in *Cinema,* and by Visconti in *Ossessione. Un colpo di pistola, Zaza* (a comedy in the French manner set during the "belle époque"), and *La donna della montagna* are films of escape. Through them Castellani managed his own flight: from the reality of the present, to be sure, but also from fascist propaganda and fascist censorship.

The opposition between "calligraphy" and neorealism must be treated cautiously, as Roy Armes points out in *Patterns of Realism.* Not only did the two tendencies share a number of temptations (to historicism, for example), but individual artists, Castellani among them, passed with apparent ease from one to the other. A "Calligrapher" as late as 1946, Castellani joined the neo-realists with *Sotto il sole di Roma,* announcing his new allegiance in the very first frame with this intertitle: "This film was inspired by events that actually took place. It was performed by non-professional actors, and shot entirely in Rome, in the neighborhoods depicted in the film." While the presence of Alberto Sordi undermined the claim of a non-professional cast, his performance as a shoe salesman (recalling, in comic mode, the shoes of *Paisà* and *Shoe Shine*), the music of Nino Rota, the theme of black marketeering, the Roman locales and dialect, and the coverage of events of early summer 1943 to the end of summer of 1944 (from the invasion of Sicily to the liberation of Rome) cast the film firmly in the honored mold of Rossellini and De Sica. The chronology of *Sotto il sole di Roma* is that of *Paisà*; it is the story of the coming of age of a group of adolescent boys, matured by destruction and death. At its conclusion, unlike the children of *Open City, Bicycle Thief,* and *Shoe Shine,* they face the future with confidence—in themselves and in the society of which they are a part.

Two films followed in the wake of *Sotto il sole di Roma* to shape a trilogy on youth and young love: *E primavera* and *Two Cents Worth of Hope.* To their scripts are linked the names of Suso Cecchi d'Amico, Cesare Zavattini, and Titina de Filippo, names in turn allied with Visconti, De Sica, and the master family of Italian comedy. Shot on location from one end of the peninsula to the other, the burning questions of the day—the *mezzogiorno,* unemployment, Communist vs. Christian Democrat—addressed in the films are cloaked in humor and, more importantly, an optimism that, as Leprohon notes in *The Italian Cinema,* official Italy found reassuring. Threatened by the bleak view of Italy exported by the post-war Italian cinema, the government reacted by passing the Andreotti Law (1948) in the same year Castellani launched what came to be known as "rosy neorealism."

The trilogy was followed by *Giulietta e Romeo.* This story of young love thwarted by parents and convention had already found expression in the contemporary working class settings of the three previous films, and was drawn from two Renaissance versions: Shakespeare's and Luigi Da Porto's. Professional and non-professional actors, including a Juliet chosen from an avalanche of responses to a talent search conducted in the neorealist style, combined to create a tension of text and performance that elicited considerable critical controversy. Once again, Castellani had adapted neorealism to his own uses. This time it was a literary neorealism, redefined to suit his inspiration, and dependent as always on the rejection of mimicry and doctrine.

—Mirella Jona Affron

CAVALCANTI, Alberto

Nationality: Brazilian. **Born:** Alberto de Almeida Cavalcanti in Rio de Janeiro, 6 February 1897. **Education:** Attended law school, Brazil, and Geneva Fine Art School, Switzerland. **Career:** Art director in Paris, early 1920s; directed first film, *Rien que les heures,* 1926; directed French language versions of American films for Paramount, Joinsville, 1929-30; joined General Post Office (GPO) Film Unit, London, 1937 (Head of Unit, 1937); joined Ealing Studios as feature director, 1940; Head of Production, Vera Cruz group, Brazil, and co-founder, Brazilian Film Institute, 1949-50; settled in Europe, 1955; director, British and French television, 1950s to 1968; film teacher, UCLA, 1963-65. **Awards:** American States Medal for Superior Artistic Achievement, 1972. **Died:** In Paris, 23 August 1982.

Films as Director:

1925 *Le Train sans yeux* (+ sc, ed)
1926 ***Rien que les heures*** (*Only the Hours*) (+ pr, sc, ed)
1927 *Yvette* (+ sc, ed); *En rade* (*Sea Fever*) (+ co-sc, ed); *La P'tite Lilie* (+ sc, ed supervisor)
1928 *La Jalousie du barbouillé* (+ sc, ed, art d); *Le Capitaine Fracasse* (+ co-sc, ed)
1929 *Le Petit Chaperon rouge* (+ sc, ed, art d); *Vous verrez la semaine prochaine* (+ sc, ed); *A michemin du ciel* (French language version of George Abbott's *Half-Way to Heaven*)
1930 *Toute sa vie* (French language version of Dorothy Arzner's *Sarah and Son*); *A cançao do berço* (Portuguese version of Dorothy Arzner's *Sarah and Son*); *Les Vacances du diable* (French language version of Edmund Goulding's *The Devil's Holiday*); *Dans une île perdue* (French language version of William Wellman's *Dangerous Paradise*)
1932 *En lisant le journal*; *Le Jour du frotteur* (+ sc, ed); *Revue Montmartroise* (+ sc); *Nous ne ferons jamais de cinéma*; *Le Truc du brésilien*; *Le Mari garçon* (*Le Garçon divorcé*)
1933 *Plaisirs défendus*; *Tour de chant* (+ sc); *Coralie et Cie* (+ sc)
1934 *Pett and Pott* (+ sound supervisor, bit role); *New Rates*
1935 *Coalface* (+ sound supervisor)
1936 *Message from Geneva*
1937 *We Live in Two Worlds* (+ pr); *The Line to Tschierva Hut* (+ pr); *Who Writes to Switzerland* (+ pr)
1938 *Four Barriers* (+ pr); *The Chiltern Country* (+ pr)
1939 *Alice in Switzerland* (+ pr); *Midsummer Day's Work* (+ pr, sc)
1940 *La Cause commune* (+ pr) (made in Britain for showing in France); *Factory Front* (+ pr) (British version of preceding film); *Yellow Caesar* (*The Heel of Italy*) (+ pr)
1941 *Young Veteran* (+ pr); *Mastery of the Sea* (+ pr)
1942 *Went the Day Well?* (*48 Hours*)
1943 *Watertight* (*Ship Safety*)
1944 *Champagne Charlie*; *Trois Chansons de la résistance* (*Trois Chants pour la France*)
1945 "The Ventriloquist's Dummy" episode of ***Dead of Night***
1947 *The Life and Adventures of Nicholas Nickleby*; *They Made Me a Fugitive* (*I Became a Criminal*)
1948 *The First Gentleman* (*Affairs of a Rogue*)
1949 *For Them That Trespass*
1952 *Simao o caolho* (*Simon the One-Eyed*) (+ pr)
1953 *O canto do mar* (*The Song of the Sea*) (+ pr, co-sc) (remake of *En rade*)
1954 *Mulher de verdade* (*A Real Woman*) (+ pr)
1955 *Herr Puntila und sein Knecht Matti* (+ co-sc)
1956 *Die Windrose* (d prologue only, collective film co-supervised with Joris Ivens)
1958 *La Prima notte* (*Les Noces vénitiennes*)
1960 *The Monster of Highgate Ponds*
1967 *Thus Spake Theodor Herzl* (*The Story of Israel*) (+ sc)

Other Films:

1923 *L'Inhumaine* (L'Herbier) (co-art d)
1924 *L'Inondation* (Delluc) (art d); *La Galerie des monstres* (Catelain) (asst d, art d); ***Feu Mathias Pascal*** (L'Herbier) (art d)
1926 *The Little People* (Pearson) (art d)
1931 *Au pays du scalp* (de Wavrin) (ed)
1934 *Windmill in Barbados* (Wright) (sound supervisor); *Granton Trawler* (Anstey) (sound supervisor); ***Song of Ceylon*** (Wright) (sound supervisor)
1935 *Book Bargain* (McLaren) (pr); *Big Money* (Watt) (pr)
1936 *Rainbow Dance* (Lye) (pr); ***Night Mail*** (Wright and Watt) (pr, sound supervisor); *Calendar of the Year* (Spice) (pr)
1937 *The Saving of Bill Blewitt* (Watt) (pr); *Roadways* (Coldstream and Legg) (pr)
1938 *North or Northwest* (Lye) (pr); *North Sea* (Watt) (pr, sound supervisor); *Distress Call* (Watt) (pr) (shortened silent version of preceding title); *Many a Pickle* (McLaren) (pr); *Happy in the Morning* (Jackson) (pr)
1939 *The City* (Elton) (pr); *Men in Danger* (Jackson) (pr); *Spare Time* (Jennings) (pr); *Health of a Nation* (*Health for the Nation, Forty Million People*) (Monck) (pr); *Speaking from America* (Jennings) (pr); *Spring Offensive* (*An Unrecorded Victory*) (Jennings) (pr); *The First Days* (Watt, Jennings, and Jackson) (pr)
1940 *Men of the Lightship* (Macdonald) (pr); *Squadron 992* (Watt) (pr); *Sea Fort* (Dalrymple) (pr); *Salvage with a Smile* (Brunel) (pr)
1941 *Guests of Honour* (Pitt) (pr); *The Big Blockade* (Frend) (assoc pr); *Merchant Seamen* (*Merchant Convoy*) (Holmes) (pr); *The Foreman Went to France* (*Somewhere in France*) (Frend) (assoc pr); *Find, Fix and Strike* (Bennett) (pr)
1942 *Greek Testament* (*The Shrine of Victory*) (Hasse) (pr)
1944 *The Halfway House* (Dearden) (assoc pr)
1950 *Caicara* (Loafer) (Celi) (pr, supervisor)
1951 *Terra sempere terra* (*Land Is Forever Land*) (Payne) (pr); *Painel* (*Panel*) (Barreto) (pr); *Santuario* (*Sanctuary*) (Barreto) (pr)
1952 *Volta redonda* (*Round Trip*) (Waterhouse) (pr); *Film and Reality* (selection and compilation)
1969 *Lettres de Stalingrad* (Katz) (role)

Publications

By CAVALCANTI: book—

Film and Reality, London, 1942; as *Film e realidade,* Rio de Janeiro, 1952.

By CAVALCANTI: articles—

"Sound in Films," in *Film* (London), November 1939.
"Cavalcanti in Brazil," in *Sight and Sound* (London), April/June 1953.
Interview with J. Hillier and others, in *Screen* (London), Summer 1972.
Cavalcanti, Alberto, in *Filme Cultura* (Rio de Janeiro), January-April 1984.

On CAVALCANTI: books—

Klaue, Wolfgang, and others, *Cavalcanti,* Berlin, 1952.
Hardy, Forsyth, editor, *Grierson on Documentary,* revised edition, London, 1966.
Lovell, Alan, and Jim Hillier, *Studies in Documentary,* New York, 1972.
Barsam, Richard, *The Non-Fiction Film,* New York, 1973.
Rotha, Paul, *Documentary Diary,* London, 1973.
Sussex, Elizabeth, *The Rise and Fall of British Documentary: The Story of the Film Movement Founded by John Grierson,* Berkeley, 1975.
Ellis, Jack C., *The Documentary Idea,* Englewood Cliffs, New Jersey, 1989.

On CAVALCANTI: articles—

De La Roche, Catherine, "Cavalcanti in Brazil," in *Sight and Sound* (London), January/March 1955.
Monegal, Emir Rodriguez, "Alberto Cavalcanti," in *Quarterly of Film, Radio, and Television* (Berkeley), Summer 1955.

Alberto Cavalcanti

Minish, Geoffrey, "Cavalcanti in Paris," in *Sight and Sound* (London), Summer 1970.
Taylor, J.R., "Surrealist Admen," in *Sight and Sound* (London), Autumn 1971.
Beylie, Claude, and others, "Alberto Cavalcanti," in *Ecran* (Paris), November 1974.
Sussex, E., "Cavalcanti in England," in *Sight and Sound* (London), August 1975.
Zapiola, G., "Medio siglo de cine en la obra del eurobrasileño Alberto Cavalcanti," in *Cinemateca Revista* (Montevideo), September 1982.
Courcier, J., obituary in *Cinéma* (Paris), October 1982.
Obituary in *Films and Filming* (London), November 1982.
Pilard, P., "Cavalcanti à Londres. Quinze ans de cinéma brittanique," in *Revue du Cinéma* (Paris), November 1983.

* * *

Alberto Cavalcanti was multi-national to a remarkable extent. Brazilian by birth, he worked in French commercial and avant-garde cinema of the 1920s, in British documentaries of the 1930s, and in British features of the 1940s. He also returned briefly to Brazil in an effort to revitalize its production, then lived in Paris during his last years, although he visited and made films elsewhere. In the long view, however, Cavalcanti may be most closely associated with British film, especially with British documentary.

Even Cavalcanti's early years in France led to that subsequent connection. Following work as a set designer, most notably for Marcel L'Herbier, he made the seminal *Rien que les heures* in 1926. Though part of the avant-garde experimentation of the 1920s, *Rien* inaugurated the "city symphonies," one of the lines picked up by John Grierson as he was molding the British documentary of the 1930s. (The other lines came from the work of Flaherty, and of the Soviets, notably Vertov, Eisenstein, and Turin.)

Before being invited by Grierson to join the General Post Office Film Unit, Cavalcanti had experience in the early sound films produced by the French studios. As he became involved in British documentary he distinguished himself, especially through his work with sound in relation to image. *Granton Trawler, The Song of Ceylon, Coal Face, Night Mail,* and *North Sea* offer evidence of his contributions. It might be argued that these films contain more sophisticated multi-layered sound and edited images—what Eisenstein called vertical montage—than that evident in narrative fiction films of the time. Cavalcanti's personal creativity became the basis for teaching other, younger members of the documentary group. Harry Watt, Basil Wright, and others have attested to Cavalcanti's significance as a teacher of conception and technique.

Though Grierson always acknowledged Cavalcanti's importance to the artistry of British documentary, there developed a split between the Grierson faction (dedicated to making films to bring about social change) and the Cavalcanti faction (more concerned with ways in which realist film technique and style could be brought to the larger audiences of the theatres). In fact, an anthology surveying the documentary film, *The Film and Reality,* co-produced by Cavalcanti and Ernest Lindgren in 1942, created a furor behind the scenes when it was released. It presented essentially an aesthetic history of documentary (Cavalcanti selected the excerpts), ending with coverage of feature fiction films embodying some of the characteristics of documentary. The Grierson group was reputedly outraged that no attention was paid to what they viewed as the dominant purpose of British documentary, which was a sort of citizenship education—communication by the government to the citizenry.

For his part, Cavalcanti said late in life that he always thought he and Grierson were up to the same thing essentially—that of course he had a social sense, as surely as did Grierson. The real trouble was that he had not received adequate screen credits for the work he had done for the GPO Film Unit during Grierson's regime. (Grierson favored the idea of anonymous collective rather than individual auteurs.)

When Cavalcanti returned to entertainment filmmaking early in the war he was missed by the documentary bunch. At the same time it must be said that Cavalcanti (like Watt, who followed him shortly) brought with him a documentary influence to Ealing Studios that extended into the wartime fiction film. The impact of his experiences in the documentary world can be seen, for example, in *The Foreman Went to France,* which he produced, and in *Went the Day Well?,* which he directed. On the other hand, Cavalcanti's finest achievement as fictional producer/director may well be *Dead of Night,* a mingling of fantasy and actuality. The surrealistic elements of the film recalled the French avant-garde.

In summary it can be said that Cavalcanti seemed always to be the artist, personal creator and, especially, consummate technician. He applied himself to the basic modes of film art—narrative fiction, avant-garde, and documentary—in a full range of capacities—set designer, sound recordist, producer, and director. A charming journeyman artist with a cosmopolitan and tasteful flair, he taught and influenced a lot of other filmmakers and was responsible for noteworthy innovation and experimentation in many of the films with which he was associated.

—Jack C. Ellis

CHABROL, Claude

Nationality: French. **Born:** Paris, 24 June 1930. **Education:** University of Paris, Ecole Libre des Sciences Politiques. **Family:** Married 1) Agnes Goute, 1952 (divorced), two sons; 2) actress Stephane Audran, 1964 (divorced), one son; 3) Aurore Pajot. **Career:** Film critic for *Arts* and for *Cahiers du Cinéma,* Paris, 1953-57 (under own name and as "Charles Eitel" and "Jean-Yves Goute"); Head of production company AJYM, 1956-61; directed first film, *Le Beau Serge,* 1958; director, *Macbeth,* Théâtre Recamier, Paris, 1967; director, French TV, 1970s. **Awards:** Golden Bear, Berlin Festival, for *Les Cousins,* 1959; D. W. Griffith Award, National Board of Review, and New York Film Critics Circle Award for Best Foreign Film, for *Story of Women,* 1989. **Agent:** c/o VMA, 40 rue Francois 1er, 75008 Paris, France. **Address:** 15 Quai Conti, 75006 Paris, France.

Films as Director:

1958 *Le Beau Serge* (*Bitter Reunion*) (+ pr, sc, bit role)
1959 *Les Cousins* (*The Cousins*) (+ pr, sc); *A double tour* (*Web of Passion*; *Leda*) (+ bit role)
1960 *Les Bonnes Femmes* (+ adapt, bit role)
1961 *Les Godelureaux* (+ co-adapt, bit role); "L'Avarice" episode of *Les Sept Péchés capitaux* (*The Seven Deadly Sins*) (+ bit role)
1962 *L'Œil du malin* (*The Third Lover*) (+ sc); *Ophélia* (+ co-sc)
1963 *Landru* (*Bluebeard*) (+ co-sc)
1964 "L'Homme qui vendit la tour Eiffel" episode of *Les Plus Belles Escroqueries du monde* (*The Beautiful Swindlers*); *Le Tigre aime la chair fraîche* (*The Tiger Likes Fresh Blood*); *La Chance et l'amour* (Tavernier, Schlumberger, Bitsch, and Berry) (d linking sequences only)
1965 "La Muette" episode of *Paris vu par ...* (*Six in Paris*) (+ sc, role); *Marie-Chantal contre le Docteur Kha* (+ co-sc, bit role); *Le Tigre se parfume à la dynamite* (*An Orchid for the Tiger*) (+ bit role)

1966 *La Ligne de démarcation* (*Line of Demarcation*) (+ co-sc)
1967 *Le Scandale* (*The Champagne Murders*); *La Route de Corinthe* (*Who's Got the Black Box?*; *The Road to Corinth*) (+ role)
1968 *Les Biches* (*The Does*; *The Girlfriends*; *Bad Girls*) (+ co-sc, role)
1969 ***La Femme infidèle*** (*Unfaithful Wife*) (+ co-sc): *Que la bête meure* (*This Man Must Die*; *Killer!*)
1970 ***Le Boucher*** (+ sc); *La Rupture* (*Le Jour des parques*; *The Breakup*) (+ sc, bit role)
1971 *Juste avant la nuit* (*Just Before Nightfall*) (+ sc)
1972 *La Décade prodigieuse* (*Ten Days' Wonder*) (+ co-sc); *Docteur Popaul* (*High Heels*) (+ co-song); *De Grey—Le Banc de Desolation* (for TV)
1973 *Les Noces rouges* (*Wedding in Blood*) (+ sc)
1974 *Nada* (*The NADA Gang*); *Histoires insolites* (series of 4 TV films)
1975 *Une Partie de plaisir* (*A Piece of Pleasure*; *Pleasure Party*); *Les Innocents aux mains sales* (*Dirty Hands*; *Innocents with Dirty Hands*) (+ sc); *Les Magiciens* (*Initiation à la mort*; *Profezia di un delitto*)
1976 *Folies bourgeoises* (*The Twist*) (+ co-sc)
1977 *Alice ou La Dernière Fugue* (*Alice or the Last Escapade*) (+ sc)
1978 *Blood Relatives* (*Les Liens de sang*) (+ co-sc); *Violette Nozière* (*Violette*)
1980 *Le Cheval d'Orgueil* (*The Horse of Pride*; *The Proud Ones*)
1982 *Les Fantômes du chapelier* (*The Hatmaker*)
1983 *Le Sang des autres* (*The Blood of Others*)
1984 *Poulet au vinaigre* (*Cop au Vin*) (+ co-sc)
1985 *Inspecteur Lavardin* (+co-sc)
1986 *Masques* (+ co-sc)
1987 *Le cri du hibou* (*The Cry of the Owl*)
1989 *Une Affaire des femmes* (*Story of Women*) (+ sc)
1990 *Jours tranquilles a Clichy* (*Quiet Days in Clichy*) (+ sc); *Docteur M* (*Club Extinction*) (+sc)
1991 *Madame Bovary* (+ sc)
1993 *Bette* (+sc); *L'oeil de Vichy* (*The Eye of the Vichy*) (doc)
1994 *L'enfer* (*Hell*)
1995 *Le ceremonie* (*The Ceremony*); *A Judgment in Stone* (+ sc)

Other Films:

1956 *Le Coup de berger* (Rivette) (co-sc, uncred co-mu, role)
1959 ***A bout de souffle*** (Godard) (tech adv); *Les Jeux de l'amour* (de Broca) (role)
1960 *Paris nour appartient* (Rivette) (role); *Saint-Tropez blues* (Moussy) (role); *Les Distractions* (Dupont) (role)
1961 *Ples v dezju* (*Dance in the Rain*) (Hladnik) (supervisor); *Les Menteurs* (Greville) (role)
1964 *Les Durs à cuire* (Pinoteau) (role)
1965 *Brigitte et Brigitte* (Moullet) (role)
1966 *Happening* (Bokanowski) (tech adv); *Zoe bonne* (Deval) (role)
1968 *La Femme ecarlate* (Valere) (role)
1969 *Et crac!* (Douchet) (role); *Version latine* (Detre) (role); *Le Travail* (Detre) (role)
1970 *Sortie de secours* (Kahane) (role)
1971 *Eglantine* (Brialy) (tech adv); *Aussi loin que l'amour* (Rossif) (role)
1972 *Piège à pucelles* (Leroi) (tech adv); *Un Meurtre est un meurtre* (Périer) (role)
1973 *Le Flipping* (Volatron) (role as interviewee)
1987 *Sale destin!* (Sylvain Madigan) (role)
1992 *Sam Suffit* (role as Mr. Denis)

Publications

By CHABROL: books—

Hitchcock, with Eric Rohmer, Paris, 1957.
La Femme Infidele, Paris, 1969.
Les Noces rouges, Paris, 1973.
Et pourtant, je tourne..., Paris, 1976.
L'adieu aux dieux (novel), Paris, 1980.
Autour d'Emma: Madame Bovary, un film de Claude Chabrol, Paris, 1991.

By CHABROL: articles—

Regular contributor to *Cahiers du Cinéma* (Paris), under pseudonyms "Charles Eitel" and "Jean-Yves Goute," 1950s.
"Tout ce qu'il faut savoir pour mettre en scène s'apprend en quatre heures," an interview with François Truffaut, in *Arts* (Paris), 19 February 1958.
"Vers un néo-romanticisme au cinéma," in *Lettres Françaises* (Paris), March 1959.
"Big Subjects, Little Subjects," in *Movie* (London), June 1962.
Interview with Gilles Jacob, in *Cinéma* (Paris), September/October 1966.
"Claude Chabrol," in *Interviews with Film Directors,* edited by Andrew Sarris, New York, 1967.
Articles anthologized in *The New Wave,* edited by Peter Graham, New York, 1968.
"*La Femme Infidèle,*" and "*La Muette,*" in *Avant-Scène du Cinéma* (Paris), no. 42, 1969.
Interview with Michel Ciment and others, in *Positif* (Paris), April 1970.
Interview with Noah James, in *Take One* (Montreal), September/October 1970.
Interview with Rui Nogueira, in *Sight and Sound* (London), Winter 1970/71.
Interview with M. Rosier and D. Serceau, in *Cinéma* (Paris), September/October 1973.
Interviews with G. Braucourt, in *Ecran* (Paris), May 1975 and February 1977.
"Chabrol's Game of Mirrors," an interview with D. Overbey, in *Sight and Sound* (London), Spring 1977.
"The Magical Mystery World of Claude Chabrol," an interview with Dan Yakir, in *Film Quarterly* (Berkeley), no. 3, 1979.
"I Fell in Love with Violette Nozière," in *Monthly Film Bulletin* (London), April 1979.
Interview with D. Simmons, in *Film Directions* (Belfast), vol. 5, no. 18, 1983.
Conversation with Georges Simenon, in *Filmkritik* (Munich), February 1983.
Interview with Jill Forbes, in *Stills* (London), June/July 1984.
"Jeu de massacre: Attention les yeux," an interview with Pierre Bonitzer and others, in *Cahiers du Cinéma* (Paris), March 1986.
"Chabrol by Chance," an interview with Claudio Lazzaro, in *World Press Review,* October 1988.
"Entretiens avec Claude Chabrol," an interview in *Cahiers du Cinéma,* December 1989.
"Conversazione con Claude Chabrol," an interview with P. Vernaglione, in *Filmcritica,* March 1989.
"Entretien avec Claude Chabrol," an interview with T. Jousse and others, in *Cahiers du Cinéma,* November 1990.
"Histoires de fuites," in *Cahiers du Cinéma,* May 1991.
"Entretien avec Claude Chabrol," an interview with T. Jousse and S. Toubiana, in *Cahiers du Cinéma,* March 1992.

On CHABROL: books—

Armes, Roy, *French Cinema Since 1946: Vol.2—The Personal Style,* New York, 1966.

Wood, Robin, and Michael Walker, *Claude Chabrol,* London, 1970.
Braucourt, Guy, *Claude Chabrol,* Paris, 1971.
Monaco, James, *The New Wave,* New York, 1976.
Moscariello, Angelo, *Chabrol,* Firenze, 1976.
Grongaard, Peter, *Chabrols Filmkunst,* Kobenhavn, 1977.
Magny, Joel, *Claude Chabrol,* Paris, 1987.
Derry, Charles, *The Suspense Thriller: Films in the Shadow of Alfred Hitchcock,* Jefferson, North Carolina, 1988.
Blanchet, Christian, *Claude Chabrol,* Paris, 1989.

On CHABROL: articles—

"New Wave" issue of *Cinéma* (Paris), February 1960.
"Chabrol Issue" of *Movie* (London), June 1963.
Gow, Gordon, "The Films of Claude Chabrol," in *Films and Filming* (London), March 1967.
Baxter, Brian, "Claude Chabrol," in *Film* (London), Spring 1969.
"Chabrol Issue" of *L'Avant-scène du Cinéma* (Paris), May 1969.
Wood, Robin, "Chabrol and Truffaut," in *Movie* (London), Winter 1969/70.
Allen, Don, "Claude Chabrol," in *Screen* (London), February 1970.
Milne, Tom, "Chabrol's Schizophrenic Spider," in *Sight and Sound* (London), Spring 1970.
Haskell, Molly, "The Films of Chabrol—A Priest among Clowns," in *Village Voice* (New York), 12 November 1970.
Milne, Tom, "Songs of Innocence," in *Sight and Sound* (London), Winter 1970/71.
Bucher, F., and Peter Cowie, "Welles and Chabrol," in *Sight and Sound* (London), Autumn 1971.
"Chabrol Issue" of *Filmcritica* (Rome), April/May 1972.
Cornand, A., "*Les Noces rouges,* Chabrol et la censure," in *Image et Son* (Paris), April 1973.
Appel, A. Jr., "The Eyehole of Knowledge," in *Film Comment* (New York), May/June 1973.
"Chabrol Issue" of *Image et Son* (Paris), December 1973.
Dawson, Jan, "The Continental Divide," in *Sight and Sound* (London), Winter 1973/74.
Le Fanu, Mark, "The Cinema of Irony: Chabrol, Truffaut in the 1970s," in *Monogram* (London), no. 5, 1974.
Walker, M., "Claude Chabrol into the '70s," in *Movie* (London), Spring 1975.
Fassbinder, Rainer Werner, "Insects in a Glass Case: Random Thoughts on Claude Chabrol," in *Sight and Sound* (London), no.4, 1976.
Harcourt, P., "Middle Chabrol," in *Film Comment* (New York), November/December 1976.
Poague, Leland, "The Great God Orson: Chabrol's '10 Days' Wonder," in *Film Criticism* (Edinboro, Pennsylvania), no. 3, 1979.
Jenkins, Steve, "And the Chabrol We Haven't Seen...," in *Monthly Film Bulletin* (London), July 1982.
Dossier on Chabrol, in *Cinématographe* (Paris), September 1982.
Bergan, Ronald, "Directors of the Decade—Claude Chabrol," in *Films and Filming* (London), December 1983.
"Chabrol Section" of *Revue du Cinéma* (Paris), May 1985.
Monthly Film Bulletin (London), August 1987.
Auld, Deborah, "I, Claude," in *Village Voice,* 8 August 1989.
Haberman, C., "Chabrol Films a Henry Miller Tale," in *New York Times,* 9 August 1989.
Pally, Marcia, "Women's Business," in *Film Comment,* September/October 1989.
Bohlen, C., "Chabrol Offers a Cool-Eyed Look at a Stormy Issue," in *New York Times,* 15 October 1989.
Fisher, William, "Occupational Hazards," in *Harper's Bazaar,* November 1989.
Borde, R., "Claude Chabrol," in *La Revue de la Cinematheque,* December/January 1989/90.
Gristwood, Sarah, "Mabuse Returns: Chabrol Pays His Respects," in *Sight and Sound,* Spring 1990.
Mayne, Richard, "Still Waving, Not Drowning," in *Sight and Sound,* Summer 1990.
Riding, A., "Flaubert Does Hollywood—Again," in *New York Times,* 13 January 1991.
Chase, Donald, "A Day in the Country," in *Film Comment,* November/December 1991.
Vaucher, Andrea R., "Madame Bovary, C'est Moi!" in *American Film,* September/October 1991.
Roth, Michael, "L'oeil de Vichy," in *American Historical Review,* October 1994.
Frodon, Jean-Michel, "Chabrol's Class Act," in *London Guardian Weekly,* 17 September 1995.

On CHABROL: film—

Yentob, Alan, *Getting Away with Murder, or The Childhood of Claude Chabrol,* for BBC-TV, London, 1978.

* * *

If Jean-Luc Godard appeals to critics because of his extreme interest in politics and film theory, if François Truffaut appeals to the popular audience because of his humanism and sentimentality, it is Claude Chabrol—film critic, filmmaker, philosopher—whose work consistently offers the opportunity for the most balanced appeal. His partisans find especially notable the subtle tone of Chabrol's cinema: his films are apparently cold and objective portraits of profoundly psychological situations; and yet that coldness never approaches the kind of fashionable cynicism, say, of a Stanley Kubrick, but suggests, rather, something closer to the viewpoint of a god who, with compassion but without sentiment, observes the follies of his creations.

Chabrol's work can perhaps best be seen as a cross between the unassuming and popular genre film and the pretentious and elitist art film: Chabrol's films tend to be thrillers with an incredibly self-conscious, self-assured style—that is, pretentious melodrama, aware of its importance. For some, however, the hybrid character of Chabrol's work is itself a problem: indeed, just as elitist critics sometimes find Chabrol's subject matter beneath them, so too do popular audiences sometimes find Chabrol's style and incredibly slow pace alienating.

Chabrol's films are filled with allusions and references to myth (as in *La Rupture,* which begins with an epigraph from Racine's *Phaedra*: "What an utter darkness suddenly surrounds me!"). The narratives of his films are developed through a sensuousness of decor, a gradual accumulation of psychological insight, an absolute mastery of camera movement, and the inclusion of objects and images—beautiful and evocative, like the river in *Le Boucher* or the lighthouse in *Dirty Hands*—which are imbued with symbolic intensity. Like Balzac, whom he admires, Chabrol attempts, within a popular form, to present a portrait of his society in microcosm.

Chabrol began his career as a critic for *Cahiers du cinéma.* With Eric Rohmer, he wrote a groundbreaking book-length study of Alfred Hitchcock, and with his friends (Truffaut, Godard, Rohmer, Jacques Rivette, and others) he attempted to turn topsy-turvy the entire cinematic value system. That their theories of authorship remain today a basic (albeit modified and continuously examined) premise certainly indicates the success of their endeavor. Before long, Chabrol found himself functioning as financial consultant and producer for a variety of films inaugurating the directorial careers of his fellow critics who, like himself, were no longer content merely to theorize.

Chabrol's career can perhaps be divided into five semi-discrete periods: 1) the early personal films, beginning with *Le Beau Serge* in 1958 and continuing through *Landru* in 1962; 2) the commercial assignments, beginning with *The Tiger Likes Fresh Blood* in 1964 and

Claude Chabrol (in checked shirt) with François Truffaut at Cannes

continuing through *The Road to Corinth* in 1967; 3) the mature cycle of masterpieces, beginning with *Les Biches* in 1968 and continuing through *Wedding in Blood* in 1973, almost all starring his wife Stephane Audran, and produced by Andre Genoves; 4) the more diverse (and uneven) accumulations of films from 1974 to the present, which have tended neither to garner automatic international release nor to feature Audran in a central role; and 5) the more recent films of higher quality, if sometimes uneven still, produced in the 1980s and 1990s by Marin Karmitz's company MK2 and including a new set of regular collaborators.

If Hitchcock's *Shadow of a Doubt,* as analyzed by Chabrol and Rohmer, is constructed upon an exchange of guilt, Chabrol's first film, *Le Beau Serge,* modeled after it, is constructed upon an exchange of redemption. Chabrol followed *Le Beau Serge,* in which a city-dweller visits a country friend, with *Les Cousins,* in which a country-dweller visits a city friend. Most notably, *Les Cousins* offers Chabrol's first "Charles" and "Paul," the names Chabrol would continue to use throughout much of his career—Charles to represent the more serious bourgeois man, Paul the more hedonistic id-figure. *A double tour,* Chabrol's first color film, is especially notable for its striking cinematography, its complex narrative structure, and the exuberance of its flamboyant style; it represents Chabrol's first studied attempt to examine and criticize the moral values of the bourgeoisie as well as to dissect the sociopsychological causes of the violence which inevitably erupts as the social and family structures prove inadequate. Perhaps the most wholly successful film of this period is the infrequently screened *L'oeil du malin,* which presents the most typical Chabrol situation: a triangle consisting of a bourgeois married couple—Hélène and her stolid husband—and the outsider whose involvement with the couple ultimately leads to violence and tragedy. Here can be found Chabrol's first "Hélène," the recurring beautiful and slightly aloof woman, generally played by Stephane Audran.

When these and other personal films failed to ignite the box office, despite often positive critical responses, Chabrol embarked on a series of primarily commercial assignments (such as *Marie-Chantal contre le Docteur Kha*), during which his career went into a considerable critical eclipse. Today, however, even these fairly inconsequential films seem to reflect a fetching style and some typically quirky Chabrolian concerns.

Chabrol's breakthrough occurred in 1968 with the release of *Les Biches,* an elegant thriller in which an outsider, Paul, disrupts the lesbian relationship between two women. All of Chabrol's films in this period are slow psychological thrillers which tend basically to represent variations upon the same theme: an outsider affecting a central relationship until violence results. In *La Femme infidèle,* one of Chabrol's most self-assured films, the marriage of Hélène and Charles is disrupted when Charles kills Hélène's lover. In the Jansenist *Que la bête meure,* Charles tracks down the unremittingly evil hit-and-run killer of his young son, and while doing so disrupts the relationship between the killer, Paul, and his sister-in-law Hélène. In *Le Boucher,* the butcher Popaul, who is perhaps a homicidal killer, attempts a relationship with a cool and frigid schoolteacher, Hélène, who has displaced her sexual energies onto her teaching of her young pupils, particularly onto one who is conspicuously given the name Charles.

In the extravagantly expressive *La Rupture,* the outsider Paul attempts a plot against Hélène in order to secure a better divorce settlement, desired by the rich parents of her husband Charles, who has turned to drug addiction to escape his repressive bourgeois existence. In *Juste avant la nuit,* it is Charles who has taken a lover, and Charles's wife Hélène who must ultimately resort to an act of calculated violence in order to keep the bourgeois surface intact. In the detective variation *Ten Days' Wonder,* the relationship between Charles and Hélène is disrupted by the intervention of a character named Théo (*Theos,* representing God), whose false image must be unmasked by the outsider Paul. And in *Wedding in Blood,* based on factual material, it is the wife and her lover who team together to plot against her husband.

Jean Renoir said that all great directors make the same film over and over; perhaps no one has taken this dictum as seriously as Chabrol; indeed, all these films represent a kind of formal geometry as Charles, Hélène, and Paul play out their fated roles in a universe strongly influenced by Fritz Lang, the structures of their bourgeois existence unable to contain their previously repressed passions. Noteworthy too is the consistency of collaboration on these films: usually with Stephane Audran, Michel Bouquet, and Jean Yanne as performers; Jean Rabier as cinematographer; Paul Gégauff as co-scriptwriter; André Génovès as producer; Guy Littaye as art director; Pierre Jansen as composer; Jacques Gaillard as editor; Guy Chichignoud on sound.

In the late 1970s and 1980s, Chabrol has increasingly explored different kinds of financing, making television films as well as international co-productions. Some of these interesting films seem quite unusual from what he has attempted before, perhaps the most surprising being *Le Cheval d'Orgueil,* an ethnographic drama chronicling the simplicity and terrible harshness of peasant life in Brittany prior to World War I with a straightforwardness and lack of sentimentality which is often riveting. Indeed, the film seems so different from much of Chabrol's work that it forces a kind of re-evaluation of his career, making him seem less an emulator of Hitchcock and more an emulator of Balzac, attempting to create his own *Comedie humaine* in a panoramic account of the society about him.

Meanwhile, without his regular collaborators, most notably Stephane Audran, Chabrol has had to establish a new "team"—now including his son, Matthieu Chabrol, as the composer, replacing the superior Pierre Jansen. Although the series of films directed for producer Marin Karmitz seems laudable and superior to Chabrol's non-Karmitz films of the 1980s and 1990s, with a few exceptions they do not quite match the unity or quality of Chabrol's earlier masterpieces.

One of the exceptions is *Une affaire des femmes,* starring Isabelle Huppert, who had previously starred in *Violette Noziere.* The story of an abortionist who ends up the last female guillotined in France (by the Vichy government), *Une Affaire des femmes,* unlike other recent Chabrol films, received international distribution as well as a variety of awards and critical recognition. Chabrol's achievement here is extraordinary: offering a complex three-dimensional portrait of a woman who is not really very likeable, *Une Affaire des femmes* turns out, by its end, to be the most fair, progressive, and passionate film ever made about abortion, dissecting the sexual politics of the "crime"—without ever resorting to polemics; and Chabrol's unswerving gaze becomes the regard of an all-knowing God. *Madame Bovary,* again with Huppert, is perhaps one notch below in quality: is it surprising that Chabrol turns *Madame Bovary* into one of his tragic bourgeois love triangles—only this time, with the protagonist called Emma, rather than Hélène? The success of these two films, as well as the earlier *Violette Noziere* and Chabrol's most recent film *La Ceremonie* (all four starring Isabelle Huppert), may indicate that Chabrol's films—so cold as an inherent result of the director's personality and formal interests—may absolutely require an extraordinary, talented, and expressive female presence in order to contribute a human, empathic dimension—else they seem slow, tedious exercises. Clearly, Stephane Audran's contributions to Chabrol's earlier masterpieces—both as fellow artist and muse—may have been seriously underestimated.

More typical of Chabrol's recent career are films like *Les Fantômes du Chapelier, Poulet au vinaigre, Inspecteur Lavardin, Masques,* and *Le cri du hibou,* which, although worthy of note, by no means measure up to Chabrol's greatest and are therefore disappointing. What becomes increasingly clear is that Chabrol is one of the most uneven great directors; and without a producer like Andre Genoves and forceful, talented collaborators on the same wavelength, Chabrol can sometimes make bad or very odd movies. The 1976 *Folies bourgeoises,* for instance, is all but unwatchable, and while *Docteur M* and *Betty* may have interesting concepts, one is a dreary re-interpretation of Fritz Lang, and the other a lifeless adaptation of a Simenon novel, containing a wooden performance by Marie Trintignant. *L'enfer* (directed in 1994) is certainly better, if still minor—a smoldering tale of growing jealousy based on the unproduced script of a master director with a somewhat kindred soul, Henri-Georges Clouzot. Nevertheless, the true cinephile loves Chabrol despite his failures—because in the midst of his overprodigious output, he can change gears and make a fascinating documentary (such as his 1993 *L'oeil de Vichy*) or can surprise everyone with a major, narrative film of startling ideas, unity, and performance (such as his 1995 *La Ceremonie*), suddenly again at the very top of his form, a New Wave exemplar for filmmakers everywhere.

—Charles Derry

CHAHINE, Youssef

Nationality: Egyptian. **Born:** Alexandria, 25 January 1926; name also spelled "Shahin." **Education:** Victoria College, and Alexandria University; studied acting at Pasadena Playhouse, California, 1946-48. **Career:** Returned to Egypt, worked with Italian documentarist Gianni Vernuccio, 1948; introduced to film production by Alvisi Orfanelli, "pioneer of the Egyptian cinema," directed first film, *Baba Amine,* 1950; introduced actor Omar Sharif, in *Sera'a fil Wadi,* 1953; voluntary exile in Libya, 1965-67. **Awards:** Special Jury Prize, Berlin Festival, for *Alexandria ... Why?,* 1979; Special Jury Prize, Berlin Festival, for *An Egyptian Story,* 1982.

Films as Director:

1950 *Baba Amine* (*Father Amine*)
1951 *Ibn el Nil* (*The Nile's Son*); *El Muharraj el Kabir* (*The Great Clown*)
1952 *Sayidet el Kitar* (*The Lady in the Train*); *Nessa bala Rejal* (*Women without Men*)
1953 *Sera'a fil Wadi* (*Struggle in the Valley*)
1954 *Shaitan el Sahara* (*Devil of the Desert*)
1955 *Sera'a fil Mina* (*Struggle on the Pier*)
1956 *Inta Habibi* (*You Are My Love*)
1957 *Wadaat Hobak* (*Farewell to Your Love*)
1958 ***Bab el Hadid*** (*Iron Gate*; *Cairo Station*; *Gare centrale*) (+ role as Kennawi); *Gamila Bohraid* (Djamila)
1959 *Hub illal Abad* (*Forever Yours*)
1960 *Bayn Ideak* (*Between Your Hands*)
1961 *Nedaa el Ochak* (*Lover's Call*); *Rajol fi Hayati* (*A Man in My Life*)
1963 *El Naser Salah el Dine* (*Saladin*)
1964 *Fajr Yum Jadid* (*Dawn of a New Day*)
1965 *Baya el Khawatim* (*The Ring Seller*)
1966 *Rimal min Zahab* (*Sand of Gold*)
1968 *El Nas wal Nil* (*People and the Nile*)
1969 *El Ard* (*The Land*)
1970 *Al Ekhtiar* (*The Choice*)
1973 *Al Asfour* (*The Sparrow*)
1976 *Awdat al Ibn al Dal* (*Return of the Prodigal Son*)
1978 *Iskindria ... Leh?* (*Alexandria ... Why?*) (+ sc)
1982 *Hadota Misreya* (*An Egyptian Story*; *La Memoire*) (+ sc)
1984 *Al Wedaa ya Bonaparte* (*Adieu Bonaparte*)
1986 *Sarikat Sayfeya* (+ ph)
1990 *Iskindiriah Kaman Oue Kaman* (*Alexandria Again and Forever*) (+ sc)
1991 *Cairo as Told by Youssef Chahine*
1994 *The Emigrant* (+ sc)

Publications

By CHAHINE: articles—

Interview with C. M. Cluny, in *Cinéma* (Paris), September/October 1973.
"Entretien avec Youssef Chahine (Le moineau)," by G. Gauthier, in *Image et Son* (Paris), December 1974.
"Youssef Chahine: Aller aussi loin qu'un peut," interview with N. Ghali, in *Jeune Cinéma* (Paris), December 1974/January 1975.
"Youssef Chahine: La memoire," an interview with Marcel Martin, in *Revue du Cinéma* (Paris), July/August 1983.
"La verité de personnages," an interview with C. Tesson, in *Cahiers du Cinéma* (Paris), June 1985.
Interview in *Cinématographe* (Paris), December 1986.
"Serge le Vaillant," in *Cahiers du Cinema* (Paris), July/August 1992.

On CHAHINE: books—

Richter, Erika, *Realistischer Film in Agypten,* Berlin, 1974.
Armes, Roy, *Third World Filmmaking and the West,* Berkeley, 1987.

On CHAHINE: articles—

Arnaud, C., "Youssef Chahine," in *Image et Son* (Paris), January 1978.
Tournes, A., "Chahine, le nationalisme demystifie: *Alexandrie pourquoi?,*" in *Jeune Cinéma* (Paris), no. 3, 1979.
Armes, Roy, "Youssef Chahine and Egyptian Cinema," in *Framework* (Norwich), Spring 1981.
Joseph, I., and C. Jages, "Le Cinéma, l'Egypte et l'histoire," in *Cahiers du Cinéma* (Paris), September 1982.
Nave, B., A. Tournes, and M. Martin, "Un film bilan: La memoire de Chahine," in *Jeune Cinéma* (Paris), April 1983.
Toubiana, Serge, "Chahine a la conque te de Bonaparte," in *Cahiers du Cinéma* (Paris), October 1984.
Dossier on Chahine, in *Revue du Cinéma* (Paris), December 1984.
Chaillet, Jean-Paul, "Soleil d'Egypte," in *Première* (Paris), May 1985.
Kieffer, A., "Youssef Chahine: Un homme de dialogue," in *Jeune Cinéma* (Paris), July/August 1985.
Tesson, C., "La Descente du Nil," in *Cahiers du Cinéma* (Paris), July/August 1986.
Guerin, N., "Youssef Chahine," in *Cinema 90,* June 1990.

* * *

Youssef Chahine is one of the most forceful and complex of Egyptian filmmakers whose progress over the forty years or so since his debut at the age of twenty-four offers remarkable insight into the evolution of Egyptian society. A series of sharply critical social studies—of which *The Sparrow* in 1975 is undoubtedly the most successful—was interrupted by a heart attack while the director was still in his early fifties. This led him to question his own personal stance and development in a manner unique in Arab cinema, and the result was the splendidly fluent autobiography *Alexandria ... Why?* in 1978, which was followed four years later by a second installment entitled *An Egyptian Story,* shot in a style best characterized as an amalgam of Fellini and Bob Fosse's *All That Jazz.*

As such references indicate, Chahine is an eclectic filmmaker whose cosmopolitan attitudes can be traced back to his origins. He was born in Alexandria in 1926 of middle-class parents. His father, a supporter of the nationalist Wafd party, was a scrupulous but financially unsuc-

Youssef Chahine: ***Iskindria ... Leh?***

cessful lawyer, and Chahine was brought up as a Christian, educated first at religious school and then at the prestigious Victoria College, where the language of tuition was English. After a year at Alexandria University he persuaded his parents to allow him to study drama for two years at Pasadena Playhouse, near Los Angeles, and on his return to Egypt he plunged into the film industry, then enjoying a period of boom in the last years of King Farouk's reign.

Alexandria ... Why? presents a vividly drawn picture of this vanished world: Alexandria in 1942, awaiting the arrival of Rommel's troops, who, it is hoped, will finally drive out the British. The film is peopled with English soldiers and Egyptian patriots, aristocrats, and struggling bourgeoises, the enthusiastic young and their disillusioned or corrupt elders. Chahine mocks the excesses of the nationalists (his terrorist patriots are mostly caricatures), leaves condemnation of Zionism to Jews, and tells love stories that cross the neatly drawn barriers separating Muslim and Jew, Egyptian aristocrat and English Tommy. The revelation of Chahine's own background and a few of his personal obsessions (as with the crucified Christ) seems to have released fresh creative powers in the director. His technique of intercutting the action with scenes from Hollywood musicals and newsreel footage from the Imperial War Museum in London is as successful as it is audacious, and the transitions of mood are brilliantly handled.

Chahine is a key figure in Third World cinema. Unlike some of the other major filmmakers who also emerged in the 1950s—such as Satyajit Ray or Lester James Peries—he has not turned his back on commercial cinema. He has always shown a keen desire to reach a wide audience, and *Alexandria ... Why?,* though personal, is by no means an inaccessible or difficult work. Chahine's strength as a filmmaker lies indeed in his ability to combine mainstream production techniques with a very individual style and approach. Though intensely patriotic, he has shown a readiness to criticize government policies with which he does not agree, such as those of the late President Sadat. It is ironic therefore that the appearance of *Alexandria ... Why?* should have coincided with the Camp David agreements between Egypt and Israel. As a result, Chahine's very personal statement of his belief in a tolerant society came to be widely criticized in the Arab world as an opportunistic political statement and a justification of Sadat's policies.

His underlying commitment to the making of an Egyptian identity, history, and memory is evident in his more recent works as well. The 1984 *Adieu Bonaparte,* a Franco-Egyptian co-production, portrays an East-West encounter through an Egyptian family during Napoleon's invasion of Egypt. Chahine's continuous efforts to reconstruct and forge an *Egyptian-ness,* "to be nothing but Egyptian," can be most clearly seen in the ways in which he strives to retell this history from a strictly Egyptian perspective and none other. Chahine's endeavor may not be unique among the whole array of Third World filmmakers who act and/or *re*act against the West. However, given his own involvement and interests in the Western arts and influences, which not too many non-Western filmmakers could in fact claim to be devoid of, it is his inventiveness in forms and consistency in content that make Chahine an important filmmaker in Egypt in particular and in the non-Western filmmaking world in general.

—Roy Armes, updated by Guo-Juin Hong

CHAPLIN, (Sir) Charles (Charlie)

Nationality: British. **Born:** Charles Spencer Chaplin in London, 16 April 1889. **Family:** Married 1) Mildred Harris, 1918 (divorced 1920); 2) Lita Grey, 1924 (divorced 1927), two sons; 3) Paulette Goddard, 1936 (divorced 1941); 4) Oona O'Neill, 1943, eight children. **Career:** Music-Hall Performer in London and provincial theatres, from 1898; engaged by Fred Karno troupe, 1907; toured United States with Karno, 1910 and 1912; signed to Keystone and moved to Hollywood, 1913; after acting in eleven Keystone comedies, began directing (thirty-five films for Keystone), 1914; signed with Essanay (fourteen films), 1915; signed with Mutual (eleven films), 1916; signed with First National (nine films), 1917; joint-founder, with Griffith, Pickford, and Fairbanks, of United Artists, 1919; left United States to visit London, reentry permit rescinded en route, 1952; moved to Vevey, on Lake Geneva, Switzerland, 1953. **Awards:** Best Actor, New York Film Critics, for *The Great Dictator,* 1940 (award refused); Honorary Oscar, "for the incalculable effect he has had in making motion pictures the art form of the country," 1971; Medallion Award, Writers Guild of America, 1971; Oscar for Best Original Dramatic Score (shared) for *Limelight,* 1972; Knighted, 1975. **Died:** In Vevey, 25 December 1977.

Films as Director, Actor and Scriptwriter:

1914 *Caught in a Cabaret* (*Jazz Waiter*; *Faking with Society*) (co-d, co-sc); *Caught in the Rain* (*Who Got Stung?*; *At It Again*); *A Busy Day* (*Lady Charlie*; *Militant Suffragette*); *The Fatal Mallet* (*The Pile Driver*; *The Rival Suitors*; *Hit Him Again*) (co-d, co-sc); *Her Friend the Bandit* (*Mabel's Flirtation*; *A Thief Catcher*) (co-d, co-sc); *Mabel's Busy Day* (*Charlie and the Sausages*; *Love and Lunch*; *Hot Dogs*) (co-d, co-sc); *Mabel's Married Life* (*When You're Married*; *The Squarehead*) (co-d, co-sc); *Laughing Gas* (*Tuning His Ivories*; *The Dentist*); *The Property Man* (*Getting His Goat*; *The Roustabout*; *Vamping Venus*); *The Face on the Bar-Room Floor* (*The Ham Artist*); *Recreation* (*Spring Fever*); *The Masquerader* (*Putting One Over*; *The Female Impersonator*); *His New Profession* (*The Good-for-Nothing*; *Helping Himself*); *The Rounders* (*Two of a Kind*; *Oh, What a Night!*); *The New Janitor* (*The Porter*; *The Blundering Boob*); *Those Love Pangs* (*The Rival Mashers*; *Busted Hearts*); *Dough and Dynamite* (*The Doughnut Designer*; *The Cook*); *Gentlemen of Nerve* (*Some Nerve*; *Charlie at the Races*); *His Musical Career* (*The Piano Movers*; *Musical Tramps*); *His Trysting Place* (*Family Home*); *Getting Acquainted* (*A Fair Exchange*; *Hullo Everybody*); *His Prehistoric Past* (*A Dream*; *King Charlie*; *The Caveman*)

1915 (for Essanay): *His New Job*; *A Night Out* (*Champagne Charlie*); *The Champion* (*Battling Charlie*); *In the Park* (*Charlie on the Spree*); *A Jitney Elopement* (*Married in Haste*); *The Tramp* (*Charlie the Hobo*); *By the Sea* (*Charlie's Day Out*); *Work* (*The Paper Hanger*; *The Plumber*); *A Woman* (*The Perfect Lady*); *The Bank*; *Shanghaied* (*Charlie the Sailor*; *Charlie on the Ocean*); *A Night in the Show*

1916 (for Essanay): *Carmen* (*Charlie Chaplin's Burlesque on Carmen*); *Police!* (*Charlie the Burglar*); (for Mutual): *The Floorwalker* (*The Store*); *The Fireman*; *The Vagabond*; *One A.M.*; *The Count*; *The Pawnshop*; *Behind the Screen*; *The Rink*

1917 (for Mutual): ***Easy Street***; *The Cure*; *The Immigrant*; *The Adventurer*

1918 (for First National): *A Dog's Life*; (for Liberty Loan Committee): *The Bond*; *Triple Trouble* (compiled from 1915 footage plus additional non-Chaplin film by Essanay after he left); (for First National): *Shoulder Arms*

1919 (for First National): *Sunnyside*; *A Day's Pleasure*

1921 ***The Kid***; (+ pr); *The Idle Class* (+ pr)

1922 *Pay Day* (+ pr); *Nice and Friendly* (+ pr) (made privately and unreleased)

1923 *The Pilgrim* (+ pr); *A Woman of Paris* (+ pr)

1925 ***The Gold Rush*** (+ pr, narration, mus for sound reissue)

1926 *A Woman of the Sea* (*The Sea Gull*) (von Sternberg) (unreleased) (pr, d additional scenes)

1927 *The Circus* (+ pr, mus, song for sound reissue)

1931 ***City Lights*** (+ pr, mus)

1936 ***Modern Times*** (+ pr, mus)

1940 ***The Great Dictator*** (+ pr, mus)

1947 *Monsieur Verdoux* (+ pr, mus); ***Limelight*** (+ pr, mus, co-choreographer)

1957 *A King in New York* (+ pr, mus)

1959 *The Chaplin Revue* (+ pr, mus) (comprising *A Dog's Life, Shoulder Arms,* and *The Pilgrim*, with commentary and music)

1967 *A Countess from Hong Kong* (+ mus)

Other Films:

1914 *Making a Living* (*A Busted Johnny*; *Troubles*; *Doing His Best*) (Lehrman) (role as reporter); *Kid Auto Races at Venice* (*The Kid Auto Race*) (Lehrman) (role as Charlie); *Mabel's Strange Predicament* (*Hotel Mixup*) (Lehrman and Sennett) (role as Charlie); *Between Showers* (*The Flirts*; *Charlie and the Umbrella*; *In Wrong*) (Lehrman) (role as Charlie); *A Film Johnnie* (*Movie Nut*; *Million Dollar Job*; *Charlie at the Studio*) (Sennett) (role as Charlie); *Tango Tangles* (*Charlie's Recreation*; *Music Hall*) (Sennett) (role as Charlie); *His Favorite Pastime* (*The Bonehead*; *His Reckless Fling*) (Nichols) (role as Charlie); *Cruel, Cruel Love* (Sennett) (role as Charlie); *The Star Boarder* (*The Hash-House Hero*) (Sennett) (role as Charlie); *Mabel at the Wheel* (*His Daredevil Queen*; *Hot Finish*) (Normand and Sennett) (role as Charlie); *Twenty Minutes of Love* (*He Loved Her So*; *Cops and Watches*) (Sennett) (role as Charlie, + sc); *The Knock Out* (*Counted Out*; *The Pugilist*) (Arbuckle) (role as Charlie); *Tillie's Punctured Romance* (*Tillie's Nightmare*; *For the Love of Tillie*; *Marie's Millions*) (Sennett) (role as Charlie); *His Regeneration* (Anderson) (guest appearance)

1921 *The Nut* (Reed) (guest appearance)

1923 *Souls for Sale* (Hughes) (guest appearance)

1928 *Show People* (King Vidor) (guest appearance)

Publications

By CHAPLIN: books—

Charlie Chaplin's Own Story, Indianapolis, 1916.
My Trip Abroad, New York, 1922.
My Autobiography, London, 1964.
My Life in Pictures, London, 1974.

By CHAPLIN: articles—

Interview with Margaret Hinxman, in *Sight and Sound* (London), Autumn 1957.
Interview with Richard Merryman, in *Life* (New York), 10 March 1967.
"Charles Chaplin parle," interviews excerpted by C. Gauteur, in *Image et Son* (Paris), November 1972.
"Chaplin est mort, vive Charlot!," interview with Philippe Soupault, text by Chaplin from 1921, and round-table discussion, in *Ecran* (Paris), March 1978.
"The INS interview with Chaplin," edited by Charles J. Maland, in *Cineaste* (New York), vol. 14, no. 4, 1986.

On CHAPLIN: books—

Delluc, Louis, *Charlot,* Paris, 1921.
Tyler, Parker, *Chaplin, Last of the Clowns,* New York, 1947.
Huff, Theodore, *Charlie Chaplin,* New York, 1951.
Bessy, Maurice, and Robert Florey, *Monsieur Chaplin ou le rire dans la nuit,* Paris, 1952.
Payne, Robert, *The Great God Pan: A Biography of the Tramp Played by Charlie Chaplin,* New York, 1952.
Sadoul, Georges, *Vie de Charlot,* Paris, 1952; published as *Vie de Charlot: Charles Spencer Chaplin, ses films et son temps,* Paris, 1978.
Mitry, Jean, *Charlot et la "fabulation" chaplinesque,* Paris, 1957.
McDonald, Gerald, and others, *The Films of Charlie Chaplin,* Secaucus, New Jersey, 1965.
Martin, Marcel, *Charlie Chaplin,* Paris, 1966; 3rd edition, Paris, 1983.
Brownlow, Kevin, *The Parade's Gone By,* London, 1968.
McCaffrey, Donald, *Four Great Comedians: Chaplin, Lloyd, Keaton, Langdon,* London, 1968.
Quigly, Isabel, *Charlie Chaplin: Early Comedies,* London, 1968.
Leprohon, Pierre, *Charles Chaplin,* Paris, 1970.
McCaffrey, Donald, editor, *Focus on Chaplin,* Englewood Cliffs, New Jersey, 1971.
Mitry, Jean, *Tout Chaplin: Tous les films, par le texte, par le gag et par l'image,* Paris, 1972.
Mast, Gerald, *The Comic Mind,* New York, 1973.
Manvell, Roger, *Chaplin,* Boston, 1974.
Lyons, T.J., *Charles Chaplin—a Guide to References and Resources,* Boston, 1977.
Sobel, Raoul, and David Francis, *Chaplin, Genesis of a Clown,* London, 1977.
McCabe, John, *Charlie Chaplin,* New York, 1978.
Nysenholc, Adolphe, *L'Age d'or du comique: sémiologie de Charlot,* Brussels, 1979.
Eisenstein, Sergei, *Film Essays and a Lecture,* edited by Jay Leyda, Princeton, New Jersey, 1982.
Gehring, Wes D., *Charlie Chaplin: A Bio-Bibliography,* Westport, Connecticut, 1983.
Robinson, David, *Chaplin: The Mirror of Opinion,* London, 1983.
Kamin, Dan, *Charlie Chaplin's One-Man Show,* Metuchen, New Jersey, 1984.
Smith, Julian, *Chaplin,* Boston, 1984.
Geduld, Harry M., *Charlie Chaplin's Own Story,* Bloomington, Indiana, 1985.
Robinson, David, *Chaplin: His Life and Art,* London, 1985.
Geduld, Harry M., *Chapliniana 1: The Keystone Films,* Bloomington, Indiana, 1987.
Mitry, Jean, *Tout Chaplin: L'Oeuvre complète presentée par le texte et par l'image,* Paris, 1987.
Saint-Martin, Catherine, *Charlot/Chaplin; ou, La Conscience du mythe,* Paris, 1987.
Epstein, Jerry, *Remembering Charlie: The Story of a Friendship,* London, 1988.
Schickel, Richard, *Schickel on Film: Encounters—critical and personal—with movie immortals,* New York, 1989.
Maland, Charles J., *Chaplin and American Culture: The Evolution of a Star,* 1990.

On CHAPLIN: articles—

Churchill, Winston, "Everybody's Language," in *Collier's* (New York), 26 October 1935.
Eisenstein, Sergei, "Charlie the Kid," and "Charlie the Grown Up," in *Sight and Sound* (London), Spring and Summer 1946.
Huff, Theodore, "Chaplin as Composer," in *Films in Review* (New York), September 1950.
Hickey, Terry, "Accusations Against Charles Chaplin for Political and Moral Offenses," in *Film Comment* (New York), Winter 1969.
Lyons, T.J., "Roland H. Totheroh Interviewed: Chaplin Films," in *Film Culture* (New York), Spring 1972.
"Chaplin Issue" of *Film Comment* (New York), September/October 1972.
"Chaplin Issue" of *Positif* (Paris), July/August 1973.
Cott, J., "The Limits of Silent Film Comedy," in *Literature/Film Quarterly* (Salisbury, Maryland), Spring 1975.
Adorno, Theodor, "Quel giorno che Chaplin mi fece l'imitazione," in *Cinema Nuovo* (Bari), July-August 1976.
"Chaplin Issue" of *Film und Fernsehen* (Berlin), March 1978.
Corliss, Richard, "Chaplin," in *Film Comment* (New York), March/April 1978.
"Pour saluter Charlot," in *Avant-Scène du Cinéma* (Paris), 1 May 1978.
"Chaplin Issue" of *University Film Association Journal* (Houston), no.1, 1979.
Sato, Tadao, "The Comedy of Ozu and Chaplin—a Study in Contrast," in *Wide Angle* (Athens, Ohio), no.2, 1979.
"Dossier: Charles Chaplin et l'opinion publique," in *Cinématographe* (Paris), January 1981.
Ingrao, P., "Chaplin: The antagonism of the comic hero," in *Film Quarterly* (Los Angeles), Fall 1981.
Everson, William K., "Rediscovery: 'New' Chaplin Films," in *Films in Review* (New York), November 1981.
Manning, H., and T.J. Lyons, "Charlie Chaplin's early life: Fact and fiction," in *Historical Journal of Film, Radio, and Television* (Abingdon, Oxon), March 1983.
Balio, Tino, "Charles Chaplin, homme d'affaires: Un artiste associé," in *Filméchange* (Paris), Spring 1983.
Millar, Gavin, "The unknown Chaplin," in *Sight and Sound* (London), Spring 1983.
Classic Images (Muscatine, Iowa), nos. 98-106, August 1983-April 1984.
Slide, Anthony, "The American Press and Public v Charles Spencer Chaplin," in *Cineaste* (New York), vol. 13, no. 4, 1984.
Maland, Charles J., "The Millionaire Tramp," in *Post Script* (Jacksonville, Florida), Spring-Summer 1984.
Jaffe, I.S., "Chaplin's labor of Performance: the circus and *Limelight,*" and R.L. Liebman, "Rabbis or rakes, schlemiels or supermen? Jewish identity in Charles Chaplin, Jerry Lewis and Woody Allen," in *Literature/Film Quarterly* (Salisbury, Maryland), July 1984.

"Chaplin Section" of *American Film* (Washington, D.C.), September 1984.

Naremore, J., "Film and the Performance Frame," in *Film Quarterly* (Los Angeles), Winter 1984-85.

Maland, Charles J., "A Documentary Note on Charlie Chaplin's Politics," in *Historical Journal of Film, Radio, and Television* (Abingdon, Oxon), vol. 5, no.2, 1985.

Heurtebise, "On first looking into Chaplin's humor," in *Sight and Sound* (London), Spring 1985.

Davis, D. William, "A Tale of Two Movies: Charlie Chaplin, United Artists, and the Red Scare," in *Cinema Journal* (Champaigne, Illinois), Fall 1987.

Florey, Robert, with Brian Naves, "Charlie Dearest," in *Film Comment* (New York), March-April 1988.

Kuriyama, Constance Brown, "Chaplin's Impure Comedy: The Art of Survival," in *Film Quarterly* (Los Angeles), Spring 1992.

Nightingale, B., "The Melancholy That Forged a Comic Genius," in *New York Times,* 22 March 1992.

Bloom, Claire, "Charles the Great," in *Vogue,* December 1992.

Ivor, Davis, "Chaplin," in *Los Angeles Magazine,* December 1992.

Combs, Richard, "Little Man, What Now?" in *Film Comment* (New York), August 1993.

On CHAPLIN: films—

Carlson, Wallace, *Introducing Charlie Chaplin,* 1915.

Abramson, Hans, "Upptäckten (Discovery)" episode of *Stimulantia,* Sweden, 1967.

Becker, Vernon, *The Funniest Man in the World,* 1967.

Hurwitz, Harry, *Chaplinesque, My Life and Hard Times,* for TV, 1967 (also released as *The Eternal Tramp*).

* * *

Charles Chaplin was the first and the greatest international star of the American silent comic cinema. He was also the twentieth century's first media "superstar," the first artistic creator and popularized creature of our global culture. His face, onscreen antics, and offscreen scandals were disseminated around the globe by new media which knew no geographical or linguistic boundaries. But more than this, Chaplin was the first acknowledged artistic genius of the cinema, recognized as such by a young and influential generation of writers and artists whose number included George Bernard Shaw, H.G. Wells, Bertolt Brecht, Pablo Picasso, James Joyce, Samuel Beckett, and the surrealist painters and poets of both Paris and Berlin. Chaplin may be the one cinema artist who might truly be called a seminal figure of the century—if only because of his influence on virtually every other recognized seminal figure of the century.

Chaplin was born in London into a theatrical family; his mother and father alternated between periods of separation and union, activities onstage and difficulties offstage (his father was an alcoholic, his mother fell victim to insanity). The young Chaplin spent his early life on the London streets and in a London workhouse, but by the age of eight he was earning his living on the stage.

Chaplin's career, like that of Buster Keaton and Stan Laurel, indicates that gifted physical comedians often develop their talents as children (as do concert pianists and ballet dancers) or never really develop them at all. By the time he was twenty years old, Chaplin had become the star attraction of the Fred Karno Pantomime Troupe, an internationally acclaimed English music-hall act, and it was on his second tour of America that a representative of the Keystone comedy film company (either Mack Sennett, comedienne Mabel Normand, or co-owner Charles Bauman) saw Chaplin. In 1913 he was offered a job at Keystone. Chaplin went to work at the Keystone lot in Burbank, California, in January of 1914.

To some extent, the story of Chaplin's popular success and artistic evolution is evident from even a cursory examination of the sheer volume of Chaplin's works (and the compensation he received). In 1914 at Keystone, Chaplin appeared in thirty-five one- and two-reel films (as well as the six-reeler *Tillie's Punctured Romance*), about half of which he directed himself, for the yearly salary of $7,800. The following year, Chaplin made fourteen one- and two-reel films for the Essanay Film Company—all of which he wrote and directed himself—for a salary of $67,000. In 1916-17, Chaplin wrote, directed and starred in twelve two-reel films for the Mutual Film company, and then signed a million-dollar contract with First National Corporation to write, direct, produce, and star in twelve more two-reel films. The contract allowed him to build his own studio, which he alone used until 1952 (it is now the studio for A&M Records), but his developing artistic consciousness kept him from completing the contract until 1923 with nine films of lengths ranging from two to six reels. Finally, in 1919, Chaplin became one of the founders of United Artists (along with Mary Pickford, Douglas Fairbanks, and D.W. Griffith), through which Chaplin released eight feature films, made between 1923 and 1952, after which he sold his interest in the company.

In his early one- and two-reel films Chaplin evolved the comic tools and means that would lead to his future success. His character of the Tramp, the "little fellow," a figure invariably garbed with derby, cane, floppy shoes, baggy pants, and tight jacket, debuted in his second Keystone film, *Kid Auto Races at Venice.* Because the tramp was a little guy, he made an easy target for the larger and tougher characters who loomed over him, but his quick thinking, agile body, and surprising ingenuity in converting ordinary objects into extraordinary physical allies helped him more than hold his own in a big, mean world. Although he was capable of lechery (*The Masquerader, Dough and Dynamite*) he could also selflessly aid the innocent woman under attack (*The New Janitor, The Tramp, The Bank*). Although he deserved her affection as a reward, he was frequently rejected for his social or sexual inadequacies (*The Tramp, The Bank, The Vagabond, The Adventurer*). Many of his early films combined his dexterous games with physical objects with deliberate attempts at emotional pathos (*The Tramp, The Vagabond, The Pawnshop*) or with social commentary on the corruption of the police, the brutality of the slums, or the selfishness of the rich (*Police, Easy Street, The Adventurer*).

Prior to Chaplin, no one had demonstrated that physical comedy could be simultaneously hilariously funny, emotionally passionate, and pointedly intellectual. While his cinema technique tended to be invisible—emphasizing the actor and his actions—he gradually evolved a principle of cinema based on framing: finding the exact way to frame a shot to reveal its motion and meaning completely, thus avoiding disturbing cuts.

Chaplin's later films evolved and featured increasingly complicated or ironic situations in which to explore the Tramp's character and the moral paradoxes of his existence. His friend and ally is a mongrel dog in *A Dog's Life*; he becomes a doughboy in *Shoulder Arms*; acquires a child in *The Kid*; becomes a preacher in *The Pilgrim*; and explores the decadent Parisian high life in *A Woman of Paris,* a comedy-melodrama of subtle visual techniques in which the Tramp does not appear.

Chaplin's four feature films between 1925 and 1936 might be called his "marriage group," in which he explores the circumstances by which the tramp might acquire a sexual-romantic mate. In *The Gold Rush* the Tramp succeeds in winning the dance-hall gal who previously rejected him, because she now appreciates his kindness and his newfound wealth. The happy ending is as improbable as the Tramp's sudden riches—perhaps a comment that kindness helps but money gets the girl. But in *The Circus,* Charlie turns his beloved over to the romantic high-wire daredevil Rex; the girl rejects him not because of Charlie's kindness or poverty but because he cannot fulfill the woman's image of male sexual attractiveness. *City Lights* builds upon this problem as it rises to a final question, deliberately and poignantly left

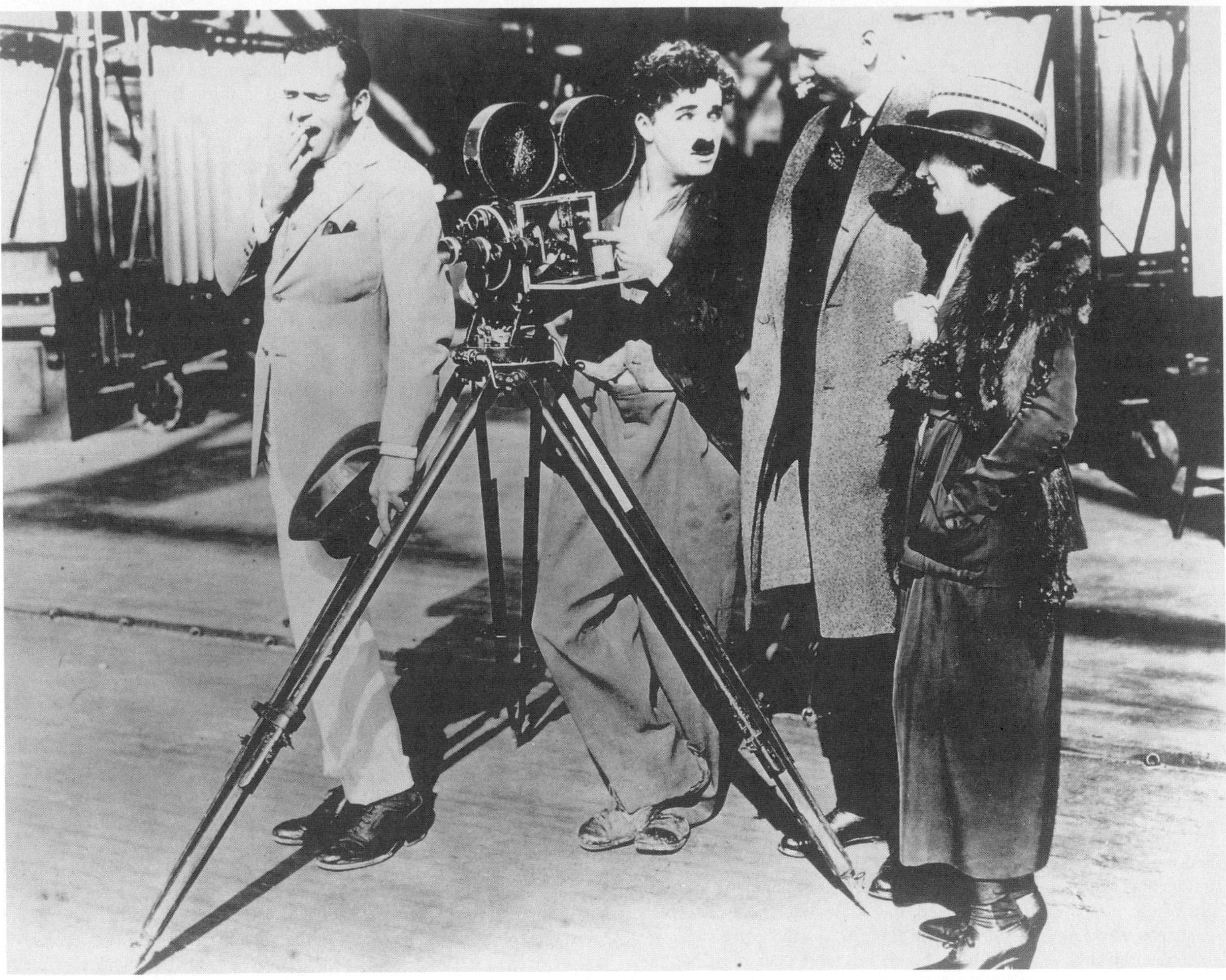

Charles Chaplin

unanswered: can the blind flower seller, whose vision has been restored by Charlie's kindness, love him for his kindness alone since her vision now reveals him to look so painfully different from the rich and handsome man she imagined and expected? And in *Modern Times*, Charlie successfully finds a mate, a social outcast and child of nature like himself; unfortunately, their marriage can find no sanctification or existence within contemporary industrial society. So the two of them take to the road together, walking away from society toward who knows where—the Tramp's final departure from the Chaplin world.

Although both *City Lights* and *Modern Times* used orchestral music and cleverly comic sound effects (especially *Modern Times*), Chaplin's final three American films were talking films—*The Great Dictator,* in which Chaplin burlesques Hitler and Nazism, *Monsieur Verdoux,* in which Chaplin portrays a dapper mass murderer, and *Limelight,* Chaplin's nostalgic farewell to the silent art of pantomime which nurtured him. In this film, in which Buster Keaton also plays a major role, Chaplin bids farewell not only to a dead movie tradition—silent comedy—but to a two-hundred-year tradition of physical comedy on both stage and screen, the tradition out of which both Keaton and Chaplin came, which would produce no clowns of the future.

Chaplin's later years were scarred by personal and political difficulties produced by his many marriages and divorces, his supposed sexual philanderings, his difficulties with the Internal Revenue Service, his outspoken defence of liberal political causes, and his refusal to become an American citizen. Although he was never called to testify before the House Un-American Activities Committee, Chaplin's films were picketed and boycotted by right-wing activist groups. When Chaplin left for a trip abroad in 1952, the State Department summarily revoked his automatic re-entry permit. Chaplin sent his young wife Oona O'Neill, daughter of the playwright Eugene O'Neill, back to America to settle their business affairs.

Chaplin established his family in Switzerland and conveyed his outrage against his former country by not returning to America for twenty years and by refusing to let any of his films circulate in America for two decades. In 1957 he made a very uneven, often embarrassing satire of American democracy, *A King in New York.* This film, like *A Countess from Hong Kong,* made ten years later, was a commercial and artistic disappointment, perhaps in part because Chaplin was cut off from the familiar studio, the experienced production team, and the painstakingly slow production methods he had been using for over three decades. In 1971 he enjoyed a triumphant return to Hollywood to accept an honorary Academy Award for a lifetime of cinematic achievement.

—Gerald Mast

CHEN Kaige

Nationality: Chinese. **Born:** Beijing, 12 August 1952; son of film director Chen Huai'ai. **Education:** Sent to work in Rubber plantation in Yunnan province to "learn from the people," as part of Cultural Revolution, 1967. **Military Service:** Served in Army. **Career:** Worked in film processing lab, Beijing, 1975-78, then studied at Beijing Film Academy, 1978-82; assigned to Beijing Film Studio, assistant to Huang Jianzhong; transferred (with Zhang Yimou and He Qun) to Guangxi Film Studios, and directed first feature, *Huang Tudi'*, 1984. **Awards:** Best Film, Berlin Film Festival, for *Yellow Earth,* 1984.

Films as Director:

1984 ***Huang Tudi'*** (*Yellow Earth*); *Qiangxing Qifei* (*Forced Take-Off*) (for TV)
1985 *Da Yuebing* (*The Big Parade*) (released in 1987)
1987 ***Haizi Wang*** (*King of the Children*)
1991 ***Ba Wang Bie Ji*** (*Farewell My Concubine*)
1995 *Temptress Moon*

Publications

By CHEN: articles—

Interview with Tony Rayns, in *Time Out* (London), 6 August 1986.
Interview in *Film Comment* (New York), July/August 1988.
Interview in *Films and Filming* (London), August 1988.
Interview with Don Ranvaud, in *Guardian* (London), 11 August 1988.
Interview in *Time Out* (London), 17 August 1988.
Interview with Jonathan Mirsky, in *New Statesman and Society* (London), 19 August 1988.
Interview in *Monthly Film Bulletin* (London), September 1988.
"La representation d'un reve," an interview with Hubert Noigret in *Positif,* March 1992.
Interview in *Positif,* November 1993.
"La longue marche," an interview with Laurent Tirard and Christophe d'Yvoire, in *Studio Magazine* (France), no. 80, 1993.

On CHEN: books—

Berry, Chris, editor, *Perspectives on Chinese Cinema,* New York, 1985.
Quiquemelle, Marie-Claire, and Jean-Loup Passek, *Le Cinema chinois,* Paris, 1985.
Armes, Roy, *Third World Filmmaking and the West,* Berkeley, 1987.
Clark, Paul, *Chinese Cinema: Culture and Politics since 1949,* Cambridge, 1987.
Semsel, George Stephen, editor, *Chinese Film: The State of the Art in the Chinese Republic,* New York, 1987.
Berry, Chris, editor, *Perspectives on Chinese Cinema,* London, 1991.

On CHEN: articles—

Hitchcock, Peter, "The Question of the Relationship of the Intellectual to the State in post-Mao China and the Position of Women," in *The Aesthetics of Alienation, or China's Fifth Generation, Cultural Studies,* January 1992.
Richard, Fréderic, "L'amour, les mirages et l'histoire: Va vie sur un fil," *Positif,* March 1992.
Koch, Ulrike, "Le seul qui puisse voir: La vie sur un fil," in *Positif,* March 1992.
Rayns, Tony, "Nights at the Opera," in *Sight and Sound,* December 1992.
Noigret, Hubert, "Dossier sur Farewell My Concubine," in *Positif,* November 1993.
Zha Jianying, "Chen Kaige and the Shadows of the Revolution," in *Sight and Sound,* February 1994.

* * *

Chen Kaige is, with Zhang Yimou, the leading voice among the Fifth Generation of Chinese filmmakers, the first group of students to have graduated following the reopening of the Beijing Film Academy in 1978 after the depredations of the Cultural Revolution. As both a participant in (as a Red Guard he denounced his own father) and a victim of the Cultural Revolution (his secondary education was curtailed and, like the protagonist of *King of the Children,* he was sent to the country to "learn from the peasants"), Chen is particularly well-placed to voice concerns about history and identity.

His films so far constitute an intelligent and powerfully felt meditation on recent Chinese history, within which, for him, the Cultural Revolution remains a defining moment. "It made," he has said, "cultural hooligans of us." He has a reputation within China as a philosophical director, and his style is indeed marked by a laconic handling of narrative and a classical reticence. This is largely deceptive: underneath is an unyielding anger and unflinching integrity.

Chen in interviews has stressed the complementary nature of his first three films. *Yellow Earth* examines the relationship of "man and the land," *The Big Parade* looks at "the individual and the group," and *King of the Children* considers "man and culture." *Yellow Earth* seems to adopt the structure of the folk ballads that provide a focus for its narrative, with its long held shots and almost lapidary editing. *The Big Parade* alternates static parade ground shots with the chaos of barrack room life, while the third film mobilises a more rhetorical style of poetic realism. Together the films act as a triple rebuttal of any heroic reading of Maoism and the revolution, precisely by taking up subjects much used in propagandist art—the arrival of the People's Liberation Army in a village, the training of new recruits, the fate of the teacher sent to the country—and by refuting their simplifications and obfuscations, shot for shot, with quite trenchant deliberation. Attention in *Yellow Earth* is focused not on the Communist Army whose soldier arrives at the village collecting songs, but on the barren plateau from which the peasantry attempts to wring a meagre existence. In the process the account of Yenan which sees it as the birthplace of Communism is marginalised. *King of the Children* banishes the bright-eyed pupils and spotless classrooms of propaganda in favour of a run-down school room, graffitied and in disrepair, from which the social fabric seems to have fallen away. Likewise *The Big Parade* banishes heroics and exemplary characters in favour of a clear-eyed look at the cost of moulding the individual into the collective.

In Chen's films what is unsaid is as important as that which is said; indeed the act of silence becomes a potent force. The voiceless appear everywhere—the almost mute brother in *Yellow Earth,* the girl's unspoken fears for her marriage ("voiced" in song), the mute cowherd in

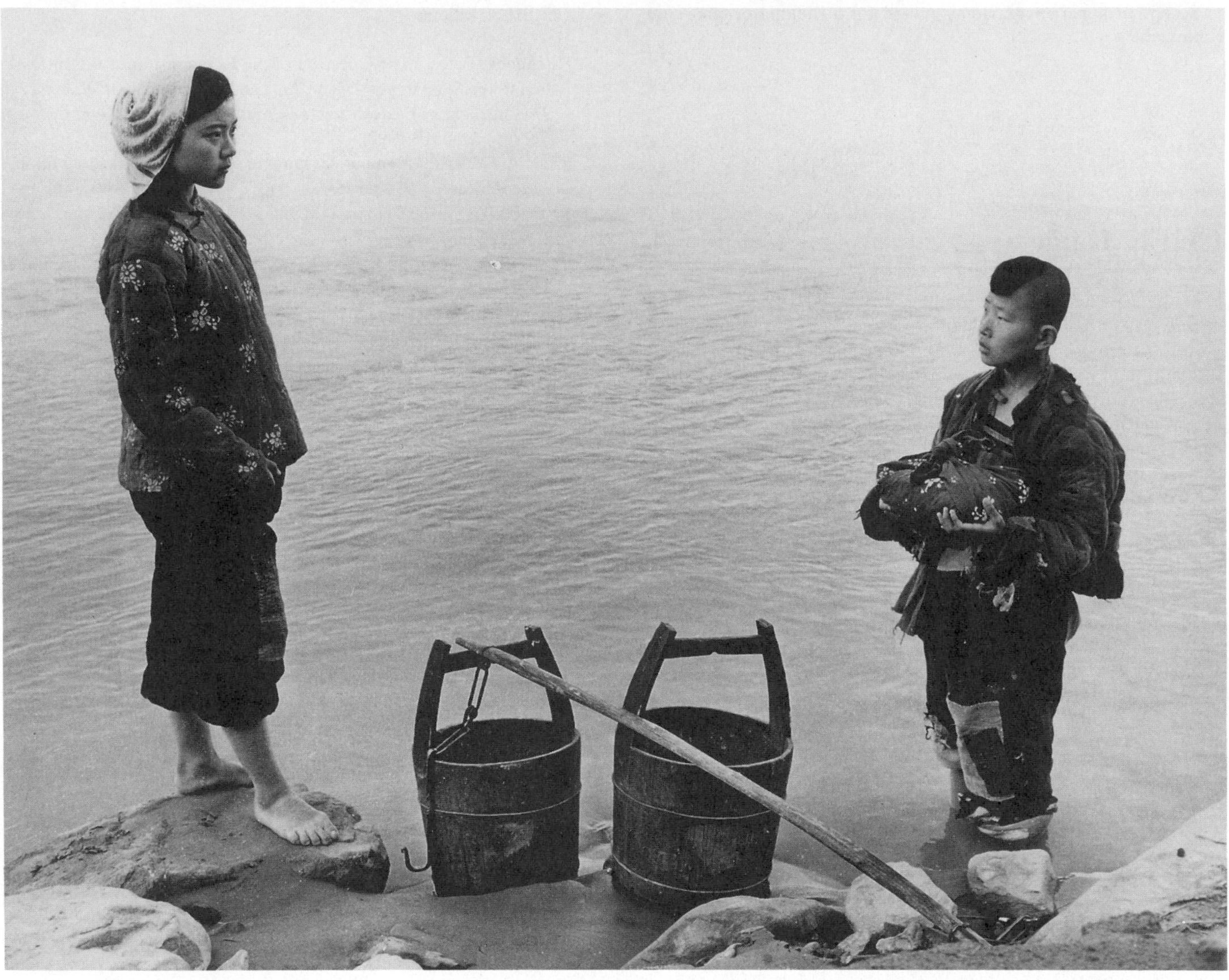

Chen Kaige: *Huang Tudi'*

King of the Children. In *Yellow Earth* the girl's voice is silenced by the force of nature as she drowns singing an anthem about the Communist Party. It is almost better, Chen implies, not to speak at all, than—as he suggests in *King of the Children*—to copy, to repeat, to "shout to make it right."

Life on a String, a leisurely allegory whose protagonists are an elderly blind musician and his young acolyte, has as tangible a sense of physical terrain as *Yellow Earth.* It also has an icy twist. Dedicatedly following his own master's instructions all his life, the old man finds himself, in the end, to have been duped. The film, fitting no fashionable niche, was largely ignored. With *Farewell My Concubine* Chen seems, superficially, to have taken a leaf from his rival Zhang Yimou's book. The film has lavish studio sets and costumes and features Zhang's favourite performer, Gong Li. Funded by Hong Kong actress Hsu Feng's Tomson Films and based on a melodramatic novel by Lilian Lee, the film traces the relationship between a young boy, sold by his prostitute mother into the brutal regime of the Peking Opera School in 1920s China, and an older, tougher boy. Deiyi is destined to play female roles, and before he is accepted he undergoes a symbolic castration. The title is taken from the title of the opera in which they make their names—set during the last days of the reign of King Chu. The film follows their fortunes up to 1977, the end of the Cultural Revolution, and closes on a note of betrayal and sacrifice. Scrupulously performed, finely filmed, the subject allows its director scope to investigate the tortuous intersection of performance, identity, self, gender, and history.

Unsurprisingly Chen's films have met with varying degrees of disapproval from the official regime. *Yellow Earth* was criticised in an anti-elitist policy. *The Big Parade* had its final sequence cut and ends with sounds of the eponymous parade in Tianenmen Square over an empty shot. *Life on a String* is banned. *Farewell My Concubine* was shown, withdrawn, then shown again. To young filmmakers in China Chen's work, and that of other Fifth Generation directors, can seem academic or irrelevant. To the rest of us, the care with which Chen Kaige observes his protagonists' struggles for integrity amid lethally shifting political tides makes for a perennially relevant body of work.

—Verina Glaessner

CHRISTENSEN, Benjamin

Nationality: Danish. **Born:** Viborg, Denmark, 28 September 1879. **Education:** Educated in medicine; entered dramatic school of the Royal Theatre, Copenhagen, 1901. **Family:** Married 1) Ellen Arctander in 1904; 2) Sigrid Stahl in 1922; 3) Kamma Winther in 1927. **Career:** Actor in Aarhus Theatre (Jutland), then Folkteatret, Copenhagen, to 1907; left stage, became agent for French champagne firm Lanson, 1907; began as film actor, 1912; directed first film, 1913; went to Germany, worked for Erich Pommer, 1923; worked in United States, 1926-34; returned to Denmark and, in 1939, went to work for Nordisk Films Kompagni; left film production, 1942, and became manager of a movie theater. **Died:** 2 April 1959.

Films as Director:

1913 *Det hemmelighedsfulde X* (*The Mysterious X*) (+ role)
1915 *Haevnens Nat* (*Blind Justice*) (+ role)
1922 *Häxan* (*Witchcraft through the Ages*) (+ sc, role as Devil and doctor)
1923 *Seine Frau, die Unbekannte* (*His Mysterious Adventure*)
1924 *Die Frau mit dem schlechten Ruf* (*The Woman Who Did*) (not completed)
1926 *The Devil's Circus*
1927 *Mockery*
1928 *Hawk's Nest*; *The Haunted House*; *House of Horror*
1929 *Seven Footprints to Satan*
1939 *Skilsmissens Børn*
1940 *Barnet*
1941 *Gaa med mig hjem*
1942 *Damen med de lyse handsker*

Other Films:

1912 *Skaebnebaeltet* (role)
1913 *Gidslet* (role); *Scenens Børn* (role); *Store Klaus og Lille Klaus* (role); *Rumaensk Blod or Søstrene Corrodi* (role); *Vingeskudt* (role)
1924 *Michael* (role)

Publications

By CHRISTENSEN: book—

Hollywood Skaebner (short stories), 1945.

Benjamin Christensen

On CHRISTENSEN: book—

Ernst, John, *Benjamin Christensen,* Copenhagen, 1967.

On CHRISTENSEN: articles—

Gillett, John, "The Mysterious X," in *Sight and Sound* (London), Spring 1966.
Higham, Charles, "Christensen Continued," in *Sight and Sound* (London), Autumn 1966.
Tessier, Max, "La Sorcellerie à travers les âges," in *Cinéma* (Paris), no. 130, 1968.
Routt, W.D., "Buried Directors," in *Focus on Film* (London), Spring 1972.

* * *

Benjamin Christensen's first film was one of the most amazing directorial debuts in the history of film. *Det hemmelighedsfulde X* is a spy melodrama about a lieutenant accused of betraying his country, but who is saved at the last minute. If the story is conventional, the handling of it shows a natural instinct for film that is way ahead of its time. Told in often very imaginatively composed pictures, the film is completely free from literary clichés in its narrative style. Throughout the length of the work, Christensen demonstrates an ability to transform the psychology of his characters into physical action. The camerawork (by Emil Dinesen) is full of significant contrasts, while the cutting is dynamic and gives the film a marvelous drive. The film was received with admiration; everybody was stunned by its remarkable visual style, and Christensen was immediately recognized as the individualist and the experimenter of the Danish film of his day. His next film, *Haevnens Nat,* was a social melodrama, burdened by a pathetic story, but also distinguished by an inventive camera style. Christensen played lead roles in both these films.

Benjamin Christensen provoked his contemporaries and set himself in opposition to the filmmaking practices of his time. He had a strong belief in himself and worked consciously with film as a new art form. He considered the director as the author of the film and stated that "like any other artist he should reveal his own individuality in his own work." Thus Christensen can be regarded as one of the first auteurs of the cinema. Carl Dreyer characterized Christensen as "a man who knew exactly what he wanted and who pursued his goal with uncompromising stubbornness."

Christensen's main work is *Häxan,* an ambitious and unique film and a pioneering achievement in both the documentary and the fiction film. In this film Christensen combined his rationalistic ideas with his passionate temperament.

Christensen was always an isolated director in the Danish film world, and after *Häxan* he left Denmark. He made an insignificant film in Germany and was seen in Dreyer's *Michael* as the master. He got an offer from Hollywood and made six films there. He used his talent for the strange and peculiar *Seven Footprints to Satan,* a witty horror comedy.

Christensen returned to Denmark in the 1930s and in 1939 he was hired by Nordisk Films Kompagni. Again Christensen showed himself to be a controversial filmmaker. Determined to break the trivial pattern of Danish cinema at that time, he made three films which dealt with topical problems arising from conflicts between generations. One film depicted children from divorce-ridden homes, another was about abortion. Christensen's last film was a spy thriller set against an international setting. It was a total failure, and Christensen left film production. For the rest of his life he lived in splendid isolation as manager of a small and insignificant cinema in the suburbs of Copenhagen.

—Ib Monty

CHYTILOVÁ, Věra

Nationality: Czech. **Born:** Ostrava, 2 February 1929. **Education:** Studied architecture at Charles University; Film Academy (FAMU), Prague, 1957-62. **Family:** Married cinematographer Jaroslav Kučera. **Career:** Assistant director on *3 Men Missing* (Ztracenci), 1956; directed first film, *Strop,* 1962; forbidden to direct or work for foreign producers, 1969-76. **Address:** c/o Barrandov Studios, Prague, Czechoslovakia.

Films as Director:

1962 *Strop* (*The Ceiling*) (+ sc); *Pytel blech* (*A Bag of Fleas*) (+ sc)
1963 *O něčem jiném* (*Something Different*; *Something Else*; *Another Way of Life*) (+ sc)
1965 "Automat Svět" (The World Cafe) segment of *Perličky na dně* (*Pearls of the Deep*) (+ co-sc)
1966 *Sedmikrásky* (*Daisies*) (+ co-sc)
1969 *Ovoce strom rajských jíme* (*The Fruit of Paradise*; *The Fruit of the Trees of Paradise*) (+ co-sc)
1977 *The Apple Game* (+ sc)
1979 *Panelstory* (*Prefab Story*) (+ co-sc)
1980 *Kalamita* (*Calamity*) (+ co-sc)
1981 *Chytilova versus Forman*
1983 *Faunovo prilis pozdni odpoledne* (*The Very Late Afternoon of a Faun*)
1985 *Praha, neklidne srace Europy* (*Prague, the Restless Heart of Europe*) (short)
1986 *Vlci bouda* (*Wolf's Hole*)
1987 *Sasek a kralovna* (*The Jester and the Queen*); *Kopytem Sem, Kopytem Tam* (*Tainted Horseplay*) (+ sc)
1991 *Mi Prazane me Rozùmeji* (*My Praguers Understand Me*)
1990 *T.G.M.—Osvoboditel* (*Tomas G. Masaryk—The Liberator*) (+ sc)
1992 *Dedictvi aneb Kurvahosigutntag* (*The Legacy*)
1993 *Kam Parenky*; *The Inheritance of Fuckoffguysgoodbye* (+ sc)

Other Films:

1958 *Konec jasnovidce* (*End of a Clairvoyant*) (role as girl in bikini)
1991 *Face of Hope* (sc)

Publications

By CHYTILOVÁ: articles—

"Neznám opravdový čin, který by nebyl riskantní" [I Don't Know Any Action That Would Not Be Risky], an interview with Galina Kopaněvová, in *Film a doba* (Prague), no. 1, 1963.
"Režijní explikace k filmu *O něčem jiném*" [The Director's Comments on *Something Different*], in *Film a Doba* (Prague), no. 1, 1964.
"*Sedmikrásky*: režijní explikace" [*Daisies*: The Directress Comments], in *Film a Doba* (Prague), no. 4, 1966.
Interview in *New York Times,* 12 March 1978.
"A Film Should Be a Little Flashlight," interview with H. Polt, in *Take One* (Montreal), November 1978.
Interview with H. Heberle and others, in *Frauen & Film* (Berlin), December 1978.
Interview with B. Eriksson-Vodakova, in *Chaplin* (Stockholm), vol. 27, no. 6, 1985.

Věra Chytilová, *Sedmikrásky*

On CHYTILOVÁ: books—

Boček, Jaroslav, *Modern Czechoslovak Film 1945-1965,* Prague, 1965.
Janoušek, Jiri, *3 Í,* Prague, 1965.
Skvorecký, Josef, *All the Bright Young Men and Women,* Toronto, 1971.
Dewey, Langdon, *Outline of Czechoslovakian Cinema,* London, 1971.
Liehm, Antonin, *Closely Watched Films,* White Plains, New York, 1974.
Liehm, Mira and Antonin, *The Most Important Art: East European Film after 1945,* Berkeley, 1977.
Habova, Milada, and Jitka Vysekalova, editors, *Czechoslovak Cinema,* Prague, 1982.
Hames, Peter, *The Czechoslovak New Wave,* Berkeley, 1985.

On CHYTILOVÁ: articles—

Boček, Jaroslav, "Podobenství Věry Chytilové" [The Parable of Věra Chytilová], in *Film a Doba* (Prague), no. 11, 1966.
Hames, P., "The Return of Vera Chytilova," in *Sight and Sound* (London), no. 3, 1979.
Martinek, Karel, "Filmový svět Véry Chytilové" [The Film World of Věra Chytilová], in *Film a Doba* (Prague), no. 3, 1982.
Zůna, Miroslav, and Vladimir Solecký, in *Film a Doba* (Prague), no. 5, 1982.
Benoit, O., "Dans la grisaille tcheque: Vera Chytilova," in *Cinéma* (Paris), May 1984.
Waller, E., in *Skrien* (Amsterdam), September-October 1984.
Manceau, Jean-Louis, "Vera Chytilova a Creteil," in *Cinéma* (Paris), 18 March 1987.
Quart, B., "Three Central European Women Directors Revisited," in *Cineaste,* vol. 19, no. 4, 1993.

* * *

So far the only important woman director of the Czech cinema is Věra Chytilová, its most innovative and probably most controversial personality. She is the only contemporary Czech filmmaker to work in the Eisensteinian tradition. She combines didacticism with often daring experimentation, based in essence on montage. Disregarding chronology and illustrative realism, she stresses the symbolic nature of images as well as visual and conceptual shock. Influenced to some extent also by cinema verité, particularly by its female representatives, and militantly feminist in her attitudes, she nevertheless made excellent use of the art of her husband, the cameraman Jaroslav Kučera, in her boldest venture to date, *Daisies.* This film, Chytilová's best known, is a dazzling display of montage, tinting, visual deformation, film trickery, color processing, etc.—a multifaceted tour de force which, among other things, is also a tribute to the classics of the cinema, from the Lumière Brothers to Chaplin and Abel Gance. It contains shots, scenes, and sequences that utilize the most characteristic techniques and motives of the masters. *Daisies* is Chytilová at her most formalist. In her later films, there is a noticeable shift towards realism. However, all the principles mentioned above still dominate the more narrative approach, and a combination of unusual camera angles, shots, etc., together with a bitterly sarcastic vision, lead to hardly less provocative shock effects.

The didactical content of these highly sophisticated and subtly formalist works of filmic art, as in Eisenstein, is naive and crude: young women should prefer "useful" vocations to "useless" ones (*The Ceiling*); extremes of being active and being inactive both result in frustration (*Something Different*); irresponsibility and recklessness lead to a bad end (*Daisies*); a sexual relationship is something serious, not just irresponsible amusement (*The Apple Game*); people should help each other (*Panel Story, The Calamity*). Given the fact that Chytilová has worked mostly under the conditions of an enforced and harshly repressive establishment, a natural explanation of this seeming incongruity offers itself: the "moral messages" of her films are simply libations that enable her, and her friends among the critics, to defend the unashamedly formalist films and the harshly satirical presentation of social reality they contain. This is corroborated by Chytilová's many clashes with the political authorities in Czechoslovakia: from an interpellation in the Parliament calling for a ban of *Daisies* because so much food—"the fruit of the work of our toiling farmers"—is destroyed in the film, to her being fired from the Barrandov studios after the Soviet invasion in 1968, and on to her open letter to President Husák printed in Western newspapers. In each instance she won her case by a combination of publicly stated kosher ideological arguments, stressing the alleged "messages" of her works, and of backstage manipulation, not excluding the use of her considerable feminine charm. Consequently, she is the only one from among the new wave of directors from the 1960s who, for a long time, had been able to continue making films in Czechoslovakia without compromising her aesthetic creed and her vision of society, as so many others had to do in order to remain in business (including Jaromil Jireš, Hynek Bočan, Jaroslav Papoušek, and to some extent Jiří Menzel).

Panel Story and *Calamity* earned her hateful attacks from establishment critics and intrigues from her second-rate colleagues, who are thriving on the absence of competition from such exiled or banned directors as Miloš Forman, Ivan Passer, Jan Němec, Evald Schorm, and Vojtěch Jasný. The two films were practically withdrawn from circulation and can be occasionally seen only in suburban theatres. The only critical film periodical, *Film a doba*, published, in 1982, a series of three articles which, in veiled terms and using what playwright Václav Havel calls "dialectical metaphysics" ("on the one hand it is bad, but on the other hand it is also good"), defended the director and her right to remain herself. In her integrity, artistic boldness, and originality, and in her ability to survive the most destructive social and political catastrophes, Chytilová was a unique phenomenon in post-invasion Czech cinema. Unfortunately, during the last years of Communist rule in Czechoslovakia, she seems to have lost something of her touch, and her latest films—such as *The Very Late Afternoon of a Faun* or *The Jester and the Queen*—are clearly not on the level of *Daisies* or *Panel Story*.

Since the "velvet revolution" she has maintained her independence as idiosyncratically as ever. Refusing to take up any comfortably accommodating position, she has been accused of nostalgia for the Communist years. This would be to misrepresent her position. A fierce campaigner for a state subsidy for the Czech film industry, she cannot but lament the extent to which the implementation of the ideology of the "free market" has been allowed to accomplish what the Soviet regime never quite could—the extinguishing of Czech film culture.

She has made a number of documentary films for television as well as a 1992 comedy about the deleterious effects of sudden wealth, which was publicly well-received but met with critical opprobrium. She has so far failed to find funding for a long-cherished project, *Face of Hope*, about the nineteenth-century humanist writer Bozena Nemcova. The continuing relevance of *Daisies*, and its depiction of philistinism in several registers, is surely the strongest argument in support of Chytilová's position. It is a film which shines with the sheer craftsmanship Czech cinema achieved in those years.

—Josef Skvorecký, updated by Verina Glaessner

CIMINO, Michael

Nationality: American. **Born:** New York, 1940. **Education:** Yale University, M.F.A. in painting, 1963. **Career:** Moved to New York, 1963; studied acting and ballet, directed documentaries, industrial films, and TV commercials, 1963-71; moved to Hollywood, worked as scriptwriter, 1971; directed first film, *Thunderbolt and Lightfoot*, 1974. **Awards:** Oscar for Best Director, and Best Director Award, Directors Guild, for *The Deer Hunter*, 1979.

Films as Director:

1974 *Thunderbolt and Lightfoot* (+ sc)
1978 ***The Deer Hunter*** (+ co-sc, co-pr)
1980 ***Heaven's Gate*** (+ sc)
1985 *Year of the Dragon* (co-sc)
1987 *The Sicilian* (+ co-pr)
1988 *Santa Anna Winds*
1990 *Desperate Hours* (+ pr)

Other Films:

1972 *Silent Running* (Trumbull) (co-sc)
1973 *Magnum Force* (Post) (co-sc)

Publications

By CIMINO: articles—

"Stalking the Deer Hunter: An Interview with Michael Cimino," with M. Carducci, in *Millimeter* (New York), March 1978.
Interview with Herb Lightman, in *American Cinematographer* (Los Angeles), November 1980.
Interview with B. Krohn, in *Cahiers du Cinéma* (Paris), June 1982.
Interview with Jean Narboni, and others, in *Cahiers du Cinéma* (Paris), November 1985.
"*L'année du dragon*: un film ambigu," an interview with G. Camy and C. Vivian, in *Jeune Cinéma* (Paris), December 1985-January 1986.

On CIMINO: books—

Bach, Steven, *The Final Cut: Dream and Disaster in the Making of "Heaven's Gate,"* New York, 1985.
Bliss, Michael, *Martin Scorsese and Michael Cimino*, Metuchen, New Jersey, 1985.
Wood, Robin, *Hollywood from Vietnam to Reagan*, New York, 1986.
Adair, Gilbert, *Hollywood's Vietnam*, London, 1989.

On CIMINO: articles—

Valley, J., "Michael Cimino's Battle to Make a Great Movie," in *Esquire* (New York), 2 January 1979.

Harmetz, A., "Oscar-winning *Deer Hunter* Is under Attack as Racist Film," in *New York Times,* 26 April 1979.

"*Heaven's Gate* Issue" of *American Cinematographer* (Los Angeles), November 1980.

"*Deer Hunter* Section" of *Literature/Film Quarterly* (Salisbury, Maryland), January 1983.

Greene, N., "Coppola, Cimino: The Operatics of History," in *Film Quarterly* (Los Angeles), Winter 1984-85.

Films and Filming (London), February 1988.

Pym, J., "Michael Cimino," in *Sight and Sound,* vol. 60, no. 1, 1990/91.

* * *

Erratic as his achievement has been, Michael Cimino is, with Martin Scorsese, one of the two most important filmmakers to have emerged in the Hollywood cinema of the 1970s. His reputation must rest, so far, essentially on two enormously ambitious and controversial films, *The Deer Hunter* and *Heaven's Gate,* and his stature will only receive due recognition when the latter is re-released (in its "original," three-and-one-half-hour version) and revalued. One can confidently prophesy that it will come as a major revelation.

In one respect, Scorsese and Cimino appear opposites of each other. Scorsese (prior, at least, to *The Last Temptation of Christ*) characteristically starts from a small, precise, concrete subject and radically explores it until it reveals strains, tensions, and contradictions central to our culture; Cimino begins with a vague and grandiose "vision" and proceeds to map in its salient features and attempts to render it concrete by developing its detail. That Scorsese's method is by far the more conducive to assured artistic success is obvious, and Cimino has yet to produce work as secure in its aim and tone as *Raging Bull* or *King of Comedy.*

We may start with *Heaven's Gate* and its critical reception: the peak of Cimino's achievement to date (it remains, for me, the greatest Hollywood film of the past fifteen years), it was almost universally savaged by the American press. The pervasive complaint was that Cimino "can't tell a story," despite the fact that he had already managed to do so very successfully, as the screenwriter of *Silent Running* and the director of *Thunderbolt and Lightfoot*; that he might wish to attempt something rather different was not considered as a possibility. Much critical and theoretical work has now been done attacking the overwhelming dominance in Hollywood cinema of the rules of classical narrative, centred on individual psychology and scene-by-scene causality: the dominance, to adopt Barthesian terminology, of the proairetic and hermeneutic codes. These form the basis of the kind of cinema to which Hollywood has so long accustomed us, but there is no reason why custom should be institutionalized as an unchallengeable and absolute system of construction, permitting no divergence.

The structure of *Heaven's Gate* is quite other, the best analogy being with architecture. Each scene or segment can be viewed as a building block enacting (though not in any obviously didactic or explicit way) a "history lesson" in the Brechtian sense of the term. Within obvious limits (the film *does* have a discernible narrative, with a beginning, middle, and end in that order), these blocks relate to each other freely *across the entire film,* rather than forming a causal a, b, c ... progression; they gradually add up to a complex structure of thematic interrelatedness. It is significant that when Cimino, after the disastrous North American premières, himself edited a two-and-one-half-hour version for general release, he produced not just a *shorter* version but a different film: not only does he use perceptibly different takes of certain shots, but whole narrative segments are transposed to different parts of the film, and one brief incident is included which he cut from the original version. This also explains why the film, in whatever version, always appears unfinished: the addition, removal, or transposition of the "blocks" could be an interminable process, the structure (freed from the strictures of narrative causality) being logically incompletable (there was once, according to Steven Bach, a five-and-one-half-hour version). It is also significant that one of the film's finest set-pieces, the magnificent roller-skating sequence, has no narrative necessity whatever, neither developing character nor furthering the plot, though it is crucial to the film's "grand design." There are no precedents in Hollywood cinema for this type of formal strategy; to find them, one must go further afield, to the Kurosawa of *High and Low* and *Ikiru,* or to the Pasolini of *Medea.*

Another initial critical objection was to the film's "Marxist content." By denying the viewer the traditional narrative pleasures of causality and close identification, Cimino transfers attention from individuals to movements, and the film's overall movement is toward the destruction of a genuinely multi-cultural, non-sexist, and *potentially* socialist America by the capitalist greed for wealth and power. In view of this, it is ironic that *The Deer Hunter* has been widely perceived as a right-wing movie. In fact, the two films are generally consistent. More intuitive than theoretical, more emotional than rational, Cimino does not have a completely consistent ideological position which the films dramatize: they seem, on the contrary, often ideologically incoherent, insufficiently *thought* (particularly the case with *Year of the Dragon,* which disintegrates under the strain of its own internal contradictions).

Though less formally radical than *Heaven's Gate, The Deer Hunter* is also characterized by great architectural strength. It is composed of five "blocks," two set in Vietnam alternating with three set in Clairton, Pennsylvania; in both sets, each block is substantially shorter than its predecessor, enacting on the formal level the theme of "dwindling" on which the action of the film is constructed. The controversial ending, in which the survivors sing "God Bless America," is neither affirmative (i.e., right wing) nor ironic (i.e., leftist): the singing is characterized by an extreme tentativeness, a failure of confidence in both an available "America" that might be blessed or a God to bless it. As in *Heaven's Gate* (and the point relates back interestingly to the work of John Ford and the whole complex American tradition for which it speaks), the "America" that might be affirmed, represented by social outsiders (in Cimino's case immigrant ethnic groups), is felt to be irredeemably lost, overwhelmed by the Nixonite/Reaganite America of corporate capitalism.

Cimino's career since *Heaven's Gate* has been as disappointing as Scorsese's since *King of Comedy.* There is perhaps a common cause: the sheer difficulty of setting up intelligent, personal, original, or challenging work in the era of endless mindless sequels and "packages," in a Hollywood dominated by precisely the kind of capitalist concern that *Heaven's Gate* assaults, more concerned with "business" than with cinema. In Cimino's case there is a more specific cause: the general distrust generated by the now almost proverbial financial catastrophe of *Heaven's Gate.* For all that, *Year of the Dragon* and *The Sicilian,* though neither can be counted an artistic success, seem far more *interesting* than *The Color of Money* or *The Last Temptation of Christ.* The former contains scenes of stunning brilliance and virtuosity, but is centrally flawed by its inability to construct a coherent attitude toward its protagonist (Mickey Rourke). The film's three most sympathetic characters—his young Chinese assistant, his wife, his mistress—are all given speeches denouncing him; he is indirectly responsible for the deaths of the first two and the gang-rape of the third. Yet Cimino also clearly wishes to affirm the character, an impulse culminating in a conclusion which even Mahler cannot save. *The Sicilian,* like *Heaven's Gate,* is an epic that precludes identification: with the possible exception of Giuliano's fiancée (a relatively minor and somewhat stereotypical role), every position dramatized in the film (including that of the hero) is shown to be severely compromised and untenable. Unlike *Heaven's Gate,* however, the detail of the film only intermittently comes alive, and then only in the supporting roles (Joss Ackland, John Turturro). Cimino seems seriously hampered by the doubtless mandatory fidelity to Mario Puzo's elephantine and cliché-ridden novel, and by the casting of Christopher Lambert, who totally lacks the charisma that alone would make Giuliano plausible. More importantly, perhaps, Cimino has shown himself in all his previous films intensely concerned with "America" (the ideological image more than the appalling reality), and relates rather distantly to a foreign environment.

Desperate Hours, a remake of William Wyler's 1955 thriller, was a surprisingly modest project for one of Hollywood's great overreachers, but one that offered the potential of grappling with American values at their core. *Desperate Hours* must be accounted partially unsatisfactory, however, and its commercial failure, with that of *The Sicilian,* has made Cimino's future in Hollywood increasingly problematic. It is, however, an enormously more interesting and challenging film than the original version. Wyler's film was "safe" in every way: his usual thoroughly sound, if thoroughly uninspired, direction, and an eminently respectable and sensible bourgeois entertainment. Cimino's film is neither safe nor sensible. It is characterized by an all-pervasive nervous tension, a relentless edginess expressed by all the characters and communicated strongly to the audience. The value and stability of bourgeois family life (a "given" in Wyler) are no longer guaranteed; the parents are separated, and can scarcely address a sentence to each other without an eruption; the children are disturbed and potentially rebellious. The corollary of this is that the gang who take over the household are no longer automatically invalidated: dangerous and vicious (with Mickey Rourke's leader prone to psychotic explosions at the slightest provocation), they nonetheless embody the justifiable revolt of the underprivileged in a society riddled with class tensions. Like Rourke's character, the film is jagged, unpredictable, incomplete. Character motivations are often unclear (Lindsay Rouse's role suffered from severe cuts), opaque, and eccentric, yet all the characters have vivid life, a spontaneity of action and reaction, beside which the conventional figures of Wyler's film seem pallid. As usual, Cimino's crime (in terms of commercial success) is to deny the audience any feeling of comfort, stability, or satisfaction; that is also what makes his films so fascinating.

There is no other filmmaker of whom my own view is quite so completely at odds with the generally accepted one. *Heaven's Gate,* above all, stands up magnificently to the test of time and repeated viewings; I have used it in film classes every year, and students greet it invariably as a revelation. Yet "accepted opinion," once established, is notoriously difficult to erode.

—Robin Wood

CLAIR, René

Nationality: French. **Born:** René Chomette in Paris, 11 November 1898. **Education:** Lycée Montaigne, and Lycée Louis-le-Grand, Paris, 1913-17. **Military Service:** Served in Ambulance Corps, 1917. **Family:** Married Bronya Perlmutter, 1926, one son. **Career:** Retired to Dominican monastery, 1918; began acting at Gaumont studios, 1920; as René Clair, became film editor of *Le Théâtre et comoedia illustré,* Paris, 1922; directed first film, *Paris qui dort,* 1923; directed for Alexander Korda in Britain, 1935-38; emigrated to United States and signed to Universal, 1940; returned to Paris, 1946. **Awards:** Honorary doctorate, Cambridge University, 1956; elected to Academie Française, 1960; Doctor *Honoris Causa,* Royal College of Arts, London, 1967; Commander of the Legion of Honour; Commander of Arts and Letters; Commander of the Italian Order of Merit. **Died:** In Neuilly, France, 15 March 1981.

Films as Director:

1923 *Paris qui dort* (+ sc, ed)
1924 ***Entr'acte***; *Le Fantôme du Moulin Rouge* (+ sc)
1925 *Le Voyage imaginaire* (+ sc)
1926 *La Proie du vent* (+ sc)
1927 ***Un Chapeau de paille d'Italie*** (+ sc)
1928 *La Tour* (+ sc); *Les Deux Timides* (+ sc)
1930 *Sous les toits de Paris* (+ sc)
1931 ***Le Million*** (+ sc); ***A Nous la liberté*** (+ sc)
1932 *Quatorze Juillet* (+ sc)
1934 *Le Dernier Milliardaire* (+ sc)
1935 *The Ghost Goes West* (+ co-sc)
1937 *Break the News* (+ co-sc)
1939 *Air pur* (+ sc) (uncompleted)
1940 *The Flame of New Orleans* (+ co-sc)
1942 Sketch featuring Ida Lupino in *Forever and a Day* (Lloyd) (+ sc); *I Married a Witch* (+ co-sc, pr)
1943 *It Happened Tomorrow* (+ co-sc)
1945 *And Then There Were None* (+ co-sc, pr)
1947 *Le Silence est d'or* (+ pr, sc)
1949 *La Beauté du diable* (+ co-sc, pr)
1952 *Les Belles-de-nuit* (+ sc, pr)
1955 *Les Grandes Manoeuvres* (+ co-sc, pr)
1957 *Porte des Lilas* (+ co-sc, pr)
1960 "Le Mariage" episode of *La Française et l'amour* (+ sc)
1961 *Tout l'or du monde* (+ co-sc, pr)
1962 "Les Deux Pigeons" episode of *Les Quatres vérités* (+ sc)
1965 *Les Fêtes galantes* (+ pr, sc)

Other Films:

1920 *Le Lys de la Vie* (Fuller) (role); *Les Deux Gamines* (Feuillade—serial) (role)
1921 *Le Sens de la mort* (Protozanoff) (role); *L'Orpheline* (Feuillade) (role); *Parisette* (Feuillade—serial) (role)
1922 *Parisette* (Feuillade) (role)
1930 *Prix de beauté* (*Miss Europe*) (Genina) (sc contribution)
1939 *Un Village dans Paris* (co-pr)
1959 *La Grande Époque* (French version of Robert Youngson's *The Golden Age of Comedy*) (narrator)

Publications

By CLAIR: books—

De fil en aiguille, Paris, 1951.
La Princesse de Chine, Paris, 1951.
Réflexion faite, Paris, 1951.
Reflections on the Cinema, London, 1953.
Comédies et commentaires, Paris, 1959.
Tout l'or du monde, Paris, 1962.
"À nous la liberté" and "Entr'acte," New York, 1970.
Four Screenplays, New York, 1970.
Cinema Yesterday and Today, New York, 1972.
Jeux d'hasard, Paris, 1976.

By CLAIR: articles—

"A Conversation with René Clair," with Bernard Causton, in *Sight and Sound* (London), Winter 1933.
"*It Happened Tomorrow,*" with Dudley Nichols, in *Theatre Arts* (New York), June 1944.

René Clair

"Television and Cinema," in *Sight and Sound* (London), January 1951.
"René Clair in Moscow," in *Sight and Sound* (London), Winter 1955/56.
"Nothing is more artificial than Neo-realism," in *Films and Filming* (London), June 1957.
"Picabia, Satie et la première d'*Entr'acte*," in *L'Avant-Scène du Cinéma* (Paris), November 1968.
"René Clair in Hollywood," an interview with R.C. Dale, in *Film Quarterly* (Berkeley, California), Winter 1970/71.
Interview in *Encountering Directors* by Charles Samuels, New York, 1972.
"A Conversation with René Clair," with John Baxter and John Gillett, in *Focus on Film* (London), Winter 1972.
"René Clair," interviews with Patrick McGilligan and Debra Weiner, in *Take One* (Montreal), January/February 1973 and May 1974.
"René Clair at 80," an interview with G. Mason, in *Literature/Film Quarterly* (Salisbury, Maryland), vol. 10, no. 2, 1982.
Interview in *Avant-Scène du Cinéma* (Paris), March 1988.

On CLAIR: books—

Viazzi, G., *René Clair,* Milan, 1946.
Bourgeois, J., *René Clair,* Geneva, 1949.
Charensol, Georges, and Roger Régent, *Un Maître du cinéma: René Clair,* Paris, 1952.
Charensol, George, *René Clair et Les Belles de nuit,* Paris, 1953.
De La Roche, Catherine, *René Clair, an Index,* London, 1958.
Mitry, Jean, *René Clair,* Paris, 1960.
Amengual, Barthélemy, *René Clair,* Paris, 1969.
Barrot, Olivier, *René Clair; ou, Le Temps mesuré,* Renens, 1985.
Greene, Naomi, *René Clair: A Guide to References and Resources,* Boston, 1985.
Dale, R.C., *The Films of René Clair,* 2 vols, Metuchen, New Jersey, 1986.

On CLAIR: articles—

Potamkin, Harry, "René Clair and Film Humor," in *Hound and Horn* (New York), October/December 1932.
Jacobs, Louis, "The Films of René Clair," in *New Theatre* (New York), February 1936.
Lambert, Gavin, "The Films of René Clair," in *Sequence* (London), no. 6, 1949.
"Clair Issue" of *Bianco e Nero* (Rome), August/September 1951.
Gauteur, Claude, "René Clair, hélas...!" in *Image et Son* (Paris), June 1963.
Beylie, Claude, "*Entr'acte*, le film sans maître," in *Cinéma* (Paris), February 1969.
Fraenkel, Helene, "*It Happened Tomorrow,*" in *Films in Review* (New York), August/September 1974.
Fischer, Lucy, "René Clair, *Le Million,* and the Coming of Sound," in *Cinema Journal* (Evanston, Illinois), Spring 1977.
Carroll, Noel, "*Entr'acte,* Paris and Dada," in *Millenium Film Journal* (New York), Winter 1977/78.
Haustrate, Gaston, "René Clair: était-il un grand cinéaste?," in *Cinéma* (Paris), April 1981.
Adair, Gilbert, "Utopia Ltd., the Cinema of René Clair," in *Sight and Sound* (London), Summer 1981.
"*Sous les toits de Paris* Issue" of *Avant-Scène du Cinéma* (Paris), 1 February 1982.
Kramer, S.P., "René Clair: Situation and Sensibility in *A nous la liberté,*" in *Literature/Film Quarterly* (Salisbury, Maryland), April 1984.
Vittorini, E., "Nella poetica di Clair una lezione di linguaggio," in *Cinema Nuovo* (Bari), March-April 1986.

On CLAIR: film—

Knapp, Hubert, and Igor Barrère, *Le Rouge est mis* (documentary on making of *Les Belles de nuit*), 1952.

* * *

During the 1930s, when the French cinema reigned intellectually preeminent, René Clair ranked with Renoir and Carné as one of its greatest directors—perhaps the most archetypally French of them all. His reputation has since fallen (as has Carné's), and comparison with Renoir may suggest why. Clair's work, though witty, stylish, charming, and technically accomplished, seems to lack a dimension when compared with the work of Renoir; there is a certain oversimplification, a fastidious turning away from the messier, more complex aspects of life. (Throughout nearly the whole of his career, Clair rejected location shooting, preferring the controllable artifice of the studio.) Critics have alleged that his films are superficial and emotionally detached. Yet, at their best, Clair's films have much of the quality of champagne—given so much sparkle and exhilaration, it would seem churlish to demand nourishment as well.

At the outset of his career, Clair directed one of the classic documents of surrealist cinema, *Entr'acte,* and this grounding in surrealism underlies much of his comedy work. The surrealists' love of sight gags (Magritte's cloud-baguettes, Duchamp's urinal) and mocking contempt for bourgeois respectability can be detected in the satiric farce of *Un Chapeau de paille d'Italie,* Clair's masterpiece of the silent era. Dream imagery, another surrealist preoccupation, recurs constantly throughout his career, from *Le Voyage imaginaire* to *Les Belles-de-nuit,* often transmuted into fantasy—touchingly poetic at its best, though in weaker moments declining into fey whimsicality.

The key films in Clair's early career, and those which made him internationally famous, were his first four sound pictures: *Sous les toits de Paris, Le Million, A Nous la liberté,* and *Quatorze Juillet.* Initially sceptical of the value of sound—"an unnatural creation"—he rapidly changed his opinion when he recognized the creative, non-realistic possibilities which the soundtrack offered. Sound effects, music, even dialogue could be used imaginatively to counterpoint and comment on the image, or to suggest a new perspective on the action. Words and pictures, Clair showed, need not, and in fact should not, be tied together in a manner that clumsily duplicates information. Dialogue need not always be audible; and even in a sound picture, silence could claim a validity of its own.

In these four films, Clair created a wholly individual cinematic world, a distinctive blend of fantasy, romance, social satire, and operetta. Song and dance are introduced into the action with no pretence at literal realism, characters are drawn largely from stock, and the elaborate sets are explored with an effortless fluidity of camera movement which would be impossible in real locations. These qualities, together with the pioneering use of sound and Clair's knack for effective pacing and brilliant visual gags, resulted in films of exceptional appeal, full of charm, gaiety, and an ironic wit which at times—notably in the satire on mechanised greed in *A Nous la liberté*—darkened towards an underlying pessimism.

As always, Clair wrote his own scripts, working closely on all four films with designer Lazare Meerson and cinematographer Georges Périnal. Of the four, *Le Million* most effectively integrated its various elements, and is generally rated Clair's finest film. But all were successful, especially outside France, and highly influential: both Chaplin (*Modern Times*) and the Marx Brothers (*A Night at the Opera*) borrowed from them.

In some quarters, though, Clair was criticized for lack of social relevance. Ill-advisedly, he attempted to respond to such criticisms; *Le Dernier Milliardaire* proved a resounding flop. This led to Clair's long exile. For thirteen years he made no films in France other than the abortive *Air pur,* and his six English-language pictures—two in Britain, four in America—have an uneasy feel about them, the fantasy strained and unconvincing. By the time Clair finally returned to France in 1946, both he and the world had changed.

The films that Clair made after World War II rarely recapture the lighthearted gaiety of his early work. In its place, the best of them display a new-found maturity and emotional depth, while preserving the characteristic elegance and wit of his previous films. The prevailing mood is an autumnal melancholy that at times, as in the elegiac close of *Les Grandes Manoeuvres,* comes near to tragedy. Characters are no longer the stock puppets of the pre-war satires, but rounded individuals, capable of feeling and suffering. More serious subjects are confronted, their edges only slightly softened by their context: *Porte des Lilas* ends with a murder, *La Beauté du diable* with a vision of the atomic holocaust. Nearest in mood to the earlier films is the erotic fantasy of *Les Belles-de-nuit,* but even this is darkly underscored with intimations of suicide.

In the late 1950s Clair came under attack from the writers of *Cahiers du cinéma,* François Truffaut in particular, who regarded him as the embodiment of the "Old Guard," the ossified *cinéma de papa* against which they were in revolt. To what he saw as Clair's emotionless, studio-bound artifice, Truffaut proposed an alternative, more "truly French" cinematic tradition, the lyrical freedom of Renoir and Jean Vigo. Clair's reputation never fully recovered from these onslaughts, nor from the lukewarm reception which met his last two films, *Tout l'or du monde* and *Les Fêtes galantes.*

Although Clair no longer commands a place among the very first rank of directors, he remains undoubtedly one of the most original and distinctive stylists of the cinema. His explorations of sound, movement, and narrative technique, liberating at the time, still appear fresh and inventive. For all his limitations, which he readily acknowledged—"a director's intelligence," he once wrote, "can be judged partly by his renunciations"—Clair succeeded in creating a uniquely personal vision of the world, which in his best films still retains the power to exhilarate and delight.

—Philip Kemp

CLARKE, Shirley

Nationality: American. **Born:** Shirley Brimberg in New York City, 1925. **Education:** Stephens College, John Hopkins University, Bennington College, and University of North Carolina. **Family:** Married lithographer Burt Clarke, one daughter. **Career:** Dancer with Martha Graham and Doris Humphrey, also chairwoman, National Dance Foundation, 1946-53; made first film, *A Dance in the Sun,* 1954; co-founder, with Jonas Mekas, Filmmakers Cooperative, 1962; worked with Public Broadcast Lab, late 1960s (fired 1969); Professor of Film and Video at U.C.L.A, 1975-85. Lives in New York City.

Films as Director:

1954 *A Dance in the Sun* (+ pr, ph, ed, co-choreo); *In Paris Parks* (+ pr, ph, ed, co-choreo)
1955 *Bullfight* (+ pr, co-ph, ed, co-choreo)
1957 *A Moment in Love* (+ pr, co-ph, ed, co-choreo)
1958 *The Skyscraper* (pr, co-d only); *Brussels "Loops"* (12 film loops made for Brussels Exposition, destroyed) (+ pr, co-ph, ed)
1959 *Bridges-Go-Round* (+ pr, co-ph, ed)
1960 *A Scary Time* (+ co-sc, ph)
1961 *The Connection* (+ co-pr, ed)
1963 *The Cool World* (+ co-sc, ed); *Robert Frost: A Lover's Quarrel with the World* (co-d)
1967 *Portrait of Jason* (+ pr, ed, voice); *Man in Polar Regions* (11-screen film for Expo '67)
1978 *Trans*; *One Two Three*; *Mysterium*; *Initiation* (all video)
1981 *Savage/Love* (video)
1982 *Tongues* (video/theatre collaboration with Sam Shepard)
1985 *Ornette, Made in America*

Other Films:

1959 *Opening in Moscow* (Pennebaker) (co-ed)
1969 *Lion's Love* (Varda) (role as herself)

Publications

By CLARKE: articles—

"The Expensive Art," in *Film Quarterly* (Berkeley), Summer 1960.
"*The Cool World,*" in *Films and Filming* (London), December 1963.
Interview with Harriet Polt, in *Film Comment* (New York), no. 2, 1964.
Interview with Axel Madsen, in *Cahiers du Cinéma* (Paris), March 1964.
Interview with James Blue, in *Objectif* (Paris), February/March 1965.
Interview with Gretchen Berg, in *Film Culture* (New York), Spring 1967.
"A Statement on Dance and Film," in *Dance Perspectives* (New York), Summer 1967.
"A Conversation—Shirley Clarke and Storm DeHirsch," in *Film Culture* (New York), Autumn 1967 and October 1968.
"Entretiens—Le Depart pour Mars," an interview with Michel Delahaye, in *Cahiers du Cinéma* (Paris), October 1968.
"Shirley Clarke: Image and Ideas," an interview with S. Rice, in *Take One* (Montreal), February 1972.
"What Directors Are Saying," in *Action* (Los Angeles), March/April 1975.

On CLARKE: books—

Hanhardt, John, and others, editors, *A History of the American Avant-Garde Cinema,* New York, 1976.
Kowalski, Rosemary A.R., *A Vision of One's Own: Four Women Film Directors,* Ann Arbor, Michigan, 1980.
Heck-Rabi, Louise, *Women Filmmakers: A Critical Reception,* Metuchen, New Jersey, 1984.
Acker, Ally, *Reel Women: Pioneers of the Cinema, 1896 to the Present,* New York, 1991.
Rabinovitz, Lauren, *Points of Resistance: Women, Power and Politics in the New York Avant-Garde Cinema, 1943-1971,* Urbana, Illinois, 1991.

On CLARKE: articles—

Breitrose, Henry, "Films of Shirley Clarke," in *Film Quarterly* (Berkeley), Summer 1960.
Archer, Eugene, "Woman Director Makes the Scene," in *New York Times Magazine,* 26 August 1962.
Pyros, J., "Notes on Woman Directors," in *Take One* (Montreal), November/December 1970.
Mekas, Jonas, in *Village Voice* (New York), 20 May 1971.

Shirley Clarke

Cooper, K., "Shirley Clarke," in *Filmmakers Newsletter* (Ward Hill, Massachusetts), June 1972.
Bebb, Bruce, "The many media of Shirley Clarke," in *Journal of University Film Association* (Carbondale, Illinois), Spring 1982.
American Film (Washington, D.C.), June 1982.

* * *

Shirley Clarke was a leader and major filmmaker in the New York film community in the 1950s and 1960s. Her films, which exemplify the artistic directions of the independent movement, are classic examples of the best work of American independent filmmaking. Clarke began her professional career as a dancer. She participated in the late 1940s in the avant-garde dance community centered around New York City's Young Men's-Young Women's Hebrew Association's (YM-YWHA) performance stage and Hanya Holm's classes for young choreographers. In 1953, Clarke adapted dancer-choreographer Daniel Nagrin's *Dance in the Sun* to film. In her first dance film, Clarke relied on editing concepts to choreograph a new cinematic space and rhythm. She then applied her cinematic choreography to a non-dance subject in *In Paris Parks,* and further explored the cinematic possibilities for formal choreography in her dance films, *Bullfight* and *A Moment in Love.*

During this time period, Clarke studied filmmaking with Hans Richter at City College of New York and participated in informal filmmaking classes with director and cinematographer Peter Glushanok. In 1955, she became an active member of Independent Filmmakers of America (IFA), a short-lived New York organization that tried to improve promotion and distribution for independent films. Through the IFA, Clarke became part of the Greenwich Village artistic circle that included avant-garde filmmakers Maya Deren, Stan Brakhage, and Jonas Mekas. It also introduced her to the importance of an economic structure for the growth of avant-garde film, a cause she championed throughout the 1960s.

Clarke worked with filmmakers Willard Van Dyke, Donn Alan Pennebaker, Ricky Leacock, and Wheaton Galentine on a series of film loops on American life for the United States Pavilion at the 1958 World's Fair in Brussels. With the leftover footage of New York City bridges, she then made her experimental film masterpiece, *Bridges-Go-Round,* utilizing editing strategies, camera choreography, and color tints to turn naturalistic objects into a poem of dancing abstract elements. It is one of the best and most widely seen examples of a cinematic Abstract Expressionism in the 1950s.

Clarke made the documentary film *Skyscraper* in 1958 with Van Dyke, Pennebaker, Leacock, and Galentine, followed by *A Scary Time* (1960), a film commissioned by the United Nations International Children's Emergency Fund (UNICEF). Clarke also began work on a public television film on Robert Frost, *A Lover's Quarrel With the World,* but due to artistic disagreements and other commitments she left the project before the film's completion while retaining a credit as co-director.

Influenced by the developing cinema-verité style in documentary films of Leacock and Pennebaker, Clarke adapted cinema verité to two feature-length dramatic films, *The Connection* and *The Cool World. The Connection* was a landmark for the emergence of a New York independent feature film movement. It heralded a new style that employed a greater cinematic realism and addressed relevant social issues in black-and-white low budget films. It was also important because Clarke made the film the first test case in the courts in a successful fight to abolish New York State's censorship rules. Her next feature film, *The Cool World,* was the first movie to dramatize a story on black street gangs without relying upon Hollywood-style moralizing, and it was the first commercial film to be shot on location in Harlem. In 1967, Clarke directed a 90-minute cinema verité interview with a black homosexual. *Portrait of Jason* is an insightful exploration of one person's character while it simultaneously addresses the range and limitations of cinema verité style. Although Clarke's features had only moderate commercial runs and nominal success in the United States, they have won film festival awards and critical praise in Europe, making Clarke one of the most highly regarded American independent filmmakers among European film audiences.

In the 1960s, Clarke also worked for the advancement of the New York independent film movement. She was one of the 24 filmmakers and producers who wrote and signed the 1961 manifesto, "Statement for a New American Cinema," which called for an economic, artistic, and political alternative to Hollywood moviemaking. With Jonas Mekas in 1962, she co-founded Film-Makers Cooperative, a non-profit distribution company for independent films. Later, Clarke, Mekas and filmmaker Louis Brigante co-founded Film-Makers Distribution Center, a company for distributing independent features to commercial movie theatres. Throughout the 1960s, Clarke lectured on independent film in universities and museums in the United States and Europe, and in 1969 she turned to video as her major medium in which to work.

—Lauren Rabinovitz

CLAYTON, Jack

Nationality: British. **Born:** Brighton, Sussex, 1 March 1921. **Family:** Married 1) actress Christine Norden; 2) Kathleen Kath; 3) Haya Haraneet. **Career:** Trained as racing ice skater. Third assistant director, assistant director, then editor, London Films, 1935-40; served in Royal Air Force Film Unit, finally Commanding Officer, 1940-46; associate producer, Romulus Films, 1950s; directed first feature, *Room at the Top,* 1958. **Awards:** Special Prize, Venice Festival, for *The Bespoke Overcoat,* 1956; Best Director Award, British Academy, for *Room at the Top,* 1959. **Address:** Heron's Flight, Highfield Park, Marlow, Buckinghamshire, England.

Films as Director:

1944 *Naples Is a Battlefield* (+ sc, co-ph—uncredited)
1955 *The Bespoke Overcoat* (+ pr)
1958 ***Room at the Top***
1961 *The Innocents* (+ pr)
1964 *The Pumpkin Eater*
1967 *Our Mother's House*
1974 *The Great Gatsby*
1983 *Something Wicked this Way Comes*
1988 *The Lonely Passion of Judith Hearne*

Other Films:

1948 *Bond Street* (Parry) (2nd unit d); *An Ideal Husband* (A. Korda) (pr mgr); *The Queen of Spades* (Dickinson) (assoc pr)
1951 *Flesh and Blood* (Kimmins) (assoc pr)
1952 *Moulin Rouge* (Huston) (assoc pr)
1953 *Beat the Devil* (Huston) (assoc pr)
1954 *The Good Die Young* (Gilbert) (assoc pr)
1955 *I Am a Camera* (Cornelius) (assoc pr)
1956 *Sailor Beware!* (*Panic in the Parlor*) (Parry) (pr); *Dry Rot* (Elvey) (pr); *Three Men in a Boat* (Annakin) (pr)

1957 *The Story of Esther Costello* (Miller) (assoc pr, 2nd unit d)
1958 *The Whole Truth* (Guillermin) (pr)

Publications

By CLAYTON: articles—

"Challenge from Short Story Films," in *Films and Filming* (London), February 1956.
"The Way Things Are," an interview with Gordon Gow, in *Films and Filming* (London), April 1974.
"I'm proud of that film," an interview with M. Rosen, in *Film Comment* (New York), July/August 1974.
"Feats of Clayton," an interview with Nick Roddick, in *Stills* (London), November-December 1983.
Interview in *American Film* (Washington, D.C.), December 1987.

On CLAYTON: book—

Craston, George M. A., *Jack Clayton: A Guide to References and Resources,* Boston, 1981.

On CLAYTON: articles—

Cowie, Peter, "Clayton's Progress," in *Motion* (London), Spring 1962.
McVay, Douglas, "The House that Jack Built," in *Films and Filming* (London), October 1967.
Houston, Penelope, "West Egg at Pinewood," in *Sight and Sound* (London), Autumn 1973.
Gregory, C. T., "There'll Always Be Room at the Top for Nothing But the Best," in *Journal of Popular Film* (Bowling Green, Ohio), Winter 1973.
Houston, Penelope, "*Gatsby,*" in *Sight and Sound* (London), Spring 1974.
"Gatsby le magnìfique," in *Avant-Scène du Cinéma* (Paris), January 1975.
Rebello, Stephen, "Jack Clayton's *The Innocents,*" in *Cinefantastique* (Oak Park, Illinois), June-July 1983.
Sinyard, Neil, "Directors of the Decade: Jack Clayton," in *Films and Filming* (London), September 1983.

* * *

Though nearly forty before directing his first feature, Clayton had a solid professional grounding as Associate Producer. His credits, though few, have been mostly major productions. Though he disclaims consciously *auteurial* choices, his films evince a heavily recognisable temperament. True, his approach is national-generational, insofar as his heavy, faintly expressionistic, blocking-in of a basic mood perpetuates the lyrical emphasis conspicuous in such "quality" films of the 1940s as *Brief Encounter, Odd Man Out,* and *Dead of Night.* His penchant for themes of melancholy, frustration, obsession, hallucination, and hauntings are also amply evident.

Clayton attracted much critical praise, and an Academy Award, with *The Bespoke Overcoat,* a "long short" brought in for £5000; writer Wolf Mankowitz adapted Gogol's tale of a haunted tailor to London's East End. Clayton's first feature was *Room at the Top,* from John Braine's novel. Laurence Harvey played the ambitious young Northerner who sacrifices his true love, played by Simone Signoret, to a cynical career-move, impregnating an industrialist's innocent daughter. Its sexual frankness (as the first "quality" film to carry the new X certificate) and its class-consciousness (its use of brand-names being as snobbery-conscious as James Bond's—though lower-class) elicited powerful audience self-recognition. It marked a major breakthrough for British cinema, opening it to other "angry young men" with their "kitchen-sink realism" and social indignation (though politically more disparate than legend has it).

Clayton kept his distance from such trends, turning down both *Saturday Night and Sunday Morning* and *The L-Shaped Room,* to select a very "literary," Victorian, ghost story, *The Innocents,* from Henry James's *The Turn of the Screw.* Deborah Kerr played the children's governess who sees ghosts by sunlight while battling to save her charges from possession by the souls of two evil, and very sexual, servants. Is the lonely governess imagining everything, or projecting her own evil? *The Pumpkin-Eater* adapted Penelope Mortimer's novel about a mother of eight (Anne Bancroft) whose new husband, a film scriptwriter, bullies her into having a hysterectomy. In *Our Mother's House,* a family of children conceal their mother's death from the authorities to continue living as a family—until their scapegrace father (Dirk Bogarde) returns and takes over, introducing, not so much "reality," as *his,* disreputable, reality.

The three films are all but a trilogy, brooding with "haunted realism" over the psychic chaos between parental—especially mother—figures and children caught in half-knowledge of sexuality, death, and individuality. Atmospheres sluggish or turbulent, strained or cavernous, envelope women or child-women enmeshed in tangles of family closeness and loneliness. If *The Innocents* arraigns Victorian fears of childhood sexuality, it acknowledges also the evil in children. *The Pumpkin Eater* balances assumptions of "excessive" maternal instinct being a neurotic defence by raising the question of whether modern superficiality is brutally intolerant of maternal desire. *Our Mother's House* concerns a "lost tribe" of children, caught between the modern, "small-family" world, infantile over-severity (with dangers of a *Lord of the Flies* situation) and adult dissipation (with Dirk Bogarde somewhat reminiscent of *The Servant*). Its echoes of other films may do it injustice.

Several years and aborted projects later came *The Great Gatsby,* an ultra-lavish version of Scott Fitzgerald's tale of the lost love of a bootlegger turned socialite. It's a 1920s yuppie story, but its glitzy surfaces and characters even wispier than their originals acquire an icy, sarcophagal air. Almost as expensive, *Something Wicked This Way Comes,* from Ray Bradbury, about an eerie carnival touring lonely prairie towns to snare unsatisfied souls, evokes children's storybook illustrations, but proved a heavy commercial failure. *The Lonely Passion of Judith Hearne* reverted to more intimate and lacerating material—Brian Moore's novel of a genteel but alcoholic spinster (Maggie Smith) courted by an opportunist (Bob Hoskins) for the money he mistakenly thinks she has.

Clayton's "family trilogy" achieves a strange osmosis of 1940s "lyrical realism" and a more "calligraphic" sensitivity, of strong material and complicated interactions between profoundly different people. The resultant tensions between a central subjectivity and "the others," emphasise the dark, confused, painful gaps between minds. If the films border on the "absurdist" experience (Pinter adapted the Mortimer), they retain the richness of "traditional" themes and forms. Critics (and collaborators) keenly discussed shifts between Mortimer's first person narration and the camera as third person, and the relegation of Fitzgerald's narrator to onlooker status. Even in the lesser films, "shifting emphases" (between gloss and core in *Gatsby,* space and emotion in *Wicked*) repay re-seeing, and Clayton's combinations of fine literary material with a troubling temperament make powerful testimony to their time and to abiding human problems.

—Raymond Durgnat

Jack Clayton

CLEMENT, René

Nationality: French. **Born:** Bordeaux, 18 March 1913. **Education:** Educated in architecture at Ecole des Beaux-Arts. **Career:** Made animated film, *Cesar chez les Gaulois,* while a student, early 1930s; directed first live-action film, *Soigne ton gauche* (with Jacques Tati), 1936; made documentaries in Arabia and North Africa, 1936-39; technical consultant on Cocteau's *La Belle et la bête,* 1946. **Awards:** Best Director Award, Cannes festival, for *La Bataille du rail,* 1946, and *Au-dela des grilles,* 1949; Academy Awards, Best Foreign Film, for *Au delà des grilles* (1949) and *Jeux interdits* (1951).

Films as Director:

1936 *Soigne ton gauche* (short)
1937 *L'Arabie interdite* (short)
1938 *La Grande Chartreuse* (short)
1939 *La Bièvre, fille perdue* (short)
1940 *Le Triage* (short)
1942 *Ceux du rail* (short)
1943 *La Grande Pastorale* (short)
1944 *Chefs de demain* (short)
1945 ***La Bataille du rail*** (*Battle of the Rails*) (+ sc)
1946 *Le Père tranquille* (*Mr. Orchid*)
1947 *Les Maudits* (*The Damned*) (+ co-adapt)
1948 *Au-delà des grilles Le Mura di Malapaga* (*The Walls of Malapaga*)
1950 *Le Chateau de verre* (+ co-sc)
1951 ***Les Jeux interdits*** (*Forbidden Games*) (+ co-sc)
1954 *Monsieur Ripois* (*Knave of Hearts*); *Lovers, Happy Lovers* (+ co-sc)
1956 *Gervais*
1958 *Barrage contre le Pacifique* (*La Diga sul Pacifico*); *This Angry Age*; *The Sea Wall* (+ co-sc)
1959 *Plein soleil* (*Purple Noon*; *Lust for Evil* (+ co-sc)
1961 *Che gioia vivere* (*Quelle joie de vivre*) (+ co-sc)
1962 *Le Jour et l'heure* (*The Day and the Hour*) (+ co-sc)
1964 *Les Félins* (*Joy House*); *The Love Cage* (+ co-sc)
1966 *Paris brûle-t-il?* (*Is Paris Burning?*)
1969 *Le Passager de la pluie* (*Rider on the Rain*)
1971 *La Maison sous les arbres* (*The Deadly Trap*)
1972 *La Course du lièvre à travers les champs* (*And Hope To Die*)
1975 *La Baby-Sitter*

Publications

By CLÉMENT: articles—

Interview with Francis Koval, in *Sight and Sound* (London), June 1950.
"On Being a Creator," in *Films and Filming* (London), October 1960.

On CLÉMENT: books—

Siclier, Jacques, *René Clément,* Brussels, 1956.
Farwagi, André, *René Clément,* Paris, 1967.
Armes, Roy, *French Cinema Since 1946: Vol.1—The Great Tradition,* New York, 1970.

On CLEMENT: articles—

Queval, Jean, in *L'Écran Français* (Paris), 16 October 1946.
Régent, Roger, in *L'Écran Français* (Paris), 14 October 1947.
Eisner, Lotte, "Style of René Clément," in *Film Culture* (New York), nos. 12 and no. 13, 1957.
Riffaud, Madeleine, in *Lettres Françaises* (Paris), 14 November 1957.
Gilson, René, in *Cinéma* (Paris), no. 44, 1960.
Mardore, Michel, in *Cinéma* (Paris), no. 62, 1962.
Bellour, Raymond, in *Lettres Françaises* (Paris), 11 June 1964.
McVay, Douglas, "The Darker Side of Life," in *Films and Filming* (London), December 1966.
"*Plein soleil* Issue" of *Avant-Scène du Cinéma* (Paris), 1 February 1981.
Dossier on *La bataille du rail,* in *Cinéma* (Paris), July-August 1982.
Oliva, L., "René Clement kdysi—a potom," in *Film a Doba* (Prague), November 1983.

* * *

René Clément was the most promising filmmaker to emerge in France at the end of World War II. He became the most technically adroit and interesting of the makers of "quality" films during the 1950s, only to see his career begin to disappoint the critics. In the years of the New Wave it was Clément, above all, who tied the older generation to the younger, especially through a film like *Purple Noon.* In a more recent phase he was associated with grand-scale dramas (*Is Paris Burning?*) and with small, personal, lyric films (*Rider on the Rain*).

Clément began his career auspiciously, helping Cocteau with *Beauty and the Beast* and directing France's only great resistance film, *La Bataille du rail.* These films showed the world his wide range. The first is a classic of fantasy while the second exhibits what can only be termed a "neo-realist" style. Because *La Bataille du rail* was shot on location with non-actors, and because its episodic story was drawn from the chronicle of everyday life, Clément, at the end of the war, was championed as France's answer to the powerful Italian school of the liberation.

For a time Clément seemed anxious to live up to this reputation. He associated himself with the progressive journal *L'Ecran francais* and sought other realist topics for his films. In *Les Maudits* he observed the plight of a group of Germans and refugees aboard a submarine. Evidently he was more concerned with the technical problems of filming in small spaces than with the moral dimensions of his plot, and this film was not a great success. But with *The Walls of Malapaga* Clément recovered his audience. This film, which won the Academy Award for best foreign film, was in fact a Franco-Italian co-production and brought together on the screen the most popular star of each country: Jean Gabin and Isa Miranda. The plot and style returned Clément to the poetic-realist films of pre-war France and continued to exhibit that tension of realism and abstraction that characterized all his work.

Unquestionably he was, along with Claude Autant-Lara, the most important figure in the French film industry during the 1950s. His *Forbidden Games* remains a classic today and is notable both for the ingenuous performances of his child actors against a natural location and for the moral incisiveness of its witty plot and dialogue, scripted by the team of Aurenche and Bost. Doubtless because he had begun working with these writers, Truffaut condemned Clément in his notorious 1954 essay, "A Certain Tendency in French Cinema," but Bazin, commenting on this essay, found Truffaut to have been too harsh in Clément's case. Indeed Bazin lobbied to have the Cannes Film Festival award its Golden Palm to Clément's next feature, *Monsieur Ripois.* Starring Gérard Philipe, this film makes extensive use of subjective camera and voice over. Shot on location in London, it is clearly an experimental project.

But Clément's experiments are always limited. Technical problems continue to interest him, but he has never relinquished his belief that a film must be well-crafted in the traditional sense of that term. This is what must always distinguish him from the New Wave filmmakers

René Clement

with whom he otherwise has something in common. His all-knowing pessimism, and his literary good taste, finally put him in the camp of the "quality" directors.

Clément, then, must be thought of as consummately French. His technical mastery sits well with his advanced political and moral ideas. He is cultured and trained. He makes excellent films both on a grand scale and on a smaller, more personal one. But finally there is something impersonal about even these small films, for, before representing himself, René Clément represents the institution of filmmaking in France. He is a good representative, perhaps the best it had after the war right up through the New Wave.

—Dudley Andrew

CLOUZOT, Henri-Georges

Nationality: French. **Born:** Niort, 20 November 1907. **Education:** Ecole Navale, Brest. **Family:** Married Vera Amado Gibson, 1950 (died 1960). **Career:** As reporter for *Paris-Midi,* offered job in film industry while interviewing Adolphe Osso, 1930; assistant to Carmine Gallone, Anatole Litvak, and others, 1930-34; contracted pleurisy, confined to sanatoriums, 1934-38; reentered film industry as writer, 1938; directed first film, *L'Assassin habite au 21,* 1942. **Awards:** Best Director, Venice Festival, for *Quai des Orfèvres,* 1947; Grand Prix, Cannes Festival, for *Le Salaire de la peur,* 1953; Prix Louis Delluc, for *Les Diaboliques,* 1955; Jury Prize, Cannes Festival, for *Le Mystère Picasso,* 1956; Oscar for Best Foreign Film, for *La Vérité,* 1960. **Died:** 12 January 1977.

Films as Director:

1931 *La Terreur des Batignolles* (short)
1942 *L'Assassin habite au vingt-et-un* (+ co-sc)
1943 *Le Corbeau* (+ co-sc)
1947 *Quai des Orfèvres* (+ co-sc)
1948 *Manon* (+ co-sc)
1949 "Le Retour de Jean" in *Retour à la vie* (+ co-sc); *Miquette et sa mère* (+ co-sc)
1952 ***Le Salaire de la peur*** (+ sc)
1954 ***Les Diaboliques*** (+ co-sc)
1955 *Les Espions* (+ co-sc)
1956 *Le Mystère Picasso*
1960 *La Vérité* (+ sc)
1968 *La Prisonnière* (+ sc)

Other Films:

1931 *Ma Cousine de Varsovie* (Gallone) (co-sc); *Un Soir de Rafle* (Gallone) (adaptation); *Je serai seule après minuit* (de Baroncelli) (co-sc): *Le Chanteur inconnu* (Tourjansky) (co-adapt)
1932 *Le Roi des palaces* (Gallone) (co-sc); *Le Dernier Choc* (de Baroncelli) (co-sc); *La Chanson d'une nuit* (French language version of Anatole Litvak's *Das Lied einer Nacht*) (co-adapt, dialogue); *Faut-il les marier?* (French version of Carl Lamac's *Die grausame Freundin,* co-d with Pierre Billon) (adapt, dialogue)
1933 *Caprice de princesse* (French version of Karl Hartl's *Ihre Durchlacht, die Verkäuferin*) (adapt, assoc d, ed, sc); *Château de rêve* (French version of Geza von Bolvary's *Das Schloss im Süden*) (sc, adapt, assoc d, ed); *Tout pour l'amour* (French version of Joe May's *Ein Lied für dich*) (sc, adapt, co-dialogue, lyrics, assoc d)
1934 *Itto d'Afrique* (Benoit-Lévy) (lyrics)
1938 *Le Révolté* (Mathot) (co-sc, lyrics, dialogue)
1939 *Le Duel* (Fresnay) (co-sc, lyrics, dialogue); *Le Monde tremblera* (*La Révolté des vivants*) (Pottier) (co-sc, lyrics, dialogue)
1941 *Le Dernier des six* (Lacombe) (lyrics, dialogue); *Les Inconnus dans la maison* (Decoin) (co-adapt, lyrics, dialogue)
1955 *Si tous les gars du monde ...* (Christian-Jaque) (co-adapt)

Publications

By CLOUZOT: books—

Le Corbeau, with Louis Chavance, Paris, 1948.
Retour à la vie, with others, Paris, 1949.
Le Cheval des dieux, Paris, 1951.

By CLOUZOT: articles—

"*Le Salaire de la peur,*" in *Avant-Scène du Cinéma* (Paris), no. 17, 1962.
"*Quai des Orfèvres,*" in *Avant-Scène du Cinéma* (Paris), no. 29, 1963.
"Voix off: Clouzot," interview with Claire Clouzot, in *Cinéma* (Paris), May 1965.
"An Interview with Henri-Georges Clouzot," with Paul Schrader, in *Cinema* (Beverly Hills), no. 4, 1969.

On CLOUZOT: books—

Chalais, François, *H.G. Clouzot,* Paris, 1950.
Lacassin, Francis, and others, *Le Procès Clouzot,* Paris, 1964.
Pilard, Philippe, *H.G. Clouzot,* Paris, 1969.
Armes, Roy, *French Cinema Since 1946: Vol.1—The Great Tradition,* New York, 1970.

On CLOUZOT: articles—

Tennant, Sylvia, "Henri-Georges Clouzot," in *Film* (London), March/April 1956.
Bianchi, Pietro, "Henri-Georges Clouzot," in *Yale French Studies* (New Haven, Connecticut), Summer 1956.
Marilen, Jacques, "Dangers et vertus de l'orfèverie," in *Positif* (Paris), November 1956.
Berger, John, "Clouzot as Delilah," in *Sight and Sound* (London), Spring 1958.
Sety, Gerard, "Clouzot: He Plans Everything from Script to Screen," in *Films and Filming* (London), December 1958.
Fontaine, A., "Clouzot sort de sa légende," in *Lettres Françaises* (Paris), July 1960.
Beylie, Claude, obituary in *Ecran* (Paris), February 1977.
Lacourbe, R., "Henri-Georges Clouzot, 1907-1977," in *Avant-Scène du Cinéma* (Paris), 15 April 1977.
Yakir, Dan, "Clouzot: the Wages of Film," in *Film Comment* (New York), November/December 1981.
Listener (London), 15 October 1987.
Ciné Revue (Paris), 29 October 1987.

* * *

Henri-Georges Clouzot

In a country like France where good taste is so admired, Henri-Georges Clouzot has been a shocking director. A film critic during the age of surrealism, Clouzot was always eager to assault his audience with his style and concerns.

Like so many others, Clouzot found his chance to move from scriptwriting to directing during the Occupation, a time when there was a paucity of directors in France. His first effort, *L'Assassin habite au 21,* was a safe film. Its script followed two similar films he had written which had been well-received by audiences. These witty police dramas were exercises in style and cleverness, befitting the epoch. *Le Corbeau,* made the next year, was in contrast a shattering film, unquestionably hitting hard at the society of the war years. Retaining all the conventions of the thriller, Clouzot systematically exposed the physical and psychological grotesqueries of every character in the film. A grim picture of small-town mores, *Le Corbeau* was condemned by the Nazis and French patriots alike.

When the war ended Clouzot found himself barred from the industry for two years by the "purification committee," an industry-appointed watchdog group that self-righteously judged complicity with the Germans. Clouzot's crime was to have made films for a German-financed company, though he was officially arraigned on charges of having maligned the French character and having demoralized the country during its dark hours. But even at this time many critics claimed that *Le Corbeau* was the only authentically engaged film made during the entire Occupation.

When he did resume his career, Clouzot's grim view of life had not improved. Both *Quai des Orfèvres* and his 1948 adaptation of *Manon* emulated American film noir with their lowlife settings. Both are extremely well acted, but ultimately small works.

Clouzot's fame in the United States came in the mid-1950s when *The Wages of Fear* and *Diabolique* gave him a reputation as a French Hitchcock, interested in the mechanics of suspense. In France, however, these films, especially *Diabolique,* were seen as only well-made studio products. His 1960 *La Vérité,* starring Brigitte Bardot, was designed to win him favor in the youth culture of the time, which was obsessed by New Wave life and movies. While the film outgrossed its New Wave competition, its cloyingly paternalistic style showed how far Clouzot was from the spontaneity of the New Wave. The cafe scenes in the film are insincere, and the inevitable indictment of society rings false.

All of Clouzot's films, even up to the 1968 *La Prisonnière* were financial successes, but in the end he ceased being the instrumental force in the film industry he had been twenty years earlier.

—Dudley Andrew

COCTEAU, Jean

Nationality: French. **Born:** Maisons-Lafitte, near Paris, 5 July 1889. **Education:** Lycée Condorcet and Fenelon, Paris. **Career:** Actor, playwright, poet, librettist, novelist, painter and graphic artist in 1920s and throughout career. Directed first film, *Le Sang d'un poète,* 1930; became manager of boxer Al Brown, 1937; remained in Paris during the Occupation, 1940. **Awards:** Chevalier de la Légion d'honneur, 1949; member, Academie Royale de Belgique, 1955; member, Academie Française, 1955; honorary doctorate, Oxford University, 1956. **Died:** In Milly-la-Foret, France, 11 October 1963.

Films as Director:

1925 *Jean Cocteau fait du cinéma* (+ sc) (neg lost?)
1930 ***Le Sang d'un poète*** (originally ***La Vie d'un poète)*** (+ ed, sc, voice-over)
1946 ***La Belle et la bête*** (+ sc)
1947 *L'Aigle à deux têtes* (+ sc)
1948 *Les Parent terribles* (+ sc, voice-over)
1950 ***Orphée*** (+ sc); *Coriolan* (+ sc, role); a 1914 "dramatic scene" by Cocteau included in *Ce siècle a cinquante ans* (Tual) (+ sc)
1952 *La Villa Santo-Sospir* (+ sc)
1960 *Le Testament d'Orphée* (*Ne me demandez pas pourquoi*) (+ sc, role as le poète)

Other Films:

1940 *La Comedie du bonheur* (L'Herbier) (co-sc)
1942 *Le Baron fantôme* (de Poligny) (sc, role as Le Baron)
1943 *L'Eternel Retour* (Delannoy) (sc); *La Malibran* (Guitry) (narration + role as Alfred de Musset)
1945 ***Les Dames du Bois de Boulogne*** (Bresson) (co-sc)
1946 *L'Amitie noire* (Villiers and Krull) (role and narration)
1947 *Ruy Blas* (Billon) (sc)
1948 *La Voix humaine* (Rossellini, from Cocteau's play); *Les Noces de sable* (Zvoboda) (sc, voice-over); *La Légende de Sainte Ursule* (Emmer) (role and narration)
1949 *Tennis* (Martin) (role + narration)
1950 *Les Enfants terribles* (Melville) (sc); *Colette* (Bellon) (role + narration); *Venise et ses amants* (Emmer and Gras) (role + narration)
1951 *Desordre* (Baratier) (role + narration)
1952 *La Couronne noire* (Saslavski) (co-sc); *8 x 8* (Richter) (role + narration)
1953 *Le Rouge est mis* (Barrère and Knapp) (role + narration)
1956 *A l'aube d'un monde* (Lucot) (role + narration); *Pantomimes* (Lucot) (role + narration)
1957 *Le Bel indifferent* (Demy, from Cocteau's play)
1958 *Django Reinhardt* (Paviot) (role + narration); *Le Musée Grevin* (Demy and Masson) (role + narration)
1959 *Charlotte et son Jules* (Godard, from same play as Demy 1957 film)
1961 *La Princesse de Cleves* (Delannoy) (co-sc)
1963 *Anna la bonne* (Jutra, from song by Cocteau)
1965 *Thomas l'imposteur* (Franju) (co-sc)
1970 *La Voix humaine* (Delouche, from Poulenc and Cocteau opera)

Publications

By COCTEAU: books—

L'Aigle à deux têtes, Paris, 1946.
Diary of a Film [La Belle et la bête], New York, 1950.
Cocteau on the Film, New York, 1954.
Jean Cocteau par lui-même, edited by André Fraigneau, Paris, 1957.
Le Sang d'un poète, with drawings, Monaco, 1957.
Le Testament d'Orphée (filmscript), Paris, 1961.
The Eagle with Two Heads, London, 1962.
The Journals of Jean Cocteau, edited by Wallace Fowlie, Bloomington, Indiana, 1964.
The Difficulty of Being, London, 1966.
Two Screenplays [The Blood of a Poet and *The Testament of Orpheus],* New York, 1968.
Beauty and the Beast, edited by Robert Hammond, New York, 1970.
Professional Secrets: An Autobiography of Jean Cocteau, edited by Robert Phelps, New York, 1970.
Cocteau on the Film, New York, 1972.
Jean Cocteau: Three Screenplays [The Eternal Return, Beauty and the Beast, and *Orpheus*], New York, 1972.
Le Testament d'Orphée; Le Sang d'un poète, Monaco, 1983.
Past Tense, Volume 1: Diaries, London, 1987.
Souvenir portraits: Paris in the Belle Epoque, translated by Jesse Browner, London, 1990.
Erotica: drawings, London, 1991.
Correspondance: Jacques-Emile Blanche, Jean Cocteau, Paris, 1993.
Les parents terribles, translated by Simon Callow, London, 1994.

By COCTEAU: articles—

Interview with Francis Koval, in *Sight and Sound* (London), August 1950.
"Conversation," in *Sight and Sound* (London), July/September 1952.
"Cocteau," in *Film* (London), March 1955.
Interview in *Film Makers on Filmmaking,* edited by Harry Geduld, Bloomington, Indiana, 1967.
"Four Letters by Jean Cocteau to Leni Riefenstahl," in *Film Culture* (New York), Spring 1973.

Jean Cocteau

"Aphorismes cinématographiques," and "Cocteau face a La Belle et la bête," in *Avant-Scène du Cinéma* (Paris), July/September 1973.

On COCTEAU: books—

Crosland, Margaret, *Jean Cocteau,* London, 1955.
Dauven, Jean, *Jean Cocteau chez les Sirènes,* Paris, 1956.
Pillaudin, Roger, *Jean Cocteau tourne son dernier film,* Paris, 1960.
Fraigneau, André, *Cocteau,* New York, 1961.
Fowlie, Wallace, *Jean Cocteau: The History of a Poet's Age,* Bloomington, Indiana, 1968.
Lannes, Roger, *Jean Cocteau,* Paris, 1968.
Sprigge, Elizabeth, and Jean-Jacques Kihm, *Jean Cocteau: The Man and the Mirror,* New York, 1968.
Gilson, René, *Cocteau,* New York, 1969.
Armes, Roy, *French Cinema Since 1946: Vol. 1—The Great Tradition,* New York, 1970.
Steegmuller, Francis, *Cocteau,* Boston, 1970.
Evans, Arthur, *Jean Cocteau and His Films of Orphic Identity,* Philadelphia, 1977.
Anderson, Alexandra, and Carol Saltus, editors, *Jean Cocteau and the French Scene,* New York, 1984.

de Miomandre, Philippe, *Moi, Jean Cocteau,* Paris, 1985.
Keller, Marjorie, *The Untutored Eye: Childhood in the Films of Cocteau, Cornell and Brakhage,* Cranbury, New Jersey, 1986.
Peters, Arthur King, *Jean Cocteau and his World: An Illustrated Biography,* London, 1987.
Marais, Jean, *L'inconcevable Jean Cocteau,* Monaco, 1993.

On COCTEAU: articles—

Lambert, Gavin, "Cocteau and Orpheus," in *Sequence* (London), Autumn 1950.
Oxenhandler, Neal, "On Cocteau," in *Film Quarterly* (Berkeley), Fall 1964.
Durgnat, Raymond, "Images of the Mind—Part 13: Time and Timelessness," in *Films and Filming* (London), July 1969.
Amberg, G., "The Testament of Jean Cocteau," in *Film Comment* (New York), Winter 1971/72.
"Cocteau Issue" of *Image et Son* (Paris), June/July 1972.
"Cocteau Issue" of *Avant-Scène du Cinéma* (Paris), July/September 1973.
Renaud, T., "Retrospective: Jean Cocteau. Un cineaste? Peut-etre. Un auteur? Certainement.," in *Cinéma* (Paris), December 1973.
Gow, Gordon, "Astonishments: Magic Film from Jean Cocteau," and "The Mirrors of Life," in *Films and Filming* (London), January and February 1978.
"Cocteau Issue" of *Avant-Scène du Cinéma* (Paris), 1 May 1983.
"Cocteau Supplement," in *Cinéma* (Paris), May 1983.
Milani, R., "Cocteau dell'immaginario," in *Filmcritica* (Florence), June 1984.
Combs, Richard, "Dream work," in *Listener* (London), 29 May 1986.
"France's anti-Cartesian," in *The Economist* (London), 9 May 1992.

* * *

Jean Cocteau's contribution to cinema is as eclectic as one would expect from a man who fulfilled on occasion the roles of poet and novelist, dramatist and graphic artist, and dabbled in such diverse media as ballet and sculpture. In addition to his directorial efforts, Cocteau also wrote scripts and dialogue, made acting appearances, and realized amateur films. His work in other media has inspired adaptations by a number of filmmakers ranging from Rossellini to Franju and Demy, and he himself published several collections of eclectic and stimulating thoughts on the film medium.

Though Cocteau took his first real steps as a filmmaker at the very beginning of the sound era, his period of greatest involvement was in the 1940s, when he contributed to the scripts of a half-dozen films, at times dominating his director (as in *L'Eternel Retour*), at other times submitting to the discipline of contributing to another's vision (as in his dialogue for Bresson's *Les Dames du Bois de Boulogne*). In addition, he directed his own adaptations of such diverse works as the fairy tale *La Belle et la bête,* his own period melodrama *L'Aigle à deux têtes,* and his intense domestic drama, *Les Parents terribles.*

But Cocteau's essential work in cinema is contained in just three wholly original films in which he explores his personal myth of the poet as Orpheus: *Le Sang d'un poète, Orphée,* and *Le Testament d'Orphée.* Though made over a period of thirty years, these three works have a remarkable unity of inspiration. They are works of fascination in a double sense. They convey Cocteau's fascination with poetry and his own creative processes, and at the same time display his openness to all the ways of fascinating an audience, utilizing stars and trickery, found material and sheer fantasy. The tone is characterized by a unique mixture of reality and dream, and his definition of *Le Sang d'un pòete* as "a realistic documentary of unreal events" is a suitable description of all his finest work.

Crucial to the lasting quality of Cocteau's work, which at times seems so light and fragile, is the combination of artistic seriousness and persistent, but unemphatic, self-mockery. For this reason his enclosed universe, with its curiously idyllic preoccupation with death, is never oppressive or constricting; instead, it allows the spectator a freedom rare in mainstream cinema of the 1930s and 1940s. In technical terms Cocteau displays a similar ability to cope with the contributions of totally professional collaborators, while still retaining a disarming air of ingenuousness, which has sometimes been wrongly characterized as amateurism.

Reviled by the Surrealists as a literary poseur in the 1920s and 1930s and distrusted as an amateur in the 1940s, Cocteau nonetheless produced films of lasting quality. In retrospect he is to be admired for the freedom with which he expressed a wholly personal vision and for his indifference to the given rules of a certain period of French "quality" filmmaking. He was one of the few French filmmakers of the past to whom the directors of the New Wave could turn for inspiration, and it is totally fitting that Cocteau's farewell to cinema, *Le Testament d'Orphée,* should have been produced by one of the most talented of these newcomers, François Truffaut.

—Roy Armes

COEN, Joel

Nationality: American. **Born:** Minneapolis, 1955. **Education:** Attended Simon's Rock College, Massachusetts, and New York University. **Family:** Married actress Frances McDormand. **Career:** Worked as an assistant film editor on *Fear No Evil* and *Evil Dead;* collaborated on screenplays with brother Ethan Coen (b. 1958); with Ethan produced first film, *Blood Simple,* 1984. **Awards:** Grand Jury Prize, U.S. Film Festival, for *Blood Simple,* 1984; Best Director Award, Cannes Film Festival, for *Barton Fink,* 1991. **Address:** c/o UTA, 9560 Wilshire Blvd., Suite 500, Beverly Hills, California 90212, U.S.A.

Films as Director and Co-scriptwriter:

(All co-written and produced by brother, Ethan Coen)

1984 *Blood Simple*
1987 *Raising Arizona*
1990 *Miller's Crossing*
1991 ***Barton Fink***
1994 *The Hudsucker Proxy*
1996 *Fargo*

Publications

On COEN: articles—

Ansen, D., "The Coens: Partners in Crime," in *Newsweek* (New York), 21 January 1985.
Breitbart, E., "Leaving the Seventies Behind: Four Independents Find Happiness Making Movies in the Manner of Hollywood," in *American Film* (Washington, D.C.), May 1985.
Edelstein, D., "Invasion of the Body Snatchers," in *American Film* (Washington, D.C.), April 1987.
Handelman, D., "The Brothers from Another Planet," in *Rolling Stone* (New York), 21 May 1987.

Joel (right) and Ethan Coen

Seidenberg, Robert, "Miller's Crossing: John Turturro Meets the Coen Brothers," in *American Film* (Washington, D.C.), March 1990.

Valot, J., "Joel Coen," in *Revue du Cinèma* (Paris), May 1990.

Sharkey, Betsy, "Movies of Their Very Own," in *New York Times Magazine,* July 8, 1990.

Richardson, J. H., "The Joel and Ethan Coen Story," in *Premiere,* October 1990.

Robertson, William Preston, "What's the Goopus?," in *American Film* (Washington, D.C.), August 1991.

Horowitz, M., "Coen Brothers A-Z: The Big Two-Headed Picture," in *Film Comment* (New York), September/October 1991.

Ferguson, K., "From Two Directions," in *Film Monthly,* February 1992.

Giavarini, J., "Joel et Ethan Coen," in *Cahiers du Cinema* (Paris), December 1992.

Clark, John, "Strange Bedfellows," in *Premiere,* April 1994.

Robertson, William Preston, "The Coen Brothers Made Easy," in *Playboy,* April 1994.

Friend, Tad, "Inside the Coen Heads," in *Vogue,* April 1994.

* * *

Although Joel Coen had worked as an assistant film editor on commercial projects and had made valuable contacts within the industry (particularly director Sam Raimi), he and brother Ethan decided to produce their first feature film independently, raising $750,000 to shoot their jointly written script for *Blood Simple,* a neo-noir thriller with a Dashiell Hammett title and a script full of homages to Jim Thompson. Though Joel received screen credit for direction and Ethan for the script, this distinction is somewhat artificial both here and in their subsequent productions. Joel and Ethan co-write their scripts and meticulously prepare storyboards in a collaborative effort unusual for the American cinema (the closest analogy perhaps comes from abroad with the British team of Powell and Pressburger).

Blood Simple was hardly the first film the brothers Coen made together. Addicted to TV and movies at an early age, they spent a good deal of their childhood writing films and then shooting them on a Super-8 camera. Movie brats in the Spielberg tradition, Ethan and Joel desired commercial success but were determined to retain control over what they produced. Hence their initial decision to make an independent film rather than continue working in an industry where Joel was already beginning to be established.

A hit with many on the art film/independent circuit but also a commercial success in art house and cable release, *Blood Simple* was the perfect choice to achieve this aim. Here was a film that succeeded because of its individual, even quirky vision. Using the film noir conventions popular with American audiences for half a century, the Coens offer a clear narrative, solidly two-dimensional characters, and the requisite amount of riveting violent spectacle (including one scene that pictures a dying man buried alive and another featuring close-ups of a white-gloved hand suddenly impaled by a knife). *Blood Simple,* however, is by no means an ordinary thriller. The plot turns expertly and unexpectedly on a number of dramatic ironies (no character knows what the spectator does, and even the spectator is sometimes taken by surprise). Unlike hardboiled narrative à la Raymond Chandler, the narrative delights in its Aristotelian neatness, in its depiction of experiences that make perfect sense, climaxing in a poetic justice that the main character and narrator, a venal private detective, finds humorous even as it destroys him. Thematically, the Coens offer a compelling analysis of *mauvaise foi* in the Sartrean vein as they develop characters doomed by bad intentions or a failure to trust and communicate (an existentialist theme that results perhaps from the fact that Ethan majored in philosophy at Princeton). *Blood Simple*'s most notable feature, however, is an expressive stylization of both sound and image that creates an experiential correlative for the viewer of the characters' confusion and disorientation. These effects are achieved by a Wellesian repertoire of tricks (wide-angle lenses, tracking set-ups, unusual framings, an artfully selected score of popular music, etc.). The film noir genre naturalizes this stylization to some degree, but *Blood Simple* exudes a riotous self-consciousness, a delight in the creation of an exciting cinema that offers moments of pure visceral or visual pleasure.

Though some critics thought *Blood Simple* a kind of pointless film-school exercise, audiences were impressed—as were the major studios who competed for releasing rights to the brothers' next project. The Coens' subsequent five films have all been made with substantial commercial backing; but these films continue to be independent in the sense that none fits into the routine categories of contemporary Hollywood production. In fact, the art cinema tradition of the seventies has been kept alive by the Coens and the few other mavericks (e.g., Quentin Tarantino) who have emerged to prominence.

The least successful of these films—*Miller's Crossing*—is the most traditional. A "realistic" drama (though the scenes of violence are highly stylized) with a well-developed plot line, this saga of Prohibition-era mobsters, like Scorsese's *Goodfellas* (released the year before), aims to debunk the romantic tradition of the gangster film most tellingly exemplified by *The Godfather* (1972). The central character, a "good guy" high up in the organization, confusingly seems more a victim of his poor circumstances than a force to be reckoned with. The plot is otherwise dependent upon unbelievable characters and unlikely twists and turns. Some elements of parody are present, but are not well integrated into the film's structure, indicating that the Coens were uncertain about how to proceed, whether to make a gangster film or send up the conventions of the genre.

The other films share a different representational regime, a magical realism that does not demand verisimilitude or logical closure, but has the virtue—for the Coens—of permitting more stylization, more moments of pure cinema. *Raising Arizona* and *The Hudsucker Proxy* offer postmodern versions of the traditional Hollywood madcap comedy; in both films, a series of zany adventures climax in romantic happiness for the male and female leads. *Raising Arizona* concerns the ultimately unsuccessful attempt of a zany and childless couple to kidnap a baby; *The Hudsucker Proxy* sends up, in mock Capra-corn style, the triumph of the virtuous, if obtuse, hero over the evil system that attempts to use him for its own purposes. *Barton Fink,* in contrast, is a darker story, heavily indebted to German Expressionism (an influence to be noted as well in the elaborately artificial sets and unnaturalistic acting of *The Hudsucker Proxy*). The film's main character is a thirties stereotype, a left-wing Jewish playwright committed to representing the miseries of what he calls "the common man." Hired away from Broadway by a Hollywood studio, he embarks unwittingly on a penitential journey that lays bare the forces of the id both in the apparently common man he meets (a salesman who is actually a serial killer) and in himself (abandoning his writing responsibility, he finds himself at film's end at the beach with the beautiful woman whose picture he first saw in a calendar).

All three of these films abound in bravura stylizations. A man dives out a skyscraper window and the camera traces the stages of his fall (*Hudsucker*); a baby's meanderings across the floor are captured by a camera literally at floor level (an elaborate mirror shot in *Arizona*); wallpaper peels off a hotel room wall revealing something warm and gooey like human flesh underneath (*Barton Fink*); exaggerated sounds—a mosquito's flight, a noisy bed, a whirling fan—perfectly express the main character's self-absorption and anxiety (*Barton Fink* again).

With *Fargo,* their 1996 release, the Coen brothers return to the crime drama. Set primarily in Minnesota, the film follows an immensely likable and very pregnant sheriff (played by Frances McDormand, Joel Coen's wife) as she pursues a couple of dimwitted and cold-blooded kidnappers. A macabre thriller veined with moments of comedy, *Fargo* features the Coen brothers' trademark cinematic flair (though the landscape mutes this somewhat) and intelligent narrative focus.

The Coens appear to have abandoned for good the stylized realism and Aristotelian narrative that made *Blood Simple* such a success. But in an era that has witnessed the commercial success of cartoonish anti-naturalism *(Dick Tracy,* the Batman films), their concern with striking visual and aural effects may provide the basis for a long career, though difficult films like *Barton Fink,* despite critical acclaim, will never gain a wide audience.

—R. Barton Palmer

COMENCINI, Luigi

Nationality: Italian. **Born:** Salo, Brescia, 8 June 1916. **Education:** Educated in architecture at Politecnico, Milan, 1934-39. **Career:** Began private cinema club with Alberto Lattuada and Mario Ferrari, mid-1930s; made first short, *La Novelletta,* 1937; film critic of *Corrente* and assistant director on several films, early 1940s; directed first feature, *Proibito rubare* (for producer Carlo Ponti), 1948; co-founder, with Lattuada, of Cineteca Italiana film archives, Milan, 1949. **Awards:** Golden Lion Award for Career Achievements, Venice Festival, 1987.

Films as Director:

1937 *La Novelletta* (short)
1946 *Bambini in cittá* (short)
1948 *Il museo dei sogni* (short); *L'ospedale del delitto* (short); *Proibito rubare* (*Guaglio*) (+ co-sc)
1949 *L'imperatore di Capri* (+ co-sc)
1951 *Persiane chiuse* (*Behind Closed Shutters*)
1952 *La tratta della bianche* (*Girls Marked Danger*) (+ co-sc); *Heidi*
1953 *Pane, amore e fantasia* (*Bread, Love and Dreams*) (+ co-sc); *La valigia dei sogni* (+ co-sc)
1954 *Pane, amore e gelosia* (*Frisky*) (+ co-sc)
1955 *La bella di Roma* (+ co-sc)
1956 *La finestra sul Luna Park* (+ co-sc)
1957 *Mariti in città* (+ co-sc)
1958 *Mogli pericolose* (+ co-sc)
1959 *Und das am Montagmorgen* (+ co-sc); *La sorprese dell'amore* (+ co-sc)
1960 *Tutti a casa* (*Everybody Go Home!*) (+ co-sc)
1961 *A cavallo della tigre* (+ co-sc)
1962 *Il commissario*
1963 *La ragazza di Bube* (*Bebo's Girl*) (+ co-sc)
1964 "Fatebenefratelli" episode of *Tre notti d'amore* (*Three Nights of Love*) (+ co-sc); "Eritrea" episode of *La mia signora* (+ co-sc); "Il trattato di eugenetica" ["Treatise in Eugenics"] episode of *Le bambole* (*The Dolls*); *Il compagno Don Camillo*
1965 *La bugiarda* (*Six Days a Week*) (+ co-adaptation)
1967 *Incompreso* (*Vita col figlio*) (+ co-sc)
1968 *Italian Secret Service* (+ co-sc)
1969 *Senza sapere niente di lei* (+ co-sc); *Infanzia, vocazione e prime esperienze di Giacomo Casanova veneziano* (+ co-sc)
1971 *Le avventure di Pinocchio* (+ co-sc)
1972 *Lo scopone scientifico*
1974 *Delitto d'amore* (+ co-sc); *Mio Dio, come sono caduta in basso!* (+ co-sc): *Educazione civica* (short)
1975 *La donna della domenica* (*The Sunday Woman*)
1976 2 episodes of *Signore e signori, buona-notte* (co-d); "L'equivoco" episode of *Basta che non si sappia in giro*; "L'ascensore" episode of *Quelle strane occasioni*
1977 *Il gatto*
1979 *L'ingorgo, una storia impossibile* (+ co-sc)
1980 *Voltati Eugenio* (+ sc)
1982 *Cercasi Gesù*
1984 *Cuore*
1986 *La Storia*
1987 *Un ragazzo di Calabria* (*A Child of Calabria*); *Run, Boy, Run*; *La Boheme*
1989 *Buon natale, buon anno* (+ sc)
1991 *Les adventures de Pinocchio*
1992 *Marcellino Pane e Vino* (+ sc)

Publications

By COMENCINI: articles—

"En guise d'autoportrait," in *Positif* (Paris), February 1974.
"Un vrai crime d'amour," an interview with Jean A. Gili, in *Ecran* (Paris), January 1975.
Interview in *Bianco e Nero* (Rome), September/December 1975.
"L'Idée de la mort," in *Positif* (Paris), December/January 1977/78.
"Les Paradoxes de Luigi Comencini," interview with D. Rabourdin and J. Roy, in *Cinéma* (Paris), May and June 1978.
"Conversation avec Luigi Comencini," with L. Codelli, in *Positif* (Paris), May 1979.
"En revoyant les notes de travail d'Eugenio," in *Positif* (Paris), January 1981.
Interview with Jean A. Gili, in *Positif* (Paris), February 1983.
Comencini, Luigi, in *Positif* (Paris), January 1984 and September 1985.
"*Cuore* Issue" of *Avant-Scène du Cinéma* (Paris), no. 345, 1985.
Interview in *Positif* (Paris), April 1987.

On COMENCINI: books—

Gili, Jean A., *Luigi Comencini*, Paris, 1981.
Tassone, Aldo, *Le Cinéma italien*, Paris, 1983.

On COMENCINI: articles—

Codelli, L., and others, "Luigi Comencini," in *Positif* (Paris), March 1974.
Tournès, A., "Comencini: le rire et les larmes," in *Jeune Cinéma* (Paris), September/October 1974.
"Comencini Issue" of *Avant-Scène du Cinéma* (Paris), 1 May 1978.
Kane, P., "Minorités impudiques," in *Cahiers du Cinéma* (Paris), May 1978.
Lefèvre, R., "Comencini pontissalien," in *Image et Son* (Paris), October 1979.
"Comencini Section" of *Cineforum* (Bergamo), June 1982.
Biofilmography in *Avant-Scène du Cinéma* (Paris), December 1985.

* * *

With more than thirty feature films, several television documentaries, and a few shorts, Luigi Comencini's work is considerable but only attracted critical attention in the 1970s. He has always enjoyed popular success in his own country, but this popularity has probably hindered his artistic status. Working within traditional genres (comedy, thrillers, melodramas), Comencini has been accused, together with his contemporaries Mario Monicelli and Dino Risi, of having betrayed the heritage of neo-realism by using it as a background adjunct to conventional story-telling.

Squeezed between the great authors (Rossellini, Fellini, Antonioni, Visconti, De Sica, Zavattini) with their obvious stylistic preoccupations and the directors of the Italian renaissance of the early 1960s (Rosi, Olmi, Pasolini, the Tavianis), Comencini has been neglected much like some of his Hollywood colleagues. Starting as a documentary filmmaker, a photographer, a movie critic for the socialist paper *Avanti*, and a co-founder of the Italian Film Archives, Comencini has had a checkered career but has finally been recognized, particularly in France, as an important artist. His work owes much to the neorealist movement, being firmly grounded in a social context, showing humanitarian preoccupations, and displaying interest in all strata of society.

The enormous success in his early career of a picturesque and charming comedy about a *carabiniere* and a beautiful country girl—*Pane, amore e fantasia* and its sequel *Pane, amore e gelosia*, starring Vittorio De Sica and Gina Lollobrigida—have given a false image of Comencini as a specialist in folksy escapism. Much more revealing is his first film, *Proibito rubare*, about the relationship between a priest and street kids in post-war Naples. The sentimentality is accompanied by a firm stand on social inequities. The subject of children proves itself

Luigi Comencini

a fruitful one for Comencini, allowing him to oppose innocence and experience and to show the dryness and hypocrisy of the adult world. Some of the best and most personal of his films deal with children: *La finestra sul Luna Park; Incompreso,* remade in 1983 by Jerry Schatzberg under the same title; *Infanzia, vocazione e prime esperienze di Giacomo Casanova Veneziano,* using the first five chapters of Casanova's memoirs to evoke the life of Venice in the eighteenth century through the eyes of a child who later becomes a libertine; *Pinocchio,* a masterful adaptation of Collodi's book; and *Voltati Eugenio,* in which a young boy severely judges his parents who had themselves been rebellious youths in the 1960s.

Like many Italians, Comencini has turned to World War II as a key experience in his country's history. *Tutti a casa* is one of the best films on this period, an epic comedy about a soldier, Schweik (Alberto Sordi), slowly becoming a resistance fighter. *La ragazze di Bube,* which tells about the love of a country girl (Claudia Cardinale) for a communist partisan who killed a fascist after the war, is also a sensitive portrait of the Mussolini period's aftermath.

Comencini displays a clarity of vision, a satiric sense, and a taste for fables and allegories in *A cavallo della tigre, La scopone scientifico, L'ingorgo, una storia impossible* and *Cercasi Gesù.* Comencini reveals himself as rational and reformist, but he is ultimately a sceptic with a philosophy close to that of the Enlightenment. However, his ironic tone does not exclude at times an emotional inspiration that leads him to melodramatic subjects set, for example, in the world of prostitution (*Pagine chiuse*) or factory work (*Delitto d'amore*). Rich in human details, varied in inspiration, and served by some of the best Italian actors, his work deserves the re-evaluation currently underway.

—Michel Ciment

CONNER, Bruce

Nationality: American. **Born:** McPherson, Kansas, 18 November 1933. **Education:** Studied at University of Wichita and at University of Nebraska, B.F.A. **Career:** Active as artist, making assemblage works, sculpture, painting and drawing, 1950s-present; moved to San Francisco, 1957; made first film, *A Movie,* to accompany exhibition of his sculpture, 1958. **Awards:** Ford Foundation Fellowship Grant, 1964; National Endowment for the Arts Fellowship Grant, 1973; American Film Institute Grant, 1974; Guggenheim Fellowship, 1975; Citation in Film, Brandeis University Creative Awards, 1979.

Films as Director (in 16mm):

1958 *A Movie*
1960-62 *Cosmic Ray*
1961-67 *Looking for Mushrooms*
1963-67 *Report*
1964 *Leader*
1964/65 *Vivian*
1965 *Ten Second Film*
1966 *Breakaway*
1967 *The White Rose*; *Liberty Crown*
1969 *Permian Strata*
1969-73 *Marilyn Times Five*
1976 *Crossroads*; *Take the 5:10 to Dreamland*
1977 *Valse Triste*
1978 *Mongoloid*
1982 *America Is Waiting*

Publications

By CONNER: articles—

Interview with Robert Brown, in *Film Culture* (New York), no. 33, 1964.
"Bruce Conner Makes a Sandwich," in *Artforum* (New York), September 1967.
"'I Was Obsessed...,'" in *Film Library Quarterly* (New York), Summer 1969.
"Excerpts from an Interview with Bruce Conner Conducted in July of 1971," with R. Haller, in *Film Culture* (New York), no.67-69, 1979.
"Amos Vogel and Bruce Conner: Two Views of the Money Crunch," in *Film Comment* (New York), September/October 1981.

On CONNER: books—

Curtis, David, *Experimental Cinema: A Fifty Year Evaluation,* New York, 1971.
Johnson, Lincoln, *Film: Space Time Light & Sound,* New York, 1974.
Sitney, P. Adams, *Visionary Film,* New York, 1974.
Hanhardt, John, and others, *A History of the American Avant-Garde Cinema,* New York, 1976.

On CONNER: articles—

O'Doherty, Brian, "Bruce Conner and His Films," in *The New American Cinema,* edited by Gregory Battcock, New York, 1967.
Belz, Carl, "Three Films by Bruce Conner," in *Film Culture* (New York), Spring 1967.
"Bruce Conner," in *Film Comment* (New York), Winter 1969.
Kelman, Ken, "The Anti-Information Film (Conner's *Report*)," in *The Essential Cinema: Essays on the Films in the Collection of Anthology Film Archives* vol.1, New York, 1975.
Fischer, Lucy, "Countdown: Some Thoughts on Bruce Conner," in *University Film Study Center Newsletter* (Cambridge, Massachusetts), no.2, 1976.
Moritz, W., and B. O'Neill, "Fallout: Some Notes on the Films of Bruce Conner," in *Film Quarterly* (Berkeley), Summer 1978.
Cook, Scott, "*Valse Triste* and *Mongoloid,*" in *Millenium Film Journal* (New York), Fall/Winter 1980/81.
Bass, William, "The Past Restructured: Bruce Conner and Others," in *Journal of University Film Association* (Carbondale, Illinois), Spring 1981.
Grindon, L., "Significance Reexamined: A Report on Bruce Conner," in *Post Script* (Jacksonville, Florida), Winter 1985.
Wide Angle (Athens, Ohio), vol. 8, nos. 3-4, 1986.
Monthly Film Bulletin (London), October and November 1987.

* * *

After graduating from the University of Nebraska, Bruce Conner moved to San Francisco to begin an exceptionally successful and still very productive career as an experimental filmmaker. Conner's production over the past thirty years manifests certain salient characteristics typical in the works of this genre. His films tend to be brief (the shortest being his 1965 *Ten Second Film*; the longest, his 1975 *Crossroads,* running 36 minutes). Beyond grant subsidy, his production is financially independent, allowing him total freedom in creativity and distribution. And his works are essentially a-collaborative, being in essence solely under Conner's control from conception through all phases of construction. However, since Conner is particularly known for the techno-structural resource of "compilation" (i.e., the use of extant or "found" footage shot by other filmmakers for various purposes), this a-collaborative characteristic deserves special qualification.

While not all of Conner's films manifest compilation (for example, each of the brief shots that form the hectic, three-minute montage of *Looking for Mushrooms* was the result of Conner's cinematography), compilation is clearly his hallmark and the intrinsic reflexivity of compilation probably accounts for the continued success of Conner's early and later films today. "Reflexivity" is indeed that contemporary preoccupation—both inside and outside the experimental film genre—with grasping and expressing the special materiality that distinguishes film from other forms such as written literature, theatre, music, etc. Since montage or editing has classically been regarded as essential to "film as film," Conner's work can best be experienced as an ongoing exploration of montage's quintessential qualities.

Early works like Conner's *A Movie* or *Cosmic Ray* easily exemplify this thesis. Constructed from bits and pieces of such films as old newsreels, animated cartoons, Hollywood features, war documentaries, academy ("count-down") leader, home movies, and 1950s pornography, the actual cinematography is at once very varied and very anonymous. Indeed, such disparate footage is largely cut together with no attempt to disguise or mitigate abrupt changes in tonality, grain, cinematographic style, or subject matter. Conner's clear exhibition of the "joints" of his montage is in contradistinction to more commercial use of library or file footage in fictive features or television news, where such visibility would prove a liability. Instead, Conner always reminds his audience that they are watching "a movie," an artifact whose very essence is bound to the extraordinary power and sometimes subtle imitations of montage.

Stylistically, Conner's earlier works—like *Report,* a 1967 review of sounds and images from the day of John F. Kennedy's shocking assassination—tend more to abrupt junctures enhanced by frenzied editing rates. The earlier films are also marked more by humor and biting ironies. Later compilation pieces such as *Crossroads* (built totally from declassified film records of early atomic bomb tests) manifest much slower pacing and more wistful moods. Comparably, *Take the 5:10 to Dreamland* employs sepia print stock to homogenize tonality, and its bittersweet representation of the past constitutes a distinct, more mature sensibility than Conner's earlier works. Still, all his production remains remarkably fresh and remarkably appealing, even to popular audiences who might otherwise find experimental production arcane or bizarre. He is doubtless one of the finest American experimental filmmakers working today.

—Edward Small

COPPOLA, Francis Ford

Nationality: American. **Born:** Detroit, Michigan, 7 April 1939. **Education:** Hofstra University, B.A., 1959; University of California, Los Angeles, M.F.A. in cinema, 1967. **Family:** Married Eleanor Neil, 1963; children: Sophia, Giancarlo (died, 1987), Roman. **Career:** Worked in various capacities for Roger Corman at American International, 1962-64; director for Seven Arts, 1964-68; founder, American Zoetrope production organization, San Francisco, 1969; director for American Conservatory Theatre and San Francisco Opera Company, 1971-72; founder, with Peter Bogdanovich and William Friedkin, Directors Company, 1972; publisher, *City* magazine, 1975-76; opened Zoetrope Studios, San Francisco, 1980. **Awards:** Oscar for Best Screenplay (with Edmund H. North), for *Patton,* 1970; Oscar for Best Screenplay (with Mario Puzo), and Best Director Award, Directors Guild of America, for *The Godfather,* 1973; Palme d'or, Cannes Festival, for *The Conversation,* 1974; Oscars for Best Director and Best Screenplay (with Puzo) for *The Godfather II,* 1975; Palme d'or and FIPRESCI Prize, Cannes Festival, 1979, for *Apocalypse Now,* 1979. **Address:** Zoetrope Studios, 916 Kearny Street, San Francisco, CA 94133, U.S.A.

Films as Director and Scriptwriter:

1962 *The Playgirls and the Bellboy* (co-d, co-sc); *Tonight for Sure* (+ pr);
1963 *The Terror* (*Lady of the Shadows*) (co-d, + assoc pr); *Dementia 13* (*The Haunted and the Hunted*) (co-sc)
1966 *You're a Big Boy Now*
1968 *Finian's Rainbow* (d only)
1969 *The Rain People*
1972 ***The Godfather*** (co-sc)
1974 *The Conversation* (+ pr); ***The Godfather, Part II*** (co-sc, + co-pr)
1979 ***Apocalypse Now*** (co-sc, + pr, role, co-mus)
1982 *One from the Heart* (co-sc, + pr)
1983 *The Outsiders* (+ pr); *Rumble Fish* (co-sc, + pr)
1984 *The Cotton Club* (co-sc)
1986 *Peggy Sue Got Married* (+ pr)
1987 *Gardens of Stone* (+ pr)
1988 *Tucker: The Man and His Dream* (+ pr)
1989 episode in *New York Stories*
1991 ***The Godfather, Part III***
1992 *Bram Stoker's Dracula* (+ co-pr)

Other Films:

1962 *The Premature Burial* (Corman) (asst-d); *Tower of London* (dialogue d); *The Magic Voyage of Sinbad* (adaptor)
1963 *The Young Racers* (Corman) (sound, 2nd unit ph—uncredited); *Battle Beyond the Sun* (Corman) (sc)
1966 *This Property Is Condemned* (Pollack) (co-sc); *Is Paris Burning? (Paris brûle-t-il?)* (Clément) (co-sc)
1967 *Reflections in a Golden Eye* (Huston) (sc)
1970 *Patton* (Schaffner) (co-sc)
1971 *THX 1138* (Lucas) (exec pr)
1973 ***American Graffiti*** (Lucas) (exec pr)
1974 *The Great Gatsby* (Clayton) (sc)
1979 *The Black Stallion* (Ballard) (exec pr)
1982 *Hammett* (Wenders) (exec pr); *The Escape Artist* (Deschanel) (exec pr)
1983 *The Black Stallion Returns* (Dalva) (exec pr)
1985 *Mishima: A Life in Four Chapters* (Schrader) (exec pr)
1987 *Tough Guys Don't Dance* (Mailer) (exec pr)
1992 *Wind* (exec pr)
1993 *The Secret Garden* (exec pr)
1994 *Mary Shelley's Frankenstein* (co-pr)
1995 *My Family, Mi Familia* (exec pr); *Haunted* (exec pr); *Don Juan DeMarco* (pr)

Publications

By COPPOLA: book—

The Cotton Club, with William Kennedy, New York, 1986.

By COPPOLA: articles—

"The Youth of Francis Ford Coppola," an interview with R. Koszarski, in *Films in Review* (New York), November 1968.
"The Dangerous Age," an interview with John Cutts, in *Films and Filming* (London), May 1969.
"The Making of *The Conversation,*" an interview with Brian De Palma, in *Filmmakers Newsletter* (Ward Hill, Massachusetts), May 1974.
Interview with Marjorie Rosen, in *Film Comment* (New York), August 1974.
"Journey Up the River," an interview with Greil Marcus, in *Rolling Stone* (New York), 1 November 1979.
Interview with O. Assayas, and others, in *Cahiers du Cinéma* (Paris), April 1982.
Coppola, Francis Ford, "Je me considere comme un compositeur de films," in *Cinéma* (Paris), April 1983.
"Ten Years of a Dreamer," interview with Gideon Bachmann, in *Stills* (London), September-October 1983.
"Idols of the King," an interview with D. Thomson and L. Gray, in *Film Comment* (New York), September-October 1983.
Interview in *American Film* (Washington, D. C.), June 1988.
"Francis Ford Coppola: Promises to Keep," an interview with Robert Lindsey, in *New York Times Magazine,* 24 July 1988.
Interview with Ric Gentry, in *Post Script* (Jacksonville, Florida), Spring-Summer 1987 and Fall 1988.
Interview in *Time Out* (London), 2 November 1988.
"Francis Ford Coppola," an interview with L. Vincenzi, in *Millimeter,* November 1990.
"Francis Ford Coppola," an interview with David Briskin, in *Rolling Stone* (New York), 7 February 1991.
"Lear et l'opera: entretien avec Francis Ford Coppola," an interview with Michel Ciment, in *Positif,* April 1991.
"A Conversation with Coppola," with P. Parisi, in *American Cinematographer,* August 1991.
"Dracula Doesn't Scare Coppola," an interview with Janet Maslin, in *New York Times,* 15 November 1992.
"His Bloody Valentine," an interview with M. Dargis, in *Village Voice* (New York), 24 November 1992.

On COPPOLA: books—

Johnson, Robert, *Francis Ford Coppola,* Boston, 1977.
Coppola, Eleanor, *Notes: On Apocalypse Now,* New York, 1979.
Pye, Michael, and Lynda Myles, *The Movie Brats: How the Film Generation Took over Hollywood,* New York, 1979.
Chaillet, Jean-Paul, and Elizabeth Vincent, *Francis Ford Coppola,* Paris, 1984, New York, 1984.
Zuker, Joel S., *Francis Ford Coppola: A Guide to References and Resources,* Boston, 1984.
Frundt, Bodo, et al., *Francis Ford Coppola,* Munich, 1985.
Chown, Jeffrey, *Hollywood Auteur: Francis Coppola,* New York, 1988.

Cowie, Peter, *Coppola: A Biography,* London, 1989, revised edition, New York, 1994.
Goodwin, Michael, and Namoi Wise, *On the Edge: The Life and Times of Francis Coppola,* New York, 1989.
Biskind, Peter, *The Godfather Companion,* New York, 1990.
Lewis, Jon, *Whom God Wishes to Destroy...: Francis Coppola and the New Hollywood,* Durham, North Carolina, 1995.

On COPPOLA: articles—

Taylor, John Russell, "Francis Ford Coppola," in *Sight and Sound* (London), Winter 1968/69.
McGillivray, D., "Francis Ford Coppola," in *Focus on Film* (London), Autumn 1972.
Pearce, Christopher, "San Francisco's Own American Zoetrope," in *American Cinematographer* (Los Angeles), October 1972.
Braudy, Susan, "Francis Ford Coppola: A Profile," in *Atlantic Monthly* (Boston), August 1976.
Bock, Audie, "Zoetrope and *Apocalypse Now,*" in *American Film* (Washington, D.C.), September 1979.
McGilligan, Patrick, "Coppola on the Beat," in *Films and Filming* (London), December 1981.
Bygrave, M., and J. Goodman, "Meet Me in Las Vegas," in *American Film* (Washington, D.C.), October 1981.
Myles, Lynda, "The Zoetrope Saga," in *Sight and Sound* (London), Spring 1982.
Benayoun, Robert, and others, "Le chat et la pendule," in *Positif* (Paris), April 1984.
Krohn, B., "Coppola des studios Zoetrope aux studios Astorias," in *Cahiers du Cinema* (Paris), December 1984.
Greene, N., "Coppola, Cimino: The Operatics of History," in *Film Quarterly* (Los Angeles), Winter 1984/85.
"Coppola Section," in *Positif* (Paris), February 1985.
"The Backdrop Is Only an Inch Away," in *Monthly Film Bulletin* (London), June 1985.
Turnquist, K., "Grape Expectations," in *American Film* (Washington, D.C.), November 1985.
Braudy, Leo, "The Sacraments of Genre: Coppola, De Palma, Scorsese," in *Film Quarterly* (Los Angeles), Spring 1986.
Post Script (Jacksonville, Florida), Spring-Summer 1987.
Kolker, Robert, "Francis Coppola," in *A Cinema of Loneliness: Penn, Kubrick, Coppola, Scorsese,* New York, 1988.
Phillips, Gene, "Francis Coppola," in *Films in Review* (New York), March 1989.
Lourdeaux, Lee, "Francis Ford Coppola," in *Italian and Irish Filmmakers in America: Ford, Capra, Coppola, Scorsese,* Philadelphia, 1990.
Bookbinder, Robert, "*The Godfather, The Godfather, Part II,*" in *The Films of the Seventies,* New York, 1990.
Grant, Edmond, "*Godfather III,*" in *Films in Review* (New York), March-April 1991.
Bawer, Bruce, "*Peggy Sue Got Married,*" in *The Screenplay's the Thing,* Hamden, Connecticut, 1992.
Cahir, Linda, "Narratological Parallels in Conrad's *Heart of Darkness* and Coppola's *Apocalypse Now,*" in *Literature/Film Quarterly* (Salisbury, Maryland), Summer 1992.
Greiff, Louis, "Conrad's Ethics and Margins of *Apocalypse Now,*" in *Literature/Film Quarterly* (Salisbury, Maryland), Summer 1992.
Ehrenstein, David, "One from the Art: *Dracula,*" in *Film Comment* (New York), January-February 1993.
Norman, Barry, "*The Godfather, The Godfather, Part II,*" in *The 100 Best Films of the Century,* New York, 1993.
Kael, Pauline, "*The Godfather, The Godfather, Part II,*" in *For Keeps,* New York, 1994.
Whalen, Tom, "Romancing Film: Images of *Dracula,*" in *Literature/Film Quarterly* (Salisbury, Maryland), Spring 1995.
Fitzgerald, Frances, "*Apocalypse Now,*" in *Past Imperfect: History According to the Movies,* edited by Mark Carnes, New York, 1995.
Phillips, Gene, "Darkness at Noon: *Apocalypse Now,*" in *Conrad and Cinema: The Art of Adaptation,* New York, 1995.

On COPPOLA: film—

Hearts of Darkness: A Filmmaker's Apocalypse (TV special), 1991.

* * *

Francis Ford Coppola became the first major American film director to emerge from a university degree program in filmmaking. He received his Master of Cinema degree from UCLA in 1968, after submitting his first film of consequence, *You're a Big Boy Now* (1967), a free-wheeling comedy about a young man on the brink of manhood, to the university as his master's thesis.

The Rain People (1969), based on an original scenario of his own, followed in due course. The plot of this tragic drama concerns a depressed housewife who impulsively decides to walk out on her family one rainy morning to make a cross-country trek in her station wagon, in the hope of getting some perspective on her life. For the first time Coppola's overriding theme, which centers on the importance of the role of a family spirit in people's lives, is clearly delineated in one of his films.

Coppola's preoccupation with the importance of family in modern society is brought into relief in his *Godfather* films, which depict an American family over a period of more than seventy years. Indeed, the thing that most attracted him to the project in the first place was the fact that the best-selling book on which the films are based is really the story of a family. It is about "this father and his sons," he says, "and questions of power and succession." In essence, *The Godfather* (1972) offers a chilling depiction of the way in which young Michael Corleone's loyalty to his flesh-and-blood family gradually turns into an allegiance to the larger Mafia family to which they in turn belong—a devotion that in the end renders him a cruel and ruthless mass murderer. With this film Coppola definitely hit his stride as a filmmaker, and the picture was an enormous critical and popular success.

The Godfather II (1974) treats events that happened before and after the action covered in the first film. The second *Godfather* movie not only chronicles Michael's subsequent career as head of the "family business," but also presents, in flashback, the early life of his father in Sicily, as well as his rise to power in the Mafia in New York City's Little Italy. *The Godfather II,* like *The Godfather,* was a success both with the critics and the public, and Coppola won Oscars for directing the film, co-authoring the screenplay, and co-producing the best picture of the year. In 1990 he made his third *Godfather* film. This trilogy of movies, taken together, represents one of the supreme achievements of the cinematic art.

In contrast to epic films like the *Godfather* series, *The Outsiders* was conceived on a smaller scale; it revolves around a gang of underprivileged teenage boys growing up in Tulsa, Oklahoma, in the 1960s. *The Outsiders* was a box-office hit, as was *Peggy Sue Got Married,* a remarkable fantasy. The title character is a woman approaching middle age who passes out at a high-school reunion and wakes up back in high school in 1960. But she brings with her on her trip down memory lane a forty-two-year-old mind, and hence views things from a more mature perspective than she possessed the first time around.

Coppola has made two films about the Vietnam War. *Apocalypse Now,* the first major motion picture about the war, is a king-sized epic shot on location in the Philippines; and it contains some of the most extraordinary combat footage ever filmed. But there are no such stunning battle sequences in its companion film, *Gardens of Stone,*

Francis Ford Coppola (right) directing Marlon Brando in *Apocalypse Now*

since it takes place state-side, and is concerned with the homefront during the same period.

His next subject was a biographical film about Preston Tucker, a maverick automobile designer, entitled *Tucker: The Man and His Dream.* Coppola contends that Tucker developed plans for a car that was way ahead of its time in terms of engineering; yet the auto industry at large stubbornly resisted his ideas. Unfortunately, Coppola comments, creative people do not always get a chance to exercise their creativity.

Coppola demonstrated once more that he had mastered his craft in making *Bram Stoker's Dracula.* In it he created a more faithful rendering of the Stoker novel than had been the case with previous film versions of the celebrated horror tale, and the film turned out to be a huge critical and popular success.

Francis Coppola is one creative person who has continued to exercise his considerable talent throughout his career. Admittedly, he has had his occasional failure, such as the off-center teen movie *Rumble Fish* (1983). But the majority of the films he has directed over the years have demonstrated that he is one of the most gifted directors to come across the Hollywood horizon since Stanley Kubrick.

Coppola himself observes that he looks upon the movies he has directed in the past as providing him with the sort of experience that will help him to make better films in the future. So the only thing for a filmmaker to do, he concludes, is to just keep going.

—Gene D. Phillips

CORMAN, Roger

Nationality: American. **Born:** Roger William Corman in Detroit, Michigan, 5 April 1926. **Education:** Attended Beverly Hills High School; Stanford University, California, engineering degree; Oxford University, one term, 1950. **Military Service:** Served in United States Navy during World War II. **Family:** Married Julie Halloran, 1969, one daughter, two sons. **Career:** Messenger boy, Twentieth Century-Fox, then television stagehand and literary agent, Hollywood, early 1950s; scriptwriter and producer, then director and producer, mainly for American International Pictures (AIP), from 1953; directed first film, *Guns West,* 1954; founder and director of production and distribution company New World Pictures, 1970-83; founded production company New Horizons Pictures, 1983, and distribution company Concorde, 1985; set up Brentwood TV company, 1990. **Address:** c/o New Horizons Production Company, 11600 San Vicente Boulevard, Los Angeles, California 90049, U.S.A.

Films as Producer and Director:

1954 *Guns West*
1955 *Apache Woman*; *Day the World Ended*
1956 *The Oklahoma Woman*; *It Conquered the World*; *Gunslinger*; *Swamp Woman*; *The Undead*

1957 *She-Gods of Shark Reef (Shark Reef); Naked Paradise; Not of This Earth; Rock All Night; Attack of the Crab Monsters; Carnival Rock; Teenage Doll; Sorority Girl (The Bad One); The Saga of the Viking Women and Their Voyage to the Waters of the Great Sea Serpent (Viking Women and the Sea Serpent; Viking Women)*
1958 *War of the Satellites* (+ role); *Machine Gun Kelly; Teenage Caveman (Out of the Darkness); I, Mobster (The Mobster); Last Woman on Earth* (+ role)
1959 *The Wasp Woman* (+ role); *A Bucket of Blood*
1960 *Ski Troop Attack* (+ role); *The Fall of the House of Usher (House of Usher); The Little Shop of Horrors* (+ role); *Creature from the Haunted Sea* (+ role); *Atlas*
1961 *Pit and the Pendulum; The Intruder (I Hate Your Guts)*
1962 *The Premature Burial; Tales of Terror; Tower of London*
1963 *The Raven; The Young Racers* (+ role); *The Haunted Palace; The Terror; X (The Man with the X-Ray Eyes)*
1964 *The Secret Invasion*; **The Masque of the Red Death**; *The Tomb of Ligeia*
1966 *The Wild Angels*
1967 *The St. Valentine's Day Massacre*
1969 *What's In It for Harry* (for TV)
1970 *Gass-s-s-s, or It Became Necessary to Destroy the World in Order to Save It*
1971 *Von Richthofen and Brown (The Red Baron)*
1989 *Frankenstein Unbound*

Films as Producer or Executive Producer:

1954 *Highway Dragnet* (Juran) (+ co-sc); *Monster from the Ocean Floor* (Ordung); *The Fast and the Furious* (Ireland and Sampson)
1955 *Beast with 1,000,000 Eyes* (Kramarsky)
1958 *Stake Out on Dope Street* (Kershner); *The Cry Baby* (Addiss); *Monster from Galaxy 27* (Kowalski); *Hot Car Girl* (Kowalski); *Night of the Blood Beast* (Kowalski); *The Brain Eaters* (Ve Sota); *Paratroop Command* (Witney); *The Wild Ride* (Berman)
1959 *Tank Commando (Tank Commandos)* (Topper); *Crime and Punishment U.S.A.* (Sanders); *High School Big Shot (The Young Sinners)* (Rapp); *Attack of the Giant Leeches (Demons of the Swamp)* (Kowalski); *Beast from a Haunted Cave* (Hellman); *T-Bird Gang (The Pay-Off)* (Harbinger); *Battle of Blood Island* (Rapp)
1961 *Night Tide* (Harrington); *The Mermaids of Tiburon (Aquasex)* (Lamb)
1962 *The Magic Voyage of Sinbad* (Posco) (re-edited version of Ptuschko's 1952 film *Sadko*); *Battle beyond the Sun* (Colchart) (re-edited version of Kozyr and Karyukov's 1960 film *Nebo zovet/The Heavens Call*)
1963 *Dementia (The Haunted and the Hunted)* (Coppola)
1965 *The Girls on the Beach* (Witney); *Sky Party* (Rafkin); *Beach Ball* (Weinrib); *The Shooting* (Hellman); *Ride in the Whirlwind* (Hellman); *Blood Bath* (Hill and Rothman)
1966 *Queen of Blood* (Harrington)
1967 *Targets* (Bogdanovich); *Devil's Angels* (Haller)
1969 *The Dunwich Horror* (Haller); *Naked Angels* (Clark); *Pit Stop* (Hill); *Paddy* (Haller)
1970 *Student Nurses* (Rothman); *Angels Die Hard!* (Compton)
1971 *Angels Hard as They Come* (Viola); *Women in Cages* (de Leon); *Private Duty Nurses* (Armitage); *The Big Doll House* (Hill); *The Velvet Vampire* (Rothman)
1972 *The Final Comedown* (Williams); *Boxcar Bertha* (Scorsese); *The Big Bird Cage* (Hill); *The Unholy Rollers* (Zimmerman); *Night Call Nurses* (Kaplan); *Fly Me* (Santiago); *The Young Nurses* (Kimbro); *The Hot Box* (Viola); *Night of the Cobra Woman* (Meyer)
1973 *I Escaped from Devil's Island* (Meyer); *The Arena* (Carver); *The Student Teachers* (Kaplan); *Tender Loving Care (Naughty Nurses)* (Edmonds)
1974 *Cheap* (Swenson); *Candy Stripe Nurses* (Holleb); *Cockfighter (Born to Kill)* (Hellman); *Big Bad Mama* (Carver); *Caged Heat* (Demme); *TNT Jackson* (Santiago); *Street Girls* (Miller); *The Woman Hunt* (Romero)
1975 *Capone* (Carver); *Death Race 2000* (Bartel); *Crazy Mama* (Demme); *Summer School Teachers* (Peeters); *Dark Town Strutters* (Witney); *Cover Girl Models* (Santiago)
1976 *Hollywood Boulevard* (Arkush and Dante); *Fighting Mad* (Demme); *Cannonball (Carquake)* (Bartel); *Jackson County Jail* (Miller); *Nashville Girl (New Girl in Town)* (Trikonis); *Moving Violation* (Dubin); *God Told Me To* (Demon) (Cohen); *Dynamite Women (The Great Texas Dynamite Chase)* (Pressman); *Eat My Dust!* (Wilson)
1977 *Black Oak Conspiracy* (Kelljan); *Grand Theft Auto* (Howard); *I Never Promised You a Rose Garden* (Page); *Thunder and Lightning* (Allen); *Andy Warhol's Bad* (Johnson); *Moonshine County Express* (Trikonis); *Dirty Duck* (Swenson); *Maniac (Assault on Paradise)* (Compton); *A Hero Ain't Nothin' But a Sandwich* (Nelson)
1978 *Deathsport* (Suso and Arkush); *Piranha* (Dante); *Avalanche* (Allen); *Outside Chance* (Miller); *The Bees* (Zacharias)
1979 *Rock 'n' Roll High School* (Arkush); *Saint Jack* (Bogdanovich)
1980 *Battle beyond the Stars* (Colchart)
1981 *Smokey Bites the Dust* (Griffith); *Galaxy of Terror* (Clark)
1982 *Forbidden World* (Holzman)
1983 *Star Child* (Cohne); *Space Raiders* (Howard Cohen); *Suburbia* (Spheeris); *Warrior and the Sorceress* (Broderick)
1984 *Love Letters* (Jones); *Deathstalker* (John Watson)
1985 *Barbarian Queen* (Oliveira); *Streetwalkin'* (Freeman)
1986 *Cocaine Wars* (Oliveira), *Big Bad Mama II* (Wynorski)
1987 *Munchies* (Hirsch); *Stripped to Kill* (Ruben); *The Lawless Land* (Hess); *Amazons* (Sessa); *Slumber Party Massacre* (Amy Jones); *Hour of the Assassin* (Llosa); *Sweet Revenge* (Sobel)
1988 *The Drifter* (Brand); *Daddy's Boys* (Minion); *Half Life* (Ruben); *Saturday the 14th Strikes Back* (Howard Cohen); *Nightfall* (Mayersberg); *Dangerous Love* (Ollstein); *Watchers* (Hess)
1989 *Two to Tango* (Oliveira); *Crime Zone* (Llosa); *Stripped to Kill* (Shea Ruben); *Dance of the Damned* (Shea Ruben); *The Terror Within* (Notz); *Time Trackers* (Howard Cohen); *Bloodfist* (Winkless); *Masque of the Red Death* (Brand); *Wizards of the Lost Kingdom II* (Griffith); *Heroes Stand Alone* (Griffiths); *Transylvania Twist* (Wynorski)
1990 *Overexposed* (Brand); *Streets* (Shea Ruben); *Morella* (Wynorski); *Cry in the Wild* (Griffiths); *Back to Back* (Kincade); *Primary Target* (Henderson); *Watchers II* (Notz); *Silk 2* (Santiago); *Full Fathom Five* (Franklin); *Bloodfist II* (Blumenthal)
1991 *Terror Within II* (Stevens); *Hollywood Boulevard* (Dante and Arkush); *Rock 'n' Roll High School Forever* (Feldman); *Futurekick* (Klaus)
1992 *Play Murder for Me* (Oliveira); *Eye of the Eagle 3* (Santiago); *In the Heat of Passion* (Flender); *Deathstalker 4* (Hill); *Bloodfist 3* (Sassone); *Immortal Sins* (Hachuel); *Berlin Conspiracy* (Winkless); *Field of Fire* (Santiago); *Dance with Death* (Moore); *Ultra Violet* (Griffiths); *Bodywaves* (Pesce); *Blackbelt* (C.P. Moore); *Sorority House Massacre 2* (Wynorski); *Munchie* (Wynorski); *Body Chemistry 2* (Simon); *Assassination Game* (Winfrey); *Final Embrace* (Sassone); *Homicidal Impulse* (Tausik); *Bloodfist 4* (Ziller)

1993 *Firehawk* (Santiago); *To Sleep with a Vampire* (Friedman); *Stepmonster* (Stanford); *Dracula Rising* (Gallo); *Carnosaur* (Simon); *800 Leagues down the Amazon* (Llosa); *Live by the Fist* (Santiago); *Dragonfire* (Jacobson)
1994 *Cheyenne Warrior* (Griffiths); *Unborn 2* (Jacobson); *Watchers 3* (Stanford); *In the Heat of Passion II* (Cyran); *Reflections in the Dark* (Purdy)
1995 *Carnosaur 2* (Morneau); *Spy Within* (Railsback); *Crazysitter* (McDonald); *Dillinger and Capone* (Purdy)

Other Films:

1967 *A Time for Killing* (*The Long Ride Home*) (Karlson) (uncredited co-d); *Wild Racers* (Haller) (uncredited 2nd unit d)
1969 *De Sade* (Enfield) (uncredited co-d)
1974 ***The Godfather, Part II*** (Coppola) (role)
1980 *The Howling* (Dante) (role)
1983 *Der Stand der Dinge* (*The State of Things*) (Wenders) (role)
1984 *Swing Shift* (Demme) (role)
1991 ***Silence of the Lambs*** (Demme) (role as FBI Director Hayden Burke)
1993 ***Philadelphia*** (Demme) (role as Mr. Laird)
1995 *Apollo 13* (Howard) (role as Congressman)

Publications

By CORMAN: book—

How I Made a Hundred Movies in Hollywood and Never Lost a Dime, with Jim Jerome, New York, 1990.

By CORMAN: articles—

Sight and Sound (London), Summer 1963.
Midi-Minuit Fantastique (Paris), no. 10-11, 1965.
Image et Son (Paris), March 1967.
"A Letter from Roger Corman," in *Take One* (Montreal), July-August 1968.
Interview in *The Film Director as Superstar,* by Joseph Gelmis, New York, 1970.
Interview with Joe Medjuck, in *Take One* (Montreal), July-August 1970.
Interview with Philip Strick, in *Sight and Sound* (London), Autumn 1970.
Interview with Charles Goldman, in *Film Comment* (New York), Fall 1971.
Séquences (Montreal), October 1974.
Millimeter (New York), December 1975.
Interview with Bill Davidson, in *New York Times Magazine,* 28 December 1975.
Interview in *Journal of Popular Film* (Washington, D.C.), vol. 5, no. 3-4, 1976.
Interview in *Cahiers du Cinéma* (Paris), January 1979.
Interviews in *Ecran Fantastique* (Paris), no. 18, 1981, and May 1984.
Interview in *Films and Filming* (London), November 1984.
Interview with Robin Wood and Richard Lippe, in *Movie* (London), Winter 1986.
Interview in *Film Comment* (New York), July-August 1988.

On CORMAN: books—

Willemen, Paul, David Pirie, David Will, and Lynda Myles, *Roger Corman: The Millenic Vision,* Edinburgh, 1970.
McCarthy, Todd, and Charles Flynn, editors, *King of the Bs,* New York, 1975.
Turroni, Guiseppe, *Roger Corman,* Florence, 1976.
di Franco, J. Philip, *The Movie World of Roger Corman,* New York, 1979.
Hillier, Jim, and Aaron Lipstadt, *Roger Corman's New World,* London, 1981.
Naha, Ed, *The Films of Roger Corman,* New York, 1982.
Bourgoin, Stéphane, *Roger Corman,* Paris, 1983.
McGee, Mark Thomas, *The Story of American International Pictures,* Jefferson, North Carolina, 1984.
Morris, Gary, *Roger Corman,* Boston, 1985.
Ottoson, Robert, *American International Pictures,* New York and London, 1985.
McGee, Mark Thomas, *Roger Corman: The Best of the Cheap Acts,* Jefferson, North Carolina, 1988.
Ray, Fred Olen, *The New Poverty Row,* Jefferson, North Carolina, 1991.

On CORMAN: articles—

Monthly Film Bulletin (London), vol. 31, 1964.
Positif (Paris), March 1964.
Dyer, Peter John, "Z Films" in *Sight and Sound* (London), Autumn 1964.
Midi-Minuit Fantastique (Paris), no. 1, 1965.
Film (London), no. 43, 1965.
French, Philip, "Incitement against Violence" in *Sight and Sound* (London), Winter 1967-68.
Wallace, Eric in *Screen Education* (London), July-August 1968.
Jeune Cinéma (Paris), February 1969.
Action (Los Angeles), July-August 1969.
Montage (London), April 1970.
Diehl, Digby, in *Show* (New York), May 1970.
Ecran Fantastique (Paris), December 1970.
Koszarski, Richard, in *Film Comment* (New York), Fall 1971.
Ciné Revue (Paris), 5 February 1976.
National Film Theatre booklets (London), December 1976 and January 1977.
Avant-Scène (Paris), 15 May 1980.
National Film Theatre booklet (London), February 1981.
Chute, David, in *Film Comment* (New York), March-April 1982.
"Corman Issue" of *Cinema Nuovo* (Turin), January-February 1984.
Goldstein, Patrick, in *American Film* (Washington, D.C.) January-February 1985.
Newman, Kim, "The Roger Corman Alumni Association," in *Monthly Film Bulletin* (London), November and December 1985.
Strick, Philip, "The Return of Roger Corman," in *Films and Filming* (London), March 1986.
Hillier, Jim, and Aaron Lipstadt, "The Economics of Independence: Roger Corman and New World Pictures 1970-80," in *Movie* (London), Winter 1986.
Hollywood Reporter, 26 March 1987.
Exline, P., "King of the B's," in *American Film* (Washington, D.C.), September 1987.
Dixon, W., article in *Postscript* (Commerce, Texas), Fall 1988.
Bourgoin, S., and F. Guerif, article in *Revue du Cinéma* (Paris), September 1989.
Garsault, A., article in *Positif* (France), February 1990.
Solman, G., "Roger Corman," in *Millimeter,* May 1990.
Peary, Gerald, "Roger Corman: They Call Him Cheap, Quick, and 'America's Greatest Independent Filmmaker,'" in *American Film,* June 1990.
Combs, R., article in *Sight and Sound* (London), Winter 1990/91.
Pede, R., and D. DuFour, article in *Film en Televisie* (Bruxelles, Belgium), May-June 1991.
Bohlin, L., and L. Holmstrom, article in *Filmrutan* (Sweden), 1992.
Jousse, T., and N. Saada, article in *Cahiers du Cinema* (Paris), January 1993.

Roger Corman

On CORMAN: film—

The Roger Corman Special (for TV), 1995.

* * *

Grand master and patron saint of the American exploitation film, Roger Corman has forged a reputation for creative filmmaking on means so minimal as to seem absurd. He began his career in the mid-1950s producing and directing Westerns, gangster movies, mythological "spectacles," teen pictures, and sci-fi/horror films distinguished largely by their five-digit budgets and shooting schedules as short as three days. By the early 1960s his business savvy and understanding of the developing "youth" market had made him the most valuable commodity at American International Pictures, and his shrewd innovations in production and distribution contributed substantially to that company's pre-eminence in the exploitation market.

Backhandedly dubbed by critics "the King of Schlock" and "the Orson Welles of Z-Pictures," Corman has become a symbol of the creativity available to those willing to accept the economic limitations of working outside the mainstream. As a producer, he was able to provide decisive career breaks for a number of actors (Jack Nicholson, Ellen Burstyn, Robert De Niro, Cindy Williams), screenwriters (Robert Towne), and directors (Francis Ford Coppola, Peter Bogdanovich, Martin Scorsese, Jonathan Demme) who were to rise toward the upper echelons of the New Hollywood. Meanwhile, Corman insisted on maintaining his own kingdom on the fringes. When AIP's growing budgets and pretenses began to tighten studio control over individual projects, Corman left and, in 1970, established his own studio, New World Pictures, which quickly usurped AIP's place in the exploitation field. Corman did not direct at New World, but instead exerted a decisive influence as producer, cultivating the drive-in/inner-city audience by developing specialized sub-genres (women's prison pictures; soft-core nurse/teacher films; hard-core action and horror movies) and a strict formula, requiring given amounts of violence, nudity, humor, and social commentary. The social element not only reflected Corman's own attitudes (a self-characterized "liberal to radical" politically, he independently financed his anti-racist *The Intruder* when no studio would put up the money), but also an understanding of the politically disfranchised groups which comprised the New World audience. At the same time, Corman used the company to provide some of the first intelligent American marketing of foreign "art films," accruing respectable successes with Bergman's *Cries and Whispers,* Fellini's *Amarcord,* Truffaut's *Adele H.,* and Kurosawa's *Dersu Uzala.*

Yet it would not be quite fair to dismiss Corman, as Andrew Sarris did in 1968, as a producer "miscast" as a director. Admittedly, at that time Corman's most accomplished, complex, and disturbing film, *Bloody Mama,* was still to be made. But Corman had hit his artistic stride in the early 1960s with a series of seven flamboyantly artificial color horror films, loosely based on Poe and ranging in tone from slightly tongue-in-cheek to openly parodic. The cycle peaked with *Masque of the Red Death,* which made ingenious use of imagery borrowed from Bergman's *Seventh Seal,* to the disbelief of American critics and the delight of the Europeans, who have always seemed willing to take Corman fairly seriously. Indeed, even in the 1950s Corman had learned to make artistic virtue of low-budget tawdriness, which contributed greatly to the existential bleakness of such tortured morality plays as *Teenage Doll* and *Sorority Girl,* and to the essential minimalism of the definitive black comedies *Bucket of Blood* and *Little Shop of Horrors.* Yet, even if one is unwilling to recognize the philosophical despair of the moralist struggling against nihilism which underlies the straight-faced lunacy of *It Conquered the World,* the visionary metaphysics of *X (The Man with the X-Ray Eyes),* and even the Urbiker picture of the 1960s, *The Wild Angels,* Corman's audacious independence has at least earned him the right to symbolize the myriad contradictions between artistic ambition and fiscal responsibility which seem inherent to commercial filmmaking.

Circumstances caused Corman to put his directorial career in the deep freeze in 1971. A rare foray into TV with *What's in It for Harry* (1969) had resulted in a film rejected as too violent by ABC, which released the film theatrically without a Corman credit. Studio interference with his youth movement paean, *Gas-s-s-s* (1970), eased his break with long-term home-base AIP, but he fared even worse when United Artists slashed his pet World War I drama, *Von Richthofen and Brown* (1971), into unrecognizability. It was critical savagery of the latter that drove him to assume mogul status full-time by forming New World Pictures, where he served as mentor to Ron Howard, Jonathan Kaplan, John Sayles, and Joe Dante, among others.

After selling New World Pictures in 1983 and then suing the purchasers for reneging on a distribution agreement, Corman returned to the pre-sold production whirl with a new outfit, Concorde/New Horizons. Although Corman is still a vital, hands-on moviemaker and a godsend to untried auteurs, his current product is indistinguishable from other direct-to-video fodder. In addition to expanding into family escapism and sexploitation noirs, Corman has been remaking his AIP classics for Showtime, along with some cable-TV originals like *Runaway Daughters* and *Suspect Device,* but none of these Cormanized revamps and remakes demonstrates the verve of the compact originals.

Cleverly conceived and infused with an undertow of nostalgic tristesse, Corman's directorial comeback, *Frankenstein Unbound,* is truly a monster movie for the backward-glancing 1990s. Responsible for precipitating an apocalypse in the future through his unchecked experimentations, a scientist travels back to the nineteenth century, where he tries to bridle Victor Frankenstein's excesses as a *mea culpa* for his own God-complex.

A cinematic Victor Frankenstein, Corman goes on robbing genre graveyards to bring new life to exploitation filmmaking. While Corman is irreplaceable as a studio chief, his *Frankenstein Unbound* is idiosyncratic enough to raise hopes for an occasional slumming into personal expression. An unselfish artist with a healthy respect for profits, Corman genuinely gets gratification out of his hired guns' success stories, and this shining example of vicarious creativity may be the only producer in Hollywood history who could be considered a father figure. As a cinematic icon, Corman's cameo appearances in his protegee's blockbusters like *Godfather: Part Two, Philadelphia,* and *Apollo 13* reveal a soft-spoken, mysterious man with immense powers of focus; he looks like the archetypical American loner who simply gets the job done.

—Ed Lowry, updated by Robert J. Pardi

COSTA-GAVRAS, Constantin

Nationality: French. **Born:** Konstantinos Gavras in Athens, Greece, on February 13, 1933 (naturalized French citizen, 1956). **Education:** the Sorbonne, Paris, and Institut des Hautes Etudes Cinématographiques. **Family:** Married Michèle Ray, 1968, one son, one daughter. **Career:** Ballet dancer in Greece, then moved to Paris, 1952; assistant to Yves Allegret, René Clair, René Clément, Henri Verneuil, and Jacques Demy, 1958-65; became naturalized French citizen, 1956; directed first film, *Compartiment tueurs,* 1966; became president of the Cinematheque Francais, 1982. **Awards:** Moscow Film Festival Prize for *Un Homme de trop;* Best Director, New York Film Critics Award, and Jury Prize, Cannes Festival, for *Z,* 1970; Oscar nominations for Best Director and Best Screenplay, for *Z,* 1970; Louis Delluc Prize for *State of Siege,*

Constantin Costa-Gavras © Andy Lane

1973; Best Director Award, Cannes Festival, for *Special Section,* 1975; Palme d'or, Cannes Festival, 1982, and Oscar for Best Screenplay (with Donald Stewart), for *Missing,* 1983; ACLUF Award for *Betrayed,* 1988. **Agent:** John Ptak, William Morris Agency, 151 El Camino Drive, Beverly Hills, CA 90212, U.S.A.

Films as Director and Scriptwriter:

1966 *Compartiment tueurs* (*The Sleeping Car Murders*)
1968 *Un Homme de trop* (*Shock Troops*)
1969 ***Z*** (co-sc)
1970 *L'Aveu* (*The Confession*)
1973 *Etat de siège* (*State of Siege*) (co-sc)
1975 *Section speciale* (*Special Section*) (co-sc)
1979 *Clair de femme* (*Womanlight*)
1982 *Missing* (co-sc)
1983 *Hanna K* (co-sc, + pr)
1985 *Family Business*
1988 *Summer Lightning* (*Sundown*); *Betrayed* (d only)
1990 *Music Box* (d only)
1993 *La Petite Apocalypse* (*The Minor Apocalypse*) (co-sc)
1995 *Les kankobals*, episode in *A propos de Nice, la suite*

Other Films:

1977 *La Vie devant soi* (*Madame Rosa*) (Mizrahi) (role as Ramon)
1985 *Spies Like Us* (Landis) (role as Tadzhik); *Thé au harem d'Archimede* (*Tea in the Harem*) (sc)

Publications

By COSTA-GAVRAS: articles—

"Costa-Gavras Talks," an interview with Dan Georgakas and Gary Crowdus, in *Take One* (Montreal), July/August 1969.
Interview with David Austen, in *Films and Filming* (London), June 1970.
"A Film is Like a Match: You Can Make a Big Fire or Nothing at All," an interview with H. Kalishman and Gary Crowdus, in *Cineaste* (New York), vol. 6, no. 1, 1973.
"Constantin Costa-Gavras: An American Film Institute Seminar on His Work," 1977.
Interview with F. Guerif and S. Levy-Klein, in *Cahiers de la Cinémathèque* (Perpignan), Spring/Summer 1978.
Interview with John Pilger, in *Time Out* (London), 8 December 1983.
"There's Always a Point of View," an interview with Dan Georgakas, in *Cineaste* (New York), vol. 16, no. 4, 1988.
Interview in *Film Comment* (New York), July-August 1988.
"Direct Action," an interview with Andrew Kopkind, in *Interview* (New York), September 1988.
"Constantin Costa-Gavras: Politics at the Box Office," an interview with Claudia Dreifus, in *The Progressive,* September 1988.

Interview in *La Revue du Cinema* (Paris), November 1988.
"Keeping Alive the Memory of the Holocaust," an interview with Gary Crowdus, in *Cineaste* (New York), February 1990.
"Black and White Movies," an interview with Sheila Johnston, in *Independent* (London), 31 May 1990

On COSTA-GAVRAS: books—

Solinas, Franco, *State of Siege,* (includes articles), New York, 1973.
Michalczyk, John J., *Costa-Gavras: The Political Fiction Film,* Philadelphia, 1984.

On COSTA-GAVRAS: articles—

Sauvaget, D., and others, "A propos de Costa-Gavras," in *Image et Son* (Paris), December 1977.
Crowdus, G., and L. Rubenstein, "The *Missing* Dossier," in *Cineaste* (New York), vol. 12, no. 1, 1982.
Wood, M., "In Search of the Missing," in *American Film* (Washington, D.C.), March 1982.
Yakir, Dan, "*Missing* in Action," in *Film Comment* (New York), March/April 1982.
Camy, G., "Costa-Gavras: Pour un certain cinéma politique," in *Jeune Cinéma* (Paris), November 1983.
Johnston, Sheila, "Costa-Gavras," in *Sight and Sound* (London), Summer 1984.
Clark, T., "Cinematheque Broadens Its Horizons," in *Variety* (New York), 1 October 1986.
"Colleagues Attack Costa-Gavras for Pic Archive Stand," in *Variety* (New York), 4 February 1987.
"4 Who've Made It," in *Variety* (New York), 25 October 1989.
Dargis, M., "Crimes of the Heart," in *Village Voice* (New York), 17 April 1990.
Crawley, T., "A Hellene in Gaul and a U.S. Favorite," in *Variety* (New York), 2 May 1990.
"Costa-Gavras Strikes a Match," in *New Yorker* (New York), 19 June 1995.

* * *

The films of Constantin Costa-Gavras are exciting, enthralling, superior examples of dramatic moviemaking, but the filmmaker is far from being solely concerned with keeping the viewer in suspense. A Greek exile when he made *Z,* set in the country of his birth, Costa-Gavras is most interested in the motivations and misuses of power: politically, he may be best described as an anti-fascist, a humanist. As such, his films are as overtly political as any above-ground, internationally popular and respected filmmaker in history.

Costa-Gavras's scenarios are often based on actual events in which citizens are deprived of human rights and expose the hypocrisies of governments to both the left and right of center. In *Z,* Greek pacifist leader Yves Montand is killed by a speeding truck, a death ruled accidental by the police. Journalist Jean-Louis Trintignant's investigation leads to a right-wing reign of terror against witnesses and friends of the deceased, and to revelations of a government scandal. *The Confession* is the story of a Communist bureaucrat (Montand) who is unjustifiably tortured and coerced into giving false testimony against other guiltless comrades. *State of Siege* is based on the political kidnapping of a United States official in Latin America (Montand); the revolutionaries slowly discover the discreetly hidden function of this "special advisor"—to train native police in the intricacies of torture. In *Special Section,* a quartet of young Frenchmen are tried and condemned by an opportunistic Vichy government for the killing of a German naval officer in occupied Paris. In *Missing,* an idealistic young American writer (John Shea) is arrested, tortured, and killed in a fascist takeover of a Latin American country. His father, salt-of-the-earth businessman Jack Lemmon, first feels it's all a simple misunderstanding. After he realizes that he has been manipulated and lied to by the American embassy, he applies enough pressure and embarrasses enough people so that he can finally bring home the body of his son.

Despite these sobering, decidedly non-commercial storylines, Costa-Gavras has received popular as well as critical success, particularly with *Z* and *Missing,* because the filmmaker does not bore his audience by structuring his films in a manner that will appeal only to intellectuals. Instead, he casts popular actors with significant box office appeal. Apart from a collective message—that fascism and corruption may occur in any society anywhere in the world—Costa-Gavras's films also work as mysteries and thrillers. He has realized that he must first entertain in order to bring his point of view to a wider, more diversified audience, as well as exist and even thrive within the boundaries of motion picture economics in the Western world. As Pauline Kael so aptly noted, *Z* is "something very unusual in European films—a political film with a purpose and, at the same time, a thoroughly commercial film." Costa-Gavras, however, is not without controversy: *State of Siege* caused a furor when it was cancelled for political reasons from the opening program of the American Film Institute theater in Washington.

Not all of Costa-Gavras's features are "political": *The Sleeping Car Murders* is a well-made, atmospheric murder mystery, while *Clair de femme* is the dreary tale of a widower and a woman scarred by the death of her young daughter. Both of these films star Yves Montand. But while Costa-Gavras's most characteristic works do indeed condemn governments that control other governments or suppress human rights, his concerns as a filmmaker have perhaps shifted towards the more personal. The two features made with scriptwriter Joe Eszterhaus, *Betrayed* and *Music Box,* focused on the relationship between the central female character and a man (a lover in *Betrayed,* a father in *Music Box*) who is subsequently revealed as a fascist.

On further review, both *Betrayed* and *Music Box* prove to be deeply flawed films. Both are set in America, and spotlight quintessentially American characters: an all-American farmer and an up-by-the-bootstraps immigrant. Yet both reveal deeply prejudicial, preconceived notions about the essence of the American character.

Betrayed covers a difficult, explosive topic: Racism and white supremacy in mainstream America. Gary Simmons (Tom Berenger) is a Vietnam war hero and widowed farmer who, outwardly at least, is a likable, salt-of-the-earth American. His mother is the type whose apple pies win blue ribbons at county fairs. His two kids, a boy and a girl, are fine, well-behaved youngsters. On the Fourth of July, this family joins with its neighbors for an afternoon of picnicking and an evening of fireworks.

Yet underneath this picture-perfect view of Main Street lies something warped and sinister. Through changing times and economic realities beyond their understanding and control, Gary and those like him have been losing their farms and their way of life. This powerlessness has been translated into a violent, horrific extremism. Gary—and, it is implied, thousands of others like him—has become a clandestine terrorist. He spouts the gospel that "the Jews are running the country." He claims that blacks are not human, but rather "mud people." In a sequence that is among the most jarring of any movie of the late 1980s, he and his cronies hunt down and kill a black man strictly for sport. Most disturbing of all, Gary's sweet, cuddly daughter repeats what she's learned from her father. On to the scene comes a government investigator (Debra Winger), posing as an itinerant farm laborer. Before she is certain of his true nature, she finds herself becoming involved with him sexually and romantically.

Betrayed is ultimately an outsider's view of the American heartland and the Vietnam veteran. While Gary and his ilk objectify blacks, Jews, Asians, and gays, Costa-Gavras and screenwriter Joe Eszterhaus are equally as guilty of objectifying white midwesterners. The film would lead you to believe that every last American farmer is a closet cross-burner. And Gary Simmons, a psycho in sheep's clothing, is yet one more superficial celluloid Vietnam veteran.

In *Music Box,* Armin Mueller-Stahl takes on the Berenger role: a Hungarian-immigrant father accused of horrible war crimes and thus faces deportation. Jessica Lange plays his devoted attorney daughter who defends him in a high-profile trial. Of course, the sweet old man eventually is shown to be guilty as charged. The generalization here is that all working-class immigrants hold equally sinister views, and equally clandestine pasts.

Costa-Gavras' most recent film, *La Petite Apocalypse (The Minor Apocalypse),* is a decidedly minor affair, a satire of 1960s radicals, capitalist greed, the demise of communism, and an overzealous media. It premiered in New York in 1995 not on a theatrical run, but as the opening film in the Sixth Annual Human Rights Watch International Film Festival.

—Rob Edelman

COSTNER, Kevin

Nationality: American. **Born:** Los Angeles, 18 January 1955. **Education:** California State University, B.S. (marketing), 1978; studied acting at South Coast Actors' Co-op, 1977-78. **Family:** Married Cindi Silva, 1975 (divorced); two daughters, one son. **Career:** Stage manager of Raleigh Studios, 1980-83; stage debut, *Invitation to March,* Costa Mesa Playhouse; screen debut, *Sizzle Beach,* 1974; directorial debut, *Dances with Wolves,* 1990. **Awards:** "Star of Tomorrow" award, National Association of Theatre Owners, 1987; Hasty Pudding Man of the Year, Harvard University, 1990; Academy Awards, Best Picture and Best Director, for *Dances with Wolves,* 1990; Director's Guild of America award, Best Director, for *Dances with Wolves,* 1990. **Agent:** Creative Artists Agency, 9830 Wilshire Blvd., Beverly Hills, CA 90212, U.S.A.

Films as Director:

1990 *Dances with Wolves* (+ co-pr, role)

Films as Actor:

1974 *Sizzle Beach*
1981 *Shadows Run Black*
1982 *Night Shift*; *Chasing Dreams*; *Frances*
1983 *Stacy's Knights*; *Table for Five*; *Testament*; ***The Big Chill*** (scenes cut)
1984 *The Gunrunner*
1985 *American Flyers*; *Fandango*; *Silverado*
1987 *The Untouchables*; *No Way Out*
1988 *Bull Durham*

Kevin Costner (center) directing *Dances with Wolves*

1989 *Field of Dreams*
1990 *Revenge* (+ exec-pr)
1991 *Truth or Dare* (cameo); *Robin Hood: Prince of Thieves*; *JFK*; *The Bodyguard*
1993 *A Perfect World*
1994 *Wyatt Earp* (+ co-pr)
1995 *Waterworld* (+ co-pr)

Other Films:

1995 *Rapa-Nui* (co-pr)

Publications

By COSTNER: articles—

"Dancing with the Wolves," *Premiere,* 1990.
"American Tongue," *Interview,* 1990.

On COSTNER: books—

Keith, Todd, *Kevin Costner: The Unauthorized Biography,* Oliver Books, 1991.
Wright, Adrian, *Kevin Costner: A Life on Film,* Warner, 1993.

On COSTNER: articles—

Schruers, F., "Kevin Costner," *Rolling Stone,* 1990.
Morais, R. C., "Kevin Costner Journeys to a New Frontier," *New York Times,* 1990.
Cohn, Lawrence, "First-time Helmers Get Their Best Shot; Tyros Score as Cost of Top Directors Soars," *Variety,* 1990.
Klein, E., "Costner in Control," *Vanity Fair,* 1992.

* * *

Kevin Costner first caught the eye of critics and the public in Lawrence Kasdan's yuppie Western *Silverado* (1985), where his co-starring role as a young, devil-may-care gunslinger all but stole the show out from under stars Kevin Kline and Scott Glenn. Reviewers compared his boyish charm and everyman quality to the early Jimmy Stewart, Gary Cooper, even Steve McQueen. Strangely, Costner has not brought such energy to a role since; he mostly appears as a somewhat softspoken, even laconic, and unperturbable type, regardless of the odds his characters are up against.

Costner had been getting steady parts in films, most of them low-budget exploitation affairs, since the early 1980s. His big break came when Lawrence Kasdan cast him in the important role of Alex, the former 1960s radical whose suicide prompts his now middle-aged college chums to reevaluate their lives, in *The Big Chill* (1983). Costner's scenes wound up on the cutting room floor; as compensation, Kasdan offered him the showiest part in *Silverado,* which panned out as Costner's big break. The role also led to his being cast as the tight-lipped crime fighter Eliott Ness in *The Untouchables* (1987), Brian De Palma's violent historical cartoon about the fall of mobster Al Capone, which was based on the hit 1960s TV series of the same name starring the equally tight-lipped Robert Stack as Ness. *The Untouchables* made Costner a superstar whose rise, in Hollywood terms, was meteoric.

Costner formed his own production company with an eye toward exercising greater creative control over the films in which he appeared. His first project in the capacity of actor-producer was the 1990 action-potboiler *Revenge,* where he exercised his control by jettisoning the ailing John Huston as director in favor of Tony Scott. The film did respectable box-office, but was not a huge hit; nevertheless, it enabled Costner to continue producing, co-producing, or executive-producing the majority of films he has made since. A notable exception was Oliver Stone's *JFK* (1991), which featured Costner's best and most multi-layered performance (as crusading New Orleans District Attorney Jim Garrison, out to expose the CIA-engineered murder of President Kennedy) since *Silverado.*

Costner's ultimate goal was not just to act and produce, but to direct as well. His superstar status and clout in the industry enabled him to achieve this goal fairly quickly. A longtime fan of Westerns in general and the Cinerama opus *How the West Was Won* (1962) in particular, he stubbornly insisted on making his directorial debut with a big-budget Western, even though the genre (excepting the occasional Clint Eastwood oater) was considered box-office poison or even dead by most Hollywood insiders. Costner proved them wrong.

For his source material, Costner chose Michael Blake's sprawling Indian saga *Dances with Wolves,* the story of a U.S. Army officer who turns his back on white civilization to live with the Sioux after the debacle of the War between the States. It is ironic, given his fondness for *How the West Was Won,* that Costner's Western expressed a very different viewpoint, portraying the Sioux as helpless victims in the path of an implacable, indeed pathological, white man menace. It could have been titled "How the West Was Lost." The theme was so relentlessly expressed that Western movie historian William K. Everson wrote: "The film is totally unbalanced in its attempts to address the wrongs inflicted on the Indian. Costner appears as a somewhat surly, Christ-like figure opposed by Indian-hating white Union officers and men who are insane, coarse, murderous and generally so ill-disciplined that it's surprising that the majority of them hadn't been court-martialed and executed long before they got to Indian country. [But] if nothing else, *Dances with Wolves* has undone much of the damage inflicted upon the epic Western by *Heaven's Gate* (1980)."

The theatrically released version of *Dances with Wolves* was three hours long (cut down from four, with the shorn footage subsequently restored on video); this also spelled doom to its box-office chances, according to industry insiders. But audiences disagreed. Captivated by Costner's epic vision, politically correct theme, or both, they made *Dances with Wolves* a smash hit that could not be ignored come Oscar time. It won the Academy Award as Best Picture, something no Western had done since *Cimarron* in 1931. It swept several other major Oscar categories as well, most sweetly for Costner the Best Director prize, making him the third actor-turned-director to win the award his first time out in less than a decade. (The other two were Robert Redford and Warren Beatty—heady company indeed.) Unlike them, however, Costner has not directed a film since, and is, perhaps, waiting for the next epic subject to come along to warrant the effort.

—John McCarty

COX, Alex

Nationality: British. **Born:** Bebington, Wirral, 15 December 1954. **Education:** Educated at Oxford University, Worcester College (Law); Bristol University (Film Production Studies); University of California, Los Angeles, Film School (Fulbright scholarship), 1981. **Family:** Divorced. **Career:** Television work includes *Red, Hot & Blue,* 1990; *Death and the Compass* (+ sc), 1990. **Address:** P.O. Box 1002, Venice, CA 90291 (home); Together Brothers Productions Inc., 9505 West Washington Boulevard, Culver City, CA 90230 (office). **Agent:** Stephanie Mann & Associates, 8323 Blackburn, No. 5, Los Angeles, CA 90048, U.S.A.

Films as Director:

1980 *Sleep Is for Sissies*
1984 *Repo Man* (+ sc, role)
1985 *Sid and Nancy* (+ co-sc)
1986 *Straight to Hell* (+ co-sc)
1987 *Walker* (+ co-ed)
1991 *Highway Patrolman* (*El Patrullero*)
1993 *Death and the Compass*
1995 *The Winner*

Other Films:

1993 ***Philadelphia*** ("Well, Did You Evah?" clip from *Red, Hot & Blue* only)
1994 *Floundering* (role); *Queen of the Night* (role); *Dead Beat* (role)

Publications

On COX: articles—

Scene, October 1986.
Village Voice, October 1986.
American Film, November 1986.
Rolling Stone, September 1987.

* * *

Best known in his native country as the host of BBC television's cult film showcase "Moviedrome" (1988-94), Alex Cox's own career as a filmmaker offers two distinct highpoints, two honourable failures, and one irredeemable embarrassment. Debuting with the made-to-measure cult hit *Repo Man*, his determinedly off-centre films play around with a standard mix-and-match of broad satire, black comedy, punk rock, casual corruption (both personal and institutional), desert landscapes, roving lawmen, and an abiding interest in south-of-the-border American cultures. Cox's anti-heroes, such as "white suburban punk" Otto, drug casualty Sid Vicious, and mercenary-turned-dictator William Walker, provoke equal amounts of amusement, contempt, and grudging sympathy. They try to kid themselves that they can find their own way through the chaotic worlds around them, only to realise that they are at best passive spectators, at worst crushed victims. In all cases, the strings are pulled elsewhere. This theme is carried through into the more restrained (and controlled) *Highway Patrolman*, an impressively low-key tale which suggests a shift in approach on Cox's part, letting the subject speak for itself rather than ramming it home with sledgehammer subtlety. More than a decade after *Repo Man*, Cox

Alex Cox

remains a definite candidate for the "not proven" file, there being no way of guessing if films one and five are the rule or the exception.

Partly inspired by Cox's own brief stint in the car repossession business, *Repo Man* offers an assured, if overstretched, blend of science-fiction parody and consumer satire, with a few jabs at dollar-hungry television evangelism. As an exceptionally mad scientist drives four dead aliens around in the trunk of a Chevy Malibu, aimless drifter Otto graduates from supermarket shelf-stacker to trainee repo(ssession) man, forsaking his thieving punk friends for the wisdom of experienced operator Harry Dean Stanton ("Repo man's always intense"). Throwing in a CIA conspiracy, mohawk haircuts, a Sid Vicious t-shirt, words of wisdom ("The more you drive, the less intelligent you are"), and a vaporized motorcycle cop (only his smoking boots remain), *Repo Man* has enough pace and invention to sustain itself, flagging only in the last twenty minutes or so. The finale, where Otto is driven off in the Chevy, which has been transformed by alien metamorphosis into a glowing flying machine, offers an amusing counterpoint to the more sentimental climax of *Close Encounters of the Third Kind.* Ignored by his parents, betrayed by his friends, cheated by his employer, beaten up by car-payment defaulters, and tortured by a one-handed government agent, Otto has little reason to stick around.

Apparently identifying with his hero, Cox accepted the "punk" director label conferred by *Repo Man,* offering a perhaps over-literal confirmation of this tag with *Sid and Nancy,* the dismal true-life story of the Sex Pistols bass player who fatally stabbed his groupie girlfriend while in the thralls of heroin addiction. For all the sex, drugs, violence, and swearing, the film amounts to little more than a standard biopic cum morality tale, complete with moment-of-death flashback structure. Described by manager/creator Malcolm McClaren as a "fabulous disaster," Vicious is depicted as a basically decent boy (kind to animals, loves his mother) who is completely unable to deal with his celebrity/notoriety and its attendant trappings. With the punk movement presented as an empty response to everything else being "boring" (even sex), *Sid and Nancy* is a predictable, overly slick road-to-ruin story, offering a heavy-handed treatment of rebel-establishment culture clash (both in the British and American scenes) and only so-so period recreation. In the title roles, Chloe Webb whines, nags, and yells her way to merciful oblivion, while Gary Oldman is too intelligent and charismatic to entirely convince as the inarticulate, pathetic Vicious. The film does carry a certain integrity, dwelling on the awkward tenderness between Sid and Nancy as well as the regular shooting-up, yet dramatizing events less than a decade old requires more sense of purpose than is exhibited here.

Having made a film about punks, Cox proceeded to make one with them, recruiting the likes of Joe Strummer, Courtney Love, Elvis Costello, Grace Jones, and The Pogues for the dismal spoof spaghetti western *Straight to Hell.* Cox claims to have made the film as a pretext for retrieving his motorbike from its Spanish location and there is nothing in the finished product to suggest otherwise.

Walker is more distinguished, if similarly self-indulgent. Cox uses the historical figure of William Walker, an amoral adventurer who in 1856 was made president of Nicaragua, to comment on America's contemporary involvement in the country's affairs, aiding the anti-government Contra forces. Ed Harris cuts an imposing figure as the articulate, arrogant Walker, leading his multi-ethnic band of mercenaries in search of supposed riches and glory, and Cox stages some impressive action sequences, yet the comic-book style never quite catches fire. Over anxious to present Walker as a symbol of American imperialism, the film rapidly abandons any pretence at understatement, throwing in a series of crass anachronisms (a limousine, a television, a helicopter, *Newsweek* magazine) for anyone who might not be getting the point. It is typical of the film's confusion that the biggest victim of capitalist aggression seems to be Walker himself, a self-styled leader of men who is nothing more than the puppet of railway and shipping magnate Cornelius Vanderbilt.

Financed with Mexican, American, and Japanese money, the belated release of *Highway Patrolman* sees Cox working on a far more naturalistic level, with laudable results. The story of a newly graduated Mexican policeman attempting to retain some sense of morality in a society where corruption is not only accepted but expected unreels with a quiet confidence. Advised to expect the worst of people before he has even left the police academy ("they're always guilty of something"), Patrolman Pedro Rojas finds his professional dilemmas mirrored by his personal life, as he splits his loyalties between his farm-owner wife and a junkie prostitute. Cox offers some memorable images of offhand corruption at work (stolen toys donated to an orphanage; a suspect pig carcass illegally sold to poor villagers), and the moments of violence carry a harrowing sense of realism.

Whether or not Cox will continue to work in restrained mode is open to question. His next announced project is an expanded cinema version of his television film *Death and the Compass,* an irritatingly overcooked Jorge Luis Borges adaptation. Hopefully the lessons of *Highway Patrolman* have made a difference.

—Daniel O'Brien

CRAVEN, Wes

Nationality: American. **Born:** Wesley Earl Craven in Cleveland, Ohio, 2 August 1939. **Education:** Wheaton College, B.A.; John Hopkins University, M.A. **Family:** Married, one son, one daughter. **Career:** College Humanities Professor, left to work as a messenger in a film production house, New York City; assistant editor for Sean Cunningham, from 1970; directed first feature, *Last House on the Left,* 1972, for $90,000 (it made $20 million); also TV director, from 1985. **Awards:** Best Director Award, Madrid Festival, 1988. **Agent:** Andrea Eastman, International Creative Management, 8899 Beverly Boulevard, Los Angeles, CA 90048, U.S.A. **Address:** c/o Alive Films, 8271 Melrose Avenue, Los Angeles, CA 90046, U.S.A.

Films as Director and Scriptwriter:

1973 *Last House on the Left* (+ ed)
1977 *The Hills Have Eyes* (+ ed)
1978 *Stranger in Our House* (*Summer of Fear*)
1981 *Deadly Blessing*
1982 *Swamp Thing*
1983 *The Hills Have Eyes, Part II*
1984 *A Nightmare on Elm Street*; *Invitation to Hell*
1985 *Chiller*
1986 *Deadly Friend*
1988 *Serpent and the Rainbow*
1989 *Shocker*
1990 *Night Visions* (for TV) (+ exec pr)
1991 *The People under the Stairs* (+ exec pr)
1994 *Wes Craven's New Nightmare* (+ pr, role as himself)
1995 *Vampire in Brooklyn*

Other Films:

1971 *Together* (*Sensual Paradise*) (Cunningham) (asst-pr); *You've Got to Walk It Like You Talk It or You'll Lose That Beat* (Cunningham) (co-ed)
1972 *It Happened in Hollywood* (Cunningham) (ed)

1986 *A Nightmare on Elm Street 3: Dream Warriors* (co-sc, exec pr)
1987 *Flowers in the Attic* (co-sc)
1990 *Bloodfist II* (advisor)
1992 *Nightmare Cafe* (TV series) (creator, exec pr, sc of pilot)
1995 *The Fear* (role as Dr. Arnold); *Wes Craven Presents Mind Ripper: Live in Horror, Die in Fear* (for TV) (exec pr)

Publications

By CRAVEN: articles—

Interview with T. Williams, in *Journal of Popular Film* (Washington, D.C.), Fall 1980.
Interviews in *Ecran Fantastique* (Paris), no. 24, 1982, and March 1985.
Interview in *Starburst* (London), April 1982.
Interview with Paul Taylor, in *Monthly Film Bulletin* (London), August 1982.
"Fairy Tales for the Apocalypse," an interview with C. Sharrett, in *Literature/Film Quarterly* (Salisbury, Maryland), vol. 13, no. 3, 1985.
Interview with E. Caron-Lowins, in *Revue du Cinéma* (Paris), April 1985.
Interview in *Cinefantastique* (Oak Park, Illinois), July 1985.
Interview in *Time Out* (London), 29 August 1985.
Interviews in *Hollywood Reporter,* 5 February and 26 August 1988.
Interview with A. Martin, in *Cinema Papers* (Melbourne), November 1988.
"Entretien avec Wes Craven," with T. Jousse and N. Saada, in *Cahiers du Cinema,* January 1993.

On CRAVEN: books—

Meyers, Richard, *For One Week Only: The World of Exploitation Films,* Piscataway, New Jersey, 1983.
McCarty, John, *Splatter Movies: Breaking the Last Taboo of the Screen,* New York, 1984.
Newman, Kim, *Nightmare Movies: A Critical History of the Horror Film from 1968,* London, 1988.
McCarty, John, *The Modern Horror Film,* Secaucus, New Jersey, 1990.
McCarty, John, *Movie Psychos and Madmen,* Secaucus, New Jersey, 1993.
McCarty, John, *The Fearmakers,* New York, 1994.

On CRAVEN: articles—

"Wes Craven," in *Image et Son* (Paris), May 1981.
Starburst (London), April and July 1985, and April 1986.
National Film Theatre Booklet (London), June 1988.
Time Out (London), 1 June 1988.
Mancini, Marc, "Professor Gore," in *Film Comment,* September-October 1989.
Biodrowski, S., "Wes Craven: Alive and Shocking," in *Cinefantastique,* vol. 22, no. 2, 1991.
Biodrowski, S., "Director Wes Craven on the Politics of Horror," in *Cinefantastique,* vol. 22, no. 5, 1992.

* * *

Of all the horror specialists who came to prominence during the 1970s, Wes Craven has had the least settled career. While Tobe Hooper and John Carpenter have had major creative slumps, George Romero and Larry Cohen have carved out their own areas of independent endeavour, and David Cronenberg and Brian De Palma have, with various levels of success, graduated to major studio projects, Craven has been bouncing between successes (*The Hills Have Eyes, A Nightmare on Elm Street*) and failures (*Swamp Thing, Deadly Friend*) with a manic energy, forced occasionally to take work on television to keep going. While his best work exhibits a canny grasp of genre and a disturbing understanding of the place of violence within society, and *Elm Street*—after a long and difficult gestation period—emerged as one of the most influential horror movies of the 1980s, his worst films literally flounder in the wake of his successes, frequently (as in *The Hills Have Eyes, Part 2* and *Shocker*) resorting to self-plagiarism to tie together blatantly misconceived projects, suggesting a desperate intellect which too often tries to find a short cut.

Craven's first movie, *Last House on the Left,* a hard-gore remake of Bergman's *The Virgin Spring,* was an ultra-low-budget sleeper that hit the drive-ins well before *The Texas Chain Saw Massacre* and served to drag the genre away from the then-tired mists of Hammer-style gothic towards the more fruitful modern fields of gritty psychosis and social unrest. As with the early films of Romero, Hooper, and Cohen, the focus of *Last House* is on the destructive potential of the family, as a group of homicidal maniacs torture a pair of innocent girls and are themselves slaughtered by the martyr heroine's "normal" parents. Filmed with a raw style and a sense of fascinated revulsion, *Last House*—still banned in the United Kingdom—is one of the strongest of horror pictures, and remains so tough that most audiences cannot take it, either when the maniacs are disembowelling their victims or the parents are fighting back. *The Hills Have Eyes* is a more expansive, more fantastically horrid re-run of the first movie, stirring in some black humour and an EC Comics-style set of inbred mutants as it replays the wagon train Western scenario out in the desert, where a vacationing family of normals clash with their degenerate mirror image. Although it tackles the same thematic territory as *Last House, The Hills Have Eyes* is a more approachable work and shows off Craven's special skills with simple action, even daring to turn the heroes' dog into a modern movie hero who relates to Rin-Tin-Tin much as Dirty Harry relates to George Dixon.

Despite these two powerful pictures, which at once demonstrated Craven's competence as a director and his flair for the intriguingly horrific, he then fell into a career hole of botched projects, including TV work and an interesting attempt to film David Morell's *First Blood. Deadly Blessing,* a hodge-podge of psychotic and demonology themes, is alarmingly inconsistent, featuring some of the best and the worst of Craven as it deals with a series of murders in a cleverly evoked Hittite community. *Swamp Thing,* an adaption of the DC comic, is a misconceived and childish superhero picture dragged under by ridiculous monster suits and an underdeveloped screenplay, although it has one memorably unchildish scene when Adrienne Barbeau takes a nude swim in the swamp. After this, it is easy to see how Craven could resort to making *The Hills Have Eyes, Part 2,* which contains an inordinate amount of flashback footage from the first film simply because the budget ran out before the movie was actually completed. Although *Deadly Friend* and *Shocker* are more expensively bad, *Hills 2* stands as Craven's worst film.

However, Craven then turned his career round, dashing off the unexceptional but acceptable *Invitation to Hell* and *Chiller* and several pretty good *Twilight Zone* segments—including "Shatterday," a Harlan Ellison story with Bruce Willis, and the disorienting "Word Play"—before finally getting the green light on *A Nightmare on Elm Street. Last House* and *Deadly Blessing* had experimented with surreal, disorienting dream sequences—a bit of nightmare dentistry, and a spider-falling-into-mouth shock—but *Elm Street* is built around such moments, and features a dreamstalking bogeyman, Freddy Krueger (Robert Englund), who somehow became a cult hero through the course of four sequels—only one of which, *A Nightmare on Elm Street, Part 3: Dream Warriors,* did Craven have anything to do with, as a writer—and a TV series. The first *Elm Street* is a seamless stalk-and-scare horror movie which fully deserved its success for its clever reassembly of the elements of teenage horror established by Carpenter with *Hal-*

loween and Stephen King in *Carrie* and *Christine.* However, it is a less rigorous, less satisfying movie than Craven's best early films, reducing their ambiguous culture clash to a simple conflict between an innocent heroine (Heather Langenkamp) and an unredeemable monster villain. Part of the disturbing quality of *Last House* and *Hills* comes from their occasionally sympathetic approaches to their villains, and in the way the heroes' violent revenge is seen to degrade them to the level of the monsters; Langenkamp's guerilla-style assault on Freddy, meanwhile, is simply a cheerable demonstration of American resourcefulness.

Leaving the *Elm Street* sequels, which had been set up by a fairly annoying last-minute logical lapse at the end of the first film, to other hands, Craven departed the independent sector for a pair of big studio projects—the execrable *Deadly Friend,* a cute-robot-cum-teen-zombie movie adapted from Diana Henstell's novel *Friend,* and *The Serpent and the Rainbow,* an interesting and seductive voodoo picture adapted from Wade Davis's nonfiction novel. Both films carry over the dream theme from *Elm Street,* in the first case to beef up a badly sagging storyline, and in the second as part of a bizarre and affecting cultural travelogue that develops the old Craven's fascination with magical and monstrous societies as opposed to individuals. However, following that experience, Craven returned to the independents, like John Carpenter before him, and produced another carbon copy of his own most successful work in *Shocker,* which is nothing but an identikit of *A Nightmare on Elm Street* with more ideas than it can handle and severe lapses of script, characterisation, and tone to pull it down between its undeniably brilliant sequences (a grand guignol electrocution, a final chase through "television land"). Craven's entire career has been like *Shocker,* with moments of startling inspiration and genre craftsmanship let down by hurried scripts and just plain wrong decisions.

Craven bounced back from the erratic *Shocker* with *The People under the Stairs.* The film fuses the time-honored "wicked stepmother" concept with Craven's familiar predilections for home-style booby-traps and nightmare sequences. The house itself is one big booby-trap, wired with explosives and rigged with electronic doors of solid steel. It is also one big, bad *Nightmare on Elm Street* dreamscape, seemingly designed by the same deranged architect responsible for the labyrinthine yet claustrophobic cabin in Sam Raimi's *The Evil Dead.*

Craven returned to Elm Street with the film-within-a-film *Wes Craven's New Nightmare.* The film brought back Freddy Krueger as well as some of the cast members of the original *Elm Street* as themselves, now victims of the horror series, which is mysteriously being acted out in "real life." Craven appears as himself in the film. Cynics viewed the film as a run-for-cover effort on Craven's part to renew the Freddy Krueger franchise following the lukewarm reception of *People under the Stairs.* Others viewed it as the ultimate Craven statement on dream psychology. It confused many, scared few, and was not a box-office winner. Craven then abandoned horror cinema's most famous street for equally tried and true genre territory with *Vampire in Brooklyn.* A mixture of comedy and splatter, it marked the latest attempt by former superstar Eddie Murphy to jump-start his fading career.

—Kim Newman, updated by John McCarty

CRICHTON, Charles

Nationality: British. **Born:** Wallasey, England, 6 August 1910. **Education:** Oundle School and Oxford University. **Career:** Began as cutter for London Film Productions, 1931; editor on major Korda productions, 1935-40; joined Ealing Studios, 1940; directed first film, *For Those in Peril,* 1944; TV director, from 1960s.

Films as Director:

1944 *For Those in Peril*
1945 *Painted Boats* (*The Girl on the Canal*); "The Golfing Story" episode of ***Dead of Night***
1946 *Hue and Cry*
1948 *Against the Wind*; *Another Shore*
1949 "The Orchestra Conductor" episode of *Train of Events*
1950 *Dance Hall*
1951 ***The Lavender Hill Mob***; *Hunted* (*The Stranger in Between*)
1952 *The Titfield Thunderbolt*
1953 *The Love Lottery*
1954 *The Divided Heart*
1956 *The Man in the Sky* (*Decision Against Time*)
1958 *Law and Disorder*; *Floods of Fear* (+ sc)
1959 *The Battle of the Sexes*
1960 *The Boy Who Stole a Million* (+ co-sc)
1964 *The Third Secret*
1965 *He Who Rides a Tiger*
1968 *Tomorrow's Island* (+ sc)
1988 *A Fish Called Wanda,* (+ co-sc)

Other Films:

1932 *Men of Tomorrow* (Sagan) (asst ed)
1933 *Cash* (*For Love or Money*) (Z. Korda) (asst ed); ***The Private Life of Henry VIII*** (A. Korda) (asst ed); *The Girl from Maxim's* (A. Korda) (asst ed)
1935 *Sanders of the River* (Z. Korda) (ed); ***Things to Come*** (Menzies) (co-assoc ed)
1937 *Elephant Boy* (Flaherty and Z. Korda) (ed); *Twenty-One Days* (*The First and the Last*; *Twenty-One Days Together*) (Dean) (ed)
1938 *Prison without Bars* (Hurst) (ed)
1940 *Old Bill and Son* (Dalrymple) (ed); *The Thief of Bagdad* (Berger, Powell, Whelan) (ed); *Yellow Caesar* (*The Heel of Italy*) (Cavalcanti) (ed)
1941 *The Big Blockade* (Frend) (co-ed); *Guests of Honour* (Pitt) (ed); *Young Veteran* (Cavalcanti) (ed); *Find, Fix and Strike* (Bennett) (ed, assoc pr)
1942 *Nine Men* (Watt) (ed, assoc pr); *Greek Testament* (*The Shrine of Victory*) (Hasse) (assoc pr)

Publications

By CRICHTON: book—

A Fish Called Wanda, with John Cleese, London, 1988.

By CRICHTON: article—

Interview in *Directing Motion Pictures,* edited by Terence Marner, New York, 1972.

On CRICHTON: books—

Balcon, Michael, *A Lifetime of Films,* London, 1969.
Barr, Charles, *Ealing Studios,* London, 1977.
Perry, George, *Forever Ealing,* London, 1981.

On CRICHTON: articles—

Tynan, Kenneth, "Ealing: The Studio in Suburbia," in *Films and Filming* (London), November and December 1955.

Charles Crichton directing *The Divided Heart*

Barr, Charles, "Projecting Britain and the British Character: Ealing Studios," in *Screen* (London), Summer 1974.

Green, Ian, "Ealing: In the Comedy Frame," in *British Cinema History*, edited by James Curran and Vincent Porter, London, 1983.

Barr, Charles, "Charles Crichton," in *Edinburgh Film Festival Booklet,* 1988.

Falk, Quentin, "*Wanda*: Cleese, Crichton, and Man-Management," in *Sight and Sound* (London), Spring 1988.

Listener (London), 13 October 1988.

* * *

The demise of Ealing Studios seemed to cast a blight on the careers of those who worked there. Within ten years of the final Ealing release virtually all the studio's leading directors—Mackendrick, Hamer, Harry Watt, Charles Frend—had shot their last film; only Basil Dearden was still active. And until recently the career of Charles Crichton appeared to have followed the same dispiriting pattern. His triumphant comeback at the age of seventy-eight, with the huge international success of *A Fish Called Wanda,* was as heartening as it was wholly unexpected.

Wanda kicks off with a jewel heist sequence notable for the wit and precision of its editing. Like several of his Ealing colleagues, Crichton started out in the cutting room, working for Korda on *Things to Come* and *The Thief of Bagdad,* and was said to be one of the finest editors in the British film industry. (Among his uncredited achievements is the rescue of Mackendrick's *Whisky Galore,* which he recut after it had been botched by its original editor.) A sense of pace and timing, the skilled editor's stock-in-trade, distinguishes all his best work.

Comedy has always been seen as Crichton's forte. His reputation, prior to *Wanda,* rested on the three comedies he directed at Ealing to scripts by T. E. B. Clarke: *Hue and Cry, The Lavender Hill Mob,* and *The Titfield Thunderbolt.* If all three seem to belong more to the writer's oeuvre than to the director's, this may be because Crichton has always been dependent in his comedies on the quality of the script. *The Lavender Hill Mob,* perhaps the archetypal comedy of the Ealing mainstream, gains enormously from Crichton's supple comic timing; but given stodgy material, as in *The Love Lottery* or *Another Shore,* his lightness of touch deserts him. Even *Titfield,* with Clarke writing some way below his best, feels sluggish and under-directed beside its two predecessors.

Though the serious side of Crichton's output, the dramas and thrillers, has attracted little attention, he often seems here less at the mercy of his script, able to make something personal even of flawed material. His one non-comedy with Clarke, the Resistance drama *Against the Wind,* has a downbeat realism and a refusal of easy heroics that recalls Thorold Dickinson's *Next of Kin* (and probably ensured its failure at the post-war box-office). *Hunted,* a killer-on-the-run thriller, builds up a complex tension as well as offering Dirk Bogarde a rare intelligent role amid the dross of his early career. Crichton's cool, unemphatic handling of the central conflict in *The Divided Heart* deftly avoids emotional overkill—though nothing, perhaps, could have prevented the film's final slide into sententiousness.

After Ealing, projects attuned to his talents became increasingly rare. Given the darker aspects of his work, black comedy was clearly well within his range, and *The Battle of the Sexes,* with Peter Sellers as the Scots clerk trying to bump off efficiency expert Constance Cummings, would have been ideal—were it not for a script that junked the quiet implacability of the original (Thurber's caustic tour-de-force *The Catbird Seat*) for cautious whimsy and a vapid happy ending. After a couple of interestingly off-beat thrillers—*The Third Secret* and *He Who Rides a Tiger*—both marred by clumsy writing and uncertainty of tone, Crichton cut his losses and retreated into television.

From there, directing corporate videos must have seemed like a further downhill step. But the company involved was John Cleese's Video Arts, and it was Cleese's enthusiastic backing—and his status as a bankable star—that enabled Crichton, after more than twenty years, to return to the cinema. *A Fish Called Wanda,* with its four ill-assorted crooks, its central portrait of respectability undermined by larcenous urges, and its running theme of internecine treachery, crosses *The Lavender Hill Mob* with *The Ladykillers*—and adds a degree of sex and violence that would certainly have alarmed Michael Balcon. But had Ealing comedy survived Balcon's death and lived on into the late 1980s, *Wanda* is most likely what it would have looked like—and its bite and vitality only inspire regret for the films left unmade during Crichton's years in the wilderness.

—Philip Kemp

CROMWELL, John

Nationality: American. **Born:** Elwood Dager in Toledo, Ohio, 23 December 1887. **Education:** Howe High School, Howe, Indiana, 1901-05. **Military Service:** 1917-18. **Family:** Married 1) Alice Indahl; 2) Marie Goff; 3) Kay Johnson; 4) Ruth Nelson; one son. **Career:** Actor on Broadway, from 1910; theatre director for William Brady, from 1913; actor and stage director, New York Repertory Theatre, 1915-19; stage actor-producer to 1928; hired by Paramount as dialogue director, 1928; directed first film, *Close Harmony,* 1929; hired by RKO, 1933; President, Screen Actors' Guild, 1944-45; returned to Broadway, 1951, and to repertory theatre, 1960s. **Died:** In Santa Barbara, California, 26 September 1979.

Films as Director:

1929 *Close Harmony* (co-d); *The Dance of Life* (co-d with Sutherland, role as doorkeeper); *The Mighty* (+ role as Mr. Jamieson)
1930 *The Street of Chance* (+ role as Imbrie); *The Texan*; *Seven Days Leave* (*Medals*); *For the Defense*; *Tom Sawyer*
1931 *Scandal Sheet*; *Unfaithful*; *Vice Squad*; *Rich Man's Folly*
1932 *The World and the Flesh*
1933 *Sneepings*; *The Silver Cord*
1934 *Of Human Bondage*; *The Fountain*; *Jalna*; *I Dream Too Much*
1936 *Little Lord Fauntleroy*; *To Mary with Love*; *Banjo on My Knee*
1937 *The Prisoner of Zenda*
1938 *Algiers*
1939 *Made for Each Other*; *In Name Only*
1940 *Abe Lincoln in Illinois* (*Spirit of the People*) (+ role as John Brown); *Victory*
1941 *So Ends Our Night*
1942 *Son of Fury*
1944 *Since You Went Away*
1945 *The Enchanted Cottage*
1946 *Anna and the King of Siam*
1947 *Dead Reckoning*; *Night Song*
1950 *Caged*
1951 *The Company She Keeps*; *The Racket*
1958 *The Goddess*
1959 *The Scavengers*
1960 *De Sista Stegen* (*A Matter of Morals*)

Other Films:

1929 *The Dummy* (R. Milton) (role as Walter Babbing)
1957 *Top Secret Affair* (*Their Secret Affair*) (Potter) (role as General Grimshaw)
1977 *Three Women* (Altman) (role)
1978 *A Wedding* (Altman) (role as cardinal)

Publications

By CROMWELL: articles—

Interview with D. Lyons, in *Interview* (New York), February 1972.
Interview with Leonard Maltin, in *Action* (Los Angeles), May/June 1973.

On CROMWELL: articles—

"*The Goddess*," in *Films in Review* (New York), May 1958.
Rotha, Paul, in *Films and Filming* (London), August 1958.
Prouse, Derek, in *Sight and Sound* (London), Autumn 1958.
Sarris, Andrew, "Likable But Elusive," in *Film Culture* (New York), Spring 1963.
Cutts, John, "The Finest Zenda of Them All," in *Cinema* (Beverly Hills), Spring 1968.
Frey, R., "John Cromwell," in *Sight and Sound* (London), Autumn 1972.
Canham, Kingsley, "John Cromwell: Memories of Love, Elegance, and Style," in *The Hollywood Professionals* (London) vol. 5, 1976.
Bleys, J.P., "John Cromwell ou la mélodie du mélodrame," in *Cahiers de la Cinémathèque* (Perpignan), no. 28, 1979.
"Cromwell Section," in *Positif* (Paris), March 1979.
Obituary in *New York Times,* 28 September 1979.
Obituary in *Cinéma* (Paris), March 1980.

* * *

John Cromwell, a fine New York actor, had a distinguished list of credits when he was hired by Paramount in 1928. Talking films were a new medium then, and Cromwell was eminently qualified to direct dialogue. He started in collaboration with Edward Sutherland on *Close Harmony* and *The Dance of Life* (from the play *Broadway*). Paramount then promoted him to solo status on such films as *The Street of Chance,* with William Powell, and *The Texan* and *Seven Days Leave,* both with Gary Cooper.

Once established as an ace director, he went over to the new RKO studios, where in 1933 he directed such movies as *The Silver Cord* (from Sidney Howard's play), starring Irene Dunne with Joel McCrea;

John Cromwell

and the adaptation of Maugham's novel *Of Human Bondage,* with Leslie Howard and Bette Davis. He met David O. Selznick at this time, and subsequently directed such Selznick films as *Little Lord Fauntleroy, The Prisoner of Zenda, Made for Each Other,* and *Since You Went Away.*

Meanwhile, Cromwell continued as director of other RKO successes, including *In Name Only,* with Cary Grant, Carole Lombard, and Kay Francis; and Robert Sherwood's *Abe Lincoln in Illinois,* starring Raymond Massey. He also directed Hedy Lamarr's American film debut with Charles Boyer in *Algiers; Victory,* from the Joseph Conrad novel; and *So Ends Our Night,* a remarkably tense melodrama of World War Two, with Fredric March, Margaret Sullavan, Glenn Ford, Frances Dee, and Erich von Stroheim.

In 1944 Harriet Parsons at RKO signed Cromwell to direct *The Enchanted Cottage,* a sensitive drama of a plain girl (Dorothy McGuire) and a scarred, crippled war veteran (Robert Young) who begin to see one another as straight and beautiful through the power of love. By this time, Cromwell was a thorough craftsman. He believed in full rehearsals with camera before any shooting took place. "For every day of full rehearsal you give me," he was fond of saying, "I'll knock off a day on the shooting schedule." At RKO they gave him three days for rehearsal, and he obligingly came in three days early. *The Enchanted Cottage* was a tricky assignment; the love story was so sensitive that it could easily slip into sentimentality, but it never did. He treated it realistically, an approach that, as he said, is "the only way to treat a fantasy. It always works."

Cromwell then directed Irene Dunne and Rex Harrison in *Anna and the King of Siam,* a film of great pictorial beauty. His best subsequent efforts were a woman's prison story, *Caged,* and *The Goddess,* a realistic story about a film star.

Cromwell was falsely accused by Howard Hughes of being a Communist during the McCarthy era. "I was never anything that suggested a Red," he said, "and there never was the slightest evidence with which to accuse me of being one." He was blacklisted, however, and the assignments ceased coming his way. He simply returned to the theatre as an actor, and was brilliant as Henry Fonda's father in the stage play of John Marquand's *Point of No Return.*

—DeWitt Bodeen

CRONENBERG, David

Nationality: Canadian. **Born:** Toronto, 15 May 1943. **Education:** University of Toronto, B.A., 1967. **Career:** After making two short films, made first feature, *Stereo,* 1969; travelled to France, directed filler material for Canadian TV, 1971. **Address:** David Cronenberg Productions, 217 Avenue Road, Toronto M5R 2J3, Canada. **Agent:** John Burnham, William Morris Agency, 151 El Camino Drive, Beverly Hills, CA 90212, U.S.A.

Films as Director and Scriptwriter:

1966 *Transfer* (short) (+ ph, ed)
1967 *From the Drain* (short) (+ ph, ed)
1969 *Stereo* (+ pr, ph, ed)
1970 *Crimes of the Future* (+ pr, ph)
1975 *Shivers* (*They Came from Within*; *The Parasite Murders*; *Frissons*)
1976 *Rabid* (*Rage*)
1978 *Fast Company* (d only); *The Brood*
1979 *Scanners*
1982 *Videodrome*
1983 *The Dead Zone* (d only)
1986 *The Fly* (co-sc, + role as gynecologist)
1988 ***Dead Ringers*** (*Twins*) (co-sc, + pr)
1991 *Naked Lunch*
1992/3 *M. Butterfly* (d only)
1996 *Crash*

Other Films:

1985 *Into the Night* (Landis) (role)
1989 *Nightbreed* (Barker) (role)
1992 *Blue* (McKellar) (role)
1994 *Trial by Jury* (Gould) (role)

Publications

By CRONENBERG: articles—

Interview in *Ecran Fantastique* (Paris), no. 2, 1977.
Interview in *Time Out* (London), 6 January 1978.
Interview in *Cinema Canada* (Montreal), September/October 1978.
Interview in *Starburst* (London), nos. 36/37, 1981.
Interview in *Films* (London), June 1981.
Interviews in *Ecran Fantastique* (Paris), June and November 1983.
Interview with S. Ayscough, in *Cinema Canada* (Montreal), December 1983.
Interview in *Starburst* (London), May 1984.
Interview with C. Tesson and T. Cazals, in *Cahiers du Cinéma* (Paris), January 1987.
Interview with Brent Lewis, in *Films and Filming* (London), February 1987.
Interview in *Film Comment* (New York), September/October 1988.
Interview in *American Film* (Washington, D.C.), October 1988.
Interview in *Cinefex* (Riverside, California), November 1988.
Interview with Derek Malcolm, in the *Guardian* (London), 29 December 1989.

On CRONENBERG: books—

McCarty, John, *Splatter Movies: Breaking the Last Taboo,* New York, 1981.
Handling, Piers, editor, *The Shape of Rage: The Films of David Cronenberg,* Toronto, 1983.
Drew, Wayne, editor, *David Cronenberg,* London, 1984.
Newman, Kim, *Nightmare Movies: A Critical History of the Horror Film from 1968,* London, 1988.
Rodley, Chris, editor, *Cronenberg on Cronenberg,* London, 1992.
Morris, Peter, *David Cronenberg: A Delicate Balance,* Toronto, 1994.

On CRONENBERG: articles—

Film Comment (New York), March/April 1980.
"Cronenberg Section" of *Cinema Canada* (Montreal), March 1981.
"Cronenberg Section" of *Cinefantastique* (Oak Park, Illinois), Spring 1981.
Sutton, M., "Schlock! Horror! The Films of David Cronenberg," in *Films and Filming* (London), October 1982.
Harkness, J., "The Word, the Flesh, and the Films of David Cronenberg," in *Cinema Canada* (Montreal), June 1983.
Sharrett, C., "Myth and Ritual in the Post-Industrial Landscape: The Films of David Cronenberg," in *Persistence of Vision* (Maspeth, New York), Summer 1986.

David Cronenberg directing Jeremy Irons in *Dead Ringers* courtesy of The Rank Organisation Plc

Edelstein, R., "Lord of the Fly," in *Village Voice* (New York), 19 August 1986.
Lucas, Tim, in *American Cinematographer* (Los Angeles), September 1986.
"*The Fly* Issue" of *Starburst* (London), January 1987.
"*The Fly* Issue" of *Ecran Fantastique* (Paris), January 1987.
Newman, Kim, "King in a Small Field," in *Monthly Film Bulletin* (London), February 1987.
Time Out (London), 11 February 1987.
Revue du Cinéma (Paris), May 1987.

* * *

David Cronenberg's breakthrough movie, *Shivers,* carries over the Burroughsian mind-and-body-bending themes of his underground pictures—*Stereo* and *Crimes of the Future*—but also benefits from the influence of Romero's *Night of the Living Dead* and Siegel's *Invasion of the Body Snatchers* in its horror movie imagery, relentless pacing, and general vision of a society falling apart. Thus the film locates Cronenberg at the centre of the thriving 1970s horror movement that produced such figures as Romero, Larry Cohen, John Carpenter, Wes Craven, and Tobe Hooper. While a mad scientist's creation—a horde of creeping parasites that look like phallic turds—infects people with a combination of venereal disease and aphrodisiac, a chilly, luxurious, modernist skyscraper apartment building becomes a Boschian nightmare of blood and carnality. An undisciplined film, *Shivers* gains from its scattershot approach. Cronenberg has since proved himself capable of more control but, in a movie about the encroachment of chaos upon order, it is appropriate that the narrative itself should break down. While strong enough in its mix of sex and violence to give fuel to critics who view Cronenberg as a reactionary moralist, it is clear that his approach is ambiguous, and that he is as concerned with the anomie of the normality disrupted as he is with the nature of the outbreak. The orgiastic solution of the blood parasites may be too extreme, but the soulless routine they replace suggests the straight world deserves to be eaten away from within.

His follow-up movies, *Rabid, The Brood,* and *Scanners,* develop the themes of *Shivers*—although his odd-man-out film, the drag-racing drama *Fast Company,* comes from this period also—and gradually struggle away from impersonal nihilism. *Rabid* is a plague story, with Marilyn Chambers quite affecting as the Typhoid Mary, while *The Brood* is an intense family melodrama about child abuse triggered by Nola (Samantha Eggar), a mad mother who can manifest her anger as murderous malformed children, and *Scanners* concerns itself with the feuds of a race of telepaths who co-exist with humanity and are unsure whether to conquer or save the world. With its exploding heads and car chases, *Scanners* is a progression away from the venereal apocalypse of the earlier films and is almost an upbeat movie after the icy down-ness of *The Brood. Scanners* has the typical early Cronenberg construction: it crams in more ideas than it can possibly deal with and tears through its overly complex plot so quickly that the holes only become apparent when it is all over. The unrelenting action of *Shivers* and *Rabid* show a society tearing itself apart; and, given the breakup of Nola's family, the incestuous cruelty of *The Brood* is inevitable; but *Scanners* follows a purposeful conflict between opposing, highly motivated sides, out of which a new world will emerge. If *The Brood* finds a balance between mind and body, *Scanners* finally achieves a hard-won harmony. *Crimes of the Future, Shivers, Rabid,* and *The Brood* all end with the persistent disease threatening to spread. In *Scanners,* for the first time in a David Cronenberg film, the Good Guys win.

Cronenberg closed this phase of his career with *Videodrome,* which summed up his work to date. Structurally reminiscent of *Shivers,* the film follows Max Renn (James Woods), a cable TV hustler whose justification for his channel's output of "softcore pornography and hardcore violence" is "better on television than in the streets." Renn is trying to track down a pirate station that is transmitting *Videodrome,* "a show that's just torture and murder. No plot. No characters. Very realistic," because he thinks "it's the coming thing." Underneath the stimulating images of sex and violence is a signal which causes a tumor in Renn's brain that makes him subject to hallucinations which increasingly take over the flow of the film, completely fracturing reality with disturbing developments of Cronenberg's by-now familiar bodily evolutions. A television set pulses with life and Renn buries his head in its mammary screen as he kisses the image of his fantasy lover (Deborah Harry). A vaginal slot grows from a rash on his stomach and the villains plunge living videocassettes into it which program him as an assassin. His hand and gun grow together to create a sickening biomechanical synthesis. Once Renn has been exposed to *Videodrome,* the film cannot hope to sustain its storyline, and, as Paul Taylor wrote in *Monthly Film Bulletin,* "becomes most akin to sitting before a TV screen while someone else switches channels at random."

After travelling so far into his own personal—and uncommercial—nightmare, Cronenberg felt the need to ease off by tackling an uncomplicated project. *The Dead Zone,* a bland but efficient adaption of Stephen King's novel, is one of the few films he has directed without having been involved in the writing. Having proved that he could work in the mainstream, Cronenberg turned to more personal projects that still somehow pass as commercial cinema, keeping up a miraculous balancing act that has put him, in a career sense, on a much more solid footing than Romero, Hooper, Cohen, Carpenter, or Craven, all of whom he has outstripped. *The Fly,* a major studio remake of the 1958 monster movie, is despite its budget and lavish special effects a quintessentially Cronenbergian movie, pruning away the expected melodrama to concentrate on a single relationship, between Seth Brundle (Jeff Goldblum), a gawky scientist whose teleportation device has set in motion a metamorphosis that turns him into an insect, and his horrified but compassionate lover (Geena Davis). *The Fly* is an even more concentrated, intimate movie than *The Brood,* with only three main characters and one major setting. Like Rabid Rose and Max Renn, Brundle remains himself as he changes, tossing away nervous remarks about his collection of dropped-off body parts, giving an amusingly disgusting TV-chef-style demonstration of the flylike manner in which the new creature eats a doughnut, humming, "I know an old lady who swallowed a fly," and treating his mutation as a voyage of discovery.

Based on a true-life *National Enquirer* headline ("Twin Docs Found Dead in Posh Pad"), *Dead Ringers* follows the lives of Beverly and Elliot Mantle (Jeremy Irons), identical twins who develop a precocious interest in the problems of sex and the female anatomy and grow up to be a world-beating team of gynecologists. Their intense relationship, when unbalanced by the presence of a third party (Genevieve Bujold), eventually leads to their destruction. The film takes fear of surgery about as far as it can go when Beverly, increasingly infuriated that women's bodies do not conform to his textbooks, brings in a Giger-ish surrealist metalworker to create a set of "Gynecological Instruments for Operating on Mutant Women." In the theatre, Beverly is kitted up in scarlet robes more suited to a mass and horrifyingly blunders through a supposedly simple operation, wielding these bizarre and distorted implements. The home stretch is profoundly depressing, and yet deeply moving, as the twins come to resemble each other more and more in their degradation. The calculating Elliot follows Beverly into drug addiction on the theory that only if the Mantle brothers really become identical can the two inadequate personalities separate from each other and get back to some kind of functioning normality. Too often genre publications sneer at filmmakers who achieve success with horror but then claim they want to move on, but notions of genre are inherently limiting, and Cronenberg is entirely justified in leaving behind the warmed-over science fiction elements of his earlier films and concentrating on a more intellectual, character-based mode. For the first time, he is able to present the inhuman condition without recourse (one slightly too blatant dream sequence apart, as in *The Fly*) to slimy special effects, borrowings from earlier horror films, and the trappings of conventional melodrama. This is not the work of someone trying for the commercial high ground, and it certainly is not by any stretch of the imagination a mainstream movie. *Dead Ringers* is not a horror film. It is a David Cronenberg film, and entering the 1990s, that put it at the cutting edge of the nightmare cinema.

Cronenberg used his commercial clout to bring to the screen William S. Burroughs' "unfilmable" novel *Naked Lunch,* a book that had long preoccupied him. While Burroughs's novel is indeed "unfilmable" ("It would cost hundreds of millions of dollars and be banned in every country on earth," Cronenberg has noted), the director had a very different and daring concept in mind. Rather than adapt the book in the traditional sense, he made a film about what it was like to be William S. Burroughs. Where *Dead Ringers* had largely eschewed the fantastic while retaining the horrific, *Naked Lunch* grows from the fantastic and relegates the horrific to a very minor position. The film is essentially a dissection of the act of creativity, which is presented in the film as subversive, cathartic, sexual, and inescapable. Whereas Cronenberg had presented art as a viable outlet for release in *Scanners,* in *Naked Lunch* he recognizes that such a release can lead to an inescapable trap for the artist. Peter Weller's Burroughs would like to be a "normal" person, but this is not to be because he is what he is—he has no choice. Many critics viewed this as self-justification on Cronenberg's part for the nightmare images he puts on the screen. They may be right. But the criticism has little bearing on the point Cronenberg is making.

With *Naked Lunch,* Cronenberg came full-circle, arriving back where he started—with an original, unsettling, dangerous, and subversive "art film" reminiscent of his earliest work. These qualities made him a seemingly natural choice to direct the film version of David Henry Hwang's bizarre, gender and identity-bending Broadway hit *M. Butterfly,* about a French diplomat's (Jeremy Lyons) love affair with a Chinese opera diva whom he never realizes is a man (and spy to boot). Remarkably, the film turned out to be rather subdued and orthodox—most non-Cronenbergian.

—Kim Newman, updated by John McCarty

CRUZE, James

Nationality: American. **Born:** Jens Cruz Bosen in Five Points, near Ogden, Utah, 27 March 1884. **Education:** Studied at "Colonel" F. Cooke Caldwell dramatic school, 1900-03. **Family:** Married 1) actress Marguerite Snow, 1913 (divorced 1924); 2) actress Betty Compson, 1924 (divorced 1930). **Career:** Left home, went to San Francisco, 1900; barker (selling snake-bite cure) for Billy Banks Travelling Stock Co., then organized own troupe, 1903; member of Belasco Company, New York, 1906; joined Thanhouser Film Company as featured player, 1911; joined Lasky Company, 1916, began directing, 1918; began production company James Cruze Inc., 1927 (James Cruze Productions Inc., 1929). **Died:** 3 August 1942.

Films as Director:

1918 *Too Many Millions*; *The Dub*
1919 *Alias Mike Moran*; *The Roaring Road*; *You're Fired*; *The Love Burglar*; *The Valley of the Giants*; *The Lottery Man*; *An Adventure in Hearts*; *Hawthorne of the U.S.A.*
1920 *Terror Island*; *Mrs. Temple's Telegram*; *The Sins of St. Anthony*; *What Happened to Jones*; *A Full House*; *Food for Scandal*; *Always Audacious*; *The Charm School*
1921 *The Dollar-a-Year Man*; *Crazy to Marry*; *Gasoline Gus*; *The Fast Freight* (*Freight Prepaid*; *Via Fast Freight*) (unreleased)
1922 *Leap Year* (*Skirt Shy*) (unreleased); *One Glorious Day*; *Is Matrimony a Failure?*; *The Dictator*; *The Old Homestead*; *Thirty Days*
1923 *The Covered Wagon*; *Hollywood*; *Ruggles of Red Gap*; *To the Ladies*
1924 *The Fighting Coward*; *The Enemy Sex*; *Merton of the Movies*; *The City That Never Sleeps*; *The Garden of Weeds*
1925 *Waking Up the Town* (+ co-story); *The Goose Hangs High*; *Welcome Home*; *Marry Me*; *Beggar on Horseback*; *The Pony Express*
1926 *Mannequin*; *Old Ironsides* (*Sons of the Sea*); *The Waiter from the Ritz* (unreleased)
1927 *We're All Gamblers*; *The City Gone Wild*; *On to Reno*
1928 *The Mating Call*; *The Red Mark*; *Excess Baggage* (+ pr)
1929 *A Man's Man* (+ pr); *The Duke Steps Out* (+ pr); *The Great Gabbo*
1930 *Once a Gentleman*; *She Got What She Wanted*
1931 *Salvation Nell*
1932 *Racetrack*; *Washington Merry-Go-Round* (*Invisible Power*); "The Condemned Man" episode (or, according to other sources, "The Streetwalker" and "The Old Ladies' Home" episodes) of *If I Had a Million*
1933 *Sailor Be Good*; *I Cover the Waterfront*; *Mr. Skitch*
1934 *David Harum*; *Their Big Moment* (*Afterwards*); *Helldorado*
1935 *Two-Fisted*
1936 *Sutter's Gold*
1937 *The Wrong Road*
1938 *Prison Nurse*; *Gangs of New York*; *Come On Leathernecks*

Other Films:

1911 *A Boy of the Revolution* (role); *The Higher Law* (Nicholls) (role); *She* (Nicholls) (role)
1912 *Dr. Jekyll and Mr. Hyde* (Henderson) (role); *The Arab's Bride* (Nicholls) (role); *On Probation* (role); *Flying to Fortune* (role); *For Sale—A Life* (role); *Into the Desert* (Nicholls) (role); *Rejuvenation* (role); *Miss Arabella Snaith* (role); *Love's Miracle* (role); *Jess* (Nicholls) (role); *The Ring of a Spanish Grandee* (role); *East Lynne* (Nicholls) (role); *Called Back* (Nicholls) (role); *Whom God Hath Joined* (Nicholls) (role); *Lucille* (role); *Undine* (role); *But the Greatest of These Is Charity* (role); *Put Yourself in His Place* (role); *Miss Robinson Crusoe* (role); *When Mercy Tempers Justice* (role); *The Thunderbolt* (role); *Cross Your Heart* (role); *The Other Half* (role); *A Militant Suffragette* (role); *The Cry of the Children* (role); *The Star of Bethlehem* (role)
1913 *The Dove in the Eagle's nest* (Marston) (role); *A Poor Relation* (role); *The Tiniest of Stars* (role); *When the Studio Burned* (Marston) (role); *Good Morning, Judge* (role); *Napoleon's Lucky Stone* (role); *The Idol of the Hour* (role); *Her Gallant Knights* (role); *For Her Boy's Sake* (role); *Cymbeline* (role); *The Woman Who Did Not Care* (role); *The Marble Heart* (role); *Her Sister's Secret* (role); *The Snare of Fate* (role); *The Lost Combination* (role); *Tannhauser* (role); *Rosie's Revenge* (role); *The Ward of the King* (role); *The Message of Headquarters* (role); *Plot Against the Governor* (Heffron) (role); *A Girl Worth While* (role)
1914 *Joseph in the Land of Egypt* (Moore) (role); *Frou Frou* (role); *The Legend of Provence* (role); *Why Reginald Reformed* (role); *The Woman Pays* (role); *Cardinal Richelieu's Ward* (role); *A Leak in the Foreign Office* (role); *The Desert Tribesman* (role); *The Cat's Paw* (role); *The Million Dollar Mystery* (Hansel) (serial) (role); *A Debut in the Secret Service* (role); *A Mohammedan Conspiracy* (role); *From Wash to Washington* (role); *Zudora* (*The Zudora Mystery*) (Sullivan) (serial) (role)
1915 *The Twenty Million Dollar Mystery* (Hansel) (serial) (role); *The Heart of Princess Mitsari* (role); *The Patriot and the Spy* (role); *His Guardian Auto* (role); *Armstrong's Wife* (role)
1916 *The Snowbird* (Carewe) (role)
1917 *What Money Can't Buy* (Tellegen) (role); *The Call of the East* (Melford) (role); *Nan of Music Mountain* (Melford) (role)
1918 *Hidden Pearls* (Melford) (role); *Wild Youth* (Melford) (role); *Believe Me Xantippe* (Crisp) (role); *The Source* (Melford) (role); *Under the Top* (Crisp) (role)
1919 *Johnny Get Your Gun* (Crisp) (role)

Publications

By CRUZE: articles—

"Jimmie Cruze," an interview with Frank Condon, in *Photoplay* (New York), September 1914.
Interview in *Motion Picture Classic* (Brooklyn), November 1918.

On CRUZE: books—

Everson, William K., and George N. Fenin, *The Western: From Silents to Cinerama,* New York, 1962; revised edition, as *The Western: From Silents to the Seventies,* 1977.
Brownlow, Kevin, *The War, The West, and the Wilderness,* New York, 1979.
Buscombe, Ed, editor, *The BFI Companion to the Western,* London, 1989.

On CRUZE: articles—

Donnell, D., "Cruze, Trail-Breaker," in *Motion Picture Classic* (Brooklyn), September 1925.
Condon, Frank, "Cruze, Director," in *Collier's* (New York), 28 March 1936.
Obituary in *New York Times,* 5 August 1942.
Obituary in *Time* (New York), 17 August 1942.
Geltzer, George, "James Cruze," in *Films in Review* (New York), June/July 1954.
Cohen, J., "Cruze's Last Efforts," in *Films in Review* (New York), August/September 1954.
Starman, R., "James Cruze—Cinema's Forgotten Director," in *Films in Review* (New York), October 1985.
Brown, Karl, "James Cruze," in *Films in Review* (New York), April 1986.

* * *

James Cruze

James Cruze was selected in the "Film Daily" annual nationwide poll as one of the top ten Hollywood directors in 1926 and 1928. During the year in between, he was the highest salaried one, earning an impressive $7,000 a week. Yet today, Cruze is no more than a footnote in film history, long deceased and long forgotten. His career did survive the advent of sound but, unlike Ford and Lubitsch and others, he did not really thrive. Cruze was far from a great director: even at his peak, his films were awkwardly constructed, unimaginative, and even monotonous. But they were extremely popular, and his career is not unworthy of reappraisal.

Cruze began working in Hollywood in front of the camera, playing leads at Pathé and Thanhouser; in the second decade of the century, he was Thanhouser's most popular male star. He first directed Wallace Reid in *Too Many Millions,* then guided the actor through romantic farces and melodramas. He also made Fatty Arbuckle comedies.

Cruze's great contribution to cinema history came in 1923 with *The Covered Wagon.* The film is stagily directed and plays quite badly today, but it was the first of its kind: a large-scale, larger-than-life western drama of epic proportion that centered on the travails of a wagon train on its way west. Previously, westerns focused mostly on character interaction and drama; while these ingredients are noticeably lacking in *The Covered Wagon,* Cruze in this film was the first to open up and explore the possibility of setting a picture in the wide open spaces of the Southwest. Additionally, the film was responsible for renewing audience interest in westerns, which despite the popularity of Tom Mix and a few others, had been in decline. Cruze later unsuccessfully tried to repeat *The Covered Wagon's* popularity with *The Pony Express, Old Ironsides,* and, during the 1930s, *Sutter's Gold,* the latter almost bankrupting Universal Pictures.

Cruze also directed two of the early satires detailing the frustrations of hopeful youngsters who trek from small towns to Hollywood in search of motion picture stardom: *Hollywood* and *Merton of the Movies.* In 1927 he organized his own independent production-distribution organization, and then made *The Great Gabbo,* one of the earliest talkies. Erich von Stroheim starred in this bizarre drama of an egomaniacal, intolerant ventriloquist whose love for a dancer is communicated via the mouth of his dummy. There have subsequently been numerous variations on this theme, most memorably in the Cavalcanti classic *Dead of Night* and the atmospheric, underrated 1960s mystery, *Devil Doll.*

Cruze's sound films are not all potboilers. He also made *Washington Merry Go Round,* a political drama; the May Robson sequence in *If I Had a Million;* Will Rogers's *David Harum;* and a solid drama, *I Cover the Waterfront.* But his star rapidly dimmed and, like so many other silent era personalities, his decline was striking. His last credits before retiring in 1938 were such Republic "B" films as *Prison Nurse, Gangs of New York,* and *Come On Leathernecks.* By the time of his death in 1942, Cruze had seen his previous wealth dwindle away to nothing. As the Associated Press reported, "James Cruze, former motion picture director and producer, once had a hilltop mansion and a million dollars, but when he died ... his estate was valued at only $1,000."

—Rob Edelman

CUKOR, George

Nationality: American. **Born:** George Dewey Cukor in New York, 7 July 1899. **Education:** DeWitt Clinton High School, New York. **Military Service:** Served in U.S. armed forces; directed film for the Signal Corps., 1943. **Career:** Stage manager on Broadway, 1919-24; manager, stock company in Rochester, New York, and director, New York City, 1924-26; stage director, New York, 1926-29; co-director for Paramount in Hollywood, 1929-32; joined RKO, began association with Katharine Hepburn, 1932; began association with writers Ruth Gordon and Garson Kanin, 1947. **Awards:** Oscar for Best Director, and Directors Guild of America Award, for *My Fair Lady,* 1964; Honorary doctorates, University of Southern California, 1968, and Loyola University, Chicago, 1976; D.W. Griffith Award, Directors Guild of America, 1981; Golden Lion, Venice Festival, 1982. **Died:** 24 January 1983.

Films as Director:

1930 *Grumpy* (co-d); *The Virtuous Sin* (co-d); *The Royal Family of Broadway* (co-d)
1931 *Tarnished Lady*; *Girls About Town*
1932 *What Price Hollywood?*; *A Bill of Divorcement*; *Rockabye*; *One Hour with You* (co-d with Lubitsch, uncredited, + dialogue director); *The Animal Kingdom* (co-d, uncredited)
1933 *Our Betters*; *Dinner at Eight*; *Little Women*; *David Copperfield* (*The Personal History, Adventures, Experience, and Observations of David Copperfield, the Younger*); *No More Ladies* (co-d, uncredited)
1936 *Sylvia Scarlett*; *Romeo and Juliet*
1937 ***Camille***
1938 *Holiday*
1939 *Zaza*; ***The Women***; ***Gone with the Wind*** (co-d, uncredited)
1940 *Susan and God*; ***The Philadelphia Story***
1941 *A Woman's Face*; *Two-Faced Woman*
1942 *Her Cardboard Lover*
1943 *Keeper of the Flame*
1944 *Gaslight*; *Winged Victory*
1945 *I'll Be Seeing You* (co-d, uncredited)
1947 *A Double Life*; *Desire Me* (co-d, uncredited)
1949 *Edward My Son*; ***Adam's Rib***
1950 *A Life of Her Own*; *Born Yesterday*
1951 *The Model and the Marriage Broker*
1952 *The Marrying Kind*; *Pat and Mike*
1953 *The Actress*
1954 *It Should Happen to You*; ***A Star Is Born***
1956 *Bhowani Junction*
1957 *Les Girls*; *Wild Is the Wind*
1958 *Hot Spell* (co-d, uncredited)
1960 *Heller in Pink Tights*; *Let's Make Love*; *Song without End* (co-d, uncredited)
1962 *The Chapman Report*
1964 *My Fair Lady*
1969 *Justine*
1972 *Travels with My Aunt*
1975 *Love among the Ruins* (for TV)
1976 *The Bluebird*
1979 *The Corn Is Green* (for TV)
1981 *Rich and Famous*

Other Films:

1929 *River of Romance* (Wallace) (dialogue d)
1930 ***All Quiet on the Western Front*** (Milestone) (dialogue d)

Publications

By CUKOR: articles—

Interview with Eric Rohmer and Jean Domarchi, in *Cahiers du Cinéma* (Paris), January 1961.

George Cukor

"Conversation with George Cukor," with John Gillett and David Robinson, in *Sight and Sound* (London), Autumn 1964.
Interview with Richard Overstreet, in *Interviews with Film Directors,* edited by Andrew Sarris, New York, 1969.
Interview, in *The Celluloid Muse,* by Charles Higham and Joel Greenberg, New York, 1972.
Interview with Gene Phillips, in *Film Comment* (New York), Spring 1972.
"Cukor and Cukor," with J. Calendo, in *Interview* (New York), December 1973.
"The Director," in *Hollywood Directors: 1914-40,* edited by Richard Koszarski, New York, 1976.
"Surviving," an interview with John Taylor, in *Sight and Sound* (London), Summer 1977.
"Dialogue on Film: George Cukor," edited by James Powers, in *American Film* (Washington, D.C.,), February 1978.
"Carry On, Cukor," with J. McBride and T. McCarthy, in *Film Comment* (New York), September/October 1981.
Interview with Gene D. Phillips, in *Films and Filming* (London), January 1982.
Interview with J.P. Le Pavec and D. Rabourdin, in *Cinéma* (Paris), March 1982.

On CUKOR: books—

Langlois, Henri, and others, *Hommage a George Cukor,* Paris, 1963.
Domarchi, Jean, *George Cukor,* Paris, 1965.
Carey, Gary, *Cukor and Company: The Films of George Cukor and His Collaborators,* New York, 1971.
Lambert, Gavin, *On Cukor,* New York, 1972.
Clarens, Carlos, *George Cukor,* London, 1976.
Phillips, Gene D., *George Cukor,* Boston, 1982.
Bernadoni, James, *George Cukor: A Critical Study and Filmography,* Jefferson, North Carolina, 1985.
Haver, Ronald, *A Star is Born: The Making of the 1954 Movie and its 1983 Restoration,* London, 1989.

On CUKOR: articles—

Houston, Penelope, "Cukor and the Kanins," in *Sight and Sound* (London), Spring 1955.
Tozzi, Romano, "George Cukor: His Success Directing Women Has Obscured His Other Directorial Virtues," in *Films in Review* (New York), February 1958.
Reid, John, "So He Became a Lady's Man," in *Films and Filming* (London), August 1960.
"Retrospective Cukor" issue of *Cahiers du Cinema* (Paris), February 1964.
Buscombe, Ed, "On Cukor," in *Screen* (London), Autumn 1973.
Grisolia, M., "George Cukor, ou comment le desir vient aux femmes," in *Cinéma* (Paris), February 1974.
McBride, J., "George Cukor: The Blue Bird," in *Action* (Los Angeles), November/December 1975.
Friedman, A., "George Cukor: A Tribute," in *Cinema* (Beverly Hills), no. 35, 1976.
Sarris, Andrew, "Cukor," in *Film Comment* (New York), March/April 1978.
Estrin, Allen, "George Cukor," in *The Hollywood Professionals,* London and New York, 1980.
Bodeen, De Witt, "George Cukor," in *Films in Review* (New York), November 1981.
Flint, Peter, obituary in *New York Times,* 26 January 1983.
Hollywood Reporter, 26 and 28 January 1983.
Kanin, Garson, "George Cukor's Loving Marriage to the Movies," in *New York Times,* 30 January 1983.
"Cukor Section" of *Casablanca* (Madrid), March 1983.
Magny, Joel, "George Cukor: Un homme qui s'affiche," in *Cinéma* (Paris), March 1983.
Taylor, John Russell, "Remembering George Cukor," in *Films and Filming* (London), March 1983.
Clarens, Carlos, "The Cukor touch," in *Film Comment* (New York), March-April 1983.
Ward, L.E., "The Films of George Cukor," in *Classic Images* (Muscatine, Iowa), December 1986.

* * *

George Cukor's films range from classics like Greta Garbo's *Camille,* to *Adam's Rib* with Spencer Tracy and Katharine Hepburn, to the Judy Garland musical *A Star Is Born.* Throughout the years he managed to "weather the changes in public taste and the pressures of the Hollywood studio system without compromising his style, his taste, or his ethical standards," as his honorary degree from Loyola University of Chicago is inscribed. Indeed, Cukor informed each of the stories he brought to the screen with his affectionately critical view of humanity. In film after film he sought to prod the mass audience to reconsider their cherished illusions in order to gain fresh insights into the problems that confront everyone. "When a director has provided tasteful entertainment of a high order consistently," noted Andrew Sarris, "it is clear that he is much more than a mere entertainer, he is a genuine artist."

Although most of Cukor's films are adaptations of preexisting novels and plays, he has always chosen material that has been consistent with his view of reality. Most often he has explored the conflict between illusion and reality in peoples' lives. The chief characters in his films are frequently actors and actresses, for they, more than anyone, run the risk of allowing the world of illusion with which they are constantly involved to become their reality. This theme is obvious in many of Cukor's best films and appears in some of his earliest work, including *The Royal Family of Broadway,* which he co-directed. In it he portrays a family of troupers, based on the Barrymores, who are wedded to their world of fantasy in a way that makes a shambles of their private lives.

The attempt of individuals to reconcile their cherished dreams with the sober realities of life continues in films as superficially different as *Dinner at Eight, The Philadelphia Story,* and *A Double Life.* Ronald Colman earned an Academy Award in the latter as an actor who becomes so identified with the parts he plays that, while enacting Othello, he develops a murderous streak of jealousy which eventually destroys him.

While it is true that Cukor was often drawn to stories about show people, his films also suggest that everyone leads a double life that moves between illusion and reality, and that everyone must seek to sort out fantasy from fact if they are to cope realistically with their problems—something Cukor's characters frequently fail to do. *Les Girls* is the most explicit of all Cukor's films in treating this theme. Here the same events are told from four different points of view at a libel trial, each version differing markedly from the others. Because Cukor allows each narrator "equal time," he is sympathetic to the way each of them has subconsciously revised their common experiences in a manner that enables him or her to live with the past in the present. As Sarris remarks, Cukor does not imply that people necessarily are liars, but rather that they tell the truth in their own fashion.

Though Cukor must have harbored some degree of affection and sympathy for the world of romantic illusion—for there is always a hint of regret in his films when actuality inevitably asserts itself in the life of one of his dreamers—his movies nonetheless remain firmly rooted in, and committed to, the workaday world of reality.

Directing his last film, *Rich and Famous,* merited Cukor the distinction of being one of the oldest filmmakers ever to direct a major motion picture. His work on that film likewise marked him as a man who had enjoyed the longest continuous career of any director in film or television. Some of the satisfaction which he derived from his long career was grounded in the fact that few directors have commanded such a large portion of the mass audience. "His movies," Richard Schickel has noted, "can be appreciated—no, liked—at one level or another by just about everyone."

For his part, Cukor once reflected that "I look upon every picture that I make as the first one I've ever done—and the last. I love each film I have directed, and I try to make each one as good as I possibly can. Mind you, making movies is no bed of roses. Every day isn't Christmas. It's been a hard life, but also a joyous one."

—Gene D. Phillips

CURTIZ, Michael

Nationality: Hungarian. **Born:** Born Mihály Kertész in Budapest, 24 December 1888. Also known as Michael Courtice. **Education:** Markoszy University and Royal Academy of Theatre and Art, Budapest. **Military Service:** Served in Hungarian infantry, 1914-15. **Family:** Married 1) actress Lucy Dorraine, 1915 (divorced 1923); 2) Bess Meredyth. **Career:** Stage actor, 1906-12; directed first Hungarian feature film, *Az utolsó bohém,* 1912; studied filmmaking at Nordisk Studios in Denmark, 1912-14; managing director, Phönix Studios, Hungary, 1917; left Hungary, worked in Swedish, French, and German film industries, 1918; director for Sascha Films, Austria, 1919; signed by Jack Warner, directed first Hollywood film, *The 3rd Degree,* 1926. **Awards:** Oscar for Best Director for *Casablanca,* 1943. **Died:** 11 April 1962.

Films as Director:

(as Mihály Kertész)

1912 *Az utolsó bohém* (*The Last Bohemian*); *Ma es holnap* (*Today and Tomorrow*) (+ role)

1913 *Rablélek* (*Captive Soul*); *Hazasodik az uram* (*My Husband Lies*)

1914 *A hercegnö Pongyolaban* (*Princess Pongyola*); *Az éjszaka rabjai* (*Slaves of the Night*) (+ role); *A Kölcsönkért csecsemök* (*Borrowed Babies*); *Bánk bán*; *A toloncz* (*The Vagrant*); *Aranyáso* (*The Golden Shovel*)

1915 *Akit ketten szeretnek* (*Loved By Two*) (+ role)

1916 *Az ezust kecske* (*The Silver Goat*) (+ co-sc); *A medikus* (*The Apothecary*); *Doktor ur* (*The Doctor*); *Farkas* (*The Wolf*); *A fekete szivarvany* (*The Black Rainbow*); *Makkhetes* (*Seven of Clubs*); *Karthauzi* (*The Carthusian*); *A Magyar föld ereje* (*The Strength of the Hungarian Soil*)

1917 *Arendás zsidó* (*John, the Tenant*); *Az ezredes* (*The Colonel*); *A föld embere* (*The Man of the Soil*); *Halálcsengö* (*The Death Bell*); *A kuruzslo* (*The Charlatan*); *A Szentjóbi erdö titka* (*The Secret of St. Job Forest*); *A senki fia* (*Nobody's Son*); *Tavasz a télben* (*Spring in Wintertime*); *Zoárd Mester* (*Master Zoard*); *Tatárjárás* (*Invasion*); *A béke ut ja* (*The Road to Peace*); *A vörös Sámson* (*The Red Samson*); *Az utolsó hajnal* (*The Last Dawn*); *Egy krajcár története* (*The Story of a Penny*)

1918 *Kilencvenkilenc* (*99*); *Judás*; *Lulu*; *Az ördög* (*The Devil*); *A napraforgós hölgy* (*The Lady with Sunflowers*); *Alraune* (co-d); *Vig özvegy* (*The Merry Widow*) (+ sc); *Varázskeringö* (*Magic Waltz*); *Lu, a kokott* (*Lu, the Cocotte*); *A Wellingtoni rejtély* (*The Wellington Mystery*); *Szamárbör* (*The Donkey Skin*); *A csunya fiu* (*The Ugly Boy*); *A skorpió* (*The Scorpion*)

1919 *Jön az öcsem* (*John the Younger Brother*); *Liliom* (unfinished)

(in Austria, as Michael Kertesz)

1919 *Die Dame mit dem schwarzen Handschuh* (*The Lady with the Black Glove*)

1920 *Der Stern von Damaskus*; *Die Dame mit den Sonnenblum* (+ sc); *Herzogin Satanella*; *Boccaccio* (+ pr); *Die Gottesgeisel*

1921 *Cherchez la femme*; *Dorothys Bekenntnis* (*Frau Dorothys Bekenntnis*); *Wege des Schreckens* (*Labyrinth des Grauens*); *Miss Tutti Frutti*

1922 *Sodom und Gomorrah: Part I. Die Sünde* (*Die Legende von Sünde und Strafe*) (+ co-sc)

1923 *Sodom und Gomorrah: Part II. Die Strafe* (*Die Legende von Sünde und Strafe*) (+ co-sc); *Samson und Dalila* (co-d); *Der Lawine* (*Avalanche*); *Der junge Medardus*; *Namenlos* (*Der Scharlatan*; *Der falsche Arzt*)

1924 *Ein Spiel ums Leben*; *Harun al Raschid*; *Die Slavenkönigin* (*Moon of Israel*)

1925 *Celimene, Poupee de Montmartre* (*Das Spielzeug von Paris*; *Red Heels*)

1926 *Der goldene Schmetterling* (*The Road to Happiness*); *Fiaker Nr. 13* (*Einspänner Nr. 13*)

(in United States, as Michael Curtiz)

1926 *The Third Degree*

1927 *A Million Bid*; *Good Time Charley*; *A Desired Woman*

1928 *Tenderloin*

1929 *Noah's Ark*; *The Glad Rag Doll*; *Madonna of Avenue A*; *Hearts in Exile*; *The Gamblers*

1930 *Mammy*; *Under a Texas Moon*; *The Matrimonial Bed* (*A Matrimonial Problem*); *Bright Lights*; *A Soldier's Plaything* (*A Soldier's Pay*); *River's End*

1931 *Dämon des Meeres* (German language version of Lloyd Bacon's *Moby Dick*); *God's Gift to Women* (*Too Many Women*); *The Mad Genius*

1932 *The Woman from Monte Carlo*; *Alias the Doctor*; *The Strange Love of Molly Louvain*; *Doctor X*; *Cabin in the Cotton*

1933 *Twenty Thousand Years in Sing Sing*; *The Mystery of the Wax Museum*; *The Keyhole*; *Private Detective 62*; *Goodbye Again*; *The Kennel Murder Case*; *Female*

1934 *Mandalay*; *British Agent*; *Jimmy the Gent*; *The Key*

1935 *Black Fury*; *The Case of the Curious Bride*; *Front Page Woman*; *Little Big Shot*; *Captain Blood*

1936 *The Walking Dead*; *Stolen Holiday*; *Charge of the Light Brigade*

1937 *Kid Galahad*; *Mountain Justice*; *The Perfect Specimen*

1938 *Gold is Where You Find It*; ***The Adventures of Robin Hood*** (co-d); *Four Daughters*; *Four's a Crowd*; *Angels with Dirty Faces*

1939 *Dodge City*; *Sons of Liberty*; *The Private Lives of Elizabeth and Essex*; *Four Wives*; *Daughters Courageous*

1940 *Virginia City*; *The Sea Hawk*; *Santa Fe Trail*

1941 *The Sea Wolf*; *Dive Bomber*

1942 *Captains of the Clouds*; ***Yankee Doodle Dandy***; ***Casablanca***

1943 *Mission to Moscow*; *This is the Army*

1944 *Passage to Marseille*; *Janie*

1945 *Roughly Speaking*; ***Mildred Pierce***

1946 *Night and Day*

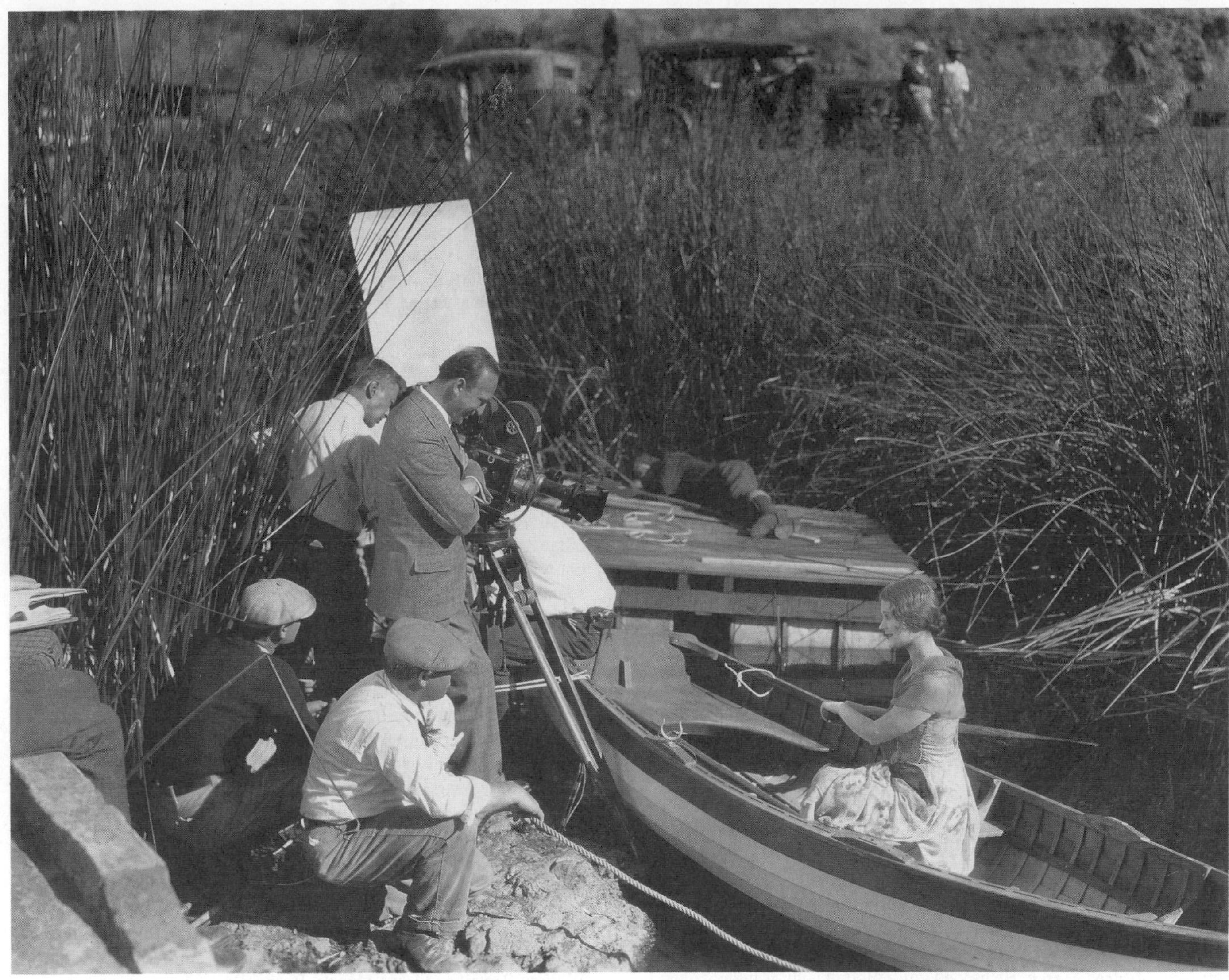

Michael Curtiz directing Dolores Costello in *Tenderloin*

1947 *Life with Father*; *The Unsuspected*
1948 *Romance on the High Seas* (*It's Magic*)
1949 *My Dream is Yours* (+ pr); *Flamingo Road* (+ exec pr); *The Lady Takes a Sailor*
1950 *Young Man with a Horn* (*Young Man of Music*); *Bright Leaf*; *Breaking Point*
1951 *Jim Thorpe—All American* (*Man of Bronze*); *Force of Arms*
1952 *I'll See You in My Dreams*; *The Story of Will Rogers*
1953 *The Jazz Singer*; *Trouble Along the Way*
1954 *The Boy from Oklahoma*; *The Egyptian*; *White Christmas*
1955 *We're No Angels*
1956 *The Scarlet Hour* (+ pr); *The Vagabond King*; *The Best Things in Life are Free*
1957 *The Helen Morgan Story* (*Both Ends of the Candle*)
1958 *The Proud Rebel*; *King Creole*
1959 *The Hangman*; *The Man in the Net*
1960 *The Adventures of Huckleberry Finn*; *A Breath of Scandal* (*Olympia*)
1961 *Francis of Assisi*
1962 *The Comancheros*

Other Films:

1913 *Atlantis* (Blom) (asst d, role)

Publications

By CURTIZ: article—

"Talent Shortage is Causing Two-Year Production Delay," in *Films and Filming* (London), June 1956.

On CURTIZ: books—

Martin, Pete, *Hollywood Without Makeup,* New York, 1948.
Anobile, Richard, editor, *Michael Curtiz's "Casablanca,"* New York, 1975.
Rosenzweig, Sidney, *"Casablanca" and other Major Films of Michael Curtiz,* Ann Arbor, Michigan, 1982.
Kinnard, Roy, and R.J. Vitone, *The American Films of Michael Curtiz,* Metuchen, New Jersey, 1986.

Mayne, Judith, *Private Novels, Public Films,* Athens, Georgia, 1988.

On CURTIZ: articles—

Martin, Pete, "Hollywood's Champion Language Assassin," in *Saturday Evening Post* (New York), 2 August 1947.

Sarris, Andrew, "Likable but Elusive," in *Film Culture* (New York), Spring 1963.

Dienstfrey, Harris, "Hitch Your Genre to a Star," in *Film Culture* (New York), Fall 1964.

Callenbach, Ernest, "Comparative Anatomy of Folk-Myth Films: *Robin Hood* and *Antonio das Mortes*," in *Film Quarterly* (Berkeley), Winter 1969/70.

Nolan, Jack Edmund, "Michael Curtiz," in *Films in Review* (New York), no. 9, 1970.

Behlmer, R., and A. Pinto, "Letters," in *Films in Review* (New York), February 1971.

Davis, John, "*Captain Blood*," in *Velvet Light Trap* (Madison, Wisconsin), June 1971.

Davis, John, "*The Unsuspected*," in *Velvet Light Trap* (Madison, Wisconsin), Summer 1972.

Davis, John, "The Tragedy of *Mildred Pierce*," in *Velvet Light Trap* (Madison, Wisconsin), Fall 1972.

Canham, Kingsley, "Michael Curtiz," in *The Hollywood Professionals, Vol. 1,* London, 1973.

Shadoian, J., "Michael Curtiz' *Twenty Thousand Years in Sing Sing*," in *Journal of Popular Film* (Bowling Green, Ohio), Spring 1973.

Davis, John, "When Will They Ever Learn?," in *Velvet Light Trap* (Madison, Wisconsin), Autumn 1975.

Berard, V.R., and P. Canniere, "Michael Curtiz: Maître du baroque," in *Image et Son* (Paris), February 1982.

Werner, G., "Fran Lidingon till *Casablanca*?" in *Chaplin* (Stockholm), vol. 26, no. 2, 1984.

* * *

The films of Michael Curtiz have come to symbolize Warner Brothers Studios of the 1930s and 1940s. Curtiz directed many favorites from that era, including *Captain Blood, The Charge of the Light Brigade, The Sea Hawk, Yankee Doodle Dandy, 20,000 Years in Sing Sing,* and *Mildred Pierce.* He helped guide Bette Davis as her popularity rose in the 1930s, and helped establish Errol Flynn as the symbol of the swashbuckling hero. James Cagney (*Yankee Doodle Dandy*) and Joan Crawford (*Mildred Pierce*) both won Oscars under Curtiz's direction. His long career and directorial strengths benefitted from the constant work available in the studios of the 1930s and 1940s. Most observers, however, note a precipitous decline in the quality of Curtiz's films after World War II.

Surely Curtiz's most famous creation for today's audience is *Casablanca,* the only film for which he received an Oscar for Best Director. This cult favorite now has achieved a life of its own and established Bogart and Bergman as modern folk heroes. Conversely, director Curtiz has been lost in the shuffle with the passage of time. The anti-auteurist argument seems to be that this particular film represents a happy "accident" of the studio system, and that its enduring popularity should not be credited to its director. What is lost in this analysis is the fact that *Casablanca* was a major hit of 1943 (finishing among the top grossing films of the year), won three Academy Awards (Best Picture, Director, and Screenplay), and earned Curtiz several awards as the year's best director. Critics of the day recognized Curtiz's input. Certainly today we should give proper credit to the director of a film that was popular upon release, continues to be popular today, and has influenced countless other works.

Curtiz has been difficult for film historians to deal with because of the length and breadth of his career. Usually overlooked is the time he spent in Europe; Curtiz did not begin with Warner Brothers until he came to the United States at the age of thirty-eight. His career began in Hungary, where he participated in the beginning of the Hungarian film industry, usually receiving credit for directing that country's first feature film.

Curtiz remained active until the outbreak of the First World War. After the war he moved to Vienna where he directed several important films, including the epic *Sodom and Gomorrah.* Scholars know little else about this part of Curtiz's career, however. Accounts of other activities lead only to contradictions; no wholly reliable list of credits exists. Sadly, historians have written off the first two decades of Curtiz's career. We know a great deal of the work of other emigrés, such as Fritz Lang and F.W. Murnau, but virtually nothing of Curtiz.

Not unexpectedly there exist several versions of why and how Warner Brothers contacted Curtiz and brought him to the United States. Regardless, from 1926 Curtiz became intertwined with all the innovations of the Warner Brothers studio. In the mid-1920s he was thrust into Warner attempts to innovate sound. His *Tenderloin* and *Noah's Ark* were two-part talkies which achieved considerable popularity and garnered millions in box-office revenues. In a key transitional year, 1930, Curtiz directed no less than six Warner Brothers talkies. In that same year Warner Brothers tried to introduce color, but with none of the success associated with the studio's efforts with sound. Curtiz's *Mammy,* one of Jolson's follow-ups to *The Jazz Singer* and *The Singing Fool,* had color sequences. In 1933 he directed the well-regarded, all-color, horror film, *The Mystery of the Wax Museum.*

Curtiz's record during the transition to sound elevated him to the top echelon of contract directors at Warner Brothers. Unlike others, Curtiz seemed not to utilize this success to push for greater freedom and independence. Instead, he seemed content to take what was assigned, executing his work in a classic style. He produced crisp flowing narratives, seeking efficiency of method. He was a conservative director, adapting, borrowing, and ultimately utilizing all the dominant codes of the Hollywood system. Stylistic innovations were left to others. Today critics praise the film noir look of *Mildred Pierce,* but this film was never thought of as one of the forerunners of that style when it was initially released. After *Mildred Pierce,* Curtiz moved on to *Night and Day,* the fictionalized life of Cole Porter starring Cary Grant, and *Life With Father,* a nostalgic, light family romance starring William Powell and Irene Dunne. Both of these latter features took in a great deal of money and earned considerable critical praise, once again demonstrating how well Curtiz could operate when called upon by his employer.

If there is a way to get a handle on the enormous output of Curtiz's career, it is through genre analysis. In the early 1930s Curtiz stuck to formula melodramas. His limited participation in Warner Brothers's social realism cycles came with films like *Black Fury,* which looked at strikebreaking. Curtiz seemed to hit his stride with Warner Brothers's Errol Flynn pirate cycle of the late 1930s. *Captain Blood* and *The Sea Hawk* stand as lasting symbols of Hollywood's ability to capture the sweep of romantic adventure. Warner Brothers also sent director Curtiz and star Flynn to the Old West in *Dodge City* and *Virginia City.*

In the early 1940s the Warner studio returned to the musical, establishing its niche with the biographical film. Curtiz participated, directing *Yankee Doodle Dandy* (which depicted George M. Cohan's life), *This Is the Army* (Irving Berlin), and the aforementioned *Night and Day* (Cole Porter). *Yankee Doodle Dandy* demonstrated how well this European emigré had taken to the United States. Curtiz would continue to deal with Americana in his films during the 1940s. For example, he touched deep American ideological strains with *Casablanca,* while *Mildred Pierce* examined the dark side of the American family. Feminist critics have noted how the portrait of a strong woman in the latter film mirrors the freedom women achieved during World War II—a freedom withdrawn after the war when the men returned home.

The family in *Mildred Pierce* is constructed in an odd, bitter way, contrasting with Curtiz's affectionate portrait in *Life with Father.*

Genre analysis is helpful, but in the end it still tells us too little of what we want to know about this important director. As critics and historians continue to go through his films and utilize the records now available at the University of Wisconsin, University of Southern California, and Princeton, more insights will come to light about Curtiz's participation in the Hollywood studio system. In the meantime, Curtiz's films will live on for the fans with continual re-screenings of *Casablanca, Mildred Pierce,* and *The Adventures of Robin Hood.*

—Douglas Gomery

DAHL, John

Nationality: American. **Born:** John Roger Dahl, in Billings, Montana, 15 June 1956. **Education:** Studied fine arts at the University of Montana, 1974-76; Montana State University, B.S. in motion-picture production (with honors), 1981; Directing Fellow at American Film Institute, Los Angeles, 1982. **Family:** Married Beth-jana Friedberg. **Career:** Made amateur films in high school; assistant director on PBS-TV action-adventure series *Powerhouse,* 1981; wrote unmade comedy film scripts; sold screenplay of *Kill Me Again* to pop-promo company Propaganda Films, which allowed him to direct it himself. **Awards:** New Generation Award, Los Angeles Film Critics Association, for *Red Rock West* and *The Last Seduction.* **Agent:** UTA, 9560 Wilshire Blvd., Suite 500, Beverly Hills, CA 90212, U.S.A.

Films as Director:

1989 *Kill Me Again* (+ co-sc)
1993 *Red Rock West* (+ co-sc)
1994 *The Last Seduction*; *Meltdown*
1995 *Unforgettable* (+ co-sc, uncredited)

Other Films:

1984 *The Dungeonmaster* (Turko) (asst d)
1987 *P.I. Private Investigations* (Dick) (co-sc, 2nd unit d)

Publications

On DAHL: articles—

Otto, Susan, "Western Noir," in *FilmMaker* (Los Angeles), Summer 1994.

Charity, Tom, "Femme at Last," in *Time Out* (London), 3 August 1994.

Francke, Lizzie, "Never a Dahl Moment," in *The Guardian* (London), 4 August 1994.

Hoberman, J., "Made-for-TV Noir," in *Premiere* (New York), December 1994.

* * *

Though John Dahl has established himself, on the basis of his first three features, as one of the leading practitioners of neo-noir, his films hardly follow the tradition of noir in its classic urban manifestation. Rather, they fit the style of the urban mainstream's country cousin: rural (or even cowboy) noir. Mainstream noir is dark alleys and rainslicked city streets; rural noir is dusty, dead-end townships in Nevada or Wyoming. Urban noir is cocktail jazz, Hammett and Chandler; rural noir is rangy guitars and Jim Thompson. During the classic period of noir, the rural variety was relatively sparse (Nicholas Ray's *They Live by Night* might qualify, or Joseph H. Lewis's *Gun Crazy*), but in recent years the style has enjoyed a revival—perhaps because its imagery is less played out, less recycled through countless commercials, than that of the urban branch. Dahl's initial trio of films show that rural noir, stylishly and wittily handled, can still prove a rich lode to mine.

Dahl identifies the essential elements of noir, common to all forms of the genre, as "deceit, betrayal, wayward desire"—usually centred around the key figure of the femme fatale. In each of his films hapless males, led on as much by their libido as by the lure of easy money, wind up duped or worse by the much smarter and far less susceptible female (although in *Red Rock West* the hero turns the tables in a last-minute twist). Due to weaknesses of casting, the anti-heroines of Dahl's first two films never quite live up to their classic models, but in *The Last Seduction*—immeasurably helped by a *tour de force* performance from Linda Fiorentino—Dahl creates a femme fatale to stand with the greatest of her kind. Avaricious and manipulative, so sure of her sexual power that she has little need for dissimulation, Fiorentino's Bridget reacts to the suckers around her with barely concealed contempt. When a small-town stud, trying to pick her up in a bar, boasts that he's "hung like a horse," she calmly unzips him and plunges her hand in to check for herself.

Scenes like this underline the difference between the classic noir treatments of a similar set-up (*The Killers* or *Out of the Past,* for example) and Dahl's brand of neo-noir: Dahl is essentially playing it for laughs, relying on our familiarity with the conventions of the genre to rework them for black comedy. Not that this implies any softening of tone; the films pull no punches in terms of emotional or physical mayhem, and their endings are unfailingly bleak. But there's a constant undertow of sly humour, inviting us to relish the sheer brazenness of Bridget's ploys or the increasingly desperate attempts of Michael Rudd, fall-guy of *Red Rock West,* to escape the eponymous burg as every circumstance conspires to drag him back there.

Dahl's chief predecessors in this field of black-comedy-tinged rural noir are Joel and Ethan Coen, who staked out the territory with their 1984 film debut, *Blood Simple.* But where the Coens hit the mark the first time around, it took Dahl longer to establish the ideal balance of tone, as he readily admits. "With the first [film] I was just getting started, with the second I was up to speed, and with the third one I was beginning to have some fun with the format. It's certainly the most humorous." In the case of *The Last Seduction* (the first of his films not scripted by himself), Dahl was particularly taken by the humour in the screenplay, and always conceived it as a black comedy—although "you don't say that too loud, because it scares off distributors and producers," he notes. "Some people originally felt they were making a sexy thriller, which is a lot easier to sell."

It would seem that audiences take to Dahl's films far more readily than the distribution networks. Despite the director's growing cult following, his two most accomplished films to date, *Red Rock West* and *The Last Seduction,* were at first denied cinematic release and premiered on cable television. In both cases, it was overseas exposure that rescued the films from HBO oblivion. *Red Rock West* opened in France and travelled via the Toronto Festival to San Francisco's Roxie cinema, where it broke house records. A telecast of *The Last Seduc-*

John Dahl: *The Last Seduction*

tion was already scheduled before the film scored a hit at the Berlin Festival, which secured it a belated U.S. release.

Although he finds noir "endlessly fascinating," Dahl denies having set out to specialise in the genre. "So after I'd made three similar films, all of a sudden I'm a genre guy. But it was completely unintentional," he explains. Even so, his tastes are clearly angled towards the downside of human nature ("a love story wouldn't exactly be my forte"). So far, Dahl has luckily escaped commercial pressures to lighten his tone; on the strength of his work to date—especially *The Last Seduction*—it is greatly to be hoped that his luck holds.

—Philip Kemp

DASSIN, Jules

Nationality: American. **Born:** Middletown, Connecticut, 12 December 1911. **Education:** Morris High School, the Bronx, New York. **Family:** Married 1) Beatrice Launer, 1933 (divorced 1962), one son, two daughters; 2) actress Melina Mercouri, 1966. **Career:** Member of Artef Players (Jewish socialist theatre collective), 1936; directed first Broadway production, *Medicine Show,* 1939; contracted to RKO (moved to MGM after eight months), Hollywood, 1940; left MGM and worked with producer Mark Hellinger, 1946; named by Edward Dmytryk and Frank Tuttle in HUAC testimony as member of Hollywood "Communist faction," 1951; subpoenaed by HUAC, 1952; moved to Europe, 1953. **Awards:** Best Director Award (shared), Cannes Festival, for *Rififi,* 1955. **Address:** 25 Anagnostopoulou St., Athens, Greece.

Films as Director:

1941 *The Tell-Tale Heart* (short)
1942 *Nazi Agent*; *The Affairs of Martha* (*Once Upon a Thursday*); *Reunion* (*Reunion in France*; *Mademoiselle France*)
1943 *Young Ideas*
1944 *The Canterville Ghost*
1946 *A Letter for Evie*; *Two Smart People*
1947 *Brute Force*
1948 ***The Naked City***
1949 *Thieves' Highway*
1950 *Night and the City*
1955 ***Du Rififi chez les hommes*** (*Rififi*) (+ co-sc, role as jewel thief under pseudonym Perlo Vita)
1958 *Celui qui doit mourir* (*He Who Must Die*) (+ co-sc)
1959 *La legge* (*La Loi*) (released in U.S. 1960 as *Where the Hot Winds Blow*) (+ sc)
1960 *Pote tin kyriaki* (*Never on Sunday*) (+ pr, sc, role)

1962 *Phaedra* (+ pr, co-sc)
1964 *Topkapi* (+ pr)
1966 *10:30 p.m. Summer* (+ co-pr, sc, bit role)
1967 *Survival 67* (+ co-pr, appearance) (documentary)
1968 *Uptight!* (+ pr, co-sc)
1971 *La Promesse de l'aube* (*Promise at Dawn*) (+ pr, sc, role as Ivan Mozhukhin under pseudonym Perlo Vita)
1974 *The Rehearsal* (+ sc)
1978 *A Dream of Passion* (+ pr, sc)
1980 *Circle of Two* (released in USA 1982)

Publications

By DASSIN: articles—

Interview with Claude Chabrol and François Truffaut, in *Cahiers du Cinéma* (Paris), April and May 1955.
Interview with Cynthia Grenier, in *Sight and Sound* (London), Winter 1957/58.
Interview with George Bluestone, in *Film Culture* (New York), February 1958.
"I See Dassin Make the Law," interview with John Lane, in *Films and Filming* (London), September 1958.
"Style and Instinct," interview with Gordon Gow, in *Films and Filming* (London), February and March 1970.
"'A Dream of Passion': An Interview with Jules Dassin," with D. Georgakas and P. Anastasopoulos, in *Cinéaste* (New York), Fall 1978.

On DASSIN: books—

Ferrero, Adelio, *Jules Dassin,* Parma, 1961.
McArthur, Colin, *Underworld USA,* London, 1972.
Schuster, Mel, *The Contemporary Greek Cinema,* Metuchen, New Jersey, 1979.
Arnold, Frank, and Michael Esser, *Hommage fur Melina Mercouri und Jules Dassin,* Berlin, 1984.
Siclier, Fabrien, and Jacques Levy, *Jules Dassin,* Paris, 1986.

On DASSIN: articles—

Alpert, Hollis, "Greek Passion," in *Saturday Review* (New York), 20 December 1958.
Hammel, F., "A Director's Return," in *Cue* (New York), 10 March 1962.
"Jules Dassin," in *Film Dope* (London), April 1976.
Horton, A., "Jules Dassin: A Multi-national Filmmaker Considered," in *Film Criticism* (Meadville, Pennsylvania), Spring 1984.

* * *

Between the mid-1940s and the late 1950s, Jules Dassin directed some of the better realistic, hard-bitten, fast-paced crime dramas produced in America, before his blacklisting and subsequent move to Europe. However, while he has made some very impressive films, his career as a whole is lacking in artistic cohesion.

Dassin's films are occasionally innovative: *The Naked City* is one of the first police dramas shot on location, on the streets of New York; *Rififi* is a forerunner of detailed jewelry heist dramas, highlighted by a thirty-five-minute sequence chronicling the break-in, shot without a word of dialogue or note of music; *Never on Sunday,* starring his wife Melina Mercouri as a happy hooker, made the actress an international star, won her an Academy Award nomination, and popularized in America the Greek *bouzouki* music. *The Naked City* and *Rififi* are particularly exciting, as well as trend-setting, while *Brute Force* remains a striking, naturalistic prison drama, with Burt Lancaster in one of his most memorable early performances and Hume Cronyn wonderfully despicable as a Hitlerish guard captain. *Thieves' Highway,* also shot on location, is a vivid drama of truck driver Richard Conte taking on racketeer Lee J. Cobb. *Topkapi* is a *Rififi* remake, with a delightful touch of comedy.

Many of Dassin's later films, such as *Brute Force* and *Thieves' Highway,* attempt to observe human nature: they focus on the individual fighting his own demons while trying to survive within a chaotic society. For example, in *A Dream of Passion,* an updating of Sophocles' *Medea,* an American woman is jailed in Greece for the murder of her three children; *Up Tight,* the filmmaker's first American-made release after the McCarthy hysteria, is a remake of *The Informer* set in a black ghetto. Unfortunately, they are all generally flawed: with the exception of *Never on Sunday* and *Topkapi,* his collaborations with Melina Mercouri (from *He Who Must Die* to *A Dream of Passion*) are disappointing, while *Up Tight* pales beside the original. *Circle of Two,* with teenager Tatum O'Neal baring her breasts for aging Richard Burton, had a limited release. Dassin's early triumphs have been obscured by his more recent fiascos, and as a result his critical reputation is now irrevocably tarnished.

The villain in his career is the blacklist, which tragically clipped his wings just as he was starting to fly. Indeed, he could not find work in Europe for five years, as producers felt American distributors would automatically ban any film with his signature. When *Rififi* opened, critics wrote about Dassin as if he were European. The *New York Herald Tribune* reported in 1961, "At one ceremony, when the award to *Rififi* was announced, (Dassin) was called to the dais, and a French flag was raised above him. 'It should have been a moment of triumph but I feel awful. They were honoring my work and I'm an American.

Jules Dassin

It should have been the American flag raised in honor.'" The blacklist thus denied Jules Dassin his roots. In 1958, it was announced that he was planning to adapt James T. Farrell's *Studs Lonigan,* a project that was eventually shelved. It is one more tragedy of the blacklist that Dassin was not allowed to follow up *Brute Force, The Naked City,* and *Thieves' Highway* with *Studs Lonigan.*

—Rob Edelman

DAVES, Delmer

Nationality: American. **Born:** San Francisco, 24 July 1904. **Education:** Studied civil engineering; received law degree from Stanford University. **Family:** Married actress Mary Lou Lender. **Career:** Lived for several months in Arizona desert among Hopi and Navajo, renounced law career, and joined Pasadena Playhouse, 1925; joined James Cruze production company as property boy, 1927; scriptwriter at Warner Bros., also actor, from 1929; directed first film, *Destination Tokyo,* 1944; formed Diamond-D productions, 1950s. **Died:** September 1977.

Films as Director and Scriptwriter:

1944 *Destination Tokyo*; *The Very Thought of You*; *Hollywood Canteen*
1945 *Pride of the Marines* (*Forever in Love, Body and Soul*)
1947 *The Red House*; *Dark Passage*
1948 *To the Victor* (d only)
1949 *A Kiss in the Dark*; *Task Force*
1950 *Broken Arrow* (d only)
1951 *Bird of Paradise*
1952 *Return of the Texan* (d only)
1953 *Treasure of the Golden Condor*; *Never Let Me Go* (d only)
1954 *Demetrius and the Gladiators* (d only); *Drum Beat*
1956 *Jubal*; *The Last Wagon*
1957 *3:10 to Yuma* (d only)
1958 *Cowboy* (d only); *Kings Go Forth* (d only); *The Badlanders* (d only)
1959 *The Hanging Tree* (d only); *A Summer Place* (+ pr)
1961 *Parrish* (+ pr); *Susan Slade* (+ pr)
1962 *Rome Adventure* (*Lovers Must Learn*) (+ pr)
1963 *Spencer's Mountain* (+ pr)
1964 *Youngblood Hawke* (+ pr)
1965 *The Battle of the Villa Fiorita* (+ pr)

Other Films:

1915 *Christmas Memories* (Leonard) (role)
1925 *Zander the Great* (Hill) (role)
1928 *The Night Flyer* (Lang) (role, prop man); *Three Sinners* (Lee) (role); *The Red Mark* (Cruze) (role, prop man); *Excess Baggage* (Cruze) (role, prop man)
1929 *So This Is College* (Wood) (co-sc, role); *A Man's Man* (Cruze) (bit role, prop man); *The Duke Steps Out* (Cruze) (role, tech adv)
1930 *The Bishop Murder Case* (Grinde and Burton) (role); *Good News* (Grinde and McGregor)
1931 *Shipmates* (Pollard) (co-adapt, co-dialogue, role, sc)
1932 *Divorce in the Family* (Riesner) (sc, role)
1933 *Clear All Wires* (Hill) (continuity)
1934 *No More Women* (Rogell) (co-sc, co-story); *Dames* (Enright) (sc); *Flirtation Walk* (Borzage) (sc)
1935 *Stranded* (Borzage) (co-sc); *Page Miss Glory* (LeRoy) (co-sc); *Shipmates Forever* (Borzage) (sc)
1936 *The Petrified Forest* (Mayo) (co-sc)
1937 *The Go Getter* (Berkeley) (sc); *Slim* (Enright) (co-sc, uncredited); *The Singing Marine* (Enright) (sc); *She Married an Artist* (Gering) (co-sc)
1938 *Professor Beware* (Nugent) (sc)
1939 *Love Affair* (McCarey) (co-sc); *Thousand Dollars a Touchdown* (Hogan) (sc)
1940 *The Farmer's Daughter* (Hogan) (story, sc); *Safari* (Edward Griffith) (sc); *Young America Flies* (Eason) (short) (sc)
1941 *The Night of January 16th* (Clemens) (co-sc); *Unexpected Uncle* (Godfrey) (co-sc)
1942 *You Were Never Lovelier* (Seiter) (co-sc)
1943 *Stage Door Canteen* (Borzage) (sc)
1955 *White Feather* (Webb) (co-sc)
1957 *An Affair to Remember* (McCarey) (co-sc) (remake of *Love Affair* 1939)
1972 *Seventy-Five Years of Cinema Museum* (Hershon and Guerra) (appearance)

Publications

By DAVES: articles—

Interview with Christopher Wicking, in *Screen* (London), July/October 1969.

On DAVES: book—

Pigenet, M., *Delmer Daves,* IDHEC, Paris, 1960.

On DAVES: articles—

Whitehall, Richard, "On the 3:10 to Yuma—Delmer Daves," in *Films and Filming* (London), April and May 1963.
Wallington, Mike, "Auteur and Genre: The Westerns of Delmer Daves," in *Cinema* (Cambridge), October 1969.
"Screenwriters Symposium," in *Film Comment* (New York), Winter 1970/71.
"Daves Issue" of *Filmkritik* (Munich), January 1975.
Rabourdin, D., "Delmer Daves ou le secreat perdu," in *Cinéma* (Paris), October 1977.
Cebe, G., obituary in *Ecran* (Paris), October 1977.
Passek, J.L., obituary in *Cinéma* (Paris), November 1977.
Ledieu, Christian, "Delmer Daves ou la raison du cœur," in *Etudes Cinématographiques* (Paris), n.d.

On DAVES: film—

Wilkinson, Hazel, director, *The Critic and "3:10 to Yuma,"* Great Britain, 1961.

* * *

Delmer Daves is perhaps best remembered for the highly successful youth-oriented movies that he made for Warner Brothers in the late 1950s and early 1960s. *A Summer Place,* the definitive teenage love film, was the most financially successful of these. Yet it is unfair to relegate Daves to the realm of glossy soap opera directors. When analyzed as a whole, the body of his work reveals some fine moments.

Pride of the Marines, Broken Arrow, and *3:10 to Yuma* are all very different films, yet each is regarded by film historians as a classic.

After an early career in films as an actor, Daves turned to screenwriting in the early 1930s and worked, often in collaboration with others, on a variety of films, the most prominent of which were *The Petrified Forest* and *Love Affair.* When he began directing he continued to write the screenplays for his own films. His directorial debut was *Destination Tokyo.* While it was not a great film, this first effort was at least a cut above the glut of wartime propaganda movies being made at the time. It was also noteworthy as the only film which Cary Grant ever made without a romantic element (or even any women in the plot).

Another war film, *Pride of the Marines,* was one of Hollywood's first attempts to dramatize the plight of the returning servicemen. On a par with such other celebrated movies as *Bright Victory* and *The Men, Pride of the Marines* simply showed the anxieties and frustrations of war veterans who were wounded both physically and psychologically by their experiences. The film was powerful, yet did not resort to over-dramatization. It also dealt, albeit briefly, with the sociological issue of minority soldiers who would return home to a nation perhaps unaware of the value of their contributions to their country.

Some of Daves's most significant movies were westerns that were sympathetic to Indians and did not glamorize traditional western themes. *Broken Arrow* is often cited as the first film to portray Indians without stereotyping them, even if most of the actors were white. *3:10 to Yuma* was one of the earliest "anti-hero" westerns and is regarded as a classic both in the United States and Europe. *Cowboy* was another atypical western. Although ostensibly a comic western, *Cowboy* had an underlying anti-macho theme ahead of its time. In the beginning of the film the main characters, played by Glenn Ford and Jack Lemmon, are opposites: Ford a traditional "he-man" cowboy, and Lemmon a tenderfoot. By the end of the film both characters become aware of the opposite sides of their own natures. At least a decade before the theme became popular, *Cowboy* showed that men's hard and soft sides could co-exist and could make entertaining subject matter for a motion picture.

Daves's final film, *The Battle of Villa Fiorita,* is regarded by most critics as a run-of-the-mill soap opera, yet even this project shows his ability to build a film around an important social theme before it became popular. In this story, which, like *Cowboy,* begins as a comedy and gradually becomes a drama, Daves's characters are faced by problems which are now visible issues of social concern: divorce, remarriage (or in this case cohabitation), and the rearing of stepchildren. In this film, like *A Summer Place* and his other well known "soap operas," Daves's writing and direction make the work much better than its subject matter would suggest. Like his contemporary Douglas Sirk, whose films have been criticized in terms similar to those directed at Daves, his films are actually richer than general critical opinion would seem to indicate.

—Patricia King Hanson

DAVIES, Terence

Nationality: British. **Born:** Liverpool, 1945. **Education:** Studied at Drama School in Coventry, 1971-73, and at National Film School, Beaconsfield, late 1970s. **Career:** Clerk and accountant in a shipping office, 1960-71; directed first film, *Children,* 1974. **Awards:** International Critics' Prize, Cannes Film Festival, for *Distant Voices, Still Lives,* 1988.

Films as Director and Scriptwriter:

1974 *Children*
1980 *Madonna and Child*
1983 *Death and Transfiguration*
1984 *Terence Davies Trilogy* (comprising three previous films)
1988 ***Distant Voices, Still Lives***
1992 *The Long Day Closes*

Publications

By DAVIES: articles—

"Voices from the Past," an interview with P. Wyeth, in *Stills* (London), March 1986.
Interview with D. Heinrich, in *Cinéma* (Paris), 1 June 1988.
Interview with Nigel Floyd, in *Monthly Film Bulletin* (London), October 1988.
Interview with Brian Baxter and A. Hunter, in *Films and Filming* (London), October 1988.
Interview, in *Time Out* (London), 5 October 1988.
"Familiar Haunts," interview with Harlan Kennedy, in *Film Comment* (New York), September/October 1988.
Interview with T. Williams, in *Cineaction,* Summer/Fall 1990.
Interview with T. Wahlstedt, in *Chaplin,* vol. 32, no. 4, 1990.
Interview with A. Skwara, in *Kino,* August 1992.
Interview with E. Sorenson, in *Chaplin,* vol. 34, no. 243, 1992/1993.

By DAVIES: books—

A Modest Pageant, Faber and Faber, 1992.

On DAVIES: articles—

Variety (New York), 21 March 1984.
Baxter, Brian, "A Film Trilogy by Terence Davies," in *Films and Filming* (London), October 1984.
Gibson, Ben, "*Death and Transfiguration,*" in *Monthly Film Bulletin* (London), October 1984.
Baxter, Brian, in *Films and Filming* (London), January 1988.
Variety (New York), 18 May 1988.
Tixeront, A., in *Cinéma* (Paris), 25 May 1988.
Wilson, David, "Family Album," in *Sight and Sound* (London), Autumn 1988.
Barker, Adam, in *Monthly Film Bulletin* (London), October 1988.
Cargin, P., in *Film,* January 1989.
Lavery, D., "Functional and Dysfunctional Autobiography: *Hope and Glory* and *Distant Voices, Still Lives,*" in *Film Criticism,* vol. 15, no. 1, 1990.
Keighron, P., "Condition Critical," in *Screen,* vol. 32, no. 2, 1991.
Kirkham, P., and M. O'Shaughnessy, "Designing Desire," in *Sight and Sound* (London), May 1992.
Segnocinema, July/August 1992.

* * *

"I make films to come to terms with my family history.... If there had been no suffering, there would have been no films." Hardly the most unusual of artistic subjects, but for Terence Davies it has been the source of perhaps the most emotionally and technically distinctive films in recent British film history. *The Terence Davies Trilogy* and *Distant Voices, Still Lives* chart what some might think unremarkable territory—working class life in northern England after the war—but do so with an artistic seriousness more usually seen as the exclusive preserve of "European" cinema.

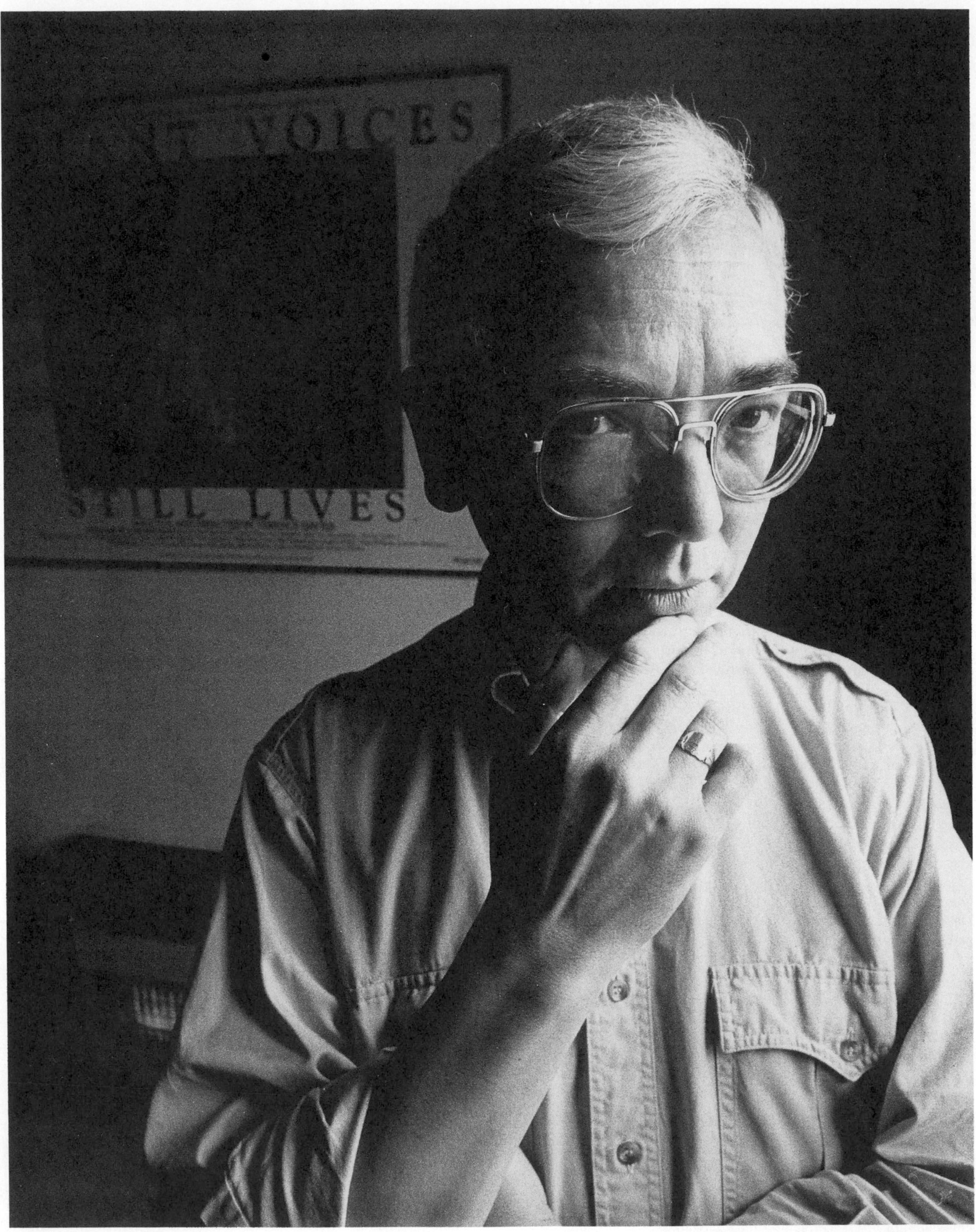

Terence Davies © Andy Lane

Born in Liverpool in 1945, the youngest of ten children (seven of whom survived infancy), Davies's early life was overshadowed by the mute malevolence and tyrannical violence of his father, for whom he still feels undiminished hatred. In a house where domesticity would cut violently to the most extreme brutality, Davies developed a sensitivity to mood and detail that was to prove intrinsic to his later filmmaking. "I have a very retentive memory, and can remember things, even atmospheres on particular days. And I think it's these details, particularly about people's behaviour, that reveal the greater truth. As a child, up to the point when my father died, because you had to gauge whether he was in a good mood or not, all my nerve endings were exposed. And when you're a child, you're like an animal, you smell things, so that now that instinct is absolutely there." His father died when young Davies was eight of a stomach cancer that was perhaps accelerated by drinking disinfectant in an effort to avoid military service.

The next few years of Davies's childhood, until his secondary school, were relatively happy, particularly because of his discovery of American musicals. Davies left school at the age of 15 and began working as a clerk and an accountant, spending his spare moments writing for the stage and radio. By the age of 26 he was shopping a script that was rejected by various television companies. It was after leaving drama school in Coventry that he applied for and received a grant from the British Film Institute Production Board to direct. *Children* received critical acclaim, including the bronze Hugo at the Chicago Film Festival. He then won a place at the National Film School, where he began his second film.

Children, Madonna and Child, and *Death and Transfiguration* took ten years for the director to complete, in part because they required three different sources of funding (including the Greater London Arts Association). His critical reputation began to build during this time. His trilogy showing the three stages in the life of Robert Tucker—from being bullied at school through a loveless middle age of masochistic homosexual fantasy to death—constituted an expiation of sexual and religious guilt. "Not having come to terms with being gay, I had prayed for forgiveness until my knees were literally raw, and I just thought, that's it. I was so angry, it seemed that even if there was a God he was just inhumane.... Although I had rejected Catholicism before I made the films, in the making of the trilogy I worked out my precise reasons for doing so." The autobiographical basis of the films, however, indicated a startling emotional maturity on the part of the filmmaker, for he explores the bleak potential future of Davies's life—a lonely death (and transfiguration) in a geriatric ward on Christmas Day.

Davies's subject matter was not to everyone's taste. Religious groups in America protested at its sexual content. And according to one critic, "It makes Ingmar Bergman look like Jerry Lewis." But its thoughtful handling of non-linear narrative and "spare and beautiful" black and white photography picked up an array of prizes.

Distant Voices, Still Lives, again made in parts with a variety of funds, confirmed the legitimacy of previous critical accolades. The film, which dealt with his family's history rather than his own, achieved a deepened emotional range and presented considerable technical innovation, winning major prizes at Cannes, Locarno, and Toronto. The desperate groping by critics to find appropriate language to describe the work underscored the originality of his achievement. "If you can readily imagine a musical version of *Coronation Street* directed by Robert Bresson, with additional dialogue by Sigmund Freud and Tommy Handley, you might know what to expect from Terence Davies:" "A proletarian Proust;" "A musical, albeit a brutal, Proustian one." Whilst 1950s revivals were not uncommon at this time, this was unmistakably something new. As Davies put it, "I remember the 1950s which have now become very fashionable and unreal, with films like *Absolute Beginners* and all those television commercials.... It was not romantic, and that's why I chose to shoot the film in that particular shade of brown, because I didn't want it to look like 'The Good Old Days.'" This colouring was achieved through a "Bleach By-Pass" operation in the laboratory and careful suppression of primary colours on the set, apart from the red of lipstick and nail-varnish. The effect is stunning. In set pieces that look like tinted photographs it captures the romance and sterility of a culture bound in working-class patriarchy, but glazed with Hollywood escapism. The father's brutality—cutting from him gently filling the children's Christmas stockings to demolishing the dinner table—is contrasted by the love songs tripping off the girls' lips, and a soundtrack featuring such songs as "Taking A Chance On Love." Scenes are overlapped through the music, and static holds are animated by sound (the incantationary Home Service Shipping Forecast in the opening shot).

Such qualities have marked Davies as the most promising director in British cinema. He shows a passionate concern with film *craft,* lamenting what he sees as the British instinct to use film as a medium for recorded theatre; primarily verbal, sentimental, and in the tight bodice of traditional narrative. His films are remarkably effective in disturbing collective memories—and myths—of British cultural life with such cinematic ingenuity.

—Saul Frampton

DE ANTONIO, Emile

Nationality: American. **Born:** Scranton, Pennsylvania, 1920. **Education:** Harvard, and Columbia University, New York. **Military Service:** Served in World War II. **Career:** Teacher of philosophy, longshoreman, and editor, 1940s and 1950s; formed G-String productions, 1958; began making compilation documentaries with *Point of Order,* 1963. **Died:** December 1989.

Films as Director:

1963 *Point of Order* (+ co-pr)
1965 *That's Where the Action Is* (for television) (+ pr)
1966 *Rush to Judgment* (+ co-pr)
1968 *In the Year of the Pig* (+ pr)
1969 *America Is Hard to See* (+ co-pr)
1971 *Millhouse: A White House Comedy* (*Millhouse: A White Comedy*) (+ pr)
1972 *Painters Painting* (+ pr)
1976 *Underground* (co-d, pr)
1983 *In the King of Prussia*
1989 *Mr. Hoover and I*

Other Films:

1961 *Sunday* (Drasin) (pr)
1965 *Drunk* (Warhol) (role)

Publications

By DE ANTONIO: articles—

Interview with Jonas Mekas, in *Village Voice* (New York), 13 November 1969.
"Radical Scavenging: An Interview with Emile de Antonio," with Bernard Weiner, in *Film Quarterly* (Berkeley), Fall 1971.

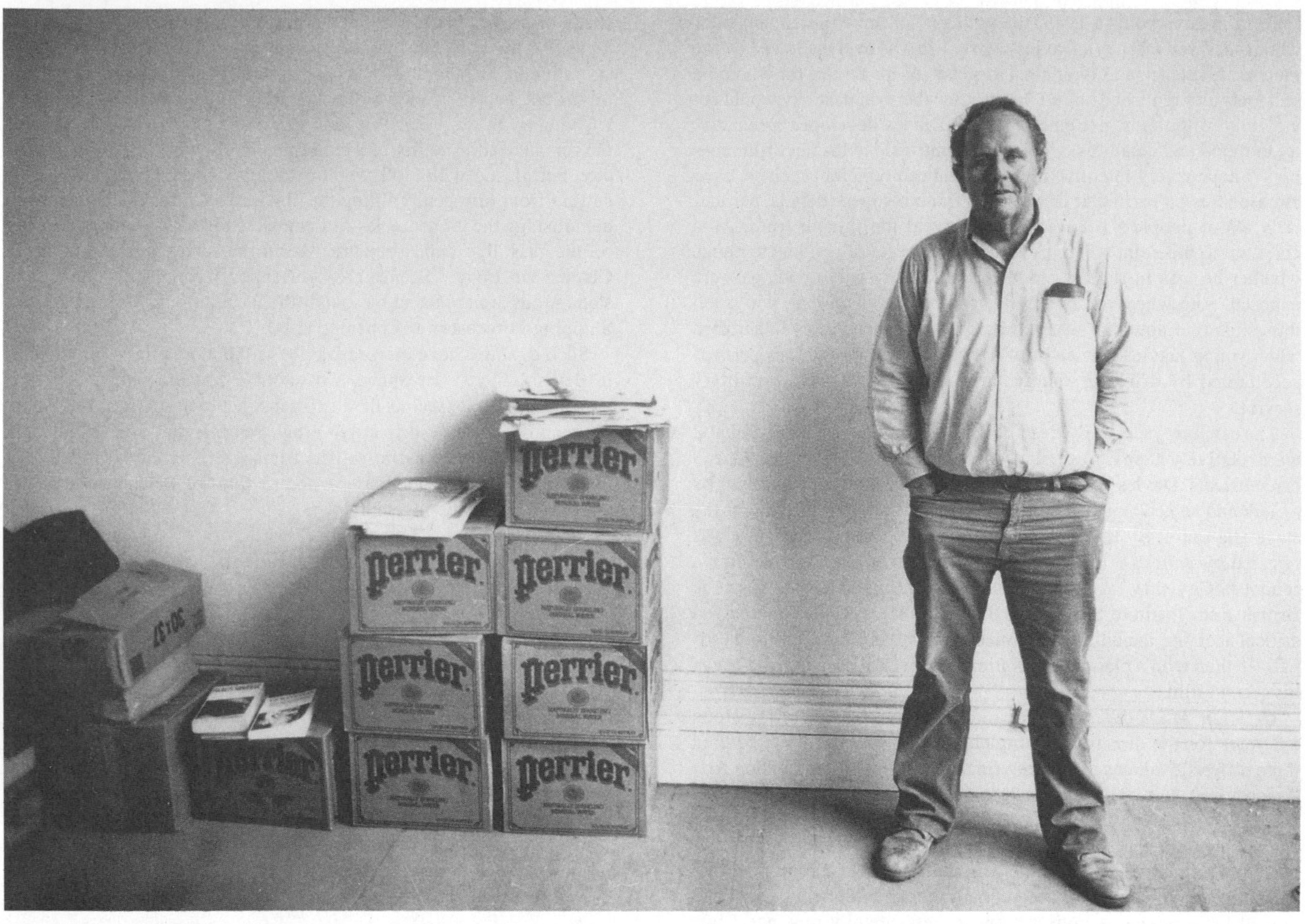

Emile De Antonio

Interview with G. O'Brien, in *Inter/View* (New York), February 1972.
"Rencontre avec Emile de Antonio," with L. Marcorelles, in *Cahiers du Cinéma* (Paris), December 1976.
"Filmer de que ne montre pas l'histoire 'officielle'," an interview with M. Euvrard, in *Cinéma Quebec* (Montreal), vol. 5, no. 19, 1977.
Interview with A. Rosenthal, in *Film Quarterly* (Berkeley), Fall 1978.
Interview in *Cineaste* (New York), vol. 12, no. 2, 1982.
"History is the theme of all my films," an interview with Gary Crowdus and Dan Georgakas, in *Cineaste* (New York), vol. 12, no. 2, 1982.
"De Antonio and the Plowshares Eight," an interview with D. Segal, in *Sight and Sound* (London), Summer 1982.
"Emile De Antonio interviews himself," in *Film Quarterly* (Los Angeles), Fall 1982.
"My brush with painting," in *American Film* (Washington, D.C.), March 1984.
"Quotations from Chairman 'Dee': Decodifying de Antonio," in *Cinema Canada* (Montreal), July-August 1984.

On DE ANTONIO: articles—

Bazelon, David, "Background of *Point of Order*," in *Film Comment* (New York), Winter 1964.
Westerbeck, Colin, Jr., "Some Out-Takes from Radical Film Making: Emile de Antonio," in *Sight and Sound* (London), Summer 1970.
Hess, J., "Political Filmmaking: Feds Harass Film Crew," in *Jump Cut* (Berkeley), September 1975.
Linfield, Susan, "De Antonio's Day in Court," in *Village Voice* (New York), 8 February 1983.
Obituary in *Variety* (New York), 27 December 1989.

* * *

A Communist with impeccable Ivy League credentials, Emile De Antonio came to filmmaking relatively late in his career. Leaving Harvard in the 1930s, he first flexed his muscles as a longshoreman on Baltimore docks. After World War II, he returned to academia, attending graduate school at Columbia University, and then teaching for a time at William and Mary College, Virginia.

The late 1950s found him in New York, engaged in get-rich-quick schemes. (With a friend, he set up "Sailor's Surplus," a mail order business.) More significantly, he became acquainted with several notable personalities in the New York art world. He went drinking with Rauschenberg and Jasper Johns and organized "galas" for the minimalist composer John Cage and the dancer Merce Cunningham. As far as his future filmmaking was concerned, this period was crucial: he was encountering the wealthy liberal arts patrons whose backing would later be so important to him.

De Antonio was a member of "The Group," a "free open organization of American cinema" set up in the summer of 1961 with the avowed aim of rejecting censorship and exploding the "myth of budget." The organization was comprised of such luminaries of the New York avant garde film scene as Jonas Mekas and Shirley Clarke. However, it was as a film producer/distributor, not as a filmmaker, that De Antonio was associated with this organization. In 1958 he had formed G String Productions to distribute the celebrated underground classic, *Pull My Daisy*.

In the early 1960s, De Antonio was given access to 188 hours worth of kinetoscopes of the McCarthy hearings. He managed to raise $75,000 from his friend Eliot Pratt, the Standard Oil heir, and set to work editing.

It took him more than two years, and he went broke in the process, but in 1964 De Antonio emerged with his first documentary, *Point of Order.* Paul Newman offered to do a narration. De Antonio turned him down. He had already evolved his film philosophy, and it held no place for narrators: "the narrator on TV becomes a super figure who has to explain to you what you've seen, or what you haven't been allowed to see. It's not the same as the jackboot of the nazis, but it is a kind of fascism of the mind."

In a sense, De Antonio was the great precursor of scratch video and sampling. He described his own method as "radical scavenging": what it entailed was expropriating footage from the television networks and editing the footage together to make a scathing critique of some aspect of American society. De Antonio devoted his energy to looking for the parapraxes, the out-takes, those never-broadcast moments that had been consigned to the deepest vaults of the network archives.

The 1960s proved to be a good period for him. Although *Point of Order* was slammed by the *New York Times,* it was successful with students, who were beginning to be politicized by the Vietnam War. Pressed as to why he did not shoot his own footage, De Antonio asked critics what chance an independent filmmaker had against the all-powerful television stations, "the ruling class of America," as he described them. An independent filmmaker would not have been allowed to get near Kennedy on that fateful day in Dallas.

Kennedy's assassination, indeed, was the subject of De Antonio's second film, *Rush to Judgment.* Sponsored in the United Kingdom by Woodfall Films, Tony Richardson's production company, this project did not endear him to the establishment. Although officially shunned, he was privately helped by "insiders" who gave him access to sensitive material. Nonetheless, the networks had an annoying tendency of destroying the most valuable, and most incriminating, footage.

His Vietnam film, *In the Year of the Pig,* was again eccentrically financed. Mrs. Orville Schell, a wealthy New York socialite, gave dinner parties at which the production money was raised, and she is credited as the film's executive producer. De Antonio managed to find an interview with U.S. General George Patton in which Patton described the young Americans in Vietnam as "a bloody good bunch of killers."

De Antonio's 1976 effort was *Underground.* He managed to track down and interview the infamous Weather Underground for this project, a fact that exasperated the authorities, who hadn't been able to get near the group. The FBI therefore tried to subpoena the film and crew.

Not long before his death, Emile De Antonio discovered that J. Edgar Hoover and the FBI had been keeping files on him for nearly thirty years. Appalled by American "secret society," he could not help but be amused at the same time. There was something pathetic and comic about this sinister man, Hoover, and his pet organization. De Antonio, in *Mr. Hoover and I,* took great pleasure in reporting FBI minutiae: the way that Hoover made all his employees wear felt hats; his admiration for the Jewish star of the television series about the FBI despite his own notorious anti-semitism; Hoover's insistence that his driver never take a left turn because of a previous car accident suffered by the FBI chief after such a turn. All of these tales appealed to De Antonio's sense of irony. "I am as much Dada as I am a Marxist," he said in an interview he conducted with himself for *Film Quarterly.*

A strange mixture of Thomas Paine and Huckleberry Finn, Emile De Antonio was a devout patriot, who defined his role as "artist" in constructively negative terms. As far as he was concerned, art was necessarily adversary, and he was determinedly critical and anarchistic. He saw such a stance as his duty.

—G.C. Macnab

DEARDEN, Basil

Nationality: British. **Born:** Basil Dear in Westcliffe-on-Sea, England, 1 January 1911. **Family:** Married actress Melissa Stribling, 1947, two sons (including scriptwriter James). **Career:** Actor in repertory, toured United States with Ben Greet Company, late 1920s; general stage manager for Basil Dean (changed name to avoid confusion), 1931-36; production manager, associate producer and scriptwriter at Ealing studios, 1936-40; co-directed several Will Hay comedies, 1941-43; directed first film, *The Bells Go Down,* 1943; worked with producer Michael Relph, 1949-71 (TV director, 1960s). **Awards:** British Film Academy Awards, with Michael Relph, for *The Blue Lamp,* 1950, and *Sapphire,* 1960. **Died:** In auto accident, 23 March 1971.

Films as Director:

1941 *The Black Sheep of Whitehall* (co-d)
1942 *The Goose Steps Out* (co-d)
1943 *The Bells Go Down*; *My Learned Friend* (co-d)
1944 *The Halfway House*; *They Came to a City*
1945 "The Hearse Driver" episode and linking story of ***Dead of Night***
1946 *The Captive Heart*
1947 *Frieda*
1948 *Saraband for Dead Lovers* (*Saraband*)
1949 "The Actor" and "The Prisoner of War" episodes of *Train of Events* (+ co-sc, Michael Relph producer); ***The Blue Lamp***
1950 *Cage of Gold*; *Pool of London*
1951 *I Believe in You* (co-d + co-pr with Michael Relph, co-sc)
1952 *The Gentle Gunman* (co-d + co-pr with Michael Relph)
1953 *The Square Ring* (co-d + co-pr with Michael Relph)
1954 *The Rainbow Jacket* (co-d + co-pr with Michael Relph); *Out of the Clouds* (co-d + co-pr with Michael Relph)
1955 *The Ship That Died of Shame* (co-d + co-pr with Michael Relph, co-sc); *Who Done It?* (co-d + co-pr with Michael Relph)
1957 *The Smallest Show on Earth*
1958 *Violent Playground*
1959 *Sapphire*; *The League of Gentlemen*
1960 *Man in the Moon*; *The Secret Partner*
1961 ***Victim***; *All Night Long* (co-d, co-pr with Relph)
1962 *Life for Ruth* (*Walk in the Shadow*)
1963 *The Mind Benders*; *A Place to Go*
1964 *Woman of Straw*; *Masquerade*
1966 *Khartoum*
1968 *Only When I Larf*; *The Assassination Bureau*
1970 *The Man Who Haunted Himself* (+ co-sc)

Other Films:

1938 *It's in the Air* (Kimmins) (asst d); *Penny Paradise* (Reed) (asst d); *This Man Is News* (MacDonald) (co-sc)
1939 *Come On, George!* (Kimmins) (asst d)
1940 *Let George Do It* (Varnel) (co-sc); *Spare a Copper* (Carstairs) (assoc pr)

Basil Dearden: *The Captive Heart*

1941 *Young Veteran* (Cavalcanti) (asst d)
1941 *Turned Out Nice Again* (Varnel) (assoc pr)
1956 *The Green Man* (Day) (supervisor, uncredited)
1957 *Davy* (Relph) (pr)
1958 *Rockets Galore* (*Mad Little Island*) (Relph) (pr)
1959 *Desert Mice* (Relph) (pr)

Publications

On DEARDEN: books—

Balcon, Michael, *A Lifetime of Films,* London, 1969.
Barr, Charles, *Ealing Studios,* London, 1977.
Perry, George, *Forever Ealing,* London, 1981.
Hill, John, *Sex, Class, and Realism: British Cinema 1956-63,* London, 1986.

On DEARDEN: articles—

Tynan, Kenneth, "Ealing: The Studio in Suburbia," in *Films and Filming* (London), November and December 1955.
"Dearden and Relph: Two on a Tandem," in *Films and Filming* (London), July 1966.
Barr, Charles, "Projecting Britain and the British Character: Ealing Studios," in *Screen* (London), Summer 1974.
Ellis, John, "Made in Ealing," in *Screen* (London), Spring 1975.

* * *

Basil Dearden is, par excellence, the journeyman-director of British cinema, standing in much the same relation to Ealing (the studio for which he directed the greater part of his output) as, say, Michael Curtiz did to Warner Brothers. More than any other director, Dearden personified the spirit of Ealing films: concerned, conscientious, socially aware, but hampered by a certain innately British caution. Dearden was the complete professional, unfailingly competent and meticulous; his films were never less than thoroughly well-constructed, and he enjoyed a reputation in the industry for total reliability, invariably bringing in assignments on schedule and under budget.

Such careful craftsmanship, though, should not be equated with dullness. Dearden's films may often have been safe, but they were rarely dull (despite the allegations of some critics). His work shows a natural flair for pace and effective action: narrative lines are clear and uncluttered, and although in many ways they have dated, his films remain eminently watchable and entertaining.

In the moral climate of the time, too, Dearden's choice of subjects showed considerable boldness. Dearden tackled such edgy topics as race (*Sapphire*), homosexuality (*Victim*), sectarian bigotry (*Life for Ruth*), and post-war anti-German prejudice (*Frieda*), always arguing for tolerance and understanding. It was perhaps inevitable, given his background and the ethos of the studio, that these "social problem" movies tended towards overly reasonable solutions. "Dearden's films," Charles Barr has pointed out in his definitive study *Ealing Studios,* "insistently *generalize* their moral lessons."

For most of his directing career Dearden worked closely with Michael Relph, who produced nearly all his films, collaborated with him on the scripts, and occasionally co-directed; after the demise of Ealing, the two men formed their own production company. Their joint output covered a wide variety of genres, including costume drama (*Saraband for Dead Lovers*) and comedy (*The Smallest Show on Earth*), as well as large scale epic (*Khartoum*). Dearden's flair for action was effectively exploited in the classic "heist" movie, *The League of Gentlemen,* and in *The Blue Lamp,* a seminal police drama and one of the first Ealing films shot almost entirely on location. Early in his career, Dearden also evinced a weakness for slightly stagey allegories in films such as *Halfway House* and *They Came To A City,* in which groups of disparate individuals are brought to a change of heart through supernatural intervention.

There can also be detected in Dearden's films, perhaps slightly unexpectedly, a muted but poetic vision of an idealized community—seen most clearly in his first film with Relph, *The Captive Heart,* a sympathetic study of prisoners-of-war. "The community," Charles Barr has noted, "is presented as part of a wider society involving all of us—and encompassing England."

In his strengths and in his weaknesses—the restraint verging on inhibition, the competent versatility tending towards lack of directorial character—Dearden was in many ways an archetypally "British" director. Anyone wishing to understand the success and limitations of post-war British cinema, and indeed of post-war British society, could do far worse than study the films of Basil Dearden.

—Theresa FitzGerald

DE FUENTES, Fernando

Nationality: Mexican. **Born:** Veracruz, 13 December 1894. **Career:** Film editor and assistant director, 1920s; first Mexican offered opportunity to direct by Compañia Nacional Productora de Peliculas, 1932; producer and director for newly formed Grovas production company, 1942; co-founder, Diana Films, 1945. **Died:** 4 July 1958.

Films as Director:

1932 *El anonimo*
1933 *El prisionero trece*; *La calandria*; *El tigre de Yautepec*; *El compadre Mendoza*
1934 *El fantasma del convento*; *Cruz diablo*
1935 *Vámonos con Pancho Villa*; *La familia Dressel*
1936 *Las mujeres mandan*; *Allá en el rancho grande*
1937 *Bajo el cielo de Mexico*; *La Zandunga*
1938 *La casa del ogro*
1939 *Papacito lindo*
1940 *Allá en el tropico*; *El jefe maximo*; *Creo en Dios*
1941 *La gallina clueca*
1942 *Asi se quiere en Jalisco*
1943 *Doña Barbara*; *La mujer sin alma*
1944 *El rey se divierte*
1945 *Hasta que perdio Jalisco*; *La selva de fuego*
1946 *La devoradora*
1948 *Jalisco canta en Sevilla*
1949 *Hipolito el de Santa*
1950 *Por la puerta falsa*; *Crimen y castigo*
1952 *Los hijos de Maria Morales*; *Cancion de cuna*
1953 *Tres citas con el destino*

Publications

On DE FUENTES: books—

Riera, Emilio Garcia, *Historia documental del cine mexicano,* vols. 1-6, Mexico City, 1969-74.
Blanco, Jorge Ayala, *La aventura del cine mexicano,* Mexico City, 1979.
Mora, Carl, *Mexican Cinema: Reflections of a Society, 1896-1980,* Berkeley, 1982.
Riera, Emilio Garcia, *Fernando de Fuentes,* Mexico City, 1984.
De los Reyes, Aurelio, *Medio siglo de cine mexicano (1894-1958),* Mexico City, 1987.

On DE FUENTES: articles—

De la Vega, Eduardo, "Fernando de Fuentes: La mirada critica sobre la Revolucion Mexicana," in *Filmoteca* (Mexico City), no. 1, 1979.
Paranagua, P.A., "Cannes 82: Homanaje a dos maestros del cine latinoamericano," in *Contracampo* (Madrid), August-September 1982.

* * *

Fernando De Fuentes

The first Mexican cineaste of note, Fernando De Fuentes is still considered the director whose interpretations of the Mexican revolution and whose contributions to typical Mexican genres have not been surpassed. Early sound film production in Mexico was dominated by foreigners: Russians who accompanied Eisenstein in the making of *Que Viva México,* Spaniards who passed through Hollywood, Cubans, and U.S. citizens who somehow ended up there. De Fuentes was one of the first Mexicans to be given a chance to direct sound films in his country.

After several false starts with "grey and theatrical melodramas," De Fuentes indicated first in *Prisionero trece* that his métier was the "revolutionary tragedy." During 1910-17, Mexico passed through a cataclysmic social revolution whose cultural expression resounded principally in the extraordinary murals of Diego Rivera, David Siquieros, and José Orozco. Fiction films did not examine this watershed event seriously until 1933 when De Fuentes made *El compadre Mendoza.* Far from the epic monumentality of revolutionary transformation painted on the walls by Rivera or Siquieros, *El compadre Mendoza* recreates the revolution from a perspective similar to Orozco's vision of individual tragedies and private pain.

Rosalio Mendoza is the owner of a large hacienda which is constantly threatened by the conflict's warring factions. In order to appease them, Mendoza pretends to support whichever group is currently visiting him—something he accomplishes by wining and dining his guests in a room conspicuously decorated with a portrait of the appropriate leader. Eventually, Mendoza and General Nieto (a follower of Emiliano Zapata's agrarian revolt) become close friends. Mendoza names his son after Nieto and asks him to be the *compadre* (godfather). But after Mendoza is ruined economically, he betrays Nieto in order to flee to Mexico City. The emphasis on fraternal bloodletting, the corruption of ideals, and disillusion in the aftermath of the revolution is powerfully conveyed in both *El compadre Mendoza* and *Vámonos con Pancho Villa.* They remain even today the best cinematic treatments of the Mexican revolution.

De Fuentes's work in traditional Mexican genres is also important. *Allá en el Rancho Grande* is the progenitor of the *charro* genre. The Mexican singing cowboy received his cinematic introduction to Mexico and the rest of Latin America in this immensely popular film. The attraction of such nostalgia for a never-existent Arcadia can be seen in the fact that in the year following the release of *Rancho Grande,* more than half of the Mexican films produced were similar pastoral fantasies, and these have continued to be a staple of Mexican cinema.

The *charro* genre's domination of Mexican cinema is almost matched by films about the Mexican mother. De Fuentes directed perhaps the most palatable of such works, *La gallina clueca.* This film starred Sara García, the character actress who is the national paradigm of the sainted, long-suffering, self-sacrificing mother. In De Fuentes's hands the overworked Oedipal melodrama is denied its usual histrionics and becomes an interesting work as well as the definitive film of this subgenre.

His better films demonstrate De Fuentes's strong narrative style, noted for its consistency and humor. They do not seem particularly dated, and De Fuentes utilizes visual techniques such as the rack focus or the dissolve particularly effectively and unobtrusively. He also makes telling use of overlay montages, à la Eisenstein or Vertov, to convey moods or concepts. In regard to singing—one of the banes of Mexican cinema—De Fuentes has been uneven. For example, in his two films on the revolution, restraint is shown and songs function well in relation to the story line. Unfortunately, *Allá en el Rancho Grande* and its various sequels are characteristically glutted with songs.

De Fuentes's career as a director went from the sublime to the ridiculous. In one year he plummeted from the heights of *Vámonos con Pancho Villa* to the depths of *Allá en el Rancho Grande.* The enormous commercial success of the latter film throughout Latin America sealed De Fuentes's fate. It was popular because De Fuentes is a talented director; but the commercial rewards for those talents came at a high price. After *Vámonos con Pancho Villa,* De Fuentes settled into the repetition of mediocre and conventional formula films.

—John Mraz

DELANNOY, Jean

Nationality: French. **Born:** Noisy-le-Sec, 8 August 1908. **Education:** Lille University; Paris University. **Career:** Began as film actor while at University (sister is actress Henriette Delannoy), late 1920s; in Service Cinématographique des Armées, then chief editor, Paramount Studios, Joinville, 1930-32; feature director, from 1935; became President of Institut des Hautes Etudes Cinématographiques (IDHEC), Paris, 1975. **Awards:** Best Film, Cannes festival, for *La Symphonie Pastorale,* 1946; International Prize, Venice Festival, for *Dieu a besoin des hommes,* 1950.

Films as Director and Co-Scriptwriter or Co-Adaptor:

1933 *Franches lippées* (short)
1934 *Une Vocation irrésistible* (short); *L'École des detectives* (short)
1935 *Paris-Deauville*
1936 *La Moule* (medium-length)
1937 *Ne tuez pas Dolly!* (medium-length)
1938 *La Vénus de l'or*
1939 *Macao, l'enfer du jeu*; *Le Diamánt noir*
1941 *Fièvres*
1942 *L'Assassin a peur la nuit*; *Pontcarral, Colonel d'Empire*
1943 *Macao, l'enfer du jeu* (partially re-shot version with Pierre Renoir in role played by Erich von Stroheim, who was forbidden by German authorities; original version of *Macao* re-released after war); *L'Éternel Retour* (*The Eternal Return*)
1944 *Le Bossu*
1945 *La Part de l'ombre* (*Blind Desire*)
1946 *La Symphonie pastorale*
1947 *Les Jeux sont faits* (*The Chips Are Down*)
1948 *Aux yeux du souvenir* (*Souvenir*)
1949 *Le Secret de Mayerling*
1950 *Dieu a besoin des hommes* (*God Needs Men*)
1951 *Le Garçon sauvage* (*Savage Triangle*)
1952 *La Minute de vérité* (*L'ora della veritá*; *The Moment of Truth*) (+ co-sc); "Jeanne (Joan of Arc)" episode of *Destinées* (*Daughters of Destiny*)
1953 *La Route Napoléon*; "Le Lit de la Pompadour" episode of *Secrets d'alcove*
1954 *Obsession*
1955 *Chiens perdus sans collier*; *Marie-Antoinette*
1956 *Notre-Dame de Paris* (*The Hunchback of Notre Dame*)
1957 *Maigret tend un piège* (*Inspector Maigret*)
1958 *Guinguette*; *Maigret et l'affaire Saint-Fiacre*
1959 *Le Baron de l'Ecluse*
1960 "L'Adolescence" episode of *La Française et l'amour* (*Love and the Frenchwoman*); *La Princesse de Clèves*
1962 *Le Rendez-vous*; *Venere imperiale* (*Vénus impériale*)
1964 *Les Amitiés particulières* (*This Special Friendship*); *Le Majordome*
1965 "Le Berceau" and "La Répétition" episodes of *Le Lit à deux places* (*The Double Bed*); *Les Sultans*
1967 *Le Soleil des voyous* (*Action Man*)

Jean Delannoy: ***La Symphonie pastorale***

1969 *La Peau de Torpedo*
1972 *Pas folle la guêpe* (+ sc)
1988 *Bernadette* (+ sc)
1990 *La passion de Bernadette*
1995 *Marie de Nazareth* (+ sc)

Other Films (partial list):

1926 *Miss Helyett* (Monca and Keroul) (role)
1927 *Casanova* (Volkoff) (role)
1929 *La Grande Passion* (Hugon) (role)
1932 *La Belle Marinière* (Lachman) (ed); *Une Étoile disparaît* (Villers) (ed); *Le Fils improvisé* (Guissart) (ed)
1933 *Le Père prématuré* (Guissart) (ed); *Les Aventures du roi Pausole* (Granowsky) (ed)
1934 *Le Roi des Champs-Elysées* (Nosseck) (ed)
1935 *Michel Strogoff* (de Baroncelli and Eichberg) (ed); *Tovaritch* (Deval) (co-ed)
1936 *Club de femmes* (Deval) (tech adv, co-ed); *Nitchevo* (de Baroncelli) (ed)

1937 *Tamara la complaisante* (Gandera) (tech adv, co-sc uncredited); *Feu!* (de Baroncelli) (ed)
1938 *Le Paradis de Satan* (Gandera) (tech adv)

Publications

By DELANNOY: book—

Bernadette: Photographies des films Bernadette et La passion de Bernadette, with text by Jacques Douyau, Paris, 1992.

By DELANNOY: article—

"Le Réalisateur," in *Le Cinéma par ceux qui le font,* Paris, 1949.

On DELANNOY: book—

Guiget, Claude, Emmanuel Papillon, and Jacques Pinturault, *Jean Delannoy: Filmographie, props, temoignanes,* Aulnay-sur-Bois, 1985.

On DELANNOY: articles—

"Jean Delannoy," in *Film Dope* (London), September 1976.
Tribute to Delannoy in *Film Francais* (Paris), 21 February 1986.

On DELANNOY: film—

Knapp, Hubert, and Igor Barrère, *Echos de plateau* (on making of *La Minute de vérité*), 1952.

* * *

Critics have not been kind to Jean Delannoy, but the public certainly has, for nearly all his films were solid box-office hits. But Delannoy, both by personal pretension and by the subject matter of his major films, demanded more serious attention. Just as André Cayatte is France's director of social problem films, so Delannoy may be considered its moral philosopher. *La Symphonie pastorale* and *God Needs Man,* made just after the war, brought him this reputation and remain his best known work, along with *Les Jeux sont faits* made in collaboration with Sartre. But more than a score of films surround this core, few of which measure up to the ambition and values for which they stand.

Delannoy flirted with the cinema in the 1920s while working at a bank. Godard would later recall these beginnings in his caricature of Delannoy "going into the Billancourt studios briefcase in hand; you would have sworn he was going into an insurance office." His initial training as an editor provided him with a sense of dramatic economy that may be the reason for his popular success and critical failure. His calculated distance, even coolness, alienated many critics, most notably the passionate New Wave cinephiles at *Cahiers du Cinéma.*

No one would have paid Delannoy any attention had he not turned away from competent studio dramas to stronger material. *Pontcarral* was his first remarkable effort, bringing him fame as a man of conviction when this Napoleonic adventure tale was interpreted as a direct call to resistance against the Nazi occupation forces.

He was then chosen to help Jean Cocteau bring to the screen *L'Éternel Retour.* Whether, as some suspect, Cocteau pushed Delannoy far beyond his usually cautious methods, or because the legendary tragedy of this Tristan and Isolde update was perfect material for the frigidity of his style, the film was a striking success, haunting in its bizarre imagery and in the mysterious implications of its plot and dialogue.

Just after the war came the films *La Symphonie pastorale* and *Dieu a besoin des hommes,* already mentioned as central to Delannoy as an auteur. Evidently, Gide, Sartre, and Queffelec inspired him to render great moral and philosophical issues in a dramatically rigorous way. Today these films seem overly cautious and pretty, even prettified. But in their day they garnered worldwide respect, the first winning the Grand Prize at Cannes in 1946 and the last the Grand Prize at Venice in 1950. The cinematic ingenuity they display, particularly in the use of geography as a moral arena (a snowy alpine village, a destitute seacoast village), and in the taut editing, gives some, though not sufficient, justification for the staginess of the weighty dialogue.

Delannoy became, perhaps, the director most maligned by *Cahiers du cinéma* because of the battle he fought with Bresson over rights to *Diary of a Country Priest* (which Bresson won) and *La Princesse de Clèves* (which Delannoy won). Accusations of his non-authenticity were borne out in the many hack productions he directed in the 1950s, including a super-production of *Notre-Dame de Paris.* While none of these films is without some merit, the 1960 *Princesse de Clèves* being full of tasteful production values, his style more and more represented the most deprecated face of the "cinema of quality."

—Dudley Andrew

DELLUC, Louis

Nationality: French. **Born:** Louis Jean René Delluc in Cadouin, Dordogne, 14 October 1890. **Education:** Lycée Henri IV, Paris, until 1909. **Family:** Married actress Eve Francis, 1919. **Career:** Editor-in-chief of *Film* magazine, 1917; began column in *Paris-Midi,* 1918; directed first film, *Fumée noire,* and co-founded *Journal de ciné-club,* 1920; helped start *Cinema* magazine and "Matinées de *Cinéma,*" 1921. From 1937, Prix Louis Delluc awarded annually (except during war years) to an outstanding French feature film. **Died:** Of tuberculosis in Paris, 22 March 1924.

Films as Director:

1920 *Fumée noire* (co-d, sc); *Le Silence* (+ sc)
1921 *Fièvre* (+ sc); *Le Chemin d'Ernoa* (*L'Américain*) (+ sc); *Le Tonnerre* (*Évangeline et la tonnerre*) (+ sc)
1922 *La Femme de nulle part* (+ sc)
1923 *L'Inondation* (+ sc)

Other Films:

1919 *La Fête espagnole* (Dulac) (sc)
1921 *Prométhée banquier* (L'Herbier) (role)

Publications

By DELLUC: books—

Cinéma et Cie, Paris, 1919.
Photogénie, Paris, 1920.
Charlot, Paris, 1921; as *Charlie Chaplin,* London, 1922.
La Jungle du cinéma, Paris, 1921.
Drames de cinéma (including *La Fête espagnole, Le Silence, Fièvre,* and *La Femme de nulle part*), Paris, 1923.
Ecrits cinématographique, edited by Pierre Lherminier, Paris, 2 vols., 1985-86.

Louis Delluc: ***La Femme de nulle part***

On DELLUC: books—

Amiguet, Philippe, *Cinéma! Cinéma!,* Lausanne, 1923.
Gance, Abel, *Prisme,* Paris, 1930.
Francis, Eve, *Temps héroïques,* Paris, 1949.
Tariol, Marcel, *Louis Delluc,* Paris, 1965.

On DELLUC: articles—

"Delluc Issue" of *Ciné-club* (Paris), March 1949.
Francis, Eve, and others, *Lettres Françaises* (Paris), 19 March 1964.
McCreary, E.C., "Louis Delluc, Film Theorist, Critic and Prophet," in *Cinema Journal* (Evanston, Illinois), Fall 1976.
McCreary, Eugene, "Film Criticism and the Historian," in *Film and History* (Newark, New Jersey), February 1981.
Régent, R., "'Le Delluc': un prix de copains," in *Avant-Scène du Cinéma* (Paris), 15 April 1981.
McCreary, Eugene, "Louis Delluc et le cinema americain," in *Cahiers de la Cinémathèque* (Perpignan), Autumn 1982.

* * *

Louis Delluc was one of the key figures in the renewal of French cinema after the collapse of the industry's world dominance in the years before World War I. Though in no sense the leader of a unified movement or faction, Delluc has considerable importance as both critic and filmmaker. His impact was crucial during the years after 1919, though he died in 1924 before the full flowering of the French film renaissance to which he had made such a contribution.

Like so many of his contemporaries, Delluc initially had literary ambitions. Abandoning his studies for a career in journalism, he wrote poetry, plays, novels and dramatic criticism. He continued to write even after he had turned to filmmaking. Delluc published—despite his early death—over a dozen literary works of various kinds, in addition to three collections of film criticism. He was also one of the few filmmakers of the early 1920s to publish a collection of his screenplays. Published under the title *Drames de cinéma,* it appeared in 1923.

The work which opened Delluc's eyes to the potential of film as an artistic medium was Cecil B. DeMille's *The Cheat,* distributed in France under the title *Forfaiture.* Though Delluc's writings show his clear awareness of the specific limitations of this particular work, which became a cult film for the cinematically-inclined French intellectuals of the period, he was very responsive to the form of cinema which it represented. This was the narrative continuity cinema that had developed during the previous five years or so in the United States, and from which French filmmakers had been shielded by the economic power of the French commercial giants, Pathé and Gaumont.

Like André Bazin some thirty years later, Delluc developed his ideas in relation to specific films—attacking the Feuillade of *La Nouvelle Mission de Judex,* while offering a keen appreciation of American and Swedish cinema and the films of French contemporaries such as Antoine, L'Herbier, and Gance. Delluc does not offer a worked-out theory of cinema, but a number of key ideas recur: the importance of cinema as a popular art, the crucial significance of rhythm and pacing in a form now based on sequences of shots instead of the long-held *plan sequences,* the importance of expressive, poetic imagery, and the choice of concrete realistic detail. All of these concepts are combined together with the need for restraint in acting. Delluc sought a cinema that would be truly the expression of its author and put stress on the inner life of its characters.

Between 1919 and 1923 Delluc scripted one film, *La Fête espagnole,* and directed seven others, from *Fumée noire* in 1920 to *L'Inondation* in 1923. With one exception, all of these were from original scripts, conceived directly for the screen. Though Delluc drew inspiration from American movies and advocated a popular cinema, he placed little emphasis on physical action. Instead, these films concentrate on the ramifications of a single incident and depict the intense interaction of a handful of characters. For none of this work did Delluc enjoy adequate resources, and he was denied the popular success which would have given him bigger budgets.

Moreover, unlike Gance and L'Herbier, Delluc did not have an instinctive flair for images, and the interest of his films lies more in their construction than their realization. Almost all contain some noteworthy stylistic exploration: the atmosphere of a single set in *Fièvre,* the use of landscape in *Le Chemin d'Ernoa,* or the interaction of past and present in *Le Silence* and his generally recognised masterpiece, *La Femme de nulle part.* Although he died at the age of 33—his contemporaries Gance and L'Herbier survived into their nineties, a factor that makes Delluc something of a figure apart—his place among the formative influences on French cinema is assured.

—Roy Armes

DELVAUX, André

Nationality: Belgian. **Born:** Héverlé, near Louvain, Belgium, 21 March 1926. **Education:** Studied at the Free University of Brussels, 1945-52; piano and composition at Royal Conservatory of Brussels. **Career:** Piano accompanist at the Belgian Cinémathèque, from 1950; head of a programme of film education for Belgian teachers, then lecturer at National Superior Institute of the Entertainment Arts (INSAS), from 1963; made first series of films as TV director, on Federico Fellini, 1960; directed first feature, *L'Homme au crane rasé,* 1966. **Awards:** Prix Louis Delluc, for *Rendez-vous à Bray,* 1972.

Films as Director and Scriptwriter:

1962 *Le Temps des ecoliers* (short)
1966 *L'Homme au crane rasé* (*Die Man die zijn Haar kort liet knippen*; *The Man Who Had His Hair Cut Short*) (co-sc)
1968 *Un Soir un train*
1971 *Rendez-vous à Bray*
1973 *Belle*
1975 *Dirk Bouts* (*Dieric Bouts*)
1979 *Femme entre chien et loup* (*Een Vrouw tussen hon en wolf*; *Woman in a Twilight Garden*)
1981 *To Woody Allen, From Europe With Love*
1983 *Benvenuta*
1985 *Babel Opera, ou la répétition de Don Juan*
1988 *L'oeuvre au noir* (*The Abyss*)

Other Films

1992 *Between Heaven and Earth* (role)

Publications

By DELVAUX: articles—

Interview, in *Image et Son* (Paris), September 1973.
Interview, in *Ecran* (Paris), November 1973.
Interview, in *The Thousand Eyes Magazine* (New York), December 1976.
Interview, in *Sight and Sound* (London), Spring 1977.
Interviews, in *Revue Belge du Cinéma* (Brussels), October and December 1977.
Interview, in *Cinéma* (Paris), July/August 1979.
Interview, in *A.I.P. & Co.* (London), July/August 1980.
Interview, in *Revue Belge du Cinéma* (Brussels), no. 20, 1981.
Interview with D. Michiels, in *Film en Televisie* (Brussels), October 1983.
Interview with T. Louis, in *Séquences* (Montreal), August 1987.
"André Delvaux Section" of *Avant-Scene du Cinema* (Paris), May 1988.
Interview, in *Revue du Cinéma* (Paris), June 1988.

On DELVAUX: books—

Pacquet, André, editor, *Le Cinéma en Belgique,* Quebec, Montreal, 1972.
Ellero, Roberto, *André Delvaux,* Venice, 1981.
Nysenholc, Adolphe, editor, *André Delvaux, ou les visages de l'imaginaire,* Brussels, 1985.

On DELVAUX: articles—

Cinéma (Switzerland), no. 4, 1974.
"Andre Delvaux," in *Film Dope* (London), September 1976.
Milne, Tom, "Countries of the Mind," in *Sight and Sound* (London), Spring 1972.
National Film Theatre Booklet (London), May 1980.
Variety (New York), September 4, 1985.
Helfgoot, H., "Andre Delvaux à pied d'oeuvre," in *Séquences* (Montréal), March 1988.
Variety (New York), 18 May 1988.
CinemAction, January 1992.
Mosley, P., "Literature, Film, Music: Julien Gracq's *Le roi cophetua* and Andre Delvaux's *Rendezvous a Bray,*" in *Literature Film Quarterly,* vol. 20, no. 2, 1992.

* * *

André Delvaux's growing body of cinema has been called one of tone, mood, and impression. Like French symbolist writers of the late nineteenth and early twentieth century, for whom aesthetic effects are sustained independently of narrative design, Delvaux writes and directs films that disperse synchronies of sound and image. Contact seems to be established with the spectator exactly when the thread of his stories is untied. Music and dialogue appear ungrounded or else alternately joined to and detached from their origins in either dialogue or visual composition. Quite often human figures seem to disappear in misty landscapes that are marked as much by sparse musical notes as physical contour. His films script effects of the dissolution of language. They are crafted through labor of collaboration with and quotation from other works of writing and art, notably Marguerite Yourcenar (*L'oeuvre au noir*) and Julien Gracq (creator of *Le roi Copheta,* which inspired *Rendez-vous à Bray*). He portrays Northern and Baroque traditions of painting that include Dirk Bouts and Caravaggio, while his affiliation with Surrealists—Ernst and others—are obvious in the graphic resemblance of the aptly entitled *Femme entre chien et loup* to Buñuel/Dali's *Un chien andalou.* Through fugacious and passing shapes the director articulates space "between" phantasm and reality.

If Delvaux's films are inspired by the epoch of the *nouvelle vague,* in which a literary cinema is proposed as an alternative to the indus-

André Delvaux directing *Belle*

trial heritage of entertainment in Hollywood, their signature is nonetheless of a Belgian, metaphysical style. The films lead to thoughts that erase boundaries usually demarcating real from imaginary worlds. He creates mental landscapes that recall the musical sense of language that had been the stuff first of Mallarmé, and later, especially, of Maeterlinck's theater. It is effective when displaced into the more immediate realm of cinema.

Perhaps the keenest impressions of his films can be felt in evanescence of sound and image. Loss of discernable forms paradoxically traces the memory of paintings and poetry that interfere with dialogue and music. Through slow montage Delvaux allows the spectator to expand the narrative field that is being viewed. In, for instance, *Rendez-vous à Bray,* soldiers of the 1870s sport uniforms with decorous colors on their epaulettes and chevrons. Set against grey mist, they set tones that immediately recall the both dreamy and lucid view of timeless death and beauty that Rimbaud—another writer of Northern French inspiration—offers in his famous sonnet, "Le dormeur du val." Film and poetry coalesce to leave fleeting sensations that conjure a moment of European history and style at the moment just prior to the beginnings of cinema.

Delvaux is not everyone's director. He asks his viewer to *read* hieroglyphs fashioned from music, painting, and literature that reach into collective memory and, no less, emerge from oblivion. His work merits extensive study for its range of sources and its meditation on the origins and the freedom of film form.

—Tom Conley

DE MILLE, Cecil B.

Nationality: American. **Born:** Cecil Blount De Mille in Ashfield, Massachusetts, 12 August 1881. **Education:** Pennsylvania Military Academy, Chester, 1896-98; American Academy of Dramatic Arts, New York, 1898-1900. **Family:** Married Constance Adams, 16 August 1902, two sons, two daughters. **Career:** Actor, playwright, stage producer, and associate with mother in De Mille Play Co. (theatrical agency), to 1913; co-founder, then Director-General, of Jesse L. Lasky Feature Play Co., 1913 (which became Paramount Pictures Corp. after merger, 1918); directed first film, *The Squaw Man,* 1914; founder, Mercury Aviation Co., 1919; established De Mille Pictures Corp., 1924; joined MGM as producer-director, 1928; co-founder, Screen Directors Guild, 1931; independent producer for Paramount, 1932; producer, Lux Radio Theater of the Air, 1936-45. **Awards:** Outstanding Service Award, War Agencies of the Government of the U.S.; Special Oscar "for 37 years of brilliant showmanship," 1949; Irving Thalberg Award, Academy, 1952; Milestone Award, Screen Producers' Guild, 1956; Chevalier de Légion d'honneur, France; Honorary doctorate, University of Southern California. **Died:** 21 January 1959.

Films as Director:

1914 *The Squaw Man* (*The White Man*) (co-d, sc, bit role); *The Call of the North* (+ sc, introductory appearance); *The Virginian*

(+ sc, co-ed); *What's His Name* (+ sc, ed): *The Man from Home* (+ sc, ed); *Rose of the Rancho* (+ sc, ed): *Brewster's Millions* (co-d, uncredited, sc); *The Master Mind* (co-d, uncredited, sc); *The Man on the Box* (co-d, uncredited, sc); *The Only Son* (co-d, uncredited, sc); *The Ghost Breaker* (co-d, uncredited, co-sc)

1915 *The Girl of the Golden West* (+ sc, ed); *The Warrens of Virginia* (+ sc, ed); *The Unafraid* (+ sc, ed); *The Captive* (+ co-sc, ed); *The Wild Goose Chase* (+ co-sc, ed); *The Arab* (+ co-sc, ed); *Chimmie Fadden* (+ co-sc, ed): *Kindling* (+ sc, ed); *Carmen* (+ sc, ed); *Chimmie Fadden Out West* (+ co-sc, ed); *The Cheat* (+ sc, ed); *The Golden Chance* (+ co-sc, ed); *The Goose Girl* (co-d with Thompson, uncredited, co-sc)

1916 *Temptation* (+ co-story, ed); *The Trail of the Lonesome Pine* (+ sc, ed); *The Heart of Nora Flynn* (+ ed); *Maria Rosa* (+ ed); *The Dream Girl* (+ ed)

1917 *Joan the Woman* (+ ed); *A Romance of the Redwoods* (+ co-sc, ed); *The Little American* (+ co-sc, ed); *The Woman God Forgot* (+ ed); *The Devil Stone* (+ ed); *Nan of Music Mountain* (co-d with Melford, uncredited); *Lost and Won*

1918 *The Whispering Chorus* (+ ed); *Old Wives for New* (+ ed); *We Can't Have Everything* (+ co-ed); *Till I Come Back to You*; *The Squaw Man*

1919 *Don't Change Your Husband*; *For Better, For Worse*; *Male and Female (The Admirable Crichton)*

1920 *Why Change Your Wife?*; *Something to Think About*

1921 *Forbidden Fruit* (+ pr); *The Affairs of Anatol (A Prodigal Knight)*; *Fool's Paradise*

1922 *Saturday Night*; *Manslaughter*; *Don't Tell Everything* (co-d with Wood, uncredited) (incorporates two reel unused *The Affairs of Anatol* footage)

1923 *Adam's Rib*; *The Ten Commandments*

1924 *Triumph* (+ pr); *Feet of Clay*

1925 *The Golden Bed*; *The Road to Yesterday*

1926 *The Volga Boatman*

1927 *The King of Kings*

1929 *The Godless Girl*; *Dynamite* (+ pr)

1930 *Madame Satan* (+ pr)

1931 *The Squaw Man* (+ pr)

1932 *The Sign of the Cross* (+ pr) (re-released 1944 with add'l footage)

1933 *This Day and Age* (+ pr)

1934 *Four Frightened People* (+ pr); *Cleopatra* (+ pr)

1935 *The Crusades* (+ pr)

1937 *The Plainsman* (+ pr)

1938 *The Buccaneer* (+ pr)

1939 *Union Pacific* (+ pr)

1940 *North West Mounted Police* (+ pr, prologue narration)

1942 *Reap the Wild Wind* (+ pr, prologue narration)

1944 *The Story of Dr. Wassell* (+ pr)

1947 *Unconquered* (+ pr)

1949 *Samson and Delilah* (+ pr, prologue narration)

1952 *The Greatest Show on Earth* (+ pr, narration, introductory appearance)

1956 *The Ten Commandments* (+ pr, prologue narration)

Other Films:

1914 *Ready Money* (Apfel) (co-sc); *The Circus Man* (Apfel) (co-sc); *Cameo Kirby* (Apfel) (co-sc)

1915 *The Country Boy* (Thompson) (co-sc); *A Gentleman of Leisure* (Melford) (sc); *The Governor's Lady* (Melford) (co-sc); *Snobs* (Apfel) (co-sc)

1916 *The Love Mask* (Reicher) (co-sc)

1917 *Betty to the Rescue* (Reicher) (co-sc, supervisor)

1923 *Hollywood* (Cruze) (guest appearance)

1930 *Free and Easy* (Sedgwick) (guest appearance)

1935 *The Hollywood You Never See* (short) (seen directing *Cleopatra*); *Hollywood Extra Girl* (Moulton) (seen directing *The Crusades*)

1942 *Star Spangled Rhythm* (Marshall) (guest appearance)

1947 *Variety Girl* (Marshall) (guest appearance); *Jens Mansson i Amerika (Jens Mansson in America)* (Janzon) (guest appearance); *Aid to the Nation* (short) (appearance)

1950 ***Sunset Boulevard*** (Wilder) (role as himself)

1952 *Son of Paleface* (Tashlin) (guest appearance)

1956 *The Buster Keaton Story* (Sheldon) (guest appearance)

1957 *The Heart of Show Business* (Staub) (narrator)

1958 *The Buccaneer* (pr, supervisor, introductory appearance)

Publications

By DE MILLE: book—

The Autobiography of Cecil B. De Mille, Englewood Cliffs, New Jersey, 1959.

By DE MILLE: articles—

"After Seventy Pictures," in *Films in Review* (New York), March 1956.
"De Mille Answers His Critics," in *Films and Filming* (London), March 1958.

By DE MILLE: plays—

The Royal Mounted (1899)
The Return of Peter Grimm, with David Belasco

On DE MILLE: books—

De Mille, William, *Hollywood Saga*, New York, 1939.
De Mille, Agnes, *Dance to the Piper*, New York, 1951.
Crowther, Bosley, *The Lion's Share*, New York, 1957.
Koury, Phil, *Yes, Mr. De Mille*, New York, 1959.
Wagenknecht, Edward, *The Movies in the Age of Innocence*, Oklahoma, 1962.
Mourlet, Michel, *Cecil B. De Mille*, Paris, 1968.
Ringgold, Gene, and De Witt Bodeen, *The Films of Cecil B. De Mille*, New York, 1969.
Essoe, Gabe, and Raymond Lee, *De Mille: The Man and His Pictures*, New York, 1970.
Higham, Charles, *Cecil B. De Mille*, New York, 1973.
Higashi, Sumiko, *Cecil B. De Mille: A Guide to References and Resources*, Boston, 1985.
Norman, Barry, *The Film Greats*, London, 1985.
Edwards, Anne, *The De Milles: An American Family*, New York, 1988.

On DE MILLE: articles—

Lardner, Ring Jr., "The Sign of the Boss," in *Screen Writer*, November 1945.
Feldman, Joseph and Harry, "Cecil B. De Mille's Virtues," in *Films in Review* (New York), December 1950.
Harcourt-Smith, Simon, "The Siegfried of Sex," in *Sight and Sound* (London), February 1951.
Johnson, Albert, "The Tenth Muse in San Francisco," in *Sight and Sound* (London), January/March 1955.
Baker, Peter, "Showman for the Millions," in *Films and Filming* (London), October 1956.

Cecil B. De Mille

Card, James, "The Greatest Showman on Earth," in *Image* (Rochester, New York), November 1956.
Arthur, Art, "C.B. De Mille's Human Side," in *Films in Review* (New York), April 1967.
"De Mille Issue" of *Présence du Cinéma* (Paris), Autumn 1967.
Ford, Charles, "Cecil B. De Mille," in *Anthologie du Cinéma,* vol. 3, Paris, 1968.
Bodeen, Dewitt, "Cecil B. De Mille," in *Films in Review* (New York), August/September 1981.
Mandell, P.R., "Parting the Red Sea (and other miracles)," in *American Cinematographer* (Los Angeles), April 1983.
D'Arc, J.V., "So let it be written ... ," in *Literature/Film Quarterly* (Salisbury, Maryland), January 1986.
Moullet, L., "Les jardins secrets de C.B.," in *Cahiers du Cinéma* (Paris), December 1991.
Eyman, Scott, "The Best Years of Their Lives," in *Film Comment* (New York), March/April 1992.

* * *

For much of his forty-year career, the public and the critics associated Cecil B. De Mille with a single kind of film, the epic. He certainly made a great many of them: *The Sign of the Cross, The Crusades, King of Kings,* two versions of *The Ten Commandments, The Greatest Show on Earth,* and others. As a result, De Mille became a symbol of Hollywood during its "Golden Age." He represented that which was larger than life, often too elaborate, but always entertaining. By having such a strong public personality, however, De Mille came to be neglected as a director, even though many of his films—not just the epics—stand out as extraordinary.

Although he made films until 1956, De Mille's masterpiece may well have come in 1915 with *The Cheat.* Even this early in his career, we can locate some of the motifs that turn up again and again in De Mille's work: a faltering upper-class marriage, the allure and exoticism of the Far East, and sexual attraction equated with hypnotic control. He also made a major aesthetic advancement in the use of editing in *The Cheat* that soon became a part of the repertoire of most filmmakers.

For the cinema's first twenty years, editing was based primarily on following action. During a chase, when actors exited screen right, the next shot had them entering screen left; or, a director might cut from a person being chased to those characters doing the chasing. In either case, the logic of the action controls the editing, which in turn gives us a sense of the physical space of a scene. But in *The Cheat,* De Mille used his editing to create a sense of psychological space. Richard Hardy, a wealthy businessman, confronts his wife with her extravagant bills, but Mrs. Hardy can think only of her lover, Haka, who is equally obsessed with her. De Mille provides a shot/counter-shot here, but the scene does not cut from Mr. Hardy to his wife, even though the logic of the action and the dialogue seems to indicate that it should. Instead, the shots alternate between Mrs. Hardy and Haka, even though the two lovers are miles apart. This sort of editing, which follows thoughts rather than actions, may seem routine today, but in 1915 it was a major development in the method of constructing a sequence.

As a visual stylist, however, De Mille became known more for his wit than for his editing innovations. At the beginning of *The Affairs of Anatol,* for instance, our first view of the title character, Anatol DeWitt Spencer, is of his feet. He taps them nervously while he waits for his wife to make breakfast. Our first view of Mrs. Spencer is also of her feet—a maid gives them a pedicure. In just seconds, and with only two shots, De Mille lets us know that this couple is in trouble. Mrs. Spencer's toenails must dry before Anatol can eat. Also from these opening shots, the viewers realize that they have been placed firmly within the realm of romantic comedy. Such closeups have no place within a melodrama.

One normally does not think of De Mille in terms of pairs of shots. Instead, one thinks on a large scale, and remembers the crowd scenes (the lions versus Christians extravaganza in *The Sign of the Cross*), the huge upper-crust social functions (the charity gala in *The Cheat*), the orgiastic parties (one of which takes place in a dirigible in *Dynamite*), and the bathrooms that De Mille turns into colossal marble shrines.

De Mille began directing in the grand style quite early in his career. In 1915, with opera star Geraldine Farrar in the lead role, he made one of the best film versions of *Carmen,* and two years later, again with Farrar, he directed *Joan the Woman.* Again and again, De Mille would refer to history as a foundation to support the believability of his stories, as if his most obvious excesses could be justified if they were at least remotely based on real-life incidents. A quick look at his filmography shows many films based on historical events (often so far back in the past that accuracy hardly becomes an issue): *The Sign of the Cross, The Crusades, Union Pacific, Northwest Mounted Police,* and others. When history was inconvenient, De Mille made use of a literary text to give his films a high gloss of acceptability and veracity. In the opening credits of *The Affairs of Anatol,* for instance, De Mille stresses that the story derives from the play by Schnitzler.

In both his silent and sound films, De Mille mixes Victorian morality with sizable doses of sex and violence. The intertitles of *Why Change Your Wife?,* for example, rail against divorce as strongly as any nineteenth century marital tract, but the rest of the film deals openly with sexual obsession, and shows two women in actual physical combat over one man. Similarly, all of De Mille's religious epics extol the Christian virtues while at the same time reveling in scenes depicting all of the deadly sins. Though it is tension between extremes that makes De Mille's films so intriguing, critics have often made this aspect of his work seem laughable. Even today De Mille rarely receives the serious recognition and study that he deserves.

—Eric Smoodin

DEMME, Jonathan

Nationality: American. **Born:** Baldwin, New York, 1944. **Education:** University of Miami. **Military Service:** U.S. Air Force, 1966. **Family:** Married director Evelyn Purcell. **Career:** Publicity writer for United Artists, Avco Embassy, and Pathe Contemporary Films, early 1960s; writer on *Film Daily,* 1968-69; worked in London, 1969; unit publicist, then writer for Roger Corman, 1970; directed first film, *Caged Heat,* 1974; also director of TV films, commercials, and music videos for recording artists Chrissie Hynde, New Order, Suzanne Vega, and others. **Awards:** Best Picture and Best Director Academy Awards, for *The Silence of the Lambs,* 1991.

Films as Director:

1974 *Caged Heat* (+ sc)
1975 *Crazy Mama*
1976 *Fighting Mad* (+ sc)
1977 *Citizen's Band* (*Handle With Care*)
1979 *Last Embrace*
1980 *Melvin and Howard*
1983 *Swing Shift* (co-d)
1984 *Stop Making Sense* (doc)
1986 *Something Wild* (+ co-pr)
1987 *Swimming to Cambodia*
1988 *Married to the Mob*; *Famous All Over Town*

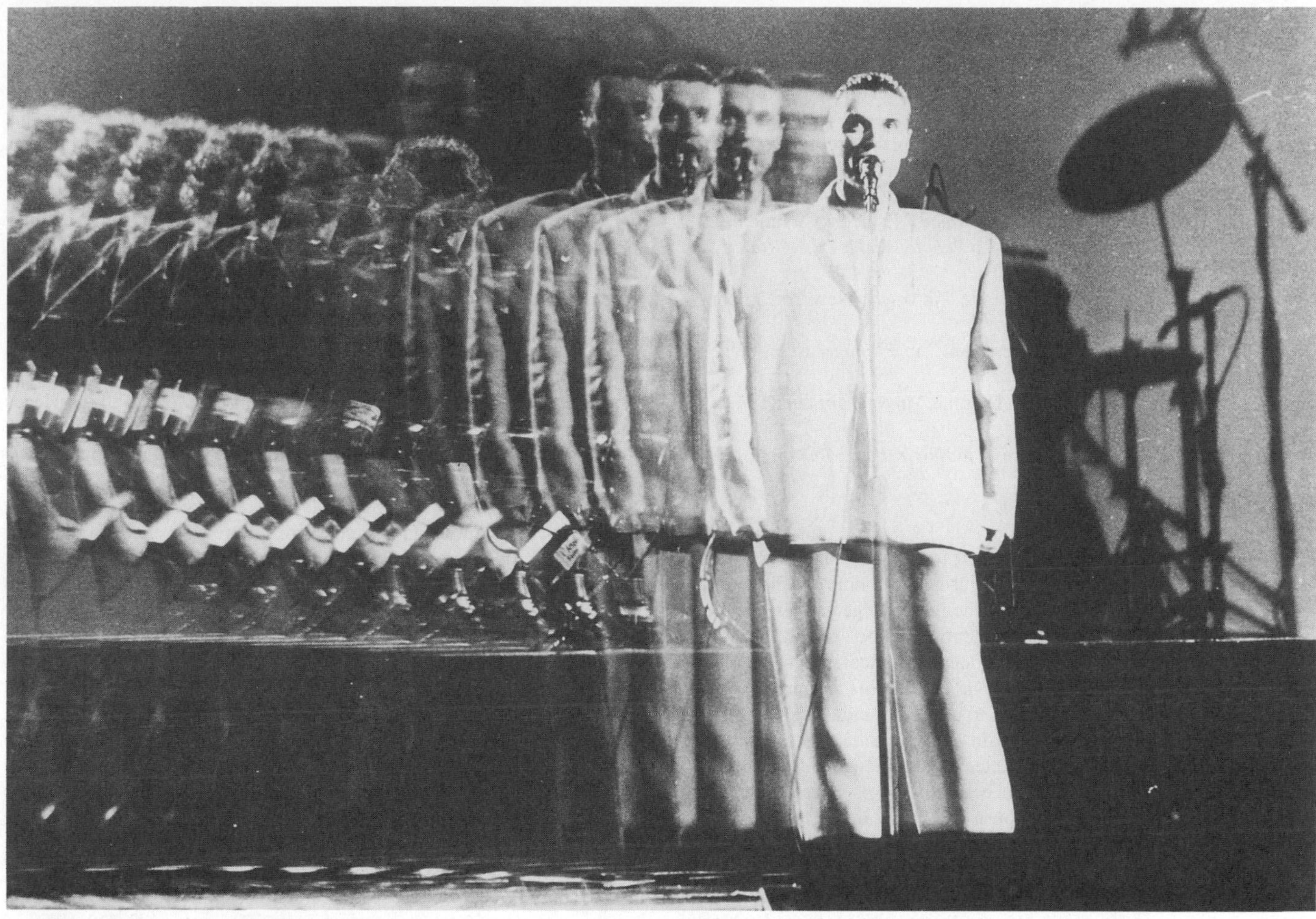

Jonathan Demme: *Stop Making Sense*

1991 ***The Silence of the Lambs***; *Cousin Bobby* (doc)
1993 ***Philadelphia*** (+ co-pr)

Other Films:

1970 *Sudden Terror* (*Eyewitness*) (Irwin Allen) (music coordinator)
1972 *Angels Hard as They Come* (Viola) (pr, co-sc); *The Hot Box* (Viola) (pr, co-sc)
1973 *Black Mama, White Mama* (Romero) (co-story)
1985 *Into the Night* (Landis) (role)
1990 *Miami Blues* (pr)
1993 *Household Saints* (Savoca) (exec pr); *Amos and Andrew* (exec pr)
1995 *Devil in a Blue Dress* (exec pr)

Publications

By DEMME: articles—

"Demme Monde," an interview with Carlos Clarens, in *Film Comment* (New York), September/October 1980.
Interview with Michael Stragow, in *American Film* (Washington, D.C.), January-February 1984.
Interview in *Time Out* (London), 1 July 1987.
Interview with Quentin Curtis in *Independent* (London), 15 June 1989.
"Identity Check," an interview with Gavin Smith in *Film Comment* (New York), January/February 1991.
"Jonathan Demme: Heavy Estrogen," an interview with Gary Indiana in *Interview* (New York), February 1991.
"Demme's monde," an interview with Amy Taubin in *Village Voice* (New York), 19 February 1991.
Interview with A. DeCurtis in *Rolling Stone* (New York), 24 March 1994.

On DEMME: articles—

Goodwin, Michael, "Velvet Vampires and Hot Mamas: Why Exploitation Films Get to Us," in *Village Voice* (New York), 7 July 1975.
Kehr, Dave, in *Film Comment* (New York), September/October 1977.
Baumgarten, Marjorie, and others, "*Caged Heat,*" in *Cinema Texas Program Notes* (Austin), Spring 1978.
Maslin, Janet, in *New York Times,* 13 May 1979.
Black, Louis, "*Crazy Mama,*" in *Cinema Texas Program Notes* (Austin), Spring 1978.
Kaplan, James, "Jonathan Demme's Offbeat America," in *New York Times Magazine,* 27 March 1988.
Schruers, Fred, "Jonathan Demme: A Study in Character," in *Rolling Stone* (New York), 19 May 1988.
Farber, J., "*Something Wild,*" in *Rolling Stone* (New York), 2 November 1989.
DeCourcey Hinds, M., "Retelling a Psychopathic Killer's Tale is No Joke," in *New York Times,* 25 March 1990.
Miller, M., "An Unlikely Director for the G-Men," in *Newsweek* (New York), 9 April 1990.

Vineberg, S., "*Swing Shift:* A Tale of Hollywood," in *Sight and Sound* (London), vol. 60, no. 1, 1990-1991.

Gramfors, R., article in *Chaplin* (Stockholm), vol. 33, no. 3, 1991.

Maslin, Janet, "How to Film a Gory Story with Restraint," in *New York Times,* 19 February 1991.

Ehrenstein, David, "Of Lambs and Slaughter: Director Jonathan Demme Responds to Charges of Homophobia," in *Advocate,* 12 March 1991.

Taubin, Amy, "Still Burning," in *Village Voice* (New York), 9 June 1992.

Gleick, E., "Only Lambs are Silent," in *People Weekly* (New York), 22 June 1992.

Cunningham, M., "Breaking the Silence," in *Vogue* (New York), January 1994.

Green, J., "The *Philadelphia* Experiment," in *Premiere* (New York), January 1994.

Tally, Ted, "Ted Tally, on Jonathan Demme," in *New Yorker,* 21 March 1994.

"Jonathan Demme's Moving Pictures," in *New Yorker,* 31 October 1994.

* * *

Jonathan Demme has proven himself to be one of the more acute observers of the inner life of America during the course of a directorial career that began in the early 1970s, though he began as just another protégé of the Roger Corman apprentice school of filmmaking. Demme's concern with character—focused particularly through the observation of telling eccentricities—is perhaps his trademark, combined with a vitality and willingness to use the frameworks of various genres to their fullest extent. A film such as *Something Wild,* for example, combines a tale of character and relationship development in an exhilarating movie which successfully mixes classic screwball comedy (you could imagine Hepburn and Tracy in the leads) with a very real menace in the closing stages that extends earlier comic confusion into the deadlier paranoia of the thriller.

Perhaps inspired by the "anything goes" aura of his Corman days, Demme has never been afraid to experiment with mood and subject matter in his films: Hitchcockian suspense in *The Last Embrace,* the possibilities of monologue in *Swimming To Cambodia,* romantic comedy in *Swing Shift,* horror in *The Silence of the Lambs,* and gangster conventions in *Married To The Mob.*

Even his earliest films—*Caged Heat* and *Fighting Mad* (which he also wrote)—showed Demme exploiting the possibilities offered by the sex-and-violence format (rampaging girl-gangs in the first, rampaging rednecks in the second) for original and highly distinctive exploration of subjects and style.

Caged Heat also gave early signs of Demme's concern with those struggling to take control of their lives—particularly, but not exclusively, women. This examination of self-determination has remained a theme throughout his work, from the women prisoners of *Caged Heat* and the munitions worker (Goldie Hawn) in *Swing Shift* to the central characters in *Something Wild* (Melanie Griffith) and *Married To The Mob* (Michelle Pfeiffer), and contributed to his reputation as a feminist filmmaker. Their struggle to establish themselves against patriarchal attitudes epitomizes, for Demme, the struggles of the underdog, which he has called "heroic." This real concern for his characters is clear in the (usually affectionate) intensity with which they—and their lives—are portrayed, and Demme recently described his films as "a little old-fashioned, at the same time as we try to make them modern."

Demme is concerned with entertaining a mass audience, and it is probably unwise to consider the low-key mood of the earlier critically-adored films *Citizen's Band* (a black comedy that explores lack of communication through a small town's obsession with CB-radio) and *Melvin And Howard* (an offbeat comedy based on a true story of a working-class man who gave a lift to a hobo Howard Hughes in the Nevada desert) as being necessarily closest to his own heart. Both films, however good they may be, were also conscious reactions to the over-the-top nature of earlier Corman-inspired work.

Misjudgment of Demme's concerns is nothing new for the filmmaker. His much-noted focus on the everyday kitsch of Americana, for example, is driven more by an understanding of its importance as a yardstick by which America consumer society measures itself ("it's our kind of fetishism") than with being a desire to be "hip." For Demme, observing kitsch is simply a form of realism in a country where the bizarre is often real.

Though much concerned with achieving an honest view of character, Demme is not uncaring about stylish direction. A sequence such as the series of out-takes used for the final credits of *Married To The Mob* is one mark of a freewheeling approach to filmmaking that has roots in the knowing wit of the French New Wave (Demme cites Truffaut as an early influence), while his pared-down vision of a Talking Heads concert in *Stop Making Sense* is a distinctive, classy example of the rock film which pointedly eschews the tacky visual trappings too often associated with the genre.

Ultimately, though, his concern is with character rather than style—content over form. Demme is concerned more with exploring humanity than with proving himself an auteur for film critics. His own description of *Married To The Mob* offers an excellent insight into what he has sought in his work. "It was intelligent fun, it didn't patronise the characters or the audience, it was good-hearted. Those are tough commodities to come by."

Since his late 1980s work, Demme has gone on to make two of the higher-profile films of the 1990s. *The Silence of the Lambs,* based on the Thomas Harris bestseller, was a film about a young FBI trainee (Jodie Foster) who locks horns with Hannibal Lecter (Anthony Hopkins), a psychopathic, cannibalistic murderer. The film, which featured fine performances and excellent direction, earned Oscars for Best Picture, Director, Actor, Actress and Adapted Screenplay—quite a haul for what is essentially a big-budget splatter film.

In quite a change of pace, Demme next directed *Philadelphia,* a film that stars Tom Hanks as Andrew Beckett, an AIDS-afflicted lawyer who fights the system after being fired from a prestigious Philadelphia law firm. Upon the film's release, gay activists complained—sometimes bitterly—that the film soft-pedals its subject. However, *Philadelphia* was not produced for those who already are highly politicized and need no introduction to the reality of AIDS. The film was made for the masses who do not live in urban gay enclaves, and who have never met—or think they have never met—a homosexual, let alone a person with AIDS. As a drama, *Philadelphia* is not without flaws. The members of Beckett's family are unfailingly supportive and understanding, a much-too-simplistic ideal in a world in which many gays and lesbians are shunned by their relatives. It also is difficult to accept the subtle changes that occur within Joe Miller (Denzel Washington), the homophobic lawyer who takes Beckett's case. But *Philadelphia* does succeed in showing that homosexuals are human beings, people who deserve to be treated fairly and civilly. It enjoyed a mainstream success with audiences who normally might be turned off by a more radical, politically loaded (let alone sexually frank) film about gays or AIDS.

—Norman Miller, updated by Rob Edelman

DEMY, Jacques

Nationality: French. **Born:** Pontchâteau (Loire-Atlantique), 5 June 1931. **Education:** Ecole des Beaux-Arts, Nantes; Ecole Technique de Photographie et de Cinématographiques, Paris. **Family:** Married director Agnes Varda, 1962; children: Mathieu and Rosalie. **Career:** Assistant to animator Paul Grimault, 1952; assistant to Georges Rouquier, 1954; made first short film, *Le Sabotier du Val de Loire,* began association with editor Anne-Marie Cotret, 1955; directed first feature, *Lola,* 1961. **Died:** 27 October, 1990, of a brain hemorrhage resulting from leukemia.

Films as Director and Scriptwriter:

1956 *Le Sabotier du Val de Loire*
1957 *Le Bel Indifférent*
1958 *Le Musée Grévin*
1959 *La Mère et l'infant* (co-d); *Ars*
1961 *Lola*
1962 "La Luxure" (Lust) episode of *Les Sept Péchés capitaux* (*Seven Deadly Sins*)
1963 *La Baie des Anges* (*Bay of the Angels*)
1964 *Les Parapluies de Cherbourg* (*The Umbrellas of Cherbourg*)
1967 *Les Demoiselles de Rochefort* (*The Young Girls of Rochefort*)
1969 *The Model Shop* (+ pr)
1971 *Peau d'ane* (*Donkey Skin*)
1972 *The Pied Piper of Hamelin* (*The Pied Piper*)
1973 *L'Évènement le plus important depuis que l'homme a marché sur la lune* (*A Slightly Pregnant Man*)
1978 *Lady Oscar*
1982 *Une Chambre en ville* (*A Room in Town*)
1985 *Parking*
1988 *Trois Places pour le 26* (*Three Places for the 26th*)

Other Films:

1954 *Lourdes et ses miracles* (Rouquier) (asst d)
1955 *Arthur Honegger* (Rouquier) (asst d)
1956 *S.O.S. Noronha* (Rouquier) (asst d)
1959 ***Les Quatre Cents Coups*** (Truffaut) (role as policeman)
1960 *Paris nous appartient* (Rivette) (role as guest at party)
1991 *Jacquot de Nantes* (role as himself)

Publications

By DEMY: articles—

"I Prefer the Sun to the Rain," in *Film Comment* (New York), Spring 1965.
Interview with Marsha Kinder, in *Film Heritage* (Dayton, Ohio), Spring 1967.
"Frenchman in Hollywood," an interview with Philip Scheuer, in *Action* (Los Angeles), November/December 1968.
"Lola in Los Angeles," in *Films and Filming* (London), April 1970.
"Cinéastes et musiciens," in *Ecran* (Paris), September 1975.
Interview and biofilmography, in *Film Dope* (London), September 1976.
Interview with G. Haustrate, in *Cinéma* (Paris), July/August 1981.
Interview with Serge Daney, Jean Narboni, and Serge Toubiana, in *Cahiers du Cinéma* (Paris), November 1982.

On DEMY: book—

Berthome, Pierre, *Jacques Demy: Les Racines du reve,* Nantes, 1982.

On DEMY: articles—

Roud, Richard, "Rondo Galant," in *Sight and Sound* (London), Summer 1964.
Billard, Ginette, "Jacques Demy and His Other World," in *Film Quarterly* (Berkeley), Fall 1964.
"Director of the Year," *International Film Guide* (London, New York), 1966.
Strick, Philip, "Demy Calls the Tune," in *Sight and Sound* (London), Autumn 1971.
Petrie, G., "Jacques Demy," in *Film Comment* (New York), Winter 1971/72.
"Journals: Gilbert Adair from Paris," in *Film Comment* (New York), March/April 1979.
"Demy Issue" of *Cinéma* (Paris), July/August 1981.
Dossier on Jacques Demy, in *Cinématographe* (Paris), October 1982.
Haustrate, Gaston, "Grand prix national du cinéma à Jacques Demy et Jean-Luc Godard," in *Cinéma* (Paris), February 1983.
Biofilmography in *Première* (Paris), November 1988.
Obituary, in *New York Times,* October 30, 1990.
Obituary, in *Variety* (New York), November 5, 1990.
Toubiana, S., "Jacques Demy ou le bel entetement," in *Cahiers du Cinéma,* December 1990.
Hogue, P., "Playing for Keeps," in *Film Comment* (New York), July/August 1991.
Hoberman, J. "The Art of Daydreaming," in *Première* (Paris), June 1993.

On DEMY: film—

Delvaux, André, *Derrière l'écran,* 1966.
Varda, Agnes, *Jacquot de Nantes* (appearance), 1991.
Varda, Agnes, *Des demoiselles ont en 25 ans (The Young Girls Turn 25),* 1993.
Varda, Agnes, *The World of Jacques Demy,* 1995.

* * *

Jacques Demy's first feature film, *Lola,* is among the early distinguished products of the New Wave and is dedicated to Max Ophüls. These two facts in conjunction define its particular character. It proved to be the first in a series of loosely interlinked films (the intertextuality is rather more than a charming gimmick, relating as it does to certain thematic preoccupations already established in *Lola* itself); arguably, it remains the richest and most satisfying work so far in Demy's erratic, frustrating, but also somewhat underrated career.

The name and character of Lola (Anouk Aimée) herself can be traced to two previous celebrated female protagonists: the Lola Montès of Max Ophüls's film of that name, and the Lola-Lola (Marlene Dietrich) of von Sternberg's *The Blue Angel*, to which Demy pays homage in a number performed by Aimée in a top hat. The explicit philosophy of Lola Montès ("For me, life is movement") is enacted in Demy's film by the constant comings and goings, arrivals and departures, and intricate intercrossings of the characters. Ophüls's work has often been linked to concepts of fate; at the same time the auteurs of the early New Wave were preoccupied with establishing Freedom—as a metaphysical principle, to be enacted in their professional methodology. The tension between fate and freedom is there throughout Demy's work. *Lola*'s credit sequence alternates the improvisatory freedom of jazz with the slow movement of Beethoven's 7th Symphony. The latter musical work is explicitly associated with destiny in the form of the huge white American car that brings back Michel, Lola's lover and father of her child, who, like his predecessors in innumerable folk songs, has left her for seven years to make his fortune. No film is more intricately and obsessively patterned, with all the characters interlinked: the middle-aged woman used to be Lola (or someone like her), her teenage daughter may become Lola (or someone like her). Yet neither resembles Lola as she is in the film: everyone is different, yet everyone is interchangeable.

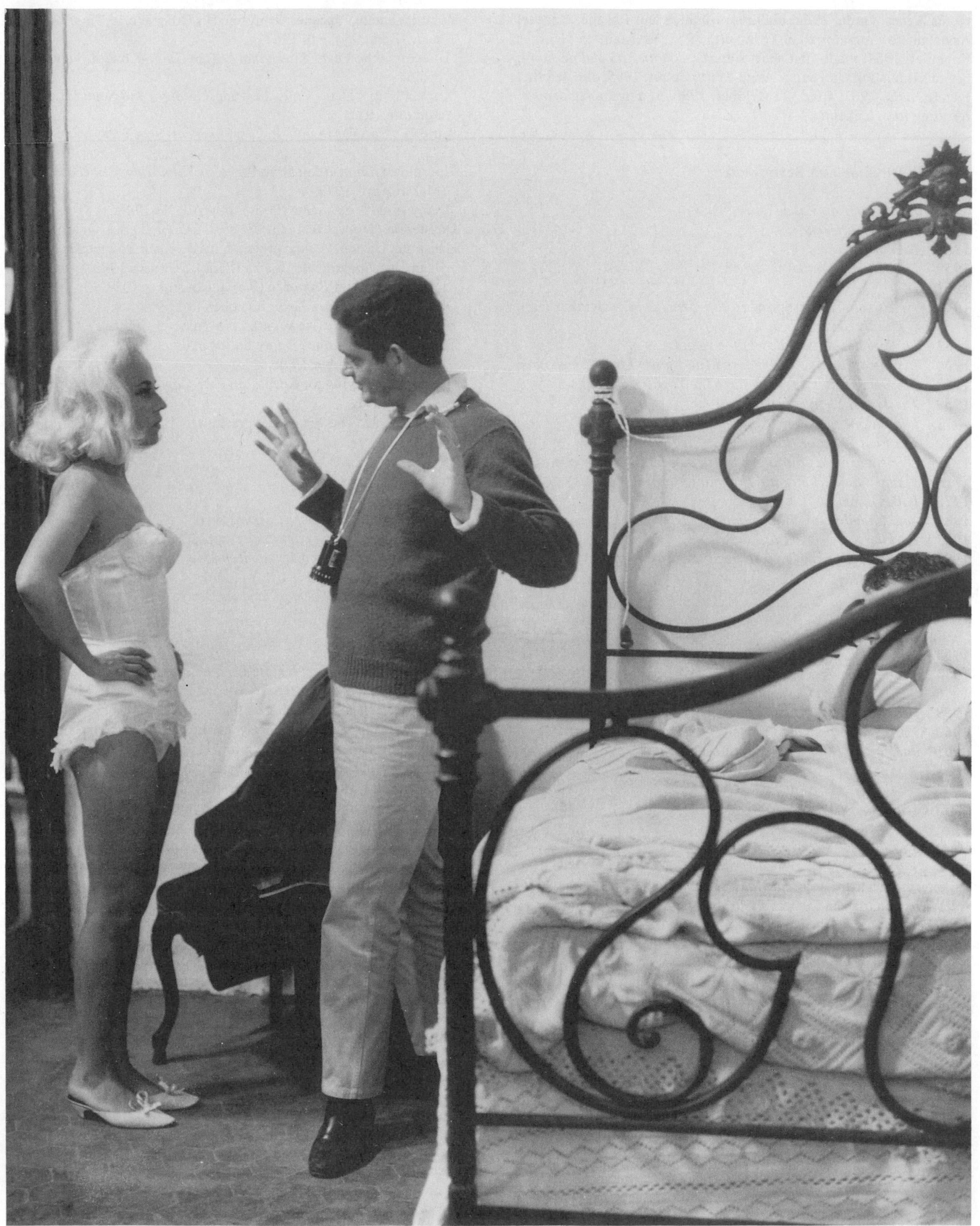

Jacques Demy directing Jeanne Moreau in *La Baie des Anges*

Two subsequent Demy films relate closely to *Lola.* In *Les Parapluies de Cherbourg,* Roland, Lola's rejected lover, recounts his brief liaison with Lola to the visual accompaniment of a flashback to the arcade that was one of their meeting-places. In addition, Lola herself reappears in *The Model Shop.* Two other films are bound in to the series as well. *Les Demoiselles de Rochefort* is linked by means of a certain cheating on the part of Demy—Lola has been found murdered and dismembered in a laundry basket, but the corpse is a different Lola. Especially poignant, as the series continues, is the treatment of the abrupt, unpredictable, seemingly fortuitous happy ending. At the end of *Lola,* Lola drives off with Michel and their child (as Roland of *Parapluies,* discarded and embittered, departs on his diamond-smuggling trip to South Africa). At the conclusion of *Le Baie des Anges*—a film that, at the time, revealed no connection with *Lola*—Jackie (Jeanne Moreau), a compulsive gambler, manages to leave the casino to follow her lover *before* she knows the result of her bet: two happy endings which are exhilarating precisely because they are so arbitrary. Then, several films later, in *Model Shop,* Lola recounts how her great love Michel abandoned her to run off with a compulsive gambler called Jackie. Thus both happy endings are reversed in a single blow.

It is not so much that Demy doesn't believe in happy endings: he simply doesn't believe in *permanent* ones (as "life is movement"). The ambivalent, bittersweet "feel" of Demy is perhaps best summed up in the end of *Les Parapluies de Cherbourg,* where the lovers, now both married to others, accidentally meet, implicitly acknowledge their love, and return with acceptance to the relationships to which they are committed.

Outside the *Lola* series, Demy's touch has been uncertain. His two fairy-tale films, *Peau d'ane* and *The Pied Piper,* unfortunately tend to confirm the common judgment that he is more a decorator than a creator. But he should not be discounted. *A Room in Town,* a return to the *Lola* mode if not to the *Lola* characters, was favorably received.

Demy's final two credits, *Parking* and *Three Places for the 26th,* are musicals which disappointed in that they were unable to capture the spark of his earlier work. Agnes Varda, his wife of almost three decades, then directed a film about Demy titled *Jacquot de Nantes,* which was released a year after his death. The film is a poignant, straight-from-the-heart record of the measure of a man's life, with Varda shifting between interviews with Demy (tenderly shot in extreme close-up), sequences from his films, and a narrative which details the youth of Demy in Nantes during the 1940s and relates how he cultivated a love of the movies. The film works best, however, as a beautiful and poignantly composed love letter. Its essence is summed up in one of its opening shots: the camera pans the content of a watercolor, focusing first on a nude woman, then on a nude man, and finally on their interlocking hands.

Jacquot de Nantes is obviously a very personal film. But it was not meant to be a tribute; rather, it was conceived and filmed when Demy was still alive. "Jacques would speak about his childhood, which he loved," Varda explained at a New York Film Festival press conference. "His memories were very vivid. I told him, 'Why don't you write about them?' So he did, and he let me read the pages. The more he wrote the more he remembered—even the names of the children who sat next to him in school. Most children do not know what they want to do when they grow up. But Jacques did, from the time he was 12. He had an incredible will. So I said, 'This [material] would make a good film.' I wrote the script, and I tried to capture the spirit of Jacques and his family, and the way people spoke and acted in [the 1940s]. We shot the film in the exact [locations] in which he grew up. I also filmed an interview with him. It's just Jacques speaking about his childhood. It's not a documentary about Jacques Demy. It's just him saying, 'Yes, this is true. This is my life.'

"He saw most of the final [version]. When Jacques 'went away,' I had to finish the film. It was difficult, but that's the only thing I know. I think the film makes Jacques very alive."

Demy was the subject of two follow-ups to *Jacquot de Nantes,* also directed by Varda: *The Young Girls Turn 25,* a sentimental reminiscence of the filming of *The Young Girls of Rochefort* and *The World of Jacques Demy,* an intensely intimate documentary-biography which includes clips from his films and interviews with those who worked with and respected him.

—Robin Wood, updated by Rob Edelman

DE PALMA, Brian

Nationality: American. **Born:** Newark, New Jersey, 11 September 1940. **Education:** Attended Columbia University, New York, and Sarah Lawrence College (writing fellowship), 1963-64. **Family:** Married 1) actress Nancy Allen, 1979 (divorced, 1984); 2) producer Gale Anne Hurd; one child. **Career:** Directed first feature, *Murder a la Mod,* 1967; also film teacher and instructor. **Awards:** Rosenthal Foundation award for *Woton's Wake,* 1963; Silver Bear Award, Berlin Festival, for *Greetings,* 1969.

Films as Director:

1961 *Icarus* (short); *660214, the Story of an IBM Card* (short)
1963 *Woton's Wake* (short)
1964 *Jennifer* (short)
1965 *Bridge That Gap* (short)
1966 *Show Me a Strong Town and I'll Show You a Strong Bank* (short); *The Responsive Eye* (doc)
1967 *Murder a la Mod* (+ sc, ed)
1968 *Greetings* (+ co-sc, ed)
1969 *The Wedding Party* (+ pr, ed, co-sc; release delayed from 1966)
1970 *Dionysus in '69* (co-d, co-ph, co-ed; completed 1968); *Hi, Mom!* (+ co-sc)
1972 *Get to Know Your Rabbit*
1973 *Sisters* (*Blood Sisters*) (+ co-sc)
1974 *Phantom of the Paradise* (+ sc)
1976 *Obsession* (+ co-sc); *Carrie*
1978 *The Fury*
1979 *Home Movies*
1980 *Dressed to Kill* (+ sc)
1981 *Blow Out* (+ sc)
1983 *Scarface*
1984 *Body Double* (+ pr, sc)
1986 *Wise Guys*
1987 *The Untouchables*
1989 *Casualties of War*
1990 *The Bonfire of the Vanities* (+ pr, role as Prison Guard)
1992 *Raising Cain* (+ sc)
1993 *Carlito's Way*
1996 *Mission: Impossible*

Publications

By DE PALMA: articles—

Interview in *The Film Director as Superstar,* by Joseph Gelmis, Garden City, New York, 1970.
Interview with E. Margulies, in *Action* (Los Angeles), September/October 1974.

"Phantoms and Fantasies," an interview with A. Stuart, in *Films and Filming* (London), December 1976.

"Things That Go Bump in the Night," an interview with S. Swires, in *Films in Review* (New York), August/September 1978.

Interview with Serge Daney and Jonathan Rosenbaum, in *Cahiers du Cinéma* (Paris), April 1982.

"Double Trouble," an interview with Marcia Pally, in *Film Comment* (New York), September/October 1984.

"Brian De Palma's Guilty Pleasures," in *Film Comment* (New York), May/June 1987.

"Brian De Palma," an interview with Robert Plunket, in *Interview* (New York), August 1992.

On DE PALMA: books—

Nepoti, Roberto, *Brian De Palma,* Florence, 1982.

Bliss, Michael, *Brian De Palma,* Metuchen, New Jersey, 1983.

Dworkin, Susan, *Double De Palma: A Film Study with Brian De Palma,* New York, 1984, revised edition, 1990.

Wood, Robin, *Hollywood from Vietnam to Reagan,* New York, 1986.

Bouzereau, Laurent, *The De Palma Cut: The Films of America's Most Controversial Director,* New York, 1988.

MacKinnon, Kenneth, *Misogyny in the Movies: The De Palma Question,* New York, 1990.

Salamon, Julie, *The Devil's Candy: The Bonfire of the Vanities Goes to Hollywood,* Boston, 1991.

On DE PALMA: articles—

Rubinstein, R., "The Making of *Sisters,*" in *Filmmakers Newsletter* (Ward Hill, Massachusetts), September 1973.

Henry, M., "L'Oeil du malin (à propos de Brian de Palma)," in *Positif* (Paris), May 1977.

Brown, R. S., "Considering de Palma," in *American Film* (Washington, D.C.), July/August 1977.

Matusa, P., "Corruption and Catastrophe: De Palma's *Carrie,*" in *Film Quarterly* (Berkeley), Fall 1977.

Garel, A., "Brian de Palma," in *Image et Son* (Paris), December 1977.

Byron, Stuart, "Rules of the Game," in *Village Voice* (New York), 5 November 1979.

Jameson, R.T., "Style vs. 'Style'," in *Film Comment* (New York), March/April 1980.

Button, S., "Visceral Poetry," in *Films* (London), November 1982.

Eisen, K., "The Young Misogynists of American Cinema," in *Cineaste* (New York), vol. 8, no. 1, 1983.

Brown, G. A., "Obsession," in *American Film* (Washington, D.C.), December 1983.

Rafferty, T., "De Palma's American Dreams," in *Sight and Sound* (London), Spring 1984.

Fisher, W., "Re: Writing: Film History: From Hitchcock to De Palma," in *Persistence of Vision* (Maspeth, New York), Summer 1984.

Denby, David, and others, "Pornography: Love or Death?" in *Film Comment* (New York), November/December 1984.

Braudy, Leo, "The Sacraments of Genre: Coppola, De Palma, Scorsese," in *Film Quarterly* (Los Angeles), Spring 1986.

Hugo, Chris, "Three Films of Brian De Palma," in *Movie* (London), Winter 1989.

White, Armond, "Brian De Palma, Political Filmmaker," Film Comment (New York), May/June 1991.

Muse, Eben J., "The Land of Nam: Romance and Persecution in Brian De Palma's *Casualties of War,*" in *Literature/Film Quarterly,* vol. 20, no. 3, 1992.

Spear, Bruce, "Political Morality and Historical Understanding in *Casualties of War,*" in *Literature/Film Quarterly,* vol. 20, no. 3, 1992.

Ingersoll, Earl G. "The Constitution of Masculinity in Brian De Palma's Film *Casualties of War,*" in *Journal of Men's Studies,* August 1995.

* * *

The conventional dismissal of De Palma—that he is a mere "Hitchcock imitator"—though certainly unjust, provides a useful starting-point, the relation being far more complex than such a description suggests. It seems more appropriate to talk of symbiosis than of imitation: if De Palma borrows Hitchcock's plot-structures, the impulse is rooted in an authentic identification with the Hitchcock thematic that results in (at De Palma's admittedly infrequent best) valid variations that have their own indisputable originality. *Sisters* and *Dressed to Kill* are modeled on *Psycho; Obsession* and *Body Double* on *Vertigo; Body Double* also borrows from *Rear Window,* as does *Blow Out.* The debt is of course enormous, but—at least in the cases of *Sister, Obsession,* and *Blow Out,* De Palma's three most satisfying films to date—the power and coherence of the films testifies to the genuineness of the creativity.

Central to the work of both directors are the tensions and contradictions arising out of the way in which gender has been traditionally constructed in a male-dominated culture. According to Freud, the human infant, while biologically male or female, is not innately "masculine" or "feminine": in order to construct the socially correct man and woman of patriarchy, the little girl's masculinity and the little boy's femininity must be repressed. This repression tends to be particularly rigorous and particularly damaging in the male, where it is compounded by the pervasive association of "femininity" with castration (on both the literal and symbolic levels). The significance of De Palma's best work (and, more powerfully and consistently, that of Hitchcock before him) lies in its eloquent evidence of what happens when the repression is partially unsuccessful. The misogyny of which both directors have been accused, expressing itself in the films' often extreme outbursts of violence against women (both physical and psychological), must be read as the result of their equally extreme identification with the "feminine" and the inevitable dread that such an identification brings with it.

Sisters is concerned single-mindedly with castration: the symbolic castration of the woman within patriarchy, the answering literal castration that is the form of her revenge. The basis concept of female Siamese twins, one active and aggressive, one passive and submissive, is a brilliant inspiration, the action of the entire film arising out of the attempts by men to destroy the active aspect in order to construct the "feminine" woman who will accept her subordination. The aggressive sister Dominique (dead, but still alive as Danielle's unconscious) is paralleled by Grace Collier (Jennifer Salt), the assertive young reporter who usurps the accoutrements of "masculinity" and eventually assumes Dominique's place in the extraordinary climactic hallucination sequence in which the woman's castration is horrifyingly reasserted. *Sister,* although weakened by De Palma's inability to take Grace seriously enough or give the character the substance the allegory demands, remains his closest to a completely satisfying film: the monstrousness of woman's oppression under patriarchy and its appalling consequences for both sexes have never been rendered more vividly. *Blow Out* rivals it in coherence and surpasses it in sensitivity: one would describe it as De Palma's masterpiece were it not for one unpardonable and unfortunately extended lapse—the entirely gratuitous sequence depicting the murder of the prostitute in the railway station, which one can account for only in terms of a fear that the film was not "spicy" enough for the box office (it failed anyway). It can stand as a fitting counterpart to *Sisters,* a rigorous dissection of the egoism fostered in the male by the culture's obsession with "masculinity." It is clear that Travolta's obsession with establishing the reality of his perceptions has little to do with an impersonal concern

Brian De Palma

for truth and everything to do with his need to establish and assert the symbolic phallus at whatever cost—the cost involving, crucially, the manipulation and exploitation of a woman, eventually precipitating her death.

Since *Body Double*—a tawdry ragbag of a film that might be seen as De Palma's gift to his detractors—De Palma seems to have abandoned the Hitchcock connection, and it is not yet clear that he has found a strong thematic with which to replace it. *The Untouchables* seems a work of empty efficiency; it is perhaps significant that one remains uncertain whether to take the patriarchal idyll of Elliott Ness's domestic life straight or as parody. *Casualties of War* is more interesting, though severely undermined by the casting of the two leads: one grasps the kind of contrast De Palma had in mind, but it is not successfully realized in that between Sean Penn's shameless mugging and Michael J. Fox's intractable blandness. Like most Hollywood movies on Vietnam, the film suffers from the inability to see Asians in terms other than an undifferentiated "otherness": it is symptomatic that the two Vietnamese girls, past and present, are played by the same actress. His return to the film of political protest (and specifically to the Vietnam War) brings De Palma's career to date full circle: his early work in an independent avant-garde (*Greetings, Hi, Mom!*) is too often overlooked. But nothing in *Casualties of War,* for all the strenuousness of its desire to disturb, achieves the genuinely disorienting force of the remarkable "Be Black, Baby" sections of *Hi, Mom!*.

Following *Casualties of War*—a film to which he had a deep personal commitment, whatever its success or failure as a comment upon the Vietnam War, violence against women, or the power of traumatic memory—De Palma seemed intent upon remaking his own public image by choosing an unusual property for him, the social satire *The Bonfire of the Vanities.* He did put a personal stamp upon the material, most notably (and paradoxically) by paying tribute to the Orson Welles of *Touch of Evil,* opening the film with an extremely long and intricate tracking shot and using distorting wide-angle lenses almost constantly (though less imaginatively than Welles). Unfortunately the visual flair did nothing to compensate for some disastrous miscastings and craven attempts to soften the book's scathing cynicism, or for the unfocused script in general and De Palma's own inability to do satiric comedy without obnoxious overemphasis. *Raising Cain,* a return to more comfortable territory—the lurid pop-Freudian thriller, the genre through which De Palma had achieved greatest fame and critical admiration—puzzled those who claimed he was merely repeating himself. But for connoisseurs it was intentionally a delicious self-parody—or at least a virtuoso filmmaker's display of his special talents—most flagrantly in a spectacularly choreographed steadicam shot in which a psychiatrist spouting endless exposition is always on the verge of walking out of the frame, and in the delirious slow-motion climax.

Carlito's Way again harked back to earlier De Palma successes, this time to crime drama, with an emotional intensity somewhere between the hallucinatory *Scarface* and the more coolly impersonal *The Untouchables.* If the film ultimately could not rise beyond the conventional trajectory of its plot—ex-hood trying to go straight is drawn back into crime by his old buddy, despite the outreach of a saintly woman—it at least boasted a brilliant impersonation of a crooked lawyer by Sean Penn and some splendid De Palma set pieces, like the chase through Grand Central Terminal. The film reminds us that De Palma is unsurpassed among film directors in portraying furies: not the collective surges of violence rendered by a Sam Peckinpah, but the private demons unleashed within or witnessed by (the same thing on dream level) "ordinary" people as well as crime kings and raving lunatics. De Palma's cinematic flourishes have often been called "operatic," but perhaps the better analogy is with the Lisztian keyboard virtuoso, someone who can tap profound emotional depths one moment but skitters over the surface at other times; who frequently improvises upon others' themes but is always unmistakably himself, for better or worse.

—Robin Wood, updated by Joseph Milicia

DEREN, Maya

Nationality: Russian/American. **Born:** Kiev, 1917, became U.S. citizen. **Education:** League of Nations School, Geneva, Switzerland; studied journalism at University of Syracuse, New York; New York University, B.A.; Smith College, M.A. **Family:** Married (second time) Alexander Hackenschmied (Hammid), 1942 (divorced); later married Teijo Ito. **Career:** Family emigrated to America, 1922; made first film *Meshes of the Afternoon,* 1943; travelled to Haiti, 1946; secretary for Creative Film Foundation, 1960. **Awards:** Guggenheim Fellowship for work in creative film, 1946. **Died:** Of a cerebral hemorrhage in Queens, New York, 13 October 1961.

Films as Director:

1943 ***Meshes of the Afternoon*** (with Alexander Hammid) (+ role); *The Witches' Cradle* (unfinished)
1944 *At Land* (+ role)
1945 *A Study in Choreography for Camera*; *The Private Life of a Cat* (home movie, with Hammid)
1946 *Ritual in Transfigured Time* (+ role)
1948 *Meditation on Violence*
1959 *The Very Eye of Night*

Publications

By DEREN: books—

An Anagram of Ideas on Art, Form and the Film, New York, 1946.
The Divine Horseman: The Living Gods of Haiti, New York, 1953.
Divine Horsemen: Voodoo Gods of Haiti, New York, 1970.

By DEREN: articles—

"Choreography of Camera," in *Dance* (New York), October 1943.
"Cinema as an Art Form," in *Introduction to the Art of the Movies,* edited by Lewis Jacobs, New York, 1960.
"Cinematography: The Creative Use of Reality," in *Daedalus: The Visual Arts Today,* 1960.
"Movie Journal," in *Village Voice* (New York), 25 August 1960.
"A Statement of Principles," in *Film Culture* (New York), Summer 1961.
"Movie Journal," in *Village Voice* (New York), 1 June 1961.
"A Lecture ... ," in *Film Culture* (New York), Summer 1963.
"Notes, Essays, Letters," in *Film Culture* (New York), Winter 1965.
"A Statement on Dance and Film," in *Dance Perspectives,* no. 30, 1967.
"Tempo and Tension," in *The Movies as Medium,* edited by Lewis Jacobs, New York, 1970.

On DEREN: books—

Hanhardt, John, and others, *A History of the American Avant-Garde Cinema,* New York, 1976.
Sitney, P. Adams, *Visionary Film,* 2d edition, New York, 1979.
Clark, Veve A., Millicent Hodson, and Catrina Neimans, *The Legend of Maya Deren: A Documentary Biography and Collected Works: Vol. 1, Pt. 1, Signatures (1917-1942),* New York, 1984.
Heck-Rabi, Louise, *Women Filmmakers: A Critical Reception,* Metuchen, New Jersey, 1984.

On DEREN: articles—

Farber, Manny, "Maya Deren's Films," in *New Republic* (New York), 28 October 1946.
"Deren Issue" of *Filmwise,* no. 2, 1961.
Obituary in *New York Times,* 14 October 1961.
Tallmer, Jerry, "For Maya Deren," in *Village Voice* (New York), 19 October 1961.
Arnheim, Rudolf, "To Maya Deren," in *Film Culture* (New York), no. 24, 1962.
Sitney, P. Adams, "The Idea of Morphology," in *Film Culture* (New York), No. 53, 54, and 55, 1971.
Cornwell, Regina, "Maya Deren and Germaine Dulac: Activists of the Avant-Garde," in *Film Library Quarterly* (New York), Winter 1971/72.
Bronstein, M., and S. Grossmann, "Zu Maya Derens Filmarbeit," in *Frauen und Film* (Berlin), December 1976.

Maya Deren in *Meshes of the Afternoon*

Camera Obscura Collective, The, "Excerpts from an interview with 'The Legend of Maya Deren' Project," in *Camera Obscura* (Berkeley, California), Summer 1979.
Mayer, T., "The Legend of Maya Deren: Champion of American Independent Film," in *Film News* (New York), September/October 1979.
"Kamera Arbeit: Der schopferische umgang mit der realitat," in *Frauen und Film* (Berlin), October 1984.
"Maya Deren Issue," of *Film Culture* (New York), 72-75, 1985.
Millsapps, J.L., "Maya Deren, Imagist," in *Literature/Film Quarterly* (Salisbury, Maryland), January 1986.
Monthly Film Bulletin (London), June and July 1988.

* * *

Maya Deren was the best-known independent, experimental filmmaker in the United States during and after World War II. She developed two types of short, subjective films: the psychodrama and the ciné-dance film. She initiated a national non-theatrical network to show her six independently-made works, which have been referred to as visual lyric poems, or dream-like trance films. She also lectured and wrote extensively on film as an art form. Her films remain as provocative as ever, her contributions to cinematic art indisputable.

Intending to write a book on dance, Deren toured with Katherine Dunham's dance group as a secretary. Dunham introduced Deren to Alexander Hammid, and the following year the couple made *Meshes of the Afternoon.* Considered a milestone in the chronology of independent film in the United States, it is famous for its four-stride sequence (from beach to grass to mud to pavement to rug). Deren acted the role of a girl driven to suicide. Continuous action is maintained while time-space unities are severed, establishing a trance-like mood by the use of slow motion, swish-pan camera movements, and well executed point-of-view shots.

In her next film, *At Land,* a woman (Deren) runs along a beach and becomes involved in a chess game. P. Adams Sitney refers to this work as a "pure American trance film." The telescoping of time occurs as each scene blends with the next in unbroken sequence, a result of preplanned editing. *At Land* is also studded with camera shots of astounding virtuosity.

Other films include Deren's first ciné-dance film, the three-minute *A Study in Choreography for Camera.* Filmed in slow motion, a male ballet dancer, partnered by the camera, moves through a variety of locales. Continuity of camera movement is maintained as the dancer's foot changes location. Space is compressed while time is expanded. According to Sitney, the film's importance resides in two fresh observations: space and time in film are *created* space and time, and the camera's optimal use is as a dancer itself. *Ritual in Transfigured Time,* another dance-on-film, portrays psycho-dramatic ritual by use of freeze frames, repeated shots, shifting character identities, body movements, and locales. *Meditation on Violence* explores Woo (or Wu) Tang boxing with the camera as sparring partner, panning and zooming to simulate human response. *The Very Eye of Night* employed Metropolitan Ballet School members to create a celestial ciné-ballet of night. Shown in its negative state, Deren's handheld camera captured white figures on a total black background. Over the course of her four dance-films Deren evolved a viable form of ciné-choreography that was adapted and adjusted to later commercial feature films. In cases such as *West Side Story,* this was done with great skill and merit.

Deren traced the evolution of her six films in "A letter to James Card," dated April 19, 1955. *Meshes* was her "point of departure" and "almost expressionist"; *At Land* depicted dormant energies in mutable nature; and *Choreography* distilled the essence of this natural changing. In *Ritual* she defined the processes of changing, while *Meditation* extends the study of metamorphosis. In *The Very Eye* she expressed her love of life and its living. "Each film was built as a chamber and became a corridor, like a chain reaction."

In 1946 Deren published *An Anagram of Ideas on Art, Form, and the Film,* a monograph declaring two major statements: the rejection of symbolism in film, and strong support for independent film after an analysis of industrial and independent filmmaking activities in the United States.

Although *Meshes* remains the most widely-seen film of its type, with several of its effects unsurpassed by filmmakers, Deren had been forgotten until recently. Her reputation now enjoys a well-deserved renaissance, for as Rudolf Arnheim eulogized, Deren was one of film's "most delicate magicians."

—Louise Heck-Rabi

DE SANTIS, Giuseppe

Nationality: Italian. **Born:** Fondi, Latina, 11 February 1917. **Education:** University of Rome and at Centro Sperimentale di Cinematografia, Rome. **Family:** Married Giovanna Valeri, 1943. **Career:** Writer for *Cinema* magazine, Rome, 1941-43; directed first feature, *Caccia tragica,* 1947. **Awards:** Golden Globe Award, Los Angeles Film Critics, for *La Strada lunga un anno,* 1958. **Address:** Piazza Faleri, 1, Fiano Romano, Italy.

Films as Director and Co-Scriptwriter:

1945 episode of *Giorni di gloria*
1947 *Caccia tragica* (*Tragic Hunt*)
1948 *Riso amaro* (*Bitter Rice*)
1949 *Non c'e pace tra gli ulivi* (*Under the Olive Tree*)
1952 *Roma ore undici* (*Rome 11 O'Clock*)
1953 *Un marito per Anna Zaccheo* (*A Husband for Anna*)
1954 *Giorni d'amore* (*Days of Love*)
1956 *Uomini e lupi* (*Men and Wolves*)
1957 *L'Uomo senza domenica*
1958 *Cesta duga godinu dana* (*La Strada lunga un anno*)
1960 *La Garçonnière*
1964 *Italiani, brava gente*
1972 *Un Apprezzato professionista di sicuro avvenire*

Other Films:

1940 *Don Pasquale* (sc)
1942 ***Ossessione*** (Visconti) (co-sc, asst d)
1943 *Desiderio* (Rossellini and Paglièro) (co-sc, asst d to Rossellini)
1945 *Il sole sorge ancora* (co-sc, asst d, role uncredited)
1946 *Ultimo amore* (co-sc)
1953 *Donne proibite* (sc)
1964 *La visita* (co-sc)

Publications

By DE SANTIS: books—

Riso amaro: un film diretto da Giuseppe de Santis, with C. Lizzani, Rome, 1978
Giuseppe De Santis verso il neorealismo, edited by Callisto Cosulich, Bologna, 1982.

By DE SANTIS: articles—

Interview with Claude Souef, in *Lettres Françaises* (Paris), November 1952.
"Una lettera di De Santis," in *Cinema Nuovo* (Turin), 15 February 1957.
Interview with Michel Delahaye and Jean Wagner, in *Cinéma* (Paris), April 1959.
"E con 'Ossessione' osai il primo giro di manovella," in *Cinema Nuovo* (Bari), June and August-October 1984.
"De Santis, entre realisme, neorealisme et realisme socialiste," in *Jeune Cinéma* (Paris), March 1985.
Hollywood Reporter, 14 July 1987.

On DE SANTIS: books—

Farnassino, Alberto, *Giuseppe De Santis,* Milan, 1978.
Masi, Stefano, *Giuseppe De Santis,* Florence, 1981.
Pacisi, Antonio, *Il cinema di Giuseppe De Santis: Tra passione e ideologia,* Rome, 1983.

On DE SANTIS: articles—

Krier, Jacques, "Giuseppe De Santis est à Paris," in *L'Écran Français* (Paris), 29 May 1950.
Lane, John, "De Santis and Italian Neo-Realism," in *Sight and Sound* (London), August 1950.
"De Santis Issue" of *Positif* (Paris), no.5, undated.
Oms, Marcel, in *Positif* (Paris), no.23, 1957.
Martini, Andrea, and Marco Melani, "De Santis," in *Il neorealismo cinematografico italiano,* Venice, 1975.
Dossier on De Santis, in *Cinema e Cinema* (Rome), January-March 1982.

* * *

For a brief period of five years, Giuseppe De Santis's film career was the most often discussed, the most highly applauded and the most commercially successful of the Italian neorealist directors. In addition, his writings in the Italian magazine *Cinema* from 1941 until 1943 took an active, prescriptive, and radical stance previously unknown to film criticism.

Like the later generation of French critics-turned-directors, such as Jean-Luc Godard or François Truffaut, De Santis's first films showed

Giuseppe De Santis

new approaches while displaying a mastery of the medium, but also succeeded in capturing popular imagination. "Popular" is the key to appreciating De Santis's work. Despite rigorous theorizing, and a profound dedication to Marxist principles, De Santis's films never appeared aloof or difficult to understand to a mass audience. He proved that the popular world was no longer something to be considered as different, but was actually the norm. While his first features are concerned with Italy, they are most significant as studies of changes in cultures and as commentaries upon filmmaking and other mass media as the modern international culture.

De Santis was the first Italian director truly to appreciate and reflect in film the effects of the mass media in various forms—newspapers, radio, television, cinema, posters, pop music, magazines, photo novels, pin-ups, advertisements, dancing. Like many of his colleagues, he displayed an admiration of American literature and cinema, but he perceived more clearly why those were popular—not merely in a commercial sense but because they were creating a new culture that international audiences found meaningful in their daily lives and habits.

Mass media, and cinema in particular, formed the modern means of education, cultural formation, and inspiration in addition to providing role models. Two aspects of this phenomenon were the star system and eroticism, joined together in Silvana Mangano's most famous performance—in *Bitter Rice*, a film nominated for an Academy Award in 1949. In this, her film debut, Mangano was transformed by De Santis into an instant star. The eroticism in the film liberated the human body from something to be leered at to something that could be celebrated and enjoyed, thus starting a trend in the Italian cinema that made stars of such women as Mangano, Gina Lollabrigida and Sophia Loren.

Ironically, the very director who freed Italian cinema from provincialism found it increasingly difficult to get his projects accepted and funded in his own country. De Santis' best works of the second half of his career were made only partially with Italian capital and often made outside the country. *La Strada lunga un anno*, about the building of a road, was filmed in and financed by Yugoslavia and indicated the possibility of a socialist cinema by joyfully depicting the solidarity of unpaid workers. Much applauded in the United States, it received the Golden Globe from the Hollywood critics as well as an Academy Award nomination. *Italiani brava gente* was the first Italian-Soviet co-production, with some American financing. Successfully and convincingly De Santis creates a gallery of characters at the Russian front during the war: a Roman, a Sicilian, a Pugliese, an Emilian played by a Soviet actor, a Milanese commandant played by Arthur Kennedy, and a Neapolitan of the medical corps played by Peter Falk. The circumstances of this production permitted De Santis to express one of his strongest beliefs: differences between people are no longer based on nationalities but on class and occupation.

—Elaine Mancini

DE SICA, Vittorio

Nationality: Italian/French (became French citizen in order to marry second wife, 1968. **Born:** Sora (near Rome), 7 July 1902. **Education:** Institut Superieur de Commerce, Rome, and University of Rome. **Family:** Married 1) Giuditta Rissone (divorced 1968); 2) Maria Mercader, 1968, two sons. **Career:** Actor in Tatiana Pavlova's Stage Company, 1923; formed own stage company with actress-wife, late 1920s; leading film actor, from 1931; directed first film, *Rose scarlette,* 1940. **Died:** In Paris, 13 November 1974.

Films as Director:

1940 *Rose scarlatte* (co-d, role as The Engineer)
1941 *Maddelena zero in condotta* (+ dialogue, role as Carlo Hartman); *Teresa Venerdi* (+ co-sc, role)
1942 *Un garibaldino al convento* (+ co-sc, role as Nino Bixio)
1943 *I bambini ci guardano* (+ co-sc)
1946 *La porta del cielo* (+ co-sc, completed 1944); ***Sciuscia*** (*Shoeshine*) (+ co-sc)
1948 ***Ladri di biciclette*** (*The Bicycle Thief*) (+ pr, co-sc)
1950 ***Miracolo a Milano*** (*Miracle in Milan*) (+ co-sc)
1952 ***Umberto D*** (+ pr, co-sc)
1953 *Stazione Termini* (*Indiscretion of an American Wife*; *Indiscretion*) (+ co-pr)
1954 *L'oro di Napoli* (*Gold of Naples*) (+ co-sc, role)
1956 *Il tetto* (*The Roof*) (+ pr)
1960 *La ciociara* (*Two Women*)
1961 *Il giudizio universale* (+ role)
1962 "La Riffa (The Raffle)" episode of *Boccacio '70*; *I sequestrati di Altona* (*The Condemned of Altona*)
1963 *Il boom*; *Ieri, oggi, domani* (*Yesterday, Today and Tomorrow*)
1964 *Matrimonio all'italiana* (*Marriage, Italian Style*)
1965 *Un Monde nouveau* (*Un Monde jeune*; *Un mondo nuovo*; *A Young World*)
1966 *Caccia alla volpe* (*After the Fox*) (+ guest role); "Un sera come le altre (A Night Like Any Other)" episode of *Le streghe* (*The Witches*)
1967 *Woman Times Seven* (*Sept fois femmes*)
1968 *Amanti* (*A Place for Lovers*) (+ co-sc)
1970 *I girasoli* (*Sunflower*); *Il giardino dei Finzi Contini* (*The Garden of the Finzi-Continis*); "Il leone" episode of *Le coppie (Les Couples)*
1972 *Lo chiameremo Andrea*
1973 *Una breve vacanza* (*A Brief Vacation*)
1974 *Il viaggio* (*The Journey*; *The Voyage*)

Other Films:

1918 *Il processo Clémenceau* (*L'Affaire Clemenceau*) (Bencivenga) (role)
1926 *La bellezza del mondo* (Almirante) (role)
1928 *La compagnia dei matti* (*La compagnie des fous*) (Almirante) (role)
1932 *La vecchia signora* (Palermi) (role); *La segretaria per tutti* (Palermi) (role); *Due cuori felici* (Negroni) (role); *Gli uomini che mascalzoni!* (Camerini) (role)
1933 *Un cattivo soggetto* (Bragaglia) (role); *Il signore desidera?* (Righelli) (role); *La canzone del sole* (German version: *Das Lied der Sonne*) (Neufeld) (role as The Secretary); *Lisetta* (Boese) (role)
1934 *Tempo massimo* (Mattoli) (role)
1935 *Darò un millione* (Camerini) (role as The Millionaire); *Amo te sola* (Mattòli) (role)
1936 *Lohengrin* (Malasomma) (role); *Ma non è una cosa seria!* (Camerini) (role); *Non ti conosco più* (Malasomma) (role); *L'uomo che sorride* (Mattoli) (role)
1937 *Hanno rapito un uomo* (Righelli) (role); *Il signor Max* (Camerini) (role); *Questi ragazzi* (Mattoli) (role)
1938 *Napoli d'altri tempi* (Palermi) (role); *L'orologio a cucù* (Mastrocinque) (role); *Partire* (Palermi) (role); *Ai vostri ordini, signora!* (Mattòli) (role); *La mazurka di papà* (Biancoli) (role); *Le due madri* (Palermi) (role); *Castelli in aria* (German version: *Ins blaue Leben*, 1939) (Genina) (role)

1939 *Grandi magazzini* (Camerini) (role); *Finisce sempre cosí* (Susini) (role); *Napoli che non muore* (Palermi) (role)
1940 *La peccatrice* (Palermi) (role); *Pazza di giola* (Bragaglia) (role); *Manon Lescaut* (Gallone) (role)
1941 *L'avventuriera del piano di sopra* (Matarazzo) (role)
1942 *Se io fossi onesto!* (Bragaglia) (role, co-sc); *La guardia del corpo* (Bragaglia) (role, co-sc)
1943 *I nostri sogni* (Cottafavi) (role, co-sc); *Non sono superstizioso, ma...!* (Bragaglia) (role, co-sc); *L'ippocampo* (Rosmino) (role, co-sc); *Diece minuti di vita* (Longanesi) (unfinished; another version made 1944 with different cast) (role); *Nessuno torna indietro* (Blasetti) (role)
1945 *Lo sbaglio di essere vivo* (Bragagalia) (role); *Il mondo vuole cosi* (Bianchi) (role)
1946 *Roma città libera* (co-sc); *Il marito povero* (Amara) (co-sc); *Abbasso la ricchezza!* (Righelli) (role, co-sc)
1947 *Sperduti nel buio* (Mastrocinque) (role as Nanzio, co-sc); *Natale al campo 119* (Francisci) (supervisor, role as The Noble Neopolitan)
1948 *Lo sconosciuto di San Marino* (Waszinsky) (role as The Proprietor); *Cuore* (Coletti) (co-sc, role as The Landlord)
1950 *Domani è troppo tardi* (Moguy) (role as Professor Landi)
1951 *Cameriera bella presenza offresi* (Pastina) (role as The Actor); "Il processo di Frine" episode of *Altri tempi* (Blasetti) (role as the Barrister); *Gli uomini non guardano il cielo* (Scarpelli) (role)
1952 *Buongiorno elefante!* (*Sabú principle ladro*) (Franciolini) (co-sc, role as Garetti); "Scena all'aperto" (role as Count) and "Don Corradino" (role as Don Corradino) episodes of *Tempi nostri* (Blasetti)
1953 ***Madame De ...*** (Ophuls) (role as Fabrizio Donati); *Pane, amore e fantasia* (Comencini) (role as Marshal Carotenuto); "Pendolin" episode of *Cento anni d'amore* (De Felice) (role); "Incidente a Villa Borghese" episode of *Villa Borghese* (Franciolini) (role); *Il matrimonio* (Petrucci) (role); "Il fine dicitore" episode of *Gran varietà* (Paolella) (role); "Le Divorce (Il divorzio)" episode of *Secrets d'alcôve* (*Il letto*) (Franciolini) (role)
1954 *Vergine moderna* (Pagliero) (role as The Banker); *L'Allegro Squadrone* (Moffa) (role as The General); *Pane, amore e gelosia* (Comencini) (role); *Peccato che sia una canaglia* (Blasetti) (role as Mr. Stroppiani)
1955 *Il segno di Venere* (Risi) (role as Alessio Spano, the Poet); *Gli ultimi cinque minuti* (*The Last Five Minutes*) (Amato) (role as Carlo); *La bella mugnaia* (Camerini) (role as The Governor); *Pane, amore e ...* (Risi) (role as Carotenuto); *Racconti romani* (Franciolini) (role); *Il bigamo* (Emmer) (role as The Barrister)
1956 *Mio figlio Nerone* (*Nero's Weekend*) (Steno) (role as Sénèquel); *Tempo di villegiatura* (Racioppi) (role as The Celebrity); *The Monte Carlo Story* (*Montecarlo*) (Taylor) (role as Count Dino Giocondo Della Fiaba); *I giorni più belli* (*I nostri anni più belli, Gli anni più belli*) (Mattòli) (role as The Banker); *Noi siamo le colonne* (D'Amico) (role as Celimontani)
1957 *Padri e figli* (Monicelli) (role as the tailor Corallo); *I colpevoli* (Vasile) (role as the barrister Vasari); *Souvenir d'Italie* (*It Happened in Rome*) (Pietrangeli) (role as The Count); *La donna che venne del mare* (De Robertis) (role as Bordigin); *Vacanze a Ischia* (Camerini) (role as Occhipinti); *I conte Max* (Bianchi) (role as Count Max Orsini Baraldo); *Amore e chiacchiere* (Blasetti) (role as Bonelli); *Il medico e lo stregone* (Monicelli) (role as Locoratolo); *Totò, Vittorio e la dottoressa* (Mastrocinque) (role as the sick nobleman); *Casino de Paris* (Hunebelle) (role as Alexandre Gordy)
1958 *A Farewell to Arms* (Vidor) (role as Count Alessandro Rinaldi); *Domenica è sempre domenica* (Mastrocinque) (role as Mr. Guastaldi); *Ballerina e buon Dio* (Leonviola) (roles as the policeman, the taxi driver, and the costume porter); *Kanonenserenade* (*Pezzo, capopezzo e capitano*) (Staudte) (role as Count Ernesto De Rossi); *Anna di Brooklyn* (Denham and Lastricati) (supervisor, co-music, role as Don Luigino); *La ragazza di Piazza S. Pietro* (Costa) (role as Armando Conforti); *Gli zitelloni* (Bianchi) (role as Professor Landi); *Pane, amore e Andulasia* (Setò) (role as Carotenuto); *La prima notte* (Cavalcanti) (role as Alfredo)
1959 *Nel blu dipinto di blu* (Volare) (Tellini) (role as Spartaco); *Il nemico di mia moglie* (Puccini) (role as The Husband); *Vacanze d'inverno* (Mastrocinque) (role as Manrizie); *Il moralista* (Bianchi) (role as The President); *Il Generale Della Rovere* (Rossellini) (role as Giovanni Bertone); *Il mondo dei miracoli* (Capuano) (role as Pietro Giordani); *Uomini e nobiluomini* (Bianchi) (role as Marquis Nicolas Peccoli); *Ferdinando I, re di Napoli* (Franciolini) (role as Ceccano); *Gastone* (Bonnard) (role as The Prince); *Les trois etc ... du colonel* (*Le tre eccetera del colonello*) (Boissol) (role as Colonel Belalcazar)
1960 *Il vigile* (Zampa) (role as The Trustee); *Le pillole di Ercole* (Salce) (role as Colonel Pietro Cuocolo); *Austerlitz* (Gance) (role as Pope Pius VII); *The Angel Wore Red* (*La sposa bella*) (Johnson) (role as General Clave); *The Millionairess* (Asquith) (role as Joe); *It Started in Naples* (Shavelson) (role as Mario Vitale); *Gli incensurati* (Giaculli) (role as comic actor); *Un amore a Roma* (Risi) (role)
1961 *Gli attendenti* (Bianchi) (role as Colonel Bitossi); *I due marescialli* (Corbucci) (role as Antonio Cotone); *Le meraviglie di Aladino* (*The Wonders of Aladdin*) (Bava and Levin) (role as The Genie); *L'onorata società* (Pazzaglia) (role as The Chef); *La Fayette* (*La Fayette, una spada per due bandiere*) (Dréville) (role as Bancroft)
1962 *Vive Henry IV, vive l'amour* (Autant-Lara) (role as Don Pedro)
1965 *The Amorous Adventures of Moll Flanders* (T. Young) (role as The Count)
1966 *Io, io, io ... e gli altri* (Blasetti) (role as Count Trepossi)
1967 *Gli altri, gli altri e noi* (Arena) (role as man on pension); *Un italiano in America* (Sordi) (role as Giuseppe's Father); *The Biggest Bundle of Them All* (Annakin) (role as Cesare Celli); *Caroline Cherie* (de la Patelliere) (role as Count de Bièvres)
1968 *The Shoes of the Fisherman* (*Les Souliers de Saint-Pierre*) (M. Anderson) (role as Cardinal Rinaldi)
1969 *If It's Tuesday, This Must Be Belgium* (M. Stuart) (role as The Shoemaker); *Una su tredici* (*12 + 1*) (Gessner and Lucignani) (role as Di Seta)
1970 *Cose di Cosa Nostra* (Steno) (role as The Lawyer); *L'Odeur des fauves* (Balducci) (role as Milord)
1971 *Trastevere* (Tozzi) (role as Enrico Formichi); *Io non vedo, tu non parli, lui non sente* (Camerini) (role as Count at the Casino)
1972 *Pinocchio* (Comencini) (for TV) (role as The Judge); *Snow Job* (*The Ski Raiders*) (Englund) (role as Dolphi); *Ettore lo fusto* (Castellari) (role as Giove); *Siamo tutti in libertà provvisoria* (Scarpelli) (role)
1973 *Storia de fratelli e de cortelli* (Amendola) (role as The Marshal); *Il delitto Matteotti* (Vancini) (role as Mauro del Giudice)
1974 *Andy Warhol's Dracula* (*Dracula cerca sangue di vergine e ... morì di sete!!, Blood for Dracula*) (Morrissey) (role as Marquis di Fiori); *C'eravamo tanto amati* (Scola) (role as himself); *Vittorio De Sica, il Regista, l'attore, l'uomo* (Gragadze) (role)

Vittorio De Sica

Publications

By DE SICA: books—

Umberto D., with Cesare Zavattini, Rome, 1954.
The Bicycle Thief, with Cesare Zavattini, New York, 1968.
Miracle in Milan, with Cesare Zavattini and others, New York, 1968.

By DE SICA: articles—

Interview with F. Koval, in *Sight and Sound* (London), April 1950.
"The Most Wonderful Years of My Life," in *Films and Filming* (London), December 1955.
"Money, the Public, and Umberto D," in *Films and Filming* (London), January 1956.
"Illiberal Censorship," in *Film* (London), January/February 1956.
"Hollywood Shocked Me," in *Films and Filming* (London), February 1956.
"I Must Act to Pay My Debts," in *Films and Filming* (London), March 1956.
"British Humor? It's the Same in Italy," in *Films and Filming* (London), April 1959.
"What's Right With Hollywood," in *Films and Filming* (London), November 1963.
Interview in *Encountering Directors*, edited by Charles Thomas Samuels, New York, 1972.
Interview with D. Lyons, in *Interview* (New York), February 1972.
"Le Jardin des Finzi-Contini," interview with G. Braucourt, in *Ecran* (Paris), February 1972.

On DE SICA: books—

Ferrara, Giuseppe, *Il nuovo cinema italiano*, Florence, 1957.
Agel, Henri, *Vittorio De Sica*, second edition, Paris, 1964.
Leprohon, Pierre, *Vittorio De Sica*, Paris, 1966.
Bazin, André, *Qu'est-ce que le cinéma*, second edition, Paris, 1975.
Mercader, Maria, *La mia vita con Vittorio De Sica*, Milan, Italy, 1978.
Anthologie du cinéma, vol. 10, Paris, 1979.
Darreta, John, *Vittorio De Sica: A Guide to References and Resources*, Boston, 1983.
Bolzoni, Francesco, *Quando De Sica era Mister Brown*, Turin, 1984.

On DE SICA: articles—

Jacobson, H.L., "De Sica's *Bicycle Thieves* and Italian Humanism," in *Hollywood Quarterly*, Fall 1949.
Hawkins, R.F., "De Sica Dissected," in *Films in Review* (New York), May 1951.
Lambert, Gavin, "The Case of De Sica," in *Sight and Sound* (London), June 1951.

Sargeant, W., "Bread, Love, and Neo-Realism," in *New Yorker,* 29 June and 6 July 1957.

Rhode, Eric, "Why Neo-Realism Failed," in *Sight and Sound* (London), Winter 1960/61.

Lane, J.F., "A Case of Artistic Inflation," in *Sight and Sound* (London), Summer 1963.

McVay, D., "Poet of Poverty," in *Films and Filming* (London), November 1964.

Comuzio, E., "De Sica o della doppia costante: il sorriso e il tarlo segreto," in *Cineforum* (Bergamo), January 1975.

Bachmann, Gideon, "Vittorio de Sica: Always a True Window," in *Sight and Sound* (London), Spring 1975.

"De Sica Issue" of *Bianco e Nero* (Rome), Fall 1975.

Passalacqua, J., "Vittorio de Sica," in *Films in Review* (New York), April 1978.

"Vittorio de Sica Issue" of *Avant-Scène du Cinéma* (Paris), 15 October 1978.

Carcassonne, P., "Dossier: le neo-realisme: De Sica 'le menteur,'" in *Cinématographe* (Paris), January 1979.

Shipman, David, "Directors of the Decade: Forties," in *Films and Filming* (London), June 1983.

"Vittorio De Sica," in *Cinema Nuovo* (Bari), February 1985.

On DE SICA: films—

De Reisner, Bika, *Meet De Sica.*

Dragadze, Peter, *Vittorio De Sica: Il regista, l'attore, l'uomo* (for TV), 1974.

* * *

The films of Vittorio De Sica are among the most enduring of the Italian post-war period. His career suggests an openness to form and a versatility uncommon among Italian directors. De Sica began acting on stage as a teenager and played his first film role in 1918. In the 1920s his handsome features and talent made him something of a matinee idol, and from the mid-1930s he appeared in a number of films by Mario Camerini, including *Gliuomini che mascalzoni!, Darò un milione,* and *Grandi magazzine.*

During his lifetime, De Sica acted in over one hundred films in Italy and abroad, using this means to finance his own directorial efforts. He specialized in breezy comic heroes, men of great self-assurance or confidence men (as in Rossellini's *Generale della Rovere*). The influence of his tenure as actor cannot be overestimated in his directorial work, where the expressivity of the actor in carefully written roles was one of his foremost technical implements. In this vein De Sica has continually mentioned the influence on his work of Charlie Chaplin. The tensive continuity between tragic and comic, the deployment of a detailed yet poetic gestural language, and a humanist philosophy without recourse to the politically radical are all elements of De Sica's work that are paralleled in the silent star's films.

De Sica's directorial debuts, *Rose scarlatte* and *Maddalena, zero in condotta,* were both attempts to bring theater pieces to the screen with suitable roles for himself. In 1943, with *I bambini ci guardano,* De Sica teamed with Cesare Zavattini, who was to become his major collaborator for the next three decades. Together they began to demonstrate elements of the post-war realist aesthetic which, more than any other director except Visconti and Rossellini, De Sica helped shape and determine. Despite the overt melodrama of the misogynistic story (a young mother destroys her family by deserting them), the filmmaker refused to narrow the perspective through an overwrought Hollywoodian mise-en-scène, preferring instead a refreshing simplicity of composition and a subdued editing style. Much of the film's original flavor can be traced to the clear, subjective mediation of a child, as promised in the title.

De Sica's intense feeling for children's sensibilities led him to imagine how children viewed the failing adult reconstruction of society after the war. *Sciuscia,* a realistic look at the street and prison life of poor, abandoned children, was the result. It is the story of how the lasting friendship of two homeless boys, who make their living shining shoes for the American G.I.'s, is betrayed by their contact with adults. At the end of the film one boy inadvertently causes the other's death. Although Zavattini insists that his creative role was minimal in this instance, the presence of his poetic imagination is evident in the figure of a beautiful white horse. This horse serves to cement the boys' mutual bond and their hope for a future. Though a miserable failure in Italy, *Sciuscia* marked De Sica's entry into international prominence; the film won a special Oscar in 1947.

For the balance of the neorealist period De Sica fought an uphill battle to finance his films through friends and acting salaries. *Ladri di biciclette* anchors searching social documentation in metaphor and a non-traditional but highly structured narrative. Workman Ricci's desperate search for his bicycle is an odyssey that enables us to witness a varied collection of characters and situations among the poor and working class of Rome. Each episode propels the narrative toward a sublimely Chaplinesque but insufficiently socially critical ending in which Ricci is defeated in his search and therefore in his attempts to provide for his family. Reduced to thievery himself, he takes his son's hand and disappears into the crowd. Like De Sica's other neorealist films, *Ladri di biciclette* gives the impression of technical nonchalance only to the indiscriminate eye, for De Sica planned his work with attention to minute details of characterization, mise-en-scène, and camera technique. During this period he preferred the non-professional actor for his or her ability to accept direction without the mediation of learned acting technique.

The story of Toto the Good in *Miracolo a Milano* remains one of the outstanding stylistic contradictions of the neorealist period (there are many), yet one which sheds an enormous amount of light on the intentions and future of the De Sica-Zavattini team. The cinematography and setting, markedly neorealist in this fable about the struggle to found a shanty town for the homeless, is undercut at every moment with unabashed clowning both in performance and in cinematic technique. Moreover, the film moves toward a problematic fairy tale ending in which the poor, no longer able to defend their happy, makeshift village from the voracious appetite of capitalist entrepreneurs, take to the skies on magic broomsticks. (The film has more special effects than anyone would ever associate with neorealism; could De Sica have left his mark on Steven Spielberg?) Still, Zavattini, who had wanted to make the film for a number of years, and De Sica defend it as the natural burlesque transformation of themes evident in their earlier work together.

By this time De Sica's films were the subject of a good deal of controversy in Italy, and generally the lines were drawn between Catholic and Communist critics. The latter had an especially acute fear (one which surfaced again with Fellini's *La Strada*) that the hard-won traits of neorealism had begun to backslide into those of the so-called "calligraphic" films of the Fascist era. These were based on an ahistorical, formal concern for aesthetic, compositional qualities and the nuances of clever storytelling. However, it was their next film, *Umberto D,* that comes closest to realizing Zavattini's ideas on the absolute responsibility of the camera eye to observe life as it is lived without the traditional compromises of entertaining narratives. The sequence of the film in which the maid wakes up and makes the morning coffee has been praised many times for its day-in-the-life directness and simplicity. *Il Tetto,* about a curious attempt to erect a small house on municipal property, is generally recognized as the last neorealist film of this original period.

Continually wooed by Hollywood, De Sica finally acquiesced to make *Stazione termini* in 1953, produced by Selznick and filmed in Rome with Jennifer Jones and Montgomery Clift. Unfortunately, neorealist representation formed only an insignificant background to this typically American star vehicle. A similar style is employed in *La ciociara,* which was created from a Moravia story about the relationship of a mother and daughter uprooted by the war. De Sica attempted to reconstruct reality in the studio during the making of this work, making use of a somewhat unsuccessful stylized lighting technique. But as usual, he obtains excellent performances in an engaging dramatic vehicle (Sophia Loren won an Oscar).

The filmmakers returned to comedic vehicles in 1954 in *L'oro di Napoli.* Human comedy emerges from the rich diversity and liveliness of Neapolitan life. Though still within the confines of realism, the film foreshadows the director's entrance into the popular Italian market for sexual satire and farce. The exactitude with which he sculpts his characters and his reluctance to reduce the scenario to a mere bunch of gags demonstrates his intention to fuse comedy and drama, putting De Sica at the top of his class in this respect—among Risi, Comencini, and Monicelli. Often with Zavattini but also with Eduardo De Filippo, Tonino Guerra, and even Neil Simon (*After the Fox*), De Sica turned out about eight such films for the lucrative international market between 1961 and 1968, the best of which are: *Il giudizio universale,* which featured an all-star cast of international comedians; *Ieri, oggi, domani* and *Matrimonio all'Italiana,* both with Loren and Mastroianni; and *Sette volte donna.*

Il giardino dei Finzi Contini, based on a Bassani novel about the incarceration of Italian Jews during the war, shows a strong Viscontian influence in its lavish setting and thematics (the film deals with the dissolution of the bourgeois family). *Una breve vacanza,* an examination of a woman who has managed to break out of the confines of an oppressive marriage during a sanitorium stay, reinstitutes the tensive relationship between comedy and tragedy of the earlier films. De Sica's last film, *Il viaggio,* is from a Pirandello novel.

—Joel Kanoff

DICKINSON, Thorold

Nationality: British. **Born:** Bristol, 16 November 1903. **Education:** Clifton College and Keble College, Oxford. **Family:** Married architect Joanna Macfadyen, 1929. **Career:** Interpreter for George Pearson in France, 1925; subsequently editor, director, and scriptwriter; programme controller, the London Film Society, 1929-39; Vice-President, Association of Cine-Technicians, 1936-53; directed first film, *High Command,* 1937; organized Army Kinematograph Service Production Group, 1942-43; Chairman of the British Film Academy, 1950-53; film advisor in Israel, 1953-54; Chief of the Film Service, Office of Public Information, United Nations, 1956-60; President of the International Federation of Film Societies, 1958-66; lecturer in film studies at Slade School of Fine Art, 1960 (first Professor of Film in Britain, 1967). **Awards:** Commander of the British Empire, 1973. **Died:** 14 April 1984.

Films as Director:

1937 *The High Command*

1938 *Spanish ABC* (short) (co-d, co-ed); *Behind the Spanish Lines* (short) (co-d, co-ed)

1939 *The Arsenal Stadium Mystery* (+ co-adapt); *The Mikado* (Schertzinger) (2nd unit d)

1940 *Gaslight* (*Angel Street*); (short films for Ministry of Information): *Westward Ho! 1940* (+ pr, co-ed); *Yesterday Is Over Your Shoulder* (+ pr, co-ed); *The Horseshoe Nail* (abandoned because of objections of Ministry of Aircraft Production)

1941 *The Prime Minister*

1942 *The Next of Kin* (+ co-sc)

1946 *Men of Two Worlds* (*Kisenga, Man of Africa*) (+ co-sc)

1948 *The Queen of Spades*

1951 *Secret People* (+ story, co-sc)

1954 *Hakarka ha a dom* (*The Red Ground*) (short) (+ co-sc, ed, bit role as man playing cards)

1955 *Hill Twenty-Four Doesn't Answer* (+ co-pr, co-sc, co-ed)

Other Films:

1926 *The Little People* (Pearson) (asst d, co-sc)

1927 *Huntingtower* (Pearson) (asst d)

1928 *Love's Option* (Pearson) (co-ed, asst d)

1929 *Auld Lang Syne* (Pearson) (co-ed, synchronization of song sequences)

1930 *The School for Scandal* (Elvey) (ed)

1931 *The Sport of Kings* (Saville) (ed); *Contraband Love* (Morgan) (ed); *Other People's Sins* (Hill) (ed); *The Great Gay Road* (Hill) (ed); *Lloyd of the CID* (*Detective Lloyd*) (twelve-episode serial) (MacRae) (ed eight episodes)

1932 *The First Mrs. Fraser* (Hill) (ed); *Karma* (Raid and Freer-Hunt) (ed); *Perfect Understanding* (Gardner) (ed)

1933 *Going Gay* (*Kiss Me Goodbye*) (Gallone, completed 1934) (ed); *For Love of You* (Gallone, completed 1934) (ed); *Loyalties* (Dean) (ed)

1934 *Java Head* (Ruben) (ed, completion of film after director fell ill); *Sing as We Go!* (Dean) (ed)

1935 *The Silent Passenger* (Denham) (ed); *Midshipman Easy* (*Men of the Sea*) (Reed) (ed, supervisor)

1936 *Whom the Gods Love* (Mozart) (Dean) (ed); *Calling the Tune* (Denham) (co-ed); *The House of the Spaniard* (Denham) (ed)

1942 (partial list for Army Kinematograph Service): *The New Lot* (Reed) (pr/spvr); *Tank Tactics* series (F.A. Young and others) (six 2-reelers) (pr/spvr); plus ten other titles

1957 *Question in Togoland* (Porter) (short for U.N.) (pr/spvr); *Out* (Rogosin) (short for U.N.) (pr/spvr); *Blue Vanguard* (McNeill) (for U.N.) (pr/spvr); *Three of Our Children* (Reed and Estelle) (short for U.N.) (pr/spvr)

1958 *Overture* (Polidoro and Singh) (short for U.N.) (pr/spvr); *Exposure* (Hughes and Singh) (short for U.N.) (pr/spvr); *Pablo Casals Breaks His Journey* (Sarma) (short for U.N.) (pr/spvr); *Big Day in Bogo* (N. Reed) (short for U.N.) (pr/spvr); *Power Among Men* (Hammid, Polidoro, and Sarma) (short for U.N.) (pr/spvr, co-sc, ed)

1959 *In Our Hands* (Sarma) (short for U.N.) (pr/spvr); *A Scary Time* (Clarke) (short for U.N.) (pr/spvr); *Workshop for Peace* (Hammid, revised version of a 1955 film) (short for U.N.) (pr/spvr)

1960 *The Farmers of Fermathe* (Polidoro) (footage from *Power Among Men,* 1958) (short for U.N.) (pr/spvr)

Publications

By DICKINSON: books—

Soviet Cinema, with Catherine de la Roche, London, 1948; reissued New York, 1972.

Screenplay of *Secret People,* in *Making a Film,* by Lindsay Anderson, London, 1952.

Thorold Dickinson

Introduction to *The Technique of Film Editing,* by Karel Reisz, London, 1952.
A Discovery of Cinema, London, 1971.

By DICKINSON: articles—

"Search for Music" and "Indian Spring," in *Penguin Film Review,* London, 1948.
"The Filmwright and the Audience," in *Sight and Sound* (London), March 1950.
"The Work of Sir Michael Balcon," in *The Year's Work in Film,* London, 1951.
"A Day in the Life of a Film," in *Sight and Sound* (London), August 1951.
"Griffith and the Development of the Silent Film," in *Sight and Sound* (London), October 1951.
"Secret People," in *Cinema* (London), 1952.
"Heaven Preserve Us from the Passive Audience!" in *Film* (London), September/October 1955.
"The Sponsoring of Films," in *Film* (London), March/April 1956.
"Conference in Paris," in *Sight and Sound* (London), Summer 1956.
"The Personal Style," in *Film* (London), March/April 1957.
"This Documentary Business," in *Film Culture* (New York), October 1957.
Interview in *Film Dope* (London), January 1977.
"Experiences in the Spanish Civil War, 1938," in *Historical Journal of Film, Radio, and Television* (Abingdon, Oxon), October 1984.

On DICKINSON: book—

Richards, Jeffrey, *Thorold Dickinson: The Man and His Films,* London, 1986.

On DICKINSON: articles—

Sainsbury, Frank, "Closeups," in *Cine-Technician* (London), August 1940.
Listener (London), 3 June 1982.
Anstey, Edgar, "Paul Rotha and Thorold Dickinson," in *Sight and Sound* (London), Summer 1984.
Obituary in *Hollywood Reporter,* 1 May 1984.
Obituary in *Revue du Cinéma* (Paris), July-August 1984.

On DICKINSON: film—

Manvell, Roger, *A Film Is Made* (BBC), 1948.

* * *

Though his work has received far less attention and acclaim than that of his contemporary Michael Powell, Thorold Dickinson has strong claims to be considered as one of British cinema's major artists. Like Powell, he belongs to the studio era of the 1940s and 1950s but marked out a highly individual path, rejecting both the literary adaptation style of Reed and Lean and the cosy conformities of Balcon's Ealing studios. Dickinson is the most English of feature directors. He learned his craft from the veteran George Pearson while still an undergraduate at Oxford and later as an editor in the mainstream of British commercial film production of the 1930s. His breakthrough to feature filmmaking came with *The High Command* in 1937, and his work soon began to show his interest in the psychological motivation of his characters and his concern with analysis of British liberal values.

The 1940 *Gaslight,* his third feature film, is his first major work. A stylish period thriller, it is a version of the play later adapted in Hollywood by George Cukor. Though overshadowed by Cukor's version, this is a fine professional piece that shows a characteristic Dickinson concern with the psychological state of the characters and their reactions under intense pressure. In a very different vein, *The Next of Kin* began as a project for a military training film before being transformed by Dickinson and his producer Balcon into a feature-length fiction which achieved considerable commercial success. Though imbued with the patriotic spirit typical of its period, *The Next of Kin* avoids the rhetoric and self-glorification so common in the 1940s. Indeed, its unsparing portrayal of a country ill-prepared for the war in which it is engaged caused it some initial problems with the film censors.

The early postwar years saw three further remarkably diverse features, all of enormous interest and power. *Men of Two Worlds* is one of the few British studies of the impact of colonialism on the educated African elite which remains viable in its analysis. In contrast to its highly constructed realism (it was researched in Tanganyika but shot in the studio), Dickinson's adaptation of Pushkin's *The Queen of Spades* has an elegant period style which shows the influence of Jean Cocteau and the German expressionists in its creation of atmosphere. Again, the director's interest in the madness which stems from the failure to control passion is evident. *Secret People,* again produced by Balcon, but in no way an "Ealing film," probed another sensitive area for the liberal conscience: the use of violence for political ends, with the focus again on questions of identity and motivation. It proved to be Dickinson's last major film as a director, though he subsequently made a fictional feature in Israel, *Hill 24 Doesn't Answer,* worked as a producer for the United Nations, and became Britain's first professor of film at the Slade School of Fine Art, London.

Dickinson's work in the feature film has a restraint and subtlety akin to that displayed by Jennings in the documentary. It is exemplary in its use of the imaginative potential of the film studio and for the director's acute moral sense. The handful of films which Dickinson directed in the course of just a dozen or so years are among the most rewarding—as well as most neglected—British films of their period.

—Roy Armes

DIEGUES, Carlos

Nationality: Brazilian. **Born:** Maceio, state of Alagoas, 19 May 1940. **Education:** Studied law, Catholic University of Rio de Janeiro. **Family:** Married entertainer Nara Leao. **Career:** Organizer of Metropolitan Union of students, also film critic and poet, early 1960s; directed first feature, *Ganga Zumba,* 1964; emigrated to France following Brazilian military takeover, late 1960s; directed *Séjour* for French TV, 1970; returned to Brazil, mid-1970s.

Films as Director:

1960 *Fuga* (short) (co-d)
1961 *Domingo* (short)
1962 "Escola de samba, alegria de viver" episode of *Cinco vêzes Favela*
1964 *Ganga Zumba* (+ co-adapt)
1965 *A 8a. Bienal de São Paulo* (short)
1966 *A grande cidade* (*The Big City*) (+ co-sc)
1967 *Oito universitários* (short)
1969 *Os herdeiros* (*The Inheritors; The Heirs*)

Carlos Diegues: ***Bye Bye Brasil***

1972 *Quando a Carnaval chegar* (*When Carnival Comes*)
1973 *Joanna Francesa* (*Jeanne la française*) (+ sc)
1976 *Xica da Silva* (*Xica*)
1977 *Chuvas de verao* (*Summer Showers*; *A Summer Rain*) (+ sc)
1978 *Os filhos do medo* (*Les Enfants de la peur*) (TV doc)
1980 ***Bye Bye Brasil*** (+ sc)
1984 *Quilombo*
1987 *Un tren para las estrellas*
1990 *Dias melhores virao* (+ sc, pr)
1994 *Rio's Love Songs* (+ sc)

Other Films:

1965 *O Circo* (Jabor) (ed)
1967 *Terra em transe* (*Land in Trance*) (Rocha) (assoc pr)
1968 *Capitu* (Saraceni) (assoc pr)
1980 *Prova de Fogo* (Altberg) (assoc pr)
1988 *Dede Mamata* (pr)

Publications

By DIEGUES: book—

Palmares: Mito e romance da utopia brasileira, with Everardo Rocha, Rio de Janeiro, 1991.

By DIEGUES: articles—

"Diegues fala de Moreau e *Joanna,*" interview, in *Filme Cultura* (Rio de Janeiro), January/February 1973.
"Carlos Diegues: 'cette chose trés simple, aimer le peuple,'" an interview with J. Delmas, in *Jeune Cinéma* (Paris), July/August 1978.
Interview with Federico De Cardenas, in *Los años de la conmoción,* by Isaac León Frías, Mexico City, 1979.
"The Mind of Cinema Novo," an interview with D. Yakir, in *Film Comment* (New York), September/October 1980.
"Le Cinéma nuovo dix ans aprés," an interview with G. Haustrate and D. Rabourdin, in *Cinéma* (Paris), November 1980.
"Adieu, cinema novo," an interview with P. A. Paranagua, in *Positif* (Paris), May 1981.
Interview with J. C. Rodrigues, in *Filme Cultura* (Rio de Janeiro), August/October 1982.
Interview with C. Espinosa Dominguez, in *Cine Cubano* (Havana), no. 104, 1983.
Interview with André Tournès, in *Jeune Cinéma* (Paris), July/August 1984.
"Cine: Arte del presente," "Sobre el cinema novo," and "Diez años de cine nacional," in *Hojas de cine: Testimonios y Documentos del Nuevo Cine Latinoamericano 1,* Mexico City, 1986.
"Choosing between Legend and History," an interview with Coco Fusco, in *Cineaste* (New York), vol. 15, no. 1, 1986.
"Schizophrenes Land," an interview with R. Braun, in *Film und Fernsehen,* vol. 18, no. 6, 1990.

On DIEGUES: books—

Johnson, Randal, *Cinema Novo x5: Masters of Contemporary Brazilian Film,* Austin, Texas, 1984.

Burton, Julianne, editor, *Cinema and Social Change in Latin America: Conversations with Filmmakers,* Austin, Texas, 1986.

Johnson, Randal, and Robert Stam, editors, *Brazilian Cinema,* Austin, Texas, 1988.

On DIEGUES: articles—

Prédal, R., "Bio-filmographie: Carlos Diegues," in *Etudes Cinématographiques* (Paris), no. 93-96, 1972.

Johnson, Randal, "*Xica de Silva*: Sex, Politics, and Culture," in *Jump Cut* (Berkeley), May 1980.

Trujillo, Marisol, "Tormento y pasión en *Los herederos* de Carlos Diegues," in *Cine Cubano* (Havana), no. 100, 1981.

Yakir, Dan, "Braziliant," in *Film Comment* (New York), May/June 1984.

Dossier on Carlos Diegues, in *Revue du Cinema* (Paris), November 1984.

Osiel, Mark, "Bye Bye Boredom: Brazilian Cinema Comes of Age," in *Cineaste* (New York), vol 15, no. 1, 1986.

Mosier, John, "Subway to the Stars," in *Americas,* January/February 1988.

Welch, Cliff, "*Quilombo,*" in *American Historical Review,* October 1992.

* * *

One of the founders of *Cinema Novo*—the movement that transformed film in Brazil and was a pivotal influence in the New Latin American Cinema—Carlos Diegues is probably the most historically minded of its adherents. Like the other directors of *Cinema Novo,* Diegues is concerned with making films which are "culturally Brazilian, and impregnated with national and Latin American problems"; and his entrance into the national reality was, as with many other members of this group, through documentary films that put him in direct contact with social problems. Diegues also shares the interest in popular culture that is characteristic of *Cinema Novo,* although he tends to emphasize the contribution of black culture, which "gave us originality. It's the element that has completely modified Brazil, which otherwise would be a mere cultural colony of Portugal and Spain."

Perhaps that which most differentiates Diegues from his *Cinema Novo* colleagues is his historical orientation. On the one hand, this can be seen in his insistent return to historical themes. But on the other hand, Diegues's conception of history is complex: he feels that the most important element in cinema is its *adecuación* (fitness) to the time in which it is made. To the degree that a film speaks to the problems and possibilities of the epoch in which it appears, it allows for the sort of "political cinema" Diegues prefers, a cinema with which the audience can interact. It is this perspective that Diegues brings to his perception of his films as corresponding to particular historical contexts.

His first works, *Samba School* and *Ganga Zumba,* are products of what Diegues describes as a "fantastic, euphoric period" in which emerged new Brazilian cinema, music, and theater. *Samba School* was typical of the early works of *Cinema Novo,* focusing on the popular culture of the slums through an analysis of the alienation represented by the schools of samba. Diegues made the film on a barebones budget and worked at practically all the production tasks, including appearing as an actor. *Ganga Zumba* was Diegues's first feature. A reconstruction of the Palmares Republic of runaway slaves in Brazil during the seventeenth century, it corresponded to the search for identity in which many Brazilian artists were then engaged. It also represented the first *Cinema Novo* film to value Afro-Brazilian culture, as well as the beginning of Diegues's interest in bringing black history to the screen: "I tried to make a black film, not a film about blacks," he stated.

The military coup of 1964, and its increasingly repressive legislation during the 1960s, changed the cultural scene profoundly. In film, an "aesthetic of silence" reigned, and Diegues perceives this as his "sick period," during which he made *The Heirs* and *Joanna Francesa* as expressions of the depressing tableau presented by the "Dantesque levels" military terrorism reached. *The Heirs* is a historical work on the period 1930-1964, which allegorically evokes the role of Getulio Vargas (a populist president-dictator who oscillated between fascism and socialism) by following the trajectory of a bourgeois family. Diegues says that his main intention was to "project a precise image of this strange, violent and sentimental, baroque and surrealist, sincere and subtle country called Brazil, whose passion torments me more than anything else in life." In *Joanna Francesa,* Diegues returned again to analyze the Revolution of 1930, this time in a film he considers a "lament" on the death of a culture and a civilization, which reflected the dolorous days through which Brazil was passing.

The liberalization of military rule led to what Diegues has described as the third phase of *Cinema Novo,* which he characterizes as "the aesthetic of life." Within this category, he places the two reconstructions, *Xica da Silva* and *Quilombo,* which continue the black history of colonial Brazil he began with *Ganga Zumba,* as well as the popular *Bye Bye Brazil.* Both *Xica da Silva* and *Quilombo* are more mythic than historic, for Diegues believes that "history is always written by the winners," and therefore a real history of blacks is either impossible or depressing. Thus, he focuses on the character of Francisca (Xica), a black slave whom a wealthy Portuguese freed and took as his lover. Little real information exists on this eighteenth-century woman because all mention of her was exorcised by the townspeople, but her love of freedom is an important myth of Brazilian popular culture.

Quilombo was made just two or three years before Brazil was liberated from military rule, and that context allowed Diegues to utilize the story of the runaway slave republic as a metaphor for the building of a utopia. With even less information available about *quilombos* than existed on Xica, Diegues allowed himself free rein; the result, as he intended, says more about the future than about the past. *Xica da Silva* was immensely popular in Brazil, but the film which has achieved the most international recognition is *Bye Bye Brazil.* In this exuberant film "dedicated to Brazilians in the twenty-first century," Diegues returns to *Cinema Novo*'s insistent concern with popular culture and concludes that the way in which culture is assimilated and re-elaborated is more important than its origin or alleged "purity." This is perhaps one of the more useful lessons Diegues has to teach his fellow filmmakers of *Cinema Novo.*

—John Mraz

DIETERLE, William

Nationality: American. **Born:** Wilhelm Dieterle in Ludwigshafen, 15 July 1893; became U.S. citizen, late 1930s. **Family:** Married 1) comedienne and writer Charlotte Hagenbruch, 1921 (died 1965); 2) Elisabeth Dieterle. **Career:** Studied acting with Paul Tietsch, Mannheim; actor in German theatre, from 1911; member of Max Reinhardt's company, Berlin, and film actor, 1920-23; directed first film, *Der Mensch am Wege,* 1923; began avant-garde Dramatisches Theater with Georg Kaiser and others, Berlin, 1924; founded Charha-Film production company, 1927; signed by Carl Laemmle to Deutsch

Universal for five films, 1929; left with wife for United States, 1930; signed seven-year contract with Warner Bros., 1931; left Warners for RKO, working as own producer; also, with Fritz Lang, financed emigration to United States of Brecht, Weill, and Helene Weigel, 1941; signed long-term contract with Hal Wallis, producing for Paramount, 1942; following McCarthyist attacks, passport confiscated, 1951 and 1953; returned to Germany, 1958; television director, from 1961. **Died:** In Ottobrunn, 9 December 1972.

Films as Director:

1923 *Der Mensch am Wege* (+ sc, role as the angel); *Die grüne Manuela* (co-d with Dupont, role)
1924 *Das Wachsfigurenkabinett* (co-d with Leni, role)
1927 *Das Geheimnis des Abbé X* (*Der Mann, der nicht lieben darf*) (+ pr, sc, role)
1928 *Die Heilige und ihr Narr* (*La Sainte et le fou*) (+ pr, role as Harro, Count of Torstein); *Geschlecht in Fesseln—Die Sexualnot der Gefangenen* (*Chaînes*; *Les Sexes enchainés*) (+ role as Franz Sommer)
1929 *Ich liebe für dich* (*Le Triomphe de la vie*) (+ role as Bergson); *Frühlingsrauschen* (*Tränen die ich dir geweint*; *Rêves de printemps*; *Nostalgie*) (+ role as Friedrich); *Das Schweigen im Walde* (*Le Silence dans la forêt*; *La Nuit de la Saint-Jean*) (+ role as Ettingen)
1930 *Ludwig der Zweite, König von Bayern* (+ co-sc, role as Ludwig II of Bavaria); *Eine Stunde glück* (+ co-sc, role as Eddy)

(Films made in United States):

1930 *Der Tanz geht weiter* (German version of William Beaudine's *Those Who Dance*) (+ role as Fred Hogan); *Die Maske fällt* (German version of Frank Lloyd's *The Way of All Men*); *Kismet* (German version of Dillon film); *Dämon des Meeres* (co-d) (German version of Curtiz's *Moby Dick*)
1931 *Die Heilige Flamme* (co-d) (German version of Archie Mayo's *The Sacred Flame*); *The Last Flight*; *Her Majesty*; *Love*
1932 *Man Wanted*; *Jewel Robbery*; *Six Hours to Live!*; *The Crash*; *Scarlet Dawn*
1933 *Lawyer Man*; *Grand Slam*; *Adorable*; *The Devil's in Love*; *Female* (co-d); *From Headquarters*
1934 *Fashions of 1934* (co-d); *Madame du Barry*; *Fog Over Frisco*; *Doctor Monica* (co-d); *The Firebird*; *The Secret Bride*
1935 *A Midsummer Night's Dream* (co-d); *Dr. Socrates*
1936 *The Story of Louis Pasteur*; *The White Angel*; *Satan Met a Lady*
1937 *The Great O'Malley*; *Another Dawn*; *The Life of Emile Zola*
1938 *Blockade*
1939 *Juarez*; *The Hunchback of Notre Dame*
1940 *Dr. Ehrlich's Magic Bullet* (*The Story of Dr. Ehrlich's Magic Bullet, The Magic Bullet*); *A Dispatch from Reuter's* (*This Man Reuter*); *All That Money Can Buy* (*The Devil and Daniel Webster*) (+ pr, co-sc)
1942 *Syncopation* (+ pr, co-sc); *Tennessee Johnson* (*The Man on America's Conscience*)
1943 *Kismet*
1944 *I'll be Seeing You* (co-d)
1945 *This Love of Ours*; *Love Letters*
1946 *Duel in the Sun* (co-d); *The Searching Wind*
1948 *Paid in Full*; *The Accused*
1949 *Portrait of Jennie* (*Tidal Wave*) (production begun 1947); *Rope of Sand*; *Volcano*
1950 *September Affair*; *Dark City*
1952 *Red Mountain* (co-d, produced in 1950); *Boots Malone*; *The Turning Point*
1953 *Salome*
1954 *Elephant Walk*
1956 *Magic Fire* (+ co-pr, shot in 1954); *One Against Many* (+ co-sc, made for television)
1957 *Peking Express* (produced in 1951); *The Loves of Omar Khayyam*
1965 *The Confession* (*Quick, Let's Get Married, Seven Different Ways*)

(after return to Germany):

1959 *Il Vendicatore* (*Dubrowsky*; *L'Aigle noir*; *Révolte sur la Volga*)
1960 *Herrin der Welt* in two parts: "Herrin der Welt" and "Angkor-Vat" (*Apocalisse sull fiume giallo*; *Les Mystères d'Angkor*) (co-d); *Die Fastnachtsbeichte*

Other Films:

1913 *Fiesko* (role)
1915 *Der Erbföster* (Oberläner) (role)
1921 *Die Geier-Wally* (Dupont) (role); *Die Hintertreppe* (Jessner and Leni) (role); *Fräulein Julie* (Basch) (role); *Die Silbermöwe* (Sauer) (role)
1922 *Frauenopfer* (Grüne) (role); *Es leuchtet meine Liebe* (Stein) (role); *Der Graf von Charolais* (Grune) (role); *Lukrezia Borgia* (Oswald) (role); *Marie-Antoinette—Das Leben einer Königin* (Meinert) (role)
1923 *Boheme—Künstlerliebe* (Righelli) (role); *Der zweite Schuss* (Krol) (role); *Die Pagode* (Fekete) (role); *Die Austreibung—Die Macht der zweiten Frau* (Murnau) (role)
1924 *Carlos und Elisabeth—Eine Herrschertragödie* (Oswald) (role); *Moderne Ehen* (Otto) (role); *Mutter und Kind* (Froehlich) (role)
1925 *Wetterleuchten* (Walther-Fein) (role); *Lena Warnstetten* (Eriksen) (role); *Die Blumenfrau von Potsdamer Platz* (Speyer) (role); *Sumpf und Moral* (Walther-Fein) (role); *Die vom Niederrhein* (Walther-Fein) (role); *Der Hahn im Korb* (Jacoby) (role); *Der Rosa Diamant* (Gliese) (role); *Die Dame aus Berlin* (von Kabdebo) (role); *Die Gesunkenen* (Walther-Fein) (role); *Gerechtigkeit* (role); *Der Traumkönig* (role)
1926 *Die Mühle von Sanssouci* (Philippini) (role); *Die Försterchristel* (Zelnik) (role); *Qualen der Nacht* (Bernhardt) (role); *Familie Schimeck* (*Wiener Herzen*) (Halm) (role); *Die Flucht in den Zirkus* (*Verurteilt nach Sibirien—Moskau 1912*) (Bonnard and Schamberg) (role); *Zopf und Schwert* (*Eine tolle Prinzessin*) (Janson) (role); *Faust—Eine Deutsche Volkssage* (Murnau) (role); *Hölle der Liebe—Erlebnisse aus einem Tanzpalais* (Rahn) (role); *Wie bliebe ich jung und schön* (*Ehegeheimnisse*) (Rahn) (role); *Der Jäger von Fall* (Seitz) (role); *Der Pfarrer von Kirchfeld* (Fleck) (role)
1927 *Unter Ausschluss der Öffentlichkeit* (Wiene) (role); *Der Zigeunerbaron* (*Sandor, Prince Vagabond*) (Zelnik) (role); *Violantha* (Froehlich) (role); *Die vom Schicksal verfolgten* (Kleinmann) (role); *Am Rande der Welt* (Grüne) (role); *Die Weber* (Zelnik) (role); *Ich habe im Mai von der Liebe geträumt* (Seits) (pr, role); *Liebesreigen* (Walther-Fein) (role); *Petronella* (Schwartz) (role); *Heimweh* (Righelli) (role); *Das Geheimnis des Abbe* (*Der Mann der nicht lieben darf*; *Behind the Altar*) (+ pr, sc, role)
1928 *Frau Sorge* (Land) (role); *Apachenliebe* (*Die Apachen von Paris*) (Malikoff) (role); *Diebe* (Heuberger) (role); *Ritter der Nacht* (*Le Gentilhomme des bas-fonds, Les Chevaliers de la nuit*) (Reichmann) (role)

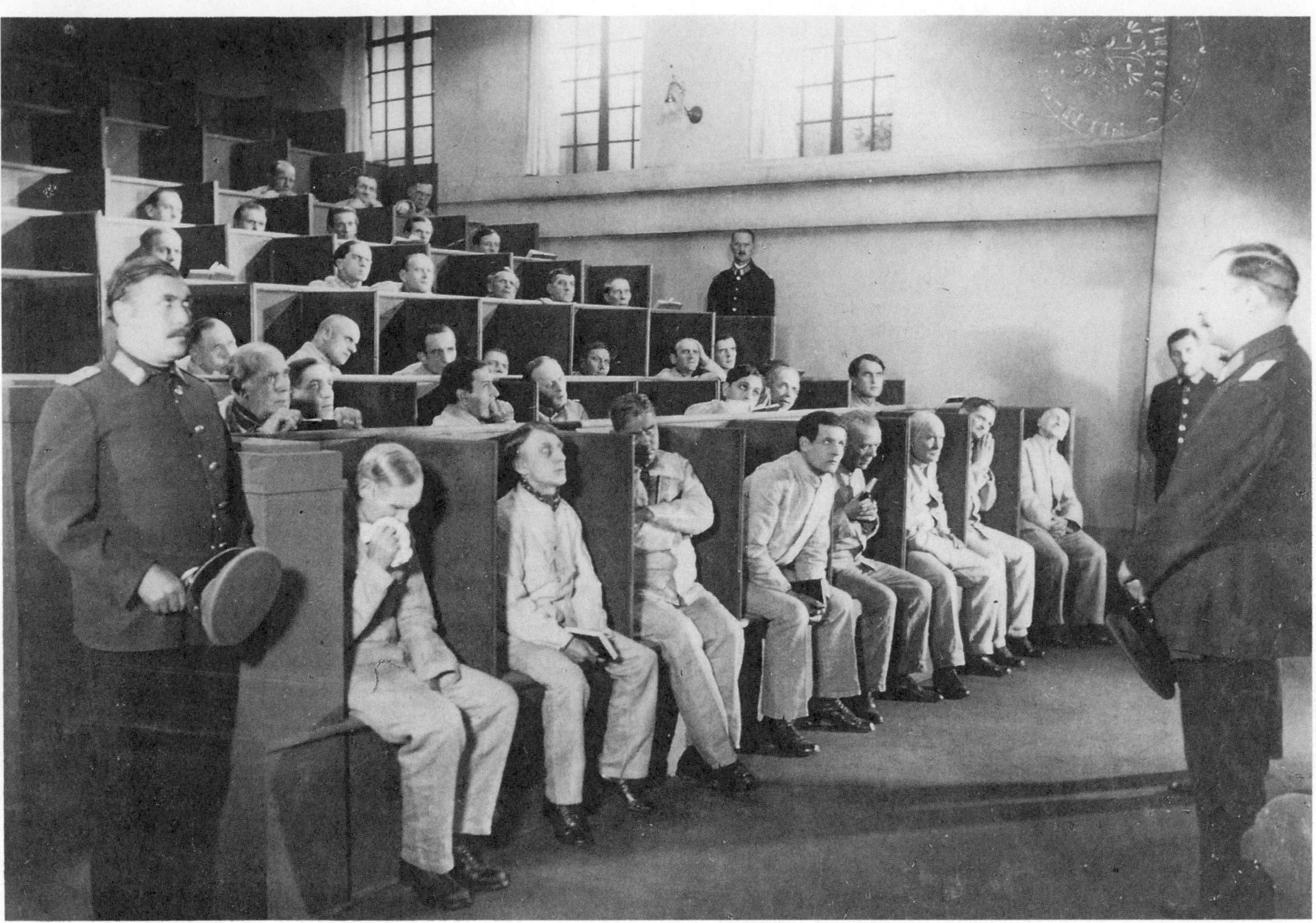

William Dieterle: ***Geschlecht in Fesseln***

Publications

By DIETERLE: book—

The Good Tidings, New York, 1950.

By DIETERLE: articles—

"The Great God Box-Office," in *Cinema Progress* (Los Angeles), February/March 1938.
"Hollywood and the European Crisis," in *Studies in Philosophy and Social Science* (New York), vol. 9, 1941.
"Do Films Have a Pedagogical Mission for the Masses?" in *Decision* (New York), March 1941.
Interview with Francis Koval, in *Sight and Sound* (London), May 1950.
"Directors in a Rut," in *Cine-Technician* (London), April 1954.
"Max Reinhardt in Hollywood," in *A Centennial Festschrift,* New York, 1973.
"William Dieterle: the Plutarch of Hollywood," an interview with T. Flinn, in *Velvet Light Trap* (Madison), Autumn 1975.

On DIETERLE: book—

Von Deutschland nach Hollywood: W. Dieterle, Berlin, 1973.

On DIETERLE: articles—

Lydo, Waldemar, "William Dieterle und der Filmschnitt," in *Reichsfilmblatt* (Berlin), 5 October 1929.
Luft, Herbert, "William Dieterle," in *Films in Review* (New York), April 1957 (see also Dieterle's response in May 1957, and Luft's response in June/July issue)
Pinto, Alfonso, and Francisco Rialp, "The Films of William Dieterle," in *Films in Review* (New York), October 1968.
Beylie, Claude, "William Dieterle l'heteroclite," in *Ecran* (Paris), February 1973.
"William Dieterle," in *Film Dope* (London), January 1977.
Dumont, Hervé, "William Dieterle 1893-1972," in *Avant-Scène du Cinéma* (Paris), 15 November 1977.
Wide Angle (Athens, Ohio), vol. 8, no. 2, 1986.

* * *

William Dieterle came from that cradle of film talent, the theatre of Max Reinhardt. Although he appeared in the film *Fiesko* in 1913, it was in Dupont's *Die Geierwally* with Henny Porten that he established himself as a screen actor. He became much sought after and appeared with Asta Nielsen in *Fraulein Julie,* Jessner's *Hintertreppe,* Oswald's *Lukretia Borgia* and *Carlos and Elizabeth,* Leni's *Waxworks,* Dupont's *Die grüne Manuela,* and Murnau's *Die Austreibung* and *Faust.*

Dieterle, who ran his own theatre in Berlin in 1924, was married to the actress Charlotte Hagenbruch, who was to be his close collaborator in both Europe and America. In 1923 he directed Marlene Dietrich in a small part. By 1928 and 1929 he was directing many films, two of which, *Die Heilige und ihr Narr* and *Geschlecht in Fesseln,* were outstanding. The latter, dealing with the sexual problems of prisoners, ran into censor trouble and was banned at one stage. Dieterle played in his own productions, including *Ludwig der Zweite,* which featured a script by his wife and design by Ernst Stern. In 1927 he appeared in Karl Grüne's unusual anti-war film *Am Rande der Welt* and Friedrich Zelnik's version of Hauptmann's *Die Weber.*

In 1930 Dieterle went to Hollywood to direct German versions of American films. Soon he was directing in English and was one of the most popular and successful of immigrant filmmakers. He directed Janet Gaynor in *Adorable,* based on a story by Billy Wilder. In 1934 he made two Bette Davis films, *Fashions of 1934* and *Fog Over Frisco.* He collaborated with his old master Reinhardt on *A Midsummer Night's Dream.* Then followed *The Story of Louis Pasteur,* for which Paul Muni won an Academy Award as best actor, and the brilliant *Juarez,* with Muni, Davis, and Brian Aherne. Another biographical film, *Dr. Ehrlich's Magic Bullet,* starred Edward G. Robinson. *Blockade* proved controversial as it touched on the Spanish Civil War.

Perhaps the best film that Dieterle made in America was *All That Money Can Buy,* based on Steven Vincent Benet's *The Devil and Daniel Webster.* This was a transposition of the Faust legend to a rural New England setting. The film was remarkable for its atmosphere and the fact that its portrayal of the supernatural really worked. It was a visually beautiful work that featured impeccable acting from a distinguished cast, including Edward Arnold as Webster and Walter Huston as Mr. Scratch, the homely and roguish Mephistopheles of the story. He directed Charles Laughton in *The Hunchback of Notre Dame* in 1939 and made two distinguished films with Jennifer Jones, *Love Letters* and *Portrait of Jenny.* But his version of *Salome* with Rita Hayworth in 1953 added nothing to his reputation and a decline set in. He returned to Germany in 1958 and later directed the Pushkin story *Dubrowsky,* which he made in Yugoslavia.

Dieterle had begun life as a carpenter in Ludwigshaven. He was a man of large stature and dynamic energy coupled with a cultured elegance which made his Hollywood home a salon where artists and writers met. In the studios he appeared with large hat and white gloves, an outfit that marked him out as *the director.* His skilled artistry enabled him to cover a wide range of subject matter, and all his films carried an air of refinement of thought and feeling.

—Liam O'Leary

DMYTRYK, Edward

Nationality: American. **Born:** Grand Forks, British Columbia, Canada, 4 September 1908, became U.S. citizen, 1939. **Education:** California Institute of Technology, 1926-27. **Family:** Married second wife, actress Jean Porter, 1948, one son. **Career:** Messenger and handy boy at Famous Players-Lasky, 1923, subsequently cutter, then editor; directed first film, *The Hawk,* 1935; directed series of films for Columbia, 1940-42, and for RKO, 1942-47; subpoenaed to appear before House Un-American Activities Committee as one of "Hollywood Ten," 1947; moved to England, 1948; forced to return to U.S., fined and given six months jail sentence for contempt of Congress, 1950; appeared as friendly witness before HUAC, and hired by producer Stanley Kramer, 1951; moved to England, 1971; taught at University of Texas, Austin, 1978; Professor of Filmmaking at University of Southern California, from 1981.

Films as Director:

1935 *The Hawk*
1939 *Television Spy*; *Emergency Squad*; *Million Dollar Legs* (co-d with Grinde, uncredited)
1940 *Golden Gloves*; *Mystery Sea Raider*; *Her First Romance*
1941 *The Devil Commands*; *Under Age*; *Sweetheart of the Campus* (*Broadway Ahead*); *The Blonde from Singapore* (*Hot Pearls*); *Secrets of the Lone Wolf* (*Secrets*); *Confessions of Boston Blackie* (*Confessions*)
1942 *Counter-Espionage*; *Seven Miles from Alcatraz*
1943 *Hitler's Children*; *The Falcon Strikes Back*; *Captive Wild Woman*; *Behind the Rising Sun*; *Tender Comrade*
1944 *Farewell, My Lovely* (*Murder My Sweet*)
1945 *Back to Bataan*; *Cornered*
1946 *Till the End of Time*
1947 ***Crossfire***; *So Well Remembered*
1949 *Obsession* (*The Hidden Room*); *Gives Us This Day* (*Salt to the Devil*)
1952 *Mutiny*; *The Sniper*; *Eight Iron Men*
1953 *The Juggler*; *Three Lives* (short)
1954 *The Caine Mutiny*; *Broken Lance*; *The End of the Affair*
1955 *Soldier of Fortune*; *The Left Hand of God*; *Bing Presents Oreste* (short)
1956 *The Mountain* (+ pr)
1957 *Raintree County*
1958 *The Young Lions*
1959 *Warlock* (+ pr); *The Blue Angel*
1962 *The Reluctant Saint* (+ pr); *Walk on the Wild Side*
1963 *The Carpetbaggers*
1964 *Where Love Has Gone*; *Mirage*
1966 *Alvarez Kelly*
1968 *Lo sbarco di Anzio* (*Anzio*; *The Battle for Anzio*); *Shalako*
1972 *Barbe-Bleue* (*Bluebeard*) (+ co-sc)
1975 *The "Human" Factor*
1976 *He Is My Brother*

Other Films:

1930 *Only Saps Work* (Gardner and Knopf) (ed); *The Royal Family of Broadway* (Cukor and Gardner) (ed)
1932 *Million Dollar Legs* (Cline) (ed)
1934 *Belle of the Nineties* (McCarey) (co-ed, uncredited); *College Rhythm* (Taurog) (co-ed)
1935 *Ruggles of Red Gap* (McCarey) (ed)
1936 *Too Many Parents* (McGowan) (ed); *Three Cheers for Love* (Ray McCarey) (ed); *Three Married Men* (Buzzell) (ed); *Easy to Take* (Tryon) (ed)
1937 *Murder Goes to College* (Riesner) (ed); *Turn Off the Moon* (Seiler) (ed); *Double or Nothing* (Reed) (ed); *Hold 'em Navy* (*That Navy Spirit*) (Neumann) (ed)
1938 *Bulldog Drummond's Peril* (Hogan) (ed); *Prison Farm* (Louis King) (ed)
1939 *Zaza* (Cukor) (ed); *Love Affair* (McCarey) (co-ed); *Some Like It Hot* (Archainbaud) (ed)
1950 *The Hollywood Ten* (Berry) (co-sc, appearance)
1968 *Hamlet* (Wirth) (dubbing d)
1976 *Hollywood on Trial* (Helpern) (role as interviewee)

Publications

By DMYTRYK: books—

It's a Hell of a Life But Not a Bad Living, New York, 1978.

Edward Dmytryk

On Screen Directing, London, 1984.
On Screen Acting, Boston, 1984.
On Filmmaking, Boston, 1986.
Cinema: Concept and Practice, Boston, 1988.

By DMYTRYK: articles—

"Reply to R. English," in *Nation* (New York), 26 May 1951.
"The Director-Cameraman Relationship," interview with Herb Lightman, in *American Cinematographer* (Los Angeles), May 1968.
"The Director and the Editor," in *Action* (Los Angeles), March/April 1969.
"Dmytryk On Film," in *Journal of University Film Association* (Carbondale, Illinois), Spring 1982.
"A Very Narrow Path: The Politics of Edward Dmytryk," an interview with L.D. Friedman, in *Literature/Film Quarterly* (Salisbury, Maryland), October 1984.
"Edward Dmytryk Remembers," an interview with J. Bawden, in *Films in Review* (New York), December 1985.

On DMYTRYK: articles—

English, R., "What Makes a Hollywood Communist?," in the *Saturday Evening Post* (Philadelphia), 19 May 1951.
Tozzi, Romano, "Edward Dmytryk," in *Films in Review* (New York), February 1962.
"The Cinema of Edward Dmytryk," in *Films Illustrated* (London), October 1971.
"Edward Dmytryk," in *Film Dope* (London), June 1977.
McClure, L., "Edward Dmytryk: The Director as Professor," in *Filmmakers Monthly* (Ward Hill, Massachusetts), January 1979.

* * *

Edward Dmytryk rose through the Hollywood ranks, beginning as a projectionist in the 1920s, working as an editor through most of the 1930s, and directing low-budget films during the first half of the 1940s before making his first A-budget film, *Tender Comrade,* in 1943. He continued to make notable films like *Crossfire* and *Farewell, My Lovely* before being subpoenaed to testify before HUAC. Dmytryk subsequently became one of the Hollywood Ten and, after completing his jail sentence, the only member of the Ten to become a friendly witness and name names. After doing one film for the King brothers, *Mutiny,* in 1952, Stanley Kramer hired him to direct four features culminating with *The Caine Mutiny.* He continued to direct films regularly through the 1950s and 1960s and later taught at U.S.C. in Los Angeles.

In many of his films Dmytryk displays much the same sensibility informing the work of Frank Capra: a faith in ordinary people, a belief in the virtues of working together, a deep reverence for traditional American ideals and heroes, and a strongly utopian bent that tends to see evil as a localized aberration capable of correction. Characters often see the light (*Hitler's Children,* or *Salt to the Devil*), find themselves transformed by the example or expectations of others *(The Left Hand of God* or *The Juggler),* or reveal a tender, committed side that is not immediately apparent *(Soldier of Fortune* or *Broken Lance).* Utopianism, then, instead of becoming a positive affirmation of values, becomes more an implicit trust in goodness that sometimes defuses dramatic conflict by rendering evil ineffective or by side-stepping intense confrontations or issues. By affirming the nobility of true love despite adversity, *Walk on the Wild Side,* for example, presents a more pollyannaish view of down-and-out Depression life in New Orleans than the Nelson Algren novel on which it is based.

Dmytryk directs with an essentially serious tone that minimizes comedy and seldom romanticizes the agrarian or non-urban ethos so dear to Capra. He also tends to work with more interiorized states of personal feeling that run counter to Capra's tendency to play conflicts out in public among a diverse, somewhat stereotyped range of characters. But, like Capra, Dmytryk dwells on the issue of faith—the need for it and the tests to which it is subjected. *Salt to the Devil, Tender Comrade, Soldier of Fortune, Raintree County, The Juggler, Broken Lance, The Left Hand of God, The Caine Mutiny, Hitler's Children*—these and other films involve tests of faith and commitment for their central characters. The characters strive to find and affirm a sense of personal dignity, whatever the odds, and usually do so within a private setting that uses the broader social context as a dramatic backdrop, even in *Hitler's Children* or *The Young Lions,* two films dealing with Nazism. Some have argued that Dmytryk's work simply deteriorated after his testimony before HUAC; it may also be that recurring themes bridge this period and offer intriguing parallels between the political climate, Dmytryk's personal view of life, and his overall film accomplishments.

—Bill Nichols

DONEN, Stanley

Nationality: American. **Born:** Columbia, South Carolina, 13 April 1924. **Education:** Studied dance at Town Theater, Columbia, then University of South Carolina, until 1940. **Family:** Married actress Yvette Mimieux, 1972. **Career:** Broadway debut in *Pal Joey,* 1940; choreographer for MGM musicals, Hollywood, 1943-49; co-directed (with Gene Kelly) first film, *On the Town,* 1949.

Films as Director:

1949 ***On the Town*** (co-d, co-chor)
1951 *Royal Wedding* (*Wedding Bells*)
1952 ***Singin' in the Rain*** (co-d, co-chor); *Love Is Better Than Ever* (*The Light Fantastic*); *Fearless Fagan*
1953 *Give a Girl a Break* (+ co-chor)
1954 *Seven Brides for Seven Brothers*; *Deep in My Heart* (+ co-chor)
1955 *It's Always Fair Weather* (co-d, co-chor)
1957 *Funny Face*; *The Pajama Game* (co-d, co-pr); *Kiss Them For Me*
1958 *Indiscreet* (+ pr); *Damn Yankees* (*What Lola Wants*) (co-d, co-pr)
1960 *Once More with Feeling* (+ pr); *Surprise Package* (+ pr); *The Grass Is Greener* (+ pr)
1963 *Charade* (+ pr)
1966 *Arabesque* (+ pr)
1967 *Two For the Road* (+ pr); *Bedazzled* (+ pr)
1969 *Staircase* (+ pr)
1974 *The Little Prince* (+ pr)
1975 *Lucky Lady* (+ pr)
1978 *Movie Movie* (+ pr)
1980 *Saturn 3* (+ pr)
1984 *Blame It On Rio*

Films as Choreographer or Co-Choreographer:

1943 *Best Foot Forward* (Buzzell)
1944 *Hey Rookie* (Barton); *Jam Session* (Barton); *Kansas City Kitty* (Lord); *Cover Girl* (Vidor)

Stanley Donen

1945 *Anchors Aweigh* (Sidney)
1946 *Holiday in Mexico* (Sidney); *No Leave, No Love* (Martin)
1947 *This Time for Keeps* (Thorpe); *Living in a Big Way* (La Cava); *Killer McCoy* (Rowland)
1948 *A Date with Judy* (Thorpe); *The Big City* (Taurog); *The Kissing Bandit* (Benedek)
1949 *Take Me Out to the Ball Game* (Berkeley) (+ co-sc)

Publications

By DONEN: articles—

"Giving Life an Up-Beat," in *Films and Filming* (London), July 1958.
"What to Do with Star Quality," in *Films and Filming* (London), August 1960.
Interview with Bertrand Tavernier and Gilbert Palas, in *Cahiers du Cinéma* (Paris), May 1963.
"Talking in the Sun," an interview with Colo and Bertrand Tavernier, in *Positif* (Paris), December 1969.
Interview with S. Harvey, in *Film Comment* (New York), July/August 1973.
Interview with Jim Hillier, in *Movie* (London), Spring 1977.

On DONEN: books—

Comden, Betty, and Adolph Green, *Singin' in the Rain* (script) New York, 1972.
Charness, Casey, *Hollywood Cine-Dance: A Description of the Interrelationship of Camerawork and Choreography in the Films of Stanley Donen and Gene Kelly,* Ann Arbor, Michigan, 1978.
Casper, Joseph Andrew, *Stanley Donen,* Metuchen, New Jersey, 1985.
Altman, Rick, *The American Film Musical,* Bloomington, Indiana, 1989.

On DONEN: articles—

Knight, Arthur, "From Dance to Film Director," in *Dance* (New York), August 1954.
Johnson, Albert, "The Tenth Muse in San Francisco," in *Sight and Sound* (London), Summer 1956.
Knight, Arthur, "Dance in the Movies," in *Dance* (New York), October 1958.
"Musical Comedy Issue" of *Cinéma* (Paris), August/September 1959.
McVay, Douglas, "Moanin' for Donen," in *New York Film Bulletin,* no.9, 1961.
Luft, Herbert, "Donen at Work," in *Films in Review* (New York), February 1961.
"Stanley Donen," in *Film Dope* (London), June 1977.
Telotte, J.P., "Ideology and the Kelly-Donen Musicals," in *Film Criticism* (Meadville, Pennsylvania), Spring 1984.
Sloman, Tony, "Feet First: Kelly and Donen," in *National Film Theater Booklet,* London, May 1990.

* * *

Stanley Donen is most frequently remembered for his work as a musical director/choreographer at MGM under the Arthur Freed Unit, a production team that Donen claims existed only in Arthur Freed's head (*Movie,* Spring 1977). With Gene Kelly, he co-directed three of the musical genre's best films: *On the Town, Singin' in the Rain,* and *It's Always Fair Weather.* Kelly was, in a sense, responsible for giving Donen his start in Hollywood; their first collaboration being the doppelganger dance in *Cover Girl.* Donen followed a path typical of that time, from Broadway dancer to Hollywood dancer and choreographer to director. As solo director, he won recognition for *Royal Wedding* (his first effort), *Seven Brides for Seven Brothers, Funny Face, The Pajama Game* and *Damn Yankees.*

Andrew Sarris believes that Donen always seems to function best as a hyphenated director or a genial catalyst; that any personal style he may possess is usually submerged under that of the performer (Kelly, Astaire, Fosse) or choreographer (Michael Kidd, Eugene Loring, Bob Fosse) and hence is difficult to assess. This view may simply reflect that period of studio production (mid 1940s to late 1950s), when there was a constant melding of creative personnel. As Jerome Delamater explains: "Performers, choreographers, and directors worked together and in many instances one cannot discern the auteur, as it were, or—more accurately—there seem to be several auteurs." Donen credits Astaire for his inspiration and it comes as no surprise that he feels his musical work is an extension of the Astaire/Rogers format (which itself is derived from the films of Clair and Lubitsch). This format is not logically grounded in reality, but functions more or less in the realm of pure emotion. Such a world of spontaneous singing and dancing can most accurately be presented in visual terms through forms of surrealism.

Donen's oeuvre demonstrates a reaction against the presentation of musical numbers on the stage, choreographing them instead on the streets of everyday life. It is this combination of a visual reality and a performing unreality (a performing reality is some type of stage that is clearly delineated from normal, day to day activity) that creates the tension inherent in surrealism. Donen geared the integrated musical towards the unreal; our functional perception of the real world does not include singing and dancing as a means of normal interpersonal communication. As he said in an interview with Jim Hillier, "A musical ... is anything but real."

Musicals possess their own peculiar internal reality, not directly connected to everyday life. Leo Braudy points out that Donen's musical films explore communities and the reaction/interaction of the people that dwell within. Even though Donen left the musical genre after *Damn Yankees* (returning to it in 1973), he continued to explore the situation of the individual in a social community, and the absurd, occasionally surrealistic experiences that we all face, in such deft comedies as *Bedazzled, Two for the Road,* and *Charade* (the last in homage to Hitchcock).

—Greg Faller

DONNER, Jörn

Nationality: Finnish. **Born:** Helsinki, Finland, 5 February 1933. **Education:** Educated in political science and Swedish literature at Helsinki University. **Family:** Married Inga-Britt Wik, 1954 (divorced); Jeanette Bonnier, 1974 (divorced); actress Harriet Andersson; five sons, one daughter. **Career:** Journalist, publisher and critic in Finland, 1950s; as conscientious objector spent eighteen months as hospital orderly in Pori, 1959-61; film critic for *Dagens Ntheter* newspaper, Stockholm, 1961; directed first feature, *En Söndag i September,* 1963; returned to Finland, acquired majority interest in FJ-Filmi, merging it with Jörn Donner Productions, 1967; curator, Swedish Film Institute, 1972-75, then executive producer, 1975-77, and president, from 1978; made *Yhdeksan Tapaa Lahesta Helsinkia (Nine Ways to Approach Helsinki)* for TV, 1982. **Address:** Jörn Donner Productions, Pohjoisranta 12, SF-00170 Helsinki, Finland.

Films as Director:

1954 *Aamua Kaupungissa* (*Morning in the City*) (+ sc, ed) (short)
1955 *Näinä Päivinä* (*In These Days*) (short) (+ sc, ed)
1956 *Porkala* (short) (+ sc, ed)
1957 *Vettä* (*Water*) (short) (+ sc, ed)
1962 *Vittnesbörd om Henne* (*Testimonies*) (short) (+ sc, ed)
1963 *En Söndag i September* (*A Sunday in September*) (+ sc)
1964 *Att Älska* (*To Love*) (+ sc)
1965 *Här Börjar Äventyret* (*Adventure Starts Here*) (+ sc)
1967 sequence in *Teenage Rebellion* (*Mondo Teeno*) (Herman) (+ sc); "Han-Hon" ("He-She"), episode no. 3 in *Stimulantia* (+ sc); *Tvärbalk* (*Rooftree*; *Crossbeam*) (+ sc, ed)
1968 *Mustaa Valkoisella* (*Black on White*) (+ exec pr, sc, ed, role as Juha Holm)
1969 *Sixty-nine* (+ exec pr, sc, role as Timo)
1970 *Naisenkuvia* (*Portraits of Women*) (+ exec pr, sc, ed, role as Pertti); *Anna* (+ exec pr, co-sc)
1971 *Perkele! Kuvia Suomesta* (*Fuck Off! Images of Finland*) (doc) (+ exec pr, sc)
1972 *Hellyys* (*Tenderness*) (+ exec pr, sc)
1973 *Baksmälla* (*Hangover*; *Sexier Than Sex*) (rev. version of *Tenderness*) (+ exec pr, sc)
1975 *The World of Ingmar Bergman* (doc) (+ exec pr, sc)
1978 *Manrape* (*Man Cannot Be Raped*) (+ exec pr, sc)
1982 *Nine Ways to Approach Helsinki*
1984 *Dirty Story*
1987 *Letters from Sweden*

Other Films:

1968 *Asfalttilampaat* (*The Asphalt Lambs*) (Niskanen) (role)
1972 *Marja pieni!* (*Poor Marja!*) (Bergholm) (pr)
1973 *Laukaus Tehtaalla* (*Shot in the Factory*) (Kivikoski) (pr); *Mommilan Veriteot 1917* (*The Mommilla Murders*) (Pennanen) (pr, ed)
1976 *Drömmen om Amerika* (*The American Dream*) (Abrahamsen) (exec pr); *Långt Borta och Nara* (*Near and Far Away*) (Ahrne) (pr)
1977 *Hemåt i Natten* (*Harri! Harri!*; *Homeward in the Night*; *Home and Refuge*) (Lindström) (pr); *Tabu* (*Taboo*) (Sjöman) (pr); *Elvis! Elvis!* (Pollak) (pr)
1978 *Bluff Stop* (exec pr)

Publications

By DONNER: books—

Filmipulmamme [Our Film Problem], with Martti Savo, Helsinki, 1953.
The Personal Vision of Ingmar Bergman, Bloomington, Indiana, 1966.
The Films of Ingmar Bergman, New York, 1972.
Huset dar jag bor: finis Finlandiae, Stockholm, 1992.

By DONNER: articles—

"After Three Films," in *Sight and Sound* (London), Autumn 1966.
"After Six Films," in *Sight and Sound* (London), Spring 1970.
"Filminstitutet som idébank," an interview with B. Heurling and L. Åhlander, in *Chaplin* (Stockholm), v.20, no.4, 1978.
"Donner on Swedish Cinema," in *Variety* (New York), 19 September 1979.
Donner, Jörn, "Dagbook fran Svenska Filmsinstitutet 1978-1982," in *Chaplin* (Stockholm), vol. 24, no. 1, 1982.
Interview in *Filmihullu*, no. 1, 1985.

On DONNER: book—

Eklund, Kaj Fredrik, *Bibliografi over mottagandet av Jorn Donners skonlitterara produktion i finalndsk och rikssvensk press 1951-1981*, Abo, Finland, 1983.

On DONNER: articles—

"Jörn Donner: An Outsider at Home," in *Films and Filming* (London), December 1968.
Reyner, L., "Jörn Donner," in *Film* (London), Spring 1969.
"Director of the Year," in *International Film Guide*, London, 1972.
"Jörn Donner," in *Film Dope* (London), June 1977.

* * *

If we look closely at the work of Jörn Donner as an artist, as an organization man, and as a social activist, it seems scarcely feasible that so many different things could be crammed into one human life. From even a limited list of his achievements the wide range of his interests and the great vitality of his personality become self-evident.

After studying political science and Swedish literature at the Helsinki University, Donner founded the journal *Arena*, devoted to literary and political matters, then worked as a reporter, undertaking a number of study trips to various countries, as well as being a literary and film critic. He has written over twenty books, including several novels as well as collections of comments, essays, studies, and short stories. In many of these he speaks about film work; indeed some of them are dedicated to filmmaking. Together with the films he has made (and the films made from his writing by other directors) he has been responsible for a unique body of outstanding and exuberant work linking two distinctive cultures—those of Finland and Sweden.

While he was in charge of Jörn Donner Productions as well as being chairman of the Filmi Oy (FJ), both companies made an extraordinary contribution to the development of Finnish film and opened the way for a whole generation of young filmmakers. Donner was also the director of the Swedish Film Institute for over seven years. All this might give the impression that administrative activities took precedence over his film directing, but this is not the case.

Jörn Donner stood at the cradle of the Swedish film movement in the 1960s when he made several important films notable for both their form and subject matter (*En Sönday i september* was his first feature film). He showed himself to be a creator of social dramas from contemporary life, giving his undivided attention to portraits of girls and women. As a rule, his films, whether in the form of serious drama or situational comedy, are intimate studies of relations between young people, of the magic of love and the clashes of social conventions. Another subject matter of his work is the liberation of women from marital and conventional ties (*Att Älska*).

Donner also often worked in his mother country, Finland, frequently returning to the same theme. "I am a writer," he says, "with very limited imagination. That's why I often go back to the past like a crab." *Tvaärbalk, Mustaa velkoisella*, and *Sixty-nine* are different versions of the same story and display what might be seen as satirical traits. "Satire takes on many forms. I do not know whether it is the right word to apply to the kind my films represent. Some people view them more as social criticism or irony."

Jörn Donner is a filmmaker who usually does not work from a cast-iron screenplay: it is more or less a sketch of situations without dialogue, and all the scenes are improvised. He tries to "mix fantasy with reality," and has also acted leading roles in his own films. Yet an important part of his film work is formed by documentaries, whether they analyze contemporary Finland or Sweden or offer a sensitive depiction of the film world, as in *Tre Scener med Ingmar Bergman*. While as a film director he sensitively analyzes and comments on

Jörn Donner

human relations in a developed society, we must not forget either his important work as a producer. In fact, when making a resume of all his work in the film business, it is clear that Jörn Donner is one of the outstanding personalities of Scandinavian cinema.

—Vaclåv Merhaut

DONSKOI, Mark

Nationality: Russian. **Born:** Mark Semyonovich Donskoi in Odessa, 6 March 1901. **Education:** Studied medicine and music, then law at University of Simferopol, to 1925; State Film School, under Eisenstein, 1926. **Military Service:** Served in Red Army during civil war, 1919-21. **Family:** Married scriptwriter Irina Sprink, 1936, two sons. **Career:** Worked in Ukrainian police force, early 1920s; after film school, joined Belgoskino studios, Leningrad, and directed first film, *Zhizn,* 1927; directed first sound film for Vostokkino, 1934; began at Soyuzdietfilm (Children's Film Studios), Moscow, 1940; worked at Kiev Studios, 1942-45; returned to Soyuzdietfilm (renamed Maxim Gorky Studios), 1946; assigned to Kiev Studios, 1949; returned to Gorky Studios, Moscow, late 1950s. **Awards:** Stalin Prize, 1941, 1946, 1948; Order of Lenin, 1944, 1971; Silver Seal, Locarno Festival, 1960; People's Artist of the Soviet Union, 1966; Hero of Socialist Labor, 1971. **Died:** 24 March 1981.

Films as Director:

1927 *Zhizn* (*Life*) (co-d, co-sc); *V bolshom gorode* (*In the Big City*) (co-d, co-sc)
1928 *Tsena cheloveka* (*The Price of Man*; *Man's Value*; *The Lesson*) (co-d)
1929 *Pizhon* (*The Fop*)
1930 *Chuzoi bereg* (*The Other Shore*); *Ogon* (*Fire*)
1934 *Pesnya o shchastye* (*Song about Happiness*) (co-d)
1938 *Detstvo Gorkovo* (*Childhood of Gorky*; *The Childhood of Maxim Gorki*) (+ co-sc)
1939 *Vlyudyakh* (*Among People*; *My Apprenticeship*; *Out in the World*) (+ co-sc)
1940 *Moi universiteti* (*My Universities*) (+ co-sc)
1941 *Romantiki* (*Children of the Soviet Arctic*) (+ co-sc)
1942 *Kak zakalyalas stal* (*How the Steel Was Tempered*; *Heroes Are Made*) (+ sc); "Mayak (Beacon, The Signal Tower)" (d only), "Kvartal (Block 14)" (+ spvr), "Sinie skali (Blue Crags)" (+ spvr) segments of *Boevi kinosbornik* (*Fighting Film Album*) no. 9
1944 *Raduga* (*The Rainbow*) (+ co-sc)
1945 *Nepokorenniye* (*Semya tarassa*; *Unvanquished*; *Unconquered*) (+ co-sc)
1947 *Selskaya uchitelnitsa* (*Varvara*; *An Emotional Education*; *Rural Institute*; *A Village School-teacher*)
1949 *Alitet ukhodit v gory* (*Zakoni Bolshoi zemli*; *Alitet Leaves for the Hills*) (+ co-sc) (film banned, partially destroyed)
1950 *Sportivnaya slava* (*Nachi chempiony*; *Sporting Fame*; *Our Champions*) (short)
1956 *Mat* (*Mother*) (+ co-sc)
1957 *Dorogoi tsenoi* (*At Great Cost*; *The Horse That Cried*)
1959 *Foma Gordeyev* (+ co-sc)
1962 *Zdravstvuitye deti* (*Hello Children*) (+ co-sc)
1966 *Serdtse materi* (*A Mother's Heart*)
1967 *Vernost materi* (*A Mother's Loyalty*)
1972 *Chaliapin*
1973 *Nadezhda*

Other Films:

1926 *Prostitutka* (*The Prostitute*) (Frelikh) (role as passerby)
1927 *Yevo prevosoditelstvo* (*His Excellency*) (Roshal) (ed)
1935 *Nevidimi chelovek* (*The Invisible Man*) (Whale) (spvr of dubbing and reediting)
1940 *Brat geroya* (*Brother of a Hero*) (Vasilchikov) (art d)

Publications

By DONSKOI: articles—

"Ceux qui savent parler aux dieux ...," in *Cinéma* (Paris), November 1959.
"Mon Idéal c'est un humanisme combattant," in *Les Lettres Françaises* (Paris), 19 December 1963.
Interview with Robert Grelier, in *Cinéma* (Paris), December 1967.
"My—propagandisty partii," in *Iskusstvo Kino* (Moscow), November 1972.
"Tret'e izmerenie," in *Iskusstvo Kino* (Moscow), December 1974.

On DONSKOI: books—

Leyda, Jay, *Kino: A History of the Russian and Soviet Film,* London, 1960.
Cervoni, Albert, *Marc Donskoi,* Paris, 1966.
Liehm, Mira and Antonin, *The Most Important Art: Eastern European Film After 1945,* Berkeley, California, 1977.

On DONSKOI: articles—

de la Roche, Catherine, "Mark Donskoi," in *Sequence* (London), Autumn 1948.
Fox, Charles, "The Gorki Trilogy—The Poetry of Cinema," in *Film* (London), February 1955.
Marcorelles, Louis, in *Cahiers du Cinéma* (Paris), no. 93, 1959.
Haudiquet, Philippe, "Mark Donskoi," in *Image et Son* (Paris), November 1964.
Gillett, John, "Mark Donskoi," in *Focus on Film* (London), March/April 1970.
"Director of the Year," in *International Film Guide,* London, 1971.
"Mark Donskoi," in *Film Dope* (London), June 1977.
Fadeeva, Y., "Mark Donskoi: Irrepressible Youth," in *Soviet Film* (Moscow), no. 3, 1979.
"Mark Donskoi," in *Avant-Scène du Cinéma* (Paris), 15 February 1979.
Zak, M., and others, "V kontekste istorii," in *Iskusstvo Kino* (Moscow), March 1981.
Cluny, C.M., "Hommage: Marc Donskoi," in *Cinéma* (Paris), May 1981.

* * *

Mark Donskoi may not be as familiar to western audiences as Eisenstein, Pudovkin, or Dovzhenko; his films are in no way as readily recalled as *Battleship Potemkin, Mother,* or *Earth.* Like other Soviet filmmakers, he propagandizes about the glories of the Bolshevik Revolution and highlights the life of Lenin. But Donskoi's great and unique contribution to Russian cinema is his adaption to the screen of Maxim Gorki's autobiographical trilogy: *The Childhood of Gorki, My Appren-*

ticeship, and *My Universities,* all based on the early life of the famed writer and shot during the late 1930s. (Years later, Donskoi adapted two other Gorki works, *Mother*—the same story filmed by Pudovkin in 1926—and *Foma Gordeyev.*)

In the trilogy, Donskoi chronicles the life of Gorki from childhood on, focusing on the experiences which alter his view of the world. At their best, these films are original and pleasing: the first presents a comprehensive and richly detailed view of rural life in Russia during the 1870s. While delineating the dreams of nineteenth-century Russian youth, Donskoi lovingly recreates the era. The characters are presented in terms of their conventional ambitions and relationships within the family structure. They are not revolutionaries, but rather farmers and other provincials with plump bodies and commonplace faces. The result is a very special sense of familiarity, of fidelity to a time and place. Of course, villains in Gorki's childhood are not innately evil, but products of a repressive czarist society. They are thus compassionately viewed. Donskoi pictures the Russian countryside with imagination, and sometimes even with grandeur.

Donskoi's later noteworthy works include *How the Steel Was Tempered,* one of the first Russian films to deal with World War II. While based on a Civil War story, the filmmaker includes only the sequences pertaining to Ukrainian resistance to German invaders in 1918, paralleling that situation to the Nazi invasion. The story also recalls the Gorki trilogy in its presentation of a boy who is changed by his encounter with life's challenges.

The Rainbow, an appropriately angry drama shot at the height of World War II, details the struggles of life in a German-occupied village. Donskoi's message in this film is that despite Nazi brutality, including the shooting of small boys, the spirit of the Soviet people will endure. This film is particularly inspirational; its approach may even have influenced Italian neorealism. *The Unvanquished,* about occupied Kiev, is a kind of sequel to *The Rainbow.* It graphically depicts the slaughter of Jews at Babi Yar.

The careers of few Russian filmmakers have outlasted that of Donskoi, who in his youth had fought in the Civil War and been imprisoned by the White Russians. His films span fifty years, though his Gorki trilogy alone would have assured him of a niche in cinema history.

—Rob Edelman

DOS SANTOS, Nelson Pereira *See* **PEREIRA DOS SANTOS, Nelson**

DOVZHENKO, Alexander

Nationality: Ukrainian. **Born:** Sosnytsia, Chernigov province of Ukraine, 12 September 1894. **Education:** Hlukhiv Teachers' Institute, 1911-14; Kiev University, 1917-18; Academy of Fine Arts, Kiev, 1919. **Military Service:** 1919-20. **Family:** Married 1) Barbara Krylova, 1920 (divorced 1926); 2) Julia Solntseva, 1927. **Career:** Teacher, 1914-19; chargé d'affaires, Ukrainian embassy, Warsaw, 1921; attached to Ukrainian embassy, Berlin; studied painting with Erich Heckel, 1922; returned to Kiev, expelled from Communist Party, became cartoonist, 1923; co-founder, VAPLITE (Free Academy of Proletarian Literature), 1925; joined Odessa Film Studios, directed first film, *Vasya-reformator,* 1926; moved to Kiev Film Studios, 1928; Solntseva began as his assistant, 1929; lectured at State Cinema Institute (VGIK), Moscow, 1932; assigned to Mosfilm by Stalin, 1933; artistic supervisor, Kiev Studio, 1940; front-line correspondent for *Red Army* and *Izvestia* in the Ukraine, 1942-43; denounced as "bourgeois nationalist," transferred to Mosfilm, 1944; theatre director, 1945-47; settled in Kakhiva, 1952. Julia Solntseva directed five films based on Dovzhenko's writings, 1958-69. **Awards:** Lenin Prize, 1935; Honored Art Worker of the Ukrainian SSR, 1939; 1st Degree Stalin Prize for *Shchors,* 1941; Order of the Red Flag, 1943; Order of the Red Labor Flag, 1955. **Died:** In Moscow, 26 November 1956.

Films as Director:

1926 *Vasya-reformator* (*Vasya the Reformer*) (co-d, sc); *Yahidka kokhannya* (*Love's Berry*; *Yagodko lyubvi*) (+ sc)
1927 *Teka dypkuryera* (*The Diplomatic Pouch*; *Sumka dipkuryera*) (+ revised sc, role)
1928 *Zvenyhora* (*Zvenigora*) (+ revised sc)
1929 ***Arsenal*** (+ sc)
1930 ***Zemlya*** (*Earth*) (+ sc)
1932 *Ivan* (+ sc)
1935 *Aerograd* (*Air City*; *Frontier*) (+ sc)
1939 *Shchors* (co-d, co-sc)
1940 *Osvobozhdenie* (*Liberation*) (co-d, ed, sc)
1945 *Pobeda na pravoberezhnoi Ukraine i izgnanie Nemetskikh zakhvatchikov za predeli Ukrainskikh Sovetskikh zemel* (*Victory in Right Bank Ukraine and the Expulsion of the Germans from the Boundaries of the Ukrainian Soviet Earth*) (co-d, commentary)
1948 *Michurin* (co-d, pr, sc)

Other Films:

1940 *Bukovyna-Zemlya Ukrayinska* (*Bucovina-Ukrainian Land*) (Solntseva) (artistic spvr)
1941 *Bohdan Khmelnytsky* (Savchenko) (artistic spvr)
1942 *Alexander Parkhomenko* (Lukov) (artistic spvr)
1943 *Bytva za nashu Radyansku Ukrayinu* (*The Battle for Our Soviet Ukraine*) (Solntseva and Avdiyenko) (artistic spvr, narration)
1946 *Strana rodnaya* (*Native Land*; *Our Country*) (co-ed uncredited, narration)

(films directed by Julia Solntseva, prepared or written by Dovzhenko or based on his writings):

1958 *Poema o more* (*Poem of an Inland Sea*)
1961 *Povest plamennykh let* (*Story of the Turbulent Years*; *The Flaming Years*; *Chronicle of Flaming Years*)
1965 *Zacharovannaya Desna* (*The Enchanted Desna*)
1968 *Nezabivaemoe* (*The Unforgettable*; *Ukraine in Flames*)
1969 *Zolotye vorota* (*The Golden Gates*)

Publications

By DOVZHENKO: books—

Izbrannoie, Moscow, 1957.
Tvori v triokh tomakh, Kiev, 1960.
Sobranie sotchinenyi (4 toma), izdatelstvo, Moscow, 1969.
Polum'iane zhyttia: spogadi pro Oleksandr a Dovzhenka, compiled by J. Solntseva, Kiev, 1973.

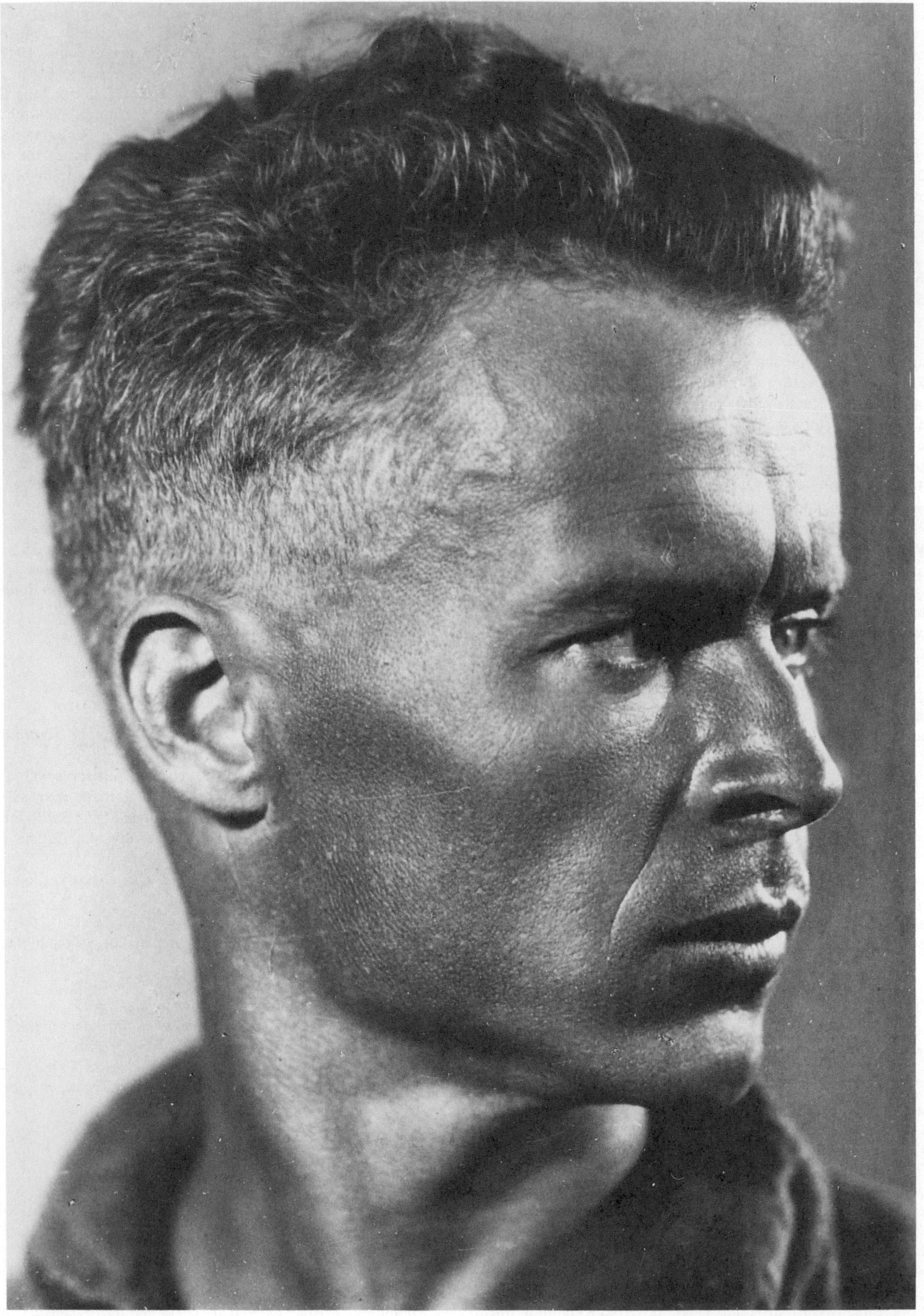

Alexander Dovzhenko

By DOVZHENKO: articles—

Interview with Georges Sadoul, in *Lettres Françaises* (Paris), 1956.
"Avtobiographia," in *Iskusstvo Kino* (Moscow), no. 5, 1958.
"Iz zapisnykh knijek," in *Iskusstvo Kino* (Moscow), nos. 1, 2, 4, 5, 1963.
Dovzhenko, Alexander, "Pis'ma raznyh let," in *Iskusstvo Kino* (Moscow), April 1984.
"Listy Aleksandra Dowzenki do zony," (Letters to Julia Solntseva 1942-52), in *Kino* (Warsaw), May 1985.

On DOVZHENKO: books—

Yourenev, R., *Alexander Dovzhenko,* Moscow, 1958.
Schnitzer, Luda, *Dovjenko,* Paris, 1966.
Mariamov, Alexandr, *Dovjenko,* Moscow, 1968.
Oms, Marcel, *Alexandre Dovjenko,* Lyons, 1968.
Amengual, Barthélemy, *Alexandre Dovjenko,* Paris, 1970.
Carynnyk, Marco, editor, *Alexander Dovzhenko: The Poet as Filmmaker,* Cambridge, Massachusetts, 1973.
Marshall, Herbert, *Masters of the Soviet Cinema: Crippled Creative Biographies,* London, 1983.
Kepley, Vance, *In the Service of the State: The Cinema of Alexander Dovzhenko,* Madison, Wisconsin, 1986.

On DOVZHENKO: articles—

"Dovzhenko at Sixty," in *Sight and Sound* (London), Autumn 1955.
Obituary in *New York Times,* 27 November 1956.
Montagu, Ivor, "Dovzhenko—Poet of Life Eternal," in *Sight and Sound* (London), Summer 1957.
"Dovzhenko Issue" of *Film* (Venice), August 1957.
Shibuk, Charles, "The Films of Alexander Dovzhenko," in *New York Film Bulletin,* nos. 11-14, 1961.
Robinson, David, "Dovzhenko," in *The Silent Picture* (London), Autumn 1970.
Carynnyk, Marco, "The Dovzhenko Papers," in *Film Comment* (New York), Fall 1971.
"Dovzhenko Issue" of *Iskusstvo Kino* (Moscow), September 1974.
Biofilmography in *Film Dope* (London), January 1978.
Trimbach, S., "Tvorchestvo A.P. Dovzhenko i narodnaia kul'tura," in *Iskusstvo Kino* (Moscow), no. 10, 1979.
Kepley, Vance, Jr., "Strike him in the eye: *Aerograd* and the Stalinist terror," in *Post Script* (Jacksonville, Florida), Winter 1983.
Bondarchuk, Sergei, "Alexander Dovzhenko," in *Soviet Film* (Moscow), January 1984.
"Dovzhenko Sections," of *Iskusstvo Kino* (Moscow), September and October 1984.
Bernard, J., "Odzak dia a mysleni Alexandra Petrovice Dovzenka," in *Film a Doba* (Prague), September and October 1984.
Pisarevsky, D., "Radiant talent," in *Soviet Film* (Moscow), September 1984.
Navailh, F., "Dovjenko: 'L'or pur et la verite'," in *Cinema* (Paris), January 1985.
Amiel, Vincent, "Hommage a Dovjenko," in *Positif* (Paris), September 1986.

On DOVZHENKO: film—

Hyrhorovych, Yevheniya (Evgeni Grigorovich), *Alexander Dovzhenko,* 1964.

* * *

Unlike many other Soviet filmmakers, whose works are boldly and aggressively didactic, Alexander Dovzhenko's cinematic output is personal and fervently private. His films are clearly political, yet at the same time he is the first Russian director whose art is so emotional, so vividly his own. His best films, *Arsenal, Earth,* and *Ivan,* are all no less than poetry on celluloid. Their emotional and poetic expression, almost melancholy simplicity, and celebration of life ultimately obliterate any external event in their scenarios. His images—most specifically, farmers, animals, and crops drenched in sunlight—are penetratingly, delicately real. With Eisenstein and Pudovkin, Dovzhenko is one of the great inventors and masters of the Russian cinema.

As evidenced by his very early credits, Dovzhenko might have become a journeyman director and scenarist, an adequate technician at best: *Vasya the Reformer,* his first script, is a forgettable comedy about an overly curious boy; *The Diplomatic Pouch* is a silly tale of secret agents and murder. But in *Zvenigora,* his fourth film, he includes scenes of life in rural Russia for the first time. This complex and confusing film proved to be the forerunner of *Arsenal, Earth,* and *Ivan,* a trio of classics released within four years of each other, all of which honor the lives and struggles of peasants.

In *Arsenal,* set in the Ukraine in a period between the final year of World War I and the repression of a workers' rebellion in Kiev, Dovzhenko does not bombard the viewer with harsh, unrealistically visionary images. Despite the subject matter, the film is as lyrical as it is piercing and pointed; the filmmaker manages to transcend the time and place of his story. While he was not the first Soviet director to unite pieces of film with unrelated content to communicate a feeling, his *Arsenal* is the first feature in which the totality of its content rises to the height of pure poetry. In fact, according to John Howard Lawson, "no film artist has ever surpassed Dovzhenko in establishing an intimate human connection between images that have no plot relationship."

The storyline of *Earth,* Dovzhenko's next—and greatest—film, is deceptively simple: a peasant leader is killed by a landowner after the farmers in a small Ukrainian village band together and obtain a tractor. But these events serve as the framework for what is a tremendously moving panorama of rustic life and the almost tranquil admission of life's greatest inevitability: death. Without doubt, *Earth* is one of the cinema's few authentic masterpieces.

Finally, *Ivan* is an abundantly eloquent examination of man's connection to nature. Also set in the Ukraine, the film chronicles the story of an illiterate peasant boy whose political consciousness is raised during the building of the Dnieper River dam. This is Dovzhenko's initial sound film: he effectively utilizes his soundtrack to help convey a fascinating combination of contrasting states of mind.

None of Dovzhenko's subsequent films approach the greatness of *Arsenal, Earth,* and *Ivan.* Stalin suggested that he direct *Shchors,* which he shot with his wife, Julia Solntseva. Filmed over a three-year period under the ever-watchful eye of Stalin and his deputies, the scenario details the revolutionary activity of a Ukrainian intellectual, Nikolai Shchors. The result, while unmistakably a Dovzhenko film, still suffers from rhetorical excess when compared to his earlier work.

Eventually, Dovzhenko headed the film studio at Kiev, wrote stories, and made documentaries. His final credit, *Michurin,* about the life of a famed horticulturist, was based on a play he wrote during World War II. After *Muchurin,* the filmmaker spent several years putting together a trilogy set in the Ukraine, chronicling the development of a village from 1930 on. He was sent to commence shooting when he died, and Solntseva completed the projects.

It is unfortunate that Dovzhenko never got to direct these last features. He was back on familiar ground: perhaps he might have been able to recapture the beauty and poetry of his earlier work. Still, *Arsenal, Ivan,* and especially *Earth* are more than ample accomplishments for any filmmaker's lifetime.

—Rob Edelman

DREYER, Carl Theodor

Nationality: Danish. **Born:** Copenhagen, 3 February 1889. **Family:** Married Ebba Larsen, 1911, two sons. **Career:** Journalist in Copenhagen, 1909-13; after writing scripts for Scandinavisk-Russiske Handelshus, joined Nordisk Films Kompagni, 1913; directed first film, *Praesidenten,* 1919; moved to Berlin, worked for Primusfilm, 1921; joined Ufa, 1924; returned to Copenhagen, 1925; hired by Société Generale de Films, Paris, 1926; left film industry, returned to journalism in Denmark, 1932; returned to filmmaking with documentary *Good Mothers,* 1942; awarded managership of a film theatre by Danish government, 1952; worked on film project on the life of Jesus, 1964-68. **Awards:** Golden Lion Award, Venice Festival, for *Ordet,* 1955. **Died:** In Copenhagen, 20 March 1968.

Films as Director:

1919 *Praesidenten* (*The President*) (+ sc, co-art d)
1920 *Prästänkan* (*The Parson's Widow*; *The Witch Woman*; *The Fourth Marriage of Dame Margaret*) (+ sc)
1921 *Blade af Satans Bog* (*Leaves from Satan's Book*) (+ co-sc, co-art d) (shot in 1919)
1922 *Die Gezeichneten* (*The Stigmatized One*; *Love One Another*) (+ sc); *Der Var Engang* (*Once Upon a Time*) (+ co-sc, ed)
1924 *Michael* (+ co-sc)
1925 *Du Skal Aere Din Hustru* (*Thou Shalt Honor Thy Wife*; *The Master of the House*) (+ co-sc, art d)
1926 *Glomdalsbruden* (*The Bride of Glomdal*) (+ sc, art d)
1928 ***La Passion de Jeanne d'Arc*** (+ co-sc)
1932 ***Vampyr*** (*The Dream of David Gray*) (+ co-sc, pr)
1942 *Mødrehjaelpen* (*Good Mothers*)
1943 ***Vredens Dag*** (*Day of Wrath*) (+ co-sc)
1945 *Två Manniskor* (*Two People*) (+ co-sc, ed)
1946 *Vandet Pa Låndet* (*Water from the Land*) (never finished) (+ sc)
1947 *Landsbykirken* (*The Danish Village Church*) (+ co-sc); *Kampen Mod Kraeften* (*The Struggle Against Cancer*) (+ co-sc)
1948 *De Naaede Faergen* (*They Caught the Ferry*) (+ sc)
1949 *Thorvaldsen* (+ co-sc)
1950 *Storstrømsbroen* (*The Bridge of Storstrøm*) (+ sc)
1954 *Et Slot I Et Slot* (*Castle within a Castle*) (+ sc)
1955 ***Ordet*** (*The Word*) (+ sc)
1964 ***Gertrud*** (+ sc)

Other Films:

1912 *Bryggerens Datter* (*The Brewer's Daughter*) (Ottesen) (co-sc)
1913 *Balloneksplosionen* (*The Balloon Explosion*) (sc); *Krigskorrespondenten* (*The War Correspondent*) (Glückstadt) (sc); *Hans og Grethe* (*Hans and Grethe*) (sc); *Elskovs Opfindsomhed* (*Inventive Love*) (Wolder) (sc); *Chatollets Hemmelighed, eller Det gamle chatol* (*The Secret of the Writing Desk*; *The Old Writing Desk*) (Davidsen) (sc)
1914 *Ned Med Vabnene* (*Lay Down Your Arms*) (Holger-Madsen) (sc)
1915 *Juvelerernes Skræk, eller Skelethaanden, eller Skelethaandens sidste bedrift* (*The Jeweller's Terror*; *The Skeleton's Hand*; *The Last Adventure of the Skeleton's Hand*) (Christian) (sc)
1916 *Penge* (*Money*) (Mantzius) (sc); *Den Hvide Djævel, eller Djævelens Protege* (*The White Devil*; *The Devil's Protegé*) (Holger-Madsen) (sc); *Den Skonne Evelyn* (*Evelyn the Beautiful*) (Sandberg) (sc); *Rovedderkoppen, eller Den røde Enke* (*The Robber Spider*; *The White Widow*) (Blom) (sc); *En Forbryders Liv og Levned, eller En Forbryders Memoirer* (*The Life and Times of a Criminal*; *The Memoirs of a Criminal*) (Christian) (sc); *Guldets Gift, eller Lerhjertet* (*The Poison of Gold*; *The Clay Heart*) (Holger-Madsen) (sc); *Pavillonens Hemmelighed* (*The Secret of the Pavilion*) (Mantzius) (sc)
1917 *Den Mystiske Selskabsdame, eller Legationens Gidsel* (*The Mysterious Lady's Companion*; *The Hostage of the Embassy*) (Blom) (sc); *Hans Rigtige Kone* (*His Real Wife*) (Holger-Madsen) (sc); *Fange Nr. 113* (*Prisoner No. 113*) (Holger-Madsen) (sc); *Hotel Paradis* (*Hotel Paradiso*) (Dinesen) (sc)
1918 *Lydia* (Holger-Madsen) (sc); *Glaedens Dag, eller Miskendt* (*Day of Joy*; *Neglected*) (Christian) (sc)
1919 *Gillekop* (Blom) (sc); *Grevindens Aere* (*The Countess' Honor*) (Blom) (sc)
1947 *De Gamle* (*The Seventh Age*) (sc)
1949 *Radioens Barndom* (ed)
1950 *Shakespeare og Kronborg* (*Hamlet's Castle*) (Roos) (sc)
1954 *Rønnes og Nexøs Genopbygning* (*The Rebuilding of Ronne and Nexø*) (sc)

Publications

By DREYER: books—

Om filmen, Copenhagen, 1959.
Five Film af Carl Th. Dreyer, edited by Ole Storm, Copenhagen, 1964.
Jesus fra Nazaret. Et filmmanuskript, Copenhagen, 1968; as *Jesus,* New York, 1972.
Four Screenplays, New York, 1970.
Oeuvres cinématographiques 1926-1934, edited by Maurice Drouzy and Charles Tesson, Paris, 1983.

By DREYER: articles—

"Lunch with Carl Dreyer," with Ragna Jackson, in *Penguin Film Review* (London), August 1947.
Interview with John Winge, in *Sight and Sound* (London), January 1950.
"Visit with Carl Th. Dreyer," with James Card, in *Image* (Rochester, New York), December 1953.
"Rencontre avec Carl Dreyer," with Lotte Eisner, in *Cahiers du Cinéma* (Paris), June 1955.
"Thoughts on My Craft," in *Sight and Sound* (London), no. 3, 1955/56.
Interview with Herbert Luft, in *Films and Filming* (London), no. 9, 1961.
"Dreyer Mosaik," in *Kosmorama* (Copenhagen), December 1963.
"Carl Dreyer nous dit: 'Le principal intérêt d'un homme: les autres hommes,'" an interview with Georges Sadoul, in *Lettres Françaises* (Paris), 24 December 1964.
Interview with Michel Delahaye, in *Cahiers du Cinéma* (Paris), no. 170, 1965.
Interview with Børge Trolle, in *Film Culture* (New York), Summer 1966.
"My Way of Working is in Relation to the Future: A Conversation with Carl Dreyer," with Carl Lerner, in *Film Comment* (New York), Fall 1966.
"Carl Dreyer: Utter Bore or Total Genius?" with Denis Duperley, in *Films and Filming* (London), February 1968.
Interview with Michel Delahaye, in *Interview with Film Directors,* edited by Andrew Sarris, New York, 1969.
"Metaphysic of Ordet," in *The Film Culture Reader,* edited by P. Adams Sitney, New York, 1970.

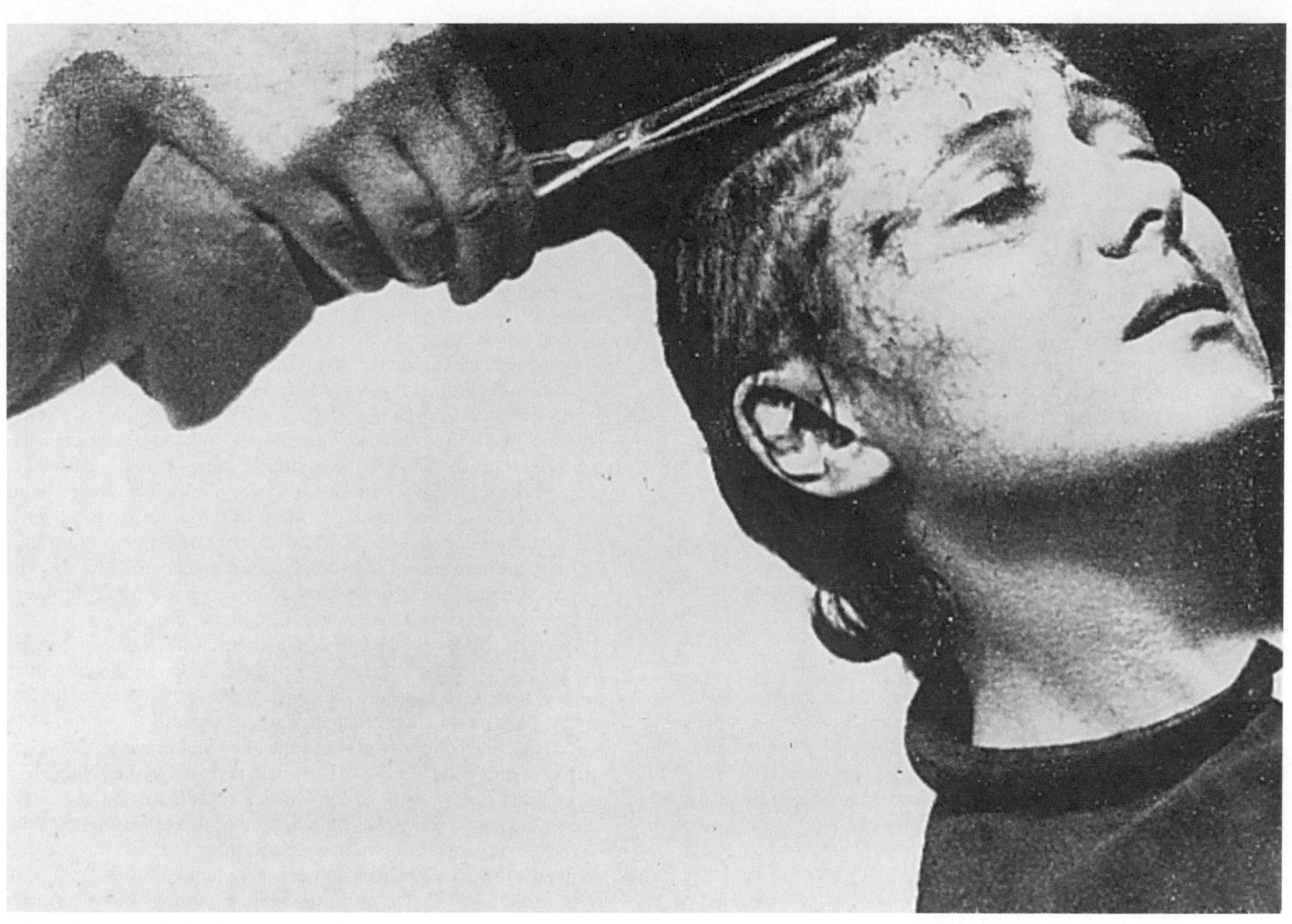

Carl Theodor Dreyer: Maria Falconetti in *La Passion de Jeanne d'Arc*

On DREYER: books—

Neergaard, Ebbe, *Carl Theodor Dreyer: A Film Director's Work,* London, 1950.
Trolle, Børge, *The Art of Carl Dreyer: An Analysis,* Copenhagen, 1955.
Sémolué, Jean, *Dreyer,* Paris, 1962.
Bowser, Eileen, *The Films of Carl Dreyer,* New York, 1964.
Monty, Ib, *Portrait of Carl Th. Dreyer,* Copenhagen, 1965.
Dyssegaard, Soren, editor, *Carl Th. Dreyer, Danish Film Director,* Copenhagen, 1968.
Milne, Tom, *The Cinema of Carl Dreyer,* New York, 1971.
Ernst, Helge, *Dreyer: Carl Th. Dreyer—en dansk filmskaber,* Copenhagen, 1972.
Schrader, Paul, *Transcendental Style in Film: Ozu, Bresson, Dreyer,* Los Angeles, 1972.
Bordwell, David, *Dreyer,* London, 1973.
Skoller, Donald, editor, *Dreyer in Double Reflection,* New York, 1973.
Nash, Mark, editor, *Dreyer,* London, 1977.
Bordwell, David, *The Films of Carl-Theodor Dreyer,* Berkeley, California, 1981.
Drouzy, M., *Carl Th. Dreyer, né Nilsson,* Paris, 1982.
Carney, Raymond, *Speaking the Language of Desire: The Films of Carl Dreyer,* Cambridge, 1989.

On DREYER: articles—

"Dreyer Issue" of *Ecran Français* (Paris), 11 November 1947.
Rowland, Richard, "Carl Dreyer's World," in *Hollywood Quarterly,* no. 1, 1950.
Duca, Lo, "Trilogie mystique de Dreyer," in *Cahiers du Cinéma* (Paris), February 1952.
Rehben, Ernst, "Carl Dreyer, poète tragique du cinéma," in *Positif* (Paris), no. 8, 1953.
Trolle, Börge, "The World of Carl Dreyer," in *Sight and Sound* (London), Winter 1955/56.
Luft, Herbert, "Carl Dreyer—A Master of His Craft," in *Quarterly of Film, Radio and Television* (Berkeley), no. 2, 1956.
Eisner, Lotte, "Réalisme et irréel chez Dreyer," in *Cahiers du Cinéma* (Paris), December 1956.
Luft, Herbert, "Dreyer," in *Films and Filming* (London), June 1961.
Cowie, Peter, "Dreyer at Seventy-Five," in *Films and Filming* (London), no. 6, 1964.
Kelman, Ken, "Dreyer," in *Film Culture* (New York), no. 35, 1964/65.
Milne, Tom, "Darkness and Light," in *Sight and Sound* (London), no. 4, 1965.
Téchiné, André, "L'Archaisme nordique de Dreyer," in *Cahiers du Cinéma* (Paris), no. 170, 1965.
Bond, Kirk, "The World of Carl Dreyer," in *Film Quarterly* (Berkeley), Fall 1965.
"Dreyer Issue" of *Kosmorama* (Copenhagen), June 1968.
"Dreyer Issue" of *Cahiers du Cinéma* (Paris), December 1968.
Amette, Jacques-Pierre, "Carl Th. Dreyer," in *Dossiers du cinéma: Cinéastes I,* Paris, 1971.

Bordwell, David, "Passion, Death and Testament: Carl Dreyer's Jesus Film," in *Film Comment* (New York), Summer 1972.
Wood, Robin, "Carl Dreyer," in *Film Comment* (New York), March/April 1974.
Vaughan, Dai, "Carl Dreyer and the Theme of Choice," in *Sight and Sound* (London), Summer 1974.
Petric, Vlada, "Dreyer's Concept of Abstraction," in *Sight and Sound* (London), Spring 1975.
De Benedictus, M., "Dreyer: La regola del pendolo," in *Bianco e Nero* (Rome), January-February 1979.
Schepelern, P., in *Kosmorama* (Copenhagen), December 1982.
Devilliers, M., "Dreyer, la chair et l'ombre," in *Cinématographe* (Paris), November 1983.
Lardeau, Yves, and C. Tesson, "Dreyer en images," in *Cahiers du Cinéma* (Paris), December 1983.
"*Gertrud* Issue" of *Avant-Scène du Cinéma* (Paris), December 1984.
"*La Passion de Jeanne d'Arc* Section," of *Skrien* (Amsterdam), November-December 1985.
Rosenbaum, Jonathan, "*Gertrud*: The Desire for the image," in *Sight and Sound* (London), Winter 1985-86.
"*Passion de Jeanne d'Arc* Issue," of *Avant-Scène du Cinéma* (Paris), January-February 1988.
Milne, Tom, "Carl Dreyer," in *Radio Times* (London), 25 February 1989.

* * *

Carl Theodor Dreyer is the greatest filmmaker in the Danish cinema, where he was always a solitary personality. But he is also among the few international directors who turned films into an art and made them a new means of expression for the artistic genius. Of Dreyer's feature films, seven were produced in Denmark, three in Germany, two in France, two in Sweden, and one in Norway.

If one tries to understand the special nature of Dreyer's art, one can delve into his early life to find the roots of his never failing contempt for pretentions and his hatred of bourgeois respectability, as well as his preoccupation with suffering and martyrdom. In his biography of Dreyer, M. Drouzy revealed the fate of Dreyer's biological mother, who died in the most cruel way following an attempted abortion. Dreyer, who was adopted by a Copenhagen family, learned about the circumstances of her death when he was eighteen years old, and Drouzy's psychoanalytical study finds the victimized woman in all of Dreyer's films. But of what value is the biographical approach to the understanding of a great artist? The work of an artist need not be the illumination of his private life. This may afford some explanation when we are inquiring into the fundamental point of departure for an artist, but Dreyer's personality is expressed very clearly and graphically in his films. We can therefore well admire the consistency which has always characterized his outlook on life.

Like many great artists, Dreyer is characterized by the relatively few themes that he constantly played upon. One of the keynotes in Dreyer's work is suffering, and his world is filled with martyrs. Yet suffering and martyrdom are surely not the fundamentals. They are merely manifestations, the results of something else. Suffering and martyrdom are the consequences of wickedness, and it is malice and its influence upon people that his films are concerned about. As early in his career as the 1921 film, *Leaves From Satan's Book,* Dreyer tackled this theme of the power of evil over the human mind. He returned to examine this theme again and again.

If the popular verdict is that Dreyer's films are heavy and gloomy, naturally the idea is suggested by the subjects which he handled. Dreyer never tried to make us believe that life is a bed of roses. There is much suffering, wickedness, death, and torment in his films, but they often conclude in an optimistic conviction in the victory of spirit over matter. With death comes deliverance. It is beyond the reach of malice.

In his delineation of suffering man, devoid of any hope before the arrival of death, Dreyer was never philosophically abstract. Though his films were often enacted on a supersensible plane, and are concerned with religious problems, his method as an artist was one of psychological realism, and his object was always the individual. Dreyer's masterly depiction of milieu has always been greatly admired; his keen perception of the characteristic detail is simply dazzling. But this authenticity in settings has never been a means towards a meticulous naturalism. He always sought to transcend naturalism so as to reach a kind of purified, or classically simplified, realism.

Though Dreyer occupied himself with the processes of the soul, he always preserved an impartiality when portraying them. One might say that he maintained a high degree of objectivity in his description of the subjective. This can be sensed in his films as a kind of presentation rather than forceful advocacy. Dreyer himself, when describing his method in *La Passion de Jeanne d'Arc,* once employed the expression "realized mysticism." The phrase indicates quite precisely his endeavours to render understandable things that are difficult to comprehend, to make the irrational appear intelligible. The meaning behind life lies in just this recognition of the necessity to suffer in order to arrive at deliverance. The characters nearly always suffered defeat in the outward world because Dreyer considered defeat or victory in the human world to be of no significance. For him the triumph of the soul over life was what was most important.

There are those who wish to demonstrate a line of development in Dreyer's production, but there is no development in the customary sense. Dreyer's world seemed established at an early period of his life, and his films merely changed in their way of viewing the world. There was a complete congruity between his ideas and his style, and it was typical of him to have said: "The soul is revealed in the style, which is the artist's expression of the way he regards his material." For Dreyer the image was always the important thing, so important that there is some justification in describing him as first and foremost the great artist of the silent film. On the other hand, his last great films were concerned with the effort to create a harmony between image and sound, and to that end he was constantly experimenting.

Dreyer's pictorial style has been characterized by his extensive and careful employment of the close-up. His films are filled with faces. In this way he was able to let his characters unfold themselves, for he was chiefly interested in the expressions that appear as the result of spiritual conflicts. Emphasis has often been given to the slow lingering rhythm in Dreyer's films. It is obvious that this dilatoriness springs from the wish to endow the action with a stamp of monumentality, though it could lead dangerously close to empty solemnity, to the formalistic.

Dreyer quickly realized the inadequacy of the montage technique, which had been regarded as the foundation of film for so many years. His films became more and more based on long uncut sequences. By the end of his career his calm, elaborating style was quite in conformity with the newer trends in the cinema.

—Ib Monty

DUIGAN, John

Nationality: Australian. **Born:** Hartney Witney, Hampshire, England, 19 June 1949. **Education:** Attended the University of Melbourne, where he studied philosophy. **Career:** Joined the Pram Factory, an innovative Melbourne drama company, late 1960s; acted in numerous short films, early 1970s; directed first film, *The Firm Man,* a nine-minute short funded by the Film and Television Board of the Australian Council for the Arts, 1974; directed first feature, *The Trespassers,* 1976; left Australia and settled in London, 1990. **Awards:** Australian Film Institute Jury Prize, 1978, for *Mouth to Mouth;* Best Screenplay, Australian Writers Guild, 1981, for *Winter of Our Dreams;* Best Director, Screenplay, and Film, Australian Film Institute Awards, and Jury Prize, Rio de Janeiro Festival, 1987, for *The Year My Voice Broke;* U.S. Humanities Prize and Best Film on a Latin American Subject, Havana Festival, 1989, for *Romero;* Best Film, Australian Film Institute Awards, 1990, for *Flirting.* **Address:** ICM, 8899 Beverly Boulevard, Los Angeles, CA 90048.

Films as Director/Screenwriter:

1974 *The Firm Man* (short) (+ pr)
1976 *The Trespassers* (+ pr)
1978 *Mouth to Mouth* (+ co-pr)
1979 *Dimboola* (d only)
1981 *The Winter of Our Dreams*
1982 *Far East*
1984 *One Night Stand*
1985 *Stop Watch* (for TV)
1987 *The Year My Voice Broke*; *Vietnam* (co-dir only) (TV miniseries); *Room to Move* (for TV)
1989 *Romero* (d only)
1990 *Flirting*
1993 *The Wide Sargasso Sea*; *Sirens* (+ role as Earnest Minister)
1995 *The Journey of August King* (d only)

Publications

By DUIGAN: books—

Badge, South Melbourne, 1975.

By DUIGAN: articles—

"John Duigan on *Mouth to Mouth,*" interview with S. Murray in *Cinema Papers* (Abbotsford, Australia), April/June 1978.
"John Duigan and *Winter of our Dreams,*" interview with S. Murray in *Cinema Papers* (Abbotsford, Australia), July/August 1981.
Interview with S. Murray in *Cinema Papers* (Abbotsford, Australia), November 1989.

On DUIGAN: articles—

"The Trespassers," photo essay in *Cinema Papers* (Abbotsford, Australia), March/April 1976.
"Yokels Curious, Not Too Resentful as to *Dimboola,*" in *Variety* (New York), 9 May 1979.
Chase, Chris, "At the Movies: Why Python Star Turned *Missionary,*" in *New York Times,* 12 November 1982.

John Duigan: Noah Taylor in *The Year My Voice Broke*

Nash, E., "*Winter's* Duigan: Audiences React," in *Film Journal* (New York), 3 December 1982.
Thompson, C., "John Duigan's Moral Tales," in *Cinema Papers* (Abbotsford, Australia), January 1988.
Van Gelder, L., "At the Movies," in *New York Times,* 2 September 1988.
Rohter, L., "*Romero* Finds a Producer: The Church," in *New York Times,* 13 November 1988.
"First Paulist Film, $4-mil *Romero,* Getting Platform Domestic Release," in *Variety* (New York), 16 August 1989.
Goldman, A. L., "A Catholic Film on a Salvadorian Murder," in *New York Times,* 24 August 1989.
Kelleher, E., "A Priest Turns Movie Producer to Salute Courageous *Romero,*" in *Film Journal* (New York), October 1989.
Malone, P., "*Romero* and Father Kieser," in *Cinema Papers* (Abbotsford, Australia), November 1989.
Tanner, Louise, "Who's in Town," in *Films in Review* (New York), November 1989.
Porter, B., "Dugian's *Flirting* with Goldwyn as Coming of Age Tale Debuts," in *Film Journal* (New York), October/November 1992.
Kythreotis, A., "Coming of Age (with Difficulty) in Australia," in *New York Times,* 8 November 1992.

* * *

John Duigan is one of the generation of Australian filmmakers who, in the 1970s and early 1980s, found themselves at the vanguard of a national cinema renaissance. At the beginning of the 1970s, the Australian Film Commission was established and the government began subsidizing the production of motion pictures. A group of young and talented directors emerged, including Bruce Beresford, Peter Weir, Gillian Armstrong, Fred Schepisi, Philip Noyce, and Duigan. With the exception of Duigan, all of these filmmakers eventually went to Hollywood, where they have made films which have not automatically been relegated to the art house ghetto and worked with stars whose reputations are international rather than local.

Duigan, however, chose to remain in Australia, living there until 1990, when he settled in England. Only two of his films have been American: *Romero,* a biography of El Salvador's martyred Bishop Oscar Romero, a specialty film in that it was financed not by a Hollywood source but by the United States Roman Catholic Church; and *The Journey of August King,* the story of a widowed farmer who helps a young runaway slave escape to freedom in 1815 North Carolina. Tellingly, these films are only directed by Duigan; he scripted most of his Australian films.

Duigan's best films have been realistic coming-of-age stories of sexual and romantic initiation, featuring characters who struggle to transcend their strict religious or provincial upbringings. From a psychological point of view, he elicits the feelings of outsiders who are sensitive in character and isolated from the mainstream. His first films are a solid foundation for his later work. *The Trespassers,* a drama of a three-cornered relationship between a young journalist and two women, mirrors changing sexual attitudes and a feminist consciousness that were byproducts of the youth culture of the late 1960s and early 1970s. *Mouth to Mouth* charts the relationships between two female miscreants and their troubled male counterparts. *Winter of Our Dreams,* the most visible of Duigan's early films, features Judy Davis as a lonely prostitute who becomes romantically involved with a married man.

The Year My Voice Broke, the film which solidified Duigan's international reputation, is the sensitive, well-handled account of Danny Embling, a young, awkward, small-town teen who is growing up in the 1960s. He develops a crush on his nubile, longtime friend, with resulting complications. *Flirting,* a follow-up to *The Year My Voice Broke,* has Danny away at a boys' boarding school. He does not fit into his regimented, inflexible environment, and he finds himself attracted to a sophisticated black African student at a nearby girls' school, who because of her race is considered an outsider. Unlike most films about teens, *The Year My Voice Broke* and *Flirting* are intelligent reflections of blossoming youth which hold interest for adults as well.

Not all of Duigan's main characters have been adolescents. Yet even those who are past their teens grapple with problems and conflicts related to sexuality and intimacy. *Sirens,* dramatically inferior to *The Year My Voice Broke* and *Flirting,* spotlights the erotic awakening of a minister's wife when she finds herself in the company of progressive artist Norman Lindsay and his frequently nude models.

And Duigan's characters do not all successfully transcend their hang-ups. Such is the case in his most ambitious film to date, *The Wide Sargasso Sea,* based on Jean Rhys's 1966 novel, which is a prequel to *Jane Eyre.* Set in the West Indies during the 1830s, it tells of the relationship between Edward Rochester and his first wife, Antoinette Cosway, a young Creole heiress with whom he enters into an arranged marriage. Antoinette in particular is another of Duigan's youthful outsiders. As a Creole, she is estranged from blacks and whites; she is hated and condescended to by blacks, and called "white nigger" by whites. Antoinette and Rochester (a proper upper-class Englishman and "damn fine gentleman") are unable to transcend their society's restrictions, or their own inner demons and inadequacies. The scenario charts the complexities of their evolving affiliation, and the pencil-thin line between their love and hate for each other. In *Flirting,* racial differences are no barrier to Duigan's protagonists. In *The Wide Sargasso Sea,* he tells an entirely different story. At one point, Rochester observes, "No matter how close we are in the dark, she is still a stranger to me, a stranger who does not think or feel as I do. I am hungry for her, but I don't understand her." And Antoinette reflects her status when she notes, "I'm not used to happiness. It makes me afraid."

Explicit depictions of sexual passion also are prominently featured in Duigan's films; *The Wide Sargasso Sea* was rated NC-17 in its theatrical release. Even when his work is dramatically flawed and obvious, as is the case with *Sirens,* the eroticism he elicits remains undeniably potent—and, in its effect, liberating.

—Rob Edelman

DULAC, Germaine

Nationality: French. **Born:** Charlotte Elisabeth Germaine Saisset-Schneider in Amiens, 17 November 1882. **Family:** Married Marie-Louis Albert Dulac, 1905 (divorced 1920). **Career:** Writer and editor for feminist journal *La Francaise,* 1909-13; offered position as camerawoman on *Caligula* by actress friend Stacia de Napierkowska, 1914; formed production company with husband and scenarist Irène Hillel-Erlanger; directed first film, *Les Soeurs enemies,* 1915; travelled to United States to observe production techniques, 1921; general secretary of Ciné-Club de France, from 1922; directed newsreels for Gaumont, 1930s. **Died:** In Paris, July 1942.

Films as Director:

1915 *Les Soeurs enemies*
1916 *Geo le mysterieux*; *Venus Victrix*; *Dans l'ouragan de la vie*
1917 *Ames de fous* (+ sc)

1918 *Le Bonheur des autres*
1919 *La Fête espagnole*; *La Cigarette* (+ co-sc)
1920 *Malencontre*; *La Belle Dame sans merci*
1921 *La Mort du soleil*
1922 *Werther* (incomplete)
1923 *La Souriante Madame Beudet* (*The Smiling Madame Beudet*); *Gossette*
1924 *Le Diable dans la ville*
1925 *Ame d'artiste* (+ co-sc); *La Folie des vaillants*
1926 *Antoinette Sabrier*
1927 ***La Coquille et le clergyman*** (*The Seashell and the Clergyman*); *L'Invitation au voyage*; *Le Cinéma au service de l'histoire*
1928 *La Princesse Mandane*; *Disque 927*; *Thèmes et variations*; *Germination d'un haricot*
1929 *Etude cinégraphique sur une arabesque*

Other Films:

1928 *Mon Paris* (Guyot) (supervision)
1932 *Le Picador* (Jacquelux) (supervision)

Publications

By DULAC: articles—

"Un Article? Mais que faut-il prouver?" in *Le Film* (Paris), 16 October 1919.
"Aux amis du cinéma," address in *Cinémagazine* (Paris), 19 December 1924.
"L'Art des nuances spirituelles," in *Cinéa-Ciné pour tous* (Paris), January 1925.
"Du sentiment à la ligne," in *Schémas,* no. 1, 1927.
"Les Esthètiques, les entraves, la cinégraphie intégrale," in *L'Art cinématographique,* Paris, 1927.
"Sur le cinéma visuel," in *Le Rouge et le noir* (Paris), July 1928.
"Jouer avec les bruits," in *Cinéa-Ciné pour tous* (Paris), 15 August 1929.
"Das Wesen des Films: Die visuelle idee," and "Das Kino der Avantgarde," in *Frauen und Film* (Berlin), October 1984.

On DULAC: book—

Heck-Rabi, Louise, *Women Filmmakers: A Critical Reception,* Metuchen, New Jersey, 1984.

On DULAC: articles—

Ford, Charles, biography in *Anthologie du cinéma* (Paris), no. 31, January 1968.
Cornwell, Regina, "Maya Deren and Germaine Dulac: Activists of the Avant-Garde," in *Film Library Quarterly* (New York), Winter 1971/72.
Van Wert, W., "Germaine Dulac: First Feminist Filmmaker," in *Women and Film* (Santa Monica, California), vol. 1, nos. 5-6, 1974.
Dozoretz, Wendy, "Dulac versus Artaud," in *Wide Angle* (Athens, Ohio), vol. 3, no. 1, 1979.
Dozoretz, Wendy, and Sandy Flitterman, in *Wide Angle* (Athens, Ohio), vol. 5, no. 3, 1983.
Flitterman, Sandy, "Theorizing the Feminine: Women as the Figure of Desire in *The Seashell and the Clergyman,*" in *Wide Angle* (Athens, Ohio), vol. 6., no. 3, 1984.
Serra, R., "La prima scrittura femminile del cinema," in *Cinema Nuovo* (Bari), August-October 1984.
Tol, I., "Films van Germaine Dulac," in *Skrien* (Amsterdam), Winter 1985-86.

* * *

Before becoming a film director, Germaine Dulac had studied music, was interested in photography, and had written for two feminist journals—all of which played a role in her development as a filmmaker. There were three phases to her filmmaking career: in commercial production, in the avant-garde, and in newsreels. In addition, filmmaking was only one phase of her film career; she also was prominent as a theorist and promoter of the avant-garde film, and as an organizer of the French film unions and the ciné-club movement. The French historian Charles Ford wrote in *Femmes Cinéastes* that Dulac was the "heart" of the avant-garde in France, that without her there would have been no avant-garde. Her role in French film history has been compared to that of Maya Deren in the United States three decades later.

Dulac learned the rudiments of filmmaking by assisting a friend who was making a film in 1914. The following year she made her first film, *Les Soeurs enemies,* which was distributed by Pathé. It was the ideal time for a woman to enter commercial production, since many men had been called into the army. After directing several other conventional story films, Dulac became more and more drawn to the avant-garde cinema, which she defined in 1927 as "lines, surfaces, volumes, evolving directly without contrivance, in the logic of their forms, stripped of representational meaning, the better to aspire to abstraction and give more space to feelings and dreams—INTEGRAL CINEMA."

It is generally reported that Dulac was introduced to the French film avant-garde movement through her friendship with Louis Delluc; but Ester Carla de Miro claims that it was in fact through Dulac that he became involved in film. Delluc wrote that Dulac's first film was worth "more than a dozen of each of her colleagues.... But the cinema is full of people ... who cannot forgive her for being an educated woman ... or for being a woman at all."

Dulac's best known and most impressive film (of the few that have been seen outside France) is *The Smiling Madame Beudet,* based on a play by Andre Obey. It depicts the life and dreams of a small-town housewife married to a coarse, if not repulsive, businessman. The film created a sensation in its day. Dulac succeeded with what was, at the time, signal originality in expressing by pictorial means the atmosphere and implications of this study of domestic conflict.

Showings of *The Seashell and the Clergyman,* based on an original screenplay by Antonin Artaud, have generally been accompanied by program notes indicating Artaud's outrage at Dulac's "feminized" direction. Yet as P. Adams Sitney points out in his introduction to *The Avant-Garde Film,* Artaud praised the actors and thanked Dulac for her interest in his script in an essay entitled "Cinema et l'abstraction." (Wendy Dozoretz has pointed out that the protest aimed against Dulac at the film's Paris opening in 1928 was based on a misunderstanding; at least one protester, Georges Sadoul, later said he had thought he was protesting against Artaud.)

At the other end of the cinema spectrum, Dulac began to use time-lapse cinematography to reveal the magical effects of tiny plants emerging from the soil with leaf after leaf unfolding and stretching to the sun. "Here comes Germaine Dulac and her lima bean," became a popular joke among film-club devotees, a joke that did not exclude admiration.

The last decade of Dulac's life was spent directing newsreels for Gaumont. She died in 1942, during the German occupation. Charles Ford, who has collected her articles, indicates that she expressed ideas in "clear and accessible language" which others often set forth "in hermetic formulas." One American writer, Stuart Liebman, sums up the opposing view: "Despite their undeniable importance for the film

Germaine Dulac

culture of the 1920s, the backward-looking character of Dulac's film theory, constituted by her nostalgia for the aesthetic discourse of the past, both defines and delimits our interest in her theoretical contributions today." The final assessment of Germaine Dulac's life and work as filmmaker and theorist may depend on the arrival of a well-documented biography, and greater access to all her writings (some short pieces are now available in English translations) and all her existing films.

—Cecile Starr

DUPONT, E.A.

Nationality: German. **Born:** Ewald André Dupont in Seitz, Saxony, 25 December 1891. **Education:** University of Berlin. **Career:** Film critic for *BZ am Mittag,* Berlin, from 1911; story editor for Richard Oswald, 1916; directed first feature, *Das Geheimnis des Amerika-Docks,* 1917; director in Hollywood, 1926; signed for British-International Pictures, London, 1928; returned to Berlin, 1931; director for Universal, Hollywood, 1933-36; signed to Paramount, 1936-37; signed for Warner Brothers, 1938; dismissed from *Hell's Kitchen,* began editing *Hollywood Tribune,* 1939; formed talent agency, 1941; returned to directing, 1951. **Died:** Of cancer in Los Angeles, 12 December 1956.

Films as Director:

1917 *Das Geheimnis des Amerika-Docks* (*The Secret of the America Dock*) (+ sc)
1918 *Es Werde Licht* (*Let There Be Light*) part 2 (co-d, co-sc); *Europa-Postlagernd* (*Post Office Europe*) (+ sc); *Mitternacht* (+ sc); *Der Schatten* (*Der lebender Schatten*) (+ sc); *Der Teufel* (+ sc); *Die Japanerin* (+ sc)
1919 *Grand Hotel Babylon* (+ sc); *Die Apachen* (*Paris Underworld*) (+ sc); *Das Derby* (+ sc); *Die Würger der Welt* (+ sc); *Die Maske* (+ sc); *Die Spione* (+ sc)
1920 *Der Mord ohne Täter* (*Murder Without Cause*) (+ co-sc); *Die weisse Pfau* (*The White Peacock*) (+ co-sc); *Herztrumpt* (+ sc); *Whitechapel* (+ sc)
1921 *Der Geier-Wally* (*Ein Roman aus den Bergen*; *Geierwally*; *The Woman Who Killed a Vulture*) (+ sc)
1922 *Kinder der Finsternis* (*Children of Darkness*) part 1—*Der Mann aus Neapel* (*The Man from Naples*) (+ co-sc); *Kinder der Finsternis* part 2—*Kämpfende Welten* (*Worlds in Struggle*) (+ co-sc); *Sie und die Drei* (*She and the Three*) (+ sc)
1923 *Die grüne Manuela* (*The Green Manuela*); *Das alte Gesetz* (*Baruch*; *The Ancient Law*)
1925 *Der Demütige und die Sängerin* (*The Humble Man and the Singer*; *La Meurtrière*) (+ co-sc); ***Variété*** (*Variety*; *Vaudeville*; *Varietes*) (+ co-sc)
1927 *Love Me and the World Is Mine* (*Implacable Destiny*) (+ co-sc)
1928 *Moulin-Rouge* (+ sc, pr); *Piccadilly* (sound version released 1929) (+ pr)
1929 *Atlantic* (+ pr); *Atlantik* (German version) (+ pr, co-sc)
1930 *Atlantis* (French version) (co-d, pr); *Cape Forlorn* (*The Love Storm*) (+ pr, co-sc); *Menschen im Käfig* (German version) (+ pr); *Le Cap perdu* (French version) (+ pr); *Two Worlds* (+ pr, co-story); *Zwei Welten* (German version) (+ pr); *Les Deux Mondes* (French version) (+ pr)
1931 *Salto Mortale* (*The Circus of Sin*)
1932 *Peter Voss, der Millionendieb* (*Peter Voss, Who Stole Millions*) (+ co-sc)
1933 *Der Läufer von Marathon* (*The Marathon Runner*)

(in United States):

1933 *Ladies Must Love*
1935 *The Bishop Misbehaves* (*The Bishop's Misadventures*)
1936 *A Son Comes Home*; *Forgotten Faces*
1937 *A Night of Mystery* (*The Greene Murder Case*); *On Such a Night*; *Love on Toast*
1939 *Hell's Kitchen* (co-d with Seiler, uncredited)
1951 *The Scarf* (*The Dungeon*) (+ sc)
1953 *Problem Girls*; *The Neanderthal Man*; *The Steel Lady* (*Secret of the Sahara*; *The Treasure of Kalifa*)
1954 *Return to Treasure Island* (*Bandit Island of Karabei*); *Miss Robin Crusoe* (co-d, uncredited)

Other Films:

1917 *Rennfieber* (*Horse Race Fever*) (Oswald) (sc); *Der Onyxkopf* (May) (sc); *Sturmflut* (Zeyn) (sc); *Die sterbende Perlen* (Meinert) (sc); *Die Faust des Riesen* parts 1 and 2 (Biebrach) (sc)
1918 *Ferdinand Lassalle* (Meinert) (sc); *Der Saratoga-Koffer* (Meinert) (sc); *Die Buchhalterin* (von Woringen) (co-sc); *Nur um tausend Dollars* (Meinert) (sc)
1927 *Madame Pompadour* (Wilcox) (sc)
1956 *Magic Fire* (Dieterle) (sc)

Publications

By DUPONT: articles—

Varieté, with Leo Birinski, in *Antologia di Bianco e nero,* Rome, 1943.
Interview with Ezra Goodman, in *Daily News* (Los Angeles), 10 April 1950.

On DUPONT: books—

Kracauer, Siegfried, *From Caligari to Hitler,* Princeton, 1947.
Eisner, Lotte, *The Haunted Screen,* Berkeley, 1968.
Luft, Herbert, *E.A. Dupont, Anthologie du Cinéma,* Paris, n.d.

On DUPONT: articles—

Weinberg, Herman, in *Take One* (Montreal), January/February 1970.
Luft, Herbert, "E.A. Dupont 1891-1956," in *Films in Review* (New York), June/July 1977.
Pinto, A., letter in *Films in Review* (New York), October 1977.
"E.A. Dupont," in *Film Dope* (London), January 1978.
"E.A. Dupont—Der Augenmensch," in *Film und Fernsehen* (East Berlin), no. 11, 1983.

* * *

Some directors are able to maintain a steady flow of talent in all their work. Others, like E.A. Dupont, are remembered for one outstanding moment in their career. *Variété,* or *Vaudeville* as it is also known, was one of the most exciting films to come from Germany in the 1920s. Dupont made many other good films, but his career as a whole is a rather tragic one. This was partly due to personal deficiencies and partly due to circumstances over which he had no control.

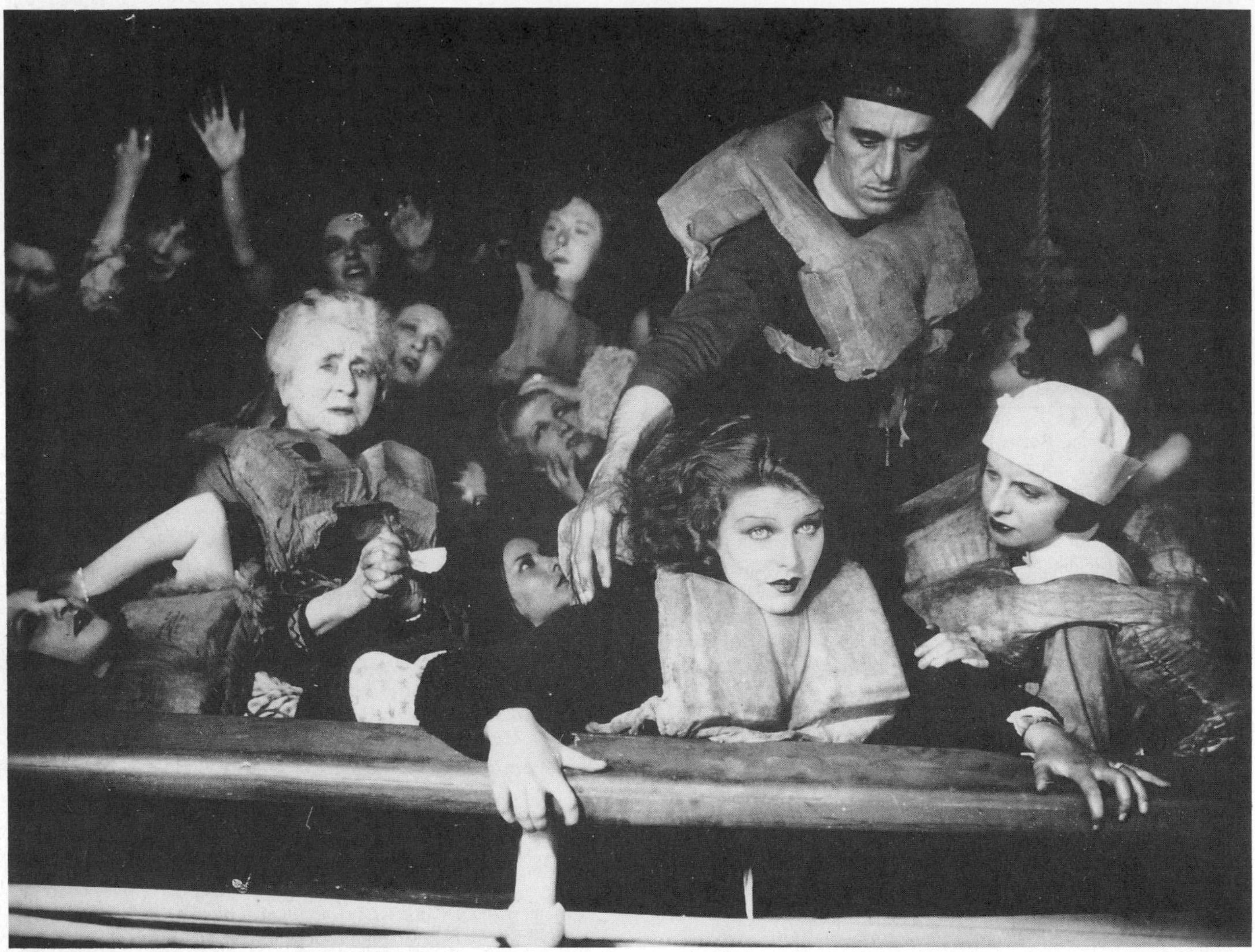

E.A. Dupont: *Atlantic*

Some European directors flourished in Hollywood; Dupont was not one of them.

Dupont had been a film critic and a film scriptwriter before becoming Richard Oswald's story editor and contributing to the latter's sensational sex film *Es werde Licht.* In 1917 he began to direct thrillers like *Das Geheimnis des America Docks* and *Europa Postlagernd.* Recognition came with *Die Geierwally* in 1921. This Henny Porten film was distinguished by the settings of Paul Leni and the camerawork of Karl Freund. It also popularized William Dieterle. Dupont had previously launched the careers of Paul Richter and Bernhardt Goetzke, later featured in the films of Fritz Lang. Freund also photographed Dupont's next film, *Kinder der Finsternis,* a film of two parts that featured striking sets by Leni.

1923 was a bumper year for Dupont. His *Die grüne Manuela,* about a young dancer who falls in love with a smuggler whose brother gives his life to ensure their happiness, won international appreciation. His next film, *Das alte Gesetz,* garnered a similar response. It told the story of a young Jew's flight from his orthodox home to seek fame in the Austrian theater. In the depiction of Jewish rituals and the life of the Austrian court and theatre, the film had a rich authenticity.

Dupont worked outside the then-current German expressionist style, being more human and realistic in his approach to filmmaking. This was evident in his tour de force *Variété,* a tale of jealousy and death amongst trapeze artists. Its powerful realism, visual fluidity, and daring techniques, coupled with the superb performances of Jannings, Lya de Putti, and Warwick Ward, made it stand out in a year rich with achievement. The virtuoso camerawork of Karl Freund contributed not merely to the spatial and temporal aspects of the film but in the revelation of motive and thought. The uninhibited sensuality depicted by the film led to censorship problems in many countries. Inevitably, Dupont went to Hollywood, where he directed a not entirely successful *Love Me and the World Is Mine* for Universal. In 1928 he made two stylish films in England: *Moulin Rouge,* which exploited the sensual charms of Olga Tschechowa, and *Piccadilly,* with Gilda Gray and Anna May Wong (Charles Laughton made his film debut in a small role).

With the coming of sound, *Atlantic,* made in German and English, proved a considerable version of the Titanic story. But the two British sound films that followed suffered from weak acting that belied the striking sets. With *Salto Mortale,* made in Germany in 1931 and featuring Anna Sten and Adolph Wohlbruch, Dupont returned to the scene of his earlier *Variété.* Two more films were made in Germany before he found himself a Jewish refugee in Hollywood. Here his career was uneven. Factory-produced B pictures gave him no scope for his talents.

Dupont was dismissed for slapping a Dead End Kid who was mocking his foreign accent. This humiliating experience played havoc with his morose and withdrawn personality. He became a film publicist, a talent agent, and wrote some scripts. He returned in 1951 to direct

The Scarf, a film of some merit for United Artists. Dupont also dabbled in television. He wrote the script for a film on Richard Wagner that was directed by his former protege William Dieterle in 1956. In December of the same year he died of cancer in Los Angeles. A sad case. Sad too to see the name of his great photographer Karl Freund on the credits of "I Love Lucy."

—Liam O'Leary

DURAS, Marguerite

Nationality: French. **Born:** Marguerite Donnadieu in Giadinh, French Indo-China, 1914. **Education:** Educated in mathematics, law and political science at the Sorbonne, Paris. **Career:** Published first novel, *Les Impudents,* 1943; subsequently novelist, journalist and playwright; directed first film, *La Musica,* 1966. **Awards:** Prix Goncourt for novel *L'Amant,* 1984, Ritz Paris Hemingway, Paris, 1986. **Address:** 5 Rue Saint-Benoît, 75006 Paris, France.

Films as Director:

1966 *La Musica* (co-d, sc)
1969 *Détruire, dit-elle* (*Destroy She Said*) (+ sc)
1971 *Jaune le soleil* (+ pr, co-ed, sc, from her novel *Abahn, Sabana, David*)
1972 *Nathalie Granger* (+ sc, music)
1974 *La Femme du Ganges* (+ sc)
1975 ***India Song*** (+ sc, voice)
1976 *Des journées entières dans les arbres* (*Days in the Trees*) (+ sc); *Son Nom de Venises dans Calcutta desert* (+ sc)
1977 *Baxter, Vera Baxter* (+ sc); *Le Camion* (+ sc, role)
1978 *Le Navire Night* (+ sc)
1978/79 *Aurelia Steiner* (4-film series): *Cesarée* (1978) (+ sc); *Les Mains négatives* (1978) (+ sc); *Aurelia Steiner—Melbourne* (1979) (+ sc); *Aurelia Steiner—Vancouver* (1979) (+ sc)
1981 *Agatha et les lectures illimitées* (*Agatha*) (+ sc)
1985 *Les Enfants* (*The Children*)

Other Films:

1959 ***Hiroshima mon amour*** (Resnais) (sc)
1960 *Moderato Cantabile* (Brook) (sc, co-adapt from her novel)
1961 *Une Aussi longue absence* (*The Long Absence*) (Colpi) (co-sc from her novel)
1964 *Nuit noire, Calcutta* (Karmitz) (short) (sc)
1965 "Les rideaux blancs" (Franju) episode of *Der Augenblick des Friedens* (*Un Instant de la paix*) (for W.German TV) (sc)
1966 *10:30 P.M. Summer* (Dassin) (co-sc uncredited, from her novel) (*Dix heures et demie du soir en été*); *La Voleuse* (Chapot) (sc, dialogue)

Publications

By DURAS: screenplays—

Hiroshima mon amour, Paris, 1959.
Moderato Cantabile, with Gérard Jarlot and Peter Brook, 1960.
Une Aussi longue absence, with Gérard Jarlot, Paris, 1961.
10:30 P.M. Summer, with Jules Dassin, Paris, 1966.
La Musica, Paris, 1966.
Detruire, dit-elle, Paris, 1969; as *Destroy, She Said,* New York, 1970.
Les rideaux blancs, Paris, 1966.
Jaune le soleil, Paris, 1971
Nathalie Granger, suivi de La Femme du Gange, Paris, 1973.
India Song—texte—theatre—film, Paris, 1975; as *India Song,* New York, 1976.
Des journées entières dans les arbres, Paris, 1976.
Son Nom de Venises dans Calcutta desert, Paris, 1976.
Le Camion, Paris, 1977.
Le Navire Night, Césarée, Les Mains négatives, Aurelia Steiner, Paris, 1979.
Vera Baxter; ou, Les Plages de l'Atlantique, Paris, 1980.
Agatha, Paris, 1981.
Les Enfants, Paris, 1985.

By DURAS: fiction—

Les Impudents, Paris, 1943.
La Vie tranquille, Paris, 1944.
Un Barrage contre le Pacifique, Paris, 1950; as *The Sea Wall,* New York, 1952; as *A Sea of Troubles,* London, 1953.
Le Marin de Gibraltar, Paris, 1952; as *The Sailor From Gibraltar,* London and New York, 1966.
Les Petits Chevaux de Tarquinia, Paris, 1953; as *The Little Horses of Tarquinia,* London, 1960.
Des journées entières dans les arbres, Paris, 1954; as *Whole Days in the Trees,* New York, 1981.
Le Square, Paris, 1955.
Moderato Cantabile, Paris, 1958, and New York, 1987.
Dix heures et demi du soir en été, Paris, 1960; as *Ten-Thirty on a Summer Night,* London, 1962.
L'Après-midi de Monsieur Andesmas, Paris, 1962; as *The Afternoon of Monsieur Andesmas,* London, 1964.
Le Ravissement de Lol V. Stein, Paris, 1964; as *The Ravishing of Lol V. Stein,* New York, 1967; as *The Rapture of Lol V. Stein,* London, 1967.
Le Vice-consul, Paris, 1966; as *The Vice-Consul,* London, 1968, New York, 1987.
L'Amante anglaise, Paris, 1967, New York, 1968.
Abahn, Sabana, David, Paris, 1970.
L'Amour, Paris, 1971.
Ah! Ernesto, with Bernard Bonhomme, Paris, 1971.
La Maladie de la mort, Paris, 1983; as *The Malady of Death,* New York, 1986.
L'Amant, Paris, 1984; as *The Lover,* New York, 1985.
Les Yeux bleus cheveux noirs, Paris, 1987; as *Blue Eyes, Black Hair,* London and New York, 1988.
Emily L., Paris, 1987, New York, 1989.

By DURAS: plays—

Théâtre 1 (includes *Les Eaux et forets, Le Square, La Musica*), Paris, 1965.
Théâtre 2 (includes *Susanna Andler; Yes, peut-étre; Le Shaga; Des journées entières dans les arbres; Un Homme est venu me voir),* Paris, 1968.
L'Homme assis dans le couloir, Paris, 1980.
L'Homme Atlantique, Paris, 1982.
Savannah Bay, Paris, 1982.
The Square, Edinburgh, 1986.
Yes, peut-etre, Edinburgh, 1986.

By DURAS: other books—

Les Parleuses, with Xaviere Gauthier, Paris, 1974.

Marguerite Duras

Étude sur l'oeuvre littéraire, théâtrale, et cinématographique, with Jacques Lacan and Maurice Blanchot, Paris, 1976.
Territoires du féminin, with Marcelle Marini, Paris, 1977.
Les Lieux de Duras, with Michelle Porte, Paris, 1978.
L'Été 80, Paris, 1980.
Outside: Papiers d'un jour, Paris, 1981, Boston 1986.
The War: A Memoir, New York, 1986.
The Physical Side, London, 1990.

By DURAS: articles—

"Conversation with Marguerite Duras," with Richard Roud, in *Sight and Sound* (London), Winter 1959/60.
"Marguerite Duras en toute liberté," interview with F. Dufour, in *Cinéma* (Paris), April 1972.
"Du livre au film," in *Image et Son* (Paris), April 1974.
"India Song, a Chant of Love and Death," interview with F. Dawson, in *Film Comment* (New York), November/December 1975.
"India Song and Marguerite Duras," interview with Carlos Clarens, in *Sight and Sound* (London), Winter 1975/76.
Interview with J.-C. Bonnet and J. Fieschi, in *Cinématographe* (Paris), November 1977.
"Les Yeux verts," special issue written and edited by Duras, of *Cahiers du Cinéma* (Paris), June 1980.
Interview with D. Fasoli, in *Filmcritica* (Florence), June 1981.
Interview with A. Grunert, in *Filmfaust* (Frankfurt), February-March 1982.
"The places of Marguerite Duras," an interview with M. Porte, in *Enclitic* (Minneapolis), Spring 1983.
Interview with P. Bonitzer, C. Tesson, and Serge Toubiana, in *Cahiers du Cinéma* (Paris), July-August 1985.
Interview with Jean-Luc Godard, in *Cinéma* (Paris), 30 December 1987.

On DURAS: books—

Bernheim, N.-L., *Marguerite Duras tourne un film,* Paris, 1976.
Ropars-Wuilleumier, Marie-Claire, *La Texte divisé,* Paris, 1981.
Trastulli, Daniela, *Dalla parola all imagine: Viaggio nel cinema di Marguerite Duras,* Geneva, 1982.
Borgomano, Madeleine, *L'Ecriture filmique de Marguerite Duras,* Paris, 1985.
Brossard, Jean-Pierre, editor, *Marguerite Duras: Cinéaste, écrivain,* La Chaux-de-Fonde, 1985.
Guers-Villate, Yvonne, *Continuité/discontinuité de l'oeuvre Durassienne,* Brussels, 1985.
Fernandes, Marie-Pierre, *Travailler avec Duras: La musica deuxième,* Paris, 1986.

Selous, Trista, *The Other Woman: Feminism and Femininity in the Work of Marguerite Duras,* New Haven, Connecticut, 1988.

On DURAS: articles—

Gollub, Judith, "French Writers Turned Film Makers," in *Film Heritage* (New York), Winter 1968/69.

"Reflections in a Broken Glass," in *Film Comment* (New York), November/December 1975.

Lakeland, M.J., "Marguerite Duras in 1977," in *Camera Obscura* (Berkeley), Fall 1977.

Van Wert, W.F., "The Cinema of Marguerite Duras: Sound and Voice in a Closed Room," in *Film Quarterly* (Berkeley), Fall 1979.

Seni, N., "Wahrnehungsformen von Zeit und Raum am Beispiel der Filme von Marguerite Duras und Chantal Akerman," in *Frauen und Film* (Berlin), September 1979.

"Marguerite Duras à l'action," in *Positif* (Paris), July/August 1980.

Andermatt, V., "Big mach (on the truck)," in *Enclitic* (Minneapolis), Spring 1980.

Lyon, E., "Marguerite Duras: Bibliography/Filmography," in *Camera Obscura* (Berkeley), Fall 1980.

Murphy, C.J., "The role of desire in the films of Marguerite Duras," in *Quarterly Review of Film Studies* (New York), Winter 1982.

Fedwik, P., "Marguerite Duras: Feminine Field of Nostalgia," in *Enclitic* (Minneapolis), Fall 1982.

Sarrut, B., "Marguerite Duras: Barrages against the Pacific," in *On Film* (Los Angeles), Summer 1983.

Murphy, C.J., "New narrative regions: The role of desire in the films and novels of Marguerite Duras," in *Literature/Film Quarterly* (Salisbury, Maryland), April 1984.

Le Masson, H., "La voix tatouee," in *Cahiers du Cinéma* (Paris), January 1985.

McWilliams, D., "Aesthetic tripling: Marguerite Duras's *Le navire Night,*" in *Literature/Film Quarterly* (Salisbury, Maryland), January 1986.

* * *

As a writer, Marguerite Duras's work is identified, along with that of such authors as Alain Robbe-Grillet and Jean Cayrol, with the tradition of the New Novel. Duras began working in film as a screenwriter, with an original script for Alain Resnais's first feature, *Hiroshima mon amour.* She subsequently wrote a number of film adaptations from her novels. She directed her first film, *La Musica,* in 1966. If *Hiroshima mon amour* remains her best known work in cinema, her later films have won widespread praise for the profound challenge they offer to conventional dramatic narrative.

The nature of narrative and the potential contained in a single text are major concerns of Duras's films. Many of her works have appeared in several forms, as novels, plays, and films. This not only involves adaptations of a particular work, but also extends to cross-referential networks that run through her texts. The film *Woman of the Ganges* combines elements from three novels—*The Ravishing of Lol V. Stein, The Vice-Consul,* and *L'Amour. India Song* was initially written as a play, taking characters from *The Vice-Consul* and elaborating on the structure of external voices developed in *Woman of the Ganges. India Song* was made as a film in 1975, and its verbal track was used to generate a second film, *Son Nom de Venises dans Calcutta desert.*

This process of transformation suggests that all works are "in progress," inherently subject to being reconstructed. This is partly because Duras's works are more concerned with the quality or intensity of experience than with events *per se.* The films present narrative rather than a linear, unambiguous sequence of events. In *Le Camion,* two characters, played by Gerard Depardieu and Duras, sit in a room as the woman describes a movie about a woman who hitches a ride with a truck driver and talks with him for an hour and twenty minutes. This conversation is intercut with scenes of a truck driving around Paris, and stopping for a female hitchhiker (with Depardieu as the driver, and Duras as the hitchhiker). Thus, the verbal description of a potential film is juxtaposed by images of what that film might be.

An emphasis on the soundtrack is also a crucial aspect of Duras's films; her verbal texts are lyrical and are as important as the images. In *India Song,* sound and image function contrapuntally, and the audience must actively assess the relation between them, reading across the body of the film, noting continuities and disjunctions. The verbal text often refers in past tense to events and characters on screen, as the viewer is challenged to figure out the chronology of events described and depicted—which name on the soundtrack corresponds to which actor, whether the voices belong to on- or off-screen characters, and so forth. In this way the audience participates in the search for a story, constructing possible narratives.

As minimal as they are, Duras's narratives are partially derived from melodrama, focusing on relations between men and women, the nature or structure of desire, and colonialism and imperialism in both literal and metaphoric terms. In pursuing these issues through non-conventional narrative forms, and shifting the burden of discovering meaning to the audience, Duras's films provide an alternative to conventional ways of watching movies. Her work is seen as exemplifying a feminine writing practice that challenges the patriarchal domination of classical narrative cinema. In an interview, Duras said, "I think the future belongs to women. Men have been completely dethroned. Their rhetoric is stale, used up. We must move on to the rhetoric of women, one that is anchored in the organism, in the body." It is this new rhetoric, a new way of communicating, that Duras strives for in her films.

—M.B. White

DUTT, Guru

Nationality: Indian. **Born:** 9 July 1925. **Education:** Educated in Calcutta; studied dancing in Uday Sankar's Art Academy, Almora, 1942-44. **Career:** Joined Prabhat Film Co., Poona, 1944; directed first film, *Baazi,* 1951; founded Guru Dutt Films, 1954; directed first Indian film in Cinemascope, *Kaagaz ke Phool,* 1959. **Died:** Committed suicide, 10 October 1964.

Films as Director:

1951 *Baazi* (*The Wager*)
1952 *Jaal* (*The Net*)
1953 *Baaz* (+ role)
1954 *Aar Paar* (*Heads or Tails*) (+ pr, role)
1955 *Mr. and Mrs. 55* (+ pr, role)
1956 *Sailaab*
1957 *Pyaasa* (*The Thirsty One*) (+ pr, role)
1959 ***Kaagaz Ke Phool*** (*Paper Flowers*) (+ pr, role)

Other Films:

1945 *Lakharani* (Bedekar) (asst d, role)
1946 *Hum ek Hain* (Santoshi) (asst d)
1947 *Mohan* (A. Banerji) (asst d)

Guru Dutt, with Waheeda Rehman in *Pyaasa*

1949 *Girls School* (Chakrabarty) (asst d)
1950 *Sangram* (Gyan Mukherji) (asst d)
1956 *C.I.D.* (pr)
1958 *12 O'Clock* (role)
1960 *Chaudhwin ka Chand* (pr, role)
1962 *Sahib, Bibi aur Ghulam* (*King, Queen, Slave*) (Abrar Alvi) (co-d, pr, role); *Sautela Bhai* (role)
1963 *Bahurani* (role); *Bharosa* (role)
1964 *Sanjh aur Savera* (role); *Suhagan* (role)

Films incomplete at the time of his death include *Professor; Raaz; Gouri; Ek Tuku Chhuua; Kaneez; Baharen Phir bhi Ayengi; Love and God* (Asif).

Publications

On DUTT: books—

Khopkar, Arun, *Guru Dutt: A Three Act Tragedy,* Marathi, n.d.
Rangoonwala, Firoze, *Guru Dutt: A Monograph,* Poona, India, 1973.
Barnouw, Erik, and S. Krishnaswamy, *Indian Film,* second edition, New York, 1980.
Gandhy, Behroze, and Paul Willemen, *Indian Cinema,* London, 1982.
Ramachandran, T.M., *70 Years of Indian Cinema (1913-1983),* Bombay, 1985.

On DUTT: articles—

Micciollo, Henri, "Guru Dutt, 1925-64," in *Avant-Scène du Cinéma* (Paris), 1975 (also as *Anthologie du Cinéma*, no. 83).
Micciollo, Henri, "Guru Dutt le tendre," in *Cinéma* (Paris), May 1985.
Tournès, André, "Un cinéaste mis à mort: Guru Dutt," in *Jeune Cinéma* (Paris), September 1985.
Cooper, Darius, "The Hindi film song and Guru Dutt," in *East West Film Journal,* June 1988.

* * *

Guru Dutt's romanticism, as director and actor, has of recent years found an enthusiastic audience abroad. In India, some of his films, notably the great *Pyaasa (The Thirsty One),* were successful in his lifetime, but others such as *Kaagaz Ke Phool (Paper Flowers)* and *Saheb, Bibi aur Ghulam (King, Queen, Slave,* co-directed by Abrar Alvi) found popularity long after his death in 1964.

Dutt's early work was marked by light thrillers such as *Baazi (The Wager), Jaal (The Net),* and *Aar Paar (Heads or Tails)*, in which dispossessed but happy-go-lucky heroes moved in a squalid, realistic world. These films were generically tied to other crime films of the period, such as Raj Kapoor's *Awara (Vagabond).* Yet they also display a certain attitude to sexuality which dominates the director's later, more poetic work: the hero is repeatedly presented as the object of the heroine's sensual desire. In *Mr and Mrs 55,* a chauvinist satire about modern women, the flighty, sensation-seeking young heroine

(Madhubala) is transformed into a woman who desperately yearns for the lover she believes has left her. In the last frames the hero, played by the director himself, emerges to bestow fulfillment on her.

This romantic enshrinement of the male hero is a major feature in *Pyaasa* and *Kaagaz Ke Phool.* These films, and Guru Dutt's screen personality as their protagonist, strongly refer to Devdas, a character of Indian literature and cinema who, thwarted in love by society's strictures, drinks his life away. *Pyaasa,* the story of an unemployed poet named Vijay, is a carefully conceived counter-cultural variation of *Devdas.* Vijay's romantic failure does not stem from social strictures, but because his beloved Meena (Mala Sinha) finds him wanting by society's criteria of success. In contrast, the prostitute Gulab (Waheeda Rehman) enshrines him in her truly worshipful gaze. "Society" is portrayed as mercenary and debasing, and it is those marginal to it who retain their moral dignity.

The film is cinematically distinguished for its inventive usage of visual and aural registers of subjectivity. The poet's point of view repeatedly transfers present images of Meena into romantic flashbacks, at once covering over and drawing attention to the passage of time and the facts of separation. Strategies of subjectivity also invest present time with a reverie about personal loss. Vijay's grief at his mother's death flows into reflections on the death of female dignity through prostitution; the routine sounds of the red light area are abruptly arrested or appropriated to the hero's intoning of Sahir Ludhianavi's great poem on the subject.

The objects of this traumatic masculine reverie are the lost feminine figures of the mother and beloved. The film moves from phases of subjectivity into modes that fix Vijay in tableaux of humiliation which expose the malignant forces at work. His masculine dignity and power are reasserted through Gulab's adoring look, but can only be realised in a space outside an irredeemable society.

In *Kaagaz Ke Phool,* the story unravels as a long flashback from the point of view of an aged film director (Dutt). Here it is the cinema itself—and the director's past glory—which has been lost and is longed for. As in *Pyaasa,* it is the denial of the hero's vision which is addressed. In *Kaagaz Ke Phool,* however, there is no compensation because the figures who could fulfil this need—a daughter (Baby Naaz) and an impossible love (Waheeda Rehman)—are subordinated to the fascination with masculine vision itself. Here Dutt works out an obsession with the idea of the sensitive male vision denied acknowledgement in society. The focus on male vision is more narcissistic, more closed in on itself than in *Pyaasa.* But it is also more uncompromising, for the conclusion suggests that the cinema finally offers the fantasy of male authority nothing but the vision of its own death.

Kaagaz Ke Phool signalled the end of a fixation. In his final directorial collaboration, *Sahib, Bibi aur Ghulam,* Dutt was able to displace attention from himself and direct it towards a remote world of decadent excess and willful female sensuality. The earlier Dutt heroes were spectators of a vision which they themselves had produced. In *Sahib,* the point of view of the Dutt character, Bhootnath, structures perception, but his own story remains a subsidiary, lighter romance to offset the darker, more compelling story of Chhoti Bahu (Meena Kumari), the neglected wife of a rentier landlord (Rehman). Bhootnath watches in fascination and even abets Chhoti Bahu in her schemes to assume the sensual image which will entice her husband away from drunken whoring. She finally fails, but the image is always somewhat in excess of the objective, as her sensuality floats free into an autoerotic register. Many years later, Bhootnath comes across her skeletal remains in the foundations of the old mansion as it is dug up. In this, his last film before his suicide in 1964, Guru Dutt no longer saw the cinema as a metaphor for an idealised male vision, but as the place in which a disturbing female sexuality had been interred.

—Ravi Vasudevan

DUVIVIER, Julien

Nationality: French. **Born:** Lille, 8 October 1896. **Education:** Lille University; studied acting in Paris. **Career:** Worked in André Antoine's Théâtre Libre, then assistant to Antoine as filmmaker, 1916; directed first film, *Haceldama ou Le Prix du Sang,* 1919; joined "Film d'Art" of Marcel Vandal and Charles Delac, 1925; made *The Great Waltz* for MGM, Hollywood, 1938; moved to United States, 1940; returned to France, 1945. **Died:** In auto accident, 26 October 1967.

Films as Director:

1919 *Haceldama ou Le Prix du Sang* (+ sc)
1920 *La Réincarnation de Serge Renaudier* (negative destroyed by fire before film shown) (+ sc)
1922 *Les Roquevillard* (+ sc); *L'Ouragan sur la montagne* (+ sc); *Der unheimliche Gast* (*Le Logis de l'horreur*) (+ sc)
1923 *Le Reflet de Claude Mercoeur* (+ sc)
1924 *Credo ou La Tragédie de Lourdes* (+ sc); *Coeurs farouches* (+ sc); *La Machine à refaire la vie* (re-released with sound, 1933) (co-d, sc); *L'Oeuvre immortelle* (+ sc)
1925 *L'Abbé Constantin* (+ sc); *Poil de carotte* (+ co-sc)
1926 *L'Agonie de Jerusalem* (+ sc); *L'Homme à l'Hispano*
1927 *Le Mariage de Mademoiselle Beulemans* (+ sc); *Le Mystère de la Tour Eiffel* (+ sc)
1928 *Le Tourbillon de Paris*
1929 *La Divine croisière* (+ sc); *Maman Colibri* (+ co-sc); *La Vie miraculeuse de Thérèse Martin* (+ sc); *Au bonheur des dames* (+ co-sc)

(Sound films):

1930 *David Golder* (+ sc)
1931 *Les Cinq Gentlemen maudits* (+ sc); *Allo Berlin? Ici Paris!* (*Hallo! Hallo! Hier spricht Berlin*) (+ sc); *Die funf verfluchten Gentlemen* (German version) (+ sc)
1932 *Poil de carotte* (remake) (+ sc); *La Tête d'un homme* (+ co-sc)
1933 *Le Petit Roi* (+ sc); *Le Paquebot 'Tenacity'* (+ co-sc)
1934 *Maria Chapdelaine* (+ sc)
1935 *Golgotha* (+ sc, adapt); *La Bandera* (+ co-sc)
1936 *L'Homme du jour* (+ co-sc); *Golem* (*Le Golem*) (+ co-sc); *La Belle Équipe* (+ co-sc)
1937 ***Pépé-le-Moko*** (+ co-sc); *Un Carnet de bal* (+ sc)
1938 *The Great Waltz* (*Toute la ville danse*) (+ sc); *La Fin du jour* (+ co-sc): *Marie Antoinette* (Van Dyke, d uncredited, sc)
1939 *La Charrette Fantôme* (+ sc)
1940 *Untel père et fils* (+ co-sc)
1941 *Lydia* (+ sc, co-story)
1942 *Tales of Manhattan* (+ co-sc)
1943 *Flesh and Fantasy* (+ co-pr)
1944 *The Imposter* (+ sc)
1946 *Panique* (+ co-sc)
1948 *Anna Karenina* (+ co-sc)
1949 *Au royaume des cieux* (+ sc, pr)
1950 *Black Jack* (+ co-sc, pr); *Sous le ciel de Paris* (+ co-sc)
1951 *Le Petit Monde de Don Camillo* (*Il piccolo mondo di Don Camillo*) (+ co-sc)
1952 *La Fête à Henriette* (+ co-sc)
1953 *Le Retour de Don Camillo* (*Il ritorno di Don Camillo*) (+ co-sc)
1954 *L'Affaire Maurizius* (+ sc)
1955 *Marianne de ma jeunesse* (+ sc)
1956 *Voice le temps des assassins* (+ co-sc)

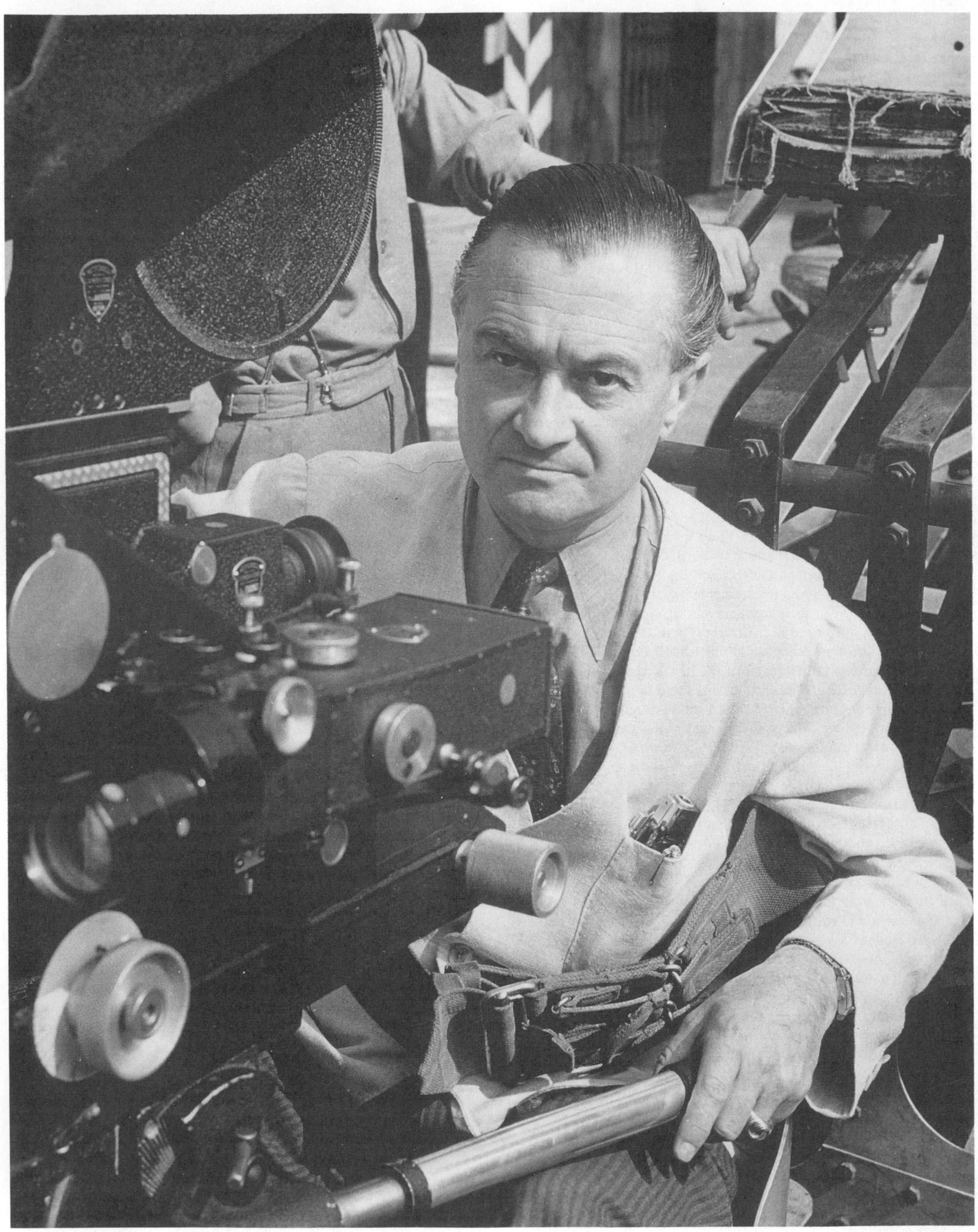

Julien Duvivier

1957 *L'Homme à l'imperméable* (+ co-sc); *Pot Bouille* (+ co-sc)
1958 *La Femme et le pantin* (+ sc, co-adapt)
1959 *Marie Octobre* (+ co-sc)
1960 *Das kunstseidene Mädchen* (*La Grande Vie*) (+ co-sc); *Boulevard* (+ co-sc)
1962 *La Chambre ardente* (+ co-sc); *Le Diable et les dix commandements* (+ co-sc)
1963 *Chair de poule* (+ co-sc)
1967 *Diaboliquement vôtre* (+ sc, co-adapt)

Other Films:

1918 *Les Travailleurs de la mer* (Antoine) (asst d)
1920 *L'Agonie des aigles* (Bernard-Deschamps) (adaptation); *La Terre* (Antoine) (asst d)
1921 *Crépuscule d'épouvante* (Etiévant) (sc)
1922 *L'Arlésienne* (Antoine) (asst d)
1924 *La Nuit de la revanche* (Etiévant) (story)
1946 *Collège swing* (*Amours, délices et orgues*) (Berthomieu) (co-sc)

Publications

By DUVIVIER: articles—

"Un Réalisateur compare deux méthodes," interview with Pierre Leprohon, in *Cinémonde* (Paris), 6 May 1946.
"De la création à la mise en scène," in *Cinémonde* (Paris), Christmas 1946.
"Julien Duvivier: 'Pourquoi j'ai trahi Zola,'" interview with Yvonne Baby, in *Lettres Françaises* (Paris), 31 October 1957.
Reminiscences in *Avant-Scène du Cinéma* (Paris), 1 February 1977.

On DUVIVIER: books—

Chirat, Raymond, *Julien Duvivier,* Lyon, 1968.
Leprohon, Pierre, "Julien Duvivier," in *Anthologie du cinéma,* vol. 4, Paris, 1969.

On DUVIVIER: articles—

Aubriant, Michel, "Julien Duvivier," in *Cinémonde* (Paris), 28 November 1952.
"Débat sur Duvivier," in *Arts* (Paris), 18 April 1956.
Epstein, Marie, "Comment ils travaillent? Julien Duvivier," in *Technique Cinématographique* (Paris), December 1958.
Marcabru, P., "Les Français à Hollywood," in *Arts* (Paris), 8 February 1961.
Obituary in *New York Times,* 30 October 1967.
Renoir, Jean, "Duvivier, le professionel," in *Le Figaro Littéraire* (Paris), 6 November 1967.
Amengual, Barthélemy, "Défense de Duvivier," in *Cahiers de la Cinémathèque* (Perpignan), Spring 1975.
"*Pépé le Moko* Issue" of *Avant-Scène du Cinéma* (Paris), 1 June 1981.
Simsolo, Noel, "A propos de Julien Duvivier," in *Image et Son* (Paris), November 1981.
"Special Mac Orlan; La Bandera, Julian Duvivier," in *L'Avant-Scène du Cinéma* (Paris), April 1982.
Douin, Jean-Luc, "Duvivier, la mauvaise reputation," in *Télérama* (Paris), 25 January 1986.

On DUVIVIER: film—

Viallaet, Pierre, and Marcel l'Herbier, *Portraits filmées ... Julien Duvivier* (for television), 1953.

* * *

No one speaks of Julien Duvivier without apologizing. So many of his fifty-odd films are embarrassing to watch that it is hard to believe he was ever in charge of his career in the way we like to imagine Renoir or Clair were in charge of theirs. But Duvivier had neither the luxury nor the contacts to direct his career. He began and remained a yeoman in the industry. A director at the Théâtre Antoine in the teens, he began his film career in 1922 and made over a score of silent films, mainly melodramas. From the first he separated himself from the experiments in narration and visual style that characterized much of that period.

Duvivier's reputation as a reputable, efficient director jumped in the sound era when he made a string of small but successful films (*David Golder, Les Cinq Gentilhommes maudits, Allo Berlin? Ici Paris!, Poil de carotte, La Tête d'un homme*). Evidently his flair for the melodramatic and his ability to control powerful actors put him far ahead of the average French director trying to cope with the problems of sound. But in this era, as always, Duvivier discriminated little among the subjects he filmed. This aspect was most evident in 1935. First came *Golgotha,* a throwback to the religious films he made in the silent era, and now completely outmoded. Duvivier struggles to energize the static tableaux the film settles into. He moves his camera wildly, but seldom reaches for a key closeup or for an authentic exchange among his actors. It is all picture postcards, or rather holy cards, set off to Jacques Ibert's operatic score.

This solemn, even bombastic, film could not be farther from the swiftness and authentic feeling of the romantic Foreign Legion film *La Bandera* made the same year. Where *Golgotha* is an official presentation of French cinema, *La Bandera* seems more intimate, more in the spirit of the times. Its success was only the first of a set of astounding films that include *La Belle Équipe, Pépé-le-Moko, Un Carnet de bal,* and *Le Fin du jour.*

It is tempting to surmise that cultural history and Julien Duvivier came for once into perfect coincidence in this age of poetic realism. Like Michael Curtiz and *Casablanca,* Duvivier's style and the actors who played out the roles of his dramas spoke for a whole generation. In France it was a better generation, vaguely hopeful with the popular front, but expecting the end of day.

Duvivier's contribution to these films extends beyond the direction of actors. Every film contains at least one scene of remarkable expressiveness, like the death of Regis in *Pépé-Le-Moko,* gunned down by his own victim with the jukebox blaring. Duvivier's sureness of pace in this era brought him a Hollywood contract even before the Nazi invasion forced him to leave France. Without the strong personality of Renoir or Clair, and with far more experience in genre pictures, Duvivier fit in rather well with American film production methods. He deplored the lack of personal control or even personal contribution in the industry, but he acquitted himself well until the Liberation.

Hoping to return to the glory years of poetic realism, Duvivier's first postwar project in France replicated the essence of its style. *Panique* featured sparse sets, an atmosphere that dominated a reduced but significant murder drama, and the evocative work of Michel Simon and Vivian Romance in an offbeat policier from Simenon. But the country had changed. The film failed, and Duvivier began what would become a lifelong search for the missing formula. With varying degrees of box office success he turned out contemporary and historical comedies and melodramas; the only one which put him in the spotlight was *Don Camillo* with Fernandel.

Believing far more in experience, planning, and hard work than in spontaneity and genius, Duvivier never relaxed. Every film taught him something and, by rights, he should have ended a better director than ever. But he will be remembered for those five years in the late 1930s, a period when every choice he made in the realms of script and direction was in tune with the romantically pessimistic sensibility of the country.

—Dudley Andrew

DWAN, Allan

Nationality: American. **Born:** Joseph Aloysius Dwan in Toronto, Canada, 3 April 1885, family moved to United States, 1893. **Education:** North Division High School, Chicago; Notre Dame University, Indiana, degree in electrical engineering, 1907. **Family:** Married 1) Pauline Bush, 1915 (divorced 1920); 2) Marie Shelton, early 1920s (died 1954). **Career:** As illuminating engineer work on mercury vapor arc light led to association with Essanay film company, 1909; wrote stories while supervising lighting; American Film Company ("Flying A") formed by Essanay staff, Dwan joined as chief scenario editor, 1910; signed to Universal Pictures, 1913; signed with Famous Players Company, New York, 1914; joined Triangle Company under supervision of D.W. Griffith, 1915; worked in England, 1932-34; trained camera units for U.S. Armed Services photographic division, 1943; contracted to Republic Pictures, 1945-54. **Died:** In Woodland Hills, California, 21 December 1981.

Films as Director (incomplete list; Dwan estimated 1,850 films):

1911 *Branding a Bad Man* and *A Western Dreamer* (split reel) (+ pr, sc); *A Daughter of Liberty* and *A Trouper's Heart* (split reel) (+ pr, sc); *Rattlesnakes and Gunpowder* and *The Ranch Tenor* (split reel) (+ pr, sc); *The Sheepman's Daughter* (+ pr, sc); *The Sagebrush Phrenologist* and *The Elopements on Double L Ranch* (split reel) (+ pr, sc); *$5,000 Reward—Dead or Alive* (+ pr, sc); *The Witch of the Range* (+ pr, sc); *The Cowboy's Ruse* and *Law and Order on Bar L Ranch* (split reel) (+ pr, sc); *The Yiddisher Cowboy* and *The Bronco Buster's Bride* (split reel) (+ pr, sc); *The Hermit's Gold* (+ pr, sc); *The Actress and the Cowboys* and *The Sky Pilot's Intemperance* (split reel) (+ pr, sc); *A Western Waif* (+ pr, sc); *The Call of the Open Range* (+ pr, sc); *The School Ma'am of Snake* and *The Ranch Chicken* (split reel) (+ pr, sc); *Cupid in Chaps* (+ pr, sc); *The Outlaw's Trail* (+ pr, sc); *The Ranchman's Nerve* (+ pr, sc); *When East Comes West* (+ pr, sc); *The Cowboy's Deliverance* (+ pr, sc); *The Cattle Thief's Brand* (+ pr, sc); *The Parting Trails* (+ pr, sc); *The Cattle Rustler's End* (+ pr, sc); *Cattle, Gold and Oil* (+ pr, sc); *The Ranch Girl* (+ pr, sc); *The Poisoned Flume* (+ pr, sc); *The Brand of Fear* (+ pr, sc): *The Blotted Brand* (+ pr, sc); *Auntie and the Cowboys* (+ pr, sc); *The Western Doctor's Peril* (+ pr, sc); *The Smuggler and the Girl* (+ pr, sc); *The Cowboy and the Artist* (+ pr, sc); *Three Million Dollars* (+ pr, sc); *The Stage Robbers of San Juan* (+ pr, sc); *The Mother of the Ranch* (+ pr, sc); *The Gunman* (+ pr, sc); *The Claim Jumpers* (+ pr, sc); *The Circular Fence* (+ pr, sc); *The Rustler Sheriff* (+ pr, sc); *The Love of the West* (+ pr, sc); *The Trained Nurse at Bar Z* (+ pr, sc); *The Miner's Wife* (+ pr, sc); *The Land Thieves* (+ pr, sc); *The Cowboy and the Outlaw* (+ pr, sc); *Three Daughters of the West* and *Caves of La Jolla* (split reel) (+ pr, sc); *The Lonely Range* (+ pr, sc); *The Horse Thief's Bigamy* (+ pr, sc): *The Trail of the Eucalyptus* (+ pr, sc); *The Stronger Man* (+ pr, sc); *The Water War* (+ pr, sc); *The Three Shell Game* (+ pr, sc); *The Mexican* (+ pr, sc); *The Eastern Cowboy* (+ pr, sc); *The Way of the West* (+ pr, sc); *The Test* (+ pr, sc); *The Master of the Vineyard* (+ pr, sc); *Sloppy Bill of the Rollicking R* (+ pr, sc); *The Sheriff's Sisters* (+ pr, sc); *The Angel of Paradise Ranch* (+ pr, sc); *The Smoke of the 45* (+ pr, sc); *The Man Hunt* (+ pr, sc); *Santa Catalina, Magic Isle of the Pacific* (+ pr, sc); *The Last Notch* (+ pr, sc); *The Gold Lust* (+ pr, sc); *The Duel of the Candles* (+ pr, sc); *Bonita of El Cajon* (+ pr, sc); *The Lawful Holdup* (+ pr, sc); *Battleships* (+ pr, sc); *Dams and Waterways* (+ pr, sc)

1912 *A Midwinter Trip to Los Angeles* (+ pr, sc); *The Misadventures of a Claim Agent* and *Bronco Busting for Flying A Pictures* (split reel) (+ pr, sc); *The Winning of La Mesa* (+ pr, sc); *The Locket* (+ pr, sc); *The Relentless Outlaw* (+ pr, sc); *Justice of the Sage* (+ pr, sc); *Objections Overruled* (+ pr, sc); *The Mormon* (+ pr, sc); *Love and Lemons* (+ pr, sc); *The Best Policy* (+ pr, sc); *The Real Estate Fraud* (+ pr, sc); *The Grubstake Mortgage* (+ pr, sc); *Where Broadway Meets the Mountains* (+ pr, sc); *An Innocent Grafter* (+ pr, sc); *Society and Chaps* (+ pr, sc); *The Leap Year Cowboy* (+ pr, sc); *The Land Baron of San Tee* (+ pr sc): *An Assisted Elopement* (+ pr, sc); *From the Four Hundred to the Herd* (+ pr, sc); *The Broken Ties* (+ pr, sc): *After School* (+ pr, sc); *A Bad Investment* (+ pr, sc); *The Full Value* (+ pr, sc); *The Tramp's Gratitude* (+ pr, sc); *Fidelity* (+ pr, sc); *Winter Sports and Pastimes of Coronado Beach* (+ pr, sc); *The Maid and the Man* (+ pr, sc); *The Cowboy Socialist* (+ pr, sc); *Checkmate* and *The Ranchman's Marathon* (split reel) (+ pr, sc); *The Coward* (+ pr, sc); *The Distant Relative* (+ pr, sc); *The Ranch Detective* (+ pr, sc); *Driftwood* (+ pr, sc); *The Eastern Girl* (+ pr, sc); *The Pensioners* (+ pr, sc); *The End of the Feud* (+ pr, sc); *The Wedding Dress* (+ pr, sc); *Mystical Maid of Jamasha Pass* (+ pr, sc); *The Other Wise Man* (+ pr, sc); *The Haters* (+ pr, sc); *The Thread of Life* (+ pr, sc); *The Wandering Gypsy* (+ pr, sc); *The Reward of Valor* (+ pr, sc); *The Brand* (+ pr, sc); *The Green Eyed Monster* (+ pr, sc); *Cupid Through Padlocks* (+ pr, sc); *For the Good of Her Men* (+ pr, sc); *The Simple Love* (+ pr, sc); *The Weaker Brother* and *Fifty Mile Auto Contest* (split reel) (+ pr, sc); *The Wordless Message* (+ pr, sc); *The Evil Inheritance* (+ pr, sc); *The Marauders* (+ pr, sc); *The Girl Back Home* (+ pr, sc); *Under False Pretences* (+ pr, sc); *Where There's a Heart* (+ pr, sc); *The Vanishing Race* (+ pr, sc); *The Fatal Mirror* and *Point Loma, Old Town* (split reel) (+ pr, sc); *The Tell Tale Shells* (+ pr, sc); *Indian Jealousy* and *San Diego* (split reel) (+ pr, sc); *The Canyon Dweller* (+ pr, sc); *It Pays to Wait* (+ pr, sc); *A Life for a Kiss* (+ pr, sc); *The Meddlers* (+ pr, sc); *The Girl and the Gun* (+ pr, sc); *The Battleground* (+ pr, sc); *The Bad Man and the Ranger* (+ pr, sc); *The Outlaw Colony* (+ pr, sc); *The Land of Death* (+ pr, sc); *The Bandit of Point Loma* (+ pr, sc); *The Jealous Rage* (+ pr, sc); *The Will of James Waldron* (+ pr, sc); *The House that Jack Built* (+ pr, sc); *Curtiss's School of Aviation* (+ pr, sc); *The Stepmother* (+ pr, sc); *The Odd Job Man* (+ pr, sc); *The Liar* (+ pr, sc); *The Greaser and the Weakling* (+ pr, sc); *The Stranger at Coyote* (+ pr, sc); *The Dawn of Passion* (+ pr, sc); *The Vengeance that Failed* (+ pr, sc); *The Fear* (+ pr, sc); *The Foreclosure* (+ pr, sc); *White Treachery* (+ pr, sc); *Their Hero Son* (+ pr, sc); *Calamity Anne's Ward* (+ pr, sc); *Father's Favorite* (+ pr, sc); *Jack of Diamonds* (+ pr, sc); *The Reformation of Sierra Smith* (+ pr, sc); *The Promise* (+ pr, sc); *The New Cowpuncher* (+ pr, sc); *The Best Man Wins* (+ pr, sc); *The Wooers of Mountain Kate* (+ pr, sc); *One, Two, Three* (+ pr, sc); *The Wanderer* (+ pr, sc); *Maiden and Men* (+ pr, sc); *God's Unfortunate* (+ pr, sc); *Man's Calling* (+ pr, sc); *The Intrusion at Lompoc* (+ pr, sc); *The Thief's Wife* (+ pr, sc); *The Would-Be Heir* (+ pr, sc); *Jack's Word* (+ pr, sc); *Her Own Country* (+ pr, sc); *Pals* (+ pr, sc); *The Animal Within* (+ pr, sc); *The Law of God* (+ pr, sc); *Nell of the Pampas* (+ pr, sc); *The Daughters of Senor Lopez* (+ pr, sc); *The Power of Love* (+ pr, sc); *The Recognition* (+ pr, sc); *Blackened Hills* (+ pr, sc); *The Loneliness of Neglect* (+ pr, sc); *Paid in Full* (+ pr, sc); *Ranch Life on the Range* (+ pr, sc); *The Man from the East* (+ pr, sc); *The Horse Thief* (+ pr, sc); *The Good Love and the Bad* (+ pr, sc)

Allan Dwan

1913 *The Fraud that Failed* (+ pr, sc); *Another Man's Wife* (+ pr, sc); *Calamity Anne's Inheritance* (+ pr, sc); *Their Masterpiece* (+ pr, sc); *His Old-Fashioned Mother* (+ pr, sc); *Where Destiny Guides* (+ pr, sc); *The Silver-Plated Gun* (+ pr, sc); *A Rose of Old Mexico* (+ pr, sc); *Building the Great Los Angeles Aqueduct* (+ pr, sc); *Women Left Alone* (+ pr, sc); *Andrew Jackson* (+ pr, sc); *Calamity Anne's Vanity* (+ pr, sc); *The Fugitive* (+ pr, sc); *The Romance* (+ pr, sc); *The Finer Things* (+ pr, sc); *Love is Blind* (+ pr, sc); *Then the Light Fades* (+ pr, sc); *High and Low* (+ pr, sc); *The Greater Love* (+ pr, sc); *The Jocular Winds* (+ pr, sc); *The Transgression of Manuel* (+ pr, sc); *Calamity Anne, Detective* (+ pr, sc); *The Orphan's Mine* (+ pr, sc); *When a Woman Won't* (+ pr, sc); *An Eastern Flower* (+ pr, sc); *Cupid Never Ages* (+ pr, sc); *Calamity Anne's Beauty* (+ pr, sc); *The Renegade's Heart* (+ pr, sc); *Matches* (+ pr, sc); *The Mute Witness* (+ pr, sc); *Cupid Throws a Brick* (+ pr, sc); *Woman's Honor* (+ pr, sc); *Suspended Sentence* (+ pr, sc); *In Another's Nest* (+ pr, sc); *The Ways of Fate* (+ pr, sc); *Boobs and Bricks* (+ pr, sc); *Calamity Anne's Trust* (+ pr, sc); *Oil on Troubled Waters* (+ pr, sc); *The Road to Ruin* (+ pr, sc); *The Brothers* (+ pr, sc); *Human Kindness* (+ pr, sc); *Youth and Jealousy* (+ pr, sc); *Angel of the Can-*

yons (+ pr, sc); *The Great Harmony* (+ pr, sc); *Her Innocent Marriage* (+ pr, sc); *Calamity Anne Parcel Post* (+ pr, sc); *The Ashes of Three* (+ pr, sc); *On the Border* (+ pr, sc); *Her Big Story* (+ pr, sc); *When Luck Changes* (+ pr, sc); *The Wishing Seat* (+ pr, sc); *Hearts and Horses* (+ pr, sc); *The Reward of Courage* (+ pr, sc); *The Soul of a Thief* (+ pr, sc); *The Marine Law* (+ pr, sc); *The Road to Success* (+ pr, sc); *The Spirit of the Flag*; *The Call to Arms* (+ sc); *Women and War*; *The Power Flash of Death* (+ sc); *The Picket Guard*; *Mental Suicide*; *Man's Duty*; *The Animal* (+ sc); *The Wall of Money*; *The Echo of a Song*; *Criminals*; *The Restless Spirit* (+ sc); *Jewels of a Sacrifice*; *Back to Life*; *Red Margaret, Moonshiner*; *Bloodhounds of the North*; *He Called Her In* (+ sc); *The Menace* (+ sc); *The Chase*; *The Battle of Wills*

1914 *The Lie*; *The Honor of the Mounted*; *Remember Mary Magdalene* (+ sc); *Discord and Harmony*; *The Menace to Carlotta*; *The Embezzler* (+ sc); *The Lamb, the Woman, the Wolf* (+ sc); *The End of the Feud*; *Tragedy of Whispering Creek*; *The Unlawful Trade*; *The Forbidden Room*; *The Hopes of Blind Alley*; *The Great Universal Mystery*; *Richelieu* (+ sc); *Wildflower*; *The Country Chairman* (+ sc); *The Small Town Girl*; *The Straight Road*; *The Conspiracy*; *The Unwelcome Mrs. Hatch*; *The Man on the Case*

1915 *The Dancing Girl*; *David Harum*; *The Love Route*; *The Commanding Officer*; *May Blossom*; *The Pretty Sister of Jose*; *A Girl of Yesterday*; *The Foundling*; *Jordan is a Hard Road* (+ sc)

1916 *Betty of Greystone*; *The Habit of Happiness* (*Laugh and the World Laughs*) (+ sc); *The Good Bad Man* (*Passing Through*); *An Innocent Magdalene*; *The Half-Breed*; *Manhattan Madness*; *Fifty-Fifty* (+ sc)

1917 *Panthea* (+ sc); *The Fighting Odds*; *A Modern Musketeer* (+ sc)

1918 *Mr. Fix-It* (+ sc); *Bound in Morocco* (+ sc); *He Comes Up Smiling*

1919 *Cheating Cheaters*; *Getting Mary Married*; *The Dark Star*; *Soldiers of Fortune*

1920 *The Luck of the Irish*; *The Forbidden Thing* (+ pr, co-sc)

1921 *A Perfect Crime* (+ pr, sc); *A Broken Doll* (+ pr, sc); *The Scoffer* (+ pr); *The Sin of Martha Queed* (+ pr, sc); *In the Heart of a Fool* (+ pr)

1922 *The Hidden Woman* (+ pr); *Superstition* (+ pr); *Robin Hood*

1923 *The Glimpses of the Moon* (+ pr); *Lawful Larceny* (+ pr); *Zaza* (+ pr); *Big Brother* (+ pr)

1924 *A Society Scandal* (+ pr); *Manhandled* (+ pr); *Her Love Story* (+ pr); *Wages of Virtue*; *Argentine Love* (+ pr)

1925 *Night Life in New York* (+ pr); *Coast of Folly* (+ pr); *Stage Struck* (+ pr)

1926 *Sea Horses* (+ pr); *Padlocked* (+ pr); *Tin Gods* (+ pr); *Summer Bachelors* (+ pr)

1927 *The Music Master* (+ pr); *West Point* (+ pr); *The Joy Girl* (+ pr); *East Side, West Side* (+ sc); *French Dressing* (+ pr)

1928 *The Big Noise* (+ pr)

1929 *The Iron Mask*; *Tide of Empire*; *The Far Call*; *Frozen Justice*; *South Sea Rose*

1930 *What a Widow!* (+ pr); *Man to Man*

1931 *Chances*; *Wicked*

1932 *While Paris Sleeps*

1933 *Her First Affaire*; *Counsel's Opinion*

1934 *The Morning After* (*I Spy*); *Hollywood Party* (uncredited)

1935 *Black Sheep* (+ sc); *Navy Wife*

1936 *Song and Dance Man*; *Human Cargo*; *High Tension*; *15 Maiden Lane*

1937 *Woman-Wise*; *That I May Live*; *One Mile from Heaven*; *Heidi*

1938 *Rebecca of Sunnybrook Farm*; *Josette*; *Suez*

1939 *The Three Musketeers*; *The Gorilla*; *Frontier Marshal*

1940 *Sailor's Lady*; *Young People*; *Trail of the Vigilantes*

1941 *Look Who's Laughing* (+ pr); *Rise and Shine*

1942 *Friendly Enemies*; *Here We Go Again* (+ pr)

1943 *Around the World* (+ pr)

1944 *Up in Mabel's Room*; *Abroad with Two Yanks*

1945 *Brewster's Millions*; *Getting Gertie's Garter*

1946 *Rendezvous with Annie* (+ co-pr)

1947 *Calendar Girl* (+ co-pr); *Northwest Outpost* (+ co-pr); *Driftwood*

1948 *The Inside Story* (+ pr); *Angel in Exile*

1949 *Sands of Iwo Jima*

1950 *Surrender* (+ co-pr)

1951 *Belle le Grand*; *The Wild Blue Yonder*

1952 *I Dream of Jeannie (With the Light Brown Hair)*; *Montana Belle*

1953 *Woman They Almost Lynched*; *Sweethearts on Parade* (+ co-pr)

1954 *Flight Nurse*; *Silver Lode*; *Passion*; *Cattle Queen of Montana*

1955 *It's Always Sunday* (for *Screen Director's Playhouse* television series); *Escape to Burma*; *Pearl of the South Pacific*; *Tennessee's Partner*

1956 *Slightly Scarlet*; *Hold Back the Night*

1957 *The River's Edge*; *The Restless Breed*

1958 *Enchanted Island*

1961 *Most Dangerous Man Alive*

Publications

By DWAN: articles—

Interview with F.T. Pope, in *Photoplay* (New York), September 1923.

"Must actors have temperament?" in *Motion Picture* (New York), February 1926.

"As It Was," in *Making Films* (New York), June 1971.

"What Directors Are Saying," in *Action* (Los Angeles), August 1971.

"Angel in Exile: Alan Dwan," interview with G. Morris and H. Mandelbaum, in *Bright Lights* (Los Angeles), no. 4, 1979.

On DWAN: books—

Brownlow, Kevin, *The Parade's Gone By,* London and New York, 1968.

Bogdanovich, Peter, *Allan Dwan, the Last Pioneer,* New York, 1971.

On DWAN: articles—

Sarris, Andrew, "Esoterica," in *Film Culture* (New York), Spring 1963.

Smith, J.M., "Allan Dwan," in *Brighton Film Review,* February 1970.

Schickel, Richard, "Good Days, Good Years," in *Harper's* (New York), October 1970.

"Six Pioneers," in *Action* (Los Angeles), November/December 1972.

Dorr, J.H., "Allan Dwan: Master of the American Folk Art of Filmmaking," in *Take One* (Montreal), September 1973.

Dorr, J., "The Griffith Tradition," in *Film Comment* (New York), March/April 1974.

Biette, J.C., "Allan Dwan, ou le cinéma nature," in *Cahiers du Cinéma* (Paris), February 1982.

McGillivray, D., obituary, in *Films and Filming* (London), March 1982.

* * *

Allan Dwan was a pioneer among pioneers. He, along with men like D.W. Griffith and Cecil B. DeMille, enjoyed careers that spanned the birth and the growth of the American motion picture industry. Active in the industry for over fifty years, Dwan participated in creating at least eight hundred films—his own estimate was 1,850. Most of these were one-to-four-reel silents, of which some two-thirds are lost, and for that reason his career remains one which has never been properly assessed. The artistic disparity of his seventy-odd sound films fail to adequately represent this technically innovative, unpretentious, avid storyteller, and his career will surely undergo considerable re-evaluation as the study of film history progresses.

It was the scientific aspect of motion pictures that first attracted Dwan to the medium, and in 1909 he joined Essanay as a lighting man. He then joined the American Flying A Company as a writer but soon found himself directing short films, mostly Westerns. He moved next to Universal, then to Famous Players, where in 1915 he introduced the dolly shot for *David Harum* and directed Mary Pickford in *The Foundling.*

That same year Dwan joined Fine Arts-Triangle, where his films were supervised by D.W. Griffith. He directed many of Griffith's top stars, including Dorothy Gish in *Betty of Greystone* and her sister Lillian in *An Innocent Magdalene.* He once stated how impressed he was with the "economy of gesture" of Griffith's players. He credits Griffith with developing his clean, spare visual style, while Griffith frequently sought out Dwan for his technical knowledge. One such request resulted in Dwan's improvising an elevator on a moving track to film the massive sets of *Intolerance.*

Dwan also established his association with Douglas Fairbanks at Fine Arts-Triangle. This professional relationship resulted in collaboration on eleven films, including *The Half-Breed, A Modern Musketeer, Bound in Morocco,* and the celebrated *Robin Hood,* described by Robert Sherwood as "the high-water mark of film production" and "the farthest step that the silent drama has ever taken along the high road to art."

In 1923 Dwan directed his favorite film, *Big Brother,* which was about underprivileged boys, and then embarked on the first of eight buoyant comedies starring Gloria Swanson, the best of which were *Zaza* and *Manhandled.* With the arrival of sound, Dwan signed a long-term contract with Fox (1930-41), where he was unfortunately relegated to their B unit except for occasional reprieves—Shirley Temple's *Heidi* and *Rebecca of Sunnybrook Farm,* and *Suez,* much admired for its typhoon sequence. He then signed with producer Edward Small, for whom he directed a delightful quartet of farces—*Up in Mabel's Room, Getting Gertie's Garter, Abroad with Two Yanks,* and *Brewster's Millions.* He then unwisely signed an exclusive deal with Republic Pictures where, except for *Sands of Iwo Jima,* his creativity was constricted by studio head Herbert Yates. Moving to RKO, he persevered despite the many obstacles of 1950s filmmaking, churning out entertaining action films.

Dwan loved moviemaking and was described as the "last of the journeyman filmmakers" by Richard Roud. Of his self-imposed retirement in 1958, Dwan explained: "It was no longer a question of 'Let's get a bunch of people together and make a picture.' It's just a business that I stood as long as I could and I got out of it when I couldn't stand it any more."

—Ronald Bowers

EASTWOOD, Clint

Nationality: American. **Born:** 31 May 1930 in San Francisco, California. **Education:** Oakland Technical High School; Los Angeles City College, 1953-54. **Military Service:** Drafted into the U.S. Army, 1950. **Family:** Married Maggie Johnson, 1953 (divorced, 1980); one son, one daughter. **Career:** Under contract with Universal, 1954-55; sporadic work in film, late 1950s; played Rowdy Yates in TV series *Rawhide,* 1959-65; went to Europe to make three highly successful westerns with Sergio Leone, 1965; returned to U.S., 1967; formed Malpaso production company and directed first film, *Play Misty for Me,* 1971; first effort as producer, *Firefox,* 1982; Mayor of Carmel, California, 1986-88. **Awards:** Chevaliers des Lettres, France, 1985; Academy Awards, Best Director and Best Picture, for *Unforgiven,* 1992; Fellowship of the British Film Institute, 1993. **Address:** Malpaso Productions, 4000 Warner Boulevard, Burbank, California 91522, USA.

Films as Director:

1971 ***Play Misty for Me*** (+ role)
1972 *High Plains Drifter* (+ role)
1973 *Breezy*
1975 *The Eiger Sanction* (+ role)
1976 *The Outlaw Josey Wales* (+role)
1977 *The Gauntlet* (+ role)
1980 *Bronco Billy* (+ role, song composer)
1982 *Firefox* (+ role, pr); *Honkytonk Man* (+ role, pr)
1983 *Sudden Impact* (+ role, pr)
1985 *Pale Rider* (+ role, pr)
1986 *Heartbreak Ridge* (+role, pr, song composer)
1987 *Bird* (+ pr)
1990 *The Rookie* (+ role); *White Hunter, Black Heart* (+ role, pr)
1992 ***Unforgiven*** (+ role, pr, music)
1993 *A Perfect World* (+ role, pr)
1995 *The Bridges of Madison County* (+role, pr)

Other Films:

1955 *Francis in the Navy* (role); *Lady Godiva* (role); *Revenge of the Creature* (role); *Tarantula* (role)
1956 *The First Travelling Saleslady* (role); *Never Say Goodbye* (role); *Star in the Dust* (role)
1957 *Escapade in Japan* (role)
1958 *Ambush at Cimarron Pass* (role); *Lefayette Escradille* (role)
1964 *A Fistful of Dollars* (role)
1965 *For a Few Dollars More* (role)
1966 ***Il Buono, il brutto, il cattivo*** (*The Good, the Bad, and the Ugly*) (Leone) (role); *Le Streghe* (role)
1967 *Hang 'em High* (role)
1968 *Coogan's Bluff* (role)
1969 *Paint Your Wagon* (role); *Where Eagles Dare* (role)
1970 *Kelly's Heroes* (role); *Two Mules for Sister Sara* (role)
1971 *The Beguiled* (role); *Dirty Harry* (role)
1972 *Joe Kidd* (role)
1973 *Magnum Force* (role)
1974 *Thunderbolt and Lightfoot* (role)
1976 *The Enforcer* (role)
1978 *Every Which Way but Loose* (role)
1979 *Escape from Alcatraz* (role)
1980 *Any Which Way You Can* (role, song composer)
1984 *City Heat* (role); *Tightrope* (role, pr)
1988 *The Dead Pool* (role, pr); *Thelonius Monk: Straight No Chaser* (exec pr)
1989 *The Pink Cadillac* (role)
1993 *In the Line of Fire* (role)

Publications

By EASTWOOD: articles—

Interview with David Thomson in *Film Comment,* September/October 1984.
Interview with C. Tesson and O. Assayas in *Cahiers du Cinema,* February 1985.
Interview with Michel Ciment and Hubert Niograt in *Positif,* July/August 1988.
Interview with Nat Hentoff in *American Film,* September 1988.
Interview with Allan Hunter in *Films and Filming,* November/December 1988.
Interview with R. Gentry in *Film Quarterly,* vol. 42, no. 3, 1989.
Interview with Michel Ciment in *Positif,* no. 351, 1990.
Interview with M. Henry in *Positif,* no. 380, 1992.

On EASTWOOD: books—

Kaminsky, Stuart, *Clint Eastwood,* New York, 1974.
Agan, Patrick, *Clint Eastwood: The Man behind the Myth,* New York, 1975.
Downing, David, and Gary Herman, *Clint Eastwood, All-American Anti-Hero: A Critical Appraisal of the World's Top Box Office Star and His Films,* London, 1977.
Ferrari, Philippe, *Clint Eastwood,* Paris, 1980.
Johnstone, Iain, *The Man with No Name: Clint Eastwood,* London, 1981; revised edition 1988.
Zmijewsky, Boris, and Lee Pfeiffer, *The Films of Clint Eastwood,* Secaucas, NJ, 1982; revised editions, 1988 and 1993.
Cole, Gerald, and Peter Williams, *Clint Eastwood,* London, 1983.
Guerif, Francois, *Clint Eastwood,* Paris, 1983.
Rider, Jeffrey, *Clint Eastwood,* New York, 1987.
Lagarde, Helene, *Clint Eastwood,* Paris, 1988.
Weinberger, Michele, *Clint Eastwood,* Paris, 1989.
Frayling, Christopher, *Clint Eastwood,* London, 1992.
Thompson, Douglas, *Clint Eastwood: Riding High,* Chicago, 1992.
Smith, Paul, *Clint Eastwood: A Cultural Production,* Minneapolis, 1993.

Clint Eastwood directing *Unforgiven*

Bingham, Dennis, *Acting Male: Masculinities in the Films of James Stewart, Jack Nicholson, and Clint Eastwood,* New Brunswick NJ, 1994.

Gallafent, Edward, *Clint Eastwood: Filmmaker and Star,* New York, 1994.

On EASTWOOD: articles—

Patterson, E., "Every Which Way but Lucid: The Critique of Authority in Clint Eastwood's Police Films," *Journal of Popular Film,* Fall 1982.

"Clint Eastwood section" of *Positif,* January 1985.

Kehr, Dave, "A Fistful of Eastwood," *American Film,* March 1985.

Chevrie, M., and D. J. Wiener, "Le dernier des cow-boys," *Cahiers du Cinema,* March 1987.

Holmlund, C., "Sexuality and Power in Male Doppelganger Cinema: The Case of Clint Eastwood and *Tightrope,*" *Cinema Journal,* vol. 26, no. 1, 1986.

Bingham, D., "Men with No Names: Clint Eastwood, the Stranger Persona, Identification and the Impenetrable Gaze," *Journal of Film and Video,* vol. 42, no. 4, 1990.

Combs, Richard, "Shadowing the Hero," *Sight and Sound,* October 1992.

Tibbetts, J. C., "Clint Eastwood and the Machinery of Violence," *Literature-Film Quarterly,* vol. 21, no. 1, 1993.

*   *   *

In 1992, after almost forty years in the business, Clint Eastwood finally received Oscar recognition. *Unforgiven* brought him the awards for Best Achievement in Directing and for Best Picture, along with a nomination for Best Actor. Indeed, this strikingly powerful Western was nominated for no less than nine Academy Awards, Gene Hackman collecting Best Supporting Actor for his performance as the movie's ruthless marshall, "Little Bill" Daggett, and Joel Cox taking the Oscar for editing. It seems appropriate, therefore, that this film, which brought him such recognition, should end with the inscription "Dedicated to Sergio and Don." For without the intervention and influence of his two "mentors," directors Sergio Leone and Don Siegel, it is difficult to imagine Eastwood achieving his present respectability, let alone emerging as the only major star of the modern era who has become a better director than he ever was an actor.

That is not to belittle Eastwood, who has always been generous in crediting Leone and Siegel, and who is certainly far more than a passive inheritor of their directorial visions. Even in his *Rawhide* days of the 1950s and early 1960s he wanted to direct; more than once Eastwood has told of his attempts to persuade that series' producers to let him shoot some of the action rather more ambitiously than was the TV norm. Not surprisingly, they were reluctant, but they did in the end allow him to make trailers for upcoming episodes. He was not to take on a full-fledged directorial challenge until 1971 and *Play Misty for Me,* but in the intervening years he had become a massive box-office attraction as an actor, first with Leone in Europe in the three famous and founding "spaghetti westerns," and then in a series of films with Siegel back in the United States, most significantly *Dirty Harry*.

It is not easy to untangle the respective influences of his mentors. In general terms, because they both contributed to the formation of Eastwood's distinctive screen persona, they helped him to crystallise an image which, as a director, he would so often use as a foil. The Italian Westerns' "man with no name," and his more anguished urban equivalent given expression in *Dirty Harry*'s eponymous anti-hero, have provided Eastwood with well-established and economical starting characters for so many of his performances. In directing himself, furthermore, he has used that persona with a degree of irony and distance. Sometimes, especially in his Westerns, that has meant leaning toward stylisation and almost operatic exaggeration (*High Plains Drifter, Pale Rider,* the last section of *Unforgiven*), though rarely reaching Leone's extremes of delirious overstatement. On other occasions, it has seen him play on the tension between the seemingly assertive masculinity of the Eastwood image and the strong female characters who are so often featured in his films (*Play Misty for Me, The Gauntlet, Heartbreak Ridge* and, in part at least, *The Bridges of Madison County*). It is, of course, notoriously difficult to both direct and star in a movie. Where Eastwood has succeeded in that combination (not always the case) it has depended significantly on his inventive building on the Eastwood persona.

It is important to give Eastwood full credit for this inventiveness in any attempt to assess his work. His better films as a director have a richness to them, not just stylistically—though in those respects he has learned well from Leone's concern with lighting and composition and from Siegel's way with in-frame movement, editing, and tight narration—but also a moral complexity which belies the one-dimensionality of the Eastwood image. The protagonists in his better films, like Josey Wales in *The Outlaw Josey Wales*, Highway in *Heartbreak Ridge,* Munny in *Unforgiven,* even Charlie Parker in the flawed *Bird,* are not simple men in either their virtues or their failings. Eastwood's fondness for narratives of revenge and redemption, furthermore, allows him to draw upon a rich generic vein in American cinema, a tradition with a built-in potential for character development and for evoking human complexity without giving way to art-film portentousness.

In these respects Eastwood is the modern inheritor of traditional Hollywood directorial values, once epitomised in the transparent style of a John Ford, Howard Hawks, or John Huston (himself the subject of Eastwood's *White Hunter, Black Heart*), and passed on to Eastwood by that next-generation carrier of the tradition, Don Siegel. For these filmmakers, as for Eastwood, the action movie, the Western, the thriller were opportunities to explore character, motivation, and human frailty within a framework of accessible entertainment. Of course, all of them were also capable of "quieter" films, harnessing the same commitment to craft, the same attention to detail, in the service of less action-driven narratives, just as Eastwood has done most recently with *The Bridges of Madison County.* But in the end their and Eastwood's real art was to draw upon Hollywood's genre traditions and make of them unique and perceptive studies of human beings under stress. Though his directorial career has been uneven, at his best Eastwood has proved a more than worthy carrier of this flame.

—Andrew Tudor

EDWARDS, Blake

Nationality: American. **Born:** William Blake McEdwards in Tulsa, Oklahoma, 26 July 1922. **Military Service:** Served in the U.S. Coast Guard, 1944-45. **Family:** Married 1) Patricia Walker, 1953, one son, one daughter; 2) actress Julie Andrews, 1969, two adopted daughters. **Career:** Created NBC radio series, *Richard Diamond, Private Detective,* for Dick Powell, 1949; as writer/director for Columbia B-picture Unit, directed first feature *Bring Your Smile Along,* 1955; directed first A-picture, *Mister Cory,* 1957; creator, *Peter Gunn,* 1958, *Mr. Lucky,* 1959, and *Dante's Inferno,* 1960, for TV; after dispute over *The Carey Treatment,* moved to Europe; signed three-picture deal with Orion, 1978, agreement terminated after *10,* 1979; directed Julie Andrews on Broadway in a stage adaptation of *Victor/Victoria,* 1995; lives in Gstaad, Switzerland. **Awards:** Writers Guild of America Award, Best-Written Comedy Adapted from Another Medium, for *The Pink Panther Strikes Again* (co-authored with Frank Waldman), 1976.

Films as Director:

1955 *Bring Your Smile Along* (+ sc)
1956 *He Laughed Last* (+ sc)
1958 *This Happy Feeling* (+ sc)
1959 *The Perfect Furlough* (+ sc); *Operation Petticoat* (+ sc)
1960 *High Time* (+ sc)
1961 ***Breakfast at Tiffany's***
1962 *Experiment in Terror* (*The Grip of Fear*) (+ pr, sc); *Days of Wine and Roses*; *Walk on the Wild Side* (Dmytryk) (d add'l scenes, uncredited)
1964 *The Pink Panther* (+ co-sc); *A Shot in the Dark* (+ sc)
1965 *The Great Race* (+ sc, co-story, bit rolc as troublemaker); *What Did You Do in the War, Daddy?* (+ sc, co-story, pr)
1967 *Gunn* (+ co-sc)
1968 *The Party* (+ co-sc, pr)
1970 *Darling Lili* (+ co-sc, co-pr)
1971 *The Wild Rovers* (+ co-pr, sc)
1972 *The Carey Treatment* (*Emergency Ward*)
1974 *The Tamarind Seed* (+ sc); *The Return of the Pink Panther* (+ co-sc, pr)
1976 *The Pink Panther Strikes Again* (+ co-sc, pr)
1978 *Revenge of the Pink Panther* (+ co-sc, pr)
1979 *10* (+ sc, pr)
1981 *S.O.B.* (+ sc, pr)
1982 *Victor Victoria* (+ co-pr, sc); *Trail of the Pink Panther* (+ pr)
1983 *Curse of the Pink Panther* (+ pr, sc); *The Man Who Loved Women* (+ pr, co-sc)
1984 *Micki and Maude* (+ pr)
1986 *A Fine Mess* (*The Music Box*) (+ sc); *That's Life* (*Crisis*) (+ co-sc)
1987 *Blind Date*
1988 *Sunset*
1989 *Skin Deep*; *Peter Gunn* (for TV)
1991 *Switch* (+ sc)
1992 *Julie* (TV series) (+ ex pr)
1993 *Son of the Pink Panther* (+ sc)

Other Films:

1942 *Ten Gentlemen from West Point* (Hathaway) (role); *Lucky Legs* (Barton) (role)
1943 *A Guy Named Joe* (Fleming) (role)
1944 *In the Meantime, Darling* (Preminger) (role); *Marshal of Reno* (Grissell) (role); *See Here, Private Hargrove* (Ruggles) (role); *Ladies Courageous* (Rawlins) (role); *The Eve of St. Mark* (Stahl) (role); *Marine Raiders* (Schuster) (role); *Wing and a Prayer* (Hathaway) (role); *My Buddy* (Sekely) (role); *The Unwritten Code* (Rotsten) (role); *Thirty Seconds over Tokyo* (LeRoy) (role); *She's a Sweetheart* (Lord) (role)

1945 *This Man's Navy* (Wellman) (role); *A Guy, a Gal, and a Pal* (Boetticher) (role); *Gangs of the Waterfront* (Blair) (role); *What Next, Corporal Hargrove?* (Thorpe) (role); *They Were Expendable* (Ford) (role); *Tokyo Rose* (Landers) (role); *Strangler of the Swamp* (Wisbar) (major role)
1946 *The Strange Love of Martha Ivers* (Milestone) (role); *Till the End of Time* (Dmytryk) (role); *The Best Years of Our Lives* (Wyler) (role)
1947 *The Beginning or the End* (Taurog) (role); *Panhandle* (co-sc, co-pr, role)
1948 *Leather Gloves* (*Loser Take All*) (Quine and Asher) (sc, role)
1949 *Stampede* (Selander) (co-sc, pr)
1952 *Sound Off* (Quine) (sc); *Rainbow Round My Shoulder* (Quine) (sc)
1953 *All Ashore* (Quine) (sc); *Cruisin' Down the River* (Quine) (sc)
1954 *Drive a Crooked Road* (Quine) (sc); *The Atomic Kid* (Martinson) (story, sc)
1955 *My Sister Eileen* (Quine) (sc)
1956 *Operation Mad Ball* (Quine) (co-sc)
1961 *The Couch* (Crump) (co-story)
1962 *The Notorious Landlady* (Quine) (co-sc)
1963 *Soldier in the Rain* (Nelson) (co-sc, pr)
1967 *Inspector Clouseau* (Yorkin) (sc)

Publications

By EDWARDS: articles—

"Un Humour sérieux," in *Cahiers du Cinéma* (Paris), May/June 1965.
"Sophisticated Naturalism," interview with Jean-Francois Hauduroy, in *Cahiers du Cinéma in English* (New York), no. 3, 1966.
"Confessions of a Cult Figure," interview with Stuart Byron, in *Village Voice* (New York), 5 August 1971.
"Dans la tradition classique," interview with C. Viviani, in *Positif* (Paris), June 1973.
Interview with P. Stamelman, in *Millimeter* (New York), January 1977.
"Riding Herd on a Chinese Fire Drill," interview, in *American Cinematographer* (Los Angeles), July 1978.
"Too Much To Do, Not Enough Time To Do It," interview with P. Lehman and W. Luhr, in *Wide Angle* (Athens, Ohio), vol. 3, no. 3, 1980.
Interview in *Hollywood Reporter,* 56th Anniversary Edition, 1986.
Interview with William Luhr and Peter Lehman in *Positif* (Paris), January 1990.

On EDWARDS: books—

Lehman, Peter, and William Luhr, *Blake Edwards,* Athens, Ohio, 1980.
Lehman, Peter, and William Luhr, *Returning to the Scene: Blake Edwards, Volume 2,* Athens, Ohio, 1989.

On EDWARDS: articles—

Haller, Robert, "*Peter Gunn*: The Private Eye of Blake Edwards," in *Film Heritage* (New York), Summer 1968.
Lightman, Herb, "*Wild Rovers*: Case History of a Film," in *American Cinematographer* (Los Angeles), July 1971.
Benayoun, Robert, "Blake Edwards ou la sophistication de l'innocence," in *Positif* (Paris), June 1973.
Luhr, William, and Peter Lehman, "You'll Never Work in Hollywood Again," in *Wide Angle* (Athens, Ohio), vol. 1, no. 4, 1977; "The Case of the Missing Lead Pipe Cinch," in *Wide Angle* (Athens, Ohio), no. 1, 1979; and "Crime in the Bedroom," in *Wide Angle* (Athens, Ohio), no. 2, 1979.
Morris, G., "Blake Edwards Takes *10,*" in *Film Comment* (New York), November/December 1979.
Kennedy, Harlan, "Blake Edwards: Life after *10,*" in *American Film* (Washington, D.C.), July/August 1981.
"Lost in Gloss or Cineaste maudit: The Strange Case of Blake Edwards," in *Monthly Film Bulletin* (London), July 1984.
Tobin, Y., and A. Masson, in *Positif* (Paris), April 1985.
Ciné Revue (Paris), 16 June 1988.
Cook, Anthony, "Survival is the Best Revenge," in *Gentlemen's Quarterly* (New York), April 1989.
Maslin, Janet, "It's Not Just a Man's World for Blake Edwards," in *New York Times,* 5 May 1991.
Legrand, G., article in *Positif* (Paris), May 1992.
Thirard, P. L., article in *Positif* (Paris), May 1992.
Weinraub, Bernard, "A Hollywood Incident Full of Sound and Furor," in *New York Times,* 28 May 1992.

On EDWARDS: Films—

Hindle, Will, *Experiment on "Experiment,"* for TV, 1962.
Anderson, Edward, *Gift of Laughter,* Great Britain, 1975.

* * *

Blake Edwards is one of the few filmmakers from the late classical period of American movies (the late 1940s and 1950s) to survive and prosper through the 1980s. If anything, Edwards's work has deepened with the passing decades, though it no longer bears much resemblance to the norms and styles of contemporary Hollywood. Edwards is an isolated figure, but a vital one.

Edwards's critical and box office reputation first peaked in the early 1960s with such films as *Operation Petticoat, Breakfast at Tiffany's, Days of Wine and Roses,* and *The Pink Panther.* But as the new, post-studio Hollywood moved away from his brand of classicism, Edwards had a string of commercial disappointments—*What Did You Do in the War, Daddy?, Gunn, The Party*—leading up to the total failure of the multi-million dollar musical *Darling Lili.* In the early 1970s, Edwards was barely visible, issuing occasional programmers—*The Wild Rovers, The Carey Treatment, The Tamarind Seed*—until he decided to revive the Inspector Clouseau character for *The Return of the Pink Panther.*

The mordant slapstick of the Panther films was back in style, and Edwards rode the success of *Return* through three more sequels, with the promise (despite the death of Clouseau's interpreter, Peter Sellers) of more to come. The success of the Panther films allowed Edwards to capitalize more personal projects, one of which—the 1979 *10*—became a sleeper hit. In his sixties, he again became a brand name, with his own production company (Blake Edwards Entertainment) and a measure of security.

For all his artistic independence, Edwards has always chosen to work within well-defined, traditional genres—the musical, the melodrama, the slapstick farce, the thriller. There is little continuity in tone between a film like *The Tamarind Seed* (a transcendent love story) and *S.O.B.* (a frenzied black farce), yet there are the more important continuities of personality. Edwards has no particular commitment to any single genre (though his greatest successes have been comedies); he varies his choices as a painter varies the colors of his palette, to alter the tonal mix. The single stylistic constant has been Edwards's use of Panavision; with very few exceptions, his films have used the widescreen format as the basic unit of organization and expression.

At their most elemental level, Edwards's films are about space—crossing it, filling it, transcending it. In his comedies, the widescreen space becomes a vortex fraught with perils—hidden traps, aggressive objects, spaces that abruptly open onto other, unexpected spaces. Edwards extends the principles of silent comedy into modern technol-

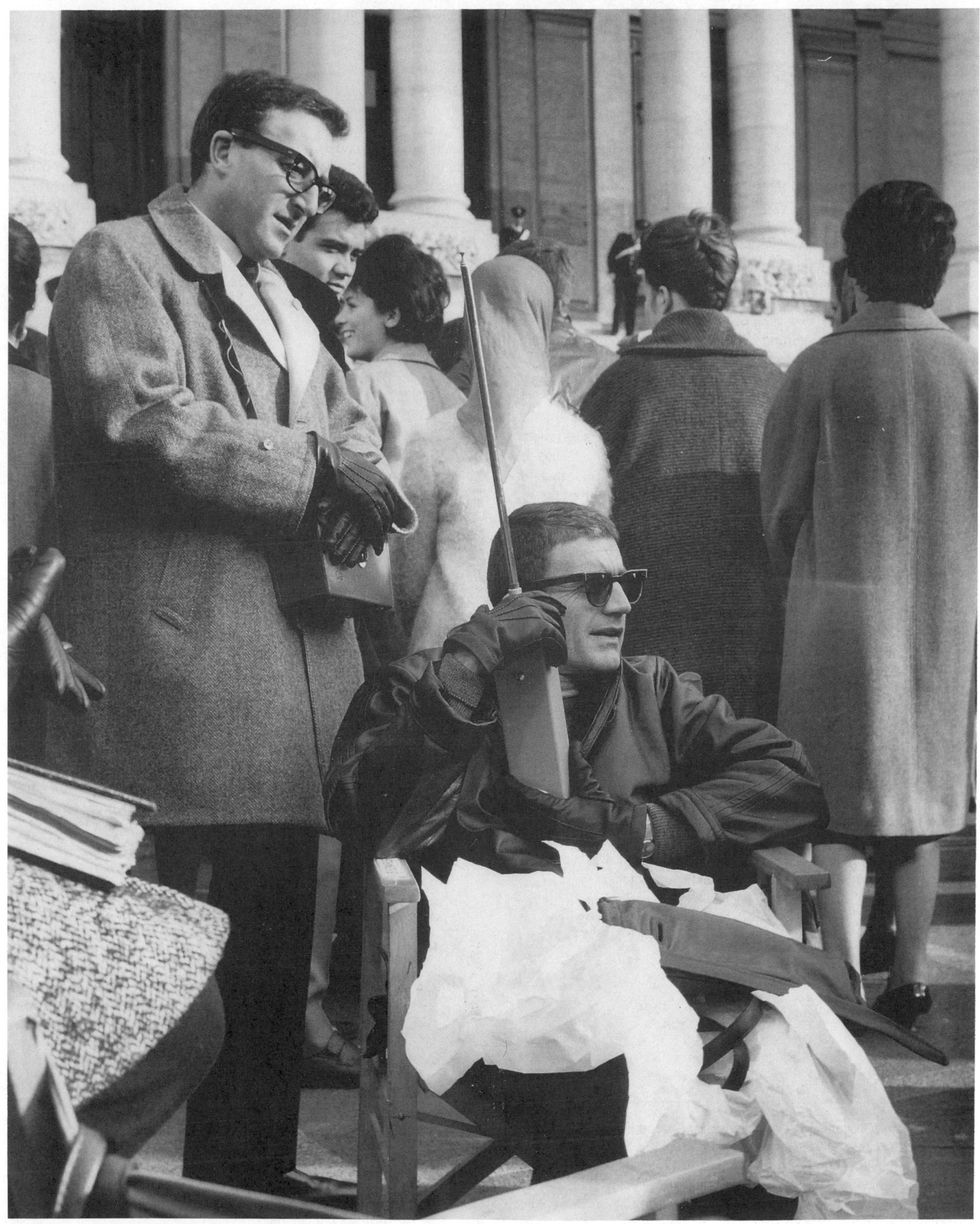

Blake Edwards (seated) with Peter Sellers on the set of *The Pink Panther*

ogy and modern absurdism; his comic heroes are isolated in the hostile widescreen space, unable to conquer it as Chaplin and Keaton could conquer the more manageable dimensions of the silent frame. (Though the Panther films employ this principle, Edwards's masterpiece in this vein is the relatively unknown 1968 film, *The Party.*)

Visually, Edwards's thrillers appear to be more dense, more furnished, more confining than his comedies (and two of the best of them, *Gunn* and *Experiment in Terror,* were photographed in the standard screen ratio); the threat comes not from empty space, but from the crowding of objects, colors, surfaces—the hard, cold *thingness* of things. This deathly solidity gives way, when the surfaces dissolve, to a more deathly chaos. In the romances, that operative space is the space between the characters; it must be collapsed, transformed, overcome. In *Darling Lili,* a room full of red roses is an emblem of love; it is not the trite symbolism of the flowers that gives the image its power, but the complete filling in of the widescreen space, its emotional conquest. In *The Tamarind Seed,* the lovers' conquest of space entails, as it does in the sublime 1930s romances of Frank Borzage, a conquest of death.

With *10* and *Victor/Victoria,* Edwards managed to blend the styles and assumptions of his comedies and romances. The strict genre divisions that once ruled his work are broken down, and with their dissolution a new humanism appears. Edwards's *10* uses its long lenses trained on Bo Derek's face (as perfect a blank, deathly surface as any in Edwards's films) to create looming, overlarge images of romantic fantasy. But when Dudley Moore finds his way back to Julie Andrews, Edwards shifts to balanced wide-screen compositions—two lovers occupying the same stable space—which convey images of a realistic, responsible romanticism. *Victor/Victoria,* with its theatrical metaphors, builds small proscenium spaces for each of its role-playing characters; as the constricting roles are cast off, these isolating spaces give way to an overall openness and warmth. The widescreen space is no longer inherently hostile, but contains the promise of closeness and comfort.

With the exception of *That's Life*—a clever domestic comedy co-scripted with his analyst—Edwards' recent output has been disappointing. For the post part, he has attempted—and failed—to recycle old material and stale comic formulas.

A perfect case-in-point is *Switch,* a poor variation of *Victor/Victoria,* in which a womanizing male is killed by a vengeful conquest and comes back to earth as a member of the opposite sex. *Blind Date* (about a yuppie on a blind date) and *Sunset* (in which Tom Mix and Wyatt Earp come together to solve a mystery) featured Bruce Willis in two of his weakest screen roles. *Skin Deep* is an erratic comedy about a hedonistic writer. Finally, *Son of the Pink Panther,* with popular Italian comedian Roberto Benigni replacing the late Peter Sellers, was a dreadful picture that quickly vanished after its theatrical release.

—Dave Kehr, updated by Audrey E. Kupferberg

EISENSTEIN, Sergei

Nationality: Russian. **Born:** Sergei Mikhailovich Eisenstein in Riga, Latvia, 23 January 1898. **Education:** Educated in St. Petersburg and at gymnasium in Riga; Institute of Civil Engineering, St. Petersburg (studied architecture), 1914-17; studied Japanese at General Staff Academy, Moscow, 1920. **Family:** Married Peta Attasheva. **Career:** Sent for officer training, 1917; poster artist on front at Minsk, then demobilized, 1920; scenic artist, then co-director of Proletkult Theatre, Moscow, 1920; designer for Vsevolod Meyerhold's "directors' workshop," 1922; directed *Stachka,* 1925; made professor at State Institute for Cinema, 1926; with Grigori Alexandrov and Edouard Tisse, travelled to Hollywood, 1929; signed for Paramount, but after work on various scripts, contract broken, 1930; refused a work permit by State Department, went to Mexico to work on *Que Viva Mexico!*; refused reentry permit to United States, after financier Upton Sinclair halts shooting and keeps uncut film; returned to U.S.S.R., 1932; began teaching at Moscow Film Institute, 1933; *Behzin Meadow* project denounced, production halted, 1937; worked on Pushkin film project, named Artistic Director of Mosfilm Studios, 1940; after finishing *Ivan the Terrible,* suffered heart attack, 1946; prepared a third part to *Ivan,* to have been made in color, 1947. **Awards:** Gold Medal, Exposition Internationale des Arts Décoratifs, Paris, for *Strike!,* 1925; Order of Lenin, 1939; Stalin Prize, 1st Class, for *Ivan the Terrible, Part I,* 1946. **Died:** In Moscow, 11 February 1948.

Films as Director:

1923 *Kinodnevik Glumova* (*Glumov's Film Diary*) (short film inserted in production of Ostrovsky's *Enough Simplicity in Every Wise Man*, Proletkult Theater, Moscow) (+ sc)

1925 ***Stachka*** (*The Strike*) (+ co-sc, ed); ***Bronenosets Potemkin*** (*The Battleship Potemkin*) (+ sc, ed)

1928 ***Oktiabr*** (*October*; *Ten Days That Shook the World*) (co-d, co-sc)

1929 *Staroe i novoe* (*Old and New*) [film produced as *Generalnaia linia* (*The General Line*), title changed before release] (co-d, co-sc)

1930 *Romance sentimentale* (co-d, sc)

1933 *Thunder Over Mexico* (unauthorized, produced by Sol Lesser from *Que Viva Mexico!* footage, seen by Eisenstein in 1947 and disowned); *Death Day* and *Eisenstein in Mexico* (also unauthorized productions by Sol Lesser from *Que Viva Mexico!* footage)

1938 ***Aleksandr Nevskii*** (*Alexander Nevsky*) (+ co-sc, set des, costume des, ed)

1939 *Time in the Sun* (produced by Marie Seton from *Que Viva Mexico!* footage); *The Ferghana Canal* (short documentary out of footage from abandoned feature subject on same subject) (+ sc)

1941 shorts edited by William Kruse for Bell and Howell from *Que Viva Mexico!* footage: *Mexico Marches*; *Conquering Cross*; *Idol of Hope*; *Land and Freedom*; *Spaniard and Indian*; *Mexican Symphony* (feature combining previous five titles); *Zapotecan Village*

1944 ***Ivan Groznyi*** (*Ivan the Terrible, Part I*) (+ sc, set des, costume des, ed)

1958 ***Ivan Groznyi II: Boyarskii zagovor*** (*Ivan the Terrible, Part II: The Boyars' Plot*) (+ sc) (completed 1946); *Eisenstein's Mexican Project* (+ sc) (unedited sequences of *Que Viva Mexico!* assembled by Jay Leyda)

1966 *Bezhin Lug* (*Bezhin Meadow*) (+ sc) (25 minute montage of stills from original film assembled by Naum Kleiman, with music by Prokofiev)

Other Films:

1924 *Doktor Mabuze—Igrok* (co-ed) (Russian version of Lang's *Dr. Mabuse der Spieler*)

1929 *Everyday* (Hans Richter) (role as London policeman)

Publications

By EISENSTEIN: books—

The Soviet Screen, Moscow, 1939.
The Film Sense, edited by Jay Leyda, New York, 1942.
Notes of a Film Director, Moscow, 1948.
Film Form, edited by Jay Leyda, New York, 1949.
Charlie Chaplin, Zurich, 1961.
Que Viva Mexico, London, 1951.
Drawings, Moscow, 1961.
Ivan the Terrible: A Screenplay, New York, 1962.
Sergei Eizenshtein, Izbrannye proizvedeniya (6 vols.), edited by P.M. Atasheva and others, Moscow, 1964-71.
Film Essays with a Lecture, edited by Jay Leyda, London, 1968.
Potemkin, New York, 1968.
The Battleship Potemkin, text by Andrew Sinclair, London, 1968.
Notes of a Film Director, New York, 1970.
Collected Works of Sergei Eisenstein, edited by Herbert Marshall, Cambridge, Massachusetts, 1971.
The Complete Works of Sergei M. Eisenstein, edited by Marcel Martin, Guy Lecouvette, and Abraham Segal, New York, 1971.
Eisenstein: Three Films, edited by Jay Leyda, New York, 1974.
The Complete Films of Eisenstein, New York, 1974.
Immoral Memories: An Autobiography, translated by Herbert Marshall, Boston, 1983.
October and Alexander Nevsky, edited by Jay Leyda, New York, 1984.
Iz tvorcheskogo naslediya S.M. Eizenshteina, edited by L. Kozlov and N. Kleiman, Moscow, 1985.
Nonindifferent Nature, edited by Herbert Marshall, Cambridge, 1987.
Eisenstein: Selected Works, Volume 1: Writings 1922-1934, edited by Richard Taylor, London, 1988.
S.M. Eisenstein: The Psychology of Composition, edited by A.Y. Upchurch, London, 1988.
Eisenstein: Selected Works, Volume 2: Towards a Theory of Montage, edited by Richard Taylor and Michael Glenny, London, 1991.

By EISENSTEIN: articles—

"Mass Movies," in *Nation* (New York), 9 November 1927.
"Mexican Film and Marxian Theory," in *New Republic* (New York), 9 December 1931.
"The Cinematographic Principle and Japanese Culture," in *Experimental Cinema,* no. 3, 1932.
"Through Theatre to Cinema," in *Theatre Arts* (New York), September 1936.
"The Mistakes of *Bezhin Lug,*" in *International Literature* (Moscow), no. 1, 1937.
"My Subject is Patriotism," in *International Literature* (Moscow), no. 2, 1939.
"Charlie the Kid," in *Sight and Sound* (London), Spring 1946.
"Charlie the Grownup," in *Sight and Sound* (London), Summer 1946.
"The Birth of a Film," in *Hudson Review* (Nutley, New Jersey), no. 2, 1951.
"Sketches for Life," in *Films and Filming* (London), April 1958.
"One Path to Colour: An Autobiographical Fragment," in *Sight and Sound* (London), Spring 1961.
Interview, in *Interviews with Film Directors,* edited by Andrew Sarris, New York, 1967.
"La Quatrième Dimension du cinéma," in *Cahiers du Cinéma* (Paris), September/October 1976.
"Sergei Eisenstein, Wilhelm Reich correspondence," edited by F. Albera, in *Screen* (London), vol. 22, no. 4, 1981.
"A Postcard and a letter from S.M. Eisenstein to Renaud De Jouvenel," in *Film Culture* (New York), nos. 70-71, 1983.

On EISENSTEIN: books—

Rotha, Paul, Ivor Montagu, and John Grierson, *Eisenstein 1898-1948,* London, 1948.
Arnheim, Rudolph, *Film as Art,* Berkeley, California, 1957.
Leyda, Jay, *Kino,* London, 1960.
Mitry, Jean, *S.M. Eisenstein,* Paris, 1961; revised edition, 1978.
Montagu, Ivor, *With Eisenstein in Hollywood,* New York, 1969.
Nizhny, Vladimir, *Lessons with Eisenstein,* New York, 1969.
Geduld, Harry, and Ronald Gottesman, *Sergei Eisenstein and Upton Sinclair: The Making and Unmaking of "Que Viva Mexico!",* Bloomington, Indiana, 1970.
Moussinac, Léon, *Sergei Eisenstein,* New York, 1970.
Brakhage, Stan, *The Brakhage Lectures,* Chicago, 1972.
Mayer, D., *Eisenstein's Potemkin: A Shot-by-shot Presentation,* New York, 1972.
Barna, Yon, *Eisenstein,* Bloomington, Indiana, 1973.
Shlovskii, V., *Eizenshtein,* Moscow, 1973.
Fernandez, Dominique, *Eisenstein,* Paris, 1975.
Swallow, N., *Eisenstein: a Documentary Portrait,* London, 1976; New York, 1977.
Ropars-Wuilleumier, Marie-Claire, and others, *Octobre, Ecriture et idéologie,* Paris, 1976.
Barthes, Roland, *Image/Music/Text,* New York, 1977.
Marshall, Herbert, editor, *Sergei Eisenstein's "The Battleship Potemkin,"* New York, 1978.
Seton, Marie, *Sergei M. Eisenstein,* London, 1978.
Aumont, Jacques, *Montage Eisenstein,* Paris, 1979.
Ropars-Wuilleumier, Marie-Claire, and others, *La Révolution figurée,* Paris, 1979.
Thompson, Kristin, *Eisenstein's Ivan the Terrible, a Neoformalist Analysis,* Princeton, 1981.
Leyda, Jay, and Zina Vignow, *Eisenstein at Work,* New York, 1982.
Marshall, Herbert, *Masters of the Soviet Cinema: Crippled Creative Biographies,* London, 1983.
Polan, Dana B., *The Political Language of Film and the Avant-Garde,* Ann Arbor, Michigan, 1985.
Yurenev, R., *Sergei Eizenshtein, Zamysli, Fil'my, Metod, vol. 1: 1898-1929,* Moscow, 1985; *vol. 2: 1930-1945,* Moscow, 1988.
Aumont, Jacques, *Montage Eisenstein,* London, 1987.
Christie, Ian, and David Elliot, editors, *Eisenstein at 90,* London, 1988.
Christie, Ian, and Richard Taylor, editors, *Eisenstein Rediscovered,* London, 1991.

On EISENSTEIN: articles—

Wilson, Edmund, "Eisenstein in Hollywood," in *New Republic* (New York), 4 November 1931.
Montagu, Ivor, "Sergei Eisenstein," in *Penguin Film Review* (London), September 1948.
Seton, Marie, "Eisenstein's Images and Mexican Art," in *Sight and Sound* (London), September 1953.
Harrah, D., "Aesthetics of the Film: The Pudovkin-Arnheim-Eisenstein Theory," in *Journal of Aesthetics and Art Criticism,* December 1954.
Knight, Arthur, "Eisenstein and the Mass Epic," in *The Liveliest Art,* New York, 1957.
Sadoul, Georges, "Entretiens sur Eisenstein," in *Cinéma* (Paris), 1960.
Leyda, Jay, "Care of the Past," in *Sight and Sound* (London), Winter 1961/62.
Leyda, Jay, "Missing Reel," in *Sight and Sound* (London), Spring 1965.
Yourenev, Rostislav, "Eisenstein," in *Anthologie du Cinéma,* Paris, 1966.

Sergei Eisenstein

Siegler, R., "Masquage, an Extrapolation of Eisenstein's Theory of Montage-as-Conflict to the Multi-image Film," in *Film Quarterly* (Berkeley, California), Spring 1968.

Wollen, Peter, "Eisenstein: Cinema and the Avant-Garde," in *Art International* (Lugano), November 1968.

Henderson, Brian, "Two Types of Film Theory," in *Film Quarterly* (Berkeley), Spring 1971.

Pleynet, M., "The 'Left' Front of Art: Eisenstein and the Old 'Young' Hegelians," in *Screen* (London), Spring 1972.

Kuleshov, Lev, "Kuleshov, Eisenstein, and the Others," in *Film Journal* (New York), Fall/Winter 1972.

Levaco, R., "The Eisenstein-Prokoviev Correspondence," in *Cinema Journal* (Evanston, Illinois), Fall 1973.

Seydor, P., "Eisenstein's Aesthetics: A Dissenting View," in *Sight and Sound* (London), Winter 1973/74.

"Eisenstein Issue" of *Cine Cubano* (Havana), no. 89-90, 1974.

Barthes, Roland, "Diderot, Brecht, Eisenstein," in *Screen* (London), Summer 1974.

Bordwell, David, "Eisenstein's Epistemological Shift," in *Screen* (London), Winter 1974/75 (see also Bordwell letter in *Screen,* Spring 1975).

Perlmutter, R., "Le Gai Savoir: Godard and Eisenstein: Notions of Intellectual Cinema," in *Jump Cut* (Berkeley, California), May/July 1975.

"Eisenstein Issue" of *Cinema Journal* (Evanston, Illinois), Fall 1977.

Gallez, D.W., "The Prokoviev-Eisenstein Collaboration," in *Cinema Journal* (Evanston, Illinois), Spring 1978.

Goodwin, J., "Eisenstein: Ideology and Intellectual Cinema," and H. Marshall, "A Note on Eisenstein's Shot Montage ...," in *Quarterly Review of Film Studies* (Pleasantville, New York), Spring 1978.

Burch, Noel, "Film's Institutional Mode of Representation and the Soviet Response," in *October* (Cambridge, Massachusetts), Winter 1979.

Gutiérrez Alea, T., "Alienation and De-Alienation in Eisenstein and Brecht," in *Cinema Papers* (Melbourne), July/August 1981.

Goodwin, J., "Plusiers Eisenstein: Recent criticism," in *Quarterly Review of Film Studies* (New York), Fall 1981.

Selden, D.L., "Vision and Violence: The Rhetoric of Potemkin," in *Quarterly Review of Film Studies* (New York), Fall 1982.

"*Alexander Nevsky* Section" of *Film Culture* (New York), no. 70-71, 1983.

Perry, T., "Sergei Eisenstein: A Career in Pictures," in *American Film* (Washington, D.C.), January/February 1983.

Bordwell, David, "Narrative and Scenography in the Later Eisenstein," in *Millenium Film Journal* (New York), Fall 1983-Winter 1984.

Hogenkamp, Bert, "De russen komen! Poedowkin, Eisenstein en Wertow in Nederland," in *Skrien* (Amsterdam), November/December 1985.

Taylor, Richard, "Eisenstein: 1898-1948-1988," in *Historical Journal of Film, Radio, and TV* (Abingdon, Oxon), Summer 1988.

Christie, Ian, "Eisenstein at 90," in *Sight and Sound* (London), Summer 1988.

"Eisenstein Lives," in *National Film Theatre Booklet* (London), September, October, and December 1988.

On EISENSTEIN: films—

Aslem, Henk, *Eisenstein in Nederland (Eisenstein in Holland),* Holland, 1930.

Attasheva, Pera (directed and scripted by), *In Memory of Eisenstein,* USSR.

Seton, Marie, and John Minchinton, *Eisenstein Survey,* Great Britain, 1952.

Katanyan, V., *S.M. Eisenstein (Sergei Eisenstein Film Biography),* USSR, 1958.

Eisenstein Directs Ivan (derived from previous film), Great Britain, 1969.
Hudsmith, Philip, *Eisenstein in Mexico,* Canada, 1977.

* * *

Eisenstein is generally considered to be one of the most important figures—perhaps *the* most important figure—in the history of cinema. But he was not only the leading director and theorist of Soviet cinema in his own lifetime, he was also a theatre and opera director, scriptwriter, graphic artist, teacher, and critic. His contemporaries called him quite simply "the Master."

Eisenstein's reputation as a filmmaker rests on only seven completed feature films, but among them *The Battleship Potemkin* has consistently been regarded as one of the greatest films ever made. The pivotal scene in the film—the massacre on the Odessa Steps—has become the most famous sequence in film history and a paradigm of the montage techniques that were central to Eisenstein's theories of filmmaking.

Like many early Soviet filmmakers, Eisenstein came to cinema by a circuitous route. Born in Riga, then a largely German-speaking provincial city of the Russian Empire, he saw his first film on a visit to Paris with his parents when he was only eight: *Les 400 farces du diable* by Méliès. He was educated at a technical grammar school so that he would follow his father's career as an engineer. Despite, or perhaps because of, his artistic bent, he was consistently given low marks at school for his drawing. Conversely, he consistently did his best in the subject of religious knowledge. In 1909 his parents separated and his mother went to live in St. Petersburg. On various visits to her, Eisenstein was entranced by his first taste of the circus and intrigued by his clandestine reading of her copies of *Venus in Furs* by Sacher-Masoch and Mirabeau's *The Torture Garden.* Reflections of this can be detected in his later work.

In 1915 Eisenstein entered the Institute for Civil Engineering in Petrograd, where he saw his first Meyerhold productions in the theatre. After the Revolution he abandoned his courses and joined the Red Army. He was assigned to a theatrical troupe, where he worked as a director, designer, and actor. In 1920 he was demobilised to Moscow and rapidly became head of design at the First Proletkult Workers Theatre. His first sets were for a production of *The Mexican,* written by Jack London, Lenin's favourite writer. In 1921 he joined Meyerhold's theatre workshop (he was later to describe Meyerhold as his "spiritual father") and worked on designs for *Puss in Boots.*

Eisenstein's first stage production, a version of Ostrovsky's *Enough Simplicity for Every Wise Man* in 1923, included his first venture into cinema, *Glumov's Diary.* This was inspired by the use of a short film in the Kozintsev and Trauberg production of Gogol's *The Wedding,* which he had seen the year before. His production of Tretyakov's *Gas Masks* in 1924 staged in the Moscow gasworks was an attempt to bridge the gap between stage "realism" and the reality of everyday life. It failed and, as Eisenstein himself put it, he "fell into cinema."

Eisenstein had already worked with Esfir Shub re-editing Fritz Lang's *Dr Mabuse* for Soviet audiences in 1923, but he made his first full-length film—*The Strike,* set in 1905—in 1925. In this film he applied to cinema the theory of the "montage of attractions" that he had first developed in *Enough Simplicity for Every Wise Man.* Eisenstein was not the first to develop the notion of montage as the essence of cinema specificity: that honour belonged to Lev Kuleshov in 1917. Unlike Kuleshov, however, Eisenstein thought that montage depended on a *conflict* between different elements from which a new synthesis would arise. This notion developed partly from his study of Japanese ideograms and partly from his own partial understanding of the Marxist dialectic. It followed from the primacy accorded to montage in this theory that the actor's role was diminished while the director's was enhanced. Eisenstein's view of the primacy of the director was to cause him serious problems on both sides of the Atlantic.

In his silent films Eisenstein used amateur actors who were the right physical types for the part, a practice he called "typage": hence an unknown worker, Nikandrov, played the role of Lenin in *October,* released in 1927. Most of thc parts in his second full-length film, *The Battleship Potemkin,* released in 1926, were played by amateurs. Even the local actors who appeared in the Odessa Steps sequence were chosen not for their professional training, but because they looked right for the parts. It was *Potemkin* that secured Eisenstein's reputation both at home and abroad, especially in Germany, where it was a spectacular commercial success and attracted far greater audiences than in the USSR itself. *Potemkin* put Soviet cinema on the world map.

After *Potemkin* Eisenstein started work on a film about collectivisation, *The General Line,* but broke off to make *October* for the tenth anniversary of the October Revolution. It was with this film that his serious problems with the authorities began. Critics were divided about the film. Some enthused about the birth of a new "intellectual cinema," based on "intellectual montage," which, like Brecht's "alienation effect," stimulated audiences to think rather than to react solely with their emotions. Other critics were troubled by what they saw as an overabundance of abstract symbolism that was, in the (officially inspired) catch-phrase of the times, "unintelligible to the millions."

When Eisenstein returned to *The General Line* and completed it in 1929, the Party's general line on agriculture had changed and Trotsky had fallen from grace: the film therefore had to be re-edited to reflect these developments, and it was finally released under the title of *The Old and the New.* The political problems Eisenstein encountered with this project were to recur in all his subsequent film work in the Soviet Union.

In 1929 Eisenstein went abroad with his assistants Alexandrov and Tisse, ostensibly to study the new medium of sound film. In his "Statement on Sound," published in the summer of 1928, he had warned against the dangers of purely illustrative sound, as in the "talkies," and argued for the application of the techniques of the montage of attractions to produce what he called "orchestral counterpoint." It was to be another ten years before he had the chance to put these ideas into effect.

Eisenstein first visited Western Europe and then travelled to Hollywood to work for Paramount. From the outset he was subjected to a hostile press campaign characterising him as a "red dog" and a Bolshevik. After rejecting several of his film projects, Paramount cancelled his contract. He went on to start filming *Que Viva Mexico!* with funds provided by the Socialist millionaire novelist Upton Sinclair. Eisenstein spent most of 1931 working on the film, but Sinclair was not satisfied either with the pace of progress or the escalating cost. Material for three-quarters of the Mexican film had, however, been shot when the project collapsed in acrimonious exchanges. Eisenstein returned to the Soviet Union in May 1932. He had accepted assurances from Sinclair that the raw footage would be shipped to Moscow so that he could edit it, but this assurance was never honoured.

The Soviet Union that Eisenstein returned to was significantly different from the country he had left three years earlier. The political and economic changes associated with the first Five-Year Plan had led to concomitant changes in Soviet cinema, which was now run by an Old Bolshevik, Boris Shumyatsky, who was determined to create a "cinema for the millions." After several abortive projects, including *Moscow,* a history of the capital, *The Black Consul,* which would have starred Paul Robeson, and a film version of Karl Marx's *Das Kapital,* Eisenstein began making his first sound feature, *Bezhin Meadow,* in 1935. The film focused on the generational conflict engendered by the collectivisation programme, but it too was dogged with problems and was eventually stopped on the orders of Shumyatsky in March 1937. Eisenstein was forced to confess his alleged errors in public. This submission, together with the dismissal of Shumyatsky in January 1938, enabled him to start filming again.

The result was Eisenstein's most popular film, *Alexander Nevsky,* made in record time and released in 1938, but it was also the film that he regarded as his least successful. Nevertheless, it contains the best, and most famous, illustration of his technique of "orchestral counterpoint" in the sequence of the Battle on the Ice. On the other hand, *Nevsky* to some extent gave Eisenstein the reputation of "court filmmaker," particularly after he was awarded the Order of Lenin. It was because of this that, after the signature of the Nazi-Soviet Pact—and the subsequent withdrawal of *Nevsky* from distribution—Eisenstein was asked to direct a new production of Wagner's *Die Walküre* at the Bolshoi Theatre.

When not filming, Eisenstein taught at the State Institute of Cinema, where he had been head of the directing department since his return to the Soviet Union and where he was made professor in January 1937, shortly before the final crisis with *Bezhin Meadow.* He also devoted an increasing amount of time and energy to his theoretical writings, but his magnum opus on *Direction,* like his other works on *Mise-en-Scène* and the theory of montage, remained unfinished at his death.

Eisenstein's last film, arguably his masterpiece of masterpieces, was also unfinished: filming of the first part of *Ivan the Terrible* was begun in 1943 in Alma-Ata, where the Moscow studios had been evacuated because of the war, and released in 1945. The film was an instant success and earned Eisenstein and his associates the Stalin Prize. While celebrating this award in February 1946, Eisenstein suffered a heart attack, a development that encouraged his premonitions of an early death at the age of fifty. He threw himself into a flurry of frenzied activity, completing his memoirs and Part 2 of *Ivan* and starting on Part 3. In Part 2, however, the historical parallels between Ivan and Stalin became too obvious and, although completed, the film was not shown until 1958.

Eisenstein died of a second, massive heart attack in February 1948, just past his fiftieth birthday. He died very much under a cloud in his own country, but has since been universally acknowledged as one of cinema's greatest creative geniuses and a towering figure in the culture of the twentieth century. Some of his most important theoretical texts are only now being properly assembled and published, both in the Soviet Union and abroad.

—Richard Taylor

EMSHWILLER, Ed

Nationality: American. **Born:** East Lansing, Michigan, 1925. **Education:** University of Michigan, Bachelor of Design, 1949; studied graphics at Ecole des Beaux-Arts, Paris, 1949-50; Art Students League, New York, 1951. **Career:** As "EMSH," active as painter and illustrator of books and magazines, 1951-64; collaborator on dance films with choreographer Alwin Nikolais, 1963-73; Ford Foundation research fellow at Center for Music Research, University of California at San Diego, 1965; Member of Board of Trustees, American Film Institute, 1969-75; artist in residence, WNET-TV/Channel 13 TV lab, New York, 1972-79; Dean of the School of Film and Video, California Institute of the Arts, Valencia, from 1979 (Provost 1981-85). **Awards:** Special Award, Oberhausen Festival, for *Relativity,* 1967; Von Stroheim Prize for most original feature, Mannheim Festival, for *Image, Flesh and Voice,* 1970; INDY Award, Association of Independent Video and Filmmakers, 1976; American Film Institute Maya Deren Award for Independent Film and Video Makers, 1987. **Addresses:** Film distributor—Filmmakers Cooperative, 175 Lexington Ave., New York, NY 10016. U.S.A.; video distributor—Electronic Arts Intermix, 84 5th Ave., New York, NY 10011, U.S.A. **Died:** July 1990.

Films as Director:

1955/58 *Paintings by Ed Emshwiller*
1959 *Dance Chromatic*; *Transformation*
1960 *Lifelines*
1960/61 *Variable Studies*
1961 *Time of the Heathen* (collaboration with Peter Kass)
1962 *Thanatopsis*
1963 *Totem* (collaboration with Alwin Nikolais); *Scrambles*
1964 *George Dumpson's Place*
1965 *Dlugoszewski Concert*; *Faces of America*
1966 *Relativity*; *Art Scene USA*
1967 *Fusion* (collaboration with Alwin Nikolais)
1968 *Project Apollo*
1969 *Image, Flesh and Voice*
1970 *Carol*; *Film with Three Dancers*; *Branches*
1971 *Choice Chance Woman Dance*; *Images* (video)
1972 *Computer Graphics No. 1* (video); *Thermogenesis* (video—short version of *Computer Graphics No. 1*); *Woe Oh Ho No*; *The Chalk Line*; *Inside the Gelatin Factory*; *Scape-Mates* (video)
1973 *Chrysalis* (collaboration with Alwin Nikolais); *Positive Negative Electronic Faces* (video—collaboration with Tony Bannon); *Identities*
1974 *Pilobolus and Joan* (video); *Interrupted Solitude*; *Crossings and Meetings* (video)
1975 *Inside Edges* (video); *Family Focus* (video)
1976 *New England Visions Past and Future* (video—collaboration with William Thompson); *Short and Very Short Films* (video—compilation of films from 1952-76); *Collisions* (video); *Self Trio* (video)
1977 *Slivers* (video) (multi-monitor installation with partly masked screens); *Sur Faces* (video); *Face Off* (video)
1978 *Dubs* (video)
1979 *Sunstone* (video—computer animation)
1982 *Passes* (video) [4-monitor installation comprised of following videotapes: *Space Passes* (1981); *Vascular Passes* (1982); *Cut Passes* (1981); *Pan Passes* (1982); *Echo Passes* (1979-82)]
1984 *Skin-matrix* (computer graphics with live video)
1986 *Vertigo* (multi-monitor concert piece)
1987 *Hungers* (multi-screen computer graphics/video, collaboration with Morton Subotnick)
1989 *The Blue Wall* (interactive computer graphics and live video installation); *Versions/Stages* (multi-screen concert piece in collaboration with Roger Reynolds); *"2x4"* (multi-media computer animation, video and performance)

Other Films (partial listing):

1961 *The American Way* (ph)
1963 *Hallelujah the Hills* (Mekas) (ph); *Film Magazine No. 1* (ph); *The Streets of Greenwood* (ph); *The Quiet Takeover* (ph)
1964 *The Opinion Makers* (ph); *The Existentialist* (ph)
1965 *Oysters* (ph)
1967 *Norman Jacobson* (ph)
1972 *Painters Painting* (de Antonio) (ph)

Publications

By EMSHWILLER: book—

Stan Brakhage, Ed Emshwiller, edited by Rochelle Reed, Washington, D.C., 1973.

By EMSHWILLER: articles—

"A Statement," in *Film Culture* (New York), Summer 1963.
Interview with James Mullins, in *Film Culture* (New York), Fall 1966.
"Cine-dance," in *Dance Perspectives* (New York), Summer 1967.
"Movies," in *New Worlds,* no. 178, 1968.
"Images from the Underground," in *Dialogue,* vol. 4, no. 1, 1971.
"AFI Seminar," in *Dialogue on Film* (Washington, D.C.), January 1973.
Interview with Scott Hammon, in *Afterimage* (Rochester, New York), September 1974.
Article, in *Directing the Film: Film Directors on Their Art,* by Eric Sherman, Washington, D.C., 1976.
"Image Maker Meets Video, or, Psyche to Physics and Back," in *The New Television,* edited by Douglas Davis and Allison Simmons, Cambridge, Massachusetts, 1977.
Interview with G. Jamison, in *Filmmakers Newsletter* (Ward Hill, Massachusetts), November 1977.
Interview with Melanie Mitzner, in *Video Systems,* February 1983.
Interview with R. Allezaud, in *Cinéma* (Paris), March 1984.
Interview with Gene Youngblood, in *Send,* Spring 1985.

On EMSHWILLER: books—

Curtis, David, *Experimental Cinema,* New York, 1971.
Mekas, Jonas, *Movie Journal: The Rise of the New American Cinema, 1959-1971,* New York, 1972.
Staples, Don, editor, *The American Cinema,* New York, 1981.

On EMSHWILLER: articles—

Mancia, Adrienne, and Willard Van Dyke, "Four Artists as Filmmakers," in *Art in America* (New York), January/February 1967.
Whitehall, Richard, "The Films of Ed Emshwiller," in *Film Quarterly* (Berkeley), Spring 1967.
Whitehall, Richard, "Relativity Re-Affirms Emshwiller's Stature," in *Filmmakers Newsletter* (Ward Hill, Massachusetts), November 1967.
Mekas, Jonas, in the *Village Voice* (New York), 25 June 1970.
Eisenhauer, Letty Lou, "Ed Emshwiller: Beginnings," in *Art and Artists* (London), March 1974.
Belloir, Dominique, in *Cahiers du Cinéma* (Paris), no. 10, 1981.
Ancona, Victor, "Combining Inner and Outer Landscapes," in *Videography,* September 1983.

* * *

Ed Emshwiller's first major film was *Dance Chromatic,* an effort which, like *Transformations* and *Life Lines,* was an admixture of animated and live action images. By the early 1970s he had completed over twenty works, many of them very famous and—for the experimental film genre—successful. His film *Relativity,* made under a Ford Grant, displays the fine craftsmanship and technical precision that helped assure an international appeal and repeated awards for his various productions. His concerns during this early period were diverse, ranging from animated graphics through dance films to live action experimental constructions—all characterized by compositional and cinematographic virtuosity that made them mainstays of American underground film. During the same period he was active as cinematographer on other artists' shorts, features, and documentaries. Further, Emshwiller himself produced or collaborated on many mixed-media productions (such as *Split 5th,* with the Denver Symphony) which were quite innovative for the time.

From the early 1970s Emshwiller extended his skill in cinematographic construction to electronic image-making. His *Images 1971* Whitney Museum video exhibition was followed by over a dozen experimental video projects that augmented his continued experimental film production. Such fluency with diverse technological resources has always marked Emshwiller's career. But because changes in technology are invariably structurally consequential, his more recent video productions—often predicated upon computer-generated or synthesized graphics—resulted in essential differences from his earlier film work. The silent three-minute *Sunstone* of 1980, an eight-month endeavor employing a digital computer, is a case in point. With its post-structuralist attention to cathode-ray tube dimensionality and to movement and radiated color, *Sunstone* is so distinct from the limbo-lighting and cinematic superimpositions of *Dance Chromatic* that audiences might find difficulty in assigning both constructions to the same author.

Thus Emshwiller's personal evolution from painter's graphics, through film and mixed media, into video provides scholars with a fine microcosmic example of the progressions that marked the larger technostructural transformation of experimental film as a historical genre.

—Edward S. Small

EPSTEIN, Jean

Nationality: French. **Born:** Warsaw, 25 March 1897. **Education:** Collège Francais, Villa Saint-Jean, Fribourg; Ecole Centrale, Lyons, degree in medicine, 1916. **Career:** Met Auguste Lumière, 1916; founder of revue, *Le Promenoir,* 1920; hired as editor by Editions de la Sirène, 1921; directed first film, *Pasteur,* for Jean Benoit-Levy, 1922; signed to Pathé, 1923; joined Alexandre Kamenska's Films Albatros, 1924; set up Les Films Jean Epstein, 1926; with sister, scenarist Marie Epstein, captured by Gestapo, saved from deportation through intervention of friends and Red Cross, early 1940s; taught at IDHEC after the war. **Died:** Of cerebral hemorrhage, in Paris, 3 April 1953.

Films as Director:

1922 *Pasteur; Les Vendanges*
1923 *L'Auberge rouge* (+ sc); *Coeur fidèle* (+ sc); *La Montagne infidèle; La Belle Nivernaise* (+ sc)
1924 *Le Lion des Mogols* (+ adaptation); *L'Affiche; La Goutte de sang* (Mariaud) (uncredited d)
1925 *Le Double Amour; Les Aventures de Robert Macaire*
1926 *Mauprat* (+ pr); *Au pays de George Sand* (+ pr)
1927 *Six et demi onze* (+ pr); *La Glace a trois faces* (+ pr)
1928 *La Chute de la maison Usher* (+ pr)
1929 *Finis terrae* (+ sc); *Sa Tête* (+ sc)
1930 *Le Pas de la mule* (+ pr)
1931 *Mor-Vran* (*La Mer des corbeaux*) (+ pr); *Notre-Dame de Paris* (+ pr); *La Chanson des peupliers* (+ pr); *Le Cor* (+ pr)
1932 *L'Or des mers* (+ sc); *Les Berceaux* (+ pr); *La Villanelle des Rubans* (+ pr); *Le Vieux Chaland* (+ pr)
1933 *L'Homme a l'Hispano* (+ sc, pr); *La Chatelaine du Liban* (+ sc, pr)
1934 *Chanson d'armor* (+ pr, adaptation); *La Vie d'un grand journal* (+ pr)
1936 *Coeur de Gueux* (+ pr, adaptation); *La Bretagne* (+ pr); *La Bourgogne* (+ pr)
1937 *Vive la vie* (+ pr); *La Femme du bout de monde* (+ pr, sc)
1938 *Les Batisseurs* (+ pr); *Eau vive* (+ pr, sc)
1939 *Arteres de France* (+ pr); *La Charrette fantôme* (Duvivier) (d superimpositions and special photographic effects)
1947 *Le Tempestaire* (+ pr, sc)
1948 *Les Feux de la mer* (+ pr); *La Bataille de l'eau lourde* (*Kampen om tungtvannet*) (Marin and Vibe-Muller) (d prologue)

Jean Epstein: ***La Chute de la maison Usher***

Other Film:

1921 *Le Tonnerre* (Delluc) (asst d)

Publications

By EPSTEIN: books—

Bonjour cinéma, Paris, 1921.
La Poésie d'aujourd'hui—Un nouvel état d'intelligence, Paris, 1921.
La Lyrosophie, Paris, 1922.
Le Cinématographe vu de l'Etna, Paris, 1926.
L'Or des mers, Valois, 1932.
Les Recteurs et la sirène, Paris, 1934.
Photogénie de l'impondérable, Paris, 1935.
L'Intelligence d'une machine, Paris, 1946.
Le Cinéma du diable, Paris, 1947.
Esprit de cinéma, Paris, 1955.

By EPSTEIN: articles—

"Jean Epstein nous parle de ses projets et du film parlant," interview with Pierre Leprohon, in *Pour vous* (Paris), 17 October 1929.
Article in *Cahiers du Cinéma* (Paris), June 1953.

On EPSTEIN: books—

Gawrak, Zbigniew, *Jan Epstein,* Warsaw, 1962.
Leprohon, Pierre, *Jean Epstein,* Paris, 1964.

On EPSTEIN: articles—

Leprohon, Pierre, "Un Poète de l'image," in *Cinémonde* (Paris), 28 February 1929.
Wunscher, Catherine, "Jean Epstein," in *Sight and Sound* (London), October/December 1953.
"Epstein Issue" of *Cinemages* (New York), edited by Gideon Bachmann, vol. 2, 1955.
Toussenot, R., "Souvenirs en l'honneur de Jean Epstein," in *L'Age Nouveau* (Paris), October 1956.
Haudiquet, Philippe, "Epstein," in *Anthologie du Cinéma,* vol. 2, Paris, 1967.
"Jean Epstein," in *Film Dope* (London), March 1978.
"Jean Epstein," in *Travelling* (Lausanne), Summer 1979.
"Cinema Rising: Epstein in the Twenties," special section in *Afterimage* (Rochester), no. 10, 1981.
"Cine-mystique," in *Millenium Film Journal* (New York), Fall 1981/ Winter 1982.

"A propos de Jean Epstein," in *Avant-Scène du Cinéma* (Paris), October 1983.

* * *

Jean Epstein belongs to the generation of 1920s French filmmakers who were drawn to the cinema by the impact of the Hollywood productions of Griffith, Chaplin, and Ince. Gifted with a precocious intelligence, Epstein was one of a number of these filmmakers who had previously been interested in literature. He had already published books on literature, philosophy, and the cinema when he made his debut as a filmmaker with a documentary on Pasteur in 1922 at the age of only twenty-five. Three fictional features in the following year, including *Coeur fidèle,* which contains virtuoso passages to rank with the work of Gance and L'Herbier, put him in the forefront of French avant-garde filmmaking.

The four films Epstein made during 1925-26 for the Albatros company run by the Russian emigré Alexandre Kamenka include two, *L'Affiche* and *Le Double Amour,* from scripts by Jean's sister Marie Epstein. The spectacular *Le Lion des Mogols,* which featured a preposterous script by its star, the great actor Ivan Mosjoukine, was followed by *Les Aventures de Robert Macaire,* an adaptation of the play parodied by Fredéric Lemaître in Carné's *Les Enfants du paradis.* None of these are generally considered to be among Epstein's best work, but they established him as a director after the controversies which had surrounded the showings of *Coeur fidèle,* and enabled him to set up his own production company in 1926.

The films which Epstein both produced and directed are varied. He began with two films in which his own artistic aspirations were balanced by the demands of commercial popularity: an adaption of George Sand's novel *Mauprat,* which had formed part of his childhood reading; and *Six et demi onze,* again from a script by his sister. But the last two films of Les Films Jean Epstein were resolutely independent works. The short feature *La Glace à trois faces* is remarkable for its formal pattern, which looks forward to experiments in narrative structure of a kind that were still striking to audiences thirty years later when Alain Resnais made *Hiroshima mon amour.* Even more accomplished in terms of acting and setting, and as intriguing in terms of narrative, is Epstein's atmospheric evocation of the dark world of Edgar Allan Poe, *La Chute de la maison Usher.* This tale of love, art, and madness is told in a marvellously controlled style which makes extensive use of slow motion and multiple superimposition. Just as the hero refuses to accept the division of life and death and, through the effort of will, summons back the woman he has killed through devotion to his art, so too Epstein's film creates a universe where castle and forest, interior and exterior interpenetrate.

After this masterly evocation of a world of northern imagination, a film that can rank with Dreyer's *Vampyr* and serves as a reminder of Epstein's part-Polish ancestry, the director largely withdrew from the world of Parisian film production. With only occasional forays into commercial filmmaking, Epstein devoted much of his efforts from the silent *Finis terrae* in 1929 to the short *Le Tempestaire* in 1947 to a masterly series of semi-documentary evocations of the Breton countryside and seascape.

Epstein is a complex and uncompromising figure whose filmmaking was accompanied by a constant theoretical concern with his chosen medium. If the central concept of his 1930s writing—*La photogénie*—remains not merely undefined but undefinable, and he makes recourse to notions of a magical or mystical essence of cinema that are unfortunately typical of the period, his theoretical work nonetheless remains of great interest. The republication of his complete works, *Ecrits sur le Cinéma,* in 1974-75, demonstrated the modernity and continuing interest of his explorations of key aspects of the relationship between the spectator and the screen.

—Roy Armes

ERICE, Victor

Nationality: Spanish. **Born:** Carranza, Spain, 1940. **Education:** Studied economics and political science at the University of Madrid; attended the Escuela Oficial de Cinematografia, also in Madrid. **Career:** Directed shorts while in film school; was film critic at the Spanish journals *Nuestro Cine* and *Cuadernos de Arte y Pensamieto;* earned international acclaim with his first full-length feature, *The Spirit of the Beehive,* 1973. **Address:** Ministry of Culture, Motion Picture Division, San Marcos 40, Madrid, Spain 28004.

Films as Director and Screenwriter:

1970 *Los Desafios* (*The Challenges*) (segment)
1973 ***El espiritu de la colmena*** (*The Spirit of the Beehive*)
1983 *El Sur* (*The South*)
1992 *El Sol del Membrillo* (*Dream of Light*; *The Quince Tree Sun*)

Publications

By ERICE: books—

Erice, Victor, and Angel Fernandez Santos, *El espiritu de la colmena,* Madrid, 1974.

By ERICE: articles—

"De geest van de bijenkorf," interview with J. Rabago in *Skoop* (Amsterdam), February 1974.
"Victor Erice over *El sur:* Ik hou niet van symbolische," interview with P. van Lierop in *Skoop* (Amsterdam), October 1983.
Interview with V. M. Foix in *Positif* (Paris), April 1984.
Interview with R. Castro in *R. Belg* (Brussels), Winter 1989.
Interview with T. Jousse and L. Giavarini in *Cahiers du Cinema* (Paris), June 1992.
Interview with J. L. Guarner in *FCR...,* November 1992.
"Victor Erice: Painting the Sun," interview with R. Morgan in *Sight and Sound* (London), 29 April 1993.
Interview with T. Perez Turrent in *Positif* (Paris), May 1993.

On ERICE: books—

Voir et lire Victor Erice: l'esprit de la ruche, Dijon, 1990.

On ERICE: articles—

Eder, Richard, "A Great Movie We May Never See," in *New York Times,* 12 September 1976.
Canby, Vincent, "Grown-up Movies about Children," in *New York Times,* 10 October 1976.
Baker, B., biography-filmography in *Film Dope* (London), March 1978.
Borelli, S., "Lo spirito di Victor Erice," in *Segnocinema* (Vicenza, Italy), March 1987.
Ehrlich, E. R., "The Name of the Child: Cinema as Social Critique," in *Film Criticism* (Meadville, Pennsylvania), no. 2, 1990.
Insdorf, Annette, "Spain also Rises," in *Film Comment* (New York), July-August 1980.
Paranagua, P. A., "La solitude de Victor Erice," in *Positif* (Paris), April 1984.
Biography-filmography in *Cahiers Cinematheque* (Paris), Winter 1984.

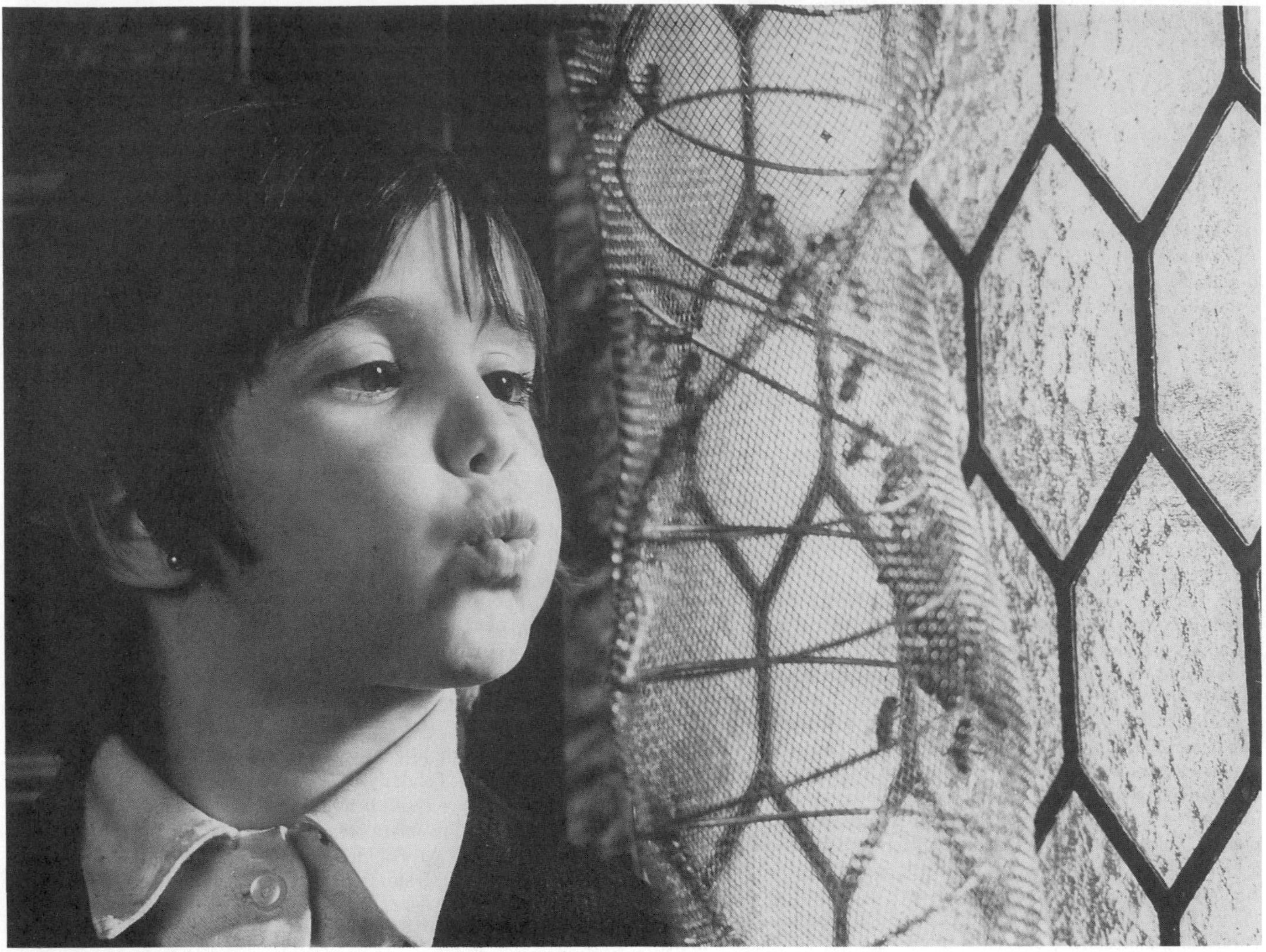

Victor Erice: Ana Torrent in *El espiritu de la colmena*

Giavarini, L. and Jousse, T., "Le songe de la lumiere," in *Cahiers du Cinema* (Paris), hors series, no. 62, 1992.

Martin-Marquez, S. L., "Monstrous Identity: Female Socialization in *El espiritu de la colmena*," in *New Orleans Review*, no. 2, 1992.

Smith, P. J., "Whispers and Rapture," in *Sight and Sound* (London), April 1993.

* * *

Such is the power of the press that a reviewer for an influential publication can laud a heretofore little-known film by an obscure director and thereby thrust that work into the international spotlight. Back in 1976, *New York Times* critic Richard Eder authored an article in praise of what was then a three-year-old film. The title of the piece was "A Great Film We May Never See." The film in question is *The Spirit of the Beehive*, directed by Victor Erice. According to Eder, it had played in Spain ("where it did not so much evade the censorship as envelop it") and on the film-festival circuit, and had been screened at the Museum of Modern Art. But it had not earned a commercial U.S. distributor. Eder discovered the film at the Telluride Festival, where his piece was filed. "It is one of the two or three most haunting films about children ever made," Eder wrote. "It is perhaps one of the two dozen best pictures made anywhere in the past half-dozen years," he added, before going on to describe it as a film "whose power to move and astonish comes in quite original and magical ways."

The Spirit of the Beehive unfolds in a Castillan village in 1940, just after the end of the Spanish Civil War. While the town has not been a battleground, its young men are nowhere to be seen as they all have gone off to fight. The focus is on two children, eight-year-old Ana and her sister, ten-year-old Isabel. They see a print of James Whale's *Frankenstein*, at which point little Ana becomes obsessed with the image of the Frankenstein monster—especially the sequence in which a small girl picks a flower and hands it to the creature. Ana asks her wiser older sister if the story is true. Isabel says yes. And so Ana sets out in and around her village in search of the monster's spirit. Its existence is authenticated for her when she finds and helps an escaped prisoner who has found refuge in a barn, prior to his being found and shot by the police.

Much of the film's allure derives from the poignancy and simplicity of its sequences, especially those focusing on Ana, which are graceful unions of image and sound. *The Spirit of the Beehive* works as a fable of childhood, an ode to the wonders of youthful imagination and the magic of the moving image, and a subtly telling portrait of life in Spain under the repressive regime of Franco. At the film's core are the constraints on Spanish society under Franco, from the time in which it is set all the way through the time in which it was made. Franco's

Spain is depicted as being in a state of inertia, with the only spark of life coming from Ana's imagination. Out of necessity, so as not to incur the fury of local censors, this commentary is ever-so-subtly drawn.

Prior to making *The Spirit of the Beehive,* Erice directed the last segment of *Los Desafios,* a three-part film, each episode of which deals with the experiences of Americans in Spain. Since then, he has worked infrequently. *El Sur,* made a full decade after *The Spirit of the Beehive,* is similar to its predecessor in that it too centers around an imaginative young girl—this one growing up in the 1950s—who fantasizes about her father. The documentary *El Sol del Membrillo* spotlights the inner workings of the creative process as it records the elaborate manner in which Spanish artist Antonio Lopez goes about painting a quince tree. A parallel exists between Lopez's exacting artistic method and Erice's, given the filmmaker's minute output over the past quarter-century.

—Rob Edelman

FÁBRI, Zoltán

Nationality: Hungarian. **Born:** Budapest, 1917. **Education:** Academy of Fine Arts and Academy of Dramatic and Film Art, Budapest, diploma 1941. **Career:** Stage designer, actor, and director; interned as prisoner of war, 1941-45; at Artists Theatre, Budapest, 1945-49; artistic director of Hunnia Studios, 1949; made first feature, 1952; began collaboration with cameraman György Illés on *Húsz óra,* 1964; President of Union of Hungarian Cinema and Television Artists, and Professor at Academy of Dramatic and Cinema Arts, Budapest. **Awards:** Moscow Festival, for *141 perc a Befejezetlen mondatból,* 1975; Grand Prize, Moscow Festival, for *Az ötödik pecsét,* 1977; received Kossuth Prize three times.

Films as Director:

1951 *Gyarmat a föld alatt* (*Colony Beneath the Earth*) (co-d)
1952 *Vihar* (*Storm*)
1954 *Eletjel* (*Vierzehn Menschenleben*; *Life Signs*)
1955 *Körhinta* (*Merry-go-Round*; *Karussell*) (+ co-sc, art d)
1956 *Hannibál tonár úr* (*Professor Hannibal*) (+ co-sc)
1957 *Bolond április* (*Summer Clouds*; *Crazy April*); *Èdes Anna* (*Anna, Schuldig?*) (+ co-sc)
1959 *Dùvad* (*The Brute*; *Das Scheusal*) (+ sc)
1961 *Két Félidö a pokolban* (*The Last Goal*) (+ art d)
1963 *Nappali sötétség* (*Darkness in Daytime*; *Dunkel bei Tageslicht*) (+ sc, art d)
1964 *Húsz óra* (*Twenty Hours*)
1965 *Vizivárosi Nyár* (*A Hard Summer*) (for TV)
1967 *Utószezon* (*Late Season*)
1968 *A Pál utcai fiúk* (*The Boys of Paul Street*) (+ co-sc)
1969 *Isten hozta, örnagy úr!* (*The Toth Family*) (+ co-sc)
1971 *Hangyaboly* (+ co-sc)
1973 *Plusz minusz egy nap* (*One Day More, One Day Less*)
1974 *141 perc a Befejezetlen mondatból* (*141 Minutes from the Unfinished Sentence*) (+ co-sc)
1976 *Az ötödik pecsét* (*The Fifth Seal*) (+ sc)
1977 *Magyarok* (*The Hungarians*) (+ sc)
1979 *Fábián Bálint találkozása Istennel* (*Balint Fabian Meets God*) (+ sc)
1981 *Requiem*

Publications

By FÁBRI: articles—

Interview with M. Ember, in *Filmkultura* (Budapest), April 1975.
"Az emberi méltóság védelme foglalkoztat," in *Filmkultura* (Budapest), September/October 1977.
"Bálint Fábián's Encounter with God," in *Hungarofilm Bulletin* (Budapest), no. 4, 1979.

On FÁBRI: articles—

Biographical note, in *International Film Guide,* London, 1965.
Hanisch, Michael, "Zoltán Fábri," in *Regiestühle,* Berlin, 1972.
Biofilmography in *Film und Fernsehen* (Berlin), no. 3, 1976.
Nemes, K., "Egy életmü—a társadalom fejlödésében," in *Filmkultura* (Budapest), September/October 1977.
Revy, E., in *Filmkultura* (Budapest), March/April 1984.

On FÁBRI: film—

Nádassy, László, director, *Fábri portré,* 1980.

* * *

Having been a theatre director and designer, Zoltán Fábri began to work in films in 1950 and quickly discovered his true vocation. In 1952 he made his first film, *Vihar,* a drama about the collectivization of a village. *Körhinta,* presented at Cannes in 1956 was astonishing for the beauty of its images and feelings, and for the appearance of a young actress, Mari Töröcsik, whom he picked again two years later for his film *Èdes Anna.*

Also in 1956 he made *Hannibál tanár úr,* the tragedy of a man broken by the pressure of his conformist milieu, with the outstanding Ernö Szabó in the main role. This film, honored at in the main role. This film, honored at the Karlovy Vary Festival in 1957, raised the problem of the heritage of a fascist past and indirectly attacked the oppressive atmosphere of the Stalinist period. Following the political events which supervened in 1956, it was excluded from Hungarian screens.

In all of his work, nourished by Hungarian literature, Fábri deals with moral problems bound up with the history of his country, making use of a vigorous realism. Besides the meticulous composition of his narratives, and precise evocation of atmosphere and the milieu where they unfold, it's necessary to underline the importance given to his work with actors and his own participation in the creation of some set designs.

Following a drama showing the present-day problems of life in the countryside, *Dúvad,* Fábri continued with *Két félidö a pokolban,* set in a concentration camp. The moral behavior of men in times of crisis, the confrontation of ideas and of characters, of cowardice and heroism, totally absorb him and are at the heart of all his films. In *Húsz óra,* made in 1964, he uses an investigation undertaken by a journalist as the starting point for a brilliant reflection on the impact in Hungary of political events in the recent past, confirming anew his abilities as an analyst and director. For this film he was again able to engage György Illés as cameraman, and they have continued a constant collaboration since.

Having given the Hungarian cinema an international audience, Fábri in 1968 directed a Hungarian-American co-production, *The Boys of Paul Street,* faithfully adapted from the popular novel by Ferenc Molnár, a touching story of childhood heroism. After *Hangyaboly,* a drama that unfolds behind the walls of a convent, with Mari Töröcsik, he made *141 perc a Befejezetlen mondatból,* then returned to a moral

Zoltán Fábri: *Hannibál tanár úr*

analysis of the wartime period with *Az ötödik pecsét,* a work of deep psychological insight, which received the Grand Prize at the Moscow Festival in 1977 and remains one of the director's best films. With *Magyarok,* and its sequel *Fábián Bálint találkozása Istennel,* he traces in epic style and more conventional form the fate of the peasants in the period between the wars. In *Requiem,* he sets against the drama of a young girl the tragic consequences of the postwar political dislocations. In attempting thus to renew his method, he succeeds once again in powerfully expressing the message of a great moralist.

Having received the Kossuth Prize three times, as well as being President of the Union of Hungarian Cinema and Television Artists, and professor at Budapest's Academy of Dramatic and Cinema Arts, Fábri is a key figure of the Hungarian cinema

—Karel Tabery

FASSBINDER, Rainer Werner

Nationality: German. **Born:** Bad Wörishofen, Bavaria, 31 May 1946. **Education:** the Rudolf Steiner School and Secondary schools in Augsburg and Munich until 1964; studied acting at Fridl-Leonhard Studio, Munich. **Family:** Married Ingrid Caven, 1970 (divorced). **Career:** Worked as decorator and in archives of *Süddeutsche Zeitung,* Munich, 1964-66; failed entrance exam to West Berlin Film and Television Academy, 1965; joined *action-theater,* Munich, with Hanna Schygulla, 1967; first original play produced (*Katzelmacher*), *action-theater* closed in May, co-founded *anti-theater,* 1968; began making films with members of *anti-theater,* 1969; worked in German theatre and radio, and as actor, 1969-82; founder, Tango Film, independent company, 1971; with Kurt Raab and Roland Petri, took over Theater am Turm (TAT), Frankfurt, 1974; TAT project failed, returned to Munich to concentrate on film work, 1975. **Awards:** Golden Bear, Berlin Festival, for *Die Sehnsucht der Veronika Voss,* 1982. **Died:** In Munich, 10 June 1982.

Films as Director (under pseudonym Franz Walsch):

1965 *Der Stadtstreicher* (*The City Tramp*) (+ sc, ed, uncredited pr, role)

1966 *Das kleine Chaos* (*The Little Chaos*) (+ sc, ed, role, uncredited pr)

1969 *Liebe ist kälter als der Tod* (*Love Is Colder than Death*) (+ sc, ed, role as Franz, uncredited pr); *Katzelmacher* (+ sc, ed, art d, role as Jorgos, uncredited pr); *Götter der Pest* (*Gods of the Plague*) (+ sc, ed, role as Porno Buyer, uncredited pr); *Warum läuft Herr R amok?* (*Why Does Herr R Run Amok?*) (co-d, co-sc, co-ed, uncredited pr)

1970 *Rio das Mortes* (+ sc, role as Discotheque-goer); *Whity* (+ sc, co-ed, role as Guest in Saloon, uncredited pr); *Die*

Niklashauser Fahrt (*The Niklashausen Journey*) (co-d, co-sc, co-ed, role as Black Monk, uncredited pr); *Der amerikanische Soldat* (*The American Soldier*) (sc, song, role as Franz); *Warnung vor einer heiligen Nutte* (*Beware of a Holy Whore*) (+ co-ed, sc, role as Sascha, uncredited pr)

(under real name):

1971 *Pioniere in Ingolstadt* (*Pioneers in Ingolstadt*) (+ sc, uncredited pr); *Das Kaffeehaus* (*The Coffee House*) (for television) (+ sc, uncredited pr); *Der Händler der vier Jahreszeiten* (*The Merchant of the Four Seasons*) (+ sc, role as Zucker, uncredited pr)

1972 *Die bitteren Tränen der Petra von Kant* (*The Bitter Tears of Petra von Kant*) (+ sc, des, uncredited pr); *Wildwechsel* (*Wild Game*) (+ sc, uncredited pr); *Acht Stunden sind kein Tag* (*Eight Hours Don't Make a Day*) (+ sc, uncredited pr) (shown on German television in five monthly segments); *Bremer Freiheit* (*Bremen Freedom*) (for television) (+ sc, uncredited pr)

1973 *Welt am Draht* (*World on a Wire*) (in two parts) (+ co-sc, uncredited pr); ***Angst essen Seele auf*** (*Fear Eats the Soul*) (+ sc, des, uncredited pr); *Martha* (+ sc, uncredited pr); *Nora Helmer* (for television) (+ sc, uncredited pr)

1974 *Fontane Effi Briest* (*Effi Briest*) (+ sc, role as narrator, uncredited pr); *Faustrecht der Freiheit* (*Fox*) (+ co-sc, role as Franz Biberkopf—'Fox,' uncredited pr); *Wie ein Vogel auf dem Draht* (*Like a Bird on a Wire*) (for television) (+ sc, uncredited pr)

1975 *Mutter Küsters Fahrt zum Himmel* (*Mother Küster's Trip to Heaven*) (+ co-sc, uncredited pr); *Angst vor der Angst* (*Fear of Fear*) (+ sc, uncredited pr)

1976 *Ich will doch nur, dass Ihr mich liebt* (*I Only Want You to Love Me*) (+ sc, uncredited pr); *Satansbraten* (*Satan's Brew*) (+ sc, uncredited pr); *Chinesisches Roulette* (*Chinese Roulette*) (+ sc, co-pr)

1977 *Bolwieser* (+ sc, uncredited pr); *Frauen in New York* (*Women in New York*); *Eine Reise ins Licht* (*Despair*)

1978 Episode of *Deutschland im Herbst* (*Germany in Autumn*) (+ sc, role, uncredited pr); ***Die Ehe der Maria Braun*** (*The Marriage of Maria Braun*) (+ story); *In einem Jahr mit dreizehn Monden* (*In a Year with Thirteen Moons*) (+ sc, ph, uncredited pr)

1979 *Die dritte Generation* (*The Third Generation*) (+ sc, ph, uncredited pr)

1980 *Berlin Alexanderplatz* (for television, thirteen episodes with epilogue) (+ sc, ph, role as himself in dream sequence, uncredited pr); *Lili Marleen* (+ sc, ph, uncredited pr)

1981 ***Lola*** (+ sc, ph, uncredited pr); *Theater in Trance* (TV documentary) (+ commentary)

1982 *Die Sehnsucht der Veronika Voss* (Veronika Voss) (+ sc, uncredited pr, ph); *Querelle* (+ sc, ph, uncredited pr)

Other Films:

1967 *Tony Freunde* (Vasil) (role as Mallard)

1968 *Der Bräutigam, die Komödiantin und der Zuhalter* (*The Bridegroom, the Comedienne and the Pimp*) (Straub) (role as the pimp)

1969 *Fernes Jamaica* (*Distant Jamaica*) (Moland) (sc); *Alarm* (Lemmel) (role as the man in uniform); *Al Capone im deutschen Wald* (Wirth) (role as Heini); *Baal* (Schlöndorff) (role as Baal); *Frei bis zum nächsten Mal* (Köberle) (role as the mechanic)

1970 *Matthias Kneissl* (Hauff) (role as Flecklbauer); *Der plötzliche Reichtum der armen Leute von Kombach* (Schlöndorff) (role as a peasant); *Supergirl* (Thome) (role as man who looks through window)

1973 *Zärtlichkeit der Wölfe* (Lommel) (role as Wittkowski)

1974 *1 Berlin-Harlem* (Lambert) (role as himself)

1976 *Schatten der Engel* (*Shadow of Angels*) (Schmid) (sc, role as Raoul, the pimp)

1978 *Bourbon Street Blues* (Sirk, Schonherr, and Tilman) (role)

1980 *Lili Marleen* (Weisenborn) (role)

Publications

By FASSBINDER: books—

Antitheater, Frankfurt, 1973.
Antitheater 2, Frankfurt, 1974.
Stücke 3, Munich, 1978.
Querelle Filmbuch, Munich 1982.
Film Befreien den Kopf: Essays und Arbeitsnotizen, edited by Michael Toteburg, Frankfurt, 1984.
Die Anarchie der Phantasie: Gesprache und Interviews, edited by Michael Toteburg, Frankfurt, 1986.
The Marriage of Maria Braun, edited by Joyce Rheuban, New Brunswick, New Jersey, 1986.
Die Kinofilme 1, Munich, 1987.

By FASSBINDER: articles—

"*Liebe ist kälter als der Tod,*" in *Film* (London), no. 8, 1969.
Interview in *Filmkritik* (Munich), August 1969.
"Imitation of Life: On the Films of Douglas Sirk," in *Douglas Sirk,* edited by Mulvey and Halliday, Edinburgh, 1972.
Interview in *Sight and Sound* (London), Winter 1974/75.
Interview in *Film Comment* (New York), November/December 1975.
"Insects in a Glass Case," in *Sight and Sound* (London), Autumn 1976.
Interview in *Cineaste* (New York), Autumn 1977.
"Ich bin das Gluck dieser Erde. Ach war' das schon wenn's so ware," an interview with B. Steinborn and R. von Naso, in *Filmfaust* (Frankfurt), April-May 1982.
Interview with P. Pawlikowski, in *Stills* (London), November/December 1982.

On FASSBINDER: books—

Limmer, Wolfgang, *Fassbinder,* Munich, 1973.
Jansen, Peter, and Wolfram Schütte, editors, *Reihe Film 2: Rainer Werner Fassbinder,* Munich, 1979.
Eckhardt, Bernd, *Rainer Werner Fassbinder: In 17 jahren 42 Filme—Stationen eines Leben fur den Deutschen Film,* Munich, 1982.
Iden, Peter, and others, *Rainer Werner Fassbinder,* Munich, 1982.
Raab, Kurt, and Karsten Peters, *Die Sehnsucht des Rainer Werner Fassbinder,* Munich, 1982.
Foss, Paul, editor, *Fassbinder in Review,* Sydney, 1983.
Hayman, Ronald, *Fassbinder: Filmmaker,* London, 1984.
Phillips, Klaus, *New German Filmmakers: From Oberhausen through the 1970's,* New York, 1984.
Katz, Robert, and Peter Berling, *Love Is Colder than Death: The Life and Times of Rainer Werner Fassbinder,* London, 1987.
Elsaesser, Thomas, *New German Cinema: A History,* London, 1989.
Lardeau, Yann, *Rainer Werner Fassbinder,* Paris, 1990.

On FASSBINDER: articles—

Wilson, David, "Anti-Cinema: Rainer Werner Fassbinder," in *Sight and Sound* (London), no. 2, 1972.

Rainer Werner Fassbinder

"Fassbinder and Sirk," in *Film Comment* (New York), November/December 1975.
"Gay Men and Film Section," in *Jump Cut* (Berkeley), no. 16, 1977.
"Fassbinder Issue" of *October* (Cambridge, Massachusetts), Summer 1982.
Dossier on Fassbinder, in *Cinéma* (Paris), July-August 1982.
Roud, Richard, "Biter Bit," in *Sight and Sound* (London), Autumn 1982.
Hoberman, J., "Explorations," in *American Film* (Washington, D.C.), September 1982.
Riley, B., and H. Kennedy, obituaries, in *Film Comment* (New York), September/October 1982.
MacBean, J.R., "The Success and Failure of Rainer Werner Fassbinder," in *Sight and Sound* (London), Winter 1982/83.
MacBean, J.R., "The Cinema as Self Portrait: The Final Films of R.W. Fassbinder," in *Cineaste* (New York), vol. 12, no. 4, 1983.
Sirk, Douglas, "Obituary for Rainer Werner Fassbinder," in *Framework* (Norwich), no. 20, 1983.
Erffmeyer, T.E., "I only want you to love me: Fassbinder, melodrama and Brechtian form," in *Journal of University Film Association* (Carbondale, Illinois), Winter 1983.
Feinstein, Herbert, "BRD 1-2-3: Fassbinder's Postwar trilogy and the Spectacle," in *Cinema Journal* (Champaign, Illinois), Fall 1983.
Katz, Robert, "Fear Ate His Soul," in *American Film* (Washington, D.C.), July/August 1985.
Krasnova, G., "Uber Rainer Werner Fassbinder," in *Beiträge zur Film und Fernsehwissenschaft* (Berlin), vol. 26, no. 2, 1985.

On FASSBINDER: films—

von Mengershausen, Joachim, *Ende einer Kommune,* West Germany, 1970.
Ballhaus, Michael, and Dietmar Buchmann, *Fassbinder produziert: Film Nr. 8,* West Germany, 1971.
Wiebel, Martin, and Ludwig Metzger, *Glashaus-TV Intern,* West Germany, 1973.
Plater, Edward M.V., "The Externalization of the Protagonist's Mind in Fassbinder's *Despair*," in *Film Criticism* (Meadville, Pennsylvania), vol. 11, no. 3, 1987.

* * *

Rainer Werner Fassbinder was the leading member of a group of second-generation, alternative filmmakers in West Germany. The first generation consisted of Alexander Kluge and others who in 1962 drafted the Oberhausen Manifesto, initiating what has come to be called the "New German Cinema." Fassbinder's most distinguishing trait within the tradition of "counter-cinema," aside from his reputation for rendering fragments of the new left ideology of the 1960s on film, was his modification of the conventions of political cinema initiated in the 1920s and subsequent tailoring of these conventions to modern conditions of Hollywood cinema. He did this to a greater degree than Godard, who is credited with using these principles as content for filmic essays on narrative.

In an interview in 1971 Fassbinder asserted what has come to represent his most convincing justification for his innovative attachment to story: "The American cinema is the only one I can take really seriously, because it's the only one that has really reached an audience. German cinema used to do so, before 1933, and of course there are individual directors in other countries who are in touch with their audiences. But American cinema has generally had the happiest relationship with its audience, and that is because it doesn't try to be 'art.' Its narrative style is not so complicated or artificial. Well, of course it's artificial, but not 'artistic.'"

This concern with narrative and popular expression (some of his productions recall the good storytelling habits of Renoir) was evident early in the theatrical beginnings of Fassbinder's career, when he forged an aesthetic that could safely be labeled a creative synthesis of Brecht and Artaud oriented toward the persuasion of larger audiences.

This aesthetic began to form with Fassbinder's turn to the stage in 1967. He had finished his secondary school training in 1964 in Augsburg and Munich. He joined the Action-Theater in Munich with Hanna Schygulla, whom he had met in acting school. After producing his first original play in 1968, the Action-Theater was closed by the police in May of that year. Fassbinder then founded the "anti-theater," a venture loosely organized around the tenets of Brechtian theater translated into terms alluring for contemporary audiences. Although the 1969 *Liebe ist kälter als der Tod* marks the effective beginning of his feature film career (*Der Stadtsreicher* and *Das kleine Chaos* constituting minor efforts), he was to maintain an intermittent foothold in the theater over the years until his premature death, working in various productions throughout Germany and producing a number of radio plays in the early 1970s. The stint with "anti-theater" was followed by the assumption of directorial control, with Kurt Raab and Roland Petri, over the Theater am Turm (TAT) of Frankfurt in 1974, and the founding of Albatross Productions for coproductions in 1975.

When TAT failed, Fassbinder became less involved in the theater, but a trace of his interest always remained and was manifested in his frequent appearances in his own films. In fact, out of the more than forty feature films produced during his lifetime, there have only been a handful or so in which Fassbinder did not appear in one way or another. Indeed, he has had a major role in at least ten of these films.

Fassbinder's mixing together of Hollywood and avant-garde forms took a variety of turns throughout his brief career. In the films made during the peak of 1960s activism in Germany—specifically *Katzelmacher, Liebe ist kälter als der Tod, Götter der Pest,* and *Warum läuft Herr R. Amok?*—theatrical conventions, principally those derived from his Brechtian training, join forces with a "minimalist" aesthetic and the indigenous energies of the *Heimatfilm* to portray such sensitive issues as the foreign worker problem, contradictions within supposedly revolutionary youth culture, and concerns of national identity. These early "filmed theater" pieces, inevitably conforming to a static, long-take style because of a dearth of funding, tended to resemble parables or fables in their brevity and moral, didactic structuring. As funding from the government increased in proportion to his success, the popular forms of filmmaking associated with Hollywood became his models. His output from 1970 through the apocalyptic events of October 1977 (a series of terrorist actions culminated in Hans-Martin Schleyer's death, etc.) is an exploration of the forms of melodrama and the family romance as a way to place social issues within the frame of sexual politics. *Whity, Der Händler der vier Jahreszeiten, Die bitteren Tränen der Petra von Kant, Martha, Faustrecht der Freiheit,* and *Frauen in New York* are perhaps the most prominent examples. A self-reflexive pastiche of the gangster film is evident as well in *Der amerikanische Soldat.* This attention to the mediation of other forms ultimately began to assume the direction of a critique of the "art film": *Warnung vor einer heiligen Nutte,* an update of *8 1/2*; *Satansbraten,* a comment on aesthetics and politics centered around the figure of Stephen George; and *Chinesisches Roulette,* a parody concerning an inbred aristocracy.

The concern with the continuation of fascism into the present day received some attention in this period (specifically in *Wildwechsel, Despair,* and *Bolwieser*), but it became the dominant structuring motivation in the final period (1977-82) of Fassbinder's career. Here there is a kind of epic recombination of all earlier innovations in service of an understanding of fascism and its implications for the immediate postwar generation. Fassbinder's segment in *Deutschland im Herbst* (a collective endeavor of many German intellectuals and filmmakers) inaugurates this period. It and *Die Ehe der Maria Braun, Lili Marleen, Lola,* and *Die Sehnsucht der Veronika Voss* may be seen as a portrayal of the consolidation of German society to conform to the "American Model" of social and economic development. *In einem Jahr mit 13 Monden, Berlin Alexanderplatz,* and *Querelle* are depictions of the crisis in sexual identity, and the criminal and counter-cultural worlds associated with that process, in relation to "capitalism in crisis." *Die dritte Generation* is a kind of cynical summation of the German new left in the wake of a decade of terrorist activities.

This final phase, perhaps Fassbinder's most brilliant cinematically, will be the one given the greatest critical attention in future years. It is the one which evinces the keenest awareness of the intellectual spaces traversed in Germany since the years of fascism (and especially since the mid-1960s), and the one which reveals the most effective assimilation of the heritage of forms associated with art and political cinema.

—John O'Kane

FEJÖS, Paul

Nationality: Hungarian. **Born:** Pál Fejös in Budapest, 24 January 1897; became U.S. citizen, 1930. **Education:** school in Veszprem and at Kecskemet; studied medicine. **Military Service:** Served on Italian front, organized plays for soldiers, 1914-18. **Career:** Set designer for opera and for Orient-Film studios, 1918; director for Studio Mobil, from 1919; travelled across Europe, worked with Max Reinhardt and Fritz Lang, left for United States, 1923; medical research assistant at Rockefeller Institute, moved to Hollywood, 1926; signed to Universal, 1928; with cameraman Hal Mohr, designed crane allowing great camera mobility, 1929; signed to MGM, 1930; invited to Paris by Pierre Braunberger, 1931; director for Films Osso in Hungary, broke MGM contract, 1932; signed to Nordisk Films, 1934; went to Madagascar, 1935-36; signed to Svensk Filmindustri, travelled to Indonesia and New Guinea, 1937; director of Viking Fund, New York, 1941; later director of Wenner-Gren Foundation for Anthropological Research. **Died:** In New York, 23 April 1963.

Films as Director:

(in Hungary):

1920 *Pan*; *Lidércnyomás* (*Nightmare*; *Hallucination*; *Lord Arthur Saville's Crime*) (+ co-sc); *Ujraélök* (*Reincarnation*); *Jóslat* (*Prophecy*)
1921 *Fekete Kapitany* (*The Black Captain*); *Arsén Lupin utolsó kalandja* (*The Last Adventure of Arsène Lupin*)
1922 *Szenzáció* (*Sensation*)
1923 *Egri csillagok* (*The Stars of Eger*) (+ sc, incomplete)

(in United States):

1928 *The Last Moment* (*Le Dernier Moment*) (+ sc, ed); *Lonesome* (*Solitude*)

1929 *Broadway*; *The Last Performance* (working title: "Erik the Great")

1930 *Captain of the Guard* (*Marseillaise*) (co-d, uncredited); *Menschen hinter Gittern* (German version of George Hill's *The Big House*)

(in France):

1931 *Fantômas* (+ co-sc)

(in Hungary):

1932 *Tavaszi zápor* (*Marie, légende hongroise*; *Une Histoire d'amour*) (+ co-sc); *Itél a Balaton* (*Storm at Balaton*)

(in Austria):

1933 *Sonnenstrahl* (*Gardez le sourire*) (+ co-pr, co-sc); *Frühlingsstimmen* (*Les Voix du printemps*)

(in Denmark):

1934 *Flugten fra millionerne* (*Flight from the Millions*; *Les Millions en fuite*) (+ sc)

1935 *Fange nr. 1* (*Prisoner No. 1*) (+ co-sc): *Det gyldne Smil* (*The Golden Smile*; *Le Sourire d'or*) (+ sc)

(in Madagascar):

1935/36 *Svarta Horisonter* (*Horizons noirs*) series: 1. *Danstävlingen i Esira* (*Dance Contest in Esira*); 2. *Skönhetsvård i djungeln* (*Beauty Care in the Jungle*); 3. *Världens mest Användbara Träd* (*The Most Useful Tree in the World*); 4. *Djungeldansen* (*Jungle Dance*); 5. *Havets Djävul* (*The Sea Devil*); 6. *Våra Faders Gravar* (*Tombs of Our Ancestors*)

(in Indonesia and New Guinea):

1937/38 *Stammen Lever an* (*The Tribe Lives On*); *Bambuå påldern på Mentawei* (*The Age of Bamboo at Mentawei*); *Hövdingens Son är död* (*The Chief's Son Is Dead*); *Draken på Komodo* (*The Dragon of Komodo*); *Byn vid den Trivsamma Brunnen* (*The Village Near the Pleasant Fountain*); *Tambora*; *Att*

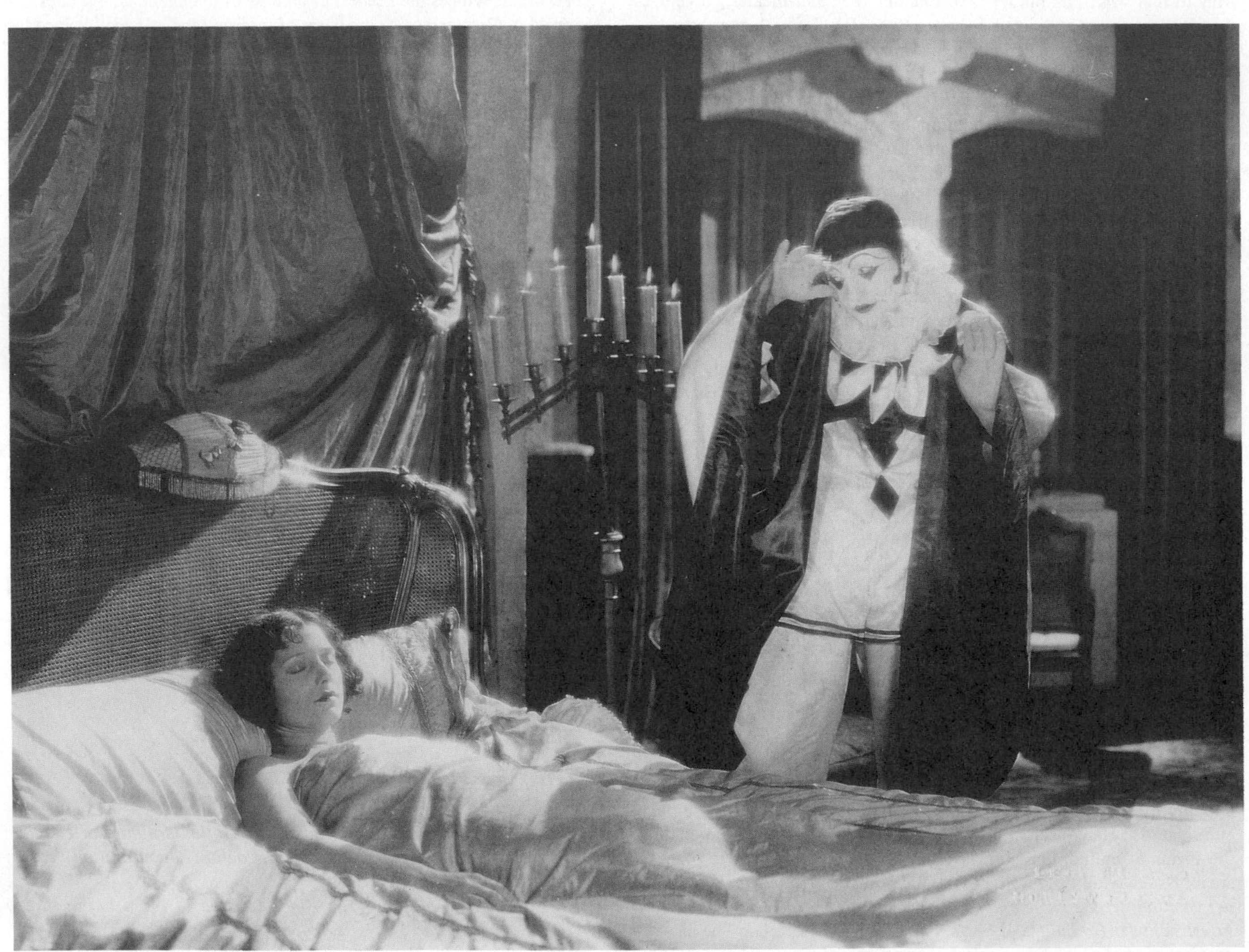

Paul Fejös: *The Last Moment*

Segla är Nödvändigt (*To Sail Is Necessary*) (completed by Åke Leijonhufvud)

(in Thailand):

1938 *En Handfull Ris* (*A Handful of Rice*); *Man och Kvinna* (*Homme et femme*) (co-d)

(in Peru):

1940/41 *Yagua* ("directed" by Yagua tribe shaman with Fejos controlling camera)

Other Films:

1923 *Land of the Lawless* (Buckinham) (adapt)
1931 *L'Amour a l'américaine* (supervision)

Publications

On FEJÖS: books—

Dodds, John, *The Several Lives of Paul Fejos*, New York, 1973.

On FEJÖS: articles—

Bréchignac, Jean-Vincent, "La Carrière de Paul Fejos," in *Pour Vous* (Paris), 31 January 1929.
Doré, Claude, "Fantômas reparait," in *Ciné-Miroir* (Paris), 22 January 1932.
Wunscher, Catherine, "Paul Fejos," in *Films in Review* (New York), March 1954.
Kraft, R., "Fejos's Broadway," letter in *Films in Review* (New York), April 1954.
Molnar, Istvan, "Fejös Pal es a *Tavaszi Zapor*," in *Filmkultura* (Budapest), October 1960.
Bidney, David, "Paul Fejos (1897-1963)," in *The American Anthropologist* (New York), February 1964.
Balint, Lajos, "Fejös Pal—A Tavolbalato," in *Filmvilag* (Budapest), 15 July 1966.
Haudiquet, Philippe, "Paul Fejos 1897-1963," in *Anthologie du Cinéma* (Paris), vol. 4, 1968.
Ban, Robert, in *Film, Szinhaz, Muzsika* (Budapest), 17 August 1968.
Petrie, Graham, "Fejos," in *Sight and Sound* (London), Summer 1978.
Petrie, Graham, "Paul Fejos in America," in *Film Quarterly* (Berkeley), no. 2, 1979.
"Fejos Issue" of *Filmkritik* (Munich), August 1979.

* * *

Few directors have had such a curious and diverse career as that of Paul Fejös, who was equally at home behind a camera directing entertainment features and documentaries or on anthropological expeditions to South America and the Far East.

After an early career in his native Hungary that embraced medicine, painting, and play production, Paul Fejös became a film director in the late teens. A trip to Paris persuaded him that he wanted to direct in the West, specifically the United States. In 1921 he arrived in America and started to work at the Rockefeller Institute. Eventually, Fejös journeyed to Hollywood—despite his penniless situation—and made his first American film, *The Last Moment*, for $5,000, borrowed from Edward Spitz. An experimental drama in which a drowning man (Otto Matiesen) relives his life, *The Last Moment* was hailed by the Hollywood intelligentsia and enabled Fejös to land a contract at Universal. The film also indicated that Fejös was to be no ordinary Hollywood-style producer. He was going to use every technical trick the cinema offered in the creation of his films, whether the works were melodramas about magicians (*The Last Performance*) or screen adaptations of popular Broadway productions (*Broadway*).

Paul Fejös's one genuine screen masterpiece (and the only one of his films which is readily available for appraisal today) is *Lonesome*, which uses cinéma vérité to provide a study of two lonely New Yorkers who spend a Saturday afternoon and evening at Coney Island. Not only are the visuals in *Lonesome* stunningly exciting, but the director manages to obtain realistic performances from his two stars, Barbara Kent and Glenn Tryon, neither of whom had previously shown much indication that they were capable of such performances.

The director's Hollywood career ended as suddenly as it had begun. There were arguments over the direction of *All Quiet on the Western Front*, a project which he cherished but which was assigned to Lewis Milestone. Fejös returned to Hungary, where he directed *Marie*, generally considered the best pre-war production from that country. He also directed films in Austria and Denmark before embarking on a documentary filmmaking trip to the Far East, China, and Japan, where he made *Black Horizons* and *A Handful of Rice*, among others. In 1941 he joined the Wenner-Gren Foundation in New York. He spent the rest of his life directing anthropological research.

—Anthony Slide

FELLINI, Federico

Nationality: Italian. **Born:** Rimini, Italy, 20 January 1920. **Education:** Catholic schools in Rimini, until 1938. **Family:** Married Giulietta Masina in Rome, 30 October 1943, one son (died). **Career:** Worked on *420* and *Avventuroso* magazines in Florence, 1938; caricature artist and writer in Rome, from 1939; through friend Aldo Fabrizi, worked as screenwriter, from 1941; worked on Rossellini's *Rome, Open City*, 1944; screenwriter and assistant director, 1946-52; formed Capitolium production company with Alberto Lattuada for *Variety Lights*, 1950; formed Federiz production company with Angelo Rizzoli (subsequently taken over by Clemente Fracazzi), 1961. **Awards:** Grand Prize, Venice Festival, 1954, New York Film Critics Circle Award, 1956, Screen Directors Guild Award, 1956, and Oscar for Best Foreign Film, 1956, for *La strada*; Oscar for Best Foreign Film, for *La notti di Cabiria*, 1957; Oscar for Best Foreign Film, 1960, Palme d'or, Cannes Festival, 1960, and New York Critics Circle Award, 1961, for *La dolce vita*; Oscar for Best Foreign Film, for *8 1/2*, 1963; Oscar for Best Foreign Film, and New York Film Critics Circle Award, for *Amarcord*, 1974; Special Prize, Cannes Festival, 1987; Special Oscar, honoring the body of his work, 1993; Honorary Doctor of Humane Letters, Columbia University, New York, 1970. **Died:** Italy, 31 October 1993.

Films as Director and Scriptwriter:

1950 *Luci del varieta* (co-d, + co-pr)
1951 *Lo Sceicco Bianco*
1953 *I Vitelloni*; "Un'agenzia matrimoniale" in *Amore in citta* (Zavattini)
1954 *La strada*

1955 *Il bidone*
1956 *La notti di Cabiria* (*Nights of Cabiria*)
1960 ***La dolce vita***
1962 "Le tentazioni del dottor Antonio" in *Boccaccio '70* (Zavattini)
1963 ***Otto e mezzo*** (*8 1/2*)
1965 *Giulietta degli spiriti* (*Juliet of the Spirits*)
1968 "Toby Dammit" (Il ne faut jamais parier sa tête contre le diable) in *Histoires extraordinaires/Tre passi nel delirio* (anthology film)
1969 *Block-notes di un regista* (*Fellini: A Director's Notebook*) (for TV) (+ narration, role); *Satyricon* (*Fellini Satyricon*)
1970 *I clowns* (*The Clowns*)
1972 *Roma* (*Fellini Roma*) (+ role)
1974 *Amarcord*
1976 *Casanova* (*Il Casanova di Federico Fellini*)
1978 *Prova d'orchestra* (*Orchestra Rehearsal*) (for TV)
1980 *La città delle donne* (*City of Women*)
1983 *E la nave va* (*And the Ship Sailed On*)
1986 *Ginger and Fred* (+ co-sc)
1987 *Intervista* (*The Interview*) (+ role)
1990 *La voce della luna* (*The Voice of the Moon*)

Other Films:

1939 *Lo vedi come ... lo vedi come sei?!* (Mattòli) (gagman)
1940 *Non me lo dire!* (Mattòli) (gagman); *Il pirata sono io!* (Mattòli) (gagman)
1941 *Documento Z3* (Guarini) (sc/co-sc, uncredited)
1942 *Avanti, c'e posto* (Bonnard) (sc/co-sc, uncredited); *Chi l'ha vistro?* (Alessandrini) (sc/co-sc); *Quarta pagina* (Manzari and Gambino) (sc/co-sc)
1943 *Apparizione* (de Limur) (sc/co-sc, uncredited); *Campo dei fiori* (Bonnard) (sc/co-sc); *Tutta la città canta* (Freda) (sc/co-sc); *L'ultima carrozzella* (Mattòli) (sc/co-sc)
1945 *Roma, città aperta* (Rossellini) (asst d, co-sc)
1946 *Paisà* (Rossellini) (asst d, co-sc)
1947 *Il delitto di Giovanni Episcopo* (Lattuada) (co-sc); *Il passatore* (Coletti) (co-sc); *La fumeria d'oppio* (*Ritorna Za-la-mort*) (Matarazzo) (co-sc); *L'ebreo errante* (Alessandrini) (co-sc)
1948 "Il miracolo" episode of *L'amore* (Rossellini) (asst d, co-sc, role as stranger mistaken for St. Joseph); *Il mulino del Po* (Lattuada) (co-sc); *In nome della legge* (Germi) (co-sc); *Senza pietà* (Lattuada) (co-sc); *La città dolente* (Bonnard) (co-sc)
1949 *Francesco, giullare di Dio* (Rossellini) (co-sc, asst d)
1950 *Il cammino della speranza* (Germi) (co-sc); *Persiane chiuse* (Comencini) (co-sc)
1951 *La città si difende* (Germi) (co-sc); *Cameriera bella presenza offresi* (Pastina) (co-sc)
1952 *Il brigante di Tacca del Lupo* (Germi) (co-sc); *Europa '51* (Rossellini) (co-sc, uncredited)
1958 *Fortunella* (De Filippo) (co-sc)
1970 *Alex in Wonderland* (Mazursky) (role as himself)
1974 *C'eravamo tanto amati* (Scola) (guest appearance)

Publications

By FELLINI: books—

Il Bidone, with Ennio Flaiano and Tullio Pinelli, Paris, 1956.
Le notti di Cabiria di Federico Fellini, edited by Lino del Fra, Rocca San Casiano, Italy, 1957.
La dolce vita di Federico Fellini, edited by Tullio Kezich, Bologna, 1960; New York, 1961.
8 1/2 di Federico Fellini, edited by Camilla Cederna, Rocca San Casciano, Italy, 1963.
Giulietta degli spiriti, edited by Tullio Kezich, Rocca San Casciano, Italy, 1965; as *Juliet of the Spirits,* New York, 1965.
La mia Rimini, Bologna, 1967.
Tre passi nel delirio, with Louis Malle and Roger Vadim, Bologna, 1968.
Fellini Satyricon di Federico Fellini, edited by Dario Zanelli, Bologna, 1969; as *Fellini Satyricon,* New York, 1970.
Il primo Fellini: Lo sceicco blanco, I vitelloni, La strada, Il bidone, edited by Renzo Renzi, Bologna, 1969.
Federico Fellini, Discussion no. 1, Beverly Hills, 1970.
I clowns, edited by Renzo Renzi, Bologna, 1970; 2nd edition, 1988.
Three Screenplays, New York, 1970.
Early Screenplays: Variety Lights, The White Sheik, New York, 1971.
Roma di Federico Fellini, Rocca San Casciano, Italy, 1972.
Amarcord, with Tonino Guerra, Milan, 1973; published as *Amarcord: Portrait of a Town,* London, 1974.
Federcord: disegni per Amarcord di Federico Fellini, edited by L. Betti and O. Del Buono, Milan, 1974.
Il Casanova di Fellini: sceneggiatura originale, with Bernardino Zapponi, Turin, 1974.
4 film: I vitelloni, La dolce vita, 8-1/2, Giulietta degli spiriti, Turin, 1974.
Fellini on Fellini, edited by Christian Strich, New York, 1976.
Fare un film, Turin, 1980.
Bottega Fellini. La città delle donne, with text by Raffaele Monti, Rome, 1981.
Federico Fellini: Intervista sul cinema, edited by Giovanni Grazzini, Rome, 1983; as *Federico Fellini: Comments on Film,* Fresno, California, 1988.
Ginger e Fred, with Tonino Guerra and Tullio Pinelli, Milan, 1986.
81/2 (Otto e mezzo), edited by Charles Affron, New Brunswick, New Jersey, 1987.
La strada, New Brunswick, New Jersey, 1987.
Fellini's Cinecitta, London, 1989.

By FELLINI: articles—

"Strada sabarrata: via libera ai vitelloni," in *Cinema Nuovo* (Turin), 1 January 1953.
"Ogni margine è bruciato," in *Cinema* (Rome), 10 August 1954.
"Enquête sur Hollywood," in *Cahiers du Cinéma* (Paris), Christmas 1955.
"A Personal Statement," in *Film* (London), January/February 1957.
"Les Femmes libres de Magliano," in *Cahiers du Cinéma* (Paris), February 1957.
Interview with George Bluestone, in *Film Culture* (New York), October 1957.
"Crisi e neorealismo," in *Bianco e Nero* (Rome), July 1958.
"Témoignage à André Bazin," in *Cahiers du Cinéma* (Paris), January 1959.
"My Sweet Life," in *Films and Filming* (London), April 1959.
"Su *La dolce vita* la parola a Fellini," in *Bianco e Nero* (Rome), January/February 1960.
"The Bitter Life—of Money," in *Films and Filming* (London), January 1961.
Interview with Enzo Peri, in *Film Quarterly* (Berkeley), Fall 1961.
"The Screen Answers Back," in *Films and Filming* (London), May 1962.
Interview with Gideon Bachmann, in *Sight and Sound* (London), Spring 1964.
"'I Was Born for the Cinema': A Conversation with Federico Fellini," with Irving Levine, in *Film Comment* (New York), Fall 1966.

Federico Fellini

Interview with Pierre Kast, in *Interviews with Film Directors,* edited by Andrew Sarris, Indianapolis, 1967.
Interview with Roger Borderie and others, in *Cahiers du Cinéma* (Paris), May/June 1971.
Interview, in *Encountering Directors* by Charles Samuels, New York, 1972.
"Huit Entretiens autour du Casanova de Fellini," with O. Volta, in *Positif* (Paris), March 1977.
"The Cinema Seen as a Woman," an interview with Gideon Bachmann, in *Film Quarterly* (Berkeley), Winter 1980/81.
Interview with Gideon Bachmann, in *Film Comment* (New York), May/June 1985.
Interview with J.-A. Gili, in *Positif* (Paris), February 1986.
Interview in *Monthly Film Bulletin* (London), November 1986.
Interview with Germaine Greer in *Interview,* December 1988.
Interview with A. Samueli in *Cahiers du Cinema* (Paris), May 1990.
Interview with Gideon Bachmann in *Film Quarterly,* Spring 1994.
Interview with Liselotte Millauer in *Interview,* January 1994.

On FELLINI: books—

Bastide, François-Régis, Juliette Caputo, and Chris Marker, editors, *La Strada,* Paris, 1955.
Renzi, Renzo, *Federico Fellini,* Parma, 1956; Lyons, 1960.
Solmi, Angelo, *Storia di Federico Fellini,* Milan, 1962.
Rondi, Brunello, *Il Cinema di Fellini,* Rome, 1965.
Budgen, Suzanne, *Fellini,* London, 1966.
Solmi, Angelo, *Fellini,* New York, 1967.
Salachas, Gilbert, *Federico Fellini: An Investigation into His Films and Philosophy,* New York, 1969.
Novi, Mario, editor, *Fellini TV: I clowns,* Rome, 1970.
Hughes, Eileen, *On the Set of Fellini Satyricon: A Behind-the-Scenes Diary,* New York, 1971.
Pecori, Franco, *Federico Fellini,* Florence, 1974.
Ketcham, Charles, *Federico Fellini: The Search for a New Mythology,* New York, 1976.
Murray, Edward, *Fellini the Artist,* New York, 1976.
Rosenthal, Stuart, *The Cinema of Federico Fellini,* London, 1976.
Alpert, Hollis, *Fellini: A Life,* New York, 1981.
Fruttero, Carlo, and Franco Lucentini, *Je te trouve un peu pale: Recit d'été avec trente fantasmes feminins de Federico Fellini,* Paris, 1982.
Costello, Donald P., *Fellini's Road,* Notre Dame, Indiana, 1983.
Burke, Frank, *Federico Fellini: Variety Lights to La Dolce Vita,* Boston, 1984.
Fava, Claudio F., and Aldo Vigano, *The Films of Federico Fellini,* Secaucus, New Jersey, 1985.
Kezich, Tullio, *Fellini,* Milan, 1987.
Ciment, Michel, *Federico Fellini,* Paris, 1988.

Grazzini, Giovanni, editor, *Federico Fellini: Comments on Film,* Fresno, California, 1988.
Bondanella, Peter, *The Cinema of Federico Fellini,* Princeton, New Jersey, 1992.
Bondanella, Peter, and Cristina Degli-Esposti, editors, *Critical Essays on Federico Fellini,* New York, 1993.
Baxter, John, *Fellini: The Biography,* New York, 1994.
Chandler, Charlotte, *I, Fellini,* New York, 1995.
Tornabuoni, Lietta, editor, *Rederico Fellini,* New York, 1995.

On FELLINI: articles—

Autera, Leonardo, editor, "Fellini e la critica," in *Bianco e Nero* (Rome), June 1957.
Taylor, John, "Federico Fellini," in *Cinema Eye, Cinema Ear,* New York, 1964.
Ross, Lillian, "Profiles: 101/2," in *New Yorker,* 30 October 1965.
Harcourt, Peter, "The Secret Life of Federico Fellini," in *Film Quarterly* (Berkeley), Spring 1966.
Walter, Eugene, "The Wizardry of Fellini," in *Films and Filming* (London), June 1966.
Eason, Patrick, "Notes on Double Structure and the Films of Fellini," in *Cinema* (London), March 1969.
Cox, Harvey, Jr., "The Purpose of the Grotesque in Fellini's Films," in *Celluloid and Symbols,* edited by Cooper and Skrade, Philadelphia, 1970.
"Fellini Issue" of *L'Arc* (Aix-en-Provence, France), no. 45, 1971.
Julia, Jacques, "Psychanalyse de Fellini," in *Cinéma* (Paris), May 1971.
Chemasi, Antonio, "Fellini's *Casanova*: The Final Nights," in *American Film* (Washington, D.C.), September 1976.
Sarne, M., "Meeting Fellini," in *Films and Filming* (London), April 1978.
Comuzio, Ermanno, "Fellini/Rota: Un matrimonio concertato," in *Bianco e Nero* (Rome), July-August 1979.
Burke, F.M. "Reason and Unreason in Federico Fellini's *I vitelloni,*" in *Literature/Film Quarterly* (Salisbury, Maryland), vol. 8, no. 2, 1980.
Fumento, R., "Maestro Fellini, studente Angelucci," in *Literature/Film Quarterly* (Salisbury, Maryland), October 1982.
Dossier on Fellini, in *Cinématographe* (Paris), January 1984.
Polan, Linda, "With Fellini," in *Sight and Sound* (London), Summer 1984.
Gilliatt, Penelope, "*La dolce vita,*" in *American Film* (Washington, D.C.), November 1985.
"Fellini Section," of *Literature/Film Quarterly* (Salisbury, Maryland), vol. 15, no. 2, 1987.
Lavery, D., "'Major Man': Fellini as an Autobiographer," in *Post Script* (Jacksonville, Florida), Winter 1987.
"Fellini Section" of *Positif* (Paris), December 1987.
Pierson, Frank, "Fellini's magical *8 1/2,*" in *American Film* (Los Angeles), June 1989.
Benigni, Roberto, article in *Positif* (Paris), May 1990.
Cavazzoni, E., article in *Cahiers du Cinema* (Paris), May 1990.
Lavaudant, G., article in *Cahiers du Cinema* (Paris), January 1991.
"New Gigs for Old Pros," in *Variety* (New York), 20 May 1991.
Young, D., "Helmer at Odds Over Ads," in *Variety* (New York), 11 November 1991.
Kauffmann, Stanley, "Regarding Fellini," in *New Republic* (Washington, D.C.), 25 May 1992.
Schneider, K.S., article in *People Weekly* (New York), 18 January 1993.
Obituary in *Times* (London), 1 November 1993.
Obituary in *New York Times,* 1 November 1993.
Obituary in *Los Angeles Times,* 1 November 1993.
Obituary in *Chicago Tribune,* 7 November 1993.
Obituary in *Newsweek* (New York), 8 November 1993.
Obituary in *Variety* (New York), 15 November 1993.
Schneider, K.S., obituary in *People Weekly* (New York), 15 November 1993.
Kauffmann, Stanley, obituary in *New Republic* (Washington, D.C.), 31 January 1994.
Schickel, Richard, "Send in the Clowns: An Aspect of Fellini," in *Film Comment* (New York), September/October 1994.

On FELLINI: films—

Goldbarb, Peter, *Fellini,* for TV, Canada, 1968.
Bachmann, Gideon, *Ciao, Federico!,* U.S., 1970.
Fellini's Cinema: Notes of a Director, Italy, 1992.

* * *

Federico Fellini is one of the most controversial figures in the recent history of Italian cinema. Though his successes have been spectacular, as in the cases of *La strada, La dolce vita,* and *Otto e mezzo,* his failures have been equally flamboyant. This has caused considerable doubt in some quarters as to the validity of his ranking as a major force in contemporary cinema, and made it somewhat difficult for him to achieve sufficient financial backing to support his highly personalized film efforts in his last years. Certainly, few directors in any country could equal Fellini's interest in the history of the cinema or share his certainty regarding the appropriate place for the body of his work within the larger film canon. Consequently, he has molded each of his film projects in such a way that any discussion of their individual merits is inseparable from the autobiographical details of his personal legend.

Fellini's early film *La sceicco bianco* gave a clear indication of the autobiographical nature of the works to follow, for it drew upon his experience as a journalist and merged it with many of the conceits he had developed in his early motion picture career as a gag writer and script writer. However, he was also an instrumental part of the development of the neorealistic film in the 1940s, writing parts of the screenplays of Roberto Rossellini's *Roma città aperta* and *Paisà,* and his reshaping of that tradition toward an autobiographical mode of expression in *La sceicco bianco* troubled a number of his former collaborators. But on his part, Fellini was seemingly just as critical of the brand of neorealism practiced by Rossellini, with its penchant for overt melodrama.

In a succeeding film, *La strada,* Fellini took his autobiographical parallels a step farther, casting his wife, Giulietta Masina, in the major female role. This highly symbolic work was variously interpreted as a manifesto on human rights, or at least a treatise on women's liberation. In these contexts, however, it roused the ire of strict neorealists who regarded it as containing too much justification for political oppression. Yet as a highly metaphorical personal parable about the relationship between a man and a woman it was a critical success and a confirmation of the validity of Fellini's autobiographical instincts. This gave him the confidence to indulge in a subtle criticism of the neorealistic style in his next film, *Il bidone.* The film served, in effect, a tongue-in-cheek criticism of the form's sentimental aspects.

In the films of Fellini's middle period, beginning in 1959 with *La dolce vita,* Fellini became increasingly preoccupied with his role as an international "auteur." As a result, the autobiographical manifestations in his films became more introspective and extended to less tangible areas of his psyche than anything that he had previously brought to the screen. *La dolce vita* is a relatively straightforward psychological extension of what might have become of Moraldo, the director's earlier biographical persona (*I vitelloni*), after forsaking his village for the decadence of Rome. But its successors increasingly explored the areas of its creator's fears, nightmares, and fantasies.

After establishing actor Marcello Mastroianni as his alter ego in *La dolce vita,* Fellini again employed him in his masterpiece, *Otto e mezzo (8 1/2),* as a vehicle for his analysis of the complex nature of artistic inspiration. Then, in a sequel of sorts, he examined the other side of the coin. In *Giulietta degli spiriti (Juliet of the Spirits),* he casts his wife as the intaglio of the Guido figure in *8 1/2.* Both films, therefore, explored the same problems from different sexual perspectives while, on the deeper, ever-present autobiographical plane, the two characters became corresponding sides of Fellini's mythic ego.

Subsequent films continued the rich, flamboyant imagery that became a Fellini trademark, but with the exception of the imaginative fantasy *Fellini Satyricon,* they have, for the most part, returned to the vantage point of direct experience that characterized his earlier works. Finally, in 1980's *La città delle donne,* which again featured Mastroianni, he returned to the larger than life examination of his psyche. In fact, a number of critics regarded the film as the ultimate statement in an ideological trilogy (begun with *8 1/2* and continued in *Juliet of the Spirits*) in which he finally attempts a rapprochement with his inner sexual and creative conflicts. Unfortunately, *City of Women* is too highly derivative of the earlier work. Consequently, it does not resolve the issues raised in the earlier two films.

Several of Fellini's films are masterpieces by anyone's standards. Yet in no other director's body of films does each work identifiably relate a specific image of the creator that he wishes to present to the world and to posterity. Whether any of the films are truly autobiographical in any traditional sense is open to debate. They definitely do not interlock to provide a history of a man, and yet each is a deliberately crafted building block in the construction of a larger than life Fellini legend which may eventually come to be regarded as the "journey of a psyche."

While the final credits on Fellini's filmography are far from his best works, they nonetheless are fitting conclusions to what is one of the legendary careers in the history of world cinema. *And the Ship Sails On* is the wildly preposterous but uniquely Felliniesque tale of the miscellaneous luminaries who come together for an ocean cruise in which they will bid farewell to a just-deceased opera performer. *Ginger and Fred* is a sweetly nostalgic film because of its union of two of Fellini's then-aging but still vibrant stars of the past, Giulietta Masina and Marcello Mastroianni. *The Voice of the Moon,* Fellini's last feature—which did not earn a U.S. distributor—works as a summation of the cinematic subjects which had concerned the film maker for the previous quarter century.

The most outstanding and revealing late-career Fellini is *Intervista,* an illuminating film (and characteristic Fellini union of reality and fantasy) about the production by a Japanese television crew of a documentary about the director. Fellini himself appears on screen, where he is shown to be shooting an adaptation of Kafka's *Amerika,* a film that appears to be a typically Felliniesque extravaganza-in-the-making, complete with eccentric extras, surreal images, and autobiographical touches. We watch the filmmaker as he casts *Amerika.* We meet his various associates and underlings, from producers to actors, from casting director to assistant director. We see how Fellini directs his performers and the steps he takes to inspire feelings and attitudes within them. And we are privy to the various crises, big and small, which are standard fare during the filmmaking process. Finally, Marcello Mastroianni and Anita Ekberg, who over thirty years before had co-starred in *La dolce vita,* appear as themselves. Mastroianni's entrance is especially magical; the sequence in which he and Ekberg (whom, he remarks, he has not seen since making *La dolce vita*) observe their younger selves in some famous clips from the film is wonderful nostalgia.

However, *Intervista* is primarily an homage to Cinecitta, the studio where Fellini shot his films. Revealingly, the filmmaker describes the studio as "a fortress, or perhaps an alibi." Fellini first came to Cinecitta in 1940, when he was a young journalist. His assignment was to interview an actress for a magazine profile. This event is dramatized in *Intervista*; at various points in the film, the narrative drifts from images of the real Fellini, an artist in the twilight of a much-honored career, to a recreation of young Federico (played by Sergio Rubini) and his initiation into the world of Cinecitta.To fully appreciate this very personal movie about the movie-making process, you must be familiar with—and an admirer of—Fellini and his work.

—Stephen L. Hanson, updated by Rob Edelman

FERNÁNDEZ, Emilio

Nationality: Mexican. **Born:** In Hondo, Coahuila, 26 March 1904. Also known as "El Indio." **Family:** Married 1) Gladys Fernández, 1941 (divorced), one daughter; 2) actress Columbia Domínguez (divorced), one daughter; 3) Gloria Cabiedes (divorced), one son; 4) Beatriz (divorced). **Career:** Took part in the rebellion of Adolfo de la Huerta against the Mexican government, captured and sentenced to prison, but escaped to United States, 1923; actor in California, returned to Mexico following amnesty, 1934; directed first film, 1941; served six months of four and one half year sentence for manslaughter, 1976. **Awards:** Best Film, Cannes Festival, for *María Candelaria,* 1946. **Died:** In Mexico City, 6 August 1986.

Films as Director and Co-Scriptwriter:

1941 *La isla de la pasión* (*Passion Island*)
1942 *Soypuro mexicano*
1943 *Flor silvestre* (+ role as Rogelio Torres); ***María Candelaria***
1944 *Las abandonadas*; *Bugambilia*
1945 *Pepita Jiménez*; *La perla* (*The Pearl*)
1946 *Enamorada*
1947 *Río Escondido* (*Hidden River*)
1948 *Maclovia*; *Salón México*; *Pueblerina*
1949 *La malquerida*; *Duelo en las montañas*; *Del odio nació el amor* (*The Torch*; *The Beloved*)
1950 *Undia de vida*; *Victimas del pecado*; *Islas Marías*; *Siempre Tuya*
1951 *La bien amada*; *Acapulco*; *El mar y tú*
1952 *Cuando levanta la niebla*
1953 *La red* (*The Net*); *Reportaje*; *El rapto*; *La rosa blanca*
1954 *La rebelión de los colgados*; *Nostros dos*
1955 *La Tierra de Fuego se apaga*
1956 *Una cita de amor*; *El imposter*
1961 *Pueblito*
1963 *Paloma herida*
1967 *Un dorado de Pancho Villa* (*A Loyal Soldier of Pancho Villa*)
1968 *El crepúsculo de un Dios*
1973 *La Choca*
1975 *Zona roja*
1977 *México norte*
1978 *Erótica*

Films as Actor:

1927 *The Gaucho* (Jones)
1933 *Flying Down to Rio* (Freeland) (as dancer)
1934 *Corazón bandolero* (Sevilla) (as Chacal); *Cruz Diablo* (De Fuentes) (as Toparca); *Tribu* (Contreras); *Janitzio* (Navarro) (as Zirahuén)
1935 *Mariá Elena* (Sevilla) (as dancer); *Celos* (Boytler)
1936 *Marijuana* (*El monstruo verde*) (Bohr) (as El Indio); *Las mujeres mandan* (De Fuentes) (as dancer); *Allá en el Rancho Grande* (De Fuentes) (as dancer); *El superloco* (Segura) (as Idúa); *El Impostor* (Kirkland)

Emilio Fernández: *Maclovia*

1937 *Adiós Nicanor* (Portas) (as Nicanor); *Las cuatro milpas* (Pereda)
1938 *Aquí llego el valentón* (*El fanfarron*) (Rivero); *Juan sin miedo* (Segura) (as Valentín)
1939 *Con los dorados de Villa* (de Anda); *Los de abajo* (*Con la División del Norte*) (Urueta)
1940 *El Charro Negro* (de Anda); *Rancho alegre* (Aguila); *El zorro de Jalisco* (Benavides) (as Ernesto)
1958 *La Cucaracha* (I. Rodríguez) (as Coronel Antonia Zeta)
1961 *Los hermanos de Hierro* (I. Rodríguez) (as Pascual Velasco)
1962 *La Bandida* (R. Rodríguez) (as Epigmenio Gómez)
1963 *El revólver sangriento* (Delgado) (as Félix Gómez); *Night of the Iguana* (Huston) (as barman, also assoc d)
1964 *Los Hermanos Muerte* (Baledón) (as Marcos Zermeño); *Yo, el valiente* (Corona Blake) (as El Cuervo); *La recta final* (Taboada) (as Lucio); *Un callejón sin salida* (Baledón) (as Antonio)
1965 *Duelo de pistoleros* (Delgado) (as Pancho Gatillo Romero); *La conquista de El Dorado* (Portillo) (as Indio Romo); *Un tipo difícil de matar* (Portillo) (as Ringo); *Los malvados* (Corona Blake) (as Emilio); *The Reward* (Bourgignon); *Return of the Seven* (Kennedy)
1966 *El silencioso* (Mariscal) (as Emilio Segura); *The Appaloosa* (Furie); *The War Wagon* (Kennedy)
1967 *El caudillo* (Mariscal); *El jinete fantasma* (Zugsmith); *Cuando corre el alazán* (Mendoza)
1968 *El Yaqui* (Martínez)
1969 ***The Wild Bunch*** (Peckinpah)
1971 *Indio* (de Anda)
1972 *Derecho de asilo* (Zeceña); *El rincón de las Virgenes* (Isaac); *Pat Garrett and Billy the Kid* (Peckinpah)
1973 *Bring Me the Head of Alfredo Garcia* (Peckinpah)
1980 *Las cabareteras* (Cisneros); *Una gallina muy ponedora* (Portillo); *Ahora mis pistolas hablan* (Orozco)
1983 *Mi abuelo, mi perro y yo* (Fernández); *Los amantes* (Vega); *Mercenarios* (Cisneros); *Under the Volcano* (Huston); *El tesoro del Amazonas* (Cardona); *Lola la trailera* (Fernández)
1985 *Cuando corrió el alazán* (Perez)

Publications

By FERNÁNDEZ: books—

En su propio espejo (Entrevista con Emilio "El Indio" Fernández), edited by Julia Tuñon, Mexico City, 1988.

By FERNÁNDEZ: articles—

"After the revolution," in *Films and Filming* (London), June 1963.
Interview in *The Mexican Cinema: Interviews with 13 Directors*, by Beatriz Reyes Navares, Albuquerque, New Mexico, 1976.

On FERNÁNDEZ: books—

Riera, Emilio García, *Historia documental del cine mexicano,* vols. 1-9, Mexico City, 1969.
Blanco, Jorge Ayala, *La aventura del cine mexicano,* Mexico City, 1979.
Mora, Carl, *Mexican Cinema: Reflections of a Society, 1896-1980,* Berkeley, 1982.
de Luna, Andrés, *La batalla y su sombra (La revolución en el cine mexicano),* Mexico City, 1984.
Blanco, Jorge Ayala, *La condición del cine mexicano,* Mexico City, 1986.
Fernández, Adela, *El Indio Fernández: Vida y mito,* Mexico City, 1986.
Taibo, Paco Ignacio, *El Indio Fernández: El cine por mis pistolas,* Mexico City, 1986.
de los Reyes, Aurelio, *Medio Siglo de cine mexicano (1896-1947),* Mexico City, 1987.

On FERNÁNDEZ: articles—

"El Indio," in *Time* (New York), 11 November 1946.
Ellis, K., "Stranger than Fiction: Emilio Fernandez' Mexico," in *Journal of Popular Film* (Washington, D.C.), Spring 1982.
Cuel, F., and J.P. Royer, "Emilio Fernandez," in *Cinématographe* (Paris), April 1982.
Tesson, C., "Portrait d'Emilio Fernandez en metteur en scène," in *Cahiers du Cinéma* (Paris), May 1982.
Mraz, John, "Of *Churros* and *Charros,*" in *Jump Cut* (Berkeley), no. 29, 1984.
Obituaries in *Hollywood Reporter,* 8 and 19 August 1986.
Obituary in *Variety* (New York), 13 August 1986.
Dávalos, Federico, "Por México: La leyenda del Indio Fernández," in *Pantalla* (Mexico City), November 1986.
Rozado, Alejandro, "Lo trágico en el cine de Emilio Fernández," in *Dicine* (Mexico City), November 1987.

* * *

If he did not already exist, it would be necessary to invent Emilio "El Indio" Fernández. His manneristic visual style, his folkloric themes and characters, and his distinctively Indian physiognomy made him an integral element of Mexico's culture of nationalism, as well as the nation's best-known director. Fleeing Mexico after the defeat of his faction in the rebellion of 1923, Fernández ended up digging ditches in Hollywood. As has been the case with so many Latin American artists and intellectuals, Fernández discovered his fatherland by leaving it: "I understood that it was possible to create a Mexican cinema, with our own actors and our own stories.... From then on the cinema became a passion with me, and I began to dream of Mexican films." Making Mexican cinema became Fernández's obsession and, as is so often true of cultural nationalism, a short-term gain was to turn into a long-term dead end.

Perhaps that which most distinguishes Fernández's films is their strikingly beautiful visual style. Fernández and Gabriel Figueroa, the cinematographer, created the classical visual form of Mexican cinema. Ironically, their expressive cinematic patriotism was significantly inspired by foreign models—the most important of which was that of Sergei Eisenstein and his cameraman Eduard Tisse. Fernández evidently saw *Qué Viva Mexico!* in Hollywood, and he later played the lead in *Janitzio,* a film influenced by Eisenstein and the documentaries of Robert Flaherty and Willard Van Dyke. He even went on to "remake" *Qué Viva Mexico!* twice with *Maria Candelaria* and *Maclovia.* Another important antecedent was Paul Strand's photography in *Los Redes,* which must itself have reflected Eisenstein's examples as well as Strand's experiences in the Film and Photo League.

Foreign models were prominent at a formal level, but nationalism was presumably communicated in the content of the visual images. The films of Fernández and Figueroa are a celebration of Mexico's natural beauty: stony Indian faces set off by dark rebozos and white shirts, *charros* and their stallions riding through majestic cactus formations, fishermen and their nets reflected in the swirling ocean tides, flower vendors in Xochimilco's canals moving past long lines of tall poplar trees; and over it all, the monumentally statuesque masses of rolling clouds made impossibly luminous by photographic filters.

In the earlier films, the incredible beauty of the visual structures functioned as a protagonist, providing context for the story and resonating with the characters' emotions. However, Fernández and Figueroa apparently became victims of their own myths, for their later films manifest a coldness and immobility which indicate an emphasis on visual form at the expense of other cinematic concerns. The dangers inherent in their "tourist" images of Mexico were ever-present, of course; but they became increasingly obvious with the petrification of the style.

Fernández's stories have been summed up by Carlos Monsivais, a leading Mexican critic, as "monothematic tragedies: the couple is destroyed by the fate of social incomprehension, Nature is the essence of the Motherland, beauty survives crime, those who sacrifice themselves for others understand the world." One is tempted to add: the Indian is a cretin, the *charro* a blustering *macho,* women are long-suffering and self-denying saints—and the revolution a confused tangle of meaningless atrocities.

Fernández's picturesque myths still retain vigor in the statist nationalism which dominates ideological discourse in Mexico. And, judging from the international attention that Fernández received for his early works, they were evidently also what the world expected from Mexican cinema. The pity is that Emilio "El Indio" Fernández did not demand a little more from himself.

—John Mraz

FERRARA, Abel

Nationality: American. **Born:** The Bronx, New York, 1951. **Education:** Attended Rockland Community College, one year; State University of New York at Purchase. **Career:** While at SUNY, made a number of shorts, including *Could This Be Love?*; formed Navaron Films with long-term collaborator Nicholas St. John.

Films as Director:

late 1970s *Nine Lives*
1979 *The Driller Killer* (+ ed, role)
1980 *Ms.45* (*Angel of Vengeance*) (+ role)
1984 *Fear City*
1985 "The Home Invaders" and "The Dutch Oven" episodes of *Miami Vice* (for TV)
1986 *Gladiator*; pilot episode of *Crime Story* (for TV)
1987 *China Girl*
1989 *Cat Chaser*
1990 *King of New York*
1992 *Bad Lieutenant*
1993 *Invasion of the Body Snatchers* (*Body Snatchers*)
1993 *Snake Eyes* (*Dangerous Game*)
1995 *The Addiction*

Publications

On FERRARA: articles—

Newman, Kim, "The Street Where I Live—Abel Ferrara," in *Monthly Film Bulletin,* January 1988.

Smith, Gavin, "In the Gutter," in *Film Comment,* July/August 1990.
Smith, Gavin, "The Gambler," in *Sight and Sound,* February 1993.
Hoban, Phoebe, "Raising Cain," in *New York,* 1 February 1993.
Adams, Mark, "Abel Ferrara: The King of New York," in *National Film Theatre Programme,* May 1993.
Article, in *Velvet Light Trap,* Autumn 1993.

* * *

According to Abel Ferrara: "There's only one kind of film to make, the kind you go all out on. Maybe some people don't like these subjects, but I don't think there can *be* any other subjects." To those horrified by the violence of his films he gives the uncompromising answer that "once you're an adult, then that's it; anything within the scope of an artist's imagination has got to be portrayed, and if you don't like it then leave." Given his in-your-face, unflinchingly brutal, yet unquestionable and still-developing sense of style, it's not surprising to discover that the director he most admires is Pasolini ("because he filmed his visions and did it without qualifications") and that the first film he remembers being taken to see was Douglas Sirk's devastating, no-holds-barred melodrama *Imitation of Life*.

Ferrara is undoubtedly one of the most notable American directors to have emerged during the 1980s. His films have aroused considerable controversy, but even those who dislike them would be hard put to deny their kinetic energy and verve, and the remarkable performances at the heart of many of them (for example, Zoe Tamerlis in *Ms.45,* Christopher Walken in *King of New York,* and above all, Harvey Keitel in *Bad Lieutenant*). To his admirers, though, he has been greeted in much the same terms that were used to hail Scorsese on the release of *Mean Streets.* Thus, Jim Shelley in the *Guardian,* "Ferrara is American cinema's most uncompromising maverick, someone who genuinely doesn't give a damn and one of the few American directors who not only has some kind of personal 'vision' but has the single-minded determination to express it." In the States *Film Comment* has championed Ferrara in much the same way as it did Scorsese in his early days; it named *Ms.45* as one of the ten best films of 1981, and in 1990 Gavin Smith compared Ferrara's films to what Scorsese and Schrader "might have made together if they had remained in orbit around *Taxi Driver's* lurid nighttime New York and carried on exploring the pulp violence of *Hardcore* and *Rolling Thunder* and the ethnic obsessions of *Mean Streets,*" praising his "way-out melodramas bursting with outrageous excess" for their "hyperbolic style, a subversive vein of sociopolitical comment, and a no-holds-barred pulp inventiveness" reminiscent of early Jonathan Demme and Larry Cohen.

Ferrara began making eight-millimeter shorts at high school with his friend Nicholas St. John, who went on to script *Driller Killer, Ms.45, Fear City, China Girl, King of New York,* and *Dangerous Game/ Snake Eyes.* Their first feature together was *Nine Lives,* a love story with fantasy elements, which they made after forming Navaron Films. Their first film to garner any attention, however, was *The Driller Killer,* which became something of a cult hit on the drive-in circuit in the States. In Britain, by contrast, this story of a New York artist who goes crazy and starts attacking derelicts with an electric drill became infamous as one of the films which started off the "video nasty" panic in the early 1980s, and soon found itself totally banned both on film and video, the victim of a particularly rabid and ill-informed campaign by an ill-matched alliance of pro-censorship campaigners and a sensation-hungry and grotesquely hypocritical tabloid press which revelled in what it purported to condemn. In all the furor of condemnation and vilification, no journalist or critic actually bothered to see the offending item, of course. The only magazine which attempted (in vain) to stem the tide of outraged censoriousness was the British Film Institute's *Monthly Film Bulletin,* which devoted several articles to this and other "videos maudits," with the present writer daring to suggest that *The Driller Killer* was a film of "very considerable merit," and horror guru Kim Newman noting that although "*The Driller Killer* has a collage of revolting sights and sounds unmatched since *Peeping Tom* and *Performance* ... there is no denying the cheapskate proficiency with which Ferrara puts his films together, or the painful accuracy of his probing for the unhealthy nerve." He also suggests that its central character, Reno (played by Ferrara himself), is "perhaps the only psycho in the movies to be driven mad by economic/environmental, rather than sexual/psychological, factors." Whatever the case, any cinema in Britain which tried to show *Driller Killer,* or any shop which tried to rent or sell a video of it, would even today risk a visit from the police, a court case, and a hate campaign by the press.

Thanks partly to the advocacy of William Friedkin, Ferrara's next film, *Ms.45,* the story of a mute young woman who is raped twice and turns into an avenging angel, was taken up and distributed by Warner Bros. In Britain, meanwhile, it was not released in cinemas and was heavily cut on video. By this time Ferrara's name spelled danger to an increasingly nervous British Board of Film Classification, although the fuss over *The Driller Killer* had brought him to the admiring attention of many horror aficionados. There followed the bigger-budget *Fear City,* starring Tom Berenger and Melanie Griffith. This story of the hunt for a psychopath who mutilates and kills strippers also failed to find a cinema release in Britain and was cut to bits on video. In the States, however, it brought Ferrara to the attention of Michael Mann, for whom he directed two first-season episodes of *Miami Vice* ("Home Invaders" and "Dutch Oven") and the pilot of *Crime Story,* all displaying his customary style and verve. *China Girl* updated *Romeo and Juliet* (and *West Side Story*) to take in a love story set against conflict between the Chinatown and Little Italy districts of New York. *Cat Chaser* remains the best adaptation of an Elmore Leonard thriller to date (Alan Sharp provided the first screenplay), even though Ferrara himself left the project before the editing was completed to work on *The King of New York.* This is one of his very finest films.

The story of a gangster with a moral streak (he wants to save a children's hospital with funds raised from drug-dealing) pitted against three cops who break every moral code in the book, this is a truly stunning contemporary "film noir" and can also be read as a wry comment on Reaganite (and Thatcherite) "trickle down" economics, or as a very dark-hued Robin Hood for our times. Christopher Walken's performance as the ambitious crook-with-a-conscience is nothing short of mesmeric. Even more remarkable, however, is Harvey Keitel as the utterly ravaged, almost deranged cop in *Bad Lieutenant,* undoubtedly Ferrara's darkest, bleakest, most tormented film, and a frighteningly intense addition to the cinema of abjection. This is also the film in which the curious religious streak, almost always present in Ferrara's work, is closest to the surface. For although *Bad Lieutenant* presents us with an appalling catalogue of human turpitude, it is, ultimately, a story of redemption, and one presented in often quite explicitly Christian terms; as Mark Kermode put it in a perceptive review of the film in *Sight and Sound,* "like *The Exorcist,* the film frequently seems to revel in obscenity, but remains draped throughout in the pious clothing of the priesthood." Similarly, *Variety* compared it to Ingmar Bergman's *The Silence* in that it "tackled the subject of God's absence from people's lives in such a sexually explicit and morbid context." The comparison with Bergman is also telling in that this harsh, tortured film, with its spare, elliptical, real-time narrative, delivers almost none of the conventional pleasures normally associated with "Hollywood" cinema, coming across instead as a particularly angst-ridden, contemporary "art movie." As such, it's a film to admire rather than like, but it does prove triumphantly (as if proof were needed) that Keitel is an absolutely major talent and that Ferrara, as well as being a fine visual stylist, is a first-class actor's director. As he himself put it: "the most fulfilling part of directing is to create a space for a performance. To be there for the actor, and to find the actors who can do it." Much of Keitel's performance seems to be improvised (for example, the infamous and queasy long-drawn-out scene in which

Abel Ferrara

he frenziedly masturbates whilst harassing two young female traffic offenders, all the while mouthing obscenities) but, just like Jack Nicholson's celebrated dope-smoking scene in *Easy Rider*, one suspects it isn't. As Ferrara himself puts it: "Improvisation is a funny concept because the basis of any great improvisation is great material, a great script, to begin with. And then it's very hard to say where it starts and stops. These scenes have been discussed and worked on and written together, so who knows where that improv begins or where there are real lines."

In a different key altogether is *Invasion of the Body Snatchers*, the third cinema version of Jack Finney's classic tale of urban paranoia, but equally successful in its own way as the other two. *Dangerous Game* reunites Ferrara with Keitel in a film-within-a-film which he has described as being like "*Who's Afraid of Virginia Woolf?* on acid." Certainly it's an extraordinarily reflexive and self-conscious work where it's often made extremely difficult to work out the reality status of the images we're watching, which is something of a new departure for Ferrara and seems to take us back into "art movie" territory. On the other hand, the remark by Keitel's Eddie Israel, the director of *Mother of Mirrors*, the film-within-the-film, that "the ultimate is pain and suffering—that's what it takes to survive" could well be taken as a distillation of the Ferrara philosophy and a summary of the import of his entire oeuvre.

—Julian Petley

FERRERI, Marco

Nationality: Italian. **Born:** Milan, 11 May 1928. **Education:** Veterinary medicine. **Family:** Married Jacqueline (Ferreri). **Career:** Dropped out of university, worked as liquor salesman, advertising agent, and journalist, late 1940s; produced two issues of filmic "magazine" *Documento mensile*, 1950-51; film actor and writer, 1952-53; optical instrument salesman in Spain, 1954; directed first feature, *El Pisito*, 1958. **Awards:** International Critics Award, Venice Festival, for *The Wheelchair*, 1960; International Critics Award, Cannes Festival, for *La Grande Bouffe*, 1973; Golden Bear Award, Berlin Film Festival, for *La Casa del Sorriso (House of Smiles)*, 1991.

Films as Director:

1958 *El Pisito* (+ co-sc)
1959 *Los chicos* (+ co-sc)
1960 *El cochecito* (*The Wheelchair*; *The Motorcart*) (+ co-sc); *Le Secret des hommes bleus* (*Caravan pour Zagora*; *El secreto de los hommes azules*) (d begun by Ferreri, completed by Edmon Agabra)
1961 "Gli adulteri (L'infidelità conjugale)" episode of *Le italiane e l'amore* (+ sc)
1963 *Una storia moderna: l'ape regina* (*The Conjugal Bed*) (+ co-sc)

1964 *La donna scimmia* (*The Ape Woman*) (+ co-sc); "Il professore" episode of *Controsesso* (+ co-sc)
1965 "L'uomo dei cinque palloncini (The Man with the Balloons)" episode of *Oggi, domani, dopodomani* (+ co-sc)
1966 *Marcia nuziale* (+ co-sc)
1967 *L'harem* (+ co-sc)
1968 *Dillinger è morto* (*Dillinger Is Dead*) (+ co-sc); *Break-Up* (revised version of episode from 1964 film *Oggi, domani, dopodomani*) (+ sc)
1969 *Il seme dell'uomo* (*The Seed of Man*) (+ co-sc)
1970 *Perché pagare per essere felici!* (documentary, for television) (+ sc)
1971 *L'udienza* (+ co-sc)
1972 *Liza* (*La cagna*) (+ co-sc)
1973 ***La grande bouffe*** (*La grande abbuffata*; *Blow-Out*) (+ sc); *Non toccate la donna bianca* (*Touche pas la femme blanche*) (+ co-sc, role)
1976 *L'ultima donna* (*La Dernière Femme*; *The Last Woman*) (+ co-sc)
1978 *Bye Bye Monkey* (*Ciao maschio*) (+ co-sc)
1979 *Chiedo asilo* (*My Asylum*) (+ sc)
1981 *Tales of Ordinary Madness* (*Storie di ordinaria follia*) (+ co-sc)
1983 *Storia di Piera* (*Piera's Story*) (+ co-sc)
1984 *Il Futuro e Donna* (*The Future Is Woman*) (+ co-sc)
1986 *Ti amo* (*I Love You*)
1987 *Come Sono Buoni I Bianchi*
1988 *Y'a bon les blancs* (*Um good, de white folks*) (+ co-sc)
1989 *La Banquet de Platon*
1991 *La Carne* (*The Flesh*; *Love Ritual*) (+ co-sc); *La Casa del Sorriso* (*House of Smiles*) (+ co-sc)
1993 *Diario di un Vizio* (*Diary of a Maniac*) (+ co-sc)
1995 *Faictz ce que vouldras* (*Do What Thou Wilt*) (+ sc)

Other Films:

1950 *Il principe ribelle* (Mercanti) (role)
1951 *Documento mensile* (two or three "issues," according to sources) (prod mgr); *Il cappotto* (Lattuada) (prod mgr)
1953 *Amore in città* (anthology film) (prod mgr); *La spiaggia* (Lattuada) (prod mgr, role)
1954 *Donne e soldati* (Malerba and Marchi) (prod mgr, co-sc, role)
1956 *Fiesta brava* (*Toro bravo*) (Cottafavi, unauthorized release) (prod mgr)
1962 *Mafioso* (Lattuada) (co-sc)
1964 *Casanova '70* (Monicelli) (role)
1967 *Il fischio al naso* (Tognazzi) (role)
1969 *Porcile* (Pasolini) (role); *Le vent d'est* (Godard) (role)
1970 *Ciao Gulliver* (Tuzii) (role); *Sortilegio* (Bonomi) (role)
1971 *Lui per lei* (Rispoli) (role)

Publications

By FERRERI: books—

Marco Ferreri: Cinema, Amiens, 1982.

By FERRERI: articles—

"Je fais du cinéma commercial parce que je ne suis pas un héros," an interview with Noel Simsolo, in *Cinéma* (Paris), January 1973.

"Touche pas la femme blanche," interview with J.A. Gili and G. Braucourt, in *Ecran* (Paris), March 1974.

"Perché ho fatto un film fisiologico," interview edited by P. Mereghetti, in *Cineforum* (Bergamo), May 1974.

Interview with P. Bonitzer and others, in *Cahiers du Cinéma* (Paris), July/August 1976.

"Marco Ferreri on *L'ultima donna,*" with R. Schar, in *Cinema Papers* (Melbourne), September/October 1976.

"Why? Why Not?," interview with P.L. Thirard, in *Positif* (Paris), June 1978.

Interview with G. Buscaglia and others, in *Framework* (Norwich), no. 12, 1980.

Interview with Dan Yakir, in *Film Comment* (New York), March/April 1983.

Interview with O. Dazat, in *Cinématographe* (Paris), May 1986.

Interview with F. Sabouraud and Serge Toubiana, in *Cahiers du Cinéma* (Paris), January 1988.

Interview with M. Ciment and others, in *Positif* (Paris), March 1988.

Interview with F. Strauss, in *Cahiers du Cinéma* (Paris), January 1992.

On FERRERI: books—

Accialini, Fulvio, and Coluccelli, Lucia, *Marco Ferreri,* Milan, 1979.

Migliarini, Angelo, *Marco Ferreri: La distruzione dell'uomo storico,* Pisa, 1984.

Maheo, Michel, *Marco Ferreri,* Paris, 1986.

Borin, Fabrizio, editor, *Marco Ferreri,* Venice, 1988.

On FERRERI: articles—

Lane, J.F., "The Face of '63—Italy," in *Films and Filming* (London), April 1963.

"*L'Audience,*" in *Avant-Scène du Cinéma* (Paris), March 1973.

Peruzzi, G., "Il Recupero del fantastico nell'opera di Marco Ferreri," in *Cinema Nuovo* (Turin), July/August 1973.

"*La Grand Bouffe,*" in *Avant-Scène du Cinéma* (Paris), January/February 1974.

Depuyper, C., "Ferreri: un cinéma de moeurs-fiction," in *Cinéma* (Paris), September/October 1974.

"Director of the Year," *International Film Guide* (London, New York), 1975.

"Marco Ferreri," in *Film Dope* (London), September 1978.

Martin, Marcel, and others, "Marco Ferreri," in *Revue du Cinéma* (Paris), July/August 1983.

"Ferreri Issue" of *Cinema Nuovo* (Bergamo), March/April 1984.

Maheo, M., "Un Corps a corps avec le mythe," in *Cinéma* (Paris), October 1984.

Crawley, T., "The Key to Love," in *Photoplay Movies & Video* (London), October 1986

Première (Paris), July 1987.

"Ferreri's Latest Satire Film Fails to Provoke Expected Controversy," in *Variety* (New York), 27 January 1988.

Career overview in *Cinéma* (Paris), November 1991.

* * *

Marco Ferreri's films are daringly excessive and outrageous, to some even obscene. But the filmmaker does not wish to shock or startle or offend the viewer solely for effect. Rather, his aim is to jar his audience into pondering his themes: the break-up of the nuclear family, the redefinition of sex roles, and the alienation inherent in modern city living. He is a social critic who captures in his images a contemporary world on the edge of social chaos. Ferreri is if anything a humanist—and a pessimist—who is so frustrated by his perceptions of society that his art can only border on the absurd.

Ferreri's early films center around the crumbling institution of marriage. In *The Conjugal Bed* (*L'Ape Regina,* the translation of which is *The Queen Bee*), a pleasant, fortyish bachelor (Ugo Tognazzi) who is unable to keep up with youthful wife Marina Vlady's sexual demands becomes an invalid and dies before the final credits. The heavy in Ferreri's works, though, is not always the wife. *The Ape Woman,* played by Annie Girardot, has her body and face covered with hair. She is exploited by a two-bit showman (Tognazzi, again) who eventually must marry her to keep her from leaving his freak show. In the film's Italian-released print, the title character dies in childbirth and her husband has her stuffed, putting her on exhibit.

Dillinger Is Dead, arguably Ferreri's masterpiece, sums up the first phase of his career. It is the surreal, ambiguous tale of an industrial designer (Michel Piccoli), disenchanted with his wife, job, and home, who polishes and fixes an old revolver, kills his mate, and escapes to Tahiti. Perhaps, however, all these events occurred only in his imagination during his drive home from work.

The filmmaker's scenarios during the 1970s expand beyond familial relationships. In *La Grande Bouffe,* a quartet of bored middle-aged men (a chef, airline pilot, judge, and television producer) eat themselves to death in an orgy of gluttony. In *Bye Bye Monkey,* Ferreri's first English-language feature, Gerard Depardieu is gang-raped by several women and a rat colony that has overrun New York City devours a baby chimp. Ben Gazzara stars in *Tales of Ordinary Madness* as a rumpled, booze-loving beat poet who rambles through a maze of hookers, nymphomaniacs, neurotics, and weirdos. *The Last Woman* is the story of a male chauvinist factory engineer (Depardieu), who appears throughout almost entirely in the nude. He has his consciousness raised by nursery school teacher Ornella Muti and, in the film's finale, slices off his sex organ with an electric carving knife. In this last film, Ferreri's characters exist in an ambience of stark, impersonal, dehumanizing factories, high-rises, shopping centers, and superhighways.

Marco Ferreri's films range from the superb (*Dillinger Is Dead*) to the dreadful (*Tales of Ordinary Madness*). But they are unified in their despair for modern society. He offers no positive solutions: his characters gorge themselves to death, or deny themselves of the sexuality that is the essence of their lives. As the filmmaker explained, "Society is finished. The values that once existed no longer exist. The family, the bourgeoisie—I'm talking about values, morals, economic relationships—they no longer serve a purpose. My films are reactions translated into images. The Roman Empire is over. We are entering the new Middle Ages. What interests me are moments when the world is dissolving and exploding."

Ferreri's more recent films are united in that they remain true to his vision of the decline of modern society. Additionally, they feature characters who find themselves in unusual sexual situations. Still, his two 1992 releases are decidedly minor affairs, with their intended tastelessness no longer seeming shocking or outrageous. *La Casa del Sorriso (House of Smiles),* which focuses on a spicy romance between a pair of seventysomethings in a rest home, is surprisingly low-key and insipid. *La Carne (The Flesh)* tells of a nightclub performer, separated from his wife, who commences a heated sexual relationship with a seductive younger woman. The twist is that the man, rather than the woman, is the sex object. But the result is obvious and silly, and the cannibalism depicted near the film's end is a limp imitation of the finale of *The Last Woman.*

Diario di un Vizio (Diary of a Maniac) is a return to form for Ferreri. It is the keenly observed story of a solitary, disturbed toilet bowl detergent salesman. Obsessed with sex, he constantly squabbles with his girlfriend. He keeps a diary, the contents of which grow more and more perverse and disturbing until it practically envelops him.

—Rob Edelman

FEUILLADE, Louis

Nationality: French. **Born:** Lunel, France, 19 February 1873. **Education:** the Institut de Brignac and at the Petit Séminaire, Carcassonne. **Military Service:** Served with French Army, 1891-95, and 1915. **Family:** Married Jeanne-Léontine Janjou, 1895 (daughter married to filmmaker Maurice Champreux). **Career:** Worked in publishing in Paris, 1898; founder of satirical journal *La Tomate,* 1903; hired as writer by Alice Guy at Gaumont Studios, 1905; replaced Guy as Director of Gaumont Productions, 1907; began series of "ciné-romans" (serials) with *Judex,* 1916; first President of the Societé des Auteurs de Films, 1917-18; moved, with Gaumont, to Nice, 1918. **Died:** In Nice, 26 February 1925.

Films as Director (Feuillade wrote and directed an estimated eight hundred films; this partial listing includes all series titles and known non-series titles):

1906 *Le billet de banque*; *C'est Papa qui prend la purge*; *Les deux Gosses*; *La Porteuse de pain*; *Mireille* (co-d); *N'te promène donc pas toute nue*

1907 *Un accident d'auto*; *La course des belles-mères*; *Un facteur trop ferré*; *L'homme aimanté*; *La légende de la fileuse*; *Un paquet embarrassant*; *La sirène*; *Le thé chez la concierge*; *Vive le sabotage*

1908 *Les agents tels qu'on nous les présente*; *Une dame vraiment bien*; *La grève des apaches*; *Nettoyage par le vide*; *Une nuit agitée*; *Prométhé*; *Le récit du colonel*; *Le roman de Sœur Louise*; *Un tic*

1909 *L'aveugle de Jerusalem*; *La chatte métamorphosée en femme*; *La cigale et la fourmi*; *Le collier de la reine*; *Les filles du cantonnier*; *Les heures*; *Histoire de puce*; *Le huguenot*; *Judith et Holopherne*; *Fra Vincenti*; *La légende des phares*; *La mère du moine*; *La mort de Mozart*; *La mort*; *La possession de l'enfant*; *Le savetier et le financier*; *Le printemps*; *Vainqueur de la course pédestre*;

1910 *Benvenuto Cellini*; *Le Christ en croix*; *Esther*; *L'Exode*; *Le festin de Balthazar*; *La fille de Jephté*; *Mil huit cent quatorze*; *Mater dolorosa*; *Maudite soit la guerre*; *Le pater*; *Le roi de Thulé*

1910/11 "Le Film Esthétique" series: (1910: *Les sept péchés capitaux, La nativité*; 1911: *La vierge d'Argos*)

1910/13 "Bébé" series (74 films, from 88 to 321 meters length) (series begins with *Bébé fume* in 1910; final title is *Bébé en vacances* in 1913)

1911 *L'aventurière, dame de compagnie*; *Aux lions les chrétiens*; *Dans la vie*; *Les doigts qui voient*; *Fidélité romaine*; *Le fils de la sunamité*; *Le fils de Locuste*; *Les petites apprenties*; *Quand les feuilles tombent*; *Sans le joug*; *Le trafiquant*

1911/13 "La vie telle qu'elle est" series: (1911: *Les vipères, Le mariage de l'aînée, Le roi Lear au village, En grève, Le bas de laine [Le Trésor], La tare, Le poison, La souris blanche, Le trust [Les batailles de l'argent], Le chef-lieu de Canton, Le destin des mères, Tant que vous serez heureux*; 1912: *L'accident, Les braves gens, Le nain, Le pont sur l'Abime*; 1913: *S'affranchir*)

1912 *Amour d'automne*; *Androclès*; *L'anneau fatal*; *L'attrait du bouge*; *Au pays des lions*; *L'Aventurière*; *La cassette de l'emigrée*; *Le chateau de la peur*; *Les cloches de Paques*; *Le cœur et l'argent*; *La course aux millions*; *Dans la brousse*; *La demoiselle du notaire*; *La fille du margrave*; *La hantise*; *Haut les mains!*; *L'homme de proie*; *La maison des lions*; *Le maléfice*; *Le mort vivant*; *Les noces siciliennes*; *Le Noël de Francesca*; *Préméditation*; *La prison sur le gouffre*; *Le témoin*; *Le tourment*; *Tyrtée*; *La vertu de Lucette*; *La vie ou la mort*; *Les yeux qui meurent*

1912/16 "Bout-de-Zan" series (53 films, from 79 to 425 meters length) [series begins with *Bout-de-Zan revient du cirque* (1912); final title is *Bout-de-Zan et la torpille* (1916)]

1912/13 "Le Détective Dervieux" series (1912: *Le Proscrit, L'oubliette*; 1913: *Le guet-apens, L'écrin du rajah*)

1913 *L'agonie de Byzance*; *L'angoisse*; *Les audaces du cœur*; *Bonne année*; *Le bon propriétaire*; *Le browning*; *Les chasseurs de lions*; *La conversion d'Irma*; *Un drame au pays basque*; *L'effroi*; *Erreur tragique*; *La gardienne du feu*; *Au gré des flots*; *L'intruse*; *La marche des rois*; *Le mariage de miss Nelly*; *Le ménestrel de la reine Anne*; *La mort de Lucrèce*; *La petite danseuse*; *Le revenant*; *La rose blanche*; *Un scandale au village*; *Le secret du forçat*; *La vengeance du sergent de ville*; *Les yeux ouverts*

1913/14 "Fantômas" series: (1913: *Fantômas, Juve contre Fantômas, La mort qui tue*; 1914: *Fantômas contre Fantômas, Le faux magistrat*)

1913/16 "La vie drôle" series (35 films, of which 26 are preserved) [series begins with *Les millions de la bonne* (1913), and includes *L'Illustre Machefer* (1914), *Le colonel Bontemps* (1915), and *Lagourdette, gentleman cambrioleur* (1916)]

1914 *Le calvaire*; *Le coffret de Tolède*; *Le diamant du Sénéchal*; *L'enfant de la roulotte*; *L'épreuve*; *Les fiancés de 1914*; *Les fiancés de Séville*; *Le gendarme est sans culotte*; *La gitanella*; *L'hôtel de la gare*; *Les lettres*; *Manon de Montmartre*; *La neuvaine*; *Paques rouges*; *La petite Andalouse*; *La rencontre*; *Severo Torelli*

1915 *L'angoisse au foyer*; *La barrière*; *Le blason*; *Celui qui reste*; *Le collier de perles*; *Le coup du fakir*; *La course a l'abîme*; *Deux Françaises*; *L'escapade de Filoche*; *L'expiation*; *Le fer a cheval*; *Fifi tambour*; *Le furoncle*; *Les noces d'argent*; *Le Noël du poilu*; *Le sosie*; *Union sacrée*

1915/16 "Les vampires" series (1915: ***La tête coupée***; ***La bague qui tue***; ***Le cryptogramme rouge***; 1916: *Le spectre*; ***L'évasion du mort***; ***Les yeux qui fascinent***; ***Satanas***; *Le maître de la foudre*; ***L'homme des poisons***; ***Les noces sanglantes***)

1916 *L'aventure des millions*; *C'est le printemps*; *Le double jeu*; *Les fiançailles d'Agénor*; *Les fourberies de Pingouin*; *Le malheur qui passe*; *Un mariage de raison*; *Les mariés d'un jour*; *Notre pauvre cœur*; *Le poète et sa folle amante*; *La peine du talion*; *Le retour de Manivel*; *Si vous ne m'aimez pas*; ***Judex*** (serial in a prologue and twelve episodes)

1917 *L'autre*; *Le bandeau sur les yeux*; *Débrouille-toi*; *Déserteuse*; *La femme fatale*; *La fugue de Lily*; *Herr Doktor*; *Mon oncle*; *La nouvelle mission de Judex* (serial in twelve episodes); *Le passé de Monique*

1918 *Aide-toi*; *Les petites marionnettes*; *Tih Minh* (serial in twelve episodes); *Vendémiaire*

1919 *Barrabas* (serial in twelve episodes); *L'engrenage*; *L'énigme (Le mot de l')*; *L'homme sans visage*; *Le nocturne*

1920 *Les deux Gamines* (serial in twelve episodes)

1921 *L'Orpheline* (serial in twelve episodes); *Parisette* (serial in twelve episodes)

1921/22 "Belle humeur" series (1921: *Gustave est médium, Marjolin ou la fille manquée, Saturnin ou le bon allumeur, Séraphin ou les jambes nues, Zidore ou les métamorphoses*; 1922: *Gaétan ou le commis audacieux, Lahire ou le valet de cœur*)

1922 *Le fils du flibustier* (serial in twelve episodes)

1923 *Le gamin de Paris*; *La gosseline*; *L'orphelin de Paris* (serial in six episodes); *Vindicta* (film released in five parts)

1924 *La fille bien gardée*; *Lucette*; *Pierrot Pierrette*; *Le stigmate* (serial in six episodes)

Other Films:

1905 *Le coup de vent* (*Le chapeau*) (sc)

1906 *La course au potiron* (sc)

Publications

By FEUILLADE: books—

Le Clos (play), with Etienne Arnaud, Paris, 1905.
Les Vampires, with George Meirs, Paris, 1916.
Judex, with Arthur Bernède, Paris, 1917 (and 1934).
La nouvelle Mission de Judex, with Arthur Bernède, Paris, 1919.
Tih Minh, with Georges Le Faure, Paris, 1919.
Barrabas, with Maurice Level, Paris, 1920.

By FEUILLADE: articles—

"Naundor, la genèse d'un crime historique," (under pseudonym P. Valergues), in *Revue mondiale* (Paris), 10 November 1904 through 25 October 1905.
Manifestos on the series "Le film esthétique" and "La vie telle qu'elle est", in *L'Anthologie du Cinéma,* edited by Marcel Lapierre, Paris, 1946.

On FEUILLADE: books—

Delluc, Louis, *Cinéma et Compagnie,* Paris, 1919.
Védrès, Nicole, *Images du cinéma français,* Paris, 1945.
Lacassin, Francis, *Louis Feuillade,* Paris, 1964.
Prédal, René, *Le Cinéma muet à Nice,* Aix-en-Provence, 1964.
Florey, Robert, *La Lanterne magique,* Lausanne, 1966.

On FEUILLADE: articles—

Beylie, Claude, "Louis Feuillade," in *Ecrans de France* (Paris), 15 May 1959.
Lacassin, F., and R. Bellour, "En effeuillant la Marguerite," in *Cinéma* (Paris), March through June 1961.
Florey, Robert, "Une Saison dans la cage à mouches avec Feuillade," in *Cinéma* (Paris), June 1962.
Fieschi, Jean-André, "Feuillade (l'homme aimanté)," in *Cahiers du Cinéma* (Paris), November 1964.
Lacassin, Francis, "Louis Feuillade," in *Sight and Sound* (London), Winter 1964/65.
Lacassin, Francis, "Les lettres de Léon Gaumont à Louis Feuillade," in *Cinéma* (Paris), no. 95, 1965.
"Feuillade," in *Anthologie du Cinéma,* vol. 2, Paris, 1967.
Roud, Richard, "Maker of Melodrama," in *Film Comment* (New York), November/December 1976.
"Louis Feuillade," in *Film Dope* (London), September 1978.
Cartier, C., and M. Oms, "Quand Louis Feuillade cinématographiait à la cité de Carcassonne," in *Cahiers de la Cinémathèque* (Paris), Winter 1979.
"*Fantômas* Issue" of *Avant-Scène du Cinéma* (Paris), 1 July 1981.
You, D., "*Fantômas* et *Judex* au tribunal: Feuillade a-t-il cédé ses droits," in *Filméchange* (Paris), Winter 1983.
Lacassin, F., "Naissance d'un héros," in *Avant-Scène du Cinéma* (Paris), April 1984.
Pithon, R., "Retour à Feuillade," in *Positif* (Paris), February 1987.
Abel, R., "Before *Fantômas*: Louis Feuillade and the Development of Early French Cinema," in *Post Script* (Jacksonville, Florida), Fall 1987.

* * *

Louis Feuillade

Louis Feuillade was one of the most solid and dependable talents in French cinema during the early twentieth century. He succeeded Alice Guy as head of production at Gaumont in 1906 and worked virtually without a break—aside from a period of war service—until his death in 1925. He produced some eight hundred films of every conceivable kind: comedies and contemporary melodramas, biblical epics and historical dramas, sketches and series with numerous episodes adding up to many hours of running time. Alhough most of these films were made from his own scripts, Feuillade was not an innovator. The years of his apprenticeship in the craft of filmmaking were those in which French producers reigned supreme, and he worked uncomplainingly in a context in which commercial criteria were paramount. For Feuillade—as for so many of his successors in the heyday of Hollywood—aesthetic strategies not rooted in sound commercial practices were inconceivable, and a filmmaker's only viable ambition was to reach the widest possible audience.

Most of Feuillade's output forms part of a series of some kind and he clearly saw films in generic terms rather than as individually sculpted works. Though not an originator in terms of the forms or styles he adopted, he made films which are among the finest examples of the various popular genres he successively explored. Before 1914 his work is enormously diverse. It included thirty comic films in the series of *La Vie drôle,* a group of seriously intended dramas in which a concern with the quality of the pictorial image is apparent (marketed under the banner of the *Film esthétique*), and a number of contemporary dramas, *La Vie telle qu'elle est,* with somewhat ambiguous claims to realism. In addition, he made some seventy-six films with a four-year-old child star, Bébé, and another fifty or so with the urchin Bout-de-Zan.

But the richest vein of Feuillade's work is the series of crime melodramas that extended from *Fantômas* in 1913-14 to *Barrabas* in 1920. Starting with his celebration of Fantômas, master criminal and master of disguise, who triumphs effortlessly over the dogged ordinariness of his opponent Inspector Juve, Feuillade went on to make his wildest success with *Les Vampires.* Made to rival the imported American serials, this series reflects the chaotic wartime state of French production. It is marked by improvised stories refusing all logic, bewildering changes of casting (necessary as actors were summoned to the war effort), economical use of real locations, and dazzling moments of total incongruity.

Les Vampires reached a level that Feuillade was never able to duplicate. Subsequent works like *Judex* and especially *La Nouvelle Mission de Judex* are marked by a new tone of moralising, with the emphasis placed on the caped avenger rather than the feckless criminals. If the later serials, *Tih Minh* and *Barrabas,* contain sequences able to rank with the director's best, Feuillade's subsequent work in the 1920s lacks the earlier forcefulness.

It was the films' supreme lack of logic, the disregard for hallowed bourgeois values—so appropriate at a time when the old social order of Europe was crumbling under the impact of World War I—which led the surrealists such as André Breton and Louis Aragon to hail *Fantômas* and *Les Vampires,* and most of Feuillade's subsequent advocates have similarly celebrated the films' anarchistic poetry. But this should not lead us to see Feuillade as any sort of frustrated artist or poet of cinema, suffocating in a world dominated by business decisions. On the contrary, the director was an archetypal middle class family man who prided himself on the commercial success of his work and conducted his personal life in accord with strictly ordered bourgeois principles.

—Roy Armes

FEYDER, Jacques

Nationality: Belgian. **Born:** Jacques Frédérix in Ixelles, Belgium, 21 July 1885, became French citizen, 1928. **Education:** the Ecole régimentaire, Nivelles, 1905. **Military Service:** Served in Belgian Army, 1917-19. **Family:** Married Françoise Rosay, 1917, three sons. **Career:** Worked in family's cannon foundry, 1906-07; theatre actor in Paris, 1911-13, and in Lyons, 1913-14; also film actor, from 1912; assistant to film director Gaston Ravel, 1914; directed first film, for Gaumont, 1916; *Les Nouveaux Messieurs* banned in France for insulting "the dignity of parliament and its ministers," accepted MGM offer and moved to Hollywood, 1928; MGM contract terminated, 1933; moved to Switzerland, 1942; producer in Paris, 1945. **Awards:** Best Foreign Film Award, New York Film Critics, and Best Direction, Venice Festival, for *La Kermesse héroïque,* 1935. **Died:** In Prangins, Switzerland, 25 May 1948.

Films as Director:

1915 *Monsieur Pinson, policier* (co-d)

1916 *Têtes de femmes, femmes de tête*; *Le Pied qui etreint* (four episodes) (+ sc); *L'Homme au foulard à pois* (+ sc); *Le Bluff* (+ sc); *Un Conseil d'ami* (+ sc); *L'Homme de compagnie*; *Tiens, vous êtes à Poitiers?* (+ sc); *Le Frère de lait* (+ sc)

1917 *L'Instinct est maître*; *Le Billard cassé* (+ sc); *Abrégeons les formalités!* (+ sc); *La Trouvaille de Bûchu* (+ sc); *Le Pardessus de demi-saison*; *Les Vieilles Femmes de l'Hospice*

1919 *La Faute d'orthographe* (+ sc)

1921 *L'Atlantide* (*Missing Husbands*) (+ sc)

1922 *Crainquebille* (+ sc, art d)

1925 *Visages d'enfants* (*Faces of Children*) (+ sc, art d); *L'Image* (+ co-sc, role); *Gribiche* (*Mother of Mine*) (+ sc)

1926 *Carmen* (+ sc)

1927 *Au pays du Roi Lépreux* (documentary) (+ sc)

1928 *Thérèse Raquin* (*Du sollst nicht Ehe brechen*; *Shadows of Fear*) (+ co-sc); *Les Nouveaux Messieurs* (*The New Gentlemen*) (+ co-sc)

1929 *The Kiss* (+ co-sc); *Anna Christie* (German version of Clarence Brown film) (+ sc)

1930 *Le Spectre vert* (French version of Lionel Barrymore's *The Unholy Night*) (+ sc); *Si l'Empereur savait ça* (French version of *His Glorious Night*) (+ sc); *Olympia* (French version) (+ sc)

1931 *Daybreak*; *Son of India*

1934 *Le Grand Jeu* (+ co-sc)

1935 *Pension Mimosas* (+ co-sc); ***La Kermesse héroïque*** (*Carnival in Flanders*) (+ co-sc)

1936 *Die klugen Frauen* (German version of *La Kermesse héroïque*) (+ sc)

1937 *Knight without Armour*

1938 *Les Gens du voyage* (+ co-sc); *Fahrendes Volk* (German version of *Les Gens du voyage*) (+ sc)

1942 *La Loi du nord* (made 1939; during Occupation titled *La Piste du nord*) (+ co-sc); *Une Femme disparait* (*Portrait of a Woman*) (+ co-sc)

Other Films:

1913 First episode of series *Protéa* (Jasset) (role)

1914 *Quand minuit sonna* (role)

1915 *Autour d'une bague* (Ravel) (role); *Les Vampires* (serial) (Feuillade) (bit role)

Jacques Feyder: *Thérèse Raquin*

1925 *Poil de carotte* (Duvivier) (sc)
1928 *Gardiens de Phare* (Grémillon) (sc)
1943 *Maturareise* (*Jeunes filles d'aujourd'hui*) (Steiner) (tech + artistic supervision)
1946 *Macadam* (*Back Streets of Paris*) (Blistène) (art d)

Publications

By FEYDER: book—

Le Cinéma, notre métier, with Françoise Rosay, Geneva, 1946.

By FEYDER: articles—

"Impressions de Hollywood, L'Ordre," in *Anthologie du Cinéma,* edited by Marcel Lapierre, Paris, 1946.
"Transposition visuelle," in *Intelligence du cinématographe,* edited by Marcel l'Herbier, Paris, 1946.
"Je crois au film parlant, Pour vous," in *L'Art du cinéma,* edited by Pierre Lherminier, Paris, 1960.
"*La Kermesse héroïque*," in *Avant-Scène du Cinéma* (Paris), no. 26, 1965.

On FEYDER: books—

Jacques Feyder ou le Cinéma concret (anthology), Brussels, 1949.
Bachy, Victor, *Jacques Feyder,* Paris, 1966.
Ford, Charles, *Jacques Feyder,* Paris, 1973.
Abel, R.D., *French Cinema: The First Wave,* Princeton, New Jersey, 1984.

On FEYDER: articles—

Chaperot, Georges, "Souvenirs sur Jacques Feyder," in *Revue du Cinéma* (Paris), 1 July 1930.
Obituary in *New York Times,* 26 May 1948.
"Feyder Issue" of *L'Ecran Français* (Paris), 8 June 1948.
"Feyder Issue" of *Ciné-Club* (Paris), 2 November 1948.
"Jacques Feyder" in *Film Dope* (London), September 1978.
"Jacques Feyder," *National Film Theatre Booklet* (London), August 1983.
Dossier on Feyder, in *Cahiers de la Cinématheque* (Perpignan), Summer 1984.

On FEYDER: film—

Antoine, Raymond, and Charles Van Der Hagen, *Jacques Feyder et son chef d'oeuvre,* Belgium, 1974.

* * *

Underneath everything Jacques Feyder did was a great love and mastery of his medium that gave integrity and style to his work. As a young man he rejected the bourgeois background of his Belgian home and became an actor. He fell in love with the talented Françoise Rosay, who became his partner for life. He acted in the cinema of Victorin Jasset, Feuillade, and Léon Gaumont, then became a scriptwriter, and finally began directing.

Feyder's individual approach to *La Faute d'orthographe* did not commend itself to Gaumont, and Feyder raised the money to make the popular novel of Pierre Benois, *L'Atlantide*. This film, despite the presence of an ill-chosen Napierkowska in the lead, was an international success. The scenes shot in the Sahara under difficult conditions balanced the picturesque and exotic interiors, depicting an underground city.

Dining out in Montmartre, Feyder and Françoise discovered a boy playing in the street. This child was little Jean Forest, whom Feyder directed with consummate skill in three films, *Crainquebille, Visages d'enfants,* and *Gribiche.* The first, based on the Anatole France story, added to Feyder's reputation, while the second, shot with simplicity and sensitivity in the Haut Valais, Switzerland, showed that Feyder possessed a remarkable skill for directing child actors. *Gribiche* was his first film for the Russian-inspired Albatros Company. It introduced the designer Lazare Meerson, working in the Art Deco style. It also featured Françoise Rosay in her first major role. Following a pictorially beautiful *Carmen,* with a recalcitrant Raquel Meller in the title role, came Feyder's masterpiece. *Thérèse Raquin* was shot in a German studio and featured Gina Manes in her greatest part. Zola's sombre bourgeois tragedy was brought vividly to life. The details of the Raquin home, the human tensions, the unspoken words, and the looming shadows created an unforgettable effect. At the end of the saga, the old dumb and paralysed woman peers through those shadows to watch the dead bodies of the murderous lovers lying on the floor. This scene remains one of the great moments of cinema.

After an irreverent satire on French politics, *Les Nouveaux Messieurs,* which succeeded in getting itself banned, Feyder set out for Hollywood. He directed Garbo in *The Kiss,* her last silent film and one of her most intelligent roles. Feyder proceeded to tackle the sound film with European versions of *Anna Christie, Le Spectre vert,* and *Olympia*. In 1931 he directed Ramon Novarro in *Son of India* and *Day Break* before returning to France. Teaming up with his fellow countryman Charles Spaak he made in quick succession *Le Grand Jeu,* one of the best films of the Foreign Legion; *Pension Mimosas,* with Rosay in a great tragic role; and the delightful, decorative, and witty *La Kermesse héroïque,* a costume film that defies the ravages of time. The latter outraged the sensibilities of his fellow Belgians even as it delighted the rest of the world.

Feyder directed *Knight without Armour* for Alexander Korda in London, Dietrich playing opposite Robert Donat. This story of the revolution in Russia featured an elegant Dietrich moving through picturesque landscapes and great buildings designed by Lazare Meerson in one of his last assignments. Feyder then went to Germany to make *Les Gens du voyage* in two versions. After this story of circus life he returned to France and made his last important film, *La Loi du nord,* with Michele Morgan. This story of a Mounted Police search for a murderer in the Far North still showed the Feyder quality. Shortly after its completion, France was invaded. Feyder chose to live in Switzerland during the war. He turned out a star vehicle for Françoise Rosay, *Une Femme disparait,* in 1941. He died in Switzerland in 1948, a year which also saw the passing of Eisenstein and Griffith. Feyder was in the company of his peers. But in 1970 René Clair could still say "Jacques Feyder does not occupy today the place his work and his example should have earned him."

—Liam O'Leary

FISHER, Terence

Nationality: British. **Born:** London, 23 February 1904. **Education:** Christ's Hospital, Horsham, Sussex. **Career:** Apprenticeship aboard training ship H.M.S. Conway, 1926-28; junior officer for P & O Lines, 1929; window-dresser for London Department Store, 1930; clapper boy, runner, then assistant film editor, at Shepherd's Bush Studios, from 1930; editor, from 1936; directed first feature, for Rank, *A Song for Tomorrow,* 1948; joined Hammer Company, 1952; also television director, on *Robin Hood* and others, from 1952. **Died:** 18 June 1980.

Films as Director:

1948 *A Song for Tomorrow*; *Colonel Bogey*; *To the Public Danger*; *Portrait from Life* (*The Girl in the Painting*)
1949 *Marry Me*; *The Astonished Heart* (+ co-d)
1950 *So Long at the Fair* (co-d)
1951 *Home to Danger*
1952 *The Last Page* (*Manbait*); *Stolen Face*; *Wings of Danger* (*Dead on Course*); *Distant Trumpet*
1953 *Mantrap* (*Man in Hiding*) (+ co-sc); *Four Sided Triangle* (+ co-sc); *Spaceways*; *Blood Orange*
1954 *Face the Music* (*The Black Glove*); *The Stranger Came Home* (*The Unholy Four*); *Final Appointment*; *Mask of Dust* (*Race for Life*); *Children Galore*
1955 *Murder by Proxy* (*Blackout*); *Stolen Assignment*; *The Flaw*
1956 *The Gelignite Gang*; *The Last Man to Hang?*
1957 *Kill Me Tomorrow*; *The Curse of Frankenstein*
1958 ***Dracula*** (*Horror of Dracula*); *The Revenge of Frankenstein*
1959 *The Hound of the Baskervilles*; *The Man Who Could Cheat Death*; *The Mummy*; *The Stranglers of Bombay*
1960 *The Brides of Dracula*; *The Two Faces of Dr. Jekyll* (*House of Fright*); *Sword of Sherwood Forest*
1961 *The Curse of the Werewolf*
1962 *The Phantom of the Opera*; *Sherlock Holmes und der Halsband des Todes*; *Sherlock Holmes and the Deadly Necklace* (English version of the preceding)
1964 *The Horror of It All*; *The Earth Dies Screaming*; *The Gorgon*
1965 *Dracula—Prince of Darkness*
1966 *Island of Terror*; *Frankenstein Created Woman*
1967 *Night of the Big Heat* (*Island of the Burning Damned*)
1968 *The Devil Rides Out* (*The Devil's Bride*)
1969 *Frankenstein Must Be Destroyed*
1973 *Frankenstein and the Monster from Hell*

Other Films:

1935 *Brown on Resolution* (*Forever England*; *Born for Glory*) (Asquith) (asst ed)
1936 *Tudor Rose* (*Nine Days a Queen*) (Stevenson) (ed); *Jack of All Trades* (*The Two of Us*) (Stevenson and Hulbert) (ed); *Where There's a Will* (Beaudine) (ed); *Everybody Dance* (Reisner) (co-ed); *Windbag the Sailor* (Beaudine) (ed)
1938 *Mr. Satan* (Woods) (ed)
1939 *On the Night of the Fire* (*The Fugitive*) (Hurst) (ed)
1940 *George and Margaret* (King) (ed)
1941 *Atlantic Ferry* (*Sons of the Sea*) (Forde) (ed); *The Seventh Survivor* (Hiscott) (ed)
1942 *Flying Fortress* (Forde) (ed); *The Peterville Diamond* (Forde) (ed); *Tomorrow We Live* (*At Dawn We Die*) (King) (supervising ed); *The Night Invader* (Mason) (supervising ed)

Terence Fisher

1943 *The Dark Tower* (Harlow) (ed); *The Hundred Pound Window* (Hurst) (supervising ed); *Candlelight in Algeria* (King) (supervising ed)
1944 *One Exciting Night* (*You Can't Do Without Love*) (Forde) (ed); *Flight from Folly* (Mason) (supervising ed)
1945 *The Wicked Lady* (Arliss) (ed)
1947 *The Master of Bankdam* (Forde) (supervising ed)

Publications

By FISHER: articles—

"Horror Is My Business," an interview with Raymond Durgnat and John Cutts, in *Films and Filming* (London), July 1964.
Interview with P. Bachmann, in *Positif* (Paris), January 1975.

On FISHER: books—

Pirie, David, *Heritage of Horror: The English Gothic Cinema 1946-1972,* London, 1973.
Eyles, Allen, Robert Adkinson, and Nicholas Fry, *The House of Horror: The Story of Hammer Films,* London, 1973; revised edition, 1981.
Bourgoin, Stéphane, *Terence Fisher,* Paris, 1984.

On FISHER: articles—

Ringel, H., "The Horrible Hammer Films of Terence Fisher," in *Take One* (Montreal), May 1973.
"*Le Cauchemar de Dracula,*" in *Avant-Scène du Cinéma* (Paris), July/September 1975.
Carrère, E., "Prométhée délivré (sur les *Frankenstein* de Terence Fisher)," in *Positif* (Paris), July/August 1977.
"Terence Fisher," in *Film Dope* (London), February 1979.
Ross, P., "Terence Fisher, le prince des ténèbres," in *Image et Son* (Paris), September 1980.
"Terence Fisher Section" of *Avant-Scène du Cinéma* (Paris), 1 November 1982.

* * *

Between 1957 and the mid-1960s Terence Fisher directed the majority of the "classic" Hammer horror films. To a certain extent, his work can be seen to have set the terms, stylistically and thematically, for British horror in general, so that even those later British horror films which attempted to be different were largely defining themselves against the "norm" created in part by Fisher at Hammer.

Before discussing Fisher's career as a filmmaker, it is worth briefly considering his place in the critical pantheon of British film directors.

Some critics, most notably David Pirie, have claimed that Fisher was an "auteur," someone whose work expressed a distinctive aesthetic and moral vision. Other critics, perhaps the majority, have been less generous, seeing Fisher as at best a "journeyman" filmmaker, a competent producer of horror potboilers.

Perhaps the truth about Fisher lies somewhere between these two critical positions. Certainly, when compared with other British horror films from the period in which he was working, Fisher's films for Hammer do exhibit distinctive and recognisable features. In particular, one can point out as marks of his authorship a pervasive compositional balance, smooth tracks, and precise, symmetrical editing patterns. These elements are in turn linked with a moral certainty whereby the forces of good and evil within the films in question are implacably and unambiguously opposed.

At the same time, Fisher's career does not offer itself as that of an "auteur." Throughout the first half of the 1950s, he made a number of films (some of them for Hammer, before its rebirth as the horror factory) in a variety of genres. While some of these contained elements of fantasy (*Stolen Face, The Four-Sided Triangle,* and *Spaceways*) or a period setting equivalent to the later Hammer horrors (most notably, the film he co-directed with Anthony Darnborough for Gainsborough Pictures, *So Long at the Fair*), the majority were competently made but essentially anonymous programme-fillers.

It is fair to say that when Fisher did eventually emerge as a director with an identifiable signature in 1957 (with *The Curse of Frankenstein*), it was as just one part, albeit an important one, of the creative team at Hammer. This team included producer-writer Anthony Hinds, producer Michael Carreras, writer Jimmy Sangster, production designer Bernard Robinson, composer James Bernard, and a number of others, all of whom contributed extensively towards the distinctive Hammer horror "look." It is against the background of this tightly knit grouping that Fisher's prolific output at the studio needs to be understood. This is not to downgrade Fisher's achievement, merely to put it in its proper context. It is significant, however, that the few films Fisher made for companies other than Hammer in the 1960s contain few or none of the qualities which one associates with the best of his work at Hammer.

The almost paternal authority of Fisher's directorial style—perhaps his main contribution to Hammer—enabled him to represent effectively and sympathetically those father figures (including Van Helsing in *Dracula* and *The Brides of Dracula* and Sherlock Holmes in *The Hound of the Baskervilles*) around which many of Hammer's horror films revolved. The orderliness of his *mise-en-scène* was also ideally suited for his recreation of the ordered Victorian and Edwardian settings in which most of the films took place.

Fisher's later work for Hammer—especially *Frankenstein Created Woman, The Devil Rides Out,* and *Frankenstein Must Be Destroyed*—reveals a further maturing of his directorial skills. These films, virtuoso variations upon and questionings of basic Hammer horror assumptions about the nature of good and evil, are dark and often despairing dramas. They show a depth of response which perhaps had not been there before, and Fisher's *mise-en-scène* has become even more precise and magisterial. They stand as a further testament, if such is needed, to Fisher's accomplishment as a director, an accomplishment which is still largely overshadowed by his association with horror, one of the most critically despised of all film genres.

—Peter Hutchings

FLAHERTY, Robert

Nationality: American. **Born:** Robert Joseph Flaherty in Iron Mountain, Michigan, 16 February 1884. **Education:** Upper Canada College, Toronto, and Michigan College of Mines. **Family:** Married Frances Hubbard, 1914. **Career:** Explorer, surveyor and prospector for Canadian Grand Trunk Railway and Canadian Mining Syndicates, 1900s; worked for industrial entrepreneur William MacKenzie, searching for iron ore deposits along Hudson Bay, 1910-16; made first travelogue film, 1915; made first feature, *Nanook of the North,* 1922; made *Moana* with backing of Paramount (then Famous Players-Lasky), 1923-25; invited to work for Irving Thalberg at MGM, quit and formed company with F.W. Murnau to produce *Tabu,* 1928; made *Industrial Britain* for John Grierson's Empire Marketing Board, 1931; moved to Aran Islands and made *Man of Aran,* 1932-34; made *The Land* for U.S. government, 1939-41; hired by Frank Capra to work in U.S. Army orientation film unit, 1942; made *Louisiana Story,* sponsored by Standard Oil, 1946-48. Robert Flaherty Foundation (later renamed International Film Seminars Inc.) established, 1953. **Awards:** International Prize, Venice Festival, for *Louisiana Story,* 1948. **Died:** 23 July 1951.

Films as Director:

1922 ***Nanook of the North*** (+ ph, ed, sc)
1925 *The Potterymaker* (*Story of a Potter*) (short) (+ ph, sc)
1926 *Moana* (*Moana: A Romance of the Golden Age. Moana: The Love Life of a South Sea Siren*) (+ co-sc, co-ph, co-ed)
1927 *The Twenty-Four-Dollar Island* (short) (+ sc, ph)
1931 ***Tabu*** (co-d, co-sc, uncredited co-ph)
1933 *Industrial Britain* (co-d, co-ph); *The English Potter* (short) (+ ph) (edited by Marion Grierson from footage shot for *Industrial Britain*); *The Glassmakers of England* (short) (+ ph) (edited from *Industrial Britain* footage); *Art of the English Craftsman* (short) (+ ph) (from *Industrial Britain* footage)
1934 ***Man of Aran*** (+ sc, co-ph)
1937 *Elephant Boy* (co-d)
1942 ***The Land*** (+ sc, co-ph, narration)
1948 ***Louisiana Story*** (+ co-sc, co-ph, pr)
1949 *The Titan* (+ sc, ph)
1967 *Studies for Louisiana Story* (+ sc, ph) (fifteen hours of outtakes from *Louisiana Story* edited by Nick Cominos)

Other Films:

1945 *What's Happened to Sugar* (David Flaherty) (pr)
1949 *The Story of Michelangelo* (co-pr)
1950 *Green Mountain Land* (short) (David Flaherty) (pr)
1951 *St. Matthew's Passion* (ed, narration) (reedited version of Ernst Marischka's 1949 *Matthaus-Passion*)

Publications

By FLAHERTY: books—

Anerca: Drawings by Enooesweetof, revised ed., Toronto, 1959.
Eskimo, by Edmund Carpenter with Frederick Varley and Flaherty, Toronto, 1959.

By FLAHERTY: articles—

Article on *North Sea,* a film by Harry Watt, in *Sight and Sound* (London), Summer 1938.
Interview with Theodore Strauss, in the *New York Times,* 12 October 1941.

Robert Flaherty: ***Man of Aran***

"How I Filmed *Nanook of the North*," in *Filmmakers on Filmmaking*, edited by Harry M. Geduld, Bloomington, Indiana, 1971.

On FLAHERTY: books—

Rotha, Paul, *The Film Till Now*, London, 1930.
Flaherty, Frances, *Elephant Dance*, New York, 1937.
Flaherty, Frances, *Sabu: The Elephant Boy*, New York, 1937.
Rotha, Paul, *Documentary Film*, New York, 1952.
Flaherty, Frances, *The Odyssey of a Film-Maker: Robert Flaherty's Story*, Urbana, Illinois, 1960.
Quintar, Fuad, *Robert Flaherty et le Documentaire Poetique: Etudès Cinématographique No. 5*, Paris, 1960.
Cuenca, Carlos Fernandez, *Robert Flaherty*, Madrid, 1963.
Klaue, Wolfgang, compiler, *Robert Flaherty*, Berlin, 1964.
Agel, Henri, *Robert J. Flaherty*, Paris, 1965.
Calder-Marshall, Arthur, *The Innocent Eye: The Life of Robert Flaherty*, London, 1970.
Griffith, Richard, *The World of Robert Flaherty*, New York, 1970.
Hardy, Forsyth, editor, *Grierson on Documentary*, revised ed., New York, 1971.
Levin, G. Roy, *Documentary Explorations: Fifteen Interviews with Filmmakers*, Garden City, New York, 1971.
Barsam, Richard, *Nonfiction Film: A Critical History*, New York, 1973.
Armes, Roy, *Film and Reality: An Historical Survey*, Baltimore, 1974.
Barnouw, Erik, *Documentary: A History of the Non-Fiction Film*, New York, 1974.
Napolitano, Antonio, *Robert J. Flaherty*, Florence, 1975.
Murphy, William T., *Robert Flaherty: A Guide to References and Resources*, Boston, 1978.
Williams, Christopher, *Realism and Cinema: A Reader*, London, 1980.
Rotha, Paul, *Robert J. Flaherty: A Biography*, Philadelphia, 1983.
Barsam, Richard, *The Vision of Robert Flaherty: The Artist as Myth and Filmmaker*, Bloomington, Indiana, 1988.

On FLAHERTY: articles—

Ramsaye, Terry, "Flaherty, Great Adventurer," in *Photoplay* (New York), May 1928.
Grierson, John, "Flaherty," in *Cinema Quarterly* (London), Autumn 1934.
Griffith, Richard, "Flaherty and the Future," in *New Movies* (New York), January 1943.
Rosenheimer, Arthur (Arthur Knight), "They Make Documentaries: No. 1—Robert Flaherty," in *Film News* (New York), April 1946.
Taylor, Robert Lewis, "Profile of Flaherty," in the *New Yorker*, 11, 18 and 25 June 1949.
Gray, Hugh, "Robert Flaherty and the Naturalist Documentary," in *Hollywood Quarterly*, Fall 1950.
Grierson, John, "Flaherty as Innovator," in *Sight and Sound* (London), October/November 1951.
"Flaherty in Review," in *Sight and Sound* (London), November/December 1951.
Huston, John, "Regarding Flaherty," in *Sequence* (London), no. 14, 1952.
George, George L., "The World of Robert Flaherty," in *Film News* (New York), no. 4, 1953.
Manvell, Roger, "Robert Flaherty, Geographer," in *The Geographical Magazine* (New York), February 1957.
Siepmann, Charles, "Robert Flaherty—The Man and the Filmmaker," in *Film Book I: The Audience and the Filmmaker*, edited by Robert Hughes, New York, 1959.
Flaherty, Frances, "Flaherty's Quest for Life," in *Films and Filming* (London), January 1959.
Bachmann, Gideon, "Bob," in *Film* (London), September/October 1959.
Van Dongen, Helen, "Robert J. Flaherty, 1884-1951," in *Film Quarterly* (Berkeley), Summer 1965.
Barnouw, Erik, "Robert Flaherty," in *Film Culture* (New York), Spring 1972.
Corliss, Richard, "Robert Flaherty: The Man in the Iron Myth," in *Film Comment* (New York), November/December 1973.
Zinnemann, Fred, "Remembering Robert Flaherty," in *Action* (Los Angeles), May/June 1976.
"Robert Flaherty," in *Film Dope* (London), February 1979.
Lee, R., "Robert Flaherty: Free Spirit," in *American Cinematographer* (Los Angeles), January 1984.
Winston, B., "The White Man's Burden," in *Sight and Sound* (London), Winter 1984/85.
"The Innocent Eye: Robert Flaherty," in *National Film Theatre Booklet* (London), September 1984.
Barsam, Richard, "The Vision of Robert Flaherty," in *Sight and Sound* (London), Autumn 1988.

On FLAHERTY: films—

Romine, Charles, producer, *Odyssey: The World of Robert Flaherty*, for CBS-TV in cooperation with the Museum of Modern Art, broadcast 17 February 1957.
Stoney, George, *How the Myth Was Made: A Study of Robert Flaherty's Man of Aran*, for television, 1978.

* * *

Robert Flaherty was already thirty-six years old when he set out to make a film, *Nanook of the North.* Before that he had established himself as a prospector, surveyor, and explorer, having made several expeditions to the sub-Arctic regions of the Hudson Bay. He had shot motion picture footage on two of these occasions, but before *Nanook*, filmmaking was only a sideline.

Yet these years in the wilderness were to have a profound effect on Flaherty's development as a filmmaker. First, the expeditions brought Flaherty into intimate contact with the Eskimo culture. Second, they enhanced his knowledge about the human condition in a natural setting. Third, the numerous evenings that he spent in isolation encouraged him to contemplate the day's events by writing in his diaries, from which he developed highly skilled powers of observation which sharpened his sense of photographic imagery and detail. Also a violinist and an accomplished storyteller, Flaherty had clearly cultivated an artistic sensibility before becoming a film director. Filmmaking became a compelling mechanism for expressing this sensibility.

Flaherty turned to filmmaking not only as a means of creation but also to communicate to the outside world his impressions of Eskimo culture. He held a profound admiration for these people, who lived close to nature and whose daily existence was an unrelenting struggle to survive. The struggle ennobled this proud race. Flaherty sought to portray their existence in a manner that would illustrate the purity and nobility of their lives, a purpose underlying each of his films.

Flaherty developed a method of working that was fairly consistent from film to film. The films about the people of Hudson Bay, Samoa, the Aran Islands, and the Louisiana Bayou demonstrate a more or less constant concern with people who live in natural settings. These geographical locations are incidental; others would have done just as well. Eskimo culture was the only one in which he was deeply versed. Nevertheless, the locations were chosen because they represented societies on the verge of change. Indeed, Flaherty has often been criticized for presenting his subjects as they existed years ago, not as he found them. But Flaherty saw his projects as the last opportunity to capture a way of life on film.

Another consistent feature of Flaherty's technique was the selection of a "cast." Although he pioneered the use of real people to re-enact their own everyday lives before the camera lens, he deliberately chose ideal types on the basis of physical appearance and even created artificial families to act before the camera.

Flaherty worked without a plot or script, allowing for a maximum of improvisation. The Flaherty method entailed total immersion in these cultures in order to discover the basic patterns of life. *Nanook* represented the least difficulty because of his thorough familiarity with Eskimo culture. However, *Moana* and *Man of Aran* represented unfamiliar territory. Flaherty had to become steeped in strange cultures. His search for struggle and conflict in Savaii misled him and he later abandoned it. Struggle was more readily apparent in the Aran Islands, in terms of conflict between man and the sea; the hunt for the basking shark which he portrayed, abandoned in practice some years earlier, helps the audience to visualize this conflict.

Flaherty's technical facility also served him well. Generally he carried projectors and film printers and developing equipment to these far off places so that he could view his rushes on a daily basis. Flaherty, a perfectionist, shot enormous quantities of footage for his films; the lack of a script or scenario contributed to this. He went to great lengths to achieve photographic excellence, often shooting when shadows were longest. In *Moana* he used the new panchromatic film stock, which was much more sensitive to color than orthochromatic film. He pioneered the use of long lenses for close-up work, a method that allowed him an intimacy with his subjects that was novel for its time.

Flaherty's films were generally well received in the popular press and magazines as well as in the more serious critical literature. *Nanook* was praised for its authenticity and its documentary value as well as its pictorial qualities. John Grierson was the first to use the term "documentary" to describe a film when he reviewed *Moana.* Subsequently, Grierson, through his filmmaking activities and writings, began to formulate a documentary aesthetic dealing with social problems and public policy, subjects that Flaherty (except for *The Land*) tried to avoid. Nevertheless, Grierson's writings, which were to influence the development of the modern sponsored film, had their foundations in Flaherty's work. Their purposes were ultimately quite different, but Grierson gave due credit to Flaherty for working with real people, shaping the story from the material, and bringing a sense of drama to the documentary film.

Man of Aran aroused the most critical responses to Flaherty's work. It was released at a time when the world was beset with enormous political, social, and economic problems, and many enthusiasts of documentary film believed it was irresponsible and archaic of Flaherty to produce a documentary that made no reference to these problems or concealed them from public view. *Louisiana Story,* on the other hand, was greeted as the culminating work of a master filmmaker. Recognized for its skillful interweaving of sound and image, one critic described the film as an audiovisual symphony. However, in today's world of pollution and oil spills it is much more difficult to accept the film's picture of the oil industry as a benign presence in the bayou.

Although Flaherty made a relatively small number of films in his long career, one would be hard pressed to find a more influential body of work. He always operated outside the mainstream of the documentary movement. Both he and Grierson, despite their contradictory purposes, can be credited with the development of a new genre and a documentary sensibility; Flaherty by his films, Grierson by his writing. Watching today's 16mm distribution prints and video cassettes, it is often difficult to appreciate the photographic excellence of Flaherty's work. Nevertheless, the clean lines are there, as well as an internal rhythm created by the deft editing touch of Helen Van Dongen. Although his films were improvised, the final product was never haphazard. It showed a point of view which he wished to share.

—William T. Murphy

FLEISCHER, Richard

Nationality: American. **Born:** Brooklyn, NY, 8 December 1916. **Education:** Brown University, B.A., 1938; Yale University, M.F.A., 1940. **Family:** Son of animation pioneer Max Fleischer; married to Mickey Fleischer. **Career:** Stage director, 1940-42; joined RKO Pathe as writer of newsreel commentaries, 1942; writer-director of *This Is America* documentary series and various documentary short subjects, and writer-producer of *Flicker Flashbacks* comedy shorts, 1942-45. **Awards:** Academy Award, Best Feature Length Documentary, 1947, for *Design for Death.* **Address:** 169 S. Rockingham Avenue, Los Angeles, CA 90049, U.S.A.

Films as Director:

1947 *Child of Divorce*; *Banjo*
1948 *Bodyguard*; *So This Is New York*
1949 *Follow Me Quietly*; *Make Mine Laughs*; *The Clay Pigeon*; *Trapped*
1950 *Armored Car Robbery*
1952 *The Narrow Margin*; *The Happy Time*
1953 *Arena*
1954 *Twenty Thousand Leagues Under the Sea*
1955 *Violent Saturday*; *The Girl in the Red Velvet Swing*
1956 *Bandido*; *Between Heaven and Hell*
1958 *The Vikings*
1959 *These Thousand Hills*; *Compulsion*
1960 *Crack in the Mirror*
1961 *The Big Gamble*
1962 *Barabbas*
1966 *Fantastic Voyage*
1967 *Doctor Dolittle*
1968 *The Boston Strangler*
1969 *Che*
1970 *Tora! Tora! Tora!*
1971 *Ten Rillington Place*; *See No Evil*; *The Last Run*
1972 *The New Centurions*
1973 *Soylent Green*; *The Don Is Dead*
1974 *The Spikes Gang*; *Mr. Majestyk*
1975 *Mandingo*
1976 *The Incredible Sarah*
1978 *Crossed Swords*
1979 *Ashanti*
1980 *The Jazz Singer*
1981 *Tough Enough*
1983 *Amityville 3-D*
1984 *Conan the Destroyer*
1985 *Red Sonja*
1987 *Million Dollar Mystery*
1989 *Call from Space*

Other Films:

1947 *Design for Death* (co-pr)

Publications

By FLEISCHER: books—

Just Tell Me When to Cry, New York, 1993.

By FLEISCHER: articles—

"Richard Fleischer on *Mandingo*," *Movie*, 1976.
"Mod men en professionel—Richard Fleischer," *Kosmorama*, 1979.
"The True Crime Films of Richard Fleischer," *Mystery Scene*, 1996.

On FLEISCHER: books—

Bourgoin, Stephane, *Richard Fleischer*, Paris, 1986.

On FLEISCHER: articles—

Salmi, M., "Richard Fleischer," *Film Dope*, 1979.
Granger, R., "Richard Fleischer the Survivor Tackles *Conan the Destroyer*," *Film Journal*, 1984.
Pulleine, T., "Directors: Richard Fleischer," *Films & Filming*, 1984.
Sammon, Paul R., "Conan the Destroyer," *Cinefantastique*, 1984.
Roberts, J., "Richard Fleischer: Filmmaking Is in His Genes," *Classic Images*, 1992.

* * *

Richard Fleischer has been in the movie business for more than half a century. The son of animation pioneer and Disney competitor Max Fleischer, he eschewed the easel for the director's chair and during his long career made some of the most popular films ever to come out of Hollywood, as well as some of its most notable flops (like 1967's *Doctor Dolittle*). His spectacular 1954 version of Jules Verne's *Twenty Thousand Leagues Under the Sea*, starring Kirk Douglas and made for Walt Disney, remains one of the formative moviegoing experiences of the baby-boom generation.

While Fleischer made films in every conceivable category, he had a preference for thrillers and crime films, and his best work falls into these genres. He cut his directorial teeth on a number of them for RKO's B-picture unit in the late 1940s, such as the excellent *Follow Me Quietly* (1949), a solidly crafted suspense thriller that runs barely an hour. His *Armored Car Robbery* (1950), the story of an intricately planned heist, was one of the first Hollywood films to defy the Motion Picture Code by examining the planning and execution of its titular crime in detail.

Fleischer followed *Armored Car Robbery* two years later with the classic Hollywood B *The Narrow Margin*, the story of a cop assigned to protect a key witness to a mob hit from being rubbed out before she can testify. Shot entirely on a studio soundstage, the film's action takes place primarily aboard a cross-country train, and its plot is full of clever twists and turns. RKO's Howard Hughes was so impressed with *The Narrow Margin* that he considered shelving it and having Fleischer immediately do a remake with a bigger budget and all-star cast. But Hughes finally decided against this and released the film Fleischer had made. It earned an Oscar nomination for Best Motion Picture Story, was profiled in *Time*, and became a "sleeper" hit that

Richard Fleischer

remains on most film buffs' short lists of the tightest, tautest low-budget films noir ever made. (It finally was remade with that bigger budget and all-star cast, albeit less successfully, by director Peter Hyams in 1990.)

It was the critical and commercial success of *The Narrow Margin* that enabled Fleischer to graduate to A films for bigger studios like Twentieth Century-Fox, for whom he remained under contract during the next three decades. It was for Fox that he made several other good thrillers, beginning with *Violent Saturday* (1954), another heist tale in which a trio of gangsters invade a small Arizona mining town. Looking forward to Peter Weir's much-acclaimed *Witness* (1985), the conclusion takes place in Amish country, where the hero is almost done in by a psychopathic gang member but ends up being saved from death by an Amish farmer, who casts aside his pacifist beliefs for a moment in order to thrust a pitchfork into the bad guy's back. The moral dilemma injected into the scene was contributed by Fleischer himself.

The same year, Fleischer all but invented today's booming true crime docudrama genre with *The Girl in the Red Velvet Swing,* the story of the scandalous Stanford White/Harry K. Thaw/Evelyn Nesbitt love triangle of America's gilded age which resulted in Thaw's imprisonment for White's murder. Though weakly scripted, the film—which starred Ray Milland, Farley Granger, and Joan Collins—benefitted from a vivid period atmosphere brought flavorfully to life by Fleischer. But the director really began to hit his stride in the burgeoning genre with 1959's *Compulsion,* a recounting of the notorious Leopold and Loeb case based on the novel by Meyer Levin, wherein the names were changed to protect the guilty. This did not stop Leopold from suing the studio for "incorporating his likeness" in the film, however, and winning his case.

The Boston Strangler (1968), the story of confessed but unconvicted serial killer Albert DeSalvo, provided an even more exhaustive examination of a complex series of crimes and glimpse into the criminal mind. Fleischer made the film cohesive through innovative use of split-screen, and the events fathomable through a tour de force performance elicited from star Tony Curtis. (DeSalvo also tried to sue, but his case was thrown out.) The director's masterpiece in the genre remains *10 Rillington Place* (1971), a realistic and disturbing look at the controversial John Reginald Christie/Timothy Evans case that rocked the British judicial system in the early 1950s and led to the abolition of capital punishment in England.

In his 1993 autobiography *Just Tell Me When to Cry,* Fleischer revealed himself a thoughtful, witty, innovative-minded, and committed filmmaker, whereas most critics see him as an "impersonal studio hack." This harsh judgment stems largely from Fleischer's seeming willingness to accept any assignment, no matter how dubious or crassly commercial (i.e, *Che, Mandingo, Conan the Destroyer, Amityville 3-D, The Jazz Singer*), just to keep working. In his book, Fleischer does not deny that he had to make a living, but offers compelling rationales for his choices of material, even the duds—and he is no shirker of responsibility for the awfulness of the latter. A director, he says, must be willing to take the blame if he wants to take the bows. And there are more than a few films on Fleischer's long resume—including the gargantuan Day of Infamy docudrama *Tora! Tora! Tora!*—for which he fully deserves some bows.

—John McCarty

FLEMING, Victor

Nationality: American. **Born:** Pasadena, California, 23 February 1883. **Career:** Car-racing driver and chauffeur, then hired as assistant cameraman at American Film Company, 1910; began working with Allan Dwan, 1911; cameraman at Triangle, under D.W. Griffith, 1915; joined photographic section of U.S. Army Signal Corps, 1917; cameraman for Walter Wanger at Versailles Peace Conference, 1919; directed first feature, 1920; contract director for MGM, from 1932. **Awards:** Oscar for Best Director, for *Gone with the Wind,* 1939. **Died:** In 1949.

Films as Director:

1919 *When the Clouds Roll By* (co-d) (private film featuring Douglas Fairbanks, Sr., made for the Duke of Sutherland)
1920 *The Mollycoddle*
1921 *Mamma'a Affair*; *Woman's Place*
1922 *The Lane That Had No Turning*; *Red Hot Romance*; *Anna Ascends*
1923 *Dark Secrets*; *The Law of the Lawless*; *To the Last Man*; *The Call of the Canyon*
1924 *Code of the Sea*; *Empty Hands*
1925 *The Devil's Cargo*; *Adventure*; *A Son of His Father*; *Lord Jim*
1926 *The Blind Goddess*; *Mantrap*
1927 *The Rough Riders* (*The Trumpet Call*); *The Way of All Flesh*; *Hula*
1928 *The Awakening*
1929 *Abie's Irish Rose*; *Wolf Song*; *The Virginian*
1930 *Common Clay*; *Renegades*
1931 *Around the World with Douglas Fairbanks* (*Around the World in Eighty Minutes with Douglas Fairbanks*) (+ role)
1932 *The Wet Parade*; *Red Dust*
1933 *The White Sister*; *Bombshell* (*Blond Bombshell*)
1934 *Treasure Island*
1935 *Reckless*; *The Farmer Takes a Wife*
1937 *Captains Courageous*; *The Good Earth* (co-d with Franklin, uncredited); *A Star Is Born* (Wellman) (d add'l scenes)
1938 *Test Pilot*; *The Crowd Roars* (Thorpe) (d add'l scenes); *The Great Waltz* (co-d with Duvivier, uncredited)
1939 ***The Wizard of Oz***; ***Gone with the Wind***
1941 *Dr. Jekyll and Mr. Hyde* (+ pr)
1942 *Tortilla Flat*
1943 *A Guy Named Joe*
1945 *Adventure*
1948 *Joan of Arc*

Other Films (incomplete listing):

1916 *His Picture in the Papers* (Emerson) (ph); *The Habit of Happiness* (*Laugh and the World Laughs*) (Dwan) (ph); *The Good Bad Man* (*Passing Through*) (Dwan) (ph); *Betty of Greystone* (Dwan) (ph); *Macbeth* (Emerson) (ph); *Little Meena's Romance* (Powell) (ph); *The Mystery of the Leaping Fish* (Emerson) (ph) (short); *The Half-breed* (Dwan) (ph); *An Innocent Magdalene* (Dwan) (ph); *A Social Secretary* (Emerson) (ph); *Manhattan Madness* (Dwan) (ph); *50-50* (Dwan) (ph); *American Aristocracy* (Ingraham) (ph); *The Matrimaniac* (Powell) (ph); *The Americano* (Emerson) (ph)
1917 *Down to Earth* (Emerson) (ph); *The Man from Painted Post* (Henabery) (ph); *Reaching for the Moon* (Emerson) (co-ph); *A Modern Musketeer* (Dwan) (ph)
1919 *His Majesty, the American* (*One of the Blood*) (Henabery) (ph)

Publications

On FLEMING: books—

Thompson, Frank, *Between Action and Cut: 5 American Directors,* Metuchen, New Jersey, 1985.

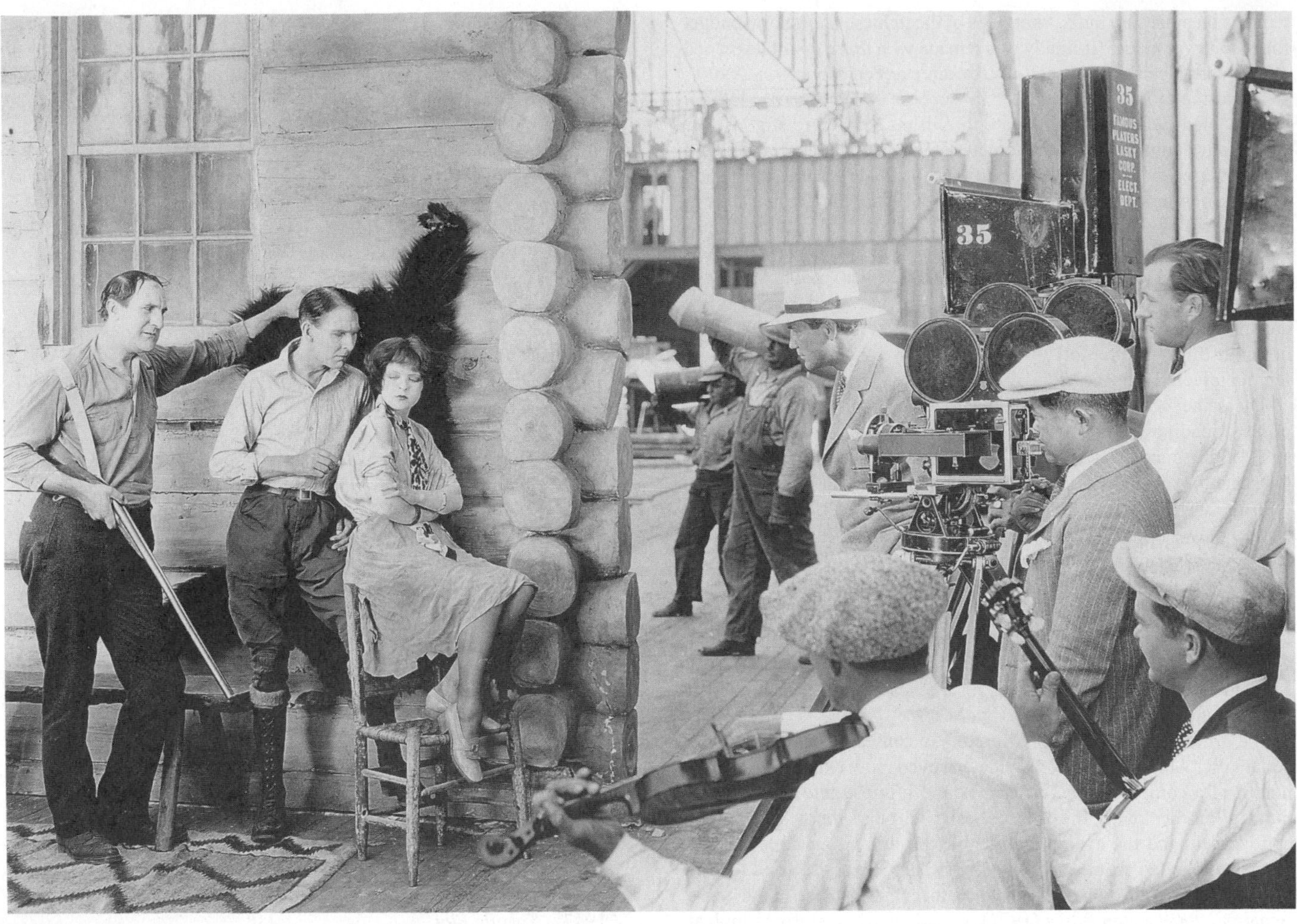

Victor Fleming (in straw hat) directing *Mantrap*

Harmetz, Aljean, *The Making of The Wizard of Oz,* London, 1989.

On FLEMING: articles—

Obituary in *New York Times,* 7 January 1949.
Reid, John, "The Man Who Made *Gone With the Wind,*" in *Films and Filming* (London), December 1967.
Reid, John, "Fleming: The Apprentice Years," in *Films and Filming* (London), January 1968.
"Checklist—Victor Fleming," in *Monthly Film Bulletin* (London), October 1977.
Brownlow, Kevin, "Victor Fleming," in *Film Dope* (London), February 1979.
Gallagher, J., "Victor Fleming," in *Films In Review* (New York), March 1983.

* * *

Victor Fleming was a successful, respected director of some of Metro-Goldwyn-Mayer's biggest and most celebrated films (*Red Dust, Captains Courageous, Test Pilot*) as well as two undisputed Hollywood classics by the standards of popular taste, *The Wizard of Oz* and *Gone with the Wind.* Ironically, it is probably the enormous continuing popularity of the latter two titles that has eclipsed Fleming's personal reputation. Correctly perceived as producer-dominated, studio-influenced cinema, both *Oz* and *Gone with the Wind* are talked and written about extensively, but never as Victor Fleming films. They are classic examples of the complicated collaborations that took place under the old studio system. Although Fleming received directorial credit (and 1939's Oscar as Best Director) for *Gone with the Wind,* others made significant contributions to the final film, among them George Cukor.

Fleming served his film apprenticeship as a cinematographer, working with such pioneers as Allan Dwan at the Flying A company and D.W. Griffith at Triangle. He photographed several Douglas Fairbanks films, among them *The Americano, Wild and Woolly,* and *Down to Earth.* He developed a skillful sense of storytelling through the camera, as well as a good eye for lighting and composition during those years. After he became a director, his critical reputation became tied to the studio at which he made the majority of his films, Metro-Goldwyn-Mayer. Known unofficially as a "producer's studio," MGM concentrated on showcasing its well-known stable of stars in suitable vehicles.

At Metro, Fleming was frequently thought of as a counterpart to George Cukor; Cukor was labelled a "woman's director," Fleming a "man's director." Besides being a close personal friend and favorite director of Clark Gable, Fleming was responsible for directing the Oscar-winning performance of Spencer Tracy in *Captains Courageous.* His flair for getting along with male stars enabled him to create an impressive group of popular films that were loved by audiences, who saw them as "Gable films" or "Tracy films." Both Henry Fonda (whose screen debut was in Fleming's *The Farmer Takes a Wife*) and Gary Cooper (whose first big screen success was in *The Virginian*) owed much of their early recognition to Fleming's talent for directing actors. Fleming had a talent for spotting potential stars and understanding the phenomenon of the star persona. In addition to his work with male actors, he also played a key role in the career development of Jean Harlow. Under Fleming's direction, she was encouraged to mix comedy with her sex appeal.

The Virginian, Fleming's first sound film, is an underrated movie which demonstrates a remarkable ability to overcome the problems of the early sound era, shooting both outdoors and indoors with equal fluidity and success. Fleming's use of naturalistic sound in this film did much to influence other early films. However, Fleming's work is not unified by a particular cinematic style, although it is coherent in thematic terms. His world is one of male camaraderie, joyous action, pride in professionalism, and lusty love for women who are not too ladylike to return the same sort of feelings. In this regard, his work is not unlike that of Howard Hawks, but Fleming lacked Hawks' ability to refine style and content into a unified vision.

Fleming's name is not well known today. Although he received directorial credit for what is possibly the most famous movie ever made in Hollywood (*Gone with the Wind*), he is not remembered as its director. His work stands as an example of the best done by those directors who worked within the studio system, allowing the film to bear the stamp of the studio rather than any personal vision.

—Jeanine Basinger

FLOREY, Robert

Nationality: French. **Born:** Paris, 14 September 1900. **Education:** Educated in Switzerland. **Career:** Actor/writer in Switzerland, 1918-19; writer for *Cinémagazine* and *La Cinématographie française,* Paris, then for Feuillade's Studios, Nice, 1920; gagman, then director of foreign publicity for Douglas Fairbanks, Mary Pickford, and Rudolph Valentino, Hollywood, 1921-23; assistant director at MGM, 1924-26; left MGM to direct *One Hour of Love* for Tiffany, 1926; director for Paramount, 1928; returned to Europe, 1929, directed for UFA; returned to Hollywood, 1932; left filmmaking, became TV director, 1950. **Awards:** French Legion d'Honneur, 1950. **Died:** 16 May 1979.

Films as Director:

1919 *Heureuse Intervention* (+ sc); *Isidore sur le lac* (+ sc); *Isidore a la deveine* (+ sc)
1923 *Valentino en Angleterre* (+ sc); *50-50* (+ sc)
1926 *One Hour of Love*; *That Model from Paris* (co-d with Gasnier, uncredited, + sc);
1927 *The Romantic Age*; *The Cohens and the Kellys* (Beaudine) (2nd unit d); *Face Value*; *Life and Death of a Hollywood Extra* (*The Life and Death of 9413—A Hollywood Extra*) (+ sc); *Johann the Coffin Maker* (+ sc); *The Loves of Zero* (+ sc)
1928 series of twenty-four shorts for Paramount featuring New York stage stars; *Night Club*; *Skyscraper Symphony* (+ sc, ph); *The Pusher-in-the-Face*; *Bonjour, New York!* (+ sc); *The Hole in the Wall*
1929 *The Cocoanuts* (+ co-d); *The Battle of Paris* (*The Gay Lady*); *Eddie Cantor* (+ sc); *La Route est belle*
1930 *L'Amour chante* (also directed German version: *Komm' zu mir zum Rendezvous*, and Spanish version: *Professor de mi Señora*); *Anna Christie* (Brown) (d New York exteriors, uncredited)
1932 *Le Blanc et le noir* (co-d); *The Murders in the Rue Morgue* (+ co-sc); *The Man Called Back*; *Those We Love*; *A Study in Scarlet* (+ sc); *The Blue Moon Murder Case*; *Girl Missing*; *Ex-lady*
1933 *The House on 56th Street*; *Bedside*; *Registered Nurse*; *Smarty* (*Hit Me Again*)
1934 *Oil for the Lamps of China* (LeRoy) (d exteriors); *Shanghai Orchid* (d exteriors); *I Sell Anything*; *I Am a Thief*; *The Woman in Red*
1935 *Go into Your Dance* (co-d with Mayo, uncredited); *The Florentine Dagger*; *Going Highbrow*; *Don't Bet on Blonds*; *The Payoff*; *Ship Cafe*; *The Rose of the Rancho* (Gering) (d add'l scenes, uncredited); *The Preview Murder Mystery*
1936 *Till We Meet Again*; *Hollywood Boulevard* (+ co-sc); *Outcast*
1937 *The King of the Gamblers*; *This Way Please*; *Mountain Music*; *Daughter of Shanghai* (*Daughter of the Orient*); *Disbarred*; *King of Alcatraz*
1938 *Dangerous to Know*; *Hotel Imperial*
1939 *The Magnificent Fraud*; *Parole Fixer*; *Death of a Champion*; *Women without Names*
1940 *Meet Boston Blackie*; *The Face Behind the Mask*
1941 *Two in a Taxi*; *Dangerously They Live*; *Lady Gangster*
1942 *The Desert Song* (+ co-sc)
1943 *Bomber's Moon* (co-d with Fuhr, uncredited); *Roger Touhy, Gangster* (*The Last Gangster*); *The Man from Frisco*
1944 *Escape in the Desert* (co-d with Blatt, uncredited); *God Is My Co-Pilot*
1945 *Danger Signal*; *The Beast with Five Fingers*;
1947 *Tarzan and the Mermaids*
1948 *Rogue Regiment* (+ sc); *Outpost in Morocco*
1949 *The Crooked Way*; *Johnny One-Eye*
1950 *The Vicious Years* (*The Gangster We Made*)

Other Films:

1918 *Le Cirque de la mort* (Lindt) (role as le detective)
1921 *L'Orpheline* (serial in twelve episodes) (Feuillade) (asst d, role as an apache); *Saturnin* (*Le Bon Allumeur*) (Feuillade) (asst d, role as un gazier); *Monte Cristo* (Flynn) (historical advisor)
1922 *Robin Hood* (Dwan) (French sub-titles)
1923 *Wine* (Gasnier) (asst d)
1924 *Parisian Nights* (Santell) (asst d, tech advisor); *The Exquisite Sinner* (von Sternberg) (asst d); *Time the Comedian* (Leonard) (asst d)
1925 *The Masked Bride* (von Sternberg) (asst d); *La Boheme* (King Vidor) (asst d); *Escape* (Rosen) (asst d); *Paris* (*Shadows of Paris*) (Goulding) (asst d, tech advisor); *Dance Madness* (Leonard) (asst d); *Toto* (Stahl) (asst d)
1926 *Monte Carlo* (*Dreams of Monte Carlo*) (Cabanne) (asst d); *Bardelys the Magnificent* (King Vidor) (asst d)
1926 *The Magic Flame* (King) (asst d)
1927 *The Woman Disputed* (King) (asst d)
1932 ***Frankenstein*** (Whale) (sc)
1947 *Monsieur Verdoux* (Chaplin) (co-assoc d)
1948 *Adventures of Don Juan* (Sherman) (sc under pseudonym Florian Roberts)

Publications

By FLOREY: books—

Filmland, Paris, 1923.
Deux ans dans les studios américains, Paris, 1924; revised edition, 1984.
Douglas Fairbanks, sa vie, ses films, ses aventures, Paris, 1926.
Pola Negri, Paris, 1926.
Adolphe Menjou, with André Tinchant, Paris, 1927.
Charlie Chaplin, Paris, 1927.

Ivan Mosjoukine, with Jean Arnoy, Paris, 1927.
Hollywood d'hier et d'aujourd'hui, Paris, 1948.
Monsieur Chaplin, or Le Rire dans la nuit, with Maurice Bessy, Paris, 1952.
La Lanterne magique, Lausanne, 1966.
Hollywood années zéro. La Prehistoire l'invention, les pionniers, naissance des mythes, Paris, 1972.
Hollywood Village: Naissance des studiós de Californie, Paris, 1986.

By FLOREY: articles—

From 1921 to 1926: several hundred articles for *Cinémagazine* (Paris); numerous articles for Parisian publications, including *Pour Vous, Saint Cinéma des Prés, Ciné-Club, Le Technicien du Film, La Cinématographie Française,* and *Cinéma*
Interview in *Film Comment* (New York), March/April 1988.

On FLOREY: books—

Bourgoin, Stéphane, *Robert Florey,* Paris, 1986.
Taves, Brian, *Robert Florey: The French Expressionist,* Metuchen, New Jersey, 1987.

On FLOREY: articles—

Spears, Jack, "Robert Florey," in *Films in Review* (New York), April 1960 (collected in his *Hollywood: The Golden Era,* New York, 1971)
Higham, Charles, "Visitors to Sydney," in *Sight and Sound* (London), Summer 1962.
Salmi, M., "Robert Florey," in *Film Dope* (London), February 1979.
Beylie, Claude, obituary in *Ecran* (Paris), 15 July 1979.
Luft, Herbert, "Robert Florey," in *Films in Review* (New York), August/September 1979.
American Cinematographer (Los Angeles), April 1987.

* * *

It is not easy to define Robert Florey's status in the history of the American film. As a list of his films quite clearly attests, he was not a major director, but he was certainly an interesting and intriguing one who seemed able to keep abreast with trends and changes in the methodology of filmmaking.

After working on a number of minor silent program features, Florey reached the peak of his artistic filmmaking career in the late 1920s with the production of four experimental shorts—*The Life and Death*

Robert Florey directing *One Hour of Love*

of 9413—A Hollywood Extra, The Loves of Zero, Johann the Coffin Maker, and *Skyscraper Symphony*—that showed a skillful understanding of editing and the influence of German expressionist cinema. The best known of these shorts is *A Hollywood Extra,* which no longer appears to survive in its entirety, but which nonetheless illustrates Florey's grasp of montage and satire. Florey never again returned to this form of filmmaking, but thanks to these shorts he was invited to direct a number of early talkies at Paramount. Aside from *Cocoanuts,* which is more Marx Brothers than Florey, these Paramount features—notably *The Battle of Paris*—again demonstrate that the director was not only totally cognizant of developments in the sound film but also was able to bring ingenuity and fluidity to the medium.

A crucial point in Florey's career came in 1931 when he was asked to script and direct *Frankenstein.* Although some elements of the Florey screenplay are utilized, his script was basically scrapped and he was replaced as director by James Whale. Had Florey been allowed to keep the assignment, he would doubtless have become a major Hollywood director. Instead he was assigned *Murders in the Rue Morgue,* which, while it contains some nice atmospheric lighting effects as well as moments of surprising brutality, never achieved the cult popularity of *Frankenstein.* For the next twenty years Robert Florey toiled away as a reliable contract director, churning out pleasant and diverting entertainments. Even when he worked as co-director with Chaplin on *Monsieur Verdoux,* Florey saw his more daring directing ideas rejected by the comedian in favor of a static filmmaking style which Chaplin favored. Florey moved exclusively into television direction in 1950, and seemed very much at ease working on programs such as *The Loretta Young Show,* whose star and content suited his own conservative temperament.

Aside from his work as a director, Robert Florey deserves recognition as a commentator on and witness to the Hollywood scene. He *loved* cinema from his first involvement in his native France as an assistant to Louis Feuillade. That love led to his arrival in Hollywood in the early 1920s as a correspondent for a French film magazine. He eventually wrote eight books on the history of the cinema, all of which are exemplary works of scholarship.

—Anthony Slide

FORD, John

Nationality: American. **Born:** Sean Aloysius O'Feeney (or John Augustine Feeney) in Cape Elizabeth, Maine, 1 February 1895. **Education:** Portland High School, Maine; University of Maine, 1913 or 1914 (for three weeks). **Military Service:** Lieutenant-Commander, U.S. Marine Corps, 1942-45 (wounded at Battle of Midway); in U.S. Naval Reserve, given rank of Admiral by President Nixon. **Family:** Married Mary McBryde Smith, 1920, one son, one daughter. **Career:** Joined brother Francis (director for Universal) in Hollywood, 1914; actor, stuntman and special effects man for Universal, 1914-17; assumes name "Jack Ford," 1916; contract director for Universal, 1917-21; signed to Fox Film Corp., 1921; began collaboration with screenwriter Dudley Nichols on *Men without Women,* 1930; assembled film crew that became Field Photographic Branch of U.S. Office of Strategic Services, 1940. **Awards:** Oscar for Best Director, and Best Direction Award, New York Film Critics, for *The Informer,* 1935; Best Direction Award, New York Film Critics, for *Stagecoach,* 1939; Oscar for Best Director, for *Grapes of Wrath,* 1940; Oscar for Best Director and Best Direction Award, New York Film Critics, for *How Green Was My Valley,* 1941; Oscar for Best Documentary, for *Battle of Midway,* 1942; Legion of Merit and Purple Heart; Annual Award, Directors Guild of America, 1952; Grand Lion Award, Venice Festival, 1971; Lifetime Achievement Award, American Film Institute, 1973. **Died:** In Palm Desert, California, 31 August 1973.

Films as Director:

1917 *The Tornado* (+ sc, role); *The Trail of Hate* (may have been directed by Francis Ford); *The Scrapper* (+ sc, role); *The Soul Herder*; *Cheyenne's Pal* (+ story); *Straight Shooting*; *The Secret Man*; *A Marked Man* (+ story); *Bucking Broadway*

1918 *The Phantom Riders*; *Wild Woman*; *Thieves' Gold*; *The Scarlet Drop* (+ story); *Hell Bent* (+ co-sc); *A Woman's Fool*; *Three Mounted Men*

1919 *Roped*; *The Fighting Brothers*; *A Fight for Love*; *By Indian Post*; *The Rustlers*; *Bare Fists*; *Gun Law*; *The Gun Packer* (*The Gun Pusher*); *Riders of Vengeance* (+ co-sc); *The Last Outlaw*; *The Outcasts of Poker Flat*; *The Ace of the Saddle*; *The Rider of the Law*; *A Gun Fightin' Gentleman* (+ co-story); *Marked Men*

1920 *The Prince of Avenue A*; *The Girl in Number 29*; *Hitchin' Posts*; *Just Pals*; *The Big Punch* (+ co-sc)

1921 *The Freeze Out*; *Desperate Trails*; *Action*; *Sure Fire*; *Jackie*

1922 *The Wallop*; *Little Miss Smiles*; *The Village Blacksmith*; *Silver Wings* (Carewe) (d prologue only)

1923 *The Face on the Barroom Floor*; *Three Jumps Ahead* (+ sc); *Cameo Kirby*; *North of Hudson Bay*; *Hoodman Blind*

1924 *The Iron Horse*; *Hearts of Oak*

1925 *Lightnin'*; *Kentucky Pride*; *The Fighting Heart*; *Thank You*

1926 *The Shamrock Handicap*; *Three Bad Men*; *The Blue Eagle*

1927 *Upstream*

1928 *Mother Machree*; *Four Sons*; *Hangman's House*; *Napoleon's Barber*; *Riley the Cop*

1929 *Strong Boy*; *Salute*; *The Black Watch*

1930 *Men Without Women* (+ co-story); *Born Reckless*; *Up the River* (+ co-sc, uncredited)

1931 *Seas Beneath*; *The Brat*; *Arrowsmith*; *Flesh*

1933 *Pilgrimage*; *Dr. Bull*

1934 *The Lost Patrol*; *The World Moves On*; *Judge Priest*

1935 *The Whole Town's Talking*; ***The Informer***; *Steamboat Round the Bend*

1936 *The Prisoner of Shark Island*; *Mary of Scotland*; *The Plough and the Stars*

1937 *Wee Willie Winkie*; *The Hurricane*

1938 *Four Men and a Prayer*; *Submarine Patrol*

1939 ***Stagecoach***; *Drums Along the Mohawk*; ***Young Mr. Lincoln***

1940 ***The Grapes of Wrath***; *The Long Voyage Home*

1941 *Tobacco Road*; *Sex Hygiene*; *How Green Was My Valley*

1942 *The Battle of Midway* (+ co-ph); *Torpedo Squadron*

1943 *December Seventh* (co-d); *We Sail at Midnight*

1945 *They Were Expendable*

1946 ***My Darling Clementine***

1947 *The Fugitive* (+ co-pr)

1948 *Fort Apache* (+ co-pr); *Three Godfathers* (+ co-pr)

1949 ***She Wore a Yellow Ribbon*** (+ co-pr)

1950 *When Willie Comes Marching Home*; *Wagonmaster* (+ co-pr); *Rio Grande* (+ co-pr)

1951 *This is Korea!*

1952 *What Price Glory*; ***The Quiet Man*** (+ co-pr)

1953 *The Sun Shines Bright*; *Mogambo*

1955 *The Long Gray Line*; *Mister Roberts* (co-d); *Rookie of the Year* (episode for *Screen Directors Playhouse* TV series); *The Bamboo Cross* (episode for *Fireside Theater* TV series)
1956 ***The Searchers***
1957 *The Wings of Eagles*; *The Rising of the Moon*
1958 *The Last Hurrah*
1959 *Gideon of Scotland Yard* (*Gideon's Day*); *Korea*; *The Horse Soldiers*
1960 *The Colter Craven Story* (episode for *Wagon Train* TV series); *Sergeant Rutledge*
1961 *Two Rode Together*
1962 ***The Man Who Shot Liberty Valance***; *Flashing Spikes* (episode for Alcoa Premiere TV series); *How the West Was Won* (directed "The Civil War" segment)
1963 *Donovan's Reef* (+ pr)
1964 *Cheyenne Autumn*
1965 *Young Cassidy* (+ co-d)
1966 *Seven Women*
1970 *Chesty: A Tribute to a Legend*

Other Films:

1914 *Lucille Love, the Girl of Mystery* (fifteen-episode serial) (Francis Ford) (role); *The Mysterious Rose* (Francis Ford) (role)
1915 ***The Birth of a Nation*** (Griffith) (role); *Three Bad Men and a Girl* (Francis Ford) (role); *The Hidden City* (Francis Ford) (role); *The Doorway of Destruction* (Francis Ford) (asst d, role); *The Broken Coin* (twenty-two-episode serial) (Francis Ford) (role)
1916 *The Lumber Yard Gang* (Francis Ford) (role); *Peg o' the Ring* (fifteen-episode serial) (Francis Ford and Jacques Jaccard) (role); *Chicken-Hearted Jim* (Francis Ford) (role); *The Bandit's Wager* (Francis Ford) (role)
1929 *Big Time* (Kenneth Hawks) (role as himself)
1971 *Vietnam! Vietnam!* (Beck, for USIA) (exec pr)

Publications

By FORD: books—

John Ford's Stagecoach, edited by Richard Anobile, New York, 1975.
My Darling Clementine, edited by Robert Lyons, New Brunswick, New Jersey, 1984.

By FORD: articles—

Interview with Lindsay Anderson, in *Sequence* (London), New Year issue 1952.
"Rencontre avec John Ford," in *Cahiers du Cinéma* (Paris), March 1955.
"Poet in an Iron Mask," interview with Michael Barkun, in *Films and Filming* (London), February 1958.
"Ford on Ford," in *Cinema* (Beverly Hills), July 1964.
"Rencontre avec John Ford," with Axel Madsen, in *Cahiers du Cinéma* (Paris), July 1965.
Interview with Jean Mitry, in *Interviews with Film Directors,* edited by Andrew Sarris, New York, 1967.
"Our Way West," interview with Burt Kennedy, in *Films and Filming* (London), October 1969.
"Notes of a Press Attache: John Ford in Paris, 1966," interview with Bertrand Tavernier, in *Film Comment* (New York), July/August 1994.

On FORD: books—

Mitry, Jean, *John Ford,* Paris, 1954.
Haudiquet, Philippe, *John Ford,* Paris, 1966.
Kitses, Jim, *Horizons West,* London, 1969.
Baxter, John, *The Cinema of John Ford,* New York, 1971.
French, Warren, *Filmguide to The Grapes of Wrath,* Bloomington, Indiana, 1973.
McBride, Joseph, and Michael Wilmington, *John Ford,* London, 1975.
Sarris, Andrew, *The John Ford Movie Mystery,* London, 1976.
Bogdanovich, Peter, *John Ford,* Berkeley, 1978.
Ford, Dan, *Pappy: The Life of John Ford,* Englewood Cliffs, New Jersey, 1979.
Sinclair, Andrew, *John Ford,* New York, 1979.
Anderson, Lindsay, *About John Ford,* London, 1981.
Caughie, John, editor, *Theories of Authorship: A Reader,* London, 1981.
Schatz, Thomas, *Hollywood Genres: Formulas, Filmmaking and the Studio System,* New York, 1981.
Reed, Joseph W., *Three American Originals: John Ford, William Faulkner, Charles Ives,* Middletown, Connecticut, 1984.
Gallagher, Tag, *John Ford: The Man and His Films,* Berkeley, 1986.
Stowell, Peter, *John Ford,* Boston, 1986.
Buscombe, Ed, editor, *The BFI Companion to the Western,* London, 1989.
Carey, Harry, Jr., *Company of Heroes: My Life as an Actor in the John Ford Stock Company,* Metuchen, New Jersey, 1994.

On FORD: articles—

McVay, Douglas, "The Five Worlds of John Ford," in *Films and Filming* (London), November 1955.
Barkun, Michael, "Notes on the Art of John Ford," in *Film Culture* (New York), Summer 1962.
Bogdanovich, Peter, "Autumn of John Ford," in *Esquire* (New York), April 1964.
"John Ford Issue" of *Présence du Cinéma* (Paris), March 1965.
"John Ford Issue" of *Cahiers du Cinéma* (Paris), October 1966.
Tavernier, Bertrand, "John Ford à Paris," in *Positif* (Paris), March 1967.
Beresford, Bruce, "Decline of a Master," in *Film* (London), Autumn 1969.
Anderson, Lindsay, "John Ford," in *Cinema* (Beverly Hills), Spring 1971.
"John Ford Issue" of *Focus on Film* (London), Spring 1971.
"John Ford Issue" of *Velvet Light Trap* (Madison, Wisconsin), August 1971.
"Special Issue Devoted to John Ford and His Towering Achievement, *Stagecoach,*" in *Action* (Los Angeles), September/October 1971.
"Ford's Stock Company Issue" of *Filmkritik* (Munich), January 1972.
Editors of *Cahiers du Cinéma,* "John Ford's *Young Mr. Lincoln,*" in *Screen* (London), Autumn 1972.
McBride, J., "Drums Along the Mekong: I Love America, I Am Apolitical," in *Sight and Sound* (London), Autumn 1972.
McBride, J., "Bringing in the Sheaves," in *Sight and Sound* (London), Winter 1973/74.
Rubin, M., "Ford and Mr. Rogers," in *Film Comment* (New York), January/February 1974.
"John Ford (1895-1973) Issue" of *Anthologie du Cinéma* (Paris), March 1975.
Dempsey, M., "John Ford: A Reassessment," in *Film Quarterly* (Berkeley), Summer 1975.
Gallagher, Tag, "John Ford: Midway. The War Documentaries," in *Film Comment* (New York), September/October 1975.
Belton, J.R., "Ceremonies of Innocence: Two Films by John Ford," in *Velvet Light Trap* (Madison), Winter 1975.

John Ford on the set of *Flesh*

Budd, M., "A Home in the Wilderness: Visual Imagery in John Ford's Westerns," in *Cinema Journal* (Evanston), Fall 1976.

Roth, W., "Where Have You Gone, My Darling Clementine?," in *Film Culture* (New York), no. 63-64, 1977.

Stowell, H.P., "John Ford's Literary Sources: From Realism to Romance," in *Literature/Film Quarterly* (Salisbury, Maryland), Spring 1977.

"John Ford Issue" of *Wide Angle* (Athens, Ohio), vol. 2, no. 4, 1978.

McCarthy, T., "John Ford and Monument Valley," in *American Film* (Washington, D.C.), May 1978.

Ellis, K., "On the Warpath: John Ford and the Indians," in *Journal of Popular Film* (Washington, D.C.), vol. 8, no. 2, 1980.

Combs, Richard, "At Play in the Fields of John Ford," in *Sight and Sound* (London), Spring 1982.

"John Ford Section" of *Casablanca* (Madrid), January 1983.

Roth, L., "Ritual Brawls in John Ford's Films," in *Film Criticism* (Meadville, Pennsylvania), Spring 1983.

Bogdanovich, Peter, "Touch of Silence for Mr. Ford," in *New York,* October 1983.

Schickel, Richard, "Ford Galaxy," in *Film Comment* (New York), March/April 1984.

Stevens, G., Jr., and Robert Parrish, "Directors at War," in *American Film* (Washington, D.C.), July/August 1985.

Gallagher, Tag, "Acting for John Ford," in *American Film* (Washington, D.C.), March 1986.

Nolley, Ken, "Reconsidering Ford's Military Trilogy," in *Literature/Film Quarterly* (Salisbury, Maryland), April 1986.

Wood, Robin, "*Drums Along the Mohawk,*" in *Cine Action!* (Toronto), no. 8, 1987.

Nolley, Ken, "Reconsidering *The Quiet Man,*" in *Cine Action!* (Toronto), no. 9, 1987.

Bernstein, Matthew, "Hollywood's 'Arty Cinema': John Ford's *The Long Voyage Home,*" in *Wide Angle* (Athens, Ohio), vol. 10, no. 1, 1988.

Card, James, "*The Searchers*: by Alan LeMay and John Ford," in *Literature/Film Quarterly* (Salisbury, Maryland), vol. 16, no. 1, 1988.

Gallagher, Tag, "John Ford's Indians," in *Film Comment* (New York), September/October 1993.

Eby, Lloyd, "The Man Who Invented Westerns Explored the American Character," in *Insight on the News,* 20 February 1995.

On FORD: films—

Haggard, Mark, *John Ford: Memorial Day 1970,* U.S., 1970.

Bogdanovich, Peter, *Directed by John Ford,* U.S., 1971.

Sanders, Denis, *The American West of John Ford,* U.K., 1971.

* * *

John Ford has no peers in the annals of cinema. This is not to place him above criticism, merely above comparison. His faults were unique, as was his art, which he pursued with a single-minded and single-hearted stubbornness for sixty years and 112 films. Ford grew up with the American cinema. That he should have begun his career as an extra in the Ku Klux Klan sequences of *The Birth of a Nation* and ended it supervising the documentary *Vietnam! Vietnam!* conveys the remarkable breadth of his contribution to film, and the narrowness of its concerns.

Ford's subject was his life and his times. Immigrant, Catholic, Republican, he spoke for the generations that created the modern United States between the Civil and Great Wars. Like Walt Whitman, Ford chronicled the society of that half century, expansionist by design, mystical and religious by conviction, hierarchical by agreement; an association of equals within a structure of command, with practical, patriotic, and devout qualities. Ford portrayed the society Whitman celebrated as "something in the doings of man that corresponds with the broadcast doings of night and day."

Mythologizing the armed services and the church as paradigms of structural integrity, Ford adapts their rules to his private world. All may speak in Ford's films, but when divine order is invoked, the faithful fall silent, to fight and die as decreed by a general, a president, or some other member of a God-anointed elite.

In Ford's hierarchy, Native and African Americans share the lowest rung, women the next. Businessmen, uniformly corrupt in his world, hover below the honest and unimaginative citizenry of the United States. Above them are Ford's elite, within which members of the armed forces occupy a privileged position. In authority over them is an officer class of career military men and priests, culminating in a few near-saintly figures of which Abraham Lincoln is the most notable, while over all rules a retributory, partial, and jealous God.

The consistency of Ford's work lies in his fidelity to the morality implicit in this structure. *Mary of Scotland*'s Mary Queen of Scots, the retiring Nathan Brittles in *She Wore a Yellow Ribbon* and outgoing mayor Frank Skeffington in *The Last Hurrah* all face the decline in their powers with a moral strength drawn from a belief in the essential order of their lives. Mary goes triumphantly to the scaffold, affirming Catholicism and the divine right of kings. Duty to his companions of the 7th Cavalry transcending all, Brittles returns to rejoin them in danger. Skeffington prefers to lose rather than succumb to modern vote-getting devices such as television.

"I make westerns," Ford announced on one well-publicized occasion. Like most of his generalizations, it was untrue. Only a third of his films are westerns, and of those a number are rural comedies with perfunctory frontier settings: *Doctor Bull, Judge Priest, Steamboat Round the Bend, The Sun Shines Bright.* Many of his family films, like *Four Men and a Prayer* and *Pilgrimage,* belong with the stories of military life, of which he made a score. A disciple of the U.S. Navy, from which he retired with the emeritus rank of Rear Admiral, Ford found in its command structure a perfect metaphor for moral order. In *They Were Expendable,* he chose to falsify every fact of the Pacific War to celebrate the moral superiority of men trained in its rigid disciplines—men who obey, affirm, keep faith.

Acts, not words, convey the truths of men's lives; public affirmations of this dictum dominate Ford's films. Dances and fights signify in their vigor a powerful sense of community; singing and eating and getting drunk together are the great acts of Fordian union. A film like *The Searchers,* perhaps his masterpiece, makes clear its care for family life and tradition in a series of significant actions that need no words. Ward Bond turns away from the revelation of a woman's love for her brother-in-law, exposed in her reverent handling of his cloak; his turn away is the instinctive act of a natural gentleman. Barred from the family life which his anger and independence make alien to his character, John Wayne clutches his arm in a gesture borrowed from Ford's first star, Harry Carey; in a memorable final image, the door closes on him, a symbol of the rejection of the eternal clan-less wanderer.

Ford spent his filmmaking years in a cloud of critical misunderstanding, with each new film unfavorably compared to earlier works. *The Iron Horse* established him as an epic westerner in the mold of Raoul Walsh, *The Informer* as a Langian master of expressionism, the cavalry pictures as Honest John Ford, a New England primitive whose work, in Lindsay Anderson's words, was "unsophisticated and direct." When, in his last decades of work, he returned to reexamine earlier films in a series of revealing remakes, the skeptical saw not a moving reiteration of values but a decline into self-plagiarism. Yet it is *The Man Who Shot Liberty Valance,* in which he deals with the issues raised in *Stagecoach,* showing his beloved populist west destroyed by law and literacy, that stands today among his most important films.

Belligerent, grandiose, deceitful, and arrogant in real life, Ford seldom let these traits spill over into his films. They express at their best a guarded serenity, a skeptical satisfaction in the beauty of the American landscape, muted always by an understanding of the dangers implicit in the land, and a sense of the responsibility of all men to protect the common heritage. In every Ford film there is a gun behind the door, a conviction behind the joke, a challenge in every toast. Ford belongs in the tradition of American narrative art where telling a story and drawing a moral are twin aspects of public utterance. He saw that we live in history, and that history embodies lessons we must learn. When Fordian man speaks, the audience is meant to listen—and listen all the harder for the restraint and circumspection of the man who speaks. One hears the authentic Fordian voice nowhere more powerfully than in Ward Bond's preamble to the celebrating enlisted men in *They Were Expendable* as they toast the retirement of a comrade. "I'm not going to make a speech," he states. "I've just got something to say."

—John Baxter

FORMAN, Milos

Nationality: Czech. **Born:** Kaslov, Czechoslovakia, 18 February 1932, became U.S. citizen, 1975. **Education:** Academy of Music and Dramatic Art, Prague, and at Film Academy (FAMU), Prague, 1951-56. **Family:** Married 1) Jana Brejchová (divorced); 2) Vera Kresadlova (divorced). **Career:** Collaborated on screenplay for Frič's *Leave It to Me,* 1956; theatre director for Laterna Magika, Prague, 1958-62; directed first feature, *Black Peter,* 1963; moved to New York, 1969, after collapse of Dubcek government in Czechoslovakia; co-director of Columbia University Film Division, from 1975: became American citizen, 1975. **Awards:** Czechoslovak Film Critics' Prize, for *Black Peter,* 1963; Grand Prix Locarno, for *Black Peter,* 1964; Czechoslovak State Prize, 1967; Oscar for Best Director, and Best Director Award, Directors Guild of America, for *One Flew Over the Cuckoo's Nest,* 1975; Oscar for Best Director, for *Amadeus,* 1984. **Agent:** Robert Lantz, 888 Seventh Ave., New York, NY 10106, U.S.A.

Films as Director:

1963 *Cerný Petr* (*Black Peter*; *Peter and Pavla*); (+ co-sc); *Konkurs* (*Talent Competition*) (+ co-sc)
1965 ***Lásky jedné plavovlásky*** (*Loves of a Blonde*) (+ co-sc); *Dobře placená procházka* (*A Well Paid Stroll*) (+ co-sc)
1967 *Hoří, má panenko* (*The Firemen's Ball*) (+ co-sc)
1970 *Taking Off* (+ co-sc)
1972 "Decathlon" segment of *Visions of Eight* (+ co-sc)

1975 *One Flew Over the Cuckoo's Nest*
1979 *Hair*
1981 *Ragtime*
1983 *Amadeus*
1989 *Valmont*

Other Films:

1955 *Nechte to na mně (Leave It to Me)* (Frič) (+ co-sc); *Dědeček automobil (Old Man Motorcar)* (Radok) (asst d, role)
1957 *Stěnata (The Puppies)* (+ co-sc)
1962 *Tam za lesem (Beyond the Forest)* (Blumenfeld) (asst d, role as the physician)
1968 *La Pine à ongles* (Carrière) (+ co-sc)
1975 *Le Mâle du siècle* (Berri) (story)
1986 *Heartburn* (Nichols) (role)
1989 *New Year's Day* (Jaglom) (role)

Publications

By FORMAN: books—

Taking Off, with John Guare and others, New York, 1971.
Milos Forman, with others, London, 1972.
Turnaround: A Memoir, with Jan Novak, New York, 1994.

By FORMAN: articles—

"Closer to Things," in *Cahiers du Cinéma in English* (New York), January 1967.
Interview with Galina Kopaněvová, in *Film a Doba* (Prague), no. 8, 1968.
Interview, in *The Film Director as Superstar,* edited by Joseph Gelmis, New York, 1970.
"Getting the Great Ten Percent," an interview with Harriet Polt, in *Film Comment* (New York), Fall 1970.
"A Czech in New York," an interview with Gordon Gow, in *Films and Filming* (London), September 1971.
Interview in *American Cinematographer* (Los Angeles), November 1972.
Interview with L. Sturhahn, in *Filmmakers Newsletter* (Ward Hill, Massachusetts), December 1975.
"Milos Forman: An American Film Institute Seminar on His Work," 1977.
Interview with T. McCarthy, in *Film Comment* (New York), March/April 1979.
Interview with Michel Ciment, in *Positif* (Paris), July/August 1979.
"How *Amadeus* was translated from play to film," an interview with M. Kakutani, in *New York Times,* 16 September 1984.

Milos Forman: *Hoří, má panenko*

"The Czech Bounces Back," interview with C. Hodenfeld in *Rolling Stone* (New York), 27 September 1984.
Interview with Michel Ciment, in *Positif* (Paris), November 1984.
Interview in *Cahiers du Cinéma* (Paris), November 1984.
Forman, Milos, "Celui a qui on pense en secret," in *Cahiers du Cinéma* (Paris), December 1984.
Interview in *Films* (London), March 1985.
Interview with T.J. Slater, in *Post Script* (Jacksonville, Florida), Spring/Summer and Fall 1985.
"What's Wrong with Today's Films," an interview with J. Kearney, in *American Film* (Washington, D.C.), May 1986.
Interview in *Première* (Paris), July 1987.
Interview with Michel Ciment, in *Positif* (Paris), December 1989.
Forman, Milos, "L'opera muet," in *Cahiers du Cinéma* (Paris), May 1991 (supplement).
Interview with Nell Scovell, in *Vanity Fair* (New York), February 1994.

On FORMAN: books—

Boček, Jaroslav, *Modern Czechoslovak Film 1945-1965,* Prague, 1965.
Skvorecký, Josef, *All the Bright Young Men and Women,* Toronto, 1971.
Henstell, Bruce, editor, *Milos Forman, Ingrid Thulin,* Washington, D.C., 1972.
Liehm, Antonín, *Closely Watched Films,* White Plains, New York, 1974.
Liehm, Antonín, *The Milos Forman Stories,* White Plains, New York, 1975.
Vecchi, Paolo, *Milos Forman,* Florence, 1981
Slater, Thomas, *Milos Forman: A Bio-Bibliography,* New York, 1987.
Liehm, Antonin, *Pribehy Milos Forman,* Prague, 1993.

On FORMAN: articles—

Dyer, Peter, "Star-Crossed in Prague," in *Sight and Sound* (London), Winter 1965/66.
Bor, Vladimír, "Formanovský film a některé předsudky" ["The Formanesque Film and Some Prejudices"], in *Film a Doba* (Prague), no. 1, 1967.
Effenberger, Vratislav, "Obraz člověka v českém film," ["The Portrayal of Man in the Czech Cinema"] in *Film a Doba* (Prague), no. 7, 1968.
"Director of the Year," *International Film Guide* (London, New York), 1969.
Combs, Richard, "Sentimental Journey," in *Sight and Sound* (London), Summer 1977.
Baker, B., "Milos Forman," in *Film Dope* (London), April 1979.
Cameron, J., "Milos Forman and *Hair*: Styling the Age of Aquarius," in *Rolling Stone* (New York), 19 April 1979.
Stein, H., "A Day in the Life: Milos Forman: Moment to Moment with the Director of *Hair,*" in *Esquire* (New York), 8 May 1979.
Holloway, Ron, "Columbia U.'s Film School Now Attracts Europe's Helmers," in *Variety* (New York), 14 January 1981.
Buckley, T., "The Forman Formula," in *New York Times,* 1 March 1981.
Kennedy, Harlan, "*Ragtime*: Milos Forman Searches for the Right Key," in *American Film* (Washington, D.C.), December 1981.
Quart, Leonard, and Barbara Quart, "*Ragtime* Without a Melody," in *Literature-Film Quarterly* (Salisbury, Maryland), vol. 10, no. 2, 1982.
Kamm, M., "Milos Forman Takes His Camera and *Amadeus* to Prague," in *New York Times,* 29 May 1983.
Jacobson, H., "Mostly Mozart: As Many Notes as Required," in *Film Comment* (New York), September/October 1984.
Harmetz, Aljean, "Film Makers in a Race Over *Les liaisons,*" in *New York Times,* 10 February 1988.
"4 Who've Made It," in *Variety* (New York), 25 October 1989.
Dudar, Helen, "Milos Forman Takes a New Look at Old Loves," in *New York Times,* 12 November 1989.
Goodman, Walter, "Forman in His Own and Others' Words," in *New York Times,* 22 December 1989.
Warchol, T., "The Rebel Figure in Milos Forman's American Films," in *New Orleans Review,* 1990.
Wharton, Dennis, "Top Directors Get Behind Film-labeling Legislation," in *Variety,* July 29, 1991.
Cohn, L., "A tale of Two Expatriate Filmmakers," in *Variety* (New York), 29 January 1992.

On FORMAN: film—

Weingarten, Mira, *Meeting Milos Forman,* U.S., 1971.

* * *

In the context of Czechoslovak cinema in the early 1960s, Milos Forman's first films (*Black Peter* and *Talent Competition*) amounted to a revolution. Influenced by Czech novelists who revolted against the establishment's aesthetic dogmas in the late 1950s rather than by Western cinema (thought the mark of late neorealism, in particular Ermanno Olmi, is visible), Forman introduced to the cinema after 1948 (the year of the Communist coup) portrayals of working-class life untainted by the formulae of socialist realism.

Though Forman was fiercely attacked by Stalinist reviewers initially, the more liberal faction of the Communist party, then in ascendancy, appropriated Forman's movies as expressions of the new concept of "socialist" art. Together with great box office success and an excellent reputation gained at international festivals, these circumstances transformed Forman into the undisputed star of the Czech New Wave. His style was characterized by a sensitive use of non-actors (usually coupled with professionals); refreshing, natural-sounding, semi-improvised dialogue which reflected Forman's intimate knowledge of the milieu he was capturing on the screen; and an unerring ear for the nuances of Czech folk-rock and music in general.

All these characteristic features of Forman's first two films are even more prominent in *Loves of a Blonde,* and especially in *The Firemen's Ball.* The latter film works equally well on one level as a realistic, humorous story and on an allegorical level that points to the aftermath of the Communist Party's decision to reveal some of the political crimes committed in the 1950s (the Slánský trial). In all these films—developed, except for *Black Peter,* from Forman's original ideas—he closely collaborated with scriptwriters Ivan Passer and Jaroslav Papousek, who later became directors in their own right.

Shortly after the Soviet invasion of Czechoslovakia in 1968, *The Firemen's Ball* was banned and Forman decided to remain in the West, where he was working on the script for what was to become the only film in which he would apply the principles of his aesthetic method and vision to indigenous American material, *Taking Off.* It is also his only American movie developed from his original idea; the rest are adaptations.

Traces of the pre-American Forman are easily recognizable in his most successful U.S. film, *One Flew Over the Cuckoo's Nest,* which radically changed Ken Kesey's story and—just as in the case of Papousek's novel *Black Peter*—brought it close to the director's own objective and comical vision. The work received an Oscar in 1975. In that year Forman became an American citizen.

The Forman touch is much less evident in his reworking of the musical *Hair,* and almost—though not entirely—absent from his version of E.L. Doctorow's novel *Ragtime.* The same is true of the box-office smash hit and multiple Oscar winner *Amadeus,* and his later adaptation, *Valmont.* Of marginal importance are the two remaining parts of Forman's oeuvre, *The Well-Paid Stroll,* a jazz opera adapted from the stage for Prague TV, and *Decathlon,* his contribution to the 1972 Olympic documentary *Visions of Eight.*

Forman is a merciless observer of the *comedie humaine* and has often been accused of cynicism, both in Czechoslovakia and in the

West. To such criticisms he answers with the words of Chekhov, pointing out that what is cruel in the first place is life itself. But apart from such arguments, the rich texture of acutely observed life and the sensitive portrayal of and apparent sympathy for people as victims—often ridiculous—of circumstances over which they wield no power, render such critical statements null and void. Forman's vision is deeply rooted in the anti-ideological, realistic, and humanist tradition of such "cynics" of Czech literature as Jaroslav Hasek (*The Good Soldier Svejk*), Bohumil Hrabal (*Closely Watched Trains*) or Josef Skvorecký (whose novel *The Cowards* Forman was prevented from filming by the invasion of 1968).

Although the influence of Forman's filmmaking methods may be felt even in some North American films, his lasting importance will, very probably, rest with his three Czech movies. *Taking Off*, a valiant attempt to show America to Americans through the eyes of a sensitive, if caustic, foreign observer, should be added to this list as well. After the mixed reception of this film, however, Forman turned to adaptations of best sellers and stage hits.

In recent years, Forman has been inactive as a director. His last release to date, *Valmont,* attempted to capture the spirit of his smash hit *Amadeus.* But *Valmont* suffers by comparison. Moreover, it was released after Stephen Frears' superior *Dangerous Liaisons,* adapted from the same Choderlos de Laclos novel. Forman remains an outstanding craftsman and a first-class actors' director; however, in the context of American cinema he does not represent the innovative force he was in Prague.

Forman has been more involved in the academic world in recent years, accepting a position as professor of film and co-chair of the film division at Columbia University's School of the Arts. He also appeared onscreen in a small role as Catherine O'Hara's husband in Mike Nichols' *Heartburn,* in which he was reunited with his *One Flew Over the Cuckoo's Nest* star, Jack Nicholson. He also played, oddly enough, an apartment house janitor in Henry Jaglom's *New Years' Day.*

—Josef Skvorecký, updated by Rob Edelman

FORSYTH, Bill

Nationality: Scottish. **Born:** Glasgow, 1947. **Education:** Studied at National Film School, Beaconsfield, Bucks., for three months, 1971. **Family:** One son, one daughter. **Career:** Left school at age sixteen and worked for documentary filmmaker Stanley Russell; set up Tree Films with Charles Gormley, 1972; producer of documentaries, 1970s; began working with Glasgow Youth Theatre, 1977; directed first feature, *That Sinking Feeling,* 1979. **Awards:** British Academy Award for Best Screenplay, for *Gregory's Girl,* 1981; BAFTA Award for Best Screenplay, 1983; Honorary Doctorate, University of Glasgow, 1983.

Films as Director and Scriptwriter:

1979 *That Sinking Feeling*
1980 ***Gregory's Girl***
1983 *Local Hero*
1984 *Comfort and Joy*
1987 *Housekeeping* (*Sylvie's Ark*)
1989 *Breaking In*
1990 *Rebecca's Daughter*
1994 *Being Human*

Publications

By FORSYTH: articles—

Interview in *Sight and Sound* (London), Autumn 1981.
"A Suitable Job for a Scot," an interview with J. Brown, in *Sight and Sound* (London), Summer 1983.
Interview with A. Hunter, in *Films and Filming* (London), August 1984.
"The Forsyth Saga," an interview with E. Stein, in *American Film* (Washington, D.C.), November 1984.
Interview with Graham Fuller, in *Listener* (London), 19 November 1987.
Interview in *Films and Filming* (London), December 1987.
Interview with L. Tanner, in *Films in Review* (New York), February 1988.

On FORSYTH: books—

Park, James, *Learning to Dream: The New British Cinema,* London, 1985.
Roddick, Nick, and Chris Auty, *British Cinema Now,* London, 1985.
Walker, Alexander, *National Heroes: British Cinema in the '70s and '80s,* London, 1985.
Dick, Eddie, editor, *From Limelight to Satellite: A Scottish Film Book,* London, 1990.
Hardy, Forsyth, *Scotland in Film,* Edinburgh, 1990.

On FORSYTH: articles—

Films Illustrated (London), August 1981.
Falk, Quentin, "Local heroes," in *Sight and Sound* (London), Autumn 1982.
Films (London), July 1983.
Nave, B., "Humour ecossais: *Local Hero,*" in *Jeune Cinema* (Paris), April 1984.
Malcomson, S.L., "Modernism Comes to the Cabbage Patch," in *Film Quarterly* (Berkeley), Spring 1985.
Pym, John, "*Housekeeping,*" in *Sight and Sound* (London), Winter 1987-88.

* * *

For a while during the early 1980s Scottish cinema was virtually synonymous with Bill Forsyth. Today his work remains among the most original and distinctive to have emerged not only from Scotland but from Britain as a whole. The Forsyth oeuvre is rooted in a gentle and extremely charming offbeat view of the world which has affinities with a variety of comic traditions including Ealing comedy, Frank Capra, Jacques Tati, and Ermanno Olmi (*Il Posto* is practically a blueprint in tone and feel of *Gregory's Girl*), but which maintains its own individuality and character. Forsyth's choice of comedy as his mode of expression was partly dictated by the fact that his first two films were made on tiny budgets. In characteristically modest fashion he regarded comedy as more appropriate, being less self-indulgent and more fun to do for everyone involved. Crucially, the comic character of these films gave them a vitality which helped them transcend their budgetary limitations and, in the case of *Gregory's Girl,* find a sizable audience outside Scotland.

Forsyth's charm lies in his attention to detail, particularly the various quirks and idiosyncrasies of his characters, which are conveyed equally effectively through both image and dialogue. These characters are often marginalised individuals caught up in circumstances they are ill equipped to deal with. Forsyth finds a great deal of humour in their predicaments but he does so in a wry and generous

Bill Forsyth

manner which is never at the expense of the characters. Instead, his approach amounts to a celebration of the human spirit with all its foibles and shortcomings.

Forsyth's acute perception of human behaviour gives his films a depth which transcends their initial charm as quirky comedies. *Gregory's Girl,* for example, is populated by dreamers lost in their various obsessions. The film centre is the first stirrings of sexuality in rather awkward male adolescents. Gregory is obsessed with the enigmatic and ultimately unobtainable Dorothy (a situation repeated in *Local Hero* with the unrequited love that Danny and McIntyre feel for Marina and Stella, respectively). But Forsyth also uncovers a variety of obsessions, ranging from a fascination with numbers to useless facts and cookery, that serve as expressions of the problems and confusions associated with adolescence; these obsession are presented as, in essence, a redirection of sexual energy.

Although equally obsessed with boys, the girls in the film are more knowing and sophisticated (Gregory constantly seeks advice on matters of the heart from his eleven-year-old sister) and wield greater control over their own destinies—Dorothy overcomes the sexist opposition of the coach to earn a place in the football team, while Susan ingeniously uses her friends to divert Gregory's romantic attentions away from Dorothy and towards herself. Forsyth obviously has a great empathy with the female point of view, and it is no coincidence that *Housekeeping,* his most mature and accomplished work, concentrates totally on the relationship between two young girls and their rather eccentric aunt.

Despite the generally upbeat ambience, Forsyth's cinema has its darker side. There are poignant moments of irony in *That Sinking Feeling,* a film which, despite its quirkiness and innocence, features a group of teenagers attempting to cope with the problems of unemployment. The film is set against a bleak and crumbling urban landscape. *Local Hero* has a rather subdued ending, which compensates for the cozy and contrived resolution reached between beachcomber Ben Knox and Happer the oil tycoon; McIntyre resumes a life in Texas that he has come to regard as shallow and meaningless.

Comfort and Joy is darker than its predecessors not only in theme but in visual style. It concentrates on one solitary character, charting his development from morbid introspection (after his girlfriend leaves him at Christmas) to fascination with the absurdities of the world around him. Despite Forsyth's intention to make a gloomier film, *Comfort and Joy* appears rather whimsical when compared to the brutality of the real Glasgow "Ice Cream Wars" which occurred at about the same time.

But Forsyth's most serious effort by far is *Housekeeping,* his first adaptation and the first film that he shot outside Scotland. In exploring the dilemma of whether to conform to social expectations or opt out altogether, it successfully mixes very real moments of tragedy and grief (it is the only Bill Forsyth film to provoke real anxiety and even tears) with lighter and more familiar Forsythian observations and character traits. *Housekeeping* marks a major development in Forsyth's career, demonstrating a greater emotional complexity and directorial assuredness. It opens out his cinema from its provincial Scottish roots while retaining the charm and warmth of his earlier work and suggests that we may not yet have seen the best of this major filmmaking talent.

Since *Housekeeping,* though, Forsyth has not made any films that rival the work of his early career. *Breaking In,* a comedy which charts the relationship between a young thief (Casey Siemaszko) and his aging mentor (Burt Reynolds), was a dud. *Being Human* is an oddity—and a box office disaster—featuring Robin Williams as five separate characters from different eras of history, each of whom are laboring to attain satisfaction in their lives. *Being Human* is an adventuresome and well-intentioned project, to be sure. But the result is maddeningly uneven, and one hopes that Forsyth will be able to recapture the spirit of his first features.

—Duncan J. Petrie, updated by Rob Edelman

FOSSE, Bob

Nationality: American. **Born:** Robert Louis Fosse in Chicago, 23 June 1927. **Education:** Amundsen High School, Chicago, graduated 1945; studied acting at American Theatre Wing, New York, 1947. **Family:** Married 1) Mary Ann Niles (divorced); 2) Joan McCracken (divorced); and 3) Gwen Verdon, 1960 (divorced). **Career:** Formed dance team, "The Riff brothers," with Charles Grass, 1940; master of ceremonies in a night club, 1942; enlisted in U.S. Navy, 1945, assigned to entertainment units in Pacific; chorus dancer in touring companies, 1948-50; Broadway debut in *Dance Me a Song,* 1950; signed to MGM, Hollywood, 1953; Broadway debut as choreographer with *The Pajama Game,* 1954; directed first film, *Sweet Charity,* 1968. **Awards:** Nine "Tony" Awards; Oscar for Best Director, and British Academy Award for Best Director, for *Cabaret,* 1972; also Emmy Award, for *Liza with a "Z,"* 1973. **Died:** Of a heart attack, in Washington, D.C., 23 September 1987.

Films as Director:

1968 *Sweet Charity* (+ chor)
1972 ***Cabaret*** (+ chor)
1974 *Lenny*
1979 *All That Jazz* (+ chor)
1983 *Star 80*

Other Films:

1953 *The Affairs of Dobie Gillis* (Weis) (role); *Kiss Me Kate* (Sidney) (role); *Give a Girl a Break* (Donen) (role)
1955 *My Sister Eileen* (Quine) (chor, role)
1957 *The Pajama Game* (Donen and Abbott) (chor)
1958 *Damn Yankees* (*What Lola Wants*) (Donen and Abbott) (chor, dancer in "Who's Got the Pain" number)
1974 *The Little Prince* (Donen) (chor "Snake in the Grass" number, role)
1976 *Thieves* (Berry) (role)

Publications

By FOSSE: articles—

"Inter/View with Bob Fosse," with L. Picard, in *Inter/View* (New York), March 1972.
"The Making of *Lenny,*" interview with S. Hornstein, in *Filmmakers Newsletter* (Ward Hill, Massachusetts), February 1975.
Interview in *Cinématographe* (Paris), March 1984.

On FOSSE: books—

Altman, Rick, *The American Film Musical,* Bloomington, Indiana, 1989.
Grubb, Kevin Boyd, *Razzle Dazzle: The Life and Work of Bob Fosse,* New York, 1989.

On FOSSE: articles—

Vallance, T., "Bob Fosse," in *Focus on Film* (London), Summer 1972.
Gardner, P., "Bob Fosse," in *Action* (Los Angeles), May/June 1974.
Badder, D.J., "Bob Fosse," in *Film Dope* (London), April 1979.
Drew, B., "Life as a Long Rehearsal," in *American Film* (Washington, D.C.), November 1979.
Braun, E., "In Camera: The Perfectionist," in *Films and Filming* (London), January 1980.
Valot, J., P. Ross, and D. Parra, "Bob Fosse," in *Revue du Cinéma* (Paris), March 1984.
Mizejewski, Linda, "Women, Monsters, and the Masochistic Aesthetic in Fosse's *Cabaret,*" in *Journal of Film and Video* (Boston), vol. 39, no. 4, 1987.
Wood, Robin, "Cloven Hoofer: Choreography as Autobiography in *All That Jazz,*" in *Post Script* (Jacksonville, Florida), Winter 1987.
Obituary in *Variety* (New York), 24 September 1987.
Obituary in *Hollywood Reporter,* 25 September 1987.
Obituary in *Films and Filming* (London), November 1987.
Kemp, P., "Degrees of Radiance," in *Cinema Papers* (Melbourne), March 1988.

* * *

Rex Reed once said of Bob Fosse (in a review of his performance as The Snake in *The Little Prince*), "The man can do anything!" Somewhat effusive, Reed's comment nonetheless has more than a kernel of truth: Fosse won eight Tonys, one Oscar, and one Emmy over the course of his career. In fact, he garnered four of the awards (the Oscar for *Cabaret,* the Emmy for *Liza with a Z,* and two Tonys for *Pippin*) in one year.

Fosse started his career as a dancer and choreographer on Broadway and divided his time almost equally between directing for the stage and for films. All of Fosse's films are musicals (with the exception of *Lenny*) and it is within this genre that he made significant contributions. The directorial choices employed by Fosse stemmed, not surprisingly, from his style of dancing and choreography: a type of eccentric jazz that isolates and exaggerates human motion, breaking it up into small components. It has been noted that there appears to be little difference between the dance material for Fosse's stage and film choreography. But the presentation of the dance is radically different. On the stage, only the performers could create the fragmentation of Fosse's choreography. In film, the use of multiple camera set-ups and editing allowed an amplification of this fragmentation, essentially obliterating the dance material and the mise-en-scène.

This style can be seen as the complete opposite of Astaire's presentation, which strives to preserve spatial and temporal integrity. "I love the camera," Fosse once said, "I love camera movement and camera angles. As a choreographer you see everything with a frame." Camera angle and camera image become more important choreographic components than the dancing. The dance routine itself is non-essential, subordinated to a more complex system of integration and commentary, as Jerome Delameter has noted.

Fosse's notions of integration and commentary drastically altered the structure of the American musical film. Reacting against thirty-odd years of the Arthur Freed musical, Fosse broke new ground in 1972 with *Cabaret.* No longer were the musical numbers "integrated" into the narrative with people singing to each other. All dance performances were logically grounded, occurring where they might be expected—on a stage, for example (and never leaving that stage, as Berkeley did)—and was distinctly separated from the narrative. The "integration" took place in the sense that each performance was a comment on the narrative action. In an interview with Glenn Loney for *After Dark,* Fosse shed some light on his approach. "I don't think there is any such thing as a realistic musical. As soon as people start to sing to each other, you've already gone beyond realism in the usual sense.... I have generally tried to make the musical more believable." Fosse did not seek to make the events more realistic, just more plausible and logical. Fosse expounded on his concepts of "believability," "integrated commentary," and visual fragmentation of performance via camera angle and editing with *All That Jazz,* a film in which musical numbers are literal hallucinations, obviously separated from the narrative but still logically grounded within it.

—Greg Faller

FOSTER, Jodie

Nationality: American. **Born:** Alicia Christian Foster in Los Angeles, California, 19 November 1962. **Education:** Attended Lycée Français, Los Angeles; Yale University, B.A., 1985. **Career:** Acted in TV commercials from the age of three; made acting debut on TV in *Mayberry R.F.D.,* 1969; made film debut in *Napoleon and Samantha,* 1972. **Awards:** U.S. National Film Critics Award, and Los Angeles Film Critics Award, for *Taxi Driver,* 1976; BAFTA Awards for Best Supporting Actress and Most Promising Newcomer, for *Taxi Driver* and *Bugsy Malone,* 1976; Academy Award for Best Actress, for *The Accused,* 1989, for *The Silence of the Lambs,* 1991. **Address:** 8942 Wilshire Blvd., Beverly Hills, California 90211, U.S.A.

Films as Director:

1991 *Little Man Tate* (+ role)
1995 *Home for the Holidays*

Films as Actress:

1972 *Napoleon and Samantha* (McEveety) (as Samantha); *Kansas City Bomber* (Freedman) (as Rita)
1973 *Tom Sawyer* (Taylor) (as Becky Thatcher); *One Little Indian* (McEveety) (as Martha)
1975 *Alice Doesn't Live Here Anymore* (Scorsese) (as Audrey); *Echoes of a Summer* (*The Last Castle*) (Taylor) (as Deirdre Striden)
1976 *Freaky Friday* (Nelson) (as Annabel Andrews); *Bugsy Malone* (Parker) (as Tallulah); ***Taxi Driver*** (Scorsese) (as Iris Steensman)
1977 *The Little Girl Who Lives Down the Lane* (Gessner) (as Ryan Jacobs)
1978 *Candleshoe* (Tokar) (as Casey Brown); *Moi, Fleur Bleue* (*Stop Calling Me Baby!*) (as Fleur Bleue)
1980 *Foxes* (Lyne) (as Jeanie); *Carny* (Kaylor) (as Donna); *Il cassoto* (*The Beach House*) (as Tersina)
1983 *O'Hara's Wife* (Bartman) (as Barbara O'Hara); *Le Sang des autres* (*The Blood of Others*) (Chabrol) (as Helene)
1984 *The Hotel New Hampshire* (Richardson) (as Franny Berry); *Mesmerized* (Laughlin) (as Victoria, + co-pr)
1987 *Siesta* (Lambert) (as Nancy)
1988 *Five Corners* (Bill) (as Linda); *The Accused* (Kaplan) (as Sarah Tobias); *Stealing Home* (Kampmann) (as Katie Chandler)
1989 *Catchfire* (*Backtrack*) (Smithee/Hopper) (as Anne Benton)
1990 ***The Silence of the Lambs*** (Demme) (as Clarice Starling)
1992 *Shadows and Fog* (as Prostitute)
1993 *Sommersby* (as Laurel); *It Was a Wonderful Life* (doc) (narrator)
1994 *Nell* (as Nell); *Maverick* (as Annabelle Bransford)

Publications

On FOSTER: articles—

Abramowitz, R., "Loving a Lie," in *Premiere,* March 1991.
Hirshey, G., "Jodie Foster," in *Rolling Stone,* 21 March 1991.
Wilson, P., "The Changing Fortunes of Jodie Foster," in *Film Monthly,* July 1991.
Cameron, J., "Burden of the Gift," in *American Film,* November/December 1991.
Rich, B. R., "Nobody's Handmaid," in *Sight and Sound,* December 1991.
Nevers, C., "Jodie Foster," in *Cahiers du Cinema,* no. 30, 1992.

* * *

A *wunderkind* stage-managed by a pushy mother who enrolled her in a French-speaking school for gifted children and succeeded in bringing her to the notice of fledgling director Martin Scorsese, Jodie Foster has in many ways lived up to her early promise, winning an Academy Award for her performance in *The Accused* and graduating with honors from Yale. After notable appearances as a child actress in *Alice Doesn't Live Here Anymore* and *Taxi Driver* (the only performance to inspire a would-be presidential assassin?), Foster suffered through the reactionary and overly conventional 1980s with few real opportunities to display her acting talents. Both *The Accused* and *Silence of the Lambs,* however, afforded her the opportunity once again to make an impression on mainstream cinema with finely crafted portraits of morally ambiguous women who, though victimized, maintain their integrity and self-respect.

Though urged by talent and inclination toward the director's chair, Foster has directed only two films. Perhaps too much was expected of her maiden effort (Foster appeared on the cover of *Time* immediately

Jodie Foster directing *Little Man Tate*

upon the release of *Little Man Tate,* which the magazine enthusiastically reviewed). Critics and audiences alike, however, generally did not like the film. Foster was undoubtedly attracted to the project to some extent by the subject matter, which has strong resonances with her own life and experiences. Fred Tate is also a *wunderkind,* whose only problem is that he needs more stimulation than his loving, if terribly low-brow, mother (played by Foster) is able to provide. Enter Jane Grierson, head of a school for gifted children, who wants to take charge of Fred's education. Dede Tate reluctantly agrees, and the remainder of the film treats the struggle between these two mothers, and their different parenting styles, for control of Fred.

Never a fan of mainstream cinema's glitz and fascination with (particularly) violent spectacle, Foster seems to have found in this story by Scott Frank the material for a dramatically effective small film. And yet Foster's handling (and the problems in Frank's screenplay) don't do the material justice. Because Fred has no conflicts, except for finding a proper environment, he is rightly displaced from the story's center. And yet the conflict between the two women is not adroitly handled. Dede's decision to let Jane have Fred is not clearly dramatized; in fact, a number of scenes that begin with some promise of illuminating the similarities and differences of the two women end confusingly. Lacking the essential Aristotelian elements of a linear movement toward a conclusion and clearly drawn characters, the film becomes tedious and pointless; it is not rescued by an improbable conclusion and out-of-place melodramatic touches along the way. If Foster's point is to make some point about a mother's need to combine career aspirations for her child with unconditional elemental love and respect, the film only confusingly endorses such a position.

Foster waited four years before directing her follow-up effort, *Home for the Holidays,* in 1995. Continuing with the theme of parent-child relationships, the film stars Holly Hunter as the estranged daughter of a dysfunctional family who returns home to attempt to make peace. *Home for the Holidays* received mixed reviews, with some critics praising its dark humor and on-target picture of family life, while others claimed that the repeated clashes between parents and siblings made it difficult to watch. At any rate, the release of the film demonstrated that the multitalented Foster does intend to continue her pursuit of a directorial career.

—R. Barton Palmer

FRAMPTON, Hollis

Nationality: American. **Born:** Wooster, Ohio, 11 March 1936. **Education:** Western Reserve University, 1954-57. **Career:** Moved to New York City, 1958; technician in film laboratories, 1961-69; primarily engaged in still photography, 1959-66; finished first released film, *Manual of Arms,* 1966; taught filmmaking at Free University of New York, 1966-67; assistant professor, Hunter College, New York, 1969-73; also lectured at School of Visual Arts and The Cooper Union, New York; associate professor, State University of New York at Buffalo, from 1973; co-designer and programmer of DEMON, an interpretative microcomputer language for audio-frequency data editing and control, 1979, and of IMAGO, a video master graphics computer language, 1980-81. **Died:** March 1984.

Films (entire body of film preserved by Royal Film Archive of Belgium):

1962 *Clouds Like White Sheep* (destroyed)
1963 *A Running Man* (destroyed)
1964 *Ten Mile Poem* (destroyed)
1965 *Obelisk Ampersand Encounter* (lost)
1966 *Manual of Arms*; *Process Red*; *Information*; *A & B in Ontario* (abandoned)
1967 *States*; *Heterodyne*
1968 *Snowblind*; *Maxwell's Demon*; *Surface Tension*
1969 *Palindrome*; *Carrots and Peas*; *Lemon*; *Prince Ruperts Drops*; *Works and Days*; *Artificial Light*
1970 *Zorn's Lemma*
1971 *Nostalgia*; *Travelling Matte*; *Critical Mass*
1972 *Special Effects*; *Poetic Justice*; *Ordinary Matter*; *Remote Control*; *Hapax Legomena*; *Apparatus Sum*; *Tiger Balm*; *Yellow Springs*
1973 *Public Domain*; *Less*
1974 *Autumnal Equinox*; *Noctiluca*; *Winter Solstice*; *Banner*
1975 *Ingenium Nobis Ipsa Puella Fecit*; *Solariumagelani*; *Drum*; *Pas de Trois*
1976 *Magellan: At the Gates of Death: Part I: The Red Gate, Part II: The Green Gate*; *Otherwise Unexplained Fires*; *Not the First Time*; *For Georgia O'Keeffe*; *Quaternion*; *Tuba*; *Procession*
1979 *More than Meets the Eye*; *Gloria!*; *The Birth of Magellan: Dreams of Magellan: Parts I-VI*
1980 *The Birth of Magellan: Mindfall: Parts I-VII*; *The Birth of Magellan: Fourteen Cadenzas*

Unfinished Projects:

1972 *Magellan*
1973 *Monsieur Phot: A Film by Joseph Cornell*
1980 *R*

Publications

By FRAMPTON: books—

Poetic Justice, Rochester, New York, 1973.
Fictcryptokrimsographs, Buffalo, New York, 1975.
Carl André—Hollis Frampton: 12 Dialogues 1962-1963, New York, 1980.
Circles of Confusion, Rochester, New York, 1983.

By FRAMPTON: articles—

Interview with Michael Snow, in *Film Culture* (New York), Winter/Spring 1970.
"For a Metahistory of Film: Commonplace Notes and Hypotheses," in *Artforum* (New York), September 1971.
"Nostalgia: Voice-Over Narration for a Film of that Name," in *Film Culture* (New York), Spring 1972.
Interview with Simon Field and Peter Sainsbury, in *Afterimage* (London), Fall 1972.
"Digressions on the Photographic Agony," in *Artforum* (New York), November 1972.
"Eadweard Muybridge: Fragments of a Tesseract," in *Artforum* (New York), March 1973.
"Incisions in History/Segments of Eternity," in *Artforum* (New York), October 1974.
Interview in *Structural Film Anthology,* edited by Peter Gidal, London, 1976.
"Notes on Composing in Film," in *October* (New York), Spring 1976.
Interview with Mitch Tuchmann, in *Film Comment* (New York), September/October 1977.
"Impromptus on Edward Weston: Everything in Its Place," in *October* (New York), Summer 1978.
"Talking about *Magellan,*" an interview with Bill Simon, in *Millenium Film Journal* (New York), Fall/Winter 1980/81.
Three Talks by Frampton, in *Millenium Film Journal* (New York), Fall/Winter 1986/87.

On FRAMPTON: books—

The Films of Hollis Frampton, Minneapolis, 1972.
Sitney, P. Adams, editor, *The Avant-Garde Film: A Reader of Theory and Criticism,* New York, 1979.
Sitney, P. Adams, *Visionary Film,* New York, 1980.
Jenkins, Bruce, and Susan Krane, *Hollis Frampton: Recollections/Recreations,* Cambridge, Massachusetts, 1984.
Macdonald, Scott, *A Critical Cinema: Interviews with Independent Filmmakers,* Berkeley, 1988.

On FRAMPTON: articles—

Field, Simon, "Alphabet as Ideogram," in *Art and Artists* (London), August 1972.
Mekas, Jonas, "Movie Journal," in *Village Voice* (New York), 4 and 11 April 1974.
Rayns, Tony, "Lines Describing an Impasse: Experimental Five," in *Sight and Sound* (London), Spring 1975.
Gunning, Tom, "The Participatory Film," in *American Film* (Washington, D.C.), October 1975.
Weinstein, Dave, "Hollis Frampton—Film as Symbol," in *Artweek* (Oakland, California), 8 May 1976.
Simon, Bill, "Reading *Zorn's Lemma,*" in *Millenium Film Journal* (New York), Spring/Summer 1978.
Jenkins, Bruce, "Frampton Unstructured: Notes for a Metacritical History," in *Wide Angle* (Athens, Ohio), Fall 1978.
Fischer, Lucy, "Frampton and the Magellan Metaphor," in *American Film* (Washington, D.C.), May 1979.
Lindemann, Bernhard, "Experimental Film as Meta-Film: Frampton's *Zorn Lemma,*" in *Enclitic* (Minneapolis), Fall 1979.
Tuchman, Mitch, "Frampton," in *Film Comment* (New York), July/August 1985.
Millenium Film Journal (New York), Fall/Winter 1984/85.

* * *

Hollis Frampton worked in poetry, painting, and photography before turning to filmmaking. In addition, he studied widely in a variety of disciplines outside of as well as within the arts. Much of the richness and complexity of his films results from influences culled from many diverse fields that he fused within single works.

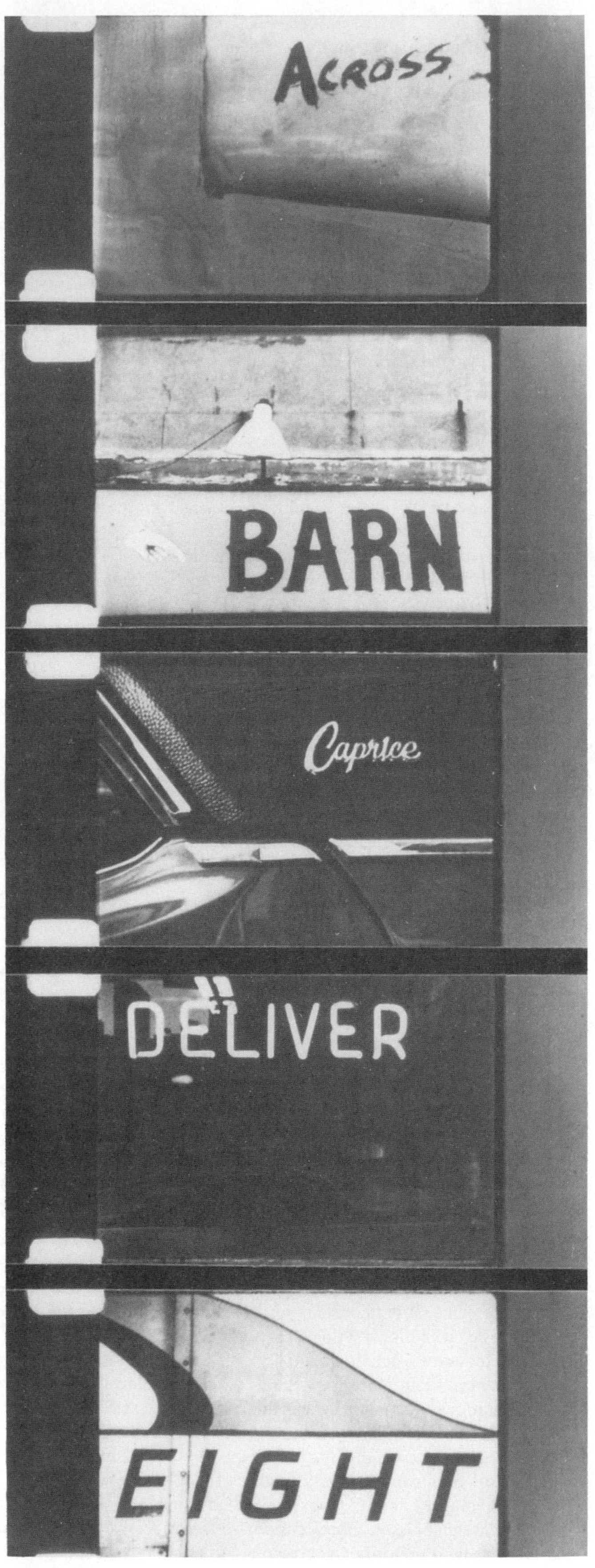

Hollis Frampton: *Zorn's Lemma*

Many of Frampton's films exhibit complex, spectacularly strict structures. *Zorn's Lemma,* his best-known work, has a long central section in which alphabetized signs are gradually replaced with wordless images. This and similar devices involve the audience in an overtly participatory way. In *Nostalgia,* we hear still photographs described before seeing them, and are thus involved with constructing a mental image from the description. This image is generally quite different from the actual photograph we then see.

Many of Frampton's pre-*Magellan* films involve game-like activities of counting, reading, guessing. While carefully controlled structures and audience participation were common to other avant-garde films and other arts in the late 1960s, Frampton's films in this mode are characterized by a unique rigor. He seeks to bring to cinema some of the precision of the sciences and mathematics.

True to the modernist tradition of which he is a part, Frampton devoted much of his cinema's energy to the act of investigating the medium itself. In a great number of early films made before *Zorn's Lemma,* he explored a vast range of cinematic possibilities, from the simplest use of black and white portrait imagery (*Manual of Arms*) to abstract shapes (*Palindrome*) to various modifications of photo imagery (*Artificial Light*). He said that film itself "is what all films are about," and much of his work can be taken as the proffering of possible alternative definitions of the medium. But by defining Frampton does not mean to delimit: not only do different films offer different definitions, each film tries to be the most perfect example of its possibility that it can. These works are characterized by their frequently spectacular photographic qualities and their absolute formal precision.

In seeking to investigate the properties of his medium, rather than place primary emphasis on the idiosyncratic qualities of his own inner vision, Frampton set different goals for himself than do Brakhage or Baillie. But an autobiographical element is often also present in Frampton's work. This element is most evident in his serial film *Hapax Legomena,* of which *Nostalgia,* is the first of seven parts. The sections that make up this work simultaneously display a range of possible interactions between film and other media (still photography, writing, video, spoken language), and tell an implied story of the birth of a filmmaker via an evolution through film-related media (photography, a film script) to cinema itself. The sequence's seventh and final section, *Special Effects,* completes this movement by presenting a moving white-outlined rectangle at the edge of a black frame. This serves as a meditation on one of cinema's essences, the frame itself. The evolution within *Hapax Legomena* can also be seen to lead to Frampton's massive, multi-part (uncompleted) *Magellan.*

Of Frampton's other areas of involvement, still photography seemed to have the strongest influence on his filmmaking. He saw in photographers like Weston the possibility that a photo image, and the sensuality of its tiniest modulations, can constitute an ineluctable mystery which is finally outside of language. The subject matter and photographic and editing styles of *Magellan*'s completed sections are many and various, but again and again the editing functions to return the viewer to a contemplation of the graphic qualities of the screen imagery, as if cinematically recreating the process of looking at a still photograph. The filmmaker's exhibition scheme for the completed film defied anything yet attempted in the medium; for instance, there was to be at least one different film for each day of the year. *Magellan*'s encyclopedic goal is perhaps best expressed by Frampton himself, who called it an attempt to record, and render comprehensible, the sights and sounds of the visible world.

—Fred Camper

FRANJU, Georges

Nationality: French. **Born:** Fougères, Brittany, 12 April 1912. **Education:** Attended religious school in Fougères. **Military Service:** In Algeria, 1928-32. **Career:** Set builder for Folies Bergères and the Casino de Paris, 1932-33; began Cercle du Cinéma programme with Henri Langlois, and directed *Le Metro,* 1934; co-founder, with Langlois, of Cinémathèque Française and *Cinématographe* magazine, 1937; executive secretary of La Fedération Internationale des Archives du Film (FIAF), from 1938; Secretary-General of the Institut de Cinématographie Scientifique, 1945-54; founder, L'Academie du Cinéma, 1946; directed first feature-length film, 1958; director for French television (including *Chroniques de France*), from 1965. **Awards:** Chevalier de la Légion d'honneur; Officier de l'ordre national du Mérite et des Arts et des Lettres. **Died:** 5 November 1987.

Films as Director:

1934 *Le Metro* (co-d, sc) (short)
1949 ***Le Sang des bêtes*** (+ sc) (short)
1950 *En passant par la Lorraine* (+ sc) (short)
1951 *Hôtel des Invalides* (+ sc) (short)
1952 *Le Grand Méliès* (+ sc) (short)
1953 *Monsieur et Madame Curie* (+ sc) (short)
1954 *Les Poussières* (+ sc) (short); *Navigation marchande* (*Marine marchande*) (+ sc) (short; disowned by Franju)
1955 *A propos d'une rivière* (*Le Saumon Atlantique*) (+ sc) (short); *Mon chien* (+ sc) (short)
1956 *Le Théâtre National Populaire* (*Le T.N.P.*) (+ sc) (short); *Sur le Pont d'Avignon* (+ sc)(short)
1957 *Notre Dame, cathédrale de Paris* (+ sc) (short)
1958 *La Première nuit* (+ sc) (short); *La Tête contre les murs* (*The Keepers*)
1959 ***Les Yeuxs sans visage*** (+ co-adapt)
1960 *Pleins feux sur l'assassin* (*Spotlight on Murder*)
1962 ***Thérèse Desqueyroux*** (+ co-sc)
1963 *Judex*
1964 *Thomas l'imposteur* (*Thomas the Imposter*) (+ co-sc)
1970 *La Faute de l'Abbé Mouret* (*The Demise of Father Mouret*) (+ co-sc)
1974 *Nuits rouges* (*L'Homme sans visage*; *Shadowman*) (+ co-mus)

Other Film:

1956 *Décembre, mois des enfants* (Storck) (co-sc)

Publications

By FRANJU: book—

De Marey à Renoir, trésors de la Cinématheque Française 1882-1939, Paris, 1981.

By FRANJU: articles—

Interview with Freddy Buache, in *Positif* (Paris), September 1957.
Interview with François Truffaut, in *Cahiers du Cinéma* (Paris), November 1959.
Interview with Jean-André Fieschi and André Labarthe, in *Cahiers du Cinéma* (Paris), November 1963.
"*Hôtel des Invalides,*" in *Avant-Scène du Cinéma* (Paris), no. 38, 1964.
"*Le Sang des bêtes,*" in *Avant-Scène du Cinéma* (Paris), no. 41, 1964.
"Réalisme et Surréalisme," in *Etudes Cinématographiques* (Paris), no. 41/42, 1965.
Interview with Tom Milne, in *Sight and Sound* (London), Spring 1975.
"*Les Yeuxs sans visage,*" in *Avant-Scène du Cinéma* (Paris), June 1977.
"A propos du *Grand Méliès,*" in *Positif* (Paris), December 1977/January 1978.
"Mystery and Melodrama: A Conversation with Georges Franju," by R. Conrad, in *Film Quarterly* (Los Angeles), Winter 1981/82.
Interview with P. Hillairet, in *Cinématographe* (Paris), October 1986.

On FRANJU: books—

Agel, Henri, *Miroirs de l'insolité dans le cinéma français,* Paris, 1957.
Durgnat, Raymond, *Franju,* Berkeley, 1968.
Vialle, Gabriel, *Georges Franju,* Paris, 1968.

On FRANJU: articles—

Grenier, Cynthia, "Franju," in *Sight and Sound* (London), Spring 1957.
Godard, Jean-Luc, "Georges Franju," in *Cahiers du Cinéma* (Paris), December 1958.
"Franju Issue" of *Image et Son* (Paris), March 1966.
Milne, Tom, "Songs of Innocence," in *Sight and Sound* (London), Winter 1970/71.
MacLochlainn, A., "The Films of Luis Buñuel and Georges Franju," in *Film Journal* (New York), Summer 1971.
Gow, Gordon, "Franju," in *Films and Filming* (London), August 1971.
Wood, Robin, "Terrible Buildings: The World of Georges Franju," in *Film Comment* (New York), November/December 1973.
"*Nuits rouges* Issue" of *Avant-Scène du Cinéma* (Paris), January 1975.
Brown, R., "Georges Franju: Behind Closed Windows," in *Sight and Sound* (London), Autumn 1983.
"Georges Franju Issue" of *Avant-Scène du Cinéma* (Paris), April 1984.
"*La Tête contre les murs* Issue" of *Avant-Scène du Cinéma* (Paris), no. 353, 1986.
Monthly Film Bulletin (London), May 1987.
Obituary in *Variety* (New York), 11 November 1987.
Tribute in *Première* (Paris), December 1987.
Tribute in *Revue du Cinéma* (Paris), January 1988.

* * *

Franju's career falls clearly into two parts, marked by the format of the films: the early period of documentary shorts, and a subsequent period of fictional features. The parts are connected by many links of theme, imagery, attitude, and iconography. Critical attention has focused primarily on the shorts, and there is some justice in this. While it is difficult to accept Noel Burch's assertion that "the magic that is so much a part of his nonfiction work no longer survives in his fiction features," it is true that nothing in the later work surpasses *Le Sang des bêtes* and *Hôtel des Invalides,* and the intensity and poetic concentration of those early masterpieces are recaptured only in intermittent moments. It is necessary to define the *kind* of documentary Franju made (it is highly idiosyncratic, and I can think of no close parallels; though Resnais's documentaries are often linked with his, the differences seem more important than the similarities).

The traditional documentary has three main modes: the factual, the lyrical, and the politically tendentious. It is the peculiar distinction of Franju's documentaries that they correspond to none of these modes. The kind of organization that structures them is essentially poetic, built upon imagery and juxtaposition, rather than on overt statement or clear-cut symbolism. *Hôtel des Invalides* might well have been expected, from its genesis, to correspond to either the second or third type of documentary (or an amalgamation of the two, a quite com-

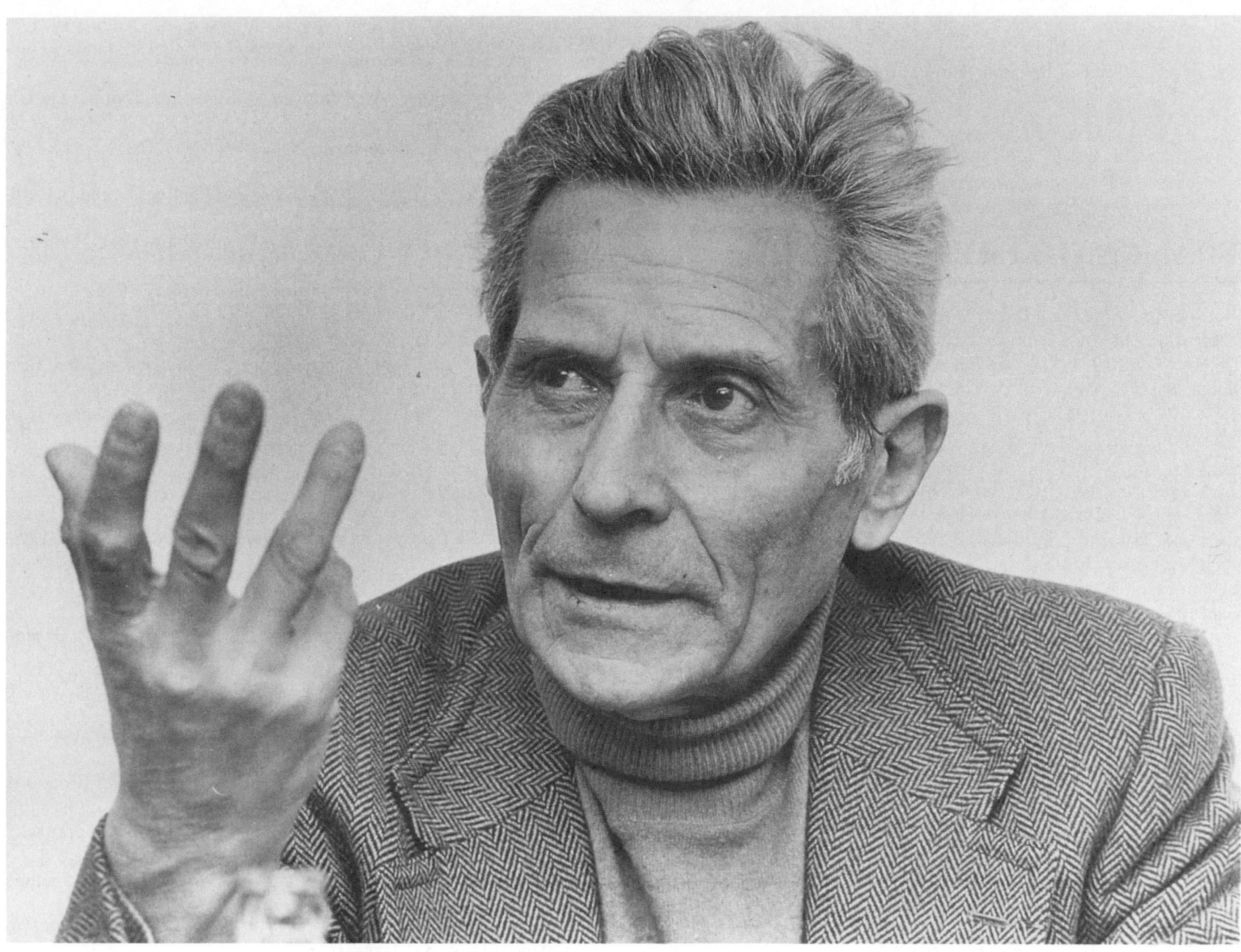

Georges Franju

mon phenomenon). It was commissioned by an organization called Forces et Voix de France, and the intention was to celebrate a national monument-institution: the Musée de L'Armée, home of Napoleon's tomb, an edifice dedicated to the glory of France and of war. Franju seized upon and made central to his film the fact that the building also houses the *victims* of war and "glory": the veterans' hospital of the film's title, peopled with the shell-shocked, the crippled, the mutilated. These wounded soldiers continue to carry military banners, wear their medals, and attend the religious ceremonies that constitute an aspect of their oppression. Beyond the skillful use of purely cinematic codes (lighting, camera movement, editing, etc.) and Maurice Jarre's music, Franju adds nothing extraneous to his raw material. The introductory commentary (spoken by Michel Simon), locating the museum in place and history, is rigorously factual and unemotional. Once inside, we have only the "authentic" commentary of the museum guides. Yet the application of cinematic codes to this material transforms its meaning totally, producing a continuous irony that modulates back and forth between the violent and the subtle: the emblems of military glory and national pride become sinister, monstrous, terrifying.

A politically tendentious documentary after all, then? Certainly not in any simple or clear-cut way. Ultimately, *Hôtel des Invalides* is no more an anti-war movie than *Le Sang des bêtes* is an appeal for vegetarianism—though those meanings can and will be read by many viewers. The film's elements of rage and protest are finally subordinated to an overriding sense of irredeemable insanity, an intimation of a world and a species so fundamentally crazy that protest is almost superfluous. The supreme irony Franju produces out of his material involves the museum's very status as a national monument: here, at the heart of civilization, regarded with pride, admiration and wonderment, stands what amounts to a monument to pain, cruelty, ugliness, death—and no one notices.

The basic problem with Franju's feature films is that he does not seem greatly interested in narrative. He has usually relied on the support of a pre-existent literary work, whose structure, characters, and movement he recreates with a generally scrupulous fidelity, delicacy, and discretion, the changes being mainly of emphasis and omission. The curious feat of *Thérèse Desqueyroux* has often been noted: a faithful, almost literal translation of a novel by a famous Catholic writer (Mauriac) that never violates the integrity of Franju's atheism. Cocteau singled out Franju as the director to whom he would most confidently entrust his work, and Franju justified that confidence fully with his version of *Thomas l'imposteur.* Nonetheless, these films are discernibly Franju's: the directorial reticence should not be mistaken for abdication. The clearest way to demonstrate the continuity of the director's work is to show how the Franjuesque iconography that is already fully developed in the documentaries recurs in the features, producing those moments of poetic density and resonance that are the films' chief distinction.

If *Les Yeux sans visage* remains the finest of Franju's feature films, it is because it is the one that permits the greatest concentration of poetry created out of the association of these elements.

—Robin Wood

FRANKENHEIMER, John

Nationality: American. **Born:** Malba, New York, 19 February 1930. **Education:** La Salle Military Academy, graduated 1947; Williams College, B.A., 1951. **Military Service:** Served in newly-formed Film Squadron, U.S. Air Force, 1951-53. **Family:** Married Carolyn Miller, 1954 (divorced, 1961), two daughters; remarried, 1964. **Career:** Assistant director, later director, CBS-TV, New York, 1953; television director, *Playhouse 90,* Hollywood, from 1955; directed first feature, *The Young Stranger,* 1957; formed John Frankenheimer Productions, 1963. **Award:** Christopher Award, 1954; Grand Prize for best film direction, Locarno Film Festival, 1955; Emmy Award for Directing for a Miniseries Or A Special, *The Burning Season,* 1994. **Address:** c/o John Frankenheimer Productions, 2800 Olympic Blvd., Suite 201, Santa Monica, CA 90404, U.S.A.

Films as Director:

1957 *The Young Stranger*
1961 *The Young Savages*
1962 *The Manchurian Candidate* (+ co-pr); *All Fall Down*; *Birdman of Alcatraz*
1963 *Seven Days in May*
1964 *The Train*
1966 *Grand Prix*; *Seconds*
1968 *The Extraordinary Seaman*; *The Fixer*
1969 *The Gypsy Moths*
1970 *I Walk the Line*; *The Horsemen*
1973 *L'Impossible Objet* (*Impossible Object*); *The Iceman Cometh*
1974 *99 44/100 Dead* (retitled *Call Harry Crown* for general release in U.K.)
1975 *French Connection II*
1976 *Black Sunday* (+ bit role as TV controller)
1979 *Prophecy*
1982 *The Challenge*
1985 *The Holcroft Covenant*
1986 *52 Pick-Up*
1987 *Across the River and Into the Trees*
1989 *Dead Bang*; *The Fourth War*
1991 *Year of the Gun*
1994 *Against the Wall* (for television)
1994 *The Burning Season* (for television)

Publications

By FRANKENHEIMER: articles—

"Seven Ways with *Seven Days in May,*" in *Films and Filming* (London), June 1964.
Interview, in *The Celluloid Muse,* edited by Charles Higham and Joel Greenberg, London, 1969.
Interview with Russell Au Werter, in *Action* (Los Angeles), May/June 1970.
Interview with J. O'Brien, in *Inter/View* (New York), August 1971.
"Filming *The Iceman Cometh,*" in *Action* (Los Angeles), January/February 1974.
"John Frankenheimer: An American Film Institute Seminar On His Work," 1977.
Interview with L. Gross and R. Avrech, in *Millimeter* (New York), July/August 1975.
Interviews with R. Appelbaum, in *Films and Filming* (London), October and November 1979.
Interview with P. Broeske, in *Films in Review* (New York), February 1983.
Interview in *Films and Filming* (London), February 1985.
"Frankly speaking," an interview with K. Ferguson, in *Photoplay Movies & Video* (London), October 1985.
"Dialogue on Film: John Frankenheimer," in *American Film* (New York), March 1989.
"Drive, he said," an interview with S. Modderno, in *Movieline* (Los Angeles), September 1989.

On FRANKENHEIMER: book—

Pratley, Gerald, *The Cinema of John Frankenheimer,* New York, 1969.

On FRANKENHEIMER: articles—

Mayersberg, Paul, "John Frankenheimer," in *Movie* (London), December 1962.
Thomas, John, "John Frankenheimer, the Smile on the Face of the Tiger," in *Film Quarterly* (Berkeley), Winter 1965/66.
Casty, Alan, "Realism and Beyond: The Films of John Frankenheimer," in *Film Heritage* (New York), Winter 1966/67.
Higham, Charles, "Frankenheimer," in *Sight and Sound* (London), Spring 1968.
Filmer, Paul, "Three Frankenheimer Films: A Sociological Approach," in *Screen* (London), July/October 1969.
Madsen, Axel, "*99 and 44/100 Dead,*" in *Sight and Sound* (London), Winter 1973/74.
Drew, B., "John Frankenheimer: His Fall and Rise," in *American Film* (Washington, D.C.), March 1977.
Combs, Richard, "A Matter of Conviction," in *Sight and Sound* (London), no. 4, 1979.
Cook, B., "The War Between the Writers and the Directors: Part II: The Directors," in *American Film* (Washington, D.C.), June 1979.
"Directors of the Decade: John Frankenheimer," in *Films and Filming* (London), February 1984.
Article by Frederic Rosen in *Video* (New York), December 1984.
Scheinfeld, Michael, "*The Manchurian Candidate,*" in *Films in Review* (New York), vol. 39, no. 11, 1988.
Levy, Shawn, "Year of the Gun: John Frankenheimer's Sinister Formula," *American Film,* November/December 1991.
Career overview in *Film* (London), February 1992.
Weinraub, Bernard, "A Director Trying to Reshoot His Career," in *New York Times,* 24 March 1994.
Zoller Seitz, Matt, "Those High-tech Shoot-em-ups Got the Formula from 'The Train,'" in *New York Times,* 30 April 1995.

* * *

The seven feature films John Frankenheimer directed between 1961 and 1964 stand as a career foundation unique in American cinema. In a single talent, film had found a perfect bridge between television and Hollywood drama, between the old and new visual technologies, between the cinema of personality and that of the corporation and the computer.

Frankenheimer's delight in monochrome photography, his instinct for new light cameras, fast stocks, and lens systems like Panavision informed *The Manchurian Candidate, Seven Days in May,* and *Seconds* with a flashing technological intelligence. No less skillful with the interior drama he had mastered as a director of live television, he turned *All Fall Down* and *The Young Savages* into striking personal explorations of familial disquiet and social violence. He seemed unerring. Even *Birdman of Alcatraz* and *The Train,* troubled projects taken over at the last minute from Charles Crichton and Arthur Penn, respectively, emerged with the stamp of his forceful technique.

Frankenheimer's career began to sour with *Seconds,* a film that was arguably too self-conscious with its fish-eye sequences and rampant paranoia. *Grand Prix,* an impressive technical feat in Super Panavision, showed less virtuosity in the performances. His choices thereafter were erratic: heavy-handed comedy, rural melodrama, a further unsuccessful attempt at spectacle in *The Horsemen,* which was shot in Afghanistan. Frankenheimer relocated in Europe, no doubt mortified that Penn, Lumet, and Delbert Mann, lesser lights of live TV drama, had succeeded where he failed.

Despite a career revival with the 1975 *French Connection II,* a sequel which equalled its model in force and skill, Frankenheimer has not hit his stride since. The director's choices remain variable in intelligence, though by staying within the area of violent melodrama he has at least ceased to dissipate his talent in the pursuit of production values. *Black Sunday* is a superior terrorist thriller, *Prophecy* a failed but worthy horror film with environmental overtones, and *The Challenge* a stylish Japanese romp in the style of *The Yakuza.* Unfortunately, new directors who grew up with the Frankenheimer work as benchmarks do such material better.

Frankenheimer's late 1980s and early 1990s features—*Dead Bang, The Fourth War,* and *Year of the Gun*—did nothing to resuscitate his career, and were quickly forgotten as they made their way to video store oblivion. Only the 1987 theatrical re-release of *The Manchurian Candidate,* after decades of unavailability, earned Frankenheimer high critical praise. Indeed, the film was atop many critics' lists as among the best to come to movie houses that year. Additionally, the emergence of the high-tech thriller genre, so popular in the 1990s, has been critically traced back to *The Train.*

In 1994 Frankenheimer returned to his roots in television by directing *Against the Wall* and *The Burning Season,* two above-average made-for-TV movies. The former is a solid prison drama which retraces the events surrounding the 1971 Attica prison riots. The latter is even better: an outstanding, politically savvy account of the life of activist Chico Mendes, who battled against the exploitation of those who toil in the Amazon rain forests of Brazil and paid for his valor with his life.

—John Baxter, updated by Rob Edelman

John Frankenheimer

FREARS, Stephen

Nationality: British. **Born:** Leicester, 1941. **Education:** Studied law at Cambridge University, 1960-63. **Career:** Assistant at the Royal Court Theatre, 1964; assistant on films, from 1966; directed first film, 1967; director and producer for TV, from 1969, including *Me! I'm Afraid of Virginia Woolf* (series of plays by Alan Bennett, 1978) and *Walter* for Channel 4, 1982; also director of TV commercials.

Films as Director:

1967 *The Burning* (+ pr)
1971 *Gumshoe*
1978 *Long Shot*
1980 *Bloody Kids*
1981 *Going Gently*
1982 *Walter*
1983 *Saigon*
1984 *The Hit*
1985 ***My Beautiful Laundrette***
1987 *Prick Up Your Ears*; *Sammy and Rosie Get Laid*
1988 *Dangerous Liaisons*
1990 ***The Grifters***
1992 *Hero*
1993 *The Snapper*

Other Films:

1966 *Morgan, a Suitable Case for Treatment* (Reisz) (asst d)
1967 *Charlie Bubbles* (Finney) (asst d)
1968 *If...* (Anderson) (asst d)
1973 *O Lucky Man!* (Anderson) (asst d)
1978 *Long Shot* (Hatton) role

Publications

By FREARS: articles—

Interview in *Time Out* (London), 10 November 1983.
Interview with P. Merigeau and F. Guerif, in *Revue du Cinema* (Paris), November 1984.
"Sheer Frears," an interview with J. Saynor, in *Stills* (London), November 1985.
Interview with Harlan Kennedy, in *Film Comment* (New York), March/April 1987.
Interview in *Inter/View* (New York), April 1987.
Interview with K.M. Chanko, in *Films in Review* (New York), October 1987.
American Film (Washington, D.C.), December 1988.
Interview with H. Merrick, in *Revue du Cinema* (Paris), January 1991.
Interview with L. Vincenzi, in *Millimeter,* February 1991.
Interview with K. Vandemaele, in *Skoop,* April 1991.
"One Foot in Hollywood," interview with Ralph Rugoff, in *Vogue,* October 1992.
"Keeping His Own Voice: An Interview with Stephen Frears," *Post Script,* vol. 11, no. 3, 1992.
"Rolling in the Isles," interview with Gregg Kilday, in *Entertainment Weekly,* 28 January 1994.

On FREARS: articles—

"Song of Experience: Stephen Frears," in *Monthly Film Bulletin* (London), May 1987.
"Stephen Frears Section" of *Positif* (Paris), November 1987.
Hunter, Mark, "Marquise de Merteiul and Comte de Valmont get Laid," in *American Film,* December 1988.
Lindsey, Robert, "The Dangerous Leap of Stephen Frears," in *New York Times Magazine,* December 18, 1988.
Dancyger, K., "The Bigger Picture: A Consideration of the Influence of Journalism and Theatre on the Feature Length Screenplay," in *Journal of Film and Video,* vol. 42, no. 3, 1990.
McDonagh, Maitland, "Straight to Hell," in *Film Comment* (New York), November/December 1990.
Merrick, H., "Un realisateur en liberte," in *Revue du Cinema* (Paris), January 1991.
Quart, L., "The Politics of Irony: The Frears-Kureishi Films," in *Film Criticism,* vol. 16, no. 1/2, 1991/92.
Regosa, M., "Stephen Frears e la fenomenologia del politico," in *Cinema Nuovo,* May/June 1992.
Joshel, S.R., "Fatal Liaisons and Dangerous Attraction: The Destruction of Feminist Voices," in *Journal of Popular Culture,* vol. 26, no. 3, 1992.
Saynor, J., "Accidental Auteur," in *Sight and Sound,* April 1993.

* * *

Stephen Frears has had two major periods as a director of feature films; he first came to public theatrical notice as the creator of 1971's *Gumshoe,* an oddly memorable crime thriller laced with parodic, self-reflexive overtones. This comedy/drama starred Albert Finney and Billie Whitelaw, and surprisingly, had a music score by the then comparatively unknown Andrew Lloyd Webber. It was a gentle, unassuming film, and had its adherents, but was soon forgotten.

During the 1980s, though, Frears directed a blistering series of features that established him as one of the more important British directors of the period. The breakthrough film was *My Beautiful Laundrette,* a movie partly funded by Channel 4 TV that also launched Daniel Day Lewis as an actor, brought Shirley Anne Field back to the screen, and gave the screenwriter Hanif Kureishi his first substantial hit.

Frears had done some other work before *My Beautiful Laundrette* put him back on the map, however. In 1978 he made *Long Shot,* a film which mirrored his own personal and professional dilemma: how to raise the money to finance a film. Made on a shoestring, the film was positively received, but did not effectively revitalize Frears's career. His 1984 film *The Hit* had a great cast (John Hurt, Terence Stamp, and Fernando Rey), and told the story of a small-time hood named Willie Parker (Stamp) who informs upon his partners-in-crime. Ten years later, Stamp suddenly finds that his long-time hiding place has been discovered by his former associates. Eric Clapton wrote the theme song for the film, but despite the favorable critical press, the film failed to catch on.

The Hit is tense, well-acted, and has an authentic air of despair and failure in its tightly constructed visuals, yet at the same time it manages to be quite funny, and oddly difficult to grasp. It reminds one of the Hammer psychological thrillers of the early 1960s, in which Jimmy Sangster's scripts kept the audience guessing throughout; it also stands up well against more contemporary works, such as *The Long Good Friday.* But it was *My Beautiful Laundrette* that really re-established Frears's career, taking him out of the grind of ordinary television production, and affording him a more luxurious canvas with which to work. Nevertheless, it is clear that his work in television prepared him for this moment: the fast pace of television production allowed Frears to wring every last value out of minimal funding.

A titillating, cheaply exotic and yet deeply romantic film, *Laundrette* is set firmly in the world of 1980s London, a barren, Thatcherite landscape of failing businesses, exploited workers, and simmering racial tension. The love affair between Johnny (Day Lewis) and the

Stephen Frears © Andy Lane

Asian Omar crosses the "barrier" of the heterosexual ruling faction and serves as an "affront" to the rigid class and racial barriers of an England caught in the grip of a pervasive economic depression. The film's look is lush, multi-hued, and dreamy; it exists outside of time, as its protagonists most truly come to life outside the structures imposed upon them. With *Laundrette,* Frears aligned himself with a strong scenarist (Kureishi) who also sought to revitalize British cinema, and the iconic structures that had come to be taken as fixed points of reference in its landscape (Kureishi stated that one of his ambitions in writing the script for the film was to make a gay-themed British movie "without Dirk Bogarde"). A surprise "art house" hit in the United States, the film revived Frears's career as a director. He was thus able to plunge into a group of new works that consolidated his reputation.

Sammy and Rosie Get Laid, another Kureishi script, was perhaps less successful than *Laundrette,* but it still did respectable business in the United States and Britain, and found several critical champions. *Sammy and Rosie* took the basic image of London in collapse posited in *Laundrette* several steps further. *Sammy and Rosie* is a clever reinterpretation of Godard's vision of the city-as-apocalypse, with a Buñuelian flair for surreal interruptions and a grimy look similar to that used by 1960s British directors like Tony Richardson and Karel Reisz.

In the same year, Frears's *Prick Up Your Ears,* an examination of the life of the playwright Joe Orton, from an Alan Bennett screenplay, received substantial critical acclaim both in England and the United States.

Frears's most successful and popular film, *Dangerous Liaisons,* owes a considerable stylistic debt to Roger Vadim's 1960 *Les liaisons dangereuses,* a modern-dress version of the same text by Laclos. Vadim's film featured Jeanne Moreau and Gerard Philipe; Frears's film, from a screenplay by Christopher Hampton, is anchored by the brilliant performances of Glenn Close and John Malkovich, and succeeds because of the sense of period verisimilitude it creates. Frears's camera seems almost a recording angel within the context of the film's narrative; it is omnipresent, but never oppressive, and maintains a discreet distance, except in the climactic dueling sequence.

Dangerous Liaisons does not strive to be sumptuous; rather, it plants the characters firmly within the context of the decor, and lets them do their work. Malkovich, in particular, has never appeared to better advantage, and the final shot of Glenn Close, after having been scorned in public, wiping her evening's make-up off her face with brutal finality while regarding herself in her dressing room mirror, is one of the most despairingly triumphant moments in recent cinema history.

Interestingly, Frears completely eschews the aggressive visual style of *Laundrette* and *Sammy and Rosie* in *Dangerous Liaisons*; rather, his camera seems entirely at the service of the actors. He frames them in introductory wide-shots in the classical studio manner before going in for intimate close-ups. In this, the film is a double period piece, recreating the British studio system and its inherent dependence upon actors, as well as the eighteenth-century period in which the fictive text is set. Perhaps because of this double classicism, the film has proven to be Frears's most accessible and popularly-praised work.

Frears further consolidated his position in film with two early 1990s releases. *The Grifters,* a noirish drama featuring Annette Bening, John Cusack, and Angelica Huston, won all-around critical and popular accolades. And in 1993, Frears switched gears yet again. *The Snapper* told the story of a working-class family in Ireland. When their eldest daughter, who is unmarried, becomes pregnant, her relationship with her father is tested. The film is ultimately a warm portrait of family imperfections and loyalties.

—Wheeler Winston Dixon

FRIČ, Martin

Nationality: Czech. **Born:** Prague, 29 March 1902. **Family:** Married actress Suzanne Marwille, 1932. **Career:** Actor in Prague and Bratislava, 1918; lab man, cameraman, and designer, 1919-21; began film acting, scriptwriting, 1922; began collaboration with Karel Lamac, 1924; billed as Mac Frič on films made during occupation, 1940s; television director, from 1961; 1st Chairman, Union of Czechoslovakian Film and Television Artists, 1965. **Awards:** Recipient of National Artist; Order of the Republic; Laureate; State Prize. **Died:** 22 August 1968.

Films as Director (partial listing):

1928 *Páter Vojtěch* (*Father Vojtech*) (+sc, role)
1929 *Varhaník v sv. Víta* (*The Organist at St. Vitus*) (+ co-sc); *Chudá holka* (*Poor Girl*) (+sc)
1930 *Vše pro lásku* (*All for love*) (+co-sc)
1931 *Der Zinker* (*The Informer*) (co-d); *On a jeho sestra* (*He and His Sister*) (co-d); *Dobrý voják Svejk* (*The Good Soldier Schweik*) (+ ed)
1932 *Kantor Ideál* (*Master Ideál*); *Sestra Angelika* (*Sister Angelica*) (+ ed)
1933 *Revisor* (*The Inspector*) (+ ed); *U snědeného krámu* (*The Emptied-out Grocer's Shop*) (+ ed); *Pobočník Jeho Výsosti* (*Adjutant to His Highness*) (+ ed); *Zivot je pes* (*A Dog's Life*) (+ co-sc); *Dvanáct křesel* (*The Twelve Chairs*) (co-d); *S vyloučením ve ejnosti* (*Closed Doors*)
1934 *Hej rup!* (*Heave-ho!*) (+ ed, co-sc); *Poslední muž* (*The Last Man*); *Mazlíček* (*Darling*) (+ ed, co-sc)
1935 *Hrdina jedné noci* (*Hero for a Night*) (+ ed); *Jánošík* (ed, co-sc); *Jedenácté přikázání* (*The Eleventh Commandment*) (+ ed); *Ať žije nebožtík* (*Long Live the Deceased*) (+ ed, co-sc)
1936 *Pater Vojtěch* (*Father Vojtech*) (remake); *Svadlenka* (*The Seamstress*); *Ulička v ráji* (*Paradise Road*)
1937 *Svět patří nám* (*The World Is Ours*) (+ co-sc, role); *Hordubalové* (*The Hordubals*)); *Lidé na kře* (*People on a Glacier*)
1938 *Krok do tmy* (*Madman in the Dark*); *Skola, základ života* (*School, the Basis of Life*)
1939 *Eva tropí hlouposti* (*The Escapades of Eva*); *Kristián* (*Christian*) (+ co-sc); *Muž z neznáma* (*The Reluctant Millionaire*)
1940 *Muzikantská Liduška* (*Liduška of the Stage*; *Musicians' Girl*); ***Baron Prášil*** (*Baron Munchhausen*); *Katakomby* (*Catacombs*); *Druhá směna* (*Second Tour*)
1941 *Těžký život dobrodruha* (*Hard Is the Life of an Adventurer*); *Hotel Modrá hv zda* (*The Hotel Blue Star*) (+ co-sc)
1942 *Barbora Hlavsová*
1943 *Experiment*; *Der zweite Schuss* (*The Second Shot*) (+ co-sc)
1944 *Počestné paní pardubické* (*The Virtuous Dames of Pardubice*); *Prstýnek* (*The Wedding Ring*)
1945 *13. revír* (*Beat 13*)
1947 *Varuj!* (*Warning!*) (+ co-sc); *Capkovy povídky* (*Tales from Capek*) (+ co-sc)
1948 *Návrat domu* (*Lost in Prague*); *Polibek ze stadionu* (*A Kiss from Stadium*) (+ co-sc)
1949 *Pětistovka* (*Motorcycles*); *Pytlákova schovanka* (*The Kind Millionaire*)
1950 *Past* (*The Trap*); *Zoceleni* (*Tempered Steel*; *Steel Town*)
1951 *Císařv pekař a Pekařuv pekař* (*The Emperor's Baker and the Baker's Emperor*) (+ co-sc); *Akce B* (*Action B*) (+ co-sc)
1953 *Tajemství krve* (*The Secret of Blood*) (+ co-sc)
1954 *Psohlavci* (*Dog-Heads*) (+ co-sc)

Martin Frič: ***Janosik***

1955 *Nechte to na mně* (*Leave It to Me*) (+ co-sc)
1956 *Zaostřit, prosím* (*Watch the Birdie!*) (+ co-sc)
1958 *Povode* (*The Flood*); *Dnes naposled* (*Today for the Last Time*)
1959 *Princezna se zlatou hvězdou* (*The Princess with the Golden Star*) (+ co-sc)
1960 *Dařbuján a Pandrhola* (*A Compact with Death*); *Bilá spona* (*The White Slide*)
1963 *Krák Králu* (*King of Kings*); *Tři zlaté vlasy děda Vševěda* (*The Three Golden Hairs of Old Man Know-All*)
1964 *Hvězda zvaná Pelyněk* (*A Star Named Wormwood*)
1966 *Lidé z maringotek* (*People on Wheels*) (+ co-sc)
1967 *Přísně tajné premiéry* (*Recipe for a Crime*; *Strictly Secret Previews*)
1968 *Nejlepší ženská mého života* (*The Best Woman of My Life*) (+ co-sc)

Publications

By FRIČ: article—

Interview, in *Closely Watched Films,* by Antonín Liehm, White Plains, New York, 1974.

On FRIČ: book—

Modern Czechoslovak film, Prague, 1965.

On FRIČ: articles—

Hrbas, J., "Martin Frič: Lidový vypráveč," (in four parts) in *Film a Doba* (Prague), January through April 1972.
Dewey, L., "Czechoslovakia: Silence into Sound," in *Film* (London), no. 60.
Taussig, P., *Film a Doba* (Prague), December 1983 and April 1984.
Bartosek, L., "Scenes from the History of Czechoslovak Cinema," in *Czechoslovak Film* (Prague), Summer 1985.

* * *

Scion of a notable middle-class Prague family, Martin Frič left the road marked out by family tradition at the age of sixteen to follow the uncertain path of a cabaret performer, actor, and filmmaker. In 1919 he designed a poster for Jan Stanislav Kolár's film *Dáma s malou nozkou* (*Lady With a Little Foot*), and thus began his years of apprenticeship. He was by turns an actor, a scenarist, a film laboratory worker, and a cameraman. Of crucial importance to the young Frič was his collaboration and friendship with Karel Lamac, the most influential director in Czech film. Lamac taught him the film trade and enabled him to become familiar with the film studios of Berlin and Paris.

In 1928 Frič made his debut with the film *Páter Vojtěch* (*Father Vojtech*) and followed it immediately with his most important film of the silent era, *Varhaník u sv. Vita* (*The Organist at St. Vitus*), which dealt with the tragedy of a man suspected of murder. In the sound era Frič quickly gained a position of prominence, chiefly through his ability to work quickly (making up to six films a year) and, no matter the circumstances, with surprising ease and dexterity. Comedy became his domain. His comedies, often produced in two language versions (German or French), featured popular comedians as well as actors and actresses whose comic talent he recognized and helped to develop. First and foremost of these was Vlasta Burián, who appeared in the situation comedies *On a jeho sestra* (*He and His Sister*) with Anny Ondrákova, *Pobočník Jeho Výsosti* (*Adjutant to His Highness*), *Dvanáct křesel* (*The 12 Chairs*), *Katakomby* (*Catacombs*), and also in the film adaptation of Gogol's *Revisor* (*The Inspector*).

Frič had much to do with shaping the film acting of Hugo Haas in such films as *Zivot je pes* (*A Dog's Life*—the first Czech screwball comedy with Adina Mandlová), *Ať žije nebožlík* (*Long Live the Deceased*), *Jedenácté přikázání* (*The Eleventh Commandment*), and *Ulička a ráji* (*Paradise Road*). Together with Voskovec and Werich he made the social comedy *Hej rup!* (*Heave-ho*) and the modern political satire *Svět patří nám* (*The World Is Ours*). Then came *Kristián* (*Christian*), a social comedy with Oldrich Nový that is undoubtedly Frič's best work.

But Frič also demonstrated his directorial abilities in infrequent excursions into other genres. His *Jánošík* (*Jánosík*), a poetic epic about a legendary highwayman, is one of the pinnacles of Czechoslovak cinematography. Frič showed sensitivity and an understanding of the atmosphere of the time in his film rendition of *U snědeného krámu* (*The Emptied-Out Grocer's Shop*), a story by the nineteenth-century Czech writer Ignát Hermann. He also made felicitous film versions of the dramas *Hordubalové* (*The Hordubals*), based on the novel by Karel Capek, *Lidé na kře* (*People on a Glacier*), and *Barbora Hlavsová.*

Following the nationalization of Czechoslovak filmmaking, Frič aided in the development of filmmaking in Slovakia with his film *Varuj...!* (*Warning!*). In 1949, in collaboration with Oldrich Nový, he fashioned his next masterpiece, *Pytlákova schovanka* (*The Kind Millionaire*), a parody of film kitsch. Following the successful costume comedy *Císařuv pekař a Pekařuv pekař* (*The Emperor's Baker and the Baker's Emperor*) with Jan Werich, and an excursion into the biographical genre with the film *Tajemství krve* (*The Secret of Blood*), Frič made a few films that were—for the first time, actually—neither a popular nor a critical success.

Frič's last creative surge came at the beginning of the 1960s. He made fine adaptations for Czechoslovak television and directed Chekhov's tales *Medved* (*The Bear*), *Slzy, které svě nevidi* (*Tears the World Can't See*), and *Námluvy* (*Courting*), and once more returned to the studios. The tragicomedy *Hvězda zvaná Pelyněk* (*A Star Named Wormwood*) and the comedy *Nejlepší ženská mého života* (*The Best Woman of My Life*), the premieres of which he did not live to see, close out his final period of creativity.

Frič's creation is the work of a solid and honest artist who demonstrated his talent in diverse genres from psychological drama to madcap comedy. He produced two masterful comedies, *Kristián* and *Pytlákova schovanka,* which can be numbered among the world's best of the period. The best proof of the quality and vitality of his creative work is the fact that almost a third of the films he made are still shown in the theaters of Czechoslovakia, where they bring pleasure to new generations of viewers.

—Vladimír Opela

FRIEDKIN, William

Nationality: American. **Born:** Chicago, 29 August 1939. **Family:** Married 1) Jeanne Moreau, 1977 (divorced); 2) Lesley-Anne Down, 1982 (divorced), one son. **Career:** Mailroom assistant, then studio floor manager, WGN-TV, Chicago, 1955; TV director, 1957-67; partner, with Francis Ford Coppola and Peter Bogdanovich, in the Directors Company, 1973 (withdrew, 1974). **Awards:** Oscar for Best Director, for *The French Connection,* 1971. **Agent:** c/o Edgar Gross International Business Management, 9696 Culver Blvd., Culver City, CA 90232, U.S.A.

William Friedkin

Films as Director:

1967 *Good Times*
1968 *The Night They Raided Minsky's*; *The Birthday Party*
1970 *The Boys in the Band*
1971 *The French Connection*
1973 *The Exorcist*
1977 *Sorcerer* (*Wages of Fear*)
1978 *The Brinks Job*
1980 *Cruising* (+ sc)
1981 *Duet for One*
1983 *The Deal of the Century*
1985 *To Live and Die in L.A.* (+ sc); *Sea Trial*
1986 *Judgement Day*
1990 *The Guardian* (+ co-sc)
1992 *Rampage* (+ co-sc)
1994 *Blue Chips*
1995 *Jade*

Publications

By FRIEDKIN: articles—

"Anatomy of a Chase," in *Take One* (Montreal), July/August 1971.
"Photographing *The French Connection,*" with Herb Lightman, in *American Cinematographer* (Los Angeles), February 1972.
Interview with M. Shedlin, in *Film Quarterly* (Berkeley), Summer 1972.
"Dialogue on Film: William Friedkin," in *American Film* (Washington, D.C.), February/March 1974.
"Mervyn Leroy Talks with William Friedkin," in *Action* (Los Angeles), November/December 1974.
Interview with R. Appelbaum, in *Films and Filming* (London), March 1979.
Interview with R. Gentry, in *Post Script* (Jacksonville, Florida), Spring/Summer and Fall 1986.

On FRIEDKIN: book—

Segaloff, Nat, *Hurricane Billy: The Career of William Friedkin,* New York, 1989.

On FRIEDKIN: articles—

Maslin, Janet, "Friedkin Defends His *Cruising,*" in *New York Times,* 18 September 1979.
"William Friedkin," in *Film Dope* (London), September 1979.
Gentry, R., "Louma Crane and William Friedkin," in *American Cinematographer* (Los Angeles), August 1985.
Bornet, J., "William Friedkin: le chaos final," in *Revue du Cinéma,* July/August 1990.

Spotnitz, F., "William Friedkin," in *American Film,* December 1990.

* * *

The success, both critical and commercial, of William Friedkin's films has been uneven since the release of his first feature in 1967. Although his works span several different genres, they share some common thematic and technical characteristics. His heroes are nontraditional and find themselves in unconventional situations or environments foreign to the average viewer. Technically, Friedkin often seems more concerned with creating mood and establishing atmosphere than with the progress of the narrative or character development. His great attention to detail and characteristic use of long establishing shot sequences do create mood and atmosphere but often do not contribute to the film as a whole.

In two of Friedkin's early films, *The Birthday Party* and *The Boys in the Band* (both based on stage productions), the use of establishing prologues works very well. *The Birthday Party* begins with an early morning shot of a deserted beach. Empty canvas beach chairs look out over an unnatural vastness of sameness—a seemingly endless grayish blue ocean that disappears into a grayish blue sky. This slightly unsettling visual sets the mood for Harold Pinter's play. To the beginning of *The Boys in the Band,* Friedkin adds a montage prologue that introduces all of the main characters. But these are the only personal interpretations evident in these two works.

In *The Night They Raided Minsky's,* Friedkin's attention to detail successfully establishes 1920s period authenticity and adds to a richness of character missing in his other works. The film was criticized, however, for having too broad a narrative told through overly long sequences that do not contribute to the story. This characteristic would prove to be a major flaw of several of Friedkin's subsequent films.

Friedkin's two most popular films, *The French Connection* and *The Exorcist,* have some aspects in common. In addition to nontraditional heroes in unusual situations, both films have broad narratives expressed through similar filmic techniques: minimal dialogue; long, detailed sequences; and documentary-style use of the camera.

The French Connection, Friedkin's most critically acclaimed work, maintains a precarious balance between becoming tedious to watch and portraying the tedium and fatigue of Jimmy Doyle and Buddy Russo's lives. Friedkin uses a long prologue to establish the drug operation in Marseilles. This sequence, filmed with little dialogue and great attention to detail, not only serves to introduce the drug operation but also to contrast the lifestyles of French narcotics dealer Alain Charnier and New York City cops Doyle and Russo. This very long sequence is followed by another that establishes the cops' personalities and beat. Consequently, it takes quite some time before the actual narrative begins.

Friedkin's ability to create atmosphere does work well in *The French Connection* because the environment itself, New York City, is one of the main characters. The city and its inhabitants are depicted in detail. The scenes—sometimes gritty, sometimes gory, sometimes dull—produce the urban reality, and at the same time reflect the reality of policework, which is also sometimes dull, but sometimes dangerous.

The Exorcist, a commercially successful film, is tedious throughout. The film plods along through an excessively long opening sequence (the significance of which is never made clear), a pseudo psychological explanation of the character Father Karras, countless close-ups of "meaningful" facial expressions, and predictable stages in both the possession and exorcism of Regan MacNeil. Friedkin does succeed at times in creating tension and suspense, but this mood is not sustained throughout the film. Apparently, the shock value of watching the disturbing physical transformation of Regan from young girl to hideous monster is enough to maintain viewer interest, since this continues to be a popular film.

Sorcerer did not follow the trend of commercial success begun by the two previous films. A remake of Clouzot's *The Wages of Fear, Sorcerer* is a good action adventure once the story finally gets underway. Like other Friedkin films, it is weighed down by several long introductory sequences. After these initial sequences, the use of documentary technique, including hand-held tracking shots, creates a reality of place that can almost be smelled and touched.

Friedkin's subsequent films contain his characteristic cinematic techniques. His filmic representation of the sadomasochistic homosexual subculture in New York City in *Cruising* is too realistic and brutal for many reviewers. *Deal of the Century,* although not commercially or critically popular, is a fair satire on the profitable business of selling arms to third world nations, using an introductory sequence very effectively to set the tone.

The Guardian, Friedkin's first horror film since *The Exorcist,* was not well received critically or at the box office. As in *The Exorcist,* Friedkin employs an unconventional situation for the narrative and uses mood and atmosphere to gradually turn reality into a nightmare. Unlike the narrative in *The Exorcist,* however, this story of a yuppie couple who hire a nanny that feeds newborns to trees is told on a much smaller scale, but still is not consistently interesting. *Jade,* Friedkin's most recent feature, has been criticized not only for unsuccessful attempts to establish mood that bog down the narrative, but also for unoriginal dialogue and stale action sequences. The screenwriter of *Jade,* Joe Eszterhas, is equally credited for the film's flaws, along with Friedkin, in many critical reviews.

—Marie Saeli

FUENTES, Fernando De *See* **DE FUENTES, Fernando**

FULLER, Samuel

Nationality: American. **Born:** Samuel Michael Fuller in Worcester, Massachusetts, 12 August 1911. **Military Service:** Served in 16th regiment of U.S. Army 1st Division, 1942-45, awarded Bronze Star, Silver Star, and Purple Heart. **Family:** Married actress Christa Lang, 1965. **Career:** Copy-boy and journalist, *New York Journal,* from 1924; crime reporter, from 1928; screenwriter in Hollywood, from 1936; screenwriter at Warner Bros., 1946-48; directed first feature, 1948; signed to 20th Century-Fox, 1951-57; TV director, 1960s.

Films as Director:

1948 *I Shot Jesse James* (+ sc)
1950 *The Baron of Arizona* (+ sc); *The Steel Helmet* (+ sc, co-pr)
1951 *Fixed Bayonets* (+ sc)
1952 *Park Row* (+ sc, co-pr)
1953 *Pickup on South Street* (+ sc) [remade in 1968 as *Cape Town Affair* (Webb)]
1954 *Hell and High Water* (+ co-sc)
1955 *The House of Bamboo* (+ co-sc, role as Japanese policeman)
1957 *Run of the Arrow* (+ pr, sc); *China Gate* (+ pr, sc); *Forty Guns* (+ pr, sc)
1958 *Verboten!* (+ pr, sc)
1959 *The Crimson Kimono* (+ pr, sc)
1960 ***Underworld USA*** (+ pr, sc)

1962 *Merrill's Marauders* (+ co-sc)
1963 ***Shock Corridor*** (+ pr, sc); *The Naked Kiss* (+ co-pr, sc)
1967 *Caine* (+ sc)
1973 *Dead Pigeon on Beethoven Street* (+ sc, role as United States Senator)
1980 *The Big Red One* (+ sc)
1982 *White Dog*
1983 *Thieves After Dark*
1989 *Street of No Return* (+ co-sc)

Other Films:

1936 *Hats Off* (Petroff) (sc)
1937 *It Happened in Hollywood* (Lachman) (sc)
1938 *Gangs of New York* (Cruze) (remade in 1945 as *Gangs of the Waterfront*) (Blair) (sc); *Adventure in Sahara* (Lederman) (sc); *Federal Man-Hunt* (Grinde) (sc)
1940 *Bowery Boy* (Morgan) (sc)
1941 *Confirm or Deny* (Lang, Mayo) (sc)
1943 *Power of the Press* (Landers) (sc)
1948 *Shockproof* (Sirk) (sc)
1951 *The Tanks Are Coming* (Seiler) (sc)
1952 *Scandal Sheet* (Karlson) (sc)
1953 *The Command* (Butler) (sc)
1965 *Pierrot le fou* (Godard) (role as himself)
1966 *Brigitte et Brigitte* (Moullet) (role as himself)
1971 *The Last Movie* (Hopper) (role as himself)
1974 *The Klansman* (Young) (sc)
1976 ***Der Amerikanische Freund*** (*The American Friend*) (Wenders) (role as The American)
1979 *1941* (Spielberg) (small role)

Publications

By FULLER: books—

Burn, Baby, Burn, New York, 1935.
Test Tube Baby, New York, 1936.
Make Up and Kiss, New York, 1938.
The Dark Page, New York, 1944 (published as *Murder Makes a Deadline,* New York, 1952).
The Naked Kiss, New York, 1964.
Crown of India, New York, 1966.
144 Piccadilly, New York, 1971.
Dead Pigeon on Beethoven Street, New York, 1973.
Il etait un fois ... Samuel Fuller: Histoires d'Ameriques, edited by Jean Narboni and Noel Simsolo, Paris, 1986.

By FULLER: articles—

"What Is Film?" in *Cinema* (Beverly Hills), July 1964.
"Samuel Fuller: Two Interviews," with Stig Björkman and Mark Shivas, in *Movie* (London), Winter 1969/70.
Interview in *The Director's Event* by Eric Sherman and Martin Rubin, New York, 1970.
Interview with Ian Christie and others, in *Cinema* (Cambridge), February 1970.
"Sam Fuller Returns," interview with Claude Beylie and J. Lourcelles, in *Ecran* (Paris), January 1975.
"War That's Fit to Shoot," in *American Film* (Washington, D.C.), November 1976.
"Three Times Sam: The Flavor of Ketchup," interview with R. Thompson, in *Film Comment* (New York), January/February 1977.
Interview with Russell Merritt and P. Lehman, in *Wide Angle* (Athens, Ohio), vol. 4, no. 1, 1980.
"Samuel Fuller—Survivor," an interview with T. Ryan, in *Cinema Papers* (Melbourne), December/January 1980/81.
"Fuller mis au défi par l'avocat du diable," in *Cahiers du Cinéma* (Paris), April 1982.
Interview with A. Hunter, in *Films and Filming* (London), November 1983.
Interview in *Monthly Film Bulletin* (London), March 1984.

On FULLER: books—

Will, David, and Peter Wollen, editors, *Samuel Fuller,* Edinburgh, 1969.
Hardy, Phil, *Samuel Fuller,* New York, 1970.
Garnham, Nicholas, *Samuel Fuller,* New York, 1971.
MacArthur, Colin, *Underworld U.S.A.,* London, 1972.
Amiel, Victor, *Samuel Fuller,* Paris, 1985.
Caprara, Valerio, *Samuel Fuller,* Florence, 1985.
Server, Lee, *Sam Fuller: Film is a Battleground,* Jefferson, North Carolina, 1994.

On FULLER: articles—

Lee, Russell, "Samuel Fuller," in *New Left Review,* January/February 1964.
Wollen, Peter, "Notes Toward a Structural Analysis of the Films of Samuel Fuller," in *Cinema* (Cambridge), December 1968.
Canham, Kingsley, "The World of Samuel Fuller," in *Film* (London), November/December 1969.
Canham, Kingsley, "Samuel Fuller's Action Films," in *Screen* (London), November/December 1969.
McArthur, Colin, "Samuel Fuller's Gangster Films," in *Screen* (London), November/December 1969.
Belton, John, "Are You Waving the Flag At Me: Samuel Fuller and Politics," in *Velvet Light Trap* (Madison, Wisconsin), Spring 1972.
McConnell, F., "*Pickup on South Street* and the Metamorphosis of the Thriller," in *Film Heritage* (New York), Spring 1973.
Cook, B., "Sam Fuller Lands with the Big One," in *American Film* (Washington, D.C.), June 1979.
Valot, J., "Love, Action, Death, Violence: Cinema Is Emotion (sur quelques films de Samuel Fuller)," in *Image et Son* (Paris), July/August 1980.
Milne, Tom, "Sam Fuller's War," in *Sight and Sound* (London), Autumn 1980.
"Fuller Section" of *Image et Son* (Paris), April 1981.
"Fuller Issue" of *Avant-Scène du Cinéma* (Paris), 1 November 1981.
Dossier on Fuller, in *Framework* (Norwich), no. 19, 1982.
Revue du Cinéma (Paris), April 1988.

* * *

Sam Fuller's narratives investigate the ways that belonging to a social group simultaneously functions to sustain and nurture individual identity and, conversely, to pose all sorts of emotional and ideological threats to that identity. Fuller's characters are caught between a solitude that is both liberating and debilitating, and a communality that is both supportive and oppressive. Unlike Howard Hawks, whose films suggest the triumph of the group over egoism, Fuller is more cynical and shows that neither isolation nor group membership is without its hardships and tensions.

Many of the films touch upon a broad kind of belonging, as in membership in a nation—specifically the United States (although *China Gate* comments on several other nationalities)—as a driving idea and ideal, national identity becoming a reflection of personal identity. For example, in Fuller films about the building of the West, such as *Forty Guns, The Baron of Arizona,* or *Run of the Arrow,* the central characters initially understand their own quests as necessarily divergent from the quest of America for its own place in the world. Even though the course of the films suggests the moral and emotional losses that such divergence leads to, the films also imply that there is something inadequate in the American quest itself, in the ways such a quest undercuts its own purity by finding strength in a malevolent violence (the readiness of "ordinary" people in *The Baron of Arizona* to lynch at a moment's notice), in mistrust and prejudice (unbridled racism in *Run of the Arrow*), or in political corruption.

Similarly, in films such as *House of Bamboo, Underworld USA,* and *Pickup on South Street,* about criminal organizations infiltrated by revenging outsiders, the narrative trajectory will begin by suggesting the moral separation of good guys and bad guys, but will then continue to demonstrate their parallelism, their interweaving, even their blurring. For example, in *Underworld USA,* the criminals and crimefighters resemble each other in their methods, in their cold calculation and determination, and in their bureaucratic organization. Tolly, the film's central character, may agree to map his own desire for revenge onto the crimefighters' desire to eliminate a criminal element, but the film resolutely refuses to unambiguously propagandize the public good over personal motives.

At a narrower level of group concern, Fuller's films examine the family as a force that can be nurturing but is often stifling and riddled with contradictions. Not accidentally, many of Fuller's films concentrate on childless or parentless figures: the family here is not given but something that one loses or that one has to grope towards. Often, the families that do exist are, for Fuller, like the nation-state, initially presenting an aura of innocent respectability but ultimately revealing a corruption and rotted perversity. Indeed, *The Naked Kiss* connects questions of political value to family value in its story of a woman discovering that her fiancé, the town's benefactor and a model citizen, is actually a child molester. Similarly, *Verboten!* maps the story of postwar America's self-image as benefactor to the world onto an anti-love love story. A German woman initially marrys a G.I. for financial support and then finds she really loves him, only to discover that he no longer loves her.

Love, to be sure, is a redemptive promise in Fuller's films but it is run through by doubt, anger, mistrust, deception. Any reciprocity or sharing that Fuller's characters achieve comes at a great price, ranging from mental and physical pain to death. For example, in *Underworld USA,* Tolly is able to drop his obsessional quest and give himself emotionally to the ex-gangster's moll, Cuddles, only when he is at a

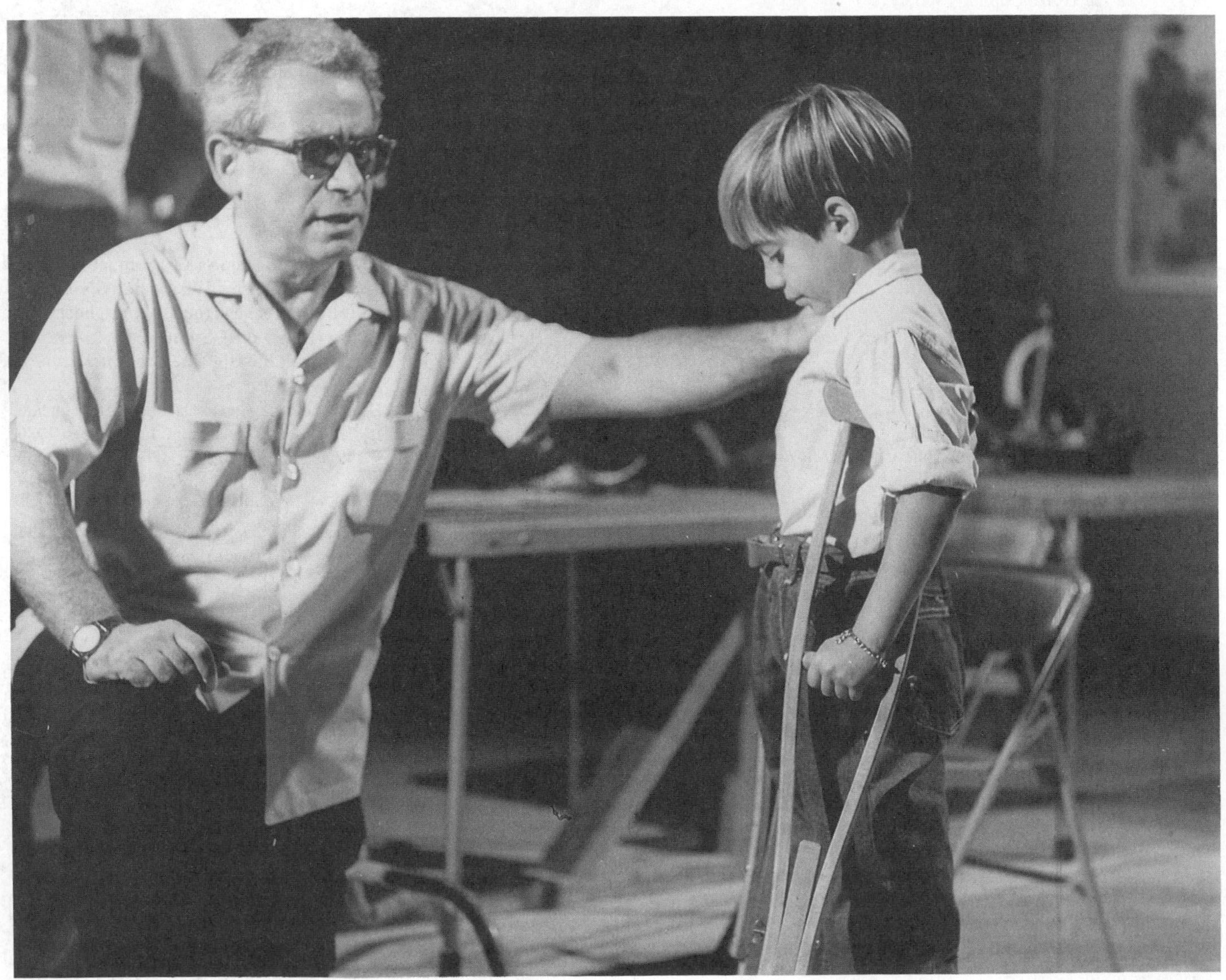

Samuel Fuller directing *The Naked Kiss*

point of no return that will lead him to his death. Against the possibility of love (which, if it ever comes, comes so miraculously as to call its own efficacy into doubt), Fuller's films emphasize a world where everyone is potentially an outsider and therefore a mystery and even a menace. No scene in Fuller's cinema encapsulates this better than the opening of *Pickup on South Street* where a filled subway car becomes the site of intrigued and intriguing glances as a group of strangers warily survey each other as potential victims and victimizers. Echoing the double-entendre of the title (the pickup is political—the passing on of a secret microfilm—as well as sexual), the opening scene shows a blending of sexual desire and aggression as a sexual come-on reveals itself to be a cover for theft, and passive passengers reveal themselves to be government agents.

In a world of distrust, where love can easily betray, the Fuller character survives either by fighting for the last vestiges of an honest, uncorrupted love (in the most optimistic of the films) or, in the more cynical cases, by displacing emotional attachment from people to ideas; to myths of masculine power in *Forty Guns*; to obsessions (for example, Johnny Barratt's desire in *Shock Corridor* to win the Pulitzer Prize even if that desire leads him to madness); to mercenary self-interest; to political or social ideals; and ultimately, to a professionalism that finally means doing nothing other than doing your job right without thinking about it. This is especially the case in Fuller's war films, which show characters driven to survive for survival's sake, existence being defined in *Merrill's Marauders* as "put(ting) one foot in front of the other."

Fuller's style, too, is one based on tensions: a conflict of techniques that one can read as an enactment for the spectator of Fuller themes. Fuller is both a director of rapid, abrupt, shocking montage, as in the alternating close-ups of robber and victim in *I Shot Jesse James,* and a director who uses extremely long takes incorporating a complex mix of camera movement and character action. Fuller's style is the opposite of graceful; his style seems to suggest that in a world where grace provides little redemption, its utilization would be a kind of lie. Thus, a stereotypically beautiful shot like the balanced image of Mount Fujiyama in *House of Bamboo* might seem a textbook example of the well-composed nature shot but for the fact that the mountain is framed through the outstretched legs of a murdered soldier.

—Dana B. Polan

GAÁL, István

Nationality: Hungarian. **Born:** Salgótarján, 25 August 1933. **Education:** Academy of Theatre and Film Art, Budapest, graduated 1959; studied at Centro Sperimentale, Rome, 1959-61. **Career:** Director and cameraman for Hungarian Newsreel Dept, 1961; directed first feature, 1964; director for Hungarian TV, from 1977.

Films as Director:

1957 *Pályamunkások* (*Surfacemen*; *Railroaders*) (+ sc, ed) (short)
1961 *Etude* (+ sc, ed) (short)
1962 *Tisza—öszi vázlatok* (*Tisza—Autumn Sketches*) (+ sc, ed) (short); *Oda—vissza* (*To and Fro*) (+ sc, ed) (short)
1964 *Sodrásban* (*The Stream*; *Current*) (+ sc, ed)
1965 *Zöldár* (*Green Flood*; *The Green Years*) (+ ed, co-sc)
1967 *Krónika* (*The Chronicle*) (+ sc, ed, ph) (short); *Keresztelö* (*Christening Party*) (+ sc, ed)
1969 *Tiz éves Kuba* (*Cuba's Ten Years*) (+ sc, ed, ph) (short)
1970 *Bartók Béla: az éjszaka zenéje* (*Béla Bartók: The Music of the Night*; *The Night Music*) (+ sc, ed) (short); *Magasiskola* (*The Falcons*) (+ sc, ed)
1971 *Holt vidék* (*The Dead Country*) (+ co-sc, ed)
1977 *Legato* (*Ties*) (+ co-sc, ed); *Naponta két vonat* (*Two Trains a Day*) (+ sc, ed) (for TV); *Vámhatár* (*Customs Frontier*) (+ ed) (for TV)
1981 *Cserepek* (*Buffer Zone*) (+ sc, ed)
1985 *Orfeusz es Eurydike* (+ sc)

Other Films:

1962 *Cigányok* (*Gypsies*) (Sára) (ed, ph) (short)
1964 *Férfiarckép* (*Portrait of a Man*) (Gyöngyössy) (co-ph) (short)
1967 *Vizkereszet* (*Twelfth Night*) (Sára) (co-sc) (short)

Publications

By GAÁL: articles—

"Un Réalisateur hongrois," interview with J. Camerlain, in *Séquences* (Paris), January 1973.
Interview in *Cinema Canada* (Montreal), April/May 1973.
"Interviewing István Gaál," in *Hungarofilm Bulletin* (Budapest), no. 4, 1977.
"A Challenge and a Trial of Strength," an interview in *Hungarofilm Bulletin* (Budapest), no. 5, 1983.

On GAÁL: book—

Petrie, Graham, *History Must Answer to Man,* London, 1978.

On GAÁL: articles—

Petrie, Graham, "István Gaál and *The Falcons,*" in *Film Quarterly* (Berkeley), Spring 1974.
Martin, M., and Y. Biro, "István Gaál, de *Remous à Paysage mort*: itinéraire d'un témoin," in *Ecran* (Paris), March 1974.
"István Gaál," in *Film Dope* (London), September 1979.
Predal, René, "István Gaál: les remous de la quarantaine," in *Jeune Cinéma* (Paris), October 1981.
Pörös, G., in *Filmkultura* (Budapest), May/June 1984.

* * *

The artistic personality of the film editor, cameraman, scriptwriter, and director István Gaál was formed by his study at the Higher School of Theatrical and Film Art in Budapest, where he arrived as a young electrical engineer determined to devote himself to the art of film. Here he shaped and precisely defined his artistic viewpoint in a classroom that is already legendary today as the meeting place of later notable personalities in Hungarian cinematography—Judit Elek, Pál Gábor, Imre Gyöngössy, Zoltán Huszárik, Ferenc Kardos, Zsolt Kérdi-Kovács, János Rózsa, István Szabó, Sándor Sára, Ferenc Kósa, and others. Gaál took his first, already conspicuous step in a creative workshop, the experimental studio of Béla Balázs. The artistic path he chose was a difficult one, because it was the specific, individual form of documentary. In the course of his creative career he returns constantly to this basic source, but at the same time he applies its elements in his not very extensive but masterfully suggestive artistic film work.

Gaál is one of the founders of the Hungarian new wave of the mid-1960s, which he inaugurated with *Sodrásban,* his deeply emotive debut. Not only did this work reflect the positive social events of the time, but the author also applied genuine elements of a subjectively motivated poetics. With every important subsequent film—and these are for the most part adaptations of his own literary work—Gaál reveals the strange world of the Hungarian countryside, a world of desolation and unromantically flat landscapes with scattered, lonely settings where solitary tree trunks, well-beams, and the whitewashed walls of old buildings occasionally loom. In this microcosm he uncovers human community, relationships, and problems of morality. In intimate episodes he manages to take up and treat delicate problems of the past and generalize them in the form of a profound philosophical drama that reveals the roots of violence and evil and the dangerous elements of apathy and indifference, despair and loneliness. At the same time, his films, with their limited dialogue and almost totally graphic conception, are poetic pictures that have dramatic tension. However, István Gaál is not the romantic poet of the countryside he may appear to be. In a brief moment and in simple fashion he suggests the atmosphere and the relationships among characters, and he is equally adept at capturing the essence of a hunting lodge in the wilderness, a depopulated village, or the smell of a provincial town. For him the environment is merely a symbolic medium, because each of his works offers a kind of parallel between the world of nature and human society, a metaphor with deep ideological and moral significance.

István Gaál: ***Sodrásban***

There is a close union of all artistic components in films under his direction—a carefully constructed script, a poetic form of screen photography, simple non-illustrative music, and dramatically motivated editing, along with prodigious acting by the noted performers whom the director gets to "shed their theatrical skin," enabling them to achieve quite a remarkable degree of expression before the camera.

In the intervals between making his fictional film works, Gaál constantly returns to the pure documentary, which is for him a starting point and perhaps also an experimental station. But he shapes his documentaries with the same fire and originality. Here again, there is an alteration between people and nature, and a struggle between the two.

In his most recent films, Gaál turns more to the inner world of his contemporaries. His works delineate masterful psychological portraits in which there is more and more reflection of history on a general plane. His films are personal, poetically veiled confessions about present-day people, their problems and their relations.

—Václav Merhaut

GAD, Urban

Nationality: Danish. **Born:** Korsør, 12 February 1879. **Education:** Educated in Copenhagen until 1897; attended art school in Paris. **Family:** Married 1) Asta Nielsen, 1912 (divorced 1918); 2) Esther Burgert Westenhagen, 1922. **Career:** Artistic advisor and playwright, Copenhagen, then directed first film, 1910; worked in German film industry, 1911-22; manager of "Grand" film theatre, Copenhagen, 1922-47. **Died:** 26 December 1947.

Films as Director:

1910 *Afgrunden* (*The Abyss*)

1911 *Den sorte Drøm*; *Hulda Rasmussen or Dyrekøbt Glimmer* (*When Passion Blinds Honesty*); *Aedel Daad or Den store Flyver* (*Generosity*); *Gennem Kamp til Sejr* (*Through Trials to Victory*); *Der fremde Vogel*; *Die Verräterin*; *Heisses Blut*; *In dem grossen Augenblick*; *Nachtfalter*; *Zigeunerblut* (*Gypsy Blood*)

1912 *Den hvide Slavehandel III or Det berygtede Hus; Das Mädchen ohne Vaterland* (*Nina, In the Hands of the Impostors*); *Der Totentanz*; *Die arme Jenny*; *Die Kinder des Generals*; *Die Macht des Goldes*; *Jugend und Tollheit*; *Komødianten*; *Wenn die Maske fällt*; *Zum Tode gehetz*

1913 *Der Tod in Sevilla*; *Die Filmprimadonna*; *Die Sünden der Vater*; *Die Suffragette*; *Engelein*; *S.I.*

1914 *Aschenbrødel*; *Das Feuer*; *Das Kind ruft*; *Die ewige Nacht*; *Die Tochter der Landstrasse*; *Engeleins Hochzeit*; *Vordertreppe und Hintertreppe*; *Weisse Rosen*; *Zapatas Bande*

1916 *Der rote Streifen*

1917 *Der breite Weg*; *Die Gespensterstunde*; *Die Vergangenheit rächt sich*; *Die verschlossene Tür*; *Klosterfriede*
1918 *Das sterbende Modell*; *Das verhängnisvolle Andenken*; *Der Schmuck des Rajah*; *Die Kleptomanin*; *Die neue Dalila*; *Vera Panina*
1919 *Das Spiel von Liebe und Tod*; *Mein Mann—der Nachtredakteur*
1920 *Der Abgrund der Seelen*; *Der Liebes-Korridor*; *So ein Mädel*; *Weltbrand*
1921 *Christian Wahnschaffe*; *Der vergiftete Brunnen*; *Die Insel der Verschollenen*
1922 *Hanneles Himmelfahrt*
1926 *Lykkehjulet* (*The Gay Huskies*)

Publications

By GAD: book—

Filmen: Dens Midler og Maal, Copenhagen, 1919; published as *Der Film: seine Mittel—seine Ziele,* 1921.

On GAD: article—

Wollenberg, H.H., obituary in *Penguin Film Review* (London), September 1948.

* * *

"The part he played in the early history of European film art can be compared with that of D.W. Griffith in America," wrote H.H. Wollenberg in his obituary of Urban Gad. These kind words are—to put it mildly—an exaggeration of Urban Gad's importance in the history and development of the film. Considering his total output, Urban Gad might better be characterized as a cultivated craftsman, who was mainly occupied with the handling of actors. Considering his background—he came from a high-society milieu with a cultural leaning—and his work as a dramatic consultant for Copenhagen theaters, this is quite natural. He was an intellectual with a great affection for and belief in the film as an artistic means of expression. His book *The Film: Its Means and Ends,* published in 1919 and two years later translated into German, was a very intelligent, open-minded, and stimulating theoretical work, remarkable qualities given the

Urban Gad: Poul Reumert and Asta Nielsen in *Afgrunden*

lack of respect that the medium of film had from most intellectuals at the time.

Gad's position in early film history is secured by one work. *Afgrunden,* his first work, was written and directed by Gad with the assistance of the experienced cameraman Alfred Lind. The story was about a young bourgeois girl who is infatuated with a circus artist. She abandons her quiet and safe life, follows the performer, and in the end she murders him in a rage of jealousy. *Afgrunden* introduced the erotic melodrama, with a background of social contrast, which became in the next few years a Danish specialty and an influence on international film. Gad had written the role of the girl for Asta Nielsen. She made her screen debut in the film and was an instant sensation. Her sensuality and frankness shocked the audience and one scene, in which Nielsen performs a gaucho dance with Poul Reumert, the leading man, was a hitherto unseen demonstration of sexual provocation. Urban Gad had created the first European film star.

Gad was known for his meticulous care when filming, and he had a reputation for being a very demanding director. In the next two films, made for Nordisk before he went to Germany, he used more sets than was customary. Gad left Denmark with Asta Nielsen. He wrote and directed thirty-four of her films until 1914, when they separated. Asta Nielsen rose to stardom, but Gad never played an important part in German film. After a couple of films in Denmark in the 1920s he left film production in 1926. For the rest of his life, though, he was held in great esteem as the manager of one of Copenhagen's most prestigious cinemas.

—Ib Monty

GANCE, Abel

Nationality: French. **Born:** Paris, 25 October 1889. **Education:** Collège de Chantilly; Collège Chaptal, Paris, baccalaureate 1906. Served with Service Cinématographique et Photographique de l'Armée, 1917. **Family:** Married (second wife) actress Odette Vérité, 1933. Daughter: Clarisse (Mme. Jacques Raynaud). **Career:** Actor at Théâtre du Parc, Brussels, 1908-09; began selling screenplays to Gaumont, 1909; formed production company, Le Film Français, 1911; artistic director of Le Film d'Art, 1917; after death of first wife, travelled to United States, 1921; patented widescreen "Polyvision" process, 1926; patented "Perspective Sonore," stereophonic sound process, 1929; directed *Marie Tudor* for television, 1965; lived in Nice, worked on screenplay for *Christophe Colomb* project, first begun in 1939, 1970s; reassembled *Napoléon* premiered in New York, 1981. **Awards:** Gold Medal, Union Française des Inventeurs, and Cinérama Gold Medal, Société des Auteurs, 1952; Théâtre de l'Empire named for Gance, Paris, 1961; Grand prix national de Cinéma, 1974; César Award, 1980; Commandeur de la Légion d'honneur; Grand officier de l'ordre national du Merité, et des Arts et des Lettres. **Died:** In Paris, 10 November 1981.

Films as Director:

1911 *La Digue, ou Pour sauver la Hollande* (+ sc)
1912 *Le Nègre blanc* (+ sc, role); *Il y a des pieds au plafond* (+ sc); *Le Masque d'horreur* (+ sc)
1915 *Un drame au Château d'Acre* (*Les Morts reviennent-ils?*) (+ sc); *Ecce Homo* (+ sc) (unfinished)
1916 *La Folie du Docteur Tube* (+ sc); *L'Enigme de dix heures* (+ sc); *Le Fleur des ruines* (+ sc); *L'Heroïsme de Paddy* (+ sc); *Fioritures* (*La Source de beauté*) (+ sc); *Le Fou de la falaise* (+ sc); *Ce que les flots racontent* (+ sc); *Le Périscope* (+ sc): *Barberousse* (+ sc); *Les Gaz mortels* (*Le Brouillard sur la ville*) (+ sc); *Strass et compagnie* (+ sc)
1917 *Le Droit à la vie* (+ sc); *La Zone de la mort* (+ sc); *Mater Dolorosa* (+ sc)
1918 *La Dixième Symphonie* (+ sc); *Le Soleil noir* (+ sc) (unfinished)
1919 ***J'Accuse*** (+ sc)
1923 *La Roué* (+ sc); *Au secours!* (+ sc)
1927 ***Napoléon*** *(Napoléon vu par Abel Gance)* (+ sc)
1928 *Marines et Cristeaux* (+ sc) (experimental footage for "Polyvision")
1931 *La Fin du monde* (+ sc)
1932 *Mater Dolorosa* (+ sc)
1934 *Poliche* (+ sc); *La Dame aux Camélias* (+ sc); *Napoléon Bonaparte* (+ sc) (sound version, with additional footage)
1935 *Le Roman d'un jeune homme pauvre* (+ sc); *Lucrèce Borgia*
1936 *Un Grande Amour de Beethoven* (*The Life and Loves of Beethoven*) (+ sc); *Jérome Perreau, héro des barricades* (*The Queen and the Cardinal*); *Le Voleur de femmes* (+ sc)
1937 *J'accuse* (*That They May Live*) (+ sc)
1939 *Louise* (+ co-sc); *Le Paradis perdu* (*Four Flights to Love*) (+ co-sc)
1941 *La Vénus aveugle* (+ sc)
1942 *Le Capitaine Fracasse* (+ co-sc)
1944 *Manolete* (+ sc) (unfinished)
1954 *Quatorze Juillet* (+ sc); *La Tour de Nesle* (+ sc)
1956 *Magirama* (+ sc, co-pr) (demonstration of "Polyvision" in color)
1960 *Austerlitz* (co-d, + co-sc)
1964 *Cyrano et d'Artagnan* (+ co-sc)
1971 *Bonaparte et la révolution* (+ sc, co-pr)

Other Films:

1909 *Le Portrait de Mireille* (Perret) (sc); *Le Glas du Père Césaire* (+ sc); *La Légende de l'arc-en-ciel* (sc); *Molière* (Perret) (role)
1909/10 Some Max Linder short comedies (role as Max's brother)
1910 *Paganini* (sc); *La Fin de Paganini* (sc); *Le Crime de Grand-père* (Perret) (sc); *Le Roi des parfums* (sc); *L'Aluminité* (sc); *L'Auberge rouge* (sc); *Le Tragique Amour de Mona Lisa* (Capellani) (sc)
1911 *Cyrano et D'Assoucy* (Capellani) (sc); *Un Clair de lune sous Richelieu* (Capellani) (sc); *L'Électrocuté* (Morlhon) (sc)
1912 *Une Vengeance d'Edgar Poe* (Capellani) (sc); *La Mort du Duc d'Enghien* (Capellani) (sc); *La Conspiration des drapeaux* (sc); *La Pierre philosophe* (sc)
1914 *L'Infirmière* (Pouctal) (sc)
1920 *L'Atre* (Boudrioz) (pr)
1929 *Napoléon auf St. Helena* (*Napoléon à Saint-Hélène*) (Pick) (sc)
1933 *Le Maître de forges* (Rivers) (sc, supervisor)
1953 *Lumière et l'invention du cinématographe* (*Louis Lumière*) (Paviot) (commentary, narration)
1954 *La Reine Margot* (Dréville) (sc)

Publications

By GANCE: books—

J'Accuse, Paris, 1922.
Napoléon vu par Abel Gance, Paris, 1927.

Abel Gance on the set of *Napoléon*

La Roué, scénario original arrangé par Jean Arroy, Paris, 1930.
Prisme, Paris, 1930.
La Fin du Monde, scénario arrangé par Joachim Renez, Paris, 1931.
Mater Dolorosa, scénario original arrangé par Joachim Renez, Paris, 1932.
Napoléon, as seen by Abel Gance, edited by B. Ballard, London, 1990.

By GANCE: articles—

"Qu'est-ce que le cinématographe? Un sixième art," in *Intelligence du cinématographe,* by Marcel L'Herbier, Paris, 1946.
"Les nouveaux chapitres de notre syntaxe," in *Cahiers du Cinéma* (Paris), October 1953.
"Départ vers la polyvision," in *Cahiers du Cinéma* (Paris), December 1954.
"Entretien avec Jacques Rivette et François Truffaut," in *Cahiers du Cinéma* (Paris), January 1955.
"*The Kingdom of the Earth,*" in *Film Culture* (New York), December 1957.
"Film as Incantation: An Interview with Abel Gance," in *Film Comment* (New York), March/April 1974.

On GANCE: books—

Arroy, Jean, *En tournant "Napoléon" avec Abel Gance,* Paris, 1927.
Daria, Sophie, *Abel Gance, hier et demain,* Paris, 1959.
Icart, Roger, *Abel Gance,* Toulouse, 1960.
Brownlow, Kevin, *The Parade's Gone By,* New York, 1969.
Kramer, Steven, and James Welsh, *Abel Gance,* Boston, 1978.
Icart, Roger, *Abel Gance; ou, Le Promethée foudroyé,* Lausanne, 1983.
King, Norman, *Abel Gance: A Politics of Spectacle,* London, 1984.
Groppali, Enrico, *Abel Gance,* Florence, 1986.

On GANCE: articles—

Epstein, Jean, "Mon ami Gance," in *Cahiers du Cinéma* (Paris), August/September 1955.
"Gance Issue" of *L'Ecran* (Paris), April/May 1958.
Lenning, Arthur, "*Napoléon* and *La Roue,*" in *The Persistence of Vision,* edited by Joseph McBride, Madison, Wisconsin, 1968.
Brownlow, Kevin, "*Bonaparte et la révolution,*" in *Sight and Sound* (London), Winter 1971/72.
Welsh, J.M., and S.P. Kramer, "Abel Gance's Accusation Against War," in *Cinema Journal* (Evanston), Spring 1975.
Gilliatt, Penelope, in *New Yorker,* 6 September 1976.
Drew, W.M., "Abel Gance: Prometheus Bound," in *Take One* (Montreal), July 1978.
Nerguy, C., and Y. Alion, "*Un Grand Amour de Beethoven,*" in *Avant-Scène du Cinéma* (Paris), 1 October 1978.
Brownlow, Kevin, "Abel Gance," in *Film Dope* (London), September 1979.
Allen, W., "*Napoléon* reconstructed," in *Stills* (London), Autumn 1981.
Obituary, in the *New York Times,* 11 November 1981.

Cluny, C.M., "Abel Gance: trop grand pour le cinéma?," in *Cinéma* (Paris), December 1981.
Lafaye, C., obituary, in *Cinéma* (Paris), January 1982.
Riley, B., obituary, in *Film Comment* (New York), January/February 1982.
Jeancolas, J.-P., "Abel Gance entre *Napoléon* et *Philippe Pétain,*" in *Positif* (Paris), June 1982.
Icart, R., C. Lafaye, and L. Martin, "Tumultueux Abel Gance," in *Revue du Cinéma* (Paris), May 1983.
King, Norman, "The Sounds of Silents," in *Screen* (London), May/June 1984.
Virmaux, A. and O., "Deux amis," in *Cinématographe* (Paris), November 1986.

On GANCE: films—

Ford, Charles, and Jacques Guillon, *Les Éloquents,* France, 1956.
Kaplan, Nelly, *Abel Gance, hier et demain (Abel Gance, Yesterday and Tomorrow),* Paris, 1964.
Brownlow, Kevin, *Abel Gance—the Charm of Dynamite,* London, 1968.

* * *

Abel Gance's career as a director was long and flamboyant. He wrote his first scripts in 1909, turning to directing a couple of years later, and made his last feature, *Cyrano et d'Artagnan,* in 1964. As late as 1971 he re-edited a four-hour version of his Napoleon footage to make *Bonaparte et la révolution,* and he lived long enough to see his work again reach wide audiences.

Gance's original aspirations were as a playwright, and throughout his life he treasured the manuscript of his verse tragedy *La Victoire de Samothrace,* written for Sarah Bernhardt and on the brink of production when the war broke out in 1914. If Gance's beginnings in the film industry he then despised were unremarkable, he showed his characteristic audacity and urge for experimentation with an early work, the unreleased *La Folie du Docteur Tube,* which made great use of distorting lenses, in 1916. He learned his craft in a dozen or more films during 1916 and 1917—the best remembered of which are *Les Gaz mortels, Barberousse,* and *Mater dolorosa.* He reached fresh heights with a somewhat pretentious and melodramatic study of a great and suffering composer, *La Dixième Symphonie.* Even more significant was his ambitious and eloquent antiwar drama, *J'Accuse,* released in 1919. These films established him as the leading French director of his generation and gave him a preeminence he was not to lose until the coming of sound.

The 1920s saw the release of just three Gance films. If *Au secours!*, a comedy starring his friend Max Linder, is something of a lighthearted interlude, the other two are towering landmarks of silent cinema. *La Roue* began as a simple melodramatic tale, but in the course of six months scripting and a year's location shooting, the project took on quite a new dimension. In the central figure of Sisif, Gance seems to have struggled to create an amalgam of Oedipus, Sisyphus, and Lear. Meanwhile portions of the film that were eventually cut apparently developed a social satire of such ferocity that the railway unions demanded its excision. The most expensive film as yet made in France, its production was again delayed when the death of Gance's wife caused him to abandon work and take a five month trip to the United States.

Like his previous work, *La Roue* had been conceived and shot in the pre-1914 style of French cinema, which was based on a conception of film as a series of long takes, each containing a significant section of the action, rather than as a succession of scenes made up of intercut shots of different lengths, taken from varying distances. But in Hollywood, where he met D.W. Griffith, Gance came into contact with the new American style of editing. Upon his return to France, Gance spent a whole year reediting his film. On its release in 1923 *La Roue* proved to be one of the stunning films of the decade. Even in its shortened version—comprising a prologue and four parts—the film had a combined running time of nearly eight hours.

Gance's imagination and energy at this period seemed limitless. Almost immediately he plunged into an even vaster project whose title clearly reflects his personal approach, *Napoléon va par Abel Gance.* If *La Roue* was particularly remarkable for its editing (certain sequences are classic moments of French 1920s avant-garde experimentation), *Napoléon* attracted immediate attention for its incredibly mobile camerawork, created by a team under the direction of Jules Kruger. *Napoléon* thus emerges as a key masterpiece of French cinema at a time when visual experimentation took precedence over narrative and the disorganization of production offered filmmakers the chance to produce extravagant and ambitious personal works within the heart of the commercial industry. Gance's conception of himself as visionary filmmaker and of Napoleon as a master of his destiny points to the roots of Gance's style in the nineteenth century and his romantic view of the artist as hero. The scope of Gance's film, bursting into triple screen effects at the moment of Napoleon's climactic entry into Italy, remains staggering even today.

The 1920s in France was a period of considerable creative freedom. Given this atmosphere, a widespread urge to experiment with the full potential of the medium was apparent. If the freedom came from the lack of a tightly controlled studio system, the desire to explore new forms of filmic expression can be traced to a reaction against the situation imposed by Pathé and Gaumont before 1914, when film was seen as a purely commercial product, underfinanced and devoid of artistic or personal expression. This had been the cinema in which Gance had made his debut, and he was one of those striving most forcefully in the 1920s both to increase the possibilities for personal expressiveness and to widen the technical scope of cinema. He pioneered new styles of cutting and camerawork, as well as widescreen and multiscreen techniques.

It is ironic, then, that the advent of the greatest technical innovation of the period left Gance stranded. The explanation for this lies less in the irrelevance of sound to his personal vision of the medium—he was pioneering a new stereophonic system with *La Fin du monde* as early as 1929—than the fact that new forms of tighter production control were implemented as a result of the greater costs associated with sound filmmaking.

The 1930s emerge as a sad era for a man accustomed to being in the forefront of the French film industry. Gance, whose mind had always teemed with new and original projects, was now reduced to remaking his old successes: sound versions of *Mater dolorosa* in 1932, *Napoléon Bonaparte* in 1934, and *J'accuse* in 1937. Otherwise, the projects he was allowed to make were largely adaptations of fashionable stage dramas or popular novels: *Le Maître de forges, Poliche, La Dame aux camélias,* and *Le Roman d'un jeune homme pauvre.* In the late 1930s he was able to treat subjects in which his taste for grandly heroic figures is again apparent: Savonarola in *Lucrèce Borgia* and the great composer—played by Harry Baur—in *Un Grand Amour de Beethoven,* but by 1942, when he made *Le Capitaine Fracasse,* Gance's career seemed to have come to an end.

Though a dozen years were to pass before he directed another feature film, Gance maintained his incredible level of energy. Refusing to be beaten, he continued his experiments with "polyvision" which were to culminate in his *Magirama* spectacle. He eventually made three further features, all historical dramas in which his zest, if not the old towering imagination, is still apparent: *La Tour de Nesle, Austerlitz,* and *Cyrano et d'Artagnan.*

The French 1920s cinema of which Gance is the major figure has consistently been undervalued by film historians, largely because its rich experimentation with visual style and expressiveness was not accompanied by an similar concern with the development of film narrative. Gance's roots were in the nineteenth century romantic tradition, and despite his literary background, he, like his contemporaries, was willing to accept virtually any melodramatic story that would allow him to pursue his visual interests. For this reason French 1920s work has been marginalized in accounts of film history that see the growth of storytelling techniques as the central unifying factor. The rediscovery of Gance's *Napoléon* in the 1980s, though—thanks largely to twenty years of effort by Kevin Brownlow—has made clear to the most skeptical the force and mastery achieved in the years preceding the advent of sound, and restored Gance's reputation as a master of world cinema.

—Roy Armes

GARCÍA BERLANGA, Luis

Nationality: Spanish. **Born:** Luis García-Berlanga Marti in Valencia, 12 July 1921. **Education:** Studied at Jesuit school, Switzerland; Valencia University; IIEC (School of Cinema), Madrid, 1947-50. **Military Service:** Served in División Azul (Blue Division) of Spanish volunteers with German forces on Russian front, early 1940s. **Career:** Painter and poet, 1942-47; with Antonio Bardem, directed first film, 1951; several projects banned by censor, 1950s; began collaboration with writer Rafael Azcona on *Plácido,* 1961; Professor at IIEC, 1970s; President of Filmoteca Nacional, 1980s.

Films as Director:

1948/49 *Paseo sobre una guerra antigua* (as IIEC student); *Tres cantos* (IIEC student); *El circo* (+ sc, ed) (IIEC student)
1951 *Esa pareja feliz* (*That Happy Couple*) (co-d, ph, co-sc)
1952 *¡Bienvenido, Mr. Marshall!* (*Welcome, Mr. Marshall*) (+ co-sc)
1953 *Novio a la vista* (*Fiancé in sight*) (+ co-sc)
1956 *Calabuch* (+ co-sc)
1957 *Los jueves, milagro* (*Thursdays, Miracle*) (+ co-sc)
1961 *Plácido* (+ co-sc)
1962 "La muerte y el leñador" ("Death and the Woodcutter") episode of *Las cuatro verdades* (+ co-sc)
1963 ***El verdugo*** (*The Executioner*; *Not On Your Life*) (+ co-sc)

Luis García Berlanga: *Plácido*

1967 *Las pirañas* (+ co-sc)
1969 *Vivan los novios* (*Long Live the Bride and Groom*) (+ co-sc)
1973 *Tamaño natural* (*Life Size*) (+ co-sc)
1978 *La escopeta nacional* (*The National Rifle*; *The Spanish Shotgun*) (+ co-sc)
1979 *Cuentos eróticos* (*Erotic Tales*) (collectively directed)
1980 *Patrimonio nacional* (+ co-sc)

Other Films:

1953 *Sangre y luces* (Muñoz) (sc) (Spanish language version of Georges Rouquier's *Sang et lumières*)
1955 *Familia provisional* (Rovira Beleta) (co-sc)
1967 *No somos de piedra* (*We Are Not Made Out of Stone*) (Summers) (role)
1968 *Sharon vestida de rojo* (Lorente) (role)
1971 *Apunte sobre Ana* (*Memorandum on Ana*) (Galán) (role)

Publications

By GARCÍA BERLANGA: articles—

"The Day I Refused to Work," in *Films and Filming* (London), December 1961.
"Cara a cara ... Bardem—Berlanga," in *Cinema 2002* (Madrid), July/August 1980.
"Berlanga Life Size," interview with Katherine Kovacs, in *The Quarterly Review of Film Studies* (Pleasantville, New York), Spring 1983.

On GARCÍA BERLANGA: books—

Santolaya, Ernesto, *Luis G. Berlanga,* Vitoria, 1979.
Perucha, Julio Pérez, *Sobre Luis G. Berlanga,* Valencia, 1981.
Higginbotham, Virginia, *Spanish Film Under Franco,* Austin, Texas, 1988.

On GARCÍA BERLANGA: articles—

Cobos, Juan, "Spanish Fighter," in *Films and Filming* (London), February 1958.
"*Grandeur nature,*" in *Avant-Scène du Cinéma* (Paris), November 1974.
Les, J. Hernandez, "Luis Berlanga aujourd'hui et hier," in *Jeune Cinéma* (Paris), April/May 1979.
Acosta, J.L., "Berlanga—B. Wilder: Buscando un punto común," in *Cinema 2002* (Madrid), April 1980.
Marías, Miguel, "El Patrimonio de Berlanga," in *Casablanca* (Madrid), April 1981.
Guarner, José Luis, "Luis G. Berlanga," in *International Film Guide 1981,* London, 1982.
"Spanish Cinema Section" of *Cinéma* (Paris), June 1984.
Screen International (London), 25 June 1988.

* * *

For many years in Spain strict censorship guidelines inhibited the development of a vital and creative film industry. The first original *auteur* of the post-Civil War period was Luis García Berlanga. When he began to make movies in the early 1950s, Berlanga and fellow filmmaker Juan Antonio Bardem were referred to as the two palm trees in the desert of Spanish film. Since then, and in spite of the fact that he could make relatively few films under Franco, Berlanga has remained one of Spain's foremost talents.

In the early years, the most important influence on Berlanga's filmmaking was Italian neo-realism. At the Conversations of Salamanca (1955) Berlanga and other young directors enthusiastically supported it as an antidote to Francoist cinema, a way of making authentic films that dealt with the everyday problems of ordinary people. From his first movie, *Esa pareja feliz,* which he co-directed with Bardem in 1951, to his "trilogy" on the Spanish aristocracy, Berlanga has remained true to the spirit of Salamanca.

In many movies he has exposed the pitfalls of Spanish society and satirized those institutions or individuals who take themselves too seriously, often using black humor to deflate their pretentions. Berlanga's sympathies are with the underdogs of whatever social class, those who are victims of fate, institutions, or other forces they cannot control. In a number of his films we follow the efforts of an individual who wants to achieve something or attain some goal, struggles to do so, and in the end is defeated, ending up in the same or in a worse situation than before. This unfortunate outcome reflects Berlanga's pessimism about a society in which the individual is powerless and in danger of being devoured. There are no winners in Berlanga's movies; all of the victories are Pyrrhic. But never one to deliver messages or lessons, Berlanga expresses his pessimistic viewpoint with such verve, vitality and humor that audiences leave the theatre elated with the spontaneity and inventiveness of his films.

Berlanga prefers working with groups of characters rather than concentrating on the fate of a single protagonist. Rarely does one individual dominate the action. Usually we move from one person to the next so that our point of view on the action is constantly shifting. This approach is supported by Berlanga's distinctive camera style. He tends to use very long takes in which the camera surreptitiously follows the movement of the characters, the shot lasting as long as the sequence. (In *Patrimonio nacional* there are some takes that last six or seven minutes.) These sequences are not, however, the carefully arranged and choreographed efforts of a Jancsó. As Berlanga explains it, until he begins shooting he has no specific setup in mind: "What I do is organize the actors' movements and then tell the cameraman how to follow them. When we bump into some obstacle, we stop shooting." In shooting the often feverish activities of his characters in this way, Berlanga gives a fluid, spontaneous feeling to his films. His predilection for these shots expresses what Berlanga calls his "god complex"—his desire to be everywhere at once and to express the totality of any scene.

In his scrutiny of contemporary Spanish life, Berlanga is also attached to much older Spanish literary and cultural traditions, most notably to that of the picaresque novel, in which a *pícaro* or rogue is thrust out into the world and forced to fend for himself. At the bottom of the social heap, the *pícaro* is afforded "a worm's eye view" of society and learns to be tricky in order to survive. The *pícaro* keeps hoping and waiting for a miracle, a sudden change in fate that will change his or her fortune in one stroke. Berlanga's *pícaros,* whether they be naive like Plácido (*Plácido*) or noble like the Marquis of Leguineche (*Patrimonio nacional*), share the same hopes and tenacious desire to survive. These characters, like Berlanga himself, are deeply attached to Spanish cultural traditions. In fact, one might even consider Berlanga to be a sort of picaresque hero who managed to survive the vagaries of the Franco regime and its system of censorship. A popular director since *Welcome Mr. Marshall,* Berlanga has gone on to even greater success since Franco's death with *La escopeta nacional,* a satiric look at a hunting party of Spain's notables during the Franco regime. In this irreverent and amusing comedy and in its two sequels, Berlanga introduced himself and his vision of his country to a new generation of Spaniards.

—Katherine Singer Kovács

GARNETT, Tay

Nationality: American. **Born:** Los Angeles, 13 June 1894. **Education:** Los Angeles High School. **Military Service:** Joined Naval Air Service, 1917; studied at Massachusetts Institute of Technology and in Navy Schools, then instructor at San Diego Air Station. **Family:** Married 1) actress Patsy Ruth Miller (divorced); 2) actress and writer Helga Moray (divorced); 3) actress Mari Aldon (divorced). **Career:** Went to Hollywood, 1920; scriptwriter, gag man (for Hal Roach and Mack Sennett), and stunt man, early 1920s; scriptwriter on De Mille unit at Pathé, 1927; directed first film, *Celebrity,* 1928; formed Thor Productions with Bert Friedlob, 1949; director for television, including *Wagon Train, Rawhide,* and *The Untouchables,* from late 1950s. **Died:** In 1977.

Films as Director:

1928 *Celebrity* (+ co-sc); *The Spieler* (*The Spellbinder*) (+ co-adapt)
1929 *The Flying Fool* (+ co-sc); *Oh, Yeah!* (*No Brakes*) (co-d, adapt, co-lyrics)
1930 *Officer O'Brien*; *Her Man* (+ co-story)
1931 *Bad Company* (+ co-sc); *One Way Passage*
1932 *Prestige* (+ co-adapt); *Okay America* (*The Penalty of Fame*)
1933 *Destination Unknown*; *S.O.S. Iceberg* (English-language version of Fanck's *S.O.S. Eisberg*; location footage shot by Fanck)
1935 *Professional Soldier*; *China Seas*; *She Couldn't Take It* (*Woman Tamer*)
1937 *Love Is News*; *Slave Ship*; *Stand-in*
1938 *Joy of Living*; *Trade Winds* (+ story)
1939 *Eternally Yours* (+ bit role as pilot)
1940 *Slightly Honorable*; *Seven Sinners*
1941 *Cheers for Miss Bishop*
1942 *My Favorite Spy*
1943 *Bataan*; *The Cross of Lorraine*
1944 *Mrs. Parkington*; *See Here, Private Hargrove* (co-d with Ruggles, uncredited)
1945 *The Valley of Decision*
1946 *The Postman Always Rings Twice*
1947 *Wild Harvest*
1948 *A Connecticut Yankee* (*A Yankee in King Arthur's Court*)
1950 *The Fireball* (+ co-sc); *Cause for Alarm!*
1951 *Soldiers Three*
1952 *One Minute to Zero*
1953 *Main Street to Broadway*
1954 *The Black Knight*
1955 *Seven Wonders of the World* (d Indian sequence only)
1960 *A Terrible Beauty* (*The Night Fighters*)
1963 *Cattle King* (*Guns of Wyoming*)
1970 *The Delta Factor* (+ pr, sc)
1975 *Challenge to be Free* (co-d, + role) (completed 1972); *Timber Tramps* (completed 1972)

Other Films:

1922 *Broken Chains* (Holubar) (co-sc, uncredited); *The Hottentot* (Horne) (co-sc)
1924 *Don't Park There!* (Wagner) (co-sc); *Off His Trolley* (Cline) (co-story); *Honeymoon Hardships* (Cedar) (co-story)
1925 *Somewhere in Wrong* (Pembroke) (titles); *The Snow Hawk* (Pembroke) (titles); *Half a Man* (Sweet) (titles); *Who's Your Friend* (Sheldon) (continuity)
1926 *That's My Baby* (Beaudine) (co-sc, uncredited); *Up in Mabel's Room* (Hopper) (co-sc); *The Strong Man* (Capra) (co-sc, uncredited); *There You Are!* (Sedgwick) (co-sc); *The Cruise of the Jasper B.* (Horne) (co-adapt)
1927 *Rubber Tires* (*10,000 Reward*) (Hale) (co-sc); *Getting Gertie's Garter* (Hopper) (co-sc, uncredited); *White Gold* (Howard) (co-sc); *Long Pants* (Capra) (co-sc, uncredited); *No Control* (Sidney) (co-sc); *The Wise Wife* (Hopper) (co-sc); *Turkish Delight* (Sloane) (sc)
1928 *Skyscraper* (Higgin) (co-sc); *The Cop* (Crisp) (sc); *Power* (Higgin) (sc)
1941 *Unexpected Uncle* (Godfrey) (pr); *Weekend for Three* (Reis) (pr)

Publications

By GARNETT: books—

A Man Laughs Back, 1935.
Light Up Your Torches and Pull Up Your Tights, New Rochelle, New York, 1973.

By GARNETT: articles—

"The Director's Problems," in *Photoplay* (New York), September 1939.
"Les 44 films de Tay Garnett," with Claude Beylie, in *Ecran* (Paris), April and May 1977.
"Tay Garnett," with J.-L. Passek, in *Cinéma* (Paris), December 1977.
"Tay Garnett Speaking," an interview with R. Fernandez, in *Velvet Light Trap* (Madison, Wisconsin), Spring 1978.

On GARNETT: articles—

Thomas, B., "Tay Garnett: A Man for All Films," in *Action* (Los Angeles), September/October 1972.
Navacelle, T., "Hommage à Tay Garnett," in *Cinéma* (Paris), January 1978.
Salmi, M., "Tay Garnett," in *Film Dope* (London), September 1979.
Viviani, C., "Tay Garnett (1898-1977)," in *Avant-Scène du Cinéma* (Paris), 1 April 1980.
Gallagher, J., "Tay Garnett," in *Films in Review* (New York), December 1981.
Classic Images (Muscatine, Iowa), November 1984.

* * *

Tay Garnett's career can best be described as chaotic. He has directed comedies and dramas, war films and women's pictures, a couple of classics, more than a couple of solid entertainments, and one too many turkeys.

Garnett's career did not develop in a cohesive manner or one that can be successfully charted. Most of his best films were made during the early part of his career. *Her Man,* a Frankie and Johnny story set in Cuba, is exceptional for its period ambience and smooth camerawork. *One Way Passage,* a sophisticated drama about a romance between terminally ill Kay Francis and con man William Powell, remains a woman's picture of the highest caliber. *China Seas,* a melodrama with Clark Gable, Jean Harlow, and a stellar cast aboard a Hong Kong-bound ship, is corny but exciting. *Stand-in* is a funny, underrated satire of Hollywood.

Garnett's one outstanding post-1940 feature is *The Postman Always Rings Twice,* a sizzling drama of adultery and murder based on the James M. Cain story that is far superior to Bob Rafelson's 1981

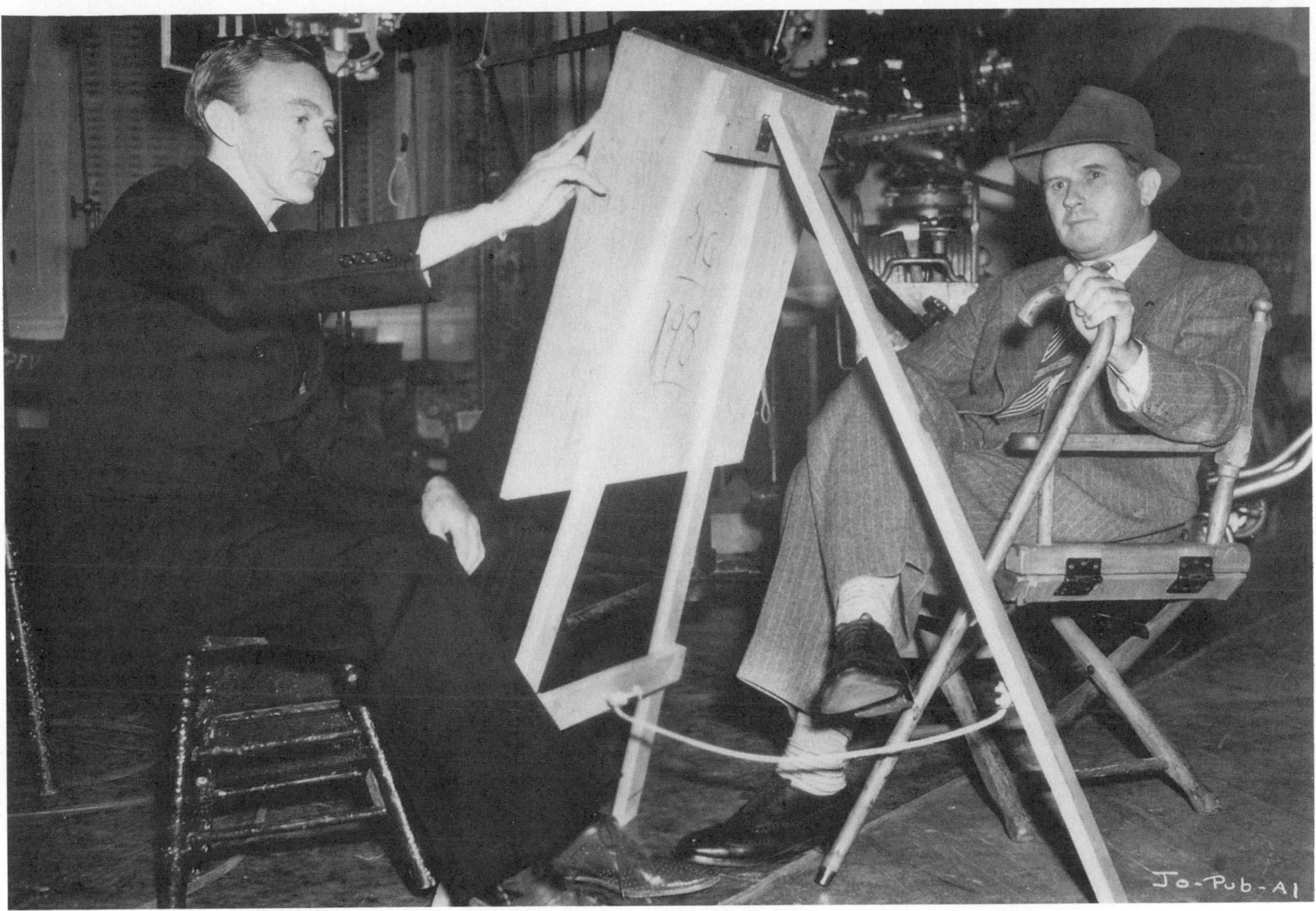

Tay Garnett (right)

remake. In fact, of all Garnett's credits, only *One Way Passage* and *The Postman Always Rings Twice* approach the level of greatness. The rest are all good examples of their respective types, but are in no way linked by any artistic vision.

However, Garnett's films are generally evenly paced. Even in his less auspicious productions the narrative flows smoothly, and there is an effective union of background and storyline. Aware that a film was sometimes unevenly paced because it was too slow, rather than too fast, Garnett often re-shot scenes, attempting to trim them down by an all-important eight or ten seconds.

Garnett was also a keen observer of actors. When necessary, he could be stern, as with Wallace Beery, a difficult star with a large ego. Yet he was particularly patient with performers (for instance, Jean Harlow) who were not naturally gifted but were willing to work and learn. As a result, he would accentuate the strengths of his actors. He insisted on casting Humphrey Bogart, then known solely for gangster roles, as a leading man in *Stand-in*.

In 1968 Andrew Sarris wrote, "inconsistency is the hobgoblin of Tay Garnett's career, and inconsistency can never be defined satisfactorily.... For the moment, Garnett's ultimate reputation is still unusually elusive." From the late 1940s on, Garnett's films do become increasingly mediocre. At their best, however, they're likable as well as competently made, and Garnett deserves to be called an entertainer—not an uncomplimentary appellation.

—Rob Edelman

GERASIMOV, Sergei

Nationality: Soviet. **Born:** Sergei Apollinarievich Gerasimov in Zlatoust, Ural region, 21 May 1906. **Education:** Leningrad Art School; studied scenic design at State Institute of Dramatic Art, Leningrad, 1920-25. **Career:** Joined FEKS group founded by Grigori Kozintsev and Leonid Trauberg, early 1920s; directed first film, 1930; head of Acting and Directing Master Class, Lenfilm Studios, 1931-41; in charge of *Fighting Film Album No. 1,* Moscow, 1941; continued war work, in charge of official films of Yalta and Berlin conferences, 1942-44; head of Central Newsreel and Documentary Studios, Moscow, 1944; Professor, Moscow Film School (VGIK), 1944-1970s; artistic supervisor, Gorki Film Studios, 1955; served as deputy to the Supreme Soviet of the RSFSR, secretary of Soviet Union of Cinematographers, and on editorial board of *Isskustvo Kino,* 1970s. **Awards:** Red Banner of Labor, 1940 and 1950; Red Star, 1944; Peoples' Artist of USSR, 1948; State prizes, for *Uchitel,* 1941, *The Young Guard,* 1949, and *Liberated China,* 1951. **Died:** 27 November 1985.

Films as Director:

1930 *Twenty-Two Misfortunes* (co-d)
1931 *The Forest* (+ sc)
1932 *Solomon's Heart* (co-d, + sc)
1934 *Do I Love You?* (+ sc)

1936 *Semero smelykh* (*The Bold Seven*)
1938 *Komsomolsk* (+ co-sc)
1939 *Uchitel* (*Teacher*) (+ sc)
1941 *Masquerade* (+ sc, role as the stranger); *Meeting with Maxim* segment of *Fighting Film Album No. 1*; *The Old Guard*
1943 *The Invincible* (*The Unconquerable*) (co-d, + co-sc); *Film-Concert Dedicated to the Twenty-Fifth Anniversary of the Red Army* (*Cine-Concert Dedicated to the Twenty-Fifth Anniversary of the Red Army*) (co-d, + co-sc)
1944 *Great Land* (*The Mainland*) (+ sc)
1947 *Molodaya gvardiya* (*Young Guard*) (+ sc)
1950 *Liberated China* (+ sc)
1951 *Selskiy vrach* (*Country Doctor*)
1954 *Nadezhda* (+ sc)
1957/58 *Tikhy Don* (*And Quiet Flows the Don*) (+ sc)
1959 *Sputnik Speaking* (*The Sputnik Speaks*) (co-d, co-sc)
1962 *Men and Beasts* (+ sc)
1967 *Zhurnalist* (*The Journalist*) (+ sc)
1969 *U ozera* (*By the Lake*) (+ sc)
1972 *Lyubit cheloveka* (*For the Love of Man*) (+ sc)
1974 *Materi i docheri* (*Mothers and Daughters*)
1984 *Lev Tolstoj*

Other Films:

1925 *Michki protiv Youdenitsa* (*Mishka Against Yudenitch*) (Kozintsev and Trauberg) (role as the spy)
1926 *Chyortovo koleso* (*The Devil's Wheel*) (Kozintsev and Trauberg) (role as the conjuror); *Shinel* (*The Cloak*) (Kozintsev and Trauberg) (role as the card-shark); *Bratichka* (*Little Brother*) (Kozintsev and Trauberg) (role as the driver)
1927 *S.V.D.* (*The Club of the Big Deed*) (Kozintsev and Trauberg) (role as Medoks); *Someone Else's Jacket* (Boris Shpis) (role as Skalkovsky)
1929 ***Novyi Vavilon*** (*The New Babylon*) (Kozintsev and Trauberg) (asst d, role as the journalist Lutreau); *Oblomok imperii* (*Fragment of an Empire*) (Ermler) (role as the Menshevik)
1931 *Odna* (*Alone*) (Kozintsev and Trauberg) (asst d, role as the chairman of the village soviet)
1932 *Three Soldiers* (*Ivanov*) (role as Commander of the Iron Regiment)
1933 *Dezertir* (*Deserter*) (Pudovkin) (role as the bonze); *Razbudite Lenochky* (*Wake Up Lenochka*) (Kudryavtseva) (role)
1935 *The Frontier* (Dubson) (role as Yakov the Tailor)
1939 *Chapayev Is with Us* (co-sc); *Vyborgskaya storona* (*New Horizons*; *The Vyborg Side*) (Kozintsev) (role as the Socialist-Revolutionary)
1944 *The Yalta Conference* (pr supervisor)
1945 *The Berlin Conference* (pr supervisor)
1955 *Damy* (Organisyan and Kulidzhanov) (artistic supervisor)
1956 *The Road of Truth* (Frid) (sc)
1958 *Memory of the Heart* (Lioznova) (sc)
1961 *Dimy Gorina* (*Career of Dima*) (Doblatyan and Mirski) (artistic supervisor)
1962 *U Krutovo Yara* (*On the Steep Cliff*) (K. and A. Morakov) (artistic supervisor)
1963 *Venski Les* (*Vienna Woods*) (Grigoriev) (artistic supervisor)
1964 *Sostyazanie* (*Controversy*) (Mansurev) (artistic supervisor)

Publications

By GERASIMOV: book—

Vospitanie kinorezhisseva, Moscow, 1978.

By GERASIMOV: articles—

"Socialist Realism and the Soviet Cinema," in *Films and Filming* (London), December 1958.
"All Is Not Welles," in *Films and Filming* (London), September 1959.
"A Clash of Conscience," in *Films and Filming* (London), March 1961.
Interview with Roger Hudson, in *Film* (London), Spring 1969.
"V dobryi chas!'," in *Iskusstvo Kino* (Moscow), no. 10, 1976.
"Soviet Cinema: Films, Personalities, Problems," with others, in *Soviet Film* (Moscow), no. 271, 1979.
"Akyual'nost' istorii," interview with G. Maslovskij, in *Iskusstvo Kino* (Moscow), September 1980.
Interview in *Isskustvo Kino* (Moscow), December 1982.
Interview in *Soviet Film* (Moscow), February 1984.
Film a Doba (Prague), May 1986.

On GERASIMOV: articles—

Vronskaya, J., "Recent Russian Cinema," in *Film* (London), Summer 1971.
"Sergei Gerasimov," in *Soviet Film* (Moscow), no. 261, 1979.
Obituary in *Variety* (New York), 4 December 1985.
Obituary in *Soviet Film* (Moscow), no. 6, 1987.

* * *

The very survival of the brilliant, original, almost iconoclastic Sergei Gerasimov through turbulent eras of Soviet history has tended to obscure the importance of his early contributions to cinema. The somewhat stern image of a grim conservative headmaster he seemed to project to students at the Moscow Film School (VGIK) in the early 1970s was an antithesis of his prewar self.

Gerasimov's career started in Leningrad when, after graduating as a theatrical designer, he joined the "Factory of Eccentric Actors" (FEKS). He became one of the strongest and most original actors in Soviet silent cinema, with a special attraction to complex roles. Together with what he learned from Kozintsev and Trauberg, who directed most of the productions in which he appeared, his deep study of acting was an important part of Gerasimov's apprenticeship as a filmmaker.

Gerasimov cut his directorial teeth on three silent productions in the early 1930s, but it was not until 1936, with his first sound film *Semero Smelykh* (*The Bold 7*), that Gerasimov came into his own as a major talent. In this and his next film (*Komsomolsk*) he broke new ground in his choice of subject and in his sincere and unusually successful attempt to portray ordinary young people as varied, breathing, living human beings rather than animated heroic sculptures. His sympathetic direction of his young cast, together with his romantic but naturalistic scripts (pitting teams of young people against the elements) achieved something approaching the elusive ideal of socialist realism.

Gerasimov's works were by far the most successful films of their genre during the 1930s. *Uchitel* (*Teacher*), released in 1939, completed his trio of lyrical but unpretentious evocations of the new Soviet generation in the Russian countryside. *Uchitel* told the tale of a young man who leaves the bright lights of the city to return to his native village as a schoolmaster. This film begins, perhaps, to show some signs of the stress imposed by the increasing rigidity of official dogma, for it does not achieve the freshness of the previous two films. Yet, sadly, some seven years later Gerasimov castigated himself for not having adhered more strictly to the party line. "I loved the film," he wrote, "and I still love it, despite the fact that it is far too polished ... and not a little too obsequious in its attitude to Art." By this time the war had intervened and Gerasimov (in 1944) had become a member of the Communist Party.

Besides Gerasimov's rural trilogy, his only other prewar feature, *Masquerade,* was a lavish version of Lermontov's verse tragedy. He had certainly set himself an uphill task in trying to combine his FEKS style with the tradition of stage drama and dialogue in verse, although his own performance as "The Stranger" was an echo of his old FEKS philosophy and the Leningrad setting was spectacular. Although successful at the time, the film was criticized by the director himself, a stern exponent of "socialist self-criticism." While he admitted that the film had helped him "refine his art," he considered it "haphazard and unplanned" and lacking sufficient appreciation of Lermontov's particular genius.

During World War II, Gerasimov was put in charge of the documentary film studios. There he brought together the talents of feature directors and documentarists and once more proved his flair for encouraging good work from others. This led to his appointment in 1944 as head of the directing and acting workshops of the Moscow Film School (VGIK). Occupying this seminal position through the following thirty years, he had an enormous influence on the whole present generation of Soviet filmmakers.

After the war Gerasimov's own work seems to have swung dramatically from his self-effacing, sympathetic form of filmmaking to the grandiose style fashionable during Stalin's final phase. Fadeev's patriotic, lyrical novel *The Young Guard* would seem to have been ideal source material for a typical Gerasimov film, yet it turned out to be bombastic, pompous, and overblown. His other huge epic, *And Quiet Flows the Don,* shown in three full-length parts, unfortunately suffered from similar grandiosity. Apart from this foray into gigantism, and a documentary on China, much of Gerasimov's post-Stalin output saw a return to his themes of the 1930s. While he remained a highly competent director, however, he never quite recaptured the freshness of approach and lightness of touch that marked his earlier work.

—Robert Dunbar

GERMI, Pietro

Nationality: Italian. **Born:** Genoa, 14 September 1914. **Education:** Instituto Nautico; studied acting and directing at Centro Sperimentale di Cinematografia, Rome. **Career:** Directed first film, *Il testimone,* 1946; retired from *Amici miei* project because of ill health, 1974. **Awards:** Oscar for Best Story and Screenplay, with Alfredo Giannetti and Ennio de Concini, for *Divorce Italian Style,* 1962; Best Film (co-recipient), Cannes Festival, for *Signore e signori,* 1966. **Died:** In Rome, 5 December 1974.

Films as Director:

1946 *Il testimone* (+ co-sc)
1947 *Gioventù perduta* (*Lost Youth*) (+ co-sc)
1949 *In nome della legge* (*Mafia*) (+ co-sc)
1950 *Il cammino della speranza* (*The Path of Hope*) (+ co-story, co-adapt)
1951 *La città si difende* (*Four Ways Out*) (+ co-sc)
1952 *La presidentessa* (*Mademoiselle Gobette*) (+ co-sc); *Il brigante di Tacca del Lupo* (+ co-sc)
1953 *Gelosia* (+ co-sc)
1954 "Guerra 1915-1918" episode of *Amori di mezzo secolo*
1956 *Il ferroviere* (*The Railroad Man*; *Man of Iron*) (+ co-sc, role)
1957 *L'uomo di paglia* (+ co-sc, role)
1962 *Divorzio all'italiana* (*Divorce Italian Style*) (+ co-sc)
1964 *Sedotta e abbandonata* (*Seduced and Abandoned*) (+ co-sc)
1965 *Signore e signori* (*The Birds, the Bees and the Italians*) (+ co-sc, co-pr)
1967 *L'immorale* (*The Climax*; *Too Much for One Man*) (+ co-sc)
1968 *Serafino* (+ co-sc, pr)
1970 *Le castagne sono buone* (*Till Divorce Do You Part*) (+ co-sc, pr)
1972 *Alfredo, Alfredo* (+ co-sc, pr)

Other Films:

1939 *Retroscena* (Blasetti) (asst d, co-sc)
1943 *Nessuno torna indietro* (Blasetti) (asst d)
1945 *I dieci comandamenti* (Chili) (co-sc)
1946 *Monte Cassino* (Gemmiti) (role)
1948 *Fuga in Francia* (Soldati) (role)
1959 *Jovanka e le altre* (*Five Branded Women*) (Ritt) (role)
1960 *Il rossetto* (Damiani) (role)
1961 *La viaccia* (Bolognini) (role); *Il sicario* (Damiani) (role)
1963 *The Directors* (pr: Greenblatt) (appearance)
1975 *Amici miei* (Monicelli) (co-sc, + credit "A Film by Pietro Germi")

Publications

By GERMI: articles—

"Man Is Not Large Enough for Man," in *Films and Filming* (London), September 1966.

On GERMI: articles—

Passek, J.L., "Pietro Germi," in *Cinéma* (Paris), February 1975.
Monicelli, M., "Pietro Germi, mon amour," in *Ecran* (Paris), September 1976.
Pattison, B., "Pietro Germi," in *Film* (London), October 1976.
"Pietro Germi," in *Film Dope* (London), December 1979.
Filméchange (Paris), Autumn 1984.

* * *

Pietro Germi, though often regarded by scholars as fundamentally a neorealist director who made a transition in mid-career to social comedy, never actually considered himself to be an adherent to the style popularized by Roberto Rossellini. Like several other Italian directors achieving prominence in the late 1940s, notably Alberto Lattuada, Alberto De Santis and, of course, Vittorio DeSica, he produced films notable for breaking with prevailing themes that dealt with the immediate aftermath of World War II. His early works addressed themselves instead to the fundamental, even timeless, social issues affecting post-war Italy and in particular, those exemplified in the poverty of the island of Sicily.

Germi's early films, notably *In nome della legge* and *Il cammino della speranza,* owe as much, if not more, to the influence of American director John Ford as they do to neorealism. In Germi's work, Sicily easily replaces Ford's Monument Valley and the island's traditional knife duels supplant the American director's classic showdowns. In all other respects, the fundamental issues in Germi's first few films differ little from a typical John Ford production like *Stagecoach.* Indeed the themes of the aforementioned Germi films (in *In nome della legge,* a clash between a young judge and the local Mafia over his attempts to enforce the law and, in *Il cammino della speranza,* the problem of illegal immigration) deal with problems not too far removed from those of the actual post-Civil War American West.

Pietro Germi

Interestingly, the fact that Germi dared to propose solutions to the problems that he examined in these and in succeeding films effectively removed him from the realm of pure neorealism which, as construed by Rossellini and his immediate followers, must limit itself merely to the exposition of a particular social condition. It cannot suggest solutions. Unfortunately, in a number of cases (*Il cammino della speranza,* in particular), the director's solutions were overly romanticized, pat, and simplistic.

During the latter part of the 1950s, Germi began to compress the scope of his social concerns to those affecting the individual and his relationship to the family unit, albeit as components of the larger society. In *Il ferroviere* and *L'uomo di Paglia,* however, he continued to be plagued by his penchant for simplistic and overly contrived solutions as well as a tendency to let the films run on too long. They are redeemed to some extent by their realistic portrayals of working class characters which. Though considered melodramatic by many reviewers at the time of their release, these characterizations have come to be more highly regarded.

Germi corrected his problems in the 1960s by changing his narrative style to one dominated by satirical devices. Yet he did not compromise his family-centered social vision. *Divorzio all'italiana,* for which he won an Academy Award for best screenplay, *Sedotta e abbandonata,* and *Signori e signore* all magnify social questions all out of proportion to reality and thus, through the chaos that results, reduce the issues to absurdity.

Divorzio all'italiana, in particular, is a craftsmanlike portrayal of the internal upheavals within a family, set in the oppressive atmosphere of a small Sicilian village. It features the deft use of a moving camera that passes swiftly, almost intimately, through endless groups of gawking townspeople. In addition, the director's use of actors, including Marcello Mastroianni and Daniella Rocca, as well as his own latent sense of humor, make the social commentary in this film quite possibly more penetrating than in his early neorealist films.

Though Germi shifted over the length of his career from social dramas to socio-moral satires, his social concerns and his favorite setting for them—Sicily—remained constant. As is not normally the case with many artists of his stature, his most polished and commercially successful efforts also turned out to be the critical equals of his earlier and more solemn ones.

—Stephen L. Hanson

GETINO, Octavio *See* **SOLANAS, Fernando E., and Octavio GETINO**

GILLIAM, Terry

Nationality: American. **Born:** Terry Vance Gilliam in Minneapolis, Minnesota, 22 November 1940. **Education:** Studied political science at Occidental College, Los Angeles. **Family:** Married make-up artist Margaret Weston; three children: Amy Rainbow, Holly du Bois, Harry Thunder. **Career:** Associate editor, *HELP* magazine, and freelance illustrator, New York, from 1962; moved to London, 1967; illustrator and animator for *Marty, We Have Ways of Making You Laugh,* and *Do Not Adjust Your Set,* for TV, 1968; member of *Monty Python's Flying Circus,* from 1969; directed first solo project, *Jabberwocky,* 1977. **Awards:** Special Award for Graphics, British Academy of Film and Television Arts, for *Monty Python's Flying Circus,* 1969; Silver Award, Montreux Festival, for *Monty Python's Flying Circus,* 1971; Best Film and Best Screenplay, Los Angeles Critics Association and Oscar nomination, Best Screenplay, for *Brazil,* 1985; Michael Balcon Award, Outstanding British Contribution to Cinema, 1987; Golden Globe nomination, Best Director, for *The Fisher King,* 1992.

Films as Director:

1975 *Monty Python and the Holy Grail* (co-d, + co-sc, anim, role)
1977 *Jabberwocky* (+ co-sc)
1981 *Time Bandits* (+ co-sc, pr)
1985 ***Brazil*** (+ co-sc)
1989 *The Adventures of Baron Munchausen* (+ co-sc)
1991 *The Fisher King*
1995 *Twelve Monkeys*

Other Films:

1971 *And Now for Something Completely Different* (co-sc, anim, role)
1979 *Monty Python's Life of Brian* (Jones) (co-sc, design, anim, role)
1982 *Monty Python Live at the Hollywood Bowl* (co-sc, role)
1983 *Monty Python's The Meaning of Life* (Jones) (co-sc, anim, d some sequences, role)
1985 *Spies Like Us* (Landis) (role)

Publications

By GILLIAM: books—

Harvey Kurtzman's Fun and Games, with Harvey Kurtzman, New York, 1965.
Monty Python's Big Red Book, London, 1972.
The Brand New Monty Python Book, London, 1973.
Sporting Relations, with Roger McGough, London, 1974.
Monty Python and the Holy Grail, London, 1977.
Jabberwocky, London, 1977.
Animations of Mortality, London, 1978.
Monty Python's Life of Brian (of Nazareth), London, 1979.
The Complete Works of Shakespeare and Monty Python, London, 1981.
Time Bandits, with Michael Palin, London, 1981.
Monty Python's The Meaning of Life, London, 1983.
The Adventures of Baron Munchausen, with Charles McKeown, New York and London, 1989.

By GILLIAM: articles—

Interview in *Inter/View* (New York), vol. 7, no. 6, 1975.
Interview in *Film Comment* (New York), November/December 1981.
Interview with D. Rabourdin, in *Cinéma* (Paris), February 1985.
Interview with Nick Roddick, in *Stills* (London), February 1985.
Interview with B. Howell, in *Films and Filming* (London), March 1985.
Interview with M. Girard and A. Caron, in *Séquences* (Montreal), April 1986.
Interview with D. Morgan, in *Sight and Sound* (London), Autumn 1988.
Interview in *Starburst* (London), April 1989.
"Terry Gilliam's Guilty Pleasures," in *Film Comment* (New York), September/October 1991.

On GILLIAM: books—

Perry, George, *Life of Python,* London, 1983.
Yule, Andrew, *Losing the Light: Terry Gilliam and the Munchausen Saga,* New York, 1991.

Terry Gilliam (left) on the set of *The Adventures of Baron Munchausen*

On GILLIAM: articles—

"*Brazil* Section" of *Revue du Cinéma* (Paris), March 1985.
"Gilliam Section" of *Positif* (Paris), March 1985.
Mathews, J., "Earth to Gilliam," in *American Film* (Los Angeles), March 1989.
Turan, Kenneth, "The Awful Adventures of Terry Gilliam," in *Gentleman's Quarterly,* March 1989.
"Gilliam Issue" of *Cinefex* (Riverside, California), May 1989.
Ellison, Harlan, "Harlan Ellison's Watching," in *Magazine of Fantasy and Science Fiction,* May 1989.
Van Gelder, L., "At the Movies," in *New York Times,* 1 June 1990.
Ciment, Michel, article in *Positif* (Paris), November 1990.
Panek, Richard, "A Writer's Dream," in *Premiere,* May 1991.
Drucker, E., "*The Fisher King,*" in *American Film* (Los Angeles), September/October 1991.

* * *

"A trilogy about the ages of Man and the subordination of magic to realism." So Terry Gilliam described the trio of films which stretched from *Time Bandits* through *Brazil* to *The Adventures Of Baron Munchausen.* Gilliam has worked resolutely in the space between the two elements of magic and reality in all his work, hardly surprising in a man who first became widely known as the provider of brilliant, surreal animation sequences for the Monty Python comedy team in the late 1960s and early 1970s.

Gilliam is very much a champion of imagination in his films in both visual and narrative terms. Despite his often surreal vision, however, the products of the imagination do not necessarily have to be fantastic. Love, for example—often a triumph of emotional imagination over reality—has been an important arena in Gilliam's battle between magic and realism—comical and childlike in *Jabberwocky,* bittersweet and adult in *Brazil.*

For Gilliam, magic counterbalances what he perceives as the sterility of the rational, a view that is manifested in extreme form in the Orwellian nightmare world of *Brazil.* If love is perhaps the emotional expression of Gilliam's magic, then visual and narrative fantasy is the conceptual. Elements of the fantastic have been ever-present in Gilliam's work from his *Monty Python* days to the spectacles of *Baron Munchausen* (an island transformed into a giant fish, a ship gliding through a desert strewn with statues). His feature films often seem, in fact, semi-conscious attempts to recreate the world of his early animations in live-action.

Fellow director Alex Cox has described Gilliam as a "highly skilled visualist," a judgement which cannot really be disputed. (It is worth noting that Gilliam's cinematographer for the dazzling *Brazil* was Roger Pratt, later to give a similar gloss to the mega-buck *Batman.*) Gilliam is often criticized, however, for opting for visual pyrotechnics at the expense of narrative solidity. The issue is clouded by Gilliam's constant return to the fairy tale/fantasy format, where the requirement of narrative sense or continuity is arguably less strict anyway. Arthurian legend in *Monty Python and The Holy Grail* (co-directed with Terry Jones), Lewis Carroll's nonsense world in *Jabberwocky,* time travel in *Time Bandits,* an insane world in *Brazil,* and eighteenth-century tall tales in *Baron Munchausen* all exemplified Gilliam's fascination with fantasy. Is Gilliam merely an escapist with a remarkably fertile imagination? In opting to undermine the bedrock of dull rationality does he fail to offer anything in return? It is, after all, perfectly possible to make films which are funny and surreal *and* which have bite—satire as opposed to escapism.

Gilliam's defense against such charges is *Brazil.* Without *Brazil,* Gilliam's output smacks a little too much of clownish entertainment. But with *Brazil* it is clear that the clown can also wear a sadder, darker face. For here, Gilliam opts to take on board the challenging burdens of rationality rather than trying merely to escape them. His vision has *weight.* If he escapes here it is through facing the deadening products of rationality and triumphing over them through a combination of acid ridicule and emotional willpower. The sights which influenced his perception of the story included a Los Angeles riot, and he has half-cryptically, half-menacingly described the setting of the film as "somewhere on the Los Angeles/Belfast border."

Brazil revealed depths to Gilliam's talent which had only been glimpsed in his blackly comic *Monty Python* animations rather than his earlier features. *Baron Munchausen,* disappointingly, proved a regression back to escapism rather than a development of the inspired mood of *Brazil* (though the pressures of an ever-escalating budget cannot have helped). Perhaps the battle he had to fight with Warner Bros. over *Brazil*—first over a re-edit (read massacre), then over even releasing the film—had warned him against attempting anything with real edge.

The Fisher King, Gilliam's follow-up to *The Adventures of Baron Munchausen,* is among his best works. The film, a dazzlingly visual allegory that offers a profound commentary on ethics in contemporary society, ponders a tarnished soul's chance to reclaim a moral lifestyle.

Its scenario (authored by Richard LaGravenese, rather than Gilliam) spotlights the plight of Jack Lucas (Jeff Bridges), a cold-hearted, self-centered radio talk show host who undergoes a personality crisis when one of his listeners, whom he has just crudely dismissed, promptly commits mass murder. Lucas is delivered from the brink of despair by a character who might have been concocted during Gilliam's early Monty Python days, an oddball street person (Robin Williams) who is consumed with finding the Holy Grail and hooking up with an evasive young woman (Amanda Plummer).

In 1995 Gilliam released *Twelve Monkeys,* a film set in post-apocalyptic America. Reminiscent of *Brazil* in its dark vision of the future, *Twelve Monkeys* concerns a criminal of the future (played by Bruce Willis) who is sent back in time to late twentieth-century America to gather information about a devastating plague that pushed survivors into a bleak underground existence. The film was more accessible to mainstream audiences than some of Gilliam's earlier films (in part because of its big-name cast, which also included Madeleine Stowe and Brad Pitt), but still featured Gilliam's signature cynicism about society's dark underbelly, evocatively presented as always.

Gilliam's films are brilliantly imaginative, though sometimes maddeningly uneven. He remains an outstanding talent who, unfortunately, works too infrequently on screen.

—Norman Miller, updated by Rob Edelman

GILLIAT, Sidney *See* **LAUNDER, Frank, and Sidney GILLIAT**

GODARD, Jean-Luc

Nationality: French. **Born:** Paris, 3 December 1930, became citizen of Switzerland. **Education:** Nyon, Switzerland; Lycée Buffon, Paris; Sorbonne, 1947-49, certificate in ethnology 1950. **Family:** Married 1) Anna Karina, 1960 (divorced); 2) Anne Wiamzensky, 1967 (divorced). **Career:** Delivery boy, cameraman, assistant editor for Zurich television, construction worker, and gossip columnist (for *Les Temps de Paris*), in Switzerland and Paris, 1949-56; founded short-lived *Gazette du cinéma,* writing as "Hans Lucas," 1950-51; critic for *Cahiers du cinéma,* from 1952; directed first film, *Opération Béton,* 1954; worked as film editor, 1956; worked in publicity department, 20th Century-Fox, Paris, with producer Georges de Beauregard, 1957; working for Beauregard, directed first feature, *A bout de souffle,* 1959; formed Anoucka films with Anna Karina, 1964; led protests over firing of Henri Langlois, director of Cinémathèque, instigated shut down of Cannes Festival, 1968; began collaboration with Jean-Pierre Gorin, editor of *Cahiers marxistes-léninistes,* 1969 (partnership terminated 1973); "reclaimed" work from 1969-72 as that of the Dziga Vertov group; established Sonimage film and video studio in Grenoble with Anne-Marie Miéville, 1974-75; moved to the Swiss town of Rolle, 1978; began the second stage of his directorial career, 1980; directed jeans advertisement, 1987. **Awards:** Best Direction Award, Berlin Festival, for *A bout de souffle,* 1960; Prix Pasinetti, 1962; Golden Lion, Venice Film Festival, for *Prenom: Carmen,* 1983; Honorary César, 1986; Lifetime Achievement Award, New York Film Critics' Circle, 1994. **Address:** 15 rue du Nord, 1180 Roulle, Switzerland.

Films as Director:

1954 *Opération Béton* (+ pr, sc) (released 1958)

1955 *Une Femme coquette* (d as 'Hans Lucas,' + sc pr, ph, bit role as man visiting prostitute)

1957 *Charlotte et Véronique ou Tous les garçons s'appellent Patrick* (+ sc)

1958 *Une Histoire d'eau* (co-d: actual shooting by Truffaut, + co-sc) (released 1961); *Charlotte et son Jules* (+ sc, dubbed voice of Jean-Paul Belmondo) (released 1961)

1959 ***A bout de souffle*** (*Breathless*) (+ sc, role as passerby who points out Belmondo to police)

1961 *Une Femme est une femme* (+ sc)

1962 "La Paresse" episode of *Les Sept Péchés capitaux* (+ sc); ***Vivre sa vie*** (*My Life to Live*) (+ sc, dubbed voice of Peter Kassowitz), "Il nuovo mondo (Le Nouveau Monde)" in *RoGoPaG* (*Laviamoci il cervello*) (+ sc, bit role)

1963 *Le Petit Soldat* (+ sc, bit role as man at railway station) (completed 1960); *Les Carabiniers* (+ sc); *Le Mépris* (+ sc, role)

1964 "Le Grand Escroc" in *Les Plus Belles Escroqueries du monde* (+ sc, narration, bit role as man wearing Moroccan chéchia); *Bande à part* (+ sc); *La Femme mariée* (*Une Femme mariée*) (+ sc); *Reportage sur Orly* (+ sc) (short)

1965 "Montparnasse—Levallois" in *Paris vu par ...* (+ sc); ***Alphaville*** (+ sc); *Une Étrange aventure de Lemmy Caution* (+ sc); *Pierrot le fou* (+ sc)

1966 *Masculin-féminin* (*Masculin féminin: quinze faits précis*) (+ sc); *Made in U.S.A.* (+ sc, voice on tape recorder)

1967 *Deux ou trois choses que je sais d'elle* (+ sc); "Anticipation" episode of *Le Plus Vieux Métier du monde* (+ sc); *La Chinoise ou Plutôt à la chinoise* (+ sc); "Caméra-oeil" in *Loin du Viêt-Nam* (+ sc, appearance); ***Le Weekend*** (*Weekend*) (+ sc)

1968 *Le Gai Savoir* (+ sc); *Cinétracts* (+ sc) (series of untitled, creditless newsreels); *Un Film comme les autres* (+ sc, voice); *One Plus One* (*Sympathy for the Devil*) (+ sc, voice); *One A.M.* (*One American Movie*) (+ sc) (unfinished)

1969 *British Sounds* (*See You at Mao*) (co-d, co-sc); *Pravda* (+ sc) (collective credit to Groupe Dziga-Vertov); *Lotte in Italia* (*Luttes en Italie*) (+ sc) (collective credit to Groupe Dziga-Vertov); "L'amore" episode of *Amore e rabbia* (+ sc) (completed 1967: festival showings as "Andante e ritorno dei figli prodighi" episode of *Vangelo 70*)
1970 *Vent d'est* (co-d, co-sc); *Jusqu'à la victoire* (*Till Victory*) (co-d, + sc) (unfinished)
1971 *Vladimir et Rosa* (+ sc, collective credit to Groupe Dziga-Vertov, role as U.S. policeman, appearance, narration)
1972 ***Tout va bien*** (co-d, + co-sc, pr); *A Letter to Jane or Investigation About a Still* (*Lettre à Jane*) (co-d, + co-sc, co-pr, narration)
1975 *Numéro deux* (+ co-sc, co-pr, appearance)
1976 *Ici et ailleurs* (co-d, + co-sc) (includes footage from *Jusqu'à la victoire*); *Comment ça va* (co-d, + co-sc)
1977 *6 x 2: sur et sous la communication* (co-d, + co-sc) (for TV)
1980 *Sauve qui peut* (*La vie; Every Man for Himself*) (+ co-sc, co-ed)
1982 *Passion* (+ sc)
1983 *Prenom: Carmen* (*First Name: Carmen*) (role)
1985 *Hail Mary*; *Detective*
1986 *Grandeur et Decadence d'un Petit Commerce du Cinema* (*The Rise and Fall of a Little Film Company*) (for TV)
1987 *Soigne ta droite* (*Keep Up Your Right*) (ed, role); episode in *Aria*; *King Lear* (role)
1990 *Nouvelle Vague* (*New Wave*) (+ sc)
1990 *Visages Suisse* (*Faces of Switzerland*) (co-d)
1991 *Allemagne Neuf Zero* (*Germany Nine Zero*) (+ sc)
1993 *Helas Pour Moi* (*Oh, Woe Is Me*) (+ sc, ed)
1994 *JLG/JLG—Autoportrait de Decembre* (*JLG/JLG—Self-Portrait in December*) (+ sc, appearance)
1995 *Deux fois cinquante ans de cinema Francais* (*2 times 50 Years of French Cinema*) (co-d, + co-sc, co-ed); *Les enfants jouent a la Russie* (*The Kids Play Russian*) (+ sc, ed, appearance)

Other Films:

1950 *Quadrille* (Rivette) (pr, role)
1951 *Présentation ou Charlotte et son steack* (Rohmer) (role)
1956 *Kreutzer Sonata* (Rohmer) (pr); *Le Coup du berger* (Rivette) (role)
1958 *Paris nous appartient* (Rivette) (Godard's silhouette)
1959 *Le Signe du lion* (Rohmer) (role)
1961 ***Cléo de cinq à sept*** (Varda) (role with Anna Karina in comic sequence); *Le Soleil dans l'oeil* (Bourdon) (role)
1963 *Schehérézade* (Gaspard-Huit) (role); *The Directors* (pr: Greenblatt) (appearance); *Paparazzi* (Rozier) (appearance); *Begegnung mit Fritz Lang* (Fleischmann) (appearance); *Petit Jour* (Pierre) (appearance)
1966 *L'Espion* (*The Defector*) (Levy) (role)
1971 *One P.M.* (*One Parallel Movie*) (Pennebaker) (includes footage from abandoned *One A.M.* and documentary footage of its making)

Publications

By GODARD: books—

Jean-Luc Godard par Jean-Luc Godard: articles, essais, entretiens, edited by Jean Narboni, Paris, 1968; published as *Godard on Godard: Critical Writings,* edited by Narboni and Tom Milne, New York, 1986.
Weekend, New York, 1972.
A bout de souffle, Paris, 1974.
Jean-Luc Godard: Three Films—"A Woman is a Woman," "A Married Woman," "Two or Three Things I Know about Her," New York, 1975.
Introduction à une véritable histoire du cinéma, Paris, 1980.

By GODARD: articles—

Contributing editor of *La Gazette du Cinéma* (Paris), 1950; regular contributor to *Cahiers du Cinéma* (Paris), 1952 through 1968, and to *Arts* (Paris), 1957 through 1960.
"*Charlotte et son Jules,*" in *Avant-Scène du Cinéma* (Paris), June 1961.
"*Une Histoire d'eau,*" in *Avant-Scène du Cinéma* (Paris), September 1961.
"*Vivre sa vie,*" in *Avant-Scène du Cinéma* (Paris), October 1962; also in *Film Culture* (New York), Winter 1962.
Interview with Tom Milne, in *Sight and Sound* (London), Winter 1962.
Interview with Herbert Feinstein, in *Film Quarterly* (Berkeley), Spring 1964.
"*La Femme mariée,*" in *Avant-Scène du Cinéma* (Paris), March 1965.
"*Les Carabiniers,*" in *Avant-Scène du Cinéma* (Paris), May 1965.
"*Deux ou trois choses que je sais d'elle,*" in *Avant-Scène du Cinéma* (Paris), May 1967.
"*A bout de souffle,*" in *Avant-Scène du Cinéma* (Paris), March 1968.
"Struggle on Two Fronts," an interview with Jacques Bontemps, in *Film Quarterly* (Berkeley), Winter 1968.
"*La Chinoise,*" in *Avant-Scène du Cinéma* (Paris), May 1971.
"*Pierrot le fou,*" in *Avant-Scène du Cinéma* (Paris), July/September 1976.
"Jean-Luc Godard ... For Himself," in *Framework* (Norwich), Autumn 1980.
"En attendant *Passion.* Le chemin vers la parole," an interview with Alain Bergala, Serge Daney, and Serge Toubiana, in *Cahiers du Cinéma* (Paris), May 1982.
Interview with Don Ranvaud and A. Farassino, in *Framework* (Norwich), Summer 1983.
"The Carrots are Cooked," an interview with Gideon Bachman, in *Film Quarterly* (Berkeley), Spring 1984.
"Genesis of a Camera," with J.P. Beauviala, in *Camera Obscura* (Berkeley), Spring/Summer 1985.
"Godard in His 'Fifth' Period," an interview with K. Dieckmann, in *Film Quarterly* (Berkeley), Winter 1985/86.
"Colles et ciseaux," in *Cahiers du Cinéma* (Paris), December 1987.
Godard, Jean-Luc, article in *Chaplin* (Stockholm), vol. 30, no. 2/3, 1988.
Interview with Alain Bergala and Serge Toubiana, in *Cahiers du Cinéma* (Paris), January 1988.
Transcript of Cannes Film Festival press conference, in *Cinema* (Paris), June 1990.
Transcript of Cannes Film Festival press conference, in *Cahiers du Cinema* (Paris), June 1990.
Interview in *Cahiers du Cinema* (Paris), November 1990.
Interview in *Cahiers du Cinema* (Paris), October 1993.
Interview with Andrew Sarris, in *Interview,* July 1994.
Interview with Scott Kraft, in *Los Angeles Times,* 2 April 1995.

On GODARD: books—

Collet, Jean, *Jean-Luc Godard,* Paris, 1963; New York, 1970.
Roud, Richard, *Jean-Luc Godard,* New York, 1967.
Mussman, Toby, editor, *Jean-Luc Godard: A Critical Anthology,* New York, 1968.
Cameron, Ian, editor, *The Films of Jean-Luc Godard,* London, 1969.
Mancini, Michele, *Godard,* Rome, 1969.
Brown, Royal, editor, *Focus on Godard,* Englewood Cliffs, New Jersey, 1972.

Jean-Luc Godard

Farassino, Alberto, *Godard,* Florence, 1974.
Monaco, James, *The New Wave,* New York, 1976.
Kawin, Bruce, *Mindscreen: Bergman, Godard, and First-Person Film,* Pinceton, New Jersey, 1978.
Lesage, Julia, *Jean-Luc Godard, a Guide to References and Resources,* Boston, 1979.
Kreidl, John Francis, *Jean-Luc Godard,* Boston, 1980.
Achard, Maurice, *Vous avez dit Godard: ou J'm'appelle pas Godard,* Paris, 1980.
MacCabe, Colin, *Godard: Images, Sounds, Politics,* London, 1980.
Walsh, Martin, *The Brechtian Aspect of Radical Cinema,* London, 1981.
Lefevre, Raymond, *Jean-Luc Godard,* Paris, 1983.
Bordwell, David, *Narration in the Fiction Film,* London, 1985.
Weis, Elisabeth, and John Belton, *Film Sound: Theory and Practice,* New York, 1985.
Andrew, Dudley, ed., *Breathless/Jean-Luc Godard,* New Brunswick, New Jersey, 1987.
Cerisuelo, Marc, *Jean-Luc Godard,* Paris, 1989.
Desbarats, Carole, and Jean-Paul Gorce, *L'Effet Godard,* Toulouse, 1989.
Douin, Jean-Luc, *Jean-Luc Godard,* Paris, 1989.
Paech, Joachim, *Passion, oder, Die Einbildungen des Jean-Luc Godard,* Frankfort, 1989.
Locke, Maryel, and Charles Warren, eds. *Jean-Luc Godard's Hail Mary: Women and the Sacred in Film,* Carbondale, Illinois, 1993.
Bellour, Raymond, and Mary Lea Bandy, *Jean-Luc Godard Son + Image,* New York, 1993.

On GODARD: articles—

Moullet, Luc, "Jean-Luc Godard," in *Cahiers du Cinéma* (Paris), April 1960.
Fieschi, Jean-André, "Godard: Cut Sequence: *Vivre sa vie,*" in *Movie* (London), January 1963.
Bellour, Raymond, "Godard or Not Godard," in *Les Lettres Françaises* (Paris), 14 May 1964.
Sarris, Andrew, and Andrew Blasi, "Waiting for Godard," in *Film Culture* (New York), Summer 1964.
Kael, Pauline, "Godard est Godard," in *The New Yorker,* 9 October 1965.
Metz, Christian, "Le Cinéma moderne et la narrative," in *Cahiers du Cinéma* (Paris), December 1966.
Bertolucci, Bernardo, "Versus Godard," in *Cahiers du Cinéma* (Paris), January 1967.
"Godard Issue" of *Image et Son/Revue du Cinéma* (Paris), December 1967.
"Godard Issue" of *Film Heritage* (Dayton, Ohio), Spring 1968.

Schickel, Richard, "The Trying Genius of M. Godard," in *Life* (New York), 12 April 1968.
Clouzot, Claire, "Godard and the U.S.," in *Sight and Sound* (London), Summer 1968.
Farber, Manny, "The Films of Jean-Luc Godard," in *Artforum* (New York), October 1968.
MacBean, James, "Politics, Poetry, and the Language of Signs in Godard's *Made in U.S.A.*," in *Film Quarterly* (Berkeley), Spring 1969.
Sainsbury, Peter, "Jean-Luc Godard," in *Afterimage* (New York), April 1970.
Goodwin, Michael, and others, "The Dziga Vertov Group in America," in *Take One* (Montreal), March/April 1971.
MacBean, James, "Godard and the Dziga Vertov Group: Film and Dialectic," in *Film Quarterly* (Berkeley), Fall 1972.
Kolkeon, R.P., "Angle and Reality: Godard and Gorin in America," in *Sight and Sound* (London), Summer 1973.
"Director of the Year," *International Film Guide* (London, New York), 1974.
Rayns, Tony, "The Godard Film Forum," in *Film* (London), January 1974.
MacCabe, Colin, "Realism and the Cinema: Notes on Some Brechtian Theses," in *Screen* (London), Summer 1974.
Lesage, Julia, "Visual Distancing in Godard," in *Wide Angle* (Athens, Ohio), no. 3, 1976.
Gilliatt, Penelope, "Profile," in *The New Yorker,* 25 October 1976.
Lefèvre, Raymond, "La Lettre et la cinématographe: L'Ecrit dans les films de Godard," in *Image et Son* (Paris), May 1977.
Forbes, Jill, "Jean-Luc Godard: Two into Three," in *Sight and Sound* (London), Winter 1980/81.
"Godard Issue" of *Camera Obscura* (Berkeley), Fall 1982.
Burgoyne, Robert, "The Political Topology of Montage: The Conflict of Genres in the Films of Godard," in *Enclitic* (Minneapolis), Spring 1983.
Lovell, Alan, "Epic Theater and Counter Cinema," and Julia Lesage, "Godard and Gorin's Left Politics," in *Jump Cut* (Berkeley), April 1983.
Dossier on Godard, in *Cinématographe* (Paris), December 1983.
"Godard Issue" of *Avant-Scène du Cinéma* (Paris), March 1984.
MacCabe, Colin, "Every Man for Himself," in *American Film* (Washington, D.C.), June 1984.
Gervais, M., "Jean-Luc Godard 1985—These Are Not the Days," in *Sight and Sound* (London), Autumn 1985.
Durgnat, Raymond, "Jean-Luc Godard: His Crucifixion and Resurrection," in *Monthly Film Bulletin* (London), September 1985.
"Godard Issue" of *Revue Belge du Cinéma* (Brussels), Summer 1986.
Wide Angle (Athens, Ohio), vol. 9, no. 1, 1987.
"Godard Issue" of *Cinéma* (Paris), 30 December 1987.
Ciment, Michel, "Je vous salue Godard," in *Positif* (Paris), February 1988.
Francois Quenin, article in *Cinéma* (Paris), June 1988.
Article in *L'avant Scene Cinéma* (Paris), April 1989.
Colette Mazabrard, article in *Cahiers du Cinéma* (Paris), May 1989.
Michael O'Pray, article in *Monthly Film Bulletin* (London), November 1989.
Stam, Robert, "The Lake, the Trees," in *Film Comment,* January/February 1991.
Riding, Alan, "What's in a Name if the Name is Godard?," in *New York Times,* 25 October 1992.
Klawans, Stuart, "Jean-Luc Godard: Son + Image," in *The Nation* (New York), 23 November 1992.
Sterritt, David, "Recognizing a Film Renegade," in *Christian Science Monitor* (New York), 27 November 1992.
Hoberman, J., "Picasso, Marx, and Coca-Cola," in *ARTnews* (New York), February 1993.
Eco, Umberto, "Do-it-yourself Godard," in *Harper's Magazine* (New York), May 1993.
Stoneman, Rod, "Bon voyage," in *Sight and Sound* (London), July 1993.
Dieckmann, Katherine, "Godard's Counter Memory," in *Art in America* (New York), October 1993.
James, Caryn, "From France, Depardieu as God and Other Joys," in *New York Times,* 18 February 1994.
Sterritt, David, "Vive la cinema! French Film Series Erupts with Energy," in *Christian Science Monitor* (New York), 25 February 1994.
Darke, Chris, "It All Happened in Paris," in *Sight and Sound* (London), July 1994.
Sterritt, David, "Ideas, not Plots, Inspire Jean-Luc Godard," in *Christian Science Monitor* (New York), 3 August 1994.

On GODARD: films—

Bazin, Janine, and others, *Jean-Luc Godard, ou le cinéma de défi,* for TV, 1964.
Doniol-Valcroze, Jacques, *Pour le plaisir,* for TV, 1965.
Thanhauser, Ralph, *Godard in America,* U.S.A., 1970.
Berckmans, Jean-Pierre, *La Longue Marche de Jean-Luc Godard,* Belgium, 1972.
Costard, Hellmuth, *Der kleine Godard,* West Germany, 1978.

* * *

If influence on the development of world cinema is the criterion, then Jean-Luc Godard is certainly the most important filmmaker of the past thirty years; he is also one of the most problematic.

Godard's career so far falls roughly into three periods: the early works from *About de souffle* to *Weekend* (1959-1968), a period whose end is marked decisively by the latter film's final caption, "Fin de Cinéma"; the period of intense politicization, during which Godard collaborated (mainly though not exclusively) with Jean-Pierre Gorin and the Dziga Vertov group (1968-1972); and the subsequent work, divided between attempts to renew communication with a wider, more "mainstream" cinema audience and explorations of the potentialities of video (in collaboration with Anne-Marie Miéville). One might also separate the films from *Masculin-Féminin* to *Weekend* as representing a transitional phase from the first to the Dziga Vertov period, although in a sense all Godard's work is transitional.

What marks the middle period off from its neighbours is above all the difference in intended audience: the Dziga Vertov films were never meant to reach the general public. They were instead aimed at already committed Marxist or leftist groups, campus student groups, and so on, to stimulate discussion of revolutionary politics and aesthetics, and, crucially, the relationship between the two.

Godard's importance lies in his development of an authentic modernist cinema in opposition to (though, during the early period, at the same time *within*) mainstream cinema; it is with his work that film becomes central to our century's major aesthetic debate, the controversy developed through such figures as Lukács, Brecht, Benjamin, and Adorno as to whether realism or modernism is the more progressive form. As ex-*Cahiers du Cinéma* critic and New Wave filmmaker, Godard was initially linked with Truffaut and Chabrol in a kind of revolutionary triumvirate; it is easy, in retrospect, to see that Godard was from the start the truly radical figure, the "revolution" of his colleagues operating purely on the aesthetic level and easily assimilable into the mainstream.

A simple way of demonstrating the essential thrust of Godard's work is to juxtapose his first feature, *Breathless,* with the excellent American remake. Jim McBride's film follows the original fairly closely, with the fundamental difference that in it all other elements are subordinated to the narrative and the characters. In Godard's film, on the contrary, this traditional relationship between signifier and signified shows a continuous tendency to come adrift, so that the *process of narration* (which mainstream cinema strives everywhere to conceal) becomes foregrounded; *A bout de souffle* is "about" a story and characters, certainly, but it is also about the cinema, about film techniques, about Jean Seberg, etc.

This foregrounding of the process—and the means—of narration is developed much further in subsequent films, in which Godard systematically breaks down the traditional barrier between fiction/documentary, actor/character, narrative film/experimental film to create freer, "open" forms. Persons appear as themselves in works of fiction, actors address the camera/audience in monologues or as if being interviewed, materiality of film is made explicit (the switches from positive to negative in *Une Femme mariée,* the turning on and off of the soundtrack in *Deux ou trois choses que je sais d'elle,* the showing of the clapper-board in *La Chinoise*). The initial motivation for this seems to have been the assertion of personal freedom: the filmmaker shatters the bonds of traditional realism in order to be able to say and do whatever he wants, creating films spontaneously. (*Pierrot le fou*—significantly, one of Godard's most popular films—is the most extreme expression of this impulse.) Gradually, however, a political motivation (connected especially with the influence of Brecht) takes over. There is a marked sociological interest in the early films (especially *Vivre sa vie* and *Une Femme mariée*), but the turning-point is *Masculin-féminin* with its two male protagonists, one seeking fulfillment through personal relations, the other a political activist. The former's suicide at the end of the film can be read as marking a decisive choice: from here on, Godard increasingly listens to the voice of revolutionary politics and eventually (in the Dziga Vertov films) adopts it as his own voice.

The films of the Dziga Vertov group (named after the great Russian documentarist who anticipated their work in making films that foreground the means of production and are continuously self-reflexive) were the direct consequence of the events of May 1968. More than ever before the films are directly concerned with their own process, so that the ostensible subjects—the political scene in Czechoslovakia (*Pravda*) or Italy (*Lotte in Italia*), the trial of the Chicago Eight (*Vladimir and Rosa*)—become secondary to the urgent, actual subject: how does one make a revolutionary film? It was at this time that Godard distinguished between making political films (i.e. films on political subjects: Costa-Gavras's *Z* is a typical example) and making films politically, the basic assumption being that one cannot put radical content into traditional form without seriously compromising, perhaps negating, it. Hence the attack on realism initiated at the outset of Godard's career manifests its full political significance: realism is a bourgeois art form, the means whereby the bourgeoisie endlessly reassures itself, validating its own ideology as "true," "natural," "real"; its power must be destroyed. Of the films from this period, *Vent d'est* (the occasion for Peter Wollen's seminal essay on "Counter-Cinema" in *After Image*) most fully realized this aesthetic: the original pretext (the pastiche of a Western) recedes into the background, and the film becomes a discussion about itself—about the relationship between sound and image, the materiality of film, the destruction of bourgeois forms, the necessity for continuous self-criticism and self-awareness.

The assumption behind the Dziga Vertov films is clearly that the revolutionary impetus of May 1968 would be sustained, and it has not been easy for Godard to adjust to its collapse. That difficulty is the subject of one of his finest works, *Tout va bien* (again in collaboration with Gorin), an attempt to return to commercial filmmaking without abandoning the principles (both aesthetic and political) of the preceding years. Beginning by foregrounding Godard's own problem (how does a radical make a film within the capitalist production system?), the film is strongest in its complex use of Yves Montand and Jane Fonda (simultaneously fictional characters/personalities/star images) and its exploration of the issues to which they are central. These issues include the relationship of intellectuals to the class struggle; the relationship between professional work, personal commitment, and political position; and the problem of sustaining a radical impulse in a non-revolutionary age. *Tout va bien* is Godard's most authentically Brechtian film, achieving radical force and analytical clarity without sacrificing pleasure and a degree of emotional involvement.

Godard's relationship to Brecht has not always been so clear-cut. While the justification for Brecht's distanciation principles was always the communication of clarity, Godard's films often leave the spectator in a state of confusion and frustration. He continues to seem by temperament more anarchist than Marxist. One is troubled by the continuity between the criminal drop-outs of the earlier films and the political activists of the later. The insistent intellectualism of the films is often offset by a wilful abeyance of systematic thinking, the abeyance, precisely, of that self-awareness and self-criticism the political works advocate. Even in *Tout va bien,* what emerges from the political analysis as the film's own position is an irresponsible and ultimately desperate belief in spontaneity. Desperation, indeed, is never far from the Godardian surface, and seems closely related to the treatment of heterosexual relations: even through the apparent feminist awareness of the recent work runs a strain of unwitting misogyny (most evident, perhaps, in *Sauve qui peut*). The central task of Godard criticism, in fact, is to sort out the remarkable and salutary nature of the positive achievement from the temperamental limitations that flaw it.

From 1980 on, Godard commenced the second phase of his directorial career. Unfortunately, far too many of his films have become increasingly inaccessible to the audiences who had championed him in his heyday during the 1960s. *Sauve qui peut (La Vie) (Every Man for Himself),* Godard's comeback film, portended his future work. It is an awkward account of three characters whose lives become entwined: a man who has left his wife for a woman; the woman, who is in the process of leaving the man for a rural life; and a country girl who has become a prostitute.

In fact, several of Godard's works might best be described as anti-movies. *Passion,* for example, features characters named Isabelle, Michel, Hanna, Laszlo and Jerzy (played respectively by Isabelle Huppert, Michel Piccoli, Hanna Schygulla, Laszlo Szabo, and Jerzy Radziwilowicz), who are involved in the shooting of a movie titled *Passion.* The latter appears to be not so much a structured narrative as a series of scenes which are visions of a Renaissance painting. The film serves as a cynical condemnation of the business of moviemaking-for-profit, as the extras are poorly treated and the art of cinema is stained by commercial considerations.

Prenom: Carmen (First Name: Carmen) is Godard's best latter-career effort, a delightfully subversive though no less pessimistic mirror of the filmmaker's disenchantment with the cinema. His Carmen is a character straight out of his earlier work: a combination seductress/terrorist/wannabe movie maker. Her uncle, played by Godard, is a once-celebrated but now weary and faded film director named, not surprisingly, Jean-Luc Godard.

It seemed that Godard had simply set out to shock in *Hail, Mary,* a redo of the birth of Christ set in contemporary France. His Mary is a young student and gas station attendant; even though she has never had sex with Joseph, her taxi-driving boyfriend, she discovers she is pregnant. Along with Scorsese's *The Last Temptation of Christ,* this became a cause celebre among Catholics and even was censured by the Pope. However, the film is eminently forgettable; far superior is *The Book of Mary,* a perceptive short about a girl and her constantly quarrelling parents. It accompanied showings of *Hail, Mary,* and is directed by long-time Godard colleague Anne-Marie Miéville.

Detective, dedicated to auteur heroes John Cassavetes, Edgar G. Ulmer, and Clint Eastwood, is a verbose, muddled film noir. Despite its title, *Nouvelle Vague (New Wave),* an observance of the lives of a wealthy and influential couple, only makes one yearn for the days of the real "Nouvelle Vague." The narrative, which focuses on the sexual and political issues that are constants in Godard's films, is barely discernable; the dialogue—including such lines as "Love doesn't die, it leaves you," "One man isn't enough for a woman—or too much," "A critic is a soldier who fires at his own regiment," "Have you ever been stung by a dead bee?"—is superficially profound.

King Lear, an excessive, grotesque updating of Shakespeare, is of note for its oddball, once-in-a-lifetime cast: Godard; Woody Allen; Norman and Kate Mailer; stage director Peter Sellars; Burgess Meredith; and Molly Ringwald. The political thriller *Allemagne Neuf Zero (Germany Nine Zero),* although as confusing as any latter-day Godard film, works as nostalgia because of the presence of Eddie Constantine. He is recast as private eye Lemmy Caution, who last appeared in *Alphaville.* Here, he encounters various characters in a reunified Germany.

Helas Pour Moi (Oh, Woe Is Me), based on the Greek legend of Alcmene and Amphitryon and a text penned by the Italian poet Leopardi, is a long-winded bore about a God who wants to perceive human feeling; those intrigued by the subject matter would be advised to see Wim Wenders' *Wings of Desire* and *Faraway, So Close. JLG/JLG—Autoportrait de Decembre (JLG/JLG—Self-Portrait in December),* filmed in and near Godard's Swiss home, is a semi-abstract biography of the filmmaker. Its structure is appropriate, given the development of Godard's cinematic style. Ultimately, it is of interest mostly to those still concerned with Godard's life and career.

—Robin Wood, updated by Rob Edelman

GÓMEZ, Sara

Nationality: Cuban. **Born:** Havana, 1943. **Education:** Conservatory of Music, Havana. **Career:** Assistant director at Instituto Cubano del Arte e industria Cinematograficos (ICAIC), under Tomás Gutiérrez Alea, Jorge Fraga, and Agnes Varda, from 1961; directed first film, *Ire a Santiago,* 1964; shot and edited first feature, *De cierta manera,* 1974; original negative, damaged in processing, restored under supervision of Gutiérrez Alea and Rigoberto Lopez, 1974-76. **Died:** Of acute asthma, 2 June 1974.

Films as Director:

1964 *Ire a Santiago*
1965 *Excursion a Vueltabajo*
1967 *Y tenemos sabor*
1968 *En la otra isla*
1969 *Isla del tesero*
1970 *Poder local, poder popular*
1971 *Un documental a proposito del transito*
1972 *Atencion prenatal*; *Ano uno*
1973 *Sobre horas extras y trabajo voluntario*
1977 ***De cierta manera*** (*One Way or Another*)

Publications

On GÓMEZ: book—

Chanan, Michael, *The Cuban Image,* London, 1985.

On GÓMEZ: articles—

Chijona, Geraldo, and Rigoberto López, in *Cine Cubano* (Havana), no. 93.
Burton, Julianne, "Individual Fulfillment and Collective Achievement," in *Cinéaste* (New York), January 1977.
Burton, Julianne, "Introduction to the Revolutionary Cuban Cinema," and Carlos Galiano, "*One Way or Another*: The Revolution in Action," in *Jump Cut* (Chicago), December 1978.
Lesage, Julia, "*One Way or Another*: Dialectical, Revolutionary, Feminist," in *Jump Cut* (Chicago), May 1979.

* * *

We shall never know all that Sara Gómez might have given to us. We have her one feature film, the marvelous *De cierta manera,* and a few short documentaries to indicate what might have been had she lived beyond the age of thirty-one. But we will never really know all that this prodigiously talented black woman was capable of.

Sara Gómez could be seen as prototypical of the new Cuban directors. Entering the Cuban Film Institute (ICAIC) at an early age, she worked as assistant director for various cineastes, including Tomás Gutiérrez Alea, whose influence marked her work as it has so many young directors. During a ten-year period (1964-74) she fulfilled the usual apprenticeship among Cuban cineastes by directing documentary films. Documentaries are seen as an important training ground for Cuban directors because they force them to focus on the material reality of Cuba and thus emphasize the use of cinema as an expression of national culture. As Gutiérrez Alea noted, "the kind of cinema which adapts itself to our interests, fortunately, is a kind of light, agile

Sara Gómez

cinema, one that is very directly founded upon our own reality." This is precisely the kind of cinema Sara Gómez went on to produce, beginning work on *De cierta manera* in 1974 and finishing the editing of the film shortly before her death of acute asthma.

Gómez's early training in documentaries and the influence of Gutiérrez Alea is evident in *De cierta manera.* The film combines the documentary and fiction forms so inextricably that they are impossible to disentangle. Through this technique, she emphasized the material reality that is at the base of all creative endeavor and the necessity of bringing a critical perspective to all forms of film.

In choosing this style, which I call "dialectical resonance," Gómez appeared to follow Gutiérrez Alea's example in the superb *Memories of Underdevelopment.* But there is a crucial difference between the two films—a difference that might be said to distinguish the generation of directors who came of age before the triumph of the revolution (e.g. Gutiérrez Alea) from those who have grown up within the revolution. In spite of its ultimate commitment to the revolutionary process, *Memories* remains in some ways the perspective of an "outsider" and might be characterized as "critical bourgeois realism." However, *De cierta manera* is a vision wholly from within the revolution, despite the fact that every position in the film is subjected to criticism—including that of the institutionalized revolution, which is presented in the form of an annoyingly pompous omniscient narration. Thus, the perspective of Gomez might be contrasted to that of *Memories* by calling it "critical socialist realism." The emphasis on dialectical criticism, struggle, and commitment is equally great in both films, but the experience of having grown up within the revolution created a somewhat different perspective.

Despite its deceptively simple appearance—a result of being shot in 16mm on a very low budget—*De cierta manera* is the work of an extremely sophisticated filmmaker. Merely one example among many of Gómez's sophistication is the way in which she combined a broad range of modern distanciation techniques with the uniquely Cuban tropical beat to produce a film that is simultaneously rigorously analytic and powerfully sensuous—as well as perhaps the finest instance to date of a truly dialectical film. Although we are all a little richer for the existence of this work, we remain poorer for the fact that she will make no more films.

—John Mraz

GORETTA, Claude

Nationality: Swiss. **Born:** Geneva, 23 June 1929. **Education:** Law coursework at Université de Genève. **Career:** With Alain Tanner, moved to London, 1955; worked at British Film institute, 1956-57; television director in Switzerland, from 1958; formed production company "Groupe de 5," with Tanner, Jean-Louis Roy, Claude Soutter, and Yves Yersin, 1968; directed first feature, *Le Fou,* 1970. **Awards:** Ecumenical Prize, Cannes Festival, for *La Dentellière,* 1977.

Films as Director and Scriptwriter:

1957 *Nice Time* (co-d, co-sc)
1970 *Le Fou* (*The Madman*) (+ co-pr)
1973 *L'Invitation* (*The Invitation*) (co-sc)
1975 *Pas si méchant que ça* (*Not as Wicked as That*; *The Wonderful Crook*) (co-sc)
1977 ***La Dentellière*** (*The Lacemaker*) (co-sc); *Jean Piaget* (*The Epistemology of Jean Piaget*)
1978 *Les Chemines de l'Exile ou Les Dernières Années de Jean-Jacques Rousseau* (*The Roads of Exile*)
1980 *La Provinciale* (*The Girl from Lorraine*); *Bonheur toi-même*
1983 *La Mort de Mario Ricci* (*The Death of Mario Ricci*)
1985 *Orfeo*
1987 *Si le soleil ne revenais pas* (*If the Sun Never Returns*); *Le Rapport du Gendarme* (for TV)
1991 *L'Ombre*; *Visages Suisses*
1994 *Het Verdriet Van Belgie*

Publications

By GORETTA: book—

La Dentellière, Paris, 1981.

By GORETTA: articles—

Interview with G. Langlois, in *Cinéma* (Paris), April 1973.
Interview with M. Boujut, in *Cinema* (Zurich), vol. 21, no. 1, 1975.
Interview with D. Maillet, in *Cinématographe* (Paris), June 1977.
Interview with Judith Kass, in *Movietone News* (Seattle), 14 August 1978.

On GORETTA: articles—

Delmas, J., "Tanner, Goretta, la Suisse et nous," in *Jeune Cinéma* (Paris), September/October 1973.
"Claude Goretta," in *Cinema* (Zurich), vol. 20, no. 1, 1974.
Milne, Tom, "Goretta's *Roads of Exile,*" in *Sight and Sound* (London), no. 2, 1979.
Milne, Tom, "Claude Goretta," in *Film Dope* (London), April 1980.
"*La Dentellière* Issue" of *Avant-Scène du Cinéma* (Paris), 15 April 1981.
Buache Freddy, "Claude Goretta," in *Revue Belge du Cinéma* (Brussels), Winter 1985.
Buache, F., article in *Cinemaction,* April 1990.

* * *

Claude Goretta's gentle comedies and sensitive depictions of provincial naifs have been among the most successful Swiss films of recent years. Although Goretta shares his countryman Alain Tanner's preoccupation with Renoiresque evocations of landscape and lovable eccentrics, there is a sharp disparity between these two idiosyncratic Swiss directors. As Goretta himself has observed, "Tanner's films always have a discourse, while mine do everything they can to avoid one."

Goretta's first film, an experimental short called *Nice Time,* was in fact made with the collaboration of Alain Tanner when both men were affiliated with the British Film Institute. This impressionistic view of Piccadilly Circus, one of the sleazier parts of central London, prefigures both directors' subsequent interest in whimsical vignettes with serious, and occasionally acerbic, sociological underpinnings.

Like many contemporary directors of note, Goretta served his apprenticeship in television. Many of his early television films were literary adaptations, including an adaptation of four Chekhov stories, *Chekov ou le miroir des vies perdues.*

Goretta's first feature film, *Le Fou,* featured one of his favorite actors, the distinguished character player, François Simon. Despite a mixed critical reception, *Le Fou* was awarded a prize as the best Swiss film of 1970 by the Swiss Critics' Association. *L'Invitation* was the first of Goretta's films to receive widespread international recognition. This unpretentious comedy about the loss of inhibitions experienced by a group of office workers during a mildly uproarious party was ecstatically reviewed by British and American critics who casually invoked the names of both Buñuel and Renoir for the sake of comparison. *Pas si méchant que ça* fared less well with both the critics and public, although Gérard Depardieu's charming portrayal of a whimsical thief was widely praised.

Le Dentellière, an incisive character study of a guileless young beautician played flawlessly by Isabelle Huppert (in her first major role), received an even more rhapsodic critical reception than *L'Invitation.* Jean Boffety's pristine cinematography and Goretta's restrained direction were singled out for praise, although several feminist critics cogently observed that Goretta's reverence for the Huppert character's enigmatic passivity was a singularly insidious example of male condescension.

Les Chemins de l'exil marked Goretta's return to his roots in documentary filmmaking. This leisurely biographical portrait of Jean-Jacques Rousseau stars François Simon as the famed *philosophe* who remains one of the most celebrated figures in Swiss cultural history. *La Provinciale* was a somewhat muddled attempt to reiterate many of the themes first explored in *La Dentellière,* although Nathalie Baye's performance was suffused with integrity. *The Death of Mario Ricci* was favorably received at the 1983 Cannes Film Festival.

—Richard Porton

GOSHO, Heinosuke

Nationality: Japanese. **Born:** Tokyo, 1 February 1902. **Education:** Keio Commerce School, graduated 1921. **Family:** Married three times. **Career:** Assistant to director Yasujiro Shimazu, Shochiku-Kamata Studio, 1923; directed first film, *Nanto no haru,* 1925; moved to Daiei Studio, 1941; returned to Shochiku-Ofuna, 1945, then to Toho until 1948; established Studio 8 Productions, affiliated with Shin-Toho, 1951; worked for several studios, from 1954; also writer for television; president of the Japanese Association of Film Directors, 1964-75; also director of the Japanese Haiku Art Association. **Awards:** Eleven films placed among Kinema Jumpo Best Films of the Year between 1927 and 1968; Mainichi Film Prize, Japan, for *One More Time,* 1947; Kun Yon-to Asahi Shoju sho Order of the Japanese Government, 1947; International Peace Prize, Berlin Festival, for *Where Chimneys Are Seen,* 1953. **Died:** 1 May 1981.

Films as Director:

1925 *Nanto no haru* (*Spring of Southern Island*) (+ sc); *Sora wa haretari* (*No Clouds in the Sky*); *Otokogokoro* (*Man's Heart*) (+ sc); *Seishun* (*Youth*) (+ sc); *Tosei tamatebako* (*A Casket for Living*)

1926 *Machi no hitobito* (*Town People*); *Hatsukoi* (*First Love*) (+ sc); *Hahayo koishi* (*Mother, I Miss You*; *Mother's Love*); *Honryu* (*A Torrent*); *Musume* (*A Daughter*) (+ sc); *Kaeranu sasabue* (*Bamboo Leaf Flute of No Return*; *No Return*); *Itoshi no wagako* (*My Loving Child*) (+ sc); *Kanojo* (*She*; *Girl Friend*) (+ sc)

1927 *Sabishiki ranbomono* (*Lonely Hoodlum*); *Hazukashii yume* (*Shameful Dream*), *Karakuri musume* (*Fake Girl*) (+ co-sc); *Shojo no shi* (*Death of a Maiden*) (+ co-sc); *Okame* (*A Plain Woman*) (+ sc); *Tokyo koshinkyoko* (*Tokyo March*)

1928 *Sukinareba koso* (*Because I Love*; *If You Like It*) (+ co-sc); *Mura no hanayome* (*The Village Bride*); *Doraku shinan* (*Guidance to the Indulgent*; *Debauchery Is Wrong*) (+ co-sc); *Kami e no michi* (*Road to God*); *Hito no yo no sugata* (*Man's Worldly Appearance*); *Kaido no kishi* (*Knight of the Street*); *Haha yo, kimi no na o kegasu nakare* (*Mother, Do Not Shame Your Name*)

1929 *Yoru no mesuneko* (*Cat of the Night*); *Shin josei kagami* (*A New Kind of Woman*); *Oyaji to sono ko* (*Father and His Son*); *Ukiyo-buro* (*The Bath Harem*) (+ sc); *Netsujo no ichiya* (*A Night of Passion*) (+ co-sc)

1930 *Dokushinsha goyojin* (*Bachelors Beware*) (+ co-sc); *Dai-Tokyo bi ikkaku* (*A Corner of Great Tokyo*) (+ add'l dialogue); *Hohoemu jinsei* (*A Smiling Life*); *Onna yo, kini no na o kegasu nakare* (*Women, Do Not Shame Your Names*); *Shojo nyuyo* (*Virgin Wanted*); *Kinuyo monogatari* (*The Kinuyo Story*); *Aiyoku no ki* (*Record of Love and Desire*)

1931 *Jokyu aishi* (*Sad Story of a Barmaid*); *Yoru hiraku* (*Open at Night*); *Madamu to nyobo* (*Next Door Madame and My Wife*; *The Neighbor's Wife and Mine*); *Shima to ratai jiken* (*Island of Naked Scandal*) (+ add'l dialogue); *Gutei kenkei* (*Stupid Young Brother and Wise Old Brother*) (+ add'l dialogue); *Wakaki hi no kangeki* (*Memories of Young Days*)

1932 *Niisan no baka* (*My Stupid Brother*) *Ginza no yanagi* (*Willows of Ginza*); *Tengoku ni musubu koi* (*Heaven Linked with Love*); *Satsueijo romansu: Renai annai* (*Romance at the Studio: Guidance to Love*); *Hototogisu* (*A Cuckoo*); *Koi no Tokyo* (*Love in Tokyo*)

1933 *Hanayome no negoto* (*The Bride Talks in Her Sleep*); *Izu no odoriko* (*Dancer of Izu*); *Jukyu-sai no haru* (*The Nineteenth Spring*); *Shojo yo sayonara* (*Virgin, Goodbye*); *Lamuru* (*L'Amour*)

1934 *Onna to umaretakaranya* (*Now That I Was Born a Woman*); *Sakura Ondo* (*Sakura Dance*); *Ikitoshi Ikerumono* (*Everything That Lives*)

1935 *Hanamuko no negoto* (*The Bridegroom Talks in His Sleep*); *Hidari uchiwa* (*A Life of Luxury*); *Fukeyo koikaze* (*Breezes of Love*); *Akogare* (*Yearning*); *Jinsei no onimotsu* (*Burden of Life*)

1936 *Oboro yo no onna* (*Woman of Pale Night*); *Shindo* (*New Way*) parts I and II; *Okusama shakuyosho* (*A Married Lady Borrows Money*)

1937 *Hanakago no uta* (*Song of the Flower Basket*) (+ adapt)

1940 *Mokuseki* (*Wood and Stone*)

1942 *Shinsetsu* (*New Snow*)

1944 *Goju-no to* (*The Five-storied Pagoda*)

1945 *Izu no musumetachi* (*Girls of Izu*)

1947 *Ima hitotabi no* (*One More Time*)

1948 *Omokage* (*A Vestige*)

1951 *Wakare-gumo* (*Drifting Clouds*) (+ co-sc)

1952 *Asa no hamon* (*Trouble in the Morning*)

1953 ***Entotsu no mieru basho*** (*Four Chimneys*; *Where Chimneys Are Seen*)

1954 *Osaka no yado* (*An Inn at Osaka*) (+ co-sc); *Niwatori wa futatabi naku* (*The Cock Crows Twice*); *Ai to shi no tanima* (*The Valley Between Love and Death*)

1955 *Takekurabe* (*Growing Up*)

1956 *Aruyo futatabi* (*Again One Night*) (+ co-sc)

1957 *Kiiroi karasu* (*Yellow Crow*; *Behold Thy Son*); *Banka* (*Elegy of the North*)

1958 *Hotaru-bi* (*Firefly's Light*); *Yoku* (*Desire*); *Ari no Machi no Maria* (*Maria of the Street of Ants*)

1959 *Karatachi nikki* (*Journal of the Orange Flower*)

1960 *Waga ai* (*When a Woman Loves*); *Shiroi kiba* (*White Fangs*)

1961 *Ryoju* (*Hunting Rifle*); *Kumo ga chigireru toki* (*As the Clouds Scatter*) (+ co-pr); *Aijo no keifu* (*Record of Love*) (+ co-pr)

1962 *Kachan kekkon shiroyo* (*Mother, Get Married*) (+ co-sc)

Heinosuke Gosho: *Madamu to nyobo*

1963 *Hyakumanin no musumetachi* (*A Million Girls*) (+ co-sc)
1964 *Osore-zan no onna* (*A Woman of the Osore Mountains*; *An Innocent Witch*)
1966 *Kachan to Juichi-nin no Kodomo* (*Mother and Eleven Children*; *Our Wonderful Years*)
1967 *Utage* (*Feast*; *Rebellion in Japan*)
1968 *Onna no misoshiru* (*Women and Miso Soup*); *Meiji haruaki* (*Seasons of Meiji*)

Publications

On GOSHO: books—

Anderson, Joseph, and Donald Richie, *The Japanese Film,* New York, 1961; revised edition, 1982.
Mellen, Joan, *The Waves at Genji's Door,* New York, 1976.
Bock, Audie, *Japanese Film Directors,* New York, 1978; revised edition, Tokyo, 1985.

On GOSHO: articles—

Anderson, J.L., and Donald Richie, "The Films of Heinosuke Gosho," in *Sight and Sound* (London), Autumn 1956.
Gillett, John, "Coca-Cola and the Golden Pavilion," in *Sight and Sound* (London), Summer 1970.
Gillett, John, "Heinosuke Gosho," in *Film Dope* (London), April 1980.
Tessier, Max, "Heinosuke Gosho," in *Image et Son* (Paris), June 1981.
"Heinosuke Gosho: A Pattern of Living," in *National Film Theatre Booklet* (London), March 1986.
Le Fanu, Mark, "To love is to suffer," in *Sight and Sound* (London), Summer 1986.
Niogret, H., "Heinosuke Gosho et la maîtrise du découpage," in *Positif* (Paris), March 1987.

* * *

Gosho began his career in 1925 as a disciple of Yasujiro Shimazu at Shochiku Studio. Young Gosho immediately proved his skill at the genre of "shomin-geki," stories of the life of ordinary people, characteristic of his mentor's work at that studio. Gosho's early films were criticized as "unsound" because they often involved characters physically or mentally handicapped (*The Village Bride* and *Faked Daughter*). Gosho's intention, however, was to illustrate a kind of warm and sincere relationship born in pathos. Today, these films are highly esteemed for their critique of feudalistic village life. Gosho was affected by this early criticism, however, and made his next films about other subjects. This led him into a long creative slump, although he continued to make five to seven films annually.

The first film by Gosho to attract attention was *Lonely Hoodlum* of 1927, a depiction of the bittersweet life of common people, Gosho's characteristic subject. In 1931 Shochiku gave him the challenge of making the first Japanese "talkie" (because many established directors had refused). The film, *Next Door Madame and My Wife,* was welcomed passionately by both audiences and critics. It is a light and clever comedy that effectively uses ambient sounds such as a baby's cries, an alarm clock, a street vendor's voice, and jazz music from next door. Because every sound had to be synchronized, Gosho explored many technical devices, and used multiple cameras, different lenses, and frequent cuts to produce a truly "filmic" result.

Gosho preferred many cuts and close-up shots, a practice he related to his studying Lubitsch carefully in his youth. Gosho's technique of creating a poetic atmosphere with editing is most successful in *Dancer of Izu,* in which he intentionally chose the silent film form after making several successful talkies.

Even after the success of these films, Gosho had to accept many projects which he did not want to do. He later reflected that only those films that he really wanted to do were well-made. For example, he found the subject of *The Living* most appealing—its protagonist tries to protest against social injustice but is unable to continue his struggle to the end.

Gosho is believed to be at his best making films depicting the human side of life in his native Tokyo (*Woman of Pale Night, Song of the Flower Basket, Where Chimneys Are Seen,* and *Comparison of Heights*). However, the director also worked in many other genres, including romantic melodrama, family drama, light comedy, and social drama. He further extended his range in such films as *An Elegy,* a contemporary love story, and *A Woman of Osore-zan,* which is unusual for its unfamiliar dark tones and its eccentricity. His experimental spirit is illustrated by his story of the treatment of a disturbed child with color-oriented visual therapy in *Yellow Crow.*

Throughout his career, Gosho expressed his basic belief in humanistic values. The warm, subtle, and sentimental depiction of likable people is characteristic both of Gosho's major studio productions and his own independent films.

—Kyoko Hirano

GOULDING, Edmund

Nationality: British. **Born:** London, 20 March 1891. **Career:** Stage debut in London, 1903; writer, actor, and director, London theatre, until 1914; New York stage debut, 1915; served with British Army in France, 1915-18; returned to America, worked as writer, 1919; hired by MGM as director/scriptwriter, 1925. **Died:** In Los Angeles, 24 December 1959.

Films as Director:

1925 *Sun-up* (+ sc); *Sally, Irene and Mary* (+ sc)
1926 *Paris* (*Shadows of Paris*) (+ sc)
1927 *Women Love Diamonds* (+ story); *Love* (*Anna Karenina*) (+ adapt, uncredited, pr, sc)
1930 "Dream Girl" episode of *Paramount on Parade* (+ role); *The Devil's Holiday* (+ sc, music, song) [foreign language versions: *Les Vacances du diable* (Cavalcanti); *La vacanza del diavolo* (Salvatori); *La fiesta del diablo* (Millar); *Sonntag des Lebens* (Mittler); *En kvinnas morgondag* (Bergman)]
1931 *Reaching for the Moon* (+ sc); *The Night Angel* (+ sc, song melodies)
1932 *Grand Hotel*; *Blondie of the Follies* (+ co-lyrics, bit role as Follies director)
1934 *Riptide*; *Hollywood Party* (co-d, uncredited)
1935 *The Flame Within* (+ sc)
1937 *That Certain Woman* (+ sc)
1938 *White Banners*; *The Dawn Patrol*
1939 *Dark Victory* (+ song); *The Old Maid*; *We Are Not Alone*
1940 *'Til We Meet Again*
1941 *The Great Lie*
1943 one episode of *Forever and a Day*; *The Constant Nymph*; *Claudia*
1946 *Of Human Bondage*; *The Razor's Edge*; *The Shocking Miss Pilgrim* (Seaton) (d several scenes while Seaton ill)
1947 *Nightmare Alley*
1949 *Everybody Does It*
1950 *Mr. Eight Hundred Eighty*
1952 *Down Among the Sheltering Palms*; *We're Not Married*
1956 *Teenage Rebel* (+ music for song *Dodie*)
1958 *Mardi Gras*

Other Films:

1911 *Henry VIII* (Parker) (role)
1914 *The Life of a London Shopgirl* (Raymond) (role)
1916 *Quest of Life* (sc, co-play basis)
1917 *The Silent Partner* (Neilan) (sc, story)
1918 *The Ordeal of Rosetta* (Chautard) (sc, story)
1919 *The Perfect Love* (Ralph Ince) (sc); *The Glorious Lady* (Irving) (sc, story); *A Regular Girl* (Young) (sc, co-story); *Sealed Hearts* (Ralph Ince) (sc, co-story); *The Imp* (Ellis) (sc, co-story)
1920 *A Daughter of Two Worlds* (Young) (sc); *The Sin That Was His* (Henley) (sc); *The Dangerous Paradise* (Earle) (sc, story); *The Devil* (Young) (sc)
1921 *Dangerous Toys* (*Don't Leave Your Husband*) (Bradley) (sc, story); *The Man of Stone* (Archainbaud) (sc, co-story); *Tol'able David* (King) (co-sc); *Peacock Alley* (Leonard) (sc)
1922 *The Seventh Day* (King) (sc); *Fascination* (Leonard) (sc); *Broadway Rose* (Leonard) (sc); *Till We Meet Again* (Cabanne) (sc); *Heroes of the Street* (Beaudine) (co-sc); *Fury* (King) (sc; d erroneously attributed to Goulding in Library of Congress Copyright Catalogue); *Three Little Ghosts* (Fitzmaurice) (role)
1923 *Dark Secrets* (Fleming) (sc); *Jazzmania* (Leonard) (sc); *The Bright Shawl* (Robertson) (sc); *Bright Lights of Broadway* (*Bright Lights and Shadows*) (Campbell) (sc); *Tiger Rose* (Franklin) (co-sc)
1924 *Dante's Inferno* (Otto) (sc); *The Man Who Came Back* (Flynn) (sc); *Gerald Cranston's Lady* (Flynn) (sc)
1925 *The Dancers* (Flynn) (sc); *The Scarlet Honeymoon* (Hale) (sc, story; some sources credit story to Fannie Davis); *The Fool* (Millarde) (sc); *Havoc* (Lee) (sc); *The Beautiful City* (Webb) (sc, story)
1926 *Dancing Mothers* (Brenon) (co-play basis)
1928 *Happiness Ahead* (Seiter) (story); *A Lady of Chance* (Leonard) (adapt)
1929 *The Broadway Melody* (Beaumont) (story)
1930 *The Grand Parade* (Newmeyer) (sc, pr, songs)
1932 *Flesh* (Ford) (story); *No Man of Her Own* (Ruggles) (co-story)
1940 *Two Girls on Broadway* (*Choose Your Partner*) (Simon) (remake of *The Broadway Melody*, 1929)
1944 *Flight from Folly* (Mason) (story basis)

Publications

By GOULDING: book—

Fury, 1922.

Edmund Goulding

By GOULDING: article—

"The Razor's Edge," in *Life* (New York), 12 August 1946.

On GOULDING: articles—

Time (New York), 19 May 1947.
Obituary, in the *New York Times,* 25 December 1959.
Sarris, Andrew, "Likable But Elusive," in *Film Culture* (New York), Spring 1963.
Brooks, Louise, "Why I Will Never Write My Memoirs," in *Film Culture* (New York), no. 67-69, 1979.
Walker, Michael, "Edmund Goulding," in *Film Dope* (London), April 1980.
Films and Filming (London), July 1983.
"Edmund Goulding: Love, Marriage, Infidelity," in *National Film Theatre Booklet* (London), January 1984.

* * *

Our sense of Edmund Goulding is, of course, skewed by his frequently revived *Grand Hotel* and *Dark Victory.* These films are viewed today not as examples of the director's art, but rather as star acting vehicles, the second also being seen as a prototypical "woman's film." It is generally assumed that such films were primarily authored by the studio and the stars. Yet, without suggesting that Goulding had a visual signature as distinctive as von Sternberg's or a thematic/ideological one as coherent as Capra's, we must recognize the director's personality in the care of the stagings and in the vitality of the performances complemented by those stagings.

Grand Hotel seems, at first, a product of MGM's collective enterprise rather than Goulding's particular imagination. The sleekness of the writing, photography, and art direction are exemplary of the studio that defined cinematic luxury. The assembly of stars—Garbo, Crawford, Beery, John and Lionel Barrymore—in a "hotel" as grand as the studio itself would seem sufficient *direction* of the film. Yet we must give Goulding credit for the exceptionally involved choreography of faces, voices, and bodies in *Grand Hotel* when we look at the same stars in other movies of the period. The film's numerous two-shots are organized with a nuance that makes us as attentive to the shifting relationships between those starry faces as we are to the faces themselves. And we need only see Garbo as directed by Clarence Brown or George Fitzmaurice to appreciate the contribution of Edmund Goulding. He is exceptionally sensitive to the time it takes the actress to register thought through her mere act of presence.

That sensitivity is not diminished when Goulding directs Bette Davis, whose rhythm is totally dissimilar to Garbo's. In *Dark Victory* and *The Old Maid* the director presides over shots that permit us to perceive star and character simultaneously, a requisite of successful screen star performance. Goulding's strength is in characterization, in creating the kind of atmosphere in which actors explore the richest areas within themselves, and in creating the visual/aural contexts that put such exploration in relief for the viewer. This is certainly the case in *The Constant Nymph.* Its precious narrative conceit—a soulful adolescent girl (Joan Fontaine) inspires an excessively cerebral composer (Charles Boyer) to write music with emotion—both reflects the emotional qualities of Goulding's films and displays the actors at their most courageous.

For Goulding, the mature Joan Fontaine is able to sustain her impersonation of an impulsive, loving girl for the whole length of a film. And in *Nightmare Alley,* Tyrone Power is pushed to expose his own persona in the most unflattering light—the "handsome leading man" as charlatan. But that exposure, one of many in the films of Goulding, is also evidence of his affinity for the dilemma of the performing artist, vulnerable in the magnifying exposures of the cinematic medium and dependent on the director's empathy if that vulnerability is to become a meaningful cinematic sign.

—Charles Affron

GREENAWAY, Peter

Nationality: British. **Born:** London, 5 April 1942. **Education:** Studied painting. **Career:** First exhibition of paintings, London, 1964; worked as a film editor for Central Office of Information, 1965-76; made first film, *Train,* 1966; made first feature, *The Falls,* 1980; *A TV Dante* broadcast, 1990. **Awards:** Special Award, British Film Institute, for *The Falls,* 1980; Best Short Film, Melbourne Festival, for *Act of God,* 1981; Best Artistic Contribution, Cannes Festival, for *Drowning by Numbers,* 1988; two prizes, Festival International du Nouveau Cinema et de la Video, for *A TV Dante,* 1990.

Films as Director:

1966 *Train*; *Tree*
1967 *Revolution*; *Five Postcards from Capital Cities*
1969 *Intervals*
1971 *Erosion*
1973 *H is for House*
1975 *Windows*; *Water*; *Water Wrackets*
1976 *Goole by Numbers*
1977 *Dear Phone*
1978 *1-100*; *A Walk Through H*; *Vertical Features Remake*
1980 *The Falls*
1981 *Act of God*; *Zandra Rhodes*
1982 ***The Draughtsman's Contract***
1983 *Four American Composers*
1984 *Making a Splash*; *A TV Dante—Canto 5*
1985 *Inside Rooms—The Bathroom*; *A Zed and Two Noughts*
1987 *The Belly of an Architect*
1988 *Drowning by Numbers*
1989 ***The Cook, the Thief, His Wife and Her Lover***; *A TV Dante*
1991 *Prospero's Books*; *M is for Man, Music, Mozart*
1992 *Rosa*
1993 *The Baby of Macon*

Publications

By GREENAWAY: books—

A Walk Through H, London, 1978.
Verticle Features Remake, London, 1979.
The Falls, London, 1980.
The Droughtsman's Contract, London, 1982.
A Zed and Two Noughts, London, 1986.
The Belly of an Architect, London, 1988.
Drowning by Numbers, London, 1988.
The Cook, the Thief, His Wife and Her Lover, London, 1989.
Fifty-five Men on Horseback, London, 1990.
Prospero's Books, New York, 1991.
Flying Out of This World, Paris, 1992; Chicago, 1994.

By GREENAWAY: articles—

Interview with K. Jaehne, in *Cineaste* (New York), vol. 13, no. 2, 1984.

Interviews with Michel Ciment, in *Positif* (Paris), February 1984 and October 1987.
Interview with E. Decaux and B. Villien, in *Cinématographe* (Paris), March 1984.
Interview with Don Ranvaud, in *Sight and Sound* (London), Summer 1987.
"Architecture and Morality," an interview with J. Clarke, in *Films and Filming* (London), October 1987.
Interview in *Post Script* (Jacksonville, Florida), Winter 1989.
Interview with Michel Ciment in *Positif* (Paris), November 1989.
Interview in *Cinema Papers* (Melbourne), March 1990.
Interview with Gary Indiana in *Interview* (New York), March 1990.
"Food for Thought," interview with Gavin Smith in *Film Comment* (New York), May/June 1990.
"Paintbox-bilder," in *Monthly Film Bulletin* (London), vol. 33, no. 5-6, 1991.
Interview with Marcia Pally in *Cineaste* (New York), vol. 18, no. 3, 1991.
Interview with Michel Ciment in *Positif* (Paris), April 1991.
"Notes de travail pour *Les livres de Prospero,*" in *Positif* (Paris), May 1991.
Interview with Michel Ciment in *Positif* (Paris), October 1991.
Interview with Lawrence Frascella in *Harper's Bazaar* (New York), November 1991.

On GREENAWAY: book—

Caux, Daniel, and others, *Peter Greenaway,* Paris, 1987.

On GREENAWAY: articles—

Simon, L., "Music and Film: An Interview with Michael Nyman," in *Millenium* (New York), Fall 1981/Winter 1982.
Kennedy, Harlan, "Peter Greenaway: His rise and *Falls,*" in *Film Comment* (New York), January/February 1982.
Brown, R., "*The Draughtsman's Contract*: From a view to death," in *Monthly Film Bulletin* (London), November 1982.
Auty, Chris, "Greenaway's Games," in *Stills* (London), May/June 1983.
Rayns, Tony, "Peter Greenaway," in *American Cinematographer* (Los Angeles), September 1983.
"*The Draughtsman's Contract* Issue" of *Avant-Scène du Cinéma* (Paris), October 1984.
Rayns, Tony, "Of Natural History and Mythology Born," in *Monthly Film Bulletin* (London), December 1985.
"Peter Greenaway Section" of *Positif* (Paris), April 1986.
Elsaesser, Thomas, and Tony Rayns, "*Drowning by Numbers*: Games of Love and Death," in *Monthly Film Bulletin* (London), October 1988.
Bohringer, R., article in *Positif* (Paris), November 1989.
De Feo, R., "Fantasy in Crimson," in *Art News* (New York), March 1990.
Trucco, T., "The Man Will Eat Literally Anything," in *New York Times,* 1 April 1990.
Acker, K., "The Color of Myth," in *Village Voice* (New York), 17 April 1990.
Van Gelder, L., "At the Movies," in *New York Times,* 29 June 1990.
Pally, Marcia, "Order vs. Chaos: The Films of Peter Greenaway," in *Cineaste* (New York), vol. 18, no. 3, 1991.
Jacobs, K., "For Peter Greenaway, Movies Are a Dutch Treat," in *New York Times,* 21 April 1991.
Clark, J., "Filmographies," in *Premiere* (New York), September 1991.
Richard, F., article in *Positif* (Paris), October 1991.
Frascella, L., "Britain's Mavericks," in *Harper's Bazaar* (New York), November 1991.
Rodman, H.A., "Anatomy of a Wizard," in *American Film* (Los Angeles), November/December 1991.

* * *

An ancient Chinese encyclopedia, according to Borges, divides animals into "(a) those that belong to the Emperor, (b) embalmed ones, (c) those that are trained, (d) suckling pigs, (e) mermaids, (f) fabulous ones, (g) stray dogs, (h) those that are included in this classification, (i) those that tremble as if they are mad, (j) innumerable ones, (k) those drawn with a very fine camel's hair brush, (l) others, (m) those that have just broken a flower vase, (n) those that resemble flies from a distance." One is tempted to add, (o) those featured in Peter Greenaway's films. The inclusion would seem appropriate for a filmmaker who has constantly displayed a fascination for the organic and the classificatory in a body of films that have themselves retained an art-house individuality within the broader criteria of popular success.

Greenaway's biography implies a deeper integration between life and his art than some critics might suggest. He grew up in post-war Essex, his father was an ornithologist—perhaps the quintessential English hobby—and the petit-bourgeois world of public respectability and private eccentricity seems to have left him with a taste for the contradictory that hallmarks his work ("The black humour, irony, distancing, a quality of being in control, an interest in landscape, treating the world as equal with an image, these are very English qualities. I can't imagine myself living abroad"). He trained as a painter rather than a filmmaker, but his first exhibition, "Eisenstein at the Winter Palace," indicated an interest that led him into film editing at the Central Office of Information, the government department responsible for informing the public in the unique "home-counties" voice of domestic propaganda.

These years also saw Greenaway developing a crop of his own absurdist works—films, art, novels, illustrated books, drawings—with titles such as *Goole by Numbers* and *Dear Phone,* as well as directing (non-absurdist) Party Political Broadcasts for the Labour Party. They also saw the introduction of his fictional alter ego, Tulse Luper, archivist, cartographer, ornithologist extraordinaire ("He's me at about 65. A know-all, a Buckminster Fuller, a McLuhan, a John Cage, a pain"). Nomenclature means a lot to Greenaway in determining where one would be filed in the unfortunate event of a statistically (im)probable end. *The Falls* is a catalogue of victims of V.U.E. (Violent Unknown Event), with characters such as Mashanter Fallack, Carlos Fallanty, Raskado Fallcastle, and Hearty Fallparco. The epitome of absurdity was perhaps reached in *Act of God,* a film based around interviews with people who'd been struck by lightning in an attempt to find out what led to such an unpredictable event.

But perhaps the most tickling piece of absurdity for Greenaway came in the commercial success of *The Draughtsman's Contract,* his first film made on a reasonable budget. It made an uncharacteristic concession to plot, characterization, and scenic coherence. A stylish, lavish, and enigmatic puzzle revolving around murder in a stately seventeenth-century English home, it soon became the subject of a mythical French film conference that discussed its title for five days, and gained popular fame as everyone asked what was it all about. But it made Greenaway's name, and briefly contested box office ratings with the likes of *E.T.* and *Gandhi,* although Greenaway's intended length was four hours—"one suspects it was originally closer to *Tristram Shandy* than *Murder at the Vicarage,*" as one critic remarked.

Greenaway's ideas tend to work in twos. *A Zed and Two Noughts* took Siamese twins separated at birth and saw them cope with their grief at the death of their wives in a study in the decomposition of zoo animals. *Belly of an Architect* silhouetted the visceral mortality of Stourley Kracklite against his plans for an exhibition on a visionary eighteenth-century architect, Etiénne-Louis Boullée. But the dialectic seems more important than the ideas themselves, as Greenaway hints: "The important thing about Boullée—and this is where he's very like a filmmaker, who tends to spend much more time on uncompleted projects than completed ones—is that very few of his buildings were constructed. I've taken that up in Kracklite's fear of committal,

Peter Greenaway

being prepared to go half-way and no further, which is Kracklite's position and maybe my position as well."

In this position Greenaway has always been most successful when casting strong leading actors. He secured Brian Dennehy as Kracklite, for instance, and the cast of arguably his most successful film, *The Cook, The Thief, His Wife and Her Lover,* included Michael Gambon (the Thief) and Helen Mirren (his Wife).

Greenaway's ideas are always sufficiently ambiguous to resist trivialisation, but invariably involve death: Death and Landscape, Death and Animals, Death and Architecture, Death and Sex, Death and Food (cannibalism). But there are factors which make them more palatable. One of them is a taste for sumptuous framing (helped by cinematographer Sacha Vierney), in which he envisages an aesthetic complexity similar to that of the golden age of Dutch art, "where those amazing manifestations of the real world that we find in Vermeer and Rembrandt are enriched by a fantastic metaphorical language." The other is his close collaboration with the composer Michael Nyman, whose insistent scores lend an inexorable quality to Greenaway's sometimes spatial fabric of ideas.

The films of Peter Greenaway continue to be consistently outrageous and challenging. *Drowning by Numbers* is a bizarre, erotic concoction about three generations of women, each named Cissie Colpitts (and played by Joan Plowright, Juliet Stevenson, and Joely Richardson). Each Cissie is saddled with a husband who is lecherous or inattentive. And each one decides to murder her mate by drowning him. Madgett the coroner (Bernard Hill), who lusts after these women, agrees to list the deaths as natural. But the heroines hold the upper hand in the story, and Madgett's fate proves to be beyond his control.

Prospero's Books is an original, daring adaptation of Shakespeare's *The Tempest,* with almost all of the dialogue spoken by 87-year-old Sir John Gielgud (cast as Prospero, a role he played many times on stage). The other actors are little more than extras and, as in many of Greenaway's works, there is a mind-boggling amount of nudity. Purist defenders of the Bard may find much to fault in *Prospero's Books.* But the film remains noteworthy both for Gielgud's splendid reading of the text and its exquisitely layered imagery and production design.

Finally, *The Baby of Macon,* which featured Julia Ormond and Ralph Fiennes prior to their ascension to stardom, is a demanding drama. It is set in the 17th century and presented as a play being performed on a vast stage. The play depicts the birth and life of a saint-like baby. In typical Greenaway fashion, there is luminous cinematography (by the filmmaker's frequent collaborator, Sacha Vierny) and production design. Some will find *The Baby of Macon* stimulating; others will think it overblown; and still others will be perplexed by it all.

There are contradictions in Greenaway's works, a fact that seems to openly provoke divided opinion. Some would suggest that the fecundity of his vision, his intellectual rigor, is the stuff of great cinema; others, while admitting his originality, would still look for evidence of a deeper engagement with film as a medium, rather than as a vehicle for ideas. Lauded in Europe, under-distributed in the United States, loved and reviled in his own country, Greenaway is, nevertheless, in an enviable position for a filmmaker.

—Saul Frampton, updated by Rob Edelman

GRÉMILLON, Jean

Nationality: French. **Born:** Bayeux, Normandy, 3 October 1901. **Education:** l'Ecole Communale de Saint-Lô, Lycée de Brest, and Ecole des Cordeliers, Dinan; Schola Cantorum, Paris (studied with Vincent d'Indy), 1920. **Military Service:** 1920-22. **Family:** Married Christiane (Grémillon). **Career:** Film titler, editor, and director of short films, from 1923; worked in Spain and Germany, 1935-38; war cinematographer, from 1939; elected president of Cinémathèque Française, 1944; president of C.G.T., film technicians union, 1946-50. **Died:** 25 November 1959.

Films as Director:

1923 *Chartres* (*Le Cathédrale de Chartres*) (+ ed); *Le Revêtement des routes* (+ ed)
1924 *La Fabrication du fil* (+ ed); *Du fil à l'aiguille* (+ ed); *La Fabrication du ciment artificiel* (+ ed); *La Bière* (+ ed); *Le Roulement à billes* (+ ed); *Les Parfums* (+ ed); *L'Étirage des ampoules électriques* (+ ed); *La Photogénie mécanique* (+ ed)
1925 *L'Education professionelle des conducteurs de tramway* (six short films) (+ ed); *L'Electrification de la ligne Paris-Vierzon* (+ ed); *L'Auvergne* (+ ed); *La Naissance des cigognes* (+ ed); *Les Aciéries de la marine et d'Homécourt* (+ ed)
1926 *La Vie des travailleurs italiens en France* (+ ed); *La Croisière de L'Atalante* (+ ed); *Un Tour au large* (+ ed, sc, music—recorded on piano rolls)
1927 *Maldone* (+ ed, co-music); *Gratuités* (+ ed)
1928 *Bobs* (+ ed)
1929 *Gardiens de phare* (+ ed)
1930 *La Petite Lise* (+ ed)
1931 *Dainah la métisse* (+ ed) (disowned due to unauthorized reediting); *Pour un sou d'amour* (no d credit on film; + ed)
1932 *Le Petit Babouin* (+ ed, music)
1933 *Gonzague ou L'Accordeur* (+ sc)
1934 *La Dolorosa*
1935 *La Valse royale* (French version of Herbert Maisch's *Königswalzer*)
1936 *Centinella alerta!* (not completed by Grémillon); *Pattes de mouches* (+ co-sc)
1937 *Gueule d'amour*
1938 *L'Etrange Monsieur Victor*
1941 *Remorques*
1943 *Lumière d'été*
1944 *Le Ciel est à vous*
1945 *Le Six Juin à l'aube* (*Sixth of June at Dawn*) (+ sc, music)
1949 *Pattes blanches* (+ co-dialogue); *Les Charmes de l'existence* (co-d, co-sc, co-commentary, music advisor)
1951 *L'Etrange Madame X*
1952 *Astrologie ou Le Miroir de la vie* (+ sc, co-music); "Alchimie" episode of *L'Encyclopédie filmée—Alchimie, Azur, Absence* (+ sc)
1954 *L'Amour d'une femme* (+ sc, dubbed actor Paolo Stoppa); *Au cœur de l'Ile de France* (+ sc, co-music)
1955 *La Maison aux images* (+ sc, music)
1956 *Haute Lisse* (+ sc, music adapt)
1958 *André Masson et les quatre éléments* (+ sc, music)

Other Film:

1951 *Désastres de la guerre* (Kast) (commentary and co-music)

Publications

By GRÉMILLON: books—

Hommage à Jacques Feyder, Paris, 1948.
Le Printemps de la Liberté, Paris, 1948.

By GRÉMILLON: articles—

"Propositions," in *Comoedia* (Paris), 27 November 1925.

Jean Grémillon: Mireille Balin and Jean Gabin in *Gueule d'amour*

"Le Cinema? Plus qu'un art ...," in *L'Ecran Français* (Paris), August 1947.
"Jacques Feyder, ce combattant," in *L'Ecran Français* (Paris), 8 June 1948.
"Conférences sur Flaherty," in *Cinéma* (Paris), no. 9-10, 1956.
"Ma rencontre avec André Masson," in *Les Lettres Françaises* (Paris), 24 November 1960.

On GRÉMILLON: books—

Jean Grémillon, Première Plan, no. 5, Paris, 1960.
Agel, Henri, "Jean Grémillon," in *Cinéma d'aujourd'hui,* no. 58, Paris, 1969.
Sellier, Geneviève, *Jean Grémillon: Le Cinéma est à vous,* Paris, 1989.

On GRÉMILLON: articles—

Hackett, Hazel, "Jean Grémillon," in *Sight and Sound* (London), Summer 1947.
Kast, Pierre, "Exercice d'un tragique quotidien ...," in *Revue du Cinéma* (Paris), August 1948.
"Grémillon Issue" of *Ciné-Club* (Paris), January/February 1951.
Laurent, F., "Sur Jean Grémillon," in *Image et Son* (Paris), February 1955.
"Gremillon Issue" of *Lettres Françaises* (Paris), 3 December 1959.
Chevassu, François, "Dossier Jean Grémillon," in *Image et Son* (Paris), January 1960.
Mayoux, Michel, "Jean Grémillon, cinéaste de la réalité," in *Cahiers du Cinéma* (Paris), February 1960.
"Grémillon Issue" of *Cinéma* (Paris), March 1960.
Clair, René, "Jean Grémillon devant l'avenir," in *Lettres Françaises* (Paris), 24 November 1960.
Vivet, J.-P., "Hommage à Jean Grémillon," in *Avant-Scène du Cinéma* (Paris), 15 September 1962.
Billard, Pierre, "Jean Grémillon," in *Anthologie du Cinéma,* vol. 2, Paris, 1967.
Siclier, Jacques, "Portrait: Jean Grémillon," in *Radio-Télé-Cinéma* (Paris), 24 November 1969.
"Jean Grémillon," in *Dossier du Cinéma* (Paris), 1971.
Le Dantec, and M. Latil, "Jean Grémillon: le réalisme et le tragique," in *Cinématographe* (Paris), no. 40, 1978.
Le Dantec, and M. Latil, "Le Cinéma de Jean Grémillon," in *Cinématographe* (Paris), no. 41, 1978.
Biofilmography, in *Film Dope* (London), October 1980.
"Jean Grémillon Section" of *Cinéma* (Paris), November 1981.
"*Le Ciel est à vous* Issue" of *Avant-Scène du Cinéma* (Paris), 15 November 1981.
"Grémillon Issue" of *Filmkritik* (Munich), April 1983.
Detassis, P., "Jean Grémillon, 'l'uomotramite' tra due epoche del cinema francese," in *Bianco e Nero* (Rome), October/December 1983.
Kast, Pierre, in *Cinéma* (Paris), December 1984.

* * *

Jean Grémillon is finally beginning to enjoy the international reputation most French film scholars always bestowed upon him. Although Americans have until recently been able to see only one or two of his dozen important works, he has generally been placed only slightly below Renoir, Clair, and Carné in the hierarchy of French classical cinema.

Evidently, no one was more versatile than Grémillon. A musician, he composed many of his own scores and supervised all aspects of his productions scrupulously. Along with the search for a romantic unity of feeling and consistency of rhythm, his films also display an attention to details and locations that derives from his earliest documentaries.

No one was more prepared than Grémillon for the poetic realist sensibility that dominated French cinema in the 1930s. Even in the silent period his *Maldone* and *Gardiens de phare* reveal a heightening of strange objects as they take on fatal proportions in these tense and dark melodramas. *La Petite Lise* displayed these same qualities, along with an incredibly imaginative and rigorous use of sound. It should be called the first poetic realist film, anticipating Carné's work in particular.

After a few years of obscurity, Grémillon re-emerged with *Gueule d'amour,* a Foreign Legion love story with Jean Gabin. Then came a series of truly wonderful films: *L'Étrange M. Victor, Remorques, Le Ciel est à vous,* and *Lumière d'été.* Spanning the period of French subjugation by the Nazis, these films capture the sensibility of the times with their wistful romanticism, the fatality of their conclusions, and their attention to social classes.

Le Ciel est à vous must be singled out as a key film of the Occupation. Enormously popular, this tale of a small-town couple obsessed with aviation has been variously interpreted as a work promoting Vichy morality (family, small-town virtues, hard work) and as a representation of the indomitable French spirit, ready to soar beyond the temporary political restraints of the Occupation. Charles Vanel and Madeleine Renaud give unforgettable performances.

Grémillon often sought mythic locations (mysterious villages in the Alps or Normandy, the evocative southern cities of Orange and Toulon) where his quiet heroes and heroines played out their destinies of passion and crime. Unique is the prominent place women hold in his dramas. From the wealthy femme fatale murdered by Gabin in *Gueule d'amour* to the independent professional woman who refuses to give up her medical career, even for love (*L'Amour d'une femme*), women are shown to be far more prepossessed than the passionate but childish men who pursue them.

It is perhaps the greatest tragedy of French cinema that Grémillon's career after World War II was derailed by the conditions of the industry. His *Sixth of June at Dawn* shows how even a documentary project could in his hands take on poetic proportions and become a personal project. Yet the final years before his death in 1959 (when he was only fifty-seven) were spent in teaching and preparing unfinanced scripts. This is a sad end for the man some people claim to have been the most versatile cinematic genius ever to work in France.

—Dudley Andrew

GRIERSON, John

Nationality: Scottish. **Born:** Deanston, Scotland, 18 April 1898. **Education:** Glasgow University, degree in philosophy, 1923. **Military Service:** Served in Royal Navy, World War I. **Family:** Married Margaret Taylor, 1930. **Career:** Travelled to United States to study press, cinema, and other mass media, 1924-27; joined Empire Marketing Board (EMB) Film Unit under Stephen Tallents, London, 1927; produced and directed *Drifters,* 1928-29; became head of General Post Office (GPO) Film Unit when EMB dissolved and its Film unit transferred to GPO, 1933; resigned from GPO to form Film Centre with Arthur Elton, Stuart Legg, and J.P.R. Golightly, 1937; Film Advisor to Imperial Relations Trust, and to Canadian, Australian, and New Zealand Governments, 1937-40; Film Commissioner of Canada, helped establish National Film Board of Canada, 1939-45; Co-coordinator of Mass Media at UNESCO, 1947; Controller, Films Division of Central Office of Information, London, 1948-50; Joint Executive Producer of Group 3, established by National Finance Company to produce feature films, 1951-54; became member of Films on Scotland Committee, 1954; produced and presented *This Wonderful World* for Scottish television, 1955-65. **Awards:** Commander of the British Empire, 1948; Golden Thistle Award, Edinburgh Film Festival, 1968. **Died:** 19 February 1972.

Films as Director:

1929 ***Drifters*** (+ sc)

Other Films:

1930 *Conquest* (pr, co-ed)
1931 *The Country Comes to Town* (Wright) (pr); *Shadow on the Mountain* (pr); *Upstream* (pr)
1931/32 *Industrial Britain* (Flaherty) (pr, co-ed)
1932 *King Log* (pr); *The New Generation* (pr); *The New Operator* (pr); *O'er Hill and Dale* (Wright) (pr); *The Voice of the World* (pr)
1933 *Aero-Engine* (pr); *Cargo from Jamaica* (Wright) (pr); *The Coming of the Dial* (pr); *Eskimo Village* (pr); *Line Cruising South* (Wright) (pr); *So This Is London* (pr); *Telephone Workers* (pr); *Uncharted Waters* (pr); *Windmill in Barbados* (Wright) (pr)
1934 *BBC: Droitwich* (Watt) (pr); *Granton Trawler* (Cavalcanti) (pr, ph); *Pett and Pott* (Cavalcanti) (pr); *Post Haste* (pr); *Six-Thirty Collection* (Watt) (pr); *Song of Ceylon* (Wright) (pr, co-sc); *Spring Comes to England* (co-pr); *Spring on the Farm* (pr); *Weather Forecast* (pr)
1935 *BBC: The Voice of Britain* (co-pr); *Coalface* (Cavalcanti) (pr); *Introducing the Dial* (pr)
1936 *Night Mail* (Watt and Wright) (pr, co-sc); *The Saving of Bill Blewett* (Watt) (pr); *Trade Tattoo* (pr)
1937 *Calender of the Year* (pr); *Children at School* (Wright) (co-pr); *Four Barriers* (pr); *Job in a Million* (pr); *Line to Tschierva Hut* (Cavalcanti) (pr); *The Smoke Menace* (co-pr); *We Live in Two Worlds* (pr)
1938 *The Face of Scotland* (Wright) (pr)
1939 *The Londoners* (co-pr)
1951 *Judgment Deferred* (exec pr); *Brandy for the Parson* (exec pr)
1952 *The Brave Don't Cry* (exec pr); *Laxdale Hall* (exec pr); *The Oracle* (exec pr); *Time Gentlemen Please* (exec pr); *You're Only Young Twice* (exec pr)
1953 *Man of Africa* (exec pr); *Orders Are Orders* (exec pr)
1959 *Seawards the Great Ships* (treatment)
1961/62 *Heart of Scotland* (treatment)

Publications

By GRIERSON: books—

Grierson on Documentary, edited by Forsyth Hardy, revised edition, London, 1966.

John Grierson (right of camera) directing *Drifters*

By GRIERSON: articles—

"Future for British Film," in *Spectator* (London), 14 May 1932.
"The Symphonic Film I," in *Cinema Quarterly* (London), Spring 1933.
"The Symphonic Film II," in *Cinema Quarterly* (London), Spring 1934.
"One Hundred Percent Cinema," in *Spectator* (London), 23 August 1935.
"Dramatising Housing Needs and City Planning," in *Films* (London), November 1939.
"Post-War Patterns," in *Hollywood Quarterly,* January 1946.
"Prospect for Documentary," in *Sight and Sound* (London), Summer 1948.
"Flaherty as Innovator," in *Sight and Sound* (London), October/December 1951.
"The Front Page," in *Sight and Sound* (London), April/June 1952.
"The BBC and All That," in *Quarterly of Film, Radio, Television* (Berkeley), Fall 1954.
"Making of *Man of Africa,*" in *Films and Filming* (London), October 1954.
"The Prospect for Cultural Cinema," in *Film* (London), January/February 1956.
"I Derive My Authority from Moses," in *Take One* (Montreal), January/February 1970.
"The Golden Years of Grierson," interview with Elizabeth Sussex, in *Sight and Sound* (London), Summer 1972.
"Grierson on Documentary: Last Interview," with Elizabeth Sussex, in *Film Quarterly* (Berkeley), Fall 1972.

On GRIERSON: books—

Rotha, Paul, *Rotha on Film,* London, 1958.
Rotha, Paul, *Documentary Film,* 4th Edition, London, 1964.
Lovell, Alan, and Jim Hillier, *Studies in Documentary,* New York, 1972.
Sussex, Elizabeth, *The Rise and Fall of British Documentary: The Story of the Film Movement Founded by John Grierson,* Berkeley, 1975.
Beveridge, J.A., *John Grierson—Film Master,* New York, 1978.
Hardy, Forsyth, *John Grierson: A Documentary Biography,* London, 1979.
Evans, Gary, *John Grierson and the National Film Board: The Politics of Wartime Propaganda,* Toronto, 1984.
Ellis, Jack C., *John Grierson: A Guide to References and Resources,* Boston, 1986.
Nelson, Joyce, *The Colonized Eye: Rethinking the Grierson Legend,* Toronto, 1988.
Ellis, Jack C., *The Documentary Idea,* Englewood Cliffs, New Jersey, 1989.

On GRIERSON: articles—

Lambert, Gavin, "Who Wants True?," in *Sight and Sound* (London), April/June 1952.

Ellis, Jack C., "The Young Grierson in America," in *Cinema Journal* (Evanston, Illinois), Fall 1968.

Ellis, Jack C., "John Grierson's First Years at the National Film Board," in *Cinema Journal* (Evanston, Illinois), Fall 1970.

Sussex, Elizabeth, "John Grierson," in *Sight and Sound* (London), Spring 1972.

James, R., "Le Rêve de Grierson," in *Cinéma Québec* (Montreal), May 1972.

Ellis, Jack C., "Grierson at University," in *Cinema Journal* (Evanston), Spring 1973.

Dickinson, T., "The Rise and Fall of the British Documentary," in *Film Comment* (New York), January/February 1977.

Goetz, W., "The Canadian Wartime Documentary," in *Cinema Journal* (Evanston), Spring 1977.

MacGann, R.D., "Subsidy for the Screen: Grierson and Group Three/ 1951-55," in *Sight and Sound* (London), Summer 1977.

Herrick, D., "The Canadian Connection: John Grierson," in *Cinema Canada* (Montreal), September/October 1978.

Cox, K., "The Grierson Files," in *Cinema Canada* (Montreal), June/ July 1979.

"John Grierson," in *Film Dope* (London), October 1980.

Ellis, Jack C., "Changing of the Guard: From the Grierson documentary to Free Cinema," in *Quarterly Review of Film Studies* (New York), Winter 1982.

Pratley, Gerald, "Only Grierson," in *Films and Filming* (London), March 1982.

Swann, P., "John Grierson and the G.P.O. Film Unit, 1933-39," in *Historical Journal of Film, Radio and TV* (Abindon, Oxon), March 1983.

Ellis, Jack C., "The Final Years of British Documentary as the Grierson Movement," in *Journal of Film and Video* (Boston), Fall 1984.

Tomaselli, K., "Grierson in South Africa: Culture, State and Nationalist Ideology in the South African Film Industry: 1940-41," in *Cinema Canada* (Montreal), September 1985.

"Grierson Issue" of *Historical Journal of Film, Radio and TV* (Abingdon, Oxon), vol. 9, no. 3, 1989.

* * *

More than any one other person, John Grierson was responsible for the documentary film as it has developed in the English-speaking countries. He was the first to use the word *documentary* in relation to film, applying it to Robert Flaherty's *Moana* while Grierson was in the United States in the 1920s.

Grierson took the term and his evolving conception of a new kind and use of film back to Britain with him in 1927. There he was hired by Stephen Tallents, secretary of the Empire Marketing Board, a unique government public relations agency intended to promote the marketing of the products of the British Empire.

The first practical application of Grierson's ideas at the EMB was *Drifters* in 1929, a short feature about herring fishing in the North Sea. Following its success, Grierson established, with the full support of Tallents, the Empire Marketing Board Film Unit instead of pursuing a career as an individual filmmaker. He staffed the Film Unit with young people, mostly middle class and well educated (many were from Cambridge University). Basil Wright, Arthur Elton, Edgar Anstey, and Paul Rotha were among the early recruits; Stuart Legg and Harry Watt came later, as did Humphrey Jennings. Alberto Cavalcanti joined the group shortly after it moved to the General Post Office and served as a sort of co-producer and co-teacher with Grierson.

The training at the EMB Film Unit and subsequently the General Post Office Film Unit was ideological as well as technical and aesthetic. The young filmmakers exposed to it came to share Grierson's broad social purposes and developed an extraordinary loyalty to him and to his goals. It was in this way that the British documentary movement was given shape and impetus.

Grierson wanted documentaries to inform the public about their nation and involve them emotionally with the workings of their government. His assumptions were as follows: if people at work in one part of the Empire are shown to people in the other parts, and if a government service is presented to the population at large, an understanding and appreciation of the interrelatedness of the modern world, and of our dependency on each other, will develop and everyone will want to contribute his or her share to the better functioning of the whole. On these assumptions was based the first phase in Grierson's lifelong activity on behalf of citizenship education. Phase one included some of the most innovative, lovely, and lasting of the British documentaries: *Drifters, Industrial Britain, Granton Trawler, Song of Ceylon, Coal Face,* and *Night Mail.*

Phase two, which began in the mid-1930s, consisted of calling public attention to pressing problems faced by the nation, insistence that these problems needed to be solved, and suggestions about their causes and possible solutions. Since these matters may have involved differing political positions (and in any case did not relate directly to the concerns of the sponsoring General Post Office), Grierson stepped outside the GPO to enlist sponsorship from private industry. Big oil and gas concerns were especially responsive to his persuasion. The subjects dealt with in this new kind of documentary included unemployment (*Workers and Jobs*), slums (*Housing Problems*), malnutrition among the poor (*Enough to Eat?*), smog (*The Smoke Menace*), and education (*Children at School*). Unlike the earlier British documentaries, these films were journalistic rather than poetic, and seemed quite unartistic. Yet they incorporated formal and technical experiments. Most notable among these was the direct interview, with slum dwellers in *Housing Problems,* for example, presaging the much later cinéma vérité method. The direct interview remains a standard technique of television documentary today.

Grierson's use of institutional sponsorship—public and private—to pay for his kind of filmmaking, rather than depend on returns from the box office, was a key innovation in the development of documentary. A second innovation, complementing the first, was nontheatrical distribution and exhibition: going outside the movie theaters to reach audiences in schools and factories, union halls and church basements.

During the ten years between *Drifters* and Grierson's departure for Canada in 1939, the sixty or so filmmakers who comprised the British documentary movement made over three hundred films. These films and the system they came out of became models for other countries. Paul Rotha, one of Grierson's principal lieutenants, went on a six-month missionary expedition to the United States in 1937, and film people from America and other countries visited the documentary units in Britain. Grierson, meanwhile, carried his ideas not only to Canada, where he drafted legislation for the National Film Board and became its first head, but to New Zealand, Australia, and later South Africa, all of which established national film boards.

The National Film Board of Canada stands as the largest and most impressive monument to Grierson's concepts and actions relating to the use of film by governments in communicating with their citizens. During his Canadian years he moved beyond national concerns to global ones. The Film Board's *The World in Action,* a monthly series for the theaters along *March of Time* lines, expressed some of these concerns. His ideas regarding the education of citizens required in a world at war, and a new world to follow, were expressed in major essays that have inspired many who have read them. "The Challenge of Peace," reprinted in *Grierson on Documentary,* is one of them.

It is for his many-faceted, innovative leadership in film and in education that Grierson is most to be valued. As a theoretician he articulated the basis of the documentary film, its form and function, its aesthetic and its ethic. As a teacher he trained and, through his writing and speaking, influenced many documentary filmmakers, not only in Britain and Canada but throughout the world. As a producer he was responsible to one extent or another for thousands of films, and he played a decisive creative role in some of the most important of them. In addition, he was an adroit political figure and dedicated civil servant for most of his life. Whether in the employ of a government or not, his central concern was always with communicating to people (of a nation and of the world) the information and attitudes that he thought would help them to lead more useful, productive, satisfying, and rewarding lives.

—Jack C. Ellis

GRIFFITH, D.W.

Nationality: American. **Born:** David Wark Griffith on Oldham County Farm, near Centerfield, Kentucky, 23 January 1875. **Education:** District schools in Oldham County, Shelby County, and Louisville, Kentucky. **Family:** Married 1) Linda Arvidson, 1906 (divorced 1936); 2) Evelyn Baldwin, 1936 (divorced 1947). **Career:** As "Lawrence Griffith," "Alfred Lawrence," "Lawrence Brayington," and "Thomas Griffith," actor in regional stock companies, 1895-99; actor in New York and in touring companies, 1899-1906; actor for Edison Company and Biograph Pictures, also sold scenarios to Biograph and American Mutascope, 1907; director and scriptwriter for Biograph (approximately 485 one- and two-reelers), 1908-13; began association with cameraman G.W. (Billy) Bitzer, and with actress Mary Pickford, 1909; supervised Mack Sennett's first films, 1910; made first film with Lillian and Dorothy Gish, *An Unseen Enemy,* 1912; joined Reliance Majestic (affiliated with Mutual), 1913; became partner in Triangle Pictures, 1915; travelled to Britain to aid war effort, 1917; engaged by Paramount, 1918; with Pickford, Fairbanks, and Chaplin, formed United Artists, 1919; built own studio at Mamaroneck, New York, 1920; directed three pictures for Paramount, 1925-26; returned to United Artists, 1927 (through 1931); directed his first talking picture, *Abraham Lincoln,* 1930; resigned as head of his own production company, resigned from United Artists Board and sold UA stock, 1932-33; returned to Hollywood to work on *One Million B.C.*, 1939. **Awards:** Director of the Year, 1931, and Special Award, 1936, from Academy of Motion Picture Arts and Sciences; Honorary Doctorate, University of Louisville, 1945. **Died:** In Los Angeles, 23 July 1948.

Films as Director and Scriptwriter:

(at Biograph):

1908 *The Adventures of Dolly*; *The Redman and the Child*; *The Tavern Keeper's Daughter*; *The Bandit's Waterloo*; *A Calamitous Elopement*; *The Greaser's Gauntlet*; *The Man and the Woman*; *For Love of Gold*; *The Fatal Hour*; *For a Wife's Honor*; *Balked at the Altar*; *The Girl and the Outlaw*; *The Red Girl*; *Betrayed by a Hand Print*; *Monday Morning in a Coney Island Police Court*; *Behind the Scenes*; *The Heart of Oyama*; *Where the Breakers Roar*; *The Stolen Jewels*; *A Smoked Husband*; *The Zulu's Heart*; *The Vaquaro's Vow*; *Father Gets in the Game*; *The Barbarian, Ingomar*; *The Planter's Wife*; *The Devil*; *Romance of a Jewess*; *The Call of the Wild*; *After Many Years*; *Mr. Jones at the Ball*; *Concealing a Burglar*; *Taming of the Shrew*; *The Ingrate*; *A Woman's Way*; *The Pirate's Gold*; *The Guerrilla*; *The Curtain Pole*; *The Song of the Shirt*; *The Clubman and the Tramp*; *Money Mad*; *Mrs. Jones Entertains*; *The Feud and the Turkey*; *The Test of Friendship*; *The Reckoning*; *One Touch of Nature*; *An Awful Moment*; *The Helping Hand*; *The Maniac Cook*; *The Christmas Burglars*; *A Wreath in Time*; *The Honor of Thieves*; *The Criminal Hypnotist*; *The Sacrifice*; *The Welcome Burglar*; *A Rural Elopement*; *Mr. Jones Has a Card Party*; *The Hindoo Dagger*; *The Salvation Army Lass*; *Love Finds a Way*; *Tragic Love*; *The Girls and a Daddy*

1909 *Those Boys*; *The Cord of Life*; *Trying to Get Arrested*; *The Fascinating Mrs. Frances*; *Those Awful Hats*; *Jones and the Lady Book Agent*; *The Drive for Life*; *The Brahma Diamond*; *Politician's Love Story*; *The Jones Have Amateur Theatricals*; *Edgar Allen Poe*; *The Roué's Heart*; *His Wife's Mother*; *The Golden Louis*; *His Ward's Love*; *At the Altar*; *The Prussian Spy*; *The Medicine Bottle*; *The Deception*; *The Lure of the Gown*; *Lady Helen's Escapade*; *A Fool's Revenge*; *The Wooden Leg*; *I Did It, Mama*; *The Voice of the Violin*; *And a Little Child Shall Lead Them*; *The French Duel*; *Jones and His New Neighbors*; *A Drunkard's Reformation*; *The Winning Coat*; *A Rude Hostess*; *The Road to the Heart*; *The Eavesdropper*; *Schneider's Anti-Noise Crusade*; *Twin Brothers*; *Confidence*; *The Note in the Shoe*; *Lucky Jim*; *A Sound Sleeper*; *A Troublesome Satchel*; *Tis an Ill Wind That Blows No Good*; *The Suicide Club*; *Resurrection*; *One Busy Hour*; *A Baby's Shoe*; *Eloping with Auntie*; *The Cricket on the Hearth*; *The Jilt*; *Eradicating Auntie*; *What Drink Did*; *Her First Biscuits*; *The Violin Maker of Cremona*; *Two Memories*; *The Lonely Villa*; *The Peach Basket Hat*; *The Son's Return*; *His Duty*; *A New Trick*; *The Necklace*; *The Way of Man*; *The Faded Lilies*; *The Message*; *The Friend of the Family*; *Was Justice Served?*; *Mrs. Jones' Lover* or *"I Want My Hat!"*; *The Mexican Sweethearts*; *The Country Doctor*; *Jealousy and the Man*; *The Renunciation*; *The Cardinal's Conspiracy*; *The Seventh Day*; *Tender Hearts*; *A Convict's Sacrifice*; *A Strange Meeting*; *Sweet and Twenty*; *The Slave*; *They Would Elope*; *Mrs. Jones' Burglar*; *The Mended Lute*; *The Indian Runner's Romance*; *With Her Card*; *The Better Way*; *His Wife's Visitor*; *The Mills of the Gods*; *Franks*; *Oh, Uncle*; *The Sealed Room*; *1776* or *The Hessian Renegades*; *The Little Darling*; *In Old Kentucky*; *The Children's Friend*; *Comata, the Sioux*; *Getting Even*; *The Broken Locket*; *A Fair Exchange*; *The Awakening*; *Pippa Passes*; *Leather Stockings*; *Fools of Fate*; *Wanted, a Child*; *The Little Teacher*; *A Change of Heart*; *His Lost Love*; *Lines of White on the Sullen Sea*; *The Gibson Goddess*; *In the Watches of the Night*; *The Expiation*; *What's Your Hurry*; *The Restoration*; *Nursing a Viper*; *Two Women and a Man*; *The Light that Came*; *A Midnight Adventure*; *The Open Gate*; *Sweet Revenge*; *The Mountaineer's Honor*; *In the Window Recess*; *The Trick That Failed*; *The Death Disc*; *Through the Breakers*; *In a Hempen Bag*; *A Corner in Wheat*; *The Redman's View*; *The Test*; *A Trap for Santa Claus*; *In Little Italy*; *To Save Her Soul*; *Choosing a Husband*; *The Rocky Road*; *The Dancing Girl of Butte*; *Her Terrible Ordeal*; *The Call*; *The Honor of His Family*; *On the Reef*; *The Last Deal*; *One Night, and Then—*; *The Cloister's Touch*; *The Woman from Mellon's*; *The Duke's Plan*; *The Englishman and the Girl*

1910 *The Final Settlement*; *His Last Burglary*; *Taming a Husband*; *The Newlyweds*; *The Thread of Destiny*; *In Old California*; *The Man*; *The Converts*; *Faithful*; *The Twisted Trail*; *Gold is Not All*; *As It Is in Life*; *A Rich Revenge*; *A Romance of the Western Hills*; *Thou Shalt Not*; *The Way of the World*; *The*

Unchanging Sea; *The Gold Seekers*; *Love Among the Roses*; *The Two Brothers*; *Unexpected Help*; *An Affair of Hearts*; *Romona*; *Over Silent Paths*; *The Implement*; *In the Season of Buds*; *A Child of the Ghetto*; *In the Border States*; *A Victim of Jealousy*; *The Face at the Window*; *A Child's Impulse*; *The Marked Time-table*; *Muggsy's First Sweetheart*; *The Purgation*; *A Midnight Cupid*; *What the Daisy Said*; *A Child's Faith*; *The Call to Arms*; *Serious Sixteen*; *A Flash of Light*; *As the Bells Rang Out*; *An Arcadian Maid*; *The House with the Closed Shutters*; *Her Father's Pride*; *A Salutary Lesson*; *The Usurer*; *The Sorrows of the Unfaithful*; *In Life's Cycle*; *Wilful Peggy*; *A Summer Idyll*; *The Modern Prodigal*; *Rose o' Salem Town*; *Little Angels of Luck*; *A Mohawk's Way*; *The Oath and the Man*; *The Iconoclast*; *Examination Day at School*; *That Chink at Golden Gulch*; *The Broken Doll*; *The Banker's Daughters*; *The Message of the Violin*; *Two Little Waifs*; *Waiter No. Five*; *The Fugitive*; *Simple Charity*; *The Song of the Wildwood Flute*; *A Child's Strategem*; *Sunshine Sue*; *A Plain Song*; *His Sister-in-law*; *The Golden Supper*; *The Lesson*; *When a Man Loves*; *Winning Back His Love*; *His Trust*; *His Trust Fulfilled*; *A Wreath of Orange Blossoms*; *The Italian Barber*; *The Two Paths*; *Conscience*; *Three Sisters*; *A Decree of Destiny*; *Fate's Turning*; *What Shall We Do with Our Old?*; *The Diamond Star*; *The Lily of the Tenements*; *Heart Beats of Long Ago*

1911 *Fisher Folks*; *His Daughter*; *The Lonedale Operator*; *Was He a Coward?*; *Teaching Dad to Like Her*; *The Spanish Gypsy*; *The Broken Cross*; *The Chief's Daughter*; *A Knight of the Road*; *Madame Rex*; *His Mother's Scarf*; *How She Triumphed*; *In the Days of '49*; *The Two Sides*; *The New Dress*; *Enoch Arden, Part I*; *Enoch Arden, Part II*; *The White Rose of the Wilds*; *The Crooked Road*; *A Romany Tragedy*; *A Smile of a Child*; *The Primal Call*; *The Jealous Husband*; *The Indian Brothers*; *The Thief and the Girl*; *Her Sacrifice*; *The Blind Princess and the Poet*; *Fighting Blood*; *The Last Drop of Water*; *Robby the Coward*; *A Country Cupid*; *The Ruling Passion*; *The Rose of Kentucky*; *The Sorrowful Example*; *Swords and Hearts*; *The Stuff Heroes Are Made Of*; *The Old Confectioner's Mistake*; *The Unveiling*; *The Eternal Mother*; *Dan the Dandy*; *The Revue Man and the Girl*; *The Squaw's Love*; *Italian Blood*; *The Making of a Man*; *Her Awakening*; *The Adventures of Billy*; *The Long Road*; *The Battle*; *Love in the Hills*; *The Trail of the Books*; *Through Darkened Vales*; *Saved from Himself*; *A Woman Scorned*; *The Miser's Heart*; *The Failure*; *Sunshine Through the Dark*; *As in a Looking Glass*; *A Terrible Discovery*; *A Tale of the Wilderness*; *The Voice of the Child*; *The Baby and the Stork*; *The Old Bookkeeper*; *A Sister's Love*; *For His Son*; *The Transformation of Mike*; *A Blot on the 'Scutcheon*; *Billy's Strategem*; *The Sunbeam*; *A String of Pearls*; *The Root of Evil*

1912 *The Mender of the Nets*; *Under Burning Skies*; *A Siren of Impulse*; *Iola's Promise*; *The Goddess of Sagebrush Gulch*; *The Girl and Her Trust*; *The Punishment*; *Fate's Interception*; *The Female of the Species*; *Just Like a Woman*; *One Is Business, the Other Crime*; *The Lesser Evil*; *The Old Actor*; *A Lodging for the Night*; *His Lesson*; *When Kings Were the Law*; *A Beast at Bay*; *An Outcast Among Outcasts*; *Home Folks*; *A Temporary Truce*; *The Spirit Awakened*; *Lena and the Geese*; *An Indian Summer*; *The Schoolteacher and the Waif*; *Man's Lust for Gold*; *Man's Genesis*; *Heaven Avenges*; *A Pueblo Legend*; *The Sands of Dee*; *Black Sheep*; *The Narrow Road*; *A Child's Remorse*; *The Inner Circle*; *A Change of Spirit*; *An Unseen Enemy*; *Two Daughters of Eve*; *Friends*; *So Near, Yet So Far*; *A Feud in the Kentucky Hills*; *In the Aisles of the Wild*; *The One She Loved*; *The Painted Lady*; *The Musketeers of Pig Alley*; *Heredity*; *Gold and Glitter*; *My Baby*; *The Informer*; *The Unwelcome Guest*; *Pirate Gold*; *Brutality*; *The New York Hat*; *The Massacre*; *My Hero*; *Oil and Water*; *The Burglar's Dilemma*; *A Cry for Help*; *The God Within*; *Three Friends*; *The Telephone Girl and the Lady*; *Fate*; *An Adventure in the Autumn Woods*; *A Chance Deception*; *The Tender Hearted Boy*; *A Misappropriated Turkey*; *Brothers*; *Drink's Lure*; *Love in an Apartment Hotel*

1913 *Broken Ways*; *A Girl's Strategem*; *Near to Earth*; *A Welcome Intruder*; *The Sheriff's Baby*; *The Hero of Little Italy*; *The Perfidy of Mary*; *A Misunderstood Boy*; *The Little Tease*; *The Lady and the Mouse*; *The Wanderer*; *The House of Darkness*; *Olaf—An Atom*; *Just Gold*; *His Mother's Son*; *The Yaqui Cur*; *The Ranchero's Revenge*; *A Timely Interception*; *Death's Marathon*; *The Sorrowful Shore*; *The Mistake*; *The Mothering Heart*; *Her Mother's Oath*; *During the Round-up*; *The Coming of Angelo*; *An Indian's Loyalty*; *Two Men of the Desert*; *The Reformers* or *The Lost Art of Minding One's Business*; *The Battle at Elderbush Gulch* (released 1914); *In Prehistoric Days* (*Wars of the Primal Tribes*; *Brute Force*); *Judith of Bethulia* (+ sc) (released 1914)

Films as Director:

(after quitting Biograph):

1914 *The Battle of the Sexes*; *The Escape*; *Home, Sweet Home*; *The Avenging Conscience*

1915 ***The Birth of a Nation*** (+ co-sc, co-music)

1916 ***Intolerance*** (+ co-music)

1918 *Hearts of the World* (+ sc under pseudonyms, co-music arranger); *The Great Love* (+ co-sc); *The Greatest Thing in Life* (+ co-sc)

1919 *A Romance of Happy Valley* (+ sc); *The Girl Who Stayed at Home*; *True-Heart Susie*; *Scarlet Days*; ***Broken Blossoms*** (+ sc, co-music arranger); *The Greatest Question*

1920 *The Idol Dancer*; *The Love Flower*; *Way Down East*

1921 *Dream Street* (+ sc); *Orphans of the Storm*

1922 *One Exciting Night* (+ sc)

1923 *The White Rose* (+ sc)

1924 *America: Isn't Life Wonderful* (+ sc)

1925 *Sally of the Sawdust*

1926 *That Royle Girl*; *The Sorrows of Satan*

1928 *Drums of Love*; *The Battle of the Sexes*

1929 *Lady of the Pavements*

1930 *Abraham Lincoln*

1931 *The Struggle* (+ pr, co-music arranger)

Publications

By GRIFFITH: books—

The Rise and Fall of Free Speech in America, Los Angeles, 1916; reprinted, 1967.

The Man Who Invented Hollywood: The Autobiography of D.W. Griffith, edited by James Hart, Louisville, Kentucky, 1972.

By GRIFFITH: articles—

"What I Demand of Movie Stars," in *Motion Picture Magazine* (Los Angeles), February 1917.

"The Motion Picture Today—and Tomorrow," in *Theatre Magazine* (New York), October 1929.

"An Old Timer Advises Hollywood," in *Liberty* (New York), 17 June 1939.

On GRIFFITH: books—

Hastings, Charles, and Herman Holland, *A Biography of David Wark Griffith,* New York, 1920.

Trauberg, Leonid, and Georg Ronen, *David Griffith,* Moscow, 1926.

Huff, Theodore, *A Shot Analysis of D.W. Griffith's Birth of a Nation,* New York, 1961.

Barry, Iris, and Eileen Bowser, *D.W. Griffith: American Film Master,* New York, 1965.

Mitry, Jean, "Griffith," in *Anthologie du Cinéma,* Paris, 1966.

Brownlow, Kevin, *The Parade's Gone By,* New York and London, 1968.

Gish, Lillian, *The Movies, Mr. Griffith, and Me,* with Ann Pinchot, Englewood Cliffs, New Jersey, 1969.

Henderson, Robert, *D.W. Griffith: The Years at Biograph,* New York, 1970.

O'Dell, Paul, *Griffith and the Rise of Hollywood,* New York, 1970.

Geduld, Harry, editor, *Focus on D.W. Griffith,* Englewood Cliffs, New Jersey, 1971.

Lahue, Kalton, *Dreams for Sale: The Rise and Fall of the Triangle Film Corporation,* New York, 1971.

Henderson, Robert, *D.W. Griffith: His Life and Work,* New York, 1972.

Bowser, Eileen, editor, *The Biograph Bulletins 1908-1912,* New York, 1973.

Niver, Kemp, *D.W. Griffith: His Biograph Films in Perspective,* Los Angeles, 1974.

Wagenknecht, Edward, and Anthony Slide, *The Films of D.W. Griffith,* New York, 1975.

Williams, Martin, *Griffith: First Artist of the Movies,* New York, 1980.

Brion, Patrick, editor, *D.W. Griffith,* Paris, 1982.

Brown, Karl, *Adventures with D.W. Griffith,* edited by Kevin Brownlow, London, 1983; revised edition, 1988.

Mottet, Jean, editor, *D.W. Griffith: Colloque International,* Paris, 1984.

Schickel, Richard, *D.W. Griffith: An American Life,* New York, 1984; also published as *D.W. Griffith and the Birth of Film,* London, 1984.

Graham, Cooper C., and others, *D.W. Griffith and the Biograph Company,* Metuchen, New Jersey, 1985.

Drew, William M., *D.W. Griffith's Intolerance: Its Genesis and Its Vision,* Jefferson, North Carolina, 1986.

Jesionowski, Joyce E., *Thinking in Pictures: Dramatic Structures in D.W. Griffith's Biograph Films,* Berkeley, 1987.

Lang, Robert, *American Film Melodrama: Griffith, Vidor, Minnelli,* New Jersey, 1989.

Elsaesser, Thomas, and Adam Barker, editors, *Early Cinema: Space-Frame-Narrative,* London, 1990.

On GRIFFITH: articles—

Gordon, Henry Stephen, "The Story of D.W. Griffith," in *Photoplay* (New York), June through November 1916.

Feldman, Joseph, "The D.W. Griffith Influence," in *Films in Review* (New York), July/August 1950.

Eisenstein, Sergei, "Dickens, Griffith and the Film Today," in *Film Form,* New York, 1949; also in *Sight and Sound* (London), June, July, and November 1950.

Stern, Seymour, "The Cold War Against D.W. Griffith," in *Films in Review* (New York), February 1956.

Pratt, George, "In the Nick of Time, D.W. Griffith and the Last-Minute Rescue," in *Image* (Rochester, New York), 2 May 1959.

"*Birth of a Nation* Issue" of *Film Culture* (New York), Summer 1965.

Batman, Richard, "D.W. Griffith: The Lean Years," in *California Historical Society Quarterly,* September 1965.

Silverstein, Norman, "D.W. Griffith and Anarchy in American Films," in *Salmagundi* (New York), Winter 1966.

Meyer, Richard, "The Films of David Wark Griffith: The Development of Themes and Techniques in 42 of His Films," in *Film Comment* (New York), Fall/Winter 1967.

Casty, Alan, "The Films of D.W. Griffith: A Style of the Times," in *Journal of Popular Film* (Bowling Green, Ohio), Spring 1972.

"Griffith Issues" of *Cahiers de la Cinémathèque* (Lyons), Spring 1972 and Christmas 1975.

"Griffith Issue" of *Ecran* (Paris), February 1973.

"Griffith Issue" of *Filmkritik* (Berlin), April 1975.

"Griffith Issue" of *Filmcritica* (Rome), May/June 1975.

"Griffith Issue" of *Films in Review* (New York), October 1975.

"Special Issues" of *Griffithiana* (Genoa), March/July 1980 and January 1982.

Merritt, Russell, "Rescued from a Perilous Nest: D.W. Griffith's Escape from Theatre into Film," in *Cinema Journal* (Evanston), Fall 1981.

Merritt, Russell, "D.W. Griffith Directs the Great War: The Making of *Hearts of the World,*" in *Quarterly Review of Film Studies* (Salisbury, Maryland), Winter 1981.

"Griffith Issue" of *Avant-Scène du Cinéma* (Paris), 15 February 1983.

"Griffith Sections" of *Positif* (Paris), December 1982, March 1983, and April 1983.

Gunning, Thom, "The Movies, Mr. Griffith, and Us," in *American Film* (Washington, D.C.), June 1984.

Corliss, Richard, and Richard Schickel, "Writing in Silence," in *Film Comment* (New York), July/August 1985.

Neilan, Marshall, and R.S. Birchard, "Griffith—An Untold Chapter," in *American Cinematographer* (Los Angeles), January 1986.

Doty, Alexander, "D.W. Griffith's Poetics of Place and the Rural Ideal," in *Journal of Comparative Poetics,* Spring 1986.

Keil, Charles, "Transition through Tension: Stylistic Diversity in the Late Griffith Biographs," in *Cinema Journal* (Evanston), Spring 1989.

Literature/Film Quarterly (Salisbury, Maryland), vol. 18, no. 2, 1990.

* * *

Perhaps no other director has generated such a broad range of critical reaction as D.W. Griffith. For students of the motion picture, Griffith's is the most familiar name in film history. Generally acknowledged as America's most influential director (and certainly one of the most prolific), he is also perceived as being among the most limited. Praise for his mastery of film technique is matched by repeated indictments of his moral, artistic, and intellectual inadequacies. At one extreme, Kevin Brownlow has characterized him as "the only director in America creative enough to be called a genius." At the other, Paul Rotha calls his contribution to the advance of film "negligible" and Susan Sontag complains of his "supreme vulgarity and even inanity"; his work "reeks of a fervid moralizing about sexuality and violence" and his energy comes "from suppressed voluptuousness."

Griffith started his directing career in 1908, and in the following five years made some 485 films, almost all of which have been preserved. These films, one or two reels in length, have customarily been regarded as apprentice works, films in which, to quote Stephen Zito, "Griffith borrowed, invented, and perfected the forms and techniques that he later used to such memorable effect in *The Birth of a Nation, Intolerance, Broken Blossoms,* and *Way Down East.*" These early "Biographs" (named after the studio at which Griffith worked) have usually been studied for their stylistic features, notably parallel editing, camera placement, and treatment of light and shadow. Their most famous structuring devices are the last-minute rescue and the cross-cut.

D.W. Griffith

In recent years, however, the Biographs have assumed higher status in film history. Many historians and critics rank them with the most accomplished work in Griffith's career. Vlada Petric, for instance, calls them "masterpieces of early cinema, fascinating lyrical films which can still affect audiences today, conveying the content in a cinematic manner often more powerful than that of Griffith's later feature films." Scholars have begun studying them for their characters, images, narrative patterns, themes, and ideological values, finding in them a distinctive signature based on Griffith's deep-seated faith in the values of the woman-centered home. Certain notable Biographs—*The Musketeers of Pig Alley, The Painted Lady, A Corner in Wheat, The Girl and Her Trust, The Battle of Elderbush Gulch, The Unseen Enemy,* and *A Feud in the Kentucky Hills*—have been singled out for individual study.

Griffith reached the peak of his popularity and influence in the five years between 1915 and 1920, when he released *The Birth of a Nation, Intolerance, Broken Blossoms,* and *Way Down East.* He also directed *Hearts of the World* during this period, a film that incorporates newsreel and faked documentary footage into an epic fictional narrative. A First World War propaganda epic, *Hearts of the World,* alone among his early spectacles, is ignored today. But in 1918 it was the most popular war film of its time, and rivalled *The Birth of a Nation* as the most profitable of all Griffith's features. Today, it is usually studied as an example of World War I hysteria or as a pioneering effort at government-sponsored mass entertainment.

Although Griffith's epics are generally grouped together, Paul Goodman points out that his films are neither so ideologically uniform nor so consistent as recent writers have generally assumed. With equal fervor Griffith could argue white supremacy and make pleas for toleration, play the liberal crusader and the reactionary conservative, appear tradition-bound yet remain open to experimentation, saturate his work in Victorian codes while struggling against a Victorian morality. Frustrated by his inability to find consistent ideological threads in Griffith's work, Norman Silverstein has called Griffith the father of anarchy in American films because his luminous movements in these epics never appear to sustain a unified whole.

Yet, as Robert Lang observes, the epics do share broad formal characteristics, using history as a chaotic background for a fictional drama that stresses separation and reunification. Whether set in the French Revolution (*Orphans of the Storm*), the American Revolution (*America*), the Civil War (*Birth of a Nation*), or in the various epochs of *Intolerance,* the Griffith epic is an action-centered spectacle that manipulates viewer curiosity with powerfully propulsive, intrinsically developmental scenes culminating in a sensational denouement.

Griffith also made a much different sort of feature during these years—the pastoral romance. These have only recently received serious critical attention. In these films, which are stripped of spectacle and historical surroundings, the cast of principal characters does not exceed two or three, the action is confined in time and space, and the story is intimate. Here, in films like *Romance of Happy Valley, True-heart Susie,* and *The Greatest Question,* Griffith experiments with alternative narrative possibilities, whereby he extends the techniques of exposition to the length of a feature film. Strictly narrative scenes in these films are suspended or submerged to convey the illusion of near-plotlessness. The main figures, Griffith implied (usually played by Lillian Gish and Bobby Harron), would emerge independent of fable; atmosphere would dominate over story line.

From the start, critics and reviewers found the near absence of action sequences and overt physical struggle noteworthy in the Griffith pastorals, but differed widely in their evaluation of it. Most of the original commentators assumed they had found a critical shortcoming, and complained about the thinness of plot, padded exposition, and frequent repetition of shots. Even Kenneth MacGowan, who alone among his contemporaries preferred Griffith's pastorals to his epics, scored the empty storyline of *The Romance of Happy Valley* for its "loose ends and dangling characters." More recent critics, on the other hand—notably Jean Mitry, John Belton, and Rene Kerdyk—have found transcendental virtues in the forswearing of event-centered plots. Ascribing to Griffith's technique a liberating moral purpose, Mitry called *True-heart Susie* "a narrative which follows characters without entrapping them, allowing them complete freedom of action and event." For John Belton, *True-heart Susie* is one of Griffith's "purest and most immediate films" because, "lacking a 'great story' there is nothing between us and the characters." Equating absence of action sequences with the elimination of formal structure, Belton concludes that "it is through the characters not plot that Griffith expresses and defines the nature of the characters' separation."

If these judgments appear critically naive (plainly these films have plots and structures even if these are less complex than in *Intolerance* and *Birth*), they raise important questions Griffith scholars continue to debate: how does Griffith create the impression that characters exist independent of action, and, in a temporal medium, how does Griffith create the impression of narrative immobility?

By and large, Griffith's films of the mid- and late-1920s have not fared well critically, although they have their defenders. The customary view—that Griffith's work became dull and undistinguished when he lost his personal studio at Mamaroneck in 1924—continues to prevail, despite calls from John Dorr, Arthur Lennig, and Richard Roud for re-evaluation. The eight films he made as a contract director for Paramount and United Artists are usually studied (if at all) as examples of late 1920s studio style. What critics find startling about them—particularly the United Artists features—is not the lack of quality, but the absence of any identifiable Griffith traits. Only *Abraham Lincoln* and *The Struggle* (Griffith's two sound films) are recognizable as his work, and they are usually treated as early 1930s oddities.

—Russell Merritt

GUERRA, Ruy

Nationality: Mozambiquian. **Born:** Lourenço Marques, Mozambique, 22 August 1931. **Education:** Educated in Mozambique and Portugal. **Career:** Attended IDHEC, Paris, 1952-54; Théâtre National Populaire, 1955; assistant director in Paris, 1956-57; invited to direct *Joana* (unrealized), in Brazil, 1958; remained in Brazil until returning to Paris, 1967; following independence of Mozambique, returned to help plan film industry, late 1970s.

Films as Director:

1954 *Les Hommes et les autres* (+ sc) (short, IDHEC diploma work)
1960 *Oros* (+ sc) (short, unfinished)
1961 *O cavalo de Oxumaire* (*The Horse of Oxumaire*) (co-d, + co-sc, unfinished)
1962 *Os cafajestes* (*The Unscrupulous Ones*) (+ co-sc)
1964 ***Os fuzis*** (*The Guns*) (+ co-sc, co-ed)
1967 "Vocabulaire" episode of *Loin du Viêt-nam* (not included in released version) (+ sc)
1969 *Sweet Hunters* (+ co-sc)
1970 *Os deuses e os mortos* (*The Gods and the Dead*) (+ co-sc, co-ed)
1978 *A queda* (*The Fall*) (co-d, + co-sc, co-music, co-ed)
1979 *Mueda, memória e massacre* (*Mueda, Memory and Massacre*) (+ co-ph, ed)
1983 *Erendira* (+ sc)
1986 *Opera do Malandro*
1988 *Fábula de la bella palomera* (*Fable of the Beautiful Pigeon-Fancier*)
1989 *Kuarup*
1991 *Me alquilo para sonar*

Other Films:

1955 *Souvenir de Paris* (Théocary) (asst d); *Chiens perdus, sans collier* (Delannoy) (asst d)
1957 *S.O.S. Noronha* (Rouquier) (asst d, role)
1958 *Le Tout pour le tout* (Dally) (asst d)
1963 *Os mendigos* (role)
1969 *Benito Cereno* (Roullet) (role)
1970 *Le Maître du temps* (Pollet) (role); *Le Mur* (Roullet) (role)
1971 *Les Soleils de l'Ile de Pâques* (Kast) (role); *O homem das estrelas* (*Man and the Stars*) (Barreto) (role)
1972 *Aguirre, der Zorn Göttes* (*Aguirre, the Wrath of God*) (Herzog) (role)

Publications

By GUERRA: articles—

Interview with J.A. Fieschi and J. Narboni, in *Cahiers du Cinéma* (Paris), April 1967.
Interview with Thomas Elsaesser, in *Monogram* (London), no. 5, 1974.
Interview with Rui Nogueira, in *Image et Son* (Paris), December 1974.
"Filmen in Mozambique," interview with F. Sartor, in *Film en Televisie* (Brussels), May/June 1981.
Interview with Michel Ciment, in *Positif* (Paris), June 1983.
Interview with Serge Toubiana, in *Cahiers du Cinéma* (Paris), December 1983.
Interview with M. Buruiana, in *24 Images* (Montréal), Winter 1987.

On GUERRA: books—

Johnson, Randal, *Cinema Novo x 5: Masters of Contemporary Brazilian Film,* Austin, Texas, 1984.

On GUERRA: articles—

Mardore, Michel, "Diaphragme à quatre," in *Cahiers du Cinéma* (Paris), November 1964.
Ciment, Michel, "Le Dieu, le diable et les fusils," in *Positif* (Paris), May 1967.

Ruy Guerra: *Os deuses e os mortos*

Zele, Van, "*Os Fuzis,*" in *Image et Son* (Paris), November 1969.
Demeure, Jacques, "Pour un réalisme magique," in *Positif* (Paris), January 1971.
"Le 'cinema nôvo' brésilien Issue" of *Études Cinématographiques* (Paris), no. 93-96, 1972.
"Ruy Guerra," in *Film Dope* (London), March 1981.
Larraz, E., "Une collection hispanique: 'Amours difficiles,'" in *Cinemaction,* October 1990.
Maslin, Janet, "Director Returns to Garcia Marquez," in *New York Times,* March 1, 1991.
Lasarte, F., "Marquez og de levende billeder," in *Kosmorama,* Fall 1991.

* * *

A truly cosmopolitan artist, Ruy Guerra was born in Mozambique of Portuguese settlers, secured his higher education in Lisbon, and studied cinema at the Paris IDHEC. He was one of the leaders of the Brazilian *cinema novo* with two films that broke new ethical and aesthetic ground, *Os cafajestes* and *Os fuzis.* He shot *Sweet Hunters* in French and in English, and went back to Mozambique after it became independent to organize the newly born cinema industry. After returning he completed a documentary, *Mueda, memória e massacre,* before going to Mexico to adapt Gabriel García Marquez's *Erendira* in 1983. Besides writing his own scripts, Guerra is the author of lyrics for Latin American pop songs (sung in particular by Baden Powell), and an actor in his own right (he took on roles in Herzog's *Aguirre* and in Serge Roullet's adaptation of *Benito Cereno*).

The product of a cultural melting pot, Guerra's style is hard to define. Very classical in form (except in the extraordinary *Os deuses e os mortes,* the epitome of Brazilian tropicalist aesthetics, which featured virtuoso camera movements and sequence shots), his style shows none of the *external* signs of modernity, such as non-chronological sequences, manipulation of the sound track, or elaborate framing. On the other hand, it displays a very unusual use of rhythm, and makes use of a great variety of tempos in a way that is akin to that found in some Japanese films, such as those of Kurosawa.

Guerra is preoccupied, even obsessed with the theme of frustration and disappointed expectations. Guerra's interest in social issues was evident in his first film, *Os cafajestes,* about penniless young loafers in Rio who blackmail a girl after having taken photos of her in the nude. *Os fuzis,* set in the northeast of Brazil, pits a sergeant and four soldiers guarding a harvest destined for town (to profit the landowner mayor) against the covetous desires of hungry peasants. Thirteen years later Guerra shot a sequel, *A queda* (*The Fall*), with the same actors to show what happened to the characters after a decade spent in the big city.

Os deuses e os mortes presents in grand operatic manner a feud between two families of farmers. This film reveals another aspect of Guerra's personality: a taste for magic and dream, an interest in myths and surrealism. The economic and the psychic are bound together in this difficult and fascinating work. *Sweet Hunters,* Guerra's most poetic film (with Sterling Hayden, Susan Strasberg, and Stuart Whitman), is set on an island where the three characters act out their obsessions and frustrated desires. Allan, a keen ornithologist, is waiting for the migration of birds, his wife Clea for the arrival of a man who has escaped from a nearby prison, and his sister for her departure.

Given his interest in dreams and legends, Guerra was a logical choice to adapt García Marquez's novella *Erendira.* The film is set in an imaginary country where a mythical and monstrous grandmother (Irene Pappas) sells her granddaughter as a prostitute. A picaresque tale of economic exploitation, with ironical characters and nightmarish situations, it offers a good synthesis of Guerra's style even if the faithfulness of his adaptation does not allow him to give full vent to his ordinarily richer and more personal inspiration.

—Michel Ciment

GUITRY, Sacha

Nationality: French. **Born:** Alexandre-Georges Pierre Guitry in St. Petersburg, Russia, 21 February 1885. **Education:** Lycée Jeanson-de-Sailly, St. Petersburg, 1894, then at twelve different schools until 1902. **Family:** Married 1) Charlotte Lysès, 1907 (divorced); 2) Yvonne Printemps, 1919 (divorced); 3) Jacqueline Delubac, 1935 (divorced); 4) Geneviève de Séréville, 1942 (divorced); 5) Lana Marconi, 1949. **Career:** Debut as actor, with father Lucien Guitry, 1904; playwright and stage actor, through 1930s; directed first feature, *Bonne Chance,* 1935; arrested for collaborating with the Nazis, released after two months, 1944; officially cleared of charges, ban on work lifted, 1947. **Awards:** Chevalier de la Légion d'Honneur, 1923; Commander of the Légion d'Honneur, 1936; elected to the Goncourt Academy, 1939; Grande Médaille d'Or de la Société des Auteurs, 1955. **Died:** In Paris, 24 July 1957.

Films as Director:

1915 *Ceux de chez nous* (+ sc, ph)
1935 *Pasteur* (co-d, + sc, role as Pasteur); *Bonne chance* (+ sc, role as Claude)
1936 *Le Nouveau Testament* (+ sc, role as Jean Marcelin); *Le Roman d'un tricheur* (*The Story of a Cheat*) (+ sc, role as the cheat); *Mon Père avait raison* (+ sc, role as Charles Bellanger); *Faisons un rêve* (+ sc, role as He)
1937 *Le Mot de Cambronne* (+ sc, role as Cambronne); *Les Perles de la couronne* (*Pearls of the Crown*) (+ sc, role as François I, Barras, Napoleon III, Jean Martin); *Désiré* (+ sc, role as Désiré Tronchais)
1938 *Quadrille* (+ sc, role as Philippe de Moranes); *Remontons les Champs-Elysées* (+ sc, role as the teacher, Louis XV, Ludovic at 54 years of age, Jean-Louis at 54, Napoleon III)
1939 *Ils étaient neuf célibataires* (+ sc, role as Jea Lécuyer)
1942 *Le Destin fabuleux de Desirée Clary* (+ sc, role as Napoleon I)
1943 *Donne-moi tes yeux* (+ sc, role as François Bressoles)
1944 *La Malibran* (+ sc, role as M. Malibran)
1948 *Le Comédien* (+ sc, role as Lucien Guitry at 40)
1949 *Le Diable boiteux* (+ sc, role as Talleyrand); *Aux deux colombes* (+ sc, role as Jean-Pierre Walter); *Toâ* (+ sc, role as Michel Desnoyers)
1950 *Le Trésor de Cantenac* (+ sc, role as Baron de Cantenac); *Tu m'as sauvé la vie* (+ sc, role as Baron de Saint-Rambert)
1951 *Deburau* (+ sc, role as Jean-Gaspard Deburau); *La Poison* (+ sc)
1952 *Je l'ai été trois fois* (+ sc, role as Jean Renneval)
1953 *La Vie d'un honnête homme* (+ sc)
1954 *Si Versailles m'etait conté* (+ sc, role as Louis XIV)
1955 *Napoléon* (+ sc, role as Talleyrand)
1956 *Si Paris nous était conté* (+ sc)
1957 *Assassins et voleurs* (+ sc); *Les Trois font la paire* (+ sc)

Other Films:

1918 *Un Roman d'amour ... et d'aventures* (Hervil and Mercanton) (role)
1931 *Le Blanc et le noir* (sc)
1935 *Les Deux coverts* (sc)
1938 *L'Accroche-coeur* (sc); *Bluebeard's Eighth Wife* (Lubitsch) (guest appearance as man leaving hotel with girl on arm)
1951 *Adhemar* or *Le Jouet de la fatalité* (sc)
1958 *La Vie à deux* (sc)

Publications

By GUITRY: books—

Si j'ai bonne mémoire, Paris, 1934.
Mémoires d'un tricheur, Paris, 1935.
De Jeanne d'Arc à Philippe Pétain, Paris, 1944.
Toutes réflexions faites, Paris, 1947.
Le Comédien, Paris, 1948.
Et Versailles vous est conté, Paris, 1954.
Théâtre, je t'adore!, Paris, 1958.
Les Femmes et l'amour, Paris, 1959.
Théâtre, Volumes I-XIV, Paris, 1959/62.
Le Cinéma et moi, Paris, 1977.
Le Petit Carnet rouge et autres souvenirs inedits, Paris, 1979.
A bâtons rompus, Paris, 1981.

On GUITRY: books—

Madis, Alex, *Sacha,* Paris, 1950.
Prince, Stéphane, *Sacha Guitry hors sa légende,* Paris, 1959.
Lauwick, Hervé, *Sacha Guitry et les femmes,* Paris, 1965.
Sicilier, Jacques, "Sacha Guitry," in *Anthologie du Cinéma II,* Paris, 1967.
Harding, James, *Sacha Guitry: The Last Boulevardier,* New York, 1968.
Lorcey, Jacques, *Sacha Guitry par les témoins de sa vie,* Paris, 1976.
Knapp, Bettina, *Sacha Guitry,* Boston, 1981.
Lorcey, Jacques, *Sacha Guitry: L'Homme et l'oeuvre,* Paris, 1982.
Lorcey, Jacques, *Sacha Guitry: Cent ans de théâtre et d'esprit,* Paris, 1985.
Simsolo, Nöel, *Sacha Guitry,* Paris, 1988.

On GUITRY: articles—

Obituary, in *New York Times,* 24 July 1957.
Marcorelles, Louis, "Sacha Guitry," in *Sight and Sound* (London), Autumn 1957.
"Guitry Issue" of *Cahiers du Cinéma* (Paris), no. 173, 1965.
"Guitry Issue" of *Revue du Cinéma* (Paris), vol. 3, 1971.
Fieschi, J., "La Mise en pièce du film," in *Cinématographe* (Paris), no. 40, 1978.
Adair, Gilbert, "Sacha, an Introduction to Guitry," in *Sight and Sound* (London), Winter 1980/81.
Dossier on Guitry, in *Cinématographe* (Paris), February 1983.
Tesson, C., "Le Convive des dernières fates," in *Cahiers du Cinéma* (Paris), January 1984.

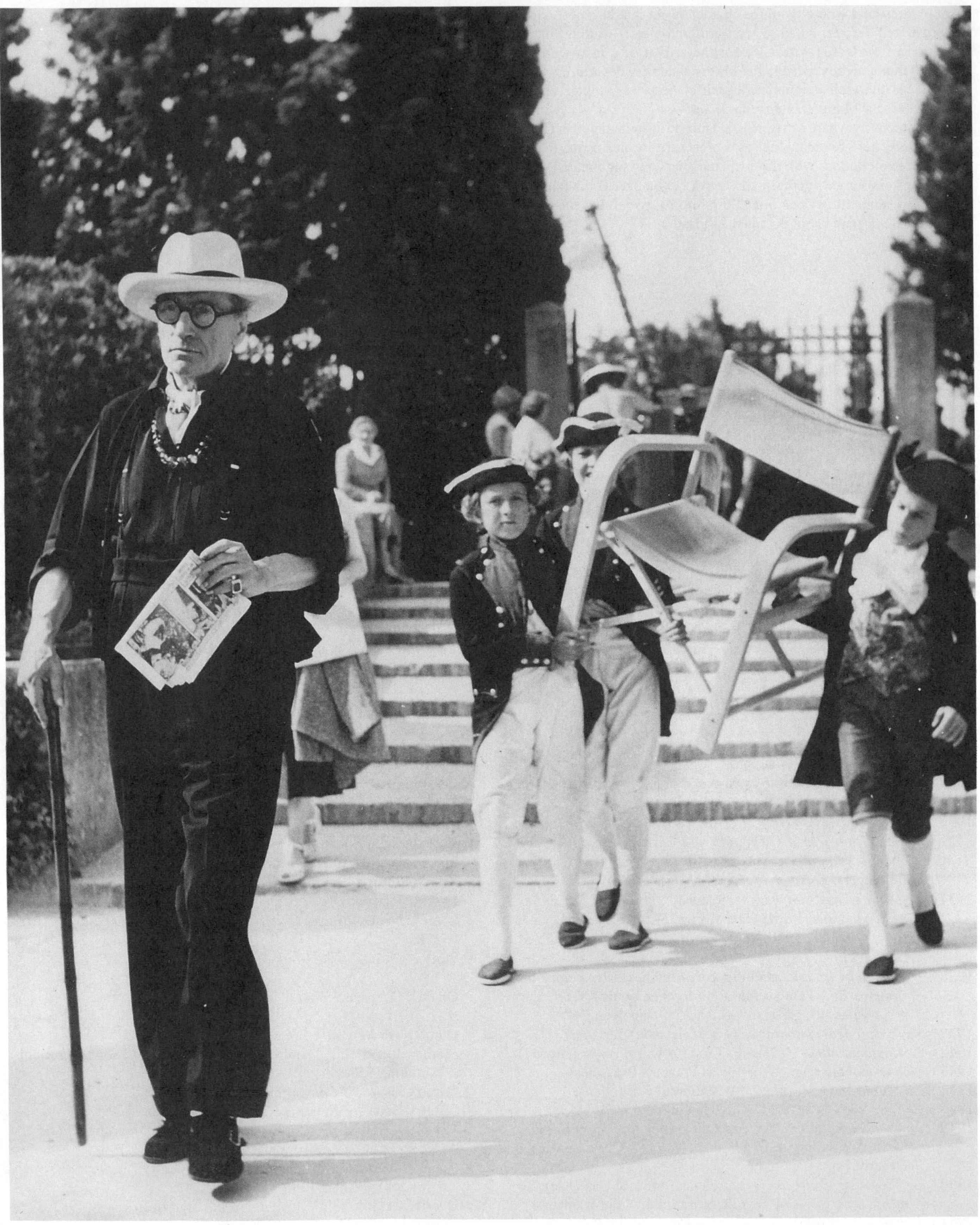

Sacha Guitry

Viviani, C., "Sur quatre films de Sacha Guitry," in *Positif* (Paris), January 1984.
Gauteur, C., "Harry Baur/Sacha Guitry ou la croisée des destins," in *Cinéma* (Paris), May 1984.
"Sacha: An introduction to Guitry," in *National Film Theatre Booklet* (London), September/October 1985.

On GUITRY: films—

Prince, Stéphane, *Le Musée de Sacha Guitry* (short)
de Givray, Claude, *Cinéastes de notre temps: Sacha Guitry,* for television, France, 1965.

* * *

Values change and time plays tricks on one's memory of how it really was. Back in the early 1930s, when talking pictures were gaining a foothold in this country and all foreign nations were exhibiting their product in America, it seemed as if there was nobody in films as charming, witty, and multi-talented as Sacha Guitry. His films, made in France, appeared at all the best art houses; he was a delightful actor, a director with a Lubitsch-like wit, and a writer of amusing sophisticated comedy. Seeing his films today in revival, however, they do not seem that funny. His features appear old-fashioned and are often dull, while his preoccupation with sex is too often mere lechery. Only two films are still diamond-bright: *Les Perles de la couronne,* which he co-directed with Christian-Jaque, and *Le Roman d'un tricheur.*

The first of the above-mentioned films has a narrative device that enables Guitry to skip back and forth from one century to another and from one country to another, and still keep the story clear and funny. In *Les Perles de la couronne* Guitry plays tricks with actual events and people. The comedy has a nice bite, and Guitry pulls off a narrative resolution that is masterly in its irony. *Le Roman d'un tricheur,* meanwhile, is a razor-sharp treatise on the rewards of dishonesty. It involves a hero who as a young boy is sent to bed without dinner as punishment for a lie he has told. Because he does not eat the meal that has been prepared, he lives while all other members of his family perish, having consumed a dish prepared from toad-stools rather than fresh mushrooms.

Sacha Guitry was once the toast of Paris. One season he had as many as three plays running simultaneously. When he turned his talents to talking pictures, the medium seemed to have been invented expressly for his convenience. His father, Lucien Guitry, was France's greatest actor, and in time his talented son wrote two plays that his father turned into pure gold—*Pasteur* and *Mon Père avait raison.* In all, Sacha Guitry wrote more than a hundred plays; his films were often adaptations of these. Most were boudoir farces, remarkable in that they always seemed to work thanks to skillful construction, though they were also generally feather light and too often highly forgettable.

Guitry married five actresses who all rose to prominence in roles he wrote before he divorced them. The one who became a star in her own right was Yvonne Printemps, the second actress he married; she finally divorced him to marry her leading man, handsome Pierre Fresnay, while Guitry that same year married a new leading lady, the beautiful Jacqueline Delubac.

In World War Two Guitry was trapped in Paris, and he was not permitted by the Nazis to act on the Parisian stage. After four years, when the Germans were forced to quit Paris, Guitry was arrested by a ridiculous quirk of fate on a charge of having collaborated with the enemy; he was released after two months, exonerated, and freed to go on with his career.

—DeWitt Bodeen

GÜNEY, Yilmaz

Nationality: Turkish. **Born:** Yilmaz Putun in village near Adana in southern Turkey, 1937. **Education:** Educated in law in Ankara; studied economics in Istanbul. **Career:** Worked for film distribution company, 1952; began working with director Atif Yilmaz, 1958; sentenced to eighteen months in prison and six months exile for publishing "communist" novel *Equations with 3 Strangers,* 1961; began career in commercial cinema, as writer and actor, known as "Cirkin kral" ("The Ugly King"), 1963; founded Güney-Filmcilik production company, 1968; arrested on charge of sheltering wanted anarchist students, imprisoned without trial for twenty-six months, 1972 (released under general amnesty, 1974); alleged to have shot judge in restaurant, sentenced to twenty-four years hard labor (later commuted to eighteen years); while in prison, allowed to continue scripting films and overseeing productions, 1974-80; films banned following military takeover, 1980; escaped to France, 1981, stripped of Turkish citizenship. **Awards:** Best Film (co-recipient), Cannes Festival, for *Yol,* 1982. **Died:** Of cancer, in Paris, 9 September 1984.

Films as Director:

1966 *At avrat silah* (*The Horse, the Woman, and the Gun*) (+ sc, role)
1967 *Bana kursun islemez* (*Bullets Cannot Pierce Me*) (+ sc, role); *Benim adim Kerim* (*My Name Is Kerim*) (+ sc, role)
1968 *Pire Nuri* (*Nuri the Flea*) (co-d, + sc, role); *Seyyit Han "Topragin Gelini"* (*Seyyit Khan, Bride of the Earth*) (+ sc, role as Seyyit Han)
1969 *Ac kurtlar* (*The Hungry Wolves*) (+ sc, role); *Bir cirkin adam* (*An Ugly Man*) (+ sc, role)
1970 *Umut* (*Hope*) (+ co-sc, role as Cabar); *Piyade Osman* (*Osman the Wanderer*) (co-d, + sc, role); *Yedi belalilar* (*The Seven No-goods*) (co-d, + sc, role)
1971 *Kacaklar* (*The Fugitives*) (+ sc, role); *Vurguncular* (*The Wrong-doers*) (+ sc, role); *Ibret* (*The Example*) (co-d, + sc, role); *Yarin son gündür* (*Tomorrow Is the Final Day*) (+ sc, role); *Umutsuzlar* (*The Hopeless Ones*) (+ sc, role); *Aci* (*Pain*) (+ sc, role); *A it* (*Elegy*) (+ sc, role as Copano lu); *Baba* (*The Father*) (+ sc, role as Cemal, the Boatman)
1974 *Arkadas* (*The Friend*) (+ sc, role as the friend); *Endise* (*Anxiety*) (co-d, + sc)
1975 *Zavallilar* (*The Poor Ones*) (co-d, + co-sc, role as Abu) (begun 1972)
1982 *Le Mur* (*The Wall*) (+ sc, role)

Other Films:

1958 *Alageyik* (*The Hind*) (Yilmaz) (co-sc, role); *Bu vatanin cocuklari* (*The Children of This Country*) (Yilmaz) (co-sc, role)
1959 *Karacaoğlanin kara sevdasi* (*Karacaoğlan's Mad Love*) (Yilmaz) (co-sc); *Tütün zamani* (Arlburnu) (role)
1960 *Clum perdesi* (*The Screen of Death*) (Yilmaz) (asst d)
1961 *Dolandiricilar* (*The King of Thieves*) (Yilmaz) (asst d); *Kizil vazo* (*The Red Vase*) (Yilmaz) (asst d); *Seni kaybederesen* (*If I Lose You*) (Yilmaz) (asst d); *Yaban gülü* (*The Desert Laughs*) (Utku) (co-sc); *Dolandiricilar sahi* (Yilmaz) (role); *Tatli-Bela* (Yilmaz) (role)
1963 *Ölüme yalniz gidilar* (*The Dead Only Perish*) (Yalinkilic) (sc); *Ikisi de cesurdu* (*Two Brave Men*) (co-sc, role)
1964 *Hergün ölmektense* (Ceylan) (sc, role); *Kamali zeybek* (*Hero with a Knife*) (Akinci) (sc, role); *Dağlarin kurdu Kocero*

Yilmaz Güney: ***Ac kurtlar***

(*Kocero, Mountain Wolf*) (Utku) (sc, role); *Halimeden mektup var* (Doğan) (role); *Kocaoğlan* (Demirel) (role); *Kara sahin* (Akinci) (role); *Mor defter* (Ergün) (role); *10 Korkusuz adam* (Basaran) (role); *Prangasiz mahkumlar* (Ariburnu) (role); *Zimba gibi delikanli* (Jöntürk) (role)

1965 *Kasimpasali* (Akinci) (sc, role); *Kasimpasali recep* (Akinci) (sc, role); *Konyakci* (*The Drunkard*) (Basaran) (sc, role); *Kirallar kirali* (*King of Kings*) (Olgac) (sc, role); *Ben öldükce yasarim* (*Sağiroğlu*) (role); *Beyaz atli adam* (Jöntürk) (role); *Dağlarin oğlu* (Atadeniz) (role); *Davudo* (Kazankaya) (role); *Gönül kusu* (Gülnar) (role); *Sayili kabadayilar* (Kazankaya) (role); *Kan Gövdeyi götürdü* (Atadeniz) (role); *Kahreden kursun* (Atadeniz) (role); *Haracima dokunma* (Kazankaya) (role); *Kanli buğday* (Ceylan) (role); *Korkuszlar* (Evin) (role); *Silaha yeminliydim* (Inci) (role); *Sokakta kan vardi* (Turkali) (role); *Tehlikeli adam* (Kazankaya) (role); *Torpido Yilmaz* (Okcugil) (role); *Ücünüzü de mihlarim* (Olgac) (role); *Yarali kartal* (Dursun) (role)

1966 *Burcak tarlasi* (Utku) (sc); *Aslanlarin dönüsü* (*Return of the Heroes*) (Atadeniz) (sc, role); *Esrefpasali* (Tokatli) (sc, role); *Hudutlarin kanunu* (*The Law of Smuggling*) (Akad) (sc, role); *Yedi dağin aslani* (*Seven Wild Lions*; *The Mountain King*) (Atadeniz) (sc, role); *Tilki Selim* (*Crafty Selim*) (Hancer) (sc, role); *Aanasi yiğit doğurmus* (Kurthan) (role); *Cirkin kiral* (Atadeniz) (role); *Kovboy Ali* (Atadeniz) (role); *Silahlarin kanunu* (Atadeniz) (role); *... Veda silahlara veda ...* (Jöntürk) (role); *Yiğit yarali olur* (Görec) (role)

1967 *At hirsizi banus* (Jöntürk) (sc, role); *Seytanin oğlu* (Aslan) (sc, role); *Balatli arif* (Yilmaz) (role); *Bomba Kemal* (Kurthan) (role); *Büyük cellatlar* (Duru) (role); *Cirkin kiral affetmez* (Atadeniz) (role); *Eskiya celladi* (Jöntürk) (role); *Ince cumali* (Duru) (role); *Kizilirmak-Karakoyun* (Akad) (role); *Kozanoğlu* (Yilmaz) (role); *Kuduz recep* (Sağirğlu) (role); *Kurbanlik katil* (Akad) (role)

1968 *Azrail benim* (*The Executioner*) (sc, role); *Kargaci Halil* (*Halil, the Crow-Man*) (Yalinkilic) (sc, role); *Aslan bey* (Yalinkilic) (role); *Beyoğlu canavari* (Görec) (role); *Canpazari* (Görec) (role); *Marmara hasan* (Aslan) (role); *Öldürmek hakkimdir* (Ergün) (role)

1969 *Belanin yedi türlüsü* (*Seven Kinds of Trouble*) (Ergün) (sc, role); *Bin defa ölürüm* (Aslan) (role); *Cifte tabancali kabadayi* (Aslan) (role); *Güney ölüm saciyor* (Aslan) (role); *Kan su gibi akacak* (Atadeniz) (role); *Kursunlarin kanunu* (Ergün) (role)

1970 *Imzam kanla yazilir* (*I Sign in Blood*) (Aslan) (sc, role); *Sevgili muhafizin* (*My Dear Bodyguard*) (Jöntürk) (sc, role); *Seytan kayaliklari* (*Devil Crag*) (Filmer) (sc, role); *Cifte yürekli* (Evin) (role); *Kanimin son damlasina kadar* (Figenli) (role); *Onu Allah affetsin* (Elmas) (role); *Son kizgin adam* (Davutoğlu) (role); *Zeyno* (Yilmaz) (role)

1971 *Cirkin ve cesur* (Ozer) (role); *Namus ve silah* (Görec) (role)

1972 *Sabte yar* (Görec) (role)

1975 *Izin* (Leave) (Gürsü) (sc); *Bir gün mutlaka* (*One Day Certainly*) (Olgac) (sc)

1978 *Sürü* (*The Herd*) (Ökten) (sc, pr supervision)

1979 *Düsman* (*The Enemy*) (Ökten) (sc, pr supervision)

1981 *Yol* (*The Way*) (sc, pr supervision, ed)

Publications

By GÜNEY: articles—

"Entretien avec Yilmaz Güney (1977)," in *Positif* (Paris), April 1980.

Interview with Michel Ciment, in *Positif* (Paris), June 1982.

Interview with Marcel Martin, in *Image et Son* (Paris), July-August 1982.

"Güney's last journey," an interview with C. Gardner, in *Stills* (London), October 1984.

On GÜNEY: books—

Armes, Roy, *Third World Filmmaking and the West,* Berkeley, 1987.

On GÜNEY: articles—

Weales, G. "Istanbul Journal," in *Film Comment* (New York), January/February 1975.

Kazan, Elia, "The View from a Turkish Prison," in *New York Times Magazine,* 4 February 1979.

"Guney Issue" of *Positif* (Paris), April 1980.

Armes, Roy, "Yilmaz Guney: The Limits of Individual Action," in *Framework* (Norwich), Summer 1981.

Elley, Derek, "Yilmaz Güney," in *International Film Guide 1983,* London, 1982.

Giles, D., and H. Sahin, "Revolutionary Cinema in Turkey: Yilmaz Güney," in *Jump Cut* (Berkeley), July 1982.

Rayns, Tony, "From Isolation," in *Sight and Sound* (London), Spring 1983.

Bassan, R., "*Le Mur*: L'Itinéraire escarpé de Yilmaz Güney," in *Revue du Cinéma* (Paris), June 1983.

Obituary in *Variety* (New York), 12 September 1984.

Finlayson, E., "Levantine Approaches: On First looking into Güney's Turkey," in *Monthly Film Bulletin* (London), October 1984.

Listener (London), 15 January 1987.

On GÜNEY: film—

Stempel, Hans, and Martin Ripken, *Besuch auf Imrali (Portrait of Yilmaz Güney),* 1979.

* * *

Yilmaz Güney's life was fully as dramatic as any of his films. The son of a rural worker, he supported himself through studies at university in Ankara and Istanbul. Though his career was interrupted by a series of arrests for political activities, he established himself as a scriptwriter and actor in the 1960s and developed a wide popular following. More than a film star in the conventional sense, he became something of a popular myth, a figure in whose sufferings and ruthless quest for vengeance the poor and oppressed could see their lives and aspirations reflected.

When Güney turned to directing in the late 1960s, his first films were in the same commercial tradition as his early hits. But the early 1970s saw a fresh burst of creativity, brought to an end by a new prison sentence of two years. After his release he completed one of his most interesting films, *Arkadas (The Friend),* in 1974, before finding himself back in prison, this time on a murder charge for which he received a sentence of twenty-four years imprisonment. But even this could not put a stop to his career. He maintained contact with the outside world and continued scripting films, some of which, like *Sürü (The Herd),* achieved international success. When he finally made his escape from Turkey in 1981 he was able to work on yet another film he had scripted, *Yol (The Way),* which won the Cannes Grand Prix in 1982.

Perhaps Güney's major achievement as an actor-director in the early 1970s was to make the transition from the heroic superman figure of his early films, such as *Ac Kurtlar (The Hungry Wolves),* to the vulnerable individual of his later work. In the series of masterly films that begin with the ironically titled *Umut (Hope)* in 1970, the failure of the isolated individual acting alone becomes the uniting thread of Güney's work. Already, in *The Hungry Wolves,* the picture of Turkish society portrayed by Güney is most remarkable for what is lacking: no concerned government to maintain the law, no self-help for the terrorized peasants, no acceptable role for women, no vision beyond instinctive revolt on the part of the bandits. These factors continue to form the background for the series of defeated individuals in both rural settings as in the bandit film *Ağıt (Elegy)* and the urban environment as in *Baba (The Father)* and *Zavallilar (The Poor Ones).* The one film which posits a set of positive values is his last completed work as a director before his arrest in 1974, *The Friend.* But even here the vision is a dark one, for the intellectual hero (played by Güney) confronts an erstwhile friend with his empty life and thereby drives him to suicide.

The next film Güney began, *Endise (Anxiety),* was completed by his friend and former assistant Serif Gören following Güney's arrest. He was to spend eight years in prison, but he continued to write film scripts indefatigably. Among his best films of this period are those which offer a vivid picture of the life of peasants in the still feudal world of his native district, Adana: *Anxiety* and *The Herd,* the latter directed by Zeki Ökten. Güney's final Turkish work, *Yol,* which he edited himself in exile, is even wider in its scope, offering an image of the whole breadth of Turkey through its intercut stories of five detainees released from prison for a week who travel home to their families. Despite Güney's strong political commitment, his films are social studies rather than overtly political tracts. He himself never failed to make the distinction between his political activity, which is directed towards revolutionary change in society, and his filmmaking. For Güney, the fictional feature film remained first and foremost a popular form, a way of communicating with a mass audience, and, as *Yol* shows, he used in an exemplary way the possibilities it offers for stating and examining the contradictions that underlie modern Turkish society.

—Roy Armes

GUTIÉRREZ ALEA, Tomás

Nationality: Cuban. **Born:** Havana, 11 December 1928. **Education:** Studied law at the University of Havana; attended Centro Sperimentale, Rome, 1951-53. **Career:** Worked with Cine-Revista newsreel organisation, late 1950s; following establishment of Instituto Cubano del Arte e Industria Cinematograficos (ICAIC) by revolutionary government, began making documentaries, 1959; later collaborated with younger filmmakers, in keeping with ICAIC policy.

Films as Director:

1955 *El megano* (co-d)
1959 *Esta tierra nuestra*
1960 *Asemblea General*
1961 *Muerte al invasor* (co-d); *Historias de la revolucion*
1962 *Las doce sillas* (*The Twelve Chairs*)
1964 *Cumbite*
1966 *La muerte de un burócrata* (*The Death of a Bureaucrat*)
1968 ***Memorias del subdesarrollo*** (*Memories of Underdevelopment*)
1971 *Una pelea cubana contra los demonios* (*A Cuban Struggle against the Demons*)
1974 *El arte del tobaco*
1976 *La última cena* (*The Last Supper*)
1979 *Los sobrevivientes* (*Survivors*) (+ co-sc)
1983 *Hasta cierto punto* (*Up to a Point*) (+ co-sc)
1988 *Cartas del parque* (*Letters from the Park*)
1993 *Fresa y chocolate* (*Strawberry and Chocolate*) (co-d)
1995 *Guantanamera* (co-d, + co-sc)

Publications

By GUTIÉRREZ ALEA: book—

Las doce sillas, Havana, 1963.

By GUTIÉRREZ ALEA: articles—

"Individual Fulfillment and Collective Achievement: An Interview with Tomás Gutiérrez Alea," with Julianne Burton, in *Cineaste* (New York), January 1977.
"Towards a Renewal of Cuban Revolutionary Cinema," an interview with Zuzana Mirjam Pick, in *Cine-Tracts* (Montreal), no. 3/4, 1978.
Interview with G. Chijona, in *Framework* (Norwich), Spring 1979.
Interview with M. Ansara, in *Cinema Papers* (Melbourne), May/June 1981.
"Dramaturgia (cinematografica) y realidad," in *Cine Cubano* (Havana), no. 105, 1983.
Interview with E. Colina, in *Cine Cubano* (Havana), no. 109, 1984.
"I Wasn't Always a Filmmaker," in *Cineaste* (New York), vol. 14, no. 1, 1985.
Interview with Gary Crowdus, in *Cineaste* (New York), vol. 14, no. 2, 1985.
Interview with J. R. MacBean, in *Film Quarterly* (Berkeley), Spring 1985.
"The Viewer's Dialectic," in *Reviewing Histories: Selections from New Latin American Cinema,* edited by Coco Fusco, Buffalo, New York, 1987.
"Another Cinema, Another World, Another Society," in *Journal of Third World Studies,* vol. 11, no. 1, 1994.
West, Dennis, "*Strawberry and Chocolate,* Ice Cream and Tolerance: Interviews with Tomás Gutiérrez Alea and Juan Carlos Tabío," in *Cineaste,* vol. 21, no. 1-2, 1995.

On GUTIÉRREZ ALEA: books—

Nelson, L., *Cuba: The Measure of a Revolution,* Minneapolis, 1972.
Myerson, Michael, editor, *Memories of Underdevelopment: The Revolutionary Films of Cuba,* New York, 1973.
Chanan, Michael, *The Cuban Image: Cinema and Cultural Politics in Cuba,* Bloomington, Indiana, 1985.
Oroz, Silvia, *Os filmes que Não Filmei: Gutiérrez Alea,* Rio de Janeiro, 1985.
Burton, Julianne, editor, *Cinema and Social Change in Latin America: Conversations with Filmmakers,* Austin, Texas, 1986.
Fornet, Ambrosio, editor, *Alea: Una retrospectiva critica,* Havana, 1987.
Douglas, María Eulalia, *Diccionario de Cineastas Cubanos: 1959-1987,* Merida, Venezuela, 1989.
Chanan, Michael, editor, *Memories of Underdevelopment, Tomás Gutiérrez Alea, Director, and Inconsolable Memories, Edmundo Desnoes, Author,* London, 1990.
Paranagua, Paulo Antonio, editor, *Le Cinema Cubain,* Paris, 1990.
Pick, Zuzana M., *The New Latin American Cinema: A Continental Project,* Austin, Texas, 1993.

On GUTIÉRREZ ALEA: articles—

Sutherland, Elizabeth, "Cinema of Revolution—Ninety Miles from Home," in *Film Quarterly* (Berkeley), Winter 1961/62.

Adler, Renata, in *New York Times*, 10, 11, and 12 February 1969.
Engel, Andi, "Solidarity and Violence," in *Sight and Sound* (London), Autumn 1969.
Crowdus, Gary, "The Spring 1972 Cuban Film Festival Bust," in *Film Society Review* (New York), March/May 1972.
Lesage, Julia, "Images of Underdevelopment," in *Jump Cut* (Chicago), May/June 1974.
Kernan, Margot, "Cuban Cinema: Tomás Gutiérrez Alea," in *Film Quarterly* (Berkeley), Winter 1976.
Burton, Julianne, "Introduction to Revolutionary Cuban Cinema," in *Jump Cut* (Chicago), December 1978.
West, Dennis, "Slavery and Cinema in Cuba: The Case of Gutiérrez Alea's *The Last Supper*," in *Western Journal of Black Studies*, Summer 1979.
Alexander, W., "Class, Film Language, and Popular Cinema," in *Jump Cut* (Berkeley), March 1985.
Burton, Julianne, "The Intellectual in Anguish: Modernist Form and Ideology in *Land in Anguish* and *Memories of Underdevelopment*," in *Ideologies and Literature*, Winter-Spring 1985.
West, Dennis, "*The Last Supper*," in *Magill's Survey of Cinema: Foreign Language Films*, edited by Frank N. Magill, Englewood Cliffs, New Jersey, 1985.
Sanchez Crespo, Osvaldo, "The Perspective of the Present: Cuban History, Cuban Filmmaking," in *Reviewing Histories: Selections from New Latin American Cinema*, edited by Coco Fusco, Buffalo, New York, 1987.
West, Dennis, "Cuba: Cuban Cinema before the Revolution and After," in *World Cinema since 1945*, edited by William Luhr, New York, 1987.
"Tomás Gutiérrez Alea," in *Film Dope* (London), March 1988.
Chanan, Michael, "Tomás Gutiérrez Alea: The Man in Havana," in *National Film Theatre Booklet* (London), October/November 1989.
Fornet, Ambrosio, "Alea: Diez notas en busca de un autor," in *Encuadre* (Venezuela), vol. 11, 1992.
Chávez, Rebeca, "Tomás Gutiérrez Alea: Entrevista filmada," in *La Gaceta de Cuba*, September-October 1993.
Padrón Nodarse, Frank, "La realidad en el cine cubano de los noventa," in *Dicine*, vol. 57, 1994.
Strawberry and Chocolate issue of *Viridiana* (Madrid), no. 7, 1994.
González, Reynaldo, "Meditation for a Debate, or Cuban Culture with the Taste of *Strawberry and Chocolate*," in *Cuba Update*, May 1994.
Mason, Joyce, "State Machismo: The Official Versions of the State of Male/Female Relations," in *Cineaction*, May 1986.
Jaramillo, Diana, "El sabor de la cubanía," in *Kinetoscopio*, May-June 1994.
Yglesias, Jorge, "La espera del futuro," in *Kinetoscopio*, November-December 1994.
Cotler, Andrés, "Contradicciones cubanas: *Fresa y chocolate*," in *La Gran Ilusion*, vol. 4, 1995.
Espinasa, JoséMaría, "*Fresa y chocolate:* Un cuento de hadas," in *Nitrato de Plata*, vol. 20, 1995.
Mraz, John, "*Memorias del subdesarrollo:* Conciencia burguesa, contexto revolucionario," in *Nitrato de Plata*, vol. 20, 1995.
Martínez Carril, Manuel, "Gutiérrez Alea observa a Cuba desde adentro," in *Cinemateca Revista*, January 1995.
Wise, Michael Z., "In Totalitarian Cuba, Ice Cream and Understanding," in *New York Times*, 22 January 1995.

* * *

The narrative and structural approaches and the style of Gutiérrez Alea's films have varied widely, but his best works show a significant thematic unity stemming from the director's position as a committed revolutionary filmmaker working within a film industry controlled by a socialist state. The director's greatest films all explore aspects of revolution. This central theme of revolution is announced in the neorealist-influenced *Historias de la revolución*, the first feature made by Gutiérrez Alea after the triumph of the Cuban revolution.

Gutiérrez Alea believes that bureaucracy is a part of revolutionary Cuba's bourgeois heritage. His *La muerte de un burócrata* is a polemical yet humorous feature on bureaucratization in a revolutionary socialist society. This masterful satire is outstanding for its dimension of playful inventiveness: credits which are typed in "bureaucratese," the humorous use of animated cartoons, and the many well-integrated parodies of renowned sequences from world cinema. *La muerte de un burócrata* demonstrates that socialist cinema need not resort to heavy-handed methods to express important themes.

Gutiérrez Alea's masterpiece, *Memorias del subdesarrollo*, is a critique of the colonized bourgeois mentality. The protagonist is a man without a future: a middle-aged bourgeois intellectual who refuses to flee to Miami but who is unable to integrate himself into the Cuban revolutionary process. Gutiérrez Alea successfully draws on historical motifs (speeches by Kennedy and Castro) and elements of other film genres (documentary and newsreel) in order to show this individual's place in the march of history.

A primary goal of Cuba's revolutionary filmmakers has been to decolonize the taste of the Cuban film-going public, which for decades had been subjected to standard Hollywood fare. In *Memorias del subdesarrollo*, Gutiérrez Alea contributes overtly to this effort by including a sequence in which clips from a pornographic film are shown in order to critique that genre. *Memorias del subdesarrollo* also features more subtle efforts at decolonization; the director subverts and questions conventional film techniques and strategies through self conscious and self-reflective devices, as when the director appears as himself in the Instituto Cubano del Arte e Industria Cinematográficos (ICAIC) commenting on this very film, and when the author of the novel *Memorias del subdesarrollo* participates in a round table on literature and underdevelopment.

In *La última cena*, Gutiérrez Alea abandons self-conscious and self-reflective techniques in favor of a realist style and a conventional chronological treatment of the story line. He uses traditional Christian motifs associated with the Last Supper and the Resurrection in order to reveal the religious ideology of the white planter class—a dead-letter Christianity which reinforced the socio-economic status quo and reconciled black slaves to a life of bondage. One of the goals of ICAIC has been to contribute to the forging of an authentic national identity through the reassessment of Cuban history. *La última cena* re-examines the historical role of blacks by depicting a slave revolt which is based on an actual incident. Gutiérrez Alea and others at ICAIC supported this film project because Cuba's tradition of black resistance (to slavery and to Spanish colonial powers) was seen as a major contribution to today's socialist Cuba, whose proclaimed objectives include an end to the oppressive legacy of colonialism and to all forms of domination.

In the 1990s, Gutiérrez Alea co-directed two important features with his younger Cuban colleague Juan Carlos Tabío. Both films, which are rather conventional stylistically, offer sharply critical examinations of revolutionary Cuban society. The Cuban box-office smash *Strawberry and Chocolate* is a comedy-drama that represents ICAIC's first major attempt to explore the difficulties of leading a gay lifestyle in a revolutionary society. The comedy *Guantanamera* satirizes a Cuban bureaucracy that is more paper-pushing than it is revolutionary.

The films of Gutiérrez Alea have been well received by Cuban audiences and by critics of many nations. Gutiérrez Alea is one of the greatest Latin American filmmakers because of his ability to mold widely different structural and stylistic approaches to a variety of significant revolutionary themes. This achievement is particularly impressive for having been accomplished in a developing country with modest financial and technical resources.

—Dennis West

GUY, Alice

Nationality: French. **Born:** Born in Saint-Mandé, 1 July 1873. Also known as Alice Guy-Blaché and Alice Blaché. **Education:** Convent du Sacré-Coeur, Viry, France 1879-85; religious school at Ferney, and brief term in Paris; studied stenography. **Family:** Married Herbert Blaché-Bolton, 1907 (divorced 1922), two children. **Career:** Secretary to Léon Gaumont, 1895; directed first film, *La Fée aux choux*, 1896 (some sources give 1900); director of Gaumont film production, 1897-1907; using Gaumont "chronophone," made first sound films, 1900; moved to United States with husband, who was to supervise Gaumont subsidiary Solax, 1907; ceased independent production, lectured on filmmaking at Columbia University, 1917; assistant director to husband, 1919-20; returned to France, 1922; moved to United States, 1964. **Awards:** Legion of Honor, 1955. **Died:** In Mahwah, New Jersey, 24 March 1968.

Films as Director and Scriptwriter:

1896 *La Fée aux choux* (*The Cabbage Fairy*)

1897 *Le Pêcheur dans le torrent*; *Leçon de danse*; *Baignade dans le torrent*; *Une nuit agitée*; *Coucher d'Yvette*; *Danse fleur de lotus*; *Ballet Libella*; *Le Planton du colonel*; *Idylle*; *L'Aveugle*

1897/98 *L'Arroseur arrosé*; *Au réfectoire*; *En classe*; *Les Cambrioleurs*; *Le Cocher de fiacre endormi*; *Idylle interrompue*; *Chez le magnétiseur*; *Les Farces de Jocko*; *Scène d'escamotage*; *Déménagement à la cloche de bois*; *Je vous y prrrends!*

1898/99 *Leçons de boxe*; *La Vie du Christ* (11 tableaux)

1899/1900 *Le Tondeur de chiens*; *Le Déjeuner des enfants*; *Au cabaret*; *La Mauvaise Soupe*; *Un Lunch*; *Erreur judiciaire*; *L'Aveugle*; *La Bonne Absinthe*; *Danse serpentine par Mme Bob Walter*; *Mésaventure d'un charbonnier*; *Monnaie de lapin*; *Les Dangers de l'acoolisme*; *Le Tonnelier*; *Transformations*; *Le Chiffonier*; *Retour des champs*; *Chez le Maréchal-Ferrant*; *Marché à la volaille*; *Courte échelle*; *L'Angélus*; *Bataille d'oreillers*; *Bataille de boules de neige*; *Le marchand de coco*

1900 *Avenue de l'Opéra*; *La petite magicienne*; *Leçon de danse*; *Chez le photographe*; *Sidney's Joujoux* series (nine titles); *Dans les coulisses*; *Au Bal de Flore* series (three titles); *Ballet Japonais* series (three titles); *Danse serpentine*; *Danse du pas des foulards par des almées*; *Danse de l'ivresse*; *Coucher d'une Parisienne*; *Les Fredaines de Pierrette* series (four titles); *Vénus et Adonis* series (five titles); *La Tarantelle*; *Danse des Saisons* series (four titles); *La Source*; *Danse du papillon*; *La Concierge*; *Danses* series (three titles); *Chirurgie fin de siècle*; *Une Rage de dents*; *Saut humidifié de M. Plick*

1900/01 *La Danse du ventre*; *Lavatory moderne*; *Lecture quotidienne*

1900/07 (Gaumont "Phonoscènes", i.e. films with synchronized sound recorded on a wax cylinder): *Carmen* (twelve scenes); *Mireille* (five scenes); *Les Dragons de Villars* (nine scenes); *Mignon* (seven scenes); *Faust* (twenty-two scenes); *Polin* series (thirteen titles); *Mayol* series (thirteen titles); *Dranem* series of comic songs (twelve titles); Series recorded in Spain (eleven titles); *La Prière* by Gounod

1901 *Folies Masquées* series (three titles); *Frivolité*; *Les Vagues*; *Danse basque*; *Hussards et grisettes*; *Charmant FrouFrou*; *Tel est pris qui croyait prendre*

1902 *La fiole enchantée*; *L'Equilibriste*; *En faction*; *La Première Gamelle*; *La Dent récalcitrante*; *Le Marchand de ballons*; *Les Chiens savants*; *Miss Lina Esbrard Danseuse Cosmopolite et Serpentine* series (four titles); *Les Clowns*; *Sage-femme de première classe*; *Quadrille réaliste*; *Une Scène en cabinet particulier vue à travers le trou de la serrure*; *Farces de cuisinière*; *Danse mauresque*; *Le Lion savant*; *Le Pommier*; *La Cour des miracles*; *La Gavotte*; *Trompé mais content*; *Fruits de saison*; *Pour secourer la salade*

1903 *Potage indigeste*; *Illusioniste renversant*; *Le Fiancé ensorcelé*; *Les Apaches pas veinards*; *Les Aventures d'un voyageur trop pressé*; *Ne bougeons plus*; *Comment monsieur prend son bain*; *La Main du professeur Hamilton ou Le Roi des dollars*; *Service précipité*, *La Poule fantaisiste*; *Modelage express*; *Faust et Méphistophélès*; *Lutteurs américains*; *La Valise enchantée*; *Compagnons de voyage encombrants*; *Cake-Walk de la pendule*; *Répétition dans un cirque*; *Jocko musicien*; *Les Braconniers*; *La Liqueur du couvent*; *Le Voleur sacrilège*; *Enlèvement en automobile et mariage précipite*

1903/04 *Secours aux naufragés*; *La Mouche*; *La Chasse au cambrioleur*; *Nos Bon Etudiants*; *Les Surprises de l'affichage*; *Comme on fait son lit on se couche*; *Le Pompon malencontreux 1*; *Comment on disperse les foules*; *Les Enfants du miracle*; *Pierrot assassin*; *Les Deux Rivaux*

1904 *L'Assassinat du Courrier de Lyon*; *Vieilles Estampes* series (four titles); *Mauvais coeur puni*; *Magie noire*; *Rafle de chiens*; *Cambrioleur et agent*; *Scènes Directoire* series (three titles); *Duel tragique*; *L'Attaque d'un diligence*; *Culture intensive ou Le Vieux Mari*; *Cible humaine*; *Transformations*; *Le Jour du terme*; *Robert Macaire et Bertrand*; *Electrocutée*; *La Rêve du chasseur*; *Le Monolutteur*; *Les Petits Coupeurs de bois vert*; *Clown en sac*; *Triste Fin d'un vieux savant*; *Le Testament de Pierrot*; *Les Secrets de la prestidigitation dévoilés*; *La Faim ... L' occasion ... L'herbe tendre*; *Militaire et nourrice*; *La Première Cigarette*; *Départ pour les vacances*; *Tentative d'assassinat en chemin de fer*; *Paris la nuit ou Exploits d' apaches à Montamartre*; *Concours de bébés*; *Erreur de poivrot*; *Volée par les bohémiens* (*Rapt d' enfant par les romanichels*); *Les Bienfaits du cinématographe*; *P tissier et ramoneur*; *Gage d'amour*; *L'Assassinat de la rue du Temple* (*Le Crime de la rue du Temple*); *Le Réveil du jardinier*; *Les Cambrioleurs de Paris*

1905 *Réhabilitation*; *Douaniers et contrebandiers* (*La Guérité*); *Le Bébé embarrassant*; *Comment on dort á Paris!*; *Le Lorgnon accusateur*; *La Charité du prestidigitateur*; *Une Noce au lac Saint-Fargeau*; *Le Képi*; *Le Pantalon coupé*; *Le Plateau*; *Roméo pris au piége*; *Chien jouant á la balle*; *La Fantassin Guignard*; *La Statue*; *Villa dévalisée*; *Mort de Robert Macaire et Bertrand*; *Le Pavé*; *Les Maçons*; *La Esmeralda*; *Peintre et ivrogne*; *On est poivrot, mais on a du cœur*; *Au Poulailler!*

1906 *La Fée au printemps*; *La Vie du marin*; *La Chaussette*; *La Messe de minuit*; *Pauvre pompier*; *Le Régiment moderne*; *Les Druides*; *Voyage en Espagne* series (fifteen titles); *La Vie de Christ* (25 tableaux); *Conscience de prêtre*; *L'Honneur du Corse*; *J'ai un hanneton dans mon pantalon*; *Le Fils du garde-chasse*; *Course de taureaux à Nîmes*; *La Pègre de Paris*; *Lèvres closes* (*Sealed Lips*); *La Crinoline*; *La Voiture cellulaire*; *La Marâtre*; *Le Matelas alcoolique*; *A la recherche d'un appartement*

1907 *La vérité sur l'homme-singe* (*Ballet de Singe*); *Déménagement à la cloche de bois*; *Les Gendarmes*; *Sur la barricade* (*L'enfant de la barricade*)

1910 *A Child's Sacrifice* (*The Doll*)

1911 *Rose of the Circus*; *Across the Mexican Line*; *Eclipse*; *A Daughter of the Navajos*; *The Silent Signal*; *The Girl and the Bronco Buster*; *The Mascot of Troop 'C'*; *An Enlisted Man's Honor*;

Alice Guy

The Stampede; *The Hold-Up*; *The Altered Message*; *His Sister's Sweetheart*; *His Better Self*; *A Revolutionary Romance*; *The Violin Maker of Nuremberg*

1912 *Mignon or The Child of Fate*; *A Terrible Lesson*; *His Lordship's White Feather*; *Falling Leaves*; *The Sewer*; *In the Year 2000*; *A Terrible Night*; *Mickey's Pal*; *Fra Diavolo*; *Hotel Honeymoon*; *The Equine Spy*; *Two Little Rangers*; *The Bloodstain*; *At the Phone*; *Flesh and Blood*; *The Paralytic*; *The Face at the Window*

1913 *The Beasts of the Jungle*; *Dick Whittington and His Cat*; *Kelly from the Emerald Isle*; *The Pit and the Pendulum*; *Western Love*; *Rogues of Paris*; *Blood and Water*; *Ben Bolt*; *The Shadows of the Moulin Rouge*; *The Eyes that Could Not Close*; *The Star of India*; *The Fortune Hunters*

1914 *Beneath the Czar*; *The Monster and the Girl*; *The Million Dollar Robbery*; *The Prisoner of the Harem*; *The Dream Woman*; *Hook and Hand*; *The Woman of Mystery*; *The Yellow Traffic*; *The Lure*; *Michael Strogoff or The Courier to the Czar*; *The Tigress*; *The Cricket on the Hearth*

1915 *The Heart of a Painted Woman*; *Greater Love Hath No Man*; *The Vampire*; *My Madonna*; *Barbara Frietchie* (co-d)

1916 *What Will People Say?*; *The Girl with the Green Eyes*; *The Ocean Waif*; *House of Cards*;

1917 *The Empress*; *The Adventurer*; *A Man and the Woman*; *When You and I Were Young*; *Behind the Mask*

1918 *The Great Adventure*

1920 *Tarnished Reputation*

Other Films:

1919 *The Divorcee* (asst d); *The Brat* (asst d)

1920 *Stronger than Death* (asst d)

Publications

By GUY: book—

Autobiographie d'une pionnière du cinéma 1873-1968, Paris, 1976; published as *The Memoirs of Alice Guy-Blaché*, edited by Anthony Slide, Metuchen, New Jersey, 1986.

By GUY: articles—

"Woman's Place in Photoplay Production," in *The Moving Picture World* (New York), 11 July 1914.

Letter in *Films in Review* (New York), May 1964.

"La Naissance du cinéma," in *Image et Son* (Paris), April 1974.

"Tournez, mesdames ...," in *Ecran* (Paris), August/September 1974.

On GUY: books—

Slide, Anthony, *Early Women Directors*, New York, 1977.

Elsaesser, Thomas, and Adam Barker, editors, *Early Cinema: Space-Frame-Narrative*, London, 1990.

On GUY: articles—

Levine, H.Z., "Madame Alice Blaché," in *Photoplay* (New York), March 1912.

Ford, Charles, "The First Female Producer," in *Films in Review* (New York), March 1964.

Smith, F.L., "Alice Guy-Blaché," in *Films in Review* (New York), April 1964.

Lacassin, Francis, "Out of Oblivion: Alice Guy-Blaché," in *Sight and Sound* (London), Summer 1971.

Mitry, Jean, "A propos d'Alice Guy," in *Ecran* (Paris), July 1976.

Deslandes, J., "Sur Alice Guy: polémique," in *Ecran* (Paris), September 1976.

Peary, Gerald, "Czarina of the Silent Screen," in *Velvet Light Trap* (Madison, Wisconsin), Winter 1977.

* * *

Alice Guy was the first person, or among the first, to make a fictional film. The story-film was quite possibly "invented" by her in 1896 when she made *La Fée aux choux (The Cabbage Fairy).* Certain historians claim that films of Louis Lumière and Georges Méliès preceded Guy's first film. The question remains debatable; Guy claimed precedence, devoting much effort in her lifetime to correcting recorded errors attributing her films to her male colleagues, and trying to secure her earned niche in film history. There is no debate regarding Guy's position as the world's first woman filmmaker.

Between 1896 and 1901 Guy made films averaging just seventy-five feet in length; from 1902 to 1907 she made numerous films of all types and lengths using acrobats, clowns, and opera singers as well as large casts in ambitious productions based on fairy and folk tales, Biblical themes, paintings, and myths. The "tricks" she used—running film in reverse and the use of double exposure—were learned through trial-and-error. In this period she also produced "talking pictures," in which Gaumont's Chronophone synchronized a projector with sound recorded on a wax cylinder.

One of these sound films, *Mireille,* was made by Guy in 1906. Herbert Blaché-Bolton joined the film crew of *Mireille* to learn directing. Alice Guy and Herbert were married in early 1907. The couple moved to the United States, where they eventually set up a studio in Flushing, New York. The Blachés then established the Solax Company, with a Manhattan office. In its four years of existence, Solax released 325 films, including westerns, military movies, thrillers, and historical romances. Mme. Blaché's first picture in the United States was *A Child's Sacrifice* (in 1910), which centers on a girl's attempts to earn money for her family. In her *Hotel Honeymoon* of 1912, the moon comes alive to smile at human lovers, while in *The Violin Maker of Nuremberg,* two apprentices contend for the affections of their instructor's daughter.

The Blachés built their own studio at Fort Lee, New Jersey, a facility with a daily printing capacity of 16,000 feet of positive film. For its inauguration in February 1912, Mme. Blaché presented an evening of Solax films at Weber's Theatre on Broadway. In that year she filmed two movies based on operas: *Fra Diavolo* and *Mignon,* each of which were three-reelers that included orchestral accompaniment. Her boldest enterprises were films using animals and autos.

Cataclysmic changes in the film industry finally forced the Blachés out of business. They rented, and later sold, their studio, then directed films for others. In 1922 the Blachés divorced. Herbert directed films until 1930, but Alice could not find film work and never made another film. She returned to France, but without prints of her films she had no evidence of her accomplishments. She could not find work in the French film industry either. She returned to the United States in 1927 to search the Library of Congress and other film depositories for her films, but her efforts in vain: only a half-dozen of her one-reelers survive. In 1953 she returned to Paris, where, at age seventy-eight, she was honored as the first woman filmmaker in the world. Her films, characterized by innovation and novelty, explored all genres and successfully appealed to both French and American audiences. Today she is finally being recognized as a unique pioneer of the film industry.

—Louise Heck-Rabi

GUZMÁN, Patricio

Nationality: Chilean. **Born:** Santiago de Chile, 11 August 1941. **Education:** Escuela oficial de cinematografia (EOC), Madrid, graduated 1969. **Career:** After writing novels, joined Filmic Institute, Catholic University in Santiago, 1965; left for Spain, 1967; returned to Chile, joined Chile-Films (national film production company), heading Documentary Film Workshops, 1970; constituted Group of the Third Year to produce *The Battle of Chile,* imprisoned shortly after September coup d'etat, 1973; moved to Cuba, 1974, completed *The Battle of Chile,* 1977; moved to Spain, 1980.

Films as Director:

1965 *Viva la libertad* (*Hail to Freedom*) (short)
1966 *Artesania popular* (*Popular Crafts*) (short); *Electroshow* (short)
1967 *Cien Metros con Charlot* (*One Hundred Meters with Chaplin*); *Escuela de sordomudos* (*School for Deafmutes*)
1968 *La tortura* (*Torture*); *Imposibrante*
1969 *Opus seis* (*Opus Six*); *El Paraiso ortopedico* (*Orthopedic Paradise*)
1970 *Elecciones municipales* (*Municipal Elections*); *El primer año* (*The First Year*)
1972 *La respuesta de Octobre* (*The Response in October*); *Comandos comunales* (*Communal Organization*); *Manuel Rodriquez* (unfinished)
1974 ***La batalla de Chile: La lucha de un pueblo sin armas*** (*The Battle of Chile: The Struggle of an Unarmed People*) Part 1: ***La insurrección de la burguesia*** (*Insurrection of the Bourgeoisie*)
1976 Part 2: ***El golpe de estado*** (*Coup d'état*)
1979 Part 3: ***El poder popular*** (*The Popular Power*)
1983 *La rosa de los vientos* (*Rose of the Winds*)
1986 *En el Nombre de Dios*
1992 *La Cruz del Sur*

Publications

By GUZMÁN: books—

La insurrección de la burgesia, edited by Racinante, Caracas, 1975.
La batalla de Chile: La lucha de un pueblo sin armas, Madrid, 1977.
El cine contra el fascismo, with P. Sempere, edited by Fernando Torres, Valencia, 1977.

By GUZMÁN: articles—

"Le Cinéma dans la politique de l'Unité Populaire," in *Jeune Cinéma* (Paris), November 1974.
"La Bataille du Chili II," interview with Marcel Martin, in *Ecran* (Paris), January 1977.
"Politics and the Documentary in People's Chile," interview with Julianne Burton, in *Socialist Review,* October 1977.
"*La batalla de Chile,*" interview with Carlos Galiano, in *Cine Cubano* (Havana), no. 91-92, 1978.
"Chile," 3: Guzmán," and "Chile," in *Framework* (Norwich), Spring and Autumn 1979.
Interview with Z. M. Pick, in *Ciné-Tracts* (Montreal), Winter 1980.

On GUZMÁN: books—

Burton, Julianne, editor, *Cinema and Social Change in Latin America: Conversations with Filmmakers,* Austin, Texas, 1986.
King, John, *Magical Realism: A History of Cinema in Latin America,* London, 1990.

On GUZMÁN: articles—

Gauthier, Guy, "Chili: la première année," in *Image et Son* (Paris), March 1973.
Gauthier, Guy, "*La Bataille du Chili,* première partie: *L'Insurrection de la bourgeoisie,*" in *Image et Son* (Paris), January 1976.
Niogret, Hubert, "*La Batalla de Chile: el golpe de estado,*" in *Positif* (Paris), July/August 1976.
Delmas, Jean, "*La Batalla de Chile,* deuxième partie: *Le Coup d'état,*" in *Jeune Cinéma* (Paris), February 1977.
West, Dennis, "*The Battle of Chile,*" in *Cineaste* (New York), vol. 11, no. 2, 1978.
West, Dennis, "Documenting the End of the Chilean Road to Socialism: *La Batalla de Chile,*" in *The American Hispanist,* February 1978.
"*La Batalla de Chile* Section" of *Cine Cubano* (Havana), March 1978.
Angry Arts group, "*Battle of Chile* in Context," and V. Wallis, "*Battle of Chile*: Struggle of People without Arms," in *Jump Cut* (Chicago), November 1979.
Mouesca, J., "El cine chileño en el exilio (1973-1983)," in *Cine Cubano* (Havana), no. 109, 1984.

* * *

Chilean director Patricio Guzmán studied fiction filmmaking in Spain in the 1960s, but he eventually dropped plans to make fiction features when he returned to Chile during the presidency of the Marxist-socialist Salvador Allende (1970-73). Guzmán is above all a political filmmaker, and the intense everyday political activities in Allende's Chile stimulated Guzmán to take to the streets and factories in order to make documentary records of those fast-paced events. In all three of his documentaries on Allende's Chile—*El primer año, La respuesta de Octubre,* and *La batalla de Chile*—the director rejected archival footage and the compilation approach in favor of immersing himself in significant political events in order to obtain actuality footage.

Guzmán's success in obtaining meaningful and abundant actuality footage is due in large part to his (and his colleagues') marked ability to understand and foresee the flow of political events. Political savvy coupled with rigorous and disciplined production techniques allowed Guzmán and his production groups to overcome formidable obstacles, including financial and technical difficulties. To film the three feature-length parts of the masterwork *La batalla de Chile,* the director and his collective had access to one 16mm Eclair camera and one Nagra tape recorder; film stock, unavailable in Chile, had been sent from abroad by a European colleague.

During his stay in Allende's Chile, Guzmán successfully combined his personal political militancy with his concept of the role of the filmmaker. Guzmán, a committed Marxist, wished to make films that would help Allende's leftist Popular Unity coalition take power. Marx and Engels (*Manifesto of the Communist Party*) viewed classes as the protagonists of history, and conflict as an inherent dimension of class societies; Guzmán follows this Marxist conception in that classes are the protagonists of his films and events are framed in terms of class conflict. In accordance with the Marxist-Leninist revolutionary view that there can be no peaceful transition to socialism before the repressive machinery of the bourgeois state is broken up and replaced, the first two parts of *La batalla de Chile* follow the military's drift to the right as well as the anti-Allende activities of the opposition-dominated legislature. Both *La respuesta de Octubre* and part three of *La batalla de Chile* center on workers organizing as a class in order to achieve self-emancipation and transform the world created by the bourgeoisie.

The style of the journalistic *El primer año* is unexceptional, and it was only with *La batalla de Chile* that Guzmán found a distinctive documentary style. This style is characterized by the frequent use of the sequence shot, which the director prefers because it is a synthetic device allowing spectators to see events unfolding in front of their eyes without breaks in the flow of the images.

El primer año and *La respuesta de Octubre* have not circulated widely outside of Allende's Chile. Inside Allende's Chile, these documentaries were well received by working-class audiences. *La respuesta de octubre* was particularly popular with workers who, heartened to see their efforts to create worker-controlled industrial zones documented on film, facilitated the documentary's distribution in the country's factories. Guzmán's international reputation as a documentary filmmaker has been secured by *La batalla de Chile,* hailed by both Marxist and non-Marxist critics in many countries as a landmark in the history of the political documentary.

—Dennis West

HAANSTRA, Bert

Nationality: Dutch. **Born:** Holten, Holland, 31 May 1916. **Education:** Academy of Arts, Amsterdam. **Career:** Painter and press photographer, from late 1930s; joined Royal Dutch Shell Film Unit, 1952; producer and manager, Shell Film Unit, Venezuela, 1956; founded production company, Bert Haanstra Filmproductie, 1960. **Awards:** Grand Prix (documentary), Cannes Festival, for *Mirror of Holland,* 1951.

Films as Director:

1948 *De Muiderkring herleeft* (*The Muyder Circle Lives Again*) (+ sc, ph, ed)
1950 *Spiegel van Holland* (*Mirror of Holland*) (+ sc, ph, ed)
1951 *Nederlandse beeldhouwkunst tijdens de late Middeleeuwen* (*Dutch Sculpture*) (+ co-ed); *Panta Rhei* (*All Things Flow*) (+ sc, ph, ed)
1952 *Dijkbouw* (*Dike Builders*) (+ sc, ed)
1954 *Ont staan en vergaan* (*The Changing Earth*) (+ sc); *De opsporing van aardolie* (*The Search for Oil*) (+ sc); *De verkenningsboring* (*The Wildcat*) (+ sc); *Het olieveld* (*The Oilfield*) (+ sc)
1955 *The Rival World* (*Strijd zonder einde*) (+ ed, sc); *God Shiva* (+ sc, pr, ed); *En de zee was niet meer* (*And There Was No More Sea*) (+ pr, sc, ed)
1957 *Rembrandt, schilder van de mens* (*Rembrandt, Painter of Man*) (+ pr, sc, ed)
1958 *Over glas gesproken* (*Speaking of Glass*) (+ pr, sc, ed); *Glas* (*Glass*) (+ co-ed, pr, sc); *Fanfare* (+ co-sc, co-ed)
1960 *De zaak M.P.* (*The M.P. Case*) (+ co-sc, co-ed, pr)
1962 *Zoo* (+ pr, sc, ed); *Delta Phase I* (+ pr, sc, ed)
1963 *Alleman* (*The Human Dutch*) (+ co-sc, narration for English and German versions)
1966 *De stem van het water* (*The Voice of the Water*) (+ co-sc, pr, ed)
1967 *Retour Madrid* (*Return Ticket to Madrid*) (+ co-pr, co-ph)
1972 *Bij de beesten af* (*Ape and Super Ape*) (+ pr, sc, ed, co-commentary, co-add'l ph, narration)
1975 *Dokter Pulder zaait papavers* (*Dr. Pulder Sows Poppies, When the Poppies Bloom Again*) (+ pr)
1978 *Nationale Parken ... noodzaak* (*National Parks ... a Necessity, National Parks in the Netherlands*) (+ pr, sc, ed)
1979 *Een pak slaag* (*Mr. Slotter's Jubilee*) (+ pr)
1983 *Vroeger kon je lachen* (*One Could Laugh in Former Days*) (+ pr, sc); *Nederland* (*The Netherlands*) (+ pr, sc, ed)

Other Films:

1949 *Myrte en de demonen* (*Myrte and the Demons*) (Schreiber) (ph); *Boer Pietersen schiet in de roos* (*Bull's Eye for Farmer Pietersen*) (Brusse) (ph)
1955 *Belgian Grand Prix* (Hughes) (co-ph)
1957 *De gouden Ilsy* (*The Golden Ilsy*) (van der Linden) (ph); *Olie op reis* (*Pattern of Supply*) (Pendry) (pr)
1959 *Paleontologie* (*Schakel met het verleden*; *Story in the Rocks*) (van Gelder) (pr, tech advisor)
1960 *Lage landen* (*Hold Back the Sea*) (Sluizer) (tech advisor)
1962 *De overval* (*The Silent Raid*) (Rotha) (co-sc, uncredited)
1968 *Pas assez* (*Not Enough*; *Niet genoeg*) (van der Velde) (ed)
1970 *Trafic* (Tati) (collaborator); *Summer in the Fields* (van der Linden) (ed)
1972 *Grierson* (Blais) (role as interviewee)
1979 *Juliana in zeventig bewogen jaren* (*Juliana in Seventy Turbulent Years*) (Kohlhaas) (advisor)

Publications

By HAANSTRA: articles—

"Gresprek met Bert Haanstra en prof. dr. G.P. Behrends," with R. du Mèe and others, in *Skoop* (Amsterdam), v.8, no.6, 1972.
"Geen klachten over hoeveelheid aandacht voor Nederlandse film," in *Skoop* (Amsterdam), February 1976.

On HAANSTRA: book—

Verdaasdonk, Dorothee, editor, *Bert Haanstra,* Amsterdam, 1983.

On HAANSTRA: articles—

"Director of the Year," in *International Film Guide,* London, 1966.
Cowie, Peter, "Bert Haanstra," in *Focus on Film* (London), Spring 1972.
"Bert Haanstra," in *Film Dope* (London), March 1981.
Bertina, B.J., "Haanstra en het onverzorgde corpus van Dorothee Verdaasdonk," in *Skoop* (Amsterdam), December 1983/January 1984.

* * *

Bert Haanstra is one of Holland's most renowned filmmakers. The twenty-eight films he has made since 1948 belong to various genres. His first films were documentaries. Typical of these, and a hallmark of Haanstra's personal style, is the frequent use of "rhyming images" and of images blending into each other. Critics responded warmly to the lyrical and pictorial qualities of Haanstra's early work. In his films about oil drilling, commissioned by Shell, Haanstra showed that instructional films can be of artistic as well as informative value.

Haanstra's first feature film, *Fanfare,* was a comedy and a big hit at the box-office. The film, however, was also praised for its artistic importance and considered by many as a turning point in Dutch film: "This film should set the tone for the future production of Dutch feature-films," wrote a critic. His second feature film, *De zaak M. P.,* was very coolly received, however, and Haanstra turned again to making documentaries.

Bert Haanstra: *Alleman*

Discussions in the 1960s about the establishment of a tradition of Dutch feature films—a tradition lacking at that time—were heavily influenced by the views on film expressed by the French *nouvelle vague* cineastes. Haanstra's long documentaries, *Alleman, De stem van het water,* and *Bij de beesten af,* show him perfectly able to catch the peculiarities of human behavior, especially those of the Dutch. These three films still enjoy a firm reputation in Holland and elsewhere. *Alleman* and *Bij de beesten af* were nominated for Academy Awards. Although the number of movie-goers in Holland has sharply decreased, Haanstra's public has remained large and loyal.

In 1975 Haanstra made his first novel-based film. *Dokter Pulder zaait papavers* gives a subtle and detailed analysis of a number of fundamental human problems: loss of love, social failure, aging, and addiction to drugs and liquor. The film is psychologically convincing and full of tension. *Een pak slaag,* again based on a novel by Anton Koolhaas, failed to interest the public. In 1983 Haanstra brought out another feature film with Simon Carmiggelt as the main character listening to the tragicomic monologues of various ordinary people. Carmiggelt's ability to render this type of monologue had won a wide audience for his daily columns, which have appeared since 1945 in a Dutch newspaper. The film, *Vroeger kon je lachen,* was well received.

By virture of Haanstra's diversity of films and of his great reputation with critics and the public, Haanstra has made an invaluable contribution to the establishment of a Dutch film tradition. He is a very important representative of the Dutch documentary school, which grew to fame in the 1960s and won countless awards at international film festivals. Haanstra's own films have won over 70 prizes; he received an Academy Award for *Glas,* a short documentary film. As a director of feature films he has convinced a large audience that Dutch films can (and should) be judged according to the same standards as important foreign films.

His films, and also his cooperation with Simon Carmiggelt and Anton Koolhaas, show that Haanstra's work is firmly rooted in Dutch culture, which, however, he transcends by taking it as an example of more general aspects of human behavior. This is beautifully exemplified in *Bij de beesten af.* Although his films do not contain explicit political statements, Haanstra is anything but a "neutral observer." By the art of montage he gives his films a deeper meaning which not infrequently embodies a critical view of human society and poignant tragicomic scenes.

—Dorothee Verdaasdonk

HALLSTROM, Lasse

Nationality: Swedish. **Born:** Stockholm, Sweden, 1946. **Family:** Married actress Lena Olin. **Career:** Made 16mm film as a teenager that was eventually screened on Swedish TV; filmed and edited inserts for Swedish TV; directed program "Shall We Dance" for Danish TV; director and producer of TV programs and feature films. **Awards:** Academy Award nominations, director and screenplay, for *My Life as a Dog*. **Agent:** International Creative Management, 8942 Wilshire Blvd., Beverly Hills, California, 90211, U.S.A.

Films as Director:

1975 *A Lover and His Lass*
1977 *ABBA—The Movie*
1979 *Father to Be*
1981 *The Rooster*
1983 *Happy We*
1985 *My Life as a Dog* (+ co-sc)
1986 *The Children of Bullerby Village*
1987 *More about the Children of Bullerby Village*
1991 *Once Around* (+ sc)
1993 *What's Eating Gilbert Grape* (+ co-exec pr)
1995 *Something to Talk About*

Other Films:

1993 *World of Film* (television special) (role)

Publications

By HALLSTROM: articles—

Interview with W. Schneider, in *Video,* June 1988.

On HALLSTROM: articles—

Powers, John, "*What's Eating Gilbert Grape,*" in *New York,* 17 January 1994.
Alleva, Richard, "*What's Eating Gilbert Grape,*" in *Commonweal,* 22 April 1994.
Schickel, Richard, "*Something to Talk About,*" in *Time,* 14 August 1995.
Travers, Peter, "*Something to Talk About,*" in *Rolling Stone,* 24 August 1995.

* * *

Lasse Hallstrom's career has been built upon the substantial foundation of a single film, *My Life as a Dog,* the film that brought him immediate international recognition and achieved (for a film in a foreign language) an appreciable popular success outside Sweden, and on the strength of which he was invited to Hollywood. The lure of Hollywood is obviously very potent—especially if you are a young filmmaker on the threshold of your career. Whether it was wise of Hallstrom to accept the invitation remains, at this point, after three Hollywood movies of varying distinction, open to discussion. Hallstrom's is the kind of gentle, somewhat diffident talent that can easily get submerged or misused in the Hollywood machinery, its businessmen's eyes on box office receipts as production costs (and stars' salaries) soar into the stratosphere.

My Life as a Dog is a minor masterpiece, and one of the finest films about childhood ever made, sensitive without sentimentality, generous but clear-sighted, disturbing in its full awareness of what W. B. Yeats called "the ignominy of boyhood," in turns painful, poignant, and hilarious. Essentially, it is a film about survival, celebrating the resilience of its young hero Ingemar while unflinchingly depicting experiences that must leave lifetime scars.

One can imagine such a film being made within the Hollywood context only in a much softened, sentimentalized, and bowdlerized form. The early sequences depict Ingemar's experiences in a family from which the father is completely absent (according to Ingemar, loading bananas somewhere abroad, a task for which the boy tries to convince himself that his father is indispensable—though this may be either pure fantasy or a lie he has been told by adults who lie to him as matter of course), and otherwise consisting of a mother who is dying of (presumably) consumption and an elder brother who has inoculated himself with insensitivity and an assumption of superiority—a "family" in which his only comfort is a dog on which he showers his otherwise unwanted attentions, and which is casually (while Ingemar is away) "put to sleep" as a mere inconvenience. A running theme is Ingemar's exposure to adult sexuality in its multitudinous variety. Especially problematic in Hollywood would be his relationship with a young girl who wants to be perceived as a boy in order to continue playing on the boys' football team, and who becomes Ingemar's sparring partner/opponent in the boxing ring—her ambivalence to her sexuality expressed in her attempts to conceal her developing breasts whilst repeatedly attracting Ingemar's attention to them. The film ends with them huddled up together on a sofa, their complicated sexual/gender problems apparently resolved.

Of Hallstrom's three Hollywood films the second, *What's Eating Gilbert Grape?,* is clearly the most successful; it is also, not coincidentally, the closest to *My Life as a Dog,* the characters so memorably incarnated by Johnny Depp and Leonardo di Caprio both relating in somewhat different ways to Ingemar, with Juliette Lewis replacing his idiosyncratic and rebellious girlfriend. Far less audacious than the Swedish film, it is nevertheless a very offbeat project for Hollywood, conceived perhaps as much for its variously eccentric stars as for its atypical director. It allows Hallstrom license to develop his favorite themes—the dysfunctional family, survival within conditions so unpromising as to appear to predetermine defeat—and his finest qualities of generosity and emotional delicacy. One might single out (because on paper they would appear particularly hazardous) Depp's scenes with Mary Steenburgen, the lonely and desperate older woman who uses him as a sexual outlet. Hazardous because such a situation has traditionally (and not only in Hollywood films) been taken as a pretext for the most vindictive and gloating cruelties at the woman's expense. Here, Hallstrom achieves the perfect balance between conflicting needs, each treated with equal sympathy: Steenburgen's sense of deprivation, Depp's need to extricate himself from a situation he has entered into because he is used to being used (everyone in the film has claims on him) and now feels to be false.

The least successful seems to me Hallstrom's Hollywood debut, *Once Around,* although it contains some wonderful scenes and fine performances: its central premise, that a wealthy and aggressive American businessman, with the kind of energy that goes into the multiplication of dollars, might legitimately incarnate the "life force," rejuvenating (with occasional setbacks) all the other characters, is quite simply inadmissible, at least as presented here, without apparent irony.

Hallstrom's most recent film, *Something to Talk About,* got a generally bad press (a side-effect, perhaps, of the current backlash against Julia Roberts, as mindless as the previous adulation); it seems to me a more interesting, intelligent, and coherent film than it has been given credit for. It does, however, raise a question: a new departure for Hallstrom (one would never, I think, guess it was his film), or evidence of his final absorption into "Hollywood" and all that word has come

Lasse Hallstrom: ***My Life as a Dog***

to convey? My present inclination is to defend it, as I think it has been misrepresented. It has been perceived, generally, as a somewhat banal account of how Dennis Quaid, the unfaithful husband, gets his comeuppance and learns to behave "correctly." In fact, Quaid is presented no more critically than the other characters. The real subject of the film (and the real meaning of its title) is that sexual and gender tensions and problems in marriage should be "something to talk about," not push under the carpet. The film's critique of marital infidelity (in the older, as well as the younger, generation) rests essentially on the old but still operative "double standard": husbands do it, wives don't. Roberts's exposure of its ubiquity, although greeted on all sides with horror, becomes an act of liberation, potentially for everyone, male and female. It is only superficially that the film can be read along conventional lines ("Husbands should be punished for infidelity"); it is open to a different reading, that our attitudes toward marriage, sex, fidelity, etc., all need to be rethought and, above all, opened to discussion. It seems to be an open question as to where Hallstrom will, or indeed can, go from here.

—Robin Wood

HAMER, Robert

Nationality: British. **Born:** Kidderminster, 31 March 1911. **Education:** Rossall and at Corpus Christi College, Cambridge. **Career:** Started as cutter for London Films, 1935; editor, from 1938, then associate producer, from 1943; directed episode of *Dead of Night,* 1945; directed first feature, *Pink String and Sealing Wax,* 1945. **Died:** 4 December 1963.

Films as Director:

1944 *Fiddlers Three* (Watt) (d of add'l scenes, assoc-pr, co-lyrics)
1945 "The Haunted Mirror" episode of ***Dead of Night***; *Pink String and Sealing Wax*
1947 *It Always Rains on Sunday* (+ co-sc); *The Loves of Joanna Godden* (Frend) (d some scenes while Frend ill)
1949 ***Kind Hearts and Coronets*** (+ co-sc); *The Spider and the Fly*
1951 *His Excellency* (+ sc)
1952 *The Long Memory* (+ co-sc)

1954 *Father Brown* (*The Detective*) (+ co-sc); *To Paris with Love*
1958 *The Scapegoat* (+ sc)
1959 *School for Scoundrels* (*How to Win without Actually Cheating*)

Other Films:

1938 *Vessel of Wrath* (*The Beachcomber*) (Pommer) (ed); *St. Martin's Lane WC2* (*Sidewalks of London*) (Whelan) (co-ed)
1939 *Jamaica Inn* (Hitchcock) (ed)
1940 *La Cause commune* (*Factory Front*) (Cavalcanti) (short) (ed); *French Communique* (Cavalcanti) (short) (ed)
1941 *Mastery of the Sea* (Cavalcanti) (short) (ed); *Turned Out Nice Again* (Varnel) (ed, uncredited); *Ships with Wings* (Nolbandov) (ed); *The Foreman Went to France* (*Somewhere in France*) (Frend) (ed)
1943 *My Learned Friend* (Dearden and Hay) (assoc-pr, uncredited); *San Demetrio London* (Frend) (assoc-pr, co-sc)
1955 *Rowlandson's England* (Hawkesworth) (short) (co-sc); *Molière* (Tildian and de Chessin) (short) (commentary for English-language version)
1962 *Fifty-Five Days at Peking* (Ray) (add'l dialogue)
1963 *A Jolly Bad Fellow* (*They All Died Laughing*) (Chaffey) (co-sc)

Publications

By HAMER: book—

Kind Hearts and Coronets, London and New York, 1974.

By HAMER: articles—

Interview with Freda Lockhart, in *Sight and Sound* (London), October/December 1951.
"A Free Hand," in *Sight and Sound* (London), Spring 1959.

On HAMER: books—

Slide, Anthony, editor, *Michael Balcon, Producer,* London, 1969.
Barr, Charles, *Ealing Studios,* London, 1977.
Perry, George, *Forever Ealing,* London, 1981.

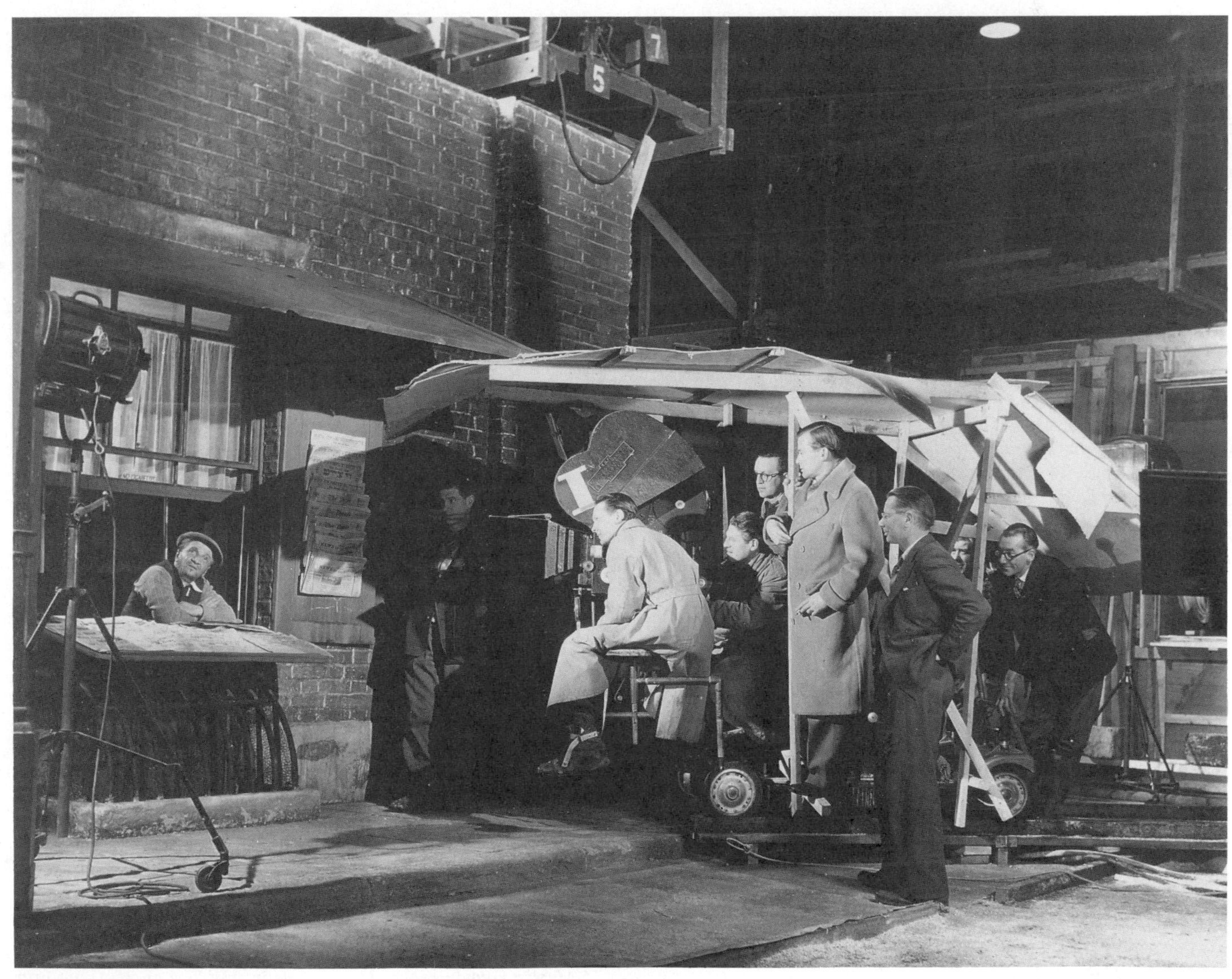

Robert Hamer (in coat, standing) directing *It Always Rains on Sunday*

Fluegel, Jane, editor, *Michael Balcon: The Pursuit of British Cinema,* New York, 1984.

Murphy, Robert, *Realism and Tinsel,* London, 1989.

On HAMER: articles—

Vincent, J., "Hamer's Potted Lifemanship," in *Films and Filming* (London), July 1959.

Barr, Charles, "Projecting Britain and the British Character: Ealing Studios," in *Screen* (London), Summer 1974.

"*It Always Rains on Sunday* Section" of *Framework* (Norwich), Winter 1978-79.

"Robert Hamer," in *Film Dope* (London), March 1981.

* * *

Rarely has a director's career risen and declined quite so abruptly as that of Robert Hamer. (Only Preston Sturges, perhaps, furnishes a comparable example.) Within the space of fifteen years, Hamer directed two films (plus an episode of *Dead of Night*) evincing increasing mastery and promise, produced one outstanding masterpiece, then went into virtually instantaneous decline wherein he produced half a dozen disappointing pictures culminating with a dismal flop. Three years later he was dead at the age of fifty-two, a development that led David Thomson to call Hamer's career "the most serious miscarriage of talent in the post-war British cinema."

Something of the forces that contributed to Hamer's sadly blighted career can be inferred from his films—especially the later ones, which often center around lonely, unattached individuals, victims of emotional atrophy. (Four of his pictures starred Alec Guinness, whose remote, withdrawn quality as an actor clearly matched Hamer's requirements.) The protagonists of *The Scapegoat, The Long Memory,* and *The Spider and the Fly* are all isolated and at odds with society, while a similarly bleak despair pervades the Chestertonian humor of *Father Brown,* preventing laughter. Only once, in *Kind Hearts and Coronets,* did Hamer strike the ideal balance between comedy and the blackness of his vision.

From the first, Hamer's films evoked a dark, dangerous world lurking below the calm surface of everyday life. This aspect, in itself, is enough to set them apart from the commonsense mainstream of Ealing Studios, for whom all Hamer's early films were made. In his *Haunted Mirror* episode from *Dead of Night,* a bland young man is drawn into a past filled with sexual jealousy and madness. The son in *Pink String and Sealing Wax* escapes from his stiflingly respectable Victorian family into a glittering night-world of drink, lust and, ultimately, murder. The exciting, threatening past, embodied in the person of her convict ex-lover, returns to confront the heroine of *It Always Rains on Sunday.* In all these films, Hamer displays an exceptional flair for the vivid recreation of atmosphere and milieu, as sure with the lush Victoriana of *Pink String* as with the contemporary East End realism of *It Always Rains on Sunday.* The latter offers a rare example of the pre-war fatalism of Carné effectively transposed to a British context.

All these elements—the black humour, the concern with suppressed passion, the sense of atmosphere, and Hamer's savagely ambiguous view of family life—come together in his one masterpiece, *Kind Hearts and Coronets.* Undoubtedly the finest black comedy ever produced by the British cinema, *Kind Hearts* blends wit, elegance, and unfailingly apt visual effects into a stylish and consistently satisfying film. The humour, both verbal and visual, is wickedly subversive, and complemented by superb performances—especially from Dennis Price, Joan Greenwood, and Alec Guinness in his famous eight-fold role.

From there on, it was all downhill. Neither *The Spider and the Fly* nor *Father Brown* could be dismissed as failures, but they never approach the sustained mastery of *Kind Hearts,* and the vitality of the early films is also lacking. Michael Balcon, the head of Ealing, felt that Hamer was "engaged on a process of self-destruction." In the light of the artistic deterioration of the later films, paralleled by the director's gradual descent into alcoholism, Balcon's verdict would, sadly, appear to be justified.

—Philip Kemp

HANI, Susumu

Nationality: Japanese. **Born:** Tokyo, 19 October 1926. **Education:** Graduated from Jiyu Gakuen, Tokyo. **Family:** Married actress Sachiko Hidari, 1960. **Career:** Began working for Kyoto News Agency, 1945; joined Iwanami Eiga production company, initially as still photographer, 1950; directed first film, 1952; producer, writer and director for TV, from 1959; formed Hani productions, mid-1960s. **Awards:** First Prize (educational short), Venice Festival, and First Prize (short film), Cannes Festival, for *Children Who Draw,* 1955; Special Jury Prize for Best Direction, Moscow festival, for *Children Hand in Hand,* 1965.

Films as Director:

1952 *Seikatsu to mizu* (*Water in Our Life*) (co-d, co-sc) *Yuki matsuri* (*Snow Festival*) (+ sc)

1953 *Machi to gesui* (*The Town and Its Drains*) (+ sc)

1954 *Anata no biru* (*Your Beer*) (+ sc); *Kyoshitsu no kodomotachi* (*Children in the Classroom*) (+ sc)

1955 *Eo kaku kodomotachi* (*Children Who Draw*) (+ sc)

1956 *Group no shido* (*Group Instruction*) (+ sc); *Soseiji gakkyu* (*Twin Sisters*) (+ sc); *Dobutsuen nikki* (*Zoo Story*) (feature) (+ sc)

1958 *Shiga Naoya* (+ sc); *Horyu-ji* (*Horyu Temple*) (+ sc); *Umi wa ikiteiru* (*The Living Sea*) (feature) (+ sc); *Nihon no buyo* (*Dances in Japan*) (+ sc): *Tokyo 1958* (co-d, co-sc, co-ed)

1960 *Furyo shonen* (*Bad Boys*)

1962 *Mitasareta seikatsu* (*A Full Life*) (+ co-sc): *Te o tsunagu kora* (*Children Hand in Hand*)

1963 *Kanojo to kare* (*She and He*) (+ co-sc)

1965 *Bwana Toshi no uta* (*The Song of Bwana Toshi*) (+ co-sc)

1966 *Andesu no hanayome* (*Bride of the Andes*) (+ sc)

1968 *Hatsuoki jig ok uhen* (*Inferno of First Love*; *Nanami: Inferno of First Love*) (+ co-sc)

1969 *Aido* (*Aido, Slave of Love*)

1970 *Mio* (+ sc, co-ed)

1972 *Gozenchu no jikanwari* (*Timetable*; *Morning Schedule*) (+ co-sc)

1981 *Afurika monogatari* (*A Tale of Africa*) (co-d)

Publications

By HANI: books—

Engishinai shuyakutachi [The Leading Players Who Do Not Act, The Non-professional Actor], 1958.

Camera to maiku no ronri [Aesthetics of Camera and Microphone], 1960.

Afurika konnan ryoko [My Travels in Africa, Report About Film Making in Africa], 1965.

Susumu Hani

Andes ryoko [Travels in the Andes, Report About Film Making in the Andes], 1966.

By HANI: articles—

Interview with James Blue, in *Film Comment* (New York), Spring 1969.
"En préparant Mio," in *Ecran* (Paris), July/August 1972.
"Susumu Hani: a decouvrir avec *Bwana Toshi,*" interview with A. Tournès, in *Jeune Cinéma* (Paris), April/May 1979.

On HANI: books—

Mellen, Joan, *Voices from the Japanese Cinema,* New York, 1975.
Sato, Tadao, *Currents in Japanese Cinema,* Tokyo, 1982.

On HANI: article—

"Susumu Hani," in *Film Dope* (London), September 1981.

* * *

Hani was born in Tokyo in 1928, the son of a famous liberal family. After schooling, he worked for a while as a journalist at Kyoto Press and entered filmmaking as a documentarist in 1950 when he joined Iwanami Productions. Most of his later dramatic features reflect his early documentary training, relying on authentic locations, amateur actors, hand-held camera techniques, and an emphasis upon contemporary social issues.

His film career comprises three areas: documentary films; narratives relating to social problems, especially among the young; and dramas focusing on the emerging woman. Of the 18 documentaries made between 1952 and 1960, the best known are *Children in the Classroom* and *Children Who Draw Pictures.* The latter won the 1957 Robert Flaherty Award.

Hani's first dramatic feature, *Bad Boys,* further develops many of his previous concerns. The film, a loose series of situations about reform school, was enacted by former inmates who improvised dialogue. For Hani, truth emerges from the juxtaposition of fiction and fact. He also believes that all people have an innate capacity for acting.

Subsequent films, which deal with the effect of post-war urban realities on the lives of the young, include *Children Hand in Hand* and *Inferno of First Love.* The former depicts young children in a provincial town and especially one backward child who becomes the butt of the other children's malicious teasing and pranks; the latter is a story of two adolescents in modern Tokyo, each of whom has been exploited, who find with each other a short-lived refuge.

Like his earlier documentaries, these films explore themes relating to broken homes, the alienation of modern society, the traumatic effects of childhood, the oppressiveness of a feudal value system, and the difficulty of escaping, even in an alternative social structure. To all these films Hani brings a deep psychological understanding of the workings of the human psyche. Finally, each of these films focuses on individual growth and self-awakening, although Hani is clear to indicate that the problems cannot be solved on a personal level. Both topics—growing self-awareness and a critique of the existing social order—connect these works with Hani's second major theme, the emergence of women.

Hani's first film on this subject was *A Full Life,* which deals with the efforts of a young wife, married to a self-involved older man, to forge a life of her own in the competitive world of modern Tokyo. After demeaning work and involvement in the student demonstrations of the early 1960s, the wife returns home, a changed woman.

Hani's other films on this topic are *She and He,* the depiction of a middle-class marriage in which the wife gains independence by her kindness to a local ragpicker, and *Bride of the Andes,* the story of a mail-order Japanese bride in Peru who finds personal growth through her relationship with South American Indians. As in *A Full Life,* none of these women are able to make a full break with their husbands. However, through personal growth (usually affected by contact with a group or person marginal to society), they are able to challenge the patriarchal values of Japanese society as represented by their husbands and to return to the relationship with new understanding and dignity. Both films starred Sachiko Hidari, who was then his wife.

Contact with a non-Japanese society and challenging Japanese xenophobia also occur in *The Song of Bwana Toshi,* which was filmed in Kenya and deals with Toshi, an ordinary Japanese man living in Central Africa. Here he cooperates with natives and rises above his isolation to establish brotherhood with foreigners.

Hani's subsequent work, *Timetable,* combines his interest in contemporary youth with his continued interest in modern women. The story deals with two high school girls who decide to take a trip together. The fiction feature, which is narrated, was filmed in 8mm and each of the major actors was allowed to shoot part of the film. Further, the audience is informed of who is shooting, thereby acknowledging the filmmaker within the context of the work. The use of 8mm is not new for Hani. More than half of his fourth film was originally shot in 8mm. Likewise, the use of a narrator dates back to *A Full Life.*

Throughout his career, Hani has concerned himself with people who have difficulty in communicating with one another. His documentaries, narratives on social problems, and dramas on emerging women have established his reputation as one of the foremost psychologists of the Japanese cinema.

—Patricia Erens

HARTLEY, Hal

Nationality: American. **Born:** 3 November 1959, in Lindenhurst, New York. **Education:** Attended Massachusetts College of Art, late 1970s; State University of New York at Purchase Film School, graduated with honors, 1984. **Career:** Free-lance production assistant, mid-1980s; worked for Action Productions (public service announcements), whose president sponsored Hartley's first feature, *The Unbelievable Truth*, 1989; this film's success at the Toronto Film Festival led to its commercial release by Miramax, 1990. **Address:** c/o True Fiction Pictures, 12 W. 27th St., New York, NY 10001, U.S.A.

Films as Director:

1984 *Kid* (short, student thesis film) (+ sc, ed, pr)
1987 *Dogs* (short); *The Cartographer's Girlfriend* (short) (+ ed, pr)
1990 *The Unbelievable Truth* (+ sc, ed, pr)
1991 *Trust* (+ sc); *Theory of Achievement* (short, for TV) (+ sc, mus); *Surviving Desire* (for TV) (+ sc, ed); *Ambition* (short, for TV) (+ sc)
1992 *Simple Men* (+ sc, co-pr, mus)
1994 *Amateur* (+ sc, pr, mus)
1995 *Flirt* (+ sc, mus, role)

Publications

By HARTLEY: books—

Simple Men and Trust (screenplays), Faber & Faber, 1992.
Amateur (screenplay), Faber & Faber, 1994.

On HARTLEY: articles—

Fuller, Graham, "Hal Hartley's World of Trouble and Desire," *Interview* (New York), September 1992.
Hogue, Peter, "Bands of Outsiders," *Film Comment* (New York), January-February 1993.
Sarris, Andrew, "Trusting Hal Hartley," *Film Comment* (New York), January-February 1993.
Bauer, Douglas, "An Independent Vision," *Atlantic Monthly* (Boston), April 1994.

* * *

Well known in Europe, but more of a cult favorite than a box-office draw in his native United States, Hal Hartley has been held in high critical esteem for his quirky feature films and shorts and, incidentally, for putting Long Island on the map of famed cinematic locales. Writing his own screenplays, punctuating the dramas with his own sparse music, and working regularly with the same actors and technicians, Hartley is a model of the resolutely independent film artist.

Hartley's screenplays are among the most distinctive features of his cinema. Reminiscent of both David Mamet (perhaps the film *House of Games* as well as certain plays) and Harold Pinter (chiefly the period of *The Homecoming*), Hartley's dialogue tends toward the laconic and the absurd: occasionally downright hilarious and almost always droll, especially when spoken by mostly humorless characters. Of the actors whom Hartley has used a number of times, Martin Donovan is supreme in his deadpan delivery of lines, with exactly the right amount of dry irony, anger, or cluelessness, as the moment calls for.

Of cinematic influences, Jean-Luc Godard has constantly been singled out. Occasionally Hartley appears to be doing a conscious homage, as in the sudden burst into dance in *Surviving Desire,* a nod to *Bande à part (Band of Outsiders)*—but a dance scene in *Simple Men,* similarly unexpected but more elaborately choreographed and integrated into the story world, seems altogether original. The stylization of violence in *Amateur* also recalls Godard, though the shoving matches of most of the earlier films seem pure Hartley. Perhaps more subtly Godardian, *Weekend* vintage, are the vacant landscapes of "Long Island" (actually Texas, for the most part) in *Simple Men,* where characters more or less stumble through their peculiar lives.

The Unbelievable Truth already has Hartley's unmistakable style and tone. With a plot suited for either soap opera or film noir in its melodrama and romantic entanglements—an ex-con returns to the town where he caused the deaths of two people, and where he is shunned by most but loved by a rebellious young woman—the film is instead a black comedy with a bent toward real romance, all centered around the question of trusting people enough to accept their versions of "the true story." Hartley's hometown of Lindenhurst, a rather ramshackle-looking small town half metamorphosed into a commuter suburb, seems the perfect pale backdrop for his oddball characters.

Trust superficially resembles *The Unbelievable Truth,* with Adrienne Shelley again as a rebellious youth and Lindenhurst as locus of American family dysfunction. It also has much of the same droll comedy as *The Unbelievable Truth,* yet a considerably darker tone overall, with its brutal parents, severely asocial hero (Martin Donovan), and unexpected violence—as in the liquor store clerk's attack upon the Shelley character. In its confident handling of mixed moods it may be Hartley's most impressive feature to date.

Simple Men, set on a more rural Long Island after a brief stop in Lindenhurst, has a wilder plot and if anything more outrageous comedy, as two sons—a criminal and a college student—follow clues in search of their long-missing father, a reputed terrorist bomber. The cynical Bill, who notes that "you don't need an ideology to knock over a liquor store," has been betrayed in love, and so is determined to seduce women by appearing to be "mysterious, thoughtful, deep, but modest" and then "throw them away." Of course he falls for a woman who claims to find him all of those things (she manages to use all four adjectives in a short conversation), although the words seem to apply much more to her. The less-experienced Dennis falls for an eccentric Rumanian who turns out to be his father's new girlfriend. When he points out that his father is a womanizer—a married man who has also stood her up—she tells him he should be more respectful. Including two actors from *The Unbelievable Truth* who essentially reprise their roles as garage mechanic and assistant—and featuring a nun who answers a question about a medallion with, "It's the Holy Blessed Virgin, you idiot," before wrestling the man to the ground—*Simple Men* often crosses the border into farce, then withdraws to a dryer detachment. Again issues of truth and reliability are central, though this film is in addition more directly concerned with masculine values and behavior than any of the others. The story is almost always focused upon the two brothers and their attitudes toward their father, or their confusion about women; the women are rarely seen apart from men observing them; the talk is very often macho, though at one point the two couples and another would-be lover preposterously launch into a discourse about Madonna and modern women's "control over the exploitation of their own bodies."

Amateur, more or less commissioned by Isabel Huppert, who stars in it, is yet more melodramatic, featuring an amnesiac (Donovan again), evidently a sadistic criminal in his "former life," who is befriended by an ex-nun who wants to write pornography (Huppert)—the pair of them having to flee various crazed and criminal types. Here the themes of trust and the knowability of a mysterious person's past are developed through the most lurid situations. *Flirt* is also concerned with issues of love and betrayal, but is also an experiment in structure: Hartley's fifth feature is actually a trilogy of short films, each using some of the same dialogue and following the same dramatic

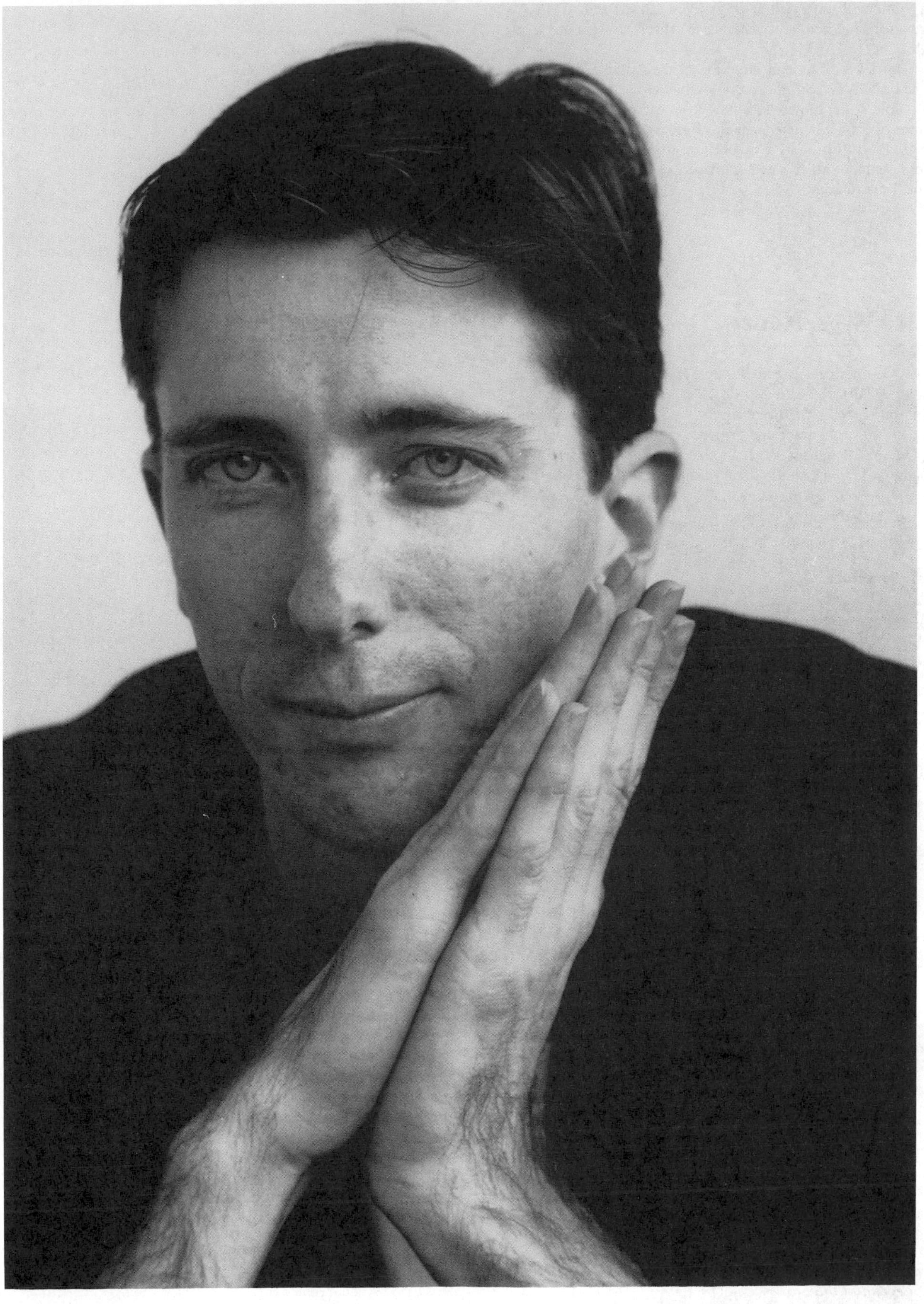

Hal Hartley

trajectory, but with different settings (New York-Berlin-Tokyo) and gender relations (according to whether the flirt is straight or gay, male or female).

All of Hartley's films call attention to their own artifice through the stylized dialogue and the actors' deliveries of it, and through the eccentric plots. *Flirt* moves to a new level of self-reflexivity in that the director plays a character named "Hal" who carries around a can of a film called "Flirt." It will be interesting to see how Hartley continues to balance artifice and dramatic passions, cool wit and melodrama, in films to come.

—Joseph Milicia

HATHAWAY, Henry

Nationality: American. **Born:** Marquis Henri Leopold de Fiennes in Sacramento, California, 13 March 1898. **Education:** Educated in California until 1912. **Military Service:** 1918-19. **Career:** Entered film industry as child actor and protégée of Allan Dwan, 1908; prop boy for Universal studios, 1912; film actor, 1912-17; assistant director for Sam Goldwyn's studio, then for Paramount, 1919-32; directed first film, *Heritage of the Desert,* for Paramount, 1932. **Died:** In Hollywood, 11 February 1985.

Films as Director:

1932 *Heritage of the Desert*; *Wild Horse Mesa*
1933 *Under the Tonto Rim*; *Sunset Pass*; *Man of the Forest*; *To the Last Man*; *The Thundering Herd*
1934 *The Last Round-Up*; *Come on Marines!*; *The Witching Hour*; *Now and Forever*
1935 *The Lives of a Bengal Lancer*; *Peter Ibbetson*
1936 *Trail of the Lonesome Pine*; *Go West, Young Man*; *I Loved a Soldier* (unfinished)
1937 *Souls at Sea*; *Lest We Forget*
1938 *Spawn of the North*
1939 *The Real Glory*
1940 *Johnny Apollo*; *Brigham Young* (*Brigham Young—Frontiersman*); *Sundown*
1941 *The Shepherd of the Hills*
1942 *Ten Gentlemen from West Point*; *China Girl*
1944 *Home in Indiana*; *Wing and a Prayer*
1945 *Nob Hill*; *The House on 92nd Street*
1946 *The Dark Corner*; *13 Rue Madeleine*
1947 *Kiss of Death*
1948 *Call Northside 777*
1949 *Down to the Sea in Ships*
1950 *The Black Rose*; *Rawhide*
1951 *You're in the Navy Now* (*U.S.S. Tea Kettle*); *Fourteen Hours*; *The Desert Fox* (*Rommel—Desert Fox*; *The Story of Rommel*)
1952 *Diplomatic Courier*; "The Clarion Call" episode of *O. Henry's Full House* (*Full House*) (d linking scenes, uncredited); *Red Skies of Montana* (co-d with Newman, uncredited)
1953 *Niagara*; *White Witch Doctor*; *The Coronation Parade*
1954 *Prince Valiant*; *Garden of Evil*
1955 *The Racers* (*Such Men Are Dangerous*)
1956 *The Bottom of the Bottle* (*Beyond the River*); *Twenty-three Paces to Baker Street*
1957 *Legend of the Lost* (+ co-pr)
1958 *From Hell to Texas* (*Manhunt*)
1959 *Woman Obsessed*
1960 *North to Alaska* (+ pr); *Seven Thieves*
1962 "The Rivers," "The Plains," and "The Outlaws" episodes of *How the West Was Won*
1963 *Rampage* (Karlson; d begun by Hathaway)
1964 *Circus World* (*The Magnificent Showman*); *Of Human Bondage* (Hughes; Hathaway began film and d add'l scenes)
1965 *The Sons of Katie Elder*
1966 *Nevada Smith* (+ pr)
1967 *The Last Safari* (+ pr)
1968 *Five Card Stud*
1969 *True Grit*
1970 *Airport* (some direction when George Seaton became ill)
1971 *Raid on Rommel*; *Shootout*
1974 *Hangup*

Other Films:

1917 *The Storm Boy* (Baldwin) (role)
1923 *The Spoilers* (Hillyer) (asst d); *To the Last Man* (Fleming) (asst d)
1924 *The Heritage of the Desert* (Willat) (asst d); *The Border Legion* (Howard) (asst d)
1925 *The Thundering Herd* (Howard) (asst d); *Wild Horse Mesa* (Seitz) (asst d)
1926 *Bachelor Brides* (*Bachelor's Brides*) (Howard) (asst d); *Mantrap* (Fleming) (asst d); *Man of the Forest* (Waters) (asst d)
1927 *Hula* (Fleming) (asst d); *The Rough Riders* (*The Trumpet Call*) (Fleming) (asst d); ***Underworld*** (*Paying the Penalty*) (von Sternberg) (asst d)
1928 *The Last Command* (von Sternberg) (asst d); *Under the Tonto Rim* (Raymaker) (asst d); *The Shopworn Angel* (Wallace) (asst d)
1929 *Sunset Pass* (Brower) (asst d); *Wolf Song* (Fleming) (asst d); *Thunderbolt* (von Sternberg) (asst d); *The Virginian* (Fleming) (asst d); *Redskin* (Schertzinger) (asst d)
1930 *Seven Days Leave* (*Medals*) (Wallace) (asst d); *The Texan* (Cromwell) (asst d); *Morocco* (von Sternberg) (asst d); *The Spoilers* (Carewe) (asst d)
1931 *Dishonored* (von Sternberg) (asst d)
1932 *Shanghai Express* (von Sternberg) (asst d)
1972 *Seventy-five Years of Cinema Museum* (Herson and Guerra) (appearance)

Publications

By HATHAWAY: articles—

Interview with Rui Nogueira, in *Focus on Film* (Washington, D.C.) v. 7.
Interview with Michel Ciment and Bertrand Tavernier, in *Positif* (Paris), March 1972.
Interview with E. Decaux and B. Villien, in *Cinématographe* (Paris), October 1983.

On HATHAWAY: articles—

Crichton, K., "Lives of a Hollywood Director," in *Collier's* (New York), 5 September 1936.
Reid, John Howard, "The Best Second Fiddle," in *Films and Filming* (London), November 1962.
Sarris, Andrew, "Likable but Elusive," in *Film Culture* (New York), Spring 1963.
Eyles, Allen, "Henry Hathaway: Filmography," in *Focus on Film* (London), January/February 1970.

Henry Hathaway

Kerbel, Michael, in *Village Voice* (New York), 18 November 1971.
Tavernier, Bertrand, "Sur Henry Leopold de Fienne, dit Hathaway," in *Positif* (Paris), February 1972.
Canham, Kingsley, "An Appreciation of Henry Hathaway," in *The Hollywood Professionals, Vol. 1,* London, 1973.
Kaminsky, Stuart, "Legend of the Lost," in *Velvet Light Trap* (Madison, Wisconsin), Winter 1975.
"Henry Hathaway," in *Film Dope* (London), September 1981.
Bawden, J., "Henry Hathaway," in *Films in Review* (New York), March 1984.
Obituary in *Variety* (New York), 20 February 1985.
Obituary in *Revue du Cinéma* (Paris), April 1985.
Ciné Revue (Paris), 27 August 1987.

* * *

Henry Hathaway had a reputation for being difficult on actors, but efficient with film. Aside from strictly biographical information, very little is generally said or known about Hathaway. To a large extent this neglect is due to film critics.

Hathaway's career can be seen in terms of four distinct periods, each period representing a change in his assignments, control, and interests. His western period (1932-34) comprises nine films, including *Wild Horse Mesa, To the Last Man,* and *Under the Tonto Rim.* "Commercial versatility" characterizes films from 1934 to 1945, including such contract projects as *Lives of a Bengal Lancer, Peter Ibbetson, Souls at Sea, Johnny Apollo,* and *Sundown.* The noir and semi-documentary films of 1945 to 1952 include *The House on 92nd Street, The Dark Corner, 14 Hours, 13 Rue Madeleine, Kiss of Death,* and *Call Northside 777.* It is the films of Hathaway's mature period, beginning with *Niagara,* in 1952, that have been most neglected by critics.

Hathaway was clearly interested in foreign or exotic locales. This was true throughout his career, but was most strikingly apparent in his mature period, when only four of his films had a contemporary or American setting. He tended to see all of his exotic settings—Africa, the Old West, Mexico—as primitive, mysterious, grotesque, and even comic, dominated by a visual unreality.

It has generally been accepted that Hathaway's one major excursion into surrealism was *Peter Ibbetson.* The evidence of the film shows, however, that the depiction of unreality, the conversion of supposedly "real" settings into personal, unreal visions, was a growing interest with Hathaway. Unreality frequently intrudes on Hathaway's films, most strikingly in his use of painted backdrops and optical effects.

Hathaway's heroes were always remarkably humble and humanly weak. They drink, wench, cheat, but always respect and believe in the unknown. They are, like John Wayne in *Legend of the Lost,* mystics in a strange landscape, God-fearing men who have either been through a terrible crisis that taught them humility or are undergoing that crisis in the course of the film.

The films in Hathaway's mature period are about specific, dangerous quests undertaken by small groups in hostile, barren lands (with this in mind, *Prince Valiant* is not an act of commercial pandering, but a quintessential Hathaway film). The quest, for the hero, is an act of communion with nature (or he learns that it should be). If the protagonist-hero is a younger man, he transgresses intentionally or by accident and is shown the way back to righteousness by an older, paternal figure. Invariably, the young protagonist or a central woman character must face the crisis of a father or husband who proves to have been less than he should have been. The woman, young man, or even villain must have the strength to accept this Jobian lesson or be destroyed by it and by their own hatred.

Hathaway's films are filled with striking mixtures of Christianity and paganism. Mystical omens and forebodings abound, and Hathaway characters frequently quote from the Old Testament to gain strength or understanding.

—Stuart M. Kaminsky

HAWKS, Howard

Nationality: American. **Born:** Howard Winchester Hawks in Goshen, Indiana, 30 May 1896. **Education:** Pasadena High School, California, 1908-13; Phillips Exeter Academy, New Hampshire, 1914-16; Cornell University, New York, degree in mechanical engineering, 1917. **Military Service:** Served in U.S. Army Air Corps, 1917-19. **Family:** Married 1) Athole (Hawks), 1924 (divorced 1941); 2) Nancy Raye Gross, 1941 (divorced), one daughter; 3) Mary (Dee) Hartford (divorced), two sons, two daughters. **Career:** Worked in property dept. of Famous Players-Lasky during vacations, Hollywood, 1916-17; designer in airplane factory, 1919-22; worked in independent production as editor, writer, and assistant director, from 1922; in charge of story dept. at Paramount, 1924-25; signed as director for Fox, 1925-29; directed first feature, *Road to Glory,* 1926; formed Motion Picture Alliance for the Preservation of American Ideals, with Borden Chase, 1944. **Awards:** Quarterly Award, Directors Guild of America, for *Red River,* 1948/49; Honorary Oscar for "A master American filmmaker whose creative efforts hold a distinguished place in world cinema," 1974. **Died:** In Palm Springs, California, 26 December 1977.

Films as Director:

1926 *The Road to Glory* (+ story); *Fig Leaves* (+ story)
1927 *The Cradle Snatchers*; *Paid to Love*; *Fazil*
1928 *A Girl in Every Port* (+ co-sc); *The Air Circus* (co-d)
1929 *Trent's Last Case*
1930 *The Dawn Patrol*
1931 *The Criminal Code*
1932 *The Crowd Roars* (+ story); *Tiger Shark*; ***Scarface: The Shame of a Nation*** (+ pr, bit role as man on bed)
1933 *Today We Live*; *The Prizefighter and the Lady* (*Everywoman's Man*) (Van Dyke; d parts of film, claim disputed)
1934 *Viva Villa!* (Conway; d begun by Hawks); *Twentieth Century*
1935 *Barbary Coast*; *Ceiling Zero*
1936 *The Road to Glory*; *Come and Get It* (co-d)
1938 ***Bringing Up Baby***
1939 *Only Angels Have Wings*
1940 ***His Girl Friday***
1941 *The Outlaw* (Hughes; d begun by Hawks); *Sergeant York*; *Ball of Fire*
1943 *Air Force*
1944 *To Have and Have Not*
1946 ***The Big Sleep***
1947 *A Song is Born* (remake of *Ball of Fire*)
1948 ***Red River*** (+ pr)
1949 *I Was a Male War Bride* (*You Can't Sleep Here*)
1952 *The Big Sky* (+ pr); "The Ransom of Red Chief" episode of *O. Henry's Full House* (episode cut from some copies) (+ pr); *Monkey Business*
1953 *Gentlemen Prefer Blondes*
1955 *Land of the Pharaohs* (+ pr)
1959 ***Rio Bravo*** (+ pr)
1962 *Hatari!* (+ pr)
1963 *Man's Favorite Sport* (+ pr)

1965 *Red Line 7000* (+ story, pr)
1966 *El Dorado* (+ pr)
1970 *Rio Lobo* (+ pr)

Other Films:

1917 *A Little Princess* (Neilan) (d some scenes, uncredited; prop boy)
1923 *Quicksands* (Conway) (story, sc, pr)
1924 *Tiger Love* (Melford) (sc)
1925 *The Dressmaker from Paris* (Bern) (co-story, sc)
1926 *Honesty—the Best Policy* (Bennett and Neill) (story, sc); ***Underworld*** (von Sternberg) (co-sc, uncredited)
1932 *Red Dust* (Fleming) (co-sc, uncredited)
1936 *Sutter's Gold* (Cruze) (co-sc, uncredited)
1937 *Captain Courageous* (Fleming) (co-sc, uncredited)
1938 *Test Pilot* (Fleming) (co-sc, uncredited)
1939 ***Gone with the Wind*** (Fleming) (add'l dialogue, uncredited); *Gunga Din* (Stevens) (co-sc, uncredited)
1943 *Corvette K-225* (*The Nelson Touch*) (Rosson) (pr)
1951 *The Thing* (*The Thing from Another World*) (Nyby) (pr)

Publications

By HAWKS: book—

Hawks on Hawks, edited by Joseph McBride, Berkeley, 1982.

By HAWKS: articles—

Interview with Jacques Becker, Jacques Rivette, and Francois Truffaut, in *Cahiers du Cinéma* (Paris), February 1956.
Interview in *Movie* (London), 5 November 1962.
"Man's Favorite Director, Howard Hawks," interview in *Cinema* (Beverly Hills), November/December 1963.
Interview with James R. Silke, Serge Daney, and Jean-Louis Noames, in *Cahiers du Cinéma* (Paris), November 1964.
Interview, in *Interviews with Film Directors,* by Andrew Sarris, New York, 1967.
Interview with Jean-Louis Comolli, Jean Narboni, and Bertrand Tavernier, in *Cahiers du Cinéma* (Paris), July/August 1967.
"Gunplay and Horses," with David Austen, in *Films and Filming* (London), October 1968.
"Do I Get to Play the Drunk this Time," an interview in *Sight and Sound* (London), Spring 1971.
Interviews with Naomi Wise and Michael Goodwin, in *Take One* (Montreal), November/December 1971 and March 1973.
"Hawks Talks," interview with J. McBride, in *Film Comment* (New York), May/June 1974.
"Hawks on Film, Politics, and Childrearing," interview with C. Penley and others, in *Jump Cut* (Berkeley), January/February 1975.
"You're goddam right I remember," interview with K. Murphy and R.T. Jameson, in *Movietone News* (Seattle), June 1977.

On HAWKS: books—

Bogdanovich, Peter, *The Cinema of Howard Hawks,* New York, 1962.
Missiaen, Jean-Claude, *Howard Hawks,* Paris, 1966.
Wood, Robin, *Howard Hawks,* London, 1968, revised 1981.
Gili, J.-A., *Howard Hawks,* Paris, 1971.
Willis, D.C., *The Films of Howard Hawks,* Metuchen, New Jersey, 1975.
Murphy, Kathleen A., *Howard Hawks: An American Auteur in the Hemingway Tradition,* Ann Arbor, Michigan, 1978.
Giannetti, Louis D., *Masters of the American Cinema,* Englewood Cliffs, New Jersey, 1981.
Mast, Gerald, *Howard Hawks, Storyteller,* New York, 1982.
Poague, Leland, *Howard Hawks,* Boston, 1982.
Belton, John, *Cinema Stylists,* Metuchen, New Jersey, 1983.
Simsolo, Noel, *Howard Hawks,* Paris, 1984.
Branson, Clark, *Howard Hawks: A Jungian Study,* Los Angeles, 1987.

On HAWKS: articles—

Rivette, Jacques, and François Truffaut, "Howard Hawks," in *Films in Review* (New York), November 1956.
Perez, Michel, "Howard Hawks et le western," in *Présence du Cinéma* (Paris), July/September 1959.
Dyer, John Peter, "Sling the Lamps Low," in *Sight and Sound* (London), Summer 1962.
Sarris, Andrew, "The World of Howard Hawks," in *Films and Filming* (London), July and August 1962.
"Hawks Issue" of *Cahiers du Cinéma* (Paris), January 1963.
"Hawks Issue" of *Movie* (London), 5 December 1962.
Comolli, Jean-Louis, "Howard Hawks ou l'ironique," in *Cahiers du Cinéma* (Paris), November 1964.
Brackett, Leigh, "A Comment on the Hawksian Woman," in *Take One* (Montreal), July/August 1971.
Wise, Naomi, "The Hawksian Woman," in *Take One* (Montreal), April 1972.
"Hawks Issue" of *Filmkritik* (Munich), May/June 1973.
Wood, Robin, "To Have (Written) and Have Not (Directed)," in *Film Comment* (New York), May/June 1973.
Haskell, Molly, "Howard Hawks: Masculine Feminine," in *Film Comment* (New York), March/April 1974.
Cohen, M., "Hawks in the Thirties," in *Take One* (Montreal), December 1975.
Richards, Jeffrey, "The Silent Films of Howard Hawks," in *Focus on Film* (London), Summer/Autumn 1976.
Durgnat, Raymond, "Hawks Isn't Good Enough," in *Film Comment* (New York), July/August 1977; see also February and March/April 1978.
"Hawks Section" of *Positif* (Paris), July/August 1977.
"Dossier: le cinéma de Howard Hawks," in *Cinématographe* (Paris), March 1978.
Rohmer, Eric, and others, "Hommage à Hawks," in *Cinema* (Paris), March 1978.
McBride, J., "Hawks," in *Film Comment* (New York), March/April 1978.
Burdick, D.M., "Danger of Death: The Hawksian Woman as Agent of Destruction," in *Post Script* (Jacksonville, Florida), Fall 1981.
McCarthy, T., "Phantom Hawks," in *Film Comment* (New York), September/October 1982.
Lev, P., "Elaborations on a Theme," in *Quarterly Review of Film Studies* (New York), Spring 1984.
Jewell, R.B., "How Howard Hawks Brought Baby Up," in *Journal of Popular Film* (Washington, D.C.), Winter 1984.
Walker, Michael, "Hawks and Film Noir: *The Big Sleep,*" in *Cine-Action!* (Toronto), no. 13/14, 1988.

On HAWKS: films—

Bogdanovich, Peter, *The Great Professional—Howard Hawks,* for television, Great Britain, 1967.
Schickel, Richard, *The Men Who Made the Movies: Howard Hawks,* for television, United States, 1973.
Blumenberg, Hans, *Ein verdammt gutes Leben (A Hell of a Good Life),* West Germany, 1978.

* * *

Howard Hawks

Howard Hawks was perhaps the greatest director of American genre films. Hawks made films in almost every American genre, and each of these films could well serve as one of the very best examples and artistic embodiments of the type: gangster (*Scarface*), private eye (*The Big Sleep*), western (*Red River, Rio Bravo*), screwball comedy (*Bringing Up Baby*), newspaper reporter (*His Girl Friday*), prison picture (*The Criminal Code*), science fiction (*The Thing*), musical (*Gentlemen Prefer Blondes*), race-car drivers (*The Crowd Roars, Red Line 7000*), and air pilots (*Only Angels Have Wings*). But into each of these narratives of generic expectations Hawks infused his particular themes, motifs, and techniques.

Born in the Midwest at almost the same time that the movies themselves were born in America, Hawks migrated with his family to southern California when the movies did; he spent his formative years working on films, learning to fly, and studying engineering at Cornell University. His initial work in silent films as a writer and producer would serve him well in his later years as a director, when he would produce and, if not write, then control the writing of his films as well. Although Hawks' work has been consistently discussed as exemplary of the Hollywood studio style, Hawks himself did not work for a single studio on a long-term contract. Instead, he was an independent producer who sold his projects to every Hollywood studio.

Whatever the genre of a Hawks film, it bore traits that made it unmistakably a Hawks film. The narrative was always elegantly and symmetrically structured and patterned. This quality was a sign of Hawks' sharp sense of storytelling as well as his sensible efforts to work closely with very talented writers: Ben Hecht, William Faulkner, and Jules Furthman being the most notable among them. Hawks' films were devoted to characters who were professionals with fervent vocational commitments. The men in Hawks' films were good at what they did, whether flying the mail, driving race cars, driving cattle, or reporting the news. These vocational commitments were usually fulfilled by the union of two apparently opposite physical types who were spiritually one: either the union of the harder, tougher, older male and a softer, younger, prettier male (John Wayne and Montgomery Clift in *Red River,* Wayne and Ricky Nelson in *Rio Bravo*), or by a sharp, tough male and an equally sharp, tough female (Cary Grant and Rosalind Russell in *His Girl Friday,* Bogart and Bacall in *To Have and Have Not* and *The Big Sleep,* John Barrymore and Carole Lombard in *Twentieth Century*). This spiritual alliance of physical opposites revealed Hawks' unwillingness to accept the cultural stereotype that those who are able to accomplish difficult tasks are those who appear able to accomplish them.

This tension between appearance and ability, surface and essence in Hawks' films led to several other themes and techniques. Characters talk very tersely in Hawks' films, refusing to put their thoughts and feelings into explicit speeches which would either sentimentalize or vulgarize those internal abstractions. Instead, Hawks' characters reveal their feelings through their actions, not by what they say. Hawks deflects his portrayal of the inner life from explicit speeches to symbolic physical objects—concrete visual images of things that convey the intentions of the person who handles, uses, or controls the piece of physical matter. One of those physical objects—the coin which George Raft nervously flips in *Scarface*—has become a mythic icon of American culture itself, symbolic in itself of American gangsters and American gangster movies (and used as such in both *Singin' in the Rain* and *Some Like It Hot*). Another of Hawks' favorite actions, the lighting of cigarettes, became his subtextual way of showing who cares about whom without recourse to dialogue.

Consistent with his narratives, Hawks' visual style was one of deadpan understatement, never proclaiming its trickiness or brilliance but effortlessly communicating the values of the stories and the characters. Hawks was a master of point-of-view, knowledgeable about which camera perspective would precisely convey the necessary psychological and moral information. That point of view could either confine us to the perceptions of a single character (Marlowe in *The Big Sleep*), ally us with the more vital of two competing life styles (with the vitality of Oscar Jaffe in *Twentieth Century,* Susan Vance in *Bringing Up Baby,* Walter Burns in *His Girl Friday*), or withdraw to a scientific detachment that allows the viewer to weigh the paradoxes and ironies of a love battle between two equals (between the two army partners in *I Was a Male War Bride,* the husband and wife in *Monkey Business,* or the older and younger cowboy in *Red River*). Hawks' films are also masterful in their atmospheric lighting; the hanging electric or kerosene lamp that dangles into the top of a Hawks frame became almost as much his signature as the lighting of cigarettes.

Hawks' view of character in film narrative was that actor and character were inseparable. As a result, his films were very improvisatory. He allowed actors to add, interpret, or alter lines as they wished, rather than force them to stick to the script. This trait not only led to the energetic spontaneity of many Hawks films, but also contributed to the creation or shaping of the human archetypes that several stars came to represent in our culture. John Barrymore, John Wayne, Humphrey Bogart, and Cary Grant all refined or established their essential personae under Hawks' direction, while many actors who would become stars were either discovered by Hawks or given their first chance to play a major role in one of his films. Among Hawks' most important discoveries were Paul Muni, George Raft, Carole Lombard, Angie Dickinson, Montgomery Clift, and his Galatea, Lauren Bacall.

Although Hawks continued to make films until he was almost seventy-five, there is disagreement about the artistic energy and cinematic value of the films he made after 1950. For some, Hawks' artistic decline in the 1950s and 1960s was both a symptom and an effect of the overall decline of the movie industry and the studio system itself. For others, Hawks' later films—slower, longer, less energetically brilliant than his studio-era films—were more probing and personal explorations of the themes and genres he had charted for the three previous decades.

—Gerald Mast

HAYNES, Todd

Nationality: American. **Born:** Los Angeles, California, 2 January 1961. **Education:** Graduated from Brown University, where he studied semiotics and art. **Career:** Founded Apparatus Productions, a non-profit organization that funds and produces short films, 1987; directed first feature, *Poison,* 1991. **Awards:** Golden Gate Award for *Superstar: The Karen Carpenter Story,* 1987; Special Jury Prize, Sundance Festival, Teddy Award, Best Feature, Berlin Festival, and Critics Award, Locarno Festival, 1991, for *Poison.* **Office:** Bronze Eye Productions, 525 Broadway, Room 701, New York, NY 10012-4015.

Films as Director:

1978 *The Suicide* (short) (+ pr)
1982 *Letter from a Friend* (short)
1983 *Sex Shop* (short)
1985 *Assassins: A Film Concerning Rimbaud* (short) (+ pr)
1987 *Superstar: The Karen Carpenter Story* (short)
1991 *Poison* (+ sc)
1993 *Dottie Gets Spanked* (short) (for TV)
1995 *Safe* (+ sc)

Other Films:

1988 *Muddy Hands* (pr); *Cause and Effect* (pr)
1989 *La Divina* (pr); *He Was Once* (pr, role)
1990 *Anemone Me* (pr); *Oreos with Attitude* (pr)
1992 *Swoon* (Kalin) (role as Phrenology Head)

Publications

By HAYNES: articles—

"Doll Boy," interview with L. Kennedy in *Village Voice* (New York), 24 November 1987.
"Cinematic/Sexual Transgression," interview with J. Wyatt in *Film Quarterly* (Berkeley, California), Spring 1993.
"We Can't Get There from Here," article in *Nation* (New York), 5 July 1993.
"Antibodies," interview with Larry Gross in *Filmmaker* (New York), Summer 1995.

On HAYNES: articles—

Laskaway, M., "*Poison* at the Box Office," in *Cineaste* (New York), no. 3, 1991.
Lanouette, J., "Todd Haynes," in *Premiere* (New York), April 1991.
James, Caryn, "Politics Nurtures *Poison,*" in *New York Times,* 14 April 1991.
Als, H., "Ruminations on Todd," in *Village Voice* (New York), 16 April 1991.

* * *

Todd Haynes is no stranger to controversy. He began his career making outrageously personal short films that comment on the manner in which pop culture impacts on the individual. One of them—*Superstar: The Karen Carpenter Story,* featuring an all-doll cast—had to be yanked from distribution because of legal complications, and now is considered an underground classic. *Poison,* Haynes's initial, equally incendiary feature, was financed in part by the New York State Council on the Arts and the National Endowment for the Arts. Because of its subject matter, this support resulted in cries of outrage from those who prefer that publicly funded art be as inoffensive as a painting of a bowl of fruit.

Whether *Poison* is or is not to one's individual taste, it is a film of high artistic aspiration. *Poison* is inspired by the writings of Jean Genet, and consists of a trio of skillfully interwoven stories. The first is a mock documentary about a seven-year-old boy who shot and killed his father and then summarily disappeared. How did this happen? Who was the boy, and why was he driven to such an act? A number of clues are offered by his mother. "I mean, I punished him," she matter-of-factly tells the camera. "His father beat him, just like any kid." Later, she observes, "He was a meek soul. People pick on meek souls."

The second story is a 1950s science-fiction movie parody, in which a brilliant scientist ingests some serum and becomes disfigured. People stare at him wherever he goes, and little girls spit at him. Eventually, he becomes the infamous "leper sex killer." In the third story, a man arrives at a prison. He is an orphan and a thief, and he is gay. In jail, which he describes as "the counterfeit world of men among men," he has found his true identity—as well as what he calls "the violence of love." *Poison* is a jarring film about what it means to be different, what it is like to be so alienated from the mainstream that you feel more at home in a prison than in the outside world. Haynes shows how you are different and victimized if you are gay, physically deformed, or a sensitive child in a dysfunctional family. *Poison* is a disturbing film. It will make you uncomfortable, but it also will make you think.

In *Safe,* Haynes' equally strong follow-up feature, he for the first time tells one story through the course of an almost-two-hour film. His heroine is Carol White (Julianne Moore), an emotionally disconnected, squeaky-clean San Fernando Valley housewife. Lately, she has been feeling run down, which she at first attributes to stress. But her body, and soon her mind, begin to deteriorate. Her doctor cannot diagnose her infirmity, instead suggesting that she see a psychiatrist. She eventually becomes convinced that the cause of her malady is environmental pollution, that she is "chemically sensitive" and "allergic to the twentieth century."

In a more conventional film, Carol not only would find a cure for her illness but would enter into an emotionally fulfilling romance with the agreeable guy (James LeGros) she meets at a New Age retreat. But Haynes had no intention of making a conventional film. He offers no easy answers to his heroine's predicament, as she declines into a frail apparition of her former self. Indeed, hovering unquestionably over her deterioration is the harsh reality of AIDS and the New Age psychobabble that the individual is responsible for his own plight, regardless of the outside forces that one cannot control but that irrevocably impact on one's physical and mental well-being. In *Safe,* Haynes has made a scary film without ghouls and gushing blood, a highly politicized story that does not overtly refer to political concerns. He subtly but chillingly captures Carol's isolation by constantly posing her alone, sitting on a couch, or standing by her pool or looking in a mirror.

At the same time, Haynes has not abandoned the short-film form. Between *Poison* and *Safe* he made *Dottie Gets Spanked,* a twenty-seven-minute examination of the carnal fantasies of a young, highly imaginative boy who is obsessed with watching television sit-coms.

—Rob Edelman

HEIFITZ, Josef

Nationality: Russian. **Born:** Josef Yefimovitch Heifitz (sometimes transliterated as Kheifits) in Minsk, Russia, 17 December 1905. **Education:** Leningrad School of Screen Arts, graduated 1927. **Family:** Married, two sons (filmmakers Vladimir and Dmitri Svetozarov). **Career:** Formed partnership with fellow student Alexander Zarkhi; they directed first film together, *A Song of Steel,* for Sovkino, 1928; joined Soyuzfilm, 1933, Lenfilm, 1935; ended partnership with Zarkhi, 1950. **Awards:** Stalin Prize, for *Razgrom Japonii,* 1945.

Films as Director:

1928 *Pesn o metallye* (*A Song of Steel*) (co-d, + co-sc, co-ed)
1930 *Veter v litso* (*Facing the Wind*) (co-d)
1931 *Polden* (*Noon*) (co-d, + co-sc)
1933 *Moya rodina* (*My Fatherland*; *My Country*) (co-d, + co-sc)
1935 *Goryachie dyenechki* (*Hectic Days*) (co-d, + co-sc)
1936 *Deputat Baltiki* (*Baltic Deputy*) (co-d, + co-sc)
1940 *Chlen pravitelstva* (*The Great Beginning*; *Member of the Government*) (co-d, + co-sc)
1942 *Yevo zovut Sukhe-Bator* (*His Name is Sukhe-Bator*) (co-d, + co-sc)
1944 *Malakhov Kurgan* (co-d, + co-sc)
1945 *Razgrom Japonii* (*The Defeat of Japan*) (co-d, + co-sc, co-ed)
1946 *Vo imya zhizni* (*In the Name of Life*) (co-d, + co-sc)

Josef Heifitz: *Dama s sobachkoi*

1948 *Dragotsennye zerna* (*The Precious Grain*) (co-d)
1950 *Ogni Baku* (*Flames over Baku*; *Fires of Baku*) (co-d) (released 1958)
1953 *Vesna v Moskve* (*Spring in Moscow*) (co-d)
1954 *Bolshaya semya* (*The Big Family*)
1956 *Dyelo Rumyantseva* (*The Rumyantsev Case*) (+ co-sc)
1958 *Dorogoi moi chelovek* (*My Dear Fellow*; *My Dear Man*) (+ co-sc)
1960 *Dama s sobachkoi* (*The Lady with the Little Dog*) (+ sc)
1962 *Gorizont* (*Horizon*)
1964 *Dyen schastya* (*A Day of Happiness*) (+ co-sc)
1967 *V gorodye S* (*In the Town of S*) (+ sc)
1970 *Saliut Maria!* (*Salute, Maria*) (+ co-sc)
1973 *Plokhoy khoroshyi chelovek* (*The Duel*; *The Bad Good Man*) (+ sc)
1976 *Edinstvennaia* (*The Only One*; *The One and Only*) (+ co-sc)
1977 *Asya* (*Love Should Be Guarded*) (+ sc)
1979 *Vpervye zamuzhem* (*Married for the First Time*) (+ co-sc)
1982 *Shurochka*
1985 *Podsudimy* (*The Accused*) (+ co-sc)
1987 *Vspomnim, Tovarisc*

Other Films:

1928 *Luna sleva* (*The Moon is to the Left*) (Ivanov) (co-sc, asst-d)
1930 *Transport ognya* (*Transport of Fire*) (Ivanov) (co-sc, asst-d)

Publications

By HEIFITZ: articles—

"Director's Notes," in *Iskusstvo Kino* (Moscow), no. 1, 1966.
Interview in *Iskusstvo Kino* (Moscow), no. 2, 1971.
Interview in *Soviet Film* (Moscow), no. 9, 1976.
Article in *Soviet Film* (Moscow), no. 11, 1978.

On HEIFITZ: books—

Christie, Ian, and Richard Taylor, editors, *The Film Factory: Russian and Soviet Cinema in Documents 1896-1939,* London, 1988.

On HEIFITZ: articles—

Soviet Film (Moscow), no. 2, 1967, and no. 2, 1971.
Panoráma, no. 4, 1976.
Lipkov, "Iosif Heifits," in *Soviet Film* (Moscow), February 1983.
"Iosif Kheifits," in *Film Dope* (London), September 1984.
Gillett, John, and Claire Kitson, "Chekhov and After: The Films of Iosif Heifitz," in *National Film Theatre Booklet* (London), December 1986.
Dobrotvorsky, S., "Father and Sons," in *Soviet Film* (Moscow), April 1987.

* * *

It is impossible to discuss the career of Iosif Heifitz without also paying tribute to Alexander Zarkhi, with whom he worked for over twenty years after they both left the Leningrad Technicum of Cinema Art in 1927. The first film they made together was *A Head Wind,* but their first collaboration to gain prominence was *Baltic Deputy,* a landmark film of "socialist" or "historic" realism that transcends the genre's usual bombastic propaganda, moral and political schematism, and impossibly perfect and idealised heroes and heroines. This film concerns an elderly professor who, despite the disapproval of his stuffy academic colleagues, joins the forces of revolution in 1917 and is eventually elected to the Petrograd Soviet by the sailors of the Baltic fleet. It contains both humour and humanistic values, and is particularly distinguished by an excellent central performance from Nikolai Cherkasov. Equally impressive, for the same reasons, is *Member of the Government.* Set during the rural collectivisation period and focusing on a young farm worker who rises to a government position despite the opposition of her husband, this film concerns the improved status of women in the USSR after 1917. A similar concentration on the social position of women can be seen in his later film, *Married for the First Time.* Vera Maretskaya is superb throughout *Member of the Government,* the first of several memorable female leading roles in Heifitz's films.

Both Zarkhi and Heifitz benefited creatively from their split in 1950, although Heifitz has undoubtedly become better known. His impressive second film on his own, *The Big Family,* is recognised as one of the forerunners of the post-Stalin rejuvenation of the Soviet cinema. This film presents the lives of a family of shipbuilders with a feeling for everyday realities, a lively, detailed texture, a concern with the problems of the individual as opposed to the masses, and generally tries to avoid producing neat, formulaic, ideologically "sound" solutions.

In 1960 Heifitz made the film for which he is probably best known, *The Lady with the Little Dog,* the first of a Chekhov trilogy including *In the Town of S* and *The Bad Good Man.* It is hardly surprising that the director should have been drawn to Chekhov, nor that his Chekhov adaptations are among his finest works, for both share an understanding of the complexity of human beings, a feeling for the minute, telling detail, and a remarkable ability to conjure an almost tangible sense of atmosphere. Indeed, in the trilogy some of the most "Chekhovian" moments are not in the original stories at all! Thus, it is hardly surprising to find Heifitz admitting (in an interview in *Soviet Film*) that "much as I love Dostoevsky I regard Chekhov as my teacher." Stressing Chekhov's concern with the importance of clear and legible writing (in both senses of the word), he adds: "I try to apply the laws of Chekhovian prose, with due adjustments to suit our time, in my films about the present. I have always considered Chekhov to be among the most modern of writers, and have never treated him as a venerable, 'moth-eaten' classic. To me Chekhov has always been an example of a social-minded writer.... The hallmark of Chekhov's approach is that, while describing these small, weak people living in an atmosphere of triviality and inaction, he preserved his faith in a better future and in the power of the human spirit. So he imparted to them an important quality—the capacity to make a critical judgment of the surrounding world and of oneself. This is the quality that I prize most highly."

Thus, in spite of his obvious relish for period feel in Chekhov (and Turgenev, in the beautiful *Asya*), Heifitz is obviously a great deal more than a "period" director. Claiming that modern Soviet filmmakers are "heirs to the humanistic tradition of Russian literature," he has said that his films are "a panorama of the better part of a century." Looking at the remarkable gallery of characters he has presented with his mix of everyday heroism and humanity, it is hard to disagree. Heifitz is not a stylistic innovator, but his films, whether set in the past or present, all exhibit an equally strong feeling for the minutiae of daily life and the humanity of their characters. In this last respect it should be pointed out that Heifitz is a masterly director of actors, and that he largely "discovered" Nikolai Cherkasov, Vera Maretskaya, Iya Savvina and Alexei Batalov, all of whom have given some of their finest performances in his films. As he himself stated, "many directors today strive for documentary realism and naturalness of tone. But in that case individuality disappears, and the human voice with its infinite inflections gives way to banality." Heifitz adds: "Directing in the cinema means above all directing the actor. The actor is the focal point of the director's efforts and experience."

—Julian Petley

HELLMAN, Monte

Nationality: American. **Born:** 12 July 1932, Greenpoint, Long Island, NY. **Education:** Gained NBC radio scholarship to Stanford University to study speech and drama; post-graduate work in film at the University of California, Los Angeles. **Family:** Married and divorced twice; one daughter, one son. **Career:** Co-founder, actor, and director, Stumptown Players Summer Theatre, Guerneville, CA, mid- to late 1950s; directed radio plays; editor's assistant on ABC-TV series *Medic,* at Ziv Studios; joined summer stock company for three summers, directed West Coast premiere of *Waiting for Godot;* directed first feature for Roger Corman, 1959; worked as editor and second unit director for Corman; made two low-budget features in Philippines for AIP, 1964; shot *The Shooting* and *Ride in the Whirlwind* back-to-back on location in Utah, 1965; directed first major-budget feature for Universal, 1971; shot Italian-produced Western in Spain, 1978. **Address:** 11075 Santa Monica Blvd, Suite 275, Los Angeles, CA 90025, U.S.A.

Films as Director:

1959 *The Beast from the Haunted Cave*
1964 *Back Door to Hell*; *Flight to Fury* (released 1967)
1965 *The Shooting*; *Ride in the Whirlwind*
1971 *Two-Lane Blacktop*
1974 *Cockfighter* (*Born to Kill*)
1978 *China 9, Liberty 37* (*I pistoleri*; *Amore piombo e furore*; *Clayton & Catherine*)
1988 *Iguana*
1989 *Silent Night, Deadly Night III: Better Watch Out*

Other Films:

1958 *Last Woman on Earth* (Corman) (2nd unit d, uncredited)
1960 *Ski Troop Attack* (Corman) (2nd unit d, uncredited); *Creature from the Haunted Sea* (Corman) (pre-credit sequence d, uncredited)
1963 *The Terror* (Corman) (location d)
1965 *Bus Riley's Back in Town* (Hart) (asst ed, uncredited)
1966 *The Wild Angels* (Corman) (ed)
1967 *A Time for Killing* (Karlson) (co-ed, uncredited)
1969 *How to Make It* (Corman) (ed)
1971 *The Christian Licorice Store* (Frawley) (role)
1973 *Pat Garrett and Billy the Kid* (Peckinpah) (co-sc, uncredited)
1974 *Shatter* (Carreras) (co-d, uncredited)
1975 *The Killer Elite* (Peckinpah) (ed)
1976 *Fighting Mad* (Demme) (ed)
1979 *Avalanche Express* (Robson) (co-d)
1986 *Monte Hellman's Life in a Day: Plunging on Alone* (role)
1991 *Sam Peckinpah, Man of Iron* (interviewee)
1992 *Warren Oates: Across the Border* (participant); ***Reservoir Dogs*** (Tarantino) (exec pr)
1993 *Killing Box* (Hickenlooper) (ed)

Monte Hellman: ***The Shooting***

Publications

By HELLMAN: books—

Interview with Steven Gaydos in *Movie Talk from the Front Lines: Filmmakers Discuss Their Work with the Los Angeles Film Critics Association,* edited by Jerry Roberts and Steven Gaydos, Jefferson, NC and London, 1995.

By HELLMAN: articles—

"Quelques principes," in *Positif* (Paris), February 1968.
"James Taylor and Monte Hellman," interview with Michael Goodwin, in *Interview* (New York), August 1971.
"Monte Hellman: A Profile," interview with Christian Braad Thomsen, in *Take One* (Montreal/Toronto), November/December 1972.
"Monte Hellman," interview with Dave Pirie and Chris Petit, in *Time Out* (London), 23 March 1973.
"Entretien avec Monte Hellman," interview with Michel Ciment, in *Positif* (Paris), May 1973.
"Monte Hellman," interview with Christian Braad Thomsen, in *Sunset Boulevard* (Hellerup, Denmark), Autumn 1973.
"Moving along with Love and Obsession," interview with Gordon Gow, in *Films & Filming* (London), October 1974.
"Corman and *Cockfighter,*" interview with Nicholas Pasquariello, in *Jump Cut* (Chicago), June 1976.
"Del 'western' e di altre cose," interview with Anna Maria and Franco Tató, in *Cinema Sessanta* (Rome), March/April 1978.
"Entretien avec Monte Hellman," interview with Bernard Boland and Philippe Jalladeau, in *Cahiers du cinéma* (Paris), July/August 1978.
"Monte Hellman," interview with Philippe Carcassone and Jacques Fieschi, in *Cinématographe* (Paris), March/April 1981.
"Le solitaire de Laurel Canyon," interview with Serge le Peron, in *Cahiers du cinéma* (Paris), April 1982.

On HELLMAN: books—

National Film Theatre, *Monte Hellman: Director,* London, 1973.
Tatum, Charles, *Monte Hellman,* Crisnée (Belgium), 1988.

On HELLMAN: articles—

Johnston, Claire, "Monte Hellman," in *Cinema* (London), August 1970.

Walker, Beverly, "Two-Lane Blacktop," in *Sight & Sound* (London), Winter 1970/71.
Salvato, Larry, "Discovering Monte Hellman: A Walking, Talking, Directing Hollywood Paradox," in *Millimeter* (New York), July/August 1975.
Toubiana, Serge, "Monte Hellman à Cannes," in *Cahiers du cinéma* (Paris), July/August 1979.
Pierson, Melissa, "Starting Over, and Over," in *Village Voice* (New York), 6 August 1981.
Krohn, Bill, "*Iguana:* Le retour de Monte Hellman: The Melville Connection," in *Cahiers du cinéma* (Paris), November 1988.
Fleming, Charles, "Missing Persons," in *Variety* (New York/Los Angeles), 11 May 1992.
Tarantino, Quentin, "A Rare Sorrow," in *Sight & Sound* (London), February 1993.
Case, Brian, "The Full Monte," in *Time Out* (London), 4 January 1995.
John Wrathall, "The Full Monte," in *Premiere* (London), February 1995.

* * *

The irony of Monte Hellman's career is that he has become far better known for not making films than for making them. Over the years he has attracted the acclaim of critics at home and abroad, and of fellow directors from Peckinpah ("the best director working today") to Tarantino ("If ever a director was due for critical rediscovery, it would be Monte Hellman"). His work, even in a lesser offering like *China 9, Liberty 37,* is unmistakably that of a skilled, highly individual creative artist. Never profligate, Hellman shoots fast and within absurdly modest budgets; he himself is known as cultured, courteous, and soft-spoken. Yet most of his near-forty years as a filmmaker have been spent in the wilderness, wrestling with abortive projects, and of the mere ten films he has so far contrived to make, none have gained proper distribution and barely half ever get shown at all. The term "director *maudit*" might have been coined for him: few filmmakers have been worse treated by the industry with less apparent reason.

Given that moviegoers so rarely get a chance to see Hellman's work, it seems strange to suggest (as does David Thomson in his *Biographical Dictionary of Film*) that his career problems can be blamed on his "lofty intransigence towards audiences." Though such downbeat and open-ended films were never destined for major box-office success, on the few occasions they have gained a showing audiences have not been lacking. His mid-1960s pair of low-budget Westerns, *The Shooting* and *Ride in the Whirlwind,* denied a release in the States, played for months in Paris to capacity houses.

It was these two Westerns that first brought Hellman to public attention. Jointly produced by Hellman and Jack Nicholson—who also acted in both films, and scripted *Whirlwind*—they were shot back-to-back over seven weeks in the Utah desert with a crew of ten, for a total cost of $150,000. Spare, laconic, and bone-dry, closer in spirit to Samuel Beckett than to Zane Grey, the films make no attempt to disguise their scanty budget; on the contrary, it is turned to account in their elemental simplicity. Hellman himself describes them as "anti-Westerns": in each, a small group of characters circle warily around each other, yoked together by dumb chance and driven on by circumstances they hardly grasp, towards an inexorable showdown. Dialogue is brief to the point of inarticulacy, and explanations are not forthcoming. "I don't see no point to it," protests someone in *The Shooting.* "There isn't any," comes the response.

This existential ambivalence left critics fascinated but uneasy. "The films are startling and discomforting in their nihilism," wrote Beverly Walker in *Sight and Sound,* adding that they "offer none of the orthodox Western entertainment values. Action is minimal, rugged individualism is out, and nobody wins." An alternative angle came from the director himself, observing that in *The Shooting* "all the characters are bigger than life ... it's bordering closely on satire."

Hellman refuses to manipulate his audience, preferring his films to remain "open to individual interpretation," and quoting Cocteau to the effect that a work of art should be "difficult to pick up." He relishes unpredictability as much in the filmmaking process as in the finished work. "What I like in making films," he told a panel of Los Angeles critics, "is to be surprised.... It's the accidents that make the film interesting." In his best movies—*The Shooting, Two-Lane Blacktop, Cockfighter*—the austerity of the narrative line is constantly snagged by a quirky, deadpan humour "dropping in like capricious rain," as Melissa Pierson put it in *Village Voice.* (It is no coincidence that all three films star Hellman's favourite actor, Warren Oates, whom he regarded as "my alter ego" and valued for his "quality of mystery." No director except Peckinpah made better use of Oates's lopsided, scuzzbag charm.)

Nearly always, Hellman's films follow the archetypal pattern of a trek, not so much a Huston-style quest as a foray into the unknown. In *Blacktop,* the nearest he has so far come to a major studio production, the cross-country motor race that ostensibly motivates the action is constantly stalled, sidetracked, and finally abandoned without a result. Far more interesting to Hellman than who wins is the maze of emotional and psychological cross-currents between his characters, underscored by the aching melancholy of Kris Kristofferson's "Me and Bobby McGee" ("Freedom's just another word for nothing left to lose"). And in *Cockfighter* Oates's Frank Mansfield achieves his nominal ambition, to become Cockfighter of the Year, with offhand indifference; whatever cryptic goal he was pursuing, it was not this. "It's a film about inner life rather than outer life," Hellman said about *Blacktop,* but the description fits *Cockfighter* equally well.

There's something of the same wry detachment in Hellman's own attitude toward the shambles of his career. ("If I'm a cult director," he once dryly commented, "what I want to know is, where's my cult?") His work since *Cockfighter* has been sparse and increasingly erratic. *China 9, Liberty 37* (the title refers to a signpost, not the score in some bizarre ideologico-sporting fixture) played a few jokey riffs on the conventions of the spaghetti Western; minor Hellman, but at least it got shown occasionally. Not so *Iguana,* a jagged allegory adapted from a Spanish novel and shot in the Canary Islands, which remains undistributed. (His only other film of the 1980s, an entry in a trashy stalk-and-slash series, can best be put down to dire financial need.)

Known as a fine editor, Hellman has often been called in to rescue troubled films, sometimes shooting uncredited footage. At other times promising assignments have slipped through his fingers: he was originally slated to direct *Pat Garrett and Billy the Kid,* and passed up *The Last Picture Show* when preoccupied with *Blacktop.* More recently, he was due to direct *Reservoir Dogs,* only to lose it when Tarantino, having sold *True Romance,* took over the reins. But as *quid pro quo* Tarantino has undertaken to back Hellman's current project, the prison drama *Red Rain.* The return of such an elusive, intriguing filmmaker to the screen is keenly awaited.

—Philip Kemp

HENNING-JENSEN, Astrid and Bjarne

Nationality: Danish. **Born:** Frederiksberg, Denmark; Astrid (née Astrid Smahl): 10 December 1914; Bjarne: 6 October 1908. **Family:** Married 6 October 1938. **Career:** Bjarne actor at various theatres, Astrid actress at "Riddersalen," Copenhagen, 1931-38; Bjarne director at Nordisk Films Kompagni, 1940-50; Astrid assistant director, 1941, then director, 1943, at Nordisk; Astrid at Norsk Film A/S, Oslo, 1950-52; Bjarne and Astrid both worked as freelance writers and directors for film, theatre, radio, and television, from early 1950s. **Awards:** Astrid: Director Prize, Venice, for *Denmark Grows Up,* 1947; Cannes Festival Prize for *Palle Alone in the World,* 1949; Catholic Film Office Award, Cannes Festival, and Technik Prize, for *Paw,* 1960; Best Director, Berlin Festival, for *Winter Children,* 1979. Bjarne: Director Prize, Venice, for *Ditte: Child of Man,* 1946. **Address:** Astrid: Frederiksberg Allé 76, DK-1820 Copenhagen V, Denmark. **Died:** Bjarne, 1995.

Films as Directors:

1940 *Cykledrengene i Tørvegraven* (Bjarne only)
1941 *Hesten paa Kongens Nytorv* (Bjarne only); *Brunkul* (Bjarne only); *Arbejdet kalder* (Bjarne only); *Chr. IV som Bygherre* (*Christian IV: Master Builder*) (Bjarne only)
1942 *Sukker* (*Sugar*) (Bjarne only)
1943 *Korn* (*Corn*) (Bjarne only); *Hesten* (*Horses*) (Bjarne only); *Føllet* (Bjarne only); *Papir* (*Paper*) (Bjarne only); *Naar man kun er ung* (*To Be Young*) (Bjarne only); *S.O.S. Kindtand* (*S.O.S. Molars*)
1944 *De danske Sydhavsøer* (*Danish Island*) (Bjarne only)
1945 *Flyktingar finner en hamn* (*Fugitives Find Shelter*); *Dansk politi i Sverige* (Astrid only); *Folketingsvalg 1945*; *Brigaden i Sverige* (*Danish Brigade in Sweden*) (Bjarne only); *Frihedsfonden* (*Freedom Committee*) (Bjarne only)
1946 *Ditte Menneskebarn* (*Ditte: Child of Man*) (Bjarne d, Astrid asst)
1947 *Stemning i April*; *De pokkers unger* (*Those Blasted Kids*); *Denmark Grows Up* (Astrid co-d only)
1948 *Kristinus Bergman*
1949 *Palle alene i Verden* (*Palle Alone in the World*) (Astrid only)
1950 *Vesterhavsdrenge* (*Boys from the West Coast*)
1951 *Kranes Konditori* (*Krane's Bakery Shop*) (Astrid only)
1952 *Ukjent mann* (*Unknown Man*) (Astrid only)
1953 *Solstik*
1954 *Tivoligarden spiller* (*Tivoli Garden Games*); *Ballettens børn* (*Ballet Girl*) (Astrid only)
1955 *Kaerlighed pa kredit* (*Love on Credit*) (Astrid only, + sc); *En saelfangst i Nordgrønland* (Bjarne only); *Hvor bjergene sejler* (*Where Mountains Float*) (Bjarne only)
1959 *Hest på sommerferie* (Astrid only); *Paw* (*Boy of Two Worlds*; *The Lure of the Jungle*) (Astrid only)
1961 *Een blandt mange* (Astrid only)
1962 *Kort år sommaren* (*Short Is the Summer*) (Bjarne only)
1965 *De blå undulater* (Astrid only)
1966 *Utro* (*Unfaithful*) (Astrid only)
1967 *Min bedstefar er en stok* (Astrid only)
1968 *Nille* (Astrid only)
1969 *Mig og dig* (*Me and You*) (Astrid only)
1974 *Skipper & Co.* (Bjarne only)
1978 *Vinterbørn* (*Winter Children*) (Astrid only, + sc, ed)
1980 *Ejeblikket* (*The Moment*) (Astrid only)
1986 *Barndommens gade* (*Street of Childhood*) (Astrid only)
1991 *In Spite Of*
1995 *Bella, My Bella*

Other Films:

1937 *Cocktail* (Astrid: role)
1938 *Kongen bød* (Bjarne: role)
1939 *Genboerne* (Bjarne: role)
1940 *Jens Langkniv* (Bjarne: role)
1942 *Damen med de lyse Handsker* (Christensen) (Bjarne: role)

* * *

Astrid and Bjarne Henning-Jensen started as stage actors, but shortly after they married in 1938 they began working in films. Bjarne Henning-Jensen directed several government documentaries beginning in 1940 and he was joined by Astrid in 1943. At that time the Danish documentary film, strongly influenced by the British documentary of the 1930s, was blooming, and Bjarne Henning-Jensen played an important part in this. In 1943 he made his first feature film, Astrid serving as assistant director. *Naar man kun er ung* was a light, everyday comedy, striving for a relaxed and charming style, but it was too cute, and it was politely received. Their next film, *Ditte Menneskebarn,* was their breakthrough, and the two were instantly considered as the most promising directors in the postwar Danish cinema. The film was an adaptation of a neoclassical novel by Martin Andersen-Nexø. It was a realistic story of a young country girl and her tragic destiny as a victim of social conditions. The novel, published between 1917 and 1921, was in five volumes, but the Henning-Jensens used only parts of the novel. The sentimentality of the book was, happily, subdued in the film, and it is a sensitive study of a young girl in her milieu. The film was the first example of a more realistic and serious Danish film and it paralleled similar trends in contemporary European cinema, even if one would refrain from calling the film neorealistic. It was a tremendous success in Denmark and it also won a certain international recognition.

Astrid and Bjarne Henning-Jensen's film was a sincere attempt to introduce reality and authentic people to the Danish film. They continued this effort in their subsequent films, but a certain facile approach, a weakness for cute effects, and a sensibility on the verge of sentimentality made their films less and less interesting. In the 1950s Bjarne Henning-Jensen returned to documentaries. In 1955 he made the pictorially beautiful *Hvor bjergene sejler,* about Greenland. He attempted a comeback to features in 1962 with a rather pedestrian adaptation of Knut Hamsun's novel *Pan* called *Kort år sommaren.* His last film, in 1974, was a failure. Astrid Henning-Jensen continued making films on her own. She made two carefully directed and attractive films in Norway, and in the 1960s she tried to keep up with the changing times in a couple of films. But it was not until the last few years that she regained her old position. In *Vinterbørn,* about women and their problems in a maternity ward, and in *Ejeblikket,* treating the problems of a young couple when it is discovered that the woman is dying of cancer, she worked competently within an old established genre in Danish films, the problem-oriented popular drama.

—Ib Monty

HEPWORTH, Cecil

Nationality: British. **Born:** Lambeth, London, 19 March 1874. **Career:** Patented hand-feed lamp for optical lantern, 1895; assistant projectionist to Birt Acres, 1896; became cameraman for Charles Urban, 1898; formed Hepwix Films at Walton-on-Thames, worked as actor and director, and patented film developing system; formed Hepworth Manufacturing Company, 1904; patented Vivaphone "Talking Film" device and became first chairman, Kinematograph Manufacturer's Association, 1910; founded British Board of Film Censors, 1911; founded Hepworth Picture Plays, 1919 (company goes bankrupt, 1923); technical advisor and producer, National Screen Service, 1936. **Died:** In Greenford, Middlesex, 9 February 1953.

Cecil Hepworth

Films as Director:

1898 *Oxford and Cambridge Boat Race* (short); *The Interrupted Picnic* (short); *Exchange Is No Robbery* (short); *The Immature Punter* (short); *The Quarrelsome Anglers* (short); *Two Fools in a Canoe* (short)
1899 *Express Train in a Railway Cutting* (short)
1900 *Wiping Something off the Slate* (short); *The Conjurer and the Boer* (short); *The Punter's Mishap* (short); *The Gunpowder Plot* (short); *Explosion of a Motor Car* (short); *The Egg-Laying Man* (short); *Clown and Policeman* (short); *Leapfrog as Seen by the Frog* (short); *How It Feels to be Run Over* (short); *The Eccentric Dancer* (short); *The Bathers* (short); *The Sluggard's Surprise* (short); *The Electricity Cure* (short); *The Beggar's Deceit* (short); *The Burning Stable* (short); *Topsy Turvy Villa* (short); *The Kiss* (short)
1901 *How the Burglar Tricked the Bobby* (short); *The Indian Chief and the Seidlitz Powder* (short); *Comic Grimacer* (short); *Interior of a Railway Carriage* (short); *Funeral of Queen Victoria* (short); *Coronation of King Edward VII* (short); *The Glutton's Nightmare* (short)
1902 *The Call to Arms* (short); *How to Stop a Motor Car* (short)
1903 *The Absent-Minded Bootblack* (short); *Alice in Wonderland* (short); *Firemen to the Rescue* (short); *Saturday's Shopping* (short)
1904 *The Jonah Man* (short)
1905 *Rescued by Rover* (short); *Falsely Accused* (short); *The Alien's Invasion* (short); *A Den of Thieves* (short)
1907 *A Seaside Girl* (short)
1908 *John Gilpin's Ride* (short)
1909 *Tilly the Tomboy* (short)
1911 *Rachel's Sin* (short)
1914 *Blind Fate* (short); *Unfit or The Strength of the Weak* (short); *The Hills Are Calling* (short); *The Basilisk*; *His Country's Bidding* (short); *The Quarry Mystery* (short); *Time the Great Healer*; *Morphia the Death Drug* (short); *Oh My Aunt* (short)
1915 *The Canker of Jealousy*; *A Moment of Darkness* (short); *Court-Martialled*; *The Passing of a Soul* (short); *The Bottle*; *The Baby on the Barge*; *The Man Who Stayed at Home*; *Sweet Lavender*; *The Golden Pavement*; *The Outrage*; *Iris*
1916 *Trelawney of the Wells*; *A Fallen Star*; *Sowing the Wind*; *Annie Laurie*; *Comin' Thro' the Rye*; *The Marriage of William Ashe*; *Molly Bawn*; *The Cobweb*
1917 *The American Heiress*; *Nearer My God to Thee*
1918 *The Refugee*; *Tares*; *Broken in the Wars*; *The Blindness of Fortune*; *The Touch of a Child*; *Boundary House*
1919 *The Nature of the Beast*; *Sunken Rocks*; *Sheba*; *The Forest on the Hill*
1920 *Anna the Adventuress*; *Alf's Button*; *Helen of Four Gates*; *Mrs. Erricker's Reputation*
1921 *Tinted Venus*; *Narrow Valley*; *Wild Heather*; *Tansy*
1922 *The Pipes of Pan*; *Mist in the Valley*; *Strangling Threads*; *Comin' Thro' the Rye* (second version)
1927 *The House of Marney*
1929 *Royal Remembrances*

Publications

By HEPWORTH: books—

Animated Photography, London, 1898.
Came the Dawn: Memories of a Film Pioneer, New York, 1951.

By HEPWORTH: articles—

"My Film Experiences," in *Pearson's Magazine* (London), 1920.
"Those Were the Days," in *Penguin Film Review* (London), no. 6, 1948.

On HEPWORTH: books—

Barnes, John, *The Beginnings of Cinema in England,* London, 1976.
Barnes, John, *Pioneers of the British Film 1894-1901,* London, 1983.

On HEPWORTH: articles—

"Cecil Hepworth Comes Through," in *Era* (London), 3 May 1935.
"Hepworth: His Studios and Techniques," in *British Journal of Photography* (London), 15 and 22 January 1971.

* * *

The son of a famous magic lanternist and photographer named T.C. Hepworth (who authored an important early volume titled *The Book of the Lantern*), Cecil Hepworth was—along with Robert W. Paul—the best known and most important of early British film pioneers. In the first twenty years of British cinema, Hepworth's place is easy to determine. He was a major figure who wrote the first British book on cinematography, *Animated Photography, the A.B.C. of the Cinematograph* (published in 1897) and who produced *Rescued by Rover,* which is to British cinema what D.W. Griffith's *The Adventures of Dollie* is to the American film industry. But as the industry grew, Cecil Hepworth failed to grow along with it, and as the English critic and historian Ernest Betts has written, "although a craftsman and a man of warm sympathies, an examination of his career shows an extremely limited outlook compared with Americans or his contemporaries."

A cameraman before turning to production in the late 1890s, "Heppy," as he was known to his friends and colleagues, founded the first major British studio at Walton-on-Thames (which was later to become Nettlefold Studios). He experimented with sound films before 1910 and was also one of the few British pioneers to build up his own stable of stars, not borrowed from the stage, but brought to fame through the cinema. Alma Taylor, Chrissie White, Stewart Rome, and Violet Hopson were his best known "discoveries." So omnipotent was Hepworth in British cinema prior to the First World War that major American filmmakers such as Larry Trimble and Florence Turner were eager to associate with him when they journeyed to England from the United States to produce films.

Hepworth's problem and the cause of his downfall was shared with many other pioneers. He did not move with the times. His films were always exquisitely photographed and beautiful to look at, but they were totally devoid of drama. The editing techniques which he had displayed in *Rescued by Rover* were forgotten by the teens. His productions were all too often like the magic lantern presentations of his father, lifeless creations featuring slow dissolves from one sequence or even one bit of action to the next, even when it was obvious to others that quick cuts were needed. Hepworth appeared to despise anything that would bring movement to his films, preferring that the camera linger on the pictorial beauty of the scene. Nowhere is this more apparent than in Hepworth's best-known feature, *Comin' thro' the Rye* (which he filmed twice, in 1916 and 1922). As Iris Barry was forced to admit, when writing of the latter version, it is "a most awful film."

Bankruptcy and a closed mind drove Cecil Hepworth from the industry which he had helped to create. He returned late in life to supervise the production of trailers for National Screen Service, and also served as chairman of the History Research Committee of the British Film Institute, at which time he also wrote his autobiography, *Came the Dawn.*

—Anthony Slide

HERZOG, Werner

Nationality: German. **Born:** Werner Stipetic in Sachrang, 5 September 1942. **Education:** Classical Gymnasium, Munich, until 1961; University of Munich, early 1960s. **Family:** Married journalist Martje Grohmann, one son. **Career:** Worked as a welder in a steel factory for U.S. National Aeronautics and Space Administration; founded Werner Herzog Filmproduktion, 1966; walked from Munich to Paris to visit film historian Lotte Eisner, 1974. **Awards:** Bundesfilmpreis, and Silver Bear, Berlinale, for *Signs of Life,* 1968; Bundespreis, and Special Jury Prize, Cannes Festival, for *Every Man for Himself and God against All,* 1975; Best Director, Cannes Festival, for *Fitzcarraldo,* 1982. **Address:** Turkenstr. 91, D-80799 Münich, Germany.

Films as Director (beginning 1966, films are produced or co-produced by Werner Herzog Filmproduktion)

1962 *Herakles* (+ pr, sc)
1964 *Spiel im Sand* (*Game in the Sand*) (unreleased) (+ pr, sc)
1966 *Die beispiellose Verteidigung der Festung Deutschkreuz* (*The Unprecedented Defense of the Fortress of Deutschkreuz*) (+ pr, sc)
1967 *Lebenszeichen* (*Signs of Life*) (+ sc, pr)
1968 *Letzte Worte* (*Last Words*) (+ pr, sc); *Massnahmen gegen Fanatiker* (*Precautions against Fanatics*) (+ pr, sc)
1969 *Die fliegenden Ärzte von Ostafrika* (*The Flying Doctors of East Africa*) (+ pr, sc); *Fata Morgana* (*Mirage*) (+ sc, pr)
1970 *Auch Zwerge haben klein angefangen* (*Even Dwarfs Started Small*) (+ pr, sc, mu arrangements); *Behinderte Zukunft* (*Handicapped Future*) (+ pr, sc)
1971 *Land des Schweigens und der Dunkelheit* (*Land of Silence and Darkness*) (+ pr, sc)
1972 ***Aguirre, der Zorn Göttes*** (*Aguirre, the Wrath of God*) (+ pr, sc)
1974 *Die grosse Ekstase des Bildschnitzers Steiner* (*The Great Ecstasy of the Sculptor Steiner*) (+ pr, sc); ***Jeder für sich und Gott gegen alle*** (*Every Man for Himself and God against All; The Enigma of Kaspar Hauser*) (+ pr, sc)
1976 *How Much Wood Would a Woodchuck Chuck* (+ pr, sc); *Mit mir will keiner spielen* (*No One Will Play with Me*) (+ pr, sc); *Herz aus Glas* (*Heart of Glass*) (+ pr, co-sc, bit role as glass carrier)
1977 *La Soufrière* (+ pr, sc, narration, appearance)
1978 *Stroszek* (+ pr, sc)
1979 *Nosferatu—Phantom der Nacht* (*Nosferatu, the Vampire*) (+ pr, sc, bit role as monk); *Woyzeck* (+ pr, sc)
1980 *Woyzeck*; *Glaube und Währung* (*Creed and Currency*)
1981 *Fitzcarraldo* (+ pr, sc)
1983 *Where the Green Ants Dream* (*Wo Die Grünen Ameisen Traümen*)
1984 *Ballade vom Kleinen Soldaten* (*Ballad of the Little Soldier*); *Gasherbrum—Der leuchtende Berg* (*Gasherbrum—The Dark Glow of the Mountains*)
1987 *Cobra Verde* (+ sc)
1988 *Wodaabe—Die Hirten der Sonne* (*Herdsmen of the Sun*); *Les Gaulois* (*The French*)
1989 *Es ist nicht leicht ein Gott zu sein* (*It Isn't Easy Being God*)
1990 *Echos aus Einem Dustern Reich* (*Echoes from a Somber Kingdom*)
1991 *Schrie aus Stein* (*Scream of Stone*); *Jag Mandir* (*The Eccentric Private Theatre of the Maharajah of Udaipur*)
1992 *Lektionen in Finsternis* (*Lessons of Darkness*)
1993 *Bells from the Deep* (*Glocken aus der Tiefe*)
1994 *Die Verwandlung der Welt in Musik* (*The Transformation of the World into Music*)

Publications

By HERZOG: books—

Werner Herzog: Drehbücher I, Munich, 1977.
Werner Herzog: Drehbücher II, Munich 1977.
Sur le chemin des glaces: Munich-Paris du. 23.11 au 14.12.1974, Paris, 1979.
Werner Herzog: Stroszek, Nosferatu: Zwei Filmerzählungen, Munich, 1979.
Cobra Verde, Munich, 1987.
Vom Gehen im Eis (Of Walking in Ice), London, 1994.

By HERZOG: articles—

"Rebellen in Amerika," in *Filmstudio* (Frankfurt), May 1964.
"Neun Tage eines Jahres," in *Filmstudio* (Frankfurt), September 1964.
"Mit den Wölfen heulen," in *Filmkritik* (Munich), July 1968.
"Warum ist überhaupt Seiendes und nicht vielmehr Nichts?," in *Kino* (West Berlin), March/April 1974.
Interview with S. Murray, in *Cinema Papers* (Melbourne), December 1974.
"Every Man for Himself," interview with D. L. Overbey, in *Sight and Sound* (London), Spring 1975.
Interview with Michel Ciment, in *Positif* (Paris), May 1975.
L'Énigme de Kaspar Hauser, cutting continuity and dialogue, in *Avant-Scène du Cinéma* (Paris), June 1976.
"Signs of Life: Werner Herzog," interview with Jonathan Cott, in *Rolling Stone* (New York), 18 November 1976.
Aguirre, la colère de Dieu, cutting continuity and dialogue, in *Avant-Scène du Cinéma* (Paris), 15 June 1978.
"I Feel That I'm Close to the Center of Things," interview with L. O'Toole, in *Film Comment* (New York), November/December 1979.
Interview with B. Steinborn and R. von Naso, in *Filmfaust* (Frankfurt), February/March 1982.
Interview with G. Bechtold and G. Griksch, in *Filmfaust* (Frankfurt), October/November 1984.
Interview in *Time Out* (London), 20 April 1988.

On HERZOG: books—

Greenberg, Alan, *Heart of Glass,* Munich, 1976.
Schütte, Wolfram, and others, *Herzog/Kluge/Straub,* Vienna, 1976.
Franklin, James, *New German Cinema: From Oberhausen to Hamburg,* Boston, 1983.
Phillips, Klaus, editor, *New German Filmmakers: From Oberhausen through the 1970's,* New York, 1984.
Corrigan, Timothy, *The Films of Werner Herzog: Between Mirage and History,* New York, 1986.
Elsaesser, Thomas, *New German Cinema: A History,* London, 1989.

On HERZOG: articles—

"Herzog Issue" of *Cinema* (Zurich), vol. 18, no. 1, 1972.
Wetzel, Kraft, "Werner Herzog," in *Kino* (West Berlin), April/May 1973.

Werner Herzog: ***Fitzcarraldo***

Bachmann, Gideon, "The Man on the Volcano," in *Film Quarterly* (Berkeley), Autumn 1977.
Dorr, John, "The Enigma of Werner Herzog," in *Millimeter* (New York), October 1977.
Walker, B., "Werner Herzog's *Nosferatu,*" in *Sight and Sound* (London), Autumn 1978.
Andrews, N., "Dracula in Delft," in *American Film* (Washington, D.C.), October 1978.
Morris, George, "Werner Herzog," in *International Film Guide 1979,* London, 1978.
Cleere, E., "Three Films by Werner Herzog," in *Wide Angle* (Athens, Ohio), vol. 3, no. 4, 1980.
Van Wert, W.F., "Hallowing the Ordinary, Embezzling the Everyday: Werner Herzog's Documentary Practice," in *Quarterly Review of Film Studies* (Pleasantville, New York), Spring 1980.
Davidson, D., "Borne Out of Darkness: The Documentaries of Werner Herzog," in *Film Criticism* (Edinboro, Pennsylvania), Fall 1980.
"Werner Herzog," in *Film Dope* (London), March 1982.
Goodwin, M., "Herzog the God of Wrath," in *American Film* (Washington, D.C.), June 1982.
Carroll, Noel, "Herzog, Presence, and Paradox," in *Persistence of Vision* (Maspeth, New York), Fall 1985.
Kennedy, Harlan, "Amazon Grace," in *Film Comment* (New York), September/October 1986.
Davidson, David, "Borne Out of Darkness: The Documentaries of Werner Herzog," in *Film Criticism* (Meadville, Pennsylvania), no. 1/2, 1987.
Mouton, Jan, "Werner Herzog's *Stroszek*: A Fairy-Tale in an Age of Disenchantment," in *Literature/Film Quarterly* (Salisbury, Maryland), vol. 15, no. 2, 1987.
Caltvedt, Lester, "Herzog's *Fitzcarraldo* and the Rubber Era," in *Film and History* (New York), vol. 18, no. 4, 1988.
"Herzog Issue" of *Post Script* (Jacksonville, Florida), Summer 1988.
Elsaesser, Thomas, "Werner Herzog: Tarzan Meets Parsifal," in *Monthly Film Bulletin* (London), May 1988.

On HERZOG: films—

Weisenborn, Christian, and Erwin Keusch, *Was ich bin sind meine Filme,* Munich, 1978.
Blank, Les, *Werner Herzog Eats His Shoe,* U.S., 1980.
Blank, Les, *Burden of Dreams,* U.S., 1982.

* * *

Werner Herzog, more than any director of his generation, has through his films embodied German history, character, and cultural richness. While references to verbal and other visual arts would be out of place in treating most film directors, they are key to understanding Herzog. For his techniques he reaches back into the early part of the twentieth century to the Expressionist painters and filmmakers; back to the Romantic painters and writers for the luminance and allegorization of landscape and the human figure; even further beyond into sixteenth-century Mannerist extremes of Mathias Günwald; and throughout his nation's heritage for that peculiarly Germanic grotesque. In all these technical and expressive veins, one finds the qualities of exaggeration, distortion, and the sublimation of the ugly.

More than any, "grotesque" presents itself as a useful term to define Herzog's work. His use of an actor like Klaus Kinski, whose singularly ugly face is sublimated by Herzog's camera, can best be described by such a term. Persons with physical defects like deafness and blindness, and dwarfs, are given a type of grandeur in Herzog's artistic vision. Herzog, as a contemporary German living in the shadow of remembered Nazi atrocities, demonstrates a penchant for probing the darker aspects of human behavior. Herzog's vision renders the ugly and horrible sublime, while the beautiful is omitted and, when included, destroyed or made to vanish (like the beautiful Spanish noblewoman in *Aguirre).*

Closely related to the grotesque in Herzog's films is the influence of German expressionism on him. Two of Herzog's favorite actors, Klaus Kinski and Bruno S., have been compared to Conrad Veidt and Fritz Kortner, prototypical actors of German expressionistic dramas and films during the teens and 1920s. Herzog's actors make highly stylized, indeed often stock, gestures; in close-ups, their faces are set in exaggerated grimaces.

The characters of Herzog's films often seem deprived of free will, merely reacting to an absurd universe. Any exertion of free will in action leads ineluctably to destruction, death, or at best frustration by the unexpected. The director is a satirist who demonstrates what is wrong with the world but, as yet, seems unable or unwilling to articulate the ways to make it right; indeed, one is at a loss to find in his world view any hope, let alone prescription, for improvement.

Herzog's mode of presentation has been termed by some critics as romantic and by others as realistic. This seeming contradiction can be resolved by an approach that compares him with those Romantic artists who first articulated elements of the later realistic approach. Critics have found in the quasi-photographic paintings of Caspar David Friedrich an analogue for Herzog's super-realism. As with these artists, there is an aura of unreality in Herzog's realism. Everything is seen through a camera that rarely goes out of intense, hard focus. Often it is as if his camera is deprived of the normal range of human vision, able only to perceive part of the whole through a telescope or a microscope.

In this strange blend of romanticism and realism lies the paradoxical quality of Herzog's talent: he, unlike Godard, Resnais, or Altman, has not made great innovations in film language; if his style is to be defined at all it is as an eclectic one; and yet, his films do have a distinctive stylistic quality. He renders the surface reality of things with such an intensity that the viewer has an uncanny sense of seeing the essence beyond. *Aguirre,* for example, is unrelenting in its concentration on filth, disease, and brutality; and yet it is also an allegory which can be read on several levels: in terms of Germany under the Nazis, America in Vietnam, and more generally on the bestiality that lingers beneath the facade of civilized conventions. In one of Herzog's romantic tricks within his otherwise realistic vision, he shows a young Spanish noblewoman wearing an ever-pristine velvet dress amid mud and squalor; further, only she of all the rest is not shown dying through violence and is allowed to disappear almost mystically into the dense vegetation of the forest: clearly, she represents that transcendent quality in human nature that incorruptibly endures. This figure is dropped like a hint to remind us to look beyond mere surface.

One finds, however, in *Fitzcarraldo,* Herzog's supreme apotheosis of the spiritual dimensions of the rain forest. As much in the production as in the substance of the film, the Western Imperialist will to reshape the wilderness is again and again met with reversals that render that will meaningless. The protagonist's titanic effort to get a riverboat over a hill from one river to another is achieved only to be thwarted by the natives who cut the ropes, sending it careening downstream through the rapids in a sacrifice to their river deity. The boat ends up uselessly back where it began: a massive symbol of human futility. Only the old gramophone shown playing records of Caruso throughout the jungle voyage offers—like the Spanish noblewoman in *Aguirre*—Herzog's vision of beauty that rarely escapes being rendered meaningless by an otherwise absurd universe.

Herzog's Australian film *Where Green Ants Dream* does penance for any taint of Western Imperialism that *Fitzcarraldo* might have given him. The director comes down hard against the modern way of life. This film is saved from tendentiousness by movements of human comedy through which a very sympathetic hero learns from the Native Australians, and by Herzog's much-loved 360-degree pans over the flatness of the Outback. This technique is also used by Herzog to convey the sense of flat immensity of sub-Saharan Africa in *Herdsmen of the Sun,* a lyrical celebration of the Wodaabe tribesmen, who bend Western gender expectations by having the men and women reverse roles in courtship. Here, too, Herzog evidences his German heritage by following in the African footsteps of his greatest—if most problematic—filmmaking compatriot: Leni Riefenstahl, whose last work was a documentary of a sub-Saharan tribe to the east of the Wodaabe.

—Rodney Farnsworth

HILL, George Roy

Nationality: American. **Born:** Minneapolis, Minnesota, 20 December 1921. **Education:** Blake School, Hopkins, Minnesota; Yale University, B.A. (Music), 1943; Trinity College, Dublin, B. Litt., 1949. **Military Service:** Served as U.S. Marine Corps transport pilot, 1943-45, and during Korean war. **Family:** Married Louisa Horton, 1951, four children. **Career:** Theatre actor, early 1950's; writer, producer, and director for US TV, 1954-57; director on and off Broadway, 1957-62; directed first film, *Period of Adjustment,* 1962; signed a 5-year contract with Universal, 1975; **Awards:** Emmy Awards for *A Night to Remember,* 1954; Best Direction Award, British Academy, for *Butch Cassidy and the Sundance Kid,* 1970; Jury Prize, Cannes Festival, for *Slaughterhouse-Five,* 1972; Academy Award for Best Director, and Director Award, Directors Guild of America, for *The Sting,* 1973. **Address:** Pan Arts Productions, 75 Rockefeller Plaza, New York, NY 10019, U.S.A.

Films as Director:

1962 *Period of Adjustment*
1963 *Toys in the Attic*
1964 *The World of Henry Orient*
1966 *Hawaii*
1967 *Thoroughly Modern Millie*
1969 *Butch Cassidy and the Sundance Kid*
1972 *Slaughterhouse-Five*
1973 *The Sting*
1975 *The Great Waldo Pepper* (+ story)
1977 *Slap Shot*
1979 *A Little Romance*
1982 *The World According to Garp*
1984 *The Little Drummer Girl*
1988 *Funny Farm*

Other Films:

1952 *Walk East on Beacon* (*Crime of the Century*) (Werker) (role)

Publications

By HILL: articles—

Interview with C. Flynn, in *Focus on Film* (London), Spring 1970.
Interview with J.-A. Gili and others, in *Ecran* (Paris), November 1972.
"Flying High: George Roy Hill," an interview with R. Appelbaum, in *Films and Filming* (London), August 1979.
Interview with B.L. Zito, in *Millimeter* (New York), October 1979.
"Butch and Millie," an interview in *Films* (London), March 1981.
Interview in *Film Comment* (New York), July/August 1988.

On HILL: books—

Goldman, William, *Adventures in the Screen Trade,* New York, 1983.
Shores, Edward, *George Roy Hill,* Boston, 1983.
Horton, Andrew, *The Films of George Roy Hill,* New York, 1984.

On HILL: articles—

"Stage to Film," in *Action* (Los Angeles), October 1968.
Thomas, B., "Award Winner," in *Action* (Los Angeles), May/June 1974.
"*L'Arnaque,*" in *Avant-Scène du Cinéma* (Paris), June 1974.
Owen, Derek, "George Roy Hill," in *Film Dope* (London), March 1982.
"George Roy Hill Section" of *Revue du Cinéma* (Paris), April 1985.
Parshall, Peter F., "Meditations on the Philosophy of Tralfamadore: Kurt Vonnegut and George Roy Hill," in *Literature/Film Quarterly* (Salisbury, Maryland), vol. 15, no. 1, 1987.

On HILL: film—

Crawford, Robert, *The Making of Butch Cassidy and the Sundance Kid,* U.S.A., 1970.

* * *

George Roy Hill has found his greatest popular success when he works with actors Paul Newman and Robert Redford. Before the emergence of films by George Lucas and Steven Spielberg, Hill's two collaborations with the duo earned him the distinction of being the only director to have made two among the ten most financially successful films.

Butch Cassidy and the Sundance Kid is an examination of the western hero, the myth and the reality. Butch and Sundance are nearly Robin Hood characters of the Old West, but they are also shown to be trapped in their criminal profession and in their own myths. Their violent deaths are inevitable, as there is no way for heroes or criminals to age. Helped considerably by the screen charm of Newman and Redford, Hill makes the pair into lovable, wisecracking rogues. The freeze frame death scene seems to be Hill's acknowledgment that the western myth must be recognized as a viable entity even though most of the action preceding their end seems to undercut the myth.

Hill's second film with Newman and Redford was *The Sting.* Illusions abound as experienced con men set up an elaborate scheme to avenge a friend's death. Redford's character's first big successful con is actually a mistake that leads to his mentor's death. Newman's character seems to be a down and out drunk but soon proves his merit as an extremely competent con man and schemer. Hill's ultimate illusion in the film is a con the film plays on the audience.

Hill again directed Redford in *The Great Waldo Pepper,* focusing on the myth and reality of the barnstorming early years of aviation. Redford's character finally achieves his goal of showing how good a pilot he is when he turns an illusion (a filmed aerial battle) into a real aerial battle. Newman's character in *Slap Shot* is similar. The most underrated film of Hill's career (mostly criticized for the profane but accurately observed locker room talk), *Slap Shot* shows the development of minor league hockey coach Reg Dunlop. Reg, late in his career, recognizes that sport in America is just an illusionary entertainment and that a sport can be manipulated to please a blood-thirsty audience. As his team wins the championship through overly aggressive play, the teams' star player, who had been reluctant to fight, breaks down and performs a strip tease, thus joining "the team" Reg has created.

Hill has not yet found great acceptance with the critics, some of whom regard his films as superficial entertainment. Critics do acknowledge Hill's skill with narrative. This ability, coupled with charismatic stars, certainly are at the base of the appeal of Hill's films.

—Ray Narducy

HILL, Walter

Nationality: American. **Born:** Long Beach, California, 10 January 1942. **Education:** Attended University of Americas, Mexico City, 1959-60; Michigan State University, B.A., 1962, M.A., 1963. **Career:** Began in films as writer; directed first film, *Hard Times,* 1975; created *Dog and Cat* TV series, 1977. **Address:** c/o Lone Wolf Co., 8800 Sunset Boulevard, Suite 210, Los Angeles, CA 90069, U.S.A.

Films as Director:

1975 *Hard Times* (*The Streetfighter*) (+ co-sc)
1978 *The Driver* (+ sc)
1979 *The Warriors* (co-sc)
1980 *The Long Riders*
1981 *Southern Comfort* (co-sc)
1982 *48 HRS.* (+ sc)
1984 *Streets of Fire* (+ sc, pr)
1985 *Brewster's Millions*
1986 *Crossroads*
1987 *Extreme Prejudice*
1988 *Red Heat* (+ sc, pr)
1989 *Johnny Handsome*; *Tales from the Crypt* (TV series) (+ co-exec pr)
1990 *Another 48 HRS.*
1992 *Trespass*
1993 *Geronimo: An American Legend* (+ pr)
1995 *Wild Bill* (+ sc)
1996 *Gundown* (+ sc)

Other Films:

1968 *The Thomas Crown Affair* (Jewison) (2nd asst-d)
1969 *Take the Money and Run* (Allen) (asst-d)
1972 *Hickey and Boggs* (Culp) (sc); *The Getaway* (Peckinpah) (sc)
1973 *The Thief Who Came to Dinner* (Yorkin) (sc); *The Mackintosh Man* (Huston) (sc)
1975 *The Drowning Pool* (Rosenberg) (co-sc)
1979 *Alien* (Scott) (co-pr)
1986 *Aliens* (Cameron) (co-pr); *Blue City* (Manning) (co-sc, pr)
1992 *Alien 3* (sc, pr)
1994 *The Getaway* (sc)

Publications

By HILL: articles—

Interview with A. J. Silver and E. Ward, in *Movie* (London), Winter 1978/79.
"Making *Alien,*" an interview with M. P. Carducci, in *Cinefantastique* (Oak Park, Illinois), no. 1, 1979.
Interview with M. Greco, in *Film Comment* (New York), May/June 1980.
Interview with Pat Broeske, in *Films in Review* (New York), December 1981.
"Dead End Streets," an interview with D. Chute, in *Film Comment* (New York), July/August 1984.
Interview with A. Hunter, in *Films and Filming* (London), October 1984.
"Walter Hill," an interview with L. Gross, in *Bomb,* Winter 1993.

On HILL: book—

Cantero, Marcial, *Walter Hill,* Madrid, 1985.

On HILL: articles—

"Walter Hill," in *Film Dope* (London), March 1982.
Sragow, M., "Don't Jesse James Me," in *Sight and Sound* (London), Summer 1982.
Rafferty, T., "The Paradoxes of Home: Three Films by Walter Hill," in *Film Quarterly* (Berkeley), Fall 1982.
Sragow, M., "Hill's Street Blues," in *American Film* (Washington, D.C.), June 1984.
Heuring, D., "*Red Heat*—Cross-Culture Cop Caper," in *American Cinematographer* (Los Angeles), June 1988.
Revue du Cinéma/Image et Son (Paris), June 1990.
Roth, P. A., "The Virtue of Violence: The Dimensions of Development in Walter Hill's *The Warriors,*" in *Journal of Popular Culture,* vol. 24, no. 3, 1990.
"Walter Hill," in *CinemAction,* January 1992.
Solman, Gregory, "At Home on the Range: Walter Hill," in *Film Comment,* March/April 1994.

* * *

Established in the early 1970s as a writer of action movies (earlier he had ambitions to illustrate comic books), Walter Hill went almost unnoticed for his first two directorial ventures. Not so with his third. *The Warriors* reportedly occasioned gang fights in the United States, while one British newspaper dubbed it "the film they mustn't show here." Replete with highly stylized violence, *The Warriors* has been described by Hill as "a comic book rock 'n' roll version of the Xenophon story." It is a precise description: the movie takes the *Anabasis* and adapts it to an appropriately mythical setting among the street gangs of modern New York. The stranded Warriors fight their way home through the subways and streets of an extraordinary fantasy city. This world, as so often in Hill's movies, is evacuated of any sense of the everyday, and is rendered with the use of the strong reds, yellows, and blues of comic book design. In its subway scenes especially, colors leap from the screen much as, say, a Roy Lichtenstein picture leaps from the canvas, its direct assault on our vision as basic as that of a comic strip.

The pleasure of the movie lies in that style, transforming its much-maligned violence into a kind of ritual dance. Given this transformation, you could as well accuse Hill of celebrating gang warfare as you could accuse Lichtenstein of condoning aerial combat in his painting *Whaam!* The fascination of Hill's cinema is that it evokes and elaborates upon mythical worlds, in the case of *The Warriors* grounded in ancient Greece and in comics, though in his other movies more often based in the cinema itself. Thus *Driver* eliminates orthodox characterization in favour of thriller archetypes: the Driver, the Detective, and the Girl, as the credits list them. They revolve around each other in a world of formally defined roles, roles made archetypal by movies themselves. *The Long Riders,* in presenting a version of the Jesse James story, traps its characters in their own movie mythology so

Walter Hill

that they even seem to be aware that they are playing out a sort of destiny born of the Western genre, a sense of fate which also imbues Hill's other outstanding Western, *Geronimo: An American Legend. Southern Comfort* manipulates and undermines the war-movie ideology of the small military group, while *48 HRS.* pursues its unstoppable and richly entertaining action in precisely the fashion of a Don Siegel cop movie—*Madigan,* say, or *Dirty Harry.*

It is as if Hill's project is to tour the popular genres, and although he has suffered a sequence of poor films in the latter half of the 1980s, in 1993 *Geronimo* triumphantly demonstrated that he remains one of the most intelligent genre directors in the modern cinema. He is highly skilled in the narrative use of chase and confrontation, adept at the montage techniques so central to action-movie tension, while offering us not a "reality" but a distillation of the rules of the genre game. In his films we are witness to the *enmything* of characters, if that neologism is not too pompous for so pleasurable an experience, a self-conscious evocation of genre but without the knowing, postmodern wink which often attends such exercises. Hill manages to take the genre seriously *and* to reflect upon it.

Inevitably such immersion in popular genre conventions, however skilled, risks critical opprobrium. Although *Geronimo* has deservedly received its share of positive comment—in part, of course, because it treats its Native Americans with more sensitivity than has generally been the case in genre cinema—*The Warriors, Southern Comfort,* and *48 HRS.* have all been dismissed as shallow and morally suspect, lacking in the "seriousness" considered necessary to redeem their almost exclusive focus upon action. This, however, is to miss the real pleasures of Hill's cinema, its visual power, its narrative force, and its absorbing concern with myth-making and myth-breaking. These, too, are qualities to which the label "serious" may properly be applied.

—Andrew Tudor

HITCHCOCK, Alfred

Nationality: British. **Born:** Alfred Joseph Hitchcock in Leytonstone, London, 13 August 1899, became U.S. citizen, 1955. **Education:** Salesian College, Battersea, London, 1908; St. Ignatius College, Stamford Hill, London, 1908-13; School of Engineering and Navigation, 1914; attended drawing and design classes under E.J. Sullivan, London University, 1917. **Family:** Married Alma Reville, 2 December 1926, daughter Patricia born 1928. **Career:** Technical clerk, W.T. Henley Telegraph Co., 1914-19; title-card designer for Famous Players-Lasky at Islington studio, 1919; scriptwriter and assistant director, from 1922; directed two films for producer Michael Balcon in Germany, 1925; signed with British International Pictures as director, 1927; directed first British film to use synchronized sound, *Blackmail,* 1929; signed with Gaumont-British Studios, 1933; moved to America to direct *Rebecca* for Selznick International Studios, decided to remain, 1939; returned to Britain to make short films for Ministry of Information, 1944; directed first film in color, *Rope,* 1948; producer and host, *Alfred Hitchcock Presents* (*The Alfred Hitchcock Hour* from 1962), for TV, 1955-65. **Awards:** Irving Thalberg Academy Award, 1968; Chevalier de la Légion d'Honneur, 1971; Commander of the Order of Arts and Letters, France, 1976; Life Achievement Award, American Film Institute, 1979; Honorary Doctorate, University of Southern California; Knight of the Legion of Honour of the Cinématheque Français; knighted, 1980. **Died:** Of kidney failure, in Los Angeles, 29 April 1980.

Films as Director:

1922 *Number Thirteen* (or *Mrs. Peabody*) (incomplete)
1923 *Always Tell Your Wife* (Croise; completed d)
1926 *The Pleasure Garden* (*Irrgarten der Leidenschaft*); *The Mountain Eagle* (*Der Bergadler*; *Fear o' God*); *The Lodger*; *A Story of the London Fog* (*The Case of Jonathan Drew*) (+ co-sc, bit role as man in newsroom, and onlooker during Novello's arrest)
1927 *Downhill* (*When Boys Leave Home*); *Easy Virtue*; *The Ring* (+ sc)
1928 *The Farmer's Wife* (+ sc); *Champagne* (+ adapt); *The Manxman*
1929 ***Blackmail*** (+ adapt, bit role as passenger on "tube") (silent version also made); *Juno and the Paycock* (*The Shame of Mary Boyle*)
1930 *Elstree Calling* (Brunel; d after Brunel dismissed, credit for "sketches and other interpolated items"); *Murder* (*Mary, Sir John greift ein!*) (+ co-adapt, bit role as passerby) *An Elastic Affair* (short)
1931 *The Skin Game* (+ co-sc)
1932 *Rich and Strange* (*East of Shanghai*) (+ co-sc): *Number Seventeen* (+ co-sc)
1933 *Waltzes from Vienna* (*Strauss's Great Waltz*; *The Great Waltz*)
1934 *The Man Who Knew Too Much*

1935 ***The Thirty-Nine Steps*** (+ bit role as passerby)
1936 *Secret Agent*; *Sabotage* (*The Woman Alone*)
1937 *Young and Innocent* (*The Girl Was Young*) (+ bit as photographer outside courthouse)
1938 ***The Lady Vanishes*** (+ bit role as man at railway station)
1939 *Jamaica Inn*
1940 *Rebecca* (+ bit role as man outside phone booth); *Foreign Correspondent* (+ bit role as man reading newspaper)
1941 *Mr. and Mrs. Smith* (+ bit role as passerby); *Suspicion*
1942 *Saboteur* (+ bit role as man by newsstand)
1943 *Shadow of a Doubt* (+ bit role as man playing cards on train)
1944 *Life Boat* (+ bit role as man in "Reduco" advertisement); *Bon Voyage* (short); *Aventure Malgache* (*The Malgache Adventure*) (short)
1945 *Spellbound* (+ bit role as man in elevator)
1946 ***Notorious*** (+ story, bit role as man drinking champagne)
1947 *The Paradine Case* (+ bit role as man with cello)
1948 *Rope* (+ bit role as man crossing street)
1949 *Under Capricorn*; *Stage Fright* (+ bit role as passerby)
1951 ***Strangers on a Train*** (+ bit role as man boarding train with cello)
1953 *I Confess* (+ bit role as man crossing top of flight of steps)
1954 *Dial M for Murder* (+ bit role as man in school reunion dinner photo); ***Rear Window*** (+ bit role as man winding clock); *To Catch a Thief* (+ bit role as man at back of bus); *The Trouble with Harry* (+ bit role as man walking past exhibition)
1955 *The Man Who Knew Too Much* (+ bit role as man watching acrobats);
1956 *The Wrong Man* (+ intro appearance)
1957 ***Vertigo*** (+ bit role as passerby)
1959 ***North by Northwest*** (+ bit role as man who misses bus)
1960 ***Psycho*** (+ bit role as man outside realtor's office)
1963 ***The Birds*** (+ bit role as man with two terriers)
1964 ***Marnie*** (+ bit role as man in hotel corridor)
1966 *Torn Curtain* (+ bit role as man in hotel lounge with infant)
1969 *Topaz* (+ bit role as man getting out of wheelchair)
1972 *Frenzy* (+ bit role as man in crowd listening to speech)
1976 *Family Plot* (+ bit role as silhouette on office window)

Other Films:

1920 *The Great Day* (Ford) (inter-titles des); *The Call of Youth* (Ford) (inter-titles des)
1921 *The Princess of New York* (Crisp) (inter-titles des); *Appearances* (Crisp) (inter-titles des); *Dangerous Lies* (Powell) (inter-titles des); *The Mystery Road* (Powell) (inter-titles des); *Beside the Bonnie Brier Bush* (*The Bonnie Brier Bush*) (Crisp) (inter-titles des)
1922 *Three Live Ghosts* (Fitzmaurice) (inter-titles des); *Perpetua* (*Love's Boomerang*) (Robertson and Geraghty) (inter-titles des); *The Man from Home* (Fitzmaurice) (inter-titles des); *Spanish Jade* (Robertson and Geraghty) (inter-titles des); *Tell Your Children* (Crisp) (inter-titles des)
1923 *Woman to Woman* (Cutts) (co-sc, asst-d, art-d, ed); *The White Shadow* (*White Shadows*) (Cutts) (art-d, ed)
1924 *The Passionate Adventure* (Cutts) (co-sc, asst-d, art-d); *The Prude's Fall* (Cutts) (asst-d, art-d)
1925 *The Blackguard* (*Die Prinzessin und der Geiger*) (Cutts) (asst-d, art-d)
1932 *Lord Camber's Ladies* (Levy) (pr)
1940 *The House Across the Bay* (Mayo) (d add'l scenes); *Men of the Lightship* (MacDonald, short) (reediting, dubbing of U.S. version)
1941 *Target for Tonight* (Watt) (supervised reediting of U.S. version)
1960 *The Gazebo* (Marshall) (voice on telephone telling Glenn Ford how to dispose of corpse)
1963 *The Directors* (pr: Greenblatt) (appearance)
1970 *Makin' It* (Hartog) (documentary appearance from early thirties)
1977 *Once Upon a Time ... Is Now* (Billington, for TV) (role as interviewee)

Publications

By HITCHCOCK: book—

Le Cinéma selon Hitchcock, with François Truffaut, Paris, 1966; published as *Hitchcock,* New York, 1985.

By HITCHCOCK: articles—

"My Own Methods," in *Sight and Sound* (London), Summer 1937.
"On Suspense and Other Matters," in *Films in Review* (New York), April 1950.
Interview with Claude Chabrol, in *Cahiers du Cinéma* (Paris), February 1955.
Interview with Catherine de la Roche, in *Sight and Sound* (London), Winter 1955/56.
"Rencontre avec Alfred Hitchcock," with François Truffaut, in *Cahiers du Cinéma* (Paris), September 1956.
"Alfred Hitchcock Talking," in *Films and Filming* (London), July 1959.
Interview with Ian Cameron and V.F. Perkins, in *Movie* (London), 6 January 1963.
"Hitchcock on Style," in *Cinema* (Beverly Hills), August/September 1963.
"*Rear Window,*" in *Take One* (Montreal), November/December 1968.
"Alfred Hitchcock: The German Years," an interview with B. Thomas, in *Action* (Los Angeles), January/February 1973.
"Hitchcock," transcript of address to Film Society of Lincoln Center, 29 April 1974, in *Film Comment* (New York), July/August 1974.
"Hitchcock," an interview with Andy Warhol, in *Inter/View* (New York), September 1974.
"Surviving," an interview with John Taylor, in *Sight and Sound* (London), Summer 1977.

On HITCHCOCK: books—

Amengual, Barthélémy, and Raymond Borde, *Alfred Hitchcock,* Paris, 1957.
Rohmer, Eric, and Claude Chabrol, *Hitchcock,* Paris, 1957.
Bogdanovich, Peter, *The Cinema of Alfred Hitchcock,* New York, 1962.
Perry, George, *The Films of Alfred Hitchcock,* London, 1965.
Wood, Robin, *Hitchcock's Films,* London, 1965; published as *Hitchcock's Films Revisited,* New York, 1989.
Douchet, Jean, *Alfred Hitchcock,* Paris, 1967.
Simsolo, Noel, *Alfred Hitchcock,* Paris, 1969.
Taylor, John Russell, *Hitch,* New York, 1978.
Bellour, Raymond, *L'Analyse du film,* Paris, 1979.
Fieschi, J.-A., and others, *Hitchcock,* Paris, 1981.
Hemmeter, Thomas M., *Hitchcock the Stylist,* Ann Arbor, Michigan, 1981.
Bazin, Andre, *The Cinema of Cruelty: From Bunuel to Hitchcock,* New York, 1982.
Narboni, Jean, editor, *Alfred Hitchcock,* Paris, 1982.
Rothman, William, *Hitchcock—The Murderous Gaze,* Cambridge, Massachusetts, 1982.
Spoto, Donald, *The Dark Side of Genius: The Life of Alfred Hitchcock,* New York, 1982.

Weis, Elisabeth, *The Silent Scream: Alfred Hitchcock's Sound Track,* Rutherford, New Jersey, 1982.
Belton, John, *Cinema Stylists,* Metuchen, New Jersey, 1983.
Phillips, Gene D., *Alfred Hitchcock,* Boston, 1984.
Douchet, Jean, *Alfred Hitchcock,* Paris, 1985.
Deutelbaum, Marshall, and Leland Poague, *A Hitchcock Reader,* Ames, Iowa, 1986.
Hogan, David J., *Dark Romance: Sexuality in the Horror Film,* Jefferson, North Carolina, 1986.
Humphries, Patrick, *The Films of Alfred Hitchcock,* Greenwich, Connecticut, 1986.
Kloppenburg, Josef, *Die Dramaturgische Funktion der Musik in Filmen Alfred Hitchcocks,* Munich, 1986.
Ryall, Tom, *Alfred Hitchcock and the British Cinema,* London, 1986.
Sinyard, Neil, *The Films of Alfred Hitchcock,* London, 1986.
Leff, Leonard J., *Hitchcock and Selznick: The Rich and Strange Collaboration of Alfred Hitchcock and David O. Selznick in Hollywood,* New York, 1987.
Modleski, Tania, *The Women Who Knew Too Much: Hitchcock and Feminist Theory,* New York, 1988.
Brill, Linda, *The Hitchcock Romance: Love and Irony in Hitchcock's Films,* Princeton, New Jersey, 1988.
Leitch, Thomas M., *Find the Director and Other Hitchcock Games,* Athens, Georgia, 1991.
Raubicheck, Walter, and Walter Srebnick, eds., *Hitchcock's Rereleased Films: From Rope to Vertigo,* Detroit, 1991.
Sharff, Stefan, *Alfred Hitchcock's High Vernacular: Theory and Practice,* New York, 1991.
Finler, Joel W., *Hitchcock in Hollywood,* New York, 1992.
Kapsis, Robert E., *Hitchcock: The Making of a Reputation,* Chicago, 1992.
Price, Theodore, *Hitchcock and Homosexuality: His 50-year Obsession with Jack the Ripper and the Superbitch Prostitute,* Metuchen, New Jersey, 1992.
Spoto, Donald, *The Art of Alfred Hitchcock: Fifty Years of His Motion Pictures,* New York, 1992.
Corber, Robert J., *In the Name of National Security: Hitchcock, Homophobia, and the Political Construction of Gender in Postwar America,* Durham, North Carolina, 1993.
Hurley, Neil P., *Soul in Suspense: Hitchcock's Fright and Delight,* Metuchen, New Jersey, 1993.
Naremore, James, *North by Northwest: Alfred Hitchcock, Director,* New Brunswick, New Jersey, 1993.
Sloan, Jane, *Alfred Hitchcock: A Guide to References and Sources,* New York, 1993.
Arginteanu, Judy, *The Movies of Alfred Hitchcock,* Minneapolis, 1994.
Gottlieb, Sidney, ed., *Hitchcock on Film: Selected Writings and Interviews,* Berkeley, California, 1995.

On HITCHCOCK: articles—

Pratley, Gerald, "Alfred Hitchcock's Working Credo," in *Films in Review* (New York), December 1952.
"Hitchcock Issue" of *Cahiers du Cinéma* (Paris), October 1953.
May, Derwent, in *Sight and Sound* (London), October/December 1954.
Bazin, André, "Alfred Hitchcock," in *Radio, Cinéma, Télévision* (Paris), 23 January 1955.
Sarris, Andrew, "The Trouble with Hitchcock," in *Film Culture* (New York), Winter 1955.
"Hitchcock Issue" of *Cahiers du Cinéma* (Paris), August/September 1956.
Pett, John, "A Master of Suspense," in *Films and Filming* (London), November and December 1959.
Cameron, Ian, "Hitchcock and the Mechanics of Suspense," in *Movie* (London), October 1962.
Higham, Charles, "Hitchcock's World," in *Film Quarterly* (Berkeley), December/January 1962/63.
Houston, Penelope, "The Figure in the Carpet," in *Sight and Sound* (London), Autumn 1963.
Truffaut, François, "Skeleton Keys," in *Film Culture* (New York), Spring 1964.
Cameron, Ian, and Richard Jeffrey, "The Universal Hitchcock," in *Movie* (London), Spring 1965.
"An Alfred Hitchcock Index," in *Films in Review* (New York), April 1966.
Sonbert, Warren, "Alfred Hitchcock: Master of Morality," in *Film Culture* (New York), Summer 1966.
Lightman, Herb, "Hitchcock Talks about Light, Camera, Action," in *American Cinematographer* (Hollywood), May 1967.
Braudy, Leo, "Hitchcock, Truffaut, and the Irresponsible Audience," in *Film Quarterly* (Berkeley), Summer 1968.
Houston, Penelope, "Hitchcockery," in *Sight and Sound* (London), Autumn 1968.
Millar, Gavin, "Hitchcock versus Truffaut," in *Sight and Sound* (London), Spring 1969.
Durgnat, Raymond, "The Strange Case of Alfred Hitchcock," in *Films and Filming* (London), February 1970 through November 1970.
Smith, J.M., "Conservative Individualism: A Selection of English Hitchcock," in *Screen* (London), Autumn 1972.
Kaplan, G., "Lost in the Wood," in *Film Comment* (New York), November/December 1972.
Poague, Lee, "The Detective in Hitchcock's *Frenzy*: His Ancestors and Significance," in *Journal of Popular Film* (Bowling Green, Ohio), Winter 1973.
Sarris, Andrew, "Alfred Hitchcock, Prankster of Paradox," in *Film Comment* (New York), March/April 1974.
Simer, D., "Hitchcock and the Well-Wrought Effect," in *Literature/Film Quarterly* (Salisbury, Maryland), Summer 1975.
Fisher, R., "The Hitchcock Camera 'I'," in *Filmmakers Newsletter* (Ward Hill, Massachusetts), December 1975.
Silver, A.J., "Fragments of a Mirror: Uses of Landscape in Hitchcock," in *Wide Angle* (Athens, Ohio), v. 1, no. 3, 1976.
Bellour, Raymond, "Hitchcock, the Enunciator," in *Camera Obscura* (Berkeley), Fall 1977.
Lehman, Ernest, "He Who Gets Hitched," in *American Film* (Washington, D.C.), May 1978.
"Hitchcock Section" of *Wide Angle* (Athens, Ohio), vol. 4, no. 1, 1980.
Combs, Richard, "Perché Hitchcock?," and Ivor Montagu, "Working with Hitchcock," in *Sight and Sound* (London), Summer 1980.
"Hitchcock Issue" of *Cinématographe* (Paris), July/August 1980.
Lehman, Ernest, "Hitch," in *American Film* (Washington, D.C.), August 1980.
Wollen, P., "Hybrid Plots in *Psycho,*" in *Framework* (Norwich, England), Autumn 1980.
Belton, John, "Alfred Hitchcock's *Under Capricorn*: Montage entranced by mise-en-scène," in *Quarterly Review of Film Studies* (New York), Fall 1981.
"Hitchcock Issue" of *Camera/Stylo* (Paris), November 1981.
Brown, R.S., "Herrmann, Hitchcock, and the Music of the Irrational," in *Cinema Journal* (Chicago), Spring 1982.
Rossi, J., "Hitchcock's *Foreign Correspondent,*" in *Film and History* (Newark, New Jersey), May 1982.
"Hitchcock Issue" of *Avant-Scène du Cinéma* (Paris), 1 December 1982.
Wood, Robin, "Fear of Spying," in *American Film* (Washington, D.C.), November 1983.
Jenkins, Steve, and Richard Combs, "Hitchcock x 2. Refocussing the Spectator: Just Enough Rope ...," in *Monthly Film Bulletin* (London), February 1984.
Sussex, Elizabeth, "The Fate of F3080," in *Sight and Sound* (London), Spring 1984.

Kehr, Dave, "Hitch's Riddle," in *Film Comment* (New York), May/June 1984.

"Hitchcock Issues" of *Revue Belge du Cinéma* (Brussels), Autumn 1984 and Winter 1984/85.

Bannon, B.M., "Double, Double, Toil and Trouble," in *Literature/Film Quarterly* (Salisbury, Maryland), January 1985.

Allen, J. Thomas, "The Representation of Violence to Women: Hitchcock's *Frenzy,*" in *Film Quarterly* (Berkeley), Spring 1985.

French, Philip, "Alfred Hitchcock—The Filmmaker as Englishman and Exile," in *Sight and Sound* (London), Spring 1985.

Kapsis, Robert E., "Alfred Hitchcock: Auteur or Hack?," in *Cineaste* (New York), vol. 14, no. 3, 1986.

Zirnite, D., "Hitchcock, On the Level: The Heights of Spatial Tension," in *Film Criticism* (Meadville, Pennsylvania), Spring 1986.

Miller, G., "Beyond the Frame: Hitchcock, Art, and the Ideal," in *Post Script* (Jacksonville, Florida), Winter 1986.

Abel, Richard, "*Stage Fright*: The Knowing Performance," in *Film Criticism* (Meadville, Pennsylvania), no. 1/2, 1987.

Anderegg, Michael, "Hitchcock's *The Paradine Case* and Filmic Unpleasure," in *Cinema Journal* (Chicago), vol. 26, no. 4, 1987.

Kapsis, Robert E., "Hollywood Filmmaking and Reputation Building: Hitchcock's *The Birds,*" in *Journal of Popular Film and TV* (Washington, D.C.), Spring 1987.

Greig, Donald, "The Sexual Differentiation of the Hitchcock Text," in *Screen* (London), Winter 1987.

Lee, Sander H., "Escape and Commitment in Hitchcock's *Rear Window,*" in *Post Script* (Jacksonville, Florida), vol. 7, no. 2, 1988.

Wood, Robin, "Symmetry, Closure, Disruption: The Ambiguity of *Blackmail,*" in *CineAction!* (Toronto), no. 15, 1988.

American Cinematographer (Los Angeles), January 1990.

Desowitz, Bill, "Strangers on Which Train?" in *Film Comment* (New York), May/June 1992.

Wood, Brett, "Foreign Correspondence: The Rediscovered War Films of Alfred Hitchcock," in *Film Comment* (New York), July/August 1993.

Green, Susan, "The Trouble with Hitch," in *Premiere,* February 1994.

On HITCHCOCK: films—

Casson, Philip, *Interview with Alfred Hitchcock,* for TV, Great Britain, 1966.

Ya'acovolitz, M., and S. Melul, *Im Hitchcock bi Yerushalayin (With Hitchcock in Jerusalem),* short, Israel 1967.

Schickel, Richard, *The Men Who Made the Movies: Alfred Hitchcock,* for TV, U.S., 1973.

* * *

In a career spanning just over fifty years (1925-1976), Hitchcock completed fifty-three feature films, twenty-three in the British period, thirty in the American. Through the early British films we can trace the evolution of his professional/artistic image, the development of both the Hitchcock style and the Hitchcock thematic. His third film (and first big commercial success), *The Lodger,* was crucial in establishing him as a maker of thrillers, but it was not until the mid-1930s that his name became consistently identified with that genre. In the meantime, he assimilated the two aesthetic influences that were major determinants in the formation of his mature style: German Expressionism and Soviet montage theory. The former, with its aim of expressing emotional states through a deformation of external reality, is discernible in his work from the beginning (not surprisingly, as he has acknowledged Lang's *Die müde Tod* as his first important cinematic experience, and as some of his earliest films were shot in German studios). Out of his later contact with the Soviet films of the 1920s evolved his elaborate editing techniques: he particularly acknowledged the significance for him of the Kuleshov experiment, from which he derived his fondness for the point-of-view shot and for building sequences by cross-cutting between person seeing/thing seen.

The extreme peculiarity of Hitchcock's art (if his films do not seem very odd it is only because they are so familiar) can be partly accounted for by the way in which these aesthetic influences from high art and revolutionary socialism were pressed into the service of British middle-class popular entertainment. Combined with Hitchcock's all-pervasive scepticism ("Everything's perverted in a different way, isn't it?"), this process resulted in an art that at once endorsed (superficially) and undermined (profoundly) the value system of the culture within which it was produced, be that culture British or American.

During the British period the characteristic plot structures that recur throughout Hitchcock's work are also established. I want here to single out three examples of his work, not because they account for *all* of the films, but because they link the British to the American period, because their recurrence is particularly obstinate, and because they seem, taken in conjunction, central to the thematic complex of Hitchcock's total *oeuvre.*

The first Hitchcock theme is the story about *the accused man*: this is already established in *The Lodger* (in which the male protagonist is suspected of being Jack the Ripper); it often takes the form of the "double chase," in which the hero is pursued by the police and in turn pursues (or seeks to unmask) the actual villains. Examples in the British period are *The 39 Steps* and *Young and Innocent.* In the American period it becomes the commonest of all Hitchcock plot structures: *Saboteur, Spellbound, Strangers on a Train, I Confess, To Catch a Thief, The Wrong Man, North by Northwest,* and *Frenzy* are all based on it.

A second Hitchcock plot device is the story about *the guilty woman*: although there are guilty women in earlier films, the structure is definitively established in *Blackmail,* Hitchcock's (and Britain's) first sound film. We may also add *Sabotage* from the British period, but it is in the American period that examples proliferate: *Rebecca* (Hitchcock's first Hollywood film), *Notorious, Under Capricorn, The Paradine Case, Vertigo, Psycho* (the first third), *The Birds,* and *Marnie* are all variations on the original structure.

It is striking to observe that the opposition of the two themes discussed above is almost complete; there are very few Hitchcock films in which the accused man turns out to be guilty after all (*Shadow of a Doubt* and *Stage Fright* are the obvious exceptions; *Suspicion* would have been a third if Hitchcock had been permitted to carry out his original intentions), and no Hitchcock film features an accused woman who turns out to be innocent (*Dial M for Murder* comes closest, but even there, although the heroine is innocent of murder, she is guilty of adultery). Second, it should be noticed that while the falsely accused man is usually (not quite always) the central consciousness of type one, it is less habitually the case that the guilty woman is the central consciousness of type two: frequently, she is the object of the male protagonist's investigation. Third, the outcome of the guilty woman films (and this may be dictated as much by the Motion Picture Production Code as by Hitchcock's personal morality) is dependent upon the *degree* of guilt: the woman can sometimes be "saved" by the male protagonist (*Blackmail, Notorious, Marnie*), but not if she is guilty of murder or an accomplice to it (*The Paradine Case, Vertigo*).

Other differences between the two types of films are also evident. One should note the function of the opposite sex in the two types, for example. The heroine of the falsely accused man films is, typically, hostile to the hero at first, believing him guilty; she subsequently learns to trust him, and takes his side in establishing his innocence. The function of the male protagonist in the guilty woman films, on the other hand, is either to save the heroine or to be destroyed (at least morally and spiritually) by her. It is important to recognize that the true nature of the guilt is always sexual, and that the falsely accused man is usually seen to be contaminated by this (though inno-

Alfred Hitchcock

cent of the specific crime, typically murder, of which he is accused). Richard Hannay in *The 39 Steps* can stand as the prototype of this: when he allows himself to be picked up by the woman in the music hall, it is in expectation of a sexual encounter, the notion of sexual disorder being displaced on to "espionage," and the film systematically moves from this towards the construction of the "good" (i.e. socially approved) couple. The very title of *Young and Innocent,* with its play on the connotations of the last word, exemplifies the same point, and it is noteworthy that in that film the hero's *sexual* innocence remains in doubt (we only have his own word for it that he was not the murdered woman's gigolo). Finally, the essential Hitchcockian dialectic can be read from the alternation, throughout his career, of these two series. On the whole, it is the guilty woman films that are the more disturbing, that leave the most jarring dissonances: here, the potentially threatening and subversive female sexuality, precariously contained within social norms in the falsely accused man films, erupts to demand recognition and is answered by an appalling violence (both emotional and physical); the cost of its destruction or containment leaves that "nasty taste" often noted as the dominant characteristic of Hitchcock's work.

It is within this context that the third plot structure takes on its full significance: the story about the *psychopath.* Frequently, this structure occurs in combination with the falsely accused man plot (see, for example, *Young and Innocent, Strangers on a Train, Frenzy,*) with a parallel established between the hero and his perverse and sinister adversary, who becomes a kind of shadowy alter ego. Only two Hitchcock films have the psychopath as their indisputably central figure, but they (*Shadow of a Doubt, Psycho*) are among his most famous and disturbing. The Hitchcock villain has a number of characteristics which are not necessarily common to all but unite in various combinations: a) Sexual "perversity" or ambiguity: a number are more or less explicitly coded as gay (the transvestite killer in *Murder!,* Philip in *Rope,* Bruno Anthony in *Strangers on a Train*); others have marked mother-fixations (Uncle Charlie in *Shadow of a Doubt,* Anthony Perkins in *Psycho,* Bob Rusk in *Frenzy*), seen as a source of their psychic disorder; (b) Fascist connotations: this becomes politically explicit in the U-boat commander of *Lifeboat,* but is plain enough in, for example, *Shadow of a Doubt* and *Rope;* (c) The subtle associations of the villain with the devil: Uncle Charlie and Smoke in *Shadow of a Doubt,* Bruno Anthony in the paddle-boat named Pluto in *Strangers on a Train,* Norman Bates' remark to Marion Crane that "no one ever comes here unless they've gotten off the main highway" in *Psycho;* (d) Closely connected with these characteristics is a striking and ambiguous fusion of power and impotence operating on both the sexual and non-sexual levels. What is crucially significant here is that this feature is by no means restricted to the villains. It is shared, strikingly, by the male protagonists of what are perhaps Hitchcock's two supreme masterpieces, *Rear Window* and *Vertigo.*

The latter aspect of Hitchcock works also relates closely to the obsession with control (and the fear of losing it) that characterized Hitchcock's own methods of filmmaking: his preoccupation with a totally finalized and story-boarded shooting script, his domination of actors and shooting conditions. Finally, it's notable that the psychopath/villain is invariably the most fascinating and seductive character of the film, and its chief source of energy. His inevitable destruction leaves behind an essentially empty world.

If one adds together all these factors, one readily sees why Hitchcock is so much more than the skillful entertainer and master craftsman he was once taken for. His films represent an incomparable exposure of the sexual tensions and anxieties (especially *male* anxieties) that characterize a culture built upon repression, sexual inequality, and the drive to domination.

—Robin Wood

HOLGER-MADSEN

Nationality: Danish. **Born:** Holger Madsen, 11 April 1878, began spelling name with hyphen, 1911. **Career:** Actor in Danish provinces, 1896-1904, and in Copenhagen, from 1904; actor in films, from 1907; directed first film, 1912; director for Nordisk Films Kompagni, 1913-20; worked in Germany, from 1920; returned to Denmark, 1930; manager of small Copenhagen cinema, 1938-43. **Died:** 30 November 1943.

Films as Director:

1912 *Kun en Tigger* (+ role)

1913 *Under Savklingens Taender* (*The Usurer's Son*) (+ role); *Under Mindernes Trae* (*Dengamle Baenk, Left Alone*); *Skaebnens Veje* (*Under Kaerlighedens Aag*; *In the Bonds of Passion*); *Det mørke Punkt* (*Staalkongens Vilje*; *The Steel King's Last Wish*); *Mens Pesten raser* (*Laegens Hustru*; *During the Plague*); *Ballettens Datter* (*Danserinden*; *Unjustly Accused*); *Elskovsleg* (*Love's Devotee*); *Prinsesse Elena* (*The Princess's Dilemma*); *Den hvide Dame* (*The White Ghost*); *Fra Fyrste til Knejpevaert* (*The Gambler's Wife*); *Millionaerdrengen* (*The Adventures of a Millionaire's Son*); *Guldet og vort Hjerte* (*Et vanskeligt Valg*; *The Heart's Voice*)

1914 *Tempeldanserindens Elskov* (*Bajaderens Haevn*; *The Bayadere's Revenge*); *Børnevennerne* (*A Marriage of Convenience*); *En Opstandelse* (*Genopstandelsen*; *A Resurrection*); *Husassistenten* (*Naar Fruen skifter Pige*; *The New Cook*); *Søvngaengersken* (*The Somnambulist*); *Opiumsdrømmen* (*The Opium Smoker's Dream*); *Den mystiske Fremmede* (*A Deal with the Devil*); *Endelig Alene* (*Alone at Last*); *Min Ven Levy* (*My Friend Levy*); *Ned med Vaabnene* (*Lay Down Your Arms*); *Trold kan taemmes* (*The Taming of the Shrew*); *De Forviste* (*Uden Faedreland*; *Without a Country*); *Et Huskors* (*Lysten styret*; *Enough of It*); *Barnets Magt* (*The Child*); *Et Haremseventyr* (*An Adventure in a Harem*); *Evangeliemandens Liv* (*The Candle and the Moth*); *Kaerlighedens Triumf* (*Testamentet*; *The Romance of a Will*); *Krig og Kaerlighed* (*Love and War*); *Spiritisten* (*A Voice from the Past*): *Det stjaalne Ansigt* (*The Missing Admiralty Plans*); *En Aeresoprejsning* (*Misunderstood*); *Liykken draeber*

1915 *Cigaretpigen* (*The Cigarette Maker*); *Hvem er Gentlemantyven* (*Strakoff the Adventurer*); *En Ildprøve* (*A Terrible Ordeal*); *Danserindens Haevn* (*Circus Arrives*; *The Dancer's Revenge*); *Danserindens Kaerlighedsdrøm* (*Den Dødsdømte*; *A Dancer's Strange Dream*; *The Condemned*); *Den frelsende Film* (*The Woman Tempted Me*); *Grevinde Hjerteløs* (*The Beggar Princess*); *Guldets Gift* (*The Tempting of Mrs. Chestney*); *Den hvide Djaevel* (*Caught in the Toils*; *The Devil's Protege*); *Hvo som elsker sin Fader or Faklen* (*Who So Loveth His Father's Honor*); *I Livets Braending* (*The Crossroads of Life*); *Manden uden Fremtid* (*The Man without a Future*); *Den omstridte Jord* (*Jordens Haevn*; *The Earth's Revenge*); *Sjaeletyven* (*The Unwilling Sinner*; *His Innocent Dupe*); *Det unge Blod* (*The Buried Secret*); *Krigens Fjende* (*Acostates første Offer*; *The Munition Conspiracy*); *En Kunstners Gennembrud* (*Den Dødes Sjael*; *The Soul of the Violin*)

1916 *For sin Faders Skyld* (*The Veiled Lady*; *False Evidence*); *Maaneprinsessen* (*Kamaeleonen*; *The Mysterious Lady*; *The May-Fly*); *Børnenes Synd* (*The Sins of the Children*); *Fange no. 113* (*Convict No. 113*); *Hans rigtige Kone* (*Which Is*

Holger-Madsen: *Himmelskibet*

Which); *Hendes Moders Løfte* (*Dødens Kontrakt*; *A Super Shylock*); *Hittebarnet* (*The Foundling of Fate*): *Hvor Sorgerne glemmes* (*Søster Cecilies Offer*; *Sister Cecilia*); *Livets Gøglespil* (*An Impossible Marriage*); *Manden uden Smil*; *Nattens Mysterium* (*Who Killed Barno O'Neal*); *Nattevandreren* (*Edison Maes Dagbog*; *Out of the Underworld*); *Pax Aeterna*; *Lydia* (*The Music Hall Star*); *Lykken* (*The Road to Happiness*; *Guiding Conscience*); *Praestens Datter*; *Testamentets Hemmelighed* (*Den Dødes Røst*; *The Voice of the Dead*; *Nancy Keith*); *Den Aereløse* (*The Infamous*; *The Prison Taint*); *Smil* (*Far's Sorg*; *Father Sorrow*; *The Beggar Man of Paris*)

1917 *Himmelskibet* (*A Trip to Mars*); *Retten sejrer* (*Justice Victorious*); *Hendes Helt* (*Vogt dig for dine Venner*)

1918 *Folkets Ven* (*A Friend of the People*); *Mod Lyset* (*Towards the Light*); *Manden, der sejrede* (*The Man Who Tamed the Victors*; *Fighting Instinct*)

1919 *Gudernes Yndling* (*Digterkongen*; *Trials of Celebrity*; *The Penalty of Fame*); *Har jeg Ret til at tage mit eget Liv* (*Flugten fra Livet*; *The Flight from Life*; *Beyond the Barricade*); *Det Störste i Verden* (*Janes gode Ven*; *The Greatest in the World*; *The Love That Lives*)

1921 *Am Webstuhl der Zeit*; *Tobias Buntschuh* (+ role); *Den dvende Stad* (*Die sterbende Stadt*)

1922 *Pømperly's Kampf mit dem Schneeschuh* (co-d)

1923 *Das Evangelium*; *Zaida, die Tragødie eines Modells*

1924 *Der Mann um Mitternacht*

1925 *Ein Lebenskünstler*

1926 *Die seltsame Nacht*; *Die Sporck'schen Jäger*; *Spitzen*

1927 *Die heilige Lüge*

1928 *Freiwild*; *Die seltsame Nacht der Helga Wansen*; *Was ist los mit Nanette*

1934 *København, Kalundborg og—?* (co-d)

1936 *Sol over Danmark*

Films as Actor:

1907 *Den sorte Hertug*

1908 *Magdalene*; *En grov Spøg* (*A Practical Joke and a Sad End*); *Verdens Herkules* (*Hercules the Athlete*); *Karneval* (*The Bank Director, Carnival*); *Svend Dyrings Hus* (*The Stepmother*); *De smaa Landstrygere* (*Sold to Thieves*); *Smaeklaasen* (*The Spring Lock*); *Natten før Kristians Fødelsdag* (*The Night Before Christian's Birthday*); *Rulleskøjterne* (*On Roller Skates*); *Sherlock Holmes I*; *Sherlock Holmes III*

1909 *Den graa Dame* (*The Gray Dame*)

1911 *Det store Fald or Malstrømmen*; *Dødssejleren or Dynamitattentatet paa Fyrtaarnet*; *Den svarte doktorn*

1912 *Paa Livets Skyggeside*

1913 *Elskovs Mast*

1931 *Praesten i Vejlby*; *Krudt med Knald*

1933 *Fem raske Piger*; *Med tuld Musik*

1934 *Lynet; 7-9-13*
1935 *Kidnapped*

* * *

The two leading directors at Nordisk Films Kompagni in the Golden Age of the Danish cinema from 1910 to 1914 were August Blom and Holger-Madsen. They were similar in many respects. They both started as actors, but unlike Blom, Holger-Madsen began as a director with companies other than Nordisk. When he came to Nordisk he worked in almost all of the genres of the period—sensational films, comedies, farces, dramas, and tragedies. Gradually, though, Holger-Madsen developed his own personality, both in content and style.

Holger-Madsen specialized in films with spiritual topics. His main film in this genre was *Evangeliemandens Liv,* in which Valdemar Psilander plays the leading part of a dissolute young man of good family who suddenly realizes how empty and pointless his life is. He becomes a Christian and starts working as a preacher among the poor and the social outcasts of the big city. He succeeds in rescuing a young man from the path of sin. Several of the cliches of the period are featured in this tale, but the characterization of the hero is largely free of sentimentality, and Holger-Madsen coached Psilander into playing the role with a mature, calm, and genuine strength of feeling. Formally the film is exquisite. The sets, the camerawork, and the lighting are executed with great care, and the film is rich in striking pictorial compositions, which was the director's forte.

Holger-Madsen had a predilection for extraordinary, often bizarre images and picturesque surroundings. With his cameraman, Marius Clausen, he emphasized the visual look of his films. His use of side light, inventive camera angles, and close-ups, combined with unusual sets, made him an original stylist. He was not very effective in his cutting technique, but he could establish marvelously choreographed scenes in which people moved in elegant patterns within the frame.

Holger-Madsen's reputation as an idealistic director led him to direct the big prestige films with pacifist themes which Ole Olsen, the head of Nordisk Films Kompagni, wanted to make in the naive hope that he could influence the fighting powers in the First World War. The films were often absurdly simple, but Holger-Madsen brought his artistic sense to the visual design of these sentimental stories. One of his most famous films is *Himmelskibet* from 1917, a work about a scientist who flies to Mars in a rocket ship. There he is confronted with a peaceful civilization. The film has obtained a position as one of the first science fiction films.

When the Danish cinema declined, Holger-Madsen went to Germany. Returning to Denmark after the 1920s, he was offered the opportunity of directing during the early sound film period, but his productions were insignificant. He was a silent film director; the image was his domain, and he was one of the craftsmen who molded and refined the visual language of film.

—Ib Monty

HOLLAND, Agnieszka

Nationality: Polish. **Born:** Warsaw, Poland, 28 November 1948. **Education:** Graduated from the Filmova Akademie Muzickych Umeni (FAMU) film school in Prague, where she studied directing. **Career:** Maintained her studies in Prague even after the Soviet invasion; was jailed by the authorities after months of harassment by police, 1970; returned to Poland and became member of film collective "X," headed by Andrzej Wajda, 1972; began career as a production assistant to director Krzysztof Zanussi on *Illumination,* 1973; worked in Polish theatre and television, 1970s; began authoring scripts of films directed by Wajda, 1979; directed first feature, *Provincial Actors,* 1979; moved to Paris after the declaration of martial law in Poland, and began making documentaries for French television, 1981; earned first major international acclaim for *Angry Harvest,* 1985; member of board of directors of Zespoly Filmowne; member of board of directors of Polish Filmmakers Association. **Awards:** Award at TV Films and Plays Festival, Olsztyn, 1976; Prize at San Remo Festival, and MIFED, Milan, 1976, for *Sunday Children;* Grand Prix, Koszalin Festival, 1979, for *Provincial Actors;* Co-winner, International Critics Prize, Cannes Festival, 1980, for *Provincial Actors;* Grand Prize, Gdansk Festival, 1981, for *The Fever;* New Cinema Grand Prize, Montreal Festival, 1981, for *A Woman Alone;* Oscar nomination, Best Foreign Language Film, 1985, for *Angry Harvest;* Golden Globe Award, Best Foreign Language Film, National Board of Review, Best Foreign Language Film, and Oscar nomination, Best Screenplay, 1990, for *Europa, Europa.* **Agent:** William Morris, 151 E. Camino Drive, Beverly Hills, CA 90212.

Films as Director/Screenwriter:

1974 *Evening at Abdon's* (*An Evening at Abdon*) (for TV)
1976 *Niedzielne Dzieci* (*Sunday Children*) (for TV)
1977 *Something for Something* (for TV); *Screen Tests* (episode in sketch film)
1979 *Aktorzy prowincjonalni* (*Provincial Actors*)
1981 *Fever* (*The Fever: The Story of the Bomb*)
1982 *A Woman Alone* (*A Lonely Woman*) (co-dir)
1984 *Bittere ernte* (*Angry Harvest*)
1988 *To Kill a Priest* (*Le complot*) (co-sc)
1990 *Europa, Europa*
1991 *Olivier, Olivier*
1993 *The Secret Garden* (d only)
1995 *Total Eclipse* (d only)

Other Films:

1978 *Dead Case* (sc); *Bez znieczulenia* (*Without Anesthesia*; *Rough Treatment*) (Wajda) (sc)
1981 *Cziowiek z zelaza* (*Man of Iron*) (Wajda) (sc)
1982 *Przesluchanie* (role as Witowska)
1983 *Danton* (Wajda) (sc)
1984 *Ein Liebe en Deutschland* (*A Love in Germany*) (Wajda) (sc)
1987 *Anna* (Bogayevicz) (sc); *Les Possedes* (sc)
1988 *La Amiga* (sc)
1990 *Korczak* (Wajda) (sc)
1993 ***Trois Couleurs: Bleu*** (Kieslowski) (additional dialogue)

Publications

By HOLLAND: articles—

"Agnieszka Holland: le cinema polonais cintinue d'exister mais un lui a coupe le souffle," interview by P. Li in *Avant-Scene Cinema* (Paris), December 1983.
"Lessons from the Past," interview by Peter Brunette in *Cineaste* (New York), no. 1, 1986.
"Off-screen: A Pole Apart," interview by J. Hoberman in *Village Voice* (New York), 18 March 1986.
"Dialogue on Film: Agnieszka Holland," in *American Film* (New York), September 1986.

Agnieszka Holland directing *Europa, Europa*

"Lekja historii," interview by J. Wroblewski in *Kino* (Warsaw), August 1989.
Holland, Agnieszka, "Felix dia Wajdy," in *Kino* (Warsaw), April 1991.
"Spotkanie z Agnieszka Holland," interview by T. Lubelshi in *Kino* (Warsaw), April 1991.
"Nowa gra," interview by Z. Benedyktow in *Kino* (Warsaw), 16 February 1992.
"Holland," interview by E. Krolikowska-Avis in *Kino* (Warsaw), October 1992.

On HOLLAND: articles—

"Agnieszka Holland," in *Avant-Scene Cinema* (Paris), December 1983.
Warchol, T., "The End of a Beginning," in *Sight and Sound* (London), no. 3, 1986.
Stone, Judy, "Behind *Angry Harvest*: Polish Politics and Exile," in *New York Times,* 16 March 1986.
Taubin, Amy, "Woman of Irony," in *Village Voice* (New York), 2 July 1991.
Quart, Barbara, "Three Central European Women Directors Revisited," in *Cineaste* (New York), no. 4, 1993
Blinken, A. J., "Going to Extremes," in *Harper's Bazaar* (New York), February 1993.
Cohen, R., "Holland without a Country," in *New York Times,* 8 August 1993.
Taubin, Amy, "Imagination among the Ruins," in *Village Voice* (New York), 17 August 1993.
Clark, J. and Hample, H. S., "Filmographies," in *Premiere* (New York), September 1993.
Quart, Barbara, "The Secret Garden of Agnieszka Holland," in *Ms.* (New York), September/October 1993.
Gaydos, Stephen, "For Holland, Less Is More," in *Variety* (New York), October 30, 1995.

* * *

The death camps were liberated decades ago. Auschwitz and Birkenau, Chelmno and Dachau—the ABCDs of the Final Solution—have long been silent memorials to the mass murder of millions. Despite this passage of time—and despite the media-induced impression that Stephen Spielberg's *Schindler's List* is the only movie ever made which confronts the mass extermination of a people during the Second World War—the Holocaust has long been a topic for filmmakers. One such filmmaker is director Agnieszka Holland.

Holland is a Polish Jew who was born scant years after the end of World War II. The legacy of that era has influenced her life, and her work. She is not so much interested in the politics of the war, in how and why the German people allowed Hitler to come to power. Rather, a common theme in her films is the manner in which individuals responded to Hitler and the Nazi scourge. This is most perfectly exemplified in what is perhaps her most distinguished film to date: *Europa, Europa,* a German-made feature based on the memoirs of Salamon Perel, who as a teenaged German Jew survived World War II by passing for Aryan in a Hitler Youth academy. This thoughtful, tremendously moving film was the source of controversy on two accounts: it depicts a Jew who compromises himself in order to insure his survival; and it was not named as Germany's official Best Foreign Language Film entrant, making it ineligible in that category for an Academy Award. However, it did earn Holland a nomination for Best Screenplay (based on material from another medium).

Even though Holland only wrote the screenplay for *Korczak*—the film was directed by her mentor, Andrzej Wajda—it too is one of her most impassioned works. Her simple, poignant script chronicles the real-life story of a truly gentle, remarkable man: Janusz Korczak (Wojtek Pszoniak), a respected doctor, writer, and children's rights advocate who operated a home for Jewish orphans in Warsaw during the 1930s. Korczak's concerns are people and not politics. "I love children," he states, simply and matter-of-factly. "I fight for years for the dignity of children." In his school, he offers his charges a humanist education. And then the Nazis invade his homeland. Given his station in life, Korczak easily could arrange his escape to freedom. But he chooses to remain with his children and do whatever he must to keep his orphanage running and his children alive, even after they all have been imprisoned in the Warsaw Ghetto.

After directing several theatrical and made-for-television features in Poland, Holland came to international attention in 1985 with *Angry Harvest,* a superb drama about a wealthy farmer who offers to shelter a Jewish woman in his cellar in World War II Poland. His repressed sexuality transforms this act of kindness into one of hypocrisy, as he attempts to abuse his guest. Films like *Angry Harvest, Korczak,* and *Europa, Europa* serve a necessary, essential purpose: they are tools that can be used to educate young people, Jew and non-Jew alike, about the exploitation and extermination of a race. They are monuments—as much to the memory of generations past as to the survival of generations to come.

Not all of Holland's films have dealt directly with the Holocaust. Another of her themes—which also may be linked to the Holocaust by its very nature—is the loss of innocence among children that occurs not by the natural progression of growing into adulthood, but by odd, jarring circumstances. *Olivier, Olivier,* like *Europa, Europa* and *Korczak,* also is a based-on-fact narrative. It is the intricate account of a country couple whose youngest offspring, Olivier, mysteriously disappears. Six years later he "reappears," but is no longer the special child who was a joy to his family. Rather, he is a Parisian street hustler who claims to have forgotten his childhood. One also can understand Holland's attraction to *The Secret Garden,* an adaptation of the Frances Hodgson Burnett children's story about a ten-year-old orphan who revitalizes a neglected garden in her uncle's Victorian mansion.

Most of Holland's films have been artistically successful. Two exceptions have been *To Kill a Priest,* an ambitious but ultimately clumsy drama about an ill-fated activist priest in Poland; and *Total Eclipse,* about the relationship between French poets Arthur Rimbaud and Paul Verlaine (and based on a play by Christopher Hampton), which was a fiasco—one of the more eagerly anticipated yet disappointing films of 1995. Thankfully, however, these failures comprise the minority of Holland's filmic output.

—Rob Edelman

HONDO, Med

Nationality: Mauritanian. **Born:** Abid Mohamed Medoun Hondo in Mauritania (formerly Mauretania), 4 May 1936. **Education:** Trained as a chef at hotel management school, Rabat, Morocco, 1954-58. **Career:** Moved to France, 1959; worked in restaurants and as Swiss cheese salesman in Paris; took drama classes, from 1965, then formed own theatre company "Shango" (named after Yoruba god of thunder); actor, then assistant director on films, from 1967; directed first feature, *Soleil O,* 1969, and set up production company Films Soleil O; helped found the African Committee of Filmmakers, 1982. **Awards:** Golden Leopard, Locarno Festival, 1970, and International Critics Prize, Pan-African Festival, Ougadougou, 1971, for *Soleil O.*

Films as Director:

1969 *Balade aux sources* (*Ballad to the Sources*) (short); *Partout ou peut-être nulle part* (*Everywhere, Nowhere Maybe*) (short); *Soleil O* (*O Sun*)
1973 *Les Bicots-nègres, vos voisins* (*The Black-Wogs, Your Neighbours*; *Arabs and Niggers, Your Neighbours*)
1977 *Nous aurons toute la mort pour dormir* (*We Have All of Death for Sleeping*; *We'll Sleep When We Die*)
1979 *Polisario, un peuple en armes* (*Polisario, A People in Arms*); *West Indies, les nègres marrons de la liberté*
1986 *Sarraounia*

Other Films:

1967 *Shock Troops* (Costa-Gavras) (role)
1968 *Tante Zita* (Enrico) (role)
1969 *A Walk with Love and Death* (Huston) (role)

Publications

By HONDO: articles—

Interview with Jean Delmas, in *Jeune Cinéma* (Paris), June/July 1970.
Interview with Michel Ciment and Paul-Louis Thirard, in *Positif* (Paris), September 1970.
"Je suis un immigré," an interview with Nourredine Ghali, in *Jeune Cinéma* (Paris), September/October 1974.
Interview, in *Filmfaust* (Frankfurt), September/October 1977.
Interview with Don Ranvaud, in *Framework* (Norwich), Spring 1978.
"What is Cinema for Us?," in *Framework* (Norwich), Autumn 1979.
"Africa: Towards a National Cinema," an interview with Anne Head, in *Screen International* (London), 23 February 1985.
Interview with Mark Reid, in *Jump Cut* (Berkeley), March 1986.
Interview with J. Leahy, in *Monthly Film Bulletin* (London), January 1988.

On HONDO: books—

Martin, Angela, editor, *African Film: The Context of Production,* London, 1982.
Pfaff, Françoise, *25 Black African Filmmakers: A Critical Study,* Westport, Connecticut, 1988.

On HONDO: articles—

Ciment, Michel, "*Soleil O,*" in *Positif* (Paris), September 1970.
"African Film Section" of *Jump Cut* (Berkeley), March 1986.
Mirmont, Roger, "Impressions d'Afrique," in *Première* (Paris), July 1986.

*   *   *

Med Hondo, born in Mauritania but living since 1959 in Paris, is one of the leading figures in African filmmaking. His theatrical background is very apparent in his first feature, *Soleil O,* which comprises a mixture of documentary observations and dramatic scenes and sketches, acted out by a small group of African and Antillean players who take on a variety of successive roles. The film explores the whole range of issues raised by the experiences of an African worker newly arrived in France, beginning with the hero's delusions ("Sweet France ... I've come home") and ending with his anguish and alienation. *Soleil O* has all the qualities and some of the defects of a well-directed piece of agit-prop: some telling points, a few good jokes, and the occasional passage of tedium. But its crucial importance lies in its assured manner of putting forward what had rarely been heard in cinema: an authentically African voice.

In *The Black-Wogs, Your Neighbours (Les bicots-nègres vos voisins)* there is the same potentially powerful collage of documentary and drama, but this time the *cinéma-vérité* elements predominate. As a result, the film raises a mass of interesting issues concerning exploitation, emigration, and culture but has only a limited audience impact, since the argument emerges as too long and undisciplined. Some of the same weaknesses characterise Hondo's documentary in support of the Polisario Front, *We Have All of Death for Sleeping* (*Nous avons toute la mort pour dormir*). There can be little doubt about the sincerity of the filmmaker's commitment or the justice of his message. But the celebration of revolution is little more than lyrical rhetoric, a preaching to the already converted.

Fortunately, Hondo's two subsequent fictional features have shown his dazzling skills as a director of drama. *West Indies* deals with some four centuries of colonial impact in the Antilles and a variety of forms of slavery and oppression. But instead of offering an alternative history as such (in terms of the names and dates of the oppressed), the film gives us visual, spatial enactments of revolt. Using the single stylised set of a slave ship (built in its entirety at an abandoned railway station), *West Indies* offers the celebratory anticipation of the dawn of liberation through the whirling colours and shapes of popular dance. The interweaving of music, sound effects, dance, declamation, and song gives *West Indies* a forceful impact.

Set in the 1890s, *Sarraounia* chronicles the exemplary resistance of the pagan queen of the Aznas to a powerful and well-armed French force which rampages across the country, threatening all who stand in its path. But the film is not the story of an individual princess and her prowess. Instead, Hondo is concerned with dramatically spelling out the unity of pagan and Moslem Africans against a violent force which disintegrates under the pressures wrought by the overweening personal ambition of the French commander. The director's confident handling of his resources and masterly sense of pace and rhythm place him in the forefront of contemporary African filmmaking.

—Roy Armes

HOU Hsiao-Hsien

Nationality: Taiwanese. **Born:** Hour Shiaw-shyan (name in pinyin, Hou Xiaoxian) in Meixian, Kuangtung (Canton) province, 8 April 1947; moved to Hualien, Taiwan, 1948. **Education:** Attended the film program of the Taiwan National Academy of the Arts, 1969-72. **Career:** Electronic calculator salesman, 1972-73; script boy, then assistant director, from 1974; scriptwriter, from 1975; directed first film, *Cute Girls,* 1979; sold house to finance *Growing Up,* 1982; actor in *When Husband Is Out of Town,* for TV, and director of music video, 1985. **Awards:** Best Director Award, Asian-Pacific Film Festival, for *A Summer at Grandpa's,* 1985; Golden Lion Award, Venice Festival, and Best Director, Golden Horse Awards, Taiwan, for *A City of Sadness,* 1989.

Films as Director:

1979 *Chiu Shih Liu Liu Tê T'a* (*Cute Girls*) (+ sc)
1980 *Feng Erh T'i T'a Ts'ai* (*Cheerful Wind*) (+ sc)
1982 *Tsai Nei Ho P'an Ch'ing Ts'ao Ch'ing* (*The Green, Green Grass of Home*) (+ sc)
1983 Episode of *Erh Tzu Tê Ta Wan Ou* (*The Sandwich Man*; *Son's Big Doll*)
1984 *Fêng Kuei Lai Tê Jen* (*The Boys from Fengkuei*) (+ co-sc); *Tung Tung Te Chia Ch'i* (*A Summer at Grandpa's*)
1985 *T'ung Nein Wang Shih* (*A Time to Live and a Time to Die*)
1986 *Lien Lien Feng Ch'eng* (*Dust in the Wind*) (+ role)
1987 *Ni Luo Ho Nü Erh* (*Daughter of the Nile*) (+ role)
1989 *Pei Ch'ing Ch'êng Shih* (*A City of Sadness*) (+ role)
1993 *The Puppetmaster*
1995 *Haonan Haonu* (*Good Men, Good Women*)

Other Films:

1974 *Yun shen Pu Chih Ch'u* (*Lost in the Deep Cloud*) (asst-d); *Chin shui Lou Tai* (*A Better Chance*) (asst-d)
1975 *Tao Hua Neu Tou Chao Kung* (*The Beauty and the Old Man*) (sc, asst-d); *Yeuh Hsia Lao Jen* (*The Matchmaker*) (sc, asst-d)
1976 *Ai Yu Ming T'ien* (*Love Has Tomorrow*) (asst-d); *Yen Shuio Han* (*The Glory of the Sunset*) (asst-d); *Nan Hai Yü Nü Hai Tê Chan Chêng* (*The War between Boys and Girls*) (asst-d)
1977 *Ts'ui Hu Han* (*The Chilly Green Lake*) (asst-d); *Yen P'o Chiang Shang* (*On the Foggy River*) (sc, asst-d); *Tsao an Taipei* (*Good Morning, Taipei*) (sc); *Pei Chih Ch'iu* (*Sadness of Autumn*) (sc)
1978 *Tso Yeh Yü Hsiao Hsiao* (*The Rushing Rain of Last Night*) (sc, asst-d); *Wo T'a Laong Erh Lai* (*I Come with the Wave*) (sc, asst-d)
1979 *T'ien Liang Hao Kê Ch'iu* (*What a Cold but Wonderful Autumn*) (sc, asst-d); *Ch'iu Lien* (*Autumn Lotus*) (sc)
1980 *P'eng P'eng I Ch'uan Hsin* (*Pounding Hearts*) (sc, asst-d)
1981 *Ch'iao Ju Ts'ai Tieh Fei Fei Fei* (*A Butterfly Girl*) (sc, asst-d)
1982 *Hsiao Pi Te Ku Shih* (*Growing Up*) (co-pr, co-sc, asst-d)
1984 *Yu Ma Ts'ai Tzu* (*Ah Fei*) (co-sc); *Hsiao Pa Pa Te T'ien K'ung* (*Out of the Blue*) (co-sc); *Ch'ing Mei Chu Ma* (*Taipei Story*) (role); *Tsui Hsiang Nien Tê Chi Chieh* (sc)

Publications

By HOU: articles—

Interview with Olivier Assayas, in *Cahiers du Cinéma* (Paris), December 1984.
Interview with Tony Rayns, in *Monthly Film Bulletin* (London), June 1988.
"Not the Best Possible Face," an interview with Tony Rayns, in *Monthly Film Bulletin* (London), June 1990.
"*City of Sadness,*" an interview in *Film,* March 1990.
"Straniero in patria," an interview with Z. Yan, in *Cinema Forum,* March 1991.
"History's Subtle Shadows," an interview with P. H. P. Chiao, in *Cinemaya,* Autumn 1993.

Hou Hsiao-Hsien: ***Pei Ch'ing Ch'êng Shih***

Interview with M. Ciment, in *Positif,* December 1993.
Interview with T. Jousse, in *Cahiers du Cinéma,* December 1993.
"*The Puppetmaster,*" an interview with F. Sartor, in *Film und Televisie + Video,* January 1994.

On HOU: articles—

"A Taiwan Tale," in *Film,* April 1989.
Huang, Vivian, "Taiwan's Social Realism," in *The Independent* (New York), January/February 1990.
Combs, Richard, "*Dust in the Wind,*" in *Monthly Film Bulletin* (London), April 1990.
Grosoli, F., "Lo sguardo diretto di Hou Xiaoxian," in *Cinema Forum,* March 1991.
"Hou's *City of Sadness* Is Key to Success," in *Variety,* 17 February 1992.
Cheshire, G., "Time Span: The Cinema of Hou Hsiao-Hsien," in *Film Comment,* November/December 1993.
Delval, D., "Le maitre de marionnettes," in *Grand Angle,* January 1994.

* * *

Hou Hsiao-hsien is the most internationally renowned of the filmmakers associated with Taiwan's "New Cinema" movement. The "New Cinema" was forged out of the country's aging industry in the early 1980s by a group of emerging filmmakers, most of whom were in their early thirties at the time. The members of this cohesive group helped each other make films, and were strongly supported in turn by a group of film critics belonging to the same generation. Their works diverged from mainstream films of the time both in style and in content; instead of the escapist romances and propaganda films in melodramatic form that dominated Taiwan's film market in the 1970s, this new wave of filmmakers used a realistic style to convey their socially concerned themes.

The experiences of life in Taiwan figure prominently in Hou's work, due to his personal background: Hou, who has lived in Taiwan for most of his life, was a year old in 1948 when he and his family, on a visit from the mainland, were forced to remain more or less permanently as a result of the Civil War. Unlike the previous generation of filmmakers, who were brought up and educated in mainland China and who hired professionals to dub all the dialogue with standard Mandarin, the official language of both Taiwan and mainland China, Hou began using large amounts of the Taiwanese dialect spoken by most of the island's inhabitants. Following *The Sandwich Man,* Hou also mixed in the dialect of the ancient Hakkas ethnic group, as well as Japanese. (Japan had occupied Taiwan for almost fifty years, previous to the Nationalist takeover.) While the previous generation of filmmakers identified with or bowed to the Nationalist strategy of mandating exclusive use of the Mandarin language to "Chinacize" the people of Taiwan, Hou and his peers, whether mainlander or islander, recognized the fact that Taiwan was not synonymous with China. Due to this break from the state-enforced ideology, the New Cinema practitioners were able to begin to face and examine the sources and manifestations of their society's problems.

Perhaps most dynamic in this rapidly industrializing country was the emotional as well as physical dislocation resulting from the urbanization of Taiwan's traditionally rural culture. The conflict between urban and rural values is a recurring theme in Hou's films. Hou, who grew up in the countryside and moved to Taipei at the beginning of his college studies, retains a strong attachment to traditional Taiwanese values. On the screen, he uses country living and sentiments in the idyllic scene structure of his films. In *A Summer at Grandpa's,* the protagonist Tung Tung, a young boy who grew up in Taipei but stayed at his grandfather's in the country while his mother was hospitalized, gained "real" childhood experiences—playing in the river and exchanging his toy car with another child's live turtle, as well as more gritty life experiences—learning of the complexities of social relationships through the rape of an insane woman and her subsequent unsuccessful pregnancy. Contrasted with the positive influences one can gain from country life in most of Hou's films are the attractions of the city, with its opportunities for a living wage and concomitant confusion of an alien social structure, and its dissimilar types of human relationships.

In *The Boys from Fengkuei,* when three young men arrive at Kaohsiung, they find that their friend's sister, who has moved to the city from their hometown, has somehow become "morally corrupted." While they wander around on the streets of the city, a stranger on a motorcycle collects their money to see an underground porno film, sending them into an empty building still under construction. Instead of a movie screen, they view the city landscape from huge holes awaiting windows. A silent long take and a long shot shows the three naive boys staring at the city—the farce turning out to be their first taste of the bitterness of the city—without anger but with a deep sense of helplessness.

That the urban experience can prove damaging to one's physical as well as mental health is illustrated in *Dust in the Wind.* The protagonist Ah-Yuan is beaten up by his boss's wife for failing to deliver a lunch box to her son, and some friends of Ah-Yuan, including his girlfriend, are injured during their work. While these country children are wounded by the city, they can always go back to their rural homes to recuperate from their mental and physical injuries. However, in *Daughter of the Nile,* when the teenaged girl Shao Yang and her brother Shao Fang settle in the city of Taipei, they become the orphans of the world. *Daughter of the Nile* is Hou's first and thus far only film that takes place entirely in Taipei. Hou's shots of the dark city illuminated by the colorful neon signs eerily demonstrate the materialism that dislocates the youths, and finally takes Shao Fang's life.

The uneasiness and the difficulties of adjusting to social changes was the other theme in almost all of Hou's directorial works. In *The Sandwich Man,* Hou used a clown costume as the symbol of this discomfort. In *Dust in the Wind,* this discomfort is transformed into physical suffering when the rural teenagers are beaten and otherwise abused by their working environment. Death also played the main metaphoric role of the transition in *A Time to Live and a Time to Die*: the deaths of protagonist Ah-ha's father, mother, and grandmother punctuate his stages of growing up as well as his ideological divergence from the Nationalist party between the years 1958 and 1966. Similarly, in *A City of Sadness,* each of the four brothers of the Lin family was killed either physically or mentally in differing political climates and social circumstances during the 1940s, their deaths indicating their failure in adjusting to the new eras.

Hou's achievement is not only in his cinematic sensitivities but also in his social consciousness. As much as he is a filmmaker, Hou is a historical and social commentator of the first order.

—Vivian Huang

HOWARD, William K.

Nationality: American. **Born:** William Kerrigan Howard in St. Mary's, Ohio, 16 June 1899. **Education:** Educated in engineering and law, Ohio State University. **Military Service:** Served with American Expeditionary Force, France, 1917-18. **Career:** Worked for film distributor, Cincinnati, then Vitagraph sales manager, Minnesota, 1916-17; sales advisor for Universal, Hollywood, 1919; assistant director, 1920, then director, for Fox, 1921; signed with Famous Players-Lasky, 1924; joined Cecil B. de Mille's Producers Distributing Corps, 1926; under contract to Fox, 1928-33; made *A Guy Could Change* for Republic, 1946. **Died:** 21 February 1954.

Films as Director:

1921 *Get Your Man* (co-d); *Play Square*; *What Love Will Do*
1922 *Extra! Extra!*; *Lucky Dan*; *Deserted at the Altar* (co-d); *Captain Fly-by-Night*
1923 *The Fourth Musketeer*; *Danger Ahead*; *Let's Go*
1924 *The Border Legion*; *East of Broadway*
1925 *The Thundering Herd*; *Code of the West*; *The Light of Western Stars*
1926 *Red Dice*; *Bachelor Brides* (*Bachelor's Brides*); *Volcano*; *Gigolo*
1927 *White Gold*; *The Main Event*
1928 *A Ship Comes In* (*His Country*); *The River Pirate*
1929 *Christina*; *The Valiant*; *Love, Live and Laugh* (dialogue scenes d by Henry Kolker)
1930 *Good Intentions* (+ co-sc, dialogue scenes d by Henry Kolker); *Scotland Yard* (*Detective Clive, Bart*)
1931 *Don't Bet on Women* (*More than a Kiss*); *Transatlantic*; *Surrender*
1932 *The Trial of Vivienne Ware*; *The First Year*; *Sherlock Holmes*
1933 *The Power and the Glory* (*Power and Glory*); *The Cat and the Fiddle*
1934 *This Side of Heaven*; *Evelyn Prentice*
1935 *Vanessa, Her Love Story*; *Rendezvous*; *Mary Burns, Fugitive*
1936 *The Princess Comes Across*; *Fire over England*
1937 *The Squeaker* (*Murder on Diamond Row*); *Over the Moon* (Freeland; d uncredited)
1939 *Back Door to Heaven* (+ pr, story)
1940 *Money and the Woman*; *Knute Rockne—All American* (*A Modern Hero*) (Bacon; d begun by Howard)
1941 *Bullets for O'Hara*
1942 *Klondike Fury*
1943 *Johnny Come Lately* (*Johnny Vagabond*)
1944 *When the Lights Go on Again*
1946 *A Guy Could Change* (+ assoc pr)

Other Films:

1920 *The Skywayman* (Hogan) (asst d)
1921 *The One-Man Trail* (Durning) (sc)
1922 *Trooper O'Neill* (Dunlap and Wallace) (sc); *The Crusader* (Mitchell) (co-sc)
1929 *Sin Town* (co-sc)
1937 *The Green Cockatoo* (*Four Dark Hours*; *Race Gang*) (Menzies) ("A William K. Howard Production")

Publications

On HOWARD: book—

Thompson, Frank, editor, *Between Action and Cut: Five American Directors,* Metuchen, New Jersey, 1985.

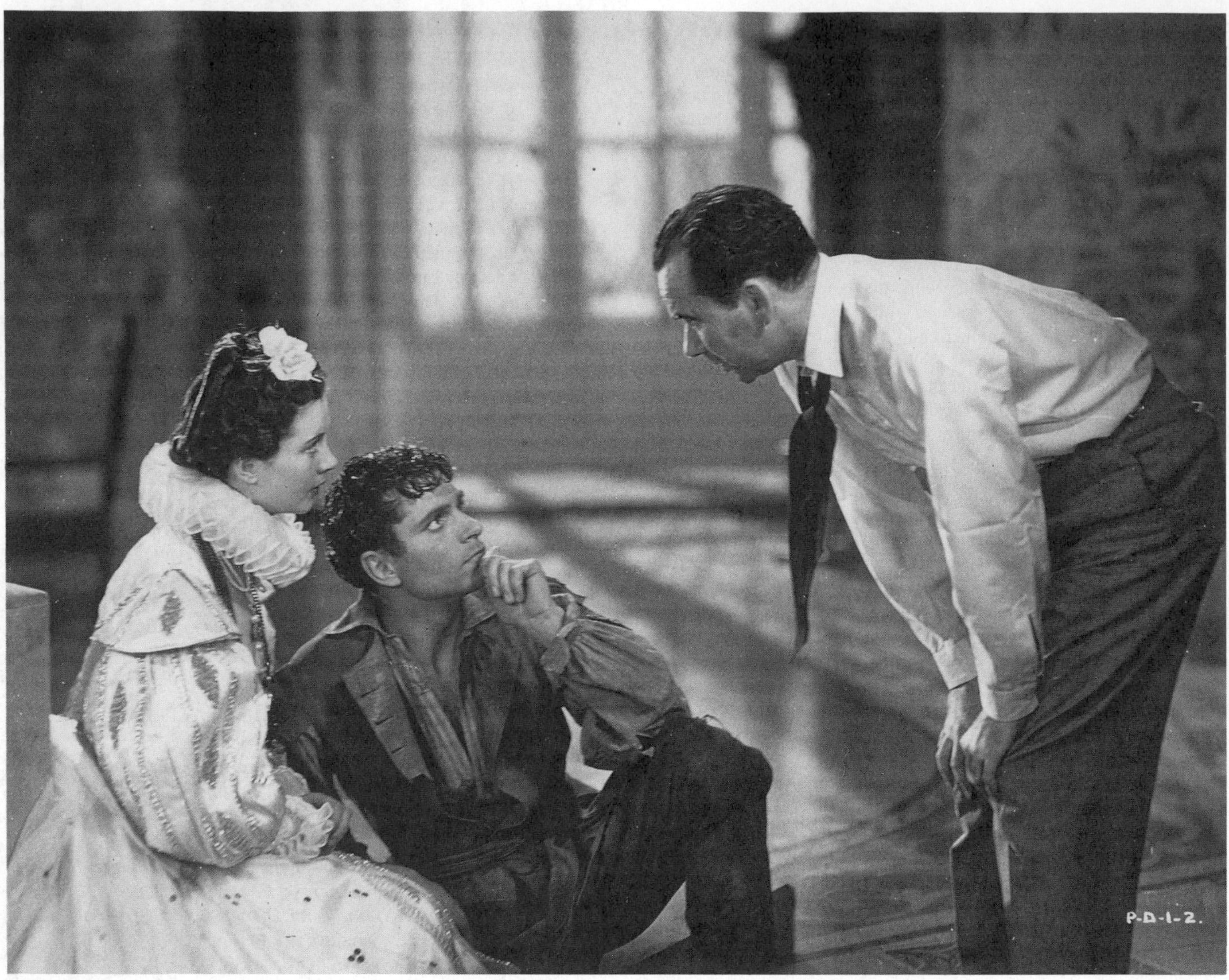

William K. Howard directing Laurence Olivier and Vivien Leigh in *Fire over England*

On HOWARD: articles—

Obituary, in *New York Times,* 22 February 1954.
Everson, William K., "William K. Howard," in *Films in Review* (New York), May 1954.
Rutherford, T.S., "William K. Howard," in *Film Dope* (London), November 1982.

* * *

For more than twenty years, William K. Howard was a reliable Hollywood director, able to turn his attention with ease to most types of features. He was not a major director, the majority of his films being no better than those turned out by his contemporaries, but Howard does deserve more than passing recognition for his work on *White Gold, Sherlock Holmes, The Power and the Glory,* and *Fire over England.*

Howard's silent features were always well-made commercial successes. The best-known of these titles included a version of Zane Grey's *The Thundering Herd,* starring Jack Holt and Tim McCoy, and a spectacular melodrama featuring Bebe Daniels, *Volcano.* Most historians agree that Howard's best silent film work is *White Gold,* which owes much to German expressionist cinema and which one historian, William K. Everson, has compared favorably to *The Last Laugh.* Certainly the film's star, Jetta Goudal gives her most impressive performance, one that is immediately reminiscent of Lillian Gish in *The Wind.* In the early 1940s Howard actively considered a remake of *White Gold.*

Curiously, William K. Howard seemed to establish far more of a visual style with his sound films than with his silent efforts. This is particularly apparent in *Sherlock Holmes* and, above all, in *The Power and the Glory.* The latter utilizes a series of flashbacks—rather like *Citizen Kane* some years later—to tell of a railroad executive's rise to power. Highly regarded at the time, the film's continuing appeal owes as much to Howard's direction as to its brilliant script by Preston Sturges. For example, it is doubtful that a lesser team than Howard and Sturges could have created the sequence in which Spencer Tracy and Colleen Moore become engaged, told as the couple climb a steeper and steeper hill with no dialogue except for the commentary by Ralph Morgan.

From 1936 through 1938 Howard worked in England, notably on *Fire over England,* based on the A.E.W. Mason historical romance set during the reign of Elizabeth I. Howard was aided by a cast which included Flora Robson (as Elizabeth), Laurence Olivier, Vivien Leigh, and Raymond Massey, not to mention the cinematography of James Wong Howe, but even so the director deserves credit for his capable handling of both sweeping historical spectacle and intimate drama.

With his return to the States, Howard settled down to directing routine melodramas. He did create something of a sensation in the film community in 1936 when he ordered his supervising producer off the set during the filming of *The Princess Comes Across,* the first time a director had enforced the policies of the fledgling Screen Directors Guild.

Contemporaries of Howard have described him as both brilliant and cynical, and it is perhaps the latter trait which enabled the director to add a reasonable amount of artistry to films which might otherwise have been nothing more than mere box office successes.

—Anthony Slide

HSIAO-HSIEN, Hou *See* **HOU Hsiao-Hsien**

HU, Chin-Ch'üan *See* **KING Hu**

HU, King *See* **KING Hu**

HUILLET, Danièle *See* **STRAUB, Jean-Marie, and Danièle HUILLET**

HUSTON, John

Nationality: Irish/American. **Born:** John Marcellus Huston, son of actor Walter, in Nevada, Missouri, 5 August 1906, became Irish citizen, 1964. **Education:** Attended boarding school in Los Angeles and at Lincoln High School, Los Angeles, 1923-24. **Military Service:** Served in Signal Corps, Army Pictorial Service, 1942-45, discharged at rank of major. **Family:** Married 1) Dorothy Jeanne Harvey, 1926 (divorced 1933); 2) Leslie Black, 1937 (divorced 1944); 3) Evelyn Keyes, 1946 (divorced 1950), one adopted son; 4) Ricki Soma, 1950 (died 1969), one son, two daughters including actress Anjelica; also son Daniel by Zoë Sallis; 5) Celeste Shane, 1972 (divorced 1977). **Career:** Doctors in St. Paul, Minnesota, diagnose Huston with enlarged heart and kidney disease; taken to California for cure, 1916; boxer in California, 1920s; actor in New York, 1924; competition horseman, Mexico, 1927; journalist in New York, 1928-30; scriptwriter and actor in Hollywood, 1930; worked for Gaumont-British, London, 1932; moved to Paris with intention of studying painting, 1933; returned to New York, editor *Midweek Pictorial,* stage actor, 1934; writer for Warner Bros., Hollywood, 1936; directed first film, *The Maltese Falcon,* 1941; with William Wyler and Philip Dunne, formed Committee for the 1st Amendment to counteract HUAC investigation, 1947; formed Horizon Pictures with Sam Spiegel, 1948; formed John Huston Productions for unrealized project *Matador,* 1952; moved to Ireland, 1955; narrator for TV, from mid-1960s; moved to Mexico, 1972. **Awards:** Legion of Merit, U.S. Armed Services, 1944; Oscar for Best Direction, for *Treasure of the Sierra Madre,* 1947. **Died:** Of pneumonia, in Newport, Rhode Island, 28 August 1987.

Films as Director:

1941 ***The Maltese Falcon*** (+ sc)
1942 *In This Our Life* (+ co-sc, uncredited); *Across the Pacific* (co-d)
1943 *Report from the Aleutians* (+ sc); *Tunisian Victory* (Capra and Boulting; d some replacement scenes when footage lost, + co-commentary)
1945 *San Pietro* (*The Battle of San Pietro*) (+ sc, co-ph, narration)
1946 *Let There Be Light* (unreleased) (+ co-sc, co-ph); *A Miracle Can Happen* (*On Our Merry Way*) (King Vidor and Fenton; d some Henry Fonda/James Stewart sequences, uncredited)
1948 ***The Treasure of the Sierra Madre*** (+ sc, bit role as man in white suit); *Key Largo* (+ co-sc)
1949 *We Were Strangers* (+ co-sc, bit role as bank clerk)
1950 ***The Asphalt Jungle*** (+ co-sc)
1951 *The Red Badge of Courage* (+ sc)
1952 ***The African Queen*** (+ co-sc)
1953 *Moulin Rouge* (+ pr, co-sc)
1954 *Beat the Devil* (+ co-pr, co-sc)
1956 *Moby Dick* (+ pr, co-sc)
1957 *Heaven Knows, Mr. Allison* (+ co-sc); *A Farewell to Arms* (Charles Vidor; d begun by Huston)
1958 *The Barbarian and the Geisha*; *The Roots of Heaven*
1960 *The Unforgiven*
1961 ***The Misfits***
1963 *Freud* (*Freud: The Secret Passion*) (+ narration); *The List of Adrian Messenger* (+ bit role as Lord Ashton)
1964 *The Night of the Iguana* (+ co-pr, co-sc)
1965 *La bibbia* (*The Bible*) (+ role, narration)
1967 *Casino Royale* (co-d, role); *Reflections in a Golden Eye* (+ voice heard at film's beginning)
1969 *Sinful Davey*; *A Walk with Love and Death* (+ role); *De Sade* (Enfield; d uncredited) (+ role as the Abbe)
1970 *The Kremlin Letter* (+ co-sc, role)
1971 *The Last Run* (Fleischer; d begun by Huston)
1972 *Fat City* (+ co-pr); *The Life and Times of Judge Roy Bean* (+ role as Grizzly Adams)
1973 *The Mackintosh Man*
1975 *The Man Who Would Be King* (+ co-sc)
1976 *Independence* (short)
1979 *Wise Blood* (+ role)
1980 *Phobia*
1981 *Victory* (*Escape to Victory*)
1982 *Annie*
1984 *Under the Volcano*
1985 *Prizzi's Honor*
1987 *The Dead*

Other Films:

1929 *The Shakedown* (Wyler) (small role); *Hell's Heroes* (Wyler) (small role)
1930 *The Storm* (Wyler) (small role)
1931 *A House Divided* (Wyler) (dialogue, sc)
1932 *Murders in the Rue Morgue* (Florey) (dialogue, sc)
1935 *It Started in Paris* (Robert Wyler) (co-adapt, sc); *Death Drives Through* (Cahn) (co-story, sc)

1938 *Jezebel* (Wyler) (co-sc); *The Amazing Dr. Clitterhouse* (Litvak) (co-sc)
1939 *Juarez* (Dieterle) (co-sc)
1940 *The Story of Dr. Ehrlich's Magic Bullet* (*Dr. Ehrlich's Magic Bullet*) (Dieterle) (co-sc)
1941 ***High Sierra*** (Walsh) (co-sc); *Sergeant York* (Hawks) (co-sc)
1946 ***The Killers*** (Siodmak) (sc, uncredited); *The Stranger* (Welles) (co-sc, uncredited); *Three Strangers* (Negulesco) (co-sc)
1951 *Quo Vadis* (LeRoy) (pre-production work)
1963 *The Cardinal* (Preminger) (role as Cardinal Glennon); *The Directors* (pr: Greenblatt, short) (appearance)
1968 *Candy* (Marquand) (role as Dr. Dunlap); *The Rocky Road to Dublin* (Lennon) (role as interviewee)
1970 *Myra Breckenridge* (Sarne) (role as Buck Loner)
1971 *The Bridge in the Jungle* (Kohner) (role as Sleigh); *The Deserter* (Kennedy) (role as General Miles); *Man in the Wilderness* (Sarafian) (role as Captain Henry)
1974 *Battle for the Planet of the Apes* (Thompson) (role as Lawgiver); ***Chinatown*** (Polanski) (role as Noah Cross)
1975 *Breakout* (Gries) (role as Harris); *The Wind and the Lion* (Milius) (role as John Hay)
1976 *Sherlock Holmes in New York* (Sagal) (role as Professor Moriarty)
1977 *Tentacles* (Hellman) (role as Ned Turner); *Il grande attacco* (*La battaglia di Mareth*; *The Biggest Battle*) (Lenzi) (role); *El triangulo diabolico de la Bermudas* (*Triangle: The Bermuda Mystery*; *The Mystery of the Bermuda Triangle*) (Cardona) (role); *Angela* (Sagal) (role)
1978 *Il visitatore* (*The Visitor*) (Paradisi) (role)
1979 *Jaguar Lives* (Pintoff) (role); *Winter Kills* (Richert) (role)
1980 *Head On* (Grant) (role); *Agee* (Spears) (role as interviewee)
1981 *To the Western World* (Kinmonth) (narrator)
1982 *Cannery Row* (Ward) (narrator)
1983 *Lovesick* (Brickman) (role as psychiatrist)

Publications

By HUSTON: books—

Frankie and Johnny, New York, 1930.
The Maltese Falcon, New York, 1974.
The Treasure of the Sierra Madre, edited by James Naremore, Madison, Wisconsin, 1979.
The Asphalt Jungle, with Ben Maddow, Carbondale, Illinois, 1980.
An Open Book, New York, 1980.
Juarez, with Aeneas Mackenzie and Wolfgang Reinhardt, Madison, Wisconsin, 1983.
Reflections in a Male Eye: John Huston and the American Experience, edited by Gaylyn Studlar and David Desser, Washington, 1993.

By HUSTON: articles—

Interview with Karel Reisz, in *Sight and Sound* (London), January/March 1952.
"How I Make Films," interview with Gideon Bachmann, in *Film Quarterly* (Berkeley), Fall 1965.
"Huston!," interview with C. Taylor and G. O'Brien, in *Inter/View* (New York), September 1972.
"Talk with John Huston," with D. Ford, in *Action* (Los Angeles), September/October 1972.
"The Innocent Bystander," interview with D. Robinson, in *Sight and Sound* (London), Winter 1972/73.
"Talking with John Huston," with Gene Phillips, in *Film Comment* (New York), May/June 1973.
Interview with D. Brandes, in *Filmmakers Newsletter* (Ward Hill, Massachusetts), July 1977.
Interview with P.S. Greenberg, in *Rolling Stone* (New York), June/July 1981.
"Dialogue on Film: John Huston," in *American Film* (Washington, D.C.), January/February 1984.
Interview with Michel Ciment and D. Allison, in *Positif* (Paris), October 1987.

On HUSTON: books—

Davay, Paul, *John Huston,* Paris, 1957.
Allais, Jean-Claude, *John Huston,* Paris, 1960.
Agee, James, *Agee on Film: Five Film Scripts,* foreword by John Huston, Boston, 1965.
Nolan, William, *John Huston, King Rebel,* Los Angeles, 1965.
Benayoun, Robert, *John Huston,* Paris, 1966; revised edition, 1985.
Cecchini, Riccardo, *John Huston,* 1969.
Tozzi, Romano, John Huston, *A Picture Treasury of his Films,* New York, 1971.
Kaminsky, Stuart, *John Huston: Maker of Magic,* London, 1978.
Madsen, Axel, *John Huston,* New York, 1978.
Giannetti, Louis D., *Masters of the American Cinema,* Englewood Cliffs, New Jersey, 1981.
Hammen, Scott, *John Huston,* Boston, 1985.
Ciment, Gilles, editor, *John Huston,* Paris, 1987.
McCarty, John, *The Films of John Huston,* Secaucus, New Jersey, 1987.
Grobel, Lawrence, *The Hustons,* New York, 1989.

On HUSTON: articles—

"Huston Issues" of *Positif* (Paris), August 1952 and January 1957.
Mage, David, "The Way John Huston Works," in *Films in Review* (New York), October 1952.
Laurot, Edouard, "An Encounter with John Huston," in *Film Culture* (New York), no. 8, 1956.
Archer, Eugene, "John Huston—The Hemingway Tradition in American Film," in *Film Culture* (New York), no. 19, 1959.
"John Huston, The Bible and James Bond," in *Cahiers du Cinema in English* (New York), no. 5, 1966.
Koningsberger, Hans, "From Book to Film—via John Huston," in *Film Quarterly* (Berkeley), Spring 1969.
"Huston Issue" of *Film Comment* (New York), May/June 1973.
Bachmann, Gideon, "Watching Huston," in *Film Comment* (New York), January/February 1976.
Jameson, R.T., "John Huston," in *Film Comment* (New York), May/June 1980.
Drew, B., "John Huston: At 74 No Formulas," in *American Film* (Washington, D.C.), September 1980.
Millar, G., "John Huston," in *Sight and Sound* (London), Summer 1981.
"John Huston," in *Film Dope* (London), January 1983.
Hachem, S., *"Under the Volcano,"* in *American Cinematographer* (Los Angeles), October 1984.
Combs, Richard, "The Man who would be Ahab: The Myths and Masks of John Huston," in *Monthly Film Bulletin* (London), December 1985.
"Huston Issue" of *Positif* (Paris), January 1986.
Taylor, John Russell, "John Huston: The Filmmaker as Dandy," in *Films and Filming* (London), August 1986.
Edgerton, G., "Revisiting the Recordings of Wars Past: Remembering the Documentary Trilogy of John Huston," in *Journal of Popular Film and TV* (Washington, D.C.), Spring 1987.

McCarthy, T., obituary, in *Variety* (New York), 2 September 1987.
Schulz-Keil, W., and B. Walker, "Huston," in *Film Comment* (New York), September/October 1987.
Buckley, M., obituary in *Films in Review* (New York), November 1987.
Combs, Richard, "John Huston: An Account of One Man Dead," in *Monthly Film Bulletin* (London), December 1987.
Literature/Film Quarterly (Salisbury, Maryland), vol. 17, nos. 2 and 4, 1989.
American Film (Washington, D.C.), June 1989.
Grobel, L., "Talent to Burn," in *Movieline,* March 1990.
Denby, D., "A Good Man is Hard to Find," in *Premiere,* July 1990.
Richards, Peter, "Huston's Killer Comedy," in *Film Comment* (New York), May/June 1991.
Hagen, W.M., "Under Huston's 'Volcano,'" in *Literature/Film Quarterly* (Salisbury, Maryland), vol. 19, no. 3, 1991.
James, C., "John Huston: The Director as Monster," in *New York Times,* 9 August 1992.
Edelman, Lee, "Plasticity, Paternity, Perversity: Freud's 'Falcon,' Huston's 'Freud,'" in *American Imago,* Spring 1994.

On HUSTON: films—

Kronick, William, *On Location: The Night of the Iguana,* for TV, U.S., 1964.
Graef, Roger, *The Life and Times of John Huston, Esquire,* Great Britain, 1967.
Joyce, Paul, *Ride This Way Grey Horse,* Great Britain, 1970.
Huston, Danny, *The Making of* The Dead, U.S., 1989.

*   *   *

Few directors have been as interested in the relationship of film to painting as has John Huston and, perhaps, none has been given as little credit for this interest. This lack of recognition is not completely surprising. Criticism of film, despite the form's visual nature, has tended to be derived primarily from literature and not from painting or, as might be more reasonable, a combination of the traditions of literature, painting, theater, and the unique forms of film itself.

In a 1931 profile in *The American Mercury* that accompanied a short story by John Huston, the future director said that he wanted to write a book on the lives of French painters. The following year, unable to or dissatisfied with work as a film writer in London, Huston moved to Paris to become a painter. He studied for a year and a half, making money by painting portraits on street corners and singing for pennies. Even after he became an established film director, Huston's continued to indulge his interest in painting, "retiring" from filmmaking from time to time to concentrate on his painting.

Each of Huston's films has reflected this prime interest in the image, the moving portrait and the use of color—as well as the poetic possibilities of natural dialogue. Each film has been a moving canvas on which Huston explores his main subject: the effect of the individual ego on the group and the possibility of the individual's survival.

Huston began exploring his style of framing in his first film, *The Maltese Falcon.* Following his sketches, he set up shots like the canvases of paintings he had studied. Specifically, Huston showed an interest in characters appearing in the foreground of a shot, with their faces often covering half the screen. Frequently, too, the person whose face half fills the screen is not talking, but listening. The person reacting thus becomes more important than the one speaking or moving.

Huston's first film as a director presented situations he would return to again and again. Spade is the obsessed professional, a man who will adhere to pride and dedication, to principle unto death. Women are a threat, temptations that can only sway the hero from his professional commitment. They may be willfully trying to deceive, as with Brigid and Iva, or they may, as in later Huston films, be the unwitting cause of the protagonist's defeat or near-defeat. In *The Asphalt Jungle,* for example, the women in the film are not evil; it is the men's obsession with them that causes disaster.

Even with changes and cuts, a film like *The Red Badge of Courage* reflects Huston's thematic and visual interests. Again, the film features a group with a quest that may result in death. These soldiers argue, support each other, pretend they are not frightened, brag, and, in some cases, die. In the course of the action, both the youth and the audience discover that the taking of an isolated field is not as important as the ability of the young men to face death without fear. Also, as in other Huston films, the two central figures in *The Red Badge of Courage,* the youth and Wilson, lie about their attitudes. Their friendship solidifies only when both confess that they have been afraid during the battle and have fled.

Visually, Huston continued to explore an important aspect of his style: the placement of characters in a frame so that their size and position reflect what they are saying and doing. He developed this technique with Bogart, Holt, and Walter Huston in *The Treasure of the Sierra Madre* and Audie Murphy and Bill Mauldin in *The Red Badge of Courage.*

Early in *The African Queen,* for instance, after Rosie's brother dies, there is a scene in which Rosie is seated on the front porch of the mission. Charlie, in the foreground, dominates the screen while Rosie, in the background, is small. As Charlie takes control of the situation and tells Rosie what must be done, he raises his hand to the rail and his arm covers our view of her. Charlie is in command.

Thematically, *Moulin Rouge* was a return to Huston's pessimism and exploration of futility. The director identified with the character of Lautrec who, like Huston, was given to late hours, ironic views of himself, performing for others, sardonic wit, and a frequent bitterness toward women. Lautrec, like Huston, loved horses, and frequently painted pictures of them.

The narrative as developed by Huston and Ray Bradbury in *Moby Dick* is in keeping with the director's preoccupation with failed quests. Only one man, Ishmael, survives. All the other men of the *Pequod* go down in Ahab's futile attempt to destroy the whale. But Huston sees Ahab in his actions and his final gesture as a noble creature who has chosen to go down fighting.

The Roots of Heaven is yet another example of Huston's exploration of an apparently doomed quest by a group of vastly different people, led by a man obsessed. In spite of the odds, the group persists in its mission and some of its members die. As in many Huston films, the quest is not a total failure; there is the likelihood of continuation, if not success, but the price that must be paid in human lives is high.

Huston's *The Misfits* again featured a group on a sad and fruitless quest. The group, on a search for horses, find far fewer than they had expected. The expedition becomes a bust and the trio of friends are at odds over a woman, Roslyn (Marilyn Monroe), who opposes the killing and capturing of the horses.

With the exception of Guido, the characters represent the least masked or disguised group in Huston's films. Perhaps it is this very element of never-penetrated disguise in Guido that upset Huston and drove him to push for a motivation scene, an emotional unmasking of the character.

As a Huston film, *Freud* has some particular interests: Huston serves as a narrator, displaying an omnipotence and almost Biblical detachment that establishes Freud as a kind of savior and messiah. The film opens with Huston's description of Freud as a kind of hero or God on a quest for mankind. "This is the story of Freud's descent into a region as black as hell, man's unconscious, and how he let in the light," Huston says in his narration. The bearded, thin look of Freud, who stands alone, denounced before the tribunal of his own people, also suggests a parallel with Christ. Freud brings a message of salvation which is rejected, and he is reluctantly denounced by his chief defender, Breuer.

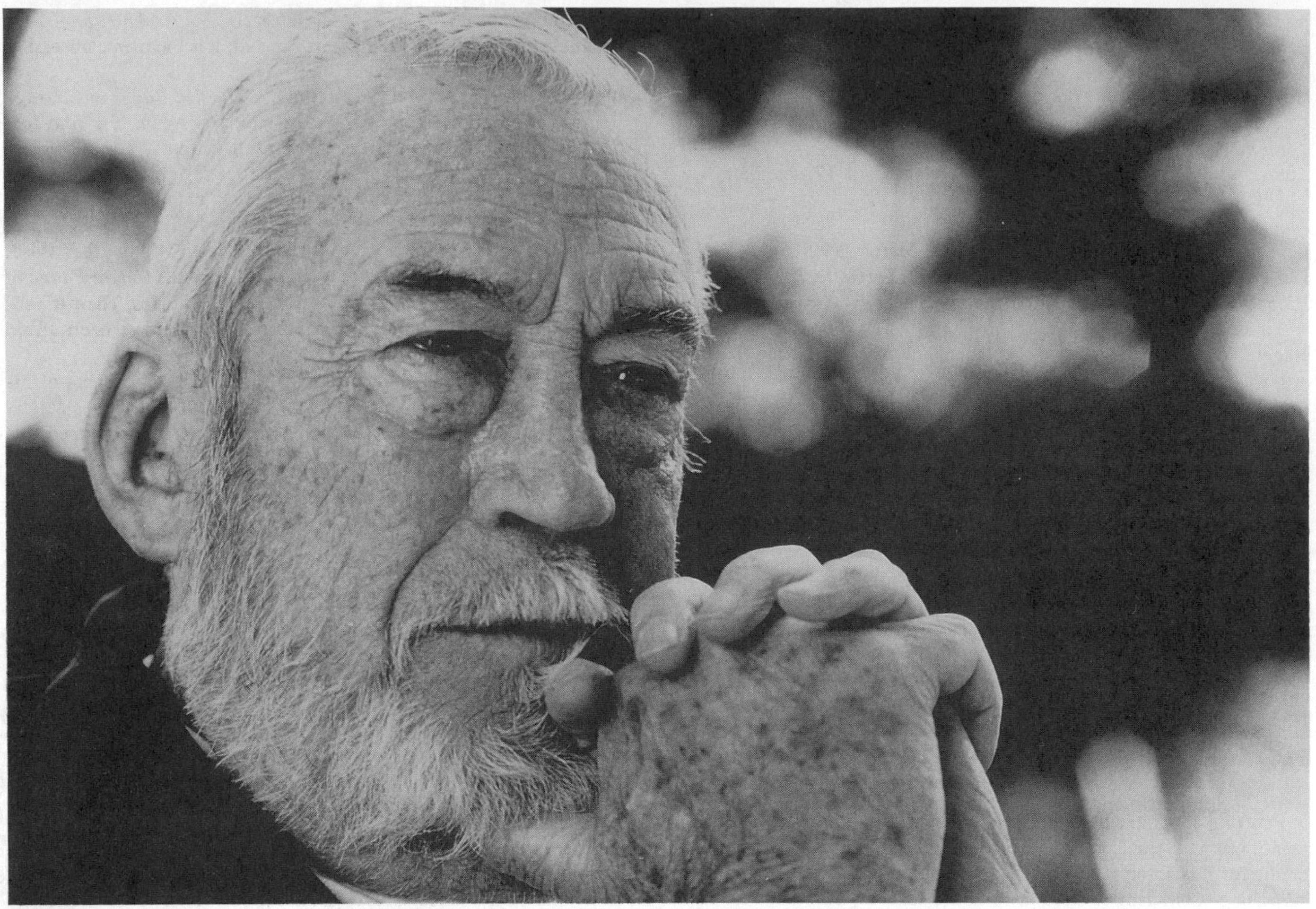

John Huston

Of all Huston's films, *The List of Adrian Messenger* is the one that deals most literally with people in disguise. George, who describes himself as unexcused evil, hides behind a romantic or heroic mask that falls away when he is forced to face the detective, who functions very much like Freud. The detective penetrates the masks, revealing the evil, and the evil is destroyed.

Huston's touch was evident in *The Night of the Iguana* in a variety of ways. First, he again took a group of losers and put them together in an isolated location. The protagonist, Shannon, once a minister, has been reduced to guiding tourists in Mexico. At the furthest reaches of despair and far from civilization, the quest for meaning ends and the protagonist is forced to face himself. Religion is an important theme. The film opens with Richard Burton preaching a sermon to his congregation. It is a startling contrast to Father Mapple's sermon in *Moby Dick.* Shannon is lost, confused, his speech is gibberish, an almost nonsensical confession about being unable to control his appetites and emotions. The congregation turns away from him.

This choice between the practical and the fantastic is a constant theme in Huston's life and films. There is also a choice between illusion and reality, a choice Huston finds difficult to make. Religion is seen as part of the fantasy world, a dangerous fantasy that his characters must overcome if they are not to be destroyed or absorbed by it. This theme is present in *The Bible, Wise Blood,* and *Night of the Iguana.*

Huston's negative religious attitude is also strong in *A Walk with Love and Death,* which includes three encounters with the clergy. In the first, Heron is almost killed by a group of ascetic monks who demand that he renounce the memory of Claudia and "repent his knowledge of women." The young man barely escapes with his life. These religious zealots counsel a move away from the pleasure of the world and human love, a world that Huston believes in.

There are clearly constants in Huston's works—man's ability to find solace in animals and nature, the need to challenge oneself—but his world is unpredictable, governed by a whimsical God or no God at all. Each of Huston's characters seeks a way of coming to terms with that unpredictability, establishing rules of behavior by which he can live.

The Huston character, like Cain or Adam, is often weak, and frequently his best intentions are not sufficient to carry him through to success or even survival. The more a man thinks in a Huston film, the more dangerous it is for his survival. Conversely, however, his films suggest that those who are carried away by emotion, or too much introspection, are doomed. Since the line between loss of control and rigidity is difficult to walk, many Huston protagonists do not survive. It takes a Sam Spade, Sergeant Allison, or Abraham, very rare men indeed, to remain alive in this director's world.

Reflections in a Golden Eye raised many questions about the sexuality inherent in many of the themes that most attracted Huston: riding horses, hunting, boxing, and militarism. The honesty with which the director handles homosexuality is characteristic of his willingness to face what he finds antithetical to his own nature. In the film, the equation of Leonora and her horse is presented as definitely sexual, and at one point Penderton actually beats the horse in a fury because he himself is impotent. Huston also includes a boxing match in the film which is not in the novel. The immorally provocative Leonora watches the match, but Penderton watches another spectator, Williams. *Reflections* becomes an almost comic labyrinth of voyeurism, with characters spying on other characters.

Huston's protagonists often represent extremes. They are either ignorant, pathetic, and doomed by their lack of self-understanding (Tully and Ernie in *Fat City,* Dobbs in *The Treasure of the Sierra Madre,* Peachy and Danny in *The Man Who Would Be King*) or intelligent, arrogant, but equally doomed by their lack of self-understanding (Penderton in *Reflections in a Golden Eye* and Ahab in *Moby Dick*). Between these extremes is the cool, intelligent protagonist who will sacrifice everything for self-understanding and independence (Sam Spade in *The Maltese Falcon,* and Freud). Huston always finds the first group pathetic, the second tragic, and the third heroic. He reserves his greatest respect for the man who retains his dignity in spite of pain and disaster.

Many of Huston's films can de divided between those involving group quests that fail and those involving a pair of potential lovers who must face a hostile world. Generally, Huston's films about such lovers end in the union of the couple or, at least, their survival. In that sense, *A Walk with Love and Death,* starring his own daughter, proved to be the most pessimistic of his love stories, and *Annie,* his most commercial venture, proved to be his most optimistic.

—Stuart M. Kaminsky

ICHIKAWA, Kon

Nationality: Japanese. **Born:** Uji Yamada in Ise, Mie Prefecture, 20 November 1915. **Education:** Ichioka Commercial School, Osaka. **Family:** Married scriptwriter Natto Wada, 1948. **Career:** Worked in animation dept. of J.O. Studios, Kyoto, from 1933; assistant director on feature-filmmaking staff, late 1930s; transferred to Tokyo when J.O. became part of Toho company, early 1940s; collaborated on scripts with wife, 1948-56; used pen name "Shitei Kuri" (after Japanese rendering of Agatha Christie), from 1957; writer and director for TV, 1958-66. **Awards:** San Giorgio Prize, Venice Festival, for *Harp of Burma,* 1956.

Films as Director:

1946 *Musume Dojoji* (*A Girl at Dojo Temple*) (+ co-sc)
1947 *Toho senichi-ya* (*1001 Nights with Toho*) (responsible for some footage only)
1948 *Hana hiraku* (*A Flower Blooms*); *Sanbyaku rokujugo-ya* (*365 Nights*)
1949 *Ningen moyo* (*Human Patterns*; *Design of a Human Being*); *Hateshinaki jonetsu* (*Passion without End*; *The Endless Passion*)
1950 *Ginza Sanshiro* (*Sanshiro of Ginza*); *Netsudeichi* (*Heat and Mud*; *The Hot Marshland*) (+ co-sc): *Akatsuki no tsuiseki* (*Pursuit at Dawn*)
1951 *Ieraishan* (*Nightshade Flower*) (+ co-sc): *Koibito* (*The Lover*) (+ co-sc); *Mukokuseki-sha* (*The Man without a Nationality*); *Nusumareta koi* (*Stolen Love*) (+ co-sc); *Bungawan Solo* (*River Solo Flows*) (+ co-sc); *Kekkon koshinkyoku* (*Wedding March*) (+ co-sc)
1952 *Rakkii-san* (*Mr. Lucky*); *Wakai hito* (*Young People, Young Generation*) (+ co-sc); *Ashi ni sawatta onna* (*The Woman Who Touched Legs*) (+ co-sc); *Ano te kono te* (*This Way, That Way*) (+ co-sc)
1953 *Puu-san* (*Mr. Pu*) (+ co-sc); *Aoiro kakumei* (*The Blue Revolution*); *Seishun Zenigata Heiji* (*The Youth of Heiji Zenigata*) (+ co-sc); *Ai-jin* (*The Lover*)
1954 *Watashi no subete o* (*All of Myself*) (+ co-sc); *Okuman choja* (*A Billionaire*) (+ co-sc); *Josei ni kansuru juni-sho* (*Twelve Chapters on Women*)
1955 *Seishun kaidan* (*Ghost Story of Youth*); *Kokoro* (*The Heart*)
1956 ***Biruma no tategoto*** (*The Burmese Harp*; *Harp of Burma*); *Shokei no heya* (*Punishment Room*); *Nihonbashi* (*Bridge of Japan*)
1957 *Manin densha* (*The Crowded Streetcar*) (+ co-sc); *Tohoku no zummu-tachi* (*The Men of Tohoku*) (+ sc); *Ana* (*The Pit*; *The Hole*) (+ sc)
1958 *Enjo* (*Conflagration*)
1959 *Sayonara, konnichiwa* (*Goodbye, Hello*) (+ co-sc); *Kagi*) (*The Key*; *Odd Obsession* (+ co-sc); *Nobi* (*Fires on the Plain*); *Jokyo II: Mono o takaku uritsukeru onna* (*A Woman's Testament, Part 2: Women Who Sell Things at High Prices*)
1960 *Bonchi* (+ co-sc); *Ototo* (*Her Brother*)
1961 *Kuroijunin no onna* (*Ten Dark Women*)
1962 *Hakai* (*The Outcast*; *The Broken Commandment*); *Watashi wa nisai* (*I Am Two*; *Being Two Isn't Easy*)
1963 *Yukinojo henge* (*An Actor's Revenge*; *The Revenge of Yukinojo*); *Taiheiyo hitoribotchi* (*My Enemy, the Sea*; *Alone on the Pacific*)
1964 *Zeni no odori* (*The Money Dance*; *Money Talks*) (+ sc)
1965 *Tokyo Orimpikku* (*Tokyo Olympiad*) (+ co-sc)
1967 *Toppo Jijo no botan senso* (*Toppo Gigio and the Missile War*) (+ co-sc)
1969 *Kyoto* (+ sc)
1970 *Nihon to Nihonjin* (*Japan and the Japanese*) (+ sc)
1972 *Ai futatabi* (*To Love Again*)
1973 *Matatabi* (*The Wanderers*) (+ pr, co-sc); "The Fastest" episode of *Visions of Eight*
1975 *Wagahai wa neko de aru* (*I Am a Cat*)
1976 *Tsuma to onna no aida* (*Between Women and Wives*) (co-d); *Inugami-ke no ichizoku* (*The Inugami Family*) (+ co-sc)
1977 *Akuma no temari-uta* (*A Rhyme of Vengeance*; *The Devil's Bouncing Ball Song*) (+ sc); *Gokumonto* (*The Devil's Island*; *Island of Horrors*) (+ co-sc)
1978 *Jo-bachi* (*Queen Bee*) (+ co-sc)
1980 *Koto* (*Ancient City*) (+ co-sc); *Hi no tori* (*The Phoenix*) (+ co-sc)
1982 *Kofuku* (*Lonely Hearts, Happiness*) (+ co-sc)
1983 *Sasame Yuki* (*The Makioka sisters*; *Fine Snow*)
1985 *Ohan*; *Biruma no tategoto* (*The Burmese Harp*)
1987 *Eiga Joyu* (*The Actress*); *Taketori Monogatari* (*Princess from the Moon*)
1991 *Tenkawa Densetsu Satsujin Jiken*
1993 *Fusa* (+ sc)
1994 *47 Ronin*

Other Film:

1970 *Dodes'ka-den* (Kurosawa) (pr)

Publications

By ICHIKAWA: book—

Seijocho 271 Banchi, with Natto Wada, Tokyo, 1961.

By ICHIKAWA: articles—

Article in *Filmmakers on Filmmaking,* edited by Harry M. Geduld, Bloomington, Indiana, 1967.
"Kon Ichikawa at the Olympic Games," an interview in *American Cinematographer* (Los Angeles), November 1972.

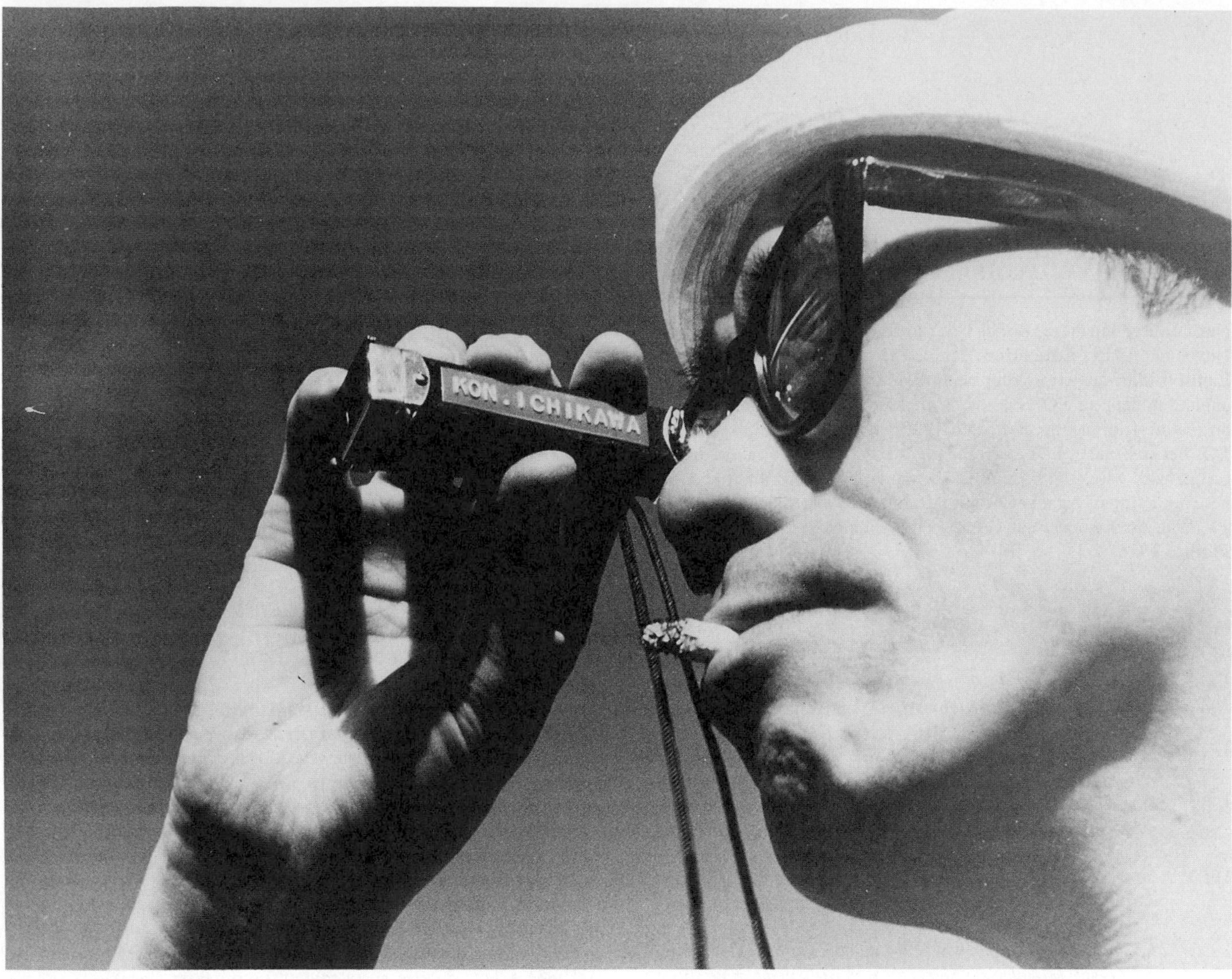

Kon Ichikawa

On ICHIKAWA: books—

Anderson, Joseph, and Donald Richie, *The Japanese Film: Art and Industry,* Rutland, Vermont, 1960; revised edition, Princeton, 1982.
Mellen, Joan, *Voices from the Japanese Cinema,* New York, 1975.
Soumi, Angelo, *Kon Ichikawa,* Florence, 1975.
Mellen, Joan, *The Wave at Kenji's Door: Japan Through Its Cinema,* New York, 1976.
Bock, Audie, *Japanese Film Directors,* New York, 1978; revised edition, Tokyo, 1985.
Burch, Noël, *To the Distant Observer: Form and Meaning in the Japanese Cinema,* Berkeley, 1979.
Allyn, John, *Kon Ichikawa: A Guide to References and Resources,* Boston, 1985.

On ICHIKAWA: articles—

Richie, Donald, "The Several Sides of Kon Ichikawa," in *Sight and Sound* (London), Spring 1966.
Milne, Tom, "The Skull Beneath the Skin," in *Sight and Sound* (London), Autumn 1966.
Tessier, Max, "Kon Ichikawa l'entomologiste," in *Jeune Cinéma* (Paris), March 1967.
Dewey, Langdon, "Kon Ichikawa," in *International Film Guide 1970,* London, 1969.
"Ichikawa Issue" of *Cinema* (Los Angeles), no. 2, 1970.
Johnson, W., "Ichikawa and *The Wanderers,*" in *Film Comment* (New York), September/October 1975.
Gillett, John, "Kon Ichikawa," in *Film Dope* (London), January 1983.

* * *

Kon Ichikawa is noted for a wry humor that often resembles black comedy, for his grim psychological studies—often of misfits and outsiders—and for the visual beauty of his films. He is noted as one of Japan's foremost cinematic stylists, and has commented, "I began as a painter and I think like one."

His early films show a perverse sense of humor as they reveal human foibles and present an objective view of corruption. In *Mr. Pu,* a projector breaks down while showing scenes of an atomic explosion. In *A Billionaire,* a family dies from eating radioactive tuna, leaving only a lazy elder son and a sympathetic tax collector. In *The Key,* a group of rather selfish, despicable people are poisoned inadvertently by a senile old maid, who becomes the only survivor. The film is a study of an old man who becomes obsessed with sex to compensate for his fears of impotency. He becomes a voyeur, and through the manipulation of the camera, we come to share in this activity. Slowly, however, he emerges as being sympathetic while the other characters are revealed in their true light.

Throughout his career Ichikawa has proven himself a consistent critic of Japanese society, treating such themes as the rebirth of militarism (*Mr. Pu*), the harshness and inhumanity of military feudalism (*Fires on the Plain*), the abuse of the individual within the family (*Bonchi* and *Her Brother*), as well as familial claustrophobia and the tendency of repression to result in perversion and outbreaks of violence (*The Key*). His films usually refuse a happy ending, and Ichikawa has been frequently criticized for an unabashed pessimism, bordering on nihilism.

Two of his most important films, *Harp of Burma* and *Fires on the Plain,* deal with the tragedies of war. The former concerns a soldier who adopts Buddhist robes and dedicates himself to burying the countless Japanese dead on Burma; the latter is about a group of demoralized soldiers who turn to cannibalism. A third work, *Tokyo Olympiad,* provided a new approach to sports films, giving as much attention to human emotions and spectator reactions as to athletic feats.

Ichikawa is a master of the wide screen and possesses a strong sense of composition, creating enormous depth with his use of diagonal and overhead shots. Often he utilizes black backgrounds to isolate images within the frame, or a form of theatrical lighting, or he blocks out portions of the screen to alter the format and ratio.

Ichikawa remains fascinated with experimental techniques. His excellent use of the freeze frame in *Kagi* reflects his case study approach to characterization. He has also done much in the way of color experimentation. *Kagi* is bathed in blues, which bleach skin tones to white, thus creating corpse-like subjects. *Her Brother* is so filtered that it resembles a black and white print with dull pinks and reds. On most of his films, Ichikawa has used cameramen Kazuo Miyagawa or Setsuo Kobayashi.

After *Tokyo Olympiad* Ichikawa encountered many studio difficulties. His projects since then include a twenty-six-part serialization of *The Tale of Genji* and *The Wanderers,* a parody of gangster films with a nod to *Easy Rider,* plus a dozen documentaries and fiction features, among which *The Inugami Family,* a suspense thriller, proved to be the biggest box office success in Japanese film history.

—Patricia Erens

IMAI, Tadashi

Nationality: Japanese. **Born:** Tokyo, 8 January 1912. **Education:** Tokyo Imperial University, until 1935. **Family:** Married in 1934 and 1955. **Career:** Assistant at J.O. Studio, Kyoto, from 1935; directed first film, *Numazu Hei-gakko,* 1939; joined Communist party, late 1940s; left Toho, helped initiate independent film production movement, 1950; "prestige director" for Toei, Daiei, and other studios, 1953 through 1960s; resumed independent production, 1969. **Awards:** Mainichi Film Competition Award, for *The People's Enemy,* 1946; five Kinema Jumpo Awards for Best Japanese Film, 1950s. **Address:** 1-4-1 Yazakicho, Fuchu City, Tokyo, Japan.

Films as Director:

1939 *Numazu Hei-gakko* (*Numazu Military Academy*); *Waga kyokan* (*Our Teacher*)
1940 *Tajiko mura* (*The Village of Tajiko*); *Onna no machi* (*Women's Town*); *Kakka* (*Your Highness*)
1941 *Kekkon no seitai* (*Married Life*)
1943 *Boro no kesshitai* (*The Suicide Troops of the Watch Tower*; *The Death Command of the Tower*)
1944 *Ikari no umi* (*Angry Sea*)
1945 *Ai to chikai* (*Love and Pledge*)
1946 *Minshu no teki* (*An Enemy of the People*; *The People's Enemy*); *Jinsei tonbo-gaeri* (*Life Is Like a Somersault*)
1947 *Chikagai nijuyo-jikan* (*Twenty-four Hours of a Secret Life*)
1949 *Aoi sanmyaku* (*Green Mountains*) parts I and II; *Onna no kao* (*A Woman's Face*)
1950 *Mata au hi made* (*Until We Meet Again*)
1951 *Dokkoi ikiteiru* (*Still We Live*)
1952 *Yamabiko gakko* (*School of Echoes*)
1953 *Himeyuri no to* (*The Tower of Lilies*; *Himeyuri Lily Tower*); *Nigori-e* (*Muddy Water*)
1955 *Aisureba koso* (*Because I Love*), episode; *Koko ni izumi ari* (*Here Is a Fountain*); *Yukiko*
1956 *Mahiru no ankoku* (*Darkness at Noon*)
1957 *Kome* (*Rice*); *Junai monogatari* (*The Story of Pure Love*)
1958 *Yoru no tsuzumi* (*The Adulteress*; *Night Drum*); *Kiku to Isamu* (*Kiku and Isamu*)
1960 *Shiroi gake* (*The Cliff*; *White Cliff*)
1961 *Are ga minato no hikari da* (*That Is the Port Light*)
1962 *Nippon no obachan* (*Japanese Grandmothers*; *The Old Women of Japan*)
1963 *Bushido zankoku monogatari* (*Bushido: Samurai Saga*; *The Cruel Story of the Samurai's Way*)
1964 *Echigo tsutsuishi oyashirazu* (*Death in the Snow*); *Adauchi* (*Revenge*)
1967 *Sato-gashi ga kazureru toki* (*When the Cookie Crumbles*)
1968 *Fushin no toki* (*The Time of Reckoning*)
1969 *Hashi no nai kawa* (*River without Bridges*)
1970 *Hashi no nai kawa* (*River without Bridges*) Part II
1971 *En to iu onna* (*A Woman Named En*)
1972 *Aa koe naki tomo* (*Ah! My Friends without Voice*); *Kaigun tokubetsu shonen hei* (*Special Boy Soldiers of the Navy*)
1974 *Kobayashi Takiji* (*The Life of a Communist Writer*)
1976 *Ani imoto* (*Mon and Ino*; *Older Brother and Younger Sister*); *Yoba* (*The Old Woman Ghost*)
1982 *Himeyuri no to* (*Himeyuri Lily Tower*) (remake)
1991 *Senso to Seishun* (*War and Youth*)

Publications

On IMAI: books—

Anderson, Joseph, and Donald Richie, *The Japanese Film,* New York, 1961; revised edition, Princeton, 1982.
Mellen, Joan, *Voices from the Japanese Cinema,* New York, 1975.
Mellen, Joan, *The Waves at Genji's Door,* New York, 1976.

On IMAI: articles—

Philippe, Pierre, "Imai: La Femme infidèle," in *Cinema* (Paris), February 1964.
Tayama, Rikiya, "Imai Tadashi," in *Image et Son* (Paris), July 1964.

Iawaski, Akira, "La Production independante," in *Cinema* (Paris), September/October 1969.

* * *

After displaying early Marxist commitment, Imai was forced to give up politics under Japan's World War II military regime. Because of the regime's ideological restriction, Imai's first works were so-called "war-collaboration" films. Some of them are nonetheless valued for Western-style action sequence technique (for example, *The Death Command of the Tower*) and for the successful depiction of the personality of an army officer (*Our Teacher*).

Imai's postwar return to Marxism surprised his audience. As early as 1946, he made a film that severely attacked corruption among the wartime rulers, and he preached on behalf of postwar democracy in *The People's Enemy.* Imai's real fame came with his record-breaking commercial success, *Green Mountains,* which became legendary for its reflection of the almost revolutionary excitement of the postwar period. The film depicts, in a light, humorous style, the struggle at a small town high school against the established institutions and values.

Until We Meet Again became another legendary film for its romantic, lyrical treatment of tragic wartime love. In particular, the scene of the young lovers kissing through the window glass became famous. The Red Purge at the time of the Korean War drove Imai out of the organized film industry. He then became one of the most active filmmakers, initiating the postwar leftist independent film production movement.

His successive films fall into two main categories—films analyzing social injustice and oppression from the Communist point of view, and meticulously made literary adaptations. The films of the first category outnumber the second. Imai was much influenced by Italian neorealism in his themes and semi-documentary method based on location shooting. The hardship and tribulations of the proletariat are depicted in *Still We Live* (about day-laborers), *Rice* (concerning farmers), and *That Is the Port Light* (about fishermen and problems between Japan and Korea). Social problems are treated in *School of Echoes* (concerning the progressive education movement in a poor mountain village), *Kiku and Isamu,* which deals with Japanese-black mixed-blood children, *Japanese Grandmother* (on the aged), and *River without Bridges I* and *II,* about discrimination against the outcast class. The mistaken verdict in a murder case is the subject of *Darkness at Noon,* which condemns the police and the public prosecutor. *Himeyuri Lily Tower,* another commercial hit, depicts tragic fighting on Okinawa toward the end of the war, showing the cruelty of both the Japanese and the American forces. *Night Drum, The Cruel Story of the Samurai's Way, Revenge,* and *A Woman Named En* focus on feudalism and its oppression from the viewpoint of its victims.

These films all embody an explicit and rather crude leftist point-of-view. However, Imai's talent at entertaining the audience with deft storytelling and comfortable pacing attracted popular and critical support for his work. Imai is especially skillful in powerful appeals to the audience's sentimentalism. His distinctive lyrical and humanistic style is valued and helps us to differentiate Imai from other more dogmatic leftist directors.

Imai is also appreciated for his depiction of details. This trait helped make his literary adaptations (e.g. *Muddy Water*) so successful that every ambitious actress was said to want to appear in Imai's films to obtain prizes. His collaboration with the excellent scenario writer, Yoko Mizuki, is indispensable to Imai's success.

Imai's unchanged formula of the poor being oppressed by the authorities became increasingly out-of-date through the 1960s and 1970s. However, his lyricism still proved to be attractive in more recent works, such as *Older Brother and Younger Sister.*

—Kyoko Hirano

IMAMURA, Shohei

Nationality: Japanese. **Born:** Tokyo, 1926. **Education:** Educated in technical school, Tokyo, until 1945; studied occidental history at Waseda University, Tokyo, graduated 1951. **Career:** Assistant director at Shochiku's Ofuna studios, 1951; moved to Nikkatsu studios, 1954; assistant to director Yuzo Kawashima, 1955-58; directed first film, *Nusumareta yokuju,* 1958; formed Imamura Productions, 1965; worked primarily for TV, from 1970; founder and teacher, Yokohama Broadcast Film Institute. **Awards:** Palme d'Or, Cannes Festival, for *The Ballad of Narayama,* 1983.

Films as Director:

1958 *Nusumareta yokujo* (*Stolen Desire*); *Nishi Ginza eki mae* (*Lights of Night*; *Nishi Ginza Station*) (+ sc); *Hateshinaki yokubo* (*Endless Desire*) (+ co-sc)
1959 *Nianchan* (*My Second Brother*; *The Diary of Sueko*) (+ co-sc)
1961 *Buta to gunkan* (*The Flesh Is Hot*; *Hogs and Warships*) (+ co-sc)
1963 *Nippon konchuki* (*The Insect Woman*) (+ co-sc)
1964 *Akai satsui* (*Unholy Desire*; *Intentions of Murder*) (+ co-sc)
1966 *Jinruigaku nyumon* (*The Pornographers: Introduction to Anthropology*) (+ co-sc, pr)
1967 *Ningen johatsu* (*A Man Vanishes*) (+ sc, role, pr)
1968 *Kamigami no fukaki yokubo* (*The Profound Desire of the Gods*; *Kuragejima: Tales from a Southern Island*) (+ co-pr, co-sc)
1970 *Nippon sengoshi: Madamu Omboro no seikatsu* (*History of Postwar Japan as Told by a Bar Hostess*) (+ co-pr, planning, role as interviewee)
1975 *Karayuki-san* (*Karayuki-san, the Making of a Prostitute*) (for TV) (+ co-pr, planning)
1979 ***Fukushu suruwa ware ni ari*** (*Vengeance Is Mine*)
1980 *Eijanaika* (*Why Not?*) (+ co-sc)
1983 ***Narayama bushi-ko*** (*The Ballad of Narayama*)
1987 *Zegen* (*The Pimp*)
1988 *Kuroi Ame* (*Black Rain*)

Other Films:

1951 *Bakushu* (*Early Summer*) (Ozu) (asst d)
1952 *Ochazuke no aji* (*The Flavor of Green Tea over Rice*) (Ozu) (asst d)
1953 ***Tokyo monogatari*** (*Tokyo Story*) (Ozu) (asst d)
1954 *Kuroi ushio* (*Black Tide*) (Yamamura) (asst d)
1955 *Tsukiwa noborinu* (*Moonrise*) (Tanaka) (asst d)
1956 *Fusen* (*The Balloon*) (Kawashima) (co-sc)
1958 *Bakumatsu Taiyoden* (*Saheiji Finds a Way*; *Sun Legend of the Shogunate's Last Days*) (Kawashima) (co-sc)
1959 *Jigokuno magarikago* (*Turning to Hell*) (Kurahara) (co-sc)
1962 *Kyupora no aru machi* (*Cupola Where the Furnaces Glow*) (Uravama) (sc)
1963 *Samurai no ko* (*Son of a Samurai*; *The Young Samurai*) (Wakasugi) (co-sc)
1964 *Keirin shonin gyojoki* (Nishimira) (co-sc)
1967 *Neon taiheiki-keieigaku nyumon* (*Neon Jungle*) (Isomi) (co-sc)
1968 *Higashi Shinaki* (*East China Sea*) (Isomi) (story, co-sc)

Publications

By IMAMURA: book—

Sayonara dake ga jinsei-da [Life Is Only Goodbye: Biography of Director Yuzo Kawashima], Tokyo, 1969.

Shohei Imamura: *Kamigami no fukaki yokubo*

By IMAMURA: articles—

"Monomaniaque de l'homme...," in *Jeune Cinéma* (Paris), November 1972.

Interview with S. Hoass, in *Cinema Papers* (Melbourne), September/October 1981.

Interview with Max Tessier, in *Revue du Cinéma* (Paris), September 1983.

Interview with C. Tesson, in *Cahiers du Cinéma* (Paris), November 1987.

Interview in *Revue du Cinéma/Image et Son* (Paris), November 1989.

On IMAMURA: books—

Imamura Shohei no eiga [The Films of Shohei Imamura], Tokyo, 1971.

Mellen, Joan, *Voices from the Japanese Cinema,* New York, 1975.

Sugiyama, Heiichi, *Sekai no eiga sakka 8: Imamura Shohei* [Film Directors of the World 8: Shohei Imamura], Tokyo, 1975.

Bock, Audie, *Japanese Film Directors,* New York, 1978; revised edition, Tokyo, 1985.

Tessier, Max, editor, *Le Cinema japonais au present: 1959-1979,* Paris, 1980.

Richie, Donald, with Audie Bock, *Notes for a Study on Shohei Imamura,* Bergamo, 1987.

Piccardi, Adriano, and Angelo Signorelli, *Shohei Imamura,* Bergamo, 1987.

On IMAMURA: articles—

Yamada, Koichi, "Les Cochons et les dieux: Imamura Shohei," in *Cahiers du Cinéma* (Paris), May/June 1965.

"Dossier on Imamura," in *Positif* (Paris), April 1982.

Gillett, John, "Shohei Imamura," in *Film Dope* (London), January 1983.

Casebier, A., "Images of Irrationality in Modern Japan: The Films of Shohei Imamura," in *Film Criticism* (Edinboro, Pennsylvania), Fall 1983.

Kehr, Dave, "The Last Rising Sun," in *Film Comment* (New York), September/October 1983.

"Imamura Section" of *Positif* (Paris), May 1985.

* * *

Outrageous, insightful, sensuous, and great fun to watch, the films of Shohei Imamura are among the greatest glories of postwar Japanese cinema, yet Imamura remains largely unknown outside of Japan. Part of the reason, to be sure, lies in the fact that Imamura has until recently worked for small studios such as Nikkatsu or on his own independently financed productions. But it may also be because Imamura's films fly so furiously in the face of what most westerners have come to expect of Japanese films.

After some amateur experience as a theater actor and director, Imamura joined Shochiku Studios in 1951 as an assistant director, where he worked under, among others, Yasujiro Ozu. His first important work, *My Second Brother,* an uncharacteristically gentle tale set among Korean orphans living in postwar Japan, earned him third place in the annual *Kinema Jumpo* "Best Japanese Film of the Year" poll, and from then on Imamura's place within the Japanese industry was established. Between 1970 and 1978, Imamura "retired" from feature filmmaking, concentrating his efforts instead on a series of remarkable television documentaries that explored little-known sides of postwar Japan. In 1978, Imamura returned to features with his greatest commercial and critical success, *Vengeance Is Mine,* a complex, absorbing study of a cold-blooded killer. In 1983, his film *The Ballad of Narayama* was awarded the Gold Palm at the Cannes Film Festival, symbolizing Imamura's belated discovery by the international film community.

Imamura has stated that he likes to make "messy films," and it is the explosive, at times anarchic quality of his work that makes him appear "uncharacteristically Japanese" when seen in the context of Ozu, Mizoguchi, or Kurosawa. Perhaps no other filmmaker anywhere has taken up Jean-Luc Godard's challenge to end the distinction between "documentary" and "fiction" films. In preparation for filming, Imamura will conduct exhaustive research on the people whose story he will tell, holding long interviews to extract information and to become familiar with different regional vocabularies and accents (many of his films are set in remote regions of Japan). Insisting always on location shooting and direct sound, Imamura has been referred to as the "cultural anthropologist" of the Japanese cinema. Even the titles of some of his films—*The Pornographers: Introduction to Anthropology* and *The Insect Woman* (whose Japanese title literally translates to "Chronicle of a Japanese Insect")—seem to reinforce the "scientific" spirit of these works. Yet, if anything, Imamura's films argue against an overly-clinical approach to understanding Japan, as they often celebrate the irrational and instinctual aspects of Japanese culture.

Strong female protagonists are usually at the center of Imamura's films, yet it would be difficult to read these films as "women's films" in the way that critics describe works by Mizoguchi or Naruse. Rather, women in Imamura's films are always the ones more directly linked to "ur-Japan,"—a kind of primordial fantasy of Japan not only preceeding "westernization" but before any contact with the outside world. In *The Profound Desire of the Gods,* a brother and sister on a small southern island fall in love and unconsciously attempt to recreate the myth of Izanagi and Izanami, sibling gods whose union founded the Japanese race. Incest, a subject which might usually be seen as shocking, is treated as a perfectly natural expression, becoming a crime only due to the influence of "westernized" Japanese who have come to civilize the island. Imamura's characters indulge freely and frequently in sexual activity, and sexual relations tend to act as a kind of barometer for larger, unseen social forces. The lurid, erotic spectacles in *Eijanaika,* for example, are the clearest indication of growing frustrations that finally explode in massive riots in the film's conclusion.

—Richard Peña

INGRAM, Rex

Nationality: Irish/American. **Born:** Reginald Ingram Montgomery Hitchcock in Dublin, 15 January 1893. **Education:** Saint Columba's College, Dublin; studied sculpture at Yale, 1911. **Military Service:** Served in Canadian Air Force (wounded in action), 1918. **Family:** Married 1) actress Doris Pawn, 1917 (divorced 1920); 2) Alice Terry, 1921. **Career:** Immigrated to United States, 1911; actor in England, 1912; assistant for Edison Co., New York, also scenario writer for Stuart Blackton and screen actor, 1913; moved to Vitagraph, 1914; hired by Fox, changed name to Rex Ingram, 1915; director for Universal, 1916; contracted by Paralta-W.W. Hodkinson Corp., 1918; joined Metro Pictures, 1920; moved to France, 1923; modernized Studios de la Victorine de Saint-Augustin, Nice, 1924; established Ingram Hamilton Syndicated Ltd. production company, London, 1928; moved to Egypt, 1934; returned to Hollywood, 1936. **Awards:** Honorary degree, Yale University; Légion d'honneur française. **Died:** In California, 1950.

Films as Director:

1916 *The Great Problem* (Truth) (+ sc); *Broken Fetters* (*A Human Pawn*) (+ sc); *Chalice of Sorrow* (*The Fatal Promise*) (+ sc); *Black Orchids* (*The Fatal Orchids*) (+ sc)
1917 *The Reward of the Faithless* (*The Ruling Passion*) (+ sc); *The Pulse of Life* (+ sc); *The Flower of Doom* (+ sc); *Little Terror* (+ sc)
1918 *His Robe of Honor*; *Humdrum Brown*
1919 *The Day She Paid*
1920 *Under Crimson Skies* (*The Beach Comber*); *Shore Acres*; *Hearts Are Trumps*
1921 ***The Four Horsemen of the Apocalypse*** (+ pr); *The Conquering Power* (*Eugenie Grandet*); *Turn to the Right*
1922 *The Prisoner of Zenda*; *Trifling Women* (+ sc) (remake of *Black Orchids*); *Where the Pavement Ends* (+ sc)
1923 *Scaramouche* (+ pr)
1924 *The Arab* (*L'Arabe*) (+ sc)
1925 *Mare Nostrum* (+ co-pr)
1926 *The Magician* (+ co-pr, sc)
1927 *The Garden of Allah*
1929 *The Three Passions* (*Les Trois Passions*) (+ sc)
1931 *Baroud* (*Love in Morocco*; *Passion in the Desert*) (+ pr, co-sc)

Other Films:

1913 *Hard Cash* (Reid) (role, sc); *The Family's Honor* (Ridgely) (sc); *Beau Brummel* (Young) (role); *The Artist's Great Madonna* (Young) (role); *A Tudor Princess* (Dawley) (role)
1914 *Witness to the Will* (Lessey) (role); *The Necklace of Ramses* (Brabin) (role); *The Price of the Necklace* (Brabin) (role); *The Borrowed Finery* (role); *Her Great Scoop* (Costello and Gaillord) (role); *The Spirit and the Clay* (Lambart) (role); *The Southerners* (Ridgely and Collins) (role); *Eve's Daughter* (North) (role); *The Crime of Cain* (Marston) (role); *The Circus and the Boy* (Johnson) (role); *David Garrick* (Young) (role); *The Upper Hand* (Humphrey) (role); *Fine Feathers Make Fine Birds* (Humphrey) (role); *His Wedded Wife* (Humphrey) (role); *Goodbye, Summer* (Brooke) (role); *The Moonshine Maid and the Man* (Gaskill) (role)
1915 *Should a Mother Tell?* (Edwards) (sc); *The Song of Hate* (Edwards) (sc, role); *The Wonderful Adventure* (Thompson) (sc); *The Blindness of Devotion* (Edwards) (sc); *A Woman's Past* (Powell) (sc); *The Galley Slave* (Edwards) (co-sc, uncredited); *The Evil Men Do* (Costello and Gaillord) (role); *Snatched From a Burning Death* (Gaskill) (role)
1916 *The Cup of Bitterness* (sc)
1923 *Mary of the Movies* (McDermot) (role as a guest)
1925 ***Greed*** (von Stroheim) (co-ed 2nd cut)

Publications

By INGRAM: articles—

Interview with L. Montanye, in *Motion Picture Classic* (Brooklyn), July 1921.

Interview with J. Robinson, in *Photoplay* (New York), August 1921.

Article in *Motion Picture Directing,* by Peter Milne, New York, 1922.

On INGRAM: books—

Predal, Rene, *Rex Ingram,* Paris, 1970.
O'Leary, Liam, *Rex Ingram, Master of the Silent Cinema,* Dublin, 1980.

On INGRAM: articles—

Obituary in *New York Times,* 23 July 1950.
Geltzer, George, "Hollywood's Handsomest Director," in *Films in Review* (New York), May 1952.
O'Laoghaire, Liam, "Rex Ingram and the Nice Studios," in *Cinema Studies* (England), December 1961.
Bodeen, Dewitt, "Rex Ingram and Alice Terry," in two parts in *Films in Review* (New York), February and March 1975.
O'Leary, Liam, "Rex Ingram," in *Film Dope* (London), July 1983.

On INGRAM: film—

Graham, Dan, *The Conquering Power: Rex Ingram 1893-1950,* 1990.

* * *

Rex Ingram's work has tended to be overlooked and forgotten as a result of his retirement from films in the early 1930s, an era when sound had taken over the world of cinema. He began his career in films in 1913, working as designer, scriptwriter, and actor for Edison, Vitagraph, and Fox. In 1916 he directed his own story, *The Great Problem,* for Universal at the age of only twenty-three. His educational background was that of an Irish country rectory and the Yale School of Fine Arts, where he studied sculpture under Lee Lawrie and developed an aesthetic sense which informed all his films.

The early films Ingram made for Universal have disappeared. His version of *La Tosca,* transferred to a Mexican setting as *Chalice of Sorrow,* and a 1922 remake of *Black Orchids* titled *Trifling Women,* earned critical attention for the quality of the acting and their visual beauty. Cleo Madison starred in both these films. The fragment that exists of *The Reward of the Faithless* shows a realism that is reminiscent of von Stroheim, who was later to acknowledge his indebtedness by allowing Ingram to do the second cutting on *Greed.* It may be noted also that greed was the theme of *The Conquering Power.* A characteristic element of Ingram's work was the use of grotesque figures like dwarfs and hunchbacks to offset the glamour of his heroes. After a period of ups and downs, he made another film for Universal in 1920, *Under Crimson Skies,* which won critical acclaim.

Rex Ingram with Alice Terry

With the release of *The Four Horsemen of the Apocalypse* in 1921 Ingram achieved top status in his profession. Ordinarily, Valentino dominates discussion of this film, but Ingram's work on the feature is of the highest quality. Armed with his team of cameraman John Seitz and editor Grant Whytock, Ingram went on to make a dazzlingly successful series of films for Metro. His financial and artistic success gave him carte blanche and his name became a box-office draw. *The Conquering Power, The Prisoner of Zenda* and *Scaramouche* featured his wife, the beautiful and talented Alice Terry, and the latter two films introduced a new star, Ramon Novarro, who also played with Alice Terry in the South Seas romance *Where the Pavement Ends.* Ingram made stars and knew how to get the best out of players. He came to be considered the equal of Griffith, von Stroheim, and DeMille.

In 1924 the formation of Metro-Goldwyn-Mayer saw a tightening up of front office control over the creative director and Ingram sought fresh fields to conquer. He made *The Arab* with Terry and Novarro in North Africa, a region that he fell in love with. He next moved to Nice, where he founded the Rex Ingram Studios and released his masterpiece *Mare Nostrum* in 1926 for "Metro-Goldwyn." (He would never allow his arch-enemy Louis B. Mayer to have a credit.) In this work Alice Terry gave her best performance as the Mata Hari-like heroine. This film as well as *The Four Horsemen,* both of which were authored by Blasco Ibañez, were later suppressed because of its anti-German sentiments.

The German-inspired *The Magician* featured Paul Wegener (the original *Golem*) and was based on a Somerset Maugham story. After *The Garden of Allah* Ingram broke with MGM in 1926. *The Three Passions,* with an industrial background, followed in 1929. His last film, *Baroud,* a sound film in which he himself played the lead, completed a distinguished career.

Ingram sold his studios in Nice, where he had reigned as an uncrowned king; as the Victorine Studios they were to become an important element in French film production. Ingram retired to North Africa and later rejoined his wife Alice Terry in Hollywood. He indulged his hobbies of sculpture, writing, and travel.

Ingram was the supreme pictorialist of the screen, a great director of actors, a perfectionist whose influence was felt not least in the films of David Lean and Michael Powell. The themes of his films ranged over many locations but his careful research gave them a realism and authenticity that balanced the essential romanticism of his work.

—Liam O'Leary

IOSELIANI, Otar

Nationality: Soviet Georgian. **Born:** 2 February 1934. **Education:** Educated in music, Tbilisi Conservatory; studied graphic art; degree in mathematics, Moscow University; studied under Alexander Dovzhenko, V.G.I.K., Moscow. **Career:** Directed first feature, *April,* 1961; failed to receive authorization for its distribution, abandoned filmmaking; returned to direct *Listopad,* 1966; **Awards:** FIPRESCI Prize, Berlin Festival, for *Pastorale,* 1982.

Films as Director:

1958 *Akvarel* (*Watercolor*) (short, for TV)
1959 *Sapovnela* (*The Song About Flowers*) (short)
1961 *April* (*Stories About Things*) (not released) (+ sc)
1964 *Tudzi* (*Cast-Iron* (+ sc) (short)
1966 *Listopad* (*When Leaves Fall*; *Falling Leaves*)
1969 *Starinnaja gruzinskaja pesnja* (*Old Georgian Song* (short)
1972 *Zil pevcij drozd* (*There Was a Singing Blackbird*; *There Lived a Thrush*) (+ co-sc)
1976 *Pastoral* (*The Summer in the Country*) (+ co-sc)
1982 *Lettre d'un cinéaste* (short, for TV)
1983 *Sept pièces pour cinéma noir et blanc* (*Seven Pieces for Black and White Cinema*)
1984 *Les Favoris de la Lune*
1988 *Un petit monastère en Toscane* (*A Little Monastery in Tuscany*)
1989 *Et la lumière fut* (*And Then There Was Light*)

Publications

By IOSELIANI: articles—

Interview with G. Kopanevová, in *Film a Doba* (Prague), May 1974.
Interview with Michel Ciment, in *Positif* (Paris), May 1978.
Interview with Serge Daney and S. Toubiana, in *Cahiers du Cinéma* (Paris), November 1979.
Interview with A. Gerber, in *Film a Doba* (Prague), February 1981.
Interview with Serge Toubiana and Alain Bergala, in *Cahiers du Cinéma* (Paris), February 1985.
Interview with Michel Ciment, in *Positif* (Paris), November 1992.

On IOSELIANI: articles—

Cereteli, K., "Stat' ja iz gazety 'Zarja Vostoka'," in *Iskusstvo Kino* (Moscow), November 1973.
"Il était une fois un merle chanteur de O. Iosseliani," in *Revue Belge du Cinéma* (Brussels), vol. 13, no. 1-2, 1975/76.
Martin, Marcel, "L'Art 'Comme la vie' d'Otar Iosseliani," in *Image et Son* (Paris), September 1980.
"Ioseliani Section" of *Positif* (Paris), January 1985.
Gauthier, G., and R. Bassan, "Otar Ioseliani," in *Revue du Cinéma* (Paris), February 1985.
Navailh, F., "Otar Ioseliani," in *Cinéma* (Paris), February 1985.
Christie, Ian, "Pastoral Hide and Seek," in *Monthly Film Bulletin* (London), March 1985.

* * *

The Georgian cinema, which has a history dating back to the 1920s, experienced a renaissance in the 1960s with Otar Ioseliani as its most remarkable representative. Together with Tarkovsky (but in a very different way) he is the young Soviet director who has been the most uncompromising and the most consistent in his aesthetic approach. Born in 1934, he studied music as well as graphic art at the Tbilisi Conservatory, and graduated from Moscow University in mathematics. But finally he chose cinema as his favorite field and graduated from VGIK after attending Alexander Dovzhenko's class. His first film, *April,* of which little is known, was not released. His second, *When Leaves Fall,* shows the characteristic elements of his style. Ioseliani, like many of his contemporaries, is hostile to the cinema of Eisenstein—to his intellectual montage and to the theoretical aspect of his work. In presenting Jean Vigo as his master, Ioseliani insists that he tries "to capture moments of passing life," and in doing so wants to reach the ultimate goal of art. In a way, his films are close to the Czech new wave (Forman, Passer, Menzel), but realism is counterbalanced by a more formal treatment, particularly in the use of sound and off-screen space.

His films also show a disregard for conventional ways of life. Ioseliani's nonconformity, stubbornness, and frankness have alienated authorities. *When Leaves Fall* takes place in a wine factory and

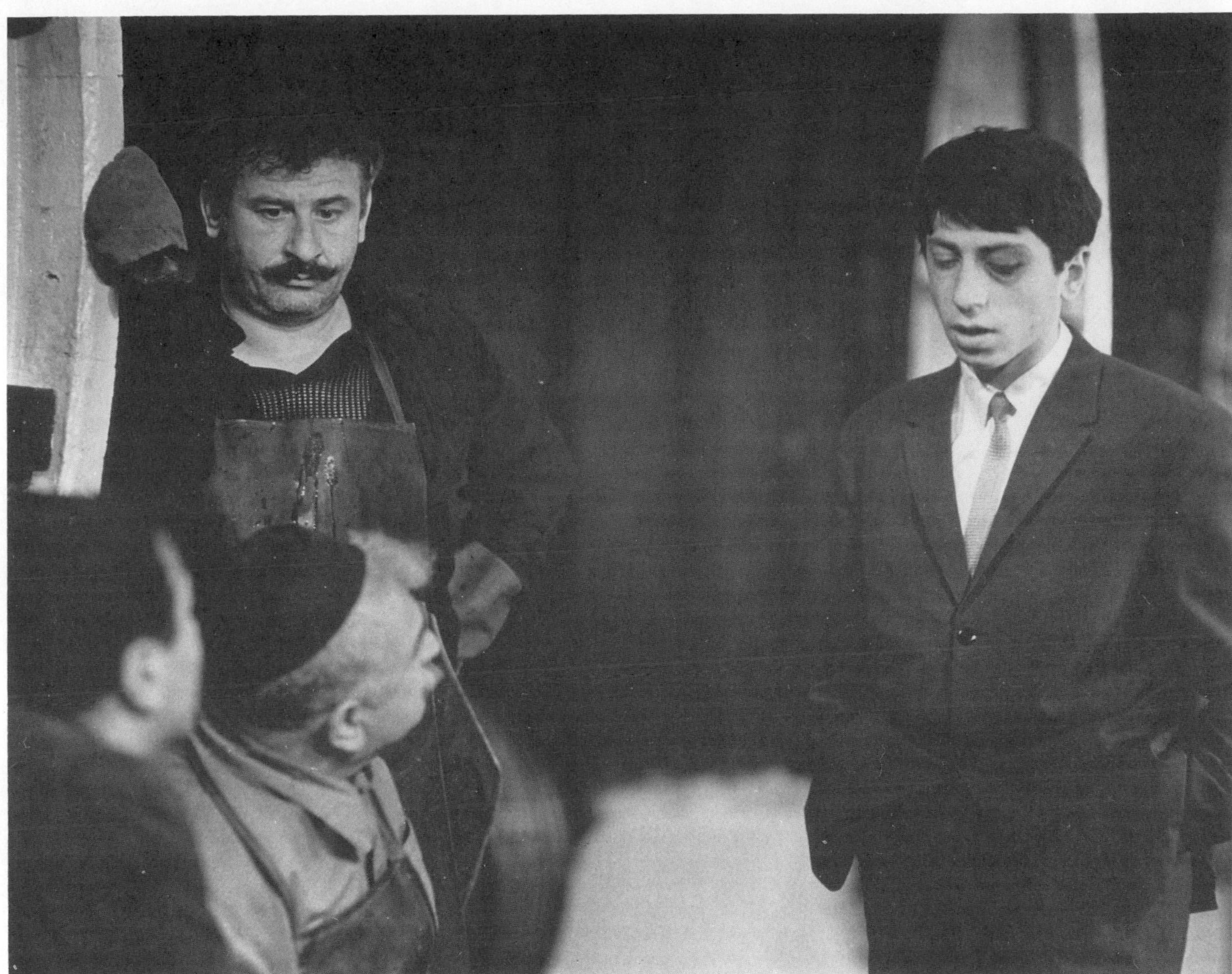

Otar Ioseliani: ***Listopad***

shows an innocent and honest young man trying to live in a bureaucratic universe. He does not wear a moustache, that Georgian symbol of bourgeois respectability.

There Was a Singing Blackbird, Ioseliani's third film, portrays the life of a musician in the Tbilisi orchestra who always arrives at the last minute to perform, being busy enjoying his life, drinking and courting girls. His behavior is an insult to an official morality based on work and duty. Ioseliani's fancifulness and sense of humor are shown at their best in this sprightly comedy that ends tragically with the hero's death. *Pastoral,* which had problems with the Moscow authorities (though the film was shown regularly in Georgia), is about a group of five musicians from the city who come to live with a peasant family. Ioseliani observes the opposition of city and country, and makes a young peasant girl the observer of this delightful conflict of manners and morals. Using many non-professionals—as in his earlier films—the director manages to show us poetically and with truthfulness the life of the Georgian people. Discarding any kind of plot, observing his characters with affection and irony, he is faithful to his anti-dogmatic stance: "Everyone is born to drink the glass of his life." Ioseliani's limited output is of a very high level indeed.

—Michel Ciment

ITAMI, Juzo

Nationality: Japanese. **Born:** Kyoto, May 15, 1933, the son of film director Mansaku Itami. **Education:** High school. **Family:** Married to actress Nobuko Miyamoto, two children. **Career:** Amateur boxer and commercial designer; became film actor, 1960 (sometimes as Ichizo Itami); subsequently stage actor, TV actor and director, TV chat-show host, author, translator, and chef; also edited magazine on psychoanalysis; began directing films at age 50, 1984; stabbed gangland-style in his home, allegedly in retaliation for his depiction of Japanese mobsters in *Mimbo No Onna (Minbo, Or the Gentle Art of Japanese Extortion/The Gangster's Moll/The Anti-Extortion Woman),* 1992. **Address:** Resides in Tokyo.

Films as Director and Scriptwriter:

1984 *Ososhiki* (*The Funeral*)
1986 ***Tampopo*** (*Dandelion*)
1987 *Marusa no onna* (*A Taxing Woman*)
1988 *Marusa no onna II* (*A Taxing Woman Returns*)

Juzo Itami

1990 *A-Ge-Man* (*A-Ge-Man—Tales of a Golden Geisha*) (+ pr)
1991 *Minbo No Onna* (*Minbo, Or the Gentle Art of Japanese Extortion*; *The Gangster's Moll*; *The Anti-Extortion Woman*)
1995 *Daibyonin* (*The Last Dance*; *The Seriously Ill*)

Films as Actor:

1960 *Kirai Kirai Kirai* (*Dislike*) (Edagawa); *Nise Daigakusei* (*The Phoney University Student*) (Masamura); *Ototo* (*Her Brother*) (Ichikawa)
1961 *Kuroi junin no onna* (*The Ten Dark Women*) (Ichikawa)
1963 *55 Days at Peking* (Nicholas Ray)
1964 *Lord Jim* (Brooks)
1966 *Otoko no kao wa rirekisho* (*A Man's Face is His History*) (Kato)
1967 *Nihon Shunka ko* (*A Treatise on Japanese Bawdy Songs*) (Oshima)
1974 *Imoto* (*My Sister, My Love*) (Fujita)
1975 *Wagahai wa nwko dearu* (*I Am a Cat*) (Ichikawa)
1980 *Kusa Meikyu* (*Labyrinth in the Field*) (Terayama); *Yugure made* (*Until Dusk*) (Kuroki)
1983 *Sasameyuki* (*The Makioka Sisters*) (Ichikawa); *Kazoku gemu* (*The Family Game*) (Morita)
1985 *The Makioka Sisters* (Ichikawa); *MacArthur's Children* (Shinoda)

Publications

By ITAMI: books—

Yoroppa taikutsu nikki (*Diary of Boring Days in Europe*), Tokyo, 1965.
Onnatachi yo! (*Listen, Women*).
Nippon sekenbanashi taikei (*Panorama of Japanese Gossips*).
Enjoy French Cooking with Me, 1987.

By ITAMI: articles—

Interview in *Cinema* (Paris), June 1985.
Interview with B. Meares, in *Cinema Papers* (Melbourne), July 1985.
Interview with Tony Rayns, in *Monthly Film Bulletin* (London), April 1988.
Interview with Alan Stanbrook, in *Films and Filming* (London), April 1988.
Interview in *Films and Filming* (London), April 1988.
Interview with L. Tanner, in *Films in Review* (New York), May 1988.

On ITAMI: articles—

Canby, Vincent, "What's so Funny About Japan?" in *New York Times*, 18 June 1989.
Sipe, Jeffrey, "Death and Taxes: A Profile of Juzo Itami," in *Sight and Sound* (London), Summer 1989.
Efron, Sonni, "Japanese Director Juzo Itami Recovering After Gangland-style Stabbing at Home," in *Los Angeles Times*, 26 May 1992.
Sterngold, James, "A Director Boasts of His Scars, and Says He is Right about Japan's Mob," in *New York Times*, 30 August 1992.
"5 Arrested in Slashing of Tokyo Film Maker," in *New York Times*, 4 December 1992.
Kuzue, Suzuki, "Juzo Itami, director extraordinaire," in *Japan Quarterly* (Tokyo), July/September 1993.
Friedland, Jonathan, "Director uses films to question authority," in *Far Eastern Economic Review* (Hong Kong), 21 October 1993.

* * *

It is probable that Itami's films convey meanings to Japanese audiences that are not readily accessible to westerners: they are pervasively concerned with rituals, customs, and practices that go back through centuries, and their interaction with contemporary economic and socio-political actualities. On the other hand, Itami is clearly aware of international cinematic practice, and his films seem made partly with an international audience in mind. Offered here is a westerner's assessment of the films: incomplete, but nonetheless valid.

A westerner, then, would situate Itami somewhere between Buñuel and Almodóvar, *The Funeral* leaning toward the former, *Tampopo* toward the latter (the two *Taxing Woman* movies, though not at all inconsistent with these in tone and attitude, stand apart from them because of their general irreverence and skepticism). Itami has not so far achieved the extraordinary distinction of Buñuel at his best (but neither did Buñuel until he was very old, and then in only a very few films). On the other hand, if *Tampopo,* in its comic-erotic audacities and its seemingly free and inconsequential handling of narrative, evokes a heterosexual Almodóvar, the comparison works very much in Itami's favour, underlining his greater maturity, discipline, and powers of self-criticism: casual *divertissement* as it may seem, *Tampopo* manifests a security of taste, tone, and attitude to which Almodóvar, with his apparently uncritical faith in the sanctity of his own impulses, cannot yet lay claim.

The Funeral can be at once "placed" and done justice to by being juxtaposed with, on the one hand, Buñuel's late films, and, on the other, Altman's *A Wedding.* Superficially, it has far more in common with the latter: a satirical view of ritualized social performances and their emptiness, exposing the manifold hypocrisies they generate. Yet the complexity of attitude—the disturbing fusion of critical rigour and emotional generosity—is closer to Buñuel. *A Wedding,* among the worst films of one of the most uneven of directors, is more complicated than complex, its proliferation of characters and incident encompassed by Altman's contempt for all of it and his desire to assert his superiority: the simplicity and unpleasantness of the attitude precludes any possibility of genuine disturbance.

A Funeral analyses the traditional elaborate rites in documentary detail and precision, while simultaneously undercutting the reverence they are supposed to express with a pervasive sense of absurdity: the old man whose death necessitates all this ceremony, expenditure, and hypocrisy was an unlovable egoist for whom no one felt any particular affection or respect while he was alive. Yet Itami, unlike Altman, never presents his characters as merely stupid, and shows no inclination to demonstrate his superiority to them. If the tone is never *not* satirical, it is also never *only* satirical. One might single out as an example the disturbing interplay of conflicting responses generated by the scene where the son-in-law has sex in the bushes with his mistress while his wife (the dead man's daughter), fully aware of what is going on, quietly distracts herself on a swing. The juxtaposition of the seduction (treated as broad comedy) and the wife's sense of troubled hurt, which takes place in the context of death that encloses the whole action, creates a complex effect capped by the abrupt appearance of Chishu Ryu as the officiating priest, and the accumulated resonances he brings with him from so many Ozu movies. If this is not exactly the tone of *Viridiana,* we are at least not far from that of *The Discreet Charm of the Bourgeoisie,* though the comparison brings with it the reflection that Itami's film has no equivalent for the three "insert narratives" of the Buñuel and the dimension of radical pain and disturbance they introduce.

A Taxing Woman and *A Taxing Woman's Return* represent a remarkably successful attempt to appropriate a popular genre (criminal investigation) for purposes of radical social criticism. For the westerner, at least, they relate interestingly to the recent wave of feminist detective fiction centered on female investigators, of which Sara Paretsky's series of novels remains the most impressive example. There is a crucial difference between Paretsky's V.I. Warshawski and the heroine of Itami's movies: the former is a "private eye," a lone operator, the latter the leader of a government-employed team. Yet the parallel is strong: in both cases the woman becomes committed not simply to the solution of a specific "case" but to the exposure of the corruption and inherent criminality of the patriarchal-capitalist power structure. The radicalism has its limitations. The fact that the "taxing woman" (Itami's wife Nobuko Miyamoto) works for the government prohibits—for all the force of her personal crusade against corporate corruption—the raising of a key question: To what ends are taxes actually used within a capitalist state? The films attack the corruption but are unable to challenge the system that produces it. Itami's commitment to feminism is also somewhat dubious: one suspects that it is more an incidental offshoot of his desire to work with his extremely talented wife (a brilliant comedienne who commands rapid and subtle shifts of tone) rather than being rooted in any firm theoretical basis.

Despite these limitations, the films (together with their wide and international commercial success) are, like Paretsky's novels, sufficient proof that popular genres can be used to dramatize radical positions, and for once the sequel actually improves on the original: tougher, darker, with an altogether bleaker ending, its powerful and disturbing rigour was doubtless made possible by the success of its more lightweight predecessor.

As Itami's career has progressed, his films have not lost their bite. *A-Ge-Man (A-Ge-Man—Tales of a Golden Geisha)* is a discerning examination of conventional male-female associations, depicted via the perceptions of a modern-era geisha. *Minbo No Onna (Minbo, Or the Gentle Art of Japanese Extortion/The Gangster's Moll/The Anti-Extortion Woman),* a rapier-witted satire of Japanese organized crime, follows a gritty lawyer who takes on a blackmailing band of yakuza. Several days after the Japanese premiere of *Minbo No Onna,* Itami was severely injured when his neck and face were slashed, allegedly by members of the yakuza. The incident served as sobering proof that Itami's brand of controversial, radical filmmaking, however high-spirited, can indeed be a dangerous business.

This tragedy, however, did not alter his cinematic style. In the aftermath of the stabbing, Itami commenced pondering the insincere, impersonal manner in which hospital patients in Japan are treated. The result was *Daibyonin (The Last Dance/The Seriously Ill),* a black comedy about a second-rate film director who is diagnosed with cancer.

—Robin Wood, updated by Rob Edelman

IVENS, Joris

Nationality: Dutch. **Born:** Georg Henri Anton Ivens in Nijmegen, Holland, 18 November 1898. **Education:** Economische Hogeschool, Rotterdam, 1916-17 and 1920-21; studied chemistry and photography at Technische Hochschule, Charlottenberg, 1922-23. **Military Service:** Lieutenant in Artillery, 1917-18. **Family:** Married 1) photographer Germaine Krull, 1937 (divorced, 1943); 2) Marceline Loridan. **Career:** Technical director for CAPI (father's firm selling photographic equipment); travelled to U.S.S.R. to meet Soviet filmmakers, 1930; made industrial documentaries in Holland, and began association with cinematographer John Fernhout (John Ferno), 1931; returned to U.S.S.R., 1932; clandestinely filmed striking Belgian miners for *Borinage,* 1933; visited New York, formed group, with Ernest Hemingway, John Dos Passos, Lillian Hellman, Fredric March, and Luise Rainer, to finance films on contemporary events, 1936; filmed *Spanish Earth* during Spanish Civil War, 1937; filmed *400 Million* in China, 1938; made industrial documentaries, U.S., 1939-40; taught at University of Southern California, 1941; invited by John Grierson to direct *Alarme!* for national Film Board of Canada, 1942; worked on *Why We Fight* series, Hollywood, 1943-44; travelled to Sydney, Australia, to make *Indonesia Calls,* regarded as traitorous act by Dutch authorities, 1945-46; moved to Prague, 1947; taught in Lodz, Poland, 1950-51; moved to Paris, 1957; taught filmmaking in Peking, 1958; filmed in Italy and Africa, 1959-60; taught filmmaking in Cuba, 1960-61; taught in Chile, 1962-63; Ivens Archive established after retrospective at Nederlands Filmmuseum, 1964; made first of Vietnam War documentaries, 1965; made 12-part documentary, *Comment Yu-Kong déplaça les montagnes,* with Marceline Loridan and others, in China, 1971-75. **Member:** Filmliga film club, Amsterdam, from 1926. **Awards:** World Peace Prize, Helsinki, 1955; Palme d'Or for Best Documentary for *La Seine a rencontre Paris,* Cannes Festival, 1958; Diploma *Honoris Causa,* Royal College of Art, London, 1978. **Died:** Of a heart attack, in Paris, 28 June 1989.

Films as Director:

1911 *De brandende straal* or *Wigwam* (*Flaming Arrow*) (+ ed, ph)
1927 *Zeedijk-Filmstudie* (*Filmstudy—Zeedijk*) (+ ed, ph)
1928 *Etudes de mouvements* (+ ed, ph); *De Brug* (*The Bridge*) (+ ed, ph)
1929 *Branding* (*The Breakers*) (co-d, ed, ph); *Regen* (*Rain*) (+ ed, ph) (sound version prepared 1932 by Helen van Dongen); *Ik-Film* (*"I" Film*) (co-d, ed, ph) (unfinished); *Schaatsenrijden* (*Skating*; *The Skaters*) (+ ed, ph) (unfinished); *Wij Bouwen* (*We Are Building*) (+ co-sc, ed, ph) [footage shot for but not used in *Wij Bouwen* used for following films: *Heien* (*Pile Driving*) (+ co-sc, ed, ph); *Nieuwe architectur* (*New Architecture*) (+ co-sc, ed, ph); *Caissounbouw Rotterdam* (+ co-sc, ed, ph); *Zuid Limburg* (*South Limburg*) (+ co-sc, ed, ph)]
1929/30 *N.V.V. Congres* (*Congres der Vakvereeinigingen*) (+ ed, ph); *Arm Drenthe* (+ ed, ph)
1930 *De Tribune film: Breken en bouwen* (*The Tribune Film: Break and Build*) (+ ed, ph); *Timmerfabriek* (*Timber Industry*) (+ co-ph, co-ed); *Film-notities uit de Sovjet-Unie* (*News from the Soviet Union*) (+ ed); *Demonstratie van proletarische solidariteit* (*Demonstration of Proletarian Solidarity*) (+ ed)
1931 *Philips-Radio* (*Symphonie industrielle, Industrial Symphony*) (+ co-ph, co-ed); *Creosoot* (*Creosote*) (+ sc, ph, ed)
1932 *Pesn o Gerojach* (*Youth Speaks*; *Song of Heroes*) (+ ed)
1933 *Zuyderzee* (+ sc, co-ph)
1934 *Misére au Borinage* (*Borinage*) (co-d, co-sc, co-ed, co-ph); ***Nieuwe Gronden*** (*New Earth*) (+ sc, co-ph, co-ed, narration)
1937 ***The Spanish Earth*** (+ sc, co-ph)
1939 *The Four Hundred Million* (*China's Four Hundred Million*) (co-d, sc)
1940 *Power and the Land* (+ co-sc): *New Frontiers* (unfinished)
1941 *Bip Goes to Town*; *Our Russian Front* (co-d); *Worst of Farm Disasters*
1942 *Oil for Aladdin's Lamp*
1943 *Alarme!* or *Branle-Bas de combat* (*Action Stations!*) (+ sc, ed) (released in shorter version *Corvette Port Arthur*)
1946 *Indonesia Calling* (+ sc, ed)
1949 *Pierwsze lata* (*The First Years*) (+ co-ed, produced 1947)
1951 *Pokoj zwyciezy swiat* (*Peace Will Win*) (co-d)
1952 *Naprozod mlodziezy* (*Freundschaft siegt*; *Friendship Triumphs*) (co-d); *Wyscig pokoju Warszawa-Berlin-Praga* (*Friedensfahrt*; *Peace Tour*) (+ sc)
1954 *Das Lied der Ströme* (*Song of the Rivers*) (+ co-sc)
1957 *La Seine a rencontré Paris* (+ co-sc); *Die Abenteuer des Till Ulenspiegel* (*The Adventures of Till Eulenspiegel*) (co-d)
1958 *Before Spring* (*Early Spring*; *Letters from China*) (+ sc, ed); *Six Hundred Million People Are with You* (+ ed)

Joris Ivens: *Misére au Borinage*

1960 *L' Italia non e un paese povero* (*Italy Is Not a Poor Country*) (+ co-sc, co-ed); *Demain à Nanguila* (*Nanguila Tomorrow*)
1961 *Carnet de viaje* (+ sc); *Pueblos en armas* (*Cuba, pueblo armado*; *An Armed Nation*) (+ sc)
1963 *... à Valparaiso* (+ sc); *El circo mas pequeño* (*Le Petit Chapiteau*)
1964 *El tren de la victoria* (*Le Train de la victoire*)
1966 *Pour le mistral* (+ co-sc); *Le Ciel, la terre* (*The Sky, the Earth*) (+ narration, appearance); *Rotterdam-Europoort* (*Rotterdam-Europort*; *The Flying Dutchman*)
1967 Hanoi footage in *Loin du Viêt-nam* (*Far from Vietnam*) (co-d)
1968 *Le Dix-septième parallèle* (*The Seventeenth Parallel*) (co-d, co-sc); *Aggrippès à la terre* (co-d); *Déterminés à vaincre* (co-d)
1969 *Rencontre avec le Président Ho Chi Minh* (co-d); (next 7 titles made as part of collective including Marceline Loridan, Jean-Pierre Sergent, Emmanuele Castro, Suzanne Fen, Antoine Bonfanti, Bernard Ortion, and Anne Rullier): *Le Peuple et ses fusils* (*The People and Their Guns*); *L' Armée populaire arme le peuple*; *La Guerre populaire au Laos*; *Le Peuple peut tout*; *Qui commande aux fusils*; *Le Peuple est invincible*; *Le Peuple ne peut rien sans ses fusils*
1976 *Comment Yukong déplaça les montagnes* (in 12 parts totalling 718 minutes) (co-d)
1977 *Les Kazaks—Minorité nationale—Sinking* (co-d); *Les Ouigours—Minorité nationale—Sinkiang* (co-d)
1988 *Une Histoire de vent* (co-d)

Other Films:

1929/30 *Jeugd-dag* (*Days of Youth*) (co-ed)
1931 Short film in *VVVC Journal* series (ed)
1956 *Mein Kind* (*My Child*) (Pozner and Machalz) (artistic supervisor)
1957 *Die Windrose* (*The Wind Rose*) (Bellon and others) (co-supervisor)
1972 *Grierson* (Blais) (role as interviewee)
1981 *Conversations with Willard Van Dyke* (Rothschild) (role as interviewee)

Publications

By IVENS: books—

Lied der Ströme, with Valdimir Pozner, Berlin, 1957.
Joris Ivens, edited by W. Klaue and others, Berlin, 1963.

Autobiografie van een Filmer, Amsterdam, 1970.
The Camera and I, Berlin, 1974.
Entretiens avec Joris Ivens, with Claire Devarrieux, Paris, 1979.
Joris Ivens: ou, La Memoire d'un regard, with Robert Destanque, Paris, 1982.

By IVENS: articles—

Numerous articles in *Filmliga* (Amsterdam), 1928-32.
"Notes on Hollywood," in *New Theatre* (New York), 28 October 1936.
"Collaboration in Documentary," in *Film* (New York), 1940.
"Apprentice to Film," in *Theatre Arts* (New York), March and April 1946.
"*Borinage*—A Documentary Experience," in *Film Culture* (New York), no. 1, 1956.
"Ik-Film," in *Skoop* (Amsterdam), no. 2, 1964.
"Ivens Issue" of *Film Culture* (New York), Spring 1972.
"Entretien avec Joris Ivens and Marceline Loridan," with J. Grant and G. Frot-Coutaz, in *Cinéma* (Paris), April 1976.
"Joris Ivens Filming in China," interview with D. Bickley, in *Filmmakers Newsletter* (Ward Hill, Massachusetts), February 1977.
Interview with E. Naaijkems and others, in *Skrien* (Amsterdam), October 1977.
Interview with E. Decaux and B. Villien, in *Cinématographe* (Paris), September 1982.
"Borinage," in *Revue Belge du Cinéma* (Brussels), Winter 1983/Spring 1984.
Interview with P. van Bueren, in *Skoop* (Amsterdam), February/March 1984.
Interview with D. Shaffer, in *Cineaste* (New York), vol. 14, no. 1, 1985.

On IVENS: books—

Hemingway, Ernest, *The Spanish Earth,* Cleveland, 1938.
Zalzman, Abraham, *Joris Ivens,* Paris, 1963.
Grelier, Robert, *Joris Ivens,* Paris, 1965.
Wegner, Hans, *Joris Ivens, Dokumentarist den Wahrheit,* Berlin, 1965.
Loridan, Marceline, *Dix-septieme Parallèle, la guerre du peuple,* Paris, 1968.
Meyer, Han, *Joris Ivens, de weg naar Vietnam,* Utrecht, 1970.
Kremeier, Klaus, *Joris Ivens, ein Filmer an den Fronten der Weltrevolution,* Berlin, 1976.
Joris Ivens; 50 jaar wereldcineast, Nederlands Filmmuseum, Amsterdam, 1978.
Passek, Jean-Loup, editor, *Joris Ivens: Cinquante ans de cinéma,* Paris, 1979.
Brunel, Claude, *Joris Ivens,* Paris, 1983.
Waugh, Thomas, editor, *"Show Us Life": Toward a History and Aesthetics of the Committed Documentary,* Metuchen, New Jersey, 1984.

On IVENS: articles—

Ferguson, Otis, "Guest Artist," in the *New Republic* (New York), 15 April and 13 May 1936.
Grenier, Cynthia, "Joris Ivens: Social Realist vs. Lyric Poet," in *Sight and Sound* (London), Spring 1958.
"Ivens Issue" of *Cine Cubano* (Havana), no. 3, 1960.
Waugh, Thomas, "How Yukong Moved the Mountains: Filming the Cultural Revolution," in *Jump Cut* (Berkeley), 30 December 1976.
Sklar, Robert, "Joris Ivens—The China Close-Up," in *American Film* (Washington, D.C.), June 1978.
Hogenkamp, B., "Joris Ivens 50 jaar wereldcineast," in *Skrien* (Amsterdam), November 1978.
van Dongen, Helen, "'Ik kwam Joris Ivens tegen': 'waarom ben je bij de film gegaan?'," in *Skoop* (Amsterdam), November 1978.
Jervis, N., "The Chinese Connection: Filmmaking in the People's Republic," in *Film Library Quarterly* (New York), no. 1, 1979.
Hogenkamp, B., "Joris Ivens and the Problems of the Documentary Film," in *Framework* (Norwich, England), Autumn 1979.
Waugh, Thomas, "Travel Notebook—A People in Arms: Joris Ivens' Work in Cuba," in *Jump Cut* (Berkeley), May 1980.
Waugh, Thomas, and P. Pappas, "Joris Ivens Defended," letters, in *Cineaste* (New York), Fall 1980.
"Ivens Issue" of *Avant-Scène du Cinéma* (Paris), 1 January 1981.
Waugh, Thomas, "Men Cannot Act in Front of the Camera in the Presence of Death," in *Cineaste* (New York), vol. 12, no. 2, 1982.
"Joris Ivens," in *Film Dope* (London), July 1983.
Revue du Cinéma/Image et Son (Paris), March 1989.
Sight and Sound (London), Autumn 1989.

On IVENS: film—

Hudon, Wieslaw, *A chacun son Borinage,* Belgium, 1978.

* * *

From his debut with *The Bridge* in 1928, Joris Ivens made over 50 documentary films. A staunch advocate of a socialist society, Ivens consistently attacked fascism and colonialism in his films made after 1930. His first two films, *The Bridge* and *Rain,* are rather abstract. Here Ivens's main concern is the elaboration of a varied, often breathtaking, rhythm of images. In this, he appears to be indebted to the French and German avant-garde films, notably those by Ruttmann and Man Ray.

In 1930 Ivens visited the U.S.S.R. at the invitation of Pudovkin. The compelling expressiveness of Russian agit-prop films had a deep influence upon Ivens in shaping his unique and powerful style. According to Ivens, films should convey social and political insights by confronting the public directly with reality. This analytical and didactic viewpoint was exemplified in *Komsomol,* the first film Ivens made in Russia. His 1934 film *Misére au Borinage* not only shows in pitiful and often violent images the miserable conditions under which the Belgian coalminers lived and worked; the film also indicates that the desperate situation of the workers follows necessarily from a specific social order. To deepen his analysis and to strengthen the urgency of his message, Ivens reconstructed a number of scenes, such as the May Day celebration. This procedure also reflects Ivens's conviction that a documentary film is an emotional presentation of facts. Ivens has said that the maker of a documentary film should be in search of truth. To attain truth, one must have solidarity with the people whose situation is depicted. Mutual confidence and understanding are essential to a good documentary film.

Ivens's techniques bear the mark of such filmmakers as Eisenstein and Pudovkin. In addition to developing specific ways of shooting and styles of montage, Ivens has always attached great importance to spoken commentary. In *Spanish Earth,* a film about the Spanish civil war, Ernest Hemingway speaks the commentary; Jacques Prévert does so in *La Seine a rencontré Paris.* Commentary plays a secondary role in the films Ivens made during the 1970s, notably in *How Yukong Moved the Mountains.* In this documentary epos about daily life in China after the cultural revolution, people tell about their own situation. Ivens's style here is descriptive, with many long sequences and with less dramatic montage.

Ivens was one of the founders in 1926 of the Dutch Film League, which united a number of intellectuals and Dutch filmmakers. Their efforts to promote quality films included publishing a review, organizing film screenings, and inviting important foreign avant-garde filmmakers to give talks. Among these were René Clair and Man Ray; Ivens's contacts with Pudovkin and Eisenstein also date to this period. Ivens's contributions to Dutch film culture are immense, although he remained a controversial figure. His manifest sympathy for the struggle of the Indonesian people against colonialism (*Indonesia Calling*) brought him into conflict with the Dutch government, and until 1956 Ivens was deprived of his Dutch passport.

His films have examined important social and political issues. From 1938 till 1945 he lived in the United States. *Power and the Land* is about the improvements in farming brought about by the use of electricity. With *Our Russian Front* Ivens intended to urge the Americans to enter World War II and to support the Russians. The film was financed by Ivens himself and some of his New York Russian friends. He hoped to make more films of this kind, but the project titled *Letters to the President* was coolly received. It led to only one film, *A Sailor on Convoy Duty to England,* which was financed by the National Film Board of Canada. In the 1950s Ivens worked in Eastern Europe and *The First Years* shows the transformation of a capitalist society into a socialist one; the film concentrates on episodes from postwar life in Bulgaria, Czechoslovakia, and Poland.

In 1956 the Dutch government returned Ivens's passport; he then took up residence in Paris. After that he worked in Latin America (Cuba, Chile) and even more extensively in Asia (Vietnam, Laos, and China). *Travel Notebook* is about daily life in Cuba; *An Armed People* shows how the militia of the Cuban people captures a small group of counter-revolutionaries. *Le Train de la victoire* is a report on the election campaign of Salvador Allende, later president of Chile. Ivens also taught Vietnamese filmmakers, and engagement with the cause of the Vietnamese people manifests itself in such films as *The Threatening Sky* and *The 17th Parallel.*

Ivens always had great influence on new technical developments in the domain of film equipment. He hailed the professionalization of the 16mm camera as a big step forward, since it enabled the camera to take part in the action. He taught at numerous film schools and advised many colleagues. In the 1950s he was an advisor to the Defa Studios (GDR) and collaborated on many films there. Together with a number of leftist French filmmakers (Jean-Luc Godard, Alain Resnais, Agnès Varda, and others), Ivens made the filmic pamphlet of solidarity *Loin du Viët-nam.*

For Ivens the documentary film provided the only possibility of surviving as an artist outside the field of commercial films. He always succeeded in financing his projects on such terms that he conserved maximum artistic freedom and full responsibility for the final product. This even holds for the two films which he made at an early stage in his career and which were commissioned by commercial firms (*Creosoot* and *Philips-Radio*).

Within his lifetime Ivens became a legend. His films comment on many events which shaped the modern world. His art, his intelligence, his sophisticated political views, and his deep sincerity account for the unique position Joris Ivens holds among documentary filmmakers.

—Dorothee Verdaasdonk

IVORY, James

Nationality: American. **Born:** Berkeley, California, 7 June 1928. **Education:** Educated in architecture and fine arts, University of Oregon; studied filmmaking at University of Southern California, M.A. 1956. **Military Service:** Corporal in U.S. Army Special Services, 1953-55. **Career:** Founder and partner, Merchant-Ivory Productions, New York, 1961; directed first feature, also began collaboration with writer Ruth Prawer Jhabvala, on *The Householder,* 1963. **Awards:** Best Foreign Film, French Academie du Cinema, and prize at Berlin Festival, for *Shakespeare Wallah,* 1968; Guggenheim Fellow, 1973; Oscar nomination, Best Director and Directors Guild nomination, for *A Room With a View,* 1987; Silver Lion, Venice Festival, for *Maurice,* 1987; Oscar nomination, Best Director, for *Howards End,* 1992; John Cassavetes Award, Independent Spirit Award, Independent Feature Project/West, 1993. **Address:** c/o Merchant-Ivory Productions, Ltd., 250 W. 57th St., Suite 1913-A, New York, NY 10107, U.S.A.

Films as Director:

1957 *Venice: Themes and Variations* (doc) (+ sc, ph)
1959 *The Sword and the Flute* (doc) (+ sc, ph, ed)
1963 *The Householder*
1964 *The Delhi Way* (doc) (+ sc)
1965 *Shakespeare Wallah* (+ co-sc)
1968 *The Guru* (+ co-sc)
1970 *Bombay Talkie* (+ co-sc)
1971 *Adventures of a Brown Man in Search of Civilization* (doc)
1972 *Savages* (+ pr, sc)
1974 *The Wild Party*
1975 *Autobiography of a Princess*
1977 *Roseland*
1979 *Hullabaloo over Georgie and Bonnie's Pictures*; *The Europeans* (+ pr, co-sc, role as man in warehouse)
1980 *Jane Austen in Manhattan*
1981 *Quartet* (+ co-sc)
1982 *Courtesans of Bombay* (doc) (+ co-sc)
1983 *Heat and Dust*
1984 *The Bostonians*
1986 ***A Room with a View***
1987 *Maurice* (+ co-sc)
1989 *Slaves of New York*
1990 *Mr. and Mrs. Bridge*
1992 ***Howards End***
1993 *The Remains of the Day*
1995 *Jefferson in Paris*

Publications

By IVORY: books—

Savages, with Ruth Prawer Jhabvala, New York, 1973.
Shakespeare Wallah: A Film, with Ruth Prawer Jhabvala, New York, 1973.
Autobiography of a Princess: Also Being the Adventures of an American Film Director in the Land of the Maharajas, New York, 1975.

By IVORY: articles—

"*Savages,*" in *Sight and Sound* (London), Autumn 1971.
Interviews with Judith Trojan, in *Take One* (Montreal), January/February 1974 and May 1975.
Interview with D. Eisenberg, in *Inter/View* (New York), January 1975.
Interview with P. Anderson, in *Films in Review* (New York), October 1984.
"The trouble with Olive," in *Sight and Sound* (London), Spring 1985.
"Dialogue on Film: James Ivory," in *American Film* (Washington, D.C.), January/February 1987.
Interviews in *Hollywood Reporter,* 31 March and 6 May 1989.
"Arachnophobia," in *Sight and Sound* (London), Autumn 1990.
Interview with G. Fuller in *Interview* (New York), November 1990.

On IVORY: books—

Pym, John, *The Wandering Company: Twenty-One Years of Merchant-Ivory Films,* London, 1983.

James Ivory

Martini, Emanuela, *James Ivory,* Bergamo, 1985.
Long, Robert Emmett, *The Films of Merchant Ivory,* New York, 1991.

On IVORY: articles—

Gillett, John, "Merchant-Ivory," in *Sight and Sound* (London), Spring 1973.
Gillett, John, "A Princess in London," in *Sight and Sound* (London), Summer 1974.
Hillgartner, D., "The Making of *Roseland,*" in *Filmmakers Newsletter* (Ward Hill, Massachusetts), January 1978.
"*Quartet* Issue" of *Avant-Scène du Cinéma* (Paris), 1 October 1981.
McFarlane, Brian, "Some of James Ivory's later films," in *Cinema Papers* (Melbourne), June 1982.
Firstenberg, J.P., "A Class Act Turns Twenty-Five," in *American Film* (Washington, D.C.), September 1987.
Monthly Film Bulletin (London), November 1987.
Harmetz, Aljean, "Partnerships Make a Movie," in *New York Times,* 18 February 1990.
"Is Good Taste Enough? The Gorgeous Films of Merchant Ivory," in *The Economist* (London), 29 February 1992.
Hirshey, G., "A Team with a View," in *Gentlemen's Quarterly* (New York), March 1992.
Dudar, Helen, "In the Beginning, the Word; At the End, the Movie," in *New York Times,* 8 March 1992.
Maslin, Janet, "Finding Realities to Fit a Film's Illusions," in *New York Times,* 12 March 1992.
Corliss, Richard, "Doing It Right the Hard Way," in *Time* (New York), 16 March 1992.
Lyons, D., "Tradition of Quality," in *Film Comment* (New York), May/June 1992.
Eller, C., "Merchant Ivory Links with Disney," in *Variety* (New York), 27 July 1992.
Ash, J., "Stick It Up Howard's End," in *Gentlemen's Quarterly* (New York), August 1994.

* * *

The work of James Ivory was a fixture in independent filmmaking of the late 1960s and 1970s. *Roseland,* for example, Ivory's omnibus film about the habitués of a decaying New York dance palace, garnered a standing ovation at its premiere at the New York Film Festival in 1977, and received much critical attention afterward. However, it was not until *A Room with a View,* Ivory's stately adaptation of E. M. Forster's novel, that Ivory gained full international recognition. The name-making films Ivory directed earlier in the 1980s—which included adaptations of two Forster works and two Henry James novels among them—linked him inextricably with the contemporary British cinema's tradition of urbane, even ultra-genteel, costume-dramas.

Ivory's independence, his influential involvement with English film, and his sustained collaborative partnership with producer Ismail Merchant invite comparisons with an earlier pairing in British cinema, Michael Powell and Emeric Pressburger. Both teams have found themselves attracted to material dealing with the effects of sexual repression or with the clash of differing cultures, as in, for example, *Black Narcissus* (Powell/Pressburger, 1947) or *The Europeans* (Ivory/Merchant, 1979). But while Powell and Pressburger worked with various forms of visual experimentation, employing heightened colors, frequently moving cameras, and various forms of cinematographic juxtaposition to achieve an opulent, metaphorical visual texture, Ivory's work represents a distinct retrenchment, a withdrawal from visual hyperbole, a comparative conservatism of visual style. An example of one of Ivory's few attempts at visual expressionism (a moment in his work that seems directly inspired by Powell, in fact) illustrates this point. In *The Bostonians,* Ivory attempts to express Olive Chancellor's hysteria by using stylized colors and superimposition in isolated dream sequences. Because the film's style is deeply rooted in naturalism, unlike that of Powell, the sequences look stilted and awkward, remarkably out of place in the context of the film.

The naturalism of Ivory's style often perfectly complements the director's interest in the dynamics of isolated communities: the drama troupe in *Shakespeare Wallah,* for example, or the dancers in *Roseland,* or the members of the New York downtown-punk scene in *Slaves of New York.* Ivory's films characteristically trace the formation of community around a common interest—or, more often, a common flaw or a shared loss—and his powers of observation are enlivened by attention to minute details of gesture and a keen sympathy for marginal characters. It is this sympathy that attracts him to works such as Evan Connell's novels *Mrs. Bridge* and *Mr. Bridge.* Ivory thus provides a densely ironic but ultimately sympathetic account of the quietly desperate middle-class lives of the Bridges in Kansas City. This sympathy accounts as well for Ivory's handling of characters such as Charlotte Bartlett in *Room with a View.* In Forster's novel, Miss Bartlett is lampooned tirelessly, emerging as one of the novel's chief examples of English hypocrisy and Forster's conception of high culture as the poison of the spirit (this is in spite of a half-hearted reprieve for the character in the novel's last pages). In the film, Maggie Smith's agile, witty performance makes the character far more appealing, and Ivory's treatment of the character (he cuts from the lovers' final union to shots of Miss Bartlett's soundless, unbending loneliness) shows that he clearly interprets her as a fully sympathetic character of great pathos.

Ivory's two Forster adaptations, *Room with a View* and *Maurice,* may well prove to be the high-water mark of his career. These two films do more than demonstrate Ivory's often bracingly literary sensibility (most of Ivory's films are adaptations that doggedly strive for extreme "faithfulness" to their source material): In the Forster adaptations, this "faithfulness" co-exists with crucial shifts of emphasis that provide, simultaneously, modern interpretations of the texts.

An example of this occurs in the scene of the murder in the square in *Room with a View.* In its use of hand-held cameras, graphic matches, and rhythmic editing, which provides mercurial shifts in the tone of the sequence from gravity to exultation, the sequence becomes one of the film's set-pieces, supplying the complexities that Forster largely avoids in his comparatively laconic treatment of the scene.

The work of Ivory, Merchant, and Jhabvala has become even more distinguished as they have aged. Upon its theatrical release, *Howards End* (directed by Ivory, produced by Merchant and scripted by Prawer Jhabvala) was justifiably hailed as the best film ever in their long and distinguished careers. This stylish work is yet another adaptation of an E. M. Forster novel. Its scenario examines a popular Ivory theme, exploring the repercussions when social classes come together at a specific point in recent history (in this case, at the close of the Edwardian era in England). Emma Thompson is altogether brilliant in the role that solidified her career. She plays a cheeky and individualistic young woman who does not come from a monied background, and who is slyly charmed by a prosperous gentleman (Anthony Hopkins) whose upper class facade hides a deceitful and heartless disposition.

The Remains of the Day is nearly as fine a film as *Howards End.* Based on the acclaimed novel by Kazuo Ishiguro, the scenario dissects the personality of an ideal servant: Stevens (Hopkins), a reserved British butler who is singlemindedly dedicated to his employer, Lord Darlington (James Fox). The time is between the World Wars. No matter that the misguided Darlington is perilously flirting with Nazism. No matter that Miss Kenton (Thompson), the new housekeeper, might be a potential romantic partner. Stevens is steadfastly absorbed in his professional role, to the exclusion of all else. He knows only to suppress his needs, feelings, and desires, all in the name of service to his master. *The Remains of the Day* essentially is a character study of Stevens, who is superbly played by the ever-reliable Hopkins. It is yet one more in a line of Ivory's meticulous period dramas.

The period drama *Jefferson in Paris* concerns the American Thomas Jefferson, one of America's founding fathers, shown here as the U.S. Ambassador to France. However, the film is several shades below the best of the previous Ivory-Merchant-Jhabvala collaborations. While *Jefferson in Paris* captures a time and place with exquisite detail, the level of detail included in the film renders the narrative all too episodic in quality. Still, Ivory offers a full-bodied portrayal of Jefferson (Nick Nolte), while depicting a large range of his personal and political involvements. Most intriguing of all is the paradox of Jefferson's disgust with the overindulgences of the French aristocracy combined with his agonized collusion in keeping the status quo with regard to the maintenance of slavery as an American "institution." In *Jefferson in Paris,* Ivory yet again depicts his theme of class differences, exploring the invisible walls that separate those classes. Only here, class is measured by the color of one's skin. Even though individuals share the same bloodlines because of sexual liaisons between master and slave, those with black skin are enslaved by those with white skin. Ivory portrays the widowed Jefferson as a man who falls in love with a married woman (Greta Scacchi), and has a sexual tryst with Sally Hemings (Thandie Newton), a teenaged slave girl. It remains uncertain if the latter affair ever happened. For this reason, *Jefferson in Paris* was the subject of debate and controversy among Jeffersonian scholars.

—James Morrison, updated by Rob Edelman

JACKSON, Peter

Nationality: New Zealander. **Born:** Wellington, New Zealand, 30 October 1961. **Family:** Unmarried; current partner co-screenwriter Fran Walsh. **Career:** Started making films when given Super 8-millimeter camera by parents at age eight; made amateur fiction shorts, including *The Dwarf Patrol, Curse of the Gravewalker, The Valley;* left school at age seventeen, failed to get job in film industry, joined local newspaper as photo-engraving apprentice; named top New Zealand photo-engraving apprentice three years running; bought 16-millimeter Bolex, 1983; started making feature film *Roast of the Day* on weekends with friends and colleagues; renamed *Bad Taste,* film took four years to shoot; finally completed after funding received from New Zealand Film Commission, 1986, enabling Jackson to quit newspaper job for full-time filmmaking; set up own studio, Wingnut Films, in Wellington, with computer-driven special effects division, WETA; after three low-budget features, international acclaim for *Heavenly Creatures* led to deal with Universal to make next project in New Zealand with U.S. funding. **Awards:** Metro Media Award, Toronto, and Silver Lion, Venice, both 1994, and Oscar nomination, Best Screenplay, 1995, all for *Heavenly Creatures.* **Agent:** UTA, 9560 Wilshire Blvd., Suite 500, Beverly Hills, CA 90212, U.S.A.

Films as Director and Co-Screenwriter:

1987 *Bad Taste* (+ pr, ph, ed, multiple roles)
1989 *Meet the Feebles* (+ pr)
1992 *Braindead*
1994 *Heavenly Creatures*
1995 *Frighteners* (+ pr)

Other Films:

1995 *Jack Brown, Genius* (Hiles) (sc, 2nd unit d, exec pr); *Good Taste* (interviewee)

Publications

By JACKSON: articles—

"Meet the Feebles," interview with Alan Jones in *Starburst* (London), May 1991.

"Peter Jackson: *Heavenly Creatures,*" interview in *Cinema Papers* (Melbourne), April 1994.

On JACKSON: articles—

Clarke, Jeremy, "Talent Force," in *Films & Filming* (London), September 1989.

Clarke, Jeremy, "Photolithographers from Outer Space," in *What's On in London,* 13 September 1989.

Floyd, Nigel, "Kiwi Fruit," in *Time Out* (London), 12 May 1993.

Maxford, Howard, "Gore Blimey!," in *What's On in London,* 12 May 1993.

McDonald, Lawrence, "A Critique of the Judgement of Bad Taste or Beyond Braindead Criticism: The Films of Peter Jackson," in *Illusions* (Wellington, NZ), Winter 1993.

Salisbury, Mark, "Peter Jackson, Gore Hound," in *Empire* (London), June 1993.

Feinstein, Howard, "Death and the Maidens," in *Village Voice* (New York), 15 November 1994.

Charity, Tom, "Gut Reaction," in *Time Out* (London), 25 January 1995.

Cameron-Wilson, James, "Natural-Born Culler," in *Times* (London), 8 February 1995.

Cameron-Wilson, James, "The Frightener," in *What's On in London,* 8 February 1995.

Atkinson, Michael, "Earthly Creatures," in *Film Comment* (New York), May/June 1995.

* * *

After his first three features, most critics thought they had Peter Jackson neatly pegged: an antipodean maverick whose films made up for their zero-budget limitations with comic gusto and creative ingenuity; films whose gross-out excesses of spurting bodily fluids and splattered guts made George Romero and Sam Raimi look like models of genteel restraint. Jackson's work, in short, seemed to be comprehensively summed up by the blithely upfront title of his debut film, *Bad Taste.* And then came his fourth film, the award-winning *Heavenly Creatures,* and suddenly all the assumptions had to be revised. Jackson himself, noting a hint of surprise behind the acclaim, pointed out that like all his work the film stemmed from his "unhealthy interest in the grotesque." But if there was continuity in terms of themes and preoccupations, *Heavenly Creatures* showed Jackson was also capable of emotional complexity, subtlety, and sophistication—qualities no one would have suspected from his previous films.

Far from striving to disguise the ramshackle, garden-shed genesis of his early work, Jackson gloried in it, making an amateurish, peculiarly New Zealander domesticity central to his humour. The Astral Investigation and Defence Service team ("I wish they'd do something about those initials") who foil predatory aliens in *Bad Taste* are as far from their jut-jawed Hollywood counterparts as could be imagined; inept, nerdish, and post-adolescent, they shamble around bickering over trivialities or moaning about filling in time-sheets. In *Braindead,* whose showdown erupts in a bland suburban home, the hero demolishes a horde of flesh-eating zombies, not with flame-thrower or pump-action shotgun, but with a rotary lawnmower—"a Kiwi icon," according to the director. It comes as no surprise to read, in the end-titles for *Bad Taste,* a credit to "Special Assistants to the Producer (Mum and Dad)."

Both *Bad Taste* and *Braindead* (whose farcical brand of ultra-physical violence Jackson dubs "splatstick") spoof well-established and much-parodied formulas within the horror genre, respectively the space-invaders movie and the zombie movie. *Meet the Feebles* is more audacious in its choice of target: the hitherto sacrosanct world of Jim Henson's Muppets. Hijacking the standard Muppet narrative framework of backstage shenanigans, Jackson gleefully subverts the perky ethos of the puppet troupe with lavish helpings of booze, filth, sex, and drugs, culminating in one of his trademark bloodbaths. He also pushes the unstated logic of Muppetry to ends that Henson would shudder to confront; if Miss Piggy can get the hots for Kermit, why shouldn't an elephant have sex with a chicken? (The resultant outlandish hybrid is wheeled on—literally—for our delectation.) Jackson further outrages Muppet conventions by making the frog character in his film a Vietnam vet with a heroin habit, while Kermit's counterpart as stage director is an effete, English-accented fox who mounts a big production number in praise of sodomy.

This fascination with outrage, with the consequences of pushing beyond the bounds of convention, carries through into *Heavenly Creatures,* Jackson's finest film to date. Based on an actual New Zealand *cause celèbre* of the 1950s, the Parker-Hulme case, the film traces the progress of two fifteen-year-old schoolgirls into an increasingly unhinged world of ritual and fantasy. Instinctive loners, Pauline and Juliet bond together to turn their outsider status into an exclusive, hermetic society tinged with lesbianism and peopled by personal icons—Mario Lanza, James Mason—along with figures from their medieval fantasy kingdom of Borovnia. Drawing on real case documents (Pauline's diaries and the girls' own Borovnian "novels"), Jackson creates a mood of intense pubescent obsession sliding steadily out of control until—as the borders between the two worlds elide—it culminates in brutal murder.

Determined not to present his heroines as the "evil lesbian killers" they were branded by contemporary press accounts, Jackson not only portrays them with sympathy and insight, but captures the richly creative energy of their shared fantasies. Their behaviour is seen as a reaction to the imagination-starved society around them, since 1950s Christchurch, all garish pastels and agonised gentility, appears no less bizarre and unbalanced a world (and a whole lot less fun) than the one the girls create for themselves. Yet the killing—of Pauline's uncomprehending, well-meaning mother—shares none of the sick-joke relish of Jackson's previous films; it is shown as clumsy, painful, and distressing.

Jackson firmly denies that *Heavenly Creatures* represents a bid to be seen as a "serious filmmaker" who wants to do "arty mainstream films." "People immediately assume that filmmakers do things because of a grand plan.... I do intend to do other splatter films," he told *Cinema Papers.* "I have intentions of doing all sorts of films. I have no interest in a 'career' as such."

For the moment, too, Jackson seems set on remaining true to his roots—rather than following other New Zealand directors (Roger Donaldson, Geoff Murphy, Jane Campion) in using his first major hit as a springboard for Hollywood—and has set up his own production base (Wingnut Films) in his native city of Wellington. "I choose to stay in New Zealand earning a fraction of what I could make in Los Angeles because I want to do whatever I feel like doing.... The freedom that I have in New Zealand is worth millions of dollars to me. It is worth more than what I could earn in Hollywood." Instead, he has used his professional clout to make Hollywood come to him, with Universal funding his next, firmly New Zealand-based production, *The Frighteners,* but leaving him full creative control. Hitherto, the departure of each successful filmmaker has repeatedly robbed New Zealand of the continuity and experience needed to build an indigenous industry. Peter Jackson, with his specifically New Zealand humour and sensibility, may be the ideal director to break the pattern.

—Philip Kemp

JANCSÓ, Miklós

Nationality: Hungarian. **Born:** Vác, Hungary, 27 September 1921. **Education:** Educated in law at Kolozsvár University, Romania, doctorate 1944; Budapest Academy of Dramatic and Film Art, graduated 1950. **Family:** Married director Márta Mészáros; son Miklos Jr. is cameraman. **Career:** Newsreel director, early 1950's; shot documentaries in China, 1957; directed first feature, *A harangok Römába mentek,* 1958; director at "25th" theatre, Budapest, 1960's. **Awards:** Hungarian Critics' Prize, for *Cantata,* 1963; Best Director Award, Cannes Festival, for *Red Psalm,* 1972; Special Prize, Cannes Festival, 1979.

Films as Director:

(of short films and documentaries):

1950 *Kezunbe vettuk a béke ugyét* (*We Took Over the Cause of Peace*) (co-d)

1951 *Szovjet mezögazdasági küldöttsek tanításai* (*The Teachings of a Soviet Agricultural Deputation*) (co-d)

1952 *1952 Május 1* (*May 1st 1952*)

1953 *Választás elótt* (*Before Election*); *Arat az Orosházi Dözsa* (*Harvest in the Cooperative "Dosza"*); *Közös útan* (*Ordinary Ways*; *On a Common Path*) (co-d)

1954 *Galga mentén* (*Along the Galgu River*); *Ösz Badacsonyban* (*Autumn in Badacsony*); *Éltetö Tisza-víz* (*The Health-Giving Waters of Tisza*; *Life-Bringing Water*); *Emberek! Ne engedjétek!* (*Comrades! Don't Put Up with It*) (co-d, co-sc); *Egy kiállitás képei* (*Pictures at an Exhibition*)

1955 *Angyalföldi fiatalok* (*Children of Angyalfold*; *The Youth of "The Land of Angels"*); *A Varsoí vit* (*Varsoí Világifjusági Találkozö I-III*; *Warsaw World Youth Meeting I-III*); *Egy délután Koppánymonostorban* (*One Afternoon in Koppanymonostor*; *An Afternoon in the Village*); *Emlékezz, ifjúság* (*Young People, Remember*)

1956 *Móricz Zsigmond* (*Zsigmond Moricz 1879-1942*)

1957 *A város peremén* (*In the Outskirts of the City*); *Dél-Kína tájain* (*The Landscapes of Southern China*); *Színfoltok Kínaböl* (*Colorful China*; *Colors of China*); *Pekingi palotái* (*Palaces of Peking*); *Kína vendégei voltunk* (*Our Visit to China*)

1958 *Derkovitz Gyula 1894-1934*; *A harangok Römába mentek* (*The Bells Have Gone to Rome*) (feature)

1959 *Halhatatlanság* (*Immortality*) (+ sc, ph); *Izotöpok a gyögyászatban* (*Isotopes in Medical Science*)

1960 first episode of *Három csillág* (*Three Stars*); *Az eladás müvészete* (*The Art of Revival*; *The Art of Salesmanship*) (co-d); *Szerkezettervezés* (*Construction Design*) (+ sc)

1961 *Az idö kereke* (*The Wheels of Time*) (+ sc); *Alkonyok és hajnalok* (*Twilight and Dawn*) (+ sc); *Indiántörténet* (*Indian Story*) (+ sc)

1963 *Oldás és kötés* (*Cantata*) (+ co-sc); *Hej, te eleven Fa ...* (*Living Tree ... An Old Folk Song*) (+ sc)

(of feature films):

1964 *Igyjöttem* (*My Way Home*)

1965 *Szegénylegények* (*The Round-Up*); *Jelenlét* (*The Presence*) (short) (+ sc); *Közelrölia: a vér* (*Close-up: The Blood*) (short)

1967 ***Csillagosok, katonák*** (*The Red and the White*) (+ co-sc)

1968 *Csend és kiáltás* (*Silence and Cry*) (+ co-sc); *Vörös Május* (*Red May*) (short)

1969 *Fényes szelek* (*The Confrontation*); *Sirokkó* (*Teli sirokkó lek*; *Winter Wind*) (+ co-sc)

1970 *Égi bárány* (*Agnus Dei*) (+ co-sc); *La pacifista* (*The Pacifist*) (+ co-sc); *Füst* (*Smoke*) (short)
1972 ***Még kér a nép*** (*Red Psalm*)
1975 *Szerelmem, Elektra* (*Elektreia*)
1976 *Vizi privati, pubbliche virtù* (*Vices and Pleasures*)
1978 *Eletünket és vérunket: Magyar rapszödia 1* (*Hungarian Rhapsody*) (+ co-sc); *Allegro barbaro: Magyar rapszödia 2* (*Allegro barbaro*) (+ co-sc)
1981 *A zsranok szíve avagy Boccaccio Magyarországon* (*The Tyrant's Heart*; *Boccaccio in Hungary*) (+ co-sc)
1984 *Omega, Omega ...* ; *Muzsika* (*Music*)
1986 *L'Aube* (*Dawn*)
1987 *Szörnyek Evadja*
1989 *Jézus Krisztus Horoszkója*
1990 *Isten hátrafelé megy* (*God Runs Backwards*)

Other Films:

1950 *A Maksimenko brigád* (*The Maximenko Brigade*) (Koza) (story)
1968 *A Pál utcai fiúk* (*The Boys of Paul Street*) (Fabri) (role)
1977 *Difficile morire* (Silva) (role)

Publications

By JANCSÓ: articles—

Interview, in *The Image Maker,* edited by Ron Henderson, Richmond, Virginia, 1971.
"L'Idéologie, la technique et le rite," interview with Claude Beylie, in *Ecran* (Paris), December 1972.
"I Have Played Christ Long Enough: A Conversation with Miklos Jancso," with Gideon Bachmann, in *Film Quarterly* (Berkeley), Fall 1974.
"Entretien ... sur *Vitam et sanguinem,*" with Michel Ciment and J.-P. Jeancolas, in *Positif* (Paris), May 1979.
"A jelenlét," interview with I. Antal, in *Filmkultura* (Budapest), November/December 1981.
Interview with L. Somogyi, in *Filmkultura* (Budapest), October 1986.
Interview in *Hungarofilm Bulletin* (Budapest), no. 2, 1988.

On JANCSÓ: books—

Taylor, John, *Directors and Directions,* New York, 1975.
Petrie, Graham, *History Must Answer to Man: The Contemporary Hungarian Cinema,* London, 1978.
Marlia, Giulio, *Lo schermo liberato: il cinema di Miklos Jancso,* Florence, 1982.
Paul, David, W., editor, *Politics, Art and Commitment in the East European Cinema,* New York, 1983.

On JANCSÓ: articles—

"Miklós Jancsó," in *International Film Guide 1969* edited by Peter Cowie, London, 1968.
Houston, Penelope, "The Horizontal Man," in *Sight and Sound* (London), Summer 1969.
Kane, P., and others, "Lectures de Jancsó: hier et aujourd'hui," in *Cahiers du Cinéma* (Paris), March and May 1969, and April 1970.
Robinson, D., "Quite Apart from Miklos Jancso," in *Sight and Sound* (London), Spring 1970.
Czigany, Lorant, "Jancsó Country: Miklos Jancso and the Hungarian New Cinema," in *Film Quarterly* (Berkeley), Fall 1972.
Bachmann, Gideon, "Jancso Plain," in *Sight and Sound* (London), Autumn 1974.
"Jancso Issue" of *Etudes Cinématographiques* (Paris), no. 104-108, 1975.
Robinson, David, "Old Jancso Customs," in *Sight and Sound* (London), no.1, 1978/79.
Biro, Y., "Landscape During the Battle," in *Millenium* (New York), Summer/Fall 1979.
Gillett, John, "Miklos Jancso," in *Film Dope* (London), July 1983.
"Special Section" of *Filmfaust* (Frankfurt), March/April 1984.
Petrie, G., "Miklós Jancsó," in *Revue Belge du Cinéma* (Brussels), Summer 1985.

On JANCSÓ: films—

Kovács, Zsolt, *Kamerával Kosztromában* (With a Camera in Kosztroma), short, 1967.
Comolli, Jean-Louis, *Miklos Jancso,* for TV, France, 1969.

* * *

Miklós Jancsó is probably the best internationally known of the directors to emerge from the new wave Hungarian cinema of the 1960s. With his hypnotic, circling camera, the recurrent—some critics say obsessive—exploration of Hungary's past, and his evocative use of the broad plains of his countries' Puszta, Jancsó fashioned a highly individual cinema within the confines of a state operated film industry. Although a prolific director of short films during the 1950s and an equally prolific director of feature films since the early 1970s, it is for his work during the middle and late 1960s that Jancsó is best known outside his own country.

Beginning with *My Way Home,* which dealt with a young Hungarian soldier caught up in the German retreat and Soviet advance during the Second World War, Jancsó discovered both a set of themes and a style which helped him to fashion his own voice. *My Way Home,* unlike most of Jancsó's films, has a hero, but this hero often behaves in a most unheroic way as he makes his way home. Set free by the chaos of the war's end, he is fired upon both by the Russians and the Germans and finally dons a Russian uniform as a protective disguise. Although clearly focused on individual figures, Jancsó's movie does contain an interesting allegory of the fate of his native country as, freed from Nazi oppression, the soldier only reluctantly dons the Russian uniform.

Szegénylegények (*The Round-Up,* literally *The Hopeless*) established Jancsó as a filmmaker of international importance. The film is set in the Hungarian plain in a fort that houses a group of peasants under surveillance following the Kossuth rebellion of 1848, and focuses on the ritual quality of the games played as tormentors and informers and rebels interchange in a mysterious, elliptical dance of human passions. Shot in black and white, the film also revealed a purity of style as each meticulously composed shot conveys Jancsó's preoccupation with humans dislodged from convention and victimised by history. In spite of its scope, however, the film won praise for its analysis of the politics of terror and of the Kafkaesque state machinery through which such terror works.

Csillagosok Katonák (1967, *The Red and the White*) and *Csend és Kiáltás* (1968, *Silence and Cry*) moved into the early twentieth century and are concerned with communist revolutions of the immediate post-World War I period. *The Red and the White* was commissioned by the Soviet government to commemorate the 50th anniversary of the October revolution. The film isolates a group of Hungarian volunteers who are fighting on the side of the reds during the Russian civil war. Once again the expansive plain provides an open background against which huddle the opposing groups, both red and white. It is interesting

Miklós Jancsó

considering the source of his commission that Jancsó refuses to choose to side with either the red or the whites but rather to present each as a mixture of compassion and understanding, barbarity and stupidity. *Silence and Cry,* operating on a smaller scale, deals with an isolated farmstead but also raises questions about people caught up in a society torn by social and political change. Here Jancsó's circling camera becomes hypnotic, and his tendency to de-psychologize his characters is at its most extreme. Jancsó explains very little in his plot, leaving the viewer to wrestle with its obscurities and ellipses.

The claustrophobic qualities of *Silence and Cry* prepared his audience for *Fényes Szelek (The Confrontation),* set in the immediate post-war world and dealing with students, both Catholic and Communist, who square off in a quadrille interweaving accusation and intimidation. Clearly the film was occasioned by the student riots and sit-ins in 1968-69 in Budapest. It pits the Marxist students as the voice of change and revolution against the conventions of the Catholic students. The plot is minimal and Jancsó's camera at its most vertiginous, hardly ever stopping in its unceasing search for the truth. The truth, of course, as it so often does, eludes us, as the confrontation finally has more to do with temporary power games than it does with ultimate reality.

In *Sirokkó (Winter Wind),* made in Yugoslavia as a Franco-Hungarian co-production, he returned to the use of color (as in *The Confrontation)* and photographed, like *Silence and Cry,* with a minimum of shots, twelve in this case. The story deals with the historical and political irony of a Croatian anarchist leader of the 1930s who is destroyed by his own forces, only later to be resurrected as a hero. *Égi Bárány (Agnus Dei),* a favorite film of Jancsó's and regarded by many Hungarians as his most nationalistic, is once again set in the broad Hungarian plain during the period of civil war, but it is far more symbolic and anticipates the new ground he would explore in his next film.

With *Még Kér a Nép (Red Psalm),* Jancsó returned to the Puszta and to the end of the last century during a period of peasant unrest. A confrontation between workers and their landowners is interrupted by the army. The subsequent action follows patterns established earlier in Jancsó's other films. But there is a difference in *Red Psalm*—the symbolic elements always present in the earlier films become foregrounded: a dead soldier is resurrected by a kiss from a young girl; the soldiers join the peasants in a Maypole dance but eventually surround the rebellious farmers and shoot them down; a girl outside the circle using a gun tied with a red ribbon guns down all of the soldiers. The mannerisms noted by a number of critics are missing here, and Jancsó seems to have found a new direction amidst old material: the symbolism of the film elevates it beyond Jancsó's usual concerns. *Red Psalm* exemplifies what is often hidden in his other films: the totality of the film, and the celebration of life in the revolution which will bring joy in the renewed possibilities for human expression and freedom.

Although Miklós Jancsó has gone on to make other films, many of them outside Hungary itself, his body of work from *My Way Home* to *Red Psalm* seems to best exemplify his unique contribution to world cinema. Like many of the other new Hungarian filmmakers, Jancsó rejected the traditions of the conservative and classic bound national cinema he inherited, turning to a more liberating and avant-garde style that allowed him not only greater artistic expression but also increased freedom from state censorship. By adopting a more modernist approach, most notably evident in his use of a minimal plot and in the dialectical tensions between the images, he has urged his audiences out of their complacency by challenging the status quo through his questioning of the uses and abuses of state power wielded in the name of the people. This has made his films truly revolutionary.

—Charles L.P. Silet

JARMAN, Derek

Nationality: British. **Born:** Northwood, Middlesex, 31 January 1942. **Education:** King's College, London, 1960-63; Slade School of Fine Art, 1963-67. **Career:** First exhibition, Lisson Gallery, London, 1967; set designer for Royal Ballet, Ballet Rambert, and English National Opera, 1968; film designer for Ken Russell on *The Devils,* 1970; began working in Super-8 film, 1971; directed first feature, *Sebastiane,* 1976; directed promo videos for The Smiths, 1986; diagnosed as being HIV-positive, 1987; revealed his condition, and began actively speaking out in favor of AIDS research, 1987; directed video and stage show for Pet Shop Boys, 1989. **Awards:** Peter Stuyvesant Award for painting, 1967; British Film Institute Award, 1990. **Died:** Of AIDS-related illnesses, 19 February 1994.

Films as Director (short Super-8 Films unless stated otherwise):

1971 *Studio Bankside*; *Miss Gaby*; *A Journey to Avebury*
1972 *Garden of Luxor* (*Burning the Pyramids*); *Andrew Logan Kisses the Glitterati*; *Tarot* (*The Magician*)
1973 *The Art of Mirrors* (*Sulphur*); *Building the Pyramids*
1974 *The Devils at the Elgin* (*Reworking the Devils*); *Fire Island*; *Duggie Fields*
1975 *Ula's Fête* (*Ula's Chandelier*); *Picnic at Ray's*; *Sebastiane Wrap*
1976 *Gerald's Film*; *Sloane Square, A Room of One's Own* (*Removal Party*); *Houston Texas*; *Sebastiane* (16mm feature)
1977 *Jordan's Dance*; *Every Woman for Herself and All for Art*
1978 *Jubilee* (16mm feature)
1979 *Broken English* (short, Super-8 and 16mm); *The Tempest* (16mm feature)
1980 *In the Shadow of the Sun* (includes re-edited versions of earlier 8mm films)
1981 *TG Psychic Rally in Heaven*
1982 *Diese Machine ist mein antihumanistisches Kunstwerk*; *Pirate Tape* (*W.S. Burroughs*); *Pontormo and Punks at Santa Croce*
1983 *Waiting for Godot* (short, Super-8 and video); *B2 Tape/Film*; *The Dream Machine*
1984 *Catalan* (for TV); *Imagining October*
1985 *The Angelic Conversation* (Super-8 and video)
1986 *The Queen Is Dead* (promo videos on Super-8); *Caravaggio* (35mm feature)
1987 "Depuis le jour" episode of *Aria* (Super-8 and 35mm); *The Last of England* (Super-8 feature)
1988 *L'Ispirazione*; *War Requiem* (35mm feature)
1990 *The Garden* (Super-8 and 16mm feature)
1991 *Edward II* (35mm feature)
1993 *Wittgenstein* (35mm feature); *Blue* (35mm feature); *Glitterbug* (video)

Other Films:

1971 ***The Devils*** (Russell) (designs)
1972 *Savage Messiah* (Russell) (designs)
1975 *The Bible* (Russell) (sc)
1979 *Nighthawks* (Peck, Hallam) (role)
1986 *Ostia* (role)
1987 *Prick Up Your Ears* (Frears) (role)
1988 *Behind Closed Doors* (role); *Derek Jarman: You Know What I Mean*; *Cactus Land* (narration)
1993 *There We Are John* (role); *Love Undefeated: Conversations with Derek Jarman*

Publications

By JARMAN: books—

Dancing Ledge, edited by Shaun Allen, London, 1984.
Caravaggio, London, 1986.
Last of England, London, 1987.
War Requiem: The Film, London, 1990.
Queer Edward II, London, 1992.
Dancing Ledge, London, 1993
At Your Own Risk: A Saint's Testament, London, 1994.
Modern Nature, London, 1994.
Blue: Text of a Film, New York, 1994.
Chroma, New York, 1995.

By JARMAN: articles—

Interviews in *Time Out* (London), November 1976 and 31 January 1985.
Interview in *Film Directions* (Belfast), vol. 2, no. 8, 1979.
Interviews with Michael O'Pray, in *Monthly Film Bulletin* (London), June 1984 and April 1986.
"Renaissance Man," an interview with M. Sutton, in *Stills* (London), April 1986.
Interview in *American Film* (Washington, D.C.), September 1986.
Interview in *Filmfaust* (Frankfurt), September/October 1986.
Interview with Anne-Marie Hewitt, in *Cinema Papers* (Melbourne), September 1987.
Interview with D. Heinrich, in *Cinéma* (Paris), 16 December 1987.
Interview in *City Limits* (London), 6 July 1989.
Interview in *Listener* (London), 16 August 1990.
Interview with P. Loewe in *Chaplin* (Stockholm), vol. 33, no. 6, 1991/1992.
Jarman, Derek, "Jag filmar mitt liv," in *Chaplin* (Stockholm), vol. 33, no. 6., 1991/1992.

On JARMAN: articles—

"Jarman Issue" of *Afterimage* (London), Autumn 1985.
Rayns, Tony, "Unnatural Lighting," in *American Film* (Washington, D.C.), September 1986.
Olofsson, A., article in *Chaplin* (Stockholm), vol. 30, no. 1, 1990.
O'Pray, M., "The art of mirrors: Derek Jarman," in *Monthly Film Bulletin* (London), January 1991.
Ball, E., "I, Camera," in *Village Voice* (New York), 29 January 1991.
McCabe, Colin, "Throne of blood," in *Sight and Sound* (London), October 1991.
O'Pray, M., "Damning desire," in *Sight and Sound* (London), October 1991.
Kennedy, Harlan, "The Two Gardens of Derek Jarman," in *Film Comment* (New York), November/December, 1993.
Obituary, in *New York Times,* 21 February 1994.
Obituary, in *Washington Post,* 21 February 1994.
Obituary, in *The Times* (London), 21 February 1994.
Obituary, in *Los Angeles Times,* 24 February 1994.
Obituary, in *Chicago Tribune,* 27 February 1994.
Obituary, in *Variety* (New York), 28 February 1994.

* * *

Since making his feature debut with *Sebastiane,* Derek Jarman has been one of Britain's most original and highly controversial filmmakers. Vilified by the self-appointed guardians of the nation's morals, he has been hailed as a genius by others. It is Jarman's uncompromising and direct approach to cinema which has resulted in such extreme and polarized evaluations of his work. Like Ken Russell, who introduced him to filmmaking by inviting him to design *The Devils* and *Savage Messiah,* Jarman has consistently assaulted comfortable, conservative assumptions of "good taste." The powerful and explicit treatment of homo-erotic passion in his work has generated the greatest hostility, with *Sebastiane,* one of the most erotic and uninhibited British films ever made, the target of a particularly nasty anti-homosexual campaign generated by the tabloid press.

Drawing on personal experience to a greater degree than most British filmmakers, Jarman's sexuality and his public school/military background have profoundly influenced his cinema. He has paid tribute to other gay artists such as Caravaggio, deducing his tragic love affair with Ranuccio Thomasoni from clues in his paintings, and Benjamin Britten, creating stunning images for his *War Requiem.* He has also interpreted the island in Shakespeare's *The Tempest* as a metaphor for homosexuality and read his sonnets as homo-erotic love poems, incorporating them into the soundtrack of *The Angelic Conversation.* Jarman's films also abound with militaristic images, particularly uniformed authority figures. Such images are often ambivalent, an echo of Jarman's own relationship with his father, who was a wing commander in the RAF.

Jarman's later work is more explicitly autobiographical. *The Last of England,* for example, is constructed around the presence of the artist: the fictional elements of the film are integrated with sequences featuring Jarman working at home and wandering around the streets with a camera. There are also fragments of old home movie footage shot by Jarman's father and grandfather, including images of the filmmaker as a child playing with his mother and sister.

Despite being regarded as subversive by many, Jarman is paradoxically a traditionalist. He is nostalgic for a world uncorrupted by the bourgeois bureaucrats and advertising executives whom he regards as forces controlling our culture. The motif of the garden, that very English symbol of personal spaces, a haven to be cherished and protected, occurs time and time again, particularly in his later work such as *The Angelic Conversation,* his section for *Aria,* and *The Garden,* the title of which relates to Jarman's own garden at Dungeness on the Kent coast.

Trained as a painter, Jarman's cinema betrays a diversity of aesthetic influences. In contrast to the dominant literary/theatrical tradition in British cinema, he draws heavily on painting and poetry. He has consistently experimented with narrative, from the cut-up collage approach of *Jubilee* to the poetic open narrative style of his Super-8 work from *Imagining October* to *The Last of England.* Such an approach requires an active participation on the part of the audience, often forcing them to impose their own coherence and meaning on the visual and aural collage. This aesthetic eclecticism is reflected in the design of Jarman's productions, which frequently eschew realism by mixing period costumes and props with modern elements, part of the director's effort to generate and communicate living ideas and concepts rather than attempt to excavate a dead past. In contrast to the clutter which characterizes much British realist cinema, the interior designs in Jarman's films are often rather austere, drawing attention to the significance of objects.

Derek Jarman sought to preserve his independence from the aesthetic and ideological compromises inherent in mainstream commercial cinema. This made the task of financing his projects extremely difficult, and he was forced to make his films on shoestring budgets. No other major British filmmaker has consistently worked with such meager resources. The seven-year struggle to raise money for *Caravaggio* prompted Jarman to return to the Super-8 film-making of his pre-*Sebastiane* days.

By the mid-1980s it was possible to make technically sophisticated experimental films by generating images on Super-8, then transferring this material to video tape for editing and post-production while

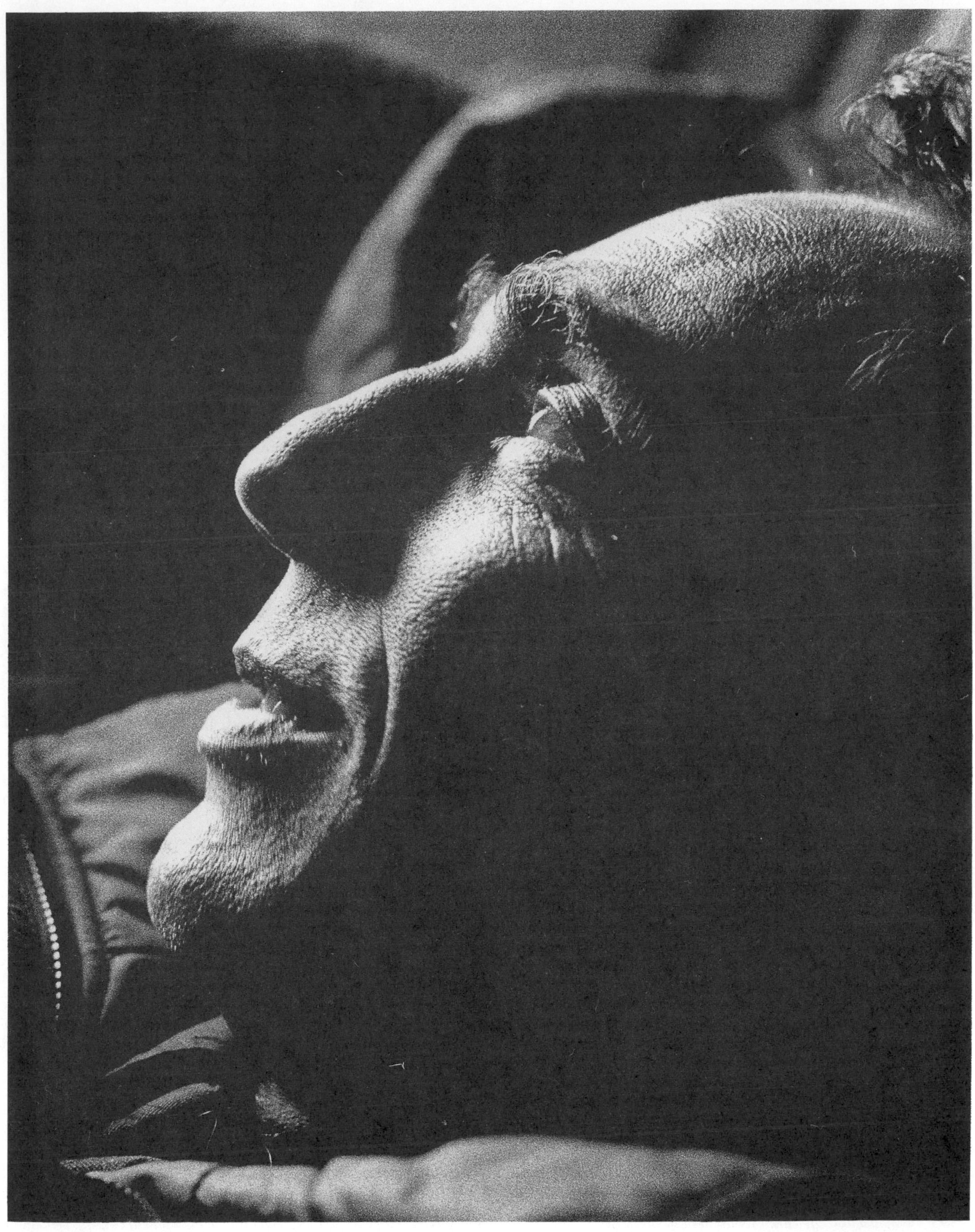

Derek Jarman © Andy Lane

maintaining the texture and quality of the Super-8 film image in the process. The results have been extremely interesting, culminating in the production of *The Last of England,* the first full-length British feature film to be made in this way. These experiments confirmed Jarman's status as a genuine innovator who constantly challenged orthodox approaches to filmmaking. His refusal to be absorbed into the mainstream ensured his integrity as an artist but kept him on the margins of a rather conservative British film culture.

Jarman's premature death—he was yet another casualty to the scourge of AIDS—robbed the film world of one of its most daring and controversial talents. Among his last films were *Wittgenstein* and *Edward II,* both pointed, characteristically outlandish Jarman concoctions which deal with the lives of famous homosexuals. The former charts the life of the influential Viennese philosopher Ludwig Wittgenstein, depicting everything from his family background to his association with Bertrand Russell and John Maynard Keynes, examining the evolution of his ideas as well as his gay relationships with younger men. The latter, detailing the undoing of the title monarch and his lover, serves as an expose of gay oppression throughout the ages. Meanwhile, *The Garden* is yet another of Jarman's jarring examinations/condemnations of homophobia. Via striking imagery, he offers comparison between the persecution of gays and the crucifixion of Christ.

Blue (not to be confused with the Krzysztof Kieslowski film of the same title) is a fitting close to Jarman's career. It is a deeply personal meditation on the artist's life in the face of his impending demise. The screen is entirely blue, and via narration Jarman exposes his soul as he considers his existence and his struggle with disease.

—Duncan J. Petrie, updated by Rob Edelman

JARMUSCH, Jim

Nationality: American. **Born:** Akron, Ohio, 1953. **Education:** Columbia University, New York, graduated 1975; New York University Graduate Film School, 1976-79, as teaching assistant to Nicholas Ray. **Career:** With help of Ray, completed first film, *Permanent Vacation,* for $10,000, 1980; made *New World* with 30 minutes of leftover film, 1982; added another hour's worth of film to it to make *Stranger than Paradise,* 1984; recording artist with "The Del-Byzanteens." **Awards:** Golden Leopard, Locarno Festival, Best Film Award, National Society of Film Critics, and Camera d'Or for Best New Director, Cannes Festival, for *Stranger than Paradise,* 1984; Palme d'Or, Cannes Festival, for *Coffee and Cigarettes (Somewhere in California),* 1993. **Address:** Lives in the Bowery, New York.

Films as Director and Scriptwriter:

1980 *Permanent Vacation* (+ sc, ed, mus)
1982 *The New World* (*Stranger than Paradise, Part One*) (short)
1984 *Stranger Than Paradise*
1986 *Down By Law*
1987 *Coffee and Cigarettes*
1989 *Mystery Train*
1989 *Coffee and Cigarettes (Memphis Version)*
1992 *Night on Earth* (+ pr)
1993 *Coffee and Cigarettes (Somewhere in California)*
1995 *Dead Man*

Other Films:

1979 *Red Italy* (Mitchel) (role)
1980 *Lightning Over Water* (*Nick's Movie*) (Wenders and Ray) (prod asst); *Underground U.S.A.* (Mitchell) (sound recordist)
1981 *Only You* (Vogel) (role); *You Are Not I* (Driver) (ph)
1982 *Burroughs* (Brookner) (sound recordist); *The State of Things* (Wenders) (featured songs by The Del-Byzanteens)
1983 *Fraulein Berlin* (Lambert) (role as Mr. Dade); *American Autobahn* (Degas) (role)
1984 *Sleepwalk* (Driver) (ph); *American Autobahn* (Degas) (role)
1986 *Straight to Hell* (Cox) (role)
1987 *Candy Mountain* (Wurlitzer, Frank) (role)
1988 *Helsinki Napoli All Night Long* (role)
1989 *Leningrad Cowboys Go America* (Kaurismaki) (role)
1990 *Golden Boat* (Ruiz) (role)
1992 *In the Soup* (Rockwell) (role)
1994 *Tigrero: A Film That Was Never Made* (Kaurismaki) (role)
1995 *Blue in the Face* (Wang, Auster) (role)

Publications

By JARMUSCH: articles—

Interview (on Nicholas Ray) with F. Vega, in *Casablanca* (Madrid), February 1983.
Interview with H. Leroux and Y. Lardeau, in *Cahiers du Cinéma* (Paris), December 1984.
Interview with H. Jacobson, in *Film Comment* (New York), January/February 1985.
Interview in *American Cinematographer* (Los Angeles), March 1985.
Interview in *American Film* (Washington, D.C.), October 1986.
Interview with Jonathan Rosenbaum, in *Cahiers du Cinéma* (Paris), November 1986.
Interview with Saskia Baron, in *Stills* (London), February 1987.
"Asphalt Jungle Jim," an interview with M. Mordue, in *Cinema Papers* (Melbourne), January 1988.
Interview in *Cineforum* (Bergamo), December 1989.
Interview in *Films and Filming* (London), December 1989.
Schoemer, Karen, "Film as Life, and Vice Versa," in *New York Times,* 30 April 1992.
"Jarmusch's Guilty Pleasures," in *Film Comment* (New York), May/June 1992.
Keogh, Peter, "Home and Away," in *Sight and Sound* (London), August 1992.

On JARMUSCH: articles—

Kiolkowski, F., "Independent Film: *Stranger than Paradise,*" in *On Film* (Los Angeles), Fall 1984.
Klady, L., "Jim Jarmusch," in *American Film* (Washington, D.C.), October 1986.
Stiller, Nikki, "A Sad and Beautiful Film," in *Hudson Review* (New York), vol. 40, no. 1, 1987.
Monthly Film Bulletin (London), January 1987.
Leibowitz, Flo, "Neither Hollywood nor Godard: The Strange Case of *Stranger than Paradise,*" in *Persistence of Vision* (Maspeth, New York), no. 6, 1988.
Pally, Marcia, article in *Film Comment* (New York), July/August 1989.
Article in *Cahiers du Cinema* (Paris), May 1991.
Bassan, Raphael, article in *La Revue du Cinema* (Paris), December 1991.

Jim Jarmusch: *Stranger than Paradise*

Schoemer, Karen, "A Director's Night on Earth, Close to Home," in *New York Times,* 1 May 1992.

Hoberman, J., "Roadside Attractions," in *Sight and Sound* (London), August 1992.

* * *

Jim Jarmusch has risen quickly to the forefront of young, independent American filmmakers. Recognition has been his from the very beginning with the release of his first film, *Stranger than Paradise,* a work that won a Camera d'Or at the 1984 Cannes Film Festival (for best "first film") and "Best Picture" from the National Society of Film Critics. The key to Jarmusch's success is a well-defined and thoughtfully conceived stylistic approach and a coherent circle of interests.

The focal point of all Jarmusch's work is the apparent contradiction that exists between the popular perception of the American Dream and what that dream actually holds for the individual who doesn't quite fit in. This contradiction is explored through the interaction of a characteristic ensemble of characters. Each of Jarmusch's films is built around a trio of characters, although *Mystery Train* varies that slightly by using three separate stories to explore this central theme. The characters are all decidedly off-beat, but all seem to have a vision or aspiration which echoes a popular perception of America. The central characters—Tom Waits' down and out disc jockey in *Down By Law,* or John Lurie's small-time pimp in the same film—are forced to confront their misconceptions and misguided dreams when they are thrown together by fate with a foreigner who views this dream as an observer. In *Down By Law,* for example, the two central characters find themselves in jail with an Italian immigrant who has murdered someone for cheating at cards. The character carries a small notebook of American slang expressions from which he quotes dutifully and incorrectly. He refers to this notebook as "everything I know about America." It is this kind of character situation that Jarmusch uses to scoff at an America he sees as misguided and woefully out of touch with itself.

Stylistically, Jarmusch's work echoes the work of the French "New Wave" filmmakers, in particular the Godard of films like *Breathless* and *Weekend.* Jump-cuts are frequently used to disconnect characters from sublime and rational passages of time and space. A sense of disenfranchisement is created in this way, separating characters from the continuity of space and time which surrounds them. In *Down By Law,* for example, Tom Waits sits in his cell, then lays on the floor, then lays across his bed, but what seems like "a day in the life" editing approach actually concludes with days having passed, not hours. Jarmusch also uses moving-camera a great deal, but unlike his predecessors in other traditions, his fluid camera style is not functional. Camera movements in films like *Down By Law* and *Mystery Train* create a visual world that is always in transition. *Down By Law* opens with camera movement first right to left down a street in a small town, then left to right. As a result, the audience is introduced, through a visual metaphor, to the collision course that is central to the film's themes.

Night on Earth, Jarmusch's most mature film to date, is an exhilarating five-part slice-of-life, each of which unravels at the same point in time in Los Angeles, New York, Paris, Rome, and Helsinki. All are set in taxis, and spotlight brief but poignant exchanges between cab driver and passenger. The best of many highlights: the sequence in which a black Brooklynite (Giancarlo Esposito) and an East German refugee (Armin Mueller-Stahl) reveal their names to each other. Jarmusch's point is that people are people, whether black or white, American or French or Finnish.

Jarmusch also is not averse to working in the short film format. In 1987 he made *Coffee and Cigarettes,* in which an American (Steven Wright) and an Italian (Roberto Benigni) meet in a cafe and converse over coffee and cigarettes. Jarmusch reworked the film's concept and structure twice more: *Coffee and Cigarettes (Memphis Version),* made two years later, in which an argument between twins Joie and Cinque Lee is intruded on by an overly-earnest waiter (Steve Buscemi); and *Coffee and Cigarettes (Somewhere in California),* made four years after that, this time featuring a barroom conversation between Iggy Pop and Tom Waits.

Jarmusch's cool style and strangers-in-a-strange-land subject matter have influenced other filmmakers. *Cold Fever,* a likable 1995 Icelandic feature co-produced and co-scripted by Jarmusch colleague Jim Stark and directed by Fridrik Thor Fridriksson, chronicles a Japanese businessman's odyssey across Iceland to perform a memorial ritual at the spot where his parents had died seven years earlier.

Like other young filmmakers of his generation, such as Spike Lee, Jim Jarmusch approaches the American way of life with a sense of hip cynicism. A product of contemporary American film school savvy, Jarmusch incorporates a sense of film history, style, and awareness in his filmmaking approach. The tradition which he has chosen to follow, the one which offers him the most freedom, is that established by filmmakers such as Chabrol, Godard, and Truffaut in the 1950s and 1960s.

—Rob Winning, updated by Rob Edelman

JENNINGS, Humphrey

Nationality: British. **Born:** Frank Humphrey Sinkler Jennings in Walberswick, Suffolk, 1907. **Education:** Perse School and Pembroke College, Cambridge, until 1934. **Career:** Joined General Post Office (GPO) film unit as scenic designer and editor, 1934; worked with Len Lye at Shell films, from 1936; returned to GPO film unit (became Crown Film Unit, 1940), 1938; became associated with Mass Observation movement, late 1930s; director for Wessex Films, 1949. **Died:** After falling from a cliff while scouting locations for film, in Poros, Greece, 1950.

Films as Director:

1938 *Penny Journey*

1939 *Spare Time* (+ sc); *Speaking from America*; *SS Ionian* (*Her Last Trip*); *The First Days* (*A City Prepares*) (co-d)

1940 *London Can Take It* (co-d); *Spring Offensive* (*An Unrecorded Victory*); *Welfare of the Workers* (co-d)

1941 *Heart of Britain* (*This Is England*); *Words for Battle* (+ sc)

1942 *Listen to Britain* (co-d, co-sc, co-ed)

1943 ***Fires Were Started*** (*I Was a Fireman*) (+ sc); *The Silent Village* (+ pr, sc)

1944 *The Eighty Days* (+ pr); *The True Story of Lilli Marlene* (+ sc); *VI* (+ pr)

1945 *A Diary for Timothy* (+ sc)

1946 *A Defeated People*

1947 *The Cumberland Story* (+ sc)

1949 *Dim Little Island* (+ pr)

1950 *Family Portrait* (+ sc)

Other Films:

1934 *Post-Haste* (ed); *Pett and Pott* (Cavalcanti) (sets ed, role as grocer); *Glorious Sixth of June* (Cavalcanti) (role as telegraph boy); *The Story of the Wheel* (ed)

1935 *Locomotives* (ed)

1936 *The Birth of a Robot* (Lye) (color direction and production)

Publications

By JENNINGS: books—

Pandaemonium 1660-1886: The Coming of the Machine as Seen by Contemporary Observers, edited by Mary-Lou Jennings and Charles Madge, London, 1985.

On JENNINGS: books—

Grierson, John, *Humphrey Jennings: A Tribute,* London, 1951.

Hardy, Forsyth, *Grierson on Documentary,* revised edition, London, 1966.

Lovell, Alan, and Jim Hillier, *Studies in Documentary,* New York, 1972.

Sussex, Elizabeth, *The Rise and Fall of British Documentary: The Story of the Film Movement Founded by John Grierson,* Berkeley, California, 1975.

Hodgkinson, Anthony, and Rodney Sheratsky, *Humphrey Jennings: More than a Maker of Films,* Hanover, New Hampshire, 1982.

Jennings, Mary-Lou, editor, *Humphrey Jennings: Film-Maker/Painter/Poet,* London, 1982.

Vaughan, Dai, *Portrait of an Invisible Man: The Working Life of Stewart McAllister, Film Editor,* London, 1983.

Aldgate, Anthony, and Jeffrey Richards, *Britain Can Take It: The British Cinema in the Second World War,* Oxford, 1986.

Tomicek, Harry, *Jennings,* Vienna, 1989.

On JENNINGS: articles—

Wright, Basil, "Humphrey Jennings," in *Sight and Sound* (London), December 1950.

Lambert, Gavin, "Jennings' Britain," in *Sight and Sound* (London), May 1951.

Védrès, Nicole, "Humphrey Jennings—A Memoir," in *Sight and Sound* (London), May 1951.

Anderson, Lindsay, "Only Connect: Some Aspects of the Work of Humphrey Jennings," in *Sight and Sound* (London), April/June 1954.

Dand, Charles, "Britain's Screen Poet," in *Films in Review* (New York), February 1955.

Strick, Philip, "Great Films of the Century: *Fires Were Started,*" in *Films and Filming* (London), May 1961.

Rhode, Eric, and Gabriel Pearson, "Cinema of Appearance," in *Sight and Sound* (London), Autumn 1961.

"Jennings Issue" of *Film Quarterly* (Berkeley), Winter 1961/62.

Millar, Daniel, "*Fires Were Started,*" in *Sight and Sound* (London), Spring 1969.
Belmans, Jacques, "Humphrey Jennings, 1907-1950," in *Anthologie du Cinéma* (Paris), vol. VI, 1971.
Sharatsky, R.E., "Humphrey Jennings: Artist of the British Documentary," special issue of *Film Library Quarterly* (New York), vol. 8, no. 3-4, 1975.
Zaniello, T.A., "Humphrey Jennings' Film *Family Portrait*: The Velocity of Imagistic Change," in *Literature/Film Quarterly* (Salisbury, Maryland), no. 1, 1979.
Eaton, Mick, "In the Land of the Good Image," in *Screen* (London), May/June 1982.
Robson, K.J., "Humphrey Jennings: The Legacy of Feeling," in *Quarterly Review of Film Studies* (New York), Winter 1982.
"Humphrey Jennings," in *Film Dope* (London), December 1983.
Colls, R., and P. Dood, "Representing the Nation: British Documentary Film 1930-45," in *Screen* (London), January/February 1985.
Nowell-Smith, Geoffrey, "Humphrey Jennings, Surrealist Observer," in *All Our Yesterdays,* edited by Charles Barr, London, 1986.

* * *

Though Jennings was (from 1934 on) part of the Grierson documentary group, he was never fully part of it. Grierson regarded him as something of a dilettante; Jennings' tastes and interests were subtler and gentler than Grierson's. It wasn't until Grierson had left England to become wartime head of the National Film Board of Canada that Jennings gained creative control over the films on which he worked. The outbreak of World War II seemed to let loose in Jennings a special poetic eloquence, and his finest work was done at the Crown Film Unit during the war years. *Listen to Britain, Fires Were Started,* and *A Diary for Timothy* are generally regarded as his masterpieces.

Jennings was part of the English intellectual aristocracy. Extremely well educated, he had done a good deal of research into English literature and cultural history. He was also a surrealist painter and poet. In his wartime films his deep-felt affection for English tradition mingles with impressionist observations of the English people under the stress of war. Rather than following the sociological line of the Griersonian documentaries of the 1930s, Jennings offered a set of cultural notations—sights and sounds, people and places—illuminated by his very special aesthetic sensibility and complete mastery of the technique of the black and white sound film. His films present an idealized English tradition in which class tensions do not appear. They record and celebrate contemporary achievement in preserving a historical heritage, along with commonplace decencies and humor in the face of an enemy threat. They also are experiments with form, of such breathtaking distinctiveness that they never really have been imitated.

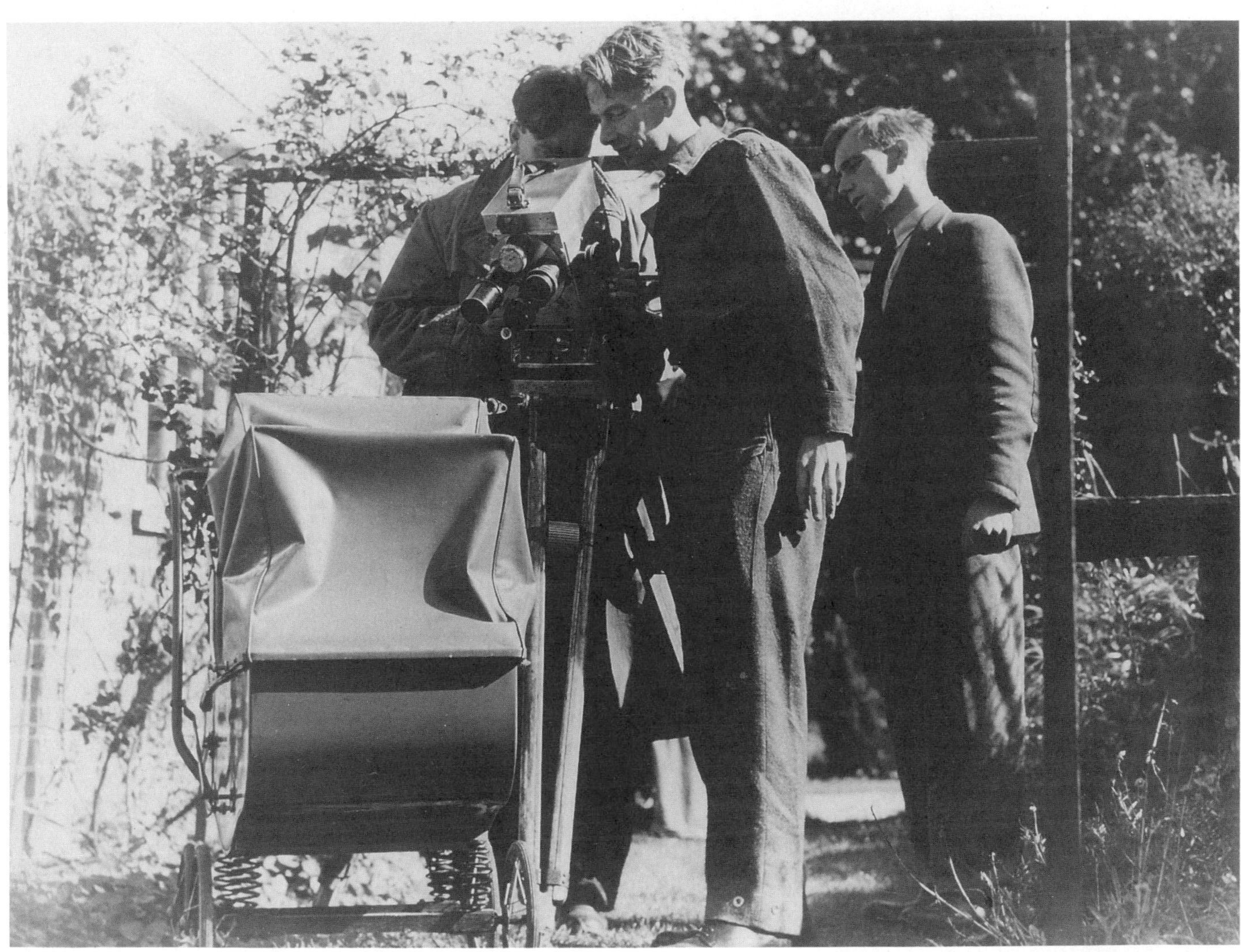

Humphrey Jennings (center) directing *A Diary for Timothy*

(Though Lindsay Anderson and other Free Cinema filmmakers would later acknowledge the importance of Jennings's work to them as inspiration, the Free Cinema films are radically different from Jennings's films in what they say about England, and are also much simpler in form.)

Listen to Britain, a short, is a unique impressionistic mosaic of images and sounds, including much music (as is usual in Jennings' work)—a sort of free-association portrait of a nation at a particular historical moment. The feature-length *Fires Were Started* carries the understated emotionality of the British wartime semi-documentary form to a kind of perfection: a very great deal about heroic effort and quiet courage is suggested through an austere yet deeply moving presentation of character and simple narrative. In *A Diary for Timothy,* which runs about forty minutes, Jennings attempted to fuse the impressionism of *Listen to Britain* with the narrativity of *Fires Were Started.* In its formal experimentation it is the most complex and intricate of all of Jennings's films.

With the Germans massed across the Channel, and bombs and then rockets being dropped on Britain, the British people needed a kind of emotional support different from the wartime psychological needs in other countries. In rising to this particular occasion Jennings became one of the few British filmmakers whose work might be called poetic. He is also one of a small international company of film artists whose propaganda for the state resulted in lasting works of art.

—Jack C. Ellis

JEWISON, Norman

Nationality: Canadian. **Born:** Toronto, Ontario, 21 July 1926. **Education:** Malvern Collegiate Institute; Victoria College, University of Toronto, B.A., 1945; studied piano and music theory at the Royal Conservatory. **Military Service:** Served in the Royal Canadian Navy. **Family:** Married Margaret Ann Dixon, 1953, two sons, one daughter. **Career:** Actor and scriptwriter in London, 1950-52; producer and director, Canadian Broadcasting Corporation, 1953-58; director for CBS, New York, won several Emmy awards, 1958-61; moved to Hollywood, 1961; after directing first feature, *40 Pounds of Trouble,* signed seven-picture contract with Universal, 1963; executive producer, *The Judy Garland Show,* for television, 1963-64; moved to MGM for *The Cincinnati Kid,* 1965; moved to the top rank of Hollywood directors with the award-winning *In the Heat of the Night,* 1968; maintains an office in London and a residence in Malibu, but primarily works out of his native Toronto, where he is the founder and co-chairman of the Canadian Center for Advanced Film Studies. **Awards:** Golden Globe and Oscar for Best Picture, for *In the Heat of the Night,* 1968; Best Director Prize, Berlin Film Festival, for *Moonstruck,* 1988. Officer, Order of Canada, 1982; Honorary LL.D, University of Western Ontario; Honored by American Civil Liberties Union, 1984. **Address:** Yorktown Productions Ltd., 18 Glouster Lane, 4th Floor, Toronto, Ontario M4X IL5, Canada.

Films as Director:

1962 *40 Pounds of Trouble*
1963 *The Thrill of It All*
1964 *Send Me No Flowers*
1965 *The Art of Love*; *The Cincinnati Kid*
1966 *The Russians Are Coming, the Russians Are Coming* (+ pr)
1967 *In the Heat of the Night*
1968 *The Thomas Crown Affair* (+ pr)
1969 *Gaily, Gaily* (*Chicago, Chicago*) (+ pr)
1971 *Fiddler on the Roof* (+ pr)
1973 *Jesus Christ Superstar* (+ co-pr, co-sc)
1975 *Rollerball* (+ pr)
1978 *F.I.S.T.* (+ pr)
1979 *... And Justice for All* (+ co-pr)
1982 *Best Friends* (+ co-pr)
1984 *A Soldier's Story* (+ co-pr)
1985 *Agnes of God* (+ co-pr)
1988 *Moonstruck* (+ co-pr)
1989 *In Country* (+ co-pr)
1991 *Other People's Money* (+ pr)
1994 *Only You* (+ pr)
1995 *Bogus* (+pr)

Other Films:

1970 *The Landlord* (Ashby) (pr)
1973 *Billy Two Hats* (Kotcheff) (co-pr)
1980 *The Dogs of War* (Irvin) (exec pr)
1984 *Iceman* (Schepisi) (co-pr)
1989 *January Man* (O'Connor) (pr)

Publications

By JEWISON: articles—

"Norman Jewison Discusses Thematic Action in *The Cincinnati Kid,*" in *Cinema* (Beverly Hills), July/August 1965.
"Turning On in Salzburg," in *Action* (Los Angeles), July/August 1969.
Interview in *Directors at Work,* edited by Bernard Kantor and others, New York, 1970.
Interview with Gordon Gow, in *Films and Filming* (London), January 1971.
Interview with C. Tadros, in *Cinema Canada* (Montreal), September 1985.
Interview in *Premiere* (New York), Autumn 1987.
Interview with L. Van Gelder, in *New York Times,* 11 December 1987.
Interview with T. Matthews, in *Box Office* (Hollywood), January 1988.
Interview with A. Hunter, in *Films and Filming* (London), April 1988.

On JEWISON: articles—

Carducci, M., "Norman Jewison Directs *Rollerball,*" in *Millimeter* (New York), March 1975.
Mariani, John., "Norman Jewison Directs *And Justice for All,*" in *Millimeter* (New York), October 1979.
Robertson, R., "Motion Pictures: The Great American Backlot," in *Millimeter* (New York), February 1988.
Rothstein, M., "In Middle America a Movie Finds Its Milieu," in *New York Times,* 6 March 1988.
Article in *American Film* (New York), July 1990.
Greenberg, J., article in *New York Times,* 6 July 1990.
De Vries, H., "A director's story," in *Premiere,* November 1991.

* * *

The very model of the modern up-market commercial director, Norman Jewison seems cut out to make the kind of prestige pictures once handled at MGM by Clarence Brown and Victor Fleming. No theme is so trashy or threadbare that he cannot elevate it by stylish technique and apt casting into a work of merit, even on occasion art.

Early work with an aging and cantankerous Judy Garland marked him as a man at ease with the cinema's sacred monsters; in the indifferent sex comedies of the early 1960s, he acquired equal skill with the pastels of Hollywood color and the demands of widescreen. A recognizable Jewison style was first evident in *The Cincinnati Kid.* Its elements—rich crimsons; the sheen of faces, tanned or sweating, in shadowed rooms; an edgy passion in performance—reappeared in *In the Heat of the Night* and *The Thomas Crown Affair,* novelettes redeemed by their visual flair and a sensual relish, not for sex, but for the appurtenances of power.

Not at home in domestic or comic realms, Jewison brought little to Ben Hecht's film memoir *Gaily, Gaily,* the literary ellipsis of *The Landlord,* or comedies like *Best Friends.* Two musicals, *Fiddler on the Roof* and *Jesus Christ, Superstar,* did, however, offer an invitation to location shooting and unconventional staging which Jewison confidently accepted. Though little liked on release, the latter shows a typical imagination and sensuality applied to the subject, which Jewison relocated in contemporary Israel to spectacular effect. *Rollerball,* his sole essay in science fiction, belongs with *Thomas Crown* in its relish for high life. The film's strength lies not in its portrayal of the eponymous gladiatorial game but its depiction of the dark glamour of life among the future power elite.

A pattern of one step forward, two steps backward, dominates Jewison's career into the 1980s. The Israel-shot western *Billy Two Hats* was a notable miscalculation, as was the Sylvester Stallone union melodrama *F.I.S.T.,* a program picture that needed to be an epic to survive. He was on surer ground in *... And Justice for All,* a dark and sarcastic comedy/drama about the idiocy of the law, with a credible Al Pacino in command. But films like the post-Vietnam melodrama *In Country* did little to enhance his reputation. It is a cause for concern that he could never put together his projected musical remake of *Grand Hotel,* whose elements seem precisely those with which he works most surely. A taint of the high-class advertising lay-out characterises Jewison's best work, just as the style and technique of that field rescues his often banal material.

Jewison's other recent films, *Other People's Money* (about an all-consumingly greedy Wall Street type, a role tailor-made for Danny De Vito) and *Only You* (the story of an incurable romantic and her quest for true love) are well-crafted and likeable but never truly memorable. The same might be said for *Moonstruck,* the biggest hit of the latter stages of his career, a popular comedy of life among New York City's ethnic Italians. The film was a box office hit and earned Cher an Academy Award. But while entertaining, on closer examination the film is all Hollywood gloss; it fails to authentically capture a true sense of its characters and their down-home ethnicity in a way that independent director Nancy Savoca, working on budgets minuscule to Jewison's, succeeds so brilliantly in doing in *True Love* and *Household Saints.* Another project that Jewison had an interest in never came to fruition. The director originally had wanted to film an account of the life of Malcolm X, but he gave up the project upon Spike Lee's protestations that only a black filmmaker could do justice to the story.

—John Baxter, updated by Rob Edelman

JIN, Xie *See* **XIE Jin**

JIREŠ, Jaromil

Nationality: Czech. **Born:** Bratislava, 10 December 1935. **Education:** Film technical school, Cmelice; the FAMU Film Faculty, Prague, graduate in photography, 1958, and direction, 1960. **Family:** Married Hana Jirešová. **Career:** Worked with Polyecran and the Magic Lantern, 1960-62; director of feature films, Barrandov Film Studio, from 1963; director of documentary films at Short Film Prague, from 1965; also TV director, from 1974, specialising in opera and ballet, late 1980s; president of Association of Czech Film Directors, from 1992. **Awards:** Great Prize, Oberhausen, for *The Romance,* 1966; Prize San Sebastian, for *The Joke,* 1969; Grand Premio, Bergamo, 1970, and Silver Hugo, Chicago, 1973, for *Valerie and the Week of Wonders;* Silver Prize, Berlin, 1982, and Best Director, Calcutta, 1983, for *Partial Eclipse;* Critics' Choice, AFI International Film Festival, for *The Labyrinth,* 1992; Great Prize, Harare, for *Helimadoe,* 1994. **Address:** Na ostrohu 42, Praha 6, 160 00, Czech Republic.

Films as Director:

1958 *Horečka* (*Fever*) (doc) (+ sc)
1959 *Strejda* (*Uncle*) (+ sc)
1960 *Sál ztracených kroku* (*The Hall of Lost Steps*) (+ sc, ph); *Stopy* (*Footprints*); *Polyekrán pro BVV* (*Polyecran for the Brno Industrial Fair*) (co-d); *La salle des pas perdus* (*The Waiting Room*) (doc)
1961 *Polyekrán pro Mezinárodní výstavu práce Turin* (*Polyecran for International Exposition of Labor Turin*) (co-d)
1962 *Houslový koncert* (*The Violin Concert*) (co-d, Magic Lantern program)
1963 *Krik* (*The Cry*) (+ co-sc)
1964 "Romance" episode of *Perličky na dně* (*Pearls in the Deep*) (+ sc)
1965 *Srub* (*The Log Cabin*) (+ sc); *Fuga* (for TV)
1966 *Občan Karel Havlíček* (*Citizen Karel Havlíček*) (doc) (+ co-sc)
1967 *Hra na krále* (*The King Game*) (+ sc)
1968 *Zert* (*The Joke*) (+ sc); *Don Juan 68* (doc) (+ sc); *Dědáček* (*Granpa*) (doc) (+ sc)
1969 *Cesta do Prahy Vincence Mošteka a Simona Pešla z Vlčnova l.p. 1969* (*The Journey of Vincenc Moštek and Simon Pešl of Vlčnov to Prague, 1969 A.D.*) (doc) (co-d, co-sc); *Tribunal* (doc)
1970 *Valerie a týden divu* (*Valerie and a Week of Wonders*) (+ sc); *Il Divino Boemo* (doc) (+ sc)
1972 *... a pozdravuji vlaštovky* (*My Love to the Swallows*) (+ sc)
1973 *Kasař* (*The Safe Cracker*) (doc) (+ sc)
1974 *Lidé z metra* (*The People from the Metro*) (+ co-sc); *Leoš Janáček* (+ sc, for TV)
1976 *Ostrov stříbrných volavek* (*The Island of Silver Herons*)
1977 *Talíře nad Velkým Malíkovem* (*Flying Saucers Over the Great Littletown*) (+ sc)
1978 *Mladý muž a bílá velryba* (*The Young Man and the White Whale*) (+ sc); *Diary of One Who's Disappeared* (for TV)
1979 *Causa králík* (*The Rabbit Case*) (+ sc)
1980 *Svět Alfonso Muchy* (*The World of Alphonse Mucha*) (doc) (+ sc); *Vtěky domů* (*Escapes Home*) (+ co-sc); *Bohuslav Martinů* (for TV)
1981 *Opera ve vinici* (*Opera in the Vineyard*) (+ sc)
1982 *Kouzelna Praha Rudolfa II* (*The Magic Prague of Rudolph II*) (doc) (+ sc); *Neúplné zatmění* (*Partial Eclipse*) (+ co-sc)
1983 *Katapult* (*Catapult*)
1984 *Prodloužený čas* (*The Prolonged Time*); *The Swan* (for TV)
1985 *Cuckoo's Egg: Milos Forman* (doc); *Eternal Faust* (for TV)
1986 *Dialogue of Forms* (ballet, for TV)
1987 *Lev s bílou hřívou* (*The Lion with the White Mane*); *I Love NY: Sidney Lumet* (doc); *F. Murray Abraham: Man and Actor* (doc)
1988 *Dialogue with Conscience of the Past* (for TV)

Jaromil Jireš

1989 *Memento Mori* (for TV); *Vive la musique et la liberté* (for TV)
1990 *Antonín Dvořák* (doc, for TV)
1991 *The Labyrinth* (+ co-sc)
1992 *Requiem for Those Who Overlived* (doc); ... *About Jaroslav Havlíček* (doc); *Mimikry* (ballet, for TV); *Music and Faith* (for TV)
1993 *Helimadoe*; *New York Diary—Alexander Hackenschmied* (doc); *GEN—Jiří Anderle* (doc); *GEN—Josef Skvorecký* (doc); *Music and Pain* (for TV); *Bambini di Praga* (for TV)
1994 *Teacher of Dance*
1995 *GEN—Miloš Kopecký* (doc); *Rodin* (doc)

Publications

By JIREŠ: articles—

Interview, in *The Image Maker,* edited by Ron Henderson, Richmond, Virginia, 1971.
Interview with E. Zaoralová, in *Film a Doba* (Prague), February 1981.
Interview with V. Kratochvilova, in *Film a Doba* (Prague), June 1985.
Interview with M. Storchova, in *Czechoslovak Film* (Prague), Autumn 1986.
Interview with J. Sitarova, in *Film a Doba* (Prague), April 1987.

On JIREŠ: books—

Janoušek, Jiří, *3 1/2 po druhé,* Prague, 1969.
Hames, Peter, *The Czechoslovak New Wave,* Berkeley, 1985.

On JIREŠ: articles—

Sarris, Andrew, "Movers," in *Saturday Review* (New York), 23 December 1967.
"Jaromil Jireš," in *Film Dope* (London), December 1983.

* * *

Having finished his studies at the Prague Film School, Jireš entered filmmaking at the end of the 1950s with several short films, the most engaging of which was *Sál ztracených kroku (The Hall of Lost Steps).* In 1963 he made his debut in feature-length films with the picture *Křik (The Cry),* which earned him a place among the ranks of young directors striving for new content and a new film language. In his debut Jireš reacts to modern film currents, above all to the stylistics of the cinéma vérité, whose elements he utilizes, conscious, of course, of the danger that this can hold for the representation of reality and the expression of truth. The story of *The Cry* suppresses traditional dramatic structure. It consists of the fragmentary memories of the two main protagonists, a husband and wife, on the day their child is to be born. Arranging individual recollections, combining fictional segments with documentary shots, and using a hidden camera, Jireš seeks to convince the viewer of man's connection with the present, the past, and the future, and his close and immediate link with the whole world. (Jireš: "We live in a time when a person's most intimate experiences are connected with the major currents of world events.") *The Cry* was very well received and won several awards; it is the first pinnacle of Jireš's creative work.

The second pinnacle was achieved in two totally disparate pictures from the early 1970s. One film was *Valerie a týden divu (Valerie and a Week of Wonders),* based on a novel by the eminent modern Czech poet Viítězslav Nezval. What interested Jireš about the novel was "the juncture of reality and dream and the playful struggle between horror and humor." The other film, ... *a pozdravuji vlaštovky (My Love to the Swallows),* is purely Jireš's own. The director was inspired by the life and death of the real-life character of Maruška Kudeříková, a young woman who fought against German fascism during the Second World War. Here, in a different connection, Jireš used the same method of alternating real-life elements and reminiscences, as in *The Cry,* but for a different purpose, namely, to demonstrate a person's inner strength, the source of her faith and hope.

The following years, in which Jireš made three pictures, were a period of stagnation. The fairy-tale film *Lidé z metra (The People from the Metro)* and *Ostrov stříbrných volavek (The Island of Silver Herons),* in which he returns to the days of the First World War, are equally undistinguished. Even less noteworthy is the fantastic tale *Talíře nad Velkým Malíkovem (Flying Saucers Over Velký Malík).*

Jireš's creative path took a new turn in 1978 with *Mladý muž a bílá velryba (The Young Man and the White Whale).* The film is an adaptation of Vladimír Páral's novel of the same name and deals with modern man's uneasy oscillation between a mask of cynicism and pure human feeling. Next came *Causa králík (The Rabbit Case),* an apparently humorous morality piece with a bitter finale on the struggle for justice against cunning and evil. The heroine of Jireš's next work, *Utěky domu (Escapes Home),* is a young woman who must face a conflict between her desire for self-fulfillment in a challenging profession and her duties as a wife and the mother of a family. In *Neúplné zatmění (Partial Eclipse),* about a little blind girl, he speculates on an emotional level about the meaning of life and the quest for human personality. All these recent films address problems of modern life in the area of the ethics of human relations.

Documentary films form an integral part of Jireš's creative work. Unlike his friends of the same generation, Jireš remained faithful to the documentary genre throughout his artistic career. This segment of his work shows great thematic breadth. We can nonetheless delineate two fundamental areas of interest for Jireš. In the 1960s his attention was drawn to the folklore of southern Moravia, where several of his short films have their setting. Jireš returned to this region and to this subject matter in a modified form in 1981 with the ballad story *Opera ve vinici (Opera in the Vineyard).* From the 1970s his documentary films turn more and more to the world of art, to music, painting, and architecture.

—Vladimir Opela [translated by Robert Streit]

JOFFÉ, Roland

Nationality: English. **Born:** London, 17 November 1945. **Education:** Attended Manchester University. **Career:** Co-founder of the Young Vic and former member of the National Theater under Laurence Olivier; moved into television and made various documentaries as well as dramatic series; started big-screen production in mid-1980's with emphases on both the grandeur of the visual and the complexity of politics and religion. **Awards:** Golden Palm, Cannes International Film Festival, for *The Mission,* 1986.

Films as Director:

1978 *The Legand Hall Bombing* (for TV); *The Spongers* (for TV)
1979 *No, Mama, No* (for TV)
1981 *United Kingdom* (for TV)
1984 *The Killing Fields*
1986 *The Mission*
1989 *Fat Man and Little Boy* (+ co-sc)
1992 *City of Joy* (+ co-pr)

Roland Joffé directing Jeremy Irons in *The Mission*

Other Films:

1991 *Made in Bangkok* (pr)

Publications

By JOFFÉ: articles—

"Entretien avec Roland Joffé," with M. Ciment, in *Positif* (Paris), February 1985.

"Light Shining in Darkness: Roland Joffé on *The Mission,*" interview with M. Dempsey, in *Film Quarterly* (Berkeley), no. 4, 1987.

On JOFFÉ: articles—

Michiels, D., "*The Spongers,*" in *Film en Television + Video* (Brussels), December 1980.

Denby, D., "Movies: Blood Brothers," in *New York,* 17 November 1984.

Kael, P., "The Current Cinema: Unreal," in *New Yorker,* 10 December 1984.

Jensen, L., "Vietnamkrigen Borte med Blaesten," in *Levende Dilleder* (Copenhagen), 15 February 1985.

Joyeux, D., "Marknadsforare med sinne for Film," in *Chaplin* (Stockholm), no. 2, 1985.

Park, J., "Bombs and Pol Pots," in *Sight and Sound* (London), no. 54, 1984/85.

Le Fanu, M., "Regard Aigu sur un Destin Funeste," in *Positif* (Paris), February 1985.

Agostinis, V., "Quando l'emozione supera il realismo della politica," in *Segnocinema* (Italy), March 1985.

Pally, M., "Red Faces," in *Film Comment* (New York), January/February 1986.

Magny, J., "Conscience Impossible," in *Cahiers du Cinema* (Paris), October 1986.

Miller, J., "*The Mission* Carries a Message from Past to Present," in *New York Times,* 26 October 1986.

Millar, G., "The Honourable Dead," in *Sight and Sound* (London), no. 4, 1986.

Mosier, J., "Tramps Abroad: The Anglo-Americans at Cannes," in *New Orleans Review,* no. 4, 1986.

Lally, K., "*Mission* Accomplished: Epic Arrives after 15-Year Struggle," in *Film Journal* (New York), January 1987.

Rodman, H. A., "Director Roland Joffé," in *Millimeter* (Cleveland), April 1987.

Pinsky, M. I., "*The Mission,* Junipero Serra, and the Politics of Sainthood," in *Jump Cut* (Berkeley), February 1988.

Rios, A., "La Pasion segun Roland Joffé," in *Cine Cubano* (Havana), no. 123, 1988.

Lee, N., "*Fat Man and Little Boy*: Birth of the Atom Bomb," in *American Cinematographer* (Hollywood), November 1989.

Kael, P., "The Current Cinema: Bombs," in *New Yorker,* 13 November 1989.

Buckley, M., "Roland Joffé," in *Films in Reviews* (New York), January/February 1990.
Root, D., "Holy Men in the Wilderness: *The Mission* and Sainte Marie among the Hurons," in *Cineaction* (Toronto), Winter/Spring 1990.
Scheck, F., "*Fat Man and Little Boy,*" in *Films in Review* (New York), March 1990.
Jenkins, S., "*City of Joy,*" in *Sight and Sound* (London), October 1992.
Romano, H., "*Cite de la Joie,*" in *Jeune Cinema* (Paris), October 1992.

* * *

Often compared with that of David Lean, the famed epic master of a generation ago, Roland Joffé's filmic career to date has proven to be an uneven one. Despite several noble attempts to render the grandeur of idealism and the complexity of politics, religions, and history, Joffé often falls short of the truly large-scale perspectives and touches of genuine humanity that underline Lean's masterpieces, such as *The Bridge on the River Kwai* and *Lawrence of Arabia.*

Having worked quite extensively in both theater and television, Joffé made his big-screen debut with 1984's *The Killing Fields,* produced by arguably the most influential British producer of the 1980s, David Puttnam. A story about an interracial friendship set in the time of the genocide in Cambodia during the mid-1970s, *The Killing Fields* strives to capture the universal spirit of humanity that binds people, despite their differences. A group of Western reporters are rescued by Dith Pran (played by Dr. Haing S. Ngor). The high drama unfolds when those Westerners realize that they are not capable of rescuing their Cambodian friend, their life saver, in return. The beautifully done cinematography and excellent soundtrack of "Nessun Dorma" from Puccini's *Turandot* nonetheless fail to save the feeble (when stripped of all its flamboyant superficiality) narrative in its attempt to document one of the most monstrous tragedies in human history.

The highly problematic, revisionist portrayal of South American history during the mid-eighteenth century in *The Mission* calls for even more scrutiny. Two Jesuit missionaries, played by high-profile Jeremy Irons and Robert De Niro, participate in the resistance against the intermingled conflicts with Spain, Portugal, the Pope, and many a merchant whose monetary concerns dictate their actions. The end result is "calamitous ...: the Battle of Caibale (1756), during which [the two Jesuit leaders], several other Jesuits, and some 1500 Indians die," according to Michael Dempsey. Speaking of the seemingly licensed fictionality of the two key Jesuit characters, Joffé refers to "liberation theology" in saying that "The film in that sense is intimately concerned with the struggle for liberation in liberation theology, and that's why the historical perspective is very important, because what it's actually saying is that these people haven't *come out of nowhere*" [emphasis mine]. It is then Joffé and his team's historical perspectives that enable them, as Dempsey aptly puts it, to "re-oppress the people with overbearing film technology and appropriate their story for a grandiose prestige spectacle."

The little-noticed *Fat Man and Little Boy,* a story about the creation of the atom bomb, failed even with the star power of Paul Newman. Following that was *City of Joy,* a story celebrating spirituality as the link that crosses all boundaries. Set in Calcutta, *City of Joy* seems to be over-fascinated with the city itself. As Joffé himself enthusiastically confessed in a publicity essay, Calcutta "taught me, in its complexity, its passion, anger and pettiness, that our individual failings are no more or less than the failings of the species; as there are no perfect individuals, there are no perfect races." In this spirit, what is being presented in this movie are two individuals, one American (Max, played by Patrick Swayze) and the other Indian (Hasari Pal, played by Om Puri). What they have in common is that they both are *not* perfect. The problematized narrative falls into an almost stereotypical treatment of interracial relationships. Max's spiritual fulfillment comes with the ability to help with Hasari's material needs (for example, the medallion which provides for her daughter's dowry), while Hasari, though sometimes distrustful and even jealous, is nonetheless a rescuer for the American, who is easily beaten by and lost in the immense (both human—the oppressive ganglord's son—and natural—the monsoon season) primitiveness of Calcutta.

After tracing Roland Joffé filmic career to date, Steven Jenkins's astute observation particularly rings true. "One has the feeling that in his striving for epic, the 'big picture' indeed, Joffé would like to be David Lean.... But the interrelationship between character and backdrop in *The Bridge on the River Kwai* and *Lawrence of Arabia* seems ideologically more complex and rigorously scrutinized than anything here." Despite the consistently stunning visuals in Joffé's films, one cannot help but feel an imbalance, one that tilts between a historical and ideological monstrosity gotten out of hand and a simple-minded heroism blown out of proportion.

—Guo-Juin Hong

JORDAN, Neil

Nationality: Irish. **Born:** Sligo County, Ireland, 25 February 1950. **Education:** Read History and literature at University College, Dublin. **Career:** Formed Irish Writers' Co-op, 1974, and had first collection of short stories, *Night in Tunisia,* published, 1976; worked as assistant on John Boorman's *Excalibur,* in fringe theatre, and as a writer, before directorial debut with *Angel,* 1982; made first American film, *High Spirits,* 1988; directed music videos for The Pogues and Kirsty MacColl. **Awards:** Guardian Prize for fiction, for *A Night in Tunisia,* 1979; Best Film and Best Director, London Critics Circle, for *The Company of Wolves,* 1984; Palme d'Or, Cannes Festival, and De Sica Award, Sorrento Festival, for *Mona Lisa,* 1986; Oscar, Best Screenplay, for *The Crying Game,* 1992. **Address:** Lives in Bray, near Dublin.

Films as Director:

1982 *Angel* (*Danny Boy*) (+ sc)
1984 *The Company of Wolves* (+ sc)
1986 ***Mona Lisa*** (+ co-sc)
1988 *High Spirits* (+ sc)
1989 *We're No Angels*
1991 *The Miracle* (+ sc)
1992 ***The Crying Game*** (+ sc)
1994 *Interview with the Vampire*

Publications

By JORDAN: books—

A Night in Tunisia, London, 1976.
The Past, London, 1980.
Dream of the Beast, London, 1983.
Mona Lisa, with David Leland, London, 1986.
High Spirits, London, 1989.

By JORDAN: articles—

Interview with M. Open, in *Film Directions* (Belfast), vol. 5, no. 17, 1982.

Neil Jordan © Andy Lane

Interviews in *Time Out* (London), 13 October 1983 and 13 September 1984.

Interview with Paul Taylor and Steve Jenkins, in *Monthly Film Bulletin* (London), September 1984.

Interview with J. Powers, in *American Film* (Washington, D.C.), July/August 1986.

"Lines Written in Dejection," in *Producer* (London), May 1987.

Interview in *City Limits* (London), 8 December 1988.

"Here Comes Mr. Jordan," interview with R. Sawhill in *Interview* (New York), December 1989.

"Neil Jordan's Guilty Pleasures," in *Film Comment* (New York), November/December 1992.

"Irish Eyes," interview with M. Glicksman in *Film Comment* (New York), January/February 1990.

Interview with Lois Gould in *New York Times Magazine,* 9 January 1994.

Interview with S. O'Shea in *Harper's Bazaar* (New York), November 1994.

On JORDAN: articles—

Barra, Alan, "Here Comes Mr. Jordan," in *American Film* (Los Angeles), January 1990.

O'Toole, F., "Neil Jordan Gets Back to Making Home Movies," in *New York Times,* 14 October 1990.

Barra, Alan, "Jordan Airs," in *Village Voice* (New York), 6 August 1991.

Hooper, J., "Pop Terrorist," in *Esquire* (New York), December 1992.

"Rules of the Game," in *New Yorker,* 7 December 1992.

McDonagh, M., "Sex, Politics, and Identity Clash in Neil Jordan's *Crying Game,*" in *Film Journal,* December 1992.

Harris, M., "The Little Movie that Could: *The Crying Game,*" in *Entertainment Weekly* (New York), 12 February 1993.

Conant, J. "Lestat, c'est moi," in *Esquire* (New York), March 1994.

* * *

The film career of Neil Jordan could be said to parallel the fortunes of the British film industry during the 1980s. He made a stunning impact with his first two films. *Angel* was arguably the most accomplished film-making debut sponsored by Channel 4, while *The Company of Wolves* was the first feature to be produced by Palace, one of the more exciting film companies to emerge in the decade. *Mona Lisa* consolidated his reputation as a distinctive and visionary filmmaker. However, by the end of the decade both Jordan and the British film industry seemed to have run out of steam. In comparison with his earlier work, the more overtly commercial *High Spirits* and *We're No Angels* can only be described as mediocre and sadly lacking in ideas. The director recovered in the early 1990s, however, with *The Crying Game,* a film that rode a wave of publicity to an unlikely level of financial success.

At its most successful, Jordan's cinema demonstrates forcefully his ability to make the familiar seem strange and in doing so to question our assumptions about the nature of the world. All his films revolve to some extent around the idea that reality is complex and multi-faceted. Jordan's characters often encounter nightmare worlds which they must negotiate rather than push aside precisely because they are unacknowledged dimensions of reality. *Angel* and *Mona Lisa,* for instance, are similar in structure; each deal with individuals who become inadvertently caught up in personal nightmares which threaten to destroy them: Danny with sectarian violence and bloody revenge and George with the hellish underworld of teenage prostitution and drug addiction.

The idea of the nightmare world is given a more literal rendition in *The Company of Wolves.* Based on a short story by Angela Carter, the film is a reworking of the Little Red Riding Hood story, a bizarre and sumptuous mixture of fairy tale, gothic horror, and Freudian psychoanalysis which betrays a rich variety of cinematic influences, from Cocteau through Michael Powell and Hammer horror to Laughton's *Night of the Hunter.* The film explicitly challenges the spurious division between reality and fantasy by setting up two distinct worlds: the "real" world of the girl asleep in bed, suffering from the onset of her first menstrual period, and the "dream world" of Rosalean and her granny, set in a magical forest which was entirely constructed in a studio. At the film's conclusion, the barrier between these two worlds is broken down; the wolves from the dream invade the sleeping girl's bedroom by smashing through a picture and the window.

It follows that symbolism is extremely important in Jordan's work. *The Company of Wolves* is rife with symbolic images relating to sexuality and procreation. *Mona Lisa* employs such devices to explore the film's central thematic concern with innocence and corruption. Images relating to childhood, and by extension innocence—the white rabbit, the silly glasses, the old woman's shoe, the dwarves—are juxtaposed with scenes of degradation, depravity, and violence. In *Angel* lost innocence is again explored. Danny's decision to swap his saxophone for a gun effectively symbolizes the idea of the heavenly musician turned avenging angel. It is precisely the ambiguity of Danny—a figure who straddles the divine/demonic divide—which gives the film its power. Initially repulsed by the violence which claims an angelic deaf-mute girl, Danny becomes a cold-blooded killer himself in his pursuit of the perpetrators. In comparison, the religious symbolism in *We're No Angels* seems rather clumsy and sentimental.

Despite being a powerful piece of cinema, there were indications in *Mona Lisa* that Jordan had begun to lose his sense of direction. The film lacks the moral ambiguity that made *Angel* so challenging. George remains a rather naive and socially inept character, his uncomplicated and thoroughly "decent" moral code at odds with the world in which he becomes involved, a world he cannot begin to understand. But his naivete is too overwhelming to be credible, and his social ineptitude borders on cliché. Unlike *Angel* and *The Company of Wolves,* the resolution of *Mona Lisa* is rather cozy and contrived; George returns to "normality," apparently none the worse for his traumatic experience.

Significantly, Jordan also attempted to lighten *Mona Lisa* by introducing comic elements, courtesy of the eccentric character Thomas, played by Robbie Coltrane. This familiar strategy in British cinema more often than not serves to blunt a film's cutting edge. *High Spirits* and *We're No Angels* demonstrate rather painfully that Jordan does not have a feel for comedy. The former relies on unimaginative stereotyping and comic cliché, while the latter descends at times into messy slapstick reminiscent of Abbott and Costello or the Three Stooges. Indeed, apart from the odd visual touch it is virtually impossible to recognise the latter film as the work of the person who made *Angel* or *The Company of Wolves.*

After the debacle of *We're No Angels,* Jordan sensibly returned to Ireland. There he directed *The Miracle,* an atmospheric, subtly sensuous coming-of-age drama. The scenario's focus is on James and Rose, alienated adolescents who perceive the world with the type of poetic cynicism that is the license of bright, bored teens. James's father is introduced as a widower who drinks too much and plays bad music in a ten-cent dance hall. One day a pretty mystery woman (Beverly D'Angelo) comes to town. James and Rose are fascinated by her, and he soon begins wooing her. But he is unaware of her true identity, and Jordan proceeds to throw a curve ball at his audience that rivals the one thrown in Jordan's next film, *The Crying Game.* It turns out that the woman is none other than James's mother.

The Crying Game was a sensation, a feature which the film media extolled as a "must-see." The praise was warranted, for *The Crying Game* is inventive and entertaining, and it spotlights what was to become one of the most talked-about celluloid plot twists in screen history. It begins as a bleak political drama in which a kidnapped black British soldier (Forest Whitaker) is held hostage by an Irish Republican Army militant (Stephen Rea). Eventually, the latter sets out to locate the former's sweetheart (Jaye Davidson), who proves to have some interesting secrets. *The Crying Game* is at once a political drama, a thriller, and a love story. It became one of the rare "art house" films to make its way into mall theaters.

Jordan's follow-up to *The Crying Game* was the much anticipated but over-produced and ultimately tedious adaptation of Anne Rice's *Interview with the Vampire.* Despite the presence of some of Hollywood's hottest actors, including Tom Cruise, Brad Pitt, Antonio Banderas, and Christian Slater, the best thing about the film was the provocative performance of young Kirsten Dunst in the role of Claudia, the child vampire.

—Duncan J. Petrie, updated by Rob Edelman

JUTRA, Claude

Nationality: Canadian. **Born:** Montreal, 11 March 1930. **Education:** Doctor of Medicine, University of Montreal, 1952. **Career:** Made first films, in collaboration with Michel Brault, 1947; worked intermittently for National Film Board, 1954-66; founded Films Cassiopée to produce *A tout prendre,* 1961. **Awards:** First Prize for experimental film, with Norman McLaren, Venice Festival, for *A Chairy Tale,* 1958; Best Film, Canadian Film Awards, for *A tout prendre,* 1964. **Died:** After apparently committing suicide, November 1986 (body found in St. Lawrence River, near Quebec City, April 1987).

Films as Director:

1947 *Le Dément du Lac Jean Jeune* (co-d)
1949 *Mouvement perpétuel* (co-d, sc)
1956 *Pierrot des bois* (+ sc, ed, role); *Les Jeunesses musicales* (+ sc)
1957 *A Chairy Tale* (*Il etait une chaise*) (co-d with Norman McLaren, role)
1958 *Les Mains nettes*
1959 *Anna la bonne*; *Félix Leclerc, troubadour*; *Fred Barry, comédien* (+ sc)
1961 *Le Niger—jeune république* (+ ed); *La Lutte* (*Wrestling*) (co-d, co-ph, co-ed, co-sound)
1962 *Québec-USA* (*L'Invasion pacifique*; *Visit to a Foreign Country*) (co-d, ed)
1963 *Les Enfants du silence* (co-d, ed, commentary); *Petit Discours de la méthode* (co-d, ed, commentary); *A tout prendre* (*Take It All*) (+ sc, ed, role)
1966 *Comment savoir* (*Knowing to Learn*); *Rouli-Roulant* (*The Devil's Toy*) (+ ph, ed, commentary)
1969 *Wow* (+ sc, co-ed); *Au coeur de la ville*
1970 *Marie-Christine*
1971 *Mon Oncle Antoine* (+ role as Fernand)
1972 *Kamouraska*
1975 *Pour le meilleur et pour le pire*
1978 *Surfacing*
1980 *By Design*
1985 *La Dame en couleurs*

Other Film:

1978 *Two Solitudes* (role)

Publications

By JUTRA: articles—

"En courant derrière Rouch," in *Cahiers du Cinéma* (Paris), November 1960, and January and February 1961.
Interview in *Cahiers du Cinéma* (Paris), April/May 1968.
"Claude Jutra: Une Exploration dans une morale pathologique," an interview with G. Langlois, in *Cinéma* (Paris), January 1973.
"Un espèce de joie dans la création," an interview with J. P. Tadros, in *Cinéma Québec* (Montreal), March/April 1973.
Interview with G. C. Koller and P. Wronski, in *Cinema Canada* (Montreal), November 1975.
"Jutra on the Tube," an interview with P. Kelman, in *Cinema Canada* (Montreal), March 1979.

On JUTRA: books—

Marsolais, Gilles, *Le Cinéma canadien,* Paris, 1968.
Chabot, Jean, *Cinéastes du Québec Quatre: Claude Jutra,* Montreal, 1970.
Beattie, Eleanor, *A Handbook of Canadian Film,* Toronto, 1973.
May, John R., and Michael Bird, editors, *Religion in Film,* Knoxville, Tennessee, 1982.

On JUTRA: articles—

Prédal, René, "Jeune Cinéma Canadien," in *Premier Plan* (Lyons), no. 45, 1967.
Blumer, Ronald, "Dr. Claude Jutra: Filmmaker," in *McGill Medical Journal* (Montreal), December 1969.
"Les honneurs siéent bien à Claude Jutra," in *Séquences* (Montréal), July 1985.
Obituary, in *Variety* (New York), 29 April 1987.
"Claude Jutra Section" of *Séquences* (Montreal), October 1987.
Billard, J. A., obituary, in *24 Images* (Montreal), no. 36, 1986/87.

* * *

Claude Jutra won his first Canadian Film Award at the age of nineteen for *Mouvement perpétuel.* At twenty-one he received his doctor of medicine from the Université de Montréal. Two years later, in 1953, he authored the first-ever teleplay to be screened on the French Radio Canada network. By the following year he was established at the National Film Board of Canada, in that era a stronghold of the Griersonian documentary approach and its technique. Jutra commuted to the Film Board, then based in Ottawa, from Montréal, where he was studying theatre at the Théatre du Nouveau Monde.

After winning acclaim at the 1957 Venice Festival with *A Chairy Tale,* an animated film using the pixilation technique of his co-director, Norman McLaren, Jutra left Canada to spend four years working in France, where he directed the short film of Jean Cocteau's *Anna, la bonne,* produced by Francois Truffaut. Jutra also spent time learning from, working with, and developing a close friendship with cinéma verité pioneer Jean Rouch.

His return to Québec in 1961, fresh from the experience and energy of the French New Wave, indubitably helped to set Jutra apart from the English Canadian filmmakers working at that time. Simultaneously, a group of French Canadian filmmakers—including Jutra's early collaborator, Michel Brault; the great Québecois proponent of cinéma verité, Pierre Perrault; and Gilles Carle, among others—had begun to carve out a separate aesthetic space for themselves within the Canadian film industry, an aesthetic space inextricable from their identity as Francophones living and working in Québec in the early years of what was then called the Quiet Revolution.

Jutra's independently made feature, *A tout prendre,* a cinéma directe film wherein the actors played "themselves," dealt with the relationship between Claude and Johanne, Jutra's African-Canadian girlfriend, and also touched upon the issue of homosexuality. The film both shocked and impressed the film industry of the early 1960s, winning the Canadian Film Awards' Best Feature Film prize for Jutra, its director, writer, co-producer, and lead player.

Mon oncle Antoine, later to be voted Canada's best film of all time, was released in 1971. Jutra's intimate, comic-poetic feature, based on the reminiscences of screenwriter Clément Perron's childhood in rural Québec, swept the Canadian Film Awards that year, winning eight prizes. The film had previously been rejected by the Cannes Festival committee and screened in English Canada without subtitles—it also suffered innumerable delays before its release.

Jutra went on to film Anne Hébert's period novel *Kamouraska,* starring Genevieve Bujold. Although the film won Best Feature and Bujold the prize for Best Actress, French and English filmmakers in Canada had come to increasing odds and the Canadian Film Awards ceremony in 1973 had been boycotted by Québecois filmmakers. Meanwhile, the National Film Board found itself unable to come to terms with the harsh and hard-hitting political work of its Francophone filmmakers—films which, at this point in the history of Québec, were an interpretation and reaction to the October Crisis of 1970. Although Jutra's work was not overtly political in the same sense as his contemporaries, he too was affected by the slump in the Québecois film industry at the time and in 1975 left Montréal for Toronto, where he spent the next six years working for CBC television and directing two features. It was, he claimed, "like working in a foreign country."

By the late 1970s, however, Jutra recognized that his once-impeccable memory had begun to slide; his mental health was at the beginning of its long decline. It was in his native Montréal, in 1984, that Jutra completed his last film, *La dame en couleur.* Work became impossible in the efforts of day-to-day survival, his affable personality and childlike energy all but submerged by what was eventually diagnosed as Alzheimer's disease.

On November 5, 1986, after having left a note for the sister who had become his caretaker, Claude Jutra disappeared from his Montréal home. Newspaper headlines in the following months speculated as to whether Jutra had left the country or had simply retreated to a secret location outside of the city. In the spring of 1987, down the St. Lawrence River from Montréal and close to Québec City, Jutra's body was discovered. Found in a personal journal alongside which were detailed descriptions of his mental decline, Jutra had written down the directions to the Jacques Cartier bridge, where he apparently took his own life at the age of fifty-six.

—Clea H. Notar

KACHYŇA, Karel

Nationality: Czech. **Born:** Vyskov, 1 May 1924. **Education:** Film Academy (FAMU), Prague, 1947-51. **Career:** Associated with co-director Vojtěch Jasný, 1949-55; after working for Armed Forces Film Studio, joined Barrandov Film Studios, 1959; associated with writer Jan Procházka, late 1950s-1970. **Awards:** Czech Film Critics Award, for *Smugglers of Death,* 1959.

Films as Director:

1950 *Není stále zamrečeno* (*The Clouds Will Roll Away*) (co-d, co-sc with Vojtěch Jasný, ph); *Vedeli si rady* (*They Know What to Do*) (co-d, co-sc, ph)
1951 *Za život radostný* (*For a Joyful Life*) (co-d, co-sc with Jasný)
1952 *Neobyčejná léta* (*Extraordinary Years*) (co-d, co-sc)
1953 *Lidé jednoho srdce* (*People of One Heart*) (co-d, co-sc, co-ph)
1954 *Stará činská opera* (*Old Chinese Opera*) (co-d, co-sc, ph); *Z čínskëo zápisniku* (*From a Chinese Notebook*) (co-d, co-sc, ph)
1955 *Dnes večer všechno skonči* (*Everything Ends Tonight*) (co-d, co-sc)
1956 *Ztracená stopa* (*The Lost Track*) (+ sc); *Křivé zrcadlo* (*Crooked Mirror*) (+ sc)
1957 *Mistrovstvi světa leteckých modelářu* (*World Championship of Air Models*) (+ sc); *Pokušeni* (*Temptation*) (+ sc, ph)
1958 *Tenkrát o vánocich* (*That Christmas*) (+ co-sc); *Ctyřikrát o Bulharsku* (*Four Times about Bulgaria*) (+ sc); *Městomä svou tvář* (*The City Has Your Face*) (+ sc)
1959 *Král Sumavy* (*The King of the Sumava*) (+ co-sc)
1960 *Práče* (*The Slinger*) (+ co-sc)
1961 *Pouta* (*The Country Doctor*; *Fetters*) (+ co-sc); *Trápeni* (*Stress of Youth*) (co-sc)
1962 *Závrat* (*Vertigo*) (+ co-sc)
1963 *Nadeje* (*Hope*) (+ co-sc)
1964 *Vysoká zed* (*The High Wall*) (+ co-sc)
1965 *Af žije republika* (*Long Live the Republic*) (+ co-sc)
1966 *Kočár do Vídně* (*Carriage to Vienna*) (+ co-sc)
1967 *Noc nevěsty* (*Night of the Bride*) (+ co-sc)
1968 *Vánoce s Alžbětou* (*Christmas with Elizabeth*) (+ co-sc)
1969 *Směšný pán* (*Funny Old Man*) (+ co-sc); *Ucho* (*The Ear*)
1970 *Už zase skáču přes kaluže* (*Jumping the Puddles Again*) (+ co-sc);
1972 *Vlak do stanice nebe* (*Train to Heaven*) (+ co-sc); *Láska* (*Love*) (+ co-sc); *Horká zima* (*Hot Winter*) (+ co-sc)
1974 *Pavlínka*; *Robinsonka* (*Robinson Girl*)
1975 *Skaredá dědina* (*The Ugly Village*); *Smrt mouchy* (*The Death of a Fly*)
1976 *Malá mořská víla* (*The Little Mermaid*) (+ co-sc)
1977 *Setkání v červenci* (*Meeting in July*)
1978 *Cekání na déšť* (*Waiting for the Rain*)
1979 *Láska mezi kapkami deště* (*Love Between the Raindrops*)
1980 *Cukrová bouda* (*Sugar Cottage*; *The Little Sugar House*)
1981 *Pozor vizita!* (*Watch Out, The Rounds!*)
1982 *Fandy, ó Fandy* (*Fandy, Oh Fandy*)
1983 *Sestricky* (*Nurses*)
1985 *Dobré svetlo* (*Good Light*)
1986 *Smrt krásnych srncu* (*Death of a Beautiful Dream*)
1987 *Kam pánové, kam jdete?* (*And What Now, Gentlemen?*)
1988 *Oznamuje se láskam vasim* (*Let It Be Known to All Your Loves*)
1989 *Blázni a devcátka* (*Young Girls, Crazy Guys*)
1990 *The Last Butterfly* (+ sc)
1992 *Ucho* (*The Ear*)
1993 *The Cow* (+ sc)

Other Film:

1952 *Věda jde s lidem* (*Science Goes with People*)

Publications

By KACHYŇA: articles—

Interview with E. Hepnerová, in *Film a Doba* (Prague), February 1976.
Interview in *Film a Doba* (Prague), January 1982.
Interview with L. Hofmanova, in *Film a Doba* (Prague), November 1986.

On KACHYŇA: books—

Bocek, Jaroslav, *Modern Czechoslovak Film 1945-65,* Prague, 1965.
Bartoskovi, Sárka and Lubos, *Filmové profily,* Prague, 1966.
Liehm, Antonin, *Closely Watched Films,* New York, 1974.
CSF—Czechoslovak Cinema, Czechoslovak Film Institute, Prague, 1982.
Hames, Peter, *The Czechoslovak New Wave,* Berkeley, 1985.

On KACHYŇA: articles—

Melounek, P., in *Film a Doba* (Prague), May 1984.
Kudriavtsev, S., in *Iskusstvo Kino,* no. 4, 1992.

* * *

Karel Kachyňa is an artist with a broad range of ideas which constitute the starting point for his thinking in images. Despite their formal variety, his works bear an individual creative stamp characterized by a play of poetic images precisely tailored to the dramatic structure of the story. Like any original artist who continuously seeks new paths of self-expression, Kachyňa has brief periods which seem to be at odds with the rest of his work. These are the exceptions, the experiments, the preparations for great artistic work to come.

At first it seemed that Kachyňa's main calling would be making documentary films. He has gone beyond these; they served as a point of departure for his dramatic films. His first creative period is characterized by innovatively conceived documentaries which not only captured the facts but also expressed the view of the filmmaker. His attempts to combine elements of fantasy, story, and style led him to the dramatic film, where he concentrated on films of wartime adventure and suspense. In so doing he did not forget what he had learned in making documentaries: to capture reality and transform it into a new artistic image in a carefully conceived story. The culmination of this period is *Král Sumavy (The King of the Sumava).*

Gradually other elements asserted themselves in his films: detailed psychological characterization and a precise portrayal of relationships against the backdrop of a given historical situation. Since he was never an independent writer of his own films, he was able to detach himself from the given material and consider it from a unique viewpoint. He was most interested in the contradiction-fraught relationships of people taking their first steps into adulthood, or the world of children on the verge of some kind of awakening, a discovery of life in the brief interval in which reality stimulates the world of thoughts, dreams, and memories and becomes itself only a framework for a profound catharsis of feelings: *Trápeni (Stress of Youth), Závral (Vertigo), Už zase skáču přes kaluže (Jumping the Puddles Again), Smrt mouchy (Death of a Fly),* and others. His films are first and foremost images interspersed with brief dialogue, where small details, objects, and nature come to life. He directs his actors, be they amateurs or professionals, in a way that enables them to live the roles they play, to create the truth of life, to shape and express their own feelings and views. His tendency to create intimate dramas, however, leads to formal refinement in which an objective view of reality is often lost.

Kachyňa has been served by several literary works which were sensitively adapted for the screen. But the foundation of his work remains the cinematic poem of feelings, for example *Pavlinka, Robinsonka,* or *Skaredá dědina (The Ugly Village).* "I like drawing-room stories set in an atmosphere of feelings, where the leading role is played by image, music, and often by what cannot even be expressed, that which is a part of our lives but is not concrete and cannot even be described. Apprehensions, hopes, dreams, someone's touch ... I would always like to have these things in my films. I think they are an essential part of the truth of life. And this truth is what film is mainly about. A film will never be a work of art unless it mirrors that truth, however subtly it may strive in other ways to express the most sublime thought," said Karel Kachyňa in one conversation. And it is this credo that he strives strictly to uphold in his own films. After a lengthy period in which he focused on the world of children at the threshold of adulthood, he has turned in his more recent works to an adult milieu.

—Vaclàv Merhaut

KADÁR, Ján

Nationality: Czechoslovak. **Born:** Budapest, 1 April 1918. **Education:** Gave up law studies to study photography at Bratislava school, 1938. **Career:** Prisoner in Nazi labor camp, early 1940s; after war, producer and director, Bratislava Studio of Short Films; scriptwriter and assistant director, Barrandov Studio, Prague, from 1947; began association with Elmar Klos (born in Brno, 26 January 1910), 1952; moved to U.S., 1969. **Awards:** Oscar for Best Foreign Language Film, for *The Shop on Main Street,* 1965; National Artist of Czechoslovakia, 1969. **Died:** In Los Angeles, 1 June 1979.

Films as Director:

1945 *Life is Rising from the Ruins*
1950 *Katka* (*Kitty*) (+ co-sc)
1952 *Unos* (*Kidnapped*) (co-d, co-sc with Elmar Klos)
1954 *Hudba z Marsu* (*Music from Mars*) (co-d, co-sc with Klos)
1957 *Tam na konečné* (*The House at the Terminus*) (co-d with Klos)
1958 *Tři přání* (*Three Wishes*) (co-d, co-sc with Klos)
1963 *Smrt si říká Engelchen* (*Death Is Called Engelchen*) (co-d, co-sc with Klos)
1964 *Obžalovaný* (*The Accused*; *The Defendant*) (co-d, co-sc with Klos)
1965 ***Obchod na korze*** (*The Shop on Main Street*; *The Shop on the High Street*) (co-d, co-sc with Klos)
1970 *The Angel Levine*
1971 *Touha zvaná Anada* (*Adrift*), *Something Is Drifting on the Water*) (completed 1969; co-d with Klos)
1975 *Lies My Father Told Me*
1978 *Freedom Road*

Other Films:

1947 *Nevité o bytě?* (*Looking for a Flat*) (sc)

Publications

By KADÁR: articles—

"Elmar Klos and Jan Kadar," interview with Jules Cohen, in *Film Culture* (New York), Fall/Winter 1967.
Interview with Robert Haller, in *Film Heritage* (Dayton, Ohio), Spring 1973.
Interview with L. Vigo, in *Image et Son* (Paris), June 1973.

On KADÁR: books—

Bocek, Jaroslav, *Modern Czechoslovak Film 1945-1965,* Prague, 1965.
Liehm, Antonin, *Closely Watched Films,* White Plains, Prague, 1974.
Hames, Peter, *The Czechoslovak New Wave,* Berkeley, 1985.

On KADÁR: articles—

"Director," in the *New Yorker,* 12 February 1966.
"The Czech Who Bounced Back," in *Films Illustrated* (London), April 1972.
Obituary, in *New York Times,* 4 June 1979.
Moret, H., obituary in *Ecran* (Paris), 15 July 1979.
Gervais, G., obituary in *Jeune Cinéma* (Paris), July/August 1979.
Keenan, Richard C., "The Sense of an Ending: Jan Kadár's Distortion of Stephen Crane's *The Blue Hotel,*" in *Literature/Film Quarterly* (Salisbury, Maryland), vol. 16, no. 4, 1988.

* * *

Ján Kadár is undoubtedly best known for his film *The Shop on the High Street,* made with his long time collaborator, Elmar Klos. This was the first Czechoslovak film to win an Academy Award and was heralded as the beginning of the Czech film renaissance of the 1960s. In fact, Kadár made his first feature, *Katka,* in 1950, and Klos was one of those who helped to draw up the plans for the nationalisation of the film industry in that decade. This, of course, was a mixed blessing, as Kadár himself pointed out: "to innovative filmmakers this was a dream—it would liberate them from commercial pressures. Instead, there was political pressure. This was the disadvantage of subsidised art."

Ján Kadár: *Lies My Father Told Me*

Katka itself ran into political difficulties. Made in Kadár's native Slovakia, it tells the story of a village girl who becomes a factory worker. However, as the director points out, at about this time "it had been decided that it was no longer necessary to urge people to leave their homes for industry. But above all, the film wasn't 'national' enough, it wasn't sufficiently steeped in folklore and Slovakism. And that was referred to as 'the bourgeois point of view.'" Expelled from the Slovak film industry, Kadár "became Czech" and began his partnership with Klos. Their first collaboration was *Kidnapped,* which Kadár later described as "an extremely naive, dogmatic, cold-war type of film" but which was nonetheless criticised at the time for "bourgeois objectivism." Saved by the intervention of V. I. Pudovkin, they went on to make *Music From Mars,* a musical satire on bureaucracy, which gave rise to complaints that they had slandered public figures.

Their next film steered clear of trouble. This was *House at the Terminus,* which posed the question of whether is it right to bring children into the world in its present state. Given the country's low and falling birth rate this was more than simply a philosophical question. By avoiding explicitly "public" problems and issues and concentrating instead on the private sphere, the film managed to avoid censure for drawing what is surely a rather depressing picture of Czech society. Peter Hames in *The Czechoslovak New Wave* speaks of its air of "gloomy desolation" and remarks that although "there is little overt political criticism, the implicit criticism is considerable, and the problems with which it deals take place in a social context. Hence loneliness, cynicism, personal and professional failure, compromise, wrongful imprisonment, and lack of faith are shown as generalised characteristics of a supposedly socialist society," one in which, that is, such problems have supposedly been eliminated.

Three Wishes, a modern version of the old fairy tale in which a character is granted his heart's desire only to find that the dream turns sour, was banned until 1963 (that is, once the process of de-Stalinization had got under way). Again, the problem seems to have been that it painted a less than ideal view of society, since it shows the central character realising his wishes by exploiting the corruption and hypocrisy he finds around him in society.

After this film, Kadár and Klos were unable to work again for two years, but during the ensuing "thaw" period they produced their most famous work, *The Shop on the High Street.* This is set in Slovakia during the period of the independent fascist state, described by one Czechoslovak critic as "a gruesomely grotesque miniature of the apocalypse of the Third Reich" and by Klos as representing "a special kind of national fascism." The story concerns an old, deaf Jewish woman and her relationship with the Slovak who is assigned to her shop as an "Aryan controller." An extremely effective picture of everyday fascism in an ordinary small community, the film may revolve around a grim and tragic theme but it is actually played largely as a gentle comedy. Kadár once claimed that his favourite directors were Chaplin, Truffaut and Fellini, and their presences can all be felt here in the quirky, offbeat humour, the mingling of the comic and tragic, and the gentle observation of its characters' failures and all-too-human shortcomings. One is also, of course, put in mind of the early works of Passer, Forman and Menzel. Like the old lady at the centre of the film, Kadár was himself Jewish, and although by his own account he never encountered anti-Semitism, *The Shop* later attracted charges of Zionism from certain quarters, particularly after Kadár's departure for the States.

With the end of the "Prague Spring," Kadár left Czechoslovakia for Vienna and from there went to America. At the time of the invasion he and Klos were working on a Czech-American co-production titled *Adrift,* which was made in collaboration with the Hungarian writer Imre Gyöngyössy, who later went on to become a director himself. On his arrival in the States, Kadár was fortunate enough to be offered the direction of *The Angel Levine,* based on a Bernard Malamud story. He then returned to Czechoslovakia to complete *Adrift.* This is an atypical Kadár film, clearly influenced by Resnais and Robbe-Grillet, about a girl who may or may not have been saved from drowning in the Danube.

In the States and Canada (where he also found work) Jewish themes in his films clearly came to the fore—hence *The Angel Levine, Lies My Father Told Me* and *Mendelstam's Witness.* Other works which must surely have had a strong personal resonance for the director were the TV movies *The Case Against Milligan,* which examines the theme of freedom of conscience, and *The Other Side of Hell,* which looks at the plight of the sane person in an insane society. While none of his later films attain the level of *The Shop on the High Street,* they nonetheless attest to the warmth and generosity of spirit that is the hallmark of Kadár's best and most typical work.

—Julian Petley

KAIGE, Chen *See* **CHEN Kaige**

KAPOOR, Raj

Nationality: Indian. **Born:** Ranbirraj Kapoor in Peshwar (now in Pakistan), 14 December 1942. **Education:** Educated in Calcutta and Bombay. **Family:** Married Krishna (Kapoor), three sons, two daughters. **Career:** Entered film industry as clapper boy, late 1930s; assistant on Bombay Talkies, then production manager, art director, and actor, Prithvi Theatres, early 1940s; first leading role, in *Neel Kamal,* 1947; directed first film, *Aag,* 1948. **Awards:** Filmfare Award for Best Director for *My Name is Joker,* 1970. **Died:** Of complications from asthma attack, in New Delhi, 2 June 1988.

Films as Director:

1948 *Aag* (*Fire*) (+ pr, role)
1949 *Barsaat* (+ role)
1951 ***Awara*** (*The Vagabond*) (+ role)
1955 *Shri 420* (*Mister 420*) (+ role)
1964 *Sangam* (+ role, pr)
1970 *Mera Naam Joker* (*My Name Is Joker*) (+ role, pr)
1974 *Bobby* (+ pr)
1978 *Satyam Shivam Sundaram* (+ pr)
1982 *Prem Rog* (+ pr)

Other Films:

1935 *Inquilab* (role)
1943 *Hamari Baat* (role); *Gowri* (role)
1946 *Valmiki* (role)
1947 *Neel Kamal* (role); *Chithod Vijay* (role); *Jail Yaatra* (role); *Dil Ki Raani* (role)
1948 *Gopinath* (role)
1949 *Andaz* (role); *Parivartan* (role); *Sunehere Din* (role)
1950 *Banwara* (role); *Banware Nayan* (role); *Dastaan* (role); *Jaan Pehchan* (role); *Pyaar* (role); *Sargam* (role)
1952 *Ambar* (role); *Anhonee* (role); *Aashiyana*; (role); *Bewafa* (role)
1953 *Dhoon* (role); *Paapi* (role); *Aah* (pr, role)
1954 *Boot Polish* (pr)
1956 *Jagte Raho* (pr, role); *Chori Chori* (role)
1957 *Ab Dilli Dur Nahin* (pr)
1958 *Sharada* (role); *Parvarish* (role); *Phir Subah Hogi* (role)
1959 *Anadi* (role); *Char Dil Char Rahen* (role); *Do Ustad* (role); *Kanhaiya* (role); *Main Nashe Me Hoon* (role)
1960 *Jis Desh Me Ganga Behti Hai* (*Where the Ganges Flows*) (pr, role); *Chaliya* (role); *Shriman Satyavadi* (role)
1961 *Nazraana* (role)
1962 *Aashik* (role)
1963 *Dil Hi To Hai* (role); *Ek Dil Sou Afsane* (role)
1964 *Dulha Dulhan* (role)
1966 *Teesri Kasam* (role)
1967 *Around the World* (role); *Diwana* (role)
1968 *Sapnon Ka Saudgar* (role)
1972 *Kal, Aaj Aur Kal* (pr, role)
1975 *Dhadram Karam* (pr); *Do Jasoos* (role)
1976 *Khaan Dost* (role)
1977 *Chandi Sona* (role)
1981 *Biwi O Biwi* (pr); *Abdullah* (role)
1982 *Gopichand Jasoos* (role)

Publications

On KAPOOR: books—

Barnouw, Erik, and S. Krishnaswamy, *Indian Film,* New York, 1965.
Sarkar, Kobita, *The Indian Cinema Today,* New Delhi, 1975.
Abbas, Ahmad, *I Am Not An Island: An Experiment in Autobiography,* New Delhi, 1977.
Burra, Rani, editor, *Looking Back 1896-1960,* New Delhi, 1981.
Willemen, Paul, and Behroze Gandhy, *Indian Cinema,* London, 1982.
Ramachandran, T.M., *70 Years of Indian Cinema,* Bombay, 1985.
Dissanayake, Wimal, and Malti Sahai, *Raj Kapoor's Films: Harmony of Discourses,* New Delhi, 1987.
Reuben, Bunny, *Raj Kapoor, The Fabulous Showman: An Intimate Biography,* Bombay, 1988.

On KAPOOR: articles—

"Special Issue" of *Film Français* (Paris), Spring 1953.
Tesson, C., "Le Rêve indien," in *Cahiers du Cinéma* (Paris), March 1985.

Raj Kapoor in *Shri 420*

Thomas, R., "Indian Cinema: pleasures and Popularity," in *Screen* (London), May/August 1985.
Hollywood Reporter, November 1985.
Obituary in *Variety* (New York), 8 June 1988.

* * *

Raj Kapoor was the best-known screen personality in India. He acted major roles in over fifty films, produced more than a dozen, and during the course of a thirty-five-year career directed six of the most popular films of the Hindi cinema—*Awara, Shri 420, Sangam, Mera Nam Joker, Bobby,* and *Satyam Shivam Sundaram*). The popularity of Raj Kapoor's work derives from a paradoxical achievement: he intensified in his films both the lavishness and the social consciousness of the Hindi cinema. His films are characterized by elaborate sets, evocative music, new stars, dramatic confrontations and narrow escapes from heartbreak. At the same time he addressed poverty, injustice, and the plight of individuals insisting on their own way against the massive force of social conventions. Indian audiences responded enthusiastically to Raj Kapoor's mixture of entertainment and serious issues; his films articulate at some level the longings of an entire people.

Raj Kapoor's first film, *Aag,* is restrained by smallness of scale; the set is modest and the fiery character of the emotional triangle in the story is rendered chiefly through high-contrast lighting. But his third and fourth films (*Awara* and *Shri 420*) disclose a fully operatic style. In *Awara,* the key court scene is played in a deep, amply lit hall; and in both *Awara* and *Shri 420,* the houses of the rich are magnificently spacious, fitted with winding stairs, high ceilings and tall, curtained windows. For music, Raj Kapoor employed the lyricist Shailendra and the composers Shankar-Jaikishen, who specialized in brightening up traditional melodies; a number of their songs for *Awara Hun, Mera Joota Hai Japani* are among the most popularly known in India. Raj Kapoor also delights in soaring camera movements, as over the courtroom in *Awara* and under the circus tent in *Mera Nam Joker.* The speed and freedom of the camera contributes to the audience's sense of dynamic progress.

Raj Kapoor's films deal with important cultural experiences: *Shri 420* is concerned with the ruthlessness confronting new migrants to the city; *Awara* with the malign influence of slum environments; *Sangam, Bobby* and *Satyam Shivam Sundaram* with tensions between spontaneous affection and social protocols for intimacy; and *Mera Nam Joker* presents the loneliness of a circus clown as an archetype for people who have been uprooted. Both plot and music invite viewers to identify with the experiences of unfortunate protagonists. Meanwhile the mise-en-scene directs the attention of viewers to the furnishings of rich houses (*Shri 420* and *Awara*), to the mountain spectacle of various Himalayan resorts (*Bobby*), to a spacious temple courtyard and a daringly costumed dancer (*Satyam Shivam Sundaram*), and to entire acts of the Soviet State Circus (*Mera Nam Joker*).

Since the time of Raj Kapoor's first films, filmmaking in India has moved toward greater generic variety and coherence. From the perspective of the new political films, Raj Kapoor's productions seem complacent; from the perspective of the new realist films, his work seems gaudy. Nonetheless, his work is certain to be remembered for its spectacular vitality.

—Satti Khanna

KASDAN, Lawrence

Nationality: American. **Born:** Miami Beach, Florida, 14 January 1949. **Education:** University of Michigan, B.A., 1970, M.A. (education), 1972. **Family:** Married Meg Goldman, 1971, two sons. **Career:** Advertising copywriter, Detroit, 1972-75, and Los Angeles, 1975-77; screenwriter, from 1977; directed first film, *Body Heat,* 1981. **Awards:** Directors Guild of America Award, for *The Big Chill,* 1983; Golden Lion Award, Berlin Film Festival, for *Grand Canyon,* 1992. **Address:** c/o Kasdan Productions, 4117 Radford Avenue, Studio City, CA 91604.

Films as Director:

1981 *Body Heat* (+ sc)
1983 ***The Big Chill*** (+ exec pr, sc)
1985 *Silverado* (+ pr, co-sc)
1988 *The Accidental Tourist*
1989 *I Love You to Death*
1991 *Grand Canyon* (+ pr, co-sc)
1994 *Wyatt Earp* (+ pr, sc)
1995 *French Kiss*

Other Films:

1980 ***The Empire Strikes Back*** (co-sc)
1981 ***Raiders of the Lost Ark*** (co-sc); *Continental Divide*
1983 ***Return of the Jedi*** (co-sc)
1987 *Cross My Heart* (pr)
1989 *Immediate Family* (exec pr)
1991 *Jumpin' at the Boneyard* (exec pr)
1992 *The Bodyguard* (pr, sc)

Publications

By KASDAN: books—

The Empire Strikes Back Notebook, edited by Diane Attias and Lindsay Smith, New York, 1980.
The Art of Return of the Jedi, with George Lucas, New York, 1983.
The Big Chill, with Barbara Benedek, New York, 1987.
Wyatt Earp: The Film and the Filmmakers, New York, 1994.

By KASDAN: articles—

Interview in *Film Comment* (New York), September/October 1981.
Interview with Minty Clinch, in *Films* (London), March 1982.
"Dialogue on Film: Lawrence Kasdan," in *American Film* (Washington, D.C.), April 1982.
Interview with P. H. Broeske, in *Films in Review* (New York), April 1984.
Interview with A. Garel and others, in *Revue du Cinéma* (Paris), December 1985.
Interview in *American Film* (Washington, D.C.), January/February 1989.

On KASDAN: articles—

"Lawrence Kasdan," in *Film Dope* (London), March 1984.
Fikejzov, M., "Lawrence Kasdan," in *Film Doba,* February 1990.
Alion, Y., "Lawrence Kasdan," in *Revue du Cinéma* (Paris) June 1990.
Kaplan, James, "Talking 'bout Their Generation," in *Entertainment Weekly,* February 14, 1992.
Griffin, Nancy, "Return of the Ride-Back Gang," in *Premiere* (New York), July 1994.

* * *

On the basis of relatively few films, Lawrence Kasdan has had a prestigious career as screenwriter and director, though one that is difficult to characterize easily. His early work is notable for toying humorously with established genres like the action-adventure serial, film noir, and the western without ever going all the way into parody. That is, he was able to convey a certain "hip" or postmodern sensibility without neglecting an appeal to some viewers' nostalgia for the past and a great many more viewers' craving for good storytelling.

His very 1980s approach to older movie genres worked splendidly in *Raiders of the Lost Ark* (written, not directed, under the Lucas-Spielberg aegis) and the hyper-sultry *Body Heat.* The latter contained gentle, knowing allusions to a film noir past while sustaining its own snappy dialogue and ingeniously structured suspense, and seemed to relish its own outrageously steamy setting, an erotic/violent Florida where only the most primitive air conditioners seem to have been invented. Less successful was *Silverado,* a kind of postmodern Western, which lacked a consistently graspable tone and effective narrative pacing. (Though the complicated narrative makes sense in outline, some of the subplots do not seem to exist in the same narrative world, like those of the heavy-handedly portrayed struggling black family and the preposterously romantic Kevin Kline-Linda Hunt relationship.) Curiously, Kasdan's most recent genre films seem to have lost that hyper-consciousness, those knowing winks. *Wyatt Earp* is utterly conventional even while seemingly schizoid in its inability to decide whether it is an old-fashioned, sweepingly grand Western, a cynical expose of the "real" Earp, or a dry chronicle of a historically significant life. And *French Kiss* is equally conventional as a romantic farce, though far more fresh and spirited than *Wyatt Earp.*

Kasdan's less classifiable dramas have some of the same quirky humor as the earlier genre pieces. *The Big Chill* was variously loved or hated for its sympathetic yet satirical portrayal of the ego crises of a spectrum of 1960s activists finding themselves in the doldrums of the early 1980s. By the standards of classical Hollywood storytelling, *The Big Chill* is pleasingly loose in structure, with its assembly of former friends in close encounters during a long weekend; but it seemed to some viewers contrived and slick in comparison to the more low-key, low-budget film by John Sayles on the same subject, *The Return of the Secaucus Seven. The Accidental Tourist,* Kasdan's first effort in adapting a literary text, also drew mixed reactions, but this time over its success or failure in adapting a highly regarded novel, and over William Hurt's extremely subdued performance. *I Love You to Death* is not much like any of the earlier films, falling into a comedy subgenre involving farcically unsuccessful efforts at murder. Some viewers found the black comedy insufficiently black or comical; certainly, one finds less of the cool, sly humor of the earlier films or even of parts of

Lawrence Kasdan directing *Body Heat*

French Kiss. With *Grand Canyon,* another experiment in creating an ensemble film with several interwoven plot strands, Kasdan is again in fine form, even if he leans too heavily toward a feel-good finale. There is a wit in the very talkiness of the film, as characters continually launch into existentialistic discussions of the random violence and miracles of life, with the film producer Davis (Steve Martin) downright Shavian in his defense of ultraviolent movies (like Major Barbara's father defending his munitions plants).

Kasdan may eventually be remembered as a starmaker. *Body Heat* introduced Kathleen Turner and the sultry persona she continued to use; it offered Mickey Rourke a memorable supporting role; and it made William Hurt a new kind of leading man, with a distinctively 1980s manner, even when playing a 1940s-style victim of a femme fatale or, as in *The Big Chill,* an erstwhile hippie. *The Big Chill* boosted the careers of Glenn Close, Kevin Kline, and Meg Tilly, as *Silverado* did that of Kevin Costner and *The Accidental Tourist* that of Geena Davis. At the same time as promoting individual talents, Kasdan seems particularly skilled in directing ensemble acting, not only throughout *The Big Chill* and *Grand Canyon,* but in the glimpses of eccentric family life in *The Accidental Tourist* and the joint murder efforts in *I Love You to Death*—arguably those films' best scenes.

Kasdan's visual style from film to film may be more difficult to characterize than his handling of genre and actors, though one may note consistently fluid camera movements and a determination to give each film a distinctive look and mood, while keeping a number of the same technical personnel. One remembers the blues, whites, and shadows of a sweltering Florida in *Body Heat;* the autumnal glow of *The Big Chill;* the conventional but still handsome Techniscope vistas of *Silverado;* the glowing landscapes of provincial France in *French Kiss;* and the pale colors and vacant widescreen spaces of *The Accidental Tourist. Grand Canyon* has so many scenes inside automobiles, with widescreen two-shots, that it makes the private vehicle seem the modern setting *par excellence* for meaningful dialogue.

Sometimes unfairly slighted as a mere spokesperson for aging babyboomers when he is not a mere genre artist, Kasdan may not have established a consistently strong individual voice, as his early films seemed to promise, but he remains a formidable craftsman whose films continue to promise future greatness.

—Joseph Milicia

KAUFMAN, Philip

Nationality: American. **Born:** Chicago, Illinois, 1936. **Education:** University of Chicago, graduated 1958; attended Harvard Law School, 1958. **Family:** Married Rose Fisher, 1958, one son, Peter. **Career:** Moved to San Francisco, then to Europe for two years while attempting to write a novel; worked on a Kibbutz in Israel; entered Universal Studios Young Directors' Program, 1969. **Awards:** Prix de la Nouvelle Critique for first feature, *Goldstein,* Cannes Film Festival, 1964. **Agent:** Creative Artists Agency, 9830 Wilshire Blvd., Beverly Hills, CA 90212, U.S.A.

Films as Director and Scriptwriter:

1964 *Goldstein*
1967 *Fearless Frank*
1972 *The Great Northfield Minnesota Raid*
1974 *The White Dawn*
1978 *Invasion of the Body Snatchers*
1979 *The Wanderers*
1983 *The Right Stuff*
1988 *The Unbearable Lightness of Being*
1990 *Henry & June*
1993 *Rising Sun*

Other Films:

1976 *The Outlaw Josey Wales* (Eastwood) (co-sc)
1981 *Raiders of the Lost Ark* (Spielberg) (co-story)

Publications

By KAUFMAN: articles—

Interview with B. Krohn, in *Cahiers du Cinéma,* no. 358, 1984.
Interview with A. Baecque, in *Cahiers du Cinéma,* no. 405, 1988.
Interview with F. Guerif, in *Revue du Cinéma,* no. 437, 1988.
Interview with M. Ciment, in *Positif,* no. 357, 1990.
Interview with Gavin Smith, in *Film Comment,* July 1993.

On KAUFMAN: articles—

Dempsey, Michael, "Invaders and Encampments: The Films of Philip Kaufman," in *Film Quarterly,* Winter 1978/79.
Goodwin, Michael, "Riding High with *The Right Stuff,*" in *American Film,* November 1983.
Sojka, Gregory S., "The Astronaut: An American Hero with *The Right Stuff,*" in *Journal of American Culture,* Spring 1984.
Lavery, David, "Departure of the Body Snatchers," in *The Hudson Review,* vol. 39, no. 3, 1986.
Klinger, Judson, "The Casting of *Henry & June,*" in *American Film,* September 1990.
Lindroth, Colette, "Mirrors of the Mind: Kaufman Conquers Kundera," in *Literature/Film Quarterly,* vol. 19, no. 4, 1991.
Fellows, Catherine, "*The Unbearable Lightness of Being* on Film," in *Cinema and Fiction: New Modes of Adapting,* edited by Colin Nicholson, Edinburgh, Scotland, 1992.
Mitchell, Sean, "Strangers in a Strange Land," in *Premiere,* August 1993.
Ehrenstein, David, "War Business," in *Sight and Sound,* October 1993.
Hendershot, Cyndy, "Vampire and Replicant: The One-Sex Body in a Two-Sex World," in *Science-Fiction Studies,* November 1995.
See, Fred G., "'Something Reflective': Technology and Visual Pleasure," in *Journal of Popular Film and Television,* Winter 1995.

* * *

Philip Kaufman has not set any records for productivity, but the few films he has made have been intelligently and independently done. His choice of topics has been eclectic. He has adapted novels as far removed as Milan Kundera's *The Unbearable Lightness of Being* and Michael Crichton's *Rising Sun.* He adapted Tom Wolfe's journalistic epic about the space program, *The Right Stuff,* brilliantly; he also adapted the personal writings of Anais Nin in *Henry & June.* His work has ranged from realism to fantasy: *The White Dawn,* for example, is a historical film about three whalers from New England marooned in the Arctic, shot in a documentary style, while *Invasion of the Body Snatchers* is a remake of the Don Siegel science-fiction classic, satirically updated. The satire that surfaces in some of Kaufman's work might be considered part of his artistic "signature," even though the satire of *The Right Stuff* can be traced back to Tom Wolfe's source. The director has asserted himself when artistic differences surfaced: Kaufman quarreled with Clint Eastwood and lost on *The Outlaw Josey Wales,* which Kaufman originally was to have directed; he quarreled with Michael Crichton and won on *Rising Sun,* changing the sidekick, the villain, the balance, the tone, and the conclusion of the novel to suit his own purposes and taking the edge off Crichton's warning about the Japanese.

Kaufman has been a risk-taker. The erotic content of *Henry & June* tested the limits of the MPAA Code and was the first film released with an NC-17 rating (No Children Under 17 Admitted), created to remove the stigma of the old "X" rating. In terms of the candid treatment of adult relationships, this constituted an artistic breakthrough, achieved by an unconventional filmmaker who was willing to take a chance and put his career on the line. But Kaufman probably has not worried too much about his career.

Born to a cultured German-Jewish family, Kaufman grew up on Chicago's North Side, studied history at the University of Chicago, and, after a year at the Harvard Law School, enrolled in the master's program in history at his alma mater. Eventually a wanderlust took Kaufman and his wife Rose to the Bay Area of San Francisco, where he held various odd jobs while attempting to write a novel; he then moved to Europe, taught in Greece and Italy, and worked on an Israeli Kibbutz. By 1962 Kaufman was back in Chicago, where he developed a screenplay from his unfinished novel, working with his friend Benjamin Manaster as co-writer, director, and producer.

Kaufman's debut feature, *Goldstein,* made for $50,000 with friends from Chicago's Second City, was, according to one source, loosely based on one of Martin Buber's *Tales of the Hassidim* and starred Lou Gilbert as Goldstein, a parody prophet. Kaufman took his film to the Cannes Film Festival in 1964, where it shared the Prix de la Nouvelle Critique with Bernardo Bertolucci's *Before the Revolution,* an incredible stroke of good fortune.

Encouraged by this success, Kaufman then wrote and directed a second Chicago film, *Fearless Frank,* in 1965, with Jon Voight making his film debut as a farm boy who goes to the city and falls in love with a gangster's moll. This film also utilized the satiric talents of the Second City players but won no prizes at Cannes in 1967. In fact, *Fearless Frank* failed to find an American distributor until American International picked it up in 1969, after Jon Voight's success in John Schlesinger's *Midnight Cowboy.* Though *Fearless Frank* was not a critical success, Jennings Lang of Universal Studios invited Kaufman into Universal's Young Directors' Program. At Universal Kaufman then wrote and directed *The Great Northfield Minnesota Raid,* starring Robert Duvall as Jesse James and Cliff Robertson as Cole Younger. This film opened to mixed reviews in 1972.

Philip Kaufman: *The Right Stuff*

Kaufman adapted his next film, *The White Dawn,* released by Paramount in 1974, from a novel by James Houston, telling the story of three whalers who survived a shipwreck in Baffin Bay in 1896 and were rescued by Eskimos. The film, starring Warren Oates, Timothy Bottoms, and Lou Gossett, was shot in northern Canada under difficult conditions, but it was not given full support by Paramount and was not widely seen. The following year Kaufman was assigned to direct *The Outlaw Josey Wales* after having worked on the script for Clint Eastwood, but Eastwood soon took over the direction himself. Kaufman got credit with Sonia Chernis for the screenplay, adapted from the Forrest Carter novel *Gone to Texas.* In 1981 Kaufman also worked as a writer when he helped George Lucas develop the original story for *Raiders of the Lost Ark,* but most of his work has involved directing.

In 1978, at a time when his Hollywood career needed a boost, Kaufman had a major windfall when he was assigned to direct the remake of Don Siegel's *Invasion of the Body Snatchers* for United Artists, working from W. D. Richter's updated screenplay adaptation of Jack Finney's novel. Kaufman moved the action to San Francisco and redefined the alien threat in a way that was disturbing, humorous, and believable. This was followed by *The Wanderers,* his adaptation of Richard Price's comic novel about Italian high-school gangs in the Bronx, set in 1963.

Kaufman's greatest success was his blockbuster hit *The Right Stuff,* which earned eight Academy Award nominations, including Best Picture. Kaufman also earned Writers Guild and Directors Guild nominations for his satiric adaptation of Tom Wolfe's account of the astronaut program. Kaufman has a talent for adaptation. Terrence Rafferty praised Kaufman's adaptation of *The Unbearable Lightness of Being* for its fidelity "to the novel as it exists in the mind of the reader," rather than to the novel as an autonomous entity (Kaufman changed and simplified the structure), claiming that "the movie's most interesting character is Philip Kaufman."

And that claim might be made for other Kaufman films as well. The adaptations are centered in the personality of the filmmaker. For example, Kaufman turned *Rising Sun* into his own reinvented story. His strength is in the whimsical, the satirical (*The Invasion of the Body Snatchers, The Right Stuff,* and *Rising Sun*), and in the erotic and the lyrical (*The Unbearable Lightness of Being* and *Henry & June*). Though the films themselves seem impossibly varied, his best work has a personal imprint. The style of his later films seems vaguely European, but his values, stressing individualism and integrity, are clearly American. Kaufman has not produced a large body of work, but his best work certainly merits critical attention.

—James M. Welsh

KAURISMAKI, Aki

Nationality: Finnish. **Born:** Finland, 4 April 1957. **Career:** Began working as co-scenarist and assistant director with his older brother, Mika Kaurismaki, 1980; co-directed *Saimaa Ilmio* with Mika, 1981; directed first feature on his own, *Crime and Punishment,* 1983; directed the music videos *Rocky VI, Thru the Wire,* and *L.A. Woman,* 1986; with Mika, runs own production company, Villealfa Film Productions, in Helsinki, operates art movie houses in Helsinki, and organized the Midnight Sun Film Festival. **Awards:** Jussi Award, Best First Film and Script, and diplomas from FILMEX, Nordische Filmtage, and Karlovy Vary Festival, 1983, for *Crime and Punishment;* Special Award, Hong Kong Festival, 1985, for *Calimari Union;* Jussi Award, Best Finnish Film, 1986, for *Shadows in Paradise.* **Address:** Villealfa Filmproductions Oy, Vainamoisenkatu 19 A, SF-00100 Helsinki, Finland.

Films as Director:

1981 *Saimma Ilmio* (*The Saimma Gesture*) (co-dir)
1983 *Rikos ja Pangaistus* (*Crime and Punishment*) (+ co-sc)
1985 *Calimari Union* (+ sc)
1986 *Varjoja Paratiisissa* (*Shadows in Paradise*) (+ sc)
1987 *Hamlet Liikemaailmassa* (*Hamlet Goes Business*) (+ sc, pr)
1988 *Ariel* (+ sc, pr)
1989 *Leningrad Cowboys Go America* (+ sc)
1990 *I Hired a Contract Killer* (+ sc, pr); *Tulitikkutehtaan Tytto* (*The Match Factory Girl*) (+ sc, pr)
1991 *Those Were the Days* (short) (+ sc, ed)
1992 *La Vie de Boheme* (*The Bohemian Life*) (+ sc, pr)
1993 *These Boots* (short) (+ sc, pr, ed)
1994 *Leningrad Cowboys Meet Moses* (+ sc, pr, ed)
1994 *Total Balalaika Show* (doc) (+ pr)
1994 *Pida huivsta kiinnim Tatjana* (*Take Care of Your Scarf, Tatiana*) (+ pr, co-sc)

Other Films:

(as co-scenarist and assistant director to brother Mika Kaurismaki)

1980 *The Liar* (+ role)
1982 *Arvottomat* (*The Worthless*) (+ role)
1984 *Klanni—tarina sammokoitten* (*The Clan—Tale of the Frogs*)
1985 *Rosso*

(as producer)

1993 *The Prodigal Son* (Aaltonen)
1994 *Iron Horsemen* (Charmant) (+ role)

Publications

By KAURISMAKI: articles—

Interview in *Cahiers du Cinema* (Paris), November 1988.
Interview with I. Ruchti in *Positif* (Paris), June 1990.
Interview with B. Fornara and L. Gandini in *Cineforum* (Bergamo), October 1990.

On KAURISMAKI: articles—

Reynaud, B., article in *Cahiers du Cinema* (Paris), November 1988.
Fisher, W., "Aki Kaurismaki Goes Business," in *Sight and Sound* (London), vol. 58, no. 4, 1989.
Stein, Elliott, "Film: Foreign Affairs," in *Village Voice* (New York), 31 January 1989.
Fornara, B., article in *Cineforum* (Bergamo), March 1989.
Hoberman, J., "Finland Goes Movies," in *Premiere* (New York), June 1989.
Strauss, F., article in *Cahiers du Cinema* (Paris), April 1990.
Dieckmann, K., "Aki Kaurismaki," in *Premiere* (New York), July 1990.
Fisher William, career overview in *Sight and Sound* (London), Autumn 1989.
Taubin, Amy, "The Finnish Line," in *Village Voice* (New York), 28 August 1990.
Causo, Massimo, article in *Cineforum* (Bergamo), September 1990.
Cohn, L., "For Aki Kaurismaki, It's Been a Very Good Year," in *Variety* (New York), 29 October 1990.
Sterritt, David, article in *Christian Science Monitor* (New York), 6 November 1990.
Pulliene, Tim, "More Time in the Bar—Aki Kaurismaki," in *Monthly Film Bulletin* (London), February 1991.
Saada, N., article in *Cahiers du Cinema* (Paris), May 1991.
De Santi, G., article in *Cineforum* (Bergamo), June 1991.
Jordahl, A. and Lahger, H., "Aki Kaurismaki," in *Chaplin* (Stockholm), vol. 32, no. 1, 1992.
Taubin, Amy, "Finnish Lines," in *Village Voice* (New York), 10 November 1992.
Sterritt, David, article in *Christian Science Monitor* (New York), 13 November 1992.

* * *

The cinema of Aki Kaurismaki is a cinema of the absurd. He and his brother, director Mika Kaurismaki, have become two of the world's most prolific and uniquely impudent movie-makers. At first, they were far outside the Finnish establishment, in that their parodies and farces lampooned the conventions of their society. Nevertheless, as they became known and respected on the international film scene, they quickly came to be regarded as the leading talents of their country's minuscule motion picture industry. Certainly, the Kaurismaki brothers' success helped educate cineastes to the fact that Scandinavian films do not only come from Sweden and Norway.

Aki and Mika Kaurismaki began collaborating in the early 1980s, but Aki was the one who initially established himself internationally. In 1990 alone, seven of his films were screened in various venues in New York City. His films are linked in that they are straightforward, serio-comic studies infused with a unique sense of the ridiculous. His characters are far removed from the mainstream, in some cases to the point of being isolated and completely alone; occasionally, they are on the road, roaming across landscapes in which they will be eternal outsiders. But their feelings of alienation or despondency rarely become the principal force at work on screen. Rather, Kaurismaki elicits a poignancy as he charts his characters' lives, with a special emphasis on the humor which symbolizes the utter absurdity of their situations.

A number of Kaurismaki's heros are dejected blue-collar loners driven to desperate acts and outrageous behavior by a repressive society. Such is the case in *Ariel,* a comical, existential road movie about a mine worker (Turo Pajala) who loses his job and sets out on an odyssey across Finland. *Ariel* offers a textbook example of the manner in which Kaurismaki drolly observes the life of a character whose very existence is outwardly depressing. In a similar vein is *The Match Factory Girl,* a sharply drawn black comedy about a dreary, oppressed young woman (Kati Outinen). Her job is tiresome, her life is going nowhere, and then she becomes involved with a man who is destined to drop her. He expects her to meekly squirm back into her shell, but her response—and her revenge—is way out of character.

Retaliation also is a prominent theme in the first film Kaurismaki directed by himself, *Crime and Punishment,* a reworking of the

Aki Kaurismaki: *Leningrad Cowboys Go America*

Dostoyevsky novel. *Crime and Punishment* is set in 1980s Helsinki, and the hero, Rahikaainen (Markku Toikka), murders a powerful businessman who was responsible for the hit-and-run death of his fiancee. By far, *Crime and Punishment* is Kaurismaki's most somber film. On the other end of the emotional scale is *I Hired a Contract Killer,* in which he brings his alienated hero to an outlandishly comic extreme. Here, he tells the story of a nebbish (Jean-Pierre Leaud) with nothing to live for who haplessly fails to kill himself. He hires a pro to do the job but changes his mind after unexpectedly falling in love, and then must hurriedly attempt to cancel the contract.

Another Kaurismaki concern is the creative lifestyle. He examines this issue in *La Vie de Boheme,* an affectionate comedy about what it means to single-mindedly devote one's life to art, regardless of the consequences and sacrifices. The film is a slice-of-life about three men, a writer (Andre Wilms), a painter (Matti Pellonpaa), and a composer-musician (Kari Vaanenen). Each is aging, has little or no money, and has not earned any kind of commercial or critical recognition. Indeed, there are no undiscovered Hemingways, Picassos, or Mozarts in the group; it would not be unfair to judge each a mediocre talent. But all three remain steadfastly committed to their work and ideals. The women in their lives remain secondary figures; each values his library, piano, and paint above everything else.

One of Kaurismaki's zaniest films is *Leningrad Cowboys Go America,* which also features characters with warped senses of their talents. But here, they revel in their awfulness as they proudly hold the mantle as "the worst rock 'n' roll band in the world." *Leningrad Cowboys* is a loopy farce that lampoons the manner in which the tackiest aspects of American pop culture have impacted on even the farthest reaches of Finland. His "cowboys" are a deadpan, perfectly dreadful band of rock musicians from the Finnish tundra, who embark on a "world tour" which will take them not to Madison Square Garden but across a vast small-town American wasteland.

Kaurismaki had only begun to mine the Leningrad Cowboys' comic possibilities. He followed *Leningrad Cowboys Go America* with two short films featuring the Cowboys in renditions of hit pop songs: *Those Were the Days,* a six-minute mini-saga of a lonesome cowpoke rambling through the streets of the Big City in the company of his donkey; and *These Boots,* a five-minute history of Finland between 1950 and 1969 as seen from the viewpoint of the Cowboys. Next came the feature-length *Leningrad Cowboys Meet Moses,* in which the Cowboys actually have a top-ten hit to their credit. They start out in Mexico, make their way through Coney Island, and end up back in Europe; their manager (Matti Pellonpaa) professes that he is Moses, and pledges to guide the boys home to the Promised Land of Siberia. Finally, in the documentary *Total Balalaika Show,* Kaurismaki presents the Leningrad Cowboys in concert before fifty thousand fans in Helsinki's Senate Square with none other than Russia's Alexandrov Red Army Chorus and Dance Ensemble—described by a *Variety* critic as "the most incongruous—and inspired—crosscultural pairing since Nureyev danced with Miss Piggy."

—Rob Edelman

KÄUTNER, Helmut

Nationality: German. **Born:** Düsseldorf, 1908. **Education:** Munich University and Munich Art School, studying poster design, graphics, and interior design. **Family:** Married actress/director Erica Balqué, 1934. **Career:** Writer and director for Munich Student Cabaret, "Die vier Nachrichter," 1931-35; stage actor and director in Germany, Austria, and Switzerland, from 1936; founder, with Wolfgang Staudte and Harald Braun, of production company Camera-Filmproduktion (later Freie Filmproduktion); later director, actor, and designer for television. **Died:** 1980.

Films as Director:

1939 *Kitty und die Weltkonferenz* (+ sc, lyrics)
1940 *Frau nach Mass* (+ sc); *Kleider machen Leute* (+ sc)
1941 *Auf Wiedersehen, Franziska!* (+ co-sc)
1942 *Anuschka* (+ adapt); *Wir machen Musik* (+ sc, lyrics)
1943 *Romanze in Moll* (+ co-sc, role)
1944 *Grosse Freiheit Nr. 7* (+ co-sc, lyrics, role)
1945 *Unter den Brücken* (+ co-sc)
1947 *In jenen Tagen* (+ co-sc, role)
1948 *Der Apfel ist ab* (+ co-sc, role)
1949 *Königskinder* (+ co-sc, role)
1950 *Epilog* (*Das Geheimnis der Orplid*) (+ co-sc, role)
1951 *Weisse Schatten* (+ co-sc)
1953 *Käpt'n Bay-Bay* (+ co-sc)
1954 *Die letzte Brücke* (+ co-sc, role); *Bildnis einer Unbekannten* (+ co-sc); *Ludwig II—Glanz und Elend eines Königs*
1955 *Des Teufels General* (+ co-sc, role); *Himmel ohne Sterne* (+ sc)
1956 *Ein Mädchen aus Flandern* (+ co-sc, role); *Der Hauptmann von Köpenick* (+ co-sc, role)
1957 *Die Zürcher Verlobung* (+ co-sc, lyrics, role); *Montpi* (+ sc, role)
1958 *The Restless Years* (*The Wonderful Years*); *A Stranger in My Arms*; *Der Schinderhannes* (+ role)
1959 *Der Rest ist Schweigen* (+ co-sc, co-pr, role); *Die Gans von Sedan* (*Sans tambour ni trompette*) (+ co-sc, role)
1960 *Das Glas Wasser* (+ sc, lyrics)
1961 *Scwarzer Kies* (+ co-sc); *Der Traum von Lieschen Müller* (*Happy-End im siebten Himmel*) (+ co-sc, lyrics)
1962 *Die Rote* (*La Rossa*) (+ sc)
1963 *Das Haus in Montevideo* (+ sc)
1964 *Lausbubengeschichten*
1970 *Die Feuerzangenbowle*

Other Films:

1932 *Kreuzer Emden* (Ralph) (role)
1939 *Schneider Wibbel* (de Kowa) (co-sc); *Salonwagen E 417* (Verhoeven) (co-sc); *Die Stimme aus dem Äther* (Paulsen) (co-sc); *Marguerite: 3—Eine Frau für Drei* (Lingen) (co-sc)
1947 *Film ohne Titel* (Jugert) (co-sc)
1951 *Nachts auf den Strassen* (Jugert) (co-sc)
1955 *Griff nach den Sternen* (Schroth) (co-sc)
1957 *Franziska* (*Auf Wiedersehen, Franziska*) (Liebeneiner) (co-sc)
1961 *Zu jung für die Liebe?* (Erica Balqué) (co-sc, role)
1972 *Versuchung in Sommerwind* (Thiele) (role)
1974 *Karl May* (Syberberg) (title role)

Publications

By KÄUTNER: books—

Von der Filmides zum Drehbuch, with Béla Balázs and others, 1949.
Abblenden, Munich, 1981.

On KÄUTNER: books—

Koschnitzki, Rudiger, *Filmographie Helmut Käutner,* Wiesbaden, 1978.
Gillett, John, *Eighteen Films by Helmut Käutner,* Goethe Institute, London, 1980.

On KÄUTNER: articles—

Cahiers du Cinéma (Paris), July 1957.
Obituary in *Filme* (Paris), no. 4, 1980.
Obituary in *Screen International* (London), 19 April 1980.
Obituary in *Cinéma* (Paris), June 1980.
Gillett, John, "Helmut Käutner," in *Film Dope* (London), March 1984.

On KÄUTNER: films—

Harmsen, Henning, *Erlebte Filmgeschichte Helmut Käutner,* for German TV, 1975.
von Troschke, Harald, *Im Gespräch porträtiert: Helmut Käutner,* for German TV, 1978.

* * *

Along with Forst and Sirk, Käutner was one of the great stylists of the cinema of the Third Reich. Admittedly the competition was extremely thin but this in no way belittles the achievement of the director, whose best work stands comparison with Ophüls and is rooted in the same rich vein of Austro-German romanticism. In particular one notices the same concern with the passing of an era, an elegance bordering on dandyism, and what Louis Marcorelles has called "a subtle perfume of death and decadence." As John Gillett puts it in the catalogue produced to accompany a pioneering season of Käutner's films at London's Goethe Institute, the work of Käutner, Ophüls, and Forst "consolidated a film-making genre notable for its attention to period detail, its elaborate costuming and art direction, and for directorial styles which used the mobile camera to achieve a uniquely filmic musical structure and rhythm."

Käutner entered cinema as a scriptwriter in 1938 (although he had appeared in a small role in Louis Ralph's *Kreuzer Emden* in 1932) having studied architecture, philosophy, theatre, and art history, worked in cabaret in Munich as both writer and performer from 1931 to 1935, and gone into "straight" theatre in 1936. Some of his more caustic cabaret sketches had annoyed the Nazis, and as he noted, "I was not really interested in the cinema. Politically I was left-wing and that meant that I was disinterested in the cinema which, since Hugenberg, had been moving in a right-wing, nationalistic direction. I really wanted to go on working in the theatre, and I had very clear-cut ideas about the theatre—others would have called it cabaret."

His first film, *Kitty und die Weltkonferenz,* a light, frothy comedy, evoked comparisons with Lubitsch, but its favourable portrait of a British minister and slightly satirical view of relations between Italy and Germany incurred Goebbels's displeasure and the film vanished from view. His next film, an adaptation of Keller's novella *Kleider Machen Leute,* in which a humble tailor finds himself mistaken for a Russian prince, could certainly be read, beneath its apparent retreat into Biedermeyer mannerism, as an allegory about Germans' exaggerated respect for figures of power and authority and their consequent readiness to fall under the Nazi spell. However, this does not seem to

Helmut Käutner (right) with cameraman Kurt Hasse

have occurred to the authorities. The film has a lightness of touch and a feeling for fantasy that anticipates both Minnelli and Cocteau, and is distinguished by some marvellous swirling camerawork in the musical scenes. On the whole Käutner avoided contemporary subjects during his Third Reich period, an exception being *Auf Wiedersehen, Franziska!,* which deals with the strains in a newsreel reporter's marriage caused by his numerous absences. The authorities insisted on an upbeat, flag-waving ending quite out of key with the film's poignant, carefully nuanced atmosphere and, like Sirk in *Stutzen der Gesellschaft,* Käutner deliberately makes the whole thing stand out a mile. The film is also distinguished by a marvellous performance by Marianne Hoppe.

Käutner's masterpiece is undoubtedly *Romanze in Moll,* a highly Ophülsian adaptation of Maupassant's *Les Bijoux.* Maupassant's dark vision of life did not endear him to the literary authorities in the Reich, and this film, though not banned, was condemned in some quarters as "defeatist" and "destructive of marriage and morals." Käutner himself acts in the film, playing the part of a resigned, world-weary poet, a role which, his films suggest, was close to his own in real life. As Francis Courtade and Pierre Cadars put it in their excellent *Histoire du Cinéma Nazi,* "Everything centres on the almost palpable re-creation of this fin-de-siécle milieu in which a woman, condemned to death by her surroundings, suffers. Composition, framing, camera movement, editing, sound, remain, from start to finish, crystal clear.... Like Claude Autant-Lara, Käutner is fanatical over details. His direction of actors is magisterial.... The overall result is an exemplary reconstruction of the style and atmosphere of the original story, and one of the two or three most faithful adaptations of Maupassant."

In spite of his difficulties with the authorities, Käutner was entrusted with an expensive and elaborate Agfacolor project in the latter days of the Reich. This was *Grosse Freiheit Nr. 7,* a melancholy, bittersweet story of disappointed love set amongst the sailors' clubs and bars of the Hamburg waterfront, with clear overtones of Carné, Clair, and in particular (through the presence of Hans Albers of *Blue Angel* fame) Von Sternberg. Apart from difficulties caused by bombing, Käutner also had to cope with Goebbels's request that the film include shots of the harbour with ships flying the Nazi flag. His response was to make copious use of artificial fog in the panoramic long shots. When the film was released Admiral Dönitz complained that its representation of German sailors visiting prostitutes and drinking was damaging to the reputation of Germany in general and Hamburg in particular, and the film was banned.

Käutner's last Third Reich film, and one of his best, was *Unter den Brücken,* which is set amongst the bargees of the River Havel and, like its predecessor, shows the clear influence of French pre-war "poetic realism": in particular there are distinct overtones of *L'Atalante.* At one time thought to be a "lost" film, *Unter den Brücken* finally turned up and revealed itself to be, in the words of the *Süddeutsche Zeitung,* "a subtle depiction of a private world, half-tones full of melancholy and a quiet sublimination of the free life ... a story told with great sensitivity which, softly but insistently, counteracts the grimness of contemporary reality with the longing for private happiness and the right to a non-regimented self-realisation."

Käutner's post-war films never reached the heights of his best work in the Third Reich, though some of them are not without interest. The main problem seems to have been a rather ill-advised turn towards social realism and "problem" subjects in films such as *In Jenen Tagen, Die Letzte Brücke, Himmel Ohne Sterne,* and *Schwarzer Kies* which simply did not suit his artistic temperament. In *Der Apfel ist Ab* and *Der Traum von Lieschen Müller* Käutner attempted to bring something of his old cabaret style into the contemporary cinema, but with mixed results. In 1957 he signed a seven-year contract with Universal in Hollywood which resulted in *The Restless Years* (*The Wonderful Years* in the UK) and *Stranger in My Arms.* In 1959 he directed a modern-day version of Hamlet entitled *Der Rest ist Schweigen,* but in the 1960s his time was increasingly taken up with more conventional literary adaptations (many of them for television), a direction already signalled in the 1950s with his productions of Zuckmayer's *Des Teufels General, Ein Mädchen aus Flandern,* and *Der Hauptmann von Köpenick.* He also played the German pulp writer Karl May in Hans-Jurgen Syberberg's film of the same name, which also included several other notables from the cinema of the Third Reich, a period which it is hard not to regard as representing Käutner's finest hour. One German critic has suggested that his films of this period are "illustrative of an inner immigration which could express its opposition only secretly and in cyphers," and it may well be that the need to proceed by allusion, understatement, ambiguity, and suggestion suited Käutner's remarkable talents peculiarly well.

—Julian Petley

KAWALEROWICZ, Jerzy

Nationality: Polish. **Born:** Gwózda (Gwozdziec), now part of Soviet Ukraine, 19 January 1922. **Education:** Film Institute, Cracow. **Family:** Married actress Lucyna Winnicka. **Career:** Assistant director and scriptwriter, 1946-51; co-directed first feature with Kazimierz Sumerski, 1952; head of Studia Kadr, from 1955. **Awards:** Premio Evrotecnica, Venice Festival, for *Night Train,* 1959; Silver Palm, Cannes Festival, for *Mother Joanna of the Angels,* 1961; Silver Bear, Berlin Festival, for *The President's Death,* 1977.

Films as Director:

1952 *Gromada* (*The Village Mill*; *Commune*) (co-d)
1954 *Celuloza* (*Cellulose*) (+ co-sc); *Pod gwiazda frygijska* (*Under the Phrygian Star*) in two parts (+ co-sc)
1956 *Cién* (*The Shadow*)
1957 *Prawdziwy koniec wielkiej wojny* (*The Real End of the Great War*) (+ co-sc)
1959 *Pociag* (*Night Train*; *Baltic Express*) (+ co-sc)
1961 ***Matka Joanna od Aniolów*** (*Mother Joanna of the Angels*) (+ co-sc)
1965 *Faraon* (*The Pharaoh*) (+ co-sc)
1968 *Gra* (*The Game*) (+ sc)
1970 *Maddalena*
1977 *Śmierć Prezydenta* (*Death of a President*) (+ co-sc)
1979 *Spotkanie na Atlantyku* (*Meeting on the Atlantic*) (+ co-sc)
1982 *Austeria* (+ co-sc)
1989 *Jeniec Europy*
1991 *Bronsteins Kinder* (+ sc)

Other Films:

1946 *Jutro premiera* (*Morning Premiere*) (asst d)
1947 *Zakazane piosenki* (*Forbidden Songs*) (asst d); *Ostatni etap* (*The Last Stage*) (asst d)
1948 *Stalowe serca* (*Steel Hearts*) (asst d); *Czarci źleb* (*The Devil's Pass*) (asst d)

Publications

By KAWALEROWICZ: articles—

"Historia i forma," interview with K. Zórawski, in *Kino* (Warsaw), September 1977.
Interview with M. Dipont, in *Kino* (Warsaw), October 1980.
Interview, in *Filmowy serwis prasowy* (Warsaw), no. 2, 1983.
Interview with G. Delmas, in *Jeune Cinéma* (Paris), May/June 1987.

On KAWALEROWICZ: books—

Grzelecki, Stanislaw, *Twenty Years of Polish Cinema,* Warsaw, 1969.
Michalek, Boleslaw, *Film—sztuka w ewolucji,* Warsaw, 1975.
Kuszewski, Stanislaw, *Contemporary Polish Film,* Warsaw, 1978.

On KAWALEROWICZ: articles—

Kornatowska, M., "Jerzy Kawalerowicz czyli milosć do geometrii," in *Kino* (Warsaw), February 1978.
Modrzejewska, E., in *Kino* (Warsaw), April 1985.
"Jerzy Kawalerowicz," in *Film Dope* (London), March 1984.
Heinrich, D., "La Pologne par le coeur," in *Cinéma* (Paris), 10 February 1988.

* * *

It is no simple matter to give a precise characterization of Kawalerowicz. His work is full of twists and turns, strange shifts, and new experiments. The films of Jerzy Kawalerowicz are uneven; it is as though the filmmaker, after momentary triumphs and outstanding artistic achievements, would lapse into a crisis that prepared him for yet another masterpiece. His films are long in preparation. Between individual works come lengthy pauses in which the director carefully absorbs raw material from a wide range of disciplines in order to personally work it into film form. Only in a very few directors' works do we find such range, from the realistic film to the profound psychological drama, from the historical epic to the political drama.

Kawalerowicz has always gone his own way, and it has not been an easy path, especially when we realize that he has never turned back, never given a particular theme further development. Although he began at the same time as Wajda and Munk, he never created a work that belonged to the "Polish school of film." After his first independent film, *Celuloza (Cellulose),* both a realistic portrayal and a literary adaptation, he never came back to this subject or form. In his next creative period he quickly turned out several films that are unusual analytic studies of human relationships, earnest pyschological examinations of lonely people marked by war *(The Real End of the Great War),* isolated while travelling on an overnight express *(Night),* or within the walls of a cloister *(Mother Joanna of the Angels).*

Jerzy Kawalerowicz: *Faraon*

Kawalerowicz demonstrates his creative mastery with these films. In fact, they initiated an entire trend of intimate dramas, popular with other directors several years later.

The historical epic *Faraon (Pharaoh),* adapted from the celebrated novel by Boleslaw Prus, is once again unusual in composition. It is a film on a grand scale, a monumental fresco, but at the same time an unusual psychological film with political and philosophical elements. In this drama of a struggle for power in ancient Egypt, the director finds room for an account of human qualities, motives, and feelings.

Emotions are the leitmotif of Kawalerowicz's work. After the grand epic *Faraon,* the filmmaker attempted a return to the intimate, psychologically-oriented film. A crisis sets in. His subsequent work fails to attain the level of his earlier pieces. There is a kind of break, a respite that will bear fruit in the later, purely political film and documentary drama *Death of a President.* The approach taken by Kawalerowicz in this film, which is the chronicle of an actual event—the assassination of President Gabriel Natutowicz in the 1930s—served as the director's credo. "When we studied the documents and the testimony and compiled the chronology of events, we ascertained that the drama of history, the drama of real events, is far more persuasive than what we ourselves could invent." Captivated by the facts, Kawalerowicz relates not only a real-life event but also a common human story that is timeless. After this film, critics expected the director to continue in this same genre, in which he had shown such mastery. But once again Kawalerowicz was experimenting with new genres and forms, though outstanding literary works and actual political or historical events, shaped into provocative dramas, remain the foundation of his creative work.

—Vaclåv Merhaut

KAZAN, Elia

Nationality: American. **Born:** Elia Kazanjoglou in Constantinople (now Istanbul), Turkey, 7 September 1909; moved with family to New York, 1913. **Education:** Mayfair School; New Rochelle High School, New York; Williams College, Massachusetts, B.A. 1930; Yale Drama School, 1930-32. **Family:** Married 1) Molly Day Thatcher, 1932 (died 1963), two sons, two daughters; 2) actress Barbara Loden, 1967 (died 1980), one son; 3) Frances Rudge, 1982. **Career:** Actor, property manager, then director, Group Theatre, New York, from 1933; stage director, including plays by Tennessee Williams and Arthur Miller,

1935 through 1960s; co-founder, with Cheryl Crawford, Actors' Studio, New York, 1948; appeared voluntarily before HUAC, admitting membership of Communist Party, 1934-36, and naming fellow members, 1952; began career as novelist, 1961; left Actors' Studio to direct newly-formed Lincoln Center Repertory Company, 1962-64. **Awards:** Many awards for theatre work; Academy Award for Best Director, and Best Direction Award, New York Film Critics, for *Gentleman's Agreement,* 1947; International Prize, Venice Festival, for *Panic in the Streets,* 1950; Special Jury Prize, Venice Festival, for *A Streetcar Named Desire,* 1951; Oscar for Best Director, and Most Outstanding Directorial Achievement, Directors Guild of America, for *On the Waterfront,* 1954; Honorary doctorates from Wesleyan University, Carnegie Institute of Technology, and Williams College. **Address:** c/o 432 W. 44th St., New York, NY 10036, U.S.A.

Films as Director:

1937 *The People of the Cumberlands* (+ sc) (short)
1941 *It's Up to You*
1945 *A Tree Grows in Brooklyn*
1947 *The Sea of Grass*; *Boomerang*; *Gentleman's Agreement*
1949 *Pinky*
1950 *Panic in the Streets*
1952 ***A Streetcar Named Desire***; *Viva Zapata!*; *Man on a Tightrope*
1954 ***On the Waterfront***
1955 ***East of Eden*** (+ pr)
1956 *Baby Doll* (+ pr, co-sc)
1957 *A Face in the Crowd* (+ pr)
1960 *Wild River* (+ pr)
1961 *Splendour in the Grass* (+ pr)
1964 *America, America* (+ sc, pr)
1969 *The Arrangement* (+ pr, sc)
1972 *The Visitors*
1976 *The Last Tycoon*
1978 *Acts of Love* (+ pr)
1982 *The Anatolian* (+ pr)
1989 *Beyond the Aegean*

Other Films:

1934 *Pie in the Sky* (Steiner) (short) (role)
1940 *City for Conquest* (Litvak) (role as Googie, a gangster)
1941 *Blues in the Night* (Litvak) (role as a clarinetist)

Publications

By KAZAN: books—

America America, New York, 1961.
The Arrangement, New York, 1967.
The Assassins, New York, 1972.
The Understudy, New York, 1974.
Acts of Love, New York, 1978.
Anatolian, New York, 1982.
Elia Kazan: A Life, New York and London, 1988.
Beyond the Aegean, New York, 1994.

By KAZAN: articles—

"The Writer and Motion Pictures," in *Sight and Sound* (London), Summer 1957.
Interview with Jean Domarchi and André Labarthe, in *Cahiers du Cinéma* (Paris), April 1962.
Article in *Cahiers du Cinéma* (Paris), December 1963/January 1964.
Interview with S. Byron and M. Rubin, in *Movie* (London), Winter 1971/72.
Interview with G. O'Brien, in *Inter/View* (New York), March 1972.
"Visiting Kazan," interview with C. Silver and J. Zukor, in *Film Comment* (New York), Summer 1972.
"All You Need to Know, Kids," in *Action* (Los Angeles), January/February 1974.
"Hollywood Under Water," interview with C. Silver and M. Corliss, in *Film Comment* (New York), January/February 1977.
"Kazan Issue" of *Positif* (Paris), April 1977.
"Visite à Yilmaz Güney ou vue d'une prison turque," with O. Adanir, in *Positif* (Paris), February 1980.
"L'Homme tremblant: Conversation entre Marguerite Duras et Elia Kazan," in *Cahiers du Cinéma* (Paris), December 1980.
Interview with Tim Pulleine, in *Stills* (London), July/August 1983.
Interview with P. Le Guay, in *Cinématographe* (Paris), February 1986.
Interview in *Time Out* (London), 4 May 1988.

On KAZAN: books—

Clurman, Harold, *The Fervent Years: The Story of the Group Theatre and the Thirties,* New York, 1946.
Tailleur, Roger, *Elia Kazan,* revised edition, Paris, 1971.
Ciment, Michel, *Kazan on Kazan,* London, 1972.
Giannetti, Louis, *Masters of the American Cinema,* Englewood Cliffs, New Jersey, 1981.
Pauly, Thomas H., *An American Odyssey: Elia Kazan and American Culture,* Philadelphia, 1983.
Michaels, Lloyd, *Elia Kazan: A Guide to References and Resources,* Boston, 1985.
Ciment, Michael, *An American Odyssey: Elia Kazan,* London, 1989.
Murphy, Brenda, *Tennessee Williams and Elia Kazan: A Collaboration in the Theatre,* Cambridge, 1992.

On KAZAN: articles—

Stevens, Virginia, "Elia Kazan: Actor and Director of Stage and Screen," in *Theatre Arts* (New York), December 1947.
Archer, Eugene, "Elia Kazan: The Genesis of a Style," in *Film Culture* (New York), vol. 2, no. 2, 1956.
Archer, Eugene, "The Theatre Goes to Hollywood," in *Films and Filming* (London), January 1957.
Neal, Patricia, "What Kazan Did for Me," in *Films and Filming* (London), October 1957.
Bean, Robin, "The Life and Times of Elia Kazan," in *Films and Filming* (London), May 1964.
Tailleur, Roger, "Elia Kazan and the House Un-American Activities Committee," in *Film Comment* (New York), Fall 1966.
"Kazan Issue" of *Movie* (London), Spring 1972.
Changas, E., "Elia Kazan's America," in *Film Comment* (New York), Summer 1972.
Kitses, Jim, "Elia Kazan: a Structural Analysis," in *Cinema* (Beverly Hills), Winter 1972/73.
Biskind, P., "The Politics of Power in *On the Waterfront,*" in *Film Quarterly* (Berkeley), Autumn 1975.
"*A l'est d'Eden* Issue" of *Avant-Scène du Cinéma* (Paris), November 1975.
Kazan Section of *Positif* (Paris), April 1981.
"Kazan Issue" of *Avant-Scène du Cinéma* (Paris), 1 July 1983.
"Elia Kazan," in *Film Dope* (London), March 1984.
Michaels, Lloyd, "Elia Kazan: A Retrospective," in *Film Criticism* (Edinboro, Pennsylvania), Fall 1985.

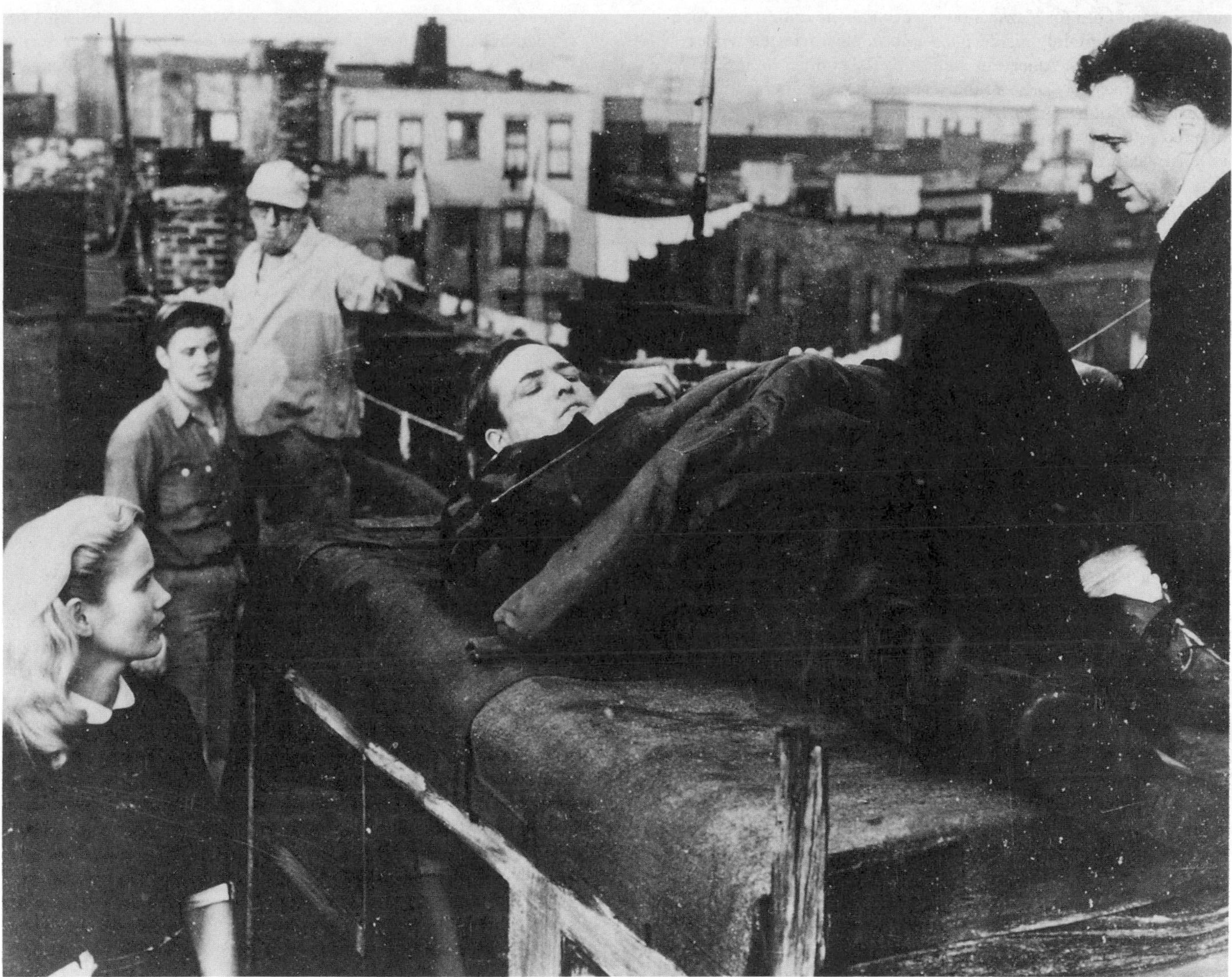

Elia Kazan (right) directing *On the Waterfront*

Neve, Brian, "The Immigrant Experience on Film: Kazan's *America America,*" in *Film and History* (New York), vol. 17, no. 3, 1987.
Nangle, J., "The American Museum of the Moving Image Salutes Elia Kazan," in *Films in Review* (New York), April 1987.
Georgakas, Dan, "Don't Call Him Gadget: Elia Kazan Reconsidered," in *Cineaste* (New York), vol. 16, no. 4, 1988.
Rathgeb, Douglas, "Kazan as Auteur: The Undiscovered *East of Eden,*" in *Literature/Film Quarterly* (Salisbury, Maryland), vol. 16, no. 1, 1988.
McGilligan, Patrick, "Scoundrel Tome," in *Film Comment* (New York), May/June 1988.
Butler, T., "Polonsky and Kazan. HUAC and the Violation of Personality," in *Sight and Sound* (London), Autumn 1988.

* * *

Elia Kazan's career has spanned more than four decades of enormous change in the American film industry. Often he has been a catalyst for these changes. He became a director in Hollywood at a time when studios were interested in producing the kind of serious, mature, and socially conscious stories Kazan had been putting on the stage since his Group Theatre days. During the late 1940s and mid-1950s, initially under the influence of Italian neorealism and then the pressure of American television, he was a leading force in developing the aesthetic possibilities of location shooting (*Boomerang, Panic in the Streets, On the Waterfront*) and CinemaScope (*East of Eden, Wild River*). At the height of his success, Kazan formed his own production unit and moved back east to become a pioneer in the new era of independent, "personal" filmmaking that emerged during the 1960s and contributed to revolutionary upheavals within the old Hollywood system. As an archetypal *auteur,* he progressed from working on routine assignments to developing more personal themes, producing his own pictures, and ultimately directing his own scripts. At his peak during a period (1950-1965) of anxiety, gimmickry, and entropy in Hollywood, Kazan remained among the few American directors who continued to believe in the cinema as a medium for artistic expression and who brought forth films that consistently reflected his own creative vision.

Despite these achievements and his considerable influence on a younger generation of New York-based filmmakers, including Sidney Lumet, John Cassavetes, Arthur Penn, Martin Scorsese, and even Woody Allen, Kazan's critical reputation in America has ebbed. The turning point both for Kazan's own work and the critics' reception of it was almost certainly his decision to become a friendly witness before the House Un-American Activities Committee in 1952. While "naming names" cost Kazan the respect of many liberal friends and colleagues (Arthur Miller most prominent among them), it ironically ushered in the decade of his most inspired filmmaking. If Abraham Polonsky, himself blacklisted during the 1950s, is right in claiming that Kazan's post-HUAC movies have been "marked by bad conscience," perhaps he overlooks how that very quality of uncertainty may be what makes films like *On the Waterfront, East of Eden,* and *America America* so much more compelling than Kazan's previous studio work.

His apprenticeship in the Group Theater and his great success as a Broadway director had a natural influence on Kazan's films, particularly reflected in his respect for the written script, his careful blocking of scenes, and, pre-eminently, his employment of Method Acting on the screen. While with the Group, which he has described as "the best thing professionally that ever happened to me," Kazan acquired from its leaders, Harold Clurman and Lee Strasberg, a fundamentally artistic attitude toward his work. Studying Marx led him to see art as an instrument of social change, and from Stanislavski he learned to seek a play's "spine" and emphasize the characters' psychological motivation. Although he developed a lyrical quality that informs many later films, Kazan generally employs the social realist mode he learned from the Group. Thus, he prefers location shooting over studio sets, relatively unfamiliar actors over stars, long shots and long takes over editing, and naturalistic forms over genre conventions. *On the Waterfront* and *Wild River,* though radically different in style, both reflect the Group's quest, in Kazan's words, "to get poetry out of the common things of life." And while one may debate the ultimate ideology of *Gentleman's Agreement, Pinky, Viva Zapata!* and *The Visitors,* one may still agree with the premise they all share, that art should illuminate society's problems and the possibility of their solution.

Above all else, however, it is Kazan's skill in directing actors that has secured his place in the history of American cinema. Twenty-one of his performers have been nominated for Academy Awards; nine have won. He was instrumental in launching the film careers of Marlon Brando, Julie Harris, James Dean, Carroll Baker, Warren Beatty, and Lee Remick. Moreover, he elicited from such undervalued Hollywood players as Dorothy McGuire, James Dunn, Eva Marie Saint, and Natalie Wood perhaps the best performances of their careers. For all the long decline in critical appreciation, Kazan's reputation among actors has hardly wavered. The Method, which became so identified with Kazan's and Lee Strasberg's teaching at the Actors Studio, was once simplistically defined by Kazan himself as "turning psychology into behavior." An obvious example from *Boomerang* would be the suspect Waldron's gesture of covering his mouth whenever he lies to the authorities. But when Terry first chats with Edie in the park in *On the Waterfront,* unconsciously putting on one of the white gloves she has dropped as he sits in a swing, such behavior becomes not merely psychological but symbolic and poetic. Here Method acting transcends Kazan's own mundane definition.

His films have been most consistently concerned with the theme of power, expressed as either the restless yearning of the alienated or the uneasy arrangements of the strong. The struggle for power is generally manifested through wealth, sexuality, or, most often, violence. Perhaps because every Kazan film except *A Tree Grows in Brooklyn* and *The Last Tycoon* (excluding a one-punch knockout of the drunken protagonist) contains at least one violent scene, some critics have complained about the director's "horrid vulgarity" (Lindsay Anderson) and "unremitting stridency" (Robin Wood), yet even his most "overheated" work contains striking examples of restrained yet resonant interludes: the rooftop scenes of Terry and his pigeons in *On the Waterfront,* the tentative reunion of Bud and Deanie at the end of *Splendor in the Grass,* the sequence in which Stavros tells his betrothed not to trust him in *America America.* Each of these scenes could be regarded not simply as a necessary lull in the drama, but as a privileged, lyrical moment in which the ambivalence underlying Kazan's attitude toward his most pervasive themes seems to crystallize. Only then can one fully realize how Terry in the rooftop scene is both confined by the *mise-en-scène* (seen within the pigeon coop) and free on the roof to be himself; how Bud and Deanie are simultaneously reconciled and estranged; how Stavros becomes honest only when he confesses to how deeply he has been compromised.

—Lloyd Michaels

KEATON, Buster

Nationality: American. **Born:** Joseph Francis Keaton in Piqua, Kansas, 4 October 1895. **Military Service:** Served in U.S. Army, France, 1918. **Family:** Married 1) Natalie Talmadge, 1921 (divorced 1932), two sons; 2) Mae Scribbens, 1933 (divorced 1935); 3) Eleanor Norris, 1940. **Career:** Part of parents' vaudeville act, The Three Keatons, from 1898; when family act broke up, became actor for Comique Film Corp., moved to California, 1917; appeared in 15 two-reelers for Comique, 1917-19; offered own production company with Metro Pictures by Joseph Schenk, 1919, produced 19 two-reelers, 1920-23; directed ten features, 1923-28; dissolved production company, signed to MGM, 1928; announced retirement from the screen, 1933; starred in 16 comedies for Educational Pictures, 1934-39; worked intermittently as gag writer for MGM, 1937-50; appeared in 10 two-reelers for Columbia, 1939-41; appeared on TV and in commercials, from 1949; Cinémathèque Française Keaton retrospective, 1962. **Died:** Of lung cancer, in Woodland Hills, California, 1 February 1966.

Films as Director and Actor:

1920 *One Week* (co-d, co-sc with Eddie Cline); *Convict Thirteen* (co-d, co-sc with Cline); *The Scarecrow* (co-d, co-sc with Cline)

1921 *Neighbors* (co-d, co-sc with Cline); *The Haunted House* (co-d, co-sc with Cline); *Hard Luck* (co-d, co-sc with Cline) *The High Sign* (co-d, co-sc with Cline); *The Goat* (co-d, co-sc with Mal St. Clair); *The Playhouse* (co-d, co-sc with Cline); *The Boat* (co-d, co-sc with Cline)

1922 *The Paleface* (co-d, co-sc with Cline); ***Cops*** (co-d, co-sc with Cline); *My Wife's Relations* (co-d, co-sc with Cline); *The Blacksmith* (co-d, co-sc with Mal St. Clair); *The Frozen North* (co-d, co-sc with Cline); *Day Dreams* (co-d, co-sc with Cline); *The Electric House* (co-d, co-sc with Cline)

1923 *The Balloonatic* (co-d, co-sc with Cline); *The Love Nest* (co-d, co-sc with Cline); *The Three Ages*; *Our Hospitality* (co-d)

1924 ***Sherlock Jr.*** (co-d); ***The Navigator*** (co-d)

1925 *Seven Chances*; *Go West* (+ story)

1926 *Battling Butler*; ***The General*** (co-d, co-sc)

1927 *College* (no d credit)

1928 *Steamboat Bill, Jr.* (no d credit); *The Cameraman* (no d credit, pr)

1929 *Spite Marriage* (no d credit)

1938 *Life in Sometown, U.S.A.*; *Hollywood Handicap*; *Streamlined Swing*

Other Films:

1917 *The Butcher Boy* (Fatty Arbuckle comedy) (role as village pest); *A Reckless Romeo* (Arbuckle) (role as a rival); *The Rough House* (Arbuckle) (role); *His Wedding Night* (Arbuckle) (role); *Oh, Doctor!* (Arbuckle) (role); *Fatty at Coney Island* (Coney Island) (Arbuckle) (role as husband touring Coney Island with his wife); *A Country Hero* (Arbuckle) (role)
1918 *Out West* (Arbuckle) (role as a dude gambler); *The Bell Boy* (Arbuckle) (role as a village pest); *Moonshine* (Arbuckle) (role as an assistant revenue agent); *Good Night, Nurse!* (Arbuckle) (role as the doctor and a visitor); *The Cook* (Arbuckle) (role as the waiter and helper)
1919 *Back Stage* (Arbuckle) (role as a stagehand); *The Hayseed* (Arbuckle) (role as a helper)
1920 *The Garage* (Arbuckle) (role as a garage mechanic); *The Round Up* (role as an Indian); *The Saphead* (role as Bertie "the Lamb" Van Alstyne)
1922 *Screen Snapshots, No. 3* (role)
1929 *The Hollywood Revue* (role as an Oriental dancer)
1930 *Free & Easy* (*Easy Go*) (role as Elmer Butts); *Doughboys* (pr, role as Elmer Stuyvesant)
1931 *Parlor, Bedroom & Bath* (pr, role as Reginald Irving); *Sidewalks of New York* (pr, role as Tine Harmon)
1932 *The Passionate Plumber* (pr, role as Elmer Tuttle); *Speak Easily* (role as Professor Timoleon Zanders Post)
1933 *What! No Beer!* (role as Elmer J. Butts)
1934 *The Gold Ghost* (role as Wally); *Allez Oop* (role as Elmer); *Le Roi des Champs Elysees* (role as Buster Garnier and Jim le Balafre)
1935 *The Invader* (*The Intruder*) (role as Leander Proudfoot); *Palookah from Paducah* (role as Jim); *One Run Elmer* (role as Elmer); *Hayseed Romance* (role as Elmer); *Tars & Stripes* (role as Elmer); *The E-Flat Man* (role as Elmer); *The Timid Young Man* (role as Elmer)
1936 *Three On a Limb* (role as Elmer); *Grand Slam Opera* (role as Elmer); *La Fiesta de Santa Barbara* (role as one of several stars); *Blue Blazes* (role as Elmer); *The Chemist* (role as Elmer); *Mixed Magic* (role as Elmer)
1937 *Jail Bait* (role as Elmer); *Ditto* (role as Elmer); *Love Nest on Wheels* (last apearance as Elmer)
1939 *The Jones Family in Hollywood* (co-sc): *The Jones Family in Quick Millions* (co-sc); *Pest from the West* (role as a traveler in Mexico); *Mooching through Georgia* (role as a Civil War veteran); *Hollywood Cavalcade* (role)
1940 *Nothing but Pleasure* (role as a vacationer); *Pardon My Berth Marks* (role as a reporter); *The Taming of the Snood* (role as an innocent accomplice); *The Spook Speaks* (role as a magician's housekeeper); *The Villain Still Pursued Her* (role); *Li'l Abner* (role as Lonesome Polecat); *His Ex Marks the Spot* (role)
1941 *So You Won't Squawk* (role); *She's Oil Mine* (role); *General Nuisance* (role)
1943 *Forever and a Day* (role as a plumber)
1944 *San Diego, I Love You* (role as a bus driver)
1945 *That's the Spirit* (role as L.M.); *That Night with You* (role)
1946 *God's Country* (role); *El Moderno Barba azul* (role as a prisoner of Mexicans who is sent to moon)
1949 *The Loveable Cheat* (role as a suitor); *In the Good Old Summertime* (role as Hickey); *You're My Everything* (role as butler)
1950 *Un Duel a mort* (role as a comic duellist); ***Sunset Boulevard*** (Wilder) (role as a bridge player)
1952 ***Limelight*** (Chaplin) (role as the piano accompanist in a music hall sketch); *L'incantevole nemica* (role in a brief sketch); *Paradise for Buster* (role)
1955 *The Misadventures of Buster Keaton* (role)
1956 *Around the World in Eighty Days* (role as a train conductor)
1960 *When Comedy was King* (role in a clip from *Cops*); *The Adventures of Huckleberry Finn* (Curtiz) (role as a lion tamer)
1963 *Thirty Years of Fun* (appearance in clips); *The Triumph of Lester Snapwell* (role as Lester); *It's a Mad, Mad, Mad, Mad World* (Kramer) (role as Jimmy the Crook)
1964 *Pajama Party* (role as an Indian chief)
1965 *Beach Blanket Bingo* (role as a would-be surfer); *Film* (role as Object/Eye); *How to Stuff a Wild Bikini* (role as Bwana); *Sergeant Deadhead* (Taurog) (role as Private Blinken); *The Rail-rodder* (role); *Buster Keaton Rides Again* (role)
1966 *The Scribe* (role); *A Funny Thing Happened on the Way to the Forum* (Lester) (role as Erronius)
1967 *Due Marines e un Generale* (*War, Italian Style*) (role as the German general)
1970 *The Great Stone Face* (role)

Publications

By KEATON: book—

My Wonderful World of Slapstick, with Charles Samuels, New York, 1960; revised edition, 1982.

By KEATON: articles—

"Why I Never Smile," in *The Ladies Home Journal* (New York), June 1926.
Interview with Christopher Bishop, in *Film Quarterly* (Berkeley), Fall 1958.
Interview with Herbert Feinstein, in *Massachusetts Review* (Amherst), Winter 1963.
Interview with Kevin Brownlow, in *Film* (London), no. 42, 1965.
"Keaton: Still Making the Scene," interview with Rex Reed, in *New York Times*, 17 October 1965.
"Keaton at Venice," interview with John Gillett and James Blue, in *Sight and Sound* (London), Winter 1965.
Interview with Arthur Friedman, in *Film Quarterly* (Berkeley), Summer 1966.
Interview with Christopher Bishop, in *Interviews with Film Directors*, edited by Andrew Sarris, New York, 1967.
"'Anything Can Happen—And Generally Did': Buster Keaton on His Silent Film Career," interview with George Pratt, in *Image* (Rochester), December 1974.
Articles from the 1920s reprinted in *Cahiers du Cinéma* (Paris), January 1979.

On KEATON: books—

Pantieri, José, *L'Originalissimo Buster Keaton*, Milan, 1963.
Turconi, Davide, and Francesco Savio, *Buster Keaton*, Venice, 1963.
Coursodon, Jean-Pierre, *Keaton et Compagnie: Les Burlesques américaines du "muet,"* Paris, 1964.
Oms, Marcel, *Buster Keaton*, Premier Plan No. 31, Lyons, 1964.
Blesh, Rudi, *Keaton*, New York, 1966.
Lebel, Jean-Pierre, *Buster Keaton*, New York, 1967.
Brownlow, Kevin, *The Parade's Gone By*, New York, 1968.
McCaffrey, Donald, *Four Great Comedians*, New York, 1968.
Robinson, David, *Buster Keaton*, London, 1968.
Denis, Michel, "Buster Keaton," in *Anthologie du Cinéma*, vol. 7, Paris, 1971.
Coursodon, Jean-Pierre, *Buster Keaton*, Paris, 1973.
Kerr, Walter, *The Silent Clowns*, New York, 1975.

Buster Keaton

Anobile, Richard, editor, *The Best of Buster,* New York, 1976.
Wead, George, *Buster Keaton and the Dynamics of Visual Wit,* New York, 1976.
Moews, Daniel, *Keaton: The Silent Features Close Up,* Berkeley, California, 1977.
Wead, George, and George Ellis, *The Film Career of Buster Keaton,* Boston, 1977.
Dardis, Tom, *Keaton: The Man Who Wouldn't Lie Down,* New York, 1979.
Benayoun, Robert, *The Look of Buster Keaton,* Paris, 1982; London, 1984.
Coursodon, Jean-Pierre, *Buster Keaton,* Paris, 1986.

On KEATON: articles—

Brand, Harry, "They Told Buster to Stick to It," in *Motion Picture Classic* (New York), June 1926.
Keaton, Joe, "The Cyclone Baby," in *Photoplay* (New York), May 1927.
Saalschutz, L., "Comedy," in *Close Up* (London), April 1930.
Agee, James, "Great Stone Face," in *Life* (New York), 5 September 1949.
Kerr, Walter, "Last Call for a Clown," in *Pieces at Eight,* New York, 1957.
Agee, James, "Comedy's Greatest Era," in *Agee on Film,* New York, 1958.
Dyer, Peter, "Cops, Custard—and Keaton," in *Films and Filming* (London), August 1958.
"Keaton Issue" of *Cahiers du Cinéma* (Paris), August 1958.
Bishop, Christopher, "The Great Stone Face," in *Film Quarterly* (Berkeley), Fall 1958.
Baxter, Brian, "Buster Keaton," in *Film* (London), November/December 1958.
Robinson, David, "Rediscovery: Buster," in *Sight and Sound* (London), Winter 1959.
Beylie, Claude, and others, "Rétrospective Buster Keaton," in *Cahiers du Cinéma* (Paris), April 1962.
Buñuel, Luis, "*Battling Butler* [*College*]," in *Luis Buñuel: An Introduction,* edited by Ado Kyrou, New York, 1963.
Lorca, Federico García, "Buster Keaton Takes a Walk," in *Sight and Sound* (London), Winter 1965.
Crowther, Bosley, "Dignity in Deadpan," in *The New York Times,* 2 February 1966.
Sadoul, Georges, "Le Génie de Buster Keaton," in *Les Lettres Françaises* (Paris), 10 February 1966.
Benayoun, Robert, "Le Colosse de silence," and "Le Regard de Buster Keaton," in *Positif* (Paris), Summer 1966.
McCaffrey, Donald, "The Mutual Approval of Keaton and Lloyd," in *Cinema Journal* (Evanston), no. 6, 1967.
Rhode, Eric, "Buster Keaton," in *Encounter* (London), December 1967.
Houston, Penelope, "The Great Blank Page," in *Sight and Sound* (London), Spring 1968.
Villelaur, Anne, "Buster Keaton," in *Dossiers du Cinéma: Cinéastes I,* Paris, 1971.
Maltin, Leonard, "Buster Keaton," in *The Great Movie Shorts,* New York, 1972.
Gilliatt, Penelope, "Buster Keaton," in *Unholy Fools,* New York, 1973.
Mast, Gerald, "Keaton," in *The Comic Mind,* New York, 1973.
Sarris, Andrew, "Buster Keaton," in *The Primal Screen,* New York, 1973.
"Keaton Issue" of *Avant-Scène du Cinéma* (Paris), February 1975.
Cott, Jeremy, "The Limits of Silent Film Comedy," in *Literature/Film Quarterly* (Salisbury, Maryland), Spring 1975.
Rubinstein, E., "Observations on Keaton's *Steamboat Bill Jr.,*" in *Sight and Sound* (London), Autumn 1975.
Everson, William, "Rediscovery: *Le Roi des Champs Elysees,*" in *Films in Review* (New York), December 1976.
Wade, G., "The Great Locomotive Chase," in *American Film* (Washington, D.C.), July/August 1977.
Valot, J., "Discours sur le cinéma dans quelques films de Buster Keaton," in *Image et Son* (Paris), February 1980.
Gifford, Denis, "Flavour of the Month," in *Films and Filming* (London), February 1984.
"Buster Keaton," in *Film Dope* (London), March 1984.
Sight and Sound (London), Spring 1985.
Cazals, T., "Un Monde à la démesure de l'homme," in *Cahiers du Cinéma* (Paris), March 1987.

* * *

Buster Keaton is the only creator-star of American silent comedies who equals Chaplin as one of the artistic giants of the cinema. He is perhaps the only silent clown whose reputation is far higher today than it was in the 1920s, when he made his greatest films. Like Chaplin, Keaton came from a theatrical family and served his apprenticeship on stage in the family's vaudeville act. Unlike Chaplin, however, Keaton's childhood and family life were less troubled, more serene, lacking the darkness of Chaplin's youth that would lead to the later darkness of his films. Keaton's films were more blithely athletic and optimistic, more committed to audacious physical stunts and cinema tricks, far less interested in exploring moral paradoxes and emotional resonances. Keaton's most famous comic trademark, his "great stone face," itself reflects the commitment to a comedy of the surface, but attached to that face was one of the most resiliently able and acrobatic bodies in the history of cinema. Keaton's comedy was based on the conflict between that imperviously dead-pan face, his tiny but almost superhuman physical instrument, and the immensity of the physical universe that surrounded them.

After an apprenticeship in the late 1910s making two-reel comedies that starred his friend Fatty Arbuckle, and after service in France in 1918, Keaton starred in a series of his own two-reel comedies beginning in 1920. Those films displayed Keaton's comic and visual inventiveness: the delight in bizarrely complicated mechanical gadgets (*The Scarecrow, The Haunted House*); the realization that the cinema itself was an intriguing mechanical toy (his use of split-screen in *The Playhouse* of 1921 allows Buster to play all members of the orchestra and audience, as well as all nine members of a minstrel troupe); the games with framing and composition (*The Balloonatic* is a comic disquisition on the surprises one can generate merely by entering, falling out of, or suppressing information in the frame); the breathtaking physical stunts and chases (*Daydreams, Cops*); and the underlying fatalism when his exuberant efforts produce ultimately disastrous results (*Cops, One Week, The Boat*).

In 1923 Keaton's producer, Joseph M. Schenck, decided to launch the comic star in a series of feature films, to replace a previously slated series of features starring Schenck's other comic star, the now scandal-ruined Fatty Arbuckle. Between 1923 and 1929, Keaton made an even dozen feature films on a regular schedule of two a year—always leaving Keaton free in the early autumn to travel east for the World Series. This regular pattern of Keaton's work—as opposed to Chaplin's lengthy laboring and devoted concentration on each individual project—reveals the way Keaton saw his film work. He was not making artistic masterpieces but knocking out everyday entertainment, like the vaudevillian playing the two-a-day. Despite the casualness of this regular routine (which would be echoed decades later by Woody Allen's regular one-a-year rhythm), many of those dozen silent features are comic masterpieces, ranking alongside the best of Chaplin's comic work.

Most of those films begin with a parodic premise—the desire to parody some serious and familiar form of stage or screen melodrama, such as the Civil War romance (*The General*), the mountain feud (*Our Hospitality*), the Sherlock Holmes detective story (*Sherlock, Jr.*), the

Mississippi riverboat race (*Steamboat Bill, Jr.*), or the western (*Go West*). Two of the features were built around athletics (boxing in *Battling Butler* and every sport but football in *College*), and one was built around the business of motion picture photography itself (*The Cameraman*). The narrative lines of these films were thin but fast-paced, usually based on the Keaton character's desire to satisfy the demands of his highly conventional lady love. The film's narrative primarily served to allow the film to build to its extended comic sequences, which, in Keaton's films, continue to amaze with their cinematic ingenuity, their dazzling physical stunts, and their hypnotic visual rhythms. Those sequences usually forced the tiny but dexterous Keaton into combat with immense and elemental antagonists—a rockslide in *Seven Chances*; an entire ocean liner in *The Navigator*; a herd of cattle in *Go West*; a waterfall in *Our Hospitality*. Perhaps the cleverest and most astonishing of his elemental foes appears in *Sherlock, Jr.* when the enemy becomes cinema itself—or, rather, cinematic time and space. Buster, a dreaming movie projectionist, becomes imprisoned in the film he is projecting, subject to its inexplicable laws of montage, of shifting spaces and times, as opposed to the expected continuity of space and time in the natural universe. Perhaps Keaton's most satisfyingly whole film is *The General*, virtually an extended chase from start to finish, as the Keaton character chases north, in pursuit of his stolen locomotive, then races back south with it, fleeing his Union pursuers. The film combines comic narrative, the rhythms of the chase, Keaton's physical stunts, and his fondness for mechanical gadgets into what may be the greatest comic epic of the cinema.

Unlike Chaplin, Keaton's stardom and comic brilliance did not survive Hollywood's conversion to synchronized sound. It was not simply a case of a voice's failing to suit the demands of both physical comedy and the microphone. Keaton's personal life was in shreds, after a bitter divorce from Natalie Talmadge. Always a heavy social drinker, Keaton's drinking increased in direct proportion to his personal troubles. Neither a comic spirit nor an acrobatic physical instrument could survive so much alcoholic abuse. In addition, Keaton's contract had been sold by Joseph Schenck to MGM (conveniently controlled by his brother, Nicholas Schenck, head of Loew's Inc., MGM's parent company). Between 1929 and 1933, MGM assigned Keaton to a series of dreary situation comedies—in many of them as Jimmy Durante's co-star and straight man. For the next two decades, Keaton survived on cheap two-reel sound comedies and occasional public appearances, until his major role in Chaplin's *Limelight* led to a comeback. Keaton remarried, went on the wagon, and made stage, television, and film appearances in featured roles. In 1965 he played the embodiment of existential consciousness in Samuel Beckett's only film work, *Film*, followed shortly by his final screen appearance in Richard Lester's *A Funny Thing Happened on the Way to the Forum*.

—Gerald Mast

KHAN, Mehboob *See* **MEHBOOB Khan**

KIEŚLOWSKI, Krzysztof

Nationality: Polish. **Born:** Warsaw, 27 June 1941. **Education:** School of Cinema and Theatre, Lodz, graduated 1969. **Career:** Worked as director of documentaries and fiction films for TV, from 1969; directed first feature for cinema, Blizna, 1976; vice-president of the Union of Polish Cinematographers, 1978-81; member of faculty of Radio and Television, University of Silesia, 1979-82; made *Dekalog*, series of short films for Polish TV, 1988-89, then gained financing to make longer versions of two episodes for cinematic release. **Awards:** First Prize, Mannheim Festival, for *Personel*, 1975; FIPRESCI Prize, Moscow Festival, for *Amator*, 1979; Diploma from the Polish Ministry of Foreign Affairs, 1979; Special Jury Prize, Cannes Film Festival, and Academy Award for Best Foreign Feature Film, for *A Short Film about Killing*, 1988. **Died:** Of a heart attack, 13 March 1996.

Films as Director:

(Documentary shorts, unless otherwise stated)

1967 *Urząd* (*The Job*)
1968 *Zdjęcie* (*The Photograph*) (for TV)
1969 *Z miasta Łodzi* (*From the City of Lodz*)
1970 *Byłem żołnierzem* (*I Was a Soldier*); *Przed rajdem* (*Before the Rally*); *Fabryka* (*Factory*)
1972 *Gospordaze* (*Workers*) (co-d); *Miedzy Wrocławiem a Zieloną Górą* (*Between Wroclaw and Zielona Gora*); *Podstawy BHP w kopalni miedzi* (*The Degree of Hygiene and Safety in a Copper Mine*); *Robotnicy 71 nic o nas bez nas* (*Workers 71*) (co-d); *Refren* (*Refrain*)
1973 *Murarz* (*Bricklayer*); *Dziecko* (*Child*); *Pierwsza miłość* (*First Love*) (for TV); *Prześwietlenie* (*X-Ray*); *Przajście podziemne* (*Pedestrian Subway*) (feature for TV)
1975 *Życiorys* (*Life Story*); *Personel* (*Personnel*) (feature for TV)
1976 *Klaps* (*Slate*); *Szpital* (*Hospital*); *Spokój* (*Stillness*) (feature for TV); *Blizna* (*The Scar*) (feature)
1977 *Nie wiem* (*I Don't Know*); *Z punktu widzenia nocnego portiera* (*Night Porter's Point of View*)
1978 *Siedem kobiet w różnym wieku* (*Seven Women of Various Ages*)
1979 *Amator* (*Camera Buff*) (feature)
1980 *Dworzec* (*The Station*); *Gadajace głowy* (*Talking Heads*)
1981 *Krótki dzień pracy* (*A Short Working Day*) (feature for TV); *Przypadek* (*Blind Chance*) (feature, released 1987)
1984 *Bez końca* (*No End*) (feature)
1988 *Krótki film o zabi janiu* (*A Short Film about Killing*) (feature); *Krótki film o milóści* (*A Short Film about Love*) (feature)
1989 ***Dekalog*** (*Decalogue*) (10 episodes for TV)
1990 *City Life* (*Episode in Netherlands*) (feature)
1991 *Podwójne życie Weroniky* (*La Double vie de Véronique*; *The Double Life of Véronique*) (feature) (+ sc)
1993-94 ***Trois couleurs Bleu*** (*Three Colours: Blue*) (feature) (+ sc); ***Trois couleurs Blanc*** (*Three Colours: White*) (feature) (+ sc); ***Trois couleurs Rouge*** (*Three Colours: Red*) (feature) (+ sc)

Publications

By KIEŚLOWSKI: book—

Decalogue, London, 1991.

By KIEŚLOWSKI: articles—

Interview, in *Jeune Cinéma* (Paris), December 1979.
Interview with H. Samsonowska, in *Kino* (Warsaw), October 1981.
Interview with S. Magela and C. Göldenboog, in *Filmfaust* (Frankfurt), April/May 1983.
Interview with Marszalek, in *Kino* (Warsaw), August 1987.
Interview with A. Tixeront, in *Cinéma* (Paris), December 1988.
Interview, in *Time Out* (London), 15 November 1989.

Krzysztof Kieślowski

Interview with B. Fornara, in *Cinema Forum,* April 1990.
Interview with P. Cargin, in *Film,* May/June 1990.
Interview with T. Sobolewski, in *Kino,* June 1990.
Interviews with M. Ciment and H. Niogret, in *Positif,* June 1991 and September 1993.
Interview with M.C. Loiselle and C. Racine, in *Images,* November/December 1991.
"Dziennik 89-90," in *Kino,* December 1991/February 1992.
Interview with V. Ostria, in *Kino,* August 1992.
Interview with Steven Gaydos, in *Variety,* 8 August 1994.

On KIEŚLOWSKI: articles—

"Krzysztof Kieslowski," in *International Film Guide 1981,* edited by Peter Cowie, London, 1980.
Zaoral, F., "Krzysztof Kieslowski," in *Film a Doba* (Prague), September 1985.
Kieslowski Section of *Positif* (Paris), December 1989.
Revue du Cinéma/Image et Son (Paris), January 1990.
Cavendish, Phil, "Kieslowski's *Decalogue,*" in *Sight and Sound* (London), Summer 1990.
Taubin, A., "Kieslowski Doubles Up," in *Village Voice,* 24 September 1991.
Hoberman, J., "Red, White, and Blue," in *Premiere,* October 1994.
Harvey, Miles, "Poland's Blue, White, and Red," in *Progressive,* April 1995.

* * *

In the late 1970s, when the conflict between the State and the citizens of Poland was imminent, a new trend emerged in cinematography—the "cinema of moral unrest." All the films in this trend have one common denominator: an unusually cutting critical view of the state of the society and its morals, human relationships in the work process, public and private life. It is more than logical that Krzysztof Kieślowski would have belonged to this trend; he had long been concerned with the moral problems of the society, and paid attention to them throughout his film career with increasing urgency. The direction of his artistic course was anticipated by his graduation film *From the City of Lodz,* in which he sketched the problems of workers, and by his participation in the stormy protest meeting of young filmmakers in Cracow in 1971, who warned against a total devaluation of basic human values.

A broad scale of problems can be found in the documentary films Kieślowski made between shooting feature films: disintegration of the economic structure, criticism of executive work, and the relationship of institutions and individuals. These documentaries are not a mere recording of events, phenomena, or a description of people and their behaviour, but always attempt instead to look underneath the surface. The director often used non-traditional means. Sometimes the word dominates the image, or he may have borrowed the stylistics of slapstick or satire, or he interfered with the reality in front of the camera by a staged element. Kieślowski did not emphasize the aesthetic function of the image, but stressed its real and literal meaning.

His feature films have a similar orientation: he concentrated on the explication of an individual's situation in the society and politics, on the outer and inner bonds of man with the objectively existing world, and on the search for connections between the individual and the general. He often placed his heroes in situations where they have to make a vital decision (in his TV films *The Staff* and *The Calm,* and in his films for theatrical release).

The Amateur is the synthesis of his attitudes and artistic search of the 1970s, and is also one of the most significant films of the "cinema of moral unrest." In the story of a man who buys a camera to follow the growth of a newborn daughter, and who gradually, thanks to this film instrument, begins to realize his responsibility for what is happening around him, the director placed a profound importance on the role of the artist in the world, on his morality, courage, and active approach to life. Here Kieślowski surpassed, to a large extent, the formulaic restrictions of the "cinema of moral unrest" resulting from the outside-the-art essence of this trend. These restrictions are also eliminated in his following films. In *The Accident* (made in 1981, released in 1987) he extended his exploration of man and his actions by introducing the category of the accidental. The hero experiences the same events (Poland in 1981) three times, and therefore is given three destinies, but each time on a different side. Two destinies are more or less given by accident, the third one he chooses himself, but even this choice is affected by the accidental element. The transcendental factor appears in *No End* (a dead man intervenes in worldly events), but the film is not an exploration of supernatural phenomena so much as a ruthless revelation of the tragic period after the declaration of the state of emergency in December 1981, and a demonstration of the professed truth that private life cannot be lived in isolation from the public sphere.

In the 1980s Kieślowski's work culminated in a TV cycle and two films with subjects from the Ten Commandments. *A Short Film about Killing* is based on the fifth commandment (Thou shalt not kill), while *A Short Film about Love* comes from the sixth. Both films and the TV cycle are anchored in the present and express the necessity of a moral revival, both of the individual and the society, in a world which may be determined by accidentality, but which does not deliver us from the right and duty of moral choice.

After the fall of communism when, as a consequence of changes in economic conditions, the production of films experienced a sharp fall in all of Eastern Europe, some Polish directors sought a solution to the ensuing crisis in work for foreign studios and in co-productions. This was the road taken by Kieślowski, and so all his films made in the 1990s were created with the participation of French producers: *The Double Life of Véronique* and the trilogy *Three Colours: Blue, Three Colours: White, Three Colours: Red*—loosely linked to the noble motto of the French Revolution: liberty, equality, fraternity. In these films Kieślowski followed up on his films from the 1980s, in which his heroes struggle with the duality of reason and feelings, haphazardness and necessity, reality and mystery. Even in these films made abroad we can also trace certain irony and sarcasm which first appeared in his films made in the 1970s in Poland.

—Blažena Urgošíková

KING, Henry

Nationality: American. **Born:** Christianburg, Virginia, 24 January 1888. **Family:** Married twice. **Career:** Worked with Empire Stock Company, travelling repertory company, also in circus, vaudeville, and burlesque, early 1900s; actor and writer for Lubin Co., Philadelphia, 1912-16; actor and director, Balbao Films, Long Beach, California, from 1916; moved to American Film Company, 1918; worked mainly for Fox, 1930-61. **Died:** In San Fernando Valley, 29 June 1982.

Films as Director:

1915 *Who Pays?*
1916 *Little Mary Sunshine*; *Joy and the Dragon*; *Pay Dirt*; *The Strained Pearl*
1917 *The Mainspring*; *The Climber*; *Southern Pride*; *A Game of Wits*; *The Mate of the Sally Ann*; *Twin Kiddies*; *Told at Twilight*; *Sunshine and Gold*
1918 *Beauty and the Rogue*; *Powers That Prey*; *Hearts or Diamonds*; *Up Romance Road*; *The Locked Heart*; *Hobbs in a Hurry*; *The Unafraid*; *Souls in Pawn*; *The Spectre of Suspicion*; *The Bride's Silence*
1919 *When a Man Rides Alone*; *Where the West Begins*; *Brass Buttons*; *Some Liar*; *Sporting Chance*; *This Hero Stuff*; *Six Feet Four*; *A Fugitive from Matrimony*; *23 1/2 Hours Leave*; *Haunting Shadows*
1920 *The White Dove*; *Uncharted Channels*; *One Hour Before Dawn*; *Help Wanted—Male*; *Dice of Destiny*
1921 *When We Were Twenty-One*; *Mistress of Shenstone*; *Salvage*; *The Sting of the Lash*; *Tol'able David*
1922 *The Seventh Day*; *Sonny*; *The Bond Boy*
1923 *Fury*; *The White Sister*
1925 *Sackcloth and Scarlet*; *Any Woman*; *Romola*
1926 *Stella Dallas*; *Partners Again*; *The Winning of Barbara Worth*
1927 *The Magic Flame*
1928 *The Woman Disputed*
1929 *She Goes to War*
1930 *Hell Harbor*; *Eyes of the World*; *Lightnin'*
1931 *Merely Mary Ann*; *Over the Hill*
1932 *The Woman in Room Thirteen*
1933 *State Fair*; *I Love You Wednesday*
1934 *Carolina*; *Marie Galante*
1935 *One More Spring*; *Way Down East*
1936 *The Country Doctor*; *Ramona*; *Lloyd's of London*
1937 *Seventh Heaven*
1938 *In Old Chicago*; *Alexander's Ragtime Band*
1939 *Jesse James*; *Stanley and Livingstone*
1940 *Little Old New York*; *Maryland*; *Chad Hanna*
1941 *A Yank in the RAF*; *Remember the Day*
1942 *The Black Swan*
1943 *The Song of Bernadette*
1944 *Wilson*
1945 *A Bell for Adano*
1946 *Margie*
1947 *Captain from Castille*
1948 *Deep Waters*
1949 *The Prince of Foxes*
1950 *Twelve O'Clock High*; *The Gunfighter*
1951 *I'd Climb the Highest Mountain*; *David and Bathsheba*
1952 *Wait 'til the Sun Shines, Nellie*; "The Gift of the Magi" episode of *O. Henry's Full House*; *The Snows of Kilimanjaro*
1953 *King of the Khyber Rifles*
1955 *Untamed*; *Love Is a Many-Splendored Thing*
1956 *Carousel*
1957 *The Sun Also Rises*
1958 *The Bravados*
1959 *This Earth Is Mine*; *Beloved Infidel*
1961 *Tender Is the Night*

Henry King: ***Stella Dallas*** **© 1937, Samuel Goldwyn, All Rights Reserved**

Publications

By KING: articles—

"Filmmakers as Goodwill Ambassadors," in *Films in Review* (New York), October 1958.
"Henry King: The Flying Director," interview with Richard Cherry, in *Action* (Los Angeles), July/August 1969.
"Pioneers '73," with C. Kirk, in *Action* (Los Angeles), November/December 1973.
Interview with S. Eyman, in *Focus on Film* (London), Winter 1976.
Interviews and article with J. Lacourcelles and P. Guinle, in *Ecran* (Paris), June and July 1978.
Interview with D. Badder, in *Sight and Sound* (London), Winter 1977/78.
Interview with Gene D. Phillips, in *Séquences* (Montreal), October 1983.

On KING: books—

Brownlow, Kevin, *The Parade's Gone By,* London, 1968.
Denton, Clive, and others, *The Hollywood Professionals Vol. 2: Henry King, Lewis Milestone, Sam Wood,* New York, 1974.
Coppedge, Walter, *Henry King's America,* Metuchen, New Jersey, 1986.

On KING: articles—

Shibuk, Charles, and Christopher North, "The Life and Films of Henry King," in *Films in Review* (New York), October 1958.
Mitchell, G.J., "Henry King," in *Films in Review* (New York), July 1964.
Pickard, Roy, "The Tough Race," in *Films and Filming* (London), September 1971.
Obituary, in *New York Times,* 1 July 1982.
Rabourdin, D., obituary, in *Cinéma* (Paris), September 1982.
"Henry King," in *Film Dope* (London), September 1984.
Reilly, J.P., "The Authenticity of Henry King," in *Films in Review* (New York), October 1984.

* * *

Henry King has been called the "pastoral poet" of American motion pictures by a small coterie of film historians, but in general his lengthy and prominent career as a director has been slighted, partly because many of his silent films remain inaccessible and partly because his interpretation of life in rural America has been overshadowed by the works of such directors as King Vidor, John Ford, and D.W. Griffith.

At their best, King's films re-created a charming and honestly sentimental America, evoking a sincere nostalgia and naturalism, and expressing an optimistic and durable view of romantic love. He presented his stories in a simple, straightforward manner, not attempting any "between-the-lines" analyses. He relied on plot and the competence of his actors to interpret his stories. Technically his films were spare and unencumbered by cinematic tricks. No technical virtuoso, he nevertheless possessed a remarkable facility for creating rustic tableaux which represented the virtues of American country life.

King came to motion pictures via acting both in theatre stock companies and, like his contemporaries John Ford and Raoul Walsh, in silent pictures. Acting led to directing, his first film of note being *23 1/2 Hours Leave,* produced by Thomas Ince. *Tol'able David,* his interpretation of life in his native rural Virginia, brought his first real acclaim, including praise from the Russian master Pudovkin. The Lillian Gish vehicle *The White Sister* was a beautifully conceived religious tragedy and one of the first major U.S. productions filmed abroad. His *Stella Dallas* remains the best and least maudlin version of that often-filmed tear-jerker and contains a remarkable performance by Belle Bennett.

With the arrival of sound, King signed a contract with Fox, where he would remain for the balance of his career, frequently working with the esteemed cinematographer Leon Shamroy. King proved a supreme studio craftsman and his first sound masterpiece was the memorable *State Fair,* starring the popular Will Rogers. The best of his many films for Fox relied heavily on nostalgia and Americana, and exhibited a steadfast earnestness (e.g., *In Old Chicago, Alexander's Ragtime Band, Jesse James,* and *Stanley and Livingstone*). In *Song of Bernadette* he transcended the sentimentality of the novel; *Wilson,* however, for all its nobility, was really more Darryl F. Zanuck than King and today is tedious to watch.

Twelve O'Clock High is a compelling depiction of a U.S. Air Force commander's breakdown and contains Gregory Peck's best performance, while *The Gunfighter* is a vivid, albeit off-beat Western. *I'll Climb the Highest Mountain,* a greatly underrated film, is the synthesis of all of King's love of ordinary country life and romance, and *The Snows of Kilimanjaro* is better Hemingway than most critics admit and was the author's favorite among the film adaptions of his writings.

Love Is a Many-Splendored Thing is another example of how King could make audiences believe in pure, romantic love, and *The Bravados,* an austere western, was his last good film: *Beloved Infidel* is an embarrassment and *Tender Is the Night,* which has its moments, was botched by David O. Selznick's meddling.

Before his death in 1982, King began to see a renewed interest in his work through numerous retrospectives. In 1969, the International Motion Picture Almanac listed what it deemed the "Greatest Hundred" films and six of King's works appeared on that list: *Tol'able David, The White Sister, Stella Dallas, Alexander's Ragtime Band, The Song of Bernadette,* and *Wilson.*

King's venerable career deserves more recognition than it has yet received; as Andrew Sarris has stated, King is a "subject for further research."

—Ronald Bowers

KING Hu

Nationality: Chinese. **Born:** Hu Chin-Ch'üan (as actor known as Chin Ch'üan; name in pinyin: Hun Jinquan) in Peking, 29 April 1931. **Education:** Hui-Wen Middle School, Peking; Peking National Art College. **Family:** Married scriptwriter Chong Ling (separated). **Career:** Moved to Hong Kong, 1949; worked in design department, Yong Hua Film Company, as actor, and as assistant director and scriptwriter, 1950-54; set designer, Great Wall Film Company, mid-1950s; radio producer, worked for Voice of America, 1954-58; actor, scriptwriter, and director for Shaw Brothers, 1958-65; director and production manager, Union (Liangbang) Film Company, 1965-70; founded King Hu Productions, 1970. **Awards:** Grand Prix, Cannes Festival, for *A Touch of Zen,* 1975.

Films as Director:

1962 *Yü T'ang Ch'un* (*The Story of Sue San*) (credited as exec d, disowned)
1963 *Liang Shan-po yü Chu Ying T'ai* (*Eternal Love*) (co-d)
1964 *Ta Ti Erh Nü* (*Children of the Good Earth*; *Sons and Daughters of the Good Earth*)
1965 *Ta Tsui Hsia* (*Come Drink with Me*) (+ co-sc, lyrics)
1967 *Lung Men K'o Chan* (*The Dragon Gate Inn*) (+ sc)
1970 *Hsia Nü* (*A Touch of Zen*) (+ sc, ed); "Nu" ("Anger") episode of *Hsi Nu Ai Le* (*Four Moods*) (+ sc)
1973 *Ying Ch'un Ko Chih Fêng Po* (*The Fate of Lee Khan*; *Trouble at Spring Inn*) (+ co-sc, pr)
1974 *Chung Lieh T'u* (*The Valiant Ones*; *Portrait of the Patriotic Heroes*) (+ sc, pr)
1978 *Shan Chung Ch'uan Chi* (*Legend of the Mountain*) (+ pr)
1979 *K'ung Shan Ling Yü* (*Raining in the Mountain*) (+ sc, pr)
1981 *Chung Shên Ta Shih* (*The Juvenizer*) (+ pr)
1983 Episode of *Ta Lun Hui* (*The Wheel of Life*)
1989 *Hsiao Ao Chiang Hu* (*The Swordsman*) (co-d)
1992 *Hua Pi Zhi Yinyang Fawang* (*Painted Skin*)

Other Films:

1958 *Hung Hu-Tzu* (*Red Beard*) (P'an Lei) (sc)
1961 *Hua T'ien-T'so* (*Bridenapping*) (Yen Chun) (sc)
1976 *Lung Men Fêng Yun* (*Dragon Gate*) (Ou-yang Chun) (sc)

Publications

By KING HU: article—

Interview with Michel Ciment, in *Positif* (Paris), May 1975.

On KING HU: articles—

Rayns, Tony, "Director: King Hu," in *Sight and Sound* (London), Winter 1975/76.
Elley, Derek, "King Hu," in *International Film Guide 1978,* London, 1977.
Tessier, Max, "King Hu dans les montagnes," in *Ecran* (Paris), July 1978.
Ooi, V., "Jacobean Drama and the Martial Arts Films of King Hu: A Study in Power and Corruption," in *Australian Journal of Screen Theory* (Kensington, New South Wales), no. 7, 1980.
Vos, J. M., and others, "King Hu," in *Film en Televisie* (Brussels), January 1980.
Bady, P., and Tony Rayns, article in *Positif* (Paris), July/August 1982.
Kennedy, Harlan, "Beyond Kung-Fu: Seven Hong-Kong Firecrackers," in *Film Comment* (New York), September/October 1983.
"King Hu Section" of *Cahiers du Cinéma* (Paris), September 1984.
Bourget, J. L., "*Hua Pi Zhi Yinyang Fawang,*" in *Positif,* November 1992.
Stratton, D., "*Painted Skin,*" in *Variety,* 9 November 1992.

* * *

King Hu is not only a master in the historical martial art film genre (known in Chinese as Wu Hsia P'ien or Wu Xia Pian), but a revolutionary of the form as well. One of the most popular genres in Chinese film history, it reached its peak in the 1970s in Hong Kong. In fact, the very first film made in China was a historical martial art film documenting Peking Opera performer T'an Hsin P'ei, who performed some fighting scenes from the opera *Ting Chun Shang* in 1906.

Influenced by Peking opera, King Hu always presents his main characters clearly and vividly in their first appearances on screens and lets the characters' interactions occur within a limited space. The presentations provide the audience with an early introduction of the main characters' backgrounds, personalities, motives, and duties, giving a clear indication of where everyone fits in the moral landscape. This restricted realm creates denser and more intensive emotional developments, paving the way to a higher dramatic climax. Such structuring can be observed at the temple in *Raining in the Mountain,* and the inn in both *The Dragon Gate Inn* and *The Fate of Lee Khan.*

Most filmmakers in this genre tend to focus on fighting scenes and on displaying various styles of kung fu. In many cases the plots are constructed simply to support the fighting, which itself is given over to such elaborate special effects as to resemble more closely a supernatural force than a manifestation of human struggle. History itself loses its meaning: it simply provides an excuse for making another "historical" martial art film. This destruction of referentiality becomes all the balder when a character from the Han dynasty wears a hat from the Ming dynasty to go with his Han dynasty robe, goes into an inn that is a mess of Tang architecture and Ching furniture. As a result, the historical martial art film genre's main function is to create an imaginary and mystical world for the audience to escape to. But King Hu's work stands out with its professionalism in art direction and the director's personal philosophy in historical backgrounding.

The Ming dynasty (1386-1644 A.D.) has been King Hu's favorite historical period, reflecting as it does two major issues of the contemporary Chinese political situation. First of all, the legitimacy of the Chinese government—should it belong to the Nationalist Party, founded by Dr. Sun Yat-sen, or the Chinese Communist Party, which enjoys the support of the majority of Chinese? King Hu never gives an answer, but he surely does not hesitate to take a Han-centric viewpoint of the Ming dynasty. In Chinese history, it is commonly perceived as an act of legitimization of authority when Chu Yuan-chang, the founding emperor of the Ming dynasty, started a revolution to overthrow the Yuan dynasty, founded by Mongolian "invaders." Chu is a Han, the majority ethnic group of China. In *The Fate of Lee Khan,* the revolutionaries led by Chu are brave, intelligent, united, self-sacrificing, and virtuous, while the Mongolians are cowardly, stupid, selfish, and morally corrupted. Although it seems to be an exception that the Mongolian lord and princess are equally brave, smart, and know the secrets of kung fu, they are cruel to their people. They even attempt to kill a traitor to Chu who offers them secret information about Chu's military power. In the end, the Mongolian lord, princess, and the traitor are killed by the revolutionaries.

Another parallel to contemporary times is the Ming dynasty's power struggles. The rivalries among corrupt officers, ministers, and eunuchs not only deceived the emperors, but ruined the welfare of the Chinese people. Facing a chaotic era like this, King Hu's solution seems to be found in *A Touch of Zen,* which won the Grand Prix de Technique Superieur at Cannes in 1975, marking a milestone in his career. King Hu expresses the limitations of scholarly and chivalric life in the first half of *A Touch of Zen,* while in the other half he initiates the audience into a surrealistic visionary world—the realm of Zen metaphysics: a monk bleeds gold and possesses extraordinary powers that seem to stem from the sun and other natural forces.

However, one may find a different philosophy in *The Swordsman,* which he co-directed with Tsui Hark, a leading figure of the Hong Kong New Wave and director of *Peking Opera Blues.* Although the artistic disputes between Tsui Hark and King Hu caused the latter to leave in the middle of production, *The Swordsman* surprisingly ends up being a combination of several filmmakers' virtues. Stylistically, there are kung fu scenes from martial art director Chen Hsiao Tung (director of *Chinese Ghost Story*), visionary special effects from Tsui Hark, and art design from King Hu, who eventually set the story in his preferred Ming dynasty. Its pace is one of the contemporary commercial Hong Kong film, much faster than King Hu's normal work. It employs Tsui Hark's cynical view of life, showing almost none of the characters to be trustworthy: they all have their own selfish ambitions, the fact of which breaks down the easy formulation of hero and villain. King Hu's specialty—the power struggles within intensive circumstances—is still in evidence, while a rather forced romantic relationship is evidence of Chen's hand.

King Hu's metaphysical Zen and the sublimation of the spiritual are not themes in *The Swordsman.* They are replaced by the nihilism of Tsui Hark, as seen when the protagonist and his girlfriend ride without a clear direction on an uncultivated field after they both encounter some of the complexities of life. Somehow more rooted in reality, King Hu subsequently prepared a film about the Chinese railroad workers' early U.S. history following immigration in the nineteenth century.

—Vivian Huang

KINOSHITA, Keisuke

Nationality: Japanese. **Born:** Hamamatsu City, Shizuoka Prefecture, 5 December 1912. **Education:** Hamamatsu Engineering School; Oriental Photography School, Tokyo, 1932-33. Military service, 1940-41. **Career:** Laboratory assistant, Shochiku's Kamata studios, 1933; camera assistant under chief cinematographer for Yasujiro Shimazu, 1934-36; assistant director, Shimazu's group, 1936-42; chief assistant to director Kozaburo Yoshimura, 1939; director, from 1943; left Shochiku, began as TV director, 1964. **Awards:** Kinema Jumpo Best Film of the Year, for *The Morning of the Osone Family,* 1946, *24 Eyes,* 1954, and *The Ballad of Narayama,* 1958. **Address:** Mamiana Mansions, #910, 44 Maniana-cho, Minato-ku, Tokyo, Japan.

Films as Director:

1943 *Hanasaku minato* (*The Blossoming Port*); *Ikite-iru Magoroku* (*The Living Magoroku*) (+ sc)
1944 *Kanko no machi* (*Jubilation Street*; *Cheering Town*); *Rikugun* (*The Army*)
1946 *Osone-ke no asa* (*Morning for the Osone Family*); *Waga koiseshi otome* (*The Girl I Loved*) (+ sc)
1947 *Kekkon* (*Marriage*) (+ story); *Fujicho* (*Phoenix*) (+ sc)
1948 *Onna* (*Woman*) (+ sc); *Shozo* (*The Portrait*); *Hakai* (*Apostasy*)
1949 *Ojosan kanpai* (*A Toast to the Young Miss*; *Here's to the Girls*); *Yotsuya kaidan, I-II* (*The Yotsuya Ghost Story, Parts I and II*); *Yabure daiko* (*Broken Drum*) (+ co-sc)
1950 *Konyaku yubiwa* (*Engagement Ring*) (+ sc)
1951 *Zemma* (*The Good Fairy*) (+ co-sc); *Karumen kokyo ni kaeru* (*Carmen Comes Home*) (+ sc); *Shonen ki* (*A Record of Youth*) (+ co-sc); *Umi no hanabi* (*Fireworks over the Sea*) (+ sc)
1952 *Karumen junjo su* (*Carmen's Pure Love*) (+ sc)
1953 *Nihon no higeki* (*A Japanese Tragedy*) (+ sc)
1954 *Onna no sono* (*The Garden of Women*) (+ sc); *Nijushi no hitomi* (*Twenty-four Eyes*) (+ sc)

Keisuke Kinoshita

1955 *Toi kumo* (*Distant Clouds*) (+ co-sc); *Nogiku no gotoki kimi nariki* (*You Were Like a Wild Chrysanthemum*) (+ sc)
1956 *Yuyake-gumo* (*Clouds at Twilight*); *Taiyo to bara* (*The Rose on His Arm*) (+ sc)
1957 *Yorokobi mo kanashimi mo ikutoshitsuki* (*Times of Joy and Sorrow; The Lighthouse*) (+ sc); *Fuzen no tomoshibi* (*A Candle in the Wind; Danger Stalks Near*) (+ sc)
1958 *Narayama bushi-ko* (*The Ballad of the Narayama*) (+ sc); *Kono ten no niji* (*The Eternal Rainbow; The Rainbow of This Sky*) (+ sc)
1959 *Kazabana* (*Snow Flurry*) (+ sc); *Sekishun-cho* (*The Bird of Springs Past*) (+ sc); *Kyo mo mata kakute arinan* (*Thus Another Day*) (+ sc)
1960 *Haru no yume* (*Spring Dreams*) (+ sc); *Fuefuki-gawa* (*The River Fuefuki*) (+ sc)
1961 *Eien no hito* (*The Bitter Spirit; Immortal Love*) (+ sc)
1962 *Kotoshi no koi* (*This Year's Love*) (+ sc); *Futari de aruita iku-haru-aki* (*The Seasons We Walked Together*) (+ sc)
1963 *Utae, wakodo-tachi* (*Sing, Young People!*); *Shito no densetsu* (*Legend of a Duel to the Death*) (+ sc)
1964 *Koge* (*The Scent of Incense*) (+ sc)
1967 *Natsukashiki fue ya taiko* (*Lovely Flute and Drum*) (+ pr, sc)
1976 *Suri Lanka no ai to wakare* (*Love and Separation in Sri Lanka*) (+ sc)
1979 *Shodo satsujin: Musukoyo* (*My Son*) (+ sc)
1983 *Kono ko o nokoshite* (*The Children of Nagasaki; These Children Survive Me*)
1986 *Yorokobi mo kanashima mo ikutoshitsuki* (*Times of Joy and Sorrow; Big Joys, Small Sorrows*)

Publications

By KINOSHITA: articles—

"Jisaku o kataru," [Keisuke Kinoshita Talks About His Films], in *Kinema Jumpo* (Tokyo), no.115, 1955.
Interview with P. Vecchi, in *Cineforum* (Bergamo), August 1984.
Interview with A. Tournès, in *Jeune Cinéma* (Paris), November-December 1986.

On KINOSHITA: books—

Anderson, Joseph, and Donald Richie, *The Japanese Film*, New York, 1961.
Mellen, Joan, *The Waves at Genji's Door*, New York, 1976.
Bock, Audie, *Japanese Film Directors*, Tokyo, 1978.
König, Regula, and Marianne Lewinsky, *Keisuke Kinoshita: Entretien, etudes, filmographie, iconographie*, Locarno, 1986.

On KINOSHITA: articles—

"Keisuke Kinoshita," in *Film Dope* (London), September 1984.
Tournès, A., "Terres inconnues du cinéma japonais," in *Jeune Cinéma* (Paris), October 1984.
Niogret, H., "Keisuke Kinoshita: Un metteur en scène de compagnie," in *Positif* (Paris), July/August 1986.
National Film Theatre Programme (London), March 1987.

* * *

Kinoshita's films are characteristic of the Shochiku Studio's work: healthy home drama and melodrama as conventionalized by the studio's two masters, Shimazu and Ozu, who specialized in depicting everyday family life. Kinoshita gravitated toward sentimentalism and a belief in the eventual triumph of good will and sincere efforts. It was agai this "planned unity" that the new generation of Shochiku direct (for example, Oshima and his group) reacted.

Kinoshita is skilled in various genres. His light satiric comedi began with his first film, *The Blossoming Port.* Although ostensibl illustrated the patriotism of two con men in a small port town, tl film demonstrated Kinoshita's extraordinary talent for witty mis en-scène and briskly-paced storytelling. His postwar comedies inclu *Broken Drum, Carmen Comes Home, Carmen's Pure Love* and *Candle in the Wind,* which captured the liberated spirit of postw democratization. *A Toast to the Young Miss* was a kind of situatio comedy that became unusually successful due to its excellent cast.

Among Kinoshita's popular romantic melodramas, *Marriage* an *Phoenix* surprised audiences with bold and sophisticated expression o love, helping pioneer the new social morality in Japanese film. *Yo Were Like a Wild Chrysanthemum* is a romantic, sentimental lov story.

The sentimental human drama became Kinoshita's most character istic film. It is typified by *24 Eyes,* which deftly appeals to the Japa nese audience's sentimentality, depicting the life of a woman teacher on a small island. This was followed by such films as *Times of Joy and Sorrow, The Seasons We Walked Together,* and *Lovely Flute and Drum.* The Shochiku Studio was proud that these films could attract "women coming with handkerchiefs to wipe away their tears."

Films of rather straightforward social criticism include *Morning for the Osone Family, Apostasy, A Japanese Tragedy, The Garden of Women, The Ballad of the Narayama,* and *Snow Flurry.* These vary from rather crude "postwar democratization" films to films that deal with such topics as the world of folklore, struggles against the feudalistic system, and current social problems.

Kinoshita is adventurous in his technical experimentation. *Carmen Comes Home* is the first Japanese color film and is sophisticated in its use of the new technology. In its sequel, *Carmen's Pure Love,* he employs tilting compositions throughout the film, producing a wry comic atmosphere. In *A Japanese Tragedy,* newsreel footage is inserted to connect the historical background with the narrative. *You Were Like a Wild Chrysanthemum,* a film presented as an old man's memory of his youth, creates a nostalgic effect by vignetting with an oval shape and with misty images. *The Ballad of the Narayama,* except for the last outdoor sequence, takes place on a set that accentuates artificiality and theatricality, with the added effect of a peculiar use of color. Kabuki-style acting, music, and storytelling create the fable-like ambience of this film. *The River Fuefuki* is entirely tinted in colors that correspond to the sentiment of each scene (e.g. red for fighting, blue for funerals, and green for peaceful village life).

After the Japanese film industry sank into a depression in the 1960s, Kinoshita successfully continued his career in TV for a long period. His skill at entertaining and his sense of experimentation have kept him popular with television audiences as well.

—Kyoko Hirano

KINUGASA, Teinosuke

Nationality: Japanese. **Born:** Teinosuke Kogame in Mie Prefecture, 1 January 1896. **Education:** Sasayama Private School. **Career:** Ran away to Nagoya, began theatrical apprenticeship, 1913; stage debut, 1915; *oyama* actor (playing female roles), Nikkatsu Mukojima studio, 1918; wrote and directed first film, 1921; moved to Makino Kinema, 1922; contract director for Shochiku Company, formed Kinugasa Motion Picture League, became involved with new actors' and techni-

cians' union, led mass walkout over plan to replace *oyama* actors with female performers, mid-1920s; travelled to Russia and Germany, 1928; returned to Japan, 1929; began association with kabuki actor Hasegawa, 1935; moved to Toho Company, 1939; moved to Daici Company, 1949, (appointed to board of directors, 1958). **Awards:** Best Film, Cannes Festival, Academy Award for Best Foreign Film, and Best Foreign Film, New York Film Critics, for *Gate of Hell*, 1954; Purple Ribbon Medal, Japan, for distinguished cultural service, 1958.

Films as Director:

1921 *Imoto no shi* (*The Death of My Sister*) (+ sc, role)
1922 *Niwa no kotori* (*Two Little Birds*) (+ sc); *Hibana* (*Spark*) (+ sc)
1923 *Hanasake jijii* (+ sc); *Jinsei o Mitsumete* (+ sc); *Onna-yo ayamaru nakare* (+ sc); *Konjiki yasha* (*The Golden Demon*) (+ sc); *Ma no ike* (*The Spirit of the Pond*) (+ sc)
1924 *Choraku no kanata* (*Beyond Decay*) (+ sc); *Kanojo to unmei* (*She Has Lived Her Destiny*) (in two parts) (+ sc); *Kire no ame* (*Fog and Rain*) (+ sc); *Kishin yuri keiji* (+ sc); *Kyoren no buto* (*Dance Training*) (+ sc); *Mirsu* (*Love*) (+ sc); *Shohin* (*Shuto*) (+ sc); *Shohin* (*Shusoku*) (+ sc); *Jashumon no onna* (*A Woman's Heresy*) (+ sc); *Tsuma no himitsu* (*Secret of a Wife*); *Koi* (*Love*); *Sabishi mura* (*Lonely Village*)
1925 *Nichirin* (*The Sun*); *Koi to bushi* (*Love and a Warrior*) (+ sc); *Shinju yoimachigusa*; *Tsukigata hanpeita*; *Wakaki hi no chuji*
1926 *Kurutta ippeiji* (*A Page of Madness*); *Kirinji*; *Teru hi kumoru hi* (*Shining Sun Becomes Clouded*); *Hikuidori* (*Cassowary*); *Ojo Kichiza*; *Oni azami*; *Kinno jidai* (*Epoch of Loyalty*); *Meoto boshi* (*Star of Married Couples*); *Goyosen*; *Dochu sugoroku bune*; *Dochu sugoroku kago* (*The Palanquin*); *Akatsuki no yushi* (*A Brave Soldier at Dawn*); *Gekka no kyojin* (*Moonlight Madness*)
1928 ***Jujiro*** (*Crossroads*) (+ sc); *Benten Kozo* (*Gay Masquerade*); *Keiraku hichu*; *Kaikokuki* (*Tales from a Country by the Sea*); *Chokon yasha* (*Female Demon*)
1931 *Reimei izen* (*Before Dawn*) (+ sc); *Tojin okichi*
1932 *Ikinokata Shinsengumi* (*The Surviving Shinsengumi*) (+ sc); *Chushingura* (*The Loyal 47 Ronin*; *The Vengeance of the 47 Ronin*) (+ sc)
1933 *Tenichibo to iganosuke* (+ sc); *Futatsu doro* (*Two Stone Lanterns*) (+ sc); *Toina no Ginpei* (*Ginpei from Koina*) (+ sc)
1934 *Kutsukate tokijiro* (+ sc); *Fuyaki shinju* (+ sc); *Ippan gatana dohyoiri* (*A Sword and the Sumo Ring*) (+ sc); *Naguraretа kochiyama* (+ sc)
1935 *Yukinojo henge* (*The Revenge of Yukinojo*; *Yukinojo's Revenge*) (+ co-sc) (in 3 parts, part 3 released 1936); *Kurayama no ushimatsu* (+ sc)
1937 *Hito hada Kannon* (*The Sacred Protector*) (+ sc) (in 5 parts); *Osaka natsu no jin* (*The Summer Battle of Osaka*) (+ sc)
1938 *Kuroda seichuroku* (+ sc)
1940 *Hebi himesama* (*The Snake Princess*) (+ sc) (in two parts)
1941 *Kawanakajima kassen* (*The Battle of Kawanakajima*) (+ sc)
1943 *Susume dokuritsuki* (*Forward Flag of Independence*)
1945 *Umi no bara* (*Rose of the Sea*)
1946 *Aru yo no tonosama* (*Lord for a Night*)
1947 "Koi no sakasu (The Love Circus)" section of *Yottsu no koi no monogatari* (*The Story of Four Loves*); *Joyu* (*Actress*) (+ co-sc)
1949 *Kobanzame* (part 2) (+ sc); *Koga yashiki* (*Koga Mansion*) (+ sc); *Satsujinsha no kao* (*The Face of a Murderer*)
1951 *Beni komori* (+ sc); *Tsuki no watari-dori* (*Migratory Birds Under the Moon*) (+ sc); *Meigatsu somato* (*Lantern Under a Full Moon*) (+ sc)
1952 *Daibutsu kaigen* (*Saga of the Great Buddha*; *The Dedication of the Great Buddha*) (+ sc); *Shurajo hibun* (+ sc) (in 2 parts)
1953 ***Jigokumon*** (*Gate of Hell*) (+ sc)
1954 *Yuki no yo ketto* (*Duel of a Snowy Night*) (+ sc); *Hana no nagadosu* (*End of a Prolonged Journey*) (+ sc); *Tekka bugyo* (+ sc)
1955 *Yushima no shiraume* (*The Romance of Yushima*; *White Sea of Yushima*) (+ sc); *Kawa no aru shitamachi no hanashi* (*It Happened in Tokyo*) (+ sc); *Bara ikutabi* (*A Girl Isn't Allowed to Love*) (+ sc)
1956 *Yoshinaka o meguru sannin no onna* (*Three Women Around Yoshinaka*) (+ sc); *Hibana* (*Spark*) (+ sc); *Tsukigata hanpeita* (in 2 parts) (+ sc)
1957 *Shirasagi* (*White Heron*; *The Snowy Heron*) (+ sc); *Ukifune* (*Floating Vessel*) (+ sc); *Naruto hicho* (*A Fantastic Tale of Naruto*) (+ sc)
1958 *Haru koro no hana no en* (*A Spring Banquet*) (+ sc); *Osaka no onna* (*A Woman of Osaka*) (+ sc)
1959 *Joen* (*Tormented Flame*) (+ sc); *Kagero ezu* (*Stop the Old Fox*) (+ sc)
1960 *Uta andon* (*The Old Lantern*) (+ sc)
1961 *Midare-gami* (*Dishevelled Hair*) (+ sc); *Okoto to Sasuke* (*Okoto and Sasuke*) (+ sc)
1963 *Yoso* (*Priest and Empress*; *The Sorcerer*) (+ sc); episode of *Uso* (*When Women Lie*; *Lies*)
1967 *Chiisana tobosha* (*The Little Runaway*) (co-d)

Other Films (incomplete listing):

1918 *Nanairo yubi wa* (*The Seven Colored Ring*) (Oguchi) (film acting debut)
1920 *Ikeru shikabane* (*The Living Corpse*) (Tanaka) (role)

Publications

By KINUGASA: articles—

Interview with H. Niogret, in *Positif* (Paris), May 1973.
"Une Page folle," interview with Max Tessier, in *Ecran* (Paris), April 1975.

On KINUGASA: book—

Anderson, Joseph, and Donald Richie, *The Japanese Film: Art and Industry*, New York, 1960; revised edition, Princeton, New Jersey, 1982.

On KINUGASA: articles—

Tessier, Max, "Yasujiro Ozu et le cinéma japonais à la fin du muet," in *Ecran* (Paris), December 1979.
Tessier, Max, obituary, in *Image et Son* (Paris), April 1982.
Obituary in *Cinéma* (Paris), June 1982.
Petric, Vlad, "*A Page of Madness*: A Neglected Masterpiece of the Silent Cinema," in *Film Criticism* (Meadville, Pennsylvania), Fall 1983.
"Teinosuke Kinugasa," in *Film Dope* (London), January 1985.
Cinema Journal (Champaign, Illinois), Autumn 1989.

* * *

Teinosuke Kinugasa made two of the most famous films ever to come out of Japan, and was, historically, the first of his country's directors known in the West. *Rashomon* brought wider interest and admiration for Japanese cinema, but some observers fondly recall

Teinosuke Kinugasa

Crossroads, which had some showings in Europe in 1929 and in New York in 1930, under the title *The Slums of Tokyo.*

On one hand, *Crossroads* is the Japanese equivalent of the German "street" films, and on the other it is the oft-told local tale of a hard-working, self-sacrificing woman suffering on behalf of her idle younger brother, who is in love with an unvirtuous woman. The pace is slow, but the film is the work of a master. As in his earlier surrealist and experimental film, *A Page of Madness,* which made a late, freak appearance in the West in 1973, he intercuts furiously to express mental agitation and to move backwards and forwards in time in a way seldom used in Western cinema until the *Nouvelle Vague* in the 1960s.

Kinugasa's films of the 1930s confirm the impression that he did not regard the camera as a mere recorder: we may be astonished by the number of glides, of overhead shots, of sudden close-ups—each correctly juxtaposed against the images on either side. It is clear that Kinugasa, along with his peers, used this "decorative" approach rather more freely with historical subjects: if you compare his most popular film, *The Revenge of Yukinojo* with Ichikawa's 1963 remake, *An Actor's Revenge,* you will find many of the shots duplicated, despite the stunning addition of colour and wide screen. (The same actor, Kazuo Hasegawa, appeared in both, but here under the pseudonym Chojiro Hayashi.)

The two films are too far apart, chronologically, to make further comparisons, but in 1947 Kinugasa directed *Actress*, while Mizoguchi tackled the same subject, based on fact, in *The Love of Sumako the Actress*. Mizoguchi's version has an intensity lacking in Kinugasa's film, which is more subtle.

Gate of Hell (1953) was the first Japanese colour film seen in the West, and only one other film had preceded it, after *Rashomon*. It bowled over almost everyone who saw it: the gold, scarlet, beige, white and green of the costumes; the mists, the moon, the sea, the distant hills. We did not know then how many Japanese films start this way, with an exposition of a country torn apart by war and revolution, nor how many concerned murderous and amorous intrigues among feudal warlords and their courtesans. *Gate of Hell* is an exquisite picture, but it remains overshadowed by Mizoguchi's (black-and-white) historical films of this period. It lacks their power and tension, their breadth and their sheer craftsmanship.

It was in this decade and into the 1960s that the Japanese cinema flowered, with a series of masterpieces by Kurosawa, Kobayashi, Ichikawa and others. Some of the older directors, including Kinugasa, continued to make films of integrity and skill: but many of their films look a little plodding beside those made by the younger generation.

—David Shipman

KLUGE, Alexander

Nationality: German. **Born:** Halberstadt, 14 February 1932. **Education:** Charlottenburger Gymnasium, Berlin, Abitur 1949; studied law and history at Freiburg, Marburg, and Johann-Wolfgang Goethe Universität, Frankfurt (degree in law, 1953). **Career:** Lawyer, novelist, and political writer, 1950s; began in films as assistant to Fritz Lang, 1958; leader and spokesman of group of German filmmakers protesting condition of German filmmaking, Oberhausen Festival, 1962; head of film division of Hochschule für Gestaltung in Ulm (known as "Institut für Filmgestaltung"), from 1962; founder, Kairos-Films, 1963. **Awards:** Berliner Kuntspreis for *Lebensläufe*, 1964; Bayrischer Staatspreis für Literatur, for *Porträt einer Bewärung* and for *Schlachtbeschreibung*; Golden Lion, Venice Festival, for *Die Artisten in der Zirkus-kuppel: ratlos*, 1967; Honorary Professor, University of Frankfurt am Main, 1973; International Critics award, Cannes Festival, for *Ferdinand the Strongman*, 1976; Fontane-Preis, 1979; Grosser Breme Literatur-preis, 1979. **Address:** Elisabethstrasse 38, 8000 Munich 40, Germany.

Films as Director:

1960 *Brutalität in Stein* (*Die Ewigkeit von gestern*; *Brutality in Stone*; *Yesterday Goes On for Ever*) (co-d) (short)
1961 *Rennen* (*Racing*) (co-d) (short)
1963 *Lehrer im Wandel* (*Teachers in Transformation*) (co-d) (short)
1964 *Porträt einer Bewährung* (*Portrait of One Who Proved His Mettle*) (short)
1966 *Pokerspiel* (short); *Abschied von gestern* (*Yesterday Girl*)
1967 *Frau Blackburn, geb. 5 Jan. 1872, wird gefilmt* (*Frau Blackburn, Born 5 Jan. 1872, Is Filmed*) (short); *Die Artisten in der Zirkuskuppel: ratlos* (*Artistes at the Top of the Big Top—Disoriented*)
1968 *Feuerlöscher E. A. Winterstein* (*Fireman E. A. Winterstein*) (short)
1969 *Die unbezähmbare Leni Peickert* (*The Indomitable Leni Peickert*); *Ein Arzt aus Halberstadt* (*A Doctor from Halberstadt*) (short)
1970 *Der grosse Verhau* (*The Big Dust-up*)
1971 *Wir verbauen 3 x 27 Milliarden Dollar in einen Angriffsschlachter* (*Der Angriffsschlachter*; *We'll Blow 3 x 27 Billion Dollars on a Destroyer*; *The Destroyer*) (short); *Willi Tobler und der Untergang der sechste Flotte* (*Willi Tobler and the Wreck of the Sixth Fleet*)
1972 *Besitzbürgerin, Jahrgang 1908* (*A Woman from the Property-owning Middle Class, Born 1908*) (short)
1973 *Gelegenheitsarbeit einer Sklavin* (*Occasional Work of a Female Slave*)
1974 *In Gefahr und grösster Not bringt der Mittelweg den Tod* (*The Middle of the Road Is a Very Dead End*)
1975 *Der starke Ferdinand* (*Strongman Ferdinand*); *Augen aus einem anderen Land*
1977 *Die Menschen, die die Staufer-Austellung vorbereiten* (*Die Menschen, die das Stauferjahr vorbereiten*; *The People Who Are Preparing the Year of the Hohenstaufens*) (co-d) (short); *'Zu böser Schlacht schleich' ich heut' Nacht so bang'* (*In Such Trepidation I Creep Off Tonight to the Evil Battle*) (revised version of *Willi Tobler and the Wreck of the Sixth Fleet*)
1979 *Die Patriotin* (*The Patriotic Woman*)
1980 *Der Kandidat* (co-d)
1983 *Krieg und Frieden* (co-d); *Die Macht der Gefühle* (*The Power of Emotions*)
1985 *Der Angriff der Gegenwart auf die Ubrige Zeit* (*The Blind Director*)
1987 *Vermischte Nachrichten* (+ sc, pr)

Other Films:

1965 *Unendliche Fahrt—aber begrenzt* (Reitz) (feature) (text)
1973 *Die Reise nach Wien* (Reitz) (sc)
1978 *Deutschland im Herbst* (*Germany in Autumn*) (Schlöndorff) (contribution)
1986 *There Must Be a Way Out: The Film World of Alexander Kluge* (Buchka) (addl d)
1989 *Schweinegeld, Ein Marchen der Gebruder Nimm* (pr)

Publications

By KLUGE: books—

Kulturpolitik und Ausgabenkontrolle, Frankfurt, 1961.
Lebensläufe, Stuttgart, 1962; 2nd edition, Frankfurt, 1974.
Schlachtbeschreibung, Olten and Freiburg, 1964; expanded edition, Munich, 1978.
Abschied von gestern, Frankfurt am Main, n.d.
Die Artisten in der Zirkuskuppel: ratlos. Die Ungläubige. Projekt Z. Sprüche der Leni Peickert, Munich, 1968.
Der Untergang der sechsten Armee—Schlachtbeschreibung, Munich, 1969.
Öffentlichkeit und Erfahrung. Zur Organisationsanalyse bürgerlicher und proletarischer öffentlichkeit, with Oskar Negt, Frankfurt, 1972.
Filmwirtschaft in der Bundesrepublik Deutschland und in Europa. Götterdämmerung in Raten, with Florian Hopf and Michael Dost, Munich, 1973.
Lernprozesse mit tödlichem Ausgang, Frankfurt, 1973.
Gelegenheitsarbeit einer Sklavin. Zur realistischen Methode, Frankfurt, 1975.
Neue Erzählungen. Hefte 1-18 "Unheimlichkeit der Zeit," Frankfurt, 1977.

Alexander Kluge directing *Abschied von Gestern*

Die Patriotin, Frankfurt, 1979.
Geschichte und Eigensinn, with Oskar Negt, 1982.
Die Macht der Gefühle, Frankfurt, 1984.
Der Angriff de Gegenwart auf die übrige zeit, Frankfurt, 1985.
Theodor Fontane, Heinrich von Kleist und Anna Wilde: Zur Grammatik der Zeit, K. Wagenbach, 1987.
Public Sphere and Experience: Toward an Analysis of the Bourgeois and Proletarian Public Sphere, with Oskar Negt, University of Minnesota Press, 1993.
Ich Schulde der Welt einen Toten: Gesprache, Rotbuch Verlag, 1995.

By KLUGE: articles—

"Medienproduktion," in *Perspektiven der kommunalen Kulturpolitik,* edited by Hoffman and Hilmar, Frankfurt, 1974.
"KINO-Gespräch mit Alexander Kluge," interview with A. Meyer, in *KINO* (Berlin), May 1974.
Interview with J. Dawson, in *Film Comment* (New York), November/December 1974.
"Film ist das natürliche Tauschverhältnis der Arbeit...," interview with B. Steinborn, in *Filmfaust* (Frankfurt), December 1977.
"Das Theater der spezialisten, Kraut und Rüben," interview with M. Schaub, in *Cinema* (Zurich), May 1978.
"Kluge Issue" of *ZEIT Magazin,* 9 March 1979.
"*Die Patriotin*: Entstehungsgeschichte—Inhalt," in *Filmkritik* (Munich), November 1979.
"Eine realistische Haltung müsste der Zuschauer haben, müsste ich jaben, müsste der Film Haben," with R. Frey, in *Filmfaust* (Frankfurt), November 1980.
"On Film and the Public Sphere," in *New German Critique,* Fall 1981-Winter 1982.
Interviews with B. Steinborn in *Filmfaust* (Frankfurt), February/March 1982 and February/March 1983.
"Zum Unterschied von Machtbar und Gewalttatig: Die Macht der Bewusstseinsindustrie und das Schicksal Unserer Offentlichkeit," in *Merkur: Deutsche Zeitschrift fur Europaisches Denken,* April 1984.
"Das Schicksal und Sei ne Gegengeschichten: Zu Zwei Textstellen aus Opern," in *Merkur: Deutsche Zeitschrift fur Europaisches Denken,* September 1984.
"Symposium on Homelessness," in *If You Lived Here: The City in Art, Theory, and Social Activism,* Bay Press, 1991.
"Film Digression," in *Writing in the Film Age: Essays by Contemporary Novelists,* University of Colorado Press, 1991.
"Resurrection," in *Art from the Ashes: A Holocaust Anthology,* Oxford University Press, 1995.

ON KLUGE: books—

Buselmeier, M., *In Gefahr und grösster Not bringt der Mittelweg den Tod. Zur Operativität bei Alexander Kluge,* Heidelberg, 1975.
Gregor, Ulrich, and others, *Herzog, Kluge, Straub,* Munich, 1976.
Kötz, M., and P. Höhe, *Sinnlichkeit des Zusammenhangs, Zur Filmstrategie Alexander Kluges,* Frankfurt, 1979.
Lewandowski, Rainer, *Alexander Kluge,* Munich, 1980.
Sandford, John, *The New German Cinema,* Totowa, New Jersey, 1980.
Franklin, James, *New German Cinema: From Oberhausen to Hamburg,* Boston, 1983.
Phillips, Klaus, *New German Filmmakers: From Oberhausen through the 1970s,* New York, 1984.
Carp, Stefanie, *Kriegsgeschichten: Zum Werk Alexander Kluges,* Munich, 1987.
Alexander Kluge: A Retrospective, Goethe Institute, 1988.
O'Kane, John Russell, *Film and Cultural Politics after the Avantgarde,* University of Minnesota, 1988.
Rentschler, Eric, *West German Filmmakers on Film: Visions and Voices,* New York, 1988.
Elsaesser, Thomas, *New German Cinema: A History,* London, 1989.
Gnam, Andrea, *Positionen der Wunschokonomie: Das Asthetische Textmodell Alexander Kluges und seine Philosophischen Voraussetzungen,* P. Lang, 1989.
Kaes, Anton. *From 'Hitler' to 'Heimat': The Return of History as Film,* Harvard University Press, 1989.
Lutze, Peter-Charles, *The Last Modernist: The Film and Television Work of Alexander Kluge,* University of Wisconsin-Madison, 1991.
Steckel, Gerd, *The Empty Space in Between: Alexander Kluge's Texts and Films Between the Traditions of Enlightenment and Romantic Discourses,* University of Minnesota, 1992.
Gruneis, Olaf, *Schauspielerische Darstellung in Filmen Alexander Kluges: Zur Ideologiekritik des Schauspielens im Film,* Die Blaue Eule, 1994.
Pavsek, Christopher Paul, *The Utopia of Film: The Critical Theory and Films of Alexander Kluge,* Duke University, 1994.
Fehrenbach, Heide, *Cinema in Democratizing Germany: Reconstructing National Identity After Hitler,* North Carolina University Press, 1995.
Huyssen, Andreas, *Twilight Memories: Marking Time in a Culture of Amnesia,* Routledge, 1995.

On KLUGE: articles—

"Kluge Issue" of *Filmkritik* (Munich), December 1976.
Moeller, H. B., and C. Springer, "Directed Change in the Young German Film: Alexander Kluge and Artists under the Big Top: Perplexed," in *Wide Angle* (Athens, Ohio), vol .2, no. 1, 1978.
Bruck, J., "Kluge's Antagonistic Concept of Realism," in *Australian Journal of Screen Theory* (Kensington, New South Wales), no. 13/14, 1983.
Tournès, A., "Kluge: L'intelligence du sentiment. Armer les entiments," in *Jeune Cinéma* (Paris), November 1983.
"Alexander Kluge," in *Film Dope* (London), January 1985.
Hansen, M., "The Stubborn Discourse: History and Storytelling in the Films of Alexander Kluge," in *Persistence of Vision* (Maspeth, New York), Fall 1985.
Steinborn, B., "Der Verfuhrerische Charme der Phantasie," in *Filmfaust* (Frankfurt), December 1985/January 1986.
Bowie, A., "Alexander Kluge: An Introduction," in *Cultural Critique,* Fall 1986.
Bruck, Jan, "Brecht's and Kluge's Aesthetics of Realism," in *Poetics: International Review for the Theory of Literature,* April 1988.
"Kluge Issue" of *October,* Fall 1988.
Huber, A, "Kluge Sites," in *Filmnews,* vol. 19, no. 9, 1989.
Rainer, Y., and Larsen, E., "We Are Demolition Artists," in *Independent,* June 1989.
"Special Issue on Alexander Kluge," *New German Critique,* Winter 1990.
Kaes, Anton, "History and Film: Public Memory in the Age of Electronic Dissemination," in *History and Memory,* no. 1, 1990.
Mantegna, Gianfranco, "Television and Its Shadow: New German Video: Kluge, Klier, Odenbach," in *Arts Magazine,* January 1991.
Bruck, J, "Kluge's Dilemmas," in *Filmnews,* vol. 22, no. 3, 1992.
Pavsek, Christopher, "The Storyteller in the Age of Mechanical Reproduction: Alexander Kluge's Reworking of Walter Benjamin," in *Found Object,* Fall 1993.
Staunton, Denis, "Vox Appeal," in *Guardian,* 8 November 1993.

* * *

Alexander Kluge, the chief ideologue of the new German cinema, is the author of various books in the areas of sociology, contemporary philosophy, and social theory. In 1962 he helped initiate, and was the spokesman for, the "Oberhausen Manifesto," in which "Das Opas Kino" ("grandpa's cinema") was declared dead.

At the same time Kluge published his first book, *Lebensläufe,* a collection of stories that presented a comprehensive cross-section of contemporary life along with its deeply rooted historical causes. His method is grounded in a rich and representative mosaic of sources: fiction, public records and reports, essays, actual occurrences, news, quotations, observations, ideas, and free associations. The method is used by Kluge as a principle of construction in his best films, such as *Abschied von gestern, Die Artisten in der Zirkuskuppel: ratlos, In Gefahr und grösster Not bringt der Mittelweg den Tod,* and in the series of collective films: *Deutschland im Herbst, Der Kandidat,* and *Krieg und Frieden.* The theme of war, in particular the Second World War, appears in all his works.

Kluge views filmmaking as another form of writing since it essentially continues the recording of his participation in the development of society and in everyday life. His unifying creative trait could be called verbal concentration, or image concentration. His filmic activity is a living extension of his comprehensive epistemological and sociological researches, which he has published, together with Oskar Negt (associated with the "Frankfurt School" of Adorno and Horkheimer), as *Öffentlichkeit und Erfahrung* (1972) and *Geschichte und Eigensinn* (1982).

Kluge's films probe reality—not by way of the fantastic fictions of Fassbinder, or film school pictures as with Wenders—but through establishing oppositions and connections between facts, artifacts, reflections, and bits of performance. The protagonists of his feature films are mostly women who seek to grasp and come to terms with their experiences. For the sake of continuity these women are played either by Alexandra Kluge, his sister, or by Hannelore Hoger. They move through the jungle of contemporary life, watching and witnessing, suffering and fighting. The director mirrors their experiences.

As a filmmaker, Kluge is unique, but not isolated. The three collective films, which together with Volker Schlöndorff, Fassbinder, Stephan Aust, and others he has devoted to the most pressing contemporary events, are something new and original in the history of world cinema. Without Kluge these would be inconceivable, since it is he who pulls together and organizes, aesthetically and ideologically, the fragments filmed by the others. He creates film forms and image structures to transform the various narrative modes and artistic conceptions into a new, conscious, mobilized art of cinema, free of fantasy. This cinema is not only non-traditional, but conveys a socio-historical content.

Without Kluge a new German cinema would be scarcely conceivable, since creative inspiration needs to be supported by a strong film-political foundation. It is thanks to him, above all, that film was officially promoted in the Federal Republic, and that film in Germany has been taken seriously in the last two decades. An untiring fighter for the interests of his colleagues, Kluge gets involved whenever the fate of the new German cinema is at stake.

Since the late 1980s, Kluge has become involved in the production of alternative programming for German television. Like the overtly political aims of his filmmaking, Kluge hopes that his efforts in the television industry will help to assemble and sustain a public sphere where open critical discourse concerning German and European politics may occur. Kluge, by means of his "Development Company for Television Producers," has been instrumental in arranging for magazines such as *Der Spiegel* and *Stern* to purchase air time on German commercial television in order for each of them to produce and broadcast independent news programs. It is Kluge's hope that "the complete editorial independence" of these productions will "offer diversity" on television, a medium that typically seeks, in formal and thematic ways, to deny the existence of a heterogeneous viewing audience. In a 1988 interview Kluge remarked: "You only need one percent of alternative television, of calmness within the television set. If you have it, people will accept that this TV world isn't the only one."

In addition to his efforts in television, Kluge recently co-authored another book with Oskar Negt, *Public Sphere and Experience: Toward an Analysis of the Bourgeois Public and Proletarian Public Sphere* (1993), in which he continues his interrogations of late-twentieth-century culture. Indeed, the proliferation of articles, books, and dissertations which have appeared in recent years examining Kluge's artistic and theoretical contributions suggest his impact on several cultural fronts. Whether on the screen or the page, the accomplishments of Alexander Kluge continue to distinguish him as a figure sincerely committed to social and political change.

—Maria Racheva, updated by Kevin J. Costa

KOBAYASHI, Masaki

Nationality: Japanese. **Born:** Hokkaido, 4 February 1916. **Education:** Educated in Oriental art at Waseda University, Tokyo, 1933-41. **Military Service:** Drafted into military service, served in Manchuria, 1942-44; following his refusal to be promoted above rank of private as expression of opposition to conduct of war, transferred to Ryukyu Islands, 1944, then interned in detention camp on Okinawa. **Career:** Assistant at Shochiku's Ofuna studios for 8 months prior to military service, 1941; returned to Shochiku, 1946; assistant director on staff of Keisuke Kinoshita, 1947-52; directed first film, 1952. **Awards:** Recipient, Special Jury Prizes, Cannes Festival, for *Seppuku,* 1963, and for *Kwaidan,* 1965.

Films as Director:

1952 *Musuko no seishun* (*My Sons' Youth*)
1953 *Magokoro* (*Sincerity*; *Sincere Heart*)
1954 *Mittsu no ai* (*Three Loves*) (+ sc); *Kono hiroi sora no dokoka ni* (*Somewhere under the Broad Sky*)
1955 *Uruwashiki saigetsu* (*Beautiful Days*)
1956 *Kabe atsuki heya* (*The Thick-Walled Room*) (completed 1953); *Izumi* (*The Spring*; *The Fountainhead*); *Anata kaimasu* (*I'll Buy You*)
1957 *Kuroi kawa* (*Black River*)
1959 ***Ningen no joken I*** (*The Human Condition Part I: No Greater Love*) (+ co-sc); ***Ningen no joken II*** (*The Human Condition Part II: Road to Eternity*) (+ co-sc)
1961 ***Ningen no joken III*** (*The Human Condition Part III: A Soldier's Prayer*) (+ co-sc)
1962 *Karami-ai* (*The Entanglement*; *The Inheritance*); ***Seppuku*** (*Harakiri*)
1964 ***Kwaidan*** (*Kaidan*)
1967 *Joiuchi* (*Rebellion*)
1968 *Nihon no seishun* (*The Youth of Japan*; *Hymn to a Tired Man*)
1971 *Inochi bo ni furo* (*Inn of Evil*; *At the Risk of My Life*)
1975 *Kaseki* (*Fossils*) (originally made for TV as 8-part series)
1983 *Tokyo saiban* (*The Tokyo Trials*) (documentary)
1985 *Shokutaku no nai ie* (*The Empty Table*)

Publications

By KOBAYASHI: articles—

"Harakiri, Kobayashi, Humanism," interview with James Silke, in *Cinema* (Beverly Hills), June/July 1963.
"Cinq japonais en quête de films: Masaki Kobayashi," interview with Max Tessier, in *Ecran* (Paris), March 1972.
Interview with Joan Mellen, in *Voices from the Japanese Cinema,* New York, 1975.
Interview with A. Tournès, in *Jeune Cinéma* (Paris), April 1985.

On KOBAYASHI: books—

Bock, Audie, *Japanese Film Directors,* New York, 1978; revised edition, Tokyo, 1985.
Blouin, Claude R., *Le Chemin détourné: Essai sur Kobayashi et le cinéma Japonais,* Quebec, 1982.

On KOBAYASHI: articles—

Richie, Donald, "The Younger Talents," in *Sight and Sound* (London), Spring 1960.
Iwabuchi, M., "Kobayashi's Trilogy," in *Film Culture* (New York), Spring 1962.
Esnault, Philippe, "L'Astre japonais," in *Image et Son* (Paris), February 1969.
Kobayashi Section of *Cinéma Québec* (Montreal), February/March 1974.
Tucker, Richard, "Masaki Kobayashi," in *International Film Guide 1977,* London, 1976.
"Masaki Kobayashi," in *Film Dope* (London), January 1985.
Gillett, John, "Masaki Kobayashi: Power and Spectacle," in *National Film Theatre Booklet* (London), July 1990.

* * *

The dilemma of the dissenter—the individual who finds himself irrevocably at odds with his society—is the overriding preoccupation of Kobayashi's films, and one which stems directly from his own experience. In 1942, only months after starting his career at Shochiku studios, Kobayashi was drafted into the Imperial Japanese Army and sent to Manchuria. A reluctant conscript, he refused promotion above the rank of private and was later a prisoner of war. Released in 1946, he returned to filmmaking, becoming assistant to Keisuke Kinoshita, whose flair for lyrical composition clearly influenced Kobayashi's own style—though he succeeded, fortunately, in shaking off the older director's penchant for excessive sentimentality.

Initially, Kobayashi's concern with social justice, and the clash between society and the individual, expressed itself in direct treatment of specific current issues: war criminals in *Kabe atsuki heya*—a subject

Masaki Kobayashi: *Seppuku*

so sensitive that the film's release was delayed three years; corruption in sport in *Anata kaimasu*; and, in *Kuroi kawa,* organized crime and prostitution rampant around U. S. bases in Japan. This phase of Kobayashi's career culminated in his towering three-part, nine-hour epic, *Ningen no joken,* a powerful and moving indictment of systematized brutality inherent in a militaristic society.

The ordeal of the pacifist Kaji, hero of *Ningen no joken* (played by Tatsuya Nakadai, Kobayashi's favorite actor), closely parallels the director's own experiences during the war. Kaji is the archetypal Kobayashi hero, who protests, struggles, and is finally killed by an oppressive and inhumane system. His death changes nothing and will not even be recorded; yet the mere fact of it stands as an assertion of indomitable humanity. Similarly, the heroes of Kobayashi's two finest films, *Seppuku* and *Joiuchi,* revolt, make their stand, and die—to no apparent avail. In these films Kobayashi turned the conventions of the *jidai-geki* (period movie) genre to his own ends, using historical settings to universalize his focus on the dissident individual. The masterly blend of style and content, with the unbending ritual of samurai convention perfectly matched by cool, reticent camera movement and elegantly geometric composition, marks in these two films the peak of Kobayashi's art.

By Japanese standards, Kobayashi has made few films, working slowly and painstakingly with careful attention to detail. From *Seppuku* onwards, an increasing concern with formal beauty has characterized his work, most notably in *Kaidan.* This film, based on four of Lafcadio Hearn's ghost stories, carried for once no social message, but developed a strikingly original use of color and exquisitely stylized visual composition.

The crisis that overtook Japanese cinema in the late 1960s hit Kobayashi's career especially hard. His uncompromising seriousness of purpose and the measured cadences of his style held little appeal for an industry geared increasingly to flashy exploitation movies. Few of his projects came to fruition, and *Kaseki* had to be made first for television, a medium he dislikes. He refused to watch the eight-hour TV transmission, regarding it merely as rough footage for his 213-minute cinema version.

Kaseki, in which a middle-aged businessman confronts the prospect of incurable cancer, seemed to mark a move away from Kobayashi's wider social concerns—as did the far weaker *Moeru aki. Tokyo saiban,* though, found him back on more characteristic ground. A *tour-de-force* of editing, it used archive and newsreel footage to make compelling drama of the Allied trials of Japanese wartime leaders. And with

Shokutaku no nai ie, Kobayashi returned to his central preoccupation, with a principled individual (Nakadai once again) standing out against daunting social pressures. Though lacking the impact of *Ningen no joken* or *Seppuku,* it evinced his undiminished skill in exploiting the tension between outward formality and inner turmoil and reaffirmed the austere integrity that informs all his work.

—Philip Kemp

KONCHALOVSKY, Andrei *See* **MIKHALKOV-KONCHALOVSKY, Andrei**

KOPPLE, Barbara

Nationality: American. **Born:** New York City, 30 July 1946. **Education:** Graduated from Northeastern University with degree in psychology. **Career:** Assisted documentary filmmakers as an editor, sound recordist, and camerawoman; spent four years in coal fields of Harlan County, Kentucky, recording struggles of unionized miners for documentary *Harlan County, U.S.A.,* 1972-76. **Awards:** Critic's Choice Award, Cannes Film Festival, 1972, for *Winter Soldier;* Academy Award for Best Feature Documentary, designation by Congress as American Film Classic in National Film Registry, Blue Ribbon, Grierson Award, and Emily Award at the American Film Festival, all 1977, all for *Harlan County, U.S.A.;* Christopher Award, 1977; Mademoiselle Award, 1977; National Endowment for the Arts Fellowships, 1970s and 1980s; Blue Ribbon, American Film and Video Festival, 1990, for *Out of Darkness;* Academy Award for Best Feature Documentary, Grand Jury Prize, Audience Award, and Filmmaker's Trophy at the Sundance Film Festival, Golden Gate Award at the San Francisco International Film Festival, Blue Ribbon at the American Film and Video Festival, Outstanding Achievement from the International Documentary Association, Los Angeles Film Critics Award, and National Society of Film Critics Award, all 1991, all for *American Dream;* Best Feature Documentary, Director's Guild of America, 1992, for *American Dream;* Metro Labor Council Award, 1992; Cine Golden Eagle, 1992; John Simon Guggenheim Memorial Foundation Fellowship, 1992; Dorothy Arzner Directing Award, Women in Film, 1993; Outstanding Directorial Achievement from Director's Guild of America, Alfred I. duPont-Columbia University Award, and Best Special Award from Television Critics Association, all 1993, all for *Fallen Champ.*

Films as Director:

1972 *Winter Soldier* (co-d)
1976 *Harlan County, U.S.A.* (+ sound, pr)
1981 *No Nukes* (co-d)
1983 *Keeping On* (+ exec pr)
1989 *Civil Rights: The Struggle Continues* (+ pr)
1990 *Out of Darkness* (co-d)
1991 *American Dream* (+ sound, co-pr)
1992 *Beyond JFK: The Question of Conspiracy* (co-d); *Locked Out: Ravenswood*
1993 *Fallen Champ: The Untold Story of Mike Tyson* (+ pr)
1994 *Century of Women* (segment d)
1995 *Prisoners of Hope* (co-d)

Other Films:

1974 *Richard III* (pr, sound, ed)
1986 *Hurricane Irene* (pr)
1995 *Nails* (segment pr)

Publications

On KOPPLE: books—

Rosenthal, Alan, *The Documentary Conscience: A Casebook in Film Making,* University of California Press, 1980.
Shulevitz, Judith, *The Women's Companion to International Films,* edited by Annette Kuhn and Susannah Radstone, University of California Press, 1994.

On KOPPLE: articles—

Dunning, Jennifer, "A Woman Film Maker in the Coal Fields," in *New York Times,* 15 October 1976.
Eder, Richard, "Film Festival: *Harlan County,*" in *New York Times,* 15 October 1976.
Verr (A. Verrill), "*Harlan County, U.S.A.,*" in *Variety,* 20 October 1976.
Maslin, J., "Rich Vein," in *Newsweek,* 1 November 1976.
"Cinema 5's Probable *Harlan County* Deal," in *Variety,* 15 December 1976.
Biskind, Peter, "*Harlan County, U.S.A.:* The Miners' Struggle," in *Jump Cut,* no. 14, 1977.
Kleinhans, Chuck, "Barbara Kopple Interview," in *Jump Cut,* no. 14, 1977.
Kaplan, E. A., "*Harlan County, U.S.A.:* The Documentary Form," in *Jump Cut,* no. 15, 1977.
Paramentier, Ernest, "*Harlan County, U.S.A.,*" in *FilmFacts,* vol. 20, no. 12, 1977.
Mills, N., "*Harlan County, U.S.A.,*" in *Dissent,* vol. 24, no. 3, 1977.
Howe, I., "Another View of *Harlan County, U.S.A.,*" in *Dissent,* vol. 24, no. 3, 1977.
Sarris, Andrew, "Films in Focus: In the Winter of His Discontent," in *Village Voice,* 31 January 1977.
Kauffmann, Stanley, "Stanley Kauffmann on Films: Importances," in *New Republic,* 12 February 1977.
Blake, R. "The Reel-y Real," in *America,* 12 February 1977.
Haleff, M., "*Harlan County, U.S.A.,*" in *Film Bulletin,* March 1977.
Westerbeck, C. L., Jr., "Women's Work," in *Commonweal,* 4 March 1977.
McCreadie, M., "*Harlan County, U.S.A.,*" in *Films in Review,* April 1977.
McNally, Judith, "The Making of *Harlan County, U.S.A.,*" in *Filmmakers Newsletter,* May 1977.
Carcassonne, P., "*Harlan County, U.S.A.,*" in *Cinematographe,* June 1977.
Giraud, T., "*Harlan County, U.S.A.,*" in *Cahiers du Cinema,* July 1977.
Henry, M., "*Harlan County, U.S.A.,*" in *Positif,* July/August 1977.
Crowdus, Gary, "Filming in Harlan (Interviews with Barbara Kopple and Hart Perry)," in *Cineaste,* Summer 1977.
Jones, E. S., "*Harlan County U.S.A.,*" in *Film News,* Summer 1977.
Aghed, J., "Entretien avec Barbara Kopple," in *Positif,* October 1977.
Bovier-Lapierre, E., "*Harlan County, U.S.A.,*" in *Cinematographe,* October 1977.
Martin, M., "Entretien avec Barbara Kopple," in *Ecran,* 15 October 1977.
Le Peron, S., and Skorecki, L., "Entretien avec Barbara Kopple," in *Cahiers du Cinema,* November 1977.
Thirard, P. L., "*Harlan County, U.S.A.,*" in *Positif,* November 1977.

Grelier, R., "*Harlan County, U.S.A.*," in *Revue du Cinema,* November 1977.
Odebrant, P., and Ohlsson, J., "*Harlan County, U.S.A.*," in *Chaplin,* vol. 20, 1978.
Vrdlovec, Z., "Harlanski revir," in *Ekran,* vol. 3, 1978.
Heijs, J., "*Harlan County, U.S.A.*," in *Skrien,* May 1978.
Forbes, J., "*Harlan County, U.S.A.*," in *Sight and Sound,* Summer 1978.
Coleman, J., "Crying Out Loud," in *New Statesman,* 2 June 1978.
King, Noel, "Recent 'Political' Documentary: Notes on *Union Maids* and *Harlan County, U.S.A.*," in *Screen,* vol. 22, 1981.
Ferrario, D., "*Harlan County, U.S.A.* di Barbara Kopple," in *Cineforum,* January 1981.
O'Connor, J. J., "TV: *Keeping On,* a Drama of Life in a Mill Town," in *New York Times,* 8 September 1983.
McCall, A., and A. Tyndall, "Sixteen Working Statements: Notes from Work on a Film in Progress," in *Millennium,* Spring/Summer 1978.
Hoberman, J., "The Non-Hollywood Hustle," in *American Film,* October 1980.
Kaplan, E. A., "Theories and Strategies of the Feminist Documentary," in *Millennium,* Fall 1982/Winter 1983.
Penley, Constance, "Documentary/Documentation," in *Camera Obscura* Spring/Summer 1985.
Sorensen, S., "Dokumentarisme," in *Film & Kino,* no. 4, 1987.
Di Mattia, J., "Of Politics and Passion," in *International Documentary,* Winter 1990/91.
Quindlen, Anna, "Our Bad Dreams," in *New York Times,* 21 October 1990.
Crowdus, Gary, "*American Dream* (Interview)," in *Cineaste,* vol. 18, no. 4, 1991.
Rossi, U., "Per una comunicazione attiva," and "Due scioperi da Oscar nel cinema off Hollywood," in *Cineforum,* September 1991.
Fink, Leon, "Motion Picture Review: *American Dream,*" in *Journal of American History,* December 1991.
Legiardi-Laura, Roland, "Barbara Kopple," in *BOMB,* Winter 1992.
Weinberg, Joel, "Union Maid," in *New York,* 9 March 1992.
Rule, S., "In Film, a Career of Trying to Balance the Inequalities of Life," in *New York Times,* 24 March 1992.
Rafferty, Terrence, "No Man's Land," in *New Yorker,* 23 March 1992.
Brown, G., "O Say Can You See?," in *Village Voice,* 24 March 1992.
Klawans, Stuart, "*American Dream,*" in *Nation,* 30 March 1992.
Kelleher, E., "Kopple's Oscar-Winning *Dream* Explores Harsh Labor Dispute," in *Film Journal,* April 1992.
Meusel, M., "*American Dream,*" in *Film Journal,* April 1992.
Linlield, Susie, "Barbara Kopple," in *Premiere,* April 1992.
Schickel, Richard, "Which Side Are You On?," in *Time,* 6 April 1992.
Powers, John, "Food for Thought," in *New York,* 13 April 1992.
Roberts, S., "*American Dream* Charts Labor's Loss," in *New York Times,* May 1992.
Karp, A., "*American Dream,*" in *Box Office,* May 1992.
Meyers, Kate, "*American* Chronicle: Barbara Kopple," in *Entertainment Weekly,* 1 May 1992.
Winokur, L.A., "Barbara Kopple (Interview)," in *Progressive,* November 1992.
Tucker, Ken, "Heavyweight *Champ,*" in *Entertainment Weekly,* February 1993.
Meyers, Kate, "Barbara Kopple's KO Punch," in *Entertainment Weekly,* 12 February 1993.
Zoglin, Richard, "*Fallen Champ,*" in *Time,* 15 February 1993.
Brock, Pope, "Barbara Kopple: A Firebrand Documentary Filmmaker Moves to TV to Tackle Her Latest Subject: Iron Mike Tyson," in *People Weekly,* 15 February 1993.
Christgau, Georgia, "The Spirit of Resistance and the Second Line," in *Labor History,* Winter 1993.
Feaster, Felicia, "*Fallen Champ,*" in *Film Quarterly,* Winter 1993/94.
Espen, Hal, "The Documentarians," in *New Yorker,* 21 March 1994.
Orvell, Miles, "Documentary and the Power of Interrogation: *American Dream* and *Roger and Me,*" in *Film Quarterly,* Winter 1994/95.

* * *

Barbara Kopple got her start in film working for Albert and David Maysles. In order to make films, she decided it was necessary to learn all aspects of their production. At the Maysles' studio, she became familiar with the craft—from getting coffee to reconstituting trims, no job was trivialized. She became an assistant editor for the Maysles and began working as editor and sound recordist for other producers.

After gaining enough experience and confidence, Kopple decided it was time to direct her own films. Her crews consisted of a camera operator and sound recordist, of which she was the sound recordist. As with most documentaries, such a small crew was an economic necessity, but it also enhanced the filmmaker's intimacy with the subject. According to Kopple, recording sound brought her "deeper into what was happening"; she was "hearing" and participating in the filmic process on multiple levels. As a technician, interviewer, and director, she is both observer and participant. In supervising post-production she becomes the storyteller.

Most of Kopple's independent films require her constant attention to fundraising. Winning the Academy Award for Best Feature-length Documentary for *Harlan County, U.S.A.* did not ensure funds for another project. While shooting *American Dream,* rather than process film, she bought freezers to store the exposed rolls until money could be raised for lab expenses. Kopple thinks "small crews are great, but sometimes it's better to have money and hire a sound recordist."

Kopple was influenced by the Maysles brothers and D. A. Pennebaker, exponents of Direct Cinema. Her method of filmmaking, though owing much to her predecessors, is very much a result of form following content. Though her style may differ slightly from film to film because of the organic strategy she employs for each story, there is an overriding consistency to her work. She gives those not normally heard a voice—the audience of most films are her subjects. Her documentaries have become emblematic of social change films.

Most of Kopple's films have no simple beginning—we enter a story that has already begun. The audience may know the outcome, yet we are engaged in the suspense of how we arrived at that point. Her films examine the antecedents of power relationships, how people are affected, respond, and make sense of their own actions and those of others. Though the chronology of a film may shift through history, intercutting past events with the contemporary, we experience the action in the present tense. Her endings are never clean, sometimes with story updates occurring under the end credits. Kopple's films create a discourse that cuts through historical time in an attempt to understand where we are today.

Kopple's films create such intimacy of identity that we feel sure she lived the experience. However, *Harlan County, U.S.A.* took only thirteen months to make. After reading about the death of Joseph Yablonski, his wife, and daughter, and the formation of Miners for Democracy, she decided to make the film and secured a $10,000 loan from Tom Brandon. The film develops small stories to contextualize a larger narrative.

The Consolidation Coal Mannington Mine Disaster of 1968, the Yablonski family murder in 1970, and the union election places the Harlan strike in a national relationship. History is seen as a growing organism and montage moves the discourse through time. John L. Lewis is cut against Carl Horn, president of Duke Power, as though they were engaged in debate. Yet the film is faithful to and references the chronology of the Harlan strike.

Kopple uses music to remind the audience of our folk storytelling tradition. In geographically isolated regions such as Harlan, music has been a way of sharing experience, creating a unifying identity. In the film music functions to evoke cultural memory and meaning. Though we may be thousands of miles from Harlan, we share a common heritage of labor struggle. The voice of the film is the voice of many. There is no one hero, but a common chorus of purpose uniting gender and race.

"Which Side Are You On" functions as *Harlan County, U.S.A.*'s theme song. The film is about choice. Kopple is asked by Duke Power's thugs to identify herself; there is no question of her allegiance. Kopple thinks that being a woman may have contributed to the local police letting her film in jail. They did not consider her a threat. There is no question that the film threatened Duke Power; the camera is beaten. And the film is very much about violence: everyday life seems harsh, and the strike heightens the brutality. The audience must look at the conflict's viscera—pieces of lung and brains in the dirt—and ultimately the death of striker Lawrence Jones. The strike may be won, but it is a momentary victory. The struggle continues without end through the credits.

Kopple continues themes developed in *Harlan County, U.S.A.* in *American Dream,* but the story and issues have become more complicated. Again she films a strike, a labor crisis, and documents the crisis of labor. At issue is whether the union movement will be destroyed by Reaganism, or whether it will transform and once again play an active role in the American drama. The film follows Local P-9 of the United Food and Commercial Workers International Union as the rank and file struggles with the International leadership and dissidents among its own membership, as well as labor's traditional antagonist, in this case Hormel and Company.

Again a strike is the motivating force for communality. But because labor is divided—brother pitted against brother—*American Dream* evokes the heartbreak of the Civil War. The labor movement has lost its innocence, yet Local P-9 seems naive. They lack a historical perspective to labor negotiations. When the strike is going well they are enthusiastic, but they succumb to moral self-righteousness when frustrated. Recognizing stasis in the International, they hire an outside labor consultant, Ray Rogers of "Corporate Campaign," whose strategy is to effect economic distress on Hormel, build solidarity with other locals, and make the strike "newsworthy." He packages the strike for television, but we are not sure which side of the camera he prefers to be on; as he seems to be playing a role from *Norma Rae* (Rogers was the organizer at J. P. Stevens). Authenticity becomes problematic.

As in *Harlan County, U.S.A.,* there is no doubt that Kopple's camera is on the side of labor. However, in *American Dream* the camera re-positions itself to show the conflicting points-of-view within the labor movement. The camera is with Local P-9 leader Jim Guyette, then with Lewie Anderson, director of the International Union's Meatpacking Division. It is in a car with dissidents as they defy the Local and go back to work. But the camera does not cross the picket line with them; it watches the dissidents go through the gate from the vantage point of the strikers.

In *American Dream,* Kopple utilizes various documentary styles. Direct Cinema techniques are combined with conventional sit-down interviews and narration. The voice of the film is that of labor, but unlike *Harlan County, U.S.A., American Dream* employs narration. Guyette and Anderson provide commentary for their own stories. And Kopple personally announces voice-over information necessary to move the story forward. As the film proceeds to its end, we are aware of a distance and dislocation of voice and character not experienced in *Harlan County, U.S.A.* The grand narrative of American labor is fractured, and we wonder if the Dream can ever be reconstructed. The film ends with an *American Graffiti*-style montage of character updates. But it is the 1980s, and although there may be personal change, one story remains the same: company profits continue to grow while workers are paid less.

Kopple thinks of herself as a filmmaker of traditional dramas, examining how people behave in moments of crisis and change. Her films question the construct of the "American Dream" and the price we pay in its attainment; how this "Dream" influences and informs our collective and individual identity and what we value; and how we are equipped to deal with and interpret issues of justice and change.

—Judy Hoffman

KORDA, Alexander

Nationality: Hungarian/British. **Born:** Sándor László Kellner in Puszta Turpósztó, Hungary, 16 September 1893; adopted surname Korda, from journalistic pseudonym "Sursum Corda" (meaning "lift up your hearts"), 1910. **Education:** Attended schools in Kisújszállás, Mezötúr, and Budapest, until 1909. **Family:** Married 1) Maria Farkas (actress Maria Corda), 1919 (divorced 1930), one son; 2) Merle Oberon, 1939 (divorced 1945); 3) Alexander Boycun, 1953. **Career:** Worked at Pathé studios, Paris, 1911; title writer and secretary, Pictograph films, Budapest, and founder of film journal *Pesti mozi,* 1912; directed first film, 1914; formed Corvin production company with Miklós Pásztory, built studio near Budapest, 1917; arrested under Horthy regime, fled to Vienna, 1919; formed Corda Film Consortium, 1920 (dissolved 1922); formed Korda-Films, Berlin, 1923; with wife, contracted to First National, Hollywood, 1927; hired by Paramount French subsidiary, 1930; moved to British Paramount, London, 1931; founder, London Films, 1932; built Denham Studios, also made partner in United Artists, 1935 (sold interest, 1944); lost control of Denham Studios, 1938; formed Alexander Korda Productions, retained position as head of London Films, 1939; based in Hollywood, 1940-43; entered partnership with MGM, 1943 (dissolved, 1946); reorganized London Films, bought controlling interest in British Lion (distributors), 1946; founder, British Film Academy (now British Academy of Film and Television Arts), 1947. **Awards:** Knighthood, 1942. **Died:** In London, 23 January 1956.

Films as Director:

1914 *A becsapott újságíró* (*The Duped Journalist*) (co-d); *Tutyu és Totyo* (*Tutyu and Totyo*) (co-d)

1915 *Lyon Lea* (*Lea Lyon*) (co-d); *A tiszti kardbojt* (*The Officer's Swordknot*) (+ sc)

1916 *Fehér éjszakák* (*White Nights*) or *Fedora* (+ sc); *A nagymama* (*The Grandmother*) (+ sc); *Mesék az írógépröl* (*Tales of the Typewriter*) (+ sc); *A kétszívü férfi* (*The Man with Two Hearts*); *Az egymillió fontos bankó* (*The One Million Pound Note*) (+ sc); *Ciklámen* (*Cyclamen*); *Vergödö szívek* (*Struggling Hearts*); *A nevetö Szaszkia* (*The Laughing Saskia*); *Mágnás Miska* (*Miska the Magnate*)

1917 *Szent Péter esernyöje* (*St. Peter's Umbrella*) (+ pr); *A gólyakalifa* (*The Stork Caliph*) (+ pr); *Mágia* (*Magic*) (+ pr); *Harrison és Barrison* (*Harrison and Barrison*) (+ pr)

1918 *Faun* (+ pr); *Az aranyember* (*The Man with the Golden Touch*) (+ pr); *Mary Ann* (+ pr)

1919 *Ave Caesar!* (+ pr); *Fehér rózsa* (*White Rose*) (+ pr); *Yamata* (+ pr); *Se ki, se be* (*Neither In Nor Out*) (+ pr); *A 111-es* (*Number 111*) (+ pr)

1920 *Seine Majestät das Bettelkind* (*Prinz und Bettelknabe*; *The Prince and the Pauper*)

Alexander Korda

1922 *Heeren der Meere* (*Masters of the Sea*); *Eine Versunkene Welt* (*Die Tragödie eines Verschollenen Fürstensohnes*) (*A Vanished World*); *Samson und Delilah* (*Samson and Delilah*) (+ pr)
1923 *Das unbekannte Morgen* (*The Unknown Tomorrow*) (+ pr)
1924 *Jedermanns Frau* (*Jedermanns Weib*) (*Everybody's Woman*) (+ pr); *Tragödie im Hause Habsburg* (*Das Drama von Mayerling*) (*Tragedy in the House of Hapsburg*) (+ pr)
1925 *Der Tänzer meiner Frau* (*Dancing Mad*)
1926 *Madame wünscht keine Kinder* (*Madame Wants No Children*)
1927 *Eine Dubarry von heute* (*A Modern Dubarry*); *The Stolen Bride*; *The Private Life of Helen of Troy*
1928 *Yellow Lily*; *Night Watch*
1929 *Love and the Devil*; *The Squall*; *Her Private Life*
1930 *Lilies of the Field*; *Women Everywhere*; *The Princess and the Plumber*
1931 *Die Manner um Lucie* (+ pr); *Rive Gauche* (French version of *Die Manner um Lucie*) (+ pr); *Marius; Zum Goldenen Anker* (German version of *Marius*)
1932 *Service for Ladies* (*Reserved for Ladies*) (+ pr)
1933 *Wedding Rehearsal* (+ pr); ***The Private Life of Henry VIII*** (+ pr); *The Girl from Maxim's* (+ co-pr)
1934 *La Dame de Chez Maxim* (French version) (+ pr); *The Private Life of Don Juan* (+ pr)
1936 *Rembrandt* (+ pr)
1941 *That Hamilton Woman* (*Lady Hamilton*) (+ pr)
1945 *Perfect Strangers* (*Vacation from Marriage*) (+ pr)
1947 *An Ideal Husband* (+ pr)

Publications

On KORDA: books—

Balcon, Michael, and others, *Twenty Years of British Films, 1925-45,* London, 1947.
Brunel, Adrian, *Nice Work: The Story of Thirty Years in British Film Production,* London, 1949.
Tabori, Paul, *Alexander Korda,* London, 1959.
Cowie, Peter, *Korda,* in *Anthologie du Cinéma* no. 6, Paris, 1965.
Nemeskurty, István, *Word and Image: A History of the Hungarian Cinema,* Budapest, 1968.
Kulik, Karol, *Alexander Korda: The Man Who Could Work Miracles,* London, 1975.
Korda, Michael, *Charmed Lives: A Family Romance,* New York, 1979.

On KORDA: articles—

Watts, Stephen, "Alexander Korda and the International Film," in *Cinema Quarterly,* Autumn 1933.
Lejeune, C.A., "Alexander Korda: A Sketch," in *Sight and Sound* (London), Spring 1935.
Harman, Jympson, "'Alex': A Study of Korda," in *British Film Yearbook 1949-50,* London, 1949.
Price, Peter, "The Impresario Urge," in *Sight and Sound* (London), November 1950.
Campbell, Colin, "The Producer: Sir Alexander Korda," in *Sight and Sound* (London), Summer 1951.
Gilliat, Sidney, and others, "Sir Alexander Korda," in *Sight and Sound* (London), Spring 1956.
Richards, Jeffrey, "Korda's Empire: Politics and Films in *Sanders of the River, The Drum,* and *The Four Feathers,*" in *Australian Journal of Screen Theory* (Kensington, New South Wales), no. 5-6, 1980.
Taylor, John Russell, "Tales of the Hollywood Raj. Alexander Korda: Showman or Spy?," in *Films and Filming* (London), July 1983.
"Alexander Korda," in *Film Dope* (London), January 1985.
Street, Sarah, "Denham Studios: The Golden Jubilee of Korda's Folly," in *Sight and Sound* (London), Spring 1986.
Street, Sarah, "Alexander Korda, Prudential Assurance and British Film Finance in the 1930s," in *Historical Journal of Film, Radio and TV* (Abingdon, Oxon), October 1986.

On KORDA: films—

Vas, Robert, *The Golden Years of Alexander Korda,* BBC TV documentary, 1968.

* * *

Alexander Korda may be Britain's most controversial film figure, but there is no doubt that his name stands everywhere for the most splendid vision of cinema as it could be, if one had money and power. Both of these Korda had, although several times he was close to bankruptcy, living on pure Hungarian charm and know-how. He at least had a dream that came near reality on several occasions.

Korda had two younger brothers, Zoltan, who worked with him as a director, and Vincent, who was an art director; both were outstanding in their fields. Alexander worked as a journalist and film magazine editor before he directed his first film in Hungary in 1914. He had labored long in the cinematic fields of Vienna and Berlin when finally in 1926 his film production of *A Modern Dubarry* earned him a contract in Hollywood with First National, where his initial film was the extravagantly beautiful *The Private Life of Helen of Troy,* starring his wife Maria Corda as Helen. It brought him instant recognition. He directed four features starring Billie Dove (who should have played Helen of Troy for him): *The Stolen Bride, The Night Watch, The Yellow Lily,* and *Her Private Life,* a remake of Zoë Akins's play, which Corinne Griffith had filmed earlier under its stage title, *Declassé.* Korda also directed a sound feature starring Griffith, *Lilies of the Field.* Alexander Korda could soon write his own ticket.

He did just that in 1931, leaving Hollywood to return to England where he set up his own production company, London Film Productions. There he was almost fully occupied with production details, and only directed eight of the many films which his company produced. It was an exciting era for an ambitious producer like Korda. His company's product was so lavish that he seemed in a fair way not only to rival Hollywood but to surpass it. His first big success was *The Private Life of Henry VIII,* starring Charles Laughton as Henry and with Merle Oberon making her debut as the unfortunate Anne Boleyn. Korda then married Oberon and started to set the stage for her stardom. Hers was not the only career Korda established, for he had much to do with the film careers of Laurence Olivier, Vivian Leigh, Robert Donat, and Leslie Howard, among others. He was the power behind it all who set up financial deals for pictures that starred these actors.

While the pictures he directed, like *Rembrandt, That Hamilton Woman,* and *Vacation from Marriage,* were done in exquisite taste, Korda was also involved in the production of such pictures as *Catherine the Great, The Scarlet Pimpernel, Elephant Boy, The Ghost Goes West, Drums, The Four Feathers, The Thief of Bagdad, The Fallen Idol,* and *The Third Man.*

Three times Korda built and rebuilt his company, and the third time it was with national aid. Even after the Korda empire collapsed he was able to secure new financial alliances which allowed him to keep producing until his death in 1956. His name stood for glory, and when, after 1947, his name ceased to appear as part of the film credits, the lustre surrounding a London Films production vanished.

—DeWitt Bodeen

KOZINTSEV, Grigori

Nationality: Russian. **Born:** Kiev, 22 March 1905. **Education:** Gymnasium, Kiev; studied Art with Alexandra Exter, Kiev; Academy of Fine Arts, Petrograd, 1919. **Career:** Scenic artist, Lenin Theatre, Kiev, 1918; sent to Petrograd by Union of Art Workers of Kiev, 1919; founder, with Leonid Trauberg and Sergei Yutkevitch, The Factory of the Eccentric Actor (FEKS), 1921; with Trauberg, made first film, 1924; with Trauberg, prepared film on life of Karl Marx (unrealized), 1939-40. **Awards:** Stalin Prize for the Maxim Trilogy, 1941; Lenin Prize for *Hamlet,* 1965. **Died:** In Leningrad, 11 May 1973.

Films as Director:

1924 *Pokhozdeniya Oktyabrini* (*The Adventures of Octyabrina*) (co-d with Leonid Trauberg, co-sc)
1925 *Michki protiv Youdenitsa* (*Mishka against Yudenitch*) (co-d with Trauberg, co-sc)
1926 *Chyortovo Koleso* (*The Devil's Wheel*) (co-d with Trauberg); *Shinel* (*The Cloak*) (co-d with Trauberg)
1927 *Bratichka* (*Little Brother*) (co-d with Trauberg, co-sc); *S.V.D.* (*Soyuz Velikogo Dela*) (*The Club of the Big Deed*) (co-d with Trauberg)
1929 ***Novyi Vavilon*** (*The New Babylon*) (co-d with Trauberg)
1931 *Odna* (*Alone*) (co-d with Trauberg, co-sc)
1935 ***Yunost Maksima*** (*The Youth of Maxim*) (co-d with Trauberg, co-sc)
1937 ***Vozvrashcheniye Maksima*** (*The Return of Maxim*) (co-d with Trauberg, co-sc)
1939 ***Vyborgskaya storona*** (*The Vyborg Side*) (co-d with Trauberg, co-sc)
1945 *Prostiye Lyudi* (*Plain People*) (released in re-edited version 1956, which Kozintsev disowned) (co-d with Trauberg, co-sc)
1947 *Pirogov*
1953 *Belinski* (+ co-sc)
1957 *Don Quixote*
1963 *Hamlet* (+ sc)
1971 ***Korol Lir*** (*King Lear*) (+ sc)

Publications

By KOZINTSEV: books—

Shakespeare: Time and Conscience, New York, 1966.
Glubokij ekran, Moscow, 1971.
King Lear: The Space of Tragedy, Berkeley, California, 1977.

By KOZINTSEV: articles—

"Deep Screen," in *Sight and Sound* (London), Summer/Autumn 1959.

Grigori Kozintsev

"The Hamlet within Me," in *Films and Filming* (London), September 1962.
"Over the Parisiana," in *Sight and Sound* (London), Winter 1962/63.
"Prostrantsvo tragedii," in *Iskusstvo Kino* (Moscow), January, April, June, August, and November 1972, and January 1973.
"A Child of the Revolution," in *Cinema in Revolution,* edited by Luda and Jean Schnitzer, New York, 1973.
"Gogoliada," in *Iskusstvo Kino* (Moscow), May, June and July 1974.
"Iz pisem raznyh let," in *Iskusstvo Kino* (Moscow), May 1983.

On KOZINTSEV: books—

Leyda, Jay, *Kino,* London, 1960.
Verdone, Mario, and Barthelemy Amengual, *La Feks,* Paris, 1970.
Rapisarda, Giusi, editor, *La FEKS: Kozintsev e Trauberg,* Rome, 1975.
Christie, Ian, and John Gillett, *Futurism, Formalism, FEKS: Eccentrism and Soviet Cinema 1918-36,* London, 1978.
Leaming, Barbara, *Grigori Kozintsev,* Boston, 1980.
Christie, Ian, and Richard Taylor, editors, *The Film Factory: Russian and Soviet Cinema in Documents 1896-1939,* London, 1988.

On KOZINTSEV: articles—

"A Meeting with Grigori Kozintsev," in *Film* (London), Autumn 1967.
Barteneva, Yevgeniya, "One Day with *King Lear,*" in *Soviet Film* (Moscow), no. 9, 1969.
Yutkevitch, Sergei, "The Conscience of the King," in *Sight and Sound* (London), Autumn 1971.
"Director of the Year," in *International Film Guide 1972,* London, 1971.
Robinson, David, "Grigori Kozintsev, 1905-1973," in *Sight and Sound* (London), Summer 1973.
Obituaries, in *Iskusstvo Kino* (Moscow), October 1973.
Hejfic, I., and others, "G.M. Kozincev, kakim my ego znali ...," in *Iskusstvo Kino* (Moscow), November 1974.
Tsikounas, M., and Leonid Trauberg, "*La Nouvelle Babylone,*" in *Avant-Scène du Cinéma* (Paris), 1 December 1978.
Shklovsky, V., and others, "Iz myslej o G.M. Kozinceve," in *Iskusstvo Kino* (Moscow), April 1980.
"Grigori Kozintsev," in *Film Dope* (London), January 1985.
Gerasimov, Sergei, and Iosif Heifitz, "Licnost' mastera," in *Iskusstvo Kino* (Moscow), March 1985.

* * *

A man of enormous enthusiasms, bursting with theories which were always intended to be put into practice as soon as possible, Kozintsev started his career at the age of fifteen by giving public performances of plays in his family's sitting room in Kiev. When he went to art school in Petrograd he met Sergei Yutkevich, and the two boys joined with Leonid Trauberg to found FEKS, the Factory of the Eccentric Actor. They produced a book on *Eccentrism,* "published in Eccentropolis (formerly Petrograd)," and they produced all sorts of street theater, an amalgam of music hall, jazz, circus, and posters, meanwhile exhibiting their paintings at avant-garde shows.

Kozintsev was barely nineteen when he and Trauberg brought all this flashy modernism, their love of tricks and devices, their commitment to a new society, and their boundless energy together in their first film, *The Adventures of Oktyabrina.* Through their next few productions the two young directors perfected their art, learned how to control the fireworks, and developed a mature style which, however, never lost its distinctive FEKS flavor.

In *The New Babylon,* a story about the Paris Commune of 1870, largely set in a fantastic department store, they reached that standard of excellence only achieved by the greatest silent films: in complete control of the medium, using Enei's brilliant art direction to the full, but peopling a gripping story with human characters only the correct degree larger than life that the medium demanded. A young composer, Shostakovich, was commissioned to write the accompanying score.

Kozintsev and Trauberg were themselves a little disappointed with their first sound film, *Alone,* a contemporary subject, although it was by no means a failure and it at least brought Shostakovich to the notice of the world at large. For the *Maxim Trilogy* they returned to a "historical-revolutionary" subject with tremendous success, building on their own experience with *New Babylon,* but completely integrating sound and dialogue rather than merely adding them to the previous recipe.

Sadly, the trilogy was really the last work of this highly successful partnership; their *Plain People,* about the wartime evacuation of a Leningrad factory to Central Asia, ran into serious official trouble and, although completed in 1945, was not released until 1956 in a version that Kozintsev refused to acknowledge.

For the rest of his independent career he remained loyal to the Leningrad studios and, perhaps because of the troubles with *Plain People,* devoted himself exclusively to historical or literary themes. After two "biopics"—*Pirogov* and *Belinski*—he turned to *Don Quixote,* which was well received at home and abroad. His *Hamlet,* with its brooding Scandinavian background, superb photography, and beautifully handled acting, won even wider international acclaim, as did his even more brooding and original *King Lear.* These films were not merely very accomplished interpretations of Shakespeare's plays: they were the result of Kozintsev's own "brooding," years of deep research and careful thought, electrified, however, by equally profound emotions—the final flowering, in fact, of that enthusiastic fifteen-year-old in Kiev.

Kozintsev himself wrote to Yutkevich after *King Lear,* "I am certain that every one of us ... in the course of his whole life, shoots a single film of *his own....* " This film of one's own "is made ... in your head, through other work, on paper ... in conversation: but it lives, breathes, somehow prolongs into old age something that began its existence in childhood!" And indeed *King Lear* still combines Kozintsev's original emotionalism with his commitment to a cause; it is no accident that, despite its humanistic values, the film can be analyzed in terms of dialectical materialism.

Kozintsev's enthusiasm never deserted him. Not long before his death, after a private London showing of *King Lear,* the director was asked a question about which translation of the play he had used. Kozintsev, waving his arms in excitement, his eyes flashing, his voice rising several octaves, launched himself into a passionate eulogy and defense of the officially discredited poet Boris Pasternak. So Kozintsev was an "eccentric actor" to the last—but, as always, with a deep concern for humanity and truth, regardless of any personal consequences.

—Robert Dunbar

KRAMER, Stanley

Nationality: American. **Born:** Stanley Earl Kramer in New York, 29 September 1913. **Education:** New York University, degree in business administration, 1933. **Military Service:** Served in U.S. Army Signal Corps, making training films, 1943-45. **Family:** Married 1) Anne Pearce, 1950, one son, one daughter; 2) Karen Sharpe, 1966, two daughters. **Career:** Apprentice writer, 20th Century-Fox, 1934; senior editor, Fox, 1938; staff writer for Colombia and Republic Pictures, 1939-40; joined MGM, 1942; with Herbert Baker and Carl Foreman, formed Screen Plays Inc., 1947; formed Stanley Kramer

Productions (became Stanley Kramer Co., 1950), 1949; Stanley Kramer Co. joined Colombia Pictures, 1951; formed Stanley Kramer Pictures Corp., 1954; directed first film, 1955. **Awards:** Academy Award for Best Director, and Best Director, New York Critics, for *The Defiant Ones,* 1958; Irving G. Thalberg Award, Academy of Motion Picture Arts and Sciences, 1961; Gallatin Medal, New York University, 1968.

Films as Director:

1955 *Not as a Stranger* (+ pr)
1957 *The Pride and the Passion* (+ pr)
1958 *The Defiant Ones* (+ pr)
1959 *On the Beach* (+ pr)
1960 *Inherit the Wind* (+ pr)
1961 *Judgement at Nuremberg* (+ pr)
1963 *It's a Mad Mad Mad Mad World* (+ pr)
1965 *Ship of Fools* (+ pr)
1967 *Guess Who's Coming to Dinner?* (+ pr)
1969 *The Secret of Santa Vittoria* (+ pr)
1970 *RPM* (+ pr)
1971 *Bless the Beasts and Children* (+ pr)
1973 *Oklahoma Crude* (+ pr)
1976 *The Domino Principle* (+ pr)
1979 *The Runner Stumbles* (+ pr)

Other Films:

1948 *So This Is New York* (Fleischer) (pr)
1949 *Champion* (Robson) (pr); *Home of the Brave* (Robson) (pr)
1950 *The Men* (Zinnemann) (pr); ***Cyrano de Bergerac*** (Gordon) (pr)
1951 *Death of a Salesman* (Benedek) (pr)
1952 *My Six Convicts* (Fregonese) (pr); *The Sniper* (Dmytryk) (pr); ***High Noon*** (Zinnemann) (pr); *The Happy Time* (Fleischer) (pr); *The Four Poster* (Reis) (pr); *Eight Iron Men* (Dmytryk) (pr); *The Member of the Wedding* (Zinnemann) (pr)
1953 *The Juggler* (Dmytryk) (pr); *The Five Thousand Fingers of Dr. T* (Rowland) (pr)
1954 *The Wild One* (Benedek) (pr); *The Caine Mutiny* (Dmytryk) (pr)
1962 *Pressure Point* (Cornfield) (pr)
1963 *A Child is Waiting* (Cassavetes) (pr)
1964 *Invitation to a Gunfighter* (Wilson) (pr)

Publications

By KRAMER: articles—

"The Independent Producer," in *Films in Review* (New York), March 1951.
"Kramer on the Future," in *Films in Review* (New York), May 1953.
"Politics, Social Comment, and My Emotions," in *Films and Filming* (London), June 1960.
"Sending Myself the Message," in *Films and Filming* (London), February 1964.
"Nine Times Across the Generation Gap," in *Action* (Los Angeles), March/April 1968.
Interview, in *Directors at Work,* edited by Bernard Kantor and others, New York, 1970.
"Stanley Kramer: The Man and His Film," interview, in *American Cinematographer* (Los Angeles), November 1979.
"Dialogue on Film: Stanley Kramer," in *American Film* (Washington, D.C.), March 1987.
"Paul Winfield and Stanley Kramer: A Conversation on the Power of Film Between an Actor Who Defied the System and a Director Who Changed It," in *American Film* (Washington, D.C), May 1991.

On KRAMER: books—

Spoto, Donald, *Stanley Kramer: Film Maker,* New York, 1978.

On KRAMER: articles—

Houston, Penelope, "Kramer and Company," in *Sight and Sound* (London), July/September 1952.
Bogdanovich, Peter, "Dore Schary—Stanley Kramer Syndrome," in *New York Film Bulletin,* no. 12-14, 1960.
Alpert, Hollis, and Arthur Knight, "Haunting Question: Producer-Director at Work," in *Saturday Review* (New York), 2 December 1961.
Tracy, Spencer, and Montgomery Clift, "An Actor's Director," in *Films and Filming* (London), January 1962.
Cowie, Peter, "The Defiant One," in *Films and Filming* (London), March 1963.
Decter, Midge, "Movies and Messages," in *Commentary* (New York), November 1965.
Omatsu, Mary, "Guess Who Came to Lunch?," in *Take One* (Montreal), v.1, no. 9, 1968.
"A Recipe for Greatness," in *Films and Filming* (London), March 1968.
McGillivray, D., "Stanley Kramer," in *Focus on Film* (London), Autumn 1973.
"Stanley Kramer," in *Film Dope* (London), January 1985.
Luft, H.G., "Stanley Kramer," in *Films in Review* (New York), March 1985.

* * *

Kramer was among the first of the successful, postwar independent producers in Hollywood. His work offers testimony to the virtues of such a position in controlling subject matter, while also confirming the power of the tacit constraints that limit social criticism in Hollywood. Films produced, or produced and directed, by Stanley Kramer remain close to the typical styles of postwar Hollywood narrative: location realism in *The Sniper, The Juggler, On the Beach,* and *Judgment at Nuremberg*; a clean narrative trajectory, except for somewhat "preachy" scenes when characters discuss the overt issues confronting them (medical care for the psychopath in *The Sniper* and *Pressure Point,* the need to support those with legal authority in *High Noon* or *The Caine Mutiny*); and a stress on the dilemmas of particular individuals via the mechanisms of psychological realism, although Kramer's characters bear a greater than average burden of representing social types and prominent social attitudes or beliefs.

Frequent attention to topical social issues gives Kramer's work its greatest distinction. These issues include criminality vs. mental illness, G.I. rehabilitation, racism, campus unrest in the sixties, juvenile delinquency, the need for and limits to legitimate authority, and the hazard of nuclear war. However, some of Kramer's work is only obliquely issue-related (*The Four Poster, Cyrano de Bergerac, It's a Mad Mad Mad Mad World,* and *The 5000 Fingers of Dr. T*). Even as fewer and fewer topical, social issue films were being produced during the 1950s, Kramer continued to bring such fare to the screen. His films are not radical or revolutionary by any means. They tend to plead for a respect for the existing institutions of law and authority, although they do point to serious flaws in need of redress. They lack the idiosyncratic, more stylistically expressive sensibility of filmmakers less overtly socially-conscious who nevertheless raise similar issues, such

Stanley Kramer

as Samuel Fuller or John Cassavetes. Even so, Kramer's films continue a long-standing Hollywood tradition of marrying topical issues to dramatic forms, a tradition in which we find many of Hollywood's more openly progressive films.

In many ways, Kramer's films address the issues those who were blacklisted during the 1950s hoped to confront. Kramer himself was not blacklisted, though he was and is still regarded as a socially concerned liberal.

In fact, Stanley Kramer's career is ripe for reinvestigation. Criticized or dismissed by the left for failing to support black-listed individuals or for not taking a sufficiently critical view of existing institutions, Kramer has also been criticized and dismissed by auteurist critics for failing to evince a personal enough stylistic signature (or the kind of fascination evoked by the romantic individualism of a Fuller or Ray). Structuralists have also overlooked his work, and so it remains a scarcely studied, poorly assessed body of very significant work—as revealing of the limits of critical approaches as it may be of Kramer's own artistic or political sensibilities.

—Bill Nichols

KUBRICK, Stanley

Nationality: American. **Born:** New York, 26 July 1928. **Education:** Attended New York City public schools; attended evening classes at City College of the City University of New York, 1945. **Family:** Married 1) Toba Metz, 1947 (divorced, 1952); 2) dancer Ruth Sobotka, 1952 (divorced), one daughter; 3) actress Suzanne Christiane Harlan, 1958, two daughters. **Career:** Apprentice photographer, *Look* magazine, New York, 1946; made first film, 1950; formed Harris-Kubrick Productions with James Harris, 1955 (dissolved 1962); worked on *One-Eyed Jacks* with Marlon Brando, 1958; planned film on Napoléon, 1969; moved to England, 1974. **Awards:** Best Direction, New York Film Critics Award, and Best Written American Comedy (screenplay) Award (with Peter George and Terry Southern), Writers Guild of America, for *Dr. Strangelove,* 1964; Oscar for Special Visual Effects, for *2001,* 1968; Best Direction, New York Film Critics, for *A Clockwork Orange,* 1971; Best Direction, British Academy Award, for *Barry Lyndon,* 1975. **Address:** P.O. Box 123, Borehamwood, Hertfordshire, England.

Films as Director:

1952 *Day of the Fight* (doc) (+ pr, sc, ph, ed); *Flying Padre* (doc) (+ sc, ph)
1953 *The Seafarers* (+ ph); *Fear and Desire* (+ pr, co-sc, ph, ed)
1955 *Killer's Kiss* (+ co-pr, co-sc, ph, ed)
1956 *The Killing* (+ co-pr, sc)
1957 ***Paths of Glory*** (+ co-pr, co-sc)
1960 *Spartacus*
1962 ***Lolita***
1964 ***Dr. Strangelove: Or, How I Learned to Stop Worrying and Love the Bomb*** (+ pr, co-sc)
1968 ***2001: A Space Odyssey*** (+ pr, co-sc, special effects designer)
1971 ***A Clockwork Orange*** (+ pr, sc)
1975 *Barry Lyndon* (+ pr, sc)
1980 *The Shining* (+ pr, co-sc)
1987 ***Full Metal Jacket*** (+ pr, co-sc)

Publications

By KUBRICK: books—

Stanley Kubrick's A Clockwork Orange, New York, 1972.
Full Metal Jacket, New York and London, 1987.

By KUBRICK: articles—

"Bonjour, Monsieur Kubrick," interview with Raymond Haine, in *Cahiers du Cinéma* (Paris), July 1957.
"Words and Movies," in *Sight and Sound* (London), Winter 1961.
"How I Learned to Stop Worrying and Love the Cinema," in *Films and Filming* (London), June 1963.
"Kubrick Reveals All," in *Cinéaste* (New York), Summer 1968.
"A Talk with Stanley Kubrick," with Maurice Rapf, in *Action* (Los Angeles), January/February 1969.
"What Directors Are Saying," in *Action* (Los Angeles), January/February and November/December 1971.
"Kubrick," an interview with Gene Phillips, in *Film Comment* (New York), Winter 1971/72.
Interview with Phillip Strick and Penelope Houston, in *Sight and Sound* (London), Spring 1972.
Interview with Michel Ciment, in *Positif* (Paris), June 1972.
"Something More," an interview with Gordon Gow, in *Films and Filming* (London), October 1975.
"Stanley Kubrick's Vietnam," an interview with Francis Clines, in *New York Times,* 21 June 1987.

On KUBRICK: books—

Austen, David, *The Cinema of Stanley Kubrick,* London, 1969.
Agel, Jerome, *The Making of Kubrick's 2001,* New York, 1970.
Kagan, Norman, *The Cinema of Stanley Kubrick,* New York, 1972, revised edition, 1993.
Walker, Alexander, *Stanley Kubrick Directs,* New York, 1972.
Devries, Daniel, *The Films of Stanley Kubrick,* Grand Rapids, Michigan, 1973.
Phillips, Gene, *Stanley Kubrick: A Film Odyssey,* New York, 1977.
Ciment, Michael, *Kubrick,* Paris, 1980, revised edition, 1987, New York, 1984.
Kolker, Robert Philip, *A Cinema of Loneliness: Penn, Kubrick, Coppola, Scorsese, Altman,* Oxford, 1980, revised edition, 1988.
Coyle, Wallace, *Stanley Kubrick: A Guide to References and Resources,* Boston, 1980.
Nelson, Thomas, *Kubrick: Inside a Film Artist's Maze,* Bloomington, Indiana, 1982.
Hummel, Christoph, editor, *Stanley Kubrick,* Munich, 1984.
Brunetta, Gian Piero, *Stanley Kubrick: Tempo, spazio, storia e mondi possibili,* Parma, 1985.
Magistrale, Anthony, et al., *The Shining Reader,* New York, 1991.
Falsetto, Mario, *Stanley Kubrick: A Narrative and Stylistic Analysis,* Westport, Connecticut, 1994.

On KUBRICK: articles—

"Twenty-nine and Running: The Director with Hollywood by the Horns," in *Newsweek* (New York), 2 December 1957.
Noble, Robin, "Killers, Kisses, and *Lolita,*" in *Films and Filming* (London), December 1960.
Burgess, Jackson, "The Antimilitarism of Stanley Kubrick," in *Film Quarterly* (Berkeley), Fall 1964.
"Stanley Kubrick," in *Cahiers du Cinéma* (Paris), December 1964/January 1965.

Bernstein, Jeremy, "Profiles: How about a Little Game?," in *New Yorker,* 12 November 1966.
Ciment, Michel, "L'Odyssee de Stanley Kubrick," in *Positif* (Paris), October 1968.
Houston, Penelope, "Kubrick Country," in *Saturday Review* (New York), 25 December 1971.
Deer, Harriet and Irving, "Kubrick and the Structures of Popular Culture," in *Journal of Popular Film* (Bowling Green, Ohio), Summer 1974.
Carducci, Mark, "In Search of Stanley K.," in *Millimeter* (New York), December 1975.
Feldmann, Hans, "Kubrick and His Discontents," in *Film Quarterly* (Berkeley), Fall 1976.
Moskowitz, Ken, "Clockwork Violence," in *Sight and Sound* (London), Winter 1976/77.
Kennedy, H., "Kubrick Goes Gothic," in *American Film* (Washington, D.C.), June 1980.
Brown, J., "Kubrick's Maze: The Monster and the Critics," in *Film Directions* (Belfast), no. 16, 1982.
Kinney, J. L., "Mastering the Maze," in *Quarterly Review of Film Studies* (New York), Spring 1984.
Combs, Richard, "Stanley Kubrick: To Be or Not To Be ... Again and Again," in *Monthly Film Bulletin* (London), July 1984.
Sklar, Robert, "Stanley Kubrick et l'industrie Hollywoodienne," in *Filméchange* (Paris), no. 38, 1987.
Rafferty, T., "Remote Control," in *Sight and Sound* (London), Autumn 1987.
Lacayo, R., "Semper fi," in *Film Comment* (New York), September/October 1987.
"Kubrick Section" of *Positif* (Paris), October 1987.
Cazals, T., "L'Homme labyrinthe," in *Cahiers du Cinéma* (Paris), November 1987.
"*Full Metal Jacket* Section" of *Literature/Film Quarterly* (Salisbury, Maryland), vol. 16., no. 4, 1988.
French, Philip, "*A Clockwork Orange,*" in *Sight and Sound* (London), Spring 1990.
Brode, Douglas, "*Spartacus, Lolita, Dr. Strangelove,*" in *The Films of the Sixties,* New York, 1990.
Bookbinder, Robert, "*Clockwork Orange,*" in *The Films of the Seventies,* New York, 1990.
Norman, Barry, "*Paths of Glory, 2001: A Space Odyssey,*" in *The 100 Best Films of the Century,* New York, 1993.
Kael, Pauline, "*Lolita, Clockwork Orange, Full Metal Jacket,*" in *For Keeps,* New York, 1994.
Stein, Michael, "The New Violence: *Clockwork Orange* and Other Films," in *Films in Review* (New York), January/February 1995.
Manchel, Frank, "What about Jack? Family Relationships in *The Shining,*" in *Literature/Film Quarterly* (Salisbury, Maryland), Winter 1995.

* * *

Few American directors have been able to work within the studio system of the American film industry with the independence that Stanley Kubrick has achieved. By steadily building a reputation as a filmmaker of international importance, he has gained full artistic control over his films, guiding the production of each of them from the earliest stages of planning and scripting through post-production. Kubrick has been able to capitalize on the wide artistic freedom that the major studios have accorded him because he learned the business of filmmaking from the ground up.

In the early 1950s he turned out two documentary shorts for RKO; he was then able to secure financing for two low-budget features which he says today were "crucial in helping me to learn my craft," but which he would otherwise prefer to forget. He made both films almost singlehandedly, doing his own camerawork, sound, and editing, besides directing the films.

Then, in 1955, he met James Harris, an aspiring producer; together they made *The Killing,* about a group of small-time crooks who rob a race track. *The Killing* not only turned a modest profit but prompted the now-legendary remark of *Time* magazine that Kubrick "has shown more imagination with dialogue and camera than Hollywood has seen since the obstreperous Orson Welles went riding out of town."

Kubrick next acquired the rights to Humphrey Cobb's 1935 novel *The Paths of Glory,* and in 1957 turned it into one of the most uncompromising antiwar films ever made. Peter Cowie is cited in *Major Film Directors of the American and British Cinema* as saying that Kubrick uses his camera in the film "unflinchingly, like a weapon," as it sweeps across the slopes to record the wholesale slaughter of a division.

Spartacus, a spectacle about slavery in pre-Christian Rome, Kubrick recalls as "the only film over which I did not have absolute control," because the star, Kirk Douglas, was also the movie's producer. Although *Spartacus* turned out to be one of the better spear-and-sandal epics, Kubrick vowed never to make another film unless he was assured of total artistic freedom, and he never has.

Lolita, about a middle-aged man's obsessive infatuation with his pre-teen step-daughter, was the director's first comedy. "The surprising thing about *Lolita,*" Pauline Kael wrote in *For Keeps,* "is how enjoyable it is. It's the first new American comedy since those great days in the 1940s when Preston Sturges re-created comedy with verbal slapstick. *Lolita* is black slapstick and at times it's so far out that you gasp as you laugh."

For those who appreciate the dark humor of *Lolita,* it is not hard to see that it was just a short step from that film to Kubrick's masterpiece in that genre, *Dr. Strangelove: Or How I Learned to Stop Worrying and Love the Bomb,* concerning a lunatic American general's decision to launch an attack inside Russia. The theme implicit in the film is man's final capitulation to his own machines of destruction. Kubrick further examined his dark vision of man in a mechanistic age in *2001: A Space Odyssey.*

Kubrick's view of life, as it is reflected in *2001,* seems to be somewhat more optimistic than it was in his previous pictures. *2001* holds out hope for the progress of mankind through man's creative encounters with the universe. In *A Clockwork Orange,* however, the future appears to be less promising than it did in *2001*; in the earlier film Kubrick showed (in the "person" of the talking computer, Hal) the machine becoming human, whereas in *A Clockwork Orange* he shows man becoming a machine through brainwashing and thought control.

Ultimately, however, the latter film only reiterates in somewhat darker terms a repeated theme in all of Kubrick's previous work: man must retain his humanity if he is to survive in a dehumanized, highly mechanized world. Moreover, *A Clockwork Orange* echoes the warning of *Dr. Strangelove* and *2001* that man must strive to gain mastery over himself if he is to master the machines of his own invention.

After a trio of films set in the future, Kubrick reached back into the past and adapted Thackeray's historical novel *Barry Lyndon* to the screen in 1975. Kubrick has portrayed Barry, an eighteenth-century rogue, and his times in the same critical fashion as Thackeray did before him. The film echoes a theme which appears in much of the director's best work, that through human error the best-laid plans often go awry; and hence man is often thwarted in his efforts to achieve his goals. The central character in *Lolita* fails to possess a nymphet exclusively; the "balance of terror" between nations designed to halt the nuclear arms race in *Dr. Strangelove* does not succeed in averting global destruction; and modern technology turns against its human instigators in *Dr. Strangelove, 2001,* and *A Clockwork Orange.* In this list of films about human failure the story of *Barry Lyndon* easily finds a place, for its hero's lifelong schemes to become

Stanley Kubrick

a rich nobleman in the end come to nothing. And the same can be said for the frustrated writing aspirations of the emotionally disturbed hero of Kubrick's provocative "thinking man's thriller," *The Shining*, derived from the horror novel by Stephen King.

It is clear, therefore, that Kubrick can make any source material fit comfortably into the fabric of his work as a whole, whether it be a remote and almost forgotten Thackeray novel, or a disturbing story about the Vietnam war by a contemporary writer, as with *Full Metal Jacket*, based on the book by Gustav Hasford. Furthermore, it is equally evident that Kubrick wants to continue to create films that will stimulate his audience to think about serious human problems, as his pictures have done from the beginning. Because of the success of his movies in the past, Kubrick can go on making films in the way he wants to, proving in the future, as he has in the past, that he values the artistic freedom which he has worked so hard to win and he has used so well.

—Gene D. Phillips

KULESHOV, Lev

Nationality: Soviet. **Born:** Lev Vladimirovich Kuleshov in Tambov, Russia, 14 January 1899. **Education:** Studied painting at Fine Arts School, Moscow, 1914-16. **Family:** Married to actress Alexandra Khokhlova. **Career:** Set designer for director Evgeni Bauer, from 1916, also began experiments with editing; first theoretical article published, 1918; helped found first National Film School, 1919, teacher from 1920; made short *agitki* and formed film workshop, 1919-21; temporarily stopped filmmaking, 1933; director of State Institute of Cinematography, Moscow, from 1944. **Awards:** Merited Artist of the RSFSR, 1935. **Died:** 29 March 1970.

Films as Director:

1918 *Proyekt inzhenera Praita* (*Engineer Prite's Project*) (+ art d)

1919 *The Unfinished Love Song* (co-d, art d); Newsreels: *Vskrytiye moshchei Sergiya Radonezhskogo* (*The Exhumation of the Holy Remains of St. Sergius of Radonezh*) (co-d); *Reviziya VTiSK v Tverskoi Gubernii* (*The VTiSK Inspection in the Tver Province*); *Ural* (+ sc); *Pervoye maya 1920 v Moskve* (*May 1, 1920 in Moscow*)

1920 *Na krasnom fronte* (*On the Red Front*) (+ sc, role)

1924 *Kavkazskiye mineralniye vody* (*Mineral Waters of the Caucasus*); ***Neobychainye priklucheniya Mistera Vesta v stranye bolshevikov*** (*The Extraordinary Adventures of Mr. West in the Land of the Bolsheviks*) (+ art d)

1925 *Luch smerti* (*Death Ray*) (+ role)

1926 *Po zakonu* (*By the Law*)

1927 *Vasha znakomaya* (*Your Acquaintance*)

1929 *Vesyolaya kanareika* (*The Happy Canary*); *Dva-Buldi-Dva* (*The Two Buldis*) (co-d); *Parovoz B-1000* (*Locomotive No. B-1000*) (unreleased)

1930 *Sorok serdets* (*Forty Hearts*)

1933 *Gorizont* (*Horizon*) (+ co-sc); *Velikii uteshitel* (*The Great Consoler*) (+ co-sc, art d)

1935 *Dokhunda* (unreleased)

1940 *Sibiriaki* (*The Siberians*)

1942 *Klyatva Timura* (*Timur's Oath*); *Uchitelnitsa Kartashova* (*The Teacher Kartashova*) (unreleased)

1944 *My s Urala* (*We Are From the Urals*) (co-d)

Other Films:

1917 *Nabat* (*The Alarm*) (Bauer) (co-art d); *Za schastyem* (*For Happiness*) (Bauer) (art d, role); *Teni lyubvi* (*Shadows of Love*) (Gromov) (art d); *Zhizn'trekh dnei* (*Three Days' Life*) (Gromov) (art d); *Korol' Parizha* (*King of Paris*) (Bauer and Rakhmanova) (art d); *Chernaya lyubov* (*Black King*) (Strizhevsky) (art d, role)

1918 *Vdova* (*The Widow*) (Komissarzhevsky) (art d); *Miss Meri* (*Miss Mary*) (Tchaikovsky) (art d); *Slyakot' bulvarnaya* (*Boulevard Slush*) (Tchaikovsky) (art d)

1919 *Thérèse Raquin* (Tchaikovsky) (art d) (unreleased); *Son Tarasa* (*Taras' Dream*) (Zhelyabuzhsky) (short) (ed); *Smelchak* (*Daredevil*) (Narakov and Turkin) (co-ed)

1930 *Sasha* (Khokhlova) (co-sc)

1934 *Krazha zreniya* (*Theft of Sight*) (Obolensky) (artistic supervisor)

1940 *Sluchai v vulkane* (*Incident in a Volcano*) (Schneider) (directorial advisor)

Publications

By KULESHOV: books—

Eisenstein: Potiemkine, with V. Shlovsky and E. Tisse, Moscow, 1926.
The Art of Cinema [in Russian], Moscow, 1929.
Fundamentals of Film Direction [in Russian], Moscow, 1941.
Traité de mise-en-scène. Les Premières Prises de vues, Paris, 1962.
Kuleshov on Film, edited by Ronald Levaco, Berkeley, 1974.
Lev Kuleshov. Selected Works: Fifty Years in Films, edited by E. Khokhlova, Moscow, 1987.
Sobranie sochinenii v trekh tomakh [Collected Works in Three Volumes], Moscow, 1987-89.

By KULESHOV: articles—

Interview with André Labarthe and Bertrand Tavernier, in *Cahiers du Cinéma* (Paris), May/June 1970.
"Souvenirs (1918-1920)," in *Cahiers du Cinéma* (Paris), July 1970.
"Selections from *Art of the Cinema*," in *Screen* (London), Winter 1971/72.

On KULESHOV: books—

Leyda, Jay, *Kino*, London, 1960.
Taylor, Richard, and Ian Christie, editors, *The Film Factory: Russian and Soviet Cinema in Documents, 1896-1939*, London and Cambridge, Massachusetts, 1988.

On KULESHOV: articles—

Sadoul, Georges, "Au début du cinéma soviétique était Lev Koulechov. Portrait d'un ami," in *Lettres Françaises* (Paris), 18 October 1962.
Sadoul, Georges, "Lev Koulechov grand théoreticien du cinéma," in *Le Techicien du Film* (Paris), January 1965.
Hill, Steven, "Kuleshov—Prophet without Honor?," in *Film Culture* (New York), Spring 1967.
"Lev Kuleshov: 1899-1970," in *Afterimage* (Rochester, New York), April 1970.
Zorkaia, Neïa, "Lev Koulechov," in *Cahiers du Cinéma* (Paris), May/June 1970.
Taylor, Richard, "Lev Kuleshov, 1899-1970," in *Silent Pictures* (London), Autumn 1970.
Levaco, Ronald, "Kuleshov," in *Sight and Sound* (London), Spring 1971.

Lev Kuleshov: ***Velikii uteshitel***

"The Classic Period of Soviet Cinema," in *Film Journal* (New York), Fall/Winter 1972.
Gromov, E., in *Iskusstvo Kino* (Moscow), September and October 1982.
Soviet Film (Moscow), no. 1, 1985.
"Lev Kuleshov," in *Film Dope* (London), March 1985.
Navailh, F., in *Cinéma* (Paris), November 1988.
Revue du Cinéma/Image et Son (Paris), February 1989.
Yampolsky, M., "Kuleshov's Experiments and the New Anthropology of the Actor," in *Inside the Film Factory: New Approaches to Russian and Soviet Cinema,* edited by Richard Taylor and Ian Christie, London and New York, 1991.

* * *

Kuleshov is known to Soviet filmmakers quite simply as the "father of Soviet cinema." He began his career in cinema before the Revolution working with Evgeni Bauer and became one of Soviet cinema's leading film directors and theorists. Vsevolod Pudovkin, who was one of his pupils, once wrote, "We make films, Kuleshov made cinema."

It was the desire to establish a theoretical foundation for the legitimacy of cinema as an art form independent of theatre that led Kuleshov to be the first to distinguish montage as the key element specific to cinema in an article written in 1917. This idea was to be taken up and developed by various schools of Soviet filmmaking, above all by Eisenstein and Vertov, but the distinctive feature of Kuleshov's theory was a belief in serial montage, a brick-by-brick construction of a filmic narrative.

In the early post-Revolutionary period, when there was a desperate shortage of everything, including film stock, Kuleshov worked at the new State Film School with a small workshop of actors, refining his techniques in the so-called "films without film." Central to these was the experiment that has become known as the "Kuleshov effect," which demonstrated that the viewer's interpretation of an individual shot is determined by the context (or sequence) in which that shot is seen. The same shot could be interpreted differently in different contexts. But Kuleshov also appreciated the importance of acting and was responsible for developing the notion of the actor as *naturshchik* or "model," deriving from the Delsartian school of acting technique. By economical and stylised gestures, refined during an intensive period of rehearsal, the *naturshchik* could convey precise meanings to the audience in accordance with the director's plan. Kuleshov would produce an "action score" for every movement in his films.

These techniques were first applied on a large scale in Kuleshov's first feature film, the highly original satirical comedy *The Extraordinary Adventures of Mr. West in the Land of the Bolsheviks* (1924), in which Pudovkin played onc of the criminals. The apotheosis of the *naturshchik* was the role of "the Countess," played by Kuleshov's wife, the extraordinary actress Alexandra Khokhlova. The film's technique also demonstrated one of Kuleshov's other preoccupations of the period, an obsession with the characteristic features of American cinema, which he dubbed *amerikanshchina,* "Americanism" or "Americanitis," and which included fast action, stylised gesture and, above all, rapid cutting and maximum economy. There are no *lacunae* in a Kuleshov film.

His next film, *The Death Ray,* a thriller, was popular with audiences but not with officialdom. On the other hand, *By the Law,* set in the Yukon during the Gold Rush and based on a story by Jack London, was a great critical success. But his next three films were variously regarded as failures: *Your Acquaintance, The Happy Canary* and *The Two Buldis.* The end of the 1920s was no time for experimentation: filmmakers were increasingly expected to fulfill the "social command" associated with the First Five-Year Plan by making films that were "accessible to the millions."

After this, Kuleshov came under increasingly frequent attack from the authorities for his alleged Formalism and his apparent inability (widely shared) to produce a film on a contemporary theme. His subsequent films include at least one further masterpiece, *The Great Consoler,* which can be understood on many different, but sometimes overlapping, levels. It confronts the problem of differing layers of reality at a time when the doctrine of socialist realism was being promulgated and a single officially inspired version of reality held up as a paradigm. *The Great Consoler* was Kuleshov's first sound film, again starring Khokhlova, and still demonstrating a fascination with experimenting to push cinema to its limits. His other, later films were less distinguished, and he complained vociferously about his treatment at the hands of the authorities. Nevertheless, in 1935 he received the title of Merited Artist of the RSFSR.

Throughout his career Kuleshov was an eminent teacher: in 1939 he was made a professor at the State Institute of Cinema, and in 1944 he became its director. His theories of cinema are expounded in Russian in his publications *The Art of Cinema* (1929), *The Rehearsal Method in Cinema* and *The Practice of Film Direction* (both 1935), and *The Foundations of Film Direction* (1941). The importance of his role as teacher can be measured by the fact that almost all these books were published at a time when he was no longer able to make films himself.

Kuleshov's career and influence have been much under-appreciated in the West. This is mainly because so much of his significance lies in his scarcely translated theoretical work, known largely by indirect repute, and in his teaching, the impact of which is almost impossible to quantify. But any Soviet film scholar asked to list the most important figures in the history of Soviet cinema will almost certainly begin with Kuleshov, whether as filmmaker, theorist, or teacher.

—Richard Taylor

KUROSAWA, Akira

Nationality: Japanese. **Born:** Tokyo, 23 March 1910. **Education:** Kuroda Primary School, Edogawa; Keika High School; studied at Doshusha School of Western Painting, 1927. **Family:** Married Yoko Yaguchi, 1945, one son (producer Hisao Kurosawa), one daughter. **Career:** Painter, illustrator, and member, Japan Proletariat Artists' Group, from late 1920s; assistant director, P.C.L. Studios (Photo-Chemical Laboratory, later Toho Motion Picture Co.), studying in Kajiro Yamamoto's production group, from 1936; also scriptwriter, from late 1930s; directed first film, *Sugata Sanshiro,* 1943; began association with actor Toshiro Mifune on *Yoidore tenshi,* and founder, with Yamamoto and others, Motion Picture Artists Association (Eiga Gei jutsuka Kyokai), 1948; formed Kurosawa Productions, 1959; signed contract with producer Joseph E. Levine to work in United States, 1966 (engaged in several aborted projects through 1968); with directors Keisuke Kinoshita, Kon Ichikawa, and Masaki Kobayashi, formed Yonki no Kai production company, 1971. **Awards:** Oscar for Best Foreign Language Film, and Grand Prix, Venice Festival, for *Rashomon,* 1951; Golden Bear Award for Best Direction and International Critics Prize, Berlin Festival, for *The Hidden Fortress,* 1959; Oscar for Best Foreign Language Film, for *Dersu Uzala,* 1976; European Film Academy Award, for "humanistic contribution to society in film production," 1978; Best Director, British Academy Award, and Palme d'Or, Cannes Festival, for *Kagemusha,* 1980; Order of Culture of Japan, 1985; British Film Institute Fellowship, 1986; Honorary Academy Award, 1989.

Films as Director:

1943 *Sugata Sanshiro* (*Sanshiro Sugata, Judo Saga*) (remade as same title by Shigeo Tanaka, 1955, and by Seiichiro Uchikawa, 1965, and edited by Kurosawa) (+ sc)
1944 *Ichiban utsukushiku* (*The Most Beautiful*) (+ sc)
1945 *Zoku Sugata Sanshiro* (*Sanshiro Sugata—Part 2*; *Judo Saga—II*) (+ sc); *Tora no o o fumu otokotachi* (*Men Who Tread on the Tiger's Tail*) (+ sc)
1946 *Asu o tsukuru hitobito* (*Those Who Make Tomorrow*); *Waga seishun ni kuinashi* (*No Regrets for Our Youth*) (+ co-sc)
1947 *Subarashiki nichiyobi* (*One Wonderful Sunday*) (+ co-sc)
1948 *Yoidore tenshi* (*Drunken Angel*) (+ co-sc)
1949 *Shizukanaru ketto* (*A Silent Duel*) (+ co-sc); *Nora inu* (*Stray Dog*) (+ co-sc)
1950 *Shubun* (*Scandal*) (+ co-sc); ***Rashomon*** (+ co-sc)
1951 *Hakuchi* (*The Idiot*) (+ co-sc)
1952 ***Ikiru*** (*To Live, Doomed*) (+ co-sc)
1954 ***Shichinin no samurai*** (*Seven Samurai*) (+ co-sc)
1955 *Ikimono no kiroku* (*Record of a Living Being*; *I Live in Fear*; *What the Birds Knew*) (+ co-sc)
1957 *Kumonosu-jo* (*The Throne of Blood*; *The Castle of the Spider's Web*) (+ co-sc, co-pr); *Donzoko* (*The Lower Depths*) (+ co-sc, co-pr)
1958 *Kakushi toride no san-akunin* (*The Hidden Fortress*; *Three Bad Men in a Hidden Fortress*) (+ co-sc, co-pr)
1960 *Warui yatsu hodo yoku nemuru* (*The Worse You Are the Better You Sleep*; *The Rose in the Mud*) (+ co-sc, co-pr); ***Yojimbo*** (*The Bodyguard*) (+ co-sc)
1962 *Sanjuro* (+ co-sc)
1963 *Tengoku to jigoku* (*High and Low*; *Heaven and Hell*; *The Ransom*) (+ co-sc)
1965 *Akahige* (*Red Beard*) (+ co-sc)
1970 *Dodesukaden* (*Dodeskaden*) (+ co-sc, co-pr)
1975 *Dersu Uzala* (+ co-sc)
1980 ***Kagemusha*** (*The Shadow Warrior*) (+ co-sc, co-pr)
1985 ***Ran*** (+ sc)
1990 *Dreams* (*Akira Kurosawa's Dreams*) (+ sc)
1991 *Hachigatsu No Kyohshikyoku* (*Rhapsody in August*) (+ sc)
1993 *Madadayo* (+ sc, ed)

Other Films:

1937 *Sengoku gunto den* (*Sage of the Vagabond*) (sc, asst dir)
1941 *Uma* (*Horses*) (Yamamoto) (co-sc)

1942 *Seishun no kiryu* (*Currents of Youth*) (Fushimizi) (sc); *Tsubasa no gaika* (*A Triumph of Wings*) (Yamamoto) (sc)
1944 *Dohyo-matsuri* (*Wrestling-Ring Festival*) (Marune) (sc)
1945 *Appare Isshin Tasuke* (*Bravo, Tasuke Isshin!*) (Saeki) (sc)
1947 *Ginrei no hate* (*To the End of the Silver Mountains*) (Taniguchi) (co-sc); *Hatsukoi* (*First Love*) segment of *Yottsu no koi no monogatari* (*Four Love Stories*) (Toyoda) (sc)
1948 *Shozo* (*The Portrait*) (Kinoshita) (sc)
1949 *Yakoman to Tetsu* (*Yakoman and Tetsu*) (Taniguchi) (sc); *Jigoku no kifujin* (*The Lady from Hell*) (Oda) (sc)
1950 *Akatsuki no dasso* (*Escape at Dawn*) (Taniguchi) (sc); *Jiruba no Tetsu* (*Tetsu 'Jilba'*) (Kosugi) (sc); *Tateshi danpei* (*Fencing Master*) (Makino) (sc)
1951 *Ai to nikushimi no kanata e* (*Beyond Love and Hate*) (Taniguchi) (sc); *Kedamono no yado* (*The Den of Beasts*) (Osone) (sc); *Ketto Kagiya no tsuji* (*The Duel at Kagiya Corner*) (Mori) (sc)
1957 *Tekichu odan sanbyakuri* (*Three Hundred Miles through Enemy Lines*) (Mori) (sc)
1960 *Sengoku guntoden* (*The Saga of the Vagabond*) (Sugie) (sc)

Publications

By KUROSAWA: books—

Ikiru, with Shinobu Hashimoto and Hideo Oguni, edited by Donald Richie, New York, 1968.
Rashomon, with Shinobu Hashimoto, edited by Donald Richie, New York, 1969; also New Brunswick, New Jersey, 1987.
The Seven Samurai, New York, 1970.
Kurosawa Akira eiga taikei [Complete Works of Akira Kurosawa], edited by Takamaro Shimaji, in 12 volumes, Tokyo, 1970/72.
Something Like an Autobiography, New York, 1982.
Ran, London, 1986.

By KUROSAWA: articles—

"Waga eiga jinsei no ki," [Diary of My Movie Life], in *Kinema jumpo* (Tokyo), April 1963.
"Why Mifune's Beard Won't Be Red," in *Cinema* (Los Angeles), July 1964.
"L'Empereur: entretien avec Kurosawa," with Yoshio Shirai and others, in *Cahiers du Cinéma* (Paris), September 1966.
Interview with Donald Richie, in *Interviews with Film Directors,* edited by Andrew Sarris, New York, 1967.
Interview with Joan Mellen, in *Voices from the Japanese Cinema,* New York, 1975.
"Tokyo Stories: Kurosawa," interview with Tony Rayns, in *Sight and Sound* (London), Summer 1981.
Interview with E. Decaux and B. Villien, in *Cinématographe* (Paris), April 1982.
"Kurosawa on Kurosawa," in *American Film* (Washington, D.C.), April 1982.
Interview with Kyoko Hirano, in *Cineaste* (New York), May 1986.
Kurosawa, Akira, "Lat oss halla ut tillsammaus," in *Chaplin* (Stockholm), vol. 30, no. 2/3, 1988.
Interview in *Time Out* (London), 9 May 1990.
Interview in *Etudes Cinematographiques* (Paris), no. 165/169, 1990.
Interview in *Cahiers du Cinema* (Paris), June 1991.
"Moments with Kurosawa," an interview with Shawn Levy and James Fee, in *American Film* (New York), January/February 1992.

On KUROSAWA: books—

Anderson, Joseph, and Donald Richie, *The Japanese Film: Art and Industry,* New York, 1960; revised edition, Princeton, New Jersey, 1982.
Sato, Tadao, *Kurosawa Akira no sekai* [The World of Akira Kurosawa], Tokyo, 1968.
Richie, Donald, *The Films of Akira Kurosawa,* Berkeley, California, 1970; revised edition, 1984.
Richie, Donald, *Japanese Cinema: Film Style and National Character,* New York, 1971.
Richie, Donald, editor, *Focus on Rashomon,* Englewood Cliffs, New Jersey, 1972.
Mesnil, Michel, *Kurosawa,* Paris, 1973.
Mellen, Joan, *The Waves at Genji's Door: Japan Through Its Cinema,* New York, 1976.
Bock, Audie, *Japanese Film Directors,* New York, 1978; revised edition, Tokyo, 1978.
Erens, Patricia, *Akira Kurosawa: A Guide to References and Resources,* Boston, 1979.
Tassone, Aldo, *Akira Kurosawa,* Florence, 1981.
Bazin, André, *The Cinema of Cruelty: From Buñuel to Hitchcock,* New York, 1982.
Sato, Tadao, *Currents in Japanese Cinema,* Tokyo, 1982.
Desser, David, *The Samurai Films of Akira Kurosawa,* Ann Arbor, Michigan, 1983.
Tassone, Aldo, *Akira Kurosawa,* Paris, 1983.
Ito, Kosuke, *Kurosawa Akira 'Ran' no sekai,* Tokyo, 1985.
Achternbusch, Herbert, and others, *Akira Kurosawa,* Munich, 1988.
Chang, Kevin K., *Kurosawa: Perceptions on Life,* Honolulu, Hawaii, 1991.
Prince, Stephen, *The Warrior's Camera: The Cinema of Akira Kurosawa,* Princeton, N.J., 1991.
Goodwin, James, editor, *Perspectives on Akira Kurosawa,* New York, 1994.

On KUROSAWA: articles—

Leyda, Jay, "The Films of Kurosawa," in *Sight and Sound* (London), October/December 1954.
Anderson, Lindsay, "Two Inches Off the Ground," in *Sight and Sound* (London), Winter 1957.
Anderson, Joseph, and Donald Richie, "Traditional Theater and the Film in Japan," in *Film Quarterly* (Berkeley), Fall 1958.
McVay, Douglas, "The Rebel in a Kimono," and "Samurai and Small Beer," in *Films and Filming* (London), July and August 1961.
"Kurosawa Issues" of *Kinema jumpo* (Tokyo), April 1963 and 5 September 1964.
"Akira Kurosawa," in *Cinema* (Los Angeles), August/September 1963.
"Kurosawa Issue" of *Études Cinématographiques* (Paris), no. 30-31, Spring 1964.
Akira, Iwasaki, "Kurosawa and His Work," in *Japan Quarterly* (New York), January/March 1965.
"Director of the Year," *International Film Guide* (London, New York), 1966.
"Akira Kurosawa: Japan's Poet Laureate of Film," in *Film Makers on Film Making,* edited by Harry Geduld, Bloomington, Indiana, 1967.
Richie, Donald, "Dostoevsky with a Japanese Camera," in *The Emergence of Film Art,* edited by Lewis Jacobs, New York, 1969.
Manvell, Roger, "Akira Kurosawa's *Macbeth, The Castle of the Spider's Web,*" in *Shakespeare and the Film,* London, 1971.
Tessier, Max, "Cinq japonais en quete de films: Akira Kurosawa," in *Ecran* (Paris), March 1972.
Mellen, Joan, "The Epic Cinema of Kurosawa," in *Take One* (Montreal), June 1972.
Kaminsky, Stuart, "The Samurai Film and the Western," in *The Journal of Popular Film* (Bowling Green, Ohio), Fall 1972.
Tucker, Richard, "Kurosawa and Ichikawa: feudalist and individualist," in *Japan: Film Image,* London, 1973.
"Kurosawa Issue" of *Kinema jumpo* (Tokyo), 7 May 1974.
Richie, Donald, "Kurosawa: A Television Script," in *1000 Eyes* (New York), May 1976.

Akira Kurosawa

Silver, Alain, "Akira Kurosawa," in *The Samurai Film,* Cranbury, New Jersey, 1977.

McCormick, Ruth, "Kurosawa: The Nature of Heroism," in *1000 Eyes* (New York), April 1977.

Ray, Satyajit, "Tokyo, Kyoto et Kurosawa," in *Positif* (Paris), December 1979.

Mitchell, G., "Kurosawa in Winter," in *American Film* (Washington, D.C.), April 1982.

Dossier on *Ran,* in *Revue du Cinéma* (Paris), September 1985.

"Kurosawa Section" of *Positif* (Paris), October 1985.

Boyd, D., "*Rashomon*: from Akutagawa to Kurosawa," in *Literature-Film Quarterly* (Salisbury, Maryland), vol. 15, no. 3, 1987.

Kusakabe, K., "Akira Kurosawa, the emperor of cinema," in *Cinema India International* (Bombay), vol. 4, no. 13, 1987.

Lannes-Lacroutz, M., "Le Sabra et la camélia," in *Positif* (Paris), March 1987.

McCarthy, T., "Kurosawa mum on next film during audience in Tokyo," in *Variety* (New York), 7 October 1987.

Prince, S., "Zen and Selfhood: Patterns of Eastern Thought in Kurosawa's Films," in *Post Script* (Jacksonville, Florida), Winter 1988.

Ostria, V., "Kurosawa en vogue," in *Cahiers du Cinema* (Paris), January 1989.

Stein, Elliot, "Film: Foreign Affairs," in *Village Voice* (New York), 31 January 1989.

Peary, G., "Akira Kurosawa," in *American Film* (New York), April 1989.

Positif (Paris), June 1990.

Biofilmography in *L'avant Scene Cinema* (Paris), June 1990.

Weisman, S.R., "Kurosawa is Sailing Unfamiliar Seas," *New York Times,* October 1, 1990.

Bibliography in *L'avant Scene Cinema* (Paris), June-July 1991.

Bourguignon, Thomas, article in *Positif* (Paris), November 1991.

Medine, David, "Law and Kurosawa's 'Rashomon," in *Literature-Film Quarterly* (Salisbury, Maryland), January 1992.

Sterngold, James, "Kurosawa, in His Own Style, is Planning His Next Film," in *New York Times,* 1 February 1992.

Helm, Leslie, "Is Kurosawa Ready to Stop Making Films? Not Yet ...," in *Los Angeles Times,* 24 June 1992.

Segers, F., "Kurosawa and Toho go way back," in *Variety* (New York), 9 November 1992.

Seltzer, Alex, "Akira Kurosawa: Seeing Through the Eyes of the Audience," in *Film Comment* (New York), May/June 1993.

Reid, T.R., "The Setting Sun of Akira Kurosawa; Japan's Famed Director Draws Yawns for Film Memoir," in *Washington Post,* 28 December 1993.

Crowl, Samuel, "The Bow is Bent and Drawn: Kurosawa's 'Ran' and the Shakespearean Arrow of Desire," in *Literature-Film Quarterly* (Salisbury, Maryland), April 1994.

Manheim, Michael, "The Function of Battle Imagery in Kurosawa's Histories and the 'Henry V' Films," in *Literature-Film Quarterly* (Salisbury, Maryland), April 1994.

James, Caryn, "Gleaning a master director's painted clues...," in *New York Times,* 5 June 1994.

On KUROSAWA: film—

Richie, Donald, *Akira Kurosawa: Film Director,* 1975.

* * *

Unquestionably Japan's best-known film director, Akira Kurosawa introduced his country's cinema to the world with his 1951 Venice Festival Grand Prize winner, *Rashomon.* His international reputation has broadened over the years with numerous citations, and when 20th Century-Fox distributed his 1980 Cannes Grand Prize winner, *Kagemusha,* it was the first time a Japanese film achieved worldwide circulation through a major Hollywood studio.

At the time *Rashomon* took the world by surprise, Kurosawa was already a well-established director in his own country. He had received his six-year assistant director's training at the Toho Studios under the redoubtable Kajiro Yamamoto, director of both low-budget comedies and vast war epics such as *The War at Sea from Hawaii to Malaya.* Yamamoto described Kurosawa as more than fully prepared to direct when he first grasped the megaphone for his own screenplay, *Sanshiro Sugata,* in 1943. This film, based on a best-selling novel about the founding of judo, launched lead actor Susumu Fujita as a star and director Kurosawa as a powerful new force in the film world.

Despite numerous battles with wartime censors, Kurosawa managed to get production approval for three more of his scripts before the Pacific War ended in 1945. By this time he was fully established with his studio and his audience as a writer-director. His films were so successful commercially that he would, until late in his career, receive a free creative hand from his producers, ever-increasing budgets, and extended schedules. In addition, he was never subjected to a project that was not of his own initiation and his own writing.

In the pro-documentary, female emancipation atmosphere that reigned briefly under the Allied Occupation of Japan, Kurosawa created his strongest woman protagonist and produced his most explicit pro-left message in *No Regrets for Our Youth.* But internal political struggles at Toho left bitterness and creative disarray in the wake of a series of strikes. As a result, Kurosawa's 1947 *One Wonderful Sunday* is perhaps his weakest film, an innocuous and sentimental story of a young couple who are too poor to get married.

The mature Kurosawa appears in the 1948 *Drunken Angel.* Here he displays not only a full command of black-and-white filmmaking technique with his characteristic variety of pacing, lighting, and camera angles for maximum editorial effect, but his first use of sound-image counterpoints in the "Cuckoo Waltz" scene, where lively music contrasts with the dying gangster's dark mood. Here too is the full-blown appearance of the typical Kurosawan master-disciple relationship first suggested in *Sanshiro Sugata,* as well as an overriding humanitarian message despite the story's tragic outcome. The master-disciple roles assume great depth in Takashi Shimura's portrayal of the blustery alcoholic doctor and Toshiro Mifune's characterization of the vain, hotheaded young gangster. The film's tension is generated by Shimura's questionable worthiness as a mentor and Mifune's violent unwillingness as a pupil. These two actors would recreate similar testy relationships in numerous Kurosawa films from the late 1940s through the mid-1950s, including the noir police drama *Stray Dog,* the doctor dilemma film *Quiet Duel,* and the all-time classic *Seven Samurai.* In the 1960s Yuzo Kayama would assume the disciple role to Mifune's master in the feudal comedy *Sanjuro* and in *Red Beard,* a work about humanity's struggle to modernize.

Kurosawa's films of the 1990s have been minor asterisks to the career of this formidable, legendary director. *Dreams (Akira Kurosawa's Dreams)* is a disappointingly uneven recreation of eight of the director's dreams; *Hachigatsu No Kyohshikyoku (Rhapsody in August)* is a slight account of the recollection of a grandmother who remembers the bombing of Nagasaki.

These films are linked to *Madadayo,* Kurosawa's most recent film to date, in that all are deeply personal and reflective. *Madadayo,* released when Kurosawa was 83 years old, is an account of 17 years in the retirement of a beloved teacher who is respected by the generations of his former students. As he ages into a "genuine old man," he remains as feisty and vigorous as ever; his favorite phrase is the film's title, the English translation of which is "not yet." But he is as equally vulnerable to the ravages of time and life's losses, as illustrated by his grieving upon the disappearance of his pet cat. *Madadayo* is a flawed film, if only because one-too-many sequences ramble. While it most decidedly is the work of an old man, it and his other latter-period work do not negate the vitality of Kurosawa's many all-time classics.

Part of Kurosawa's characteristic technique throughout his career has involved the typical Japanese studio practice of using the same crew or "group" on each production. He consistently worked with cinematographer Asakazu Nakai and composer Fumio Hayasaka, for example. Kurosawa's group became a kind of family that extended to actors as well. Mifune and Shimura were the most prominent names of the virtual private repertory company that, through lifetime studio contracts, could survive protracted months of production on a Kurosawa film and fill in with more normal four-to-eight-week shoots in between. Kurosawa was thus assured of getting the performance he wanted every time.

Kurosawa's own studio contract and consistent box-office record enabled him to exercise creativity never permitted lesser talents in Japan. He was responsible for numerous technical innovations as a result. He pioneered the use of long lenses and multiple cameras in the famous final battle scenes in the driving rain and splashing mud of *Seven Samurai.* He introduced the first use of widescreen in Japan in the 1958 samurai entertainment classic *Hidden Fortress.* To the dismay of leftist critics and the delight of audiences, he invented realistic portrayals of swordfighting and other violence in such extravagant confrontations as those of *Yojimbo,* which spawned the entire Clint Eastwood spaghetti western genre in Italy. Kurosawa further experimented with long lenses on the set in *Red Beard;* and accomplished breathtaking work with his first color film *Dodeskaden,* now no longer restorable. A firm believer in the importance of motion picture science, Kurosawa pioneered the use of Panavision and multi-track Dolby sound in Japan with *Kagemusha.* His only reactionary practice is his editing, which he does entirely himself on an antique Moviola, better and faster than anyone else in the world.

Western critics have most often chastised Kurosawa for using symphonic music in his films. His reply to this is to point out that he and his entire generation grew up on music that was more Western in quality than native Japanese. As a result, native Japanese music can sound artificially exotic to a contemporary audience. Nevertheless, he has succeeded in his films in adapting not only boleros and elements of Beethoven, but snatches of Japanese popular songs and musical instrumentation from Noh theater and folk song.

Perhaps most startling of Kurosawa's achievements in a Japanese context, however, have been his innate grasp of a story-telling technique that is not culture bound, and his flair for adapting Western classical literature to the screen. No other Japanese director would have dared to set Dostoevski's *Idiot,* Gorki's *Lower Depths,* or Shakespeare's *Macbeth (Throne of Blood)* and *King Lear (Ran)* in Japan. But he also adapted works from the Japanese Kabuki theater (*Men Who Tread on the Tiger's Tail*) and used Noh staging techniques and music in both *Throne of Blood* and *Kagemusha.* Like his counterparts and most admired models, Jean Renoir, John Ford, and Kenji Mizoguchi, Kurosawa has taken his cinematic inspirations from the full store of world film, literature, and music. And yet the completely original screenplays of his two greatest films, *Ikiru,* the story of a bureaucrat dying of cancer who at last finds purpose in life, and *Seven Samurai,* the saga of seven hungry warriors who pit their wits and lives against marauding bandits in the defense of a poor farming village, reveal that his natural story-telling ability and humanistic convictions transcend all limitations of genre, period, and nationality.

—Audie Bock, updated by Rob Edelman

KUSTURICA, Emir

Nationality: Yugoslavian (Bosnia-Herzegovina). **Born:** Sarajevo, Yugoslavia, 24 November 1955. **Education:** Studied film direction at FAMU (Prague Film School) in Czechoslovakia. **Career:** Produced amateur films while attending secondary school; moved to Czechoslovakia to study film, 1973; directed *Guernica,* his diploma film, 1978; directed two television films and played guitar in a rock band, late 1970s; directed first feature, *Do You Remember Dolly Bell?,* 1981; earned international acclaim with *When Father Was Away on Business,* 1985; came to the United States and began teaching a film directing course at Columbia University, 1988. **Awards:** Golden Lion, Venice Festival, 1981, for *Do You Remember Dolly Bell?*; Palme d'Or and co-winner, International Critics Prize, Cannes Festival, and Oscar nomination, Best Foreign Language Film, 1985, for *When Father Was Away on Business;* Best Director, Cannes Festival, and Roberto Rossellini Career Achievement Award, 1988, for *Time of the Gypsies;* Palme d'Or, Cannes Festival, 1995, for *Underground.* **Agent:** CAA, 9830 Wilshire Blvd., Beverly Hills CA 90212.

Films as Director:

1978 *Guernica*; *Nevjeste dolaze* (*The Brides Are Coming*) (for TV)
1980 *Bife Titanic* (*The Titanic Bar*) (for TV) (+ sc)
1981 *Sjecas li se Dolly Bell?* (*Do You Remember Dolly Bell?*)
1985 *Otac na sluzbenoh putu* (*When Father Was Away on Business*)
1988 ***Dom za vesanje*** (*Time of the Gypsies*) (+ co-sc)
1993 *Arizona Dream*
1995 *Underground* (+ co-sc, role)

Other Film:

1987 *Strategija svrake* (*The Magpie Strategy*) (sc); *Zivot Radina* (sc)

Publications

By KUSTURICA: articles—

Interview with P. Elhem in *Visions* (Brussels), Summer 1985.
Interview with L. Codelli in *Positif* (Paris), October 1985.
"Emir Kusturica," an interview with M. Martin and D. Parra in *La Revue du Cinema* (Paris), October 1985.
"Winner from the Balkans," an interview with Kenry Kamm in *New York Times,* 24 November 1985.
Interview with A. Crespi in *Cineforum* (Bergamo), June 1989.
Interview with M. Ciment and L. Codelli in *Positif* (Paris), November 1989.
Interview with I. Katsahnias in *Cahiers du Cinema* (Paris), November 1989.
"Time for Kusturica," an interview with Arlene Pachasa in *American Film* (New York), August 1990.
Interview with T. Jousse and V. Ostria in *Cahiers du Cinema* (Paris), May 1992.
"A Bosnian Movie Maker Laments the Death of the Yugoslav Nation," an interview with David Binder in *New York Times,* 25 October 1992.

On KUSTURICA: articles—

McCarthy, Todd, "Yugo Director Kusturica Planning 'Spirit-Wrestlers,'" *Variety* (New York), 2 October 1985.
Downey, M., article in *Chaplin* (Stockholm), vol. 28, no. 1, 1986.
Horton, Andrew, "The New Serbo-Creationism," *American Film* (Washington, D.C.), January/February 1986.
Cade, Michel, article in *Cahiers du Cinema* (Paris), March 1987.
Report on retrospective at Montpellier Film Festival, in *Cinema* (Paris), October 1989.

Emir Kusturica (left) directing Davor Dujmovic and Elvira Sali (right) in *Dom za vesanje*

Katsahnias, I., article in *Cahiers du Cinema* (Paris), June 1989.
Gili, J. A., article in *Positif* (Paris), November 1989.
Ahlund, J., "Emir Kusturica: regissor med hog kroppstemperatur," *Chaplin* (Stockholm), vol. 32, no. 5, 1990.
Insdorf, Annette, article in *New York Times,* 4 February 1990.
Jousse, T., and V. Ostria, article in *Cahiers du Cinema* (Paris), May 1991.
Williams, Michael, and Deborah Young, "Iron Curtain Alums Test West's Mettle," *Variety* (New York), 29 June 1992.
Maslin, Janet, "Two Films on Strife in Balkans Win Top Prizes at Cannes," *New York Times,* 29 May 1995.
Turan, Kenneth, "A Requiem for Yugoslavia Takes Cannes Prize," *Los Angeles Times,* 29 May 1995.
Klady, Leonard, and Todd McCarthy, "*Underground* Mines Cannes D'or," *Variety* (New York), 5 June 1995.

* * *

Emir Kusturica's films are concerned with a universal humanism. While they come out of a specific part of the world—in which the political situation plays no small role in affecting his characters' lives—they are timeless stories in that they deal with basic human needs, wants, desires, feelings, and experiences.

Do You Remember Dolly Bell?, Kusturica's first feature, is an insightful, bittersweet comedy about Dino (Slavko Stimac), an adolescent who goes about losing his virginity and experiencing first love. There may be political and social implications within the story: Dino's father is a Muslim-Marxist who fervently believes in a communist utopia despite the fact that he and his family reside in one crowded room; and the scenario is rife with jabs at Communist Party bureaucracy. During the course of the story Dino's father dies, which symbolically mirrors Kusturica's conviction that the failure of communism to improve peoples' lives is irrevocable. Still, the film mainly is a coming-of-age comedy not dissimilar to scores of other cinematic rite-of-passage chronicles. Undoubtedly, its gently ironic style was influenced by Kusturica's having attended the Prague Film School, where he studied with Jiri Menzel.

Kusturica was to emerge as a force on the international film scene with his next feature, *When Father Was Away on Business,* which won him a Cannes Film Festival Palme d'Or. It is the fresh, winning account of what happens when a philandering, indiscreet Yugoslavian man, Mesha Malkoc (Miki Manojlovic), is sent into exile for three years, with the scenario unravelling through the eyes and perceptions of Malik (Moreno D'E Bartolli), his six-year-old son. Politics and history impact on the story, which is set in the early 1950s after Marshal Tito, Yugoslavia's ruler, had split with Stalin. This resulted in the country's expulsion from the Soviet Socialist Bloc. In Yugoslavia, individual loyalties were harshly divided between Tito and Stalin, leading to mass denunciations and betrayals which often had nothing to do with political leanings. Such is the case with the father in *When Father Was Away on Business.* The spitefulness of one of Mesha's girlfriends, along with that of his brother-in-law, results in his arrest during a family party. But all Malik knows is that his father has been whisked away from the family, and his mother is left to struggle along as a seamstress in order to feed and clothe her children.

The scenario eventually takes Malik and his family to the salt mine where Mesha is being held. The camp is filled with prisoners who, like Mesha, have been incarcerated for reasons having nothing to do with political ideology. There, Malik also comes of age, but in an altogether different manner than depicted in *Do You Remember Dolly Bell?* Primarily, his maturation results from his interaction with an incurably ill young girl. *When Father Was Away on Business* is a major work, one of the finest films of the 1980s.

Kusturica's next feature, *Time of the Gypsies,* is another coming-of-age story as well as a flavorful account of gypsy life. It tells of an innocent young boy (Davor Dujmovic) who wishes to make a better life for himself, but finds he can only accomplish this by becoming involved in a criminal lifestyle. In telling his story, Kusturica offers a bitter condemnation of a society's exploitation of children. *Arizona Dream,* Kusturica's first American film, was a major disappointment. It features Johnny Depp as a recently orphaned young man who returns to his Arizona hometown for the wedding of his uncle (Jerry Lewis). The movie only received a limited theatrical distribution in the United States.

The civil war that has bitterly divided his homeland was bound to influence Kusturica's work. In 1995 he won a second Cannes Palme d'Or for *Underground,* a French-German-Hungarian-produced allegorical epic of Yugoslavia between 1941 and 1992. As he charts the camaraderie and conflict between two Belgrade men, Marko and Blacky, Kusturica bitterly censures both the postwar communist domination of his homeland and the bloody present-day civil war in which, in his view, all sides are culpable.

—Rob Edelman

LA CAVA, Gregory

Nationality: American. **Born:** Towanda, Pennsylvania, 10 March 1892. **Education:** Educated in Rochester, New York; Art Institute of Chicago; Art Students League and National Academy of Design, New York. **Family:** Married (second time) Grace Carland, 1941, one son. **Career:** Cartoonist for American Press Association, New York, then head of animated cartoon unit, Hearst Enterprises, 1917; worked on *Mutt and Jeff* series, then *Torchy* stories for Johnny Hines, from 1921; director, from 1922, then writer and director for Paramount, from 1924 (moved to Hollywood 1929); director for First National, 1929, then Pathé, 1930; signed with 20th Century Pictures, 1933, then freelance, from 1934; hired by Mary Pickford company to direct *One Touch of Venus,* then left set after dispute, 1948. **Awards:** New York Film Critics Circle Award, for *Stage Door,* 1937. **Died:** In 1952.

Films as Director:

(partial list)

1917 *Der Kaptain Discovers the North Pole* ("Katzenjammer Kids" series) (co-d) (animated short)
1919 *How Could William Tell?* ("Jerry on the Job" series) (animated short)
1920 *Smokey Smokes (and) Lampoons* ("Judge Rummy Cartoons" series) (animated short); *Judge Rummy in Bear Facts* (animated short); *Kats Is Kats* ("Krazy Kat Cartoon") (animated short)
1922 *His Nibs* (5 reels); *Faint Heart* (2 reels); *A Social Error* (2 reels)
1923 *The Four Orphans* (2 reels); *The Life of Reilly* (2 reels); *The Busybody* (2 reels); *The Pill Pounder* (2 reels); *So This Is Hamlet?* (2 reels); *Helpful Hogan* (2 reels); *Wild and Wicked* (2 reels); *Beware of the Dog* (2 reels); *The Fiddling Fool* (2 reels)
1924 *The New School Teacher* (+ co-sc); *Restless Wives*
1925 *Womanhandled*
1926 *Let's Get Married*; *So's Your Old Man*; *Say It Again*
1927 *Paradise for Two* (+ pr); *Running Wild*; *Tell It to Sweeney* (+ pr); *The Gay Defender* (+ pr)
1928 *Feel My Pulse* (+ pr); *Half a Bride*
1929 *Saturday's Children*; *Big News*
1930 *His First Command* (+ co-sc)
1931 *Laugh and Get Rich* (+ sc, co-dialogue); *Smart Woman*
1932 *Symphony of Six Million*; *Age of Consent*; *The Half Naked Truth* (+ co-sc)
1933 *Gabriel over the White House*; *Bid of Roses* (+ co-dialogue); *Gallant Lady*
1934 *Affairs of Cellini*; *What Every Woman Knows* (+ pr)
1935 *Private Worlds* (+ co-sc); *She Married Her Boss*
1936 *My Man Godfrey* (+ pr, co-sc)
1937 *Stage Door*
1939 *Fifth Avenue Girl* (+ pr)
1940 *Primrose Path* (+ pr, co-sc)
1941 *Unfinished Business* (+ pr)
1942 *Lady in a Jam* (+ pr)
1947 *Living in a Big Way* (+ story, co-sc)

Publications

On LA CAVA: articles—

Article in *Life* (New York), 15 September 1941.
Obituary in *New York Times,* 2 March 1952.
Sarris, Andrew, "Esoterica," in *Film Culture* (New York), Spring 1963.
Beylie, Claude, "Enfin, La Cava vint ...," in *Ecran* (Paris), May 1974.
McNiven, R., "Gregory La Cava," in *Bright Lights* (Los Angeles), no. 4, 1979.
"Gregory La Cava," in *Film Dope* (London), March 1985.

* * *

Although many of his individual films are periodically reviewed and reassessed by film scholars, Gregory La Cava remains today a relatively under-appreciated director of some of the best "screwball comedies" of the 1930s. Perhaps his apparent inability to transcend the screwball form or his failure with a number of straight dramas contributed to this lack of critical recognition. Yet, at his best, he imposed a vitality and sparkle on his screen comedies that overcame their often weak scripts and some occasionally pedestrian performances from his actors.

The great majority of La Cava's films reflect an instinctive comic sense undoubtedly gained during his early years as a newspaper cartoonist and as an animator with Walter Lantz on such fast and furious cartoons as those in "The Katzenjammer Kids" and "Mutt and Jeff" series. La Cava subsequently became one of the few directors capable of transferring many of these techniques of animated comedy to films involving real actors. His ability to slam a visual gag home quickly sustained such comedies as W.C. Fields's *So's Your Old Man* and *Running Wild.* Yet his real forte emerged in the sound period when the swiftly paced sight gags were replaced by equally quick verbal repartee.

La Cava's "screwball comedies" of the 1930s were characterized by improbable plots and brilliantly foolish dialogue but also by a dichotomous social view that seemed to delight in establishing satirical contrasts between the views of themselves held by the rich and by the poor. Although treated in varying degrees in *Fifth Avenue Girl, She Married Her Boss,* and *Stage Door,* La Cava's classic treatment of this subject remains *My Man Godfrey.* Made during the depths of the Depression, it juxtaposes the world of the rich and frivolous with the plight of the real victims of the economic disaster through the sharply satiric device of a scavenger hunt. When one of the hunt's objectives turns out to be "a forgotten man," in this case a hobo named Godfrey Parke (William Powell), it provides a platform for one of the Depression's victims to lash out at the upper class as being composed of frivolous "nitwits." The film seemingly pulls its punches at the end, however, when one socialite, Irene Bullock (Carole Lombard), achieves some realization of the plight of the less fortunate, and the hobo

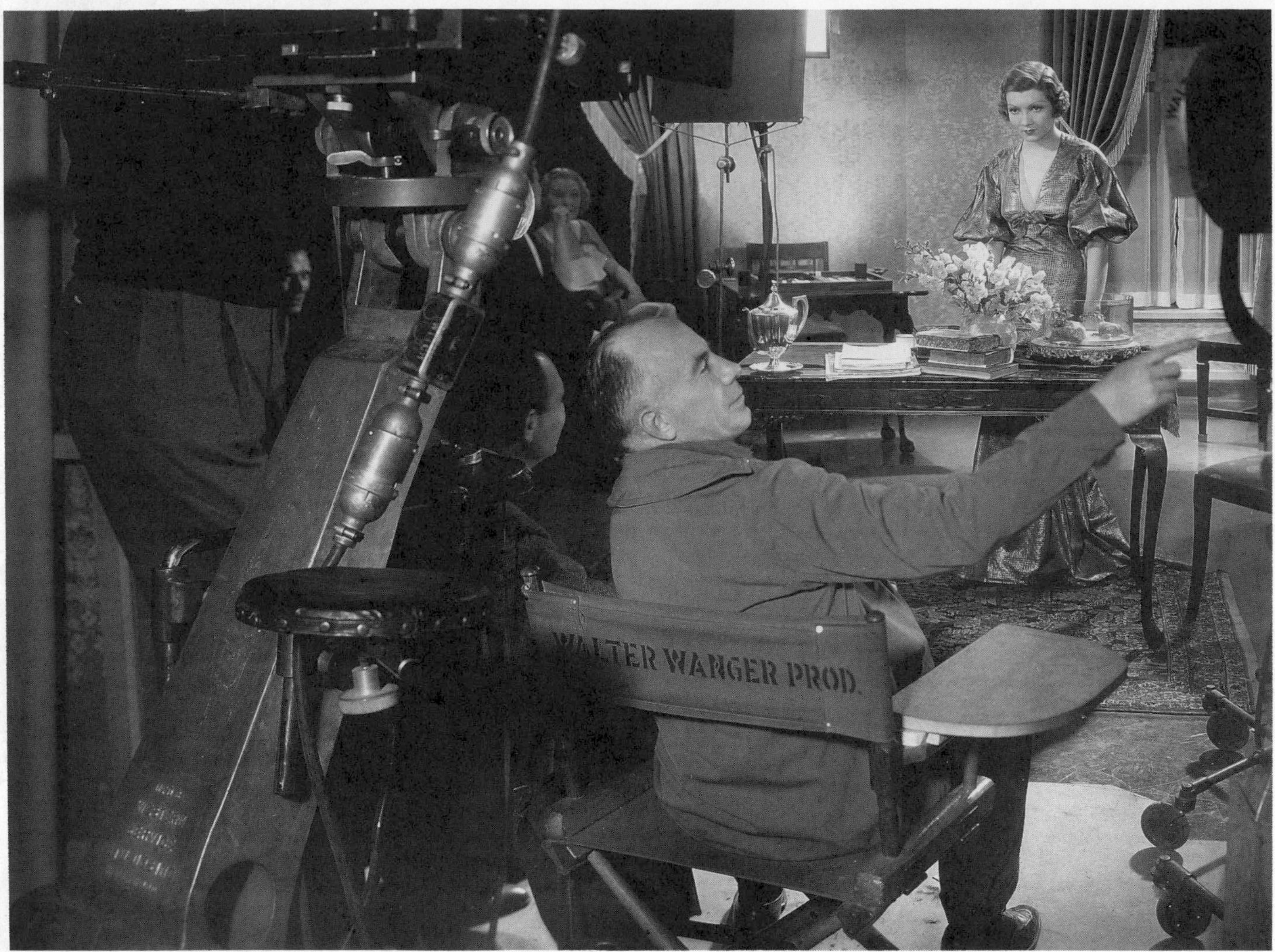

Gregory La Cava directing Claudette Colbert in *Private Worlds*

Godfrey turns out to be a formerly wealthy Harvard man who actually renews his fortune through his association with her, although he has been somewhat tempered by his experience with the hoboes.

La Cava, perhaps more than other directors working in the screwball genre, was able, by virtue of doing much of the writing on his scripts, to impose his philosophical imprint upon the majority of his films. While he was often required to keep a foot in both the conservative and the liberal camps, his films do not suffer. On the contrary, they maintain an objectivity that has allowed them to grow in stature with the passage of years. *My Man Godfrey, Stage Door,* and *Gabriel over the White House,* which is only now being recognized as a political fantasy of great merit, give overwhelming evidence that critical recognition of Gregory La Cava is considerably overdue.

—Stephen L. Hanson

LANG, Fritz

Nationality: German/American. **Born:** Vienna, 5 December 1890, became U.S. citizen, 1935. **Education:** Studied engineering at the Technische Hochschule, Vienna. **Family:** Married (second time) writer Thea von Harbou, 1924 (separated 1933). **Career:** Cartoonist, fashion designer, and painter in Paris, 1913; returned to Vienna, served in army, 1914-16; after discharge, worked as scriptwriter and actor, then moved to Berlin, 1918; reader and story editor for Decla, then wrote and directed first film, *Halbblut,* 1919; worked with von Harbou, from 1920; visited Hollywood, 1924; *Das Testament des Dr. Mabuse* banned by Nazis, 1933; offered post as supervisor of Nazi film productions by Goebbels, but fled Germany; after working in Paris and London, went to Hollywood, 1934; signed with Paramount, 1940; co-founder, then president, Diana Productions, 1945; quit Hollywood, citing continuing disputes with producers, 1956; directed two films in India, 1958-59, before last film, directed in Germany, 1960. **Awards:** Officier d'Art et des Lettres, France. **Died:** In Beverly Hills, 2 August 1976.

Films as Director:

1919 *Halbblut* (*Half Caste*) (+ sc); *Der Herr der Liebe* (*The Master of Love*) (+ role); *Hara-Kiri*; *Die Spinnen* (*The Spiders*) Part I: *Der Goldene See* (*The Golden Lake*) (+ sc)

1920 *Die Spinnen* (*The Spiders*) Part II: *Das Brillantenschiff* (*The Diamond Ship*) (+ sc); *Das Wandernde Bild* (*The Wandering Image*) (+ co-sc); *Kämpfende Herzen* (*Die Vier um die Frau*; *Four around a Woman*) (+ co-sc)

1921 *Der müde Tod: Ein Deutsches Volkslied in Sechs Versen* (*The Weary Death*; *Between Two Worlds*; *Beyond the Wall*; *Destiny*) (+ co-sc)

1921/22 ***Dr. Mabuse, der Spieler*** (*Dr. Mabuse, the Gambler*; *The Fatal Passions*) in two parts: ***Ein Bild der Zeit*** (*Spieler aus Leidenschaft*; *A Picture of the Time*) and ***Inferno—Menschen der Zeit*** (*Inferno des Verbrechens*; *Inferno—Men of the Time*) (+ co-sc)

1924 ***Die Nibelungen*** in two parts: ***Siegfrieds Tod*** (*Death of Siegfried*) and ***Kriemhilds Rache*** (*Kriemhild's Revenge*) (+ co-sc, uncredited)

1927 ***Metropolis*** (+ co-sc, uncredited)

1928 *Spione* (*Spies*) (+ pr, co-sc, uncredited)

1929 *Die Frau im Mond* (*By Rocket to the Moon*; *The Girl in the Moon*) (+ pr, co-sc, uncredited)

1931 ***M, Mörder unter Uns*** (*M*) (+ co-sc, uncredited)

1933 ***Das Testament des Dr. Mabuse*** (*The Testament of Dr. Mabuse*; *The Last Will of Dr. Mabuse*) (+ co-sc, uncredited) (German and French versions)

1934 *Liliom* (+ co-sc, uncredited)

1936 ***Fury*** (+ co-sc)

1937 ***You Only Live Once***

1938 *You and Me* (+ pr)

1940 *The Return of Frank James*

1941 *Western Union*; *Man Hunt*; *Confirm or Deny* (co-d, uncredited)

1942 *Moontide* (co-d, uncredited)

1943 *Hangmen Also Die!* (+ pr, co-sc)

1944 *Ministry of Fear*; *The Woman in the Window*

1945 *Scarlet Street* (+ pr)

1946 *Cloak and Dagger*

1948 *Secret Beyond the Door* (+ co-pr)

1950 *House by the River*; *An American Guerrilla in the Philippines*

1952 *Rancho Notorious*; *Clash by Night*

1953 *The Blue Gardenia*; ***The Big Heat***

1954 *Human Desire*

1955 *Moonfleet*

1956 *While the City Sleeps*; ***Beyond a Reasonable Doubt***

1959 *Der Tiger von Eschnapur* (*The Tiger of Bengal*) and *Das Indische Grabmal* (*The Hindu Tomb*) (+ co-sc) (released in cut version as *Journey to the Lost City*)

1960 *Die Tausend Augen des Dr. Mabuse* (*The Thousand Eyes of Dr. Mabuse*) (+ pr, co-sc)

Other Films:

1917 *Die Hochzeit im Ekzentrik Klub* (*The Wedding in the Eccentric Club*) (May) (sc); *Hilde Warren und der Tod* (*Hilde Warren and Death*) (May) (sc, four roles); *Joe Debbs* (series) (sc)

1918 *Die Rache ist mein* (*Revenge Is Mine*) (Neub) (sc); *Herrin der Welt* (*Men of the World*) (May) (asst d); *Bettler GmbH* (sc)

1919 *Wolkenbau und Flimmerstern* (*Castles in the Sky and Rhinestones*) (d unknown, co-sc); *Totentanz* (*Dance of Death*) (Rippert) (sc); *Die Pest in Florenz* (*Plague in Florence*) (Rippert) (sc); *Die Frau mit den Orchiden* (*The Woman with the Orchid*) (Rippert) (sc); *Lilith und Ly* (sc)

1921 *Das Indische Grabmal* (in 2 parts: *Die Sendung des Yoghi* and *Der Tiger von Eschnapur*) (co-sc)

1963 *Le Mépris* (*Contempt*) (Godard) (role as himself)

Publications

By LANG: articles—

"The Freedom of the Screen," 1947 (reprinted in *Hollywood Directors 1941-1976*, by Richard Koszarski, New York, 1977).

"Happily Ever After," 1948 (collected in *Film Makers on Film Making*, edited by Harry Geduld, Bloomington, Indiana, 1969).

"Fritz Lang Today," interview with H. Hart, in *Films in Review* (New York), June/July 1956.

"The Impact of Television on Motion Pictures," interview with G. Bachmann, in *Film Culture* (New York), December 1957.

Interview with Jean Domarchi and Jacques Rivette, in *Cahiers du Cinéma* (Paris), September 1959.

"On the Problems of Today," in *Films and Filming* (London), June 1962.

"Fritz Lang Talks about Dr. Mabuse," interview with Mark Shivas, in *Movie* (London), November 1962.

"Was bin ich, was sind wir?," in *Filmkritik* (Munich), no.7, 1963.

"La Nuit viennoise: Une Confession de Fritz Lang," edited by Gretchen Berg, in *Cahiers du Cinéma* (Paris), August 1965 and June 1966.

Interview with Axel Madsen, in *Sight and Sound* (London), Summer 1967.

"Autobiography," in *The Celluloid Muse: Hollywood Directors Speak*, by Charles Higham and Joel Greenberg, London, 1969.

"Interviews," in *Dialogue on Film* (Beverly Hills), April 1974.

Interview with Gene Phillips, in *Focus on Film* (London), Spring 1975.

"Fritz Lang Gives His Last Interview," with Gene Phillips, in *Village Voice* (New York), 16 August 1976.

On LANG: books—

Kracauer, Siegfried, *From Caliari to Hitler: A Psychological History of the German Film*, Princeton, New Jersey, 1947.

Courtade, Francis, *Fritz Lang*, Paris, 1963.

Moullet, Luc, *Fritz Lang*, Paris, 1963.

Eibel, Alfred, editor, *Fritz Lang*, Paris, 1964.

Bogdanovich, Peter, *Fritz Lang in America*, New York, 1969.

Eisner, Lotte, *The Haunted Screen: Expressionism in the German Cinema and the Influence of Max Reinhardt*, Berkeley, 1969.

Jensen, Paul, *The Cinema of Fritz Lang*, New York, 1969.

Johnston, Claire, *Fritz Lang*, London, 1969.

Grafe, Frieda, Enno Patalas, and Hans Prinzler, *Fritz Lang*, Munich 1976.

Eisner, Lotte, *Fritz Lang*, edited by David Robinson, New York, 1977.

Armour, Robert, *Fritz Lang*, Boston, 1978.

Ott, Frederick, *The Films of Fritz Lang*, Secaucus, New Jersey, 1979.

Jenkins, Stephen, editor, *Fritz Lang: The Image and the Look*, London, 1981.

Kaplan, E. Ann, *Fritz Lang: A Guide to References and Resources*, Boston, 1981.

Maibohm, Ludwig, *Fritz Lang: Seine Filme—Sein Leben*, Munich, 1981.

Dürrenmatt, Dieter, *Fritz Lang: Leben und Werk*, Basle, 1982.

Humphries, Reynold, *Fritz Lang: Cinéaste Américain*, Paris, 1982.

Humphries, Reynold, *Fritz Lang: Genre and Representation in His American Films*, Baltimore, 1988.

On LANG: articles—

Wilson, Harry, "The Genius of Fritz Lang," in *Film Quarterly* (Berkeley), Summer 1947.

Truffaut, François, "Aimer Fritz Lang," in *Cahiers du Cinéma* (Paris), January 1954.

Lambert, Gavin, "Fritz Lang's America," in *Sight and Sound* (London), Summer 1955.

Demonsablon, Phillipe, "La Hautaine Dialectique de Fritz Lang," and Michel Mourlet, "Trajectoire de Fritz Lang," in *Cahiers du Cinéma* (Paris), September 1959.

Franju, Georges, "Le Style de Fritz Lang," in *Cahiers du Cinéma* (Paris), November 1959.

Taylor, John, "The Nine Lives of Dr. Mabuse," in *Sight and Sound* (London), Winter 1961.

Sarris, Andrew, "Fritz Lang," in *Film Culture* (New York), Spring 1963.

Rhode, Eric, "Fritz Lang (The German Period, 1919-1933)," in *Tower of Babel* (London), 1966.

Fritz Lang (center) directing *Human Desire*

"Lang Issue" of *Image et Son* (Paris), April 1968.
Joannides, Paul, "Aspects of Fritz Lang," in *Cinema* (London), August 1970.
Burch, Noel, "De *Mabuse* à *M*: Le Travail de Fritz Lang," in special issue of *Revue d'esthétique* (Paris), 1973.
Appel, Alfred Jr., "Film Noir: The Director Fritz Lang's American Nightmare," in *Film Comment* (New York), November/December 1974.
Gersch, Wolfgang, and others, "*Hangmen Also Die!*: Fritz Lang und Bertolt Brecht," in *Filmkritik* (Munich), July 1975.
Sarris, Andrew, "Fritz Lang (1890-1976) Was the Prophet of Our Paranoia," in *Village Voice* (New York), 16 August 1976.
Overby, David, "Fritz Lang, 1890-1976," in *Sight and Sound* (London), Autumn 1976.
Kuntzel, Thierry, "The Film-Work," in *Enclitic* (Minneapolis), Spring 1978.
Willis, Don, "Fritz Lang: Only Melodrama," in *Film Quarterly* (Berkeley), Winter 1979/80.
Magny, Joel, and others, "Actualité de Fritz Lang," in *Cinéma* (Paris), June 1982.
Neale, Steve, "Authors and Genres," in *Screen* (London), July/August 1982.
Duval, B., "Le crime de M. Lang. Portrait d'un Fritz en artisan de Hollywood," in *Image et Son* (Paris), November 1982.
McGivern, William P., "Roman Holiday," in *American Film* (Washington, D.C.), October 1983.
Rotondi, C.J., and E. Gerstein, "The 1984 Review. The 1927 review. Fritz Lang: The Maker of *Metropolis*," in *Films in Review* (New York), October 1984.
"Lang section" of *Positif* (Paris), November 1984.
"*Der Tiger von Eschnapur* Issue" of *Avant-Scène du Cinéma* (Paris), April 1985.
"*Das indische Grabmal* Issue" of *Avant-Scène du Cinéma* (Paris), May 1985.
"Fritz Lang," in *Film Dope* (London), November 1985.
Giesen, R., "Der Trickfilm," in *Cinefex* (Riverside, California), February 1986.
Bernstein, M., "Fritz Lang, Incorporated," in *Velvet Light Trap* (Madison, Wisconsin), no. 22, 1986.
Pelinq, M., in *Jeune Cinéma* (Paris), April/May and June/July 1989.

On LANG: films—

Luft, Friedrich, and Guido Schütte, *Künstlerporträt: Fritz Lang,* for TV, Germany, 1959.
Fleischmann, Peter, *Begegnung mit Fritz Lang,* Germany, 1963.
Leiser, Erwin, *Das war die Ufa,* Germany, 1964.
Leiser, Erwin, *Zum Beispiel Fritz Lang,* for TV, Germany, 1968.
Dütsch, Werner, *Die Schweren Träume des Fritz Lang,* for TV, Germany, 1974.

* * *

Fritz Lang's career can be divided conveniently into three parts: the first German period, 1919-1933, from *Halbblut* to the second Mabuse film, *Das Testament des Dr. Mabuse*; the American period, 1936-1956, from *Fury* to *Beyond a Reasonable Doubt*; and the second German period, 1959-60, which includes the two films made in India and his last film, *Die tausend Augen des Dr. Mabuse.*

Lang's apprentice years as a scriptwriter and director were spent in the studios in Berlin where he adopted certain elements of expressionism and was imbued with the artistic seriousness with which the Germans went about making their films. In Hollywood this seriousness would earn Lang a reputation for unnecessary perfectionism, a criticism also thrown at fellow émigrés von Stroheim and von Sternberg. Except for several films for Twentieth Century-Fox, Lang never worked long for a single studio in the United States, and he often preferred to work on underbudgeted projects which he could produce, and therefore control, himself. The rather radical dissimilarities between the two studio worlds within which Lang spent most of his creative years not surprisingly resulted in products which look quite different from one another, and it is the difference in look or image which has produced the critical confusion most often associated with an assessment of Lang's films.

One critical approach to Lang's work, most recently articulated by Gavin Lambert, argues that Lang produced very little of artistic interest after he left Germany; the *Cahiers du cinéma* auteurists argue the opposite, namely that Lang's films made in America are superior to his European films because the former were clogged with self-conscious artistry and romantic didacticism which the leanness of his American studio work eliminated. A third approach, suggested by Robin Wood and others, examines Lang's films as a whole, avoiding the German-American division by looking at characteristic thematic and visual motifs. Lang's films can be discussed as exhibiting certain distinguishing features—economy, functional precision, detachment—and as containing basic motifs such as the trap, a suppressed underworld, the revenge motive, and the abuse of power. Investigating the films from this perspective reveals a more consistent development of Lang as a creative artist and helps to minimize the superficial anomalies shaped by his career.

In spite of the narrowness of examining only half of a filmmaker's creative output, the sheer number of Lang's German movies which have received substantial critical attention as "classic" films has tended to submerge the critical attempt at breadth and comprehensiveness. Not only did these earlier films form an important intellectual center for the German film industry during the years between the wars, as Siegfried Kracauer later pointed out, but they had a wide international impact as well and were extensively reviewed in the Anglo-American press. Lang's reputation preceded him to America, and although it had little effect ultimately on his working relationship, such as it was, with the Hollywood moguls, it has affected Lang's subsequent treatment by film critics.

If Lang is a "flawed genius," as one critic has described him, it is less a wonder that he is "flawed" than that his genius had a chance to develop at all. The working conditions Lang survived after his defection would have daunted a less dedicated director. Lang, however, not only survived but flourished, producing films of undisputed quality: the four war movies, *Man Hunt, Hangmen Also Die!, Ministry of Fear,* and *Cloak and Dagger,* and the urban crime films of the 1950s, *Clash by Night, The Blue Gardenia, The Big Heat, Human Desire,* and *While the City Sleeps.*

These American films reflect a more mature director, tighter mise-en-scène, and more control as a result of Lang's American experience. The films also reveal continuity. As Robin Wood has written, the formal symmetry of his individual films is mirrored in the symmetry of his career, beginning and ending in Germany. All through his life, Lang adjusted his talent to meet the changes in his environment, and in so doing produced a body of creative work of unquestionable importance in the development of the history of cinema.

—Charles L.P. Silet

LATTUADA, Alberto

Nationality: Italian. **Born:** Milan, 13 November 1914. Educated in architecture. **Family:** Married Carla Del Poggio, 1945 (divorced). **Career:** Co-founder of avant-garde journal *Camminare,* 1933; helped found *Corrente*; with Mario Ferreri and Luigi Comencini, founder of Cineteca Italiana, Italian film archive, 1940; directed first film, 1942; opera director, from 1970. **Address:** Via N. Paganini, 7 Rome, Italy.

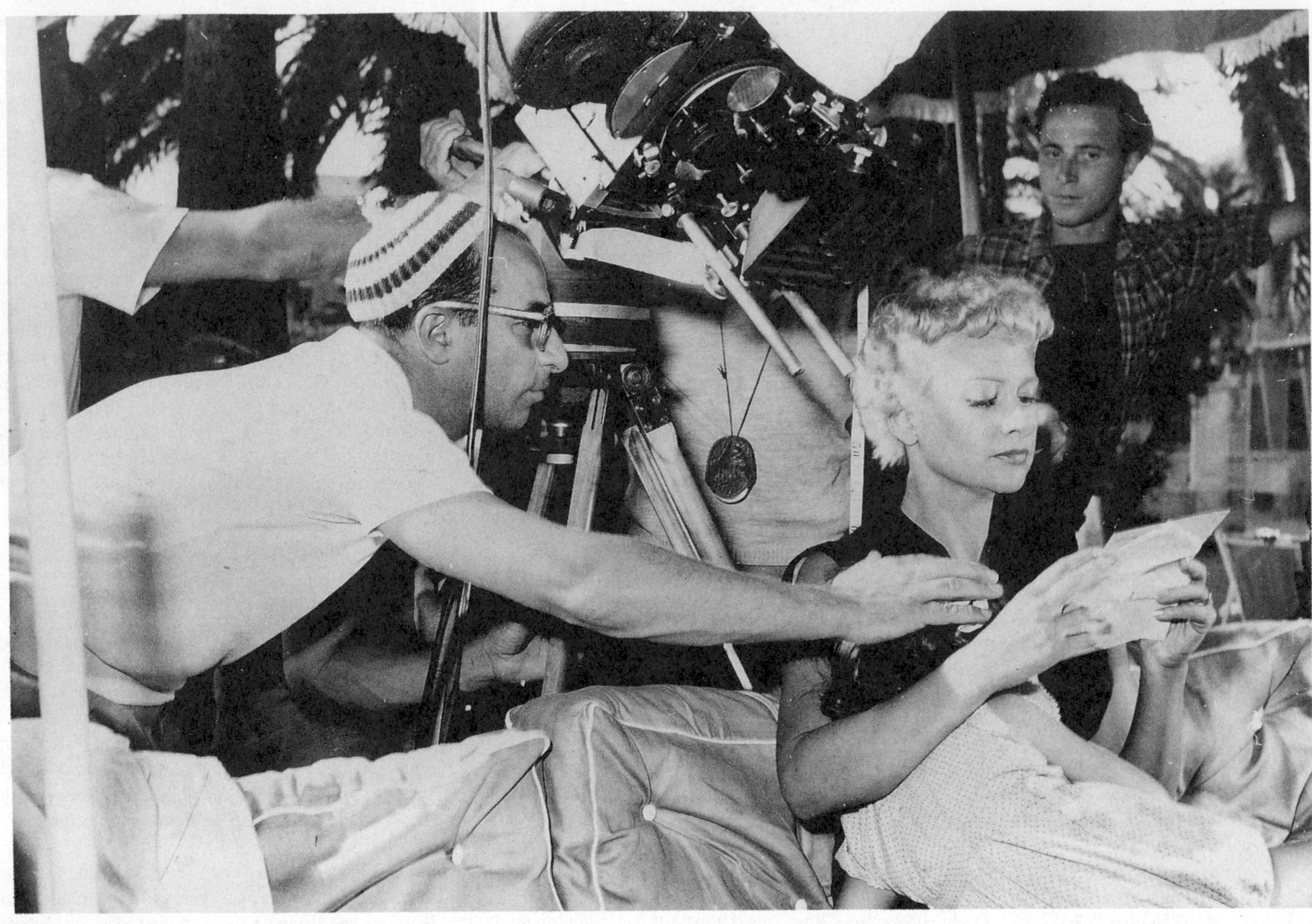

Alberto Lattuada directing Martine Carol in *La spiaggia*

Films as Director and Co-Scriptwriter:

1942 *Giacomo l'idealista*
1945 *La freccia nel fianco*; *La nostra guerra* (documentary)
1946 *Il bandito*
1947 *Il delitto di Giovanni Episcopo* (*Flesh Will Surrender*)
1948 *Senza pietà* (*Without Pity*)
1949 *Il mulino del Po* (*The Mill on the Po*)
1950 *Luci del varietà* (*Variety Lights*) (co-d, co-pr)
1952 *Anna*; *Il cappotto* (*The Overcoat*)
1953 *La lupa* (*The She-Wolf*); "Gli italiani si voltano" episode of *Amore in città* (*Love in the City*)
1954 *La spiaggia* (*The Beach*); *Scuola elementare*
1956 *Guendalina*
1958 *La tempesta* (*Tempest*)
1960 *I dolci inganni*; *Lettere di una novizia* (*Rita*)
1961 *L'imprevisto*
1962 *Mafioso*; *La steppa*
1965 *La mandragola* (*The Love Root*)
1966 *Matchless*
1967 *Don Giovanni in Sicilia* (+ co-pr)
1968 *Fräulein Doktor*
1969 *L'amica*
1970 *Venga a prendere il caffe ... da noi* (*Come Have Coffee With Us*)
1971 *Bianco, rosso e ...* (*White Sister*)
1973 *Sono stato io*
1974 *Le farò da padre ...* (*Bambina*)
1976 *Cuore di cane*; *Bruciati da cocente passione* (*Oh Serafina!*)
1978 *Cosi come sei*
1980 *La cicala*
1983 *Cristoforo Colombo* (*Christopher Columbus*)
1987 *Una spina nel cuore* (+ sc)
1988 *Fratelli*

Other Films:

1935 *Il museo dell'amore* (asst d)
1936 *La danza delle lancette* (collaborator on experimental short)
1941 *Piccolo mondo antico* (Soldati) (asst d)
1942 *Si signora* (asst d, co-sc)
1958 *Un eroe dei nostri tempi* (Monicelli) (role)

Publications

By LATTUADA: books—

Occhio quadrate, album of photos, Milan, 1941.
La tempesta, Bologna, 1958.
La steppa, Bologna, 1962.

Gli uccelli indomabili, Rome, 1970.
Cuore di cane, Bari, 1975.
A proposito di Cosi come sei, edited by Enrico Oldrini, Bologna, 1978.
Diario di un grane amatore, Milan, 1980.
Feuillets au vent, Paris, 1981.
La massa, Rome, 1982.
La luna be partita, Calcata, 1992.

By LATTUADA: articles—

"We Took the Actors into the Streets," in *Films and Filming* (London), April 1959.
"Alberto Lattuada: du néoréalisme au réalisme magique," interview with A. Tournès, in *Jeune Cinéma* (Paris), December/January 1974/75.
"*Moi et le diable*: je ne puis vivre ni avec toi ni sans toi," in *Positif* (Paris), June 1978.
Interview with G. Volpi, in *Positif* (Paris), September and October 1978.
"Alberto Lattuada: une foi dans la beauté," interview with C. Depuyper and A. Cervoni, in *Cinéma* (Paris), April 1981.
Interview with L. Codelli, in *Films and Filming* (London), July 1982.
"Conversazione con Alberto Lattuada," interview with G. Turroni, in *Filmcritica* (Rome), June 1991.

On LATTUADA: books—

De Sanctis, Filippo Mario, *Alberto Lattuada,* Parma, 1961, and Lyons, 1965.
Bruno, Edoardo, *Lattuada o la proposta ambigua,* Rome, 1968.
Broher, J.J., *Alberto Lattuada,* Brussels, 1971.
Turroni, Giuseppe, *Alberto Lattuada,* Milan, 1977.
Zanellato, Angelo, *L'uomo: il cinema di Lattuada,* Padua, 1978.
Bruno, Edoardo, *Italian Directors: Alberto Lattuada,* Rome, 1981.
Camerini, Claudio, *Alberto Lattuada,* Florence, 1982.
Cosulich, Callisto, *I film di Alberto Lattuada,* Rome, 1985.

On LATTUADA: articles—

Turroni, G., "Film e figurazione: la riflessione metalinguistica," in *Filmcritica* (Rome), January 1979.
Duval, Bernard, "Lattuada: un précursor perpetuel," in *Image et Son* (Paris), July 1979.
"Alberto Lattuada," in *Film Dope* (London), November 1985.

* * *

One of the most consistently commercially successful directors in Italy, Lattuada has continued to enjoy a freedom of subject matter and style despite ideological shifts and methodological changes. His main films during the neorealist period, which he claims never to have taken part in, succeeded in further establishing the Italian cinema in the international market and, unlike many of his colleagues' works, also proved popular in the domestic market. *Il bandito* and *Il mulino del Po,* for example, combined progressive ideology, realistic detail (due to location shooting and attention to quotidian activities), and tight narrative structure through careful attention to editing. In fact, Lattuada's entire career has demonstrated an on-going interest in editing, which he considers more fundamental than the script and which gives his films a strictly controlled rhythm with no wasted footage. He shoots brief scenes that, he claims, are more attractive to an audience and that can be easily manipulated at the editing stage.

Lattuada's background stressed the arts, and his films display a sophisticated cultural appreciation. As a boy, he took an active interest in his father's musicianship in the orchestra of La Scala in Milan. As a young man, Lattuada worked as a film critic, wrote essays on contemporary painters, co-founded cultural magazines, and worked as an assistant director and scriptwriter. Lattuada co-scripts most of his films and occasionally produces them. He also co-founded what became the Milan film archive, the Cineteca Italiana.

As a director, Lattuada is often called eclectic because of his openness to projects and his ability to handle a wide variety of subject matter. His major commercial successes have been *Bianco, rosso e ...,* which he wrote especially for Sophia Loren; *Matchless,* a parody of the spy genre; *Anna,* the first Italian film to gross over one billion lire in its national distribution; *La spiaggia,* a bitter satire of bourgeois realism; and *Mafioso,* starring Alberto Sordi and filmed in New York, Sicily, and Milan.

Lattuada has also filmed many adaptations of literary works that remain faithful to the original but are never simply static reenactments. These range from the comically grotesque *Venga a prendere ...*; a version of Brancati's satirical *Don Giovanni in Sicilia*; the horror film *Cuore di cane,* taken from a Bulgakov novel; the spectacular big-budget *La tempesta,* from two Pushkin stories; and Chekhov's metaphorical journey in *La steppa.* His 1952 version of *The Overcoat* is considered his masterpiece for its portrayal of psychological states and the excellence of Renato Rascel's performance. Lattuada is famous for his handling of actors, and has launched the career of many an actress, including Catherine Spaak, Giulietta Masina and Nastassia Kinski.

Notwithstanding the diversity of subject matter he has directed, Lattuada's main interest has been pubescent sexuality, the passage of a girl into womanhood, and the sexual relationship of a couple as the primary attraction they have for each other. Thus, his films deal with eroticism as a central theme and he chooses actresses whose physical beauty and sensuousness are immediately apparent. This motif appeared in Lattuada's work as early as his second feature and has been his main preoccupation in his films since 1974.

His films have been critically well-received in Italy, although rarely given the attention enjoyed by some of his contemporaries. In France, however, his work is highly acclaimed; *Il bandito* and *Il cappotto* received much praise at the Cannes festivals when they were shown. With a few exceptions, his more recent work is little known in Britain and the United States, although when *Come Have Coffee with Us* was released commercially in the U.S. ten years after it was made, it enjoyed a fair success at the box office and highly favorable reviews.

—Elaine Mancini

LAUNDER, Frank, and Sidney GILLIAT

LAUNDER. Nationality: British. **Born:** Hitchin, Hertfordshire, 1906. **Education:** Brighton. **Career:** Civil servant, then actor, in Brighton; studio assistant, 1928; first collaboration with fellow writer Sidney Gilliat, 1935; with Gilliat, wrote radio serials *Crooks Tour* and *Secret Mission 609,* 1939; co-directed first film, *Millions Like Us,* 1943; formed Individual Pictures production company with Gilliat, 1944 (dissolved 1950).

GILLIAT. Nationality: British. **Born:** Edgeley, Cheshire, 1908. **Education:** London University. **Career:** Hired by Walter Mycroft, film critic of *London Evening Standard* (edited by Gilliat's father) and scenario chief at British International Pictures, Elstree, as studio assistant, 1928; gagman and dogsbody for director Walter Forde, 1929-30; collaborator with Frank Launder (see above), from 1935; president, Screen Writers Association, 1936; director, British Lion, 1958-72; chairman of Shepperton Studios, from 1961; also co-founder of TV commercial company, Littleton Park Film Productions; wrote opera libretto for *Our Man in Havana,* 1963. **Died:** 1994.

Films Directed, Produced, and Written by Launder and Gilliat:

1943 *Millions Like Us* (Launder and Gilliat)
1944 *Two Thousand Women* (Launder)
1945 *The Rake's Progress* (*The Notorious Gentleman*) (Gilliat)
1946 *Green for Danger* (Gilliat); *I See a Dark Stranger* (Launder)
1947 *Captain Boycott* (Launder)
1948 *The Blue Lagoon* (Launder); *London Belongs to Me* (*Dulcimer Street*) (Gilliat)
1950 *State Secret* (*The Great Manhunt*) (Gilliat); *The Happiest Days of Your Life* (Launder)
1951 *Lady Godiva Rides Again* (Launder)
1952 *Folly to Be Wise* (Launder)
1953 *The Story of Gilbert and Sullivan* (*The Great Gilbert and Sullivan*) (Gilliat)
1954 *The Constant Husband* (Gilliat); *The Belles of St. Trinian's* (Launder)
1955 *Geordie* (*Wee Geordie*) (Launder)
1956 *Fortune Is a Woman* (*She Played with Fire*) (Gilliat)
1957 *Blue Murder at St. Trinian's* (Launder)
1959 *The Bridal Path* (Launder); *Left, Right and Centre* (Gilliat)
1960 *The Pure Hell of St. Trinian's* (Launder)
1961 *Only Two Can Play* (Gilliat)
1965 *Joey Boy* (Launder)
1966 *The Great St. Trinian's Train Robbery* (Launder and Gilliat)

Films Written by Launder and Gilliat:

1936 *Seven Sinners* (de Courville); *Twelve Good Men* (Ince)
1938 ***The Lady Vanishes*** (Hitchcock)
1939 *Inspector Hornleigh On Holiday* (Forde)
1940 *They Came by Night* (Lachman); *Night Train to Munich* (Reed)
1942 *The Young Mr. Pitt* (Reed)
1956 *The Green Man* (Day) (+ pr)

Other Films—Launder:

1928 *Cocktails* (Banks) (titles)
1929 *Under the Greenwood Tree* (Lachman) (co-sc)
1930 *The Compulsory Husband* (Banks) (dialogue/dubbing); *Song of Soho* (Lachman) (co-sc); *Harmony Heaven* (Bentley) (additional dialogue); *The W Plan* (Saville) (additional dialogue); *The Middle Watch* (Walker) (co-sc); *Children of Change* (Esway) (co-sc); *How He Lied to Her Husband* (Lewis) (sc)
1931 *Keepers of Youth* (Bentley) (sc); *Hobson's Choice* (Bentley) (co-sc); *A Gentleman of Paris* (Hill) (co-sc); *The Woman Between* (Mander) (co-sc)
1932 *After Office Hours* (Bentley) (co-sc); *The Last Coupon* (Bentley) (co-sc); *Arms and the Man* (Lewis) (co-sc, uncredited); *Josser in the Army* (Lee) (sc)
1935 *Emil and the Detectives* (Rosmer) (co-sc); *Rolling Home* (R. Ince) (sc); *So You Won't Talk* (Beaudine) (co-sc); *Mr. What's His Name* (Ince) (co-sc); *Educated Evans* (Beaudine) (co-sc); *Windbag the Sailor* (Beaudine) (sc editor)
1937 *Good Morning Boys* (Varnel) (sc editor); *Bank Holiday* (Reed) (sc editor); *O-Kay for Sound* (Varnel) (sc editor); *Doctor Syn* (Neill) (sc editor); *Oh, Mr. Porter!* (Varnel) (story)
1938 *Owd Bob* (Stevenson) (sc editor); *Strange Boarders* (Mason) (sc editor); *Convict 99* (Varnel) (sc editor); *Alf's Button Afloat* (Varnel) (sc editor); *Hey! Hey! U.S.A.!* (Varnel) (sc editor); *Old Bones of the River* (Varnel) (sc editor)
1939 *Ask a Policeman* (Varnel) (sc editor); *A Girl Must Live* (Reed) (sc); *The Frozen Limits* (Varnel) (sc editor)
1940 *Inspector Hornleigh Goes To It* (Forde) (story)
1969 *An Elephant Called Slowly* (Hill) (sc uncredited)
1980 *Wildcats of St. Trinian's* (d, sc)

Other Films—Gilliat:

1928 *Toni* (Maude) (titles); *Champagne* (Hitchcock) (titles); *Adams's Apple* (Whelan) (titles); *Weekend Wives* (Lachman) (titles); *The Manxman* (Hitchcock) (research)
1929 *The Tryst* (short) (co-d); *Would You Believe It?* (Forde) (asst d, + role)
1930 *Red Pearls* (Forde) (asst d); *You'd Be Surprised* (Forde) (asst d, + role); *The Last Hour* (Forde) (asst d); *Lord Richard in the Pantry* (Forde) (sc); *Bed's Breakfast* (Forde) (sc)
1931 *3rd Time Lucky* (Ford) (additional dialogue); *The Ghost Train* (Forde) (additional dialogue); *A Gentleman of Paris* (Hill) (sc); *The Happy Ending* (Webb) (co-sc, uncredited); *A Night in Marseilles* (Night Shadows) (de Courville) (sc); *Two Way Street* (King) (sc)
1932 *Lord Babs* (Forde) (additional dialogue); *Jack's the Boy* (Forde) (sc continuity); *Rome Express* (Forde) (sc); *For the Love of Mike* (Banks) (co-sc)
1933 *Sign Please* (Rawlins—short) (sc); *Post Haste* (Cadman—short) (sc); *Facing the Music* (Hughes) (co-story); *Falling for You* (Hulbert and Stevenson) (story); *Orders Is Orders* (Forde) (co-sc); *Friday the Thirteenth* (Saville) (co-story)
1934 *Jack Ahoy!* (Forde) (co-sc) *Chu-Chin-Chow* (Forde) (co-sc); *My Heart Is Calling* (Gallone) (adapt/dialogue)
1935 *Bulldog Jack* (*Alias Bulldog Drummond*) (Forde) (co-sc); *King of the Damned* (Forde) (co-sc)
1936 *Tudor Rose* (Stevenson) (assoc pr); *Where There's a Will* (Beaudine) (sc); *The Man Who Changed His Mind* (*The Man Who Lived Again*) (Stevenson) (co-sc, assoc pr); *Strangers on a Honeymoon* (de Courville) (co-sc)
1937 *Take My Tip* (Mason) (co-sc); *A Yank at Oxford* (Conway) (story)
1938 *Strange Boarders* (Mason) (co-sc); *The Gaunt Stranger* (*The Phantom Strikes*) (Forde) (sc)
1939 *Ask a Policeman* (Varnel) (story); *Jamaica Inn* (Hitchcock) (sc)
1940 *The Girl in the News* (Reed) (sc)
1941 *The Ghost Train* (Forde) (additional dialogue); *Kipps* (*The Remarkable Mr. Kipps*) (Reed) (sc); *Mr. Proudfoot Shows a Light* (Mason—short) (story); *You're Telling Me!* (Peak—short) (sc); *From the Four Corners* (Havelock-Allan—short) (sc, uncredited)
1942 *Unpublished Story* (French) (co-sc); *Partners in Crime* (short) (co-d, sc)
1944 *Waterloo Road* (d, sc)
1957 *The Smallest Show on Earth* (Dearden) (pr)
1972 *Ooh ... You Are Awful* (*Get Charlie Tully*) (Owen) (co-exec pr); *Endless Night* (d, sc)

Publications

On LAUNDER AND GILLIAT: books—

Durgnat, Raymond, *A Mirror for England,* 1971.
Brown, Geoff, *Launder and Gilliat,* London, 1977.

On LAUNDER AND GILLIAT: articles—

Sight and Sound (London), Autumn 1946, December 1949, and Autumn 1958.

Sidney Gilliat and Frank Launder

Films and Filming (London), July 1963.
Brown, Geoff, in *National Film Theatre Booklet* (London), November/December 1977.
Films Illustrated (London), November 1979.
"Frank Launder," in *Film Dope* (London), November 1985.
Tobin, Y., "Launder et Gilliat: retrospective," in *Positif,* July-August 1990.

* * *

Launder and Gilliat's chosen specialty was intelligent entertainment with a distinctive British flavor. Each had their individual style and preferences. Frank Launder favored the breezy implausibilities of farce (*The Happiest Days of Your Life,* the *St. Trinian's* films), tempered with a dose of Celtic whimsy (*Geordie, The Bridal Path,* parts of *I See a Dark Stranger*). Sidney Gilliat leaned more towards caustic social comedy (*The Rake's Progress, Only Two Can Play*) and rigorously detailed thrillers (*State Secret*). But they functioned admirably as a team: first as screenwriters (working in tandem from 1935), then, from 1943, as writer-producer-directors—though only on their first feature, *Millions Like Us,* did they attempt joint direction, side by side.

Both separately entered the industry in lowly capacities in 1928, and gradually worked up the ladder during the 1930s, serving in various studio script departments. As a team they earned their reputation with thrillers. *Seven Sinners,* their first collaboration, established their talent for concocting ingenious plot twists, expertly balancing comedy with suspense, and stamping even the most minor character with individuality. Subsequent films refined the formula: *The Lady Vanishes,* for instance (their script was substantially written before Hitchcock came on board as director), and *Night Train to Munich,* one of several scripts directed by Carol Reed. Both these films featured Charters and Caldicott—comic, imperturbable Englishmen, played by Basil Radford and Naunton Wayne, who bumbled obliviously round a jittery Europe, babbling about cricket scores and picking up *Mein Kampf* at a German station bookstall only after a fruitless request for *Punch.*

Charters and Caldicott make an appearance in *Millions Like Us,* laying beach mines. But this was only for old times' sake: the film belonged firmly to the women factory workers, whose hopes and problems were explored in a rich tapestry of individual plot-lines. Few other British feature films of World War II evoke the Home Front's daily round with quite the same nose for detail or emotional pull. Gilliat's next production, *Waterloo Road,* slipped into melodrama at times, but still maintained a strong realistic atmosphere in its triangular drama of an AWOL soldier, the soldier's roving wife, and a muscle-flexing local spiv.

In 1944 Launder and Gilliat launched their own company, Individual Pictures. They began on a high level, working from their own original scripts. Gilliat's *The Rake's Progress* offered a biting satirical treatment of a profligate charmer (Rex Harrison, ideally cast) washed up on the rocks of the 1930s. Launder's marvelous *I See a Dark Stranger* wrapped up its far-fetched story about a naive Irish girl persuaded to spy for Germany with Hitchcockian panache. Subsequent films followed a more obviously commercial path, though Gilliat's *Green for Danger* and *State Secret* demonstrated his witty way with thriller conventions, while *The Happiest Days of Your Life,* adapted from John Dighton's popular play, displayed Launder's happy ability to keep the wildest farce on an even keel.

Artistically, the 1950s and 1960s proved less rewarding. The *St. Trinian's* series, inspired by the hideous schoolgirls featured in Ronald Searle's cartoons, began briskly enough within *The Belles of St. Trinian's,* but the formula and humor coarsened drastically as the sequels followed. The pleasant whimsy of *Geordie*—Launder's tale of the amazing growth of an undersized Scot and his exploitation by others—was no match for the barbed blarney that lit up *I See a Dark Stranger,* while Gilliat's gift for social comedy appeared stunted in *The Constant Husband* and *Left, Right and Centre.*

Much of their energies were by this time being spent in boardroom activities: as directors of British Lion, they nursed several films by other filmmakers through the production process, including the lively prison comedy *Two-Way Stretch.* But Gilliat managed a confident return to form in *Only Two Can Play,* a lively version of Kingsley Amis's novel about a philandering Welsh librarian, fully alert to the comic drabness of provincial life.

After *Endless Night,* an elegant diversion adapted from Agatha Christie, was unfairly mauled by the critics, Gilliat retired from filmmaking in the early 1970s. Launder, however, unwisely returned in 1980 with *The Wildcats of St. Trinian's*—one of the few films in the team's long career which seemed out of step with audience's tastes.

—Geoff Brown

LEACOCK, Richard

Nationality: British. **Born:** the Canary Islands, 18 July 1921. **Education:** Educated in England, then studied physics at Harvard University, graduated 1943. **Career:** Began making documentaries in the Canaries, 1935; moved to U.S., 1938; served as combat photographer, World War II; worked on documentaries with Robert Flaherty, Louis de Rochemont, John Ferno, and Willard Van Dyke, among others, from late 1940s; worked with Robert Drew of Time-Life, then formed partnership with D.A. Pennebaker, 1960s; founder then Head of Department of Film at Massachusetts Institute of Technology, from 1969.

Films as Director and Cinematographer:

1935 *Canary Bananas*
1938 *Galápagos Islands*
1944/49 *Pelileo Earthquake*
1951 *The Lonely Boat*
1954 *Toby and the Tall Corn*
1955 *How the F-100 Got Its Tail*
1958 *Bernstein in Israel*
1959 *Bernstein in Moscow*; *Coulomb's Law*; *Crystals*; *Magnet Laboratory*; *Points of Reference*
1960 ***Primary*** (co-d, co-ph, ed); *On the Pole* (co-d, co-ph, co-ed); *Yanqui No* (co-d, co-ph)
1961 *Petey and Johnny* (co-d, co-ph); *The Children Were Watching* (co-d, co-ph)
1962 *The Chair* (co-d, co-ph); *Kenya, South Africa* (co-d, co-ph)
1963 *Crisis* (co-d, co-ph); *Happy Mother's Day* (co-d, co-ph, co-ed)
1964 *A Stravinsky Portrait* (+ ed); *Portrait of Geza Anda* (+ ed); *Portrait of Paul Burkhard* (+ ed); *Republicans—The New Breed* (co-d, co-ph)
1965 *The Anatomy of Cindy Fink* (co-d, co-ph); *Ku Klux Klan—The Invisible Empire*
1966 *Old Age—The Wasted Years*; *Portrait of Van Cliburn* (+ ed)
1967 *Monterey Pop* (+ co-ph); *Lulu*
1968 *Who's Afraid of the Avant-Garde* (co-d, co-ph, co-ed); *Hickory Hill*
1969 *Chiefs* (+ ed)
1970 *Queen of Apollo* (+ ed)
1986 *Impressions de L'Ile des Morts* (co-d)

Other Films:

1940 *To Hear Your Banjo Play* (Van Dyke, W.) (ph)
1946 *Louisiana Story* (Flaherty) (ph, assoc pr)
1944/49 *Geography Films Series* (ph)
1950 *New Frontier* (*Years of Change*) (ph, ed)
1951 *The Lonely Night* (ph)
1952 *Head of the House* (ph)
1954 *New York* (ph)
1958 *Bullfight at Málaga* (ph)
1959 *Balloon* (co-ph)
1968 *Maidstone* (co-ph)
1971 *Sweet Toronto* (co-ph); *One P.M.* (co-ph); *Keep On Rockin'* (co-ph)

Publications

By LEACOCK: articles—

"To Far Places with Camera and Sound-Track," in *Films in Review* (New York), March 1950.
"Richard Leacock Tells How to Boost Available Light," with H. Bell, in *Popular Photography* (Boulder, Colorado), February 1956.
"The Work of Ricky Leacock: Interview," in *Film Culture* (New York), no.22-23, 1961.
"For an Uncontrolled Cinema," in *Film Culture* (New York), Summer 1961.
Interview, in *Movie* (London), April 1963.
"Ricky Leacock on *Stravinsky* Film," in *Film Culture* (New York), Fall 1966.
"On Filming the Dance," in *Filmmakers Newsletter* (Ward Hill, Massachusetts), November 1970.
"Richard Leacock,"in *Documentary Explorations* edited by G. Roy Levin, Garden City, New York, 1971.
"Remembering Frances Flaherty," in *Film Comment* (New York), November/December 1973.
"Leacock at M.I.T.," an interview with L. Marcorelles, in *Sight and Sound* (London), Spring 1974.
"(Richard) Leacock on Super 8, Video Discs and Distribution," interview with M. Sturken, in *Afterimage* (Rochester, New York), May 1979.
Interview with H. Naficy, in *Literature/Film Quarterly* (Salisbury, Maryland), vol. 10, no. 4, October 1982.

On LEACOCK: books—

Issari, M. Ali, *Cinéma Verité,* East Lansing, Michigan, 1971.
Mamber, Stephen, *Cinéma Verité in America: Studies in Uncontrolled Documentary,* Cambridge, Massachusetts, 1974.

Issari, M. Ali, and Doris A. Paul, *What is Cinéma Verité?* Metuchen, New Jersey, 1979.

On LEACOCK: articles—

Callenbach, Ernest, "Going Out to the Subject," in *Film Quarterly* (Berkeley), Spring 1961.

Bachmann, Gideon, "The Frontiers of Realist Cinema: The Work of Ricky Leacock," in *Film Culture* (New York), Summer 1961.

Mekas, Jonas, "Notes on the New American Cinema," in *Film Culture* (New York), no.24, 1962.

Blue, James, "One Man's Truth," in *Film Comment* (New York), Spring 1965.

Vanderwildt, A., "Richard Leacock Uses Super-8," in *Lumiere* (Melbourne), September 1973.

"Richard Leacock," in *Film Dope* (London), November 1985.

Barsam. R.M., "American Direct Cinema: The Re-Presentation of Reality," in *Persistence of Vision* (Maspeth, New York), Summer 1986.

* * *

As cinematographer, producer, director, and editor, Richard Leacock has been an important contributor to the development of the documentary film, specifically in *cinéma verité,* now often called *direct cinema.*

For direct cinema filming, the lightweight 16-millimeter camera, handheld and synced to a quiet recorder, allows the filmmaker to intrude as little as possible into the lives of those being filmed. From the very beginning of his interest in this kind of filming, Leacock has been an active experimenter and an inventor of mobile 16-millimeter equipment for filming events, lifestyles, ongoing problematic situations, and other varieties of live history. At Massachusetts Institute of Technology, where he heads the department of film, he has developed super-8 sync-sound equipment and related technology. As a patient, courteous and informative lecturer to hundreds of teachers in many workshops, he has demonstrated this equipment and its use for TV, shown his films, and indirectly taught many youngsters who went on to work in film, TV, and related fields.

At fourteen, Leacock, already an active still photographer, impressed his schoolmates in England with a 16-minute film made on his home island. An indicator, perhaps, of his later concentration on non-subjective filming, his 1935 *Canary Bananas* is still a good, straightforward silent film about what workers do on a banana plantation. Leacock's later work on diverse topics, including the life of a traveling tent show entertainer, communism and democracy in South America, excitement about quintuplets in South Dakota, the mind and work of an artist, and opera attest to the breadth of his interests.

Leacock treasures his experience as photographer with poetic filmmaker/explorer Robert Flaherty on *Louisiana Story,* which was commissioned by Standard Oil to show preliminary steps in searching and drilling for oil, but emerged as a film poem about a boy in the bayou. Leacock stated that he learned from Flaherty how to discover with a camera. But having realized how difficult Flaherty's ponderous unsynced equipment had made direct shooting, Leacock later joined a group, led by Robert Drew of Time-Life in 1960, committed to making direct cinema films for TV.

An example of the Drew unit's work was *Primary,* an account of the campaign of Democratic Senators John F. Kennedy and Hubert Humphrey in the Wisconsin presidential primary that Leacock worked on with Donn Alan Pennebaker, Robert Drew, and Terry Filgate. Critics called this film an excellent report on the inner workings of a political campaign as well as an appealing glimpse of the personal lives of candidates and their families. But Leacock was dissatisfied because the camera people could never get in to film such vital behind-the-scenes activities as public relations methods.

Leacock has frequently indicated his own and other documentarists concerns about obstacles to achieving direct cinema. Leacock, always critical of his own work, is concerned about distribution problems and thoughtful about the role of films in effecting social change. He has dedicated his life to creating less expensive, more manageable apparatus, to portraying art and artists, to experimenting, to letting situation and event tell their own story, and to teaching.

—Lillian Schiff

LEAN, David

Nationality: British. **Born:** Croydon, Surrey, 25 March 1908. **Education:** Leighton Park Quaker School, Reading. **Family:** Married 1) Kay Walsh, 1940 (divorced 1949); 2) Ann Todd, 1949 (divorced 1957); 3) Leila Matkar, 1960 (divorced 1978); 4) Sandra Hotz, 1981 (marriage dissolved 1985). **Career:** Clapperboard boy at Lime Grove Studios under Maurice Elvey, 1926; camera assistant, then cutting room assistant, 1928; chief editor for Gaumont-British Sound News, 1930, then for British Movietone News, from 1931; editor for British Paramount, from 1934; invited by Noel Coward to co-direct *In Which We Serve,* 1942; co-founder, with Ronald Neame and Anthony Havelock-Allan, Cineguild, 1943 (dissolved 1950); began association with producer Sam Spiegel, 1956; returned to filmmaking after fourteen-year absence to make *A Passage to India,* 1984. **Awards:** British Film Academy Award for *The Sound Barrier,* 1952; Commander Order of the British Empire, 1953; Best Direction, New York Film Critics, 1955; Oscar for Best Director, and Best Direction, New York Film Critics, for *The Bridge on the River Kwai,* 1957; Oscars for Best Director and Best Film, for *Lawrence of Arabia,* 1962; Officier des Arts et des Lettres, France, 1968; Fellow of the British Film Institute, 1983; Fellow of the American Film Institute, 1989. **Died:** In London, 16 April 1991.

Films as Director:

1942 *In Which We Serve* (co-d)
1944 *This Happy Breed* (+ co-adapt)
1945 *Blithe Spirit* (+ co-adapt); ***Brief Encounter*** (+ co-sc)
1946 ***Great Expectations*** (+ co-sc)
1948 *Oliver Twist* (+ co-sc)
1949 *The Passionate Friends* (*One Woman's Story*) (+ co-adapt)
1950 *Madeleine*
1952 *The Sound Barrier* (*Breaking the Sound Barrier*) (+ pr)
1954 *Hobson's Choice* (+ pr, co-sc)
1955 *Summer Madness* (*Summertime*) (+ co-sc)
1957 *The Bridge on the River Kwai*
1962 ***Lawrence of Arabia***
1965 *Doctor Zhivago*
1970 *Ryan's Daughter*
1984 ***A Passage to India***

Other Films:

1935 *Escape Me Never* (Czinner) (ed)
1936 *As You Like It* (Czinner) (ed)
1937 *Dreaming Lips* (Czinner) (ed)
1938 *Pygmalion* (Asquith and Howard) (ed)
1939 *French Without Tears* (Asquith) (ed)

1941 *Major Barbara* (Pascal) (ed)
1942 *49th Parallel* (Powell) (ed); *One of Our Aircraft Is Missing* (Powell) (ed)

Publications

By LEAN: articles—

"*Brief Encounter*," in *The Penguin Film Review* (New York), no. 4, 1947.
"David Lean on What You Can Learn from Movies," in *Popular Photography* (Boulder, Colorado), March 1958.
"Out of the Wilderness," in *Films and Filming* (London), January 1963.
Interview, in *Interviews with Film Directors,* edited by Andrew Sarris, New York, 1967.
Interview with S. Ross, in *Take One* (Montreal), November 1973.
Interview with Graham Fuller and Nick Kent, in *Stills* (London), March 1985.
Interview with J.-L. Sablon, in *Revue du Cinéma* (Paris), June 1989.

On LEAN: books—

Phillips, Gene, *The Movie Makers,* Chicago, 1973.
Pratley, Gerald, *The Cinema of David Lean,* New York, 1974.
Silver, Alain, and James Ursini, *David Lean and His Films,* London, 1974.
Castelli, Louis P., and Caryn Lynn Cleeland, *David Lean: A Guide to References and Resources,* Boston, 1980.
Anderegg, Michael A., *David Lean,* Boston, 1984.
Sesti, Mario, *David Lean,* Florence, 1988.
Silverman, Stephen M., *David Lean,* London, 1989.
Silver, Alain, *David Lean and His Films,* Los Angeles, 1992.

On LEAN: articles—

Lejeune, C.A., "The Up and Coming Team of Lean and Neame," in *New York Times,* 15 June 1947.
Holden, J., "A Study of David Lean," in *Film Journal* (New York), April 1956.
Watts, Stephen, "David Lean," in *Films in Review* (New York), April 1959.
"David Lean, Lover of Life," in *Films and Filming* (London), August 1959.
Alpert, Hollis, "The David Lean Recipe: A Whack in the Guts," in *New York Times Magazine,* 23 May 1965.
Lightman, Herb, "On Location with *Ryan's Daughter,*" in *American Cinematographer* (Los Angeles), August 1968.
Kael, Pauline, "Bolt and Lean," in *New Yorker,* 21 November 1970.
Thomas, B., "David Lean," in *Action* (Los Angeles), November/December 1973.
Pickard, Ron, "David Lean: Supreme Craftsman," in *Films in Review* (New York), May 1974.
Andrews, George, "A Cinematographic Adventure with David Lean," in *American Cinematographer* (Los Angeles), March 1979.
Kennedy, Harlan, and M. Sragow, "David Lean's Right of *Passage,*" in *Film Comment* (New York), January/February 1985.
Combs, Richard, "David Lean: Riddles of the Sphinx," in *Monthly Film Bulletin* (London), April 1985.
Levine, J.P., "Passage to the Odeon: Too Lean," in *Literature/Film Quarterly* (Salisbury, Maryland), vol. 14, no. 3, 1986.
"David Lean," in *Film Dope* (London), March 1986.
McInerney, J.M., "Lean's *Zhivago*: A Re-Appraisal," in *Literature/Film Quarterly* (Salisbury, Maryland), vol. 15, no. 1, 1987.
"Master of Spectacle: David Lean Leaves a Legacy of Movie Epics," obituary in *Maclean's,* 29 April 1991.
Horton, Robert, "Jungle Fever," in *Film Comment* (New York), September/October 1991.
McFarlane, B., "David Lean's 'Great Expectations': Meeting Two Challenges," in *Literature/Film Quarterly* (Salisbury, Maryland), vol. 20, no. 1, 1992.
Sragow, Michael, "David Lean's Magnificient 'Kwai,'" in *Atlantic Monthly,* February 1994.

* * *

There is a trajectory that emerges from the shape of David Lean's career, and it is a misleading one. Lean first achieved fame as a director of seemingly intimate films, closely based on plays of Noel Coward. His first directorial credit was shared with Coward, for *In Which We Serve.* In the 1960s he was responsible for extraordinarily ambitious projects, for an epic cinema of grandiose effects, difficult location shooting, and high cultural, even literary, pretention. But, in fact, Lean's essential approach to the movies never changed. All of his films, no matter how small or large their dimensions, demonstrate an obsessive cultivation of craft, a fastidious concern with production detail that defines the "quality" postwar British cinema. That craft and concern are as hyperbolic in their devices as is the medium itself. Viewers surprised at the attention to detail and composition in *Ryan's Daughter,* a work whose scope would appear to call for a more modest approach, had really not paid attention to the truly enormous dimensions of *Brief Encounter,* a film that defines, for many, intimist cinema.

Lean learned about the movies during long years of apprenticeship, gaining particularly important experience as an editor. It is clear, even in the first films he directed with (and then for) Coward, that his vision was not bound to the playwright's West End proscenium. *This Happy Breed,* a lower class version of *Cavalcade,* makes full use of the modest terraced house that is the film's prime locus. The nearly palpable patterns of the mise-en-scène are animated by the highly professional acting characteristic of Lean's early films. Watching the working out of those patterns created by the relationship between camera, decor, and actor is like watching choreography at the ballet, where the audience is made aware of the abstract forms of placement on the stage even as that placement is vitalized by the individual quality of the dancer. The grief of Celia Johnson and Robert Newton is first expressed by the empty room that they are about to enter, then by the way the camera's oblique backward movement respects their silence.

It is in *Brief Encounter* that the fullness of the director's talent becomes clear. This story of chance meeting, love, and renunciation is as apparently mediocre, conventional, and echoless as Flaubert's *Madame Bovary.* What could be more boringly middle-class than the romantic longing of a nineteenth-century French provincial housewife or the oh-so-tasteful near adultery of two "decent" Britishers? In both cases, the authorial interventions are massive. Lean conveys the film's passion through the juxtaposition of the trite situation against the expressionistic violence of passing express trains and the wrenching departure of locals, against the decadent romanticism of the Rachmaninoff score, and most emphatically against one of the most grandiose and hyperbolic exposures of an actress in the history of film. The size of Celia Johnson's eyes finally becomes the measure of *Brief Encounter,* eyes whose scope is no less expansive than Lawrence's desert or Zhivago's tundra.

Lean's next two successes were his adaptations (with Ronald Neame) of Charles Dickens novels, *Great Expectations* and *Oliver Twist.* Again, intimacy on the screen becomes the moment of gigantic display. The greatness of Pip's expectations are set by the magnitude of his frightful encounter with an escaped convict who, when he emerges into the frame, reminds us all what it is like to be a small child in a world of oversized, menacing adults. A variation of this scale is also seen in Pip's meeting with mad Miss Havisham, in all her gothic splendor.

David Lean

Lean's next few films seem to have more modest ambitions, but they continue to demonstrate the director's concern with expressive placement. Of his three films with his then-wife Ann Todd, *Madeleine* most fully exploits her cool blond beauty.

A significant change then took place in the development of his career. Lean's reputation as a "location" director with a taste for the picturesque was made by *Summertime,* an adaptation of the play *The Time of the Cuckoo,* in which the city of Venice vies with Katharine Hepburn for the viewer's attention. It is from this point that Lean must be identified as an international rather than an English director. The subsequent international packages that resulted perhaps explain the widespread (and unjust) opinion that Lean is more of an executive than a creator with a personal vision.

The personality of Lean is in his compulsive drive to the perfectly composed shot, whatever the cost in time, energy, and money. In this there is some affinity between the director and his heroes. The Colonel (Alec Guinness) in *The Bridge on the River Kwai* must drive his men to build a good bridge, even if it is for the enemy. Lawrence (Peter O'Toole) crosses desert after desert in his quest for a self purified through physical ordeal, and viewers must wonder about the ordeals suffered by the filmmakers to photograph those deserts. The same wonder is elicited by the snowy trek of Dr. Zhivago (Omar Sharif) and the representation of life in early twentieth-century Russia.

That perfectly composed shot is emblemized by the principal advertising image used for *Ryan's Daughter*—an umbrella floating in air, suspended over an oceanside cliff. This is a celebration of composition per se, composition that holds unlikely elements in likely array. Composition is an expressive tension, accessible to viewers as it simultaneously captures the familiar and the unfamiliar. It is the combination that makes so many viewers sensitive to *Brief Encounter,* where middle-class lives (the lives of filmgoers) are filled with overwhelming passion and overwhelming style. Laura and Alex fall in love when they go to the movies.

—Charles Affron

LECONTE, Patrice

Nationality: French. **Born:** Paris, France, 12 November 1947. **Education:** Studied at the Institute des Hautes Etudes Cinematographiques. **Career:** Directed first feature, *Les veces etaient fermes de l'interieur,* 1976; often worked with producer Christian Fechner, and actors from the Cafe Splendide, the famed Parisian comedy cafe theater; cemented his international reputation with *Monsieur Hire,* 1989; has directed many commercials for French television, including ads for Peugeot and Carlsberg beer. **Address:** French Film Office, 745 Fifth Avenue, New York, NY 10151.

Films as Director and Screenwriter:

1976 *Les veces etaient fermes d'interieur*
1978 *Les bronzes*
1981 *Viens chez moi, j'habite chez une copine* (*Come to My Place, I'm Living at My Girlfriend's*)
1982 *Ma femme's appelle reviens* (*Singles*)
1983 *Circulez y a rien a voir* (*Move Along, There's Nothing to See*)
1985 *Les Specialistes* (*The Specialists*)
1986 *Tandem*
1989 *Monsieur Hire*
1990 *Le mari de la coiffeuse* (*The Hairdresser's Husband*)
1991 *Contre l'oubli* (*Against Oblivion*) (co-d)
1992 *Le batteur du bolero*
1993 *Le tango* (*Tango*); *Yvonne's Perfume*
1995 *Lumiere et compagnie* (*Lumiere and Company*) (short Lumiere film)

Other Films:

1984 *Moi vouloir toi* (*Me Want You*) (Dewolf) (co-sc)
1994 *The Son of Gascogne* (role)

Publications

By LECONTE: articles—

Leconte, Patrice, "Recontre: Leconte/Stevenin a propos de Passe-montagne," in *Cinematographe* (Paris), January 1979.
"20 questions aux cineastes," in *Cahiers du Cinema* (Paris), May 1981.
Interview with P. Carcassonne in *Cinematographe* (Paris), January 1983.
Leconte, Patrice, and F. Cuel, "Rencontre avec Claude Ventura," in *Cinematographe* (Paris), March 1983.
Interview with D. Dubroux in *Cahiers du Cinema* (Paris), May 1985.
Interview with M. Ciment in *Positif* (Paris), July/August 1986.
Interview with F. Aude in *Positif* (Paris), May 1991.
Interview with S. Brisset in *Presence* (Paris), January/February 1993.
Interview with F. Aude in *Positif* (Paris), March 1993.

On LECONTE: articles—

Fieschi, J., article in *Cinematographe* (Paris), July 1979.
de Klerk, N., article in *Skrien* (Amsterdam), December 1991/January 1992.
Kelleher, T., "Triton's *Hairdresser's Husband* Leconte's Light Comic Return," in *Film Journal* (New York), July 1992.

* * *

In 1989 Patrice Leconte earned international acclaim upon the release of *Monsieur Hire,* a sharp, clever thriller. Yet for almost a decade and a half, he had been thriving as a director of light, strictly commercial satires—smashingly successful at home but little-known outside France—which were crammed with physical slapstick, plays-on-words, and other assorted shenanigans. These films were amusing and nonsensical, with his casts including Josiane Balasko, Michel Blanc, Bernard Giraudeau, and other prominent actors from the French theater and cinema. A typical Leconte film of this period is *Les Bronzes,* a farce which chides Club Med-style vacation villages by contrasting two single males. One (Blanc) is hopelessly unsuccessful with the opposite sex, even in such ready-made surroundings. The other (Thierry Lhermitte) is a stud who finds it all-too-easy to seduce women.

So it seemed astonishing when Leconte directed *Monsieur Hire,* a film that was anything but funny. It is a psychological thriller, based on the same Georges Simenon novel that inspired Duvivier's *Panique,* in which Blanc appears as the title character—a bald, eccentric, middle-aged loner. The film is a revealing portrait of French-style provincialism in that M. Hire resides in a Parisian suburb where the status quo reigns, and where anyone who is different is viewed with suspicion. And M. Hire is different indeed. So he is the logical suspect after a young girl is brutally murdered, and is summarily and mercilessly hounded by the cop on the case. *Monsieur Hire* may be linked to a film like *Les Bronzes* in that both deal with men who obsess over women, seeing them not as human beings but as objects. Here, M. Hire has a voyeuristic obsession with Alice (Sandrine Bonnaire), his pretty young neighbor. But M. Hire is no comically inept male; rather, he is a lonely, affection-starved soul who eventually strikes up a friendship with the free-spirited Alice. Of course, M. Hire is not the kind of man

Patrice Leconte

to attract such a woman. Because he is blinded by his feelings for Alice and oblivious to her true nature, he ends up being manipulated and victimized.

Leconte's follow-up, *The Hairdresser's Husband,* works as a companion piece to *Monsieur Hire.* It is the deceptively simple story of Antoine, who as a young boy on the edge of puberty does not spend his time with other kids, riding bicycles or indulging in sports. Instead, he is constantly at the town barbershop, where he is smitten with the buxom haircutter. As a middle-aged man, Antoine (Jean Rochefort) can describe the woman in minute detail. Back when he was a boy, he decided that his sole goal in life would be to marry a hairdresser. And so he does. He proposes to the beautiful Mathilde (Anna Galiena) while she cuts his hair for the first time. She accepts, and they are wed. Both are content and the days pass, one after the other, as if in a dream. If all of this sounds slight, it is not. The film, as it focuses on Antoine and Mathilde's love and their attempt to shelter themselves from all that is bad in life, is crammed with profoundly deep layers of emotion. Like *Monsieur Hire,* it is a concise, knowing allegory about romantic obsession and how a man can be fascinated by a woman. The difference between the two films is that, here, love brings him peace. But how fragile is that peace? All lovers are destined to be separated by death, if not by cruel fate. In *Monsieur Hire,* a man is thwarted in his attempt to find his idealized love, to the point where his life becomes enveloped by tragedy. While a different (yet not dissimilar) man does find love in *The Hairdresser's Husband,* Leconte is worldly enough to know that, because of the very nature of human existence, such happiness is fated to be only temporary.

In *Tango,* a third Leconte feature, the filmmaker returned to his comic roots, but with a devilish twist. *Tango* is the story of a woman-hater (Philippe Noiret) who believes that "wife-killing isn't really murder." Via blackmail, he coerces another man (Richard Bohringer), who had killed his own wife and her lover, into murdering the mate of his nephew (Thierry Lhermitte), who is tired of married life and wants the freedom to play around. What sounds like a thriller actually is a freewheeling, ingeniously structured, pitch-black comedy about the manner in which men are endlessly fascinated by women but dislike being tied down by them. In this regard, *Tango* is an extension of the characters and themes explored in *Monsieur Hire* and *The Hairdresser's Husband.* These three films are evidence that Leconte has matured as a filmmaker, and that his days making frivolous farces are forever past.

—Rob Edelman

LEDUC, Paul

Nationality: Mexican. **Born:** Mexico City, 11 March 1942. **Education:** Studied architecture and theatre, Universidad Nacional Autónoma de México; attended Institut des hautes études cinématographiques (IDHEC), Paris, 1965-66. **Career:** Film critic in Mexico, early 1960s; worked for French TV, then returned to Mexico, 1967.

Films as Director:

1968 *Comunicados del comité nacional de huelga* (3 shorts)
1969 *Parto psicoprofiláctico* (doc short)
1973 *Reed: México insurgente* (*Reed: Insurgent Mexico*)
1974 *Sur, sureste 2604* (short); *El mar*
1975 *Bach y sus intérpretes*
1978 *Etnocidio: notas sobre el Mezquital*; *Estudios para un retrato* (*Francis Bacon*) (doc short); *Puebla hoy* (doc); *Monjas coronadas* (doc short)
1979 *Historias prohibidas de Pulgarcito*
1981 *Complot petrolero*; *La cabeza de la hidra*
1982 *Como ves?* (*Whaddya Think?*)
1984 *Frida: Naturaleza vita* (*Frida*)
1989 *Barroco* (*Baroque*)
1990 *Latino Bar*
1993 *Dollar Mambo*

Publications

By LEDUC: articles—

Interview with Nelson Carro, in *Imagenes* (Mexico City), October 1979.
Interview with Enrique Pineda Barnet, in *Cine Cubano* (Havana), no. 104, 1983.
"Caminar por el continente," in *Cine Cubano* (Havana), no. 105, 1983.
Interview with Dennis West, in *Cineaste* (New York), vol. 26, no. 4, 1988.
"Nuevo cine latinoamericano: Dramaturgia y autocrítica," in *Pantalla* (Mexico City), August 1985.
Interview with Dennis West, in *Cineaste* (New York), vol. 16, no. 4, 1988.

On LEDUC: books—

Blanco, Jorge Ayala, *La búsqueda del cine mexicano,* Mexico City, 1974.
Sánchez, Alberto Ruy, *Mitologia de un cine en crisis,* Mexico City, 1981.
Mora, Carl, *Mexican Cinema: Reflections of a Society, 1896-1980,* Berkeley, 1982.
Blanco, Jorge Ayala, *La condicíon del cine mexicano,* Mexico City, 1986.
Costa, Paola, *La "aperatura" cinematográfica,* Puebla, 1988.
Ramirez Berg, Charles, *Cinema of Solitude: A Critical Study of Mexican Film, 1967-1983,* Austin, 1992.

On LEDUC: articles—

Espinasa, José María, "El cine mexicano hoy," in *Hojas de cine,* vol. 2, Mexico City, 1988.
Bejar, Ruth, "*Frida*," in *American Historical Review,* October 1989.
Koivunen, A. "Myytti Naisesta jaa Elamaan," in *Filmihullu* (Helsinki), no. 5, 1989.
Pick, Z. M., "Territories of Representation," in *Iris* (Paris), Summer 1991.
Kieffer, A., "Baroque mexicain et Revolution: Paul Leduc," in *Jeune Cinema,* January/February 1992.
Mauro, S., "*Latino Bar,*" in *Segnocinema* (Italy), July/August, 1992.
Palant, V., "*Latino Bar,*" in *Revista del Cinmetografo* (Rome), July/August 1992.
Pezzuto, A., "*Latino Bar,*" in *Film* (Italy), no. 4, 1992.
Gill, J. A., "*Latino Bar,*" in *Positif* (Paris), September 1992.

* * *

Generally acknowledged as the most talented and socially conscious of contemporary Mexican directors, Paul Leduc has been forced to make his films on the margins of commercial cinema. Leduc began his career in a university department of film studies, an initiation increasingly prevalent among the younger generation of Mexican filmmakers. His first films were documentaries, a typical beginning for directors of the "New Latin American Cinema." Then Leduc was able to take some advantage of a novel situation: during the reign of President Luis Echeverria (1970-76) the Mexican government actively intervened as a producer of cinema, the only time since the 1930s (e.g., *Redes*) that it has attempted to create some sort of alternative to the wretched fare provided by the country's commercial film industry. The government paid for the amplification of *Reed: Insurgent Mexico* to 35mm and co-produced *Mezquital* with the Canadian National Film Board. Since that time, however, Leduc has funded his films independently, through universities and unions, and with collective efforts.

Reed: Insurgent Mexico is perhaps Leduc's most accomplished fiction film, and was the first really distinctive work of the "New Cinema" movement in Mexico. Although the film was shot on a minuscule budget in 16mm, it has an exquisite sepia tone which reproduces the ambience of antique revolutionary photographs. Deliberately undramatic, *Reed* demystified the Mexican revolution (1910-17) in a way that had not been seen since Fernando De Fuentes's masterpieces of 1933-35. One Mexican critic, Jorge Ayala Blanco, described *Reed* as "raging against, incinerating, and annihilating the spider web that had been knitted over the once-living image of the revolution, while briefly illuminating the nocturnal ruins of our temporal and cultural distance from the men who participated in that upheaval." The film is a dramatization of John Reed's famous account of the revolution, *Insurgent Mexico,* with Reed as the main protagonist. Although the film is a beautiful and important work, it does not really rise above the level of a vignette (perhaps too greatly influenced by the book's form), nor does it achieve the heights of De Fuentes's films.

Leduc's following works reflected his concern for actuality. *Etnocidio: notas sobre el Mezquital* is probably the best documentary on the extermination of the native peoples in Latin America, allowing the Otomi Indians of the Mezquital region in Mexico to relate their experiences with "civilization." The film is an interesting example of collaborative effort, for the "script" was written by Roger Bartra, Mexico's leading rural sociologist, who based it on his years of research in the area. *Historias prohibidas* is a flawed work that Leduc made in a collective, but it does contain a lively analysis of El Salvador's history. *Complot petrolero* is a made-for-TV thriller about an attempt by right-wing elements (including the CIA and anti-Castro Cubans) to take over the oil and uranium resources of Mexico. Actually a miniseries totaling three-and-one-half hours, it has never been shown on Mexican television, which is largely dominated by series and made-for-TV movies imported from the United States.

Just when it appeared that Leduc was firmly settled in the aesthetic of realism, he directed a highly expressionist, lyrical work on the painter Frida Kahlo, *Frida: Naturaleza viva.* An experimental film which keeps words, whether spoken or written, to an absolute minimum, the movie has been most controversial. And, while one must admire Leduc for risking a break with traditional cinematographic styles, the absence of dialogue reduces pivotal figures of history and culture such as Diego Rivera, León Trotsky, David Alfaro Siqueiros, André Breton, and Frida Kahlo to caricatures of themselves. Instead of using the film to develop these characters in political or personal terms, Leduc takes the easy way out, allowing them to remain at the lowest common denominator of the popular stereotypes fomented in mass culture.

Other critical views of Leduc's *Frida,* however, suggest a different reading: objects such as Frida's dress become political iconography that proposes "a self-conscious affirmation of a *mestizo* identity but also a specifically Mexican rearrangement of the indigenous. From this perspective, as Pick observes, "the 'alternative modernism' ... intimated by Frida Kahlo's dress, its effect as representation and self-representation, embodies a distinctly Latin American way to affirm cultural identity." It is exactly in such a retainment of "the political problematic that has characterized the last three decades of Latin American filmmaking." Leduc's rejection of social realism may thus be viewed as a step forward, towards a realm of expressionism that crystallizes the political by ways of, according to Jean Franco, "a struggle over meanings and the history of meanings, histories that have been acquired and stored with unofficial institutions."

In general, Mexico has proven to be a difficult context for Leduc, who appropriately describes cinema there as "a perfect disaster, composed of *churros*—vulgar, cheap, and badly made films." Dominated by the "fastbuck" mentality typical of dependent capitalism, Mexican commercial cinema has offered few opportunities for Leduc to direct the kind of films which interest him.

—John Mraz, updated by Guo-Juin Hong

LEE, Ang

Nationality: Taiwanese. **Born:** Taiwan; moved to United States, 1978. **Education:** Attended theater program, University of Illinois. **Career:** Directed first two features in the United States, 1991-93; returned to Taiwan to direct *Eat Drink Man Woman,* 1994. **Awards:** Golden Bear Award at Berlin Film Festival, 1993, for *The Wedding Banquet;* Golden Bear Award at Berlin Film Festival, Best Director from New York Film Critics, and Best Director and Best Picture from National Board of Review, all 1995, all for *Sense and Sensibility.*

Films as Director:

1991 *Pushing Hands*
1993 *Hsi Yen* (*The Wedding Banquet*)
1994 *Eat Drink Man Woman* (+ co-sc)
1995 *Sense and Sensibility*

Publications

By LEE: articles—

"Dinner for Two," an interview in *Filmmaker,* vol. 1, no. 4, 1993.
"Ang Lee Returned to His Native Taiwan to Make *Eat Drink Man Woman,*" an interview with Steven Rea, in *Knight-Ridder/Tribune News Service,* 19 August 1994.

On LEE: articles—

Shapiro, M., "Ang Lee," in *Independent,* May 1993.

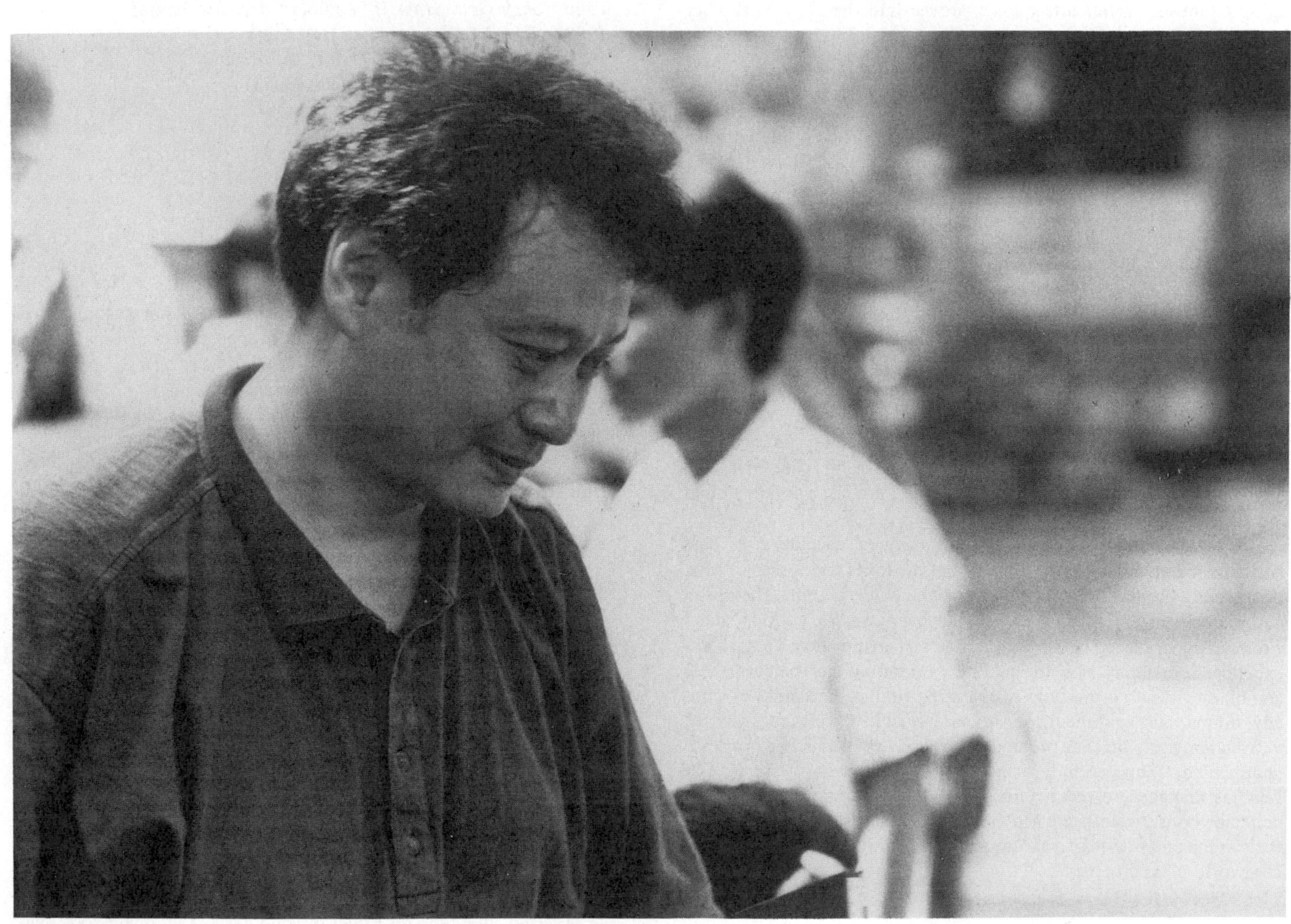

Ang Lee directing *Eat Drink Man Woman* © Buena Vista UK International

Hornaday, A., "A Director's Trip from Salad Days to a *Banquet,*" in *New York Times,* 1 August 1993.
Noh, D., "Ang Lee's *Wedding Banquet* Serves Up a Mix of Cultures," in *Film Journal,* September 1993.
Berry, C., "Taiwanese Melodrama Returns with a Twist in *The Wedding Banquet,*" in *Cinemaya,* Autumn 1993.
Hamlin, Suzanne, "Le Grand Exces Spices Love Poems to Food," in *New York Times,* 31 July 1994.
Kauffman, Stanley, "*Eat Drink Man Woman,*" in *New Republic,* 5 September 1994.
Schickel, Richard, "*Sense and Sensibility,*" in *Time,* 18 December 1995.

* * *

In the space of only five years and four films, Taiwanese film director Ang Lee has grown from art-house phenomenon to major studio director. Lee's first three films, a sort of trilogy of charming family dramas, established him as a talented director with a particularly deft hand at creating character-driven studies of human nature. His fourth film, *Sense and Sensibility* (1995) marked his emergence from relative anonymity into the film world spotlight. A delightful adaptation of the Jane Austen novel, *Sense and Sensibility* won a number of well-deserved awards, including Best Director from the New York Film Critics, and Best Director and Best Picture from the National Board of Review (it was also nominated for seven Oscars).

Lee's first feature was *Pushing Hands,* a 1991 film in which an aging Chinese martial arts master moves into the New York City home of his son and daughter-in-law. The relationship between the old man, who speaks no English, and the daughter-in-law, who speaks no Chinese, is a difficult one, full of resentment and misunderstanding, but both try to make the arrangement work. *Pushing Hands,* a languidly paced comedy drama that first displayed Lee's fondness for filming scenes in which food figures prominently, was followed by *The Wedding Banquet,* another film that explored family relationships. The Oscar-nominated film concerns a Chinese father who visits his son in America, only to find him engaged in an elaborate marital charade to mask his homosexuality.

In 1994 Lee released *Eat Drink Man Woman,* the first of his movies to be shot entirely in Taiwan. It is an enjoyable tale of a master chef at a Taipei hotel and his relationship with his three adult daughters, all of whom are grappling with one problem or another. The action centers around the immense, sumptuous Sunday feasts that he prepares for his daughters; Stanley Kauffmann remarks that "the preparation of these dishes, their wonderful appearance, their almost tasteable succulence are the film's true base and being. The stories, the hassle and hustle of the characters' troubles, are just garnish around the dishes."

Lee's next film was *Sense and Sensibility,* an adaptation of Jane Austen's nineteenth-century novel about the loves and losses of Mrs. Dashwood (Gemma Jones) and her two daughters (Emma Thompson and Kate Winslet) as they try to find happiness in various social circles of upper-class English society. Lee's smart direction, Thompson's excellent screenplay, and the picture's uniformly fine performances combine to create a thoroughly charming film. A fine meld of comedy, drama, and sentiment, *Sense and Sensibility* whisked away the veil of anonymity that had previously covered Lee. As Richard Schickel commented, "You certainly wonder how a Taiwan-born director like Lee has managed to reach across time and cultures to deliver these delicate goods undamaged. Maybe some of that whoosh of delight one feels at the end of *Sense and Sensibility* is for him, and his emergence as a world-class director."

—Kevin Hillstrom

LEE, Spike

Nationality: American. **Born:** Shelton Jackson Lee in Atlanta, Georgia, 20 March 1957; son of jazz musician Bill Lee. **Education:** Morehouse College, B.A., 1979; New York University, M.A. in Filmmaking; studying with Martin Scorsese. **Family:** Married lawyer Tonya Linette Lewis, 1993; one son, Satchel. **Career:** Set up production company 40 Acres and a Mule; directed first feature, *She's Gotta Have It,* 1986; also directs music videos and commercials for Nike/Air Jordan; Trustee of Morehouse College, 1992. **Awards:** Student Directors Academy Award, for *Joe's Bed-Stuy Barbershop: We Cut Heads,* 1980; U.S. Independent Spirit Award for First Film, New Generation Award, Los Angeles Film Critics Association, and Prix de Jeunesse, Cannes Film Festival, all for *She's Gotta Have It,* 1986; U.S. Independent Spirit Award, Best Picture, L.A. Film Critics, and Best Picture, Chicago Film Festival, all for *Do the Right Thing,* 1989; Essence Award, 1994. **Address:** 40 Acres and a Mule, 124 Dekalb Avenue, Suite 2, Brooklyn, NY 11217-1201, U.S.A.

Films as Director, Scriptwriter, and Editor:

1977 *Last Hustle in Brooklyn* (Super-8 short)
1980 *The Answer* (short)
1981 *Sarah* (short)
1982 *Joe's Bed-Stuy Barbershop: We Cut Heads* (+ role)
1986 *She's Gotta Have It* (+ role as Mars Blackmon)
1988 *School Daze* (+ role as Half Pint)
1989 *Do the Right Thing* (+ role as Mookie)
1990 *Mo' Better Blues* (+ role as Giant)
1991 *Jungle Fever* (+ role as Cyrus)
1992 ***Malcolm X*** (+ role as Shorty)
1994 *Crooklyn* (+ role as Snuffy)
1995 *Clockers* (+ role as Chucky)
1996 *Girl 6* (+ role as Jimmy)

Other Films:

1993 *The Last Party* (*Youth for Truth*) (doc) (appearance); *Seven Songs for Malcolm X* (doc) (appearance); *Hoop Dreams* (doc) (appearance)
1994 *DROP Squad* (exec pr, appearance)
1995 *New Jersey Drive* (exec pr); *Tales from the Hood* (exec pr)

Publications

By LEE: books—

Spike Lee's She's Gotta Have It: Inside Guerilla Filmmaking, New York, 1987.
Uplift the Race: The Construction of School Daze, New York, 1988.
Do the Right Thing: A Spike Lee Joint, with Lisa Jones, New York, 1989.
Mo' Better Blues, with Lisa Jones, New York, 1990.
Five for Five: The Films of Spike Lee, New York, 1991.
By Any Means Necessary: The Trials and Tribulations of the Making of Malcolm X, with Ralph Wiley, New York, 1993.

By LEE: articles—

Interview in *New York Times,* 10 August 1986.
Interview in *Village Voice* (New York), 12 August 1986.
"Class Act," in *American Film* (Washington, D.C.), January/February 1988.

"Entretien avec Spike Lee," in *Cahiers du Cinema,* June 1989.
"Bed-Stuy BBQ," an interview with M. Glicksman, in *Film Comment,* July/August 1989.
"I Am Not an Anti-Semite," in *New York Times,* 22 August 1990.
Interview with Mike Wilmington, in *Empire* (London), October 1990.
"Entretien avec Spike Lee," with A. de Baecque and N. Saada, in *Cahiers du Cinema,* June 1991.
Interview with M. Cieutat and Michael Ciment in *Positif,* July/August 1991.
"The Rolling Stone Interview: Spike Lee," with David Breskin, in *Rolling Stone,* July 1991.
"Spike Speaks," an interview with Lisa Kennedy, in *Village Voice,* 11 June 1991.
"Playboy Interview: Spike Lee," with Elvis Mitchell, in *Playboy,* July 1991.
"He's Gotta Have It," an interview with Janice M. Richolson, in *Cineaste,* no. 4, 1991.
"Generation X," an interview with H. L. Gates, Jr., in *Black Film Review,* no. 3, 1992.
"Just Whose Malcolm Is It, Anyway?" interview in *New York Times,* 31 May 1992.
"United Colors of Benetton," in *Rolling Stone,* 12 November 1992.
"Words with Spike Lee," an interview with J. C. Simpson, in *Time,* 23 November 1992.
Interview with David Breskin, in *Inner Views: Filmmakers in Conversation,* Boston, 1992.
"Entretien avec Spike Lee," with B. Bollag, in *Positif,* February 1993.
"Doing the Job," an interview with J. Verniere, in *Sight and Sound,* February 1993.
"Our Film Is Only a Starting Point," an interview with George Crowdus and Dan Georgakas, in *Cineaste,* no. 4, 1993.
"De qui parler?" an interview with V. Amiel and Jean-Pierre Coursodon, in *Positif,* February 1993.
"Is *Malcolm X* the Right Thing?" an interview with Lisa Kennedy, in *Sight and Sound,* February 1993.
"The Lees on Life," an interview with Lynn Darling, in *Harper's Bazarr,* May 1994.
"Spike Lee: The Do-The-Right-Thing Revolution," an interview with Henry Louis Gates, in *Interview,* October 1994.
"Spike on Sports," an interview with Daryl Howerton, in *Sport,* February 1995.

On LEE: books—

Spike Lee and Commentaries on His Work, Bloomington, Indiana, 1992.
Patterson, Alex, *Spike Lee,* New York, 1992.
Bernotas, Bob, *Spike Lee: Filmmaker,* Hillside, New Jersey, 1993.
Lee, David, *Malcolm X, Denzel Washington: A Spike Lee Joint,* New York, 1992.
Chapman, Kathleen, *Spike Lee,* Mankato, Minnesota, 1994.
Hardy, James Earl, *Spike Lee,* New York, 1996.

On LEE: articles—

Tate, G., "Spike Lee," in *American Film* (Washington, D.C.), September 1986.
Glicksman, M., "Lee Way," in *Film Comment* (New York), September/October 1986.
Taylor, C., "The Paradox of Black Independent Cinema," in *Black Film Review,* no. 4, 1988.
Crouch, Stanley, "*Do the Right Thing,*" in *Village Voice,* 20 June 1989.
Davis, Thuliani, "We've Gotta Have It," in *Village Voice,* 20 June 1989.
Davis, T., "Local Hero," in *American Film,* July/August, 1989.
Sharkey, B., and T. Davis, "Knocking on Hollywood's Door," in *American Film* (Washington, D.C.), July/August 1989.
McDowell, J., "Profile: He's Got to Have It His Way," in *Time,* 17 July 1989.
Orenstein, Peggy, "Spike's Riot," in *Mother Jones,* September 1989.
Norment, L., "Spike Lee: The Man behind the Movies and the Controversy," in *Ebony,* October 1989.
Kirn, Walter, "Spike It Already," in *Gentlemens Quarterly,* August 1990.
George, N., "Forty Acres and an Empire," in *Village Voice,* 7 August 1990.
Hentoff, Nat, "The Bigotry of Spike Lee," in *Village Voice,* 4 September 1990.
O'Pray, Michael, "Do Better Blues—Spike Lee," in *Monthly Film Bulletin* (London), October 1990.
Perkins, E., "Renewing the African American Cinema: The Films of Spike Lee," in *Cineaste,* no. 4, 1990.
Baecque, A. de, "Spike Lee," in *Cahiers du Cinema,* May 1991.
Boyd, T., "The Meaning of the Blues," in *Wide Angle,* no. 3/4, 1991.
Breskin, D., "Spike Lee" in *Rolling Stone,* 11-25 July 1991.
Bates, Karen Grigsby, "They've Gotta Have Us," in *New York Times Magazine,* 14 July 1991.
Gilroy, Paul, "Spiking the Argument," in *Sight and Sound,* November 1991.
Grenier, Richard, "Spike Lee Fever," in *Commentary,* August 1991.
Hamill, Pete, "Spike Lee Takes No Prisoners," in *Esquire,* August 1991.
Backer, Houston A. Jr., "Spike Lee and the Commerce of Culture," in *Black American Literature Forum,* Summer 1991.
Whitaker, Charles, "Doing the Spike Thing," in *Ebony,* November 1991.
Johnson, A., "Moods Indigo: A Long View, Part 2," in *Film Quarterly,* Spring 1991.
Klein, Joe, "Spiked Again," in *New York,* 1 June 1992.
Elise, Sharon, "Spike Lee Constructs the New Black Man: Mo' Better," in *Western Journal of Black Studies,* Summer 1992.
Weinraub, B., "Spike Lee's Request: Black Interviewers Only," in *New York Times,* 29 October 1992.
Harrison, Barbara G., "Spike Lee Hates Your Cracker Ass," in *Esquire,* October 1992.
Wiley, R., "Great 'X'pectations," in *Premiere,* November 1992.
Reden, L., "Spike's Gang," in *New York Times,* 7 February 1993.
Hooks, Bill, "Male Heroes and Female Sex Objects: Sexism in Spike Lee's *Malcolm X,*" in *Cineaste,* no. 4, 1993.
Johnson, Victoria E., "Polyphone and Cultural Expression: Interpreting Musical Traditions in *Do the Right Thing,*" in *Film Quarterly,* Winter 1993.
Horne, Gerald, "Myth and the Making of *Malcolm X,*" in *American Historical Review,* April 1993.
Hirschberg, Lynn, "Living Large," in *Vanity Fair,* September 1993.
Pinsker, Sanford, "Spike Lee: Protest, Literary Tradition, and the Individual Filmmaker," in *Midwest Quarterly,* Autumn 1993.
Norment, Lynn, "A Revealing Look at Spike Lee's Changing Life," in *Ebony,* May 1994.
Rowland, Robert C., "Social Function, Polysemy, and Narrative-Dramatic Form: A Case Study of *Do the Right Thing,*" in *Communication Quarterly,* Summer 1994.
Hooks, Bell, "Sorrowful Black Death Is Not a Hot Ticket," in *Sight and Sound,* August 1994.
Lee, Jonathan Scott, "Spike Lee's *Malcolm X* as Transformational Object," in *American Imago,* Summer 1995.

* * *

Spike Lee is the most famous African-American to have succeeded in breaking through the Hollywood establishment to create a notable career for himself as a major director. What makes this all the more notable is that he is not a comedian—the one role in which Hollywood

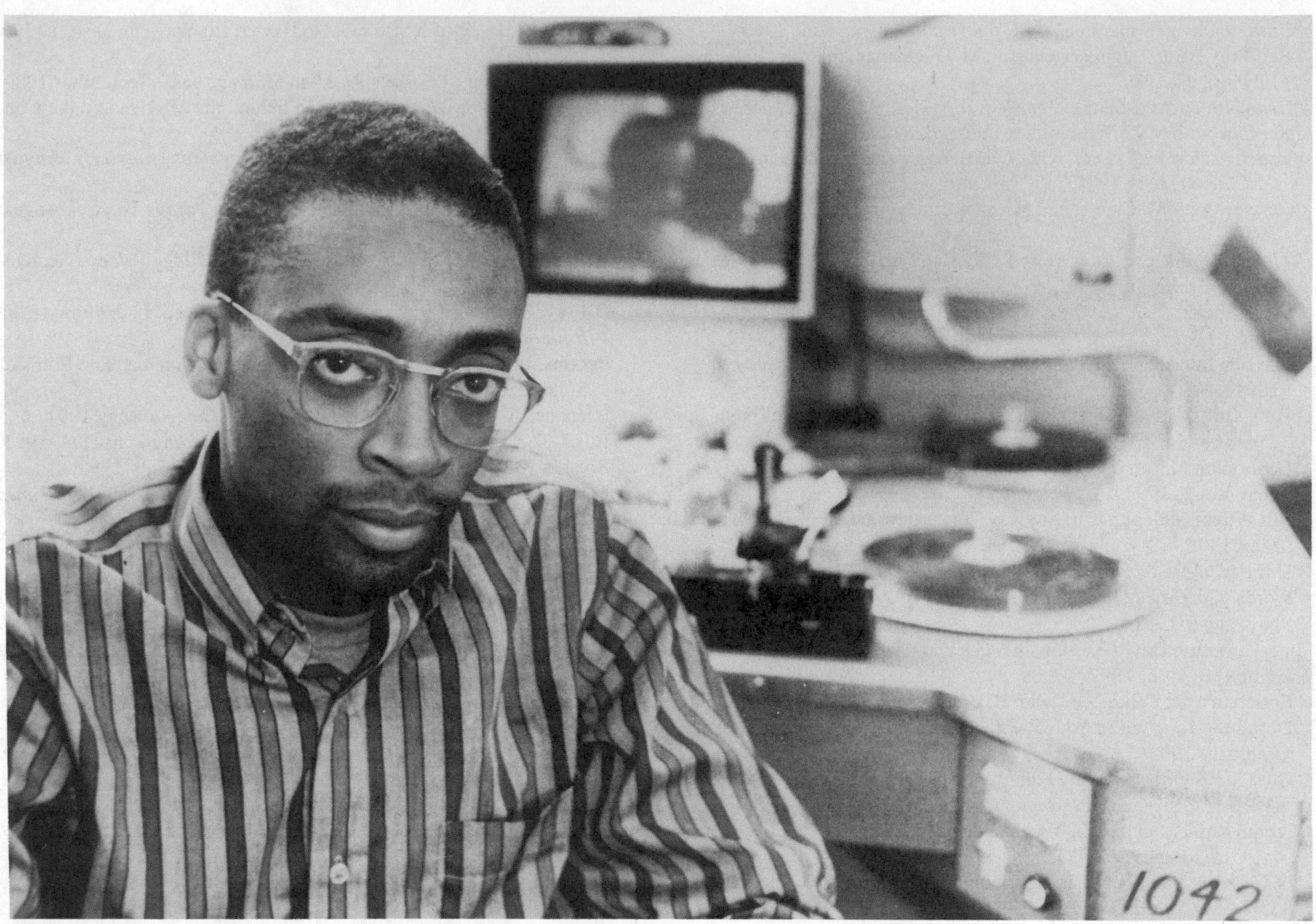

Spike Lee

has usually allowed blacks to excel—but a prodigious, creative, multi-faceted talent who writes, directs, edits, and acts, a filmmaker who invites comparisons with American titans like Woody Allen, John Cassavetes, and Orson Welles.

His films, which deal with different facets of the black experience, are innovative and controversial even within the black community. Spike Lee refuses to be content with presenting blacks in their "acceptable" stereotypes: noble Poitiers demonstrating simple moral righteousness are nowhere to be found. Lee's characters are three-dimensional and often vulnerable to moral criticism. His first feature film, *She's Gotta Have It,* dealt with black sexuality, unapologetically supporting the heroine's promiscuity. His second film, *School Daze,* drawing heavily upon Lee's own experiences at Morehouse College, examined the black university experience and dealt with discrimination within the black community based on relative skin colors. His third film, *Do the Right Thing,* dealt with urban racial tensions and violence. His fourth film, *Mo' Better Blues,* dealt with black jazz and its milieu. His fifth film, *Jungle Fever,* dealt with interracial sexual relationships and their political implications, by no means taking the traditional, white liberal position that love should be color blind. His sixth film, *Malcolm X,* attempted no less than a panoramic portrait of the entire racial struggle in the United States, as seen through the life story of the controversial activist. Not until his seventh film, *Crooklyn,* primarily an autobiographical family remembrance of growing up in Brooklyn, did Spike Lee take a breath to deal with a simpler subject and theme.

Lee's breakthrough feature was *She's Gotta Have It,* an independent film budgeted at $175,000 and a striking box-office success: a film made by blacks for blacks which also attracted white audiences. *She's Gotta Have It* reflects the sensibilities of an already sophisticated filmmaker and harkens back to the early French New Wave in its exuberant embracing of bravura technique—intertitles, black-and-white cinematography, a sense of improvisation, characters directly addressing the camera—all wedded nevertheless to serious philosophical/sociological examination. The considerable comedy in *She's Gotta Have It* caused many critics to call Spike Lee the "black Woody Allen," a label which would increasingly reveal itself as a rather simplistic, muddle-headed approbation, particularly as Lee's career developed. (Indeed, in his work's energy, style, eclecticism, and social commitment, he more resembles Martin Scorsese, a Lee mentor at the NYU film school.) Even to categorize Spike Lee as a black filmmaker is to denigrate his talent, since there are today virtually no American filmmakers (except Allen) with the ambitiousness and talent to write, direct, and perform in their own films. And Lee edits as well.

Do the Right Thing, Lee's third full-length feature, is one of the director's most daring and controversial achievements, presenting one sweltering day which culminates in a riot in the Bedford Stuyvesant section of Brooklyn. From its first images—assailing jump cuts of a woman dancing frenetically to the rap "Fight the Power" while colored lights stylistically flash on a location ghetto block upon which Lee has constructed his set—we know we are about to witness something deeply disturbing. The film's sound design is incredibly dense and complex, and the volume alarmingly high, as the film continues to assail us with tight close-ups, extreme angles, moving camera, colored lights, distorting lenses, and individual scenes directed like high operatic arias.

Impressive, too, is the well-constructed screenplay, particularly the perceptively drawn Italian family at the center of the film who feel so besieged by the changing, predominantly black neighborhood around them. A variety of ethnic characters are drawn sympathetically, if unsentimentally; perhaps never in American cinema has a director so accurately presented the relationships among the American urban underclasses. Particularly shocking and honest is a scene in which catalogs of racial and ethnic epithets are shouted directly into the camera. The key scene in *Do the Right Thing* has the character of Mookie, played by Spike Lee, throwing a garbage can through a pizzeria window as a moral gesture which works to make the riot inevitable. The film ends with two quotations: one from Martin Luther King Jr., eschewing violence; the other from Malcolm X, rationalizing violence in certain circumstances.

Do the Right Thing was one of the most controversial films of the last twenty years. Politically conservative commentators denounced the film, fearful it would incite inner-city violence. Despite widespread acclaim the film was snubbed at the Cannes Film Festival, outraging certain Cannes judges; despite the accolades of many critics' groups, the film was also largely snubbed by the Motion Picture Academy, receiving a nomination only for Spike Lee's screenplay and Danny Aiello's performance as the pizzeria owner.

Both *Mo' Better Blues* and the much underrated *Crooklyn* owe a lot to Spike Lee's appreciation of music, particularly as handed down to him by his father, the musician Bill Lee. *Crooklyn* is by far the gentler film, presenting Lee's and his siblings' memories of growing up with Bill Lee and his mother. Typical of Spike Lee, the vision in *Crooklyn* is by no means a sentimental one, and the father comes across as a proud, if weak, man; talented, if failing in his musical career; loving his children, if not always strong enough to do the right thing for them. The mother, played masterfully by Alfre Woodard, is the stronger of the two personalities; and the film—ending as it does with grief—seems Spike Lee's version of Fellini's *Amarcord*. For a white audience, *Crooklyn* came as a revelation: the sight of black children watching cartoons, eating Trix cereal, playing hopscotch, and singing along with the Partridge family, seemed strange—because the American cinema had so rarely (if ever?) shown a struggling black family so rooted in popular-culture iconography all Americans could relate to. Scene after scene is filled with humanity, such as the little girl stealing groceries rather than be embarrassed by using her mother's food stamps. *Crooklyn*'s soundtrack, like so many other Spike Lee films, is unusually cacophonous, with everyone talking at once, and its improvisational style suggests Cassavetes or Scorsese. Lee's 1995 film, *Clockers*, which deals with drug dealing, disadvantage, and the young "gangsta," was actually produced in conjunction with Scorsese, whose own work, particularly the seminal *Meanstreets*, Lee's work often recalls.

Another underrated film from Lee is *Jungle Fever* (from 1991). Taken for granted is how well the film communicates the African-American experience; more surprising is how persuasively and perceptively the film communicates the Italian-American experience, particularly working-class attitudes. Indeed, one looks in vain in the Hollywood cinema for an American director with a European background who presents blacks with as many insights as Lee presents his Italians. And certainly unforgettable, filmed expressively with nightmarish imagery, is the film's set-piece in which we enter a crack house and come to understand profoundly and horrifically the tremendous damage being done to a component of the African-American community by this plague. *Jungle Fever*, like *Do the Right Thing*, basically culminates in images of Ruby Dee screaming in horror and pain, a metaphor for black martyrdom and suffering.

Nevertheless, the most important film in the Spike Lee *oeuvre* (if not his best) is probably *Malcolm X*—important because Lee himself campaigned for the film when it seemed it would be given to a white director, creating then an epic with the sweep and majesty of a David Lean and a clear political message of black empowerment. If the film on the whole seems less interesting than many of Lee's films (because there is less Lee there), the most typical Lee touches (such as the triumphant coda which enlists South African President Nelson Mandela to play himself and teach young blacks about racism and their future) seem among the film's most inspired and creative scenes. If more cautious and conservative, in some ways the film is also Lee's most ambitious: with dozens of characters, historical reconstructions, and the biggest budget in his entire career. *Malcolm X* proved definitively to fiscally conservative Hollywood studio executives that an African-American director could be trusted to direct a high-budget "A film." The success of *Malcolm X*, coupled with the publicity machine supporting Spike Lee, helped a variety of young black directors—like John Singleton, the Wayans brothers, and Mario Van Peebles—all break through into mainstream Hollywood features.

And indeed, Lee seems often to be virtually everywhere. On television interview shows he is called upon to comment on every issue relevant to black America: from the O. J. Simpson verdict to Louis Farrakhan and the Million Man March. In bookstores, his name can be found on a variety of published books on the making of his films, books created by his own public relations arm particularly so that others can read about the process, become empowered, find their own voices, and follow in Lee's filmic footsteps. On the basketball court, Lee can be found very publicly attending the New York Knicks' games. On MTV, he can be found in notable commercials for Nike basketball shoes. On college campuses, he can be found making highly publicized speeches on the issues of the day. And on the street, his influence can be seen even in fashion trends—such as the ubiquitous "X" on a variety of clothing the year of *Malcolm X*'s release. There may be no other American filmmaker working today who is so willing to take on all comers, so politically committed to make films which are consistently and unapologetically in-your-face. Striking, too, is that instead of taking his inspiration from other movies, as do the gaggle of Spielberg imitators, Lee takes his inspiration from real life—whether the Howard Beach or Yusuf Hawkins incidents, in which white racists killed blacks, or his own autobiographical memories of growing up black in Brooklyn.

As Spike Lee has become a leading commentator on the cultural scene, there has been an explosion of Lee scholarship, not all of it laudatory: increasing voices attack Lee and his films for either homophobia, sexism, or anti-Semitism. Lee defends both his films and himself, pointing out that because characters espouse some of these values does not imply that he himself does, only that realistic portrayal of the world *as it is* has no place for political correctness. Still, some of the accusers point to examples which give pause: Lee's insistence on talking only to black journalists for stories about *Malcolm X*, but refusing to meet with a black journalist who was gay; the totally cartoonish portrait of the homosexual neighbor in *Crooklyn*, one of the few characters in that film who is given no positive traits to leaven the harsh criticism implied by Lee's treatment or to make him seem three-dimensional. Similar points have been made regarding Lee's attitudes toward Jews (particularly in *Mo' Better Blues*) and women. At one point, Lee even felt the need to defend himself in the *New York Times* in a letter to the editor entitled, "Why I Am Not an Anti-Semite."

Interesting, almost as an aside, is Lee's canny ability to use certain catch phrases in his films which help both to attract and delight audiences. In *She's Gotta Have It*, there was the constant refrain uttered by Spike Lee as Mars Blackmon, "Please baby, please baby, please baby, baby, baby, please...."; in *Do the Right Thing*, the disc jockey's "And that's the truth, Ruth." Lee's fusion of popular forms and audience-pleasing entertainment with significant cultural commentary is particularly impressive coming from a filmmaker still so young. Notable also is the director's assembly—in the style of Bergman and Chabrol and Woody Allen in their prime—of a consistent stable of very talented collaborators, including his father, Bill Lee, as musical composer, production designer Wynn Thomas, producer Monty Ross, and cinematographer Ernest Dickerson, among others. He has also used many of the same actors from one film to another, including Wesley Snipes, Denzel Washington, his sister Joie Lee, John Turturro, Samuel L. Jackson, Ossie Davis, and Ruby Dee, helping to create a climate which propelled several to stardom and inspired a new wave of high-level attention to a variety of breakout African-American performers.

—Charles Derry

LEFEBVRE, Jean-Pierre

Nationality: Canadian. **Born:** Montreal, 17 August 1942. **Education:** Educated in French Literature, University of Montreal. **Career:** Staff writer for *Objectif* (Montreal), 1960-67; Professor of French, 1963-65; formed Cinak production company, 1969; initiated "Premières Oeuvres" section of Office National du Film, 1969-71; President of Association des Réalisateurs de Films du Quebec, 1974.

Films as Director and Scriptwriter:

1964 *L'Homoman* (short) (+ pr, ph)
1965 *Le Révolutionnaire* (+ pr)
1966 *Patricia et Jean-Baptiste* (+ pr); *Mon Oeil* (*My Eye*) (unrealized)
1967 *Il ne faut pas mourir pour ça* (*Don't Let It Kill You*) (+ pr); *Mon Amie Pierrette*
1968 *Jusqu'au coeur*
1969 *La Chambre blanche* (*House of Light*)
1970 *Un Succès commercial* (*Q-bec My Love*)
1971 *Les Maudits sauvages* (*Those Damned Savages*); *Ultimatum*
1973 *On n'engraisse pas les cochons à l'eau claire*; *Les Dernières Fiançailles* (*The Last Betrothal*)
1975 *Le Gars des vues*; *L'Amour blessé*
1977 *Le Vieux Pays ou Rimbaud est mort*
1978 *Avoir 16 ans*
1982 *Les Fleurs sauvages* (*The Wild Flowers*)
1983 *Au Rythme de mon coeur* (*To the Rhythm of My Heart*)
1984 *Le Jour "S ... "*
1987 *Laliberté* (*Alfred Laliberté, sculpteur*)
1988 *La Boîte à soleil* (*The Box of Sun*)

Publications

By LEFEBVRE: book—

Parfois quand je vis (poems), Montreal, 1970.

By LEFEBVRE: articles—

"Complexes d'une technique," in *Objectif* (Montreal), March 1961.
"L'Equipe française souffre-t-elle de Roucheole?," with Jean-Claude Pilon, in *Objectif* (Montreal), August 1962.
"Les Années folles de la critique ou petite histoire des revues de cinéma au Québec," in *Objectif* (Montreal), October/November 1964.
"La Crise du language et le cinéma canadien," in *Objectif* (Montreal), April/May 1965.
"La Méche et la bombe," in *Cahiers du Cinéma* (Paris), March 1966.
"Les Paradis perdus du cinéma canadien, chapitre 1: notes en guise d'introduction à une préface éventuelle," in *Objectif* (Montreal), November/December 1966.
Interview with Michel Delahaye, in *Cahiers du Cinéma* (Paris), January 1967.
"Les Paradis perdus du cinéma canadien, chapitre 2: illustration existentielle du chapitre 1 à partir de données oniriques," in *Objectif* (Montreal), May 1967.
"Les Paradis perdus du cinéma canadien, chapitre 3: Saint Gabiaz, priez pour nous," in *Objectif* (Montreal), August/September 1967.
"Les Quatres Saisons," in *Cahiers du Cinéma* (Paris), April/May 1968.
Interview with M. Amiel, in *Cinéma* (Paris), December 1972.
Interviews with J.-P. Tadros, in *Cinéma Québec* (Montreal), December 1973/January 1974, and no. 6, 1977.
"Des lois et des cadres: La Guerre des gangs," in *Cinéma Québec* (Montreal), no. 4, 1976.
"Commission d'enquête sur le cinéma organisé," in *Cinéma Québec* (Montreal), no. 5, 1976.
Interview with René Prédal, in *Jeune Cinéma* (Paris), February 1978.
Interviews with B. Samuels and S. Barrowclough, in *Cinema Canada* (Montreal), May 1982.
"Un Métier merveilleusement périlleux," in *Copie Zéro* (Montreal), October 1984.
Interview with C. Racine, in *24 Images* (Montreal), Autumn 1984/Winter 1985.
"La leçon de l'ami Moreau," in *Copie Zéro* (Montreal), March 1986.

On LEFEBVRE: books—

Marsolais, Gilles, *Le Cinéma canadien,* Paris, 1968.
Cinéastes de Québec 3: Jean-Pierre Lefebvre, Ottawa, 1970.
Bérubé, Renald, and Yvan Patry, editors, *Jean-Pierre Lefebvre,* Montreal, 1971.
Barrowclough, Susan, editor, *Jean-Pierre Lefebvre: The Quebec Connection,* London, 1981.
Harcourt, Peter, *Jean-Pierre Lefebvre,* Ottawa, 1981.

On LEFEBVRE: articles—

Fraser, Graham, "The Gentle Revolutionary," in *Take One* (Montreal), October 1967.
Larsen, André, "Le Sens de la contestationet Jean-Pierre Lefebvre," in *Le Cinéma Québecois: Tendences et prolongements,* Cahiers Ste-Marie, 1968.
La Rochelles, Real, and Gilbert Maggi, "Political Situation of Quebec Cinema," in *Cineaste* (New York), Summer 1972.
Gauthier, G., "Sur deux films de Jean-Pierre Lefebvre," in *Image et Son* (Paris), January 1975.
Barrowclough, Susan, "The Films of Jean-Pierre Lefebvre," in *Ciné-Tracts* (Montreal), Winter 1982.
Bessette, M., "Jean Pierre Lefebvre: au rythme de son coeur," in *Copie Zero* (Montreal), October 1988.
Loiselle, M.-C "Le pouvoir de l'imaginaire," *24 Images* (Montreal), Autumn 1991.

* * *

There is a filmmaker who has been invited to present his work at the Cannes Film Festival Director's Fortnight more often than any other filmmaker in the world. His career began, not in film school or under the aegis of a state-funded film organization, but instead as a poet, a critic and as a student and then professor of French literature. With eighteen films to his credit in a career of just over twnety-four years, he has barely reached the age of fifty. The filmmaker is Jean Pierre Lefebvre, a French Canadian, born and educated in Montreal, Quebec, respected and lauded by Francophone film audiences and critics, and yet still relatively unknown in the English language film world and in the world of commercial cinema.

In many ways Lefebvre is the archetypal Francophone intellectual. His large film oeuvre is stamped with the imprint of a philosopher, a humourist, a poet, an observer, and a humble yet assured commentator on the state of things. Lefebvre's films play with the idea of relationships: relationships among individuals, between individuals and their surroundings, and between individuals and the language they use and personalize through poetic and colloquial misuse. He is concerned also with the relationship of the elements of film language and the relationship between the film spectator and what is projected on the screen. Lefebvre plays with sound, words and images, succeeding in drawing the spectator's attention to the possibilities contained within language, film language, and the situation in which we confront these vehicles for communication. As the Canadian film critic Peter Harcourt observed of Lefebvre's technique, "the extended takes give us time not only to experience an action but also to think about what we may be feeling."

The work of Lefebvre is also indicative of an intellectual and artistic movement endemic to French Canadians of Quebecois origin, and in particular to those who came of age during the 1960s. Quebecois culture, which had been colonized, both literally and metaphorically, by the French, the English, the Church, and the Americans, made its voice heard at home and on the international front through demonstrations, civil disobedience, and the radical presence of the Front de Liberation du Quebec. Quebecois culture began to assert itself through its vocal and visible difference, a difference that hinged greatly on the language of the Quebecois population. Lefebvre describes the role of film in this historic situation: "In the late 1950s and 1960s, cinema was terribly important for naming our society, for making it exist in people's mind."

Working within the constraints of small budgets, Lefebvre has constructed film works that speak of a specific political time and place, just as they speak of the universal, philosophical, and humourous personal and sexual conditions. Lefebvre's wife and collaborator, the late Marguerite Duparc, acted as editor and producer on many of Lefebvre's works as well as co-directing Cinak, the production company set up by Lefebvre in the late 1960s. Duparc was known to sacrifice her own creative projects in order to ensure that monetary assistance would be concentrated on Lefebvre's own works. The situation for fiction filmmakers in Quebec during the 1970s and 1980s was economically difficult.

Lefebvre's work is "political" in the personal, formal, and aesthetic sense and not always in the easily identifiable party political sense. His style varies with the subject matter he tackles, as he adapts the structure of his features to the nature of the narratives and the queries they pose. Similar in some ways to Godard and Bresson, two filmmakers to whose work Lefebvre's has been compared, Lefebvre often experiments with sound and image. At the same time, he stands apart from his contemporaries in the Quebecois film industry and cannot be grouped with any particular indigenous movement. Nevertheless, the film work of Lefebvre continues to attract critical and public attention for its continuing commitment to the politics and the beauty of language, of Quebecois culture, and of the fine art of cinema.

—Clea H. Notar

LEIGH, Mike

Nationality: British. **Born:** Salford, Lancashire, 20 February 1943. **Education:** Attended North Grecian Street County Primary School, Salford, and Salford Grammar School; studied at the Royal Academy of Dramatic Art, London, 1960-62, Camberwell School of Arts and Crafts, London, 1963-64, Central School of Art and Design, London, 1964-65, and London Film School, 1965. **Family:** Married actress Alison Steadman, 1973; two sons. **Career:** Founded, with David Halliwell, the production company Dramagraph, London, 1965; associate director, Midlands Art Centre for Young People, Birmingham, 1965-66; actor, Victoria Theatre, Stoke-on-Trent, Staffordshire, 1966; assistant director, Royal Shakespeare Company, 1967-68; lecturer, Sedgley Park and De La Salle colleges, Manchester, 1968-69, London Film School, 1970-73; founded Thin Man Films, with producer Simon Channing-Wilson, 1989; directed TV advertisements, 1991. **Awards:** Grands Prix, Chicago and Locarno festivals, 1972, for *Bleak Moments;* International Critics Prize, Venice, 1988, for *High Hopes;* Best Film Prize, National Society of Film Critics, 1991, for *Life Is Sweet;* Best Direction Prize, Cannes Film Festival, 1993, for *Naked.* **Agent:** Peters, Fraser and Dunlop, 503-4 The Chambers, Chelsea Harbour, London SW1O OXF, England. **Address:** Lives in Muswell Hill, North London.

Films as Director:

(Feature films)

1971 *Bleak Moments*
1988 *High Hopes*
1990 ***Life Is Sweet***
1993 ***Naked***

(Television films)

1972 *A Mugs Game*; *Hard Labour*
1975 *The Permissive Society*; group of five 5-minute films: *The Birth of the 2001 FA Cup Final Goalie*; *Old Chums*; *Probation*; *A Light Snack*; *Afternoon*
1976 *Nuts in May*; *Plays for Britain* (title sequence only); *Knock for Knock*; *The Kiss of Death*
1977 *Abigail's Party*
1978 *Who's Who*
1980 *Grown-Ups*
1982 *Home Sweet Home*
1983 *Meantime*
1985 *Four Days in July*
1987 *The Short and Curlies*
1992 *A Sense of History*

Publications

On LEIGH: books—

Clements, Paul, *The Improvised Play: The Work of Mike Leigh,* London, 1983.
Coveney, Michael, *The World According to Mike Leigh,* New York, 1996.

On LEIGH: articles—

Taylor, John Russell, "Giggling beneath the Waves: The Uncosy World of Mike Leigh," in *Sight and Sound,* Winter 1982/83.

Boyd, William, "Seeing Is Believing," in *New Statesman,* 17 September 1982.

French, Sean, "Life on the Edge without a Script," in *Observer Magazine,* 8 January 1989.

Ruchti, Isabelle, "Mike Leigh, miniaturiste du social," in *Positif,* April 1989.

Kermode, Mark, "Inherently and Inevitably Awful: Mike Leigh," in *Monthly Film Bulletin,* March 1991.

Cieutat, Michel, "Glauques esperances," in *Positif,* September 1991.

Kennedy, Harlan, "Mike Leigh about His Stuff," in *Film Comment,* September/October 1991.

Hoberman, J., "Cassavetes and Leigh: Poets of the Ordinary," in *Premiere,* October 1991.

Adams, Mark, "A Long Weekend with Mike Leigh," in *National Film Theatre Programme,* May 1993.

Naked Issue of *L'Avant-Scene du Cinema,* November 1993.

Berthin-Scaillet, Agnes, "Lignes de fuite," in *Positif,* November 1993.

Medhurst, Andy, "Mike Leigh: Beyond Embarrassment," in *Sight and Sound,* November 1993.

Ellickson, Lee, and Richard Porton, "I Find the Tragicomic Things in Life," in *Cineaste,* vol. 20, no. 3, 1994.

Smith, Gavin, "Worlds Apart," in *Film Comment,* September/October 1994.

Paletz, Gabriel M., and David L. Paletz, "Mike Leigh's *Naked* Truth," in *Film Criticism,* Winter 1994/95.

* * *

Like Ken Loach and Stephen Frears, Mike Leigh had built up a remarkable body of television work years before he became known to a wider international audience with his film *High Hopes.* Indeed, even as early as 1982 the BBC screened a retrospective of his work, and devoted a whole edition of its arts programme *Arena* to him as well. By contrast, Americans had to wait another ten years to see what had led up to *High Hopes,* when the New York Museum of Modern Art staged a retrospective in 1992. In fact, *High Hopes* was only Leigh's second feature in seventeen years, the first being *Bleak Moments,* which was largely funded by Albert Finney's company Memorial Enterprises (also behind Stephen Frears's *Gumshoe* in 1971) at a time when the British cinema had almost ceased to exist—or, as Leigh puts it, "was alive and well and hiding-out in television, mostly at the BBC."

So, as the critic Sean French put it in an article on the director in the *Observer:* "For years Leigh has been making better and more penetrating films than anyone else about the class system (*Nuts in May* and *Grown-Ups*), unemployment (*Meantime*), Northern Ireland (*Four Days in July*), and family life under Thatcher (*High Hopes*). By almost any reckoning Leigh should be considered one of our major film directors, yet he is virtually ignored in most considerations of British cinema." With the release of *Naked* this situation may have improved somewhat, but now it is hard to avoid the conclusion that although Leigh may be better known in Britain than he was formerly, he is now, like Ken Loach, actually more highly regarded abroad than in his own country.

Mike Leigh

That Leigh has found it difficult to make feature films is certainly a sad comment on the sickly state of the British film industry. But as he himself admits, his approach to filmmaking could seem off-putting even to the most sympathetic of financiers: "I only accept a project if nobody else wants to know what it's going to be. I come along and say 'I've got no script, I really don't know what I'm going to do, just give me the money and I'll bugger off and do it.'" And doing it is time-consuming—the rehearsals for *High Hopes* took a not untypical fifteen weeks.

It is impossible to discuss Leigh's work without discussing his working methods, even though there's an unfortunate tendency amongst critics to fetishise these to the point of ignoring what the work thus produced is actually all about. Leigh himself has referred to such writings as "an albatross, a media preoccupation," but since misunderstandings abound and are often used as a basis on which to attack his work, it is important to understand what he is doing. In fact, his methods have changed little since he developed them in the theatre in the mid-1960s. As he put it in 1973: "I begin with a general area which I want to investigate. I choose my actors and tell them that I don't want to talk to them about the play. (There is no play at this stage.) I ask them to think of several people of their own age. Then we discuss these people till we find the character I want." Each actor then builds up his or her own character through a lengthy process of research and improvisation, both in the rehearsal room and in real locations. Only when the actors have fully "'found' their characters are they brought together and the all-important relationships are formed between the characters: the play is what happens to the characters, what they make for themselves. Behaviour dictates situation."

For Leigh there is no great mystique about improvisation; as he put it in 1980: "Improvisation is actually a practical way of investigating real-life going on the way real life actually operates. That's all." At the same time, however, he is utterly opposed to the notion of improvisation as "some kind of all-in anarchic democracy." To quote from the same 1980 interview: "It is a question of discovering what the film or play is about by making the film. It isn't a committee job nor is it 'let's just see what happens and go along with it.' Nor is it a question of shooting a lot of footage in which actors improvise. In my films 98 percent is structured." The main work, therefore, is done in research, improvisation, and rehearsal long before the cameras appear; by that time "there's very much a script. It just so happens that I don't start with a document, that's all. What finally appears on screen is only very, very rarely improvised in front of the camera. For the most part it's arrived at through a long process, and it's finally pinned down and rehearsed and very disciplined, while the quality of the language and the imagery is heightened.... Improvisation and research are simply tactics, a means to an end and not an end in themselves." It is for these reasons that most of his television films carry the unique credit "devised and directed by Mike Leigh," and the theatre critic Benedict Nightingale once described him as "part composer, part conductor, part catalyst." And whatever the critical misunderstandings surrounding Leigh's method, it certainly brings results. His cast lists have included some of Britain's finest younger actors, such as Alison Steadman, Anthony Sher, Jim Broadbent, Gary Oldman, Tim Roth, Lindsay Duncan, David Thewlis, Frances Barber, and Jane Horrocks, many of whom have done some of their best work for him.

Given Leigh's improvisatory methods, it is no surprise to find that films such as *On the Waterfront, Rebel without a Cause,* and *Shadows* were early influences. Rather more interesting, however, is his citing of the playwrights Beckett and Pinter and the artists Hogarth, Gilray, and Rowlandson as major inspirations. This points us towards a central fact of Leigh's oeuvre: that it is absolutely not naturalistic, and that critics who have tried to pigeonhole it as such are largely to blame for the tired old saw that Leigh cannot portray "real people" without sneering or laughing at them, or being condescending. Perhaps the best way to describe Leigh's work is as distilled or heightened realism, which certainly does not preclude elements of humour and even caricature in his depiction of character. For example, the frightful yuppies the Booth-Braines in *High Hopes* and the appalling Jeremy in *Naked* are certainly caricatures but they are entirely, indeed all too, believable, as is the terrifying Beverly in *Abigail's Party.* For all the demotic, quotidian surface appearances of his films, Leigh expresses a remarkably consistent and personal view through them. In his work, implicitly, a great deal is suggested about the way life might, or should, be by showing, in a particular way, the world as it actually is. Speaking at the time of the release of *High Hopes* Leigh talked revealingly of "distilling my metaphor out of an absolutely tangible, real and solid and plausible and vulnerable and unheroic and unexotic kind of world," and not for nothing in that film does he have his most positive characters, Cyril and Shirley, visit the tomb of Karl Marx in Highgate Cemetery, on which is written: "The philosophers have only interpreted the world in various ways. The point however is to change it." Not that Leigh offers any easy answers, and certainly not Marxist ones—something else which has hardly endeared him to the Left in Britain. Or as he puts it: "For me the whole experience of making films is one of discovery. What is important, it seems to me, is that you share questions with the audience, and they have to go away with things to work on. That's not a cop out. It is my natural, instinctive way of storytelling and sharing ideas, predicaments, feelings and emotions." On the other hand, as a perceptive article in *Cineaste* remarked: "Although Leigh resolutely refuses to engage in sloganeering, his films are acutely political since they consistently articulate an often hilarious critique of everyday life. This critique is always rooted in the idiosyncracies of individual characters."

Mike Leigh, then, is very much an "auteur." If anything could sum up his vision it might be Thoreau's famous remark about the mass of people living "lives of quiet desperation," and one is also reminded of Chekov in the way his films seem constantly to hover between comedy and tragedy, with despair lurking never very far beneath the surface. As he himself once remarked, "there's no piece that isn't, somewhere along the way, a lamentation for the awfulness of life." In more specifically English terms other reference points might be Alan Ayckbourn (however much Leigh would disagree), Alan Bennett, and Victoria Wood. Although his films are often taken to be about "Englishness"—or even more specifically, about life under the appalling social experiment commonly known as Thatcherism (although much of Leigh's work actually predates the egregious regime)—their success abroad suggests that they tap into rather more universal doubts and fears about the human condition. This is certainly the case with *Naked,* which, through Johnny's rantings and ravings about chaos theory, Nostradamus, Revelations, and God knows what else, achieves much more than a particularly rancid glimpse of a squalid corner of this septic isle and exudes an imminent, all-pervasive sense of geo-political doom.

On the other hand there is something quintessentially English about Leigh's films,. and maybe that is why certain English people do not like them. As the novelist William Boyd observed in a piece on Leigh in the *New Statesman,* on the occasion of the above-mentioned BBC retrospective: "Any edginess or unease prompted by his observations can only be a sign that certain truths are too uncomfortable for some critics to acknowledge. Ostrich complexes are easily fostered; complacency is a very tolerable frame of mind." And not for nothing did Vincent Canby once describe Leigh as not only "the most innovative of contemporary English filmmakers" but "also the most subversive." Whether it's the cruelly, painfully funny examination of preternatural shyness and sexual ineptitude of *Bleak Moments,* the suburban Strindberg of *Abigail's Party,* or the excruciating family row into which *High Hopes* gradually boils up, the vision of England that emerges, though leavened by absurdity, humour, and moments of human warmth and togetherness, is hardly an attractive one, to put it mildly. As Andy Medhurst put it in one of the better British pieces on

Leigh: "This England is specific, palpable and dire, though aspects of it are at the same time liable to inspire a kind of wry resignation.... If anything, Englishness is revealed as a kind of pathological condition, emotionally warping and stunting, to which the only response can be a kind of damage limitation. What many of Leigh's films suggest is that to be English is to be locked in a prison where politeness, gaucheness and anxiety about status form the bars across the window.... His best films (*Bleak Moments, Grown-Ups, Meantime*) exemplify his skills as a choreographer of awkwardness, a geometrician of embarrassments, able to orchestrate layers of accumulated tiny cruelties and failures of communication until they swell into a crescendo of extravagant farce."

—Julian Petley

LELOUCH, Claude

Nationality: French. **Born:** Paris, 30 October 1937. **Family:** Married Christine Cochet, 1968 (divorced), one son, two daughters; married Maie-Sophie Pochat (aka Marie-Sophie L.), three children. **Career:** Maker of short films as "cinereporter," 1956-58; served in Service-Cinéma des Armées (S.C.A.), 1958-60; founder, Les Films 13 production company, 1960; made some 250 "scopitones," 2-3 minute mini-musicals shown on a type of jukebox, 1960-62; directed first feature, 1962. **Awards:** Prize at Cannes' Amateur Film Festival, for *La Mal du siecle,* 1953; Oscars for Best Foreign Film and Best Story and Screenplay, and Palme d'Or, Cannes Festival, for *Un Homme et une femme,* 1966; Grand Prix du Cinéma français, for *Vivre pour vivre,* 1967; Prix Raoul Levy, 1970. **Address:** 15 avenue Hoche, 75008 Paris, France.

Films as Director:

1953 *Le Mal du siècle* (+ pr, sc, ed); *USA en vrac* (+ pr, sc, ed)
1957 *Quand le rideau se lève* (+ pr, sc, ed)
1959 *La Guerre du silence* (+ pr, sc, ed); *Les Mécaniciens de l'armée de l'air* (+ pr, sc, ed); *S.O.S. hélicoptère* (+ pr, sc, ed)
1960 *Le Propre de l'homme* (*The Right of Man*) (+ pr, sc, role as Claude); *La Femme spectacle* (*Night Women*) (+ pr, sc)
1964 *Une Fille et des fusils* (*To Be a Crook*) (+ pr, sc, ph); *Vingt-quatre heures d'amant* (+ pr, sc)
1965 *Les Grands Moments* (+ pr, sc, ph); *Jean-Paul Belmondo* (+ pr, sc); *Pour un maillot jaune* (+ pr, sc)
1966 *Un Homme et une femme* (*A Man and a Woman*) (+ co-ed, ph, sc)
1967 *Vivre pour vivre* (*Live for Life*) (+ pr, sc); episode of *Loin du Vietnam* (*Far From Vietnam*)
1968 *Treize jours en France* (*Grenoble*) (+ co-ph, pr, sc); *La Vie, l'amour, la mort* (*Life Love Death*) (+ co-sc, pr)
1969 *Un Homme qui me plaît* (*Love Is a Funny Thing*) (+ co-pr, co-sc)
1970 *Le Voyou* (*The Crook*) (+ pr, sc)
1971 *Smic Smac Smoc* (+ ph, pr, sc); *Glories of Iran*
1972 *L'Aventure c'est l'aventure* (*Money Money Money*) (+ co-sc, pr); *La Bonne année* (*Happy New Year*) (+ co-pr, co-sc, ph)
1973 "The Losers" episode in *Visions of Eight* (+ co-sc, pr)
1974 *Toute une vie* (*And Now My Love*) (+ pr, sc); *Mariage* (*Marriage*) (+ co-sc, pr)
1975 *Le Chat et la souris* (*Cat and Mouse*) (+ pr, sc); *Le Bon et les méchants* (*The Good and the Bad*) (+ pr, sc)
1976 *Rendez-vous* (+ pr, sc); *Si c'était à refaire* (*If I Had to Do It All Over Again*) (+ ph, pr, sc)
1977 *Another Man, Another Chance* (+ co-pr, sc)
1978 *Robert et Robert* (+ pr, sc)
1979 *À nous deux* (*An Adventure for Two; Us Two*) (+ pr, sc)
1981 *Les Uns et les autres* (+ pr, sc)
1982 *Edith et Marcel* (*Edith and Marcel*) (+ pr, sc); *Bolero*
1984 *Vive la Vie!*
1985 *Partir, revenir* (*Going and Coming Back*) (+ pr, sc)
1986 *Un Homme et une femme: Vingt ans déja* (*A Man and a Woman: Twenty Years Later*)
1987 *Attention Bandits* (*Bandits*)
1988 *L'Itinéraire d'un enfant gâté* (*Itinerary of a Spoiled Child*) (+ co-pr, sc)
1990 *Il y a des Jours ... et des Lunes* (*There Were Days and Moons*) (+ co-pr, sc)
1992 *La belle histoire* (*The Beautiful Story*) (+ pr, sc)
1993 *Tout ca ... pour ca!* (*All That ... For This?!*) (+ pr, sc)
1995 *Les miserables* (+ sc, pr, co-ph)

Other Films:

1988 *Happy New Year* (Avildsen) (role)

Publications

By LELOUCH: books—

A Man and a Woman, with Pierre Uytterhoeven, New York, 1971.
Ma vie pour un film, with Yonnick Flot, Paris, 1986.

By LELOUCH: articles—

"*Un homme et une femme* Issue" of *Avant-Scène du Cinéma* (Paris), December 1966.
"Claude Lelouch at the Olympic Games," an interview, in *American Cinematographer* (Los Angeles), November 1972.
Interview with J. Craven, in *Filmmakers Newsletter* (Ward Hill, Massachusetts), March 1974.
Interview with P. Lev, in *Take One* (Montreal), August 1977.
Interview with S. McMillin, in *Filmmakers Newsletter* (Ward Hill, Massachusetts), February 1978.
Interview with Tim Pulleine, in *Sight and Sound* (London), Summer 1983.
Interview with P. Carcassonne, in *Cinématographe* (Paris), May 1984.
Interview and filmography in *La Revue du Cinema* (Paris), March 1988.
Interview with M. Elia, in *Séquences* (Montreal), March 1989.
Interview in *Cahiers du Cinema* (Paris), May 1990.

On LELOUCH: books—

Armes, Roy, *French Cinema Since 1946: Vol.2—The Personal Style,* New York, 1966.
Guidez, Guylaine, *Claude Lelouch,* Paris, 1972.
Ronchetti, Pierluigi, *Claude Lelouch,* Citta di Castello, Italy, 1979.
Tonnerre, Jerome, *Lelouch filme les uns et les autres: histoire d'un tournage,* Paris, 1982.
Lev, Peter, *Claude Lelouch, Film Director,* New York, 1983.
Alberti, Olympia, *Lelouch Passion,* Paris, 1987.

On LELOUCH: articles—

"Lelouch: table ronde," in *Cinéma* (Paris), May 1965.
Comolli, Jean-Louis, "Claude Lelouch, ou la bonne conscience retrouvée," in *Cahiers du Cinéma* (Paris), June 1966.

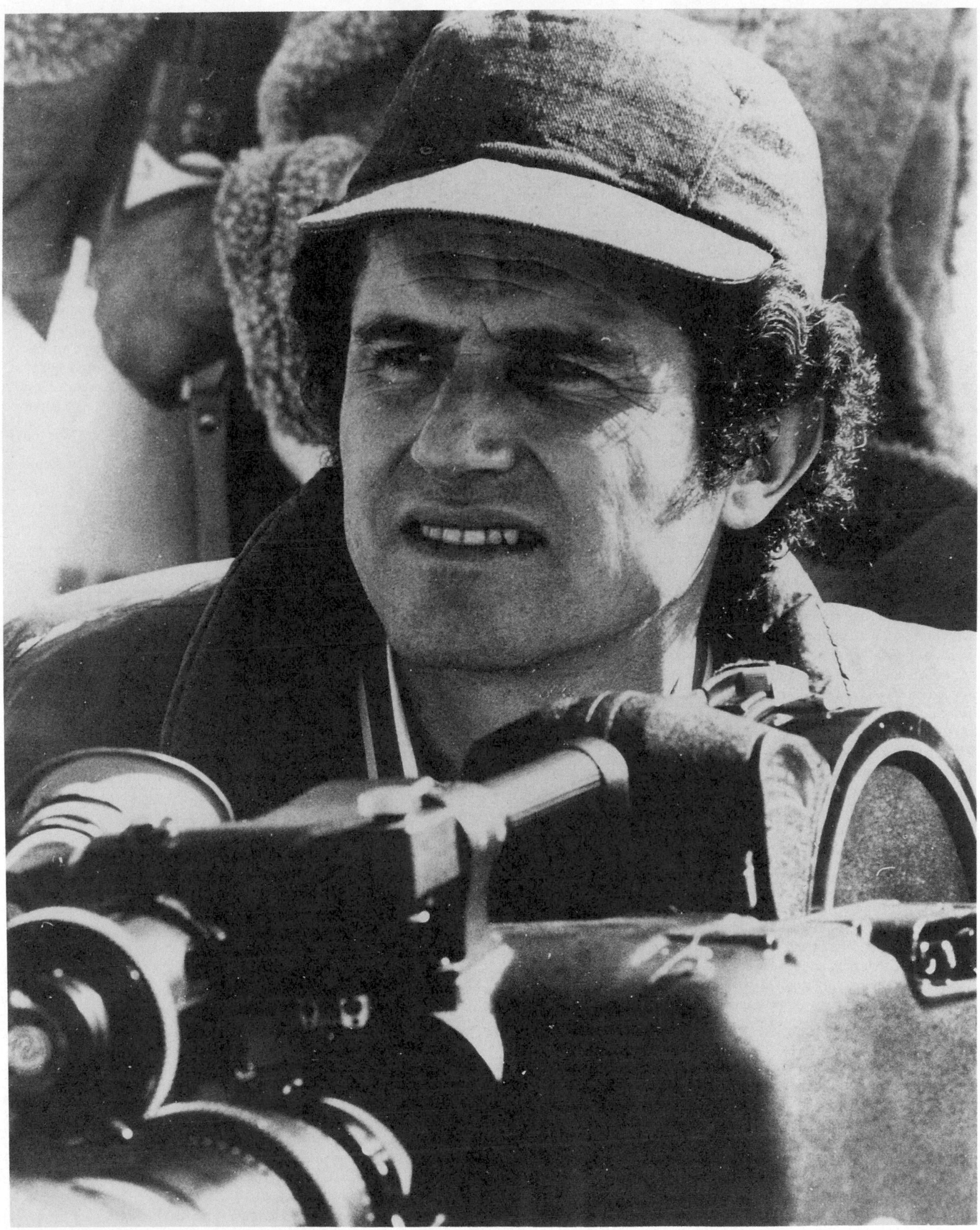

Claude Lelouch

Perisset, Maurice, "Le Cas Lelouch," in *Cinéma* (Paris), May 1969.
Carroll, Kathleen, article in *Daily News* (New York), 2 December 1973.
Garel, A., "A propos de *Toute une vie* ou Lelouchiens si vous saviez," in *Image et Son* (Paris), January 1975.
Eyles, A., "*And Now My Love*," in *Focus on Film* (London), Summer 1975.
Lardine, Bob, article in *Daily News* (New York), 24 July 1977.
Lewis, Flora, article in *The New York Times*, 14 July 1978.
Profile in *Millimeter* (New York), October 1982.
Johnston, Sheila, "The Ins and Outs of Claude Lelouch," in *Stills* (London), July/August 1983.
"Claude Lelouch," in *Film Dope* (London), March 1986.
Hunter, Allan, "A Man and a Woman: Twenty Years Later," in *Films and Filming* (London), August 1986.
Miller, Judith, article in *New York Times*, 14 August 1986.
Elia, M., "Claude Lelouch," in *Séquences* (Montreal), April 1987.

* * *

The films of Claude Lelouch may be classified under three diverse headings: romance, crime, and liberal politics. Occasionally, they focus on one specific area; more often, the categories will be combined.

A Man and a Woman is a pure and simple love story. Despite Lelouch's many commercial successes, he is most identified with this glossy, gimmicky, tremendously popular tale of script girl Anouk Aimée, a widow, and her widower counterpart, race car driver Jean-Louis Trintignant. *A Man and a Woman* became one of the most beloved romantic films of its time, a favorite of young couples. The scenario may be a soap opera, photographed on what some critics perceive as postcard-pretty locations; still, it is emotionally touching and truthful. Most significantly, there is refreshingly flexible camera work. Lelouch, who also served as photographer for the film (besides co-editing the film and co-authoring the screenplay), uses his camera like a paintbrush, with total ease and freedom.

More typically, Lelouch mixes several genres together in his work. He combines love and politics in *Live for Life,* the story of television journalist Yves Montand, whose work takes him to Vietnam and Africa; this character leaves devoted wife Annie Girardot for fashion model Candice Bergen. The filmmaker combines love and crime in *Happy New Year,* in which two robbers plan a caper and one falls for the proprietress of a nearby antique store. He blends crime and politics in *Money, Money, Money,* in which a gang of crooks realize that the changing times will allow them to gain greater profits by committing political crimes.

Lelouch has always had one eye on box office receipts, once too often selecting his subject matter with commercial potential being the sole consideration. Early in his career he directed *Night Woman,* a relatively erotic film about, as the filmmaker explains, "all the kinds of women one wouldn't like to marry," in the hope of earning a financial success. His first box office hit, however, was *To Be a Crook,* the story of four men and a deaf-and-dumb girl who become kidnappers and murderers; highlighted are gunfights and a striptease.

Lelouch does have political concerns: he participated (with Alain Resnais, Jean-Luc Godard, Joris Ivens, William Klein, and Agnes Varda) in the anti-war compilation film *Far From Vietnam.* And he has made quite a few delightfully clever entertainments: *Happy New Year*; *Money, Money, Money*; and *Cat and Mouse,* a mystery-comedy about a police inspector's efforts to uncover a rich philanderer's killer. Other films include *The Crook* and *And Now My Love,* which utilizes comedy, music, and drama to unite lovers Marthe Keller and Andre Dussollier. Yet he will all too often repeat himself, with uninspired results. For example, *Live for Life,* the follow-up to *A Man and a Woman,* is just too frilly, a slickly photographed soap opera lacking the warmth of its predecessor. *Another Man, Another Chance* is a blatant rip-off of *A Man and a Woman,* with James Caan the widower and Genevieve Bujold the widow.

None of Lelouch's recent films have in any way upgraded his status in the pantheon of filmmakers. *Un Homme et une Femme: Vingt ans deja (A Man and a Woman: Twenty Years Later)* is an uninspired attempt to capture the spark of its predecessor. *L'Itineraire d'un enfant gate (Itinerary of a Spoiled Child)* is the contrived tale of an industrialist who sets off on a sailing trip around the world, while *Attention Bandits (Bandits)* is the by-the-numbers account of a young woman who learns that her father, with whom she's been corresponding for years, is in prison for a crime he did not commit. *Il y a des Jours ... Et des lunes (There Were Days and Moons)* has a clever premise—the lives of various people are controlled by time reversing itself—but the result is instantly forgettable. *La Belle histoire* is an ambitious but muddled epic, whose scenario covers the biblical era in ancient Rome to the present. In the equally unimpressive *Tout Ca ... Pour Ca! (All That ... For This?!),* a woman attorney attempts to discern the truth from three jailed working class crooks, whose problems stem from the women in their lives; in a parallel story, a married judge has an affair with an equally married woman lawyer. Conversely, *Les miserables,* an ambitious, three-hour-long epic "freely adapted" from the Victor Hugo novel, was Lelouch's best film in years. Despite his many successes, however, Claude Lelouch ultimately cannot be ranked with the top filmmakers of his generation.

—Rob Edelman

LENI, Paul

Nationality: German. **Born:** Stuttgart, 8 July 1885. **Career:** Painter and stage designer, and member of avant-garde movement associated with publication *Der Sturm,* Berlin, 1900s; production designer, from 1914; directed first film, 1916; also worked as scenarist and actor; hired for Universal in Hollywood by Carl Laemmle, 1927. **Died:** Of blood poisoning, 2 September 1929.

Films as Director:

1916 *Das Tagebuch des Dr. Hart*
1917 *Dornröschen* (+ sc)
1919 *Platonische Ehe* (+ co-prod des); *Prinz Kuckuk* (+ co-prod des)
1920 *Patience* (+ sc, prod des)
1921 *Fiesco* (*Die Verschwöhrung zu Genua*) (+ co-prod des); *Das Gespensterschiff* (+ prod des); *Hintertreppe* (*Backstairs*) (co-d, prod des); *Komödie der Leidenschaften* (+ prod des)
1924 *Das Wachsfigurenkabinett* (*Waxworks*) (+ prod des)
1927 *The Cat and the Canary* (in US); *The Chinese Parrot* (in US)
1928 *The Man Who Laughs* (in US)
1929 *The Last Warning* (in US)

Other Films:

1914 *Das Panzergewölbe* (May) (prod des)
1915 *Der Katzensteg* (Mack) (prod des); *Das achte Gebot* (Mack) (prod des)
1917 *Das Rätsel von Bangalor* (assoc d, co-sc)
1920 *Der weisse Pfau* (Dupont) (co-prod des, co-sc); *Die Schuld der Lavinia Morland* (May) (co-prod des, role); *Veritas Vincit* (May) (co-prod des)
1921 *Die Geier Wally* (Dupont) (prod des); *Kinder der Finsternis* (Dupont) (prod des)
1922 *Frauenopfer* (Grüne) (prod des)

Paul Leni

1923 *Tragödie der Liebe* (May) (prod des)
1925 *Die Frau von vierzig Jahren* (Oswald) (prod des); *Der Farmer aux Texas* (May) (prod des); *Der Tänzer meiner Frau* (Korda) (prod des)
1926 *Manon Lescaut* (Robinson) (costumes); *Fiaker Nr. 13* (Kertesz) (prod des); *Wie einst im Mai* (Wolff) (prod des); *Der goldene Schmetterling* (Kertesz) (prod des)

Publications

By LENI: article—

"L'image comme action," in *Cinématographe* (Paris), February 1982.

On LENI: books—

Kracauer, Siegfried, *From Caligari to Hitler,* Princeton, 1947.
Eisner, Lotte, *The Haunted Screen: Expressionism in the German Cinema and the Influence of Max Reinhardt,* Berkeley, 1969.
Willett, John, *Art and Politics in the Weimar Period: The New Sobriety 1917-1933,* New York, 1978.
Bock, Hans-Michael, *Paul Leni: Grafik, Theater, Film,* Frankfurt, 1986.

On LENI: articles—

Buache, Freddy, "Paul Leni 1885-1929," in *Anthologie du Cinéma* (Paris), vol. 4, 1968.
"Paul Leni," in *Film Dope* (London), March 1986.

* * *

Siegfried Kracauer, in *From Caligari to Hitler,* calls Leni "one of the outstanding film directors of the post-World War I era," and refers to the Jack-the-Ripper episode of *Waxworks* as being "among the greatest achievements of film art." Yet Leni's name is familiar only to film scholars today.

Leni predates Hitchcock as a maker of thrillers; the screen cliches of trembling hands intent on murdering unsuspecting innocents, and corpses falling from opened doors, were first presented in his *The Cat and the Canary.* Excluding the films of Lon Chaney, he was the foremost practitioner of utilizing make-up to create grotesque creatures, silent-screen monsters who terrified audiences by looks alone.

Leni's death from blood poisoning at age forty-four denied the cinema what might have developed into a major career. Leni commenced his work in the German cinema as a painter, set designer, and art director, most notably collaborating with Max Reinhardt. These concerns carry through into his own films: his sets are strikingly stylized, dreamlike, and expressionistic.

Leni's attempt to go beyond the limits of photographed reality utilizing set and costume design was never more successfully realized than in *Das Wachsfigurenkabinett (Waxworks).* The film, with its distorted sets and ingenious lighting, is as profound an example of surreal cinematic madness as *The Cabinet of Dr. Caligari.* Three of the best-known actors in the post-World War I German cinema starred as the wax-work villains: Emil Jannings, Conrad Veidt, and Werner Krauss. Each appears in a separate episode as, respectively, Haroun-al-Raschid, Ivan the Terrible (who places hourglasses near each of his poison victims, so that they will know the exact moment of their deaths), and Jack the Ripper (a sequence that, in its dreaminess, is extremely Caligari-like). Veidt's Ivan allegedly influenced Sergei Eisenstein's conception of the character.

Like many foreign talents of the period, Leni ended up in Hollywood. As a result of his success with *Waxworks,* he was signed by Universal's Carl Laemmle. His first project was *The Cat and the Canary,* the original haunted house movie and quite unlike its successor: here, heiress Laura La Plante and her nervous cronies spend a night in an old dark house. To his credit, Leni did not sensationalize the material. The film's chills result from atmosphere, from stylized, expressionistic set design. The mansion, seen in the distance, is eerily gothic; inside are long, winding corridors and staircases. *The Cat and the Canary* is not just a chiller, in that Leni adds charming touches of humor to the scenario. Paul Leni made only four features in Hollywood. His final one, prophetically titled *The Last Warning,* was his only talkie.

—Rob Edelman

LEONE, Sergio

Nationality: Italian. **Born:** Rome, 3 January 1929. **Education:** Attended law school, Rome. **Family:** Son of director Vincenzo Leone; married Carla (Leone), 1960, three daughters. **Career:** Assistant to, then second unit director for, Italian filmmakers and American directors working in Italy, such as LeRoy, Walsh, and Wyler, 1947-56; scriptwriter, from late 1950s; directed first feature, *Il colosso di Rodi,* 1961; headed own production company, Rafran Cinematografica, 1970s. **Died:** In Rome, April 1989.

Films as Director:

1961 *Il colosso di Rodi* (*The Colossus of Rhodes*) (+ co-sc)
1964 *Per un pugno di dollari* (*A Fistful of Dollars*) (+ co-sc)
1965 *Per qualche dollaro in più* (*For a Few Dollars More*) (+ co-sc)

Sergio Leone on the set of *C'era una volta il West*

1966 ***Il buono il brutto il cattivo*** (*The Good, the Bad, and the Ugly*) (+ co-sc)
1968 ***C'era una volta il West*** (*Once upon a Time in the West*) (+ co-sc)
1972 *Giù la testa* (*Duck, You Sucker*; *Il était une fois la révolution*) (+ co-sc)
1975 *Un genio due compari e un pollo* (+ co-sc)
1984 ***Once upon a Time in America*** (+ co-sc)

Other Films:

1958 *Nel segno di Roma* (*Sign of the Gladiator*) (co-sc)
1959 *Gli ultimi giorni di Pompeii* (*The Last Days of Pompeii*) (Bonnard) (co-sc, uncredited co-d)
1961 *Sodoma e Gommorra* (*Sodom and Gomorrah*) (Aldrich) (2nd unit d, co-d according to some sources)
1973 *My Name is Nobody* (story idea)
1978 *Il gatto* (pr)

Publications

By LEONE: books—

Conversations avec Sergio Leone, edited by Noel Simsolo, Paris, 1987.

By LEONE: articles—

Interview, in *Take One* (Montreal), January/February 1972.
"Il était une fois la révolution," interview with G. Braucourt, in *Ecran* (Paris), May 1972.
"Pastalong Cassidy Always Wears Black," with Cynthia Grenier, in *Oui* (Chicago), April 1973.
Interview with M. Chion and others, in *Cahiers du Cinéma* (Paris), May 1984.
Interview with J.P. Domecq and J.A. Gili, in *Positif* (Paris), June 1984.
Interview with M. Corliss and E. Lomenzo, in *Film Comment* (New York), July/August 1984.
Interview with G. Graziani, in *Filmcritica* (Florence), October/November 1984.

On LEONE: books—

Lambert, Gavin, *Les Bons, les sales, les méchants et les propres de Sergio Leone,* Paris, 1976.
Frayling, Christopher, *Spaghetti Westerns: Cowboys and Europeans: From Karl May to Sergio Leone,* London, 1981.
Cèbe, Gilles, *Sergio Leone,* Paris, 1984.
De Fornari, Oreste, *Tutti i Film di Sergio Leone,* Milan, 1984.

Cumbow, Robert C., *Once upon a Time: The Films of Sergio Leone,* Metuchen, New Jersey, 1987.
Cressard, Gilles, *Sergio Leone,* Paris, 1989.
Mininni, Francesco, *Sergio Leone,* Paris, 1989.

On LEONE: articles—

Witonski, Peter, "Meanwhile ... Back at Cinecitta," in *Film Society Review* (New York), Fall 1965.
Sarris, Andrew, in *Village Voice* (New York), 19 and 26 September 1968.
Frayling, Christopher, "Sergio Leone," in *Cinema* (London), August 1970.
Kaminsky, Stuart, in *Take One* (Montreal), January/February 1972.
Jameson, Richard, "Something To Do with Death," in *Film Comment* (New York), March/April 1973.
Garel, A., and F. Joyeux, "Il etait une fois ... le western: de Sergio Leone," in *Image et Son* (Paris), July 1979.
Nicholls, D., "Once upon a Time in Italy," in *Sight and Sound* (London), Winter 1980/81.
Mitchell, T., "Leone's America," in *Sight and Sound* (London), Summer 1983.
"Sergio Leone," in *Film Dope* (London), March 1986.
Cohn, L., obituary in *Variety* (New York), 3 May 1989.
Bertolucci, Bernardo, obituary in *Film Comment* (New York), July/August 1989.
Thomson, D., "Leonesque," in *American Film* (Washington, D.C.), September 1989.

* * *

Not since Franz Kafka's *America* has a European artist turned himself with such intensity to the meaning of American culture and mythology. Sergio Leone's career is remarkable in its unrelenting attention to both America and American genre film. In France, Truffaut, Godard, and Chabrol have used American film as a touchstone for their own vision, but Leone, an Italian, a Roman who began to learn English only after five films about the United States, devoted most of his creative life to this examination.

Leone's films are not realistic or naturalistic visions of the American nightmare or fairy tale, but comic nightmares about existence. The feeling of unreality is central to Leone's work. His is a world of magic and horror. Religion is meaningless, a sham which hides honest emotions; civilization is an extension of man's need to dominate and survive by exploiting others. The Leone world, while not womanless, is set up as one in which men face the horror of existence. In this, Leone is very like Howard Hawks: as in Hawks's films, death erases a man. A man who dies is a loser, and the measure of a man is his ability to survive, to laugh or sneer at death. This is not a bitter point in Leone films. There are few lingering deaths and very little blood. Even the death of Ramon (Gian Maria Volonte) in *Fistful of Dollars* takes place rather quickly and with far less blood than the comparable death in *Yojimbo.* A man's death is less important than how he faces it. The only thing worth preserving in Leone's world is the family—and his world of American violence is such a terrible place that few families survive. In *Fistful of Dollars,* Clint Eastwood's primary emotional reaction is to attempt to destroy the family of the woman Ramon has taken. In the later films, *The Good, the Bad, and the Ugly* and *Once upon a Time in the West, Duck, You Sucker* and *Once upon a Time in America,* family life is minimal and destroyed by self-serving evil, not out of hatred but by a cold, passionless commitment to self-interest. Leone's visual obsessions contribute to his thematic interests. Many directors could work with and develop the same themes and characters, but Leone's forte lies in the development of these themes and characters in a personal world. No director, with the possible exception of Sam Fuller, makes as extensive use of the close-up as does Leone, and Leone's close-ups often show only a portion of the face, usually the eyes of one of the main characters. It is the eyes of these men that reveal what they are feeling—if they are feeling anything.

Such characters almost never define their actions in words. Plot is of minimal interest to Leone. What is important is examination of the characters, watching how they react, what makes them tick. It appears almost as if everything is, indeed, happening randomly, as if we are watching with curiosity the responses of different types of people, trying to read meaning in the slightest flick of an eyelid. The visual impact of water dripping on Woody Strode's hat, or Jack Elam's annoyed reaction to a fly, is of greater interest to Leone than the gunfight in which the two appear in *Once upon a Time in the West.*

The use of the pan in Leone films is also remarkable. The pan from the firing squad past the church and to the poster of the governor, behind which Rod Steiger watches in bewilderment through the eyes of the governor's image, is a prime example in *Duck, You Sucker.* The shot ties the execution to the indifferent church, to the non-seeing poster, and to Steiger's reaction in one movement.

The apparent joy and even comedy of destruction and battle in Leone films is often followed immediately by some intimate horror, some personal touch that underlines the real meaning of the horror which moments before had been amusing. The death of Dominick and his final words, "I slipped," in *Once upon a Time in America* undercut the comedy and zest for battle. There is little dialogue; the vision of the youthful dead dominates as it does in the cave scene in *Duck, You Sucker,* in which Juan's family lies massacred.

At the same time, Leone's fascination with spontaneous living, his zeal for existence in the midst of his morality films, can be seen in his handling of details. For example, food in his films is always colorful and appetizing and people eat it ravenously.

The obsession of Leone protagonists and villains, major and minor, with the attainment of wealth can be seen as growing out of a dominant strain within American genres, particularly western and gangster films. The desire for wealth and power turns men into ruthless creatures who violate land and family.

Leone's films are explorations of the mythic America he created. Unlike many directors, he did not simply repeat the same convention in a variety of ways. Each successive film takes the same characters and explores them in greater depth, and Leone's involvement with this exploration is intense.

—Stuart M. Kaminsky

LEROY, Mervyn

Nationality: American. **Born:** San Francisco, 15 October 1900. **Education:** Attended night school, 1919-1924. **Family:** Married 1) Doris Warner, 1933 (divorced), one son, one daughter; 2) Kathryn Spiegel, 1946. **Career:** Newsboy, from 1910; hired to portray newsboy in film *Barbara Fritchie,* 1912; film extra and vaudeville performer (as "The Singing Newsboy," later, with Clyde Cooper, as "Leroy and Cooper: Two Kids and a Piano"), 1912-1919; through cousin Jesse Lasky, got job in films, folding costumes, 1919; also film actor, to 1924; gag writer and comedy construction specialist for director Alfred E. Green, 1924; directed first film, *No Place to Go,* for First National, 1927; hired by MGM as producer and director, 1938; started own production company, 1944. **Awards:** Special Oscar, for *The House I Live In,* 1945; Victoire du Cinéma français, for *Quo Vadis,* 1954; Irving Thalberg Academy Award, 1975. **Died:** In Beverly Hills, 13 September 1987.

Mervyn Leroy and writer Sally Benson with set designs for *Little Women*

Films as Director:

1927 *No Place to Go*
1928 *Flying Romeos*; *Harold Teen*; *Oh, Kay!*
1929 *Naughty Baby* (*Reckless Rosie*); *Hot Stuff*; *Broadway Babies* (*Broadway Daddies*); *Little Johnny Jones*
1930 *Playing Around*; *Showgirl in Hollywood*; *Numbered Men*; *Top Speed*; *Little Caesar*; *Too Young to Marry*; *Broad-Minded*; *Five Star Final* (*One Fatal Hour*); *Tonight or Never*
1932 *High Pressure*; *Heart of New York*; *Two Seconds*; *Big City Blues*; *Three on a Match*; ***I Am a Fugitive from a Chain Gang***
1933 *Hard to Handle*; *Tugboat Annie*; *Elmer the Great*; *Gold Diggers of 1933*; *The World Changes*
1934 *Heat Lightning*; *Hi, Nellie!*; *Happiness Ahead*
1935 *Oil for the Lamps of China*; *Page Miss Glory*; *I Found Stella Parish*; *Sweet Adeline*
1936 *Anthony Adverse*; *Three Men on a Horse*
1937 *The King and the Chorus Girl*; *They Won't Forget*
1938 *Fools for Scandal*
1940 *Waterloo Bridge*; *Escape* (+ pr)
1941 *Blossoms in the Dust* (+ pr); *Unholy Partners*; *Johnny Eager*
1942 *Random Harvest*
1944 *Madame Curie*
1945 *Thirty Seconds Over Tokyo*
1946 *Without Reservations*
1948 *Homecoming*
1949 *Little Women* (+ pr); *Any Number Can Play*
1950 *East Side, West Side*; *Quo Vadis?*
1952 *Lovely to Look At*; *Million Dollar Mermaid* (*The One-Piece Bathing Suit*)
1953 *Latin Lovers*
1954 *Rose Marie* (+ pr)
1955 *Strange Lady in Town* (+ pr); *Mister Roberts* (co-d)
1956 *The Bad Seed* (+ pr); *Toward the Unknown* (*Brink of Hell*) (+ pr)
1958 *No Time for Sergeants* (+ pr); *Home before Dark* (+ pr)
1959 *The FBI Story* (+ pr)
1960 *Wake Me When It's Over* (+ pr)
1961 *The Devil at Four O'Clock* (+ pr); *A Majority of One* (+ pr)
1962 *Gypsy* (+ pr)
1963 *Mary, Mary* (+ pr)
1965 *Moment to Moment* (+ pr)

Other Films:

(partial list)

1920 *Double Speed* (Wood) (role as juvenile)
1922 *The Ghost Breaker* (Green) (role as a ghost)
1923 *Little Johnny Jones* (Rosson and Hines) (role as George Nelson); *Going Up* (Ingraham) (role as bellboy); *The Call of the Canyon* (Fleming) (role as Jack Rawlins)
1924 *In Hollywood with Potash and Perlmutter* (*So This is Hollywood*) (gag-writer); *Broadway after Dark* (Bell) (role as Carl Fisher); *The Chorus Lady* (Ralph Ince) (role as Duke)
1925 *Sally* (gag-writer); *The Desert Flower* (gag-writer); *The Pace That Thrills* (gag-writer); *We Moderns* (gag-writer)
1926 *Irene* (gag-writer); *Ella Cinders* (gag-writer); *It Must Be Love* (gag-writer); *Twinkletoes* (gag-writer)
1927 *Orchids and Ermines* (gag-writer)
1932 *The Dark Horse* (Green) (uncredited help)
1937 *The Great Garrick* (Whale) (pr)
1938 *Stand Up and Fight* (W.S. Van Dyke) (pr); *Dramatic School* (pr); *At the Circus* (pr)
1939 ***The Wizard of Oz*** (Fleming) (pr)
1945 *The House I Live In* (pr)
1947 *Desire Me* (Cukor) (uncredited direction)
1949 *The Great Sinner* (Siodmak) (uncredited direction and editing)
1968 *The Green Berets* (Wayne and Kellogg) (assisted Wayne)

Publications

By LEROY: books—

It Takes More Than Talent, as told to Alyce Canfield, New York, 1953.
Mervyn LeRoy: Take One, as told to Dick Kleiner, New York, 1974.

By LEROY: articles—

"The Making of Mervyn LeRoy," in *Films in Review* (New York), May 1953.
"What Directors Are Saying," in *Action* (Los Angeles), May/June 1970.
"Mervyn LeRoy Talks with William Friedkin," in *Action* (Los Angeles), November/December 1974.

On LEROY: articles—

Surtees, Robert, "The Filming of *Quo Vadis* in Italy," in *American Cinematographer* (Hollywood), October 1951.
Sarris, Andrew, "Likable, but Elusive," in *Film Culture* (New York), Spring 1963.
"Should Directors Produce?," in *Action* (Los Angeles), July/August 1968.
Campbell, Russell, "*I Am a Fugitive From a Chain Gang,*" in *Velvet Light Trap* (Madison, Wisconsin), June 1971.
Kaminsky, Stuart, "*Little Caesar* and Its Role in the Gangster Film Genre," in *Journal of Popular Film* (Bowling Green, Ohio), Summer 1972.
Canham, Kingsley, "Mervyn LeRoy: Star-making, Studio Systems, and Style," in *The Hollywood Professionals,* vol. 5, London, 1976.
Veillon, O.R., "Mervyn LeRoy à la Warner," in *Cinématographe* (Paris), October 1982.
"Mervyn Le Roy revisited," in *Image et Son* (Paris), December 1982.
"Mervyn Leroy," in *Film Dope* (London), September 1986.
Obituary in *Films and Filming* (London), November 1987.

* * *

The career of Mervyn LeRoy, one of the most successful in the heyday of the studio system, is a reflection of that system. When at Warner Brothers, through most of the 1930s, LeRoy was a master of the style dominant at that studio, demonstrated in the fast-paced toughness of films like his *Little Caesar* and *I Am a Fugitive from a Chain Gang.* As producer-director at MGM, until the mid-1950s, he presided over lushly romantic vehicles for Greer Garson and Vivien Leigh. Prolific, versatile (at home in action films, women's films, musicals, historical spectacles), LeRoy's fluency marks him as the kind of director who validates collaborative creativity. Sensitive to the particular individuals with whom he works, and to the wide-ranging needs of the various materials he treats, LeRoy offers us an image of the Hollywood technique during the development of the classic Hollywood narrative.

This often makes it difficult to locate that which is LeRoy's specific contribution to films as dissimilar as the taut courtroom drama *They Won't Forget* (that featured the memorable debut of Lana Turner, the "sweater girl" under personal contract to the director) and the colossal pageantry of *Quo Vadis?,* where decor completely submerges character. But if LeRoy lacks the recognizable visual and thematic coherence we notice in the works of "auteurs" (Welles, Ford, Griffith), it would be incorrect to characterize him as a director without a personal vision, or at least an affinity for specific subjects. Some of his best-remembered films contain narrative configurations that display the protagonists in situations of pathetic isolation. It is as if the director's eye and the spectator's eye spied a character in a state of embarrassing vulnerability. At the end of *I Am a Fugitive,* a film about a man wrongly charged with a crime and perpetually hounded by the police, the hero confesses that he must now steal to live. Staged in a dark alley, the last words emerge from total blackness that ironically hides the speaker's face in this moment of painful revelation. (It has been said that the blackout was due to a power failure on the set. This in no way lessens the significance of the decision to leave the scene in, as shot.) In *Random Harvest,* one of the most popular films LeRoy made at MGM, the director repeatedly finds ways to underscore the pain of the wife who "plays" at being the secretary of her husband, an amnesia victim who has forgotten her identity. Here, as in *Waterloo Bridge,* where the heroine represents one thing to the audience (a prostitute) and another to the hero (his long-lost fiancée), the staging exploits this ironic brand of double identity.

In a film made at Warners in 1958, *Home before Dark,* the dual representation of character is extended into the figure of the schizophrenic (Jean Simmons) who, wishing to be like her sister, appears in a crowded nightclub wearing an oversized gown and garishly inappropriate makeup. This sort of embarrassing exposure reaches a theatrical peak in *Gypsy,* where the mother of the striptease artists does her own "turn" on the bare stage of an empty theater, stripping down to her raw ambition and envy.

—Charles Affron

LESTER, Richard

Nationality: American. **Born:** Philadelphia, 19 January 1932. **Education:** William Penn Charter School, Germanstown, Pennsylvania; University of Pennsylvania, B.S. in Clinical Psychology, 1951. **Family:** Married dancer and choreographer Deirdre Vivian Smith, 1956, one son, one daughter. **Career:** Music editor, assistant director, then director, CBS-TV, Philadelphia, 1951-54; director and composer, ITV, London, 1955-57, then producer, 1958; director, Courtyard Films, Ltd., from 1967; also composer, musician, and, from 1960, director of TV commercials. **Awards:** Palme d'Or, Cannes Festival, for *The Knack,* 1965; Gandhi Peace Prize, Berlin Festival, for *The Bed Sitting Room,* 1969. **Address:** c/o Twickenham Studios, St. Margarets, Middlesex, England.

Films as Director:

1959 *The Running, Jumping and Standing Still Film* (+ ph, mu, co-ed)
1962 *It's Trad, Dad* (*Ring-a-Ding Rhythm*)
1963 *The Mouse on the Moon*
1964 ***A Hard Day's Night***
1965 *The Knack—and How to Get It*; *Help!*
1966 *A Funny Thing Happened on the Way to the Forum*
1967 *Mondo Teeno* (*Teenage Rebellion*) (doc) (co-d); *How I Won the War* (+ pr)
1968 *Petulia*
1969 *The Bed Sitting Room* (+ co-pr)
1974 *The Three Musketeers* (*The Queen's Diamonds*); *Juggernaut*
1975 *The Four Musketeers* (*The Revenge of Milady*); *Royal Flash*
1976 *Robin and Marian* (+ co-pr); *The Ritz*
1979 *Butch and Sundance: The Early Days*; *Cuba*
1980 *Superman II* (U.S. release 1981)
1983 *Superman III*
1984 *Finders Keepers* (+ exec pr)
1989 *Return of the Musketeers*
1991 *Get Back* (doc)

Publications

By LESTER: articles—

"In Search of the Right Knack," in *Films and Filming* (London), July 1965.
"Lunch with Lester," with George Bluestone, in *Film Quarterly* (Berkeley), Summer 1966.
"Richard Lester and the Art of Comedy," in *Film* (London), Spring 1967.
Interview with Ian Cameron and Mark Shivas, in *Movie* (London), Winter 1968/69.
"What I Learned from Commercials," in *Action* (Los Angeles), January/February 1969.
"Running, Jumping and Standing Still: An Interview with Richard Lester," with Joseph McBride, in *Sight and Sound* (London), Spring 1973.
"The Pleasure in the Terror of the Game," interview with Gordon Gow, in *Films and Filming* (London), October 1974.
"Richard Lester: Doing the Best He Can," interview with Gerald Pratley, in *Film* (London), February 1975.
"Deux Entretiens avec Richard Lester," with Michel Ciment, in *Positif* (Paris), November 1975.
Interview with J. Brosnan, in *Sight and Sound* (London), Summer 1983.
Interview with E. Vincent, in *Cinématographe* (Paris), July/August 1986.

On LESTER: books—

Rosenfeldt, Diane, *Richard Lester: A Guide to References and Resources,* Boston, 1978.
Sinyard, Neil, *The Films of Richard Lester,* London, 1985.

On LESTER: articles—

"Richard Lester," in *New Yorker,* 28 October 1967.
Gelmis, Joseph, "Richard Lester," in *The Film Director as Superstar,* Garden City, New York, 1970.
Kantor, Bernard, and others, editors, "Richard Lester," in *Directors at Work,* New York, 1970.
McBride, Joseph, "Richard Lester," in *International Film Guide 1975,* London, 1974.
Monaco, James, "Some Late Clues to the Lester Direction," in *Film Comment* (New York), May 1974.
Armes, Roy, "The Return of Richard Lester," in *London Magazine,* December/January 1974/75.
Thomas, Bob, "Richard Lester: *Robin and Marian,*" in *Action* (Los Angeles), November/December 1975.
Maillet, D., "Richard Lester," in *Cinématographe* (Paris), March 1977.
Lefèvre, R., "Richard Lester: Un odyssée en apesanteur," in *Revue du Cinéma* (Paris), February 1983.
"Richard Lester," in *Film Dope* (London), September 1986.

* * *

It is ironic that *A Hard Days Night,* the one film guaranteed to ensure Richard Lester his place in cinema history, should in many ways reflect his weaknesses rather than his strengths. If the film successfully captures the socio-historical phenomenon that was the Beatles at the beginning of their superstardom, it is as much due to Alun Owen's "day in the life" style script, which provides the ideal complement to (and restraint on) Lester's anarchic mixture of absurd/surreal humour, accelerated motion, and cinema verité, to name but a few ingredients. Lester made a mark on cinema through his innovative utilisation of the techniques of television advertisements and pop shows. His inability to entirely dispense with these methods, regardless of the subject matter to which they were applied, wrecked too many of his later projects.

The Knack stands as a supreme example of style (or styles) obliterating content. Bleached imagery, choruses of schoolboys reciting the litany of the "knack," disapproving members of the older generation talking straight to the camera, seem randomly assembled to no apparent end. Worse is the lack of taste. Can the sight of Rita Tushingham running down a street crying "rape" to an assortment of indifferent individuals have ever seemed funny? *How I Won the War* fails along similar lines. Realistic battlefields and bloodshed clash with a ridiculous plot (soldiers sent to construct a cricket pitch on enemy territory) and characters who are peculiar rather than likeable. One does not doubt Lester's sincerity in his aim of making his audience ashamed of watching men die for their entertainment, but his lack of judgement is disconcerting. Even the more controlled *Petulia* is afflicted by a surfeit of flashbacks and flashforwards, its often intriguing examination of unhappy relationships in an out-of-control society weighed down by a relentless determination to Say Something Important. All this is a far cry from the skillfully orchestrated physical comedy of *A Funny Thing Happened on the Way to the Forum* or the opening section of *Superman III,* both free from a desire to preach.

Where Lester's major strength as a director lies is in his ability to produce personal works within the confines of an established genre, such as the swashbuckler (*The Three Musketeers/The Four Musketeers*), the western (*Butch and Sundance: The Early Days*), and the fantasy (*Superman II*). If we wish to seek out underlying themes in his work these later films provide fertile ground (the mythical hero surrendering his power for human love in *Superman II,* Robin Hood attempting to regain his heroic status in a world no longer interested in heroes in *Robin and Marian*) while avoiding the collapse into uneasy self-importance or significance suffered by earlier work. Occasional lapses into heavy-handedness (the priest blessing the cannons for use in a religious war while muttering to himself in Latin in *The Four Musketeers,* the overly bloody beating inflicted on the mortal Clark Kent in *Superman II*) can be discounted as minor flaws.

It is this talent for creating something original out of conventional material that gives Lester his distinction, rather than his misguided, if bold attempts at "serious" comedy (with all the accompanying cin-tic tricks which ultimately produce only weariness in the viewer). ugh it may seem paradoxical, Lester is a director who needs a firm ndation to work from before his imagination can be let loose. ly, he has had little opportunity to demonstrate this since the high-file Superman films, following the misfiring farce *Finders Keepers* h two slightly threadbare attempts at recapturing former glories. *urn of the Musketeers* appears to have been ill-fated from the start, h the accidental death of Lester regular Roy Kinnear during film-. Moments of inspired action and slapstick could not disguise an rall feeling of deja vu (the film went straight to cable television in United States). *Get Back* amounts to little more than an adequate, taid record of Paul McCartney's 1989-90 world tour, though Lester's of footage from the Beatles' heyday serves as a poignant reminder both the overall 1960s cultural explosion and his own emergence as of the cinema's most outlandish frontrunners.

—Daniel O'Brien

EVINSON, Barry

ationality: American. **Born:** Baltimore, Maryland, 1942. **Educa-on:** Studied Broadcast Journalism, American University, Washing-n, D.C. **Family:** Married 1) screenwriter and actress Valerie Curtin ivorced, 1982); 2) Diana Mona; three sons, one daughter. **Career:** omedy performer and writer, Los Angeles, from mid-1960s; writer r TV, including "Carol Burnett Show" and "Marty Feldman Show," inning three Emmy awards, from 1970; directed first feature, *Diner,* 982. **Awards:** Oscar for Best Director, for *Rain Man,* 1988.

ilms as Director and Scriptwriter:

982 *Diner*
984 *The Natural*
985 *Young Sherlock Holmes*
987 *Tin Men*; *Good Morning, Vietnam*
988 *Rain Man*
990 *Avalon*
991 *Bugsy* (+ pr)
992 *Toys* (+ pr)
993 *Homicide: Life on the Street* (TV pilot) (+ exec pr)
994 *Jimmy Hollywood* (+ pr, role); *Disclosure* (+ pr)

Other Films:

1974 *Street Girls* (Miller) (co-sc, asst ph)
1976 *Silent Movie* (Brooks) (co-sc, role as executive)
1978 *High Anxiety* (Brooks) (co-sc, role as bellhop)
1979 *... And Justice For All* (Jewison) (co-sc)
1980 *Inside Moves* (Donner) (co-sc)
1981 *History of the World, Part 1* (Brooks) (role as column salesman)
1982 *Best Friends* (Jewison) (co-sc)
1984 *Unfaithfully Yours* (Zieff) (co-sc)
1993 *Wilder Napalm* (pr)
1994 *Quiz Show* (Redford) (role as Dave Garroway)

Publications

By LEVINSON: books—

Avalon; Tin Men; Diner: Three Screenplays, New York, 1990.
Levinson on Levinson, edited by David Thompson, London, 1992.

By LEVINSON: articles—

Interview with Stephen Farber, in *New York Times,* 18 April 1982.
Interview with R. Ward, in *American Film* (Washington, D.C.), June 1982.
Interview in *Inter/View* (New York), July 1984.
Interview in *Screen International* (London), 27 October 1984.
Interview with M. Cieutat and G. Gressard, in *Positif* (Paris), March 1989.
Interview with Alex Ward, in *New York Times Magazine,* 11 March 1990.
Interview with M. Chyb, in *Filmowy Serwis Prasowy,* vol. 36, no. 5/6, 1990.

On LEVINSON: articles—

"Barry Levinson," in *Film Dope* (London), September 1986.
Alion, Y., "Barry Levinson," in *Revue du Cinéma,* July/August 1990.
Rothstein, M., "Barry Levinson Reaches Out to a Lost America," in *New York Times,* 30 September 1990.
Yagoda, B., "Baltimore, My Baltimore," in *American Film,* November 1990.
"Retrospective," in *Film Journal,* October/November 1991.
McDonnell, Terry, "The New Barry Levinson Show," in *Esquire,* February 1992.
Carter, B., "Pure Baltimore, Right Down to the Steamed Crabs," in *New York Times,* 24 January 1993.
Schwed, Mark, "Kill or Be Killed," in *TV Guide,* 30 January 1993.
Lehman, Susan, "A Man and His *Toys,*" in *Premiere,* February 1993.
Fretts, Bruce, "The Dead Beat," in *Entertainment Weekly,* 5 February 1993.
Kornbluth, Jesse, "Wary Levinson," in *Premiere,* April 1994.

* * *

Although his most lucrative Oscar-winning film, *Rain Man,* was set in conservative Cincinnati, Los Angeles, Las Vegas, and several points in between, Barry Levinson has never forgotten his roots and is still regarded by Marylanders as the ultimate Baltimore filmmaker. *Diner,* the film that launched his directing career in 1982, was based in the Baltimore suburb of Forest Park, where he grew up. So was *Tin Men,* made five years later. And in 1989, at the age of forty-seven, following the success of *Rain Man* and *Good Morning, Vietnam,* Levinson was back again in Baltimore, to the delight of the Maryland Film Commission, shooting *Avalon.*

It could not have been otherwise, since *Avalon* is based upon Levinson's own family immigrating to Baltimore from Russia in 1914. Baltimore is his city and his most personal films have focussed upon ordinary people he might have met there growing up during the 1940s and 1950s—the youngsters of *Diner,* the aluminum siding hucksters of *Tin Men.* Levinson has internalized the values of middle-America and has succeeded most brilliantly when filming stories about characters who live by those values.

If some of the critics were disturbed that Robert Redford's Roy Hobbs was not as seriously flawed as the original character in Bernard Malamud's *The Natural,* it is perhaps because Levinson's interpretation of the character is governed by assumptions different from Malamud's and because Levinson's orientation is decidedly more optimistic. The fidelity of Levinson's *The Natural* can be and has been challenged on pedantic grounds. The film might better be regarded not as an adaptation, but as an interpretation that will stand on its own, regardless of its source.

Levinson told the *New York Times Magazine* that he does not consider himself as a writer or a "writer-director." As Alex Ward rightly suggested, however, Levinson can be considered an American *auteur*

Richard Lester

Barry Levinson

who will leave his personal imprint on any project he touches, through sentimental touches (in *The Natural* or *Tin Men,* for example), quirky casting, or inspired comedic improvisation. He has an unfailing sense of what might constitute the right touch in a given dramatic situation. "I don't like other people directing what I write," Levinson told Ward, "but I don't mind directing something somebody else wrote."

In fact, after moving to the West Coast from American University in Washington, D.C., Levinson worked for over two years as a writer for Mel Brooks on two pictures, *Silent Movie* and *High Anxiety* (also making his screen debut as an insane bellhop in the *Psycho* parody scene). While working with Brooks on *High Anxiety* he first met Mark Johnson, who later became the Executive Producer of *Diner.* At that point Levinson had already won three Emmy Awards for his network television writing with the "Tim Conway Show" and "Carol Burnett Show."

Levinson collaborated with Valerie Curtin (whom he met at the Comedy Store in Los Angeles) on two feature film scripts, ... *And Justice for All* (for Norman Jewison) and *Inside Moves* (for Richard Donner), before writing the script for *Diner.* His debut film as director is about young men "hanging out" in Baltimore over Christmas of 1959, one of them (Steve Guttenberg) enjoying his last days of bachelorhood before getting married. Mel Brooks told him that the script idea resembled *I vitelloni,* but Levinson had not even seen Fellini's film. Levinson told Stephen Farber of the *New York Times* that the Guttenberg character was based upon his cousin Eddie, who "loved fried bologna sandwiches" and "slept until 2:30 in the afternoon." The cast also featured Mickey Rourke and talented newcomers Kevin Bacon and Ellen Barkin. It was the lowest-budgeted "sleeper" produced by MGM that year. It started slowly after being reviewed in *Rolling Stone* and the *New Yorker,* then gradually built a following and staying power. (The president for distribution at MGM/UA referred to it as "Lazarus.") Vincent Canby in the *New York Times* called it the "happiest surprise of the year to date," and Levinson was "discovered."

Levinson also collaborated with Valerie Curtin in writing *Best Friends* (starring Burt Reynolds and Goldie Hawn) and a remake of the Preston Sturges classic *Unfaithfully Yours.* The screenplay for ... *And Justice for All,* meanwhile, was nominated for an Academy Award, demonstrating the quality of the Levinson-Curtin team. Levinson also directed the high-spirited fantasy *Young Sherlock Holmes,* but aside, perhaps, from *Rain Man* and *The Natural,* Levinson will best be remembered for his Baltimore pictures, drawn from his own experience and marked with his own special brand of compassionate humor and nostalgia. As a personal filmmaker he is perhaps the nearest American equivalent to François Truffaut.

During the 1990s Levinson scored a popular and critical success working with author James Toback on *Bugsy,* starring Warren Beatty as larger-than-life gangster Benjamin (Bugsy) Siegel and Annette Bening as Virginia Hill. The film was much admired for its snappy dialogue and named best picture of 1991 by the Los Angeles Film Critics, who also voted Levinson Best Director and Toback Best Screenwriter. *Bugsy* later earned ten Academy Award nominations, including Best Picture and Best Director.

In 1992 Levinson misfired with *Toys,* an odd antiwar fable written by Levinson and Valerie Curtain, starring Robin Williams, Joan Cusack, and Michael Gambon. Levinson had the project in mind for years and was able to direct it after the success of *Bugsy.* The idea that children can be conditioned by the kinds of toys they are given was workable, but the fantasy was too bizarre to be taken seriously. Levinson also misfired in 1994 with *Jimmy Hollywood,* starring Joe Pesci as a loser and hustler, which was described in *Variety* as "an oddball attempt to mix offbeat comedy with social commentary."

In 1994 Levinson reclaimed his Hollywood clout with his expert direction of *Disclosure,* starring Michael Douglas and Demi Moore and adapted by Paul Attanasio from the popular novel by Michael Crichton, who also worked with Levinson as producer. The controversial novel, concerning sexual harassment in the workplace, helped to generate interest in the film. But a far more important collaboration between Levinson and Paul Attanasio started in 1993 on the NBC television police series *Homicide: Life on the Street,* adapted from *Baltimore Sun* reporter David Simon's published memoir about policework in Levinson's hometown. The series was hailed by critics as the best police drama on television, giving it prominence over the flashier yet more conventional *NYPD Blue.* As executive producer of the series Levinson also directed the pilot in 1993 and the season finale in 1995, thus helping *Homicide* to establish and maintain its quality and authenticity as an outstanding reality-based detective drama. Arguably, the series represents the director's best work since *Avalon* while setting a new standard for television drama.

—James M. Welsh

LEWIN, Albert

Nationality: American. **Born:** Brooklyn, New York, 23 September 1894; grew up in Newark, New Jersey. **Education:** New York University, B.A. in English; Harvard University, M.A. in English; attended Columbia University. **Military Service:** U.S. Army, 1918. **Family:** Married Mildred Mindlin, 17 August 1918; no children. **Career:** English instructor, University of Missouri, 1916-18; assistant national director, American Jewish Relief Committee, 1918-22; drama and film critic, *The Jewish Tribune,* 1921-22; entered films as a New York-based reader for Samuel Goldwyn, 1921; moved to Culver City, continued as a reader, then trained as script clerk with King Vidor and Victor Sjöström and worked unofficially as an assistant editor, 1922-23; hired as writer by Metro Pictures, 1924; promoted to head of Metro-Goldwyn-Mayer (MGM) story department, 1927; promoted to production supervisor, 1929; after death of mentor, Irving Thalberg, moved to Paramount as producer, 1937-40; quit Paramount, founded independent production company with David Loew, 1940; Loew-Lewin released its second production, and Lewin's first as director, *The Moon and Sixpence,* after which Lewin returned to MGM as a director, 1942; quit MGM after release of his second directorial film, *The Picture of Dorian Gray,* and revived Loew-Lewin, 1945; dissolved Loew-Lewin again, after one film, Lewin's third as director, *The Private Affairs of Bel Ami,* and returned to MGM as an executive, 1948; wrote and directed *Pandora and the Flying Dutchman* while on sabbatical from MGM, 1950-51; retired from films after a near-fatal heart attack, 1959. **Awards:** As producer, received best picture Academy Award for *Mutiny on the Bounty,* 1935. **Died:** In New York City, 9 May 1968, of pneumonia.

Films as Director:

1942 *The Moon and Sixpence* (+ co-exec pr, sc)
1945 *The Picture of Dorian Gray* (+ sc)
1947 *The Private Affairs of Bel-Ami* (+ co-exec pr, sc)
1951 *Pandora and the Flying Dutchman* (+ co-pr, sc)
1954 *Saadia* (+ pr, sc)
1957 *The Living Idol* (+ co-pr, sc)

Other Films:

1924 *Bread* (continuity)
1925 *The Fate of a Flirt* (continuity)
1926 *Ladies of Leisure* (story, continuity); *Blarney* (co-scenarist); *Tin Hats* (continuity)
1927 *A Little Journey* (scenarist); *Altars of Desire* (continuity); *Spring Fever* (co-scenarist); *Quality Street* (co-scenarist, co-adapter)
1928 *The Actress* (co-scenarist)
1929 *The Kiss* (production supervisor, uncredited); *Devil-May-Care* (production supervisor, uncredited)
1931 *The Guardsman* (production supervisor, uncredited); *The Cuban Love Song* (production supervisor, uncredited)
1932 *Red-Headed Woman* (production supervisor, uncredited); *Smilin' Through* (production supervisor, uncredited)
1934 *What Every Woman Knows* (production supervisor, uncredited)
1935 *China Seas* (assoc pr); *Mutiny on the Bounty* (assoc pr)
1937 *The Good Earth* (assoc pr); *True Confession* (pr)
1938 *Spawn of the North* (pr)
1939 *Zaza* (pr)
1940 *So Ends Our Night* (co-exec pr)

Publications

By LEWIN: book—

The Unaltered Cat (novel), Charles Scribner's Sons, 1967.

By LEWIN: articles—

"Fine Art and the Films," in *The Temptation of Saint Anthony: Bel Ami International Art Competition,* The American Federation of Arts, 1946.
Interview in *The Real Tinsel,* Bernard Rosenberg and Harry Silverstein, eds., Macmillan, 1970.
"'Peccavi!': The True Confession of a Movie Producer," in *Theatre Arts,* September 1941.

On LEWIN: book—

Felleman, Susan, *Botticelli in Hollywood: Albert Lewin, Director,* Twayne, 1997.

On LEWIN: articles—

Arkadin [John Russell Taylor], "Film Clips," *Sight and Sound,* Winter 1967-68.
Arnaud, Claude, "Les statues meurent aussi," *Cinématographe,* January 1982.
Combs, Richard, "Retrospective: The Picture of Dorian Gray," *Monthly Film Bulletin,* November 1985.
Felleman, Susan, "How High Was His Brow? Albert Lewin, His Critics and the Problem of Pretension," *Film History,* Winter 1995-96.
Garsault, Alain, "Albert Lewin: un créateur à Hollywood," *Positif,* July-August 1989.
McVay, Douglas, "The Private Affairs of Bel Ami (1947)," *Movietone News,* 13 March 1981.

Albert Lewin with Claudette Colbert

Milne, Tom, "You Are a Professor, Of Course," *Monthly Film Bulletin,* November 1985.

Török, Jean-Paul, ed., "Pandora," *l'Avant-Scène du Cinéma,* 1 April 1980.

* * *

A genuine Hollywood highbrow, Albert Lewin trod the line between the commercially viable and the artistically daring in his own inimitable way. Friends with the likes of writers Djuna Barnes and Robert Graves, artist Man Ray and director Jean Renoir, Lewin had given up a nascent career as scholar and critic to pursue the grail of movies. Impressed especially by the most stylized and fantastic aspects of silent cinema, from Sjöström to Stroheim, Caligari to Keaton, Lewin left New York for Hollywood in 1922 and—just prior to Sam Goldwyn and Louis B. Mayer—joined Metro Pictures early in 1924. He impressed Irving Thalberg with his combination of erudition and sense and soon made himself indispensable at the Metro-Goldwyn-Mayer (MGM) story department, where he came to be known as Thalberg's story brain. He thrived first as a writer, then a producer at MGM until Thalberg's death. After a brief and unhappy stint as a producer at Paramount, he embarked upon his career as a director, he claimed, out of financial necessity. Lewin and his college fraternity brother, David Loew, had founded their own independent production company, and Loew urged Lewin to direct his own adaptation of W. Somerset Maugham's *The Moon and Sixpence* (1942) as an economic measure.

The result was a commercial and critical success. Lewin's adaptation of Maugham's strange novel about a milquetoast English stockbroker and family man turned passionate painter and fierce misanthrope (his protagonist, Charles Strickland, was based on the French painter Paul Gauguin) was made on the cheap, but includes several original turns and stylistic and thematic signatures that would return faithfully in Lewin's films, particularly his next two, more lavish productions: *The Picture of Dorian Gray* (1945) and *The Private Affairs of Bel Ami* (1947). All three films feature suave, cynical George Sanders, who clearly represented a kind of ego ideal for Lewin, in variations on what would become his standard film persona.

The three black-and-white films from the 1940s are united not only by Sanders and their fin-de-siècle European settings, but also by the fact that all are essentially morality plays—albeit rather perverse and ambiguous ones—in which art, decadence, and sexual thrall are viewed through the prism of a very pictorial, complex, and studied mise-en-scène. *The Picture of Dorian Gray,* the most elaborate of the three, is a film of stunning self-consciousness and density—a psychosexual horror film, enacted with choreographic precision in exquisite and mannered late-Victorian interiors. Hurd Hatfield plays the eponymous protagonist with chilling circumspection and Sanders is persuasive uttering the Wildean epigrams of Lord Henry Wotton. Harry Stradling's cinematography won the film's only Academy Award; it along with the sets and costumes realizes Lewin's Beardsleyesque visual conception perfectly, while Herbert Stothart's score employs Chopin's Twenty-fourth Prelude evocatively.

The musical score, this time by Darius Milhaud, was also a strength of Lewin's next film, *The Private Affairs of Bel Ami,* based on Guy de Maupassant's novel *Bel-Ami.* This story of a narcissistic and calculating Parisian bounder whose successes are achieved through a series of sexual liaisons secured Lewin's reputation, according to the *Times,* for achieving "censor-proof depravity." Subtly feminist, this film revolves around a (rather wooden) male object of female desire (Sanders, again, as Georges Duroy, a.k.a. *bel ami*) and features impressive performances from its female cast, including Ann Dvorak, Angela Lansbury, and Katherine Emery. Russell Metty's cinematography and Gordon Wiles's set design contribute to *Bel Ami*'s measured, almost anaesthetic contemplation of desire and duplicity. Here, as in *Dorian Gray,* the characters move—or are moved—around on patterned floors like chessmen on a checkerboard. The metaphysical implications of this trope are reiterated in *Bel Ami* by a host of symbols: Punch and Judy, dolls and games, and by a somewhat heavy-handed moral coda.

Notably, these films each include the revelation in color insert of a painting. In the original prints of *The Moon and Sixpence* black-and-white photography changed to sepia when the scene changed from Europe to Tahiti and then, momentarily, to color when the painter Strickland's "masterpiece" (in fact a mediocre Gauguinesque pastiche) was revealed near the end. In *Bel Ami* it is a shockingly anachronistic painting of *The Temptation of St. Anthony* by Surrealist Max Ernst that erupts from the screen in color. The technique is put more in the service of the narrative in *The Picture of Dorian Gray,* where Technicolor enhances the vivid senescence and putrefaction of Ivan Albright's rendition of the titular portrait.

Lewin continued to highlight art works in his color films of the 1950s, including in what is arguably his masterpiece, the singular *Pandora and the Flying Dutchman* (1951), a heady melange of Greek myth, German legend, Shakespearean and Jacobean drama, Romantic poetry, and Surrealist imagery, all spiced up with bullfighting, flamenco dancing, jazz combos, and speed-racing! From an original story, this dazzling film, often deliberately Surrealist and sometimes inadvertently camp, was shot on Spain's Costa Brava and features Ava Gardner (divinely beautiful as costumed by Beatrice Dawson and photographed by Jack Cardiff) and James Mason in the title roles. Its uneven reception—most Anglo-American critics cringed, while the French swooned—is a testimony to its audacity.

Lewin's last two films, made under considerable budget and casting restraints by MGM, were almost unanimously (and fairly) deemed failures. *Saadia* (1954), based on a minor French novel of colonial Morocco, despite the authenticity and beauty of its location ambience, is an awkward blend of romantic cliché and intellectual speculation. *The Living Idol* (1957), from an original script, like Lewin's later novel *The Unaltered Cat,* is an even uneasier synthesis of formulaic romance, sensational supernaturalism, and almost laughable pedantry, in which the plot seems a flimsy armature upon which its director's pet intellectual obsessions are top-heavily disposed.

Albert Lewin was a dilettante in the fullest sense of the word. His profound enthusiasms for the other arts are manifest in his films, several of which have artist-protagonists and all of which incorporate literary allusion, scenes of song and dance (e.g., Tahitian, Indonesian, Parisian, Andalusian, Moroccan, and Mexican), and manifold art objects. But Lewin's (real and anticipated) battles with the Hays Office and his sense of popular taste seem to have led him to add, as sops to the censors and the box office, plot elements and characters for their strictly comedic, sentimental, or moralizing values. Even his best films are thus occasionally weakened by an anomalous scene or banal figure. And, especially in his original scripts, his literary and dilettantish impulses were wont to run amok. But his efforts resulted in a few films of real distinction, of proto-Godardian reflexivity, visual intricacy, and literary pith. In the United States, where critics and audiences are often alienated by such qualities, Lewin's reputation has languored, while in Europe, where his influence on directors like Godard and Antonioni has been claimed, it has borne up rather better.

—Susan Felleman

LEWIS, Jerry

Nationality: American. **Born:** Joseph Levitch in Newark, New Jersey, 16 March 1926. **Education:** Irvington High School, New Jersey, through tenth grade. **Family:** Married 1) singer Patti Palmer, 1944, five sons; 2) Sandra Pitnick, 1983. **Career:** Stage debut in 1931;

developed comic routines and attracted Irving Kaye as manager, 1942; began working with Dean Martin at Atlantic City club, 1946; with Martin, signed by Hal Wallis for Paramount, 1948; acted in first feature, also founded production company to direct series of pastiches of Hollywood films (later Jerry Lewis Productions), 1949; chairman of Muscular Dystrophy Association of America, raising funds from annual telethons, from 1952; started solo career, 1956; signed seven-year contract with Paramount-York, 1959; after abandonment of *The Day the Clown Cried,* left films for eight years, 1972; appeared on Broadway as the devil in revival of *Damn Yankees,* 1995. **Awards:** Commander of the Order of Arts and Letters, and Commander of the Legion of Honour, France, 1984; Nobel Peace Prize nomination, 1978, for work for the Muscular Dystrophy Association. **Agent:** Jeff Witjas, William Morris Agency, 151 El Camino Drive, Beverly Hills, CA 90212, U.S.A. **Address:** Jerry Lewis Films Inc., 3160 W. Sahara Avenue #16-C, Las Vegas, NV 89102, U.S.A.

Films as Director:

(partial list)

1949 *Fairfax Avenue* (short pastiche of *Sunset Boulevard*); *A Spot in the Shade* (short pastiche of *A Place in the Sun*); *Watch on the Lime* (pastiche); *Come Back, Little Shicksa* (pastiche); *Son of Lifeboat* (pastiche); *The Re-Inforcer* (pastiche); *Son of Spellbound* (pastiche); *Melvin's Revenge* (pastiche); *I Should Have Stood in Bedlam* (pastiche of *From Here to Eternity*); *The Whistler* (pastiche)
1960 *The Bellboy* (+ sc, pr, role as Stanley)
1961 *The Ladies' Man* (+ sc, pr, roles as Herbert H. Heebert and his mother, Mrs. Heebert); *The Errand Boy* (+ sc, role as Morty S. Tachman)
1963 *The Nutty Professor* (+ sc, roles as Julius F. Kelp and Buddy Love)
1964 *The Patsy* (+ sc, role as Stanley Belt)
1965 *The Family Jewels* (+ pr, sc, roles as Willard Woodward, Uncle James Peyton, Uncle Eddie Peyton, Uncle Julius Peyton, Uncle Shylock Peyton, Uncle Bugs Peyton)
1966 *Three on a Couch* (+ pr, roles as Christopher Prise, Warren, Ringo Raintree, Rutherford, Heather)
1967 *The Big Mouth* (+ pr, sc, roles as Gerald Clamson, Sid Valentine)
1970 *One More Time*; *Which Way to the Front?* (+ pr, roles as Brendan Byers III, Kesselring)
1972 *The Day the Clown Cried* (+ principal role) (not completed)
1980 *Hardly Working* (+ sc, principal role)
1982 *Cracking Up* (*Smorgasbord*) (+ sc, principal role)

Other Films:

1949 *My Friend Irma* (Marshall) (role as Seymour)
1950 *My Friend Irma Goes West* (Walker) (role as Seymour)
1951 *At War with the Army* (Walker) (role as Soldier Korwin); *That's My Boy* (Walker) (role as "Junior" Jackson)
1952 *Sailor Beware* (Walker) (role as Melvin Jones); *Jumping Jacks* (Taurog) (role as Hap Smith)
1953 *The Stooge* (Taurog) (role as Ted Rogers); *Scared Stiff* (Marshall) (role as Myron Myron Mertz); *The Caddy* (Taurog) (role as Harvey Miller)
1954 *Money from Home* (Marshall) (role as Virgil Yokum); *Living It Up* (Taurog) (role as Homer Flagg); *Three Ring Circus* (Pevney) (role as Jerry Hotchkiss)
1955 *You're Never Too Young* (Taurog) (role as Wilbur Hoolick); *Artists and Models* (Tashlin) (role as Eugene Fullstack)
1956 *Pardners* (Taurog) (role as Wade Kingsley Jr.); *Hollywood or Bust* (Tashlin) (role as Malcolm Smith)
1957 *The Delicate Delinquent* (McGuire) (pr, role as Sidney Pythias); *The Sad Sack* (Marshall) (role as Meredith T. Bixby); *The Geisha Boy* (Tashlin) (pr, role as Gilbert Wooley)
1958 *Rock-a-Bye Baby* (Tashlin) (pr, role as Clayton Poole)
1959 *Don't Give Up the Ship* (Taurog) (role as John Paul Steckley VII)
1960 *Visit to a Small Planet* (Taurog) (role as Kreton); *Cinderfella* (Tashlin) (pr, role as Fella); *Li'l Abner* (Frank) (brief appearance)
1962 *It's Only Money* (Tashlin) (role as Lester March)
1963 *It's a Mad, Mad, Mad, Mad, World* (Kramer) (role as man who drives over Culpepper's hat); *Who's Minding the Store?* (Tashlin) (role as Raymond Phiffier)
1964 *The Disorderly Orderly* (Tashlin) (role as Jerome Littlefield)
1965 *Boeing Boeing* (Rich) (role as Robert Reed)
1966 *Way Way Out* (Douglas) (role as Peter Matamore)
1967 *Don't Raise the Bridge, Lower the River* (Paris), (role as George Lester)
1969 *Hook, Line and Sinker* (Marshall) (pr, role as Peter Ingersoll, alias Dobbs)
1981 *Rascal Dazzle* (doc) (narration)
1982 *The King of Comedy* (Scorsese) (role as Jerry Langford); *Slapstick* (Paul) (role)
1984 *Retenex-moi ... ou je fais un malheur* (*To Catch a Cop*) (Gerard) (role as Jerry Logan); *Par ou t'est rentre? On t'a pas vu sortir* (Clair) (role); *Slapstick of Another Kind* (Paul) (role)
1989 *Cookie* (Seidelman) (role)
1992 *American Dreamers* (role); *Mr. Saturday Night* (role); *Arizona Dream* (role as Leo Sweetie)
1995 *Funny Bones* (Chelsom) (role as George Fawkes)

Publications

By LEWIS: books—

The Total Film-Maker, New York, 1971.
Jerry Lewis in Person, New York, 1982.

By LEWIS: articles—

"Mr. Lewis Is a Pussycat," interview with Peter Bogdanovich, in *Esquire* (New York), November 1962.
"America's Uncle: Interview with Jerry Lewis," with Axel Madsen, in *Cahiers du Cinéma in English* (New York), no.4, 1966.
Interview in *Directors at Work,* edited by Bernard Kantor and others, New York, 1970.
"Five Happy Moments," in *Esquire* (New York), December 1970.
"Dialogue on Film: Jerry Lewis," in *American Film* (Washington, D.C.), September 1977.
Interview with D. Rabourdin, in *Cinéma* (Paris), April 1980.
Interview with Serge Daney, in *Cahiers du Cinéma* (Paris), May 1983.
"The King of Comedy," an interview with T. Jousse and V. Ostria, in *Cahiers du Cinéma,* July/August 1993.
"Thank You Jerry Much," an interview with Graham Fuller, in *Interview,* April 1995.

On LEWIS: books—

Gehman, Richard, *That Kid—The Story of Jerry Lewis,* New York, 1964.
Simsolo, Noel, *Le Monde de Jerry Lewis,* Paris, 1969.

Maltin, Leonard, *Movie Comedy Teams,* New York, 1970.
Recasens, Gerard, *Jerry Lewis,* Paris, 1970.
Marx, Arthur, *Everybody Loves Somebody Sometime (Especially Himself): The Story of Dean Martin and Jerry Lewis,* New York, 1974.
Cremonini, Giogio, *Jerry Lewis,* Firenza, 1979.
Marchesini, Mauro, *Jerry Lewis: Un comico a perdere,* Verona, 1983.
Benayoun, Robert, *Bonjour Monsieur Lewis: journal ouvert, 1957-1980,* Paris, 1989.
Lewis, Patti, *I Laffed Till I Cried: Thirty-Six Years of Marriage to Jerry Lewis,* Waco, Texas, 1993.
Neibaur, James L., *The Jerry Lewis Films: An Analytical Filmography of the Innovative Comic,* Jefferson, North Carolina, 1995.
Levy, Shawn, *King of Comedy: The Life and Art of Jerry Lewis,* New York, 1996.

On LEWIS: articles—

Farson, Daniel, "Funny Men: Dean Martin and Jerry Lewis," in *Sight and Sound* (London), July/September 1952.
Kass, Robert, "Jerry Lewis Analyzed," in *Films in Review* (New York), March 1953.
Hume, Rod, "Martin and Lewis—Are Their Critics Wrong?," in *Films and Filming* (London), March 1956.
Taylor, John, "Jerry Lewis," in *Sight and Sound* (London), Spring 1965.
Sarris, Andrew, "Editor's Eyrie," in *Cahiers du Cinéma in English* (New York), no. 4, 1966.
Schickel, Richard, "Jerry Lewis Retrieves a Lost Ideal," in *Life* (New York), 15 July 1966.
Camper, Fred, "Essays in Visual Style," in *Cinéma* (London), no. 8, 1971.
Vialle, G., and others, "Jerry Lewis," in *Image et Son* (Paris), no. 278, 1973.
Coursodon, J. P., "Jerry Lewis's Films: No Laughing Matter?," in *Film Comment* (New York), July/August 1975.
LeBour, F., and R. DeLaroche, "Which Way to Jerry Lewis?," in *Ecran* (Paris), July 1976.
Shearer, H., "Telethon," in *Film Comment* (New York), May/June 1979.
McGilligan, P., "Recycling Jerry Lewis," in *American Film* (Washington, D.C.), September 1979.
Jerry Lewis Section of *Casablanca* (Madrid), June 1983.
Polan, Dana, "Being and Nuttiness: Jerry Lewis and the French," in *Journal of Popular Film and Television* (Washington, D.C.), Spring 1984.
Liebman, R. L., "Rabbis or Rakes, Schlemiels or Supermen? Jewish Identity in Charles Chaplin, Jerry Lewis, and Woody Allen," in *Literature/Film Quarterly* (Salisbury, Maryland), vol. 12, no. 3, July 1984.
"Jerry Lewis," in *Film Dope* (London), September 1986.
Bukatman, S., "Paralysis in Motion: Jerry Lewis's Life as a Man," in *Camera Obscura,* May 1988.
Reynaud, B., "Qui a peur de Jerry Lewis? Pas nous, pas nous," in *Cahiers du Cinéma,* February 1989.
Kruger, Barbara, "Remote Control," in *Artforum,* November 1989.
Bukatman, S., "Session: Jerry Lewis," in *Quarterly Review of Film Studies,* no. 4, 1989.
Selig, Michael, "The Nutty Professor: A 'Problem' in Film Scholarship," in *Velvet Light Trap,* Fall 1990.
Angeli, Michael, "God's Biggest Goof," in *Esquire,* February 1991.
Woodcock, J. M., "The Name Dropper Drops Jerry Lewis, Part I," in *American Cinemeditor,* no. 3, 1991.
Hoberman, J., "Before There Was 'Scarface' There Was ... Rubberface," in *Interview,* February 1993.
Bolte, Bill, "Jerry's Got to Be Kidding," in *Utne Reader,* March 1993.
Wolff, C., "Highs, Lows, Joy, and Regret, All in a Single Day's Living," in *New York Times,* 5 August 1993.
Rapf, Joanna E., "Comic Theory from a Feminist Perspective: A Look at Jerry Lewis," in *Journal of Popular Culture,* Summer 1993.
Bennetts, Leslie, "Letter from Las Vegas: Jerry vs. the Kids" in *Vanity Fair,* September 1993.
Krutnik, Frank, "Jerry Lewis: The Deformation of the Comic," in *Film Quarterly,* Fall 1994.
Haller, Beth, "The Misfit and Muscular Dystrophy," in *Journal of Popular Film and Television,* Winter 1994.
Castro, Peter, "Hellza Poppin," in *People Weekly,* 27 March 1995.
Krutnik, Frank, "The Handsome Man and His Monkey: The Comic Bondage of Dean Martin and Jerry Lewis," in *Journal of Popular Film and Television,* Spring 1995.

* * *

In France, Jerry Lewis is called "Le Roi de Crazy" and adulated as a genius by filmmakers as respectable as Alain Resnais, Jean-Luc Godard, and Claude Chabrol. In America, Jerry Lewis is still an embarrassing and unexplained paradox, often ridiculed, awaiting a persuasive critical champion. This incredible gulf can in part be explained by American access, on television talk shows and Lewis's annual muscular dystrophy telethon, to Lewis's contradictory public persona: egotistical yet insecure, insulting yet sentimental, juvenile yet adult, emotionally naked yet defensive. Were not the real Lewis apparently so hard to love, the celluloid Lewis might be loved all the more. And yet a Lewis cult thrives among American cinephiles; and certainly *The Bellboy, The Errand Boy, The Nutty Professor,* and *Which Way to the Front?* appear today to be among the most interesting and ambitious American films of the 1960s.

Lewis's career can be divided into four periods: first, the partnership with singer Dean Martin, which resulted in a successful nightclub act and popular series of comedies, including *My Friend Irma* and *At War with the Army,* as well as several highly regarded films directed by former cartoonist and Lewis mentor Frank Tashlin; second (after professional and personal tensions fueled by Lewis's artistic ambitions irrevocably destroyed the partnership), an apprenticeship as a solo comedy star, beginning with *The Delicate Delinquent* and continuing through Tashlin's *Cinderfella*; third, the period as the self-professed "total filmmaker," inaugurated in 1960 with *The Bellboy* and followed by a decade of Lewis films directed by and starring Lewis, which attracted the attention of auteurist critics in France and overwhelming box-office response in America, culminating with a string of well-publicized financial failures, including *Which Way to the Front?* and the unreleased, near-mythical *The Day the Clown Cried,* in which clown Lewis leads Jewish children to Nazi ovens; and finally, the period as valorized, if martyred auteur, exemplified by Lewis's work as an actor in Martin Scorsese's *The King of Comedy* and Lewis's sporadic, unsuccessful attempts to re-establish his own directorial career.

Lewis's appeal is significantly rooted in the American silent film tradition of the individual comedian: like Chaplin, Lewis is interested in pathos and sentiment; like Keaton, Lewis is fascinated by the comic gag which could only exist on celluloid; like Harry Langdon, Lewis exhibits, within an adult persona, childish behavior which is often disturbing and embarrassing; like Stan Laurel, whose first name Lewis adopts as an *homage* in several of his films, Lewis is the lovable innocent often endowed with almost magical qualities. What Lewis brings uniquely to this tradition, however, is his obsession with the concept of the schizophrenic self; his typical cinema character has so many anxieties and tensions that it must take on other personalities in order to survive. Often, the schizophrenia becomes overtly autobiographical, with the innocent, gawky kid escaping his stigmatized existence by literally becoming "Jerry Lewis," beloved and successful comedian (as in *The Bellboy* and *The Errand Boy*) or romantic leading man, perhaps representing the now absent Dean Martin (as in *The Nutty Professor*). Jerry Lewis's physical presence on screen in his idiot persona emphasizes movement disorders in a way which relates provocatively to his highly publicized work for the Muscular Dystrophy

Jerry Lewis on the set of *The Nutty Professor*

Association. Schizophrenia is compounded in *The Family Jewels:* what Jean-Pierre Coursodon calls Lewis's "yearning for self-obliteration" is manifested in seven distinct personalities. Ultimately, Lewis escapes by turning himself into his cinema, as evidenced by the credits in his failed comeback film, which proudly announce: "Jerry Lewis is ... *Hardly Working.*" This element of cinematic escape and schizophrenia is especially valued by the French, who politicize it as a manifestation of the human condition as influenced by American capitalism.

Much must also be said about the strong avant-garde qualities to Lewis's work: his interest in surrealism; his experimentalism and fascination with self-conscious stylistic devices; his movement away from conventional gags toward structures apparently purposely deformed; his interest in plotlessness and ellipsis; the reflexivity of his narrative; his studied use of extended silence and gibberish in a sound cinema; the ambiguous sexual subtext of his work; and finally, his use of film as personal revelation.

The last decade has seen a slight diminution of Lewis's reputation as a director (Lewis having directed television situation comedies, but no features), but an augmentation of his reputation as an actor and icon. His *King of Comedy* appearance now seems definitely a major performance in the American cinema, as does the Scorsese film a major statement about the American lust for celebrity. Ever since that film, a variety of younger directors have used Lewis as icon and/or as reflexive comment on the Lewis career. Perhaps Lewis's most interesting showcase is his 1995 performance as a Las Vegas comedian in *Funny Bones,* directed by Peter Chelsom. It is hard not to see *Funny Bones* as a deadly look at the Las Vegas side of the Lewis persona, complete with the jazzy, Sinatra score and the institutional insincerity: Lewis is the funny father who overshadows his psychologically wounded and relatively untalented son, his own celebrity having a dark, depressing underside and a deleterious effect on family life.

Lewis as George Fawkes admits that he was not true to his talent and confesses, "It kills me that I used writers, instead of using me." The film's philosophy—"I never saw anything funny that wasn't terrible, that didn't cause pain"—seems a natural segue to other recent events in the Lewis life: his autobiography, written in 1982, chronicled, among other things, his addiction to Percodan and his driven personality. His ex-wife, Patti Lewis, followed with her own autobiography—whose title tells it all: *I Laffed Till I Cried: Thirty-Six Years of Marriage to Jerry Lewis.* And although Lewis has dedicated his life to raising hundreds of millions of dollars for the Muscular Dystrophy Association, he has been virulently attacked by many adults with the disease—particularly in 1992 and 1993—who claim he publicly demonstrates a patronizing, demeaning attitude and exploits them with a pity which makes their lives in society harder, not easier. Lewis responded by attacking his accusers equally virulently, thus creating great pathos and bitterness all around: yet another fold in that seamless garment which is Lewis's life and art. Comic performances in films by younger French directors added little to Lewis's reputation, but a recurring role in the TV series *Wiseguy* in 1989 and a triumphant Broadway appearance as the devil in *Damn Yankees* in 1995, which reprised all his "Jerry Lewis" shtick, have been well received. Perhaps only Lewis's death will allow any definitive American evaluation of his substantial career.

—Charles Derry

LEWIS, Joseph H.

Nationality: American. **Born:** New York, 6 April 1907 (other sources say 1900). **Education:** De Witt Clinton High School. **Military Service:** Served in U.S. Army Signal Corps, 1943-44. **Career:** Camera boy at MGM, 1926; editor and director of title sequences at Mascot studio (became Republic, 1935), 1930s; director, from 1937; director in charge of second units at Universal and Republic, 1940s; TV director, from late 1950s; subject of retrospective, Edinburgh Film Festival, 1980.

Films as Director:

1937 *Navy Spy* (co-d); *Courage of the West*; *Singing Outlaw*
1938 *The Spy Ring* (*International Spy*); *Border Wolves*; *Last Stand*
1939 *Two Fisted Rangers* (*Forestalled*)
1940 *Blazing Six Shooters* (*Stolen Wealth*); *The Man from Tumbleweeds*; *Texas Stagecoach* (*Two Roads*); *The Return of Wild Bill* (*False Evidence*); *Boys of the City*; *That Gang of Mine*; *Pride of the Bowery* (*Here We Go Again*)
1941 *Invisible Ghost*; *Criminals Within*; *Arizona Cyclone*; *The Mad Doctor of Market Street*
1942 *Bombs Over Burma* (+ co-sc); *The Silver Bullet*; *Boss of Hangtown Mesa*
1943 *Secret of a Co-ed* (*Silent Witness*)
1944 *Minstrel Man*
1945 *The Falcon in San Francisco*; *My Name is Julia Ross*
1946 *So Dark the Night*
1947 *The Swordsman*
1948 *The Return of October* (*Date with Destiny*)
1949 *Undercover Man*; *Gun Crazy* (*Deadly as the Female*)
1950 *A Lady Without Passport*
1952 *Retreat, Hell!*; *Desperate Search*
1953 *Cry of the Hunted*
1954 *The Big Combo*
1955 *Man on a Bus*; *A Lawless Street*
1956 *7th Cavalry*
1957 *The Halliday Brand*
1958 *Terror in a Texas Town*

Other Films:

1934 *In Old Santa Fe* (Howard) (sup ed)
1935 *Behind the Green Lights* (Cabanne) (ed); *The Miracle Rider* (Eason and Shaefer) (ed); *One Frightened Night* (Cabanne) (ed); *The Headline Woman* (*The Woman in the Case*) (Nigh) (ed); *Ladies Crave Excitement* (Grindé) (ed); *The Adventures of Rex and Rinty* (Eason and Beebe); *Harmony Lane* (Santley) (sup ed); *Streamline Express* (Fields) (ed); *Waterfront Lady* (Santley) (sup ed); *Confidential* (Cahn) (sup ed); *$1000 a Minute* (Scotto) (sup ed)
1936 *Hitch Hike Lady* (*Eventful Journey*) (Scotto) (sup ed); *The Leavenworth Case* (Collins) (sup ed); *Darkest Africa* (*Hidden City*) (Eason and Kane) (sup ed); *The House of a Thousand Candles* (Lubin) (sup ed); *Laughing Irish Eyes* (Santley) (sup ed); *The Harvester* (Santley) (sup ed); *Undersea Kingdom* (Eason and Kane) (sup ed); *The Devil on Horseback* (Wilbur) (ed)
1946 *The Jolson Story* (Green) (d production numbers)
1953 *The Naked Jungle* (Haskin) (begun by Lewis)

Publications

By LEWIS: articles—

Interview with L. Ruhmann, and others, in *Velvet Light Trap* (Madison, Wisconsin), Summer 1983.

On LEWIS: books—

Sarris, Andrew, *The American Cinema,* New York, 1968.
Flynn, C., and T. McCarthy, *Kings of the Bs,* New York, 1975.
Shadoian, Jack, *Dreams and Dead Ends,* Cambridge, Massachusetts, 1977.
Silver, Alain, and Elizabeth Ward, *Film Noir,* New York, 1979.
Wicking, C., *The American Vein,* New York, 1979.

On LEWIS: articles—

Anderson, Lindsay, "*Gun Crazy,*"in *Sequence* (London), Autumn 1950.
Flinn, T., "*The Big Heat* and *The Big Combo,*" in *Velvet Light Trap* (Madison, Wisconsin), no. 11, 1974.
Bogdanovich, Peter, Paul Schrader, and others, in *Cinema* (Los Angeles), Fall 1971.
Lewis Section of *Positif* (Paris), July/August 1975.
Lewis Sections of *Monthly Film Bulletin* (London), March and April 1980.
Pulleine, Tim, "Joseph Lewis," in *Films and Filming* (London), October 1983.
Sattin, R., "Joseph H. Lewis: Assessing an (Occasionally) Brilliant Career," in *American Classic Screen,* November/December 1983.
Kerr, Paul, "My name is Joseph H. Lewis," in *Screen* (London), July/October 1983, also January/February 1984.
Hunter, Allan, "Joseph H. Lewis at the NFT," in *Films and Filming* (London), September 1985.
Tesson, Charles, "Joseph Lewis ou la loi du genre," and "*Get Me a Gun,*" in *Cahiers du Cinéma* (Paris), November 1985 and January 1986.
"Joseph H. Lewis," in *Film Dope* (London), September 1986.
Cocks, Jay, and Martin Scorcese, "Maverick Movie Makers Inspire Their Successors," in *New York Times,* May 12, 1991.
Stein, E., "The King of the B's," *Village Voice* (New York), May 28, 1991.

* * *

Joseph H. Lewis simultaneously supports and confounds the critical methodology of authorship. His forty-one features in twenty-one years provide enough examples of strong visual creativity, originality, and intelligence under the severe budgetary constraints of B film production to warrant bestowing the title "auteur." Yet, banal scripts, meager production values, and unaccomplished actors seem to deny him the opportunity to articulate a "consistent world view," reducing Lewis to a "metteur en scene." This dichotomy between a recognizable (if inconsistent) personal style and a lack of personally revealing (or expressive) thematic content forms the core of the Lewis debate.

Lewis labored for many studios, adapting to many genres, but began his best work while at Columbia after World War II. In 1945 and 1946, he directed *My Name is Julia Ross* and *So Dark the Night, films noir* that precipitated his first important critical recognition. Until 1955, with a few exceptions, he continued surveying *film noir,* directing *Undercover Man, A Lady Without Passport,* and the *noir*-influenced *Desperate Search* and *Cry of the Hunted,* culminating his fluency in the genre with two "undisputed masterpieces," *Gun Crazy* and *The Big Combo.* The critical favor awarded these films, and their eventual cult status, pushes Lewis into an intimate association with *film noir,* even though he directed many more Westerns.

His *films noir,* like his other films, were co-features or B movies slotted for the second half of a double bill. They were typically based on weak scripts with witless dialogue, ran under 90 minutes (many under 75), and received little distribution marketing. They were shot in less than two or three weeks, with miniscule budgets, on inexpensive black and white film stock, without stars or accomplished actors, using a few minimal sets or locations, and without rehearsed crowd scenes. These limitations functioned as a catalyst for his ingenuity. Improvising practical solutions to production limitations, Lewis devised a complex and unique visual style—a combination of Bresson and Ophuls—upon which his reputation and signature rest. His films emphasize images, employing low key lighting, high contrast, location shooting, long takes, camera movement, great depth of focus with dominating foreground objects, choreographed violence and sexuality, montage, off-screen action, sound manipulation, and a reduction of dialogue to a minimum. Each aspect ultimately accommodates a dual purpose, economic and aesthetic.

The use of low-key lighting served three practical economic purposes associated with B movie making: it cost less than high key lighting; it allowed the construction of only partial sets; and it concealed meager production values. It also served a vital aesthetic purpose by providing a striking visual style differentiating film noir from other genres. High contrast images resulted from the use of cheap black and white film stocks, yet underscored the visual play of blinding light cutting through opaque darkness. Location shooting reduced the dependence on sets and sound stage work while evoking a gritty urban realism. The combination of exceptionally long takes, great depth of focus with dominating foreground objects, and camera movement reduced shooting schedules and post-production expenses. They also added a documentary "time" and "atmosphere" to the realism of the films. The depiction of violence and sexuality through montage, off-screen space, and sound manipulation intensified their effect on the spectator while requiring neither complete performance nor extensive set construction and circumventing the Production Code. The reduction of dialogue hid the limited acting skills of his performers and returned the emphasis of his films to the visual. Examples of the combined utilization of these techniques include: the celebrated 4-minute Hampton robbery one-take and the robbery sequence in *Gun Crazy*; the torture by hearing-aid, the "kissing" shot, and the climax in *The Big Combo*; the report of the girl's death in *So Dark the Night*; and Rocco's assassination in *Undercover Man.* In other words, due to economic factors, Lewis's *films noir* represent the genre reduced to its visual essence.

Lewis's visual style stands without question. Whether or not this textual surface supports a consistent thematic content initiates a heated debate. Is he, as Richard Combs claims, "a stylistic authority operating in a vacuum," or as Richard Sattin explains, someone with visual intelligence and style who doesn't recognize the need for theme? Or is he, as Andrew Sarris states in Lewis's description under "Expressive Esoterica," a "somber personality revealed through a complex visual style?" Traditional analyses see his films betraying efforts to construct thematic coherence because their pleasure exists only as complex textual surfaces. More recent approaches can note the pleasure of his films' complex textual surfaces precisely activating the thematic concerns of *film noir* as well as inaugurating a disturbing and fascinating exploration of Existentialism.

The primacy of textual surface derived from the economic limitations of B movie making denies Lewis the luxury of psychologizing characters, character motivation, and events. Consequently, behavior finds its truest and clearest (and only) expression in action. Action is readily observable and objectively presentable as "pure" textuality. The accent on action as textual surface offers no judgement on or explanation of existence, only description. The world described is Existential, devoid of logic, justice, and order.

Lewis approached these Existential themes by eliding individual identity with social action. These themes find their sharpest focus in Lewis's masterpieces, *Gun Crazy* and *The Big Combo,* but appear in all his *films noir* and his late Westerns (*A Lawless Street, The Halliday Brand,* and *Terror in a Texas Town*).

Lewis's film career ended in 1958, coinciding with the death of "classical" *film noir.* His intensification and fusing of textuality and Existentialism within the genre pushed *film noir* to its logical extreme. His work, however, influenced a budding French movement, the *Nouvelle Vague* (a comparison between *Gun Crazy* and its focus on *l'amour fou* and Godard's *A bout de souffle* and *Pierrot le fou* would prove an interesting study), and may even stand as the base for today's technologically driven and production design oriented action-adventure films.

—Greg S. Faller

L'HERBIER, Marcel

Nationality: French. **Born:** Paris, 23 April 1888. **Education:** Lycée Voltaire, Sainte-Marie de Monceau; University of Paris. **Military Service:** Served with Service Auxiliaire, 1914-17, and with Section Cinématographique de l'Armée, 1917-18. **Career:** Scriptwriter, from 1917; directed first film, *Rose-France,* 1918; organized Cinégraphic production company, 1922; secretary general of Association des Auteurs de Films, 1929; co-founder, Cinémathèque Française, 1936; co-founder (1937) then president, Syndicat des Techniciens, from 1938; founder and president of Institut des Hautes Etudes Cinématographiques (IDHEC), French film school, 1943; president of Comité de Défense du Cinéma Français, 1947; producer for television, 1952-62. **Awards:** Commandeur de Légion d'Honneur et des Arts et Lettres. **Died:** 26 November 1979.

Films as Director:

1918 *Phantasmes* (+ sc) (incomplete); *Rose-France* (+ sc)
1919 *Le Bercail* (+ sc); *Le Carnaval des vérités* (+ sc)
1920 *L'Homme du large* (+ sc); *Villa Destin* (+ sc)
1921 *El Dorado* (+ sc); *Prométhée ... banquier*
1922 *Don Juan et Faust* (+ sc)
1923 *Résurrection* (+ sc) (incomplete)
1924 *L'Inhumaine* (*The New Enchantment*) (+ co-sc)
1925 ***Feu Mathias Pascal*** (*The Late Mathias Pascal*) (+ sc)
1926 *Le Vertige* (+ sc)
1927 *Le Diable au coeur* (*L'Ex-Voto*) (+ sc)
1928 *Nuits de Prince* (+ sc)
1929 ***L'Argent*** (+ sc); *L'Enfant de l'amour* (+ sc)
1930 *La Femme d'une nuit* (*La donna d'una notte*) (+ sc); *La Mystère de la chambre jaune* (+ sc)
1931 *Le Parfum de la dame en noir* (+ sc)
1933 *L'Epervier* (*Les Amoureux; Bird of Prey*) (+ sc)
1934 *Le Scandale*; *L'Aventurier* (+ sc); *Le Bonheur* (+ sc)
1935 *La Route impériale* (+ sc); *Veille d'armes* (*Sacrifice d'honneur*) (+ co-sc)
1936 *Les Hommes nouveux* (+ sc); *La Porte du large* (*The Great Temptation*) (+ sc); *Nuits de feu* (*The Living Corpse*) (+ co-sc)
1937 *La Citadelle du silence* (*The Citadel of Silence*) (+ sc); *Forfaiture* (+ sc)
1938 *La Tragédie impériale* (*Rasputin*) (+ sc); *Adrienne Lecouvreur*; *Terre de feu*; *La Brigade sauvage* (*Savage Brigade*) (completed by J. Dreville)
1939 *Entente cordiale*; *Children's Corner* (short); *La Mode rêvée* (short) (+ sc)
1940 *La Comédie du bonheur* (+ sc)
1941 *Histoire de rire* (*Foolish Husbands*)
1942 *La Nuit fantastique*; *L'Honorable Catherine*
1943 *La Vie de Bohême*
1945 *Au petit bonheur*
1946 *L'Affaire du collier de la Reine* (*The Queen's Necklace*)
1947 *La Révoltée* (*Stolen Affections*) (+ sc)
1948 *Les Derniers Jours de Pompéi* (*The Last Days of Pompeii*) (+ co-sc)
1953 *Le Pére de mademoiselle* (co-d)
1963 *Hommage à Debussy* (short)
1967 *Le Cinéma du diable* (anthology film)

Other Films:

1917 *Le Torrent* (Hervil) (sc); *Bouclette* (*L'Ange de minuit*) (Mercanton and Hervil) (sc)
1932 *Le Martyre de l'Obèse* (Chenal) (supervisor)
1933 *La Bataille* (Farkas) (supervisor)
1938 *Terra di fuoco* (Ferroni) (Italian version of *Terre de feu*) (supervisor)
1943 *Le Loup des Malveneur* (Radot) (supervisor)
1947 *Une Grande Fille tout simple* (Manuel) (supervisor)

Publications

By L'HERBIER: books—

Au jardin des jeux secrets, Paris, 1914.
L'Enfantement du mort, Paris, 1917.
Intelligence du cinématographe (anthology), Paris, 1947 (revised 1977).
La Tête qui tourne, Paris, 1979.

By L'HERBIER: articles—

Interview, in *Cahiers du Cinéma* (Paris), no. 202, 1968.
Interview with J. Fieschi and others, in *Cinématographe* (Paris), no. 40, 1978.
"Un Cinéaste ...," in *Avant-Scène du Cinéma* (Paris), 1 January 1980.
Interview, in *Cinémagazine,* reprinted in *Avant-Scène du Cinéma* (Paris), 15 October 1981.

On L'HERBIER: books—

Jaque-Catelain présente Marcel L'Herbier, Paris, 1950.
Burch, Noël, *Marcel L'Herbier,* Paris, 1973.
Hommage à Marcel L'Herbier en cinq films de l'art muet, brochure for retrospective, Paris, 1975.
Brossard, Jean-Pierre, editor, *Marcel L'Herbier et son temps,* La Chaux-de-Fonds, Switzerland, 1980.
Canosa, Michele, *Marcel L'Herbier,* Parma, 1985.

On L'HERBIER: articles—

"The Big Screens," in *Sight and Sound* (London), Spring 1955.
Roud, Richard, "Memories of Resnais," in *Sight and Sound* (London), Summer 1969.
Blumer, R.H., "The Camera as Snowball: France 1918-1927," in *Cinema Journal* (Evanston), Spring 1970.
Article on five films of L'Herbier, in *Ecran* (Paris), no. 43, 1976.
"L'Herbier Issue" of *Avant-Scène du Cinéma* (Paris), 1 June 1978.
Trosa, S., "Archeologie du cinéma," in *Cinématographe* (Paris), December 1978.
Obituary, in *New York Times,* 28 November 1979.
Fieschi, J., "Marcel L'Herbier," in *Cinématographe* (Paris), December 1979.

Obituary, in *Image et Son* (Paris), January 1980.
"Marcel L'Herbier," in *Film Dope* (London), September 1986.

* * *

Marcel L'Herbier was one of the most prominent members of the French 1920s avant-garde. His direct involvement with filmmaking extended into the 1950s and he made important contributions to the organization of the industry, to the foundation of the film school, the IDHEC, and to early television drama.

Like so many of his generation L'Herbier turned to cinema after an early enthusiasm for literature and the theatre, and in his case it was Cecil B. DeMille's *The Cheat* with Sessue Hayakawa which opened his eyes to the unrealized potential of the new medium. He came to prominence in the years 1919-22 with a series of films made for Léon Gaumont's "Pax" series. Among the half-dozen films made for Gaumont, two at least stand out as artistic and commercial successes: *L'Homme du large,* a melodrama shot partly on location on the Brittany coast, where the director's interest in visual effects and symbolism is very apparent; and *El Dorado,* a Spanish drama in which L'Herbier's use of cinema to convey the mental and psychological states of characters finds perfect expression. *El Dorado* achieved a success to match that of Gance's *La Roue* the following year.

Difficulties with Gaumont over the production of the ambitious *Don Juan et Faust* led L'Herbier to set up his own company, Cinégraphic, in 1922. He was able to assist the debuts of young filmmakers such as Jaque Catelain and Claude Autant-Lara as well as produce the last film of Louis Delluc, *L'Inondation.* His own films were made largely in co-production and ranged widely in style and approach. The celebrated but controversial *L'Inhumaine,* partly financed by its star the singer Georgette Leblanc, aimed to offer a mosaic of the decorative modern art of 1925, with sets produced by four very individual designers, including Fernand Léger and Robert Mallet-Stevens. In total contrast, *Feu Matthias Pascal* was essentially an experiment with complex narrative structures, co-produced with the Albatros company which had been set up by Russian exiles and starring the great silent actor, Ivan Mosjoukine. L'Herbier's eclectic approach and love of juxtapositions are very apparent in these films, together with his immense visual refinement. After a couple of commercial works he made his silent masterpiece, an updating of Zola's *L'Argent,* in 1929. Inspired by the scope of Gance's *Napoléon,* L'Herbier created a strikingly modern work marked by its opulent, oversized sets and a complex, multi-camera shooting style.

L'Herbier was in no way hostile to the coming of sound, but despite a pair of interesting adaptations of comic thrillers by Gaston Leroux, *Le Mystére de la chambre jaune* and *Le Parfum de la dame en noir,* L'Herbier was largely reduced to the role of efficient but uninspired adaptor of stage plays in the 1930s. During the occupation years L'Herbier again came to prominence with his delicately handled, dreamlike *La Nuit fantastique,* but his subsequent work, which included a spectacular version of *Les Derniers Jours de Pompei* in 1948, attracted little critical favor. In more recent years, however, L'Herbier's reputation has benefitted from the revival of interest in the experimental aspects of French 1920s cinema. Though to some extent overshadowed by the towering figure of Abel Gance, L'Herbier emerges as a figure of considerable interest. In particular the work of the critic and theorist Noël Burch has emphasized the modernity of the approach to shooting and to narrative construction displayed in his ambitious *L'Argent.* There seems little doubt that French 1920s cinema offers a rich and largely unexplored area for future film studies and that L'Herbier's reputation can only benefit from fresh investigation of his varied 1920s oeuvre.

—Roy Armes

Marcel L'Herbier: *L'Inhumaine*

LINKLATER, Richard

Nationality: American. **Born:** Austin, Texas, 1965. **Career:** Founded Austin Film Society, 1987; directed first feature, *It's Impossible to Learn to Plow by Reading Books,* 1988. **Awards:** Silver Bear Award for Best Director, Berlin Film Festival, 1995.

Films as Director:

1988 *It's Impossible to Learn to Plow by Reading Books*
1991 *Slacker* (+ pr, sc, role)
1993 *Dazed and Confused* (+ pr, sc)
1995 *Before Sunrise* (+ sc)

Other Films:

1995 *The Underneath* (role as Ember Doorman)

Publications

By LINKLATER: books—

Slacker, St. Martin's Press, 1992.
Dazed and Confused, St. Martin's Press, 1993.

By LINKLATER: articles—

"Slacker," an interview with C. Gore, in *Film Threat,* no. 22, 1990.
"The Six Million Dollar Slacker," an interview with C. Gore, in *Film Threat,* 29 April 1993.
"Richard Linklater's Hot List," interview in *Rolling Stone,* 13 May 1993.
"Richard Linklater: The Austin Auteur Refuses to Play by Hollywood's Rules—and Wins," an interview with Robert Draper, in *Texas Monthly,* September 1995.

On LINKLATER: articles—

Horton, R., "Stranger Than Texas," in *Film Comment,* July-August 1990.
Shulevitz, J., "City Slacker," in *Village Voice,* 9 July 1991.
"A $23,000 Film Is Turning into a Hit," in *New York Times,* 7 August 1991.
Dargis, M., "In the Loop," in *Village Voice,* 29 December 1992.
Kelleher, E., "*Dazed and Confused* Recalls '70s Teen Days," in *Film Journal,* August 1993.
Brown, David, and Jessica Shaw, "Look Back in Languor," in *Entertainment Weekly,* 8 October 1993.

* * *

Once, in Hollywood, directors were *anonymous* (despite the fact that their names appeared on many films): I was not aware of Howard Hawks or Leo McCarey until very late in their careers, despite the fact that I had seen a number of their films. Then, in the brief heyday of the Auteur theory, directors became briefly *important:* some filmgoers, at least, became aware of their names. In contemporary Hollywood, directors are largely *superfluous.* Aside from one or two tenacious *auteurs* like Scorsese, what does it matter anymore who directed what? Hollywood films today are, for the most part, produced by cine-illiterate corporations and directed (apparently) by anyone who happens to wander onto the set. They are made by technicians, the directors of "stunts," and the special-effects department.

It is in this context that the careers of several courageous young independent filmmakers, with the nerve to reveal certain seemingly obsolete or unwelcome qualities like integrity, conscience, and personal vision, have to be considered: I have in mind especially Todd Haynes, Gregg Araki, and Richard Linklater. All three are clearly *auteurs* in that their films are thematically and stylistically consistent and recognizable; but the same could be said of Ken Russell or David Lynch, so that one should add that their work is also distinguished by real intelligence. It is certainly arguable that *Safe* (Haynes), *The Doom Generation* (Araki), and *Before Sunrise* (Linklater) are, Scorsese aside, the three best American films of the 1990s. Each now has a following, and so long as their living arrangements don't require a house in Beverly Hills and more than one swimming pool, there seems no reason why they should not continue to make the finest American films currently being produced.

One may begin at (so far) the end, with *Before Sunrise,* an oasis in the desert of contemporary Hollywood where one may again breathe fresh air and drink unpolluted water. A film built upon the long take, by a director who trusts and works with his actors for character and nuance, instead of relying on TV-style editing; a film that expresses, at every point, a refinement, a grace, a sensibility one believed long ago destroyed by the advance of corporate capitalism; incidentally, a film that begins with Purcell (*Dido and Aeneas*) and (almost) ends with Bach (the Goldberg Variations): one could not predict such a film, not only from the Hollywood context, but from Linklater's previous work, intelligent and distinctive as that is. One also wonders whether anything like it can be done again, given the feebleness of public response and the half-hearted polite interest of most reviewers. At least it was honored at the Berlin Film Festival, but I have not found it on a single critic's list of the best films of 1995 (except my own private one, where it has first place).

With its Vienna setting, including a visit to the Prater, and its overriding concern with the redefinition of romantic love, it seems inevitable to compare it with an earlier masterpiece, a film of equal delicacy, subtlety, and emotional fineness, Ophuls's *Letter from an Unknown Woman*—the differences being, of course, more important than the parallels. In *Letter,* "romantic love" entailed lifetime commitment (even when unreciprocated), an existence sustained solely by illusion, and ultimate tragedy; but the basis for that was the subordinate position of women, their complementary options of wife or prostitute, both selling their services. "Romantic love," as fantasy, represented the heroine's only means of transcending the ignominy of her situation. *Before Sunrise* redefines romantic love in a world where the lovers meet on a level of full equality, where permanence of any kind and on either side is uncertain and no longer necessarily desirable. Everyone with whom I have discussed the film asks what is implied by the ending: Will they or won't they keep their date in Vienna six months later? I think the more interesting question the film raises implicitly is, Would it be better if they did or if they didn't? Is it better to imprison yourself in the still-dominant conventions of "the couple" (marriage, family, permanence), or to keep fresh the memory of one perfect, magical night, and go on from there? The film's refusal to answer *either* question perhaps accounts for its commercial failure: audiences still seem to resent being left in a state of uncertainty, even though most of their members live in one.

Despite its extreme difference, *Before Sunrise* has certain aspects in common with its two predecessors, *Slacker* and *Dazed and Confused.* All three take place in less than twenty-four hours; each presents a world in which nothing is certain anymore and where no future is guaranteed; although each is situated within a single town or city, all three are about wandering; in all three, the characters are essentially or literally homeless, if only for the time period of the film. In *Slacker,* the only home besides cheap, impermanent apartments is

Richard Linklater directing Ethan Hawke and Julie Delpy in *Before Sunrise*

that of the first character (aside from Linklater himself, the stranger whose arrival in town initiates the chain of interlocking, overlapping episodes), who is arrested and removed from it for deliberately running down and killing his own mother. In *Dazed and Confused,* home is something to be escaped from, and in *Before Sunrise* two people, strangers without money in a foreign city, spend the night wandering the streets. Their attraction to each other clearly has little to do with any possible domestic future.

All three films are distinguished by Linklater's complex relationship to the characters and the action, delicately poised between sympathy and critical distance. His characters are neither indulged nor held up to ridicule, they are presented generously but quite unsentimentally. The various "slackers" of the first film are frequently bizarre and slightly absurd, but this is understood in terms of their alienation from a culture that offers them no hope and breeds paranoia. *Dazed and Confused* (the least unconventional of the three, and the one commercial success) is at once modeled on and an antidote to *American Graffiti,* without a vestige of that film's condescending, audience-flattering "cuteness." It also never descends into nostalgia for "the best days of your life." It depicts quite uncompromisingly the brutality and stupidity of initiation rituals, the variously corrupted and brutalized seniors using the (relatively) innocent young as the victims of their own frustrations, their acquired sadism, the physical cruelty of the males echoed in the females' desire to humiliate their juniors. Indeed, "initiation," in a very real sense, is enacted in one of the plot-threads, wherein a freshman learns, as a way to "belonging," the destructive behavior of his elders. One character, despite severe pressures from both his coach and his peers, manages to preserve his integrity—by refusing to sign a paper promising to forswear drugs and alcohol. In the context Linklater creates, it is a heroic gesture.

Finally, one must acknowledge Linklater's brilliant work with actors, whether the huge cast of non-professionals in *Slacker,* the multiple narratives of *Dazed and Confused,* or the marvelously subtle, flexible and nuanced performances of Ethan Hawke and Julie Delpy in *Before Sunrise.*

—Robin Wood

LITTIN, Miguel

Nationality: Chilean. **Born:** Palmilla (Colchagua), Chile, 9 August 1942. **Education:** Theatre School of the University of Chile, Santiago. **Family:** Married Eli Menz. **Career:** TV director and producer, 1963; stage director and actor, and assistant on several films, 1964-67; founding member, Committee of the Popular Unity Filmmakers, 1969; named director of national production company Chile Films by Salvador Allende, 1970; made weekly newsreels for Chile Films, 1970-71; emigrated to Mexico following coup d'etat, 1973; member of Executive Committee of Latin American Filmmakers, 1974. **Awards:** Chilean Critics Prize, for *El Chacal de Nahueltoro,* 1970.

Films as Director and Scriptwriter:

1968 *Por la tierra ajena* (*On Foreign Land*)
1969 ***El chacal de Nahueltoro*** (*The Jackal of Nahueltoro*)
1971 *Compañero Presidente*
1973 *La tierra prometida* (*The Promised Land*)
1975 *El recurso del método* (*Viva el Presidente*; *Reasons of State*) (co-sc)
1980 *La viuda de Montiel* (*Montiel's Widow*)
1982 ***Alsino y el cóndor*** (*Alsino and the Condor*)
1985 *Actas de Marusia* (*Letters from Marusia*)
1986 *Acta General de Chile* (*General Statement on Chile*)
1990 *Sandino* (+ sc)
1994 *Los Naufragos*

Other Films:

1965 *Yo tenía un camarada* (*I Had a Comrade*) (Soto) (role)
1966 *Mundo mágico* (*Magic World*) (Soto) (role); *ABC do amor* (*The ABC of Love*) (role)

Publications

By LITTIN: books—

Cine chileno: La tierra prometida, Caracas, 1974.
El Chacal de Nahueltoro: La tierra prometida, Mexico City, 1977.

By LITTIN: articles—

"Film in Chile," an interview in *Cineaste* (New York), Spring 1971.
Interview with M. Torres, in *Cine Cubano* (Havana), no. 76/77, 1972.
"Culture populaire et lutte impérialiste," an interview with J.-R. Huleu and others, in *Cahiers du Cinéma* (Paris), July/August 1974.
Interview with Marcel Martin, in *Ecran* (Paris), November 1977.
"Cine Chileno en exilio," an interview with Gastón Ancelovici, in *Contracampo* (Madrid), December 1979.
Interview with Emilia Palma, in *Cine Cubano* (Havana), no. 100, 1981.
"Lo desmesurado, el espacio real del sueño americano," in *Cine Cubano* (Havana), no. 105, 1983.
"Coming Home," in *American Film* (Washington, D.C.), January/February 1986.

On LITTIN: books—

Bolzoni, Francesco, *El cine de Allende,* Valencia, 1974.
Chanan, Michael, editor, *Chilean Cinema,* London, 1976.
García Marquéz, Gabriel, *Clandestine in Chile: The Adventures of Miguel Littin,* New York, 1987.

On LITTIN: articles—

Wilson, David, "Aspects of Latin American Political Cinema," in *Sight and Sound* (London), Summer 1972.
Burton, Julianne, "*The Promised Land,*" in *Film Quarterly* (Berkeley), Fall 1975.
Scott, R., "The Arrival of the Instrument in Flesh and Blood: Deconstruction in Littin's *Promised Land,*" in *Ciné-Tracts* (Montreal), Spring/Summer 1978.
Kovacs, K.S., "Miguel Littin's *Recurso del método*: the aftermath of Allende," in *Film Quarterly* (Berkeley), Spring 1980.
Le Pennec, Françoise, "Cinéma du Chili: en exil ou sur place," in *Cinéma* (Paris), February 1983.
Mouesca, J., "El cine chileno en el exilio (1973-1983)," in *Cine Cubano* (Havana), no. 109, 1984.
"Miguel Littin," in *Film Dope* (London), September 1986.

* * *

"Each of my movies corresponds to a moment in Chilean political life." From this manifesto-like stance in his earlier career, Miguel Littin's cinematic concerns have widened geographically but maintained their political orientation. Certainly it is an attitude that has earned him detractors. But it is fair to say that his best work has been provoked by *contradictions* offered to socialist ideals through the lessons of history. Squaring this circle, or for Littin, seeing how imperialism, dictatorship, and subjugation are self-perpetuating, allows us to trace the fine line in his work between political sentimentality and genuine cinematic ingenuity.

El chacal de Nahueltoro courageously addresses the notion of ideology in the true story of an illiterate peasant who murders his common-law wife and her five children. Taking this popular personification of Evil, Littin shows the irony of a peasant who only achieves self-enlightenment at the point of judicial persecution, only becomes literate to sign his death warrant, and only becomes a good Catholic in time to die one. But the film seeks to avoid the perpetuation of bourgeois forms itself: flashbacks culminate at a point midway through the film when the crime is actually committed; the real dialogue of the peasant is used; and handheld camera shots and journalistic techniques simultaneously invoke sensations of authenticity and manipulation.

The film pitched Littin into the leading ranks of Latin American directors, an achievement he followed with *La tierra prometida.* Again closely historically detailed, it tells the story of a popular revolt that is finally massacred by the army. But it moved to a larger cinematic scope, starring the peasants of the Santa Cruz region, and invoked the ambiguity of folk symbolism in an allegory of the weaknesses in Allende's Popular Unity. Two months after it was made a similar military coup put an end to Allende's government.

After the coup, Littin went to Mexico and looked back on Chile's recent, violent history in *Actas de Marusia.* This film documents the roots of right-wing domination in an English Mining Company's exploitation of a small Chilean town at the start of the century, ending in torture, hostage-taking, and mass-murder. For some, however, the film was too one-sided, one critic calling it "nothing so much as a Stalinist hymn to the glories of suicidal sacrifice." Nonetheless its ochre-toned intensity gained it an Academy Award nomination as Best Foreign Film.

From here his career took a different turn. The emerging fashion for Latin American "magic realism" in European and American literary tastes saw Littin making a parallel *rapprochement* with "western" intellectual culture—the previous agent of cultural contamination. *El recurso del método,* based on a Carpentier novel, was archly thoughtful, quoting from Descartes in its portrayal of an exiled Latin American dictator. But again it detailed Littin's concern with the forms of ideology that condone dictatorship—here in the delusion of subjectivity: "The dictator can seem nice and understandable in his behaviour, but at the same time he reveals the extent to which he himself has been destroyed by the ideology of imperialism. ... Therefore I didn't want to stress the individual." Mirrors, paintings, and lamps refract the lighting, rendering illumination and identification uncertain: "It is a play of reflections between truths, lies, ambiguities, and from the joining of all these elements, the spectator will be able to draw a conclusion, to become aware of what a dictatorship is." *El recurso del método* struck the plangent note of the exiled Littin's own political pessimism, a note that was echoed in *La viuda de Montiel,* which showed the widow of a local tyrant gradually becoming aware of her previous self-delusions. In spite of Garciá Márquez providing the story, the film failed to take off.

But *Alsino y el cóndor,* taking as its subject a boy's dream of flying, did take off, showing Littin's return to contemporary Latin American realities in the context of Somoza's Nicaragua of 1979. Some saw the film's clear political sympathies as hampering it at the Academy Awards where it was nominated for Best Foreign Film. But the film cinematically transcended its political objectives in a powerful, emotive vision of a country torn by civil war, seen through the eyes of a crippled child.

That innocent eye is one Littin tried to capture when he surreptitiously returned to Chile after twelve years in exile to secretly film life under Pinochet. He was disguised as an Uruguayan businessman and covertly directed four film crews. The resulting four-part documentary, *Acta General de Chile,* is a testament to Littin's flexibility and bravado.

Littin's place in Latin American film history is ensured, for reasons that go beyond the aesthetic. Paradoxically, what has earned him posterity has often cost him aesthetically. Responsiveness to a changing political climate renders him an unpredictable director, but nonetheless bodes well for the future.

—Saul Frampton

LITVAK, Anatole

Nationality: Russian/American. **Born:** Mikhail Anatol Litvak in Kiev, 21 May 1902; became U.S. citizen, 1940. **Education:** University of Leningrad, Ph.D. in philosophy, 1921; attended State School of Theatre, 1922. **Military Service:** Joined Special Services Film Unit, U.S. Army, 1942, working with Frank Capra. **Family:** Married 1) Miriam Hopkins, 1937 (divorced 1939); 2) Sophie Steur, 1949. **Career:** Theatre director and assistant director, then art director, Nordkino film studios, Leningrad, from 1923; moved to Paris, then editor for G.W. Pabst at Ufa studios, Berlin, 1925; assistant to emigré director Alexander Volkoff, 1926-30; directed first film, 1930; moved to Paris, 1933; contract director at Warners in Hollywood, 1937-41; returned to Paris following military service, 1949. **Awards:** Croix de guerre; Légion d'honneur; International Prize, Venice Festival, for *The Snake Pit,* 1949. **Died:** In Paris, 15 December 1974.

Films as Director:

1923 *Tatiana* (short)
1924 *Hearts and Dollars* (short)
1930 *Dolly macht Karriere*
1931 *Nie wieder Liebe* (+ co-adapt); French version *Calais-Douvres*
1932 *Coeur de Lilas* (+ sc); *Das Lied einer Nacht*; English version *Be Mine Tonight*
1933 *Cette vielle canaille* (+ co-adapt); *Sleeping Car*
1935 *L'Equipage* (+ co-sc)
1936 *Mayerling*
1937 *The Woman I Love*; *Tovarich*
1938 *The Amazing Dr. Clitterhouse*; *The Sisters*
1939 *Confessions of a Nazi Spy*
1940 *Castle on the Hudson*; *City for Conquest*; *All This and Heaven Too*
1941 *Out of the Fog*; *Blues in the Night*
1942 *This Above All*; ***Why We Fight*** series—No. 2: ***The Nazis Strike*** (co-d)
1943 ***Why We Fight*** series—No. 3: ***Divide and Conquer*** (co-d)
1944 ***Why We Fight*** series—No. 7: ***The Battle of Russia*** (+ co-sc); No. 8: ***The Battle of China*** (co-d)
1945 ***Why We Fight*** series—No. 9: ***War Comes to America*** (+ co-sc)
1947 *The Long Night*
1948 *Sorry, Wrong Number* (+ co-pr); *The Snake Pit* (+ co-pr)
1951 *Decision before Dawn* (+ co-pr)
1954 *Act of Love* (+ co-sc)
1955 *The Deep Blue Sea* (+ co-pr)
1956 *Anastasia*
1957 *Mayerling* (remake for TV)
1959 *The Journey* (retitled after release as *Some of Us May Die*) (+ pr)
1961 *Aimez-vous Brahms?* (*Goodbye Again*) (+ pr, appearance in nightclub scene)
1962 *Le Cocteau dans la plaie* (*Five Miles to Midnight*)

Anatole Litvak

1966 *10:30 P.M. Summer* (+ pr)
1967 *The Night of the Generals*
1970 *The Lady in a Car with Glasses and a Gun* (*La Dame dans l'auto avec des lunettes et un fusil*) (+ co-pr)

Other Films:

1925 *Samii yunii pioner* [A Very Young Pioneer] (Derzhavin) (co-sc)
1927 *Casanova* (*The Loves of Casanova*) (asst d to Alexander Volkoff)
1929 *Sheherazade* (*Secrets of the Orient*) (asst d to Volkoff)
1930 *Der weisse Teufel* (*The White Devil*) (asst d to Volkoff, d dialogue and musical sequences)
1932 *La Chanson d'une nuit* (French version of *Das Lied einer Nacht*) (Clouzot and Colombier) (artistic supervisor)
1947 *Meet Me at Dawn* (co-play basis)

Publications

By LITVAK: article—

"A Cutter at Heart," interview with Allen Eyles and Barrie Pattison, in *Films and Filming* (London), February 1967.

On LITVAK: book—

Roddick, Nick, *A New Deal in Entertainment: Warner Brothers in the 1930s,* London, 1983.

On LITVAK: articles—

Article on production of *The Snake Pit,* in *Time* (New York), 20 December 1948.
Nolan, Jack, "Anatole Litvak," in *Films in Review* (New York), November 1967.
Obituary in *Ecran* (Paris), February 1975.
"Anatole Litvak," in *Film Dope* (London), September 1986.

* * *

Anatole Litvak was a minor, commercially successful director whose personal and professional life can be characterized in one word: disingenuous. He was a multi-lingual cosmopolitan who possessed an anti-establishment political consciousness. He understood the technique and potential of the film medium—for example, he used location shooting and realistic documentary effects as early as the 1930s; he emphasized realistic sound effects over dialogue in sound films; and he capably used camera tracking shots and pans. Yet his films were erratic in quality and uneven in content; his intelligence and talents never found a satisfying cinematic expression.

Litvak acted and directed at the State School of Theatre and probably was assistant director and/or set decorator for at least nine silent Russian films at Leningrad's Nordkino studios. He was evasive about his background and life in Russia. Little is known except that he fled to Berlin in 1925, where he was an editor on G.W. Pabst's *Die freudlose Gasse,* worked as general assistant to Russian emigré director Nicholas Alexander Bolkoff, claims to have been one of the many editors on Abel Gance's *Napoléon,* and made his directorial debut with Ufa's *Dolly macht Karriere* in 1929. Two years later he directed *Nie wieder Liebe,* which was filmed simultaneously in a French version entitled *Calais-Douvres,* with Max Ophüls as Litvak's assistant. He went to Paris to direct *Coeur de lilas,* in which he used natural street sounds which he found to be "another support for a film's images, heightening their pictoral values, underscoring their visual beauty."

Paris became his home after he fled Hitler's Germany, and a favorite locale for his films—thirteen of his thirty-seven pictures were set in Paris. It was also the city where he directed *Mayerling,* the internationally popular film which brought him to Hollywood.

Upon arriving in Hollywood he directed *The Woman I Love* for RKO (a remake of *L'Equipage,* which he had directed in Paris with Annabella and Charles Vanel) starring Miriam Hopkins, whom he later married. Litvak then signed a four-year contract with Warner Brothers, and while that studio was deeply entrenched in its politically conscious period—an atmosphere which would have seemed very well suited to his temperament—he was apparently too independent, if not overtly iconoclastic, to fit into the studio mold. For the most part his films there were sophisticated women's fare—*Tovarich, The Sisters,* and *All This and Heaven Too.* One exception was the now-dated, anti-Nazi propaganda film *Confessions of a Nazi Spy.* Here Edward G. Robinson played a FBI agent who breaks up a ring of Nazi spies in the United States, and Litvak used newsreels of actual U.S. Nazi rallies for a docu-drama effect.

During World War II he directed or co-directed for the U.S. Army's Special Services Film Unit and was in charge of motion picture operations during the Normandy invasion. His war efforts brought him the *Légion d'honneur* and the *Croix de guerre.*

Following the war Litvak produced and directed his two best and most popular American films—*Sorry, Wrong Number* and *The Snake Pit,* a starkly realistic depiction of life in an insane asylum. Litvak then left the United States to live and work in Paris for the remainder of his career. There he produced and directed what is probably his best film—*Decision before Dawn,* a compelling drama about German prisoners of war who returned to spy in their native Germany in an effort to defeat Nazism.

Thereafter, Litvak's films were star-studded trifles with the exception of the immensely dramatic and moving *Anastasia,* which was Ingrid Bergman's return to mainstream films. The most notable of Litvak's late films was the sadistic and lurid *The Night of the Generals* starring Peter O'Toole. His last picture was a non-entity entitled *The Lady in the Car with Glasses and a Gun.*

—Ronald Bowers

LOACH, Ken

Nationality: British. **Born:** Kenneth Loach in Nuneaton, Warwickshire, 17 June 1937. **Education:** Read law at Oxford University. **Military Service:** Two years in the Royal Air Force. **Family:** Married Lesley Ashton (Loach), three sons (one deceased), two daughters. **Career:** Actor with repertory company, Birmingham, then joined BBC, 1961; director of *Z Cars* for TV, 1962; directed *Wednesday Play* for TV, 1965; first collaboration with producer Tony Garnett was *Up the Junction,* 1965; with Garnett, set up Kestrel Films production company, 1969; freelanced, though working mainly for Central TV, from 1970s; lives in London. **Awards:** TV Director of the Year Award, British TV Guild, 1965; Special Jury Prize, Cannes Festival, for *Hidden Agenda,* 1990.

Films as Director and Co-Scriptwriter:

1967 *Poor Cow*
1969 *Kes*
1971 *The Save the Children Fund Film* (short); *Family Life*
1979 *Black Jack*
1981 *Looks and Smiles*
1986 *Fatherland* (*Singing the Blues in Red*)
1990 ***Hidden Agenda***
1991 *Riff Raff*
1993 *Raining Stones*
1994 *Ladybird Ladybird*
1995 ***Land and Freedom***

Films for Television:

1964 *Catherine*; *Profit By Their Example*; *The Whole Truth*; *The Diary of a Young Man*
1965 *Tap on the Shoulder*; *Wear a Very Big Hat*; *Three Clear Sundays*; *Up the Junction*; *The End of Arthur's Marriage*; *The Coming Out Party*
1966 *Cathy Come Home*
1967 *In Two Minds*
1968 *The Golden Vision*
1969 *The Big Flame*; *In Black and White* (not transmitted)
1971 *The Rank and File*; *After a Lifetime*
1973 *A Misfortune*
1976 *Days of Hope* (in four parts)
1977 *The Price of Coal*
1979 *The Gamekeeper*
1980 *Auditions*
1981 *A Question of Leadership*
1983 *The Red and the Blue*; *Questions of Leadership* (in four parts, not transmitted)
1984 *Which Side Are You On?*
1985 *Diverse Reports: We Should Have Won*
1989 *Split Screen: Peace in Northern Ireland*

Publications

By LOACH: articles—

"Spreading Wings at Kestrel," an interview with P. Bream, in *Films and Filming* (London), March 1972.
Interview with M. Amiel, in *Cinéma* (Paris), December 1972.
Interview with J. O'Hara, in *Cinema Papers* (Melbourne), April 1977.
"A Fidelity to the Real," an interview with L. Quart, in *Cineaste* (New York), Fall 1980.
Interview with Julian Petley, in *Framework* (Norwich), no. 18, 1982.
Interview with Robert Brown, in *Monthly Film Bulletin* (London), January 1983.
"The complete Ken Loach," an interview with P. Kerr, in *Stills* (London), May/June 1986.

Ken Loach directing *Family Life*

"Getting it right!" an interview with G. Ambjornsson, in *Chaplin* (Stockholm), vol. 29, no 3, 1987.
Interview in *Film Dope* (London), February 1987.
"Voice in the Dark," an interview with Gavin Smith, in *Film Comment* (New York), March/April 1988.
Interview in *Cinema* (Paris), June 1990.
Interview in *La Revue du Cinema* (Paris), November 1991.
Interview in *Cahiers du Cinema* (Paris), November 1991.
Petley, Julian, and Sheila McKechnie, "Why Cathy will never come home again," in *New Statesman & Society* (London), 2 April 1993.
"Sympathetic Images," an interview with Gavin Smith, in *Film Comment* (New York), March/April 1994.
Interview with Geoffrey Mcnab, in *Sight and Sound* (London), November 1994.

On LOACH: articles—

Taylor, John, "The *Kes* Dossier," in *Sight and Sound* (London), Summer 1970.
"Tony Garnett and Ken Loach," in *Documentary Explorations: Fifteen Interviews with Filmmakers,* by G. Roy Levin, New York, 1971.
McAsh, Iain, "One More Time," in *Films Illustrated* (London), December 1978.
Petley, Julian, "Questions of Censorship," in *Stills* (London), November 1984.
Kerr, Paul, "The Complete Ken Loach," in *Stills* (London), May/June 1986.
Fatherland Section of *Jeune Cinéma* (Paris), January/February 1987.
Petley, Julian, "Ken Loach—Politics, Protest and the Past," in *Monthly Film Bulletin* (London), March 1987.
"Kenneth Loach," in *Film Dope* (London), February 1987.
Nave, B., "Portrait d'un cinéaste modeste: Ken Loach," in *Jeune Cinéma* (Paris), October/November 1987.
Grant, Steve, "Troubles Shooter," in *Time Out* (London), 2 January 1991.
Pannifer, Bill, "Agenda Bender," in *Listener* (London), 3 January 1991.
Malcolm, Derek, "Straight Out of Britain, Tales of Working-Class Life," in *New York Times,* 31 January 1993.
Fuller, G., "True Brit," *Village Voice* (New York), 9 February 1993.

* * *

Ken Loach is not only Britain's most political filmmaker, he is also its most censored—and the two are not entirely unconnected. Loach's career illustrates all too clearly the immense difficulties facing the radical filmmaker in Britain today: the broadcasting organisations' position within the state makes them extraordinarily sensitive sites from which to tackle certain fundamental political questions (about labour relations, "national security," or Northern Ireland, for example), while the film industry, though less subject to political interference and self-censorship, simply finds Loach's projects too "uncommercial," thanks to its habitually poverty-stricken state. And what other filmmaker, British or otherwise, has found one of his films the subject of vitriolic attacks by sections of his own country's press at a major international film festival—as happened at Cannes in 1990 with *Hidden Agenda*?

For all the obvious *political* differences with Grierson, Loach is the chief standard bearer of the British cinematic tradition that started with the documentary movement in the 1930s. His quintessentially naturalistic approach was apparent even in his earliest works (in his contributions to the seminal BBC police series *Z Cars,* for instance) but really came to the fore with *Up the Junction* and *Cathy Come Home.* In the days when television drama was still finding its way beyond the proscenium arch and out from under the blanket of middle-brow, middle-class, literary-based classics, *Cathy's* portrayal of a homeless family hounded by the forces of a pitiless bureaucracy caused a sensation and led directly to the founding of the housing charity Shelter. Indeed, one critic described it as "effecting massive, visceral change in millions of viewers in a single evening." Typically, however, Loach himself has been far more circumspect, arguing that the film was *socially* as opposed to *politically* conscious, that it made people aware of a problem without giving them any indication of what they might do about it. He concludes that "ideally I should have liked *Cathy* to lead to the nationalisation of the building industry and home ownership. Only political action can do anything in the end"—a point of view to which he has remained faithful throughout his career.

Accordingly, in *The Big Flame, The Rank and File,* and the four-part series *Days of Hope,* Loach turned to more directly political subjects. It is in these dramas that Loach begins his project of giving voice to the politically silenced and marginalised. As he put it, "I think it's a very important function to let people speak who are usually disqualified from speaking or who've become non-persons—activists, militants, or people who really have any developed political ideas. One after the other in different industries, there have been people who've developed very coherent political analyses, who are really just excluded. They're vilified—called extremists and then put beyond the pale."

Such views made enemies across the spectrum of political ideologies but, typically, Loach's critics cloaked what were basically *political* objections in apparently *aesthetic* rhetoric. In particular, Loach was dragged into the much-rehearsed argument that the "documentary-drama" form dishonestly and misleadingly blurs the line between fact and fiction and, in particular, presents the latter as the former. Loach himself dismisses such criticisms as "ludicrous" and a "smokescreen," citing the numerous uncontroversial disinterrings of Churchill, Edward VII, and others and concluding that "It's an argument that's always dragged out selectively when there's a view of history, a view of events, that the Establishment doesn't agree with—it's not really the form which worries them at all. It's such an intellectual fraud that it doesn't bear serious consideration."

Loach's work, especially *Days of Hope,* was also drawn into a more serious debate which raged at one time in the pages of *Screen* about whether films with "progressive" political content can be truly "progressive" if they utilise the allegedly outworn and ideologically dubious conventions of realism. Loach's response was to accuse such critics of "not seeing the woods for the trees. The big issue which we tried to make plain to ordinary folks who aren't film critics was that the Labour leadership had betrayed them fifty years ago and were about to do so again. That's the important thing to tell people. It surprised me that critics didn't take the political point, but a rather abstruse cinematic point.... Even the more serious critics always avoid confronting the content of the film and deciding if they think it is truthful. They'll skirt around it by talking about realism and the Function of Film or they'll do a little paragraph while devoting all their space to some commercial film they pretend to dislike."

With the coming of the 1980s Loach began to shift increasingly into documentary proper, abandoning dramatic devices altogether. This was partly a result of the increasing difficulty, both economic and political, that he had in making the kind of films in which he was most interested, but was also related to the advent of Thatcherism in 1979. As he himself explained, "There were things we wanted to say head on and not wrapped up in fiction, things that should be said as directly as one can say them. Thatcherism just felt so urgent that I thought that doing a fictional piece for TV, which would take a year just to get commissioned and at least another year to make, was just too slow. Documentaries can tackle things head on, and you can make them faster than dramas too—though with hindsight it's just as hard, if not harder, to get them transmitted."

Indeed, Loach had major problems with his analysis of the relationship between trade union leaders and the rank and file in *A Question of Leadership* and the series *Questions of Leadership,* the first of which was cut in order to include a final "balancing" discussion and broadcast in only one ITV region, while the second was never broadcast at all after numerous legal wrangles over alleged defamation. Similarly, Loach's coal dispute film, *Which Side Are You On?,* was banned by the company (London Weekend Television) which commissioned it. It was finally televised, but only after it could be "balanced" by a programme less sympathetic to the striking miners than Loach's. It says a great deal about the system of film and television programme making in Britain that one of the country's most experienced and politically conscious directors was, and remains, unable to produce a full-scale work about one of the most momentous political events in the country's recent history.

Exactly the same could be said about Loach and Northern Ireland. Revealingly, the initial idea for what was to become *Hidden Agenda* came from David Puttnam when he was studio boss at Columbia, after two of Loach's long-cherished Irish projects, one with the BBC and the other with Channel 4, had foundered. However, Loach has borne his treatment at the hands of the British establishment with remarkable fortitude. With his particular political outlook he would presumably be surprised if things were otherwise. Nor does he have an inflated view of the role of film and the filmmaker. As his remarks about *Cathy* clearly testify, Loach is a great believer in the primacy of the political. And, as he himself concludes, "filmmakers have a very soft life really, in comparison to people who have to work for a living. And so it's easy to be a radical filmmaker. The people who really are on the front line aren't filmmakers. We're in a very privileged position, very free and good wages—if you can keep working."

As Ken Loach ages, his films remain consistently provocative and politically savvy, with a deep respect for and understanding of his struggling, working class characters. *Riff Raff* features a prototypical Loach hero: an unemployed blue collar worker who comes to London and lands a job on a construction site. However, the film is no dry, pedantic political tract. While it is never less than pointed in its depiction of the never-ending conflict between the classes, it also is piercingly funny. Comic asides also highlight *Raining Stones,* an otherwise intense drama depicting the efforts of an out-of-work laborer to scrape together funds to feed his family. He is a proud man, who will not accept charity; however, trouble comes when he unwittingly borrows money from a loan shark to pay for his daughter's communion dress. With vivid irony, Loach graphically depicts the sense of hopelessness of honorable laborers who desire nothing more than the right to a suitable job, for suitable pay.

Loach's concerns are not solely with the male working class. *Ladybird Ladybird* is a trenchant, based-on-fact drama about a profoundly distressed single mother with a sad history of being exploited by men. He also is interested in the impact of history on the individual; in *Land and Freedom,* he abandons his usual British working class setting to tell the story of a jobless but passionate Liverpudlian Communist who treks to Barcelona during the Spanish Civil War to do battle for "land and freedom." The film works best as a potent look at political idealism in the face of the reality of a heartless, brutal enemy.

—Julian Petley, updated by Rob Edelman

LORENTZ, Pare

Nationality: American. **Born:** Clarksburg, West Virginia, 11 December 1905. **Education:** Wesleyan College; University of West Virginia. **Family:** Married Eliza Meyer. **Career:** Writer and film critic for *McCall's, Town and Country,* and Ring features, 1930s; directed first film, *The Plow That Broke the Plains,* for the U.S. Resettlement Agency, 1936; director of U.S. Film Service, 1938-40; directed shorts for RKO, 1941; made 275 navigational films for U.S. Air Force, 1941-45; chief of film section of War Department's Civil Affairs Division, 1946-47; film consultant, New York, 1960s. **Awards:** "Saluted" by Academy of Motion Pictures Arts and Sciences, 1981.

Films as Director and Scriptwriter:

1936 *The Plow That Broke the Plains*
1937 ***The River***
1940 *The Fight for Life*
1946 *Nuremberg Trials*

Other Films:

1939 *The City* (Steiner and Van Dyke) (co-sc)

Publications

By Lorentz: book—

FDR's Moviemaker: Memoirs and Scripts, Reno, Nevada, 1992.

By LORENTZ: article—

"The Narration of *The River,*" in *Film Comment* (New York), Spring 1965.

On LORENTZ: books—

Snyder, Robert L., *Pare Lorentz and the Documentary Film,* Norman, Oklahoma, 1968. Republished Reno, Nevada, 1993, with new Preface.
Barsam, Richard, *Non-Fiction Film,* New York, 1973.
MacCann, Richard Dyer, *The People's Films,* New York, 1973.
Barnouw, Erik, *Documentary—A History of the Non-Fiction Film,* New York, 1974.
Alexander, William, *Film on the Left: American Documentary Film from 1931-42,* Princeton, New Jersey, 1981.
Ellis, Jack C., *The Documentary Idea,* Englewood Cliffs, New Jersey, 1989.

On LORENTZ: articles—

Goodman, Ezra, "The American Documentary," in *Sight and Sound* (London), Autumn 1938.
White, W.L., "Pare Lorentz," in *Scribner's* (New York), January 1939.
Black, C.M., "He Serves Up America: Pare Lorentz," in *Collier's* (New York), 3 August 1940.
Van Dyke, Willard, "Letter from *The River,*" in *Film Comment* (New York), Spring 1965.
"Conscience of the Thirties," in *Newsweek* (New York), 5 August 1968.
Harmetz, Aljean, "Hollywood Hails Lorentz, Documentary Pioneer," in *New York Times,* 22 October 1981.
"Pare Lorentz," in *Film Dope* (London), February 1987.

On LORENTZ: film—

"Pare Lorentz on Film," in four instalments produced by WGBH in Boston for NET network.

* * *

In the United States it was Pare Lorentz who was in a position for leadership in relation to documentary film comparable to that of John Grierson in Britain and later in Canada. Lorentz was founding head and leader of the short-lived government program, which began in 1935, became the United States Film Service in 1938, and ended in 1940. He established American precedent for the government use of documentaries, which would be continued during World War II (by the Armed Forces and the Office of War Information) and afterwards (by the United States Information Agency, now International Communication Agency). From Lorentz's efforts five large and important films resulted, the first three of which he directed: *The Plow that Broke the Plains, The River, The Fight for Life, Power and the Land* (directed by Joris Ivens), and *The Land* (directed by Robert Flaherty).

In *The Plow that Broke the Plains* and *The River,* Lorentz developed an original, personal style of documentary that also became a national style. In his two mosaic patterns of sight (carefully composed images shot silent) and sound (symphonic music, spoken words, noises), no one element says much by itself. Together they offer form and content that resemble epic poems. They seem close to the attitudes of American populism and are rooted in frontier tradition. The sweeping views of a big country, the free verse commentaries with their chanted litany of place names and allusions to historic events, make one think of Walt Whitman. The use of music is quite special, with composer Virgil Thomson sharing more fully than usual in the filmmaking process; a sort of operatic balance is achieved between the musical score and the other elements. Thomson made his scores for these two films into concert suites which have become part of the standard orchestral repertoire.

In *The Fight for Life,* Lorentz is much less sure in his control of its narrative form than he was of the poetic form of the two preceding films. He seems to have been much more comfortable with land and rivers than with people. *Fight for Life* is about the work of the Chicago Maternity Center delivering babies among the impoverished. It is an interesting film, if curiously flawed by melodramatic excesses. It is important in its innovations and might be regarded as a prototype for the postwar Hollywood semi-documentaries; for example, *The House on 92nd Street, Boomerang, Call Northside 777.*

In contributing two lasting masterpieces to the history of documentary—*The Plow* and, especially, *The River*—Lorentz joins a very select company of the artists of documentary. (Flaherty and Jennings would be other members of that company.) Some would argue that *The River* is the finest American documentary to date—aesthetically and in terms of expressing aspects of the American spirit.

However, Lorentz had major limitations, politically, if not artistically. First, he relied on the impermanent partisan backing of the party in power. Lorentz had the support of President Franklin Roosevelt and the films were associated with Democratic policies. When the balance in Congress shifted to Republican in 1940, the United States Film Service was not allowed to continue. Second, even within the New Deal context Lorentz opted for a few big films sponsored by agencies related to one department (four of the five films were on agricultural subjects), rather than many smaller films from various departments that would have broadened the base of sponsorship and made for a steady flow of film communication. Third, he was creating art at public expense—making personal films à la Flaherty—with no real commitment to public service. (Lorentz disliked the term documentary and considered much of Grierson's work in England too school-teacherish; instead Lorentz was trying to create, he said, "films

Pare Lorentz: ***The River***

of merit.") Finally, Lorentz remained aloof in Washington. He made no efforts to seek sponsorship for documentary filmmaking outside the government; he had no real connection with the New York City filmmakers responsible for the nongovernmental documentaries of the 1930s (though some of them had worked with him on the government films).

However one chooses to look at the matter, it would be generally agreed that documentary in the United States remained a non-movement of individual rivalries, competitiveness, and political differences. The closing down of the U.S. Film Service proved a great waste. Shortly after its demise the United States entered World War II and government filmmaking on a vast scale had to be started from scratch. It was the Hollywood filmmakers, without documentary experience, who assumed leadership in the wartime government production. Lorentz spent the war making films as guides to navigation for the U.S. Air Corps. His film on the Nuremberg war-crimes trials became his last, as he chose to work instead mainly as a "film consultant."

—Jack C. Ellis

LOSEY, Joseph

Nationality: American. **Born:** La Crosse, Wisconsin, 14 January 1909. **Education:** Dartmouth College, New Hampshire, B.A., 1929; Harvard University, M.A. in English literature, 1930. **Career:** Stage director, New York, 1932-34; attended Eisenstein film classes, Moscow, 1935; staged Living Newspaper productions and other plays for Federal Theater Project, New York, 1947; hired by Dory Schary for RKO, 1948; blacklisted, moved to London, 1951; began collaboration with writer Harold Pinter and actor Dirk Bogarde, 1963; directed *Boris Godunov,* Paris, Opera, 1980. **Awards:** Chevalier de l'Ordre des Arts et des Lettres, 1957; International Critics Award, Cannes Festival, for *Accident,* 1967; Palme d'Or, Cannes Festival, for *The Go-Between,* 1971; Honorary Doctorate, Dartmouth College, 1973. **Died:** In London, 22 June 1984.

Films as Director:

1939 *Pete Roleum and His Cousins* (short) (+ p, sc)
1941 *A Child Went Forth* (short) (+ co-p, sc); *Youth Gets a Break* (short) (+ sc)
1945 *A Gun in His Hand* (short)
1949 *The Boy with Green Hair*
1950 *The Lawless*
1951 *The Prowler*; *M*; *The Big Night* (+ co-sc)
1952 *Stranger on the Prowl* (*Encounter*) (d as "Andrea Forzano")
1954 *The Sleeping Tiger* (d as "Victor Hanbury")
1955 *A Man on the Beach*
1956 *The Intimate Stranger* (*Finger of Guilt*) (d as "Joseph Walton")
1957 *Time without Pity*
1958 *The Gypsy and the Gentleman*
1959 *Blind Date* (*Chance Meeting*)
1960 *The Criminal* (*The Concrete Jungle*)
1962 *Eve*
1963 *The Damned* (*These Are the Damned*); ***The Servant*** (+ co-p)
1964 *King and Country* (+ co-p)
1966 *Modesty Blaise*
1967 *Accident* (+ co-p)
1968 *Boom!*; *Secret Ceremony*
1970 *Figures in a Landscape*; *The Go-Between*
1972 *The Assassination of Trotsky* (+ co-p)
1973 *A Doll's House*
1975 *Galileo* (+ co-sc); *The Romantic Englishwoman*
1977 *Mr. Klein*
1979 *Don Giovanni*
1982 *The Trout*
1985 *Steaming*

Publications

By LOSEY: books—

Losey on Losey, edited by Tom Milne, New York, 1968.
Le Livre de Losey: entretiens avec le cinéaste, edited by Michel Ciment, Paris, 1979; as *Conversations with Losey,* London, 1985.

By LOSEY: articles—

"A Mirror to Life," in *Films and Filming* (London), June 1959.
"Entretiens," in *Cahiers du Cinéma* (Paris), September 1960.
Interview with Penelope Houston and John Gillett, in *Sight and Sound* (London), Autumn 1961.
"The Monkey on My Back," in *Films and Filming* (London), October 1963.
"Speak, Think, Stand Up," in *Film Culture* (New York), Fall/Winter 1970.
"Losey and Trotsky," interview with Tony Rayns, in *Take One* (Montreal), March 1973.
Interview with Gene Phillips, in *Séquences* (Montreal), April 1973.
"Something More," interview with Gordon Gow, in *Films and Filming* (London), October 1975.
"The Reluctant Exile," interview with Richard Roud, in *Sight and Sound* (London), no. 3, 1979.
"Dialogue on Film: Joseph Losey," in *American Film* (Washington, D.C.), November 1980.
Interview with Michel Ciment, in *Positif* (Paris), October 1982.
"Screenwriters, Critics and Ambiguity," an interview with J. Weiss, in *Cineaste* (New York), vol. 13, no. 1, 1983.
Interview with Allen Eyles, in *Stills* (London), May 1985.

On LOSEY: books—

Leahy, James, *The Cinema of Joseph Losey,* New York, 1967.
Ledieu, Christian, *Joseph Losey,* Paris, 1970.
Hirsch, Foster, *Joseph Losey,* Boston, 1980.

On LOSEY: articles—

"Losey Issue" of *Cahiers du Cinéma* (Paris), September 1960.
Jacob, Gilles, "Joseph Losey, or The Camera Calls," in *Sight and Sound* (London), Spring 1966.
Ross, T.J., "Notes on an Early Losey," in *Film Culture* (New York), Spring 1966.
Durgnat, Raymond, "Puritan Maids," in *Films and Filming* (London), April and May 1966.
Phillips, Gene, "The Critical Camera of Joseph Losey," in *Cinema* (Beverly Hills), Spring 1968.
Strick, Philip, "The Mice in the Milk," in *Sight and Sound* (London), Spring 1969.
Gow, Gordon, "Weapons," in *Films and Filming* (London), October 1971.
Combs, Richard, "Losey, Galileo, and the Romantic Englishwoman," in *Sight and Sound* (London), Summer 1975.
Legrand, G., "Pro-positions à propos de Losey," in *Positif* (Paris), October 1976.

Phillips, Gene, "The Blacklisting Era: Three Cases," in *America* (New York), 18 December 1976.
Houston, B., and Marcia Kinder, "The Losey-Pinter Collaboration," in *Film Quarterly* (Berkeley), Fall 1978.
McCarthy, T., obituary, in *Variety* (New York), 27 June 1984.
Amiel, M., obituary, in *Cinéma* (Paris), September 1984.
Roud, Richard, "Remembering Losey," in *Sight and Sound* (London), Winter 1984/85.
Elsaesser, Thomas, "Joseph Losey: Time Lost and Found," in *Monthly Film Bulletin* (London), June 1985.
"Losey section" of *Positif* (Paris), July/August 1985.
"Joseph Losey," in *Film Dope* (London), February 1987.

* * *

Joseph Losey's career spanned five decades and included work in both theater and film. Latterly an American expatriate living in Europe, the early years of his life as a director were spent in the very different milieus of New Deal political theater projects and the paranoia of the Hollywood studio system during the McCarthy era. He was blacklisted in 1951 and left America for England where he continued making films, at first under a variety of pseudonyms. His work is both controversial and critically acclaimed, and Losey has long been recognized as a director with a distinctive and highly personal cinematic style.

Although Losey rarely wrote his own screenplays, preferring instead to work closely with other authors, there are nevertheless several distinct thematic concerns which recur throughout his work. It is his emphasis on human interaction and the complexity of interior thought and emotion that makes a Losey film an intellectual challenge, and his interest has always lain with detailed character studies rather than with so-called "action" pictures. Losey's domain is interior action and his depiction of the physical world centers on those events which are an outgrowth or reflection of his characters' inner lives. From *The Boy with Green Hair* to *The Trout,* his films focus on individuals and their relationships to themselves, to those around them, and to their society as a whole.

One of Losey's frequent subjects is the intruder who enters a pre-existing situation and irrevocably alters its patterns. In his earlier films, this situation often takes the form of a community reacting with violence to an individual its members perceive as a threat. The "boy with green hair" is ostracized and finally forced to shave his head by the inhabitants of the town in which he lives; the young Mexican-American in *The Lawless* becomes the object of a vicious manhunt after a racially motivated fight; and the child-murderer in Losey's 1951 version of *M* inspires a lynch mob mentality in the community he has been terrorizing. In each of these cases, the social outsider who, for good or evil, does not conform to the standards of the community evokes a response of mass rage and suspicion. And as the members of the group forsake their individuality and rational behavior in favor of mob rule, they also forfeit any hope of future self-deception regarding their own capacity for unthinking brutality.

In Losey's later films, the scope of the "intruder" theme is often narrowed to explore the effect of a newcomer on the relationship of a husband and wife. *The Sleeping Tiger, Eve, Accident, The Romantic Englishwoman,* and *The Trout* all feature married couples whose lives are disrupted and whose relationships are shattered or redefined by the arrival of a third figure. In each of these films, either the husband or the wife is strongly attracted to the outsider. In *The Sleeping Tiger, Eve,* and *The Trout,* this attraction leads to tragedy and death for one of the partners, while the couples in *Accident* and *The Romantic Englishwoman* are forced to confront a serious rift in a seemingly untroubled relationship. A further level of conflict is added by the fact that the intruder in all of the films is either of a different social class (*The Sleeping Tiger, Eve, The Trout*) or a different nationality (*Accident, The Romantic Englishwoman*) than the couple, representing not only a sexual threat but a threat to the bourgeois status quo as well.

Joseph Losey

This underlying theme of class conflict is one which runs throughout Losey's work, emerging as an essential part of the framework of films as different as *The Lawless, The Servant,* and *The Go-Between.* Losey's consistent use of film as a means of social criticism has its roots in his theatrical work of the 1930s and his association with Bertolt Brecht. The two collaborated on the 1947 staging of Brecht's *Galileo Galilei,* starring Charles Laughton—a play which twenty-seven years later Losey would bring to the screen—and Brecht's influence on Losey's own career is enormous. In addition to his interest in utilizing film as an expression of social and political opinions, Losey has adapted many of Brecht's theatrical devices to the medium as well. The sense of distance and reserve in Brechtian theatre is a keynote to Losey's filmic style, and Brecht's use of a heightened dramatic reality is also present in Losey's work. The characters in a Losey film are very much of the "real" world, but their depiction is never achieved through a documentary-style approach. We are always aware that it is a drama that is unfolding, as Losey makes use of carefully chosen music on the soundtrack, or photography that borders on expressionism, or deliberately evokes an atmosphere of memory to comment on the characters and their state of mind. It is this approach to the intellect rather than the emotions of the viewer that ties Losey's work so closely to Brecht.

Losey's films are also an examination of illusion and reality, with the true nature of people or events often bearing little resemblance to their outer appearances. The friendly community that gives way to mob violence, the "happy" marriage that unravels when one thread is plucked; these images of actual versus surface reality abound in Losey's work. One aspect of this theme manifests itself in Losey's fascination with characters who discover themselves through a relationship which poses a potential threat to their position in society. Tyvian, in *Eve*, can only acknowledge through his affair with a high-class prostitute that his fame as a writer is actually the result of plagiarism, while Marian, in *The Go-Between*, finds her true sexual nature, which her class and breeding urge her to repress, in her affair with a local farmer.

Several of Losey's films carry this theme a step further, offering characters who find their own sense of identity becoming inextricably bound up in someone else. In *The Servant*, the complex, enigmatic relationship between Tony and his manservant, Barrett, becomes both a class struggle and a battle of wills as the idle young aristocrat slowly loses control of his life to the ambitious Barrett. This is an idea Losey pursues in both *Secret Ceremony* and *Mr. Klein*. In the former, a wealthy, unbalanced young girl draws a prostitute into a destructive fantasy in which the two are mother and daughter, and the prostitute finds her initial desire for money becoming a desperate need to believe the fantasy. Alain Delon in *Mr. Klein* portrays a man in occupied France who becomes obsessed with finding a hunted Jew who shares his name. At the film's conclusion, he boards a train bound for the death camps rather than abandon his search, in effect becoming the other *Mr. Klein*. Losey emphasizes his characters' identity confusion cinematically, frequently showing them reflected in mirrors, their images fragmented, prism-like, or only partially revealed.

Losey's choice of subject led to his successful collaboration with playwright Harold Pinter on *The Servant*, *Accident*, and *The Go-Between*, and Losey once hoped to film Pinter's screenplay of Proust's *Remembrance of Things Past*. Their parallel dramatic interests served both men well, and their work together is among the finest in their careers. Yet if Losey found his most nearly perfect voice in Pinter's screenplays, his films with a wide variety of other writers have still resulted in a body of work remarkably consistent in theme and purpose. His absorbing, sometimes difficult films represent a unique and uncompromising approach to cinema, and guarantee Losey's place among the world's most intriguing directors.

—Janet E. Lorenz

LUBITSCH, Ernst

Nationality: German/American. **Born:** Berlin, 28 January 1892; became U.S. citizen, 1936. **Education:** Attended the Sophien Gymnasium. **Family:** Married 1) Irni (Helene) Kraus, 1922 (divorced 1930); 2) Sania Bezencenet (Vivian Gaye), 1935 (divorced 1943), one daughter. **Career:** Taken into Max Reinhardt Theater Company, 1911; actor, writer, then director of short films, from 1913; member of Adolph Zukor's Europäischen Film-Allianz (Efa), 1921; joined Warner Brothers, Hollywood, 1923; began association with Paramount, 1928; began collaboration with writer Ernest Vajda, 1930; head of production at Paramount, 1935 (relieved of post after a year); left Paramount for three-year contract with 20th Century-Fox, 1938; suffered massive heart attack, 1943. **Awards:** Special Academy Award (for accomplishments in the industry), 1947. **Died:** In Hollywood, 29 November 1947.

Films as Director:

1914 *Fräulein Seifenschaum* (+ role); *Blindkuh* (+ role); *Aufs Eis geführt* (+ role)
1915 *Zucker und Zimt* (co-d, co-sc, role)
1916 *Wo ist mein Schatz?* (+ role); *Schuhpalast Pinkus* (+ role as Sally Pinkus); *Der gemischte Frauenchor* (+ role); *Der G.m.b.H. Tenor* (+ role); *Der Kraftmeier* (+ role); *Leutnant auf Befehl* (+ role); *Das schönste Geschenk* (+ role); *Seine neue Nase* (+ role)
1917 *Wenn vier dasselbe Tun* (+ co-sc, role); *Der Blusenkönig* (+ role): *Ossis Tagebuch*
1918 *Prinz Sami* (+ role); *Ein fideles Gefängnis*; *Der Fall Rosentopf* (+ role); *Der Rodelkavalier* (+ co-sc); *Die Augen der Mumie Mâ*; *Das Mädel vom Ballett*; *Carmen*
1919 *Meine Frau, die Filmschauspielerin; Meyer aus Berlin* (+ role as apprentice); *Das Schwabemädle; Die Austernprinzessin; Rausch; Madame DuBarry*; *Der lustige Ehemann* (+ sc); *Die Puppe* (+ co-sc)
1920 *Ich möchte kein Mann sein!* (+ co-sc); *Kohlhiesels Töchter* (+ co-sc); *Romeo und Julia im Schnee* (+ co-sc); *Sumurun* (+ co-sc); *Anna Boleyn*
1921 *Die Bergkatze* (+ co-sc)
1922 *Das Weib des Pharao*
1923 *Die Flamme*; *Rosita*
1924 *The Marriage Circle*; *Three Women; Forbidden Paradise* (+ co-sc)
1925 *Kiss Me Again* (+ pr); *Lady Windermere's Fan* (+ pr)
1926 *So This Is Paris* (+ pr)
1927 *The Student Prince in Old Heidelberg* (+ pr)
1928 *The Patriot* (+ pr)
1929 *Eternal Love* (+ pr); *The Love Parade* (+ pr)
1930 *Paramount on Parade* (anthology film); *Monte Carlo* (+ pr)
1931 *The Smiling Lieutenant* (+ pr)
1932 *The Man I Killed* (*Broken Lullaby*) (+ pr); *One Hour with You* (+ pr); ***Trouble in Paradise*** (+ pr); *If I Had a Million* (anthology film)
1933 *Design for Living* (+ pr)
1934 *The Merry Widow* (+ pr)
1936 *Desire* (co-d, pr)
1937 *Angel* (+ pr)
1938 *Bluebeard's Eighth Wife* (+ pr)
1939 ***Ninotchka*** (+ pr)
1940 *The Shop Around the Corner* (+ pr)
1941 *That Uncertain Feeling* (+ co-pr)
1942 ***To Be or Not to Be*** (co-source, co-pr)
1943 *Heaven Can Wait* (+ pr)
1946 *Cluny Brown* (+ pr)
1948 *That Lady in Ermine* (co-d)

Other Films:

1913 *Meyer auf der Alm* (role as Meyer)
1914 *Die Firma Heiratet* (Wilhelm) (role as Moritz Abramowski); *Der Stolz der Firma* (Wilhelm) (role as Siegmund Lachmann); *Fräulein Piccolo* (Hofer) (role); *Arme Marie* (Mack) (role); *Bedingung—Kein Anhang!* (Rye) (role); *Die Ideale Gattin* (role); *Meyer als Soldat* (role as Meyer)
1915 *Robert und Bertram* (Mack) (role); *Wie Ich Ermordert Wurde* (Ralph) (role); *Der Schwarze Moritz* (Taufstein and Berg) (role); *Doktor Satansohn* (Edel) (role as Dr. Satansohn); *Hans Trutz im Schlaraffenland* (Wegener) (role as Devil)

Publications

By LUBITSCH: articles—

"American Cinematographers Superior Artists," in *American Cinematographer* (Los Angeles), December 1923.

"Concerning Cinematography ... as Told to William Stull," in *American Cinematographer* (Los Angeles), November 1929.

Ernst Lubitsch

"Lubitsch's Analysis of Pictures Minimizes Director's Importance," in *Variety* (New York), 1 March 1932.

"Hollywood Still Leads ... Says Ernst Lubitsch," interview with Barney Hutchinson, in *American Cinematographer* (Los Angeles), March 1933.

"A Tribute to Lubitsch, with a Letter in Which Lubitsch Appraises His Own Career," in *Films in Review* (New York), August/September 1951.

Letter to Herman Weinberg (10 July 1947), in *Film Culture* (New York), Summer 1962.

On LUBITSCH: books—

Verdone, Mario, *Ernst Lubitsch,* Lyon, 1964.

Baxter, John, *The Hollywood Exiles,* New York, 1976.

Poague, Leland, *The Cinema of Ernst Lubitsch: The Hollywood Films,* London, 1977.

Weinberg, Herman, *The Lubitsch Touch: A Critical Study,* 3rd revised edition, New York, 1977.

Carringer, R., and B. Sabath, *Ernst Lubitsch: A Guide to References and Resources,* Boston, 1978.

Paul, William, *Ernst Lubitsch's American Comedy,* New York, 1983.

Prinzler, Hans Helmut, and Enno Patalas, editors, *Lubitsch,* Munich, 1984.

Cahiers du Cinéma/Cinématheque Française: Ernst Lubitsch, Paris, 1985.

Petrie, Graham, *Hollywood Destinies: European Directors in Hollywood 1922-31,* London, 1985.

Bourget, Eithne, and Jean-Loup, *Lubitsch: ou, La Satire Romanesque,* Paris, 1987.

Nacache, Jacqueline, *Lubitsch,* Paris, 1987.

On LUBITSCH: articles—

Merrick, Mollie, "Twenty-five Years of the 'Lubitsch Touch' in Hollywood," in *American Cinematographer* (Los Angeles), July 1947.

"E. Lubitsch Dead: Film Producer, 55," in *New York Times,* 1 December 1947.

"Ernst Lubitsch: A Symposium," in *Screen Writer,* January 1948.

Wollenberg, H.H., "Two Masters: Ernst Lubitsch and Sergei M. Eisenstein," in *Sight and Sound* (London), Spring 1948.

"Lubitsch section" of *Revue du Cinéma* (Paris), September 1948.

"The Films of Ernst Lubitsch," special issue of *Film Journal* (Australia), June 1959.

"A Tribute to Lubitsch (1892-1947)," in *Action!* (Los Angeles), November/December 1967.

Eisenschitz, Bernard, "Lubitsch (1892-1947)," in *Anthologie du Cinéma* vol. 3, Paris, 1968.

"Lubitsch section" of *Cahiers du Cinéma* (Paris), February 1968.

Eisner, Lotte, "Lubitsch and the Costume Film," chapter 4 in *The Haunted Screen,* Berkeley, 1969.

Weinberg, Herman, "Ernst Lubitsch: A Parallel to George Feydeau," in *Film Comment* (New York), Spring 1970.

Sarris, Andrew, "Lubitsch in the Thirties," in *Film Comment* (New York), Winter 1971/72 and Summer 1972.

Mast, Gerald, "The 'Lubitsch Touch' and the Lubitsch Brain," in *The Comic Mind: Comedy and the Movies,* Indianapolis, Indiana, 1973; revised edition, 1979.

McBride, J., "The Importance of Being Ernst," in *Film Heritage* (New York), Summer 1973.

Schwartz, N., "Lubitsch's Widow: The Meaning of a Waltz," in *Film Comment* (New York), March/April 1975.

Horak, Jan-Christopher, "The Pre-Hollywood Lubitsch," in *Image* (Rochester, New York), December 1975.

Whittemore, Don, and Philip Cecchettini, "Ernst Lubitsch," in *Passport to Hollywood: Film Immigrants: Anthology,* New York, 1976.

Baxter, John, "The Continental Touch," in *American Film* (Washington, D.C.), September 1976.

Bond, Kirk, "Ernst Lubitsch," in *Film Culture* (New York), no. 63-64, 1977.

Gillett, John, "Munich's Cleaned Pictures," in *Sight and Sound* (London), Winter 1977/78.

Truffaut, François, "Lubitsch Was a Prince," in *American Film* (Washington, D.C.), May 1978.

McVay, D., "Lubitsch: The American Silent Films," in *Focus on Film* (London), April 1979.

Traubner, R., "Lubitsch Returns to Berlin," in *Films in Review* (New York), October 1984.

"Lubitsch section" of *Cinéma* (Paris), April 1985.

"Lubitsch section" of *Positif* (Paris), June and July/August 1986.

"Ernst Lubitsch," in *Film Dope* (London), February 1987.

Nave, B., "Aimer Lubitsch," in *Jeune Cinéma* (Paris), May/June 1987.

* * *

Ernst Lubitsch's varied career is often broken down into periods to emphasize the spectrum of his talents—from an actor in Max Reinhardt's Berlin Theater Company to head of production at Paramount. Each of these periods could well provide enough material for a sizeable book. It is probably most convenient to divide Lubitsch's output into three phases: his German films between 1913 and 1922; his Hollywood films from 1923 to 1934; and his Hollywood productions from 1935 till his death in 1947.

During the first half of Lubitsch's filmmaking decade in Germany he completed about nineteen shorts. They were predominantly ethnic slapsticks in which he played a "Dummkopf" character by the name of Meyer. Only three of these one- to five-reelers still exist. He directed eighteen more films during his last five years in Germany, almost equally divided between comedies—some of which anticipate the concerns of his Hollywood works—and epic costume dramas. Pola Negri starred in most of these historical spectacles, and the strength of her performances together with the quality of Lubitsch's productions brought them both international acclaim. Their *Madame Dubarry* (retitled *Passion* in the United States) was not only one of the films responsible for breaking the American blockade on imported German films after World War I, but it also began the "invasion" of Hollywood by German talent.

Lubitsch came to Hollywood at Mary Pickford's invitation. He had hoped to direct her in *Faust,* but they finally agreed upon *Rosita,* a costume romance very similar to those he had done in Germany. After joining Warner Brothers, he directed five films that firmly established his thematic interests. The films were small in scale, dealt openly with sexual and psychological relationships in and out of marriage, refrained from offering conventional moral judgments, and demystified women. As Molly Haskell and Marjorie Rosen point out, Lubitsch created complex female characters who were aggressive, unsentimental, and able to express their sexual desires without suffering the usual pains of banishment or death. Even though Lubitsch provided a new and healthy perspective on sex and increased America's understanding of a woman's role in society, he did so only in a superficial way. His women ultimately affirmed the status quo. The most frequently cited film from this initial burst of creativity, *The Marriage Circle,* also exhibits the basic narrative motif found in most of Lubitsch's work—the third person catalyst. An essentially solid relationship is temporarily threatened by a sexual rival. The possibility of infidelity serves as the occasion for the original partners to reassess their relationship. They acquire a new self-awareness and understand the responsibilities they have towards each other. The lovers are left more intimately bound than before. This premise was consistently reworked until *The Merry Widow* in 1934.

The late 1920s were years of turmoil as every studio tried to adapt to sound recording. Lubitsch, apparently, was not troubled at all; he considered the sound booths nothing more than an inconvenience, something readily overcome. Seven of his ten films from 1929 to 1934 were musicals, but not of the proscenium-bound "all-singing, all-dancing" variety. Musicals were produced with such prolific abandon during this time (what better way to exploit the new technology?) that the public began avoiding them. Film histories tend to view the period from 1930 to 1933 as a musical void, yet it was the precise time that Lubitsch was making significant contributions to the genre. As Arthur Knight notes, "He was the first to be concerned with the 'natural' introduction of songs into the development of a musical-comedy plot." Starting with *The Love Parade,* Lubitsch eliminated the staginess that was characteristic of most musicals by employing a moving camera, clever editing, and the judicial use of integrated musical performance, and in doing so constructed a seminal film musical format.

In 1932 Lubitsch directed his first non-musical sound comedy, *Trouble in Paradise.* Most critics consider this film to be, if not his best, then at least the complete embodiment of everything that has been associated with Lubitsch: sparkling dialogue, interesting plots, witty and sophisticated characters, and an air of urbanity—all part of the well-known "Lubitsch Touch." What constitutes the "Lubitsch Touch" is open to continual debate, the majority of the definitions being couched in poetic terms of idolization. Andrew Sarris comments that the "Lubitsch Touch" is a counterpoint of poignant sadness during a film's gayest moments. Leland A. Poague sees Lubitsch's style as being gracefully charming and fluid, with an "ingenious ability to suggest more than he showed...." Observations like this last one earned Lubitsch the unfortunate moniker of "director of doors," since a number of his jokes relied on what unseen activity was being implied behind a closed door.

Regardless of which romantic description one chooses, the "Lubitsch Touch" can be most concretely seen as deriving from a standard narrative device of the silent film: interrupting the dramatic interchange by focusing on objects or small details that make a witty comment on or surprising revelation about the main action. Whatever the explanation, Lubitsch's style was exceptionally popular with critics and audiences alike. Ten years after arriving in the United States he had directed eighteen features, parts of two anthologies, and was recognized as one of Hollywood's top directors.

Lubitsch's final phase began when he was appointed head of production at Paramount in 1935, a position that lasted only one year. Accustomed to pouring all his energies into one project at a time, he was ineffective juggling numerous projects simultaneously. Accused of being out of step with the times, Lubitsch updated his themes in his first political satire, *Ninotchka,* today probably his most famous film. He continued using parody and satire in his blackest comedy, *To Be or Not to Be,* a film well liked by his contemporaries, and today receiving much reinvestigation. If Lubitsch's greatest talent was his ability to make us laugh at the most serious events and anxieties, to use comedy to make us more aware of ourselves, then *To Be or Not to Be* might be considered the consummate work of his career.

Lubitsch, whom Gerald Mast terms the greatest technician in American cinema after Griffith, completed only two more films. At his funeral in 1947, Mervyn LeRoy presented a fitting eulogy: "he advanced the techniques of screen comedy as no one else has ever done. Suddenly the pratfall and the double-take were left behind and the sources of deep inner laughter were tapped."

—Greg S. Faller

LUCAS, George

Nationality: American. **Born:** Modesto, California, 14 May 1944. **Education:** Attended Modesto Junior College; University of Southern California Film School, graduated 1966. **Career:** Six-month internship at Warner Bros. spent as assistant to Francis Ford Coppola, 1967-68; co-founder, with Coppola, American Zoetrope, Northern California, 1969; directed first feature, *THX-1138,* 1971; established special effects company, Industrial Light and Magic, at San Rafael, California, 1976; formed production company Lucasfilm, Ltd., 1979; founded post production company Sprocket Systems, 1980; built Skywalker Ranch, then executive producer for Disneyland's 3-D music space adventure, *Captain EO,* 1980s. **Awards:** New York Film Critics Award for Best Screenwriting (with Gloria Katz and Willard Huyck), 1973. **Address:** c/o Lucasfilm, Ltd., P.O. Box 2009, San Rafael, California 94912, U.S.A.

Films as Director and Scriptwriter:

(Short student films)

1965-67 *Look at Life*; *Freiheit*; *1.42.08*; *Herbie* (co-d); *Anyone Lived in a Pretty How Town* (co-sc); *6.18.67* (doc); *The Emperor* (doc); *THX 1138:4EB*

1968 *Filmmaker* (doc)

(Feature films)

1971 *THX 1138* (co-sc)

1973 ***American Graffiti*** (co-sc)

1977 ***Star Wars*** (+ exec pr)

Films as Executive Producer:

1979 *More American Graffiti* (Norton) (+ story)

1980 ***The Empire Strikes Back*** (Kershner) (+ story); *Kagemusha (The Shadow Warrior)* (Kurosawa) (of int'l version)

1981 ***Raiders of the Lost Ark*** (Spielberg) (+ story); *Body Heat* (Kasdan) (uncredited)

1982 *Twice upon a Time* (Korty and Swenson)

1983 ***Return of the Jedi*** (Marquand) (+ co-sc, story)

1984 *Indiana Jones and the Temple of Doom* (Spielberg) (+ story)

1985 *Mishima* (Schrader)

1986 *Howard the Duck* (Huyck); *Labyrinth* (Henson); *Captain EO* (Coppola) (+ sc)

1988 *Willow* (Howard) (+ story); *Tucker: The Man and His Dream* (Coppola); *The Land before Time*

1989 *Indiana Jones and the Last Crusade* (Spielberg) (+ story)

1994 *Radioland Murders* (Mel Smith) (+ story)

Publications

By LUCAS: book—

American Graffiti: A Screenplay, with Gloria Katz and Willard Stuyck, New York, 1973.

By LUCAS: articles—

"*THX-1138,*" in *American Cinematographer* (Los Angeles), October 1971.

"The Filming of *American Graffiti,*" an interview with L. Sturhahn, in *Filmmakers Newsletter* (Ward Hill, Massachusetts), March 1974.

Interview with S. Zito, in *American Film* (Washington, D.C.), April 1977.

Interview with Robert Benayoun and Michel Ciment, in *Positif* (Paris), September 1977.

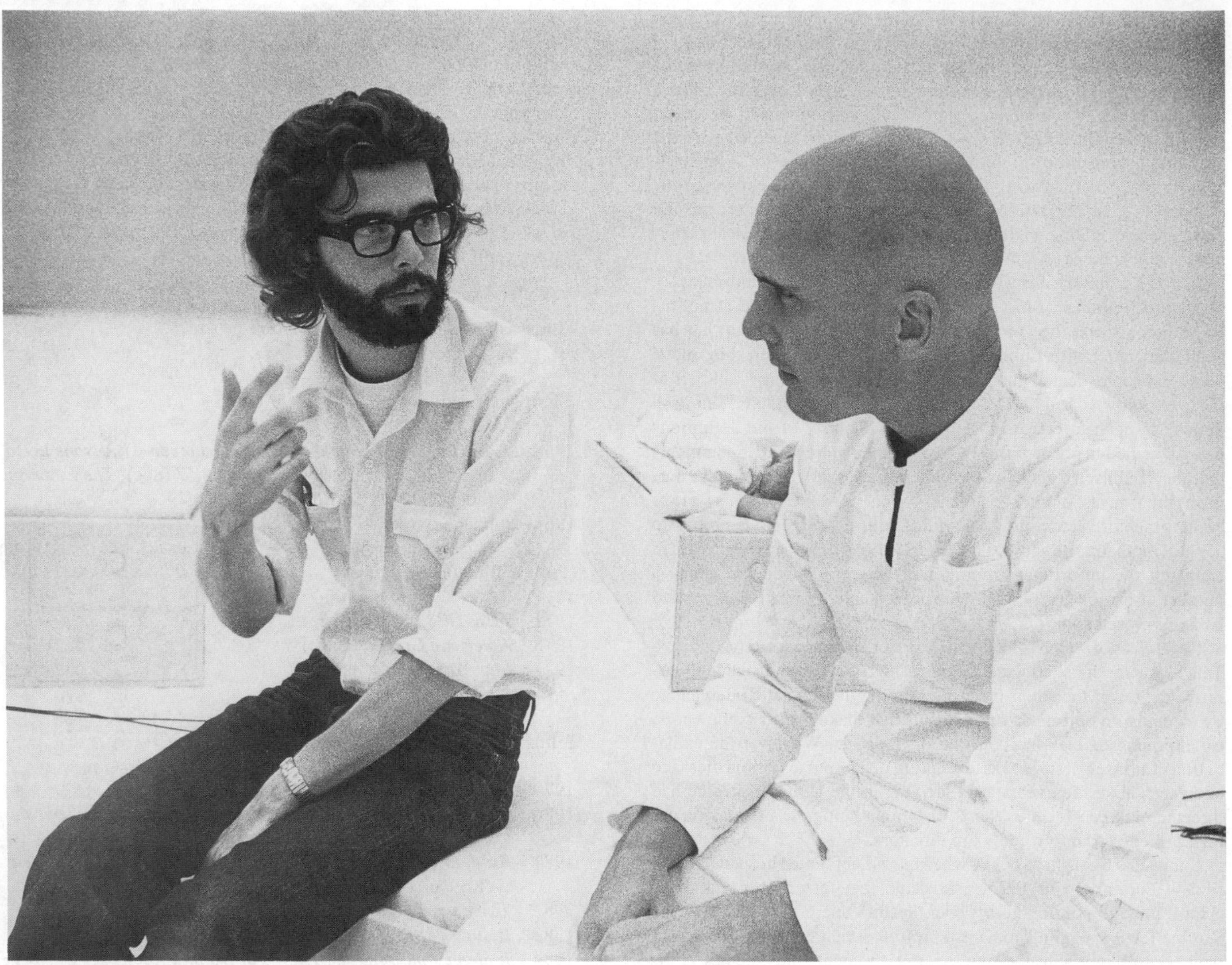

George Lucas (left) with Robert Duvall on the set of *THX 1138*

Interview with Audie Bock, in *Take One* (Montreal), no. 6, 1979.
Interview with M. Tuchman and A. Thompson, in *Film Comment* (New York), July/August 1981.
Interview with David Sheff, in *Rolling Stone* (New York), 5 November/10 December 1987.

On LUCAS: books—

Smith, Thomas G., *Industrial Light and Magic: The Art of Special Effects,* New York, 1986.
Champlin, Charles, *George Lucas, The Creative Impulse: Lucasfilm's First Twenty Years,* New York, 1992.
Carrau, Bob, *Monsters and Aliens from George Lucas,* New York, 1993.
Cotta Vaz, Mark, and Shinji Hata, *From Star Wars to Indiana Jones: The Best of Lucasfilm Archives,* San Francisco, 1994.

On LUCAS: articles—

Farber, Steven, "George Lucas: The Stinky Kid Hits the Big Time," in *Film Quarterly* (Berkeley), Spring 1974.
"Behind the Scenes of *Star Wars,*" in *American Cinematographer* (Los Angeles), July 1977.
Fairchild, B. H., Jr., "Songs of Innocence and Experience: The Blakean Vision of George Lucas," in *Literature/Film Quarterly* (Salisbury, Maryland), no. 2, 1979.
Pye, Michael, and Lynda Myles, "The Man Who Made *Star Wars,*" in *Atlantic Monthly* (Greenwich, Connecticut), March 1979.
Harmetz, A., "Burden of Dreams: George Lucas," in *American Film* (Washington, D.C.), June 1983.
Garsault, A., "Les paradoxes de George Lucas," in *Positif* (Paris), September 1983.
Schembri, J., "Robert Watts: Spielberg, Lucas and the Temple of Doom," in *Cinema Papers* (Melbourne), October/November 1984.
"George Lucas," in *Film Dope* (London), February 1987.
Star Wars Section of *Variety* (New York), 3 June 1987.
Kearney, J., and J. Greenberg, "The Road Warrior," in *American Film* (Washington, D.C.), June 1988.
Kaplan, David A., "The Force of an Idea Is with Him," in *Newsweek,* 31 May 1993.
Marx, Andy, "The Force Is with Him: *Star Wars* Savant Lucas Plans Celluloid," in *Variety,* 4 October 1993.
Marx, Andy, "Lucas Dishes Future Media at Intermedia," in *Variety,* 7 March 1994.
King, Thomas, "Lucasvision," in *Wall Street Journal,* March 1994.

Weintraub, Bernard, "The Ultimate Hollywoodian Lives an Anti-Hollywood Life," in *New York Times,* 20 October 1994.

Biskind, Peter, "'Radio' Days," in *Premiere,* November 1994.

Weiner, Rex, "Lucas the Loner Returns to 'Wars'," in *Variety,* 5 June 1995.

Groves, M., "Digital Yoda," in *Los Angeles Times,* June 1995.

* * *

In whatever capacity George Lucas works—director, writer, producer—the films in which he is involved are a mixture of the familiar and the fantastic. Thematically, Lucas's work is often familiar, but the presentation of the material usually carries his unique mark. His earliest commercial science-fiction film, *THX 1138,* is not very different in plot from previous stories of futuristic totalitarian societies in which humans are subordinate to technology. What is distinctive about the film is its visual impact. The extreme close-ups, bleak sets, and crowds of "properly sedated" shaven-headed people moving mechanically through hallways effectively produce the physical environment of this cold, well-ordered society. The endless whiteness of the vast detention center without bars could not be more oppressive.

Although not a special effects film, *American Graffiti,* Lucas's second feature, does show his attention to detail and his interest in archetypal themes. Within the 24-hour period of the film, the hero potential is brought forth from within the main characters, either through courageous action or the making of courageous decisions. The film captures America on the verge of transition from the 1950s to the brave new world of the 1960s. Lucas does this visually by recreating the 1950s on screen down to the smallest detail, but he also communicates through his characters the feeling that their lives will never be the same again.

The combination of convention, archetype, and fantasy comes together fully in Lucas's subsequent films—the *Star Wars* and *Indiana Jones* series. On one level the *Star Wars* trilogy is a fairy tale set in outer space, as suggested in the opening title: "A long time ago in a galaxy far, far away...." The basic plot conventions of the fairy tale are present: a princess in distress, a powerful evil ruler, and courageous knights. The trilogy is also a tale of the emergence of the hero within and the quest by which individuals realize their true selves, for the princess is really a Shaman, the evil ruler a self divided in need of healing, and the knights latent heroes who do not realize themselves as such at the beginning of the tale.

Scenes, especially from *Star Wars* and *The Empire Strikes Back,* look and sound like *Flash Gordon* episodes. Members of the Empire—the Emperor, Darth Vadar, the storm troopers—are an easily identifiable evil in their dark, drab clothing and cloaked or helmeted faces. Their movements are accompanied by a menacing, martial film score of the type that ushered Ming the Merciless on screen. Another reference that associates the Empire with a great evil is that the storm troopers in several scenes resemble the rows of assembled storm troopers on review in *Triumph of the Will.* In contrast to these images of darkness, the rebel forces and their habitats are colorful and full of life.

The *Star Wars* trilogy is also very much science fiction. The special effects developed to realize Lucas's futuristic vision brought about technological advances in motion picture photography. The workshop formed for the production of *Star Wars,* Industrial Light and Magic, continues on as an independent special effects production company. While working on *Star Wars,* John Dykstra developed the Dykstraflex camera, for which he received an Academy Award. The camera was used in conjunction with a computer to achieve the accuracy necessary in photographing multiple-exposure visual effects. Another advancement in motion-control photography was developed for *The Empire Strikes Back*—Brian Edlund's Empireflex camera.

Lucas and Steven Spielberg then set out to make a film based on the romantic action/adventure movies of the 1940s. The successful result was *Raiders of the Lost Ark.* Indiana Jones, based on the rough-edged, worldly-wise screen heroes of those earlier adventure films, is set to such mythic tasks as the quest for the Ark of the Covenant and the quest for the Holy Grail. Jones's enemies on these quests (which occur in the first and the last films of the series), the Nazis, are representatives of the dark side of this universe and carry legendary status of their own. As in the *Star Wars* trilogy, the main characters, including the extraordinary Indiana, face challenges that will bring forth qualities and strengths they had not yet realized. The dialogue in *Indiana Jones and the Last Crusade* especially emphasizes the theme of the hero within. At one point the senior Jones tells Indiana that "The search for the cup of Christ is the search for the divine in all of us"; later in the film Indiana is challenged to look within himself by the enemy as he is told, "It's time to ask yourself what you believe."

Radioland Murders is set in the world of live radio broadcasts of the late 1930s. All the conventional character types are here—from the inept director and his highly competent assistant to the golden-voiced booth announcer to the ever-creative sound-effects man. This romantic comedy/murder mystery was directed by Mel Smith, produced by Lucas, and based on an original story by Lucas. The narrative contains all the heroic challenges to spirit and character of more epic films condensed into a much smaller space and a much shorter time period. The action takes place within a few prime-time hours as a new radio network premieres. The broadcast carries on to a successful completion in spite of the murders of cast and crew, the police investigation, set breakdowns, and ego clashes. This universe of carefully contained chaos sometimes appears to be on the verge of spinning out of control, but it never does. The narrative, the broadcast, and the main characters persevere to the finish.

Lucas's films contain references to genre conventions and to earlier films. Also familiar in his work are the archetypal figures from myths and legends. At the same time, the films are fantastic and unfamiliar, filled with stunning visuals and exotic settings produced by innovative special effects.

—Marie Saeli

LUMET, Sidney

Nationality: American. **Born:** Philadelphia, 25 June 1924. **Education:** Professional Children's School, New York; Columbia University extension school. **Military Service:** Served in Signal Corps, U.S. Army, 1942-46. **Family:** Married 1) Rita Gam (divorced); 2) Gloria Vanderbilt, 1956 (divorced, 1963); 3) Gail Jones, 1963 (divorced, 1978); 4) Mary Gimbel, 1980; two daughters. **Career:** Acting debut in Yiddish Theatre production, New York, 1928; Broadway debut in *Dead End,* 1935; film actor, from 1939; stage director, off-Broadway, from 1947; assistant director, then director, for TV, from 1950. **Awards:** Directors Guild Awards, for *Twelve Angry Men,* 1957, and *Long Day's Journey into Night,* 1962. **Address:** c/o LAH Film Corporation, 1775 Broadway, New York, NY 10019, U.S.A.

Films as Director:

1957 ***Twelve Angry Men***
1958 *Stage Struck*
1959 *That Kind of Woman*
1960 *The Fugitive Kind*
1962 *A View from the Bridge*; *Long Day's Journey into Night*
1964 *Fail Safe*

1965 *Pawnbroker*; *Up from the Beach*; *The Hill*
1966 *The Group* (+ pr)
1967 *The Deadly Affair* (+ pr)
1968 *Bye Bye Braverman* (+ pr); *The Seagull* (+ pr)
1969 *Blood Kin* (doc) (co-d, co-pr)
1970 *King: A Filmed Record ... Montgomery to Memphis* (doc) (co-d, co-pr); *The Appointment*; *The Last of the Mobile Hot Shots*
1971 *The Anderson Tapes*
1972 *Child's Play*
1973 *The Offense*; *Serpico*
1974 *Lovin' Molly*; *Murder on the Orient Express*
1975 *Dog Day Afternoon*
1977 *Equus*; *Network*
1978 *The Wiz*
1980 *Just Tell Me What You Want* (+ pr)
1981 *Prince of the City*
1982 *Deathtrap*; *The Verdict*
1983 *Daniel*
1984 *Garbo Talks*
1986 *Power*; *The Morning After*
1988 *Running on Empty*
1989 *Family Business*
1990 *Q & A* (+ sc)
1992 *A Stranger among Us*
1993 *Guilty as Sin*

Other Films:

1939 *One Third of a Nation* (Murphy) (role as Joey Rogers)
1940 *Journey to Jerusalem* (role as youthful Jesus)
1990 *Listen Up! The Lives of Quincy Jones* (role)

Publications

By LUMET: book—

Making Movies, New York, 1995.

By LUMET: articles—

Interview with Peter Bogdanovich, in *Film Quarterly* (Berkeley), Winter 1960.
"Sidney Lumet," in *Cahiers du Cinéma* (Paris), December 1963/January 1964.
"Keep Them on the Hook," in *Films and Filming* (London), October 1964.
Interview with Luciano Dale, in *Film Quarterly* (Berkeley), Fall 1971.
"Sidney Lumet on the Director," in *Movie People: At Work in the Business,* edited by Fred Baker, New York, 1972.
Interview with Susan Merrill, in *Films in Review* (New York), November 1973.
Interviews with Gordon Gow, in *Films and Filming* (London), May 1975 and May 1978.
Interview with Dan Yakir, in *Film Comment* (New York), December 1978.
Interview with Michel Ciment and O. Eyquem, in *Positif* (Paris), February 1982.
"Delivering *Daniel,*" an interview with Richard Combs, in *Monthly Film Bulletin* (London), January 1984.
Interview with K. M. Chanko, in *Films in Review* (New York), October 1984.
Interview with M. Burke, in *Stills* (London), February 1987.
"Sidney Lumet: Lion on the Left," an interview with G. Smith, in *Film Comment* (New York), July/August 1988.
"That's the Way It Happens," an interview with Gavin Smith, in *Film Comment* (New York), September/October 1992.

On LUMET: books—

Bowles, Stephen, *Sidney Lumet: A Guide to References and Resources,* Boston, 1979.
De Santi, Gualtiero, *Sidney Lumet,* Florence, 1988.
Cunningham, Frank R., *Sidney Lumet: Film and Literary Vision,* Lexington, Kentucky, 1991.
Boyer, Jay, *Sidney Lumet,* New York, 1993.

On LUMET: articles—

Petrie, Graham, "The Films of Sidney Lumet: Adaptation as Art," in *Film Quarterly* (Berkeley), Winter 1967/68.
Rayns, Tony, "Across the Board," in *Sight and Sound* (London), Summer 1974.
Sidney Lumet Section of *Cinématographe* (Paris), January 1982.
Chase, D., "Sidney Lumet Shoots *The Verdict,*" in *Millimeter* (New York), December 1982.
Shewey, D., "Sidney Lumet: the Reluctant Auteur," in *American Film* (Washington, D.C.), December 1982.
"TV to Film: A History, a Map, and a Family Tree," in *Monthly Film Bulletin* (London), February 1983.
"Sidney Lumet," in *Film Dope* (London), June 1987.
Tempel, M. van den, "Chroniqueur van New York," in *Skoop,* May 1991.
Fleming, M., "New York Banks on Hudson Studio," in *Variety,* 15 June 1992.

* * *

Although Sidney Lumet has applied his talents to a variety of genres (drama, comedy, satire, caper, romance, and even a musical), he has proven himself most comfortable and effective as a director of serious psychodramas and was most vulnerable when attempting light entertainments. His Academy Award nominations, for example, have all been for character studies of men in crisis, from his first film, *Twelve Angry Men,* to *The Verdict.*

Lumet was, literally, a child of the drama. At the age of four he was appearing in productions of the highly popular and acclaimed Yiddish Theatre in New York. He continued to act for the next two decades but increasingly gravitated toward directing. At twenty-six he was offered a position as an assistant director with CBS television. Along with John Frankenheimer, Robert Mulligan, Martin Ritt, Delbert Mann, George Roy Hill, Franklin Schaffner, and others, Lumet quickly won recognition as a competent and reliable director in a medium where many faltered under the pressures of producing live programs. It was in this environment that Lumet learned many of the skills that would serve him so well in his subsequent career in films: working closely with performers, rapid preparation for production, and working within tight schedules and budgets.

Because the quality of many of the television dramas was so impressive, several of them were adapted as motion pictures. Reginald Rose's *Twelve Angry Men* brought Lumet to the cinema. Although Lumet did not direct the television production, his expertise made him the ideal director for this low-budget film venture. *Twelve Angry Men* was an auspicious beginning for Lumet. It was a critical and commercial success and established Lumet as a director skilled at adapting theatrical properties to motion pictures. Fully half of Lumet's complement of films have originated in the theater. Another precedent set by *Twelve Angry Men* was Lumet's career-long disdain for Hollywood.

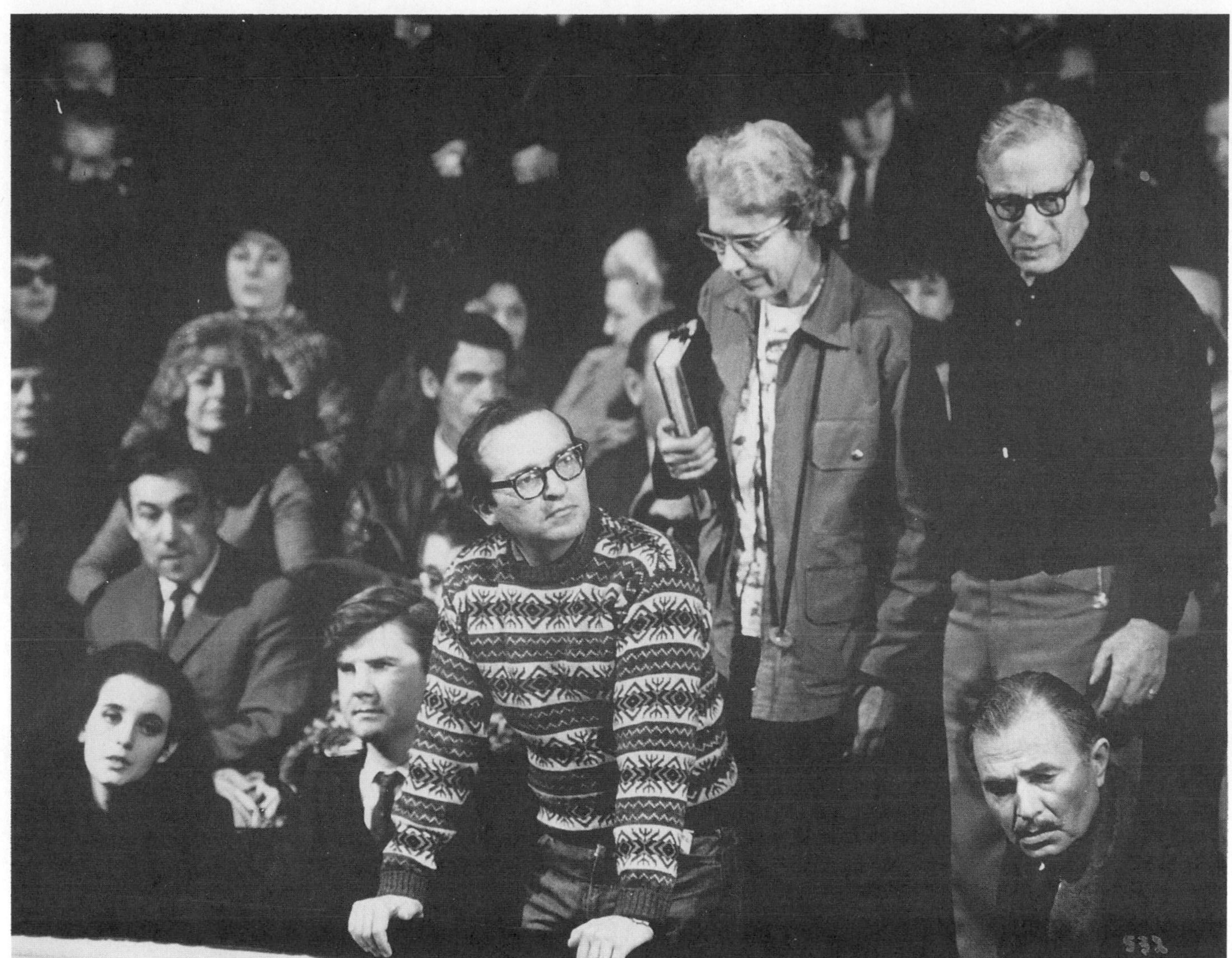

Sidney Lumet (center) directing *The Deadly Affair*

Lumet prefers to work in contemporary urban settings, especially New York. Within this context, Lumet is consistently attracted to situations in which crime provides the occasion for a group of characters to come together. Typically these characters are caught in a vortex of events they can neither understand nor control but which they must work to resolve. *Twelve Angry Men* explores the interaction of a group of jurors debating the innocence or guilt of a man being tried for murder; *The Hill* concerns a rough group of military men who have been sentenced to prison; *The Deadly Affair* involves espionage in Britain; *The Anderson Tapes* revolves around the robbery of a luxury apartment building; *Child's Play,* about murder at a boy's school, conveys an almost supernatural atmosphere of menace; *Murder on the Orient Express, Dog Day Afternoon,* and *The Verdict* all involve attempts to find the solution to a crime, while *Serpico* and *Prince of the City* are probing examinations of men who have rejected graft practices as police officers.

Lumet's protagonists tend to be isolated, unexceptional men who oppose a group or institution. Whether the protagonist is a member of a jury or party to a bungled robbery, he follows his instincts and intuition in an effort to find solutions. Lumet's most important criterion is not whether the actions of these men are right or wrong but whether the actions are genuine. If these actions are justified by the individual's conscience, this gives his heroes uncommon strength and courage to endure the pressures, abuses, and injustices of others. Frank Serpico, for example, is the quintessential Lumet hero in his defiance of peer group authority and the assertion of his own code of moral values.

Nearly all the characters in Lumet's gallery are driven by obsessions or passions that range from the pursuit of justice, honesty, and truth to the clutches of jealousy, memory, or guilt. It is not so much the object of their fixations but the obsessive condition itself that intrigues Lumet. In films like *The Fugitive Kind, A View from the Bridge, Long Day's Journey into Night, The Pawnbroker, The Seagull, The Appointment, The Offense, Lovin' Molly, Network, Just Tell Me What You Want,* and many of the others, the protagonists, as a result of their complex fixations, are lonely, often disillusioned individuals. Consequently, most of Lumet's central characters are not likable or pleasant, and sometimes not admirable figures. And, typically, their fixations result in tragic or unhappy consequences.

Lumet's fortunes have been up and down at the box office. One explanation seems to be his own fixation with uncompromising studies of men in crisis. His most intense characters present a grim vision of idealists broken by realities. From Val in *A View from the Bridge* and Sol Nazerman in *The Pawnbroker* to Danny Ciello in *Prince of the City,* Lumet's introspective characters seek to penetrate the deepest regions of the psyche.

Lumet's recently published memoir about his life in film, *Making Movies,* is extremely lighthearted and infectious in its enthusiasm for the craft of moviemaking itself. This stands in marked contrast to the tone and style of most of his films. Perhaps Lumet's signature as a director is his work with actors—and his exceptional ability to draw high-quality, sometimes extraordinary performances from even the most unexpected quarters: Melanie Griffith's believable undercover policewoman in *A Stranger among Us* and Don Johnson's smooth-talking sociopath in *Guilty as Sin.* These two latest examples of the "Lumet touch" with actors demonstrate that he has not lost it.

—Stephen E. Bowles, updated by John McCarty

LUMIÈRE, Louis

Nationality: French. **Born:** Besançon, 5 October 1864. **Education:** L'école de la Martinière, Besançon, degree 1880; attended Conservatoire de Lyon, 1880-81. **Career:** Chemist and inventor, son of an industrialist specialising in photographic chemistry and the making of emulsions; after seeing Edison Kinetoscope demonstrated in Paris, developed with brother Auguste Lumière (1862-1954) the "Cinématographe Lumière," incorporating invention of claw driven by eccentric gear for advancing film, 1894; projected first film, showing workers leaving the Lumière factory, 1895; projected first program for a paying audience at Grand Café, Boulevard des Capucines, Paris, 28 December 1895; Société du Cinématographe Lumière formed, 1896; projected film onto 16 by 21 foot screen at Paris Exposition, 1900; company ceased film production, 1905; subsequently invented and manufactured photographic equipment; worked on stereo projection method, from 1921; première of "cinéma en relief" in Paris, 1936. **Died:** In Bandol, France, 6 June 1948.

Films as Director:

1896-1900 Directed about 60 films and produced about 2000, mostly documentaries

1894 or 95 *La Sortie des usines* (version no. 1)

1895 *La Sortie des usines* (version no. 2); ***L'Arroseur arrosé*** *(Le Jardinier)*; *Forgerons*; *Pompiers*; *Attaque du feu*; *Le Repas de bébé* (*Le Déjeuner de bébé. Le Gouter de bébé*); *Pêche aux poissons rouges*; *La Voltige*; *Débarquement* (*Arrivée des congressistes à Neuville-sur-Saône*); *Discussion de M. Janssen et de M. Lagrange*; *Saut à la couverture* (*Brimade dans une caserne*); *Lyon, place des Cordeliers*; *Lyon, place Bellecour*; *Récréation à la Martinière*; *Charcuterie mécanique*; *Le Maréchalferrant*; *Lancement d'un navire à La Ciotat*; *Baignade en mer*; *Ateliers de La Ciotat*; *Barque sortant du port* (*La Sortie du port*); *Arrivée d'un train à La Ciotat*; *Partie d'ecarté*; *Assiettes tournantes*; *Chapeaux à transformations* (*Trewey: Under the Hat*); *Photographe*; *Démolition d'un mur* (*Le Mur*); *Querelle enfantine*; *Aquarium*; *Bocal aux poissons-rouges*; *Partie de tric-trac*; *Le Dejeuner du chat*; *Départ en voiture*; *Enfants aux jouets*; *Course en sac*; *Discussion*

1896-97 *Barque en mer*; *Baignade en mer*; *Arrivée d'un bateau à vapeur*; *Concours de boules*; *Premiers pas de Bébé*; *Embarquement pour le promenade*; *Retour d'une promenade en mer*; *Marché*; *Enfant et chien*; *Petit frèree et petite soeur*; *Douche aprés le bain*; *Ronde enfantine*; *Enfants au bord de la mer*; *Bains en mer*; *Touristes revenant d'une excursion*; *Scènes d'enfants*; *Laveuses*; *Repas en famille*; *Bal d'enfants*; *Leçon de bicyclette*; *Menuisiers*; *Radeau avec baigneurs*; *Le Goûter de bébé*

1900 *Inauguration de l'Exposition universelle*; *La Tour Eiffel*; *Le Pont d' Iéna*; *Danses espagnoles* and other films shown on large screen at Paris Exposition 1900

1936 *Arrivée d'un train en gare de La Ciotat* and other films presented in "cinéma en relief" program

Publications

By LUMIÈRE: books—

Cinématographe Auguste et Louis Lumière: Catalogue des Vues, first through seventh lists, Lyon, France, 1897-98.

Catalogue des vues pour cinématographe, Lyon, 1907.

By LUMIÈRE: articles—

"Lumière—The Last Interview," with Georges Sadoul, in *Sight and Sound* (London), Summer 1948.

"Bellecour—Monplaisir," with H. Bitomsky, in *Filmkritik* (Munich), August 1978.

On LUMIÈRE: books—

Kubnick, Henri, *Les Frères Lumière,* Paris, 1938.

Bessy, Maurice, and Lo Duca, *Louis Lumière, inventeur,* Paris, 1948.

Leroy, Paul, *Au seuil de paradis des images avec Louis Lumière,* Paris, 1948.

Sadoul, Georges, *Histoire générale du cinéma* vols. 1 and 2, Paris, 1949.

Pernot, Victor, *A Paris, il y a soixante ans, naissait le cinéma,* Paris, 1955.

Mitry, Jean, *Filmographie Universelle* vol. 2, Paris, 1964.

Sadoul, Georges, *Louis Lumière,* Paris, 1964.

Chardère, Bernard, and others, *Les Lumières,* Paris, 1985.

Rittaud-Hutinet, *Le Cinéma des origins: frères Lumière et leur opérateurs,* Seyssel, 1985.

Sauvage, Leo, *L'Affaire Lumière,* Paris, 1985.

Redi, Riccardo, editor, *Lumière,* Rome, 1986.

André, Jacques and Marie, *Uns Saison Lumière à Montpelier,* Perpignan, 1987.

On LUMIÈRE: articles—

Browne, Mallory, "Artisan in Light," in *Christian Science Monitor* (Boston), 7 August 1935.

"Lumière Jubilee," in *Time* (New York), 18 November 1935.

Deutelbaum, M., "Structural Patterning in the Lumière Films," in *Wide Angle* (Athens, Ohio), no. 1, 1979.

Decaux, E., "Lieux du cinéma: lettre du Chateau Lumière," in *Cinématographe* (Paris), January 1979.

Vaughan, Dai, "Let There Be Lumière," in *Sight and Sound* (London), Spring 1981.

Dubois, P., "Le gros plan primitif," in *Revue Belge du Cinéma* (Brussels), Winter 1984/85.

Rinieri, D., "Lumière fut," in *Cinématographe* (Paris), September 1985.

"Louis Lumière: 8 Films de la soirée du Grand café," in *Avant-Scène du Cinéma* (Paris), November 1984.

Louis Lumière: poster for *L'Arroseur arrosé*

Masson, André, "Lumière!," in *Positif* (Paris), January 1986.
Chardère, B., and others, "Les Droits des films Lumière," in *Filmèchange* (Paris), Autumn 1986.
Gorki, Maxim, and P. Delpeut, in *Versus* (Nijmegen), no. 2, 1988.
Chardère, B., "Les sorties des usines Lumière. Jamais deux sans trois," in *Positif* (Paris), June 1989.

* * *

Few directors since Louis Lumière have enjoyed such total control over their films. As inventor of the *cinématographe,* the first camera-cum-projector, he determined not only the subjects but also the aesthetics of early cinema. A scientist devoted to the plastic arts, Lumière initially specialised in outdoor photography. This experience, coupled with an appreciation of framing, perspective, and light values in a composition, informed his pioneering films.

To promote the *cinématographe,* he made demonstration shorts which, because of the camera's limited spool capacity, lasted less than a minute. If art refines itself through constraint, Lumière's films are excellent models. He overcame the *cinématographe's* technical limitations to achieve tightly structured views of contemporary life, both public and private.

Though Lumière's role in establishing the cinema has been dutifully recorded together with the audience's thrilled disbelief at his moving images, his contribution to film practice deserves more recognition. His first film, *La Sortie des usines,* pictures employees leaving his photographic factory. Framed by the open gates, they disperse before the camera set at a medium close-up distance, and with the closure of the gates the sequence ends. The film does not result from a casual pointing of the camera at the chosen subject: all has been pre-planned, from the placing of the hidden camera to the squaring of the action's duration with the available footage.

Over the next two years or so, Lumière experimented with diverse subjects and filming techniques. His themes reflect an unquestioning confidence in the permanence of contemporary political and social structures. Whether recording aspects of city life or the calmer pleasures of the seaside, the work of the artisan, fireman, or soldier, more personal family subjects or rehearsed comic episodes, his films imply a well-ordered, contented society where individuals cheerfully perform their allotted roles. Images of social deprivation or discontent are noticeably absent.

Scenes featuring family or friends are often filmed in medium close-up, with the single framing here reinforcing the intimacy and denying a world outside. Immaculate children, invariably in white, are shown feeding (*Repas de bébé*), learning to walk (*Premiers pas de bébé*), playing with toys (*Enfants aux jouets*), arguing (*Querelle enfantine*), dancing (*Bal d'enfants*), or delightfully trying to catch goldfish (*Pêche aux poissons rouges*). In *Concert,* Madame Lumière plays a violin, while card games involve family friends (*Partie d'écarté* and *Partie de tric-trac*). A cat lapping milk (*Déjeûner du chat*) is filmed in close-up and in *Aquarium* the fish tank fills the frame to create the illusion of underwater photography.

In films such as *Place des Cordeliers* and *Place Bellecour* the atmosphere of public squares alive with horse-drawn carriages and bustling crowds is captured, while in films such as *Baignade en mer* the novelties of sea-bathing are recorded. Other films prefigure newsreels by documenting particular events. The first of these, *Débarquement,* records photographers arriving for their conference and was projected the next day. Similar events include a street sack race (*Course en sac*), the demolition of a wall (*Démolition d'un mur*), the launching of a ship (*Lancement d'un navire à La Ciotat*), and various arrivals or departures, such as *Touristes revenant d'une excursion,* or *Arrivée d'un bateau à vapeur.* An early triumph was *Barque sortant du port,* where glistening waves and a sudden swell rocking the boat impressed themselves on a public familiar only with static images. Sequences capturing movement were an immediate attraction.

Lumière's most celebrated arrival subject was the train entering La Ciotat station (*Arrivée d'un train à la Ciotat*). Here the dramatic resources of depth of field are exploited, with the platform and the track forming strong diagonals reaching into the distance. The train, first pictured in longshot, thrusts itself towards the camera to create a dynamic close-up. So powerful was the illusion of the train's immanence that the first audiences reportedly feared for their safety. The creative use of perspective was also fundamental to the depiction of ploughing in *Labourage* and to the sack race in *Course en sac.*

Documentaries concerning artisans or the military reveal a studied composition. The camera is positioned to make actions comprehensible, whether in terms of shoeing horses (*Maréchal-ferrant*), shaping iron bars (*Forgerons*), or horsemanship (*Voltige*). Cooperation with the fire service produced a more substantial documentary. Recognising the dramatic potential of his subject, Lumière portrayed a full-scale fire practice in four linked films: *Sortie de la Pompe, Mise en Batterie, Attaque du feu,* and *Sauvetage.*

Comic sketches required careful preparation. In *L'Arroseur arrosé* a young prankster soaks an unsuspecting gardener by interrupting, then releasing, the water supply to a hose. All is tightly organized in time and space to meet the limitations of the fixed camera. In *Photographe* the innocent subject is again drenched, while in *Charcuterie mécanique* (which ridicules American mechanisation long before Tati's postman in *Jour de fête*) a pig is converted into sausages which then magically transform themselves into a pig again. Although Lumière renounced filmmaking, he extended his influence through trained operators, such as Promio, Mesguish, and Doublier. His impact on early cinema is evident in the way others, notably Méliès, imitated his subjects. His abiding presence in French film culture is witnessed in various homages: in *Les Mistons* Truffaut affectionately alludes to *L'Arroseur arrosé,* while in *Les Carabiniers* Godard parodies *L'Arrivée d'un train à la Ciotat* and *Le Repas de bébé.*

—R F. Cousins

LYNCH, David

Nationality: American. **Born:** Missoula, Montana, 20 January 1946. **Education:** High school in Alexandria, Virginia; Corcoran School of Art, c. 1964; Boston Museum School, 1965; Pennsylvania Academy of Fine Art, 1965-69; American Film Institute Centre for Advanced Studies, studying under Frank Daniel, 1970. **Family:** Married 1) Peggy Reavey, 1967 (divorced, 1974), one daughter, writer/director Jennifer Lynch; 2) Mary Fisk, 1977 (divorced, 1987), one son, Austin. **Career:** Spent five years making *Eraserhead,* Los Angeles, 1971-76; worked as paperboy and shed-builder, late 1970s; invited by Mel Brooks to direct *The Elephant Man,* 1980; with Mark Frost, made *Twin Peaks* for video (two-hour version) and as TV series, 1989. **Awards:** National Society of Film Critics Awards for Best Film and Best Director, for *Blue Velvet,* 1986; Palme d'Or, Cannes Festival, for *Wild at Heart,* 1990.

Films as Director and Scriptwriter:

1968 *The Alphabet* (short)
1970 *The Grandmother* (short)
1978 ***Eraserhead***
1980 *The Elephant Man* (co-sc)
1984 *Dune*
1986 ***Blue Velvet***
1988 episode in *Les Français vus par ...*
1990 *Wild at Heart*
1991 *Storyville*
1992 *Twin Peaks: Fire Walk with Me* (+ co-pr, role as Gordon Cole)

Other Films:

1988 *Zelly and Me* (role as Willie)
1991 *The Cabinet of Dr. Ramirez* (exec pr)
1994 *Nadja* (exec pr, role as Morgue Attendant)

Publications

By LYNCH: books—

Welcome to Twin Peaks: An Access Guide to the Town, with Richard Saul Wurman and Mark Frost, London, 1991.
Images, New York, 1994.

By LYNCH: articles—

Interview with Serge Daney and Charles Tesson, in *Cahiers du Cinéma* (Paris), April 1981.
Interview with D. Chute, in *Film Comment* (New York), September/October 1986.
Interview with K. Jaehne and L. Bouzereau, in *Cineaste* (New York), vol. 15, no. 3, 1987.
Interview with A. Caron and M. Girard, in *Séquences* (Montreal), February 1987.
Interview with D. Marsh and A. Missler, in *Cinema Papers* (Melbourne), March 1987.
Interview with Jane Root, in *Monthly Film Bulletin* (London), April 1987.
Interview with D. Breskin, in *Rolling Stone,* September 6, 1990.
Interview with M. Ciment and H. Niogret, in *Positif,* October 1990.

On LYNCH: book—

Kaleta, Kenneth C., *David Lynch,* New York, 1993.

On LYNCH: articles—

Hinson, H., "Dreamscapes," in *American Film* (Washington, D.C.), December 1984.
David Lynch section of *Revue du Cinéma* (Paris), February 1987.
Combs, Richard, "Crude Thoughts and Fierce Forces," in *Monthly Film Bulletin* (London), April 1987.
French, Sean, "The Heart of the Cavern," in *Sight and Sound* (London), Spring 1987.

David Lynch

"David Lynch," in *Film Dope* (London), June 1987.
McDonagh, M., "The Enigma of David Lynch," in *Persistence of Vision* (Maspeth, New York), Summer 1988.
Gehr, R., "The Angriest Painter in the World," in *American Film* (Washington, D.C.), April 1989.
Saada, N., "David Lynch," in *Cahiers du Cinéma,* June 1990.
Zimmer, J., "David Lynch," in *Revue du Cinéma,* July/August 1990.
Woodward, Robert B., "Wild at Heart ... Weird on Top," in *Empire* (London), September 1990.
Hoberman, J., and Jonathan Rosenbaum, "Curse of the Cult People," in *Film Comment,* January/February 1991.
Sante, Luc, "The Rise of the Baroque Directors," in *Vogue,* September 1992.
Jankiewicz, P., "Lynch's Hall of Freaks," in *Film Threat,* October 1992.
Hampton, Howard, "David Lynch's Secret History of the United States," in *Film Comment,* May/June 1993.

* * *

The undoubted perversity that runs throughout the works of David Lynch extends to his repeated and unexpected career turns: coming off the semi-underground *Eraserhead* to make the semi-respectable *The Elephant Man,* with a distinguished British cast; then bouncing into a Dino de Laurentiis mega-budget science-fiction fiasco, *Dune;* creeping back with the seductive and elusive small-town mystery of *Blue Velvet;* capping that by transferring his uncompromising vision of lurking sexual violence to American network television in *Twin Peaks;* and alienating the viewers of that bizarre soap with the rambling, intermittently stupefying, road movie *Wild at Heart.* Although there are recognisable Lynchian elements, with both *Eraserhead* and *Blue Velvet*—his two most commercially and critically successful movies—leaking images and ideas into the pairs of movies that followed them up, Lynch has proved surprisingly difficult to pin down. Given one Lynch movie, it has been—until the slightly too self-plagiaristic *Wild at Heart*—almost impossible to predict the next step. A painter and animator—his first films are Svankmajer-style shorts *The Grandmother* and *Alphabet*—Lynch came into the film industry through the back door, converting his thesis movie into *Eraserhead* on a shooting schedule that stretched over some years and required the eternal soliciting of money from friends, like Sissy Spacek, who had gone on to do well.

Eraserhead is one of the rare cult movies that deserves its cult reputation, although it is a hard movie to sit still through for a second time around. Set in a monochrome fantasy world that suggests the slums of Oz, it follows a pompadoured drudge, Henry (John Nance), through his awful life in a decaying apartment building, with occasional bursts of light relief from the fungus-cheeked songstress behind the radiator, and winds up with two extraordinarily bizarre and horrid fantasy sequences, one in which Henry's head falls off and is mined for indiarubber to be used in pencil erasers, and the other in which he cuts apart his skinned fetus of a mutant child and is deluged with a literal tide of excrement. Without really being profound, the film manages to worm its way into the hearts of the college crowd, cannily appealing—in one of Lynch's trademarks—to intellectuals who relish the multiple allusions and evasive "meanings" of the film, and to horror movie fans who just like to go along with the extreme imagery. With *The Elephant Man,* also in black and white and laden with the steamy industrial imagery of *Eraserhead,* Lynch, cued perhaps by the poignance of John Hurt's under-the-rubber performance and the presence of the sort of cast (Anthony Hopkins, John Gielgud, Freddie Jones, Michael Elphick) one would expect from some BBC-TV Masterpiece Theatre serial, opts for a more humanist approach, mellowing the sheer nastiness of the first film. In the finale, as the mutant John Merrick attends a lovingly recreated Victorian magic show, Lynch even pays homage to the gentle magician whose *The Man with the Indiarubber Head* might be cited as a precursor to *Eraserhead,* Georges Méliès.

Dune is a folly by anyone's standards, and the re-cut television version—which Lynch opted to sign with the Director's Guild pseudonym Allan Smithee—is no help in sorting out the multiple plot confusions of Frank Herbert's pretentious and unfilmable science-fiction epic. Hoping for a fusion of *Star Wars* and *Lawrence of Arabia,* De Laurentiis—who stuck by Lynch throughout the troubled $40 million production—wound up with a turgid mess, overloaded with talented performers in nothing roles, that only spottily seems to have engaged Lynch's interest, mostly when there are monsters on screen or when Kenneth McMillan is campily overdoing his perverse and evil emperor act. *Dune* landed Lynch in the doldrums, and his comeback movie, also for the forgiving De Laurentiis, was very carefully crafted to evoke the virtues and cult commercial appeal of *Eraserhead* without seeming a throwback. Drawing on *Shadow of a Doubt,* Lynch made a small-town mystery that deigns to work on a plot level, and then shot it through with his own cruel insights into the teeming, insectoid nightmare that exists beneath the red, white, and blue prettiness of the setting, coaxing sinister meaning out of resonant pop songs like "Blue Velvet" and "In Dreams," and establishing the core of a repertory company—Kyle MacLachlan of *Dune,* Isabella Rossellini, Laura Dern—who would recur in his next projects. *Blue Velvet,* far more than the muddy *Dune,* established Lynch as a master of colour in addition to his black and white skills, and also, through his handling of human monster Dennis Hopper's abuse of Rossellini, as a chronicler of extreme emotions, often combining sex and violence in one disturbing, yet undeniably appealing package.

Twin Peaks, a television series Lynch devised and for which he directed the pilot film, is a strange offshoot of *Blue Velvet,* set in a similar town and with MacLachlan again the odd investigator of a crime the nature of which is hard to define. Although it lacks the explicit tone of the earlier film, in which Dennis Hopper is given to basic outbursts like "baby wants to fuck!," *Twin Peaks* is also insidiously fascinating, using the labyrinthine plot convolutions of the typical soap opera—among other things, the show is a lineal descendant of *Peyton Place*—in addition to the puzzle-solving twists of the murder mystery to probe under the surface of a folksy America of junk food and picket fences. As a reaction to the eerie restraint of *Twin Peaks, Wild at Heart* is an undisciplined, half-satisfactory movie, a road film which evokes Elvis in Nicolas Cage's subtly overwrought performance and straggles along towards its *Wizard of Oz* finale, passing by the high points of Lynch's career (featuring players and jokes from all his earlier movies) as it plays out its couple-on-the-run storyline in a surprisingly straightforward and above-board manner. With Willem Dafoe's dirty-teeth monster replacing Dennis Hopper's gas-sniffing gangster, *Wild at Heart* echoes the violent and sexual excesses of *Blue Velvet,* including one exploding head stunt out of *The Evil Dead* and many heavy-metal-scored, heavy-duty sex scenes, but suffers perhaps from its relative predictability.

Both a genuine artist and a cunning commercial survivor, Lynch appeared—in the minds of many critics—to be one of the best hopes for cinema in the 1990s. As of 1995, however, Lynch's promise as a savior had yet to be fulfilled. Unable to get the ill-fated *Twin Peaks* out of his system after it went unceremoniously off the air without a resolution, Lynch launched a theatrical version of his TV show, *Twin Peaks: Fire Walk with Me.* Ironically, it turned out to be a prequel to the events portrayed in the series rather than a sequel, so to date we are still left without a resolution to the labyrinthine mysteries surrounding the puzzle of "who killed Laura Palmer?" Overlong and oddly underheated, it was a commercial bomb, even with hardcore *Peaks* fans.

—Kim Newman, updated by John McCarty

MACKENDRICK, Alexander

Nationality: Scottish. **Born:** Boston, 1912. **Education:** Glasgow School of Art. **Career:** Commercial artist, animator of advertising films, also worked in Holland with George Pal, 1930s; made short propaganda films for Ministry of Information, World War II; later head of documentary and newsreel department of Psychological Warfare Branch, Rome; joined Ealing Studios as scriptwriter, 1946; directed first feature, *Whisky Galore,* 1946; signed contract with Hecht-Lancaster (Harold Hecht and Burt Lancaster) to make *Sweet Smell of Success* in U.S., 1956; Dean, Film Dept. of California Institute of the Arts, Valencia, from 1969; resigned Deanship, continued to teach at CalArts, from 1978.

Films as Director:

1949 *Whisky Galore* (*Tight Little Island*) (+ co-sc)
1951 *The Man in the White Suit* (+ co-sc)
1952 *Mandy* (*The Story of Mandy*; *Crash of Silence*)
1954 *The Maggie* (*High and Dry*) (+ story)
1955 *The Ladykillers*
1957 ***Sweet Smell of Success***
1963 *Sammy Going South* (*A Boy Ten Feet Tall*)
1965 *A High Wind in Jamaica*
1967 *Oh Dad, Poor Dad, Mamma's Hung You in the Closet and I'm Feelin' So Sad* (Quine) (d add'l scenes); *Don't Make Waves*

Other Films:

1950 ***The Blue Lamp*** (Dearden) (add'l dialogue)

Publications

By MACKENDRICK: article—

Interview with Bernard Cohn, in *Positif* (Paris), February 1968.
Interview with Kate Buford, in *Film Comment* (Los Angeles), May-June 1994.

On MACKENDRICK: books—

Balcon, Michael, *A Lifetime of Films,* London, 1969.
Barr, Charles, *Ealing Studios,* London, 1977.
Perry, George, *Forever Ealing,* London, 1981.
Kemp, Philip, *Lethal Innocence: The Cinema of Alexander Mackendrick,* London, 1991.

On MACKENDRICK articles—

Cutts, John, "Mackendrick Finds the Sweet Smell of Success," in *Films and Filming* (London), June 1957.
"Alexander Mackendrick," in *Films and Filming* (London), January 1963.
Sarris, Andrew, "Oddities and One-Shots," in *Film Culture* (New York), Spring 1963.
"Mackendrick Issue" of *Dialogue on Film* (Washington, D.C.), no. 2, 1972.
Barr, Charles, "Projecting Britain and the British Character: Ealing Studios," in *Screen* (London), Summer 1974.
Goldstone, P., "Focus on Education: The Mackendrick Legacy," in *American Film* (Washington, D.C.), March 1979.
"Alexander Mackendrick," in *Film Dope* (London), June 1987.
Kemp, Philip, "Mackendrick Land," in *Sight and Sound* (London), Winter 1988/89.

* * *

In 1955 Alexander Mackendrick made *The Ladykillers,* the last of his four Ealing comedies. Two years later, in Hollywood, came his brilliantly acid study of corruption and betrayal, *Sweet Smell of Success.* At first glance, the gulf is prodigious. Yet on closer examination, it narrows considerably: the apparent contrast between the two films becomes little more than a matter of surface tone. For behind the comedies that Mackendrick made for Ealing can be detected a mordant humor, a pessimism, and even an instinct for cruelty that sets them apart from the gentle sentimentality of their stablemates (Hamer's *Kind Hearts and Coronets* always excepted). The mainstream of Ealing comedy, even including such classics as *Passport to Pimlico* and *The Lavender Hill Mob,* presents (as Charles Barr has pointed out) "a whimsical daydream of how things might be." There is little of that daydream about Mackendrick's films; at times—as in *The Ladykillers*—they edge closer to surrealist nightmare.

In *Whisky Galore* the English outsider, Captain Waggett, is subjected by islanders to continual humiliation, unalleviated even in their triumph by the slightest friendly gesture. Similarly Marshall, the American tycoon in *The Maggie,* is abused, exploited, and physically assaulted by the Scots he encounters. Both workers and bosses in *The Man in the White Suit* turn violently upon Sidney Stratton, the idealistic inventor; and *The Ladykillers* culminates in a whole string of brutal murders. Not that this blackness detracts in the least from the effectiveness of the comedy. Rather, it lends the films a biting edge that makes them all the funnier, and may well explain why they have dated far less than most other Ealing movies.

A constant theme of Mackendrick's films is the clash between innocence and experience. Innocence connotes integrity, but also blindness to the interests of others; experience brings shrewdness, but also corruption. Generally, innocence is defeated, but not always: in *The Ladykillers* it is serenely innocent Mrs. Wilberforce who survives—as does Susan Hunsecker in *Sweet Smell of Success,* albeit at a price. Children feature prominently in Mackendrick's films—especially *Mandy, Sammy Going South, The Maggie*—and often embody the principle of innocence, though again not always. In *A High Wind in Jamaica,* against all audience expectations, it is the pirates, not the children they capture, who prove to be the innocents and who suffer death for it. As so often with Mackendrick's characters, they are

Alexander Mackendrick directing Tony Curtis in *Sweet Smell of Success*

doomed by their lack of perception; trapped, like the deaf heroine of *Mandy,* in a private world, they see only what they expect to see.

Mackendrick established a reputation as an exacting and perfectionist director, bringing to his films a visual acuteness and a flair for complex fluid composition to support the tight dramatic structure. After *Sweet Smell of Success,* though, the quality of his work is generally considered to have declined, and he has made no films since 1967. A planned project on *Mary Queen of Scots* (intriguingly outlined by Mackendrick as "a sophisticated French lady landed in Boot Hill") never materialised. From 1969 to 1978 he headed an outstanding film department at the California Institute of the Arts; but the withdrawal of such a subtle and individual director from active filmmaking is greatly to be regretted.

—Philip Kemp

MADSEN, Holger *See* **HOLGER-MADSEN**

MAKAVEJEV, Dušan

Nationality: Yugoslavian. **Born:** Belgrade, 13 October 1932. **Education:** Studied psychology at Belgrade University, graduated 1955; studied direction at the Academy for Theatre, Radio, Film, and Television, Belgrade. **Military Service:** 1959-60. **Family:** Married Bojana Marijan, 1964. **Career:** Experimental filmmaker for Kino-Club, 1955-58; joined Zagreb Films, 1958; worked for Avala films, 1961; went to United States on Ford Foundation Grant, 1968; worked in United States, since 1974; instructor of film at various universities, including Columbia, Harvard, and New York.

Films as Director:

(shorts and documentaries):

1953 *Jatagan Mala* (+ sc)
1955 *Pečat* (*The Seal*) (+ sc)
1957 *Antonijevo razbijeno ogledalo* (*Anthony's Broken Mirror*) (+ sc)
1958 *Spomenicima ne treba verovati* (*Don't Believe in Monuments*) (+ sc); *Slikovnica pčelara* (*Beekeeper's Scrapbook*) (+ sc);

Prokleti praznik (*Damned Holiday*) (+ sc); *Boje sanjaju* (*Colors Are Dreaming*) (+ sc)

1959 *Sto je radnički savjet?* (*What Is a Workers' Council?*)

1961 *Eci, pec, pec* (*One Potato, Two Potato ...*) (+ sc); *Pedagoška bajka* (*Educational Fairy Tale*) (+ sc); *Osmjeh 61* (*Smile 61*) (+ sc)

1962 *Parada* (*Parade*) (+ sc); *Dole plotovi* (*Down with the Fences*) (+ sc); *Ljepotica 62* (*Miss Yugoslavia 62*) (+ sc); *Film o knjizi A.B.C.* (*Film about the Book*) (+ sc)

1964 *Nova igračka* (*New Toy*) (+ sc); *Nova domaća zivotinja* (*New Domestic Animal*) (+ sc)

(feature films):

1966 *Covek nije tica* (*Man Is Not a Bird*) (+ sc)

1967 *Ljubavni Slučaj, tragedija sluzbenice PTT* (*Love Affair; Switchboard Operator; An Affair of the Heart*) (+ sc)

1968 *Nevinost bez zaštite* (*Innocence Unprotected*) (+ sc)

1971 ***WR—Misterije organizma*** (*WR—Mysteries of the Organism*) (+ sc)

1974 *Sweet Movie* (+ co-sc)

1981 *Montenegro* (*Or Pigs and Pearls*) (+ sc)

1985 *The Coca-Cola Kid*

1989 *Manifesto* (*For a Night of Love*)

1993 *The Gorilla Bathes at Noon*

1995 *A Hole in the Soul* (+ sc, role as himself)

Publications

By MAKAVEJEV: books—

A Kiss for Komradess Slogan, 1964.

Nevinost bez zaštite [Innocence Unprotected], Zagreb, 1968.

WR—Mysteries of the Organism, New York, 1972.

Shooting the Actor, or, The Choreography of Confusion, with Simon Callow, London, 1990.

By MAKAVEJEV: articles—

"Fight Power with Spontaneity and Humor: An Interview with Dušan Makavejev," with Robert Sutton and others, in *Film Quarterly* (Berkeley), Winter 1971/72.

Interview with R. Colacielo, in *Interview* (New York), February 1972.

Interview with G. Braucourt, in *Ecran* (Paris), September/October 1972.

"Let's Put the Life Back in Political Life," interview with C. B. Thompson, in *Cinéaste* (New York), vol. 6, no. 2, 1974.

Interview with Robert Benayoun and Michel Ciment, in *Positif* (Paris), June 1974.

Interview with Edgardo Cozarinsky and Carlos Clarens, in *Film Comment* (New York), May/June 1975.

"Film Censorship in Yugoslavia," in *Film Comment* (New York), July/August 1975.

Interview with F. La Polla, in *Cineforum* (Bergamo), June/July 1986.

"Innocence Unprotected," an interview with R. Stoneman, in *Sight and Sound,* July 1992.

On MAKAVEJEV: book—

Taylor, John, *Directors and Directions,* New York, 1975.

On MAKAVEJEV: articles—

Wood, Robin, "Dušan Makavejev," in *Second Wave,* New York, 1970.

Oppenheim, O., "Makavejev in Montreal," in *Sight and Sound* (London), Spring 1970.

"Makavejev and the Mysteries of the Organism," in *Film* (London), Autumn 1971.

Robinson, David, "Joie de Vivre at the Barricades: The Films of Dušan Makavejev," in *Sight and Sound* (London), Autumn 1971.

MacBean, J. R., "Sex and Politics," in *Film Quarterly* (Berkeley), Spring 1972.

Vogel, Amos, "Makavejev: Toward the Edge of the Real ... and Over," in *Film Comment* (New York), November/December 1973.

"Dušan Makavejev," in *Fifty Major Filmmakers* edited by Peter Cowie, South Brunswick, New Jersey, 1974.

"Sweet Movie," in *Avant-Scène du Cinéma* (Paris), October 1974.

Schaub, M., "Unbeschützte und verlorene Unschuld, Dušan Makavejevs Spekulationen," in *Cinema* (Zurich), vol. 21, no. 2, 1975.

Perlmutter, R., "The Cinema of the Grotesque," in *Georgia Review* (Athens, Ohio), no. 1, 1979.

Cavell, Stanley, "On Makavejev on Bergman," in *Critical Inquiry* (Chicago), no. 2, 1979.

Kral, Petr, "Perles et Cochons: Les Fantasmes de Madame Jordan: Montenegro," in *Positif* (Paris), March 1982.

Eagle, Herbert, "Yugoslav Marxist Humanism and the Films of Dušan Makavejev," in *Politics, Art, and Commitment in the East European Cinema,* edited by David W. Paul, London, 1983.

"Dušan Makavejev," in *Film Dope* (London), December 1987.

Makavejev section of *Filmvilag,* vol. 33, no. 8, 1990.

Forgacs, I., "Ezt mondta Makavejev...," in *Filmkultura,* no. 12, 1993.

* * *

Before making his first feature film, *Man Is Not a Bird,* Makavejev had developed his filmmaking skills and formulated his chief thematic and formal concerns by producing a number of 35mm experimental shorts and documentaries. His second feature, *Love Affair,* furthered Makavejev's reputation and situated him within a growing community of Eastern European filmmakers committed to exploring the potential of the film medium by opening it up to new subject matter and experimenting with non-conventional narrative forms. *Love Affair* deals with the romance between a Hungarian-born switchboard operator, Isabella, and Ahmed, an Arab sanitation engineer, and the breakdown of the relationship, Isabella's death, and Ahmed's arrest for her murder. However, this straightforward plot is only the skeleton which supports the rest of the film. Influenced by Eisenstein and Godard, Makavejev builds an elaborate, Brechtian amalgam of documentary-like examinations of rat extermination, interviews with a sexologist and criminologist, actual stock footage of the destruction of church spires during the October Revolution, as well as almost quaint digressions on how mattress stuffing is combed and how strudel is made. Makavejev questions the nature of sexual relationships in a changing, post-revolutionary, but still puritanical society by juxtaposing ostensibly unrelated images. For example, the razing of the church spires is intercut with and comments on Isabella's seduction of Ahmed and the destruction of his archaic sexual inhibitions.

Innocence Unprotected also manifests Makavejev's interest in the dialectics of montage, the ability to create new ideas by juxtaposing incongruous or contradictory images. In this film, Makavejev rescues a little bit of "unprotected innocence" from oblivion by incorporating the original *Innocence Unprotected,* the first Serbian "all-talking" feature, into a new cinematic context. This 1940s romance-adventure—filmed by a well-known local strongman-daredevil during the Nazi Occupation, censored by the occupation government, and ironically later denounced as being Nazi-inspired—is intercut with interviews Makavejev conducted with members of the original production crew as well as newsreel footage from the period of the occupation. Moreover, Makavejev hand-tints portions of the original film to contribute to the critical distance created by the archaic quality of the footage. Perhaps more than any of his other films, *Innocence Unprotected* shows Makavejev's loving interest in traditional Yugoslavian folk culture and humor.

WR—Mysteries of the Organism deals with the sexuality of politics and the politics of sexuality. A radical condemnation of both the sterility of Stalinism and the superficial commercialism of Western capitalism, *WR* is certainly a document of its time—of Yugoslavia attempting to follow its "other road" to socialism while America fights in Vietnam and Moscow invades Czechoslovakia. Makavejev looks to Wilhelm Reich (the "WR" of the title) for enlightenment. Reich was, early in his career, one of the first to recognize the profound interconnections between socio-political structure and the individual psyche. His radical sexual ideas alienated the psychoanalytic profession and his unorthodox medical theories and practices eventually led to his imprisonment in the United States.

Although elaborate cross-cutting blends the two sections of the film, roughly the first half of *WR* is devoted to a documentary study of Wilhelm Reich's life in the United States. Interviews with Reich's therapists, Reich's relatives, even people who knew him casually, including his barber, are intercut with an examination of American sexual mores circa 1970 via interviews with Jackie Curtis, Barbara Dobson, one of the editors of *Screw* magazine, and others. The second half of the film is primarily a fictional narrative set in Belgrade, which concerns the love affair between a young female admirer of Reich (Milena) and a rather priggish and prudish Soviet ice skater named Vladimir Ilyich. Freed of his inhibitions by Milena's persistence, Vladimir makes love to her and then, unable to deal with his sexuality, decapitates her with his ice skate. However, after death, Milena's severed head continues to speak. Vladimir sings a song with a lyric written by a Soviet citizen critical of his government. *WR* ends with a photo of the smiling Reich—a sign of hope, a contradictory indication of the possibility for change and new beginnings.

WR was never released in Yugoslavia, and Makavejev made his two subsequent films, *Sweet Movie* and *Montenegro,* in the United States and Europe. Like *WR, Sweet Movie* has two parts. In the first a beauty contestant, Miss World, is wedded to and violated by Mr. Kapital and, after other humiliations, ends up in Otto Muehl's radical therapy commune. Miss World is taken in and nurtured by actual commune members who engage in various types of infantile regressions (including carrying their excrement displayed on dinner plates) as therapy. The second part of the film is an allegorical commentary on the East. A ship, with a figurehead of Karl Marx, sails about under the command of Anna Planeta, who seduces and murders young men and boys, while providing for their rebirth out of a hold filled with white sugar and corpses.

Montenegro continues this development of allegory in favor of Makavejev's earlier documentary interests. Marilyn, an American-born Swedish housewife, is lured into a world peopled by earthy and sexually active Yugoslavian immigrants who run a club called Zanzibar as an almost anarchistic communal venture. Like the heroes and heroines of Makavejev's earlier films, Marilyn cannot deal with her newly acquired sexual freedom, and she—like Ahmed, Vladimir Ilyich, and Anna Planeta—kills her lovers. *Montenegro's* linear plot contrasts sharply with the convoluted narrative structure and elaborate montage techniques characteristic of Makavejev's earlier works. While being accused of making needlessly ambiguous films with scenes of gratuitous violence and sexuality, Makavejev has consistently explored the interrelationship of sexual life and socioeconomic structure while experimenting with narrative forms that challenge traditional notions of Hollywood filmmaking.

Makavejev's seventeen years as a "knapsack director," during his exile following *WR,* were echoed in films about displaced persons, immigrants, and "nowhere men in nowhere lands." As one of his characters says, "The place which is nowhere is a true home." Another character similarly notes, "Everyone has to come from somewhere," prompting a third to reply, "Not me! I come from here!" After *Sweet Movie,* several promising projects foundered in the choppy sea of international co-financing, until Swedish producer Bo Jonsson, visiting Makavejev at Harvard University, proposed a "high-quality comedy with a popular appeal and measured eroticism," in which the director could add his "little somethings." They soon grew into the rich ethnico-socio-political dimensions of *Montenegro (Or Pigs and Pearls).* The pearl necklace of its Swedish-American heroine (Susan Ansprach) symbolizes her ego and commodity fetishism; "pigs" emblemise the funky, ego-despoiling, unbridled instincts of work-immigrants from Southeast Europe (promptly polluted by consumerism's *teasing* of real, biological, desire).

Makavejev's second comedy in the genre (comedy with psycho-political infill) came four years later, from Australia. *The Coca-Cola Kid, not* sponsored by that corporation's marketing division, concerns an enterprising young salesman who succeeds in prising open a tiny regional market, a sort of "last valley," hitherto monopolised by a local dynast's soft drink; but himself succumbs to its values. Though ten years in preparation with Australian novelist Frank Moorhouse, its *Local Hero*-type story and backwoods setting inspired less intricate detail, and a thinner intellectual texture, than the culturally mixed settings of Makavejev's richest films.

His long exile ended with *Manifesto (For a Night of Love),* by far the best of the art-house films funded, through the good offices of American Zoetrope's Tom Luddy, by Cannon-Globus (others were by Godard and Norman Mailer). As Bolsheviks of different classes and ideologies fumble their Revolution in 1920 Ruritania, Makavejev hilariously re-explores his abiding subject matter, shared with the Yugoslavian *Praxis* group of Marxist-humanist writers. His characters can only steer erratically between the four cardinal points of a spiritual compass: True Socialism (which Marxist bureaucratic classes too easily make oppressive), individualism (which Western capitalism makes smilingly rapacious); man's bodily instincts (commonly selfish and barbaric, *pace* Wilhelm Reich); and idealism (which may only camouflage the cold, abstract logic of power). Whereas "idealistic" Freudians (whether bourgeois or radical, or, like Reich, both) claim love and sex are natural but deny egoism and power, Makavejev understands that *both* instinct and idealism may spread, not just love and desire, but terror and violence. And after all, Mother Nature, like Anna Planeta, is a serial murderess: whatever lives will be killed, by *something.* Similarly, biological instincts involve, as much as sex, *food;* whence much play on bodies and nourishment. In *WR,* egg yolks, transferred unbroken from hand to hand, suggest an optimum of "communal kindness"; but even food may be over-refined (like, in *Sweet Movie,* consumerist chocolate, and the white sugar of revolutionary purity). Hence political history weighs like a nightmare on the minds of the living. And subsequent "tribal" massacres, in the former Yugoslavia and around the world, corroborate Makavejev's pessimism. Though faint hopes, and pity for history's victims, remain, his "laughter" at "mankind's follies" is more wistful, bitter, and tragic than many spectators perceive.

In his latest, largely German film, *The Gorilla Bathes at Noon,* a Red Army officer, storming Berlin in 1945, suddenly finds himself in the reunified city near a Lenin statue, which he loyally pickets, as it is marked for demolition with yellow paint, like the egg on Marxism's face. This fantasy gambit presages a return to the *Wit/Sweet Movie* genre of allegorical cinema, although the plot becomes uncertain where to go. The problem, perhaps, was topicality, for the consequences of political collapse were not yet clear enough to work on. And perhaps Makavejev's cultural background, a sort of Freudo-Marxist-Marcusian humanism, uneasily mixing economism and instinct theory, and concentrating on capitalism, cannot quite get to terms with the wider resurgence of nationalism, ethnicity, and "tribal" psychology. Though to these things the films' human stories are very sensitive.

Some spectators find that Makavejev's mixture of caricature and pessimism rather freeze their "rooting interest" in his characters, compared with his early dramas. It is a perennial problem in "serious satire." Nonetheless, Makavejev's sparkling and poetic inventions make him Eisenstein's true heir and the great reinvigorator of "intellectual cinema," integrating montage editing as one instrument in an entire orchestra, with "non-synch" sound, voice-over, music, colour, calligraphic camera, comic symbolism, dramatic fables, and visual sensuality, all weaving arguments so sophisticated that Eisenstein's look prehistoric. Where Godard faltered and fell, the Nowhere Man from ex-communist former Yugoslavia continues to blaze new trails of "philosophical cinema."

—Gina Marchetti, updated by Raymond Durgnat

MALICK, Terrence

Nationality: American. **Born:** Waco, Texas, 30 November 1943. **Education:** Harvard University, B.A., 1966; Oxford University on Rhodes Scholarship; Center for Advanced Film Studies, American Film Institute, 1969. **Career:** Journalist for *Newsweek, Life,* and the *New Yorker,* late 1960s; lecturer in philosophy, Massachusetts Institute of Technology, 1968; directed first feature, *Badlands,* 1973. **Awards:** Best Director Awards, National Society of Film Critics and New York Film Critics, 1978, and Cannes Festival, 1979, for *Days of Heaven.* **Agent:** c/o Evarts Ziegler Associates, Inc., 9255 W. Sunset Boulevard, Los Angeles, CA 90069, U.S.A.

Films as Director and Screenwriter:

1973 ***Badlands*** (+ pr, role as architect)
1978 ***Days of Heaven***

Other Films:

1969 *Lanton Mills* (short) (sc)
1972 *Pocket Money* (Rosenberg) (sc)
1974 *The Gravy Train* (co-sc, under pseudonym David Whitney)
1982 *Deadhead Miles* (Zimmerman) (co-sc) (filmed 1970)

Publications

By MALICK: articles—

"The Filming of *Badlands,*" an interview with G. R. Cook, in *Filmmakers Newsletter* (Ward Hill, Massachusetts), June 1974.
"Malick on *Badlands,*" an interview with B. Walker, in *Sight and Sound* (London), Spring 1975.
Interview with Michel Ciment, in *Positif* (Paris), June 1975.

On MALICK: articles—

Johnson, William, "*Badlands,*" in *Film Quarterly* (Berkeley), Spring 1974.
Fox, Terry Curtis, "The Last Ray of Light," in *Film Comment* (New York), September/October 1978.
Hodenfield, Chris, "Terrence Malick: *Days of Heaven*'s Image Maker," in *Rolling Stone* (New York), 16 November 1978.
Combs, Richard, "The Eyes of Texas," in *Sight and Sound* (London), Spring 1979.
Maraval, P., "Dossier: Hollywood '79: Terrence Malick," in *Cinématographe* (Paris), March 1979.
Donough, P., "West of Eden: Terrence Malick's *Days of Heaven,*" in *Post Script* (Jacksonville, Florida), Fall 1985.
"Terrence Malick," in *Film Dope* (London), December 1987.
Vancher, Andrea, "Absence of Malick," in *American Film,* February 1991.

* * *

Though he has directed only two feature films, Terrence Malick has received the kind of critical attention normally reserved for more experienced and prolific filmmakers. His career reflects a commitment to quality instead of quantity—an unusual and not always profitable gamble in the film industry.

In 1972, Malick wrote the screenplay for *Pocket Money,* which starred Paul Newman and Lee Marvin, a film memorable more for character study than story. The following year, Malick made his first feature, *Badlands.* The film was an amazing debut. Based loosely on the sensational Starkweather-Furgate murder spree, *Badlands* concerns Kit Carruthers, a twenty-five-year-old James Dean look-alike, and Holly Sargis, his fifteen-year-old girlfriend. After murdering Holly's father, they begin a flight across the northeastern United States, killing five others along the way.

This disturbing and beautiful film is narrated by Holly (Sissy Spacek), who unemotionally describes the couple's actions and feelings. Her partner in crime, Kit (Martin Sheen), is a likeable, unpredictable, and romantic killer who is so confident of his place in American history as a celebrity that he marks the spot where he is arrested, and gives away his possessions as souvenirs to police officers.

Days of Heaven, Malick's long-awaited second feature, was released five years later. The film was critically acclaimed in the United States, and Malick was named best director at the Cannes Film Festival. *Days of Heaven* is a homage to silent films (the director even includes a glimpse of Chaplin's work), with stunning visual images and little dialogue. Moving very slowly at first, the film's pace gradually accelerates as the tension heightens. Its plot and style elaborate on that of *Badlands:* the flight of two lovers following a murder, and the use of unemotional narration and offbeat characterizations.

Malick now lives in Paris, and as critics wait for his next endeavor, some wonder how the director will remain profitable to any studio with his lapses between projects, his aversion to interviews, and his refusal to help in the marketing of his films. Paramount, however, is confident of Malick's value, and has continued to send the director scripts plus a yearly stipend.

In the 1990s, Malick has not revived his career, perhaps because conditions within the industry would make it difficult for him to continue his attempts to create an American art cinema. Unlike Welles, whose lack of productivity must be traced in large measure to studio hostility to his methods and work, Malick cannot blame anyone but himself for a talent and interests that have been wasted now for almost two decades.

—Alexa Foreman, updated by R. Barton Palmer

Terrence Malick (right) with Martin Sheen on the set of *Badlands*

MALLE, Louis

Nationality: French. **Born:** Thumeries, France, 30 October 1932. **Education:** Collège des Carmes; Institut d'Études Politiques at the Sorbonne, Paris, 1951-53; Institut des Hautes Études Cinématographiques (IDHEC), 1953-54. **Family:** Married 1) Anne-Marie Deschodt, one son, one daughter (divorced 1967); 2) actress Candice Bergen, 1980, one daughter. **Career:** Assistant and cameraman to Jacques Cousteau, 1954-55; assistant to Robert Bresson on *Un Condamné à mort s'est échappé,* 1956; cameraman on Tati's *Mon Oncle,* 1957; directed first film, 1958; reported from Algeria, Vietnam, and Thailand for French Television, 1962-64; moved to India, 1968; moved to the United States, 1976; returned to France to make *Au revoir les enfants,* 1987. **Awards:** Palme d'Or, Cannes Festival, 1956, and Oscar for Best Documentary, 1957, for *The Silent World*; Prix Louis Delluc for *Ascenseur pour l'échafaud,* 1958; special jury prize, Venice Festival, for *Les Amants,* 1958; special jury prize, Venice Festival, for *Le Feu follet,* 1963; Italian Critics Association Best Film Award, for *The Fire Within,* 1964; Grand Prix du Cinema Francais, 1965, and Czechoslovakian best film award, 1966, for *Viva Maria*; Grand Prize, Melbourne Film Festival, for *Calcutta,* 1970; Prix Raoul Levy and Prix Méliès for *Lacombe, Lucien,* 1974; five Academy Award nominations, including best picture and best director, for *Atlantic City,* 1980; Golden Lion, Venice Festival, and Prix Louis Delluc, for *Au revoir les enfants,* 1987; British Academy of Film and Television Arts Awards nomination, best director, and Felix Award, European Film Awards, for *Au revoir les enfants,* 1988; elected Film Academy Fellow, British Academy of Film and Television Arts, 1991. **Died:** Of lymphoma, in Beverly Hills, California, 23 November 1995.

Films as Director:

1956 *Le Monde du silence* (*The Silent World*) (co-d, ph)
1958 *Ascenseur pour l'échafaud* (*Elevator to the Gallows*; *Frantic*) (+ pr, co-sc); *Les Amants* (*The Lovers*) (+ pr, co-sc)
1960 *Zazie dans le Métro* (*Zazie*) (+ pr, co-sc)
1962 *Vie privée* (*A Very Private Affair*) (+ pr, co-sc)
1963 *Le Feu follet* (*The Fire Within*; *A Time to Live, a Time to Die*) (+ pr, sc)
1965 *Viva Maria* (+ co-pr, co-sc)
1967 *Le Voleur* (*The Thief of Paris*) (+ pr, co-sc)
1968 "William Wilson" episode of *Histoires extraordinaires* (*Spirits of the Dead*) (+ pr, sc)
1969 *Calcutta* (+ pr, sc); *L'Inde fantôme* (*Phantom India*) (+ pr, sc) (six-hour feature presentation of TV documentary)
1971 ***Le Souffle au coeur*** (*Murmur of the Heart*) (+ pr, sc)
1972 *Humain trop humain* (+ pr, sc)
1973 *Lacombe, Lucien* (+ pr, co-sc)
1975 *Black Moon* (+ pr, co-sc)
1978 *La Petite* (+ pr, sc); *Pretty Baby* (+ pr, co-story)
1980 *Atlantic City* (+ pr, sc)
1981 *My Dinner with Andre* (+ pr, sc)
1984 *Crackers* (+ pr, sc)
1985 *Alamo Bay* (+ pr, sc); *God's Country* (+ pr, sc)
1986 *And the Pursuit of Happiness* (+ pr, sc)
1987 *Au Revoir les enfants* (*Goodbye, Children*) (+ pr, sc)
1990 *Milou en Mai* (*May Fools*) (+ pr, sc)
1992 *Damage*
1994 *Vanya on 42nd Street*

Other Films:

1969 *La Fiancée du pirate* (Kaplan) (role)

Publications

By MALLE: books—

Lacombe, Lucien, with Patrick Modiano, New York, 1975.
Louis Malle par Louis Malle, with S. Kant, Paris, 1978.
Au revoir les enfants, Paris, 1989.
Milou en mai, with Jean-Claude Carrière, Paris, 1990.
Malle on Malle, Paris, 1993.

By MALLE: articles—

"Avec *Pickpocket,* Bresson a trouvé," in *Arts* (Paris), 3 January 1960.
"*Les Amants,*" (text) in *L'Avant-Scène du Cinéma* (Paris), 15 March 1961.
"*Le Feu follet,*" (text) in *L'Avant-Scène du Cinéma* (Paris), 15 October 1963.
"Louis Malle: Murmuring From the Heart," with N. Pasquariello, in *Inter/View* (New York), July 1972.
"*Phantom India,*" with E.L. Rodrigues, in *Film Heritage* (New York), Fall 1973.
"Louis Malle on *Lacombe Lucien,*" in *Film Comment* (New York), September/October 1974.
"Like Acid," interview with Gordon Gow, in *Films and Filming* (London), December 1975.
"From *The Lovers* to *Pretty Baby,*" interview with Dan Yakir, in *Film Quarterly* (Berkeley), Summer 1978.
"Creating a Reality That Doesn't Exist," interview with A. Horton, in *Literature/Film Quarterly* (Salisbury, Maryland), no. 2, 1979.
Interview with P. Carcassonne and J. Fieschi, in *Cinématographe* (Paris), March/April 1981.
Interview in *Post Script* (Jacksonville, Florida), Autumn 1982 and Winter 1983.
Interview in *Jeune Cinema* (Paris), June/July 1987.
Interview in *Cineforum* (Bergamo), June/July 1987.
Interview in *Cahiers du Cinema* (Paris), October 1987.
Interview with Robert Benayoun, and others, in *Positif* (Paris), October 1987.
"Focus: *Au Revoir les Enfants,*" an interview with D. Chase, in *American Film* (New York), January/February 1988.
"Off screen: Louis Malle, Remembrance of Things Past," interview with Stephen Harvey, in *The Village Voice* (New York), 23 February 1988.
"Movies: Childhood's End," interview with Elvis Mitchell, in *Rolling Stone* (New York), 24 March 1988.
"Dialogue on Film: Louis Malle," in *American Film* (Washington, D.C.), April 1989.
Interview with Candice Bergen in *Interview* (New York), June 1990.
"My Discussion with Louis," an interview with George Hickenlooper, in *Cineaste* (New York), vol. 18, no. 2, 1991.
Interview with Andre Gregory in *Vogue,* November 1994.

On MALLE: books—

Chapier, Henri, *Louis Malle,* Paris, 1964.

On MALLE: articles—

Strick, P., "Louis Malle," in *Film* (London), Spring 1963.
Ledieu, Christian, "Louis Malle détruit son passé à chaque nouveau film," in *Arts* (Paris), 9 October 1963.
Gow, Gordon, "Louis Malle's France," in *Films and Filming* (London), August 1964.
Price, James, "Night and Solitude: The Cinema of Louis Malle," in *London Magazine,* September 1964.

Louis Malle

"Director of the Year," *International Film Guide* (London, New York), 1965.

Lej, Russell, "Louis Malle," in the *New Left Review* (New York), March/April 1965.

McVay, D., "Louis Malle," in *Focus on Film* (London), Summer 1974.

"Black Moon," in *Avant-Scène du Cinéma* (Paris), December 1975.

Rollet, R.T., and others, "The Documentary Films of Louis Malle," in special Malle issue of *Film Library Quarterly* (New York), vol. 9, no. 4, 1977.

Article in *Cahiers du Cinema* (Paris), July/August 1987.

Chemasi, A., "*Pretty Baby*: Love in Storyville," in *American Film* (Washington, D.C.), November 1977.

"Louis Malle," in *Film Dope* (London), December 1987.

Indsorf, Annette, "Coming Home," in *Premiere* (New York), February 1988.

Denby, David, "Murmurs of an Expatriate's Heart," in *Premiere* (New York), May 1988.

"*Au revoir les enfants* Issue" of *Avant-Scène du Cinéma* (Paris), July 1988.

Prédal, René, "L'oeuvre de Louis Malle, ou les étapes d'une évolution personnelle," in *Jeune Cinéma* (Paris), September/October 1988.

Chase, D., article in *Millimeter* (New York), January 1989.

Roud, Richard, "Malle x 4," in *Sight and Sound* (London), Spring 1989.

Chutnow, P., "Louis Malle Diagnoses His *Murmur of the Heart,*" in *New York Times,* 19 March 1989.

"Louis Malle Works Both Sides of the Pond," in *Variety,* 21 March 1990.

Bernstein, R., "Malle Uncorks the '68 Crop", in *New York Times,* 17 June 1990.

Bishop, K., "My dejeuner with Louis," in *American Film* (New York), July 1990.

Weinraub, Bernard, "Louis Malle Cuts a Film and Grows Indignant," in *The New York Times,* 22 December 1992.

Guare, John, article in *New Yorker* (New York), 21 March 1994.

* * *

In the scramble for space and fame that became the *nouvelle vague,* Louis Malle began with more hard experience than Godard, Truffaut, or Chabrol, and he showed in *Ascenseur pour l'échafaud* that his instincts for themes and collaborators were faultless. Henri Decaë's low-light photography and Malle's use of Jeanne Moreau established him as emblematic of the new French cinema. But the *Cahiers* trio with their publicist background made artistic hay while Malle persisted in a more intimate voyage of discovery with his lovely star. As the cresting new wave battered at the restrictions of conventional narrative technique, Malle created a personal style, sexual and emotional, which was to sustain him while flashier colleagues failed. Of the new wave survivors, he is the most old-fashioned, the most erotic, and, arguably, the most widely successful.

Re-viewing reveals *Ascenseur* as clumsy and improbable, a failure redeemed only by the Moreau and Maurice Ronet performances. A flair for coaxing the unexpected from his stars had often saved Malle from the consequences of too-reverent respect for production values, a penchant for burnished low-lit interiors being his most galling stylistic weakness. But playing Bardot against type in *Vie privée* as a parody of the harried star, and using Moreau as one of a pair of comic Western trollops (in *Viva Maria*) provided an indication of the irony that was to make his name.

Thereafter Malle became a gleeful chronicler of the polymorphously perverse. Moreau's hand falling eloquently open on the sheet in *Les Amants* as she accepts the joy of cunnilingus is precisely echoed in her genuflection to fellate a yoked George Hamilton in *Viva Maria.* Incest in *Souffle au coeur,* child prostitution in *Pretty Baby,* and, in particular, the erotic and sadomasochistic overtones of Nazism in *Lacombe, Lucien* found in Malle a skillful, committed, and sensual celebrant.

Malle's Indian documentaries of 1969 belong more to the literature of the mid-life crisis than to film history. *Black Moon* likewise explores an arid emotional *couloir.* Malle returned to his richest sources with the U.S.-based films of the late 1970s and after. *Pretty Baby, Atlantic City, My Dinner with Andre,* and *Alamo Bay* delight in overturning the stones under which closed communities seethe in moist darkness. The ostensible source material of the first, Bellocq's New Orleans brothel photographs, receives short shrift in favour of a lingering interest in the pre-pubescent Brooke Shields. *Atlantic City* relishes the delights of post-climactic potency, giving Burt Lancaster one of his richest roles as the fading ex-strong-arm man, dubbed "Numb Nuts" by his derisive colleagues. He seizes a last chance for sexual passion and effective action as the friend and protector of Susan Sarandon's character, an ambitious nightclub croupier.

My Dinner with Andre focuses with equal originality on the social eroticism of urban intellectuals. A globe-trotting theatrical voluptuary reviews his thespian conquests to the grudging admiration of his stay-at-home colleague. An account of theatrical high-jinks in a Polish wood with Jerzy Grotowski and friends becomes in Andre Gregory's fruity re-telling, and with Malle's lingering attention, something very like an orgy. Again, production values intrude on, even dominate the action; mirrors, table settings, the intrusive old waiter, and even the food itself provide a rich, decorated background that adds considerably to the sense of occasion. Malle sends his audiences out of the cinema conscious of having taken part in an event as filling as a five-course meal.

Given this general richness, it may be by contrast that certain of Malle's quieter, less vivid works shine. *Zazie dans le Métro,* his fevered version of Queneau's farce, marked his first break with the stable pattern of the new wave. Compared with Godard's *Une Femme est une femme,* it shows Malle as the more skillful of the two at remaking the genre film. The terse *Le Feu follet,* a vehicle for Maurice Ronet adapted from F. Scott Fitzgerald's *Babylon Revisited,* showed Malle moving towards what had become by then the standard "new" French film, characterized by the work of the so-called "Left Bank" group of Resnais, Varda, Rivette, and Rohmer. But again Malle found in the character a plump, opulent self-regard that turned *Le Feu follet,* despite its black and white cinematography and solemn style, into a celebration of self-pity, with Ronet at one point caressing the gun with which he proposes to put an end to his life. Like the relish with which Belmondo's gentleman thief in *Le Voleur* savours the objects he steals, Malle's love of physicality, of weight and color and texture, seems so deeply rooted as to be almost religious. (And Malle did, after all, work as assistant to Bresson on *Un Condamné à mort s'est échappé.*)

The latter stages of Malle's career included one well-publicized fiasco and two very different but equally brilliant films. The former is *Damage,* a boring adaptation of Josephine Hart's best-seller, crammed with boring sex footage of Jeremy Irons (as a British politician) and Juliette Binoche (as his son's girlfriend, with whom he commences an affair). The film is of note only for the hubbub created when Malle was forced to edit footage to earn the film an R (rather than NC-17) rating, and for Miranda Richardson's brief but riveting presence as Irons' rejected wife.

Au revoir les enfants, on the other hand, is as fine a film as Malle ever has made. It is set at that point in time, if such a moment can be measured, in which childhood inevitably and irrevocably ends. The film is a heartbreaking autobiographical drama which tells the story of Julien Quentin, a universal 11-year-old: a spirited prankster who attends a rural Catholic boarding school in Occupied France. Julien senses something unusual about a new classmate, a sweet-faced, bushy-haired, exceptionally intelligent boy called Jean Bonnet. Jean really is a Jew, in hiding at Julien's school. And Julien is oblivious to what Jean knows all to well: In Occupied France, it's highly dangerous—and nearly always fatal—to be Jewish. The film, ultimately, is a story of heroes and villains, of those who will risk their all to shelter the needy and those who will collaborate with the enemy to fill their pockets or gain a false sense of power. Malle slowly, carefully introduces you to his characters, so the resulting impact of the unfolding events is that much more profound. One example of Malle's mastery: Julien and Jean become lost in a forest, and are come upon by German soldiers. Jean's sense of all-encompassing terror, revealed in a split second as he panics and runs, is explicitly real. Additionally, there is a sequence in which the students come together for some entertainment and laugh at Chaplin cavorting in *The Immigrant.* Here, Malle communicates how film can be a true universal language, how the genius of an artist such as Chaplin is timeless. In its overall setting and view of life and loyalty in Occupied France, *Au revoir les enfants* is related thematically to *Lacombe, Lucien.* Julien's feelings for his mother, as personified by his sniffing for her scent after reading one of her letters, mirrors the intense mother-son relationship in *Murmur of the Heart.*

Vanya on 42nd Street, which reunites Wallace Shawn and Andre Gregory, the entire cast of *My Dinner With Andre,* is as stunningly original as the earlier film. The setting is a crumbling theater in midtown Manhattan that once was home to the Ziegfeld Follies. The film opens with actors converging on the theater, where they will rehearse a stage production of an adaptation by David Mamet of Chekhov's *Uncle Vanya.* Gregory is the director, while Shawn plays the title role. As the rehearsal proceeds, *Vanya on 42nd Street* becomes at once a highly cinematic example of filmed theater and an intimate look at the illusion that is the theater.

Sensual and perverse, Malle is an unlikely artist to have sprung from the reconstructed film-buffs of the *nouvelle vague.* It is with his early mentors—Bresson, Cousteau, Tati—that he seems, artistically and spiritually, to belong, rather than with Melville, spiritual hero of the *Cahiers* group, and there is a strong flavour of essentially French autobiographical soul searching in his *Au revoir les enfants* and *Milou en mai.* If Truffaut turned into the René Clair of the new French cinema, Malle may yet become its Max Ophüls.

—John Baxter, updated by Rob Edelman

MAMOULIAN, Rouben

Nationality: American. **Born:** Tiflis, Caucasia, Russia, 8 October 1897; became U.S. citizen, 1930. **Education:** Lycée Montaigne, Paris; gymnasium in Tiflis; University of Moscow; Vakhtangov Studio Theatre, Moscow. **Family:** Married Azadia Newman, 1945. **Career:** Stage director in London, from 1920; production director of Eastman Theater, Rochester, New York, 1923-26; directed *Porgy* on Broadway,

Rouben Mamoulian

1927; signed to Paramount, directed first film, 1929; stage director, especially of musicals, through the 1940s. **Awards:** Best Direction, New York Film Critics, for *The Gay Desperado,* 1936; Award of Excellence, Armenian American Bicentennial Celebration, 1976. **Died:** In Los Angeles, 4 December 1987.

Films as Director:

1929 *Applause*
1931 *City Streets*
1932 ***Dr. Jekyll and Mr. Hyde*** (+ pr); *Love Me Tonight* (+ pr)
1933 *Song of Songs* (+ pr); *Queen Christina*
1934 *We Live Again*
1935 *Becky Sharp*
1936 *The Gay Desperado*
1937 *High, Wide and Handsome*
1939 *Golden Boy*
1940 *The Mark of Zorro*
1941 *Blood and Sand*
1942 *Rings on Her Fingers*
1948 *Summer Holiday*
1957 *Silk Stockings*

Publications

By MAMOULIAN: books—

Abigail, New York, 1964.
Hamlet Revised and Interpreted, New York, 1965.
Rouben Mamoulian: Style Is the Man, edited by James Silke, Washington, D.C., 1971.

By MAMOULIAN: articles—

"Some Problems in the Direction of Color Pictures," in *International Photographer,* July 1935; also in *Positif* (Paris), September 1986.
"Controlling Color for Dramatic Effect," in *American Cinematographer* (Los Angeles), June 1941; also in *Hollywood Directors 1941-1976,* edited by Richard Koszarski, Oxford, 1977.
"Bernhardt versus Duse," in *Theatre Arts* (New York), September 1957.
"Painting the Leaves Black," an interview with David Robinson, in *Sight and Sound* (London), Summer 1961.
Interview with Jean Douchet and Bertrand Tavernier, in *Positif* (Paris), no. 64-65, 1965.
Article in *Interviews with Film Directors,* by Andrew Sarris, Indianapolis, 1967.
Interview in *The Celluloid Muse,* edited by Charles Higham and Joel Greenberg, London, 1969.
"*Dr. Jekyll and Mr. Hyde,*" an interview with T.R. Atkins, in *Film Journal* (New York), January/March 1973.
"Bulletin Board: Mamoulian on Griffith," in *Action* (Los Angeles), September/October 1975.
Interview with J.A. Gallagher and M.A. Amoruco, in *Velvet Light Trap* (Madison, Wisconsin), no. 19, 1982.
Interview with H.A. Hargrave, in *Literature/Film Quarterly* (Salisbury, Maryland), vol. 10, no. 4, October 1982.
"Dialogue on Film: Rouben Mamoulian," in *American Film* (Washington, D.C.), January/February 1983.

On MAMOULIAN: books—

Milne, Tom, *Rouben Mamoulian,* London, 1969.
Prinzler, Hans Helmut, and Antje Goldau, *Rouben Mamoulian: Eine Dokumentation,* Berlin, 1987.

On MAMOULIAN: articles—

Horgan, P., "Rouben Mamoulian: The Start of a Career," in *Films in Review* (New York), August/September 1973.
McCarthy, T., obituary, in *Variety* (New York), 9 December 1987.
Hanke, K., "Rouben Mamoulian," in *Films in Review* (New York), August/September 1988.

* * *

Rouben Mamoulian is certainly one of the finest directors in American film history. While not considered strictly an *auteur* with a unifying theme running through his films, the importance of each of his movies on an individual basis is significant. Mamoulian did not have a large output, having completed only sixteen assignments in his twenty-year career in motion pictures, principally because he was also very active in the theater. His most famous stage successes were the highly innovative productions of Richard Rodgers and Oscar Hammerstein II's musicals *Oklahoma!* and *Carousel* in the mid-1940s.

Mamoulian's first film, *Applause,* is a poignant story of a third-rate vaudevillian played by the popular singer Helen Morgan. The first film to utilize two sound tracks instead of one to produce a better quality sound, *Applause* is also noteworthy for its innovative use of a moving camera.

Mamoulian's third film, *Dr. Jekyll and Mr. Hyde,* is still regarded by most historians as the definitive film version of the Robert Louis Stevenson novella, as well as being one of the best horror films of all time. Yet it would be doing the film a disservice to call it "just" a horror movie. The use of light and shadows, the depth of emotion expressed by the main character, and the evocation of the evil hidden in all men make it a classic. For the time it was a very sensual film. Miriam Hopkins as Ivy Pearson is not just a girl from the lower strata of society, as the character was in other versions. In Mamoulian's film she is deliberately sensual. Fredric March, in a truly magnificent performance, is troubled by his desire for Ivy long before he turns into Hyde, which is especially evident in the erotic dream sequence. What Mamoulian was able to do in this film is show the simultaneous existence of good and evil in Jekyll before it erupts into the drug-induced schizophrenic manifestation of Mr. Hyde.

Becky Sharp, although not particularly noteworthy for its dramatic style, is today remembered as being the first film in the three-strip Technicolor process. Unusually for a director more closely associated with the stage than film, Mamoulian tried to learn and perfect virtually all of the techniques of filmmaking, and he could be accomplished in almost any genre: horror, musical, swashbuckler, or historical drama. Perhaps the only genre at which he was not successful was light comedy. His only real comedy, *Rings on Her Fingers,* is entertaining, but does not live up to the standards which he set in his other films. The three previous films, *Golden Boy, The Mark of Zorro,* and *Blood and Sand,* were all very successful films which are still applauded by critics and audiences alike.

Mamoulian's last film, *Silk Stockings,* was a very popular adaption of the musical play derived from *Ninotchka,* with a lively score by Cole Porter. The combination of Cyd Charisse and Fred Astaire in the lead roles was naturally responsible for a great part of the movie's success, and Mamoulian's direction and staging allowed their talents to be shown to their best advantage. *Silk Stockings* has a variety of delightful "specialty" numbers which do not detract from the main action, notably "Stereophonic Sound," as well as some charming character roles played by Peter Lorre, Jules Munshin, and George Tobias.

Rouben Mamoulian was one of the most talented, creative filmmakers of all time, and while his films are few, virtually every one is a tribute to his genius.

—Patricia King Hanson

MANKIEWICZ, Joseph L.

Nationality: American. **Born:** Joseph Leo Mankiewicz in Wilkes-Barre, Pennsylvania, 11 February 1909. **Education:** Stuyvesant High School, New York; Columbia University, B.A., 1928. **Family:** Married 1) Elizabeth Young, 1934 (divorced 1937), one son; 2) Rosa Stradner, 1939 (died 1958), two sons; 3) Rosemary Matthews, 1962, one daughter. **Career:** Reporter for *Chicago Tribune,* and stringer for *Variety* in Berlin, 1928; with help of brother Herman, became junior writer at Paramount, 1929; writer for MGM, 1933, then producer, from 1935; contract taken over by Twentieth Century-Fox, 1943; directed *La Bohème* for Metropolitan Opera, New York, 1952; formed Figaro Inc., independent production company, 1953. **Awards:** Academy Awards for Best Director and Best Screenplay, for *A Letter to Three Wives,* 1949, and for Best Director and Best Screenplay, for *All about Eve,* 1950. **Died:** 5 February 1993.

Films as Director:

1946 *Dragonwyck* (+ sc); *Somewhere in the Night* (+ co-sc)
1947 *The Late George Apley*; *The Ghost and Mrs. Muir*
1948 *Escape*
1949 *A Letter to Three Wives* (+ sc); *House of Strangers* (+ co-sc, uncredited)
1950 *No Way Out* (+ co-sc); ***All about Eve*** (+ sc)
1951 *People Will Talk* (+ sc)
1952 *Five Fingers* (+ dialogue, uncredited)
1953 *Julius Caesar* (+ sc)
1954 *The Barefoot Contessa* (+ sc)
1955 *Guys and Dolls* (+ sc)
1958 *The Quiet American* (+ sc)
1959 *Suddenly, Last Summer*
1963 *Cleopatra* (+ co-sc)
1967 *The Honey Pot* (+ co-p, sc)
1970 *There Was a Crooked Man ...* (+ pr)
1972 *Sleuth*

Other Films:

1929 *Fast Company* (Sutherland) (sc, dialogue)
1930 *Slightly Scarlet* (co-sc); *The Social Lion* (Sutherland) (sc, adaptation and dialogue); *Only Saps Work* (Gardner and Knopf) (sc, dialogue)
1931 *The Gang Buster* (Sutherland) (sc, dialogue); *Finn and Hattie* (Taurog) (sc, dialogue); *June Moon* (Sutherland) (co-sc); *Skippy* (Taurog) (co-sc); *Newly Rich* (*Forbidden Adventure*) (co-sc); *Sooky* (Taurog) (co-sc)
1932 *This Reckless Age* (sc); *Sky Bride* (co-sc); *Million Dollar Legs* (Cline) (co-sc); "Rollo and the Roadhogs" and "The Three Marines" sketches of *If I Had a Million* (sc)
1933 *Diplomaniacs* (co-sc); *Emergency Call* (co-sc); *Too Much Harmony* (Sutherland) (sc); *Alice in Wonderland* (McLeod) (co-sc)
1934 *Manhattan Melodrama* (Van Dyke, W.S.) (co-sc); *Our Daily Bread* (Vidor) (sc, dialogue); *Forsaking All Others* (Van Dyke, W.S.) (sc)
1935 *I Live My Life* (Van Dyke, W.S.) (sc)
1936 *Three Godfathers* (pr); **Fury** (Lang) (pr, co-story, uncredited); *The Gorgeous Hussy* (Brown) (pr); *Love on the Run* (Van Dyke, W.S.) (pr)
1937 *The Bride Wore Red* (Arzner) (pr); *Double Wedding* (pr)
1938 *Mannequin* (Borzage) (pr); *Three Comrades* (Borzage) (pr); *The Shopworn Angel* (pr); *The Shining Hour* (Borzage) (pr); *A Christmas Carol* (pr)
1939 *The Adventures of Huckleberry Finn* (*Huckleberry Finn*) (pr)
1940 *Strange Cargo* (Borzage) (pr); ***The Philadelphia Story*** (Cukor) (pr)
1941 *The Wild Man of Borneo* (pr); *The Feminine Touch* (Van Dyke, W.S.) (pr)
1942 *Woman of the Year* (Stevens) (pr); *Cairo* (Van Dyke, W.S.) (pr); *Reunion in France* (pr)
1944 *The Keys of the Kingdom* (Stahl) (pr, co-sc)

Publications

By MANKIEWICZ: books—

More about All about Eve, with Gary Carey, New York, 1972.

By MANKIEWICZ: articles—

"Putting on the Style," in *Films and Filming* (London), January 1960.
"Measure for Measure: Interview with Joseph L. Mankiewicz," with Jacques Bontemps and Richard Overstreet, in *Cahiers du Cinema in English* (New York), February 1967.
"Auteur de films! Auteur de films!," in *Positif* (Paris), September 1973.
Interview with Michel Ciment, in *Positif* (Paris), September 1973.
Interview with A. Charbonnier and D. Rabourdin, in *Cinéma* (Paris), June 1981.
Interview with David Shipman, in *Films and Filming* (London), November 1982.

On MANKIEWICZ: books—

Taylor, John, *Joseph L. Mankiewicz: An Index to His Work,* London, 1960.
Brodsky, Jack, and Nathan Weiss, *The Cleopatra Papers: A Private Correspondence,* New York, 1963.
Geist, Kenneth, *Pictures Will Talk,* New York, 1978.
Dick, Bernard F., *Joseph L. Mankiewicz,* Boston, 1983.
La Polla, Franco, *L'Insospettabile Joseph Leo Mankiewicz,* Venice, 1987.

On MANKIEWICZ: articles—

Nugent, Frank, "All about Joe," in *Collier's* (New York), 24 March 1951.
Reid, John, "Cleo's Joe," in *Films and Filming* (London), August and September 1963.
Göw, Gordon, "Cocking a Snook," in *Films and Filming* (London), November 1970.
Springer, John, "The Films of Joseph Mankiewicz," in *Films in Review* (New York), March 1971.
Segond, J., "More about Joseph L. Mankiewicz," in *Positif* (Paris), September 1973.
Geist, K., "Mankiewicz: The Thinking Man's Director," in *American Film* (Washington, D.C.), April 1978.
Tesson, Charles, "All about Mankiewicz," in *Cahiers du Cinéma* (Paris), October 1980.
Charbonnier, A., "Dossier-auteur (II): Joseph L. Mankiewicz—le temps et la parole," in *Cinéma* (Paris), July/August 1981.
Farber, S., and M. Green, "Family Plots," in *Film Comment* (New York), July/August 1984.
Buckley, M., and J. Nangle, "The Regency Salutes the Brothers Mankiewicz," in *Films in Review* (New York), October and November 1984.
"Joseph L. Mankiewicz," in *Film Dope* (London), December 1987.

* * *

Joseph L. Mankiewicz

Few of Mankiewicz's contemporaries experimented so radically with narrative form. In *The Barefoot Contessa,* Mankiewicz (who wrote most of the films he directed) let a half-dozen voice-over narrators tell the Contessa's story, included flashbacks within flashbacks, and even showed one event twice (the slapping scene in the restaurant) from two different points of view. Multiple narrators tell the story in *All about Eve,* too, and in the non-narrated framing story for that film, Mankiewicz uses slow motion to make it seem as if the elapsed time between the beginning of the film and the end is only a few seconds. For much of the film, *The Quiet American* also has a narrator, and he seems almost totally omniscient. Apparently, he looks back at events with a firm understanding of their development and of the motivation of the people involved. But in the end, we find out that the narrator was wrong about practically everything, and so gave us an inaccurate account of things. *A Letter to Three Wives* is made up, primarily, of several lengthy flashbacks, and hallucinogenic flashback sequences provide the payoff to the story in Mankiewicz's adaption of the Tennessee Williams play *Suddenly Last Summer.*

Mankiewicz's films, then, stand out in part because of the way they tell their stories. But there are also thematic motifs that turn up again and again, and one of the most important is the impact of the dead upon the living. Frequently, a dead character is more important in a Mankiewicz film than any living one. *The Late George Apley,* of course, concerns someone who has already died. Understanding a mother's dead son is the key for the psychiatrist in *Suddenly Last Summer.* In *The Ghost and Mrs. Muir,* it is the presence of the non-corporeal sea captain that makes the film so entertaining. *The Barefoot Contessa* opens with the Contessa's funeral, and then various mourners tell us what they know about the woman who has just been buried. And, of course, a famous funeral scene forms the centerpiece of another Mankiewicz film: Mark Antony's oration in *Julius Caesar.* It is Antony's stirring performance as a eulogist that turns his countrymen against Brutus.

Indeed, Mankiewicz's films deal constantly with the notion of effective and highly theatrical performance. *All about Eve,* for instance, is all about performing, since it concerns people who work on the Broadway stage. The barefoot contessa goes from cabaret dancer to Hollywood star. In *The Honey Pot,* an aging man pretends to be dying, to see how it affects his mistress. And in *Sleuth,* one marvels at the number of disguises worn by one man in his attempt to gain revenge on another.

Perhaps because he began as a screenwriter, Mankiewicz has often been thought of as a scenarist first and a director only second. But not only was he an eloquent scriptwriter, he was also an elegant visual stylist whose talents as a director far exceeded his reputation. He is one of the few major American directors who was more appreciated during the early years of his career than during the later stages. He won consecutive Best Director Academy Awards in 1949 and 1950 (for *A Letter to Three Wives* and *All about Eve*), but after the 1963 disaster *Cleopatra,* Mankiewicz's standing as a filmmaker declined rapidly.

—Eric Smoodin

MANN, Anthony

Nationality: American. **Born:** Anton or Emil Bundsmann in Point Loma or San Diego, California, 1907. **Education:** Educated in New York City public schools. **Family:** Married 1) Mildred Kenyon, 1931 (divorced 1956), one son, one daughter; 2) Sarita Montiel, 1957 (marriage annulled 1963); 3) Anna (Mann), one son. **Career:** Began work in theatre following father's death, 1923; production manager for Theater Guild, New York, from late 1920s, then director, 1933; director for Federal Theater Project, New York, 1936-38; talent scout for David Selznick, and casting director, Hollywood, 1938; assistant director at Paramount, 1939; signed to Republic Pictures, 1943, to R.K.O., 1945, then to MGM, 1949; withdrew from *Spartacus* after quarrelling with Kirk Douglas, 1960. **Died:** During shooting of last film, in Germany, 29 April 1967.

Films as Director:

1942 *Dr. Broadway*; *Moonlight in Havana*
1943 *Nobody's Darling*
1944 *My Best Gal*; *Strangers in the Night*
1945 *The Great Flamarion*; *Two O'Clock Courage*; *Sing Your Way Home*
1946 *Strange Impersonation*; *The Bamboo Blonde*
1947 *Desperate*; *Railroaded*
1948 *T-Men* (+ co-sc, uncredited); *Raw Deal*; *He Walked by Night* (co-d, uncredited)
1949 *Reign of Terror* (*The Black Book*); *Border Incident*
1950 *Side Street*; *Devil's Doorway*; *The Furies*; *Winchester '73*
1951 *The Tall Target*
1952 *Bend of the River*
1953 *The Naked Spur*; *Thunder Bay*
1954 *The Glenn Miller Story*
1955 *The Far Country*; *Strategic Air Command*; *The Man from Laramie*; *The Last Frontier*
1956 *Serenade*
1957 *Men in War*; *The Tin Star*
1958 *God's Little Acre*; *Man of the West*
1961 *Cimarron*; *El Cid*
1964 *The Fall of the Roman Empire*
1965 *The Heroes of Telemark*
1968 *A Dandy in Aspic* (co-d)

Publications

By MANN: articles—

Interview, in *Cahiers du Cinéma* (Paris), March 1957.
"Now You See It: Landscape and Anthony Mann," interview with J.H. Fenwick and Jonathan Green-Armytage, in *Sight and Sound* (London), Autumn 1965.
"A Lesson in Cinema," interview with Jean-Claude Missiaen, in *Cahiers du Cinema in English* (New York), December 1967.
Interview with Christopher Wicking and Barrie Pattison, in *Screen* (London), July/October 1969.
"Empire Demolition," in *Hollywood Directors 1941-1976,* edited by Richard Koszarski, New York, 1977.

On MANN: books—

Missiaen, Jean-Claude, *Anthony Mann,* Paris, 1964.
Kitses, Jim, *Horizons West,* Bloomington, Indiana, 1970.
Wright, Will, *Sixguns and Society,* Berkeley, California, 1975.
Basinger, Jeanine, *Anthony Mann,* Boston, 1979.

On MANN: articles—

Reid, J.H., "Mann and His Environment," in *Films and Filming* (London), January 1962.
Reid, J.H., "Tension at Twilight," in *Films and Filming* (London), February 1962.

Anthony Mann directing *The Man from Laramie*

Wagner, Jean, "Anthony Mann," in *Anthologie du Cinéma* (Paris), vol. 4, 1968.

Handzo, Stephen, "Through the Devil's Doorway: The Early Westerns of Anthony Mann," in *Bright Lights* (Los Angeles), Summer 1976.

Smith, Robert, "Mann in the Dark," in *Bright Lights* (Los Angeles), Fall 1976.

"Special Mann Double Issue" of *Movietone News* (Seattle), Fall 1978.

Miller, Don, "Eagle-Lion: The Violent Years," in *Focus on Film* (London), November 1978.

Willeman, Paul, "Anthony Mann—Looking at the Male," in *Framework* (Norwich, England), Summer 1981.

Pulleine, Tim, "History, Drama, Abstraction: Mann's Route to Madrid," and "Mann's Route to Madrid, Part II," in *Monthly Film Bulletin* (London), March and April 1982.

"Anthony Mann," in *Film Dope* (London), December 1987.

* * *

Though he incidentally directed films in various genres (the musical, the war movie, the spy drama), Anthony Mann's career falls into three clearly marked phases: the early period of low-budget, B-feature films noir; the central, most celebrated period of westerns, mostly with James Stewart; and his involvement in the epic (with Samuel Bronston as producer). All three periods produced distinguished work (in particular, *El Cid* has strong claims to be considered the finest of all the wide screen historical epics of the 1950s and 1960s, and the first half of *The Fall of the Roman Empire* matches it), but it is the body of work from the middle period in which Mann's achievement is most consistent and on which his reputation largely depends.

The first of the Stewart westerns, *Winchester '73,* contains most of the major components Mann was to develop in the series that followed. There is the characteristic use of landscape—never for the superficial beauty or mere pictorial effect that is a cliché of the genre, nor to ennoble the human figures through monumental grandeur and harmonious man-in-nature compositions, as in the classical westerns of Ford. In Mann, the function of landscape is primarily dramatic, and nature is felt as inhospitable, indifferent, or hostile. If there is a mountain, it will have to be climbed, arduously and painfully; barren rocks provide a favourite location for a shoot-out, offering partial cover but also the continued danger of the ricochet. The preferred narrative structure of the films is the journey, and its stages are often marked by a symbolic progression in landscape, from fertile valley to bare rock or snow-covered peak, corresponding to a stripping-away of the trappings of civilization and civilized behavior. *Bend of the River* represents the most systematic treatment of this prior to *Man of the West. Winchester '73* also establishes the Mann hero ("protagonist" might be a better word): neurotic, obsessive, driven, usually motivated by a desire for revenge that reduces him emotionally and morally to a brutalized condition scarcely superior to that of the villain. Hero and villain, indeed, become mirror reflections of one another: in *Winchester '73* they are actually brothers (one has murdered the father, the other seeks revenge); in *Bend of the River,* both are ex-gunfighters, Stewart bearing the mark around his neck of the hangman's noose from which, at the beginning of the film, he saves Arthur Kennedy. Violence in Mann's westerns is never glorified: it is invariably represented as ugly, disturbing, and painful (emotionally as much as physically), and this is true as much when it is inflicted by the heroes as by the villains.

Mann's supreme achievement is certainly *Man of the West,* the culmination of the Stewart series despite the fact that the Stewart role is taken over by Gary Cooper. It remains one of the great American films and one of the great films *about* America. It carries to their fullest development all the components described above, offering a magnificently complete realization of their significance. Cooper plays Link Jones (the "link" between the old West and the new), a reformed outlaw stranded in the wilderness while on a mission to hire a teacher for the first school in the new township of Good Hope. Link is sucked back into involvement with his old gang of "brother," "cousins," and monstrous adoptive father Dock Tobin (Lee J. Cobb), and forced into more and more excessive violence, as he destroys his doubles in order finally to detach himself, drained and compromised, from his own roots.

—Robin Wood

MANN, Michael

Nationality: American. **Born:** Chicago, Illinois, 5 February 1943. **Education:** University of Wisconsin, 1965; London Film School, 1967. **Family:** Married to artist Summer Mann. **Career:** Directed shorts, commercials, and documentaries in England, 1967-72; wrote episodes for television series *Starsky and Hutch* and *Police Story* and created *Vega$* and *Miami Vice;* directorial debut, *The Jericho Mile* (TV movie), 1979; screen debut, *Thief,* 1981. **Awards:** Directors Guild of America Best Director Award, 1980, for *The Jericho Mile;* Emmy Award for Outstanding Writing in a Limited Series or Special, 1980, for *The Jericho Mile.* **Agent:** Jeff Berg, International Creative Management, 8899 Beverly Blvd., Los Angeles, CA 90048, U.S.A.

Films as Director and Screenwriter:

1979 *The Jericho Mile* (TV movie)
1981 *Thief* (+ exec-pr)
1983 *The Keep*
1986 *Manhunter* (+ pr)
1989 *L.A. Takedown* (TV movie) (+ exec-pr)
1992 *The Last of the Mohicans* (co-sc, pr)
1995 *Heat*

Other Films:

1978 *Vega$* (TV movie) (sc); *Straight Time* (sc, uncredited)
1980 *Swan Song* (TV movie) (sc)
1986 *Band of the Hand* (exec-pr)
1990 *Drug Wars: The Camarena Story* (TV mini-series) (exec-pr, co-sc)
1992 *Drug Wars: The Cocaine Cartel* (TV mini-series) (exec-pr)

Publications

By MANN: articles—

"Four-Minute Mile: Michael Mann Interviewed," *Films & Filming,* 1980.

"An Interview with the Director of *Thief,*" *Rolling Stone,* 1981.

"Castle *Keep,*" *Film Comment,* 1983.

"Wars and Peace," *Sight & Sound,* 1992.

On MANN: articles—

Greco, M., "Up and Coming: Michael Mann," *Film Comment,* 1980.

Murphy, K., "Communion," *Film Comment,* 1991.

Smith, G., "Mann Hunters," *Film Comment,* 1992.

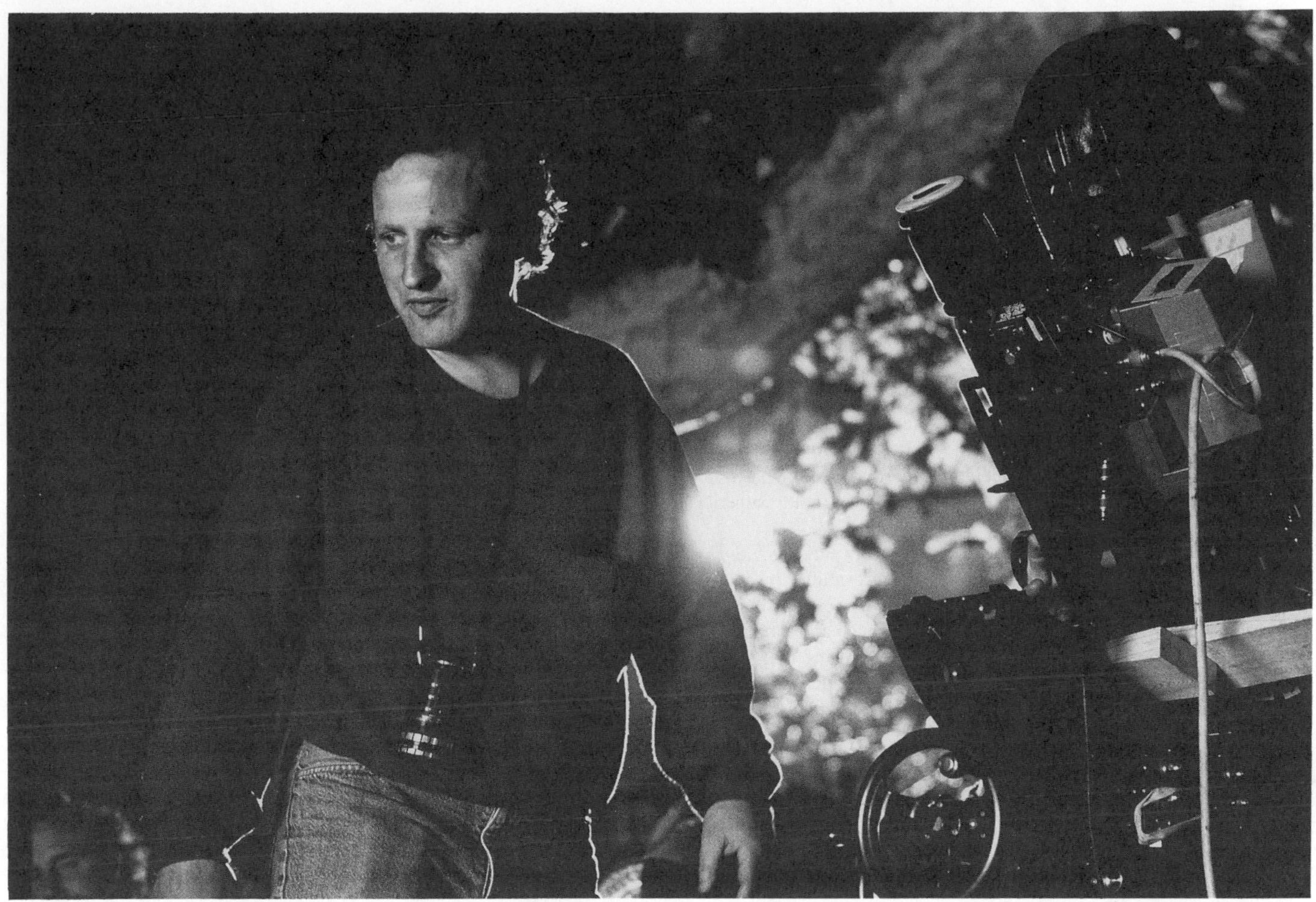

Michael Mann directing *Thief*

Ansen, David, and D. Foote, "Mann in the Wilderness," *Newsweek,* 1992.

Schruers, F., "Mann Overboard," *Premiere,* 1992.

Hooper, J., "Mann and Mohican," *Esquire,* 1992.

Lombardi, John, "What a Piece of Work Is Mann," *Gentleman's Quarterly,* 1992.

* * *

Michael Mann's cinematic milieu is the mean streets of urban neo-noir. His stylistic signature is a hip, almost neon look, the images sharply edited and backed by adrenalin-pumping music. Given the razzle-dazzle MTV approach he brings to his craft, it is ironic that he started out wanting to be a writer. However, while attending the University of Wisconsin and majoring in English literature, he took a film course for a fast *A* and got hooked on moviemaking instead.

Mann transferred to the London Film School in 1965 for training and graduated two years later. Like a number of contemporary directors, he got his start making television commercials, and he has carried over many of the stylistic ingredients of commercials into his subsequent film work.

Mann paid his dues in Hollywood writing episodes for TV cop shows of the 1970s, such as *Starsky and Hutch* and Joseph Wambaugh's *Police Story*; for the ABC network he wrote the pilot episode of *Vega$,* a short-lived Robert Urich private-eye series whose setting lent itself naturally to Mann's "neon look." By this time a specialist in the genre the French call *roman policier,* Mann had little difficulty convincing the network to give him a shot at writing and directing a feature film in similar vein for its growing made-for-TV movie division. The result was *The Jericho Mile* (1979), which replaced the sun-drenched mean streets of *Starsky and Hutch* and the often rain-slicked ones of *Police Story* with the pallid walls of Folsom Prison. A hard-hitting drama about a convicted murderer (Peter Strauss) who survives the brutality of his surroundings and regains his self-respect by striving to become an Olympic runner, the well-received film added considerable luster to the often maligned TV movie form and won Mann an Emmy award. It also landed him a contract to make his theatrical film debut.

Turning again to his chosen milieu—the seedy world of crime and criminals—Mann wrote and directed *Thief* (1981), the gritty tale of a safecracker who tries to make one last score and go straight, only to dig himself in even deeper. James Caan played the title role in the doom-laden thriller, a thematic and stylistic throwback to the classic films noir of the 1940s, but updated with the hip look and, especially, sound (courtesy here of Tangerine Dream) that are Mann's trademark.

Mann segued from *Thief* to *The Keep* (1983), based on F. Paul Wilson's novel about German soldiers who encounter a vampiric presence in the title fortress during World War II. Mann again brought considerable stylistic verve to the fantastic drama, but perhaps because he was in unfamiliar territory—the Carpathian mountains rather than the streets of L.A. and Chicago—the film failed to come together. Critics and audiences found it to be incomprehensible. It went belly-up at the box office and Mann went back to TV to create *Miami Vice,* one of the most influential cop series of the 1980s, and *Crime Story.* The former was a glitzy *roman policier* aimed at the MTV generation, while the latter was a period noir series with a neo-noir look aimed at older viewers. Mann also directed a mini-series docudrama about the murder of narcotics agent Enrique Camarena called *The Drug Wars* (1990).

In between his TV work, Mann returned to the big screen to make one of his best and most underrated films, *Manhunter* (1986), based on the novel *Red Dragon* by Thomas Harris, in which the author introduced his master serial killer character Hannibal "the Cannibal" Lecter to the public. (He is played in the film by Brian Cox.) Produced by Dino De Laurentis's DEG Entertainment, *Manhunter* failed to get much of a promotional boost due to DEG's financial collapse and went nowhere at the box office. It was left to director Jonathan Demme and star Anthony Hopkins to make "Hannibal the Cannibal" a household name with *Silence of the Lambs* (1991), their Academy Award-winning screen version of Harris's sequel to *Red Dragon.* Mann partisans as well as many thriller fans consider *Manhunter* to be the superior work, however.

As he had done with *The Keep,* Mann shifted gears entirely with *The Last of the Mohicans* (1992), this time more successfully. It remains his best film, a harshly beautiful—and definitive—version of James Fenimore Cooper's oft-filmed novel about the French and Indian War. Mann refused to take the politically correct route of making his Native American characters helpless, long-suffering victims. Instead, the film restores their dignity by restoring their historical fearsomeness as warriors, something the movies have been timid about doing for decades. In fact, Wes Studi's ferocious and very human villain Magua lingers in the memory more than does the film's hero, Hawkeye, played by Daniel Day-Lewis. Though the film's milieu is atypical of Mann, its kinetic mixture of sight and sound (the music score is remarkable) is all Mann. A moving saga of America's past, it is one of the most exciting adventure movies of recent times.

Mann's most recent film is *Heat* (1995), a return to the mean streets of urban America. It stars Al Pacino and Robert De Niro as opposing forces (albeit without much screen time together). A sprawling, almost three-hour crime drama, it has been hailed by many critics as Mann's most ambitious study of his traditional milieu to date.

—John McCarty

MARKER, Chris

Nationality: French. **Born:** Christian François Bouche-Villeneuve in Neuilly sur Seine (one source says Ulan Bator, Mongolia), 29 July 1921. **Military Service:** During World War II, resistance fighter, then joined American army. **Career:** Novelist, poet, playwright, and journalist, from late 1940s; formed SLON film cooperative (Société pour le Lancement des Oeuvres Nouvelles), 1967. **Awards:** Golden Bear, Berlin Festival, for *Description d'un combat,* 1961; International Critics Prize, Cannes Festival, for *Le Joli Mai,* 1963.

Films as Director:

1952 *Olympia 52* (+ sc, co-ph)
1953 *Les Statues meurent aussi* (co-d, co-sc)
1956 *Dimanche à Pekin* (+ sc, ph)
1958 *Lettre de Sibérie* (*Letter from Siberia*) (+ sc)
1960 *Description d'un combat* (+ sc); *Les Astronautes* (co-d, sc)
1961 *Cuba Si!* (+ sc, ph)
1963 ***Le Joli Mai*** (+ sc)
1964 *La Jetée* (completed 1962) (+ sc)
1965 *Le Mystère Koumiko* (*The Koumiko Mystery*) (+ sc)
1966 *Si j'avais quatre dromadaires* (+ sc)
1968 *La Sixième Face du Pentagone* (collaboration with Francois Reichenbach) (+ sc)
1969 *A bientôt j'espère* (+ sc)
1970 *La Bataille des dix millions* (*Cuba: Battle of the Ten Million*) (+ sc); *Les Mots ont un sens* (+ sc)
1973 *Le Train en marche* (+ sc)
1977 *Le Fond de l'air est rouge* (in 2 parts) (+ sc)
1983 ***Sans soleil*** (*Sunless*)
1984 *2084* (+ sc)
1985 *A.K.* (*A.K.: The Making of Kurosawa's Ran*) (+ sc)
1986 *Hommage à Simone Sihnoret* (+ sc)
1989 *L'Heritage de la Chouette* (for TV, 13-part series) (+ sc, pr)
1993 *Le Dernier Bolchevik* (*The Last Bolshevik*) (+ sc)

Other Films:

1957 *Le Mystère de l'atelier* (commentary, collaborator on production)
1967 *Loin du Vietnam* (*Far from Vietnam*) (Resnais) (pr, ed)
1970 *L'Aveu* (*The Confession*) (Costa-Gavras) (asst ph)
1973 *Kashima Paradise* (commentary)
1975/76 ***La batalla de Chile*** (*The Battle of Chile*) (Guzmá) (co-pr)
1976 *La Spirale* (contributor)
1988 *Les Pyramides bleues* (artistic advisor)

Publications

By MARKER: books—

Le Coeur net, Lausanne, 1950.
Giraudoux par lui-même, Paris, 1952.
Coreennes, photographs, Paris, 1962.
Commentaires, Paris, 1962.
La Jetée: ciné roman, New York, 1992.

By MARKER: articles—

"Kashima Paradise," interview with G. Braucourt and Max Tessier, in *Ecran* (Paris), November 1974.

On MARKER: articles—

Cameron, Ian, "I Am Writing to You from a Far Country ...," in *Movie* (London), October 1962.
Graham, Peter, "Cinéma Vérité in France," in *Film Quarterly* (Berkeley), Summer 1964.
Jacob, Gilles, "Chris Marker and the Mutants," in *Sight and Sound* (London), Autumn 1966.
Roud, Richard, "SLON," in *Sight and Sound* (London), Spring 1973.
Valade, P., "Un Programme Chris Marker," in *Jeune Cinéma* (Paris), February 1975.
"Si j'avais quatre dromadaires. La Solitude du chanteur de fond," in *Avant-Scène du Cinéma* (Paris), March 1975.
Roud, Richard, "The Left Bank Revisited," in *Sight and Sound* (London), Summer 1977.
Hennebelle, Guy, "Le Fond de l'air est rouge," in *Ecran* (Paris), December 1977.

Chris Marker: ***Le Mystère Koumiko***

Gaggi, S., "Marker and Resnais: Myth and Reality," in *Literature/Film Quarterly* (Salisbury, Maryland), no. 1, 1979.
Van Wert, W. F., "Chris Marker: The SLON Films," in *Film Quarterly* (Berkeley), no. 3, 1979.
Rafferty, T., "Marker Changes Trains," in *Sight and Sound* (London), Autumn 1984.
Durgnat, Raymond, "Resnais & Co.: Back to the Avant-Garde," in *Monthly Film Bulletin* (London), May 1987.
Bensmaia, R, "Du photogramme au pictogramme: a propos de 'La Jeteé' de Chris Marker," in *Iris* (Paris), no. 8, 1989.
Leeuwn, T. van, "Conjuctive Structure in Documentary Film and Television," in *Continuum,* no. 5, 1991.

* * *

Chris Marker's principal distinction may be to have developed a form of personal essay within the documentary mode. Aside from his work little is known about him; he is elusive bordering on mysterious. Born in a suburb of Paris, he has allowed a legend to grow up about his birth in a "far-off country." Marker is not his name; it is one of a half-dozen aliases he has used. He chose "Marker," it is thought, in reference to the Magic Marker pen.

He began his career as a writer (publishing poems, a novel, and various essays and translations) and journalist (whose travels took him all over the world). He is the writer of all his films and cinematographer on many of them. Their verbal and visual wit almost conceal the philosophical speculation and erudition they contain. Their commentaries are a kind of stream of consciousness; their poetry is about himself as well as about the subjects—his reactions to what he and we are seeing and hearing.

Marker is the foreign correspondent and inquiring reporter. He is especially interested in transitional societies, in "Life in the process of becoming history," as he has put it. His films are not only set in specific places, they are about the cultures of those places. Though he has tended to work in socialist countries more than most Western filmmakers, he is also fascinated by Japan. Concerned with leftist issues, he remains a member of the intellectual Left, politically committed but not doctrinaire. "Involved objectivity" is his own phrase for his approach.

In *Le Joli Mai,* for example, Marker interviews Parisians about their ambitions, their political views, their understanding of the society they live in. His sample is a cross section—a street-corner clothing salesman, a clerk, a house painter, a black student, a young couple wanting to get married, an Algerian worker—with a substantial working-class representation. The interviewees find that work offers no satisfaction. Its goal is money; what happiness money will bring is by no means certain. Marker insists to one interviewee who opts for material success that his view of life is "a trifle limited." "No interest in other things?" Marker asks.

This exchange is characteristic. Marker's tone is frequently ironical and implicitly judgmental. He engages in argument with the interviewees and makes known his disappointment in some of their answers. The interviews assume the form of a dialectic.

In the second half of *Le Joli Mai* Marker breaks away from individuals and interviews altogether. Instead he deals with news events—a police charge which crushed eight people to death in the Métro, the half-million mourners at their funeral, violent responses to the acquittal of General Salan (former commander-in-chief of French forces in Algeria), massive railroad and Renault strikes—intercut with nightclub revelry. The events refer back to those interviewed in the first half who felt themselves "unfree" to alter or even to question the social system.

The Koumiko Mystery, set amidst the 1964 Tokyo Olympics, begins but never stays with them for long. Its real subject is a young Japanese woman named Koumiko Moroaka, her city (Tokyo), her country, and the Far East as a whole. If, in a sense, Koumiko is protagonist, there is also an antagonist of sorts. The Western world and its influences are seen again and again in images on television screens, in the tastes evident in department store windows. Part of the film is photographed directly off black-and-white television screens. In this way the concerns and attitudes of the larger world are isolated. The rest of the film, which is in color, is wholly personal.

Marker's fascination with foreign, particularly Japanese, cultures is evident in the making of *Sans soleil* and *A.K.* The former is an idiosyncratic travelogue about Japan, narrated by a fictional cameraman, while the latter is a documentary about Akira Kurosawa's (arguably Japan's most renowned filmmaker) making of *Ran.* In both films, Marker's point of view remains that of an observer, a bystander. It is exactly through such deliberate distance and distanciation that the filmmaker contemplates issues that have dominated his work to date: How do various cultures perceive and sustain themselves and each other in the increasingly intermingled modern age? How, on the other hand, can one find the space of him/herself when time, place, and memory are obscured, constructed, and forgotten? In the case of *Sans soleil,* not only are images of Japan—purposefully inserted with those of Guinea Bissau, Ireland, Iceland, and elsewhere—robbed of any consistency and specificity, but memories and perceptions are also fictionalized and therefore called into ultimate question.

Following the failure of communism, as most brutally indicated by the disintegration of the former Soviet Union, comes "one of the most trenchant commentaries Marker has ever allowed himself," according to David Thomson, in his 1993 film *Le Dernier Bolchevik* (*The Last Bolshevik*). Although this film still maintains a sense of "involved objectivity" stylistically, it also may suggest a stark disillusionment of a sort in Marker, the Marxist-inspired documentarist. There is, however, no reason to stop anticipating further works by Marker that demonstrate the willingness to impose his own shaping intelligence and imagination on his materials. His films will continue to be most valued for what he perceives and understands about what he is observing, and for their whimsical juggling of forms, their tweaking of conventions and expectations, and their idiosyncratic style.

—Jack C. Ellis, updated by Guo-Juin Hong

MARKOPOULOS, Gregory

Nationality: American. **Born:** Toledo, Ohio, 12 March 1928. **Education:** University of Southern California. **Career:** Completed first experimental films, 1948; lecturer on film at University of Athens, Greece, 1954-55; worked on *Serenity,* 1955-60; writer on film, from early 1960s.

Films as Director:

1947 *Du sang de la volupté et de la mort* (trilogy comprising *Psyche, Lysis,* and *Charmides*)
1948 *The Dead Ones*
1949 *Flowers of Asphalt*
1950 *Swain*
1951 *Arbres aux champignons*
1953 *Eldora*
1955-61 *Serenity*
1963 *Twice a Man*
1965 *The Death of Hemingway*
1966 *Galaxie*; *Through a Lens Brightly: Mark Turbyfill*; *Ming Green*
1967 *Himself as Herself*; *Eros, O Basileus*; *The Iliac Passion*; *Bliss*; *The Divine Damnation*; *Gammelion*
1968 *Mysteries*
1969 *Index Hans Richter*
1970 *Genius*
1971 *Doldertal 7*; *Hagiographia*; *35 Boulevard General Koenig*

Publications

By MARKOPOULOS: books—

Quest for Serenity, New York, 1965.
A Bibliography Containing the Marvelous Distortions of My Films as Reviewed in Books, Programs, Periodicals and Newspapers during Thirty-three Years: 1945-1978, St. Moritz, 1978.

By MARKOPOULOS: articles—

"On *Serenity,*" in *Film Culture* (New York), Summer 1961.
"Toward a New Narrative Form in Motion Pictures," in *Film Comment* (New York), Fall 1963.
Interview with Robert Brown, in *Film Culture* (New York), Spring 1964.
"Random Notes During a Two-Week Lecture Tour of the United States," in *Film Culture* (New York), Fall 1964.
"The Driving Rhythm," in *Film Culture* (New York), Spring 1966.
"From 'Fanshawe' to 'Swain,'" in *Film Culture* (New York), Summer 1966.
"'Galaxie' (Production and Critical Notes)," in *Film Culture* (New York), Fall 1966.
"The Film-Maker as Physician of the Future," in *Film Culture* (New York), Spring 1967.
"Gregory Markopoulos: Free Association—Rough Transcription for Paper on Levels of Creative Consciousness," interview with David Brooks, in *Film Culture* (New York), Summer 1967.
"Correspondences of Smells and Visuals," in *Film Culture* (New York), Autumn 1967.
"Index to the Work of Gregory Markopoulos, Years 1967/70," with Jonas Mekas, in *Film Culture* (New York), Spring 1971.
"The Adamantine Bridge," in *Film Culture* (New York), Spring 1972.

On MARKOPOULOS: book—

Sitney, P. Adams, *Visionary Film: The American Avant-Garde 1943-1978,* New York, 1979.

On MARKOPOULOS: articles—

Filmwise 3 & 4: Gregory Markopoulos, Spring 1963.
Kelman, K., "Portrait of the Young Man as Artist: From the Notebook of Robert Beavers," in *Film Culture* (New York), no. 67/69, 1979.

Ehrenstein, David, "The Markopoulos Affair," *Film Comment* (Los Angeles), July-August 1993.

* * *

Gregory J. Markopoulos made his first film (a version of *A Christmas Carol*) in 1940 with a borrowed 8-millimeter silent movie camera. By the time he left the University of Southern California in 1947, he completed a trilogy titled *Du sang de la volupté et de la mort* (comprising *Psyche, Lysis,* and *Charmides*). His first 35-millimeter film was *The Dead Ones* in 1948. With these beginnings, Markopoulos became one of the best-known of the avant-garde of the post-World War II period, although his output in the 1950s was limited to four films—*Flowers of Asphalt, Arbres aux champignons, Eldora,* and *Serenity.*

Elements of homoeroticism pervade many of the Markopoulos experiments and they are as audacious and outrageous as the works of Adolfas and Jonas Mekas. In his trilogy, a battering ram becomes a phallic symbol. When the film was shown to a class at New York University in 1951, it caused Henry Hart, then the far-right editor of *Films in Review* magazine, to berate professor George Amberg for allowing it to be shown. Hart described some of the images included in the films—"a male nipple, a painted and coiffeured male head, a buttock ... and quite a few suggestions that abnormal perceptions and moods are desirable." Markopoulos soon became a much talked-about and controversial filmmaker.

The first Markopoulos film of the 1960s was *Serenity,* a drama about the Greco-Turkish War of 1921-22, shot in Greece and released in 1962. This was followed by *Twice a Man,* a recreation of the Greek myths of Hippolytus, Phaedra, and Asclepius dealing openly for the first time (for Markopoulos) with male homosexuality.

Galaxie consisted of 30 three-minute 16-millimeter silent clips of his friends (Parker Tyler, Jonas Mekas, W. H. Auden, Allen Ginsberg, Shirley Clarke, Maurice Sendak, Susan Sontag, and Gian Carlo Menotti, among others) with an electronic "clang" ending each segment as the only sound on the film. Markopoulos's subsequent films are in 16-millimeter.

Single-frame editing and superimpositions were used in *Himself as Herself,* a strange film about a half man/half woman shot in and around Boston and released in 1967. In March of that year, *Eros, O Basileus* appeared, consisting of nine sequences involving a young man representing Eros. *The Markopoulos Passion,* a dramatic movie filmed over a three-year period, was finally released in 1968 as *The Iliac Passion,* a version of the Prometheus legend set in New York City.

Until 1981, he resided in St. Moritz, and there published a 1978 folio entitled *A Bibliography Containing the Marvelous Distortions of My Films as Reviewed in Books, Programs, Periodicals and Newspapers during Thirty-Three Years: 1945-1978.* He has been a leader in the avant-garde film movement for nearly forty years.

—James L. Limbacher

MARSHALL, Penny

Nationality: American. **Born:** New York City, 15 October 1942 (some sources say 1943). **Education:** Attended the University of New Mexico, majored in math and psychology. **Family:** Married 1) Michael Henry (divorced); 2) actor/director Rob Reiner (divorced); one daughter, Tracy. **Career:** Began acting in the 1960s, appearing in stock productions; made network acting debut on *The Danny Thomas Hour,* 1967-68; auditioned unsuccessfully for the role of Gloria on the television sitcom *All in the Family,* 1970; initially attracted notice for recurring role as Jack Klugman's secretary on TV's *The Odd Couple,* 1971-75; acted on television series, including *The Mary Tyler Moore Show, Taxi, Mork and Mindy,* and *Happy Days,* 1970s; became a television star on *Laverne and Shirley,* 1976; directed commercials, several episodes of *Laverne and Shirley,* two episodes of *The Tracey Ullman Show,* and TV pilot *Working Stiffs,* late 1970s-1980s; made stage debut in off-Broadway play *Eden Court,* 1985; directed first feature, *Jumpin' Jack Flash,* 1986; signed a three-picture deal with Columbia Pictures, 1990. **Agent:** Creative Artists Agency, 1888 Century Park East, Suite 1400, Los Angeles, CA 90067, U.S.A.

Films as Director:

1986 *Jumpin' Jack Flash*
1988 *Big*
1990 *Awakenings* (+ co-exec pr)
1992 *A League of Their Own* (+ exec pr)
1994 *Renaissance Man* (+ co-exec pr)

Films as Actress:

1968 *The Savage Seven* (Rush); *How Sweet It Is!* (Paris)
1970 *The Grasshopper* (Paris)
1971 *The Feminist and the Fuzz* (Paris) (for TV)
1972 *Evil Roy Slade* (Paris) (for TV); *The Crooked Hearts* (Sandrich) (for TV); *The Couple Takes a Wife* (Paris) (for TV)
1975 *How Come Nobody's on Our Side?* (Michaels); *Let's Switch* (Rafkin) (for TV)
1978 *More Than Friends* (Burrows) (for TV)
1979 *1941* (Spielberg)
1984 *Love Thy Neighbor* (Bill) (for TV)
1985 *Movers & Shakers* (Asher); *Challenge of a Lifetime* (Mayberry) (for TV)
1991 *The Hard Way* (Badham)
1993 *Hocus Pocus* (Ortega)
1995 *Get Shorty* (Sonnenfeld)

Other Films:

1993 *Calendar Girl* (Whitesell) (exec pr)

Publications

By MARSHALL: articles—

Interview with Burt Prelutsky, in *TV Guide* (Radnor, Pennsylvania), 22 May 1976.
Interview with Marty Friedman, in *New York,* 26 October 1981.
"The Marshall Plan," with Carol Caldwell, in *Interview* (New York), January 1991.
Interview with Iain Blair, in *Chicago Tribune,* 3 February 1991.
Interview with Larry Rohter, in *New York Times,* 17 March 1991.
"Making It in the Majors," with Peggy Orenstein, in *New York Times Magazine,* 24 May 1992.
Interview in *Vanity Fair* (New York), May 1994.
"Penny Marshall Marshals Her Wits and Fishes for Dish with Carrie Fisher," with Carrie Fisher, in *Interview* (New York), May 1994.

On MARSHALL: books—

Acker, Ally, *Reel Women: Pioneers of the Cinema, 1896 to the Present,* New York, 1991.
Edelman, Rob, *Great Baseball Films,* New York, 1994.

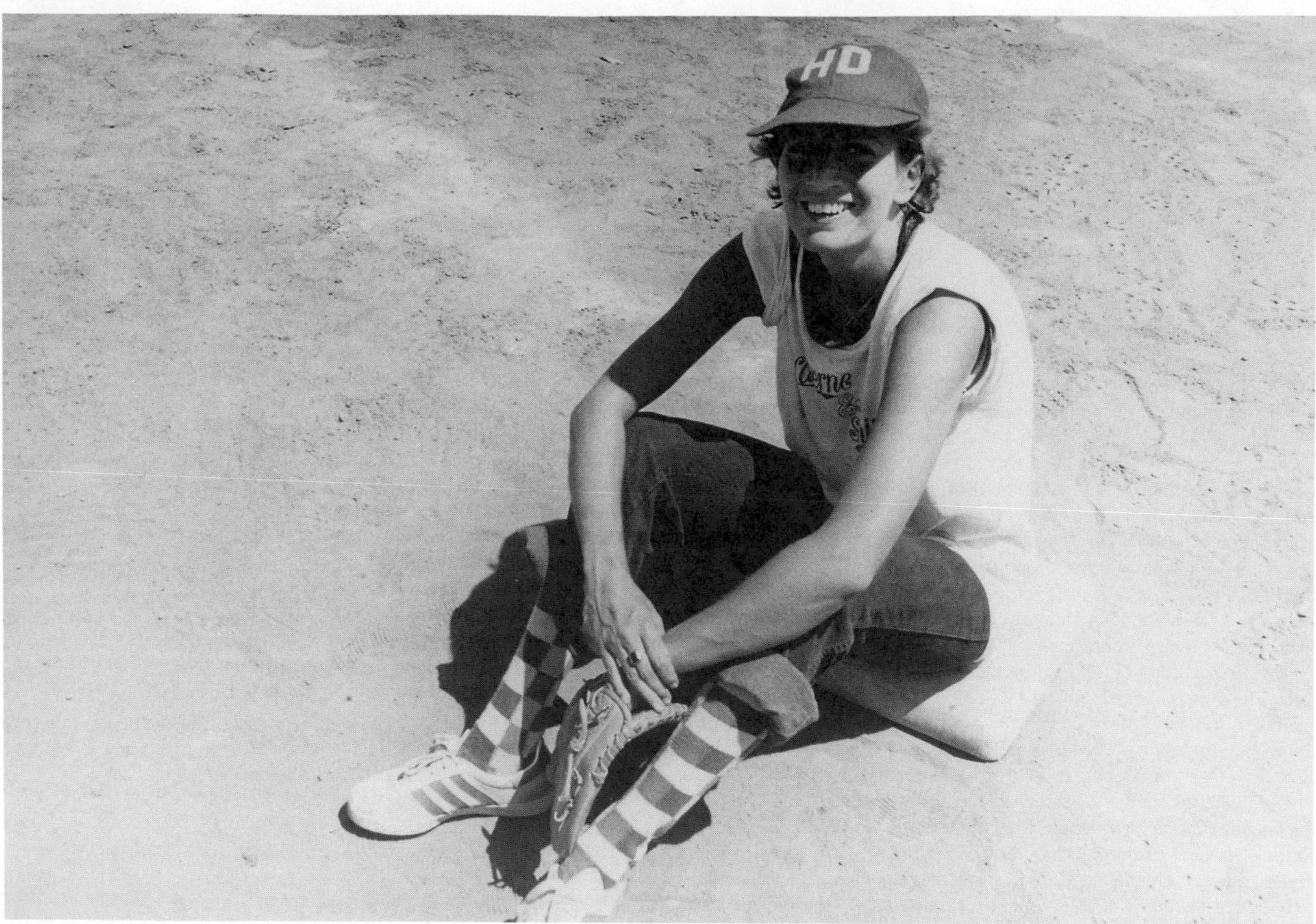

Penny Marshall

On MARSHALL: articles—

Cunneff, Tom, "Penny Marshall," in *People* (New York), 15 August 1988.

Walters, Harry F., article in *New York Woman,* December 1990.

Morgenstern, Joseph, "Penny from Heaven," in *Playboy* (Chicago), January 1991.

Wolf, J., "*Laverne & Shirley's* Strange Brew," in *TV Guide* (Radnor, Pennsylvania), 13 March 1995.

* * *

Had Penny Marshall not had show business connections—she is the younger sister of director-producer-writer Garry Marshall—she might not have been allowed the opportunities she received first as an actress, then as a director. But this can be said for any second- or third-generation Hollywood name, from Bridges to Fonda, Carradine to Sheen. Besides, had Marshall lacked the requisite abilities, her career might not have flourished as it has in both venues. Marshall has become one of a generation of actors—Ron Howard and Rob Reiner, her former husband, are others who come to mind—who first earned popularity as stars of television situation comedies, and then went on to forge major careers behind the cameras.

Marshall cut her teeth as an actress, appearing first in a handful of features and made-for-television movies, then in a quartet of television situation comedies: *The Odd Couple* (as Myra Turner, 1971-75, co-produced by brother Garry); *The Bob Newhart Show* (Miss Larson, 1972-73); *Paul Sand in Friends and Lovers* (Janice Dreyfuss, 1974-75); and, most notably, *Laverne and Shirley* (Laverne De Fazio, 1976-83, co-created and produced by brother Garry), a spin-off of *Happy Days.* The success of the latter made Marshall a household name. In 1978, she co-starred with Reiner in *More Than Friends,* a made-for-TV romantic comedy based on their courtship.

Marshall initially began directing episodes of *Laverne and Shirley.* Her feature-film directorial debut, *Jumpin' Jack Flash,* was inauspicious: one of Whoopi Goldberg's pitifully unfunny post-*Color Purple* fiascos. More recently, she made *Renaissance Man,* an overlong (at 129 minutes), generic comedy about an advertising man (Danny DeVito) who finds himself suddenly unemployed, and accepts a job tutoring a bunch of none-too-bright Army recruits. In between, however, Marshall made a trio of popular features which firmly established her as a leading Hollywood director. Each is a commercially viable film which combines solid entertainment value with a humanistic, life-affirming story line.

Big is by far the best in a string of late 1980s fantasy-comedies (including *Like Father Like Son, Vice Versa,* and *18 Again*) which are variations on the same theme: the souls of young people are transferred into the bodies of their elders (and vice versa). *Big* is the story of a pre-teen boy who, like many kids, wishes he were older. Miraculously, this request is granted—and the boy, now trapped in the body of a man almost three times his age, is thrust into the adult world. The adult is played by Tom Hanks, giving a performance which earned him his first Academy Award nomination and solidified his status as an A-list movie star. The based-on-fact *Awakenings* features superlative performances by Robin Williams (as Oliver Sacks, a reticent research doctor working in a hospital ward which houses the chronically ill) and Robert De Niro (as a patient who awakens from a thirty-year coma). *A League of Their Own* mixes fiction with fact as it tells the story of the trailblazing women athletes who played professional baseball in the All American Girls Professional Baseball League during the 1940s and 1950s.

Along with fellow TV refugees Reiner and Howard, Marshall has been able to entertain audiences while making them think and feel: an impressive accomplishment in an era dominated by crass, in-your-face, assembly-line Hollywood product.

—Rob Edelman

MAURO, Humberto

Nationality: Brazilian. **Born:** Volta Grande, Minas Gerais, 30 April 1897. **Education:** Educated in engineering. **Career:** Began filmmaking at Cataguases, small town near birthplace, and participated in founding of production company Sul América Filme (later Brasil Filme S.A.), 1925; received top prize of Rio de Janeiro film publication *Cinearte* for *Thesouro perdido,* 1927; hired by *Cinearte* publisher Adhemar Gonzaga to direct for his Cinedia Studios, Rio, 1930; made short fiction films and documentaries for *Instituto Nacional de Cinema Educativo* (INCE), from 1937.

Films as Director:

(partial list)

1925 *Valadão, o cratera* (*Valadao the Disaster*) (+ sc, ph)
1926 *Na primavera da vida* (*In the Springtime of Life*) (+ sc)
1927 *Thesouro perdido* (*Tesouro perdido*; *Lost Treasure*) (+ sc)
1928 *Brasa dormida* (*Sleeping Ember*; *Extinguished Cinders*) (+ sc)
1929 *Sangue Mineiro* (*Minas Blood*; *Blood of Minas*) (+ sc)
1930 *Labios sem beijos* (*Lips without Kisses*)
1932 *Ganga bruta* (*Rough Diamond*) (+ sc)
1934 *Favela dos meus amores* (*Favela of My Loves*) (+ sc); *Cidade mulher*
1937 *O descobrimento do Brasil* (+ sc)
1939 *Um apólogo* (shorts for Instituto Nacional de Cinema Educativo) (+ sc)
1940 *Argila* (*Clay*); *Bandeirantes* (short for Instituto Nacional de Cinema Educativo) (+ sc)
1942 *O despertar da redentora* (short for Instituto Nacional de Cinema Educativo) (+ sc)
1944 *O segredo das Asas* (medium-length film) (+ pr, sc)
1945-56 "Brasilianas" series (includes *Manhã na Roça* and *Engenhos e usinas*) (shorts for Instituto Nacional de Cinema Educativo) (+ sc)
1952 *O canto da saudade* (*The Song of Sadness*) (+ pr, sc)
1956 *Meus oito anos* (shorts for Instituto Nacional de Cinema Educativo) (+ sc)
1964 *A velha a Fiar* (short for Instituto Nacional de Cinema Educativo) (+ sc)

Publications

On MAURO: articles—

Article, in *Filme Cultura* (Rio de Janeiro), October/November 1967.

Paranagua, P. A., "Cannes 82: homenaje a dos maestros del cine latinoamericano," in *Contracampo* (Madrid), August/September 1982.

Gomes, P. E. S., "Mauro et deux autres grands," in *Positif* (Paris), April 1987.

* * *

One of the greatest of all Latin American filmmakers, Humberto Mauro was a fascinating, deeply original talent whose best work exhibited a lyrical integration of characters and environment reminiscent of Dovzhenko. Trained as an engineer, Mauro was living in Cataguases—a small city in the state of Minas Gerais, north of Rio, which produced an impressive number of important writers and artists in that era—when friends encouraged him to make a short documentary, *Valadão, o cratera,* in 1925. After another amateur experience, on the fiction feature *In the Springtime of Life,* Mauro attempted his first professional production with *Lost Treasure,* an exciting adventure story clearly influenced by the American westerns Mauro would continue to love all his life. *Lost Treasure* received some small circulation around Brazil, and in 1927 was awarded *Cinearte* magazine's "Best Brazilian Film of the Year," the first such award ever given. His next film, *Sleeping Ember,* also made in Cataguases, was one of his very finest; here Mauro demonstrated his extraordinary talent for eliciting sensitive, nuanced performances from non-professional actors, a feature of many of his best works.

Humberto Mauro

Lost Treasure and *Sleeping Ember* brought Mauro to the attention of Adhemar Gonzaga and Carmen Santos, two film enthusiasts who had plans to found a professional film studio in Rio. In 1930, Mauro moved to Rio, where he became the principal director at Gonzaga's fledgling Cinedia Studios in the early 1930s. Curiously, he continued to make silent films, even though the first Brazilian talkie, Luiz de Barro's *The End of the Hicks,* premiered in 1929. Mauro's final silent feature, *Rough Diamond*—released with a musical soundtrack—is unquestionably his masterpiece. After murdering his wife on their honeymoon night upon discovering she wasn't a virgin, a man attempts to piece together his life and his relations with women. Some of the film's blatantly Freudian symbolism seems too contrived, and the plot's resolution isn't totally satisfying, but these shortcomings are more than made up for by the film's many exquisite passages.

After a few more studio films, notably the now-lost *Favela of My Loves,* Mauro began working as filmmaker-in-residence for the National Institute of Educational Cinema, a newly-founded branch of the Ministry of Education. For the next 30 years, Mauro would continue to work for this agency, producing well over 100 documentaries on a variety of subjects. During this period, he occasionally did return to work on features—*Clay,* with Carmen Santos, in 1940, and the tender pastoral romance, *The Song of Sadness,* in 1952.

Unlike other Brazilian directors, Mario Peixoto for instance, Mauro was able, happily, to cope with the seemingly insurmountable difficulties of working in a film industry as beleaguered as that of Brazil. Mauro's greatest strength lay in his sensitivity for the people and places of his native state of Minas Gerais; curiously, by concentrating on mostly regional themes and ways of life, Mauro created the single body of film work of international significance before the explosion of Cinema Novo in the early 1960s. That generation of filmmakers—Glauber Rocha, Nelson Pereira dos Santos, Joaquim Pedro—lionized Mauro, regarding him as the spiritual grandfather of their movement to create a truly Brazilian cinema.

—Richard Peña

MAYSLES, Albert and David Paul

Nationality: American. **Born:** Albert born in Brookline, Massachusetts, 26 November 1926; David Paul born in Brookline, 10 January 1932. **Education:** Albert attended Brookline High School; Syracuse University, New York, degree in psychology; Boston University, M.A. in psychology. David attended Brookline High School; Boston University, degree in psychology. **Military Service:** During World War II, Albert served in U.S. Army Tank Corps, David served in the Army at Headquarters, Military Intelligence school, Oberammergau, Germany. **Family:** David married Judy (Maysles), one son, one daughter. **Career:** Albert taught psychology at Boston University, from late 1940s, then travelled to Russia to make first film, 1955; David worked as production assistant on *Bus Stop* and *The Prince and the Showgirl,* 1956; they make first film together, 1957; David worked as reporter on *Adventures on the New Frontier* for TV, late 1950s and early 1960s; Albert worked as cameraman for Richard Leacock, 1960; formed production company together and made first film, 1962; Albert worked as cameraman on one section of Godard's *Paris vu par,* and the brothers received Guggenheim Fellowship in experimental film, 1965; continued making full-length documentaries and industrial and corporate promotional films together, from 1970. **Awards:** Academy Award nomination, Best Dramatic Short, for *Christo's Valley Curtain,* 1972; Emmy Award, for *Horowitz Plays Mozart,* 1987. **Died:** David Maysles died in New York, 3 January 1987.

Films as Directors:

1955 *Psychiatry in Russia* (Albert only)
1957 *Youth in Poland*
1960 ***Primary*** (Albert only, co-d)
1962 *Showman*
1964 *What's Happening: The Beatles in the USA* (*Yeah Yeah Yeah, The Beatles! The First U.S. Visit*)
1965 *Meet Marlon Brando*
1966 *With Love From Truman*
1969 *Salesman* (co-d)
1970 *Gimme Shelter* (co-d)
1972 *Christo's Valley Curtain* (co-d)
1975 *Grey Gardens* (co-d)
1977 *Running Fence* (co-d)
1980 *Muhammad and Larry*
1984 *Islands* (co-d)
1986 *Vladimir Horowitz: the Last Romantic*; *Ozawa* (co-d)
1987 *Horowitz Plays Mozart* (Albert only, co-d)
1989 *Jessye Norman Sings Carmen* (Albert only, co-d)
1991 *Christo in Paris* (Albert only)
1992 *Baroque Diet* (Albert only); *Sports Illustrated: Swimsuit '92* (Albert only)
1993 *Abortion: Desperate Choices* (Albert only, co-d)

Publications

By the MAYSLES: articles—

Interview, in *Movie* (London), April 1963.
Interview with Bob Sitton, in *Film Library Quarterly* (New York), Summer 1969.
"Albert and David Maysles," in *Documentary Explorations,* edited by G. Roy Levin, Garden City, New York, 1971.
Interview with R. P. Kolker, in *Sight and Sound* (London), Autumn 1971.
"*Gimme Shelter*: Production Notes," in *Filmmakers Newsletter* (Ward Hill, Massachusetts), December 1971.
"Financing the Independent Non-fiction Film," interview, in *Millimeter* (New York), June 1978.
"'Truthful Witness': An Interview with Albert Maysles," with H. Naficy, in *Quarterly Review of Film Studies* (Pleasantville, New York), Spring 1981.
Diamond, Jamie, "Albert Maysles' Camera Sees and Says It All," in *New York Times,* 13 February 1994.

On the MAYSLES: books—

Issari, M. Ali, *Cinema Verité,* Ann Arbor, Michigan, 1971.
Issari, M. Ali, and Doris A. Paul, *What is Cinema Verité,* Metuchen, New Jersey, 1979.

On the MAYSLES: articles—

Heleff, Maxine, "The Maysles Brothers and Direct Cinema," in *Film Comment* (New York), no. 2, 1964.
Blue, James, "Thoughts on Cinéma Vérité and a Discussion with the Maysles Brothers," in *Film Comment* (New York), no. 4, 1964.
"Maysles Brothers," in *Film Culture* (New York), Fall 1966.
Steele, Robert, "*Meet Marlon Brando,*" in *Film Heritage* (Dayton, Ohio), Fall 1966.
Rosenthal, Alan, "*Salesman,*" in *The New Documentary in Action: A Casebook in Film Making,* Berkeley, California, 1971.
Sadkin, David, "*Gimme Shelter*: A Corkscrew or a Cathedral?," in *Film News* (New York), December 1971.

Safier, A. M., "Shooting Hidden Camera/Real People Spots," in *Millimeter* (New York), April 1979.

Robson, K. J., "The Crystal Formation: Narrative Structure in *Grey Gardens*," in *Cinema Journal* (Chicago), Winter 1983.

Barsam, R. M., "American Direct Cinema: The Re-Presentation of Reality," in *Persistence of Vision* (Maspeth, New York), Summer 1986.

Obituary, in *Variety* (New York), 7 January 1987.

Biofilmography, in *Film Dope* (London), March 1989.

Elliott, Stuart, "In Creating a Spot, Many Say There's Nothing Like the Real Thing," in *The New York Times*, 26 November 1993.

* * *

Shooting unobtrusively in sync sound with no instructions to the subject, the Maysles brothers made films in what they preferred to call "direct cinema." Albert, gifted photographer and director of all their projects, carried the lightweight, silent camera that he perfected on his shoulder, its accessories built in and ready for adjustment. Maysles characters, who occasionally talk to the filmmakers on screen, seem astonishingly unaware that strangers and apparatus are in the room.

David, the soundman, carried a sensitive directional mike and a Nagra recorder unattached to the camera. He was often involved in the editing and as producer had final say. During the shooting a story might become apparent, or a dominant character may surface. These elements may become clear only as the editors examine, cut, and structure the vast amounts of footage that they receive in the dailies.

In 1962, a time when Albert had acquired brief experience in documentary filmmaking and David had garnered a similar amount of experience in Hollywood feature films, they formed a partnership committed to direct cinema. Commercials and industrial filmmaking supported their preferred activity from time to time.

The company's production of two feature documentaries (which they distributed commercially), *Salesman,* a study of four bible salesmen, and *Grey Gardens,* an essay on two eccentric women, fed the constant discussions between documentarists and critics about whether objectivity is at all possible in documentaries. Both films were charged with dishonesty, exploitation, and tastelessness, but other quarters praised the Maysles' sensitivity, rapport with their subjects, and choice of situations that viewers could identify with.

The Maysles sought to answer the criticism and describe their philosophy and working methods at screenings of their films, in articles, and in letters to editors. Their instinct took them, they said, to situations related to closeness between human beings, and pointed out that they could not do films about people they dislike. They looked on their work as a discovery of how people really are, first spending time with them to get acquainted, then filming their lives as lived. All their subjects agreed to the project under consideration beforehand, and several have spoken of their satisfaction with the finished film and their good relationship with Albert and David, whom they trusted.

The Maysles did not deny that their choices affected their creation in some way. Their methodology, for example, meant that much footage must be discarded. They emphasized that nothing was staged, a structure that eventually emerges from the material. In their own work they saw a relationship to Truman Capote's concepts and methods for his "non-fiction novel": discarding preconceptions about their subjects, while concentrating on learning about them and understanding their motivations and feelings.

Albert and David Maysles have an important place in the history of the documentary for many reasons. They produced a large, varied, evocative body of work in their chosen style, as very active members of their own small company. Despite some severe criticism of their work, they are admired, and probably envied for qualities that Americans value. Directly influential or not on documentaries today, their work is certainly part of the flow of films that aim to show the truth about contemporary problems. While many other filmmakers' reports and studies embrace large communities, or even whole countries, Maysles productions are about individuals and their concerns, which often illuminate larger aspects of society as well as its general attitudes toward non-traditional behavior.

Since David Maysles' death, Albert has continued turning out documentaries, mostly collaborating with Susan Froemke, Charlotte Zwerin, and Deborah Dickson. His subjects are as varied as when he worked with his brother, ranging from classical music (*Horowitz Plays Mozart, Jessye Norman Sings Carmen*) to social issues (*Abortion: Desperate Choices,* which traces the history of abortion in America) to attempts by artists to realize their visions. The last of these efforts, *Christo in Paris,* chronicles the artist Christo's efforts to wrap Paris' Pont-Neuf Bridge; two decades earlier, Albert and David had made *Christo's Valley Curtain,* in which the artist tried to hang an orange curtain over a valley.

—Lillian Schiff, updated by Rob Edelman

MAZURSKY, Paul

Nationality: American. **Born:** Irwin Mazursky in Brooklyn, New York, 25 April 1930. **Education:** Brooklyn College, degree 1951; studied acting with Paul Mann, Curt Conway, and Lee Strasberg. **Family:** Married Betsy Purdey, 1953, two daughters. **Career:** Night-club comedian, actor, and director, off-Broadway, from 1954; joined Second City in Los Angeles, 1959; writer, with Larry Tucker, for *The Danny Kaye Show* for TV, 1964-67; co-creator of *The Monkees* for TV, 1965; directed first film, *Bob and Carol and Ted and Alice,* 1969. **Address:** c/o Telecote Productions, Inc., 280 South Beverly Drive, Suite 311, Beverly Hills, CA 90212, U.S.A.

Films as Director:

1969 *Bob and Carol and Ted and Alice* (+ co-sc)
1970 *Alex in Wonderland* (+ co-sc, role as Hal Stern)
1973 *Blume in Love* (+ sc, pr, role as Hellman)
1974 *Harry and Tonto* (+ co-sc, pr)
1976 *Next Stop Greenwich Village* (+ sc, co-pr)
1978 *An Unmarried Woman* (+ sc, co-pr, role as Hal)
1980 *Willie and Phil* (+ sc)
1982 *The Tempest* (+ sc)
1984 *Moscow on the Hudson* (+ co-sc, pr, role)
1986 *Down and Out in Beverly Hills* (+ co-sc, pr, role)
1988 *Moon Over Parador* (+ co-sc, pr, role)
1989 *Enemies: A Love Story* (+ co-sc, pr, role as Leon Tortshiner)
1990 *Scenes from a Mall* (+ co-sc, pr, role as Dr. Hans Clava)
1993 *The Pickle* (+ sc, pr, role as Butch Levine)

Other Films:

1951 *Fear and Desire* (Kubrick) (role)
1955 *Blackboard Jungle* (Brooks) (role as Emmanuel Stoken)
1966 *Deathwatch* (Morrow) (role as petty thief)
1968 *I Love You Alice B. Toklas* (Averback) (co-sc)
1976 *A Star Is Born* (Pierson) (role as John Norman's manager)
1979 *A Man, a Woman, and a Bank* (Black) (role)
1985 *Into the Night* (Landis) (role)
1988 *Punchline* (Seltzer) (role); *Scenes from the Class Struggle in Beverly Hills* (Bartel) (role)

1990 *Taking Care of Business* (Hiller) (exec pr)
1992 *Man Trouble* (role as Lee Mac Greevy)
1993 *Carlito's Way* (role as Judge Feinstein)
1994 *Love Affair* (role as Herb Stillman)
1995 *Miami Rhapsody* (role as Vic)

Publications

By MAZURSKY: book—

The Tempest: A Screenplay, with Leon Capetanos, New York, 1982.

By MAZURSKY: articles—

"Paul Mazursky Seminar," in *Dialogue on Film* (Washington, D.C.), November 1974.
Interview with N. Pasquariello, in *Millimeter* (New York), vol. 3, no. 5, 1975.
Interview with Max Tessier, in *Ecran* (Paris), July 1976.
Interview with Terry Fox, in *Film Comment* (New York), March/April 1978.
Interview with R. Appelbaum, in *Films and Filming* (London), August 1978.
Interview with James Monaco, in *American Film* (Washington, D.C.), July/August 1980.
Interview with M. Tuchman, in *Film Comment* (New York), January/February 1986.
Interview with G. Midding and others, in *Filmbulletin,* vol. 32, no. 3, 1990.

On MAZURSKY: articles—

Burgess, John, in *Film Society Review* (New York), May 1970.
Cocks, J., "Portrait of the Artisan," in *Time* (New York), 18 January 1971.
Corliss, Richard, "Paul Mazursky: The Horace with the Heart of Gold," in *Film Comment* (New York), March/April 1975.
Jacobs, Diane, "Paul Mazursky," in *Hollywood Renaissance,* New York, 1977.
Fieschi, J., "Dossier: Hollywood 79: Paul Mazursky," in *Cinématographe* (Paris), March 1979.
Mascuch, P., "Directors Series: Paul Mazursky," in *Films in Review* (New York), November 1980.
Siegel, J.E., "Bourgeois Blues," in *American Film* (Washington, D.C.), May 1984.
Silvester, Christopher, "You Look Like a Nice Boy to Me, He Said," in *20/20* (London), April 1990.

* * *

It is no small irony that Paul Mazursky's best film is one he wrote (with Larry Tucker), but was not given the chance to direct. *I Love You Alice B. Toklas,* like most of Mazursky's work, stages a humorous, if somewhat predictable, encounter between deadening forms of everyday life (especially the monotonous regularity of heterosexual monogamy) and the bewildering, if attractive, otherness of nonconformity. Directed by Hy Averback (at the insistence of star Peter Sellers, who would not work with a novice), this film records the fall of its main character, seduced by free love and marijuana brownies, into a late 1960s California underworld of unlimited self-indulgence, social honesty, and brotherly tolerance. Recovering his desire for a comfortable working life and marriage to the right girl, the Sellers character almost decides to go straight, but refuses at the very end to choose between the extremes his culture offers, the discontents of which have been equally and mercilessly exposed.

Paul Mazursky

The commercial and critical success of *Alice* gave Mazursky an entree into New Hollywood directing. Unlike the film school whiz-kids (Coppola, Scorsese, Lucas, Spielberg, and company) who came into prominence at this same time, Mazursky had spent many years in show business, developing not only an acting career (which he has continued, if in a more limited way, after turning to directing) but a fair reputation as a writer (among other credits he wrote, with Tucker, the pilot episode of *The Monkees*). Like the more famous talents of the Hollywood Renaissance, however, Mazursky has manifested an abiding interest not only in a critical social realism, but also in the European art film, which, through imitation and *hommage,* he has attempted to domesticate for the general American audience. His cinema, at the same time, favors the writer and the actor; not interested in or capable of an individual, arresting visual style, his films are based on literate scripts and afford excellent opportunities for affecting performance. And yet, unlike *Alice,* they usually retreat from the harsh conclusions which their initially penetrating analyses of contemporary life should require.

Bob and Carol and Ted and Alice, for example, offers an upwardly mobile California couple whose lives, following what appears to be a marathon Essalen encounter session, find a new direction. Taking the message of absolute honesty and non-stop self-expression to heart, they resolutely transform their social selves, experimenting with free love and attempting to loosen up their best friends, a more traditional couple who use up their energy in self-defeating games and manipulations. The foursome, now mixed, eventually winds up in a luxurious resort bed together, but are unable, presumably because of a residual conservatism, to consummate their contemplated new relationship. The film, however, offers this ideological dead-end as a triumph, as a happy ending whose import is hardly clear. Traditional marriage, with its jealousies and lies, has been mercilessly satirized, but open mar-

riage, Mazursky seems to suggest, does not suit basic human needs. And yet Mazursky's relentless tenderness toward his characters, a sentimentality that surfaces as his desire to make the spectator identify with their predicament, blunts this critique by focussing attention on a relief-filled retreat from choice (the irony that the characters are set free to enjoy themselves in Las Vegas is not underlined).

Bob and Carol made a good deal of money during its initial release in 1969, perhaps because it dared to deal with some of the conflicts of the developing sexual revolution; it has not worn well. Most of Mazursky's subsequent films re-stage the same dramatic and ideological conflicts with mixed results. *Harry and Tonto* begins by challenging notions of ageing, but winds up confirming a whole range of social stereotypes: despite an occasional bitter note, the film exudes a warm, accepting humanism that trivializes its criticism of socially acceptable self-indulgence and mindless role-playing (the main character finds his niche as a lovably cantankerous septuagenarian who likes cats). *An Unmarried Woman* cuts its richly pampered Upper East Side heroine adrift from her cheating husband only to enmesh her in a suitably vague conventional fantasy—having to choose between wonderful sex and a bohemian lifestyle with a handsome artist, on the one hand, and the self-fulfilling exploration of the world of work (whose details are deliberately left rather vague), on the other. *Alex in Wonderland* strikes an autobiographical note with its portrait of a director, naturally enamored of Fellini, in search of a powerful theme for his next project. Compared to Woody Allen's similar *hommage* (*Stardust Memories*), the film lacks biting humor and fails to find interesting reflexes for Fellini's modernist technique and intellectual seriousness. *Willie and Phil* cannot create American equivalents for Truffaut's cinema of interpersonal conflict and triumph, while *Down and Out in Beverly Hills,* based on a classic Renoir study of the venality and selfishness that cut across class lines, becomes an unintentional comedy of integration, constructing a cinematic world that sentimentalizes the inauthentic, the mindless, and the hypocritical. Like its director, the film's main character has his heart in the right place and is a reasonable success in his chosen field, even if he is unable to master the madness of the world around him without romanticizing its foibles and absurdities.

In the late 1980s and early 1990s, Mazursky has continued to find success with chronicles of contemporary American life that emphasize its contradictions and absurdities. Like *Down and Out in Beverly Hills, Scenes from a Mall* (with its deliberate Bergmanesque echoes) centers on marital problems among the haute bourgeoisie, in this case an upscale California two-career couple whose relationship disintegrates and reestablishes itself during a nightmarish odyssey through a suburban mall. The film is not only an homage to Bergman but, with its hyperconscious and motor-mouth main characters, an homage to Woody Allen, who plays the self-doubting but good-hearted husband he might have created himself. Though certainly funny and often inventive, *Scenes from a Mall* depends too heavily on its script (which bogs down in repetition halfway through) and the engaging style of Allen and Bette Midler. Mazursky does little more than stage their encounter, and except for brief moments never uses the mall inventively to create more of a cinematic experience. Though it suffered from a poor release, *The Pickle* offers Mazursky at his best, with a chronicle of the absurdities of contemporary filmmaking, especially its deal making and artistic compromises. Here the script is well constructed and allows Mazursky to do what he does best: direct the actors.

Mazursky's most memorable recent film, however, is his most untypical. *Enemies: A Love Story,* based on an Isaac Bashevis Singer story, offers a tragi-comic narrative of a man who, falling victim to circumstance and his own desires, winds up with two wives and a mistress he would like to marry. Set in a post-Shoah New York, the film offers the character's failure to settle down as, in part, the result of an entire culture's displacement and ruin (the deadly aspects of which have not ended, as one of his women kills herself, doin the Nazis were never able to accomplish). Coaxing fine perforı from a largely unknown ensemble cast (Ron Silver plays the Mazursky successfully evokes a bygone era by using nicely d sets (camp in the Catskills, Brooklyn streets, a Coney Island and a photographic style that emphasizes the human drama p out within them. *Enemies: A Love Story* deserves to be consi like *The Godfather* and *Avalon,* one of the most engaging and etrating cinematic interpretations of postwar America.

—R. Barton Pa

McCAREY, Leo

Nationality: American. **Born:** Los Angeles, 3 October 1898. **Ed cation:** Los Angeles High School; University of Southern Califorı Law School. **Family:** Married Stella Martin, 1920, one daught **Career:** Lawyer in San Francisco and Los Angeles, 1916-17; thi assistant to Tod Browning, then script supervisor, at Universal, 191 19; supervisor and director of about 300 comedy shorts for Hal Roac studios, 1923-28; gagman for Our Gang series, 1923-24; teamed Sta Laurel and Oliver Hardy, 1927; signed with Fox Studios, 1930; signed with Paramount, 1933; formed Rainbow Productions with Bing Crosby and others, 1946. **Awards:** Oscar for Best Direction for *The Awful Truth,* 1937; Oscars for Best Direction and Best Original Story for *Going My Way,* 1944. **Died:** 5 July 1969.

Films as Director:

1921 *Society Secrets* (+ pr)

1924 *Publicity Pays* (+ co-sc); *Young Oldfield* (+ co-sc); *Stolen Goods* (+ co-sc); *Jeffries Jr.* (+ co-sc); *Why Husbands Go Mad* (+ co-sc); *A Ten Minutes Egg* (+ co-sc); *Seeing Nellie Home* (+ co-sc); *Sweet Daddy* (+ co-sc); *Why Men Work* (+ co-sc); *Outdoor Pajamas* (+ co-sc); *Sittin' Pretty* (+ co-sc); *Too Many Mamas* (+ co-sc); *Bungalow Boobs* (+ co-sc); *Accidental Accidents* (+ co-sc); *All Wet* (+ co-sc); *The Poor Fish* (+ co-sc); *The Royal Razz* (+ co-sc)

1925 *Hello Baby* (+ co-sc); *Fighting Fluid* (+ co-sc); *The Family Entrance* (+ co-sc); *Plain and Fancy Girls* (+ co-sc); *Should Husbands Be Watched?* (+ co-sc); *Hard Boiled* (+ co-sc); *Is Marriage the Bunk?* (+ co-sc); *Bad Boy* (+ co-sc); *Big Red Riding Hood* (+ co-sc); *Looking for Sally* (+ co-sc); *What Price Goofy?* (+ co-sc); *Isn't Life Terrible* (+ co-sc); *Innocent Husbands* (+ co-sc); *No Father to Guide Him* (+ co-sc); *The Caretaker's Daughter* (+ co-sc); *The Uneasy Three* (+ co-sc); *His Wooden Wedding* (+ co-sc)

1926 *Charley My Boy* (+ co-sc); *Mama Behave* (+ co-sc); *Dog Shy* (+ co-sc); *Mum's the Word* (+ co-sc); *Long Live the King* (+ co-sc); *Mighty Like a Moose* (+ co-sc); *Crazy Like a Fox* (+ co-sc); *Bromo and Juliet* (+ co-sc); *Tell 'em Nothing* (+ co-sc); *Be Your Age* (+ co-sc)

1928 *We Faw Down* (*We Slip Up*); *Should Married Men Go Home?* (+ co-sc, supervisor); *Two Tars* (+ story, supervisor); *Should Women Drive?* (+ co-sc); *A Pair of Tights* (+ co-sc); *Blow By Blow* (+ co-sc); *The Boy Friend* (+ co-sc); *Came the Dawn* (+ co-sc); *Do Gentlemen Snore?* (+ co-sc); *Dumb Daddies* (+ co-sc); *Going Ga-ga* (+ co-sc); *Pass the Gravy* (+ co-sc); *Tell It to the Judge* (+ co-sc); *That Night* (+ co-sc)

Leo McCarey

1929 *Liberty* (+ co-sc); *Wrong Again* (+ co-sc); *Dad's Day* (+ co-sc); *Freed 'em and Weep* (+ co-sc); *Hurdy Gurdy* (+ co-sc); *Madame Q* (+ co-sc); *Sky Boy* (+ co-sc); *The Unkissed Man* (+ co-sc); *When Money Comes* (+ co-sc); *Why Is Plumber* (+ co-sc)
1929 *The Sophomore* (+ co-sc); *Red Hot Rhythm* (+ co-sc)
1930 *Wild Company*; *Part Time Wife* (+ co-sc)
1931 *Indiscreet*
1932 *The Kid from Spain*
1933 ***Duck Soup***
1934 *Six of a Kind*; *Belle of the Nineties* (*It Ain't No Sin*); *Ruggles of Red Gap*
1935 *The Milky Way*
1937 *Make Way for Tomorrow* (*The Years Are So Long*; *When the Wind Blows*) (+ pr); *The Awful Truth*
1938 *Love Affair*
1940 *My Favorite Wife* (+ co-sc)
1942 *Once upon a Honeymoon* (+ pr)
1944 *Going My Way* (+ pr, story)
1945 *The Bells of Saint Mary's* (+ pr, story)
1948 *Good Sam* (+ pr, co-story)
1952 *My Son John* (+ pr, story, co-sc)
1957 *An Affair to Remember* (+ co-sc)
1958 *Rally 'round the Flag, Boys!* (+ pr, co-sc)
1961 *Satan Never Sleeps* (*China Story*) (+ pr, co-sc)

Other Films:

1927 *Second Hundred Years* (story)
1938 *The Cowboy and the Lady* (co-story)

Publications

By McCAREY: articles—

"What Makes a Box Office Hit?," in *Cinema* (Los Angeles), June 1947.

On McCAREY: books—

Gehring, Wes, *Leo McCarey and the Comic Anti-Hero in American Film,* New York, 1980.
Poague, Leland, *Wilder and McCarey,* New York, 1980.

On McCAREY: articles—

Carroll, Sidney, "Everything Happens to McCarey," in *Esquire* (New York), May 1943.
"Leo McCarey Section" of *Cahiers du Cinéma* (Paris), February 1965.
Crosby, Bing, and David Butler, "Remembering Leo McCarey," in *Action* (Los Angeles), September/October 1969.
Smith, H. Allen, "A Session with McCarey," in *Variety* (New York), January 1970.
Lloyd, P., "Some Affairs to Remember: The Style of Leo McCarey," in *Monogram* (London), no. 4, 1972.
Lourcelles, Jacques, "Leo McCarey," in *Anthologie du Cinéma,* vol. 7, Paris, 1973.
Richards, Jeffrey, "Great Moments: Leo McCarey," in *Focus on Film* (London), Spring 1973.
Silver, C., "Leo McCarey: From Marx to McCarthy," in *Film Comment* (New York), September/October 1973.
Morris, George, "McCarey and McCarthy," in *Film Comment* (New York), January/February 1976.
Gehring, Wes, "Leo McCarey: The Man behind Laurel and Hardy," in *Films in Review* (New York), November 1979.
Everson, William K., and others (letters), "McCarey/Laurel and Hardy," in *Films in Review* (New York), February 1980; also letter from Wes Gehring, April 1980.
Shipman, David, "Directors of the Decade," in *Films and Filming* (London), April 1983.
Bourget, J.L., "Rally Once Again: Leo McCarey à la télévision," in *Positif* (Paris), April 1985.
"Leo McCarey," in *Film Dope* (London), June 1987.

* * *

Leo McCarey has always presented *auteur* criticism with one of its greatest challenges and one that has never been convincingly met. The failure to do so should be seen as casting doubt on the validity of *auteurism* (in its cruder and simpler forms) rather than on the value of the McCarey oeuvre. He worked consistently (and apparently quite uncomplainingly) within the dominant codes of shooting and editing that comprise the anonymous "classical Hollywood" style; the films that bear his name as director, ranging from *Duck Soup* to *The Bells of St. Mary's,* from Laurel and Hardy shorts to *My Son John,* from *The Awful Truth* to *Make Way for Tomorrow* (made the same year!), resist reduction to a coherent thematic interpretation. Yet his name is on some of the best—and best-loved—Hollywood films (as well as on some that embarrass many of even his most fervent defenders).

In fact, it might be argued that McCarey's work validates a more sophisticated and circumspect *auteur* approach: not the author as

divinely inspired individual creative genius, but the author as the animating presence in a project within which multiple determinants—collaborative, generic, ideological—complexly interact. The only adequate approach to a McCarey film would involve the systematic analysis of that interaction. A few notes can be offered, however, towards defining the "animating presence."

McCarey's formative years as an artist were spent working with the great clowns of the late silent/early sound period: Harold Lloyd, Mae West, W.C. Fields, the Marx Brothers and (especially) Laurel and Hardy, for whom he was "supervising manager" for many years, personally directing two of their greatest shorts (*Liberty* and *Wrong Again*). His subsequent career spans (with equal success) the entire range of American comedy from screwball (*The Awful Truth*) to romantic (*An Affair to Remember*). The director's congenial characteristic seems to have been a commitment to a spontaneous, individualist anarchy which he never entirely abandoned, accompanied by a consistent skepticism about institutions and restrictive forms of social organization, a skepticism which produces friction and contradiction even within the most seemingly innocuous, conservative projects. *Going My Way* and *The Bells of St. Mary's* are usually rejected outright by the intelligentsia as merely pious and sentimental, but their presentation of Catholicism is neither simple, straightforward, nor uncritical, and it is easy to mistake for sentimentality, in contexts where you expect to find it anyway (such as Hollywood movies about singing priests), qualities such as tenderness and generosity. The celebration of individualism is of course a mainspring of American ideology, yet, pushed far enough in certain directions, it can expose contradictions *within* that ideology: its oppressive response to many forms of individuality, for example.

Make Way for Tomorrow (which, understandably, remained McCarey's favorite among his own films) is exemplary in this respect. Taking as its starting point an apparently reformable social problem (with Lee Grant's *Tell Me a Riddle* it is one of the only important Hollywood films about the aged), and opening with an unassailably respectable Biblical text ("Honor thy father and thy mother"), it proceeds to elaborate what amounts to a systematic radical analysis of the constraints, oppression, and divisiveness produced by capitalist culture, lending itself to a thoroughgoing Marxist reading that would certainly have surprised its director. Typically, the film (merely very good for its first three-quarters) suddenly takes off into greatness at the moment when Victor Moore asks the ultimate anarchic question "Why not?", and proceeds to repudiate his family in favour of rediscovering the original relationship with his wife before they become absorbed into the norms of democratic-capitalist domesticity. The process is only completed when, in one of the Hollywood cinema's most poignant and subversive moments, he "unmarries" them as they say their last farewell at the train station: "It's been a pleasure knowing you, Miss Breckenridge."

—Robin Wood

MEHBOOB Khan

Nationality: Indian. **Born:** Mehboob Khan Ramzan Khan in Bilmora, in the Gandevi Taluka of Baroda State, India, 1909. **Family:** Married 1925, one son. **Career:** Extra at Imperial Film Studio, Bombay, from 1927; actor of "bit" parts for subsidiary, Sagar Movietone, from 1931; directed first film, for Sagar Film Co., 1935; established Mehboob Productions, 1943; built Mehboob Studios, 1952. **Died:** Of a heart attack, on hearing of Nehru's death, 27 May 1964.

Films as Director:

1935 *Judgement of Allah* (*Alhilal*) (+ sc)
1936 *Deccan Queen*; *Manmohan*
1937 *Jagirdar*
1938 *Hum Tum Aur Woh* (*We Three*); *Watan*
1939 *Ek Hi Rasta* (*The Only Way*)
1940 *Alibaba*; *Aurat* (*Woman*)
1941 *Bahen* (*Sister*)
1942 *Roti* (*Bread*)
1943 *Najma* (+ pr); *Taqdeer* (+ pr)
1945 *Humayun* (+ pr)
1946 *Anmol Ghadi* (*Priceless Watch*) (+ pr)
1947 *Elan* (+ pr)
1948 *Anokhi Ada* (*A Special Charm*) (+ pr)
1949 *Andaz* (*Style*) (+ pr)
1952 *Aan* (*Pride*) (+ pr)
1954 *Amar* (+ pr)
1957 ***Bharat Mata*** (*Mother India*)(+ pr)
1962 *Son of India* (+ pr)

Other Films:

1927 *Alibaba and Forty Thieves* (Misra) (role as thief)
1929 *Maurya Patan* (*Fall of Mauryas*) (Choudhury) (role)
1930 *Mewad No Mawali* (*Rogues of Rajasthan*) (Vakil) (role)
1931 *Dilawar* (Torney) (role); *Abul Hasan* (Ghosh) (role)
1932 *Romantic Prince* (*Meri Jaan*) (Ghosh)
1933 *Premi Pagal* (*Mad Cap*) (Mir) (role); *Bulbule Baghdad* (Vakil) (role)
1934 *Grihalaxmi* (Badami) (role); *Nautch Girl* (*Dancing Girl*) (Desai) (role); *Sati Anjana* (Rathod) (role)
1956 *Awaz* (Sarhady) (pr); *Paisa Hi Paisa* (Mehrish) (pr)

Publications

On MEHBOOB: books—

Barnouw, Erik, and S. Krishnaswany, *Indian Film,* New York, 1965.
Willemen, Paul, and Behroze Ghandy, *Indian Cinema,* London, 1982.
Pfleiderer, Beatrice, and Lothar Lutze, *The Hindi Film: Agent and Re-Agent of Cultural Change,* New Delhi, 1985.
Ramachandran, T.M., *70 Years of Indian Cinema (1913-1983),* Bombay, 1985.

On MEHBOOB: articles—

Film Quarterly (Berkeley), Autumn 1960.
Ray, Satyajit, "Under Western Eyes," in *Sight and Sound* (London), Autumn 1982.
Tesson, Charles, "Le rêve indien," in *Cahiers du Cinéma* (Paris), March 1985.
Thomas, R., "Indian Cinema: Pleasures and Popularity," in *Screen* (London), May/August 1985.

* * *

The urbane director K.A. Abbas once referred to Mehboob as the "great rustic" of the Hindi cinema. Indeed, a certain mythology developed around Mehboob—that of the man with popular roots. This image owed much to stories about his origins (the small town boy who worked his way up through the Bombay studios), and to certain films which dwelt on the travails of the poor and the destitute, such as *Aurat (Woman)* and *Roti (Bread).*

In fact, however, Mehboob's output as director was quite varied. After he founded his own company, Mehboob Productions, in 1943, he made historical works *(Humayun)* and fantasy spectaculars *(Aan/Pride).* Even films such as *Anmol Ghadi (Priceless Watch)* and *Anokhi Ada (A Special Charm),* which appeared to address the class divide, were variations of the triangular love story, the favoured convention of the Hindi cinema.

In these films social representation becomes incidental to the basic plot because the narrative spaces of a simple rural life or of urban destitution are constructed in an idealised rather than in a realistic way. The lighting style of such scenes show them as composed of smooth studio surfaces, and there is an indifference to the more squalid details of characterisation. The emphasis lies in the fullness of melodramatic sentiments—of loss and of romantic longing—which occasion the use of lushly orchestrated songs. All this is a pleasurable closing off of the cinema and its audience from social references, a tendency in Mehboob's work best represented by his venture into the swashbuckling colour film *Aan.*

Elements of this romantic mode are observable even in Mehboob's "social" films. In *Aurat* and its later colour version, *Mother India,* rural life is often conveyed as a series of spectacularly choreographed scenes of harvesting, festivals, and the romantic engagement of its characters. *Andaz (Style),* on the other hand, invites the audience to soak in the luxuries of the modern, upper-class settings in which its characters live.

In this sense, Mehboob was not simply a popularly rooted "rustic" artist, but engaged in creations of high artifice and escapism. However, these elements were often integrated with quite powerful constructions of meaning. *Aurat,* for example, achieves an almost anthropological view of gender roles. This is accomplished not by the accuracy of its observations about rural life, but by using the grim struggles of rural life as a way of drawing out the role performed by Indian women. This provides the basis for the film's main interest, the melodrama of the unrelieved suffering of a woman (Sardar Akhtar) on behalf of her sons (Surendra and Yakub). The subsequent version of this film, *Mother India,* is an interesting contrast. The focus is still on the suffering of the mother (Nargis); but this capacity to suffer is transformed into a distinctly mythical power which moves beyond her immediate family to inspire the whole village community. In both films the woman is the bearer of a patriarchal inheritance for her son, but *Mother India* may have represented a new, mythicised role model for women, one whose power often co-exists uneasily with its conservative functions.

Perhaps most interesting is *Andaz,* a drama, at least implicitly, of illicit desire. The story is about Nina (Nargis) who, while faithful to her absent fiancé (Raj Kapoor), relates vivaciously to an attractive young man (Dilip Kumar). The heroine is shown to be a naive innocent who cannot perceive that relaxed social relations between men and women can lead to misunderstanding, and this generates the tragic events that follow. Yet the narration moves beyond, or perhaps deeper into, its own fascination with the settings and mores of its upper class characters, introducing an interesting, fantastical ambiguity. Nina's denials that she is attracted to a man other than her husband are put into doubt for the audience through scenes depicting the hallucinations and dreams that assail the heroine. In this way the "rustic" Mehboob was surprisingly well equipped to convey certain strikingly modern problems of sexuality and desire.

—Ravi Vasudevan

MEKAS, Jonas

Nationality: Lithuanian. **Born:** Semeniskiai, 24 December 1922. **Education:** Gymnasium, Birzai, Lithuania, graduated 1942; studied philosophy and literature, Johannes Gutenberg University, Mainz, and University of Tübingen. **Family:** Married Hollis Melton, 1974; children: Oona and Sebastian. **Career:** During German occupation, taken, with brother Adolfas, to forced labor camp near Hamburg, 1944; they escaped, 1945; lived in displaced persons camps, 1945-49; while studying in Germany, edited Lithuanian emigré literary magazine *Zvilgsniai* (Glimpses), and wrote collections of short stories and poetry; moved to New York, 1949; worked in factories and shops in various capacities, through 1950s; founded *Film Culture* magazine, 1955, remains editor-in-chief; began "Movie Journal" column for *Village Voice,* 1958; shot first film, *Guns of the Trees,* and helped organize New American Cinema Group, 1960; organized The Film-Makers Cooperative, 1961; organized the Film-Makers Cinematheque, arrested and charged with showing obscene film (Jack Smith's *Flaming Creatures*), given six-month suspended sentence, 1964; co-founder with P. Adams Sitney, then acting director, Anthology Film Archives, 1970. **Awards:** Documentary Award, Venice Festival, for *The Brig,* 1965. **Address:** c/o Anthology Film Archives, 32 Second Avenue, New York, NY 10003, U.S.A.

Films as Director:

1961 *Guns of the Trees*
1963 *Film Magazine of the Arts*
1964 *The Brig*; *Award Presentation to Andy Warhol*
1966 *Report from Millbrook*; *Hare Krishna*; *Notes on the Circus*; *Cassis*
1968 *Walden (Diaries, Notes, and Sketches)*
1969 *Time & Fortune Vietnam Newsreel*
1972 *Reminiscences of a Journey to Lithuania*
1976 *Lost, Lost, Lost*
1978 *In Between*
1980 *Paradise Not Yet Lost, or Oona's Fifth Year*
1981 *Notes for Jerome*
1986 *He Stands in the Desert Counting the Seconds of His Life*
1990 *Self Portrait*; *Scenes from the Life of Andy Warhol*
1993 *Jonas in the Desert*

Publications

By MEKAS: articles—

Founder of *Film Culture* magazine, 1955, contributes regularly and remains its editor-in-chief.
Contributor of weekly column, "Movie Journal," to *Village Voice* (New York), since 1958.
Statement, in *Film Comment* (New York), Winter 1964.
Interview with B. L. Kevles, in *Film Culture* (New York), Fall 1965.
Interview with Gerald Barrett, in *Literature/Film Quarterly* (Salisbury, Maryland), Spring 1973.
Interview with Antonin Liehm, in *Thousand Eyes* (New York), October 1976.

On MEKAS: book—

James, David E., *To Free the Cinema: Jonas Mekas and the New York Underground,* Princeton, New Jersey, 1992.

On MEKAS: articles—

Harrington, Stephanie, "Pornography Is Undefined at Film-Critic Mekas's Trial," in *The Village Voice* (New York), 18 June 1964.
Levy, Alan, "Voice of the Underground Cinema," in *New York Times Magazine,* 19 September 1965.

Jonas Mekas

Simon, Bill, "New Forms in Film," in *Artforum* (New York), October 1972.
Tompkins, Calvin, "Profile: All Pockets Open," in *New Yorker,* 6 January 1973.
Goldstein, R., "Give It Away on 2nd Avenue," in *Village Voice* (New York), 29 January 1979.
MacDonald, S., "Lost Lost Lost over *Lost Lost Lost,*" in *Cinema Journal* (Champaign, Illinois), Winter 1986.
Ruoff, J. K., "Home Movies of the Avant-Garde: Jonas Mekas and the New York Art Scene," *Cinema Journal,* vol. 30, no. 3, 1991.
Siegel, F., "In Praise of Extraordinary Cinema: Anthology Film Archives," in *Boxoffice,* October 1992.
Rollet, P., "Les exils de Jonas Mekas," in *Cahiers du Cinema* (Paris), January 1993.
Sitney, P. Adams, "Three Filmmakers as Culture Heroes," in *Yale Review* (New Haven, Connecticut), October 1994.

* * *

Born in Lithuania in 1922, Jonas Mekas was a poet and resistance worker against both the German and Soviet occupations during the Second World War. After some years in a German camp for displaced persons, he and his brother, Adolfas, also a filmmaker, immigrated to New York, where they later founded the journal *Film Culture.* Initially hostile to the American avant-garde, Mekas became its champion and spokesman in the 1960s. Throughout that decade he exerted great influence through *Film Culture,* his "Movie Journal" column in the *Village Voice,* and his founding of the Film-makers Cooperative (in 1962) to distribute independent films, and the Film-makers Cinematheque (in 1963) as a New York showcase.

His first film, *Guns of the Trees,* a 35-millimeter feature, describes aspects of Beat culture in New York through the lives of four fictional characters. It reflects his hopes, at that time, for the establishment of a feature-length narrative cinema on the model of the French and Polish "New Waves." By the time he made *The Brig* with his brother, directly filming Ken Brown's stage play in the Living Theatre Production as if it were a documentary, he had already shifted his energies to his ongoing cinematic diary. The diary had actually begun in the mid-1950s when he reached the United States, but it took the liberating inspiration of Stan Brakhage and Marie Menken for Mekas to acknowledge that his artistic talent was focused outside of the feature film tradition he had been espousing.

The first installment of his *Diaries, Notes, and Sketches,* the nearly three-hour-long *Walden,* records his life, with numerous portraits of his friends and colleagues, in the mid-1960s. Its techniques are characteristic of the filmmaker's mature work: staccato, single-frame flashes, composed directly in the camera, are counterpointed to longer sketches of weddings, trips to the circus, meetings. Printed intertitles often occur. Long passages have musical accompaniment. The filmmaker repeatedly breaks in on the soundtrack to offer private reflections and aphorisms.

In 1976 Mekas released *Lost, Lost, Lost,* another three-hour section of the megadiary. This time, he went back to his initial experiments with the camera, in a more conventional and leisurely style, to document the aspirations and frustrations of his life as an exile dreaming of the re-establishment of an independent Lithuanian republic. Bits of this material had already appeared in his masterly and moving *Reminiscences of a Journey to Lithuania,* a three-part film made with the help of German television. The middle section of that film describes the emotional reunion of both brothers with their mother, then almost ninety years old, when they returned home for their first visit since the war. The film opens with a summary of Mekas's initial experiences in America and ends with a recognition of the impossibility of recovering the past, as he joins a group of his friends, mostly artists, in Vienna.

That elegiac tone is sustained and refined in *Notes for Jerome,* the record of his visits to the estate of Jerome Hill, in Cassis, France, in the late 1960s, and edited after Hill's death in 1972. Mekas married Hollis Melton in 1974; their first child, Oona, was born the next year. *Paradise Not Yet Lost, or Oona's Fifth Year* deals with his family life, but continues the theme of lost childhood which permeates Mekas's vision. It is filmed in the style of *Walden,* as is *In Between,* which records the years between *Lost, Lost, Lost* and *Walden.*

—P. Adams Sitney

MÉLIÈS, Georges

Nationality: French. **Born:** Paris, 8 December 1861. **Education:** the Lycée Imperial, Vanves, 1868-70; Lycée Louis-le-Grand, Paris, 1871-80; **Family:** Married 1) Eugénie Genin, 1885, children: Georgette and André; 2) Fanny Manieux (born Charlotte-Stéphanie Faës, stage name Jahanne D'Arcy), 1925. **Career:** Introduced to illusionism by English conjuror John Maskelyne, 1884; bought Théâtre Robert-Houdin, Paris, began to present performance of magic and illusionism, and began association with technician Eugène Calmels, 1888; attended première of Cinematographe Lumière, 1895; bought Animatographe projector in London, developed camera with Lucien Reulos, built first studio at Montreuil, began shooting first film *Partie des cartes,* "Star Film Company" begun, 1896; transformed theatre into cinema, 1897; brother Gaston Méliès opens Star Film branch in New York, 1903; second Montreuil studio built, 1905; studio closes temporarily due to American competition, 1909; returned to stage as magician, 1910 (last performance 1920); Méliès retrospective, Paris, after "rediscovery" by Leon Druhot, 1929; given an apartment at Chateau d'Orly by the Mutuelle du Cinéma, 1932. **Awards:** Legion of Honour, 1933. **Died:** In Paris, 21 January 1938.

Films as Director, Producer, Scenarist, Art Director and Actor:

1896 (seventy-eight films, two extant): *Une Nuit terrible* (*A Terrible Night*); *Escamotage d'une dame chez Robert-Houdin* (*The Vanishing Lady*)

1897 (fifty-two films, four extant): *Entre Calais et Douvres* (*Between Calais and Dover*); *L'Auberge ensorcelée* (*The Bewitched Inn*); *Aprés le bal* (*After the Ball*); *Danse au sérail* (*Dancing in a Harem*); *Combat naval en Grèce*

1898 (thirty films, eight extant): *Visite sous-marine du Maine* (*Divers at Work on the Wreck of the Maine*); *Panorama pris d'un train en marche* (*Panorama from Top of a Moving Train*); *Le Magicien*; *Illusions fantasmagoriques* (*The Famous Box Trick*); *La Lune à un mètre* (*The Astronomer's Dream*); *Un Homme de tête* (*The Four Troublesome Heads*); *La Tentation de Saint-Antoine* (*The Temptation of Saint Anthony*); *Salle à manger fantastique* (*A Dinner Under Difficulties*)

1899 (thirty-four films, four extant): *Cléopâtre* (*Robbing Cleopatra's Tomb*); *L'Impressioniste fin de siècle* (*An Up-To-Date Conjurer*); *Le Portrait mystérieux* (*A Mysterious Portrait*); *L'Affaire Dreyfus* (*The Dreyfus Affair*)

1900 (thirty-three films, seven extant): *Les Miracles de Brahmane* (*The Miracles of Brahmin*); *L'Exposition de 1900* (*Paris Exposition, 1900*); *L'Homme orchestre* (*The One-Man Band*); *Le Rêve de Noël* (*The Christmas Dream*); *Gens qui pleurent et gens qui rient* (*Crying and Laughing*); *Nouvelles*

Luttes extravagantes (*The Wrestling Sextette*); *Le Malade hydrophobe* (*The Man with Wheels in His Head*)

1901 (twenty-nine films, four extant): *Le Brahmane et le papillon* (*The Brahmin and the Butterfly*); *Dislocations mystérieuses* (*Extraordinary Illusions*); *Le Charlatan* (*Painless Dentistry*; *Barbe-Bleue* (*Blue Beard*)

1902 (twenty-three films, five extant): *L'Homme à la tête de caoutchouc* (*The Man with the Rubber Head. India Rubber Head*); *Eruption volcanique à la Martinique* (*The Eruption of Mount Pelée*); ***Le Voyage dans la lune*** (*A Trip to the Moon*); *Le Sacré d'Édouard VII* (*The Coronation of Edward VII*); *Les Trésors de Satan* (*The Treasures of Satan*)

1903 (twenty-nine films, twenty-eight extant): *La Corbeille enchantée* (*The Enchanted Basket*); *La Guirlande merveilleuse* (*The Marvellous Wreath*); *Les Filles du Diable* (*Beelzebub's Daughters*); *Un Malheur n'arrive jamais seul* (*Misfortune Never Comes Alone*); *Le Cake-walk infernal* (*The Infernal Cake Walk*); *La Boîte à malice* (*The Mysterious Box*); *Le Puits fantastique* (*The Enchanted Well*); *L'Auberge du bon repos* (*The Inn Where No Man Rests*); *La Statue animée* (*The Drawing Lesson*); *La Flamme merveilleuse* (*The Mystical Flame*); *Le Sorcier* (*The Witch's Revenge*); *L'Oracle de Delphes* (*The Oracle of Delphi*); *Le Portrait spirite* (*A Spiritualist Photographer*); *Le Mélomane* (*The Melomaniac*); *Le Monstre* (*The Monster*); *Le Royaume des Fées* (*The Kingdom of the Fairies*); *Le Chaudron infernal* (*The Infernal Cauldron*); *Le Revenant* (*The Apparition*); *Le Tonnerre de Jupiter* (*Jupiter's Thunderbolts*; *La Parapluie fantastique* (*Ten Ladies in One Umbrella*); *Tom Tight et Dum Dum* (*Jack Jaggs and Dum Dum*); *Bob Kick, l'enfant terrible* (*Bob Kick the Mischievous Kid*); *Illusions funambulesques* (*Extraordinary Illusions*); *L'Enchanteur Alcofrisbas* (*Alcofrisbas, the Master Magician*); *Jack et Jim*; *La Lanterne magique* (*The Magic Lantern*); *La Rêve du maître de ballet* (*The Ballet Master's Dream*); *Faust aux enfers* (*The Damnation of Faust*)

1904 (thirty-five films, nineteen extant): *Le Bourreau turc* (*The Terrible Turkish Executioner*); *Au Clair de la lune ou Pierrot malheureux* (*A Moonlight Serenade, or The Miser Punished*); *Un Bonne Farce avec ma tête* (*Tit for Tat*); *Le Coffre enchanté* (*The Bewitched Trunk*); *Les Apparitions fugitives* (*Fugitive Apparitions*); *Le Roi du maquillage* (*Untamable Whiskers*); *La Rêve d'horloger* (*The Clockmaker's Dream*); *Les Transmutations imperceptibles* (*The Imperceptible Transformations*); *Un Miracle sous l'inquisition* (*A Miracle Under the Inquisition*); *Benvenutto Cellini ou une curieuse évasion* (*Benvenuto Cellini, or a Curious Evasion*); *La Damnation du Docteur Faust* (*Faust and Marguerite*); *Le Thaumaturge chinois* (*Tchin-Chao, the Chinese Conjurer*); *Le Merveilleux éventail vivant* (*The Wonderful Living Fan*); *Sorcellerie culinaire* (*The Cook in Trouble*); *La Sirène* (*The Mermaid*); *Le Rosier miraculeux* (*The Wonderful Rose Tree*); *Le Voyage à travers l'impossible* (*The Impossible Voyage*); *Le Juif errant* (*The Wandering Jew*); *La Cascade de Feu* (*The Firefall*)

1905 (twenty-two films, eleven extant): *Les Cartes vivants* (*The Living Playing Cards*); *Le Diable noir* (*The Black Imp*); *Le Menuet lilliputien* (*The Lilliputian Minuet*); *Le Bacquet de Mesmer* (*A Mesmerian Experiment*); *Le Palais des mille et une nuits* (*The Palace of the Arabian Nights*); *La Compositeur toqué* (*A Crazy Composer*); *La Chaise à porteurs enchantée* (*The Enchanted Sedan Chair*); *Le Raid Paris-Monte Carlo en deux heures* (*An Adventurous Automobile Trip*); *Un Feu d'artifice improvisé* (*Unexpected Fireworks*); *La Légende de Rip van Winkle* (*Rip's Dream*); *Le Tripot clandestin* (*The Scheming Gambler's Paradise*)

1906 (eighteen films, ten extant): *Une Chute de cinq étages* (*A Mix-up in the Galley*); *La Cardeuse de Matelas* (*The Tramp and the Mattress-Makers*); *Les Affiches en goguette* (*The Hilarious Posters*); *Histoire d'un crime* (*A Desperate Crime*); *L'Anarchie chez Guignol* (*Punch and Judy*); *L'Hôtel des voyageurs de commerce* (*A Roadside Inn*); *Les Bulles de savon animées* (*Soap Bubbles*); *Les 400 Farces du Diable* (*The Merry Frolics of Satan*); *L'Alchimiste Prarafaragamus ou la Cornue infernale* (*The Mysterious Retort*); *La Fée caraboose ou le Poignard fatal* (*The Witch*)

1907 (nineteen films, seven extant): *La Douche d'eau bouillanie* (*Rogue's Tricks*)); *Le Mariage de Victorine* (*How Bridget's Lover Escaped*); *Le Tunnel sous la manche ou Le Cauchemar franco-anglais* (*Tunnelling the English Channel*); *L'Eclipse du soleil en pleine lune* (*The Eclipse, or the Courtship of the Sun and the Moon*); *Pauvre John ou Les Aventures d'un buveur de whiskey* (*Sight-Seeing Through Whiskey*); *La Colle universelle* (*Good Glue Sticks*); *Ali Barbouyou et Ali Bouf à l'huile* (*Delirium in a Studio*)

1908 (sixty-eight films, twenty-one extant): *Le Tambourin fantastique* (*The Knight of the Black Art*); *Il y a un dieu pour les ivrognes* (*The Good Luck of a Souse*); *La Génie de feu* (*The Genii of Fire*); *Why the Actor Was Late*; *Le Rêve d'un fumeur d'opium* (*The Dream of an Opium Fiend*); *La Photographie electrique à distance* (*Long Distance Wireless Photography*); *Salon de coiffure* (*In the Barber Shop*); *Le Nouveau Seigneur du village* (*The New Lord of the Village*); *Sideshow Wrestlers*; *Lulli ou le violon brisé* (*The Broken Violin*); *The Woes of Roller Skates*; *Le Fakir de Singapoure* (*The Indian Sorcerer*); *The Mischances of a Photographer*; *His First Job*; *French Cops Learning English*; *A Tricky Painter's Fate*; *Au patys des jouets* (*Grandmother's Story*); *Buncoed Stage Johnnie*; *Not Guilty*; *Hallucinations pharmaceutiques* (*Pharmaceutical Hallucinations*); *La Bonne Bergère et la méchante princesse* (*The Good Shepherdess and the Evil Princess*)

1909 (nine films, none extant)

1910 (thirteen films, three extant): *Hydrothérapie fantastique* (*The Doctor's Secret*); *Le Locataire diabolique* (*The Diabolic Tenant*); *Les Illusions fantaisistes* (*Whimsical Illusions*)

1911 (two films, one extant): *Les Hallucinations du Baron Münchausen* (*Baron Münchausen's Dream*)

1912 (four films, three extant): *La conquête du Pôle* (*The Conquest of the Pole*); *Cendrillon ou la pantoufle mystérieuse* (*Cinderella or the Glass Slipper*); *Le Chevalier des neiges* (*The Knight of the Snows*)

Publications

By MÉLIÈS: articles—

"En marge de l'histoire du cinématographe," in *Ciné Journal* (Paris), August 1926.

"Les Phénomènes du spiritisme," in *Journal de l'Association Française des artistes prestidigitateurs* (Paris), July/August 1936.

"The Silver Lining," in *Sight and Sound* (London), Spring 1938.

"A Letter from Georges Méliès to Merritt Crawford, Esq.," in *Film Culture* (New York), no. 70-71, 1983.

"*Le Livre magique* and *Le Voyage dans la lune*," in *Avant-Scène du Cinéma* (Paris), November 1984.

On MÉLIÈS: books—

Warwick Film Catalogue, London, 1901.

Star Film Catalogue, New York-Paris, 1905.
Ford, Charles, *Georges Méliès,* Brussells, 1959.
Bessy, Maurice, and Lo Duca, *Georges Méliès, Mage,* Paris, 1961.
Exposition commémorative du Centenaire de Georges Méliès, exhibition catalogue, Paris, 1961.
Sadoul, Georges, *Georges Méliès,* Paris, 1961.
Deslandes, Jacques, *Le Boulevard du cinéma à l'époque de Georges Méliès,* Paris, 1963.
Kyrou, Ado, *De Méliès a l'expressionisme, le surréalisme au cinéma,* Paris, 1963.
Malthête-Méliès, Madeleine, *Georges Méliès, créateur du spectacle cinématographique, 1861-1938,* Paris, 1966.
Malthête-Méliès, Madeleine, *Méliès, l'enchanteur,* Paris, 1973.
Hammond, Paul, *Marvellous Méliès,* New York, 1975.
Brakhage, Stan, *Film Biographies,* Berkeley, California, 1977.
Frazer, John, *Artificially Arranged Scenes: The Films of Georges Méliès,* Boston, 1979.
Usai, Paolo Cherci, *Georges Méliès,* Florence, 1983.
Jenn, Pierre, *Georges Méliès cinéaste: Le montage cinématographique chez Georges Méliès,* Paris, 1984.
Malthête-Méliès, Madeleine, *Méliès et la naissance du spectacle cinématographique,* Paris, 1984.
Sadoul, Georges, *Lumière et Méliès,* Paris, 1984.
Langlois, Henri, and others, *Méliès: Un homme d'illusions,* Paris, 1986.
Redi, Riccardo, editor, *Verso il Centenario: Méliès,* Rome, 1987.
Crawford, Merritt, and John Mulholland, *Georges Méliès, Film Pioneer,* New York, not dated.

On MÉLIÈS: articles—

Cavalcanti, Alberto, "Father of the Fantasy Film," in *The Listener* (London), 2 June 1938.
Sadoul, Georges, "An Index to the Creative Work of Georges Méliès," in *Sight and Sound* (London), no. 11, 1947.
Eisner, Lotte, "Tribute to Mme Méliès," in *Film* (London), January/February 1957.
Stephenson, Ralph, "Commemorating Méliès," in *Sight and Sound* (London), Autumn 1961.
Stephenson, Ralph, "A Film a Day," in *Films and Filming* (London), December 1961.
Bessy, Maurice, "Méliès," in *Anthologie du Cinéma,* vol. 2, Paris, 1967.
"An Interview with Madeleine Méliès," in *Film Culture* (New York), Winter/Spring 1970.
Franju, Georges, "Le Classicisme de Méliès et Zecca," in *Cinéma* (Paris), January 1971.
Hammond, Paul, "A Georges Méliès Scrapbook," in *Cinéma* (Beverly Hills), Summer 1971.
Kovacs, Katherine, "Georges Méliès and La Féerie," in *Cinema Journal* (Evanston, Illinois), Fall 1976.
Franju, Georges, "A propos du 'Grand Méliès'," in *Positif* (Paris), December/January 1977/78.
Barnouw, Eric, "The Magician and the Movies," in *American Film* (Washington, D.C.), April 1978.
McInroy, P., "The American Méliès," in *Sight and Sound* (London), no. 4, 1979.
Haleff, M., "André Méliès Interviewed," in *Film Culture* (New York), no. 67-69, 1979.
Bezombes, R., "Les Burlesque de Méliès," in *Cinématographe* (Paris), April 1979.
Questerbert, M.C., "Revoir Méliès: Méliès et la proliferation," and interview with Albert Levy, in *Cahiers du Cinéma* (Paris), April 1979.
Courant, G., "Point d'histoire: Méliès: la fin d'un mythe?," in *Cinéma* (Paris), May 1979.
Quevrain, M.A.M., "L'Idéologie de Méliès et son epoque," in *Cinéma* (Paris), September 1979.
Veillon, O.R., "Portrait de l'artiste en magicien," in *Cinématographe* (Paris), January 1981.
Williams, L., "Film Body: An Implantation of Perversions," in *Ciné-Tracts* (Montreal), Winter 1981.
Hammond, P., "Georges, this is Charles," in *Afterimage* (London), no. 8-9, Spring 1981.
"*Le Grand Méliès,*" in *Avant-Scène du Cinéma* (Paris), April 1984.
Dubois, P., "Le gros plan primitif," in *Revue Belge du Cinéma* (Brussels), Winter 1984/85.
Masson, André, "Le Cinéma des incomparables: sur Georges Méliès," in *Positif* (Paris), April 1985.
Gaudrealt, André, "Theatricality, Narrativity and Trickality: Reevaluating the Cinema of Georges Méliès," in *Journal of Popular Film and Television* (Washington, D.C.), Fall 1987.
Barnes, John, "Méliès: An NFA discovery," in *Sight and Sound* (London), Spring 1989.

On MÉLIÈS: films—

Cavalcanti, Alberto, *Film and Reality,* 1943.
Franju, Georges, *Le Grand Méliès,* 1952.
Malthête-Méliès, Madeleine, *Georges Méliès,* 1969.
Montgomery, Patrick, *Georges Méliès: Cinema Magician,* 1977.

* * *

Georges Méliès, prestidigitator and master illusionist in the Parisian theatre of the late nineteenth century, turned to the cinema and made some five hundred films of every kind fashionable at the time between 1896 and 1912. Of these less than ninety survive, though working drawings (Méliès was a prolific and considerable graphic artist) remain to supplement his work.

Born in Paris in 1861, Méliès as a youth habitually attended the Théâtre Robert-Houdin, a first-floor establishment with two hundred seats and a stage carefully devised to present Jean-Eugène Robert-Houdin's technically advanced forms of conjuring and illusion. He was also influenced by visits to Maskelyne and Cooke's Egyptian Hall in London, where for a while his father, a wealthy bootmaker, sent him to work. Maskelyne presented spectacular dramatic shows involving illusions of the kind Méliès was himself to develop when, in 1888, after selling his share in his late father's business to his brothers, he was able to buy the Théâtre Robert-Houdin and take over as showman illusionist. In addition, he exhibited lantern-slide shows with an illusion of movement achieved by continuities of superimposition.

After seeing the celebrated Cinématographe Lumière in Paris in December 1895, Méliès could not rest until he had obtained equipment for himself. He acquired his first motion picture apparatus in 1896 from R.W. Paul in London, and presented his first film show at the Robert-Houdin on 4 April 1896, using Edison's kinetoscope loops; his own initial ventures into filmmaking—moving snapshots much like Lumière's—were exhibited in the fall.

In his first year Méliès made seventy-eight films, all but one running about one minute; the exception, *The Devil's Castle,* was a vampire film that was three minutes in length. Within a year, by March 1897, he had constructed a glass studio in the garden of his house in Montreuil, near Paris, its equipment modelled on that for the stage in the Théâtre Robert-Houdin. He then turned the theater over, in part at least, to screening programs made up exclusively of films. With his staff he built the sets, designed and made the costumes, photographed and processed the films, using cameras made mainly by Gaumont, Lumière, and Pathé. He sold the prints outright to fairground and music-hall showmen, initially in France and England. He worked at a furious pace and became known as a tough employer of both artists

Georges Méliès (left) with Carl Laemmle, 1935

and technicians. At first he used non-professional players, often performing himself.

Although he was to try his hand at every kind of film, Méliès' more lasting reputation was for burlesque, magical pantomime, and stage-derived illusion. But like other producers of the era, he also made money from bogus newsreel reconstruction, theatrical melodrama, adaptions from literary sources, historical costume drama, and even so-called "stag" films (mild strip-teases) and advertising films. Among his staged newsreels were films that purported to provide coverage of the Greco-Turkish war (1897) and American involvement in Cuba and the Philippines (1898). He even reconstructed *The Eruption of Mount Pelée* on Martinique in 1902, using models, and *The Coronation of Edward VII* before the event even took place; the coronation was in any case postponed.

It is well-known that Méliès was an exponent of trick photography, inspired, according to Georges Sadoul, the French film historian, by the publication in 1897 of Albert Allis Hopkins' *Magic, Stage Illusions and Scientific Diversions, Including Trick Photography.* On the other hand, his most reliable biographer, Paul Hammond, claims Méliès would have been familiar with such devices long before. His standard techniques included duplex photography (through which a single man could appear as himself and a double in a single frame) and spirit (ghost) photography using multiple images. These techniques enabled him to make films projecting stage illusions like *The Vanishing Lady* and *The Astronomer's Dream*—dream films are recurrent in his catalogue—and *The Four Troublesome Heads,* in which a magician repeatedly removes his head. Méliès was to specialize in comic dismemberment of heads and limbs.

By the turn of the century Méliès was handling historical subjects, including *Joan of Arc.* He even made a pro-Dreyfus film of 13 minutes, *The Dreyfus Affair.* Méliès also pursued literary adaptions, such as *The Damnation of Faust,* and provided coverage (backed by phonograph recordings) of the comedian-singer Paulus in a series of films, using for the first time electric arc-lights. He even made *Christ Walking on the Water* as well as simple travel or view films, including panoramas of Paris for the 1900 World Fair. He also reproduced in modern form the past glories of celebrated ghost and skeleton exhibitions, such as *Pepper's Ghost* of London in 1862 and Robertson's *Fantasmagorie* of Paris in 1794. His mildly pornographic "stag" films included *After the Ball* and *The Bridegroom's Dilemma,* in which the actress Jahanne d'Arcy (Méliès' mistress, who became his second wife in 1925) appeared.

Most of Méliès' more celebrated films depended on illusion, comic burlesque, and pantomime. These films included *The Man with the Rubber Head,* in which Méliès' own head is seen expanding to giant size and exploding; the delightfully absurd *A Trip to the Moon,* with acrobats playing the Selenites and hand-waving dancing girls sitting on stars; *The Melomaniac,* in which Méliès conjures with numerous images of his own head, creating musical notes out of them; the space-travelling burlesque *The Impossible Voyage* (length twenty-four minutes); the pantomimic *The Merry Frolics of Satan,* with its animated, skeleton puppet horse; a ninety-one-minute version of *Hamlet; The Conquest of the Pole,* with its man-eating Giant of the Snows, a vast marionette; and *Cinderella and the Glass Slipper,* produced in association with Pathé and cut by his order from fifty-four to thirty-three minutes.

Until around 1909 Méliès remained a largely successful filmmaker. In 1900 he was elected president of the International Convention of Cinematograph Editors (a position he held until 1912), and in 1904 he became president of the Chambre Syndicale de la Prestidigitation. There were agencies for his Star Film company in Berlin, Barcelona, London, and New York. Some of his films were available at double or treble cost in hand-tinted color prints. But the introduction of the practice of renting films, advocated by Pathé and other well-financed producers, was finally to defeat Méliès. He began to turn his attention back to theatrical presentation, producing pantomimes in Paris.

His brother Gaston, based by this time in America, began to produce live-action films for Star, including Westerns in Texas and California, even for a while employing Francis Ford, John Ford's older brother, and later in 1912 touring the South Seas and Far East to make travelogues. (Gaston was to die of food poisoning in Algeria in 1914.) Georges Méliès ceased filmmaking in 1912, his kind of work outdated and unwanted, and by 1914, a widower in his sixties, he was forced to rent his properties or see them taken over for war purposes, though one of his studios was converted into a vaudeville theater and run from 1917 to 1923 by his daughter, Georgette. Méliès gave his last show in the Théâtre Robert-Houdin in 1920, by which time he was deeply in debt. Many of his negatives and prints were destroyed for scrap.

As an artist of stage and screen, Méliès was at once illusionist and pantomimist; in his films, human beings became comic creatures with fantastic costumes and make-up, liable to disintegrate or reshape into anything. Méliès' world was one of ceaseless change, a product partly of fairground magic and of costume tableaux vivants. Chaplin described him as an "alchemist of light." His sets, often beautifully painted in trompe-l'oeil with deceptive perspective, were essentially theatrical. His remarkable drawings, many happily preserved, show what a magnificent cartoon animator he could have become with his Protean imagination for the grotesque and the marvellous. As it was, adopting the cinema in the very year of its birth, he endowed it with the work of his highly individualist imagination, an imagination unlike that of any other filmmaker of his time. The best study of him in English is that by Paul Hammond, *Marvellous Méliès.*

—Roger Manvell

MELVILLE, Jean-Pierre

Nationality: French. **Born:** Jean-Pierre Grumbach in Paris, 20 October 1917. **Education:** The Lycées Condorcet and Charlemagne, Paris, and Michelet, Vanves. **Military Service:** Began military service, 1937; evacuated to England after Dunkirk, then served with Free French Forces in North Africa and Italy. **Career:** Founder, O.G.C. (Organisation générale cinématographique) as production company, 1945; built own studio, Paris, 1949 (destroyed by fire, 1967). **Awards:** Prix René-Jeanne for *Le cercle rouge,* 1970; Chevalier de la Légion d'honneur; Chevalier des Arts et des Lettres. **Died:** In Paris, 2 August 1973.

Films as Director:

1946 *Vingt quatre heures de la vie d'un clown* (+ sc, pr)
1948 *Le Silence de la mer* (+ pr, sc)
1950 *Les Enfants terribles* (+ co-sc, pr, art d)
1953 *Quand tu liras cette lettre* (+ sc)
1956 *Bob le flambeur* (+ pr, co-art d, sc)
1959 *Deux hommes dans Manhattan* (+ pr, sc, role as Moreau)
1963 *Léon Morin, prêtre* (+ sc); *Le Doulos* (+ sc); *L'Ainé des Ferchaux* (+ sc)
1966 *Le Deuxième Souffle* (+ sc)
1967 ***Le Samourai*** (+ sc)
1969 *L'Armée des ombres* (+ sc)
1972 *Le Cercle rouge* (+ sc); *Un Flic* (+ sc)

Other Films:

1948 *Les Dames du Bois de Boulogne* (Bresson) (role)
1949 ***Orphée*** (Cocteau) (role as hotel director)

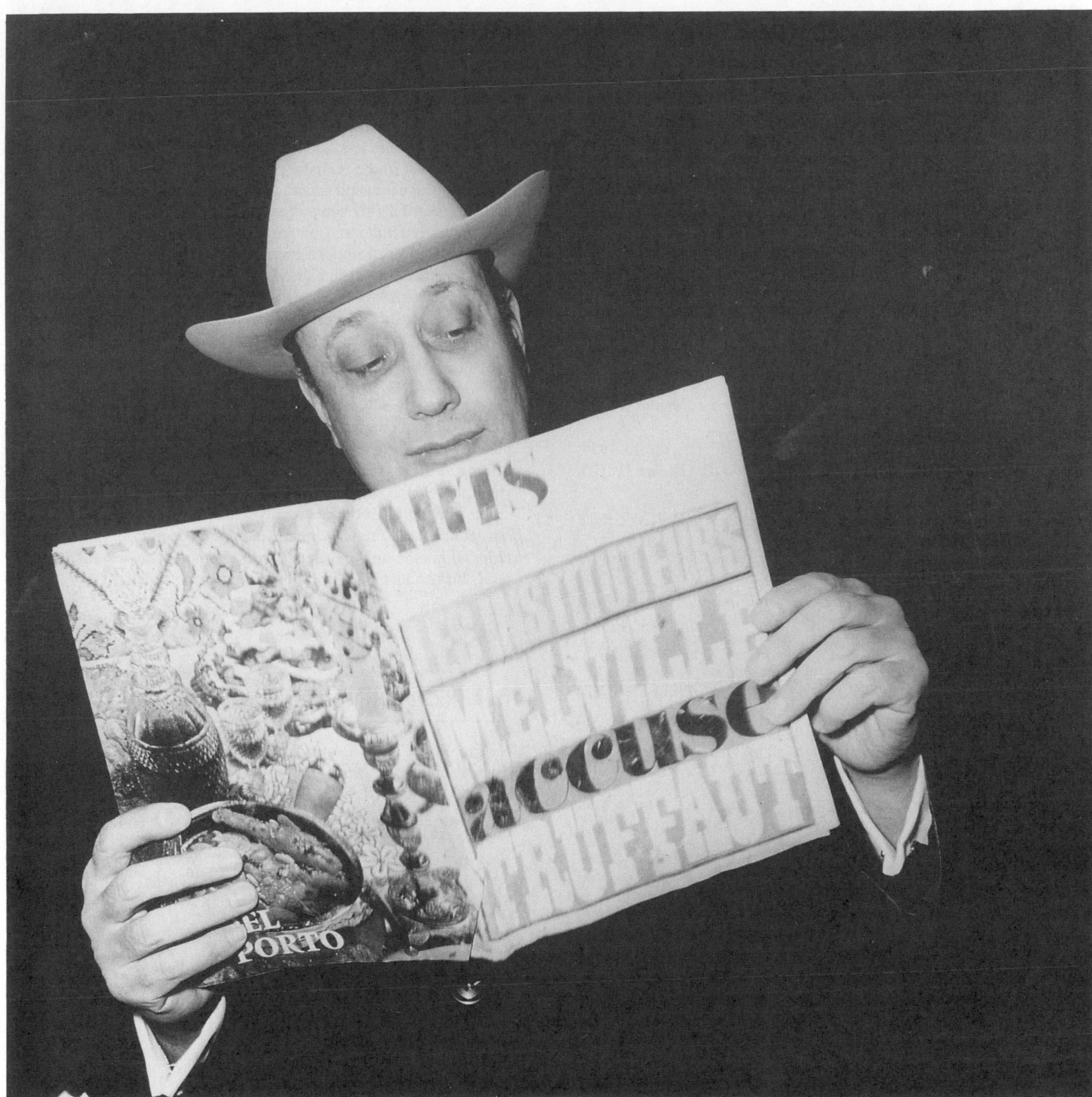

Jean-Pierre Melville

1957 *Un Amour de poche* (role as police commissioner)
1960 ***A bout de souffle*** (Godard) (role as the writer Parvulesco)
1962 *Landru* (Chabrol) (role as Georges Mandel)

Publications

By MELVILLE: articles—

Interview with Claude Beylie and Bertrand Tavernier, in *Cahiers du Cinéma* (Paris), October 1961.

"Finding the Truth Without Faith," in *Films and Filming* (London), March 1962.

"*Léon Morin, prêtre*: Découpage intégrale," in *Avant-Scène du Cinéma* (Paris), no. 10.

Interview with Eric Brietbart, in *Film Culture* (New York), Winter 1964/65.

"*Le Doulos*: Découpage intégrale," in *Avant-Scène du Cinéma* (Paris), no. 24.

Interview with Michel Dancourt, in *Arts* (Paris), 25 April 1966.

"A Samurai in Paris," interview with Rui Nogueira and François Truchaud, in *Sight and Sound* (London), Summer 1968.

"Apres Un Flic, Jean-Pierre Melville a-t-il besoin d'un deuxième souffle?," interview with R. Elbhar, in *Séquences* (Montreal), April 1973.
Interview with F. Guérif, in *Cahiers du Cinématheque* (Paris), Spring/Summer 1978.

On MELVILLE: books—

Wagner, Jean, *Jean-Pierre Melville,* Paris, 1964.
Armes, Roy, *French Cinema Since 1946: Vol.2—The Personal Style,* New York, 1966.
Nogueira, Rui, *Melville on Melville,* London, 1971.
McArthur, Colin, *Underworld U.S.A.,* London, 1972.
Nogueira, Rui, *Le Cinéma selon Melville,* Paris, 1973.
Zimmer, Jacques, and Chantal de Béchade, *Jean-Pierre Melville,* Paris, 1983.

On MELVILLE: articles—

Chabrol, Claude, "Saluer Melville?," in *Cahiers du Cinéma* (Paris), October 1956.
Beylie, Claude, "Melville le flambeur," in *Cinéma* (Paris), no. 40, 1959.
Domarchi, Jean, "Plaisir à Melville," in *Cahiers du Cinéma* (Paris), December 1959.
Ledieu, Christian, "Jean-Pierre Melville," in *Études Cinématographiques* (Paris), no. 6 and 7, 1960.
Porcile, François, "Melville ou l'amour du cinéma," in *Cinéma-texte* (Paris), January 1963.
Austen, David, "All Guns and Gangsters," in *Films and Filming* (London), June 1970.
Beylie, Claude, "Quand tu liras cette lettre ...," in *Ecran* (Paris), September/October 1973.
Renaud, T., "Il fut quand même Melville ...," in *Cinéma* (Paris), September/October 1973.
"L'Armée des ombres," in *Image et Son* (Paris), 1978.
Schlöndorff, Volker, "A Parisian-American in Paris," in *Village Voice* (New York), 6 July 1982.

* * *

The career of Jean-Pierre Melville is one of the most independent in modern French cinema. The tone was set with his first feature film, *Le Silence de la mer,* made quite outside the confines of the French film industry. Without union recognition or even the rights to the novel by Vercors which he was adapting, Melville proceeded to make a film which, in its counterpointing of images and a spoken text, set the pattern for a whole area of French literary filmmaking extending from Bresson and Resnais down to Duras in the 1980s. *Les Enfants terribles,* made in close collaboration with Jean Cocteau, was an equally interesting amalgam of literature and film, but more influential was *Bob le flambeur,* a first variation on gangster film themes which emerged as a striking study of loyalty and betrayal.

But by the time that the New Wave directors were drawing from *Bob le flambeur* a set of stylistic lessons which were to be crucial to their own breakthrough—economical location shooting, use of natural light, improvisatory approaches, and use of character actors in place of stars—Melville himself had moved in quite a different direction. *Léon Morin, prêtre* marks Melville's decision to leave this directly personal world of low-budget filmmaking for a mature style of solidly commercial genre filmmaking that used major stars and tightly wrought scripts to capture a wide audience.

This style is perfectly embodied in the trio of mid-1960s gangster films which constitute the core of Melville's achievement in cinema. Melville's concern with the film as a narrative spectacle is totally vindicated in these films, each of which was built around a star performance: Jean-Paul Belmondo in *Le Doulos,* Lino Ventura in *Le Deuxième Souffle,* and Alain Delon in *Le Samourai.* Drawing on his 1930s viewing and his adolescent reading of American thrillers, Melville manipulated the whole mythology of the gangster film, casting aside all pretence of offering a social study. His criminals are idealized figures, their appearance stylized with emphasis on the belted raincoat, soft hat, and ever-present handgun. Their behavior oddly blends violence and ritualized politeness, and lifts them out from their settings. Melville had no interest in the realistic portrayal of life. He disregarded both psychological depth and accuracy of location and costume. The director instead used his stars to portray timeless, tragic figures caught up in ambiguous conflicts and patterns of deceit, relying on the actor's personality and certainty of gesture to fill the intentional void.

Le Samourai, a perfect distillation of the cinematic myth of the gangster, remains Melville's masterpiece. Subsequent attempts to widen his range included an effort to transpose his characters into the world of Occupation and Resistance in *L'Armée des ombres,* as well as a film—*Le Cercle rouge*—that combined his particular gift for atmosphere with a *Rififi*-style presentation of the mechanics of a robbery. These films are interesting but flawed works. Melville's frustration and dissatisfaction was reflected in his last work, *Un Flic,* which completed the passage towards abstraction begun in the mid-1960s. It offers a derisory world lacking even the human warmth of loyalty and friendship which the director had earlier celebrated. In retrospect, it seems likely that Melville's reputation will rest largely on his ability, almost unique in French cinema, to contain deeply-felt personal attitudes within the tight confines of commercial genre production. Certainly his thrillers are unequalled in European cinema.

—Roy Armes

MENZEL, Jiří

Nationality: Czech. **Born:** Prague, 23 February 1938. **Education:** Film Academy (FAMU), Prague, 1957-62. **Career:** Assistant director on Věra Chytilová's *Something Different,* 1963; director at Barrandov Studios, from 1965; also stage director for Drama Club and Semafor Theatre, Prague, from 1967. **Awards:** Academy Award for Best Foreign Film, for *Closely Watched Trains,* 1967; Grand Prize, Karlovy Vary Festival, for *Capricious Summer,* 1968. **Address:** Solidarita E/31, 100 00 Praha 10, Czechoslovakia.

Films as Director:

1965 *Zločin v dívčí škole* (*Crime at a Girls' School*) (+ co-sc); *Smrt pana Baltisbergra* (*The Death of Mr. Baltisberger*) (+ co-sc)
1966 ***Ostře sledované vlaky*** (*Closely Watched Trains*) (+ co-sc, role as the doctor)
1968 *Rozmarné léto* (*Capricious Summer*) (+ co-sc, role as the magician Arnoštek); *Zločin v šantánu* (*Crime in a Night Club*) (+ co-sc)
1969 *Skřivánci na niti* (*Larks on a String*) (+ co-sc)
1975 *Kdo hledá zlaté dno* (*Who Seeks the Gold Bottom*)
1977 *Na samotě u lesa* (*Seclusion Near a Forest*) (+ co-sc)
1979 *Báječni muži s klikou* (*Magicians of the Silver Screen*) (+ co-sc, role as the director)
1980 *Postřižny* (*Short Cut; Cutting It Short*) (+ co-sc)
1983 *Slavnosti sněženek*
1985 *Prague*; *Vesnicko ma strediskova* (*My Sweet Little Village*)
1989 *Konec starych casu* (*The End of the Good Old Days*)
1990 *Havel's Audience with History* (for TV)
1991 *Opera Zebracka* (*The Beggar's Opera*) (+ pr, sc)
1995 *The Life and Extraordinary Adventures of Private Ivan Chonkin*

Other Films (incomplete listing):

1964 *Courage for Every Day* (role as guest in a pub); *If One Thousand Clarinets* (role as soldier Schulze); *A Place in a Crowd* (role as a secretary of the SCM); *The Defendant* (role as the young defense lawyer)
1965 *Wandering* (role as Dohnal); *Nobody Shall Be Laughing* (role as a bicyclist)
1967 *Dita Saxová* (role as the shy suitor)
1977 *The Apple Game* (Chytilová) (role as the doctor)

Publications

By MENZEL: book—

Closely Watched Trains (script), with Bohumil Hrabal, New York, 1977.

By MENZEL: articles—

"O režii a herectvi, o filmu a dicadle—Rozhovor s Jiřim Menzelem," interview with K. Pošová, in *Film a Doba* (Prague), December 1977.
Interview with A. Tournès, in *Jeune Cinéma* (Paris), May/June 1987.
Interview with M. Buruiana and J. Beaulieu, in *Séquences* (Montreal), September 1988.
"Hallo, hast du jetzt Zeit?" an interview with G. Kopanevova, in *Film und Fernsehen,* vol. 18, no. 11, 1990.
"Med smilet som vapen," an interview with K. Lochen, in *Film & Kino,* no. 8, 1990.
"Jiří Menzel: le printemps de Prague, la normalisation et la revolution de velours," an interview with D. Sauvaget, in *Revue du Cinema,* June 1990.
"Tragizm i humor to bliznieta," an interview with L. Szigeti, in *Kino,* March 1991.
"Jiří Menzel," an interview with R. Filac-Schindlerova, in *Ekran,* vol. 17, no. 4, 1992.
"End of the Line," an interview with R. Carver, in *Sight and Sound,* May 1993.

On MENZEL: books—

Skvorecký, Josef, *All the Bright Young Men and Women,* Toronto, 1971.
Liehm, Antonin, *Closely Watched Films,* White Plains, New York, 1974.
Stoil, Michael, *Cinema beyond the Danube,* Metuchen, New Jersey, 1974.
Liehm, Mira and Antonin, *The Most Important Art,* Berkeley, 1977.
Skvorecký, Josef, *Jiří Menzel and the History of the Closely Watched Trains,* Boulder, Colorado, 1982.
Hames, Peter, *The Czechoslovak New Wave,* Berkeley, 1985.

On MENZEL: articles—

Liehm, A. J., "Zádný strach o Jiřího Menzela" [Never Fear for Jiří Menzel], in *Film a Doba* (Prague), no. 1, 1967.
Kolodny, Irving, "The Man Who Made *Closely Watched Trains,*" in *Action* (Los Angeles), May/June 1968.
Crick, P., "Three East European Directors," in *Screen* (London), March-April 1970.
Bluestone, George, "Jirí Menzel and the Second Prague Spring," in *Film Quarterly,* Fall 1990.
Cazals, P., "Jours tranquilles en Tchecoslovaquie," in *Cahiers du Cinema,* December 1990.
Ahlund, J., "Hemvavd surrealist gor tragedin till fars," in *Chaplin,* vol. 33, no. 4, 1991.
Schutte, O., "Wenn wir filme machen, koennen wir nicht zufrieden sein, wenn das Kino leer ist," in *Filmbulletin,* vol. 35, no. 2, 1993.

* * *

Jiří Menzel's chief claim to a firm place in the history of the Czech cinema to date is his masterpiece, *Closely Watched Trains.* He received an Oscar for it in 1967, and the film was the biggest box-office success of all the works of the New Wave in Czechoslovakia. Banned from the industry after the Soviet invasion of 1968, Menzel eventually saved his career by recanting and publicly dissociating himself from his pre-invasion films, including *Closely Watched Trains.* However, even in his humiliation he scored one important point against the establishment: he refused to return his Oscar to Hollywood as the authorities had demanded (he was supposed to explain that he "did not accept awards from Zionists") and merely made a repentance movie, *Who Seeks the Gold Bottom,* a social realist formula story about workers building a huge dam.

Like Milos Forman, Menzel was influenced by Czech novelists rather than by Western filmmakers, and for a considerable time worked under the tutelage of his teacher from the Film Academy, Otakar Vávra, and his admired older colleague Věra Chytilová. Except for *Crime in a Night Club,* which was based on an original idea by novelist Josef Skvorecký, his pre-invasion films are adaptions of novels and short stories by Czech authors, either modern classics (*Capricious Summer* from a novella by Vladislav Vančura), or his contemporaries (Bohumil Hrabal's *Closely Watched Trains, The Death of Mr. Baltisberger,* and *Larks on a String,* and Skvorecký's *Crime at a Girls' School*). Except for *Capricious Summer,* all these films were banned, *Larks on a String* even before release. After three hesitant efforts following his recantation, all developed from original ideas, Menzel found his old self in another adaption of Hrabal, *Short Cut.* An even less subliminal anti-establishment message is contained in *The Snowdrop Festival,* whose hero sacrifices his life for a pot of tripe soup. Menzel's recent, very amusing comedy *My Sweet Little Village,* and another adaptation of Vančura, *The End of Old Times,* though largely apolitical, show him as the supreme craftsman of contemporary Czech cinema.

Except in his black comedies (*Crime at a Girls' School, Crime in a Night Club*), Menzel is essentially a realist whose method could, perhaps, be described by the theories of André Bazin: he reveals rather than describes reality. There is very little of the formalist elements of movie making, and if, occasionally, there are some (for example, the opening montage in *Closely Watched Trains*), they are used mainly for comic effect. Menzel even dropped the achronological structure of the novella from which he made *Closely Watched Trains,* and replaced it with linear narrative. However, there is inventive use of subtle symbolism (for example, the clocks and their chiming in *Closely Watched Trains*), excellent work with actors, both professional and non-professional, and superb editing. The trend towards subtle symbolism culminates in *Short Cut,* a Rabelaisian tribute to *elan vital* which, however, hides a caustic, encoded comment on "goulash socialism," on the Marxist refutation of Freud (the commanding image of the pretty girl sitting on a high chimney), and on various smaller malpractices of "Realsozialismus" such as jamming foreign broadcasts. The nearly subliminal nature of such satirical stabs, apparent also in *The Snowdrop Festival,* is a nut too hard for the censors to crack.

Unlike his mentor Chytilová's crude defensive moral statements, the messages of Menzel's pre-1968 works (and of *Short Cut* and *The Snowdrop Festival*) are—in the light of establishment philosophy—extremely provocative. In a way, his entire *oeuvre* is one continuous eulogy of sex—a subject at best tolerated by Marxist aestheticians in Czechoslovakia. The shock value of *Closely Watched Trains* is the combination of commendable resistance heroism with an embarrass-

Jiří Menzel: *Postřižny*

ing sexual problem: an anathema in socialist realism. Similarly, the "crime" in *Crime at a Girls' School* turns out to be not murder but loss of virginity, and the "philosophical" ruminations of the three elderly Don Juans in *Capricious Summer* concentrate on a young artiste. The main theme of *Short Cut*—characterized by the phallic symbolism of the chimney which dominates the small central Bohemian Sodom—is simply the joy of sex. Considering that sex has always been the most dangerous enemy of puritanical revolutions, Menzel's message is clear. It is a much less acceptable one than the moralizing of Chytilová, whose eccentric form and merciless vision, on the other hand, stand against everything the government watchdogs would like to see. The two artists, taken together, represent the two basic headaches any repressive aesthetic necessarily faces—the objectionable form, and the objectionable content. The survival of Menzel and Chytilová in a national cinema so full of victims demonstrates that, with perseverance, intelligence, cunning, and good luck, art can occasionally triumph over censorship.

—Josef Skvorecký

MÉSZÁROS, Márta

Nationality: Hungarian. **Born:** Budapest, 19 September 1931. **Education:** VGIK (Film School), Moscow, 1957. **Family:** Married 1), divorced 1959; 2) director Miklós Jancsó (divorced); 3) actor Jan Nowicki. **Career:** Emigrated with family to U.S.S.R., 1936; returned to Hungary, 1946; worked at Newsreel Studio, Budapest, 1954; worked for the Alexandru Sahia documentary studio, Bucharest, Romania, 1957-59; made science popularization shorts and documentary shorts, Budapest, 1959-68; joined Mafilm Group 4, mid-1960s; directed first feature, 1968.

Films as Director:

(short films in Hungary):

1954 *Ujra mosolyognak* (*Smiling Again*)
1955 *Albertfalvai történet* (*A History of Albertfalva*); *Tul a Kálvintéren* (*Beyond the Square*); *Mindennapi történetek* (*Everyday Stories*)
1956 *Országutak vándora* (*Wandering on Highways*)

(short films in Romania):

1957 *Sa zimbeasca toti copiii*
1958 *Femeile zilelor noastre*; *Popas in tabara de vara*
1959 *Schimbul de miine*

(short films in Hungary):

1959 *Az élet megy tovább* (*Life Goes On*)
1960 *Az eladás müvészete* (*Salesmanship*); *Riport egy TSZ-elnökröl* (*Report on the Chairman of a Farmers' Co-Operative*); *Rajtunk is mulik* (*It Depends on Us Too ...*)
1961 *Szívdobogás* (*Heartbeat*); *Vásárhelyi szinek* (*Colors of Vásárhely*); *Danulon gyártás* (*Danulon Production*); *A szár és a gyökér fejlödése* (*The Development of the Stalk and the Root*)
1962 *Tornyai János* (*János Tornyai*); *Gyermekek, könyvek* (*Children, Books*); *Kamaszváros* (*A Town in the Awkward Age*); *Nagyüzemi tojástermelés* (*Mass Production of Eggs*); *A labda varásza* (*The Spell of the Ball*)
1963 *1963.julius 27.szombat* (*Saturday, July 27, 1963*); *Munka vagy hivatás?* (*Work or Profession?*); *Szeretet* (*Care and Affection*)
1964 *Festök városa—Szentendre* (*Szentendre—Town of Painters*)); *Bóbita* (*Blow-Ball*); *Kiáltó* (*Proclamation*)
1965 *15 perc 15 évröl* (*Fifteen Minutes on Fifteen Years*)
1966 *Borsós Miklós* (*Miklós Borsós*); *Harangok városa—Veszprém* (*Veszprém—Town of Bells*)

(feature films):

1968 *Eltávozott nap* (*The Girl*) (+ sc); *Mészáros László emlékére* (*In Memoriam László Mészáros*) (short); *A "holdudvar"* (*Binding Sentiments*) (+ sc)
1970 *Szép lányok, ne sirjatok* (*Don't Cry, Pretty Girls*))
1971 *A lörinci fonóban* (*At the Lörinc Spinnery*) (short)
1973 *Szabad lélegzet* (*Riddance, Free Breathing*) (+ sc)
1975 *Örökbefogadás* (*Adoption*) (+ co-sc)
1976 *Kilenc hónap* (*Nine Months*)
1977 *Ök ketten* (*The Two of Them*))
1978 *Olyan, mint otthon* (*Just Like at Home*)
1979 *Utközben* (*En cours de route*)
1980 *Örökseg* (*The Heiresses*)
1981 *Anya és leánya* (*Mother and Daughter*) (+ co-sc)
1982 *Nema Kiáltás* (*Silent Cry*) (+ sc); *Napló gyermekeimnek* (*Diary For My Children*)
1983 *Délibábok országa* (*The Land of Mirages*)
1987 *Napló szerelmeimnek* (*Diary for My Loves*) (+ sc)
1988 *Piroska és a farkas* (*Bye-Bye Red Riding Hood*)
1989 *Utinapló* (docu)
1990 *Napló apámnak, anyámnak* (*Diary For My Father and My Mother*)
1993 *A Magzat*

Publications

By MÉSZÁROS: articles—

Interviews in *Filmkultura* (Budapest), November/December 1972 and March/April 1977.
Interview in *Hungarofilm Bulletin* (Budapest), no. 2, 1977.
Interview with T. Giraud and D. Villain, in *Cahiers du Cinéma* (Paris), January 1978.
Interview with C. Clouzot and others, in *Ecran* (Paris), 15 January 1979.
Interview with L. Bonneville, in *Séquences* (Montreal), September 1988.
Interview with A. Troshin, in *Film und Fernsehen*, vol. 18, no. 9, 1990.

On MÉSZÁROS: books—

Portuges, Catherine, *Screen Memories: The Hungarian Cinema of Márta Mészáros*, Bloomington, Indiana, 1993.

On MÉSZÁROS: articles—

Elley, Derek, "Hiding It Under a Bushel: Breaking Free," in *Films and Filming* (London), February 1974.
Elley, Derek, "Márta Mészáros," in *International Film Guide 1979*, London, 1978.
Martineau, B.H., "The Films of Marta Mészáros or, the Importance of Being Banal," in *Film Quarterly* (Berkeley), Fall 1980.
"Hungarian Film Section" of *Filmfaust* (Frankfurt), January/February 1984.
"Diary for My Loves," in *Hungarofilm Bulletin* (Budapest), no. 2, 1987.

Márta Mészáros

Portuges, C., "Retrospective Narratives in Hungarian Cinema: The 1980s 'Diary' Trilogy of Marta Meszaros," in *Velvet Light Trap,* Spring 1991.

Quart, B., "Three Central European Women Directors Revisited," in *Cineaste,* no. 4, 1993.

Waller, Marguerite R., "Fetus," in *American Historical Review,* October 1994.

* * *

Márta Mészáros is one of few contemporary woman filmmakers consistently making films both critically and commercially successful for an international audience. Her eight feature films made from 1968 to 1979 are concerned with the social oppression, economic constraints, and emotional challenges faced by Hungarian women. Mészáros explains: "I tell banal, commonplace stories, and then in them the leads are women—I portray things from a woman's angle."

Trained in filmmaking on a scholarship at Moscow's film school, she worked at Newsreel Studios in Budapest, made four short films at the Bucharest Documentary Studios, married a Romanian citizen in 1957, and was divorced in 1959. She returned to Budapest, where she made more than 30 documentaries before attempting a feature. Mészáros's documentaries deal with subjects as diverse as science (*Mass Production of Eggs*), a Hungarian hero (*Saturday, July 27th, 1963*), orphans (*Care and Affection*), and artists (*Szentendre—Town of Painters,* which she considers her best documentary.)

In the mid-1960s Mészáros joined Mafilm Group 4, where she met Miklós Jancsó, whom she later married. She wrote and directed her first feature, *The Girl,* in 1968. A hopeless mood pervades this story of the quest by an orphan girl for her biological parents, who had abandoned her. The girl leaves her textile factory job to comfort her mother, who introduces her as her niece to her husband and relatives. The girl meets a man whom she believes is her father. The man neither confirms nor denies this. The girl returns home and attends a factory dance where she meets a young man who is interested in her. As with most Mészáros features the film is open-ended, lacking a conventional plot. Dialogue is sparse. Derek Elley asserts that *The Girl* is a model to which Mészáros adheres in her subsequent features; her visual compositions are "carefully composed, rarely showy," and "characterisation never remains static."

In *Binding Sentiments* the conflicts between an aging mother and her son's fiancée are delineated with understated solemnity and subtle humor. A semi-musical, *Don't Cry, Pretty Girls,* lightheartedly captures the romance between a rural girl and a city musician in a hostel and youth camp setting. Mészáros's short *Woman in the Spinnery* studies the working status and conditions of the factory worker, the same subjects that she explores in *Riddance.* In this generation gap tale, a pair of lovers must deceive the young man's parents, who object to his love for a girl who was raised in a children's home with no family. *Riddance* urges assertiveness and truth to oneself, and shows little sympathy for the older generation.

A fortyish woman wants a child from her unmarried lover in *Adoption.* She meets a teenager raised by the state who wants to marry her boyfriend. The relationship which develops between these two women and the man in their lives becomes the subject of Mészáros's most illuminating work.

A factory woman with one child has an affair with an engineer in *Nine Months.* The conflicts in their relationship are never resolved; they cannot agree on the terms and conditions of a life together; neither can surrender enough self to form a partnership. The woman leaves him to bear her second child alone. The actual birth of Lila Monari's child was photographed for the film.

The aptly titled *Two Women* depicts a friendship. Juli has a daughter and a husband attempting to find a cure for his alcoholism. Mari directs a hostel for working women, and tolerates a lackluster husband. Juli and Mari enjoy a greater rapport with each other than with the men in their lives. Situations depicting humiliation of and discrimination against women recur. The subject of Mészáros's next film, about a young man's attraction to a little girl, makes *Just Like at Home* a departure from her focus on women. In this film, Andras returns to Budapest after study in the U.S. and strikes up a friendship with a ten-year-old Zsuzsi, whose parents agree that she live with Andras in Budapest and be educated there. Their chaste friendship endures despite the intrusion of Andras's lady friend. Andras learns more from Zsuzsi than she learns from him, to the bewilderment of their parents.

In *The Heiresses* Mészáros used a period setting for the first time. A young, sterile woman marries a military officer during the World War II era. Because she needs an heir to inherit her father's money, she persuades a Jewish woman to bear a child sired by her husband. After the birth, the woman and her husband become deeply attached, and a second child is born. Then the wife "turns in" the Jewish woman (Jews were deported from Hungary in 1944), the husband is arrested, and the wife is given custody of the second child.

Mészáros's films deal with realities usually ignored in Eastern European cinema: the subordination of women, conflicts of urban and rural cultures, antagonism between the bureaucracy and its employees, alcoholism, the generation gap, dissolution of traditional family structures, and the plight of state-reared children. In her unpretentious works, she creates a composite picture of life in Hungary today.

In Derek Elley's words, she "has created a body of feature work which, for sheer thematic and stylistic homogeneity, ranks among the best in current world cinema." Her features examine emotional struggles "in the search for human warmth and companionship in a present-day, industrialised society."

—Louise Heck-Rabi

MICHEAUX, Oscar

Nationality: American. **Born:** Metropolis, Illinois, 1884. **Family:** Married actress Alice Russell, 1929. **Career:** Pullman porter, then farmer, South Dakota, to 1914; published *The Homesteader,* 1914; founder, Western Book and Supply Company, Sioux City, Iowa, 1915; founded Micheaux Film and Book Corporation (later Micheaux Pictures Corporation), based in Sioux City and Chicago, to produce film version of *The Homesteader,* 1918; established office in New York City, 1921; company filed for bankruptcy, 1928, reorganized 1929; directed first "all-talkie," *The Exile,* 1931. **Died:** In Charlotte, North Carolina.

Films as Director, Producer, Scriptwriter and Editor:

(partial list)

1919 *The Homesteader*; *Circumstantial Evidence*
1920 *Within Our Gates*
1921 *Deceit*; *The Gunsaulus Mystery*
1922 *The Dungeon*
1924 *Son of Satan*; *Birthright*
1925 *Body and Soul*
mid-1920s *The House Behind the Cedars*
1928 *Easy Street*
1930 *A Daughter of the Congo*
1931 *The Exile*
1932 *Ten Minutes to Live*; *The Girl from Chicago*
1936 *Swing*; *Underworld*; *Temptation*
1937 *Miracle in Harlem*
1938 *God's Stepchildren*
1939 *Lying Lips*; *Birthright* (sound version)
1940 *The Notorious Elinor Lee*
1948 *The Betrayal*

Publications

By MICHEAUX: article—

Article in *Philadelphia Afro-American,* 24 January 1925.

On MICHEAUX: book—

Sampson, Henry, *Blacks in Black and White,* Metuchen, New Jersey, 1977.

On MICHEAUX: articles—

Cox, Clinton, "We Were Stars in Those Days," in *New York Sunday News,* 9 March 1975.

Fontenot, Chester J., Jr., "Oscar Micheaux, Black Novelist and Film Maker," in *Vision and Refuge,* edited by Frederick C. Luebke, Lincoln, Nebraska, 1982.

Bowser, P., "Oscar Micheaux, le pionnier," in *CinémAction* (Paris), January 1988.

Grupenhoff, R., "The Rediscovery of Oscar Micheaux, Black Film Pioneer," in *Journal of Film and Video* (Boston), Winter 1988.

Green, J.R., and Neal, H., Jr., "Oscar Micheaux and Racial Slur: A Response to 'The Rediscovery of Oscar Micheaux'," in *Journal of Film and Video* (Boston), Fall 1988.

* * *

Until the late 1940s, film roles for blacks in Hollywood were clichéd and demeaning: mammies, butlers, maids, Pullman porters, all decimating the English language while happily, mindlessly serving their white masters. As a result, independent filmmakers—a majority of whom were white—produced approximately three hundred "race" films especially for ghetto audiences. Easily the most famous and prolific of these filmmakers was a black man, Oscar Micheaux, a one-man production and distribution company who shot over thirty features between 1918 and 1948.

Micheaux's origins—and even an accurate list of his films—cannot be clearly determined, at least from existing volumes on the black cinema, but several facts are certain. Micheaux was a vigorous promoter who toured the nation's black ghettos, establishing contact with community leaders and convincing theater owners to screen his films. He would then dispatch his actors for personal appearances.

Micheaux's budgets were meager, between $10,000 and $20,000 per feature, and he economized on sets, shooting schedules, and behind-the-scenes personnel. He often filmed a complete feature on a single set, which may have been a private home or office. Scenes were rarely shot in more than one take; if an actor blew his lines, he just recovered his composure and completed his business. As a result, production values and performances were generally dreadful.

Some of Micheaux's films do attempt to address serious issues. *Within Our Gates* features a sequence in which a black is lynched. *Birthright* (the 1939 version) is the tale of a black Harvard graduate who experiences opposition from those of his own race as well as whites. *God's Stepchildren* centers on a light-skinned black who tries to pass for white. Because of this subject matter, Micheaux was occasionally threatened by local censors.

However, the filmmaker was concerned mostly with entertaining and earning profits, not with controversy. Actors' screen personas were modelled after those of contemporary Hollywood stars: Lorenzo Tucker was the "Black Valentino" and, after the advent of sound, the "colored William Powell"; Bee Freeman became the "sepia Mae West"; Slick Chester the "colored Cagney"; Ethel Moses the "negro Harlow." Plotlines also mirrored those of Hollywood products: *The Underworld* is a gangster film; *Temptation,* a De Mille-like sex epic; *Daughter of the Congo,* a melodrama set in Africa. Micheaux also directed the first all-talking black independent feature, *The Exile,* and 26-year-old Paul Robeson made his screen debut in a Micheaux melodrama, *Body and Soul.*

—Rob Edelman

MICKLIN SILVER, Joan *See* **SILVER, Joan Micklin**

MIKHALKOV, Nikita

Nationality: Russian. **Born:** Nikita Sergeyevich Mikhalkov-Konchalovsky in Moscow, 21 October 1945. **Education:** Studied acting at the Stanislavsky Theater Children's Studio and the Chuksin School of the Vakhtangov Theater; studied directing under Mikhail Romm at VGIK, the State Film Institute in Moscow. **Family:** Married 1) Anastasya Vertinskaya (divorced), 2) Tatyana Mikhalkova; two sons, two daughters; Mikhalkov's great-grandfather is the painter Sourikov; his grandfather is the painter Konchalovski; his father is Sergei Mikhalkov, a writer and former chairman of the USSR Writers Union; his mother is poet Natalia Konchalovskaia; his brother is director Andrei Konchalovski. **Career:** Began performing on stage and screen, making his movie debut in 1964; directed first short film, *I'm Coming Home,* 1968; submitted his VGIK diploma film, *A Quiet Day at the End of the War,* 1970; secured his international reputation with *A Slave of Love,* 1976. **Awards:** Grand Prix, San Sebastian Festival, for *An Unfinished Piece for Mechanical Piano,* 1977; Oscar nomination, Best Foreign Film, and Prize at Venice Festival, for *Urga,* 1990; Oscar, Best Foreign Language Film, and Jury Prize, Cannes Festival, for *Burnt by the Sun,* 1994. **Address:** Malaya Gruzinskaya 28, Apt. 10, 123557 Moscow, Russia.

Films as Director and Screenwriter:

1968 *I'm Coming Home* (short)
1970 *A Quiet Day at the End of the War* (diploma film)
1974 *Svoi sriedi chougikh* (*At Home Among Strangers*; *A Stranger Among His Own People*) (+ role)
1976 *Raba lubvi* (*A Slave of Love*) (+ role)
1977 *Neokontchennaya piesa dlia mekhanitcheskogo pianino* (*An Unfinished Piece for Mechanical Piano*) (+ role)
1979 *Pyat vecheroc* (*Five Evenings*) (d only)
1980 *Oblomov* (*Several Days in the Life of I. I. Oblomov*)
1982 *Rodnya* (*Family Relations*; *Family Ties*; *Kinfolk*) (d only) (+ role)
1983 *Bes svideteley* (*Without Witness*; *A Private Conversation*)
1987 *Oci ciornie* (*Dark Eyes*)
1990 *Urga* (*Close to Eden*)
1993 *Anna: 6-18* (+ co-pr, appearance)
1994 ***Outomlionnye solntsem*** (*Burnt by the Sun*) (+ co-pr, role)

Other Films (incomplete listing):

1964 *Ya shagayu po Moskve* (*Meet Me in Moscow*; *I'm Wandering Through Moscow*) (Danelia) (role as Kolka)
1967 *Csillagosok, katonak* (*The Red and the White*) (Jancso) (role as White Officer)
1969 *Dvorianckoe gnezdo* (*A Nest of Gentry*; *A Nest of Noblemen*) (Konchalovski) (role as Prince Nelidov)
1971 *Krasnaya palatka* (*The Red Tent*) (Kalatozov) (role as Chuknovsky, Icebreaker Pilot); *Sport Sport Sport* (Klimov) (appearance); *Pesnya Manshuk* (*Song of Manchuk*) (Begalin)
1978 ***Siberiade*** (Konchalovski) (role as Alexei); *Nenavist* (*Hatred*) (Gasparov) (co-sc)
1983 *Polioty vo sne naiavou* (*Flights of Fancy*; *Dream Flight*) (Balayan) (role as Director); *Vokzal dla dvoish* (*Station for Two*) (Ryazanov) (role as Vera's Boyfriend)
1984 *Jestoki romans* (*Cruel Romance*; *Ruthless Romance*) (Ryazanov) (role as Sergei Paratov)

Publications

By MIKHALKOV: books—

Griffiths, Trevor, Aleksandr Artemovich Adabashian, and Nikita Mikhalkov, *Piano: A New Play for Theatre Based on the Film Unfinished Piece for Mechanical Piano,* London, 1990.

By MIKHALKOV: articles—

"Nikita Mikhalkov: Directing Means Taking a Stand," interview with E. Barteneva in *Soviet Film* (Moscow), no. 231, 1976.
Interview with A. Lipkow in *Film und Fernsehen* (Berlin), vol. 5, no. 7, 1977.
Interview with L. Bajer and J. Plazewski in *Kino* (Warsaw), February 1977.
Interview with P. Hoff in *Film und Fernsehen* (Berlin), vol. 8, nos. 2/3, 1980.
"A Soviet Director Confronts *Oblomov,*" interview with R.W. Apple in *New York Times,* 8 March 1981.
Interview with H. Willemse and O. Surkova in *Skoop* (Amsterdam), December 1984/January 1985.
Interview with Z. Kiraly in *Filmvilag* (Hungary), vol. 28, no. 9, 1985.
Mikhalkov, Nikita, "*Oblomov* vagy Stolz," in *Filmvilag* (Hungary), vol. 30, no. 7, 1987.
Interview with K. Jaehne in *Cineaste* (New York), vol. 16, nos. 1/2, 1987/1988.
Interview with P. Taggi in *Segnocinema* (Vicenza, Italy), May 1987.
Interview in *Film und Fernsehen* (Berlin), vol. 17, no. 5, 1989.

Nikita Mikhalkov: Silvana Mangano and Marcello Mastroianni in *Oci ciornie*

Interview with J. Houdek and K. Rihova in *Film A Doba* (Prague), August 1990.

Interview with U. Koch in *Film Bulletin* (Winterhur, Switzerland), vol. 33, nos. 5/6, 1991.

Interview with J. Gazda in *Kino* (Warsaw), March 1991.

"Un Russe au pays de Soviets," interview with T. Bourguignon and O. Kohn in *Positif* (Paris), October 1991.

Mikhalkov, Nikita, "Jak narodzila sie *Urga,*" in *Kino* (Warsaw), February 1992.

Interview with P. Murat in *Kino* (Warsaw), February 1992.

"Into a New World," interview with E. Tsymbal in *Sight and Sound* (London), November 1992.

On MIKHALKOV: books—

Borelli, Sauro, *Nikita Mikhalkov,* Florence, 1981.

Sandler, A. M., and Annette Mikhailovna, *Nikita Mikhalkov: Sbornik,* Moscow, 1989.

On MIKHALKOV: articles—

Jaehne, K., "Rehabilitating the Superfluous Man: The Films in the Life of Nikita Mikhalkov," in *Film Quarterly* (Berkeley, California), Summer 1981.

Kopanevova, G., article in *Film a Doba* (Prague), July 1981.

Grenier, Richard, "A Soviet New Wave," in *Commentary* (New York), July 1981.

Forgacs, I., article in *Filmkultura* (Budapest), vol. 22, no. 11, 1986.

Lipkov, A., article in *Filmkultura* (Budapest), vol. 22, no. 11, 1986.

Stuart, J., "Mikhalkov to Lens First Non-Soviet Pic on Russian Locale," in *Variety* (New York), 16 July 1986.

Bilkova, M., article in *Film a Doba* (Prague), October 1986.

"Italo-Soviet Pic Mostly a Breeze," in *Variety* (New York), 22 October 1986.

Canby, Vincent, "Film View: The Brothers Konchalovsky-Mikhalkov," in *New York Times,* 24 May 1987.

Amiel, V., article in *Positif* (Paris), September 1987.

Kral, P., article in *Positif* (Paris), September 1987.

Bennetts, Leslie, "An Unlikely Match for a Movie," in *New York Times,* 29 September 1987.

Jaehne, K., "The Brothers M-K," in *Film Comment* (New York), September/October 1987.

Harvey, Andrew, "Infidelity: Italian (and Russian) Style," in *Vogue* (New York), October 1987.

Biography-filmography in *L'Avant Scene Cinema* (Paris), November 1987.

Gold, R., "Dubbed Version of *Dark Eyes* Aimed at Widened U.S. Audience," in *Variety* (New York), 2 March 1988.

Goodwin, D., "Honor among Poets," in *Monthly Film Bulletin* (London), August 1988.

Brashinsky, M., "The Anthill in the Year of the Dragon," in *New Orleans Review,* vol. 17, no. 1, 1990.

Biography-filmography in *Film Dope* (London), January 1990.

"Feature Hits Going to the Dogs," in *Variety* (New York), 2 May 1990.

Gazda, J., article in *Kino* (Warsaw), March 1991.
Haviarova, M., article in *Kino* (Warsaw), March 1991.
Kopanevova, G., article in *Kino* (Warsaw), March 1991.
"Pair Who Split a Name Share the Honors," in *Variety* (New York), 24 June 1991.
Sorenson, E., article in *Chaplin* (Stockholm), vol. 34, no. 1, 1992.
Young, Deborah, and Michael Williams, "Iron Curtain Alums Test West's Mettle," in *Variety* (New York), 29 June 1992.
Hoberman, J., "Out and Inner Mongolia," in *Premiere* (New York), October 1992.
Jacobson, H., "Life on the Steppes: Isn't It Romantic?," in *New York Times,* 25 October 1992.
Ball, E., "Through a Glasnost Darkly," in *Village Voice* (New York), 3 November 1992.
Epstein, Robert, "Director Nikita Mikhalkov's Declaration of Independence," in *Los Angeles Times,* 5 November 1992.
Carr, Jay, "Preserving Paradise," in *Boston Globe,* 14 February 1993.
Murray, Steve, "Improvisation Pays for Oscar-nominated *Eden,*" in *Atlanta Journal and Constitution,* 15 March 1993.
Maslin, Janet, "A Dark Comedy Wins at Cannes," in *New York Times,* 24 May 1994.
Stanley, Alessandra, "Surviving and Disturbing in Moscow," in *New York Times,* 21 March 1995.
Lipman, Masha, "Russians Beam over *Sun's* Oscar," in *Washington Post,* 29 March 1995.
Filipov, David, "Post-Soviet Screen Struggle," in *Boston Globe,* 12 April 1995.
Thomas, Kevin, "Welcome Rays from *Sun,*" in *Los Angeles Times,* 22 April 1995.
Leydon, Joe, "From Stalin to Oscar," in *Boston Globe,* 14 May 1995.

* * *

Although he did not come to prominence as a director until the mid-1970s, Nikita Mikhalkov ranks among the most gifted Russian filmmakers of the entire post-World War II era. His films are highly emotional examinations of what it means to be Russian amid the swirl of politics and turmoil that has characterized his homeland during the twentieth century. In fact, he presently finds himself one of the few Russian directors whose career has flourished since the disintegration of the USSR. While Mikhalkov's equally celebrated brother, director Andrei Konchalovsky, decided to leave their homeland in the early 1980s and work in the West, Mikhalkov chose to remain in Russia. From that vantage point he watched his international reputation expand while steadfastly continuing to make films that are uniquely Russian in subject matter and flavor.

Burnt by the Sun serves as a high point of Mikhalkov's career in that it earned him a Cannes Film Festival prize and an Academy Award. It also is the work of an artist completely freed from censorial restriction; the film is dedicated to all those who were "burnt by the betraying sun of the revolution." The year is 1936, and the filmmaker himself (who began his career as an actor) stars as Sergei Kotov, aging hero of the Bolshevik Revolution. Sergei and his family enjoy an idyllic existence at their country house. The fact of Joseph Stalin's tyranny seems a fantasy. But all of this is certain to change upon the arrival of Dimitri, the ex-lover of Sergei's young wife, Maroussia. He begins enticing Sergei and Maroussia's daughter, Nadia (played by Nadia Mikhalkov, the director's real-life offspring). The fact that Dimitri is employed by Stalin's governmental police does not bode well for Sergei. Ultimately, *Burnt by the Sun* is the statement of an artist attempting to explore and understand the unpleasantries in the not-too-distant political past of his cherished homeland.

A number of Mikhalkov's other films deal directly with the political history of post-revolutionary Russia. *At Home among Strangers,* his very first effort out of film school, is set in the 1920s, during a civil war which occurred directly after the revolution. It is a "Russian Western" about some brigands who steal gold that is meant to be used for the purchase of wheat to feed the hungry. The hero is a revolutionary who is thought to be disloyal to the cause, and who infiltrates the gang.

Mikhalkov firmed up his international reputation with his third feature, *A Slave of Love.* It is set in Southern Russia in the late teens, during the filming of an inconsequential movie melodrama. The story involves the transformation of Olga, a spoiled, class-conscious actress, as she falls in love with a Bolshevik cameraman. This funny and poignant film is effective as a reflection of both the early years of movie-making and the 1917 Bolshevik Revolution.

At Home among Strangers and *A Slave of Love* make for a fascinating contrast to *Burnt by the Sun.* The first two—made when the Soviets were still in power—depict the heroics of the revolution, and characters who become inspired by the revolutionary spirit; the latter spotlights the cruel reality of life under Stalin, and the plight and fate of one once-heroic but now-deluded revolutionary. Meanwhile, other Mikhalkov films are set in pre-Revolutionary times. *Oblomov (A Few Days in the Life of I. I. Oblomov)*—arguably his most deeply layered and emotionally complex film—is a lyrical adaptation of the famous Russian novel written by Ivan Goncharov in 1858. The title character is a thirtyish civil servant and absentee landlord who decides to retire to a listless existence in bed. The flashback sequences of Oblomov as a boy in his mother's arms are nothing short of wonderful. Mikhalkov has adapted other works from literary sources, most especially Chekhov; in fact, *A Slave of Love* was praised by critics for its Chekhovian cleverness. *An Unfinished Piece for Player Piano* is an affecting account of the various goings-on one lazy summer afternoon at the country estate of a general's widow. The many guests include husbands, wives, and former lovers, and the film—an adaptation of *Platonov,* Chekhov's first play—is noteworthy for its gallery of finely realized characterizations.

Despite his loyalty to Russia, Mikhalkov has not worked exclusively in his homeland. He went to Italy to film *Dark Eyes,* featuring Marcello Mastroianni in a role he was born to play: Romano, a likably charming but lazy lothario whose soul is sadly hollow, and who cannot comprehend that he has allowed life to pass him by. The scenario is loosely based on several Chekhov short stories. And *Close to Eden* is a bright comedy set in a contemporary China where ancient customs conflict with modern values. The story concerns a peasant couple who reside in a small village amid the expansive steppes of Inner Mongolia. They are the parents of three children. Chinese law forbids them to have a fourth, so the husband—a shepherd who reveres Genghis Khan—sets out to procure birth control.

Regarding his affinity for Chekhov's works, Mikhalkov once observed that the writer "feels very close to me because he offers no answers to the questions he poses. Chekhov's characters seek an answer which they never find. I too don't know the answer. I'm not even sure that knowing it would make me any happier. What is important is the search for the truth; that is happiness." This statement relates not just to Chekhov but to the manner in which Mikhalkov has attempted to depict and, ultimately, understand the changing face of Russia.

—Rob Edelman

MIKHALKOV-KONCHALOVSKY, Andrei

Nationality: Russian (also known as Andrei Konchalovsky). **Born:** Moscow, 1937; brother of director Nikita Mikhalkov. **Education:** Educated as pianist, Moscow Conservatoire, 1947-57; State Film School (VGIK) under Mikhail Romm, diploma 1964. **Family:** Married 1)

Natalya Arinbasarova; 2) 1969 (divorced), one child. **Career:** Scriptwriter for Andrei Tarkovsky, early 1960s; directed first film, 1965; moved to U.S.A. at invitation of Jon Voight, 1980. **Awards:** Special Jury Prize, Cannes Festival, for *Siberiade,* 1979. **Address:** Lives in Malibu, California.

Films as Director:

1961 *Malchik i golub* (*The Boy and the Pigeon*) (short)
1965 *Pyervy uchityel* (*The First Teacher*) (+ co-sc) (diploma film)
1967 *Istoriya Asi Klyachinoi, kotoraya lyubila, da nye vyshla zamuzh* (*Asya's Happiness*) (+ sc) (not released until 1988)
1969 *Dvoranskoye gnezdo* (*A Nest of Gentlefolk*) (+ co-sc)
1970 *Dyadya Vanya* (*Uncle Vanya*) (+ sc)
1974 *Romans o ul jublennyh* (*The Romance of Lovers*) (+ sc)
1978 ***Siberiade*** (*The Siberiad*) (+ sc)
1984 *Maria's Lovers*
1986 *Runaway Train*
1987 *Duet for One* (+ co-sc); *Shy People*
1989 *Homer and Eddie; Tango & Cash*
1991 *The Inner Circle* (+ sc)
1994 *Kourotchka Riaba* (+ sc, pr)

Other Films:

1961 *Katok i skripka* (*The Steamroller and the Violin*) (Tarkovsky) (sc)
1964 ***Andrei Rublev*** (Tarkovsky) (sc)
1969 *Tashkent—gorod khlyebny* (*Tashkent—City of Bread*) (sc); *Pyesn o Manshuk* (*The Song of Manshuk*)
1970 *The End of the Chieftain* (sc)

Publications

By MIKHALKOV-KONCHALOVSKY: articles—

Interview with Don Ranvaud in *Monthly Film Bulletin* (London), January 1985.
Interview with Michel Ciment and André Masson, in *Positif* (Paris), November 1984.

Andrei Mikhalkov-Konchalovsky directing Julie Andrews and Alan Bates in *Duet for One*

Interview with B. Paskin, in *Films and Filming* (London), April 1986.
Interview with K. Jaehne, in *Cineaste* (New York), vol. 16, no. 1/2, 1987/88.
Interview with Barteneva, in *Soviet Film* (Moscow), June 1988.
Interview with L. Farrah, in *Films and Filming* (London), September 1988.
"Andrei Konchalovsky: ne pas savoir quand commence le reve," interview with F. Guerif in *Revue du cinema* (Paris), July/August 1990.
Interview with A. Lipkov, in *Cine Cubano,* no. 131, 1990.

On MIKHALKOV-KONCHALOVSKY: articles—

Ciment, Michel, "Andrei Konchalovski ou les silences d'un jeune maître," in *Positif* (Paris), November 1969.
Flake, C., "Stranger in a Strange Land," in *American Film* (Washington, D.C.), December 1985.
Jaehne, K., "The Brothers Mikhalkov-Konchalovsky," in *Film Comment* (New York), September/October 1987.
Sauvaget, D., "Les 'Mikhalkov-Kontchalovsky,'" in *Revue du Cinema* (Paris), October 1991.
Brandmeier, T., "Die russischen Brueder Andrei Konchalovsky und Nikita Michalkov," in *EPD Film,* October 1991.
Meier, A, and D. Remnick, "On location with 'Petestroika,'" in *Premiere,* February 1992.

* * *

Probably the most gifted of the young Soviet directors who appeared in the 1960s, Andrei Mikhalkov-Konchalovsky did not manage to maintain his artistic level when cultural policy stiffened after the passage of the relatively liberal Khrushchev era. Andrei belongs to one of the most established families in Moscow. His grandfather was a famous pianist, his uncle a painter, his father (Sergei) a writer and the head of the writers' union, his brother (Nikita) an actor and a film director. Andrei studied music, but realizing he would not become a new Richter, he went to the V.G.I.K. (film school) in Moscow, where he graduated after studying with Mikhail Romm. Together with Andrei Tarkovsky, he wrote the script of the short film *The Streamroller and the Violin* and *Andrei Rublev,* both directed by Tarkovsky.

Konchalovsky's first film as director was the masterly *The First Teacher,* from a novel by Tenguiz Aitmatov, shot on the Central Asian steppes. Using mostly non-professionals except for the lead characters, Konchalovsky conveyed in lyrical terms the contradictions of his story: in the years following the Revolution, a young Russian soldier attempts to educate the people of a newly conquered land. The conflict of the old and the new and also the one between Asia and Europe, the beauty of tradition and the need for change, were expressed with a deft simplicity of style and a rare quality of emotion.

Konchalovsky went even further in his attempt to free the Russian cinema from its academic straitjacket by shooting his next film, *Asya's Happiness,* in an actual peasant collective. Utilizing a script that served merely as a canvas, several cameras, and improvisation techniques (which he compared in some respects to Altman's method in *Nashville*), he gave an astonishing force to his rural melodrama. Asya is pregnant by a man that she loves but who is indifferent to her, while she is courted by a man from the town whom she does not like. The realism of the film probably so shocked the censors that the film was banned and was never shown in the USSR.

Konchalovsky, following a well-known pattern, next directed literary adaptations from Turgenev (*A Nest of Gentlefolk*) and from Chekhov (*Uncle Vanya*). His love for Russia and for the past, coupled with his great cultural awareness and sensitivity, give these films an elegance and a real emotional impact, though they sometimes indulge—particularly in the first film—in a certain mannerism. *The Romance of Lovers* is a mawkish story *à la* Lelouch which was heavily attacked—and deservedly so—by the critics, but enjoyed huge popular success. *Siberiade,* a kind of Soviet *Novecento* (the story of two families since the 1917 Revolution) shows the director's ability to command a huge production. The early years of the colonization of Siberia allow him to express again his lyrical temperament, but the parts of the film concerned with more recent periods avoid controversial material (the camps, etc.), show dangerous signs of academicism, and make us regret an absence of the freedom, energy, and invention of his first films.

—Michel Ciment

MILESTONE, Lewis

Nationality: American. **Born:** Family name Milstein; born in Chisinau, near Odessa, Russia, 30 September 1895, became U.S. citizen and changed name to Milestone, 1919. **Education:** Jewish schools in Kishinev, Russia; University of Ghent, Belgium; engineering college in Mitweide, Germany. **Family:** Married Kendall Lee Glaezner, 1935 (died 1978). **Military Service:** Served in U.S. Army Signal Corps photography section, 1917-19. **Career:** Emigrated to United States, 1913; photographer's assistant, 1915; after military service, became assistant to Henry King, Hollywood, 1919; worked at Ince and Sennett studios, 1920-21; assistant editor at Fox, 1922; editor at Warner Brothers, 1923; signed contract with Howard Hughes's Caddo Company, 1927; production head for United Artists, 1932; compiled documentary with Joris Ivens, *Our Russian Front,* 1942; appeared as unfriendly witness before House Un-American Activities Committee, 1946; directed series for television, 1957-58. **Awards:** Oscar for Best Comedy Direction, for *Two Arabian Knights,* 1927; Oscar for Best Direction, for *All Quiet on the Western Front,* 1930. **Died:** In Los Angeles, 25 September 1980.

Films as Director:

1925 *Seven Sinners* (+ co-sc)
1926 *The Caveman*; *The New Klondike*
1927 *Two Arabian Knights*
1928 *The Garden of Eden*; *The Racket*
1929 *Betrayal*; *New York Nights*
1930 ***All Quiet on the Western Front***
1931 *The Front Page*
1932 *Rain*
1933 *Hallelujah, I'm a Bum*
1934 *The Captain Hates the Sea*
1935 *Paris in the Spring*
1936 *Anything Goes*; *The General Died at Dawn*
1939 *The Night of Nights*
1940 *Of Mice and Men* (+ pr); *Lucky Partners*
1941 *My Life with Caroline*
1942 *Our Russian Front* (co-d, co-pr, ed)
1943 *Edge of Darkness*; *The North Star*
1944 *The Purple Heart*
1946 *A Walk in the Sun* (+ pr); *The Strange Love of Martha Ivers*
1948 *Arch of Triumph* (+ co-sc); *No Minor Vices* (+ pr)
1949 *The Red Pony* (+ pr)
1951 *Halls of Montezuma*
1952 *Kangaroo*; *Les Miserables*
1953 *Melba*; *They Who Dare*
1957 *La Vedova* (*The Widow*)

Lewis Milestone (extreme right, above the camera) directing *The Garden of Eden*

1959 *Pork Chop Hill*
1960 *Ocean's Eleven* (+ pr)
1962 *Mutiny on the Bounty*

Publications

By MILESTONE: articles—

Interview with Herbert Feinstein, in *Film Culture* (New York), September 1964.
Interview, in *The Celluloid Muse: Hollywood Directors Speak,* by Charles Higham and Joel Greenberg, Chicago, 1969.
Interview with Digby Diehl, in *Action* (Los Angeles), July/August 1972.
"The Reign of the Director," in *Hollywood Directors: 1914-1940,* edited by Richard Koszarski, New York, 1976.
"First Aid for a Sick Giant," in *Hollywood Directors: 1941-1976,* edited by Richard Koszarski, New York, 1977.

On MILESTONE: books—

Denton, Clive, and others, *The Hollywood Professionals—Vol. 2: Henry King, Lewis Milestone, Sam Wood,* New York, 1974.
Parker, David, and Burton Shapiro, *Close Up: The Contract Director,* Metuchen, New Jersey, 1976.
Millichap, Joseph, *Lewis Milestone,* Boston, 1981.

On MILESTONE: articles—

Goodman, Ezra, "Directed by Lewis Milestone," in *Theater Arts* (New York), February 1943.
Reisz, Karel, "Milestone and War," in *Sequence* (London), 1950.
Ferguson, Otis, "Lewis Milestone 'Action!'," in *Film Comment* (New York), March/April 1974.
Everson, William, "Thoughts on a Great Adaptation," in *The Modern American Novel and the Movies,* edited by Gerald Peary and Roger Shatzkin, New York, 1978.
Jameson, R.T., "Style vs. 'Style'," in *Film Comment* (New York), March/April 1980.
Mitchell, G.J., "Making *All Quiet on the Western Front,*" in *American Cinematographer* (Los Angeles), September 1985.

* * *

Lewis Milestone is undoubtedly best remembered for his classic statement against the horrors of war, *All Quiet on the Western Front,* for which he won an Academy Award. The film, coming so early in his career, raised high hopes that subsequent efforts would expand upon the brilliant potential exhibited in his first effort. In the minds of many, his following work, with the exception of 1931's *The Front Page,* failed to live up to this early promise.

Through films like *Rain, Of Mice and Men, Pork Chop Hill,* and *Mutiny on the Bounty,* Milestone achieved a lesser reputation. He came to be known as a competent journeyman director and an excellent craftsman who, with good actors and a strong script, was capable of producing solid, entertaining films. The fundamental charge leveled against him by most critics was that he maintained a lackadaisical attitude toward run-of-the-mill projects.

Such assessments, however, overlook the outstanding achievement of at least one film, the much undervalued *A Walk in the Sun.* In this film the director's inspired use of sound, coupled with some shifts in perspective, turned a routine war drama into a small classic that compares favorably with his best work. Stylistically and thematically, it expands on the innovations of *All Quiet on the Western Front* and, at the same time, represents perhaps the most creative use of sound since it was introduced to films.

Milestone's experimentation with what the audience hears began with a unique approach to the film's narration; he added a brooding, recurring ballad as accompaniment. The ballad functions much like a chorus in a Greek play by introducing and commenting on the action. The sentiments of the song are then fleshed out through the audible thoughts and the dialogues and monologues of individual soldiers. The war is perceived through sound, allowing the audience to experience it as the fighting men do. Modern war is fought against an enemy that the average soldier rarely sees. Instead, bomb blasts, strafing from the air, and mortar fire are heard as soldiers crouch in foxholes, fearing to lift their eyes. *A Walk in the Sun,* by its very refusal to gratify the eye with images of battle and by its emphasis on the small talk of soldiers, creates a microcosm of war that effectively epitomizes the men who must fight all wars. Through Milestone's inspired use of previously-overlooked audio techniques, he achieves the sensitivity of treatment in delineating his characters that many critics had found lacking in his work.

Milestone has yet to receive the critical reassessment that he undoubtedly deserves. Films as diverse as *A Walk in the Sun* and *The Strange Love of Martha Ivers* indicate that his later films contain moments of high achievement comparable to his two great early efforts. They also suggest a greater correlation between his technical innovations and his sensitively-handled theme of men in groups than many scholars give him credit for.

—Stephen L. Hanson

MILLER, Claude

Nationality: French. **Born:** Paris, 20 February 1942. **Education:** IDHEC Film School, Paris, 1962-63. **Military Service:** National service in Le Service cinématographique de l'armée, 1964. **Family:** Married writer Annie Miller. **Career:** Worked in various capacities for other directors, including René Allio, Robert Bresson, Marcel Carné, Jacques Demy, Jean-Luc Godard, and François Truffaut, from 1965; directed six-part series *Traits de mémoire* for TV, 1974; directed first feature, 1976; also director of TV advertisements.

Films as Director and Co-Scriptwriter:

1967 *Juliet dans Paris* (short)
1969 *La Question ordinaire* (short)
1971 *Camille ou la Comédie catastrophique* (short)
1976 *La meilleure façon de marcher* (*The Best Way of Walking*) (+ co-adapter, co-dialogue)
1977 *Dites-lui que je l'aime* (*This Sweet Sickness*) (+ co-adapter, co-dialogue)
1981 *Garde à vue* (*Under Suspicion*) (co-adapter)
1983 *Mortelle randonnée* (*Deadly Circuit*)
1985 *L'Effrontée* (*An Impudent Girl*) (+ co-dialogue)
1988 *La Petite Voleuse* (*The Little Thief*) (+ co-adapter, co-dialogue)
1992 *L'Accompagnatrice* (*The Accompanist*) (+ co-adapter, co-dialogue)
1994 *Le Sourire* (*The Smile*) (+ co-exec pr)
1995 *Les Enfants de Lumiere*

Other Films:

1964 *Patrouille en zone minée* (short) (for the Service Cinématographique de l'armée); *Transmission de la divi-*

sion 59 (short; co-directed with Bernard Stora) (for the Service Cinématographique de l'armée)

1965 *Trois Chambres à Manhattan* (Carné) (asst d); *Nick Carter et la trèfle rouge* (Savignac) (asst d); *Le Dimanche de la vie* (Herman) (asst d)

1966 *Au Hasard, Balthazar* (Bresson) (asst d); *Martin Soldat* (Deville) (asst d)

1967 *Les Demoiselles de Rochefort* (Demy) (asst d); *2 ou 3 Choses que je sais d'elle* (Godard) (asst d, role); "Anticipation" episode of *Le Plus vieux métier du monde* (Godard) (asst d); *La Chinoise ou plutôt à la chinoise* (Godard) (asst d); *Week-end* (Godard) (asst d)

1968 *L'Ecume des jours* (Belmont) (production manager); *Baisers volés* (Truffaut) (production manager); *Pierre et Paul* (Allio) (production manager)

1969 *La Sirène du Mississipi* (Truffaut) (production manager); *L'Enfant sauvage* (Truffaut) (production manager, role)

1970 *Domicile conjugal* (Truffaut) (production manager)

1971 *Les Deux Anglaises et le continent* (Truffaut) (production manager); *La Voix du large* (short) (Porcile) (production manager)

1972 *Une Belle fille comme moi* (Truffaut) (production manager)

1973 *Elle court, elle court la banlieue* (Pirès) (asst d); *La Nuit américaine* (Truffaut) (production manager); *Les Gaspards* (Tchernia) (production manager)

1975 *L'Histoire d'Adèle H.* (Truffaut) (production manager)

1976 *L'Ordinateur des pompes funèbres* (Pirès) (role)

1978 *La Tortue sur le dos* (Béraud) (co-sc, co-dialogue, role)

1979 *Félicité* (Pascal) (role)

1981 *Plein Sud* (Béraud) (co-sc, co-dialogue, role)

1987 *Vent de panique* (Stora) (co-sc)

Publications

By MILLER: articles—

Interviews in *Positif* (Paris), March 1976, November 1981, January 1986, February 1989, and September 1994.

Interviews in *Cinématographe* (Paris), April/May 1976, October 1981, July/August 1982, and October 1986.

Interview in *Cinéma,* April 1976.

Interview in *Film Français,* December 1976.

Interview in *Jeune Cinéma,* November 1977.

Interviews in *Cinéma Français* (Paris), October 1977 and March 1978.

Interviews in *Sight and Sound* (London), Winter 1977/78 and Spring 1978.

Interviews in *Cahiers du Cinéma* (Paris), May 1981 and May 1985.

Interview in *24 Images,* December 1981.

Interview in *Télérama,* September 1985.

Interviews in *Première* (Paris), December 1985, February 1988, and January 1989.

Interview in *Revue du Cinéma,* January 1986.

Interview with L. Bonneville, in *Séquences* (Montreal), April 1986.

Interview with G. Legrand and O. Curchod, in *Positif* (Paris), February 1989.

Interview in *American Film,* October 1989.

On MILLER: articles—

"*La meilleure façon de marcher* Issue" of *Avant-Scène du Cinéma* (Paris), no. 168, 1976.

"*Garde à vue* Issue" of *Avant-Scène du Cinéma* (Paris), no. 228, 1982.

Article in *Revue du Cinéma,* June 1984.

Article in *Cahiers du Cinéma,* May 1985.

Claude Miller Section of *Positif* (Paris), January 1986.

Chevassu, F., "Sur cinq films de Claude Miller," in *Revue du Cinéma* (Paris), January 1989.

Article in *Film Comment,* July/August 1989.

Ellero, R., "Il cinema secondo Miller," in *Segno,* July 1990.

Article in *Positif,* September 1994.

Article in *Studio Magazine,* September 1994.

* * *

In character-centred films which sympathetically portray the tribulations of insecure or emotionally disturbed individuals, Claude Miller reveals close affinities with his mentor François Truffaut. He shares not only his humanitarian vision and refusal to moralise, but also his concern for carefully wrought narratives with an economical, resonant style.

After theoretical studies at IDHEC and work with the army film unit, Miller pursued his training under Carné, Bresson, and Demy. However, the most formative experiences came as assistant to Godard (from *2 ou 3 Choses que je sais d'elle* to *Weekend*) and as production manager for Truffaut (from *Baisers volés* to *L'Histoire d'Adèle H.*). Godardian aesthetics and political perspectives distinguish Miller's two early shorts: *Juliet dans Paris* and *La Question ordinaire.* The first portrays, in deliberately disquieting detail, the feline vampirism of a seemingly demure female; the second confronts Fascism by counterposing ideological statement and shocking images of torture. Miller's third short, *Camille ou la Comédie catastrophique,* signals the emergence of a less self-conscious and more personal style. Primarily an exploration of sexual attitudes, the film exposes the inadequacies of two salacious seducers humiliated by the willing Camille. This debunking of male posturing anticipates Miller's first feature, *La Meilleure façon de marcher.*

It is the feature films which reveal striking similarities with Truffaut's cinema. Miller's preference for working with a team of trusted collaborators (photographer Bruno Nuytten, scriptwriter Luc Béraud), or a given actress (Charlotte Gainsbourg), is much in the Truffaut tradition. Film as a form of personal statement is likewise common to Miller's conceptions. Thus, where the adaptation of a thriller is involved (*Dites-lui que je l'aime, Garde à vue, Mortelle randonnée*), the narrative is refocused to provide insight into the novel's tortured souls rather than a simple illustration of their evil deeds. This emphasis on the psychological aligns these adaptations with Miller's more self-evidently personal works: *La Meilleure façon de marcher, L'Effrontée,* and *Le Sourire,* and from Truffaut's unrealized scenario, *La Petite Voleuse.*

For Miller no individual is unredeemable, and his portrayal of human frailties eschews facile condemnation. In *La Meilleure façon de marcher,* a moral Fascism is seen as the defence mechanism of males insecure about their own their sexual orientation. Highsmith's psychotic murderer David becomes the pitiful, emotionally inadequate, and humiliated individual of *Dites-lui que je l'aime.* In *Garde à vue,* the rape investigation transforms itself into an examination of the personal relationships of detective and suspect alike, and both, in their common humanity, are found wanting. A more extreme case of symbiotic pairing, which again blurs traditional moralities, occurs in *Mortelle randonnée,* where the detective colludes with a multiple murderess who resembles his dead daughter. In *La Petite Voleuse,* as in Truffaut's *400 Coups,* social circumstances largely determine the main character's descent into crime. Throughout Miller invites understanding of the misfit.

Frequently, the nature or expression of sexuality lies at the core of the narrative matrix. For Miller's male characters sex is either a clumsy or a violent act, a humiliating fiasco, or for the sexagenarian of *Le Sourire,* a final assertion of self. By contrast the director's females are more at ease with their sexuality. In *L'Effrontée* and *La*

Petite Voleuse, where the delicately observed transitional stages of adolescence are thematic, the heroines readily anticipate their first sexual experiences, disastrous though they are. In *L'Accompagnatrice,* Sophie similarly accepts the disappointment of her first brief love affair as part of a maturing awareness of the fickle nature of adult relationships.

With the exception of his early self-conscious shorts, the flashy *Mortelle Randonnée,* and the more assertive style of *Le Sourire,* Miller's work is characterised by understatement and stylistic sobriety: his films are concerned with sentiment rather than sensation. Acts of violence such as the murders of *Dites-lui que je l'aime* or the knife incident in *La Meilleure Façon de marcher* are dramatically necessary, but not dramatised for effect. Self-effacing camerawork is the norm, with close-ups used unemphatically and special effects more generally confined to his advertising work. Music, however, forms an integral part of Miller's creation and assumes a particular importance both in mood and structure, perhaps no more so than in *L'Accompagnatrice* and *Le Sourire.*

Economy is the hallmark of Miller's expositions and narrative development: subject, characters, and locations are succinctly established through juxtaposed scenes of symbolic resonance. The ensuing narrative is constructed elliptically, and resolutions may even be in summary form, as in the photocollage ending of *Garde à vue.*

Locations are rarely specific. Indeed there is often a deliberate amalgamation of settings, as in *L'Effrontée,* to achieve generality. Places have importance not as geographical references but as symbolic elements in the exploration of character. The contrastive locations, ordinary house/luxurious mansion, of *L'Effrontée* represent the pubescent heroine's reality and her dream; in *L'Accompagnatrice,* the protagonist is dazzled by the glamorous life-style of wealthy Nazi sympathizers and, rejecting her own modest background, plays along with their values; in *Dites-lui que je l'aime,* the dark, rainy streets are metaphorical expressions of David's desperate mood. The presence of water in a Miller film is frequently associated with sexuality, has connotations of evil, and is invariably a harbinger of fatalities. The lake in *Le Sourire* and the swimming pools of *La Meilleure Façon de marcher, Dites-lui que je l'aime,* and *L'Effrontée* become synonymous with humiliation and death.

Period settings are left equally vague to suggest universality, and in this respect, Miller's uncommon use of epilogues *(La Meilleure Façon de marcher, Dites-lui que je l'aime)* constitutes a distancing from the immediate events with a prolongation of the temporal perspective. *La Petite Voleuse* and *L'Accompagnatrice* are exceptions: the moral dilemmas posed by the Occupation are integral to the thematics of *L'Accompagnatrice,* while the moral climate of the postwar years is essential to the dynamics of *La Petite Voleuse.*

The director's recent films may be seen as works of transition and renewal. *L'Accompagnatrice* testifies to enduring thematic concerns with personal values in a morally fluid society which challenges notions of integrity, fidelity, and compromise. However, Miller's customary freshness is lacking and the film comes close to cliché and dullness. A new directness marks the referential *Le Sourire,* which, entirely scripted by Miller, signals a return to the more personal statements of *La Meilleure Façon de marcher* or *L'Effrontée,* and through its obsessional phobic images of blood and vomiting to the early Godardian short *Juliet dans Paris.* The opening, contrastive locations—the clinic representing order and the fairground social disruption—and the constant mood switches through alternating jazz and classical scores recall Miller at his most accomplished.

Miller's cinema is a gallery of perceptively drawn portraits, in which delicately observed details register the elusive complexities of human nature. His vulnerable, often misguided characters, functioning in societies where ambiguity or difference are barely tolerated, are invariably bruised and humiliated in their progress towards mature self-knowledge. Yet the director's optimism determines that, for the most part, they grow in strength through their experiences. Claude Miller, who emerged as one of the most promising new French directors of the 1980s, continues to provide intermittent evidence of an exceptional talent, even though his latest films have not entirely fulfilled expectations.

—R. F. Cousins

MILLER, George

Nationality: Australian. **Born:** Brisbane, Australia, 3 March 1945. **Education:** University of New South Wales, M.D. **Family:** Married Sandy Gore, 1985, one daughter. **Career:** Physician, St. Vincent's Hospital, Sydney; began collaboration with writer/producer Byron Kennedy, 1971; directed first feature, *Mad Max,* 1979; producer/director of *The Dismissal* for TV, 1982. **Awards:** Best Director, Australian Film Institute, 1982; Best Foreign Film, Los Angeles Film Critics, 1983. **Address:** 30 Orwell Street, King's Cross, Sydney, New South Wales 2011, Australia.

Films as Director:

1971 *Violence in the Cinema: Part I* (short) (+ co-sc)
1973 *Devil in Evening Dress* (doc) (+ sc)
1979 *Mad Max*
1981 *Mad Max II (The Road Warrior)*
1983 "Nightmare at 20,000 Feet" episode in *Twilight Zone—The Movie*
1985 *Mad Max III: Beyond Thunderdome* (co-d, + co-sc, pr)
1987 *The Witches of Eastwick*
1992 *Lorenzo's Oil* (+ co-sc, co-pr)

Other Films:

1973 *Frieze, an Underground Film* (short) (ed)
1980 *Chain Reaction* (Barry) (assoc pr, collaborator on waterfall scenes)
1987 *The Riddle of the Stinson* (pr); *The Clean Machine* (pr); *Fragments of War* (pr)
1988 *Dead Calm* (exec pr); *The Year My Voice Broke* (exec pr)
1989 *Flirting* (exec pr)

Publications

By MILLER: articles—

"Production Report *Mad Max:* George Miller, Director," an interview with P. Beilby and S. Murray, in *Cinema Papers* (Melbourne), May/June 1979; also September/October 1979.
"The Ayatollah of the Movies," an interview with D. Chute, in *Film Comment* (New York), July/August 1982.
Interview with P. Broeske, in *Films in Review* (New York), October 1982.
Interview with Tony Crawley, in *Starburst* (London), no. 51, 1983.
Interview with T. Ryan, in *Cinema Papers* (Melbourne), January 1988.
"*Lorenzo's Oil,*" an interview with S. Murray, in *Cinema Papers,* April 1993.

On MILLER: book—

Mathews, Sue, *35mm Dreams,* Ringwood, Victoria, 1984.

On MILLER: articles—

Samuels, B., "Dr. George Miller: Mephisto in a Polka-Dot Tie," in *Cinema Canada* (Toronto), February 1983.
George Miller Section of *Positif* (Paris), December 1985.
Rodman, H. A., "George Miller," in *Millimeter,* May 1989.
Griffin, N., "Tell Me Where It Hurts," in *Premiere,* December 1992.
Maslin, J., "Parents Fighting to Keep Their Child Alive," in *New York Times,* 30 December 1992.
O'Brien, G., "The Doctor and the 'Miracle,'" in *New York Times,* 24 January 1993.

* * *

Along with contemporaries Peter Weir, Bruce Beresford, and Gillian Armstrong, George Miller helped to bring Australian film to the international forefront by the mid-1980s with his brilliant trilogy of *Mad Max, Mad Max II* (*The Road Warrior* in the United States), and *Mad Max: Beyond Thunderdome.* In a desolate Australian space, sometime in the future, the police have their hands full trying to keep the roads safe from suicidal, maniacal gangs. Cop Mel Gibson quits, but then seeks revenge when his wife and child are murdered. *Mad Max* was almost lost when it was released in the late 1970s, but with the success of the sequel, the style and bleak outlook were seen to represent a *tour de force* of genre filmmaking. We have little doubt what will happen; but the way the story unspools is what attracted audiences around the world. George Miller made *Mad Max* and made fellow countryman Mel Gibson an international star.

The greatness of the *Mad Max* films come from the images of burnt out men and women in a post-apocalyptic world of desolate highways. Characters are dressed in what was left after the "end of the world," including football uniform parts from American-style teams and other assorted bits and pieces of clothing. Miller seems to have patterned his hero after a Japanese samurai, but more insight can be gained by comparing these three films with the westerns of Sergio Leone, such as *Once upon a Time in the West.* The director's inventions make mundane stories into something altogether new and fresh.

For audiences the trilogy was *Dirty Harry* thrown into a desert of madness. Miller's style of directing has been called mathematical in nature, building a movie in the same manner prescribed by the early Sergei Eisenstein and utilized by the mature Hitchcock. Many argued that Miller, an Australian, outdid Steven Spielberg, the Hollywood wunderkind. And in the early 1980s *Mad Max* became a pop cult craze.

With the third installment Miller moved into mainstream Hollywood. Thus while it had the usual cast of unknown character actors and actresses placed in the sweeping, endless desert of the Australian outback, Tina Turner was cast as the ruler of Bartertown, a primitive community in the bleak futuristic post-Atomic world. Mel Gibson, again as Max, battled to the death in the Roman-style arena of Thunderdome. Miller proved he could continue the *Mad Max* appeal even though his partner of the first two, Byron Kennedy, died in 1983.

And although Miller was chosen by Spielberg for a segment of *Twilight Zone: The Movie,* he continued to work in Australia, on miniseries such as "The Dismissal." In the late 1980s Miller changed courses and directed the hit *The Witches of Eastwick* for Warner Bros. With Jack Nicholson and Cher, *The Witches of Eastwick* offered a lively, colorful fantasy set in a New England town. This was a popular film, far from the visceral violence of *Mad Max.* Miller's segment for *Twilight Zone: The Movie,* "Nightmare at 20,000 Feet," was the ultimate white-knucklers' airplane paranoid fantasy, with a computer technician staring out the window seeing a gremlin sabotaging the engines. John Lithgow turned in a bravura performance in a role originally played by William Shatner. The Miller segment, of the four, was the one most often praised in a movie now most associated with the grim tragedy of the filming of the John Landis episode. In 1992 Miller directed the acclaimed film *Lorenzo's Oil,* a tear-jerker starring Susan Sarandon as a mother fighting to save her terminally ill son.

Miller took a strange path to directorial success, but once one sees and analyzes the *Mad Max* trilogy, it makes sense. After graduating with a degree in medicine from the University of New South Wales in 1970, this "self-confessed movie freak" spent eighteen months in the emergency room of a large city hospital dealing with auto accident victims. Perhaps this is where he developed his strange view of the world.

Finally, no portrait of the talented Miller, with much of his creative future still ahead of him, should end without noting that this George Miller is *not* the same George Miller, also an Australian, who made a reputation as the director of *The Man from Snowy River* (1982).

—Douglas Gomery

MINNELLI, Vincente

Nationality: American. **Born:** Chicago, 28 February 1910. **Education:** The Art Institute of Chicago, mid-1920s. **Family:** Married 1) Judy Garland, 1945 (divorced 1951), daughter Liza; 2) Georgette Magnani, 1954 (divorced 1958), one daughter; 3) Denise Giganti, 1961 (divorced 1971); 4) Lee M. Anderson, 1982. **Career:** Child actor, Minnelli Brothers Dramatic Tent Show, 1913-18; billboard painter, then window dresser, Marshall Field's department store, Chicago, 1929; assistant stage manager and costume designer, Balaban and Katz theatre chain, Chicago, then set and costume designer, Paramount Theater, New York, 1931-33; art director, Radio City Music Hall, New York, 1934; director of ballets and musicals for the stage, then signed as producer/director, Paramount Pictures, Hollywood, 1936; bought out contract after eight months and returned to New York as theatre director; joined MGM under auspices of Arthur Freed, 1940; directed sequences in *Babes on Broadway,* 1941, and *Panama Hattie,* 1942; directed first feature, *Cabin in the Sky,* 1942; returned to stage directing with *Mata Hari,* 1967, closed after two-week run. **Awards:** Academy Award for Best Director for *Gigi,* 1958; Order of Arts and Letters, France, for contribution to French culture. **Died:** In Beverly Hills, California, 25 July 1986.

Films as Director:

1942 *Cabin in the Sky*
1943 *I Dood It* (*By Hook or By Crook*)
1944 ***Meet Me in St. Louis***
1945 *The Clock* (*Under the Clock*); *Yolanda and the Thief*
1946 *Ziegfeld Follies* (co-d); *Undercurrent*
1947 *Till the Clouds Roll By* (Whorf) (Judy Garland sequences only)
1948 *The Pirate*
1949 *Madame Bovary*
1950 *Father of the Bride*
1951 ***An American in Paris***; *Father's Little Dividend*
1952 *Lovely to Look At* (LeRoy) (fashion show sequence only)
1953 "Mademoiselle" episode of *The Story of Three Loves*; *The Bad and the Beautiful*; ***The Band Wagon***
1954 *The Long, Long Trailer*; *Brigadoon*

1955 *The Cobweb*; *Kismet*
1956 *Lust for Life*; *Tea and Sympathy*
1957 *Designing Woman*; *The Seventh Sin* (Neame; replaced Neame as director, refused credit)
1958 *Gigi*; *The Reluctant Debutante*
1959 *Some Came Running*
1960 *Home from the Hill*; *Bells Are Ringing*
1962 *The Four Horsemen of the Apocalypse*; *Two Weeks in Another Town*
1963 *The Courtship of Eddie's Father*
1964 *Goodbye Charlie*
1965 *The Sandpiper*
1970 *On a Clear Day You Can See Forever*
1976 *A Matter of Time*

Publications

By MINNELLI: book—

I Remember It Well, with Hector Arce, New York, 1974.

By MINNELLI: articles—

Interview with Charles Bitsch and Jean Domarchi, in *Cahiers du Cinéma* (Paris), August/September 1957.
"So We Changed It," in *Films and Filming* (London), November 1958.
"The Rise and Fall of the Musical," in *Films and Filming* (London), January 1962.
"Rencontre avec Vincente Minnelli," with Jean Domarchi and Jean Douchet, in *Cahiers du Cinéma* (Paris), February 1962.
"On the Relationship of Style to Content in *The Sandpiper,*" in *Cinema* (Los Angeles), July/August 1965.
Interview, in *The Celluloid Muse: Hollywood Directors Speak,* edited by Charles Higham and Joel Greenberg, London, 1969.
"Vincente Minnelli and Gigi," interview with Digby Diehl, in *Action* (Los Angeles), September/October 1972.
"The Nostalgia Express," interview with Gideon Bachmann, in *Film Comment* (New York), November/December 1976.
"Two Weeks in Another Town," interview with P. Lehman and others, in *Wide Angle* (Athens, Ohio), no. 1, 1979.

On MINNELLI: books—

Truchaud, Francois, *Vincente Minnelli,* Paris, 1966.
Knox, Donald, *The Magic Factory: How M-G-M Made "An American in Paris,"* New York, 1973.
Delameter, J., *Dance in the Hollywood Musical,* Ann Arbor, Michigan, 1981.
Guerif, François, *Vincente Minnelli,* Paris, 1984.
Brion, Patrick, and others, *Vincente Minnelli,* Paris, 1985.
Harvey, Stephen, *Directed by Vincente Minnelli,* New York, 1989.
Lang, Robert, *American Film Melodrama: Griffith, Vidor, Minnelli,* Princeton, New Jersey, 1989.

On MINNELLI: articles—

Harcourt-Smith, Simon, "Vincente Minnelli," in *Sight and Sound* (London), January/March 1952.
Johnson, Albert, "The Films of Vincente Minnelli," in *Film Quarterly* (Berkeley), Winter 1958 and Spring 1959.
McVay, Douglas, "The Magic of Minnelli," in *Films and Filming* (London), June 1959.
Shivas, Mark, "Minnelli's Method," in *Movie* (London), June 1962.
Mayersberg, Paul, "The Testament of V. Minnelli," in *Movie* (London), October 1962.
Torok, Jean-Paul, and Jacques Quincey, "V.M. ou Le Peintre de la vie rêvée," in *Positif* (Paris), March 1963.
"Minnelli Issue" of *Movie* (London), June 1963.
Galling, Dennis, "V.M. is One of the Few Hollywood Directors Who Has an Art Sense," in *Films in Review* (New York), March 1964.
Nowell-Smith, G., "Minnelli and Melodrama," in *Australian Journal of Screen Theory* (Kensington, New South Wales), no. 3, 1977.
McVay, D., "Minnelli and *The Pirate,*" in *Velvet Light Trap* (Madison), Spring 1978.
Simsolo, Noël, "Sur quelques films de Minnelli," in *Image et Son* (Paris), October 1981.
Telotte, J. P., "Self and Society: Vincente Minnelli and Musical Formula," in *Journal of Popular Film* (Washington, D.C.), Winter 1982.
McCarthy, T., obituary in *Variety* (New York), 30 July 1986.
Harvey, S., obituary in *Film Comment* (New York), September/October 1986.
Taylor, John Russell, "Tribute to Minnelli," in *Films and Filming* (London), October 1986.
Gourget, J. L., "L'oeuvre de Vincente Minnelli," in *Positif* (Paris), December 1986.
Thomas, Nick, "Vincente Minnelli," in *Annual Obituary 1986,* London and Chicago, 1989.
Goldmann, A., "'Madame Bovary' vue par Flaubert, Minnelli et Chabrol," *Cinemaction,* vol. 65, no. 4, 1992.

* * *

Between 1942 and 1962, Vincente Minnelli directed twenty-nine films (and parts of several others) at Metro-Goldywn-Mayer, eventually becoming the studio's longest-tenured director. Brought to Hollywood following a tremendously successful career as a Broadway set designer and director of musicals, he was immediately placed at the helm of MGM's biggest musical productions, beginning with the all-black *Cabin in the Sky.* Over the next decade-and-a-half, he gained a reputation as the premiere director at work in the genre. This reputation was based on a remarkable series of productions, including *Meet Me in St. Louis, The Pirate, An American in Paris,* and *The Band Wagon,* and culminating with a Best Director's Academy Award for *Gigi.* Yet Minnelli's career was by no means restricted to musicals. During the same period he also directed a series of successful comedies and melodramas with flair and stylistic elegance.

If anything, Minnelli's accomplishments as a stylist, which were recognized from the beginning of his Hollywood career, worked against his being taken seriously as a director-auteur. By the late 1950s he had been dubbed (by critic Albert Johnson) "the master of the decorative image," which seemed, at the time, the highest compliment which might be paid a director of musicals. Indeed, Minnelli's films are impeccably crafted—filled with lushly stylized sets, clever and graceful performances, and a partiality for long tales. Minnelli also utilized a fluid mobile camera suited to the filming of dance, mounting and preserving performance spatially, even as the camera involves the audience in the choreographed movement. Yet it also informs the non-musical sequences of Minnelli's films with the same kind of liberal sensibility associated with contemporaries like Otto Preminger and Nicholas Ray, one that allows both the characters and the eyes of the audience a certain freedom of movement within a nearly seamless time and space. An accompanying theatricality (resulting from a tendency to shoot scenes from a fourth-wall position) blends with Minnelli's specifically cinematic flourishes in a clever realization of the themes of art and artificiality, themes which run throughout his films.

Stylization and artifice are necessarily addressed by musical films in general, and Minnelli's films do so with great verve—most thoroughly in the baroque otherworldliness of *Yolanda and the Thief,* and most

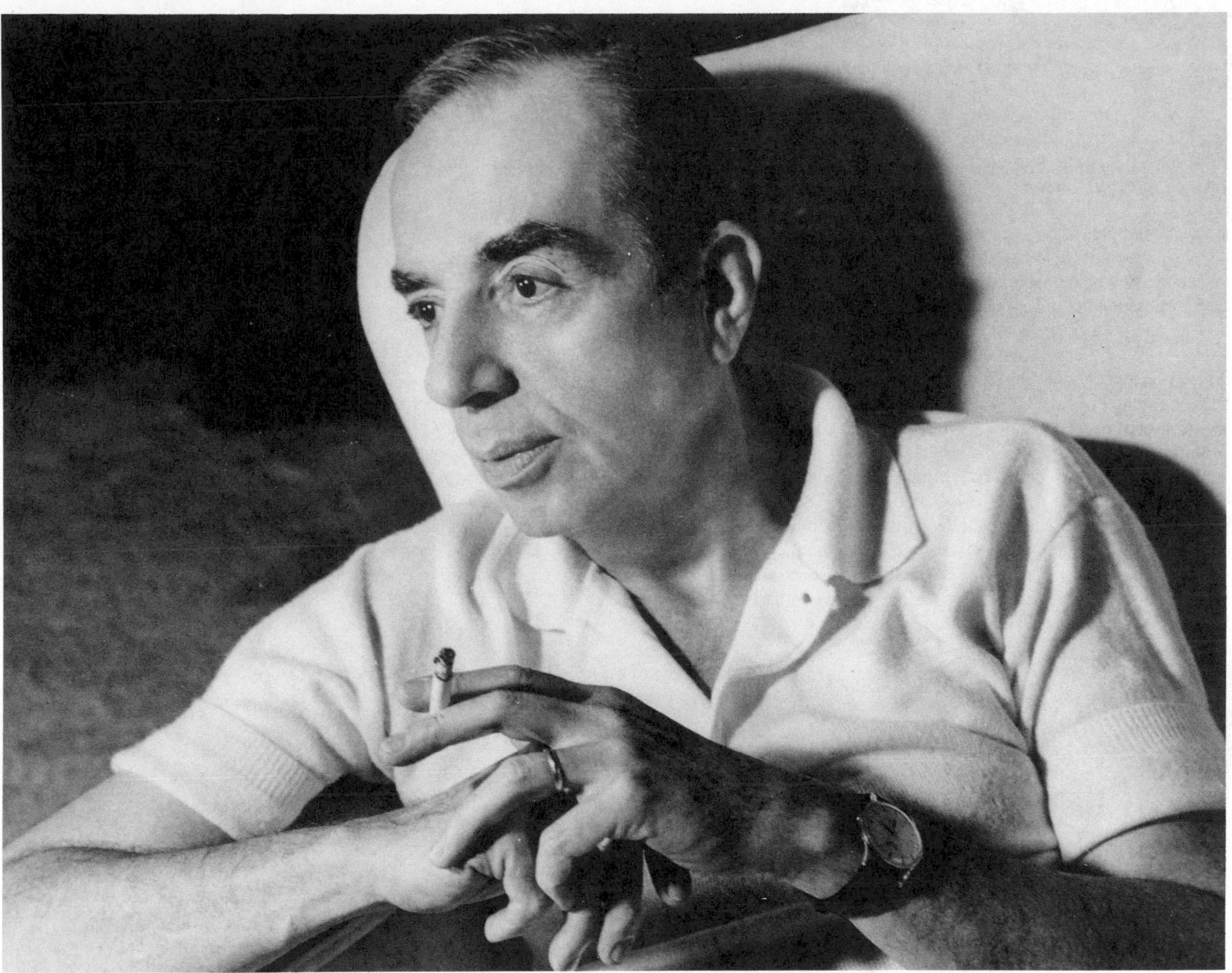

Vincente Minnelli

brilliantly in the interplay of character and actor, stage and screen in *The Band Wagon.* But an equal concern with levels of unreality informs most of his films. This is perhaps most evident in the Pirandellian meditation on Hollywood, *The Bad and the Beautiful,* and its bizarre, Cinecitta-made quasi-sequel, *Two Weeks in Another Town.* This exploration surely reaches a kind of limit in Minnelli's last film, *A Matter of Time.* This story of an aspiring actress, played by Liza Minnelli, becomes an examination of his own daughter's talents and persona (haunted by the ghost of Judy Garland), making the film into the director's own *Vertigo,* a fitting conclusion to a career devoted to the interplay of various levels of fantasy.

Filmic fantasy is almost always present in Minnelli's films, even when they address the most mundane human problems in basically realistic settings. Virtually every Minnelli film contains a fantasy sequence, a moment in which the narrative recedes in order to allow a free play of symbols on an almost exclusively formal level. In Minnelli's musicals, this is invariably an extended "ballet." The most memorable of these ballets may be the twenty-minute number which concludes *An American in Paris,* but the most powerful example might be Judy Garland's erotic fantasy of Gene Kelly as "Mack the Black" in *The Pirate.* In *Meet Me in St. Louis,* the burst of pure style occurs in the non-musical, and surprisingly horrific, Halloween sequence. In the comedy *Father of the Bride,* it is a tour-de-force dream sequence in which all of Spencer Tracy's fatherly anxieties are unleashed. The position is filled by a hallucinatory chase through a carnival in *Some Came Running,* by fantastic visions of the title figures in *The Four Horsemen of the Apocalypse,* and by mad car rides in both *The Bad and the Beautiful* and *Two Weeks in Another Town.* Such extra-narrative sequences serve to condense and resolve plot elements on a visual/emotional plane, providing the only escape routes from the exigencies of a world which Minnelli otherwise depicts as emotionally frustrating, overly complex, and terribly delicate.

Indeed, Andrew Sarris quite rightly noted that "Minnelli had an unusual, sombre outlook for musical comedy," a fact which seems responsible for the unexpected depth of most of his films. Certainly one of the factors responsible for the continued interest in *Meet Me in St. Louis* is the overt morbidity of its nostalgic tone. Yet Minnelli's troubled perspective is probably most evident in the existential isolation of his characters, and in the humanistic, yet stoic, attitude he adopts in treating equally their petty jealousies and their moral fears. A genuinely pained sense of the virtual impossibility of meaningful human contact informs the machinations of such stylized melodramas as *Some Came Running, Home from the Hill,* and *The Four Horsemen.* And the tenuousness of love and power is nowhere more artfully rendered than in his generic masterpiece, *The Cobweb,* where an argument over drapes for the rec room of a mental hospital reveals a network of neuroses amongst the staff and their families that is as deep-seated as the disorders of the patients.

At worst, Minnelli has been cited as the epitome of Hollywood's "middlebrow" aspirations toward making art accessible to the mass audience. At best, he was championed by the British critics at *Movie* during the early 1960s as one of Hollywood's consummate auteurs. For one such critic, V. F. Perkins, Minnelli's films provided some of the best examples of classical narrative style, which naturalized meaning through understated flourishes of mise-en-scène. It is certainly this capacity which enabled Minnelli to employ a forty-foot trailer as an effortless metaphor for the marriage of newlyweds Lucille Ball and Desi Arnaz (*The Long, Long Trailer*), to critique the manipulations of parental love by consumer culture through depiction of an increasingly overblown wedding (*Father of the Bride*), and to displace a child's incapacity to deal with his mother's death onto his horror at the discovery of his dead goldfish (*The Courtship of Eddie's Father*).

We must certainly categorize Minnelli as something more than a decorative artist, for the stylistic devices of his films are informed with a remarkably resilient intelligence. Even if we are finally to conclude that, throughout his work, there is a dominance of style over theme, it ultimately serves only to confirm his contribution to the refinement of those techniques by which Hollywood translates meanings into style and presents both as entertainment.

—Ed Lowry

MIZOGUCHI, Kenji

Nationality: Japanese. **Born:** Tokyo, 16 May 1898. **Education:** Aohashi Western Painting Research Institute, Tokyo, enrolled 1914. **Career:** Apprentice to textile designer, 1913; newspaper illustrator, Kobe, 1916; assistant director to Osamu Wakayama, 1922; directed first film, 1923; began association with art director Hiroshi Mizutani on *Gio matsuri,* 1933; began collaboration with writer Yoshikata Yoda on *Naniwa ereji,* 1936; member of Cabinet Film Committee, from 1940; elected president of Japanese directors association, 1949; signed to Daiei Company, 1952. **Awards:** International Prize, Venice Festival, for *The Life of Oharu,* 1952. **Died:** Of leukemia, in Kyoto, 24 August 1956.

Films as Director:

1923 *Ai ni yomigaeru hi* (*The Resurrection of Love*); *Furusato* (*Hometown*) (+ sc); *Seishun no yumeji* (*The Dream Path of Youth*) (+ sc); *Joen no chimata* (*City of Desire*) (+ sc); *Haizan no uta wa kanashi* (*Failure's Song is Sad*) (+ sc); *813* (*813: The Adventures of Arsene Lupin*); *Kiri no minato* (*Foggy Harbor*); *Chi to rei* (*Blood and Soul*) (+ sc); *Yoru* (*The Night*) (+ sc); *Haikyo no naka* (*In the Ruins*)

1924 *Toge no uta* (*The Song of the Mountain Pass*) (+ sc); *Kanashiki hakuchi* (*The Sad Idiot*) (+ story); *Gendai no joo* (*The Queen of Modern Times*); *Josei wa tsuyoshi* (*Women Are Strong*); *Jinkyo* (*This Dusty World*); *Shichimencho no yukue* (*Turkeys in a Row*); *Samidare zoshi* (*A Chronicle of May Rain*); *Musen fusen* (*No Money, No Fight*); *Kanraku no onna* (*A Woman of Pleasure*) (+ story); *Akatsuki no shi* (*Death at Dawn*)

1925 *Kyohubadan no joo* (*Queen of the Circus*); *Gakuso o idete* (*Out of College*) (+ sc); *Shirayuri wa nageku* (*The White Lily Laments*); *Daichi wa hohoemu* (*The Earth Smiles*); *Akai yuhi ni terasarete* (*Shining in the Red Sunset*); *Furusato no uta* (*The Song of Home*); *Ningen* (*The Human Being*); *Gaijo no suketchi* (*Street Sketches*)

1926 *Nogi Taisho to Kuma-san* (*General Nogi and Kuma-san*); *Doka o* (*The Copper Coin King*) (+ story); *Kaminingyo haru no sayaki* (*A Paper Doll's Whisper of Spring*); *Shin ono ga tsumi* (*My Fault, New Version*); *Kyoren no onna shisho* (*The Passion of a Woman Teacher*); *Kaikoku danji* (*The Boy of the Sea*); *Kane* (*Money*) (+ story)

1927 *Ko-on* (*The Imperial Grace*); *Jihi shincho* (*The Cuckoo*)

1928 *Hito no issho* (*A Man's Life*)

1929 *Nihombashi* (+ sc); *Tokyo koshinkyoku* (*Tokyo March*); *Asahi wa kagayaku* (*The Morning Sun Shines*); *Tokai kokyogaku* (*Metropolitan Symphony*)

1930 *Furusato* (*Home Town*); *Tojin okichi* (*Mistress of a Foreigner*)

1931 *Shikamo karera wa yuku* (*And Yet They Go*)

1932 *Toki no ujigami* (*The Man of the Moment*); *Mammo Kenkoku no Reimei* (*The Dawn of Manchukuo and Mongolia*)

1933 *Taki no Shiraito* (*Taki no Shiraito, the Water Magician*); *Gion matsuri* (*Gion Festival*) (+ sc); *Jimpuren* (*The Jimpu Group*) (+ sc)

1934 *Aizo toge* (*The Mountain Pass of Love and Hate*); *Orizuru osen* (*The Downfall of Osen*)

1935 *Maria no Oyuki* (*Oyuki the Madonna*); *Gubijinso* (*Poppy*)

1936 ***Naniwa ereji*** (*Osaka Elegy*) (+ story); *Gion no shimai* (*Sisters of the Gion*) (+ story)

1937 *Aienkyo* (*The Straits of Love and Hate*)

1938 *Aa furusato* (*Ah, My Home Town*); *Roei no uta* (*The Song of the Camp*)

1939 ***Zangiku monogatari*** (*The Story of the Last Chrysanthemum*)

1944 *Danjuro sandai* (*Three Generations of Danjuro*); *Miyamoto Musashi* (*Musashi Miyamoto*)

1945 *Meito Bijomaru* (*The Famous Sword Bijomaru*); *Hisshoka* (*Victory Song*) (co-d)

1946 *Josei no shori* (*The Victory of Women*); *Utamaro o meguru gonin no onna* (*Utamaro and His Five Women*)

1947 *Joyu Sumako no koi* (*The Love of Sumako the Actress*)

1948 *Yoru no onnatachi* (*Women of the Night*)

1949 *Waga koi wa moenu* (*My Love Burns*)

1950 *Yuki Fujin ezu* (*A Picture of Madame Yuki*)

1951 *Oyu-sama* (*Miss Oyu*); *Musashino Fujin* (*Lady Musashino*)

1952 ***Saikaku ichidai onna*** (*The Life of Oharu*)

1953 ***Ugetsu monogatari*** (*Ugetsu*); *Gion bayashi* (*Gion Festival Music*)

1954 ***Sansho dayu*** (*Sansho the Bailiff*); *Uwasa no onna* (*The Woman of the Rumor*); *Chikamatsu monogatari* (*A Story from Chikamatsu; Crucified Lovers*)

1955 *Yokihi* (*The Princess Yang Kwei-fei*); *Shin Heike monogatari* (*New Tales of the Taira Clan*)

1956 ***Akasen chitai*** (*Street of Shame*)

Publications

By MIZOGUCHI: articles—

Texts, in *Cahiers du Cinéma* (Paris), May 1959.

"Kenji Mizoguchi," in *Positif* (Paris), November 1980.

"Table ronde avec Kenji Mizoguchi" in *Positif* (Paris), December 1980 and January 1981.

On MIZOGUCHI: books—

Anderson, Joseph, and Donald Richie, *The Japanese Film: Art and Industry,* New York, 1960.
Ve-Ho, *Kenji Mizoguchi,* Paris, 1963.
Mesnil, Michel, *Mizoguchi Kenji,* Paris, 1965.
Iwazaki, Akira, "Mizoguchi," in *Anthologie du Cinéma,* vol. 3, Paris, 1968.
Yoda, Yoshikata, *Mizoguchi Kenji no hito to geijutsu* [Kenji Mizoguchi: The Man and His Art], Tokyo, 1970.
Mesnil, Michel, editor, *Kenji Mizoguchi,* Paris, 1971.
Mellen, Joan, *Voices from the Japanese Cinema,* New York, 1975.
Mellen, Joan, *The Waves at Genji's Door: Japan Through Its Cinema,* New York, 1976.
Bock, Audie, *Japanese Film Directors,* New York, 1978; revised edition, Tokyo, 1985.
Freiberg, Freda, *Women in Mizoguchi Films,* Melbourne, 1981.
Serceau, Daniel, *Mizoguchi: De la revolte aux songes,* Paris, 1983.
Andrew, Dudley, *Film in the Aura of Art,* Princeton, New Jersey, 1984.
McDonald, Keiko, *Mizoguchi,* Boston, 1984.

On MIZOGUCHI: articles—

Mizoguchi issue of *Cinéma* (Paris), no. 6, 1955.
Anderson, Joseph, and Donald Richie, "Kenji Mizoguchi," in *Sight and Sound* (London), Autumn 1955.
Rivette, Jacques, "Mizoguchi vu d'ici," in *Cahiers du Cinéma* (Paris), no. 81, 1958.
Godard, Jean-Luc, "L'Art de Kenji Mizoguchi," in *Art* (Paris), no. 656, 1958.
Mizoguchi issue of *L'Ecran* (Paris), February/March 1958.
Mizoguchi issue of *Cahiers du Cinéma* (Paris), March 1958.
"Dossier Mizoguchi," in *Cahiers du Cinéma* (Paris), August/September 1964.
"The Density of Mizoguchi's Scripts," in interview with Yoshikata Yoda, in *Cinema* (Los Angeles), Spring 1971.
Wood, Robin, "Mizoguchi: The Ghost Princess and the Seaweed Catcher," in *Film Comment* (New York), March/April 1973.
"Les Contes de la lune vague après la pluie," special Mizoguchi issue of *Avant-Scène du Cinéma* (Paris), 1 January 1977.
Cohen, R., "Mizoguchi and Modernism," in *Sight and Sound* (London), Spring 1978.
Legrand, G., and others, special Mizoguchi section, in *Positif* (Paris), November 1978.
Sato, Tadao, and Dudley Andrew, "On Kenji Mizoguchi," in *Film Criticism* (Edinboro, Pennsylvania), Spring 1980.
Andrew, Dudley, "Kenji Mizoguchi: La Passion de la identification," in *Positif* (Paris), January 1981.
Leach, J., "Mizoguchi and Ideology," in *Film Criticism* (Edinboro, Pennsylvania), Fall 1983.

* * *

By any standard Kenji Mizoguchi must be considered among the world's greatest directors. Known in the West for the final half-dozen films which crowned his career, Mizoguchi considered himself a popular as well as a serious artist. He made eighty-five films during his career, evidence of that popularity. Like John Ford, Mizoguchi is one of the few directorial geniuses to play a key role in a major film industry. In fact, Mizoguchi once headed the vast union governing all production personnel in Japan, and was awarded more than once the industry's most coveted citations. But it is as a meticulous, passionate artist that Mizoguchi will be remembered. His temperament drove him to astounding lengths of research, rehearsal, and execution. Decade after decade he refined his approach while energizing the industry with both his consistency and his innovations.

Kenji Mizoguchi

Mizoguchi's obsessive concern with ill-treated women, and his maniacal pursuit of a lofty notion of art, stemmed from his upbringing. His obstinate father, unsuccessful in business, refused to send his older son beyond primary school. With the help of his sister, a onetime geisha who had become the mistress of a wealthy nobleman, Mizoguchi managed to enroll in a western-style art school. For a short time he did layout work and wrote reviews for a newspaper, but his real education came through the countless books he read and the theater he attended almost daily. In 1920 he presented himself as an actor at Nikkatsu studio, where a number of his friends worked. He moved quickly into scriptwriting, then became an assistant director, and finally a director. Between 1922 and 1935, he made fifty-five films, mostly melodramas, detective stories, and adaptations. Only six of these are known to exist today.

Though these lost films might show the influences his work had on the development of other Japanese films, German expressionism, and American dramatic filmmaking (not to mention Japanese theatrical style and western painting and fiction), Mizoguchi himself dismissed his early efforts, claiming that his first real achievement as an artist came in 1936. Working for the first time with scriptwriter Yoshikata Yoda, who would be his collaborator on nearly all his subsequent films, he produced *Osaka Elegy* and *Sisters of the Gion,* stories of exploited women in contemporary Japan. Funded by Daiichi, a tiny independent company he helped set up to bypass big-studio strictures, these films were poorly distributed and had trouble with the censors on account of their dark realism and touchy subject. While these films effectively bankrupted Daiichi, they also caused a sensation among the critics and further secured Mizoguchi's reputation as a powerful, if renegade, force in the industry.

Acknowledged by the wartime culture as Japan's chief director, Mizoguchi busied himself during the war mainly with historical dramas which were ostensibly non-political, and thus acceptable to the wartime government. Under the Allied occupation Mizoguchi was encouraged to make films about women, in both modern and historical settings, as part of America's effort to democratize Japanese society. With Yoda as scriptwriter and with actress Kinuyo Tanaka as star, the next years were busy but debilitating for Mizoguchi. He began to be considered old-fashioned in technique, even if his subjects were of a volatile nature.

Ironically, it was the West which resuscitated this most oriental director. With his critical and box-office reputation on the decline, Mizoguchi decided to invest everything in *The Life of Oharu,* a classic seventeenth-century Japanese picaresque story, and in 1951 he finally secured sufficient financing to produce it himself. Expensive, long, and complex, *Oharu* was not a particular success in Japan, but it gained an international reputation for Mizoguchi when it won the grand prize at Venice. Daiei Films, a young company that took Japanese films and aimed them at the export market, then gave Mizoguchi virtual carte blanche in his filmmaking. Under such conditions, he was able to create his final string of masterpieces, beginning with *Ugetsu,* his most famous film.

Mizoguchi's fanatic attention to detail, his insistence on multiple rewritings of Yoda's scripts, and his calculated tyranny over actors are legendary, as he sought perfection demanded by few other film artists. He saw his later films as the culmination of many years' work, his style evolving from one in which a set of tableaux were photographed from an imperial distance and then cut together (one scene/one shot) to one in which the camera moves between two moments of balance, beginning with the movements of a character, then coming to rest at its own proper point.

It was this later style which hypnotized the French critics and through them the West in general. The most striking oppositions in his themes and dramas (innocence vs. guilt, good vs. bad) unroll like a seamless scroll until in the final camera flourish one feels the achievement of a majestic, stoic contemplation of life.

More recently Mizoguchi's early films have come under scrutiny, both for their radical stylistic innovations (such as the shared flashbacks of the 1935 *Downfall of Osen*) and for the radical political positions which they virtually shriek (in the final close-ups of *Sisters of the Gion* and *Osaka Elegy,* for instance). When charges of mysticism are levelled at Mizoguchi, it is good to recall that his final film, *Street of Shame,* certainly helped bring about the ban on prostitution in Japan in 1957.

A profound influence on the New Wave directors, Mizoguchi continues to fascinate those in the forefront of the art (Godard, Straub, Rivette). Complete retrospectives of his thirty-one extant films in Venice, London, and New York resulted in voluminous publications about Mizoguchi in the 1980s. A passionate but contemplative artist, struggling with issues crucial to cinema and society, Mizoguchi will continue to reward anyone who looks closely at his films. His awesome talent, self-discipline, and productivity guarantee this.

—Dudley Andrew

MOLANDER, Gustaf

Nationality: Swedish. **Born:** Helsingfors (now Helsinki), Finland, 18 November 1888. **Education:** Royal Dramatic Theatre, Stockholm. **Family:** Married to Karin (Molander), 1910-18. **Career:** Member of Swedish National Theatre Company, Helsingfors, directed by father, 1910-11; stage actor in Stockholm, 1913-26; began writing film scripts for Mauritz Stiller, 1917; directed first film, 1920; director for Svensk Filmindustri, from 1923; introduced Ingrid Bergman, 1935. **Died:** In Stockholm, 20 June 1973.

Films as Director:

1920 *Bodakunden* (*King of Boda*) (+ sc)
1922 *Thomas Graals myndling* (*Thomas Graal's Ward*) (+ sc); *Pärlorna* (*The Amateur Film*) (+ sc)
1924 *33.333* (+ sc); *Polis Paulus påskasmäll* (*Constable Paulus's Easter Bomb*) (+ sc)
1925 *Ingmarsarvet* (*The Ingmar Inheritance*) (+ co-sc)
1926 *Till Österland* (*To the Orient*) (+ co-sc); *Hon den enda* (*She's the Only One*); *Hans engelska fru* (*His English Wife*)
1927 *Förseglade löppar* (*Sealed Lips*)
1928 *Parisiskor* (*Women of Paris*); *Synd* (*Sin*)
1929 *Hjärtats triumf* (*Triumph of the Heart*)
1930 *Charlotte Löwenskjöld* (*Charlotte Löwensköld*); *Fridas visor* (*Frida's Songs*)
1931 *Från yttersta skären*; *En natt* (*One Night*)
1932 *Svarta rosor* (*Black Roses*); *Kärlek och kassabrist* (*Love and Deficit*) (+ co-sc); *Vi som går köksvägen* (*We Go Through the Kitchen*) (+ co-sc)
1933 *Kära släkten* (*Dear Relatives*) (+ co-sc)
1934 *En stilla flirt* (*A Quiet Affair*) (+ co-sc); *Fasters miljoner* (*My Aunt's Millions*); *Ungkarlspappan* (*Bachelor Father*) (+ co-sc)
1935 *Under falsk flagg* (*Under False Colors*) (+ co-sc); *Swedenhielms* (+ co-sc); *Bröllöpsresan* (*The Honeymoon Trip*) (+ co-sc)
1936 *På solsidan* (*On the Sunny Side*) (remade for television, 1966); *Intermezzo* (+ co-sc); *Familjens hemlighet* (*The Family Secret*)
1937 *Sara lär sig folkvett* (*Sara Learns Manners*); *Dollar* (+ co-sc)
1938 *En kvinnas ansikte* (*A Woman's Face*) (+ co-sc); *En enda natt* (*One Single Night*) (+ co-sc); *Ombyte förnöjer* (+ co-sc)
1939 *Emilie Högqvist* (+ co-sc)
1940 *En, men ett lejon* (*One But a Lion*); *Den ljusnande framtid* (*Bright Prospects*) (+ co-sc)
1941 *I natt eller aldrig* (*Tonight or Never*); *Striden går vidare* (*The Fight Goes On*) (+ co-sc)
1942 *Jacobs stege* (*Jacob's Ladder*); *Rid i natt* (*Ride Tonight!*) (+ sc)
1943 *Det brinner en eld* (*There Burned a Flame*); *Älskling, jag ger mig* (*Darling I Surrender*); *Ordet* (*The Word*)
1944 *Den osynliga muren* (*The Invisible Wall*); *Kejsaren av Portugallien* (*The Emperor of Portugal*) (+ co-sc)
1945 *Galgamannen* (*Mandragora*) (+ co-sc)
1946 *Det är min modell* (*It's My Model*)
1947 *Kvinna utan ansikte* (*Woman without a Face*)
1948 *Nu börjar livet* (*Life Begins Now*) (+ co-sc); *Eva* (+ co-sc)
1949 *Kärleken segrar* (*Love Will Conquer*)
1950 *Kvartetten som sprängdes* (*The Quartet That Split Up*)
1951 *Fästmö uthyres* (*Fiancée for Hire*); *Frånskild* (*Divorced*)
1952 *Trots* (*Defiance*) (+ sc); *Kärlek* (*Love*) (+ co-sc)
1953 *Glasberget* (*Unmarried*) (+ co-sc)
1954 *Herr Arnes pengar* (*Sir Arne's Treasure*) (+ co-sc) (remake)
1955 *Enhörningen* (*The Unicorn*) (+ co-sc)
1957 *Sången om den eldröda blommon* (*Song of the Scarlet Flower*) (remake)
1967 "Smycket (The Necklace)" episode of *Stimulantia* (shot 1965)

Other Films:

1917 *Terje Vigen* (Sjöstrom) (co-sc); *Thomas Graals bästa film* (*Thomas Graal's Best Film*) (Stiller) (co-sc)

Gustaf Molander: Ingrid Bergman in *Intermezzo* © 1936 AB Svensk Filmindustri

1918 *Thomas Graals bästa born* (*Thomas Graal's First Child*) (Stiller) (sc); *Sängen om den eldröda blommon* (*Song of the Scarlet Flower*) (Stiller) (sc)
1919 ***Herr Arnes pengar*** (*Sir Arne's Treasure*) (Stiller) (sc)
1923 *Mälarpirater* (*Pirates on Lake Mälar*) (sc)

* * *

Gustav Molander was a screenwriter/director whose work remains largely unknown outside his native Sweden. Although his career spanned nearly fifty years and resulted in over sixty feature films, he is best remembered as the man who "discovered" Ingrid Bergman and who wrote and directed *Intermezzo,* the film which brought that remarkably beautiful and talented actress to the attention of producer David O. Selznick.

Molander was a cultivated man whose career was mostly devoted to making elegant comedies and romantic dramas. Along with Victor Seastrom and Mauritz Stiller, he was one of the noted directors of Sweden's "golden age of cinema," from 1913 to 1924. Although not as artistically creative as those two masters, he was a respected journeyman director. Further, unlike Seastrom and Stiller, he chose not to emigrate to Hollywood, refusing Selznick's invitation in 1937.

In 1917 Molander had written the screenplay for Seastrom's milestone, *Terje Vigen,* which concerned the English blockade of Norway during the Napoleonic wars. He also wrote the scripts for three important films directed by Mauritz Stiller—*Thomas Graal's Best Film, Thomas Graal's Best Child,* and the sophisticated sex comedy *Erotikon.* These three films starred Karin Molander, Molander's vivacious wife, who later married Lars Hanson.

Molander began directing with *King of Boda,* and very often wrote his own screenplays. He was also the director of the Royal Dramatic Theatre, and it was he who, in the spring of 1923, suggested the young Greta Gustaffsson—later Garbo—for Stiller's *Gösta Berlings Saga.*

Following the decline of Sweden's "golden age," much of Molander's creativity was directed toward launching the career of Ingrid Bergman. He directed her first screen test, encouraged her, and directed her in seven films, most notably *Intermezzo,* which he wrote especially for her. Years later he would modestly state: "The truth is nobody discovered her. Nobody launched her. She discovered herself."

Molander's first film with the young actress was the intelligent romantic comedy, *Swedenhielms,* about a wealthy girl who is engaged to the son of a brilliant but impoverished scientist, played by the great Gosta Ekman. *On the Sunny Side* was a charming, lightweight comedy co-starring Bergman and Lars Hanson. *Intermezzo,* again with Hanson, followed, after which Bergman went to Hollywood to film the United States version of that romantic classic about the love between a beautiful young pianist and a famous, married violinist. That film made an international star of Ingrid Bergman, but she still returned to her native Sweden to star in three more films directed by Molander. *Dollar* was a sophisticated farce in which Bergman played an actress; *A Woman's Face* told the dramatic story of a facially-scarred criminal (the film was later re-made with Joan Crawford); and *En enda natt,* another elegant film which dealt with illegitimacy and extra-marital sex.

During World War II, Molander directed several anti-Nazi dramas as well as an ambitious religious allegory, *The World,* remade by Carl Dreyer in 1955. Molander also helped launch the career of another young Swedish actress from the Royal Dramatic Theatre, Signe Hasso. Molander's post-World War II career consisted mostly of rather pedestrian filmic renderings of plays and novels which relied heavily on dialogue, such as the turgid remaking of *Sir Arne's Treasure.* Molander's version of that popular novel by Selma Lagerlof bore little comparison to Stiller's masterful 1919 production. Two exceptions to this stagnant period in Molander's career were *Eva* and *Divorce,* both derived from scripts by Ingmar Bergman.

After *Song of the Scarlet Flower,* Molander retired, but he interrupted his retirement in 1964 to direct Ingrid Bergman one last time in *Stimulantia,* a four-episode film released in 1967. The Molander segment was entitled "The Necklace" and was based on Guy de Maupassant's short story. Upon completion of that film a reporter asked, "And what are your plans for the future?" Molander replied, "The graveyard." Molander died in 1973. While little-known outside Sweden, his lengthy career spanned the history of Swedish cinema.

—Ronald Bowers

MORETTI, Nanni

Nationality: Italian. **Born:** Brunico, Bolzano, Italy, 19 August 1953. **Education:** Self-taught. **Career:** Made his first amateur film, *La sconfitta,* 1973; directed additional amateur films *Pate de bourgeois,* 1973, and *Come parli frate,* 1974, shot on Super 8mm, which were screened in local cine-clubs and amateur festivals; directed first feature, *Sono un autarchico,* 1976; started production company, Sacher Films, and an art house cinema, Nuovo Sacher, which screens independent films from across the globe. **Awards:** Special Jury Prize, Berlin Festival, for *The Mass Is Ended,* 1986; Best Director, Cannes Festival, for *Caro Diario,* 1994.

Films as Director/Screenwriter/Actor:

1976 *Lo sono un autarchico* (*I Am Self-Sufficient*) (+ pr)
1978 *Ecce bombo*
1981 *Sogni d'oro* (*Sweet Dreams*)
1984 *Bianca* (co-sc)
1985 *La massa e finita* (*The Mass Is Ended*) (co-sc)
1989 *Palombella rossa* (*Red Lob*) (co-sc)
1990 *La cosa* (*The Thing*) (doc) (d and sc only)
1993 *Isole*
1994 *Caro Diario* (*Dear Diary*) (+ co-pr)

Other Films:

1988 *Domani accadra* (*It'll Happen Tomorrow*) (Luchetti) (pr)
1991 *Il portaborse* (*The Factotum*) (Luchetti) (co-pr, role)

Publications

By MORETTI: articles—

"Nanni Moretti," interview by F. Cuel and B. Villien in *Cinematographie* (Paris), November 1981.
"Conversation con Nanni Moretti," interview by M. Garriba in *Filmcritica* (Rome), April/May 1984.
"Entretien avec Nanni Moretti," interview by S. Toubiana in *Cahiers du Cinema* (Paris), November 1989.
"Nous voudrions que ce soir ca se termaine bien: entretien avec Nanni Moretti," interview by J. A. Gilli in *Positif* (Paris), December 1989.
"Entretien avec Nanni Moretti," interview with S. Toubiana and N. Saada in *Cahiers du Cinema* (Paris), May 1991.

On MORETTI: articles—

Davis, M. S., "Meet the Golden Boys Who Make Italy's New Film Comedies," in *New York Times,* 6 December 1981.
Strauss, F., "Je suis un autarcique," in *Cahiers du Cinema* (Paris), November 1989.
Jousse, T., "Le corps du defi," in *Cahiers du Cinema* (Paris), December 1989.
"Nanni Moretti," profile in *International Film Guide* (London, Hollywood), 1992.

* * *

Most Americans have never heard of Nanni Moretti, an Italian-born director-comedian who made his first film in 1973 at age twenty and has been a regular on the international film festival circuit since the early 1980s. This lack of recognition is not without irony, since his style of visually refined physical humor may be linked to the comic techniques of some of America's most beloved funnymen (including Buster Keaton, Charlie Chaplin, and the Marx Brothers). But Moretti's cinematic concerns involve much more than making his audiences laugh. He has been compared to Woody Allen in that both filmmakers have intellects, and both fill their work with philosophical deliberations.

Moretti is especially concerned with the political situation in his country, and the manner in which politics and politicians affect the lives of citizens. *Palombella rossa* is a typical Moretti film: both an off-the-wall satire and a pensive allegory about the choices, both personal and political, an individual makes in his life. It is the story of Michele, a character who often appears in Moretti's films in different guises (and is played by the filmmaker). By 1990s' standards, Michele is an anachronism in that he is a staunch communist. He also is a politician and a water-polo player. Much of the film is set during a water-polo match in which Michele constantly debates the merits of his politics with various individuals, from his teenaged daughter to journalists and political activists. All the while, the screen version of *Dr. Zhivago,* Boris Pasternak's contemplation of communism, airs on a nearby TV set. There also are flashbacks to Michele's youth. He is shown to be haunted by the more painful of his childhood memories, which adds insight into his present-day character.

Despite all this, Michele primarily is a comical creation. In his first appearance on screen, he drives his car and trades funny faces with some children in the back seat of the auto in front of him. This diversion results in his crashing into another car, causing a brief bout of amnesia that sets the stage for the goings-on during the water-polo match.

On one level, *Palombella rossa* serves as an examination of the state of communism in Italy; the athletic contest slowly degenerates into chaos, which may be seen as a reflection of the political state of Italy. But one thing is clear: Moretti is lampooning all political theorists and blowhards, those who are pro- or anti-communist/fascist/capitalist but who end up becoming tangled in their own rhetoric. And even more specifically, the film serves as his shout of despair for the collapse of communism and the corruption of the true, ideologically pure communist objective: a fair and equitable economic system in which all people, rather than certain individuals, might thrive.

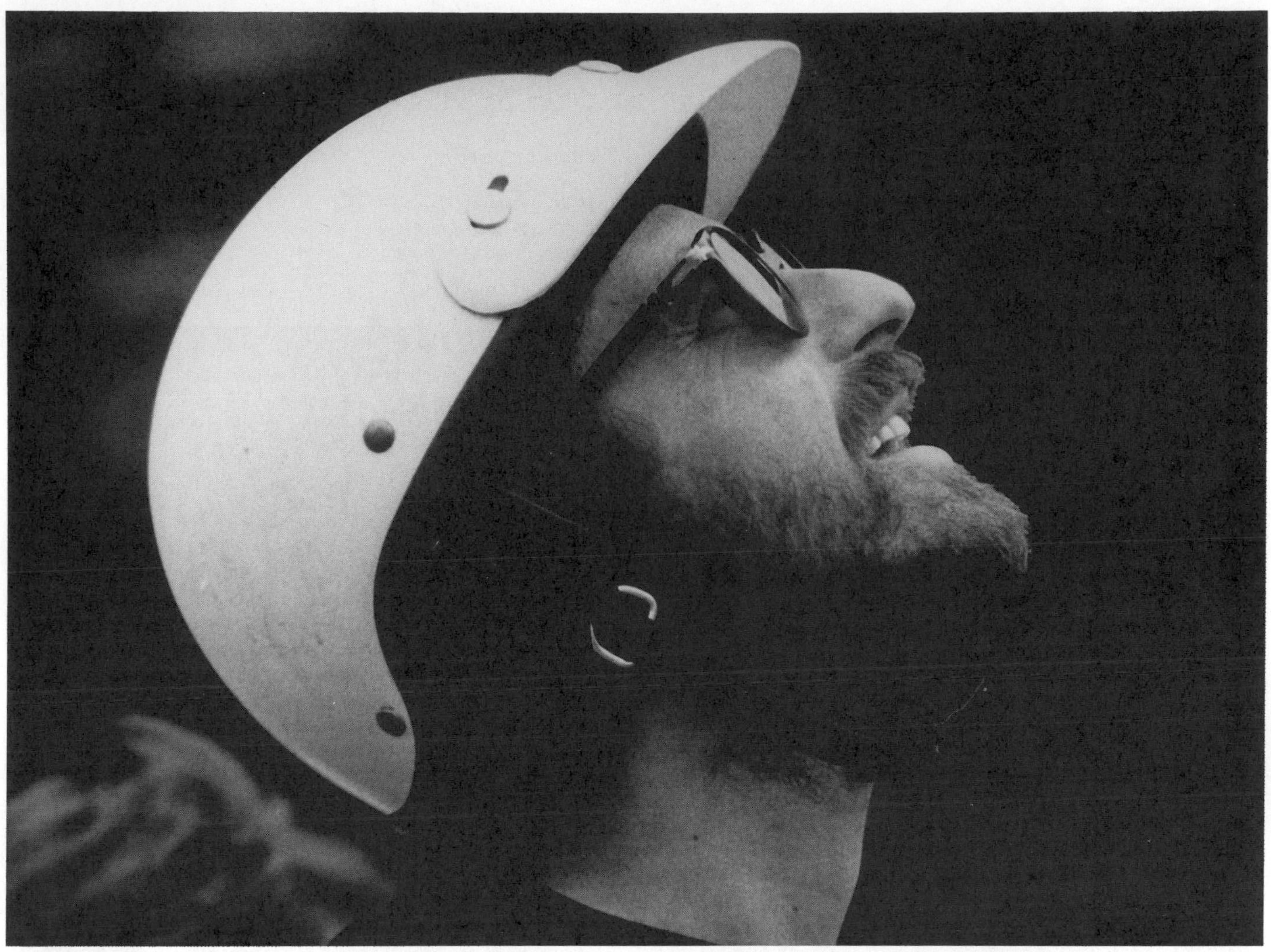

Nanni Moretti in *Caro Diario*

Moretti also overtly deals with politics in his first feature, *I Am Self-Sufficient,* in which he spoofs the totalitarian ideal while chronicling the goings-on in a theater group; he also appears as an actor in Daniel Luchetti's *Il Portaborse,* an impassioned assault on corruption within Italy's Socialist party. In his other films, however, Moretti focuses on additional issues with which he is intrigued. In *The Mass Is Over,* a speculation on the meaning of love, he plays a young cleric whose sense of priestly duty is jarred by the fact that his predecessor had broken his vows.

Moretti further spotlights this theme in *Bianca,* in which he plays a high school mathematics teacher who is consumed by the idea of romantic love. In this film, Moretti also drolly scrutinizes Europeans' fixation with American pop culture, as his teacher is employed in the "Marilyn Monroe" alternative high school, where each classroom comes complete with a jukebox. In the autobiographical *Sweet Dreams,* he plays a filmmaker who shares a complex relationship with his mother. As he is lauded by those who desire to collaborate with him on future projects and censured as a fraud by those put off by his opinions, Moretti reflects on the varied manner in which he is viewed as a filmmaker.

Moretti's most widely distributed film to date is *Caro Diario.* It is divided into three distinctly personal sections, each of which mirrors the director's concerns about his culture and, ultimately, his own survival. In the first, Moretti rides around Rome on a Vespa and makes off-the-wall observations about what he sees and feels. He pronounces that he is obsessed with Jennifer Beals, of *Flashdance* fame. This plays itself out on screen with the sudden appearance of Beals, who just so happens to be on the same street as Moretti at that very moment; as a cinematic effect, this also coincides with the manner in which Woody Allen employed Marshall McLuhan in *Annie Hall.* Moretti also savages pompous film critics who know nothing of real life, and who extol such films as *Henry: Portrait of a Serial Killer,* and he ponders why he has never visited the spot where Pier Paolo Pasolini was murdered.

In Part 2, Moretti goes island-hopping in Southern Italy. Here, he spotlights the same concerns he had dealt with earlier in *Bianca,* and ponders a most relevant contemporary question: How long can a man exist without a television set? Part 3 is the most serious segment. Here, Moretti restages his own cancer treatment. A sequence he filmed as he readied himself for a real chemotherapy treatment precedes re-enactments of him enduring uncomfortable itches and visiting numerous doctors. Each one offers different diagnoses. Each one hands him prescriptions for different pills, and the poor guy ends up with so many that he could open his own drugstore. Once again, Moretti manages to joke about a most serious situation, and in doing so pulls off quite a feat: finding humor in his own mortality.

—Rob Edelman

MORRIS, Errol

Nationality: American. **Born:** Hewlett, New York, 5 February 1948. **Education:** Graduated from the University of Wisconsin-Madison, 1969; graduate work at Princeton University and the University of California-Berkeley. **Family:** Married Julia Sheehan, an art historian; one son. **Career:** After leaving graduate school, held several jobs before beginning work on *Gates of Heaven.* **Awards:** Golden Horse award for Best Foreign Film, Taiwan International Film Festival, 1988, for *The Thin Blue Line;* Grand Jury Prize and Filmmaker's Prize, Sundance Film Festival, 1992, for *A Brief History of Time.* **Agent:** ICM, 8942 Wilshire Blvd., Beverly Hills, CA 90211, U.S.A. **Address:** Fourth Floor Productions, 678 Massachusetts Ave., Cambridge, MA 02139, U.S.A.

Films as Director:

1978 *Gates of Heaven*
1982 *Vernon, Florida*
1988 *The Thin Blue Line*

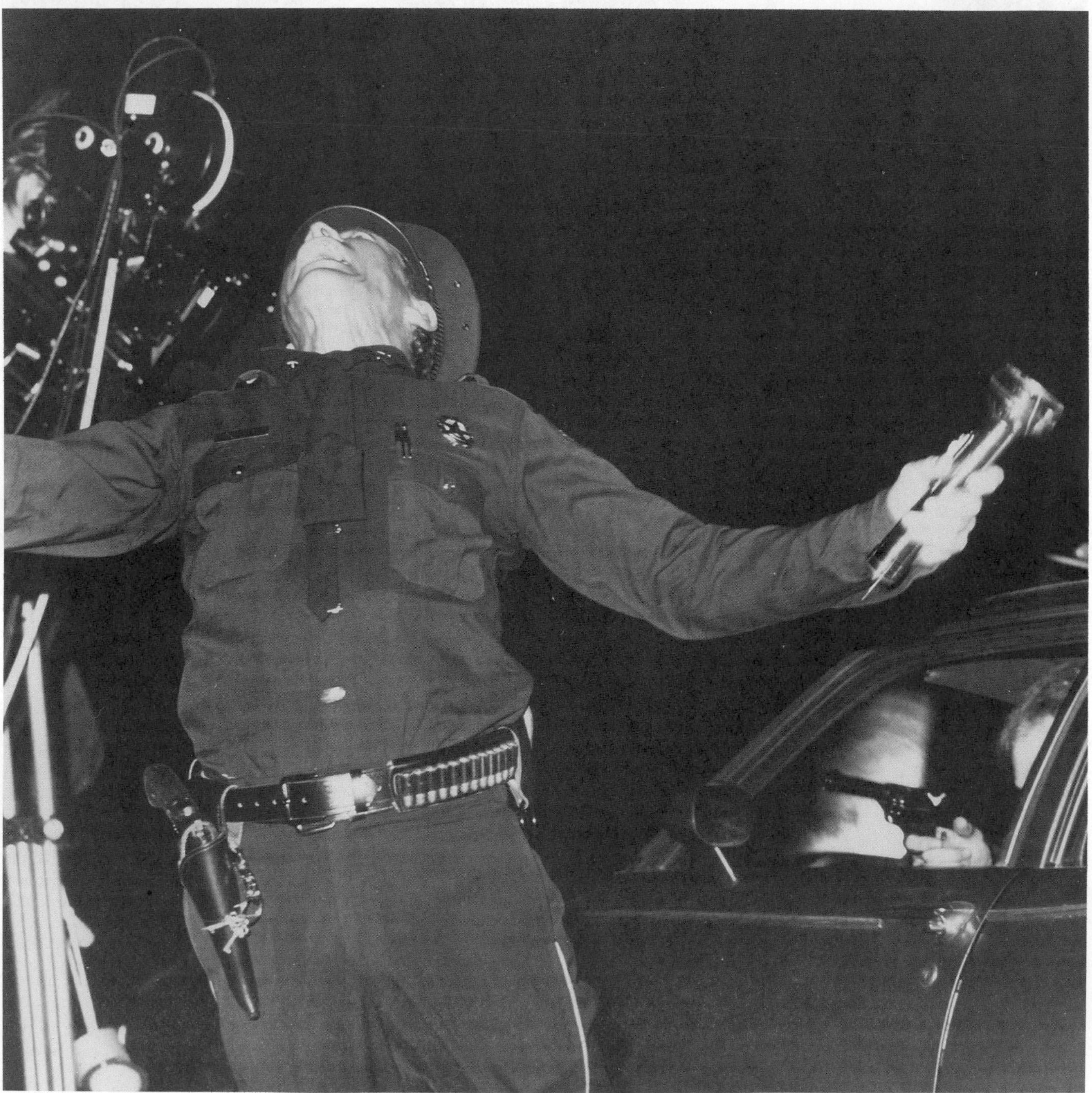

Errol Morris filming *The Thin Blue Line* courtesy of J&M Entertainment Ltd.

1992 *A Brief History of Time*; *The Dark Wind*
1996 *Fast, Cheap & Out of Control*

Publications

On MORRIS: articles—

Hoberman, J., "Errol Morris: Ordinary Weirdos," *Village Voice,* 30 June 1987.

Hopkins, E., "Cameos: Director Errol Morris," *Premiere,* December 1987.

Dieckmann, K., "Private Eye," *American Film,* January-February 1988.

Hoberman, J., "Off-screen: Errol Morris Deep in the Heart...," *Village Voice,* 30 August 1988.

Kelleher, E., "Director Morris Goes Private Eye for Miramax's *The Thin Blue Line,*" *Film Journal,* September-October 1988.

Bates, P., "Truth Not Guaranteed," *Cineaste,* no. 1, 1989.

Algar, N., "Errol Morris, Believe It or Not," *Monthly Film Bulletin,* April 1989.

Lack, R., "The Shape of Time," *Sight and Sound,* May 1992.

Chua, L., "Truth and Consequences," *Village Voice,* 22 September 1992.

* * *

Errol Morris's provocative work challenges documentary conventions. His unique style surfaces in his first film, *Gates of Heaven,* where he examines two California pet cemeteries: one a failure, and the other a successful enterprise run by a man and his two adult sons. Rather than employing an objective reportorial style in which information is presented and opposing sides are given an opportunity to present their positions, Morris allows the narrative to unfold slowly through the interwoven testimony of the participants. Quite unlike the typical, tightly controlled, interview-based documentary in which participants respond to direct questioning, in *Gates of Heaven* participants ramble on about issues both related and unrelated to the topic. As the interviews progress, the distinctive personalities of the participants emerge. The viewer is required to piece the narrative together, as the film's point of view remains ambiguous. Are the pet cemetery entrepreneurs, both successful and unsuccessful, compassionate individuals trying to help bereaved pet owners, or are they curious oddities, pandering to a few marginal individuals obsessed with their departed pets? The audience is left to decide.

Vernon, Florida, Morris's subsequent film, focuses on the residents of a small Florida community. It is a simple film which again employs the unstructured interview, the personal narrative, introduced in *Gates of Heaven.* The town's residents reflect on many facets of their lives. By conventional standards, their vivid personalities and their rural lifestyle appear quirky and eccentric. What emerges is a film that attempts neither to judge its subjects nor to tell the audience what to think.

The Thin Blue Line, dealing with the arrest and conviction of Randall Adams for the murder of a Dallas police officer in 1976, is Morris's best known and most distinctive film. The film created quite a stir when it was released, for several reasons. For example, although the film leaves the viewer with a clear sense that Randall Adams is innocent, it does not present that information directly. In a conventional documentary film, the most plausible scenario is represented and supported. Different opinions are introduced, but one clear position is taken. Morris defies that convention by illustrating conflicting interpretations, and in so doing he calls into question the very nature of the construction of truth. The audience is forced to confront the ambiguity caused by conflicting accounts. This confrontation disrupts the seamlessness of the conventional documentary and is disquieting to many viewers.

Morris also drew attention by using a series of highly stylized reenactments to illustrate the narratives told by various individuals. Reenactments have fallen out of favor as a documentary convention, and some critics feel Morris's use of reenactments detracts from the film's objectivity. Documentary has a long history of using reenactments, although they usually serve to represent typical rather than specific actions or activities. Today, viewers of documentary films expect to see evidence recorded on the scene from the historical world rather than reenacted scenarios. The introduction of cinema verite in the 1960s and the ubiquitous presence of on-the-scene reporting in the evening news has given rise to these expectations. Reenactments nowadays appear unfamiliar, unrealistic, even manipulative to many viewers. Morris takes reenactments an additional step by illustrating conflicting points of view instead of a typical or most plausible perspective.

Morris was hired to direct *A Brief History of Time,* but the film retains many characteristics of his earlier personal work. The film is based on scientist Stephen Hawking's book of the same title, and Hawking's computer-synthesized voice provides the structuring voice-over narration for the film. Hawking is presented as an ordinary man with extraordinary characteristics, including extreme physical limitations and a soaring intellect. As with the subjects in Morris's earlier work, Hawking represents himself, and his personal narrative is embellished by the recollections of friends, family, and colleagues. Hawking's synthesized voice on the soundtrack coupled with images of Hawking confined to a wheelchair, lips immobile, eyes animated, reveal powerful elements of character, personality, and intellect resulting in a complex, multifaceted portrait of the man and the scientist.

Morris's work is unfettered by slavish adherence to current documentary conventions. He does not appear in his films, but his presence is felt in their structure and style. Morris allows the individuals represented to recount their own, often equivocal narratives, which are then carefully woven into the finished product through editing. The result is not a typical "objective" or journalistic documentary with an easily accessible perspective. The viewer is made aware of the process of documentary construction through interviews that last a little too long or through the presentation of conflicting points of view without obvious resolution. The viewer is challenged and required to participate in crafting the narrative and forming an opinion about the individuals and issues presented. Morris brings a new vigor and a new insight to documentary filmmaking by playing with conventions and experimenting with new forms of representation.

—Elizabeth Cline

MULLIGAN, Robert

Nationality: American. **Born:** The Bronx, New York, 23 August 1925. **Education:** Attended theological seminary; studied radio communications, Fordham University, New York. **Military Service:** Marine radio operator, World War II. **Career:** Worked in editorial department of the *New York Times,* late 1940s; began working in TV as messenger for CBS, then TV director on *Suspense, TV Playhouse, Playhouse 90,* and others, mid-1950s; directed first feature film, *Fear Strikes Out,* 1957; founded Pakula-Mulligan Productions with Alan J. Pakula, 1962 (dissolved 1969). **Awards:** Academy Award nomination for Best Director, for *To Kill a Mockingbird,* 1962. **Agent:** Robert Stein, United Talent Agency, 9560 Wilshire Boulevard, 5th Floor,

Beverly Hills, California 90210, U.S.A. **Address:** c/o J. V. Broffman, 5150 Wilshire Boulevard #505, Los Angeles, California 90036, U.S.A.

Films as Director:

1957 *Fear Strikes Out*
1960 *The Rat Race*
1961 *The Great Imposter*; *Come September*
1962 *The Spiral Road*; *To Kill a Mockingbird*
1963 *Love with the Proper Stranger*
1965 *Baby the Rain Must Fall*
1966 *Inside Daisy Clover*
1967 *Up the Down Staircase*
1968 *The Stalking Moon*
1971 *The Pursuit of Happiness*; *Summer of '42*
1972 *The Other* (+ pr)
1975 *The Nickel Ride* (+ pr)
1978 *Blood Brothers*
1979 *Same Time, Next Year* (+ co-pr)
1982 *Kiss Me Goodbye* (+ co-pr)
1988 *Clara's Heart* (+ co-pr)
1991 *Man in the Moon*

Publications

By MULLIGAN: articles—

Interview with Michel Ciment, in *Positif* (Paris), January 1973.
Interview with J. A. Gili, in *Ecran* (Paris), October 1974.
"Time for Thought," an interview with R. Appelbaum, in *Films and Filming* (London), January 1975.
"Je n'ai pas peur du silence," an interview with M. Henry and A. Garsault, in *Positif* (Paris), December 1991.
"Entretien avec Robert Mulligan," with H. Merrick, in *Revue du Cinema,* January 1992.

On MULLIGAN: book—

Belton, John, *Cinema Stylists,* Metuchen, New Jersey, 1983.

On MULLIGAN: articles—

Godfrey, Lionel, "Flawed Genius: The Work of Robert Mulligan," in *Films and Filming* (London), January 1967.
Taylor, John, "Inside Robert Mulligan," in *Sight and Sound* (London), Autumn 1971.
Falonga, M., "Mysterious Islands: *Summer of '42,*" in *Film Heritage* (New York), Fall 1972.
"TV to Film: A History, a Map and a Family Tree," in *Monthly Film Bulletin* (London), February 1983.
Barra, Allen, "Distant Replay," in *Village Voice* (New York), 17 May 1988.
Walker, M., "Robert Mulligan," in *Film Dope,* March 1991.
Edinger, Catarina, "Dona Flor in Two Cultures," in *Literature/Film Quarterly,* vol. 4, 1991.
Kelleher, E., "Mulligan Addresses the Heart via MGM's *Man in the Moon,*" in *Film Journal,* October/November 1991.
Garsault, A., "L'amer paradis de l'enfance," in *Positif* (Paris), December 1991.
Piazzo, P., "Un artisan sensible," in *Jeune Cinema,* February/March 1992.
Strick, Philip, "*The Man in the Moon,*" in *Sight and Sound* (London), March 1992.

*   *   *

In an era in which consistent visual style seems perhaps too uniformly held as the prerequisite of the valorized auteur, one can all too easily understand why Robert Mulligan's work has failed to evince any passionate critical interest. His films all look so different; for instance, *To Kill a Mockingbird,* with its black-and-white measured pictorialism; *Up the Down Staircase,* photographed on location with a documentary graininess; *The Other,* with its heightened Gothic expressionism rather conventional to the horror genre, if not to Mulligan's previous work; and *The Summer of '42,* with a pastel prettiness which suffuses each image with the nostalgia of memory. If some would claim this visual eclecticism reflects the lack of a strong personality, others could claim that Mulligan has too much respect for his material to impose arbitrarily upon it some monolithic consistency and instead brings to his subjects the sensibility of a somewhat self-effacing Hollywood craftsman. Yet there are certainly some sequences in Mulligan's work which spring vividly to mind: the silent, final seduction in *The Summer of '42*; the almost surreal walk home by a child dressed as a ham in *To Kill a Mockingbird*; the high school dance in *Up the Down Staircase*; the climactic camera movement in *The Other,* from Niles to that empty space where Holland, were he not imaginary, would be sitting.

Even Mulligan's two biggest critical successes, *To Kill a Mockingbird* and *The Summer of '42,* both examples of the kind of respectable Hollywood filmmaking which garners Academy Award nominations, have not yet been greeted by any significant critical cult. And yet, if Mulligan's good taste has been steadfastly held against him, it must be noted that his films, albeit generally ignored, hold up remarkably well. Mulligan has a strong sense of narrative; and all his films are imbued with human values and a profound compassion which make for compelling audience identification with Mulligan's characteristic protagonists. Mulligan's tendency is to work in less familiar movie genres (such as Hollywood exposé, the family drama, the teacher film, the cinematic *Bildungsroman*), but to avoid—through sincerity and human insight—that emphasis on the purely formal which sometimes makes genre works "go dead" for their audiences upon repeated viewings. Perhaps it is American mistrust of male emotional expression which contributes to Mulligan's facile dismissal by many; certainly it appears that those critics who attacked as sentimental *The Summer of '42,* Mulligan's tasteful and bittersweet paean to lost virginity, failed to assess negatively those same qualities in so many of the French New Wave films, especially, for instance, the Antoine Doinel cycle by François Truffaut, which were instead praised for their lyrical and compassionate exploration of human interaction. Is nostalgia somehow more acceptable when it is French?

Certainly Mulligan seems especially interested in the deviant, the outsider, the loner: the mentally unbalanced Jimmy Peirsall in *Fear Strikes Out*; the enlightened attorney whose values put him in conflict with a bigoted community in *To Kill a Mockingbird*; the ex-convict trying to accustom himself to life outside the penitentiary in *Baby the Rain Must Fall*; the character of Ferdinand Demara, based on real life, who, in *The Great Imposter,* succeeds by the sheer force of his skillful impersonations in insinuating himself into a variety of environments in which he would otherwise never be accepted; the students in *Up the Down Staircase* who, psychologically stunted and economically deprived, may—even with a committed teacher's help—never fit into mainstream society. Like Truffaut, Mulligan has an extraordinary insight into the world of the child or adolescent and the secret rituals of that world. Mulligan's children never display that innocence conventionally associated with children, instead participating in often traumatic ceremonies of passage. One thinks of the child through whose eyes the innate racism of small-town America is seen in *To Kill a Mockingbird*; the precocious child-star in *Inside Daisy Clover*; the lost and often already jaded students in *Up the Down Staircase*; the pubescent adolescents who learn about sex and morality in *The Summer of '42*; and the irrevocably evil child, Niles, and his twin, Holland, in *The Other.*

Robert Mulligan

Unfortunately, despite the high quality of Robert Mulligan's films, there has been not even a minor re-evaluation of the director as a significant artist who has a consistency of themes (such as his association of puberty with violence)—this neglect despite the fact that *To Kill a Mockingbird* remains one of the most well-respected and emotionally engaging films in the American cinema, a movie which continues to please audiences whether they remember it from their past or whether they see it today for the first time. Not even the consistently fine performances elicited by Mulligan from his players (Anthony Perkins in *Fear Strikes Out,* Gregory Peck and Mary Badham in *To Kill a Mockingbird,* Sandy Dennis in *Up the Down Staircase,* Jennifer O'Neil in *The Summer of '42,* Richard Gere in *Blood Brothers,* Neil Patrick Harris in *Clara's Heart,* and indeed, all the children and adolescents who populate Mulligan's world) have served to summon ongoing critical attention. Ultimately, Mulligan's taste may be too fine and his feelings too sentimental to attract contemporary regard in a culture which thrives on the sexy, profane conflicts of a *Pulp Fiction.* And certainly, even at Mulligan's best or near-best, one sensed a subtlety or indirection when he dealt with things sexual: such as the homosexual orientation of Robert Redford's character in the underrated and fascinating Hollywood exposé *Inside Daisy Clover.* One suspects that if Mulligan may have never really had the gusto to publicize himself in the Sammy Glick-style, he neither had the opportunism or hypocrisy to jump on any passing bandwagon.

In any case, his recent films, though laudable and interesting, are hardly the works that would attract critical or popular attention. In 1982's curiously unengaging *Kiss Me Goodbye,* a reworking of the Brazilian film *Donna Flor and Her Two Husbands,* Mulligan does not seem to be especially inspired by the romantic comedy form, despite the film dealing with typical Mulligan themes of loss and grief. *Clara's Heart,* in 1988, reprised Mulligan's coming-of-age theme and, like *To Kill a Mockingbird,* dealt with personal relationships between whites and blacks, in this case, the friendship of a young white boy and the black woman who becomes his nanny. Although the narrative develops with surprising turns, the film was unjustly ignored, with Whoopi Goldberg giving a sensitive, often surprising, performance. Ultimately, *Clara's Heart* had too much heart and not enough cynicism to be successful; even though it dealt (if gently) with violence, divorce, rape, and incest, *Clara's Heart* faded in the glare of more trendy and explicit contemporary films like *Do the Right Thing.* Mulligan's final film to date, *Man in the Moon,* which had a few ardent critical supporters in 1991, is once again a coming-of-age story imbued with feelings of hopefulness and loss, nostalgia and regret. Although beautifully photographed in an older, Hollywood style by Freddie Francis, *Man in the Moon*—though a period piece—seems almost purposely set in a cultural vacuum so that Mulligan can avoid dealing with a contemporary America from which he seems rather alienated. The result is a film which, despite good performances from everyone, particularly the adolescent leads, seems somewhat dead and unconnected, certainly not the film to ignite a critical re-evaluation of Mulligan's work.

—Charles Derry

MUNK, Andrzej

Nationality: Polish. **Born:** Cracow, 16 October 1921. **Education:** Educated in engineering and law, 1946-48; State Cinema School, Lodz, degree 1950. **Family:** Married Joanna Prochnik. **Career:** Labourer, also active in resistance, World War II; general secretary of Z.N.M.S., organization of socialist students, late 1940s; director at documentary film studio, Warsaw, 1950-55; teacher at State Film School, Lodz, from 1957. **Died:** In auto accident, 20 September 1961.

Films as Director:

1949 *Kongres kombatantów* (*Congress of Fighters*) (co-d)
1950 *Sztuka młodych* (*Art of Youth*) (co-d, sc); *Zaczęło się w Hiszpanii* (*It Began in Spain*) (+ ed)
1951 *Kierunek Nowa Huta* (*Direction: Nowa Huta*); *Nauka bliżej życia* (*Science Closer to Life*) (+ co-ph)
1952 *Bajka w Ursusie* (*The Tale of Ursus*) or *Poemat symfoniczny "Bajka" Stanisława Moniuszki* (*The Symphonic Poem "Fable" of Stanislas Moniuszko*); *Pamiętniki chłopów* (*Diaries of the Peasants*) (+ sc)
1953 *Kolejarskie słowo* (*A Railwayman's Word*) (+ sc)
1954 *Gwiazdy muszą płonąć* (*The Stars Must Shine*) (co-d, co-sc)
1955 *Niedzielny poranek* (*Sunday Morning*; *Un Dimanche Matin*; *Ein Sonntagmorgen in Warschau*) (+ sc); *Błękitny krzyż* (*Men of the Blue Cross*; *Les Hommes de la croix bleue*; *Die Männer vom blauen Kreuz*) (+ sc)
1956 *Człowiek na torze* (*Man on the Track*; *Un Homme sur la voie*; *Der Mann auf den Schienen*) (+ co-sc)
1957 ***Eroica*** (*Eroica—Polen 44*)
1958 *Spacerek staromiejski* (*A Walk in the Old City of Warsaw*) (+ sc)
1959 *Kronika jubileuszowa* or *Polska kronika filmowa nr 52 A-B* (+ sc)
1960 *Zezowate szczęście* (*Bad Luck*; *De la veine a revendre*; *Das schielende Glück*) (+ role as bureaucrat)
1963 *Pasażerka* (*The Passenger*; *La Passagère*; *Die Passagierin*) (+ co-sc) (film assembled posthumously by Witold Lesiewicz)

Publications

By MUNK: articles—

"Expérience du cinéma polonais," interview with P.L. Thirard, in *Les Lettres Françaises* (Paris), no. 790, 1959.
"National Character and the Individual," in *Films and Filming* (London), vol. 8, no. 2, 1961.
"Naszych twórców ączy jedna cecha—poważne podejście do tematu i poważne traktowanie odbiorcy," [That which unites our filmmakers is a serious attitude toward the subject and the public] in *Ekran* (Warsaw), no. 22, 1961.
"Le dernier entretien avec ... ," in *Cinéma* (Paris), no. 71, 1962.

On MUNK: books—

Haudiquet, Philippe, *Nouveaux cinéastes polonais,* Premier Plan no. 27, Lyon, 1963.
Andrzej Munk, collective work, Warsaw, 1964.
Historia Filmu Polskiego IV, Warsaw, 1981.

On MUNK: articles—

Sadoul, Georges, "Andrzej Munk," in *Les Lettres Françaises* (Paris), no. 894, 1961.
Haudiquet, Philippe, "Andrzej Munk," in *Image et Son* (Paris), January 1964.
Special Munk issue of *Études Cinématographiques* (Paris), no. 45, 1965.
Brzozowski, Andrzej, "Munk et *La Passàgere,*" in *Cahiers du Cinéma* (Paris), no. 163, 1965.
Plazewsky, Jerzy, "Andrzej Munk," in *Anthologie du cinéma,* vol. 3, Paris, 1968.

Andrzej Munk

Amette, Jacques-Pierre, "Andrzej Munk," in *Dossiers du cinéma,* Cinéastes 1, Paris, 1971.
Profile of Munk, in *Illuzjon* (Warsaw), no. 3, 1986.

* * *

Andrzej Munk is one of the creators of the so-called Polish school of filmmaking and one of the most important Polish film directors. He belongs to the skeptical generation of directors who spent their early youth in the difficult years of the Second World War and embarked on filmmaking in the 1950s with no rosy illusions—but with a sense of responsibility for themselves, their actions, and the time in which they lived, a time which shaped them but was also transformed by them. Their common trait is their critical view of the present and recent events in their people's history (the defeat of Poland in September 1939, the Warsaw Uprising of 1944, the postwar disputes and struggles over the fate of Poland, and the years marked by the cult of personality).

In comparison with others in his generation and members of the "school," Munk stands out as a perceptive analyst and rationalist with a sober and searching view of people and events, a view which is only seldom presented metaphorically. Andrzej Munk adopted this view at the outset of his film career in the Documentary Film Studio, where he made several short pictures. Some of these were attributable to the prevailing schematic conception of socialist realism, but three of them (*Kolejarskie słowo, Gwiazdy muszą płonąć, Niedzielny poranek*) showed the rudiments of Munk's later approach to the dramatic film. Munk termed these films dramatic reportage, for they combine the authenticity of reality with certain dramatic elements. This step is further developed in Munk's first long film, *Błękitny krzyż,* about a successful action by the mountain service to rescue wounded partisans from territory still occupied by German units. The result, however, did not match the potential. Alongside successful sequences were others which shattered the unity of the work; dramatic sequences clashed with the paradocumentary parts.

Munk resolved this contradiction in his very next film, *Człowiek na torze,* which is the first manifestation of Munk's style based on rational reflection and analysis. Through a system of successive returns to the past, the director analyzes individual situations in the human fate of a railway worker who faces a conflict between his own sense of responsibility and the demands of society; the director's purpose is then to combine these forces in a synthesis that reveals the truth that is sought. His next two films, *Eroica* and *Zezowate szczęście*—both films are key works in the Polish film school—reveal another salient feature of Munk's artistic personality; added to his critical insight are irony, sarcasm, and, in the context of the Polish filmmaking of the time, a unique sense of comic exaggeration in exposing the function of certain national myths. In the tragic-grotesque stylization of *Eroica* he criticizes the superficiality of the prevalent conception of heroism (Wajda does the same thing in a tragic key), while in the film *Zezowate szczęście* he engages in a polemic concerning the simplistic depiction of the hero in contemporary Polish films by making his hero a man who constantly adapts to various changes in the social situation.

Munk's last major work is *Pasażerka,* produced only after his death in a reworking by Witold Lesiewicz. It returns once again to the Second World War, to the horrible environment of a concentration camp, and confronts this period with postwar recollections. Despite the cogency of the Lesiewicz reconstruction, in which already completed film clips alternate with stills from the unfinished sequences, it is impossible to make a safe guess as to where Munk's future path would have taken him. He was unmistakably tending toward a certain change in his artistic methods. But his work is closed. It is not extensive—a few short pictures, five dramatic films, one of them unfinished. Nevertheless, right up to the present time, the strength of the artistic appeal of his work has exercised an influence on subsequent generations of young filmmakers and viewers. It continues to attract them with its individual, unifying style, whose components are a perfect composition of shots, meaningful camera movement, eloquent montage, sober action, laconic dialogue, and counterpoint of image and sound; it is a style that serves precisely what Munk wished to communicate to the viewer.

—B. Urgošíková

MURNAU, F.W.

Nationality: German. **Born:** Friedrich Wilhelm Plumpe in Bielefeld, Germany, 28 December 1888. **Education:** Educated in philology, University of Berlin; art history and literature, University of Heidelberg. **Military Service:** Served in German army, from 1914; transferred to air force, interned in Switzerland following crash landing, 1917. **Career:** Attended Max Reinhardt theater school, 1908, later joined company; founder, with other Reinhardt school colleagues, Murnau Veidt Filmgesellschaft, 1919; invited by William Fox to Hollywood, 1926; returned to Germany, 1927; sailed to Tahiti with Robert Flaherty to prepare *Tabu,* 1929. **Died:** In auto accident, California, 11 March 1931.

Films as Director:

1919 *Der Knabe in Blau* (*Der Todessmaragd*; *The Boy in Blue*)
1920 *Satanas*; *Sehnsucht* (*Bajazzo*); *Der Bucklige und die Tanzerin* (*The Hunchback and the Dancer*); *Der Januskopf* (*Schrecken*; *Janus-Faced*); *Abend ... Nacht ... Morgen*
1921 *Der Gang in die Nacht*; *Schloss Vogelöd* (*Haunted Castle*); ***Nosferatu—Eine Symphonie des Grauens*** (*Nosferatu the Vampire*)
1922 *Marizza, genannt die Schmuggler-Madonna*; *Der Brennende Acker* (*Burning Soil*); *Phantom*
1923 *Die Austreibung* (*Driven from Home*)
1924 *Die Finanzen des Grossherzogs* (*The Grand Duke's Finances*); *Der Letzte Mann* (*The Last Laugh*)
1926 *Tartüff*; *Faust*
1927 ***Sunrise*** (*Sunrise: A Song of Two Humans*)
1928 *Four Devils*
1930 *Die zwolfte Stunde—Eine Nacht des Grauens* (*Nosferatu the Vampire*; *Nosferatu*) (adapted for sound); *Our Daily Bread*
1931 ***Tabu*** (+ co-pr, co-sc)

Publications

By MURNAU: book—

Sunrise (Sonnenaufgang), Ein Drehbuch von Carl Mayer mit handschriftlichen Bemerkungen von Friedrich Wilhelm Murnau, German Institute for Film Studies, Wiesbaden, 1971.

By MURNAU: articles—

"The Ideal Picture Needs No Titles," in *Theatre Magazine* (New York), January 1928.
"Étoile du Sud," in *La Revue du Cinéma* (Paris), May 1931.
"Turia, an Original Story," and "*Tabu* (*Tabou*), a Story of the South Sea," with Robert Flaherty, in *Film Culture* (New York), no. 20, 1959.

On MURNAU: books—

Jameux, Charles, *Murnau,* Paris, 1965.
Domarchi, Jean, "Murnau," in *Anthologie du cinéma,* vol. 1, Paris, 1966.
Kracauer, Siegfried, *From Caligari to Hitler,* New York, 1966.
Eisner, Lotte, *The Haunted Screen,* Berkeley, California, 1969.
Eisner, Lotte, *Murnau,* Berkeley, California, 1973.
Petrie, Graham, *Hollywood Destinies: European Directors in America 1922-1931,* London, 1985.
Berg-Ganschow, Uta, and others, editors, *F.W. Murnau 1888-1988,* Bielefeld, 1988.

On MURNAU: articles—

Josephson, Matthew, "F.W. Murnau—The German Genius of the Films," in *Motion Picture Classic* (New York), October 1926.
Astruc, Alexandre, "Le Feu et la glace," in *Cahiers du Cinéma* (Paris), December 1952; in *Cahiers du Cinéma in English* (New York), January 1966.
Wood, Robin, "*Tabu,*" in *Film Culture* (New York), Summer 1971.
Dorr, J., "The Griffith Tradition," in *Film Comment* (New York), March/April 1974.
"L'Aurore," special Murnau issue of *Avant-Scène du Cinéma* (Paris), June 1974.
"Per una ri-lettura critica di F.W. Murnau," special Murnau issue of *Filmcritica* (Rome), July 1974.
Audibert, L., "Dossier: Le Pont traversé," in *Cinématographe* (Paris), January 1977.
Latil Le Dantec, M., "De Murnau à Rohmer: les pièges de la beauté," in two parts, in *Cinématographe* (Paris), January and February 1977.
Special Murnau issue of *Avant-Scène du Cinéma* (Paris), July/September 1977.
Mitry, Jean, and others, "Griffith, Murnau et les historiens," in *Avant-Scène du Cinéma* (Paris), 15 March 1978.
Gehler, F., "F.W. Murnau, Hollywood and die Südsee," in *Film und Fernsehen* (Berlin), May 1981.
Cardullo, B., "*Der letzte Mann* Gets the Last Laugh: F.W. Murnau's Comic Vision," in *Post Script* (Jacksonville, Florida), Fall 1981.
Murnau Section of *Casablanca* (Madrid), October 1981.
Elsaesser, Thomas, "Secret Affinities," in *Sight and Sound* (London), Winter 1988/89.

* * *

F.W. Murnau (left) with cameraman Charles Rosher

F.W. Murnau was studying with Max Reinhardt when the First World War began. He was called up for military service, and after achieving his lieutenancy, he was transferred to the air service, where he served as a combat pilot. But his plane was forced down in Switzerland, where he was interned for the duration. Through the German Embassy, however, he managed to direct several independent stage productions, and he began his lifelong dedication to the motion picture, compiling propaganda film materials and editing them. This experience made it possible for him to enter the reborn film industry after peace as a full-fledged director.

Murnau's first feature film as director was *The Boy in Blue,* produced in 1919, and he made twenty-one full-length features from that year until 1926, when Fox Studios brought him to Hollywood. Unfortunately, most of the pictures he made in his native country no longer exist except in fragmentary form. They are tempting to read about, especially items like *Janus-Faced,* a study of a Jekyll and Hyde personality, which he made in 1920 with Conrad Veidt and Bela Lugosi. Critics found it more artistic than the John Barrymore version of the story made at about the same time in Paramount's New York studios.

Extant today in a complete version is *Nosferatu,* which was subtitled "a symphony of horror." It was a more faithful version of Bram Stoker's *Dracula* than any made thereafter, and the film, starring the incredibly gaunt and frightening Max Schreck as the vampire, is still available.

The next Murnau film that is still viewable is *The Last Laugh,* which starred Emil Jannings. At the time of its release, it was noted as being a picture without subtitles, told almost completely in pantomime. Its real innovation was the moving camera, which Murnau used brilliantly. The camera went everywhere; it was never static. Audiences watched spellbound as the camera moved upstairs and down, indoors and out, although the film told only the simple story of a proud commissionaire reduced in his old age to menial work as a lavatory attendant. The camera records, nevertheless, a very real world in an impressionistic way. In fact, Murnau, because of his skill with the moving camera, was generally known as the Great Impressionist, for he gave a superb impression of actual reality.

That title fit Murnau even more aptly in his next two features, both of which also starred Emil Jannings. They are *Tartuffe,* a screen adaption of Moliere's black comedy, in which Lil Dagover and Werner Krauss were also featured. It is topped by what must be the most definitive film version of Goethe's *Faust.* The film starred Jannings as Mephistopheles, with the handsome Swedish favorite, Gosta Ekman, in the title role; Camilla Horn as Marguerite; the great Parisian star Yvette Guilbert as Marthe; and a young William Dieterle as Valentine. Again, the camera not only moved, it soared, especially in the sequence where Faust is shown the world which will be his if he sells his soul to the devil. Murnau was a master of light and shadow, and his work is always brilliantly choreographed as it moves from lightness to the dark.

It came as no surprise when in 1926 Murnau was invited to Hollywood, where the red carpet at Fox was unrolled for him. He was allowed to bring his cameraman, writers, and other craftsmen to work with him, and his initial feature was called *Sunrise,* subtitled "a song of two human beings." The two stars were Janet Gaynor and George O'Brien, playing a young farm couple who make their first trip to the big city, which was constructed on the Fox lot, so that Murnau and his camera could follow them everywhere indoors and out of doors and onto a moving streetcar. Again, the story was very simple, adapted from a Hermann Suderman novel, *A Trip to Tilsit,* and simply proved that real love will always be triumphant.

Sunrise was highly praised by all critics, and was one of three pictures which brought Janet Gaynor an Academy Award as Best Actress in the 1927-28 year. Quite naturally, awards also went to cinematographers Charles Rosher and Karl Struss and to interior decorator Harry Oliver, while *Sunrise* was given a special award for its Artistic Quality of Production, a category never again specified.

For all that, *Sunrise* was not a box-office success, and the studio moved in to supervise Murnau closely on his next two productions. *Four Devils* was a circus story of four young aerialists that gave Murnau's camera a chance to fly with them from one performing trapeze to another. All prints of *Four Devils* are unfortunately lost, which is a fate common to most of the last great silent films. Murnau began shooting on his final film at Fox, called *Our Daily Bread,* with Charles Farrell and Mary Duncan, but he was not allowed to finish the picture. The overwhelming popularity of the talking screen was allowed to flaw it, for the only version of it now shown is called *City Girl,* and is only effective when it is recognizably silent and all Murnau. As a part-talkie, the film is crude and not at all Murnau.

Murnau then allied himself with Robert Flaherty, and the two men journeyed to the South Seas to make *Tabu.* Flaherty, however, withdrew, and *Tabu* is pure Murnau; some praise it as his greatest film. Murnau returned to California and was on the eve of signing at Paramount, which treated directors like Mamoulian, Lubitsch, and von Sternberg very kindly in their talking debuts. Unfortunately, Murnau lost his life in a motor accident on the Pacific Coast highway. He was only forty-two years old at the time, and after the success of *Tabu,* a new fame might have been his.

—DeWitt Bodeen

NARUSE, Mikio

Nationality: Japanese. **Born:** Tokyo, 1905. **Education:** Educated in Tokyo technical school, 1918-20. **Family:** Married actress Sachiko Chiba, 1937 (separated 1942), one child. **Career:** Prop man for Shochiku film company at Tokyo Kamata studios, 1920; assistant to director Yoshinobu Ikeda, 1921-28; comedy writer under pen name "Chihan Miki"; joined staff of Heinosuke Gosho, 1929; directed first film (now lost), 1930; left Shochiku, joined P.C.L. studios (later Toho Company), 1934; left Toho to freelance, 1945. **Died:** 1969.

Films as Director:

1930 *Chambara fufu* (*Mr. and Mrs. Swordplay*); *Junjo* (*Pure Love*); *Fukeiki jidai* (*Hard Times*) (+ story); *Ai wa chikara da* (*Love Is Strength*); *Oshikiri shinkonki* (*A Record of Shameless Newlyweds*) (+ story)

1931 *Nee kofun shicha iya yo* (*Now Don't Get Excited*); *Nikai no himei* (*Screams from the Second Floor*) (+ sc); *Koshiben gambare* (*Flunky, Work Hard!*) (+ sc); *Uwaki wa kisha ni notte* (*Fickleness Gets on the Train*) (+ sc); *Hige no chikara* (*The Strength of a Moustache*) (+ sc); *Tonari no yane no shita* (*Under the Neighbors' Roof*)

1932 *Onna wa tamoto o goyojin* (*Ladies, Be Careful of Your Sleeves*) (+ sc); *Aozora ni naku* (*Crying to the Blue Sky*); *Eraku nare* (*Be Great!*) (+ sc); *Mushibameru haru* (*Motheaten Spring*); *Chokoreito garu* (*Chocolate Girl*); *Nasanu naka* (*Not Blood Relations*)

1933 *Kimi to wakarete* (*Apart from You*) (+ sc); *Yogoto no yume* (*Every Night Dreams*) (+ story); *Boku no marumage* (*A Man with a Married Woman's Hairdo*); *Sobo* (*Two Eyes*)

1934 *Kagirinaki hodo* (*Street Without End*)

1935 *Otome-gokoro sannin shimai* (*Three Sisters with Maiden Hearts*) (+ sc); *Joyu to shijin* (*The Actress and the Poet*); *Tsuma yo bara no yo ni* (*Wife! Be Like a Rose*) (+ sc); *Sakasu gonin-gumi* (*Five Men in the Circus*); *Uwasa no musume* (*The Girl in the Rumor*) (+ sc)

1936 *Tochuken Kumoemon* (*Kumoemon Tochuken*) (+ sc); *Kimi to iku michi* (*The Road I Travel with You*) (+ sc); *Asa no namikimichi* (*Morning's Tree-lined Street*) (+ sc)

1937 *Nyonin aishu* (*A Woman's Sorrows*) (+ co-sc); *Nadare* (*Avalanche*) (+ sc); *Kafuku I, II* (*Learn from Experience, Parts I, II*)

1938 *Tsuruhachi tsurujiro* (*Tsuruhachi and Tsurujiro*) (+ sc)

1939 *Hataraku ikka* (*The Whole Family Works*) (+ sc); *Magokoro* (*Sincerity*) (+ sc)

1940 *Tabi yakusha* (*Traveling Actors*) (+ sc)

1941 *Natsukashi no kao* (*A Face from the Past*) (+ sc); *Shanhai no tsuki* (*Shanghai Moon*); *Kideko no shasho-san* (*Hideko the Bus Conductor*) (+ sc)

1942 *Haha wa shinazu* (*Mother Never Dies*)

1943 *Uta andon* (*The Song Lantern*)

1944 *Tanoshiki kana jinsei* (*This Happy Life*) (+ co-sc); *Shibaido* (*The Way of Drama*)

1945 *Shori no hi made* (*Until Victory Day*); *Sanjusangendo toshiya monogatari* (*A Tale of Archery at the Sanjusangendo*)

1946 *Urashima Taro no koei* (*The Descendants of Taro Urashima*); *Ore mo omae mo* (*Both You and I*) (+ sc)

1947 *Yottsu no koi no monogatari, II: Wakare mo tanoshi* (*Four Love Stories, Part II: Even Parting Is Enjoyable*); *Haru no mezame* (*Spring Awakens*) (+ co-sc)

1949 *Furyo shojo* (*Delinquent Girl*) (+ sc); *Ishinaka sensei gyojoki* (*Conduct Report on Professor Ishinaka*); *Ikari no machi* (*The Angry Street*) (+ co-sc); *Shiroi yaju* (*White Beast*) (+ co-sc); *Bara gassen* (*The Battle of Roses*)

1951 *Ginza gesho* (*Ginza Cosmetics*); *Maihime* (*Dancing Girl*); *Meshi* (*Repast*)

1952 *Okuni to Gohei* (*Okuni and Gohei*); *Okasan* (*Mother*); *Inazuma* (*Lightning*)

1953 *Fufu* (*Husband and Wife*); *Tsuma* (*Wife*); *Ani imoto* (*Older Brother, Younger Sister*)

1954 *Yama no oto* (*Sound of the Mountain*); *Bangiku* (*Late Chrysanthemums*)

1955 *Ukigumo* (*Floating Clouds*); *Kuchizuke, III: Onna doshi* (*The Kiss, Part III: Women's Ways*)

1956 *Shu-u* (*Sudden Rain*); *Tsuma no kokoro* (*A Wife's Heart*); *Nagareru* (*Flowing*)

1957 *Arakure* (*Untamed*)

1958 *Anzukko* (+ co-sc); *Iwashigumo* (*Herringbone Clouds*)

1959 *Kotan no kuchibue* (*Whistling in Kotan*; *A Whistle in My Heart*)

1960 *Onna ga kaidan o agaru toki* (*When a Woman Ascends the Stairs*); *Musume tsuma haha* (*Daughters, Wives and a Mother*); *Yoru no nagare* (*Evening Stream*) (co-d); *Aki tachinu* (*The Approach of Autumn*)

1961 *Tsuma toshite onna toshite* (*As a Wife, as a Woman*; *The Other Woman*)

1962 *Onna no za* (*Woman's Status*); *Horoki* (*A Wanderer's Notebook*; *Lonely Lane*)

1963 *Onna no rekishi* (*A Woman's Story*)

1964 *Midareru* (*Yearning*)

1966 *Onna no naka ni iru tanin* (*The Stranger within a Woman*; *The Thin Line*); *Hikinige* (*Hit and Run*; *Moment of Terror*)

1967 *Midaregumo* (*Scattered Clouds*; *Two in the Shadow*)

Publications

On NARUSE: books—

Bock, Audie, *Japanese Film Directors,* Tokyo, 1978.

Burch, Noel, *To the Distant Observer,* London, 1979.

Ritchie, Donald, *The Japanese Movie,* revised edition, Tokyo, 1982.

Sato, Tadao, *Currents in Japanese Cinema: Essays,* translated by Gregory Barrett, Tokyo, 1982.

Bock, Audie, *Mikio Naruse: un maître du cinéma japonais,* Locarno, 1983.

On NARUSE: articles—

Bock, Audie, "Mikio Naruse," in *Film Criticism* (Meadville, Pennsylvania), no. 55, 1979.

Interim, L., "Mikio Naruse le quatrième grand," in *Cahiers du Cinéma* (Paris), February 1983.

Niogret, H., "Mikio Naruse et l'agencement des émotions," in *Positif* (Paris), January 1984.

Tessier, Max, and Y. Mizuki, "Mikio Naruse," in *Revue du Cinéma* (Paris), February 1984.

Lopate, P., "A Taste for Naruse," in *Film Quarterly* (Berkeley), Summer 1986.

* * *

Mikio Naruse belongs in the second echelon of Japanese directors of his generation, along with Gosho, Ozu, and Kinoshita. This group ranks behind Mizoguchi, Kurosawa, Ichikawa, and Kobayashi, who broke out beyond the bounds of the conventions of the Japanese cinema, whereas Naruse and the others were mostly content to work within it. This is not to say that all of them did not tackle contemporary as well as historical subjects. And certainly Gosho, Ozu, Kinoshita, and Naruse were no less accomplished technically, though it might be noted that the last two did not respond to the challenge of the wide screen in as exciting a fashion as did Kurosawa and Kobayashi.

The homogeneity of Japanese cinema and the concomitant audience acceptance of remake after remake (at least while Naruse was working) enables us to categorise these directors: Naruse's domestic comedies share themes and situations with those of Gosho and Kinoshita, and his domestic dramas are not unlike those of middle-period Ozu, after he had lost the freshness and urgency of his early work, but before he had atrophied. But Naruse, although most of his (lost) silent films were simple slapsticks, was not later prolific in comedy. He was, however, occasionally drawn out into greater subjects, particularly towards the end of his career, and in rising to the occasion his career parallels that of Gosho, for both their filmographies contain some unexpected masterpieces. Most comments on Naruse emphasise that he was a pessimist because of his orphaned childhood, but most Japanese films tend to examine the shackles—rather than the joys—of family life or life in the geisha-house. His best films are suffused with a melancholy, with a desire for what might-have-been, which becomes, as art, warming and enlightening—and despairing rather than depressing.

It is true, however, that the few silent films made by Naruse that survive are chiefly tragedies of a not particularly high order. *Apart From You* (1933) and *Every Night Dreams* (1933) make it clear that the meek shall not inherit the earth. Naruse wrote the screenplay of the first, in which an adolescent geisha is determined that her younger sister will not follow her into that way of life; and he provided the story of the second, in which a barmaid is confronted with her useless husband, who had walked out on her some years previously. The men are weak but dangerous; the women are strong but compromised. Both are simple films, but *Street Without End* (1934) is of a richness and complexity rare for the period, despite the limitations of soap opera imposed by the newspaper serial on which it was based. It is one of the earliest surviving examples of a film that showcases the talents of a particular local star—usually female, as in this case—permitting audiences to sympathise to the ultimate with her difficulties. Naruse brings truth to this tale which, shot at an amazing number of urban locations, also including an underlying theme concerning the survival of feudalism in modern city life.

For his first sound film Naruse adapted a novel by Yasunari Kawabata, *Three Sisters With Maiden Hearts* (1935). No better constructed than the works of Ozu and Mizoguchi at this point, Naruse used flashbacks within flashbacks to complicate matters, but also displayed an imaginative use of sound. *Wife! Be Like a Rose* (1935) concerns a girl's renewed relationship with her father, who had left his self-centred wife to live happily in the country with another woman. This elegant, subtle domestic drama, which contains more humour than hitherto, was Naruse's twenty-fifth film, one of the few to survive from this period. This was a transitional film for him, for it rejects melodrama entirely. This change in emphasis by Naruse can be seen again in *Tsuruhachi and Tsurujiro* (1938), which details the destructive relationship of a man-woman shamizen team, while *The Whole Family Works* (1939) makes Western domestic dramas of the period look horrendously melodramatic.

Indeed, Naruse's pictures over the next few years cannot escape a charge of monotony. The martial subjects demanded by the authorities during World War II did not interest him, nor, it would seem, did those taken on during the Occupation, after he had left Toho. With *Repast* (1951), the story of a failing marriage, he began a series of domestic dramas which were to constitute a compassionate body of work, more sustained than either Ozu or Gosho, also concentrating on *shomin-geki*. *Repast* was based on a novel by Fumiko Hayashi, and he was to turn to her work again for four more of his best movies—*Lightning* (1952), *Late Chrysanthemums* (1954), *Floating Clouds* (1955), and the autobiographical *Lonely Lane* (1962). Hayashi was somewhat more optimistic than Naruse, but he finds in her work that life must go on, if imperfectly, and then asks why. The unanswerable questions, particularly in his studies of married life, bring him close to Bergman—though Bergman was considerably less interested in the banality of everyday existence.

It is interesting to compare Naruse's version of Saisei Muroo's novel *Older Brother Younger Sister* (1953) with those made in 1936 by Sotoji Kimura and in 1976 by Tadashi Imai. Each is of its period and each presents the riverside neighbourhood vividly, but Naruse's film is by far the best, infused with an intensity and a sensitivity that the others lack.

As his peers accepted the challenge presented in the 1950s by the international reception of the Japanese cinema, so did Naruse, but the relatively minor *Mother* (1952) was the only one of his films then seen in the West. *Floating Clouds,* from Hayashi's novel about life in the immediate postwar period, is perhaps his richest and most compelling film, an example of a director at his most confident working on completely congenial material.

Perhaps an equally successful achievement is *Flowing* (1956), a haunting study of the disillusionments which come to aging geishas. Unlike his contemporaries, Naruse had not seemed interested in geishas or prostitutes, except as an escape from poverty. His marital dramas looked away from sex, which he seemed to think was more a preoccupation for the young, while many of his women look yearningly at other women, only because they might be preferable to men.

Towards the end of his career Naruse was to widen his range, perhaps in response to Ozu's restriction of his own. He took to colour and the wide screen with *Herringbone Clouds* (1958), one of his rare rural dramas, about the break-up of feudal family rules under the pressure of modern times. Thereafter he worked chiefly in monochrome and wide screen, producing more rewarding work than some of his colleagues, for whom mere prettiness was enough. Some of them were content to turn out tear-jerkers with very popular stars, but while Naruse continued to work with his preferred actress, Hideko Takemine, he did so with a rigour which others could well have emulated. In *When a Woman Ascends the Stairs* (1960) she has a tough time managing a bar in the Ginza, not least because of amorous complications, and in *Yearning* (1964), again widowed, she is running a small grocer's shop in the face of the new competition, thrusting supermarkets. As films, both are schematic (as can happen with aging directors), but in *Yearning* a passion develops when Takemine refuses to submit to the romantic and sexual demands of her brother-in-law. As he pursues her to a small spa town, Naruse brings to the fore his mastery of the medium (loca-

Mikio Naruse

tions, photography, acting, editing), delving into the mysteries and mixed motives of his two protagonists. In the telling a good film has become a great one.

Naruse made only three more films. The last two, *Hit and Run* (1966) and *Scattered Clouds* (1967), were both thrillers set among people much more affluent than we had been accustomed to from this director. It is exhilarating to see them, not only for the supremacy of what was for him a new form but because, like all great filmmakers, he could still surprise his admirers.

—David Shipman

NEILAN, Marshall

Nationality: American. **Born:** San Bernadino, California, 11 April 1891. Known as "Mickey" Neilan. **Education:** Educated one year, Harvard Military Academy, Los Angeles. **Family:** Married 1) Gertrude Bambrick, 1913 (divorced 1921), one son; 2) Blanche Sweet, 1922 (divorced 1929). **Career:** Messenger boy for California Fruit Growers Assn., blacksmith's helper, employee of Santa Fe Railway, and boy actor for Belasco Stock Company, Los Angeles, and Barney Bernard Stock Company, San Francisco, 1902-1908; salesman for Simplex Motor Car Co., Los Angeles, and chauffeur to entrepreneur Oliver Morosco, 1908; sometime driver for D.W. Griffith at Biograph, 1909-10 and 1911; began acting at Kalem Studios, Santa Monica, 1911; joined Allan Dwan's company, American (Flying A); hired by Griffith at Biograph, 1913; signed as director for Kalem, also acted for Dwan, 1914; wrote for and starred opposite Mary Pickford, 1915; directed first feature, *The Cycle of Fate,* at Selig Chicago studios, 1916; hired by Samuel Goldwyn as Blanche Sweet's director at Lasky Company, 1917; directed series of Mary Pickford films 1917-18; began directing for First National, 1920; contracted to Goldwyn Company, 1922-24; did some writing and 2nd Unit directing, worked briefly as agent, 1930s; filed for bankruptcy, 1933 (and 1937); on payroll of 20th Century-Fox as writer, World War II. **Died:** In Hollywood, 27 October 1958.

Films as Director (Features):

1916 *The Cycle of Fate*; *The Prince Chap*; *Country That God Forgot*
1917 *Those Without Sin*; *The Bottle Imp*; *Tides of Barnegat*; *The Girl at Home*; *Silent Partner*; *Freckles*; *The Jaguar's Claws*; *Rebecca of Sunnybrook Farm*; *The Little Princess*
1918 *Stella Maris*; *Amarilly of Clothes-Line Alley*; *M'liss*; *Hit-the-Trail Holliday*; *Heart of the Wilds*; *Out of a Clear Sky*
1919 *3 Men and a Girl*; *Daddy-Long-Legs*; *The Unpardonable Sin*; *In Old Kentucky*
1920 *Her Kingdom of Dreams*; *The River's End*; *Don't ever Marry* (co-d); *Go and Get It*; *Dinty* (co-d)
1921 *Bob Hampton of Placer*; *Bits of life* (co-d); *The Lotus Eater*
1922 *Penrod* (co-d); *Fools First*; *Minnie* (co-d); *Stranger's Banquet*
1923 *Eternal Three* (co-d); *The Rendezvous*
1924 *Dorothy Vernon of Haddon Hall*; *Tess of the D'Urbervilles*
1925 *Sporting Venus*; *The Great Love*
1926 *Mike*; *The Skyrocket*; *Wild Oats Lane*; *Diplomacy*; *Everybody's Acting*
1927 *Venus of Venice*; *Her Wild Oats*
1928 *3-Ring Marriage*; *Take Me Home*; *Taxi 13*; *His Last Haul*
1929 *Black Waters*; *The Awful Truth*; *Tanned Legs*; *The Vagabond Lover*
1930 *Sweethearts on Parade*
1934 *Chloe*; *Social Register*; *The Lemon Drop Kid*
1935 *This is the Life*
1937 *Sing While You're Able*; *Swing It, Professor*

Other Films:

From 1911 Numerous supporting then leading roles through late teens
1956 *A Face in the Crowd* (Kazan) (role as Senator Fuller)

Publications

By NEILAN: articles—

Interviews in *Motion Picture Classic* (Brooklyn), April/May 1920 and December 1921.

On NEILAN: books—

Milne, Peter, *Motion Picture Directing: The Facts and Theories of the Newest Art,* New York, 1922.
Spears, Jack, *Hollywood: The Golden Era,* New York, 1971.

On NEILAN: articles—

Cohn, A.A., "Director 'Mickey'," in *Photoplay* (New York), September 1917.
St. Johns, Adela, in *Photoplay* (New York), March 1923.
Obituary in *New York Times,* 28 October 1958.
Obituary in *Time* (New York), 10 November 1958.
Gribbel, J., "Marshall Neilan," in *Films in Review* (New York), March 1960.
Spears, Jack, "Marshall Neilan," in *Films in Review* (New York), November 1962.
Lewis, K., "Blanche Sweet and Marshall Neilan," in *Films in Review* (New York), June/July 1981.

* * *

In the late 1910s, Marshall Neilan was hailed as the "youngest director genius of the industry." Yet, by the coming of sound he was reduced to directing "B" features, and at the age of forty-six he was unemployable. His was an extraordinary career, begun out of a zest for the excitement which film directing offered, It ended, though, as a drinking problem and a failure to work within the studio system took their toll. During the height of his career, Marshall Neilan could afford to insult the studio bosses—he inscribed one photograph with the words, "May you never miss the love that Louis B. Mayer does"—but when his drinking and his volatile temper got the better of him, the industry was happy to forget Neilan's successes and assign him to the depths of ignominy reserved for those unable to come to terms with the studio system.

From leading man to the likes of Blanche Sweet (whom he was to marry), Marguerite Clark, Mary Pickford, and Ruth Roland—and Neilan was a handsome leading man—he became one of Hollywood's most talented directors, equally at home with the comedy of *Daddy-Long-Legs,* the pathos of *Stella Maris,* and the militaristic propaganda of *The Unpardonable Sin.* Neilan was particularly at ease directing Mary Pickford (whom he directed in seven features), who later said, "I can truthfully say that no director, not even the great D.W. Griffith or Cecil DeMille, could wring the performance from me that Mickey did." As Jack Spears has written, Marshall Neilan was "the boy wonder of Hollywood," a director who could do no wrong as far as the stars, the public, or the critics were concerned. All of his films seemed destined to be automatic box-office successes, and all displayed Neilan's remarkable understanding of lighting and emotional audience involvement. Despite his quick temper and apparent private lack of decency (particularly after the ever more frequent bouts of drinking), Neilan was able to come to the set and produce a film of exquisite tenderness and charm.

Through the 1920s Marshall Neilan was able to keep a hold on the medium, directing such major achievements as *Dorothy Vernon of Haddon Hall* and *Tess of the D'Urbervilles,* but the coming of sound found Neilan not only at a low personal ebb (following his divorce from Blanche Sweet), but also apprehensive about the future. He simply destroyed his own career (although *Social Register* illustrates that Neilan could produce a competent and pleasurable little picture), and it was depressing to see this once-great director reduced to playing a small role in Elia Kazan's 1956 *A Face in the Crowd.*

—Anthony Slide

NEMEC, Jan

Nationality: Czech. **Born:** Prague, 12 July 1936. **Education:** Film Faculty, Academy of Music and Arts (FAMU), Prague, 1955-60. **Family:** Married 1) Ester Krumbachová (divorced); 2) Marta Kubisová. **Career:** While at film academy, assistant to directors Vaclav Krska and Martin Frič; co-scripted two features, also five shorts and five mini-musicals for TV, with then-wife, 1964-66; after *Martyrs of Love,* blacklisted by Barrandov Studios for political reasons, 1966; filmed entry of Soviet forces into Prague, footage broadcast around the world (later used in both U.S. and Soviet propaganda films), 1968; made only film following Soviet invasion, a short documentary about intensive care unit, Prague, 1972; able to leave Czechoslovakia, worked with Veronika Schamoni in Germany, 1974, then moved to U.S.A.; occasionally lectured on cinema at American universities; returned to Czechoslovakia, 1989, to direct *V žáru královské lásky* (*In the Light of the King's Love*). **Address:** 21607 Rambla Vista, Malibu, California, 90265, U.S.A.

Films as Director:

1960 *Sousto* (*The Loaf*; *A Loaf of Bread*; *A Bite to Eat*; *The Morsel*)

1963 *The Memory of Our Day*

1964 *Demanty noci* (*Diamonds of the Night*) (+ co-sc); "Pdvodnici" (The Liars, Impostors) segment of *Perličky na dně* (*Pearls of the Deep*)

1966 ***O slavnosti a hostech*** (*The Party and the Guests*; *Report on the Party and the Guests*) (+ co-sc)

1967 *Mučedníci lásky* (*Martyrs of Love*) (+ co-sc); *Mother and Son* (short) (+ co-sc)

Jan Nemec: *O slavnosti a hostech*

1968 *Oratorio for Prague* (*Oratorium for Prague*) (doc) (+ co-sc)
1972 *Between Three and Five Minutes* (doc short) (+ co-sc)
1975 *Le Décolleté dans le dos* (+ co-sc); *Metamorphosis* (short) (+ co-sc); *The Czech Connection* (+ co-sc)
1988 *True Stories: Peace in Our Time?*
1989 *The Poet Remembers*
1991 *V žáru královské lásky* (*In the Light of the King's Love*; *The Flames of Royal Love*)

Other Films:

1988 *The Unbearable Lightness of Being* (special consultant, role)

Publications

On NEMEC: books—

Skvorecký, Josef, *All the Bright Young Men and Women,* Toronto, 1971.
Liehm, Antonin, *Closely Watched Films,* White Plains, New York, 1974.
Stoil, Michael, *Cinema beyond the Danube,* Metuchen, New Jersey, 1974.
Liehm, Mira and Antonin, *The Most Important Art,* Berkeley, 1977.
Habova, Milada, and Jitka Vysekalova, editors, *Czechoslovak Cinema,* Prague, 1982.
Hames, Peter, *The Czechoslovak New Wave,* Berkeley, 1982.

On NEMEC: articles—

Skvorecký, Josef, "Unnepsegrol, bevonulasrol," in *Filmvilag,* vol. 33, no. 3, 1990.
Varga, G., "A nonkonformizmus lova," in *Filmvilag,* vol. 33, no. 7, 1990.
Durgnat, R., "Jan Nemec," in *Film Dope,* December 1991.

* * *

Jan Nemec's Czech filmography includes three shorts, three features, and a segment of a compilation work. All three features were co-scripted by his then-wife, Ester Krumbachová. He reached international fame with the 1968 screening of *The Party and the Guests* at the New York Film Festival, which followed a two-year struggle to screen the film within Czechoslovakia. After completing *The Martyrs of Love* in 1966, Nemec was blacklisted by Barrandov Studios for political reasons and was unable to work in Czechoslovakia. He immigrated to the West in 1974, settling first in Paris, then in Germany, and finally in the United States, but he was unable to re-establish his film career despite the fact that he was one of the foremost talents of the Czech New Wave.

Thematically all of Nemec's films deal with obstacles to human freedom and the ways in which men and women cope with these limitations. He has stated, "In *Diamonds of the Night* man is not free as a result of that most external of pressures called war. In *The Party and the Guests,* it is a lack of freedom that people bring on themselves by being willing to enter into any sort of collaborative relationship. In *Martyrs of Love,* it is a matter of a lack of freedom or opportunity to act out one's own folly, one's own madness, or dreams of love and human happiness." Within the context, Nemec is most concerned with the psychological effects of these restrictions.

Stylistically Nemec developed a highly metaphoric cinema utilizing several experimental techniques. He calls this style "dream realism." His works function as political and psychological parables. His first feature, *Diamonds of the Night,* based on a novel by Holocaust survivor Arnost Lustig, follows two Jewish boys who jump from a Nazi transport on its way to the concentration camps. As the boys wander through the forest looking for food, time shifts back and forth. There are memories of war-torn Prague, distorted visions of elongated trams, and menacing looks of strangers. The boys hallucinate about falling trees and swarming ants. Eventually they are arrested by the Home Guard, composed of old men more concerned with drinking and singing than with the boys. The film ends ambiguously with the fate of the two still an open question. Jaroslav Kučera's hand-held camera creates tension as the boys scamper like animals or stare subjectively into the impassive faces of their captors.

The Party and the Guests begins with a summer picnic. Suddenly a group of men appear, forcing the picnickers to obey new rules. Next they are feted at an elaborate banquet. Only one man is unwilling to participate in the festivities. At the end, accompanied by a menacing dog, the group sets out to capture the nonconformist. Here again are the themes of impersonal group control, conformity, man's indifference, and the casual use of violence, and Nemec again creates a surreal world where the extraordinary takes on the look of everyday events.

Nemec's last major work, *Martyrs of Love,* is composed of three comic stories about young men in pursuit of romance. Their inability to achieve their goal ultimately turns comedy into sadness. In creating the dream-like world of the film, Nemec used only minimal dialogue. The images are accompanied by a jazzy score, reflecting the passion for American music among young Czechs during the 1960s.

Nemec's short works deal with the same themes developed in his features. His graduation film, *The Loaf of Bread,* portrays a group of prisoners who steal a loaf of bread from their Nazi captors. Here Nemec depicts human beings under stress. As he has commented, "I am concerned with man's reactions to the drastic situation in which, through no fault of his own, he may find himself." *Mother and Son,* made in Holland in 1967, deals with the death of a sadistic soldier, who has beaten and executed prisoners. When young boys try to desecrate his grave, his old mother staunchly protects it. The film ironically concludes with the title, "Love between one human being and another is the only important thing in life."

Nemec's contribution to *Pearls from the Deep* is an episode entitled "The Poseurs." Here two senile patients at a private clinic ramble on about their former achievements, despite their failing memories. Nemec's shots of the mortuary, the place where they will ultimately reside, provide a sad and chilling commentary on all human life. Nemec's remaining works are *Metamorphosis,* an adaptation of the Kafka story filmed in Germany in 1957, and *The Czech Connection,* made the same year.

—Patricia Erens

NEWELL, Mike

Nationality: British. **Born:** St. Albans, England, 28 March 1942. **Education:** Studied at Cambridge University; studied directing at Granada Television. **Career:** Directed for the stage and television before making his feature film debut with *The Man in the Iron Mask* (which played in the United States as a made-for-television movie), 1977; directed his first feature to open theatrically in the United States, *The Awakening,* 1980; came to international prominence as the director of *Dance with a Stranger,* 1985. **Awards:** David Lean Award for Best Achievement in Directing, BAFTA, for *Four Weddings and a Funeral,* 1994. **Agent:** Alan Greenspan, ICM, 8942 Wilshire Blvd., Beverly Hills, CA 90211, U.S.A.

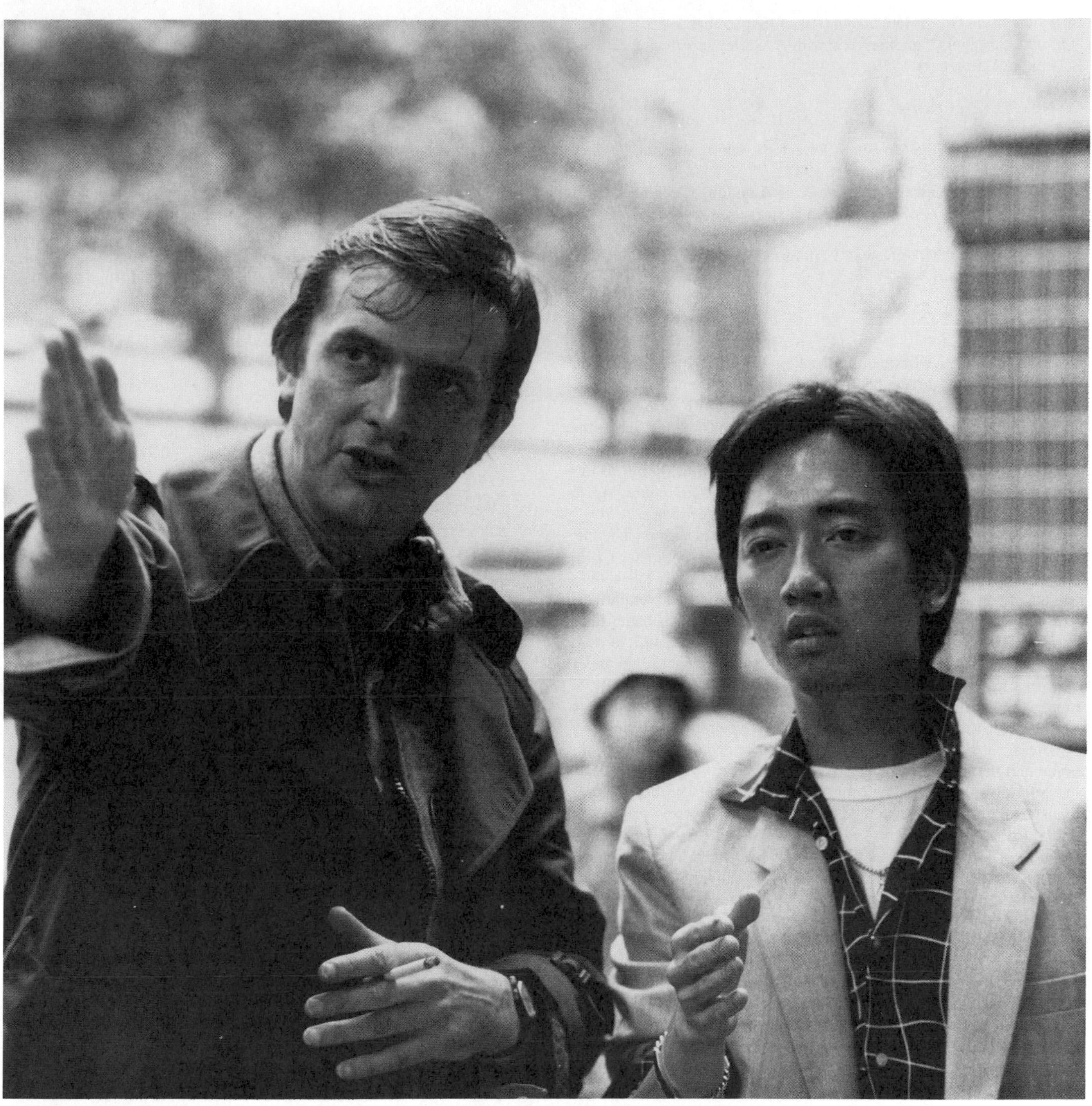

Mike Newell directing David Tse in *Soursweet*

Films as Director:

1970s *Big Soft Nelly* (for TV); *Mrs. House* (for TV); *The Gift of Friendship* (for TV)
1977 *The Man in the Iron Mask* (played on TV in the U.S.)
1980 *The Awakening*
1983 *Blood Feud* (for TV); *Bad Blood*
1985 *Dance with a Stranger*
1986 *The Good Father*
1987 *Amazing Grace and Chuck*
1988 *Soursweet*
1990 *Common Ground* (for TV)
1991 *Enchanted April* (for TV; played theatrically in the U.S.)
1992 *Into the West*
1994 *Four Weddings and a Funeral*
1995 *An Awfully Big Adventure*

Publications

By NEWELL: articles—

Interview in *Stills* (London), March 1985.

Interview by F. Guerif in *Cinema* (Paris), September 1985.
"Oriental Strangers," an interview with A. Sibley in *Films & Filming* (London), February 1989.

On NEWELL: articles—

Darnton, Nina, "At the Movies: A Director Looking Back on *Father*," in *New York Times*, 13 February 1987.
Baker, B., "Mike Newell," in *Film Dope* (London), December 1991.
Clarity, J. F., "*Into the West* Taps Irish History," in *New York Times*, 29 December 1991.
Benenson, L. H., "Mike Newell Lightens Up," in *New York Times*, 9 August 1992.

* * *

Mike Newell is a workmanlike director-for-hire whose films are an eclectic lot. He has directed both historical and contemporary dramas, as well as comedies, romances, horror films, films with serious themes, and films which are solely escapist-oriented. He has worked across the globe, from the United States (*The Awakening, Amazing Grace and Chuck*) to Ireland (*Into the West*), New Zealand (*Bad Blood*) to England (*Dance with a Stranger, The Good Father, Enchanted April, Four Weddings and a Funeral, An Awfully Big Adventure*).

Generally, Newell's American films have been his least memorable. *The Awakening* is an instantly forgettable horror entry. *Amazing Grace and Chuck* is a well-intentioned but unsuccessful morality tale about a Little Leaguer who decides to stop playing the game he loves until the world powers agree to eliminate all nuclear weapons. His better films begin with *Dance with a Stranger,* the based-on-fact account of Ruth Ellis (Miranda Richardson, in a star-making performance), a divorcee and prostitute-turned-nightclub- manager who was found guilty of murdering her lover and became the last woman ever to be hanged in England. *The Good Father* is an equally incisive drama about an angry middle-aged man (Anthony Hopkins) who is deeply hurt by his divorce and the loss of his son in a custody battle. *Into the West* is an ingratiating fable about two motherless brothers who escape their dreary Dublin existence on the back of a magical horse.

Newell is best-known for *Enchanted April* and *Four Weddings and a Funeral,* both of which came out of nowhere to earn huge commercial success. *Enchanted April,* based on a 1922 novel by Elizabeth von Arnim, is a lyrical, beautifully scripted (by Peter Barnes), acted, and directed period piece, and was one of the surprise art-house hits of 1992. It tells the story of a quartet of British women who wish a respite from their lives, and come together to rent a picturesque Italian villa. Lottie Wilkins (Josie Lawrence) and Rose Arbuthnot (Miranda Richardson), both trapped in unsatisfying marriages, respond to a newspaper ad offering the villa for rent. Their roommates are Lady Caroline Dester (Polly Walker), a beautiful socialite in need of a break from the constant attention of male admirers; and Mrs. Fisher (Joan Plowright), an assertive older woman who relishes dropping the names of the legendary authors she had met decades earlier through her father. During their brief time together, the women undergo profound changes and come in contact with their true natures. This is a sparkling filmization of the novel which manages to keep the book's mystical shading, an element which may have been misinterpreted in another director's hands.

There is much to savor in *Four Weddings and a Funeral,* an offbeat romantic comedy depicting the title events and how they affect a small circle of friends and acquaintances. Hugh Grant (in the role which brought him to Hollywood) offers a charming performance as Charles, who at the first wedding meets and becomes smitten with a flirtatious American, Carrie (Andie MacDowell). The question remains throughout the story: Will one of the trio of other weddings end up being theirs? Between the laughs, the scenario explores a number of very personal issues. How does it feel to be single and lonely at a ceremony in which two people are proclaiming their love until death they do part? What are the pros and cons of settling into marriage with someone you don't really love, rather than remaining on your own to await your true love (whom you may never be fated to meet)? Then there is the sheer unpredictability of life. Given the film's title, it is no great revelation when one character suddenly dies. The point is that the deceased could be any of the characters. You never know when your time is up, so you might as well feel "the highest capacity of joy" while you can. In spite of the inclusion of the funeral, *Four Weddings and a Funeral* is anything but depressing. It is filled with enormous charm and laugh-out-loud humor. Just prior to the release of *Four Weddings and a Funeral,* Newell also directed Hugh Grant in *An Awfully Big Adventure,* an unconventional mood piece about a theatre troupe in post-World War II England that had a hard time finding an audience.

—Audrey E. Kupferberg

NIBLO, Fred

Nationality: American. **Born:** Federico Nobile in York, Nebraska, 6 January 1874. **Family:** Married Josephine Cohan (died 1916); one son; 2) actress Enid Bennett, 1917, three children. **Career:** Vaudeville performer, blackface monologuist, through 1907; shot travelogues on round-the-world cruise, 1907; company manager and actor for George M. Cohan and Sam Harris; took American repertory company to Australia, 1912-15; directed film for Australian theatrical company J.C. Williamson, 1915; joined Ince company, Hollywood, 1918; co-founder, Academy of Motion Picture Arts and Sciences, 1928. **Died:** In New Orleans, 11 November 1948.

Films as Director:

1915 *Get-Rich-Quick Wallingford* (+ role)
1918 *Coals of Fire*; *The Marriage Ring*; *When Do We Eat?*; *A Desert Wooing*; *Fuss and Feathers*
1919 *Happy Though Married*; *The Haunted Bedroom*; *Partners Three*; *The Virtuous Thief*; *Stepping Out*; *What Every Woman Learns*
1920 *The Woman in the Suitcase*; *The False Road*; *Her Husband's Friend*; *Dangerous Hours*; *Sex*; *Hairpins*; *The Mark of Zorro*
1921 *Silk Hosiery*; *Mother o' Mine*; *Greater than Love*; *The Three Musketeers*
1922 *The Woman He Married*; *Rose o' the Sea*; *Blood and Sand*
1923 *The Famous Mrs. Fair*; *Strangers of the Night* (+ co-pr)
1924 *Thy Name Is Woman*; *The Red Lily* (+ story)
1926 *Ben-Hur*; *The Temptress*
1927 *Camille* (+ pr); *The Devil Dancer* (+ pr)
1928 *The Enemy* (+ pr); *Two Lovers* (+ pr); *The Mysterious Lady*; *Dream of Love*
1930 *Redemption* (+ pr); *Way Out West*
1931 *Donovan's Kid*; *The Big Gamble*
1932 *Two White Arms*; *Diamond Cut Diamond* (co-d); *Blame the Woman*

Other Films:

1915 *Officer 666* (role)
1930 *Free and Easy* (Sedgwick) (role)

Fred Niblo with his wife Enid Bennett

1940 *Ellery Queen, Master Detective* (Bellamy) (role); *I'm Still Alive* (role)
1941 *Life with Henry* (Reed) (role)
1944 *Four Jills in a Jeep* (Seiter) (co-sc)

Publications

By NIBLO: articles—

Interview with M. Cheatham, in *Motion Picture Classic* (Brooklyn), July 1920.
"Sketch," with K. McGaffey, in *Motion Picture Classic* (Brooklyn), October 1921.
"The Filming of *Ben Hur*," interview with R. Wharton, in *Classic Film/Video Images* (Indiana, Pennsylvania), Winter 1978.

On NIBLO: book—

Brownlow, Kevin, *The Parade's Gone By,* New York, 1968.

On NIBLO: articles—

Obituary, in *The New York Times,* 12 November 1948.
Obituary, in *Variety* (New York), 12 November 1948.
Route, W.D., "Buried Directors," in *Focus* (Chicago), Spring 1972.

* * *

Fred Niblo directed some of the most legendary stars of the 1920s in some of that decade's biggest films: *Blood and Sand* (with Valentino); *The Mark of Zorro* and *The Three Musketeers* (Fairbanks); and *Ben Hur.* He guided Garbo through *The Temptress* (replacing her mentor, Mauritz Stiller) and *The Mysterious Lady.* He worked with Lillian Gish, Ronald Colman, Conrad Nagel, Lionel Barrymore, Vilma Banky, and Norma Talmadge. Valentino, Fairbanks, and Garbo first come to mind at the mention of their films with Niblo. The other actors' best work was done elsewhere, for other more rightfully distinguished filmmakers.

Niblo's one distinction is his credit on *Ben Hur,* the cinema's first real super-spectacle. *Ben Hur* is the *Cleopatra* of its day, a boondoggle that ran way over budget and took two years to complete. It was begun by the Goldwyn Company, and passed along when Goldwyn, Loew's Metro, and Louis B. Mayer joined together to form Metro-Goldwyn-Mayer. *Ben Hur* was initially shot on location in Italy. The dissatisfied studio ordered a revised script. Ramon Novarro replaced George Walsh in the title role and Niblo, the choice of Mayer and Irving Thalberg, took over for Charles Brabin. The Coliseum was rebuilt several blocks from the MGM lot; inside the studio, Roman galleys floated inside a large tank. Eventually, the budget climbed to $3 million—perhaps even higher—with over one million feet of film shot.

Niblo not so much directed as coordinated *Ben Hur,* and the result was all effect and no drama. Sometimes the film is confusing, and even tiring, yet it is also at its best thrilling. The image of Novarro and Francis X. Bushman (as Messala) racing their chariots remains one of the best-recalled of the silent era. This sequence is supposed to have influenced the staging of the same scene in William Wyler's far superior remake.

Ultimately, Niblo's career success was more a case of luck than any inherent talent or aesthetic vision. In 1917 he married Enid Bennett, who worked for Thomas Ince; the following year, he began making films for Ince. Later, Niblo was hired by Mayer, who liked him and brought him along to MGM. Niblo's career as an A-film director did not last many years past *Ben Hur.* He made only a handful of films during the 1930s, even working in Britain before retiring in 1941. In his later years, he took small roles in films—he had commenced his career as an actor, in vaudeville, on tour, and Broadway—and was employed as a radio commentator and master of ceremonies.

Before *Don Juan, The Jazz Singer,* and the demise of silent movies, Niblo made some intriguing prognostications. He foresaw the advent of sound, declaring that motion picture music would be synchronized by radio to replace the live piano; subtitles would be synchronized and broadcast in the same way, in the actual voices of the actors. He predicted other advances as well, including the use of color cinematography, three-dimensional screens to prevent distortion, and theaters specializing in children's films.

While Niblo may have been a decent technician at best in the director's chair, he was far more adept with a crystal ball.

—Rob Edelman

NICHOLS, Mike

Nationality: American. **Born:** Michael Igor Peschkowsky in Berlin, 6 November 1931; became U.S. citizen, 1944. **Education:** University of Chicago, 1950-53; studied acting with Lee Strasberg, 1954. **Family:** Married 1) Patricia Scott, 1957 (divorced), one daughter; 2) Margot Callas, 1974 (divorced); 3) Annabel (divorced), two children; 4) Diane Sawyer, 1988. **Career:** Member of Compass Players improvisational theatre group, Chicago, 1955-57; partnership with Elaine May, 1957-61; director on Broadway, from 1963; produced *The Family* for TV, 1976. **Awards:** 7 Tony Awards; Academy Award for Best Direction, for *The Graduate,* 1968. **Office:** c/o Marvin B. Meyer, Rosenfeld, Meyer and Sussman, 9601 Wilshire Blvd., Beverly Hills, CA 90210, U.S.A.

Films as Director:

1966 *Who's Afraid of Virginia Woolf?*
1967 *The Graduate*
1970 *Catch-22*
1971 *Carnal Knowledge* (+ pr)
1973 *The Day of the Dolphin*
1975 *The Fortune* (+ co-pr)
1980 *Gilda Live*
1983 *Silkwood* (+ co-pr)
1986 *Heartburn* (+ co-pr)
1988 *Biloxi Blues*; *Working Girl*
1990 *Postcards from the Edge* (+ co-pr)
1991 *Regarding Henry* (+ co-pr)
1994 *Wolf*

Publications

By NICHOLS: articles—

Interview with Barry Davy, in *Films and Filming* (London), November 1968.
Interview with Lillian Hellman, in *New York Times,* 9 August 1970.
Interview in *The Film Director as Superstar,* by Joseph Gelmis, New York, 1971.
Interview with D. Kennedy, in *Listener* (London), 16 March 1989.
Interview with Richard Combs, in *Sight and Sound* (London), Spring 1989.
"Without Cutaways: Mike Nichols Interviewed," by Gavin Smith, in *Film Comment,* May/June 1991.
"Mike Nichols: Working Man," an interview with Stephen Greco, in *Advocate,* 5 May 1992.

On NICHOLS: books—

Kiley, Frederick, and Walter McDonald, editors, *A "Catch-22" Casebook,* New York, 1973.
Schuth, H. Wayne, *Mike Nichols,* Boston, 1978.

On NICHOLS: articles—

Rice, Robert, "A Tilted Insight," in *New Yorker,* 15 April 1961.
Bart, Peter, "Mike Nichols, Moviemaniac," in *New York Times,* 1 July 1967.
Lightman, Herb, "On Location with *Carnal Knowledge,*" in *American Cinematographer* (Los Angeles), January 1971.
Brown, John, "Pictures of Innocence," in *Sight and Sound* (London), Spring 1972.
Rich, Frank, "The Misfortune of Mike Nichols: Notes on the Making of a Bad Film," in *New York Times,* 11 July 1975.
Sarris, Andrew, "After *The Graduate,*" in *American Film* (Washington, D.C.), July/August 1978.
Fieschi, J., "Hollywood 79: Mike Nichols," in *Cinématographe* (Paris), March 1979.
Combs, Richard, "Mike Nichols: Comedy in Four Unnatural Acts," in *Monthly Film Bulletin* (London), May 1989.
Farber, Stephen, "Waiting for Mike," in *Connoisseur,* June 1991.
Christiansen, Richard, "Behind the Camera with Mike Nichols," in *Chicago Tribune,* 7 July 1991.
Hale, C., "Mike Nichols," in *Film Dope,* December 1991.
Buck, Joan Juliet, "Live Mike," in *Vanity Fair,* June 1994.

* * *

The films of Mike Nichols are guided by an eye and ear of a satirist whose professional gifts emerge from a style of liberal, improvisational comedy that originated in a Chicago theater club and developed into a performing partnership with Elaine May in the late 1950s and early 1960s. In clubs and recordings, on radio, television, and Broadway, Nichols and May routines gnawed hilariously close to the bone. Aimed at literate, self-aware audiences, their skits (sometimes anticipating key elements of Nichols's films) gleefully anatomized men and women dueling in post-Freudian combat, by turns straying from the marriage bond and clinging to it for dear life.

Before directing *Who's Afraid of Virginia Woolf?* for the screen in 1966, Nichols earned a reputation as a skillful Broadway director with

Mike Nichols

particular flair for devising innovative stage business and eliciting unusually polished performances from his casts. That sure theatrical sense, honed by his subsequent direction of Broadway plays by writers as diverse as Neil Simon, Anton Chekhov, Lillian Hellman, David Rabe, and Tom Stoppard, combines in his best films with the sardonic attitude toward American life underlying even the gentlest of his collaborations with Elaine May.

Many of Nichols's major films begin as comedies and evolve into mordant, generically ambiguous dissections of the American psyche. Their central characters exist in isolation from the landscapes they inhabit, often manufacturing illusions to shield themselves against reality (George and Martha in *Virginia Woolf,* Sandy and Jonathan in *Carnal Knowledge*) or fleeing with mounting desperation societies whose values they alone perceive as neurotic (Benjamin in *The Graduate*) or murderous (Yossarian in *Catch-22*).

Martha and George, Edward Albee's Strindbergian couple, flail at each other on their New England campus and reveal a tormented relationship that concludes with a glimmer of hope but seems nevertheless to imply the futility of monogamy, a view reenforced by *Carnal Knowledge* and *The Graduate.* Until he dates Elaine Robinson, Ben Braddock is segregated by script and camera from the company of friends: in a packed airplane, on the Berkeley campus teeming with students, surrounded by his parents' partying guests, Ben is alone. His detachment, italicized by numerous shots within the film, permits him to function as the funnel for *The Graduate's* social satire. In this respect he is Nichols's surrogate, but the director complicates the viewer's empathetic response to Ben by scrutinizing him rather as an experimenting scientist scrutinizes a mouse darting about a maze, especially as he scampers in frantic pursuit of Elaine.

In Dustin Hoffman's memorable screen debut, Ben became the moralistic spokesman for a generation that mistrusted anyone over thirty and vowed never to go into plastics. But like some other Nichols heroes Ben may be himself more than a little crazy, the inevitable child of a Southern California lifestyle that leads him to anticipate instant gratification. Nichols, moreover, intentionally undermines the comic resolution toward which the film has been heading through ambivalent shots of Ben and Elaine on their departing bus, implicating them in mutual recognition of a colossal mistake. At film's end, Ben Braddock still has considerable cause to be "worried about [his] future."

For Yossarian, worrying about the future means literally staying alive. To survive a catch-22 universe he behaves like a lunatic, but the more bizarrely he acts the more sanely is he regarded according to the military chop-logic that drives him toward madness. In *Catch-22* time is fractured (in Buck Henry's screenplay) to retain the basic storytelling method of Joseph Heller's novel. Flashbacks occur within flashbacks. Conversations are inaudible (as in the opening scene), incidents only partially revealed (as in the first Snowden sequences), to be played later in the film with deleted elements restored.

Fond of foreground shooting, long takes, and distorting close-ups to intensify the sense of his characters' entrapment, Nichols also frequently employs overlapping sound and a spare, modernistic mise-en-scène (the latter at times reminiscent of Antonioni) to convey an aura of disorientation and sterility. In the underpraised and misunderstood *Carnal Knowledge,* Nichols uses whiteouts (also prominent in *Catch-22*) and Bergmanesque talking heads as structural and thematic devices to increase the viewer's alienation from the two central characters and to ridicule notions of male sexual fantasy at the core of the film. Visually and textually (in Jules Feiffer's original screenplay) Jonathan and Sandy are the most isolated and self-deluded of Nichols's characters.

Things are seldom what they initially seem in this director's work. Like Nick and Honey, misled by George and Martha's pretense of hospitality in *Who's Afraid of Virginia Woolf?,* the viewer may be easily duped by a deceptively comic tone, enticing visual stylization, and innovative storytelling technique into misreading the bleak vision that the films usually harbor. *The Day of the Dolphin* is certainly more than just a story of talking dolphins. The film has mythic qualities, concerns good and evil, and has a painful ending. Even *The Fortune,* a farce in the screwball tradition, hinges on the attempted murder by the film's two heroes of its heroine, whose fate hangs in the balance at the final fadeout.

Nichols directs literate, intelligent scripts that pull few punches in their delineations of sexual subjects (*Virginia Woolf, The Graduate, Carnal Knowledge, Heartburn*) and political ones (*Catch-22, Day of the Dolphin, Silkwood, Working Girl*). While *The Graduate* continues to be regarded as an American classic, Nichols is sometimes undervalued for his film work because he prefers the New York theater and because his contributions to his pictures are periodically credited to their writers' screenplays (Buck Henry, Jules Feiffer) or their theatrical and literary sources (Edward Albee, Joseph Heller, Charles Webb). But Nichols is very much the auteur who works intimately with his collaborators on all aspects of his films, principally the writing. As with many auteurs, Nichols uses many of the same people over and over again, both in cast and on crew.

The films uphold Nichols's original reputation as a gifted director of actors: Hoffman in *The Graduate,* Elizabeth Taylor and Richard Burton in *Who's Afraid of Virginia Woolf?,* Jack Nicholson in *Carnal Knowledge, The Fortune, Heartburn,* and *Wolf,* George C. Scott in *The Day of the Dolphin,* Alan Arkin in *Catch-22,* Meryl Streep in *Silkwood, Heartburn,* and *Postcards from the Edge.* They also reveal, even in their intermittent self-indulgence, a director of prodigious versatility and insight.

Nichols's films are purely fiction during the first phase of his film directing career, beginning with *Who's Afraid of Virginia Woolf?* in 1966, and including *The Graduate, Catch-22, Carnal Knowledge, The Day of the Dolphin,* and ending with *The Fortune* in 1975. After seven years, the second phase begins with *Silkwood* in 1983, and this and the next seven films are closer to reality. These films are also much more hopeful and optimistic, as the characters often shed their illusions, change for the better, and achieve inner peace. *Silkwood* is based on a real person, Karen Silkwood. In Nichols's adaptation of the nuclear plant worker's story, Karen (Meryl Streep) gains a new awareness and tries to help herself and her friends even though she dies. *Heartburn* was written by Nora Ephron and was influenced by her own experiences. Although Rachel (Meryl Streep) finds her illusions about her perfect marriage shattered, she and her children move on to try again. In *Biloxi Blues,* a grown up Eugene (Matthew Broderick) thinks that his army experiences were the happiest time of his life, and some may have been inspired by writer Neil Simon's time in the army. *Working Girl* is an incisive look into the contemporary subculture of working women in Manhattan. Tess (Melanie Griffith) achieves her move up in the business world even though she has far to go. *Postcards from the Edge,* about a daughter's relationship with her famous Hollywood mother, was written by Carrie Fisher, who is certainly familiar with the Hollywood scene and the daughter of Debbie Reynolds, although the film is not autobiographical. Suzanne Vale (Meryl Streep) gets stronger and stronger throughout the film as she is finally able to shed her illusions and understand reality. *Regarding Henry* may be partially related to an incident in Nichols's life, when he states that he gained a new appreciation of life after recovering from an illness. In the film, the character of Henry (Harrison Ford) is wounded in the head, and as he recovers, he also gains a new appreciation of life.

It seems no coincidence that in 1988 Nichols married Diane Sawyer, a television news personality who deals in reality images, since Nichols himself, as shown by the films in his second phase, was now concerned more with reality than illusion.

In 1994, Nichols directed *Wolf,* which may mark the beginning of a new phase of his work. Nichols in *Wolf* tackles profound questions about aging, death, and what lies beyond concrete knowledge. Elaine

May, his old partner from his comedy days, helped with the script (uncredited). *Wolf* concerns a middle aged New York City book editor, Will Randall (Jack Nicholson), who is bitten by a wolf. Will's senses become more acute, he fights for and regains his job, he falls in love with the publishing company owner's daughter, Laura Alden (Michelle Pfeiffer), and slowly realizes that he is becoming a wolf. Nichols directs a film about transformation and possible immortality.

So from *Who's Afraid of Virginia Woolf?* to *Wolf,* Nichols has transformed from a great director to an even greater director, and has obtained a type of immortality himself, for many of his films are of such artistic merit that they will be preserved forever.

—Mark W. Estrin, updated by H. Wayne Schuth

NILSSON, Leopoldo Torre *See* **TORRE NILSSON, Leopoldo**

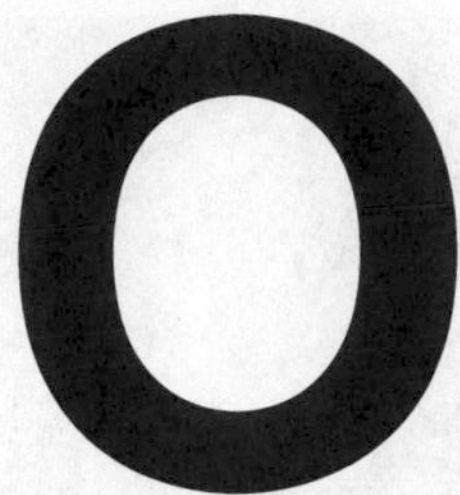

OLIVEIRA, Manoel de

Nationality: Portuguese. **Born:** Manoel Cândido Pinto de Oliveira in Oporto, 10 December 1908. **Family:** Married Maria Isabel Carvalhais, 1940, four children. **Career:** Athlete and racing car driver, 1920-27; directed first film, 1929, then returned to sporting activities, 1930s; directed first feature, *Aniki-Bóbó,* 1941; unable to make films, worked in agriculture, 1943-71; full-time filmmaker, from 1972.

Films as Director:

1931 *Douro, faina fluvial* (*Hard Labor on the River Douro*) (short) (+ pr, sc, ed)
1939 *Miramar praia das rosas* (short) (+ pr, sc, ed); *Ja se fabricam automovels em Portugal* (short) (+ pr, sc, ed)
1940 *Famalicão* (short) (+ pr, sc, ed)
1942 *Aniki-Bóbó* (+ sc)
1956 *O pintor e a cidade* (*The Painter and the Town*) (+ pr, sc, ed, ph)
1959 *O pão* (*Bread*) (+ ed, ph, sc)
1960 *O coracão* (*The Heart*) (short) (+ sc)
1963 *Acto da primavera* (*The Passion of Jesus*) (+ pr, ed, ph, sc); *A caça* (*The Hunt*) (+ ph, ed, sc)
1965 *As pinturas de meu irmão Júlio* (*Pictures of My Brother Julio*) (short) (+ pr, ph, ed)
1972 *O passado e o presente* (*Past and Present*) (+ co-pr, ed)
1975 *Benilde ou a Virgem Mãe* (*Benilde: Virgin and Mother*) (+ ed)
1978 ***Amor de perdicão*** (*Doomed Love*) (+ sc)
1981 *Francisca*
1982 *Memórias e confissoes* (*Memories and Confessions*) (to be released only after de Oliveira's death)
1983 *Lisboa Cultural* (*Cultural Lisbon*)
1984 *Nice à propos de Jean Vigo*
1985 *O Sapato de cetim* (*Le Soulier de satin*; *The Satin Slipper*) (+ sc)
1986 *O Meu Caso—Repeticoes* (*Mon Cas*) (+ sc)
1988 *Os Canibais* (*The Cannibals*); *A Bandeira Nacional* (*The National Flag*) (doc short)
1990 *Não ou a Vã Glória de Mandar* (*Non or the Vain Glory of Command*) (+ sc, ed)

Other Films:

1933 *A Canção de Lisboa* (Telmo) (role)

Publications

By OLIVEIRA: book—

Aniki-Bóbó, Porto, 1963.

By OLIVEIRA: articles—

"O cinema e o capital," in *Movimento* (Lisbon), October 1933.
Interview with Paulo Rocha, in *Critica* (Lisbon), March 1972.
Interview with João Botelho and Cabral Martins, in *M* (Lisbon), August/September 1975.
"A propos de Benilde ou a Virgem-Mãe," in *Image et Son* (Paris), February 1977.
"Los Paisajes pintados," an interview with F. Llináa and S. Zunzunegui, in *Contracampo* (Madrid), January 1981.
Interview with Richard Peña, in *Journal of Film and Video* (Carbondale, Illinois), Summer 1983.
Interview with Charles Tesson and others, in *Cahiers du Cinéma* (Paris), January 1986.
"Le cinema de demain," in *Cahiers du Cinéma* (Paris), May 1991 (sup).
Bassan, R., "La divine comedie," in *Revue du Cinema,* May 1992.
Borlee, G., "La divine comedie," in *Grand Angle,* July 1992.
Interview, in *Cahiers du Cinéma* (Paris), April 1993.
Interview with J. A. Gili, in *Positif,* September 1993.

On OLIVEIRA: books—

Manoel de Oliveira, Ciné-Club of Estremoz, 1955.
Manoel de Oliveira, with "Diálogo com Manoel de Oliveira," Cinemateca Portuguesa, Lisbon, 1981.
França, J. A., L. Pina, and A. Costa, *Introdução à obra de Manoel de Oliveira,* Lisbon, 1982.
Passek, Jean-Loup, *Le cinéma portugais,* Paris, 1982.
Lardeau, Yann, *Manoel de Oliveira,* Paris, 1988.

On OLIVEIRA: articles—

Demeure, Jacques, "Manoel de Oliveira," in *Positif* (Paris), no. 25-26, 1957.
Biette, J.C., "Notes sur l'oeuvre de Manoel de Oliveira," in *Cahiers du Cinéma* (Paris), February 1966.
Daney, Serge, "Notes sur les films de Manuel de Oliveira," in *Cahiers du Cinéma* (Paris), May 1977.
Magny, J., "Dossier-auteur Manoel de Oliveira," in *Cinéma* (Paris), March 1980.
Gillett, John, "Manoel de Oliveira," in *Sight and Sound* (London), Summer 1981.
Fonseca, M. S., "Manoel de Oliveira, o cinema e a crueldade," in *Expresso* (Lisbon), October 1981.
Lehmann, I., "Die Tetralogie der 'amours frustrés.' Zu Manoel de Oliveiras Filmen über Liebe und Tod," in *Frauen und Film* (Berlin), February 1982.
Degoudenne, L., and J. Noel, "Les cannibales," *Grand Angle,* June 1990.
Baecque, A. de, "Comment on filme l'histoire," in *Cahiers du Cinéma* (Paris), October 1990.
Bierinckx, C., "New York Stories ... en een Beetje Portugal," in *Film en Televisie & Video,* February 1991.
Asselberghs, H., and K. van Daele, "Artistieke produktiestrategieen," in *Andere Sinema,* September/October 1991.

Manoel de Oliveira

Bogaert, P. van, "O dia do desespero," *Andere Sinema,* November/December 1992.

Rollet, S., "Entre presence et absence," in *Positif,* September 1993.

* * *

Simultaneously rugged and tender, the tortured work of Manoel de Oliveira, in which a personal vision is transformed into a unique expression of Portuguese culture, finds its only counterpart in that of Carl Th. Dreyer. The radical aesthetic and ethical programs of both filmmakers met with incomprehension. In addition, one finds a tragic fusion of profane desire and an aspiration toward the sacred in the work of both directors.

No man is a prophet in his own country; Oliveira, an artist of magnitude disproportionate to such a diminutive nation, confirms this aphorism. He found no favor under the Salazar regime; instead, he was condemned by its pettiness to silence and inactivity. Persecution did not cease with the death of the dictator. Oliveira continued to be charged with "not being natural" and was accused of the sin of "elitism." This is the reason there are so many films that Oliveira *did not* make. Only relatively late in his career did international acclaim force a measure of national recognition.

The first phase of Oliveira's work, what he calls "the stage of the people," was dominated by an intense dialogue between documentary and fiction. From the very beginning Oliveira refused to subjugate himself to "genres" and "schools" of filmmaking. An unmistakable movement toward fiction, toward the autonomy of the cinema vis à vis *the real,* can be seen in his documentaries from *Douro* to *Pinturas.* In registering its images, Oliveira's camera approaches quotidien reality as a stage. Through montage, the world can be fixed, cut, and reproduced as a series of fragments.

The second phase of Oliveira's career began in 1972 and was characterized by a more complete expression of the impulse towards fiction. His work featured a concomitant change of objectives: the "stage of the people" is replaced by the "stage of the bourgeoisie." This phase comprises four films, from *O Passado e o presente* to *Francisca,* known as the "Tetralogy of Frustrated Loves." Alluringly romantic, possessed in particular by the love of perdition as expressed in the Portuguese literature of the time, these films attain an aesthetic refinement unsurpassed in European cinema.

In the 1930s Oliveira belonged to the cinematic vanguard. From 1940 to 1963 this cinematic craftsman anticipated many of the innovative aesthetic experiments of later filmmakers—from Italian neorealism to the cinema of Straub—without reducing his work to mere formalism. With the "Tetralogy," a risky and original project makes its appearance: the destruction of the narrative grammar which relies on the shot/countershot, and the destruction of psychological correspondences through the creation, in these films, of a "point of view belonging to no one." Refusing to identify itself with either the characters or the spectator, the camera alters spatial relationships in an effort not exactly to neutralize itself, but to situate itself in a space without a subject in order to fix faces and voices. His attention to "Voices" is important because, since these films were adapted from literary works, they resolutely assume the literary nature of the *text,* to which long and fixed shots or the repetition of such shots confer a temporality without parallel in the history of the cinema. The obsessive use of the studio is also underscored, re-enforcing a sense of enclosure and restriction. A similar emphasis is placed on the style or *representation* which situates actors and objects on the same level; their function is simply to be present.

Linking this formal experimentation with undeniably vigorous fiction, *Francisca* is Oliveira's masterpiece. In *Francisca,* a grandiose synthesis of literary, musical, and pictorial materials, a tellurian identification is revealed which is the origin of desire, fear, guilt, and perdition—the principle themes of Oliveira. After all, such an identification echoes an entire culture which, at its best, transcends a tormented pessimism and bitter irony, though it retains only the consolation of melancholy. This culture is Portuguese and Oliveira is its filmmaker.

—Manuel Dos Santos Fonseca

OLMI, Ermanno

Nationality: Italian. **Born:** Bergamo, 24 July 1931. **Education:** Attended Accadémia d'Arte Drammatica, Milan. **Family:** Married Loredana Detto, three children. **Career:** Worked for electric company Edisonvolta S.p.A., Milan, from 1949; director and supervisor of over forty shorts and documentaries for, or sponsored by, Edisonvolta, 1952-61; directed first feature, semi-documentary *Il tempo si è fermato,* 1959; formed production company "22 December S.p.A." with Tullio Kezich and others, 1961; TV director, from 1964; co-founded Hypothesis Cinema, a school for aspiring directors; formed Ipotesi Cinema, a workshop for young filmmakers, at Bassano del Grappa, 1980s.

Films as Director:

1953 *La digi sul ghiaccio* (short/doc) (+ spvr)
1954 *La pattuglia di passo San Giacomo* (short/doc) (+ spvr)
1955 *Società Ovesticino-Dinamo* (short/doc) (+ spvr); *Cantiere d'inverno* (short/doc) (+ spvr); *La mia valle* (short/doc) (+ spvr); *L'onda* (short/doc) (+ spvr); *Buongiorno natura* (short/doc) (+ spvr)
1956 *Michelino la B* (short/doc) (+ spvr); *Construzione meccaniche riva* (short/doc) (+ spvr)
1958 *Tre fili fino a Milano* (short/doc) (+ spvr); *Giochi di Colonia* (short/doc) (+ spvr); *Venezia città minore* (short/doc) (+ spvr)
1959 *Il tempo si è fermato* (*Time Has Stopped*; *Time Stood Still*) (+ sc, spvr)
1960 *Il grande paese d'Acciaio* (short/doc) (+ spvr)
1961 *Le grand barrage* (short/doc) (+ spvr); *Un metro lungo cinque* (short/doc) (+ spvr); ***Il posto*** (*The Sound of Trumpets*; *The Job*) (+ sc)
1963 *I fidanzati* (*The Fiancés*; *The Engagement*) (+ pr, sc)
1965 *... e venne un uomo* (*A Man Called John*; *And There Came a Man*) (+ co-sc)
1968 *Un certo giorno* (*One Fine Day*) (+ sc, ed)
1969 *I recuperanti* (*The Scavengers*) (+ co-sc, ph) (for TV)
1971 *Durante l'estate* (*During the Summer*; *In the Summertime*) (+ co-sc, ph, ed) (for TV)
1974 *La circostanza* (*The Circumstance*) (+ pr, sc, ph, ed) (for TV)
1978 ***L'albero degli zoccoli*** (*The Tree of the Wooden Clogs*) (+ sc, ph, ed)
1983 *Cammina, cammina* (*Keep Walking*)
1984 *Milano '83* (doc)
1987 *Lunga Vita alla Signora* (*Long Live the Lady!*) (+ sc, co-ph)
1988 *La leggenda del santo bevitore* (*The Legend of the Holy Drinker*) (+ sc, ed)
1992 *Lungo il fiume* (*Along the River*) (+ sc, ed)
1993 *Il segreto del bosco vecchio* (*The Secret of the Old Forest*) (+ sc)
1994 *Genesis: The Creation and the Flood* (+ sc)

Other Films:

1955 *La tesatura meccanica della linea a 220.000 volt* (short/doc) (spvr); *San Massenza* (*Cimego*) (short/doc) (spvr)
1956 *Pantano d'avio* (short/doc) (spvr); *Peru—Istituto de Verano* (short/doc) (spvr); *Fertilizzanti complessi* (short/doc) (spvr)
1957 *Fibre e civilta* (short/doc) (spvr); *Progresso in agricoltura* (short/doc) (spvr); *Campi sperimentali* (short/doc) (spvr)
1958 *Colonie Sicedison* (short/doc) (spvr); *Bariri* (short/doc) (spvr); *Il frumento* (short/doc) (spvr)
1959 *El frayle* (short/doc) (spvr); *Fertiluzzanti produtti dalla Societa del Gruppo Edison* (short/doc) (spvr); *Cavo olio fludio 220.000 volt* (short/doc) (spvr); *Auto chiese* (short/doc) (spvr); *Natura e chimica* (short/doc) (spvr)
1961 *Il pomodoro* (short/doc) (spvr); *Il sacco in Plypac* (short/doc) (spvr); *Po: forza 50.000* (short/doc) (pr)
1962 *Una storia milanese* (E. Visconti) (role)

Publications

By OLMI: book—

Il ragazzo dell Bovisa, Milan, 1986.

By OLMI: articles—

Interview with Gideon Bachmann, in *Nation* (New York), 25 May 1964.
"Ermanno Olmi, A Conversation with John Francis Lane," in *Sight and Sound* (London), Summer 1970.
Interview with A. Tassone, in *Cinéma* (Paris), January 1976.
Interview with M. Devillers and others, in *Cinématographe* (Paris), no. 40, 1978.
Interview with J. A. Gili and L. Codelli, in *Positif* (Paris), November 1983.
Interview with Don Ranvaud, in *Monthly Film Bulletin* (London), October 1988.
"Ermanno Olmi: non sono un divo," an interview with F. Cattaneo, in *Cinematografo,* January 1993.

On OLMI: books—

Samuels, Charles Thomas, *Encountering Directors,* New York, 1972.
Tassone, Aldo, *Parla il cinema italiano, II,* Milan, 1980.
Witcombe, Roger, *The New Italian Cinema,* New York, 1983.
Bondanella, Peter, *Italian Cinema: From Neorealism to the Present,* New York, 1983, reprinted, 1990.

Ermanno Olmi

Liehm, Mira, *Passion and Defiance: Film in Italy from 1942 to the Present,* Berkeley, 1984.
Dillon, Jeanne, *Ermanno Olmi,* Florence, 1986.
Marcus, Millicent, *Italian Film in the Light of Neorealism,* Princeton, 1986.
Tabanelli, Giorgio, *Ermanno Olmi: nascita del documentario poetica,* Rome, 1987.
Brunetta, Gian Piero, *Cent'anni di cinema italiano,* Rome, 1991.
Sitney, P. Adams, *Vital Crises in Italian Cinema,* Austin, 1995.

On OLMI: articles—

Lane, J. F., "The Triumph of Italy's Realism," in *Films and Filming* (London), December 1961.
Solomos, G. P., "Ermanno Olmi," in *Film Culture* (New York), Spring 1962.
Kauffman, Stanley, "A Fine Italian Hand," in *New Republic* (New York), 15 February 1964.
Houston, Penelope, "The Organisation Man," in *Sight and Sound* (London), Spring 1964.
Walsh, M., "Ermanno Olmi," in *Monogram* (London), Summer 1971.
Gervais, M., "Ermanno Olmi: Humanism in the Cinema," in *Sight and Sound* (London), Autumn 1978.
Special section on *L'Albero degli zoccoli,* in *Positif* (Paris), September 1978.
Elley, Derek, "Ermanno Olmi," in *International Film Guide 1981,* London, 1980.
De Santi, G., "Il tradimento e la vendetta dei chierici," in *Cineforum* (Bergamo), January/February 1984.
Kennedy, Harlan, "Searching for the Star Child," in *Film Comment* (New York), September/October 1984.
Kieffer, A., "A la recherche d'Olmi," in *Jeune Cinéma* (Paris), February/March 1988.

Keates, J., "Inn the cascina," in *Sight and Sound* (London), Winter 1988/89.

Kinder, Marsha, "The Subversive Potential of the Pseudo-Iterative," in *Film Quarterly,* Winter 1989/90.

Casagrande, L., "Ermanno Olmi," in *Film en Televisie + Video,* January 1991.

* * *

Ermanno Olmi, born in Bergamo in 1931, is the Italian filmmaker most committed to and identified with a regional heritage. His films are distinctly Lombardian; for the most part they describe life in Milan, the provincial capital (for example, *Il posto, Un certo giorno, Durante l'estate* and *La circonstanza*). He has also filmed in the Lombardian Alps (*Il tempo si è fermato*), and his native Bergamo (*L'albero degli zoccoli*), but even when he ventures to Sicily, it is to make a film of a Milanese worker temporarily assigned to the south who longs for home (*I fidanzati*), and when he makes a semi-documentary biography (*... e venne un uomo*), it is of the Lombardian Pope, John XXIII.

Furthermore, his work bears affinities to the central literary figure of the Lombardian tradition, Alessandro Manzoni, whose great historical novel, *I promessi sposi,* is variously reflected in at least three of Olmi's films: most directly in *I findanzati,* whose very title recasts the 1827 novel, but also in the idealization of a great ecclesiastic (*... e venne un uomo*), and in the vivid recreation of a past century (*L'albero degli zoccoli),* which portrays peasant life in the late nineteenth century rather than Manzoni's seventeenth. The most significant Manzonian characteristic of Olmi's cinema is its Catholicism: of all the major Italian filmmakers he has the least problematic relationship with the Church. He embodies the spirit of the "opening to the Left" which has characterized both religious and parliamentary politics in Italy since the early 1960s. For the most part, his films center upon an individual worker caught between employment and an individual quest to assert dignity through labor. Quite often this tension carries over from work to the conjugal or preconjugal love life of the protagonist.

Like Pasolini, Rosi, and Bertolucci, Olmi is a filmmaker nurtured by postwar neorealism. Like his great precursors, Rossellini, De Sica, and Visconti, he has worked extensively with amateur actors, chosen simplified naturalistic settings, eschewed elaborate artifices or lighting, and employed an ascetic camera style. What mobility his camera has comes largely from his extensive use of the zoom lens. In contrast, however, to the first generation of neorealists, he has a high tolerance for abstraction and ambiguity in his storytelling. Dramatic and emotional moments are consistently understated. Instead of a mobile camera, he has relied heavily upon montage (especially in the intercutting of scenes between Milan and Sicily in *I fidanzati*) and even more on the overlapping of sounds. In fact, Olmi's meticulous attention to sound, his isolation and manipulation of auditory details, tends to transform his realistically photographed scenes into psychologically inflected domains of space and time.

After *L'albero degli zoccoli,* the predominately latent religiosity in his cinema became more manifest. *Cammina, cammina* recounts a version of the story of the Three Wise Men seeking the Christ child. *La leggenda del santo bevitore* turns the last days of a Parisian clochard into a parable of divine intervention. Its plot is perhaps more characteristic of Rohmer than Olmi, but the filmmaker uses it to reimagine the simple daily activities of proletarian life through the eyes of a drunkard bewildered by his sudden streak of good fortune. Similarly, in a wholly secular mode, *Lunga Vita alla Signora* returns to the topos of *Il tempo si e fermato* and *Il posto* after nearly thirty years to glimpse the intricacies of an affluent family reunion from the perspective of a naive adolescent in his first job as a busboy in an elegant Alpine hotel.

Olmi released two films in 1992, *Lunga il fiume,* a poetic documentary on the Po River, and *Il segreto del Bosco vecchio,* a fable adapted from Dino Buzzati, set in the Dolomites before the First World War, in which a sentient forest, with talking animals and winds, defeats the plans of a retired colonel for its commercial exploitation. Both films celebrate nature as a conduit of Divinity. The commentary of *Lunga il fiume* even allegorizes the outpouring of the river into the Adriatic as a type of Jesus's kenosis and death.

Throughout the 1980s Olmi directed a workshop for young filmmakers, Ipotesi Cinema, at Bassano del Grappa. In the face of radically reduced film production and the domination of television in Italy, Ipotesi Cinema was a utopian project for helping filmmakers find alternative modes of production and financing without compromising the originality of their ideas.

—P. Adams Sitney

OPHULS, Marcel

Nationality: French/American. **Born:** Frankfurt-am-Main, Germany, 1 November 1927, son of director Max, became citizen of France, 1938, and of the U.S.A., 1950. **Education:** Hollywood High School, graduated 1945; Occidental College; University of California at Berkeley; studied philosophy, the Sorbonne. **Military Service:** Served with Occupation forces in Japan during World War II. **Family:** Married Regina Ackermann, 1956, three daughters. **Career:** Moved to France, 1932, and to Hollywood, 1941; performed with theater unit, Tokyo, 1946; 3rd assistant director, using name "Marcel Wall," Paris, from 1951; radio and TV story editor for Sudwestfunk, Baden-Baden, West Germany, also director for radio, stage and TV, 1956-59; returned to Paris, 1960; TV journalist and director of *Zoom,* TV news magazine, 1966-68; directed first major documentary, *Munich, or Peace in Our Time,* 1967; senior story editor at NDR TV, Hamburg, 1968-71; Senior Visiting Fellow, Council of the Humanities, Princeton University, 1973-74; staff producer at CBS News, then ABC News, 1975-78; returned to Europe, 1979; Secretary General, French Filmmakers' Society, and on Board of Directors, Societé des gens de lettres. **Awards:** Prix de Dinard, Prix Georges Sadoul, British Film Academy Award, National Society of Film Critics Special Award, and Special Citation, New York Film Critics, for *The Sorrow and the Pity,* 1971; Oscar for Best Documentary, for *Hotel Terminus,* 1988. **Address:** 10 rue Ernest Deloison, Neuilly-sur-Seine, France.

Films as Director:

1960 *Matisse, or The Talent for Happiness* (+ sc)

1961 German episode of *L'Amour à vingt ans* (*Love at Twenty*) (+ sc)

1963 *Peau de banane* (*Banana Skin/Banana Peel*) (+ co-sc)

1964 *Feu à volonté* (*Faites vos jeux*; *Fire at Will*) (+ co-sc)

1966 *Till Eulenspiegel* (co-d, co-sc, quit during filming) (in two parts, for German TV)

1967 *Munich, ou La Paix pour cent ans* (*Munich, or Peace in Our Time*) (for French TV) (+ sc)

1969 ***Le Chagrin et la pitié*** (*The Sorrow and the Pity*) (for TV, in two parts, 4.5 hours long) (+ sc)

1970 *Clavigo* (for TV); *The Harvest of My Lai* (for TV) (+ sc)

1971 *America Revisited* (for TV, in two parts) (+ sc); *Zwei ganze tage* (*Two Whole Days*) (for TV)

1972 *A Sense of Loss* (+ sc)

1976 *The Memory of Justice* (+ sc)
1988 *Hotel Terminus: The Life and Times of Klaus Barbie*
1990 *November Days: Voices and Choices* (for TV)
1994 *The Troubles We've Seen: A History of Journalism in Wartime*

Other Films:

(partial list)

1953 *Moulin Rouge* (Huston) (asst d)
1954 *Un Acte d'amour* (*Act of Love*) (Litvak) (asst d); *Marianne de ma jeunesse* (Duvivier) (asst d)
1955 *Lola Montès* (Max Ophüls) (asst d)

Publications

By OPHULS: articles—

"*The Sorrow and the Pity, A Sense of Loss,* a Discussion with Marcel Ophuls," with B.J. Demby, in *Filmmakers Newsletter* (Ward Hill, Massachusetts), December 1972.
"Why Should I Give You Political Solutions?" an interview in *Film Critic* (New York), November/December 1973.
"Politics and Autobiography," an interview with D. Yergin, in *Sight and Sound* (London), Winter 1973/74.
"Marcel Ophuls Tells Us We Cannot Afford to Forget," an interview with Terry Fox, in *Village Voice* (New York), 11 October 1976.
"*Memory of Justice,*" an interview with P. Lehman and others, in *Wide Angle* (Athens, Ohio), vol. 2, no. 2, 1978.
"A War Over Justice," an interview with F. Manchel, in *Literature/Film Quarterly* (Salisbury, Maryland), Winter 1978.
"Changing the Rules of the Game," in *American Film* (Washington, D.C.), May 1984.
"Joy to the World!" an interview with Michel Ciment, in *American Film* (New York), September 1988.
Interview with F. Strauss, in *Cahiers du Cinéma* (Paris), September 1988.
Interview with Graham Fuller, in *Listener* (London), 10 November 1988.
Ophuls, Marcel, "*La Ronde* de le droit d'auteur," in *Positif* (Paris), January 1990.
Ophuls, Marcel, "A monsieur le delegue general," in *Positif* (Paris), December 1991.
Ophuls, Marcel, "Correspondance inedite de Max Ophuls," in *Positif* (Paris), November 1992.

On OPHULS: articles—

"Jean-Pierre Melville Talks to Rui Nogueira About *Le Chagrin et la pitié,*" in *Sight and Sound* (London), Winter 1971/72.
"La Chagrin et la pitié," special Ophuls issue of *Avant-Scène du Cinéma* (Paris), July/September 1972.

* * *

Marcel Ophuls' 1974 film, *A Memory of Justice,* which examines war crimes by juxtaposing the Nuremburg Trials with the conflict in Vietnam, managed to please neither the critic Pauline Kael ("I feel a pang of guilt, because I think it's a very bad film—chaotic and plodding, and with an excess of self-consciousness which at times Ophuls seems to mistake for art") nor David Puttnam, one of its British producers, who claimed that the work was far too "personal" and who apparently urged Ophuls to be more "fascist" in his approach. Ophuls was not inclined to be seduced by Radical Chic: he refused to make glib parallels between Auschwitz and the My Lai massacre, and thus enraged his backers. The film was overlong (Ophuls had been contracted to make a four-hour, thirty-minute documentary and had come up with four hours and thirty-eight minutes), over-budget, and featured pubic hair in a sauna sequence which had the BBC, the project's co-sponsor, throwing up its arms in horror. Puttnam elbowed Ophuls off the production after a stormy meeting in the Ritz Bar and called in another director, Lutz Becker, to recut the footage. The film was "rescued" by an intrepid production assistant who stole a scratch print and smuggled it over to America, where it was watched in darkened Manhattan viewing rooms by Mike Nichols, Lillian Hellman, Susan Sontag, and other New York cultural luminaries. A wealthy backer bought back the negative. The movie was premiered in its intended form, acclaimed as a masterpiece by some, and savaged by Kael.

Ophuls is closely associated with polemical documentaries that court controversy and split the critics, so it seems surprising that his first feature was made in France under the aegis of François Truffaut. It starred Jeanne Moreau and Jean-Paul Belmondo, and had a title no more contentious than *Banana Skin.* One forgets that the filmmaker spent his school days at Hollywood High. Ophuls claims the two directors who really influenced him were his father, Max, and Truffaut. His grounding was in fiction. He worked for his father on *Lola Montès,* was on the crew of Huston's *Moulin Rouge,* and spent a three-year apprenticeship in the 1950s on 2nd Features. He has always taken a determinedly personal approach toward documentary, and is full of disdain for filmmakers who use it as a smokescreen behind which to hide their own lack of creative ability. *Hotel Terminus,* his 1988 investigation into the Klaus Barbie affair, was, he claims, structured along the lines of TV's *Columbo,* with Ophuls the interviewer casting himself as the detective in the dirty raincoat.

If the director's follow-up to *Banana Skin, Feu a Volonte* (1964), had not been such a failure, it is quite conceivable that Ophuls would have turned into a filmmaker along the lines of Chabrol and Rivette. As it was, he was lured away (or fled) into the world of TV journalism, working for *60 Minutes* in Germany and learning about reportage and interview techniques. *The Sorrow and the Pity,* the film which established his name, was originally intended for French TV. When French broadcasters refused to show it, however, the film found a new lease on life in the country's art houses.

As a documentary maker, Ophuls examines how the past is mediated and constructed by the present: he is interested in the past as fiction, not as actuality, in the "process of recollection, in things like choice, selective memory, rationalization." He does not try to maintain the charade of impartiality: he is an egotist who inserts himself, his character and feelings, into the films he makes. He is polite in his anger, willing to shake Barbie's hand or to listen to Albert Speer's side of the story. Often, the most startling information he garners is the incidental, the discursive: Klaus Barbie was kind to animals, for example, and was much liked by cats. Always with an eye on a profit, the Nazi tried to charge journalists for interviews when he was waiting to be extradited from Bolivia. Hannah Arendt's old cliche about the banality of evil finds new currency in Ophuls' work. Like Claud Lanzmann, he is loath to allow us the easy convenience of forgetting.

Ophuls' photography is often ramshackle and his work has been accused of lacking structure. Rather than employ commentary or voice-over, he allows his interviewees to tell their myriad different stories in their own voices. However, he is a consummate editor who believes that films are made in the cutting room. He is not above using editing to make his point and to caricature the opinions he disagrees with. For example, in his film about sectarian violence in Belfast, *A Sense of Loss,* he manages to make a whole galaxy of Protestant grotesques while his representations of Catholics are generally favourable. He is a quixotic director who will continue to infuriate

critics by intruding into his documentaries when they feel he should be behind the camera, paring his fingernails.

A great admirer of the comedies of Ernst Lubitsch, in particular *To Be Or Not To Be,* Ophuls has lectured on Hollywood comedy at Princeton University and probably feels somewhat burdened by his reputation as the maker of grave, earnest, and very long films which go down well with the liberal intellectuals of Greenwich Village. (Woody Allen queues to see *The Sorrow and the Pity* in *Annie Hall.*) It seems to have eluded his critics that he too has a sense of humour.

Ophuls continued to tackle demanding subject matter in his documentaries in the late 1980s and 1990s. *Hotel Terminus: The Life and Times of Klaus Barbie,* his first film in twelve years, picks up where *The Sorrow and the Pity* leaves off, providing an investigation of the whos, hows, and whys of the Second World War. It is the provocative account of the life of, and four-decade-long manhunt for, the notorious Gestapo chief Klaus Barbie, known as the "Butcher of Lyon." Especially telling is the information Ophuls reveals regarding Barbie's post-war activities, and the manner in which his escape to South America was arranged by American counterintelligence officers.

The title tells all in Ophuls' latest documentary, *The Troubles We've Seen: A History of Journalism in Wartime,* in which he examines the politics and ethics of his subject. He especially is intrigued by the combination of fearlessness, egotism, and benevolence often found in the best war correspondents.

—G. C. Macnab, updated by Rob Edelman

OPHÜLS, Max

Nationality: Born Max Oppenheimer in Saarbrucken, Germany, 6 May 1902, became French citizen, 1938. **Family:** Married actress Hilde Wall in 1926, one son, director Marcel Ophuls. **Career:** Acting debut, 1919; began as stage director, 1924; began working at Burgtheater, Vienna, 1926; dialogue director to Anatole Litvak at UFA, 1929; directed first film, 1930; with family, left Germany, 1932; directed in France, Italy, and Holland, 1933-40; worked in Switzerland, 1940, then moved to Hollywood, 1941; "rediscovered" by Preston Sturges, 1944; returned to France, 1949; directed for German radio, mid-1950s. **Died:** In Hamburg, 26 March 1957.

Films as Director:

1930 *Dann schon lieber Lebertran* (+ co-adaptation)
1932 *Die verliebte Firma*; *Die verkaufte Braut* (*The Bartered Bride*)
1933 *Die lachende Erben* (produced 1931); *Liebelei*; *Une Histoire d'amour* (French version of *Liebelei*)
1934 *On a volé un homme*; *La Signora di tutti* (+ co-sc)
1935 *Divine* (+ co-sc)
1936 *Komedie om Geld* (+ co-sc); *Ave Maria* (short); *La Valse brillante* (short); *La Tendre Ennemie* (*The Tender Enemy*) (+ co-sc)
1937 *Yoshiwara* (+ co-sc)
1938 *Werther* (*Le Roman de Werther*) (+ co-adaptation)
1940 *Sans lendemain*; *De Mayerling à Sarajevo* (*Mayerling to Sarajevo*); *L'Ecole des femmes* (unfinished)
1946 *Vendetta* (co-d, uncredited)
1947 *The Exile*
1948 ***Letter from an Unknown Woman***
1949 *Caught*; *The Reckless Moment*
1950 ***La Ronde*** (+ co-sc)
1952 *Le Plaisir* (*House of Pleasure*) (+ co-sc)
1953 ***Madame de ...*** (*The Earrings of Madame De*) (+
1955 ***Lola Montès*** (*The Sins of Lola Montes*) (+ co-sc)

Publications

By OPHÜLS: books—

Novelle, by Goethe, radio adaptation, Frankfurt am Main,
Max Ophüls par Max Ophüls, Paris, 1963.

By OPHÜLS: articles—

"Hollywood, petite île ...," in *Cahiers du Cinéma* (Paris), 1955.
"Le Dernier Jour de tournage," in *Cahiers du Cinéma* (Pa 1956.
Interview with Jacques Rivette and François Truffaut, in *C Cinéma* (Paris), June 1957.
"Les Infortunes d'un scenario," and "Mon experience," in *C Cinéma* (Paris), March 1958.
"*La Ronde*: Scenario et adaptation," with Jacques Natanson, *Scène du Cinéma* (Paris), April 1963.
"Memory and Max Ophüls," in *Interviews with Film Directo* by Andrew Sarris, New York, 1967.
"*Lola Montès*: Scenario et adaptation," with Jacques Natanson, *Scène du Cinéma* (Paris), January 1969.
Interview with Robert Aldrich, in *The Celluloid Muse,* edited by Higham and Joel Greenberg, Chicago, 1971.
"Interview with Ophüls (1950)," with Francis Koval, in *Maste of the French Cinema,* edited by John Weightman, New York
"*Madame de ...* Issue" of *Avant Scène du Cinéma* (Paris), n 1986.

On OPHÜLS: books—

Roud, Richard, *Max Ophüls: An Index,* London, 1958.
Annenkov, Georges, *Max Ophüls,* Paris, 1962.
Beylie, Claude, *Max Ophüls,* Paris, 1963; revised edition, 1984.
Willemen, Paul, editor, *Ophüls,* London, 1978.
Williams, Alan, *Max Ophüls and the Cinema of Desire,* New Yo 1980.
Guérin, William, *Max Ophüls,* Paris, 1988.
Asper, Helmut G., and others, *Max Ophüls,* Munich, 1989.

On OPHÜLS: articles—

Truffaut, François, "Une Certaine Tendence du cinéma français," in *Cahiers du Cinéma* (Paris), January 1954.
Archer, Eugene, "Ophüls and the Romantic Tradition," in *Yale French Studies* (New Haven), no. 17, 1956.
Tributes to Ophüls, in *Sight and Sound* (London), Summer 1957.
"Ophüls Issue" of *Cahiers du Cinéma* (Paris), March 1958.
Beylie, Claude, "Max Ophüls," in *Anthologie du Cinéma* (Paris), June 1965.
"Max Ophüls," in *Retrospektive* [1] edited by Peter Schumann, Berlin, 1966.
Williams, Forrest, "The Mastery of Movement," in *Film Comment* (New York), Winter 1969.
Koch, Howard, "Script to Screen with Max Ophüls," in *Film Comment* (New York), Winter 1970/71.
"Ophüls Issue" of *Film Comment* (New York), Summer 1971.
Camper, Fred, "Distance and Style: The Visual Rhetoric of Max Ophüls," in *Monogram* (London), no. 5, 1974.

)phuls Issues" of *Filmkritik* (Munich), November and December 1977.
pecial Ophüls section, in *Positif* (Paris), July/August 1980.
)phüls Issue," of *Movie* (London), Summer 1982.
och, G., "Die Schnitzler-Verfilmungen von Max Ophüls," in *Frauen und Film* (Berlin), October 1982.
ouseman, John, "Houseman, Ray and Ophüls," in *Sight and Sound* (London), Autumn 1986.
miel, V., "Ophüls les yeux fermés," in *Positif* (Paris), December 1986.
Iorrison, James, "Ophüls and Authorship: A Reading of *The Reckless Moment*," in *Film Criticism* (Edinboro, Pennsylvania), vol. 11, no. 3, 1987.
)oane, Mary Ann, "The Abstraction of a Lady: *La Signora di tutti*," in *Cinema Journal* (Champaign, Illinois), vol. 28, no. 1, 1988.

* * *

Max Ophüls' work falls neatly into three periods, marked by geographical locations and diverse production conditions, yet linked by common thematic concerns and stylistic/formal procedures: the pre-Second World War European period (during which he made films in four countries and four languages); the four Hollywood films of the late 1940s (to which one might add the remarkable Howard Hughes-produced *Vendetta,* on which he worked extensively in its early pre-production phases and which bears many identifiable Ophülsian traces, both thematic and stylistic); and the four films made in France in the 1950s. It is these latter films on which Ophüls' current reputation chiefly rests, and in which certain stylistic traits (notably the long take with elaborately mobile camera) are carried to their logical culmination.

Critical estimation of Ophüls has soared during the past twenty years; prior to that, the prevailing attitude was disparaging (or at best condescending), and the reasons for this now seem highly significant, reflecting far more on the limitations of the critics than of the films. The general consensus was that Ophüls' work had distinctive qualities (indeed, this would be difficult to deny), but was overly preoccupied with "style" (regarded as a kind of spurious, slightly decadent ornamentation) and given over to trivial or frivolous subjects quite alien to the "social" concerns considered to characterize "serious" cinema. In those days, the oppression of women within the patriarchal order was not identified as a "social concern"—especially within the overwhelmingly male-dominated field of film criticism. Two developments have contributed to the revaluation of Ophüls: the growth of *auteur* criticism in the 1960s and of feminist awareness, and I shall consider his work in relation to these phenomena.

1. *Ophüls and auteurism.* One of the first aims of auteur criticism was to dethrone the "subject" as the prime guarantee of a film's quality, in favor of style, mise-en-scène, the discernible presence of a defined directorial "voice": in Andrew Sarris's terms, the "how" was given supremacy over the "what." "Subject," in fact, was effectively redefined as what the auteur's mise-en-scène created. Ophüls was a perfect rallying-point for such a reformulation of critical theory. For a start, he offered one of the most highly developed and unmistakable styles in world cinema, consistent through all changes of time and place (though inevitably modified in the last two Hollywood melodramas, *Caught* and *The Reckless Moment*). Ophüls works were marked by elaborate tracking-and-craning camera movements, ornate décor, the glitter of glass and mirrors, objects intervening in the foreground of the image between characters and camera. His style can be read in itself as implying a meaning, a metaphysic of entrapment in movement, time, and destiny. Further, this style could be seen as developing, steadily gaining in assurance and definition, through the various changes in cultural background and circumstances of production—from, say, *Liebelei* through *Letter from an Unknown Woman* to *Madame de ...* Ophüls could be claimed (with partial justice) as a major creative artist whose personal vision transcended the most extreme changes of time and place.

The stylistic consistency was underlined by an equally striking thematic consistency. For example, the same three films mentioned above, though adapted from works by fairly reputable literary figures (respectively, Arthur Schnitzler, Stefan Zweig, Louise de Vilmorin), all reveal strong affinities in narrative/thematic structure: all are centered on romantic love, which is at once celebrated and regarded with a certain irony. Similarly, all three works move towards a climactic duel in which the male lover is destroyed by an avenging patriarch, an offended husband. All three films also feature patriarchal authority embodied in military figures. Finally, style and theme were perceived as bound together by a complicated set of visual motifs recurring from period to period. The eponymous protagonist of Ophüls' last film, *Lola Montès,* declares "For me, life is movement"; throughout his work, key scenes take place in vehicles of travel and places of transition (carriages, trains, staircases, and railway stations figure prominently in many of the films). Even a superficially atypical work like *The Reckless Moment* (set in modern California rather than the preferred "Vienna, 1900" or its equivalent) contains crucial scenes on the staircase, in moving cars, on a ferry, at a bus station. Above all, the dance was recognized as a central Ophülsian motif, acquiring complex significance from film to film. The romantic/ironic waltz scene in *Letter from an Unknown Woman,* the fluid yet circumscribed dances of *Madame de ...*, the hectic and claustrophobic *palais de danse* of *Le Plaisir,* the constricted modern dance floor of *Caught,* and the moment in *De Mayerling à Sarajevo* where the lovers are *prevented* from attending the ball: all of the above scenes are reminders that "life is movement" is not the simple proposition it may at first appear.

There is no doubt that the development of *auteur* theory enormously encouraged and extended the appreciation of Ophüls' work. In its pure form (the celebration of the individual artist), however, auteurism tends towards a dangerous imbalance in the evaluation of specific films: a tendency, for example, to prefer the "typical" but slight *La Ronde* (perhaps the film that most nearly corresponds to the "primitive" account of Ophüls) to a masterpiece like *The Reckless Moment,* in which Ophüls' engagement with the structural and thematic materials of the Hollywood melodrama results in an amazingly rich and radical investigation of ideological assumptions.

2. *Ophüls and Feminism.* Nearly all of Ophüls' films are centered on a female consciousness. Before the 1960s this tended merely to confirm the diagnosis of them as decorative, sentimental, and essentially frivolous: the social concerns with which "serious" cinema should be engaged were those which could be resolved within the patriarchal order, and more fundamental social concerns that threatened to undermine the order itself simply could not be recognized. The films belong, of course, to a period long before the eruption of what we now know as radical feminism; they do not (and could not be expected to) explicitly engage with a feminist politics, and they are certainly not free of a tendency to mythologize women. In retrospect, however, from the standpoint of the feminist theory and consciousness that evolved in the 1970s, they assume a quite extraordinary significance: an incomparably comprehensive, sensitive, and perceptive analysis of the position of women (subject to oppression) within patriarchal society. The films repeatedly present and examine the options traditionally available to women within our culture—marriage, prostitution (in both the literal and the looser sense), romantic love—and the relationship between those options. *Letter from an Unknown Woman,* for example, dramatizes marriage (Lisa's to von Stauffer, her mother's to the "military tailor") and prostitution ("modelling") as opposite cultural poles, then goes on to show that they really amount to the same thing: in both cases, the women are selling themselves (this opposition/parallel is brilliantly developed through the three episodes of *Le Plaisir*). Essentially, *Letter from an Unknown Woman* is an enquiry into the validity of romantic love as the only possible means

Max Ophüls

of transcending this illusory dichotomy. Clearly, Ophüls is emotionally committed to Lisa and her vision; the extraordinary complexity and intelligence of the film lies in its simultaneous acknowledgement that romantic love can only exist as narcissistic fantasy and is ultimately both destructive and self-destructive.

Far from being incompatible, the auteurist and feminist approaches to Ophüls demand to be synthesized. The identification with a female consciousness and the female predicament is the supreme characteristic of the Ophülsian thematic; at the same time, the Ophüls style—the commitment to grace, beauty, sensitivity—amounts to a celebration of what our culture defines as "femininity," combined with the force of authority, the drive, the organizational (directorial) abilities construed as masculine. In short, the supreme achievement of Ophüls' work is its concrete and convincing embodiment of the collapsibility of our culture's barriers of sexual difference.

—Robin Wood

OSHIMA, Nagisa

Nationality: Japanese. **Born:** Kyoto, 31 March 1932. **Education:** Studied political history at Kyoto University, graduated 1954. **Career:** Student leader, involved in left-wing activities, early 1950s; assistant director at Shochiku Ofuna Studios, from 1954; film critic and editor-in-chief of film magazine *Eiga hihyo,* from 1956; directed first film, 1959; left Shochiku after *Night and Fog in Japan* pulled from circulation, founded production company Sozosha, 1961 (dissolved 1973); made TV documentaries, early 1960s; created Oshima Productions, 1975; acquitted on obscenity charge relating to *Realm of the Senses,* 1976.

Films as Director:

1959 *Ai to kibo no machi* (*A Town of Love and Hope*) (+ sc); *Asu no taiyo* (short)
1960 *Seishun zankoku monogatari* (*Cruel Story of Youth*; *Naked Youth, a Story of Cruelty*) (+ sc); *Taiyo no hakaba* (*The Sun's Burial*) (+ co-sc); *Nihon no yoru to kiri* (*Night and Fog in Japan*) (+ co-sc)
1961 *Shiiku* (*The Catch*)
1962 *Amakusa shiro tokisada* (*Shiro Tokisada from Amakusa*; *The Rebel*) (+ co-sc)
1964 *Chiisana boken ryoko* (*Small Adventure*; *A Child's First Adventure*) (+ co-sc); *Watashi wa Bellet* (collective direction, advertising film)
1965 *Etsuraku* (*Pleasures of the Flesh*) (+ sc); *Yunbogi no nikki* (*The Diary of Yunbogi*) (+ pr, sc, ph) (short)
1966 *Hakuchu no torima* (*Violence at Noon*)
1967 *Ninja bugeicho* (*Band of Ninja*) (+ co-pr, co-sc); *Nihon shunkako* (*A Treatise on Japanese Bawdy Song*; *Sing a Song of Sex*)) (+ co-pr, co-sc); *Muri-shinju: Nihon no natsu* (*Japanese Summer: Double Suicide*) (+ co-sc)
1968 ***Koshikei*** (*Death by Hanging*) (+ co-pr, co-sc); *Kaettekita yopparai* (*Three Resurrected Drunkards*; *A Sinner in Paradise*) (+ co-sc)
1969 *Shinjuku dorobo nikki* (*Diary of a Shinjuku Thief*) (+ co-sc); ***Shonen*** (*Boy*)
1970 *Tokyo senso sengo hiwa* (*He Died after the War*; *The Man Who Left His Will on Film*) (+ co-sc)
1971 *Gishiki* (*The Ceremony*) (+ co-sc)
1972 *Natsu no imoto* (*Summer Sister*) (+ co-sc)
1976 ***Ai no corrida*** (*In the Realm of the Senses*; *Empire of the Senses*) (+ sc)
1978 *Ai no borei* (*Empire of Passion*; *The Phantom of Love*) (+ co-pr, sc)
1983 *Merry Christmas, Mr. Lawrence*
1986 *Max, Mon Amour* (+ co-sc); *Yunbogi no Nikki* (+ sc, ph)
1991 *Kyoto, My Mother's Place* (+ sc)
1995 *One Hundred Years of Japanese Cinema* (+ sc)

Other Films:

1956 *Shinkei gyogun* (sc) (unproduced but published)
1959 *Tsukimiso* (Iwaki) (sc); *Donto okoze* (Nomura) (co-sc); *Jusan nichi no kinyobi* (unproduced) (sc)
1969 *Yoiyami semareba* (Jissoji) (sc)

Publications

By OSHIMA: books—

Sengo eiga: Hakai to sozo [Postwar Film: Destruction and Creation], Tokyo, 1963.
Taikenteki sengo eizo ron [A Theory of the Postwar Image Based on Personal Experience], Tokyo, 1975.
Écrits (1956-1978): Dissolution et jaillissement, translated by Jean-Paul Le Pape, Paris, 1980.
Cinema, Censorship, and the State : The Writings of Nagisa Oshima, 1956-1978, edited and with an introduction by Annette Michelson, translated by Dawn Lawson, Cambridge, Massachusetts, 1992.

By OSHIMA: articles—

"Situation et sujet du cinéma japonais (1)," in *Positif* (Paris), October 1972.
"Je suis constamment concerné par le temps où je vis ...," an interview with Noel Simsolo, in *Cinéma* (Paris), November 1972.
Interview with R. McCormick, in *Cineaste* (New York), vol. 6, no. 2, 1974.
"Oshima Uncensored," an interview with M. de la F. McKendry, in *Interview* (New York), November 1976.
"Ecrits," in *Positif* (Paris), May 1978 and November 1979.
"L'Empire de la passion," an interview with Max Tessier, in *Ecran* (Paris), September 1978.
"Currents in Japanese Cinema: Nagisa Oshima, Sachiko Hidari," with S. Hoass, in *Cinema Papers* (Melbourne), September/October 1979.
Interview with P. Lehman, in *Wide Angle* (Athens, Ohio), vol. 4, no. 2, 1980.
"Tokyo Stories: Oshima," an interview with Tony Rayns, in *Sight and Sound* (London), Summer 1981.
Interview with Pascal Bonitzer and others, in *Cahiers du Cinéma* (Paris), June/July 1983.
Interview with Nick Roddick, in *Stills* (London), July/August 1983.
"Oshima and Bowie: Culture Shock," an interview with Tadao Sato, in *American Film* (Washington, D.C.), September 1983.
"Campaigner in the World of the Absurd," an interview with S. Suga, in *Framework* (Norwich), no. 26-27, 1985.
"Entretien avec Nagisa Oshima," with K. Ueno, in *Cahiers du Cinéma* (Paris), November 1990.
"Kyoto, la ville de ma mere," an interview with M. Borgese and others, in *Jeune Cinéma,* April/May 1992.

On OSHIMA: books—

Sato, Tadao, *Oshima Nagisa no sekai* [The World of Nagisa Oshima], Tokyo, 1973.

Bock, Audie, *Japanese Film Directors,* New York, 1978; revised edition, Tokyo, 1985.

Tessier, Max, editor, *Le Cinéma Japonais au présent: 1959-1979,* Paris, 1980.

Sato, Tadao, *Currents in Japanese Cinema,* Tokyo, 1982.

Magrelli, Enrico, and Emanuela Martini, *Il Rito, il rivolta: Il cinema di Nagisa Oshima,* Rome, 1984.

Polan, Dana B., *The Political Language of Film and the Avant-Garde,* Ann Arbor, Michigan, 1985.

Danvers, Louis, and Charles Tatum, *Nagisa Oshima,* Paris, 1986.

Desser, David, *Eros Plus Massacre: An Introduction to the Japanese New Wave Cinema,* Bloomington, Indiana, 1988.

Nolletti, Arthur Jr., and David Desser, eds., *Reframing Japanese Cinema: Authorship, Genre, History,* Bloomington and Indianapolis, Indiana, 1992.

On OSHIMA: articles—

Cameron, Ian, "Nagisa Oshima," in *Movie* (London), Winter 1969/70.

"Director of the Year," in *International Film Guide 1971,* London, 1970.

"La Cérémonie," special issue of *Avant-Scène du Cinéma* (Paris), May 1973.

McCormick, R., "Ritual, the Family and the State: A Critique of Nagisa Oshima's *The Ceremony,*" in *Cineaste* (New York), vol. 6, no. 2, 1974.

Dawson, J., "Nagisa Oshima: Forms and Feelings under the Rising Sun," in *Cinema Papers* (Melbourne), September/October 1976.

McCormick, R., "In the Realm of the Senses," in *Cineaste* (New York), Winter 1976/77.

High, P. B., "Oshima: A Vita Sexualis on Film," in *Wide Angle* (Athens, Ohio), vol. 2, no. 4, 1978.

Hughes, J., "Oshima in Paris: Reaching for the Flame," in *Take One* (Montreal), September 1978.

Polan, Dana, "Politics as Process in Three Films by Nagisa Oshima," in *Film Criticism* (Edinboro, Pennsylvania), Fall 1983.

Lehman, P., "The Mysterious Orient, the Crystal Clear Orient," and M. Turim, "Oshima's Tales of Youth and Politics," in *Journal of Film and Video* (Boston), Winter 1987.

"Oshima Issue" of *Wide Angle* (Athens, Ohio), vol. 9, no. 2, 1987.

Bagh, P. von, "Kolme Tuntematonta Misesta," in *Filmihulu* (Helsinki), no. 5, 1989.

Lehman, P., "Oshima," in *Filmihulu* (Helsinki), no. 5, 1989.

Coates, P., "Repetition and Contradiction in the Films of Oshima," in *Quarterly Review of Film and Video,* vol. 11, no. 4, 1990.

Michelson, A., "Oshima's Choice," in *New York Review of Books,* November 19, 1992.

Stren, L., "Roads to Freedom," in *Sight and Sound* (London), February 1993.

* * *

Oshima, the Godard of the East, spent much of the 1980s engaged in international co-productions. He directed *Merry Christmas, Mr. Lawrence* in 1983 for Jeremy Thomas, who was later to produce *The Last Emperor* for Bertolucci, and he combined with Luis Buñuel's old scriptwriter, Jean-Claude Carrière, on *Max, Mon Amour*—an Ionesco-like anatomy of bourgeois mores in which Charlotte Rampling has an affair with an ape.

These European excursions seem a world apart from the early work of the former student activist and leader of the Japanese New Wave of the late 1950s. Back in those days, Oshima was telling cruel stories of youth, using the ingredients of American teenage exploitation movies, namely sex and violence, to make a trenchant critique of postwar Japanese society. Railing against the U.S.-Japan Security Pact, and despairing of the old left communists' ability to make a meaningful intervention as the country experienced its "economic miracle," Oshima mobilized delinquency and nihilism. Unlike the French *nouvelle vague,* who tended merely to aestheticize the exploits of their young petty criminals and misfits—the Antoine Doinels and Jean Paul Belmondos—and who took until 1968 to become obstreperously political, Oshima was engaged from the outset.

He learned his craft as an assistant-director at the Shochiku Studios, where he directed his first features. However, the controversy surrounding his fourth film, *Night and Fog in Japan* (the title was deliberately designed to echo Resnais's "gas chamber" documentary), pushed him toward working as an independent. A despairing indictment of the disunity of the Japanese left—the old left were felt to have betrayed the new—*Night and Fog* is as notable for its formal characteristics as for its topical content. For a start, it contains only 43 shots. (Compare this to his 1966 work, *Violence at Noon,* which is a masterpiece of frenetic cutting, boasting over 2,000 shots in its 90-odd minutes, and you realize that Oshima is a formalist jackdaw, ready to experiment in whatever way he thinks fit.) And it was made in CinemaScope. Oshima, like Godard in *A bout de souffle,* has a penchant for hand-held camera shots. These, though, are rather more jarring when used in 70mm than in 16mm.

Cast out on his own when Shochiku withdrew *Night and Fog* only three days after its release, Oshima remained active in both film and television throughout the 1960s. His first independent movie, *The Catch,* set the tone for much that was to follow. It tells the story of a black American POW, held hostage by a small village. While waiting for the military police to remove their "catch," the villagers make the man a scapegoat for all their own problems, eventually murdering him.

In its concern with racism and brutality, whether institutional or practiced by private individuals, *The Catch* anticipates Oshima's most famous film of the 1960s, and the one that finally brought his work to the attention of the West. Shown out of competition at Cannes, *Death by Hanging* is as gruesome a film about capital punishment as one could ever wish to see. Based, like many of this director's works, on a "true story"—of a young Korean sentenced to death for the brutal murder and rape of a Japanese high school girl—the film operates on several levels, both formally and thematically. Japanese racism toward Koreans—for so long the untouchables of Japanese society—the mindless bureaucracy involved in state licensed murder, and good old adolescent existential angst are amongst its narrative components. As Noel Burch has observed, the film's style is constantly shifting: it starts as drama-documentary, shot in sober black and white, but it later develops into a self-reflexive avant-garde text in which the audience is addressed directly. It uses theatrical masquerade, paying homage to the tradition of Japanese kabuki theatre. Its early "classical realism" is utterly usurped. The Korean fails to die when he is hanged. The officials—wardens, priests, police—must recreate his crime for him because he has lost his memory. In their bid to remind him of his guilt, they actually repeat his murder.

Jean Genet, the French vagabond thief and writer, is Oshima's constant inspiration. With its emphasis on crime, sexuality and role playing, *Death by Hanging* is akin to Genet's *The Balcony.* Oshima borrowed a Genet title for his *Diary of a Shinjuku Thief,* and his rather more whimsical *Three Resurrected Drunkards,* an exemplary modernist text that literally starts again halfway through (at the 1983 Edinburgh Film Festival there was a minor riot from patrons certain that the projectionist was accidentally replaying the opening reel), looks at the question of Korean immigration in terms of costume and identity. (Three Korean immigrants steal the clothes of three drunken Japanese youths. The three Japanese, with nothing to wear and no money, become "honorary" Koreans and are appropriately persecuted.)

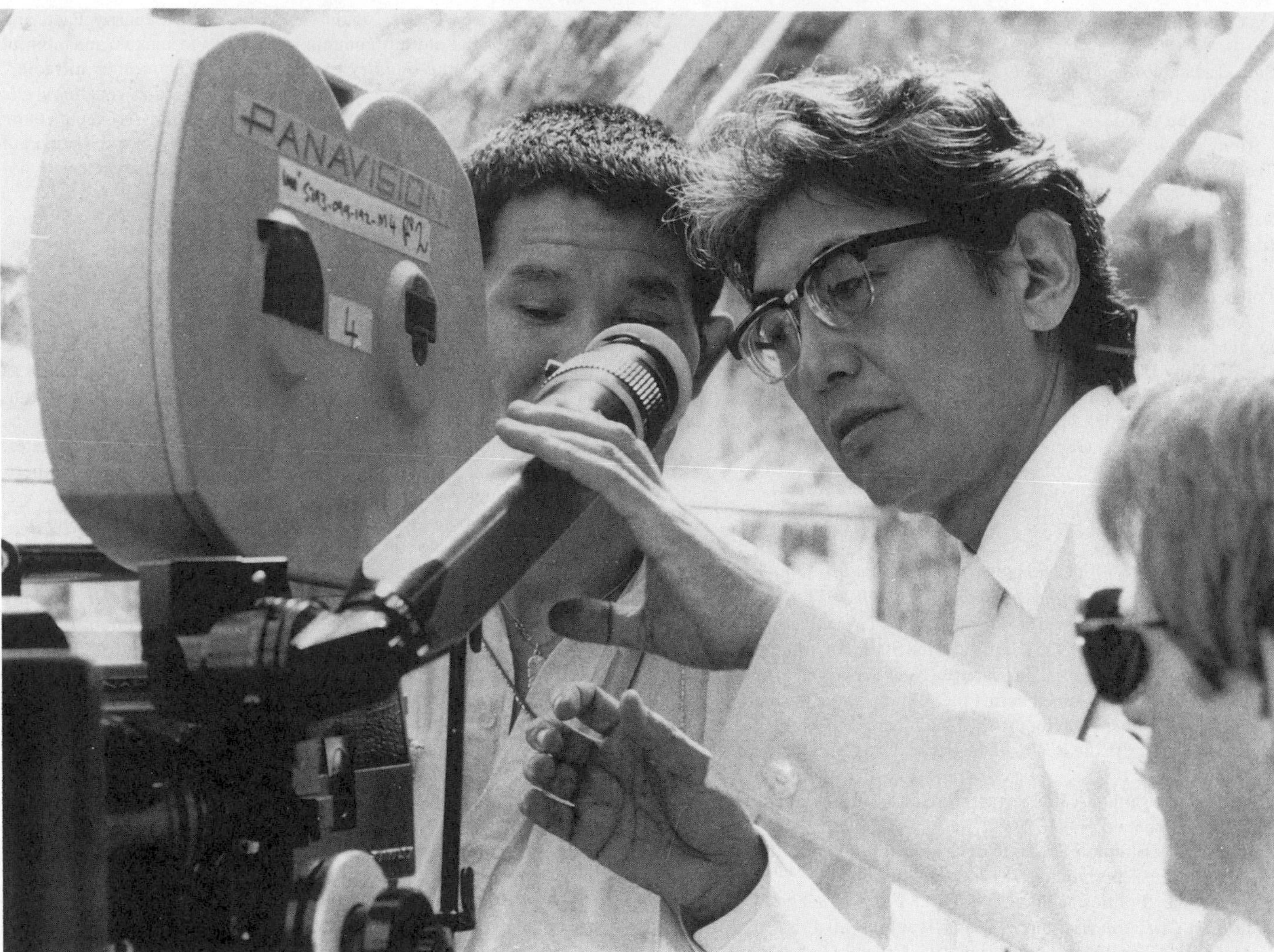

Nagisa Oshima

It is perhaps unfortunate that Oshima's best known film remains *In the Realm of the Senses,* a work customarily shown in late-night double-bills with *Last Tango in Paris* and, like the Brando vehicle, generally esteemed as the perfect marriage between art and pornography. Another "true story," this time of the notorious case of Abe Sada, who strangled and castrated her lover, Kichizo, and was arrested with his genitals in her pocket, it marks Oshima's most intimate meshing of the political with the sexual. Politics constitute the film's structuring absence. It is 1936, the high point of Japanese militarism; the two lovers' retreat into the realm of the senses must always be seen against this historical backcloth. The links between political and sexual repression are obvious, but it seems somewhat glib to view this innately tragic story as being about a straightforward liberation of female sexuality, a sort of "geisha's revenge." A familiar male response to the movie, as to Bataille's novel *The Story of Eye,* is to welcome it as a scathing critique of the male gaze: instead of being a film about a couple making love, it is transmogrified, becoming a film about what it means to be a spectator of a film about a couple making love. And, of course, it sells out every time it shows.

Almost five years after *In the Realm of the Senses* and *Empire of Passions* (1978) came another international co-production, *Merry Christmas, Mr. Lawrence,* in 1983. Pop icons David Bowie and Ryuichi Sakamoto were cast in this film, aptly helping produce what critic Janet Muslin called a "curiously dislocated quality." This highly stylized picture is filled with erotic tensions, though this time ones homoerotic and interracial in the era of war and confrontation. Repressed sexual energy, in the form of the platonic kisses Bowie (a POW) placed upon Sakamoto's (the commander of the camp) cheeks, was released probably more in the viewer's displaced projection than in the digests; Sakamoto's character was relieved of his command while Bowie was brutally executed.

Max, Mon Amour (1986) proved to be ill-received—it took three years for it to be released in Britain—and since then Oshima has been working mainly for television as a talk show host. The once ardent advocate and leader of the Japanese New Wave seems to occupy a different orbit that puzzles his admirers and critics alike.

—G. C. Macnab, updated by Guo-Juin Hong

OZU, Yasujiro

Nationality: Japanese. **Born:** Tokyo, 12 December 1903. **Education:** the Uji-Yamada (now Ise) Middle School, Matsuzaka, graduated 1921. **Career:** Teacher, 1922-23; after introduction from uncle, began as assistant cameraman at Shochiku Motion Picture Co., 1923; assistant director, 1926; directed first film, 1927; military service in China, 1937-39; made propaganda films in Singapore, 1943; interned for six months as British POW, 1945. **Died:** In Kamakura, 12 December 1963.

Films as Director:

1927 *Zange no yaiba* (*The Sword of Penitence*)
1928 *Wakodo no yume* (*The Dreams of Youth*) (+ sc); *Nyobo funshitsu* (*Wife Lost*); *Kabocha* (*Pumpkin*); *Hikkoshi fufu* (*A Couple on the Move*); *Nikutai bi* (*Body Beautiful*) (+ co-sc)
1929 *Takara no yama* (*Treasure Mountain*) (+ story); *Wakaki hi* (*Days of Youth*) (+ co-sc); *Wasei kenka tomodachi* (*Fighting Friends, Japanese Style*); *Daigaku wa deta keredo* (*I Graduated, But ...*); *Kaisha-in seikatsu* (*The Life of an Office Worker*); *Tokkan kozo* (*A Straightforward Boy*) (+ co-story)
1930 *Kekkon-gaku nyumon* (*An Introduction to Marriage*); *Hogaraka ni ayume* (*Walk Cheerfully*); *Rakudai wa shita keredo* (*I Flunked, But ...*) (+ story); *Sono yo no tsuma* (*That Night's Wife*); *Erogami no onryo* (*The Revengeful Spirit of Eros*); *Ashi ni sawatta koun* (*Lost Luck*); *Ojosan* (*Young Miss*)
1931 *Shukujo to hige* (*The Lady and the Beard*); *Bijin aishu* (*Beauty's Sorrows*); *Tokyo no gassho* (*Tokyo Chorus*)
1932 *Haru wa gofujin kara* (*Spring Comes from the Ladies*) (+ story); *Umarete wa mita keredo* (*I Was Born, But ...*) (+ story); *Seishun no yume ima izuko* (*Where Now Are the Dreams of Youth?*); *Mata au hi made* (*Until the Day We Meet Again*)
1933 *Tokyo no onna* (*A Tokyo Woman*) (+ story); *Hijosen no onna* (*Dragnet Girl*) (+ story); *Dekigokoro* (*Passing Fancy*) (+ story)
1934 *Haha o kowazu-ya* (*A Mother Should Be Loved*); *Ukigusa monogatari* (*A Story of Floating Weeds*)
1935 *Hakoiri musume* (*An Innocent Maid*); *Tokyo no yado*
1936 *Daigaku yoi toko* (*College Is a Nice Place*) (+ story); *Hitori musuko* (*The Only Son*) (+ story)
1937 *Shukujo wa nani o wasuretaka* (*What Did the Lady Forget?*) (+ co-story)
1941 *Toda-ke no kyodai* (*The Brothers and Sisters of the Toda Family*) (+ co-sc)
1942 *Chichi ariki* (*There Was a Father*) (+ co-sc)
1947 *Nagaya no shinshi roku* (*The Record of a Tenement Gentleman*) (+ co-sc)
1948 *Kaze no naka no mendori* (*A Hen in the Wind*) (+ co-sc)
1949 ***Banshun*** (*Late Spring*) (+ co-sc with Kogo Noda)
1950 *Munekata shimai* (*The Munekata Sisters*) (+ co-sc with Kogo Noda)
1951 *Bakushu* (*Early Summer*) (+ co-sc with Kogo Noda)
1952 *Ochazuke no aji* (*The Flavor of Green Tea over Rice*) (+ co-sc with Kogo Noda)
1953 ***Tokyo monogatari*** (*Tokyo Story*) (+ co-sc with Kogo Noda)
1956 *Soshun* (*Early Spring*) (+ co-sc with Kogo Noda)
1957 *Tokyo boshoku* (*Twilight in Tokyo*) (+ co-sc with Kogo Noda)
1958 ***Higanbana*** (*Equinox Flower*) (+ co-sc with Kogo Noda)
1959 *Ohayo* (+ co-sc with Kogo Noda); *Ukigusa* (*Floating Weeds*) (+ co-sc with Kogo Noda)
1960 *Akibiyori* (*Late Autumn*) (+ co-sc with Kogo Noda)
1961 *Kohayagawa-ke no aki* (*The End of Summer*) (+ co-sc with Kogo Noda)
1962 ***Samma no aji*** (*An Autumn Afternoon*) (+ co-sc with Kogo Noda)

Publications

On OZU: books—

Anderson, Joseph, and Donald Richie, *The Japanese Film: Art and Industry,* New York, 1960.
Richie, Donald, *Five Pictures of Yasujiro Ozu,* Tokyo, 1962.
Richie, Donald, *Japanese Cinema: Film Style & National Character,* New York, 1971.
Sato, Tadao, *Ozu Yasujiro no Geijutsu* [The Art of Yasujiro Ozu], Tokyo, 1971.
Satomi, Jun, and others, editors, *Ozu Yasujiro—Hito to Shigoto* [Yasujiro Ozu: the Man and His Work], Tokyo, 1972.
Schrader, Paul, *Transcendental Style in Film: Ozu, Bresson, Dreyer,* Berkeley, California, 1972.
Burch, Noël, *Theory of Film Practice,* New York, 1973.
Tessier, Max, "Yasujiro Ozu," in *Anthologie du cinéma,* vol. 7, Paris, 1973.
Richie, Donald, *Ozu,* Berkeley, California, 1974.
Schrader, Leonard, and Haruji Nakamura, editors, *Masters of Japanese Film,* Tokyo, 1975.
Bock, Audie, *Japanese Film Directors,* New York, 1978; revised edition, Tokyo, 1985.
Burch, Noël, *To the Distant Observer,* Berkeley, 1979.
Tessier, Max, editor, *Le Cinéma japonais au présent: 1959-79,* Paris, 1980.
Sato, Tadao, *Currents in Japanese Cinema,* Tokyo, 1982.
Bordwell, David, *Ozu and the Poetics of Cinema,* Princeton, New Jersey, 1988.

On OZU: articles—

"Ozu Issues" of *Kinema Jumpo* (Tokyo), June 1958 and February 1964.
Ryu, Chishu, "Yasujiro Ozu," in *Sight and Sound* (London), Spring 1964.
Iwasaki, Akira, "Ozu," in *Film* (London), Summer 1965.
"Ozu Spectrum," in *Cinema* (Beverly Hills), Summer 1970.
Rosenbaum, Jonathan, "Ozu," in *Film Comment* (New York), Summer 1972.
Zeaman, Marvin, "The Zen Artistry of Yasujiro Ozu: The Serene Poet of Japanese Cinema," in *Film Journal* (New York), Fall/Winter 1972.
Branigan, Edward, "The Space of *Equinox Flower,*" in *Screen* (London), Summer 1976.
Thompson, Kristin, and David Bordwell, "Space and Narrative in the Films of Ozu," in *Screen* (London), Summer 1976.
Thompson, Kristin, "Notes on the Spatial System of Ozu's Early Films," in *Wide Angle* (Athens, Ohio), vol. 1, no. 4, 1977.
Bergala, Alain, "L'Homme qui se lève," in *Cahiers du Cinéma* (Paris), May 1980.
"Le Cinéma toujours recommencé de Yasujiro Ozu," special section, in *Cinéma* (Paris), January 1981.
Bock, Audie, "Ozu Reconsidered," in *Film Criticism* (Edinboro, Pennsylvania), Fall 1983.
Berta, R., "A la recherche du regard," in *Cahiers du Cinéma* (Paris), December 1985.
Geist, Kathe, "Narrative Style in Ozu's Silent Films," in *Film Quarterly* (Berkeley), Winter 1986/87.
Lehman, P., "The Mysterious Orient, the Crystal Clear Orient ...," in *Journal of Film and Video* (Boston), Winter 1987.

* * *

Throughout his career, Yasujiro Ozu worked in the mainstream film industry. Obedient to his role, loyal to his studio (the mighty Shochiku), he often compared himself to the tofu salesman, offering nourishing

Yasujiro Ozu

but supremely ordinary wares. For some critics, his greatness stems from his resulting closeness to the everyday realities of Japanese life. Yet since his death another critical perspective has emerged. This modest conservative has come to be recognized as one of the most formally intriguing filmmakers in the world, a director who extended the genre he worked within and developed a rich and unique cinematic style.

Ozu started his career within a well-established genre system, and he quickly proved himself versatile, handling college comedies, wistful tales of office workers, even gangster films. By 1936, however, he had started to specialize. The "home drama," a Shochiku specialty, focused on the trials and joys of middle-class or working-class life—raising children, finding a job, marrying off sons and daughters, settling marital disputes, making grandparents comfortable. It was this genre in which Ozu created his most famous films and to which he is said to have paid tribute on his deathbed: "After all, Mr. President, the home drama."

Ozu enriched this genre in several ways. He strengthened the pathos of family crisis by suggesting that many of them arose from causes beyond the control of the individual. In the 1930s works, this often led to strong criticism of social forces like industrialization, bureaucratization, and Japanese "paternalistic" capitalism. In later films, causes of domestic strife tended to be assigned to a mystical supernature. This "metaphysical" slant ennobled the characters' tribulations by placing even the most trivial action in a grand scheme. The melancholy resignation that is so pronounced in *Tokyo Story* and *An Autumn Afternoon* constituted a recognition of a cycle of nature that society can never control.

To some extent, the grandiose implications of this process are qualified by a homely virtue: comedy. Few Ozu films wholly lack humor, and many involve outrageous sight gags. As a genre, the home drama invited a light touch, but Ozu proved able to extend it into fresh regions. There is often an unabashed vulgarity, running to jokes about eating, bodily functions, and sex. Even the generally sombre *Autumn Afternoon* can spare time for a gag about an elderly man run ragged by the sexual demands of a young wife. *Ohayo* is based upon equating talk, especially polite vacuities, with farting. Ozu also risked breathtaking shifts in tone: in *Passing Fancy,* after a tearful scene at a boy's sickbed, the father pettishly says that he wishes his son had died. The boy responds that the father was looking forward to a good meal at the funeral.

Ozu developed many narrative tendencies of the home drama. He exploited the family-plus-friends-and-neighbors cast by creating strict parallels among characters. If family A has a son of a certain type, family B will have a daughter of that type, or a son of a different sort. The father may encounter a younger or older man, whom he sees as representing himself at another point in his life. The extended-family format allowed Ozu to create dizzying permutations of comparisons. The sense is again of a vast cycle of life in which an individual occupies many positions at different times.

Ozu had one of the most distinctive visual styles in the cinema. Although critics have commonly attributed this to the influence of other directors or to traditions of Japanese art, these are insufficient to account for the rigor and precision of Ozu's technique. No other Japanese director exhibits Ozu's particular style, and the connections to Japanese aesthetics are general and often tenuous. (Ozu once remarked: "Whenever Westerners don't understand something, they simply think it's Zen.") There is, however, substantial evidence that Ozu built his unique style out of deliberate imitation of and action against Western cinema (especially the work of Chaplin and Lubitsch).

Ozu limited his use of certain technical variables, such as camera movement and variety of camera position. This can seem a willful asceticism, but it is perhaps best considered a ground-clearing that let him concentrate on exploring minute stylistic possibilities. For instance, it is commonly claimed that every Ozu shot places the camera about three feet off the ground, but this is false. What Ozu keeps constant is the perceived *ratio* of camera height to the subject. This permits a narrow but nuanced range of camera positions, making every subject occupy the same sector of each shot. Similarly, most of Ozu's films employ camera movements, but these are also systematized to a rare degree. Far from being an ascetic director, Ozu was quite virtuosic, but within self-imposed limits. His style revealed vast possibilities within a narrow compass.

Ozu's compositions relied on the fixed camera-subject relation, adopting angles that stand at multiples of 45 degrees. He employed sharp perspectival depth; the view down a corridor or street is common. Ozu enjoyed playing with the positions of objects within the frame, often rearranging props from shot to shot for the sake of minute shifts. In the color films, a shot will be enhanced by a fleck of bright and deep color, often red; this accent will migrate around the film, returning as an abstract motif in scene after scene.

Ozu's use of editing is no less idiosyncratic. In opposition to the 180-degree space of Hollywood cinema, Ozu employed a 360-degree approach to filming a scene. This "circular" shooting space yields a series of what Western cinema would consider incorrect matches of action and eyelines. While such devices crop up in the work of other Japanese filmmakers, only Ozu used them so rigorously—to undermine our understanding of the total space, to liken characters, and to create abstract graphic patterns. Ozu's shots of objects or empty locales extend the concept of the Western "cutaway": he will use them not for narrative information but for symbolic purposes or for temporal prolongation. Since Ozu early abjured the use of fades and dissolves, cutaways often stand in for such punctuations. And because of the unusually precise compositions and cutting, Ozu was able to create a sheerly graphic play with the screen surface, "matching" contours and regions of one shot with those of the next.

Ozu's work remains significant not only for its extraordinary richness and emotional power, but also because it suggests the extent to which a filmmaker working in popular mass-production filmmaking can cultivate a highly individual approach to film form and style.

—David Bordwell

PABST, G.W.

Nationality: Austrian. **Born:** Georg Wilhelm Pabst in Raudnitz, Bohemia, 27 August 1885. **Education:** Educated in engineering at technical school, Vienna, and at Academy of Decorative Arts, Vienna, 1904-06. **Military Service:** Interned as prisoner of war, Brest, 1914-18. **Family:** Married Gertrude (Pabst), one son. **Career:** Actor, from 1906; travelled to United States with German language troupe, 1910; returned to Europe, prisoner of war, 1914-18; directed season of expressionist theatre in Prague, 1919; artistic director Neuen Wiener Bühne also joined Carl Froelich's film production company, 1920; directed first film, 1923; formed Volksverband für Filmkunst (Popular Association for Film Art) with Heinrich Mann, Erwin Piscator, and Karl Freund, 1928; studied sound film techniques in London, 1929; moved to Hollywood, 1933, returned to France, 1935; planned to emigrate to United States on outbreak of war, but illness forced him to remain in Austria; formed Pabst-Kiba Filmproduktion in Vienna, 1949; worked in Italy, 1950-53. **Awards:** Légion d'honneur, 1931; Best Director, Venice Festival, for *Der Prozess,* 1948. **Died:** In Vienna, 29 May 1967.

Films as Director:

1923 *Der Schatz* (*The Treasure*) (+ co-sc)
1924 *Gräfin Donelli* (*Countess Donelli*)
1925 *Die freudlose Gasse* (*The Joyless Street*); *Geheimnesse einer Seele* (*Secrets of a Soul*)
1926 *Man spielt nicht mit der Liebe* (*One Does Not Play with Love*)
1927 *Die Liebe der Jeanne Ney* (*The Love of Jeanne Ney*)
1928 *Abwege* (*Begierde*) [Crisis (Desire)]; ***Die Büchse der Pandora*** (*Pandora's Box*)
1929 *Die weisse Hölle vom Pitz-Palu* (*The White Hell of Pitz-Palu*) (co-d); ***Das Tagebuch einer Verlorenen*** (*Diary of a Lost Girl*) (+ pr)
1930 *Westfront 1918*; *Skandal um Eva* (*Scandalous Eva*)
1931 ***Die Dreigroschenoper*** (*The Threepenny Opera*); ***Kameradschaft*** (*Comradeship*)
1932 *L'Atlantide* (*Die Herrin von Atlantis*)
1933 *Don Quichotte*; *Du haut en bas* (*High and Low*)
1934 *A Modern Hero*
1936 *Mademoiselle Docteur* (*Salonique, nid d'espions*)
1938 *Le Drame de Shanghai*
1939 *Jeunes Filles en détresse*
1941 *Komödianten* (+ co-sc)
1943 *Paracelsus* (+ co-sc)
1944 *Der Fall Molander* (unfinished and believed destroyed)
1947 *Der Prozess* (*The Trial*)
1949 *Geheimnisvolle Tiefen* (+ pr)
1952 *La Voce del silenzio*
1953 *Cose da pazzi*
1954 *Das Bekenntnis der Ina Kahr*
1955 *Der Letzte Akt* (*The Last Ten Days*; *Ten Days to Die*); *Es geschah am 20 Juli* (*Jackboot Mutiny*)
1956 *Rosen für Bettina*; *Durch die Walder, durch die Auen*

Other Films:

1921 *Im Banne der Kralle* (Frohlich) (role)

Publications

By PABST: book—

Classic Film Scripts: Pandora's Box (Lulu), translated by Christopher Holme, New York, 1971.

By PABST: articles—

"Censor the Censor!," an interview with Beatrix Moore, in *Sight and Sound* (London), Winter 1938/39.
"Le Réalisme est un passage," in *Revue du Cinéma* (Paris), October 1948.
"Über zwei meiner Filme," in *Filmkunst* (Vienna), 1960.
"*The Threepenny Opera,*" edited by Roger Manvell, in *Masterpieces of the German Cinema,* New York, 1973.

On PABST: books—

Kracauer, Siegfried, *From Caligari to Hitler,* Princeton, New Jersey, 1947.
Joseph, Rudolph, editor, *Der Regisseur: G.W. Pabst,* Munich, 1963.
Buache, Freddy, *G.W. Pabst,* Premier Plan No. 39, Lyons, 1965.
Amengual, Barthélémy, *Georg Wilhelm Pabst,* Paris, 1966.
Aubry, Yves, and Jacques Pétat, "G.W. Pabst," in *Anthologie du Cinéma,* vol. 4, Paris, 1968.
Eisner, Lotte, *The Haunted Screen,* Berkeley, 1969.
Hull, David, *Film in the Third Reich,* Berkeley, 1969.
Atwell, Lee, *G.W. Pabst,* Boston, 1977.
Brooks, Louise, *Lulu in Hollywood,* New York, 1981.

On PABST: articles—

Bryher, "G.W. Pabst: A Survey," in *Close Up* (London), December 1927.
Moore, John, "Pabst, Dovjenko: A Comparison," in *Close Up* (London), September 1932.
Potamkin, Harry, "Pabst and the Social Film," in *Hound & Horn* (New York), January-March 1933.
Rotha, Paul, "Pabst, Pudovkin and the Producers," in *Sight and Sound* (London), Summer 1933.
Bachmann, Gideon, editor, "Six Talks on G.W. Pabst," in *Cinemages* (New York), no. 3, 1955.
"Pabst Issue" of *Filmkunst* (Vienna), no. 18, 1955.
Card, James, "The Intense Isolation of Louise Brooks," in *Sight and Sound* (London), Summer 1958.
Stanbrook, Alan, "Brecht et le cinéma," in *Cahiers du Cinéma* (Paris), December 1960.
Luft, Herbert, "G.W. Pabst," in *Films in Review* (New York), February 1964.

G.W. Pabst directing *La Voce del silenzio*

Brooks, Louise, "Pabst and Lulu," in *Sight and Sound* (London), Summer 1965.

Rotha, Paul, "Thoughts on Pabst," in *Films and Filming* (London), February 1967.

Eisner, Lotte, "Meeting with Pabst," in *Sight and Sound* (London), Autumn 1967.

Stuart, John, "Working with Pabst," in *Silent Picture* (London), Autumn 1970.

"*Loulou* Issue" of *Avant-Scène du Cinéma* (Paris), 1 December 1980.

Petat, J., "Pabst, aujourd'hui?—une réévaluation nécessaire," in *Cinéma* (Paris), April 1981.

Elsaesser, Thomas, "Lulu and the Meter Man," in *Screen* (London), July/October 1983.

Horak, J.C., "G.W. Pabst in Hollywood, or Every Modern Hero Deserves a Mother," in *Film History* (Philadelphia), vol. 1, no. 1, 1987.

* * *

Bryher, writing in *Close Up* in 1927, noted that "it is the thought and feeling that line gesture that interest Mr. Pabst. And he has what few have, a consciousness of Europe. He sees psychologically and because of this, because in a flash he knows the sub-conscious impulse or hunger that prompted an apparently trivial action, his intense realism becomes, through its truth, poetry."

Pabst was enmeshed in the happenings of his time, which ultimately engulfed him. He is the chronicler of the churning maelstrom of social dreams and living neuroses, and it is this perception of his time which raises him above many of his contemporary filmmakers.

Like other German directors, Pabst drifted to the cinema through acting and scripting. His first film, *Der Schatz,* dealt with a search for hidden treasure and the passions it aroused. Expressionist in feeling and design, it echoed the current trend in German films, but in *Die freudlose Gasse* he brought clinical observation to the tragedy of his hungry postwar Europe. For Pabst the cinema and life grew closer together. In directing the young Greta Garbo and the more experienced Asta Nielsen, Pabst was beginning his gallery of portraits of women, to whom he would add Brigitte Helm, Louise Brooks, and Henny Porten.

Geheimnisse einer Seele carried Pabst's interest in the subconscious further, dealing with a Freudian subject of the dream and using all the potential virtues of the camera to illuminate the problems of his central character, played by Werner Krauss. *Die Liebe der Jeanne Ney,* based on a melodramatic story by Ilya Ehrenburg, reflected the upheavals and revolutionary ideas of the day. It also incorporated a love story that ranged from the Crimea to Paris. Through his sensitive awareness of character and environment Pabst raised the film to great heights of cinema. His individual style of linking image to create a smoothly flowing pattern induced a rhythm which carried the spectator into the very heart of the matter.

Two Pabst films have a special significance. *Die Büchse der Pandora* and *Das Tagebuch einer Verlorenen* featured the American actress Louise Brooks, in whom Pabst found an ideal interpreter for his analysis of feminine sensuality.

Between the high spots of Pabst's career there were such films as *Grafin Donelli,* which brought more credit to its star, Henny Porten, than to Pabst. *Man spielt nicht mit der Liebe* featured Krauss and Lily Damita in a youth and age romance. *Abwege*, a more congenial picture that took as its subject a sexually frustrated woman, gave Pabst the opportunity to direct the beautiful and intelligent Brigitte Helm. His collaboration with Dr. Arnold Fanck on *Die weisse Hölle vom Pitz-Palu* resulted in the best of the mountain films, aided by Leni Riefenstahl and a team of virtuoso cameramen, Angst, Schneeberger, and Allgeier.

The coming of sound was a challenge met by Pabst. Not only did he enlarge the scope of filmmaking techniques, but he extended the range of his social commitments in his choice of subject matter. Hans Casparius, his distinguished stills cameraman and friend, has stressed the wonderful teamwork involved in a Pabst film. There were no divisions of labor; all were totally involved. *Westfront 1918, Die Dreigroschenoper*, and *Kameradschaft* were made in this manner when Pabst began to make sound films. Vajda the writer, cameraman Fritz Arno Wagner (who had filmed *Jeanne Ney*) and Ernö Metzner, another old colleague, worked out the mise-en-scène with Pabst, assuring the smooth, fluid process of cinema. With Pabst the cinema was still a wonder of movement and penetrating observation. The technical devices used to ensure this have been described by the designer Metzner.

Westfront 1918 was an uncompromising anti-war film which made *All Quiet on the Western Front* look contrived and artificial. Brecht's *Die Dreigroschenoper*, modified by Pabst, is still a stinging satire on the pretensions of capitalist society. *Kameradschaft*, a moving plea for international cooperation, shatters the boundaries that tend to isolate people. All these films were studio-made and technically stupendous, but the heart and human warmth of these features were given by G.W. Pabst.

When Germany was in the grip of growing Nazi domination, Pabst looked elsewhere to escape from that country, of which he had once been so much a part.

L'Atlantide was based on the Pierre Benoit novel of adventure in the Sahara. The former success of Jacques Feyder, Pabst's work featured Brigitte Helm as the mysterious Antinea. *Don Quixote* with Chaliapin did not fulfil its promise. *A Modern Hero*, made in Hollywood for Warner Brothers, had little of Pabst in it. On his return to France he handled with some competence *Mademoiselle Docteur, Le Drame de Shanghai*, and *Jeunes Filles en détresse*.

In 1941 circumstances compelled him to return to his estate in Austria. He was trapped, and if he was to make films, it had to be for the Nazi regime. *Komödianten* was a story of a troupe of players who succeed in establishing the first National Theatre at Weimar. Its leading player was Pabst's old friend Henny Porten, who gave an excellent performance. The film won an award at the then Fascist-controlled Venice Biennale. *Paracelsus*, again an historical film, showed Pabst had lost none of his power. For his somewhat reluctant collaboration with the Nazis, Pabst has been savagely attacked, but it is hard to believe that any sympathy could have ever existed from the man who made *Kameradschaft* for the narrow chauvinists who ruled his country.

After the war Pabst made *Der Prozess*, dealing with Jewish pogroms in nineteenth-century Hungary. It was a fine film. After some work in Italy he made *Der letze Akt*, about the last days of Hitler, and *Es geschah am 20 Juli*, about the generals' plot against Hitler. Both were films of distinction.

Pabst died in Vienna in 1967, having been a chronic invalid for the last ten years of his life. As Jean Renoir said of him in 1963: "He knows how to create a strange world, whose elements are borrowed from daily life. Beyond this precious gift, he knows how, better than anyone else, to direct actors. His characters emerge like his own children, created from fragments of his own heart and mind."

—Liam O'Leary

PAGNOL, Marcel

Nationality: French. **Born:** Aubagne, near Marseilles, 25 (or 28) February 1895. **Education:** Lycée Thiers, Marseilles; University of Montpellier, degree in letters. **Military Service:** Served with French Infantry, 1914-17, and in 1940. **Family:** Married Jacqueline Bouvier, 1945, two sons. **Career:** Founded literary magazine *Fortunio*, 1911; teacher of English, from 1912; appointed professor at Lycée Condorcet, Paris, 1922; resigned teaching position after success of play *Marius*, 1929; created film company and founded magazine *Les Cahiers du film*, 1931; opened studio at Marseilles, 1933; directed first film, 1934; President of Society of French Dramatic Authors and Composers, 1944-46. **Awards:** Member, Academie française, 1947. Officer of the Légion d'honneur. **Died:** 18 April 1974.

Films as Director:

1934 *Le Gendre de Monsieur Poirier* (+ pr, sc); *Jofroi* (+ pr, sc); *L'Article 330* (+ pr, sc); *Angèle* (+ pr, sc)
1935 *Merlusse* (+ pr, sc); *Cigalon* (+ pr, sc)
1936 *Topaze* (second version) (+ pr, sc); ***César*** (+ pr, sc)
1937 *Regain* (+ pr, sc)
1938 *Le Schpountz* (+ pr, sc); ***La Femme du boulanger*** (+ pr, sc)
1940 *La Fille du puisatier* (+ pr, sc)
1945 *Naïs* (+ pr, sc)
1948 *La Belle Meunière* (+ pr, sc)
1951 *Topaze* (third version) (+ pr, sc)
1952 *Manon des sources* (+ pr, sc)
1954 *Les Lettres de mon moulin* (+ pr, sc)
1967 *Le Curé de Cucugnan* (for television) (+ pr, sc)

Other Films:

1931 ***Marius*** (Korda) (sc)
1932 ***Fanny*** (Allégret) (co-pr, sc)
1933 *Topaze* (Gasnier) (original play) (sc); *Un Direct au coeur* (Lion) (co-author of original play, sc); *L'Agonie des aigles* (Richebé) (co-pr, sc)
1934 *Tartarin de Tarascon* (Bernand) (sc)
1939 *Monsieur Brotonneau* (Esway) (pr, sc)
1950 *Le Rosier de Madame Husson* (Boyer) (sc)
1953 *Carnaval* (Verneuil) (pr, sc)
1962 *La Dame aux camélias* (Gir) (sc)
1986 *Jean de Florette* (Berri) (original story); *Manon des sources* (Berri) (original story)

Publications

(related to cinema)

By PAGNOL: books—

Les Sermons de Pagnol, edited by Robert Morel, Paris, 1968.
Confidences, Paris, 1981.
Inédits, edited by J. and F. Pagnol, Paris, 1986.

By PAGNOL: articles—

"Je n'ai pas changé de métier," an interview with Michel Gorel, in *Cinémonde* (Paris), 17 August 1933.

Marcel Pagnol

"Cinématurgie de Paris," in *Les Cahiers du Film* (Paris), 16 December 1933, 15 January 1934, and 1 March 1934; collected in *Cahiers du Cinéma* (Paris), no. 173.

"Il n'y a rien de plus bête que la technique," an interview with Maurice Bessy, in *Cinémonde* (Paris), 6 October 1938.

"Mon ami Rene Clair," in *Cinémonde* (Paris), 23 April 1946.

"Adieu à Raimu," in *L'Ecran Française* (Paris), 3 October 1951.

Interview with J.A. Fieschi and others, in *Cahiers du Cinéma* (Paris), December 1965.

Interview with Claude Beylie and Guy Braucourt, in *Cinéma* (Paris), March 1969.

On PAGNOL: books—

Clair, René, *Cinéma d'hier, cinéma d'aujourd'hui,* Paris, 1970.

Domeyne, P., *Marcel Pagnol,* Paris, 1971.

Beylie, Claude, *Marcel Pagnol,* Paris, 1972.

Castans, Raymond, *Marcel Pagnol m'a raconté ...,* Paris, 1975.

Leprohon, Pierre, *Marcel Pagnol,* Paris, 1976.

Castans, Raymond, and André Bernard, *Les films du Marcel Pagnol,* Paris, 1982.

Beylie, Claude, *Marcel Pagnol: ou, Le cinéma en liberté,* Paris, 1986.

Pompa, Dany, *Marcel Pagnol,* Paris, 1986.

Beylie, Claude, *Les années Pagnol,* Paris, 1989.

On PAGNOL: articles—

Fernandel, "Mon ami Marcel Pagnol," in *Ciné-France* (Paris), 19 November 1937.

Alpert, Hollis, "Homage à Pagnol," in *Saturday Review* (New York), 24 December 1955.

Bazin, André, "Le Cas Pagnol," in *Qu'est-ce que le cinéma?* (same author), Paris, 1959.

"Spécial Guitry-Pagnol" issue of *Cahiers du Cinéma* (Paris), 1 December 1965.

Polt, Harriet, "The Marcel Pagnol Trilogy," in *Film Society Review* (New York), October 1967.

Delahaye, Michel, "La Saga Pagnol," in *Cahiers du Cinéma* (Paris), June 1969.

Ford, Charles, "Marcel Pagnol," in *Films in Review* (New York), April 1970.

"Pagnol Issue" of *Avant-Scène du Cinéma* (Paris), July/September 1970.

Gauteur, C., "Marcel Pagnol inconnu?," in *Image et Son* (Paris), September 1973.

Gévaudan, F., "Marcel Pagnol: Un Cinéaste mineur?," in *Cinéma* (Paris), June 1974.

Beylie, Claude, "Le Rire qui vient du coeur," in *Télérama* (Paris), 28 January 1976.

Turk, E.B., "Pagnol's Marseilles Trilogy," in *American Film* (Washington, D.C.), October 1980.

Bergan, Ronald, "Marcel Pagnol," in *Films and Filming* (London), November 1984.

* * *

"The art of the theatre is reborn under another form and will realize unprecedented prosperity. A new field is open to the dramatist enabling him to produce works that neither Sophocles, Racine, nor Molière had the means to attempt." With these words, Marcel Pagnol greeted the advent of synchronous sound to the motion picture, and announced his conversion to the new medium. The words also served to launch a debate, carried on for the most part with René Clair, in which Pagnol argued for the primacy of text over image in what he saw as the onset of a new age of filmed theater.

At the time Pagnol reigned supreme in the Parisian theater world. His plays, *Topaze* and *Marius,* both opened in the 1928-29 season to the unanimous acclaim of the critics and the public. Their success vindicated the theories of a group of playwrights which had gathered around Paul Nivoix, the drama critic for *Comoedia.* They were determined to develop an alternative to the predictable theater of the boulevards and the impenetrable experiments of the surrealist avant-garde. The group pursued a dramatic ideal based on the well-made, naturalistic plays of Scribe and Dumas *fils.* The formula featured crisp dialogue, tight structures, and devastating irony. Its renewed popular appeal did not escape the notice of Bob Kane, the executive producer of the European branch of Paramount Pictures. Kane secured the rights for the screen versions of two plays, retaining Pagnol as writer for *Marius,* to be directed by Alexander Korda, but he then excluded him from any participation in the *Topaze* project. This neglect spurred the volatile young ex-schoolmaster from Provence to undertake his own productions.

With Pierre Braunberger and Roger Richebe, Pagnol produced and adapted his play *Fanny,* a sequel to *Marius,* and hired Marc Allégret to direct. Then, in 1933, he formed his own production company, modelled on United Artists, which would control the production and distribution of all his future projects. At the same time he founded *Les Cahiers du film,* dedicated to the propagation of "cinematurgie," Pagnol's theories of filmed theater.

Jofroi and *Angèle,* the first two projects over which Pagnol exercised complete artistic control, established the tone for much of his ensuing career. Adapted from stories by Jean Giono and set in Provence in the countryside surrounding Marseilles, where Pagnol was born and raised, the films treat the manners and lifestyle of the simple farmers and shopkeepers of the south and are executed with the precise principles of dramatic structure Pagnol had developed in his years with Nivoix. *Angèle* is especially notable because it was shot on location on a farm near Aubagne. The film established a precedent followed by Jean Renoir in making *Toni,* a film produced and distributed by Pagnol's company, regarded by many as a forerunner of Italian neorealism. This is the formula to which Pagnol would return with increasing success in *Regain* and *Le Femme du boulanger*: a story or novel by Giono honed by Pagnol into a taut drama, elaborating the myths and folkways of "le coeur meridonale" and pivoting on the redemptive power of woman; set on location in Provence; and peopled with the excellent repertory company Pagnol had assembled from the Marseille music halls (including Raimu, Fernandel, Fernand Charpin, Orane Dumazis, and Josette Day).

Even after a formal break with Giono in an ugly squabble over money in 1937, Pagnol continued to exploit the formula in *La Fille du puisatier* and his masterpiece, *Manon des sources.* Running three hours and more, these films, even more than before, reflected how the pace and flavor of the south colored Pagnol's approach to filmmaking. As Fernandel has put it: "With Marcel Pagnol, making a film is first of all going to Marseille, then eating some bouillabaisse with a friend, talking about the rain or the beautiful weather, and finally if there is a spare moment, shooting...." Along with Clair and Cocteau, Pagnol was inducted into the Academie Française. Every year his status grows among historians of cinema who once ridiculed his "canned theater."

—Dennis Nastav

PAKULA, Alan J.

Nationality: American. **Born:** The Bronx, New York, 7 April 1928. **Education:** Attended Bronx High School of Science; studied drama, Yale University, degree 1948. **Family:** Married 1) actress Hope Lange (divorced 1969); 2) Hannah Cohn Boorstin, 1973, five stepchildren.

Career: Assistant, cartoon department, Warner Bros., also stage director at Circle Theatre, Los Angeles, 1948; apprentice to producer-director Don Hartman at MGM, then at Paramount, from 1950; as producer, founded Pakula-Mulligan Productions with director Robert Mulligan, 1962 (active through 1969). **Awards:** Best Director, London Film Critics, 1971, for *Klute;* Best Direction, New York Film Critics, 1976, for *All the President's Men;* Eastman Award for Continued Excellence in Filmmaking, 1981. **Address:** Pakula Productions, Inc., 330 W. 58th Street, New York, NY 10019, U.S.A.

Films as Director:

1969 *The Sterile Cuckoo*
1971 ***Klute*** (+ co-pr)
1972 *Love and Pain and the Whole Damn Thing* (+ pr)
1974 *The Parallax View* (+ pr)
1976 *All the President's Men*
1978 *Comes a Horseman*
1979 *Starting Over* (+ co-pr)
1981 *Rollover*
1982 *Sophie's Choice* (+ sc, co-pr)
1986 *Dream Lover* (+ co-pr)
1987 *Orphans* (+ pr)
1989 *See You in the Morning* (+ sc, pr)
1990 *Presumed Innocent* (+ co-sc)
1992 *Consenting Adults* (+ pr)
1993 *The Pelican Brief* (+ sc, pr)

Other Films:

1957 *Fear Strikes Out* (Mulligan) (pr); *To Kill a Mockingbird* (Mulligan) (pr)
1963 *Love with a Proper Stranger* (Mulligan) (pr)
1965 *Baby the Rain Must Fall* (Mulligan) (pr)
1966 *Inside Daisy Clover* (Mulligan) (pr)
1967 *Up the Down Staircase* (Mulligan) (pr)
1968 *The Stalking Moon* (Mulligan) (pr)

Publications

By PAKULA: articles—

Interview with Tom Milne, in *Sight and Sound* (London), Spring 1972.
Interviews with Michel Ciment, in *Positif* (Paris), March 1972 and October 1976.
Interview with A. C. Bobrow, in *Filmmakers Newsletter* (Ward Hill, Massachusetts), September 1974.
"Making a Film about Two Reporters," in *American Cinematographer* (Los Angeles), July 1976.
"Dialogue on Film: Alan J. Pakula," in *American Film* (Washington, D.C.), December/January 1978/79 and November 1985.
"A Walk with Good and Evil," an interview with A. M. Bahiana, in *Cinema Papers,* December 1990.
"Alan J. Pakula: Mester i seksuell besettelse," an interview with F. Johnsen, in *Film and Kino,* no. 7, 1990.

On PAKULA: articles—

Jameson, R. T., "The Pakula Parallax," in *Film Comment* (New York), September/October 1976.
Carcassonne, P., "Dossier: Hollywood 79: Alan J. Pakula," in *Cinématographe* (Paris), March 1979.
Sinyard, Neil, "Pakula's Choice: Some Thoughts on Alan J. Pakula," in *Cinema Papers* (Melbourne), July 1984.
Seidenberg, R., "*Presumed Innocent,*" in *American Film,* August 1990.
Downey, S. D., and K. Rasmussen, "The Irony of *Sophie's Choice,*" in *Women's Studies in Communication,* vol. 14, no. 2, 1991.

* * *

Now considered by many a major cinematic stylist, Alan J. Pakula began his career as a producer. The quality of his films is rather uneven, ranging from the acclaimed *Fear Strikes Out* and *To Kill a Mockingbird* to the universally panned *Inside Daisy Clover.* Critic Guy Flatley noted that Pakula is affectionately acknowledged within the film industry as an "actor's director," eliciting "richly textured performances" from Liza Minnelli in *The Sterile Cuckoo*; Maggie Smith in *Love and Pain and the Whole Damn Thing*; Warren Beatty in *The Parallax View*; Robert Redford, Dustin Hoffman, and Jason Robards, Jr. in *All the President's Men*; Jane Fonda, James Caan, and Robards in *Comes a Horseman*; and Burt Reynolds, Candice Bergen, and Jill Clayburgh in *Starting Over.* Many filmgoers are surprised upon discovering that it was Pakula who directed all these films.

Pakula's self-effacement is deliberate. In the Oscar-winning *Sophie's Choice* (for Meryl Streep as best actress), the director's name is less known than the actors who worked so effectively under his direction, and far less known than the tragic personal, social, and historical themes of the film. Pakula stresses the psychological dimension of his films. *Klute,* one of his most celebrated efforts, is highlighted by his use of taped conversation to both reveal character and heighten suspense. The film is noted for "visual claustrophobia" and unusual, effective mise-en-scène. For her performance, Jane Fonda received an Academy Award.

Klute was Pakula's first "commercial and critical gold." As one critic writes, "the attention to fine, authentic detail in *Klute* reflected the careful research done by both the director and the actress in the Manhattan demimonde, and many of the shadings of the complex character of the prostitute were developed improvisationally during the filming by ... Fonda in collaboration with Pakula." Critical response to *Klute* is represented by such writers as Robin Wood, who said, "If it is too soon to be sure of Pakula's precise identity as an auteur, it remains true that *Klute* belongs, like any other great movie, to its director." Characteristically, Pakula believes that "the auteur theory is half-truth because filmmaking is very collaborative." Pakula's other films have had equal success: *All the President's Men,* for example, was the top-grossing film of 1976, and won four Academy Awards. It was nominated for best picture and best director, as well. Even the critic known as "Pakula's relentless nemesis," Stanley Kauffmann, "relented a little" concerning *All the President's Men.*

Alan J. Pakula is a filmmaker whose work most notably features tautness in both narrative and performance; he is a director of "moods," and is often "congratulated for the moods he sustains." He has described his approach to filmmaking as follows: "I am oblique. I think it has to do with my own nature. I like trying to do things which work on many levels, because I think it is terribly important to give an audience a lot of things they may not get as well as those they will, so that finally the film does take on a texture and is not just simplistic communication."

Although he has remained active in recent years, Pakula has not produced—with one exception—work of real significance since *Sophie's Choice* (itself more of an actors' than director's film). *See You in the Morning* attempts to recycle the melodramatic poignancy of *Klute* and *The Sterile Cuckoo,* but does not rediscover the stylistic finesse that made these earlier films so successful. *See You in the Morning*'s examination of family and personal breakdown is heavy-handed and hence strangely unaffecting.

The Pelican Brief, based on John Grisham's amateurish novel about the corrupt Washington establishment, makes no good sense, but is

Alan J. Pakula

also strangely unexciting and unsuspenseful. Unlike Hitchcock, Pakula here proves unable to forge a masterful thriller from a marginal literary source; *The Pelican Brief,* it must be said, also fails to create the paranoid atmosphere that is the hallmark of Pakula's earlier, more successful forays into the political thriller (*The Parallax View* is the best of these). *Consenting Adults* is a domestic thriller centering on an unfaithful suburban husband who falls victim to a psychopath eager to perpetrate insurance fraud and steal his wife. The first part of this film offers a chilling version of contemporary upscale suburban life; but the film's second half descends into sub-Hitchcockian third-rate twists and turns that fail to engage or excite.

Only in *Presumed Innocent* does Pakula recapture some of his earlier success. Despite numerous plot inconsistencies (the legacy of Scott Turow's novel), *Presumed Innocent* is compelling viewing because Pakula takes pains to fashion a detailed setting (heightened by fine character performances); he also astutely directs Harrison Ford in the lead role.

—Deborah H. Holdstein, updated by R. Barton Palmer

PARADZHANOV, Sergei

Nationality: Soviet Georgian. **Born:** Tiflis (Tbilisi), Soviet Georgia, 1924. Transliterations of name include "Paradjanov" and "Parajanov." **Education:** Kiev Conservatory of Music, 1942-45; studied under Igor Savchenko at Moscow Film Institute (V.G.I.K.), graduated 1951. **Family:** Married Svetlana (Paradzhanova), early 1950s (divorced after 2 years), one son. **Career:** Began as director at Kiev Dovzhenko Studio, 1953; following international success of *Shadows of Our Forgotten Ancestors,* ten filmscripts rejected by authorities through 1974; indicted for a variety of crimes, convicted of trafficking in art objects, sentenced to six years hard labor, 1974; released after international and Russian protests to Supreme Soviet, 1978. **Awards:** British Film Academy Award for *Shadows of Our Forgotten Ancestors,* 1966. **Died:** In Yerevan, of cancer, 20 July 1990.

Films as Director and Scriptwriter:

1951 *Moldavskaia skazka* (*Moldavian Fairy Tale*) (short)
1954 *Andriesh* (co-d)
1958 *Pervyi paren* (*The First Lad*)
1961 *Ukrainskaia rapsodiia* (*Ukrainian Rhapsody*)
1963 *Tsvetok no kamne* (*Flower on the Stone*)
1964 *Dumka* (*The Ballad*)
1965 ***Teni zabytykh predkov*** (*Shadows of Our Forgotten Ancestors*) (co-sc)
1969 *Sayat nova* (*The Color of Pomegranates*; *The Blood of the Pomegranates*) (released 1972)
1978 *Achraroumès* (*Retour à la vie*)
1985 *Legenda o Suramskoj kreposti* (*The Legend of the Suram Fortress*)

1986 *Arabeski na temu Pirosmani* (doc)
1988 *Ashik kerib*

Publications

By PARADZHANOV: articles—

"Perpetual Motion," and "*Shadows of Our Forgotten Ancestors,*" in *Film Comment* (New York), Fall 1968.
Interview with H. Anassian, in *Le Monde* (Paris), 27 January 1980.
Interview with M. Vartanov, in *Cahiers du Cinéma* (Paris), March 1986.
Interview with C. Tesson, in *Cahiers du Cinéma* (Paris), July/August 1988.

On PARADZHANOV: articles—

Marshall, Herbert, "The Case of Sergo Paradjanov," in *Sight and Sound* (London), Winter 1974/75.
Liehm, Antonin, "A Certain Cowardice," in *Film Comment* (New York), July/August 1975.
"Film Names Bid Soviets Be Kind to Paradzhanov," in *Variety* (New York), 17 November 1976.
Fargier, J.P., "Libérons Paradjanian," in *Cahiers du Cinéma* (Paris), August/September 1977.
Grenier, Richard, "A Soviet Filmmaker's Plight," in the *New York Times,* 16 July 1981.
Barsky, V., "Uber Sergj Paradschanow und seine Filme," in *Filmfaust* (Frankfurt), October/November 1985.
Stanbrook, Alan, "The Return of Paradjanov," in *Sight and Sound* (London), Autumn 1986.
"Ukrainian Rhapsody—Sergei Paradjanov," in *Monthly Film Bulletin* (London), November 1986.
Williamson, A., "Prisoner: The Essential Paradjanov," in *Film Comment* (New York), May/June 1989.
Rayns, Tony, "*Ashik kerib,*" in *Monthly Film Bulletin* (London), September 1989.
Alekseychuk, Leonid, "A Warrior in the Field," in *Sight and Sound* (London), Winter 1990/91.

* * *

The cinema, like heaven, has many mansions, and the place occupied by Sergei Paradzhanov is a very rich one indeed. This dissident, highly individual film creator made films startling in their beauty, deeply imbued with ethnic consciousness, as unique in their style as, say, the work of Miklos Jancsó.

Paradzhanov was unmistakably a dissident. Not for him the systematic social realism of the authorities. Like his distinguished predecessors Eisenstein and Dovzhenko, it was the poetry of life that he sought. His films must be taken in their totality, for the cumulative effect is stunning. His beautiful images, created with the eye of a painter, while striking in themselves, progress with the steady tempo of tableaux vivants.

When Paradzhanov's *Teni zabytykh predkov (Shadows of Our Forgotten Ancestors)* burst upon world screens, it was quite evident that a major artist had appeared in Soviet cinema. This film, more flexible than his later stylized creations, revealed a powerful individuality. A tale of life in an ancient Carpathian village, it revealed also a sensitive feeling for nature and landscapes and an awareness of religious forces as it probed into the recesses of the inherited mind.

It was inevitable that Paradzhanov's work would not be appreciated by lesser men. He was uncompromising even when pressures and persecution pursued him. His personal lifestyle and his dogged pursuit of an ideal made him a marked man for bureaucratic tyranny, and after his *Sayat nova (The Colour of Pomegranates)* was completed in 1972 he was driven from the cinema. He was sentenced to six years in a labour camp for charges ranging from homosexuality and fraud to incitement to suicide. After several years under duress, world opinion forced the Soviet authorities to release him. He knew shame and beggary until with great determination he won his way back to making films once more.

The Colour of Pomegranates (or *The Blood of the Pomegranates*) evokes the life of the eighteenth-century Armenian poet Arution Sayadian. In it the images are almost an *embarras de richesses.* The bleeding pomegranates, the struggling fish, details of utensils and native crafts, the boy swinging from the bellrope, pages of hundreds of books blown in the wind, the stately horseman parading back and forth, and the blazing colours of textiles in the dye-works scene pile up in a series of unforgettable impressions.

More sombre in tone is the *Legenda o Suramskoj kreposti (The Legend of the Suram Fortress),* made in 1984 when Paradzhanov returned to the Georgian Film Studio. It is again a series of episodes integrated in mood and feeling and characteristically poetic in approach. His last film, *Ashik kerib,* is suitably dedicated to Tarkovsky and tells the tale of a Turkish minstrel and his frustrated love. Again rich images prevail and the idiosyncratic style persists.

Paradzhanov was a poet of the Eastern Soviet Republics. A Georgian, born in Tiflis, he was steeped in the culture and traditions of his native region. His concern with its past was the source of his creative strength and his independence of mind. He lived, thankfully, to see repressive forces at least temporarily dissipated, bringing freedom to himself as an artist. Yet it is a great pity that in the West he is known by only a few, if important, key films. The future will no doubt bring a greater knowledge of his work.

—Liam O'Leary

PARKER, Alan

Nationality: English. **Born:** Islington, London, 14 February 1944. **Family:** Married Annie Inglis, 1966; four children. **Career:** Mailboy, later writer and director, for advertising industry, London, from mid-1960s; with producer Alan Marshall, set up Alan Parker Film Company to make advertisements, 1970; directed *The Evacuees* for TV, and first feature, *Bugsy Malone,* 1975; founding member and vice-chairman, Directors Guild of Great Britain, and member, British Screen Advisory Council; directed *The Turnip Head's Guide to British Cinema* for Thames TV, 1986; signed deal with Tri-Star Pictures, 1989; also cartoonist and novelist. **Awards:** British Academy Award for Best Screenplay, for *Bugsy Malone,* 1984; Special Jury Prize, Cannes Festival, for *Birdy,* 1984; Michael Balcon Award for Outstanding Contribution to Cinema (with Alan Marshall), 1984; BAFTA Award for Best Director, for *The Commitments,* 1991. **Agent:** c/o Judy Scott-Fox, William Morris Agency, Inc., 151 El Camino Drive, Beverly Hills, CA 90212, U.S.A. **Address:** Lives in Richmond, Surrey, and Los Angeles.

Films as Director:

1973 *Footsteps* (short) (+ sc); *Our Cissy* (short) (+ sc)
1976 *Bugsy Malone* (+ sc)
1978 ***Midnight Express***
1980 *Fame*
1981 *Shoot the Moon*

1982 *Pink Floyd—The Wall*
1985 *Birdy*
1987 *Angel Heart* (+ sc)
1988 *Mississippi Burning*
1990 *Come See the Paradise* (+ sc)
1991 *The Commitments* (+ role as record producer)
1994 *The Road to Wellville* (+ pr, sc)

Other Films:

1971 *Melody* (sc)

Publications

By PARKER: books—

Bugsy Malone, London, 1976.
Puddles in the Rain, London, 1977.
Hares in the Gate (cartoons), London, 1983.
A Filmmaker's Diary, London, 1984.

By PARKER: articles—

Interviews in *Time Out* (London), 23 July 1976 and 11 August 1978.
Interviews in *Focus on Film* (London), April 1980.
Interview in *Cinema* (London), August 1982.
"Alan Parker on *Pink Floyd—The Wall,*" in *American Cinematographer* (Los Angeles), October 1982.
Cartoons, in *Sight and Sound* (London), Summer 1983.
"Britain's Angry Young Man," an interview with A. Horton, in *Cineaste* (New York), vol. 15, no. 2, 1986.
Interview in *Literature/Film Quarterly* (Salisbury, Maryland), vol. 15, no. 3, 1987.
"The Making of *Angel Heart,*" in *Films and Filming* (London), September and October 1987.
"Dialogue on Film: Alan Parker," in *American Film* (Washington, D.C.), January-February 1988.
Interview in *American Film* (Washington, D.C.), September 1990.
"Paradise Lost: Production of the Motion Picture *Come See the Paradise,*" in *Premiere,* January 1991.

On PARKER: articles—

Roddick, Nick, "Alan Parker: From Bugsy to Birdy," in *Cinema Papers* (Melbourne), July 1985.
Houston, Penelope, "Parker, Attenborough, Anderson," in *Sight and Sound* (London), Summer 1986.
Smith, Gavin, "Mississippi Gambler: Alan Parker Rides Again," in *Film Criticism* (Meadville, Pennsylvania), vol. 24, no. 6, 1988.
Stam, H., "Het ernstige onderwerp en het grote publiek," in *Skoop,* April 1989.
"Alan Parker," in *Film a Doba,* January 1990.

Alan Parker (right) directing Brad Davis in *Midnight Express*

Zimmer, J., "Alan Parker," in *Revue du Cinema,* July-August 1990.
Apted, M., "One on One: Michael Apted and Alan Parker," in *American Film,* September 1990.
Kirk, P., "Working for High Standards," in *Boxoffice,* January 1991.
Chase, D., "Alan Parker," in *Millimeter,* February 1991.
Lally, K., "Director Parker Makes Hearty *Commitments,*" in *Film Journal,* August 1991.
Dibbell, J., "Straight outta Dublin," in *Village Voice,* August 20, 1991.
Fuller, Graham, article in *Interview,* August 1991.
Kauffmann, Stanley, article in *New Republic,* September 16, 1991.
Maslin, Janet, article in *New York Times,* October 28, 1994.
Denby, David, "The Road to Wellville," in *New York,* November 14, 1994.

* * *

Of all his fellow graduates from the prolific British commercials school of the 1960s (Ridley and Tony Scott, Hugh Hudson, and others), Alan Parker appears to have made far and away the most successful complete transition to theatrical filmmaking. Which is not to say that his movies to date—from *Bugsy Malone* to *Come See the Paradise*—have all been wholly successful in either box-office terms, critical reception or, blissfully, both at the same time. However, what Parker has managed always to achieve, with admittedly varying degrees of success, is that elusive blend of strong story and elegant frame, a symbiosis that tends regularly to elude other directors schooled in (and too often hamstrung by) the purely visual.

Two themes could be said to dominate Parker's work: children and controversy. After an award-winning teleplay, *The Evacuees,* about the bittersweet plight of evacuated London children during World War II, he made his feature debut with *Bugsy Malone,* an ingenious gangster spoof substituting kids for adults and cream balls for bullets. It was energetic and surprisingly un-quaint, ingredients that also characterised his high-voltage *Fame,* centering on a group of ambitious students at the New York High School for the Performing Arts. In between, though, controversy had first raised its head in the form of *Midnight Express,* an ultimately reprehensible and unashamedly manipulative piece of docudrama, unhappily dignified by sheer technique, about the supposed fate of a young American jailed for drug offences in Turkey.

Later, after both *Angel Heart,* a labyrinthine Faustian tale which was briefly threatened with an American "X" rating, and *Mississippi Burning,* a powerful Civil Rights drama that was accused of blatant Hollywood-isation, Parker's unquenchable passion and his admitted preference for "the theatrical edge" have continued to be, rather unfairly, mistaken for a filmmaking arrogance that tends to help make him less than a darling to those critics whom he has always termed "the Sight & Sound mafia."

Shoot the Moon, Parker's most personal film about marital mishaps and muddled offspring, and *Birdy,* which seamlessly transposed novelist William Wharton's post-World War II traumas to a post-Vietnam setting, best demonstrate his theatrical style carefully crafted into (though never subsuming) strong content. Especially the latter, which deals with two emotionally damaged young men whose bond transcends the scars resulting in a message—common to much of Parker's work—that is joyously life-affirming.

In 1991 Parker released *The Commitments,* a film based on a novel by Irish writer Roddy Doyle. The film, which garnered mixed reviews, told the story of the efforts of a ragtag group of musicians with widely varied individual agendas and their efforts to launch a successful band. 1994's *The Road to Wellville,* meanwhile, despite an impressive cast headed by Anthony Hopkins, was a decidedly unsuccessful adaptation of T. Coraghessan Boyle's novel.

—Quentin Falk

PASOLINI, Pier Paolo

Nationality: Italian. **Born:** Bologna, 5 March 1922. **Education:** School Reggio Emilia e Galvani, Bologna, until 1937; University of Bologna, until 1943. **Military Service:** Conscripted, 1943; regiment taken prisoner by Germans following Italian surrender; escaped and took refuge with family in Casarsa. **Career:** Formed "Academiuta di lenga furlana" with friends, publishing works in Friulian dialect, 1944; secretary of Communist Party cell in Casarsa, 1947; accused of corrupting minors, sacked from teaching post, moved to Rome, 1949; teacher in Ciampino, suburb of Rome, early 1950s; following publication of *Ragazzi di vita,* indicted for obscenity, 1955; co-founder and editor of review *Officina* (Bologna); prosecuted for "vilification of the Church" for directing "La ricotta" episode of *Rogopag,* 1963. **Awards:** Special Jury Prize, Venice Festival, for *Il vangelo secondo Matteo,* 1964. **Died:** Bludgeoned to death in Ostia, 2 November 1975; buried at Casarsa.

Films as Director:

1961 ***Accattone*** (+ sc)
1962 *Mamma Roma* (+ sc)
1963 "La ricotta" episode of *Rogopag* (+ sc); *La rabbia* (part one) (+ sc)
1964 *Comizi d'amore* (+ sc); *Sopralluoghi in Palestina* (+ sc); ***Il vangelo secondo Matteo*** (*The Gospel According to Saint Matthew*) (+ sc)
1966 *Uccellacci e uccellini* (*The Hawks and the Sparrows*) (+ sc); "La terra vista dalla luna" episode of *Le Streghe* (*The Witches*) (+ sc)
1967 "Che cosa sono le nuvole" episode of *Cappriccio all'italiana* (+ sc); *Edipo re* (*Oedipus Rex*) (+ sc)
1968 *Teorema* (+ sc); "La sequenza del fiore di carta" episode of *Amore e rabbia* (+ sc)
1969 *Appunti per un film indiano* (+ sc); *Appunti per una Orestiade africana* (*Notes for an African Oresteia*) (+ sc); *Porcile* (*Pigsty; Pigpen*) (+ sc); *Medea* (+ sc)
1971 *Il decameron* (*The Decameron*) (+ sc, role as Giotto)
1972 *12 dicembre* (co-d, sc); *I racconti di Canterbury* (*The Canterbury Tales*) (+ sc, role)
1974 ***Il fiore delle mille e una notte*** (*A Thousand and One Nights*) (+ sc)
1975 ***Salò o le 120 giornate di Sodome*** (*Salo—The 120 Days of Sodom*) (+ co-sc)

Other Films:

1954 *La donna del fiume* (co-sc)
1955 *Il prigioniero della montagna* (co-sc)
1956 *Le notti di Cabiria* (Fellini) (co-sc)
1957 *Marisa la civetta* (Bolognini) (co-sc)
1958 *Giovanni Mariti* (Bolognini) (co-sc)
1959 *La notte brava* (Bolognini) (co-sc)
1960 *La canta delle marane* (sc); *Morte di un amico* (co-sc); *Il bell' Antonio* (Bolognini) (co-sc); *La giornata balorda* (Bolognini) (co-sc); *La lunga notte del '43* (co-sc); *Il carro armato dell '8 settembre* (co-sc); *Il gobbo* (role)
1961 *La ragazza in vetrina* (co-sc)
1962 *La commare secca* (Bertolucci) (sc)
1966 *Requiescat* (role)
1969 *Ostia* (co-sc)
1973 *Storie scellerate* (co-sc)

Publications

By PASOLINI: books—

Poesie e Casarsa, Bologna, 1942.
Dov'è la mia patria, Casarsa, 1949.
I parlanti, Rome, 1951.
Tal cour di un frut, Tricesimo, 1953.
Del "diario" (1945-47), Caltanissetta, 1954.
Il canto popolare, Milan, 1954.
La meglio gioventù, Florence, 1954.
Ragazzi di vita, Milan, 1955; published as *The Ragazzi,* New York, 1968.
L'usignolo della Chiesa Cattolica, Milan, 1958.
Una vita violenta, Milan, 1959.
Donne di Roma, Milan, 1960.
Passione e ideologia (1948-1958), Milan, 1960; Turin, 1985.
Roma 1950, diario, Milan, 1960.
Sonetto primaverile (1953), Milan, 1960.
Accattone, Rome, 1961.
Il sogno di una cosa, Milan, 1962.
La violenza, with drawings by Attardi and others, Rome, 1962; published as *A Violent Life,* New York, 1968.
L'odore dell'India, Milan, 1962.
Mamma Roma, Milan, 1962.
Il vantone di Plauto, Milan, 1963.
Il vangelo secondo Matteo, Milan, 1964.
Alì degli occhi azzurri, Milan, 1965.
Poesie dimenticate, Udine, 1965.
Uccellacci e uccellini, Milan, 1965.
Edipo re, Milan, 1967; published as *Oedipus Rex,* London, 1971.
Teorema, Milan, 1968.
Pasolini on Pasolini, interviews by Oswald Stack, London, 1969.
Medea, Milan, 1970.
Poesie, Milan, 1970.
Empirismo eretico, Milan, 1972.
Calderón, Milan, 1973.
Il padre selvaggio, Turin, 1975.
La divina Mimesis, Turin, 1975.
La nuova gioventù, Turin, 1975.
Scritti corsari, Milan, 1975.
Trilogia della vita, edited by Giorgio Gattei, Bologna, 1975.
I turcs tal Friùl, Udine, 1976.
L'arte del Romanino e il nostro tempo, Brescia, 1976.
Lettere agli amici (1941-1945), Milan, 1976.
L'Experience hérétique: langue et cinéma, Paris, 1976.
"Volgar" eloquio, edited by A. Piromalli and D. Scarfoglio, Naples, 1976.
Affabulazione, Pilade, Milan, 1977.
Le belle bandiere: dialoghi 1960-65, Rome, 1977.
San Paolo, Turin, 1977.
I disegni, 1941-1975, Milan, 1978.
Poems, edited by Norman Macafee and Luciano Martinengo, New York, 1982.
Lettere, 1940-1954: Con una cronologia della vita e delle opere, edited by Nico Naldini, Turin, 1986.
Lettere, 1955-1975: Con una cronologia della vita e delle opere, edited by Nico Naldini, Turin, 1988.

By PASOLINI: articles—

"Intellectualism ... and the Teds," in *Films and Filming* (London), January 1961.
"Cinematic and Literary Stylistic Figures," in *Film Culture* (New York), Spring 1962.
"Pier Paolo Pasolini: An Epical-Religious View of the World," in *Film Quarterly* (Berkeley), Summer 1965.
Interview with James Blue, in *Film Comment* (New York), Fall 1965.
"Pasolini—A Conversation in Rome," with John Bragin, in *Film Culture* (New York), Fall 1966.
Interview in *Interviews with Film Directors,* edited by Andrew Sarris, New York, 1967.
"Montage et sémiologie selon Pasolini," in *Cinéma* (Paris), March 1972.
"Pasolini Today," an interview with Gideon Bachmann, in *Take One* (Montreal), September 1974.
"The Scenario as a Structure Designed to Become Another Structure," in *Wide Angle* (Athens, Ohio), vol. 2, no. 1, 1978.
"Toto," in *Cahiers du Cinéma* (Paris), March 1979.

On PASOLINI: books—

Gervais, Marc, *Pier Paolo Pasolini,* Paris, 1973.
Taylor, John, *Directors and Directions,* New York, 1975.
Siciliano, Enzo, *Vita di Pasolini,* Milan, 1978.
Bertini, Antonio, *Teoria e tecnica del film in Pasolini,* Rome, 1979.
Snyder, Stephen, *Pier Paolo Pasolini,* Boston, 1980.
Bellezza, Dario, *Morte di Pasolini,* Milan, 1981.
Bergala, Alain, and Jean Narboni, editors, *Pasolini cinéaste,* Paris, 1981.
Gerard, Fabien S., *Pasolini: ou, Le mythe de la barbarie,* Brussels, 1981.
Boarini, Vittorio, and others, *Da Accattone a Salo: 120 scritti sul cinema di Pier Paolo Pasolini,* Bologna, 1982.
Siciliano, Enzo, *Pasolini: A Biography,* New York, 1982.
De Giusti, Luciano, *I film di Pier Paolo Pasolini,* Rome, 1983.
Carotenuto, Aldo, *L'autunno della conscienza: Ricerche psicologiche su Pier Paolo Pasolini,* Turin, 1985.
Michalczyk, John J., *The Italian Political Filmmakers,* Cranbury, New Jersey, 1986.
Schweitzer, Otto, *Pier Paolo Pasolini: Mit Selbstzeugnissen und Bilddokumenten,* Hamburg, 1986.
Klimke, Cristoph, *Kraft der Vergangenheit: Zu Motiven der Filme von Pier Paolo Pasolini,* Frankfurt, 1988.
Greene, Naomi, *Pier Paolo Pasolini: Cinema as Heresy,* Princeton, New Jersey, 1990.

On PASOLINI: articles—

Lane, John, "Pasolini's Road to Calvary," in *Films and Filming* (London), March 1963.
Hitchens, Gordon, "Pier Paolo Pasolini and the Art of Directing," in *Film Comment* (New York), Fall 1965.
Bragin, John, "Pier Paolo Pasolini: Poetry as a Compensation," in *Film Society Review* (New York), January, February, and March 1969.
Macdonald, Susan, "Pasolini: Rebellion, Art and a New Society," in *Screen* (London), May/June 1969.
Armes, Roy, "Pasolini," in *Films and Filming* (London), June 1971.
Prono, F., "La Religione del suo tempo in Pier Paolo Paslini," in *Cinema Nuovo* (Turin), January/February 1972.
Bachmann, Gideon, "Pasolini in Persia: The Shooting of *1001 Nights,*" in *Film Quarterly* (Berkeley), Winter 1973/74.
Di Giammatteo, F., editor of special issue "Lo Scandalo Pasolini," in *Bianco e Nero* (Rome), vol. 37, no. 1-4, 1976.
Barthes, Roland, "Sade-Pasolini," in *Le Monde* (Paris), 16 June 1976.
"Pier Paolo Pasolini Issues" of *Etudes Cinématographiques* (Paris), no. 109-111, 1976, and no. 112-114, 1977.
Escobar, R., "Pasolini e la dialettica dell'irrealizzabile," in *Bianco e Nero* (Rome), July/September 1983.
MacBean, J.R., "Between Kitsch and Fascism: Notes on Fassbinder, Pasolini, Homosexual Politics, the Exotic ... ," in *Cineaste* (New York), vol. 13, no. 4, 1984.

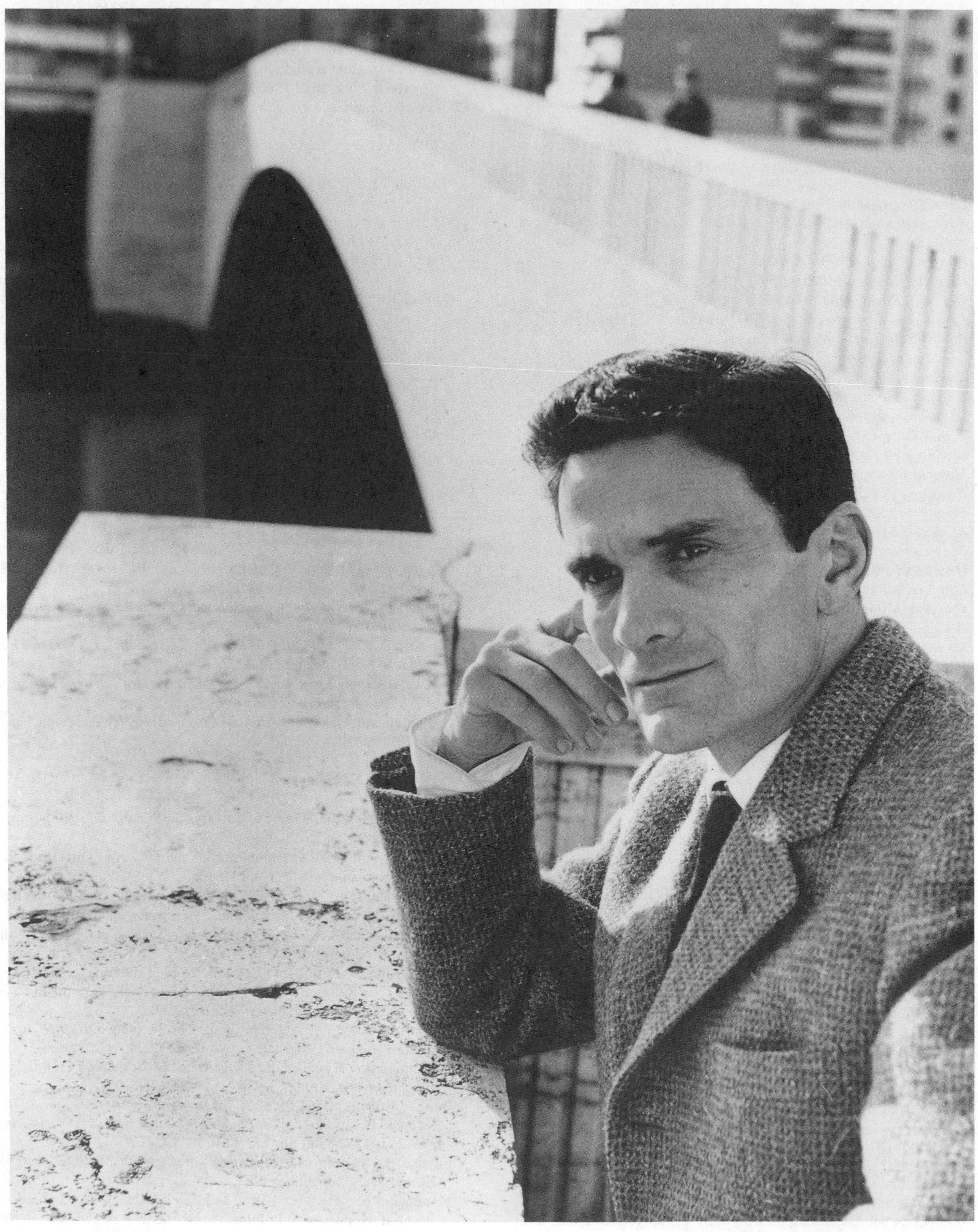

Pier Paolo Pasolini

Greene, N., "Reading Pasolini Today," in *Quarterly Review of Film Studies* (New York), Spring 1984.

Neupert, Richard, "A Cannibal's Text: Alternation and Embedding in Pasolini's *Pigsty*," in *Film Criticism* (Meadville, Pennsylvania), vol. 12, no. 3, 1988.

* * *

Pier Paolo Pasolini, poet, novelist, philosopher, and filmmaker, came of age during the reign of Italian Fascism, and his art is inextricably bound to his politics. Pasolini's films, like those of his early apprentice Bernardo Bertolucci, began under the influence of neorealism. He also did early scriptwriting with Bolognini and Fellini. Besides these roots in neorealism, Pasolini's works show a unique blend of linguistic theory and Italian Marxism. But Pasolini began transcending the neorealist tradition even in his first film, *Accattone* (which means "beggar").

The relationship between Pasolini's literary work and his films has often been observed, and indeed Pasolini himself noted in an introduction to a paperback selection of his poetry that "I made all these films as a poet." Pasolini was a great champion of modern linguistic theory and often pointed to Roland Barthes and Erich Auerbach in discussing the films many years before semiotics and structuralism became fashionable. His theories on the semiotics of cinema centered on the idea that film was a kind of "real poetry" because it expressed reality with reality itself and not with other semiotic codes, signs, or systems.

Pasolini's interest in linguistics can also be traced to his first book of poetry, *Poems of Casarsa,* which is written in his native Friuli dialect. This early interest in native nationalism and agrarian culture is also a central element in Pasolini's politics. His first major poem, "The Ashes of Gramsci" (1954), pays tribute to Antonio Gramsci, the Italian Marxist who founded the Italian Communist party. It created an uproar unknown in Italy since the time of D'Annunzio's poetry and was read by artists, politicians, and the general public.

The ideas of Gramsci coincided with Pasolini's own feelings, especially concerning that part of the working class known as the subproletariat, which Pasolini described as a prehistorical, pre-Christian, and pre-bourgeois phenomenon, one which occurs for him in the South of Italy (the Sud) and in the Third World.

This concern with "the little homelands," the indigenous cultures of specific regions, is a theme linking all of Pasolini's films, from *Accattone* to his final black vision, *Salò*. These marginal classes, known as *cafoni* (hicks or hillbillies), are among the main characters in Pasolini's novels *Ragazzi de vita* (1955) and *A Violent Life* (1959), and appear as protagonists in many of his films, notably *Accattone, Mamma Roma, Hawks and Sparrows,* and *The Gospel According to Saint Matthew.* To quote Pasolini: "My view of the world is always at bottom of an epical-religious nature: therefore even, in fact above all, in misery-ridden characters, characters who live outside of a historical consciousness, these epical-religious elements play a very important part."

In *Accattone* and *The Gospel,* images of official culture are juxtaposed against those of a more humble origin. The pimp of *Accattone* and the Christ of *The Gospel* are similar figures. When Accattone is killed at the end of the film, a fellow thief is seen crossing himself in a strange backward way, it is Pasolini's indictment of how Christianity has "contaminated" the subproletarian world of Rome. Marxism is never far away in *The Gospel*; it is evident, for instance, in the scene where Satan, dressed as a priest, tempts Christ. In *The Gospel,* Pasolini has put his special brand of Marxism even into camera angles and has, not ironically, created one of the most moving and literal interpretations of the story of Christ. A recurrent motif in Pasolini's filmmaking, and especially prominent in *Accattone* and *The Gospel,* is the treatment of individual camera shots as autonomous units; the cinematic equivalent of the poetic image. It should also be noted that *The Gospel According to Saint Matthew* was filmed entirely in southern Italy.

In the 1960s Pasolini's films became more concerned with ideology and myth, while continuing to develop his epical-religious theories. *Oedipus Rex* (which has never been distributed in the United States) and *Medea* reaffirm Pasolini's attachment to the marginal and pre-industrial peasant cultures. These two films indict capitalism as well as communism for the destruction of these cultures, and the creation of a world which has lost its sense of myth.

In *Teorema* ("theorem" in Italian), which is perhaps Pasolini's most experimental film, a mysterious stranger visits a typical middle class family, sexually seduces mother, father, daughter, and son, and destroys them. The peasant maid is the only character who is transformed because she is still attuned to the numinous quality of life which the middle class has lost. Pasolini has said about this film: "A member of the bourgeoisie, whatever he does, is always wrong."

Pigpen, which shares with *Teorema* the sulphurous volcanic location of Mount Etna, is a double film. The first half is the story or parable of a fifteenth-century cult of cannibals and their eventual destruction by the church. The second half concerns two former Nazis-turned-industrialists in a black comedy of rank perversion. It is the film closest in spirit to the dark vision of *Salò.*

In the 1970s Pasolini turned against his elite international audience of intellectuals and film buffs and embraced the mass market with his "Trilogy of Life": *Decameron, Canterbury Tales,* and *Arabian Nights.* The *Decameron* was his first major European box-office hit, due mainly to its explicit sexual content. All three films are a celebration of Pasolini's philosophy of "the ontology of reality, whose naked symbol is sex." Pasolini, an avowed homosexual, in *Decameron,* and especially *Arabian Nights,* celebrates the triumph of female heterosexuality as the epitome of the life principle. Pasolini himself appears in two of these films, most memorably in the *Decameron* as Giotto's best pupil, who on completion of a fresco for a small town cathedral says, "Why produce a work of art, when it's so much better just to dream about it."

As a result of his growing political pessimism Pasolini disowned the "Trilogy" and rejected most of its ideas. His final film, *Salò,* is an utterly clinical examination of the nature of fascism, which for Pasolini is synonymous with consumerism. Using a classical, unmoving camera, Pasolini explores the ultimate in human perversions in a static, repressive style. *Salò,* almost impossible to watch, is one of the most horrifying and beautiful visions ever created on film. Pasolini's tragic, if not ironic, death in 1975 ended a visionary career that almost certainly would have continued to evolve.

—Tony D'Arpino

PASTRONE, Giovanni

Nationality: Italian. Also known as Piero Fosco. **Born:** At Montechario d'Asti, 11 September 1883. **Career:** Administrative assistant, Carlo Rossi & Company, Turin, 1905; company reorganized as Itala Film, became adminstrative director, 1907; director, from 1910; production supervisor of Itala, from 1914; left film industry, worked on medical research, early 1920s. **Died:** In Turin, 27 June 1959.

Films as Director:

1910 *Agnese Visconti* (+ pr); *La caduta di Troia* (+ pr)
1912 *Padre* (co-d, pr)

Giovanni Pastrone: *Cabiria*

1914 ***Cabiria*** (+ pr)
1915 *Il fuoco* (+ pr); *Maciste* (+ pr)
1916 *Maciste alpino* (co-d, pr); *Tigre reale* (+ pr)
1919 *Hedda Gabler* (+ pr)
1923 *Povere bimbe* (+ pr)

Publications

On PASTRONE: books—

Margadonna, Ettore, *Cinema ieri ed oggi,* Milan, 1932.
Palmieri, Eugenio, *Vecchio cinema italiano,* Venice, 1940.
Prolo, Maria, *Storia del cinema muto italiano,* Milan, 1951.
Usai, Paola Cherchi, editor, *Giovanni Pastrone: gli anni d'oro del cinema a Torino,* Turin, 1986.

On PASTRONE: articles—

Caudana, Mino, "Vita laboriosa e geniale di Giovanni Pastrone," in *Film* (Rome), 25 February and 4 March 1939.
"Omaggio a Pastrone" issue of *Centrofilm* (Turin), no. 12, 1961.
Verdone, Mario, "Pastrone, ultimo incontro," in *Bianco e Nero* (Rome), June 1961.
Special Pastrone and Griffith issue of *Bianco e Nero* (Rome), May/August 1975.

* * *

The firm Carlo Rossi and Company (of Turin) began to manufacture films and apparatus in 1907, drawing their personnel from the Pathé Company of Paris. When Rossi left the Company, Sciamengo and Giovanni Pastrone took over what was by then Itala Films, and Pastrone soon proved himself an active and inspired manager. The services of the French comedian André Deed were acquired by the company in 1908. The comedian's role as Cretinetti proved a goldmine. Another valuable addition to the company was Segundo de Chomon, a Spanish cameraman who was a master of special effects. His first film for Itala was the sensational thriller *Tigris* in 1912.

In the meantime, Pastrone's ambitions led him into direction, and in 1910 he made *Agnese Visconti* and the sensational *Caduta del Troia,* which reached American cinemas in spite of an embargo on foreign films. His film *Padre* introduced the famous actor Ermete Zacconi to the screen. In 1913 Pastrone conceived a vast project set in the time of the Punic Wars, when Scipio conquered Carthage. Armed with a showman's instinct, Pastrone approached d'Annunzio and secured the approval and prestige of the great man's name for a tidy sum. Pastrone, under the name Piero Fosco, directed the film *Cabiria* with a script duly credited to the famous author, D'Annunzio.

Pastrone did his homework for the film with dynamic thoroughness. The period behavior, architecture, and costumes were patiently researched. Vast structures were built. Shooting took six months, ranging from the Itala studios in Turin to Tunisia, Sicily, and the Val de Lanzo, where Hannibal is reputed to have crossed the Alps. Not only was the film spectacular but, artistically, it broke new ground. The striking camerawork by de Chomon made use of travelling shots with remarkable skill, and the effects of the eruption of Mount Etna and the naval battle of Syracuse were awe-inspiring. The character of the strong man Maciste became a legend of the cinema. Later, Pastrone directed this ex-dock laborer in a further adventure, *Maciste,* and in the same year, he directed Pina Menichelli and Febo Mari in *Il Fuoco,* the love story of a young painter and a wealthy woman. The film's erotic atmosphere caused it to be banned and prompted clerical demonstrations against the film.

In 1916 Pastrone again directed Menichelli in a work by Verga, *Tigre reale,* and in 1919 he directed his former star of *Cabiria,* Itala Almirante Manzini, in *Hedda Gabler.* Before he retired at about that time he made several more films with his creation, Maciste. He abandoned the cinema to pursue research in therapeutic medicine.

—Liam O'Leary

PEARSON, George

Nationality: British. **Born:** London, 1875. **Career:** Producer/director for British Pathé, from 1913; joined G.B. Samuelson, 1914; joined Gaumont, 1915; formed Welsh Pearson Company with partner T.A. Welsh, 1918; went to United States to supervise first Anglo-American co-production, *Journey's End,* 1929; producer, director and writer for newly formed Colonial Film Unit, 1940; retired, 1955. **Awards:** Order of the British Empire. **Died:** 6 February 1973.

Films as Director:

1913 *Fair Sussex* (doc); *In Dickens Land* (doc); *Rambles Through Hopland* (doc); *Lynmouth* (doc); *Where History Has Been Written* (doc); *Kentish Industries* (doc); *Wonderful Nights of Peter Kinema* (series of shorts); *A Lighter Burden* (short); *Mr. Henpeck's Dilemma* (short); *The Fool*; *Sentence of Death*; *Heroes of the Mine*
1914 *A Fishergirl's Folly* (short); *The Live Wire*; *A Study in Scarlet*; *Christmas Day in the Workhouse* (short); *A Son of France* (short); *Incidents in the Great European War*; *The Cause of the Great European War*; *The Life of Lord Roberts VC*
1915 *Buttons* (short); *For the Empire* (short); *A Cinema Girl's Romance*; *The True Story of the Lyons Mail*; *John Halifax Gentleman*; *Ultus the Man from the Dead*
1916 *Ultus and the Grey Lady*; *Ultus and the Secret of the Night*; *Sally Bishop*
1917 *Ultus and the Three Button Mystery*; *The Man Who Made the Army* (doc); *Canadian Officers in the Making* (doc)
1918 *The Better 'ole*; *The Kiddies in the Ruins*
1919 *Hughie at the Victory Derby* (short)
1920 *Garryowen*; *Nothing Else Matters*
1921 *Mary find the Gold*; *Squibs*
1922 *Mord Em'ly*; *The Wee MacGregor's Sweetheart*; *Squib Wins the Calcutta Sweep*
1923 *Love Life and Laughter*; *Squibs M.P.*; *Squibs' Honeymoon*
1924 *Reveille*
1925 *Satan's Sister*
1926 *The Little People*; *Blinkeyes*
1927 *Huntingtower*
1928 *Love's Option*
1929 *Auld Lang Syne*
1931 *East Lynne on the Western Front*
1932 *The Third String*
1933 *A Shot in the Dark*; *The Pointing Finger*
1934 *River Wolves*; *Four Masked Men*; *Whispering Tongues*; *Open All Night*
1935 *Ace of Spades*; *That's My Uncle*; *Gentleman's Agreement*; *Once a Thief*; *Jubilee Window*; *Checkmate*
1936 *The Secret Voice*; *Wednesday Luck*; *Murder by Rope*
1937 *The Fatal Hour*; *Midnight at Madame Tussaud's*
1938 *Souvenirs* (short); *Old Soldiers* (short); *Mother of Men* (short)
1940 *Land of Water* (doc); *Take Cover* (doc); *Rural School* (doc); *A British Family in Peace and War* (doc)
1941 *British Youth* (doc); *An African in London* (doc)

Other Films:

1912 *Peg Woffington* (sc)
1919 *Pallard the Punter* (sc); *Angel Esquire* (sc)
1930 *Journey's End* (Whale) (supervising pr)
1932 *The Good Companions* (Saville) (assoc pr)
1936 *Shipmates o' Mine* (sc)
1937 *Command Performance* (sc)
1938 *Follow Your Star* (sc)

Publications

By PEARSON: book—

Flashback: An Autobiography of a British Film Maker, London, 1957.

By PEARSON: article—

"Lambeth Wall to Leicester Square," in *Sight and Sound* (London), Winter 1938/39.

On PEARSON: books—

Low, Rachael, *History of the British Film, 1914-18,* London, 1950
Low, Rachael, *History of the British Film, 1918-29,* London, 1971.

On PEARSON: articles—

"Pearson Issue" of *Silent Picture* (London), Spring 1969.
Slide, Anthony, "Tribute to George Pearson," in *International Film Guide 1974,* London, 1973.
Peet, S., "George Pearson: 1875-1973," in *Sight and Sound* (London), Spring 1973.
Slide, Anthony, "Journey's End," letter, in *Films in Review* (New York), March 1975.

* * *

George Pearson was a quiet, scholarly man, as far removed from the public image of a film director as it was possible to be. A schoolmaster for a time, he did not enter a film studio until he was thirty-six years old. Once Pearson decided he wanted to be a director, however, he quickly became one of the best of the British silent cinema. Pearson never ceased expressing his admiration for D.W. Griffith, and he modeled his directorial style after the master, using the cinema to arouse an audience through emotion rather than technical virtuosity.

The director's first films offered little out of the ordinary for British silent shorts until 1914, when he was given the opportunity to direct *A Study in Scarlet,* the first major adaptation of a Sherlock Holmes story. *A Study in Scarlet* is also noteworthy for its ambitious use of locations, with the Cheddar Gorge standing in for the Rocky

George Pearson

Mountains and the Southport Sands for the Salt Lake desert. With the "Ultus" series, produced between 1915 and 1917, George Pearson showed a grasp of the mystery film genre which led to a comparison with France's Louis Feuillade.

In 1918 George Pearson formed his own company in partnership with Tommy Welsh, and produced and directed *The Better 'ole,* based on the cartoons of Bruce Bairnsfather. The film was perhaps the first to treat the First World War in the comic terms of the participating soldiers, and was widely reviewed and released in the United States, one of the first British features to receive international recognition. With *Nothing Else Matters,* George Pearson discovered Betty Balfour, who quickly became the British silent cinema's most popular star. She worked with Pearson on more than half-a-dozen films, including the "Squibs" series, which told of the comic adventures of a cockney flower seller, and *Reveille,* a moving study of the after-effects of the First World War on a group of working-class Londoners.

With the coming of sound, George Pearson's career took a downward plunge. He was kept busy in the 1930s directing a series of low-budget, quota-quickie films that display little evidence of Pearson's earlier talent. With the Second World War, Pearson was back in demand in his old profession as a teacher with the Colonial Film Unit, educating young filmmakers from the emerging nations. Pearson's value to the British film industry as an instructor should not be overlooked, for many technicians learned their craft with him, notably Thorold Dickinson and Alberto Cavalcanti, who were associated with Pearson on *The Little People.* It was Thorold Dickinson who noted, "between Cecil Hepworth and Alfred Hitchcock, George Pearson was the outstanding personality in British silent cinema."

—Anthony Slide

PECKINPAH, Sam

Nationality: American. **Born:** David Samuel Peckinpah in Fresno, California, 21 February 1925. **Education:** Fresno State College, B.A. in Drama 1949; University of Southern California, M.A. 1950. **Family:** Married 1) Marie Selland, 1947, four children; 2) Begonia Palacios, 1964 (divorced), one child; 3) Joie Gould, 1972 (divorced). **Military Service:** Enlisted in Marine Corps, 1943. **Career:** Director/producer in residence, Huntington Park Civic Theatre, California, 1950-51; propman and stagehand, KLAC-TV, Los Angeles, then assistant editor at CBS, 1951-53; assistant to Don Siegel, from 1954; writer for television, including "Gunsmoke" and "The Rifleman," late 1950s; worked on scripts at Walt Disney Productions, 1963. **Died:** Of a heart attack, 28 December 1984.

Films as Director:

1961 *The Deadly Companions* (*Trigger Happy*)
1962 ***Ride the High Country*** (*Guns in the Afternoon*) (+ co-sc, uncredited)
1965 *Major Dundee* (+ co-sc)
1966 *Noon Wine* (+ sc)
1969 ***The Wild Bunch*** (+ co-sc)
1970 *The Ballad of Cable Hogue*
1971 *Straw Dogs* (+ co-sc)
1972 *Junior Bonner*; *The Getaway*
1973 *Pat Garrett and Billy the Kid*
1974 *Bring Me the Head of Alfredo Garcia* (+ co-sc)
1975 *The Killer Elite*
1977 *Cross of Iron*
1978 *Convoy*
1983 *The Osterman Weekend*

Other Films:

1956 ***Invasion of the Body Snatchers*** (Siegel) (role as Charlie the meter reader)
1978 *China 9 Liberty 37* (Hellmann) (role)
1980 *Il Visitatore* (Paradise) (role)

Publications

By PECKINPAH: articles—

"A Conversation with Sam Peckinpah," with Ernest Callenbach, in *Film Quarterly* (Berkeley), Winter 1963/64.
"Peckinpah's Return," an interview with Stephen Farber, in *Film Quarterly* (Berkeley), Fall 1969.
"Talking with Peckinpah," with Richard Whitehall, in *Sight and Sound* (London), Autumn 1969.
"Playboy Interview: Sam Peckinpah," with William Murray, in *Playboy* (Chicago), August 1972.
"Don Siegel and Me," in *Don Siegel: Director,* by Stuart Kaminsky, New York, 1974.
"Mort Sahl Called Me a 1939 American," in *Film Heritage* (New York), Summer 1976.

On PECKINPAH: books—

Kitses, Jim, *Horizons West,* Bloomington, Indiana, 1970.
Evans, Max, *Sam Peckinpah: Master of Violence,* Vermilion, South Dakota, 1972.
Wurlitzer, Rudolph, *Pat Garrett and Billy the Kid,* New York, 1973.
Caprara, Valerio, *Peckinpah,* Bologna, 1976.
Butler, T., *Crucified Heroes: The Films of Sam Peckinpah,* London, 1979.
McKinney, Doug, *Sam Peckinpah,* Boston, 1979.
Seydor, Paul, *Peckinpah: The Western Films,* Urbana, Illinois, 1980.
Simmons, Garner, *Peckinpah: A Portrait in Montage,* Austin, Texas, 1982.
Arnols, Frank, and Ulrich von Berg, *Sam Peckinpah: Eine Outlaw in Hollywood,* Frankfurt, 1987.
Buscombe, Ed, editor, *The BFI Companion to the Western,* London, 1989.

On PECKINPAH: articles—

McArthur, Colin, "Sam Peckinpah's West," in *Sight and Sound* (London), Autumn 1967.
Sassone, Rich, "The Ballad of Sam Peckinpah," in *Filmmakers Newsletter* (Ward Hill, Massachusetts), March 1969.
Blum, William, "Toward a Cinema of Cruelty," in *Cinema Journal* (Evanston, Illinois), Spring 1970.
Reisner, Joel, and Bruce Kane, "Sam Peckinpah," in *Action* (Los Angeles), June 1970.
Shaffer, Lawrence, "*The Wild Bunch* versus *Straw Dogs,*" in *Sight and Sound* (London), Summer 1972.
Andrews, Nigel, "Sam Peckinpah: The Survivor and the Individual," in *Sight and Sound* (London), Spring 1973.
Madsen, A., "Peckinpah in Mexico," in *Sight and Sound* (London), Spring 1974.
Macklin, Anthony, editor, special Peckinpah issue of *Film Heritage* (New York), Winter 1974/75.

Sam Peckinpah

Miller, Mark, "In Defense of Sam Peckinpah," in *Film Quarterly* (Berkeley), Spring 1975.

Pettit, Arthur, "Nightmare and Nostalgia: The Cinema West of Sam Peckinpah," in *Western Humanities Review* (Salt Lake City), Spring 1975.

Kael, Pauline, "Notes on the Nihilist Poetry of Sam Peckinpah," in the *New Yorker,* 12 January 1976.

Humphries, R., "The Function of Mexico in Peckinpah's Films," in *Jump Cut* (Berkeley), August 1978.

Fuller, Sam, "A Privilege to Work in Films: Sam Peckinpah Among Friends," in *Movietone News* (Seattle), February 1979.

Jameson, R.T., and others, "Midsection: Sam Peckinpah," in *Film Comment* (New York), January/February 1981.

McCarthy, T., obituary, in *Variety* (New York), 2 January 1985.

Murphy, K., "No Bleeding Heart," in *Film Comment* (New York), March/April 1985.

Bryson, J., "Sam Peckinpah," in *American Film* (Washington, D.C.), April 1985.

Engel, L.W., "Sam Peckinpah's Heroes: Natty Bumppo and the Myth of the Rugged Individual Still Reign," in *Literature/Film Quarterly* (Salisbury, Maryland), January 1988.

Roth, Paul A., "Virtue and Violence in Peckinpah's *The Wild Bunch,*" in *Post Script* (Jacksonville, Florida), vol. 7, no. 2, 1988.

Sharrett, Christopher, "Peckinpah the Radical: *The Wild Bunch* Reconsidered," in *CineAction!* (Toronto), no. 13-14, 1988.

* * *

It is as a director of westerns that Sam Peckinpah remains best known. This is not without justice. His non-western movies often lack the sense of complexity and resonance that he brings to western settings. He was adept at exploiting this richest of genres for his own purposes, explaining its ambiguities, pushing its values to uncomfortable limits. *Ride the High Country, Major Dundee,* and *The Wild Bunch* are the work of a filmmaker of high ambitions and rare talents. They convey a sense of important questions posed, yet finally left open and unanswered. At their best they have a visionary edge unparalleled in American cinema.

His non-westerns lose the additional dimensions that the genre brings, as in, for example, *Straw Dogs.* A polished and didactic parable about a besieged liberal academic who is forced by the relentless logic of events into extremes of violence, it is somehow too complete, its answers too pat, to reach beyond its own claustrophobic world. Though its drama is entirely compelling, it lacks the referential framework that carries Peckinpah's westerns far beyond the realm of tautly-directed action. Compared to *The Wild Bunch,* it is a one-dimensional film.

Nevertheless, *Straw Dogs* is immediately recognizable as a Peckinpah movie. If a distinctive style and common themes are the marks of an *auteur,* then Peckinpah's right to that label is indisputable. His concern with the horrors and the virtues of the male group was constant, as was his refusal to accept conventional movie morality. "My father says there's only Right and Wrong, Good and Evil, with nothing in between. But it's not that simple, is it?" asks Elsa in *Ride the High Country.* Judd's reply could almost be Peckinpah's: "No. It should be, but it isn't".

In traditional westerns, of course, right and wrong are clearly distinguishable. The westerner, as Robert Warshow has characterised him, is the man with a code. In Peckinpah's westerns, as in some of his other movies such as *Cross of Iron,* it is the code itself that is rendered problematic. Peckinpah explores the ethic rather than taking it for granted, plays off its elements one against the other, and uses his characters as emblems of those internal conflicts. He presents a world whose moral certainty is collapsing, leaving behind doomed variations on assertive individualism. In some modern westerns that theme has been treated as elegy; in Peckinpah it veers nearer to tragedy. His is a harsh world, softened only rarely in movies like *The Ballad of Cable Hogue* and *Junior Bonner.*

Peckinpah's richest achievements remain the two monumental epics of the 1960s, *Major Dundee* and *The Wild Bunch.* In both, though *Major Dundee* was butchered by its producers both before and after shooting, there is ample evidence of Peckinpah's ability to marshall original cinematic means in the service of a morally and aesthetically complex vision. It has become commonplace to associate Peckinpah with the rise of explicit violence in modern cinema, and it is true that few directors have rendered violence with such horrific immediacy. But his cinema is far more than that: his reflections upon familiar western themes are technically sophisticated, elaborately constructed, and, at their best, genuinely profound.

—Andrew Tudor

PENN, Arthur

Nationality: American. **Born:** Philadelphia, 27 September 1922. **Education:** Black Mountain College, North Carolina, 1947-48; studied at Universities of Perugia and Florence, 1949-50; trained for the stage with Michael Chekhov. **Military Service:** Enlisted in Army, 1943; joined Soldiers Show Company, Paris, 1945. **Family:** Married actress Peggy Maurer, 1955, one son, one daughter. **Career:** Assistant director on *The Colgate Comedy Hour,* 1951-52; TV director, from 1953, working on *Gulf Playhouse: 1st Person* (NBC), *Philco Television Playhouse* (NBC), and *Playhouse 90* (CBS); directed first feature, *The Left-Handed Gun,* 1958; director on Broadway, from 1958. **Awards:** Tony Award for stage version of *The Miracle Worker;* two Sylvania Awards. **Address:** c/o 2 West 67th Street, New York, NY 10023, U.S.A.

Films as Director:

1958 *The Left-Handed Gun*
1962 *The Miracle Worker*
1965 *Mickey One* (+ pr)
1966 *The Chase*
1967 ***Bonnie and Clyde***
1969 *Alice's Restaurant* (+ co-sc)
1970 *Little Big Man* (+ pr)
1973 "The Highest" in *Visions of 8*
1975 *Night Moves*
1976 *The Missouri Breaks*
1981 *Four Friends*
1985 *Target*
1987 *Dead of Winter*
1989 *Penn and Teller Get Killed* (+ pr)
1993 *The Portrait* (for TV)

Publications

By PENN: articles—

"Rencontre avec Arthur Penn," with André Labarthe and others, in *Cahiers du Cinéma* (Paris), October 1965.

Arthur Penn on the set of *Little Big Man*

"*Bonnie and Clyde*: Private Morality and Public Violence," in *Take One* (Montreal), vol. 1, no. 6, 1967.
Interview with Michael Lindsay, in *Cinema* (Beverly Hills), vol. 5, no. 3, 1969.
Interview in *The Director's Event* by Eric Sherman and Martin Rubin, New York, 1970.
"Metaphor," an interview with Gordon Gow, in *Films and Filming* (London), July 1971.
"Arthur Penn at the Olympic Games," an interview in *American Cinematographer* (Los Angeles), November 1972.
"Night Moves," an interview with T. Gallagher, in *Sight and Sound* (London), Spring 1975.
"Arthur Penn ou l'anti-genre," an interview with Claire Clouzot, in *Ecran* (Paris), December 1976.
Interview with R. Seidman and N. Leiber, in *American Film* (Washington, D.C.), December 1981.
Interview with A. Leroux, in *24 Images* (Montreal), June 1983.
Interview with Richard Combs, in *Monthly Film Bulletin* (London), August 1986.
"1968-1988," in *Film Comment* (New York), August 1988.
"L'Amerique qui change: entretien avec Arthur Penn," with P. Merenghetti, in *Jeune Cinema,* October/November 1990.
"The Importance of a Singular, Guiding Vision," an interview with Gary Crowdus and Richard Porton, in *Cineaste* (New York), 1993.

On PENN: books—

Wood, Robin, *Arthur Penn,* New York, 1969.
Marchesini, Mauro, and Gaetano Stucchi, *Cinque Film di Arthur Penn,* Turin, 1972.
Cawelti, John, editor, *Focus on Bonnie and Clyde,* Englewood Cliffs, New Jersey, 1973.
Carlini, Fabio, *Arthur Penn,* Milan, 1977.
Kolker, Robert Phillip, *A Cinema of Loneliness: Penn, Kubrick, Coppola, Scorsese, Altman,* Oxford, 1980; revised edition, 1988.
Zuker, Joel S., *Arthur Penn: A Guide to References and Resources,* Boston, 1980.
Giannetti, Louis D., *Masters of the American Cinema,* Englewood Cliffs, New Jersey, 1981.
Haustrate, Gaston, *Arthur Penn,* Paris, 1986.
Vernaglione, Paolo, *Arthur Penn,* Florence, 1988.
Kindem, Gorham, *The Live Television Generation of Hollywood Film Directors,* Jefferson, North Carolina, and London, 1994.

On PENN: articles—

Hillier, Jim, "Arthur Penn," in *Screen* (London), January/February 1969.
Gelmis, Joseph, "Arthur Penn," in *The Film Director as Superstar,* New York, 1970.
Wood, Robin, "Arthur Penn in Canada," in *Movie* (London), Winter 1970/71.
Margulies, Lee, "Filming the Olympics," in *Action* (Los Angeles), November/December 1972.
"*Le Gaucher* Issue" of *Avant-Scène du Cinéma* (Paris), November 1973.
Byron, Stuart, and Terry Curtis Fox, "What *Is* a Western?," in *Film Comment* (New York), July/August 1976.
Butler, T., "Arthur Penn: The Flight from Identity," in *Movie* (London), Winter 1978/79.
Penn Section of *Casablanca* (Madrid), March 1982.
"TV to Film: A History, a Map and a Family Tree," in *Monthly Film Bulletin* (London), February 1983.
Gallagher, J., and J. Hanc, "Penn's Westerns," in *Films in Review* (New York), August/September 1983.
Camy, G., "Arthur Penn: Un regard sévère sur les U.S.A. des années 60-70," in *Jeune Cinéma* (Paris), April 1985.
Andrew, Geoff, "*The Shootist,*" in *Time Out* (London), 13 August 1986.
Matheson, Nigel, "Arthur Penn," in *City Limits* (London), 21 August 1986.
Richards, P., "Arthur Penn: A One-Film Director?" in *Film,* October 1987.
Knowles, Peter C., "Genre and Authorship: Two Films of Arthur Penn," in *CineAction!* (Toronto), Summer/Autumn 1990.
McCloy, Sean, "Focus on Arthur Penn," in *Film West* (Dublin), July 1995.

* * *

Arthur Penn has often been classed—along with Robert Altman, Bob Rafelson, and Francis Coppola—among the more "European" American directors. Stylistically, this is true enough. Penn's films, especially after *Bonnie and Clyde,* tend to be technically experimental, and episodic in structure; their narrative line is elliptical, undermining audience expectations with abrupt shifts in mood and rhythm. Such features can be traced to the influence of the French New Wave, in particular the early films of François Truffaut and Jean-Luc Godard, which Penn greatly admired.

In terms of his thematic preoccupations, though, few directors are more utterly American. Repeatedly, throughout his work, Penn has been concerned with questioning and re-assessing the myths of his country. His films reveal a passionate, ironic, intense involvement with the American experience, and can be seen as an illuminating chart of the country's moral condition over the past thirty years. *Mickey One* is dark with the unfocused guilt and paranoia of the McCarthyite hangover, while the stunned horror of the Kennedy assassination reverberates through *The Chase.* The exhilaration, and the fatal flaws, of the 1960s anti-authoritarian revolt are reflected in *Bonnie and Clyde* and *Alice's Restaurant. Little Big Man* reworks the trauma of Vietnam, while *Night Moves* is steeped in the disillusioned malaise that pervaded the Watergate era.

As a focus for his perspective on America, Penn often chooses an outsider group and its relationship with mainstream society. The Indians in *Little Big Man,* the Barrow Gang in *Bonnie and Clyde,* the rustlers in *The Missouri Breaks,* the hippies in *Alice's Restaurant,* the outlaws in *The Left-Handed Gun,* are all sympathetically presented as attractive and vital figures, preferable in many ways to the conventional society which rejects them. But ultimately they suffer defeat, being infected by the flawed values of that same society. "A society," Penn has commented, "has its mirror in its outcasts."

An exceptionally intense, immediate physicality distinguishes Penn's work. Pain, in his films, unmistakably *hurts,* and tactile sensations are vividly communicated. Often, characters are conveyed primarily through their bodily actions: how they move, walk, hold themselves, or use their hands. Violence is a recurrent feature of his films—notably in *The Chase, Bonnie and Clyde,* and *The Missouri Breaks*—but it is seldom gratuitously introduced, and represents, in Penn's view, a deeply rooted element in the American character which has to be acknowledged.

Penn established his reputation as a director with *Bonnie and Clyde,* one of the most significant and influential films of its decade. But since 1970 he has made only a handful of films, none of them successful at the box office. *Night Moves* and *The Missouri Breaks,* both poorly received on initial release, now rank among his most subtle and intriguing movies, and *Four Friends,* though uneven, remains constantly stimulating with its oblique, elliptical narrative structure.

But since then Penn seems to have lost his way. Neither *Target,* a routine spy thriller, nor *Dead of Winter,* a reworking of Joseph H. Lewis's cult B-movie *My Name Is Julia Ross,* offered material worthy of his distinctive talents. *Penn and Teller Get Killed,* a spoof psycho-killer vehicle for the bad-taste illusionist team, got few showings outside the festival circuit. His only recent directorial work is *The*

Portrait, a solidly crafted adaptation for television of Tina Rowe's Broadway hit, *Painting Churches.*

"It's not that I've drifted away from film," Penn told Richard Combs in 1986. "I'm very drawn to film, but I'm not sure that film is drawn to me." Given the range, vitality, and sheer unpredictability of his earlier work, the estrangement is much to be regretted—especially if, as looks increasingly likely, it turns out to be permanent.

—Philip Kemp

PEREIRA DOS SANTOS, Nelson

Nationality: Brazilian. **Born:** São Paolo, 1928. **Education:** Educated in law; studied at IDHEC, Paris. **Career:** Journalist, editor at *Jornal do Brasil,* late 1940s; directed first feature, *Rio, quarenta graus,* 1955; teacher of cinema, University of Brasilia, from 1956; collaborated on short films with I. Rozemberg and J. Manzon, 1958-60; director of Department of Cinematographic Art, Federal University of Nitéroi, from 1968; participated in founding of filmmakers' cooperative, late 1970s; also editor and co-director of film revue *Luz e Açao.*

Films as Director and Scriptwriter:

1950 *Juventude* (short); *Atividades politicas em Sao Paolo* (short)
1955 *Rio, quarenta graus* (*Rio, 40 Degrees*)
1957 *Rio, zona norte* (*Rio, zone nord*)
1958 *Soldados do fogo* (short)
1960 Part of a documentary on Karl Gass made in East Germany
1961 *Mandacaru vermelho* (+ co-pr, role)
1962 *O Bôca de Ouro*; *Ballet do Brasil* (short)
1963 ***Vidas secas*** (*Barren Lives*); *Um môco de 74 anos* (short)
1964 *O Rio de Machado de Assis* (short)
1965 *Fala Brasilia*
1966 *Cruzada ABC*
1967 *El justiciero* (*Le Justicier*) (+ co-pr)
1968 *Fome de amor* (*Soif d'amour*); *Abastecimento, nova política* (short)
1969 *Azyllo muito louco* (*L'Alieniste*) (co-d)
1971 ***Como era gostoso o meu frances*** (*How Tasty Was My Little Frenchman*) (+ co-pr)
1972 *Quem e beta* (*Pas de violence entre nous*)
1974 *O Amuleta de Ogum* (*The Amulet of Ogum*); *Tenda dos milagres* (*Tent of Miracles*)
1980 *Na estrada da vida* (*On the Highway of Life*)
1984 *Memorias do carcere* (*Memories of Jail*)
1986 *Jubiaba*

Other Films:

1951 *O scai* (Nanni) (asst d)
1952 *Agulha no palheiro* (Viany) (asst d)
1953 *Balança mas nao caid* (Vanderlei) (asst d)
1958 *O grande momento* (Santos) (pr)
1962 *Barravento* (Rocha) (ed); *Pedreira de São Diogo* (Hirszman) (ed)

Publications

By PEREIRA DOS SANTOS: articles—

Interview with Leo Murray, in *Cahiers du Cinéma* (Paris), March 1966.
Interview with Fedéric de Cárdenas and Max Tessier, in *Etudes Cinématographiques* (Paris), no. 93-96, 1972.
Interview with J. Frenais, in *Cinéma* (Paris), October 1976.
Interview with A. Lima, in *Filme Cultura* (Rio de Janeiro), February 1979.
Interview with Agustin Mahieu, in *Cine Libre* (Madrid), no. 6, 1983.
Interview with Richard Peña, in *Framework* (Norwich), no. 29, 1985.
Interview with Robert Stam, and others, in *Cineaste* (New York), vol. 14, no. 2, 1985.
"Manifesto por un cinema popular," in *Hojas de cine,* by Marcelo Beraba, Mexico City, 1986.

On PEREIRA DOS SANTOS: books—

Rocha, Glauber, *Revisao critica do cinema brasiliero,* Rio de Janeiro, 1963.
Frías, Isaac Léon, *Los años de la conmoción,* Mexico City, 1979.
Johnson, Randal, and Robert Stam, editors, *Brazilian Cinema,* Rutherford, New Jersey, 1982.
Johnson, Randal, *Cinema Novo x 5,* Austin, Texas, 1984.
Burton, Julianne, editor, *Cinema and Social Change in Latin America,* Austin, Texas, 1986.

On PEREIRA DOS SANTOS: articles—

Lefèvre, Raymond, "*Vidas secas,*" in *Cinéma* (Paris), November 1965.
Monteiro, José, "Nelson Pereira dos Santos," in *Filme Cultura* (Rio de Janeiro), September/October 1970.
Kinder, Marsha, "*Tent of Miracles,*" in *Film Quarterly* (Berkeley), Summer 1978.
"Dossier criticos: *Barre Pesada,*" in *Filme Cultura* (Rio de Janeiro), February 1979.
Xavier, I., and others, "Cerimonia da purificaçao," in *Filme Cultura* (Rio de Janeiro), April/August 1984.
Paranagua, P. A., "Nelson Pereira dos Santos: Trajectoire d'un dépouillement," in *Positif* (Paris), December 1985.
Peña, Richard, "After *Barren Lives*: The Legacy of Cinema Novo," in *Reviewing Histories,* edited by Coco Fusco, Buffalo, New York, 1987.
Mraz, John, "What's Popular in the New Latin American Cinema?," in *Studies in Latin American Popular Culture,* no. 7, 1988.

* * *

Considered to be the "mentor" and "conscience" of *Cinema Novo* (New Cinema)—the movement that fundamentally transformed the theory and practice of film in Brazil and Latin America—Nelson Pereira dos Santos encapsulates many of its ideals in his works. The most important of these is the reaction against the domination of Brazilian screens by foreign films and imported cinematic models, for *Cinema Novo* is the result of efforts by directors such as Pereira, Glauber Rocha, and Carlos Diegues to make a genuinely "popular cinema." This concept has been used in a variety of ways, but to Pereira it represents a combination of commercial success and a concern with national identity. Thus, though he criticized early *Cinema Novo* works because they were inaccessible to the general public, he also feels that marketability is not the only criteria by which to judge what is "popular." For Pereira, films must also affirm the principles of Brazilian popular culture, which he sees as dramatically different from "superficial, elitist cultural forms that follow antiquated, colonized models."

The first film to embody the principles of *Cinema Novo* was *Rio, 40 Degrees,* which Pereira dos Santos made in 1955. Greatly influenced by Italian neo-realism, *Rio* was made in the streets of that city and outside studios, and was immersed in Brazil's reality. The storyline presents the poles of Brazilian society, contrasting the lives of the

Nelson Pereira dos Santos directing *Como era gostoso a meu frances*

upper and the lower classes through the device of following the activities of five peanut vendors who leave their slum houses to sell their wares in different parts of Rio.

Aside from the thematic focus on everyday life, Pereira believes the structure of the production also reflected the film's innovative approach to storytelling. The work was made with an absolute minimum of technical resources (a camera and some lights); the crew was composed of friends who did whatever was required of them, rather than technicians who worked only in their specialty; and the film was shot on location, in the places where the stories take place. However, in spite of such low-budget strategies, production of *Rio* was still expensive enough to sink Pereira deeply in debt. As a consequence, he was unable to make another feature for four years.

When Pereira did return to feature production, it was to make another "classic" of *Cinema Novo, Barren Lives.* During 1957 and 1958, the filmmaker had directed documentaries in the Brazilian northeast, where he was greatly struck by the extreme drought conditions typical of that region. At the time, there was much debate about Brazil's agrarian problems, and Pereira participated in that discussion by adapting Graciliano Ramos' book *Vidas secas* to the screen. Pereira's experience in making documentaries there served him well, for he was aware that the usual camera filters transformed the arid countryside into an exotic garden. He worked closely with Luiz Carlos Barreto, one of the finest Brazilian cameramen of the time, to produce an austere kind of photography, achieved through high-contrast film shot without filters, which reflected the reality of the area. Pereira further struggled against the sentimentalized and picturesque vision so often rendered of such regions by creating a soundtrack in which harsh noises punctuate the narrative.

History is an important source of national identity, and Pereira has directed two historical films of uncommon power and beauty: *How Tasty Was My Little Frenchman* and *Prison Memories. My Little Frenchman* was made at a time when government censorship made it difficult to produce films on contemporary problems; as Pereira noted: "The government financed historical films, but it wanted the history to be within official parameters—the hero, the father of the country, all those things we have been told since elementary school." This was a seemingly impossible task, but one that Pereira turned to his own uses by making a work that subverted "official history" by focusing on the Indian perspective of the "discovery" of America and through incorporating contradictions between the images shown and the discourses of government officials in the film. With *Prison Memories,* Pereira returned to Graciliano Ramos for inspiration. Freely adapting the book, in which Ramos described his experiences as a political prisoner during the 1930s, Pereira turned the jail into a metaphor for "the prison of social and political relations which oppress the Brazilian people." In his contemporary and historical cinema, Nelson Pereira dos Santos has explored the depths of Brazilian reality as well as the heights to which that nation's culture is capable of rising.

—John Mraz

PERIES, Lester James

Nationality: Sri Lankan. **Born:** Colombo, Ceylon (now Sri Lanka), 5 April 1919. **Education:** Catholic priests' college until 1938. **Family:** Married director and editor Sumitra Gunawardana. **Career:** Worked in theatre and on radio, during World War II; sent to London by parents, 1946; returned to Ceylon and joined Government Film Unit, 1952; with cameraman William Blake and editor Titus De Silva (Titus Thotawatte), quit Film Unit to make first Sinhalese-language feature shot on location, *Rekava,* 1955.

Films as Director:

1949 *Soliloquy* (short)
1950 *Farewell to Childhood* (short); *A Sinhalese Dance* (short)
1954 *Conquest in the Dry Zone* (short)
1955 *Be Safe or Be Sorry* (short)
1956 *Rekava* (*The Line of Destiny*; *The Line of Life*) (+ pr, sc)
1960 *Sandesaya* (*The Message*) (+ co-sc)
1961 *Too Many Too Soon* (short)
1962 *Home from the Sea* (short)
1964 *Forward into the Future* (short); *Gamperaliya* (*Changes in the Village*)
1966 *Delovak Athara* (*Between Two Worlds*) (+ co-sc)
1967 *Ran Salu* (*The Yellow Robe*)
1968 *Golu Hadawatha* (*Silence of the Heart*)
1969 *Steel* (short); *Akkara Paha* (*Five Acres of Land*)
1970 *Forty Leagues from Paradise*; *Nidhanaya* (*The Treasure*)
1971 *Kandy Perahera* (*The Procession of Kandy*) (short)
1972 *Desa Nisa* (*The Eyes*)
1973 *The God King*
1976 *Madol Duwa* (*Enchanted Island*)
1978 *Ahasin Polawatha* (*White Flowers for the Dead*)
1979 *Pinhamy* (short); *Veera Puran Appu* (*Rebellion*)
1980 *Baddegama* (*Village in the Jungle*) (+ co-sc)
1982 *Kaliyugaya* (*The Time of Kali*)
1983 *Yuganthayo* (*End of an Era*)

Publications

By PERIES: articles—

"A Filmmaker in Ceylon," in *Sight and Sound* (London), Autumn 1957.
Interview with M. Sibra, in *Cinéma* (Paris), December 1976.
Interview with A. J. Gunawardana, in *Sight and Sound* (London), Summer 1977.
"A la découverte de Lester James Peries au Festival de La Rochelle," an interview and article with I. Jordan and J. P. Hautin, in *Positif* (Paris), October 1980; (also November 1980).

On PERIES: book—

Coorey, Philip, *The Lonely Artist,* Colombo, Ceylon (Sri Lanka), 1970.

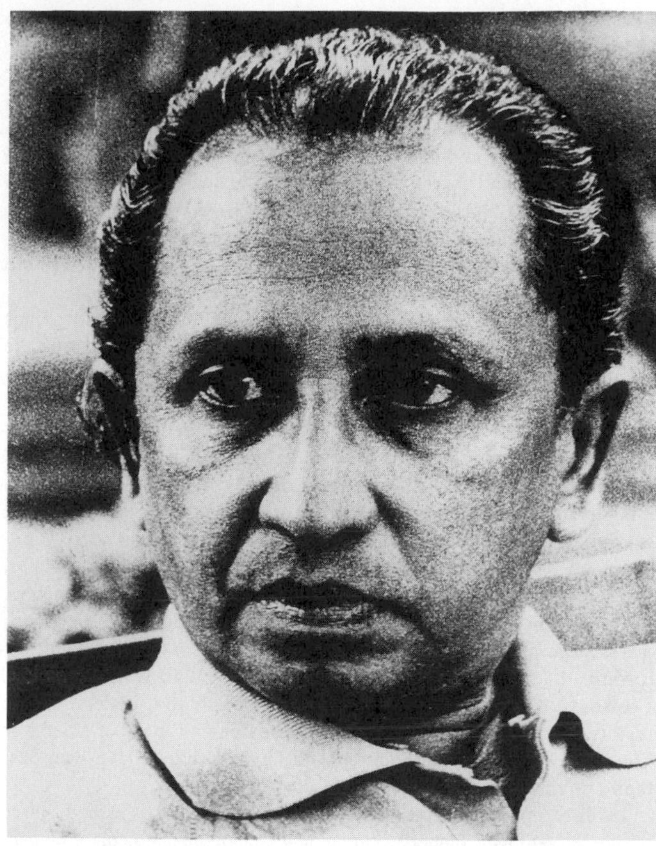

Lester James Peries

On PERIES: articles—

Gunawardana, A. J., "A Personal Cinema," in *Drama Review* (New York), Spring 1971.
Gauthier, G., "Lester James Peries: cinéaste de Sri Lanka," in *Image et Son* (Paris), March 1981.
Elley, Derek, "Lester James Peries," in *International Film Guide 1983,* London, 1982.
Robinson, D., "Bombay/Colombo/Calcutta," in *Sight and Sound* (London), Summer 1985.

* * *

The film industry of Sri Lanka (formerly Ceylon), like those of many small countries, suffers from the proximity of a similar but much larger and more prolific industry which dominates both the home market and potential export markets. For Sri Lankan filmmakers and their audience, film means Indian film, in particular the fantasy-formula movies so beloved of South Indian (Tamil) cinema. Home production has tended to rehash these movies in a Sinhalese version. When Lester James Peries broke away from the Government Film Unit, which largely made documentaries, with the aim of making "films that truly reflected the life of the people of this country ... valid in terms of cinema as it is generally accepted in other countries," he initiated a revolution in the Sinhalese industry simply, as Philip Coorey remarks in his authoritative study of Peries, *The Lonely Artist,* by "making his films in the way he thought best."

"The way he thought best" took Peries out of the studio-bound industry, with its painted backcloths and equally painted actors, into a world of real locations and real people. His first film, *Rekava* (*The Line of Destiny*), was a commercial failure, though critically well-received abroad. As yet, Sri Lankan audiences were not prepared to accept a realistic view of themselves, instead preferring fantasies. But the barrier had been broken, and despite this setback, Peries and his associates persisted, encouraging others to break with the tradition.

In his subsequent films, Peries has endeavoured "to explore human relationships as truly as I can, even if that truth be unpalatable, to do so with sympathy and compassion"—thus producing films with both local relevance and universal significance. Such works as *Gamperaliya* (*Changes in the Village*), *Nidhanaya* (*The Treasure*), and *Baddegama* (*Village in the Jungle*) are characterized by warmth, visual lyricism, and a powerful narrative instinct which occasionally (by Western standards) verges on melodrama.

With some justification, critics have accused Peries of making films which are too slow, too uncommitted. His preoccupation is with the internal conflict of his characters, rather than with the external situations which have precipitated their angst. His is a contemplative cinema—in Coorey's words, "he eavesdrops on the inner and exterior life of his characters." Peries may not specifically condemn social conditions, or make political exposés of the corrupt influences in Sri Lankan society, but by concentrating on the lives of his characters he subtly shows how Sri Lanka, and to some extent every society, imposes on people—through superstition, caste and/or class systems, and social mores—a way of life which can lead to much unhappiness, gross stupidity, and a general waste of human potential. A more serious charge against Peries might be that his films show a tendency towards the sentimental. The slow, lyrical style of his work can lead to a softness of approach, where a harder edge might give better dramatic results. However, such attempts at a more dynamic style of cinema as *The God King* (a co-production with Great Britain) have been less than convincing—although still fascinating.

In his compassionate portrayal of his people, Peries has earned a place beside Satyajit Ray, Flaherty, Renoir, and Ozu in the pantheon of humanist filmmakers. But his most distinctive achievement has been the creation, virtually single-handedly, of a truly Sri Lankan cinema.

—Theresa FitzGerald

PERRAULT, Pierre

Nationality: Canadian. **Born:** Montreal, 29 June 1927. **Education:** Educated in classical studies, Collège de Montréal and Collège Grasset, then at Collège Sainte-Marie; studied law, Universities of Montreal, Paris, and Toronto. **Family:** Married Yolande Simard, 1951; two children. **Career:** Practiced law in Montreal, 1954-56; scriptwriter for Société Radio-Canada, from 1956; directed *Au pays de Neufve-France* for TV, 1959-60; directed (with Michel Brault), first feature, *Pour la suite du monde,* 1963.

Films as Director:

1963 *Pour la suite du monde* (co-d)
1967 *Le Règne du jour*
1969 *Les Voitures d'eau*; *Le Beau Plaisir*
1970 *Un Pays sans bon sens*; *L'Acadie, L'Acadie!* (co-d)
1976 *Le Retour à la terre*; *Un Royaume vous attend*; *Le Goût de la farine*
1977 *C'était un Québécois en Bretagne, madame!*
1979 *Le Pays de la terre sans arbre*; *Gens d'Abitibi*
1982 *La Bête lumineuse*
1983 *Les Voiles bas et en travers*
1986 *Grande allure*

Publications

By PERRAULT: books—

Portulan (poems), Montreal, 1961.
Ballades du temps précieux (poems), Montreal, 1963.
Toutes Isles (stories), Montreal, 1963.
Au coeur de la rose (play), Montreal, 1964.
Le Règne du jour, Montreal, 1968.
Les Voitures d'eau, Montreal, 1969.
En désespoir de cause (poems), Montreal, 1971.
Un Pays sans bon sens, Montreal, 1972.
Chouennes (poems), Montreal, 1975.
Discours sur la condition sauvage et québécoise, Montreal, 1977.
Gélivures (poems), Montreal, 1977.
La Bête lumineuse, Montreal, 1982.
Caméramages, Paris, 1983.

By PERRAULT: articles—

"Discours sur la parole," in *Culture Vivante* (Quebec), no. 1, 1966; also in *Cahiers du Cinéma* (Paris), no. 191, 1967.
"La Parole est à Perrault," an interview with M. Basset, in *Cahiers de la Cinémathèque* (Paris), Spring 1972.
"La Femme dans le cinéma québécoise," with G. Gauthier, in *Image et Son* (Paris), January 1973.
"Pierre Perrault et Bernard Gosselin: le gout de la parole québécoise," an interview with P. Demers, in *Cinéma Québec* (Montreal), no. 5, 1976.
Interview with J. Bouthillier Lévesque, in *Positif* (Paris), October 1977.
"Il suono del diretto," an interview with M. Dall'Asta, in *Cinema and Cinema,* January-April 1991.

On PERRAULT: articles—

"Perrault Issue" of *Image et Son* (Paris), January 1972.
La Rochelle, R., and G. Maggi, "The Political Situation of Quebec Cinema," in *Cineaste* (New York), Summer 1972.
Martin, M., and P. Staran, "Trois Aspects du cinéma québécois," in *Ecran* (Paris), April 1977.
Ohlin, P., "The Film as Word (Perrault)," in *Ciné-Tracts* (Montreal), Spring/Summer 1978.
Dansereau, F., and others, "Faut-il bruler le cinéma quebecois?; le leçon du direct," in *Image et Son* (Paris), February 1979.
Clandfield, D., "Le Film ethnographique comme métaculture: la contribution de Pierre Perrault," in *Copie Zéro* (Montreal), October 1981.
Pevere, Geoff, "Aching to Speak: Power and Language in Pierre Perrault's *La Bête Lumineuse,*" in *CineAction!* (Toronto), no. 8, 1987.

* * *

Canadian Pierre Perrault—along with Americans Richard Leacock and Frederick Wiseman, and France's Jean Rouch—has been the most exemplary practitioner of cinema-verité, or candid-eye camera, which revolutionized cinema in the 1960s and introduced new ways of looking at reality. Living in Quebec, he has suffered from a relative isolation so that his important work is not well known outside France or his own country. Colleague Jean Rouch defines his originality well when he states that "it is Bresson's camera coming out of Dziga Vertov's brain and falling on Flaherty's heart: it is *Man of Aran* with direct sound, *Farrebique* with a travelling camera."

The work of Pierre Perrault can be considered an ethnological investigation of the Canadian French community. It could have been achieved only by a man with wide cultural interests. Born in 1927 in

Montreal, Perrault has been a lawyer, an athlete, a poet, and a playwright. He also worked on the radio, which explains his great interest in the spoken word (he did 300 broadcasts on the subject of popular traditions). His first documentary work (13 thirty-minute films for TV in 1959-1960), traditional in style, concerns the Northern side of the Saint Lawrence River and prefigures his major work, the trilogy *Pour la suite du monde, Le Règne du jour,* and *Les Voitures d'eau.* These films center on the Ile aux Coudres (an island which is a microcosm of the French Canadian community), the conflicts of generations, and their search for an identity. With the major contribution of cameraman Michel Brault (who co-directed *Pour la suite du monde* and later *L'Acadie, l'Acadie*), Perrault has made his camera a participant in the life of his people while also attempting to catch their true selves in concrete action. For *Pour la suite du monde,* he asked the islanders to resume sea-hog fishing thirty-eight years after it had been abandoned. Like Flaherty he lived with the community before starting to shoot and asked them to collaborate on the film, thus making it possible for them to express their worries and their passions, going beyond surface realism toward their fantasies and even a collective unconscious.

The development of cinema techniques, particularly lightweight camera equipment and extremely faithful sound recording, have allowed a remarkable flexibility to the film shape, and made possible the recording of people as they see themselves and not as an outsider would see them. The importance of speech (the French Canadians' fight for their autonomy is based on a defense of their language) is paramount in Perrault's work, but we also witness *physically* the problems faced by the islanders. In *Pour la suite du monde,* we see the shaping of a human community through a collective project; in *Le Règne du jour,* the burial of French culture as a model to follow; in *Les Voitures d'eau,* the necessity to adapt an ancient technique of building boats to a more modern usage. Later Perrault's films become much more politicized, even violent. *Un Pays sans bon sens* is a new affirmation of the Quebec identity on the occasion of a trip to French Brittany, and *L'Acadie, l'Acadie* tells of the student fights at Moncton University.

In the 1970s Perrault pursued his investigation of ethnic communities, particularly in a cycle of four films centered on the Abitibi region (*Un Royaume vous attend, Le Retour à la terre, C'était un Québecois en Bretagne, madame!,* and *Gens d'Abitibi*). *La Bête lumineuse,* a totally new experience, is about a hunting party which is given a mythological dimension, very much like Faulkner in his short story "The Bear." The chase of an animal which we never see and which will never be captured becomes a truculent saga where the members of the group reveal themselves through speech and behavior. Faithful to his methods, Perrault adds one more fascinating chapter to his human comedy.

—Michel Ciment

PETERSEN, Wolfgang

Nationality: German. **Born:** Emden, Germany, 14 March 1941. **Education:** Studied theater arts in Berlin and Hamburg at various drama schools, and at the Film and TV Academy in Berlin, where he directed short films. **Career:** Worked as assistant director at Jungen Theater, Hamburg, 1960; completed studies in film and theater and worked as stage director and actor at the Ernst Deutsch Theatre in Hamburg, 1964-1969; directed six 100-minute episodes for West German TV series *Tatort (Scene of the Crime),* 1971-1976; directed first feature film, *Einer von uns beiden,* 1973; earned initial international acclaim with *Die Konsequenz,* 1977; directed first American feature, *Enemy Mine,* 1985. **Awards:** Prix Futura, Berlin Festival, for *Smog,* 1972; German National Film Prize, Best New Director, for *Einer von uns beiden,* 1973; Prix Italia and Best Director, Monte Carlo Television Festival, for "Reifenzeugnis" (episode of *Tatort*), 1977; Oscar nominations, Best Director and Best Adapted Screenplay, Directors Guild nomination, and Bavarian Film Award for Best Director, all for *Das Boot,* 1983. **Agent:** CAA, 9830 Wilshire Blvd., Beverly Hills, CA 90212, U.S.A.

Films as Director:

1970 *Ich Werde Dich Toten Wolf* (*I Will Kill You, Wolf*) (doc)
1972 *Smog* (for TV)
1973 *Einer von uns beiden* (*One of Us*; *One or the Other*); *Van Der Valk and the Rich* (for TV)
1974 *Auf's kreuz gelegt* (*Pinned to the Ground*) (for TV); *Stadt im tal* (*Town in the Valley*) (for TV)
1975 *Stellenweise glatteis* (*Icy in Spots*) (for TV)
1976 *Hans im gluck* (*Hans' Good Fortune*) (for TV); *Vier genen die bank* (*Four against the Bank*) (for TV)
1977 *Die Konsequenz* (*The Consequence*) (+ co-sc); *Plannbung* (*The Rehearsal*) (for TV)
1978 *Schwarz und Weiss wie Tage und Nachte* (*Black and White Like Day and Night*) (for TV) (+ co-sc)
1981 ***Das Boot*** (*The Boat*) (+ sc) (originally a TV mini-series)
1982 *Reifezeugnis* (*For Your Love Only*) (+ co-sc)
1984 *The NeverEnding Story* (+ co-sc)
1985 *Enemy Mine*
1991 *Shattered* (+ sc, co-pr)
1993 *In the Line of Fire* (+ co-exec pr)
1995 *Outbreak* (+ co-pr)

Publications

By PETERSEN: articles—

Interview with T. MacTrevor, in *Cine Revue* (Brussels), 22 November 1984.
Interview with P. Pawlikowski, in *Stills* (London), April 1985.
Interview with D. Osswald, in *Cinema Papers* (Melbourne), May 1986.

On PETERSEN: articles—

Naha, Ed, article in *New York Post,* 16 February 1982.
Curtin, John, article in *New York Times,* 15 July 1984.
Article in *Variety,* 25 July 1984.
Pourroy, J., article in *Cinefex* (Riverside, California), February 1986.
Honeycutt, Kirk, article in *Los Angeles Times,* 17 June 1990.
Chutnow, Paul, article in *New York Times,* 6 October 1991.
Weinraub, Bernard, "Great Expectations Help Two Directors Enjoy the Summer," in *New York Times,* 6 July 1993.
Anderson, John, article in *Newsday* (Melville, New York), 8 July 1993.

* * *

In a review of Wolfgang Petersen's first theatrical feature, *Einer von uns beiden*—a suspense drama of romance, blackmail, and murder—a *Variety* critic noted that "After some 20 tv pix, many of them detective stories, Wolfgang Petersen is recognized as West Germany's leading action director in the Hollywood vein."

Not all of Petersen's early films fit into the action genre. *The Consequence,* for example, is a drama which charts the romantic

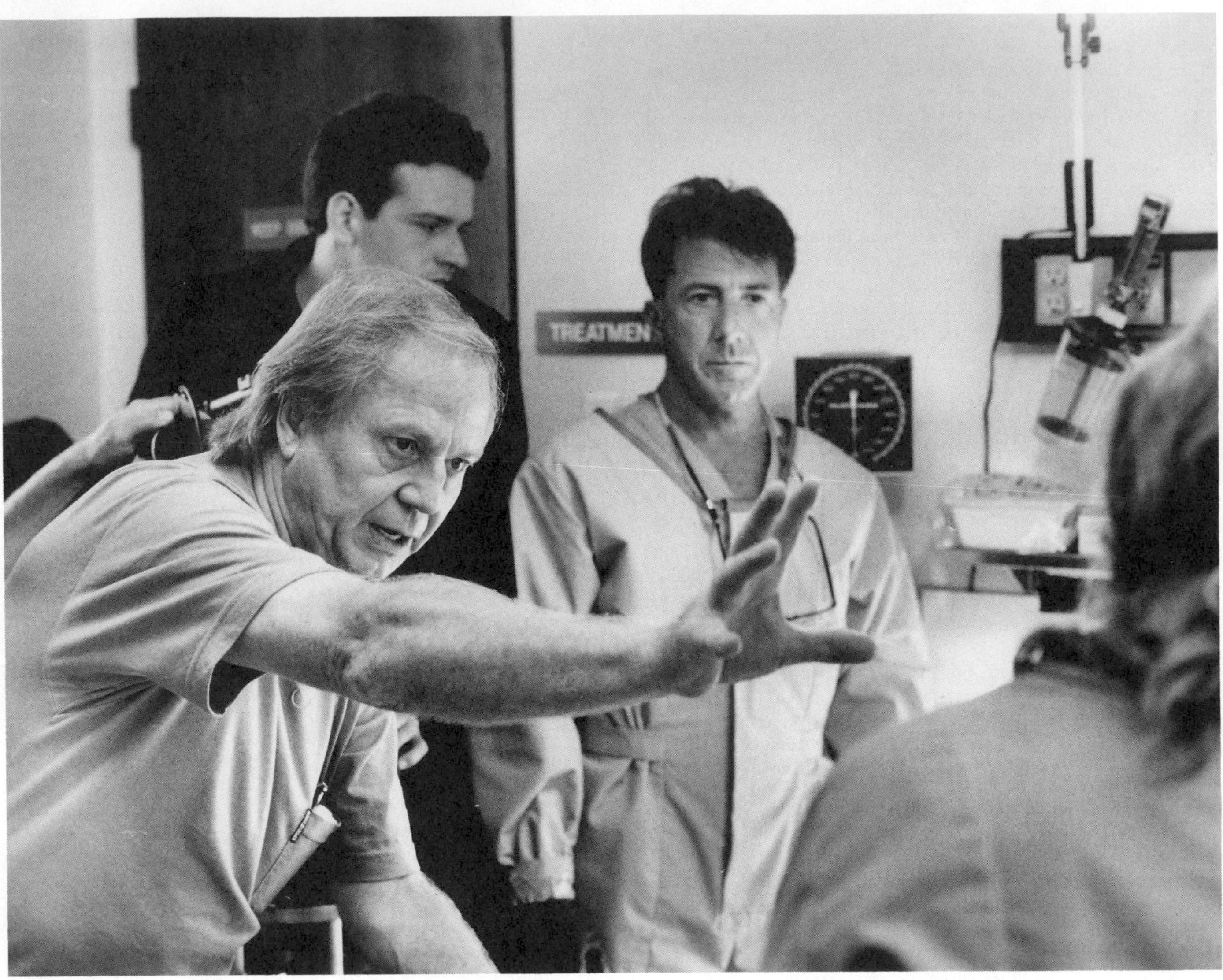

Wolfgang Petersen (left) with Dustin Hoffman directing *Outbreak*

relationship between an imprisoned gay male and the son of one of his guards. But *Das Boot,* the film which brought Petersen to international prominence, might easily have been a Hollywood-produced submarine movie spectacle. At the time of its release, *Das Boot* was the most expensive German film ever made; it originally was shot as a six-hour television mini-series, and was to become the highest-grossing foreign-language film ever released in the United States.

Das Boot is a breathtakingly filmed drama detailing the plight of a German U-boat patrolling the Atlantic during World War II. What is especially impressive about the film is that its scenario runs its course entirely within the tight confines of the vessel. With skill and precision, Petersen uses a Steadicam to visually capture the manner in which the claustrophobic quarters and the constant fear of going into battle affect the crew members, without allowing the lack of space to hamper his directorial style. Furthermore, the film takes on an antiwar aura in that there is an ever-present sense of the wastefulness of war, and the needlessness for the men to have to endure their experience aboard the U-boat. Ironically, Americans who see the film come to empathize with the various characters and pull for their survival—even though, at the time in which the film is set, Germany was America's enemy. *Das Boot* is at once an action-spectacle with a provocative point-of-view, a tremendously thrilling entertainment—and an impressive Hollywood calling card for Petersen.

The director's next noteworthy production (as well as first English-language feature) is *The NeverEnding Story,* a German-British-made fantasy about a boy who envisions the story he is reading in a book. Petersen effectively employs his skills as an action director as the book comes alive and a young hero takes on an evil wizard who has threatened to destroy the Kingdom of Fantasia. Unfortunately, the filmmaker faltered in his first two American-made films. *Enemy Mine* is a middling science fiction tale, while *Shattered* is a just-adequate Hitchcock clone about a car crash victim attempting to patch together his life after becoming an amnesiac.

With *In the Line of Fire,* Petersen redeemed himself and proved that he is capable of making a smashingly entertaining, financially successful, big-budget Hollywood nail-biter. Clint Eastwood plays one of his best roles in a non-Eastwood directed film as an aging Secret Serviceman, haunted by his failure to come between President John F. Kennedy and an assassin's bullet in November 1963, who now must contend with a sadistic killer who aspires to murder the current U.S. Chief Executive. The director's follow-up, *Outbreak,* is another topical thriller, in which an army researcher

(Dustin Hoffman) races against time to halt the spread of a killer virus. The film's limitations have to do with the script; what starts out as a credible thriller soon degenerates into a cartoon-like fantasy littered with counterfeit heroics. But Petersen's direction consistently is first-rate.

—Audrey E. Kupferberg

PETRI, Elio

Nationality: Italian. **Born:** Eraclio Petri in Rome, 29 January 1929. **Education:** University of Rome. **Career:** Film critic for Communist daily *L'Unita,* 1950s; scriptwriter and assistant director, through 1950s; directed first feature, 1961. **Awards:** Academy Award for Best Foreign-Language Film, for *Investigation of a Citizen Above Suspicion,* 1970; Best Film (*ex aequo*), Cannes Festival, for *The Working Class Goes to Paradise,* 1972. **Died:** 1982.

Films as Director:

1954 *Nasce un campione* (short) (+ co-sc)
1957 *I sette Contadini* (short) (+ co-sc)
1961 *L'assassino* (*The Lady Killer of Rome*) (+ co-sc)
1962 *I giorni contati* (+ co-sc)
1963 *Il maestro di Vigevano*
1964 "Peccato nel pomeriggio" (Sin in the Afternoon) episode of *Alta infedelta* (*High Infidelity*)
1965 *La decima vittima* (*The Tenth Victim*) (+ co-sc)
1967 *A ciascuno il suo* (*We Still Kill the Old Way*) (+ co-sc)
1968 *Un tranquillo posto di campagna* (*A Quiet Place in the Country*) (+ co-sc)
1970 *Indagine su un cittadino al di sopra di ogni sospietto* (*Investigation of a Citizen above Suspicion*) (+ co-sc); "Documenti su Giuseppe Pinelli" episode of *Ipotesi* (+ co-sc)
1971 *La classe operaia va in paradiso* (*The Working Class Goes to Heaven*; *Lulu the Tool*) (+ co-sc)
1973 *La proprietà non è piú un furto* (+ co-sc)
1976 *Todo modo* (+ co-sc)
1978 *Le Mani sporche* (for TV) (+ sc)
1979 *Le buone notizie* (+ co-sc, pr)

Other Films:

1952 *Roma ore undici* (*Rome Eleven O'Clock*) (De Santis) (co-sc)
1953 *Un marito per Anna Zaccheo* (*A Husband for Anna*) (De Santis) (co-sc)
1954 *Giorni d'amore* (*Days of Love*) (De Santis) (co-sc)
1956 *Uomini e lupi* (*Men and Wolves*) (De Santis) (co-sc)
1957 *L'Uomo senza domenica* (De Santis) (co-sc)
1958 *Cesta duga godinu dana* (*La strada lunga un anno*) (De Santis) (co-sc)
1960 *La Garconnière* (De Santis) (co-sc)

Publications

By PETRI: books—

L'assassino, Milan, n.d.
Roma ora undici, Rome and Milan, 1956.
Indagine su un cittadino al di sopra ogni sospetto, with Ugo Pirro, Rome, 1970.

By PETRI: articles—

Interview with G. Haustrate, in *Cinéma* (Paris), July/August 1972.
"Cinema Is Not for an Elite but for the Masses," an interview with Joan Mellen, in *Cinéaste* (New York), vol. 6, no. 1, 1973.
"*Todo modo,*" an interview with J. A. Gili, in *Ecran* (Paris), January 1977.
"L'Enfer selon Petri: bonnes nouvelles," an interview with A. Tournès and A. Tassone, in *Jeune Cinéma* (Paris), September/October 1980.

On PETRI: books—

Gili, Jean, *Elio Petri,* Nice, 1973.
Michalczyk, John J., *The Italian Political Filmmakers,* Cranbury, New Jersey, 1986.

On PETRI: articles—

MacBean, James in *Film Quarterly* (Berkeley), Spring 1972 and Spring 1973.
Alemanno, R., "Da Rosi a Peteri todo modo dentro il contesto," in *Cinema Nuovo* (Bari), July/August 1976.
Roy, J., obituary, in *Cinéma* (Paris), January 1983.
Savioli, A., "I trent'anni di Elio Petri," in *Bianco e Nero* (Rome), October/December 1983.
Elio Petri Section of *Jeune Cinéma* (Paris), December 1983/January 1984.

* * *

In his brief career, Elio Petri became renowned as one of the major political filmmakers of the 1960s and 1970s. He was also among the directors who achieved an international stature for the Italian cinema for the third time in its history. From his first feature, an original variation on the police thriller, he maintained a consistently high quality of style and poignant subject matter. Even with the bitterness, grotesqueness, and complexity of his films, many of them achieved a huge commercial success.

The Tenth Victim, for example, a stylized science-fiction collage of Americanisms which concentrates on the voracious rapport between a man (Marcello Mastroianni) and a woman (Ursula Andress), plays repeatedly on American television. *Investigation of a Citizen above Suspicion* (which won the Oscar for best foreign film) and *The Working Class Goes to Heaven* have enjoyed continued success with contemporary audiences through repertory screenings and 16mm distribution. With *Investigation,* Petri wanted to make a film against the police and the mechanisms that guaranteed immunity to the servants of power, yet intended no precise political references. His claim was that the state manifests itself through the police. Like his earlier film, *A ciascuno il suo,* it opens with a murder committed by a police official (Gian Maria Volonté), but, because of his position and manipulation of the system, it remains a crime without punishment. The film brilliantly studies the psychopathology of power, whereas with his other enormous success, *The Working Class Goes to Heaven,* Petri wanted to return to what he considered was the real basis of Italian neorealism—a popular hero. Filmed in a factory whose director was serving a prison sentence, it investigates the reasons why a worker is driven to strike. Again the protagonist was played by Volonté (whose name in the film, Massa, means "the masses"). Although he is a highly individualized character, Petri continually stresses that his actions, thoughts, goals, and even his sexuality are determined by society and its rules.

Elio Petri

Two common themes running throughout Petri's work have been the alienation of modern man and investigations of the socio-political relationships between an individual and his/her society. Petri usually employs a highly stylistic form which he often describes as expressionist. This is most obvious, for example, in *Todo modo,* aptly described as a celebration of death. Quite grotesque, the film was not well received in Italy, where, despite its extreme stylization, it was read as a precise analogy of the ruling political party.

Petri began his film career as a scriptwriter, most notably for Giuseppe De Santis's *Rome Eleven O'Clock*: Petri often stated that De Santis was his only mentor, and like him, Petri directed relatively few films, carefully chosen for content and precisely planned in style and detail. Filmmaking was, in his opinion, the most popular tool with which a culture could understand itself. Thus, he is considered not an artisan, but an auteur, a filmmaker who closely identified the filmmaking process with personal, social, moral, and political duties.

—Elaine Mancini

PETROVIC, Aleksandar

Nationality: Serbian. **Born:** Paris, 14 January 1929. **Education:** Educated at FAMU, Prague, 1947-48; studied history of art at Belgrade University, graduated 1955. **Career:** After FAMU, worked as an assistant director to Rene Clair and several Yugloslav directors; film critic and theoretician, 1949; lecturer in film direction at Academy of Theater, Film, Radio and Television, Belgrade, from 1962; spent several years as chairman of Union of Yugoslav Film Workers. **Awards:** Grand Prix, Karlove Vary International Film Festival, and Academy Award nomination, 1966, for *Tri* (*Three*); Palme d'Or, Cannes International Film Festival, and Academy Award nomination, 1967, for *Skupljaci Perja* (*I Even Met Happy Gypsies*); CIDALC Prize, Venice Film Festival, 1972, for *Maestro i Margerita* (*The Master and Margaret*). **Died:** Exact date unavailable.

Films as Director:

(Short documentaries)

1956 *Let nad mocvarom* (*Flight over the Swamp*) (+ sc)
1957 *Petar Dobrovic* (co-d with Vicko Raspor)
1958 *Putevi* (*The Life and Work of Sava Sumanovic*) (+ sc)
1960 *Rat—ratu* (*The War against the War*) (+ sc)
1964 *Zapisnik* (*Protocol*) (+ sc)
1965 *Sabori* (*Orthodox Churches*) (+ sc)

(Features)

1955 *Uz druga je drug* (*A Friend Next to a Friend*) (co-d with Raspor)
1958 *Jedini izlaz* (*The Only Way Out*) (co-d with Raspor)
1961 *Dvoje* (*Two*) (+ sc)
1963 *Dani* (*Days*) (+ sc)
1965 *Tri* (*Three*) (+ co-sc)
1967 ***Skupljaci Perja*** (*I Even Met Happy Gypsies*) (+ sc)
1968 *Bice skoro propast sveta* (*It Rains in My Village*) (+ co-pr, sc)
1972 *Maestro i Margerita* (*The Master and Margaret*) (+ co-pr, co-sc)
1977 *Gruppenbild mit Dame* (*Group Portrait with Lady*) (+ co-pr, co-sc)
1988 *La guerre la plus glorieuse* (*The Most Glorious War: Migrations*) (+ co-pr, co-sc)

Other Films:

1989 *Private War* (assistant production manager)

Publications

By PETROVIC: books—

Novi film I, 1971.
Novi film II, 1965-1970.
Film noir, 1988.

By PETROVIC: article—

Interview in *UNESCO Courier,* July/August 1994.

On PETROVIC: books—

Dositejeva traganja: 1739-1989, 1989.

On PETROVIC: articles—

Haye, B., "Yugo Helmer Brings Marathon *Migrations* Back Home to Shoot," in *Variety,* June 1988.

Aleksandar Petrovic

Horton, A., "The Rise and Fall of the Yugoslav Partisan Film: Cinematic Perceptions of a National Identity," in *Film Criticism,* no. 2, 1988.
Holloway, R., "Gruppenbild mit Dame," in *Variety,* May 1977.

* * *

After Aleksandar Petrovic went to film school at FAMU in Prague, he worked as an assistant director to Rene Clair and numerous Yugoslav directors. His initial foray into his own film work was as a director of short documentaries and a film critic. In the 1960s, he became a leading figure of the new Yugoslav cinema. He first garnered critical acclaim for his war film *Three.* He won the Palme d'Or at Cannes in 1967 for his film *I Even Met Happy Gypsies.* In an interview with the *UNESCO Courier* Petrovic said of the film, "If the true measure of humanity is the amount of freedom that people manage to win for themselves in this life, then Gypsies are truly men." The hero in the film is a character out of a Dostoyevsky novel who does not think about the ramifications of what he does and therefore has freedom.

Petrovic often dealt with mysticism in his films. This is most apparent in his epic film *Group Portrait with Lady.* When the film showed at Cannes, Petrovic had legal problems with a song he was using. Subsequently the song was cut from the film, and the matter never went to court. *Group Portrait with Lady* is based on a popular novel, as was another of his films, *The Master and Margaret.* In the 1970s, Petrovic experienced political problems with the former Yugoslav authorities. However, in the 1980s he returned and started production on *The Most Glorious War: Migrations.* The film went over budget and well over the expected number of weeks in production. It is based on a historical novel that follows a Serbian mercenary regiment in the eighteenth century. Petrovic died in the late 1980s or early 1990s, but an exact date is unavailable.

—Anita Gabrosek

PHALKE, Dadasaheb

Nationality: Indian. **Born:** Dhundiraj Govind Phalke in Trymbakeshwar, near Nasik, 30 April 1870. **Education:** Studied drawing at J.J. School of Arts, Bombay; art studies at Kalabhavan, Baroda. **Family:** Married first wife in 1885 (she died in 1900); married Saraswatabai (Phalke), daughter Mandakini. **Career:** Portrait photographer and scene painter, from 1900; draughtsman and photographer, Government of India's Archaelogical Department, 1903; opened Phalke Engraving and Printing Works, 1905; left business, saw *Life of Christ* in Bombay, inspired to make films, 1910; made short film, *Growth of a Pea Plant,* 1911; suffered temporary blindness; travelled to London to buy filmmaking equipment, met Cecil Hepworth, 1912; returned to build studio in Bombay, then made first feature film and first Indian film, *Raja Harishchandra,* released April 1913; "Phalke's Films" incorporated into the Hindustan Film Company, 1917; daughter played role of boy Krishna in *Kaliya Mardan,* 1918; retired to Benares, 1919; recalled to direct, 1922; attempted to set up business selling enamel boards, 1933; recalled for last film as director, *Gangavataran,* 1934 (completed 1936). **Died:** In Nasik, 16 February 1944.

Films as Director, Scriptwriter, Producer, and Cinematographer:

(partial list: Phalke made approximately one hundred feature films and twenty-two shorts)

1911 *Growth of a Pea Plant* (short)
1913 *Raja Harishchandra*
1914 *Mohini Bhasmasur*; *Pithache Panje* (short); *Savitri Stayavan*
1914/15 *Soulagna Rasa*; *Mr. Sleepy's Good Luck*; *Agkadyanchi Mouj* (anim); *Animated Coins* (anim); *Vichitra Shilpa* (*Inanimate Animated*) (anim); *Sinhasta Parvani*; *Kartiki Purnima Festival*; *Ganesh Utsava*; *Glass Works* (doc); *Talegaon* (doc); *Bird's Eye View of Budh Gaya* (doc); *Rock-Cut Temples of Ellora* (doc); *How Films Are Made* (short); *Prof. Kelpha's Magic* (+ role)
1916/17 *Raja Harishchandra* (new version); *Lanka Dahan*
1918 *Shree Krishna Janma*; *Kaliya Mardan*
1923 *Sati Mahananda*
1932 *Setu Bandhan*
1937 *Gangavataran*
1965 *Raja Harishchandra: D.G. Phalke (1870-1944): The First Indian Film Director* (compiled by Prof. Satish Bahadur)

Publications

By PHALKE: articles—

Four articles in *Navyug* (Bombay), September 1983.
Interview reprinted in *Close Up* (India), July 1968.

On PHALKE: books—

Barnouw, Erik, and S. Krishnasway, *Indian Film,* New York, 1965.
Ramachandran, T.M., *70 Years of Indian Cinema (1913-1983),* Bombay, 1985.

On PHALKE: articles—

Close Up (India), January/March 1979.
Cinema Vision, January 1980.
Rajadhyaksha, A., "Neo-traditionalism," in *Framework* (Norwich), no. 32-33, 1986.

* * *

In 1912 Dadasaheb Phalke made *Raja Harishchandra,* conventionally considered India's first feature film. Between 1912 and 1917, despite problems relating to finance and the import of equipment because of the war, Phalke and Co. (as the director's concern was called) managed to remain in production. Given such historical facts, Phalke's grand claim that he started the Indian film industry is actually quite a reasonable one.

Phalke brought an impressive string of qualifications to the cinema: painter, printer, engraver, photographer, drama teacher, and magician. The last distinction is particularly notable. He explained that his decision to make Hindu mythological films was due not only to his religious-minded audiences, but also because such subjects allowed him "to bring in mystery and miracles." The mythological aspect of the works he pursued was especially suited to fulfil the early fascination with the cinema as magical toy: hence the extensive use of dissolves and superimpositions to herald miraculous happenings in the handful of Phalke's films that have survived.

The Phalke biography is instructive for the insights it provides about media history. A well-known early story is that Phalke's immersion in intense viewing and experimentation led to ill health and temporary blindness. There is a revelatory, metaphorical aspect to the loss and recovery of sight in a man who declared that he would bring images of revered Indian deities to the screen, just as Christ's image had been presented in the West. Earlier, as photographer and printer, Phalke had been involved in the mass production of the famous religious paintings of Raja Ravi Varma. Phalke's work therefore wove into the early history of cultural self-representation through new media technologies, a period intimately related to the creation of a mass market in indigenous imagery and identity.

Equally important was Phalke's relationship with the theatre. At the time Phalke's first films were released in Bombay, it was said that the cinema was displacing traditional entertainments, such as the theatre and circus, because of its astounding popularity. When Phalke took his films to Poona in 1913, they were screened at a theatre which normally exhibited performances of *Tamasha,* a western Indian dramatic form.

Theatre also left its mark on the new entertainment. In *Raja Harischandra,* the priest as comic character—a staple of the western Indian stage—was used. Moreover, it was because of the development of the theatrical tradition that Phalke was able get the women performers he sought for his female roles—even prostitutes had refused to associate themselves with films. A lay-off in a theatrical company briefly secured for him the services of Durgabhai Gokhale and her daughter, Kamalabhai, the first women actresses of the Indian cinema.

For financial reasons, Phalke and Co. merged with the Hindustan Film Company in 1918. Except for the period 1919-22, Phalke continued to work with this company till 1932, when it was wound up. In his working life as director, which spanned the ages of forty-two to sixty-four, Phalke made some 122 feature films and shorts, concluding his career with *Gangavataran,* the only one planned as a talkie. Thereafter he conceived of various schemes, such as setting up a production unit for short films for the Prabhat company, but nothing came of these ideas, and the last years of his life were spent in relative obscurity.

—Ravi Vasudevan

PIALAT, Maurice

Nationality: French. **Born:** Puy de Dôme, 31 August 1925. **Education:** Studied Art at Ecole des Arts Décoratifs and Ecole des Beaux Arts, Paris. **Career:** Exhibited work at salons, 1945-47; actor and assistant stage director to Michel Vitold, from 1955; worked in TV, made films, from 1960; directed first feature, 1967. **Awards:** Jean Vigo Prize, for *L'enfance nue,* 1967; Prix Louis Delluc, and César for Best Film, for *A nos amours,* 1983; Palme d'Or, Cannes Festival, for *Sous le soleil de Satan,* 1987.

Films as Director:

1960 *L'amour existe* (short)
1961 *Janine* (for TV)

1962 *Maitre Galip* (for TV)
1967 *L'enfance nue* (+ sc)
1971 *La maison des bois* (for TV) (+ role)
1972 *Nous ne vieillirons pas ensemble* (+ sc, pr)
1974 *La gueule ouverte* (+ sc, pr)
1979 *Passe ton bac d'abord*
1979 *Loulou*
1983 *A nos amours* (*To Our Loves*)
1985 *Police* (+ co-sc)
1987 *Sous le soleil de Satan* (*Under Satan's Sun*) (+ co-sc, role)
1991 *Van Gogh* (+ sc)

Other Film:

1969 *Que la bete meure* (Chabrol) (role)

Publications

By PIALAT: book—

Nous ne vieillirons pas ensemble, Paris, 1972.

By PIALAT: articles—

Interview in *Image et Son* (Paris), March 1972.
Interviews in *Positif* (Paris), May 1974 and October 1980.
Interviews in *Cahiers du Cinéma* (Paris), October 1979 and December 1983.
Interview with E. Carrère and M. Sineux, in *Positif* (Paris), January 1984.
Interview with Michel Ciment and others, in *Positif* (Paris), October 1985.
Interview with Serge Toubiana and Alain Philippon, in *Cahiers du Cinéma* (Paris), September 1987.
Interview with L. Vachaud, in *Positif* (Paris), November 1991.
Interview with Michel Ciment and M. Sineux, in *Positif* (Paris), May 1992.
Interview with C. Collard, in *Cahiers du Cinéma* (Paris), April 1993.

On PIALAT: books—

Magny, Joel, *Maurice Pialat,* Paris, 1992.
Toffetti, Sergio, and Aldo Tassone, *Maurice Pialat: L'enfant sauvage,* Torino, 1992.

On PIALAT: articles—

Bonitzer, Pascal, "Le rayonnement Pialat," in *Cahiers du Cinéma* (Paris), May 1981.
Dossier on Pialat, in *Cinématographe* (Paris), November 1983.
Pialat Section of *Cahiers du Cinéma* (Paris), December 1983.
Gras, P., "Maurice Pialat," in *Revue du Cinéma* (Paris), September 1985.

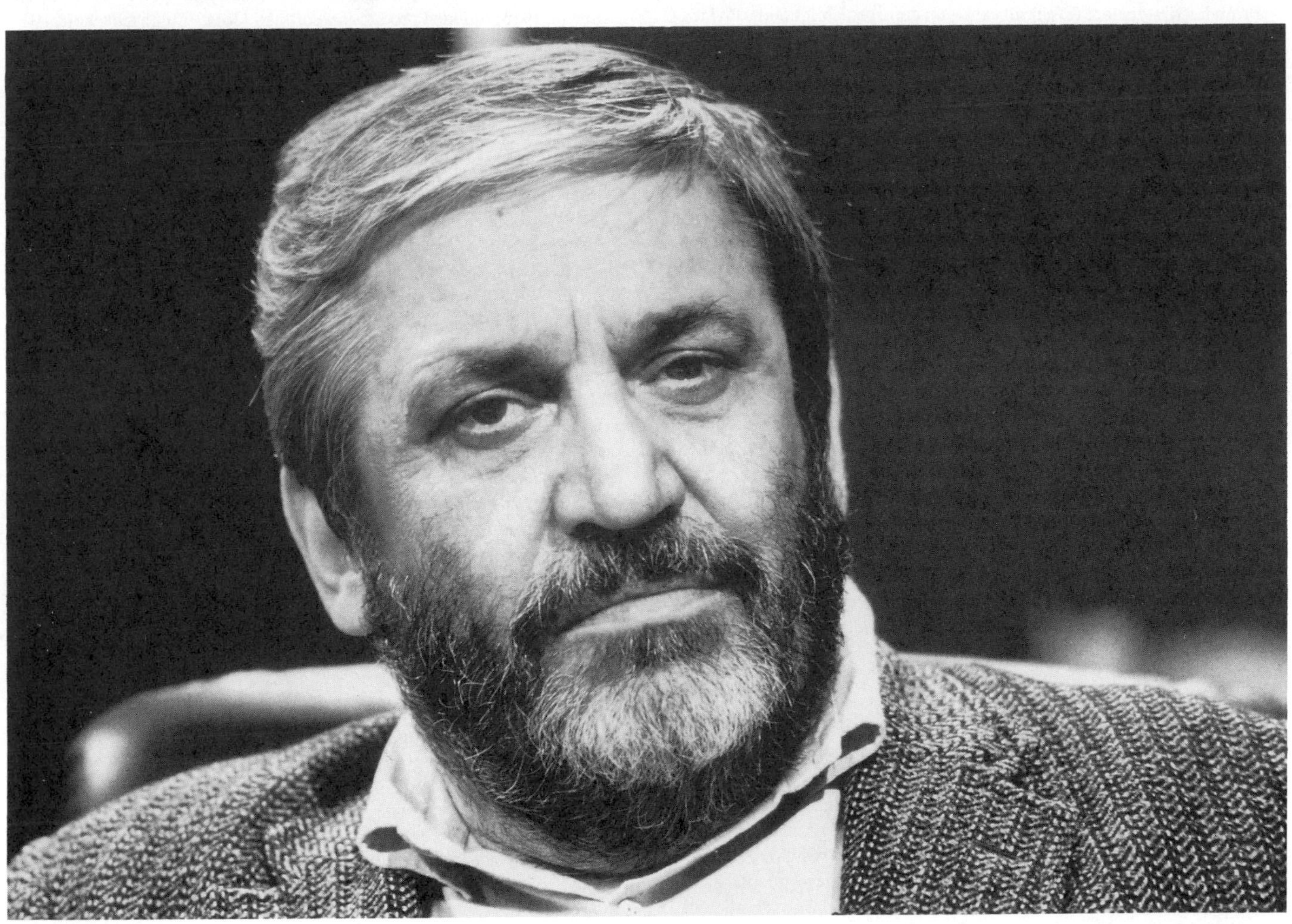

Maurice Pialat

Vincendeau, Ginette, "Pialat le terrible," in *Monthly Film Bulletin* (London), March 1986.

Martin, Marcel, and G. Lenne, "Le silence de Dieu: Critiques dans l'auditorium—perplexes," in *Revue du Cinéma* (Paris), September 1987.

Chevassu, F., "Les droles de chemins de Maurice Pialat," in *Revue du Cinéma* (Paris), December 1990.

Vrdlovec, Z., "Maurice Pialat," in *Ekran* (Ljubljana), vol. 16, no. 9/10, 1991.

Jousse, T., "L'affaire *Van Gogh,*" in *Cahiers du Cinéma* (Paris), June 1991.

Rouyer, P., "Quelques jours avec lui," in *Positif* (Paris), November 1991.

Roy, A., "Petit dictionnaire pour Maurice Pialat," in *Revue de la Cinematheque* (Montreal), March/April 1993.

* * *

Described by Alain Bergala in *Cahiers du Cinéma* as "Renoir's true heir today," Maurice Pialat is squarely in the tradition of French *auteur* cinema. Like Renoir, Feyder, and Grémillon in the 1930s, and Godard, Resnais, Varda, and a few others after the war, Pialat is an artisan who works both within and against the French film industry. He has often acknowledged his "debt" to Renoir, as well as to Pagnol, in terms of both working methods and a certain conception of realism. However, unlike the benign humanism of these two predecessors, Pialat's work is marked by harshness, violence, and conflict, both on and off screen.

From his first feature (*L'enfance nue,* on deprived childhood), Pialat's films have shown an almost ethnographic concern with unglamorous areas of French society: difficult adolescents (*Passe ton bac d'abord*), semi-hooligans (*Loulou*), the bitter breakdown of a couple (*Nous ne vieillirons pas ensemble*) and cancer (*La gueule ouverte*), combining a quasi *cinéma-vérité* approach with the reworking of deeply personal matters. Although Pialat has claimed to be "fed up with realism," and even though he has made forays into genre films with *Police* and *Sous le soleil de Satan,* his cinema is still within a realistic idiom, fusing the New Wave (and neo-realist) concern with location shooting and contemporary setting with the "intimate" realism of the central European cinema of the 1960s. His films draw on basic realist strategies such as the use of non-professional or little-known actors (sometimes alongside stars like Gérard Depardieu, and on occasion—Renoir-style—the charismatic Pialat himself), the frequent recourse to improvisation and colloquial language, hand-held camerawork, long takes, and shooting without a finished script. If these strategies traditionally produce a sense of immediacy and authenticity, they often combine, in Pialat's films, with a rare violence.

Pialat has earned a reputation as a "difficult" director. To some extent, this is an inherent part of the myth of *auteur* cinema which stresses the romantic pains of creation. Yet Pialat's career is littered with well-publicized working and personal conflicts: with actors Gérard Depardieu (*Loulou*) and Sophie Marceau (*Police*), with scriptwriter Catherine Breillat over *Police,* and with technicians on many occasions. But part of his method consists precisely of inscribing his own personal relationships within the fabric of his films, as epitomised in *A nos amours* by the Pialat/Bonnaire couple (on several professional and personal levels).

"*Pialat le terrible,*" as he was dubbed by a French paper, sometimes makes headlines, and occasionally the courtrooms. This would be mere gossip if it did not echo the very subject matter of his films. In the same way as Sam Fuller defined cinema as "a battleground," Pialat's filmmaking might be described as belonging to the boxing ring. He has repeatedly stated his preference for situations where people have rows, where they clash, where "there is trouble," and this is borne out by all his films, where conflict is the preferred element, a type of conflict which moreover assumes a great physicality. In Pialat's cinema, contact is more likely to be made through violence than through tenderness, particularly within the family, where the boxing ring overlaps with the Oedipal stage. This is true both thematically (families and couples tearing each other apart) and in the way Pialat's films address their spectators. A predominance of indoor scenes shot in claustrophobic medium close-ups, and the deliberate inclusion of "flawed" episodes, of moments of rupture or tension in the films, are ways of capturing "the truth" of characters or situations, sometimes with little regard for narrative continuity. Pialat does not pull his punches, and his cinema, in the words of editor Yann Dedet, "tends more towards emotion than comprehension."

If Pialat's films, in their bleak examination of some of the least palatable aspects of contemporary French society and personal emotions, make for difficult viewing, their reward lies in an emotional and documentary power rare in French cinema today.

—Ginette Vincendeau

PICK, Lupu

Nationality: Romanian. Also known as "Lupu-Pick." **Born:** Iasi (Jassy), 2 January 1886. **Family:** Married Edith Pasca. **Career:** Actor in Romania, 1914; emigrated to Germany, acted in Hamburg and Berlin, 1915; founded production company Rex Filmgesellschaft, 1917; directed first film, 1918; elected President of DACHO (German actors' union), 1930. **Died:** In Berlin, 9 March 1931.

Films as Director:

1918 *Der Weltspiegel*; *Die Liebe des van Royk*; *Die Rothenburger*; *Die tolle Heirat von Laló*; *Mister Wu*

1919 *Der Seelenverkäufer*; *Herr über Leben und Tod*; *Kitsch*; *Marionetten der Leidenschaft*; *Mein Wille ist Gesetz*; *Tötet nicht mehr!*; *Misericordia* (+ pr)

1920 *Der Dummkopf* (*The Idiot*) (+ role); *Niemand weiss es*

1921 *Aus den Erinnerungen eines Frauenarztes* Part 2; *Grausige Nächte*; *Scherben* (*Shattered*)

1922 *Zum Paradies der Damen*

1923 *Sylvester* (*New Year's Eve*); *Der verbotene Weg* (+ role)

1924 *La Péniche tragique*

1925 *Das Haus der Lüge*

1926 *Das Panzergewölbe* (*Armored Vault*) (+ co-sc)

1928 *Eine Nacht in London* (*A Night in London*) (+ pr)

1929 *Napoléon a Sainte-Hélène* (*Napoleon auf St. Helena*)

1931 *Les Quatres Vagabonds*; *Gassenhauer*

Other Films:

1915 *Schlemihl* (Oswald) (role); *Hoffmanns Erzählungen* (Oswald) (role); *Die Pagode* (Mr. Wu) (role)

1916 *Nächte des Grauens* (Robison) (role); *Homunculus* series (role)

1917 *Die Fremde* (role)

1917/18 *Es werde Licht* (three episodes) (role)

1922 *Fliehende Schatten* (Lamprecht) (co-sc, role)

1923 *Stadt in Sicht* (role)

1926 *Alte Herzen, neue Zeiten* (role)

1928 *Spione* (Lang) (role)

Lupu Pick: *Scherben*

Publications

On PICK: books—

Kracauer, Siegfried, *From Caligari to Hitler: A Psychological History of the German Film,* Princeton, New Jersey, 1947.

Borde, Raymond, Freddy Bauche, François Courtade, and Marcel Tariol, *Le Cinéma réaliste allemand,* Paris, 1959.

Eisner, Lotte, *The Haunted Screen: Expressionism in the German Cinema and the Influence of Max Reinhardt,* translated by Robert Greaves, Berkeley and Los Angeles, 1969.

Manvell, Roger, and Heinrich Fraenkel, *The German Cinema,* New York, 1971.

* * *

Lupu Pick, a pioneer of the German *Kammerspielfilm* that led the way from expressionism to the new realism of the late 1920s, came to the cinema from the Berlin stage, where he worked as an actor under Piscator and Reinhardt. His first films as a director were segments of an adventure series for popular actor Bernd Aldor.

Two films that Pick created with scriptwriter Carl Mayer, *Scherben* and *Sylvester,* are the basis of his reputation. *Scherben* was the first German experiment in filmmaking without intertitles. Pick and Mayer adapted the name of Reinhardt's smallest stage—which had come to represent the intimacy and concentration of the plays staged there—in the subtitle of their first film together: *Scherben, ein deutsches Filmkammerspiel.* Critics often attribute the success of *Scherben* and *Sylvester* to Mayer. Indeed, Mayer wrote many of the films usually counted as *kammerspielfilme,* working with Murnau, Jessner, and Gerlack. But Pick undeniably contributed his unique interpretation of Mayer's scripts.

Scherben uses a single intertitle and is distinguished by the extended use of a moving camera, especially in long tracking shots along railway ties. This movement contrasts sharply with the stationary plot, the slow movement of the actors, and the long-held, still shots. At times masks seem to be used in response to the expressionist punctuation Mayer used in his scripts. Diagonal slash masks isolate an image just as Mayer's one word sentences are set off by exclamation marks.

Pick created a new, non-expressionist style, concentrating on naturalistic detail rather than on abstraction. Perhaps it was this enthusiasm for naturalism which led Pick to linger over the process of mechanical tasks and everyday events. Yet his work remains tied to the expressionist movement. The actors in his films, especially his wife Edith Posca and Werner Krauss, operated within the range of theatrical expressionist style. Shot at Pick's own Rex Studios in Berlin, *Scherben* is to a great extent manufactured in the studio, although its intent and its effect involve a realist illusion.

Unlike filmmakers truly caught up in expressionism, Pick was concerned with portraying individual psychology. In his attempts to construct a drama without language he developed a system of irises and dissolves that was quite different from the psychological editing style then developing in Hollywood. Rather than cut to a reaction, Pick often masked the frame, isolating a single character. At other times he would compose a shot so that an object, framed in relation to a character, could represent a thought. While the style that Pick developed may have had little influence on subsequent filmmaking, it was nevertheless a bold experiment in film narrative in its time.

Originally Pick and Mayer had planned a trilogy that would include *Scherben, Sylvester,* and *Der letze Mann,* but a disagreement over the character of the doorman in the third film led to Pick's departure from the project.

The films Pick made after his collaboration with Mayer are not remembered by many. He continued to work as an actor, both on stage and in films. His best known role is that of Dr. Matsumoto in Lang's *Spione.* Pick made a single sound film, *Gassenhauer,* reportedly an experiment in asynchronous sound.

—Ann Harris

POLANSKI, Roman

Nationality: Polish. **Born:** Paris, 18 August 1933. **Education:** Krakow Liceum Sztuk Plastycznych (art school), 1950-53; State Film School, Lodz, 1954-59. **Family:** Married 1) actress Barbara Kwiatkowska, 1959 (divorced 1961); 2) actress Sharon Tate, 1968 (died 1969); 3) actress Emmanuelle Seigner, 1989. **Career:** Returned to Poland, 1936; actor on radio and in theatre, from 1945, and in films, from 1951; joined filmmaking group KAMERA as assistant to Andrzej Munk, 1959; directed first feature, *Knife in the Water,* 1962, denounced by Polish Communist Party chief Gomulka, funding for subsequent films denied, moved to Paris, 1963; moved to London, 1964, then to Los Angeles, 1968; wife Sharon Tate and three friends murdered in Bel Air, California, home by members of Charles Manson cult, 1969; opera director, from 1974; convicted by his own plea of unlawful sexual intercourse in California, 1977; committed to a diagnostic facility, Department of Correction; upon completion of study, returned to Paris; also stage actor and director. **Awards:** Silver Bear, Berlin Film Festival, for *Repulsion,* 1965; Golden Bear, Berlin Festival, for *Cul-de-Sac,* 1966; César Award, for *Tess,* 1980. **Address:** Lives in Paris.

Films as Director and Scriptwriter:

1955/57 *Rower* (*The Bike*) (short)
1957/58 *Morderstwo* (*The Crime*) (short)
1958 *Rozbijemy zabawe* (*Break Up the Dance*) (short); *Dwaj ludzie z szasa* (*2 Men and a Wardrobe*) (short) (+ role)
1959 *Gdy spadaja anioly* (*When Angels Fall*) (short) (+ role as old woman)
1961 *Le Gros et le maigre* (*The Fat Man and the Thin Man*) (short) (co-sc, + role as servant)
1962 *Ssaki* (*Mammals*) (short) (co-sc, + role); ***Nóz w wodzie*** (*Knife in the Water*) (co-sc)
1963 "La Rivière de diamants" ("A River of Diamonds") episode of *Les Plus Belles Escroqueries du monde* (*The Most Beautiful Swindles in the World*) (co-sc)
1964 ***Repulsion*** (co-sc)
1965 *Cul-de-sac* (co-sc)
1967 *The Fearless Vampire Killers* (*Pardon Me, But Your Teeth Are in My Neck; Dance of the Vampires*) (co-sc, + role as Alfred)
1968 ***Rosemary's Baby***
1972 *Macbeth* (co-sc)
1973 *What?* (*Che?*; *Diary of Forbidden Dreams*) (co-sc, + role as Mosquito)
1974 ***Chinatown*** (d only, + role as man with knife)
1976 *Le Locataire* (*The Tenant*) (co-sc, + role as Trelkovsky)
1979 *Tess* (co-sc)
1985 *Pirates* (co-sc)
1988 *Frantic* (co-sc)
1992 *Bitter Moon* (co-sc + pr)
1993 *Death and the Maiden*

Other Films:

1953 *Trzy opowiesci* (*Three Stories*) (Nalecki, Poleska, Petelski) (role as Maly)
1954 *Pokolenie* (*A Generation*) (Wajda) (role as Mundek)
1955 *Zaczárowany rower* (*The Enchanted Bicycle*) (Sternfeld) (role as Adas)
1956 *Koniec wojny* (*End of the Night*) (Dziedzina, Komorowski, Uszycka) (role as Maly)
1957 *Wraki* (*Wrecks*) (Petelski) (role)
1958 *Zadzwoncie do mojej zony* (*Phone My Wife*) (Mach) (role)
1959 *Lotna* (Wajda) (role as bandsman)
1960 *Niewinni czarodzieje* (*Innocent Sorcerors*) (Wajda) (role as Dudzio); *Ostroznie yeti* (*The Abominable Snowman*) (Czekalski) (role); *Do Widzenia do Jutra* (*See You Tomorrow*) (Morgenstern) (role as Romek); *Zezowate szczescie* (*Bad Luck*) (Munk) (role)
1964 *Do You Like Women?* (Léon) (co-sc)
1968 *The Woman Opposite* (Simon) (co-sc)
1969 *A Day at the Beach* (Hessera) (pr); *The Magic Christian* (McGrath) (role)
1972 *Weekend of a Champion* (Simon) (pr, role as interviewer)
1974 *Blood for Dracula* (Morrissey) (role as a villager)
1991 *Back in the U.S.S.R.* (Serafian) (role as Kurilov)
1994 *Gross Fatigue* (role as himself)
1995 *A Simple Formality* (role as Inspector)

Publications

By POLANSKI: books—

What?, New York, 1973.
Three Films, London, 1975.
Roman (autobiography), London, 1984.
Polanski par Polanski, edited by Pierre-André Boutang, Paris, 1986.

By POLANSKI: articles—

Interview with Gretchen Weinberg, in *Sight and Sound* (London), Winter 1963/64.
"Landscape of a Mind: Interview with Roman Polanski," with Michel Delahaye and Jean-André Fieschi, in *Cahiers du Cinema in English* (New York), February 1966.

Interview with Michel Delahaye and Jean Narboni, in *Cahiers du Cinéma* (Paris), January 1968.
"Polanski in New York," an interview with Harrison Engle, in *Film Comment* (New York), Fall 1968.
Interview with Joel Reisner and Bruce Kane, in *Cinema* (Los Angeles), vol. 5, no. 2, 1969.
"Satisfaction: A Most Unpleasant Feeling," an interview with Gordon Gow, in *Films and Filming* (London), April 1969.
Interview, in *The Film Director as Superstar,* by Joseph Gelmis, Garden City, New York, 1970.
"Playboy Interview: Roman Polanski," with Larry DuBois, in *Playboy* (Chicago), December 1971.
"Andy Warhol Tapes Roman Polanski," in *Inter/View* (New York), November 1973.
"Dialogue on Film: Roman Polanski," in *American Film* (Washington, D.C.), August 1974.
"Roman Polanski on Acting," with D. Brandes, in *Cinema Papers* (Melbourne), January 1977.
"*Tess,*" an interview with Serge Daney and others, in *Cahiers du Cinéma* (Paris), December 1979.
Interview with P. Pawlikowski and L. Kolodziejczyk, in *Stills* (London), April/May 1984.
Interview with O. Darmon, in *Cinématographe* (Paris), May 1986.
"Roman Oratory," an interview with Andrea R. Vaucher, in *American Film,* April 1991.
"At the Point of No Return," an interview with Rider McDowell, in *California,* August 1991.
"Entretien avec Roman Polanski," with A. de Baecque and T. Jousse, in *Cahiers du Cinéma,* May 1992.
"Roman Polanski's *Bitter Moon,*" an interview with Stephen O'Shea, in *Interview,* March 1994.

On POLANSKI: books—

Butler, Ivan, *The Cinema of Roman Polanski,* New York, 1970.
Kane, Pascal, *Roman Polanski,* Paris, 1970.
Belmans, Jacques, *Roman Polanski,* Paris, 1971.
Bisplinghoff, Gretchen, and Virginia Wexman, *Roman Polanski: A Guide to References and Resources,* Boston, 1979.
Kiernan, Thomas, *The Roman Polanski Story,* New York, 1980.
Leaming, Barbara, *Polanski: The Filmmaker as Voyeur: A Biography,* New York, 1981; also published as *Polanski: His Life and Films,* London, 1982.
Paul, David W., *Politics, Art, and Commitment in the Eastern European Cinema,* New York, 1983.
Dokumentation: Polanski und Skolimowski: Das Absurde im Film, Zurich, 1985.
Wexman, Virginia Wright, *Roman Polanski,* Boston, 1985.
Jacobsen, Wolfgang, and others, *Roman Polanski,* Munich, 1986.
Avron, Dominique, *Roman Polanski,* Paris, 1987.
McCarty, John, *The Modern Horror Film,* Secaucus, New Jersey, 1990.
Preljocaj, Angelin, *Roman Polanski,* Paris, 1992.
McCarty, John, *Movie Psychos and Madmen,* Secaucus, New Jersey, 1993.
McCarty, John, *The Fearmakers,* New York, 1994.

On POLANSKI: articles—

Haudiquet, Philippe, "Roman Polanski," in *Image et Son* (Paris), February/March 1964.
Brach, Gérard, "Polanski via Brach," in *Cinéma* (Paris), no. 93, 1965.
McArthur, Colin, "Polanski," in *Sight and Sound* (London), Winter 1968.
McCarty, John, "The Polanski Puzzle," in *Take One* (Montreal), May/June 1969.
Tynan, Kenneth, "Polish Imposition," in *Esquire* (New York), September 1971.
"Le Bal des vampires," special Polanski issue of *Avant-Scène du Cinéma* (Paris), January 1975.
Leach, J., "Notes on Polanski's Cinema of Cruelty," in *Wide Angle* (Athens, Ohio), vol. 2, no. 1, 1978.
Kennedy, H., "*Tess*: Polanski in Hardy Country," in *American Film* (Washington, D.C.), October 1979.
"L'Univers de Roman Polanski," special section, in *Cinéma* (Paris), February 1980.
Sinyard, Neil, "Roman Polanski," in *Cinema Papers* (Melbourne), November/December 1981.
Polanski Section of *Kino* (Warsaw), July 1986.
Polanski Section of *Positif* (Paris), May 1988.
Sutton, M., "Polanski in Profile," in *Films and Filming* (London), September 1988.
Ansen, David, "The Man Who Got Away," in *Newsweek,* 28 March 1994.
Weschler, Lawrence, "Artist in Exile," in *New Yorker,* 5 December 1994.
Davis, Ivor, "Out of Exile?" in *Los Angeles Magazine,* January 1995.
Heilpern, John, "Roman's Tortured Holiday," in *Vanity Fair,* January 1995.

* * *

As a student at the Polish State Film School and later as a director working under government sponsorship, Roman Polanski learned to make films with few resources. Using only a few trained actors (there are but three characters in his first feature) and a hand-held camera (due to the unavailability of sophisticated equipment) Polanski managed to create several films which contributed to the international reputation of the burgeoning Polish cinema. These same limitations contributed to the development of a visual style which was well suited to the director's perspective on modern life: one which emphasized the sort of precarious, unstable world suggested by a hand-held camera, and the sense of isolation or removal from a larger society which follows the use of only small groupings of characters. In fact, Polanski's work might be seen as an attempt to map out the precise relationship between the contemporary world's instability and tendency to violence and the individual's increasing inability to overcome his isolation and locate some realm of meaning or value beyond himself.

What makes this concern with the individual and his psyche especially remarkable is Polanski's cultural background. As a product of a socialist state and its official film school at Lodz, he was expected to use his filmmaking skills to advance the appropriate social consciousness and ideology sanctioned by the government. However, Polanski's first feature, *Knife in the Water,* drew the ire of the Communist Party and was denounced at the Party Congress in 1964 for showing the negative aspects of Polish life. Although less an ideological statement than an examination of the various ways in which individual desires and powers determine our lives, *Knife in the Water* and the response it received seem to have precipitated Polanski's subsequent development into a truly international filmmaker. In a career that has taken him to France, England, Italy, and the United States in search of opportunities to write, direct, and act, he has consistently shown more interest in holding up a mirror to the individual impulses, unconscious urges, and the personal psychoses of human life than in dissecting the different social and political forces he has observed.

The various landscapes and geographies of Polanski's films certainly seem designed to enhance this focus, for they pointedly remove his characters from most of the normal structures of social life as well

Roman Polanski

as from other people. The boat at sea in *Knife in the Water,* the oppressive flat and adjoining convent in *Repulsion,* the isolated castle and flooded causeway of *Cul-de-sac,* the prison-like apartments of *Rosemary's Baby* and *The Tenant,* and the empty fields and deserted manor house in *Tess* form a geography of isolation that is often symbolically transformed into a geography of the mind, haunted by doubts, fears, desires, or even madness. The very titles of films like *Cul-de-sac* and *Chinatown* are especially telling in this regard, for they point to the essential strangeness and isolation of Polanski's locales, as well as to the sense of alienation and entrapment which consequently afflicts his characters. Brought to such strange and oppressive environments by the conditions of their culture (*Chinatown*), their own misunderstood urges (*Repulsion*), or some inexplicable fate (*Macbeth*), Polanski's protagonists struggle to make the unnatural seem natural, to turn entrapment into an abode, although the result is typically tragic, as in the case of *Macbeth,* or absurd, as in *Cul-de-sac.*

Such situations have prompted numerous comparisons, especially of Polanski's early films, to the absurdist dramas of Samuel Beckett. As in many of Beckett's plays, language and its inadequacy play a significant role in Polanski's works, usually forming a commentary on the absence or failure of communication in modern society. The dramatic use of silence in *Knife in the Water* actually "speaks" more eloquently than much of the film's dialogue of the tensions and desires which drive its characters and operate just beneath the personalities they try to project. In the conversational clichés and banality which mark much of the dialogue in *Cul-de-sac,* we can discern how language often serves to cloak rather than communicate meaning. The problem, as the director most clearly shows in *Chinatown,* is that language often simply proves inadequate for capturing and conveying the complex and enigmatic nature of the human situation. Detective Jake Gittes's consternation when Evelyn Mulwray tries to explain that the girl he has been seeking is both her daughter and her sister—the result of an incestuous affair with her father—points out this linguistic inadequacy for communicating the most discomfiting truths. It is a point driven home at the film's end when, after Mrs. Mulwray is killed, Gittes is advised not to try to "say anything." His inability to articulate the horrors he has witnessed ultimately translates into the symptomatic lapse into silence also exhibited by the protagonists of *The Tenant* and *Tess,* as they find themselves increasingly bewildered by the powerful driving forces of their own psyches and the worlds they inhabit.

Prompting this tendency to silence, and often cloaked by a proclivity for a banal language, is a disturbing force of violence which all of Polanski's films seek to analyze—and for which they have frequently been criticized. Certainly, his own life has brought him all too close to this most disturbing impulse, for when he was only eight years old Polanski and his parents were interned in a German concentration camp where his mother died. In 1969 his wife Sharon Tate and several friends were brutally murdered by Charles Manson's followers. The cataclysmic violence in the decidedly bloody adaptation of *Macbeth,* which closely followed his wife's death, can be traced through all of the director's features, as Polanski has repeatedly tried to depict the various ways in which violence erupts from the human personality, and to confront in this specter the problem of evil in the world. The basic event of *Rosemary's Baby*—Rosemary's bearing the offspring of the devil, a baby whom she fears yet, because of the natural love of a mother for her own child, nurtures—might be seen as a paradigm of Polanski's vision of evil and its operation in our world. Typically, it is the innocent or unsuspecting individual, even one with the best of intentions, who unwittingly gives birth to and spreads the very evil or violence he most fears. The protagonist of *The Fearless Vampire Killers,* for example, sets about destroying the local vampire and saving his beloved from its unnatural hold. In the process, however, he himself becomes a vampire's prey and, as a concluding voice-over solemnly intones, assists in spreading this curse throughout the world.

It is a somber conclusion for a comedy, but a telling indication of the complex tone and perspective which mark Polanski's films. He is able to assume an ironic, even highly comic attitude towards the ultimate and, as he sees it, inevitable human problem—an abiding violence and evil nurtured even as we individually struggle against these forces. The absurdist stance of Polanski's short films, especially *Two Men and a Wardrobe* and *The Fat and the Lean,* represents one logical response to this paradox. That his narratives have grown richer, more complicated, and also more discomfiting in their examination of this situation attests to Polanski's ultimate commitment to understanding the human predicament and to rendering articulate that which seems to defy articulation. From his own isolated position—as a man effectively without a country—Polanski tries to confront the problems of isolation, violence, and evil, and to speak of them for an audience prone to their sway.

After a highly publicized 1977 sex scandal resulted in his flight from the United States and subsequent exile, Polanski surprised many by doing an apparent about face in terms of subject matter, and creating one of his most restrained and visually beautiful films: the aforementioned *Tess.* It was based on the classic Thomas Hardy novel of innocence destroyed, *Tess of the D'Urbervilles.* Polanski dedicated the movie to the memory of his murdered wife, Sharon Tate. *Tess* was followed by *Pirates,* a parody of the swashbuckling adventure films starring Errol Flynn that Polanski had enjoyed as a youth. Walter Matthau starred in the film as the comically villainous Captain Red, a role Polanski had written for Jack Nicholson. When *Pirates* failed at the box-office, Polanski returned to the cinema of fear with *Frantic,* a Hitchcock-style thriller with a Polanski touch, starring Harrison Ford. The story of a man inadvertently trapped in a nightmare situation in a foreign land, *Frantic* drew upon many of Polanski's favorite themes. But as a bid for critical and commercial success, it failed to repeat the performance of his earlier fear-films. The master of psychological suspense was not to be counted out yet, though. In 1992, Polanski bounced back with the film his fans had been clamoring for for years—a potent and powerful synthesis of all the absurdist comedies, parodies, thrillers, fear-films, and detective yarns Polanski had made in the past: *Bitter Moon.* He followed it up with the taut and well-reviewed but only modestly successful *Death and the Maiden.*

Roman Polanski's importance as a filmmaker hinges upon a uniquely unsettling point of view. All his characters try continually, however clumsily, to connect with other human beings, to break out of their isolation and to free themselves of their alienation. Could it be that his nightmarish films serve much the same purpose? Perhaps they too are the continuing efforts of a terrified young Jewish boy, adrift in a war-torn land, to connect with the rest of humanity—even after all these years.

—J. P. Telotte, updated by John McCarty

POLLACK, Sydney

Nationality: American. **Born:** Lafayette, Indiana, 1 July 1934. **Education:** South Bend Central High School; studied with Sanford Meisner, Neighborhood Playhouse, New York. **Military Service:** U.S. Army, 1957-59. **Family:** Married Claire Griswold, 1958, three children. **Career:** Actor on Broadway and for TV, also acting instructor, from 1955; TV director in Los Angeles, from 1960; directed first film, 1965; also produced his own films, from 1975. **Awards:** Emmy Award for *The Game,* 1966; Oscars for Best Film and Best Direction, for *Out of Africa,* 1986.

Films as Director:

1965 *The Slender Thread*
1966 *This Property Is Condemned*
1968 *The Swimmer* (Perry) (d one sequence only); *The Scalphunters*
1969 *Castle Keep*; *They Shoot Horses, Don't They?*
1972 *Jeremiah Johnson*
1973 *The Way We Were*
1975 *Three Days of the Condor*; *The Yakuza* (*Brotherhood of the Yakuza*) (+ pr)
1976 *Bobby Deerfield* (+ pr)
1979 *The Electric Horseman*
1981 *Absence of Malice* (+ pr)
1982 *Tootsie* (+ co-pr, role as George Fields)
1985 *Out of Africa* (+ pr)
1990 *Havana* (+ co-pr)
1993 *The Firm* (+ pr)
1995 *Sabrina* (+ pr)

Other Films:

1961 *The Young Savages* (Frankenheimer) (dialogue coach)
1962 *War Hunt* (Sanders) (role as Sergeant Van Horn)
1963 ***Il gattopardo*** (*The Leopard*) (Visconti) (supervisor of dubbed American version)
1973 *Scarecrow* (Schatzberg) (pr)
1980 *Honeysuckle Rose* (Schatzberg) (exec pr)
1984 *Songwriter* (Rudolph) (pr); *Sanford Meisner—The Theater's Best Kept Secret* (doc) (exec pr)
1988 *Bright Lights, Big City* (Bridges) (pr)
1990 *Presumed Innocent* (Pakula) (pr); *White Palace* (Mandoki) (exec pr)
1992 ***The Player*** (Altman) (role); *Death Becomes Her* (role); *Husbands and Wives* (Allen) (role)

Publications

By POLLACK: book—

Out of Africa: The Shooting Script, with Kurt Luedke, New York, 1987.

By POLLACK: articles—

Interview with G. Langlois, in *Cinéma* (Paris), July/August 1972.
"Nos Plus Belles Années," an interview with Max Tessier, in *Ecran* (Paris), April 1974.
Interview with L. Salvato, in *Millimeter* (New York), June 1975.
"Sydney Pollack: The Way We Are," an interview with Patricia Erens, in *Film Comment* (New York), September/October 1975.

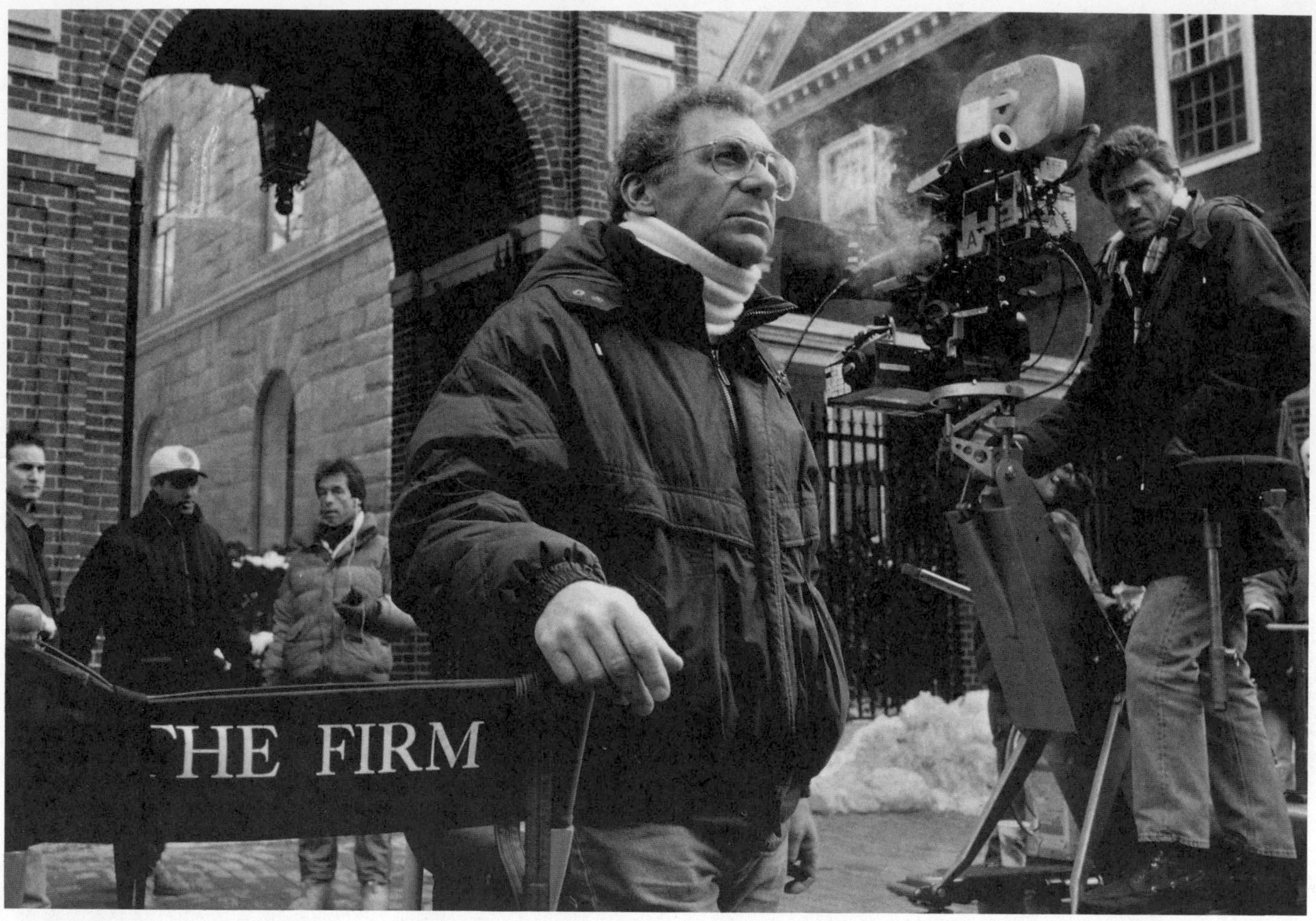

Sydney Pollack on the set of *The Firm*

"Dialogue on Film: Sydney Pollack," in *American Film* (Washington, D.C.), April 1978.

"Sydney Pollack, An Actor's Director," an interview with P. Childs, in *Millimeter* (New York), December 1979.

Interview with P. Carcassonne and J. Fieschi, in *Cinématographe* (Paris), March/April 1981.

Interview with T. Ryan and S. Murray, in *Cinema Papers* (Melbourne), May/June 1983.

Interview in *Post Script* (Jacksonville, Florida), Fall 1983.

Interview with J. A. Gili and M. Henry, in *Positif* (Paris), April 1986.

"Dialogue on Film: Sydney Pollack," in *American Film* (Washington, D.C.), December 1986.

"Sydney Pollack," an interview with A. Dutertre, in *Revue du Cinéma* (Paris), March 1991.

"Le papillon et l'ouragan: entretien avec Sydney Pollack," with M. Henry, in *Positif* (Paris), March 1991.

"Intervista a Sydney Pollack fra produzione e regia," with F. La Polla, in *Cineforum* (Bergamo), July/August 1991.

"J'espere que c'est a cause de Tootsie!" an interview with M. Henry, in *Positif* (Paris), December 1992.

On POLLACK: books—

Gili, Jean A., *Sydney Pollack,* Nice, 1971.

Taylor, William R. *Sydney Pollack,* Boston, 1981.

Leon, Michele, *Sydney Pollack,* Paris, 1991.

On POLLACK articles—

Madsen, Axel, "Pollack's Hollywood History," in *Sight and Sound* (London), Summer 1973.

Massuyeau, M., "Dossier: Hollywood 79: Sydney Pollack," in *Cinématographe* (Paris), March 1979.

"*Le Cavalier électrique* Issue" of *Avant-Scène du Cinéma* (Paris), 15 June 1980.

Camy, G., "Sydney Pollack: Souvenirs d'Amérique," in *Jeune Cinéma* (Paris), May/June 1986.

Wharton, Dennis, "Top Directors Get Behind Film-Labeling Legislation," in *Variety* (Paris), 29 July 1991.

Bart, Peter, "Filmers Face the Future," in *Variety* (Paris), 15 November 1993.

* * *

Sydney Pollack is especially noted for his ability to elicit fine performances from his actors and actresses and has worked with leading Hollywood stars, including Robert Redford (who has appeared in five Pollack films), Jane Fonda, Barbra Streisand, Dustin Hoffman, Paul Newman, and Burt Lancaster, among others. Though Pollack has treated a cross-section of Hollywood genres, the majority of his films divide into male-action dramas and female melodramas. Among the former are *The Scalphunters, Castle Keep, Jeremiah Johnson, Three Days of the Condor,* and *The Yakuza.* Among the latter are *The Slender Thread, This Property Is Condemned, The Way We Were,* and *Bobby Deerfield.*

The typical Pollack hero is a loner whose past interferes with his ability to function in the present. Throughout the course of the narrative, the hero comes to trust another individual and exchanges his isolation for a new relationship. For the most part, Pollack's heroines are intelligent women, often with careers, who possess moral strength, although in several cases they are victims of emotional weakness. Pollack is fond of portraying the attraction of opposites. The central issue in all of Pollack's work focuses on the conflict between cultural antagonists. This can be racial, as in *The Slender Thread, The Scalphunters,* or *Jeremiah Johnson* (black vs. white; white vs. Indian); religious, as in *The Way We Were* (Protestant vs. Jew); geographic, as in *This Property Is Condemned* and *The Electric Horseman* (city vs. town); nationalistic, as in *Castle Keep* (Europe vs. America; East vs. West); or based on gender differences, as in *Tootsie* (feminine vs. masculine).

Pollack's films do not possess a readily identifiable visual style. However, his works are generally noteworthy for their total visual effect, and he frequently utilizes the helicopter shot. Structurally the plots possess a circular form, often ending where they began. Visually this is echoed in the circular dance floor of *They Shoot Horses, Don't They?,* but is also apparent in *Jeremiah Johnson* and *The Way We Were.*

Along with Sidney Lumet, Pollack is one of Hollywood's foremost liberals. His work highlights social and political issues, exposing organized exploitation rather than individual villainy. Most prominent among the issues treated are racial discrimination (*The Scalphunters*), the destructiveness of war (*Castle Keep*), the Depression (*They Shoot Horses, Don't They?*), Hollywood blacklisting (*The Way We Were*), CIA activities (*Three Days of the Condor*), commercial exploitation (*The Electric Horseman*), media exploitation (*Absence of Malice*), and feminism (*Tootsie*). Although Pollack has often been attacked for using these themes as background, rather than delving deeply into their subtleties, the French critics, among others, hold his work in high esteem.

Over the years, Pollack's cache in the Hollywood community has steadily risen. Unlike Lumet, to whom his work and directorial approach bear many similarities, he is not a New York director who occasionally works in Hollywood, but a Hollywood insider. His films make money and score multiple Oscar nominations. He is instantly forgiven for a failure like *Havana,* his sweeping attempt to recall the filmmaking styles of the Old Hollywood and such pictures as *Casablanca.* Because of all this, an American Film Institute Life Achievement Award cannot be long in coming for him.

Pollack began his career as an actor and frequently appears, sometimes unbilled, in the films of other directors—though, ironically, not his own films a la Hitchcock (for whose legendary TV series Pollack both acted and directed). Woody Allen gave this former actor a particularly juicy part in *Husbands and Wives.*

But Pollack prefers to direct, and with his standing in the industry he is able to command big budgets and big stars—and choice properties—for his work. His *The Firm,* based on the runaway best-seller by lawyer turned novelist John Grisham, and starring Tom Cruise, was a sizable hit, the film's alteration of the book's ending not even a minus with Grisham fans. His latest, *Sabrina,* is, surprisingly, Pollack's first outright romantic comedy, a remake of the 1954 Billy Wilder gem, with Harrison Ford, Julia Ormond, and Greg Kinnear taking the respective roles of Humphrey Bogart, Audrey Hepburn, and William Holden.

—Patricia Erens, updated by John McCarty

POLONSKY, Abraham

Nationality: American. **Born:** New York City, 5 December 1910. **Education:** City College of New York; Columbia University, law degree. **Career:** Lawyer with Manhattan firm, then quit to write; signed with Paramount, late 1930s; served in Europe with Office of Strategic Services (O.S.S.), World War II; moved to Enterprise Productions, 1947; directed first feature, 1948; spent year in France, 1949; signed with Twentieth Century-Fox, 1950; called to testify before House Un-American Activities Committee, invoked Fifth Amendment, 1951; blacklisted until 1968; also novelist.

Films as Director and Scriptwriter:

1948 *Force of Evil*
1970 *Tell Them Willie Boy Is Here*
1971 *Romance of a Horsethief*

Other Films:

1947 *Golden Earrings* (Leisen) (sc); *Body and Soul* (Rossen) (sc)
1951 *I Can Get It For You Wholesale* (Gordon) (sc)
1968 *Madigan* (Siegel) (sc)
1979 *Avalanche Express* (Robson) (sc)
1982 *Monsignor* (sc)
1991 *Guilty by Suspicion* (sc)

Publications

By POLONSKY: book—

To Illuminate Our Time: The Blacklisted Teleplays of Abraham Polonsky, Los Angeles, 1993.

By POLONSKY: articles—

"Abraham Polonsky and *Force of Evil,*" an interview with William Pechter, in *Film Quarterly* (Berkeley), Spring 1962.
Interview in *Interviews with Film Directors,* by Andrew Sarris, New York, 1967.
Interview with William Pechter, in *Film Quarterly* (Berkeley), Winter 1968/69.
Interview with Jim Cook and Kingsley Canham, in *Screen* (London), Summer 1970.
"How the Blacklist Worked," in *Film Culture* (New York), Fall/Winter 1970.
"Making Movies," in *Sight and Sound* (London), Spring 1971.
"Nuits blanches pendant la liste noir: Extrait de journal," in *Positif* (Paris), December/January 1977/78.
"Tutkijasta tekijaksi," an interview with P. von Bagh, in *Filmihullu,* no. 3, 1991.

On POLONSKY: articles—

Canham, Kingsley, "Polonsky," in *Film* (London), Spring 1970.
Butler, T., "Polonsky and Kazan: HUAC and the Violation of Personality," in *Sight and Sound* (London), Autumn 1988.
Neve, Brian, "Fellow Traveller," in *Sight and Sound* (London), Spring 1990.

* * *

Abraham Lincoln Polonsky's filmography is quite thin: his second film as director, *Tell Them Willie Boy Is Here,* was released twenty-one years after his first, *Force of Evil.* "I was a left-winger," he told *Look* magazine in 1970. "I supported the Soviet Union. In the middle 1940s, we'd have meetings at my house to raise money for strikers and radical newspapers." For these crimes—and, equally, for the less-than-superficially patriotic qualities of his protagonists—a promising, perhaps even major, directorial career was squelched in its infancy by the insidious Hollywood blacklist.

A discussion of Polonsky would be incomplete without noting his collaborations with John Garfield, the American cinema's original anti-hero. Polonsky scripted *Body and Soul,* one of the best boxing films of all time, and both authored and directed *Force of Evil,* a "B film" ignored in its time, but now a cult classic highly regarded for its use of blank verse dialogue.

Garfield stars in *Force of Evil* as a lawyer immersed in the numbers racket. When his brother, a small-time gambler, is murdered by his gangster boss, he hunts the hood down and turns himself in to the police. In *Body and Soul,* the actor portrays a poor boy with a hard, knockout punch who rises in the fight game while alienating his family, friends, and the girl he loves. In the end he reforms, defying the mob by refusing to throw a fight. "What are you gonna do, kill me?" he chides the chief thug, "Everybody dies." With that, he walks off into the night with his girl. The final cut of *Body and Soul* is as much Polonsky's as it is director Robert Rossen's. Polonsky claimed to have prevented Rossen from altering the film's finale.

Both of Polonsky's protagonists become casualties of their desire for success. They seek out the all-American dream, but are corrupted in the process. They can only attain status by throwing fights, aligning themselves with lawbreakers. Fame and money, fancy hotels and snazzy suits, come not by hard work and honesty but by cheating, throwing the fight, fixing the books—the real American way.

Polonsky, and Garfield, were blacklisted as much for the tone of their films as their politics. Polonsky's heroes are cocky, cynical loner-losers, estranged from society's mainstream, who break the rules and cause others extreme sorrow—not the moral, honest, often comic-book caricatures of American manhood that dominated Hollywood cinema. In addition, Polonsky created a character in *Body and Soul,* a washed-up boxer (lovingly played by Canada Lee), who was one of the earliest portraits of a black man as a human being with emotions and feelings, a man exploited. *Body and Soul* and *Force of Evil* played the nation's moviehouses in 1947 and 1948, when anything less than a positive vision of America was automatically suspect.

Polonsky's plight is particularly sad. His passport was revoked, and he could not escape to find work abroad. Years after others who had been blacklisted had returned to the good graces of the cinema establishment, he toiled in obscurity writing television shows and perhaps dozens of film scripts—some Academy Award winners—under assumed names. His first post-blacklist directorial credit, *Willie Boy,* is a spiritual cousin of his earlier work. It is the tale of a nonconformist Paiute Indian (Robert Blake, who played Garfield as a child in *Humoresque*), victimized by an insensitive society after he kills in self-defense. The parallels between Polonsky and his character's fate are clear.

Before the blacklist, Polonsky had hoped to film Thomas Mann's novella, *Mario and the Magician*; in 1971, he was again planning this project, among others. None was ever completed. But most significantly, the films that he might have made between 1948 and 1969—the prime years of his creative life—can now only be imagined.

—Rob Edelman

PONTECORVO, Gillo

Nationality: Italian. **Born:** Gilberto Pontecorvo in Pisa, 19 November 1919. **Education:** Studied chemistry, University of Pisa. **Military Service:** Journalist, and partisan fighter, Milan (commanded 3rd Brigade), World War II. **Career:** Youth secretary, Italian Communist Party, 1946; Paris correspondent for Italian journals, late 1940s; began in films as assistant to Yves Allegret on *Les Miracles n'ont lieu qu'une fois,* 1951; made ten shorts, 1953-55; left Communist Party following invasion of Hungary, 1956; organizer of Venice Film Festival. **Awards:** Golden Lion, Venice Festival, for *The Battle of Algiers,* 1966. **Address:** via Paolo Frisi 18, Rome, Italy.

Films as Director:

1955 "Giovanna" episode of *Die Windrose*
1957 *La grande strada azzurra* (*La lunga strada azzurra*; *The Long Blue Road*) (+ co-sc)
1960 *Kapò* (+ co-sc)
1966 ***La battaglia di Algeri*** (*The Battle of Algiers*) (+ co-sc, co-mus)
1969 *Queimada* (*Burn!*)
1979 *Ogro* (*Operation Ogro*)
1988 *The Devil's Bishop*

Other Films:

1946 *Il sole sorge ancora* (Vergano) (role as partisan)

Publications

By PONTECORVO: articles—

Interview with Guy Hennebelle, in *Cinéma* (Paris), December 1965.
"*The Battle of Algiers*: An Adventure in Filmmaking," in *American Cinematographer* (Los Angeles), April 1967.
Interview with Joan Mellen, in *Film Quarterly* (Berkeley), Fall 1972.
"Using the Contradictions of the System," an interview with H. Kalishman, in *Cineaste* (New York), vol. 6, no. 2, 1974.
Interview with C. Lucas, in *Cineaste* (New York), Fall 1980.
"Che cosa mi sta a cuore," in *Cinema Nuovo,* November/December 1992.
"Fest Topper's Trip down Memory Lane," an interview with David Rooney, in *Variety,* August 28, 1995.

On PONTECORVO: books—

Mellen, Joan, *Filmguide to "The Battle of Algiers,"* Bloomington, Indiana, 1973.
Solinas, Franco, *Gillo Pontecorvo's "The Battle of Algiers": A Film Written by Franco Solinas,* New York, 1973.
Michalczyk, John J., *The Italian Political Filmmakers,* Cranbury, New Jersey, 1986.

On PONTECORVO: articles—

Wilson, David, "Politics and Pontecorvo," in *Sight and Sound* (London), Fall 1970.
Young, Deborah, "Pontecorvo Roars into Role as Fest Chief," in *Variety,* March 2, 1992.
Branbergen, A., "De stad moet onze prima donna zijn," in *Skoop,* September 1992.
Young, Deborah, "Fest Topper Crusading for Filmmakers," in *Variety,* September 6, 1993.

* * *

Gillo Pontecorvo is concerned with the oppressed, those kept down by the unjust and cruel use of power—and who will eventually rebel against the oppressor. "I've always wanted to look at man during the

Gillo Pontecorvo directing *Kapò*

hardest moments of his life," the filmmaker has stated. An examination of his filmography indicates that he has been true to his goals and ideals.

Kapò, for example, is the story of a young Jewish girl and her attempt to survive in a Nazi concentration camp. But Pontecorvo's masterpiece is *The Battle of Algiers,* a meticulous re-creation of the historical events surrounding the successful rebellion against the French by Algeria between 1954 and 1962. Shot in authentic locales with both actors and non-professionals in a cinéma-vérité style, Pontecorvo's black-and-white images seem like newsreels rather than staged sequences; the viewer can easily forget that the film is not a documentary. Additionally, the villains (chiefly the French Colonel Mathieu, played by Jean Martin) are not sadistic, one-dimensional imperialists, thugs and goons who abuse the rights of those they have colonized. While Mathieu is far from benevolent, he is believable and sympathetic, as much the victim of an exploitative society as the Algerians; the colonel even admits that the Algerians are destined to win—this is a lesson of history—and his job is just to temporarily put off the inevitable.

The same is true for the most visible tyrant in *Burn!,* Sir William Walker (Marlon Brando), a confused, self-destructive British adventurer who betrays the slaves who revolt on a Portuguese-controlled, sugar-producing Caribbean island in the mid-nineteenth century. Both Walker and Mathieu are depicted as human beings—with misguided values, perhaps, but human beings nonetheless. However, while *The Battle of Algiers* is a near-flawless film, the scenario of *Burn!* is muddled in that Walker's motives are never really clear. Both films are potent politically in that the imperialists are not caricatured, yet at the same time it is clear that Pontecorvo sides with the Algerians and the slaves. At the beginning of *The Battle of Algiers,* for example, a tortured Algerian is held up by French paratroopers. Despite all that follows, this sequence is in and of itself a political statement, one that sets the tone for all that follows.

Pontecorvo is a Marxist: in 1941, at the age of twenty-two, he became a member of the Italian Communist Party. His initial film, the "Giovanna" episode from *Die Windrose,* is a women's rights movie shot in East Germany. And, in *The Battle of Algiers,* he deals specifically with partisans of the Algerian National Liberation Front who, via their actions, increase the political awareness of their fellow citizens. Here Pontecorvo illustrates how a group of individuals can unite into a political force and defeat a common enemy. This is achieved by violent means: if freedom is to be earned, suffering and physical force and even the deaths of innocent people may be necessary. Gillo Pontecorvo is a filmmaker whose art is scrupulously true to his politics.

—Rob Edelman

PORTER, Edwin S.

Nationality: American. **Born:** Edwin Stratton Porter in Connellsville, Pennsylvania, 21 April 1869. **Military Service:** Served in U.S. Navy, assisted in development of gunnery range finder, 1893-96. **Career:** Left school at age fourteen, worked as sign painter, theater cashier and stagehand; after military stint, worked for Raff & Gammon, marketers of Edison Vitascope; helped arrange first New York screening of motion pictures, 1896; invented and manufactured projector, 1898; business ruined by fire, rejoined Edison Company, 1900; director and cameraman, then supervisor of production at Edison studio, New York City; quit Edison, founded Defender Pictures, 1909; organized Rex Film Company, 1910; sold interest in Rex, founded "Famous Players in Famous Plays" company, 1912, with Adolph Zukor; director general and treasurer, supervisor and director at Famous Players until 1915; became President of Precision Machine Corp., manufacturer of Simplex projector, which he helped develop, from 1915. **Died:** 30 April 1941.

Films as Director:

(partial list, also frequently sc, ph and ed)

1899 *The America's Cup Race*

1900 *Why Mrs. Jones Got a Divorce*; *Animated Luncheon*; *An Artist's Dream*; *The Mystic Swing*; *Ching Lin Foo Outdone*; *Faust and Marguerite*; *The Clown and the Alchemist*; *A Wringing Good Joke*; *The Enchanted Drawing*

1901 *Terrible Teddy the Grizzly King*; *Love in a Hammock*; *A Day at the Circus*; *What Demoralized the Barber Shop*; *The Finish of Bridget McKeen*; *Happy Hooligan Surprised*; *Martyred Presidents*; *Love by the Light of the Moon*; *Circular Panorama of the Electric Tower*; *Panorama of the Esplanade by Night*; *The Mysterious Cafe*

1902 *Uncle Josh at the Moving Picture Show*; *Charleston Chain Gang*; *Burlesque Suicide*; *Rock of Ages*; *Jack and the Beanstalk*; *Happy Hooligan Turns Burglar*; *Capture of the Biddle Brothers*; *Fun in a Bakery Shop*

1903 *The Life of an American Fireman*; *The Still Alarm*; *Arabian Jewish Dance*; *Razzle Dazzle*; *Seashore Frolics*; *Scenes in an Orphans' Asylum*; *The Gay Shoe Clerk*; *The Baby Review*; *The Animated Poster*; *The Office Boy's Revenge*; *Uncle Tom's Cabin*; *The Great Train Robbery*; *The Messenger Boy's Mistake*; *Casey and His Neighbor's Goat*

1904 *The Ex-Convict*; *Cohen's Advertising Scheme*; *European Rest Cure*; *Capture of Yegg Bank Burglars*; *City Hall to Harlem in Fifteen Seconds via the Subway Route*; *Casey's Frightful Dream*; *The Cop Fools the Sergeant*; *Elephant Shooting the Chutes at Luna Park*

1905 *The Kleptomaniac*; *Stolen by Gypsies*; *How Jones Lost His Roll*; *The Little Train Robbery*; *The White Caps*; *Seven Ages*; *The Life of an American Policeman*

1906 *The Dream of a Rarebit Fiend*; *The Life of a Cowboy*; *Three American Beauties*; *Kathleen Mavourneen*

1907 *Daniel Boone*; *Lost in the Alps*; *The Midnight Ride of Paul Revere*; *Laughing Gas*; *Rescued from an Eagle's Nest*; *The Teddy Bears*

1908 *Nero and the Burning of Rome*; *The Painter's Revenge*; *The Merry Widow Waltz Craze*; *The Gentleman Burglar*; *Honesty Is the Best Policy*; *Love Will Find a Way*; *Skinny's Finish*; *The Face on the Barroom Floor*; *The Boston Tea Party*; *Romance of a War Nurse*; *A Voice from the Dead*; *Saved by Love*; *She*; *Lord Feathertop*; *The Angel Child*; *Miss Sherlock Holmes*; *An Unexpected Santa Claus*

1909 *The Adventures of an Old Flirt*; *A Midnight Supper*; *Love Is Blind*; *A Cry from the Wilderness*; *Hard to Beat*; *On the Western Frontier*; *Fuss and Feathers*; *Pony Express*; *Toys of Fate*; *The Iconoclast*; *Hansel and Gretel*; *The Strike*; *Capital versus Labor*

1910 *All on Account of a Laundry Mark*; *Russia—the Land of Oppression*; *Too Many Girls*; *Almost a Hero*; *The Toymaker on the Brink and the Devil*

1911 *By the Light of the Moon*; *On the Brink*; *The White Red Man*; *Sherlock Holmes Jr.*; *Lost Illusions*

1912 *A Sane Asylum*; *Eyes That See Not*; *The Final Pardon*; *Taming Mrs. Shrew*

1913 *The Prisoner of Zenda* (co-d); *His Neighbor's Wife*; *The Count of Monte Cristo* (co-d); *In the Bishop's Carriage* (co-d); *A Good Little Devil* (co-d)

Edwin S. Porter: *The Great Train Robbery*

1914 *Hearts Adrift*; *Tess of the Storm Country*; *Such a Little Queen* (co-d)
1915 *The Eternal City* (co-d); *Zaza* (co-d); *Sold* (co-d); *The Prince and the Pauper* (co-d); *Bella Donna* (co-d)
1916 *Lydia Gilmore* (co-d)

Publications

By PORTER: article—

Statement, in *Filmmakers on Filmmaking,* edited by Harry Geduld, Bloomington, Indiana, 1967.

On PORTER: books—

Balshofer, Fred, and Arthur Miller, *One Reel a Week,* Berkeley, 1967.
Pratt, George, *Spellbound in Darkness,* Greenwich, Connecticut, 1973.
Salt, Barry, *Film Style and Technology: History and Analysis,* London, 1983.
Burch, Noël, *Life to Those Shadows,* Berkeley, 1990.
Elsaesser, Thomas, and Adam Barker, editors, *Early Cinema: Space-Frame-Narrative,* London, 1990.

On PORTER: articles—

Sadoul, Georges, "English Influences on the Work of Edwin S. Porter," in *Hollywood Quarterly,* Fall 1947.
Spears, Jack, "Edwin S. Porter," in *Films in Review* (New York), June/July 1970.
Burch, Noël, "Porter, or Ambivalence," in *Screen* (London), Winter 1978/79.
Schulberg, Budd, letter, in *Variety* (New York), 9 May 1979.
Gaudreault, André, "Detours in Film Narrative: The Development of Cross-Cutting," in *Cinema Journal* (Evanston), Fall 1979.
Musser, Charles, "Early Cinema of Edwin Porter," in *Cinema Journal* (Evanston), Fall 1979.
Ranvaud, Don, "After *The Great Train Robbery* ...," in *Monthly Film Bulletin* (London), December 1983.
Pearson, R., "The Filmmaker as Scholar and Entertainer: An Interview with Charles Musser," in *Cineaste* (New York), vol. 8, no. 3, 1984.

On PORTER: film—

Musser, Charles, *Before the Nickelodeon,* United States, 1984.

* * *

In the annals of film history, Edwin S. Porter is often credited as the first American film director. Although this may not be true in the literal sense, it is not unjustified to give Porter this title. Porter was first and foremost an engineer, an inventor, and a cameraman. In the early days of filmmaking, "cameraman" was synonymous with "director," and Porter found himself handling both jobs. As his own editor, he also discovered new ways of creating a narrative. While most early motion pictures were composed of a single shot showing only one continuous action from beginning to end, Porter began to combine and juxtapose his filmed images, creating new meanings as one scene "psychologically" led into another. Porter became one of the first American directors to tell a story in his films.

Porter acknowledged an influence in his filmmaking from Georges Méliès, the French filmmaker whose "trick films" were extremely popular in the United States. A designer of motion picture cameras, Porter was able to study and discover the secrets to many of Méliès's "tricks." Most importantly, Porter was struck by the fact that these films told a story. However, while Méliès's films told a straightforward, linear narrative, Porter expanded this idea with the use of cross-narrative (parallel action) to depict two simultaneous events or points of view.

Porter's first film of major importance was *The Life of an American Fireman,* made in 1902 or early 1903. This film was largely composed of stock shots from earlier Edison Company films. Racing fire engines were a popular subject for early filmmakers and Porter had much footage at his disposal. To complement these stock shots, Porter filmed additional footage that depicted a mother and child trapped in a burning building. By editing these scenes together Porter created the story of the mother and child's rescue by the firefighters. Porter intercut the scenes of mother and child with stock footage of the racing fire engines, thereby creating a dramatic tension—will the firefighters rescue the two victims from the burning building in time? While this technique of storytelling may seem blasé by today's standards, it was innovative and exciting to 1903 audiences.

Porter continued to develop his film editing techniques in his best known and most popular film, *The Great Train Robbery.* On its most simplistic level, the film is a story of crime, pursuit, and capture. But it is perhaps the first great American chase film, a form still popular today. Again Porter edited his film using cross-cutting to show events that were supposedly occurring at the same time: the bandits begin their escape while the posse organizes a pursuit. *The Great Train Robbery* was an enormously popular film at a time when nickelodeons were just opening across the country, and the film did a great deal of repeat business.

Surprisingly, after *The Great Train Robbery,* Porter did little else to advance the art of filmmaking. In 1912 he formed the Famous Players Film Co. with Adolph Zukor and David Frohman, acting as director-general of the company. However, his films of this period (such as *The Count of Monte Cristo* and *The Prisoner of Zenda*) contain none of the energy of his earlier films. In fact, they took several steps backward technically, for they were photographed in a very stagy, single point-of-view manner. Apparently, Porter was never really interested in directing films. He soon sold his shares in Famous Players and became more involved in designing motion picture cameras and projectors, including the Simplex. Still, Porter's one important contribution to filmmaking—a freer style of editing—was a turning point in the development of film as a narrative art form.

—Linda J. Obalil

POTTER, Sally

Nationality: British. **Education:** Attended London School of Contemporary Dance. **Career:** Began making 8-millimeter films in 1968; performed and choreographed for the Strider Dance Company; founded Limited Dance Company, 1974; toured Britain and U.S.A. in performance shows, both solo and in collaboration, including the Feminist Improvising Group (FIG); released short feminist comedy *Thriller,* funded by the Arts Council of Great Britain, 1979; formed Marx Bros. group with Lindsay Cooper and Georgie Born, 1980; choreographed solo dances for Maedee Dupres; lectured on feminism and feminism and cinema; made first feature film, *Gold Diggers,* financed by the British Film Institute, 1983; made films for television. **Address:** Adventure Pictures, Blackbird Yard, London E2.

Films as Director:

1968-73 *Hors d'oeuvres* (8mm short); *Play* (16mm short); *The Building* (expanded cinema event)
1979 *Thriller* (short) (+ pr, sc); *The London Story* (short) (+pr, sc)
1983 *The Gold Diggers* (+ co-sc, co-ed, composer of lyrics, performer of song "Seeing Red," choreographer)
1986 *Tears Laughter Fear and Rage* (for TV)
1988 *I Am an Ox—Women in Soviet Cinema* (for TV)
1993 *Orlando* (+ sc)

Publications

By POTTER: articles—

Interview with Valentina Agostinis, *Framework,* no. 14, Spring 1981.
"Gold Diggers and Fellow Travellers," *National Film Theatre Programmes* (London), 1 May 1984.
"The Gold Diggers," an interview with Pam Cook, *Framework,* no. 24, Spring 1984.
"Das Schwarze in Weissen," an interview with Claudia Hoff, *Frauen und Film,* no. 37, October 1984.
"Like Night and Day," an interview with Sheila Johnston, *Monthly Film Bulletin,* vol. 51, no. 604, 1984.
"Immortal Longing," an interview with Walter Donohue, *Sight and Sound,* vol. 3, no. 3, March 1993.
"Demystifying Traditional Notions of Gender," an interview with Pat Dowell, *Cineaste,* vol. 20, no. 1, July 1993.
"Debate: A Conversation with Sally Potter," an interview with Penny Florence, *Screen,* vol. 34, no. 3, Autumn 1993.

On POTTER: article—

Glaessner, Verina, "Fire and Ice," in *Sight and Sound,* vol. 2, no. 4, August 1992.

* * *

Sally Potter's career so far exemplifies the best and the worst features of British film culture: the best in its imaginativeness, inventiveness, and biting integrity; the worst in the extreme parsimony, both financial and critical, in which it existed. Potter's work in performance art, dance, and at the London Film Makers' Co-op was both culturally and financially "on the margins." Aware of these categories of "avant garde" or "independent," "feminist" or "experimental," Potter has in quite serious ways never accepted them. Quite early on she spoke of herself as working within "avant garde show business." Performance art and dance brought her into intimate contact with audiences, and she maintained this contact when she turned to film—regularly travelling with her films, watching and rewatching with different audiences, and involving herself in discussions afterwards. In various ways the idea of "the big screen" and the richness of the history of classical narrative cinema has been from the beginning part of her project. When making *Thriller,* a short but disconcerting deconstruction of *La Boheme,* she has said that she always asked herself, as she shot and then edited it, how it would look on the big screen in a Leicester Square cinema.

Sally Potter: Tilda Swinton (left) with Quentin Crisp in *Orlando*

Changes in the structure of funding independent films in Britain during the 1980s enabled Potter to make her first feature film, *The Gold Diggers.* Using Colette Lafont, with whom she had worked in *Thriller,* and dramatic landscapes of "virginal purity" in Iceland, which she had visited with her performance group, she put together a film in which the circulation of finance and the circulation of images are both scrutinised. Lafont plays a computer programmer in a bank who becomes fascinated by gold—the touchstone of value, the basis of the calculations that appear daily on her screen. Julie Christie plays an actress on the run from her image. The film's radical quality extended to its mode of production. All participants took a salary of £30 per day and the film was shot with an all-women crew, including Babette Mangolte on camera, who had had previous experience with Chantal Ackerman and Yvonne Rainer. The film was shot in black and white. Christie brought with her memories of her role within the traditional cinema epic, David Lean's *Doctor Zhivago,* but also a sense of the new, postwar woman from her work in British cinema of the sixties (*Billy Liar, Darling*). Lafont was deliberately cast against the stereotype of the black woman who is primarily a physical and sensual being. In the course of the action each woman attempts to locate a value system of her own, her own kind of gold. The film is full of affectionate references to cinema history and to the representations of women within it. Its very English quality lies in what has been called its narrative of "Alice in Wonderland-like inconsequentiality." In this lack of narrative seriousness, and in the sense in which its twin protagonists are experienced almost as a single entity, the film nicely prefigures *Orlando.*

With *Orlando* Potter seemed to be attempting to film the unfilmable, so much of the charm and persuasiveness of Virginia Woolf's thinly veiled love letter to Vita Sackville West—and to history and to language—lies in its literary mode of address, the joy of words on paper. In the event Potter's intellectual adventurousness, allied to her equally strong awareness of the cinema's potential for magic, proved precisely right. Its rich, late-twentieth-century nouveau-rococo mise-en-scene (well within the English tradition of masque and display, explored also by Derek Jarman and Peter Greenaway), its quirky humour and laconic way with big themes, were purely cinematic. Central to the success of the film was the casting of Tilda Swinton as the protagonist who lives for 400 years, changing gender in the process—a role which Potter had envisaged for her from the beginning. The intelligent performance Swinton gives provides the film with an unshakable focus.

Financial necessity again nudged Potter towards radical production solutions. Funding was cobbled together from a handful of European sources, which included Russia. From Russia also came Elem Klimov's miraculous cinematographer Alexei Rodionov, the strange landscapes of Khiva, and St. Petersburg's snow. There is a sense in *Orlando* of everything—discourses on Englishness and the foreign, history and class, gender and identity—being thrown into the air to fall almost where they will. Gender, argues Orlando, is not central to the person but inconsequential. "Same person," says Orlando, "different sex."

Visual excitement comes not from narrative drive and the surrender to the merely sensational. "I edit," Potter has said, "not to narrative, but to an idea." Likewise her early work on performance and display inhibits her from an automatic recourse to the well-nigh ubiquitous language of the tight closeup with its concomitant fetishising of body parts at the expense of the person. Craft, a sense of timing, the awareness that an audience finds pleasure in a whole complex of feelings and ideas—"ethics too are pleasurable"—all play a part.

As the language of commercial cinema becomes more homogenous across the world, films which keep alive other ways of representation and response become increasingly valuable, and indeed necessary. Potter's work so far does so with considerable wit and aplomb.

—Verina Glaessner

POWELL, Michael, and Emeric PRESSBURGER

POWELL. Nationality: British. **Born:** Michael Latham Powell at Bekesbourne, near Canterbury, Kent, 30 September 1905. **Family:** Married 1) Frances Reidy, 1943 (died 1983), two sons; 2) editor Thelma Schoonmaker, 1984. **Career:** Worked in various capacities on films of Rex Ingram, Léonce Perret, Alfred Hitchcock, Lupu Pick, from 1922; director, from 1931; Senior Director in Residence, Zoetrope Studios, 1981.

PRESSBURGER. Nationality: Hungarian/British. **Born:** Imre Pressburger in Miskolc, Hungary, 5 December 1902. **Education:** Studied at Universities of Prague and Stuttgart. **Career:** Contract writer for UFA, Berlin, 1930, later in France and, from 1935, in England, for Alexander Korda's London Films. Powell and Pressburger began collaboration on *The Spy in Black,* 1939; formed "The Archers," as producing, directing, and writing team, 1942 (disbanded 1956); also set up Vega Productions Ltd.; **Awards:** (joint) British Film Institute Special Award, 1978; Fellowship, BAFTA, 1981; Fellowship, British Film Institute, 1983; (Powell) honorary doctorate, University of East Anglia, 1978; Golden Lion, Venice Festival, 1982. **Died:** Pressburger died in Suffolk, 5 February 1988; Powell died in Gloucestershire, 19 February 1990.

Films by Powell and Pressburger:

(Powell as director, Pressburger as scriptwriter)

1939 *The Spy in Black* (*U-Boat*)
1940 *Contraband* (*Blackout*)
1941 *49th Parallel* (*The Invaders*)
1942 *One of Our Aircraft Is Missing*
1972 *The Boy Who Turned Yellow*

(produced, directed and scripted by "The Archers")

1943 ***The Life and Death of Colonel Blimp***; *The Volunteer*
1944 *A Canterbury Tale*
1945 *I Know Where I'm Going*
1946 ***A Matter of Life and Death*** (*Stairway to Heaven*)
1947 ***Black Narcissus***
1948 ***The Red Shoes***
1949 *The Small Back Room* (*Hour of Glory*)
1950 *Gone to Earth* (*The Wild Heart*); *The Elusive Pimpernel* (*The Fighting Pimpernel*)
1951 *The Tales of Hoffman*
1955 *Oh! Rosalinda* (*Fledermaus '55*)
1956 *The Battle of the River Plate* (*Pursuit of the Graf Spee*); *Ill Met By Moonlight* (*Intelligence Service*; *Night Ambush*)

Other Films Directed by Powell:

1931 *Two Crowded Hours*; *My Friend the King*; *Rynox*; *The Rasp*; *The Star Reporter*
1932 *Hotel Splendide*; *C.O.D.*; *His Lordship*; *Born Lucky*
1933 *The Fire-Raisers* (+ co-sc)
1934 *The Night of the Party*; *Red Ensign* (+ co-sc); *Something Always Happens*; *The Girl in the Crowd*
1935 *Lazybones*; *The Love Test*; *The Phantom Light*; *The Price of a Song*; *Someday*
1936 *The Man Behind the Mask*; *Crown Versus Stevens*; *Her Last Affair*; *The Brown Wallet*
1937 *Edge of the World* (+ sc)
1939 *The Lion Has Wings* (co-d)
1940 *The Thief of Bagdad* (co-d)
1941 *An Airman's Letter to His Mother* (short)
1955 *The Sorceror's Apprentice* (short)
1956 *Luna de miel* (*Honeymoon*) (+ pr)
1960 ***Peeping Tom*** (+ pr, role)
1961 *Queen's Guards* (+ pr)
1964 *Bluebeard's Castle*
1966 *They're a Weird Mob* (+ pr)
1968 *Sebastian* (Greene) (co-pr only)
1969 *Age of Consent* (+ pr)
1974 *Trikimia* (*The Tempest*) (+ pr, sc)
1978 *Return of the Edge of the World* (doc for television) (+ pr)

Other Films Written By Pressburger:

1953 *Twice Upon a Time* (+ d, pr)
1957 *Miracle in Soho* (Amyes) (+ pr)

Publications

By POWELL: books—

A Waiting Game, London, 1975.
The Red Shoes (with Pressburger), London, 1978.
A Life in Movies: An Autobiography, London, 1986.
Edge of the World, London, 1990.

By PRESSBURGER: books—

Killing a Mouse on Sunday, London, 1961
The Glass Pearls, London, 1966.
The Red Shoes (with Powell), London, 1978.

By POWELL and PRESSBURGER: articles—

"Michael Powell: The Expense of Naturalism," an interview with R. Collins and Ian Christie, in *Monogram* (London), no. 3, 1972.
Powell interview with R. Lefèvre and R. Lacourbe, in *Cinéma* (Paris), December 1976.
"Powell and Pressburger: The War Years," an interview with D.J. Badder, in *Sight and Sound* (London), no. 1, 1979.
"Michael Powell," an interview with Oliver Assayas, in *Cahiers du Cinéma* (Paris), March 1981.
"Michael Powell's Guilty Pleasures," in *Film Comment* (New York), July/August 1981.

Michael Powell (left) and Emeric Pressburger during the making of *A Canterbury Tale* courtesy of The Rank Organisation Plc

Powell interview with T. Williams, in *Films and Filming* (London), November 1981.
Powell, Michael, "Leo Marks and Mark Lewis," in *Cinématographe* (Paris), December 1983.
"Powell's Life," an interview with Allan Hunter, in *Films and Filming* (London), October 1986.
Powell, Michael, "Dance, Girl, Dance," in *American Film* (Washington, D.C.), vol. 12, no. 5, 1987.

On POWELL and PRESSBURGER: books—

Durgnat, Raymond, *A Mirror for England: British Movies from Austerity to Affluence,* London, 1970.
Gough-Yates, Kevin, *Michael Powell,* London, 1971.
Armes, Roy, *A Critical History of British Cinema,* London, 1978.
Christie, Ian, editor, *Powell, Pressburger, and Others,* London, 1978.
Cosandey, Roland, editor, *Retrospective: Powell and Pressburger,* Locarno, 1982.
Gottler, Fritz, and others, *Living Cinema: Powell and Pressburger,* Munich, 1982.
Christie, Ian, *Arrows of Desire: The Films of Michael Powell and Emeric Pressburger,* London, 1985.
Martini, Emanuela, editor, *Powell and Pressburger,* Bergamo, 1986.
Murphy, Robert, *Realism and Tinsel: British Cinema and Society 1939-48,* London, 1989.

On POWELL and PRESSBURGER: articles—

Green, O.O., "Michael Powell," in *Movie* (London), Autumn 1965.
Gough-Yates, Kevin, "Private Madness and Public Lunacy," in *Films and Filming* (London), February 1972.
Everson, William K., "A Meeting of Two Great Visual Stylists," in *Films in Review* (New York), November 1977.
Taylor, John Russell, "Michael Powell—Myths and Supermen," in *Sight and Sound* (London), Autumn 1978.
Andrews, Nigel, and Harlan Kennedy, "Peerless Powell," in *Film Comment* (New York), May/June 1979.
Everson, William K., "Michael Powell," in *Films in Review* (New York), August/September 1980.
Thompson, D., "The Films of Michael Powell: A Romantic Sensibility," in American Film (Washington, D.C.), November 1980.
"*Question de vie ou de mort* Issue" of *Avant-Scène du Cinéma* (Paris), 15 December 1980.
Durgnat, Raymond, "Aiming at the Archers," in *Positif* (Paris), February 1981.
McVay, D., "Cinema of Enchantment: The Films of Michael Powell," and "Michael Powell, Three Neglected Films," *Films and Filming* (London), December 1981 and January 1982.
Christie, Ian, "Alienation Effects: Emeric Pressburger and British Cinema," and "Powell and Pressburger: Putting Back the Pieces," in *Monthly Film Bulletin* (London), October and December 1984.
Brennan, M., "Powell and Pressburger at the NFT," in *Film and Filming* (London), October 1985.
Baron, Saskia, "The Archer at 80," in *Cinema Papers* (Melbourne), July 1986.
Boyd-Bowman, S., "Heavy Breathing in Shropshire," in *Screen* (London), November/December 1986.
McCarthy, T., obituary of Pressburger, in *Variety* (New York), 10 February 1988.
Bergan, Ronald, "Emeric Pressburger," in *Film and Filming* (London), April 1988.
Cardiff, Jack, "Michael Powell," in *Films and TV Technician* (London), April 1990.
Millar, Gavin, "Cox's Orange Pippin," in *Sight and Sound* (London), Summer 1990.

On POWELL and PRESSBURGER: film—

Millar, Gavin, *The Archers,* for "Arena," BBC TV, 1981.

* * *

Between the years 1942 and 1957, English director Michael Powell and his Hungarian partner, Emeric Pressburger, formed one of the most remarkable partnerships in cinema. Under the collaborative pseudonym "The Archers," the two created a series of highly visual and imaginative treatments of romantic and supernatural themes that have defied easy categorization by film historians. Although both were listed jointly as director, screenwriter, and frequently as producer, and the extent of each one's participation on any given film is difficult to measure, it is probably most accurate to credit Powell with the actual visualization of the films, while Pressburger functioned primarily as a writer. The latter, in fact, had no background as a director before joining Powell. He had drifted through the Austrian, German, and French film industries as a screenwriter before traveling to England in 1936.

Many of the gothic, highly expressionistic characteristics of the films produced by the partnership seem to trace their origins to Powell's apprenticeship at Rex Ingram's studio in Nice in the 1920s. There he performed various roles on at least three of the visionary director's silent productions: *Mare Nostrum* (1926), *The Magician* (1926), and *The Garden of Allah* (1927). Working on these films and subsequently on his own features in the 1930s, Powell developed a penchant for expressionism that manifested itself in several rather unique ways. The most fundamental of these was in his use of the fantasy genre, as illustrated by *A Matter of Life and Death,* with its problematic juxtaposition of psychiatry and mysticism. Another manifestation was an almost philosophical sadism that permeated his later films, such as *Peeping Tom,* with a camera that impales its photographic subjects on bayonet-like legs. The mechanical camera itself, in fact, represents still another Powell motif: the use of machines and technology to create or heighten certain aspects of fantasy. For example, the camera obscura in *A Matter of Life and Death* and the German warship in the *Pursuit of the Graf Spee* (which is revealed through a slow camera scan along its eerie structure, causing it to turn into a metallic killer fish) effectively tie machines into each film's set of symbolic motifs. In doing so, a technological mythology is created in which these objects take on near-demonic proportions.

Finally, the use of color, which most critics cite as a trademark of the Powell-Pressburger partnership, is shaped into an expressionistic mode. Powell chose his hues from a broad visual palette, and brushed them onto the screen with a calculated extravagance that became integrated into the themes of the film as a whole. In the better films, the visual and technological aspects complement each other in a pattern of symbolism. The mechanical staircase which descends from the celestial vortex in *A Matter of Life and Death,* for example, blends technology and fantasy as no other image has. Similarly, when the camera replaces the young pilot's eye in the same film and the pink and violet lining of an eyelid descends over it, the effect is extravagant, even a bit bizarre, but it effectively serves notice that the viewer is closing his eyes to external reality and entering another world. The audience is left to decide whether that world is supernatural or psychological.

This world has been most palatable in popular Powell-Pressburger fantasies like *The Red Shoes,* a ballet film used as an allegory for the artist's unremitting dedication to his art; and *The Tales of Hoffman,* in which the moody eccentricities of style have been kept in bounds by the built-in circumscriptions of the fantasy genre. At least one critic, however, has noted a strange morbidity in *The Red Shoes* derived from the directors' use of certain peculiarities of color, a criticism that has been magnified when some of Powell's and Pressburger's fantastic techniques occur in more realistic films. Their appearance in otherwise veracious contexts usually upsets normal audience expectations. *Black Narcissus* and Powell's *Peeping Tom* both created some problems for critics, for both films went to extremes in the exaggeration of otherwise plausible storylines.

Thematically, Powell and Pressburger operate in a limbo somewhere between romance and realism. The former, characterized by technical effects, camera angles and movements, and the innovative use of color, often intrudes in the merest of details in fundamentally naturalistic films. In the eyes of some, this weakens the artistic commitment to realism. On the other hand, the psychological insights embodied in serious fantasies like *A Matter of Life and Death* are too often dismissed as simply entertainment. Most of the Powell-Pressburger efforts are, in fact, attempts at fundamental reconciliations between modern ideas and the irrational, between science and savagery, or between religion and eroticism. This dichotomy usually occurs in one character's mind—as with Peter Carter in *A Matter of Life and Death* or the sex-obsessed nun in *Black Narcissus*—and hinges upon a second character such as *A Matter of Life and Death*'s Dr. Frank Reeves, who effects a degree of movement between the two sides of the dichotomy, particularly through his own death.

Although such mergings of reality and fantasy met with approval by the moviegoing public, Powell and Pressburger were less successful with the British film establishment. In a sense they were alienated from it through their exercise of a decidedly non-British flamboyance. To some degree, the Clive Candy character in *The Life and Death of Colonel Blimp* embodies the British film community during the period after the war. Powell and Pressburger's visual and thematic extravagances of style conflicted with the self-consciousness of the film industry's strivings for a rigid postwar realism not to be embellished by colorful and expressionistic ventures.

The team broke up in 1957 after *Ill Met by Moonlight,* and although Pressburger subsequently made some films by himself, they were not well received. Powell, though, continued in the vein established by his collaboration with the Hungarian director. *Luna de Miel* and *The Queen's Guards* pursue all of the philosophical concerns of his earlier efforts, while *Peeping Tom,* which is now regarded as his masterpiece, indicates a certain morbid refinement of his thematic interests. Unfortunately, the film was perhaps ahead of its time—a problem that plagued the director and his collaborator for most of their careers.

—Stephen L. Hanson

PREMINGER, Otto

Nationality: American. **Born:** Vienna, 5 December 1905, became U.S. citizen, 1943. **Education:** University of Vienna, LL.D, 1926. **Family:** Married 1) Marion Deutsch (stage name Marion Mill), 1932 (divorced); 2) Mary Gardner, 1951 (divorced 1959); 3) Hope (Preminger), 1960, two children; also one son by Gypsy Rose Lee. **Career:** Actor with Max Reinhardt company, 1924; joined theater in der Josefstadt, 1928 (succeeding Reinhardt as director, 1933); invited to Hollywood by Joseph Schenck, 1935; contract with Fox broken, moved to New York, 1937; director on Broadway, 1938-41 (and later); returned to Hollywood as actor, 1942; signed seven-year contract with Fox, 1945; independent producer, from early 1950s. **Died:** Of cancer, in New York City, 23 April 1986.

Films as Director:

1931 *Die grosse Liebe*
1936 *Under Your Spell*
1937 *Danger, Love at Work*
1943 *Margin for Error* (+ role as Nazi consul Rudolf Forster)
1944 *In the Meantime, Darling* (+ pr); ***Laura*** (+ pr)
1945 *Royal Scandal*; *Fallen Angel* (+ pr)
1946 *Centennial Summer* (+ pr)
1947 *Forever Amber*; *Daisy Kenyon* (+ pr)
1948 *That Lady in Ermine*
1949 *The Fan* (*Lady Windermere's Fan*) (+ pr); *Whirlpool* (+ pr)
1950 *Where the Sidewalk Ends* (+ pr); *The Thirteenth Letter* (+ pr)
1952 *Angel Face*
1953 *The Moon Is Blue* (+ co-pr)
1954 *River of No Return*; *Carmen Jones* (+ pr)
1955 *The Man with the Golden Arm* (+ pr); *The Court Martial of Billy Mitchell* (*One Man Mutiny*)
1957 *Saint Joan* (+ pr); *Bonjour Tristesse* (+ pr)
1959 *Porgy and Bess*; ***Anatomy of a Murder*** (+ pr)
1960 *Exodus* (+ pr)
1962 *Advise and Consent* (+ pr)
1963 *The Cardinal* (+ pr)
1964 *In Harm's Way* (+ pr)
1965 *Bunny Lake Is Missing* (+ pr)
1966 *Hurry Sundown* (+ pr)
1968 *Skidoo* (+ pr)
1970 *Tell Me That You Love Me, Junie Moon* (+ pr)
1971 *Such Good Friends* (+ pr)
1975 *Rosebud* (+ pr)
1980 *The Human Factor* (+ pr)

Other Films:

1942 *The Pied Piper* (role); *They Got Me Covered* (role)
1945 *Where Do We Go from Here* (role)
1953 *Stalag 17* (Wilder) (role as camp commandant)
1981 *Unsere Leichen Leben Noch* (Von Prauheim) (role)

Publications

By PREMINGER: book—

Preminger: An Autobiography, Garden City, New York, 1977.

By PREMINGER: articles—

"Recontre avec Otto Preminger," with Jacques Rivette, in *Cahiers du Cinéma* (Paris), December 1953.
"Movie Critic Versus Movie Director," with Bosley Crowther, in *Esquire* (New York), October 1958.
"Your Taste, My Taste ... and the Censors," in *Films and Filming* (London), November 1959.
Interview with Jacques Doniol-Valcroze and Eric Rohmer, in *Cahiers du Cinéma* (Paris), July 1961.
"Sex and Censorship in Literature and the Arts," with Norman Mailer and others, in *Playboy* (Chicago), July 1961.
"*The Cardinal* and I," in *Films and Filming* (London), November 1963.
Interview with Ian Cameron and others, in *Movie* (London), Summer 1965.
Interview in *Interviews with Film Directors,* edited by Andrew Sarris, New York, 1967.
"Otto Preminger auteur de force," an interview with D. Lyons, in *Inter/View* (New York), July 1972.
Interview with Gene Phillips, in *Focus on Film* (London), August 1979.
"Cult and Controversy," an interview with Gordon Gow, in *Films and Filming* (London), November 1979.

Otto Preminger

On PREMINGER: books—

Preminger, Marion Mill, *All I Want Is Everything,* New York, 1957.
Lourcelles, Jacques, *Otto Preminger,* Paris, 1965.
Pratley, Gerald, *The Cinema of Otto Preminger,* New York, 1971.
Frischauer, Willi, *Behind the Scenes of Otto Preminger,* London, 1973.

On PREMINGER: articles—

Gehman, Richard, "Otto Preminger," in *Theater Arts* (New York), January 1961.
"Preminger Issue" of *Présence du Cinéma* (Paris), February 1962.
"Preminger Issue" of *Movie* (London), September 1962.
"Preminger Issues" of *Interciné* (Toulouse), no. 1, and no. 2, 1963.
"Preminger Issue" of *Movie* (London), no. 4, 1963.
Sarris, Andrew, "Preminger's Two Periods—Studio and Solo," in *Film Comment* (New York), Summer 1965.
Ross, Lillian, "Profiles: Anatomy of a Commercial Interruption," in the *New Yorker,* 19 February 1966.
Bogdanovich, Peter, "Otto Preminger," in *On Film,* 1970.
Borok, B., "*Laura*: The Story Behind the Picture," in *Thousand Eyes* (New York), November 1976.
Lacourcelles, J., "*Laura* Issue" of *Avant-Scène du Cinéma* (Paris), July/September 1978.
Wegner, H., "From Expressionism to Film Noir: Otto Preminger's *Where the Sidewalk Ends,*" in *Journal of Popular Film* (Washington, D.C.), Summer 1983.
McCarthy, T., obituary, in *Variety* (New York), 30 April 1986.
Luft, H.G., in *Films in Review* (New York), August/September 1986.
Lippe, Richard, "At the Margins of *Film Noir*: Preminger's *Angel Face,*" in *CineAction*! (Toronto), no. 13-14, 1988.
Sarris, Andrew, "Otto Preminger," in *American Film* (Washington, D.C.), June 1989.

* * *

The public persona of Austrian-born Otto Preminger has epitomized for many the typical Hollywood movie director: an accented, autocratic, European-born disciplinarian who terrorized his actors, bullied his subordinates, and spent millions of dollars to ensure that his films be produced properly, although economically. Before the *Cahiers du Cinéma* critics began to praise Preminger, it may have been this public persona, more than anything else, which impeded an appreciation of Preminger's extraordinarily subtle style or thematic consistencies.

Preminger's career can be divided into two periods. Throughout the first period, Preminger worked as a studio director for Twentieth Century-Fox, where he had several well-publicized conflicts with Darryl F. Zanuck and found it difficult to conform to studio demands or to collaborate without retaining overall artistic control. His evocative and romantic mystery *Laura,* his breakthrough film, was produced during this period. Among the other eclectic assignments he directed at Fox, the most interesting include a series of film noir features in the late 1940s: *Whirlpool, Where the Sidewalk Ends, The Thirteenth Letter,* and *Angel Face.*

Throughout the second and far more interesting period of Preminger's career, Preminger worked as one of the first notable independent producer-directors, in the process successfully undermining the studio system in various ways. He fought against institutional censorship by releasing several films without the Motion Picture Association seal (for example, *The Moon is Blue*) and he explored controversial subjects the studios might have been hesitant to touch (such as criticism of the War Department in *The Court Martial of Billy Mitchell* or homosexuality in *Advise and Consent*). Preminger also championed the independent producers movement by exploiting the Paramount Divorcement Decree and aggressively marketing and arranging exhibition for his films

Preminger incorporated fresh and authentic backgrounds by promoting location shooting away from Hollywood. He worked diligently to discover new performers (such as Jean Seberg) and to develop properties (such as *Carmen Jones* and *Hurry Sundown*) which would allow the casting of Hollywood's under-used black performers. Finally, he even helped to break the studio blacklist by hiring and publicly crediting Dalton Trumbo as screenwriter on *Exodus.*

Preminger's tastes have always been as eclectic as the disparate sources from which his films have been adapted. Throughout the 1950s and 1960s, however, Preminger's films grew in pretention, displaying considerable interest in monolithic institutions (the military in *The Court Martial of Billy Mitchell* and *In Harms's Way*; the Senate in *Advise and Consent*; the Catholic Church in *The Cardinal*; the medical profession in *Such Good Friends*) as well as the examination of social and political problems (drug addiction in *The Man with the Golden Arm*; Jewish repatriation in *Exodus*; racial prejudice in *Hurry, Sundown*; political terrorism in *Rosebud*). A consistent archetype in Preminger's films is the quest for truth; indeed, the director's recurring image is the courtroom.

What has especially fascinated Preminger's admirers is the subtlety of his mise-en-scène; his most typical effort is a widescreen film with long takes, no pyrotechnical montage, few reaction shots, fluid and simple camera movements, and careful yet unselfconscious compositions. Preminger's style, though apparently invisible, is one which forces the audience to examine, to discern, to arrive at some ultimate position. Several critics have written persuasively on the ambiguity associated with Preminger's apparent objectivity, including Andrew Sarris, who has characterized Preminger as a "director who sees all problems and issues as a single-take two-shot, the stylistic expression of the eternal conflict, not between right and wrong, but between the right-wrong on one side and the right-wrong on the other, a representation of the right-wrong in all of us as our share of the human condition."

If Preminger's formula floundered in the 1970s and 1980s, an era in which the American cinema seemed dominated by mainstream genre works and overt escapism, one cannot help but feel nostalgia and profound respect for Preminger's serious subjects and artistry. Indeed, his series of films beginning with *Bonjour, Tristesse* in 1957 and continuing through *Porgy and Bess, Anatomy of a Murder, Exodus, Advise and Consent, The Cardinal, In Harm's Way, Bunny Lake Is Missing,* and *Hurry, Sundown* in 1966, constitute one of the longest strings of ambitious, provocative films in American cinema.

—Charles Derry

PRESSBURGER, Emeric *See* **POWELL, Michael, and Emeric PRESSBURGER**

PROTAZANOV, Yakov

Nationality: Russian. **Born:** Yakov Alexandrovitch Protazanov in Moscow, 4 February 1881. **Education:** Commercial school, Moscow. **Career:** Film actor, from 1905; translator, then writer of scenarios and director, Gloria studios, from 1909; moved to Ermoliev company, began collaboration with actor Ivan Mozhukhin, 1915; Ermoliev studios moved to Yalta, 1918, then to Istanbul and Marseilles, 1919-20;

moved to Paris, worked in France and Germany, 1920-22; returned to Russia, joined Mezhrabpom-Rus Studio, Moscow, 1923. **Awards:** Merited Artist of the RSFSR, 1935. **Died:** In Moscow, 8 August 1945.

Films as Director:

1909 *The Fountains of Bakhisarai*
1911 *Pesnya katorzhanina* (*The Prisoner's Song*) (+ sc)
1912 *Anfisa*; *Ukhod velikovo startza* (*Departure of a Grand Old Man*) (co-d)
1913 *Razbitaya vaza* (*The Shattered Vase*) (+ sc); *Klyuchi shchastya* (*Keys to Happiness*) (co-d); *Kak khoroshi, Kak svezhi byli rozi* (*How Fine, How Fresh the Roses Were*) (+ sc)
1915 *Petersburgskiye trushchobi* (*Petersburg Slums*) (co-d, co-sc); *Voina i mir* (*War and Peace*) (co-d, co-sc); *Plebei* (*Plebeian*) (+ sc); *Nikolai Stavrogin* (+ sc)
1916 *Pikovaya dama* (*The Queen of Spades*); *Zhenshchina s kinzhalom* (*Woman with a Dagger*); *Grekh* (*Sin*) (co-d)
1917 *Prokuror* (*Public Prosecutor*); *Andrei Kozhukhov* (+ sc); *Ne nado krovi* (*Blood Need Not Be Spilled*) (+ sc); *Prokliatiye millioni* (*Cursed Millions*); *Satana likuyushchii* (*Satan Triumphant*)
1918 *Otets Sergii* (*Father Sergius*)
1919 *Taina koroloevy* (*The Queen's Secret*) (+ sc)
1920/23 *L'Angoissante aventure*; *L'Amour et la loi* (*Love and Law*); *Pour une nuit d'amour*; *Justice d'Abord*; *Le Sens de la mort*; *L'Ombre du pêché*; *Der Liebes Pielgerfahrt*
1924 *Aelita*
1925 *Yevo prizyv* (*Broken Chains*; *His Call*); *Zakroichik iz Torzhka* (*Tailor from Torzhok*)
1926 *Protsess o tryokh millyonakh* (*The Three Million Case*) (+ co-sc)
1927 *Sorok pervyi* (*The 41st*)
1928 *Byelyi orel* (*The White Eagle*) (+ co-sc); *Dondiego i Pelaguya* (*Don Diego and Pelagea*)
1929 *Chiny i liudi* (*Ranks and People*) (+ co-sc); *The Man From the Restaurant*
1930 *Prazdnik svyatovo Iorgena* (*The Feast of St Jorgen*) (+ sc)
1931 *Tommy* (+ sc)
1934 *Marionetki* (*Marionettes*)
1937 *Bespridannitsa* (*Without Dowry*) (+ co-sc)
1938 *Pupils of the Seventh Grade*
1941 *Salavat Yulayev*
1943 *Nasreddin v Bukhare* (*Nasreddin in Bukhara*)

Publications

On PROTAZANOV: books—

Yakov Protazanov, Moscow, 1957.
Leyda, Jay, Kino, *A History of the Russian and Soviet Film,* London, 1960.
Lebedev, Nikolai, *Il cinema muto sovietico,* Turin, 1962.
Robinson, David, and others, editors, *Silent Witnesses,* London, 1989.

On PROTAZANOV: articles—

Alisova, N., "Priobzcenie k poesii," in *Iskusstvo Kino* (Moscow), April 1973.
Raizman, Yuli, and others, "Protazanov," in *Soviet Film* (Moscow), no. 6, 1981.
Vajsfel'd, I., and others, "Effect Protazanova," in *Iskusstvo Kino* (Moscow), August 1981.
Tumanova, N., "Zabytaja stat'ja Jakova Protazanova," in *Iskusstvo Kino* (Moscow), July 1984.

Yakov Protazanov

Robinson, David, "Evgeni Bauer and the Cinema of Nikolai II," in *Sight and Sound* (London), Winter 1989/90.

* * *

As a pioneer of the czarist cinema, as a director who filmed in Moscow, Yalta, Paris, and Berlin, and as one who worked under various social systems and managed to survive, Yakov Protazanov has a unique place in the story of the Russian cinema.

Originally intended for a commercial career, Protazanov fell under the spell of films and began his apprenticeship with Gloria Films in Moscow, later to become Thiemann and Reinhardt. The cinema in Russia had been socially acceptable from the beginning and enjoyed the patronage of imperial circles. From script-writing and acting Protazanov moved into directing. In 1911 he made *Pesnya katorzhanina* (*The Prisoner's Song*) with Vladimir Shaternikov, an actor he was to use many times. The following year Andreyev scripted for him an adaptation of his play *Anfisa.* The same year he made *Ukhod velikovo startza* (*The Departure of a Grand Old Man*), thereby antagonising Countess Tolstoy, who objected to the depiction of her husband as played by Shaternikov. The film was subsequently banned. A happier venture was *Klyuchishchastya* (*Keys to Happiness*), written by a popular novelist, A. Verbitskaya. The wide appeal of this film made it a great box-office success throughout Russia.

By the time of World War I, Protazanov had directed some forty films covering a wide range of material, from the perfervid, morbid, and even decadent themes so popular in Russia at the time to historical spectacles and films based on the literary heritage of his country. In *Kak khoroshi, kak svezhi byli rosi* (*How Fine, How Fresh the Roses Were*) of 1913 he was inspired by Turgenev. He utilized Shaternikov once again in the film, casting him as Lev Tolstoy.

After his experiences as a soldier Protazanov joined the Ermoliev Company, as did his former colleague Vladimir Gardin. In 1915 they shared the direction of the elaborate *Voina i mir* (*War and Peace*) and a serial called *Petersburgskiye trushchobi* (*Petersburg slums*), while Protazanov directed a version of Strindberg's *Froken Julie* under the title *Plebei* (*Plebian*). In these three films the lead was taken by Olga Preobrazhenskaya, herself to become a director of distinction in later years.

Ermoliev's greatest actor was Ivan Mozhukin, whose knowledge and interest in the whole field of cinema transcended his interpretive skills. Protazanov directed him in *Nicolai Stavrogin* (based on Dostoievsky) in 1915 and the following year in *Pikovaya dama* (*The Queen of Spades*). The latter film was a milestone in Mozhukin's career. The script, incidentally, was written by a young Fedor Otsep. Other important Protazanov films with Mozhukin were *Prokuror* (*Public Prosecutor*), *Satana likuyushchii* (*Satan Triumphant*), *Andrei Kozhukov,* and *Otets Sergii* (*Father Sergius*). The last film is undoubtedly his masterpiece. Tolstoy's story of the spiritual struggles of a young officer of the Imperial Court who gives up a life of pleasure to become a monk was a *tour de force* for Mozhukin. The actor's transition from youth to age, the authenticity of the settings, and the cohesion of the film help to make it one of the great classics of the cinema.

On a very different level was *Taina koroloevy* (*The Queen's Secret*), a film based on a novel by Elinor Glynn that again featured Mozhukin. This work was filmed in Moscow and Yalta, for with the coming of the Revolution many film artists fled to the south. Ermoliev transferred his studio to Yalta, bringing all his equipment, technicians, and artists with him. Here Protazanov made three films, but political unrest soon made work impossible. Ermoliev and all his people embarked on a British ship at Odessa which took them to Constantinople, where Protazanov continued with the direction of the film *L'Angoissante Aventure,* from a script by Mozhukin. This ambulatory film went on from Constantinople to Marseilles and Paris, where Ermoliev's production continued at Méliès' old studio at Monteuil. In spite of the circumstances under which it was made, *L'Angoissante Aventure* was a quite ingenious comedy that effectively utilized the diverse talents of Mozhukin. The film ranged from comedy to tragedy, but was resolved by the typically Russian device of being a dream.

Protazanov's *Justice d'Abord* was a remake of *Prokuror,* but he broke away from Ermoliev and his company. He adapted novels by Zola and Paul Bourget before going to Berlin, where he made *Liebes Pilgerfahrt.* Invited back to Russia to make a film of *Taras Bulba,* he instead directed *Aelita* for Mezhrabpom-Russ. This fantasy, in which life on Mars is compared with contemporary Russia, featured extraordinary sets by Alexandra Exter of the Kamerny Theatre. *Yevo prizyv* (*His Call*) was released the following year. A propaganda film with a human face, the work showed that Protazanov was still his own man. *Protsess o tryoch millyonakh* (*The Three Million Case*) of 1926 and subsequent films like *Sorok pervyi* (*The 41st*), *Byelyi orel* (*The White Eagle*), *Dondiego i Pelaguya* (a satiric comment on bureaucracy), *Chiny i Liudi* (*Ranks and People,* a compendium of three Chekhov stories), and *Prazdnik svyatovo Iorgena* (*The Feast of St Jorgen,* a satirical anti-religious film) all established him as an artist who could hold his own with the new young school of Russian film directors.

In *Sorok pervyi,* a story of the fighting in Turkestan, a young girl partisan is torn between love and duty and has to kill a young White officer, the only man she ever loved. Set in a memorable landscape of sandy desert, the film develops with a powerful impact. *Tommy,* which was released in 1931, was Protazanov's first sound film. It tells of a British soldier's reaction to a group of partisans.

A recipient of official honours, Protazanov continued to be regarded as an outstanding creative artist, and many of his films were set in far-flung locations in outlying Soviet republics. When the centre of Soviet film production moved to Alma Ata in the Urals during the German invasion of Russia in World War II, Protazanov moved with it. His last film, though, was filmed on location in Uzbekistan. *Nazreddin ve Bukhare* (*Nazreddin in Bukhara*) was a delightful comedy that featured Meyerhold's great actor Lev Sverdlin in the title role, where he gave a performance reminiscent of Fairbanks' in *Thief of Bagdad.* When Protazanov died in 1945 he was working on a script based on a play by Ostrovsky. A prolific creator of films, he remains known as a great man of the cinema.

—Liam O'Leary

PUDOVKIN, Vsevolod

Nationality: Russian. **Born:** Vsevolod Illarionovitch Pudovkin in Penza, 16 February 1893. **Education:** Educated in physics and chemistry, Moscow University; entered State Cinema School, 1920. **Military Service:** Enlisted in artillery, 1914; wounded and taken prisoner, 1915; escaped and returned to Moscow, 1918. **Family:** Married actress and journalist Anna Zemtsova, 1923. **Career:** Worked as writer and chemist, 1919-20; worked on agit films, 1920-21; student at Lev Kuleshov's studio, from 1922; quit State Cinema Institute to join Kuleshov's Experimental Laboratory, 1923; began collaboration with cinematographer Anatoly Golovnia and scriptwriter Nathan Zarkhi, 1925; with Alexandrov, signed Eisenstein's "Manifesto on Audio-Visual Counterpoint," 1928; travelled to England and Holland, 1929; joined Communist Party, 1932; after car accident, taught theoretic studies at V.G.I.K., 1935; joined Mosfilm studios, 1938. **Awards:** Order of Lenin, 1935. **Died:** In Riga, 30 June 1953.

Films as Director:

1921 *Golod ... golod ... golod* (*Hunger ... Hunger ... Hunger*) (co-d, co-sc, role)
1925 *Shakhmatnaya goryachka* (*Chess Fever*) (co-d)
1926 *Mekhanikha golovnovo mozga* (*Mechanics of the Brain*) (+ sc); ***Mat*** (*Mother*)
1927 ***Konyets Sankt-Peterburga*** (*The End of St. Petersburg*)
1928 ***Potomok Chingis-khan*** (*The Heir to Genghis-Khan*; *Storm Over Asia*)
1932 *Prostoi sluchai* (*A Simple Case*) (revised version of *Otchen kharacho dziviosta* (*Life's Very Good*); first screened in 1930)
1933 *Dezertir* (*Deserter*)
1938 *Pobeda* (*Victory*) (co-d)
1939 *Minin i Pozharsky* (co-d)
1940 *Kino za XX liet* (*Twenty Years of Cinema*) (co-d, co-ed)
1941 *Suvorov* (co-d); *Pir v Girmunka* (*Feast at Zhirmunka*) (co-d) (for "Fighting Film Album")
1942 *Ubitzi vykhodyat na dorogu* (*Murderers Are on Their Way*) (co-d, co-sc)
1943 *Vo imya rodini* (*In the Name of the Fatherland*) (co-d)
1946 *Amiral Nakhimov* (*Admiral Nakhimov*)
1948 *Tri vstrechi* (*Three Encounters*) (co-d)
1950 *Yukovsky* (co-d)
1953 *Vozvrachenia Vassilya Bortnikov* (*The Return of Vasili Bortnikov*)

Vsevolod Pudovkin

Other Films:

1920 *V dni borbi* (*In the Days of Struggle*) (role)
1921 *Serp i molot* (*Sickle and Hammer*) (asst d, role)
1923 *Slesar i kantzler* (*Locksmith and Chancellor*) (co-sc)
1924 ***Neobychainye priklucheniya Mistera Vesta v stranye bolshevikov*** (*Extraordinary Adventures of Mr. West in the Land of the Bolsheviks*) (Kuleshov) (co-sc, asst, role as the 'Count')
1925 *Luch smerti* (*The Death Ray*) (Kuleshov) (design, role); *Kirpitchiki* (*Little Bricks*) (role)
1928 *Zhivoi trup* (*A Living Corpse*) (role as Feodor Protassov)
1929 *Vessiolaia kanareika* (*The Cheerful Canary*) (role as the illusionist); ***Novyi vavilon*** (*The New Babylon*) (Kozintsev and Trauberg) (role as shop assistant)
1944 ***Ivan Grozny*** (*Ivan the Terrible*) (Eisenstein) (role as Nikolai the fanatic)

Publications

By PUDOVKIN: books—

Film Technique, translated by Ivor Montagu, London, 1933.
Film-Acting, translated by Ivor Montagu, London, 1935.
Film Technique and Film Acting, New York, 1949.
Textes choisis, Moscow, 1955.
Sobranie sochinenii v trekh tomakh, Moscow, 1974.

By PUDOVKIN: articles—

"Scénario et mise en scène," in *Revue du Cinéma* (Paris), 1 September 1930.
"Poudovkine parle du montage," with René Lévy, in *Revue du Cinéma* (Paris), 1 December 1931.
"A Conversation with V.I. Pudovkin," with Marie Seton, in *Sight and Sound* (London), Spring 1933.
"The Global Film," in *Hollywood Quarterly,* July 1947.
"Two Conversations with Pudovkin," with C.H. Waddington, in *Sight and Sound* (London), Winter 1948/49.
"Stanislavsky's System in the Cinema," in *Sight and Sound* (London), January/March 1953.

On PUDOVKIN: books—

Bryher, Winifred, *Film Problems of Soviet Russia,* London, 1929.
Yezuitov, N., *Poudovkine, "Pouti Tvortchestva," "Les Voies de la création",* Moscow, 1937.
Mariamov, A., *Vsevolod Pudovkin,* Moscow, 1952.
Leyda, Jay, *Kino: A History of the Russian and Soviet Film,* London, 1960.
Schnitzer, Luda and Jean, *Vsevolod Poudovkine,* Paris, 1966.
Amengual, Barthélemy, *V.I. Poudovkine,* Premier Plan, Lyon, 1968.
Dart, Peter, *Pudovkin's Films and Film Theory,* New York, 1974.
Marshall, Herbert, *Masters of the Soviet Cinema: Crippled Creative Biographies,* London, 1983.
Masi, Stefano, *Vsevolod I. Pudovkin,* Florence, 1985.
Taylor, Richard, and Ian Christie, editors, *The Film Factory: Russian and Soviet Cinéma in Documents 1896-1939,* London, 1988.

On PUDOVKIN: articles—

Potamkin, Harry, "Pudovkin and the Revolutionary Film," in *Hound and Horn* (New York), April/June 1933.
Rotha, Paul, "Pabst, Pudovkin and the Producers," in *Sight and Sound* (London), Summer 1933.
Leyda, Jay, "Index to the Creative work of Vsevolod Pudovkin," in *Sight and Sound* (London), November 1948.
Sadoul, Georges, "Un Humaniste et un lyrique," in *Les Lettres Françaises* (Paris), 9 July 1953.
"Pudovkin Issue" of *Cahiers du Cinéma* (Paris), August/September 1953.
Weinberg, Herman, "Vsevolod Pudovkin," in *Films in Review* (New York), August/September 1953.
Wright, Basil, "V.I. Pudovkin: 1893-1953," in *Sight and Sound* (London), October/December 1953.
Herring, Robert, "Film Image—Pudovkin," in *Cinemage* (New York), May 1955.
Bizet, Jacques-André, "Les Théories du langage et de l'expression filmiques selon Poudovkine," in *Le Cinéma Pratique* (Paris), September/October and November/December 1966 and March 1967.
"Pudovkin Issue" of *Iskusstvo Kino* (Moscow), February 1973.
Hudlin, E., "Film Language: Pudovkin and Eisenstein and Russian Formalism," in *Journal of Aesthetic Education* (Urbana, Illinois), no. 2, 1979.
Burns, P.E., "Linkage: Pudovkin's Classics Revisited," in *Journal of Popular Film and Television* (Washington, D.C.), Summer 1981.
Pudovkin Section of *Iskusstvo Kino* (Moscow), February 1983.
Kepley, Vance, Jr., "Pudovkin and the Classical Hollywood tradition," in *Wide Angle* (Athens, Ohio), vol. 7, no. 3, 1985.
Jurenev, R., "Neskol'ko povsednevnyh vstrec," in *Iskusstvo Kino* (Moscow), August 1985.
Hogenkamp. Bert, "De russen komen! Poedowkin, Eisenstein en Wertow in Nederland," in *Skrien* (Amsterdam), November/December 1985.

* * *

Vsevolod Illarionovitch Pudovkin's major contribution to the cinema is as a theorist. He was fascinated by the efforts of his teacher, the filmmaker Lev Kuleshov, in exploring the effects of montage. As Pudovkin eventually did in his own work, Kuleshov often created highly emotional moments by rapidly intercutting shots of diverse content. Of course, the results could be manipulated. In *The End of St. Petersburg,* for instance, Pudovkin mixed together shots of stock market speculation with those depicting war casualties. Occasionally, Pudovkin's images are uninspired: the above sequence looks static, even simplistic, today. Nevertheless, while other filmmakers may have advanced this technique, Pudovkin was one of the first to utilize it in a narrative.

Pudovkin's essays on film theory, "The Film Scenario" and "Film Director and Film Material," remain just as valuable as any of his works; these texts have become primers in film technique. Pudovkin wrote that it is unnecessary for a film actor to overperform or overgesture as he might in the theater. He can underplay in a film because the director or editor, via montage, is able to communicate to the viewer the pervading feeling in the shots surrounding the actor. Meanwhile, the actor may concentrate on his or her internal emotions, transmitting the truths of the character in a more subtle manner.

Beyond this, contended Pudovkin, an actor on screen is at the mercy of his director. The performer could be directed to cry without knowing his character's motivations; the shots placed around him will pass along the cause of his grief. A non-actor could even be made to give a realistic performance as a result of perceptive editing. Pudovkin often integrated his casts with both actors and non-actors; the latter were utilized when he felt the need for realism was greater than the need for actors with the ability to perform. In *Chess Fever,* a two-reel comedy, Pudovkin even edited in shots of Jose Raoul Capablanca, a famous chess master, to make him seem an active participant in the scenario. As the filmmaker explained, "the foundation of film art is editing." He noted that "the film is not shot, but built up from separate strips of celluloid that are its raw material."

Pudovkin's first significant credit, *The Death Ray,* was directed by Kuleshov. But he designed the production, wrote the scenario, assisted his teacher, and acted in the film. Before the end of the 1920s, he completed his three great silent features, which remain his best-remembered films: *Mother, The End of St. Petersburg,* and *The Heir to Genghis-Khan.* While they were each concerned with various aspects of the Revolution, they are not totally propagandistic: each film deals with human involvements, conflicts, and the effect that ideas and actions have on the lives of those involved. This is illustrated perfectly in *Mother,* based on a Maxim Gorky novel. Set during the 1905 Revolution, the film chronicles the plight of the title character (Vera Baranovskaya), who accidently causes her politically active worker son (Nikolai Batalov) to be sentenced to prison. Eventually, Batalov is shot during an escape attempt and Baranovskaya, whose political consciousness has been raised, is trampled to death by the cavalry attacking a workers' protest.

Baranovskaya also appears in *The End of St. Petersburg,* filmed to mark the tenth anniversary of the 1917 Revolution. The work centers on the political education of an inexperienced young peasant (Ivan Chuvelyov). This film is significant in that it is one of the first to satisfactorily blend a fictional scenario into a factual setting. Typically, Pudovkin cast real pre-Revolution stockbrokers and executives as stockbrokers and executives.

The Heir to Genghis-Khan (more commonly known as *Storm Over Asia*) is not as successful as the others, but is still worthy of note. The film, set in Central Asia, details the activities of partisan revolutionaries and the English army of occupation in Mongolia (called the White Russian army in foreign prints). It focuses on a young Mongol trapper (Valeri Inkizhinov) whose fate is not dissimilar to that of Pudovkin's other heroes and heroines: he is radicalized by unfolding events after he is cheated out of a prized fox fur by a European merchant.

Pudovkin continued making films after the advent of sound. *A Simple Case,* revised from his silent *Life's Very Good,* was scheduled to be the Soviet cinema's first sound feature; instead, the honor went to Nikolai Ekk's *The Road to Life.* Pudovkin was not content to just add sound to his scenarios. His initial talkie was *Deserter,* in which he experimented with speech patterns: by editing in sound, he contrasted the conversational dialogue of different characters with crowd noises, traffic sounds, sirens, music, and even silence. But Pudovkin did not abandon his concern for visuals: *Deserter* contains approximately three thousand separate shots, an unusually high number for a feature film.

Pudovkin did make other sound films. His *Minin and Pozharsky,* released at the beginning of World War II, takes place in the seventeenth century, when Moscow was controlled by King Sigismund; it was the first major Soviet film to depict Poland as an invader. Nevertheless, his çinematic language is essentially one that is devoid of words, relying instead on visual components.

—Rob Edelman

RAFELSON, Bob

Nationality: American. **Born:** New York City, 1933. **Education:** Attended Dartmouth College. **Family:** Married Toby, one son. **Military Service:** Served with Occupation forces in Japan; worked as disc jockey for military radio station. **Career:** Advisor to Shochiku Films on American market; also worked as rodeo rider and horse breaker, and as jazz musician in Mexico; reader and story editor for David Susskind's *Play of the Week,* late 1950s; with Bert Schneider created TV pop group The Monkees, 1966, also directed episodes of their TV show; with Schneider and Steve Blauner formed BBS Productions, and directed first feature, *Head,* featuring The Monkees, 1968. **Awards:** Best Direction, New York Film Critics, for *Five Easy Pieces,* 1970.

Films as Director and Co-Producer:

1968 *Head* (+ co-sc)
1970 ***Five Easy Pieces*** (+ co-story)
1973 *The King of Marvin Gardens* (pr, + co-story)
1977 *Stay Hungry* (+ co-sc)
1980 *Brubaker* (d 10 days only, then replaced by Stuart Rosenberg)
1981 *The Postman Always Rings Twice*
1987 *Black Widow*
1989 *Mountains of the Moon* (+ co-sc)
1992 *Man Trouble*
1994 *Wet*

Other Films:

1969 ***Easy Rider*** (Hopper) (co-pr)
1971 ***The Last Picture Show*** (Bogdanovich) (co-pr)
1972 *Drive, He Said* (Nicholson) (co-pr)

Publications

By RAFELSON: articles—

Interview with M. Grisolia, in *Cinéma* (Paris), June 1973.
"Staying Vulnerable," an interview with John Taylor, in *Sight and Sound* (London), no. 4, 1976.
"Raising Cain," an interview with D. Thompson, in *Film Comment* (New York), March/April 1981.
Interview with Rob Edelman, in *Films in Review* (New York), May 1981.
"Prodigal's Progress," an interview with Richard Combs and John Pym, in *Sight and Sound* (London), Autumn 1981.
Interview with F. Ramasse and M. Henry, in *Positif* (Paris), May 1987.

On RAFELSON: articles—

"Bob Rafelson," in *New Yorker,* 24 October 1970.
Lefanu, M., "Notes sur trois films de Bob Rafelson ...," in *Positif* (Paris), May 1978.
Carcassonne, P., "Dossier: Hollywood 79: Bob Rafelson," in *Cinématographe* (Paris), November 1979.
McGilligan, P., "The Postman Rings Again," in *American Film* (Washington, D.C.), April 1981.
Milne, Tom, "Bob Rafelson," in *International Film Guide 1983,* London, 1982.
Grimes, T., "BBS: Auspicious Beginnings, Open Endings," in *Movie* (London), Winter 1986.

* * *

Bob Rafelson is a neglected director mainly because he lays bare the myths essential to America. He does not sugarcoat the bitter dose of his satire, as do Coppola and Altman. A distaste on the part of mainstream critics has caused attacks upon, but mostly the neglect of, Rafelson's *The King of Marvin Gardens,* which is his most representative film. *Head* is bound by the conventions of the teenage-comedy genre and shows few marks of Rafelson's authorship; *Stay Hungry* is a minor work which sustains his standard theme of the drop-out—this time it is a Southern aristocrat who falls into the underworld, which is ambiguously mixed with the business world above. Something of a popular success, *Five Easy Pieces* certainly demands attention.

Five Easy Pieces was the first expression of the burned-out liberalism that was to become the hallmark of American films of the 1970s. Rafelson's film expresses the intelligentsia's dissatisfaction with its impotency in light of an overweening socio-economic structure. Either capitulating or dropping out seemed the only choices. The film's protagonist seeks escape, from a successful but unsatisfying career as a concert pianist, in the world of the working class—first as an oilfield worker and then, at the end of the film, as a logger. The film centers on his foray into the bourgeois bohemia of his family's home—a sort of *ad hoc* artist colony under the aegis of his sister. The world we see is both figuratively and literally one of cripples. His sister's lover is in traction. His father is a paralytic. All are emblems of a pseudoclass, without a vital motive force, that the protagonist rejects, but cannot replace. The protagonist's sole contribution to an intellectual discussion among his sister's friends is an obscene comment on the senselessness of their phrase-weaving. In the largest sense, *Five Easy Pieces* is about the American intellectual's self-hatred, his disorientation in an essentially anti-intellectual society, and his resulting inability to feel comfortable with his capacity to think and to create.

The King of Marvin Gardens cuts through the American dream—the belief that every man can achieve riches by ingenuity. The protagonist becomes drawn into his brother's success dream. Rafelson sets the film in pre-boom Atlantic City—an emblem of economic desolation. The locale's aptness is affirmed by the scene of the protagonist's sister-in-law throwing her make-up into a fire. Her ageing face, without make-up, is seen against the dilapidated facade of boardwalk hotels. Her gesture (and in Rafelson's uncommitted world we daren't ask for more) of defiance is directed against what has been the female share of the American Dream: the male has traditionally taken for himself the power that comes of wealth and left woman the illusion called "glamour." Another symbol is the blowing up of an old hotel; it

Bob Rafelson with Jack Nicholson on the set of *Five Easy Pieces*

collapses in a heap like the dream of entrepreneurship the protagonist momentarily shares with his brother.

Rafelson's elliptical style creates tension and interest in the opening moments of thrillers like *The Postman Always Rings Twice, Black Widow,* and *Man Trouble,* but this style makes for occasional plot confusion. It is often hard to tell whether the ellipses are accidental or part of aesthetic strategy. In one instance, whatever the intent, an ellipsis poetically seems to suggest a shudder of horror at the human condition and a desire to drop out entirely from it: Rafelson suddenly presents us with the strangely clipped, abrupt walkout of the protagonist at the end of *Black Widow.* The films focus on what is the main theme of Rafelson's films of the 1980s and 1990s: betrayal from those closest to you, especially from within the family group. Rafelson cannot ever be said to have been caught up in the recent sentimentalism about the traditional family structure. In his filmic vision, he places no trust in the values found there.

Only in the unconventional pairing between the explorer Burton and a liberated aristocrat (exhilaratingly played by Fiona Shaw) in *Mountains of the Moon* does one find a positive vision of marriage and human trust, achieved only after the hero drops out from the competitive struggle for grants toward explorations and for credit from the findings. Burton experiences betrayal from Spekes, his boon companion during the exploration of the mountains at the source of the Nile River. While the film tries but fails to exonerate Burton of any deep complicity in British imperialism, it does pointedly show how powerful English interests seek in every possible way to harm his career and discount his accomplishments because he is of Irish birth. The socio-historical impact is otherwise weakened by the narrative. Whereas Rafelson's thrillers benefit from elliptical expositions, they play considerable havoc with much of the first half of *Mountains of the Moon.*

Rafelson has failed to gain audience popularity and rare critical approval because he does not soften brutal political deconstruction with dazzling techniques. He devotes his attention not only to the straightforward expression of his themes but to getting brilliant acting out of his casts. He forces them to explore the darker sides of their characters—each a microcosm of society.

—Rodney Farnsworth

RAINER, Yvonne

Nationality: American. **Born:** San Francisco, 1934. **Career:** Modern dancer, then choreographer, New York, from 1957; co-founder of Judson Dance Theater, 1962; presented choreographic work in U.S. and Europe, 1962-75; began to integrate slides and short films into dance performances, 1968; completed first feature-length film, *Lives of Performers,* 1972; teacher at New School for Social Research, New York, California Institute of the Arts, Valencia, and elsewhere. **Awards:** Maya Deren Award, American Film Institute, 1988; Guggenheim Fellowship, 1969, 1989; MacArthur Fellowship, 1990-95; Wexner Prize, 1995. **Address:** 72 Franklin St., New York, NY 10013, U.S.A.

Films:

1967 *Volleyball (Foot Film)* (short)
1968 *Hand Movie* (short); *Rhode Island Red* (short); *Trio Film* (short)
1969 *Line*
1972 *Lives of Performers*
1974 *Film about a Woman Who ...*
1976 *Kristina Talking Pictures*
1980 *Journeys from Berlin/1971*
1985 *The Man Who Envied Women*
1990 *Privilege*

Publications

By RAINER: books—

Work 1961-73, New York, 1974.
The Films of Yvonne Rainer, by Rainer and others, Bloomington, Indiana, 1989.

By RAINER: articles—

"A Quasi Survey of Some 'Minimalist' Tendencies in the Quantitatively Minimal Dance Activity Midst the Plethora, or An Analysis of *Trio A,*" in *Minimal Art,* edited by Gregory Battcock, New York, 1968.
Interview in *Monthly Film Bulletin* (London), May 1977.
"More Kicking and Screaming from the Narrative Front/Backwater," in *Wide Angle* (Athens, Ohio), vol. 7, no. 1/2, 1985.
Interview with Mitch Rosenbaum, in *Persistence of Vision* (Maspeth, New York), Summer 1988.
"Script of Privilege," in *Screen Writings: Scripts and Texts by Independent Filmmakers,* edited by Scott MacDonald.

On RAINER: books—

Green, Shelley, *Radical Juxtaposition: The Films of Yvonne Rainer.*

On RAINER: articles—

Koch, Stephen, "Performance: A Conversation," in *Artforum* (New York), December 1972.
Borden, Lizzie, "Trisha Brown and Yvonne Rainer," in *Artforum* (New York), June 1973.
Michelson, Annette, "Yvonne Rainer: The Dancer and the Dance," and "Yvonne Rainer: *Lives of Performers,*" in *Artforum* (New York), January and February 1974.
"Yvonne Rainer: An Introduction, in *Camera Obscura* (Berkeley), Fall 1976.
Rosenbaum, Jonathan, "The Ambiguities of Yvonne Rainer," in *American Film* (Washington, D.C.), March 1980.
Rich, B.R., "Yvonne Rainer," in *Frauen und Film* (Berlin), October 1984.
Vincendeau, Ginette, and B. Reynaud, "Impossible Projections," in *Screen* (London), Autumn 1987.
Cook, Pam, "Love and Catastrophe—Yvonne Rainer," in *Monthly Film Bulletin* (London), August 1987.

* * *

Although Yvonne Rainer made her first feature-length film in 1972, she had already been prominent in the New York avant-garde art scene for nearly a decade. She moved to New York from San Francisco in 1957 to study acting, but started taking dance lessons and soon committed herself to dance. By the mid-1960s, she emerged as an influential dancer and choreographer, initially drawing the attention of critics and audiences through her work with the Judson Dance Theater.

Rainer saw a problem inherent in dance as an art form, namely its involvement with "narcissism, virtuosity and display." Her alternative conception was of the performance as a kind of work or task, as opposed to an exhibition, carried out by "neutral 'doers'" rather than performers. Thus the minimalist dance that she pioneered, which depended on ordinary movements, departed radically from the dramatic, emotive forms of both its classical and modern dance precursors.

Rainer was not long content with merely stripping dance of its artifice and conventions. She became interested in psychology and sexuality, in the everyday emotions that people share, and grew dissatisfied with abstract dance, which she found too limited to express her new concerns. To communicate more personal and emotional content, Rainer began experimenting with combining movements with other media, such as recorded and spoken texts, slides, film stills, and music, creating a performance collage. Language and narrative became increasingly important components of her performance.

Rainer's first films, shorts made to be part of these performances in the late 1960s, were "filmed choreographic exercises," as she wrote in 1971, "that were meant to be viewed with one's peripheral vision ... not to be taken seriously." Her interest in the narrative potential of film and the director's dominance of the medium drew Rainer further into filmmaking.

Her first two feature films, *Lives of Performers* and *Film about a Woman Who ...*, both with cinematographer Babette Mangolte, originated as performance pieces. In these and her two other films, *Kristina Talking Pictures* and *Journeys from Berlin/1971,* Rainer interweaves the real and the fictional, the personal and the political, the concrete and the abstract. She preserves the collagist methods of her performances, juxtaposing personal recollections, previous works, historical documents, and original dialogue and narration, her soundtracks often having the same richness, and the same disjunction, as the visual portions of her films.

Like Brecht, Rainer believes that an audience should contemplate what they see; they should participate in the creative process of the film rather than simply receive it passively. Thus, instead of systematically telling a story, she apposes and layers narrative elements to create meaning. The discontinuity, ambiguity, and even contradiction that often result keep Rainer's audience at a distance, so they can examine the feminist, psychological, political, or purely emotional issues she addresses. Consistent with her dance and performance, Rainer's films are theoretical, even intellectual, not dramatic, sentimental, or emotional, despite her subject matter, which is often controversial and emotion-laden.

—Jessica Wolff

RAY, Nicholas

Nationality: American. **Born:** Raymond Nicholas Kienzle in Galesville, Wisconsin, 7 August 1911. **Education:** Educated in architecture and theater, University of Chicago. **Family:** Married 1) Jean Evans, 1930 (divorced); 2) Gloria Grahame, 1948 (divorced 1952); 3) dancer Betty Schwab (divorced); 4) Susan (Ray), four children. **Career:** Director, Frank Lloyd Wright's Taliesin Playhouse, early 1930s;

in Theater of Action, 1935-37; joined John Houseman's Phoenix Theater, accident results in loss of sight in right eye, 1938; named War Information Radio Program Director by Houseman, 1942; director on Broadway, 1943; assistant to Elia Kazan in Hollywood, 1944; directed first film, *They Live By Night*, 1948; walked off set of *55 Days at Peking*, moved to Paris, 1962; teacher of filmmaking at State University of New York, Binghamton, 1971-73. **Died:** In New York, 16 June 1979.

Films as Director:

1948 ***They Live By Night*** (first released in Britain as ***The Twisted Road***, U.S. release 1949); *A Woman's Secret*
1949 *Knock on Any Door*
1950 ***In a Lonely Place***; *Born to Be Bad*
1951 *The Flying Leathernecks*
1952 *On Dangerous Ground*; *The Lusty Men*
1954 ***Johnny Guitar***
1955 *Run for Cover*; ***Rebel Without a Cause*** (+ story)
1956 *Hot Blood*; *Bigger than Life*
1957 *The True Story of Jesse James*; *Bitter Victory* (+ co-sc)
1958 *Wind Across the Everglades*; *Party Girl*
1959 *The Savage Innocents* (+ sc)
1961 *King of Kings*
1963 *55 Days at Peking* (co-d)
1975 *You Can't Go Home Again* (+ sc, unfinished)
1981 *Lightning over Water* (*Nick's Movie*) (co-d, role as himself)

Other Films:

1977 ***Der Amerikanische Freund*** (*The American Friend*) (Wenders) (role)
1979 *Hair* (Forman) (role)

Publications

By RAY: articles—

"Portrait de l'acteur en jeune homme," in *Cahiers du Cinéma* (Paris), no. 66, 1956.
"Story into Script," in *Sight and Sound* (London), Autumn 1956.
Interview with Charles Bitsch, in *Cahiers du Cinéma* (Paris), November 1958.
"Conversation with Nicholas Ray and Joseph Losey," with Penelope Houston, in *Sight and Sound* (London), Autumn 1961.
Interview with Jean Douchet and Jacques Joly, in *Cahiers du Cinéma* (Paris), January 1962.
Interview with Adriano Aprà and others, in *Movie* (London), May 1963.
Interview in *Interviews with Film Directors*, edited by Andrew Sarris, New York, 1967.
"Nicholas Ray Today," an interview with J. Greenberg, in *Filmmakers Newsletter* (Ward Hill, Massachusetts), January 1973.
"Nicholas Ray: Rebel!," an interview with M. Goodwin and N. Wise, in *Take One* (Montreal), January 1977.
"On Directing," in *Sight and Sound* (London), Autumn 1990.

On RAY: books—

McArthur, Colin, *Underworld U.S.A.*, London, 1972.
Kreidl, John, *Nicholas Ray*, Boston, 1977.
Masi, Stefano, *Nicholas Ray*, Florence, 1983.
Allan, Blaine, *Nicholas Ray: A Guide to References and Resources*, Boston, 1984.
Hillier, Jim, editor, *Cahiers du Cinéma 1: Neo-realism, Hollywood, New Wave*, London, 1985.
Erice, Victor, and Jos Oliver, *Nicholas Ray y su tiempo*, Madrid, 1986.
Giuliani, Pierre, *Nicholas Ray*, Paris, 1987.
Wagner, Jean, *Nicholas Ray*, Paris, 1987.

On RAY: articles—

Archer, Eugene, "Generation Without a Cause," in *Film Culture* (New York), vol. 2, no. 1, 1956.
Perkins, Victor, "The Cinema of Nicholas Ray," in *Movie Reader*, edited by Ian Cameron, New York, 1972.
Wood, Robin, "Film Favorites," in *Film Comment* (New York), September/October 1972.
Rosenbaum, Jonathan, "Circle of Pain: The Cinema of Nicholas Ray," in *Sight and Sound* (London), Autumn 1973.
"*Johnny Guitar* Issue" of *Avant-Scène du Cinéma* (Paris), March 1974.
Biskind, Peter, "Rebel Without a Cause: Nicholas Ray in the Fifties," in *Film Quarterly* (Berkeley), Fall 1974.
Lederer, Joseph, "Film as Experience: Nicholas Ray—The Director Turns Teacher," in *American Film* (Washington, D.C.), November 1975.
Cocks, J., "Director in Aspic," in *Take One* (Montreal), January 1977.
Thomson, D., "In a Lonely Place," in *Sight and Sound* (London), no. 4, 1979.
Obituary, in *The New York Times*, 18 June 1979.
Beylie, Claude, obituary, in *Ecran* (Paris), 15 September 1979.
Farrell, T., and others, "Nicholas Ray: The Last Movies," in *Sight and Sound* (London), Spring 1981.
Rosenbaum, Jonathan, "Looking for Nicholas Ray," in *American Film* (Washington, D.C.), December 1981.
Eisenschitz, B., "Nicholas Ray, téléaste," in *Cahiers du Cinéma* (Paris), January 1985.
Houseman, John, "Houseman, Ray and Ophüls," in *Sight and Sound* (London), Autumn 1986.

* * *

"The cinema is Nicholas Ray." Godard's magisterial statement has come in for a good deal of ridicule, not by any means entirely undeserved. Yet it contains a core of truth, especially if taken in reverse. Nicholas Ray is cinema in the sense that his films work entirely (and perhaps only) as *movies*, arrangements of space and movement charged with dramatic tension. Few directors demonstrate more clearly that a film is something beyond the sum of its parts. Consider only the more literary components—dialogue, plot, characterisation—and a film like *Party Girl* is patently trash. But on the screen the visual turbulence of Ray's shooting style, the fractured intensity of his editing, fuse the elements into a valid emotional whole. The flaws are still apparent, but have become incidental.

Nor is Ray's cinematic style in any way extraneous, imposed upon his subjects. The nervous tension within the frame also informs his characters, vulnerable violent outsiders at odds with society and with themselves. The typical Ray hero is a loner, at once contemptuous of the complacent normal world and tormented with a longing to be reaccepted into it—to become (like Bowie and Keechie, the young lovers of *They Live by Night*) "like real people." James Dean in *Rebel Without a Cause*, Robert Ryan in *On Dangerous Ground*, Robert Mitchum in *The Lusty Men*, all start by rejecting the constraints of the nuclear family, only to find themselves impelled to recreate it in substitute form, as though trying to fill an unacknowledged void. In one achingly elegiac scene in *The Lusty Men*, Mitchum prowls around the tumbledown shack that was his childhood home, "looking for something I thought I'd lost."

Ray's grounding in architecture (he studied at Taliesin with Frank Lloyd Wright) reveals itself in an exceptionally acute sense of space,

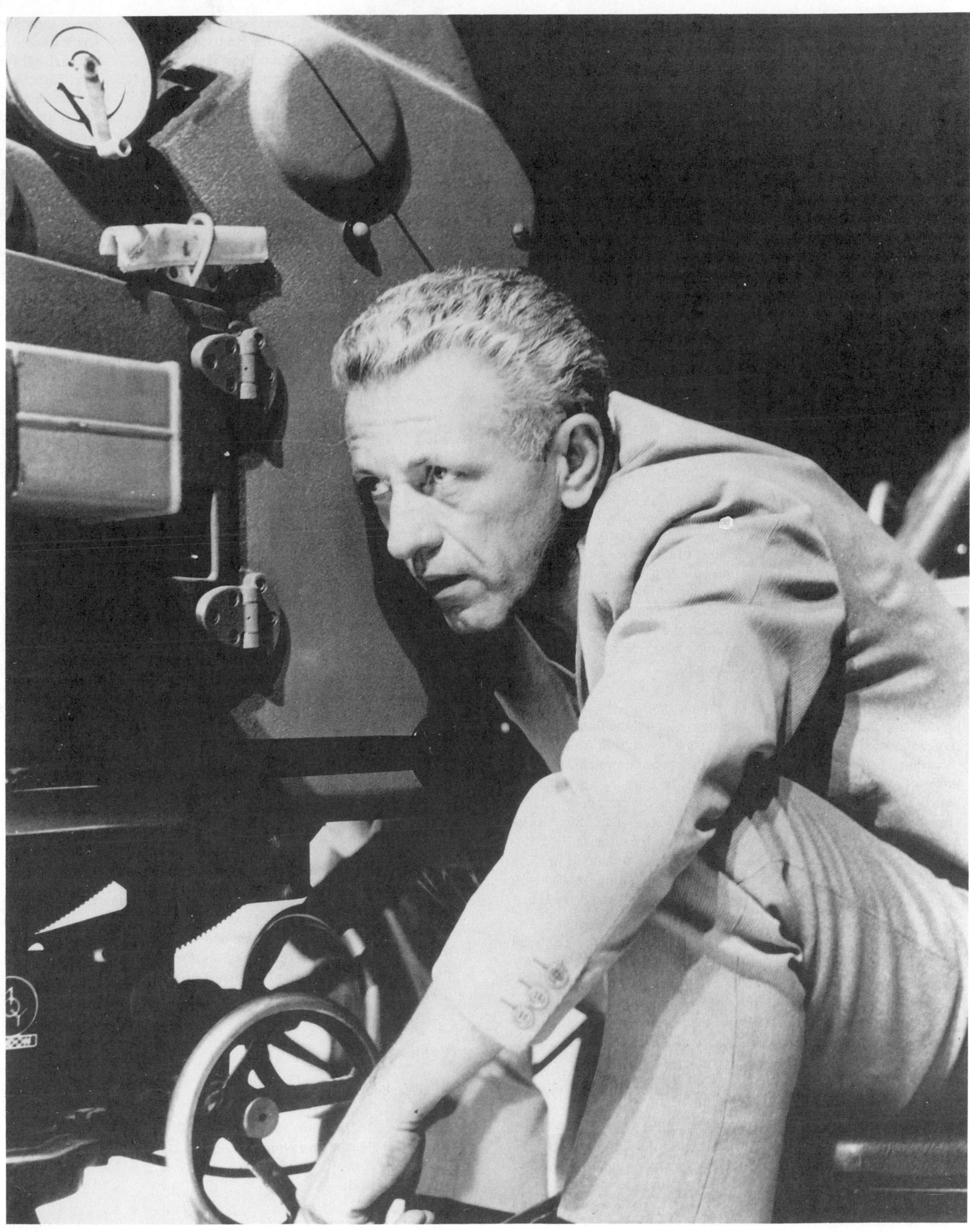

Nicholas Ray

often deployed as an extension of states of mind. In his films the geometry of locations, and especially interiors, serves as a psychological terrain. Conflict can be played out, and tension expressed, in terms of spatial areas (upstairs and downstairs, for example, or the courtyards and levels of an apartment complex) pitted against each other. Ray also credited Wright with instilling in him "a love of the horizontal line"—and hence of the CinemaScope screen, for which he felt intuitive affinity. Unlike many of his contemporaries, who found it awkward and inhibiting, Ray avidly explores the format's potential, sometimes combining it with lateral tracking shots to convey lyrical movement, at other times angling his camera to create urgent diagonals, suggesting characters straining against the constrictions of the frame.

Equally idiosyncratic is Ray's expressionist use of colour, taken at times to heights of delirium that risk toppling into the ridiculous. In *Johnny Guitar,* perhaps the most flamboyantly baroque Western ever made, Joan Crawford is colour-coded red, white, or black according to which aspect of her character—whore, victim, or gunslinger—is uppermost in a given scene. Similarly, the contrast in *Bigger Than Life* between the hero's respectable job as a schoolteacher and his déclassé moonlighting for a taxi firm is signalled by an abrupt cut from the muted grey-browns of the school to a screenful of gaudy yellow cabs that hit the audience's eyes with a visual slap.

Nearly all Ray's finest films were made in the 1950s, their agonized romanticism cutting across the grain of that decade's brittle optimism. "The poet of American disenchantment" (in David Thomson's phrase), Ray viewed social conventions as a trap, from which violence or madness may be the only escape. In *Bigger Than Life,* James Mason's smalltown teacher, frustrated by his low social status, gains the feelings of power and superiority he aspires to from a nerve drug. Under its influence the character is transformed into a hideous parody of the dominant father-figure enjoined by society. Similarly—but working from the opposite perspective—*In a Lonely Place* subverts Bogart's tough-guy persona, revealing the anguish and insecurity that underlie it and, as V.F. Perkins puts it, making "violence the index of the character's weakness rather than strength."

"I'm a stranger here myself." Ray often quoted Sterling Hayden's line from *Johnny Guitar* as his personal motto. His career, as he himself was well aware, disconcertingly mirrored the fate of his own riven, alienated heroes. Unappreciated (or so he felt) in America, and increasingly irked by the constraints of the studio system, he nonetheless produced all his best work there. In Europe, where he was hailed as one of the world's greatest directors, his craft deserted him: after two ill-starred epics, the last sixteen years of his life trickled away in a mess of incoherent footage and abortive projects. Victim of his own legend, Ray finally took self-identification with his protagonists to its ultimate tortured conclusion—collaborating, in *Lightning Over Water,* in the filming of his own disintegration and death.

—Philip Kemp

RAY, Satyajit

Nationality: Indian. **Born:** Calcutta, 2 May 1921. **Education:** Attended Ballygunj Government School; Presidency College, University of Calcutta, B.A. in economics (with honors), 1940; studied painting at University of Santiniketan, 1940-43. **Family:** Married Bijoya Das, 1949; one son. **Career:** Commercial artist for D. J. Keymer advertising agency, Calcutta, 1943; co-founder, Calcutta Film Society, 1947; met Jean Renoir making *The River,* 1950; completed first film, *Pather Panchali,* 1955; composed own music, from *Teen Kanya* (1961) on; made first film in Hindi (as opposed to Bengali), *The Chess Players,* 1977; editor and illustrator for children's magazine *Sandesh,* 1980s. **Awards:** Grand Prize, Cannes Festival, 1956, Golden Gate Award, San Francisco International Film Festival, 1957, Film Critics Award, Stratford Festival, 1958, and President of India Gold Medal, all for *Pather Panchali*; Gold Lion, Venice Festival, 1957, Best Direction, San Francisco International Film Festival, 1958, and President of India Gold Medal, all for *Aparajito;* Selznick Award and Sutherland Trophy, 1960, for *Apur Sansar;* Silver Bear for Best Direction, Berlin Festival, for *Mahanagar,* 1964, and for *Charulata,* 1965; Special Award of Honour, Berlin Festival, 1966; Decorated Order Yugoslav Flag, 1971; Golden Bear Award, Berlin Film Festival, 1973, for *Distant Thunder;* D.Litt, Oxford University, 1978; Life Fellow, British Film Institute, 1983; Legion of Honour, France, 1989; Indian Awards, Best Picture and Best Director, 1991, for *Agantuk;* Academy Award for lifetime achievement in cinema, 1992. **Died:** Of heart failure, 23 April 1992, in Calcutta.

Films as Director and Scriptwriter:

1955 ***Pather Panchali*** (*Father Panchali*) (+ pr)
1956 ***Aparajito*** (*The Unvanquished*) (+ pr)
1957 *Parash Pathar* (*The Philosopher's Stone*)
1958 *Jalsaghar* (*The Music Room*) (+ pr)
1959 ***Apur Sansar*** (*The World of Apu*) (+ pr)
1960 *Devi* (*The Goddess*) (+ pr, mus)
1961 *Teen Kanya* (*Two Daughters*) (+ pr); *Rabindranath Tagore* (doc)
1962 *Abhijan* (*Expedition*); *Kanchanjanga* (+ pr)
1963 *Mahanagar* (*The Big City*)
1964 ***Charulata*** (*The Lonely Wife*)
1965 *Kapurush-o-Mahapurush* (*The Coward and the Saint*); *Two* (short)
1966 *Nayak* (*The Hero*)
1967 *Chiriakhana* (*The Zoo*)
1969 *Goopy Gyne Bagha Byne* (*The Adventures of Goopy and Bagha*)
1970 *Pratidwandi* (*The Adversary*); *Aranyer Din Ratri* (*Days and Nights in the Forest*)
1971 *Seemabaddha*; *Sikkim* (doc)
1972 *The Inner Eye* (doc)
1973 *Asani Sanket* (*Distant Thunder*)
1974 *Sonar Kella* (*The Golden Fortress*)
1975 *Jana Aranya* (*The Middleman*)
1976 *Bala* (doc)
1977 *Shatranj Ke Khilari* (*The Chess Players*)
1978 *Joi Baba Felunath* (*The Elephant God*)
1979 *Heerak Rajar Deshe* (*The Kingdom of Diamonds*)
1981 *Sadgati* (*Deliverance*) (for TV); *Pikoo* (short)
1984 *Ghare Bahire* (*The Home and the World*) (+ pr, mus)
1989 *Ganashatru* (*An Enemy of the People*)
1990 *Shakha Proshakha* (*Branches of the Tree*)
1991 *Agantuk* (*The Visitor*)

Publications

By RAY: books—

Our Films, Their Films, New Delhi, 1977.
The Chess Players and Other Screenplays, London, 1989.

By RAY: articles—

"A Long Time on the Little Road," in *Sight and Sound* (London), Spring 1957.

"Satyajit Ray on Himself," in *Cinema* (Beverly Hills), July/August 1965.
"From Film to Film," in *Cahiers du Cinéma in English* (New York), no. 3, 1966
Interview, in *Film Makers on Filmmaking,* by Harry M. Geduld, Bloomington, Indiana, 1967.
Interview, in *Interviews with Film Directors,* edited by Andrew Sarris, New York, 1967.
Interview with J. Blue, in *Film Comment* (New York), Summer 1968.
"Conversation with Satyajit Ray," with F. Isaksson, in *Sight and Sound* (London), Summer 1970.
"Ray's New Trilogy," an interview with C. B. Thomsen, in *Sight and Sound* (London), Winter 1972/73.
"Dialogue on Film: Satyajit Ray," in *American Film* (Washington, D.C.), July/August 1978.
Interview with Michel Ciment, in *Positif* (Paris), May 1979.
Interview with U. Gupta, in *Cineaste* (New York), vol. 12, no. 1, 1982.
"Under Western Eyes," in *Sight and Sound* (London), Autumn 1982.
"Bridging the Home and the World," an interview with A. Robinson, in *Monthly Film Bulletin* (London), September 1984.
Interview with Charles Tesson, in *Cahiers du Cinéma* (Paris), July/August 1987.
Interview with Derek Malcolm, in *Sight and Sound* (London), Spring 1989.
"To Western Audiences, the Filmmaker Satyajit Ray Is Synonymous with Indian Cinema," an interview with Gowri Ramnarayan, in *Interview,* June 1992.

On RAY: films—

Satyajit Ray, 1982.
Satyajit Ray: Introspections, 1991.

On RAY: books—

Seton, Marie, *Portrait of a Director,* Bloomington, Indiana, 1970.
Wood, Robin, *The Apu Trilogy,* New York, 1971.
Taylor, John Russell, *Directors and Directions: Cinema for '70s,* New York, 1975.
Rangoonwalla, Firoze, *Satyajit Ray's Art,* Shahdara, Delhi, 1980.
Satyajit Ray: An Anthology, edited by Chidananda Das Gupta, New Delhi, 1981.
Willemen, Paul, and Behroze Gandhy, *Indian Cinema,* London, 1982.
Armes, Roy, *Third World Filmmaking and the West,* Berkeley, 1987.
Nyce, Ben, *Satyajit Ray: A Study of His Films,* New York, 1988.
Robinson, Andrew, *Satyajit Ray: The Inner Eye,* London, 1989.
Tesson, Charles, *Satyajit Ray,* Paris, 1992.

On RAY: articles—

Gray, H., "The Growing Edge: Satyajit Ray," in *Film Quarterly* (Berkeley, California), Winter 1958.
Rhode, Eric, "Satyajit Ray: A Study," in *Sight and Sound* (London), Summer 1961.
Stanbrook, Alan, "The World of Ray," in *Films and Filming* (London), November 1965.
Hrusa, B., "Satyajit Ray: Genius behind the Man," in *Film* (London), Winter 1966.
Glushanok, Paul, "On Ray," in *Cineaste* (New York), Summer 1967.
Malik, A., "Satyajit Ray and the Alien," in *Sight and Sound* (London), Winter 1967/68.
Mehta, V., "Profiles," in *New Yorker,* 21 March 1970.
Thomsen, Christian Braad, "Ray's New Trilogy," in *Sight and Sound* (London), Winter 1972/73.
Dutta, K., "Cinema in India: An Interview with Satyajit Ray's Cinematographers," in *Filmmakers Newsletter* (Ward Hill, Massachusetts), January 1975.
Hughes, J., "A Voyage in India: Satyajit Ray," in *Film Comment* (New York), September/October 1976.
"*Pathar Panchali* Issue" of *Avant-Scène du Cinéma* (Paris), 1 February 1980.
Armes, Roy, "Satyajit Ray: Astride Two Cultures," in *Films and Filming* (London), August 1982.
Robinson, A., "Satyajit Ray at Work," in *American Cinematographer* (Los Angeles), September 1983.
Ray, B., "Ray off Set," in *Sight and Sound* (London), Winter 1983/84.
Das Gupta, Chidananda, and Andrew Robinson, "A Passage from India," in *American Film* (Washington, D.C.), October 1985.
Robinson, Andrew, "The Music Room," in *Sight and Sound* (London), Autumn 1989.
Armand, M., "Satyajit Ray au present," in *Cahiers du Cinema,* July/August 1990.
Sengupta, Shuddhabarata, "Reflections on Satyajit Ray," *World Press Review,* April 1992.
Schickel, Richard, "Days and Nights at the Art House," in *Film Comment,* May/June 1992.
Andersson, K., "Satyajit Ray," in *Cinema Papers,* May/June 1992.
Chatterjee, D., "Entretien avec Satyajit Ray," in *Cahiers du Cinema,* June 1992.

* * *

From the beginning of his career as a filmmaker, Satyajit Ray has been interested in finding ways to reveal the mind and thoughts of his characters. Because the range of his sympathy is wide, he has been accused of softening the presence of evil in his cinematic world. But a director who aims to represent the currents and cross-currents of feeling within people is likely to disclose to viewers the humanness even in reprehensible figures. In any case, from the first films of his early period, Ray devises strategies for rendering inner lives; he simplifies the surface action of the film so that the viewer's attention travels to (1) the reaction of people to one another, or to their environments, (2) the mood expressed by natural scenery or objects, and (3) music as a clue to the state of mind of a character. In the *Apu Trilogy* the camera often stays with one of two characters after the other character exits the frame to see their silent response. Or else, after some significant event in the narrative, Ray presents correlatives of that event in the natural world. When the impoverished wife in *Pather Panchali* receives a postcard bearing happy news from her husband, the scene dissolves to water skates dancing on a pond. As for music, in his films Ray commissioned compositions from India's best classical musicians—Ravi Shankar, Vilayat Khan, Ali Akbar Khan—but since *Teen Kanya* has been composing his own music and has progressed towards quieter indication through music of the emotional experience of his characters.

Ray's work can be divided into three periods on the basis of his cinematic practice: the early period, 1955-66, from *Pather Panchali* through *Nayak*; the middle period, 1969-1977, from *Googy Gyne Bagha Byne* through *Shatranj Ke Khilari*; and the recent period, from *Joy Baba Felunath* and through *Sadgati* and *Ghare Bahire.* The early period is characterized by thoroughgoing realism: the mise-en-scène are rendered in deep focus; long takes and slow camera movements prevail. The editing is subtle, following shifts of narrative interest and cutting on action in the Hollywood style. Ray's emphasis in the early period on capturing reality is obvious in *Kanchanjangha,* in which 100 minutes in the lives of characters are rendered in 100 minutes of film time. *The Apu Trilogy, Parash Pather, Jalsaghar,* and *Devi* all exemplify what Ray had learned from Hollywood's studio era, from Renoir's mise-en-scène, and from the use of classical music in Indian

Satyajit Ray: *Pather Panchali*

cinema. *Charulata* affords the archetypal example of Ray's early style, with the decor, the music, the long takes, the activation of various planes of depth within a composition, and the reaction shots all contributing significantly to a representation of the lonely wife's inner conflicts. The power of Ray's early films comes from his ability to suggest deep feeling by arranging the surface elements of his films unemphatically.

Ray's middle period is characterized by increasing complexity of style; to his skills at understatement Ray adds a sharp use of montage. The difference in effect between an early film and a middle film becomes apparent if one compares the early *Mahanagar* with the middle *Jana Aranya,* both films pertaining to life in Calcutta. In *Mahanagar,* the protagonist chooses to resign her job in order to protest the unjust dismissal of a colleague. The film affirms the rightness of her decision. In the closing sequence, the protagonist looks up at the tall towers of Calcutta and says to her husband so that we believe her, "What a big city! Full of jobs! There must be something somewhere for one of us!" Ten years later, in *Jana Aranya,* it is clear that there are no jobs and that there is precious little room to worry about niceties of justice and injustice. The darkness running under the pleasant facade of many of the middle films seems to derive from the turn in Indian politics after the death of Nehru. Within Bengal, many ardent young people joined a Maoist movement to destroy existing institutions, and more were themselves destroyed by a ruthless police force. Across India, politicians abandoned Nehru's commitment to a socialist democracy in favor of a scramble for personal power. In *Seemabaddha* or *Aranyer Din Ratri* Ray's editing is sharp but not startling. In *Shatranj Ke Khilari,* on the other hand, Ray's irony is barely restrained: he cuts from the blue haze of a Nawab's music room to a gambling scene in the city. In harsh daylight, commoners lay bets on fighting rams, as intent on their gambling as the Nawab was on his music.

Audiences in India who have responded warmly to Ray's early films have sometimes been troubled by the complexity of his middle films. A film like *Shatranj Ke Khilari* was expected by many viewers to reconstruct the splendors of Moghul India as the early *Jalsaghar* had reconstructed the sensitivity of Bengali feudal landlords and *Charulata* the decency of upper class Victorian Bengal. What the audience found instead was a stern examination of the sources of Indian decadence. According to Ray, the British seemed less to blame for their role than the Indians who demeaned themselves by colluding with the British or by ignoring the public good and plunging into private pleasures. Ray's point of view in *Shatranj* was not popular with distributors and so his first Hindi film was denied fair exhibition in many cities in India.

Ray's more recent style, most evident in the short features *Pikoo* and *Sadgati,* pays less attention than earlier to building a stable geography and a firm time scheme. The exposition of characters and situations is swift: the effect is of great concision. In *Pikoo,* a young boy is sent outside to sketch flowers so that his mother and her lover can pursue their affair indoors. The lover has brought along a drawing pad and colored pens to divert the boy. The boy has twelve colored pens in his packet with which he must represent on paper the wealth of colors in nature. In a key scene (lasting ten seconds) the boy looks at a flower, then down at his packet for a matching color. Through that action of the boy's looking to match the world with his means,

Ray suggests the striving in his own work to render the depth and range of human experience.

In focussing on inner lives and on human relations as the ground of social and political systems, Ray continues the humanist tradition of Rabindranath Tagore. Ray studied at Santiniketan, the university founded by Tagore, and was close to the poet during his last years. Ray has acknowledged his debt in a lyrical documentary about Tagore, and through the Tagore stories on which he has based his films *Teen Kanya, Charulata,* and the recent *Ghare Bahire.* As the poet Tagore was his example, Ray has become an example to important younger filmmakers (such as Shyam Benegal, M. S. Sathyu, G. Aravindan), who have learned from him how to reveal in small domestic situations the working of larger political and cultural forces.

—Satti Khanna

REDFORD, Robert

Nationality: American. **Born:** Charles Robert Redford, Jr., 18 August 1937, in Santa Monica, California. **Education:** Attended University of Colorado and Pratt Institute of Design; studied painting in Europe; studied acting at American Academy of Dramatic Arts. **Family:** Married Lola Van Wagenen, September 12, 1958 (divorced), two daughters and one son. **Career:** Worked for International Business Machines, Inc. (IBM), and Standard Oil, 1950s; founder, Wildwood Enterprises (a production company), Universal City, California; owner, Sundance (a ski resort), Provo, Utah; founder, Sundance Institute (for independent filmmakers); fundraiser, Institute for Resource Management; chairman, Provo Canyon Sewer District Committee, 1976. **Awards:** Emmy Award nomination, best supporting actor, National Academy of Television Arts and Sciences, 1962, for "Voice of Charlie Pont" on *Alcoa Premiere;* Golden Globe Award, new male film star of the year, Hollywood Foreign Press Association, 1966, for *Inside Daisy Clover;* British Academy Award, best leading actor, British Academy of Film and Television Arts, 1970, for *Butch Cassidy and the Sundance Kid* and *Tell Them Willie Boy Is Here;* Hasty Pudding Man of the Year Award, Hasty Pudding Theatricals, 1970; Academy Award nomination, best actor, Academy of Motion Picture Arts and Sciences, 1973, for *The Sting;* Golden Apple Award, male star of the year, Hollywood Women's Press Club, 1973; Golden Globe Awards, male world film favorite, 1975, 1977, and 1978; Academy Award nomination, best short feature, for *The Solar Film;* Academy Award, best director, Golden Globe Award, Outstanding Directorial Achievement Award for Feature Films, Directors Guild of America, and best director awards from the National Board of Review of Motion Pictures and the New York Film Critics' Circle, all 1980, all for *Ordinary People;* L.H.D., University of Colorado, 1987; Audubon Medal, National Audubon Society, 1989, for "lifetime campaign for environmental protection"; Dartmouth Film Society award, 1990; D. Univ., University of Massachusetts, 1990; Golden Globe Award nomination, best director, 1993, for *A River Runs through It;* New York Film Critics' Circle Award and Academy Award nomination, best picture, 1995, for *Quiz Show.* **Agent:** Creative Artists Agency, 9830 Wilshire Blvd., Beverly Hills, California 90212, U.S.A. **Address:** Box 837, Provo Canyon, Utah 84601, U.S.A. (home); Wildwood Enterprises, 100 Universal City Plaza, Universal City, California 91608, U.S.A. (office).

Films as Director:

1980 *Ordinary People*
1988 *The Milagro Beanfield War* (+ pr)
1992 *A River Runs through It* (+ narr, pr)
1994 *Quiz Show*

Other Films:

1962 *War Hunt* (role)
1965 *Situation Hopeless—But Not Serious* (role)
1966 *Inside Daisy Clover* (role); *The Chase* (role); *This Property Is Condemned* (role)
1967 *Barefoot in the Park* (role); *Downhill Racer* (role, pr)
1969 *Butch Cassidy and the Sundance Kid* (role)
1970 *Tell Them Willie Boy Is Here* (role); *Little Fauss and Big Halsey* (role)
1972 *Jeremiah Johnson* (role); *The Hot Rock* (role); *The Candidate* (role, pr)
1973 *The Way We Were* (role); *The Sting* (role)
1974 *The Great Gatsby* (role); *The Great Waldo Pepper* (role)
1975 *Three Days of the Condor* (role); *A Bridge Too Far* (role)
1976 *All the President's Men* (role)
1979 *The Electric Horseman* (role)
1980 *Brubaker* (role)
1984 *The Natural* (role, pr)
1985 *Out of Africa* (role)
1986 *Legal Eagles* (role)
1987 *Promised Land* (exec pr)
1988 *Some Girls* (exec pr)
1990 *Havana* (role)
1992 *Sneakers* (role); *Incident at Oglala* (*Leonard Peltier: A True Story*) (narr, exec pr)
1993 *Indecent Proposal* (role)

Publications

By REDFORD: books—

The Outlaw Trail, New York, 1978.
(Editor and author of introduction) Richard Friedenberg, *A River Runs through It: Bringing a Classic to the Screen,* Livingston, Montana, 1992.

By REDFORD: articles—

Interview in *Saturday Evening Post* (Indianapolis, Indiana), November 1980.
Interview in *Film Comment* (New York), February 1988.
Interview in *Esquire* (New York), September 1992.
Interview in *Harper's Bazaar* (New York), October 1992.
Interview in *Interview* (New York), September 1994.
Interview in *Ladies' Home Journal* (Des Moines, Iowa), October 1994.

On REDFORD: books—

Reed, Donald A., *Robert Redford: A Photographic Portrayal of the Man and His Films,* N.p., 1975.
Spada, James, *The Films of Robert Redford,* New York, 1977.
Downing, David, *Robert Redford,* New York, 1982.

On REDFORD: articles—

Hubener, A., "Sundance," in *Chaplin* (Stockholm), vol. 34, no. 3, 1992.
McCarthy, T., "The Rundown on Redford," in *Variety* (New York), 3 February 1992.
Weinraub, B., "Robert Redford Speaks His Mind on Truth, Justice, and Hollywood," in *New York Times,* 4 May 1992.

James, C., "Pursuing Art and Angst at Bob's Movie Camp," in *New York Times,* 19 July 1992.

Weinraub, B., "Achieving a State of Grace by Water," in *New York Times,* 29 September 1992.

On REDFORD: television special—

Robert Redford and Sydney Pollack: The Men and Their Movies (also known as *Robert Redford: The Man, the Movies, and the Myth),* 1990.

* * *

There is a certain compatibility between the four films Robert Redford has chosen to direct and many of those in which he has appeared as an actor: middle-of-the-road entertainments, thoughtful within certain limits, never descending to vulgarity or stupidity but never transcending the bourgeois tenets of "good taste" (even when he played an escaped convict, an outlaw, or a con-man he remained attractive, even lovable). His commitment to cinema has, however, produced one startling anomaly, the Sundance Festival, the existence and continued flourishing of which are largely due to his championship. Sundance has become a veritable hotbed of radicalism and experimentation, launching the careers of most of the important American directors of the younger generation. It is greatly to Redford's credit that he has lent his name and prestige to an enterprise so alien to the spirit of his own work as actor and director.

So far, little of Sundance has rubbed off: Redford's films are formally and stylistically conservative and, in content, safely "within the ideology." The great progressive movements of our time—feminism, black activism, gay liberation—have had no discernible influence on them. They have, however, assurance, intelligence, and integrity. In *Hollywood from Vietnam to Reagan* I attacked *Ordinary People* as deeply reactionary, using it merely as a foil to highlight the radicalism of Scorsese's *King of Comedy.* Seeing it again ten years later has given me a new respect for it, though without revealing my previous analysis as "wrong," exactly. Perhaps I have mellowed over the years, but I am able today to feel more sympathy for the sorrows and tribulations of heterosexual males. For a start, the film is consummately acted by its three principals (Donald Sutherland, Timothy Hutton, Mary Tyler Moore), for all of whom it provides outstanding roles: Redford has managed to turn his long experience of being directed into a highly sensitive ability to direct others. Stripped of its characters' individual psychology, it remains the "textbook" Oedipal drama I previously described: the Son learns to renounce the Mother and iden-

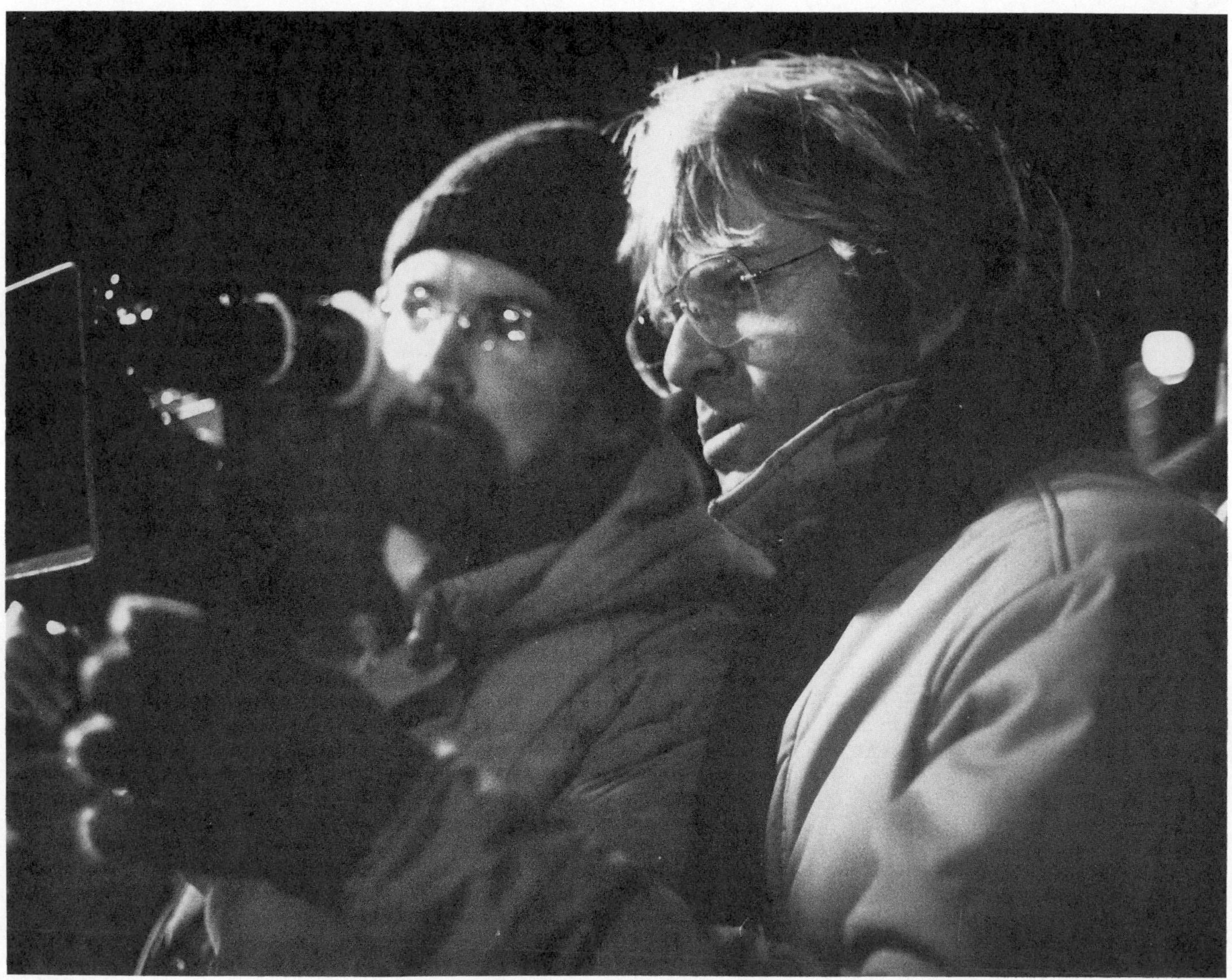

Robert Redford (right) directing *Ordinary People*

tify with the Father (guided by a second Father, the psychiatrist), and is then rewarded with the acquisition of a suitably supportive Woman of his own. But here individual psychology is all, and the particularity with which the characters are realized partly transcends the ideological banality. The developing relationship between father and son—crucial to the son's salvation—is treated very movingly; it is a pity that this is achieved at the expense of the women. The main burden of guilt and failure is imposed on Mary Tyler Moore (though her final exit from a family in which she no longer has a function is sufficiently disturbing somewhat to undercut the ending's sense of plenitude). Elizabeth McGovern, on the other hand, for all the likability of both the actress and the character, is reduced to little more than the necessary "good girl."

It is logical to link Redford's third film, *A River Runs through It,* to *Ordinary People:* both are father-son movies, the female roles marginalized and of little interest. Aside from offering what is perhaps the definitive young Brad Pitt performance, as the son who cannot conform to the family's severely limited but here celebrated way of life, the film (though very polished, achieving exactly what it sets out to achieve) seems chiefly of interest to aficionados of fly-fishing. Its immediate predecessor, *The Milagro Beanfield War,* is, in contrast, the least successful but the most interesting of the first three films. One has the impression that it is at least half an hour too short, that too much was left on the cutting-room floor, so that some of the narrative threads are underdeveloped (Melanie Griffith's role, especially, has become perfunctory to the point of absurdity). But the film displays an impressive ability to handle multiple narrative lines and sustain interest in all of them, and it contains the only female character in Redford's work so far (Sonia Braga) who is both strong and a positive force, retaining a degree of independence.

Which brings us to *Quiz Show,* clearly Redford's most distinguished film to date and in many ways a new departure. It is easy to link the film to *All the President's Men,* in which Redford played one of the crusaders against political corruption. But there is a crucial difference: here, the corruption is not merely political, it permeates every aspect of American culture through the all-powerful media bought up and controlled by the capitalist hegemony.

The "quiz show," which is supposed to be about knowledge, is not merely fraudulent but exposed as yet another "show" of personalities: the conventionally attractive, self-confident (he comes from a cultivated, upper-class background), and above all Aryan contender is recruited to supersede the edgy, odd-looking, Jewish contender with bad teeth. "Image" is all that matters: not merely to the TV audience but to van Doren's university class. Corruption pervades the entire culture. Even the "disinterested" crusader is contaminated: it is suggested that he too is motivated by the desire for "success": not the ambition to be a successful human being, but the success of becoming another media celebrity.

The central figure, Charles van Doren (Ralph Fiennes) is initially a person of integrity. His corruption by the forces of capitalism is (as portrayed) hideously and frighteningly convincing: the lure is not only wealth but fame, for which, as the "son of a famous father," he has a psychological need. The irony of which is that his father despises everything his son is doing to gain his respect. Conversely, Stempel (John Turturro), the quiz show's reigning champion, succumbs to the exactly parallel (though opposite) temptation to give an answer he knows to be wrong. At this point his wife exits abruptly from the studio audience: the closest Redford has come to a powerful feminist statement, although she too is compromised, finally, by her readiness to place her family's welfare above the revelation of truth. But the film's most brilliant touch is that, in a movie where Ralph Fiennes delivers one of the finest, most detailed characterizations in modern cinema, his character gives himself away to the investigator by his momentary and almost imperceptible failure to act convincingly on camera.

The ending resolutely refuses reassurance: what we are sent out of the theater with is the seemingly endless desire of the American public to be allowed to remain in a state of mystification, a view that might be dismissed as cynical but is in fact amply confirmed by today's political/social realities. The film demonstrates that you don't have to align yourself, in America today, with a radical movement in order to make a radical film. You have merely to look about you and record what you see. As Nadine Gordimer puts it in *A Son's Story,* "what the oppressors call subversion is the exposure of the rot in the State."

—Robin Wood

REED, Carol

Nationality: British. **Born:** Putney, London, 30 December 1906, son of actor Herbert Beerbohm Tree. **Education:** King's School, Canterbury. **Family:** Married 1) Diana Wynyard (divorced); 2) actress Penelope Ward, two sons. **Career:** Actor on London stage, from 1924; dramatic advisor to author Edgar Wallace, 1927; stage director, from 1929; dialogue director for Associated Talking Pictures, 1932; directed first feature, 1933; served in British Army Film Unit, World War II; began collaboration with writer Graham Greene, 1946. **Awards:** Best British Film Award, British Film Academy, for *Odd Man Out,* 1947; Best British Film Award, British Film Academy, and Best Direction, New York Film Critics, for *The Fallen Idol,* 1948; Best British Film Award, British Film Academy, and Quarterly Award, Directors Guild of America, for *The Third Man,* 1949; Knighted, 1952; Oscar for Best Director, for *Oliver!,* 1968. **Died:** In London, 1976.

Films as Director:

1933 *Midshipman Easy* (*Men of the Sea*)
1936 *Laburnum Grove*; *Talk of the Devil* (+ story)
1937 *Who's Your Lady Friend?*
1938 *Bank Holiday* (*Three on a Week-End*); *Penny Paradise*
1939 *Climbing High*; *A Girl Must Live*; *The Stars Look Down*
1940 *Night Train to Munich* (*Night Train*); *The Girl in the News*
1941 *Kipps* (*The Remarkable Mr. Kipps*); *A Letter from Home* (short documentary)
1942 *The Young Mr. Pitt*; *The New Lot*
1944 *The Way Ahead*
1945 *The True Glory* (collaboration with Garson Kanin)
1947 ***Odd Man Out***
1948 *The Fallen Idol*
1949 ***The Third Man***
1951 *Outcast of the Islands*
1953 *The Man Between*
1955 *A Kid for Two Farthings*
1956 *Trapeze*
1958 *The Key*
1960 *Our Man in Havana*
1963 *The Running Man* (+ pr)
1965 *The Agony and the Ecstasy* (+ pr)
1968 *Oliver!*
1970 *Flap*
1972 *Follow Me* (*The Public Eye*)

Other Film:

1937 *No Parking* (Raymond) (story)

Carol Reed

Publications

By REED: article—

Interview in *Encountering Directors,* by Charles Samuels, New York, 1972.

On REED: books—

Greene, Graham, *The Third Man,* London and New York, 1968; published as *The Third Man: A Film by Graham Greene and Carol Reed,* New York, 1984.

Phillips, Gene D., *Graham Greene: The Films of His Fiction,* New York, 1974.

DeFelice, James, *Filmguide to Odd Man Out,* Bloomington, Indiana, 1975.

Armes, Roy, *A Critical History of the British Cinema,* London, 1978.

Moss, Robert F., *The Films of Carol Reed,* New York, 1987.

Phillips, Gene D., *Major Film Directors of the American and British Cinema,* Cranbury, New Jersey, 1989.

Wapshott, Nicholas, *The Man Between: A Biography of Carol Reed,* London, 1990.

On REED: articles—

Goodman, E., "Carol Reed," in *Theatre Arts* (New York), May 1947.

Wright, Basil, "The Director: Carol Reed," in *Sight and Sound* (London), Summer 1951.

De La Roche, Catherine, "A Man with No Message," in *Films and Filming* (London), December 1954.

Sarris, Andrew, "Carol Reed in the Context of His Time," in two parts, in *Film Culture* (New York), no. 10, 1956 and no. 11, 1957.

Sarris, Andrew, "First of the Realists," and "The Stylist Goes to Hollywood," in *Films and Filming* (London), September and October 1957.

Fawcett, Marion, "Sir Carol Reed," in *Films in Review* (New York), March 1959.

Voigt, M., "Pictures of Innocence: Sir Carol Reed," in *Focus on Film* (London), Spring 1974.

Obituary, in *Cinéma* (Paris), June 1976.

Phillips, Gene D., "Carol Reed," in *Films in Review* (New York), August/September 1982.

Kemp, Philip, "Fallen Idol," in *Sight and Sound* (London), Spring 1988.

Lefèvre, Raymond, and Claude Beylie, "Carol Reed, un cinéaste au carrefour des influences," in *Avant-Scène du Cinéma* (Paris), March 1989.

Driver, Paul, "A *Third Man* Cento," in *Sight and Sound* (London), Winter 1989/90.

* * *

Carol Reed came to films from the theater, where he worked as an assistant to Edgar Wallace. He served his apprenticeship in the film industry first as a dialogue director, and then graduated to the director's chair via a series of low-budget second features.

Reed's early films, such as *Midshipman Easy,* are not remarkable, but few British films before World War II were. In the 1920s and 1930s British distributors were more interested in importing films from abroad, especially from America, than in encouraging film production at home. As a result British films were, with rare exceptions, bargain-basement imitations of Hollywood movies. In 1938, however, the British government stipulated that producers must allocate sufficient funds for the making of domestic films in order to allow an adequate amount of time for preproduction preparation, shooting, and the final shaping of each picture. Directors like Carol Reed took advantage of this increased support of British production to produce films which, though still modestly made by Hollywood standards, demonstrated the artistry of which British filmmakers were capable. By the late 1930s, then, Reed had graduated to making films of considerable substance, like *Night Train to Munich.*

"For the first time," Arthur Knight has written, "there were English pictures which spoke of the British character, British institutions—even social problems such as unemployment and nationalization—with unexpected frankness and awareness." An outstanding example of this new trend in British film making was Reed's *The Stars Look Down,* an uncompromising picture of life in a mining community that brought the director serious critical attention on both sides of the Atlantic.

Reed went on to work on some of the best documentaries to come out of the war, such as the Academy Award-winning *The True Glory.* He also directed the documentary-like theatrical feature *The Way Ahead,* an unvarnished depiction of army life. The experience gained by Reed in making wartime documentaries not only influenced his direction of *The Way Ahead,* but also was reflected in his post-war cinematic style, enabling him to develop further in films like *Odd Man Out* the strong sense of realism which had first appeared in *The Stars Look Down.* The documentary approach that Reed used to tell the story of *Odd Man Out,* which concerns a group of anti-British insurgents in Northern Ireland, was one to which audiences were ready to respond. Wartime films, both documentary and fictional, had conditioned moviegoers in Britain and elsewhere to expect a greater degree of realism in post-war cinema, and Reed provided it.

The more enterprising British producers believed that films should be made to appeal primarily to the home market rather than to the elusive American market. Yet the films that Carol Reed and some others were creating in the post-war years—films which were wholly British in character and situation—were the first such movies to win wide popularity in the United States. Among these, of course, was *Odd Man Out,* the first film which Reed both produced and directed, a factor which guaranteed him a greater degree of creative freedom than he had enjoyed before the war.

For the first time, too, the theme that was to appear so often in Reed's work was perceptible in *Odd Man Out.* In depicting for us in this and other films a hunted, lonely hero caught in the middle of a crisis usually not of his own making, Reed implies that man can achieve maturity and self-mastery only by accepting the challenges that life puts in his way and by struggling with them as best he can.

The Fallen Idol was the first of a trio of masterful films which he made in collaboration with novelist-screenwriter Graham Greene, one of the most significant creative associations between a writer and a director in the history of film. The team followed *The Fallen Idol* with *The Third Man,* which dealt with the black market in post-war Vienna, and, a decade later, *Our Man in Havana.* Commenting on his collaboration with the director, Greene has written that the success of these films was due to Reed, "the only director I know with that particular warmth of human sympathy, the extraordinary feeling for the right face for the right part, the exactitude of cutting, and not the least important, the power of sympathizing with an author's worries and an ability to guide him."

Because most of the films which Reed directed in the next decade or so were not comparable to the post-war films mentioned above, it was thought that he had passed his peak for good. *Oliver!* in fact proved that Reed was back in top form. In her *New Yorker* review of the film, Pauline Kael paid Reed a tribute that sums up his entire career in the cinema: "I applaud the commercial heroism of a director who can steer a huge production and keep his sanity and perspective and decent human feelings as beautifully intact as they are in *Oliver!.*"

A genuinely self-effacing man, Reed was never impressed by the awards and honors that he garnered throughout his career (he was knighted in 1952). Summarizing his own approach to filmmaking some time before his death at age sixty-nine in 1976, he said simply, "I give the public what *I* like, and hope they will like it too." More often than not, they did.

—Gene D. Phillips

REINER, Rob

Nationality: American. **Born:** 6 March 1945. **Education:** Attended University of California, Los Angeles. **Family:** Son of actor/director Carl Reiner; married 1) actress/director Penny Marshall, 1971 (divorced); 2) Michele Singer, 1989. **Career:** Worked as actor and improvisational comedian beginning in 1965; worked as comedy writer for television variety shows, 1968; played key role of Michael Stivic in television series *All in the Family,* 1971-1978; appeared in wide variety of television comedy as guest performer throughout 1970s and 1980s; directed first film, *This Is Spinal Tap,* 1984; directed breakthrough film, *Stand By Me,* 1986; co-founded Castle Rock Entertainment. **Awards:** Emmy awards for Best Supporting Actor, 1974 and 1978, for *All in the Family.* **Agent:** Jane Sindell, Creative Artists Agency, 9830 Wilshire Boulevard, Beverly Hills, California 90212, U.S.A. **Address:** Castle Rock Entertainment, 335 N. Maple Drive, Suite 135, Beverly Hills, California 90210-3867, U.S.A.

Films as Director:

1984 *This Is Spinal Tap* (+ co-sc, co-songs, role)
1985 *The Sure Thing*
1986 *Stand by Me*
1987 *The Princess Bride* (+ co-pr)
1989 *When Harry Met Sally* (+ co-pr)
1990 *Misery* (+ co-pr)
1992 *A Few Good Men*
1995 *North* (+ pr); *The American President* (+ pr)

Films as Actor:

1967 *Enter Laughing* (Carl Reiner) (as Clark Baxter)
1970 *Halls of Anger* (Paul Bogart) (as Leaky Couloris); *Where's Poppa* (Carl Reiner) (as Roger)
1971 *Summertree* (Anthony Newly) (as Don)
1974 *Thursday's Game* (James L. Brooks) (for TV)
1975 *How Come Nobody's on Our Side* (Richard Michaels) (as Miguelito)
1977 *Fire Sale* (Alan Arkin) (as Russel Fikus)
1979 *More Than Friends* (Jim Burrows) (for TV) (+ co-sc, co-exec pr)
1982 *Million Dollar Infield* (Hal Cooper) (for TV) (+ co-sc, co-pr)
1987 *Throw Momma from the Train* (Danny DeVito) (as Joel)
1990 *Postcards from the Edge* (Mike Nichols) (as Joe Pierce); *Likely Stories, Volume 1* (comedy sketches for cable TV)
1991 *Regarding Henry* (Mike Nichols)
1993 *Sleepless in Seattle* (Nora Ephron) (as Jay)
1994 *Bullets over Broadway* (Woody Allen) (as Sheldon Flender); *Mixed Nuts* (as Dr. Kinsky)

Publications

By REINER: articles—

"Prince Rob," an interview with Harlan Jacobson, in *Film Comment,* September 1987.
"Reiner's Reason," an interview with April Bernard, in *Interview,* July 1989.
"L'homme qui racontait des histoires," an interview with I. Katsahnias, in *Cahiers du Cinema,* October 1989.
"Rob Reiner on Stephen King," an interview with G. Wood, in *Cinefantastique,* No. 4, 1991.
"Entretiens avec Rob Reiner et William Goldman," an interview with I. Katsahnias, in *Cahiers du Cinema,* No. 4, 1991.
"Rob Reiner Makes a Comedy of Youthful Manners," an interview with R. Alexander, in *New York Times,* February 24, 1985.
Interview with D. Rosenthal, in *Playboy,* July 1985.

On REINER: book—

Dunne, Michael, "Jim Henson and Rob Reiner: Kermit's Dad Meets Rob Petrie's Son," in *Metapop: Self-Referentiality in Contemporary American Popular Culture,* University Press of Mississippi, 1992.

On REINER: articles—

Harmetz, A., "Reiner Has Last Laugh with His Rock Spoof," *New York Times,* April 25, 1984.
Kilday, Gregg, "Rob Reiner Grows Up," *Vanity Fair,* July 1989.
Lloyd, Robert, "Pals," *American Film,* July/August 1989.
Weber, B., "Can Men and Women Be Friends?" *New York Times,* July 9, 1989.
Gray, M., "Love Story," *Films and Filming,* December 1989.
Katsahnias, I., "Les fictions fatales" *Cahiers du Cinema,* October 1989.
Sharkey, B., "Misery's Company Loves a Good Time," *New York Times,* June 17, 1990.
Valot, J., "Rob Reiner," *Revue du Cinema,* September 1990.
Bernard, Rita, "From Screwballs to Cheeseballs: Comic Narrative and Idelogy in Capra and Reiner," *New Orleans Review,* No. 3, 1990.
Kermode, Mark, "Misery," *Sight and Sound,* May 1991.
Silveman, J., "Rob Reiner's Latest Hat Trick," *New York Times,* July 21, 1991.
Stefancic, M., Jr., "Rob Reiner," *Ekran,* No. 3, 1991.
Goldman, Steven, "Masters of the Numbers Game," *Guardian,* January 2, 1993.
Biskind, Peter, "A Few Good Menshes," *Premiere,* January 1993.
Newman, Kim, "A Few Good Men," *Sight and Sound,* January 1993.
Bruzzi, Stella, "Court Etiquette," *Sight and Sound,* February 1993.
Rhodes, Joe, "On Comedy, Books, and Toupees," *Los Angeles Times,* June 16, 1993.

* * *

Rob Reiner is a show business kid who has learned much from his famous father, Carl Reiner, creator of the American television series *The Dick Van Dyke Show* and director of many comedy films—most notably *Where's Poppa* and *The Jerk.* Beginning his career as an actor, Rob Reiner's most notable role was as Michael Stivic in the long-running American television series *All in the Family.* Michael Stivic was the not-too-bright comic foil for his right-wing, racist father-in-law, Archie Bunker. Thus, from the beginning of Reiner's career, several elements become apparent that are important to his development as a director: 1) a profound sympathy for the actor and the concomitant empathy to elicit skillful performances; 2) a deep understanding of comedy and satire and, more generally, an innate feel for timing and structure; and 3) an inherently liberal, humanistic sensibility.

If Reiner's facility as a comic gives him great abilities of observation, its negative side is that his career has been by and large a series of very skillful imitations of other directors and other styles. In this context, it is hard to think of Reiner as a major Hollywood artist, no matter how successful his films. Indeed, Reiner would have made an

Rob Reiner directing James Caan in *Misery*

extraordinary director at the heyday of the studio system, taking on the A-assignments with dazzling ability. So if Reiner has not yet demonstrated himself to be an *auteur*—like Woody Allen, with whom he has been compared, or like David Lynch, who seems a polar opposite—he is definitely a *metteur en scene,* like Sydney Lumet, Norman Jewison, or Sydney Pollack.

Reiner's first film was a mock documentary, *This Is Spinal Tap,* directed in 1984 and perhaps still one of his finest films. The basic concept of the mock documentary had been undertaken by many before, most notably by Peter Watkins in the 1960s or more popularly by Woody Allen in *Zelig* the year before. Reiner's sincerity is apparent in that all satire inherently admits its basis in imitation: and *This Is Spinal Tap* satirizes the documentary genre, as well as rock documentary and rock bands themselves. A young, hip movie with surprising subtlety, *This Is Spinal Tap* became a cult film and one of the few Reiner films more popular today than when it was released. Some elements of the rock satire include the early, tragic death of a band member (in this case, a drummer), the physical transformation of the band (a short-lived foray into Kiss-like makeup), the girlfriend involved in the band who virtually destroys it (a la Yoko Ono or Linda McCartney), and of course, life on the road (which includes the most brilliant pseudo-verite repartee). Throughout, the film's deadpan rhythms are virtually perfect—for instance, Spinal Tap's manager, Ian, intones, "There's no sex and drugs for Ian, David. I find lost luggage!"

This Is Spinal Tap was followed by a modest, dramatic film, *The Sure Thing,* a sweet and low-budget coming-of-age story which showed Reiner's abilities to get very good, charming performances—in this case, from his leads Daphne Zuniga and John Cusack. *The Sure Thing,* if slight, was well-observed, a kind of contemporary *It Happened One Night* offering a fairly credible view of college students, a not inconsiderable task, rarely accomplished. However, Reiner's breakthrough film was the higher-budget *Stand by Me.* A fully realized film based on a very short, uncharacteristic story by Stephen King, *Stand by Me* presented a day or so in the lives of four pre-adolescent boys. A derivative coming-of-age story which seemed to emulate Francois Truffaut (*Les Mistons*) or outright imitate Robert Mulligan (*Summer of '42*), *Stand by Me* is very entertaining, if manipulative, and designed to appeal to the nostalgia of the yuppie—filled to the brim with references to Pez candy, Walt Disney's Goofy, the *Wagon Train* television series, and so forth. By the revelations at the end, which propel the characters to their adult fates through the use of voice-over narration, the director clearly has the audience exactly where he wants them for the film's final, sentimental line: "I never had any friends later on like the ones I had when I was twelve. Jesus, does anyone?" If *Stand by Me* holds up in the future, it will be as much for the unusually skillful performances Reiner has elicited from his very young actors, including wonderful work from the late River Phoenix in one of his first films.

The Princess Bride was a huge success in 1987. In this film, Reiner told a whimsical fantasy story, changing his style yet again—recalling Spielberg or Walt Disney, even. But an even bigger success came in 1989 with *When Harry Met Sally,* an absolutely hilarious comedy which made Billy Crystal and Meg Ryan breakaway movie stars. *When Harry Met Sally* attempted to answer, definitively, the philosophical question: Can straight men and women ever be true friends without sex causing problems? (No.) Virtually every commentator praising the film noted how overwhelmingly it imitated early Woody Allen (the funny period)—the style of joke, the use of music, the characterizations, the philosophical musings, everything. Indeed, it is not farfetched to call *When Harry Met Sally* the best Woody Allen film that Allen never made. While the film added to Reiner's reputation in Hollywood and endeared him to audiences, it also began to raise some doubts about his sincerity as an artist, with no personal sensibility clearly emerging.

Misery followed in 1990. Again based on Steven King material, *Misery* was in yet another style—showing Reiner to be the most clever fast study in all of Hollywood—this time emulating Hitchcock and his thrillers, if without Hitchcock's moral sophistication. The story of a woman who keeps a famous writer her prisoner, *Misery* made Kathy Bates an Academy Award-winning star, and her line "I'm your biggest fan" a kind of cultural catch-phrase. *A Few Good Men,* released the next year, was a military courtroom drama evoking *The Caine Mutiny Court Martial, A Soldier's Story,* and several contemporary films of the Reagan/Bush era, like *Top Gun,* which got great mileage out of men in uniforms. One senses that after having presented James Caan as a weak, passive man in *Misery,* and after having worked with young people and/or comedians in so many other films, Reiner was eager to show that he could make a man's man kind of film: a solid, Hawksian drama. And indeed, multiple Academy Award nominations followed; the somewhat liberal, anti-establishment theme attracted enough attention to divert from the essential pot-boiler nature of the project. Probably lasting more than the film's reputation will be the impressive scenery-chewing of Jack Nicholson in the key supporting role.

The critical and popular failure of the sentimental and vapid *North* in 1985 represented a surprise in the Reiner career, which, through seven films, had shown a steady increase in assurance and judgment, as well as in critical and popular success. *North* was a juvenile effort uneasily combining a Spielberg-like narrative about a boy who travels across the world to pick out better parents with trite references for their own sake to television and popular culture. Thankfully for Reiner, *North* was followed in late 1995 by a very strong film, *The American President*—a funny and moving romantic comedy with deft performances by Annette Bening and Michael Douglas. *The American President* emerges from Reiner's sympathies for President Bill Clinton, the first liberal Democrat in the White House in twelve years, who was elected in 1992 with great Hollywood support and subsequently excoriated by virulently right-wing commentators over character issues for most of his presidency. *The American President,* which wears its liberalism proudly on its sleeve, also clearly attacks the growing domination of the Republican Party by the "Christian Coalition" and its mean-spirited intolerance—as represented by Bob Munson, a Kansas Senator played by Richard Dreyfuss who is a clear composite of Kansas Senator Bob Dole and others like Phil Gramm, Newt Gingrich, and Pat Buchanan. The film abounds with fetching parallels to people around Clinton (his young advisor George Stephanopoulos, his daughter Chelsea, and so forth) as well as apparent insights into life in the White House. Certainly, most of Reiner's films have been derivative of other directors, and this time it is Frank Capra, although the influence is acknowledged cheerfully and clearly in the dialogue, and Frank Capra III even serves as the film's first assistant director. Somehow, the Capra vision does not rankle here, not only because it is so suited and similar to Reiner's (although Capra's is darker and more complex), but because it is totally clear that the progressive Reiner believes passionately in his material, which gives the popular form that the film takes a great, contemporary resonance. By the film's end, when the corrupt right-wingers see their influence waning as the president finally gives the speech so many have wished Clinton had given, it is hard—if you a possess a liberal vision—not to be moved by Reiner's popular entertainment. Interesting, too, is that Reiner offscreen has started taking on the role as spokesperson for liberal Hollywood; indeed, in response to Senator Dole's 1995 (very selective) attacks on Hollywood for trashing American cultural values, Reiner has become one of Hollywood's most eloquent and public defenders.

Finally, it is necessary to comment on Reiner's overall persona as a performer—for he is a genuinely talented actor and comic, clever and canny, who has given a variety of skillful, light performances (notably in Nora Ephron's *Sleepless in Seattle,* as well as in Woody Allen's *Bullets over Broadway*). With a remarkable lack of self-consciousness, Reiner seems to be making a recent acting career from a variety of deviously satirical self-portraits, as in Mike Nichols's *Postcards from the Edge*—a film which comically presents the relationship between a parent and adult child in the film industry (based on Debbie Reynolds and Carrie Fisher) and which undoubtedly resonates for Reiner. Ultimately, as a performer as well as a director, Reiner is nothing if not likeable, and seems giving, open, and unpretentious.

—Charles Derry

REISZ, Karel

Nationality: Czechoslovakian/British. **Born:** Ostrava, Czechoslovakia, 21 July 1926. **Education:** Leighton Park School, Reading, England, 1938-44; Emmanuel College, Cambridge, 1945-47. **Family:** Married 1) Julia Coppard (divorced); 2) Betsy Blair, 1963, three sons. **Career:** Arrived in England as refugee from Nazi threat, 1938; joined Czechoslovakian wing of R.A.F., 1944-45; teacher in London grammar school, 1947-49; film critic for *Sequence* and *Sight and Sound,* from 1950; programme director for National Film Theatre, London, 1952-55; "officer of commercials" for Ford Motor Co. in England, 1956-57; directed first feature, 1960.

Films as Director:

1956 *Momma Don't Allow* (co-d)
1959 *We Are the Lambeth Boys* (doc)
1960 ***Saturday Night and Sunday Morning***
1964 *Night Must Fall* (+ co-pr)
1966 *Morgan, a Suitable Case for Treatment* (*Morgan!*)
1968 *Isadora* (*The Loves of Isadora*)
1974 *The Gambler*
1978 *Who'll Stop the Rain* (*Dog Soldiers*)
1981 *The French Lieutenant's Woman*
1985 *Sweet Dreams*
1989 *Everybody Wins*

Other Films:

1957 *Every Day Except Christmas* (Anderson) (co-pr)
1963 *This Sporting Life* (Anderson) (pr)

Publications

By REISZ: book—

The Technique of Film Editing, revised by Gavin Miller, London, 1968.

By REISZ: articles—

"Hollywood's Anti-Red Boomerang," in *Sight and Sound* (London), January/March 1953.
"Stroheim in London," in *Sight and Sound* (London), April/June 1954.
"Experiment at Brussels," in *Sight and Sound* (London), Summer 1958.
"Karel Reisz and Experimenters: An Exchange of Correspondence," in *Films and Filming* (London), December 1961.
"How to Get into Films—By the People Who Got in Themselves," in *Films and Filming* (London), July 1963.
"Desert Island Films," in *Films and Filming* (London), August 1963.
Interview with Gene D. Phillips, in *Cinema* (Los Angeles), Summer 1968.
"Outsiders," an interview with Gordon Gow, in *Films and Filming* (London), January 1979.
"Karel Reisz: permanence d'un personnage: le mal adapté," an interview with J. Grissolange, in *Jeune Cinéma* (Paris), October 1979.
Interview with B. Gilbert, in *Stills* (London), Winter 1982.

On REISZ: books—

Barsam, Richard, *Non-Fiction Film,* New York, 1973.
Walker, Alexander, *Hollywood U.K.: The British Film Industry in the 60's,* New York, 1974.

Karel Reisz

Leyda, Jay, editor, *Voices of Film Experience,* New York, 1977.
Armes, Roy, *A Critical History of the British Cinema,* New York, 1978.
Gaston, Georg, *Karel Reisz,* Boston, 1980.

On REISZ: articles—

Lambert, Gavin, "Free Cinema," in *Sight and Sound* (London), Spring 1956.
Hoggart, Richard, "*We Are the Lambeth Boys,*" in *Sight and Sound* (London), Summer/Autumn 1959.
"Karel Reisz: Free Czech," in *Films and Filming* (London), February 1961.
Zito, Stephen, "*Dog Soldiers*: Novel into Film," in *American Film* (Washington, D.C.), September 1977.
"Reisz Issue" of *Positif* (Paris), November 1978.
Kennedy, H., "Minute Reisz: Six Earlier Films," in *Film Comment* (New York), September/October 1981.
Armes, Roy, "Karel Reisz," in *International Film Guide,* edited by Peter Cowie, London, 1982.
"*Saturday Night and Sunday Morning* Issue" of *Avant-Scène du Cinéma* (Paris), 15 October 1982.
Lebouc, G., "Chacun sa chance," in *Grand Angle* (Mariembourg, Belgium), October 1990.
Grandmaire, G., "Filmographie de Karel Reisz," in *Revue du Cinema* (Paris), June 1991.
Lefevre, R., "Karel Reisz," in *Revue du Cinema* (Paris), June 1991.
McKee, A. L., "She Had Eyes a Man Could Drown In: Narrative, Desire and the Female Gaze in *The French Lieutenant's Woman,*" in *Literature Film Quarterly* (Salisbury, Maryland), vol. 20, no. 2, 1992.

* * *

Karel Reisz came to filmmaking from the world of academia and scholarship. He had taught in an English grammar school, written film criticism, co-edited with Lindsay Anderson the last issue of the slightly snooty magazine *Sequence,* and written a theoretical textbook still in use today on film editing techniques (without having spent one working day in the industry). With such a background, it was obvious he would have preconceived notions about filmmaking, but they were notions without regard to established filmmaking practices. Reisz wanted to improve the British film industry (also the critical aim of *Sequence*). He had his first opportunity to do so with two documentary shorts, *Momma Don't Allow* (co-directed with Tony Richardson) and *We Are the Lambeth Boys.* In these films, Reisz depicted contemporary Britain from a working-class viewpoint, and when they were first screened at London's National Film Theatre, they were presented along with films from Lindsay Anderson and others as "British Free Cinema." In fact, these films were to herald a new wave in British filmmaking, which reached its zenith with Reisz's first feature, *Saturday Night and Sunday Morning.*

Jack Clayton's *Room at the Top* paved the way for *Saturday Night and Sunday Morning,* a study of a tough, young machinist, played by Albert Finney, who takes out his frustrations with his work and his life through sex and alcohol. He is the quintessential British rebel, the English answer to James Dean, who takes his revenge on society by impregnating his boss's wife. It is an uninhibited, fresh, and frank look at British working-class existence, and it brought critical fame to Karel Reisz.

The only problem was that Reisz seemed temporarily unable to follow up on that first success. (Reisz's output is pathetically small: a sign perhaps not so much of a careful director as a director with whom producers feel uneasy.) Next, Reisz directed Albert Finney again in *Night Must Fall,* which had worked as a classic melodrama in the 1930s but had little relevance to the 1960s. The unconventionality of *Morgan* also seemed strained, and even a little pretentious (a claim that also can easily be made regarding Reisz's outdated study of a Vietnam vet, *Who'll Stop the Rain?*). It was not until *Isadora* that Reisz began to demonstrate a new side to his work, a romantic side, perhaps born of his Czech background (he did not come to Britain until he was twelve).

Both *Isadora* and *The French Lieutenant's Woman* showed that Reisz had discovered how to successfully blend romanticism and the realism of his first films. In *Isadora* it is perhaps a little more subtly accomplished than in *The French Lieutenant's Woman,* where the two elements fight against each other for existence.

As to his directorial techniques, Reisz appears to be very willing to listen to others. He is quoted as saying, "For me the great thing about a film is to allow everyone to make their contribution and to keep the process fluid. The process of adaptation is a free process and the process of rehearsal is a free process and the process of shooting is a free process." Free process, free cinema, and a healthy freedom in his choice of subjects have marked Reisz's career to date.

—Anthony Slide

RENOIR, Jean

Nationality: French/American. **Born:** Paris, 15 September 1894, son of painter Auguste Renoir, became citizen of United States (naturalized) in 1946, retained French citizenship. **Education:** Collége de Sainte-Croix, Neuilly-sur-Seine, 1902; Ecole Sainte-Marie de Monceau, 1903; Ecole Massina, Nice, until 1912; University of Aix-en-Provence, degree in mathematics and philosophy, 1913. **Military Service:** Served in French cavalry, 1914-15; transferred to French Flying Corps, 1916, demobilized 1918. **Family:** Married 1) Andrée Madeleine Heuschling ("Dédée," took name Catherine Hessling following 1924 appearance in *Catherine*), 1920 (divorced 1930); 2) Dido Freire, 1944, one son. **Career:** Worked as potter and ceramicist, 1920-23; directed first film, *La Fille de l'eau,* 1924; joined Service Cinématographique de l'Armée, *La Règle du jeu* banned by French government as demoralizing, 1939; Robert Flaherty arranged Renoir's passage to United States, 1940; signed with 20th Century-Fox, 1941; signed with Universal, then terminated contract, 1942; re-established residence in Paris, retained home in Beverly Hills, 1951; active in theatre through 1950s; Compagnie Jean Renoir formed with Anna de Saint Phalle, 1958; taught theatre at University of California, Berkeley, 1960. **Awards:** Prix Louis Delluc, for *Les Bas-Fonds,* 1936; Chevalier de la Légion d'honneur, 1936; International Jury Cup, Venice Biennale, for *La Grande Illusion,* 1937; New York Critics Award, for *Swamp Water,* 1941; Best Film, Venice Festival, for *The Southerner,* 1946; Grand Prix de l'Academie du Cinéma for *French Cancan,* 1956; Prix Charles Blanc, Academie Française, for *Renoir,* biography of father, 1963; Honorary Doctorate in Fine Arts, University of California, Berkeley, 1963; Fellow of the American Academy of Arts and Sciences, 1964; Osella d'Oro, Venice Festival, 1968; Honorary Doctorate of Fine Arts, Royal College of Art, London, 1971; Special Oscar for Career Accomplishment, 1975. **Died:** In Beverly Hills, California, 12 February 1979.

Films as Director:

1925 *La Fille de l'eau* (+ pr)
1926 *Nana* (+ pr, adaptation)
1927 *Catherine* (*Une vie sans joie*; *Backbiters*) (co-d, co-pr, sc, role as sub-prefect); *Sur un air de Charleston* (*Charleston-Parade*) (+ pr, ed); *Marquitta* (+ pr, adaptation)

1928 *La Petite Marchande d'allumettes* (*The Little Match Girl*) (co-d, co-pr, sc)
1928 *Tire au flanc* (+ co-sc); *Le Tournoi dans la cité* (*Le Tournoi*) (+ adaptation)
1929 *Le Bled*
1931 *On purge bébé* (+ co-sc); *La Chienne* (+ co-sc)
1932 *La Nuit du carrefour* (*Night at the Crossroads*) (+ sc); ***Boudu sauvée des eaux*** (*Boudu Saved from Drowning*) (+ co-sc)
1933 *Chotard et cie* (+ co-sc)
1934 *Madame Bovary* (+ sc)
1935 *Toni* (*Les Amours de Toni*) (+ co-sc)
1936 ***Le Crime de Monsieur Lange*** (*The Crime of Monsieur Lange*) (+ co-sc); *La Vie est à nous* (*The People of France*) (co-d, co-sc); *Les Bas-Fonds* (*Underworld*; *The Lower Depths*) (+ adaptation)
1937 ***La Grande Illusion*** (*Grand Illusion*) (+ co-sc)
1938 *La Marseillaise* (+ co-sc); ***La Bête humaine*** (*The Human Beast*; *Judas Was a Woman*) (+ co-sc)
1939 ***La Règle du jeu*** (*Rules of the Game*) (+ co-sc, role as Octave)
1941 *La Tosca* (*The Story of Tosca*) (co-d, co-sc); *Swamp Water*
1943 *This Land Is Mine* (+ co-p, co-sc)
1944 *Salute to France* (*Salut à France*) (co-d, co-sc)
1945 ***The Southerner*** (+ sc)
1946 ***Une Partie de campagne*** (*A Day in the Country*) (+ sc) (filmed in 1936); *The Diary of a Chambermaid* (+ co-sc)
1947 *The Woman on the Beach* (+ co-sc)
1951 *The River* (+ co-sc)
1953 ***Le Carrosse d'or*** (*The Golden Coach*) (+ co-sc)
1955 *French Cancan* (*Only the French Can*) (+ sc)
1956 *Elena et les hommes* (*Paris Does Strange Things*) (+ sc)
1959 *Le Testament du Docteur Cordelier* (*The Testament of Dr. Cordelier*; *Experiment in Evil*) (+ sc); *Le Déjeuner sur l'herbe* (*Picnic on the Grass*) (+ sc)
1962 *Le Caporal épinglé* (*The Elusive Corporal*; *The Vanishing Corporal*) (co-d, co-sc)
1970 *Le Petit Théâtre de Jean Renoir* (*The Little Theatre of Jean Renoir*) (+ sc)

Other Films:

1927 *Le Petit Chaperon rouge* (Cavalcanti) (co-sc, role as the Wolf)
1930 *Die Jagd nach dem Gluck* (Gliese) (role as Robert)
1937 ***The Spanish Earth*** (Ivens) (wrote commentary and narration for French version)
1971 *The Christian Licorice Store* (Frawley) (role as himself)

Publications

By RENOIR: books—

This Land Is Mine, in *Twenty Best Film Plays,* edited by Gassner and Nichols, New York, 1943.
The Southerner, in *Best Film Plays—1945,* edited by Gassner and Nichols, New York, 1946.
Renoir: Souvenirs de mon père, Paris, 1948; published as *Renoir, My Father,* New York, 1958.
Orvet, Paris, 1955.
The Notebooks of Captain George, Boston, 1966.
La Grande Illusion, London, 1968; Paris, 1974.
Rules of the Game, New York, 1970.
Ecrits 1926-1971, edited by Claude Gauteur, Paris, 1974.
My Life and My Films, New York, 1974.
Jean Renoir: Essays, Conversations, Reviews, edited by Penelope Gilliatt, New York, 1975.
Oeuvres de cinéma inédités, edited by Claude Gauteur, Paris, 1981.
Lettres d'Amérique, edited by Dido Renoir and Alexander Sesonske, Paris, 1984.
Renoir on Renoir: Interviews, Essays and Remarks, Cambridge, 1989.

By RENOIR: articles—

"Jean Renoir à Hollywood," an interview with Paul Gilson, in *L'Ecran Française* (Paris), 15 August 1945.
Interview with Jacques Rivette and François Truffaut, in *Cahiers du Cinema* (Paris), April 1954; reprinted in part as "Renoir in America," in *Sight and Sound* (London), Autumn 1954.
"*Paris-Provence*: Inspiration pour un film," in *Cahiers du Cinéma* (Paris), May 1954.
"Enquête sur la censure et l'éroticisme: le public a horreur de ça," in *Cahiers du Cinéma* (Paris), December 1954.
"*French Cancan,*" in *Cahiers du Cinéma* (Paris), May 1955.
"Nouvel entretien avec Jean Renoir," with Jacques Rivette and François Truffaut, in *Cahiers du Cinéma* (Paris), Christmas 1957; also in *La Politique des auteurs,* by André Bazin and others, Paris, 1972.
"Le Testament du Docteur Cordelier," in *L'Avant-Scène du Cinéma* (Paris), July 1961.
"Jean Renoir: propos rompus," an interview with Jean-Louis Noames, in *Cahiers du Cinéma* (Paris), May 1964.
"*La Grande Illusion,*" in *L'Avant-Scène du Cinéma* (Paris), January 1965.
"*La Règle du jeu,*" in *L'Avant-Scène du Cinéma* (Paris), October 1965.
"Renoir at 72," an interview with Axel Madsen, in *Cinema* (Los Angeles), Spring 1966.
"The Situation of the Serious Filmmaker," in *Film Makers on Film Making,* edited by Harry Geduld, Bloomington, Indiana, 1967.
"My Next Films," an interview with Michel Delahaye and Jean-André Fieschi, in *Cahiers du Cinema in English* (New York), March 1967.
Interview with Rui Nogueira and François Truchaud, in *Sight and Sound* (London), Spring 1968.
"C'est la révolution! (Crème de beauté)," in *Cahiers du Cinéma* (Paris), May 1968.
"Conversation with Jean Renoir," with Louis Marcorelles, in *Interviews with Film Directors,* edited by Andrew Sarris, New York, 1969.
Interview with James Silke, in *The Essential Cinema,* edited by P. Adams Sitney, New York, 1975.
Articles and interview, in special Renoir issue of *Positif* (Paris), September 1975.
"*La Chienne,*" in *L'Avant-Scène du Cinéma* (Paris), October 1975.

On RENOIR: books—

Davay, Paul, *Jean Renoir,* Brussels, 1957.
Cauliez, Armand-Jean, *Jean Renoir,* Paris, 1962.
Analyses des films de Jean Renoir, Institut des Hautes Etudes Cinématographiques, Paris, 1966.
Bennett, Susan, *Study Unit 8: Jean Renoir,* London, 1967.
Poulle, François, *Renoir 1938 ou Jean Renoir pour rien. Enquête sur un cinéaste,* Paris, 1969.
Leprohon, Pierre, *Jean Renoir,* New York, 1971.
Braudy, Leo, *Jean Renoir: The World of His Films,* New York, 1972; 2nd edition, 1989.
Bazin, André, *Jean Renoir,* edited by François Truffaut, Paris, 1973.
Mast, Gerald, *Filmguide to The Rules of the Game,* Bloomington, Indiana, 1973.
Durgnat, Raymond, *Jean Renoir,* Berkeley, California, 1974.
Beylie, Claude, *Jean Renoir: le spectacle, la vie,* Paris, 1975.
Faulkner, Christopher, *Jean Renoir: A Guide to References and Resources,* Boston, 1979.
Sesonske, Alexander, *Jean Renoir: The French Films 1924-1939,* Cambridge, Massachusetts, 1980.

Jean Renoir

Serceau, Daniel, *Jean Renoir,* Paris, 1985.
Bertin, Celia, *Jean Renoir,* Paris, 1986.
Faulkner, Christopher, *The Social Cinema of Jean Renoir,* Princeton, New Jersey, 1986.
Vincendeau, Ginette, and Keith Reader, *La Vie est a Nous: French Cinema of the Popular Front 1935-1938,* London, 1986.
Viry-Babel, Roger, *Jean Renoir: Le Jeu et la Règle,* Paris, 1986.
Beylie, Claude, and Maurice Bessy, *Jean Renoir,* Paris, 1989.

On RENOIR: articles—

"Renoir Issue" of *Cahiers du Cinéma* (Paris), January 1952.
Brunius, Jacques, "Jean Renoir," in *En marge du cinéma français,* Paris, 1954.
"Renoir Issue" of *Cahiers du Cinéma* (Paris), Christmas 1957.
Rohmer, Eric, "Jeunesse de Jean Renoir," in *Cahiers du Cinéma* (Paris), December 1959.
Belanger, Jean, "Why Renoir Favors Multiple Camera, Long Sustained Take Technique," in *American Cinematographer* (Los Angeles), March 1960.
Dyer, Peter, "Renoir and Realism," in *Sight and Sound* (London), Summer 1960.
Callenbach, Ernest, and Roberta Schuldenfrei, "The Presence of Jean Renoir," in *Film Quarterly* (Berkeley), Winter 1960.
Russell, Lee, (Peter Wollen), "Jean Renoir," in *New Left Review,* May/June 1964.
Millar, Daniel, "The Autumn of Jean Renoir," in *Sight and Sound* (London), Summer 1968.
Godard, Jean-Luc, "Jean Renoir and Television," in *Godard on Godard,* London, 1972.
Diehl, Digby, "Directors Go to Their Movies: Jean Renoir," in *Action* (Los Angeles), May/June 1972.
Fofi, Goffredo, "The Cinema of the Popular Front in France (1934-38)," in *Screen* (London), Winter 1972/73.
Harcourt, Peter, "A Flight from Passion: Images of Uncertainty in the Work of Jean Renoir," in *Six European Directors,* Harmondsworth, England, 1974.
Gauteur, Claude, editor, "*La Règle du jeu* et la critique en 1939," in *Image et Son* (Paris), March 1974.
Greenspun, Roger, "House and Garden: Three Films by Jean Renoir," in *Film Comment* (New York), July/August 1974.
Thomas, P., "The Sorcerer's Apprentice: Bazin and Truffaut on Renoir," in *Sight and Sound* (London), Winter 1974/75.
"Renoir Issue" of *Cinema* (Zurich), vol. 21, no. 4, 1975.
Willis, D., "Renoir and the Illusion of Detachment," in *Sight and Sound* (London), Autumn 1977.
Beylie, Claude, "Jean Renoir (1894-1979)," in special Renoir issue of *Avant-Scène du Cinéma* (Paris), 1 July 1980.
Strebel, Elizabeth Grottle, "Jean Renoir and the Popular Front," in *Feature Films as History,* edited by K.R.M. Short, London, 1981.
Sesonske, A., "Discovering America: Jean Renoir 1941," in *Sight and Sound* (London), Autumn 1981.
Rothman, William, "The Filmmaker within the Film: The Role of Octave in *The Rules of the Game,*" in *Quarterly Review of Film Studies* (New York), Summer 1982.
Turvey, G., "1936, the Culture of the Popular Front and Jean Renoir," in *Media, Culture and Society* (London), October 1982.
Lourié, Eugene, "Grand Illusions," in *American Film* (Washington, D.C.), January/February 1985.
Everson, William K., "Deana Durbin and Jean Renoir," in *Films in Review* (New York), August/September 1986 (see also June/July and October 1987).

On RENOIR: films—

Gritti, Roland, *L'Album de famille de Jean Renoir,* Paris, 1956.
Braunberger, Gisèle, *La Direction d'acteurs par Jean Renoir,* Paris, 1970.

* * *

Jean Renoir's major work dates from between 1924 and 1939. Of his 21 films the first six are silent features that put forward cinematic problems that come to dominate the entire oeuvre. All study a detachment, whether of language and image, humans and nature, or social rules and real conduct. Optical effects are treated as problems coextensive with narrative. He shows people who are told to obey rules and conventions in situations and social frames that confine them. A sensuous world is placed before everyone's eyes, but access to it is confounded by cultural mores. In Renoir's work, nature, like a frame without borders, isolates the impoverished subjects within limits at once too vast and too constricting for them. Inherited since the Cartesian revolution, and the growth of the middle class after 1789, bourgeois codes of conduct do not fit individuals whose desires and passion know no end.

The patterns established in the films appear simple, and they are. Renoir joins optical to social contradictions in the sense that every one of his films stages dramas about those who cannot conform to the frame in which they live. For the same reason his work also studies the dynamics of love in cinematography that marks how the effect is undeniably "scopic"—grounded in an impulse to see and thus to hold. Sight conveys the human wish to contain whatever is viewed, and to will to control what knows no border. As love cannot be contained, it becomes tantamount to nature itself.

The director has often been quoted as saying that he spent his life making one film. Were it fashioned from all of his finished works—including those composed in the 1920s or 1940s or 1960s in France, America, or India—it would tell the story of a collective humanity whose sense of tradition is effectively gratuitous or fake. The social milieu of many of his films is defined by a scapegoat who is killed in order to make that tradition both firm and precarious. All of Renoir's central characters thus define the narratives and visual compositions in which they are found. Boudu (Michel Simon), who escapes the confinement of bourgeois ways in *Boudu sauvé des eaux,* is the opposite of Lestingois (Charles Granval), ensconced in a double-standard marriage *à la* Balzac. Boudu, a tramp, a trickster, and a refugee from *La Chienne* (1931), changes the imagination of his milieu by virtue of his passage through it. The effect he leaves resembles that of Amédée Lange (René Lefevre) in *Le Crime de Monsieur Lange,* who gives life to a collective venture—an emblem of Leon Blum's short-lived Popular Front government launched in 1936—that lives despite his delusions about the American West and the pulp he writes. Lange is the flip side of Jacques Lantier (Jean Gabin) of *La Bête humaine* (1938), a tragic hero whose suicide prefigures André Jurieux's (Roland Toutain's) passion of *La Règle du jeu* (1939).

Boudu floats through the frame in ways that the migrant laborers of *Toni* or the souls of *La Vie est à nous* cannot. The latter are bound to conventions of capital exploitation that incarcerate humanity. In these and other films the characters all "have their reasons," that is, they have many contradictory drives that cannot be socially reconciled but that are individually well founded and impeccably logical on their own terms. When Renoir casts his characters' plural "reasons" under an erotic aura, he offers superlative studies of love. His protagonists wish to find absolution for their passion at the vanishing points of the landscapes—both imaginary and real—in which they try to move. The latter are impossible constructs, but their allure is nonetheless tendered within the sensuous frame of deep-focus photography, long takes, and lateral reframing. Rosenthal and Maréchal (Marcel

Dalio and Gabin) seek an end to war when they tramp into the distance of a snowscape at the end of *La Grande Illusion.* Lange and Florelle (Valentine) wave goodbye as they walk into the flat horizon of Belgium. But Jurieux can imagine love only as a picture-postcard when he and Christine (Nora Grégor), he hopes in desperation, will rejoin his mother in snowy Alsace. Or Lantier can be imagined jumping from his speeding locomotive into a space where the two tracks of the railroad converge, at infinity, beyond the line between Paris and Le Havre. In *Une Partie de campagne,* Henri (Georges Darnoux), frustrated beyond end at the sight of melancholy Juliette (Sylvia Bataille) rowing upstream with her husband sitting behind her in their skiff, looks tearfully at the lush Marne riverside. Sitting on the trunk of a weeping willow arched over the current, he flicks his cigarette butt in the water, unable to express otherwise the fate he has been dealt.

These scenes are shot with an economy that underscores the pathos Renoir draws from figures trapped in situations too vast for their ken or their lives. If generalization can seek an emblem, Renoir's films appear to lead to a *serre,* the transparent closure of the greenhouse that serves as the site of the dénouement of *La Règle du jeu.* The "serre" is literally what constricts, or what has deceptive depth for its beholder. It is the scene where love is acted out and extinguished by the onlooker. The space typifies what Renoir called "the feeling of a frame too narrow for the content" of the dramas he selected from a literary heritage (*Madame Bovary, The Lower Depths*) or wrote himself, such as *Rules.*

Renoir's films have an added intensity and force when viewed in the 1990s. They manifest an urgent concern for the natural world and demonstrate that we are the "human beast" destroying it. Clearly opposed to the effects of capitalism, Renoir offers glimpses of sensuous worlds that seem to arch beyond history. A viewer of *La Fille de l'eau* (1924), *Boudu,* or *Toni* surmises that trees have far more elegance than the characters turning about them, or that, echoing Baudelaire's pronouncements in his *Salons* of 1859, landscapes lacking the human species are of enduring beauty. Renoir puts forth studies of the conflict of language and culture in physical worlds that possess an autonomy of their own. His characters are gauged according to the distance they gain from their environments or the codes that tell them how to act and to live. Inevitably, Renoir's characters are marked by writing. Boudu, a reincarnation of Pan and Nature itself, can only read "big letters." By contrast, Lantier is wedded to his locomotive, a sort of writing machine he calls "la lison." The urbane La Chesnaye (Dalio) in *Rules* cannot live without his writing, the "dangerous supplements" of mechanical dolls, a calliope, or human toys. These objects reflect in the narrative the filmic apparatus that crafted Renoir's work as a model of film writing, a "caméra-stylo," or *ciné-écriture.* Use of deep focus and long takes affords diversity and chance. With the narratives, they constitute Renoir's signature, the basis of the concept and practice of the *auteur.*

Renoir's *oeuvre* stands as a monument and a model of cinematography. By summoning the conditions of illusion and artifice of film, it rises out of the massive production of poetic realism of the 1930s in France. He develops a style that is the very tenor of a vehicle studying social contradiction. The films implicitly theorize the limits that cinema confronts in any narrative or documentary depiction of our world.

—Tom Conley

RESNAIS, Alain

Nationality: French. **Born:** Vannes, Brittany, 3 June 1922. **Education:** St.-François-Xavier, Vannes; studied acting under René Simon, Paris, 1940-42; attended Institut des Hautes Etudes Cinématographiques (IDHEC), Paris, 1943-45. **Military Service:** Served with occupation army in Germany and Austria. **Family:** Married Florence Malraux, 1969. **Career:** Member of travelling theatrical company, Les Arlequins, 1945; directed first feature, *Ouvert pour cause d'inventaire,* in 16mm, 1946; worked as film editor, 1947-58; worked in New York City, 1970-72; directed first film in English, *Providence,* 1977. **Address:** 70 rue des Plantes, 75014 Paris, France.

Films as Director:

1946 *Ouvert pour cause d'inventaire* (short); *Schéma d'une identification* (short)
1947 *Visite à Lucien Coutaud* (short); *Visite à Félix Labisse* (short); *Visite à Hans Hartung* (short); *Visite à César Domela* (short); *Visite à Oscar Dominguez* (short); *Portrait d'Henri Goetz* (short); *La Bague* (short); *Journée naturelle* (short); *L'Alcool tue* (short) (+ ph, ed)
1948 *Les Jardins de Paris* (short) (+ ph, ed); *Châteaux de France* (short) (+ sc, ph, ed); *Van Gogh* (short); *Malfray* (short) (co-d); *Van Gogh* (+ ed)
1950 *Gauguin* (short) (+ ed); *Guernica* (short) (co-d, ed)
1953 *Les Statues meurent aussi* (short) (co-d, co-sc, ed)
1955 ***Nuit et brouillard*** (*Night and Fog*) (short)
1956 *Toute la mémoire du monde* (short) (+ ed)
1957 *Le Mystère de l'Atelier Quinze* (short) (co-d)
1958 *Le Chant de Styrène* (short) (+ ed)
1959 ***Hiroshima mon amour***
1961 ***L'Année dernière à Marienbad*** (*Last Year at Marienbad*)
1963 *Muriel, ou le temps d'un retour*
1966 *La Guerre est finie* (*The War is Over*)
1967 *Loin du Viêt-Nam* (*Far from Vietnam*) (co-d)
1968 *Je t'aime, je t'aime* (+ co-sc)
1974 *Stavisky*
1977 *Providence*
1980 *Mon Oncle d'Amérique*
1983 *La Vie est un roman* (*Life Is a Bed of Roses*)
1984 *L'Amour à mort*
1986 *Mélo*
1989 *I Want to Go Home*
1992 *Gershwin* (video)
1993 *Smoking; No Smoking*

Other Films:

1945 *Le Sommeil d'Albertine* (ed)
1947 *Paris 1900* (ed)
1948 *Jean Effel* (ed)
1952 *Saint-Tropez, devoir de vacances* (ed)
1955 *La Pointe courte* (ed)
1957 *L'Oeil du maître* (ed); *Broadway by Light* (ed)
1958 *Paris à l'automne* (ed)

Publications

By RESNAIS: books—

Repérages, Paris, 1974.

By RESNAIS: articles—

Interview with François Truffaut, in *Arts* (Paris), 20 February 1956.
"A Conversation with Alain Resnais," with Noël Burch, in *Film Quarterly* (Berkeley), Spring 1960.

Alain Resnais directing Delphine Syrig in *L'Année dernière à Marienbad*

Interview with André Labarthe and Jacques Rivette, in *Cahiers du Cinéma* (Paris), September 1961; reprinted in English in *Films and Filming* (London), February 1962.
Interview with Penelope Houston, in *Sight and Sound* (London), Winter 1961/62.
"Trying to Understand My Own Film," in *Films and Filming* (London), February 1962.
Interview with Marcel Martin, in *Cinéma* (Paris), December 1964 and January 1965.
Interview with Adrian Maben, in *Films and Filming* (London), October 1966.
"Last Words on Last Year: Discussion with Alain Resnais and Alain Robbe-Grillet," in *Films and Filming* (London), March 1969.
Interview with Win Sharples, Jr., in *Filmmaker's Newsletter* (Ward Hill, Massachusetts), December 1974.
"Conversations with Alan Resnais," with James Monaco, in *Film Comment* (New York), July/August 1975.
Interview with S. Daney and others, in *Cahiers du Cinéma* (Paris), May 1983.
Interview with A. Finnane, in *Cinema Papers* (Melbourne), December 1984.
Interview with Robert Benayoun, and others, in *Positif* (Paris), September 1986.

On RESNAIS: books—

Cordier, Stéphane, editor, *Alain Resnais, ou la création au cinéma,* Paris, 1961.
Pinguad, Bernard, *Alain Resnais,* Lyon, 1961.
Alain Resnais, Premier Plan no. 18, October 1961.
Bournoure, Gaston, *Alain Resnais,* Paris, 1962.
Cowie, Peter, *Antonioni, Bergman, Resnais,* London, 1963.
Armes, Roy, *The Cinema of Alain Resnais,* London, 1968.
Ward, John, *Alain Resnais, or the Theme of Time,* New York, 1968.
Bertetto, Paolo, *Resnais: Alain Resnais,* Italy, 1976.
Kreidl, John Francis, *Alain Resnais,* Boston, 1977.
Monaco, James, *Alain Resnais: The Role of Imagination,* New York, 1978.
Benayoun, Robert, *Alain Resnais: Arpenteur de l'imaginaire,* Paris, 1980; revised edition, 1986.
Sweet, Freddy, *The Film Narratives of Alain Resnais,* Ann Arbor, Michigan, 1981.
Vergerio, Flavio, *I film di Alain Resnais,* Rome, 1984.
Roob, Jean-Daniel, *Alain Resnais: Qui êtes-vous?,* Lyons, 1986.
Oms, Marcel, *Alain Resnais,* Paris, 1988.
Riambau, Esteve, *La ciencie y la ficcion: El cine de Alain Resnais,* Barcelona, 1988.
Thomas, François, *L'Atelier de Alain Resnais,* Paris, 1989.

On RESNAIS: articles—

Marcorelles, Louis, "Rebel with a Camera," in *Sight and Sound* (London), Winter 1960.
"*Nuit et brouillard* Issue" of *Avant-Scène du Cinéma* (Paris), February 1961.
Kael, Pauline, "Fantasies of the Art House Audience," in *Sight and Sound* (London), Winter 1961/62.
Taylor, John Russell, "Alain Resnais" in *Cinema Eye, Cinema Ear,* New York, 1964.
Stanbrook, Alan, "The Time and Space of Alain Resnais," in *Films and Filming* (London), January 1964.
"*Guernica* Issue" of *Avant-Scène du Cinéma* (Paris), June 1964.
"*Toute la mémoire du monde* Issue" of *Avant-Scène du Cinéma* (Paris), October 1965.
"Resnais Issue" of *L'Avant-Scène du Cinéma* (Paris), Summer 1966.
Roud, Richard, "Memories of Resnais," in *Sight and Sound* (London), Summer 1969.
Armes, Roy, "Resnais and Reality," in *Films and Filming* (London), May 1970.
Harcourt, Peter, "Memory is Kept Alive with Dream," in *Film Comment* (New York), November/December 1973.
Harcourt, Peter, "Toward a Certainty of Doubt," in *Film Comment* (New York), January/February 1974.
"Resnais Issue" of *Cinéma* (Paris), July/August 1980.
Rosenbaum, Jonathan, "In Search of the American Uncle," in *American Film* (Washington, D.C.), May 1981.
Dossier on Resnais, in *Cinématographe* (Paris), April 1982.
Brown, R., "Everyone Has His Reasons," in *Monthly Film Bulletin* (London), May 1984.
Parra, D., "Alain Resnais, cinéaste de la limpidité," in *Revue du Cinéma* (Paris), September 1984.
Moses, John W., "Vision Denied in *Night and Fog* and *Hiroshima Mon Amour,*" in *Literature/Film Quarterly* (Salisbury, Maryland), vol. 15, no.3, 1987.
"*Mélo* Issue" of *Avant-Scène du Cinéma* (Paris), April 1987.
Durgnat, Raymond, "Resnais & Co.: Back to the Avant-Garde," in *Monthly Film Bulletin* (London), May 1987.
Forbes, Jill, "Resnais in the 80s," in *Sight and Sound* (London), Summer 1987.
Tomasulo, Frank P., "The Intentionality of Consciousness: Subjectivity in Resnais's *Last Year at Marienbad,*" in *Post Script* (Jacksonville, Florida), vol. 7, no. 2, 1988.
Prédal, René, "L'oeuvre de Alain Resnais: Regard du cinéaste et place du spectateur," in *Jeune Cinéma* (Paris), April/May 1989.
McGilligan, Patrick, article in *Sight and Sound* (London), vol. 59, no. 3, 1990.

* * *

Alain Resnais is a prominent figure in the modernist narrative film tradition. His emergence as a feature director of international repute is affiliated with the eruption of the French New Wave in the late 1950s. This association was signaled by the fact that his first feature, *Hiroshima mon amour,* premiered at the Cannes Film Festival at the same time as François Truffaut's *Les 400 coups.* However, Resnais had less to do with the group of directors emerging from the context of the *Cahiers du cinéma* than he did with the so-called Left Bank group, including Jean Cayrol, Marguerite Duras, Chris Marker, and Alain Robbe-Grillet. This group provided an intellectual and creative context of shared interest. In the course of his film career Resnais frequently collaborated with members of this group. Marker worked with him on several short films in the 1950s; Cayrol wrote the narration for *Nuit et brouillard* and the script for *Muriel*; Duras scripted *Hiroshima mon amour*; and Robbe-Grillet wrote *L'Année dernière à Marienbad.* All of these people are known as writers and/or filmmakers in their own right; their association with Resnais is indicative of his talent for fruitful creative collaboration.

Resnais began making films as a youth in 8 and 16mm. In the early 1940s he studied acting and filmmaking, and after the war made a number of 16mm films, including a series about artists. His first film in 35mm was the 1948 short, *Van Gogh,* which won a number of international awards. It was produced by Pierre Braunberger, an active supporter of new talent, who continued to finance his work in the short film format through the 1950s. From 1948-58 Resnais made eight short films, of which *Nuit et brouillard* is probably the best known. The film deals with German concentration camps, juxtaposing past and present, exploring the nature of memory and history. To some extent the film's reputation and the sustained interest it has enjoyed is due to its subject matter. However, many of the film's formal strategies and thematic concerns are characteristic of Resnais's work more generally. In particular, the relationship between past and present, and the function of memory as the mechanism of traversing temporal distance, are persistent preoccupations of Resnais's films. Other films from this period similarly reveal familiar themes and traits of Resnais's subsequent work. *Toute la memoire du monde* is a documentary about the Bibliothèque Nationale in Paris. It presents the building, with its processes of cataloguing and preserving all sorts of printed material, as both a monument of cultural memory and as a monstrous, alien being. The film almost succeeds in transforming the documentary film into a branch of science fiction.

Indeed, Resnais has always been interested in science fiction, the fantastic, and pulp adventure stories. If this interest is most overtly expressed in the narrative of *Je t'aime, je t'aime* (in which a human serves as a guinea pig for scientists experimenting with time travel), it also emerges in the play of fantasy/imagination/reality pervading his work, and in many of his unachieved projects (including a remake of *Fantômas* and *The Adventure of Harry Dickson*).

Through editing and an emphasis on formal repetition, Resnais uses the medium to construct the conjunctions of past and present, fantasy and reality, insisting on the convergence of what are usually considered distinct domains of experience. In *Hiroshima mon amour* the quivering hand of the woman's sleeping Japanese lover in the film's present is directly followed by an almost identical image of her nearly-dead German lover during World War II. Tracking shots through the streets of Hiroshima merge with similar shots of Nevers, where the woman lived during the war. In *Stavisky,* the cutting between events in 1933 and a 1934 investigation of those events presents numerous, often conflicting versions of the same thing; one is finally convinced, above all else, of the indeterminacy and contingency of major historical events. And in *Providence,* the central character is an aged writer who spends a troubled night weaving stories about his family, conjoining memory and fantasy, past, present, and future, in an unstable mix.

The past's insistent invasion of the present is expressed in many different ways in Resnais's films. In *Nuit et brouillard,* where the death camps are both present structures and repressed institutions, it is a question of social memory and history; it is an individual and cultural phenomenon in *Hiroshima mon amour,* as a French woman simultaneously confronts her experiences in occupied France and the Japanese experience of the atomic bomb; it is construed in terms of science fiction in *Je t'aime, je t'aime* when the hero is trapped in a broken time-machine and continuously relives moments from his past; and it is a profoundly ambiguous mixture of an individual's real and imagined past in *L'Année dernière à Marienbad* (often considered Resnais's most avant-garde film) as X pursues A with insistence, recalling their love affair and promises of the previous year, in spite of A's denials. In all of these films, as well as Resnais's other work, the past is fraught with uncertainty, anxiety, even terror. If it is more comfortable to ignore, it inevitably erupts in the present through the workings of the psyche, memory traces, or in the form of documentation and artifacts.

In recent years, Resnais' presence on the international film scene barely has been noticed. While serious and provocative in intention, none of his films have measured up to his earlier work. However, in the early 1980s, he did direct two strikingly original films which are outstanding additions to his filmography.

In *Mon Oncle d'Amerique,* Resnais probes human responses and relations by illustrating the theories of Henri Laborit, a French research biologist. The scenario's focus is on the intertwined relationship between three everyday characters: a Catholic farm boy who has become a textile plant manager (Gerard Depardieu); a former young communist who now is an actress (Nicole Garcia); and a conformist (Roger Pierre) who is married to his childhood sweetheart. *La vie est un roman (Life Is a Bed of Roses)* is a bewitching allegory contrasting the accounts of a rich man (Ruggero Raimondi) constructing a "temple of happiness" around the time of World War I, and a seminar on education being held at that location decades later. Resnais' points are that there are no easy answers to complex dilemmas and, most tellingly, that individuals who attempt to dictate to others their concepts of perfection are as equally destructive as those whose actions result in outright chaos.

Resnais's filmic output has been relatively small. He nonetheless stands as a significant figure in modernist cinema. His strategies of fragmented point-of-view and multiple temporality, as well as his use of the medium to convey past/present and fantasy/imagination/reality as equivocal and equivalent modes of experience have amplified our understanding of film's capacity for expression.

—M. B. White, updated by Rob Edelman

RICHARDSON, Tony

Nationality: British. **Born:** Cecil Antonio Richardson in Shipley, West Yorkshire, 5 June 1928. **Education:** Wadham College, Oxford University, degree in English, 1952. **Family:** Married actress Vanessa Redgrave, 1962 (divorced 1967); three daughters, actresses Natasha and Joely, and Katherine Grimond. **Career:** President of Oxford University Drama Society, 1949-51; producer and director for BBC TV, 1953; formed English Stage Company with George Devine, 1955; began collaboration with writer John Osborne on first production of *Look Back in Anger* at the Royal Court Theatre, London, 1956; with Osborne, formed Woodfall Productions, 1958; directed first feature, *Look Back in Anger,* 1959; continued to work as stage director; director for TV, including *Penalty Phase* (1986), *Shadow on the Sun* (1988), and *Phantom of the Opera* (1990). **Awards:** Oscar for Best Direction, and New York Film Critics Award for Best Direction, for *Tom Jones,* 1963. **Died:** November 1991.

Films as Director:

1955 *Momma Don't Allow* (co-d)
1959 ***Look Back in Anger***
1960 *The Entertainer*
1961 *Sanctuary*; *A Taste of Honey* (+ pr, co-sc)
1962 *The Loneliness of the Long Distance Runner* (+ pr)
1963 ***Tom Jones*** (+ pr)
1965 *The Loved One*; *Mademoiselle*
1967 *The Sailor from Gibraltar* (+ co-sc)
1968 *Red and Blue*; *The Charge of the Light Brigade*
1969 *Laughter in the Dark* (*La Chambre obscure*); *Hamlet*
1970 *Ned Kelly* (+ co-sc)
1973 *A Delicate Balance*; *Dead Cert*
1977 *Joseph Andrews* (+ co-sc)
1978 *Death in Canaan*
1982 *The Border*
1984 *Hotel New Hampshire* (+ sc)
1985 *Turning a Blind Eye* (doc)
1990 *Blue Sky*

Other Films:

1960 ***Saturday Night and Sunday Morning*** (Reisz) (pr)
1964 *Girl with Green Eyes* (Davis) (exec pr)

Tony Richardson directing *A Taste of Honey*

Publications

By RICHARDSON: book—

The Long-Distance Runner: An Autobiography, 1993.

By RICHARDSON: articles—

"The Films of Luis Buñuel," in *Sight and Sound* (London), January/March 1954.

"The Metteur-en-Scène," in *Sight and Sound* (London), October/December 1954.

"The Method and Why: An Account of the Actor's Studio," in *Sight and Sound* (London), Winter 1956/57.

"The Man behind an Angry-Young-Man," in *Films and Filming* (London), February 1959.

"Tony Richardson: An Interview in Los Angeles," with Colin Young, in *Film Quarterly* (Berkeley), Summer 1960.

"The Two Worlds of Cinema: Interview," in *Films and Filming* (London), June 1961.

Article, in *Film Makers on Film-making* edited by Harry M. Geduld, Bloomington, Indiana, 1967.

"Within the Cocoon," an interview with Gordon Gow, in *Films and Filming* (London), June 1977.

On RICHARDSON: books—

Villelaur, Anne, *Tony Richardson, Dossiers du Cinema,* Cineastes I, Paris, 1971.

Lovell, Alan, and Jim Hillier, *Studies in Documentary,* New York, 1972.

Walker, Alexander, *Hollywood, England: The British Film Industry in the 60s,* London, 1975.

Hill, John, *Sex, Class and Realism: British Cinema 1956-63,* London, 1986.

On RICHARDSON: articles—

Houston, Penelope, "Two New Directors," in *Sight and Sound* (London), Winter 1958/59.

"Director," in *New Yorker,* 12 October 1963.

Moller, David, "Britain's Busiest Angry Young Man," in *Film Comment* (New York), Winter 1964.

Lellis, George, "Recent Richardson," in *Sight and Sound* (London), Summer 1969.

Villelaur, Anne, "Tony Richardson," in *Dossiers du Cinéma 1,* Paris, 1971.

Gomez, Joseph, "*The Entertainer*: From Play to Film," in *Film Heritage* (Dayton, Ohio), Spring 1973.

Broeske, P., "The Company of Birds," in *Stills* (London), October 1984.

Barron, J., "Tony Richardson, Director of *Tom Jones,* Dead at 63," in *New York Times,* 16 November 1991.
"The End," in *Skoop,* December 1991/January 1992.
Brandlmeier, T., "Tony Richardson," in *EPD Film,* January 1992.

* * *

Tony Richardson belongs to that generation of British film directors which includes Lindsay Anderson and Karel Reisz, all of them university-trained middle-class artists who were sympathetic to the conditions of the working classes and determined to use cinema as a means of personal expression, in line with the goals of the "Free Cinema" movement. After Oxford, he enrolled in a directors' training program at the British Broadcasting Corporation before turning to theatre and founding, with George Devine, the English Stage Company in 1955 at London's Royal Court Theatre—a company that was to include writers Harold Pinter and John Osborne. Among Richardson's Royal Court productions were *Look Back in Anger, A Taste of Honey,* and *The Entertainer,* dramatic vehicles that he would later transform into cinema.

Also in 1955, working with Karel Reisz, Richardson co-directed his first short film, *Momma Don't Allow,* funded by a grant from the British Film Institute and one of the original productions of the "Free Cinema" movement. Richardson's realistic treatment of the works of John Osborne (*Look Back in Anger*), Shelagh Delaney (*A Taste of Honey*), and Alan Sillitoe (*Loneliness of the Long-Distance Runner*) would infuse British cinema with the "kitchen sink" realism Richardson had helped to encourage in the British theatre. Indeed, Richardson's link with the "Angry Young Men" of the theatre was firmly established before he and John Osborne founded their film production unit, Woodfall, in 1958 for the making of *Look Back In Anger.*

Richardson's strongest talent has been to adapt literary and dramatic works to the screen. In 1961 he turned to Hollywood, where he directed an adaptation of Faulkner's *Sanctuary,* which he later described as arguably his worst film. His most popular success, however, was *Tom Jones,* his brilliant adaptation and abridgement of Henry Fielding's often rambling eighteenth-century novel, which in other hands would not have been a very promising film project but which, under Richardson's direction, won four Academy Awards in 1963. In 1977 Richardson tried to repeat his earlier success by adapting Fielding's other great comic novel, *Joseph Andrews,* to the screen, but though the story was effectively shaped by Richardson and the casting was splendid, the film was not the overwhelming commercial success that *Tom Jones* had been. Nonetheless, Vincent Canby singled out *Joseph Andrews* as "the year's most cheerful movie ... and probably the most neglected movie of the decade."

Other adaptations and literary collaborations included *The Loved One* (Evelyn Waugh), *Mademoiselle* (Jean Genet), *The Sailor from Gibraltar* (Marguerite Duras), *Laughter in the Dark* (Nabokov), and *A Delicate Balance* (Albee). Perhaps Richardson's most enduring dramatic adaptation, however, is his rendering of *Hamlet,* filmed in 1969, remarkable for the eccentric but effective performance by Nicol Williamson as Hamlet which it captures for posterity, and also for Anthony Hopkins's sinister Claudius. Filmed at the Roundhouse Theatre in London where it was originally produced, it is a brilliant exercise in filmed theatre in the way it keeps the actors at the forefront of the action, allowing them to dominate the play as they would do on stage. Richardson has defined cinema as a director's medium, but his *Hamlet* effectively treats it as an actor's medium, as perhaps no other filmed production has done.

Other Richardson films seem to place a premium upon individualism, as witnessed by his treatment of the legendary Australian outlaw *Ned Kelly* (starring Mick Jagger, a project Karel Reisz had first undertaken with Albert Finney). This concern for the individual can also be discerned ten years later in *The Border,* a film Richardson completed for Universal Pictures in 1982, starring Jack Nicholson as a guard on the Mexican-American border, a loner who fights for human values against a corrupt constabulary establishment. Unfortunately *The Border,* which turned out to be a caricatured and flawed melodrama, did not reflect the director's intentions in its released form, since Universal Studios apparently wanted—and got—"a much more up-beat ending where Nicholson emerges as a hero." That a talented director of considerable vision, intelligence, and accomplishment should experience such an impasse is a sorry commentary. Nonetheless, Richardson migrated to the Hollywood Hills by choice and claimed to prefer California to his native England.

—James M. Welsh

RICHTER, Hans

Nationality: German. **Born:** Berlin, 1888. **Education:** Berlin Academy for Fine Arts, 1908; Weimar Academy of Art, 1909. **Military Service:** 1915-16. **Career:** Collaborator on *Aktion* journal, from 1915; joined Dada group in Zurich, 1916; with Viking Eggeling, returned to Germany, 1918-19; experimental focus shifts completely to film, 1920; publisher of art magazine, *G,* 1923-26; immigrated to United States, 1940; director of Film Institute, City College of New York, 1942. **Died:** In Locarno, 1976.

Films as Director:

1921-24 *Rhythmus 21* (+ graphic artist, ph) (original title: *Film ist Rhythmus*)
1923-24 *Rhythmus 23* (+ graphic artist)
1925 *Rhythmus 25* (+ graphic artist)
1926 *Filmstudie* (+ graphic artist, co-ph)
1927-28 *Inflation* (+ graphic artist, sc); *Vormittagsspuk* (*Ghosts Before Breakfast*) (co-d and graphic work, co-story, role)
1928-29 *Rennsymphonie* (*Race Symphony*) (+ sc); *Zweigroschenzauber* (*Two-Penny Magic*) (+ sc); *Alles dreht sich, alles bewegt sich* (*Everything Turns; Everything Revolves*) (+ co-sc); *Forty Years of Experiment* Part 1 (comprised of experimental films and film fragments by Richter from 1921-30) (+ sc)
1944-47 *Dreams That Money Can Buy* (+ sc)
1954-57 *8 x 8* (+ sc)
1956-61 *Dadascope* (+ sc)
1963 *Alexander Calder* (+ sc)

Publications

By RICHTER: books—

Filmgegner von heute—Filmfreunde von morgen, Berlin, 1929 (reprinted Zurich, 1968).
Hans Richter by Hans Richter, edited by Cleve Gray, London, 1971.
Der Kampf um den Film, Munich and Vienna, 1976.
The Struggle for the Cinema: Towards a Socially Responsible Cinema, edited by Jürgen Romhild, Aldershot, Hampshire, 1986.

By RICHTER: articles—

"The Avant-Garde Film Seen From Within," in *Hollywood Quarterly,* Fall 1949.

"Thirty Years of Experimental Films," an interview with Herman Weinberg, in *Films in Review* (New York), December 1951.
"Eight Free Improvisations on the Game of Chess," in *Film Culture* (New York), January 1955.
"*8 x 8*: A Sequence from Hans Richter's Latest Experimental Film," in *Film Culture* (New York), Winter 1955.
"Hans Richter on the Nature of Film Poetry," an interview with Jonas Mekas, in *Film Culture* (New York), no. 11, 1957.
"From Interviews with Hans Richter During the Last Ten Years," in *Film Culture* (New York), no. 31, 1963/64.
"Learning from Film History," in *Filmmakers Newsletter* (Ward Hill, Massachusetts), November 1973.

On RICHTER: books—

Joray, Marcel, editor, *Hans Richter,* Neuchâtel, 1965.
O'Konor, Louise, *Viking Eggeling, 1880-1925, Artist and Filmmaker: Life and Work,* Stockholm, 1971.
Russett, Robert, and Cecile Starr, *Experimental Animation,* New York, 1976.

On RICHTER: articles—

Young, Vernon, "Painter and Cinematographer Hans Richter: A Retrospective of Four Decades," in *Arts Magazine* (New York), September 1959.

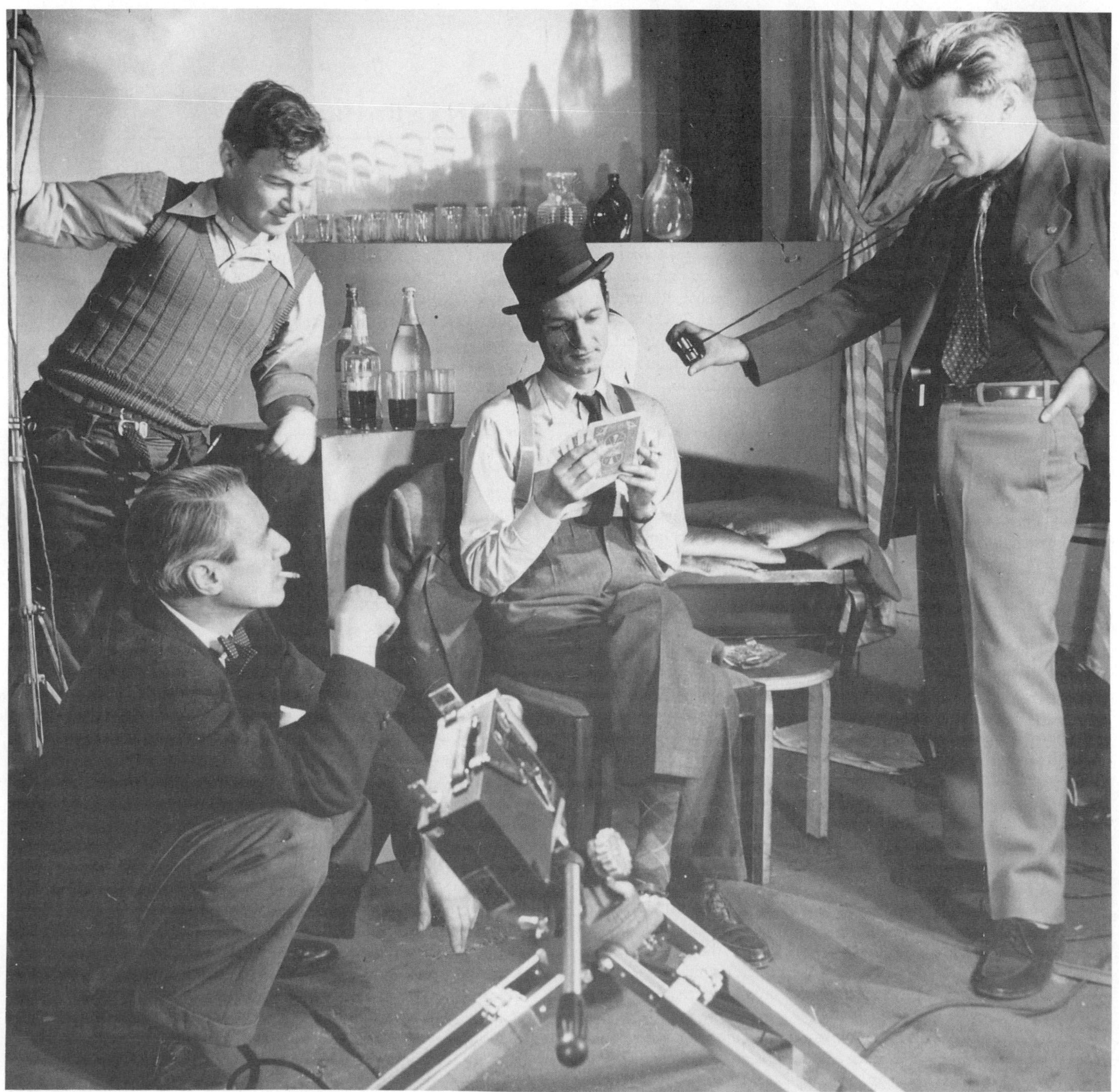

Hans Richter (bottom left) directing *Dreams That Money Can Buy*

Gray, C., "Portrait: Hans Richter," in *Art in America* (New York), January 1968.
Codroico, R., and L. Pezzolato, "Richter e l'uomo visibile," in *Cinema Nuovo* (Turin), July/August 1972.
Bassan, H., and M. Roudevitch, "Se souvenir de Hans Richter," in *Ecran* (Paris), May 1977.

* * *

Like many other filmmakers of the European avant-garde, Richter was initially a painter, influenced by such movements as futurism and cubism. Like his colleague Viking Eggeling, Richter came to extend his theoretical concerns beyond the limitations of paint and canvas to abstract scrolls and then to film. As a result of his published theoretical writings (such as *Universelle Sprache,* with Viking Eggeling) and about a dozen films realized over four decades, today he is highly regarded as a very early influence upon that major genre of production generally termed "experimental film." Perhaps his most famous and most influential film was his first, *Rhythmus 21.*

Typical of experimental production, *Rhythmus 21* is a brief, acollaborative work, realized outside the financial and organizational constraints of the film industry. A silent black and white film that runs less than two minutes, it is an animated exploration of simple cut-out paper squares of various sizes and shades. The film's aesthetic force draws upon structures and strategies common to non-representational painting or graphic design. Part of the film's value comes from its explicit remove from theatrical or fictive prototypes, which dominated cinema in the 1920s as fully as today. Certainly, *Rhythmus 21*'s value is as much predicated upon the later influence of its non-narrative structure (especially in international experimental film) as upon the lively dynamics of its simple yet stunning metamorphoses of shapes and tonalities.

Richter went on to construct a number of companion pieces (e.g. *Rhythmus 23*). His later film work took on more representational elements, as in his 1926 *Film Study,* which employed animated suns, clouds, eyes, etc., with a somewhat surrealistic exchange of imagery. This embrace of film's representational resources grew more pronounced for Richter. By 1930 he had largely ceased his concern with animated records of graphic materials, turning in other directions. *Vormittagsspuk (Ghosts Before Breakfast)* is a zany Dada story dependent upon shots of real objects and people, while *Alles dreht sich, alles bewegt sich (Everything Revolves, Everything Moves)* embodies a somewhat documentary examination of a fairground. Still, such works clearly fall under the classification of the experimental genre, in part due to their fascination with mental imagery—dream, fantasy, and reverie. This same concern also marks Richter's post-war production, such as the still surreal yet somewhat Jungian *Dreams That Money Can Buy.*

Richter's experimental film production occurred during an extraordinarily long career. As recently as the 1960s he was still realizing new pieces, such as *Dadascope.* Yet his influence and importance to film historians and experimental filmmakers probably centers upon his early abstract, animated work. *Rhythmus 21* remains one of the best-known and most influential products of the European avant-garde.

—Edward S. Small

RIEFENSTAHL, Leni

Nationality: German. **Born:** Helene Berta Amalie Riefenstahl in Berlin, 22 August 1902. **Education:** Studied Russian Ballet at the Mary Wigmann School for Dance, Dresden, and Jutta Klamt School for Dance, Berlin. **Family:** Married Peter Jacob, 1944 (divorced 1946). **Career:** Dancer, from 1920; appeared in "mountain films" directed by Arnold Franck, from 1936; established own production company, Riefenstahl Films, 1931; first film, *Das blaue Licht,* released, 1932; appointed "film expert to the National Socialist Party" by Hitler, 1933; detained in various prison camps by Allied Forces on charges of pro-Nazi activity, 1945-48; charges dismissed by Berlin court, allowed to work in film industry again, 1952; suffered serious auto accident while working in Africa, 1956; commissioned by *The Times* (London) to photograph the Munich Olympics, 1972; honored at Telluride Film Festival, Colorado (festival picketed by anti-Nazi groups), 1974; was the subject of the documentary *The Wonderful, Horrible Life of Leni Riefenstahl,* directed by Ray Muller, 1993. **Awards:** Silver Medal, Venice Festival, for *Das Blaue Licht,* 1932; Exposition Internationale des Arts et des Techniques, Paris, Diplome de Grand Prix, for *Triumph des Willens,* 1937; Polar Prize, Sweden, for *Olympia,* 1938. **Address:** 20 Tengstrasse, 8000 Munich 40, Germany.

Films as Director:

1932 *Das blaue Licht* (*The Blue Light*) (+ co-sc, role as Junta)
1933 *Sieg des Glaubens* (*Victory of the Faith*)
1935 ***Triumph des Willens*** (*Triumph of the Will*) (+ pr, ed); *Tag der Freiheit: unsere Wermacht* (+ ed)
1938 ***Olympia*** (*Olympische Spiele 1936*) (+ sc, co-ph, ed)
1944 *Tiefland* (*Lowland*) (+ sc, ed, role as Marta) (released 1954)

Films as Actress:

1926 *Der heilige Berg* (Fanck)
1927 *Der grosse Sprung* (Fanck)
1929 *Das Schiscksal derer von Hapsburg* (Raffé); *Die weisses Hölle vom Piz Palü* (Fanck)
1930 *Stürme über dem Montblanc* (Fanck)
1931 *Der weiss Rausch* (Fanck)
1933 *S.O.S. Eisberg* (Fanck)

Publications

By RIEFENSTAHL: books—

Kampf in Schnee und Eis, Leipzig, 1933.
Hinter den Kulissen des Reichsparteitagsfilms, Munich, 1935 (uncredited ghost writer Ernst Jaeger).
Schönheit im Olympischen Kampf, Berlin, 1937.
The Last of the Nuba, New York, 1974.
Jardins du corail, Paris, 1978.
Memoiren, Munich, 1987 (also published as *The Sieve of Time: The Memoirs of Leni Riefenstahl,* London, 1992, and *Leni Riefenstahl: A Memoir,* New York, 1994).
Wonders Under Water, London, 1991.
Leni Riefenstahl: Life, Tokyo, 1992.
Olympia, London, 1994.

By RIEFENSTAHL: articles—

"An Interview with a Legend," with Gordon Hitchens, in *Film Comment* (New York), Winter 1965.
Interview with Michel Delahaye, in *Interviews with Film Directors,* edited by Andrew Sarris, New York, 1967.
"A Reply to Paul Rotha," with Kevin Brownlow, in *Film* (London), Spring 1967.

"Statement on Sarris-Gessner Quarrel about *Olympia,*" in *Film Comment* (New York), Fall 1967.
Interview with Herman Weigel, in *Filmkritik* (Munich), August 1972.
"Why I Am Filming *Penthesilea,*" in *Film Culture* (New York), Spring 1973.
"Leni Riefenstahl: A Memoir," in *New York,* 13 September 1993.

On RIEFENSTAHL: books—

Cadars, Pierre, and Francis Courtade, *Histoire du cinema Nazi,* Paris, 1972.
Fanck, Arnold, *Er furte Regie mit Gletschern, Sturmen, Lawinen,* Munich, 1973.
Hull, David Stewart, *Film in the Third Reich,* New York, 1973.
Leiser, Erwin, *Nazi Cinema,* London, 1974.
Barsam, Richard, *Filmguide to "Triumph of the Will,"* Bloomington, Indiana, 1975.
Infield, Glenn, *Leni Riefenstahl, the Fallen Film Goddess,* New York, 1976.
Ford, Charles, *Leni Riefenstahl,* Paris, 1978.
Hinton, David, *The Films of Leni Riefenstahl,* Metuchen, New Jersey, 1978.
Infield, G. B., *Leni Riefenstahl et le troisieme Reich,* Paris, 1978.
Berg-Pan, Renata, *Leni Riefenstahl,* Boston, 1980.
Heck-Rabi, Louise, *Women Filmmakers: A Critical Reception,* Metuchen, New Jersey, 1984.
Graham, Cooper C., *Leni Riefenstahl and Olympia,* Metuchen, New Jersey, 1986.
Hinton, David B., *The Films of Leni Riefenstahl,* Metuchen, New Jersey, 1991.
Deutschmann, Linda, *Triumph of the Will: The Image of the Third Reich,* Wakefield, New Hampshire, 1991.

On RIEFENSTAHL: articles—

"The Case of Leni Riefenstahl," in *Sight and Sound* (London), Spring 1960.
Gunston, David, "Leni Riefenstahl," in *Film Quarterly* (Berkeley), Fall 1960.
Berson, Arnold, "The Truth about Leni," in *Films and Filming* (London), April 1965.
Gregor, Ulrich, "A Comeback for Leni Riefenstahl," in *Film Comment* (New York), Winter 1965.
Brownlow, Kevin, "Leni Riefenstahl," in *Film* (London), Winter 1966.
Rotha, Paul, "I Deplore...," in *Film* (London), Spring 1967.
Corliss, Richard, "Leni Riefenstahl—A Bibliography," in *Film Heritage* (Dayton, Ohio), Fall 1969.
Richards, J., "Leni Riefenstahl: Style and Structure," in *Silent Pictures* (London), Autumn 1970.
Alpert, Hollis, "The Lively Ghost of Leni," in the *Saturday Review* (New York), 25 March 1972.
"Riefenstahl Issue" of *Film Culture* (New York), Spring 1973.
Barsam, R. M., "Leni Riefenstahl: Artifice and Truth in a World Apart," in *Film Comment* (New York), November/December 1973.
Sontag, Susan, "Fascinating Fascism," in the *New York Review of Books,* 6 February 1975.
Sokal, Harry R., "Über Nacht Antisemitin geworden?," in *Der Spiegel* (Germany), no. 46, 1976.
"Zur Riefenstahl-Renaissance," special issue of *Frauen und Film* (Berlin), December 1977.
Fraser, J., "An Ambassador for Nazi Germany," in *Films* (London), April 1982.
Horton, W. J., "Capturing the Olympics," in *American Cinematographer* (Los Angeles), July 1984.
Loiperdinger, M., and D. Culbert, "Leni Riefenstahl, the SA, and the Nazi Party Rally Films, Nuremberg 1933-1934: *Sieg des Glaubens* and *Triumph des Willens,*" in *Historical Journal of Film, Radio and TV* (Abingdon, Oxon), vol. 8, no. 1, 1988.
Lopperdinger, M. and D. Culbert, "Leni Riefenstahl's *Tag der Freiheit:* The 1935 Nazi Party Rally Film," in *Historical Journal of Film, Radio and TV* (Abingdon, Oxon), vol. 12, no. 3, 1992.
Schiff, Stephen, "Leni's *Olympia,*" in *Vanity Fair* (New York), September 1992.
Harshaw, Tobin, "Why Am I Guilty?" in *New York Times Book Review,* 26 September 1993.
Corliss, Richard, "Riefenstahl's Last Triumph," in *Time* (New York), 18 October 1993.
Hoberman, J., "Triumph of the Swill," in *Premiere* (New York), December 1993.

On RIEFENSTAHL: films—

The Wonderful, Horrible Life of Leni Riefenstahl, 1993.
The Night of the Film-makers, 1995.

* * *

The years 1932 to 1945 define the major filmmaking efforts of Leni Riefenstahl. Because she remained a German citizen making films in Hitler's Third Reich, two at the Fuhrer's request, she and her films were viewed as pro-Nazi. Riefenstahl claims she took no political position and committed no crimes. In 1948, a German court ruled that she was a follower of, not active in, the Nazi Party. Another court in 1952 reconfirmed her innocence of war crimes. But she is destined to remain a politically controversial filmmaker who made two films rated as masterpieces.

She began to learn filmmaking while acting in the mountain films of Arnold Fanck, her mentor. She made a mountain film of her own, *The Blue Light,* using smoke bombs to create "fog." She used a red and green filter on the camera lens, over her cameraman's objections, to obtain a novel magical effect. This film is Riefenstahl's own favorite. She says it is the story of her own life. Hitler admired *The Blue Light* and asked her to photograph the Nazi Party Congress in Nuremburg. She agreed to make *Victory of the Faith,* which was not publicly viewed. Hitler then asked her to film the 1934 Nazi Party rally.

Triumph of the Will, an extraordinary work, shows Hitler arriving by plane to attend the rally. He proceeds through the crowded streets of Nuremburg, addresses speeches to civilians and uniformed troops, and reviews a five-hour parade. The question is: Did Riefenstahl make *Triumph* as pro-Nazi propaganda or not? "Cinematically dazzling and ideologically vicious," is R. M. Barsam's judgment. According to Barsam, three basic critical views of *Triumph* exist: 1) those who cannot appreciate the film at all, 2) those who can appreciate and understand the film, and 3) those who appreciate it in spite of the politics in the film.

Triumph premiered 29 March 1935, was declared a masterpiece, and subsequently earned three awards. *Triumph* poses questions of staging. Was the rally staged so that it could be filmed? Did the filming process shape the rally, give it meaning? Riefenstahl's next film, *Olympia,* posed the question of financing. Did Nazi officialdom pay for the film to be made? Riefenstahl claims the film was made independently of any government support. Other opinions differ.

The improvisatory techniques Riefenstahl used to make *Triumph* were improved and elaborated to make *Olympia.* She and her crew worked sixteen-hour days, seven days a week. *Olympia* opens as *Triumph* does, with aerial scenes. Filmed in two parts, the peak of Olympia I is Jesse Owens's running feat. The peak of Olympia II is the diving scenes. In an interview with Gordon Hitchens in 1964, Riefenstahl revealed her guidelines for making *Olympia.* She decided to make two films instead of one because "the form must excite the content and give it shape.... The law of film is architecture, balance. If the image is weak, strengthen the sound, and vice-versa; the total impact on the viewer should be 100 percent." The secret of *Olympia*'s success, she

Leni Riefenstahl directing *Olympia*

affirmed, was its sound—all laboratory-made. Riefenstahl edited the film for a year and a half. It premiered 20 April 1938 and was declared a masterpiece, being awarded four prizes.

Riefenstahl's career after the beginning of World War II is comprised of a dozen unfinished film projects. She began *Penthesilea* in 1939, *Van Gogh* in 1943, and *Tiefland* in 1944, releasing it in 1954. Riefenstahl acted the role of a Spanish girl in it while co-directing with G. W. Pabst this drama of peasant-landowner conflicts. Visiting Africa in 1956, she filmed *Black Cargo,* documenting the slave trade, but her film was ruined by incorrect laboratory procedures. In the 1960s, she lived with and photographed the Mesakin Nuba tribe in Africa.

Riefenstahl's *Triumph of the Will* and *Olympia* are two of the greatest documentaries ever made. That is indisputable. And it also is indisputable that they are among the most notorious and controversial. Each has been lauded for its sheer artistry, yet damned for its content and vision of Adolph Hitler and a German nation poised on the edge of totalitarian barbarism. After years as a name in the cinema history books, Riefenstahl was back in the news in 1992. *Memoirnen,* her autobiography, was first published in English as *The Sieve of Time: The Memoirs of Leni Riefenstahl,* and she was the subject of a documentary, Ray Muller's *The Wonderful, Horrible Life of Leni Riefenstahl.* Clearly, Riefenstahl had written the book and participated in the documentary in an attempt to have the final word regarding the debate over her involvement with Hitler and the Third Reich.

The documentary, which is three hours in length, traces Riefenstahl's undeniably remarkable life, from her success as a dancer and movie actress during the 1920s to her career as a director, her post-World War II censure, and her latter-day exploits as a still photographer. Still very much alive at age ninety-one, Riefenstahl is shown scuba diving, an activity she first took up in her seventies.

Riefenstahl is described at the outset as a "legend with many faces" and "the most influential filmmaker of the Third Reich." The film goes on to serve as an investigation of her life. Was she an opportunist, as she so vehemently denies, or a victim? Was she a "feminist pioneer, or a woman of evil?" Riefenstahl wishes history to view her as she views herself: not as a collaborator but as an artist first and foremost, whose sole fault was to have been alive in the wrong place at the wrong moment in history, and who was exploited by political forces of which she was unaware.

Upon meeting Hitler, she says, "He seemed a modest, private individual." She was "ignorant" of his ideas and politics, and "didn't see the danger of anti-Semitism." She claims to have acquiesced to making *Triumph of the Will* only after Hitler agreed that she would never have to make another film for him. To her, shooting *Triumph* was just a job. She wanted to make a film that was "interesting, one that was not with posed shots.... It had to be filmed the way an artist, not a politician, sees it." The same holds true for *Olympia,* which features images of perfectly proportioned, God-like German athletes. When queried regarding the issue of whether these visuals reflect a fascist aesthetic, Riefenstahl refuses to answer directly, replaying again that art and politics are separate entities.

"If an artist dedicates himself totally to his work, he cannot think politically," Riefenstahl says. Even in the late 1930s, she chose not to leave Germany because, as she observes, "I loved my homeland." She

Arturo Ripstein: ***La Reina de la noche***

claims that she hoped that reports of anti-Semitism were "isolated events." And her image of Hitler was "shattered much too late.... My life fell apart because I believed in Hitler. People say of me, 'She doesn't want to know. She'll always be a Nazi.' [But] I was never a Nazi."

"What am I guilty of?" Riefenstahl asks. "I regret [that I was alive during that period]. But I was never anti-Semitic. I never dropped any bombs." Explained director Muller, after a New York Film Festival screening of the film, "She was an emancipated woman before there was even such a term. She has a super ego, which has been trod upon for half a century.... [She is] an artist and a perfectionist. I believe that she was purposefully blind not to look in the direction that would get her into trouble."

In this regard, *The Wonderful, Horrible Life of Leni Riefenstahl* ultimately works as a portrait of denial. As Muller so aptly observes, "Any artist has a great responsibility. Anyone who influences the public has this. She is possessed with her art. She says, 'I'm only doing my thing.' I think this is irresponsible. She may be obsessed and possessed, and a genius. But that does not exempt her from responsibility."

In 1995, Riefenstahl briefly resurfaced in Edgar Reitz's *The Night of the Film-Makers,* consisting of interviews with German filmmakers from Frank Beyer to Wim Wenders. Eric Hansen, writing in *Variety,* summed up the essence of her appearance by noting, "Names like the ninety-two-year-old Leni Riefenstahl and young director Detlev Buck are allowed only a few self-glorifying or sarcastic comments."

Perhaps the final word on Riefenstahl is found in Istvan Szabo's *Hanussen,* a 1988 German-Hungarian film. Much of *Hanussen* is set in Germany between the world wars. One of the minor characters is a celebrated, egocentric woman artist, a member of the political inner circle, who surrounds herself with physical beauty while remaining callously unconcerned with all but her own vanity. Clearly, this character is based on Riefenstahl.

—Louise Heck-Rabi, updated by Rob Edelman

RIPSTEIN, Arturo

Nationality: Mexican. **Born:** Mexico City, 1943. **Family:** Son of Alfredo Ripstein, one of Mexico's most accomplished producers, credited with more than 180 films. **Career:** Began directorial career at the age of twenty-one, with the debut of *A Time to Die* (screenplay by Gabriel García Márquez, adapted from his own short story). **Awards:** Grand prize, San Sebastian Film Festival, 1993, for *The Beginning and the End.*

Films as Director:

1965 *Tiempo de Morir* (*A Time to Die*)
1966 *H.O.*

1968 *Los Recuerdos del Porvenir*
1969 *La Hora de los Ninos*
1970 *El Naufrago de la Calle de la Providencia* (co-d with Rafael Castanedo)
1971 *Autobiografia* (+ sc, pr)
1972 *El Castillo de la Pureza* (*The Castle of Purity*) (+ sc)
1974 *El Santo Oficio* (*The Holy Office*) (+ sc)
1975 *Foxtrot* (+ sc)
1976 *Lecumberri* (+ sc)
1977 *El Lugar sin Limites* (*The Place without Limits*; *Hell without Limits*)
1978 *Cadena Perpetua* (*Vicious Circle*) (+ sc)
1980 *La Tia Alexandra*
1983 *La Seduccion*; *Rastro de la Muerte*
1984 *El Otro* (*The Other*)
1985 *El Imperio de la Fortuna* (*In the Realm of Fortune*)
1989 *Mentiras Piadosos* (*White Lies*)
1991 *La Mujer del Puerto* (*Woman of the Port*)
1992 *La Concha de Oro* (*The Beginning and the End*)
1994 *La Reina de la Noche* (*The Queen of the Night*)

Publications

By RIPSTEIN: article—

Interview with N. Ghali, in *Revue du Cinema* (France), April 1975.

On RIPSTEIN: book—

Ramirez Berg, Charles, *Cinema of Solitude: A Critical Study of Mexican Film, 1967-1983,* Austin, 1992.

On RIPSTEIN: articles—

Cornand, A., "*Le Chateau de la purete,*" in *Revue du Cinema* (France), 1974.

Pick, Z. M., "Decouverted'un autre Cinema Mexicain," in *Positif* (Paris), no. 157, 1974.

Lajeunesse, J., "*Le saint Office,*" in *Revue de Cinema* (France), October 1974.

Hobermen, J., "Film: Hostage to Fortune," in *Village Voice* (New York), 24 March 1987.

Greenbaum, R., "New Directors, New Films—1987 (Part 2)," in *Films in Reviews* (New York), December 1987.

Vega Alfaro, E. de la, "Fichero de Cineastas Nacionales," in *Dicine* (Mexico City), November/December 1987.

Berg, C. R., "Cracks in the Macho Monolith: Machismo, Man, and Mexico in Recent Mexican Cinema," in *New Orleans Review,* no. 16, 1989.

Brandlmeier, T., "Muenchen: Ripstein und Andere," in *EPD Film* (Postfach, Germany), August 1989.

Orejel, A., "*Mentiras Piadosas,*" in *Dicine* (Mexico City), January 1990.

Carro, N. "Cineastas y Testimonios del Cine Mexicano," in *Dicine* (Mexico City), September 1990.

Uhlig, M. A., "Mexico's Film Industry Looks for a Breakthrough," in *New York Times,* 22 January 1991.

Loffreda, P., "*La Mujer del Puerto,*" in *Cineforum* (Bergamo, Italy), June 1991.

* * *

With more than twenty directorial works that span almost thirty years, Arturo Ripstein is one of the best-known Mexican directors whose fame reaches beyond the international film festival circuit. Son of one of Mexico's most accomplished film producers, Ripstein literally grew up on the backlots of studios. He was not only able to observe the techniques of some master filmmakers, such as Luis Buñuel and Emilio Fernández, but was also taken on as an assistant director by the former. With such a filmmaking background since adolescence, Ripstein made his directorial debut, *A Time to Die,* at the age of twenty-one.

A Time to Die is a Gabriel García Márquez screenplay adapted from his own short story. Following this came a series of collaborations with other Latin American talents, such as Carlos Fuentes, Manuel Puig, José Donoso, Juan Rulfo, Elena Garros, Julio Alejandro, José Emilio Pacheco, Vincete Leñero, and Silvina Ocampo. As such closeness with literary works may suggest, Ripstein's films are often precise in their realism yet tacit as well as articulate in their aesthetic visions.

His 1985 *In the Realm of Fortune* depicts the rise and fall of an ambitious peasant in the world of gambling. As the hero, Dionsio, gradually ascends from slavish poverty into affluence, Ripstein captures "superbly the sleazy, smoke-drenched atmosphere of the world of cheap carnivals, opportunistic women, cock fights and nights-long card games," according to Richard Greenbaum. It is in this world that Ripstein sets out to paint a ghastly portrait of obsession, the downfall of a human being, and fate like a pendulum oscillating between the lucky and the luckless. By the end of the movie, Dionsio commits suicide after losing everything—his wife and his fortune—except for the ornate silver coffin he wishes to be buried in. As his young daughter, Bernardina, sings in a carnival (just like her mother did to find a husband) at the very end of the movie, one cannot help but wonder: if poverty is the eternal reality of the luckless and luck does not last, how does one transcend a world driven by materialism? The content is grim and the tonality dark. Deliverance, however, is not out of the question, for, through an understanding of material obsession as such, one needs not emphasize or identify with Dionsio to *feel.*

In 1992, Ripstein started a project collaborating with yet another Nobel Prize winner, Naguib Mahfouz, on his novel *The Beginning and the End.* A story originally written in the 1940s about the social collapse of a Cairo family due to the death of the father, it takes on a universal quality under the pen of Ripstein's longtime working companion, Paz Alicia Garcíadiego (who also wrote the screenplays for *In the Realm of Fortune, White Lies,* and *Woman of the Port*). The parallels drawn between Cairo and Mexico City are uncanny. As Ripstein himself puts it, "Mexico City, an enormous urban center, noisy, dusty, like Cairo, is destroyed and reconstructed daily.... They are cities conquered by accelerated urban development, irrational modernization." In the filmmaker's vision, "the family is the guardian of retired values [and] is responsible that destiny is carried out." While the camera work almost renders a mythic texture, the soundtrack provides "a tragic breath," "an operatic tone." Recognized for its compelling treatment of a family story and rigorous artistic probing, *The Beginning and the End* was awarded the Grand Prize at the San Sebastian Film Festival in 1993.

Ripstein and Garcíadiego's 1994 collaboration, *The Queen of the Night,* is an "imaginary biography of the sentimental life of Lucha Reyes." Set between 1939 and 1944, the famed folk singer's life is chronicled in all its intensity as a "descent into the hell of alcohol, sexual excess and jealousy," writes Jorge Rufinelli. Another puissant theme of neurotic obsession and self-destruction recalls not only Dionsio's lost battle with luck but also *The Beginning and the End*'s eerie picture of a domineering mother. Family as well as interpersonal relationships are articulated not in terms of inevitable sufferings *per se,* but rather, through the alluring singing of Reyes, in terms of an intensity closer to the overpowering force of life. Therefore, with Ripstein's incisive and sure hand, "melodramatic themes are filtered through a rigorous aesthetic vision, so that [in *The Queen of the Night*] sentimentalism ends up becoming its opposite."

In his fourth decade of an outstanding filmmaking career, there is no reason not to anticipate more masterpieces from Arturo Ripstein. This must have been a painstaking lifelong process for the filmmaker. However, as Ripstein reminds us, "all art is painful. Pained by humanity."

—Guo-Juin Hong

RISI, Dino

Nationality: Italian. **Born:** Milan, 23 December 1917. **Education:** Educated in medicine, specializing in psychiatry. **Career:** Assistant to Mario Soldati and Alberto Lattuada, early 1940s; emigrated to Switzerland, studied filmmaking with Jacques Feyder, 1944; after liberation, returned to Milan as documentary maker and film critic, from 1946; with support of producer Carlo Ponti, directed first feature, *Vacanze col gangster,* 1952. **Address:** Residence Aldrovandi, via Aldrovandi, Rome, Italy.

Films as Director:

1946 *I bersaglieri della signora* (doc short); *Barboni* (doc short); *Verso la vita* (doc short)
1947 *Pescatorella* (doc short); *Strade di Napoli* (doc short); *Tigullio minore* (doc short); *Cortili* (doc short)
1948 *Costumi e bellezze d'Italia* (doc short); *Cuore rivelatore* (doc short); *1848* (doc short); *La fabbrica del Duomo* (doc short); *Segantini, il pittore della montagna* (doc short)
1949 *La città dei traffici* (doc short); *Caccia in brughiera* (doc short); *La montagna di luce* (doc short); *Vince il sistema* (doc short); *Terra ladina* (doc short); *Il siero della verità*; *Seduta spiritica*
1950 *L'isola bianca* (doc short); *Il grido della città* (doc short); *Buio in sala* (doc short); *Fuga in città* (doc short)
1952 *Vacanze col gangster* (*Vacation with a Gangster*) (+ co-sc, story)
1953 *Il viale della speranza* (*Hope Avenue*) (+ co-sc); "Paradiso per 4 ore" (Paradise for Four Hours) episode of *Amore in città* (*Love in the City*) (+ co-sc)
1955 *Il segno di Venere* (*The Sign of Venus*) (+ co-sc); *Pane, amore e ...* (*Scandal in Sorrento*) (+ co-sc)
1956 *Poveri ma belli* (*Poor but Beautiful*) (+ co-sc)
1957 *La nonna Sabella* (*Grandmother Sabella*) (+ co-sc); *Belle ma povere* (*Beautiful but Poor*; *Irresistible*) (+ co-sc)
1958 *Venezia, la luna e tu* (*I due gondolieri*; *Venice, the Moon, and You*) (+ co-sc); *Poveri milionaire* (*Poor Millionaires*) (+ co-sc)
1959 *Il vedovo* (*The Widower*) (+ co-sc); *Il mattatore* (*Love and Larceny*)
1960 *Un amore a Roma* (*Love in Rome*); *A porte chiuse* (*Behind Closed Doors*) (+ co-sc)
1961 *Una vita difficile* (*A Difficult Life*)
1962 *La marcia su Roma* (*The March to Rome*); *Il sorpasso* (*The Easy Life*; *The Overtaking*) (+ co-sc)
1963 *Il successo* (*The Success*) (co-d with Morassi, uncredited); *I mostri* (*The Monsters*; *Opiate '67*; *Fifteen from Rome*) (+ co-sc); *Il giovedi* (*Thursday*) (+ co-sc)
1964 *Il gaucho* (*The Gaucho*); "La telefonata" (The Telephone Call) episode of *Le bambole* (*The Dolls*)
1965 "Una giornata decisiva" (A Decisive Day) episode of *I complessi* (*The Complexes*) (+ co-sc); *L'ombrellone* (*The Parasol*; *Weekend Italian Style*) (+ co-sc)
1966 "Il marito di Attilia (or) Nei secoli fedele" (Attilia's Husband or Forever Faithful) episode of *I nostri mariti* (*Our Husbands*); *Operazione San Gennaro* (*Operation San Gennaro*; *Treasure of San Gennaro*) (+ co-sc)
1967 *Il tigre* (*The Tiger and the Pussycat*) (+ co-sc); *Il profeta* (*The Prophet*; *Mr. Kinky*) (+ co-sc)
1968 *Straziami ma di baci saziami* (*Tear Me But Satiate Me with Your Kisses*) (+ co-sc)
1969 *Vedo nudo* (*I See Everybody Naked*) (+ co-sc); *Il giovane normale* (*The Normal Young Man*) (+ co-sc)
1970 *La moglie del prete* (*The Priest's Wife*) (+ co-sc)
1971 *Noi donne siamo fatte cosi* (*Women: So We Are Made*) (+ co-sc)
1972 *In nome del popolo italiano* (*In the Name of the Italian People*)
1973 *Mordi e fuggi* (*Bite and Run*) (+ co-sc); *Sesso matto* (*Mad Sex*; *How Funny Can Sex Be?*) (+ co-sc)
1974 *Profumo di donna* (*Scent of a Woman*) (+ co-sc)
1975 *Telefoni bianchi* (*White Telephones*; *The Career of a Chambermaid*) (+ co-sc)
1976 *Anima persa* (*Lost Soul*) (+ co-sc)
1977 *La stanza del vescovo* (*The Bishop's Room*) (+ co-sc); *I nuovi mostri* (*The New Monsters*; *Viva Italia*) (co-d)
1978 *Primo amore* (*First Love*) (+ co-sc)
1979 *Caro Papa* (*Dear Father*) (+ co-sc)
1980 *Sunday Lovers* (co-d); *Sono fotogenico* (*I Am Photogenic*) (+ co-sc)
1981 *Fantasmo d'amore* (*Ghost of Love*) (+ co-sc)
1982 *Sesso e violentieri* (*Sex and Violence*) (+ co-sc)
1984 *Le Bon Roi Dagobert* (*Dagobert*); *E la vita continua*
1985 *Scemo di guerra*
1987 *Teresa*; *Il commissario Lo Gatto* (*Inspector Lo Gatto*)
1990 *Tolgo il disturbo*; *Come un bambino*
1991 *Vita Coi Figli*; *Sposa di Cristo*

Other Films:

1941 *Piccolo mondo antico* (Soldati) (asst d)
1942 *Giacomo l'idealista* (Lattuada) (asst d)
1951 *Anna* (Lattuada) (co-sc); *Totò e i re di Roma* (Steno and Monicelli) (co-sc)
1952 *Gli eroi della domenica* (Camerini) (co-sc)
1956 *Montecarlo* (Taylor) (co-sc)

Publications

By RISI: articles—

Interviews with L. Codelli, in *Positif* (Paris), September 1972, November 1974, and October 1975.
"Sous le rire, des choses graves...," an interview with J. A. Gili, in *Ecran* (Paris), November 1974.
Interview with A. Tassone, in *Cinéma* (Paris), January 1976.
"Le Cinéma: Dessins," in *Positif* (Paris), December 1977/January 1978.
Interview with D. Fasoli, in *Filmcritica* (Florence), May 1982.
"Dino Risi, le maestro," an interview with S. Garel, in *Cinema 90,* June 1990.

On RISI: book—

Vigano, A., *Dino Risi,* Milan, 1977.

On RISI: articles—

Garel, A., "Sur quatre films de Dino Risi," in *Image et Son* (Paris), November 1974.

Dino Risi on the set of *La moglie del prete*

"*Parfum de femme,*" in *Avant-Scène du Cinéma* (Paris), December 1975.
"*Une Vie difficile* Issue" of *Avant-Scène du Cinéma* (Paris), 15 February 1977.
Codelli, L., and A. Vigano, "Minimaximes," special section, in *Positif* (Paris), June 1978.
Turroni, G., "Film e figurazione: la riflessione metalinguistica," in *Filmcritica* (Rome), January 1979.
Codelli, Lorenzo, "Dino Risi," in *International Film Guide 1983,* London, 1982.
"Dino Risi," in *CinemAction!* (Toronto), January 1992.

* * *

No other genre of Italian filmmaking has proliferated as successfully as the Italian comedy, a mixture of sexual farce, romantic comedy, and biting social satire. Dino Risi is one of the prime movers in this field. Brother of the poet and documentary filmmaker Nelo Risi, he began work as a journalist before studying filmmaking with Jacques Feyder and becoming a screenwriter. Between 1946 and 1949 he directed thirteen shorts and documentaries. Although Risi worked on important neorealist films (as assistant to Alberto Lattuada), his real interests were always determined by an unswerving belief that cinema meant entertainment and enjoyment for the ticket buyer. Undoubtedly, he was one of the youthful forces who helped steer the industry away from the provocative criticism of the neorealist film and toward the superficial but expertly devised comedies in which it would become mired by the late 1950s. Moving out of the catastrophic postwar period and into the surefooted capitalism of the "economic miracle," Italian audiences sought out more of the lighter fare, putting Risi in the mainstream of surefire profit-makers.

Generally adhering to simplicity of story line and concentrating on a representation of the "little man," the unexceptional character finding himself in a frustrating, misapprehending world, Risi's work often suggests the influence of neorealist dramaturgy. In "Paradiso per quattro ore," an episode in *Amore in città,* Risi's camera has all the scrutinizing inquisitiveness of direct cinema, and his capacity to draw characters deftly and economically rivals that of Fellini. By means of such characterizations, he sets up a group of satirical situations at a teenage dance which abjure any need for larger narrative structures. Couples are physically mismatched or too well-matched; "Gregory Peck," the local teenage sheik, enters and takes command of the field with feigned suavity; a mother checks out each boy who asks her daughter to dance, approving only the best-dressed. This brief episode is the first of a series of particularly Risian character studies, films composed of a quick succession of effective vignettes illustrating the defects and eccentricities of the Italian male—often starring the well-balanced, polished acting duet of Vittorio Gassman and Ugo Tognazzi, who alternately played friends and adversaries and who brought a sense of personal tragedy to their work as well, in *I mostri, Vedo nudo, Sesso matto,* and *I nuovi mostri.*

In 1955 Risi made *Pane, amore, e...,* taking over from Comencini the popular series about the adventures of a *bersaglieri* marshall played by Vittorio De Sica and helping with it to launch the career of Sophia Loren. This was followed by *Poveri ma belli* and *Belle ma povere,* the story of two young "spivs" who court each other's sisters.

Seven films later, in 1961, Risi's satire assumed a serious edge and jettisoned much farcical frivolity. In *Una vita difficile* he takes stock of Italy's politico-economic transition in the story of a former partisan working as a left-wing journalist (Alberto Sordi) who finds himself set upon by government, family, and colleagues alike. *La marcia su Roma* is a wry look at Mussolini's famous march to power, depicting the cowardice and selfishness of the King who made it easy for Mussolini. Tognazzi plays an incorruptible magistrate who destroys evidence that would acquit the dishonest industrialist (Gassman) in *In nome del popolo italiano.* Several films, including *Il gaucho* and *Telefoni bianchi,* reflect Risi's desire to turn the satirical weapon of film on the film industry itself. The high calibre of the director's projects can often be attributed to excellence in the script stage due to the work of writers like Ennio Flaiano, Age and Scarpelli, Bernadino Zapponi, and Ettore Scola.

—Joel Kanoff

RITT, Martin

Nationality: American. **Born:** New York City, 2 March 1902. **Education:** Dewitt Clinton High School, New York City; attended Elon College, North Carolina; St. John's University, Brooklyn. **Military Service:** Served in U.S. Army Air Corps, 1942-46. **Career:** Member, Elia Kazan's Group Theater, 1937-42; stage director, New York City, from 1946; director and actor, live productions for CBS TV, 1948-51; blacklisted by television industry when a Syracuse grocer charged him with donating money to Communist China, 1951; taught acting at Actor's Studio, directed stage plays, 1951-56; directed first film, *Edge of the City,* 1957. **Died:** Of cardiac disease, in Santa Monica, California, 8 December 1990.

Films as Director:

1957 *Edge of the City* (*A Man Is Ten Feet Tall*); *No Down Payment*
1958 *The Long Hot Summer*
1959 *The Sound and the Fury*; *The Black Orchid*
1960 *Jovanka e le altri* (*Five Branded Women*)
1961 *Paris Blues*
1962 *Adventures of a Young Man* (*Hemingway's Adventures of a Young Man*)
1963 *Hud* (+ co-pr)
1964 *The Outrage*
1966 *The Spy Who Came in from the Cold* (+ pr)
1967 *Hombre* (+ co-pr)
1968 *The Brotherhood*
1970 *The Molly Maguires* (+ co-pr); *The Great White Hope*
1971 *Sounder*
1972 *Pete 'n' Tillie*
1974 *Conrack* (+ co-pr)
1976 *The Front* (+ pr)
1978 *Casey's Shadow*
1979 *Norma Rae*
1981 *Back Roads*
1983 *Cross Creek*
1985 *Slugger's Wife*
1986 *Murphy's Romance*
1987 *Nuts*
1989 *Stanley and Iris* (*Letters*; *Union Street*)

Other Films:

1944 *Winged Victory* (Cukor) (role as Gleason)
1975 *Der Richter und sein Henker* (*End of the Game*) (Schell) (role)

Publications

By RITT: articles—

"It's the Freedom That Counts," in *Films and Filming* (London), May 1961.

"Martin Ritt—Conversation," in *Action* (Los Angeles), March/April 1971.
"The Making of *Conrack*," an interview with B.J. Demby, in *Filmmakers Newsletter* (Ward Hill, Massachusetts), April 1974.
"Paranoia Paradise," an interview with A. Stuart, in *Films and Filming* (London), March 1977.
Interview with D. Chase, in *Millimeter* (New York), June 1979.
"Portrait of a Director: The Completely Candid Martin Ritt," an interview with D.S. Reiss, in *Filmmakers Monthly* (Ward Hill, Massachusetts), April 1981.
"Dialogue on Film: Martin Ritt," in *American Film* (Washington, D.C.), November 1983.
Interview with P. McGilligan, in *Film Comment* (New York), January/February 1986.

On RITT: book—

Whitaker, Sheila, *The Films of Martin Ritt*, London, 1972.

On RITT: articles—

Young, Colin, "The Hollywood War of Independence," in *Film Quarterly* (Berkeley), Spring 1959.
"Personality of the Month," in *Films and Filming* (London), April 1960.
Lightman, Herb, "The Photography of *Hud*," in *Action* (Los Angeles), July 1963.
McVay, Douglas, "The Best and Worst of Martin Ritt," in *Films and Filming* (London), December 1964.
Field, Sydney, "*Outrage*: A Print Documentary on Hollywood Film-Making," in *Film Quarterly* (Berkeley), Spring 1965.
Farber, Stephen, "*Hombre* and *Welcome to Hard Times*," in *Film Quarterly* (Berkeley), Fall 1967.
Cook, B., "Norma Rae's Big Daddy," in *American Film* (Washington, D.C.), April 1980.
Trainor, Richard, "Blacklist," in *Sight and Sound* (London), Summer 1988.

* * *

As his roots in the Group Theater would indicate, Martin Ritt was a man with a social conscience. He had himself known misfortune: he was blacklisted during the McCarthy years of the 1950s, an odious practice that he poignantly attacks in *The Front*. Often, the characters in his films are underdogs, victims of racism or sexism or capitalism who live lives of quiet dignity while struggling and occasionally triumphing over adversity.

Most refreshingly, Ritt's films are inhabited by odd couplings, characters from diverse backgrounds who unite for a common good while in the process expanding their own awareness. In *Norma Rae*, for example, Southern cotton mill worker Sally Field and New York Jewish labor organizer Ron Leibman form a curious coalition as they unionize a factory. In a hilarious sequence that symbolizes the cinema of Martin Ritt, Field joins the Lower East Side and Dixie when she petulantly utters the Yiddish word *kvetch* while complaining to Leibman. (The director also deals with the hardships of overworked, underpaid employees in *The Molly Maguires*, set in the Pennsylvania coal mines of the 1870s.)

Blacks and whites regularly align themselves in Ritt films, from easy-going, hard-working railroad yard worker Sidney Poitier befriending confused army deserter John Cassavetes in *Edge of the City* to schoolteacher Jon Voight educating underprivileged black children in *Conrack*. In all of these, the black characters exist within a white society, their identities irrevocably related to whites. The exception is *Sounder*, released after Hollywood had discovered that black audiences do indeed attend movies; it was produced at a point in time when blacks on movie screens were able to exist solely within a black culture. *Sounder* pointedly details the struggles of a black family to overcome adversity and prejudice. Although he spent his youth in New York City, Ritt set many of his films in the South, including *Sounder, Conrack, Norma Rae, The Long Hot Summer,* and *The Sound and the Fury*—the latter two based on William Faulkner stories.

Martin Ritt

While Ritt's films are all solidly crafted, they are in no way visually distinctive; Ritt cannot be called a great visual stylist, and is thus not ranked in the pantheon of his era's filmmakers.

—Rob Edelman

RIVETTE, Jacques

Nationality: French. **Born:** Jacques Pierre Louis Rivette in Rouen, 1 March 1928. **Education:** Lycée Corneille, Rouen. **Career:** Moved to Paris, began writing for *Gazette du cinéma,* 1950; writer for *Cahiers du Cinéma,* from 1952; worked on films in various capacities, 1952-56; directed first film in 35mm, *Le Coup de berger,* 1956, co-scripted with Chabrol, and featuring Godard and Truffaut in small roles; first feature, *Paris nous appartient,* released 1961; editor-in-chief, *Cahiers du Cinéma,* 1963-65; director for French TV, from late 1960s. **Awards:** Berlin Film Award, for *The Gang of Four,* 1989.

Films as Director:

1950 *Aux Quatre Coins*; *Le Quadrille*
1952 *Le Divertissement*

Jacques Rivette: ***Céline et Julie vont en bateau***

1956 *Le Coup de berger* (+ co-sc)
1961 *Paris nous appartient* (*Paris Belongs to Us*) (+ role as party guest)
1966 *La Religieuse* (*Suzanne Simonin, la religieuse de Denis Diderot*; *The Nun*) (+ co-sc); *Jean Renoir, le patron* (for TV)
1968 *L'Amour fou* (+ co-sc)
1971 *Out 1: noli me tangere* (for TV, never released)
1974 *Out 1: ombre* (+ co-sc); *Céline et Julie vont en bateau* (*Céline and Julie Go Boating*) (+ co-sc)
1976 *Duelle* (*Twilight*) (+ co-sc); *Noroît* (*Northwest*) (+ co-sc)
1979 *Merry-Go-Round* (+ co-sc) (released 1983)
1981 *Le Pont du Nord* (*North Bridge*); *Paris s'en va*
1984 *L'Amour par terre*
1985 *Hurlevent* (*Wuthering Heights*)
1989 *La Bande des quatre*
1990 *Belle noiseuse* (+ sc)
1991 *La Belle Noiseuse*
1993 *Divertimento*
1994 *Jeanne la Pucelle*
1995 *Haut Bas Fragile* (+ sc)

Other Films:

1955 *French Cancan* (Renoir) (asst); *Une Visite* (Truffaut) (ph)
1960 ***Chronique d'un été*** (*Chronicle of a Summer*) (Morin and Rouch) (role as Marilu's Boyfriend)

Publications

By RIVETTE: articles—

Regular contributor to *Cahiers du Cinéma* (Paris), 1952-69, and to *Arts* (Paris), 1950s.
Interviews, in *Sight and Sound* (London), Autumn 1963 and Autumn 1974.
Interview, in *Les Lettres Françaises* (Paris), April 1966.
Interview, in *Cahiers du Cinéma* (Paris), September 1968.
Interview, in *Film Comment* (New York), September/October 1974.
Interview, in *Film Quarterly* (Berkeley), Winter 1974/75.
Interview with S. Daney and J. Narboni, in *Cahiers du Cinéma* (Paris), May 1981.
Interview with P. Carcassonne and others, in *Cinématographe* (Paris), March 1982.

On RIVETTE: books—

Armes, Roy, *French Cinema Since 1946: Vol 2—The Personal Style,* New York, 1966.
Monaco, James, *The New Wave,* New York, 1976.
Rosenbaum, Jonathan, editor, *Rivette: Texts and Interviews,* London, 1977.

On RIVETTE: articles—

Burch, Noël, "Qu'est-ce que la Nouvelle Vague?," in *Film Quarterly* (Berkeley), Winter 1959.

Tyler, Parker, "The Lady Called A: or, If Jules and Jim Had Only Lived at Marienbad," in *Film Culture* (New York), Summer 1962.

Stein, E., "Suzanne Simonin, Diderot's Nun," in *Sight and Sound* (London), Summer 1966.

Lloyd, P., "Jacques Rivette and *L'Amour Fou*," in *Monogram* (London), Summer 1971.

"Rivette Issue" of *Cinéma* (Paris), March 1975.

Bassan, Raphaël, "Sur l'oeuvre de Jacques Rivette," in *Image et Son* (Paris), October 1981.

Chevrie, M., "Jacques Rivette, la ligne et l'aventure," in *Cahiers du Cinéma* (Paris), October 1984.

Blanchet, C., "Jacques Rivette: Une poétique du complot," in *Cinéma* (Paris), November 1984.

Magny, Joel, and others, "Côte cour, côte jardin," in *Cahiers du Cinéma* (Paris), February 1989.

Arecco, S., "Quel luogo supremo in cui il tempo e abolito ...," in *Filmcritica,* March 1990.

Roberti, B., "Il gioco infinito della 'messa in scena,'" in *Filmcritica,* March 1990.

Sabouraud, F., "Jue de pistes," in *Cahiers du Cinéma* (Paris), October 1990.

"Jacques Rivette," in *Cahiers du Cinéma* (Paris), June 1991.

Bassan, R., "La belle noiseuse," in *Revue du Cinema,* September 1991.

Riding, A., "One Artist Looks at Another in 'La belle noiseuse,'" in *New York Times,* 13 October 1991.

Sartor, F., "Rivette, Piccoli & Beart," in *Film en Televisie & Video,* November 1991.

Feldvoss, M., "Die schoene Querulantin, Divertimento," in *EPD Film,* March 1992.

Giavarini, L., "Ombre portee," in *Cahiers du Cinéma* (Paris), June 1992.

Lane, Anthony, "Back to the Easel," in *New Yorker,* September 20, 1993.

* * *

In the days when the young lions of the New Wave were busy railing against "Le Cinéma du papa" in magazine articles and attending all-night screenings of Frank Tashlin and Jerry Lewis movies at La Cinémathèque, Jacques Rivette was quite the keenest cinephile of them all. He made a short as early as 1950, worked as an assistant director for Becker and Renoir, and wrote endless essays for *Gazette du cinéma* and *Cahiers du cinéma,* which he would later edit. If his films seem academic and acutely self-reflexive, we must remember that he is somebody who has spent an eternity theorizing about cinema.

Rivette's first feature, *Paris nous appartient,* clocks in at a mere 140 minutes, and takes as its theme the abortive attempt by a group of French actors to mount a production of Shakespeare's *Pericles.* Rivette's fascination with the play-within-the-film, a leitmotif of his work, is given an initial, and not entirely successful, airing here. The film seems stage-bound, literary, and rather earnest, something which Rivette himself would later acknowledge: "I am very unhappy about the dialogue, which I find atrocious."

After his second feature, *La Religieuse,* was briefly banned (although it did make money) on account of its perceived anti-clericalism, Rivette decided to abandon conventional narrative cinema. Unlike Godard, who never managed to fully overcome the cult of personality (even *Tout Va Bien* and his other post-1968 collaborations with Gorin are inevitably treated as the great Jean-Luc's personal statements), Rivette easily evolved a kind of collective cinema, where the director's role was on a par with that of the actors. He gave his actors the task of improvising his/her dialogue and character and let the narrative stumble into being. A haphazard and risky working method, Rivette found this infinitely preferable to rigidly conforming to a preconceived script. As a result, Rivette's films rarely appear polished and finished.

The subject matter of Rivette films is often rehearsal: they explore the process of creation, rather than the finished artefact itself. *L'Amour fou,* an account of a company's attempts to produce Racine's *Andromaque* while the director and his actress-wife have a break-up, stops short of opening night.

In Rivette's monumental work *Out,* which lasts a full thirteen hours but has only ever seen the commercial light of day as *Ombre,* a four-hour shadow of itself, Rivette takes his theory of Direct Cinema as far as it will go. Determined to make a film "which, instead of being predicated on a central character presented as the conscience, reflecting everything that happens in the action, would be about a collective," the director assembled a large cast of actor/characters, amongst them Juliet Berto and Jean-Pierre Leaud. The film opens as a documentary. Only very gradually does Rivette allow a fictional narrative to emerge through the interaction of the cast. He describes *Out* as being "like a game ... a crossword."

Rivette commissioned Roland Barthes to write for *Cahiers du cinéma.* Rivette share Barthes' well-chronicled suspicion of authors, and he is also a fervent "intertextualist": his films abound in references to other books and films. *The Hunting of the Snark,* Aeschylus, Balzac, Shakespeare, and Edgar Allen Poe are all liable to be thrown into the melting pot. He mixes 16mm and 35mm film stock in *L'Amour fou,* where he actually depicts a television crew filming the same rehearsals that he is filming: a case of Chinese boxes, perhaps, that goes some way to explaining his unpopularity with certain British critics. Harold Hobson in the *Sunday Times* described the director's 1974 film, *Céline et Julie vont en bateau,* as a "ghastly exhibition of incompetent pretentiousness" while David Robinson suggested that *L'Amour par terre* offered the director's "now accustomed fey and onanistic silliness."

It should be noted that both of the films attacked above offered strong parts for women. Rivette, more than most of his New Wave contemporaries, has provided opportunities for actresses. He is hardly the most prolific director, and the length of his films has often counted against him. Nonetheless, his clinical, self-reflexive essays in film form, coupled with the sophisticated games he continues to play within the "house of fiction," reveal him as a cinematic purist whose commitment to the celluloid muse has hardly diminished since the heady days of the 1950s.

—G. C. Macnab

ROCHA, Glauber

Nationality: Brazilian. **Born:** Vitoria da Conquista, Bahia, Brazil, 14 March 1938. **Education:** Studied law, 1959-61. **Career:** Founder, "Lemanja-Filmes" production company, 1957; directed first feature, *Barravento,* 1962; went into exile, 1970; directed in Italy, France, and Spain, early 1970s; returned to Brazil, 1976. **Died:** In Rio de Janeiro, 22 August 1981.

Films as Director:

1957 *Um dia na rampa* (short) (co-d)
1958 *O patio* (short); *A cruz na praça* (short)
1962 *Barravento* (*The Turning Wind*) (+ co-sc)
1964 ***Deus e o diablo na terra do sol*** (*Black God, White Devil*) (+ co-pr, sc)
1965 *Amazonas Amazonas* (doc) (+ sc); *Maranhão 66* (doc) (+ sc)
1967 *Terra em transe* (*Land in Anguish*) (+ sc)

1968 *Cancer* (+ sc) (completed in Cuba, 1973-4)
1969 ***Antônio das Mortes*** (*O dragão da maldade contra o santo querreiro*) (+ co-pr, sc, art d)
1970 *Der leone have sept cabecas* (*The Lion Has Seven Heads*) (+ co-sc, co-ed); *Cabezas cortadas* (*Severed Heads*) (+ sc)
1975 *Claro* (+ sc)
1978 *Di* (doc short)
1979 *Jorjamado no cinema* (doc short)
1980 *A idade da terra* (*The Age of the Earth*) (+ sc)

Other Films:

1965 *A grande feira* (d of pr); *Menino de engenho* (pr)
1966 *A grande cidade* (co-pr)

Publications

By ROCHA: books—

Revisao critica do cinema brasiliero, Rio de Janeiro, 1962.
Revoluçao do cinema novo, Rio de Janeiro, 1981.
Riverao Sussuarana, Rio de Janeiro, 1981.
O seculo do cinema, Rio de Janeiro, 1983.

By ROCHA: articles—

"Un cinéma en transe," in *Image et Son* (Paris), January 1968.
Interview with M. Delahaye and others, in *Cahiers du Cinéma* (Paris), July 1969.
"Cinema Novo vs. Cultural Colonialism: An Interview with Glauber Rocha," in *Cineaste* (New York), Summer 1970.
Interview with Gordon Hitchens, in *Film Quarterly* (Berkeley), Fall 1970.
"Beginning at Zero: Notes on Cinema and Society," in *The Drama Review* (Cambridge, Massachusetts), Winter 1970.
Interview in *Afterimage* (London), no. 3, 1971.
"Lumière, magie, action," in *Positif* (Paris), December 1974.
Interviews in *Los años de la conmoción,* by Isaac Léon Frías, Mexico City, 1979.
"Humberto Mauro and the Historical Position of Brazilian Cinema," and "Hunger vs Profit Aesthetic," in *Framework* (Norwich), Autumn 1979.
"The History of Cinema Novo," in *Framework* (Norwich), Summer 1980.
"Epistolario: Cartas de Glauber Rocha," in *Cine Cubano* (Havana), no. 101, 1982.
"The Aesthetics of Hunger" and "Down With Populism," in *25 Years of the New Latin American Cinema,* edited by Michael Chanan, London, 1983.
"*Deus e o diablo na terra do sol,*" in *Filme Cultura* (Rio de Janeiro), January/April 1984.
"Cinema Novo and the Dialectics of Popular Culture," an interview in *Cinema and Social Change in Latin America,* by Julianne Burton, Austin, Texas, 1986.
"Revisión crítica del cine brasileño," "No al populismo," and "Estética de la violencia," in *Hojas de cine: Testimonios y documentos del Nuevo Cine Latinoamericano,* Mexico City, 1986.

On ROCHA: books—

Gerber, Raquel, editor, *Glauber Rocha,* Rio de Janeiro, 1977.
Johnson, Randal, and Robert Stam, *Brazilian Cinema,* New Brunswick, New Jersey, 1982.
Hollyman, Burnes, *Glauber Rocha and the Cinema Novo in Brazil: A Study of His Critical Writings and Films,* New York, 1983.
Johnson, Randal, *Cinema Novo X 5,* Austin, Texas, 1984.
Armes, Roy, *Third World Filmmaking and the West,* Berkeley, 1987.
Pierre, Sylvie, *Glauber Rocha,* Paris, 1987.
King, John, *Magical Reels: A History of Cinema in Latin America,* London, 1990.

On ROCHA: articles—

Callenbach, Ernest, "Comparative Anatomy of Folk Myth Films: *Robin Hood* and *Antonio das Mortes,*" in *Film Quarterly* (Berkeley), Winter 1969/70.
"Rocha Issue" of *Etudes Cinématographiques* (Paris), no. 97-99, 1973.
Gardies, R., "Structural Analysis of a Textual System: Presentation of a Method," in *Screen* (London), Spring 1974.
Cinema Novo Section of *Jump Cut* (Chicago), June 1976.
Van Wert, W.F., "Ideology in the Third World Cinema: A Study of Ousmane Sembene and Glauber Rocha," in *Quarterly Review of Film Studies* (Pleasantville, New York), no. 2, 1979.
Bruce, Graham, "Music in Glauber Rocha's Films," in *Jump Cut* (Berkeley), May 1980.
Armes, Roy, "The Incoherence of Underdevelopment," in *Films and Filming* (London), November 1981.
Rocha Section of *Cahiers du Cinéma* (Paris), November 1981.
Rocha Sections of *Cine Cubano* (Havana), nos. 100 and 101, 1982.
Rocha Section of *Film Cultura* (Rio de Janeiro), August/October 1982.
Paranagua, P., "Luis Buñuel et Glauber Rocha," in *Positif* (Paris), October 1983.
Burton, Julianne, "Modernist form in *Land in Anguish* and *Memories of Underdevelopment,*" in *Post Script* (Jacksonville, Florida), Winter 1984.
Gomes, P.E. Sallès, "Glauber Rocha," in *Positif* (Paris), April 1987.

* * *

"A camera in your hand and an idea in your head" was how Glauber Rocha described the minimalist conditions in which the filmmakers of Brazil's *Cinema Novo* (New Cinema) began. Though the origins of *Cinema Novo* can be traced to Nelson Pereira dos Santos's movie, *Rio 40 Degrees* (1955), the "official" starting point for the movement which redefined Brazilian and Latin American film is 1962, when Rocha directed *Barravento.* Rocha was *Cinema Novo*'s principle theorist and most flamboyant practitioner, developing many of its key concepts and realizing them on the screen.

The most important element in Rocha's theory of filmmaking was his recurrent insistence on discovering a filmic language of a uniquely Brazilian and Latin American quality, ending the practice endemic to neo-colonies of aping Hollywood and European cinema. This new idiom was to arise out of working directly within the reality of Latin America; thus, in one of his best-known essays, he argued that its core was an aesthetic of hunger and violence: "Hunger is the essence of our society ... and hunger's most noble cultural manifestation is violence." Rocha was looking for a popular, but not a populist, form of expression, and he felt that this would lead to new acting styles, different ways of using music and color, and innovative forms of montage.

If the base of Rocha's cinema was the traditional culture of Brazil, modern influences were also important. One of these was the Cuban revolution, which offered the example of radical social transformation in Latin America and made possible the birth of a truly Cuban cinematography. Another was the New Wave in France, from whence sprang the concept of the director as "auteur" which so influenced Rocha. Adherents of this concept pioneered the path he traveled from critic to filmmaker. However, Rocha clearly distinguished between the cinema of Europe, which expressed the existential anguish of the developed world, and the epic cinema which he believed more appropriate to articulating the social and economic crises of Latin America. As he pithily polemicized: "We're not interested in neurotics' problems, we're interested in the problems faced by those who are lucid."

After some short films, and relatively extensive experience as a critic, Rocha burst onto the international cinematic scene with *Barravento.* Although in later years he was to express dissatisfaction with the film, even disclaiming authorship because he had taken it over from another director half-way through the shooting, at the time he called it the "first great denunciation realized in Brazilian cinema." Filmed in a neo-realist style that was characteristic of many *Cinema Novo* directors—though this was the only instance in which Rocha employed this form—the movie focused on the harsh living conditions of a fishing village. If the work's realism is at odds with Rocha's later theatricality, the film nonetheless contains many of the elements found throughout his oeuvre. For example, the narrative leaps and the fighting which is choreographed as dancing presage the reflexivity of Rocha films that followed. Also present is the dialectic of the traditional and the modern, for while Rocha criticizes the mysticism that is part of the fishing people's underdevelopment, he also shows how their popular culture provides them with a defense against the ravages of capitalism.

The films that came after *Barravento* are extravagant and operatic, expressive of Rocha's search for a cinematic tropicalism equivalent to the magic realism contained in the work of Latin American writers such as Gabriel García Márquez and Alejo Carpentier. One of the unique formal elements in Rocha's work is the combination of this tropicalism with the self-reflexivity of the New Wave through such strategies as the placing of a film within a film in *Land in Anguish* and the use of highly stylized violence in *Antonio das Mortes.* In both of these films he also pricks the audience's critical sense by making the perspective of the works larger than that of their central protagonist, thus cutting back against the very identification that he simultaneously foments in the films. This sort of systematic contradiction is characteristic of Rocha's efforts to realize a dialectical form, and is perhaps most evident in the counter-point he consistently established between image and sound.

Rocha's concern with thematic dialectics is most apparent in his explorations of Brazilian popular culture, which he perceived as representing both a permanent rebellion against oppression and the evasion of social problems. His interest in resolving this contradiction and turning popular culture and myth into a progressive force is portrayed in *Black God, White Devil* and *Antonio das Mortes* through the conflict between the *cangaceiros,* the social bandits of the Brazilian Northeast, and Antonio, the killer hired to eradicate the law-breakers but who ends up embodying their social ideals. That it is popular—not populist—culture which offers the only possibility for national liberation is made explicit by Rocha in *Land in Anguish,* where he contrasts traditional values to those of liberal populism, which is shown to lead inevitably to co-option by the bourgeoisie. Rocha's efforts to form a genuinely Brazilian cinema, founded on authentic themes and expressed through an idiom peculiar to Latin America, led him to make beautiful and moving films which continue to speak for his ideals.

—John Mraz

RODRIGUEZ, Robert

Nationality: Mexican-American. **Born:** Austin, Texas, 1968. **Education:** Attended the University of Texas in Austin. **Family:** Married Elizabeth Avellan. **Career:** Began producing short videos at age twelve, with a camera purchased by his father, 1980; while in college, produced thirty low-budget super-8 and video shorts (the best-known of which is *Bedhead*), and created a cartoon strip, "Los Hooligans," based on his younger siblings, which ran for three years in the school newspaper, early 1990s; began directing first feature, *El Mariachi,* while still a University of Texas student, 1991. **Awards:** Audience Award, Sundance Festival, Independent Spirit Award, Best First Feature, Independent Spirit Award nomination, Best Director, Special Award for "exceptional directorial debut," National Board of Review, all 1993, all for *El Mariachi.*

Films as Director and Screenwriter:

1991 *El Mariachi* (+ co-pr, photo, ed)
1994 *Roadracers* (for TV)
1995 *Desperado* (+ ed); "The Misbehavers" segment of *Four Rooms* (+ ed)
1996 *From Dusk Till Dawn* (d only, + co-exec prod, ed)

Publications

By RODRIGUEZ: articles—

"On the Movie with Robert Rodriguez," an interview with Peter Travers, in *Rolling Stone* (New York), 18 March 1993.
"Suite Talk," an interview with Graham Fuller, in *Interview* (New York), October 1995.
"Four x Four," an interview with Peter Biskind, in *Premiere* (New York), November 1995.

On RODRIGUEZ: articles—

Broderick, P., "A Film for a Song," in *Filmmaker* (New York), vol. 1, no. 2, 1992/1993.
Chambers, V., "Robert Rodriguez," in *Premiere* (New York), January 1993.
Barrios, Greg, "A Borrowed Camera, $7,000 and a Dream," in *New York Times,* 21 February 1993.
Benson, Sheila, "Robert Rodriguez: Bordering on the Big Time," in *Interview* (New York), 8 March 1993.
Corliss, Richard, and Georgia Harbison, "Few Bucks, Very Big Bang," in *Time* (New York), 8 March 1993.
Lida, D., "The Almighty Peso," in *Village Voice* (New York), 9 March 1993.
Larsen, E., "Robert Rodriguez," in *Independent* (New York), May 1993.
Korman, Kenneth, "Mr. Mariachi," in *Video* (New York), December 1993.
Cohen, Jason, "A Killer Sequel," in *Texas Monthly* (Austin, Texas), August 1995.
Fuller, Graham, "A Spaghetti Western That's Good, Bad, Ugly, and the Funniest Film of the Summer," in *Interview* (New York), August 1995.
Clark, John, "Major League?," in *Premiere* (New York), September 1995.

* * *

In the 1990s, $7,000 is not a lot of money. It won't buy a house. It won't buy a new car. And, usually, it won't finance a movie. There are exceptions, however: *El Mariachi,* Robert Rodriguez's amazingly well-crafted, independently produced action film, which not only cost $7,000 to make but earned a theatrical release from a major studio, Columbia Pictures. The film's subsequent success established Rodriguez, just as *Slacker, Gas Food Lodging,* and *She's Gotta Have It* (to name three independent features of consequence) had respectively thrust Richard Linklater, Allison Anders, and Spike Lee into the limelight as fashionably idiosyncratic filmmakers.

The *El Mariachi* scenario is right out of pulp fiction, with the title character (played by Carlos Gallardo) an innocent young man who arrives in a small Mexican town. He is clad mostly in black, and his sole possession is a guitar. He is a mariachi, a singing troubadour, and he hopes to find a job entertaining in a bar. What our hero does not know is that another man, also wearing black and carrying a guitar case, also has arrived in town. Only inside his case is a mini-arsenal. He has come to murder a drug dealer who has cheated him out of money and unsuccessfully tried to have him killed. The heart of the scenario charts what happens when the drug dealer's henchmen mistake the mariachi for the assassin. In this regard, *El Mariachi* is strictly a formula action film. It is like a Western in that seemingly everyone in the town sports a firearm. No law enforcement officials are in sight, and there is an excessive amount of gunplay as well as many, many corpses.

The story surrounding the making of *El Mariachi* is a publicist's dream. From pre-production through post-production, Rodriguez served as practically a one-person film crew. In the opening credits, you learn that he directed, scripted, photographed, edited, and co-produced the film. In the closing credits, he is credited with the following: Additional Editing; Camera Operator; Co-Dolly Grip; Co-Special Effects; Sound/Music Editor; and Still Photographer. His lead actor has almost as many behind-the-scenes responsibilities. During the shoot, Carlos Gallardo sometimes would push Rodriguez and his camera in a borrowed wheelchair in order to achieve the required camera movement for a specific scene.

Rodriguez made the film (which he partially financed by serving as a guinea pig on a medical research project) with the intention of releasing it to the Spanish-language home video market. He modestly hoped that any success it enjoyed would allow him to direct additional low-budget, direct-to-video features.

What makes *El Mariachi* noteworthy beyond its bargain-basement budget is the manner in which Rodriguez (who was twenty-four years old when he made the film) cut corners during and after his shoot. He uses basic cinematic techniques—camera movement, music, sound effects, and especially editing—to tell his story as well as to create suspense and dramatic tension. There are over 2,000 separate shots in the movie; according to Rodriguez, the film's fast-paced editing was the result of his minuscule budget, which did not allow for the filming of complicated, drawn-out scenes. In fact, the film's rhythm is the direct result of its editing. (However, it must be noted that after purchasing the theatrical rights to *El Mariachi,* Columbia Pictures spent $100,000 to transfer the film from 16mm to 35mm and improve its sound and color).

All of this makes for great copy. But where does Rodriguez stand in relation to contemporary filmmakers? While his stylistic influences range from Sergio Leone and Sam Peckinpah to John Woo, his primarily link is to Quentin Tarantino. Both won kudos by creating action-oriented genre pieces which are at once nihilistic and super-hip, and which feature in-your-face cartoon violence and stratospheric body counts.

While *El Mariachi* is an impressive first feature, Rodriguez's subsequent work has been disappointing. When he chose to rework *El Mariachi* as *Desperado*—made on a budget quite a bit higher than $7,000—he did not have to cast an unknown in the lead role. At his disposal was super-hunk Antonio Banderas. In *From Dusk Till Dawn,* a road movie about two murderous brothers who contend with vampires, his cast includes George Clooney and Harvey Keitel. Fellow cinema wunderkind Tarantino acts in both films, and scripted *From Dusk Till Dawn.* However, while *Desperado* and *From Dusk Till Dawn* are flashy, and dazzlingly visual, they lack the allegorical qualities and narrative strengths of the best Leone and Peckinpah films. At their core, they are pointless exercises in violence, with set pieces which ramble on through their often bloody conclusions. *Desperado* and *From Dusk Till Dawn* seem designed to appeal to the tastes and sensibilities of video game-addicted adolescent boys.

Rodriguez's contribution to *Four Rooms,* an ensemble feature with segments also directed by Tarantino, Anders, and Alexandre Rockwell, is equally lackluster. His featurette, *The Misbehavers,* follows what happens when two perversely incorrigible youngsters are left in the care of a hotel bellboy (Tim Roth) by their gangster father (also played by Banderas).

From a purely cinematic standpoint, Robert Rodriguez has a plenitude of talent, and *El Mariachi* is a noteworthy debut feature, even a minor classic. However, at this very early stage of his career, one hopes that he will mature as an artist, and that the content of his scenarios eventually will match his visual flair.

—Rob Edelman

ROEG, Nicolas

Nationality: British. **Born:** Nicolas Jack Roeg in London, 15 August 1928. **Education:** Mercers School. **Family:** Married 1) Susan Rennie Stephens; 2) actress Theresa Russell. **Career:** Junior at Marylebone Studio, dubbing French films and making tea, from 1947; hired at MGM's Borehamwood Studios as part of camera crew on *The Miniver Story,* 1950; camera operator, from 1958; directed first feature (with Donald Cammell), *Performance,* 1970. **Address:** c/o Hatton and Baker, 18 Jermyn Street, London SW1Y 6HN, England.

Films as Director:

1970 *Performance* (co-d, + ph)
1971 ***Walkabout*** (+ ph)
1973 ***Don't Look Now***
1976 *The Man Who Fell to Earth*
1980 *Bad Timing*
1981 *Dallas Through the Looking Glass*
1982 *Eureka*
1985 *Insignificance*
1986 *Castaway*
1987 Episode in *Aria*
1988 *Track 29*
1989 *The Witches*; *Sweet Bird of Youth* (for TV)
1992 *Cold Heaven*
1993 *Heart of Darkness* (for TV)
1994 *Two Deaths*
1995 *Full Body Massage* (for TV)

Other Films:

(as camera operator)

1958 *A Woman Possessed* (Max Varnel); *Moment of Indiscretion* (Max Varnel); *The Man Inside* (Gilling)
1959 *The Great Van Robbery* (Max Varnel); *Passport to Shame* (Rakoff); *The Child and the Killer* (Max Varnel)
1960 *The Trials of Oscar Wilde* (Hughes); *Jazz Boat* (Hughes)

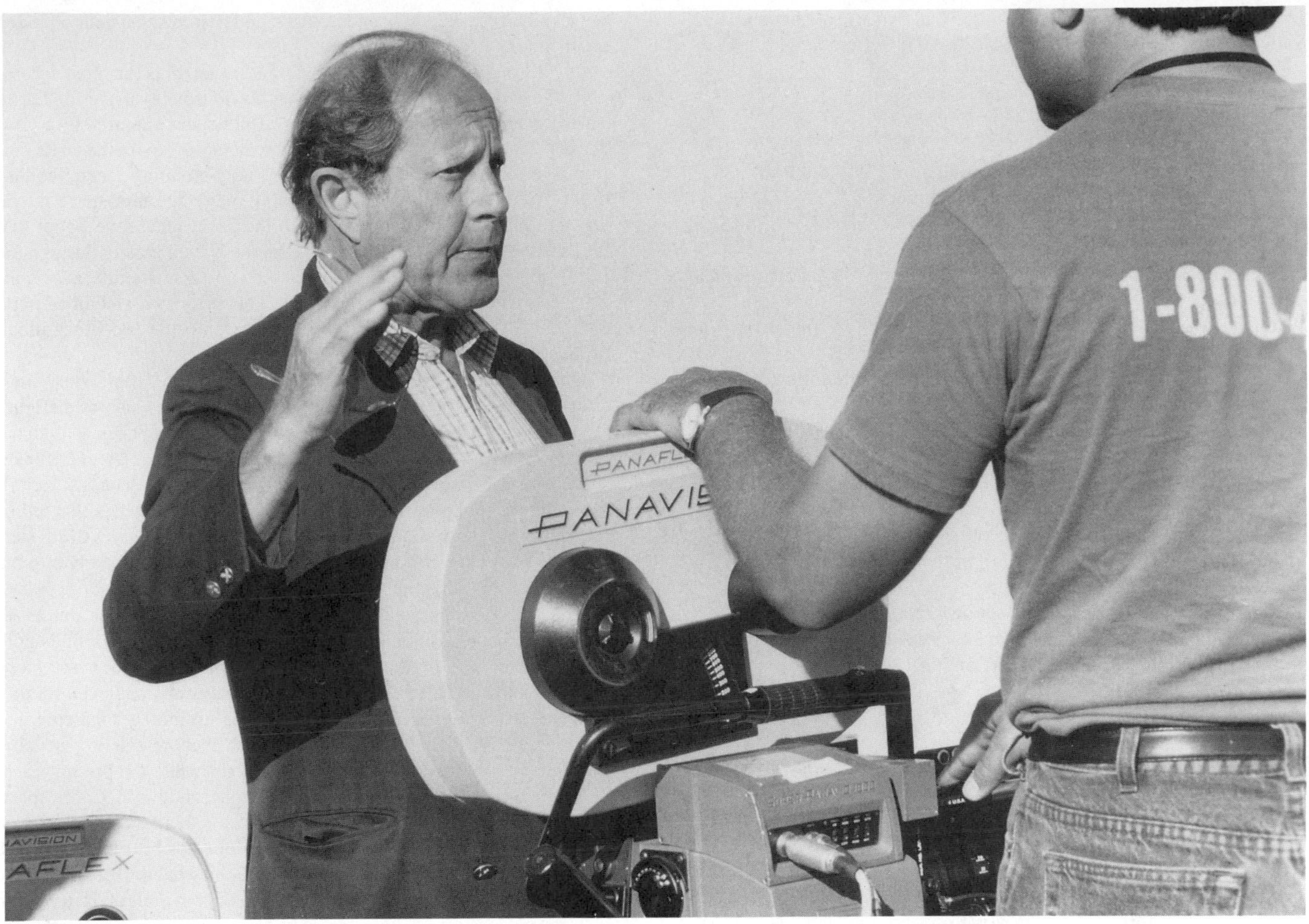

Nicolas Roeg

1961 *The Sundowners* (Zinnemann); *Information Received* (Lynn)
1962 ***Lawrence of Arabia*** (Lean) (2nd unit ph); *Dr. Crippen* (Lynn)

(as lighting cameraman)

1963 *The Caretaker* (Donner); *Just For Fun* (Flemyng); *Nothing But the Best* (Donner)
1964 ***The Masque of the Red Death*** (Corman); *The System* (*The Girl Getters*) (Winner); *Every Day's a Holiday* (Hill); *Victim Five* (*Code Seven, Victim Five*) (Lynn)
1965 *Judith* (Mann) (2nd unit ph)
1966 *A Funny Thing Happened on the Way to the Forum* (Lester); *Farenheit 451* (Truffaut)
1967 *Far from the Madding Crowd* (Schlesinger); *Casino Royale* (Huston et al) (some sections only)
1968 *Petulia* (Lester)

Publications

By ROEG: articles—

Interview with Gordon Gow, in *Films and Filming* (London), January 1972.
"*Don't Look Now*," an interview with Tom Milne and Penelope Houston, in *Sight and Sound* (London), Winter 1973/74 and Winter 1974/75.
"Nick Roeg ... and the Man Who Fell to Earth," with John Lifflander and Stephan Shroyer, in *Inter/View* (New York), March 1976.
"Roegian Thought Patterns," an interview with J. Padroff, in *Films* (London), September 1981.
Interview with Harlan Kennedy, in *Film Comment* (New York), March/April 1983.
Interview with Richard Combs, in *Sight and Sound* (London), Winter 1984/85.
Interview with Brian Baxter in *Films and Filming* (London), July 1985.
"Private Lives," an interview with G. Fuller, in *Stills* (London), June/July 1985.
Interview with Nick Roddick, in *Cinema Papers* (Melbourne), September 1985.
Interview, in *La Revue du Cinema* (Paris), October 1985.
"Roeg Time," an interview with A. Alvarez, in *Interview* (New York), July 1988.

On ROEG: books—

Feineman, Neil, *Nicolas Roeg,* Boston, 1978.
Houston, Beverle, and Marsha Kinder, *Self and Cinema: A Transformalist Perspective,* Pleasantville, New York, 1980.
Walker, John, *The Once and Future Film: British Cinema in the '70s and '80s,* London, 1983.
Lanza, Joseph, *Fragile Geometry: The Films, Philosophy, and Misadventures of Nicolas Roeg,* New York, 1989.
Sinyard, Neal, *The Films of Nicolas Roeg,* London, 1991.

Izod, John, *The Films of Nicolas Roeg: Myth and Mind,* London, 1992.
Salwolke, Scott, *Nicolas Roeg, Film By Film,* Jefferson, North Carolina, 1993.

On ROEG: articles—

Kleinhans, Chuck, "Nicolas Roeg: Permutations Without Profundity," in *Jump Cut* (Chicago), September/October 1974.
Mayersberg, Paul, "Story So Far ... *The Man Who Fell to Earth,*" in *Sight and Sound* (London), Autumn 1975.
Kolker, Robert, "The Open Texts of Nicolas Roeg," in *Sight and Sound* (London), Spring 1977.
Kennedy, H., "The Illusions of Nicholas Roeg," in *American Film* (Washington, D.C.), January/February 1980.
Cros, Jean-Louis, and Raymond Lefevre, "Pour rehabiliter Nicholas Roeg," in *Image et Son* (Paris), June 1981.
Gomez, J., "Another Look at Nicholas Roeg," in *Film Criticism* (Edinboro, Pennsylvania), Fall 1981.
Pursell, M., "From Gold Nugget to Ice Crystal: The Diagenetic Structure of Roeg's *Eureka,*" in *Literature/Film Quarterly* (Salisbury, Maryland), vol. 11, no. 4, October 1983.
Heaton, L., "A True Castaway," in *Photoplay Movies & Video* (London), February 1987.
Bernhard, S., "Right on Track," in *American Film* (New York), April 1988.
Barker, Adam, "What the Detective Saw, or A Case of Mistaken Identity," in *Monthly Film Bulletin* (London), July 1988.

* * *

Nicolas Roeg is a visual trickster who plays havoc with conventional screen narratives. Choosing an oblique storytelling formula, he riddles his plots with ambiguous characters, blurred genres, distorted chronologies, and open-ended themes to invite warring interpretations.

Even the most facile Roeg synopsis betrays alienation and incongruity, with characters getting caught in bewildering and hostile situations. His first effort, *Performance* (with co-director Donald Cammell) offers a dark look at the last days of a pursued gangster (James Fox) who undergoes a psychosexual identity change while hiding out with a has-been rock star (Mick Jagger). This psychedelic cornucopia of androgynous sex, violence, and Borges allusions blessed and cursed Roeg with the lingering label "cult director."

We had already been warned of Roeg's charming peculiarities during his cinematographer days. Such notable films as *Far from the Madding Crowd* and *Fahrenheit 451* had odd, even anachronistic looks that sometimes ran contrary to the story proper. In fact, the latter film barely resembles Truffaut at all and looks more Roegish with its dreamy color schemes and chilly atmospherics.

Even Roeg's relatively tame second feature, *Walkabout,* based on a novel by James Vance Marshall, has narrative trap doors. Jarring cross-cuts, sensuous photography, and Edward Bond's enigmatic script are more satisfying to mystics than humanists. Marshall's novel is much more clear in its tale of two Australian children (Jenny Agutter and Lucien John) who get lost in the outback and are saved by an aborigine (David Gumpilil). Roeg's version is a more complex and fatalistic expose of people from separate cultures who have no hope of connecting.

Roeg flaunts a talent for shattering a relatively simple story into heady fragments with his adaptation of Daphne du Maurier's *Don't Look Now.* The tragedy of a couple (Julie Christie and Donald Sutherland) haunted in Venice by a psychic (Hilary Mason) claiming to communicate with their drowned daughter turns into something more than just a proto-Hitchcock thriller. As in most Roegian journeys, we emerge from *Don't Look Now* more discombobulated than we were at the start. Is the psychic a fraud? Is there foul play among the Venetian authorities? Could the occult implications be just a ruse? Roeg operates on a logic that is more visceral than intellectual. Instead of outright clues, we get recurrent shapes, sounds, colors, and gestures that belie a hidden order linking people and events.

Of all Roeg's work, *The Man Who Fell to Earth* is the most accomplished and de-centered. A space alien (David Bowie) arrives on Earth, starts a multi-million dollar enterprise and is later captured by a government-corporate collusion. What threatens to be another trite sci-fi plot becomes, in Roeg's hands, a visually stunning mental conundrum. All the continuity gaffes plaguing many an outer-space movie are here intentionally exacerbated to the point where we doubt that the "visitor" is really an alien at all. We see events mostly through the alien's abstruse viewpoint as days, months, years, even decades transpire sporadically and inconsistently. The story is a sleight-of-hand distraction that forces our attention more onto the transitory mood of loneliness and dissociation.

Unlike a purely experimental director who would flout story-lines altogether, Roeg retains the bare bones of old genres only to disfigure them. His controversial *Bad Timing* could easily have been an updated "Inner Sanctum" spin-off with its pathological lovers (Art Garfunkel and Theresa Russell) and the voyeuristic detective (Harvey Keitel) snooping for foul play. But the film unfolds with vignettes that tell us one thing and show another. Time and motive—the staples of mysteries—are so deviously jumbled that we can only resign ourselves to the Roeg motto that "nothing is what it seems."

Roeg's under-appreciated and least-seen *Eureka* starts out as an adventure about a Yukon prospector (Gene Hackman) who finds gold and becomes one of the world's richest men. But soon the story splinters into soap opera, romance, murder mystery, and even splatter film—a tortuous, visionary, frustrating, and ultimately mad epic.

Since *Eureka,* Roeg has been more skittish about re-entering the labyrinth. Films like *Insignificance* (about a night when the prototypes of Albert Einstein, Marilyn Monroe, Joe DiMaggio, and Joe McCarthy meet) and *Castaway* (based on Lucy Irvine's ordeal with a lover on a deserted island) have shades of the older Roeg films but lack his gift for reckless lust. The "Twilight Zone" teasers reemerge somewhat in *Track 29,* where he teams with absurdist scriptwriter Dennis Potter in a tale about a woman beleaguered by a man her own age who claims to be her illegitimate son. Once more, Roeg treats us to another story about frustrated love and the fragile border between "reality" and hallucination.

The career of Nicolas Roeg has in recent years been in sad decline. By far his best work in this latter period was the made-for-television feature *Heart of Darkness,* a moody, shadowy adaptation of the famed Joseph Conrad novella. *Cold Heaven* is a muddled drama about a husband who may or may not have been killed in a grisly accident just as his wife is set to leave him.

Though a well-intentioned expose of the horror of war, *Two Deaths,* his most recent film, shows no evidence of a return to form. It is set during a bloody conflict. Several aristocratic types sit in a room awaiting the start of a dinner party. They complain about trifling matters, while on the streets around them blood flows like the wine they will enjoy with their meal. All too obviously, before the night is over the violence outside will intrude on their lives, with much moralizing and sermonizing along the way. Roeg beats you over the head with unsubtle symbolism: the guests slurp down oysters while a woman bleeds to death outside, and he even uses the cliched image of a dead dove.

—Joseph Lanza, updated by Rob Edelman

ROHMER, Eric

Nationality: French. **Born:** Jean-Marie Maurice Scherer in Tulle, 4 April 1920. **Career:** Literature teacher at lycée, Nancy, 1942-50; film critic, from 1948; founder, with Godard and Rivette, *La Gazette* *du cinéma,* Paris, 1950; Co-wrote book on Alfred Hitchcock with Claude Chabrol, 1957; editor-in-chief of *Cahiers du cinéma,* 1957-63; directed first feature, *Le Signe du lion,* 1959; made the "Six contes moraux" (Six Moral Tales), 1962-73; with *La Femme de l'aviator,* began new series, "Comédies et proverbes," 1980; began new series, "Tales of the Four Seasons," 1989. **Awards:** Prix Max Ophüls, for *My Night at Maud's,* 1970; Prix Louis Delluc, and Prix Méliès, for *Claire's Knee,* 1971; Special Jury Prize, Cannes Festival, for *The Marquise of O ...,* 1976; Silver Bear and share of International Critics Prize, Berlin Festival, for *Pauline at the Beach,* 1983; Officier des Arts et des Lettres. **Address:** 26 av. Pierre-1er-de-Serbie, 75116 Paris, France.

Films as Director and Scriptwriter:

1950 *Journal d'un scélérat*
1951 *Présentation ou Charlotte et son steak* (*Charlotte and Her Steak*)
1952 *Les Petites Filles modèles* (co-d) (unfinished)
1954 *Bérénice*
1956 *La Sonate à Kreutzer* (*The Kreutzer Sonata*)
1958 *Véronique et son cancre*
1959 *Le Signe du lion* (*Sign of the Lion*; *The Sign of Leo*)
1963 *La Boulangerie de Monceau* (first of the "Contes moraux"; following five films identified by "CM" and number assigned by Rohmer); *La Carrière de Suzanne* (*Suzanne's Profession*) (CM no. 2)
1964 *Nadja à Paris*
1964-69 Films for educational television: *Les Cabinets de physique au XVIIIème siècle*; *Les Métamorphoses du paysage industriel*; *Perceval*; *Don Quichotte*; *Edgar Poë*; *Pascal*; *La Bruyère*; *Mallarmé*; *La Béton dans la ville*; *Les Contemplations*; *Hugo architecte*; *Louis Lumière*
1965 Films for television series "Cinéastes de notre temps": *Carl Dreyer, Le Celluloid et la marbre*; "Place de l'étoile" episode of *Paris vu Par ...* (*Six in Paris*)
1966 *Une Étudiante d'aujourd'hui*
1967 *La Collectionneuse* (CM no. 4) (+ sc); *Fermière à Montfaucon*
1969 *Ma Nuit chez Maud* (*My Night at Maud's*) (CM no. 3)
1970 *Le Genou de Claire* (*Claire's Knee*) (CM no. 5)
1972 *L'Amour l'après-midi* (*Chloe in the Afternoon*) (CM no. 6)
1976 *La Marquise d'O ...* (*The Marquise of O ...*)
1978 *Perceval le Gaullois*
1980 *La Femme de l'aviateur* (*The Aviator's Wife*)
1982 *Le Beau Mariage* (*The Perfect Marriage*)
1983 *Loup y es-tu?* (*Wolf, Are You There?*); *Pauline à la plage* (*Pauline at the Beach*)
1984 *Les Nuits de la pleine lune* (*Full Moon in Paris*)
1986 *Le Rayon vert* (*The Green Ray*)
1987 *L'Ami de mon amie* (*My Girlfriend's Boyfriend*; *Boyfriends and Girlfriends*); *Quatre Aventures de Reinette et Mirabelle* (*Four Adventures of Reinette and Mirabelle*)
1989 *Conte de printemps* (*A Tale of Springtime*)
1992 *Un Conte d'hiver* (*A Tale of Winter*)
1993 *L'Arbre, le maire et la Mediatheque* (*The Tree, The Mayor, and the Mediatheque*)
1995 *Les rendez-vous de Paris*

Other Films:

1954 *Berenice* (role)
1993 *Francois Truffaut: portraits voles* (*Francois Truffaut: Stolen Portraits*) (Toubiana, Pascal) (appearance)

Publications

By ROHMER: books—

Hitchcock, with Claude Chabrol, Paris, 1957; Oxford, 1992.
Six contes moraux, Paris, 1974.
The Marquise of O, New York, 1985.
Le Gout de la beauté, edited by Jean Narboni, Paris, 1989.
A Taste for Beauty, Cambridge, 1990.

By ROHMER: articles—

Interview with Graham Petrie, in *Film Quarterly* (Berkeley), Summer 1971.
"Eric Rohmer Talks About Chloe," in *Inter/View* (New York), November 1972.
"Programme Eric Rohmer," an article and interview with Claude Beylie, in *Ecran* (Paris), April 1974.
"*La Marquise d'O ...,*" in *Avant-Scène du Cinéma* (Paris), October 1976.
"Rohmer's Perceval," an interview with G. Adair, in *Sight and Sound* (London), Autumn 1978.
"Rehearsing the Middle Ages," an interview with N. Tesich-Savage, in *Film Comment* (New York), September/October 1978.
"Un Allegorie policière," with Claude Chabrol, in *Avant-Scène du Cinéma* (Paris), June 1980.
Interview with Pascal Bonitzer and Serge Daney, in *Cahiers du Cinéma* (Paris), May 1981.
"Comedies and Proverbs," an interview with F. Ziolkowski, in *Wide Angle* (Athens, Ohio), vol. 5, no. 1, 1982.
"Eric Rohmer on Film Scripts and Film Plans," an interview with R. Hammond and J. P. Pagliano, in *Literature-Film Quarterly* (Salisbury, Maryland), vol. 10, no. 4, October 1982.
Interview with A. Carbonnier and Joel Magny, in *Cinéma* (Paris), January 1984.
Interview with H. Niogret, and others, in *Positif* (Paris), November 1986.
Interview with Serge Toubiana and Alain Philippon, in *Cahiers du Cinéma* (Paris), February 1987.
Rohmer, Eric, "L'homme a la sacoche," in *Cahiers du Cinema* (Paris), November 1989.
Rohmer, Eric, "Lettre d' Eric Rohmer, a Jacques Davila," in *Cahiers du Cinema* (Paris), March 1990.
Rohmer, Eric, "Nestor Almendros, naturellement," in *Cahiers du Cinema* (Paris), April 1990.
Interview with A. de Baecque and others, in *La Revue du Cinema* (Paris), April 1990.
Interview with G. Legrand and F. Thomas, in *Positif* (Paris), April 1990.
Rohmer, Eric, "La pensee et la parole," in *Avant Scene Cinema* (Paris), May 1990.
Interview with A. Danton, in *Cahiers du Cinema* (Paris), February 1992.
Interview, in *Cahiers du Cinema* (Paris), May 1993.
Rockwell, John, "Eric Rohmer Writes His Own *Winter Tale,* in *New York Times,* 27 March 1994.

On ROHMER: books—

Mellen, Joan, *Women and Sexuality in the New Film,* New York, 1973.
Vidal, Marion, *Les contes moraux d'Eric Rohmer,* Paris, 1977
Angeli, G., *Eric Rohmer,* Milan, 1979.
Mancini, Michele, *Eric Rohmer,* Florence, 1982.
Estève, Michel, *Eric Rohmer 2,* Paris, 1986.
Magny, Joel, *Eric Rohmer,* Paris, 1986.
Crisp, C. G., *Realist and Moralist,* Bloomington, Indiana, 1988.
Bonitzer, Pascal, *Eric Rohmer,* Paris, 1991.

Eric Rohmer: ***Ma Nuit chez Maud***

Showalter, E., editor, *My Night at Maud's: Eric Rohmer, Director,* New Brunswick, New Jersey, 1993

On ROHMER: articles—

"Eric Rohmer," in *Film* (London), Spring 1968.

Clarens, Carlos, "L'Amour Sage," in *Sight and Sound* (London), Winter 1969/70.

"Director of the Year," in *International Film Guide 1972,* London, 1971.

Nogueira, Rui, "Eric Rohmer: Choice and Chance," in *Sight and Sound* (London), Summer 1971.

Mellen, Joan, "The Moral Psychology of Rohmer's Tales," in *Cinema* (Beverly Hills), Fall 1971.

"Director of the Year," *International Film Guide* (London, New York), 1972.

Amiel, M., and others, "Dossier-auteur: Eric Rohmer à la recherche de l'absolu," in *Cinéma* (Paris), February 1979.

Fieschi, J., and others, "Dossier: le cinéma d'Eric Rohmer," in *Cinématographe* (Paris), February 1979.

"*Pauline à la plage* Issue" of *Avant-Scène du Cinéma* (Paris), no. 310, 1983.

Borchardt, E., "Eric Rohmer's *The Marquise of O* ... and the Theory of the German Novella," in *Literature/Film Quarterly* (Salisbury, Maryland), vol. 12, no. 2, April 1984.

Bergala, Alain, and Alain Philippon, "Eric Rohmer, la Grace et la Rigeur," in *Cahiers du Cinéma* (Paris), October 1984.

"Rohmer Issue" of *Avant-Scène du Cinéma* (Paris), January 1985.

"*Le Rayon Vert* Issue" of *Avant-Scène du Cinéma* (Paris), December 1986.

Pym, John, "Silly Girls," in *Sight and Sound* (London), Winter 1986/87.

Elia, M., "Les jeux de la liberté et du hasard dans les films d'Eric Rohmer," in *Séquences* (Montreal), August 1987.

Aumont, Jacques, "L'extraordinaire et le solide," in *Avant-Scène du Cinéma* (Paris), December 1987.

Cossardeaux, C., article in *Cahiers du Cinema* (Paris), January 1988.

Sarris, Andrew, "Films in Focus: Rohmer Resurgent," in *Village Voice* (New York), 19 July 1988.

Teyssedre, A., article in *Cahiers du Cinema* (Paris), April 1990.

Mayne, Richard, "Still Waving, Not Drowning," in *Sight and Sound* (London), Summer 1990.

Durgnat, Raymond, "Eric Rohmer: The Enlightenment's Last Gleaming," in *Monthly Film Bulletin* (London), July 1990.

Rosenbaum, Ron, "Eric Rohmer's Cinema of Snooze," in *Madamoiselle,* July 1991.

Taboulay, C., article in *Cahiers du Cinema* (Paris), February 1992.

Noel, B., article in *Positif* (Paris), May 1992.

Dalle Vacche, Angela, "Painting Thoughts, Listening to Images: Eric Rohmer's *The Marquise of O...,*" in *Film Quarterly* (Berkeley), Summer 1993.

* * *

By virtue of a tenure shared at *Cahiers du Cinéma* during the 1950s and early 1960s, Eric Rohmer is usually classified with Truffaut, Godard, Chabrol, and Rivette as a member of the French New Wave. Yet, except for three early shorts made with Godard, Rohmer's films seem to share more with the traditional values of such directors as Renoir and Bresson than with the youthful flamboyance of his contemporaries. Much of this divergence is owed to an accident of birth. Born Jean-Marie Maurice Scherer in Tulle in 1920, Rohmer was at least ten years older than any of the other critic/filmmakers in the *Cahiers* group. By the time he arrived in Paris in 1948, he was an established teacher of literature at the lycée in Nancy and had published a novel, *Elizabeth* (1946), under the pseudonym Gilbert Cordier. When he joined the *Cahiers* staff in 1951 Rohmer had already spent three years as a film critic with such prestigious journals as *La Revue du cinéma* and Sartre's *Les Temps modernes.* Thus Rohmer's aesthetic preferences were more or less determined before he began writing for *Cahiers.*

Still, the move proved decisive. At *Cahiers* he encountered an environment in which film critics and filmmaking were thought of as merely two aspects of the same activity. Consequently, the critics who wrote for *Cahiers* never doubted that they would become film directors. As it turned out, Rohmer was one of the first to realize this ambition. In 1951 he wrote and directed a short 16mm film called *Charlotte and Her Steak* in which Godard, the sole performer, plays a young man who tries to seduce a pair of offscreen women. Two of his next three films were experiments in literary adaptation. These inaugurated his long association with Barbet Schroeder, who produced or co-produced all of Rohmer's subsequent film projects.

In 1958 filmmaking within the *Cahiers* group was bustling. Rivette, Truffaut, and Chabrol were all shooting features. Rohmer, too, began shooting his first feature, *Sign of the Lion.* The result, however, would not be greeted with the same enthusiasm that was bestowed on Godard and Truffaut. Rohmer has always maintained that his films are not meant for a mass audience but rather for that small group of viewers who appreciate the less spectacular qualities of the film medium. Unfortunately, *Sign of the Lion* failed to find even this elite audience. And while Truffaut's *The 400 Blows* and Godard's *Breathless* were establishing the *Cahiers* group as a legitimate film force, it was not until 1963 that Rohmer was able to secure funding for a film of any length. That same year he ended his association with *Cahiers du Cinéma.* The journal had for some time been moving away from the aesthetic policies of Bazin and towards a more leftist variety of criticism. Rohmer had always been viewed as something of a reactionary and was voted down as co-director. He chose to leave the magazine and devote his entire career to making films. At just this moment Barbet Schroeder was able to find money for a short 16mm film.

While writing the scenario for *Suzanne's Profession,* Rohmer conceived the master plan for a series of fictional films, each a variation on a single theme: a young man, on the verge of committing himself to one woman, by chance meets a second woman whose charms cause him to question his initial choice. As a result of this encounter, his entire way of thinking, willing, desiring, that is to say, the very fabric of his moral life starts to unwind. The young man eventually cleaves to his original choice, his ideal woman against whom he measures all his other moral decisions, but the meeting with the second woman (or, as is the case in *Claire's Knee,* a trinity of women) creates a breathing space for the young man, a parenthesis in his life for taking stock. The vacillations of the young man, who often functions as the film's narrator, comprise the major action of the six films, known as "Six Moral Tales."

Rohmer recognizes the irony in his use of cinema, a medium which relies on objective, exterior images, to stage his interior moral dramas. But by effecting minute changes in the exterior landscape, he expresses subtle alterations in his protagonist's interior drama. This explains why Rohmer pays such scrupulous attention to rendering surface detail. Each film in the "Six Moral Tales" was shot on the very location and at the exact time of year in which the story is set. Rohmer was forced to postpone the shooting of *My Night at Maud's* for an entire year so that Jean-Louis Trintignant would be available during the Christmas season, the moment when the fiction was scripted to begin. The painter Daniel in *La Collectioneuse* is played by Daniel Pommereulle, a painter in real life. The Marxist historian and the priest who preaches the sermon at the end of *My Night at Maud's* are, in real life, historian and priest. The female novelist of *Claire's Knee* is a novelist and the married couple of *Chloe in the Afternoon* are portrayed by husband and wife. Such attention to detail allowed Rohmer to realize an advance in the art of cinematic adaption with his next two films, *The Marquise of O ...* and *Perceval.*

As he entered the 1980s, Rohmer completed two films of a new series of moral tales which he calls "Parables." In contrast to the "Six Moral Tales," the "Parables" are not played out on the interior landscape of a single character but rather engage an entire social milieu. In *The Aviator's Wife,* a young postal clerk trails his mistress around Paris to spy on her affair with another man. During his peregrinations, he meets a young female student and loses track of his mistress. He decides he prefers the company of the young student, only to discover her in the arms of another man. *The Perfect Marriage* chronicles the attempts of a young Parisian woman to persuade the man whom she had decided will make her a perfect husband that she will, in turn, make him the perfect wife. She discovers, too late, that he has been engaged to another woman all along.

Emerging from the crucible of the French New Wave, Rohmer has forged a style that combines the best qualities of Bresson and Renoir with distinctive traits of the Hollywood masters. And though he was never as flamboyant as Godard or Truffaut, Rohmer's appeal has proved much hardier. The international success that met *My Night at Maud's* and *The Marquise of O ...* built a following that awaited the new set of moral dilemmas limned by each further installment of the "Parables" with eagerness and reverence.

During the 1980s, Rohmer went on to complete his "Comedies and Proverbs" series. His films include: *Pauline at the Beach,* a clever, sharply observed comedy which compares the dishonesty of adult alliances and the forthrightness of adolescence; *Full Moon in Paris,* which details the plight of a willful young woman and her involvement with different men; *Four Adventures of Reinette and Mirabelle,* which insightfully contrasts the lives of two young women, one from the country and the other from the city; and *My Girlfriend's Boyfriend,* which also follows what happens when two very different women begin a friendship and then start playing amorous games with a pair of men. Here, Rohmer proves a master at writing dialogue for characters whose romantic feelings change with the setting sun.

Rohmer then began a new series, called "Tales of the Four Seasons." Its initial entry, *A Tale of Springtime,* is a typically refreshing Rohmer concoction. The filmmaker tells the story of Jeanne, a high school philosophy teacher with time on her hands who meets and befriends a younger woman. The latter's father has a girlfriend her age, whom she despises, so she decides to play cupid for Jeanne and her dad. Rohmer's dialogue is typically casual yet revealing. Beneath what may seem like superficial chatter, much is divulged regarding the characters' wants, needs, and desires. *A Tale of Springtime* is a film about everyday feelings and reactions—and Rohmer transforms these everyday feelings and reactions into art. His characters find themselves in uncomfortable or comic situations that are nonetheless of a real-life quality that can be related to on a universal level.

Rohmer's follow-up, *A Tale of Winter*, is the bittersweet story of a hairdresser who has an affair while on holiday but accidently gives her lover the wrong address when they part. They lose touch, and she has his baby. All that remains of the child's father are some photos and memories, her undying love—and the baby. Two ardent but very different suitors have become her boyfriends, and she cannot decide which one to marry. Rohmer's point, beautifully illustrated, is that one should not settle for second best in love. Follow your heart, and allow it to lead you to your true destiny.

A Tale of Winter is flawed, if only because Rohmer's heroine is far too flaky; she is constantly wavering and unfairly leading on the two suitors in a manner that makes it difficult to sympathize with her plight. Still, Rohmer's thesis is well-taken; even middle-of-the-road Rohmer is far more engaging than the works of most other filmmakers.

—Dennis Nastav, updated by Rob Edelman

ROMERO, George A.

Nationality: American. **Born:** The Bronx, New York, February 4, 1940. **Education:** Studied art, design, and theater at Carnegie-Mellon Institute, Pittsburgh. **Career:** Maker of short 8mm films, from 1954; actor/director in Pittsburgh, 1960s; directed first feature, 1968; established "Latent Image" to produce commercial/industrial films, early 1970s; worked extensively as TV director, 1970s; began collaboration with make-up artist Tom Savini on *Martin,* 1977; began association with writer Stephen King on *Creepshow,* 1982; executive producer, *Tales From the Dark Side,* for TV, 1983. **Address:** Lives in Pittsburgh, Pennsylvania, U.S.A.

Films as Director:

1954/6 *The Man from the Meteor* (short); *Gorilla* (short); *Earthbottom* (short)
1958 *Curly* (short); *Slant* (short)
1960/62 *Expostulations* (short)
1968 *Night of the Living Dead* (*Night of the Flesh Eaters*) (+ co-sc, ph, ed)
1972 *There's Always Vanilla* (*The Affair*) (+ ph)
1973 *Hungry Wives* (*Jack's Wife*; *Season of the Witch*) (+ sc, ph, ed); *The Crazies* (*Code Name: Trixie*) (+ sc, ed)
1977 *Martin* (+ sc, ed)
1978 *Zombies* (*Dawn of the Dead*) (+ sc, co-ed, role as TV director)
1981 *Knightriders* (+ sc, co-ed)
1982 *Creepshow* (+ co-ed)
1985 *Day of the Dead* (+ sc)
1988 *Monkey Shines* (+ sc)
1990 *Due occhi diabolici* (*Two Evil Eyes*) (+ sc); *Dark Half* (+ sc, pr)
1993 *The Dark Half* (+ sc, ex prod)

Other Films:

1986 *Flight of the Spruce Goose* (Majewski) (role)
1987 *Creepshow 2* (Gornick) (sc)
1990 *Night of the Living Dead* (Savini) (sc); *Tales from the Dark Side—The Movie (Cat From Hell episode)* (Harrison) (sc)
1990 *Night of the Living Dead* (Savini) (sc, co-exec prod)
1991 ***The Silence of the Lambs*** (Demme) (role)

Publications

By ROMERO: books—

Martin (novelization, with Susanna Sparrow), New York, 1977.
Dawn of the Dead (novelization, with Susanna Sparrow), New York, 1979.

By ROMERO: articles—

"Filming *Night of the Living Dead,*" an interview with A. B. Block, in *Filmmakers Newsletter* (Ward Hill, Massachusetts), January 1972.
"George Romero from *Night of the Living Dead* to *The Crazies,*" in *Inter/View* (New York), April 1973.
Interview with D. Chase, in *Millimeter* (New York), October 1979.
"The McDonaldization of America," an interview with J. Hanners and H. Kloman, in *Film Criticism* (Edinboro, Pennsylvania), Fall 1982.

By ROMERO: articles—

Interview, in *L'Ecran Fantastique* (Paris), July 1982.
Interview, in *Cinefantastique* (Oak Park, Illinois), October 1985.
Interview, in *L'Ecran Fantastique* (Paris), December 1986.
Interview, in *Cinefantastique* (Oak Park, Illinois), May 1988.
Interview, in *Cinefantastique* (Oak Park, Illinois), March 1989.

On ROMERO: books—

McCarty, John, *Splatter Movies: Breaking the Last Taboo,* New York, 1981.
Hoberman, Jay, and Jonathan Rosenbaum, *Midnight Movies,* New York, 1983.
Wood, Robin, *Hollywood From Vietnam to Reagan,* New York, 1986.
Gagne, Paul R., *"The Zombies That Ate Pittsburgh": The Films of George A. Romero,* New York, 1987.
Newman, Kim, *Nightmare Movies: A Critical History of the Horror Film From 1968,* London, 1988.

On ROMERO: articles—

McCollough, P., "A Pittsburgh Horror Story," in *Take One* (Montreal), November 1974.
Stewart, Robert M., "George Romero: Spawn of EC," in *Monthly Film Bulletin* (London), February 1980.
Yakir, Dan, article in *American Film* (Washington, D.C.), May 1981.
Vernieri, J., "A Day with the Dead," in *Film Comment* (New York), May/June 1985.
Profile, in *Millimeter* (New York), August 1985.
Rosenbaum, Jonathan, article in *Cahiers du Cinema* (Paris), February 1989.
Profile, in *Cineforum* (Bergamo), July-August 1989.
"Twilight's Last Gleaming: George A. Romero," in *Monthly Film Bulletin* (London), February 1990.
Grant, B. K., "Taking Back the *Night of the Living Dead*: George Romero, Feminism & the Horror Film," *Wide Angle,* vol. 14, no. 1, 1992.
Caruso, Giacomo, article in *Cineforum* (Bergamo), March 1993.

* * *

Between 1968 and 1979, George A. Romero produced a body of work comparable in distinction to that of Larry Cohen in the same period: both are centered in the horror genre, both extremely uneven, but they achieve in certain instances an impressive intensity and concentration. Above all, both are rooted in (and appear significantly dependent upon) the disturbances in American society during that period.

Romero's first film, *Night of the Living Dead,* is a landmark in the evolution of the American horror film. It proved decisively that significant and commercially successful work in that genre could be produced outside Hollywood, on a low budget, independent of major studios. Thematically, it drew together the twin attitudes that underlie and motivate what must now be regarded as the golden age of horror film: general disillusionment with authority/government (this is the period of Vietnam), and specific disillusionment with the institution whereby authority/domination structures are transmitted, the patriarchal nuclear family. The film opens with a brother and sister driving to a remote country graveyard over which flies the American flag; they are reluctantly honoring a dead father neither of them cares about on behalf of an invalid mother. They bicker in a repetition of childhood behavior patterns: brother taunts sister, who responds with bitterness and helpless frustration. The first zombie to appear in the film then lurches forward to attack sister and kill brother, serving as the emanation of family tensions and the embodiment of the "living dead" that is the legacy of the American past. The film follows through from this premise with exemplary rigor, paralleling the zombies and the authorities as equally mindless and destructive, flouting all generic expectations (the young couple, traditionally the guarantee of the perpetuation of the family, are killed and devoured, the hero is mistaken for a zombie and casually shot down by the sheriff's posse), tracing the progress of the nuclear family's self-destruction, as zombie-daughter kills and eats her parents and "dead" brother leads the final assault on his sister.

The sequel, *Dawn of the Dead,* is even more remarkable, and among the few outstanding American films of the 1970s. Here the zombies are associated with entrapment in consumer-capitalism, from whose structures and characteristic relationship patterns the surviving humans must learn to extricate themselves or succumb to the "living dead." The heroine, Fran, ultimately rejects marriage (clearly depicted as an institution for the oppression of women); her lover—a traditional male needing the support of a subordinated woman for the confirmation of his identity—becomes a zombie. The ending of the film centers on two emblems of male authority: the surviving male surrenders his rifle to the zombies while the pregnant Fran (cast earlier as helpless and dependent) flies the helicopter for their escape. The two have become mutually supportive but no future love-relationship is suggested. They fly off to an uncertain destination and a precarious future in which new male/female relationships must be constructed.

Romero's achievement thus far is centered on those two films, though around them are grouped several related early works which are more distinguished than their neglect suggests. *The Crazies* takes up concerns from *Night of the Living Dead* and tentatively anticipates the more forward-looking potential of *Dawn of the Dead; Jack's Wife* and *Martin* are a closely linked pair of minor works concerned with their eponymous protagonists' striving for identity and dignity in a debased, materialistic world that offers them no recognition or autonomy, and their flight into roles (witch and vampire, respectively) that offer false prestige and worse entrapment.

Since *Dawn of the Dead,* Romero's career seems to have lost its sense of direction. Its powerful radical impulse, rooted in the Vietnam/Watergate syndrome of disillusionment, protest, and subversion, did not sustain itself into the Reagan era. One may feel some sympathy (though little admiration) for the attempt in *Knight Riders* to convey liberal attitudes (and, regrettably, liberal platitudes) to the youth audience, but the film remains essentially a remake of *Alice's Restaurant,* ten years too late and with all the complexities ironed out. Nothing, however, had prepared one for *Creepshow,* a five-part anthology film made in collaboration with Stephen King, virtually indistinguishable from the British Amicus horror films of the 1970s. The same pointlessness, the same moral squalor is present: nasty people doing nasty things to other nasty people.

As the years have passed, Romero has been unable to rekindle his mantle as an innovative horror master. Most recently he scripted and co-executive produced a remake of *Night of the Living Dead,* directed by his longtime collaborator, Tom Savini. This color version copied the original practically scene-by-scene, but the result was a major disappointment, at best run-of-the-mill and at worst preposterous. He then directed *The Dark Half,* a tepid shocker from source material by Stephen King, about a college teacher who publishes best-sellers under a pseudonym. A student discovers and threatens to expose his double identity; eventually, his "alter ego" takes on a life of its own and commences a killing spree.

Despite this lackluster record, Romero maintains his place in the horror film pantheon if only for the first *Night of the Living Dead* and his major influence on David Cronenberg, Wes Craven, Tobe Hooper, and other contemporary horror masters.

—Robin Wood, updated by Rob Edelman

ROOS, Jørgen

Nationality: Danish. **Born:** Gilleleje, 14 August 1922. **Family:** Married Naomi Silberstein, 1957. **Career:** Cameraman, 1939-47; founder, Copenhagen film club, with painter Albert Mertz; scriptwriter, director, and cameraman on documentaries, from 1947; co-founder, Association of Danish Film Directors, 1956. **Awards:** Silver Bear, Berlin Festival, for *Knud,* 1966. **Address:** Ved Amagerport 5, DK-2300 Copenhagen S, Denmark.

Films as Director:

(documentaries, unless indicated)

1942 *Flugten* (*The Flight*) (co-d with Albert Mertz)
1943 *Kaerlighed paa Rulleskøjter* (co-d with Mertz); *Hjertetyven* (*Thief of Hearts*) (co-d with Mertz)
1944 *Richard Mortensens bevaegelige Maleri*; *Historien om en Mand* (*Story of a Man*) (co-d with Mertz) (unfinished)
1947 *Paa Besøg hos Kong Tingeling* (co-d with Mertz); *Goddag Dyr!* (co-d with Mertz); *Isen brydes* (co-d); *Johannes V. Jensen*; *Opus 1*; *Reflexfilm*
1948 *Mikkel*
1949 *Paris på to måder*; *Jean Cocteau*; *Tristan Tzara, dadaismens fader*; *Det definitive afslag på anmodningen om et kys* (co-d)
1950 *Spiste horisonter* (co-d); *Johannes Jørgensen i Assisi*; *Shakespeare og Kronborg* (*Hamlet's Castle*)
1951 *Historien om et slot, J. F. Willumsen*
1952 *Den strømlinjede gris*; *Slum*; *Feriebørn*
1953 *Lyset i natten*; *Spaedbørnet*; *The Newborn* (*Goddag børn*); *Skyldig—ikke skyldig*
1954 *Kalkmalerier*; *Inge bliver voksen*; *Avisen*; *Martin Andersen Nexos sidste rejse*; *Johannes Jørgensen i Svendborg*
1955 *Mit livs eventyr* (*My Life Story*)
1956 *Sølv*
1957 *Ellehammer*; *Johannes Larsen*

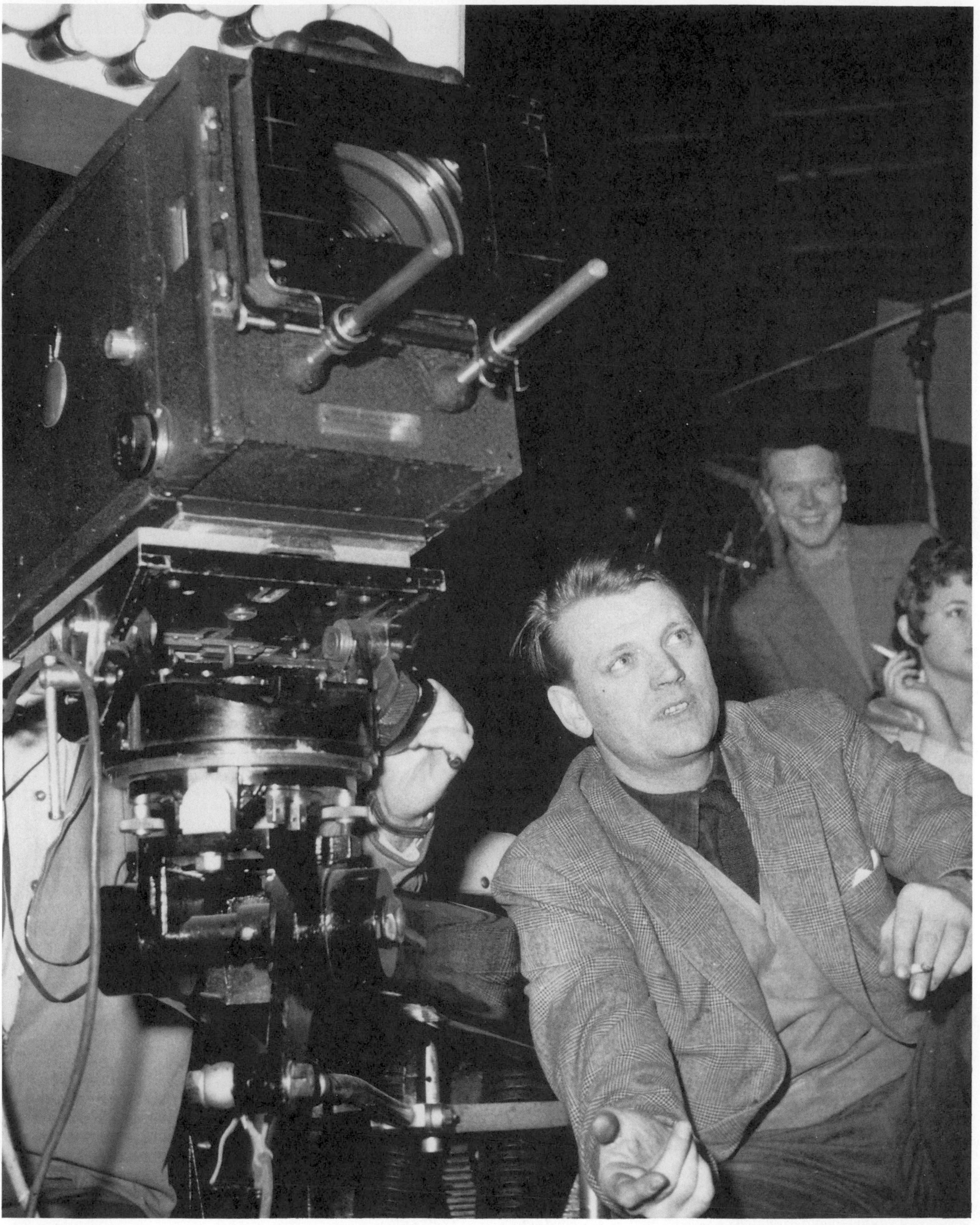

Jørgen Roos

1958 *Magie du diamant* (*Magic of the Diamond*); *6-dagesløbet* (*The Six Days*) (feature)
1959 *Friluft* (*Pure Air*)
1960 *En by ved navn København* (*A City Called Copenhagen*); *Danish Design*; *Staphylokok-faren*
1961 *Føroyar Faerøerne*; *Hamburg*
1962 *Vi haenger i en tråd*
1963 *Oslo*
1965 *Støj*
1966 *Carl Th. Dreyer*; *Knud*; *Sisimiut*
1967 *En fangerfamilie i Thuledistriktet*; *17 minutter Grønland*; *Grønlandske dialektoptagelser og trommedanse fra Thuledistriktet*; *Et år med Henry*
1968 *Ultima Thule*
1969 *Det er tilladt at vaere åndssvag*
1970 *Kaláliuvit* (*Er du grønlaender*)
1971 *Andersens hemmelighed*
1972 *Huse til mennesker*; *Udflytterne*; *To maend i ødemarken*; *Ulrik fortaeller en historie*
1974 *I den store pyramide*; *J. Th. Arnfred*
1975 *Andersen hos fotografen*
1977 *14 dage i jernalderen*; *Monarki og demokrati*
1978 *Carl Nielsen 1865-1931*
1979 *Nuuk 250 år*
1980 *Slaedepatruljen Sirius*; *Grønland*
1982 *Knud Rasmussens mindeekspedition til Kap Seddon*
1984 *Lille Cirkus*; *De unge gamle*
1985 *Harald Sæverud—1 en alder af 88 år*
1988 *Chr. IV—Tegselver icke mig*
1989 *Den levende virkelighed*; *Victor Brockdorff—en portrætskitse*

Other Film:

1971 *Er i bange* (*Are You Afraid*) (Carlsen) (ph)

* * *

Jørgen Roos is the unrivalled master of the Danish documentary film, having worked for more than forty years in this field. He has won international recognition and has received prizes at international short film festivals. Only once has he tried to direct a feature film.

Roos started out as a cameraman, taught by his brother, Karl Roos, and Theodor Christensen, the pioneer of the documentary film in Denmark. Karl Roos and Theodor Christensen were both active filmmakers, and also eminent film theoreticians. Christensen was influenced by the British documentary movement and considered himself a committed documentary filmmaker. Jørgen Roos was inspired by those two and he acquired a wide knowledge of the theory and the history of cinema. After having worked as a cameraman, he made his first experimental film in 1942 with the painter Albert Mertz, and this pair created the most interesting and original Danish avant-garde films of the 1940s. Since 1952 Roos has made numerous documentaries for governmental institutions and private companies. Besides these commissioned films he has worked on projects of his own, and in recent years he has had his own production company.

To the commissioned film Roos has brought a fresh and unconventional approach, and his way of solving the official tasks is often witty, surprising, and keen. His films are always one-man projects. He writes his own scripts, directs, and is often cameraman. And he is always the editor, because it is in the cutting room that he gives his films their definitive and personal form. Roos is superior in the short form: his editing is rhythmical, and his films have a fascinating, fast-moving drive. He likes to tease, to find unusual points of view, and he has an eye for the curious. His brilliant technique, however, can lead him into the superficial.

In 1955 Roos made one of his best films, *Mit livs eventyr,* about Hans Andersen. In this film he brought the iconographic technique to perfection, and he used it in later films. One of his most popular and widely known films is *A City Called Copenhagen,* from 1960, an untraditional and ironic tourist film. Roos was asked to make similar city portraits of Hamburg and Oslo, and has portrayed Danish personalities such as Nobel laureate Johannes V. Jensen, Carl Th. Dreyer, Greenland explorer Knud Rasmussen, and composer Carl Nielsen. In the last twenty or so years Roos has shown a special interest in Greenland. He has lost his heart to this exceptional country and he has explored both the old and the new Greenland in many films. The cool and detached view which was characteristic of Jørgen Roos's films has been replaced by a deep-felt commitment to the land which he, more than anyone else, has brought to the screen.

—Ib Monty

ROSI, Francesco

Nationality: Italian. **Born:** Naples, 15 November 1922. **Education:** Studied law, Naples University. **Military Service:** 1942. **Career:** Radio journalist in Naples, early 1940s; worked in theatre as actor, stage designer, and assistant director, Rome, from 1946; assistant director and script collaborator, through 1956, also dubbing director for Italian versions of foreign films; directed first film, *La sfida,* 1957. **Awards:** Special Jury Prize, Venice Festival, for *La sfida,* 1958; Silver Bear for Best Direction, Berlin Festival, for *Salvatore Giuliano,* 1963; Golden Lion, Venice Festival, for *Le mani sulla città,* 1963.

Films as Director and Co-Scriptwriter:

1958 *La sfida* (*The Challenge*)
1959 *I magliari*
1961 ***Salvatore Giuliano***
1963 *Le mani sulla città* (*Hands over the City*)
1965 *Il momento della verità* (*The Moment of Truth*) (co-d)
1967 *C'era una volta* (*More than a Miracle*)
1970 *Uomini contro*
1972 *Il caso Mattei* (*The Mattei Affair*)
1973 *A proposito Lucky Luciano* (*Lucky Luciano*)
1976 *Cadaveri eccelenti* (*Illustrious Corpses*)
1979 ***Cristo si è fermato a Eboli*** (*Christ Stopped at Eboli*)
1981 *Tre fratelli* (*Three Brothers*)
1984 *Carmen* (*Bizet's Carmen*)
1988 *Cronaca di una morte annunciata* (*Chronicle of a Death Foretold*)
1990 *Dimenticare Palermo* (*To Forget Palermo*)
1993 *Neapolitan Diary*
1996 *La Tregua* (*The Truce*)

Other Films:

1947 ***La terra trema*** (Visconti) (asst d)
1949 *La domenica d'agosto* (Emmer) (asst d)
1950 *Tormento* (Matarazzo) (asst d)
1951 *I figli di nessuno* (Matarazzo) (asst d); *Parigi e sempre parigi* (Emmer) (asst d, co-sc); *Bellissima* (Visconti) (asst, co-sc)

1952 *Camicie Rosse* (supervised post-production after director Goffredo Alessandri abandoned project); *I vinti* (Antonioni) (asst d); *Processo alla città* (Zampa) (sc)
1954 *Carosello Napoletano* (Giannini) (asst d); *Proibito* (Monicelli) (asst d); *Senso* (Visconti) (asst d)
1955 *Racconti Romani* (Franciolini) (co-sc)
1956 *Il bigamo* (Emmer) (asst d, co-sc)

Publications

By ROSI: articles—

Interview with Gideon Bachmann, in *Film Quarterly* (Berkeley), Spring 1965.
"Moments of Truth," an interview with John Lane, in *Films and Filming* (London), September 1970.
Interviews with Michel Ciment, in *Positif* (Paris), January 1974, February 1979, and March 1990.
Interview with Gary Crowdus, in *Cineaste* (New York), vol. 7, no. 1, 1975.
Interviews in *Sight and Sound* (London), Summer 1976 and Winter 1981/82.
"Un Débat d'idées, de mentalités, de moralités," in *Avant-Scéne du Cinéma* (Paris), May 1976.
"Sono lo psicologo del film e non del personaggio," an interview with F. Durazzo Baker, in *Cinema Nuovo* (Bari), October 1979.
"Personalizing Political Issues," an interview with Gary Crowdus, in *Cineaste* (New York), vol. 12, no. 2, 1982.
Interview with M. Kimmel, in *Films in Review* (New York), May 1982.
"Chronicle of a Film Foretold," an interview with Michel Ciment, in *Sight and Sound* (London), Winter 1986/87.
"Guardian Lecture with Francesco Rosi," an interview with D. Malcolm, in *Film* (London), April/May 1988.
"Filmare Palermo," an interview with A. Piersanti, in *Rivista ddel Ceinematografo* (Rome), July/August 1992.
"Le kid at La Terra Tremble," in *Positif* (Paris), June 1994.
"Et Dourant, Naples est une ville legere," an interview with Philippe Piazzo, in *Télérama* (Paris), 29 June 1994.
"Il etait une fois le cinema," in *Positif* (Paris), July/August 1994.
Interview with Howard Feinstein, in *Film Comment* (New York), January/February 1995.

On ROSI: books—

Michalczyk, John J., *The Italian Political Filmmakers*, Cranbury, New Jersey, 1986.
Ciment, Michel, editor, *Le Dossier Rosi*, Paris, 1987.
Gesu, Sebastiano, *Francesco Rosi*, Italy, 1991.

On ROSI: articles—

Lane, John, "A Neapolitan Eisenstein," in *Films and Filming* (London), August 1963.
Rosi Section of *Image et Son* (Paris), June/July 1976.
Alemanno, R., "Da Rosi a Petri todo modo dentro il contesto," in *Cinema Nuovo* (Bari), July/August 1976.
Rosi Section of *Thousand Eyes* (New York), November 1976.
Rosi Section of *Positif* (Paris), May 1980.
"Francesco Rosi Issue" of *Cinéma* (Zurich), vol. 28, no. 2, 1982.
"*Tre fratelli* Issue" of *Avant-Scène du Cinéma* (Paris), 1 June 1982.
Ciment, Michel, "Rosi in a New Key," in *American Film* (Washington, D.C.), September 1984.
Lennon, Peter, "A 'Cinema Fanatic' with a Social Conscience," in *Listener* (London), 14 May 1987.
Rosi Sections of *Positif* (Paris), May and June 1987.
Crowdus, Gary, "Francesco Rosi: Italy's Postmodern Neorealist," in *Cineaste* (New York), October 1994.
Klawans, Stuart, "Illustrious Rosi," in *Film Comment* (New York), January/February 1995.

* * *

The films of Francesco Rosi stand as an urgent riposte to any proposal of aesthetic puritanism as a *sine qua non* of engaged filmmaking. From *Salvatore Giuliano* to *Illustrious Corpses* and *Chronicle of a Death Foretold,* he uses a mobilisation of the aesthetic potential of the cinema not to decorate his tales of corruption, complicity, and death, but to illuminate and interrogate the reverberations these events cause. If one quality were to be isolated as especially distinctive and characteristic it would have to be the sense of intellectual passion, of direction propelled by an impassioned sense of inquiry. This can be true in a quite literal way in *Salvatore Giuliano,* in which any "suspense" accruing to Giuliano's death is put aside in favour of a search for another kind of knowledge; and *The Mattei Affair,* in which the soundtrack amasses evidence which is presented virtually in opposition to the images before us; or, in a more metaphoric sense, *Christ Stopped at Eboli,* which represents an inquiry into the social conditions of the South of Italy.

Rosi traces the evolution of his style to his early experience as an assistant on Rosselini's *Terra Trema,* where he learnt the value of immediacy, improvisation, and the use of non-professional performers. It was a mode of filmmaking that suited the exploration of concerns found within a particular current in Italian thought. It finds expression in the writings of Carlo Levi and Leonardo Sciascia, both of whom deal with the issue of the South and both of whose work Rosi has adapted for the screen, along with, latterly, that of Primo Levi. It is a current that also finds political expression in the work of Antonio Gamsci. Rosi's films are perhaps above all the films of an industrialising Italy, the Italy of Fiat, that exists dialectically with that of the peasant South.

Throughout his work there is an abiding interest in the social conditions in which individuals live their lives and their expression at the public or civic level, licit or illicit. Concern with organised crime and its social roots—though free from any taint of sociologizing—appears as a major thread through films as diverse as *Salvatore Giuliano, Hands over the City, The Mattei Affair, Lucky Luciano,* and *Chronicle of a Death Foretold.* Although Rosi uses the appurtenances of the thriller or the gangster film (in *Lucky Luciano,* for instance), his interests, as Michel Ciment has pointed out, are not at all with whodunnit but with what the crime reveals about the social context of individual lives. *Lucky Luciano,* for example, is not (unlike *The Godfather*) in the business of creating monsters but of creating a way of understanding the men who are thus mythologised. It is a tribute to Rosi's virtuosity and commitment that the trajectory he describes is not a whit less exciting.

He may examine the mesh of the individual and his context from the point-of-view of the public sphere (*Illustrious Corpses*) or the private (*Three Brothers* or *Christ Stopped at Eboli*). The issue might be the ruthless mechanics of market forces in *Hands over the City,* or the process whereby the Mafia is set in place in *The Mattei Affair.* But above all Rosi remains a pre-eminent craftsman of the cinema in his acute and responsive relationship with his regular or occasional collaborators, especially with his cinematographers and musicians.

Of recent films, *Forget Palermo* was criticised for superficiality and some awkwardness in its casting of James Belushi. Rosi argues that its initially touristical mode was part of its point. The film follows an American "man of power" to his Sicilian roots. His honeymoon trip cannot be innocent of political implications and the tangled web of drugs and finance is meticulously revealed.

Francesco Rosi

Neapolitan Diary was a more personal exploration of the same theme, taking Rosi himself back to the city of his birth and back to the location for *Hands over the City.* It is harsh and lucid, but never without hope of change, not even in bleak interviews with school-aged drug dealers. The South, urges Rosi, is not other than Italy but the place where the nation's problems outcrop most painfully. Primo Levi's *The Truce,* the subject of Rosi's most recent film, follows the homeward journey of a mixed group of Auschwitz prisoners. In it Rosi has said he sees a foreshadowing of the tensions that have frighteningly emerged in Europe since the fall of the Wall.

If his most recent films may be less wholly satisfying than, say, the urgent definitiveness of *Hands over the City,* or less rigorously aesthetic than *Illustrious Corpses,* they still reveal a rare and vital intellectual commitment to cinema as a platform for debate and testimony—a form, he has said, of active participation in public life.

—Verina Glaessner

ROSSELLINI, Roberto

Nationality: Italian. **Born:** Rome, 8 May 1906. **Family:** Married 1) Marcella de Marquis (marriage annulled), two children; 2) actress Ingrid Bergman, 1950 (divorced), three children, including actress Isabella; 3) screenwriter Somali Das Gupta (divorced), one son. **Career:** Worked on films, in dubbing and sound effects, then as editor, from 1934; directed first feature, *La nave bianca,* 1940; technical director in official film industry, while simultaneously shooting documentary footage of Italian resistance fighters, 1940-45; accepted offer from Howard Hughes to make films for RKO with Ingrid Bergman in Hollywood, 1946; apparently fell out of public favour over scandal surrounding relationships with Bergman and later Das Gupta; television director of documentaries, 1960s. **Died:** 4 June 1977.

Films as Director:

1936 *Daphne* (+ sc)
1938 *Prelude à l'apres-midi d'une faune* (+ sc)
1939 *Fantasia sottomarina* (+ sc); *Il tacchino prepotente* (+ sc); *La vispa Teresa* (+ sc)
1941 *Il Ruscello di Ripasottile* (+ sc); *La nave bianca* (+ co-sc)
1942 *Un pilota ritorna* (+ co-sc); *I tre aquilotta* (uncredited collaboration)
1943 *L'uomo della croce* (+ co-sc); *L'invasore* (+ supervised production, sc); *Desiderio* (+ co-sc) (confiscated by police and finished by Marcello Pagliero in 1946)
1945 ***Roma, città aperta*** (*Rome, Open City*) (+ co-sc)
1946 ***Paisà*** (*Paisan*) (+ co-sc, pr)
1947 *Germania, anno zero* (*Germany, Year Zero*) (+ co-sc) *L'amore* (*Woman, Ways of Love*) (+ sc); *Il miracolo* (*The Miracle*) (+ co-sc); *La macchina ammazzacattivi* (+ co-sc, pr); ***Stromboli, terra di dio*** (*Stromboli*) (+ co-sc, pr)
1950 *Francesco—giullare di Dio* (*Flowers of St. Francis*) (+ co-sc)
1952 "L'Invidia" episode of *I sette peccati capitali* (*The Seven Deadly Sins*) (+ co-sc); *Europa '51* (*The Greatest Love*) (+ co-sc)
1953 *Dov'è la libertà* (+ co-sc); ***Viaggio in Italia*** (*Voyage to Italy, Strangers*); *The Lonely Woman* (+ co-sc); "Ingrid Bergman" episode of *Siamo donne*
1954 "Napoli '43" episode of *Amori di mezzo secolo* (+ sc); *Giovanna d'Arco al rogo* (*Joan of Arc at the Stake*) (+ sc); *Die Angst* (*Le Paura*; *Fear*); *Orient Express* (+ sc, production supervision)
1958 *L'India vista da Rossellini* (ten episodes) (+ sc, pr); *India* (+ co-sc)
1959 *Il Generale della Rovere* (+ co-sc)
1960 *Era notte a Roma* (+ co-sc); *Viva l'Italia* (+ co-sc)
1961 *Vanina Vanini* (*The Betrayer*) (+ co-sc); *Torino nei centi'anni*; *Benito Mussolini* (*Blood on the Balcony*) (+ sc, production supervision)
1962 *Anima nera* (+ sc); "Illibatezza" episode of *Rogopag* (+ sc)
1966 *La Prise de pouvoir par Louis XIV* (*The Rise of Louis XIV*)
1967 *Idea di un'isola* (+ pr, sc)
1968 *Atti degli apostoli* (co-d, co-sc, ed)
1970 *Socrate* (*Socrates*) (+ co-sc, ed)
1972 *Agostino di Ippona*
1975 *Blaise Pascal*; *Anno uno*
1978 *Il Messia* (*The Messiah*) (+ co-sc)

Other Films:

1938 *Luciano Serra, pilota* (sc)
1963 *Le carabiniere* (co-sc)
1964 *L'eta del ferro* (sc, pr)
1967 *La lotta dell'uomo per la sua sopravvivenza* (sc, pr)

Publications

By ROSSELLINI: books—

Era notte a Roma, with others, Bologna, 1961.
Le Cinéma révélé, edited by Alain Bergala, Paris, 1984.
Il mio metodo: Scritti e intervisti, edited by Adriano Apra, Venice, 1987.
Quasi un autobiografie, Milan, 1987.

By ROSSELLINI: articles—

"*Paisà*: Sixth Sketch," with others, in *Bianco e Nero* (Rome), October 1947.
Interview with Francis Koval, in *Sight and Sound* (London), February 1951.
"Coloquio sul neo-realismo," with Mario Verdone, in *Bianco e Nero* (Rome), February 1952.
Interview with Maurice Schèrer and François Truffaut, in *Cahiers du Cinéma* (Paris), July 1954.
"Dix ans de cinéma," in *Cahiers du Cinéma* (Paris), August/September and November 1955, and January 1956.
"Cinema and Television: Interview," with André Bazin, in *Sight and Sound* (London), Winter 1958/59.
"Censure et culture," in *Cinéma* (Paris), October 1961.
"Conversazione sulla cultura e sul cinema," in *Filmcritica* (Rome), March 1963.
"Intervista con Roberto Rossellini," with Adriano Aprá and Maurizio Ponzi, in *Filmcritica* (Rome), April/May 1965.
Interview with Jean Collet and Claude-Jean Philippe, in *Cahiers du Cinéma* (Paris), September 1966.
"Conversazione con Roberto Rossellini," with Michele Mancin, Renato Tomasino, and Lello Maiello, in *Filmcritica* (Rome), August 1968.
"La decisione di Isa," in *Bianco e Nero* (Rome), January/March 1985.

On ROSSELLINI: books—

Hovald, Patrice, *Roberto Rossellini,* Paris, 1958.
Steele, Joseph Henry, *Ingrid Bergman: An Intimate Portrait,* New York, 1959.
Mida, Massimo, *Roberto Rossellini,* Parma, 1961.

Roberto Rossellini (right) directing *Era notte a Roma*

Verdone, Mario, *Roberto Rossellini,* Paris, 1963.
Guarner, José Luis, *Roberto Rossellini,* translated by Elizabeth Cameron, New York, 1970.
Baldelli, Pio, *Roberto Rossellini,* Rome, 1972.
Menon, Gianni, *Dibattio su Rossellini,* Rome, 1972.
Rondolino, Gianni, *Roberto Rossellini,* Florence, 1974.
Ranvaud, Don, *Roberto Rossellini,* London, 1981.
Cahiers du Cinéma 1, The 1950s: Neo-Realism, Hollywood, New Wave, edited by Jim Hillier, London, 1985.
Serceau, Michel, *Roberto Rossellini,* Paris, 1986.
Aprà, Adriano, *Rosselliniana,* Rome, 1987.
Brunette, Peter, *Roberto Rossellini,* Oxford, 1987.
Gansera, Rainer, and others, *Roberto Rossellini,* Munich, 1987.
Rossi, Patrizio, *Roberto Rossellini: A Guide to References and Resources,* Boston, 1988.
Bergala, Alain, and Jean Narboni, editors, *Roberto Rossellini,* Paris, 1990.

On ROSSELLINI: articles—

Venturi, Lauro, "Roberto Rossellini," in *Hollywood Quarterly,* Fall 1949.
Harcourt-Smith, Simon, "The Stature of Rossellini," in *Sight and Sound* (London), April 1950.
Truffaut, François, "Rossellini," in *Arts* (Paris), January 1955.
Rivette, Jacques, "Lettre sur Rossellini," in *Cahiers du Cinéma* (Paris), May 1955.
Fieschi, Jean-André, "Dov'e Rossellini?," in *Cahiers du Cinéma* (Paris), May 1962.
Sarris, Andrew, "Rossellini Rediscovered," in *Film Culture* (New York), no. 32, 1964.
Casty, Alan, "The Achievement of Roberto Rossellini," in *Film Comment* (New York), Fall 1964.
Aprà, Adriano, "Le nouvel âge de Rossellini," in *Cahiers du Cinéma* (Paris), August 1965.
"*Roma, città aperta* Issue" of *Avant-Scène du Cinéma* (Paris), 1971.
MacBean, J.R., "Rossellini's Materialist Mise-en-Scene," in *Film Quarterly* (Berkeley), Winter 1971/72.
"Rossellini Issue" of *Screen* (London), Winter 1973/74.
Norman, L., "Rossellini's Case Histories for Moral Education," in *Film Quarterly* (Berkeley), Summer 1974.
Wood, Robin, "Rossellini," in *Film Comment* (New York), July/August 1974.
"Rossellini Issue" of *Filmcritica* (Rome), May/June 1976.
Walsh, M., "*Rome, Open City; The Rise to Power of Louis XIV:* Reevaluating Rossellini," in *Jump Cut* (Chicago), no. 15, 1977.
Hughes, J., "In Memoriam: Roberto Rossellini," in *Film Comment* (New York), July/August 1977.
Lawton, H., "Rossellini's Didactic Cinema," in *Sight and Sound* (London), Autumn 1978.
Ranvaud, Don, "Documentary and Dullness: Rossellini According to the British Critic," in *Monthly Film Bulletin* (London), February 1981.
Brunette, Peter, "Rossellini and Cinematic Realism," in *Cinema Journal* (Champaign, Illinois), Fall 1985.

"*Viaggio in Italia* Issue" of *Avant-Scéne du Cinéma* (Paris), June 1987.
Tournès, A., "Rossellini: Le courage d'être humblement un homme," in *Jeune Cinéma* (Paris), January/February 1988.
Gallagher, Tag, "Rossellini, Neo-Realism, and Croce," in *Film History* (Philadelphia), vol. 2, no. 1, 1988.
Truffaut, François, and others, "Roberto Rossellini," in *Cahiers du Cinéma* (Paris), July/August 1988.

* * *

Roberto Rossellini has been so closely identified with the rise of the postwar Italian style of filmmaking known as neorealism that it would be a simple matter to neatly pigeonhole him as merely a practitioner of that technique and nothing more. So influential has that movement been that the achievement embodied in just three of his films—*Roma, città aperta; Paisà;* and *Germania, anno zero*—would be enough to secure the director a major place in film history. To label Rossellini simply a neorealist, however, is to drastically undervalue his contribution to the thematic aspects of his art.

At its most basic level, Rossellini's dominant concern appears to be a preoccupation with the importance of the individual within various aspects of the social context that emerged from the ashes of World War II. In his early films, which a number of historians have simplistically termed fascist, his concern for the individual was not balanced by an awareness of their social context. Thus, a film like his first feature, *La nave bianca,* while it portrays its sailors and hospital personnel as sensitive and caring, ignores their ideological and political milieu. It is *Roma, città aperta,* despite its carry-over of the director's penchant for melodrama, that is properly considered Rossellini's "rite of passage" into the midst of the complex social issues confronting the individual in postwar Europe. The crude conditions under which it was shot, its authentic appearance, and certain other naturalistic touches lent it an air of newsreel-like veracity, but its raw power was derived almost entirely from the individuals that Rossellini placed within this atmospheric context. With the exception of Anna Magnani and Aldo Fabrizi, the cast was made up of nonprofessionals who were so convincing that the effect upon viewers was electric. Many were certain that what they were viewing must have been filmed as it was actually occurring.

Despite legends about how Rossellini's neorealistic style arose as a result of the scarcity of resources and adverse shooting conditions that were present immediately after the war, the director had undoubtedly begun to conceive the style as early as his aborted *Desiderio* of 1943, a small-scale forerunner of neorealism which Rossellini dropped in mid-shooting. Certainly, he continued the style in *Paisà* and *Germania anno zero,* the remaining parts of his war trilogy. In both of these features, he delineates the debilitating effects of war's aftermath on the psyche of modern man. The latter film was a particularly powerful statement on the effect of Nazi ideology on the mind of a young boy, in part because it simultaneously criticizes the failure of traditional social institutions like the church to counter fascism's corrupting influence.

The Rossellini films of the 1950s shed many of the director's neorealistic trappings. In doing so he shifted his emphasis somewhat to the spiritual aspects of man, revealing the instability of life and of human relationships. *Stromboli, Europa '51, Voyage to Italy,* and *La paura* reflect a quest for a transcendent truth akin to the secular saintliness achieved by the priest in *Open City.* In the 1950s films, however, his style floated unobtrusively between involvement and contemplation. This is particularly obvious in his films with Ingrid Bergman, but is best exemplified by *Voyage to Italy* with its leisurely-paced questioning of the very meaning of life. Every character in the film is ultimately in search of his soul. What little action there is has relatively little importance since most of the character development is an outgrowth of spiritual aspirations rather than a reaction to events. In this sense, its structure resembled the kind of neorealism practiced by De Sica in *Umberto D* (without the excessively emotional overtones) and yet reaffirms Rossellini's concern for his fellow men and for Italy. At the same time, through his restriction of incident, he shapes the viewer's empathy for his characters by allowing the viewer to participate in the film only to the extent of being companion to the various characters. The audience is intellectually free to wander away from the story, which it undoubtedly does, only to find its involvement in the character's spiritual development unchanged since its sympathy is not based upon the physical actions of a plot.

Such an intertwining of empathetic involvement of sorts with a contemplative detachment carried over into Rossellini's historical films of the 1960s and 1970s. His deliberately obtrusive use of zoom lenses created in the viewer of such films as *Viva l'Italia* and *Agostino di Ippona* a delicate distancing and a constant but subtle awareness that the director's point of view was inescapable. Such managing of the viewer's consciousness of the historical medium turns his characters into identifiable human beings who, though involving our senses and our emotions, can still be scrutinized from a relatively detached vantage point.

This, then, is the seeming contradiction central to Rossellini's entire body of work. As most precisely exemplified in his early, pure neorealistic films, his camera is relentlessly fixed on the physical aspects of the world around us. Yet, as defined by his later works, which both retain and modify much of this temporal focus, the director is also trying to capture within the same lens an unseen and spiritual landscape. Thus, the one constant within all of his films must inevitably remain his concern for fundamental human values and aspirations, whether they are viewed with the anger and immediacy of a *Roma, città aperta* or the detachment of a *Viaggio in Italia.*

—Stephen L. Hanson

ROSSEN, Robert

Nationality: American. **Born:** Robert Rosen in New York City, 16 March 1908. **Education:** Attended New York University. **Family:** Married Sue Siegal, 1954, three children. **Career:** Staged plays for Washington Square Players, later the Theater Guild, 1920s; actor, stage manager, and director in New York City, 1930-35; writer under contract to Mervyn LeRoy and Warner Bros., 1936-45; member of Communist Party in Hollywood, 1937-45; directed first feature, *Johnny O'Clock,* 1947; subpoenaed by House Un-American Activities Committee (HUAC), hearing suspended after arrest of Hollywood 10, 1947; produced first film, 1949; blacklisted after refusing to cooperate when called again to testify before HUAC, 1951-53; allowed to work again after naming names, 1953. **Awards:** Best Direction, New York Film Critics, for *The Hustler,* 1961. **Died:** 18 February 1966.

Films as Director:

1947 *Johnny O'Clock* (+ sc); *Body and Soul*
1949 ***All the King's Men*** (+ sc, pr)
1951 *The Brave Bulls* (+ pr)
1955 *Mambo* (+ co-sc)
1956 *Alexander the Great* (+ sc, pr)
1957 *Island in the Sun*
1959 *They Came to Cordura* (+ co-sc)
1961 ***The Hustler*** (+ co-sc, pr)
1964 *Lilith* (+ co-sc, pr)

Other Films:

1937 *Marked Woman* (Bacon) (co-sc); *They Won't Forget* (LeRoy) (co-sc)
1938 *Racket Busters* (co-sc)
1939 *Dust Be My Destiny* (sc); ***The Roaring Twenties*** (Walsh) (co-sc)
1940 *A Child is Born* (Bacon) (sc)
1941 *Blues in the Night* (Litvak) (sc); *The Sea Wolf* (Curtiz) (sc); *Out of the Fog* (Litvak) (co-sc)
1943 *Edge of Darkness* (Milestone) (sc)
1946 *A Walk in the Sun* (Milestone) (sc); *The Strange Love of Martha Ivers* (Milestone) (sc)
1947 *Desert Fury* (sc)
1949 *The Undercover Man* (pr)

Publications

By ROSSEN: articles—

"The Face of Independence," in *Films and Filming* (London), August 1962.

"Lessons Learned in Combat: Interview," with Jean-Louis Noames, in *Cahiers du Cinéma in English* (New York), January 1967.

On ROSSEN: books—

Hearings Before the Committee on Un-American Activities, House of Representatives, 1953 Volume, Washington, D.C., 1953.

Casty, Alan, *The Films of Robert Rossen,* New York, 1969.

On ROSSEN: articles—

"Rossen Issue" of *Films in Review* (New York), June/July 1962.

Cohen, Saul, "Robert Rossen and the Filming of *Lilith,*" in *Film Comment* (New York), Spring 1965.

Casty, Alan, "The Films of Robert Rossen," in *Film Quarterly* (Berkeley), Winter 1966/67.

"Rossen Issue" of *Cahiers du Cinéma in English* (New York), January 1967.

Casty, Alan, "Robert Rossen," in *Cinema* (Beverly Hills), Fall 1968.

Dark, C. "Reflections of Robert Rossen," in *Cinema* (London), August 1970.

Wald, M., "Robert Rossen," in *Films in Review* (New York), August/September 1972.

Robert Rossen

Neve, Brian, "The Screenwriter and the Social Problem Film, 1936-38: The Case of Robert Rossen at Warner Brothers," in *Film and History* (Newark, New Jersey), February 1984.

Combs, Richard, "The Beginner's Rossen," in *Monthly Film Bulletin* (London), January 1986.

Nolletti, Arthur, "The Fissure in the Spider Web: A Reading of Rossen's *Lilith,*" in *Film Criticism* (Meadville, Pennsylvania), vol. 11, no. 1/2, 1987.

* * *

Robert Rossen died as he was beginning to regain a prominent position in the cinema. His premature death left us with a final film which pointed to a new, deepening devotion to the study of deteriorating psychological states.

As a contract writer for Warner Bros. in the late 1930s and early 1940s, Rossen worked on many excellent scripts which showed a strong sympathy for individuals destroyed by or battling "the system." His first produced screenplay, *Marked Woman,* a little-known and highly underrated Bette Davis vehicle, deserves serious attention for its study of prostitution racketeering and its empowerment of women to overthrow corruption. His fifth film, *The Roaring Twenties,* is a thoughtful study of the obsessive drive for power and money amidst the harshness of the post-World War I period and the beginnings of the Great Depression. While his early scripts occasionally displayed an idealism which bordered on naiveté, Rossen deserves credit for his commitment to the depiction of economic and social injustice.

According to Alan Casty in *The Films of Robert Rossen,* Rossen was invited to direct his own screenplay for *Johnny O'Clock,* a tale of murder among gamblers, at the insistence of the film's star, Dick Powell. Rossen followed this poorly-received directorial debut with two of his most critically and financially successful films: *Body and Soul* and *All the King's Men,* two male-centered studies of corruption and the drive for success. The first of these films is centered in the boxing ring, the second in the political arena. The success of *Body and Soul* (from a screenplay by Abraham Polonsky) allowed Rossen the financial stability to set up his own company with a financing and releasing contract through Columbia Pictures. As a result, he wrote, directed, and produced *All the King's Men,* which was awarded the Best Picture Oscar in 1949.

These back-to-back successes apparently triggered an unfortunate increase in directorial ego: production accounts of the later films detail Rossen's inability to openly accept collaboration. This paranoia was exacerbated by his deepening involvement in House Un-American Activities Committee (HUAC) proceedings. Despite a 1953 reprieve after providing names of alleged Communists to the committee, he was unable to revive his Hollywood career, although he continued to work. He seemed a particularly unlikely candidate to direct his next three films: the Ponti-DeLaurentis melodrama *Mambo,* the historical epic *Alexander the Great,* and the interracial problem drama, *Island in the Sun.* The last of his 1950s films, *They Came to Cordura,* is an interesting film which should have succeeded. Its failure so obsessed Rossen that he spent many years unsuccessfully trying to re-edit it for re-release.

Rossen's final films, *The Hustler* and *Lilith,* show a return to form, due in great part to the atmospheric cinematography of Eugene Schufftan. Rossen, firmly entrenched in the theatrical values of content through script and performance, had previously worked with strong cinematographers (especially James Wong Howe and Burnett Guffey), but had worked from the conviction that content was the prime area of concern. As he told *Cahiers du Cinéma,* "Technique is nothing compared to content." In *The Hustler,* a moody film about winners and losers set in the world of professional pool-playing, the studied script was strongly enhanced by Schufftan's predominantly claustrophobic framings. Schufftan, long a respected European cameraman (best known for his work on Lang's *Metropolis* and Carné's *Quai des brumes*), had been enthusiastically recommended to Rossen by Jack Garfein, who had brought Schufftan back to America for his *Something Wild.*

Schufftan's working posture was one of giving the director what he asked for, and production notes from the set of *The Hustler* indicate he gave Rossen what he wanted while also achieving results that one feels were beyond Rossen's vision. There was no denying Schufftan's influence in the film's success (it won him an Oscar), and Rossen wisely invited him to work on his next film.

Lilith, an oblique and elliptical film in which a psychiatric worker ends up seeking help, signalled an advance in Rossen's cinematic sensibility. While several of the purely visual passages border on being overly symbolic, one feels that Rossen was beginning to admit the communicative power of the visual. Less idealistic and with less affirmative endings, these last two films showed a deeper sense of social realism, with Rossen striving to portray the effect of the psychological rather than social environment on his characters. Rossen's last project, which went unrealized because of his death, would have allowed him to portray both the social and psychological problems of people living in the vicinity of Cape Canaveral (Cape Kennedy). Such a project would have provided him with a further opportunity to break away from his tradition of dialogue-bound character studies.

—Doug Tomlinson

ROTHA, Paul

Nationality: British. **Born:** Paul Thompson in London, 3 June 1907. **Education:** Highgate School; Slade School of Fine Art, London, 1923-25. **Family:** Married 1) Margaret Louise Lee, 1930 (divorced 1939); 2) Margot Rose Perkins, 1943; 3) actress Constance Smith. **Career:** Painter, designer, book illustrator, 1925; art critic, *Connoisseur,* 1927-28; property man, 1928, then assistant designer, British International Pictures Ltd.; author and film historian, from 1930; producer, Empire Marketing Board, 1932; directed first film, *Contact,* 1932; director of productions, Strand Films, 1936-38; Rockefeller Foundation Fellow, 1937-38; set up Associated Realist Film Productions and founded *Documentary News Letter,* 1939; managing director, Paul Rotha Productions Ltd., 1941-76; made 100 documentaries for British Ministry of Information, World War II; Head of Documentary Film Department, BBC, 1953-55; lecturer on documentary films, United States, 1953-54; member of board, Isotype Institute, from 1959; Simon Senior Research Fellow, University of Manchester, 1967-68. **Awards:** Gold Medals: Venice Festival, 1934, Brussels Festival, 1935, and Leipzig Festival, 1962; British Film Academy Awards for *The World is Rich,* 1947, and *World Without End,* 1953. **Member:** Fellow, British Film Institute, 1951; Honorary Member (posthumous), ACTT, 1984. **Died:** 7 March 1984.

Films as Director and Scriptwriter:

(documentary unless indicated)

1932 *Contact*
1933 *The Rising Tide* (reissued as *Great Cargoes,* 1935); *Shipyard*
1935 *Death on the Road*; *Face of Britain*
1936 *The Future's in the Air*; *Cover to Cover*; *The Way to the Sea*; *Peace of Britain*
1937 *Statue Parade*; *Today We Live*; *Here is the Land*

1939 *New Worlds for Old*; *Roads Across Britain* (co-d with Sidney Cole)
1940 *The Fourth Estate* (not shown until 1964); *Mr. Borland Thinks Again*
1943 *World of Plenty*
1944 *Soviet Village*
1945 *Total War in Britain*; *Land of Promise*
1946 *A City Speaks*
1947 *The World is Rich*
1950 *No Resting Place* (feature)
1953 *World Without End* (co-d with Basil Wright)
1953/55 *Hope for the Hungry*; *The Waiting People*; *No Other Way*; *The Wealth of Waters*; *The Virus Story*
1958 *Cat and Mouse* (feature)
1959 *Cradle of Genius*
1961 *Das Leben von Adolf Hitler* (*The Life of Adolf Hitler*)
1962 *De Overval* (*The Silent Raid*) (feature)

Publications

By ROTHA: books—

The Film Till Now: A Survey of the Cinema, London, 1930; 2nd edition, with Richard Griffith, 1949; 3rd edition, 1960; 4th edition, 1967.
Celluloid: The Film Today, London, 1931.
Documentary Film: The Use of the Film Medium to Interpret Creatively and in Social Terms the Life of the People as it Exists in Reality, London, 1936; 2nd edition, 1939; 3rd edition, 1952.
Movie Parade, London, 1936; published as *Movie Parade: 1888-1949: A Pictorial Survey of World Cinema*, with Roger Manvell, 1950.
World of Plenty: The Book of the Film, with Eric Mowbray, London, 1945.
Eisenstein, 1898-1948, with others, London, 1948.
Portrait of a Flying Yorkshireman: Letters from Eric Knight to Paul Rotha (editor), London, 1952.
Television in the Making (editor), London, 1956.
Rotha on the Film, London, 1958.
The Innocent Eye, with others, London, 1963.
Documentary Diary: An Informal History of the British Documentary Film 1928-1939, London, 1973.
Richard Winnington: Film Criticism and Caricature, London, 1975.
Robert J. Flaherty: A Biography, edited by Jay Ruby, Philadelphia, 1983.

By ROTHA: articles—

"The Lament," in *Sight and Sound* (London), Autumn 1938.
Documentary News Letter (London), 1939-1946.
"Television and the Future of Documentary," in *Quarterly Review of Film, Radio and TV* (New York), Summer 1955.
"The Critical Issue," with others, in *Sight and Sound* (London), August 1958.
Films and Filming (London), July 1966 to May 1967 (monthly column).
Letter in *Film and TV Technician* (London), February 1983 (reply, July 1983).

On ROTHA: books—

Wright, Basil, *The Long View*, London, 1974.
Sussex, Elizabeth, *The Rise and Fall of British Documentary: The Story of the Film Movement Founded By John Grierson*, Berkeley, 1975.
Morris, Paul, editor, *Paul Rotha*, London, 1982.
Ellis, Jack C., *The Documentary Idea*, Englewood Cliffs, New Jersey, 1989.

On ROTHA: articles—

"Rotha and the World," in *Quarterly Review of Film, Radio and TV* (New York), Fall 1955.
Film Forum (London), January 1963.
Hollywood Reporter, 23 June 1978.
"British Cinema: Paul Rotha," in *National Film Theatre Booklet* (London), August 1979.
Powell, Dilys, obituary, in *Film and TV Technician* (London), April 1984.
Obituary in *Revue du Cinéma* (Paris), May 1984.
Anstey, Edgar, "Paul Rotha and Thorold Dickinson," in *Sight and Sound* (London), Summer 1984.
"Paul Rotha," in *Annual Obituary 1985*, London and Chicago, 1985.

* * *

Paul Rotha's position in the British documentary movement has always been somewhat equivocal. Unlike other members of the group, he served only briefly in the government units Grierson assembled in the 1930s. Before that he had trained as a painter and designer, and his book, *The Film Till Now*—the first aesthetic history of film in English, perhaps in any language—had already been published. After six months at the Empire Marketing Board Film Unit, he continued in documentary as an independent producer. His ability to obtain private sponsorship was unusual for those early years, when documentary was just becoming a recognized mode.

Rotha's films were frequently innovative and experimental, with his creative impulse more akin to conceptual art than to personal expression, often mixing forms and styles. Though original in their combinations, their aspects derived from precedents that attracted Rotha. *Shipyard*, for example, takes a hard look at the cycles of work followed by unemployment that characterized the British shipbuilding industry. (In this respect the film makes one think of Joris Ivens' *Borinage*, which concerned the miserable conditions in the mining region of Belgium.) But it also contains extended passages of visual artistry of the giant ship in stages of construction—silhouettes of the hull frame and the like—that seem to stem from the "city symphonies" of early documentary, or perhaps from Ivens' *The Bridge* (1928).

World of Plenty (1943) and its sequel, *The World is Rich* (1947), seem equally original and yet, as Rotha acknowledged, their inspiration came from the sort of Depression theater called "The Living Newspaper" he had seen while on a trip to the United States in the late 1930s to spread the documentary gospel. They are intelligent, imaginative, and finally a bit too clever, the rhetorical devices attracting as much attention as the argument itself. *World Without End* is unusual because it couples footage about the work of UNESCO shot by Basil Wright in Thailand with that of Rotha in Mexico, an undertaking reminiscent of D.W. Griffith's monumental *Intolerance*. But somehow it evokes no real (or deep) sympathy for the people and their problems.

Of Rotha's three fiction features, the first, *No Resting Place*, is clearly in the semi-documentary tradition which Harry Watt had carried from the wartime Crown Film Unit over to commercial features. A film about the lives of itinerant tinkers, it was shot on location in Ireland and used non-actors as well as little-known professionals.

Rotha's compilation *The Life of Adolf Hitler*, again skillful and intelligent, follows a vein much mined by American and British television. (Rotha was head of BBC-TV documentary during 1953-55.) Specifically, it recalls "The Twisted Cross" (1956) of NBC's *Project XX* series.

In addition to his filmmaking, Rotha wrote constantly; his energy was prodigious, his output prolific. Apart from books and articles and

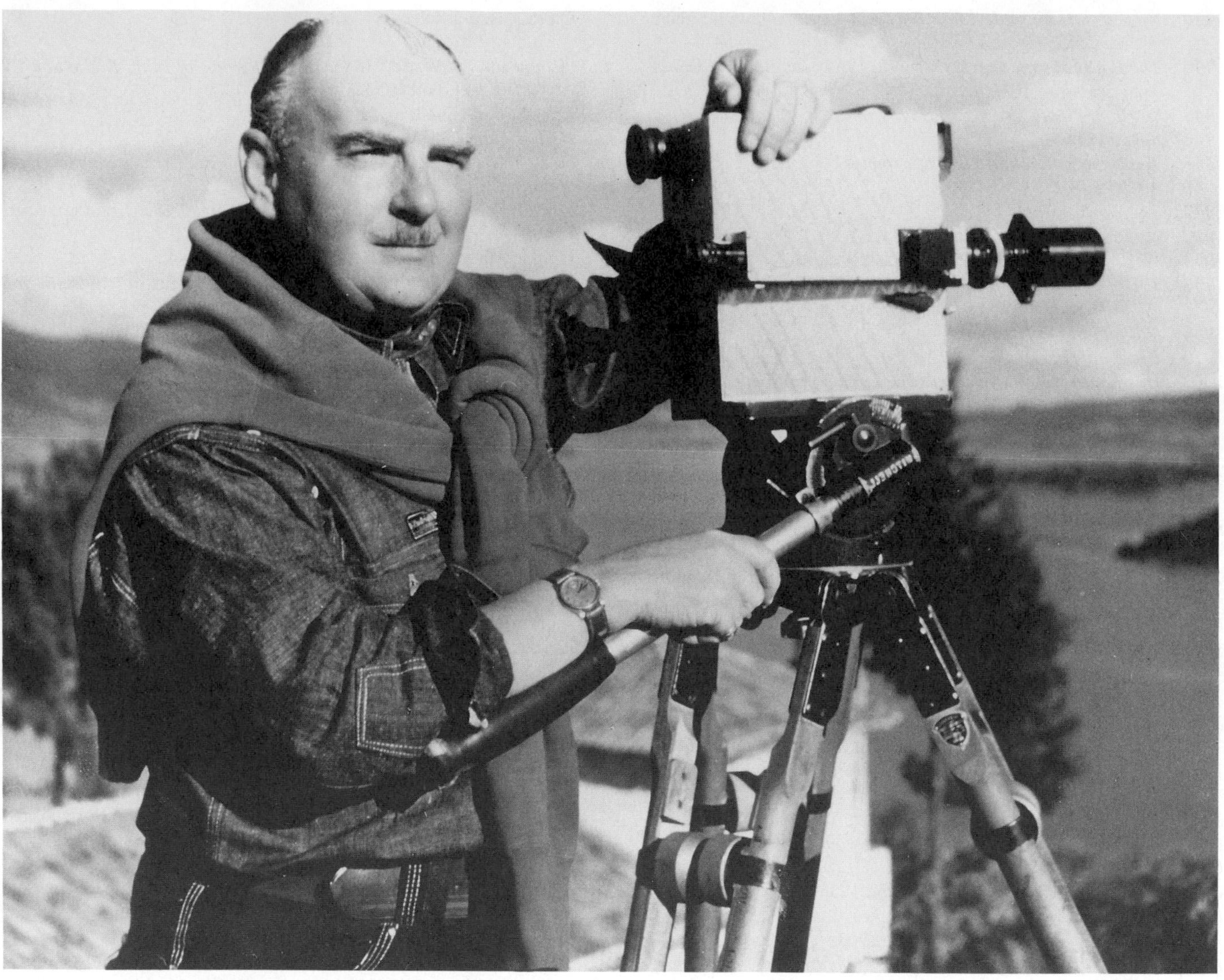

Paul Rotha

reviews devoted to the entertainment film (some of them anthologized in *Rotha on the Film*) is the equally large body of writing related to the British documentary of the 1930s. At the time he was acknowledged as the historian of the movement, in large part because *Documentary Film* and *Documentary Diary* provide such a comprehensive picture of the subject. A special labor of love is his *Robert J. Flaherty: A Biography.*

One other aspect of Rotha's role in relation to documentary deserves comment. He set himself up alongside Grierson rather than be cast as one of the loyal group members who followed Grierson. Although his politics may have been much like those of other documentarians, he maintained an outspokenness that those working at government units did not permit themselves. As a result, Rotha is honored by young left-wing film scholars and filmmakers who tend to dismiss Grierson and the documentary movement he formed as a tool of the Establishment.

Rotha was something of a maverick and gadfly. A testy and quirky man, he was given to self-promotion. But as Grierson once said in defending Rotha to documentary colleagues after he had made some contentious public outburst, "He is one of us." Rotha would no doubt have agreed, but on his own terms.

—Jack C. Ellis

ROUCH, Jean

Nationality: French. **Born:** Jean Pierre Rouch in Paris, 31 May 1917. **Education:** Lycée Henri IV, Paris, degree in literature; Ecole nationale des ponts et chaussées, Paris, degree in civil engineering. **Family:** Married Jane Margaret Gain, 1952. **Career:** Became first to make descent of Niger River by dugout canoe, also began making ethnographic films during trip, 1946-47; director of research at Centre Nationale de la Recherche Scientifique, 1966-86; Sécretaire Général du Comité du Film Ethnographique, 1972; President of La Cinémathéque française, 1987-91. **Awards:** Prize Festival du Film Maudit, Biarritz, for *Initiation à la danse,* 1949; Prix du Reportage, Paris Short Film Festival, for *Circoncision,* 1950; Critics Prize, Venice Film Festival, for *Les Maîtres fous,* 1955; Prix Delluc, for *Moi, un Noir,* 1959; Prizes at Cannes, Manheim, and Venice Festivals for *Chronique d'un été,* 1961; Golden Lion Prize, Venice, for *La Chasse au lion,* 1965.

Films as Director:

1947 *Au pays des mages noirs* (co-d, sc, ph)
1948 *Hombori*; *Les Magiciens de Wanzerbé* (co-d, pr, ph)

1949 *Initiation à la danse des Possédés*; *La Circoncision* (+ pr, ph)
1950 *Chasse à l'hippopotame*
1951 *Bataille sur le grand fleuve* (+ ph); *Cimetière dans la falaise*; *Yenendi: les Hommes qui font la pluie* (+ ph); *Les Gens du mil* (+ ph)
1952 *Les Fils de l'eau* (compilation of earlier films; released 1958)
1953 *Mammy Water* (+ sc, ph)
1954 *Les Maîtres fous* (+ ph, narration)
1957 *Baby Ghana*; *Moi, un noir* (+ sc, ph)
1958 *Moro Naba* (+ ph); *La royale goumbé* (+ ph); *Sakpata* (co-d, + ph)
1961 *La Pyramide humaine* (+ sc, co-ph); ***Chronique d'un été*** (*Chronicle of a Summer*) (co-d, co-sc); *Les Ballets de Niger*
1962 *La Punition* (co-d); *Urbanisme africain* (+ sc); *Le Mil*; *Les Pêcheurs du Niger* (+ sc); *Abidjan, port de pêche* (+ sc)
1963 *Le Palmier à l'huile*; *Les Cocotiers*; *Monsieur Albert Prophète*; *Rose et Landry*
1964 "Véronique et Marie-France" (also known as "La Fleur de l'âge ou les adolescents") episode of *Les Veuves de quinze ans* (*The Adolescents*; *That Tender Age*) (+ sc); "Gare du nord" episode of *Paris vu par* (*Six in Paris*) (+ sc)
1965 *La Chasse au lion à l'arc* (*The Lion Hunters*) (+ sc, ph, narration); *La Goumbe des jeunes noceurs* (+ sc, ph) (released 1967); *L'Afrique et la recherche scientifique*; *Alpha noir*; *Tambours de pierre*; *Festival de Dakar*; *Hampi*; *Musique et danse des chasseurs Gow*; *Jackville*
1966 *Batteries Dogon—éléments pour une étude des rythmes* (co-d); *Fêtes de novembre à Bregbo*; *Dongo Horendi*; *Dongo Yenendi*; *Koli-Koli*; *Sigui année zero* (co-d)
1967 *Jaguar* (+ ph); *Daudo Sorko*; *Sigui: l'enclume de Yougo*; *Tourou et Bitti*
1968 *Pierres chantantes d'Ayorou*; *Wanzerbe*; *Sigui 1968—les danseurs de Tyogou* (co-d); *Un Lion nommé l'Américain*
1969 *Sigui 1969—la caverne de Bongo*
1970 *Yenendi de Yantalla*; *Mya—la mère*; *Sigui 1970—Les clameurs d'Amani* (co-d)
1971 *Petit à petit* (+ co-sc, ph); *Porto Novo—la danse des reines* (co-d); *Sigui 1971—la dune d'Idyeli* (co-d); *Architectes Ayorou*; *Yenendi de Simiri*
1972 *Horendi*; *Sigui 1972—les pagnes de lame* (co-d); *Yenendi de Boukoki*; *Tanda Singui*
1973 *L'Enterrement du Hogon*; *VW—Voyou*; *Dongo Hori*; *Sécheresse à Simiri*; *Boukoki*; *Hommage à Marcel Mauss: Taro Okamoto*
1974 *Cocorico, Monsieur Poulet* (+ co-sc); *Pam Kuso Kar*; *Sigui 1973—l'auvent de la circoncision*; *La 504 et les foudroyers* (co-d); *Ambara Dama* (co-d); *Sécheresse à Simiri* (continuation of 1973 film); *Toboy Tobaye*
1975 *Souna Kouma*; *Initiation*
1976 *Babatou ou les trois conseils* (+ ph); *Médecines et médecins* (co-d); *Rhythme de travail*
1977 *Makwayela*; *Ciné-Portrait de Margaret Head* (*Margaret Head: Portrait of a Friend*); *Isphahan: Lettre Persanne 1977*; *Fête des Gandyi Bi à Simiri*; *Le Griot Badye* (co-d); *Hommage à Marcel Mauss: Marcel Levy*; *Hommage à Marcel Mauss: Germaine Dieterlen*
1978 *Simi Siddo Kuma*
1979 *Funérailles à Bongo: Le Vieux Anai* (co-d)
1982 *Yenendi Gengel*
1983 *Portrait de Raymond Depardon*
1984 *Dionysos*
1986 *Folie ordinaire d'une fille de Cham* (*The Ordinary Madness of a Daughter of Cham*)
1987 *Enigma* (co-d)
1988 *Brise-Glace* (*Icebreaker*) (co-d); *Boulevards d'Afrique—bac ou mariage*
1990 *Cantate pour deux généraux* (doc)

Other Films:

1953 *Alger—Le Cap* (adviser)
1961 *Niger, jeune républiquem* (adviser)
1976 *Chantons sous l'Occupation* (co-ph)

Publications

By ROUCH: articles—

"A propos des films ethnographiques," in *Positif* (Paris), nos. 15/16, 1955.
"Migrations au Ghana (Gold Coast)—Enquête 1953-55," in *Journal de la Société des Africanistes,* no. 26, 1956.
Interview, in *Movie* (London), April 1963.
"Jean Rouch in Conversation," with James Blue, in *Film Comment* (New York), Fall/Winter 1967.
"Situation et tendances du cinéma en Afrique," in *Catalogue des Films Ethnographiques sur l'Afrique noire* (Unesco), 1967.
"Le Film ethnographique," in *Ethnologie générale, Encyclopédie de la Pléiade,* Paris, 1968.
"Je suis mon premier spectateur," an interview with L. Marcorelles, in *Avant-Scène du Cinéma* (Paris), March 1972.
"The Camera and the Man," in *Principles of Visual Anthropology,* edited by Paul Hockings, The Hague, 1975.
Interview in *Ecran* (Paris), March 1977.
"Ciné-transe: The Vision of Jean Rouch," an interview with D. Yakir, in *Film Quarterly* (Berkeley), Spring 1978.
"The Politics of Visual Anthropology," an interview with D. Georgakas and others, in *Cineaste* (New York), Summer 1978.
"Jean Rouch: A Pastoral Perspective," interview with H. Naficy, in *Quarterly Review of Film Studies* (Pleasantville, New York), no. 3, 1979.
"Note sur les problèmes techniques soulevés par l'expérience Super 8," in *Cahiers du Cinéma* (Paris), January 1979.
Jean Rouch Section of *Framework* (Norwich, England), Autumn 1979.
"Superserious-8: Chronicle of a Master," an interview with T. Treadway, in *Filmmakers Monthly* (Ward Hill, Massachusetts), June 1981.
Interview with Enrico Fulchignoni, in *Positif* (Paris), January 1982.
Interview with A. Rodrig, in *Cinématographe* (Paris), April 1985.

On ROUCH: books—

Armes, Roy, *French Cinema Since 1946: Vol. 2—The Personal Style,* New York, 1966.
Issari, M. Ali, *Cinéma Vérité,* East Lansing, Michigan, 1971.
Marsolais, Gilles, *Jean Rouch,* Cinémathèque Québecoise, 1973.
Marsolais, Gilles, *L'Aventure du Cinéma direct,* Paris, 1974.
Barnouw, Erik, *Documentary: A History of the Non-Fiction Film,* New York, 1974.
Issari, M. Ali, and Doris A. Paul, *What Is Cinéma Vérité?,* Metuchen, New Jersey, 1979.
Eaton, Mick, *Anthropology—Reality—Cinema: The Films of Jean Rouch,* British Film Institute, 1979.
Prédal, René, ed., *Jean Rouch, un griot gaulois,* Conde-sur-Noireau, France, 1982.
Gauthier, Guy, *L'Avènement du cinéma direct,* Conde-sur-Noireau, France, 1990.
Stoller, Paul, *The Cinematic Griot: The Ethnography of Jean Rouch,* Chicago, 1992.

Jean Rouch

On ROUCH: articles—

Tanner, Alain, "Recording Africa," in *Sight and Sound* (London), Summer 1956.
Jutra, Claude, "En courant derrière Rouch," in *Cahiers du Cinéma* (Paris), November 1960, January 1961, and February 1961.
Sandell, Roger, "Films by Jean Rouch," in *Film Quarterly* (Berkeley), Winter 1961/62.
Graham, Peter, "Cinéma Vérité in France," in *Film Quarterly* (Berkeley), Summer 1964.
Blue, James, "The Films of Jean Rouch," in *Film Comment* (New York), Fall/Winter 1967.
MacDougall, David, "Prospects of the Ethnographic Film," in *Film Quarterly* (Berkeley), Winter 1969/70.
"Jean Rouch," in *Documentary Explorations,* edited by G. Roy Levin, Garden City, New York, 1971.
Ensault, Philippe, "Jean Rouch ou les aventures d'un nègre blanc," in *Image et Son* (Paris), no. 249, 1971.
Fieschi, J. A., "Dérives de la fiction: notes sur le cinéma de Jean Rouch," in *Cinéma, théories, lectures,* Paris, 1973.
Berman, Bruce, "Jean Rouch: A Founder of *Cinéma Vérité* Style," in *Film Library Quarterly,* vol. 11, no. 4, 1978.
"*Moi, un noir* Issue" of *Avant-Scène du Cinéma* (Paris), 1 April 1981.
Howes, Arthur, "Jean Rouch, Anthropological Film-maker," in *Undercut* (London), Summer 1983.

* * *

A prolific and innovative ethnographic filmmaker as well as a pioneer of *cinéma vérité* and improvised film psychodrama, Jean Rouch has not only redefined documentary film practice but also stimulated radical developments in fiction film. It was as a civil engineer preferring West Africa to the German occupation that Rouch came to anthropology through observation of Songhay rituals. After the liberation, his untutored enthusiasm found an intellectual framework at the Musée de l'Homme, where he studied social anthropology under Marcel Mauss and ethnography under Marcel Griaule, the initiator of film recording in fieldwork. It was at Griaule's instigation that in 1946 Rouch descended the Niger in a dugout canoe with a 16mm camera to make the first of over eighty ethnographic films.

Rouch's early films dutifully followed Griaule's lead in providing celluloid records of cultural practice. Typically, the self-effacing camera discreetly captured events which a later commentary interpreted for a posited Western audience. However, inspired by Flaherty's example, Rouch began to incorporate his subjects' perspective (*Cimetière dans la falaise*). Rather than make generalist exotic documentaries, he focused on particular aspects of African culture, sometimes in collaboration with fellow ethnographers. In the early years (1950-52), Rouch worked closely with Roger Rosfelder on migration, while in the period 1966-73, he made eight films with Germaine Dieterlen on the Sigui festivals of the Dogon.

Salient among the subjects covered during five decades of filming are: funeral rituals (*Cimetière dans la falaise; Moro Naba; Funérailles du vieil Anai; L'Enterrement de Hogon; Souna Kouma; Pam Kusoka; Ambara Dama; Simir Siddo Kuma*), hunting (*La Chasse à l'hippopotame; Musique et danse des chasseurs Gow; La Chasse au lion à l'arc; Un Lion nommé l'Américain, Koli-Koli*), fishing (*Au Pays des mages noires; Bataille sur le grand fleuve; Mammy Water; Abidjan—port de pêche; Les Pêcheurs de Niger*), spiritual practices (*Les Magiciens de Wanzerbe; Monsieur Albert, prophète; Jackville*), possession rituals (*Initiation à la danse des possédés; Les Maîtres fous*), rain-making rituals (*Yenendi; les hommes qui font la pluie; Dongo Yendi; Dauda Sorko; Yenendi de Ganghel, Yenendi de Yantalla; Yenendi de Simiri; Yenendi de Boukoki*), and celebrations (*Baby Ghana; Fêtes de l'indépendance de Niger; La Goumbé des jeunes noceurs*).

Apart from the rituals dealing with possession, rain-making, and funerals, the most celebrated ethnographic films concern the Gow lion-hunters: *La Chasse au lion à l'arc* and *Un lion nommé l'Américain.* Filming over a seven-year period Rouch earned the trust of the tribal hunters to capture not only their techniques but, most importantly, the intimate lion hunt rituals and their meaning for the Gow hunters.

Rouch's evolution as an ethnographic filmmaker and his progressive exploration of subjectivity can be traced through key films. In the possession rituals of *Les Maîtres fous,* participants adopt the personas of their colonial masters. Rouch conveys both collective and personal responses in the self-induced hysteria which culminates in the eating of a sacrificial dog. Inserted satirical images of the British governor break with the tradition of presenting only the pro-filmic event while the commentary indicates the violence as a politically therapeutic act. This combination of socio-political and psychological insights brought a new dimension to the ethnographic film. The powerful exteriorisation of violence and role-play had particular meaning for two creative artists: Peter Brook staging his *Marat/Sade,* and Jean Gênet in his conception of *Les Noirs.*

Rouch's first feature film, *Moi, un Noir,* has thematic links with *Les Maîtres fous.* Observation of the daily lives of migrant workers includes their fantasies as they talk to the camera in the guise of their self-attributed movie-star pseudonyms. Discovering himself through the film's rushes, "Edward G. Robinson" is stimulated to talk openly about his problems and ambitions. The valuable perceptions derived from this participatory technique reinforced the importance of including the subjective conscious alongside objective observation in the ethnographic film.

As a means to gather further insights into issues of racial and cultural difference, Rouch regularly experimented with improvised dramas: *Jaguar; Cocorico, Monsieur Poulet; Les Adolescents; La Punition;* or the indicative *La Pyramide humaine.* In this film Rouch set up the situation of a white girl attempting to integrate with black classmates. With the camera providing the catalyst, pupils developed scenes from their own experiences to create a form of cathartic psychodrama, but the experiment was flawed by the lack of synchronized sound, and efforts to recreate raw emotions for a later sound-track proved difficult.

At the suggestion of the sociologist Edgar Morin, Rouch applied his investigative documentary approach to a group of Parisians questioned about happiness (*Chronique d'un été*). With lightweight sound equipment and a special wide-angled camera developed by fellow cinematographer Michel Brault, Rouch achieved a sense of immediacy and intimacy previously lacking. Despite reservations about the interview sample (mostly Morin's friends) and the *post hoc* shaping implicit in editing twenty-five hours of recording to the ninety-minute feature, *Chronique d'été* was lauded as the new realism, or in Rouch's terms, *cinéma vérité.*

The approach differs from the didacticism or idealism of scripted documentaries and implies a new directness and truthfulness (the term is borrowed from Vertov's *kino-pravda).* Whereas the contemporary "direct" cinema movement maintained the camera's invisibility, *cinéma vérité* foregrounded the technology, insisting that the elicited information is generated by the interview situation itself. The interventionist approach was geared to stimulate spontaneity, and with it, revelation.

The influence of the film was considerable. Radical filmmakers like Jacques Rozier, Chris Marker, and Jean-Luc Godard adapted the approach, so that hand-held cameras, actors addressing the camera, improvisation, or the undisguised directorial voice became staple elements.

The experiment of *Chronique d'un été* was extended in *La punition,* where Rouch also brought into play the techniques of *La Pyramide humaine.* Non-professional actors were wired for sound and left to improvise around the theme of a girl's encounters with three men in

Paris. Rouch's aim was to maximise *cinéma vérité* spontaneity and, in order to reduce intervention through editing, filming was conducted in ten-minute takes over a single weekend. This attempt at convergence between film time and narrative time was only partially successful, and Rouch returned to the question in his "real life" drama of a fatal quarrel in *Gare du Nord,* one of the episodes in *Paris vu par....*

In subsequent films Rouch explored cultural issues through folk tales or contemporary African drama. In *Babatou ou les trois conseils,* he draws on war chronicles and a fairy tale to articulate views on slavery, while in *Cocorico, Monsieur Poulet,* a Nigerian tale about a travelling chicken dealer is retold through the collective improvisation of non-professional actors. A stage play is the source both for *Folie ordinaire d'une fille de Cham,* in which two female inmates of a mental institution act out their frustrations born of gender, race, religion, and upbringing, and for *Boulevards d'Afrique,* based on a Senegalese musical comedy, in which a young woman challenges her parent's cultural assumptions about an arranged marriage.

Rouch's most recent work confirms the continuing vitality of his eclectic interests. In the powerful *Cantate pour deux généraux,* he returns to a possession ritual in which Africans perform voodoo rites on Napoleon's grave to release the spirit of a black general. With *Brise-Glace,* he produced a wordless documentary about a Swedish ice-breaker in the North sea, while his current project, *Madame l'eau* has taken him to Holland.

As a self-tutored ethnographic filmmaker, Rouch pioneered approaches which in turn radicalised several areas of filmmaking in the 1960s. His interactive approach to documentary, which evolved into extemporized psychodramas, brought fresh insights into cultural difference, while the French tradition of scripted documentary (encapsulated in Rouquier's *Farrebique*) was jolted into a new form of directness by *Chronique d'un été.* Latter-day film and TV documetarists as well as radical filmmakers such as Godard attest to his influence in sociological film essays (*Masculin et féminin*). After half a century as a filmmaker, academic, and author, Rouch's commitment to promoting film as an instrument of enthnographical research remains undiminished. In 1978, as a mark of his international standing, he was himself the subject of a TV documentary, *Jean Rouch and His Camera in the Heart of Africa,* but there are no greater monuments to his life's work than the unique corpus of films produced for the Musée de l'Homme and the worldwide host of filmmakers who have followed his stimulating cross-disciplinary approach to filmmaking.

—R. F. Cousins

ROY, Bimal

Nationality: Indian. **Born:** Dacca, 12 July 1909. **Family:** Married to Manobina Bimal Roy, four children. **Career:** Assistant cameraman, New Theatres studio, under Nitin Bose, 1932; cameraman for director P.C. Barua, 1935-42; directed first film, *Udayer Pathey,* 1944; moved to Bombay, after World War II; formed Bimal Roy Productions, 1952; president of the Indian Motion Picture Producers' Association, 1960-62. **Died:** In 1966.

Films as Director:

1943 *Bengal Famine* (short) (+ ph)
1944 *Udayer Pathey* (+ sc, ph)
1945 *Hamrahi* (+ sc, ph)
1948 *Anjangarh* (+ sc)
1949 *Mantra-Mughdha*
1950 *Pahela Admi* (+ sc)
1952 *Maa*
1953 *Parineeta*; ***Do Bigha Zamin****/Two Acres of Land* (*Calcutta Cruel City*)
1954 *Baap Beti*; *Biraj Bahu*; *Naukri* (+ pr); *Devdas* (+ pr)
1958 *Yahudi*; *Madhumati*
1959 *Sujata*
1960 *Parakh*
1962 *Prem Patra*
1963 *Bandini*

Other Films:

1934 *Dadu Mansoor* (ph)
1935 *Devdas* (ph); *Nalla Thangal* (ph)
1936 *Manzil* (ph); *Grihadaha* (ph); *Maya* (ph)
1937 *Mukti* (ph)
1938 *Abhagin* (ph)
1939 *Badi Didi* (ph); *Haar Jeet* (ph)
1942 *Meenakshi* (ph)
1955 *Amanat* (Arbind Sen) (pr)
1956 *Parivar* (Asit Sen) (pr)
1957 *Aparadhi Kaun* (pr)
1960 *Usne Kaha Tha* (pr)
1961 *Kabuliwala* (Hemen Gupta) (pr); *Immortal Stupa* (doc) (pr)
1964 *Benazir* (pr); *Life and Message of Swami Vivekananda* (doc) (pr)
1967 *Gautama the Buddha* (doc) (pr)
1968 *Do Dooni Char* (pr)

Publications

On ROY: books—

Barnouw, Erik, and S. Krishnaswamy, *Indian Film,* New York, 1980.
da Cuncha, Uma, editor, *The New Generation: 1960-1980,* New Delhi, 1981.
Willemen, Paul, and Behroze Ghandy, *Indian Cinema,* London, 1982.
Ramachandran, T.M., *70 Years of Indian Cinema (1913-1983),* Bombay, 1985.

On ROY: articles—

Seton, Marie, "The Indian Film," in *Film* (London), March 1955.
Ray, S.K., "New Indian Directors," in *Film Quarterly* (Berkeley), Fall 1960.
Sarha, Kolita, "Discovering India," in *Films and Filming* (London), December 1960.
Roy, Manobina, "The Bimal Roy Only I Knew," in *The Illustrated Weekly of India,* 3 August 1980.
Tesson, Charles, "Le rêve Indien," in *Cahiers du Cinéma* (Paris), March 1985.

* * *

Among Indian filmgoers Bimal Roy is regarded as a filmmaker of extraordinary integrity, as someone whose life and work are of a piece—a landowner's son who relinquished claims to the family property, a producer who provided unheard-of medical and pension benefits to his employees, and a filmmaker who steadily addressed the difficult social issues of casteism and the landless poor.

Bimal Roy started out as cameraman for New Theaters in Calcutta and worked on the famous Bengali film *Devdas* (1935), but the Second World War and the consequent decline of the Bengali film industry led him, like many other Bengali filmmakers, to the chief production center of Bombay. Here, Roy earned a national reputation for the realism of his film *Do Bigha Zamin.* The film tells the story of a poor peasant who tries to hold on to his two acres of farming land against the machinations of his landlord. The peasant fails to keep the land despite a heart-rending effort to make extra money as a rickshaw puller in Calcutta. Towards the end, the film piles misfortune on misfortune, but the early part of the film is modest and sober. The actor Balraj Sahni gives a quietly dignified performance as the peasant, while the small domestic gestures between him and his wife are rendered naturally. Against the convention of most Hindi melodramas, *Do Bigha Zamin* ends on a note of despair, a note appropriate to the condition of marginal farmers in a newly-independent India.

Do Bigha Zamin was followed by the popular *Madhumati* and *Yahudi. Madhumati* dealt with the odd intimations of familiarity with strange places which Hindus attribute to acquaintance in a prior incarnation. *Yahudi* examined the prejudice against Jews within the Roman Empire, a transposition of India's caste-related problems to the context of Rome. Both films revealed Roy's special skills as cameraman-director. Although Roy preferred to keep his camera static, he calculated the orbit of view very precisely and blocked movements at several elevations to lighten the sense of a fixed perspective.

Roy's next film, *Sujata,* harnessed all his energies as a filmmaker of conscience to a single end—that of exposing the evils of the caste system. *Sujata* tells the story of an outcaste girl who is raised "almost like a daughter" in a high-caste family. While the orphaned girl is young, she can be included in her new family without too much discrimination between her and the family's real daughter, but when the real daughter becomes marriageable, there is pressure on the family to get the untouchable girl out of the way. Bimal Roy's camera views the family tensions with salutary detachment. The camera maintains a middle distance as the outcaste girl runs to her "father" to ask why she cannot sleep in a pretty bed like her sister; the camera maintains the same distance as the now older young woman walks near the windows of her room reflecting on arbitrary social distinctions. Where other Indian directors would cut from one dramatic scene to the next, Roy edits to include the undramatic moments which add substance to the drama. In a key scene by the river, Roy holds the camera on Sujata as she leans against a wall, thinking (presumably) about the man she dare not hope to marry. When the man she is thinking of appears, her few words to him derive force from the pondering Roy has included in the sequence. Things turn out well at the end of *Sujata,* but not in the way of romances. No high birth or secret treasure is discovered to make the outcaste woman grander than she is. The social resistance to according her full status is strong; only an equally strong habit of self-respect in the woman and a strong act of *choosing* her by the young man allow their love to flower.

There are no art theaters in India. The older movies for which there is demand play in small commercial theaters in the morning. It is an indication of the enduring quality of Roy's work that *Do Bigha Zamin* and *Sujata* feature in these morning shows for *aficionados* of the cinema.

—Satti Khanna

RUDOLPH, Alan

Nationality: American. **Born:** Los Angeles, 18 December 1943, son of actor and film/TV director Oscar Rudolph. **Education:** Studied accounting at UCLA. **Career:** Began work in the Paramount Pictures mailroom, mid-1960s; joined Directors Guild Training Program, 1967; assistant director for TV and films, late 1960s; directed first feature, *Premonition,* 1970 (released 1972); worked with Robert Altman at Lion's Gate, from 1973; Altman produced *Welcome to L.A.* and *Remember My Name.*

Films as Director:

1970 *Premonition* (+ sc) (released 1972)
1973 *Terror Circus* (*Barn of the Naked Dead*) (+ sc)
1976 *Welcome to LA* (+ sc)
1978 *Remember My Name* (+ sc)
1980 *Roadie* (+ co-story)
1982 *Endangered Species* (+ co-sc)
1983 *Return Engagement*
1984 *Choose Me* (+ sc); *Songwriter*
1985 *Trouble in Mind* (+ sc)
1987 *Made in Heaven*
1988 *The Moderns* (+ co-sc)
1989 *Love at Large* (+ sc)
1991 *Mortal Thoughts*
1993 *Equinox*
1994 *Mrs. Parker and the Vicious Circle* (+ co-sc)

Other Films:

1954 *The Rocket Man* (Rudolph) (role)
1973 *The Long Goodbye* (Altman) (asst d)
1974 *California Split* (Altman) (asst d)
1975 ***Nashville*** (Altman) (asst d)
1976 *Buffalo Bill and the Indians, or Sitting Bull's History Lesson* (Altman) (co-sc)
1990 *The Hollywood Mavericks* (Dauman) (appearance)
1992 ***The Player*** (Altman) (appearance)

Publications

By RUDOLPH: book—

Buffalo Bill and the Indians; or, Sitting Bull's History Lesson, with Robert Altman, New York, 1976.

By RUDOLPH: articles—

Interview in *Film Comment* (New York), January/February 1977.
"Add Romance and a Crazed World," in *Monthly Film Bulletin* (London), August 1985.
Interview with Brian Baxter, in *Films and Filming* (London), September 1986.
Interview with Karen Jaehne, in *Film Criticism* (Meadville, Pennsylvania), vol. 24, no. 2, 1988.
Interview with Richard Trainor, in *Sight and Sound* (London), Autumn 1988.
Interview with Richard Combs and Tom Milne, in *Monthly Film Bulletin* (London), March 1989.
Interview with Louise Tanner in *Films in Review* (New York), April 1990.
Interview with Gavin Smith in *Film Comment* (New York), May/June 1993.
"The Producer as Gambler," in *Film Comment* (New York), March/April 1994.

On RUDOLPH: articles—

Milne, Tom, " ... as suggestive as a neon orchid," in *Sight and Sound* (London), Summer 1985.

Farber, S., "Five Horsemen After the Apocalypse," in *Film Comment* (New York), July/August 1985.
Garel, A., and F. Guérif, "Alan Rudolph," in *Revue du Cinéma* (Paris), July/August 1985.
Rensin, D., "The Man Who Would Be Different," in *American Film* (Washington, D.C.), March 1986.
Jaehne, K., "Time for *The Moderns,*" in *Film Comment* (New York), March/April 1988.
Taylor, Paul, "Meet All the People—Alan Rudolph," in *Monthly Film Bulletin* (London), November 1990.
Nordstrom, V., article in *Chaplin* (Stockholm), vol. 33, no. 1, 1991.
Orman, T., "'Everything Means Something, Cynthia': Alan Rudolph's *Mortal Thoughts,*" in *Cineaction,* Fall 1992.
Appelo, Tim, "Finding Dorothy Parker's Voice," in *Entertainment Weekly,* 23 December 1994.

* * *

Alan Rudolph's films are populated with mysterious wanderers, musicians, painters, and journalists, people who have flirted with success without ever achieving it and who exist in a timeless, bohemian limbo. It is clear that he identifies with his protagonists. Never as trenchant a satirist as his early mentor, Robert Altman, Rudolph imbues his work with a strong romantic streak. At his worst, he is simply trite and maudlin. At his best, he weaves elaborate fantasies as colourful and eyecatching as anything Coppola ever managed at Zoetrope.

Rudolph's filmmaking career can be divided into two halves. Stunned by Altman's *McCabe and Mrs Miller,* the young Rudolph quickly attached himself to the shirt tails of the great director, co-scripting *Buffalo Bill and the Indians,* Altman's bicentennial savaging of Wild West mythology, and also working on *The Long Goodbye.*

Altman's film company produced *Welcome to LA,* Rudolph's first feature as a director. While the film was not a particularly scathing critique of Californian social mores, it nevertheless introduces themes and motifs which would be further explored in subsequent Rudolph works. For example, the film features a Kerouac-like lonesome traveller as hero. Keith Carradine plays a whisky drinking songwriter, just arrived in town, who dresses—somewhat incongruously—like the straw man in the Wizard of Oz, with a goatee beard and a tweed hat. But despite his unlikely garb, he manages to seduce everyone from Lauren Hutton to Geraldine Chaplin. Rudolph has spoken of the importance of music to his films. *Welcome to LA* boasts a truly awful soundtrack, comprising the songs which the Carradine character is supposed to have written. This may be an elaborate joke on the director's part. After all, Carradine is ostensibly a failed songwriter, and his music isn't meant to be any good.

Rudolph's second feature, *Remember My Name,* bombed at the box office. Undeterred, he geared up to start work on a third project, a long cherished movie chronicling the lives and fast times of the American artists and literati in 1920s Paris. Five weeks before the cameras were due to roll, though, the financiers pulled the plug on *The Moderns,* and Rudolph was cast out into the wilderness of work as a contract director.

Between 1978 and 1984, Rudolph was employed on several "routine" movies, directing a vehicle for the overweight American rocker Meatloaf, and making a romantic melodrama about cow killing in the U.S. Midwest, *Endangered Species.* He also found time to direct a highly provocative documentary, *Return Engagement,* which records a staged encounter between two disgraced figures from the recent American past—Timothy Leary, the psychedelic Harvard academic, and G. Gordon Liddy, mastermind behind the Watergate break-in. Although seemingly from opposite ends of the political spectrum, Leary and Liddy turn out to have a great deal in common. They are *bona fide* American anti-heroes, not at all dissimilar from the fictional characters with which Rudolph fills his films. As such, they hold an obvious attraction for the director.

Choose Me, based on a radio show and shot in less for a month for under $750,000, is quintessential Rudolph, and its success marked his return to the mainstream. It centers on a singles bar where glamorous strangers strike up acquaintance. Genevieve Bujold, a Rudolph regular, plays a DJ agony aunt, offering solace and advice to the town's yearning and heartbroken populace. There is something theatrical and stylized about the movie. The sets could be from a Minnelli musical. The mysterious journalist with a dubious past (Keith Carradine again) is reminiscent of the figure in innumerable ads. But Rudolph manages to create characters, even as the movie risks becoming an exercise in glamorous facades. In spite of the rain, the neon and the mist, and the soul music soundtrack, this is an absorbing story about sexual jealousy, and it is also genuinely mysterious: all in all, quite a coup for under a million dollars.

The follow up, *Trouble in Mind,* involves yet more tampering with Keith Carradine's coiffure: the actor, playing a young married delinquent making his first steps in organized crime, sports a lanky 1950s quiff. This contrasts with Kris Kristofferson's beard and the bald pate of a villain played by Divine, on leave from John Waters. A meticulous stylist, Rudolph is one of the few directors capable of portraying character through hairstyles. A camp *film noir,* not that far removed in its narrative from *Big Heat, Trouble in Mind* manages again to blend visual extravagance with downbeat subject matter. The same cannot be said for *Made in Heaven,* a flimsy and mawkish love story, which in spite of its passing nods to the Sturges/Capra vision of small-town America, and its celestial chicanery (early parts of the film are set in heaven, for this is yet another variation on *Heaven Can Wait*) seems toothless and bland in comparison with its two predecessors. Again, Rudolph didn't have full artistic control: "The writer-producers said they wanted me but it turned out they didn't want the darker touches I would have added."

Finally, ten years later than scheduled, Rudolph managed to make *The Moderns* in 1988. This was not the simple-minded evocation of Gertrude Stein's tea parties and Hemingway's alcoholism that some critics presumed. Based on "memoir, gossip, innuendo and lies," it attempted to question the premises on which aesthetic judgments are made. What is originality, and what constitutes forgery? These rather obvious questions seemed especially relevant in a decade when art prices were shooting through the roof. The Rudolph repertory company turned out in force, with Bujold, Carradine, and Geraldine Chaplin all cast. Playing on stereotypes of 1920s modernism, and caricaturing American attitudes toward Europe (*The Moderns* recreates Paris in Montreal) this was a far more tongue-in-cheek creation than its detractors realized.

Rudolph's films are like those of his mentor Altman in that, taken as a whole, they are always interesting and consistently crammed with style. Occasionally brilliant, in the final analysis they are widely—and maddeningly—uneven. Take *Love at Large,* the story of a private detective and his various encounters after he is hired by a mystery woman. As much as you try to like the film because the characters are, on their surfaces, so intriguing, the result is more chaotic than coherent. The same can be said for *Mortal Thoughts,* about a murder investigation, and *Equinox,* about two lookalikes—one a powerless car mechanic and the other a gangland thug—whose lives coincide.

Rudolph's most interesting recent film is *Mrs. Parker and the Vicious Circle,* a recollection of life among the 1920s New York intelligencia. At its core is the character of the writer-humorist Dorothy Parker, portrayed by Jennifer Jason Leigh. For all her surface cynicism and tenacity, Parker is depicted as a fragile, sensitive lost soul, a woman who gained a certain measure of professional success but who found elusive any level of personal contentment. The "vicious circle" of the title is the daily luncheon gathering of fabled

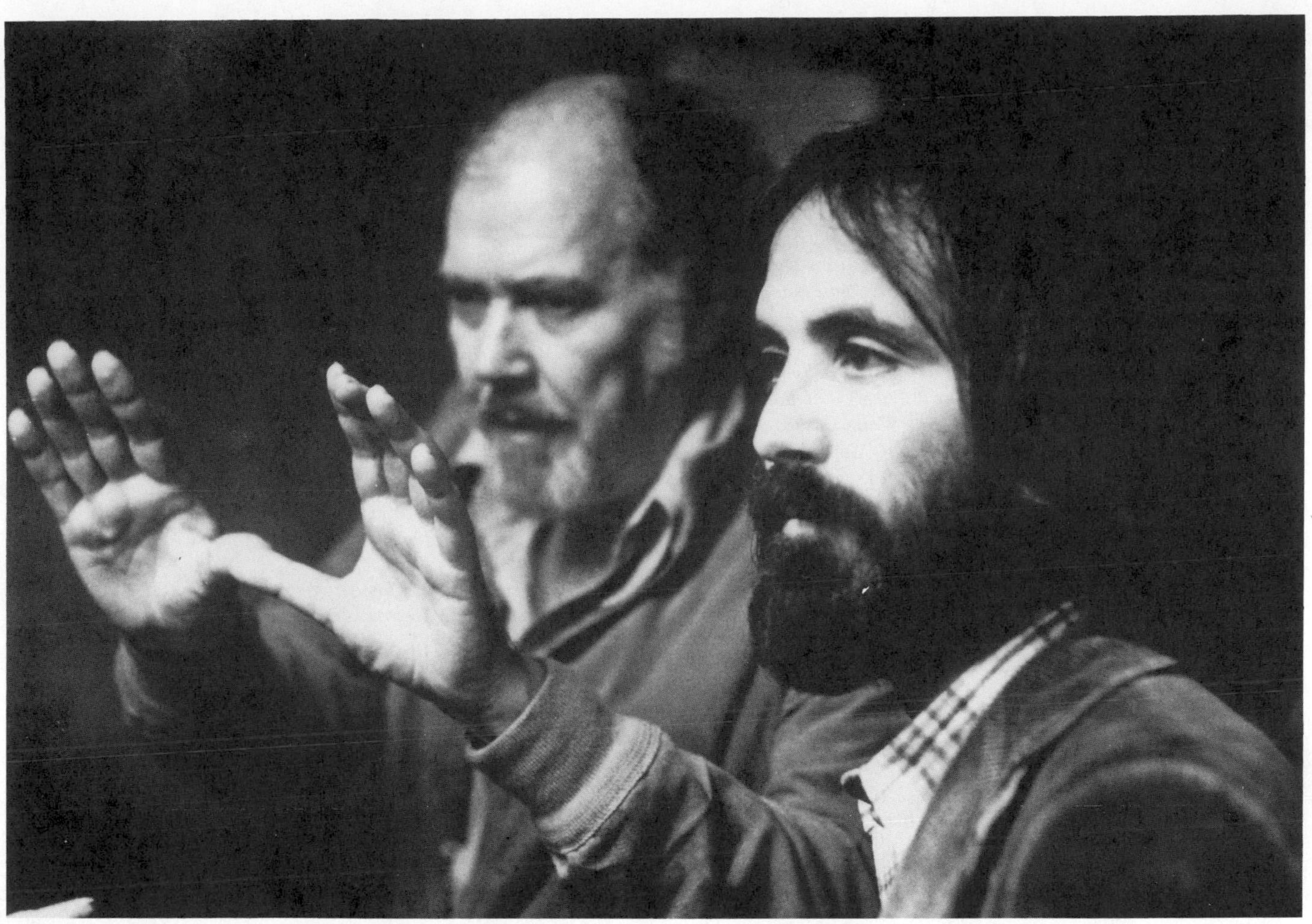

Alan Rudolph (right) with Robert Altman

writers, editors, and wits at the Algonquin Hotel's Round Table. Parker is one of the regulars. Others include Robert Benchley (Campbell Scott), with whom Parker shares a close friendship and an unconsummated sexual attraction, and Charles MacArthur (Matthew Broderick), with whom she has an ill-fated affair. Flitting in and out of the story are Alexander Woollcott, Edna Ferber, Robert Sherwood, and Marc Connelly, among many others. It is Rudolph's contention that these celebrity scribes frittered away their talents on drink and idle chatter, while the true and lasting writers of the generation (such as Hemingway and Faulkner) were devoting their energies to their work.

Parker aficionados criticized the facts as presented in the film, contending it was unlikely that Parker and Benchley (who was less physically attractive than depicted onscreen) lived with a sexual tension between them. As the on-screen Parker reads her poetry and sits with her friends at the Algonquin, she often appears as a sad sack, an alcoholic bore. Yet in fact she was a true wit, with people flocking to be in her company. Onscreen, her voice is grating and slurring; it is the voice of a drunk. Yet in the biography *You Might as Well Live: The Life and Times of Dorothy Parker,* she is described as "possessed of a voice surprisingly rich and full for so small a person."

Rudolph's wildest—and best—film to date remains *Choose Me,* a comedy-drama with an evocative from-midnight-til-dawn feel. *Choose Me* serves as the best illustration of themes which remain constant throughout his work, exploring how some individuals choose to play different roles as they relate to others, and how chance acquaintances and occurrences affect peoples' lives forever.

Rudolph is something of an anomaly among contemporary American filmmakers. In spite of his extravagant visual sense, he seems to work best on small budgets. Although his films seem destined for art houses, the cheerful, upbeat romanticism of some of his stories and his insistence on creating happy couples suggest he is a populist at heart.

—G. C. Macnab, updated by Rob Edelman

RUIZ, Raul

Nationality: Chilean. **Born:** Puerto Montt, Chile, 25 July 1941. **Education:** Studied law, theology, and theatre; spent year at Documentary Film School of Santa Fe, Argentina, 1966. **Family:** Married to filmmaker and editor Valeria Sarmiento. **Career:** Prolific writer of stage plays, 1956-62; shot first film *La maleta* (unfinished) at Grupo Cine Experimental, University of Chile, 1960; directed first feature, *Los tres triste tigres,* 1968; film advisor to the Socialist Party in Allende's coalition, 1971-72; forced into exile following Pinochet's coup, 1973; moved to Germany, then to France, 1974; filmmaker with France's National Audiovisual Institute, from 1977; director for TV, 1980s; director, La Maison de la Culture, Le Havre, 1985-88. **Awards:** Grand Prix, Locarno Festival, for *Tres Tristes Tigres,* 1969; César Award, for *Colloque de chiens,* 1978.

Films as Director and Scriptwriter:

1960 *La maleta* (unfinished)
1967 *El tango del viudo* (unfinished)
1968 *Los tres triste tigres* (*Tres Tristes Tigres*; *Three Sad Tigers*)
1969 *Militarismo y tortura* (doc short); *La cate naria* (unfinished)
1970 *Que hacer?* (co-d)
1971 *La colonia penal* (*The Penal Colony*); *Ahor te vamos a llamar hermano* (*Now We Will Call You Brother*) (short); *Nadie dijo nada* (*Nobody Said Nothing*); *Mapuches* (doc short)
1972 *Los minuteros* (*The Minute Hands, The Street Photographer*) (short)
1973 *La expropriación* (*The Expropriation*) (completed in Germany); *Nueva canción Chileña* (*New Chilean Song*) (short); *El realismo socialista* (*Socialist Realism*); *Palomilla brava* (*Bad Girl*); *Palomita blanca* (*Little White Dove*) (co-d, unfinished due to coup); *Abastecimiento* (*Supply*) (short)
1974 *Diálogo de exilados* (*Dialogue of Exiles*)
1975 *El cuerpo repartido y el mundo al revez* (*Mensch verstreut und Welt verkehrt*; *The Scattered Body and the World Turned Upside Down*)
1976 *Sotelo* (doc short)
1977 *Colloque de chiens* (*Dog's Language*) (short); *La Vocation suspendue* (*The Suspended Vocation*)
1978 *L'Hypothèse du tableau volé* (*The Hypothesis of a Stolen Painting*); *Les Divisions de la nature* (short)
1979 *De Grands Evènements et des gens ordinaires* (*Of Great Events and Ordinary People*); *Petit Manuel d'histoire de France* (*Short History of France*); *Images du débat* (*Images of Debate*); *Jeux* (*Games*); *Rue des archives 79*
1980 *Le Jeu de l'oie* (*Snakes and Ladders*) (short); *La Ville nouvelle* (*The New Town*) (short); *L'Or gris* (*Grey Gold*); *Teletests* (short); *Pages d'un catalogue* (*Pages from a Catalogue*) (short); *Fahlstrom* (short)
1981 *Le Territoire* (*The Territory*); *Le Borgne* (serial); *Het dak van de walvis* (*On Top of the Whale*; *The Whale's Roof*)
1982 *Les Trois Couronnes du Matelot* (*The Sailor's Three Crowns*); *Classification des plantes* (short); *Les Ombres chinoise* (*Chinese Shadows*) (short); *Querelle de jardins* (*The War of the Gardens*) (short)
1983 *Bérénice*; *La Ville des pirates* (*City of Pirates*); *Point de fuite*; *Voyage autour d'une main* (short); *Le retour d'un amateur de bibliothèque* (short, for TV); *La présence réelle* (*The Real Presence*)
1985 *L'Éveillé du pont de l'Alma*; *Les Destins de Manoel* (*Manuel's Destinies*); *Dans un miroir* (*In a Mirror*); *Richard III*
1986 *Mammame*; *Régime sans pain*; *L'Ile au trésor* (*Treasure Island*)
1987 *Memoire des apparences*; *Vie est un songe*; *La chouette aveugle*
1988 *Brise-Glace* (*Icebreaker*) (co-d)
1989 *Allegory*
1990 *The Golden Boat*
1991 *Treasure Island*

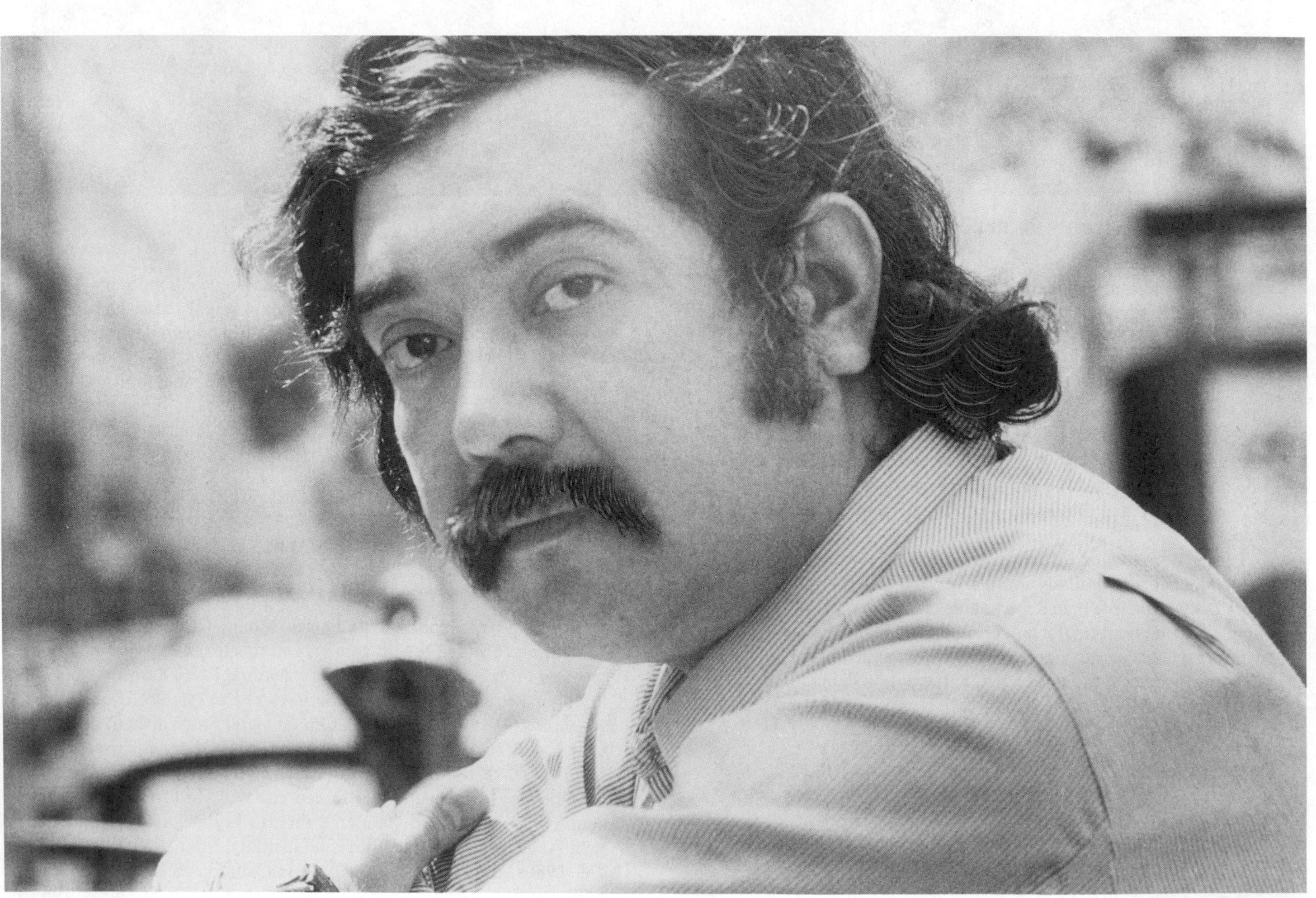

Raul Ruiz

1992 *Dark at Noon*
1994 *The Secret Journey: Lives of Saints and Sinners*; *Fado, Majeur et Mineur*

Publications

By RUIZ: articles—

"Chili: le cinema de l'unité populaire," an interview with H. Ehrmann, in *Ecran* (Paris), February 1974.
"Notes sur *La Vocation suspendue,*" in *Positif* (Paris), December/January 1977/78.
"Les Relations d'objets au cinéma," in *Cahiers du Cinéma* (Paris), April 1978.
Interview with Don Ranvaud, in *Framework* (Norwich, England), Spring 1979.
"Filters, Exile and Cunning: Problems of Time, Space and Perception," an interview with Ian Christie, in *Monthly Film Bulletin* (London), December 1984.
Interview with Alain Philippon, in *Cahiers du Cinéma* (Paris), May 1985.
Interview with D. Ehrenstein, in *Film Quarterly* (Berkeley), Fall 1986.
Interview with E. Spigland, in *Persistance of Vision,* no. 8, 1990.

On RUIZ: books—

Buci-Glucksmann, Christine, and Fabrice Revault d'Allonnes, *Raoul Ruiz,* Paris, 1987.
King, John, *Magical Reels: A History of Cinema in Latin America,* London, 1990.

On RUIZ: articles—

Pick, Zuzana, "Le Cinéma chilien sous le signe de l'Unité Populaire (1970-1973)," in *Positif* (Paris), January 1974.
Roud, Richard, "Turning Points: Ruiz & Truffaut," in *Sight and Sound* (London), Summer 1978.
"Exile and Cunning: Raul Ruiz," special section, in *Afterimage* (Rochester, New York), no. 10, 1981.
"Raul Ruiz Issue" of *Cahiers du Cinéma* (Paris), March 1983.
Raul Ruiz Section of *Positif* (Paris), December 1983.
Mouesca, J., "El cine chileño en el exilio (1973-1983)," in *Cine Cubano* (Havana), no. 109, 1984.
Raul Ruiz Section of *Casablanca* (Madrid), January 1984.
Adair, Gilbert, "Raúl: Sheheruizade, or 1001 Films," in *Sight and Sound* (London), Summer 1984.
Rosenbaum, Jonathan, "Beating the Labyrinth," in *Monthly Film Bulletin* (London), January 1985.
Christie, Ian, "Raul Ruiz and the House of Culture," in *Sight and Sound* (London), Spring 1987.
Pick, Z., "Le cinema chilien de l'exil: le cas de Raoul Ruiz," in *Cinemaction,* July 1990.
Reynaud, B., "Ruiz sur l'Hudson," in *Cahiers du Cinéma* (Paris), July/August 1990.
Codelli, L., "Raul Ruiz," in *Ekran,* no. 4/5, 1991.
Jayamanne, L., "The Case for Ruiz ...," in *Filmnews,* no. 9, 1991.
Strauss, F., "Horreur baroque," in *Cahiers du Cinéma* (Paris), February 1992.
Martin, A., and C. Tuckfield, "Never One Space: The Cinema of Raul Ruiz," in *Cinema Papers,* January 1993.
Piazzo, P., and F. Richard, "Entretien avec Raul Ruiz," in *Positif,* February 1993.

* * *

A prodigious storyteller, Raul Ruiz is also a prolific manufacturer of moving images. This Chilean filmmaker, now living in exile in Paris, has molded his films by a deeply personal concern with representation and discourse. His innovative and experimental work thus defies any attempt at classification.

The cinema of Ruiz is a cinema of ideas. He has unmasked ideological stereotypes (*Three Sad Tigers, Nobody Said Nothing,* and *Dialogue of Exiles*), has exposed the contradictions of despotic institutions (*The Suspended Vocation*), and unveiled his own tortured world (*The One-Eyed Man*) torn between his cultural origins and the false cosmopolitanism of forced exile (*The Whale's Roof*). His mise-en-scéne is preoccupied with representation (*The Hypothesis of a Stolen Painting* and *The Divisions of Nature*) and the fragmentation of reality (*The Sailor's Three Crowns*). His narrative is imbued with an intense research into performance and the ambiguity of the spoken language. His storylines never appear to enjoy a privileged position within the overall narrative of his films (*The Expropriation*). The voice-over narration (*The War of the Gardens*), the commentary (*The Divisions of Nature*), or even the dialogue (*The Penal Colony*), by detaching themselves from the image track, acquire an independent life or serve to lure the spectator into the willful contradictions that Ruiz wants to explore. The spoken language, saturated with Chilean slang, often makes his films incomprehensible for non-Chilean spectators. In France, though, Ruiz has found an audience for whom simulations of Cartesian logic are the playful components of a fictional labyrinth.

Few filmmakers have taken better advantage of commissioned work. His video essays and documentary films for television and the Centre Beaubourg are original experiments with technology and narrative which inform the strategies of his feature work. A didactic comparison of French- and English-style gardens is displaced in favour of a playful suspense story (*The War of the Gardens*). A commissioned film on Beaubourg's cartography exhibition becomes a diabolic snakes-and-ladders game (*Snakes and Ladders*).

Ruiz has a passionate affair with technology. Working with innovative directors of photography—Diego Bonancina in Chile, Sacha Vierny and Henri Alekan in France—he has brought back the magic of French poetic realism to explore a world of manipulation, impotence, and violence. He favors the use of lighting, filters, and mirrors that deform filmic reality into a kaleidoscopic maze that traps his performers (*Snakes and Ladders*) and turns familiarity into fantastic exoticism (*The Territory*). Ruiz's originality stems from personal paradox. He is an exiled filmmaker in search of a territory, mastering a new language while stubbornly upholding his roots, and confined in a culture he recognizes as having colonized his own.

Ruiz's contribution to Chilean cinema has been openly acknowledged since *Three Sad Tigers* in 1969. His innovative approach to film, his independence, and his critical stance on political reductionism have often set him apart from the mainstream. A name rarely mentioned in discussions on the new Latin American cinema, Ruiz retrospectives in Madrid, Edinburgh, London, Rotterdam, and Paris have finally brought him public recognition. After years of relative obscurity, critical acclaim has earned him a leading position within the French avant-grade.

Chilean cinema in exile has found in Ruiz a respected and vital representative. A total filmmaker, for whom theater, music, literature, and visual arts are familiar territory, Ruiz successfully combines intellectual inquiry with Latin American hedonism.

—Zuzana Mirjam Pick

RUSSELL, Ken

Nationality: British. **Born:** Henry Kenneth Alfred Russell in Southampton, England, 3 July 1927. **Education:** Attended Pangbourne Nautical College, 1941-44. **Family:** Married 1) Shirley Ann Kingdom, 1957 (divorced), four sons, one daughter; 2) Vivian Jolly, 1984, one daughter. **Military Service:** Served in merchant navy, 1945, and in Royal Air Force, 1946-49. **Career:** Dancer with Ny Norsk ballet, 1950; actor with Garrick players, from 1951; documentary maker for the BBC's *Monitor,* from 1959; directed first feature, *French Dressing,* 1963; TV director for *Omnibus,* from 1966, and for *South Bank Show,* from 1983. **Address:** Old Tinsleys, Main Road, East Boldre, Brockinhurst, Hampshire SOH2 7WT, England.

Films as Director:

1957 *Amelia and the Angel* (amateur short)
1958 *Peep Show* (amateur short); *Lourdes* (amateur short)
1959 *Poet's London* (for TV); *Gordon Jacob* (for TV); *Guitar Craze* (for TV); *Variations on a Mechanical Theme* (for TV); untitled film on Robert McBryde and Robert Colquhoun (for TV); *Portrait of a Goon* (for TV)
1960 *Marie Rambert Remembers* (for TV); *Architecture of Entertainment* (for TV); *Cranks at Work* (for TV); *The Miners' Picnic* (for TV); *Shelagh Delaney's Salford* (for TV); *A House in Bayswater* (for TV); *The Light Fantastic* (for TV)
1961 *Old Battersea House* (for TV); *Portrait of a Soviet Composer* (for TV); *London Moods* (for TV); *Antonio Gaudi* (for TV)
1962 *Pop Goes the Easel* (for TV); *Preservation Man* (for TV); *Mr. Chesher's Traction Engines* (for TV); *Lotte Lenya Sings Kurt Weill* (co-d) (for TV); *Elgar* (for TV)
1963 *French Dressing*; *Watch the Birdie* (for TV)
1964 *Lonely Shore* (for TV); *Bartok* (for TV); *The Dotty World of James Lloyd* (for TV); *Diary of a Nobody* (for TV)
1965 *The Debussy Film* (for TV); *Always on Sunday* (for TV)
1966 *Don't Shoot the Composer* (for TV); *Isadora Duncan, the Biggest Dancer in the World* (for TV)
1967 *Billion Dollar Brain*; *Dante's Inferno* (for TV)
1968 *Song of Summer* (for TV)
1969 *Women in Love*
1970 *The Music Lovers* (+ pr); *The Dance of the Seven Veils* (for TV)
1971 ***The Devils*** (+ sc, co-pr); *The Boy Friend* (+ pr, sc)
1972 *Savage Messiah* (+ pr)
1974 *Mahler* (+ sc); *Tommy* (+ co-pr, sc)
1975 *Lisztomania* (+ sc)
1977 *Valentino* (+ co-sc)
1978 *Clouds of Glory, Parts I and II* (for TV)
1980 *Altered States*
1983 *Ken Russell's View of the Planets* (for TV)
1984 *Crimes of Passion*; *Elgar* (for TV); *Vaughan Williams* (for TV)
1986 *Gothic*
1987 episode in *Aria*
1988 *Salome's Last Dance* (+ sc); *The Lair of the White Worm* (+ sc); *Ken Russell's ABC of British Music* (for TV)
1989 *The Rainbow* (+ co-sc); *Ken Russell—A British Picture* (for TV)
1990 *Strange Affliction of Anton Bruckner* (for TV)
1991 *Whore* (+ co-sc); *Prisoner of Honor* (for TV)
1993 *Lady Chatterly* (+ co-sc) (for TV)
1994 *The Insatiable Mrs. Kirsch* (+ sc)

Other Films:

1991 *The Russia House* (Schepisi) (role as Walter)

Publications

By RUSSELL: books—

An Appalling Talent: Ken Russell, with John Baxter, London, 1973.
A British Picture: An Autobiography, London, 1989.
Altered States: An Autobiography, New York, 1990.
The Lion Roars: Ken Russell on Film, London, 1993; Winchester, Massachusetts, 1994.

By RUSSELL: articles—

"Shock Treatment: Interview," with Gordon Gow, in *Films and Filming* (London), July 1970.
Interview with Gene D. Phillips, in *Film Comment* (New York), Fall 1970.
"Ken Russell Writes on Raising Kane," in *Films and Filming* (London), May 1972.
"Savage Saviour: Interview," with Peter Buckley, in *Films and Filming* (London), October 1972.
"Ideas for Films," in *Film* (London), January/February 1973.
"Ken Russell," with B. Wiener and C. Hemphill, in *Interview* (New York), March 1975.
"Fact, Fantasy, and the Films of Ken Russell," with Gene Phillips, in *Journal of Popular Film* (Bowling Green, Ohio), vol. 5, no. 3-4, 1976.
"With Ken Russell on the Set of *Valentino,*" with Herb Lightman, in *American Cinematographer* (Los Angeles), November 1977.
Interview with R. Gentry, in *Post Script* (Jacksonville, Florida), Spring/Summer 1983.
"Something Wilde," an interview with D. Nicholson, in *Films and Filming* (London), July 1988.
"Next of Ken," an interview with Graham Fuller, in *Film Comment* (New York), May/June 1989.
"Tis Pity She's a *Whore,*" an interview with J. Saynor, in *Interview* (New York), May 1991.

On RUSSELL: books—

Wilson, Colin, *Ken Russell: A Director in Search of a Hero,* London, 1974.
Atkins, Thomas, ed., *Ken Russell,* New York, 1976.
Gomez, Joseph, *Ken Russell: The Adaptor as Creator,* London, 1976.
Rosenfeldt, Diane, *Ken Russell: A Guide to Reference Sources,* Boston, 1978.
Phillips, Gene D., *Ken Russell,* Boston, 1979.
Hanke, Ken, *Ken Russell's Films,* Metuchen, New Jersey, 1984.

On RUSSELL: articles—

Dempsey, Michael, "The World of Ken Russell," in *Film Quarterly* (Berkeley), Spring 1972.
Fisher, Jack, "Three Paintings of Sex: The Films of Ken Russell," in *Films Journal* (New York), September 1972.
Kolker, Robert, "Ken Russell's Biopics: Grander and Gaudier," in *Film Comment* (New York), May/June 1973.
Farber, Stephen, "Russellmania," in *Film Comment* (New York), November/December 1975.
Gomez, Joseph, "*Mahler* and the Methods of Ken Russell's Films on Composers," in *Velvet Light Trap* (Madison, Wisconsin), Winter 1975.
Gilliatt, Penelope, "Genius, Genia, Genium, Ho Hum," in *New Yorker,* 26 April 1976.
Dempsey, Michael, "Ken Russell, Again," in *Film Quarterly* (Berkeley), Winter 1977/78.

Ken Russell on the set of *The Boy Friend*

Yacowar, Maurice, "Ken Russell's *Rabelais,*" in *Literature/Film Quarterly* (Salisbury, Maryland), Winter 1980.

Vlasopolos, Anca, "Ken Russell's *Clouds of Glory,*" in *Literature/Film Quarterly* (Salisbury, Maryland), Winter 1980.

Corliss, Richard, "Dark Nights of the Libido: *Crimes of Passion* and Other Films," in *Time* (New York), 29 October 1984.

Ackerman, Diane, "Why Horror Movies Still Gnaw: *Gothic* and Other Films," in *New York Times,* 5 April 1987.

Jaehne, Karen, "Wormomania: Ken Russell's Best Laid Planaria," in *Film Criticism* (Meadville, Pennsylvania), vol. 24, no. 6, 1988.

Billington, Michael, "Just Right for D. H. Lawrence," in *New York Times,* 30 April 1989.

Gomez, Joseph, "The Elusive Gold at the End of *The Rainbow,*" in *Literature/Film Quarterly* (Salisbury, Maryland), Spring 1990.

Bookbinder, Robert, "*Women in Love,*" in *The Films of the Seventies,* New York, 1990.

Tibbetts, John, "The Lyre of Light: Ken Russell's Biopics," in *Film Comment* (New York), March/April 1992.

Hadleigh, Boze, "*The Music Lovers,*" in *The Lavender Screen: Homosexuality on Film,* New York, 1993.

Kael, Pauline, "*Women in Love, Savage Messiah, Valentino,*" in *For Keeps,* New York, 1994.

* * *

British director Ken Russell was forty-two when his film of D. H. Lawrence's *Women in Love* placed him in the ranks of movie directors of international stature. For more than a decade before that, however, British television viewers had been treated to a succession of his skilled TV biographies of great artists like Frederick Delius (*Song of Summer*) and Isadora Duncan. Russell has always gravitated toward the past in choosing subjects for filming because, as he says, "topics of the moment pass and change. Besides, we can be more dispassionate and therefore more truthful in dealing with the past. And to see the past from the vantage point of the present is to be able to judge the effect of the past on the present."

His first TV documentaries, like that on Edward Elgar, correspond to what he calls "the accepted textbook idea of what a documentary should be; you were supposed to extol the great artists and their work. Later I turned to showing how great artists transcended their personal problems and weakness in creating great art." But this more realistic approach, exemplified in his telefilm about Richard Strauss (*Dance of the Seven Veils*) and his feature film *The Music Lovers,* about Tchaikovsky, upset some of the members of the audience for both his TV and theatrical films.

As Russell advanced from the small screen to the large in continuing to turn out what have come to be called his biopics, he has almost singlehandedly revolutionized the whole concept of the conventional film biography—to the point where the genre will never be quite the same again. One need only recall the heavily romanticized Hollywood screen biographies on subjects like Cole Porter to grasp how Russell's biopics have come to grips with the problems of an artist's life in relation to his work in a way that makes for much more challenging and entertaining films than the sugar-coated Hollywood screen biographies.

In addition to experimenting with the nature of biographical films, Russell has at the same time been seeking by trial and error to discover in all of his films, biopics or not, to what extent a motion picture can be cut loose from the moorings of conventional storytelling; and his mind-bending science-fiction thriller *Altered States* is an excellent example of this experimentation. If these experiments in narrative technique account for occasional lapses in narrative logic, as in *Lisztomania,* his biopic about Franz Liszt, they also account for the intricate and arresting blend of past and present, fact and fantasy, that characterize his best work.

Among his outstanding films must surely be numbered his screen adaptations of Lawrence's two companion novels, *Women in Love* (1969) and *The Rainbow* (1989), which focus on the personal lives of two sisters as they struggle to carve out their destinies in the modern world. The two films, taken together, represent Russell's finest achievement in the cinema.

Other films of his later career that deserve mention include *The Lair of the White Worm,* based on Bram Stoker's neglected novel about a female vampire who parallels Stoker's male vampire in *Dracula.* Russell turned Stoker's *Lair* into a bloodcurdling horror show. In addition, there is *Whore,* which, like his earlier *Crimes of Passion,* explores with unvarnished realism the grim life of a prostitute. Last but not least, mention must be made of Russell's *Lady Chatterly,* his superb four-hour TV version of Lawrence's controversial novel *Lady Chatterly's Lover,* which depicts a sensational love affair that reaches across the British class barriers. This telefilm, of course, is linked with his two previous Lawrence adaptations and marks another milestone in his career.

Although Russell has often been looked upon as a maverick who makes films that are perhaps more subjective and personal than many directors working today, it is worth noting he is the only British director in history ever to have three films playing first-run engagements in London simultaneously: *The Music Lovers, The Devils,* and *The Boy Friend.* Indeed, this provocative and fascinating director has already assured himself a place in the history of world cinema.

—Gene D. Phillips

RUTTMANN, Walter

Nationality: German. **Born:** Frankfurt am Main, 28 December 1887. **Education:** Goethe-Gymnasium, Abitur 1905; architectural studies in Zurich, from 1907; studied painting in Munich, 1909. **Military Service:** Served as artillery lieutenant on Eastern Front, World War I; suffered nervous breakdown, sent to sanatorium until 1917. **Career:** Began filmmaking, 1919; moved to Berlin, 1923; worked with Lotte Reiniger and Carl Koch on *The Adventures of Prince Achmed,* 1923-26; worked with G. W. Pabst and Abel Gance in Paris, 1929-31. **Died:** In Berlin, 15 July 1941.

Films as Director:

1921 *Opus I*

1920-23 *Opus II, III, IV*

1923 "Der Falkentraum (Dream of Hawks)" sequence in ***Die Nibelungen*** part 1 (Lang)

1924 Abstract Alps dream sequence for *Lebende Buddhas* (Wegener)

1925-26 *Opus V*

1926-27 ***Berlin, die Sinfonie der Grossstadt*** (*Berlin, Symphony of a Great City*)

1928 "Tönende Welle" episode for *Das weisse Stadion* (Fanck)

1929 *Melodie der Welt* (*World Melody*); *Des Haares und der Liebe Wellen* (short fiction film)

1930 *Weekend* (*Wochenende*)

1931 *In der Nacht* (*In the Night*); *Feind im Blut* (documentary)

1932-33 *Acciaio*

1933 *Blut und Boden*

1934 Short film incorporated into *Altgermanische Bauernkultur*; *Metall des Himmels*; Prologue to ***Triumph des Willens*** (*Triumph of the Will*) (Riefenstahl)

1935 *Kleiner Film einer grossen Stadt—Die Stadt Düsseldorf am Rhein*; *Stadt Stuttgart, 100. Cannstatter Volksfest*; *Stuttgart, die Grossstadt zwischen Wald und Reben*
1936 *Schiff in Not*
1937 *Mannesmann*
1938 *Henkel, ein deutsches Werk in seiner Arbeit*; *Weltstrasse See—Welthafen Hamburg*; *Im Dienste der Menschheit*
1940 *Deutsche Waffenschmiede* (*Waffenkammern Deutschland*); *Deutsche Panzer*; *Aberglaube*
1941 *Ein Film gegen die Volkskrankheit Krebs—jeder Achte ...*

Other Films:

1923-26 *Die Abenteuer des Prinzen Achmed* (*The Adventures of Prince Achmed*) (Reiniger) (collaborated on making abstract, moving backgrounds)

Publications

On RUTTMANN: books—

Kracauer, Siegfried, *A Psychological History of the German Film*, Princeton, New Jersey, 1974.
Russett, Robert, and Cecile Starr, *Experimental Animation*, New York, 1976.
Film as Film: Formal Experiment in Film, 1910-1975, exhibition catalog, London, 1979.

On RUTTMANN: articles—

Falkenberg, Paul, "Sound Montage: A Propos de Ruttmann," in *Film Culture* (New York), no. 22-23, 1961.
Cowie, Peter, "*Berlin,*" in *Films and Filming* (London), August 1961.
"Walter Ruttmann," in *Travelling* (Lausanne), Summer 1979.
Fulks, Barry A., "Walter Ruttmann, the Avant-Garde Film, and Nazi Modernism," in *Film and History* (Newark, New Jersey), May 1984.
Brandt, H.J., "Walter Ruttmann: Vom Expressionismus zum Faschismus," (three parts) in *Filmfaust* (Frankfurt), October/November 1985, December 1985/January 1986, and February/March 1986.

* * *

Walter Ruttmann is often associated with the films of others: he created the "Dream of the Hawks" sequence in Fritz Lang's *Die Nibelungen,* and directed several sequences in Paul Wegener's *Lebende Buddhas.* Later on, he assisted in the editing of Leni Riefenstahl's *Olympia.* Easily his own most influential work is *Berlin, Symphony of a Great City,* one of the outstanding abstract documentaries of the 1920s.

Berlin is a visual essay on an average working day in the city, from dawn to the dead of night. The quiet, seemingly abandoned metropolis comes alive as a train makes its way through the suburbs, workers travel on their way to factories, the wheels of industry are set in motion, and everyday occurrences unfold in cafes and on streets. Night approaches, and Berlin becomes lit up like a birthday cake. Boys flirt with girls, chorus girls dance, an orchestra performs Beethoven. Lovers seek out privacy in a hotel. And it will all begin again with the sunrise.

Berlin is indeed a symphony, with Ruttmann stressing the movement of people and machinery in what amounts to a visual tapestry. The key is in the editing: for example, shots of people walking on a street are followed by those of cows' legs. Ruttmann makes no social commentary, as rich and poor, man and animal, exist side by side. His sole interest is the imagery, the creation of visual poetry—even when he contrasts poor children and the food in a restaurant.

Walter Ruttmann

Ruttman's use of montage was influenced by the Russian filmmaker Dziga Vertov. Yet while Vertov's newsreels depicted the progress of a post-Revolutionary Soviet society, the life in Berlin could just as well be the life in Brussels or Amsterdam or Paris. Ruttmann is concerned with the details of daily reality edited together to form a unified whole, but he never comments or editorializes on the lives of his subjects.

The filmmaker, who appropriately began his career as an abstract painter, preceded *Berlin* with a series of experimental "Opus" films. Siegfried Kracauer describes *Opus I* as "a dynamic display of spots vaguely recalling X-ray photographs." Additionally, Ruttmann realized that the advent of sound in motion pictures was inevitable. As a result, he attempted to attune his images to the soundtracks that he felt would ultimately outweigh visual components in importance. In *World Melody,* made after *Berlin,* music and sound effects are orchestrated to relate to the images; *In der Nacht* is a union of imagery and Schumann's music.

As Ruttmann did not exhibit a social conscience in his early work, it is perhaps not surprising that, by the end of his life, he had been coopted as a propagandist. An artist whose work was initially apolitical, Ruttmann neither protested nor went into exile with the advent of National Socialism. Instead, he conformed. His last documentaries were odes to Nazism and Germany's military might.

—Rob Edelman

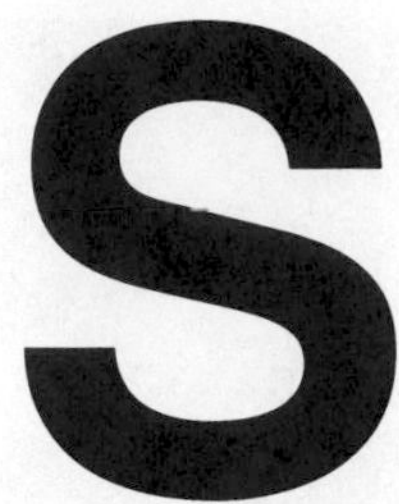

SANDERS-BRAHMS, Helma

Nationality: German. **Born:** Helma Sanders in Emden, Germany, 20 November 1940; added her mother's maiden name to her own to differentiate herself from another New German Cinema filmmaker, Helke Sander. **Education:** Studied acting in Hanover, Germany; studied drama and literature at Cologne University. **Career:** Worked as an announcer and interviewer for a Cologne television station, 1960s; began directing shorts and documentaries for German television, 1970; directed first feature, *Gewelt,* 1971; made *Erdbeben in Chile,* her first film for the Filmverlag der Autoren, set up by thirteen New German Cinema directors as a production and distribution cooperative, 1974.

Films as Director and Screenwriter:

1970 *Angelika Urban, verkauferin, verlobt* (*Angelika Urban, Salesgirl, Engaged*) (short)
1971 *Gewalt* (*Violence*); *Die industrielle Reservarmee* (*The Industrial Reserve Army*) (doc)
1972 *Der angestellte* (*The Employee*)
1973 *Die machine* (*The Machine*) (doc)
1974 *Die letzten tage von Gomorrah* (*The Last Days of Gomorrah*); *Erdbebenin Chile* (*Earthquake in Chile*)
1975 *Unter dem pflaster ist der strand* (*The Sand under the Pavement*)
1976 *Shirins hochzeit* (*Shirin's Wedding*)
1977 *Heinrich*
1980 *Deutschland bleiche mutter* (*Germany, Pale Mother*) (+ pr); *Vringsveedeler triptichon* (*The Vringsveedel Tryptych*) (doc)
1981 *Die beruhrte* (*No Mercy No Future*; *No Exit No Panic*) (+ pr, costumes, makeup)
1984 *Flugel und fesseln* (*L'Avenir d'Emilie*; *The Future of Emily*)
1986 *Laputa*
1987 *Felix* (co-dir)
1988 *Geteilte liebe* (*Divided Love*; *Manoever*) (+ pr)
1992 *Apfelbaume* (*Apple Trees*)
1995 *Lumiere et compagnie* (*Lumiere and Company*) (short Lumiere film)

Other Films:

1981 *Der Subjektive Faktor* (role)
1995 *The Night of the Filmmakers* (appearance)

Publications

By SANDERS-BRAHMS: articles—

"Misunderstood Mother and Forgotten Father," interview with G. Vincendeau in *Monthly Film Bulletin* (London), May 1985.
Interview with C. Racine in *Sequences* (Montreal), February 1987.
Interview with Peter Brunette in *Film Quarterly* (Berkeley, California), Winter 1990.
Sanders-Brahms, Helma, and S. Toubiana, "Menace a l'est," in *Cahiers du Cinema* (Paris), September 1990.
Interview with E. Richter and R. Richter in *Film und Fernsehen* (Berlin), vol. 19, no. 8/9, 1991.

On SANDERS-BRAHMS: articles—

Silberman, M., "Women Filmmakers in West Germany: A Catalog," in *Camera Obscura* (Los Angeles), Autumn 1980.
Aude, F., article in *Positif* (Paris), November 1981.
Silberman, M., "Women Working: Women Filmmakers in West Germany: A Catalog (Part 2)," in *Camera Obscura* (Los Angeles), Fall 1983.
Article in *Film a Doba* (Prague), June 1985.
Bammer, A., "Through a Daughter's Eyes: Helma Sanders-Brahms's *Germany, Pale Mother,*" in *New German Critique,* Fall 1985.
Fjordholm, H., article in *Z Filmtidsskrift* (Oslo), vol. 4, no. 5, 1986.
Desjardins, M., "*Germany, Pale Mother* and the Maternal: Towards a Feminist Spectatorship," in *Spectator,* vol. 8, no. 1, 1987.
Elsaesser, T., "Public Bodies and Divided Selves: German Women Filmmakers in the 1980s," in *Monthly Film Bulletin* (London), December 1987.
Hyams, B., "Is the Apolitical Woman at Peace? A Reading of the Fairy Tale in *Germany, Pale Mother,*" in *Wide Angle* (Baltimore, Maryland), vol. 10, no. 3, 1988.
Kinder, M., "Ideological Parody in the New German Cinema: Reading *The State of Things, The Desire of Veronika Voss,* and *Germany Pale Mother* as Postmodernist Rewritings of *The Searchers, Sunset Boulevard,* and *Blonde Venus,*" in *Quarterly Review of Film and Video* vol. 12, no. 1/2, 1990.
Kindred, Jack, "German Helmer Quits Fest over Yank Invasion," in *Variety* (New York), 14 February 1990.

* * *

The films of Helma Sanders-Brahms have been programmed with some amount of relish at film festivals and in art houses and cinematheques, but it is a safe bet that they never will be mainstream movie fare. They are not engrossing dramas in which the audience can become emotionally involved in the onscreen action. Instead, Sanders-Brahms presents, from a distance, observable archetypes of life, often with a deliberate pacing. Rather than directing actors to express emotion, she prefers "pent-up" performers who hide their real feelings. In fact, actor Heinrich Giskes found himself so emotionally "pent-up" while shooting a scene for *Heinrich* that he broke a glass over his director's head as soon as she yelled cut.

Sanders-Brahms is a rebel to Hollywood conventions. She avoids casting glamorous leading ladies or hunky actors in order to sell tickets, and her films are often very slowly paced. She does not make "road movies," because she does not revel in what she calls "the poetry of the road, the journey. The autobahn and the factory assembly line are the same thing, the same prison."

Helma Sanders-Brahms

A producer and writer in addition to director, Sanders-Brahms is a member of the New German Cinema movement, and as such she builds her scripts around the concerns of the political left. Many of her films present themes pertaining to the plight of the worker in Germany: the inequities of modern working conditions; how workers have been pitted against one another in order to attain Germany's capitalist "economic miracle"; and how the Gastarbeiter ("guest worker," or foreign migrant worker in Germany) is exploited. *Shirin's Wedding* addresses the Gastarbeiter problem, focusing on the suffering of a Turkish woman. As a child, Shirin was betrothed to Mahmud, but he left for Germany to become a Gastarbeiter. To escape an arranged marriage, Shirin travels to Germany to find Mahmud. She obtains work in a factory in Cologne and later as a cleaner, a job which disappears after she is raped by her boss. She winds up a prostitute, with Mahmud paying to have sex with her. Eventually, she is killed by a pimp's bullet. In *Die Beruhrte,* the daughter of a bourgeois family seeks sexual partners in the streets, including black migrant workers, derelicts, and aged, crippled cast-offs of society. In these neglected people, she sees the essence of Christ. Finally, *Apfelbaume* shows the destruction of a family whose members are adversely affected by the politics of reunification.

Other motifs in Sanders-Brahms's work are the independent woman under fire and the mother-daughter relationship. She herself was raised by her self-reliant mother while her father was away fighting in Hitler's armies. He did not return until she was five years old. Much of her perception of her parents' relationship and her own childhood is depicted in *Germany, Pale Mother,* one of her best-known films. The mother is shown as a strong and independent woman who gives birth to her daughter (played by Sanders-Brahms's own baby girl) during an air raid. When the war ends, this woman is expected to file away her independence in order to be an obedient wife. She does so, but her frustrations take hold in the form of a disease which paralyzes her face and, in a gut-wrenching scene, calls for the removal of all her teeth. *The Future of Emilie* tells of an actress who lives a single, unconventional lifestyle. She returns to her parents' home to retrieve her daughter, only to be told by her own mother that she is a bad influence on the child. In a powerful scene the actress and her little girl visit the beach, where they spin fantasy adventures with each other. The movie makes reference to the myth of an Amazon queen, a woman who has killed off the man she loves and is living quite nicely without the company of men. Sanders-Brahms's point is that, in modern society, there are women who also are living well without men, but they are brainwashed into thinking that they would be better off with male partners.

Sanders-Brahms's us-against-them brand of feminism mirrors the early 1970s, when the modern feminist movement was new and women who had grown up in a male-dominated society were feeling confrontational. Indeed, *Felix,* released in 1987, might have been made in the early 1970s. It is the politically loaded story of an egocentric, hypocritical modern male whose lack of self-awareness borders on the ridiculous. He has just been left by his lover, and he finds himself cast adrift in a world in which women no longer need men, or want men. *Felix* is filmed in four episodes, each shot by a different woman director—Christel Buschmann, Helke Sander, and Margarethe von Trotta, in addition to Sanders-Brahms. All are guilty of stereotyping men as jabbering idiots, and women as collectively sensitive, sensuous, and perceptive—practically perfect.

Sanders-Brahms's films are united in that they are reflective of the society in which she came of age. Along with her fellow members of the New German Cinema, she has a mission: to point out what is wrong with the world as she sees it.

—Audrey E. Kupferberg

SANJINÉS, Jorge

Nationality: Bolivian. **Born:** La Paz, Bolivia, 31 July 1936. **Education:** Studied filmmaking and philosophy at Catholic University in Santiago, Chile, late 1950s. **Career:** Made first film, *Sueños y realidades,* with Oscar Soria, in Bolivia, 1961; named head of Bolivian Film Institute, 1965; left Bolivia following coup led by Hugo Banzer, 1972; returned to Bolivia, 1979. **Address:** c/o Consejo Nacional del Cine, Casilla 9933, La Paz, Bolivia.

Films as Director:

1961 *Sueños y realidades* (co-d)
1963 *Revolución*; *Una día Paulino* (co-d)
1965 *Aysa*
1966 *Ukamau*
1969 ***Yawar mallku*** *(Blood of the Condor)*
1971 *El coraje del pueblo*
1974 *El enemigo principal*
1976 *Fuera de aquí*
1983 *Las banderas del amanecer* (co-d)
1989 *La Nacion Clandestina* (+ sc)
1995 *Para recibir el canto de los pajaros* (+ sc)

Publications

By SANJINÉS: articles—

"Cinema and Revolution," an interview in *Cineaste* (New York), Winter 1970/71.
"*Ukamau* and *Yawar Mallku*: An Interview with Jorge Sanjinés," in *Afterimage* (London), Summer 1971.
"Sobre *Fuera de Aquí!,*" and "Llamado del Grupo *Ukamau,*" in *Cine Cubano* (Havana), no. 93, 1980.
"El Cine revolucionario en Bolivia," in *Cine Cubano* (Havana), no. 99, 1981.
"Faire du cinéma un instrument de liberation," an interview with G. Gervais, in *Jeune Cinéma* (Paris), March 1982.
"Nuestro principal destinatario," in *Cine Cubano* (Cuba), no. 105, 1983.
"Revolutionary Cinema: The Bolivian Experience," in *Cinema and Social Change in Latin America: Conversations with Filmmakers,* edited by Julianne Burton, Austin, Texas, 1986.
"El plano secuencia integral," in *Cine Cubano* (Cuba), no. 125, 1989.
"Voraussetzung fuer das Verstaendnis sind Interesse an und Achtung gegenueber der anderen Kultur," an interview with R. Nierich and P. B. Schumann, in *Filmbulletin,* vol. 33, no. 4, 1991.

On SANJINÉS: books—

Gisbert, Carlos D. Mesa, and others, *Cine Boliviano: Del realizador al critico,* La Paz, 1979.
Gisbert, Carlos D. Mesa, *La aventura del cine boliviano 1952-85,* La Paz, 1985.
Armes, Roy, *Third World Filmmaking and the West,* Berkeley, 1987.

On SANJINÉS: articles—

Wilson, David, "Aspects of Latin American Political Cinema," in *Sight and Sound* (London), Summer 1972.
Campbell, Leon G., and Carlos Cortes, "Film as Revolutionary Weapon: A Jorge Sanjinés Retrospective," in *History Teacher,* May 1979.
Ledgard, M., "Jorge Sanjinés: El cine urgente," in *Hablemos de Cine* (Lima), June 1981.
West, Dennis, "Film and Revolution in the Andes," in *New Scholar* (San Diego), vol. 8, no. 1/2, 1982.
West, Dennis, "Alternative Cinema in Latin America," in *Roads to Freedom: The Struggle Against Dependence in the Developing World,* edited by Edwin G. Clausen and Jack Bermingham, Brookfield, Vermont, 1989.
Ruggle, W., "Die eigene Identitaet zurueckerobern," in *Filmbulletin,* vol. 33, no. 4, 1991.

* * *

The Bolivian Jorge Sanjinés has become internationally recognized as a leading filmmaker in spite of the fact that his country has few significant filmmaking traditions or production facilities. Working outside of a film-industry context, Sanjinés has doggedly overcome formidable obstacles, including economic ones. For instance, to finance the fiction feature *Yawar mallku* Sanjinés and other members of his Ukamau production group sold personal belongings and accepted contributions. After finishing *Yawar mallku,* members of the Ukamau collective toured the Bolivian highlands with a 16mm print and portable projection equipment in an effort to reach the film's intended audience—the Indian peasantry.

Sanjinés is a militant filmmaker whose primary goal is to bring a revolutionary Marxist political agenda to peasant and working-class audiences. His principal films respond to a militant Marxist aesthetic by examining oppressed collective protagonists (for example, an Andean peasant community) in their historical situations, by educating viewers to an understanding of those situations, and by inspiring audiences to transform the political and socioeconomic status quo in order to build a higher stage of society. The depiction of oppression in these films has in some cases been based on documented historical events.

Sanjinés's works offer a defense of the Andean Indian way of life and expose and attack the Indians' enemies. *Yawar mallku* denounces a Progress Corps (read Peace Corps) pediatrics clinic that sterilizes unsuspecting Andean women, while in the documentary reconstruction *El coraje del pueblo,* Bolivian government and military officials responsible for the massacres of Indian miners are specifically identified. The fiction feature *El enemigo principal* illustrates the exploitation and brutality suffered by indigenous peasants at the hands of powerful landowners and links the power of the landowners to U.S. imperialism. The mise-en-scène of these films reflects Sanjinés's defense of the Indian way of life. For instance, in *El enemigo principal* the Inca heritage of the modern Andean Indian pervades the mise-en-scène: the predominance of Quechua dialogue, the centuries-old custom of chewing coca leaves, the trapezoidal niches and doors characterizing Inca masonry, the ancient agricultural ritual, the everyday work of spinning and weaving.

The structural, narrative, and stylistic approaches used by Sanjinés have evolved in accordance with his basic goal of optimum communication with his peasant and working-class audiences. When exhibiting *Yawar mallku* to Indians in remote areas, Sanjinés drew on an Inca oral tradition; and before showing the film he first had a narrator introduce the story and the characters to the cinematically unsophisticated audiences. Later, in *El enemigo principal,* Sanjinés built a narrator into the film itself: a well-known Indian peasant leader periodically appears to speak, in Quechua, directly to viewers in order to introduce the characters and events which will follow. From peasant reaction to his early films, Sanjinés found that unsophisticated viewers were shocked when a close shot follows an establishing shot. Therefore, in *El enemigo principal* outdoor group scenes appear initially in long shot; and then the camera slowly zooms in, much as a spectator would approach. Although *Yawar mallku* involved an Indian community in the filming, Sanjinés later sought from indigenous groups an even more active collective participation in an effort to make films "from the people, to the people." In *El coraje del pueblo,* survivors of the army's 1967 massacre of miners actively participated in the filmmaking by re-creating their own activities before and during the bloodbath.

Since the appearance of *Yawar mallku,* Sanjinés has been a well-known and controversial figure in Bolivia; but he has at times been banished from his native country by right-wing regimes because of his highly political filmmaking activities. International critical opinion considers Sanjinés one of the leading Latin American militant filmmakers because of his oft-demonstrated ability to make aesthetically and politically significant feature films—both documentaries and fiction features—in spite of extremely limited technical and financial resources.

SAURA, Carlos

Nationality: Spanish. **Born:** Huesca, 4 January 1932. **Education:** Studied filmmaking at Instituto de Investigaciones y Experiencas Cinematográficos (IIEC), Madrid, 1952-57. **Career:** Professional photographer, 1950-53; teacher at IIEC, from 1957, left for political reasons, 1964; directed first feature, *Los golfos,* 1960. **Awards:** Silver Bear, Berlin Festival, for *La caza,* 1966, and *Peppermint frappé,* 1968; Special Jury Award, Cannes Festival, for *La prima Angelica,* 1974, and *Cria cuervos,* 1976; Golden Bear, Berlin Festival, for *Hurry, Hurry,* 1981. **Address:** Iberoamericana Films, Velazquez 12, Madrid 28001.

Films as Director and Scriptwriter:

1957 *La tarde del domingo* (*Sunday Afternoon*) (short)
1958 *Cuenca* (short)
1960 *Los golfos* (*The Hooligans*) (+ role)
1964 *Llanto por un bandido* (*Lament for a Bandit*)
1966 *La caza* (*The Hunt*; *The Chase*)
1967 *Peppermint frappé*
1968 *Stress es tres, tres* (*Stress is Three, Three*)
1969 *La madriguera* (*The Honeycomb*; *The Net*)
1970 *El jardín de las delicias* (*The Garden of Delights*)
1973 *Ana y los lobos* (*Ana and the Wolves*)
1974 *La prima Angélica* (*Cousin Angelica*)
1976 **Cria cuervos** (*Raise Ravens*)
1977 *Elisa, vida mía* (*Elisa, My Love*)
1978 *Los ojos vendados* (*Blindfold*)
1979 *Mamá cumple cien años* (*Mama Turns a Hundred*)
1980 *Deprisa, deprisa* (*Hurry, Hurry*)
1981 *Dulces horas* (*Sweet Hours*); *Bodas de sangre* (*Blood Wedding*)
1982 *Antonieta*
1983 *Carmen*
1984 *Los zancos* (*The Stilts*)
1985 *El amor brujo* (*Love the Magician*)
1987 *El dorado*
1989 *La noche oscura* (*The Dark Night*)
1990 *Ay! Carmela*
1992 *Sevillanas*; *Marathon*
1993 *Dispara!* (*Shoot!*)
1995 *Flamenco*

Publications

By SAURA: articles—

Interviews with E. Brasó, in *Positif* (Paris), May and October 1974.
Interview with G. Braucourt, in *Thousand Eyes* (New York), October 1976.
Interview with M. Capdenac and others, in *Ecran* (Paris), July 1977.
"El cumpleaños de Saura," interview with J.L. Guerin, in *Cinema 2002* (Madrid), January 1980.
"Carlos Saura: bodas de prisa," interview with M. Pereira, in *Cine Cubano* (Havana), no.99, 1981.
Interview with Nick Roddick in *Stills* (London), September/October 1983.
Saura, Carlos, "Brief an ein kind auf der treppe," in *Film und Fernsehen* (Berlin), vol. 12, no 1., 1984.
Saura, Carlos, "Die Rueckkehr nach Spanien," in *Film und Fernsehen* (Berlin), vol. 12, no. 1, 1984.

On SAURA: books—

Brasó, Enrique, *Carlos Saura,* Madrid, 1974.
Gubern, Roman, *Homenaje a Carlos Saura,* Huelva, 1979.
Arnold, Frank, and others, *Carlos Saura,* Munich, 1981.
Oms, Marcel, *Carlos Saura,* Paris, 1981.
Eichenlaub, Hans M., *Carlos Saura,* Freiburg, 1984.
Hopewell, John, *Out of the Past: Spanish Cinema After Franco,* London, 1986.
Higginbotham, Virginia, *Spanish Film Under Franco,* Austin, Texas, 1988.
Vidal, Agustin Sanchez, *El cine de Carlos Saura,* Zaragoza, 1988.
D'Lugo, Marvin, *The Films of Carlos Saura: The Practice of Seeing,* Princeton, New Jersey, 1991.

On SAURA: articles—

"*Anne et des loups* Issue" of *Avant-Scène du Cinéma* (Paris), November 1974.
"*Cria cuervos* Issue" of *Avant-Scène du Cinéma* (Paris), 15 October 1978.
Kinder, Marcia, "Carlos Saura: The Political Development of Individual Consciousness," in *Film Quarterly* (Berkeley, California), no. 3, 1979.
Kovács, Katherine, "Loss and Recuperation in *The Garden of Delights,*" in *Cine-Tracts* (Montreal), Summer/Fall 1981.
Tate, S., "Carlos Saura, Spain and *Mama Turns One Hundred,*" in *Cinema Papers* (Melbourne), April 1982.
Bartholomew, G., "The Development of Carlos Saura," in *Journal of Film and Video* (Carbondale, Illinois), Summer 1983.
D'Lugo, M., : "Carlos Saura: Constructive Imagination in Post-Franco Cinema," in *Quarterly Review of Film Studies* (New York), Spring 1983.
Kinder, Marcia, "The Children of Franco in the New Spanish Cinema," in *Quarterly Review of Film Studies* (New York), Spring 1983.
Insdorf, Annette, "*Soñar con tus ojos*: Carlos Saura's Melodic Cinema," in *Quarterly Review of Film Studies* (New York), Spring 1983.

Carlos Saura: ***Carmen***

Clarens, Carlos, "Is There Film after Bunuel?" in *Village Voice* (New York), 6 January 1984.
Hernandez, V., "Lectura e interpretacion, el contexto y la referencia en el cine de Carlos Saura," in *Contracampo* (Madrid), Winter 1984.
Schumacher, E., "Saura's New Film Returns to Flamenco," in *New York Times,* 15 December 1985.
Rabal, F., "Freund meiner Freund," in *Film und Fernsehen* (Berlin), vol. 14, no. 7, 1986.
Hopewell, John, "Mr. Carlosawa: Carlos Saura at the National Film Theatre," in *Sight and Sound* (London), Autumn 1986.
Hunter, A., "A Spanish Point of View," in *Films and Filming* (London), September 1986.
"Carlos Saura Joins with Gomez on Ambitious $5.5-mil *El Dorado,*" in *Variety* (New York), 22 October 1986.
D'Lugo, Marvin, "Historical Reflexivity: Carlos Saura's Anti-*Carmen,*" in *Wide Angle* (Baltimore, Maryland), vol. 9, no. 3, 1987.
Moore, L., "Can Saura Save Olympic Epic?," in *Variety* (New York), 31 August 1992.

* * *

Over the past three decades, Carlos Saura has attained international stature while exploring quintessentially Spanish themes. Saura was one of the first Spanish filmmakers to deal with the Spanish Civil War and its aftermath. In several films he explored the impact of the war years and of the postwar period on the men and women of his generation, those who were born in the 1930s and who suffered emotional and psychological damage that affected them well into their adult years. In a number of movies, we witness the efforts of Saura's adult protagonists to resurrect their past memories in order to come to terms with them once and for all. In the course of their recollections, we see the negative effects not only of the war, but also of the repressive system of education and of the confining family structures that were consolidated by the triumph of Franco in the postwar period.

Until Franco's death in 1975, it was not possible to express this viewpoint openly. Films were censored first at the script stage and again upon completion. Nothing controversial was allowed. Even in the 1960s, a period of liberalization when some experimentation was allowed and the New Spanish Cinema movement was born, Saura and the other young directors associated with this movement walked a delicate and difficult line, trying to convey their ideas while avoiding the hurdles imposed by the censor.

It was in this atmosphere that Saura developed his cinematic style and method of working. In order to deal with taboo subjects, he (and the other young directors of that time) resorted to tactics of allusion, association, and allegory. In one of Saura's first movies, *The Hunt,* a hunting party arranged by four former comrades-in-arms under Franco is used to represent the legacy of the Civil War and the moral bankruptcy it has engendered. In other movies, Saura destroys the chronological sequence of events in order to show the impact of the past and its continued importance in explaining the present. Actions and events taking place in the present often recall or evoke corresponding past moments, and Saura's protagonists come to exist in several temporal dimensions simultaneously. We participate in their memories, dreams, and visions as Saura creates a fluid movement from present to past and in and out of dreams. What is original about these shifts in time and perspective is that Saura dispenses with the dissolves and soft-focus shots usually used to effectuate a time change in films. In his movies, present and past, reality and fantasy are deliberately fused together. Dream figures seem to be as palpable and as concrete as any of the "real" actors on screen. The audience learns to distinguish them through a series of narrative clues, changes in clothing, and the actors' voices and facial expressions.

This method places substantial demands upon the actors with whom Saura works closely. He has often used the same actors in several movies. Saura has also worked with the same producer and crew for most of his career, which helps explain the significant continuity of his films. Sometimes images or sequences from one movie recur in later ones. As Saura himself has said, "Every film is a consequence of the film before."

Every film is also a consequence of the particular political and social climate prevailing in Spain. With the death of Franco and the subsequent abolition of film censorship that resulted from restoration of democratic rule, Saura moved away from the complex, nonlinear narrative forms he had cultivated under Franco and began to make simpler, almost documentary-like movies. One of these, which dealt with juvenile delinquents in Madrid, was shot with nonprofessional actors from the slums of the capital (*De prisa, de prisa*). Two others are filmed versions of flamenco ballets that are based upon well-known literary works (*Bodas de sangre* and *Carmen*). In these as in other movies which contain references to Spanish plays, poems, and paintings, Saura affirms his ties to Spanish cultural traditions and shows their relevance to the Spain of today.

El amor brujo is the third of Saura's "Spanish folk films," following *Bodas de sangre* and *Carmen.* In it, he combines music, dance, and melodrama in telling the story of a pair of gypsies who have been promised to each other by their respective families; as their wedding approaches, each becomes involved in other romances.

Despite an occasional foray into what for Saura is unusual territory—*Dispara!* is a cliched, unconvincing psychological drama about a rape victim who murders her attackers—the filmmaker has continued creating highly political films which explore facets of recent Spanish history, and non-narrative cinematic essays which celebrate Spanish culture. In the former category is *Ay, Carmela!,* a pointed yet endearing, extremely entertaining farce in which Carmen Maura has one of her best roles in a film not directed by Pedro Almodovar. She plays an entertainer who brings diversion to the partisans during the Spanish Civil War, and who ends up caught behind enemy lines with her husband and their assistant. The film works best as a comic reminiscence of what it means to be politically and morally correct, yet still be on the losing side of a conflict. *Flamenco* is a loving, exquisitely detailed ode to flamenco music, consisting of lively performances by an array of talented singers, dancers, and guitarists of all ages. *Flamenco* is a film that Gene Kelly would love; it leaves audience members clapping after each number, entranced by the joy and energy put forth by the performers, the best of whom are nothing short of dazzling. There are no English subtitles in *Flamenco.* None are needed.

—Katherine Singer Kovács, updated by Rob Edelman

SAUTET, Claude

Nationality: French. **Born:** Montrouge, Paris, 23 February 1924. **Education:** Ecole des Arts Decoratif, entered IDHEC, 1948. **Career:** Music critic for newspaper *Combat,* late 1940s; assistant director to Pierre Montazel, Gut Lefranc, Georges Franju, and Jacques Becker, 1950s; also TV producer; directed first feature, *Classe tous risques,* 1960.

Films as Director and Scriptwriter:

1951 *Nous n'irons plus au bois* (short)
1956 *Bonjour sourire* (d only)
1960 *Classe tous risques* (*The Big Risk*)
1965 *L'Arme à gauche* (*Guns for the Dictator*)
1970 *Les Choses de la vie* (*The Things of Life*)
1971 *Max et les ferrailleurs*

Claude Sautet directing Romy Schneider in *Les Choses de la vie*

1972 *César et Rosalie* (*Cesar and Rosalie*)
1974 *Vincent, François, Paul ... et les autres*
1976 *Mado*
1978 *Une Histoire simple*
1980 *Un Mauvais Fils* (*A Bad Son*)
1983 *Garçon*
1988 *Quelques Jours avec moi*
1992 ***Un Coeur en Hiver*** (*A Heart in Winter*) (co-sc)
1995 *Nelly & Monsieur Arnaud* (*Nelly & Mr. Arnaud*) (co-sc); *Les Enfants de Lumiere*

Other Films:

(incomplete listing)

1954 *Touchez pas au Grisbi* (*Grisbi*)
1959 ***Les Yeux sans visages*** (*Eyes without a Face*) (Franju) (asst d)

Publications

By SAUTET: book—

Conversations avec Claude Sautet, Institute Lumiere, 1994.

By SAUTET: articles—

Interviews with Claude Beylie, in *Ecran* (Paris), December 1972 and November 1974.
"Claude Sautet, c'est la vitalité," with François Truffaut, in *Avant-Scène du Cinéma* (Paris), December 1974.
Interviews with Michel Ciment and others, in *Positif* (Paris), December 1976 and January 1979.
"Romy Schneider: une actrice qui depasse le quotidien," in *Avant-Scène du Cinéma* (Paris), 15 March 1979.
Interview with G. Legrand and I. Jordan in *Positif* (Paris), December 1983.
"Je ne prevoyais pas ce debordement emotionnel," an interview with M. Sineux and Y. Tobin, in *Positif* (Paris), September 1992.
Interview in *Jeune Cinéma* (Paris), October 1992.

On SAUTET: book—

Korkmaz, Joseph, *Le Cinéma de Claude Sautet,* Paris, 1985.

On SAUTET: articles—

Sineux, M., "Entretien avec Philippe Sarde sur Claude Sautet et quelques autres," in *Positif* (Paris), January 1979.

"Claude Sautet Issue" of *Avant-Scène du Cinéma* (Paris), January 1984.
Thomas, Kevin, "The Musical Style of Claude Sautet," in *Los Angeles Times,* 18 June 1993.
Arnold, Gary, "Sex and Violins," in *Washington Times,* 11 July 1993.
Arnold, Gary, "Montand, Schneider and the Little White Lie," in *Washington Times,* 11 July 1993.
Elley, Derek, "Film Reviews—Nelly & Mr. Arnaud," in *Variety* (New York), 18 September 1995.

* * *

The career of Claude Sautet was slow in getting underway, but by the 1970s he had virtually become the French cinema's official chronicler of bourgeois life. He had made his directing debut with a solidly constructed thriller, *Classe tous risques,* in 1960, but a second film, *L'Arme à gauche,* did not follow until 1965 and was markedly less successful. Despite numerous scriptwriting assignments, his directing career did not really get underway until he completed *Les Choses de la vie* in 1969. This set the pattern for a decade of filmmaking.

The core of any Sautet film is a fairly banal emotional problem—a man caught between two women in *Les Choses de la vie* or a married woman confronted with a former lover in *César et Rosalie.* Around this situation Sautet weaves a rich pattern of bourgeois life: concerns with home and family, with money and possessions, give these films their particular tone. This is a cinema of warm, convincingly depicted characters for whom Sautet clearly has great affection and more than a touch of complicity. Problems and motivations are always explicitly set out, for this is a style of psychological realism in which the individual, not the social, forms the focus of attention.

The director's style is a sober, classical one, built on the model of Hollywood narrative traditions: action, movement, vitality. Though his style can encompass such set pieces as the boxing match in *Vincent, Francois, Paul ... et les autres,* Sautet is more concerned with the unfolding of a strong and involving narrative line. A key feature of all his work are the confrontation scenes which offer such excellent opportunities for the talented stars and solid character players who people his films.

Sautet's films from the mid-1970s to early 1980s—*Mado, Une Histoire simple,* and *Une Mauvais Fils*—are all characterized by a total assurance and a mastery of the medium. This mastery, however, is exercised within very precise limits—not in terms of the subject matter, which widens to take in the problems of affluence, women's independence, and juvenile delinquency, but in the manner in which such issues of the moment are approached. Sautet's classicism of form and ability to communicate directly with his audience is not accompanied by the resonances of social criticism which characterize the best North American cinema. Seeking to move his audience rather than enlighten it, Sautet uses powerful actors cast to type in carefully constructed roles, but any probing of the essential contradictions is avoided by a style of direction which keeps rigidly to the surface of life, the given patterns of bourgeois social behaviour. His approach is therefore condemned to a certain schematism, particularly in the handling of dialogue scenes, but his work gets its sense of vitality from the vigor with which the group scenes—the meals and excursions—and the typical locations of café or railway station are handled. Sautet offers a facsimile of life, a reflection of current problems or issues, but contained within a form calculated not to trouble the spectator after he has left the cinema. This conformism may seem limiting to the contemporary critic, but it will offer future generations a rare insight into the manner in which the French middle classes liked to see themselves in the 1970s.

In his most recent features, the popularly and critically well-received *Un Coeur en Hiver* (1992) and *Nelly & Monsieur Arnaud* (1995), Sautet continues to offer versions of French middle-class bourgeois life in the 1990s. In keeping with Sautet's thematic and stylistic terrain, *Un Coeur* and *Nelly* both focus on a small group of individuals as they undergo a set of personal and emotional situations. Again, while one senses a touch of Sautet's complicity with the bourgeois world he represents, these films do not simply offer the conservative resolutions that characterize so many of the bourgeois Hollywood productions of the 1980s and 1990s. As we watch *Un Coeur* and *Nelly,* we proceed along the interior, emotional topographies of characters like the remote and ostensibly affectless Stephan in *Un Coeur.* The tension which builds throughout *Un Coeur* as a result of Stephan's unwillingness and/or incapacity to love does not find its release, however, through the union of Stephan and Camille by the film's end: Camille continues her relationship with Maxim, Stephan remains alone. As a result, Sautet powerfully succeeds in having *us* experience the frustration these characters feel, because *Un Coeur* resists consummating a formulaic relationship with its audience via a happy ending as Hollywood films are likely to do.

Nelly & Monsieur Arnaud affects its audience in similar ways. Comparable to *Un Coeur, Nelly*'s presentation of the emotional firings and mis-firings between Nelly, Arnaud, Vincent, and Jerome draw the viewer into a narrative that resists uncomplicated closure; because of this, the world of *Nelly & Monsieur Arnaud* is more likely to resemble the reality its audience will encounter once the credits role and the lights go up. Derek Elley aptly comments in *Variety* that Sautet, in his films, "is more interested in the what-could-have-happened than the what-actually-has." *Nelly,* he concludes, "will delight those who don't like their T's crossed and I's dotted." While neither a revolutionary cinema nor one which simply gives way to Hollywood narrative conventions, Claude Sautet's films endure as poignant and insightful tales depicting the often beguiling world of human affairs.

—Roy Armes, updated by Kevin J. Costa

SAVILLE, Victor

Nationality: British/American. **Born:** Victor Salberg in Birmingham, England, 25 September 1897, became U.S. citizen, 1950. **Education:** King Edward VI Grammar School, Birmingham. **Military Service:** Wounded at Battle of Loos, 1915, and invalided out of the Army, 1916. **Family:** Married Phoebe Vera Teller, 1920, two children. **Career:** Manager of small cinema in Coventry, then joined Features and Newsreels Dept. of Pathé Frères, London, 1917; formed Victory Motion Pictures with Michael Balcon, 1919; producer for Gaumont, 1926-27; founder, independent production company Burlington Film Co., and directed first film, *The Arcadians,* 1927; director for Michael Balcon, 1930-35; formed Victor Saville Productions, Ltd., 1936; signed contract with MGM, 1937, worked in Hollywood, from 1939; joined Columbia, made *Tonight and Every Night,* then rejoined MGM, 1943; formed Parklane Productions, 1952; returned to London, 1960. **Died:** In London, 8 May 1979.

Films as Director:

1927 *The Arcadians* (+ pr)
1928 *Tesha* (*Woman in the Night*)
1929 *Kitty*; *Woman to Woman*
1930 *The W Plan*; *A Warm Corner*
1931 *The Sport of Kings*; *Michael & Mary*; *Sunshine Susie* (*The Office Girl*)
1932 *The Faithful Heart*; *Love on Wheels*
1933 *The Good Companions*; *I Was a Spy*; *Friday the Thirteenth*

Victor Saville

1934 *Evergreen*; *Evensong*; *The Iron Duke*
1935 *The Dictator* (*The Loves of a Dictator*); *Me and Marlborough*; *First a Girl*
1936 *It's Love Again*
1937 *Dark Journey* (+ pr); *Storm in a Teacup* (co-d, pr)
1938 *South Riding* (+ pr)
1943 *Forever and a Day* (co-d)
1945 *Tonight and Every Night* (+ pr)
1946 *The Green Years*
1947 *Green Dolphin Street*; *If Winter Comes*
1949 *The Conspirator*
1950 *Kim*
1951 *Calling Bulldog Drummond*
1952 *Twenty-four Hours of a Woman's Life* (*Affair in Monte Carlo*)
1954 *The Long Wait*
1955 *The Silver Chalice*

Other Films:

1923 *Woman to Woman* (*Cutts*) (co-pr with Michael Balcon); *The White Shadow* (Cutts) (co-pr with Balcon)
1924 *The Prudes Fall* (Cutts) (co-pr with Balcon)
1926 *Mademoiselle from Armentieres* (Elvey) (pr)
1927 *Roses of Picardy* (Elvey) (pr); *The Glad Eye* (Elvey) (pr); *The Flight Commander* (Elvey) (pr)
1931 *Hindle Wakes* (Elvey) (pr)
1937 *Action for Slander* (Whelan) (pr)
1938 *The Citadel* (Vidor) (pr)
1939 *Goodbye, Mr. Chips* (Wood) (pr); *Earl of Chicago* (Thorpe) (pr)
1940 *The Mortal Storm* (Borzage) (pr); *Bitter Sweet* (Van Dyke) (pr)
1941 *A Woman's Face* (Cukor) (pr); *Dr. Jekyll and Mr. Hyde* (Fleming) (pr); *Smilin' Through* (Borzage) (pr); *The Chocolate Soldier* (Del Ruth) (pr)
1942 *White Cargo* (Thorpe) (pr); *Keeper of the Flame* (Cukor) (pr)
1943 *Above Suspicion* (Thorpe) (pr)
1953 *I, the Jury* (Essex) (pr)
1955 ***Kiss Me Deadly*** (Aldrich) (exec pr)
1961 *The Greengage Summer* (Gilbert) (pr)
1962 *Mix Me a Person* (Norman) (exec pr)

Publications

On SAVILLE: books—

Balcon, Michael, *A Lifetime of Films,* London, 1969.
Rollins, Cyril, *Victor Saville,* London, 1972.
Perry, George, *The Great British Picture Show,* London, 1974.
Armes, Roy, *A Critical History of the British Cinema,* London, 1978.

On SAVILLE: articles—

Obituary, in the *New York Times,* 10 May 1979.
Obituary, in *Variety* (New York), 16 May 1979.

* * *

A former film salesman who became a producer in partnership with Michael Balcon—both men were born in Birmingham—Victor Saville began his directorial career in the late 1920s in England, and during the next decade became firmly established as one of that country's more stylish filmmakers. Unlike his contemporaries in the British film industry, Saville never made films that were particularly English in content or style; his manner of directing was quite definitely borrowed from Hollywood, and he understood the need for glamour and sophistication in order to appeal to the international film market.

One of Victor Saville's earliest films, *Tesha* (released in the United States as *Woman in the Night*) is notable for its mature subject matter: a married woman who has a child by her husband's best friend. *Kitty* is a curiosity as one of Britain's first talkies, with the sound sequences shot at the Paramount Astoria Studios on Long Island. It was in the 1930s, however, that Victor Saville hit his stride as a director, with a series of romantic comedies featuring Jessie Matthews *(The Good Companions, Friday the Thirteenth, Evergreen, First a Girl,* and *It's Love Again)* and a brilliant First World War spy melodrama, *I Was a Spy,* which made an international star of Madeleine Carroll.

MGM recognized the international quality of Victor Saville's work and selected him to produce its first two prestigious British productions, *The Citadel* and *Goodbye, Mr. Chips.* These films led to Saville's arrival in the United States, where he produced (but did not direct) a string of quality films, notably *Bitter Sweet, Dr. Jekyll and Mr. Hyde, Smilin' Through,* and *Keeper of the Flame.* As with all of Saville's American films, they were solid, slightly dull, but always well-made entertainment pictures. The same may be said of the U.S. features which Saville directed, particularly *Green Dolphin Street* and *Kim,* which are heavy on production values and light on any originality in direction.

Victor Saville once remarked that films must "bounce off the times we live in," a philosophy which his early work upholds. If his later films have any linking continuity it is that they were derived from popular literary works. One project which never saw the light of day, however, was Victor Saville's planned production of Agatha Christie's long-running play, *The Mousetrap,* which he had hoped to produce with Tyrone Power starring under the direction of Billy Wilder.

—Anthony Slide

SAYLES, John

Nationality: American. **Born:** John Thomas Sayles in Schenectady, New York, 28 September 1950. **Education:** Williams College, Williamstown, Massachusetts, B.S. in psychology, 1972. **Career:** First novel published, 1975; writer for Roger Corman's New World Pictures, from 1977; first film as director, *The Return of the Secaucus Seven,* 1980; directed own plays *New Hope for the Dead* and *Turnbuckle,* Off-Off-Broadway, 1981; writer and director for TV, from 1980; director of promo videos for Bruce Springsteen, including "Born in the U.S.A." and "I'm on Fire."

Films as Director and Scriptwriter:

1980 *The Return of the Secaucus Seven* (+ ed, role as Howie)
1981 *Lianna* (+ ed, role as Jerry)
1983 *Baby, It's You*
1984 *The Brother from Another Planet* (+ ed, role as bounty hunter)
1987 *Matewan* (+ role as preacher)
1988 *Eight Men Out* (+ role as Ring Lardner)
1991 *City of Hope* (+ ed, song, role as Carl)
1992 *Passion Fish* (+ ed)
1994 *The Secret of Roan Inish*
1995 *Lone Star* (+ pr)

Other Films:

1978 *Piranha* (Dante) (sc)

1979 *The Lady in Red* (*Kiss Me and Die*; *Guns, Sin, and Bathtub Gin*) (Teague) (sc)
1980 *Battle beyond the Stars* (Murakami) (sc); *The Howling* (Dante) (co-sc); *Alligator* (Teague) (sc)
1982 *The Challenge* (Frankenheimer) (co-sc)
1984 *Hard Choices* (King) (role as Don)
1985 *The Clan of the Cave Bear* (Chapman) (sc); *Enormous Changes at the Last Minute* (Bank, Hovde) (sc)
1987 *Wild Thing* (Reid) (sc); *Something Wild* (Demme) (role as motorcycle cop)
1989 *Breaking In* (Forsyth) (sc)
1992 *Straight Talk* (Kellman) (role as Guy Girardi); ***Malcolm X*** (Lee) (role as FBI man); *Matinee* (Dante) (role as phoney moral crusader)
1993 *A Safe Place* (Lang) (sc); *My Life's in Turnaround* (Schaeffer, Ward) (role as film producer)
1994 *Men of War* (sc); *Bedlam* (Maclean) (sc)
1995 *Apollo 13* (Howard) (sc)

Publications

By SAYLES: books—

The Pride of the Bimbos, New York, 1975.
Union Dues, New York, 1977.
The Anarchists' Convention, New York, 1979.
Thinking in Pictures: The Making of the Movie "Matewan," New York, 1987.
Los Gusanos, New York, 1991.

By SAYLES: articles—

"Ways of Looking at the World," an interview with Hunter Cordaiy, in *Metro* (Melbourne), Summer 1978/79.
Interview with T. Crawley, in *Monthly Film Bulletin* (London), December 1982.
Interview with D. Popkin, in *Cineaste* (New York), vol. 13, no. 1, 1983.
Interview with Paul Kerr, in *Monthly Film Bulletin* (London), January 1984.
Interview with Richard Laermer, in *Films in Review* (New York), February 1985.
"Dialogue on Film: John Sayles," in *American Film* (Washington, D.C.), May 1986.
Interview with Pat Aufderheide, in *Cineaste* (New York), vol. 15, no. 4, 1987.
"Color Bars," in *American Film* (Los Angeles), vol. 13, no. 6, April 1988.
"Sayles on TV," an interview with Patrick Goldstein, in *Interview* (New York), March 1990.
"Low-budget Operator Who Has a Wealth of Creativity to Draw On," an interview with David Robinson, in *The Times* (London), 29 August 1991.
"Screening the Disenfranchised," an interview with Alan Hunter, in *Impact* (London), October 1991.
"Where the Hope Is," an interview with Gary Crowdus and Leonard Quart, in *Cineaste* (New York), December 1991.
"S'il y a un espoir, il est dans la fusion," an interview with Michael Henry, in *Positif* (Paris), November 1992.
"John Sayles's Committed Cinema," an interview with Harlan Jacobson, in *Interview* (New York), April 1993.
"Sayles Talk," an interview with Trevor Johnston, in *Sight and Sound* (London), September 1993.
Interview in *American Cinematographer* (Los Angeles), February 1995.

On SAYLES: articles—

Levine, H., "Features for Under a Million: John Sayles," in *Millimeter* (New York), February 1982.
Osborne, David, "John Sayles: from Hoboken to Hollywood—and Back," in *American Film* (Washington, D.C.), October 1982.
Milligan, P., "Sayles Management," in *Film Directions* (London), Summer 1984.
Valen, M., "John Sayles," in *Films and Filming* (London), September 1984.
Vecsey, George, "John Sayles Mines the Coal Wars," in *New York Times*, 23 August 1987.
Fishbein, Leslie, "John Sayles' *Matewan*: Violence and Nostalgia," in *Film and History* (Newark, New Jersey), vol. 18, no. 3, 1988.
Isaacs, Neil D., "John Sayles and the Fictional Origin of *Matewan,*" in *Literature/Film Quarterly* (Salisbury, Maryland), vol. 16, no. 4, 1988.
Lardner, Ring, Jr., "Foul Ball," in *American Film* (Los Angeles), vol. 13, no. 9, 1988.
Newman, Kim, "Red Sayles in the Sunset," in *City Limits* (London), 13 April 1989.
Wilson, David, "Of Anarchists and Alligators" in *Monthly Film Bulletin* (London), June 1989.
Rose, Cynthia, "The Urbane Guerilla," in *Independent* (London), 24 August 1990.
Davis, Thulani, "Blue-Collar Auteur," in *American Film* (Los Angeles), June 1991.
Andrew, Geoff, "Sayles Talk," in *Time Out* (London), 23 October 1991.
Malcolm, Derek, "Why Sayles Refuses to Sell Out," in *Guardian* (London), 12 November 1991.
Thompson, Ben, "Sex, Lies and Urban Renewal," in *New Statesman & Society* (London), 15 November 1991.
Grogan, Johnny, "True Saylesmanship," in *Film Ireland* (Dublin), April/May 1993.
Sarris, Andrew, "Baby It's You: An Honest Man Becomes a True Filmmaker," in *Film Comment* (New York), May/June 1993.
Jackson, Kevin, "Making Movies against the Tide," in *Independent* (London), 19 June 1993.
Charity, Tom, "Sayles Pitch," in *Time Out* (London), 25 August 1993.
Gritten, David, "Hollywood? Not for Me, Thanks," in *Daily Telegraph* (London), 30 August 1993.
Francke, Lizzie, "Passion Player," in *Guardian* (London), 3 September 1993.

* * *

No other American director has so successfully straddled both Hollywood and independent filmmaking as John Sayles. While his fellow independents have tended to restrict themselves either in terms of audience (Jim Jarmusch, Henry Jaglom) or creative scope (Woody Allen), Sayles has continued to make highly individual, idiosyncratic films of increasingly ambitious range, aimed firmly at a mainstream audience, without compromising his own socially subversive outlook.

Even before launching out as a director, Sayles had established his reputation both as a novelist and as a provider of witty, literate scripts for genre movies—*Alligator, The Howling, The Lady in Red*—into whose conventions he deftly introduced sharp touches of political allegory. His own films, though, have steered clear of generic formulae, remaining (in subject matter as in treatment) fresh and quirkily unpredictable. The first of them, *The Return of the Secaucus Seven,* observed the reunion of a bunch of ex-1960s radicals with an affection, and a relaxed humour, that Kasdan's glossier treatment in *The Big Chill* never quite matched. "There was a realism there," Roger Corman noted, "which more money might have obscured." The film picked up several awards and rapidly became a cult favourite.

Secaucus, for all its small-scale subject and slightly shaggy charm, established the priorities of all Sayles's work to date: in his own words,

John Sayles

"the acting, and believing in the characters and caring about them." His films, situated (as Pat Aufderheide put it) "at the intersection of culture and politics," favour ensemble playing over star performances, communication over sensation, and the exploration of character and ideas over pictorial values or technical bravura. "I don't regard anything I do as art. That's a foreign world to me. I regard it as a conversation. Very often in a conversation, you tell a story to illustrate something you think or feel," Sayles has stated.

Even so, Sayles's work has developed steadily in terms of visual as well as dramatic complexity. His early films, such as *Secaucus* and *Lianna,* a sympathetic account of a married woman awakening to her lesbian nature, were criticised in some quarters for their static camerawork. Sayles, while readily conceding his lack of technical experience, pointed out that "Fluid camera work takes money. Unless it's an action movie, why cut away from good actors?" More recently, however, from *Matewan* onwards, he has adopted a more sophisticated and even elegant shooting style, though never at the expense of the story. The long, intricate tracking shots of *City of Hope* map out social connections and tensions as graphically as anything in Ophuls; while in *Matewan* scenes of nocturnal wood-smoky encampments in the Appalachian foothills, shot by Haskell Wexler in dark, grainy tones, recall elements of late Ford—*Wagonmaster,* say, or *The Horse Soldiers.*

Not that Sayles (unlike his "movie brat" contemporaries) is interested in strewing his pictures with allusive film-buff references. "I want people to leave the theater thinking about their own lives, not about other movies," he noted. His work draws its resonance from his social concerns, from his sense of character as a product of historical and cultural influences, from his acute ear for dialogue and his insight into the political process. The mismatched young couple of *Baby It's You* are no less constrained by the pressures of their class and environment (small-town 1960s New Jersey) than the West Virginian miners of *Matewan,* the baseball professionals of *Eight Men Out,* or the hostile urban factions of *City of Hope.* By contrast, the two women in *Passion Fish,* both maimed by life and thrown together in prickly proximity, surmount their backgrounds and prejudices to achieve tentative friendship. Sayles's hope is that we, as viewers, will extrapolate from what we see, grasping its relevance to our own situation. "If storytelling has a positive function, it's to put us in touch with other people's lives, to help us connect and draw strength or knowledge from people we'll never meet, to help us see beyond our own experience."

Sayles's sympathy for his characters can sometimes verge on sentimentality, as in *The Brother from Another Planet,* his least satisfactory though perhaps most likeable film—or in *The Secret of Roan Inish,* a rather too consciously poetic treatment of Celtic legend. His attitude to the movie industry, though, displays a clear-eyed realism, and an integrity which has so far resisted the lure—and the attendant compromises—of Hollywood mega-budgets. In his work as a director, Sayles has steadily extended and deepened his personal vision of his country's history. If he can sustain the balancing act, funding his own staunchly independent work with lucrative scripting for other people's movies, he looks set to become one of the most original and incisive cinematic interpreters of the American myth.

—Philip Kemp

SCHAFFNER, Franklin J.

Nationality: American. **Born:** Tokyo, 30 May 1920. **Education:** Franklin and Marshal College; studied law at Columbia University. **Military Service:** Served in U.S. Navy, 1942-46. **Family:** Married Helen Jean Gilchrist, 1948, two daughters. **Career:** Assistant director, *March of Time* series, late 1940s; television director for CBS, 1949-62, work included *Studio One, Ford Theater,* and *Playhouse 90*; with Worthington Miner, George Roy Hill, and Fielder Cook, formed "Unit Four" production company, 1955; directed *Advise and Consent* on Broadway, 1961; signed three-picture contract with 20th Century-Fox and directed first feature, *A Summer World* (incomplete), 1961; television counselor to President Kennedy, 1961-63; president, Gilchrist Productions, 1962-68; president, Franklin Schaffner Productions, from 1969; president, Directors Guild of America, 1987-89. **Awards:** Three Emmy Awards; Oscar for Best Director, and Directors Guild Award, for *Patton,* 1970. **Died:** Of cancer, in Santa Monica, California, 2 July 1989.

Films as Director:

1961 *A Summer World* (incomplete)
1963 *The Stripper* (*Woman of Summer*)
1964 *The Best Man*
1965 *The War Lord*
1967 *The Double Man* (+ role)
1968 *Planet of the Apes*
1970 *Patton* (*Patton—Lust for Glory*; *Patton: A Salute to a Rebel*)
1971 *Nicholas and Alexandra* (+ pr)
1973 *Papillon* (+ co-pr)
1977 *Islands in the Stream*
1978 *The Boys from Brazil*
1981 *Sphinx* (+ exec pr)
1982 *Yes, Giorgio*
1987 *Lionheart*
1989 *Welcome Home*

Publications

By SCHAFFNER: book—

Worthing Miner: Interviewed by Franklin J. Schaffner, Metuchen, New Jersey, 1985.

By SCHAFFNER: articles—

Interview with Gerald Pratley, in *Cineaste* (New York), Summer 1969.
Interview with R. Feiden, in *Inter/View* (New York), March 1972.
"Chronicler of Power," an interview with Kathe Geist, in *Film Comment* (New York), September/October 1972.
Interview with R. Appelbaum, in *Films and Filming* (London), February 1979.
Interview with D. Castelli, in *Films Illustrated* (London), May 1979.

On SCHAFFNER: book—

Kim, Erwin, *Franklin J. Schaffner,* Metuchen, New Jersey, 1986.

On SCHAFFNER: articles—

Wilson, David, "Franklin Schaffner," in *Sight and Sound* (London), Spring 1966.
Sarris, Andrew, "Director of the Month—Franklin Schaffner: The Panoply of Power," in *Show* (Hollywood), April 1970.
Lightman, Herb, "On Location with *Islands in the Stream,*" in *American Cinematographer* (Los Angeles), November 1976.
"Franklin J. Schaffner," in *Kosmorama* (Copenhagen), Autumn 1977.
Cook, B., "The War Between the Writers and the Directors: Part II: The Directors," in *American Film* (Washington, D.C.), June 1979.
"TV to Film: a History, a Map and a Family Tree," in *Monthly Film Bulletin* (London), February 1983.
Obituary, in *Variety* (New York), 5 July 1989.

* * *

Franklin J. Schaffner has often been referred to as an "actors' director." A former actor himself, he spent over a decade directing television drama before making his first film. This experience proved invaluable when he arrived in Hollywood. All his films starred well-established professionals such as Fonda, Heston, Brynner, Scott, Hoffman, Peck, and Olivier.

Schaffner's first film, *The Stripper,* was based on William Inge's play *A Loss of Roses.* Producer Jerry Wald died while it was being made, and after completion the film was taken out of Schaffner's hands and re-edited. As a result the character of the "stripper," played by Joanne Woodward, was sadly lacking in contrast. Schaffner's experience working on political television programs proved beneficial when he directed his second film, *The Best Man,* a story of two contenders for the presidential nomination at a political convention in Los Angeles. Set mainly in hotel rooms and corridors, it could have become very static. But Schaffner accepted the challenge and turned out a compelling drama.

After the intimacy of *The Best Man* came the vastness of *The War Lord.* A medieval costume picture, the film was a complete change for Schaffner, but he succeeded in capturing the visual splendor of the outdoor sequences—particularly in the first few minutes—and the excitement and gusto of the battle scenes. Although an "action" film, it had a literate script—but once again Schaffner's film was cut by the studio. The director's next work was *The Double Man,* an average spy drama. His first big financial success was *Planet of the Apes,* in which he had to produce realistic performances from actors in monkey suits. Handled by another director, it could easily have been turned into a farce, but Schaffner's craftsmanship made it a science fiction satire.

In 1970 Schaffner directed George C. Scott in the role of General Patton. Twenty-seven years earlier Schaffner himself had taken part in the landings in Sicily under Patton. The film was shot in 70mm, but he insisted on cutting it in 35mm to avoid being influenced by the scope of 70mm. Scott's performance was widely praised, but he refused an Academy Award (Schaffner accepted his).

It was his interest in history that first attracted Schaffner to *Nicholas and Alexandra.* Here he told what was basically an intimate story of two people, but two people surrounded by the overflowing retinue of the court and the boundless expanse of the countryside. Schaffner used the contrast to great effect, and the film was nominated for an Oscar.

Papillon is the only film which Schaffner directed in sequence, and this was not by choice. Dalton Trumbo was rewriting the script as the film was being shot, often just managing to keep up with the production. This film marked the second time that Schaffner had worked with cinematographer Fred Koenekamp, and they were teamed again for his next feature, *Islands in the Stream.* This time he faced the problem of space and isolation, having to fill the large screen for a long time with just one man. He also found it necessary to use two cameras for some of the action sequences, something which he never did if he could avoid it. Several studios turned down *The Boys from Brazil* because it was impossible to cast, but Schaffner thought it would work if he cast against type. So Gregory Peck, always known as a

Franklin J. Schaffner: Steve McQueen and Dustin Hoffman in *Papillon*

"good guy," played Mengele—the German doctor intent on producing clones of Hitler. Olivier, who had earlier played a German war criminal in *Marathon Man,* was the Jewish doctor trying to track down the Nazi. In the early 1980s Schaffner made *Sphinx,* an adventure story set amongst the pyramids, and *Yes, Giorgio,* his first "musical," with Luciano Pavarotti.

Schaffner had a reputation for getting the best out of his actors and coping well with intimate dramas. Yet he also achieved success with large-scale epics and has been compared with David Lean because of the beauty of his compositions and the breadth of his dramatic power. He reveled in films about men struggling to achieve a certain goal. A craftsman, he did his homework and prepared each scene before arriving on the set.

—Colin Williams

SCHEPISI, Fred

Nationality: Australian. **Born:** Frederic Alan Schepisi in Melbourne, Victoria, 26 December 1939. **Education:** Briefly attended seminary school. **Family:** Married 1) Joan Ford, 1960, four children; 2) casting director Rhonda Finlayson, 1973, two children; 3) Mary Rubin, 1984, one child. **Career:** Director, producer, and writer at Carden Advertising, Melbourne, from 1955; television production manager, Paton Advertising Service, Melbourne, 1961-64; Victorian manager of Cinesound Productions, Melbourne, 1964-65; managing director of The Film House, Melbourne, making advertising shorts and documentaries, 1965-79 (chairman from 1979); first feature, *The Devil's Playground,* won six Australian Film Institute awards, 1976; moved to United States, 1979; returned to Australia to make *A Cry in the Dark,* 1988; Governor of the Australian Film Institute. **Awards:** Best Director, Australian Film Awards, for *The Devil's Playground,* 1976. **Address:** P.O. Box 317, South Melbourne VIC 3205, Australia. **Agent:** c/o Sam Cohn, International Creative Management, 40 W. 57th Street, New York, NY 10019, U.S.A.

Films as Director:

1970 *The Party* (short)
1973 "The Priest" episode of *Libido*
1976 *The Devil's Playground* (+ sc, pr)
1978 *The Chant of Jimmie Blacksmith* (+ sc, pr)
1981 *Barbarosa*
1984 *Iceman*
1985 *Plenty*
1987 *Roxanne*
1988 *A Cry in the Dark* (*Guilty by Suspicion*; *Evil Angels*)
1990 *The Russia House* (+ pr)
1992 *Mr. Baseball* (+ co-pr)
1993 *Six Degrees of Separation* (+ co-pr)
1994 *I.Q.* (+ co-pr)

Publications

By SCHEPISI: articles—

Interview in *Cinema Papers* (Melbourne), January 1978.
"Le sauvage qui n'avait pas été enfant," an interview with V. Amiel and others, in *Positif* (Paris), February 1983.
Interview with M. Magill in *Films in Review* (New York), January 1984.
Interview with B. Lewis in *Films and Filming* (London), December 1985.
Interview in *Screen International* (London), 4 January 1986.
"Dialogue on Film: Fred Schepisi," in *American Film* (Washington D.C.), July/August 1987.
"The Making of *Evil Angels,*" interview with P. Hawker in *Cinema Papers* (Melbourne), November 1988.
"Fred Schepisi," interview with S. Murray in *Cinema Papers* (Melbourne), August 1990.

On SCHEPISI: books—

Tulloch, John, *Australian Cinema: Industry, Narrative and Meaning,* Sydney and London, 1982.
Hall, Sandra, *The New Australian Cinema in Review,* Adelaide, 1985.
Moran, Albert, and Tom O'Regan, editors, *An Australian Film Reader,* Sydney, 1985.
Mathews, Sue, *35mm Dreams: Conversations with Five Directors About the Australian Film Revival,* Ringwood, Australia, 1987.
McFarlane, Brian, *Australian Cinema 1970-85,* London, 1987.

On SCHEPISI: articles—

Bromby, Robin, "Test for Australia," in *Sight and Sound* (London), Spring 1979.
Stratton, D., "Man of Plenty," in *Cinema Papers* (Melbourne), March 1986.
Taitz, N., "Fred Schepisi Puts Gossip on Trial," in *New York Times,* 6 November 1988.
Lewis, B., article in *Films & Filming* (London), May 1989.
Matthews, T., article in *Box Office* (Hollywood), November 1990.
Koch, N., "No Tea, No Sympathy," in *New York Times,* 23 August 1992.
Schiff, Stephen, "A Cinematic Gallant," in *New Yorker,* 20 December 1993.

* * *

More than any other director of the Australian new wave, Fred Schepisi reflects, in his deal-making expertise, his emphasis on production values, even in his choice of New York as an adoptive base, the values of his home city, Melbourne, traditionally Australia's capital of political conservatism, old money, the church, and the law.

Schepisi's first two features assaulted Australia's endemic provincialism. *The Devil's Playground,* a story of sexual repression and dead belief set in a Catholic seminary, is based on Schepisi's 18 adolescent months in a monastery. (The theme was rehearsed in *The Priest,* his episode of the sketch film *Libido,* written by lapsed Catholic novelist Thomas Keneally.) The film's gloomy, sensual elegance is typical of Schepisi's later work, but his adolescent hero's moral and religious doubts are dealt with sketchily. Schepisi prefers to emphasize the celibate staff's problems with sex and drink, especially in a memorable scene in which priest Arthur Dignam spies on naked girls at a public swimming pool.

The Chant of Jimmie Blacksmith, again based on Thomas Keneally's work, is a period drama concerning the true story of nineteenth-century renegade aboriginal Jimmie Governor, who revolted against the dehumanization of his race at the hands of whites. Schepisi's use of landscape echoes the westerns of Anthony Mann, underlining the similarities between his film and Hollywood's pro-Indian dramas like *Broken Arrow* and *Tell Them Willie Boy is Here.* In a film that, like Schepisi's later *A Cry in the Dark,* mixes, sometimes uneasily, social protest with wide screen melodrama, an inexperienced Tommy Lewis rampages bloodily but unconvincingly across rural Australia as the ill-used part-aboriginal driven to massacre by corruption in law, religion, and the state.

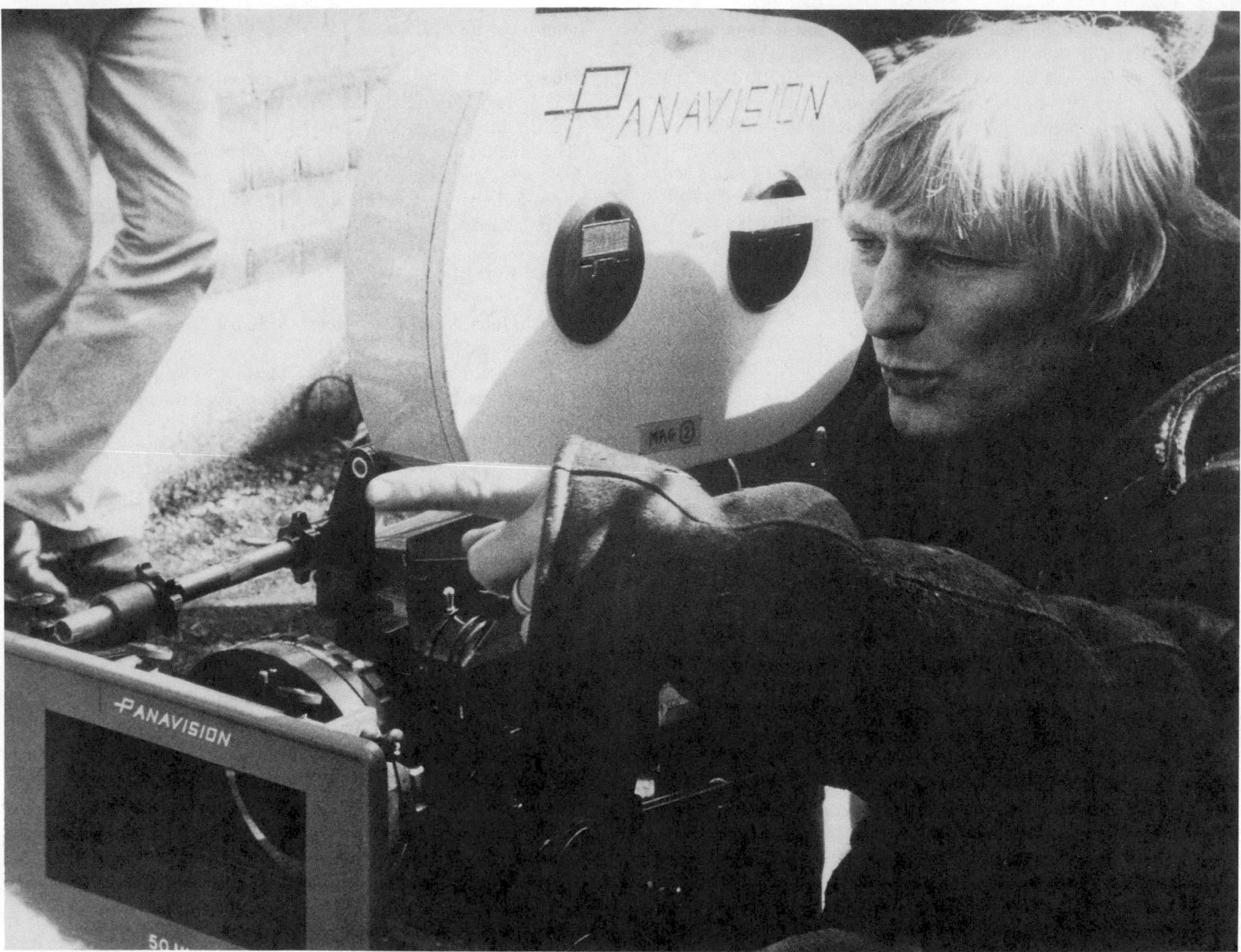

Fred Schepisi

A highly successful producer of TV commercials and documentaries, the pragmatic Schepisi conformed more comfortably than most Australian directors to Hollywood. Though his first American production, the revenge western *Barbarosa,* has all the earmarks of a test piece, he extracted good performances from an aging Gilbert Roland and the project's co-producers, Willie Nelson and a famously aggressive Gary Busey. ("I am the first director he hasn't destroyed," Schepisi said proudly.) Schepisi proved equally decisive in *Ice Man,* a piece of Green science-fiction in which John Lone's defrosted Neanderthal beguiles technocrat Tim Hutton with earth magic and Ice Age mythology.

Schepisi's first hit was an adaptation of David Hare's play *Plenty.* As the ex-Resistance heroine who finds only disillusionment in Britain's post-war affluence, Meryl Streep replaced Kate Nelligan, who created the role on stage. The casting turned *Plenty* into a star vehicle, winning international success at the cost of Hare's more precise political arguments, though Schepisi, as impatient as only an Australian can be with the British, manipulates Sir John Gielgud, Charles Dance, and especially Ian McKellen in waspish parodies of imperial privilege.

Confirmed now as a technician able to tame any project or performer, Schepisi made *Roxanne,* a comedy version of Rostand's *Cyrano de Bergerac,* reset in the Pacific Northwest as a vehicle for comic Steve Martin. In the wake of its enormous success, he returned to Australia to film *A Cry in the Dark (Evil Angels),* the sensational true story of a young mother's trial and imprisonment for infanticide. Lindy Chamberlain insisted a wild dog had stolen her baby Azaria from Ayers Rock, one of Australia's most famous desert tourist sites. But the lack of a body, combined with Lindy's own unusual religious affiliations—she was a Seventh Day Adventist—fueled rumors that the child had been sacrificed in some arcane rite. She was freed only after investigators decisively discredited the forensic evidence.

In a typical calculated risk, Schepisi cast Meryl Streep as Lindy and used the film to reprise *The Chant of Jimmie Blacksmith.* Australia itself becomes the villain, and Chamberlain was portrayed as another victim—like Blacksmith and the boy of *The Devil's Playground*—of national bigotry and ignorance. *A Cry in the Dark* depicts Australia's press as vulgar and meretricious, and its police as malicious and bumbling. Far from resenting either the imported star or the national slur, Australians greeted the film with enthusiasm, and the Streep name guaranteed a modest international success.

Schepisi debated further Australian-based projects, but with the local industry's financial base crumbling in the financial freeze of the late 1980s, he returned to New York (though much of the film was shot on location in Moscow) to direct another in his growing string of high-budget international projects, John le Carré's *The Russia House.*

Schepisi has evolved into a proficient director whose recent films, while made on big budgets with international stars, are for the most part not nearly as interesting as his early-career work in Australia. *The*

Russia House, which starred Sean Connery and Michele Pfeiffer, is an uneven spy drama; conversely, *I.Q.*, with Tim Robbins, Meg Ryan and Walter Matthau, is a lightly likable fantasy-romance in which a fictionalized Albert Einstein plays cupid for his brainy niece.

Mr. Baseball features Tom Selleck as a spoiled, aging American baseball star who goes to play in Japan. The film's production was controversial in that it originally was intended strictly as a comedy. But when the Matsushita Electric Industrial Company acquired MCA, Inc., the owner of Universal Pictures (the film's releasing company), *Mr. Baseball* became a more serious, complex film about an American hero who must become humbled and learn to accept Japanese customs before he is allowed success. Schepisi's involvement with *Mr. Baseball* seems incidental; it is a well-directed film, to be sure, but then again it would be no matter what its ultimate storyline or point of view.

The theme of relations between peoples of different cultures is continued in *Six Degrees of Separation,* among Schepisi's better post-Australian films. It is a provocative version of John Guare's play, in which a well-off Manhattan couple is taken in by a gracious young con artist who eases himself into their household by pawning himself off as the son of actor Sidney Poitier. Schepisi does an especially fine job of capturing the setting's upper-class urban ambiance and various New York City vistas.

—John Baxter, updated by Rob Edelman

SCHLESINGER, John

Nationality: British. **Born:** John Richard Schlesinger in London, 16 February 1926. **Education:** Uppingham School and Balliol College, Oxford, 1945-50. **Career:** Maker of short films, from 1948; actor with Colchester Repertory Company then Ngaio Marsh's Touring Company, 1950-52; directed 24 short documentaries for BBC TV series *Tonight* and *Monitor,* 1956-61; directed first feature, *A Kind of Loving,* 1962; associate director, National Theatre, London, from 1973; opera director, 1980s; also director for TV, work includes *Separate Tables,* 1982, and *An Englishman Abroad,* 1983. **Awards:** Best Direction, New York Film Critics, for *Darling,* 1965; Oscar for Best Director, Best Direction Award, British Film Academy, and Directors Award, Directors Guild of America, for *Midnight Cowboy,* 1969; Best Direction Award, British Film Academy, for *Sunday, Bloody Sunday,* 1970; Commander of the British Empire, 1970; British Film and TV Academy Award, for *An Englishman Abroad,* 1983. **Agent:** c/o Duncan Heath, 76 Oxford Street, London W1R 1RB, England.

Films as Director:

1961 *Terminus* (doc) (+ sc)
1962 *A Kind of Loving*
1963 *Billy Liar*
1965 *Darling* (+ sc)
1967 *Far from the Madding Crowd*
1969 ***Midnight Cowboy*** (+ co-pr)
1971 ***Sunday, Bloody Sunday***
1972 "Olympic Marathon" section of *Visions of Eight*
1975 *The Day of the Locust*
1976 *Marathon Man*
1979 *Yanks*
1980 *Honky Tonk Freeway*
1981 *Privileged* (consultant d only)
1985 *The Falcon and the Snowman* (+ pr)
1987 *The Believers* (+ pr)
1988 *Madame Sousatzka*
1990 *Pacific Heights*
1991 *A Question of Attribution*
1993 *The Innocent*
1996 *Eye for an Eye*; *Cold Comfort Farm*

Other Films:

1953 *Single-Handed* (*Sailor of the King*) (Boulting) (role)
1955 *The Divided Heart* (Crichton) (role as ticket collector)
1956 *The Last Man to Hang?* (Fisher) (role as Dr. Goldfinger)
1957 *The Battle of the River Plate* (*Pursuit of the Graf Spee*) (Powell and Pressburger) (role); *Brothers in Law* (Boulting) (role)
1986 *Fifty Years of Action!* (appearance as himself)

Publications

By SCHLESINGER: articles—

"How to Get into Films by the People Who Got in Themselves," in *Films and Filming* (London), July 1963.
"John Schlesinger," in *Directors in Action,* edited by Bob Thomas, Indianapolis, 1968.
Interview with David Spiers, in *Screen* (London), Summer 1970.
Interview with Valerie Wade, in *Interview* (New York), July 1974.
Interview with Gene D. Phillips, in *Film Comment* (New York), May/June 1975.
"Dialogue on Film: John Schlesinger," with James Powers, in *American Film* (Washington, D.C.), December 1979.
"John Schlesinger," interview with John Study, in *Films in Review* (New York), October 1981.
"Spies Like Us," interview with Stephen Rebello, in *Saturday Review* (New York), January/February 1985.
"Treason to Believe," interview with Graham Fuller in *Stills* (London), April 1985.
"Dialogue on Film: John Schlesinger," in *American Film* (Washington D.C.), November 1987, January 1991.
Interview with L. Farrah in *Films and Filming* (London), May 1988.

On SCHLESINGER: books—

Brooker, Nancy J., *John Schlesinger: A Guide to References and Resources,* Boston, 1978.
Phillips, Gene D., *John Schlesinger,* Boston, 1981.
Salizzato, Claver, *John Schlesinger,* Florence, 1986.

On SCHLESINGER: articles—

Phillips, Gene D., "John Schlesinger, Social Realist," in *Film Comment* (New York), Winter 1969.
Hall, William, "John Schlesinger, Award Winner," in *Action* (Los Angeles), July/August 1970.
"John Schlesinger at the Olympic Games," in *American Cinematographer* (Hollywood), November 1972.
Perry, George, *The Great British Picture Show,* London, 1974.
Walker, Alexander, "A Kind of Stoicism," in *Hollywood UK: The British Film Industry in the Sixties,* London, 1974.
Rand, Kenn, "Behind the Scenes of *Day of the Locust,*" in *American Cinematographer* (Hollywood), June 1975.
Sherman, Eric, "John Schlesinger," in *Directing the Film: Film Directors on their Art,* Boston, 1976.

John Schlesinger

Phillips, Gene D., "Exile in Hollywood: John Schlesinger," in *Literature/Film Quarterly* (Salisbury, Maryland), Spring 1977.

Phillips, Gene D., "On *Yanks* and Other Films," in *Focus on Film* (London), Fall 1978.

Gross, Sheryl, "Guilt and Innocence in *Marathon Man,*" in *Literature/Film Quarterly* (Salisbury, Maryland), January 1980.

Welsh, James, "Hardy and Schlesinger: *Far from the Maddening Crowd,*" in *Literature/Film Quarterly* (Salisbury, Maryland), Spring 1988.

Fuller, Graham, "An Englishman Abroad," in *Cinema Papers* (Melbourne), July 1985.

Allmendinger, Blake, "From Silent Movies to the Talkies in *The Day of the Locust,*" in *Literature/Film Quarterly* (Salisbury, Maryland), Spring 1988.

Phillips, Gene D., *Major Film Directors of the American and British Cinema,* Cranbury, New Jersey, 1989.

Brode, Douglas, "*Darling, Midnight Cowboy,*" in *The Films of the Sixties,* New York, 1990.

Bookbinder, Robert, "*Day of the Locust, Marathon Man,*" in *The Films of the Seventies,* New York, 1990.

Murphy, Robert, "*Far from the Maddening Crowd,*" in *Sixties British Cinema,* London, 1992.

Hadleigh, Boze, "*Midnight Cowboy, Sunday, Bloody Sunday,*" in *The Lavender Screen: Homosexuality on Film,* New York, 1993.

Russell, Ken, "*Sunday, Bloody Sunday,*" in *The Lion Roars: Ken Russell on Film,* Winchester, Massachusetts, 1994.

Kael, Pauline, "The Hollywood Novel: *Day of the Locust* and Other Films," in *Literature/Film Quarterly* (Salisbury, Maryland), Winter 1995.

* * *

John Schlesinger began his professional career by making short documentaries for the BBC. His first major venture in the cinema was a documentary for British Transport called *Terminus,* about twenty-four hours at Waterloo Station, which won him an award at the Venice Film Festival. Schlesinger's documentaries attracted the attention of producer Joseph Janni; together they formed a creative association which has included several of Schlesinger's British films, beginning with *A Kind of Loving,* which won the Grand Prize at the Berlin Film Festival.

Schlesinger began directing feature films in Britain at the point when the cycle of low-budget, high-quality movies on social themes (called "Kitchen Sink" dramas) was in full swing. Because these films were made outside the large studio system, Schlesinger got used to developing his own film projects. He has continued to do so while directing films in Hollywood, where he has worked with increasing regularity in recent years, starting with his first American film, *Midnight Cowboy.*

"I like the cross-fertilization that comes from making films in both England and America," he explains. "Although I am English and I do like to work in England, I have gotten used to regarding myself more and more as mid-Atlantic." As a matter of fact, foreign directors like Lang and Hitchcock and Schlesinger, precisely because they are not native Americans, are sometimes able to view American life with a vigilant, perceptive eye for the kind of telling details which homegrown directors might easily overlook or simply take for granted. Indeed, reviews of *Midnight Cowboy* by and large noted how accurately the British-born Schlesinger had caught the authentic atmosphere not only of New York City, but also of Miami Beach and the Texas Panhandle, as surely as he had captured the atmosphere of a factory town in his native England in *A Kind of Loving.*

"Any film that is seriously made will reflect the attitudes and problems of society at large," he says, and consequently possess the potential to appeal to an international audience, as many of his films have. "But it is inevitable that a director's own attitudes will creep into his films. For my part I try in my movies to communicate to the filmgoer a better understanding of other human beings by exploring the hazards of entering into a mutual relationship with another human being, which is the most difficult thing on earth to do, because it involves a voyage of discovery for both parties." Hence his prime concern as a director with examining complex human relationships from a variety of angles—ranging from the social outcasts of *Midnight Cowboy* to members of the jet set in *Darling.*

Among the standout films of his later career are: *Marathon Man,* a thriller about a young American Jew who finds himself pitted against a Nazi war criminal in New York; *The Falcon and the Snowman,* the true story of two young Americans who betrayed their country to the Russians; and *Madame Sousatzka,* which concerns a dedicated, demanding London piano teacher, whose exacting standards threaten to drive her most promising pupil away. Significantly, Schlesinger's acutely observed depiction of the ramshackle old rooming house where Madame lives, with its colorful assortment of diverse tenants, lends to the film an authentic atmosphere that recalls Schlesinger's social ("Kitchen Sink") dramas.

Given the great success of *Marathon Man,* Schlesinger went on to make a trio of superior thrillers: *Pacific Heights,* in which a hapless young landlord is victimized by a psychotic tenant; *The Innocent,* a story of international intrigue about a young English technician sent by British Intelligence to work on a secret operation in Berlin after World War II; and *Eye for an Eye,* a dark study wherein a vengeful mother vows to bring to justice the brute who raped and murdered her daughter. This trilogy of suspense films clearly established Schlesinger as a worthy successor to Hitchcock in the thriller genre.

In sum, John Schlesinger is a member of the international community of filmmakers who speak to an equally international audience. That is the way the world cinema has been developing, and directors like Schlesinger have helped to lead it there.

—Gene D. Phillips

SCHLÖNDORFF, Volker

Nationality: German. **Born:** Wiesbaden, 31 March 1939. **Education:** Lycée Henri IV, Paris; studied political science and economics; studied film directing at IDHEC, Paris. **Family:** Married filmmaker Margarethe von Trotta, 1969. **Career:** Assistant to various French directors, 1960-64; returned to Germany, 1965; formed Hallelujah-Film with Peter Fleischmann, went into partnership with German TV stations, 1969; formed Bioskop-Film with Reinhard Hauff, 1973; opera director, from 1974. **Awards:** FIPRESCT Prize, Cannes Festival, for *Young Törless,* 1966; Oscar for Best Foreign-Language Film, and Best Film, Cannes Festival *(ex aequo),* for *The Tin Drum,* 1979.

Films as Director:

1960 *Wen kümmert's ...* (*Who Cares ...*) (short, unreleased)
1966 *Der junge Törless* (*Young Törless*) (+ sc)
1967 *Mord und Totschlag* (*A Degree of Murder*) (+ co-sc)
1969 *Michael Kohlhaas—Der Rebell* (*Michael Kohlhaas—The Rebel*) (+ co-sc)
1970 *Baal* (for TV) (+ sc); *Ein unheimlicher Moment* (*An Uneasy Moment*) (short; originally episode of uncompleted feature *Paukenspieler,* filmed 1967); *Der plötzlicher Reichtum der armen Leute von Kombach* (*The Sudden Fortune of the Poor People of Kombach*) (+ co-sc)
1971 *Die Moral der Ruth Halbfass* (*The Moral of Ruth Halbfass*) (+ co-sc); *Strohfeuer* (*A Free Woman*; *Strawfire*; *Summer Lightning* (+ co-sc)
1974 *Übernachtung in Tirol* (*Overnight Stay in the Tyrol*) (for TV) (+ co-sc)
1975 *Georginas Grunde* (*Georgina's Reasons*) (for TV); *Die verlorene Ehre der Katharina Blum* (*The Lost Honor of Katharina Blum*) (co-d, co-sc)
1976 *Der Fangschuss* (*Coup de grâce*)
1977 *Nur zum Spass—Nur zum Spiel* (*Only for Fun—Only for Play*), *Kaleidoskop Valeska Gert* (*Kaleidoscope Valeska Gert*) (doc) (+ sc)
1978 *Deutschland im Herbst* (*Germany in Autumn*) (co-d)
1979 ***Die Blechtrommel*** (*The Tin Drum*) (+ co-sc)
1980 *Der Kandidat* (*The Candidate*) (doc) (+ co-sc)
1981 *Die Fälschung* (*The Forgery*) (+ sc); *Circle of Deceit*
1983 *Krieg und Frieden* (*War and Peace*) (doc)
1984 *Swann in Love* (*Un Amour de Swann*)
1985 *Death of a Salesman*
1987 *Vermischte Nachrichten* (*Odds and Ends*) (co-d); *A Gathering of Old Men* (for TV)
1990 *The Handmaid's Tale*
1991 *Last Call from Passenger Faber* (*Voyager*) (+ co-sc)

Publications

By SCHLÖNDORFF: book—

Die Blechtrommel als Film, Frankfurt, 1979.

By SCHLÖNDORFF: articles—

"Volker Schloendorff: The Rebel," interview with Rui Nogueira and Nicoletta Zalaffi, in *Film* (London), Summer 1969.
"Feu de paille," interview with M. Martin, in *Ecran* (Paris), February 1973.
"Melville und der Befreiungskampf in Baltikum," interview with H. Wiedemann, in *Film und Ton* (Munich), December 1976.
"*Die Blechtrommel,*" in *Film und Ton* (Munich), June 1979.
"The Tin Drum: Volker Schlöndorff's 'Dream of Childhood', interview with J. Hughes, in *Film Quarterly* (Berkeley), Spring 1981.
"The Limits of Journalism," an interview with A. Auster and L. Quart in *Cineaste* (New York), vol. 12, no. 2, 1982.
Interview with B. Steinborn in *Filmfaust* (Frankfurt), February/March 1983.
"Director's Chair," an interview with D. DeNicolo in *Interview* (New York), March 1990.
"The Last Days of Max Frisch," in *New York Times Book Review,* April 1992.

On SCHLÖNDORFF: books—

Lewandowski, Rainer, *Die Filme von Volker Schlöndorff,* Hildesheim, 1981.
Franklin, James, *New German Cinema: From Oberhausen to Hamburg,* Boston, 1983.
Phillips, Klaus, editor, *New German Filmmakers: From Oberhausen through the 1970s,* New York, 1984.
Elsaesser, Thomas, *New German Cinema: A History,* London, 1989.

On SCHLÖNDORFF: articles—

"*Le Coup de grâce* Issue" of *Avant-Scène du Cinéma* (Paris), 1 February 1977.

Eichenlaub, H.M., "Den deutschen Film international machen: Volker Schlöndorff und *Die Blechtrommel*," in *Cinema* (Zurich), no. 2, 1979.

Holloway, Ronald, "Volker Schlöndorff," in *International Film Guide 1982*, London, 1981.

Rickey, C., "The War Lovers," in *American Film* (Washington D.C.), January/February 1982.

"*Un Amour de Swann* Issue" of *Avant-Scène du Cinéma* (Paris), no. 321/322, 1984.

Horton, Andrew, "Black like Mich," in *Film Comment* (New York), March/April 1987.

Van Gelder, L., "At the Movies," in *New York Times*, 16 March 1990.

Strauss, F., article in *Cahiers du Cinema* (Paris), September 1991.

Lally, K., article in *Film Journal*, December 1991.

Tagliabue, J., "A Director Who Pursues His Inner Demons," in *New York Times*, 26 January 1992.

On SCHLÖNDORFF: film—

Private Conversation (doc about the making of *Death of a Salesman*), Blackwood, 1985.

* * *

In discussions of the New German Cinema, Volker Schlöndorff's name generally comes up only after the mention of Fassbinder, Herzog, Wenders, and perhaps Straub, Syberberg, or von Trotta. Though his work certainly merits consideration alongside that of any of his countrymen, there are several reasons why he has stood apart from them.

As a teenager, Schlöndorff moved to France to study, earning academic honors and a university degree in economics and political science. He enrolled at IDHEC with an interest in film directing but chose instead to pursue an active apprenticeship within the French film industry. Eventually he served as assistant director to Jean-Pierre Melville, Alain Resnais, and Louis Malle. Schlöndorff then returned to Germany and scored an immediate triumph with his first feature, *Young Törless.* Like his mentor Louis Malle, then, he ushered in his country's new wave of film artists, but also like Malle, Schlöndorff's eclectic range of projects has defied easy categorization, causing his

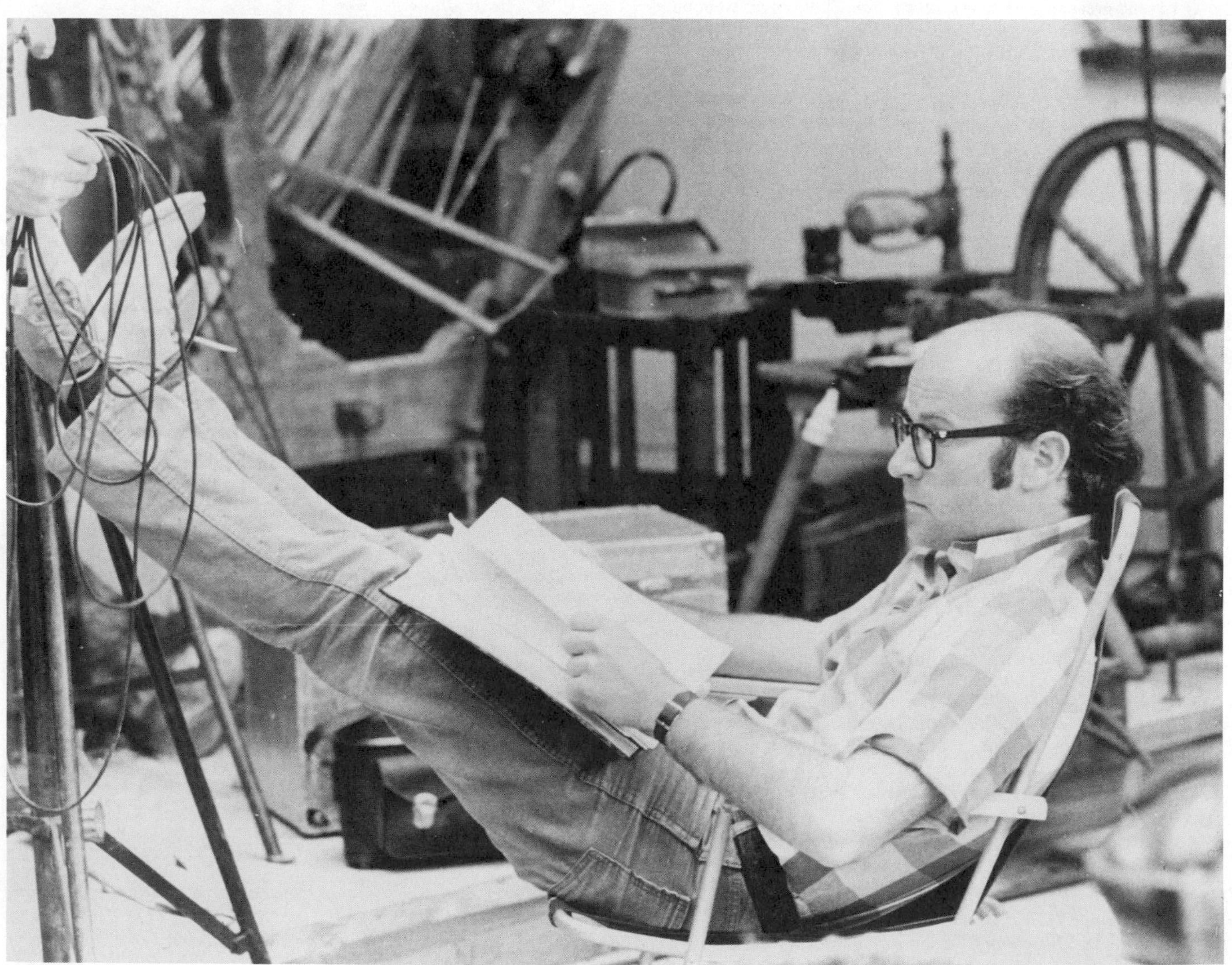

Volker Schlöndorff

work to seem less personal than that of almost any other German filmmaker. The thorough professional training received during his decade in France also set Schlöndorff apart. His time there instilled in him an appreciation for the highly-crafted, polished filmmaking that marks his style. (The quality of the photography in his work—both black and white and in color, whether by Sven Nykvist, Franz Rath, or Igor Luther—has been consistently exceptional.) While most of his contemporaries declared their antipathy toward the look and production methods of the declining German film industry of the 1960s, Schlöndorff endeavored successfully to make larger-scaled features. Toward this end he helped form and continues to operate two production companies—Hallelujah-Film and Bioskop-Film—and has regularly obtained financing from German television and a variety of international producers. Yet he has met shooting schedules of just three weeks, and his wide career includes shorts, documentaries, and television films (one is a production of Brecht's *Baal* with Fassbinder in the title role). In the mid-1970s he even turned to directing opera: Janaček's *Katya Kabanova* and a work by Hans Werner Henze.

Intellectual, literate, and fluent in several languages, Schlöndorff has chiefly been attracted to the adaption of literary works—a practice which has yielded mixed results: *Young Törless,* from Robert Musil, remains one of his best films, and there is much to praise in *The Tin Drum,* the New German Cinema's foremost commercial success, which Günter Grass helped to adapt from his novel. Despite strengths in each, though, the director's adaptations of Kleist's *Michael Kohlhaas* and Marguerite Yourcenar's *Coup de grace* turned out unevenly for quite different reasons. The admirable *Lost Honor of Katharina Blum* comes from a Heinrich Böll story, while the problematic *Circle of Deceit* was based on the novel by Nicolas Born.

Among "original" projects, on the other hand, are *A Degree of Murder,* a failure by all accounts; the fine *A Free Woman*; and the excellent *Sudden Wealth of the Poor People of Kombach.*

Despite the variety of his subjects, Schlöndorff is almost invariably drawn to material that allows him expression as social critic. All the films cited above share this characteristic. Some of his projects have been courageously political: *Katharina Blum* is an undisguised attack on Germany's powerful right-wing, scandal-mongering press, which serves large-scale social repression. As notable are his leading contributions to three collaborative documentaries: *Germany in Autumn,* a response to the authoritarian climate in the country in the wake of the Baader-Meinhof affair; *The Candidate,* a work shot during the election campaign that examines the career of ultra-conservative Christian Social Unionist Franz Josef Strauss; and *War and Peace,* an agit-prop film essay on the deployment of new American nuclear missiles in the Federal Republic.

Schlöndorff's major theme is the temptation toward moral and political equivocation within an ambiguous or malignant social order, and his films are wryly or skeptically realistic about any hoped-for solutions, even courting controversy. *A Free Woman* chastens unbridled feminist idealism; *Circle of Deceit* (made prior to the Israeli invasion of Lebanon) refuses to take sides in the Lebanese conflict.

Margarethe von Trotta, to whom Schlöndorff is married, has performed in a number of her husband's films and is a frequent collaborator on his scripts; interestingly, her own work as director is characterized not only by a polish equal to Schlöndorff's and similar political inspiration but also by a compelling intelligence and power of evocation.

Throughout the 1980s and early 1990s, Schlöndorff has continued directing films based on fine literature. They feature characters in moral conflict who are spooked by their pasts, uncertain of their futures, and unable to control their impulses and their fates.

Swann in Love, based on Marcel Proust's "Remembrances of Things Past," is the elegantly sensual story of a wealthy gentleman (Jeremy Irons) who thrives in the finest circles of high society but risks everything over his erotic obsession with a courtesan. *Death of a Salesman,* superbly adapted from the 1984 Broadway revival of the Arthur Miller play, is the saga of Willy Loman (Dustin Hoffman), the tragic, desperate travelling salesman to whom "attention must be paid." *The Handmaid's Tale,* scripted by Harold Pinter from Margaret Atwood's bestseller, is an intriguing science fiction chiller told from a woman's point of view. It is set in the future, when white women are coerced into birthing babies who will make up a new, "pure" generation. The story focuses on one such female (Natasha Richardson) who must contend with the advances of the powerful "commander" (Robert Duvall). Finally, *Voyager,* based on the Max Frisch book *Homo Faber,* is a pensive drama about two very different romances—one in the past, the other in the present—experienced by Walter Faber (Sam Shepard), a repressed American traveler.

—Herbert Reynolds, updated by Rob Edelman

SCHOEDSACK, Ernest B.

Nationality: American. **Born:** Ernest Beaumont Schoedsack in Council Bluffs, Iowa, 8 June 1893. **Military Service:** Served in photographic dept. of U.S. Signal Corps. in France, 1916, then captain in Red Cross photographic unit. **Family:** Married actress Ruth Rose, 1926, one son. **Career:** Worked with engineering road gangs in San Francisco area, then secured job as cameraman for Mack Sennett through brother Felix (G.F.) Schoedsack, early 1910s; freelance newsreel cameraman, Europe, then returned to United States, 1922; collaborated with Merian C. Cooper and newspaper correspondent Marguerite Harrison on first film, *Grass,* 1925; suffered severe eye injury while testing photographic equipment for U.S. Army Air Corps, World War II. **Died:** 23 December 1979.

Films as Director:

1925 *Grass* (doc) (co-d, co-pr, co-sc, co-ph)
1927 *Chang* (doc) (co-d, co-pr)
1929 *The Four Feathers* (co-d, co-pr)
1931 *Rango* (+ pr)
1932 *The Most Dangerous Game* (*The Hounds of Zaroff*) (co-d, co-pr)
1933 ***King Kong*** (co-d, co-pr); *Son of Kong*; *Blind Adventure*
1934 *Long Lost Father*
1935 *The Last Days of Pompeii*
1937 *Trouble in Morocco*; *Outlaws of the Orient*
1940 *Dr. Cyclops*
1949 *Mighty Joe Young*
1952 *This Is Cinerama* (d prologue only, uncredited)

Publications

By SCHOEDSACK: articles—

"*Grass*: The Making of an Epic," in *American Cinematographer* (Hollywood), February 1983.

On SCHOEDSACK: books—

Goldner, Orville, and George Turner, *The Making of King Kong,* Cranbury, New Jersey, 1975.

Gottesman, Ronald, and Harry Geduld, editors, *The Girl in the Hairy Paw,* New York, 1976.

Ernest B. Schoedsack: poster for *King Kong*

On SCHOEDSACK: articles—

Boone, Andrew R., "Prehistoric Monsters Roar and Hiss for the Sound Film," in *Popular Science Monthly* (New York), 1933.

"The Making of the Original *King Kong,*" in *American Cinematographer* (Los Angeles), January 1977.

"RKO: They Also Served," in *Monthly Film Bulletin* (London), December 1979.

Goimard, J., "Cooper et Schoedsack: une longue collaboration," in *Avant-Scène du Cinéma* (Paris), November 1982.

* * *

Ernest B. Schoedsack's initial fame as a filmmaker came from his work in the documentary mode directing "natural dramas," as he and his partner Merian C. Cooper called their films. Schoedsack's spirit for adventure in these pictures can be traced to the kind of life he himself led. He began his film career simply enough as a cameraman with the Mack Sennett Keystone Studios. When World War I broke out Schoedsack enlisted with the photographic section of the Signal Corps. He was stationed in France, where he gained a great deal of film experience as a newsreel cameraman. With the signing of the Armistice, Schoedsack decided to remain in Europe and aid the Poles in their battle against the Russians. While in Poland Schoedsack continued to make newsreels. This occupation, however, was primarily a cover to disguise the fact that he was smuggling supplies and Poles out of Russian-occupied territory.

It was in Poland that Schoedsack met his future partner Merian C. Cooper. Like Schoedsack, Cooper was an American who wanted to help the Polish people in their struggle for freedom. Cooper's exploits during the Russian-Polish conflict resulted in his imprisonment by the Russians as a spy. Fortunately he managed to escape before he could be executed. The true-life adventures of both Cooper and Schoedsack make it easy to see why these two sought out the most distant, difficult, and dangerous locations they could find for their films.

Their first motion picture collaboration, titled *Grass,* concerned the yearly migration of the Bakhtiari tribes in Persia as they crossed over the Zardeh Kuh mountain range to find grazing land for their sheep and cattle. Although the trip was long and treacherous, Cooper and Schoedsack made the journey with the tribesmen, filming every step of the way. Back home *Grass* was an extremely successful film, and, along with *Nanook of the North,* helped to set the style for documentary travelogues.

Their next project together, *Chang,* was a documentary film set in China, but with a more centralized story line than *Grass.* This film dealt with one man's efforts to protect his family from the dangers of nature. In order to help dramatize the story, some events in the film were staged. For example, the climactic elephant stampede toward the end of the film was directed at a mock village so that no lives would be endangered. Audiences in America were none the wiser, however, and *Chang* played to large crowds on Broadway.

With each successive film Cooper and Schoedsack moved more and more toward fiction, although their films still retained a documentary look. For example, their next film, *The Four Feathers,* included background scenes filmed in Africa, while the principal actors were filmed on a Hollywood stage. Eventually Cooper and Schoedsack moved their filmmaking partnership entirely to Hollywood and away from real locations. They continued to make films in the documentary style, though, as shown by their most famous film of all, *King Kong.*

As a work of fiction, *King Kong* is a fantasy version of Cooper and Schoedsack's ultimate documentary adventure—a journey to a faraway uncharted island in search of the "Eighth Wonder of the World." The film was the box-office surprise of 1933 and it is still popular today.

After *King Kong* Schoedsack directed little of note. He directed two more giant ape pictures, *Son of Kong* and *Mighty Joe Young.* An accident during World War II left Schoedsack partially blinded, but his documentary films alone earned Schoedsack an important place in the tradition of non-fiction filmmaking.

—Linda J. Obalil

SCHORM, Evald

Nationality: Czechoslovakian. **Born:** Prague, 15 December 1931. **Education:** FAMU Film Faculty, Prague, 1957-62. **Family:** Married Blanka Schormová, one son. **Career:** Construction worker, 1949-56; assistant director to Zdenek Podskalsky, 1961; began making documentaries at Short Film, Prague, from 1962; senior lecturer at FAMU Film Faculty, 1962-71; television director, from 1963; director for theatre and opera, from 1967. **Died:** In Prague, 14 December 1988.

Films as Director:

1959 *Kdo své nebe neunese* (*Too Much to Carry*) (short); *Blok 15* (*Block 15*) (+ co-sc)

1961 "Kostelník" [Sexton] shot in *Zurnál FAMU* (*The FAMU Newsreel*); *Jan Konstantin* (+ sc, ed); *Turista* (*The Tourist*) (+ co-sc)

Evald Schorm

1962 *Země zemi* (*Country to Country*) (+ sc); *Helsinky 62* (*Helsinki 62*) (+ sc); *Stromy a lidé* (*Trees and People*) (+ sc)
1963 *Komorní harmonie* (*Chamber Harmony*) (for television) (+ sc); *Zeleznič áři* (*Railwaymen*) (+ sc); *Zit svuj život* (*To Live One's Life*) (+ sc)
1964 *Proč?* (*Why?*) (+ sc); *Každý den odvahu* (*Every Day Courage*; *Courage for Every Day*); "Dum radosti" [House of Pleasure] episode of *Perličky na dně* (*Pearls in the Deep*)
1965 *Zrcadlení* (*Reflection*) (+ co-sc); *Odkaz* (*Heritage*) (+ sc); *Sukovo trio* (*Suk's Trio*) (for television) (+ sc)
1966 *Zalm* (*The Psalm*) (+ co-sc); *Návrat ztraceného syna* (*The Return of the Prodigal Son*) (+ co-sc); *Gramo von Balet* (for television) (+ co-sc); *Pět holek na krku* (*Five Girls to Cope With*)
1967 *Král a žena* (*The King and the Woman*) (for television)
1968 *Carmen nejen podle Bizeta* (*Carmen, Not According to Bizet*) (+ co-sc); "Chlebové střevičky" [Shoes Made of Bread] episode of *Pražské noci* (*Prague Nights*) (+ co-sc); *Faŕ ař uv konec* (*The Priest's End*) (+ co-sc)
1969 *Rozhovory* (*Dialogues*) (for television) (+ co-sc); *Den sedmý, osmá noc* (*Seventh Day, Eighth Night*) (+ co-sc)
1970 *Psi a lidé* (*Dogs and People*); *Koncert pro studenty* (*Concert for Students*) (for television); *Z mého života* (*From My Life*) (for television); *Lítost* (*Regret*) (for television); *Sestry* (*Sisters*) (for television) (+ sc)
1971 *Lepší pán* (*A Well-To-Do Gentleman*) (for television)
1972 *Úklady a láska* (*Intrigue and Love*) (for television)
1974 *Laska v barvách karnevalu* (*Love in Mardi Gras Colors*) (co-d, Magic Lantern program)
1976 *Etuda o zkoušce* (*An Essay on Rehearsing*) (+ sc)
1977 *Kouzelný cirkus* (*The Magic Circus*) (co-d, co-sc, Magic Lantern program)
1978 *Sněhová královna* (*The Snow Queen*) (Magic Lantern program)
1980 *Noční zkouška* (*The Night Rehearsal*)) (Magic Lantern program)
1988 *Vlastně se nic nestalo*

Other Films:

1961 *Spadla s měsíce* (*She Fell from the Moon*) (asst d)
1966 ***O slavnosti a hostech*** (*A Report on the Party and the Guests*) (Němec) (role as husband); *Hotel pro cizince* (*Hotel for Strangers*) (Máša) (role as chaplain)
1968 *Zert* (*The Joke*) (Jireš) (role as Kostka)
1969 *Bludiště moci* (*The Labyrinth of Power*) (for television) (Weigl) (role as form)
1974 *Bástyasétány 74* (*Bastion Promenade 74*) (Gazdag) (role as Master Rudolf)
1978 *Město mé naděje* (*The Town of My Hope*) (collaborator)
1980 *Útěky domu* (*Escapes Home*) (Jireš) (role as Jílek)
1987 *Krajina Shábytkem* (Smyczek) (role)

Publications

By SCHORM: articles—

Interview in *Film a Doba* (Prague), no. 2, 1966.
Interview with Claude Sembain, in *Image et Son* (Paris), no. 221, 1968.

On SCHORM: books—

Janoušek, Jiří, *3-1/2 po druhé,* Prague, 1969.
Liehm, Mira and Antonin, *The Most Important Art: East European Film after 1945,* Berkeley, 1977.
Bernard, Jan, *Evald Schorm,* Prague, 1979.
Habova, Milada, and Jitka Vysekalova, editors, *Czechoslovak Cinema,* Prague, 1982.
Hames, Peter, *The Czechoslovak New Wave,* Berkeley, 1985.

* * *

It was a noteworthy class that studied directing together at the Prague FAMU under the leadership of Otakar Vávra—Věra Chytilová, Jiří Menzel, Jan Schmidt, and Evald Schorm. Each of these individuals had a personal but emphatic influence on the development of Czech cinema. Evald Schorm finished his studies with the short film *Turista (The Tourist),* in which he attempts to depict the inner world of a worker who has failed both in his work and in his personal life. Upon receiving his certification, Schorm went off to Krátký film Praha and made, in rapid succession, *Helsinky 62,* a report on the Eighth World Youth Festival; *Země zemi (Country to Country),* which saw the beginning of years of collaboration with cameraman Jan Spáta and composer Ivan Klusák; *Zit svuj život (To Live One's Life),* an attempt at a portrait of the modern Czech photographer Josef Sudek; and the film *Proč? (Why?),* in which he tries to portray the conflict between the stated wishes of society and the facts of life, to expose the tension between appearance and substance. In the documentary inquiry *Zrcadlení (Reflection),* produced later in his career, Schorm shows his interest in man at the boundary between life and death, his view on questions of the meaning of life, values, the way one lives, and one's attitude toward death.

Schorm made his full-length debut in 1964 with *Každý den odvahu (Courage for Every Day).* In this film he captures the inner crisis of a man who had devoted a piece of his life to false ideals, a man at the turning point between youth and maturity, and his disillusionment. Then came *Návrat ztraceného syna (The Return of the Prodigal Son),* the drama of a neurotic trying to find himself, his lost inner values and confidence. His next film, *Pět holek na krku (Five Girls to Cope With),* portrays the hopes and anxieties of a young girl growing up without friendships, sympathy, or love during the period when a person's character is being molded. The film is an analysis of the mechanisms of envy, malice, and hostility and their effect on the human soul. The farce *Farářuv konec (The Priest's End),* which deals with a bogus priest, and the parable *Psi a lidé (Dogs and People)* mark the end of Schorm's work in fictional feature films.

In the 1970s Schorm collaborated in film only rarely. His major creative domain became opera and theater directing. His direction of works by Shakespeare, Dostoevsky, Brecht, and Hrabal confirmed his standing as one of the most important Czech theatrical directors of our time.

Schorm's film oeuvre has met with varying critical responses both in Czechoslovakia and abroad. His documents are a meditation on a theme provided by real life, essays that strive for a more profound, philosophical expression of reality. His works inquire into the meaning of man's world and life and examine man's relationship to society and to history. Schorm was a sensitive diagnostician of social life; his approach was characterized by emotional subtlety, integrity, and humility. He persistently and repeatedly pursued the meaning of things, and the essence and truth about man and his world. Perhaps it is this creative type that best embodies the words of the writer Karel Capek: " ... passionately and patiently you demand better vision and better hearing, clearer understanding and greater love. You create so you can recognize in your work the form and the perfection of things. Your service to things is a divine service."

—Vladimír Opěla

SCHRADER, Paul

Nationality: American. **Born:** Grand Rapids, Michigan, 22 July 1946. **Education:** Educated in Ministry of Christian Reformed religion at Calvin College, Grand Rapids, Michigan, graduated 1968; took summer classes in film at Columbia University, New York; University of California at Los Angeles Film School, M.A., 1970. **Family:** Married actress Mary Beth Hurt, 1983, one daughter, one son. **Career:** Moved to Los Angeles, 1968; writer for *Los Angeles Free Press,* then became editor of *Cinema* magazine; first script to be filmed, *The Yakuza,* 1974; directed first feature, *Blue Collar,* 1977. **Awards:** First Prize, Paris Festival, for *Blue Collar,* 1978. **Address:** Schrader Productions, 1501 Broadway, Suite 1405, New York, NY 10019, U.S.A. **Agent:** Jeff Berg, International Creative Management, 8899 Beverly Blvd., Los Angeles, CA 90048, U.S.A.

Films as Director and Scriptwriter:

1977 *Blue Collar*
1978 *Hardcore*
1979 *American Gigolo*
1981 *Cat People* (d only)
1985 *Mishima: A Life in Four Chapters*
1987 *Light of Day*
1988 *Patty Hearst* (d only)
1990 *The Comfort of Strangers* (d only)
1992 *Light Sleeper*
1994 *Witch Hunt* (d only)

Other Films:

1974 *The Yakuza* (Pollack) (co-sc)
1976 ***Taxi Driver*** (Scorsese) (sc); *Obsession* (De Palma) (co-sc)
1977 *Rolling Thunder* (Flynn) (sc); ***Close Encounters of the Third Kind*** (Spielberg) (co-sc, uncredited)
1978 *Old Boyfriends* (Tewkesbury) (co-sc, exec pr)
1980 ***Raging Bull*** (Scorsese) (co-sc)
1986 *The Mosquito Coast* (Weir) (sc)
1988 *The Last Temptation of Christ* (Scorsese) (sc)
1995 *City Hall* (Becker) (co-sc)

Publications

By SCHRADER: books—

Transcendental Style in Film: Ozu, Bresson, Dreyer, Berkeley, 1972.
Schrader on Schrader, edited by Kevin Jackson, London, 1989.
Cleopatra Club, New York, 1995.

By SCHRADER: articles—

Editor of *Cinema* (Beverly Hills), early 1970s.

"Robert Bresson, Possibly," in *Film Comment* (New York), September/October 1977.

Interview with Gary Crowdus and D. Georgakas, in *Cineaste* (New York), Winter 1977/78.

"Paul Schrader's Guilty Pleasures," in *Film Comment* (New York), January/February 1979.

Interview with M.P. Carducci, in *Millimeter* (New York), February 1979.

Interview with Mitch Tuchmann, in *Film Comment* (New York), March/April 1980.

"Truth with the Power of Fiction," interview with Tim Pulleine in *Sight and Sound* (London), Autumn 1984.

Interview with Michel Ciment, in *Positif* (Paris), June 1985.

"The Japanese Way of Death," interview with David Thomson in *Stills* (London), June/July 1985.

Interview with Allan Hunter, in *Films and Filming* (London), November 1985.

Interview with Karen Jaehne, in *Film Quarterly* (Berkeley), Spring 1986.

Interview with Glenn Rechler, in *Cineaste* (New York), vol. 17, no. 1, 1989.

Paul Schrader

"Dialogue on Film: Paul Schrader," in *American Film* (Los Angeles), July/August 1989.

Schrader, Paul, "Does the Letter Still Rate? Porn Has the X, Let's Use an A," in *New York Times,* 5 August 1990.

"To Hell with Paul Schrader," interview with L. De Coppet, in *Interview* (New York), March 1992.

"Awakenings," interview with Gavin Smith, in *Film Comment* (New York), March/April 1992.

On SCHRADER: articles—

Toubiana, Serge, and L. Bloch-Morhange, "Trajectoire de Paul Schrader," in *Cahiers du Cinéma* (Paris), November 1978.

Cuel, F., "Dossier: Hollywood 79: Paul Schrader," in *Cinématographe* (Paris), March 1979.

Wells, J., "*American Gigolo* and Other Matters," in *Film Comment* (New York), March/April 1980.

Sinyard, Neil, "Guilty Pleasures: The Films of Paul Schrader," in *Cinema Papers* (Melbourne), December 1982.

Eisen, K., "The Young Misogynists of American Cinema," in *Cineaste* (New York), vol 13, no. 1, 1983.

Gehr, Richard, "Citizen Paul," in *American Film* (Los Angeles), vol. 13, no. 10, 1988.

Fraser, Peter, "*American Gigolo* and Transcendental Style," in *Literature/Film Quarterly* (Salisbury, Maryland), vol. 16, no. 2, 1988.

Combs, Richard, "Patty Hearst and Paul Schrader: A Life and a Career in 14 Stations," in *Sight and Sound* (London), Summer 1989.

Kennedy, Harlan, "The Discomforts of Paul Schrader," in *Film Comment* (New York), July/August 1990.

Freedman, S.G., "A Fallen Calvinist Pursues His Vision of True Heroism," in *The New York Times,* 25 August 1991.

Lopate, P., "With Pen in Hand, They Direct Movies," in *New York Times,* 16 August 1992.

* * *

While it is doubtless fanciful and recherché to read Paul Schrader's movies as unmediated reflections of his own life and feelings, it is nonetheless true that the director/screenwriter's "religious fascination with the redeeming hero" echoes his extreme fascination with himself. The incredible urge that his characters have to confess (Schrader frequently resorts to voice-overs and interior monologues), exemplified by Travis Bickle's mutterings in *Taxi Driver,* Christ's musings on the cross during his *Last Temptation,* and Patty Hearst's thoughts about her abduction, suggest that his films are firmly rooted in self-analysis. The recent book *Schrader on Schrader,* and the filmmaker's enthusiasm for the bio-pic (*Mishima, Patty Hearst*), a genre that had been more or less moribund since the time of Paul Muni, testify that he does indeed share the Calvinist urge to account for everything, to make his art out of the introspective inventory of his, or somebody else's, life.

Appropriately, for a confirmed fan of the films of Bresson, the image of the condemned man/woman attempting to escape his/her fate is a leitmotif in Schrader's work. He seems obsessed with prison metaphors, with images of captivity. In *Patty Hearst,* Natasha Richardson is locked up in a cupboard. In *Cat People,* Nastassia Kinski ends up behind bars, in a zoo—a human captive in a panther's body. Richard Gere, in *American Gigolo,* is "framed" (he is "framed" for a murder he did not commit and "framed" as the object of the gaze—the camera seems to love him), and the last time we see him, he is reaching out for Lauren Hutton but is separated from her by the glass panel in the prison interview booth. Christ, predictably, ends up on the cross: he too is trapped. A last, sad image of *Raging Bull* is of Jake La Motta (Robert De Niro) banging his head against his cell wall. Schrader's work abounds in figures cabined, cribbed, and confined. Travis Bickle, that emissary from 1970s America, is a prisoner in the city, a prisoner in his own body, a prisoner behind the wheel of his taxi, a slave to pornography and junk food, and he is trying, in his mildly psychotic way, to free Jodie Foster's child prostitute, who is similarly trapped. Season Hubley in *Hardcore* is whisked away from a Calvinist Convention, kidnapped by a snuff movie producer, and needs an Ahab/John Wayne figure (George C. Scott) from the suburbs to rescue her, to try to reincarcerate her within the family. Even Schrader's Venice in *The Comfort of Strangers,* studio-built and full of interminable dark corridors, seems more like San Quentin than a beautiful European city on water.

An American of Dutch/German extraction, Schrader had a strict religious upbringing in Grand Rapids, Michigan. He did not watch as much TV as one might expect, and when it came to the cinema, he was cruelly deprived: incredibly, he saw his first film, *The Absent-Minded Professor,* when he was seventeen. Then came the revelation of *Wild in the Country,* a lurid Elvis Presley vehicle which gave him his vision on the Road to Damascus: he was captured by the celluloid muse. His Calvinist background combined with his early career as film historian/critic (he was a Pauline Kael protegé, a "Paulette" as he describes it, and it was Kael's influence which got him into the film course at UCLA) make him among the more academically inclined of mainstream Hollywood filmmakers. Few of his contemporaries have been fellows of the American Film Institute or have written ineffably unfathomable monographs on transcendental style in the movies of Ozu, Bresson, and Dreyer. He straddles two mutually exclusive cultures, traditions, discourses. On the one hand, he is the film scholar and expert in European and Japanese Cinema. On the other, he is the hack Hollywood director and screenwriter. It is a tension which he seems to enjoy. Is he the artist locked up in a commercial catacomb or is he the popular filmmaker, hampered by his own notions of art? Is he, perhaps, just plain religious freak and show-off? "The reason I put that Bressonian ending onto *American Gigolo* was a kind of outrageous perversity, saying I can make this fashion-conscious, hip Hollywood movie and at the end claim it's really pure; and in *Cat People* I can make this horror movie and say it was about Dante and Beatrice."

Sometimes Schrader seems too clever by half. Kael, attacking *Patty Hearst,* suggested he lacked a basic instinct for moviemaking: "he doesn't reach an audience's emotions." This is probably unfair. His own scripts have a relentless narrative drive, generally toward some kind of judgement day (witness his work with Scorsese). When he is directing another writer's scenario, he can lose that obsessive will to destruction, salvation, damnation. Both *Patty Hearst* and *The Comfort of Strangers*—though it must be taxing for any director to try to animate a Pinter script—lack the momentum, the frenetic desire to tell a story of the films which he wrote himself.

Apparently, he worked with Spielberg on early drafts of *Close Encounters,* but Spielberg elbowed him off the project because Schrader did not share his Capra-like love of the common man and wanted to make the protagonist a crusading religious fruitcake *à la* Travis Bickle. Whatever one's reservations about Schrader's evangelism or his tedious self-obsession, he is undoubtedly one of Hollywood's most formally arresting filmmakers. He pays enormous attention to set design. (He has worked frequently with Scarfiotti, Bertolucci's designer on *The Conformist.*) He seems equally at home with the lush, magical opulence of New Orleans in *Cat People*, the sober, almost drama-doc look of *Patty Hearst*, the glossy, superficial Los Angeles, all hotels, restaurants, and expensive apartments, of *American Gigolo*, or the stagy, elaborate sets on *Mishima.* Edgy, prowling tracks (the opening shot of *The Comfort of Strangers* is a virtuoso effort in camera peripeteia to rival the first few minutes of Welles' *Touch of Evil*), a predilection for high angle shots (humans as bugs), and his discerning use of music (he has worked with Philip Glass and Giorgio Moroder, among others) show him as a filmmaker with a consummate love of his craft.

Yet Schrader thrives on controversy. He was sacked from his job as film critic for the *Los Angeles Free Press* because he gave a debunking review to *Easy Rider. American Gigolo* was attacked as being homophobic. *Mishima* provoked an outcry in Japan. *The Last Temptation of Christ* brought the moral majority out to the picket line. Apparently a student radical in the 1960s, Schrader caricatures the Symbionese Liberation Army, Patty Hearst's abductors, as idiotic mouthers of revolutionary platitudes. His films seem to abound in right-wing visionaries (Travis Bickle, George C. Scott in *Hardcore,* Mishima, Christopher Walken in *The Comfort of Strangers*) and, while he does not straightforwardly endorse their viewpoints, he respects their right to be individuals and their struggle for redemption, a struggle which invariably leaves onlookers dead and dying in the crusading hero's wake. Social historians of American culture and politics in the 1970s and 1980s will find rich pickings in the Schrader *oeuvre.*

Schrader continued his cinematic explorations of characters attempting to purge themselves of their excesses and sins in *Light Sleeper,* a knowing, sobering film set amid the strata of the New York City drug culture. Symbolically, its scenario is set during a sanitation strike, allowing the streets to be strewn with garbage. Willem Dafoe plays John LeTour, a forty-year-old ex-junkie and "mid-level drug dealer" whose clientele consists of upscale New Yorkers willing to pay big bucks for top-quality product. Both LeTour and Ann (Susan Sarandon), his boss, are fascinating characters. Within the confines of her world, Ann is a celebrity, a legend: the Mayflower Madam of the drug trade. She dresses like a high-powered business executive, dines in fancy restaurants, and tools around town in a chauffeured limousine. She also is shifting from drug dealing to marketing cosmetics. LeTour, too, yearns to go straight: he is having trouble sleeping, and he fears he has run out of luck. However, his redemption will not come easily, a fact that quickly becomes apparent when he runs into Marianne (Dana Delany), his ex-girlfriend and also a former junkie.

On occasion in *Light Sleeper,* Schrader waxes nostalgic about the "good old days" of drug use, "before crack came," when cocaine was the drug of choice. Otherwise, he graphically depicts the ravages of drugs. His junkies are unromanticized and ultimately pathetic. Despite its top-of-the-line cast, *Light Sleeper* was too unsexy a film to earn the widespread hype enjoyed by many of Schrader's earlier films. For this reason, the name Paul Schrader no longer holds the pull and allure it did back in the days of *Taxi Driver* or *American Gigolo.*

—G.C. Macnab, updated by Rob Edelman

SCHROEDER, Barbet

Nationality: French. **Born:** Teheran, Iran, 26 August 1941. **Education:** Degree in philosophy from the Sorbonne, Paris. **Career:** Film critic, *Cahiers du Cinéma, L'air de Paris,* 1958-63; assistant to director Jean-Luc Godard for *The Soldiers,* 1968; owner and principal of Les Films du Losange, since 1963. **Awards:** Academy Award nomination, Best Director, and Golden Globe nominations, Best Director and Best Film, for *Reversal of Fortune,* 1990. **Agent:** Creative Artists Agency, 9830 Wilshire Blvd., Beverly Hills, CA 90212-1804, U.S.A. **Address:** 8033 Sunset Blvd., Suite 51, Hollywood, CA 90069, U.S.A.

Films as Director:

1969 *More* (+ co-sc)
1971 *Sing-Sing* (doc)
1972 *La vallée* (*The Valley Obscured by Clouds*) (+ co-sc)
1974 *General Idi Amin Dada* (doc)
1975 *Maitresse* (*Mistress*) (+ sc)
1978 *Koko: A Talking Gorilla* (doc)
1983 *Les tricheurs* (*Cheaters*) (+ co-sc)
1985 *The Charles Bukowski Tapes*
1987 *Barfly*
1990 *Reversal of Fortune*
1992 *Single White Female*
1995 *Kiss of Death*
1996 *Before and After*

Other Films:

1960 *The Soldiers* (role)
1962 *La boulangere de Monceau* (pr, role)
1963 *La carriere de Suzanne* (pr)
1964 *Mediterrannée* (pr)
1965 *Six in Paris: Chabrol, Douchet, Godard, Pollet, Rohmer, Rouch* (pr, role)
1966 *The Collector* (pr)
1967 *Tu imagines Robinson* (pr)
1968 *My Night at Maud's* (pr)
1971 *Claire's Knee* (pr)
1972 *Chloe in the Afternoon* (pr); *Out One* (co-pr)
1973 *The Mother and the Whore* (co-pr)
1974 ***Celine et Julie vont en bateau: Phantom Ladies Over Paris*** (*Celine and Julie Go Boating*) (pr, role)
1975 *Flocons d'or* (co-pr); *The Marquiese of O* (pr)
1977 *Le passe-montagne* (pr); *Chinese Roulette* (co-pr); *The American Friend* (co-pr)
1978 *Perceval* (pr); *The Rites of Death* (co-pr); *Roberte* (role)
1979 *Le navire night* (pr)
1981 *Le pont du nord* (pr)
1983 *Improper Conduct* (pr)
1990 *The Golden Boat* (role)
1994 *Beverly Hills Cop III* (role); *La reine Margot* (role)

Publications

By SCHROEDER: articles—

"Double Whammy," an interview with G. Fuller, in *Interview,* August 1992.
Interview with J. Temmerman, in *Skoop,* December 1992/January 1993.

On SCHROEDER: articles—

Angeli, M., "Single German Male," in *Movieline,* August 1992.
Brantley, B., "Barbet's Feast," in *Vanity Fair,* September 1992.
Schruers, F., "A Symphony of Mirrors," in *Premiere,* September 1992.
Krohn, B., "Barbet Schroeder," in *Cahiers du Cinéma,* December 1992.

* * *

Barbet Schroeder's film career began in the 1960s, after stints as a philosophy student (at the Sorbonne), journalist (for *Cahiers du Cinéma*), and promoter of jazz concerts. Acting roles in the early 1960s gave way to his ambition to direct, and after assisting Jean-Luc Godard with *Les carabiniers* in 1963, Schroeder started his own production company. Les Films du Losange proved to be a film company of some note; it provided support to the efforts of both Rivette and Rohmer, and later, Wenders and Fassbinder.

Barbet Schroeder with Faye Dunaway and Mickey Rourke on the set of *Barfly*

A number of Schroeder's early directorial efforts were documentaries, but his first feature was *More* (1969), a tale of a German grad student's crush on an American in Paris. He followed that with the documentary *Sing-Sing* and the feature *La vallée,* the latter starring Bulle Ogier as a diplomat's wife. In 1974 Schroeder released *General Idi Amin Dada,* a fascinating and disturbing documentary on the tyrannical dictator of Uganda. *Maîtresse,* a 1976 film starring Ogier as a professional dominatrix and Gerard Depardieu as her boyfriend, was a controversial film for its time—a nervy look at sexuality and power and their relationship to one another.

Schroeder continued to work throughout the late 1970s and early 1980s, but remained relatively unknown in the United States. A series of interviews with cult poet Charles Bukowski, however, led the two men to corroborate on *Barfly* (1987). Bukowski's semi-autobiographical screenplay traces the life of a literate drunk drowning himself in liquor. *Barfly* attracted some notice, but it was 1990's *Reversal of Fortune* that established Schroeder as a commercially successful director.

A critically acclaimed account of the Claus von Bulow murder case, *Reversal of Fortune* boasted a fine cast (led by Jeremy Irons's performance as a decidedly odd and eccentric von Bulow) and an appropriately murky narrative that painted an unfavorable picture of the lives of its subjects. Schroeder's next film was *Single White Female* (1992), a popular but ultimately unremarkable psychological thriller. *Kiss of Death* (1995) was Schroeder's attempt to update the 1947 film that starred Victor Mature and Richard Widmark. The results are mixed, but the noirish film does benefit from the casting of Nicholas Cage as Little Junior, a psychotic crook of dangerous unpredictability. Schroeder then turned to *Before and After* (1996), a tense drama featuring Meryl Streep and Liam Neeson as the parents of a boy accused of brutally murdering his girlfriend.

—Kevin Hillstrom

SCHROETER, Werner

Nationality: German. **Born:** Georgenthal, Thuringia, 7 April 1945. **Education:** Educated in Bielefeld and Heidelberg, and Naples; studied psychology at Mannheim; left Munich Television and Film Academy after a few weeks. **Career:** Worked as journalist, then began making 8mm films, 1967; director for TV, from 1970; release of first film to theatres, *The Kingdom of Naples,* 1978; also director for opera and theatre, and actor in several films. **Awards:** Golden Bear, Berlin Festival, for *Palermo or Wolfsburg,* 1980.

Films as Director:

1967 *Verona* (*Zwei Katzen*) (short)

1968 *Callas Walking Lucia* (short); *Callas Text mit Doppelbeleuchtung* (short); *Maria Callas Porträt* (short); *Mona Lisa* (short); *Maria Callas singt 1957 Rezitativ und Arie der Elvira aus Ernani 1844 von Giuseppe Verdi* (short); *La morte d'Isotta*; *Himmel Hoch* (short); *Paula—"je reviens"*; *Grotesk—Burlesk—Pittoresk* (co-d with Rosa von Praunheim); *Faces* (short); *Aggressionen* (short); *Neurasia*; *Argila*; *Virginia's Death* (short)
1969 *Eika Katappa*; *Nicaragua*
1970 *Der Bomber-pilot* (for TV); *Anglia*
1971 *Salome* (for TV); *Macbeth* (for TV); *Funkausstellung 1971—Hitparade* (for TV)
1972 *Der Tod der Maria Malibran* (*The Death of Maria Malibran*) (for TV)
1973 *Willow Springs* (for TV)
1974 *Der Schwarze Engel* (*The Black Angel*) (for TV)
1975 *Johannas Traum* (short)
1976 *Flocons d'or* (*Goldflocken*; *Goldflakes*)
1978 *Regno di Napoli* (*Neapolitanische Geschwister*; *Kingdom of Naples*)
1980 *Palermo oder Wolfsburg* (*Palermo or Wolfsburg*); *Weisse Reisse* (*White Journey*); *Die Generalprobe* (*La Répétition générale*; *The Dress Rehearsal*)
1982 *Der Tag der Idioten* (*Day of Idiots*); *Das Liebeskonzil* (*Lovers' Council*)
1983 *Der lachende Stern* (*The Smiling Star*)
1985 *De l'Argentine* (*About Argentina*); *Der Rosenkönig* (*Rose King*); *A la recherche du soleil* (for TV)
1991 *Malina*

Publications

By SCHROETER: book—

Liebeskonzil. Filmbuch, with Oskjar Panizza and Antonio Salines, Munich, 1982.

By SCHROETER: articles—

Interview with Gérard Courant and Jean-Claude Moireau, in *Cahiers du Cinéma* (Paris), January 1980.
Interview with Alain Carbonnier and Noël Simsolo, in *Cinéma* (Paris), March 1984.
Interview with A. Wilink, in *EPD Film,* January 1991.
Interview, in *Kino; Film der Bundesrepublik Deutschland,* no. 2, 1991.

On SCHROETER: books—

Schmid, Eva, and Frank Scurla, editors, *Werner Schroeter. Filme 1968-70,* Bochum, 1971.
Jansen, Peter W., and Wolfram Schütte, editors, *Werner Schroeter,* Munich, 1980.
Courant, Gérard, editor, *Werner Schroeter,* Paris, 1982.
Elsaesser, Thomas, *New German Cinema: A History,* London, 1989.

On SCHROETER: articles—

Wenders, Wim, "Filme von Werner Schroeter," in *Filmkritik* (Munich), May 1969; reprinted in *Emotion Pictures: Reflections on the Cinema,* London, 1990.
Grafe, Frieda, "Schauplatz für Sprache: Neurasia," in *Filmkritik* (Munich), no. 3, 1970.
Greenberg, Alan, "Notes on Some European Directors," in *American Film* (Washington, D.C.), vol. 3, no. 1, 1977.
Corrigan, Timothy, "Werner Schroeter's Operatic Cinema," in *Discourse* (Berkeley), Spring 1981.
Indiana, Gary, "Scattered Pictures: The Movies of Werner Schroeter," in *Art Forum* (New York), March 1982.
Kuhlbrodt, Dietrich, "Werner Schroeter," in *CineGraph. Lexikon zum deutschsprachigen Film,* edited by Hans-Michael Bock, Munich, 1984.
Bassan, R., and M. Martin, "Werner Schroeter," in *Revue du Cinéma* (Paris), February 1984.
Corrigan, Timothy, "On the Edge of History: The Radiant Spectacle of Werner Schroeter," in *Film Quarterly* (Berkeley), Summer 1984.
Kunze, Barbara, "Focusing on the Abstract," in *World Press Review,* April 1991.
Danton, A., "Le desert et les roses," in *Cahiers du Cinéma* (Paris), September 1991.
Bernink, M., "De ruimte van het operateske," in *Skrien,* February/March 1992.

* * *

Werner Schroeter's hyper-melodramatic films tend to provoke either intense admiration or outraged hostility. He is one of the most controversial filmmakers associated with the New German Cinema. His emotionally charged, performance-inspired cinema draws on and radically reinterprets nineteenth-century Italian *bel canto* opera and the music of German Romanticism. Schroeter's central figure is always the outsider—the homosexual, the mad person, the foreigner—and his major theme is the yearning for self-realization through passionate love and artistic creativity.

Schroeter's concept of cinema relies on intense stylization, deploying manneristic prolonged gestures. The characters are framed in sumptuous tableaux compositions, and the visuals are underscored by a highly manipulated soundtrack. Images, music, and sound are non-synchronized in Schroeter's early films: the performers mime exaggeratedly to the lyrics or spoken words on the soundtrack. The songs, arias, and literary citations (mostly from Lautréamont) give rise to stories which repeat distilled moments of desire, loss, and death.

Schroeter is not interested in reproducing an illusion of reality with psychologically motivated actions; instead, he seeks to create visions for a psychic reality. He wants to break with conventional viewing habits, hence his predilection for fragmentation, non-synchronization, extended duration, and deliberately over-the-top acting. At its best, this approach to cinema simultaneously involves the spectator through the music, whilst distancing through anti-naturalist conventions (which should not be confused with Brechtian distanciation techniques). Schroeter's cinema of excess and artifice occupies a transitional space between the avant-garde and art cinema, neither quite abstract nor quite narrative.

Music, which is central in all of Schroeter's films, is more important for its content than the mood it conveys: the music comments, but also contradicts at times. Juxtaposing classical with popular music is a major characteristic of Schroeter's cinema. For example, he puts Maria Callas, the opera diva, side by side with Caterina Valente, the German popular singer. This blurs the hierarchical distinction between "high" and "low" culture, between art and kitsch. Yet Schroeter has been accused of elitism—of making films for "culture vultures"—since his complex system of citing from pop, opera, and literature sources demands a high degree of cultural literacy from the spectator. Moreover, with Schroeter one can never be quite certain whether he parodies or celebrates.

Over the years, and thanks to major retrospectives in London, Paris, and New York, Schroeter has gained an international cult following. Though his cinema is marginal in terms of general audience appeal, Schroeter has been a seminal presence in the New German Cinema of the 1970s. Fassbinder, Herzog, and Wenders have acknowledged him as a decisive influence on their work. His impact on Syberberg is so apparent that Fassbinder has even leveled charges of plagiarism.

Eika Katappa, a radical appropriation of famous nineteenth-century opera scenes, won the Josef von Sternberg prize (as "the most idiosyncratic film") in 1969 at the Mannheim Film Festival and provided Schroeter with a major breakthrough. As a consequence he entered the world of television, and during the 1970s his films were produced almost exclusively by a small experimental television department. It is rather ironic that Schroeter's "total cinema" (owing more to the spectacle than to the narrative arts) found a home in television.

Der Tod der Maria Malibran, sublime and bizarre, is considered by many (including Michel Foucault and Schroeter himself) to be one of his best films, but it is also the most difficult. The historical figure of the singer Maria Malibran provides merely a starting point for a dense network of references and allusions encompassing Goethe, Lautréamont, Elvis Presley, and Janis Joplin. With *Regno di Napoli* Schroeter shifted towards art cinema, and it became his first commercial release. It was received with an unusual consensus of critical acclaim. Many who had regarded Schroeter as a filmmaker of fantastic fables were surprised subsequently at his politically hard-hitting documentaries. *The Laughing Star* is an extraordinary collage documentary on Marcos's corrupt regime, while *Zum Beispiel Argentinien* denounces Galtieri's dictatorship.

Schroeter's gay sensibility is expressed as an aesthetic approach that could be described as "high camp." His conception has frequently been compared to and contrasted with (not always favourably) Rosa von Praunheim's much more militant stance. Schroeter insists on the romantic version of homosexuality. In most of his films we get the gay historical subtext, rather than thematic treatment. *Der Rosenkönig,* an excessive and entrancing hallucinatory fable of oedipal and homosexual passion, is his most explicit gay film. It also marked the beginning of a six-year gap in fiction filmmaking for the director. Only in 1990 did he begin shooting his new film, *Malina.*

During the 1980s Schroeter became much more widely known as a theatre and opera director, staging a range of productions in Germany and in other countries. Some of these works are highly acclaimed, but all are controversial; indeed, his theatre and opera efforts proved even more controversial than his films.

—Ulrike Sieglohr

SCHUMACHER, Joel

Nationality: American. **Born:** New York, NY, 29 August 1939. **Education:** Attended the Fashion Institute of Technology; graduated with honors from the Parsons School of Design. **Career:** Worked as design-display artist at Henri Bendel department store while attending the Parsons School of Design, early 1960s; became a fashion designer and opened his own boutique, Paraphernalia, 1960s; worked on television commercials and designed packaging and clothing for the Revlon Group, 1960s; moved to Los Angeles and entered movies as a costume designer, 1972; designed costumes for *The Time of the Cuckoo,* presented at the Ahmanson Theatre in Los Angeles, 1974; made directorial debut with made-for-television movie *The Virginia Hill Story,* 1974; made theatrical film debut with *The Incredible Shrinking Woman,* 1981; executive produced television pilot, *Now We're Cookin',* 1983; directed first stage production, *Speed-the-Plow,* in Chicago, 1989; directed music video *The Devil Inside* for rock group INXS; co-executive produced and directed pilot episode of the television series *2000 Malibu Road,* 1992. **Agent:** CAA, 9830 Wilshire Blvd., Beverly Hills, CA 90212, U.S.A.

Films as Director:

1974 *The Virginia Hill Story* (for TV) (+ sc)
1979 *Amateur Night at the Dixie Bar and Grill* (for TV) (+ sc)
1981 *The Incredible Shrinking Woman*
1983 *D.C. Cab* (+ sc)
1985 *St. Elmo's Fire* (+ co-sc)
1987 *The Lost Boys*
1989 *Cousins*
1990 *Flatliners*
1991 *Dying Young*
1993 *Falling Down*
1994 *The Client*
1995 *Batman Forever*

Other Films:

1972 *Play It As It Lays* (Perry) (costumes); *The Last of Sheila* (Ross) (costumes)
1973 *Sleeper* (Allen) (costumes); *Blume in Love* (Mazursky) (costumes)
1974 *Killer Bees* (Harrington) (for TV) (production designer)
1975 *The Prisoner of Second Avenue* (Frank) (costumes)
1976 *Sparkle* (O'Steen) (sc); *Car Wash* (Schultz) (sc)
1978 *Interiors* (Allen) (costumes); *The Wiz* (Lumet) (sc)
1986 *Slow Burn* (Chapman) (for TV) (co-exec pr)
1987 *Foxfire* (Taylor) (for TV) (co-exec pr)

Publications

By SCHUMACHER: articles—

Interview in *Interview* (New York), September 1977.
Interview with Janet Maslin in *New York Times,* 21 June 1985.
"Joel Schumacher," an interview with A. Michaels in *Cinefantastique* (Oak Park, Illinois), January 1990.
"Schumacher's Cat-Related Theory," an interview with Susan Morgan in *Interview* (New York), July 1990.
"A Director, His Life Redeemed, Savors the Summit of Success," an interview with Bernard Weinraub in *New York Times,* 3 March 1993.
"Visual Flair, a Hip Sensibility, and a Past," an interview with Bernard Weinraub in *New York Times,* 11 June 1995.

On SCHUMACHER: articles—

Talley, Andrea Leon, article in *Women's Wear Daily* (New York), 17-24 October 1975.
Silverman, Stephen, article in *New York Post,* 4 August 1987.
Farrow, Moira, "Making *Cousins:* An Excursion," in *New York Times,* 5 February 1989.
Lew, Julie, article in *New York Times,* 16 June 1991.
Brennan, Susan, article in *Newsday* (Melville, New York), 23 February 1993.

* * *

Joel Schumacher's background as a fashion designer, display artist, and package designer prepared him for his entry into the film industry as a costume designer. Similarly, he was primed for his career as a feature film director by his work as scriptwriter on several features, and especially as scriptwriter-director of two impressive made-for-television movies: *The Virginia Hill Story* (a variation on Warren Beatty's *Bugsy,* as a based-on-fact chronicle of mobster Bugsy Siegel's

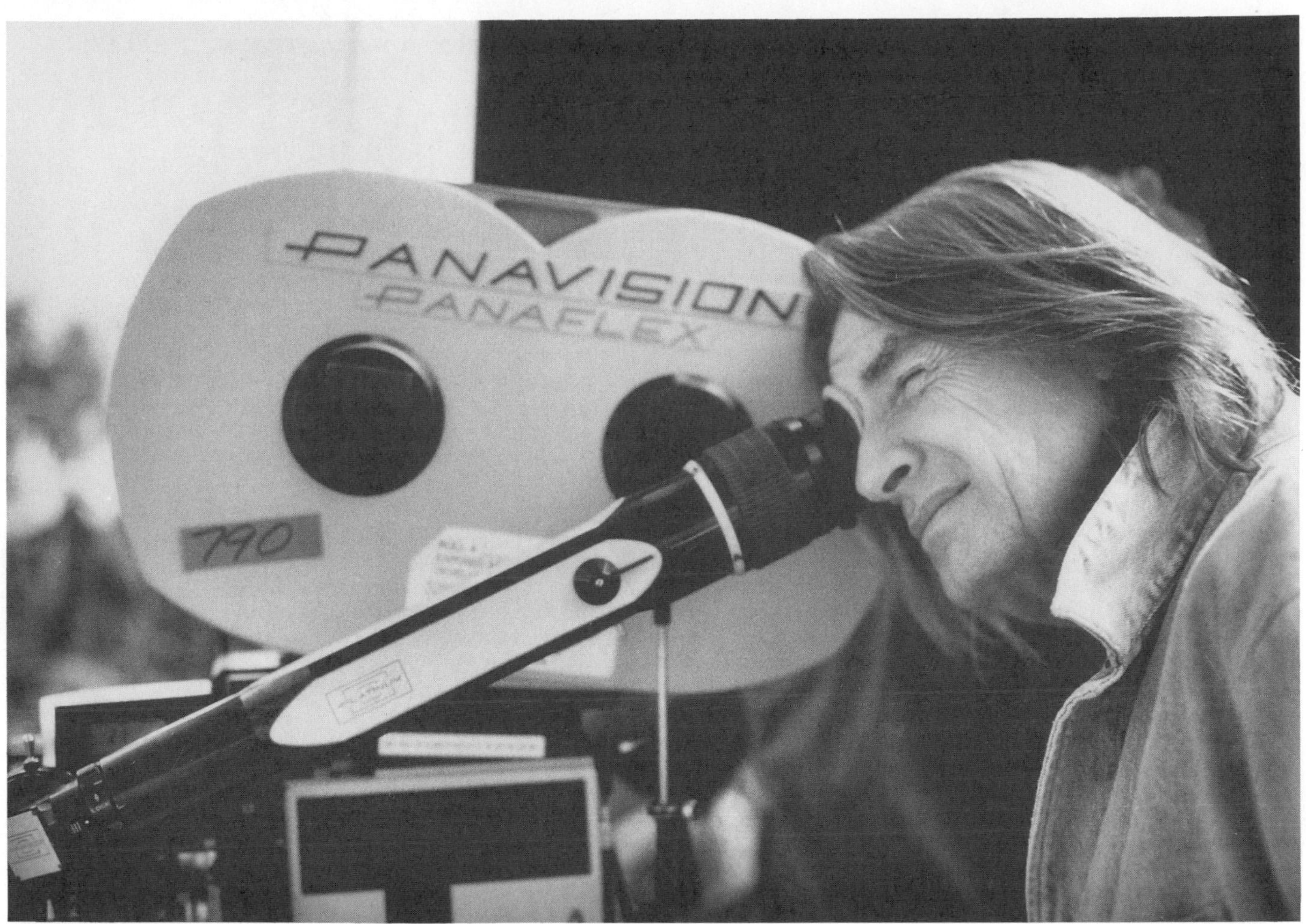

Joel Schumacher on the set of *Falling Down*

moll), and *Amateur Night at the Dixie Bar and Grill* (a well-done comedy-drama spotlighting various characters involved in a talent show at a Southern roadhouse).

All of Schumacher's films have been generic Hollywood product, filled with all the gloss their budgets could buy. His debut feature is *The Incredible Shrinking Woman,* a distaff reworking of the 1950s science-fiction cult classic *The Incredible Shrinking Man.* Lily Tomlin plays a housewife whose continuous exposure to chemical products results in her beginning to shrink. The film starts out as a wickedly clever spoof of the plight of the American housewife; as Tomlin becomes smaller, she symbolically takes up residence in a dollhouse. But the film soon degenerates into a frantic and silly farce. While *The Incredible Shrinking Man* is a classic of its kind, *The Incredible Shrinking Woman* became yet another forgettable Hollywood comedy.

Among Schumacher's better works are *Dying Young,* a deeply moving chronicle of a fatally ill cancer patient and the woman who befriends him; *Cousins,* an amiable Americanization of Jean-Charles Tachella's smash-hit French romantic comedy *Cousin-Cousine; Flatliners,* a fast-paced drama about medical students who make themselves temporarily legally dead so that they may experience afterlife episodes; *The Client,* a slick but solid adaptation of the John Grisham best-seller about a lawyer who represents an eleven-year-old boy who has come to know more than he ought to about Mafia dealings; and the entertaining (if special effects-laden) *Batman Forever,* in which the famed superhero goes up against the Riddler and Two-Face.

The second wrung of Schumacher's credits includes *D.C. Cab,* a so-so comedy about a taxi company operated by oddballs; *The Lost Boys,* about a gang of adolescent vampires; and *St. Elmo's Fire,* a brat-pack soap opera. Perhaps his most unique work is *Falling Down,* an allegory in which Michael Douglas stars as a stressed-out Modern Man who goes haywire while stuck in traffic on a Los Angeles freeway and begins a violence-laden odyssey across the city. Like *The Incredible Shrinking Woman,* the film is an attempt to make a statement about the perils of contemporary American society. And also like its predecessor, the result is only intermittently successful.

As the years have gone by, Schumacher's proficiency has allowed him to be assigned more prestigious, higher-budgeted projects. In his better work, he has been able to combine surface gloss with strong dramatic elements.

—Audrey E. Kupferberg

SCOLA, Ettore

Nationality: Italian. **Born:** Trevico, Avellino, 10 May 1931. **Education:** Studied law, University of Rome. **Career:** Scriptwriter on films with Ruggero Maccari, from 1953; directed first film, *Se permette parliamo di donne,* 1964. **Awards:** César Award, for *C'eravamo tanto amati,* 1975; Best Director, Cannes Festival, for *Brutti, sporchi*

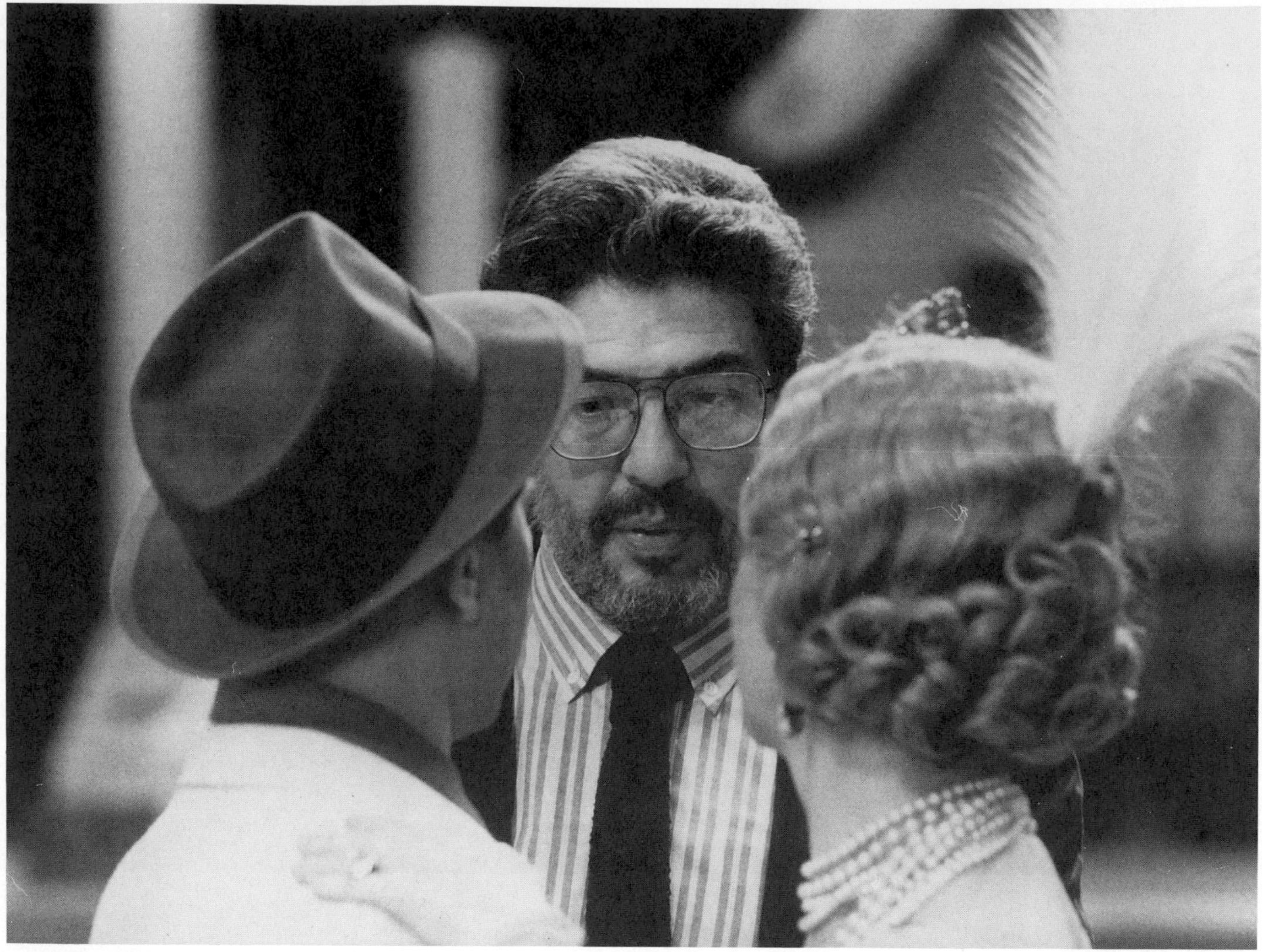

Ettore Scola on the set of *Le Bal*

e cattivi, 1976; Special Jury Prize, Cannes Festival, for *Una giornata particolari,* 1977; Best Screenplay, Cannes Festival, for *La terrazza,* 1980; Grand Jury Prize for Body of Work, Cannes Festival, 1981.

Films as Director:

1964 *Se permette parliamo di donne* (*Let's Talk About Women*) (+ co-sc); *La congiuntura* (+ co-sc)
1965 "Il vittimista" episode of *Thrilling* (+ co-sc)
1966 *L'arcidiavolo* (*Il diavolo innamorato*; *The Devil in Love*) (+ co-sc)
1968 *Il commissario Pepe* (+ co-sc); *Riusciranno i nostri eroi a trovare il loro amico misteriosamente scomparso in Africa?* (+ co-sc)
1970 *Dramma della gelosia—Tutti i particolari in cronaca* (*The Pizza Triangle: A Drama of Jealousy, and Other Things*) (+ co-sc)
1971 *Permette? Rocco Papaleo* (*Rocco Papaleo*) (+ co-sc)
1972 *La piú bella serata della mia vita* (+ co-sc)
1973 *Trevico-Torino ... Viaggio nel Fiat Nam* (+ co-sc)
1974 *C'eravamo tanto amati* (*We All Loved Each Other So Much*) (+ co-sc)
1976 *Brutti, sporchi e cattivi* (*Down and Dirty*) (+ co-sc); one episode of *Signori e signore, buonanotte* (+ co-sc)
1977 *Una giornata particolare* (*A Special Day*) (+ co-sc); one episode of *I nuovi mostri* (*The New Monsters*; *Viva Italia!*) (+ co-sc)
1979 *Che si dice a Roma* (+ co-sc)
1980 *La terrazza* (+ co-sc)
1981 *Passione d'amore* (+ co-sc)
1982 *Il mondo nuovo* (+ co-sc); *La Nuit de Varennes* (+ co-sc)
1984 *Le Bal* (+ co-sc)
1985 *Maccheroni* (*Macaroni*)
1987 *Famiglia* (*The Family*)
1989 *Splendor* (*The Last Movie*)
1990 *Che ora e*
1991 *Viaggio di Capitan Fracassa*
1993 *Mario, Maria e Mario*
1995 *Romanzo di un Giovane Povero* (*Diary of a Poor Young Man*) (+ sc)

Other Films:

1954 *Un americano a Roma* (Steno) (co-sc with Ruggero Maccari); *Due notti con Cleopatra* (*Two Nights with Cleopatra*) (co-sc with Maccari); *Una Parigina a Roma* (co-sc with Maccari)
1956 *Lo scapolo* (Pietrangeli) (co-sc with Maccari)
1958 *Nata di marzo* (co-sc with Maccari)

1960 *Il mattatore* (*Love and Larceny*) (co-sc with Maccari); *Adua e le compagne* (*Love à la Carte*) (co-sc with Maccari); *Fantasmi a Roma* (*Ghosts of Rome*) (co-sc with Maccari); "La storia di un soldato" ("The Soldier") episode of *L'amore difficile* (*Erotica*; *Of Wayward Love*) (Manfredi) (co-sc with Maccari)
1962 *Anni ruggenti* (*Roaring Years*) (Zampa) (co-sc with Maccari); *Il sorpasso* (*The Easy Life*) (Risi) (co-sc with Maccari)
1963 *I mostri* (*The Monsters*; *Opiate '67*; *Fifteen from Rome*) (Risi) (co-sc with Maccari); *La visita* (co-sc with Maccari)
1964 *Il gaucho* (*The Gaucho*) (Risi) (co-sc); *Alta infedeltà* (*High Infidelity*) (co-sc); *Il magnifico cornuto* (*The Magnificent Cuckold*) (co-sc)
1965 *Io la conoscevo bene* (Pietrangeli) (co-sc); *Made in Italy* (Loy) (co-sc)
1966 *Follie d'estate* (co-sc)
1967 *Le dolci signore* (*Anyone Can Play*) (Zampa) (co-sc); *Il Profeta* (sc)
1971 *Noi donne siamo fatte cosi* (*Women: So We Are Made*) (Risi) (co-sc)
1988 *Vacanza* (Guillot) (pr); *Mitico Gianluca* (Lazotti) (pr); *O samba* (Constantin) (pr)

Publications

By SCOLA: articles—

"Se permettete parliamo di Scola," with J. A. Gili, in *Ecran* (Paris), November 1976.
Interview with Aldo Tassone, in *Image et Son* (Paris), November 1977.
Interview with Dan Yakir, in *Film Comment* (New York), March/April 1983.
Interview with Mario Monicelli, in *Chaplin* (Stockholm), 1983.
Interview with A. Cornand and others, in *Revue du Cinéma* (Paris), February 1984.
"Monsieur le President ovvero un modo meno nevrotico di stare a Cannes," in *Bianco e Nero* (Rome), July/September 1988.
"Visuelle Stenogramme," in *Film und Fernsehen* (Potsdam, Germany), January 1989.
Interview with H. M. Fendel, in *EPD Film* (Frankfurt), August 1990.
"A Place for the Soul," in *Chaplin* (Stockholm), 1992.

On SCOLA: books—

Gili, Jean, *Le Cinema Italien,* Paris, 1978.
Tassone, Aldo, *Parla il Cinema Italiano: Volume 1,* Milan, 1979.
Bondanella, Peter, *Italian Neorealism to the Present,* New York, 1983.
Liehm, Mira, *Passion and Defiance: Film in Italy from 1942 to the Present,* Los Angeles and London, 1984.
De Santi, Pier Marco, and Rossano Vittori, *I film di Ettore Scola,* Rome, 1987.
Ellero, Roberto, *Ettore Scola,* Florence, 1988.

On SCOLA: articles—

Gili, J., article in *Ecran* (Paris), April and November 1976.
Haustrate, G., "Un haut lieu de partage," in *Cinema* (Paris), August/September 1976.
Carcassone, P., article in *Cinematographe* (Paris), October 1977.
Micheli, S., "Ein besonderer Tag," in *Film und Fernsehen* (Potsdam, Germany), April 1978.
Ieperen, A. V., "Comedie makt realitet verdraaglijk," in *Skoop* (Netherlands), May 1978.
Andersson, W., "Brutti, sporchi, cattivi & una giornata particolare," in *Filmrutan* (Sweden), 1978.
Gili, J., and others, "Une Journee Particuliere," in *Avant-Scene* (Paris), 15 June 1979.
Zaoral, Z., article in *Film a Doba* (Czechoslovakia), October 1985.
Blum, Doris, "Scola's World," in *World Press Review* (excerpted from *Die Welt*) (Bonn), January 1986.
Bassan, R., and R. Lefevre, "*Macaroni:* Wilder's Touch," in *Revue du Cinema* (Paris), February 1986.
"*Macaroni* Issue" of *Avant-Scène du Cinéma* (Paris), April 1986.
De Santi, P. M., "Scola e Scarpelli dal disegno al film," in *Bianco e Nero* (Rome), July/September 1986.
Quenin, F. Navailh, "Le Choix d'Ettore: determinant," in *Cinema* (Paris), 4 May 1988.
Bjorkman, S., "Nostalgi och satir," in *Chaplin* (Stockholm), 1989.
Anttila, E., "Scola: Suuren perinteen haltja," in *Filmihullu* (Helsinki), June 1990.
Douin, J. L., "Pain, Amour, et Dialectique," in *Telerama* (Paris), 17 February 1993.

* * *

Revered more in the international film community than in American cineaste circles, chameleon director Ettore Scola's name is inexcusably absent from several English-language reference works. With Scola, one has to dig deep for the auteurist consistencies that make less elusive artists easier to pigeonhole. While Scola's fascination with political attitude and social change dictated by purely personal psychology never varies, he skips the light fantastic through such specialties as historical epic (*La Nuit de Varennes*), the musical (*Le Bal*), screwball comedy (*A Drama of Jealousy*), domestic drama (*The Family*), and grand romance (*Passione d'Amore*). In each case, the director gives established genres a uniquely invigorating spin. Critic Stephen Harvey compares Scola to Joseph Mankiewicz, and that pithy summation of Scola as a Mankiewicz seasoned with oregano sheds light on how Scola's comic screenwriting background (over fifty screenplays) informs his later career as a filmic maestro.

Before directing his first feature in 1964, Scola was a writer and illustrator for satirical magazines, a scriptor for radio, and a screenwriter for movies, mainly comedies, directed by Nanni Loy, Antonio Pietrangeli, and Dino Risi, among others. Often constructed as star vehicles, his scripts contributed to the fame of such Italian mainstays as Vittorio Gassman, Ugo Tognazzi, and Alberto Sordi. From this particular brand of Italian comedy—bungling incompetents muddling through desperate situations, war's grotesqueries, life's ironies—Scola's work has progressed to complex studies of his countrymen dealing with their history and social environment.

Although Scola's directorial debut, *Let's Talk About Women,* echoed his film-star showcase scripts, the bold *A Drama of Jealousy (The Pizza Triangle)* established him as a quirky chronicler of *amore* as a no-win situation; the film is a sort of "Waiting for Cupid" where every day is a luckless Valentine's Day. *C'eravamo tanto amati,* a tribute to Vittorio De Sica, is not only about the difficult, frustrating post-World War II years of three men whose class differences overwhelm the close bond they formed while fighting for the Resistance. It is also a complex survey of thirty years of Italian cinema and its relationship to Italian history, photographed in various appropriate cinematic styles. *La Terazza* also dissects the Italy-Cinema symbiosis as it scrutinizes the mores of Italian intellectuals, now middle-aged and no longer creative, forever failing to measure up to their heroic past.

In even his earliest directorial efforts, details of costume and milieu are integrated into Scola's cinema of ideas compellingly, because inveterate sketch artist Scola is graced with a visual sensibility that will reach its apotheosis in *La Nuit de Varennes* and *Passione d'Amore.* In *Riusciranno,* set in modern Angola, an Italian bourgeois explores twentieth-century Africa in a nineteenth-century concept of a safari outfit, while *Brutti, sporchi e cattivi* (literally "dirty, nasty and bad") satirizes the unavoidably disgusting appearance of the inhabitants of an impoverished village in a movie Scola had intended to introduce with comments by Pasolini.

What is most striking about Scola's oeuvre, however, is his gift for compression. Restricting his observations deliberately to confined areas (for example, the coaches in *La Nuit de Varennes,* the microcosmic dance hall in *Le Bal,* the family domicile that survives decades of unrest in *The Family*), Scola forces his encaged protagonists to reveal the inner turmoil that informs their societal stances. Nowhere is this economy more apparent than in *Una giornata particolare,* which demonstrates oppression in a super-organized society that devalues individuality. Moving deeper and deeper inside the confined setting, a fluid camera concentrates on the facade and interior of a workers' dwelling on 6 May 1938, when Mussolini welcomes Hitler to Rome. As the radio blares Il Duce's doctrinaire self-confidence, two trapped members of this society—a domestically repressed housewife and an anti-fascist homosexual—meet by chance and share their humanity for a few hours. Whereas in *The Family,* the family unit struggles to withstand the winds of war and upheaval, in the stylish *Le Bal,* the decades-shifting dancers merely reflect the changes transpiring outside their social cocoon. Telescoping the French Revolution inside a few coaches, without portraying starving hordes or the king trying to escape the rabble's wrath, Scola's *La Nuit de Varennes* forces the opportunity for rumination upon an upper class facing a climate hostile to them. In a masterfully compact fashion, Scola continues to examine the past in order to interpret the present. Particularly in *The Family,* Scola avoids the epic sweep of traditional political cavalcades in favor of an intimate revisionism of history.

In all Scola's films, the choreography of history steps in partnership with his simpatico actors, gliding camerawork, and updated neorealistic melancholy. Even taking his overcooked Hollywood debut, *Macaroni,* into consideration, and the failure of his last films to secure American releases, Scola's place in humanist film history is unassailable. Unlike many screenwriters who turn director to ensure an unedited venue for their glorious dialogue, when Scola has something to say he lets his *mise-en-scene* do the talking. His manner of working liberates film stars from their confining personas and challenges moviegoers to experience the ambiguous passions of his characters. As in that embryonic *Fatal Attraction* for the nineteenth century, *Passione d'Amore* (newly minted as a Sondheim musical, *Passion*), Scola's relentless pursuit of beauty is an all-consuming mission, one that makes this filmmaker sympathetic with misfits like Fosca, whose emotional deprivation in *Passione d'Amore* is not categorized as a negative, but as an occasion for greater sensitivity. Scola revisits the impersonal past to give it a human face.

—Lillian Schiff, updated by Robert J. Pardi

SCORSESE, Martin

Nationality: American. **Born:** Flushing, New York, 17 November 1942. **Education:** Cardinal Hayes High School, Bronx, 1956-60; New York University, B.A., 1964, M.A., 1966. **Family:** Married 1) Laraine Brennan, 1965 (divorced), one daughter; 2) Julia Cameron (divorced), one daughter; 3) Isabella Rossellini, 1979 (divorced 1983); 4) Barbara DeFina, 1985. **Career:** Film Instructor, NYU, 1968-70; directed TV commercials in England, and first feature, *Who's That Knocking at My Door?,* 1968; directed *Boxcar Bertha* for producer Roger Corman, 1972; directed *The Act* on Broadway, 1977; director for TV of "Mirror, Mirror" for *Amazing Stories,* 1985; directed promo video for Michael Jackson's "Bad," 1987. **Awards:** Best Director, National Society of Film Critics, and Palme d'Or, Cannes Festival, for *Taxi Driver,* 1976; Best Director, National Society of Film Critics, for *Raging Bull,* 1980; Best Director, Cannes Festival, for *The Color of Money,* 1986; Best Director, National Society of Film Critics, for *Goodfellas,* 1990.

Films as Director:

1963 *What's a Nice Girl Like You Doing in a Place Like This?* (short) (+ sc)
1964 *It's Not Just You, Murray* (short) (+ co-sc)
1967 *The Big Shave* (short) (+ sc)
1968 *Who's That Knocking at My Door?* (+ sc, role as gangster)
1970 *Street Scenes* (doc)
1972 *Boxcar Bertha* (+ role as client of bordello)
1973 *Mean Streets* (+ co-sc, role as Shorty the Hit Man)
1974 *Italian-American* (doc) (+ co-sc)
1975 *Alice Doesn't Live Here Anymore* (+ role as customer at Mel and Ruby's)
1976 ***Taxi Driver*** (+ role as passenger)
1977 *New York, New York*
1978 *The Last Waltz* (doc)
1979 *American Boy* (doc) (+ sc)
1980 ***Raging Bull***
1983 ***The King of Comedy*** (+ role as assistant)
1985 *After Hours* (+ role as disco patron)
1986 *The Color of Money*
1988 *The Last Temptation of Christ*
1989 "Life Lessons" episode in *New York Stories*
1990 ***GoodFellas*** (+ sc); *Man in Milan* (doc)
1991 *Cape Fear*
1993 ***Age of Innocence*** (+ sc, role)
1995 *Casino* (+ sc)

Other Films:

1965 *Bring on the Dancing Girls* (sc)
1967 *I Call First* (sc)
1970 *Woodstock* (ed, asst d)
1976 *Cannonball* (Bartel) (role)
1979 *Hollywood's Wild Angel* (Blackwood) (role); *Medicine Ball Caravan* (assoc pr, post prod spvr)
1981 *Triple Play* (role)
1982 *Bonjour Mr. Lewis* (Benayoun) (role)
1990 *Dreams* (Kurosawa) (role); ***The Grifters*** (Frears) (pr); *Fear No Evil* (Winkler) (role); *The Crew* (Antonioni) (exec pr); *Mad Dog and Glory* (McNaughton) (exec pr)
1991 *Guilty by Suspicion* (role as Joe Lesser)
1993 *Jonas in the Desert* (role)
1994 *Quiz Show* (Redford) (role as sponsor); *Naked in New York* (exec pr)
1995 *Search and Destroy* (exec pr, role as accountant); *Clockers* (Lee) (pr)

Publications

By SCORSESE: books—

Scorsese on Scorsese, edited by Ian Christie and David Thompson, London, 1989.
Goodfellas, with Nicholas Pileggi, London, 1990.
The Age of Innocence: A Portrait of the Film Based on the Novel by Edith Wharton, New York, 1993.

By SCORSESE: articles—

"The Filming of *Mean Streets,*" an interview with A.C. Bobrow, in *Filmmakers Newsletter* (Ward Hill, Massachusetts), January 1974.
Interview with M. Carducci, in *Millimeter* (New York), vol. 3, no. 5, 1975.
Interview with M. Rosen, in *Film Comment* (New York), March/April 1975.
Martin Scorsese Seminar, in *Dialogue on Film* (Washington, D.C.), April 1975.
"Scorsese on *Taxi Driver* and Herrmann," an interview with C. Amata, in *Focus on Film* (London), Summer/Autumn 1976.
Interview with Jonathan Kaplan, in *Film Comment* (New York), July/August 1977.
Interview with Richard Combs and Louise Sweet, in *Sight and Sound* (London), Winter 1977/78.
"Martin Scorsese's Guilty Pleasures," in *Film Comment* (New York), September/October 1978.
Interview with Paul Schrader, in *Cahiers du Cinéma* (Paris), April 1982.
Interview with B. Krohn, in *Cahiers du Cinéma* (Paris), May 1986.
"Body and Blood," an interview with Richard Corliss, in *Film Criticism* (Meadville, Pennsylvania), vol. 24, no. 5, 1988.
Interview with Chris Hodenfield, in *American Film* (Washington, D.C.), March 1989.
"Entretien avec Martin Scorsese," with H. Niogret, in *Positif* (Paris), October 1990.
"Scorsese sur Scorsese," an interview with P. Rollet and others, in *Cahiers du Cinéma* (Paris), October 1990.
Interview with A. Decurtis, in *Rolling Stone* (New York), November 1, 1990.
"Martin Scorsese: Gangster and Priest," an interview with A. M. Bahiana, in *Cinema Papers* (Melbourne), December 1990.
Interview with David Rensin, in *Playboy* (Chicago, Illinois), April 1991.
Interviews with Graham Fuller, in *Interview* (New York), November 1991 and October 1993.
"Martin Scorsese's Mortal Sins," an interview with Marcelle Clements, in *Esquire* (New York), November 1993.
Interview with Gavin Smith, in *Film Comment* (New York), November/December 1993.

On SCORSESE: books—

Kolker, Robert Phillip, *A Cinema of Loneliness: Penn, Kubrick, Coppola, Scorsese, Altman,* Oxford, 1980; revised edition, 1988.
Bliss, Michael, *Martin Scorsese and Michael Cimino,* Metuchen, New Jersey, 1986.
Arnold, Frank, and others, *Martin Scorsese,* Munich, 1986.
Cietat, Michel, *Martin Scorsese,* Paris, 1986.
Domecq, Jean-Philippe, *Martin Scorsese: Un Rêve Italo-Américan,* Renens, Switzerland, 1986.
Weiss, Ulli, *Das Neue Hollywood: Francis Ford Coppola, Steven Spielberg, Martin Scorsese,* Munich, 1986.
Wood, Robin, *Hollywood from Vietnam to Reagan,* New York, 1986.
Weiss, Marian, *Martin Scorsese: A Guide to References and Resources,* Boston, 1987.
Kelly, Mary P., *Martin Scorsese: A Journey,* New York, 1991.
Ehrenstein, David, *The Scorsese Picture: The Art and Life of Martin Scorsese,* New York, 1992.
Keyser, Lester J., *Martin Scorsese,* New York, 1992.
Connelly, Marie K., *Martin Scorsese: An Analysis of His Feature Films,* Jefferson, North Carolina, 1993.

On SCORSESE: articles—

Gardner, P. "Martin Scorsese," in *Action* (Los Angeles), May/June 1975.
Scorsese Section of *Positif* (Paris), April 1980.
"Martin Scorsese vu par Michael Powell," in *Positif* (Paris), April 1981.
Rickey, C., "Marty," in *American Film* (Washington, D.C.), November 1982.
Rafferty, T., "Martin Scorsese's Still Life," in *Sight and Sound* (London), Summer 1983.
Braudy, Leo, "The Sacraments of Genre: Coppola, De Palma, Scorsese," in *Film Quarterly* (Berkeley), Spring 1986.
Bruce, B., "Martin Scorsese: Five Films," in *Movie* (London), Winter 1986.
"Scorsese Issue" of *Film Comment* (New York), September/October 1988.
Jenkins, Steve, "From the Pit of Hell," in *Monthly Film Bulletin* (London), December 1988.
Williams, T., "*The Last Temptation of Christ:* A Fragmented Oedipal Trajectory," in *CineAction* (Toronto), Winter/Spring 1990.
Morgan, D., "The Thriller in Scorsese," in *Millimeter* (New York), October 1991.
Biskind, Peter, "Slouching Toward Hollywood," in *Premiere* (New York), November 1991.
Stanley, A., "From the Mean Streets to Charm School," in *New York Times,* 28 June 1992.
Murphy, Kathleen, "Artist of the Beautiful," in *Film Comment* (New York), November/December 1993.
Schrader, Paul, "Paul Schrader on Martin Scorsese," in *New Yorker,* 21 March 1994.

* * *

At present, with regard to the Hollywood cinema of the last fifteen years, two directors appear to stand head-and-shoulders above the rest, and it is possible to make large claims for their work on both formal and thematic grounds: Scorsese and Cimino. The work of each is strongly rooted in the American and Hollywood past, yet is at the same time audacious and innovative. Cimino's work can be read as at once the culmination of the Ford/Hawks tradition and a radical rethinking of its premises; Scorsese's involves an equally drastic rethinking of the Hollywood genres, either combining them in such a way as to foreground their contradictions (western and horror film in *Taxi Driver*) or disconcertingly reversing the expectations they traditionally arouse (the musical in *New York, New York,* the boxing movie and "biopic" in *Raging Bull*). Both directors have further disconcerted audiences and critics alike in their radical deviations from the principles of classical narrative: hence *Heaven's Gate* is received by the American critical establishment with blank incomprehension and self-defensive ridicule, while Scorsese has been accused (by Andrew Sarris, among others) of lacking a sense of structure. Hollywood films are not expected to be innovative, difficult, and challenging, and must suffer the consequences of authentic originality (as opposed to the latest in fashionable *chic* that often passes for it).

The Cimino/Scorsese parallel ends at this shared tension between tradition and innovation. While *Heaven's Gate* can be read as the answer to (and equal of) *Birth of a Nation,* Scorsese has never ventured into the vast fresco of American epic, preferring to explore relatively small, limited subjects (with the exception of *The Last Temptation of Christ*), the wider significance of the films arising from the implications those subjects are made to reveal. He starts always from the concrete and specific—a character, a relationship: the vicissitudes in the careers and love-life of two musicians (*New York, New York*); the violent public and private life of a famous boxer (*Raging Bull*); the crazy aspirations of an obsessed nonentity (*King of Comedy*). In each case, the subject is remorselessly followed through to a point where it reveals and dramatizes the fundamental ideological tensions of our culture.

His early works are divided between self-confessedly personal works related to his own Italian-American background (*Who's That Knock-*

ing at my Door?, Mean Streets) and genre movies (*Boxcar Bertha, Alice Doesn't Live Here Anymore*). The distinction was never absolute, and the later films effectively collapse it, tending to take as their starting point not only a specific character but a specific star: Robert De Niro. The Scorsese/De Niro relationship has proved one of the most fruitful director/star collaborations in the history of the cinema; its ramifications are extremely complex. De Niro's star image is central to this, poised as it is on the borderline between "star" and "actor"—the charismatic personality, the self-effacing impersonator of diverse characters. It is this ambiguity in the De Niro star persona that makes possible the ambiguity in the actor/director relationship: the degree to which Scorsese identifies with the characters De Niro plays, versus the degree to which he distances himself from them. It is this tension (communicated very directly to the spectator) between identification and repudiation that gives the films their uniquely disturbing quality.

Indeed, Scorsese is perhaps the only Hollywood director of consequence who has succeeded in sustaining the radical critique of American culture that developed in the 1970s through the Reagan era of retrenchment and recuperation. Scorsese probes the tensions within and between individuals until they reveal their fundamental, cultural nature. Few films have chronicled so painfully and abrasively as *New York, New York* the impossibility of successful heterosexual relations within a culture built upon sexual inequality. The conflicts arising out of the man's constant need for self-assertion and domination and the woman's bewildered alterations between rebellion and complexity are—owing to the peculiarities of the director/star/character/spectator relationship—simultaneously experienced and analysed.

Raging Bull goes much further in penetrating to the root causes of masculine aggression and violence, linking socially approved violence in the ring to socially disapproved violence outside it, violence against men to violence against women. It carries to its extreme that reversal of generic expectations so characteristic of Scorsese's work: a boxing melodrama/success story, it is the ultimate anti-*Rocky*; a filmed biography of a person still living, it flouts every unwritten rule of veneration for the protagonist, celebration of his achievements, triumph after tribulation, etc. Ostensibly an account of the life of Jake LaMotta, it amounts to a veritable case history of a paranoiac, and can perhaps only be fully understood through Freud. Most directly relevant to the film is Freud's assertion that every case of paranoia, without exception, has its roots in a repressed homosexual impulse; that the primary homosexual love-objects are likely to be father and brothers; that there are four "principle forms" of paranoia, each of which amounts to a *denial* of homosexual attraction (see the analysis of the Schreber case and its postscript). *Raging Bull* exemplifies all of this with startling (if perhaps largely inadvertent) thoroughness: all four of the "principle forms" are enacted in Scorsese's presentation of LaMotta, especially significant being the paranoid's projection of his repressed desires for men onto the woman he ostensibly loves. The film becomes nothing less than a statement about the disastrous consequences, for men and women alike, of the repression of bisexuality in our culture.

King of Comedy may seem at first sight a slighter work than its two predecessors, but its implications are no less radical and subversive: it is one of the most complete statements about the emotional and spiritual bankruptcy of patriarchal capitalism today that the cinema has given us. The symbolic Father (once incarnated in figures of mythic force, like Abraham Lincoln) is here revealed in his essential emptiness, loneliness, and inadequacy. The "children" (De Niro and Sandra Bernhard) behave in exemplary Oedipal fashion: he wants to *be* the father, she wants to screw the father. The film moves to twin climaxes. First, the father must be reduced to total impotence (to the point of actual immobility) in order to be loved; then Bernhard can croon to him "You're gonna love me/like nobody's loved me," and remove her clothes. Meanwhile, De Niro tapes his TV act which (exclusively concerned with childhood, his parents, self-depreciation) culminates in a joke about throwing up over his father's new shoes, the shoes he is (metaphorically) now standing in. We see ambivalence towards the father, the hatred-in-rivalry of "brother" and "sister," the son's need for paternal recognition (albeit in fantasy) before he can announce himself to the woman he (very dubiously) loves; and the irrelevance of the mother (a mere, intermittently intrusive, off-screen voice) to any "serious"—i.e., Oedipal patriarchal—concerns. Thus *King of Comedy* constitutes one of the most rigorous assaults we have on the structures of the patriarchal nuclear family and the impossible desires, fantasies, frustrations, and violence those structures generate: an assault, that is, on the fundamental premises of our culture.

Since 1990, Scorsese has made four films which, taken together, establish him definitively as the most important director currently working in Hollywood. *Goodfellas, Cape Fear, The Age of Innocence,* and *Casino* reveal an artist in total command of every aspect of his medium—narrative construction, *mise-en-scène,* editing, the direction of actors, set design, sound, music, etc. Obviously, he owes much to the faithful team he has built up over the years, each of whom deserves an individual appreciation; but there can be no doubt of Scorsese's overall control at every level, from the conceptual to the minutiae of execution, informed by his sense of the work as a totality to which every strand, every detail, contributes integrally. If the films continue to raise certain doubts, to prompt certain reservations, it is not on the level of realization, but on moral and philosophical grounds. Let it be said at once, however, that *The Age of Innocence,* which in advance seemed such an improbable project—provoking fears that it would not transcend the solid and worthy but fundamentally dull literary adaptations of James Ivory—is beyond all doubts and reservations a masterpiece of nuance and refinement, alive in its every moment.

The other three films all raise the much-debated issue of the presentation of violence. There seem to be two valid ways of presenting violence (as opposed to the violence as "fun" of *Pulp Fiction,* violence as "aestheticized ballet" of John Woo's films, or violence as "gross out" in the contemporary horror movie). One way is to refuse to show it, always locating it (by a movement of the camera or the actors) just off-screen (Lang in *The Big Heat,* Mizoguchi in *Sansho Dayu),* leaving our imaginations free to experience its horror: a method almost totally absent from modern Hollywood. The other is to make it as explicit, ugly, painful, and disturbing as possible so that it becomes quite impossible for anyone other than an advanced criminal psychotic to enjoy it. The latter is Scorsese's method, and he cannot be faulted for it in the recent work. It was still possible, perhaps, to get a certain "kick" out of the violence in *Taxi Driver,* because of our ambiguous relationship to the central character, but this is no longer true of the violence in *Goodfellas* or *Casino.* An essential characteristic of the later films is the rigorous distance Scorsese constructs between the audience and *all* the characters: identification, if it can be said to exist at all, flickers only sporadically—is always swiftly contradicted or heavily qualified.

Yet herein lies what is at least a potential problem of these films. One can analyze the ways in which this distance is constructed, especially through the increasing fracturing of the narrative line, the splitting of voice-over narration among different characters in both *Goodfellas* and *Casino;* but isn't alienation, for many of us, inherent in the characters themselves and the subject matter? Scorsese has insisted that the characters of *Casino* are "human beings": fair enough. But he seems to imply that if we cannot feel sympathetic to them we are somehow assuming an unwarranted moral superiority. One might retort (to take an extreme case—but the Pesci character is already pretty extreme) that Hitler and Albert Schweitzer were both "human beings": may we not at least discriminate between them? One can feel a certain compassion for the characters (even Joe Pesci) as people caught up in a process they think they can control but which really controls *them;* but can one say more for them than that?

Martin Scorsese

Beyond that, though connected with it, is the films' increasing inflation: not merely their length (*Goodfellas* plays for almost two-and-a-half hours, *Casino* for almost three) but its accompanying sense of grandeur: for Scorsese, apparently, the grandeur of his subjects. One is invited to lament, respectively, the decline of the Mafia and of Las Vegas. But suppose one cannot see them, in the first place, in terms other than those of social disease? The films strike me as too insulated, too enclosed within their subjects and milieux: the Mafia and Las Vegas are never effectively "placed" in a wider social context. Scorsese's worst error seems to be the use in *Casino* of the final chorus from Bach's *St. Matthew Passion:* an error not merely of "tease" but of sense, comparable in its enormity to Cimino's use of the Mahler "Resurrection" symphony at the end of *Year of the Dragon.* If it is possible to lament the decline of Las Vegas, it surely cannot be inflated into the lament of Bach's cheer for the death of Christ on the cross.

One cannot doubt the authenticity of Scorsese's sense of the tragic. Yet it is difficult not to feel that he has not yet found for it (to adopt T. S. Eliot's famous formulation) an adequate "objective correlative."

—Robin Wood

SCOTT, Ridley

Nationality: English. **Born:** South Shields, County Durham, 1939. **Education:** Studied at West Hartlepool College of Art and at the Royal College of Art, London. **Family:** Married, three children. **Career:** Set designer, then director for BBC TV, including episodes of *Z-Cars* and *The Informer,* 1966-67; set up production company Ridley Scott Associates, directed close to 3,000 commercials, from 1967; directed first feature, *The Duellists,* 1977. **Awards:** Special Jury Prize, Cannes Festival, for *The Duellists,* 1977; Venice Film Festival Award for commercial work.

Films as Director:

1977 *The Duellists*
1979 *Alien*
1982 ***Blade Runner***
1985 *Legend*
1987 *Someone to Watch over Me* (+ exec-pr)
1989 *Black Rain*
1991 ***Thelma and Louise*** (+ co-pr)
1992 *1492: The Conquest of Paradise* (+ pr)
1996 *White Squall*

Other Films:

1994 *The Browning Version* (co-pr); *Monkey Business* (exec pr)

Publications

By SCOTT: articles—

"Ridley Scott cinéaste du décor," an interview with O. Assayas and S. LePéron, in *Cahiers du Cinéma* (Paris), September 1982.
"Designer Genes," an interview with Harlan Kennedy, in *Films* (London), September 1982.
Interview with Hubert Niogret, in *Positif* (Paris), September 1985.
Interview with Sheila Johnston, in *Films and Filming* (London), November 1985.
Interview with Raphael Bassan and Raymond Lefevre, in *Revue du Cinéma* (Paris), February 1986.
Interview with M. Buckley, in *Films in Review* (New York), January 1987.
"*Thelma and Louise* Hit the Road for Ridley Scott," an interview with M. McDonagh, in *Film Journal* (New York), June 1991.
"Ridley Scott's Road Work," an interview with A. Taubin, in *Sight and Sound* (London), July 1991.
"*1492: Conquest of Paradise,*" an interview with A. M. Bahiana, in *Cinema Papers* (Melbourne), October 1992.
"Myth Revisited," an interview with M. Moss, in *Boxoffice* (Chicago), October 1992.

On SCOTT: book—

Kernan, Judith B., ed., *Retrofitting "Blade Runner": Issues in Ridley Scott's "Blade Runner" and Philip K. Dick's "Do Androids Dream of Electric Sheep?,"* Bowling Green, Ohio, 1991.

On SCOTT: articles—

"*Blade Runner* Issue" of *Cinefex* (Riverside, California), July 1982.
"*Blade Runner* Issues" of *Starburst* (London), September/November 1982.
Kellner, Douglas, Flo Leibowitz, and Michael Ryan, "*Blade Runner*: A Diagnostic Critique," in *Jump Cut* (Chicago), no. 29, 1983.
Caron, A., "Les archétypes chez Ridley Scott," in *Jeune Cinéma* (Paris), March 1983.
Durgnat, Raymond, "Art for Film's Sake," in *American Film* (Washington, D.C.), May 1983.
Milmo, Sean, "Ridley Scott Makes the Details Count," in *Advertising Age* (Chicago), 21 June 1984.
Doll, Susan, and Greg Faller, "*Blade Runner* and Genre: Film Noir and Science Fiction," in *Literature/Film Quarterly* (Salisbury, Maryland), no. 2, 1986.
Rosen, Barbara, "How the Man Who Made *Alien* Invaded Madison Avenue," in *Business Week* (New York), 24 March 1986.
Davis, Brian, "Ridley Scott: He Revolutionized TV Ads," in *Adweek* (Chicago), 2 October 1989.
Zimmer, J., "Ridley Scott," in *Revue du Cinéma* (Paris), September 1990.
"The Many Faces of *Thelma & Louise*" (8 short articles), in *Film Quarterly* (Berkeley), Winter 1991/92.
Wilmington, Mike, "The Rain People," in *Film Comment* (New York), January/February 1992.
Wollen, Peter, "Cinema's Conquistadors," in *Sight and Sound* (London), November 1992.
Strick, Philip, "*Blade Runner*: Telling the Difference," in *Sight and Sound* (London), December 1992.
Torry, Robert, "Awaking to the Other: Feminism and the Ego-ideal in *Alien,*" in *Women's Studies* (Champaign, Illinois), vol. 23, no. 4, 1994.

* * *

Ridley Scott has enjoyed more critical acclaim and financial success as a director of television commercials than he has as a feature filmmaker. Ironically, the very element that has made him an award-winning director of commercials—his emphasis on visual design to convey the message—has often been at the core of the criticism aimed at his films.

Though Scott began his career directing popular TV programs for the BBC, he found that his meticulous attention to detail in terms of

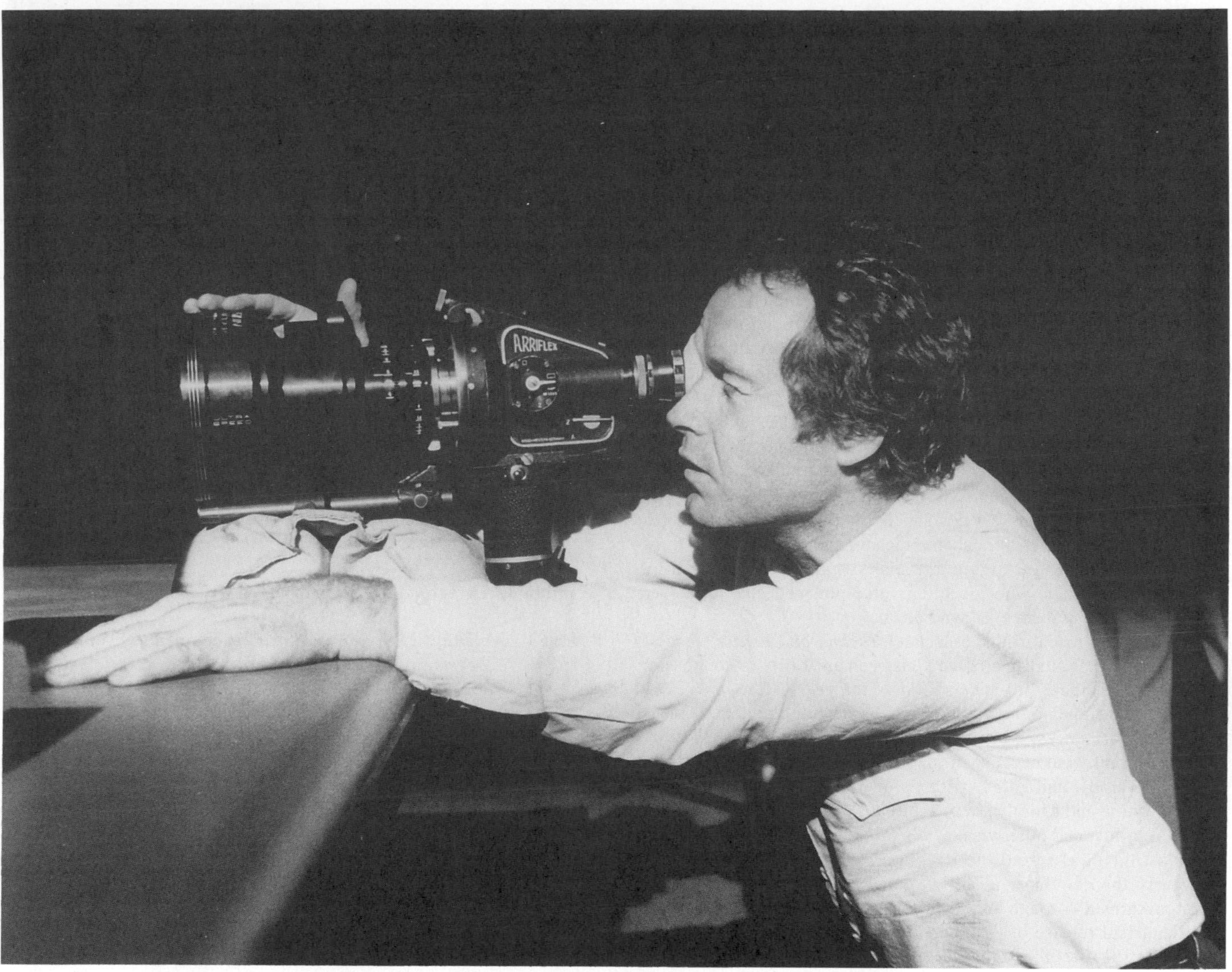

Ridley Scott

set design and props was more suited to making commercials. Scott honed his craft and style on hundreds of ad spots for British television during the 1970s, as did future film directors Alan Parker, Hugh Hudson, Adrian Lyne, and Tony Scott (Ridley's brother). In 1979, Scott became a fixture in the American television marketplace with a captivating commercial for Chanel No. 5 entitled "Share the Fantasy." Still innovative in this arena, Scott continues to spark controversy with his "pocket versions of feature films"—his term for commercials.

Scott approaches his feature films with the same emphasis on mise-en-scène that distinguishes his commercials, prompting some critics to refer to him as a visual stylist. Scott assumes control over the visual elements of his films as much as possible, rather than turn the set design completely over to the art director or the photography over to the cinematographer. Because his first feature, *The Duellists,* was shot in France, Scott was able to serve as his own cinematographer for that film—a luxury not allowed on many subsequent films due to union rules.

Hallmarks of Scott's style include a detailed, almost crowded set design that is as prominent in the frame as the actors, a fascination with the tonalities of light, a penchant for foggy atmospheres backlit for maximum effect, and a reliance on long lenses, which tend to flatten the perspective. While these techniques are visually stunning in themselves, they are often tied directly to plot and character in Scott's films.

Of all Scott's films, *Blade Runner* and *Legend* make the fullest use of set design to enhance the theme. In *Blade Runner,* the polluted, dank metropolis teems with hordes of lower-class merchants and pedestrians, who inhabit the streets at all hours. Except for huge, garish neon billboards, fog and darkness pervade the city, suggesting that urban centers in the future will have no daylight hours. This pessimistic view is in sharp contrast to the sterile, brightly lit sets found in conventional science-fiction films. Inherent in the set design is a critique of our society, which has allowed its environment to be destroyed. The overwrought set design also complements the feverish attempts by a group of androids to find the secret to longer life. *Blade Runner* influenced the genre with its dystopian depiction of the future, though the cluttered set design and low-key lighting were used earlier by Scott in the science-fiction thriller *Alien.*

Legend, a fairy tale complete with elves, goblins, and unicorns, employs a simple theme of good and evil, which is reinforced through images of light and darkness. The magical unicorns, for example, have coats of the purest white; an innocent, virginal character is costumed in flowing, white gowns; sunbeams pour over glades of white flowers; and light shimmers across silver streams as the unicorns gallop through the forest. In contrast, a character called Darkness (actually the Devil) looks magnificently evil in an array of blood reds and wine colors; the sinister Darkness resides in the dark, dismal bowels of the Earth, where no light is allowed to enter; and a corrupted world is symbolized by a charred forest devoid of flowers and leaves and black clouds that cover the sky. The forest set was constructed entirely inside the studio and is reminiscent of those huge indoor sets created for Fritz Lang's *Siegfried.*

In *Black Rain,* Scott once again reinforced the film's theme through its mise-en-scène, though here he made extensive use of actual locations instead of relying so much on studio sets. *Black Rain* follows the story of two New York detectives tracking a killer through the underworld of Osaka, Japan. The two characters are frequently depicted against the backdrop of Osaka's ornate neon signs and ultramodern architecture. Shot through a telephoto lens and lit from behind, the characters seem crushed against the huge set design, which serves as a metaphor for their struggle to penetrate the culture in order to track their man.

Though Scott has forged a style that is recognizably his own, his approach to filmmaking has a precedent in German Expressionist filmmaking. The Expressionists were among the first to use the elements of mise-en-scène (set design, lighting, props, costuming) to suggest traits of character or enhance meaning. Similarly, Scott's techniques are stunning yet highly artificial, a trait often criticized by American reviewers, who too often value plot and character over visual style, and realism over symbolism.

Scott's more recent films, especially *Thelma and Louise,* suggest that his strongest quality all along has been an ability to create film myths that resonate in viewers' minds for years afterwards. *The Duellists* continues to be a haunting film despite the actors' inadequate performances, not just because of the splendidly Romantic cinematography but because of the starkness of the tale itself (from Joseph Conrad); and *Alien,* with its own duel between a no-nonsense heroine and a hidden evil, continues to be an object of critical study, feminist and otherwise. *Blade Runner,* perhaps most of all of Scott's films, has seized the imagination of both movie fans and scholarly theoreticians: a 1991 volume of critical studies of the film contains a 44-page annotated bibliography, and this is before the theatrical release of the "Director's Cut," which had aficionados debating the merits of its eliminating Deckard's noiresque voiceovers and the hopeful green hills at the end, and of adding a brief shot of a unicorn. One might attribute the relative failures of *Someone to Watch over Me* and *Black Rain,* despite their visual swank, to their inability to transcend tired generic conventions, while the more recent *1492: The Conquest of Paradise* seems most successful in its mythic moments—notably Columbus's first glimpse of the New World as mists sweep aside—rather than in its efforts to document the Spanish extermination of native peoples while partially exonerating Columbus himself.

Thelma and Louise, with its near-hallucinatory, flamboyantly archetypal American Western settings (bearing little relation to such specificities as "Arkansas"), debuted with much debate about how feminist it actually was in its characterizations of two "dangerous women" and in its delineations of the patriarchal causes of their doomed flight. But whatever conclusions might be drawn about the film's polemics, those unforgettable shots of Thelma and Louise whooping in delight as they light out for the territory in their T-bird convertible—red hair flying, sunglasses glinting—seem destined to enter American mythology (granted that it is too soon to rank the pair alongside Huck and Jim on the raft). Closer to tall tale than high tragedy, *Thelma and Louise* is memorable due not only to the script and the seemingly inevitable casting of the leads, but to Scott's realization of landscapes, from the rainy night highways (a background wash of massive dark trucks and blinding lights) to Monument Valley and other vast spaces populated by little more than swarms of police vehicles. It may well be a defining film of the early 1990s, as *Blade Runner* now seems to be for the early 1980s.

—Susan Doll, updated by Joseph Milicia

SEMBENE, Ousmane

Nationality: Senegalese. **Born:** at Ziguinchor, Senegal, 8 January 1923. **Military Service:** Joined Free French Forces fighting in Africa, 1942, demobilized at Marseilles, 1946. **Career:** Worked as mechanic, 1937-38; after military service, returned to Senegal, then moved to France, 1948; docker in Marseilles, and Secretary General of black workers organization in France; published first novel, *Le Docker noir,* 1956; returned to Senegal, 1960; studied cinema in Moscow under Sergei Gerasimov and Mark Donskoi, 1962; made first film, *L'Empire Sonrai,* 1963; founding editor, *Kaddu* newspaper, 1972. **Awards:** Dakar Festival of Negro Arts prize, 1966; Cannes Film Festival prize, 1967; Venice Film Festival prize, 1969; Atlanta Film Festival prize, 1970.

Films as Director and Scriptwriter:

1963 *Songhays* (*L'Empire Sonrai*) (documentary, unreleased); *Borom Sarret*
1964 *Niaye*
1966 ***La Noire de...*** (*The Black Girl from...*)
1968 *Mandabi* (*The Money Order*)
1970 *Tauw* (*Taw*)
1971 *Emitai*
1974 ***Xala*** (*Impotence*)
1977 *Ceddo* (*The People*)
1987 *Camp de Thiaroye*
1992 *Guelwaar*

Other Films:

1983 *Camera d'Afrique* (Boughedir) (role)

Publications

By SEMBENE: books—

Le Docker noir, Paris, 1956.
O pays, mon beau peuple, Paris, 1957.
Les Bouts de bois de Dieu, Paris, 1960.
Voltaïque, Paris, 1962.
L'Harmattan, Paris, 1964.
Vehi Ciosane ou blanche genèse suivi de *Mandat,* Paris, 1965.
Xala, Paris, 1973; Westport, Connecticut, 1976.
Le Dernier de l'Empire, Paris, 1981; as *The Last of the Empire,* London, 1983.
Niiwan; Taaw, Paris, 1987.

By SEMBENE: articles—

Interview with Guy Hennebelle, in *Jeune Cinéma* (Paris), November 1968.
"Film-makers Have a Great Responsibility to our People," interview with H. D. Weaver, Jr., in *Cineaste* (New York), vol. 6, no. 1, 1973.

Interview with G. M. Perry, in *Film Quarterly* (Berkeley), Spring 1973.
"Ousmane Sembene, Carthage et le cinéma africain," and "Problématique du cinéaste africain: l'artiste et la révolution," interviews with T. Cheriaa, in *Cinéma Québec* (Montreal), August 1974.
Interview with C. Bosseno, in *Image et Son* (Paris), September 1979.
Interview with A. Tournès, in *Jeune Cinéma* (Paris), November/December 1988.
Interview with M. T. Oldani, in *Filmcritica* (Rome), June 1991.
Interview with E. Castiel, in *Séquences* (Montreal), July/August 1993.

On SEMBENE: books—

Vieyra, Paulin Soumanou, *Ousmane Sembene, cinéaste: Première période 1962-71,* Paris, 1972.
Vieyra, Paulin Soumanou, *Le Cinéma africain: des origines à 1973,* Paris, 1975.
Martin, Angela, editor, *African Films: The Context of Production,* London, 1982.
Moore, Carried Dailey, *Evolution of an African Artist: Social Realism in the Work of Ousmane Sembene,* Ann Arbor, Michigan, 1984.
Pfaff, Françoise, *The Cinema of Ousmane Sembene,* Westport, Connecticut, 1984.
Armes, Roy, *Third World Filmmaking and the West,* Berkeley, 1987.
Downing, John D. H., editor, *Film and Politics in the Third World,* New York, 1987.
Pfaff, Françoise, *25 Black African Filmmakers: A Critical Study,* Westport, Connecticut, 1988.
Gadjigo, Samba, ed., *Ousmane Sembene: Dialogues with Critics and Writers,* Amherst, Massachusetts, 1993.
Tsabedze, Clara, *African Independence from Francophone and Anglophone Voices: A Comparative Study of the Post-independence Novels by Ngugi and Sembene,* New York, 1994.

On SEMBENE: articles—

Ghali, N., "Ousmane Sembene," in *Cinématographe* (Paris), April 1976.
Van Wert, William, "Ideology in the Third World Cinema: A Study of Ousmane Sembene and Glauber Rocha," in *Quarterly Review of Film Studies* (Pleasantville, New York), Spring 1979.
Armes, Roy, "Ousmane Sembene: Questions of Change," in *Ciné Tracts* (Montreal), Summer-Fall 1981.

Ousmane Sembene

Landy, M., and others, "Ousmane Sembene's Films," in *Jump Cut* (Berkeley), July 1982.

Landy, M., "Political Allegory and 'Engaged Cinema': Sembene's *Xala,*" in *Cinema Journal* (Champaign, Illinois), Spring 1984.

Turvey, G., "*Xala* and the Curse of Neo-Colonialism," in *Screen* (London), May/August 1985.

Dauphin, G., "Into Africa," in *Village Voice* (New York), 18 September 1990.

Diawara, M., "Camp de Thiaroye," in *Black Film Review* (Washington, D.C.), vol. 6, no. 3, 1991.

Rosen, P., "Making a Nation in Sembene's 'Ceddo,'" *Quarterly Review of Film and Video* (New York), vol. 13, no. 1/3, 1991.

Kindem, G. H., and M. Steele, "Women in Sembene's Films," *Jump Cut* (Berkeley), May 1991.

Atkinson, Michael, "Ousmane Sembene: 'We Are No Longer in the Era of Prophets,'" in *Film Comment* (New York), July/August 1993.

* * *

Ousmane Sembene is one of the most important literary figures of sub-Saharan Africa and, at the same time, its premier filmmaker. Born in 1923 in Senegal, he received little formal education. His first literary work, autobiographical in nature, dates from 1956. It featured as its backdrop the port city of Marseilles, where he worked as a docker. Sembene came to film by necessity: painfully aware that he could not reach his largely illiterate compatriots by means of a written art form, he studied film in Moscow in 1961 and began to work in this medium shortly thereafter.

It is interesting and important to note that four of Sembene's films are based on texts, written by Sembene, which first appeared as novels or short stories. Between 1963 and 1977 he produced eight films while publishing three works of fiction. Following *Borom Sarret* and *Niaye,* Sembene made *La Noire de ...,* the first feature-length film to come out of sub-Saharan Africa: it received several awards. While technically flawed, it is still a powerful piece dealing with the issue of neocolonialism in post-independence Africa, a common theme in Sembene's work. His next film, *Mandabi (The Money Order),* marked an important breakthrough for Sembene: it is his first film in color, but, more importantly, it is the first work to use an African language—in this case Wolof, rather than French—and this allowed him to reach his primary audience in an even more direct manner than previously possible. His use of African languages continues with the creation of *Emitai,* which is made in Diola. *Emitai* was the first full-length film by Sembene which was not an adaptation of a written text.

The conditions of filmmaking in Africa are difficult and the lack of trained personnel and financial support have discouraged many African artists from working in this medium. Sembene has managed to overcome these problems and has even made a virtue of certain necessities: his almost exclusive reliance on non-professional actors and actresses, including those playing leading roles, is an example of this. He is thus able to increase both the general force of the film—the audience can more easily identify with his actors than with "stars"—and testify to his belief in the common man and the collective heroism of the masses.

Sembene's films are not innovative in a technical sense; instead, their power and critical success stem from their compelling portraits of Third World men and women struggling against forces, both internal and external, which threaten their dignity and, in fact, their very existence. Sembene clearly sees himself as a Marxist-Leninist and sees art as necessarily both functional and politically committed. But this does not mean that he is a mere propagandist and, in fact, his art transcends narrow definition. His art is clearly African in character despite his extensive contacts with the West: the filmmaker is the descendant of the traditional *griot,* recording the history of his society, criticizing its faults, finding strength in its people in the face of the denigration of African society and culture inherent in all forms of colonialism.

—Curtis Schade

SEN, Mrinal

Nationality: Indian. **Born:** East Bengal (now Bangladesh), 4 May 1923. **Education:** Studied physics in Calcutta. **Family:** Married Gita Shome, 1953; one son. **Career:** Freelance journalist and medical representative in Uttar Pradesh; involved with Indian People's Theatre Association, sponsored by Communist Party of India, 1943-47; directed first film, *Raat Bhore,* 1956; jury member at numerous international film festivals; chairman of Gov. Council Film and Television Institute of India, 1983-85. **Awards:** Silver Bear, Berlin Festival, for *Akaler Sandhane,* 1981.

Films as Director:

(in Bengali unless indicated)

1956 *Raat Bhore* (*The Dawn*; *Night's End*)
1959 *Neel Akasher Neechey* (*Under the Blue Sky*)
1960 *Baishey Shravana* (*The Wedding Day*)
1961 *Punnascha* (*Over Again*)
1962 *Abasheshey* (*And at Last*)
1964 *Pratinidhi* (*The Representative*; *Two Plus One*)
1965 *Akash Kusum* (*Up in the Clouds*)
1967 *Matira Manisha* (*Two Brothers*) (+ co-sc, in Bengali); *Moving Perspectives* (doc)
1969 *Bhuvan Shome* (*Mr. Shome*)) (+ pr, sc, in Hindi)
1970 *Ichhapuran* (*The Wish-Fulfillment*) (+ sc, in Bengali, also Hindi version)
1971 *Interview*
1972 *Calcutta 71* (+ sc); *Ek Adhuri Kahani* (*An Unfinished Story*)
1973 *Padatik* (*The Guerilla Fighter*)
1974 *Chorus*
1976 *Mrigaya* (*The Royal Hunt*) (+ co-sc, in Hindi)
1977 *Oka Oorie Katha* (*The Outsiders*) (+ co-sc, in Telugu)
1978 *Parashuram* (*The Man with the Axe*)
1979 *Ek Din Pratidin* (*And Quiet Rolls the Dawn*)
1980 ***Akaler Sandhane*** (*In Search of Famine*)
1981 *Chalachitra* (*The Kaleidoscope*)
1982 *Kharij* (*The Case Is Closed*)
1983 *Khandahar* (*The Ruins*)
1985 *Tasveer Apni Apni*
1986 *Genesis*
1989 *Ek din achanak* (+ sc)
1990 *Calcutta, My El Dorado* (doc) (+ pr)
1991 *World Within, World Without*
1992 *Mahaprithivi* (+ sc)
1994 *The Confined* (+ sc)

Publications

By SEN: books—

In Search of Famine, Calcutta, 1983; London, 1990.
The Ruins (Khandahar), Calcutta, 1984.

By SEN: articles—

"Introducing Mrinal Sen," interview with U. Gupta, in *Jump Cut* (Berkeley), no. 12/13, 1976.

"Mrinal Sen: cineasta de los humildes," interview with M. Pereira, in *Cine Cubano* (Havana), no. 99, 1981.

Interview with S. S. Chakravarty, in *Ciné-Tracts* (Montreal), 1981.

Interview with Michel Ciment, in *Positif* (Paris), January 1982.

"New Visions in Indian Cinema," an interview with U. Gupta, in *Cineaste* (New York), vol. 11, no. 4, winter 1982.

"Mrinal Sen," in *Cinema in India,* vol. 4, no. 3, 1991.

On SEN: books—

da Cunha, Uma, editor, *The New Generation 1960-1980: An Examination of India's New Cinema,* New Delhi, 1981.

Willemen, Paul, and Behroze Gandhy, *Indian Cinema,* London, 1982.

Hauff, Reinhard, *Hauff on Sen: Ten Days in Calcutta: A Portrait of Mrinal Sen,* Calcutta, 1987.

On SEN: articles—

Williams, Forrest, "The Art Film in India: Report on Mrinal Sen," in *Film Culture* (New York), Winter/Spring 1970.

"Mrinal Sen," in *International Film Guide 1982,* edited by Peter Cowie, London, 1981.

Malcolm, D., "Guerrilla Fighter," in *Sight and Sound* (London), Autumn 1981.

Vreeswijk, L., and others, "Sen dossier," special section, in *Skrien* (Amsterdam), October 1981.

Bassan, Raphael, "Mrinal Sen," in *Revue du Cinéma* (Paris), March 1985.

Roddick, Nick, "Original Sen," in *Cinema Papers* (Melbourne), July 1986.

Sen, J., "Silence! Work in Progress," in *Cinema in India,* vol. 2, no. 2, 1991.

Krishen, P., "Knocking at the Doors of Public Culture: India's Parallel Cinema," in *Public Culture,* vol. 4, no. 1, 1991.

Datta, B., "The Rhythm of Acting," in *Cinema in India,* vol. 3, no. 2, 1992.

On SEN: film—

Hauff, Reinhard, *Ten Days in Calcutta: A Portrait of Mrinal Sen,* 1987.

* * *

Mrinal Sen's work is distinguished by the attention he pays to the lives of the underprivileged in India. The style of his films varies considerably, and even within individual films his achievement is uneven, but the body of his work adds up to an important attempt in India at making political films, films which point to prevailing injustices and urge people to change society. Sen is India's pre-eminent activist filmmaker.

Sen's early films testify to the influences of the Italian neorealists and of Satayajit Ray's first films. Sen filmed people at the ragged edge of society, using natural locations and employing non-professional actors. Nothing in his films touched up the drabness of poor villages. Unlike Ray, however, Sen's attitude had less humanism in it than political urgency. In a strong film like *Baishey Shravana,* Sen suggests that a bourgeois mentality makes bad conditions worse by interposing the claims of respectability on matters of survival.

Although Sen established a reputation in Bengal with *Baishey Shravana,* he came to be known throughout India for the comic *Bhuvan Shome,* made in Hindi in 1969. The film describes a railway official's encounter with the wife of a ticket collector under fire for accepting bribes. The prudish railway official (played in a restrained slapstick manner by Utpal Dutt) is charmed by a country girl while on holiday in Gujarat and only later discovers that the girl is married to the offending ticket collector. The film is shot among sand dunes and sugarcane fields and reveals Sen's skill at sustaining a simple narrative. To some critics, *Bhuvan Shome* remains Sen's best film, an example of his little-used talents as a confectioner of cinema.

Conditions of near civil war in Calcutta in the late 1960s led to three Sen films known as the Calcutta trilogy—*Interview, Calcutta 71,* and *Padatik.* In these films, Sen moved away from the surface realism of his previous work, turning instead to allegorical characters and symbolic utterances. Sen returned to conventional narrative with the Hindi film *Mrigaya* in 1976. Since that time he has continued to present stories about marginal people, framing the story so that the viewer is led to discover his or her own complicity with oppression.

In 1980 Sen directed *Akaler Sandhane,* which describes the adventure of a film crew out to film a story about the Bengal famine of 1943. The villages in which the crew works are no more prosperous in 1980 than they were forty years before; an afternoon's shopping for the film team cleans out the village vegetable market. *Akaler Sandhane* is intensively effective in its portrayal of the film-within-film. At one point the actors recreate the dire poverty of a disabled peasant's household. The wife has sold herself to the landlord in order to bring home a potful of rice. Sen cuts from a chilling night scene of the lame husband beating his wife to the crowd of onlookers; it is an open question whether the dissipation of intensity which follows this distancing serves a necessary political purpose.

Communist critics generally favor Sen's work; liberal critics point to characteristic weakness of structure. But Sen's compassion and energy are never contested. In film after film he probes the fate of those people—tribals (*Mrigaya*), outcasts (*Oka Oorie Katha*), pavement dwellers (*Parashuram*), working women (*Ek Din Pratidin*), servants (*Kharij*)—who are treated as if they were sub-human. Sen's more recent films affect a subdued tone and, unlike the Calcutta trilogy, trust the audience to draw its own moral from the films. Outside of India, too, critics discern a new phase of maturity in Sen's work.

—Satti Khanna

SENNETT, Mack

Nationality: Canadian. **Born:** Mikall (Michael) Sinnott in Danville, Quebec, 17 January 1880. **Career:** Burlesque performer and chorus boy on Broadway, 1902-08; actor in Biograph films, 1908-10; director of Biograph shorts, from 1910, moved to Hollywood; formed Keystone Production Company with Charles Bauman and Adam Kessel, 1912; Keystone absorbed into Triangle Film Corporation with Thomas Ince's and D.W. Griffith's production companies, 1915; formed production company Mack Sennett Comedies following collapse of Triangle, 1917, though films released by Paramount; associated with Pathé, 1923-28, and with Educational Films, 1929-32, also returned to directing; producer and director of shorts for Paramount, from 1932, and experimented with early color process called "Natural Color"; returned to Educational Films, 1935, then retired to Canada; held nominal position at 20th Century-Fox from 1939. **Awards:** Special Oscar for contributions to screen comedy, 1937. **Died:** 1960.

Films as Director:

1910 *The Lucky Toothache* (+ sc, role); *The Masher* (+ sc, role)

1911 *Comrades* (+ role); *Priscilla's April Fool Joke*; *Cured*; *Priscilla and the Umbrella*; *Cupid's Joke*; *Misplaced Jealousy*; *The Country Lovers*; *The Manicure Lady* (+ role); *Curiosity*; *A Dutch Gold Mine* (+ role); *Dave's Love Affair*; *Their Fates Sealed*; *Bearded Youth*; *The Delayed Proposal*; *Stubbs' New Servants*; *The Wonderful Eye*; *The Jealous Husband*; *The Ghost*; *Jinks Joins the Temperance Club*; *Mr. Peck Goes Calling*; *The Beautiful Voice*; *That Dare Devil* (+ role); *An Interrupted Game*; *The Diving Girl*; *$500,000 Reward* (+ role); *The Baron*; *The Villain Foiled*; *The Village Hero* (+ role); *The Lucky Horseshoe*; *A Convenient Burglar*; *When Wifey Holds the Purse Strings*; *Too Many Burglars*; *Mr. Bragg, A Fugitive*; *Trailing the Counterfeit* (+ role); *Josh's Suicide*; *Through His Wife's Picture*; *The Inventor's Secret*; *A Victim of Circumstances*; *Their First Divorce Case* (+ role); *Dooley Scheme*; *Won Through a Medium*; *Resourceful Lovers*; *Her Mother Interferes*; *Why He Gave Up*; *Abe Gets Even with Father*; *Taking His Medicine*; *Her Pet*; *Caught with the Goods* (+ role); *A Mix-up in Raincoats*; *The Joke on the Joker*; *Who Got the Reward*; *Brave and Bold*; *Did Mother Get Her Wash*; *With a Kodak*; *Pants and Pansies*; *A Near-Tragedy*; *Lily's Lovers*; *The Fatal Chocolate* (+ role); *Got a Match*; *A Message from the Moon*; *Priscilla's Capture*; *A Spanish Dilemma* (+ role); *The Engagement Ring*; *A Voice from the Deep*; *Hot Stuff*; *Oh, Those Eyes*; *Those Hicksville Boys*; *Their First Kidnapping Case* (+ role); *Help, Help*; *The Brave Hunter*; *Won by a Fish*; *The Leading Man*; *The Fickle Spaniard*; *When the Fire Bells Rang*; *The Furs*; *A Close Call*; *Helen's Marriage*; *Tomboy Bessie*; *Algy, the Watchman*; *Katchem Kate*; *Neighbors*; *A Dash through the Clouds*; *The New Baby*; *Trying to Fool*; *One Round O'Brien*; *The Speed Demon*; *His Own Fault*; *The Would Be Shriner* (+ role); *Willie Becomes an Artist*; *The Tourists*; *What the Doctor Ordered*; *An Interrupted Elopement*; *The Tragedy of a Dress Suit*; *Mr. Grouch at the Seashore*; *Through Dumb Luck*

1912 *Cohen Collects a Debt* (*Cohen at Coney Island*) (+ pr); *The Water Nymph* (+ pr); *Riley and Schultz* (+ pr); *The New Neighbor* (+ pr); *The Beating He Needed* (+ pr); *Pedro's Dilemma* (+ pr, role); *Stolen Glory* (+ pr, role); *The Ambitious Butler* (+ pr, role); *The Flirting Husband* (+ pr); *The Grocery Clerk's Romance* (+ pr); *At Coney Island* (+ pr, role); *Mabel's Lovers* (+ pr); *At It Again* (+ pr, role); *The Deacon's Troubles* (+ pr); *A Temperamental Husband* (+ pr); *The Rivals* (+ pr, role); *Mr.* (+ pr, role); *A Desperate Lover* (+ pr); *A Bear Escape* (+ pr, role); *Pat's Day Off* (+ pr, role); *Brown's Seance* (+ pr); *A Family Mixup* (+ pr, role); *A Midnight Elopement* (+ pr); *Mabel's Adventures* (+ pr); *Useful Sheep* (+ pr); *Hoffmeyer's Legacy* (+ pr); *The Drummer's Vacation* (+ pr); *The Duel* (+ pr, role); *Mabel's Strategem* (+ pr)

1913 *Saving Mabel's Dad* (+ pr); *A Double Wedding* (+ pr); *The Cure That Failed* (+ pr); *How Hiram Won Out* (+ pr); *For Lizzie's Sake* (+ pr); *Sir Thomas Lipton Out West* (+ pr); *The Mistaken Masher* (+ pr, role); *The Deacon Outwitted* (+ pr); *The Elite Ball* (+ pr); *Just Brown's Luck* (+ pr); *The Battle of Who Run* (+ pr, role); *The Jealous Waiter* (+ pr); *The Stolen Purse* (+ pr, role); *Mabel's Heroes* (+ pr, role); *Her Birthday Present* (+ pr); *Heinze's Resurrection* (+ pr); *A Landlord's Troubled* (+ pr); *Forced Bravery* (+ pr); *The Professor's Daughter* (+ pr); *A Tangled Affair* (+ pr); *A Red Hot Romance* (+ pr); *A Doctored Affair* (+ pr); *The Sleuth's Last Stand* (+ pr, role); *A Deaf Burglar* (+ pr); *The Sleuths at the Floral Parade* (+ pr, role); *A Rural Third Degree* (+ pr); *A Strong Revenge* (+ pr, role); *The Two Widows* (+ pr); *Foiling Fickle Father* (+ pr); *Love and Pain* (+ pr); *The Man Next Door* (+ pr); *A Wife Wanted* (+ pr); *The Rube and the Baron* (+ pr, role); *Jenny's Pearls* (+ pr); *The Chief's Predicament* (+ pr); *At Twelve O'Clock* (+ pr); *Her New Beau* (+ pr, role); *On His Wedding Day* (+ pr); *The Land Salesman* (+ pr); *Hide and Seek* (+ pr); *Those Good Old Days* (+ pr); *A Game of Poker* (+ pr); *Father's Choice* (+ pr); *A Life in the Balance* (+ pr); *Murphy's I.O.U.* (+ pr); *A Dollar Did It* (+ pr); *Cupid in the Dental Parlor* (+ pr); *A Fishy Affair* (+ pr); *The Bangville Police* (+ pr); *The New Conductor* (+ pr); *His Chum, the Baron* (+ pr); *That Ragtime Band* (+ pr); *Algie on the Force* (+ pr); *His Ups and Downs* (+ pr); *The Darktown Belle* (+ pr); *A Little Hero* (+ pr); *Mabel's Awful Mistake* (+ pr, role); *The Foreman and the Jury* (+ pr); *The Gangster* (+ pr); *Barney Oldfield's Race for a Life* (+ pr, role); *Passions—He Had Three* (+ pr); *Help! Help! Hydrophobia!* (+ pr); *The Hansom Driver* (+ pr, role); *The Speed Queen* (+ pr); *The Waiter's Picnic* (+ pr); *The Tale of the Black Eye* (+ pr); *Out and In* (+ pr); *A Bandit* (+ pr); *Peeping Pete* (+ pr); *His Crooked Career* (+ pr, role); *For Love of Mabel* (+ pr); *Safe in Jail* (+ pr); *The Telltale Light* (+ pr); *Love and Rubbish* (+ pr); *A Noise from the Deep* (+ pr); *The Peddler* (+ pr); *Love and Courage* (+ pr); *Professor Bean's Removal* (+ pr); *Cohen's Outing* (+ pr); *The Firebugs* (+ pr); *Baby Day* (+ pr); *Mabel's New Hero* (+ pr); *Mabel's Dramatic Career* (+ pr, role); *The Gypsy Queen* (+ pr); *Willie Minds the Dog* (+ pr); *When Dreams Come True* (+ pr); *Mother's Boy* (+ pr); *The Bowling Match* (+ pr); *The Speed Kings* (+ pr); *Love Sickness at Sea* (+ pr, role); *A Muddy Romance* (+ pr); *Cohen Saves the Flag* (+ pr); *Zuzu the Band Leader* (+ pr)

1914 *In the Clutches of the Gang* (+ pr); *Mabel's Strange Predicament* (co-d, pr); *Love and Gasoline* (+ pr); *Mack at it Again* (+ pr, role); *Mabel at the Wheel* (+ pr, role); *The Knockout* (+ pr); *A New York Girl* (+ pr, role); *His Talented Wife* (+ pr, role); *Tillie's Punctured Romance* (+ pr, feature); *The Fatal Mallet* (co-d with Chaplin, pr, role)

1915 *Hearts and Planets* (+ pr, role); *The Little Teacher* (+ pr, role); *My Valet* (+ pr, role); *A Favorite Fool* (+ pr); *Stolen Magic* (+ pr, role)

1921 *Oh, Mabel Behave* (co-d, pr, role)

1927 *A Finished Actor* (co-d, pr)

1928 *The Lion's Roar* (+ sc, pr)

1929 *The Bride's Relation* (+ pr); *The Old Barn* (+ pr); *Whirls and Girls* (+ pr); *Broadway Blues* (+ pr); *The Bee's Buzz* (+ pr); *Girl Crazy* (+ pr); *The Barber's Daughter* (+ pr); *Jazz Mamas* (+ pr); *The New Bankroll* (+ pr); *The Constable* (+ pr); *Midnight Daddies* (+ pr); *The Lunkhead* (+ pr); *The Golfers* (+ pr); *A Hollywood Star* (+ pr); *Scotch* (+ pr); *Sugar Plum Papa* (+ pr); *Bulls and Bears* (+ pr); *Match Play* (+ pr); *Honeymoon Zeppelin* (+ pr); *Fat Wives for Thin* (+ pr); *Campus Crushes* (+ pr); *The Chumps* (+ pr); *Goodbye Legs* (+ pr); *Average Husband* (+ pr); *Vacation Loves* (+ pr); *The Bluffer* (+ pr); *Grandma's Girl* (+ pr); *Divorced Sweethearts* (+ pr); *Racket Cheers* (+ pr); *Rough Idea of Love* (+ pr)

1931 *A Poor Fish* (+ pr); *Dance Hall Marge* (+ pr); *The Chiseler* (+ pr); *Ghost Parade* (+ pr); *Hollywood Happenings* (+ pr); *Hold 'er Sheriff* (+ pr); *Monkey Business in America* (+ pr); *Movie-Town* (+ pr, role); *The Albany Bunch* (+ pr); *I Surrender Dear* (+ pr); *Speed* (+ pr); *One More Chance* (+ pr)

1932 *Hypnotized* (+ pr, sc)

1935 *Ye Olde Saw Mill* (+ pr, sc); *Flicker Fever* (+ pr); *Just Another Murder* (+ sc, pr); *The Timid Young Man* (+ pr); *Way Up Thar* (+ pr)

Other Films:

(incomplete list)

1908 *Balked at the Altar* (Griffith) (role); *Father Gets in the Game* (Griffith) (role); *The Song of the Shirt* (Griffith) (role); *Mr. Jones at the Ball* (Griffith) (role)

1909 *Mr. Jones Has a Card Party* (Griffith) (role); *The Curtain Pole* (Griffith) (role); *The Politician's Love Story* (Griffith) (role); *The Lonely Villa* (Griffith) (role); *The Way of a Man* (Griffith) (role); *The Slave* (Griffith) (role); *Pippa Passes* (Griffith) (role); *The Gibson Goddess* (Griffith) (role); *Nursing a Viper* (Griffith) (role)

1910 *The Dancing Girl of Butte* (Griffith) (role); *All on Account of the Milk* (Griffith) (role); *The Englishman and the Girl* (Griffith) (role); *The Newlyweds* (Griffith) (role); *An Affair of Hearts* (Griffith) (role); *Never Again!* (Griffith) (role); *The Call to Arms* (Griffith) (role); *An Arcadian Maid* (Griffith) (role)

1911 *The Italian Barber* (Griffith) (role); *Paradise Lost* (Griffith) (role); *The White Rose of the Wilds* (Griffith) (role); *The Last Drop of Water* (Griffith) (role)

1912 *The Brave Hunter* (role)

1913 *Their First Execution* (pr); *Hubby's Job* (pr); *Betwixt Love and Fire* (pr); *Toplitsky and Company* (pr); *Feeding Time* (pr); *Largest Boat Ever Launched Sidewalks* (pr); *Rastus and the Game-Cock* (pr); *Get Rich Quick* (pr); *Just Kids* (pr); *A Game of Pool* (pr); *The Latest in Life Saving* (pr); *A Chip Off the Old Block* (pr); *The Kelp Industry* (pr); *Fatty's Day Off* (pr); *Los Angeles Harbour* (pr); *The New Baby* (pr); *What Father Saw* (pr); *The Faithful Taxicab* (pr); *Billy Dodges Bills* (pr); *Across the Alley* (pr); *The Abalone Industry* (pr); *Schnitz the Tailor* (pr); *Their Husbands* (pr); *A Healthy Neighborhood* (pr); *Two Old Tars* (pr); *A Quiet Little Wedding* (pr); *The Janitor* (pr); *The Making of an Automobile Tire* (pr); *Fatty at San Diego* (pr); *A Small Town Act* (pr); *The Milk We Drink* (pr); *Wine* (pr); *Our Children* (pr); *Fatty Joins the Force* (pr); *The Woman Haters* (pr); *The Rogues' Gallery* (pr); *The San Francisco Celebration* (pr); *A Ride for a Bride* (pr); *The Horse Thief* (pr); *The Gusher* (pr); *Fatty's Flirtation* (pr); *Protecting San Francisco from Fire* (pr); *His Sister's Kids* (pr); *A Bad Game* (pr); *Some Nerve* (pr); *The Champion* (pr); *He Would A Hunting Go* (pr)

1914 *A Misplaced Foot* (pr); *A Glimpse of Los Angeles* (pr); *Love and Dynamite* (pr); *Mabel's Stormy Love Affair* (pr); *The Under Sheriff* (pr); *A Flirt's Mistake* (pr); *How Motion Pictures Are Made* (pr); *Too Many Brides* (pr); *Won in a Closet* (pr); *Rebecca's Wedding Day* (pr); *Little Billy Triumphs* (pr); *Mabel's Bare Escape* (pr); *Making A Living* (pr); *Little Billy's Strategy* (pr); *Kid Auto Races at Venice* (pr); *Olives and their Oil* (pr); *A Robust Romeo* (pr); *Raffles* (pr); *Gentleman Burglar* (pr); *A Thief Catcher* (pr); *Twixt Love and Fire* (pr); *Little Billy's City Cousin* (pr); *Between Showers* (pr); *A Film Johnnie* (pr); *Tango Tangles* (pr); *His Favorite Pastime* (pr); *A Rural Demon* (pr); *The Race* (*How Villains Are Made*) (pr); *Across the Hall* (pr); *Cruel, Cruel Love* (pr); *Barnyard Flirtations* (pr); *A Back Yard Theater* (pr); *Chicken Chaser* (pr); *The Star Boarder* (pr); *Fatal High* (pr); *The Passing of Izzy* (pr); *A Bathing Beauty* (*A Bathhouse Beauty*) (pr); *Twenty Minutes of Love* (pr); *Where Hazel Met the Villain* (pr); *Bowery Boys* (pr); *Caught in a Cabaret* (pr); *When Villains Wait* (pr); *Caught in the Rain* (pr); *A Busy Day* (pr); *The Morning Papers* (pr); *A Suspended Ordeal* (pr); *Finnegan's Bomb* (pr); *Mabel's Nerve* (pr); *The Water Dog* (pr); *When Reuben Fooled the Bandits* (pr); *Acres of Alfalfa* (pr); *Our Large Birds* (pr); *The Fatal Flirtation* (pr); *The Alarm* (pr); *The Fatal Mallet* (pr); *Her Friend the Bandit* (pr); *Our Country Cousin* (pr); *Mabel's Busy Day* (pr); *A Gambling Rube* (pr); *A Missing Bride* (pr); *Mabel's Married Life* (pr); *The Eavesdropper* (pr); *Fatty and the Heiress* (pr); *Caught in Tights* (pr); *Fatty's Finish* (pr); *Love and Bullets* (pr); *Row-Boat Romance* (pr); *Laughing Gas* (pr); *Love and Salt Water* (pr); *World's Oldest Living Thing* (pr); *Mabel's New Job* (pr); *The Sky Pirate* (pr); *The Fatal Sweet Tooth* (pr); *Those Happy Days* (pr); *The Great Toe Mystery* (pr); *Soldiers of Misfortune* (pr); *The Property Man* (pr, role); *A Coat's Tale* (pr); *The Face on the Barroom Floor* (pr); *Recreation* (pr); *The Yosemite* (pr); *Such a Cook* (pr); *That Minstrel Man* (pr); *Those Country Kids* (pr); *Caught in a Flue* (pr); *Fatty's Gift* (pr); *The Masquerader* (pr); *Her Last Chance* (pr); *His New Profession* (pr); *The Baggage Smasher* (pr); *A Brand New Hero* (pr); *The Rounders* (pr); *Mabel's Latest Prank* (pr); *Mabel's Blunder* (pr); *All at Sea* (pr); *Bombs and Bangs* (pr); *Lover's Luck* (pr); *He Loved the Ladies* (pr); *The New Janitor* (pr); *Fatty's Debut* (pr); *Hard Cider* (pr); *Killing Hearts* (pr); *Fatty Again* (pr); *Their Ups and Downs* (pr); *Hello Mabel* (pr); *Those Love Pangs* (pr); *The Anglers* (pr); *The High Spots on Broadway* (pr); *Zipp, the Dodger* (pr); *Dash, Love and Splash* (pr); *Santa Catalina Islands* (pr); *The Love Thief* (pr); *Stout Heart But Weak Knees* (pr); *Shot in the Excitement* (pr); *Doug and Dynamite* (pr); *Gentlemen of Nerve* (pr); *Lovers' Post Office* (pr); *Curses! They Remarked* (pr); *His Musical Career* (pr); *His Trysting Place* (pr); *An Incompetent Hero* (pr); *How Heroes Are Made* (pr); *Fatty's Jonah Day* (pr); *The Noise of Bombs* (pr); *Fatty's Wine Party* (pr); *His Taking Ways* (pr); *The Sea Nymphs* (pr); *His Halted Career* (pr); *Among the Mourners* (pr); *Leading Lizzie Astray* (pr); *Shotguns That Kick* (pr); *Getting Acquainted* (pr); *Other People's Business* (pr); *His Prehistoric Past* (pr); *The Plumber* (pr); *Ambrose's First Falsehood* (pr); *Fatty's Magic Pants* (pr); *Hogan's Annual Spree* (pr); *A Colored Girl's Love* (pr); *Wild West Love* (pr); *Fatty and Minnie-He-Haw* (pr); *His Second Childhood* (pr); *Gussle the Golfer* (pr); *Hogan's Wild Oats* (pr); *A Steel Rolling Mill* (pr); *The Knockout* (Chaplin) (role)

1915 *A Dark Lover's Play* (pr); *Hushing the Scandal* (pr); *His Winning Punch* (pr); *U.S. Army in San Francisco* (pr); *Giddy, Gay and Ticklish* (pr); *Only A Farmer's Daughter* (pr); *Rum and Wall Paper* (pr); *Mabel's and Fatty's Wash Day* (pr); *Hash House Mashers* (pr); *Love, Speed, and Thrills* (pr); *Mabel and Fatty's Simple Life* (pr); *Hogan's Messy Job* (pr); *Fatty and Mabel at the San Diego Exposition* (pr); *Colored Villainy* (pr); *Mabel, Fatty and the Law* (pr); *Peanuts and Bullets* (pr); *The Home Breakers* (pr); *Fatty's New Role* (pr); *Hogan the Porter* (pr); *Caught in the Park* (pr); *A Bird's a Bird* (pr); *Hogan's Romance Upset* (pr); *Hogan's Aristocratic Dream* (pr); *Ye Olden Grafter* (pr); *A Glimpse of the San Diego Exposition* (pr); *A Lucky Leap* (pr); *That Springtime Fellow* (pr); *Hogan Out West* (pr); *Ambrose's Sour Grapes* (pr); *Wilful Ambrose* (pr); *Fatty's Reckless Fling* (pr); *From Patches to Plenty* (pr); *Fatty's Chance Acquaintance* (pr); *Love in Armor* (pr); *Beating Hearts and Carpets* (pr); *That Little Band of Gold* (pr); *Ambrose's Little Hatchet* (pr); *Fatty's Faithful Fido* (pr); *A One Night Stand* (pr); *Ambrose's Fury* (pr); *Gussie's Day of Rest* (pr); *When Love Took Wings* (pr); *Ambrose's Lofty Perch* (pr); *Droppington's Devilish Dream* (pr); *The Rent Jumpers* (pr); *Droppington's Family Tree* (pr); *The Beauty Bunglers* (pr); *Do-Re-Mi-Fa* (pr); *Ambrose's Nasty Temper* (pr); *Fatty and Mabel View-*

ing the World's Fair at San Francisco (pr); *Love, Loot and Crash* (pr); *Gussie Rivals Jonah* (pr); *Their Social Splash* (pr); *A Bear Affair* (pr); *Mabel's Wilful Way* (pr); *Gussie's Backward Way* (pr); *A Human Hound's Triumph* (pr); *Our Dare Devil Chief* (pr); *Crossed Love and Swords* (pr); *Miss Fatty's Seaside Lover* (pr); *He Wouldn't Stay Down* (pr); *For Better—But Worse* (pr); *A Versatile Villain* (pr); *Those College Girls* (pr); *Mabel Lost and Won* (pr); *Those Bitter Sweets* (pr); *The Cannon Ball* (pr); *A Home Breaking Hound* (pr); *Foiled by Fido* (pr); *Court House Crooks* (pr); *When Ambrose Dared Walrus* (pr); *Dirty Work in a Laundry* (pr); *Fido's Tin-Type Tangle* (pr); *A Lover's Lost Control* (pr); *A Rascal of Wolfish Ways* (pr); *The Battle of Ambrose and Walrus* (pr); *Only a Messenger Boy* (pr); *Caught in the Act* (pr); *His Luckless Love* (pr); *Viewing Sherman Institute for Indians at Riverside* (pr); *Wished on Mabel* (pr); *Gussie's Wayward Path* (pr); *Settled at the Seaside* (pr); *Gussie Tied to Trouble* (pr); *A Hash House Fraud* (pr); *Merely a Married Man* (pr); *A Game Old Knight* (pr); *Her Painted Hero* (pr); *Saved by Wireless* (pr); *Fickle Fatty's Fall* (pr); *His Father's Footsteps* (pr); *The Best of Enemies* (pr); *A Janitor's Wife's Temptation* (pr); *A Village Scandal* (pr); *The Great Vacuum Robbery* (pr); *Crooked to the End* (pr); *Fatty and the Broadway Stars* (pr, role); *A Submarine Pirate* (pr); *The Hunt* (pr)

1916 *The Worst of Friends* (pr); *Dizzy Heights and Daring Hearts* (pr); *The Great Pearl Tangle* (pr); *Fatty and Mabel Adrift* (pr); *Because He Loved Her* (pr); *A Modern Enoch Arden* (pr); *Perils of the Park* (pr); *A Movie Star* (pr); *His Hereafter* (pr); *He Did and He Didn't* (*Love and Lobsters*) (pr); *Love Will Conquer* (pr); *His Pride and Shame* (pr); *Fido's Fate* (pr); *Better Late Than Never* (pr); *Bright Lights* (pr); *Cinders of Love* (pr); *Wife and Auto Troubles* (pr); *The Judge* (pr); *A Village Vampire* (pr); *The Village Blacksmith* (pr); *A Love Riot* (pr); *Gipsy Joe* (pr); *By Stork Delivery* (pr); *An Oily Scoundrel* (pr); *A Bathhouse Blunder* (pr); *His Wife's Mistake* (pr); *His Bread and Butter* (pr); *His Last Laugh* (pr); *Bucking Society* (pr); *The Other Man* (pr); *The Snow Cure* (pr); *A Dash Of Courage* (pr); *The Lion and the Girl* (pr); *His Bitter Pill* (pr); *Her Marble Heart* (pr); *Bathtub Perils* (pr); *The Moonshiners* (pr); *Hearts and Sparks* (pr); *His Wild Oats* (pr); *Ambrose's Cup of Woe* (pr); *The Waiter's Ball* (pr); *The Surf Girl* (pr); *A Social Club* (pr); *Vampire Ambrose* (pr); *The Winning Punch* (pr); *His Lying Heart* (pr); *She Loved a Sailor* (pr); *His Auto Ruination* (pr); *Ambrose's Rapid Rise* (pr); *His Busted Trust* (pr); *Tugboat Romeos* (pr); *Sunshine* (pr); *Her Feathered Nest* (pr); *No One to Guide Him* (pr); *Her First Beau* (pr); *His First False Step* (pr); *The Houseboat* (pr); *The Fire Chief* (pr); *Love on Skates* (pr); *His Alibi* (pr); *Love Comet* (pr); *A la Cabaret* (pr); *Haystacks and Steeples* (pr); *A Scoundrel's Toll* (pr); *The Three Slims* (pr); *The Girl Guardian* (pr); *Wings and Wheels* (pr); *Safety First Ambrose* (pr); *Maid Mad* (pr); *The Twins* (pr); *Piles of Perils* (pr); *A Cream Puff Romance* (pr); *The Danger Girl* (pr); *Bombs* (pr); *His Last Scent* (pr); *The Manicurist* (pr)

1917 *The Nick of Time Baby* (pr); *Stars and Bars* (pr); *Maggie's First False Step* (pr); *Villa of the Movies* (pr); *Dodging His Doom* (pr); *Her Circus Knight* (pr); *Her Fame and Shames* (pr); *Pinched in the Finish* (pr); *Her Nature Dance* (pr); *Teddy at the Throttle* (pr); *Secrets of a Beauty Parlor* (pr); *A Maiden's Trust* (pr); *His Naughty Thought* (pr); *Her Torpedoed Love* (pr); *A Royal Rogue* (pr); *Oriental Love* (pr); *Cactus Nell* (pr); *The Betrayal of Maggie* (pr); *Skidding Hearts* (pr); *The Dog Catcher's Love* (pr); *Whose Baby* (pr); *Dangers of a Bride* (pr); *A Clever Dummy* (pr); *She Needed a Doctor* (pr); *Thirst* (pr); *His Uncle Dudley* (pr); *Lost a Cook* (pr); *The Pawnbroker's Heart* (pr); *Two Crooks* (pr); *A Shanghaied Jonah* (pr); *His Precious Life* (pr); *Hula Hula Land* (pr); *The Late Lamented* (pr); *The Sultan's Wife* (pr); *A Bedroom Blunder* (pr); *Roping Her Romeo* (pr); *The Pullman Bride* (pr); *Are Waitresses Safe* (pr); *An International Sneak* (pr); *That Night* (pr); *Taming Target Center* (pr)

1918 *The Kitchen Lady* (pr); *His Hidden Purpose* (pr); *Watch Your Neighbors* (pr); *It Pays to Exercise* (pr); *Sheriff Nell's Tussle* (pr); *Those Athletic Girls* (pr); *Friend Husband* (pr); *Saucy Madeline* (pr); *His Smothered Love* (pr); *The Battle Royal* (pr); *Love Loops the Loop* (pr); *Two Tough Tenderfeet* (pr); *Her Screen Idol* (pr); *Ladies First* (pr); *Her Blighted Love* (pr); *She Loved Him Plenty* (pr); *The Summer Girls* (pr); *Mickey* (pr); *His Wife's Friend* (pr); *Sleuths* (pr); *Beware the Boarders* (pr); *Whose Little Wife Are You* (pr); *Her First Mistake* (pr); *Hide and Seek Detectives* (pr); *The Village Chestnut* (pr)

1919 *Cupid's Day Off* (pr); *Never Too Old* (pr); *Rip & Stitch, Tailors* (pr); *East Lynne with Variations* (pr); *The Village Smithy* (pr); *Reilly's Wash Day* (pr); *The Foolish Age* (pr); *The Little Widow* (pr); *When Love is Blind* (pr); *Love's False Faces* (pr); *Hearts and Flowers* (pr); *No Mother to Guide Him* (pr); *Trying to Get Along* (pr); *Among Those Present* (pr); *Yankee Doodle in Berlin* (pr); *Why Beaches Are Popular* (pr); *Treating 'em Rough* (pr); *A Lady's Tailor* (pr); *Uncle Tom Without the Cabin* (pr); *The Dentist* (pr); *Back to the Kitchen* (pr); *Up in Alf's Place* (pr); *Salome vs. Shenandoah* (pr); *His Last False Step* (pr); *The Speak Easy* (pr)

1920 *The Star Boarder* (pr); *Ten Dollars or Ten Days* (pr); *Gee Whiz* (pr); *The Gingham Girl* (pr); *Down on the Farm* (pr); *Fresh from the City* (pr); *Let 'er Go* (pr); *By Golly* (pr); *You Wouldn't Believe It* (pr); *Married Life* (pr); *The Quack Doctor* (pr); *Great Scott* (pr); *Don't Weaken* (pr); *It's a Boy* (pr); *Young Man's Fancy* (pr); *His Youthful Fancy* (pr); *My Goodness* (pr); *Movie Fans* (pr); *Fickle Fancy* (pr); *Love, Honor, and Behave* (pr); *A Fireside Brewer* (*Home Brew*) (pr); *Bungalow Troubles* (pr)

1921 *Dabbling in Art* (pr); *An Unhappy Finish* (pr); *On a Summer's Day* (pr); *A Small Town Idol* (pr, sc); *Wedding Bells Out of Tune* (pr); *Officer Cupid* (pr); *Away from the Steerage* (*Astray from the Steerage*) (pr); *Sweetheart Days* (pr); *Home Talent* (pr, sc); *She Sighed by the Seaside* (pr); *Hard Knocks and Love Taps* (pr); *Made in the Kitchen* (pr); *Call a Cop* (pr); *Love's Outcast* (pr); *Molly O* (pr, sc)

1922 *By Heck* (pr); *Be Reasonable* (pr); *Bright Eyes* (pr); *The Duck Hunter* (pr); *On Patrol* (pr); *Step Forward* (pr); *Gymnasium Jim* (pr); *The Crossroads of New York* (pr, sc); *Oh Daddy!* (pr); *Home-Made Movies* (pr); *Ma and Pa* (pr); *Bow Wow* (pr); *Love and Doughnuts* (pr); *When Summer Comes* (pr)

1923 *Suzanna* (pr); *The Shriek of Araby* (pr, sc); *Where is My Wandering Boy This Evening* (pr); *Nip and Tuck* (pr); *Pitfalls of a Big City* (pr); *Skylarking* (pr); *Down to the Sea in Shoes* (pr); *The Extra Girl* (pr, co-sc); *Asleep at the Switch* (pr); *One Cylinder Love* (pr); *The Dare-Devil* (pr); *Flip Flops* (pr); *Inbad the Sailor* (pr)

1924 *Ten Dollars or Ten Days* (remake, pr); *One Spooky Night* (pr); *Picking Peaches* (pr); *The Half-Back of Notre Dame* (pr); *Smile Please* (pr); *Scarem Much* (pr); *Shanghaied Ladies* (pr); *The Hollywood Kid* (pr); *Flickering Youth* (pr); *Black Oxfords* (pr); *The Cat's Meow* (pr); *Yukon Jake* (pr); *The Lion and the Souse* (pr); *His New Mama* (pr); *Romeo and Juliet* (pr); *Wall Street Blues* (pr); *The First Hundred Years* (pr); *East of the Water Plug* (pr, sc); *Lizzies of the Field* (pr);

The Luck of the Foolish (pr); *Three Foolish Wives* (pr); *Little Robinson Corkscrew* (pr); *The Hansom Cabman* (*Be Careful*) (pr); *Riders of the Purple Cows* (pr); *The Reel Virginian* (*The West Virginian*) (pr); *Galloping Bungalows* (pr); *All Night Long* (pr); *Love's Sweet Piffle* (pr); *The Cannon Ball Express* (pr); *Feet of Mud* (pr); *Off His Trolley* (pr); *Bull and Sand* (pr); *Watch Out* (pr); *Over Here* (pr); *The Lady Barber* (pr); *North of 57* (pr); *Love's Intrigue* (pr); *The Stunt Man* (pr)

1925 *The Sea Squaw* (pr); *The Plumber* (pr); *The Wild Goose Chaser* (pr); *Honeymoon Hardships* (pr); *Boobs in the Woods* (pr); *The Beloved Bozo* (pr); *Water Wagons* (pr); *His Marriage Wow* (pr); *The Raspberry Romance* (pr); *Bashful Jim* (pr); *Giddap* (pr); *Plain Clothes* (pr); *Breaking the Ice* (pr); *The Marriage Circus* (pr); *The Lion's Whiskers* (pr); *Remember When* (pr); *He Who Gets Smacked* (pr); *Skinners in Silk* (pr); *Good Morning, Nurse!* (pr); *Super-Hooper-Dyne Lizzies* (pr); *Don't Tell Dad* (pr); *Isn't Love Cuckoo* (pr); *Sneezing Breezes* (pr); *Cupid's Boots* (pr); *Tee for Two* (pr); *The Iron Nag* (pr); *Lucky Stars* (pr); *Cold Turkey* (pr); *Butter Fingers* (pr); *There He Goes* (pr); *Hurry, Doctor* (pr); *A Rainy Knight* (pr); *Love and Kisses* (pr); *Over There-Abouts* (pr); *Good Morning, Madam* (pr); *A Sweet Pickle* (pr); *Dangerous Curves Behind* (pr); *The Soapsuds Lady* (pr); *Take Your Time* (pr); *The Window Dummy* (pr); *From Rags to Britches* (pr); *Hotsy Toty* (pr)

1926 *The Gosh-Darn Mortgage* (pr); *Wide Open Faces* (pr); *Hot Cakes for Two* (pr); *Whispering Whiskers* (pr); *Saturday Afternoon* (pr); *Funnymooners* (pr); *Trimmed in Gold* (pr); *Gooseland* (pr); *Circus Today* (pr); *Meet My Girl* (pr); *Spanking Breezes* (pr); *Wandering Willies* (pr); *Hooked at the Altar* (pr); *A Love Sundae* (pr); *Soldier Man* (pr); *The Ghost of Folly* (pr); *Fight Night* (pr); *Hayfoot, Strawfoot* (pr); *A Yankee Doodle Dude* (pr); *Muscle-Bound Music* (pr); *Oh, Uncle!* (pr); *Puppy Lovetime* (pr); *Ice Cold Cocos* (pr); *A Dinner Jest* (pr); *A Sea Dog's Tale* (pr); *Baby's Pets* (pr); *A Bachelor Butt-in* (pr); *Smith's Baby* (pr); *Alice Be Good* (pr); *When a Man's a Prince* (pr); *Smith's Vacation* (pr); *Hubby's Quiet Little Game* (pr); *Her Actor Friend* (pr); *Hoboken to Hollywood* (pr); *The Prodigal Bridegroom* (pr); *The Perils of Petersboro* (pr); *Smith's Landlord* (pr); *Love's Last Laugh* (pr); *Smith's Visitor* (pr); *Should Husbands Marry* (pr); *Masked Mamas* (pr); *A Harem Knight* (pr); *Smith's Uncle* (pr); *Hesitating Houses* (pr); *The Divorce Dodger* (pr); *A Blonde's Revenge* (pr); *Flirty Four-Flushers* (pr); *Smith's Picnic* (pr)

1927 *Kitty from Killarney* (pr); *Smith's Pets* (pr); *Should Sleepwalkers Marry* (pr); *Pass the Dumpling* (pr); *A Hollywood Hero* (pr); *Smith's Customer* (pr); *Peaches and Plumbers* (pr); *Plumber's Daughter* (pr); *A Small Town Princess* (pr); *A Dozen Socks* (pr); *The Jolly Jilter* (pr); *Smith's Surprise* (pr); *Smith's New Home* (pr); *Broke in China* (pr); *Smith's Kindergarten* (pr); *Crazy to Act* (pr); *Smith Fishing Trip* (pr); *His First Flame* (pr); *Pride of Pickeville* (pr); *Cured in the Excitement* (pr); *Catalina, Here I Come* (pr); *The Pest of Friends* (pr); *Love's Languid Lure* (pr); *College Kiddo* (pr); *Smith's Candy Shop* (pr); *The Golf Nut* (pr); *Smith's Pony* (pr); *A Gold Digger of Weepah* (pr); *Smith's Cook* (pr); *Daddy Boy* (pr); *For Sale a Bungalow* (pr); *Smith's Cousin* (pr); *The Bull Fighter* (pr); *Fiddlesticks* (pr); *Smith's Modiste Shop* (pr); *The Girl from Everywhere* (pr); *Love in a Police Station* (pr); *Hold that Pose* (pr)

1928 *Smith's Holiday* (pr); *Run, Girl, Run* (pr); *The Beach Club* (pr); *Love at First Sight* (pr); *Smith's Army Life* (pr); *The Best Man* (pr); *The Swan Princess* (pr); *Smith's Farm Days* (pr); *The Bicycle Flirt* (pr); *The Girl From Nowhere* (pr); *His Unlucky Night* (pr); *Smith's Restaurant* (pr); *The Goodbye Kiss* (pr); *The Chicken* (pr); *Taxi for Two* (pr); *Caught in the Kitchen* (pr); *A Dumb Waiter* (pr); *The Campus Carmen* (pr); *Motor Boat Mamas* (pr); *The Bargain Hunt* (pr); *Smith's Catalina Rowboat Race* (*Catalina Rowboat Race*) (pr); *A Taxi Scandal* (pr); *Hubby's Latest Alibi* (pr); *A Jim Jam Janitor* (pr); *The Campus Vamp* (pr); *Hubby's Weekend Trip* (pr); *The Burglar* (pr); *Taxi Beauties* (pr); *His New Stenographer* (pr)

1929 *Clunked on the Corner* (pr); *Baby's Birthday* (pr); *Uncle Tom* (pr); *Calling Hubby's Bluff* (pr); *Taxi Spooks* (pr); *Button My Back* (pr); *Ladies Must Eat* (pr); *Foolish Husbands* (pr); *Matchmaking Mamas* (pr); *The Rodeo* (pr); *Pink Pajamas* (pr); *The Night Watchman's Mistake* (pr); *The New Aunt* (pr); *Taxi Dolls* (pr); *Don't Get Jealous* (pr); *Caught in a Taxi* (pr); *A Close Shave* (pr); *The Big Palooka* (pr); *Motoring Mamas* (pr); *Clancy at the Bat* (pr); *The New Half-Back* (pr); *Uppercut O'Brien* (pr)

1930 *He Trumped Her Ace* (pr); *Radio Kisses* (pr); *Hello Television* (pr); *Take Your Medicine* (pr); *Don't Bite Your Dentist* (pr); *Strange Birds* (pr); *A Hollywood Theme Song* (pr)

1931 *No, No, Lady* (pr); *One Yard to Go* (pr); *The College Vamp* (remake, pr); *The Bride's Mistake* (pr); *The Dog Doctor* (pr); *Just a Bear* (*It's a Bear*) (pr); *Ex-Sweeties* (pr); *In Conference* (pr); *The Cowcatcher's Daughter* (pr); *Slide, Speedy, Slide* (pr); *Fainting Lover* (pr); *Too Many Husbands* (pr); *The Cannonball* (pr); *The Trail of the Swordfish* (pr); *Poker Windows* (pr); *The World Flier* (pr); *Who's Who in the Zoo* (pr); *Taxi Troubles* (pr); *The Great Pie Mystery* (pr); *Wrestling Swordfish* (pr); *All American Kickback* (pr); *Half Holiday* (pr); *The Pottsville Palooka* (pr)

1932 *Playgrounds of the Mammals* (pr); *Dream House* (pr); *The Girl in the Tonneau* (pr); *Shopping with Wife* (pr); *Lady! Please!* (pr); *Heavens! My Husband!* (pr); *The Billboard Girl* (pr); *The Flirty Sleepwalker* (pr); *Speed in the Gay Nineties* (pr); *Man-Eating Sharks* (pr); *Listening In* (pr); *The Spot in the Rug* (pr); *Divorce a la Mode* (pr); *The Boudoir Brothers* (pr); *Freaks of the Deep* (pr); *The Candid Camera* (pr); *Sea Going Birds* (pr); *Hatta Marri* (pr); *Alaska Love* (pr); *For the Love of Ludwig* (pr); *Neighbor Trouble* (pr); *His Royal Shyness* (pr); *Young Onions* (pr); *The Giddy Age* (pr); *Lighthouse Love* (pr); *Hawkins and Watkins* (pr); *The Singing Plumber* (pr); *Courting Trouble* (pr); *False Impressions* (pr); *Bring Back 'em Sober* (pr); *A Hollywood Double* (pr); *The Dentist* (pr); *Doubling in the Quickies* (pr); *The Lion and the House* (pr); *Human Fish* (pr)

1933 *Blue of the Night* (pr); *The Wrestlers* (*A Wrestler's Bride*) (pr); *Don't Play Bridge with Your Wife* (pr); *The Singing Boxer* (pr); *Too Many Highballs* (pr); *Easy on the Eyes* (pr); *A Fatal Glass of Beer* (pr); *Caliente Love* (pr); *Sing, Bing, Sing* (pr); *The Plumber and the Lady* (pr); *Sweet Cookie* (pr); *The Pharmacist* (pr); *Uncle Jake* (pr); *Dream Stuff* (pr); *Roadhouse Queen* (pr); *See You Tonight* (pr); *Daddy Knows Best* (pr); *Knockout Kisses* (pr); *Husband's Reunion* (pr); *The Big Fibber* (pr); *The Barber Shop* (pr)

1939 *Hollywood Cavalcade* (role)

1949 *Down Memory Lane* (role)

Publications

By SENNETT: book—

Mack Sennett: King of Comedy, as Told to Cameron Shipp, New York, 1954.

By SENNETT: article—

Interview with T. Dreiser, in *Photoplay* (New York), August 1928.

On SENNETT: books—

Lejeune, C.A., *Mack Sennett,* London, 1931.
Fowler, Gene, *Father Goose: the Story of Mack Sennett,* New York, 1934.
Chevallier, Jacques, *Le Cinéma burlesque américain, 1912-30,* Paris, 1964.
Turconi, David, *Mack Sennett,* Paris, 1966.
Geduld, Harry M., editor, *Film Makers on Filmmaking,* Bloomington, Indiana, 1967.
Lahue, Kalton C., *Dreams for Sale: The Rise and Fall of the Triangle Film Corporation,* New York, 1971.
Lahue, Kalton C., *Mack Sennett's Keystone: The Man, the Myth, and the Comedies,* South Brunswick, New Jersey, 1971.
Pratt, George C., *Spellbound in Darkness,* Greenwich, Connecticut, 1973.
Mast, Gerald, *The Comic Mind: Comedy and the Movies,* Chicago, 1974; revised edition, 1979.

On SENNETT: articles—

Carr, H.C., "Mack Sennett—Laugh Tester," in *Photoplay* (New York), May 1915.
Carr, H., "The Secret of Making Film Comedies," in *Motion Picture Classic* (Brooklyn), October 1925.
Manners, D., "Defense of Low-Brow Comedy," in *Motion Picture Classic* (Brooklyn), October 1930.
Agee, James, "Comedy's Greatest Era," in *Life* (New York), 5 September 1949.
Knight, Arthur, "Era of Great Comedians," in the *Saturday Review* (New York), 18 December 1954.
Dyer, Peter John, "Cops, Custard, and Keaton," in *Films and Filming* (London), August 1958.
"Sennett Issue" of *Cinéma* (Paris), August/September 1960.
"Sennett Issue" of *Image et Son* (Paris), April 1964.
Durgnat, Raymond, "The World of Comedy: Breaking the Laugh Barrier," in *Films and Filming* (London), October 1965.
Giroux, Robert, "Mack Sennett," in *Films in Review* (New York), December 1968.
Hoffner, J.R., "King of Keystone," in *Classic Film Collector* (Indiana, Pennsylvania), Summer 1971.
Bodeen, Dewitt, "All the Sad Young Bathing Beauties," in *Focus on Film* (London), Autumn 1974.
"Mack Sennett Section" of *Cinema Nuovo* (Bari), April 1984.
Stempel, T., "The Sennett Screenplays," in *Sight and Sound* (London), Winter 1985/86.

* * *

Mack Sennett was the outstanding pioneer and primitive of American silent comedy. Although Sennett's name is most commonly associated with the Keystone Company, which he founded in 1912, Sennett's film career began four years earlier with the Biograph Company, the pioneering film company where D.W. Griffith established the principles of film narrative and rhetoric. Sennett and Griffith were colleagues and contemporaries, and Sennett served as actor, writer, and assistant under Griffith in 1908 and 1909. In 1910 he began his career as director of his own films under Griffith's supervision.

Sennett became associated with comic roles and comic films from the beginning under Griffith. In his first major role for Griffith, *The Curtain Pole* in 1908, Sennett played a comically drunk Frenchman who visits chaos upon all he meets in a desperate race through town to replace a broken curtain rod. The film contains several traits that would become associated with the mature Sennett style: the breathless chase, the reduction of human beings to venal stereotypes, the reduction of human society and its physical surroundings to chaotic rubble, and a fondness for games concerning the cinema mechanism itself, manifested in the use of accelerated (by undercranking) and reverse motion. In other roles for Griffith, Sennett consistently played the comic rube or dumb servant—roles that took advantage of Sennett's shambling bulk and oafish facial expressions.

According to legend, Sennett founded the Keystone Company when he conned his bookies, Adam Kessel and Charles Bauman, to go double or nothing on his gambling debts and stake him to a film company. Kessel and Bauman, however, had been out of the bookmaking business and in the moviemaking business for at least five years as owners of Thomas Ince's flourishing New York Motion Picture Company. Between late 1912 and early 1914, Sennett assembled a troupe of the finest raucous physical comedians and burlesque clowns in the film business. From Biograph he brought the pretty Mabel Normand, who was also an extremely agile and athletic physical comedienne, and the loony Ford Sterling, with his big-gesturing burlesque of villainy and lechery. Among the other physical comedians he found in those years were the burly Mack Swain, the tiny Chester Conklin, the round Fatty Arbuckle, and the cross-eyed Ben Turpin. He also discovered such future comic stars as Charles Chaplin, Harold Lloyd, and Harry Langdon, as well as the future director of sound comedies, Frank Capra. Perhaps more important than any artistic contribution was Sennett's managerial ability to spot comic talent and give it the opportunity to display itself.

At the root of Sennett's comic style was the brash, the vulgar, and the burlesque. His films parodied the serious film and stage hits of the day, always turning the serious romance or melodrama into outrageous nonsense. There were no serious moral, psychological, or social issues in Sennett films, simply raucous burlesque of social or emotional material. His short comedies were exuberantly impolite and often made public jokes out of ethnic, sexual, or racial stereotypes. Among the characters around whom he built film series were the Germans Meyer and Heinie, the Jewish Cohen, and the black Rastus. Many of these films were so brashly vulgar in their stereotypical humor that they cannot be shown in public today. As indicators of social attitudes of the 1910s, these films seem to suggest that the still largely immigrant American society of that time was more willing to make and respond to jokes openly based on ethnic and sexist stereotypes than they are today in an era of greater sensitivity to the potential harm of these stereotypes. In defense of Sennett's making sport of ethnic types, it must be said that the method and spirit was consistent with his films' refusal to take any social or psychological matters seriously.

Sennett's Keystone films were extremely improvisational; a typical formula was to take a camera, a bucket of whitewash, and four clowns (two male, two female) out to a park and make a movie. Sennett's aesthetic was not so much an art that conceals art but an art that derides art. His many Keystone films reveal the same contempt for orderly, careful, well-crafted art that one can see in the Marx Brothers' Paramount films or W.C. Fields's Universal films two decades later. The one conscious artistic tool which Sennett exploited was speed—keeping the actors, the action, the gags, the machines, and the camera in perpetual speeding motion. The typical Keystone title might be something like *Love, Speed, and Thrills* or *Love, Loot, and Crash.*

Among other Sennett inventions were the Keystone Kops, a burlesque of attempts at social order, and the Bathing Beauties, a burlesque of attempts at pornographic sexuality. Sennett served his apprenticeship in the American burlesque theater, and he brought to the Keystone films that same kind of entertainment which took place at the intersection of vulgar lunacy and comic pornography.

Sennett's most memorable films include a series of domestic films starring Mabel Normand, married either to Fatty Arbuckle or Charlie

Mack Sennett

Chaplin; a series of films pairing the beefy Mack Swain and the diminutive Chester Conklin; a series featuring Ben Turpin as a cross-eyed burlesque of romantic movie stars; a series built around remarkably athletic automobiles and rampaging jungle beasts starring Billy Bevan; and a series of short films featuring the pixieish child-clown Harry Langdon. Sennett also produced and personally directed the first comic feature film produced in America (or anywhere else), *Tillie's Punctured Romance,* starring Chaplin, Normand, and stage comedienne Marie Dressler in her first film role.

Sennett ceased to direct films after 1914, becoming the producer and overseer of every comic film made by his company for the next two decades. Although the Keystone Company folded by the late 1910s, Sennett's immensely long filmography is a testament to the sheer number of comic films he produced, well into the sound era. Sennett's real importance to film history, however, derives from that crucial historical moment between 1912 and 1915, a period when a comic assumption, the evolution of film technique, and a collection of talented physical clowns all came together under Sennett's stewardship to create a unique and memorable type of comedy that has assumed its place not only in the history of cinema, but in the much longer history of comedy itself.

—Gerald Mast

SHAHINE, Youssef *See* **CHAHINE, Youssef**

SHERIDAN, Jim

Nationality: Irish. **Born:** Dublin, 6 February 1949. **Education:** Graduated from University College in Dublin; attended the New York University film school. **Career:** Worked as director-writer at the Lyric Theatre in Belfast and Abbey Theatre in Dublin, originated Children's Theatre Company in Dublin, and operated and wrote plays for the Project Arts Center, a Dublin alternative theater, 1970s-early 1980s; came to New York and became artistic director of the Irish Arts Center, 1982; made screen directorial debut with *My Left Foot,* 1989. **Awards:** Fringe Award for Best Play, Edinburgh Festival, 1983, for *Spike in the First World War*; Academy Award nominations, Best Picture, Best Director, and Best Screenplay, and Best Film, New York Film Critics Circle, 1989, for *My Left Foot*; Academy Award nominations, Best Picture, Best Director, and Best Screenplay, 1993, for *In the Name of the Father.*

Films as Director and Screenwriter:

1989 *My Left Foot* (co-sc)
1990 *The Field*
1993 *In the Name of the Father* (co-sc, + pr)

Other Films:

1993 *Into the West* (Newell) (sc)

Publications

By SHERIDAN: book—

My Left Foot, with Shane Connaughton, London, 1989.

On SHERIDAN: articles—

Mueller, Matt, "Paternal Affairs," in *Premiere* (New York), December 1993.
Boynton, Graham, "London Burning," in *Vanity Fair* (New York), January 1994.
Giles, Jeff, "Fathers, Sons and the IRA," in *Newsweek* (New York), 31 January 1994.
George, Terry, "Terry George on Jim Sheridan," in *New Yorker,* 21 March 1994.
Bland, E. L., "In the Name of the Truth," in *Time* (New York), 21 March 1994.
Grenier, Richard, "In the Name of the IRA," in *Commentary* (New York), April 1994.
O'Brien, C., "Patriot Games: The Distortions of *In the Name of the Father,*" in *New Republic* (Washington, D.C.), 9 May 1994.

* * *

The cinema of Jim Sheridan is at once deeply personal, humanistic, and politically committed. His scenarios (taken from real-life as well as fiction) are heartrending, and his characters, all vividly realized, are individuals determined to triumph over seemingly insurmountable obstacles. Sheridan's films are rooted in the culture, history, and politics of his native Ireland and, commercially as well as creatively, he has been at the vanguard of his country's film industry. In 1990, *The Field,* which he directed and scripted, was the number one box office champion in Ireland—the initial instance where an Irish film bested all foreign competition.

Perhaps Sheridan's best film to date is his first, *My Left Foot,* which movingly charts the triumph of an extraordinary individual. At his death in 1981, Christy Brown (played by Daniel Day-Lewis) was one of Ireland's foremost artistic and literary figures. Yet for Brown, it was no small achievement just to master the mundane. He was born with cerebral palsy, and he titled his autobiography *My Left Foot* because it was with this limb that he painted his pictures and wrote his stories. Sheridan's telling of Brown's life is so effective because he avoids mawkishness: by no means is Brown a cardboard cripple, a stereotypical figure to be pitied or feared. He is a complex character, with the wants, needs, and contradictions of any other man.

Like Sheridan's other heroes, Christy Brown is a man of the working class; his father was a Dublin bricklayer. *My Left Foot* reflects the importance of the familial bond as, without doubt, the love and support Brown receives from his family are crucial in enabling him to flourish as an artist.

If *My Left Foot* is the story of a man who transcends his physical limitations, *The Field* and *In the Name of the Father* tell of ordinary souls thrust into extraordinary situations. *The Field,* based on a play by John B. Keane, spotlights the plight of Bull McCabe (Richard Harris), an aging, charismatic peasant who has rented a field and devoted his life to developing it into a top-quality parcel of land. Even though he does not legally own the field, he has nurtured it as one would his own child. Then, he must contend with the news that the wealthy widow who owns the land plans to sell it at auction. The scenario pointedly reflects on Ireland's history and culture: it is set during the 1930s, with the memory of famine lingering in the minds of all the citizenry; and it offers a vivid portrait of traditional Irish village life. Furthermore, a focal point of the story is McCabe's conviction that he has come to own the land. This belief is distilled from Irish tribal laws which, to his mind, transcend contemporary law.

In the Name of the Father, based on Gerry Conlon's autobiographical book *Proved Innocent,* is an even more straightforward saga of blind injustice. It is the story of Conlon (Daniel Day-Lewis), an unfocused young Belfast man who, along with others (including several of his equally guiltless family members), is arrested by the British authorities and falsely charged with the 1974 terrorist bombing of a London pub. Conlon and three others came to be known as the Guildford Four, who spent over fifteen years in prison until their convictions were reversed. *In the Name of the Father* is provocative in its anti-British feel, as Conlon and company clearly are innocents who are railroaded by an unfeeling power structure which is unconcerned with smoking out the true culprits—and which withholds decisive evidence that would have exonerated the accused. The scenario reflects on the Irish-British conflict regarding the plight of Northern Ireland, while focusing on the manner in which the dissension adversely and tragically affects one Irish family. Beyond the politics of *In the Name of the Father,* the film is motivated by humanistic and familial concern. For years, Conlon shares a jail cell with his father, Giuseppe. Previously, the son had no admiration for his father, but as time passes they become united, resulting in a solid and poignant bond.

Like *The Field, In the Name of the Father* spotlights the individual's thirst for fairness. Gerry Conlon, like Bull McCabe, is keenly aware that he is a victim of injustice. In both cases, each man stubbornly persists in a single-minded pursuit of truth— just as Christy Brown perseveres in his determination to be viewed as a man without an affliction.

Sheridan's films are uniformly well-acted. Daniel Day-Lewis and Brenda Fricker (cast as Christy Brown's ever-supportive mother) won Oscars for their performances in *My Left Foot.* Richard Harris was nominated for *The Field,* while Day-Lewis, Pete Postlethwaite (as Giuseppe Conlon), and Emma Thompson (as the lawyer who uncovers the chicanery on the part of the Crown) were cited for *In the Name of the Father.*

—Rob Edelman

SHINDO, Kaneto

Nationality: Japanese. **Born:** Hiroshima Prefecture, 28 April 1912. **Family:** Married first wife, 1939 (died 1940); second wife (divorced late 1940s); actress Nobuko Otowa. **Career:** Joined art section of Shinko-Kinema Tokyo Studio, 1928; moved to scenario department, 1939; moved to Koa Film, from 1942 (absorbed by Shochiku-Ofuna Studio, 1943); with director Kosaburo Yoshimura, left Shochiku to form independent production company Kindai Eiga Kyokai, with producer Hisao Itoya, director Tengo Yamada, and actor Taiji Tonoyama, 1950; directed first film, 1951; became president of Japanese Association of Scenario Writers, 1972. **Awards:** Grand Prix, Moscow Festival, for *Naked Island,* 1960; Asahi Prize, Japan, for activities in independent film production, 1975. **Address:** 4-8-6 Zushi, Zushi-City, Kanagawa, Japan.

Films as Director:

1951 *Aisai monogatari* (*Story of My Loving Wife*) (+ sc)
1952 *Nadare* (*Avalanche*) (+ sc); *Genbakuno-ko* (*Children of the Atomic Bomb*) (+ sc)
1953 *Shukuzu* (*Epitome*) (+ sc); *A Life of a Woman* (+ sc)
1954 *Dobu* (*Gutter*) (+ co-sc)
1955 *Ookami* (*Wolves*) (+ sc)
1956 *Gin-Shinju* (*Silver Double Suicide*) (+ sc); *Ruri no kishi* (*Bank of Departure*) (+ sc); *Joyu* (*An Actress*) (+ sc)
1957 *Umi no yarodomo* (*Guys of the Sea*) (+ sc)
1958 *Kanashimi wa onna dakeni* (*Sorrow Is Only for Women*) (+ sc)
1959 *Dai go fukuryu-maru* (+ co-sc); *Hanayome san wa sekai-ichi* (*The World's Best Bride*) (+ sc); *Rakugaki kokuban* (*Graffiti Blackboard*) (+ sc)
1960 ***Hadaka no shima*** (*Naked Island*; *The Island*) (+ sc)
1962 *Ningen* (*Human Being*) (+ sc)
1963 *Haha* (*Mother*) (+ sc)
1964 *Onibaba* (+ sc)
1965 *Akuto* (*A Scoundrel*) (+ sc)
1966 *Honno* (*Instinct*) (+ sc); *Totsuseki iseki* (*Monument of Totsuseki*) (+ sc); *Tateshina no shiki* (*Four Seasons of Tateshina*) (+ sc)
1967 *Sei no kigen* (*Origin of Sex*) (+ sc)
1968 *Yabu no naka no kuroneko* (*A Black Cat in the Bush*) (+ sc); *Tsuyomushi onna (&) yawamushi otoko* (*Strong Woman and Weak Man*) (+ sc)
1969 *Kagero* (*Heat Haze*) (+ co-sc)
1970 *Shokkaku* (*Tentacles*) (+ sc); *Hadaka no jukyu-sai* (*Naked Nineteen-year-old*) (+ co-sc)
1972 *Kanawa* (*Iron Ring*) (+ sc); *Sanka* (*A Paean*) (+ sc)
1973 *Kokoro* (*Heart*) (+ sc)
1974 *Waga michi* (*My Way*) (+ sc)
1975 *Aru eiga-kantoku no shogai: Mizoguchi Kenji no kiroku* (*Life of a Film Director: Record of Kenji Mizoguchi*) (doc) (+ sc)
1977 *Chikuzan hitori-tabi* (*Life of Chikuzan*) (+ sc)
1982 *Hokusai manga* (*Hokusai, Ukiyoe Master*) (+ sc)
1984 *Chiheisen* (*The Horizon*)
1987 *A Deciduous Tree*
1988 *Sakur Tai 8-6*

Other Films:

(partial list: has written over 200 scripts)

1939 *Nanshin josei* (*South Advancing Women*) (Ochiai) (sc)
1946 *Machiboke no onna* (*Woman Who Is Waiting*) (Makino) (sc); *Josei no shori* (*The Victory of Women*) (Mizoguchi) (sc)
1947 *Anjo-ke no butokai* (*The Ball of the Anjo Family*) (Yoshimura) (sc)
1948 *Yuwaku* (*Seduction*) (Yoshimura) (sc); *Waga shogai no kagayakeru hi* (*My Life's Bright Day*) (Yoshimura) (sc)
1949 *Waga koi wa moenu* (*My Love Burns*) (Mizoguchi) (co-sc); *Shitto* (*Jealousy*) (Yoshimura) (sc); *Mori no Ishimatsu* (*Ishimatsu of Mori*) (Yoshimura) (sc); *Ojosan kanpai* (*Toast to a Young Miss*) (Kinoshita) (sc)
1951 *Itsuwareru seiso* (*Deceiving Costume*) (Yoshimura) (sc); *Genji monogatari* (*Tale of Genji*) (Yoshimura) (sc)
1955 *Bijo to kairyu* (*The Beauty and the Dragon*) (Yoshimura) (sc)
1958 *Hadaka no taiyo* (*Naked Sun*) (Ieki) (sc); *Yoru no tsuzumi* (*Night Drum*) (Imai) (co-sc)
1963 *Shitoyakana kemono* (*Soft Beast*) (Kawashima) (sc)
1964 *Kizudarake no sanga* (*Mountains and Rivers with Scars*) (Yamamoto) (sc)
1967 *Hanaoko Seishu no tsuma* (*Seishu Hanaoka's Wife*) (Masumura)
1972 *Gunki hatameku shitani* (*Under the Military Flag*) (Fukasaku) (sc)
1987 *Eiga Joyu* (sc)
1988 *Hachi-Ko* (sc)

Publications

On SHINDO: books—

Mellen, Joan, *Voices from the Japanese Cinema,* New York, 1975.

Kaneto Shindo: *Hadaka no shima*

Mellen, Joan, *The Waves at Genji's Door,* New York, 1976.
Anderson, Joseph, and Donald Richie, *The Japanese Film,* expanded edition, Princeton, 1982.

On SHINDO: article—

"Kaneto Shindo," in *CinemAction!* (Toronto), January 1992.

* * *

Kaneto Shindo began his career in film as a scenario writer. An episode portraying his study of scenario writing, under the perfectionist director Kenji Mizoguchi, is included in his own first film as a director, *Story of My Loving Wife.* The rigorous influence of his mentor on Shindo's style is seen in both his scenarios and his direction. Such persistent influence, by one director on another, on mise-en-scène and writing, is rarely found in the work of other filmmakers.

Shindo became a very successful scenario writer mainly for Kosaburo Yoshimura's films at Shochiku. However, after this team was subjected to commercial pressure from the studio, they left to produce their own films, establishing Kindai Eiga Kyokai, or the Society of Modern Film. Thus, they have been able to pursue their own interests and concerns in choosing subjects and styles.

Shindo, a Hiroshima native, frequently deals with the effects of the atomic bomb. He traced Hiroshima's aftermath, in *Children of the Atomic Bomb,* based on the compositions of Hiroshima children. This subject could be treated only after the American Occupation ended. *Mother* focuses on a surviving woman's decision to become a mother after much mental and physical trauma. *Instinct* deals with a middle-aged survivor whose sexual potency is revived by the love of a woman. *Dai go fukuryu-maru* is about the tragedy of the fishermen heavily exposed to nuclear fallout after American testing in the South Pacific. Shindo condemns nuclear weapons for causing such misery to innocent people, but also strongly affirms the survivor's will to live.

Shindo's best-known film internationally, *Naked Island,* is experimental in not using any dialogue but only music. It also uses local people except for a professional actor and actress who play a couple living on a small island. We are impressed with the hardship of their farming life as well as with the beauty of their natural surroundings throughout the cycle of the seasons. The joy, sorrow, anger, and desperation of the hardworking couple is silently but powerfully expressed in a semi-documentary manner.

The peaceful atmosphere of this film is in contrast to many of Shindo's more obsessive works, such as *Epitome, Gutter, Sorrow Is Only for Women, Onibaba,* and *A Scoundrel.* These convey a claustrophobic intensity by using only a few small settings for the action, with much close-up camera work.

In 1975, Shindo expressed his lifelong homage to his mentor, Mizoguchi, in a unique documentary: *The Life of a Film Director: Record of Kenji Mizoguchi.* In this film, he brought together many interesting and honest accounts of Mizoguchi by interviewing people who had worked for this master. These personal recollections, along with sequences from Mizoguchi's films, are a testimony to the greatness of Mizoguchi's art, and to his intriguing personality.

Like Mizoguchi, Shindo creates many strong female figures who, by virtue of their love and the power of their will, try to "save" their male counterparts. While Mizoguchi's women seem to rely more on their generous compassion to sustain their men, Shindo's women tend to inspire and motivate their men by their own energy and power. In much the same way, Shindo's own energy and perseverance have supported his artistic vision through four decades of independent filmmaking.

—Kyoko Hirano

SHINODA, Masahiro

Nationality: Japanese. **Born:** Gifu Prefecture, 9 March 1931. **Education:** Studied drama and literature at Waseda University, Tokyo, graduated 1952. **Family:** Married actress Shima Iwashita. **Career:** Assistant director at Shochiku-Ofuna Studios, from 1953; began as director of "youth" films, 1960; left Shochiku, 1965; directed first film for independent production company Hyogen-sha [Expression Company], *Clouds at Sunset,* 1967. **Address:** 1-11-13, Kitasenzoku, Ota-Ku, Tokyo, Japan.

Films as Director:

1960 *Koi no katamichi kippu* (*One Way Ticket to Love*) (+ sc); *Kawaita mizuumi* (*Dry Lake*; *Youth in Fury*)
1961 *Yuhi ni akai ore no kao* (*My Face Red in the Sunset*; *Killers on Parade*); *Waga koi no tabiji* (*Epitaph to My Love*) (+ co-sc); *Shamisen to otobai* (*Love Old and New*)
1962 *Watakushi-tachi no kekkon* (*Our Marriage*) (+ co-sc); *Yama no sanka: moyuru wakamono-tachi* (*Glory on the Summit: Burning Youth*); *Namida o shishi no tategami ni* (*Tears on the Lion's Mane*) (+ co-sc)
1963 *Kawaita hana* (*Pale Flower*) (+ co-sc)
1964 *Ansatsu* (*Assassination*)
1965 *Utsukushisa to kanashimi to* (*With Beauty and Sorrow*); *Ibun sarutobi sasuke* (*Samurai Spy*; *Sarutobi*)
1966 *Shokei no shima* (*Punishment Island*; *Captive's Island*)
1967 *Akanegumo* (*Clouds at Sunset*)
1969 *Shinju ten no Amijima* (*Double Suicide*)
1970 *Buraikan* (*The Scandalous Adventures of Buraikan*)
1971 *Chinmoku* (*Silence*)
1972 *Sapporo Orimpikku* (*Sapporo Winter Olympic Games*)
1973 *Kaseki no mori* (*The Petrified Forest*)
1974 *Himiko*
1975 *Sakura no mori no mankai no shita* (*Under the Cherry Blossoms*) (+ co-sc)
1976 *Nihon-maru* (*Nihon-maru Ship*) (doc); *Sadono kuni ondekoza* (*Sado's Ondeko-za*) (doc)
1977 *Hanare goze Orin* (*The Ballad of Orin*) (+ co-sc)
1979 *Yashagaike* (*Demon Pond*)
1980 *Aku Ryoto* (*Devil's Island*)
1984 *Setouchi Shonen Yakyudan* (*MacArthur's Children*)
1986 *Yari no Gonza* (*Gonza, the Spearman*)
1989 *Maihime* (*Die Tänzerin. The Dancer*)
1990 *Shonnenjidai* (*Takeshi*)

Publications

By SHINODA: articles—

Interview in *American Film* (New York), May 1985.
"*MacArthur's Children,*" interview with R. Silberman and K. Hirano in *Cineaste* (New York), vol. 14, no. 3, 1986.

On SHINODA: books—

Sekai no eiga sakka 10: Shinoda Masahiro, Yoshida Yoshishige [Film Directors of the World 10: Masahiro Shinoda and Yoshishige Yoshida], Tokyo, 1971.
Richie, Donald, *Japanese Cinema: Film Style and National Character,* New York, 1971.
Mellen, Joan, *Voices from the Japanese Cinema,* New York, 1975.
Mellen, Joan, *The Waves at Genji's Door,* New York, 1976.
Bock, Audie, *Japanese Film Directors,* Tokyo, 1978; revised edition, Tokyo, 1985.

* * *

After his debut with *One Way Ticket to Love* in 1960, Masahiro Shinoda (along with Oshima and Yoshida) was termed a "Japanese Nouvelle Vague" director. However, Shinoda's devotion to sensual modernism contrasted with Oshima's direct expression of his political concerns. Shinoda's early films center on the fickle and frivolous entertainment world, petty gangsters, or confused student terrorists, ornamented by pop-art settings and a sensibility which may be largely attributed to his scenario writer, poet Shuji Terayama.

Being an intellectual and ideologue, Shinoda analyzes the fates of his marginal but likable characters with a critical eye on the social and political milieu. Even his work on Shochiku Studio home drama and melodrama projects show his critical views of the social structure.

His indulgent aestheticism, which appears in his films as incomparable sensuality, has been connected with images of death and destruction (*Assassination, With Beauty and Sorrow, Clouds at Sunset, Double Suicide, The Ballad of Orin*) and of degradation (*Silence, The Petrified Forest, Under the Cherry Blossoms*). This stance again contrasts with that of Oshima, whose sexual and political outlook ultimately affirms the value of life and survival. Shinoda's fundamental pessimism, represented by the image of falling cherry blossoms in his films, is rooted in the ephemerality of life.

The stylistic aspect of Shinoda's work originated in his long interest in the Japanese traditional theater. *Double Suicide* received the highest acclaim for his bold art direction (elaborate calligraphy on the set was done by his cousin, Toko Shinoda), ambitious experimentation as in his use of men dressed in black (recalling traditional Japanese puppeteers) appearing to lead the characters to their destinies, and the double roles of the contrasting and competing heroines, the prostitute and the wife. This black-and-white film presents a most imaginative adaptation of Bunraku, the Japanese puppet play. *The Scandalous Adventures of Buraikan* is an elaborate and colorful adaptation of Kabuki drama, playful in spirit. *Himiko* recalls the origin of Japanese theater in the primordial Japanese tribe's rituals, making use of avant-garde dancers. The two leading female roles in *Demon Pond* are played by the popular young Kabuki actor Tamasaburo Bando.

Masahiro Shinoda

Another unique aspect of Shinoda's work is his interest in sports. As an ex-athlete, he was well qualified for the assignment of making the official documentary *Sapporo Winter Olympic Games,* and a documentary on runners, *Sado's Ondeko-za.* In these films, he succeeds in conveying in a beautiful visual manner the emotions of athletes in lonely competition.

Shinoda has also played an important role as the head of an independent film production firm, Hyogen-sha, or Expressive Company, since he left Shochiku in 1965. Thus he has pursued his own concerns in choices of subjects and methods of expression, mostly through the adaption of traditional and modern Japanese literary works. He has developed many talented collaborators—actress Shima Iwashita (to whom he is married), music composer Toru Takemitsu, art directors Jusho Toda and Kiyoshi Awazu, and poet Taeko Tomioka, working as his scenario writer.

—Kyoko Hirano

SHUB, Esther

Nationality: Soviet Ukrainian. **Born:** Esfir Ilyianichna Shub in Chernigovsky district, Ukraine, 3 March 1894. **Education:** Studied literature, Moscow; Institute for Women's Higher Education, Moscow. **Career:** Administrator with Theatre Dept. of Narkompros (People's Commissariat of Education), collaborated on stage work with Meyerhold and Mayakovsky; joined film company Goskino, re-editing imported films for Soviet distribution and producing compilation and documentary films, 1922; directed first "compilation film," *The Fall of the Romanov Dynasty,* 1927; taught montage for Eisenstein class at VGIK (film school), 1933-35; left Goskino to become chief editor of *Novosti Dnya (The News of the Day)* for Central Studio for Documentary Film, Moscow, 1942. **Awards:** Honored Artist of the Republic, 1935. **Died:** In Moscow, 21 September 1959.

Films as Director:

1927 *Padenye dinastii romanovykh* (*The Fall of the Romanov Dynasty*) (+ sc, ed); *Veliky put'* (*The Great Road*) (+ sc, ed)
1928 *Rossiya Nikolaya II i Lev Tolstoi* (*The Russia of Nicholas II and Lev Tolstoy*) (+ sc, ed)
1930 *Segodnya* (*Today*) (+ sc, ed)
1932 *K-SH-E* (*Komsomol—Leader of Electrification*; *Komsomol—The Guide to Electrification*) (+ sc, ed)
1934 *Moskva stroit metro* (*Moscow Builds the Subway*; *The Metro By Night*) (+ sc, ed)
1937 *Strana Sovietov* (*Land of the Soviets*) (+ sc, ed)

1939 *Ispaniya* (*Spain*) (+ sc, ed)
1940 *Kino za XX liet* (*20 let sovetskogo kino*; *Twenty Years of Cinema*) (co-d, co-ed, sc)
1941 *Fashizm budet razbit* (*Fascism Will Be Destroyed*; *The Face of the Enemy*) (+ sc, ed)
1942 *Strana rodnaya* (*The Native Country*) (+ sc, ed)
1946 *Po tu storonu Araksa* (*Across the Araks*) (+ sc, ed); *Sud v Smolenske* (*The Trial in Smolensk*) (+ sc, ed)

Other Films:

1922-25 Edited 200 foreign fiction films and ten Soviet films, final one being *The Skotinins* (Roshal)
1926 *Krylya kholopa* (*Wings of a Serf*) (ed)

Publications

By SHUB: books—

Krupnyn planom [In the Close-Up], Moscow, 1959.
Zhizn moya—kinematogra [My Life—Cinema], Moscow, 1972.

By SHUB: articles—

"Road from the Past," in *Sovietskoye Kino* (Moscow), November/December 1934.
"Kuleshov, Eisenstein, and the Others: Part 1: On Kuleshov," interview with S.P. Hill, in *Film Journal* (New York), Fall/Winter 1972.

On SHUB: books—

Leyda, Jay, *Kino: A History of the Russian and Soviet Film,* New York, 1973.
Waugh, Thomas, editor, *"Show Us Life": Toward a History and Aesthetics of the Committed Documentary,* Metuchen, New Jersey, 1984.
Taylor, Richard, and Ian Christie, editors, *The Film Factory: Russian and Soviet Cinema in Documents 1896-1939,* London, 1988.

On SHUB: articles—

Halter, R., "Esther Shub—ihre Bedeutung für die Entwicklung des Dokumentarfilms," in *Frauen und Film* (Berlin), October 1976.

Esther Shub: ***Padenye dinastii romanovykh***

Petric, Vlada, "Esther Shub: Cinema Is My Life," in *Quarterly Review of Film Studies* (Pleasantville, New York), Fall 1978.

* * *

In Russia, as directors traditionally do their own editing, famous film editors are rare. A great exception to this rule was Esther Shub. After gaining her reputation and experience in the early 1920s on the strength of her re-editing of foreign productions and a dozen Soviet features, she became, largely on her own initiative, a pioneer of the "compilation film," producing work that has seldom since been equalled. She brought to this genre far more than her speed, industry and flair; she brought a positive genius for using all sorts of ill-considered odd bits of old footage as a painter uses his palette, using them as they had all been especially shot for her. In creating her first two brilliant compilations, *The Fall of the Romanov Dynasty* and *The Great Road,* about the first decade of the revolution (both released in 1927), she scavenged everywhere with indefatigable determination. Old newsreels, amateur footage shot by the imperial family and their friends, official footage from a pair of official imperial cinematographers, storage facilities (cellars, vaults, and closets) of wartime cameramen were all investigated by Shub. She even managed to purchase valuable material from the United States. All of this was against the original reluctance of her studios to go ahead with these projects, and they refused to recognize her rights as author when she had finished the films.

Shub originally planned a film biography of Tolstoy as her third work, but even she failed to dig out more than a few hundred feet of material. Undaunted, she wove the footage she did secure in with other early fragments with great effect, emerging with *The Russia of Nicholas II and Lev Tolstoy.*

With the advent of sound Shub made an abrupt change in her methods. For *K-SH-E (Komsomol—Leader of Electrification)* she created her own version of the Communist Hero—young, passionate and dedicated, complete with high-necked Russian blouse and leather jerkin. She forsook her cutting table to become a sort of investigative journalist, deliberately turning her back on archival material, sweeping generalizations, and bravura montage. Instead, she forged a new, original style of ultra-realism, pre-dating by 30 years many of the practices and theories of cinema verité. Forty years later a Soviet film historian was to chide her for "indulging herself with a contemporary enthusiasm for the future of sound film and with the peculiar cult for film-apparatus." This was because she opened the film in a sound studio full of every kind of cinematic machinery with what she termed a "parade of film techniques," and occasionally cut back to this theme throughout the production. She purposely included shots in which people looked into the lens, screwed up their eyes at the arc-lamps, stumbled and stuttered in front of cameras and microphones visible in the scenes, and, in general, tried to augment reality by reminding the audience that the crew and camera were actually *there* instead of pretending that they were part of some all-seeing, omnipotent but unobtrusive eye.

Another important Shub film was *Spain,* a history of the Spanish Civil War. This work was seen once again as an "editor's film." Put together from newsreels and the frontline camera work of Roman Karmen and Boris Makaseyev, the film featured a commentary by Vsevolod Vishnevski, who also collaborated on the script. In the following year Pudovkin collaborated with Shub on her compilation *Twenty Years of Cinema,* a history of the Soviet industry. She continued her documentary work through the war years and into the late 1940s.

Although as a woman and an editor she perhaps suffered some bureaucratic indifference and obstruction ("they only join pieces of film together"), Shub was an influential filmmaker who deserves at least a niche in the Soviet film pantheon alongside such other originals (in both senses) as Pudovkin and Eisenstein, who certainly appreciated her work.

—Robert Dunbar

SIEGEL, Don

Nationality: American. **Born:** Chicago, 26 October 1912. **Education:** Jesus College, Cambridge University, England; Royal Academy of Dramatic Art, London. **Family:** Married 1) actress Viveca Lindfors, 1948 (divorced 1953), one son; 2) actress Doe Avedon, 1957 (divorced), four children; 3) Carol Rydall. **Career:** Actor with the Contemporary Theater, Los Angeles, 1930; joined Warner Bros. as film librarian, 1934, later assistant editor, then joined insert department; set up montage department at Warners, 1939; 2nd unit director for Michael Curtiz, Raoul Walsh, and others, 1940-45; directed first film, *Star in the Night,* 1945, and first feature, *The Verdict,* 1946; worked for Howard Hughes at RKO, 1948-51; producer and director for TV, from 1961; executive producer for *Trial and Error,* for TV, 1988. **Awards:** Oscars for Best Short Subject, for *Star in the Night,* and for Best Documentary, for *Hitler Lives?,* 1946. **Died:** Of cancer, after a long illness, 20 April 1991, in Nipoma, California.

Films as Director:

1945 *Star in the Night*; *Hitler Lives?*
1946 *The Verdict*
1949 *Night unto Night*; *The Big Steal*
1952 *No Time for Flowers*; *Duel at Silver Creek*
1953 *Count the Hours* (*Every Minute Counts*); *China Venture*
1954 *Riot in Cell Block 11*; *Private Hell 36*
1955 *An Annapolis Story* (*The Blue and the Gold*)
1956 ***Invasion of the Body Snatchers***; *Crime in the Streets*
1957 *Spanish Affair*; *Baby Face Nelson*
1958 *The Gun Runners*; *The Line-Up*
1959 *Edge of Eternity* (+ co-pr, role as man at the pool); *Hound Dog Man*
1960 *Flaming Star*
1962 *Hell Is for Heroes*
1964 *The Killers* (+ pr, role as short-order cook in diner); *The Hanged Man*
1967 *Stranger on the Run*
1968 *Madigan*
1969 *Coogan's Bluff* (+ pr, role as man in elevator); *Death of a Gunfighter* (uncredited co-d)
1970 *Two Mules for Sister Sara*
1971 *The Beguiled* (+ pr); **Dirty Harry** (+ pr)
1973 *Charley Varrick* (+ pr, role as Murph)
1974 *The Black Windmill* (+ pr)
1976 *The Shootist*
1977 *Telefon*
1979 *Escape from Alcatraz* (+ pr, role as doctor)
1980 *Rough Cut*
1982 *Jinxed!*

Other Films:

1940 *City for Conquest* (Litvak) (montage d)
1941 *Blues in the Night* (Litvak) (montage d)
1942 ***Casablanca*** (Curtiz) (art d)
1943 *Edge of Darkness* (Milestone) (set d); *Mission to Moscow* (Curtiz) (art d); *Northern Pursuit* (Walsh) (special effects d)
1944 *The Adventures of Mark Twain* (Rapper) (ph)
1971 ***Play Misty For Me*** (Eastwood) (role as Marty the bartender)
1978 *Invasion of the Body Snatchers* (Kaufman) (cab driver)
1985 *Into the Night* (Landis) (role as embarrassed man)

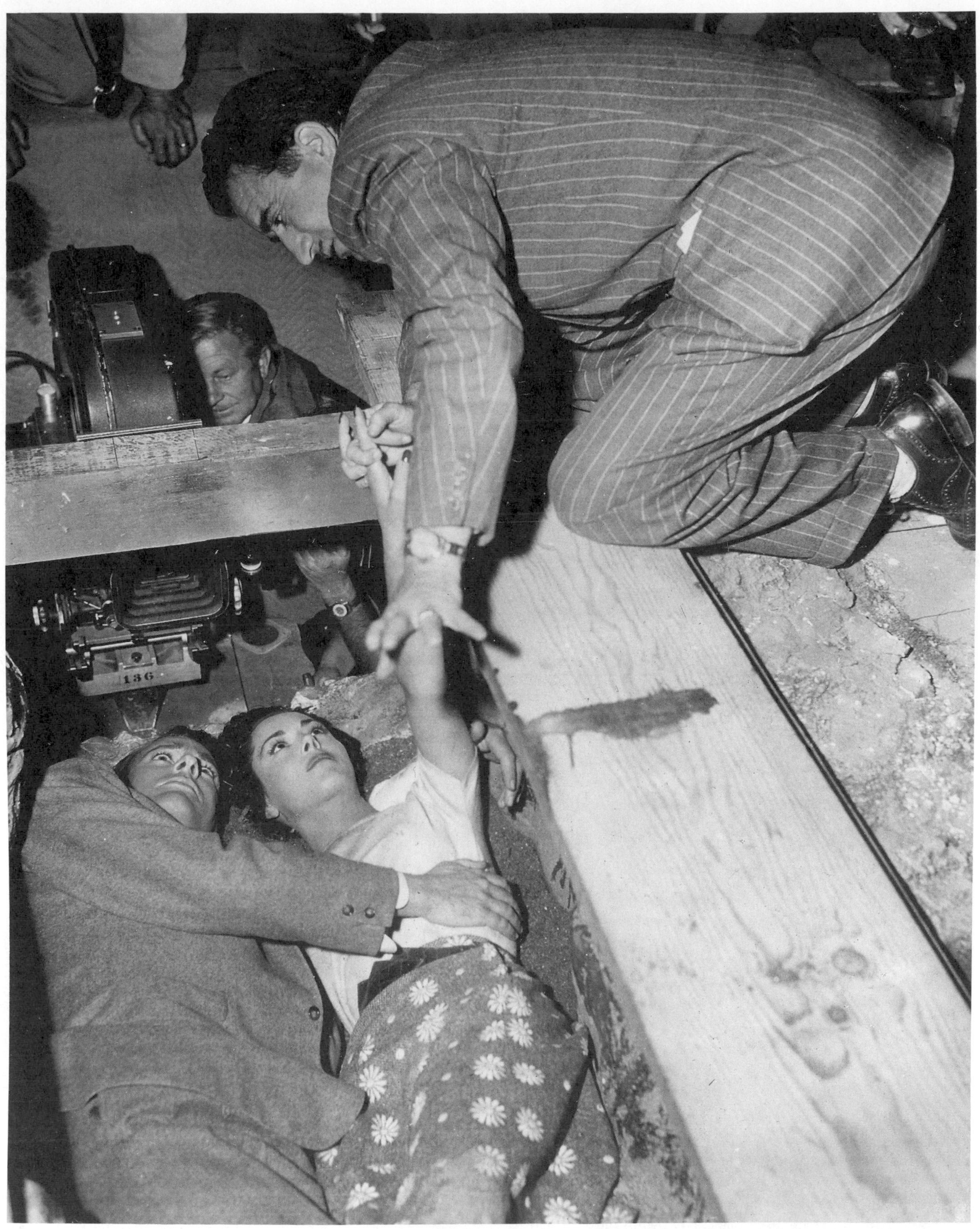

Don Siegel directing Kevin McCarthy and Dana Wynter in *Invasion of the Body Snatchers*

Publications

By SIEGEL: book—

A Siegel Film: An Autobiography, foreword by Clint Eastwood, London, 1993.

By SIEGEL: articles—

Interview with Peter Bogdanovich, in *Movie* (London), Spring 1968.
"The Anti-Heroes," in *Films and Filming* (London), January 1969.
"Conversation with Donald Siegel," with Leonard Maltin, in *Action* (Los Angeles), July/August 1971.
Interview with Sam Fuller, in *Interview* (New York), May 1972.
Interview with Stuart Kaminsky, in *Take One* (Montreal), June 1972.
"Stimulation," interview with Gordon Gow, in *Films and Filming* (London), November 1973.
"The Man Who Paid His Dues," interview with B. Drew, in *American Film* (Washington, D.C.), December 1977/January 1978.

On SIEGEL: books—

McArthur, Colin, *Underworld, U.S.A.,* London, 1972.
Kaminsky, Stuart M., *Don Siegel: Director,* New York, 1974.
Kaminsky, Stuart M., *American Film Genres,* Dayton, Ohio, 1974; revised edition, Chicago, 1983.
Belton, John, *Cinema Stylists,* Metuchen, New Jersey, 1983.
Vaccino, Roberto, *Donald Siegel,* Florence, 1985.

On SIEGEL: articles—

Austen, David, "Out for the Kill," in *Films and Filming* (London), May 1968.
Mundy, Robert, "Don Siegel: Time and Motion, Attitudes and Genre," in *Cinema* (London), February 1970.
Kael, Pauline, "Saint Cop," in *New Yorker,* 15 January 1972.
Gregory, Charles T., "The Pod Society Vs. the Rugged Individualist," in *Journal of Popular Film* (Bowling Green, Ohio), Winter 1972.
Pirie, D., "Siegel's Bluff," in *Sight and Sound* (London), Autumn 1973.
Kass, Judith M., "Don Siegel," in *The Hollywood Professionals,* vol. 4, London, 1975.
Allombert, Guy, "Donald Siegel: cinéaste de la violence et du antihéros," in *Image et Son* (Paris), May 1976.
Chase, A., "The Strange Romance of 'Dirty Harry' Callahan and Ann Mary Deacon," in *Velvet Light Trap* (Madison), Winter 1977.
Combs, R., "Less Is More: Don Siegel from the Block to the Rock," in *Sight and Sound* (London), Spring 1980.
Combs, Richard, "Count the Hours: The Real Don Siegel," in *Monthly Film Bulletin* (London), February 1984.
Sarris, Andrew, "Don Siegel: The Pro," in *Film Comment,* September/October 1991.
Eastwood, Clint, "The Padron," in *Film Comment,* September/October 1991.

* * *

Don Siegel's virtues—tightly constructed narratives and explosive action sequences—have been apparent from the very beginning. Even his B pictures have an enviable ability to pin audiences to their seats through the sheer force and pace of the events they portray. Unlike some action-movie specialists, however, Siegel rarely allows the action to overcome the characterization. The continuing fascination of *Riot in Cell Block 11,* for instance, stems as much from its central character's tensions as from the violent and eventful story. Dunn is a paradigmatic Siegel protagonist, caught between a violent inclination and the strategic need for restraint. Such incipient personal instability animates many Siegel films, finding material expression in the hunts and confrontations which structure their narratives. His people react to an unpleasant world with actions rather than words, often destroying themselves in the process. They rarely survive with dignity.

Siegel's singular distinction, however, lies in his refusal to strike conventional moral postures in relation to this depressing and often sordid material. Though one cannot fail to be involved in and excited by his action-packed stories, there is always a clear sense that he remains outside of them as something of a detached observer. In the 1950s that seeming "objectivity" gave him a minor critical reputation as a socially conscious and "liberal" director, though this was a liberalism by implication rather than a direct and paraded commitment. In retrospect the 1950s movies seem best described as individualistic, antagonistic to unthinking social conformity, rather than liberally sentimental after the fashion of "socially concerned" Hollywood movies of the period. These films are generalized warnings, not exercises in breast-beating. Their spirit is that of Kevin McCarthy's cry to his unheeding fellows in Siegel's original ending to *Invasion of the Body Snatchers* (United Artists added an epilogue): "You're next!"

In the 1960s and 1970s Siegel's reputation and his budgets grew. He struck out in new directions with such films as *Two Mules for Sister Sara* and *The Beguiled,* though his major concerns remained with action and with his emotionally crippled "heroes." The three cop movies (*Madigan, Coogan's Bluff,* and *Dirty Harry*) are representative, the latter especially encouraging the critical charge that Siegel had become a law-and-order ideologue. Its "wall-to-wall carpet of violence" (Siegel's description) easily lent itself to a "tough cop against the world" reading. Yet, just as his earlier films cannot be reduced to simple liberal formulae, so the later movies are far more complex than much criticism has suggested. A colleague remarks of Madigan: "For him everything's either right or wrong—there's nothing in between." In exploring his characters' doomed attempts to live by such absolutes Siegel refuses to make their mistake. And though he does not presume to judge them, that does not mean that he approves of their actions. As the less frenetic films like *The Shootist* and *Escape from Alcatraz* make clear, his appreciation of character and morality is far more subtle than that.

More than any other action director of his generation Siegel has avoided the genre's potential for reductive simplification. He has combined entertainment with perception, skilled filmmaking economy with nicely delineated characters, and overall moral detachment with sympathy for his hard-pressed protagonists. His movie world may often seem uncongenial, but its creator has never appeared callous or unconcerned. His films have achieved much-deserved commercial success; his skill and subtlety have deserved rather more in the way of critical attention.

—Andrew Tudor

SILVER, Joan Micklin

Nationality: American. **Born:** Omaha, Nebraska, 24 May 1935. **Education:** Studied at Sarah Lawrence College, New York, B.A., 1956. **Family:** Married Raphael D. Silver, three daughters. **Career:** Freelance writer for an educational film company, New York, from 1967; directed first feature, *Hester Street,* 1974; directed *Chilly Scenes of Winter* for United Artists, 1979, studio changed the title and the ending, but released it in its original form in 1982; director for stage and TV, 1980s.

Films as Director:

1972 *Immigrant Experience: The Long Long Journey* (short)
1974 *Hester Street* (+ sc)
1976 *Bernice Bobs Her Hair* (for TV)
1977 *Between the Lines*
1979 *Chilly Scenes of Winter* (*Head Over Heels*) (+ sc)
1985 *Finnegan, Begin Again* (for TV)
1988 *Crossing Delancey*
1990 *Loverboy*
1991 "Parole Board" segment of *Prison Stories: Women on the Inside*
1992 *Big Girls Don't Cry ... They Get Even* (*Stepkids*); *A Private Matter* (for TV)

Other Films:

1972 *Limbo* (*Women in Limbo*) (Robson) (co-sc)
1979 *On the Yard* (Silver) (prod)

Publications

By SILVER: book—

A—My Name Is Still Alice: A Musical Revue, with Julianne Boyd, London, 1993.

By SILVER: articles—

Interview in *Image et Son* (Paris), November 1975.
"Dialogue on Film: Joan Micklin Silver," in *American Film* (Los Angeles), May 1989.
Interview with Graham Fuller in the *Independent* (London), 7 April 1989.
Interview in *American Film* (Los Angeles), May 1989.

On SILVER: books—

Cohen, Sarah Blacher, *From Hester Street to Hollywood: The Jewish-American Stage and Screen,* Bloomington, Indiana, 1983.
Squire, Jason, E., *The Movie Business Book,* Englewood Cliffs, New Jersey, 1983.
Wood, Robin, *Hollywood from Vietnam to Reagan,* New York, 1986.

* * *

Undoubtedly, the impact of the feminist movement during the 1960s and early 1970s was instrumental in making it possible for women to establish themselves as directors by the latter half of the 1970s. Joan Micklin Silver was one of the first to do so. Silver's films aren't explicitly feminist in content, but she consistently displays an awareness of and sensitivity to women's identities and concerns.

As in her initial effort, *Hester Street,* Silver's films have tended to be intimate character studies centred on heterosexual relationships that are in a transitional process. In several of the films, Silver, while not minimizing her significance, decentres the film's female protagonist: in *Finnegan, Begin Again,* for example, the Robert Preston character dominates the narrative. But the two most striking examples are the films featuring John Heard, *Between the Lines* and *Chilly Scenes of Winter.* In both films, Heard plays a character with similar characteristics: a tendency to be possessive about the woman he professes to love and a casting of the relationship in the terms of romantic love. In *Chilly Scenes of Winter,* Heard imbues the film with his consciousness. His fantasy regarding a meeting with the Mary Beth Hurt character is visualized and he frequently directly addresses the viewer, providing access to his mental and/or emotional responses to a specific situation. By the film's conclusion, Heard has relinquished his romantic passion, but not without undergoing a considerable psychic and emotional strain. While Hurt rejects Heard and his overwhelming demands, she appears, on the other hand, to have no clearly formed idea of what she either wants or needs from a love relationship. Interestingly, the film does not imply that Hurt's uncertainty is a negative condition—she is just beginning to discover that she can explore the range of sexual and/or romantic involvements available to a contemporary woman.

In *Chilly Scenes of Winter,* the most complex and disturbing of her films, Silver indicates that from Hurt's point of view romantic love is oppressive and destructive; in *Crossing Delancey,* Silver employs a woman, the Amy Irving character, to investigate what could be called a romantic "perception" about possible relationships. Irving rejects the Peter Riegert character before she gets to know him on the grounds that the conditions of their meeting and his profession preclude the possibility of a romance between them. To an extent, Irving's rejection is motivated by her desire to distance herself from her Jewish ghetto origins. In Silver's films, a character's attitude to his or her origins, profession, etc., is often shown to be a contributing factor in the shaping of the romantic fantasy. In the Heard films, the character is frustrated by (*Between the Lines*) or indifferent to (*Chilly Scenes of Winter*) his professional life. In *Crossing Delancey,* it is only after Irving distinguishes between her romantic notions of appropriate partners and the reality of the Riegert character that a romance between the two can develop.

With *Lover Boy,* Silver addresses another aspect of the thematic: a young man, played by Patrick Dempsey, learns gradually through his experiences as the paid lover of a number of frustrated married women that sexual desire, pleasure, and fulfillment are enriched by having a romantic attitude towards intimate relationships (in courting women, Dempsey's musical tastes move from heavy metal to Fred Astaire). Silver's films feature a continual probing of what the romantic means—the various dimensions of the concept and its possible significance to both of the sexes. As a concept, the romantic ideal is not gender specific, and it is treated as something that can be either negative or positive in application.

In *Hollywood From Vietnam to Reagan,* Robin Wood argues that *Chilly Scenes of Winter,* to be fully appreciated, needs to be read in relation to the generic expectations it in part fulfills but also undermines. Wood's contention that the film belongs to the classical Hollywood tradition of the light comedy is well-taken; essentially, the same can be said of both *Crossing Delancey,* which is a reworking of the classical romantic comedy, and *Lover Boy,* which has its antecedents in the 1930s screwball comedy. (Similarly, Silver's graceful but unobtrusive mise-en-scène is a reflection of the classical filmmaking tradition.) In making this claim, it is important to indicate that the films are not evoking these classical genres for nostalgic purposes; instead, the films, while utilizing the structural strengths and comic potentials of the generic formulas, are offering a contemporary vision of the tensions underpinning heterosexual relations, and Silver's films predominantly respond to these tensions in a progressive manner. From this perspective, Silver's films can be compared to Woody Allen's light romantic comedies (*Annie Hall, Manhattan, Broadway Danny Rose*), though of the two directors, Silver is much less sentimental and precious about her characters (particularly in her treatment of the films' male protagonists).

Silver mostly has been idle in the 1990s. However, as more women directors emerge both outside and within the Hollywood establishment, she has come to be regarded as an elder statesman of women filmmakers. One of this new breed is her daughter, Marisa, whose films include *Old Enough, Permanent Record, Vital Signs,* and *He Said, She Said* (the latter co-directed with Ken Kwapis).

Silver's lone feature after *Loverboy* is *Big Girls Don't Cry ... They Get Even,* released in 1992 but screened the preceding year as *Stepkids.* It is a comedy which charts the plight of Laura (Hilary Wolf), a teen with a large family—and big problems. While a genial, generally likable film, it is far from Silver's best work, as it often plays like a television situation comedy, complete with overly adorable or precocious children and a too neatly wrapped-up finale.

In the last twenty years, Silver has produced a small but personal and distinguished body of work. She remains an underrated filmmaker; in part, this may be due to the fact that her films are not big budget projects or star vehicles. (Consistently, her films are conceived as ensemble pieces and contain beautifully judged performances.) It may also be due to the fact that the tone of Silver's films tends to be decidedly off-beat: although the films are clearly "serious" examinations of the complexities of heterosexual relations, Silver infuses the films with a slightly absurdist humour. On the one hand, this may produce a distancing effect that alienates the viewer. But it also allows the viewer to take a more contemplative attitude towards her depiction of the often aching pleasures involved in love relationships.

—Richard Lippe, updated by Rob Edelman

SIODMAK, Robert

Nationality: American/German. **Born:** Memphis, Tennessee, 8 August 1900. **Education:** University of Marburg, Germany. **Career:** Actor with German repertory companies, 1920-21; bank worker, 1921-23; titler for imported American films, 1925; editor for Herbert Nossen and Seymour Nebenzal, 1926-28; hired by Erich Pommer to scout for writers for UFA, 1928; directed first feature, 1930; following attack by Goebbels on film *Brennende Geheimnis,* moved with brother Curt to Paris, 1933; moved to Hollywood, 1940, signed two-year contract with Paramount, then moved to Universal under seven-year contract; after filming *The Crimson Pirate* in England and Spain, remained in Europe, from 1952. **Died:** In 1973.

Films as Director:

1929 *Menschen am Sonntag* (*People on Sunday*) (doc) (co-d)
1930 *Abschied* (*So sind die Menschen*)
1931 *Der Mann der seinen Mörder sucht* (*Looking for His Murderer*); *Voruntersuchung* (*Inquest*)
1932 *Stürme der Leidenschaft* (*The Tempest*; *Storm of Passion*); *Quick* (*Quick—König der Clowns*)
1933 *Brennende Geheimnis* (*The Burning Secret*) (+ pr); *Le Sexe faible*
1934 *La Crise est finie* (*The Slump Is Over*)
1936 *La Vie parisienne*; *Mister Flow* (*Compliments of Mr. Flow*)
1937 *Cargaison blanche* (*Le Chemin de Rio*; *French White Cargo*; *Traffic in Souls*; *Woman Racket*)
1938 *Mollenard* (*Hatred*); *Ultimatum* (co-d; completed for Robert Wiene)
1939 *Pièges* (*Personal Column*)
1941 *West Point Widow*
1942 *Fly by Night*; *The Night Before the Divorce*; *My Heart Belongs to Daddy*
1943 *Someone to Remember*; *Son of Dracula*
1944 *Phantom Lady*; *Cobra Woman*; *Christmas Holiday*
1945 *The Suspect*; *Uncle Harry* (*The Strange Affair of Uncle Harry*; *The Zero Murder Case*); *The Spiral Staircase*
1946 ***The Killers***; *The Dark Mirror*
1947 *Time Out of Mind* (+ pr)
1948 *Cry of the City*
1949 *Criss Cross*; *The Great Sinner*
1950 *Thelma Jordan*; *Deported*
1951 *The Whistle at Eaton Falls*
1952 *The Crimson Pirate*
1954 *Le Grand Jeu* (*Flesh and Woman*)
1955 *Die Ratten*
1956 *Mein Vater der Schauspieler*
1957 *Nachts wann der Teufel kam* (*The Devil Strikes at Night*)
1959 *Dorothea Angermann*; *The Rough and the Smooth* (*Portrait of a Sinner*)
1960 *Katya* (*Un Jeune Fille un seul amour, Magnificent Sinner*); *Mein Schulefreund*
1962 *L'Affaire Nina B* (*The Nina B Affair*); *Tunnel 28* (*Escape from East Berlin*)
1964 *Der Schut*
1965 *Der Schatz der Azteken*; *Die Pyramide des Sonnengottes*
1968 *Custer of the West* (*A Good Day for Fighting*)
1968/69 *Der Kampf um Rom* (in two parts)

Other Films:

1936 *Le Grand Refrain* (*Symphonie d'amour*) (Mirande) (supervisor)
1945 *Conflict* (*Bernhardt*) (co-story)

Publications

By SIODMAK: article—

"Hoodlums: The Myth and the Reality," with Richard Wilson, in *Films and Filming* (London), June 1959.

On SIODMAK: books—

McArthur, Colin, *Underworld U.S.A.,* London, 1972.
Dumont, Hervé, *Robert Siodmak: Le maitre du Film Noir,* Lausanne, 1981.

On SIODMAK: articles—

Marshman, D., "Mister Siodmak," in *Life* (New York), August 1947.
Taylor, John, "Encounter with Siodmak," in *Sight and Sound* (London), Summer/Autumn 1959.
Nolan, Jack, "Robert Siodmak," in *Films in Review* (New York), April 1969.
Flinn, Tom, "Three Faces of Film Noir," in *Velvet Light Trap* (Madison, Wisconsin), Summer 1972.
Beylie, Claude, "Robert Siodmak l'éclectique," in *Ecran* (Paris), May 1973.
"Robert Siodmak," in *Monthly Film Bulletin* (London), June 1978.
Masson, André, "Des genres creux, du clinquant, du simili," in *Positif* (Paris), September 1982.
Telotte, J.P., "Siodmak's Phantom Women and Noir Narrative," in *Film Criticism* (Meadville, Pennsylvania), Spring 1987.

* * *

Robert Siodmak is an example of the UFA-influenced German directors who moved to Hollywood when war threatened Europe. Less well known than his compatriots Billy Wilder and Fritz Lang, Siodmak demonstrated his cinematic skills early in his career with his innova-

Robert Siodmak

tive movie *Menschen am Sonntag,* which featured a non-professional cast, hand-held camera shots, stop motion photography, and the sort of flashbacks that later became associated with his work in America.

Siodmak carried with him to Hollywood the traditions and skills of his German film heritage, and became a major influence in American *film noir* of the 1940s. Deep shadows, claustrophobic compositions, elegant camera movements, and meticulously created settings on a grand scale mark the UFA origins of his work. Such themes as the treachery of love and the prevalence of the murderous impulse in ordinary people recur in his American films. The use of the flashback is a dominant narrative device, reflecting his fatalistic approach to story and character. *The Killers* (1946 version) presents a narrative that includes multiple flashbacks, each one of which is a part of the total story and all of which must be accumulated to understand the opening sequence of the film. This opening, based directly on Ernest Hemingway's famous short story, is a masterful example of film storytelling.

A typical Siodmak film of his *noir* period is *Phantom Lady,* a mini-masterpiece of mood and character that creates intense paranoia through the use of lighting and setting. Two key sequences demonstrate Siodmak's method. In the first, the heroine follows a man into the subway, a simple action that sets off feelings of danger and tension in viewers, feelings that grow entirely out of sound, light, cutting, and camera movement. In the second, one of the most famous sequences in *film noir,* Siodmak uses jazz music and cutting to build up a narrative meaning that is implicitly sexual as the leading lady urges a drummer to a faster and faster beat.

Siodmak's work is frequently discussed in comparison with that of Alfred Hitchcock, partly because they shared a producer, Joan Harrison, for a period of time. Harrison produced two Siodmak films for Universal, *The Suspect* and *Uncle Harry.* In both films a seemingly ordinary, innocent man is drawn into a tangled web of murder, while retaining the audience's sympathy. *Criss Cross,* arguably Siodmak's best *noir* work, ably demonstrates his ability to create depth of characterization through music, mood, and action, particularly in a scene in which Burt Lancaster watches his ex-wife, Yvonne DeCarlo, dance with another man. His fatal obsession with his wife and the victim/victimizer nature of their relationship is capably demonstrated through purely visual means.

In later years, Siodmak turned to such action films as *The Crimson Pirate* and *Custer of the West,* the former a celebrated romp that was one of the first truly tongue-in-cheek anti-genre films of its period. Although Siodmak's films were successful both critically and commercially in their day, he has never achieved the recognition which the visual quality of his work should have earned him. An innovative and cinematic director, he explored the criminal or psychotic impulses in his characters through the ambience of his elegant mise-en-scène. The control of all cinematic tools at his command—camera angle, lighting, composition, movement, and design—was used to establish effectively a world of fate, passion, obsession, and compulsion. Although his reputation has been elevated in recent years, his name deserves to be better known.

—Jeanine Basinger

SIRK, Douglas

Nationality: German/American. **Born:** Claus Detlev Sierk in Skagen, Denmark, 26 April 1900. **Education:** Studied law, philosophy, and art history in Copenhagen, Munich, Jena, and Hamburg until 1922. **Career:** Dramaturg for Deutsches Schauspiele, Hamburg, 1921; director for Chemnitz "Kleinez Theater," 1922; artistic director, Bremen Schauspielhaus, 1923-29; director of Altes Theater, Leipzig, 1929-36; directed first film, as Detlef Sierck, for UFA, 1935; head of Leipzig drama school, 1936; left Germany, worked on scripts in Austria and France (notably Renoir's *Partie de campagne,* 1937); signed for Warners in Hollywood, 1939, but inactive, 1940-41; contract as writer for Columbia, 1942; director for Universal, from 1950; returned to Europe, 1959; active in theatre in Munich and Hamburg, 1960s. **Died:** Of cancer, in Lugano, Switzerland, 14 January 1987.

Films as Director:

(as Detlef Sierck)

1935 *It Was een April* (Dutch version); *April, April* (German version); *Das Madchen vom Moorhof*; *Stutzen der Gesellschaft*
1936 *Schlussakkord* (*Final Accord*) (+ co-sc); *Das Hofkonzert* (+ co-sc); *La Chanson du souvenir* (*Song of Remembrance*) (co-d) (French version of *Das Hofkonzert*)
1937 *Zu neuen Ufern* (*To New Shores, Paramatta, Bagne de femmes*) (+ co-sc); *La Habanera*
1939 *Boefje* (+ co-sc)

(as Douglas Sirk)

1943 *Hitler's Madman*
1944 *Summer Storm* (+ co-sc)
1946 *A Scandal in Paris*
1947 *Lured*
1948 *Sleep My Love*
1949 *Slightly French*; *Shockproof*
1950 *Mystery Submarine*
1951 *The First Legion* (+ co-pr); *Thunder on the Hill*; *The Lady Pays Off*; *Weekend with Father*
1952 *No Room for the Groom*; *Has Anybody Seen My Gal?*; *Meet Me at the Fair*; *Take Me to Town*
1953 *All I Desire*; *Taza, Son of Cochise*
1954 *Magnificent Obsession*; *Sign of the Pagan*; *Captain Lightfoot*
1955 ***All That Heaven Allows***; *There's Always Tomorrow*
1956 *Never Say Goodbye* (Hopper) (d uncredited, completed film); ***Written on the Wind***
1957 *Battle Hymn*; *Interlude*; *The Tarnished Angels*
1958 *A Time to Love and a Time to Die*
1959 *Imitation of Life*

(for Munich Film School)

1975 *Talk to Me Like the Rain*
1977 *Sylvesternacht*
1979 *Bourbon Street Blues*

Other Films:

1937 *Liebling der Matrosen* (Hinrich) (co-sc as Detlef Sierck)
1938 *Dreiklang* (Hinrich) (story as Detlef Sierck)
1939 *Accordfinal* (Bay) (supervision, uncredited); *Sehnsucht nach Afrika* (Zoch) (role)
1986 *My Life for Zarah Leander* (Blackwood) (doc) (role)

Publications

By SIRK: articles—

Interview with Serge Daney and Jean-Louis Noames, in *Cahiers du Cinema* (Paris), April 1967.

"Douglas Sirk," with interview with D. Rabourdin and others, in *Cinema* (Paris), October 1978.

Interview with M. Henry and Y. Tobin in *Positif* (Paris), September 1982.

On SIRK: books—

Halliday, Jon, *Sirk on Sirk,* New York, 1972.

Edinburgh Film Festival 1972: Douglas Sirk, Edinburgh, 1972.

Bourget, Jean-Loup, *Douglas Sirk,* Paris, 1984.

Gledhill, Christine, editor, *Home Is Where the Heart Is: Studies in Melodrama and the Woman's Film,* London, 1987.

Laüfer, Elisabeth, *Skeptiker des Lichts: Douglas Sirk und seine Filme,* Frankfurt, 1987.

Sirk in Germany, Goethe Institute, London, 1988.

Mulvey, Laura, *Visual and Other Pleasures,* London, 1989.

On SIRK: articles—

Comolli, Jean-Louis, "L'Aveugle et le miroir, ou l'impossible cinema de Douglas Sirk," in *Cahiers du Cinema* (Paris), April 1967.

"Sirk Issue" of *Screen* (London), Summer 1971.

Bourget, E., and J. L. Bourget, "Sur Douglas Sirk," in *Positif* (Paris), April and September 1972.

Willemen, P., "Towards an Analysis of the Sirkian System," in *Screen* (London), Winter 1972/73.

"Fassbinder on Sirk," in *Film Comment* (New York), November/December 1975.

McCourt, J., "Douglas Sirk: Melo Maestro," in *Film Comment* (New York), November/December 1975.

Stern, M., "Patterns of Power and Potency, Repression and Violence," in *Velvet Light Trap* (Madison, Wisconsin), Fall 1976.

Degenfelder, P., "Sirk's The Tarnished Angels: 'Pylon' Recreated," in *Literature/Film Quarterly* (Salisbury, Maryland), Summer 1977.

Mulvey, Laura, "Notes on Sirk and Melodrama," in *Movie* (London), Winter 1977/78.

Honickel, T., "Idol der Munchner Filmstudenten: Douglas Sirk wieder in der HFF," in *Film und Ton* (Munich), February 1979.

Pulleine, T., "Stahl into Sirk," in *Monthly Film Bulletin* (London), November 1981.

"Douglas Sirk Issue" of *Positif* (Paris), September 1982.

Feuer, Jane, "Melodrama, Serial Form and Television Today," in *Screen* (London), January/February 1984.

Bourget, J.L, "Vers de nouveaus rivages. Les débuts américains de Douglas Sirk," in *Positif* (Paris), July/August 1984.

Heung, Marina, "'What's the Matter with Sara Jane?': Daughters and Mothers in *Imitation of Life,*" in *Cinema Journal* (Champaign, Illinois), vol. 26, no. 3, 1987.

Obituary, in *Variety* (New York), 21 January 1987.

Bourget, J.L., "Rêverie; sur les sources scandinaves de Sirk," in *Positif* (Paris), September 1987.

Petley, Julian, "Sirk in Germany," in *Sight and Sound* (London), Winter 1987/1988.

Hunter, Ross, "Magnificent Obsessions," in *American Film* (Los Angeles), April 1988.

Klinger, Barbara, "Much Ado About Excess: Genre, Mise-en-Scène and the Woman in *Written on the Wind,*" in *Wide Angle* (Baltimore), vol. 11, no. 4, 1989.

* * *

Douglas Sirk's critical reputation has almost completely reversed from the time when he was a popular studio director at Universal in the 1950s. He was regarded by contemporary critics as a lightweight director of soap operas who showcased the talents of Universal name stars such as Rock Hudson and Lana Turner. His films often were labelled "women's pictures," with all of the pejorative connotations that term suggested. After his last film, *Imitation of Life,* Sirk retired to Germany, leaving behind a body of work that was seldom discussed, but which was frequently revived on television late shows.

Standard works of film criticism either totally ignored or briefly mentioned him with words such as "not a creative film maker" (quoted from his brief entry in Georges Sadoul's *Dictionary of Film Makers*). In the early 1970s, however, a few American critics began to re-evaluate his works. The most important innovators in Sirk criticism in this period were Jon Halliday, whose lengthy interview in book form, *Sirk on Sirk,* has become a standard work, and Andrew Sarris, whose program notes on the director's films were compiled into the booklet *Douglas Sirk—The Complete American Period.* From the time of these two works, it became more and more appropriate to speak of Sirk in terms of "genius" and "greatness." By 1979, Sirk was even honored by BBC Television with a "Sirk Season" during which his now loyal following was treated to a weekly installment from the Sirk *oeuvre* as it now fashionably could be called.

Critics today see Sirk's films as more than melodramas with glossy photography and upper-middle-class houses. The word "expressionist" is frequently used to describe his technique, an indication not only of the style of Sirk's work in the United States, but also his background in films within the framework of German expressionism in the 1920s and early 1930s.

Sirk, who was born in Denmark, but emigrated to Germany in the teens, began work in the theater, then switched to films in the mid-1930s. Known for his "leftist" leanings, Sirk left Germany with the rise of Nazism, and eventually came to the United States in the early 1940s.

The first part of Sirk's American career was characterized by low-budget films which have faded into oblivion. His first well-known film was *Sleep My Love,* a variation on the *Gaslight* theme starring Don Ameche and Claudette Colbert. Soon he began directing films that starred several of the "hot" new Universal stars, among them Hudson and John Gavin, as well as many of the *grandes dames* of the 1930s and 1940s, such as Barbara Stanwyck, Lana Turner, and Jane Wyman. Although today he is known primarily for his dramas, Sirk did make a few lighter pieces, among them *Has Anybody Seen My Gal?,* a musical comedy set in the 1920s, and remembered by movie buffs as one of the first James Dean movies.

Many critics consider *Written on the Wind* to be Sirk's best film. It was also the one which was best received upon its initial release. All of Sirk's movies deal with relationships which are complicated and often at a dead-end. In *Written on the Wind,* the film's central characters are unhappy despite their wealth and attractiveness. They have little to interest them and seek outlets for their repressed sexuality. One of the four main characters, Kyle Hadley (Robert Stack), has always lived in the shadow of his more virile friend Mitch Wayne (Rock Hudson). He hopes to forget his own feelings of inadequacy by drinking and carousing, but his activities only reinforce his problems. Sexuality, either in its manifestation or repression, is a strongly recurrent theme in all of Sirk's works, but perhaps no where is it more blatantly dramatized than in *Written on the Wind,* where sex is the core of everyone's problems. Mitch is the only truly potent figure in the film, and thus he is the pivotal figure. Hudson's role as Mitch is very similar to that of Ron Kirby in *All That Heaven Allows.* Ron and Mitch both exhibit a strong sense of sexuality that either attracts or repels the other characters and initiates their action.

Kyle's feelings of sexual inadequacy and jealousy of Mitch are interrelated; Mitch is the manly son Kyle's father always wanted and the virile lover his wife Lucy (Lauren Bacall) loves. Kyle admires Mitch, yet hates him at the same time. Similarly, Carey Scott in *All That Heaven Allows* desires the earthy gardener Ron, yet she is shocked at her own sexuality, an apparent rejection of the conventions of her

Douglas Sirk directing *Interlude*

staid upper-middle-class milieu. In *There's Always Tomorrow,* Clifford Groves (Fred MacMurray) is faced with a similar situation. He seeks sexual and psychological freedom from his stifling family with Norma Vail (Barbara Stanwyck), yet his responsibilities and sense of morality prevent him from finding the freedom he seeks.

It is an ironic key to Sirk's popular acclaim now that exactly the same stars whose presence seemed to confirm his films as being "programmers" and "women's pictures" have ultimately added a deeper dimension to his works. By using popular stars of the 1930s through 1950s—stars who often peopled lightweight comedies and unregenerate melodramas, Sirk revealed another dimension of American society. His films often present situations in which the so-called "happy endings" of earlier films are played out to their ultimate (and often more realistic) outcomes by familiar faces. For example, in *There's Always Tomorrow,* Clifford and his wife Marion (Joan Bennett) might very well have been the prototypes for the main characters of a typical 1930s comedy in which "boy gets girl" in the last reel. Yet, in looking at them after almost 20 years of marriage, their lives are shallow. The happy ending of a youthful love has not sustained itself. Similarly, in *All That Heaven Allows,* the attractive middle-aged widow of a "wonderful man" has few things in life to make her happy. Whereas she was once a supposedly happy housewife, the loving spouse of a pillar of the community, her own identity has been suppressed to the point that his death means social ostracism. These two examples epitomize the cynicism of Sirk's view of what was traditionally perceived as the American dream. Most of Sirk's films depict families in which a house, cars, and affluence are present, but in which sexual and emotional fulfillment are not. Many of Sirk's films end on a decidedly unhappy note; the ones that do end optimistically for the main characters are those in which traditions are shattered and the strict societal standards of the time are rejected.

—Patricia King Hanson

SJÖBERG, Alf

Nationality: Swedish. **Born:** Stockholm, 21 June 1903. **Education:** Studies at the Royal Dramatic Theater. **Career:** Stage actor, from 1925; stage director, from 1927 (chief director, Royal Dramatic Theater, from 1930); directed first film, *Den starkaste,* 1929; returned to filmmaking, 1940. **Awards:** Best Film (*ex aequo*), Cannes Festival, for *Fröken Julie,* 1951. **Died:** In Stockholm, 17 April 1980.

Films as Director:

1929 *Den starkaste* (*The Strongest*) (+ story)
1940 *Med livet som insats* (*They Staked Their Lives*) (+ co-sc); *Den blomstertid* (*Blossom Time*) (+ sc)
1941 *Hem från Babylon* (*Home from Babylon*) (+ co-sc)
1942 *Himlaspelet* (*The Road to Heaven*) (+ co-sc)
1944 *Hets* (*Torment*); *Kungajakt* (*The Royal Hunt*)
1945 *Resan bort* (*Journey Out*) (+ sc)
1946 *Iris och lö jtnantsh järta* (*Iris and the Lieutenant*) (+ sc)
1949 *Bara en mor* (*Only a Mother*) (+ co-sc)
1951 ***Fröken Julie*** (*Miss Julie*) (+ sc)
1953 *Barabbas* (+ co-sc)
1954 *Karin Mansdotter* (+ sc)
1955 *Vildfåglar* (*Wild Birds*) (+ co-sc)
1956 *Sista paret ut* (*Last Pair Out*)
1960 *Domaren* (*The Judge*) (+ co-sc)
1966 *On* (*The Island*)
1969 *Fadern* (*The Father*)

Publications

By SJÖBERG: articles—

Interview in *Chaplin* (Stockholm), December 1965.
"Ingmar Bergman's Schooldays," an interview with Peter Cowie in *Monthly Film Bulletin* (London), April 1983.

On SJÖBERG: books—

Cowie, Peter, *Swedish Cinema,* New York, 1966.
Lundin, Gunnar, *Filmregi Alf Sjöberg,* Lund, 1979.

On SJÖBERG: articles—

Chaplin (Stockholm), no. 7, 1969.
Obituary, in *Variety* (New York), 30 April 1980.
"Bergman on Sjöberg," in *National Film Theatre Booklet* (London), September 1982.
Werner, Gosta, "Alf Sjoberg som filmskapare," in *Chaplin* (Stockholm), vol. 25, no. 3, 1983.

* * *

Along with Sjöström, Stiller, and Bergman, Sjöberg must be counted as one of the most significant directors of the Swedish cinema, and indeed as the most important in that long period between the departure of Sjöström and Stiller for Hollywood and the establishment of Bergman as a mature talent. However, it is hard not to agree with the judgement of Peter Cowie when he states that Sjöberg "is hampered by a want of thematic drive, for he is not preoccupied, like Bergman, with a personal vision. He has not created a world to which one returns with an immediate feeling of recognition and empathy. Each of his films is a solitary achievement, illuminating for a moment the universe of Strindberg, Lagerkvist and others with a cinematic expertise that rarely falters.... If one concludes that Sjöberg's most successful accomplishments are founded on the inspiration of others ..., it is not to deny his impeccable craftsmanship, his uncanny grasp of historical period, and his gift for describing his characters compellingly within their environment."

After studying with Greta Garbo at Stockholm's famous Dramatic Theatre School, Sjöberg rapidly made a name for himself as a theatre director, becoming chief director at the Stockholm Theatre by 1930. In the late 1920s he encountered the films of Eisenstein and Pabst, but the chief influence on his early films would appear to be the fatalism and melancholy of French "poetic realism" of the 1930s. However, in his first film, *The Strongest,* an epic tale of the seal hunters of Arctic Norway, the influences would appear to be an intriguing blend of Jack London, Robert Flaherty, the Sjöström of *The Outlaw and His Wife* and, in the remarkably fluidly edited bear-hunt that climaxes the film, *Eisenstein.* All this was too much for a cinema industry preoccupied with feeble studio comedies and light dramas, and Sjöberg was unable to make another film for ten years. Instead he confined his experiments in mise-en-scène to the theatre.

In *They Stake Their Lives,* a sombre story of the underground in an unidentified Baltic totalitarian state, and *The Royal Hunt,* which deals with Russian attempts to overthrow Gustav III of Sweden in the late eighteenth century, there are clear references to the Nazi threat. In more general terms these films deal with the theme of power and domination, one of the threads that runs through much of the director's work. More important, however, is *The Road to Heaven,* a film very

Alf Sjöberg

much in the Sjöström/Lagerlöf tradition that is generally regarded as one of the finest of the period 1920-1950 and an important milestone in the revival of the Swedish cinema at this time. A sort of Swedish *Pilgrim's Progress,* it draws heavily on the same kind of Swedish peasant art which influenced *The Seventh Seal,* though it is both more nationalistic and more specifically and directly Christian in inspiration than that work. As Forsyth Hardy has pointed out, "it helped to give spiritual structure to the revival of the Swedish cinema."

Frenzy signalled a new departure both for Swedish cinema in general and Sjöberg's work in particular, as well as the arrival of a powerful new talent in the form of its scriptwriter—Ingmar Bergman. In its story of a tyrannical schoolmaster (aptly nicknamed Caligula) who torments one of his students beyond endurance, Sjöberg clearly found a subject close to his heart, one which went beyond the obvious theme of youthful ardour vs. oppressive, reactionary middle and old age. The story allowed him to explore power relationships (with all their distinctly sexual ramifications) in a more general way. Sjöberg created a remarkably claustrophobic and sombre atmosphere to match Bergman's agonised screenplay—there are few sets, less still exterior shots, and the harsh lighting at times recalls the German silent cinema.

One of the themes explored in *Frenzy* is the destructive effect of outdated class divisions, and the evils of class society are also very much to the fore in *Only a Mother,* which is set among the "stataren," rural communities where farm labourers and their families were forced to endure almost serf-like conditions. The social dimension of Sjöberg's work at this time is a reminder that Sweden had recently introduced the full apparatus of a welfare state. At the same time, the director is still much preoccupied with formal matters, experimenting here with deep focus, huge close-ups, and sharply angled interior shots.

Sjöberg's best known film is probably *Miss Julie,* which transforms Strindberg's by then rather outdated condemnation of the class system into a study of power relationships between the sexes. Here the sadomasochistic element comes right to the fore, which earned the film a rather risqué reputation in Anglo-Saxon countries. In addition to instituting considerable modifications to the original story, Sjöberg also experimented with rapid transitions between past and present, often without the aid of cuts, and the film also contains a rare example of the flash-forward. Like *Iris and the Lieutenant* and *Only a Mother, Miss Julie* is also an indictment of the position of women under a stern patriarchal order. Strindberg was also the inspiration behind *Karin Mansdotter,* parts of which were based on his play *Erik XIV.* Beginning with a bizarre (and rather out of place) parody of cinematic costume drama, the film is beautifully shot, mostly on location in some of Sweden's most spectacular castles, by Sven Nykvist.

In his later work Sjöberg returned to contemporary Swedish society. The struggle between the sexes is continued in *Wild Birds* and the Bergman-scripted *The Last Pair Out.* At the same time, the director's concern with social injustice is evident in *The Judge,* an indictment of dubious legal activities, and *The Island,* in which the central character urges his apathetic fellow islanders to fight government plans to take away their land and turn it into a gunnery range. It has to be admitted, however, that Sjöberg's later work does not show him at his best; characters too often come across as mere puppets, there are too many wordy passages, and Sjöberg often seems unable to sustain any consistency of mood or refrain from exaggerated melodramatics. Still, his dramatically resonant use of settings, and the way in which he controls his characters' movements within them, remain interesting, reminding one that Sjöberg, at his best, has been compared to Emile Zola.

—Julian Petley

SJÖSTRÖM, Victor

Nationality: Swedish. **Born:** Victor David Sjöström in Silbodal, Sweden, 20 September 1879; also known as Victor Seastrom. **Education:** Attended high school in Uppsala, Sweden. **Family:** Married 1) Sascha St. Jagoff, 1900 (died 1916); 2) Lili Bech, 1916; 3) actress Edith Erastoff, 1922 (died 1945), two children. **Career:** Lived in Brooklyn, New York, from 1880; returned to Sweden to live with aunt, 1887; stage actor and director in Sweden and Finland, from 1896; formed own theater company, 1911; film director for Svenska Biograf film studio, Stockholm, from 1912; director for MGM, Hollywood, from 1923; worked under "Americanized" name, "Seastrom"; returned to Sweden as actor, 1930; artistic director, Svensk Filmindustri, 1943-49. **Died:** In Stockholm, 3 January 1960.

Films as Director:

1912 *Trädgårrdsmaästaren* (*The Gardener*) (+ role); *Ett Hemligt giftermaål* (*A Secret Marriage*); *En sommarsaga* (*A Summer Tale*)

1913 *Lö jen och tårar* (*Ridicule and Tears*); *Blodets röst* (*Voice of the Blood*) (+ sc, role) (released 1923); *Lady Marions sommarflirt* (*Lady Marion's Summer Flirt*); *Äktenskapsbrydån* (*The Marriage Agency*) (+ sc); *Livets konflikter* (*Conflicts of Life*) (co-d, role); *Ingeborg Holm* (+ sc); *Halvblod* (*Half Breed*); *Miraklet*; *På livets ödesvägar* (*On the Roads of Fate*)

1914 *Prästen* (*The Priest*); *Det var i Maj* (*It Was in May*) (+ sc); *Kärlek starkare än hat* (*Love Stronger Than Hatred*); *Dömen icke* (*Do Not Judge*); *Bra flicka reder sig själv* (*A Clever Girl Takes Care of Herself*) (+ sc); *Gatans barn* (*Children of the Street*); *Högfjällets dotter* (*Daughter of the Mountains*) (+ sc); *Hjärtan som mötas* (*Meeting Hearts*)

1915 *Strejken* (*Strike*) (+ sc, role); *En av de många* (*One of the Many*) (+ sc); *Sonad oskuld* (*Expiated Innocence*) (+ co-sc); *Skomakare bliv vid din läst* (*Cobbler Stay at Your Bench*) (+ sc)

1916 *Lankshövdingens dottrar* (*The Governor's Daughters*) (+ sc); *Rösen på Tistelön* (*Havsgammar*; *The Rose of Thistle Island*; *Sea Eagle*); *I. Prövningens stund* (*Hour of the Trial*) (+ sc, role); *Skepp som motas* (*Meeting Ships*); *Hon segrade* (*She Conquered*) (+ sc, role); *Therese* (+ co-sc)

1917 *Dödskyssen* (*Kiss of Death*) (+ co-sc, role); *Terje Vigen* (*A Man There Was*) (+ co-sc, role)

1918 *Berg-Ejvind och hans hustru* (*The Outlaw and His Wife*) (+ co-sc, role); *Tösen från stormyrtorpet* (*The Lass from the Stormy Croft*) (+ co-sc)

1919 *Ingmarsönerna, Parts I and II* (*Sons of Ingmar*) (+ sc, role); *Hans nåds testamente* (*The Will of His Grace*)

1920 *Klostret I Sendomir* (*The Monastery of Sendomir*) (+ sc); *Karin Ingmarsdotter* (*Karin, Daughter of Ingmar*) (+ co-sc, role); *Mästerman* (*Master Samuel*) (+ role)

1921 ***Körkarlen*** (*The Phantom Chariot*; *Thy Soul Shall Bear Witness*) (+ sc, role as David Holm)

1922 *Vem dömer* (*Love's Crucible*) (+ co-sc); *Det omringgade huset* (*The Surrounded House*) (+ co-sc, role)

1923 *Eld ombord* (*The Tragic Ship*) (+ role)

1924 *Name the Man*; *He Who Gets Slapped*

1925 *Confessions of a Queen*; *The Tower of Lies*

1927 *The Scarlet Letter*

1928 *The Divine Woman*; ***The Wind***; *Masks of the Devil*

1930 *A Lady to Love*

1931 *Markurells I Wadköping* (+ role)

1937 *Under the Red Robe*

Other Films:

1912 *Vampyren* (Stiller) (role as Lt. Roberts); *De svarta maskerna* (Stiller) (role as the Lieutenant); *I livets vår* (Garbagni) (role)
1913 *Nar karlekan dodar* (Stiller) (role as the painter); *Barnet* (Stiller) (role as medical student)
1914 *För sin kädleks skull* (Stiller) (role as Borgen); *Högfjällets dotter* (Stiller) (role); *Guldspindeln* (Magnusen) (role); *Thomas Graals bästa film* (Stiller) (role as Thomas Graal); *Thomas Graals bästa barn* (Stiller) (role as Thomas Graal)
1934 *Synnove Solbakken* (T. Ibsen) (role)
1935 *Valborgsmaässoafton* (Edgren) (role)
1937 *John Ericsson* (role)
1939 *Gubben Kommer* (Lindberg) (role); *Mot nya tider* (Wallen) (role)
1941 *Striden går vidare* (Molander) (role)
1943 *Det brinner en eld* (Molander) (role); *Ordet* (Molander) (role)
1944 *Kejsaren av Portugalien* (Molander) (role)
1947 *Rallare* (Mattson) (role)
1940s *Farlig vår* (Mattson) (role)
1950 *Till Glädje* (Bergman) (role); *Kvartetten som sprängdes* (Molander) (role)
1952 *Hård klang* (Mattson) (role)
1955 *Nattens väv* (Mattson) (role)
1957 ***Smultronstället*** (*Wild Strawberries*) (Bergman) (role as Professor)

Publications

On SJÖSTRÖM: books—

Idestam-Almquist, Bengt, *Den Svenska Filmens Drama: Sjöström och Stiller,* Stockholm, 1938.
Hardy, Forsyth, *Scandinavian Film,* London, 1951.
Lauritzen, Einar, *Swedish Film,* New York, 1962.
Jeanne, Rene, and Charles Ford, *Sjöström et l'ecole suédois,* Paris, 1963.
Cowie, Peter, *Swedish Cinema,* London, 1966.
Pensel, Hans, *Seastrom and Stiller in Hollywood,* New York, 1969.
Petrie, Graham, *Hollywood Destinies: European Directors in Hollywood 1922-31,* London, 1985.
Forslund, Bengt, *Victor Sjöström: His Life and His Work,* New York, 1988.

On SJÖSTRÖM: articles—

Vaughn, Dai, "Victor Sjöström and D.W. Griffith," in *Film* (London), January/February 1958.
"Bergman on Victor Sjöström," in *Sight and Sound* (London), Spring 1960.
Turner, Charles L., "Victor Sjöström," in *Films in Review* (New York), May and June 1960.
Wood, Robin, "Essays on the Swedish Cinema (Part 2)," in *Lumiere* (Melbourne), April/May 1974.
Gillett, John, "Swedish Retrospect," in *Sight and Sound* (London), Summer 1974.
Milne, Tom, "Lost and Found," in *Sight and Sound* (London), Autumn 1975.
Beylie, Claude, and M. Martin, "Sjöström, Stiller et L'Amérique," in *Ecran* (Paris), September 1978.
Torbacke, J., "Vem såg Victor Sjöström mästerverk?," in *Chaplin* (Stockholm), vol. 22, no. 6, 1980.
"Victor Sjostrom Issue" of *Avant-Scene du Cinéma* (Paris), July/August 1984.
Niogret, H., "Notes sur quelques films de Victor Sjostrom," in *Positif* (Paris), September 1987.
Viviani, C., "Trois films américains pour connaître Victor Sjöström," in *Positif* (Paris), June 1989.

* * *

With a career in film that in many ways paralleled that of his close friend Mauritz Stiller, Victor Sjöström entered the Swedish film industry at virtually the same time (1912), primarily as an actor, only to become almost immediately, like Stiller, a film director. Whereas Stiller had spent his youth in Finland, however, Sjöström had spent six formative years as a child in America's Brooklyn. Once back in Sweden after an unhappy childhood, his training for the theater proved fruitful. He became a well-established actor before entering the film industry at the age of 32. "The thing that brought me into filmmaking was a youthful desire for adventure and a curiosity to try this new medium," he once said in an interview. The first films in which he appeared in 1912 were Stiller's *The Black Masks* and *Vampyren.*

Although Sjöström proved excellent as an actor in comedy, his innate seriousness of outlook was reflected in the films he directed. He developed a deep response to nature and the spectacular northern landscape, capturing the expanses of ice, snow, trees, and mountains in all their (to him as to other Scandinavians) mystical force. One of his earliest films was *Ingeborn Holm,* which exposed the cruelties of the forced labor system to which the children of paupers were still subjected. This film was produced partially outdoors; Sjöström's pantheistic response to nature was developed in *Terje Vigen,* his adaptation of Ibsen's ballad poem, with its narrative set in the period of the Napoleonic confrontation with Britain. Sjöström himself played Terje, the bitter Norwegian sailor who had been imprisoned for a while by the British for attempting to break through their blockade at sea in order to bring food through to the starving people, including his wife and son, in his village. He fails in this attempt and they die as a consequence. Terje's obsessive desire for vengeance is later purged as a result of his response to his British captor's child, whom he rescues in a storm.

Sjöström became a prolific director. He completed nearly 30 films between 1912 and 1918, the year he directed *The Outlaw and His Wife.* Of that film, French critic and filmmaker Louis Delluc wrote in 1921: "Here without doubt is the most beautiful film in the world. Victor Sjöström has directed it with a dignity that is beyond words ... it is the first love duet heard in the cinema. A duet that is entire life. Is it a drama? ... I don't know.... People love each other and live. That is all." In this film a rich widow abandons her estate to live in the mountains with her outlaw lover until, hounded by his pursuers, they die together in the snow. It is typical of the Swedish film that winter, after the symbolic summer of love, should become the synonym for death.

Sjöström's intense feeling for nature expanded still further in his first adaptation of a novel by Selma Lagerlöf who, as a writer in the grand tradition, became one of the primary inspirers of the Swedish cinema of this period. This adaptation was from *The Lass from the Stormy Croft* and featured a magnificent rustic setting which seems at once to transcend and embody the exigencies of human passion—the frustration of the poor peasant girl with her illegitimate child and the troubles that afflict the son of a landowner (played by Lars Hanson in his first important film role) who tries to befriend her. As Carl Dreyer, who in the same year made *The Parson's Widow* in Sweden, commented, "Selma Lagerlöf's predilection for dreams and supernatural events appealed to Sjöström's own somewhat sombre artistic mind."

Sjöström's most famous film before his departure for Hollywood in 1923 was *The Phantom Chariot* (also known as *Thy Soul Shall Bear Witness*), also based on a novel by Selma Lagerlöf. The legend had it that the phantom chariot came once each year, on New Year's Eve,

Victor Sjöström (left)

St. Sylvester's Night, to carry away the souls of sinners. In the film the central character is David Holm, a violent and brutalized man who is brought to relive his evil past on St. Sylvester's Night, especially the ill-treatment he had given his wife, until his conscience is awakened. As Holm recalls his wicked deeds in flashback he is haunted by the approach of the chariot, and is saved just in time through reunion with his wife, whose imminent suicide he prevents. Holm is played brilliantly by Sjöström himself, while Julius Jaenzen's multi-exposure camerawork emphasizes the distinction between body and soul in visuals that surpass virtually all that had been achieved in cinematography by 1920.

In the postwar era, Swedish films, with their comparatively heavy themes, began to prove less popular as exports. Sjöström, like Stiller, left for America on the invitation of Louis B. Mayer at MGM. He was to remain in Hollywood six years, directing nine films under the name of Victor Seastrom. Of these, *The Scarlet Letter,* with Lillian Gish as Hester Prynne and Lars Hanson as the priest, and *The Wind,* also with Lillian Gish and Lars Hanson, are the more significant; the latter now ranks as a masterpiece of the silent cinema. Lillian Gish said of Sjöström that "his direction was a great education for me ... the Swedish school of acting is one of repression." In *The Wind* she plays a sensitive girl from Kentucky forced into marriage with a coarse cattleman from Texas, a repellent marriage which, along with the harsh Texan environment, finally drives her nearly insane and impels her to kill a male intruder in self-defense. The film, shot in the Mojave region, suffered from re-editing by the studio and the imposition of a sound track.

Sjöström's single attempt to recreate Sweden in America was *The Tower of Lies* (with Lon Chaney and Norma Shearer), an adaptation of Selma Lagerlöf's novel *The Emperor of Portugal,* which at least one American reviewer praised for, "its preservation of the simplicity of treatment in *Thy Soul Shall Bear Witness.*"

Sjöström returned to Sweden in 1928 and directed one good sound film, *Markurells i Wadköping,* in which he starred as a grim man, much like Terje Vigen, who is finally purged of his desire for revenge. Apart from directing a lame period romance in England called *Under the Red Robe,* with Raymond Massey and Conrad Veidt, Sjöström concentrated on his career as an actor, giving at the age of 78 a great performance as the aged professor in Bergman's *Wild Strawberries.*

—Roger Manvell

SKOLIMOWSKI, Jerzy

Nationality: Polish. **Born:** Warsaw, 5 May 1938. **Education:** Educated in literature and history at Warsaw University, diploma 1959; Warsaw University and State Superior Film School in Lodz, 1960-64. **Career:** Published first collection of poetry, *Quelque part près de soi,* 1959; directed first feature (as film student), *Rysopis,* 1964; *Rece de gory* banned by Polish authorities, left Poland, 1967; moved to United States, 1984. **Awards:** Grand Prix for Grand Prize, Bergamo International Film Festival, 1966, for *Barrier*; Golden Bear, Berlin Film Festival, 1967, for *Le Depart*; Special Jury Grand Prize, Cannes Festival, 1978, for *The Shout*; British Film Award and Best Screenplay, Cannes Festival, for *Moonlighting,* 1982; Special Prize, Venice Film Festival, 1985, for *The Lightship.*

Films as Director:

1960 *Oko wykol* (*L'Oeil Torve*) (short) (+ sc); *Hamles* (*Le Petit Hamlet*) (short) (+ sc); *Erotyk* (*L'Érotique*) (short)(+ sc)
1961 *Boks* (*Boxing*) (short) (+ sc); *Piednadze albo zycie* (*La Bourse ou la vie*) (short) (+ sc); *Akt* (short) (+ sc)
1964 *Rysopis* (*Identification Marks: None*) (+ sc, pr, art d, ed, role as Andrzej Leszczyc)
1965 *Walkower* (*Walkover*) (+ sc, co-ed, role as Andrzej Leszczyc)
1966 *Bariera* (*Barrier*) (+ sc)
1967 *Le Départ* (+ co-sc); *Rece do gory* (*Hands Up!*) (+ sc, co-art d, role as Andrzej Leszczyc)
1968 *Dialog* (*Dialogue*) (+ sc, art d)
1970 *The Adventures of Gerard* (+ co-sc); *Deep End* (+ co-sc)
1971 *King, Queen, Knave* (+ co-sc)
1978 *The Shout* (+ co-sc)
1982 *Moonlighting* (+ sc, co-pr)
1984 *Success is the Best Revenge*
1985 *The Lightship*
1989 *Torrents of Spring* (+ sc)
1991 *Ferdydurke* (+ sc)
1992 *30 Door Key*

Other Films:

1959 *Niewinni czardodziejе* (*Innocent Sorcerers*) (Wajda) (co-sc)
1960 ***Noz w wodzie*** (*Knife in the Water*) (Polanski) (co-sc); *Przy Jaciel* (*A Friend*) (co-sc)
1981 *Falschung* (Schlöndorff) (role)
1985 *White Knights* (Hackford) (role)

Publications

By SKOLIMOWSKI: books—

Quelque part près de soi, Np, 1958.
La Hache et le ciel, Np, 1959.

By SKOLIMOWSKI: articles—

"Passages and Levels: Interview with Jerzy Skolimowski," with Michel Delahaye, in *Cahiers du Cinema in English* (New York), December 1967.
"'An Accusation That I Throw in the Face of My Generation'—A Conversation with the Young Polish Director, Jerzy Skolimowski," in *Film Comment* (New York), Fall 1968.
"Jerzy Skolimowski: A Conversation," with Peter Blum, in *Film Culture* (New York), Fall 1968.
Interview with Michel Ciment and Bernard Cohn, in *Positif* (Paris), February 1972.
"Skolimowski's Cricket Match," interview with Philip Strick, in *Sight and Sound* (London), Summer 1978.
"Jerzy Skolimowski," an interview with P. Carcassonne and others, in *Cinématographe* (Paris), June 1978.
Interview with K.L. Geist in *Films in Review* (New York), vol. 33, no. 9, November 1982.
Interview with Dan Yakir in *Film Comment* (New York), November/December 1982.
Interviews in *Cahiers du Cinéma* (Paris), January 1983 and Summer 1984.
Interview with E. Carrière and Michel Ciment in *Positif* (Paris), February 1986.
"*Under Western Eyes*: Skolimowski's Conradian Progress," interview with Richard Combs in *Monthly Film Bulletin* (London), May 1986.
"Jade do Polski robic 'Ferdydurke,'" interview with V. Remy in *Kino* (Warsaw), June 1990.
Interview with S. Mizrahi in *Positif* (Paris), March 1992.

Jerzy Skolimowski

On SKOLIMOWSKI: books—

Borin, Fabrizio, *Jerzy Skolimowski,* Florence, 1987.

On SKOLIMOWSKI: articles—

Toeplitz, Krzysztof-Teodor, "Jerzy Skolimowski: Portrait of a Debutant Director," in *Film Quarterly* (Berkeley), Fall 1967.
Thomsen, Christian, "Skolimowski," in *Sight and Sound* (London), Summer 1968.
Bean, Robin, "Adventures of Yurek," in *Films and Filming* (London), December 1968.
"Director of the Year," in *International Film Guide 1970,* London, 1969.
Lefèvre, R., "Jerzy Skolimowski ou la poésie du dérisoire," in *Cinéma* (Paris), September/October 1973.
Powers, J., "*Under Western Eyes,*" in *American Film* (Washington, D.C.), December 1986.
Fuksiewicz, J., "Des Polonais a l'Quest," in *CinemAction* (Conde-sur-Noireau, France), July 1990.
Saada, N., "Skolimowski tourne *Ferdydurke,*" in *Cahiers du Cinema* (Paris), March 1991.
Miodek, M., "*Ferdydurke,*" in *Filmowy Serwis Prasowy,* vol. 38, no. 3, 1992.
Mizrahi, S., "La porte de la maturite," in *Positif* (Paris), March 1992.

* * *

Together with Roman Polanski, Jerzy Skolimowski is the most remarkable representative of the second generation of the Polish new wave. Younger than Wajda, Munk, or Kawalerowicz. These two did not share the hope for a new society after World War II. They are more skeptical filmmakers, to the point of cynicism at times. With Polanski, Skolimowski wrote *Knife in the Water,* which deals precisely with the relationship between two generations, after having also collaborated on the script of Wajda's *Innocent Sorcerers,* one of the director's rare attempts at portraying Poland's youth.

A student in ethnography, a poet, an actor, and a boxer, Skolimowski went to the Lodz film school (1960-1964) and graduated with a diploma work that brought world attention to his talent. That film, *Rysopis (Identification Marks: None),* and its totally controlled sequel *Walkover,* reveal an astonishing flexible style as it follows a central character, Andrzej Leszczyc, played by Skolimowski himself. Without resorting to a subjective camera, the director nevertheless makes us see reality through his hero. He refuses dramatic plot twists, filming instead in a manner very much like a jazz musician—all rhythm and improvisation. *Rysopis* tells of the few hours before being called up for military service, while *Walkover* provides an account of the time preceding a boxing match. A limited number of shots (39 and 29, respectively!) give an extraordinary sense of fluidity, of life caught in its most subtle shifts.

Bariera is a much more literary and symbolic work. It offers the same themes and milieu (young people, often students), although with a dreamlike atmosphere. The film's somnambulistic quality reappears later in Skolimowski's work, though integrated into its realistic surface. "Our cynical and indifferent generation still possesses romantic aspirations," says one of the characters, a statement that accurately sums up the filmmaker's ambivalent attitude towards life.

If *Bariera* was, according to Skolimowski, influenced by Godard's *Pierrot le fou,* his next film, *Le Départ,* shot in Belgium, borrowed two actors, Jean-Pierre Léaud and Catherine Duport, from the French director's *Masculin féminin.* The film deals with a young hairdresser who dreams of becoming a rally driver, and his relationship with a girl. The same sensitive portrait of youth is found again in a more accomplished work, *Deep End,* a brilliant portrayal of a London swimming bath attendant and his tragic love affair.

The titles of Skolimowski's films (*Walkover, Barrier, Departure, Hands Up, Deep End*) suggest the relationship to sports, movement, and physical effort that characterize his nervous and dynamic style. *Hands Up,* banned for fifteen years by the Polish authorities because of its bleak symbolic portrayal of a group of people shut up inside a railway carriage, prompted Skolimowski to work in the West, though he has always returned regularly to his home country. But difficulties associated with an international career appeared quickly with the failure of *The Adventures of Gerard,* a spoof on Conan Doyle's Napoleonic novel, and the more evident one of *King, Queen, Knave,* a film based on Nabokov's novel that was shot in Munich.

However, Skolimowski came back to the forefront of European filmmaking with *The Shout* and *Moonlighting.* The former, adapted from a Robert Graves short story, has a sense of the absurd which verges on creating a surrealistic atmosphere—a classic component of Polish culture. This film, which concerns a love triangle between a kind of sorcerer, the woman he is in love with, and her husband, is an intense, haunting piece of work.

Moonlighting, arguably Skolimowski's best film to date, was written and shot within a few months and looks deceptively simple. The tale of four Polish workers sent from Warsaw to refurbish the house a rich Pole has bought in London gradually reveals layers of meaning, commenting on contacts between East and West and repression in Poland. The nightmare emerges slowly from a close scrutiny of reality, confirming that Skolimowski's materialism and lucidity do not contradict but rather refine his unique poetic sensibility.

Subsequent films included *Success, The Lightship, Torrents of Spring,* and *30 Door Key.* Of these, *The Lightship* was notable for its depiction of a grim power struggle between characters played by Klaus Maria Brandauer and Robert Duvall. *Torrents of Spring,* meanwhile, a visually lavish drama about a nineteenth-century Russian aristocrat and his love for two women, was based on an Ivan Turgenev story.

—Michel Ciment

SNOW, Michael

Nationality: Canadian. **Born:** Michael James Aleck Snow in Toronto, Ontario, 10 December 1929. **Education:** Upper Canada College, Toronto, 1946-51; Ontario College of Art, Toronto, 1951-55. **Family:** Married filmmaker Joyce Wieland, 1959. **Career:** Independent artist, musician, filmmaker, and photographer, Toronto, from 1955; worked at Graphic Films, Toronto, and directed first film, animated short *A to Z,* 1955-56; moved to New York City, 1962; worked in several media, began concentrating on film, from mid-1960s; represented Canada at Venice Biennale with films and other art works, 1970; professor of advanced film studies, Yale University, 1970; returned to Toronto, 1971; visiting artist, Nova Scotia College of Art & Design, Halifax, 1970, 1974, and Ontario College of Art, 1973, 1974, 1976. **Awards:** Guggenheim Fellowship, 1972; LL.D., Brock University, St. Catherine's, Ontario, 1975; Order of Canada, 1981; Independent Experimental Film Award, Los Angeles Film Critics Association, 1983. **Address:** c/o The Isaacs Gallery, 179 John Street, Toronto, Ontario M5T 1X3, Canada.

Films as Director:

1956 *A to Z* (short)
1964 *New York Eye and Ear Control* (*A Walking Woman Work*)
1965 *Short Shave*

1966/67 ***Wavelength***
1967 *Standard Time*
1968/69 (*Back and Forth*); *One Second in Montreal*; *Dripping Water* (with Joyce Wieland)
1970 *Side Seat Paintings Slides Sound Film*
1970/71 *La Region centrale* (*The Central Region*)
1972/76 *Breakfast* (*Table Top Dolly*)
1974 *Two Sides to Every Story* (2-screen)
1972/74 *Rameau's Nephew by Diderot Thanx to Dennis Young by Wilma Schoen*
1980/81 *Presents*
1982 *So Is This*
1984 *Funnel Piano*
1988 *Seated Figures*
1990 *See You Later* (*Au Revoir*)
1991 *To Lavoisier Who Died in the Reign of Terror*

Other Films:

1988 *I Will Not Make Any More Boring Art* (MacGillivray) (doc) (role)

Publications

By SNOW: books—

Michael Snow: A Survey, exhibition catalogue, Art Gallery of Toronto, 1970.
Cover to Cover, Halifax, 1973.
Collected Writings of Michael Snow, Waterloo, 1994.
The Michael Snow Project: Music/Sound: 1948-1993 (editor), Toronto, 1995.
Screen Writings: Scripts and Texts by Independent Filmmakers, edited by Scott MacDonald, Berkeley, 1995.

By SNOW: articles—

"Letter from Michael Snow," in *Film Culture* (New York), no. 46, 1967.
"Conversation with Michael Snow," with Jonas Mekas and P. Adams Sitney, in *Film Culture* (New York), Autumn 1967.
"Michael Snow on 'La Region Centrale,'" in *Film Culture* (New York), Spring 1971.
"Passage," in *Artforum* (New York), September 1971.
"The Life and Times of Michael Snow," interview with J. Medjuck, in *Take One* (Montreal), April 1972.
"Snow's Sinema Soufflé," including interview with A. Ibranyi-Kiss, in *Cinema Canada* (Montreal), May/June 1975.
"Michael Snow in San Francisco," interview with P. Adams Sitney and others, in *Cinemanews* (San Francisco), no. 2/4, 1979.
Interview with Jonas Mekas and P. Adams Sitney, in *Cahiers du Cinéma* (Paris), January 1979.
"The 'Presents' of Michael Snow," an interview with Jonathan Rosenbaum, in *Film Comment* (New York), May/June 1981.
Interview with F. Ziolkowski, in *On Film* (Los Angeles), Spring 1984.
Interview with P. Lehman, in *Wide Angle* (Baltimore, Maryland), vol. 7, nos. 1/2, 1985.
"Letters: A Disturbing Omission," in *MacLean's,* 26 March 1990.

On SNOW: books—

Gidal, Peter, *Structural Film Anthology,* London, 1976.
Hanhardt, John, and others, *A History of the American Avant-Garde,* New York, 1976.
Le Grice, Malcolm, *Abstract Film and Beyond,* London, 1977.
Sitney, P. Adams, *Visionary Film: The American Avant-Garde 1943-1978,* New York, 1979.
Cornwell, Regina, *Snow Seen: Films and Photographs of Michael Snow,* Toronto, 1980.
Elder, Bruce, *Image and Identity: Reflection on Canadian Film and Culture,* Waterloo, 1989.
James, David, *Allegories of Cinema: American Film in the Sixties,* Princeton, 1989.
Testa, Bart, ed., *Spirit in the Landscape,* Toronto, 1989.
Mellencamp, Patricia, *Indiscretions: Avant-Garde Film, Video and Feminism,* Bloomington, 1990.
MacDonald, Scott, *A Critical Cinema—2,* Berkeley, 1992.
Wees, William, *Light Moving in Time: Studies in the Visual Aesthetics of Avant-Garde Film,* Berkeley, 1992.
Bordwell, David, and Kristin Thompson, *Film Art: An Introduction,* New York, 1993.
MacDonald, Scott, *Film: Motion Studies,* London, 1993.
Peterson, James, *Dreams of Chaos, Visions of Order: Understanding the American Avant-Garde Cinema,* Detroit, 1994.
Dompierre, Louise, Philip Monk, and Dennis Reid, *The Michael Snow Project: Visual Art 1951-1993,* Toronto, 1995.
Shedden, Jim, ed., *Presence and Absence: The Films of Michael Snow 1956-1991,* Toronto, 1995.

On SNOW: articles—

Michelson, Annette, "Toward Snow," in *Artforum* (New York), June 1971.
Mekas, Jonas, "A Note on Michael Snow, Written in a Minnesota Snowstorm," in *Take One* (Montreal), April 1972.
Skoller, Donald, "Aspects of Cinematic Consciousness...," in *Film Comment* (New York), September/October 1972.
Simon, Bill, "New Forms in Film," in *Artforum* (New York), October 1972.
Marcorelles, L., and T. Raneri, "Snow Storms Italy," in *Cinema Canada* (Montreal), February/March 1973.
Hayum, A., "A Casing Shelved," in *Film Culture* (New York), Spring 1973.
Heath, S., "Narrative Space," in *Screen* (London), no. 3, 1976.
Cornwell, R., "Hitting on 'A Lot of Near Mrs.,'" in *Film Reader* (Evanston, Illinois), no.3, 1978.
Bloch, L., "Digne (A propos de Michael Snow)," in *Cahiers du Cinéma* (Paris), July/August 1978.
Michelson, A., "About Snow," in *October* (Cambridge, Massachusetts), Spring 1979.
Elder, R. B., "All Things in Their Times," in *Ciné-Tracts* (Montreal), Summer/Fall 1982.
"Michael Snow Issue" of *Afterimage* (London), Winter 1982/83.
Brakhage, Stan, "Some Words on the North," in *American Book Review* (Boulder, Colorado), May/June 1988.
Hoolboom, Mike, "On the Road," in *Millennium Film Journal* (New York), Winter 1989/Spring 1990.
Camper, Fred, "Look Closer—What Do You See?," in *Chicago Reader,* 5 June 1992.
Young, Pamela, "Snow Storm: A Sprawling Retrospective Spotlights a Prolific Creator," in *Maclean's* (Toronto), 21 March 1994.

* * *

After studies at the Ontario College of Art, Michael Snow simultaneously pursued careers as a jazz musician and an artist, making sculpture, paintings, and photography. He began to make films while working for a commercial film company in Canada, but his first important film, *New York Eye and Ear Control,* was made in New York, as an extension of his attempt to represent a graphic image (his "Walking Woman" outline) in a wide range of media. The film is notable for its use of a powerful jazz soundtrack.

In *Wavelength,* he built the entire film around the exploration of the illusionary properties of the zoom lens. That set the program for his most ambitious cinematic works, several of which examine the range of possibilities inherent in a given technique. In , the entire film consists of panning movements, first horizontally, then vertically, and finally a superimposed recapitulation for both. *One Second in Montreal* brought the film composed wholly of stills to a new intensity of stasis, testing the possibilities of perceptual distinctions when shots are held unusually long, but for varying lengths of time.

The Central Region employs a specially built, remote-controlled equatorial mount to perform intricate movements, sweeping the entire desolate landscape of the zone of northern Canada where it was set up, to present the visible world as if it were the inside of a great sphere. This three-hour-long film without human presence develops the tensions between cinematic time, as emphasized by the unequivocally mechanical camera gyrations, and the natural cycle of the solar day.

Rameau's Nephew by Diderot (Thanx to Dennis Young) by Wilma Schoen takes on an encyclopedic range of topics related to picture and sound, with a Duchampian "study" of language most prominent. For 285 minutes, in apparently 24 distinct sections, the film explores the human body as a source of sound. The inherent independence of picture and sound in all films becomes the justification for the invention of a series of totally improbable environments born of the disembodiment of sound: someone plays a sink, a voice roves around a room filled with people, a male/female urinating context is grotesquely simplified, a chair guffaws wildly, a piano moans out an orgasm, and so on. Like all of Snow's major films, this, his longest, takes a technical fact as the generating force for a wholly cinematic presentation of space.

Rameau's Nephew was the turning point in Snow's career. In the course of its production he gradually shifted the center of his activities from New York to Toronto, and in the years following filmmaking has played a subsidiary role to his sculpture, music, and holography. *Rameau's Nephew* was also a transition insofar as Snow shifted his attention from baroque examinations of camera movement to another dimension of cinema. In his subsequent film, *Presents,* he directed his attention to editing. In that field the challenge of his rivals for preeminence among the avant-garde filmmakers of his generation, especially Stan Brakhage, was so great that the uniqueness of Snow's achievement was not as apparent as in his earlier work. However, the dimension of parody, which had been latent in the earlier films and emerged in full force in the Menippean comedy of *Rameau's Nephew,* continues to animate *Presents* and all of his later work. Beginning with *Rameau's Nephew* it is apparent that Snow is having fun making films, and that intellectually stimulating fun is often infectious. Thus *Presents* begins with a hilarious palinode of his own in which the stage clumsily rocks back and forth, rather than the camera, before entering upon an extended series of very short takes, each glimpsing a different place.

None of the films Snow made in Canada have had the influence and resonance of the work of his astonishing decade in New York. This may be due, in part, to the fact that most of these works extend, refine, and parody types first presented in the 1960s and 1970s by other avant-garde filmmakers (in several instances themselves influenced by Snow and under his mentorship): Hollis Frampton's film in words, *Poetic Justice* (1972), precedes Snow's purely verbal *So Is This* (1982), and his *Palindrome* (1969) first explored the color effects of chemical decompositions of the image which Snow elaborated on in *To Lavoisier Who Died in the Reign of Terror* (1991); Ernie Gehr's *Field* (1970) reduces a landscape to fluctuating horizontal bands by sweeping the camera close to the ground, while Snow's *Seated Figures* (1988) projects the vertical shadows of an audience (together with their sounds) against a complex fugue of horizontal sweeps; and Snow's *See You Later (Au Revoir)* (1990) recalls a series of three-minute Fluxus films Peter Moore shot with different artists in the mid 1960s using a 2,000 frames-per-second camera.

In 1993 the Art Gallery of Toronto mounted a massive exhibition of Snow's work in several media and published *The Michael Snow Project* in several volumes.

—P. Adams Sitney

SODERBERGH, Steven

Nationality: American. **Born:** 14 January 1963, in Atlanta, GA. **Education:** High school graduate, 1980. **Family:** Married Betsy Brantley; one daughter. **Career:** Did odd jobs while writing scripts and directing short films, 1980-85; directed *90125,* a Yes concert film, for MTV, 1986; first feature, *sex, lies, and videotape,* a surprise international success, 1989. **Awards:** Grammy Award for Best Director, 1986, for *90125;* Palme d'Or for Best Feature Film, Cannes International Film Festival, 1989, and Independent Spirit awards for Best Feature and Best Director, 1990, for *sex, lies, and videotape.* **Agent:** Pat Dollard, United Talent Agency, 9560 Wilshire Blvd., Beverly Hills, CA 90212, U.S.A.

Films as Director:

1986 *90215* (doc; for TV)
1989 *sex, lies, and videotape* (+ sc, ed)
1991 *Kafka* (+ ed)
1993 *King of the Hill* (+ sc); "The Quiet Room" (episode of TV series *Fallen Angels*)
1995 *The Underneath* (+ co-sc, uncredited)

Other Films:

1993 *Suture* (exec pr)

Publications

By SODERBERGH: book—

sex, lies, and videotape (journal and screenplay), Harper & Row, 1990.

On SODERBERGH: articles—

Minsky, Terri, "Hot Phenom," *Rolling Stone* (New York), May 18, 1989.
Jacobson, Harlan, "Truth or Consequences," *Film Comment* (New York), July-August 1989.
Gabriel, Trip, "Steven Soderbergh: The Sequel," *New York Times Magazine,* 3 November 1991.
Werckmeister, O. K., "Kafka 007," *Critical Inquiry,* Winter 1995.

* * *

Steven Soderbergh's work is difficult to characterize as a whole, considering the remarkable variety among his first four features: a contemporary sexual drama/comedy; a fantasy thriller set in Kafka's Prague; a portrait of a child growing up in Depression-era America; and a remake of a classic film noir. Following the sensational success

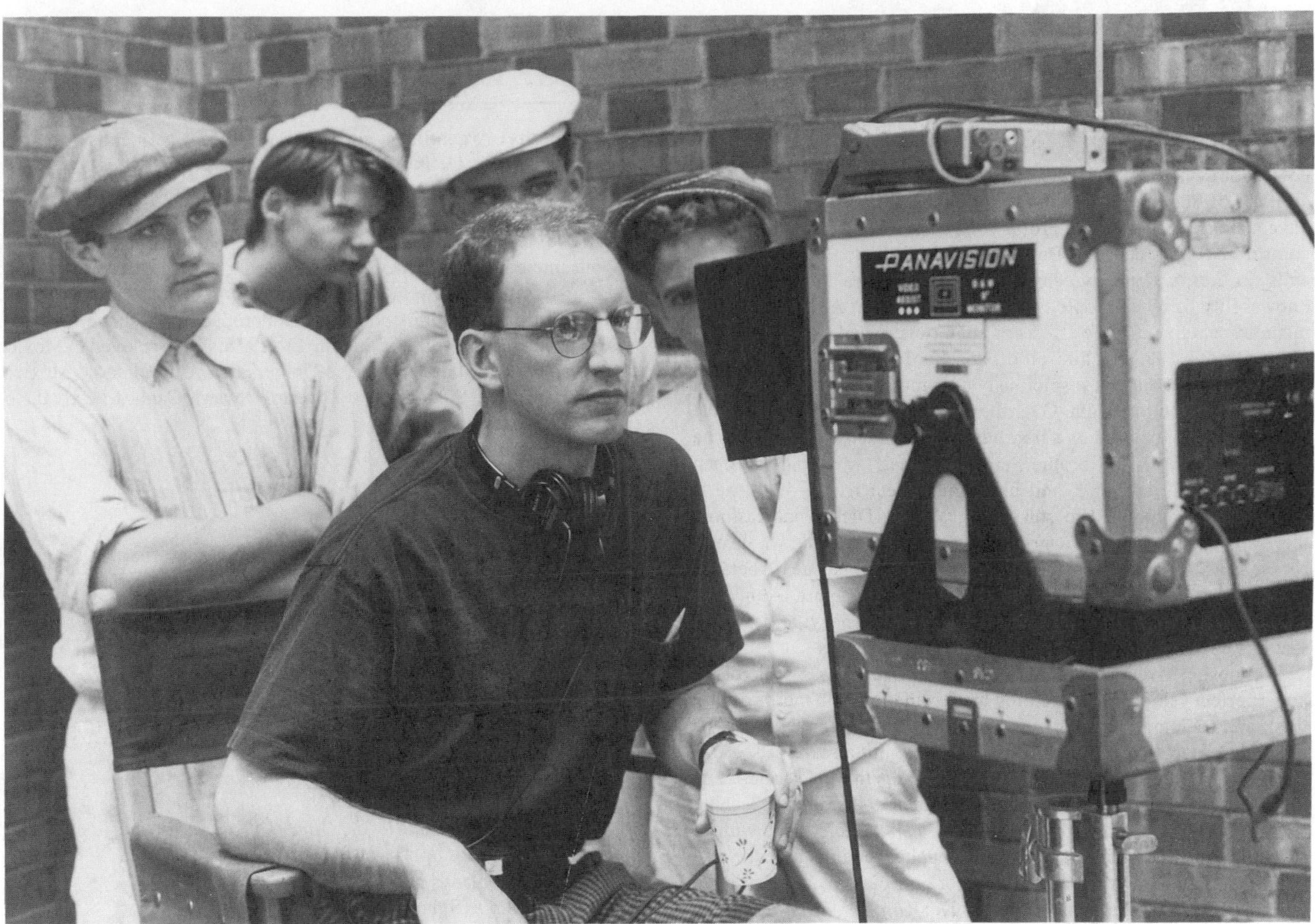

Steven Soderbergh directing *King of the Hill*

of his first feature, *sex, lies, and videotape,* Soderbergh was often compared to other young independent American filmmakers, notably Jim Jarmusch and Hal Hartley. However, as subsequent films have shown, his film style is much less immediately identifiable (or from a Hollywood viewpoint, less eccentric) than those others'. Overall, one can say that his narrative techniques tend to be concise and polished in ways reminiscent of classic Hollywood rather than European models, yet fresh, with unusual overall structures and surprising turns from scene to scene; his cinematography is always superb, notably in framing and lighting, though extremely varied from film to film to match the subject matter and mood. Unfortunately, Soderbergh has not continued to receive the critical and popular attention awarded to his first feature, or attracted enthusiasts (e.g., Internet fan clubs) as have Hartley and some others; yet he remains in his own way a daring artist whose projects have been far from predictable.

sex, lies, and videotape is more than a highly accomplished debut film—it is quite simply a remarkably accomplished film. In portraying a budding relationship between a man who is impotent, except when watching his own video interviews with women on sexual topics, and a woman who finds that her husband and sister are having an affair behind her back, the writer/director manages to create neither low farce nor soap-operatic psychodrama. Actually, the film is rather touchingly romantic, in a witty, gentle, unsoppy sort of way. Soderbergh deftly introduces the four main characters through a montage of scenes linked by a voiceover of Ann speaking to her therapist; he moves the story forward with some striking closeups and high angle shots, while unobtrusively establishing a world for each character through decor (including Graham's mostly empty spaces). And he brilliantly structures the climactic scene of Ann taking hold of Graham's camera: he postpones the second half of it until later, when her unfaithful but furious husband seizes the tape and begins to watch it, and Soderbergh cuts from the tape itself to a flashback of Ann and Graham making the tape. As for Soderbergh's handling of the actors, one might simply note that the film immeasurably boosted the careers of James Spader and Andie MacDowell and gave Laura San Giacomo a strong debut. If Peter Gallagher's performance is merely solid—perhaps because his character is conceived more as a simple type than the other three—Soderbergh did later provide the actor with one of his best, most subtle screen roles, in *The Underneath.*

Striking into new territory for his eagerly anticipated second feature, Soderbergh created a work uneasily occupying a space between a European art film and a plot-driven Hollywood suspense film. *Kafka* has a script that derives from two different kinds of paranoid world—the literary one of Franz Kafka and the cinematic one of the political-conspiracy thriller—and a visual style inspired by Carol Reed's *The Third Man* (rather more than by Orson Welles's eccentric version of Kafka's *The Trial*), and perhaps too blatantly by Terry Gilliam's *Brazil* in the color sequence inside the Castle. The film does have astonishingly handsome black-and-white cinematography, some quite terrifying moments involving a shrieking killer, and some droll slapstick humor in the antics of a pair of office assistants. But there is an awkwardness in having a protagonist who on one level is the "real" Franz Kafka—shown as a drudge in an insurance office who writes agonized letters to his father and also fantastic stories like "Metamorphosis" and others alluded to—but on another level is a reluctant movie hero drawn into uncovering a sinister organization that turns out to be diabolical in a much more conventional way than anything in an actual Kafka story.

King of the Hill has its terrifying moments too, notably in the figure of a snarly bellboy trying to evict the young hero from the hotel room where his father has more or less abandoned him. Indeed, all three of Soderbergh's features following *sex, lies, and videotape* have a single isolated male protagonist trapped in a world out of his control or comprehension. But *King of the Hill* also particularly recalls *sex, lies, and videotape* in its concern with lies and the doubtful knowability of other people. The plot, based upon A. E. Hotchner's memoir, centers upon the efforts of an impoverished twelve-year-old (Jesse Bradford) to pass himself off at school as well-to-do, and upon his need to trust that his suspiciously undemonstrative father (Jeroen Krabbe) will return to him. Overall, the story line is rather dark: the boy not only is exposed as a liar, but loses contact with everyone he loves—in turn, his kid brother, sickly mother, travelling-salesman father, the girl next door, and his roguish best friend—until he is nearly literally reduced to starvation. Yet, in Dickensian fashion, there are also warm and downright comical moments and whole episodes, as well as a number of reunions. Soderbergh manages to balance the bleak and joyful elements skillfully, for the most part, though one might wish the cinematography did not have that hazy golden glow that has become too commonly used for period pieces.

In choosing to remake the classic film noir *Criss Cross,* Soderbergh had a perfect vehicle for continuing his fascination with motifs of lies, trust, and seemingly cosmic entrapment within the conventions of a genre that specializes in such concerns. Most impressively, *The Underneath* has the true noir feel, without aping the black-and-white visuals of the Robert Siodmak original or other 1940s films, or leaning toward parody a la *Body Heat,* or making a slick melodrama with an unambiguously decent protagonist and an upbeat ending (as in the case of Barbet Schroeder's remake of another noir classic, *Kiss of Death,* which opened at the same time as *The Underneath*). Selecting widescreen Panavision with some very unsettling compositions, and constructing a far more complex flashback structure than the original film had, Soderbergh flawlessly plays out the drama of an ex-gambling addict still obsessed with his ex-wife (now married to a gangster) and drawn into an armored car robbery that betrays his kindly mentor. There is a telling moment when Michael's new girlfriend, sensing his mind on other things, remarks, "You're not very present tense": a perfect description of a film noir hero trapped in webs of the past and fearing the future. In the film's fluid flashback structure we indeed see Michael's life fluctuating between three time lines, and we gradually put the puzzle together: his selfish or addictive past (marked by his having a beard); his ethical/familial/sexual entanglements when he returns to his hometown; and (in what may be considered flashforwards) the day of the robbery, marked by bluish lighting and time subtitles, like "6:02 p.m." Only at the violent moment of the robbery, more than an hour into the film, are we fully "caught up" in time; and at this point Soderbergh proceeds to a daring seven minutes of subjective-viewpoint shots as various characters address a delirious Michael in his hospital bed. This is followed by a set piece of suspense, involving a possible assassin, that may derive from the earlier film or the novel but is so superbly gauged that it is a classic in itself.

Receiving mixed reviews and low attendance at its opening, *The Underneath* quickly disappeared from theatres—an undeserved fate for one of the best of the neo-noirs, and perhaps Soderbergh's most accomplished work after *sex, lies, and videotape.* One can only hope that the director will continue to explore his favorite—or obsessive—themes of honesty and (self-) deceit in ways that use Hollywood traditions with a new vigor.

—Joseph Milicia

SOLANAS, Fernando E., and Octavio GETINO

Nationality: Argentinian. **Born:** Solanas born in Buenos Aires, 16 February 1936; Getino born in Spain, moved to Argentina, 1952. **Education:** Solanas studied law, theater, and musical composition. **Career:** Getino active as writer, also made short documentary *Trasmallos,* early 1960s; Solanas worked in advertising, early 1960s; both entered Cine Liberación group, making underground films, 1966; Perón returned to power, Getino accepted post on national film board, 1973; following military coup against Perón, Solanas moved to Paris, Getino moved to Peru, working for TV, 1976; Getino moved to Mexico as member of Film Dept. of the Universidad Autónoma de México, 1982. **Awards:** Solanas, Best Director Award, Cannes Festival, for *Sur,* 1988.

Films as Directors:

1968 ***La hora de los hornos*** (*The Hour of the Furnaces*) (Solanas d, co-sc, co-ph, ed, mus; Getino co-sc, sound)
1971 *Perón: actualización politica y doctrinaria para la toma del poder*; *Perón: La revolución justicialista* (both films made as part of Grupo de Cine Liberación)
1973 *El familiar* (Getino only)
1976 *Los hijos de Fierro* (Solanas only)
1978 *La familia Pichilin* (Getino only)
1979 *La mirada de los otros* (*Régard des autres*)) (doc) (Solanas only)
1986 *Tangos—el exilio de Gardel* (*Tangos—l'exil de Gardel*) (Solanas only)
1988 *Sur* (Solanas only)
1992 *El Viaje* (Solanos only)

Publications

By SOLANAS AND GETINO: books—

Cine, cultura y descolonización, Mexico City, 1973.
Getino, Octavio, *Notas sobre cine argentino y latinoamericano,* Mexico City, 1984.

By SOLANAS AND GETINO: articles—

"Cinema as a Gun," an interview with Solanas by Gianni Volpi and others, in *Cineaste* (New York), Fall 1969.
"Fernando Solanas: An Interview," in *Film Quarterly* (Berkeley), Fall 1970.
Getino, Octavio, and Fernando Solanas, "Towards a Third Cinema," in *Cineaste* (New York), Winter 1971.
Solanas, Fernando, and others, "Situation et perspectives du cinéma d'Amérique Latine," in *Positif* (Paris), June 1972.
"Dar espacio a la expresión popular," Solanas interview, in *Cine Cubano* (Havana), no. 86/88, 1973.
"Argentina: Fernando Solanas," an interview with Don Ranvaud, in *Framework* (Norwich), Spring 1979.
Solanas, Fernando, and others, "Round Table: The Cinema: Art Form or Political Weapon," in *Framework* (Norwich), Autumn 1979.
"Godard on Solanas/Solanas on Godard," in *Reviewing Histories,* edited by Coco Fusco, Buffalo, New York, 1987.
"The Tango of Esthetics and Politics," interview with Solanas by Coco Fusco, in *Cineaste* (New York), vol. 16, nos. 1/2, 1987/1988.

Fernando E. Solanas

Interview with Paranagua, in *Positif,* December 1988.
"De *La hora de los hornos* a *Sur*: Entrevista con Fernando Solanas," with Luis Gastelum, in *Dicine* (Mexico City), September 1989.

On SOLANAS AND GETINO: books—

Pick, Zuzana Mirjam, *Latin American Filmmakers and the Third Cinema,* Ottawa, 1978.
King, John, and Nissa Torrents, editors, *The Garden of Forking Paths: Argentine Cinema,* London, 1988.
Pines, Jim, and Paul Willemen, editors, *Questions of Third Cinema,* London, 1989.
King, John, *Magical Reels: A History of Cinema in Latin America,* London, 1990.

On SOLANAS AND GETINO: articles—

Matthews, John, "... And After?: A Response to Solanas and Getino," in *Afterimage* (London), Summer 1971.
Wilson, David, "Aspects of Latin American Political Cinema," in *Sight and Sound* (London), Summer 1972.
Burton, Julianne, "The Camera as 'Gun': Two Decades of Culture and Resistance in Latin America," in *Latin American Perspectives,* Winter 1978.
Hennebelle, Guy, "Le Réalisme magique et les élans du coeur," in *Ecran* (Paris), 15 March 1979.
Stam, Robert, "*Hour of the Furnaces* and the Two Avant-Gardes," in *Millennium* (New York), Fall/Winter 1980/81.
"Solanas Issue" of *Avant-Scène du Cinéma* (Paris), January/February 1989.
Evora, J. A., "Milagro en la Torre de Babel," in *Cine Cubano,* no. 129, 1990.
Chanan, M., "Le troisieme cinema de Solanas et Getino," in *Cinemaction,* July 1991.
Paranagua, P. A., "Solanas, victime d'un attentat," in *Positif,* July/August 1991.
Arlyck, R., "Argentine Filmmaker Fights Menem 'Mafia,'" in *The Independent,* October 1991.
Pelko, S., "Fernando Solanas: izumitelj poti," in *Ekran,* no. 6/7, 1992.
Vicari, D., "La volonta di crescere nel viaggio di Fernando Solanas," in *Cinema Nuovo,* March/April 1993.

* * *

Originators of the pivotal "third cinema" concept, Solanas and Getino demonstrated its practice in the only really important film they were to make—the influential *La hora de los hornos.* "Third cinema" was the product of a very specific context: the world-wide insurrections during the late 1960s. While U.S. students were protesting against the Vietnam War, Argentina moved close to genuine social revolution for the first time in its history. Solanas and Getino participated in that movement as cineastes, but they made it clear that their concern was with social change, not film art, in their first declaration as the Cine Liberacion Group: "Our commitment as cineastes in a dependent country is not with universal culture or art or abstract man; before anything else it is with the liberation of our country and the Latin American peoples."

As intellectuals and artists in a neo-colonial situation, Solanas and Getino were greatly influenced by the "Third Worldism" of the period, frequently citing ideologists from the African (Frantz Fanon) and Asian (Mao Tse-Tung) struggles. They contrasted "third cinema" to the "first cinema" of the Hollywood industry and to the auteurist "second cinema" in various ways, distinguishing it first of all by its ideological commitment to anti-imperialism and the struggle for socialism. Against the consumerism provoked by the hermetic narrative structures of Hollywood, they proposed a cinema which would require active audience participation. Thus, a film was important as a "detonator" or a "pretext" for assembling a group, not as an experience that was born and that died on the screen. Likening themselves to guerrillas who open paths with machete blows, they perceived cinema as a provisional tool: "Our time is one of hypothesis rather than thesis, a time of works in process—unfinished, unordered, violent works made with the camera in one hand and a rock in the other."

The most realized description of "third cinema" can be found near the end of their often-reprinted essay, "Towards a Third Cinema." There they summarize it in the following manner: "The third cinema above all counters the film industry of a cinema of characters with one of themes, that of individuals with that of masses, that of the author with that of the operative group, one of neocolonial misinformation with one of information, one of escape with one that recaptures the truth, that of passivity with that of aggressions. To an institutionalized cinema, it counterposes a guerilla cinema; to movies as shows, it opposes a film act ... to a cinema made for the old kind of human being, it proposes a *cinema fit for a new kind of human being, for what each one of us has the possibility of becoming.*"

Given their concern to produce a cinema of information rather than one of fantasies to be consumed, Solanas and Getino naturally turned to the documentary. However, they conceived of the documentary as "not fundamentally one which illustrates, documents, or passively establishes a situation; rather it attempts to intervene in the situation as an element providing thrust or rectification ... it provides discovery through transformation." *La hora de los hornos* may be a bit too didactic at times, but it was certainly more "revolutionary" than the documentaries they were to make as the official cineastes they became on the return of Juan Perón, the urban populist who was President of Argentina (1946-55 and 1973-74).

Because of the timeliness of *La hora de los hornos* and the extensive publication of Solanas' and Getino's theoretical writings and interviews, they have received attention which may be disproportionate to that given to other Latin American cineastes of greater achievement, most notably the Cubans. Nonetheless, the French film critic Guy Hennebelle argued that "third cinema" is the concept that seems to be "most viable" as a counterpoint to traditional film study, stating, "according to this perspective, a veritable 'counter-history' of the seventh art is yet to be written." In both their writings and their cinematic practice, Solanas and Getino have provided an alternative and a clearly articulated challenge to bourgeois cinema.

—John Mraz

SOLAS, Humberto

Nationality: Cuban. **Born:** Havana, December 1942. **Education:** Studied architecture, 1957. **Career:** Involved in insurrectionary movement against Batista government, 1957-59; member of Instituto Cubano de Arte e Industria Cinematografico (ICAIC), from 1959; directed first film in collaboration with Hector Veitia, under supervision of Joris Ivens, 1961; Licenciatura in History, University of Havana, 1978.

Films as Director:

1961 *Casablanca*
1962 *Minerva traduce el mar* (co-d)
1963 *Variaciones*; *El retrato*
1964 *El acoso*

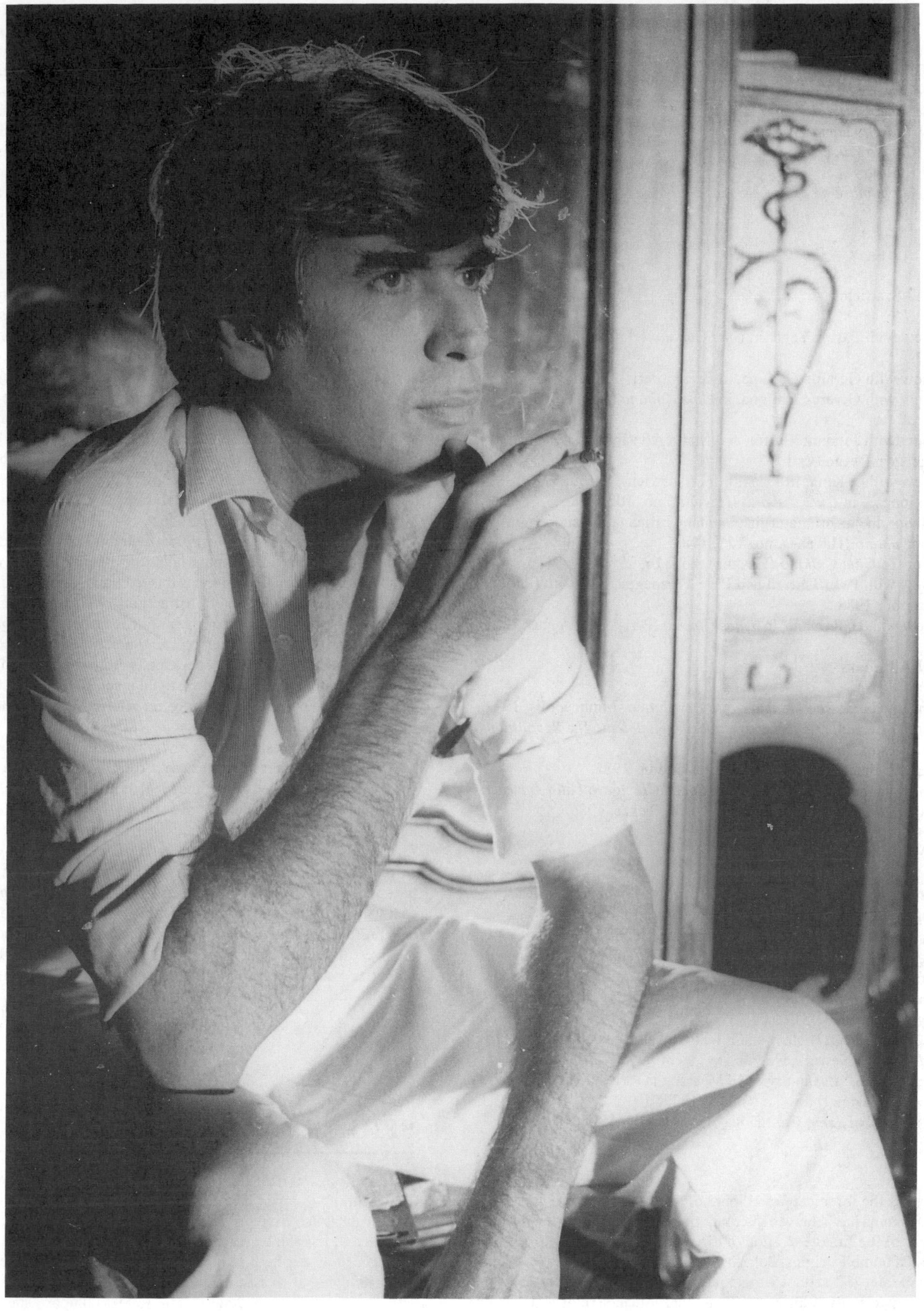

Humberto Solas

1965 *La acusation*; *Manuela*
1968 ***Lucía***
1972 *Un dia de Noviembre*
1974 *Simparele*
1975 *Cantata de Chile* (+ sc)
1977 *Nacer en Leningrado* (short)
1978 *Wilfredo Lam*
1982 *Cecilia Valdés*
1983 *Amada*
1986 *Un hombre de exito* (*A Successful Man*) (+ sc)

Publications

By SOLAS: articles—

Interview with Pastor Vega, in *Cine Cubano* (Havana), no. 42/44, 1967.
Interview with Gerardo Chijona, in *Ecran* (Paris), January 1977.
Interview with Gerardo Chijona, in *Cine Cubano* (Havana), March 1978.
Interview with Julianne Burton and Marta Alvear, in *Jump Cut* (Chicago), December 1978.
Interview with J. King, in *Framework* (Norwich), Spring 1979.
"Reflexiones," in *Cine Cubano* (Havana), no. 102, 1982.
"Alrededor de una dramaturgia cinematográfica latinoamericano," in *Cine Cubano* (Havana), no. 105, 1983.
Interview in *Cine Cubano* (Havana), no. 116, 1986.
Interview with P. L. Thirard and P. A. Paranagua, in *Positif* (Paris), December 1988.
Interview with H. Romano, in *Jeune Cinéma* (Paris), July/August 1993.

On SOLAS: books—

Nelson, L., *Cuba: The Measure of a Revolution,* Minneapolis, 1972.
Myerson, Michael, *Memories of Underdevelopment: The Revolutionary Films of Cuba,* New York, 1973.
Chanan, Michael, *The Cuban Image,* London, 1985.
Burton, Julianne, editor, *Cinema and Social Change in Latin America: Conversations with Filmmakers,* Austin, Texas, 1986.

On SOLAS: articles—

Sutherland, Elizabeth, "Cinema of Revolution—Ninety Miles from Home," in *Film Quarterly* (Berkeley), Winter 1961/62.
Adler, Renata, article in *New York Times,* 10, 11, and 12 February 1969.
Engel, Andi, "Solidarity and Violence," in *Sight and Sound* (London), Autumn 1969.
Biskind, P., "*Lucía*: Struggles with History," in *Jump Cut* (Chicago), July/August 1974.
Mraz, John, "*Lucía*: History and Film in Revolutionary Cuba," in *Film and History* (Newark, New Jersey), February 1975.
Kovacs, Steven, "*Lucía*: Style and Meaning in Revolutionary Film," in *Monthly Review* (New York), June 1975.
"Solas Issue" of *Jump Cut* (Chicago), December 1978.

* * *

Perhaps the foremost practitioner of the historical genre for which Cuban cinema has achieved international acclaim, Humberto Solas is a member of the first generation of directors to mature under the revolution. Of humble origins, Solas became an urban guerrilla at age fourteen and later left school altogether because "it was a very unstable time to try to study. Either Batista (dictator of Cuba) closed down the university, or we did." Prior to the triumph of the revolution, being a filmmaker "seemed like an unrealizable dream," but Solas financed a short film out of his savings and was invited to join the Cuban Film Institute (ICAIC) soon after its founding in 1959. Although it is customary for Cuban directors to serve an extensive apprenticeship in documentaries, Solas directed several early fiction shorts as well. He considers his imitation of European film styles in these works to be typical of feelings of cultural inferiority and alienation in the underdeveloped world, and affirms that "Neither me, nor my generation, nor my country can be seen in any of these films."

Historical subjects proved to be Solas's avenue to Cuban and Latin American reality. He believes that the importance attached to historical films in Cuba derives from the fact that "Our history had been filtered through a bourgeois lens. We lack a coherent, lucid, and dignified appreciation of our national past." *Manuela,* a medium-length film on the guerrilla war in the mountains, was the first of Solas's works to embody "more genuinely Cuban forms of expression." His continuing search for national (and Latin American) cinematic idioms and themes led him to direct his masterpiece to date, *Lucía,* at age twenty-six. Focusing on three periods of Cuban history through the characters of representative women, Solás used three different film styles to portray forms of experience and cognition during these epochs. In his later films, Solas interpretively analyzed the history of Haiti (*Simparele*), Chile (*Cantata de Chile*), and slavery in Cuba (*Cecilia Valdés*). These works are marked by an exciting blend of music, dance, documentary footage, primitive painting, and the re-enactment of historical events in an operatic style.

Solas considers his films "historical melodramas," in which a Marxist perspective provides a materialistic explanation for events and personal psychology. He contrasts this to common melodrama and its "particular world of valorative abstractions" which determine events, but lack the power to explain them. For example, although the travails suffered by the heroines of *Lucía* are experienced personally, they are depicted as deriving specifically from the colonial and neocolonial situation of Cuba (and vestigial machismo), rather than from any "eternal passions" which have no relationship to concrete historical circumstances.

For Solas, historical cinema is always a dialogue about the present, and he has often chosen women as a central metaphor in his films because, as a dominated group, they feel more deeply and reflect more immediately the contradictions of society—for example, the maintenance of archaic forms such as *machismo* in a revolutionary situation. As Solas states: "The sad masquerade of limited, archetyped, and suffocating human relations in defense of private property is most transparent in the case of the women—half of humanity. The pathetic carnival of economic exploitation begins there." To Solas, the past is only present insofar as it continues to condition (for both good and bad) the lives of people today. It is about this past/present that Humberto Solas has made and continues to make beautiful and moving cinema.

—John Mraz

SPHEERIS, Penelope

Nationality: American. **Born:** New Orleans, LA, 2 December 1945. **Education:** School of Theater, Film, and Television, University of California at Los Angeles, M.F.A. **Family:** One daughter, whose father died of a heroine overdose in 1974. **Career:** Voted Most Likely to Succeed by her high school classmates; made several short films while studying at UCLA, early 1970s; worked as an actress and film editor, early 1970s; founded Rock 'n' Reel, a company specializing in rock music promotion, 1974; produced short films directed by Albert

Brooks and presented on *Saturday Night Live,* mid-late 1970s; entered the motion picture industry as producer of Brooks's feature *Real Life,* 1979; directed first theatrical feature, the documentary *The Decline of Western Civilization,* 1981; directed first fictional feature, *Suburbia,* 1984; co-created, co-wrote, and directed television series *Danger Theater,* 1993. **Agent:** The Gersh Agency, 232 North Canon Drive, Beverly Hills, CA 90210, U.S.A.

Films as Director:

1981 *The Decline of Western Civilization* (doc) (+ sc, pr)
1984 *Suburbia* (*The Wild Side*) (+ sc)
1985 *The Boys Next Door*
1986 *Hollywood Vice Squad*
1987 *Dudes*
1988 *The Decline of Western Civilization II: The Metal Years* (doc) (+ sc)
1991 *Prison Stories: Women on the Inside* (for TV) (episode of three-part film)
1992 *Wayne's World*; *Lifers Group: World Tour* (doc short)
1993 *The Beverly Hillbillies*
1994 *The Little Rascals* (+ sc)
1995 *Black Sheep*

Other Films:

1979 *Real Life* (Brooks) (pr)
1987 *Summer Camp Nightmare* (*The Butterfly Revolution*) (Dragin) (co-sc)
1990 *Wedding Band* (Raskov) (role)

Publications

By SPHEERIS: articles—

"Is There Life after Punk?," an interview with Peter Occhiogrosso in *American Film* (Washington, D.C.), April 1985.
Spheeris, Penelope, "Western Civilization Declines Again," in *Premiere* (New York), June 1988.
"Dialogue on Film," with Penelope Spheeris and Danny Elfman, in *American Film* (New York), February 1991.

On SPHEERIS: articles—

Gold, Richard, article in *Variety* (New York), 26 December 1984.
Wickenhaver, J., article in *Millimeter* (New York), April 1987.
Occhiogrosso, Peter, article in *Premiere* (New York), October 1987.
Milward, John, article in *Newsday* (Melville, New York), 17 June 1988.
Maslin, Janet, "Film View: Penelope Spheeris Finds the Heart of Rock," in *New York Times,* 26 June 1988.
Willman, Chris, article in *Los Angeles Times,* 1 March 1992.
Diamond, Jamie, "Penelope Spheeris: From Carny Life to *Wayne's World,*" in *New York Times,* 12 April 1992.
Cohn, Lawrence, "Truth-Tellers Start to Tell Tales," in *Variety* (New York), 11 May 1992.

* * *

Unlike many women directors, Penelope Spheeris does not make films that are sensitive at their core, that focus on women and their relationships and emotions. Rather, her films—at least the group she made in the first section of her career—are hard-edged and in-your-face brutal. In terms of subject matter, they often deal with male adolescent angst as it exists within a grim, realistic urban environment. If none are particularly distinguished, they certainly are linked thematically, and by their solemn and depressing outlook.

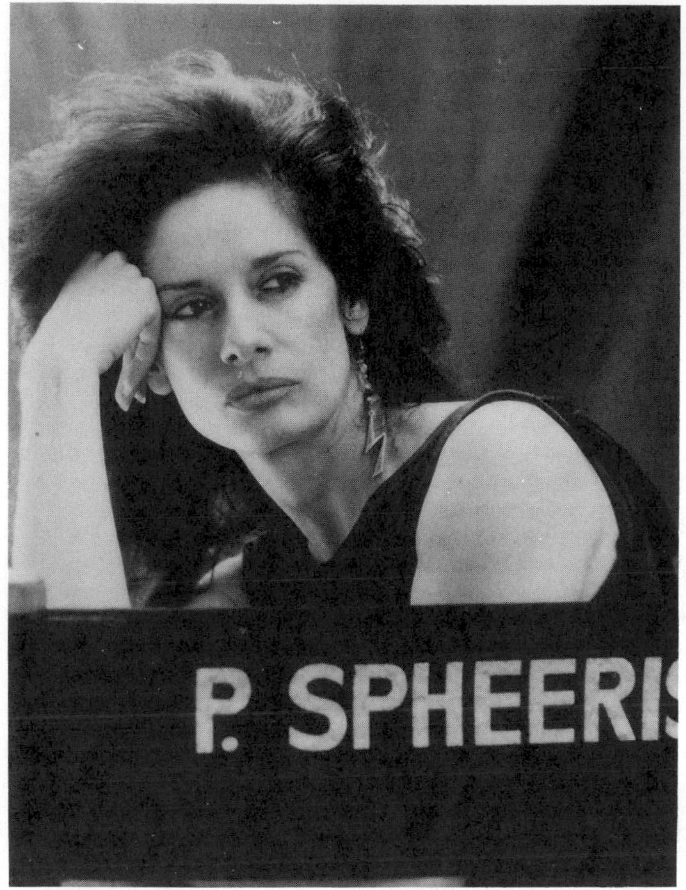

Penelope Spheeris

Suburbia, Spheeris's first non-documentary feature, details the plight of a group of teen runaways residing on the edge of Los Angeles. It opens with a pack of wild dogs tearing a baby to shreds. *The Boys Next Door* is the saga of two teen boys who become serial killers. It included footage which had to be edited out in order to avoid an X rating. *Dudes* focuses on some young urban punk rockers who cross paths with murderous Southwestern rednecks. Not all of Spheeris's young protagonists are male, however. One of the characters in *Hollywood Vice Squad* is a runaway girl who has become a heroin-addicted prostitute.

Spheeris has admitted that her preoccupation with alienation and brutality is directly related to the incidents in her life. "I look at violence in a realistic way because I've experienced a lot of it in my own life," she once told an interviewer. While she grew up in a travelling side show called the Magic Empire Carnival, there was nothing enchanted about her childhood. When she was seven years old, her father was murdered. Her younger brother died at the hands of a drunken driver. Her mother, an alcoholic, was married nine times. And her lover, the father of her daughter Anna, overdosed on heroin in 1974. Perhaps the infant being torn apart at the beginning of *Suburbia* is a representation of innocent young Penelope Spheeris, whose childhood purity was ripped from her at a too-young age.

As a child, Spheeris became captivated by rock music as an expression of youthful rebellion. This interest led her into a career in the music industry (as she formed her own company, Rock 'n' Reel, which produced short promotional films for such groups as the Doobie Brothers) and to the subject matter of her initial feature, the one which established her as a director. It is the 1981 documentary *The Decline of Western Civilization,* which records the late 1970s punk rock scene in Los Angeles. Featured are groups with such names as Circle Jerks, Fear, X, and Catholic Discipline, which are made up of rockers who are alienated not only from the core of straight American society but from the established, old guard in the rock 'n roll hierarchy; to these rockers, the Beatles, Rolling Stones, or Kinks are as much a part of the mainstream as Spiro Agnew. Six years later, Spheeris made *The Decline of Western Civilization Part II: The Metal Years,* which contrasted several veterans of the heavy metal scene (including Ozzy Osbourne, Gene Simmons, and members of Aerosmith) to younger punk wannabes. Indeed, Spheeris's attraction to individuals so far outside even the farthest degrees of the establishment may be traced to one of the films she made while a student at the UCLA Film School, *Hats Off to Hollywood,* about the romance between a drag queen and a lesbian.

Spheeris's first mega-hit came with *Wayne's World,* based on the nonsensical but nonetheless popular *Saturday Night Live* skit featuring Mike Myers and Dana Carvey as self-proclaimed "party dudes" who have their own cable TV show. Despite the film's box-office success, it is too often idiotic and dull. Her features since then, like *The Beverly Hillbillies* and *The Little Rascals,* are even bigger disappointments, and far removed from the spirit of her earlier work: the first is a poorly done version of the silly but funny 1960s TV sit-com, and the second a pale reworking of the beloved Hal Roach one- and two-reel comedies.

—Rob Edelman

SPIELBERG, Steven

Nationality: American. **Born:** Cincinnati, Ohio, 18 December 1947. **Education:** California State College at Long Beach, B.A. in English, 1970. **Family:** Married 1) actress Amy Irving (divorced 1989), one son, one daughter; 2) actress Kate Capshaw, one daughter. **Career:** Won amateur film contest with 40-minute film *Escape to Nowhere,* 1960; on strength of film *Amblin',* became TV director for Universal, late 1960s; TV work included episodes of *Marcus Welby, M.D., Columbo,* and *Night Gallery,* and TV films, including *Duel,* then given theatrical release; directed first feature, *The Sugarland Express,* 1974; formed own production company, Amblin Productions; produced television series *Amazing Stories,* late 1980s, and *seaQuest DSV* and others, 1990s; formed new Hollywood studio DreamWorks SKG, with David Geffen and Jeffrey Katzenberg, 1995. **Awards:** David Di Donatello Award (Italy) for Best Foreign Director, Kinema Jumpo Award (Japan) for Best Foreign Director, National Society of Film Critics Award for Best Director, and L.A. Film Critics Award for Best Director, for *E.T.,* 1982; Directors Guild Award for Best Director, and British Academy of Film and Television Arts Award for Best Director, for *The Color Purple,* 1985; Irving G. Thalberg Award for body of work, Motion Picture Academy, 1986; D. W. Griffith Award, National Board of Review, for *Empire of the Sun,* 1987; Academy Awards for Best Director and Best Film, L.A. Film Critics Best Film, New York Film Critics Circle Best Film, D. W. Griffith Award for Best Film, and National Society of Film Critics Best Film and Director, for *Schindler's List,* 1993; Golden Lion for Career Achievement, Venice Film Festival, 1993; Life Achievement Award, American Film Institute, 1995. **Agent:** Jay Moloney, Creative Artists Agency, 9830 Wilshire Boulevard, Beverly Hills, CA 90212, U.S.A. **Address:** Amblin Entertainment/Dreamworks SKG, 100 Universal City Plaza, Bungalow 477, Universal City, CA 91608-1085, U.S.A.

Films as Director, Scriptwriter, and Producer:

1969 *Amblin'* (short)
1971 ***Duel*** (for TV)
1972 *Something Evil* (for TV)
1974 *The Sugarland Express* (+ co-story)
1975 ***Jaws***
1977 ***Close Encounters of the Third Kind*** (2nd version released 1980) (+ story)
1979 *1941*
1981 ***Raiders of the Lost Ark***
1982 ***E.T.—The Extraterrestrial*** (co-pr)
1983 episode of *The Twilight Zone—The Movie* (co-pr)
1984 *Indiana Jones and the Temple of Doom*
1986 *The Color Purple* (co-pr)
1987 *Empire of the Sun* (co-pr)
1989 *Indiana Jones and the Last Crusade*
1990 *Always* (co-pr)
1991 *Hook*
1993 *Jurassic Park* (+ co-exec pr); ***Schindler's List*** (+ co-exec pr)

Other Films:

1973 *Ace Eli and Rodger of the Skies* (Erman) (story)
1978 *I Wanna to Hold Your Hand* (Zemeckis) (pr)
1980 *Used Cars* (Zemeckis); *The Blues Brothers* (Landis) (role)
1981 *Continental Divide* (Apted) (co-exec pr)
1982 *Poltergeist* (Hooper) (co-pr, co-story, co-sc)
1984 *Gremlins* (Dante) (co-exec pr)
1985 *Back to the Future* (Zemeckis) (co-exec pr); *Young Sherlock Holmes* (Levinson) (co-exec pr); *Goonies* (Donner) (co-exec pr)
1986 *The Money Pit* (Benjamin) (co-exec pr); *An American Tail* (Bluth) (co-exec pr); *Innerspace* (Dante) (co-exec pr); ** batteries not included* (Matthew Robbins) (co-exec pr)
1988 *Who Framed Roger Rabbit?* (Zemeckis) (co-exec pr); *The Land Before Time* (Bluth) (co-exec pr)
1989 *Dad* (Goldberg) (co-exec pr); *Back to the Future, Part II* (Zemeckis) (co-exec pr); *Joe vs. the Volcano* (Shanley) (co-exec pr)
1990 *Arachnophobia* (Frank Marshall) (co-exec pr); *Back to the Future, Part III* (Zemeckis) (co-exec pr); *Gremlins 2: The New Batch* (Dante) (co-exec pr)
1991 *Cape Fear* (Scorsese) (exec pr); *An American Tail: Fievel Goes West* (Nibbelink) (co-pr)
1993 *We're Back: A Dinosaur's Tail* (co-exec pr); *Trail Mix-up* (exec pr)
1994 *I'm Mad* (exec pr)
1995 *To Wong Foo, Thanks for Everything, Julie Newmar* (Kidron) (co-exec pr); *Balto* (exec pr); *Casper* (exec pr)

Publications

By SPIELBERG: book—

The Sugarland Express—Spielberg, Barwood and Robbins, Zsigmond, edited by Rochelle Reed, Washington, D.C., 1974.

By SPIELBERG: articles—

Steven Spielberg Seminar, in *Dialogue on Film* (Washington, D.C.), July 1974.

"From Television to Features," an interview with M. Stettin, in *Millimeter* (New York), March 1975.

"Close Encounter of the Third Kind: Director Steve Spielberg," with C. Austin, in *Filmmakers Newsletter* (Ward Hill, Massachusetts), December 1977.
"The Unsung Heroes or Credit Where Credit Is Due," in *American Cinematographer* (Los Angeles), January 1978.
Interview with Mitch Tuchman, in *Film Comment* (New York), January/February 1978.
"Directing *1941*," in *American Cinematographer* (Los Angeles), December 1979.
"Of Narrow Misses and Close Calls," in *American Cinematographer* (Los Angeles), November 1981.
Interview with T. McCarthy, in *Film Comment* (New York), May/June 1982.
"Dialogue on Film: Steven Spielberg," in *American Film* (Washington, D.C.), June 1988.
"A Revealing Interview with Steven Spielberg," in *Film Threat* (Beverly Hills), vol. 19, 1989.
"Always," an interview with S. Royal, in *American Premiere Magazine* (Beverly Hills), no. 6, 1989/90.
"China and the Oscars," written with Kathleen Kennedy, *New York Times,* 25 March 1991.
"A Close Encounter with Steven Spielberg," an interview with D. Shay, in *Cinefex* (Riverside, California), February 1993.

On SPIELBERG: books—

Pye, Michael, and Lynda Myles, *The Movie Brats: How the Film Generation Took Over Hollywood,* London, 1979.
Kolker, Robert Phillip, *A Cinema of Loneliness: Penn, Kubrick, Scorsese, Spielberg, Altman,* Oxford, 1980; revised edition, 1988.
Crawley, Tony, *The Steven Spielberg Story,* London, 1983.
Goldau, Ant Je, and Hans Helmut Prinzler, *Spielberg: Film als Spielzeug,* Berlin, 1985.
Mott, Donald R., and Cheryl McAllister Saunders, *Steven Spielberg,* Boston, 1986.
Smith, Thomas G., *Industrial Light and Magic: The Art of Special Effects,* London, 1986.
Weiss, Ulli, *Das Neue Hollywood: Francis Ford Coppola, Steven Spielberg, Martin Scorsese,* Munich, 1986.
Godard, Jean-Pierre, *Spielberg,* Paris, 1987.
Sinyard, Neil, *The Films of Steven Spielberg,* London, 1987.
Slade, Darren, and Nigel Watson, *Supernatural Spielberg,* London, 1992.
Taylor, Philip M., *Steven Spielberg: The Man, His Movies, and Their Meaning,* New York, 1992; revised, 1994.
Somazzi, Claud, *Steven Spielberg: Dreaming the Movies,* Santa Cruz, 1994.
Brode, Douglas, *The Films of Steven Spielberg,* New York, 1995.
Oskar Schindler and His List: The Man, the Book, the Film, the Holocaust, and Its Survivors, Forest Dale, Vermont, 1995.
Ferber, Elizabeth, *Steven Spielberg: A Biography,* New York, 1996.
Sanello, Frank, *Spielberg: The Man, the Movies, the Myth,* Dallas, 1996.

On SPIELBERG: articles—

Eyles, A., "Steven Spielberg," in *Focus on Film* (London), Winter 1972.
Cumbow, R. C., "The Great American Eating Machine," in *Movietone News* (Seattle), 11 October 1976.
Cook, B., "Close Encounters with Steven Spielberg," in *American Film* (Washington, D.C.), November 1977.
Jameson, R. T., "Style vs. 'Style'," in *Film Comment* (New York), March/April 1980.
Geng, Veronica, "Spielberg's Express," in *Film Comment* (New York), July/August 1981.
Auty, Chris, "The Complete Spielberg?," in *Sight and Sound* (London), Autumn 1982.
Turner, G. E., "Steven Spielberg and *E.T.—the Extra-Terrestrial,*" in *American Cinématographer* (Los Angeles), January 1983.
McGillivray, D., "The Movie Brats: Steven Spielberg," in *Films and Filming* (London), May 1984.
Smetak, J. R., "Summer at the Movies, Steven Spielberg: Gore, Guts and PG-13," in *Journal of Film and Popular Television* (Washington, D.C.), Spring 1986.
Britton, Andrew, "Blissing Out: The Politics of Reaganite Entertainment," in *Movie* (London), Winter 1986.
Combs, Richard, "Master Steven's Search for the Sun," in *Listener* (London), February 1988.
"Cinematheque Honors Spielberg," in *New York Times,* 3 April 1989.
Griffin, Nancy, "Manchild in the Promised Land," in *Premiere* (New York), June 1989.
Abbott, Diane, "Steven Spielberg," in *American CinemEditor* (Encino, California), no. 1, 1990.
Cientat, M., "Le phenomene Spielberg ou la nouvelle cinephilie," in *Cinemaction* (Conde-sur-Noireau), January 1990.
Torry, Robert, "Politics and Parousia in Close Encounters of the Third Kind," in *Literature/Film Quarterly* (Salisbury, Maryland), no. 3, 1991.
Peacock, John, "When Folk Goes Pop: Consuming the Color Purple," in *Literature/Film Quarterly* (Salisbury, Maryland), no. 3, 1991.
Greenberg, Harvey Roy, "Raiders of the Lost Text: Remaking as Contested Homage in *Always,*" in *Journal of Popular Film and Television* (Washington, D.C.), Winter 1991.
Gordon, Andrew, "Steven Spielberg's *Empire of the Sun:* A Boy's Dream of War," in *Literature/Film Quarterly* (Salisbury, Maryland), no. 4, 1991.
Schruers, Fred, "Peter Pandemonium," in *Premiere* (New York), December 1991.
Davis, Ivor, "I Won't Grow Up!" in *Los Angeles Magazine,* December 1991.
Wood, G., "On Spielberg: A Tale of Two Steves," in *Cinefantastique* (Forest Park, Illinois), no. 4, 1991.
Green, C., and others, "Steven Spielberg: A Celebration," in *Journal of Popular Film* (Washington, D.C.), no. 4, 1991.
Andrews, S., "The Man Who Would Be Walt," in *New York Times,* 26 January 1992.
Sheehan, Henry, "The Panning of Steven Spielberg," in *Film Comment* (New York), May 1992.
Sheehan, Henry, "Spielberg II," in *Film Comment* (New York), July/August 1992.
Perlez, J., "Spielberg Grapples with the Horror of the Holocaust," in *New York Times,* 13 June 1993.
Wollen, Peter, "Theme Park and Variations," in *Sight and Sound* (London), July 1993.
Secher, Andy, "Directing the Dinosaurs," in *Lapidary Journal* (San Diego, California), July 1993.
Jameson, L., "Spielberg's Theory of Devolution," in *Film Threat* (Beverly Hills), August 1993.
Place, Vanessa, "Supernatural Thing," in *Film Comment* (New York), September/October 1993.
Gellately, Robert, "Between Exploitation, Rescue, and Annihilation: Reviewing *Schindler's List,*" in *Central European History* (Atlanta, Georgia), no. 4, 1993.
Richardson, John H., "Steven's Choice," in *Premiere* (New York), January 1994.
Maser, Wayne, "The Long Voyage Home," in *Harper's Bazaar* (New York), February 1994.
Gourevitch, Philip, "A Dissent on *Schindler's List,*" in *Commentary* (New York), February 1994.
White, Armond, "Toward a Theory of Spielberg History," in *Film Comment* (New York), March 1994.

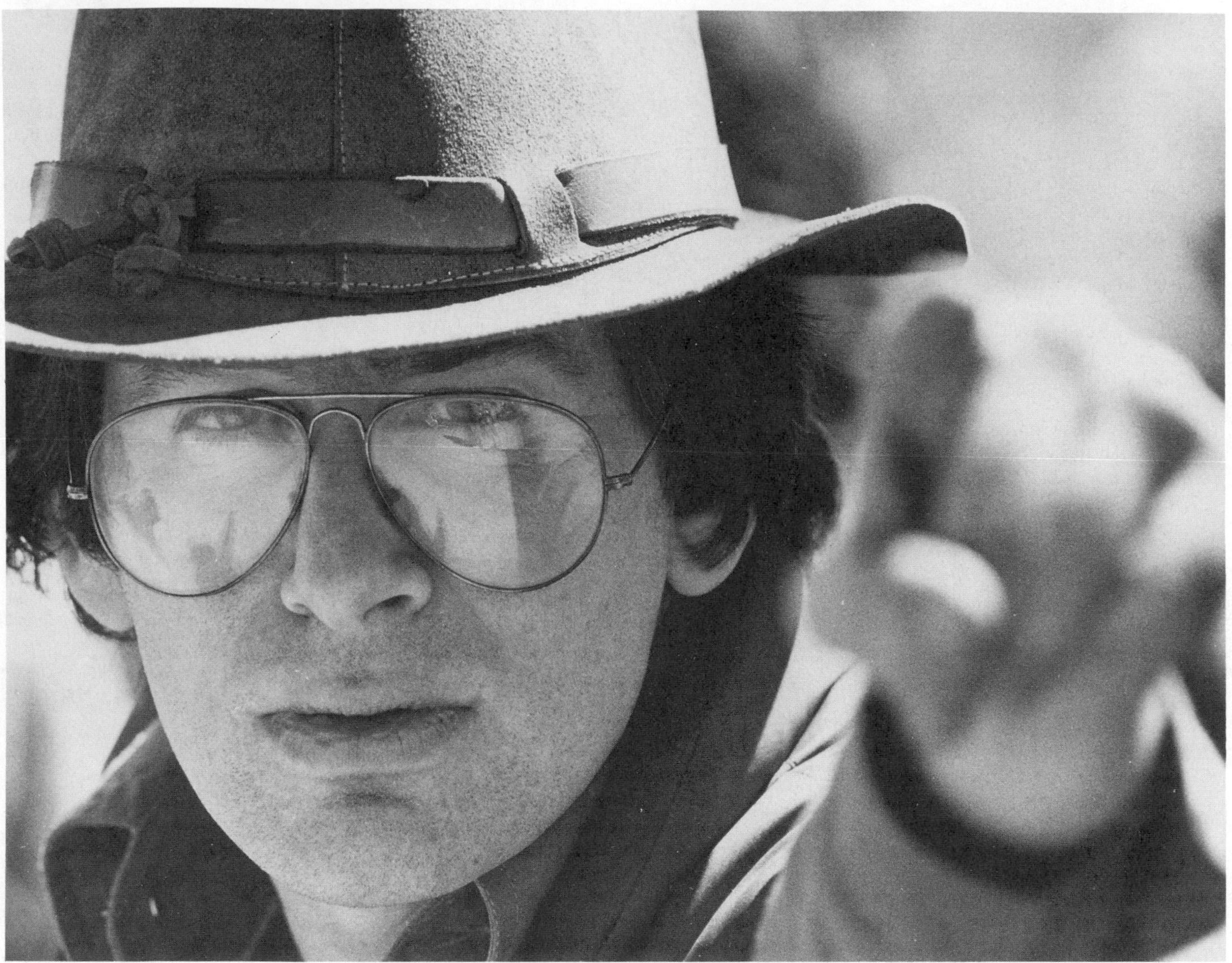

Steven Spielberg

Louvish, Simon, "Witness," in *Sight and Sound* (London), March 1994.
"*Schindler's List:* Myth, Movie, and Memory," roundtable discussion in *Village Voice* (New York), 29 March 1994.
Thomson, David, "Presenting Enamelware," in *Film Comment* (New York), March 1994.
Schiff, Stephen, "Behind the Camera: Seriously Spielberg," in *New Yorker,* 21 March 1994.
Nagorski, Andrew, "*Schindler's List* and the Polish Question," in *Foreign Affairs* (New York), July 1994.
Epstein, Jason, "Rethinking *Schindler's List,*" in *Utne Reader* (Minneapolis, Minnesota), July 1994.
Lane, Randall, "I Want Gross," *Forbes* (New York), 26 September 1994.
O'Shaughnessy, Elise, "The New Establishment," in *Vanity Fair* (New York), October 1994.
Manchel, Frank, "A Reel Witness: Steven Spielberg's Representation of the Holocaust in *Schindler's List,*" *Journal of Modern History* (Chicago), March 1995.
Corliss, Richard, "Hey, Let's Put on a Show!" in *Time* (New York), 27 March 1995.
Masters, Kim, "What's Ovitz Got to Do With It?" in *Vanity Fair* (New York), April 1995.
Hartman, Geoffrey, "The Cinema Animal: On Spielberg's *Schindler's List,*" in *Salmagundi* (Saratoga Springs, New York), Spring 1995.
Griffin, Nancy, "In the Grip of *Jaws,*" in *Premiere* (New York), October 1995.

* * *

Perhaps any discussion of Steven Spielberg must inevitably begin with the consideration that, as of 1996, Spielberg remains the most commercially successful director the world has yet seen—an incredible, if mind-boggling proposition which, in another time, might have immediately made the director's films ineligible for serious critical consideration. Yet the fact that Spielberg's combined films have grossed well over one billion dollars attests to their power in connecting to the mass audience and offers the analyst an immediate conundrum which may take a more distanced generation of critics and filmgoers to answer fully: What does Spielberg know? And why has so much of his work invited such audience approval?

Spielberg has worked in a variety of genres: the television film *Duel* is a thriller; *Jaws* is a horror film; *1941* is a crazy comedy; *Close Encounters of the Third Kind* is a science-fiction film; *Raiders of the Lost Ark* is an adventure film patterned after film serials of the early

1950s; *E.T.—The Extraterrestrial* is a fantasy/family film combining elements from *The Wizard of Oz, Lassie,* and *Peter Pan; The Color Purple* is a social drama; *Empire of the Sun* is an expansive wartime epic. And yet virtually all of Spielberg's films are united by the same distinctive vision: a vision imbued with a sense of wonder which celebrates the magic and mystery that imagination can reveal as an alternative to the humdrum and the everyday. The artistic consistency within Spielberg's work is demonstrated further by his narratives, which are structurally similar. In the typical Spielberg film, an Everyman protagonist has his conception of the world enlarged (often traumatically) as he comes face to face with some extraordinary and generally non-human antagonist who is often hidden from the rest of the world and/or the audience until the narrative's end. In *Duel,* a California businessman named Mann finds himself pitted against the monstrous truck whose driver's face is never shown; in *Jaws,* the water-shy sheriff must face an almost mythological shark whose jaws are not clearly shown until the final reel; in *Close Encounters,* a suburban father responds to the extrasensory messages sent by outer-space creatures who are not revealed until the last sequence of the film; in *Raiders of the Lost Ark,* Indiana Jones quests for the Lost Ark which does not let forth its Pandora's Box of horrors until summoned up by those who would attempt to profit from it; and, of course, in *E.T.,* a small boy whose life is already steeped in imagination keeps secret his adoption of a playful extra-terrestrial (although one could easily argue that the non-human antagonist here is not really the sensitive E.T., but the masked and terrifying government agents who, quietly working behind the scenes throughout the narrative, finally invade the suburban house and crystallize the protagonist's most horrific fears). Structural analysis even reveals that *Poltergeist,* the Spielberg-produced, Tobe Hooper-directed film which relates to Spielberg's career in the same way the Howard Hawks-produced, Christian Nyby-directed *The Thing* related to Hawks's career, is indeed a continuation of the Spielberg canon. In *Poltergeist,* a typical American family ultimately discovers that the antagonists responsible for the mysterious goings-on in their suburban home are the other-worldly ghosts and skeletons not shown until the end of the film, when the narrative also reveals the villainy of the real estate developer who had so cavalierly disposed of the remains from an inconveniently located cemetery.

Technically proficient and dazzling, Spielberg's films are voracious in their synthesis of the popular culture icons which have formed the director's sensibilities: Hitchcock movies, John Wayne, comic books, *Bambi,* suburban homes, fast food, the space program, television. His vision is that of the child-artist—the innocent and profound imagination that can summon up primeval dread from the deep, as well as transcendent wonder from the sky. If Spielberg's films are sometimes attacked for a certain lack of interest in social issues or "adult concerns," they may be defended on the grounds that his films—unlike so many of the "special effects" action films of the 1970s and 1980s—derive from a sensibility which is sincerely felt. A more subtle attack on Spielberg would hold that his interest in objects and mechanical effects (as in *1941* and *Raiders of the Lost Ark*), though provocative, may not always be in perfect balance with his interest in sentiment and human values. Spielberg himself acknowledges his debt to Walt Disney, whose theme "When You Wish upon a Star," a paean to faith and imagination, dictates the spirit of several Spielberg films. And yet certainly if intellectual and persuasive critical constructions be sought to justify our enjoyment of Spielberg's cinema, they can easily be found in the kind of mythic, Jungian criticism which analyzes his very popular work as a kind of direct line to the collective unconscious. *Jaws,* for instance, is related to the primal fear of being eaten as well as to the archetypal initiation rite; *Close Encounters* is constructed according to the archetypal form of the quest and its attendant religious structures of revelation and salvation; and of course *E.T.* has already been widely analyzed as a re-telling of the Christ story—complete with a sacred heart, a ritual death, a resurrection brought about by faith, and an eventual ascension into heaven as E.T. returns home.

If Spielberg is especially notable in any other way, it is perhaps that he represents the most successful example of what has been called the film-school generation, which is increasingly populating the new Hollywood: a generation which has been primarily brought up on television and film, rather than literature, and for whom film seems apparently to have replaced life as a repository of significant experience. And yet if the old Hollywood's studio system is dead, it has been partially replaced by a solid, if informal matrix of friendships and alliances: between Spielberg and a fraternity that includes George Lucas, Francis Ford Coppola, Lawrence Kasdan, John Milius, Bob Zemeckis, Robert Gale, Hal Barwood, Matthew Robbins, Melissa Mathison, and Harrison Ford.

It is noteworthy that Hollywood, though consistently accused of a preference for box-office appeal over critical acclaim, has nevertheless refused (until *Schindler's List* in 1994) to valorize publicly Spielberg's work, despite his popular and critical success. The Academy of Motion Picture Arts and Sciences has consistently chosen to pass over Spielberg's films and direction—in 1975 bypassing *Jaws* in favor of *One Flew over the Cuckoo's Nest* and Milos Forman; in 1977, bypassing *Close Encounters* for *Annie Hall* and Woody Allen; in 1981 bypassing *Raiders of the Lost Ark* for *Chariots of Fire* and Warren Beatty (as director of *Reds*); in 1982 bypassing *E.T.* for *Gandhi* and Richard Attenborough; and in 1985 bypassing *The Color Purple* for *Out of Africa* and Sydney Pollack.

More than requiring an explanatory footnote in film history texts, these "slights" made it clear that the industry of the time had come to hold Spielberg responsible for the juvenilization of the American cinema in the late 1970s and 1980s. If the Coppolas and the Scorseses attempted to remake Hollywood to their own vision of a freer, more European, artistic sensibility (and by and large failed), should Spielberg now be held responsible for betraying earlier victories and turning Hollywood into a Disneyland? And although Spielberg became the richest man in Hollywood, the most commercially savvy, the man everyone most wanted to make a deal with, the most influential, he could not easily become anything at all like its most serious, respected artist. Spielberg's longtime insistence on avoiding adult themes, instead taking refuge in nostalgia, special effects, remakes, and sequels, seemed to be directly responsible for rather perniciously preventing non-Spielberg-like films from being produced. As well, the overwhelming number of Spielberg imitators, many producing films under Spielberg's own auspices, have largely contributed commercially successful hackwork.

Hollywood noted the irony, too, that it was in the Spielberg production of *The Twilight Zone* movie (directed by John Landis) that two children and actor Vic Morrow should have been killed in a clearly avoidable accident in which the children's employment violated child-labor law. *The Color Purple,* although conforming to Spielberg's typical pattern of the hidden antagonist, backed off from an explicit representation of Celie's lesbianism, turning her instead into a cute *E.T.*-like creature. Thus the confrontation of the hidden antagonist (Celie's true nature) became a kind of missing climax in a film which many critics ridiculed. After *The Color Purple,* when receiving the Irving Thalberg award from the Motion Pictures Academy, Spielberg gave a widely quoted speech which seemed surprisingly to admit responsibility for the state of American film culture: "I think in our romance with technology and our excitement at exploring all the possibilities of film and video, I think we have partially lost something.... It's time to renew our romance with the word; I'm as culpable as anyone in exalting the image at the expense of the word.... Only a generation of readers will spawn a generation of writers." Spielberg's speech was followed by arguably his finest work: from a screenplay by famed dramatist Tom Stoppard, *Empire of the Sun,* set in Asia during

World War II, includes some of Spielberg's most startling set-pieces (such as a crowd sequence which rivals Eisenstein's use of montage in "The Odessa Steps" sequence of *Potemkin,* or an unusually expressive evocation of the atomic bombing at Hiroshima), as well as more adult themes relating to war and peace, community integration and disintegration. Nevertheless, when this film was overshadowed in many ways by Bertolucci's Asia epic, *The Last Emperor,* Spielberg seemed to beat a hasty retreat into safer material.

Always, a remake of *A Guy Named Joe* in which Spielberg portrayed adult relationships within a fantasy context including helpful ghosts, was both a critical and financial failure. Even more distressing was the critical failure of the 1991 *Hook,* in which Spielberg's professed appreciation for the word disappeared under the weight of charmless Hollywood juveniles having onscreen food fights amidst special effects gleefully presented by Spielberg as artistic entertainment. Although critics had for years suggested that the source material *Peter Pan* would provide Spielberg his most natural material (a boy not wanting to grow up), many were stunned when Spielberg's version finally arrived: bloated, overlong, overproduced, looking more like a vapid amusement park ride or a multimillion dollar commercial for a new attraction at the Universal Studio Tour than a film. Its artistic message—that its adult Peter Pan should work less and spend more quality time with his children—was in ludicrous contradiction to the herculean effort required by all, including its director, to devote themselves to such a high-budget, effects-heavy project; thus the film emerges as the most cynical, hypocritical attempt to play on audience sentiment to attract box-office in the Spielberg *oeuvre.*

The year 1993 marked a turning point for Spielberg—with the release of two films in the same year that could not have been more different. *Jurassic Park,* a cinefantastique wonder showing dinosaurs wreaking havoc in a contemporary theme park, was a roller-coaster ride which fast became the most commercially successful film of all time, bypassing even Spielberg's own *E.T.* Although the special effects were mostly marvelous and definitely the reason for the film's appeal (can anyone who has seen the film ever forget the startlingly graceful images of apatosaurs grazing in the forest?), many critics were startled by a certain desultoriness in the construction of the narrative: loose ends here and there, scenes which seemed not all to pay off. And indeed, deficiencies may be attributed to Spielberg losing some interest in the project—for the other Spielberg film released in 1993 was the film which would finally, irrevocably answer his critics: a black-and-white film photographed in a radically different camera style, devoid of the famous Spielberg backlighting as well as his traditional over-the-top orchestrations, using virtually unknown actors, and all on the single most unremittingly serious subject of the contemporary world: the Holocaust. Spielberg's *Schindler's List* was his most striking, overwhelming work; with it, he finally won his Academy Awards for film and director, as well as best film awards from the L.A. and New York critics groups, the Board of Review, and the National Society of Film Critics—a startlingly unanimous achievement. For a serious film, *Schindler's List* was also amazingly successful with the public, which was powerfully moved and horrified by the film. Based on the real-life story of Oskar Schindler, a German industrialist who actually saved over a thousand Jews by employing them at his factory, *Schindler's List,* keeping with the Spielberg ethos, emphasized the most hopeful components of the story without minimizing or denying its horrifying components. The film's coda, which showed the actors along with their real-life counterparts who survived because of Schindler visiting the gravesite of the real Schindler, was criticized by some, but this strategy insisted the audience understand the story as historical and gave the film an even greater emotional depth. Although time will tell whether *Schindler's List* will retain its instant reputation as a great, towering achievement comparable to, say, Alain Resnais's short *Night and Fog,* the definitive Holocaust film, the film has—according to his own testimony—altered Spielberg's life, sensibility, and career. The first artistic work that allowed Spielberg directly to explore his Jewish heritage, *Schindler's List* so consumed him that he has since embarked on what he has called his most important life's work: a video project documenting the survivors of the Holocaust for educational purposes. In interviews given before his multiple Academy Award wins, Spielberg has also said that he could no longer imagine going back to directing the kinds of films he made before *Schindler's List.*

On other fronts, Spielberg has continued to consolidate his position in Hollywood as its most powerful man. His company, Amblin, has stepped up television production, either Spielberg and/or Amblin involved in television series as disparate as *Amazing Stories, seaQuest,* the top-rated drama *ER,* and the children's show *The Animaniacs.* Spielberg has continued to help produce the films of others, and at least one of those post-*Schindler* films, *To Wong Foo, Thanks for Everything, Julie Newmar,* though a traditional Hollywood film in its warmth and sentiment, took on a non-traditional subject: homophobia in America. More monumentally, in one of the most publicized entertainment stories of 1994, Spielberg has formed a new Hollywood studio called DreamWorks SKG in partnership with two of the other most powerful men in Hollywood, Jeffrey Katzenberg and David Geffen. As Spielberg moves closer and closer to being a modern-day mogul in the style of Walt Disney or Cecil B. DeMille, will his *Schindler's* conversion continue and he devote himself to serious, revealing, personal projects requiring no apology, or will the lure of big bucks for future installments of Indiana Jones and other popular entertainments prove too great a temptation for DreamWorks to forego? Perhaps Spielberg will find some way of mediating these apparently contradictory goals with enough integrity and skill to retain his popular appeal as well as his newfound critical respectability as a serious artist.

—Charles Derry

STAHL, John M.

Nationality: American. **Born:** New York City, 21 January 1886. **Education:** Educated in New York City public schools. **Family:** Married Roxana Wray, 1932. **Career:** Actor on stage and later in films, from 1901; hired by Vitagraph Studio, Brooklyn, as director, 1914; moved to Hollywood, worked for Louis B. Mayer in independent productions, then at MGM, 1917; vice-president and directorial producer, Tiffany-Stahl Studios, 1928; sold interest in studio and joined Universal, 1930. **Died:** 12 January 1950.

Films as Director:

(incomplete listing prior to 1918)

1914 *The Boy and the Law*
1917 *The Lincoln Cycle* (14-reeler distributed in six chapters including *My Mother, My Father, My Self, The Call to Arms*)
1918 *Scandal Mongers*; *Wives of Men* (+ sc); *Suspicion*
1919 *Her Code of Honor*; *A Woman Under Oath*
1920 *Greater Than Love*; *Women Men Forget*; *The Woman in His House*; *Sowing the Wind*; *The Child Thou Gavest Me* (+ pr)
1922 *The Song of Life*; *One Clear Call* (+ pr); *Suspicious Wives*
1923 *The Wanters* (+ pr); *The Dangerous Age* (+ pr)
1924 *Why Men Leave Home*; *Husbands and Lovers* (+ pr)
1925 *Fine Clothes*
1926 *Memory Lane* (+ pr, co-sc); *The Gay Deceiver*

1927 *Lovers?* (+ pr); *In Old Kentucky* (+ pr)
1930 *A Lady Surrenders*
1931 *Seed*; *Strictly Dishonorable*
1932 *Back Street*
1933 *Only Yesterday*
1934 *Imitation of Life*
1935 *Magnificent Obsession*
1937 *Parnell*
1938 *Letter of Introduction* (+ pr)
1939 *When Tomorrow Comes* (+ pr)
1941 *Our Wife*
1942 *The Immortal Sergeant*
1943 *Holy Matrimony*
1944 *The Eve of St. Mark*; *The Keys of the Kingdom*
1946 *Leave Her to Heaven*
1947 *Forever Amber* (replaced by Otto Preminger); *The Foxes of Harrow*
1948 *The Walls of Jericho*
1949 *Father Was a Fullback*; *Oh, You Beautiful Doll*

Publications

By STAHL: article—

"Oh, the Good Old Days," in *The Hollywood Reporter,* 16 May 1932.

On STAHL: books—

Glèdhill, Christine, editor, *Home Is Where the Heart Is: Studies in Melodrama and the Woman's Film,* London, 1987.

On STAHL: articles—

Obituary, in *The New York Times,* 14 January 1950.
Sarris, Andrew, "Esoterica," in *Film Culture* (New York), Spring 1963.
Morris, G., "John M. Stahl: The Man Who Understood Women," in *Film Comment* (New York), May/June 1977.
Pulleine, Tim, "Stahl into Sirk," in *Monthly Film Bulletin* (London), November 1981.
Renov, Michael, "*Leave Her to Heaven*: The Double Bind of Post-War Women," in *Journal of the University Film and Video Association,* Winter 1983.

* * *

John Stahl was a key figure in the development of the Hollywood "women's melodrama" during the 1930s and 1940s, and quite possibly in the 1910s and 1920s as well. Although he began directing in 1914, and apparently made as many films before sound as after, only two of his silents (*Her Code of Honor* and *Suspicious Wives*) seem to have survived. Yet this is hardly the only reason that the ultimate critical and historical significance of his work remains to be established. More pertinent is the critical disrepute of the "tearjerker" genre in which he worked almost exclusively—a genre which had to await the discovery of Douglas Sirk's melodramas and the reworking of the form by R.W. Fassbinder to attract serious critical attention.

Comparisons between Sirk's baroquely aestheticized and Stahl's straightforwardly unadorned treatments of equally improbable plots is somewhat useful, and virtually inevitable, given that Sirk remade three of Stahl's classic 1930s "weepies": *Imitation of Life* (1934/1959), *Magnificent Obsession* (1935/1954), and *When Tomorrow Comes* (1939), which became *Interlude* (1957). In a genre focusing on the problems presented by the social/sexual order for the individual (most frequently, the bourgeois female), Sirk tended to abstract dramatic conflicts in the direction of Brecht, while Stahl chose to emphasize the effects of social rigidities through the emotions of his characters.

Stahl's career seemed to flourish most at Universal in the 1930s with the production of the highly accomplished *Back Street, Only Yesterday,* and the three films Sirk remade, all of which present emotionally similar heroines buffeted by twists of fate which wreak havoc on their socially-determined modes of behavior. In his version of Fannie Hurst's *Back Street* (remade in 1941 and 1961), Stahl encourages sympathy for Irene Dunne, an independent working woman who gives up everything to be "kept" in isolation by the respectable married man she loves. Audacious contradictions emerge from the very simplicity with which Stahl presents outrageous plot twists. Dunne meets the "kept woman" next door to her back street apartment, for example, only when the woman literally catches on fire and must be rescued. Recognizing a sister in shame, Dunne counsels the injured woman against allowing herself to be exploited by the man she loves; yet what seems to be a dawning moment of self-awareness on the part of our heroine is instantly obscured by a romantic haze when her own lover walks through the door in the middle of her diatribe. Similarly powerful contradictions abound in *Imitation of Life* (based on another Hurst novel), where best friends Claudette Colbert and Louise Beavers find themselves incapable, despite their best intentions, of breaking the social conventions which keep the black woman subservient to the white, even when the former is responsible for the latter's wealth and success.

Given material such as the Fannie Hurst novels, the "inspirational" message of Lloyd C. Douglas's *Magnificent Obsession,* and the hopelessly romantic *Only Yesterday* (virtually remade as Max Ophüls' *Letter from an Unknown Woman*), and considering the period during which Stahl worked, the point of reference seems not to be Sirk so much as Stahl's better-appreciated contemporary Frank Borzage. It is Borzage's unrelenting romanticism which is usually assumed to characterize the "weepies" of the 1920s and 1930s; yet Stahl's work offers another perspective. While he clearly encourages emotional identification with his heroines, Stahl seems more interested in exposing their romantic illusions than in relishing them. In fact, his meditative restraint in such situations has prompted George Morris to suggest that "it is Carl Th. Dreyer whom Stahl resembles more than directors like Sirk or Borzage."

Yet ultimately, Stahl's visual style seems largely dependent upon studio and cinematographer, a fact most clearly demonstrated by *Leave Her to Heaven,* a preposterously plotted drama of a psychotically duplicitous woman shot in Technicolor by Leon Shamroy on the modernesque sets of 20th Century-Fox, where the director's mise-en-scène emerges as florid and baroque as Sirk in his heyday—and a full decade earlier.

It seems that Stahl's films represent something of a missing link between Borzage's romanticism and Sirk. Certainly, an examination of his work expands an understanding of the variety of Hollywood's strategies in personalizing overtly ideological questions of sex, status, and money. In fact, if film scholars are serious about studying the melodrama in any depth, then the films of John Stahl remain a top and current priority.

—Ed Lowry

STAUDTE, Wolfgang

Nationality: German. **Born:** Saarbrücken, 9 October 1906. **Education:** Educated as engineer. **Career:** Stage actor for Max Reinhardt and Erwin Piscator, until 1933; film actor, from 1931; writer and director of advertising films and shorts, 1930s; directed first feature,

Akrobat schö-ö-ön, for Tobis Film, also co-founder, with Harald Braun and Helmut Kaütner, "Freie Film-Produktion-GmbH," 1943; worked for DEFA Studios, East Germany, 1945; worked in West Germany, from 1953; television director, from 1970s. **Awards:** Silver Lion, Venice Festival, for *Ciske de Rat,* 1955. **Died:** Of heart failure, in Zigarski, 19 January 1984.

Films as Director:

1943 *Akrobat schö-ö-ön* (+ sc)
1944 *Ich hab' von Dir geträumt*
1945 *Frau über Bord*
1946 ***Die Mörder sind unter uns*** (*The Murderers Are Among Us*) (+ sc)
1948 *Die seltsamen Abenteuer des Herrn Fridolin B* (+ sc)
1949 *Rotation* (+ co-sc); *Schicksal aus zweiter Hand* (+ sc); *Der Untertan* (*The Submissive*) (+ co-sc)
1953 *Die Geschichte des kleinen Muck* (*The Story of Little Mook*) (+ co-sc)
1954 *Leuchtfeuer* (+ co-sc)
1955 *Ciske—Ein Kind braucht Liebe* (*Ciske—A Child Wants Love*) (+ sc)
1957 *Rose Bernd*
1958 *Kanonen-Serenade* (*The Muzzle*) (+ co-sc); *Madeleine und der Legionär*; *Der Maulkorb*
1959 *Rosen für den Staatsanwalt* (*Roses for the Prosecutor*) (+ story)
1960 *Kirmes* (*Kermes*) (+ sc); *Der letzte Zeuge* (*The Last Witness*)
1962 *Die glücklichen Jahre der Thorwalds* (co-d)
1963 *Die Dreigroschenoper* (*The Threepenny Opera*)
1964 *Herrenpartie* (*Me's Outing*); *Das Lamm* (*The Lamb*)
1966 *Ganovenehre* (*Hoodlum's Honor*)
1968 *Heimlichkeiten* (+ co-sc)
1970 *Die Herren mit der weissen Weste* (*Those Gentlemen Who Have a Clean Sheet*)
1971 *Fluchtweg St. Pauli—Grossalarm fur die Davidswache*
1972 *Verrat ist kein Gesselschaftsspiel* (for TV); *Marya Sklodowska-Curie. Ein Mädchen, das die Welt verändert* (for TV)
1973 *Nerze Nachts am Strassenrand* (for TV); *The Seawolf*
1974 *Ein herrliches Dasein*
1976 *Zwei Erfahrungen Reicher* (for TV)
1978 *Des Verschollene Inka-Gold* (for TV); *Zwischengleis* (*Memories*)

Other Films:

1931 *Gassenhauer* (Pick) (role)
1945 *Der Mann, dem man den Namen stahl* (co-sc)
1949 *Das Beil von Wandsbek* (co-sc)
1950 *Geheimnis des blauen Zimmers* (role); *Tannenberg* (role); *Der Choral von Leuthen* (role); *Heimkehr ins Glück* (role); *Pechmarie* (role); *Die Bande von Hoheneck* (role); *Schwarzer Jäger Johanna* (role); *Stärker als Paragraphen* (role); *Gleisdreieck* (role); *Susanne im Bade* (role); *Am seidenen Faden* (role); *Lauter Lügen* (role); *Pour le mérite* (role); *Mordsache Holm* (role); *Spiel im Sommerwind* (role); *Das Gewehr über* (role); *Die fremde Frau* (role); *Drei Unteroffiziere* (role); *Brand im Ozean* (role); *Legion Condor* (role); *Blutsbrüderschaft* (role); *Aus erster Ehe* (role); ***Jud Süss*** (role); *Jungens* (role); *Friedemann Bach* (role); *... reitet für Deutschland* (role); *Das grosse Spiel* (role)

Publications

By STAUDTE: article—

"Aber wenn geschlagen wird im diesem Land ...," interview, in *Film und Fernsehen* (Berlin), no. 5, 1979.

On STAUDTE: articles—

Bachmann, J., "Wolfgang Staudte," in *Film* (London), Summer 1963.
"Kurt Maetzig, Wolfgang Staudte," in *Information* (Wiesbaden), no. 3-6, 1976.
Karkosch, K., "Wolfgang Staudte," in *Film und Ton* (Munich), March 1976.

* * *

Wolfgang Staudte is one of the few important German directors of the postwar years. *Die Mörder sind unter uns,* the first German postwar film, remains today among the director's best works. In the film, a surgeon, Hans Mertens, returns home from the war, becomes an alcoholic, and lives hopelessly among the ruins. His girlfriend Susanne has survived a concentration camp and attempts to help him overcome his apathy. The apathy is quickly dispelled by the appearance of an industrialist, formerly a Nazi, whose outlook remains unchanged and who, just as before the war, uses deceptive phrases to justify the new situation.

This contemporary material was realized by Staudte in a thoroughly realistic style with expressionistic strokes in a manner that suggests analogies with Rossellini's *Paisà.* An English critic identified the director as a successor to Lang and Pabst. A phrase in the film—"The murderers are among us"—became a symbolic expression for the spirit of the time, in which progressive German intellectuals sought every means to reckon with the fascist past. It was not by chance that the film was made in the Soviet sector of Berlin and produced by the newly-founded DEFA studios. Staudte's efforts to interest cultural officials in the western zones in his project met with no success. This was also the case with *Rotation* and *Der Untertan,* a satiric version of Heinrich Mann's novel of the same title, set in an actual embassy.

Staudte was a political artist because, as he said, he was a political person. He had perfect command of a variety of means of expression and narrative forms, and used a rich palette of symbolic images in realistically-structured filmic space. His films often led to comparisons with René Clément and Rossellini. Only his own country—the media and public as well as the authorities—could not accept him and systematically and conclusively thwarted him.

In the beginning Staudte was repeatedly labelled a communist because of his association with DEFA. He was urged to make West German films. In 1951 he decided to do so, and so began an unhappy period for him which consisted of attempts "to improve the world with the money of people who already find the world to be just fine." He was regularly reproached for fouling his own nest, and was reluctantly reduced to making entertainment films. In its headlong rush toward economic development, West German society wanted to see neither fundamental analysis of the Nazi past, nor pessimistic mistrust directed against the new, American-oriented NRD-model.

Years of harassment by the press and cultural authorities went by with Staudte working away, often in vain, writing unengaging comedies. He nevertheless made a few masterpieces: *Rosen für den Staatsanwalt, Kirmes,* and *Herrenpartie.* These films are united by Staudte's conviction that the present and the past are bound together and that man today remains inseparable from yesterday. The most imposing of these films is *Herrenpartie*: it confronts two worlds—that of today's German bourgeoisie, which would gladly bury Nazi memories, and that of a village of Yugoslavian widows who, despite everything, are better able to behave humanely than the Germans.

In the latter part of his career, Wolfgang Staudte directed television detective stories. His case demonstrates that the new German cinema has worthy predecessors who nevertheless remain unappreciated even by their colleagues.

—Maria Racheva

Wolfgang Staudte

STERNBERG, Josef von *See* **VON STERNBERG, Josef**

STEVENS, George

Nationality: American. **Born:** George Cooper Stevens in Oakland, California, 18 December 1904. **Family:** Married Joan (Stevens) (divorced), one son. **Military Service:** Joined U.S. Army Signal Corps, became head of Special Motion Pictures Unit assigned to photograph activities of 6th Army, 1943; Unit awarded citation from General Eisenhower, 1945. **Career:** Actor and stage manager for father's theatrical company, 1920-21; moved to Hollywood, 1921, worked as assistant and 2nd cameraman, then cameraman; joined Hal Roach as cameraman for Laurel and Hardy shorts, 1927; director of two-reel shorts for Roach, from 1930, and for RKO and Universal, from 1932; directed first feature, *The Cohens and Kellys in Trouble,* 1933; also producer, from 1938; resumed career after military service during World War II. **Awards:** Oscars for Best Director, for *A Place in the Sun,* 1951, and *Giant,* 1956; Irving G. Thalberg Award, Academy of Motion Picture Arts and Sciences, 1953. **Died:** In Paris, 9 March 1975.

Films as Director:

1930 *Ladies Past*
1931 *Call a Cop !*; *High Gear*; *The Kick-Off*; *Mama Loves Papa*
1932 *The Finishing Touch*; *Boys Will Be Boys*; *Family Troubles*
1933 *Should Crooners Marry*; *Hunting Trouble*; *Rock-a-bye Cowboy*; *Room Mates*; *A Divorce Courtship*; *Flirting in the Park*; *Quiet Please*; *Grin and Bear It*; *The Cohens and the Kellys in Trouble*
1934 *Bridal Bail*; *Ocean Swells*; *Bachelor Bait*; *Kentucky Kernels*
1935 *Laddie*; *The Nitwits*; *Alice Adams*; *Annie Oakley*
1936 *Swing Time*
1937 *Quality Street*; *A Damsel in Distress*
1938 *Vivacious Lady* (+ pr)
1939 *Gunga Din* (+ pr)
1940 *Vigil in the Night* (+ pr)
1941 *Penny Serenade* (+ pr)
1942 *Woman of the Year*; *The Talk of the Town* (+ pr)
1943 *The More the Merrier* (+ pr)
1948 *I Remember Mama* (+ co-pr)

George Stevens

1951 ***A Place in the Sun*** (+ pr)
1952 *Something to Live For* (+ pr)
1953 ***Shane*** (+ pr)
1956 ***Giant*** (co-pr)
1959 *The Diary of Anne Frank* (+ pr)
1965 *The Greatest Story Ever Told* (+ pr)
1970 *The Only Game in Town*

Other Films:

(partial list)

1924 *The White Sheep* (cameraman); *The Battling Oriole* (cameraman)
1925 *Black Cyclone* (cameraman)
1926 *The Devil Horse* (cameraman); *The Desert's Toll* (cameraman); *Putting Pants on Philip* (cameraman)
1927 *No Man's Law* (cameraman); *The Valley of Hell* (cameraman); *Lightning* (cameraman); *The Battle of the Century* (cameraman)
1928 *Leave 'em Laughing* (cameraman); *Two Tars* (McCarey) (cameraman); *Unaccustomed as We Are* (cameraman)
1929 *Big Business* (cameraman)

Publications

By STEVENS: articles—

Interview, in *Cinema* (Beverly Hills), December/January 1965.
"George Stevens: Shorts to Features: Interview," with Leonard Maltin, in *Action* (Los Angeles), November/December 1970.

On STEVENS: books—

Richie, Donald, *George Stevens: An American Romantic,* New York, 1970.
Phillips, Gene D., *The Movie Makers: Artists in the Industry,* Chicago, 1973.
Petri, Bruce, *A Theory of American Film: The Films and Techniques of George Stevens,* New York, 1987.

On STEVENS: articles—

"Best Director in Hollywood," in *Time* (New York), 16 February 1942.
Houston, Penelope, "*Shane* and George Stevens," in *Sight and Sound* (London), Fall 1953.
Cecil, N., "George Stevens: Letter," in *Films in Review* (New York), February 1954.
Archer, E., "George Stevens and the American Dream," in *Film Culture* (New York), no. 1, 1957.
Luft, Herbert, "George Stevens," in *Films in Review* (New York), November 1958.
Stasey, Joanne, "Hollywood Romantic," in *Films and Filming* (London), July 1959.
Silke, J.R., "The Costumes of George Stevens," in *Cinema* (Beverly Hills), November/December 1963.
Bartlett, N., "Sentiment and Humanism," in *Film* (London), Spring 1964.
"Stevens Issue" of *Cinema* (Beverly Hills), December/January 1964/65.
McVay, D., "Greatest Stevens," in *Films and Filming* (London), April 1965.
Stanbrook, Alan, "The Return of Shane," in *Films and Filming* (London), May 1966.
Beresford, Bruce, "George Stevens," in *Film* (London), Summer 1970.
"Stevens Issue" of *Dialogue on Film* (Washington, D.C.), no. 1, 1972.
Obituary, in *Action* (Los Angeles), March/April 1975.
Beylie, Claude, obituary, in *Ecran* (Paris), May 1975.
"Stevens Issue" of *Dialogue on Film* (Washington, D.C.), May/June 1975.
"A George Stevens Album," in *Action* (Los Angeles), May/June 1975.
Petri, Bruce, "George Stevens: The Wartime Comedies," in *Film Comment* (New York), July/August 1975.
McGilligan, P., and J. McBride, "George Stevens: A Piece of the Rock," in *Bright Lights* (Los Angeles), no. 4, 1979.
Adair, Gilbert, "Directors of the Decade: Forties," *Films and Filming* (London), June 1983.
Combs, Richard, "Slow Burner," in *Listener* (London), 12 February 1987.

* * *

Katharine Hepburn had originally been responsible for bringing George Stevens to the attention of those in the front office. He had directed a great many two-reelers for Hal Roach, and was just entering films as a director of features when Hepburn met him, liked him, and asked that he be assigned as director to her next film, *Alice Adams.* It was a giant step forward for Stevens, but *Alice Adams,* from the Booth Tarkington novel, was a project right up his alley.

Two years later Stevens directed Hepburn again in a charming version of Barrie's play, *Quality Street,* and then in 1941 Hepburn again got him over to MGM to direct her and Spencer Tracy in *Woman of the Year,* the first film the two actors did together.

In the first half of his film career Stevens directed a Barbara Stanwyck feature, *Annie Oakley,* one of the best Astaire-Rogers dancing romances, *Swing Time,* and a delightful Ginger Rogers feature, *Vivacious Lady.* Astaire was never more debonair than in the adaption of Wodehouse's novel *A Damsel in Distress,* with George Burns and Gracie Allen. Stevens then really hit his stride as director of *Gunga Din,* a Kiplingesque glorification of romantic derring-do that featured Cary Grant, Victor McLaglen, and Douglas Fairbanks Jr. Two romances, *Vigil in the Night,* starring Carole Lombard, and *Penny Serenade,* co-starring Irene Dunne with Cary Grant, added to his reputation as an ideal director for romance, especially the weepy sort. His final feature before departing for wartime Europe was one of his best. *The More the Merrier* was a very funny comedy concerning the wartime housing situation in the nation's capital.

After the war, Stevens decided that he would like to produce and direct something that glorified America's past, preferably a comedy. Fortunately, Stevens had been named by Irene Dunne as one of those she would like to work for as the projected star of *I Remember Mama.*

The film was in production for six months and went far over schedule and budget. Stevens was a perfectionist who was determined not to be caught short of any piece of film he needed when making his first cut. He shot a master scene fully, with moving camera, and then shot and kept shooting the same scene from every conceivable angle. For a montage sequence involving Sir Cedric Hardwicke, Stevens spent nearly ten days shooting footage of Sir Cedric reading aloud while the family listened. He overshot, and it was expensive, but the end result was as nearly perfect as any movie could be. Because of the excessive production cost (over $3 million), *I Remember Mama* did not realize the profit it might have earned, although it premiered and played five continuous weeks at Radio Music City Hall, gathering rave notices and honors for all concerned.

Stevens had proved that he was back in form and at the top. He moved over to Paramount, where he made two of his best pictures—*A Place in the Sun,* from Theodore Dreiser's American classic, and *An American Tragedy,* with three perfectly-cast players: Montgomery Clift, Elizabeth Taylor, and Shelly Winters. He then served as the producer-director of one of the most remarkable westerns ever filmed, *Shane.* Told through the eyes of a young boy, the film has a disarming innocence in spite of its violence.

Stevens moved over to Warner Bros. to film *Giant,* Edna Ferber's novel about Texas. *Giant* featured Elizabeth Taylor, Rock Hudson, and James Dean. It was Dean's final credit, for he was killed in an auto crash directly after the shooting of his scenes was finished. Stevens' last three features—*The Diary of Anne Frank, The Greatest Story Ever Told,* and *The Only Game in Town*—were released by 20th Century-Fox. The last one, the best of the three, was virtually sloughed off in its release. When asked what the story was about, Stevens replied, "It's about an aging hooker and a losing gambler, if you think the world is ready for that." He had become embittered. The climate had changed in Hollywood, and it was difficult to get a first-class release for a picture made with the kind of extravagance Stevens was accustomed to.

—De Witt Bodeen

STEVENSON, Robert

Nationality: British/American. **Born:** Buxton, Derbyshire, 1905, became U.S. citizen, 1940. **Education:** Attended Shrewsbury School; St. John's College, Cambridge University, degree in Mechanical Sciences, 1926. **Military Service:** Served as motion picture producer with U.S. War Dept., from 1942; major in U.S. Army reserve, 1946-53. **Family:** Married actress Anna Lee, 1933 (divorced 1944). **Career:** Editor of *Granta* magazine, 1927; scriptwriter, Gaumont British and Gainsborough Studios, from 1929; directed first film, *Happy Ever After,* for UFA in Germany, 1932; signed by David O. Selznick, moved to Hollywood, 1939; director for RKO, late 1940s and early 1950s; director for Walt Disney Productions, 1956-77; also producer, writer, and director for television, from 1950s. **Died:** In Santa Barbara, California, 30 April 1986.

Films as Director:

1932 *Happy Ever After* (co-d)
1933 *Falling For You* (co-d)
1936 *Jack of All Trades* (co-d); *Tudor Rose* (*Nine Days a Queen*); *The Man Who Changed His Mind* (*The Man Who Lived Again*)
1937 *King Solomon's Mines*; *Non-Stop New York*
1938 *Owd Bob* (*To the Victor*)
1939 *The Ware Case*; *A Young Man's Fancy*; *Return to Yesterday*
1940 *Tom Brown's Schooldays*
1941 *Back Street*
1942 *Joan of Paris*
1944 *Forever and a Day* (co-d); *Jane Eyre*
1947 *Dishonoured Lady*
1948 *To the Ends of the Earth*
1949 *I Married a Communist* (*The Woman on Pier 13*)
1950 *Walk Softly, Stranger*
1951 *My Forbidden Past*
1952 *The Las Vegas Story*
1957 *Johnny Tremain*; *Old Yeller*
1959 *Darby O'Gill and the Little People*
1960 *Kidnapped*; *The Absent-Minded Professor*
1962 *In Search of the Castaways*
1963 *Son of Flubber*
1964 *The Misadventures of Merlin Jones*; *Mary Poppins*
1965 *The Monkey's Uncle*; *That Darn Cat*
1967 *The Gnome Mobile*
1968 *Blackbeard's Ghost*
1969 *The Love Bug*
1971 *Bedknobs and Broomsticks*
1974 *Herbie Rides Again*; *The Island at the Top of the World*
1975 *One of Our Dinosaurs is Missing*
1976 *The Shaggy D.A.*

Publications

By STEVENSON: book—

Darkness in the Land, London, 1938.

By STEVENSON: articles—

Interviews, in *Film Weekly* (London), 6 August 1938 and 8 April 1939.
Interview, in *American Film* (Washington, D.C.), March 1978.

On STEVENSON: books—

Maltin, Leonard, *The Disney Films,* New York, 1973; revised edition, 1984.
Holliss, Richard, and Brian Sibley, *The Disney Studio Story,* London, 1988.

On STEVENSON: articles—

Films in Review (New York), August-September 1969.
Films Illustrated (London), March 1975.
"British Cinema: Robert Stevenson," in *National Film Theatre Booklet* (London), January 1979.
Obituary, in *Variety* (New York), 7 May 1986.

* * *

A poll in the trade magazine *Variety* in 1977, the year he retired from filmmaking at the age of 72, named Robert Stevenson as "the most commercially successful director in the history of films." Though by now surpassed, this accolade reflected a long career at the Walt Disney studios where he directed such huge international successes as *Mary Poppins* and *The Love Bug,* aimed squarely at the family audience. Yet such prominence came only after a series of almost separate careers.

The British film industry that Robert Stevenson joined in the late 1920s was still far from respectable, and had become notorious for its cheap, low-quality "quota quickies," films produced in response to the 1927 Cinematograph Act. Yet Stevenson, with his first-class degree in mechanical sciences from Cambridge University, was one of a new breed of well-educated, bright young men introduced into the industry by the more far-sighted producers of the day. Their diverse talents were to enhance greatly the standing of British cinema. Some went into the documentary field, encouraged by John Grierson, but Stevenson, along with others like Carol Reed and Anthony Asquith, chose to enter the mainstream of feature-film production. In 1929 he started as a scriptwriter for Gainsborough-Gaumont-British, then under the control of Michael Balcon, later the head of Ealing Studios.

By 1932 Stevenson had directed his first film, *Happy Ever After,* a typical product of the studio that was nonetheless an amiable star vehicle for the popular comic pairing of Jack Hulbert and Cicely Courtneidge. In 1936 he wrote and directed *Tudor Rose,* an historical costume drama in the style of Alexander Korda's internationally successful *The Private Life of Henry VIII.* It won him critical as well as popular acclaim, and he enhanced his reputation with several other noteworthy films in the late 1930s, including an ambitious version of

Robert Stevenson directing Anna Lee and Cedric Hardwicke in *King Solomon's Mines* courtesy of The Rank Organisation Plc

King Solomon's Mines with Paul Robeson. By 1939 he was named by fellow director Anthony Asquith, in an article in *Film Weekly,* as one of a new breed of directors who were developing a discernibly British style. Ironically, it was at this point that Stevenson, the leading director at Gaumont-British after the departure of Alfred Hitchcock to America, also chose to go, along with his actress wife Anna Lee, to Hollywood.

There was some resentment in England towards those filmmakers who remained in the United States after the outbreak of World War II. Interestingly, though, two of Stevenson's best films from this period (when he was under contract to David O. Selznick) were adaptations of classic English novels; *Tom Brown's Schooldays,* starring Freddie Bartholomew, and an atmospheric version of *Jane Eyre,* co-directed by Orson Welles. In 1940, however, Stevenson had become an American citizen. In addition to making documentary films for the U.S. War Department, he served in the U.S. Army, remaining a major in the U.S. Reserve for several years after the war.

Stevenson continued making films throughout this period, including *To the Ends of the Earth,* a fine thriller made for RKO in 1948 that featured the dimly-lit sets and complicated plot twists characteristic of American cinema of the time. His next film, however, *I Married a Communist,* was more characteristic of the anti-Red paranoia of its producer Howard Hughes. It proved a disaster at the box office.

After only three more films, Stevenson left RKO in 1952 to start a career as a writer and director for the new medium of television. He directed over 100 productions for American television, including *Playhouse of the Stars, General Electric Theater,* and *Alfred Hitchcock Presents* (an ironic reunion with his former colleague at Gaumont-British), before accepting, at the age of 51, an unexpected offer from Walt Disney. As he later recalled, "I was hired for six weeks, and stayed for 20 years."

It was a period of Stevenson's career that was as successful as it was (initially, at least) unlikely. He had shown himself to be a versatile and technically adept director, but he was as surprised as anyone by his phenomenal career at the Disney studios. At Disney he directed no less than eleven major box-office hits, including *The Absent-Minded Professor, The Love Bug, Mary Poppins, Bedknobs and Broomsticks,* and *One of Our Dinosaurs Is Missing.* These films were all enjoyable, live-action comic fantasies, deliberately broad in their appeal. They typically combined frenzied action, eccentric characters, and impressive special effects, often blending animation and film. The success of these well-made films owed much to Stevenson's old-fashioned insistence on the importance of a good story, and his skill as a craftsman in deftly pacing the narrative. He also possessed an instinctive awareness of what made an audience laugh, revealing a consistently popular touch rare enough in Hollywood, let alone for an Englishman of his upper-middle-class background.

Apart from an Academy Award nomination for *Mary Poppins* in 1964 (which won five Oscars and brought the studio over $30 million), Stevenson retained a low profile outside the industry, although he remained hugely respected within it. Of his work, he once said, "When I'm directing a picture, what I have in mind is a happy audience, enjoying it in a movie house." Such a deceptively simple statement reflects his modest and unpretentious approach, but belies the skill with which Robert Stevenson was able to keep audiences happy.

—Nicholas Thomas

STILLER, Mauritz

Nationality: Swedish/Russian (became citizen of Sweden, 1921). **Born:** Mosche Stiller in Helsinki, Finland, 17 July 1883. **Career:** Actor in Finland, from 1899; moved to Sweden to avoid Russian military draft, worked as actor in Sweden, from 1904; manager of avant-garde theatre Lilla Teatern, Stockholm, 1911; hired as film director (also writer and actor) for newly-formed Svenska Biograf film studio, Stockholm, 1912; began collaboration with Greta Gustafsson (Greta Garbo), 1923; moved to Hollywood under contract to MGM, 1925; fired by MGM before completing a film, hired by Erich Pommer at Paramount to direct *Hotel Imperial,* then returned to Sweden, 1927. **Died:** 8 November 1928.

Films as Director:

1912 *Mor och dotter* (*Mother and Daughter*) (+ sc, role as Count Raoul de Saligny); *När svärmor regerar* (*When the Mother-in-Law Reigns*) (+ sc, role as the pastor); *Vampyren* (*Vampire*) (+ sc); *Barnet* (*The Child*); *De svarta makerna* (*The Black Masks*) (+ co-sc); *Den tryanniske fästmannen* (*The Tyrannical Fiancée*) (+ sc, role as Elias Petterson)

1913 *När kärleken dödar* (*When Love Kills*) (+ co-sc); *När larmhlockan ljuder* (*When the Alarm Bell Rings*); *Den okända* (*The Unknown Woman*) (+ sc); *Bröderna* (*Brothers*) (+ co-sc); *Den moderna suffragetten* (*The Suffragette*) (+ sc); *Pålivets ödesväger* (*The Smugglers*); *Mannekägen* (*The Model*) (+ sc); *För sin kärleks skull* (*The Stockbroker*) (+ sc); *Gränsfolken* (*The Border Feud*); *Livets konflikter* (*Conflicts of Life*) (+ sc); *Kammarjunkaren* (*Gentleman of the Room*) (+ sc)

1914 *Lekkamraterna* (*The Playmates*) (+ sc); *Stormfågeln* (*The Stormy Petrel*); *Det röda tornet* (*The Master*) (+ co-sc); *Skottet* (*The Shot*); *När konstnärer älska* (*When Artists Love*)

1915 *Hans hustrus förflutna* (*His Wife's Past*); *Hämnaren* (*The Avenger*); *Madame de Thèbes* (*The Son of Destiny*); *Mästertjuven* (*The Son of Fate*); *Hans bröllopsnatt* (*His Wedding Night*); *Minlotsen* (*The Mine Pilot*); *Dolken* (*The Dagger*) (+ co-sc); *Lyckonälen* (*The Motorcar Apaches*) (+ co-sc)

1916 *Balettprimadonnan* (*Anjuta, the Dancer*); *Kärlek och journalistik* (*Love and Journalism*); *Kampen om hans hjärta* (*The Struggle for His Heart*); *Vingarne* (*The Wings*) (+ co-sc)

1917 *Thomas Graals bästa film* (*Thomas Graal's Best Picture*); *Alexander den Store* (*Alexander the Great*) (+ sc)

1918 *Thomas Graals bästa barn* (*Thomas Graal's First Child*) (+ co-sc); *Sången om den eldröda blomman* (*Song of the Scarlet Flower, The Flame of Life*)

1919 *Fiskebyn* (*The Fishing Village*); ***Herr Arnes Pengar*** (*Sir Arne's Treasure*) (+ co-sc)

1920 ***Erotikon*** (*Bonds That Chafe*) (+ co-sc); *Johan* (+ sc)

1921 *De Landsflyktige* (*The Exiles*) (+ co-sc)

1922 *Gunnar Hedes saga* (*Gunnar Hede's Saga, The Old Mansion*) (+ sc)

1923 ***Gösta Berlings saga*** (*The Story of Gösta Berling*; *The Atonement of Gösta Berling*) (+ co-sc)

1926 *The Temptress* (finished by Fred Niblo) (+ sc)

1927 *Hotel Imperial* (+ co-sc); *The Woman on Trial*; *Barbed Wire* (finished by Rowland Lee) (+ sc)

1928 *The Street of Sin* (finished by Ludvig Berger) (+ sc)

Publications

On STILLER: books—

Idestam-Almquist, Bengt, *Den Svenska Filmens Drama: Sjöström och Stiller,* Stockholm, 1938.

Hardy, Forsyth, *Scandinavian Film,* London, 1951.
Waldekranz, Rune, *Swedish Cinema,* Stockholm, 1959.
Lauritzen, Einar, *Swedish Film,* New York, 1962.
Cowie, Peter, *Swedish Cinema,* London, 1966.
Pensel, Hans, *Seastrom and Stiller in Hollywood,* New York, 1969.
Werner, Gösta, *Mauritz Stiller och hans filmer,* Stockholm, 1969.
Petrie, Graham, *Hollywood Destinies: European Directors in Hollywood 1922-31,* London, 1985.

On STILLER: articles—

Idestam-Almquist, Bengt, "Stiller, a Pioneer of the Cinema," in *Biografbladet* (Stockholm), Fall 1950.
Idestam-Almquist, Bengt, "The Man Who Found Garbo," in *Films and Filming* (London), August 1956.
Sjöström, Victor, "As I Remember Him," in *Film Comment* (New York), Summer 1970.
Wood, Robin, "Essays on the Swedish Cinema (Part 2)," in *Lumiere* (Melbourne), April/May 1974.
Gillett, John, "Swedish Retrospect," in *Sight and Sound* (London), Summer 1974.
Robertson, J., "Mauritz Stiller," in *Monthly Film Bulletin* (London), December 1977.
Beylie, Claude, and M. Martin, "Sjöström, Stiller et l'Amérique," in *Ecran* (Paris), September 1978.
Sopocy, M., "Oltre il realisimo. 'Griffithiana'," in *Quarterly Review of Film Studies* (New York), September 1986.

* * *

Like the other two distinguished pioneers of the early Swedish cinema, Sjöström and Sjöberg, Mauritz Stiller had an essentially theatrical background. But it must be remembered that he was reared in Finland of Russian-Jewish stock, did not emigrate to Sweden until he was 27, and remained there only 15 years before going to Hollywood. He responded relatively late to the Swedish cultural tradition, so heavily influenced by the country's extreme northern climate and landscape, and by the fatalistic, puritanical literary and dramatic aura exerted most notably by the Swedish dramatist Strindberg and the Nobel prize-winning novelist Selma Lagerlöf. The latter's works—*Herr Arne's Treasure, Gunnar Hede's Saga,* and *Gösta Berlings Saga*—were inspired by tradition and legend, and were all to be adapted by Stiller for the silent screen.

After establishing himself as a talented stage actor, Stiller's work on film began in 1912. He immediately proved to be a meticulous craftsman, with a strong visual instinct and a polished sense of timing and rhythm. His early work showed how much he had learned technically from the considerable number of D.W. Griffith's short narrative films shown in Sweden. For example, *The Black Masks,* made in 1912, is noted by Forsyth Hardy as having, "over a hundred scenes, a constantly changing combination of interiors and exteriors, close-ups and panoramic shots." In 1913 Stiller even made a film based on the activities of Mrs. Pankhurst called *Den moderna suffragetten,* reflecting his reputation in the theater for avant-garde subjects.

Stiller also proved adept at comedy, as his films *Love and Journalism, Thomas Graal's Best Film*—one of the earliest films about filmmaking—and *Thomas Graal's First Child* reveal, with their skirmishing and coquetry that characterize the relationship of the sexes. Stiller insisted, however, on restraint in acting style; he was an autocratic perfectionist, and Emil Jannings, Germany's leading actor, termed him "the Stanislavski of the cinema." The second of these films had a complex structure, full of flashbacks and daydreams; the director Victor Sjöström starred in all three, as well as in other of Stiller's films. In some of his earliest efforts, Stiller made appearances himself.

Mauritz Stiller

The climax to Stiller's career in the production of elegant and graceful comedies of sex manners was *Erotikon*; though better known, because of its alluring title, than its predecessors, it is somewhat less accomplished. Elaborately staged and full of sexual by-play—the wife of a preoccupied professor has two lovers in hot pursuit, a young sculptor and an elderly baron—it includes a specially commissioned ballet performed by the opera in Stockholm. These sophisticated silent films rank alongside the early comedies of Lubitsch, whose work in this genre in Germany in fact succeeded them. Lubitsch readily acknowledged his debt to Stiller.

Again like Lubitsch (with whose career Stiller's can best be compared at this stage), Stiller also worked on epic-style, historical subjects. He took over the adaptation of Selma Lagerlöf's novel *Sir Arne's Treasure* from Sjöström, its original director. This was essentially an eighteenth-century story of escape and pursuit—three Scottish mercenaries in the service of King John III are imprisoned for conspiracy. They abscond in the depths of winter, undertaking a desperate journey overland to flee the country. In the process they become increasingly violent and menacing until they come upon Arne's mansion. They steal his treasure, burn his house, and slaughter its inhabitants except for an orphan girl. The orphan Elsalill, who survives the massacre, is a haunted figure half-attracted to the leader of the Scottish renegades. But she eventually betrays him and dies in the final confrontation in which the Scots are recaptured. The long, snake-like column of black-robed women moving over the icy waste in the girl's funeral procession is Stiller's concluding panoramic scene; one of the best-known spectacular shots in early cinema, it still appears in most history books. The film illustrates grandly the response of the early Swedish filmmakers to the menacing magnificence of the northern winter landscape.

After completing *Erotikon* Stiller moved on to *Johan,* a dark and satiric study of the triangular relationship of husband, wife, and the visitant, stranger-lover. Set in the desolate expanse of the countryside, the film includes a climax worthy of Griffith as the guilty couple, chased by the husband, ride the rapids in a small boat. Stiller then crowned his career in Sweden with two further adaptations of Lagerlöf's work: *Gunnar Hedes Saga* and *Gösta Berlings Saga.* In the former—in every way an outstanding film of its period in its immixture of dream and actuality—the hero, the violinist Nils (Einar Hansson), is inspired to emulate his father, who made a fortune by driving a vast herd of reindeer south from the Arctic circle. Nils's adventure in realizing this dream only leads to severe injury resulting in amnesia; back home in the forests of the south he experiences hallucinations from which the girl who loves him finally liberates him. The film's duality is striking: the realism of the trek with the reindeer, which involved panoramic shots of the great herds and brilliant tracking shots of the catastrophic stampede which leads to Nils's accident, is in marked contrast to the twilit world of his hallucinations.

Gösta Berling's Saga, on the other hand, though famous for its revelation of the star quality of the young drama student, Greta Garbo, and its melodramatic story of the defrocked priest (Lars Hanson) fatally in love with Garbo's Italian girl, is clumsy in structure compared with *Gunnar Hede's Saga,* and was later destructively cut for export to half its original length of four hours.

Stiller travelled in 1925 to America at the invitation of Louis B. Mayer of MGM on the strength of his reputation as a sophisticated European director, but mostly (it would seem) because he was Garbo's Svengali-like and obsessive mentor. He very soon fell out with Mayer, who endured him because he wanted Garbo as a contract player. All but mesmerized by Stiller, Garbo insisted that he direct her in *The Temptress*; the inevitable difficulties arose and he was withdrawn from the film.

Stiller's best film in America was made at Paramount. *Hotel Imperial,* which starred Pola Negri, concerned a wartime love affair between a hotel servant and an Austrian officer and was notable for its spectacular, composite hotel set over which the camera hung suspended from an overhead rail. After finishing a second film with Negri, *The Woman on Trial,* Stiller never managed to complete another film; the respiratory illness that was undermining his health forced him to part from Garbo and return to Sweden, where he died in 1928 at the age of 45.

—Roger Manvell

STONE, Oliver

Nationality: American. **Born:** New York City, 1946. **Education:** Studied at Yale University, dropped out, 1965; studied filmmaking under Martin Scorsese, New York University, B.F.A., 1971. **Military Service:** Volunteered for 25th Infantry Division, U.S. Army, 1967, awarded Bronze Star for Valor, and the Purple Heart with Oak Leaf Cluster. **Family:** Married 1) Majwa Sarkis, 1971 (divorced 1977); 2) Elizabeth Burkit Cox, 1981. **Career:** Teacher at Free Pacific Institute, Cholon, Vietnam, 1965; joined U.S. Merchant Marine, 1966; taxi driver in New York City, 1971; directed first film, *Seizure,* 1974. **Awards:** Oscar for Best Screenplay Adaptation, and Writers Guild Award, for *Midnight Express,* 1979; Directors Guild of America Award, Oscar for Best Director, and Golden Globe Award for Best Director, for *Platoon,* 1987, and for *Born on the Fourth of July,* 1989.

Films as Director and Scriptwriter:

1974 *Seizure*
1981 *The Hand*
1986 ***Salvador*** (+ pr, co-sc); *Platoon*
1987 *Wall Street* (co-sc)
1988 *Talk Radio* (co-sc)
1989 *Born on the Fourth of July* (co-sc)
1991 *The Doors* (co-sc, + uncredited role as film professor); *JFK* (+ pr)
1993 *Heaven and Earth* (+ pr)
1994 *Natural Born Killers*
1995 *Nixon* (+ pr)

Other Films:

1978 ***Midnight Express*** (Parker) (sc)
1982 *Conan the Barbarian* (Milius) (co-sc)
1983 *Scarface* (De Palma) (sc)
1985 *Year of the Dragon* (Cimino) (sc)
1986 *8 Million Ways to Die* (Ashby) (co-sc)
1991 *The Iron Maze* (exec pr)
1992 *South Central* (exec pr); *Zebrahead* (exec pr)
1993 *Dave* (role as himself); *The Last Party* (role as himself); *The Joy Luck Club* (exec pr); *Wild Palms* (for TV) (exec pr)
1994 *The New Age* (exec pr)
1995 *Indictment: The McMartin Trial* (for TV) (exec pr)

Publications

By STONE: books—

Platoon and Salvador: The Screenplays, with Richard Boyle, Cranbury, New Jersey, 1987.
Oliver Stone's Heaven and Earth, with Michael Singer, Boston, 1993.
JFK: The Book of the Film, with Zachary Sklar, New York, 1992.

By STONE: articles—

Interview with Nigel Floyd, in *Monthly Film Bulletin* (London), January 1987.
Interview with Pat McGilligan, in *Film Comment* (New York), January/February 1987.
Interview with M. Burke, in *Stills* (London), 29 February 1987.
Interview with Louise Tanner, in *Films in Review* (New York), March 1987.
Interview with M. Sineux and Michel Ciment, in *Positif* (Paris), April 1987.
Interview with Alexander Cockburn, in *American Film* (Washington D.C.), December 1987.
Interview with Gary Crowdus, in *Cineaste* (New York), vol. 16, no. 3, 1988.
Interview with M. Tessier and others, in *Revue du Cinéma* (Paris), April 1989.
Interview with Mark Rowland, in *American Film* (Washington, D.C.), March 1991.
Interview with David Breskin, in *Rolling Stone* (New York), 4 April 1991.
Interview in *Time* (New York), 23 December 1991.
Interview with David Ansen, in *Newsweek* (New York), 23 December 1991.
Interview with Jeff Yarbrough, in *Advocate* (New York), 7 April 1992.
Interview with Gavin Smith, in *Film Comment* (New York), January/February 1994.
Interview with Gregg Kilday, in *Entertainment Weekly* (New York), 14 January 1994.
Interview with Graham Fuller, in *Interview* (New York), September 1994.
Interview with Nathan Gardels, in *New Perspectives* (Toronto), Spring 1995.

On STONE: books—

Beaver, Frank, *Oliver Stone: Wakeup Cinema,* New York, 1994.
Riordan, James, *Stone: The Controversies, Excesses, and Exploits of a Radical Filmmaker,* New York, 1994.

On STONE: articles—

Chase, Chris, "Good Fortune Has Creator of *Hand* Nervous," in *New York Times,* 15 May 1981.
Sklar, Robert, and others, "*Platoon* on Inspection: A Critical Symposium," in *Cineaste* (New York), vol. 15, no. 4, 1987.
Peary, Gerald, "The Ballad of a Haunted Soldier," in *Maclean's* (Toronto), 30 March 1987.
Boozer, Jack, Jr., "*Wall Street*: The Commodification of Perception," in *Journal of Popular Film and Television* (Washington, D.C.), vol. 17, no. 3, 1989.
Corliss, Richard, "Who Cares?," in *Film Criticism* (Meadville, Pennsylvania), vol. 25, no. 1, 1989.
Jones, G., "Trash Talk: Oliver Stone's *Talk Radio,*" in *Enclitic* (Los Angeles), vol. 11, no. 2, 1989.
Wrathall, J., "Greeks, Trojans and Cubans—Oliver Stone," in *Monthly Film Bulletin* (London), October 1989.
Denby, David, "Days of Rage," in *New York,* 18 December 1989.
Klawans, Stuart, "*Born on the Fourth of July,*" in *Nation* (New York), 1 January 1990.
Kauffman, Stanley, "The Battle after the War," in *New Republic* (New York), 29 January 1990.
Simon, John, "Wild Life," in *National Review* (New York), 5 February 1990.
Hoberman, J., "Out of Order," in *Sight and Sound* (London), Spring 1991.
Horton, Robert, "Riders on the Storm," in *Film Comment* (New York), May/June 1991.
Schiff, Stephen, "The Last Wild Man," in *New Yorker,* 8 August 1994.

On STONE: film—

Oliver Stone: Inside Out (for TV), 1992.

* * *

Anyone attempting with any degree of success, both artistic and commercial, to make overtly political movies that sustain a left-wing position within the Hollywood cinema of the 1980s and 1990s deserves at least our respectful attention. In fact, Oliver Stone's work dramatizes, in a particularly extreme and urgent form, the quandary of the American left-wing intellectual.

Platoon and *Wall Street* provide a useful starting point, as they share the same basic structure. A young man (Charlie Sheen, in both films) has to choose in terms of values between the Good Father (Willem Dafoe, Martin Sheen) and the Bad Father (Tom Berenger, Michael Douglas); he learns to choose the Good Father and destroy the Bad. The opposition is very similar in both cases: the Good Father is a liberal with a conscience, aware of the impossibility of changing or radically affecting the general situation but committed to the preservation of his personal integrity; the Bad Father has no conscience and no integrity to preserve, and this, combined with a total ruthlessness, is what equips him to survive (until the dénouement) and makes him an insidiously seductive figure. The Bad Father is completely adapted to a system that the Good Father can protest against but do nothing to change. The young man can exact a kind of individual justice by destroying the Bad Father, but the system remains intact.

Platoon and *Wall Street* do not represent Stone's work at its best: their targets are a bit too obvious, the characteristic rage comes too easily, tinged with self-righteousness, so that the alienating aspects of his manner—the heavy stylistic rhetoric, the emotional bludgeoning—are felt at their most obtrusive. But the two films encapsulate the quandary—one might say the *blockage*—that is treated more complexly elsewhere: what does one fight for within a system one perceives as totally corrupt but in which the only alternative to capitulation is impotence?

The fashionable buzz-phrase "structuring absence" becomes resonant when applied to Stone's films: in the most literal sense, his work so far is structured precisely on the absence of an available political alternative, which could only be a commitment to what is most deeply and hysterically taboo in American culture, a form of Marxist socialism. There is a curious paradox here which Americans seem reluctant to notice: Lincoln's famous formula, supposedly one of the foundations of American political ideology, "Government of the people, by the people and for the people," could only be realized in a system dubbed, above all else, "un-American" (American capitalism, as Stone sees very clearly, is government *by* the rich and powerful *for* the rich and powerful). In both *Salvador* and *Born on the Fourth of July* the protagonist declares, at a key point in the development, "I am an American, I love America," and we must assume he is speaking for Stone. But we must ask, *which* America does he love, since the American actuality is presented in both films as unambiguously and uniformly hateful? What is being appealed to here is clearly a *myth* of America, but the films seem, implicitly and with profound unease, to recognize that the myth cannot possibly be realized, that capitalism *must* take the forms it has historically taken. Hence the sense one takes from the films of a just but impotent rage: without the availability of the alternative there is no way out.

This is nowhere clearer than in *Salvador,* one of Stone's strongest, least flawed works and a gesture of great courage within its social-political context. While in American capitalist democracy it is still possible to make a film like *Salvador* (the equivalent in Stalinist Russia would have been unthinkable), it is not possible for the film to go further than it does, to take the necessary, logical step. Impotent rage is permissible, the promotion of a constructive alternative is not. Stone's films can be acceptable, even popular, even canonized by Academy Awards precisely because their ultimate effect, beyond the rage, is to suggest that things *cannot* be changed (as indeed they cannot, while one remains within the system). *Salvador* offers a lucid and cogent analysis of the political situation, a vivid dramatization of historical events (the death of Romero, the rape and murder of the visiting Nicaraguan nuns), and an outspoken denunciation of American intervention. Neither does it chicken out at the end: the final scene, where the protagonist at last gets his lover and her two children over the border into the "land of the free," to have them abruptly and brutally sent back by American security officers, is as chilling as anything that modern Hollywood cinema has to offer. But the film's attitude to the concept of a specifically *socialist* revolution (as opposed to a vague notion of people "fighting for their freedom") is thoroughly cagy and equivocal. Nothing is done to demystify the habitual American conflation of socialism and Marxism with Stalinism.

All the film can say is that the threat of a general "Communist" takeover is either imaginary or grossly exaggerated (if it were not, presumably the horrors we are shown would all be justified or at least pardonable), that the Salvadoreans, like good Americans, just want their liberty, and that America, in its own interests, has betrayed its founding principles by intervening on the wrong side.

Born on the Fourth of July recapitulates the earlier film's force, rage, and outspokenness, and also its impasse. It seems to be weakened, however, by its final construction of its protagonist as a redeemer-hero. Ron Kovic, by the end of the film, in realizing (with whatever irony) his mother's dream that he would one day speak before thousands of people saying wonderful things, at once regains his full personal integrity and sense of self-worth and offers an appar-

Oliver Stone on the set of *Natural Born Killers*

ent political escape by revealing the "truth." But recent history has shown many times that the revelation of truth can be very readily mythified and absorbed into the system (the Oscar awards and nominations for Stone's movies represent an exact equivalent).

Talk Radio received no such accolades and seems generally regarded as a minor, marginal work. On the contrary, it is arguably Stone's most completely successful film to date and absolutely central to his work, to the point of being confessional. It has been taken as more an Eric Bogosian movie than a Stone movie. We can credit Stone with firmer personal integrity and higher ambitions than are evidenced by Barry Champlain (Bogosian's character), but, that allowance made, Stone has found here the perfect "objective correlative" for his own position, his own quandary. Champlain's rage, toppling over into hysteria, parallels the tone of much of Stone's work and identifies one of its sources, the frustration of grasping that no one really listens, no one understands, no one *wants* to understand; the sense of addressing a people kept in a state of mystification so complete, by a system so powerful and pervasive, that no formal brainwashing could improve on it (this "reading" of the American public is resumed in *Born on the Fourth of July*). The film is indeed revelatory, and very impressive in its honesty and nakedness.

In the 1990s, Stone's career entered a new phase as the director became even more commercially successful while raising the ante of political controversy. His earlier films, especially *Platoon,* had successfully exploited classic realist techniques—especially the device of a likeable main character—to arouse audience sympathy for a radical point of view: that the system deals in death, not life, and counts as enemies all who oppose it, including "good" Americans. Classic realism, however, leads the spectator toward emotional catharses that blunt the point of such political perceptions; furthermore, the narrative closure required in such texts suggests a victory for the protagonists of good will even as the political problems so tellingly enunciated are transcended. Of Stone's recent films, only *Heaven and Earth,* which completes his Vietnam trilogy, remains more or less within the regime of classic realism. Based on the autobiographical novels of Le Ly Hayslip, *Heaven and Earth* also offers a main character—a young Vietnamese woman—who is both sympathetic and socially typical, who offers, in short, an ideal emotional and narrative vantage point for the representation—poignant if not objective or detailed—of Vietnamese history since 1953. Le Ly is abused and manipulated by the successive regimes in her village—French, South Vietnamese, Viet Cong—only to be "rescued" by a burned-out GI who takes her to an America concerned only with materialism and its own comfort. This ambitious film never individualizes, hardly humanizes its main character (who heroically resists Americanization by an entrepreneurship that allows her to live alone and return to Vietnam). With its startling visual stylization, artful use of disorienting editing, and expressionistic mise-en-scène, *Heaven and Earth* treats its subject with an operatic grandeur. The abandonment of realism (with its carefully restrained stylization) for expressionism is also evident in *The Doors,* which takes as its subject yet another—for Stone—heroic rebel of the 1960s, musician/poet Jim Morrison. Here visual and aural stylizations are motivated by Stone's desire to pay homage to the psychodelism of the period, even as they "express" the artistic rebellion of Morrison's music. As in *Heaven and Earth,* the film is less about a character than a *zeitgeist,* but many reviewers and spectators were disappointed by Stone's lack of emphasis on narrative and complex character.

A further, though never complete rejection of realism is to be found in the three Stone films that have found the most commercial success, even as they have aroused the greatest political controversy (making Stone a frequent guest on TV talk shows to defend his latest work and simultaneously plug it). *Natural Born Killers,* though ostensibly set in the 1990s, actually constructs its own, nightmarish version of American reality. Following Brecht, Stone here revives an American myth—the outlaw couple a la Bonnie and Clyde—but empties the outrageously violent attack on family and society perpetrated by Mickey and Mallory of all emotional content through two defamiliarizing techniques: a fragmentary, Eisensteinian montage that prevents any scene from achieving a reality effect; and acting that avoids naturalism at all costs. If *Platoon* uses the violence of war for melodramatic effect, *Natural Born Killers* eschews emotion of any kind to make a political point: the murderous connection between the deep-seated pathology of American family life and the reprehensible tendency for the media to exploit the desire of the abused and battered to find some kind of identity and self-worth. The result is the most intellectually profound and cerebral contemplation of violence in American life since Peckinpah's *The Wild Bunch.*

Stone, however, has not been satisfied to transcend the historical through mythopoeia and stylistic virtuosity (in the manner of, say, Jim Morrison). His conception of the film director's social role is the most enlarged since the time of D. W. Griffith, whose career his own has in part mirrored. What the Civil War was for Griffith's generation, the Kennedy assassination has been for Stone's: a defining historical event, seen rightly or wrongly as the source of subsequent developments. *JFK* is Stone's attempt to argue that case: not simply to advance yet another conspiracy theory, but to identify the death of Kennedy as the beginning of a deterioration in American life that has not yet come to an end. Like Griffith, Stone attempted a paradoxical recreation of history: a film that, he argues, is "true" to the facts and yet, making use of dramatic license, creates its own facts as an interpretation, a possible version of history. Like Griffith, Stone has been much attacked for so doing, even as his film has reopened interest in an event and its aftermath for a new generation. *JFK* uneasily joins two stylistic regimes: a classic realist narrative (the pursuit of the truth by a sympathetically presented main character, district attorney Jim Garrison) and a highly rhetorical, expressionistic recreation of the events under investigation. Of course, Garrison, like Stone's other heroes, fails to do more than the right thing: the vaguely evoked fascistic cabal of southern businessmen and loose cannon Cubans emerges unscathed after pinning the rap on hapless Lee Harvey Oswald. Like *Heaven and Earth, JFK* ultimately turns nostalgically toward a past as yet unspoiled by the fall into political violence. *Nixon,* in contrast, is less oriented toward an event and an era than toward political biography. In the extensively annotated published screenplay, Stone answers his expected critics by pointing to the historical record as a source for the film's material. In that book, Stone insists that his story of Nixon is a classically tragic tale of the essentially good man who overreaches and thereby dooms himself to disgrace. The resulting film, however, is disappointingly simplistic. Nixon becomes a bumbling, foul-mouthed fool whose physical and political gaffes define his relations with others (their constant disapproval is evoked by numerous reaction shots). This interpretation is very much at odds with the substance of the political record and does nothing to explain the shifting tides of popular sentiment that swept Nixon into office and returned him for a second term. Choosing a subject for which he could feel little sympathy, Stone reveals in *Nixon* the limits of his political vision, which, like Griffith's, depends too much on the melodramatic opposition of heroes to villains.

—Robin Wood, updated by R. Barton Palmer

STORCK, Henri

Nationality: Belgian. **Born:** Ostend, 5 September 1907. **Family:** Married photographer Virginia Lierens. **Career:** Began making films in 8mm, 1927; organized cine-club in Ostend, made first "reportages," 1928; assistant in France to Pierre Billon, Jean Croillon, and Jean Vigo, 1931; with Joris Ivens, made *Borinage,* 1933; began making films about art and folklore, 1936; directed first Belgian-international co-production, *Le Banquet des fraudeurs,* 1951; president (for fifteen years), Association Belge des Auteurs de Films et Auteurs de Television, and co-founder, Royal Film Archive of Belgium.

Films as Director:

1927-28 amateur films on Ostend

1929-30 *Pour vos beaux yeux*; *Images d'Ostende*

1930 *Une Pêche au hareng*; *Le Service de sauvetage sur la côte belge*; *Les Fêtes du centenaire*; *Trains de plaisir*; *Tentative de films abstraits*; *La Mort de Vénus*; *Suzanne au bain*; *Ostende, reine des plages*

1931 *Une Idylle à la plage*

1932 *Travaux du tunnel sous l'Escaut*; *Histoire du soldat inconnu*; *Sur les bords de la caméra*

1933 *Trois Vies une corde*; *Misère au Borinage* (co-d, co-ph)

1934 *Création d'ulcères artificiels chez le chien*; *La Production sélective du réseau à soixante-dix*

1935 *Electrification de la ligne Bruxelles-Anvers*; *L'Île de Pâques*; *Le Trois-Mâts*; *Cap du sud*; *L'Industrie de la tapisserie et du meuble sculpté*; *Le Coton*

1936 *Les Carillons*; *Les Jeux de l'été et de la mer*; *Sur les routes de l'ete*; *Regards sur la Belgique ancienne*

1937 *La Belgique nouvelle*; *Un ennemi public*; *Les Maisons de la misère*

1938 *Comme une lettre à la poste*; *La Roue de la fortune*; *Terre de Flandre*; *Vacances*; *Le Patron est mort*

1939 *Voor Recht en Vrijheid te Kortrijk*

1940 *La Foire internationale de Bruxelles*

1942-44 *Symphonie paysanne* (co-d, ph)

1944 *Le Monde de Paul Delvaux* (+ ph)

1947 *La Joie de revivre*

1947-48 *Rubens*

1949 *Au carrefour de la vie*

1950 *Carnavals*

1951 *Le Banquet des fraudeurs* (feature)

1952 *La Fenêtre ouverte*

1953 *Herman Teirlinck*

1954 *Les Belges et la mer*; *Les Portes de la maison*; *Le Tour du monde en bateau-stop*

1955 *Le Trésor d'Ostende*

1956 *Décembre, mois des enfants*

1957 *Couleur de feu*

1957-60 *Les Seigneurs de la forêt*

1960 *Les Gestes du silence*

1961 *Les Dieux du feu*; *L'Énergie et vous*

1962 *Variation sur le geste*; *Le Bonheur d'être aimée* (+ co-pr, co-sc); *Les Malheurs de la guerre*

1963 *Plastiques*

1964 *Matières nouvelles*

1965 *Le Musée vivant*

1966 *Jeudi on chantera comme dimanche*

1968 *Forêt secrète d'Afrique*

1969-70 *Paul Delvaux ou les femmes défendues* (+ ed)

1969-72 *Fêtes de Belgiques*

Henri Storck

1974-75 *Fifres et tambours d'Entre-Sambre-et-Meuse*; *Les Marcheurs de Sainte Rolende*; *Les Joyeux Tromblons*
1985 *Permeke* (+ sc)

Other Film:

1975 ***Jeanne Dielman, 23 Quai du commerce, 1080 Bruxelles*** (Akerman) (role as 1st caller)
1987 *Henri Storck: Ooggetuige* (consultant)

Publications

By STORCK: articles—

Interview, in *Documentary Explorations,* by G. Roy Levin, New York, 1972.
Interview with Bert Hogenkamp, in *Skrien* (Amsterdam), July/August 1977.
Interview with J. P. Everaerts in *Film en Televisie* (Brussels), September 1987.
Interviews with A. Tournès in *Jeune Cinéma* (Paris), May/June and July/August 1988.

On STORCK: articles—

Blakeston, Oswell, "The Romantic Cinema of Henri Storck," in *Architectural Review* (New York), May 1931.
Bassan, R., "Storck le touche-à-tout," in *Ecran* (Paris), September 1977.
Grelier, R., "Henri Storck," in *Image et Son* (Paris), September 1977.
Davay, P., "Henri Storck à l'honneur," in *Amis du Film et de la Télévision* (Brussels), January 1979.
"Storck Issue" of *Revue Belge du Cinéma* (Brussels), August 1979.
De Bongnie, J., "Storck vu par un jeune Hudon," in *Amis du Film et de la Télévision* (Brussels), November 1979.
"Storck Section" of *Revue Belge du Cinéma* (Brussels), Winter/Spring 1983/84.
Vrielynck, R., "Sincerite et bon sens," in *Plateau,* vol. 7, no. 3, 1986.

* * *

After growing up in the seaside town of Ostend, Henri Storck naturally chose the beach and the sea, with the surrounding sand dunes, as background and subject for many of his early films. He became friendly with Ostend's resident and visiting artists, and they all apparently absorbed creative strength from the solid tradition of Flemish paintings as well as physical stamina from the invigorating North Sea air. Primarily a documentarist, Storck's prolific output of over seventy films does include a couple of fiction films: *Une Idylle à la plage,* a short film about adolescent love; and *Le Banquet des fraudeurs,* a feature film with a thriller framework.

Storck has described the work of his mentor, Charles DeKeukeleire, another Belgian film pioneer, as having "lyrical expression, faithfulness to authentic reality, and a sense of rhythm in editing." These words are just as applicable to Storck's own *oeuvre. Borinage,* a film about a coal miners' strike in the Borinage—a district southwest of Brussels—is a powerful revelation of the miners' living conditions. The film cinematically echoes the feelings that Van Gogh expressed in his drawings of an earlier period. *Borinage* is full of strong, intense images. A daring project, made in collaboration with Joris Ivens, the film had to be shot covertly in order to evade the police. Banned from public showing in Belgium and Holland at the time it was released, *Borinage* became a time-tested classic and an inspiration to the "Grierson boys" in England. *Symphonie paysanne,* made in a completely different style, depicted the passage of the seasons on a Belgian farm. This pastoral eulogy again demonstrated Storck's ability to express his humane sensibility in a cinematic manner.

After the war, Storck immensely enhanced a developing genre—films analyzing the visual arts. *Rubens* (made in collaboration with Paul Haesaerts) and *The World of Paul Delvaux* are outstanding examples which were immediately recognized as *tours de force. The Open Window* and *The Sorrows of the War* were also worthy contributions to this category. A later film about Delvaux, *Paul Delvaux or the Forbidden Women,* was, to Storck's great amusement, promoted on Times Square as a pornographic film. In his films about art, Storck was particularly innovative in his use of camera movement to display the details of the art works, and in some films used animated lines to demonstrate their structures of composition. Henri Storck's humanistic vision is revealed by his films and crosses all national and cultural boundaries.

—Robert Edmonds

STRAUB, Jean-Marie, and Danièle HUILLET

Nationality: French, German. **Born:** Jean-Marie Straub born in Metz, 8 January 1933. **Career:** Straub organized a film society in his hometown, late 1940s; studied literature at the Universities of Strasbourg and Nancy, 1950-54; moved to Paris and began collaboration with Huillet, who was to become his wife, 1954; worked as assistant to

French directors Abel Gance, Jean Renoir, Jacques Rivette, Robert Bresson, and Alexandre Astruc, 1954-58; left France to avoid military service in the Algerian conflict, 1958 (received amnesty, 1971); Straub and Huillet moved to Munich, 1959; collaborated on their first film, *Machorka-Muff,* 1963; moved to Italy, 1969.

Films as Directors:

1963 *Machorka-Muff* (Straub: d, co-ed, co-sound; Huillet: sc, co-ed, co-sound)
1965 *Nicht versöhnt oder Es hilft nur Gewalt, wo Gewalt herrscht* (*Es hilft nicht, wo Gewalt herrscht*), (*Not Reconciled*) (Straub: d, co-ed, co-ph; Huillet: sc, co-ed, co-ph)
1968 ***Chronik der Anna Magdalena Bach*** (*Chronicle of Anna Magdalena Bach*) (Straub: d; Huillet: sc); *Der Bräutigam, die Komödiantin und der Zuhälter* (*The Bridegroom, the Comedienne and the Pimp*) (Straub: d, co-ed; Huillet: sc, co-ed)
1969 *Othon* (*Les Yeux ne veulent pas en tout temps se fermer ou Peut-être qu'un jour Rome se permettra de choisir à son tour*), (*Die Augen wollen sich nicht zu jeder Zeit schliessen oder Vielleicht eines Tages wird Rom sich erlauben, seinerseits zu wählen*), (*Eyes Do Not Want to Close at All Times or Perhaps One Day Rome Will Permit Herself to Choose in Her Turn, Othon*) (co-d, co-ed; Huillet + sc, Straub + role under pseudonym Jubarithe Semaran); *Einleitung zu Arnold Schoenberg Begleit Musik zu einer Lichtspielscene* (*Introduction to Arnold Schoenberg's Accompaniment for a Cinematographic Scene*) (+ co-pr, co-ed; Huillet + sc) (for TV)
1972 *Geschichtsunterricht* (*History Lessons*) (+ co-pr, co-ed; Huillet + sc)
1975 *Moses und Aron* (*Moses and Aaron*) (+ co-ed; Huillet + sc)
1976 *Fortini/Cani* (*I cani del Sinai*) (+ co-ed; Huillet + sc)
1977 *Toute révolution est un coup de dés* (*Every Revolution Is a Throw of the Dice*) (Huillet + sc)
1979 *Della nube alla resistenza* (*From the Cloud to the Resistance*) (Huillet + sc)
1983 *Trop tot, trop tard* (*Too Early, Too Late*)
1985 *Klassenverhältnisse* (*Class Relations*)
1987 *Tod des Empedokles* (*The Death of Empedocles*)
1989 *Schwarze Sunde* (*Black Sin*); *Cézanne*
1992 *Antigone*

Other Films (Straub):

1954 *La Tour des Nesle* (Gance) (asst d)
1955 *French Cancan* (Renoir) (asst d)
1956 *Eléna et les hommes* (Renoir) (asst d); *Le Coup de Berger* (Rivette) (asst d); ***Un Condamné à mort s'est échappé*** (Bresson) (asst d)
1958 *Une Vie* (Astruc) (asst d)

Jean-Marie Straub and Danièle Huillet: *Moses und Aron*

Publications

By STRAUB AND HUILLET: books—

Klassenverhältnisse, edited by Wolfram Schütte, Frankfurt, 1984.

By STRAUB AND HUILLET: articles—

"Frustration of Violence," in *Cahiers du Cinema in English* (New York), January 1967.
"*Moses und Aron* as an Object of Marxist Reflection," interview with J. Rogers, in *Jump Cut* (Chicago), no. 12-13, 1976.
"Decoupage di Fortini/Cani," in *Filmcritica* (Rome), November/December 1976.
Interview with R. Gansera, in *Filmkritik* (Munich), September 1978.
Interview with Serge Daney and J. Narboni, in *Cahiers du Cinéma* (Paris), November 1979.
Interview with H. Hurch and B. Brewster, in *Undercut* (London), Spring 1983.
Interview with H. Farocki in *Filmkritik* (Munich), May 1983.
Interview with S. Blum and J. Prieur, in *Camera/Stylo* (Paris), September 1983.
Interview with E. Bruno and R. Rosetti, in *Filmcritica* (Rome), September 1984.
Interview with M. Blank and others, in *Filmkritik* (Munich), September/October 1984.
Interview with A. Bengala and others, in *Cahiers du Cinema* (Paris), October 1984.
Interview with P. Toulemonde, in *Cinematographe* (Paris), November 1984.
Interview with E. Szekely in *Filmvilag* (Budapest), vol. 28, no. 8, 1985.
Interview with G. Baratta and G. Latini in *Filmcritica* (Rome), January/February 1987.
Straub. J.M., article in *Cahiers du Cinema* (Paris), October supplement 1987.
Rossellini, R., and Straub, J.M., "Rapporto tra film e conoscenza," in *Filmcritica* (Rome), December 1987.
Interview with C. Desbarats in *Cinema 88* (Paris), 6/13 January 1988.
Interview with H. Hurch in *Andere Sinema* (Antwerp), September/October 1989.
Interview with P. Willemsen in *Andere Sinema* (Antwerp), September/October 1989.
Straub, J.M., "Senza titolo," in *Filmcritica* (Rome), December 1989.

On STRAUB AND HUILLET: books—

Roud, Richard, *Jean-Marie Straub,* London, 1971.
Walsh, Martin, *The Brechtian Aspect of Radical Cinema,* London, 1981.
Franklin, James, *New German Cinema: From Oberhausen to Hamburg,* Boston, 1983.
Phillips, Klaus, *New German Filmmakers: From Oberhausen through the 1970s,* New York, 1984.
Rosetti, Riccardo, editor, *Straub-Huillet Film,* Rome, 1984.
Elsaesser, Thomas, *New German Cinema: A History,* London, 1989.

On STRAUB AND HUILLET: articles—

Baxter, B., "Jean-Marie Struab," in *Film* (London), Spring 1969.
Engel, Andi, "Jean-Marie Straub," in *Second Wave,* New York, 1970.
Walsh, M., "Political Formations in the Cinema of Jean-Marie Straub," in *Jump Cut* (Chicago), November/December 1974.
"*Moses und Aron* Issue" of *Cahiers du Cinéma* (Paris), October/November 1975.
"Straub and Huillet Issue" of *Enthusiasm* (London), December 1975.
Bonitzer, P., "J.-M.S. et J.-L.G.," in *Cahiers du Cinéma* (Paris), February 1976.
Dermody, S., "Straub/Huillet: The Politics of Film Practice," in *Cinema Papers* (Melbourne), September/October 1976.
"Danièle Huillet Jean-Marie Straub's *Fortini/Cani,*" special issue of *Filmkritik* (Munich), January 1977.
Simsolo, Noel, "Jean-Marie Straub et Danièle Huillet," in *Cinéma* (Paris), March 1977.
Bennett, E., "The Films of Straub Are Not 'Theoretical'," in *Afterimage* (Rochester), Summer 1978.
Rosenbaum, Jonathan, "Jean-Luc, Chantal, Danielle, Jean-Marie and the Others," in *American Film* (Washington, D.C.), February 1979.
Daney, Serge, "Le Plan Straubien," in *Cahiers du Cinéma* (Paris), November 1979.
Magisos, M., "Not Reconciled: The Destruction of Narrative Pleasure," in *Wide Angle* (Athins, Ohio), vol. 3, no. 4, 1980.
Sauvaget, D., article in *Revue du Cinema* (Paris), April 1980.
Blank, R., article in *Skrien* (Amsterdam), Summer 1981.
Durgnat, Raymond, "From Caligari to Hitler," in *Film Comment* (New York), Summer 1981.
Graziani, G. and others, article in *Filmcritica* (Rome), September/October 1981.
Goldschmidt, D., article in *Cinematographe* (Paris), March 1982.
Mitry, Jean, article in *Cinematographe* (Paris), September 1982.
Simons, J., article in *Skrien* (Amsterdam), September 1982.
Lange, M., and others, article in *Filmkritik* (Munich), January 1983.
Ranieri, N., article in *Cinema Nuovo* (Torino), August/October 1983.
Maderna, M., article in *Segnocinema* (Vicenza), January 1984.
Hoberman, J., "Once Upon a Time in Amerika," in *Artforum* (New York), September 1984.
Bergala, A., article in *Cahiers du Cinema* (Paris), October 1984.
Ehrenstein, D., and others, "Reagan at Bitburg: Spectacle and Memory," in *On Film* (Los Angeles), Spring 1985.
Rosetti, R., article in *Filmcritica* (Rome), October 1985.
Kamiah, J., article in *Filmcritica* (Rome), January/February 1987.
Chevrie, M., article in *Cahiers du Cinema* (Paris), April 1989.
Dominicus, M., and J. de Putter, article in *Skrien* (Amsterdam), February/March 1990.
Petley, Julian, "Straub/Huillet's *Empedocles,*" in *Sight and Sound* (London) Summer 1990.

* * *

The films of Jean-Marie Straub and Danièle Huillet are best understood in the context of contemporary developments in radical, materialist cinema. They offer what many people see as a genuine alternative to both dominant narrative cinema and conventional art movies. Their work is formally austere and demands attentive, intellectual participation from audiences. However, it must be acknowledged that many people find their films nearly impenetrable and absolutely boring. This is explained in part by the fact that the films do not rely on standard narrative construction or conventional characters. While the films of Straub and Huillet are by no means "abstract" it is nearly impossible to (re)construct a unified, imaginary, referential "world" through them.

In a sense their work might be explained in terms of strategies of displeasure, a wilful refusal to captivate audiences with a coherent fictional world. Instead they promote a distanciated, intellectual interaction between viewer and film. Because of this insistence on critical distance, audiences must work with the film in a dialectical process of meaning construction. (In fact, Straub is notoriously critical of "lazy" viewers who are unwilling to engage in this activity.)

Straub and Huillet's films directly address the nature of cinematic signification and its political implications. This includes breaking away from conventional assumptions and practices of dominant narrative cinema. Their films exploit all channels of the medium—music, sounds, words, and images—as equivalent carriers of meaning, rather than privileging the "visual" or relegating music and sound effects to the task of support material. Thus, there are times when extremely long, static shots accompany lengthy, complex verbal passages (a singularly "uncinematic" practice according to conventional canons of film aesthetics). Sequences may be developed along the lines of montage construction, juxtaposing graphic material, verbal material, and moving images. Both of these strategies are used in *Introduction to Schoenberg's "Accompaniment for a Cinematographic Scene"*; and the starting point for this short film was a piece of music written by the composer. The major texts, read on-screen (though interrupted at intervals by black frames), are a letter from Schoenberg to Kandinsky explaining his reasons for not participating in the Bauhaus, and a text by Brecht elaborating the relationship between fascism and capitalism. The readings of these texts take up most of the film, which includes Straub and Huillet as on-camera narrators "placing" the texts. The film then concludes with a montage sequence. The political aspect of the film derives not only from the logical argument advanced, the Brecht analysis standing as a critique of Schoenberg's "liberal" position, but also from the film's rejection of documentary norms. At the same time it has been pointed out that Schoenberg's music stands in relation to classical rules of harmonic composition in the same manner that Straub and Huillet films stand in relation to the conventions of dominant cinema.

The incorporation of musical works and verbal texts, as both a source for and signifying material within their films, is an important aspect of their work. The figure of Bertolt Brecht is perhaps the most pervasive presence in Straub and Huillet's films. His writing is included in *Introduction to Schoenberg* and provided the source for *History Lessons*. More crucially, the strategies of deconstruction and distanciation in their films derive from principles advanced in Brechtian theory. These include concepts of alienation and anti-illusionism elaborated in Brecht's theory of epic theater. Straub and Huillet have developed these ideas in the context of their films and their persistent concern with the politics of cinematic expression.

Straub and Huillet will probably never be as well-known to cineastes as fellow New German filmmakers Rainer Werner Fassbinder, Volker Schlondorff, Werner Herzog, or Wim Wenders. But their minimalist films remain important contributions to the New German cinema, and they have been a meaningful voice for the art crowd in Germany. As with all gifted and dedicated film artists whose works are unconventionally structured, their cinematic output remains worthy of study by serious film students and equally worthy of viewing by discerning audiences.

—M.B. White, updated by Rob Edelman

STROHEIM, Erich von *See* **VON STROHEIM, Erich**

STURGES, John

Nationality: American. **Born:** Oak Park, Illinois, 3 January 1911. **Education:** Attended Marin Junior College, California. **Career:** Worked in blueprint department, RKO-Radio Pictures, 1932; assistant to designer Robert Edmond Jones on first Technicolor films, and production assistant to David O. Selznick; worked in RKO cutting rooms, from 1935; served in Army Air Corps, directed about 45 documentaries, 1942-45; signed as director for Columbia, and directed first feature, 1946; joined MGM, 1949; began working on independent productions, 1960; co-founder The Mirisch Company. **Awards:** Outstanding directorial achievement, Directors Guild of America, for *Bad Day at Black Rock,* 1955. **Died:** 1993.

Films as Director:

1946 *The Man Who Dared*; *Shadowed*
1947 *Alias Mr. Twilight*; *For the Love of Rusty*; *Keeper of the Bees*
1948 *Best Man Wins*; *The Sign of the Ram*
1949 *The Walking Hills*
1950 *Mystery Street*; *The Capture*; *The Magnificent Yankee*; *Right Cross*
1951 *Kind Lady*; *The People Against O'Hara*; *It's a Big Country* (co-d)
1952 *The Girl in White*
1953 *Jeopardy*; *Fast Company*; *Escape from Fort Bravo*
1954 *Bad Day at Black Rock*
1955 *Underwater*; *The Scarlet Coat*
1956 *Backlash*
1957 *Gunfight at the O.K. Corral*
1958 *The Old Man and the Sea* (took over direction from Fred Zinnemann); *The Law and Jake Wade*
1959 *Last Train from Gun Hill*; *Never So Few*
1960 *The Magnificent Seven*
1961 *By Love Possessed*
1962 *Sergeants Three*; *A Girl Named Tamiko*
1963 *The Great Escape*
1965 *The Satan Bug*; *The Hallelujah Trail*
1967 *The Hour of the Gun*
1968 *Ice Station Zebra*
1969 *Marooned*
1972 *Joe Kidd*
1973 *Valdez il mezzosangue* (*Chino*; *The Valdez Horses*)
1974 *McQ*
1976 *The Eagle Has Landed*

Publications

By STURGES: articles—

"How the West Was Lost!," in *Films and Filming* (London), December 1962.

On STURGES: articles—

Anderson, Joseph, "When the Twain Meet: *Seven Samurai* vs. *The Magnificent Seven,*" in *Film Quarterly* (Berkeley), Spring 1962.
Cherry, Richard, "Capsule of John Sturges," in *Action* (Los Angeles), November/December 1969.
Jones, D., "The Merit of Flying Lead," in *Films and Filming* (London), February 1974.
Jones, D., "The Power of the Gun," in *Films and Filming* (London), February 1974.

* * *

John Sturges had a long and varied career in film. In the thirties he was an editor and then a producer. After working on documentaries during the war, he began directing in 1946. Popular film critics either pass over his work or they demean it. Andrew Sarris regards him as a mislabeled "expert technician" whose career was anything but

John Sturges

"meaningful." Sturges has had success at the box office with some of the many action films he did. *Gunfight at the OK Corral, The Magnificent Seven,* and *The Great Escape* were all major winners with audiences.

Sturges's films frequently deal with a group of men working towards a specific goal. In *The Great Escape* this theme is emphasized as each of the characters tries to escape from a German P.O.W. camp unsuccessfully. Only when they work together as a unit can success be achieved. While the goals are usually attained, the attempt is often costly. In several of the films, the group is decimated by the end of the mission. In *Marooned* only two of the astronauts survive and *The Magnificent Seven* is reduced to three by the end of the battle.

Sturges's work does not exclude women but the women are usually shown only as fringe characters. They are identified by the men they are associated with and react to what the men do or say. This is particularly clear in *Marooned.* In one sequence, each astronaut's wife is allowed a moment to talk to her husband via a television hook-up and say good-bye as the astronauts are trapped in their capsule in outer space.

Sturges held a respected position in the film industry. His successes at the box office helped him to gain that respect, but he also showed an excellent eye for casting. His films have begun and furthered the careers of many actors. Steve McQueen's progress toward stardom can be traced in his films with Sturges—*Never So Few, The Magnificent Seven,* and *The Great Escape.* James Coburn, Charles Bronson, Ernest Borgnine, and Lee Marvin received career boosts from their roles in Sturges's films. Unlike Andrew Sarris, Hollywood appreciated Sturges's handling of wide-screen formats in his films of the 1950s. It is thought that he was one of the first directors to develop the wide screen as a technique rather than use it as a gimmick. It is also very clear from Sturges's films that Hollywood felt confident in giving Sturges a project with a large cast and big budget. He capably handled large-scale projects, was able to deal with star egos (he directed "rat pack" films with Frank Sinatra), and produced commercial successes. Hollywood could not have asked for more.

—Ray Narducy

STURGES, Preston

Nationality: American. **Born:** Edmund P. Biden in Chicago, 29 August 1898; adopted by mother's second husband, Solomon Sturges. **Education:** Educated in Chicago (Coulter School); Lycée Janson, Paris; Ecole des Roches, France; Villa Lausanne, Switzerland; and in Berlin and Dresden. **Family:** Married 1) Estelle Mudge (divorced 1928); 2) Eleanor Post Hutton, 1932 (annulled 1932); 3) Louise Sergeant Tervis (divorced); 4) actress Anna Nagle (known professionally as Sandy Mellen), three sons. **Career:** Managed mother's cosmetic shop in Deauville, then New York, early 1910s; runner for Wall Street brokerage firm, 1914; enlisted in Air Corps, attended School of Military Aeronautics, Austin, Texas, 1917; returned to cosmetic business in New York, invented kissproof lipstick, 1919; turned business over to mother, worked in various jobs and as inventor; playwright, from 1927; *The Guinea Pig* ran 16 weeks on Broadway, 1929; scriptwriter from 1930, moved to Hollywood, 1932; directed own screenplays, from 1940; also manager of Sturges Engineering Company, producing diesel engines; began association with Howard Hughes, 1944; moved to Paris, 1949. **Awards:** Oscar for Best Original Screenplay, for *The Great McGinty,* 1940; Laurel Award for Achievement (posthumously), Writers Guild of America, 1974. **Died:** At the Algonquin Hotel, New York, 6 August 1959.

Films as Director and Scriptwriter:

1940 *The Great McGinty*; *Christmas in July*
1941 ***The Lady Eve***; ***Sullivan's Travels***
1942 *The Palm Beach Story*
1944 *Hail the Conquering Hero*; *The Miracle of Morgan's Creek*; *The Great Moment*
1947 *Mad Wednesday* (+ pr)
1948 *Unfaithfully Yours* (+ pr)
1949 *The Beautiful Blonde from Bashful Bend* (+ pr)
1951 *Vendetta* (co-d with Ferrer, uncredited)
1957 *Les Carnets du Major Thompson* (*The French, They Are a Funny Race*)

Other Films:

1930 *The Big Pond* (Henley) (co-sc, co-dialogue); *Fast and Loose* (Newmeyer) (sc, dialogue)
1931 *Strictly Dishonorable* (Stahl) (sc, play basis)
1933 *The Power and the Glory* (Howard) (sc); *Child of Manhattan* (Buzzell) (sc, play basis)
1934 *Thirty Day Princess* (Gering) (co-sc); *We Live Again* (Mamoulian) (co-sc); *Imitation of Life* (Stahl) (co-sc, uncredited)
1935 *The Good Fairy* (Wyler) (sc); *Diamond Jim* (Sutherland) (co-sc)
1936 *Next Time We Love* (Edward Griffith) (co-sc, uncredited); *One Rainy Afternoon* (Lee) (lyrics for "Secret Rendezvous")
1937 *Hotel Haywire* (Archainbaud) (sc); *Easy Living* (Leisen) (sc)
1938 *Port of Seven Seas* (Whale) (sc); *If I Were King* (Lloyd) (sc)
1940 *Remember the Night* (Leisen) (sc)
1947 *I'll Be Yours* (Seiter) (screenplay basis)
1951 *Strictly Dishonorable* (Frank and Panama) (play basis)
1956 *The Birds and the Bees* (Taurog) (screenplay basis)
1958 *Rock-a-bye Baby* (Tashlin) (screenplay basis); *Paris Holiday* (Oswald) (role as Serge Vitry)

Publications

By STURGES: books—

5 Screenplays by Preston Sturges, edited by Brian Henderson, Berkeley, 1985.
Preston Sturges by Preston Sturges, edited by Sandy Sturges, New York, 1990.

By STURGES: articles—

"Conversation with Preston Sturges," with Gordon Gow, in *Sight and Sound* (London), Spring 1956.
Interview, in *Interviews with Film Directors,* edited by Andrew Sarris, New York, 1967.

On STURGES: books—

Cywinski, Ray, *Satires and Sideshows: The Films and Career of Preston Sturges,* Ann Arbor, Michigan, 1981.
Gordon, James R., *Comic Structures in the Films of Preston Sturges,* Ann Arbor, Michigan, 1981.
Curtis, James, *Between Flops: A Biography of Preston Sturges,* New York, 1982.
Cywinski, Ray, *Preston Sturges: A Guide to References and Resources,* Boston, 1984.

Dickos, Andrew, *Intrepid Laughter: Preston Sturges and the Movies,* Metuchen, New Jersey, 1985.

Spoto, Donald, *Madcap: The Life of Preston Sturges,* Boston, 1990.

On STURGES: articles—

Ericsson, Peter, "Preston Sturges," in *Sequence* (London), Summer 1948.

Kracauer, Siegfried, "Preston Sturges or Laughter Betrayed," in *Films in Review* (New York), February 1950.

King, Nel, and G.W. Stonier, "Preston Sturges," in *Sight and Sound* (London), Summer/Autumn 1959.

Farber, Manny, and W.S. Poster, "Preston Sturges: Success in the Movies," and Eric Jonsson, "Preston Sturges and the Theory of Decline," in *Film Culture* (New York), no. 26, 1962.

Houston, Penelope, "Preston Sturges," in *Sight and Sound* (London), Summer 1965.

Budd, Michael, "Notes on Preston Sturges and America," in *Film Society Review* (New York), January 1968.

Sarris, Andrew, "Preston Sturges in the Thirties," in *Film Comment* (New York), Winter 1970/71.

Corliss, Richard, "Preston Sturges," in *Cinema* (Beverly Hills), Spring 1972.

Rubenstein, E., "The Home Fires: Aspects of Sturges's Wartime Comedy," in *Quarterly Review of Film Studies* (New York), Spring 1982.

Rebello, S., and J. Curtis, "King of Comedy: the Rise of Preston Sturges," in *American Film* (Washington, D.C.), May 1982.

Rubinstein, E., "The End of Screwball Comedy: *The Lady Eve* and *The Palm ...,*" in *Post Script* (Jacksonville, Florida), Spring-Summer 1982.

"Preston Sturges Issue" of *Positif* (Paris), July/August 1984.

Schickel, Richard, "Preston Sturges: Alien Dreamer," in *Film Comment* (New York), November/December 1985.

Henderson, B., "Sturges at Work," in *Film Quarterly* (Berkeley), Winter 1985/1986.

Brown, Geoff, "Preston Sturges Inventor," in *Sight and Sound* (London), Autumn 1986.

Sarris, Andrew, "Comedies With Bite," in *American Film* (Washington, D.C.), October 1986.

Shokoff, James, "A Knockenlocker by Any Other Word: The Democratic Comedy of Preston Sturges," in *Post Script* (Jacksonville, Florida), vol. 8, no. 1, 1988.

* * *

As a screenwriter, Preston Sturges stands out for his narrative inventiveness. All of the amazing coincidences and obvious repetitions in such comedies as *Easy Living* and *The Good Fairy* show Sturges's mastery of the standard narrative form, as well as his ability to exaggerate it and shape it to his own needs. Moreover, in *The Power and the Glory* (an early model for *Citizen Kane*), Sturges pioneered the use of voice-over narration to advance a story.

Along with John Huston, Sturges was one of the first of the sound-era screenwriters to become a director, and those films that he made from his own screenplays take even further the narrative experiments he began as a writer in the 1930s. He continued making comedies, but often he combined them with elements that more properly belonged to social dramas in the Warner Brothers tradition, even though Sturges himself worked primarily for Paramount. *The Great McGinty,* for instance, deals with big-city political corruption. *Christmas in July,* despite its happy end, analyzes an American dream perverted by dishonesty and commercial hype. And *Sullivan's Travels,* even as it mixes aspects of *It Happened One Night* and *I Am a Fugitive From a Chain Gang,* examines the uses of comedy in a society burdened by poverty and social injustice.

With *The Palm Beach Story* and *The Lady Eve,* Sturges goes from combining genres to parodying the standard narrative form. Traditionally, in the classical narrative, elements repeat from scene to scene, but with slight differences each time. The story, then, becomes a series of episodes that are similar, but not obviously so. *The Palm Beach Story,* however (although we cannot be sure of this until the end), deals with two sets of twins, one pair male and the other female, and Sturges takes full advantage of a practically infinite number of possibilities for doubling and repetition.

In *The Lady Eve,* there are no twins to call our attention to how Sturges exaggerates the typical narrative. But the central female character, Jean, changes her identity and becomes Eve Harrington, an English aristocrat, so she can double-cross the man who jilted her when he found out she made her living as a con artist. So in this film, too, Sturges provides us with some obvious doubling. In fact, *The Lady Eve* divides neatly into two very similar parts: the shipboard romance of Charles and Jean, and then the romance, on land, of Charles and Jean-as-Eve. In this second half, the film virtually turns into a screwball comedy version of *Vertigo.* Charles falls in love with a woman who looks exactly like another woman he had loved and lost, and who, indeed, really is that woman.

The Lady Eve is most interesting in the way that it stands narrative convention on its head. Charles Pike, a wealthy ale heir, looks for snakes on the Amazon, but as soon as he leaves the jungle and heads back to civilization, the hunter becomes the hunted. This inversion itself is hardly remarkable, either in literature or the cinema. What does stand out as unusual is that the predators are all women. Pike boards a luxury liner steaming back to the United States, and every unmarried woman on board decides to end the voyage engaged to him, to "catch" him just as Charles had been trying to capture reptiles. Few films from this period feature such active, aggressive female characters.

Sturges works out the notion of feminine entrapment not only in his script but also through his visual style. On board, Jean plots to get Charles, and Sturges shows us her predatory skill by letting her capture Pike's image. In the dining room, Jean watches as various women attempt to attract Pike's attention. She does not want him to see her staring, so she turns away from Pike's table and holds a mirror to her face, as if she were giving a quick re-arrangement to her makeup. But instead she uses the mirror to watch Charles. Sturges cuts to a close-up of the mirror, and so we share Jean's point of view. As spectators, we are used to an appreciative male gaze, and are accustomed to a woman as the subject of that gaze. But here, once again, Sturges reverses our expectations. In his tale it is the woman who plays the voyeur. As an added show of her strength, it is Jean who apparently controls the images through her possession of the mirror. She thus captures an unknowing Charles within the frame of a looking-glass.

Sturges's most interesting achievement may be his 1948 film, *Unfaithfully Yours.* Here, he shows the same event three times. While fairly common in literature, this sort of narrative construction is extremely rare in the cinema. But even in literature, the repeated event almost always comes to us from the points of view of different characters. In Sturges's films, we see the event the first and second time through the eyes of the same man: an orchestra conductor plots revenge on his wife, whom he suspects of infidelity, and he imagines two different ways of accomplishing his goal. Then, the next repetition, rather than being imaginary, actually depicts the conductor's attempts to murder his wife. So, since the conductor acts once again as the main character, even this last repetition comes to us from his point of view. The film stands out, then, as a remarkable case study of the thoughts and actions of a single character, and as one more of Sturges's experiments in narrative repetition.

During the early and mid-1940s, critics hailed Sturges as a comic genius. But after *Unfaithfully Yours,* over the last eleven years of his life, Sturges made only two more films. Upon leaving Paramount, he set out to make films for Howard Hughes, but the attempt was an ill-fated one, and Sturges's standing in the critical community declined

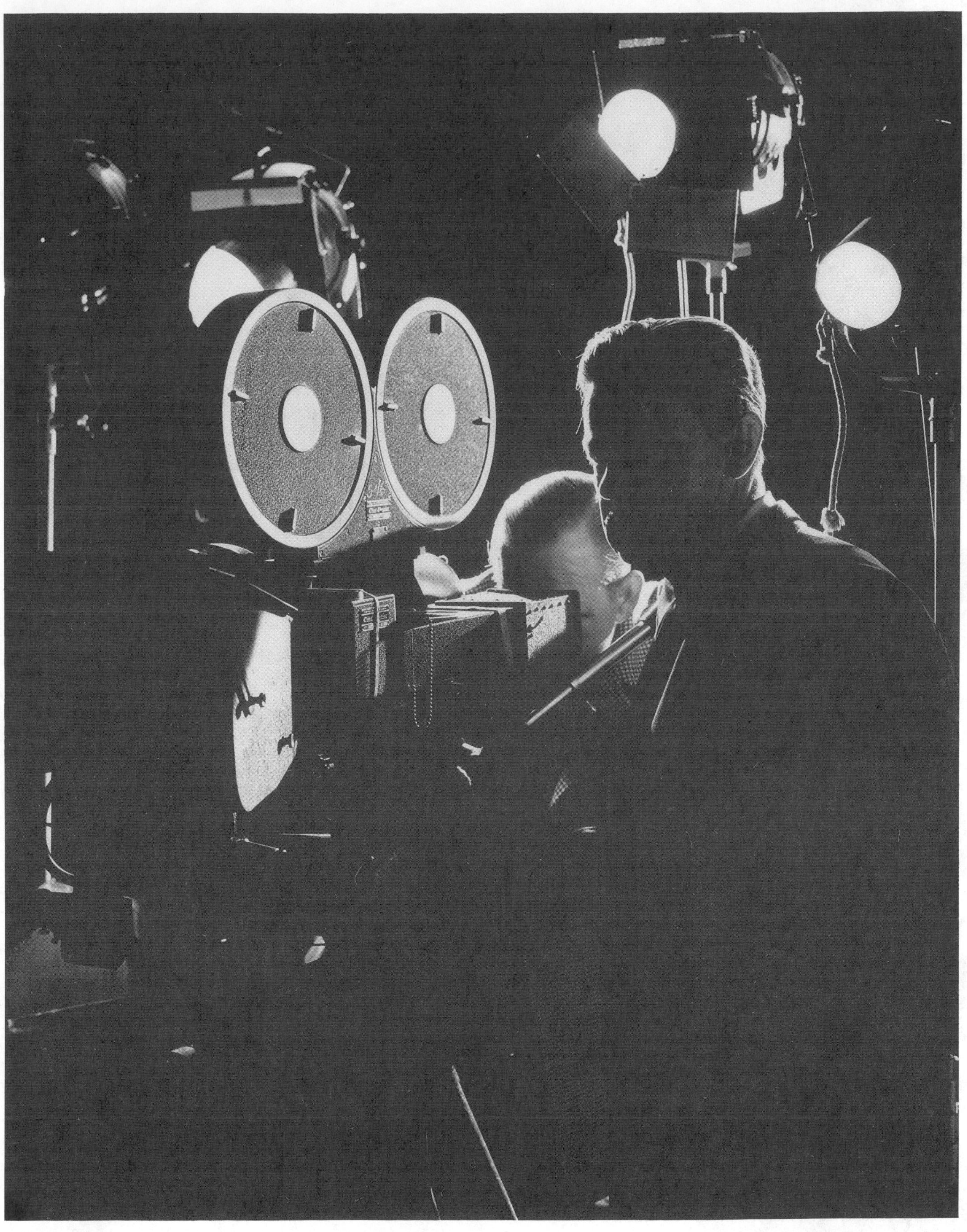

Preston Sturges

Arne Sucksdorff: ***Det stora äventyret***

rapidly. For several years, though, a reevaluation has been underway. Sturges's sophisticated handling of sexual relations (which the heiress in *The Palm Beach Story* refers to as "Topic A") make his films seem remarkably contemporary. And there can be no doubting Sturges's screenwriting abilities. But only recently have critics come to appreciate Sturges's consummate skills as a filmmaker.

—Eric Smoodin

SUCKSDORFF, Arne

Nationality: Swedish. **Born:** Stockholm, 3 February 1917. **Education:** Studied painting with Otto Skold and photography with Rudolf Klein-Rogge, Reimannschule, Berlin. **Family:** Married Astrid Bergman (divorced); remarried. **Career:** First two films attracted attention of Svensk Filmindustri, which produced next eleven shorts, from 1940; directed first feature, 1953; moved to Brazil, taught at film school, Rio de Janeiro. **Awards:** Oscar for Best Short Subject, for *Symphony of a City,* 1948; Prize for Superior Technique, Cannes Festival, for *The Great Adventure,* 1954.

Films as Director:

1939 *En Augustirapsodi* (*An August Rhapsody*) (short)
1940 *Din tillvaros land* (*This Land Is Full of Life*; *Your Own Land*) (short)
1941 *En Sommersaga* (*A Summer's Tale*) (short)
1943 *Vinden från våster* (*Wind from the West*) (short); *Sarvtid* (*Reindeer People*) (short)
1944 *Trut!* (*Gull!*) (short)
1945 *Gryning* (*Dawn*) (short); *Skugger över snön* (*Shadows on the Snow*) (short)
1947 *Människor i stad* (*Symphony of a City*; *Rhythm of a City*) (short); *Den drömda dalen* (*Soria-Moria*; *Tale of the Fjords*; *The Dream Valley*) (short) (+ ph)
1948 *Uppbrott* (*The Open Road*) (short) (+ ph, ed); *En kluven värld* (*A Divided World*) (short) (+ sc)
1950 *Strandhugg* (*Going Ashore*) (short) (+ sc); *Ett horn i norr* (*The Living Stream*) (short)
1951 *Indisk by* (*Indian Village*) (short) (+ pr); *Vinden och floden* (*The Wind and the River*) (short) (+ ph)
1953 *Det stora äventyret* (*The Great Adventure*)
1957 *En djungelsaga* (*The Flute and the Arrow*)
1961 *Pojken i trädet* (*The Boy in the Tree*)
1965 *Mitt hem är Copacabana* (*My Home Is Copacabana*)
1971 Antarctic animal sequences in *Forbush and the Penguins*

Publications

By SUCKSDORFF: article—

Interview and article, in *Cinema* (Beverly Hills), July/August 1965.

On SUCKSDORFF: book—

Sundgren, Nils, *The New Swedish Cinema,* Stockholm, 1970.

On SUCKSDORFF: articles—

Hardy, Forsyth, "The Films of Arne Sucksdorff," in *Sight and Sound* (London), Summer 1948.
Knight, Arthur, "Producer-Director-Writer-Photographer Emerges as a New Talent through a Series of Short Subjects," in *New York Times,* 21 November 1948.
Ericsson, Peter, "Arne Sucksdorff," in *Sequence* (London), Spring 1949.
Ulrichsen, E., "Arne Sucksdorff," in *Films in Review* (New York), October 1953.
De La Roche, Catherine, "Arne Sucksdorff's Adventures," in *Sight and Sound* (London), October/December 1953.
De La Roche, Catherine, "Film-Maker on His Own," in *Sight and Sound* (London), November 1954.
"Arne Sucksdorff," in *Image* (Rochester, New York), May 1955.

* * *

Swedish filmmaker Arne Sucksdorff is what the French film critics call an *auteur,* or author of his work. He wrote, shot, edited, and/or supervised his films, and they bear the stamp of his personality. His films, taken as a whole, have similar themes and style, and they reflect his personal vision.

Sucksdorff, as a young man, studied both biology and art. After working with still photography, he combined his knowledge and love of nature with filmmaking. Working primarily in the documentary and semi-documentary traditions in the 1940s and 1950s, he used the images and sounds of reality and shaped them as would a poet. His films are often set in the country, and his characters are often wild animals and children (non-actors). He prefers black and white to color. Unlike Walt Disney's "true life adventures," where nature is often seen as comforting and even fun, and unlike Robert Flaherty's romantic films, where outdoor life is presented as it should be, Sucksdorff shows how things are. "This is life," says Sucksdorff, "and whether we like it or not, this is the way life goes on." The spider web is almost a signature in a Sucksdorff film. It is at once beautiful and dangerous. A shadowy forest may hide a beautiful deer or a hungry bear. Animals chase and kill each other for survival. They prey upon each other. But life has its beautiful moments, too, and it is, as in the title of his most famous film, the great adventure.

Sucksdorff had considerable technical skill. Each frame of film is beautifully composed, from an extreme close-up of a gull's eye to an extreme long shot of an island cliff. Sucksdorff often used great depth-of-field and high-contrast lighting (the moon on a snowy lake) in order to create a poetic, yet realistic, mood. He also took great care in capturing foreground and background action for a sense of excitement. He spent months in the wilderness waiting for birds on the wing, rabbits washing their faces, and lynxes stalking their prey. He made much use of natural sounds, music, and narration with little, if any, dialogue. He then spent months in the cutting room on even his short films in order to present his vision. His technical skill, however, was never used to show off, but to help us see the natural world in new ways.

Svensk Filmindustri sponsored many of his early films, which often cost as much as a feature. His most famous short film is *Symphony of a City,* where people in Stockholm (rather than animals in the wilderness) are seen, sometimes through the eyes of a child. The fishing nets look like spider webs. There is beauty in the docks and a cathedral, but also disquiet in crowds, traffic, and the precarious angles of faces.

Sucksdorff's most personal statement is the feature-length *The Great Adventure,* produced by his own company and filmed in central Sweden. The adventure of the title is life, and Sucksdorff presents it (as he does in many other films) through the eyes of young animals and children (his son and his son's friend). In the film, a fox must care for her young; two boys save an otter from a hunter and care for it. In spring, the young foxes are grown and the otter needs to be free. Although there is sorrow as the otter leaves for the wilderness, there is joy in seeing the cranes fly free overhead. Soon the boys will also be grown in the great adventure of life.

Sucksdorff went on to make *The Flute and the Arrow,* about the ancient Muria tribe in Central India. Surprisingly, he then made a dramatic fiction feature, *The Boy in the Tree,* and was shaken when it was unsuccessful. He left Sweden and spent some years as a teacher of film in Rio de Janeiro. Several of his students became the leading directors of the Brazilian Cinema Novo. Sucksdorff's film *My Home Is Copacabana* is about children in Rio and their gift for survival.

Sucksdorff's films of the 1940s and 1950s are the most critically acclaimed. Since many were made on his own and distributed in 16mm through the non-theatrical film industry to schools and libraries, his films live primarily in the classroom rather than on television or in theatres. But what more appropriate place for films that show "the way life goes on."

—H. Wayne Schuth

SYBERBERG, Hans-Jurgen

Nationality: German. **Born:** Nossendorf, Pomerania, 8 December 1935. **Education:** Educated in literature and art history, Munich. **Career:** Lived in East Berlin, then moved to West Germany, 1953; made 8mm films of Brecht's Berliner Ensemble at work, 1950s (blown up for release on 35mm, 1970); made 185 current affairs and documentary shorts for Bavarian Television, 1963-66; formed own production company, 1965; made five feature-length "character portraits" on Fritz Kortner and others, 1965-69; directed first feature, *Scarabea,* 1968; made "German Trilogy," 1972-77; began working exclusively on projects with German actress Edith Clever after the release of *Parsifal,* 1983.

Films as Director:

1965 *Fünfter Akt, siebte Szene. Fritz Kortner probt Kabale und Liebe* (*Act Five, Scene Seven. Fritz Kortner Rehearses Kabale und Liebe*); *Romy. Anatomie eines Gesichts* (*Romy. Anatomy of a Face*) (doc)
1966 *Fritz Kortner spricht Monologe für eine Schallplatte* (*Fritz Kortner Recites Monologues for a Record*) (doc); *Fritz Kortner spricht Shylock* (*Fritz Kortner Recites Shylock*) (short; extract from *Fritz Kortner spricht Monologe ...*); *Fritz Kortner spricht Faust* (*Fritz Kortner Recites Faust*) (short; extract from *Fritz Kortner spricht Monologe ...*); *Wilhelm von Kobell* (short, doc)
1967 *Die Grafen Pocci—Einige Kapitel zur Geschichte einer Familie* (*The Counts of Pocci—Some Chapters Towards the History of a Family*) (doc); *Konrad Albert Pocci, der Fussballgraf vom Ammerland—Das vorläufig letzte Kapitel einer Chronik der Familie Pocci* (*Konrad Albert Pocci, the Football Count*

from the Ammerland—Provisionally the Last Chapter of a Chronicle of the Pocci Family) (extract from the preceding title)

1968 *Scarabea—Wieviel Erde braucht der Mensch?* (*Scarabea—How Much Land Does a Man Need?*)

1969 *Sex-Business—Made in Passing* (doc)

1970 *San Domingo*; *Nach Meinem letzten Umzug* (*After My Last Move*); *Puntila* and *Faust* (shorts; extracts from the preceding title)

1972 *Ludwig II—Requiem für einen jungfräulichen König* (*Ludwig II—Requiem for a Virgin King*); *Theodor Hierneis oder: Wie man ehem. Hofkoch wird* (*Ludwig's Cook*)

1974 *Karl May*

1975 *Winifred Wagner und die Geschichte des Hauses Wahnfried von 1914-1975* (*The Confessions of Winifred Wagner*)

1977 ***Hitler. Ein Film aus Deutschland*** (*Hitler, a Film from Germany*; *Our Hitler*) (in four parts: 1. ***Hitler ein Film aus Deutschland*** [*Der Graal*]; 2. ***Ein deutscher Traum***; 3. ***Das Ende eines Wintermärchens***; 4. ***Wir Kinder der Hölle***)

1983 *Parsifal*

1985 *Die Nacht*

1987 *Penthesilea*

1989 *Die Marquise Von O*

Publications

By SYBERBERG: books—

Zum Drama Friedrich Durrenmatts; zwei modellinterpretationen zur Wesensdentung des modernen Dramas, Munich, 1963.

Le Film, musique de l'avenir, Paris, 1975.

Syberberg Filmbuch, Munich, 1976.

Hitler, ein Film aus Deutschland, Reinbek bei Hamburg, 1978.

Die Freudlose Gesellschaft: Notizen aus dem Letzten Jahr, Munich, 1981.

Parsifal, ein Filmessay, Munich, 1982.

Der Wald Steht Schwarz und Schweiger, Neue Notizen aus Deutschland, Zurich, 1984.

By SYBERBERG: articles—

Interview with A. Tournès, in *Jeune Cinéma* (Paris), December/January 1972/73.

"Forms of Address," interview and article with Tony Rayns, in *Sight and Sound* (London), Winter 1974/75.

Interview with M. Martin, in *Ecran* (Paris), July 1978.

"Form ist Moral: 'Holocaust' Indiz der grössten Krise unserer intellektuellen Existenz," in *Medium* (Frankfurt), April 1979.

Interview with B. Erkkila, in *Literature-Film Quarterly* (Salisbury, Maryland), October 1982.

Interview with I. Schroth, in *Filmfaust* (Frankfurt), October/November 1985.

"Sustaining Romanticism in a Postmodernist Cinema," an interview with Christopher Sharrett, in *Cineaste* (New York), vol. 15, no. 3, 1987.

Sybergerg, Hans-Jurgen, "S'approprier le monde," in *Cahiers du Cinema* (Paris), May 1991 (supplement).

Berlin Snell, Marilyn, "Germany's New Nostalgia: How Benign?," in *Harper's Magazine* (New York), March 1993.

On SYBERBERG: books—

Franklin, James, *New German Cinema: From Oberhausen to Hamburg,* Boston, 1983.

Phillips, Klaus, editor, *New German Filmmakers: From Oberhausen through the 1970s,* New York, 1984.

Rentschler, Eric, editor, *West German Filmmakers on Film: Visions and Voices,* New York, 1988.

Elsaesser, Thomas, *New German Cinema: A History,* London, 1989.

Santner, Eric L., *Stranded Objects: Mourning, Memory and Film in Postwar Germany,* Ithaca, New York, 1990.

Socci, Stefano, *Hans Jurgen Syberberg,* Florence, 1990.

On SYBERBERG: articles—

Pym, John, "Syberberg and the Tempter of Democracy," in *Sight and Sound* (London), Autumn 1977.

Sauvaget, D., "Syberberg: dramaturgie, anti-naturaliste et germanitude," in *Image et Son* (Paris), January 1979.

"Syberberg Issue" of *Revue Belge du Cinéma* (Brussels), Spring 1983.

Article, in *Sight and Sound* (London), Spring 1985.

Rockwell, John, "An Elusive German Director Re-emerges in Edinburgh," in *New York Times,* 2 September 1992.

* * *

The films of Hans-Jürgen Syberberg are at times annoying, confusing, and overlong—but they are also ambitious and compelling. In no way is he ever conventional or commercial: critics and audiences have alternately labelled his work brilliant and boring, absorbing and pretentious, and his films today are still rarely screened. Stylistically, it is difficult to link him with any other filmmaker or cinema tradition. In this regard he is an original, the most controversial of all the New German filmmakers and a figure who is at the vanguard of the resurgence of experimental filmmaking in his homeland.

Not unlike his contemporary, Rainer Werner Fassbinder, Syberberg's most characteristic films examine recent German history: a documentary about Richard Wagner's daughter-in-law, a close friend of Hitler (*The Confessions of Winifred Wagner*); his trilogy covering 100 years of Germany's past (*Ludwig II: Requiem for a Virgin King, Karl May,* and, most famously, *Hitler, A Film From Germany,* also known as *Our Hitler*). These last are linked in their depictions of Germans as hypocrites, liars, and egocentrics, and in the final part he presents the rise of the Third Reich as an outgrowth of German romanticism.

Even more significantly, Syberberg is concerned with the cinema's relationship to that history. *Our Hitler,* seven hours and nine minutes long, in four parts and 22 specific chapters, is at once a fictional movie, a documentary, a three-ring circus (the "greatest show on earth"), and a filmed theatrical marathon. The Führer is presented with some semblance of reality, via Hans Schubert's performance. But he is also caricatured, in the form of various identities and disguises: in one sequence alone, several actors play him as a house painter, Chaplin's Great Dictator, the Frankenstein monster, Parsifal (Syberberg subsequently filmed the Wagner opera), and a joker. Hitler is also portrayed as an object, a ventriloquist's doll, and a stuffed dog. In all, twelve different actors play the role, and 120 dummy Führers appear in the film. The result: Syberberg's Hitler is painted as both a fascist dictator who could have risen to power at any point in time in any number of political climates (though the filmmaker in no way excuses his homeland for allowing Hitler to exist, let alone thrive), and a monstrous movie mogul whose *Intolerance* would be the Holocaust.

Syberberg unites fictional narrative and documentary footage in a style that is at once cinematic and theatrical, mystical and magical. His films might easily be performed live (*Our Hitler* is set on a stage), but the material is so varied that the presence of the camera is necessary to thoroughly translate the action. The fact that his staging has been captured on celluloid allows him total control of what the viewer sees at each performance. Additionally, the filmmaker is perceptibly aware of how the everyday events that make up history are ultimately comprehended by the public via the manner in which they are presented in the media. History is understood more by catch-words and generalities than facts. As a result, in this age of mass media, real events can easily become distorted and trivialized. Syberberg demonstrates this in *Our Hitler* by presenting the Führer in so many disguises that the viewer is often desensitized to the reality that was this mass murderer.

"Aesthetics are connected with morals," Syberberg says. "Something like *Holocaust* is immoral because it's a bad film. Bad art can't do good things." He commented that "my three sins are that I believe Hitler came out of us, that he is one of us; that I am not interested in money, except to work with; and that I love Germany." *Our Hitler,* and his other films, clearly reflect these preferences.

In recent years, Syberberg has remained relatively inactive as a filmmaker. None of his latter work has earned him the visibility, let alone the acclaim, of his earlier films. Since *Parsifal,* his version of the Wagnerian opera which was his most widely-seen film, he has collaborated only with one of that film's stars, Edith Clever. Their artistic ventures have included a number of theatrical monologues, a few of which have been videotaped or filmed. The series commenced with *Die Nacht,* a six-hour-long examination of how an individual may act or what an individual may ponder deep into the night.

Syberberg, however, has spoken out on issues relating to his homeland. He especially is troubled by the Americanization of world culture, and has hypothesized that the resurgence of neo-Nazism in Germany, especially among the nation's youth, is a natural response to the hollowness of the capitalist culture which enveloped Germany in the post-World War II years. Thus, even in the wake of German unification, the memory of Hitler—despite the fact that he ultimately brought catastrophe and anguish to Germany—continues to influence and mold the national psyche.

—Rob Edelman

SZABÓ, István

Nationality: Hungarian. **Born:** Budapest, 18 February 1938. **Education:** Academy of Theatre and Film Art, Budapest, graduated 1961. **Career:** Directed two shorts for Béla Balázs Studio, 1961-63; directed first feature, *Almodozások kora,* 1964. **Awards:** Silver Bear, Berlin Festival, for *Confidence,* 1980; Oscar for Best Foreign Film, David di Donatello Prize, Hungarian Film Critics Award, and Best Screenplay Award and FIPRESCI Prize, Cannes Festival, for *Mephisto,* 1982.

Films as Director:

1961 *Koncert* (*Concert*) (short) (+ sc): *Variációk egy témára* (*Variations on a Theme*) (short) (+ sc)
1963 *Te* (*You ...*) (short) (+ sc)
1964 *Álmodozások kora* (*The Age of Daydreaming*) (+ sc)
1966 *Apa* (*Father*) (+ sc)
1967 *Kegyelet* (*Piety*) (short) (+ sc)
1970 *Szerelmesfilm* (*Love Film*) (+ sc)
1971 *Budapest, amiért szeretem* (*Budapest, Why I Love It*) (series of shorts: *Alom a házröl* (*Dream About a House*), *Duna—halak—madarak* (*The Danube—Fishes—Birds*), *Egy tukor* (*A Mirror*), *Léanyportre* (*A Portrait of a Girl*), *Tér* (*A Square*), *Hajnal* (*Dawn*), *Alkony* (*Twilight*) (+ sc)
1973 *Tüzoltó utca 25* (*25 Fireman's Street*) (+ sc)
1974 *Ösbemutató* (*Premiere*) (+ sc)
1976 *Budapesti mesék* (*Budapest Tales*) (+ sc)
1977 *Várostérkép* (*City Map*) (short) (+ sc)
1979 *Bizalom* (*Confidence*) (+ sc); *Der grüne Vogel* (*The Green Bird*) (+ sc)
1981 ***Mephisto*** (+ sc)
1984 *Bali*
1985 *Redl Ezredes* (*Colonel Redl*)
1988 *Hanussen*
1990 *Meeting Venus* (+ sc)
1992 *Sweet Emma, Dear Bobe* (+ sc)

Publications

By SZABÓ: articles—

Interview with Yvette Biro, in *Cahiers du Cinéma* (Paris), July 1966.
"Hungarian Director Szabo Discusses His Film Father," with Robert Siton, in *Film Comment* (New York), Fall 1968.
"Conversation with István Szabó," in *Hungarofilm Bulletin* (Budapest), no. 5, 1976.
"Mit adhat a magyar film a világnak?," interview, in *Filmkultura* (Budapest), January/February 1978.
"The Past Still Plays a Major Role," interview, in *Hungarofilm Bulletin* (Budapest), no. 2, 1979.
"Dreams and Nightmares," interview with L. Rubenstein in *Cineaste* (New York), vol. 12, no. 2, 1982.
"*Mephisto*: Istvan Szabo and 'the Gestapo of Suspicion,'" interview with J.W. Hughes in *Film Quarterly* (Berkeley), Summer 1982.
"I'd Like to Tell a Story," in *Hungarofilm Bulletin* (Budapest), vol. 2, no. 84, 1984.
Interview with Karen Jaehne in *Stills* (London), December 1985/January 1986.
Interview with R. Pede in *Film en Televisie + Video* (Brussels, Belgium), November 1991.
Interview with A. Crespi in *Cineforum* (Bergamo, Italy), April 1992.
Interview with K. Csala in *New Hungarian Quarterly* (Budapest), vol. 33, no. 125, 1992.
Interview with L. Joris in *Film en Televisie + Video* (Brussels, Belgium), no. 432, May 1993.

On SZABÓ: book—

Petrie, Graham, *History Must Answer to Man: The Contemporary Hungarian Cinema,* London, 1978.

On SZABÓ: articles—

Jaehne, Karen, "Istvan Szabo: Dreams of Memories," in *Film Quarterly* (Berkeley), Fall 1978.
Hirsch, T., "Filmek családfája," in *Filmkultura* (Budapest), March/April 1981.
"*Colonel Redl* Issue" of *Avant-Scène du Cinéma* (Paris), March 1986.
Christensen, Peter G., "Collaboration in Istvan Szabo's *Mephisto,*" in *Film Criticism* (Meadville, Pennsylvania), vol. 12, no. 3, 1988.
Gyertyan, E., "In Search of a Trilogy," in *New Hungarian Quarterly* (Budapest), vol. 29, no. 112, 1988.
Rutkowski, A. M., "Opera Europa," in *Kino* (Warsaw), July 1990.
Mills, M. C., "The Three Faces of *Mephisto*: Film, Novel, and Reality," in *Literature Film Quarterly* (Salisbury, Maryland), vol. 18, no. 4, 1990.
Blomkvist, M., "Maste det regna pa var karlek?" in *Chaplin* (Stockholm), vol. 33, no. 5, 1991.
Lefebvre, P., "La tentation de Venus," in *Grand Angle* (Mariembourg, Belgium), September/October 1991.

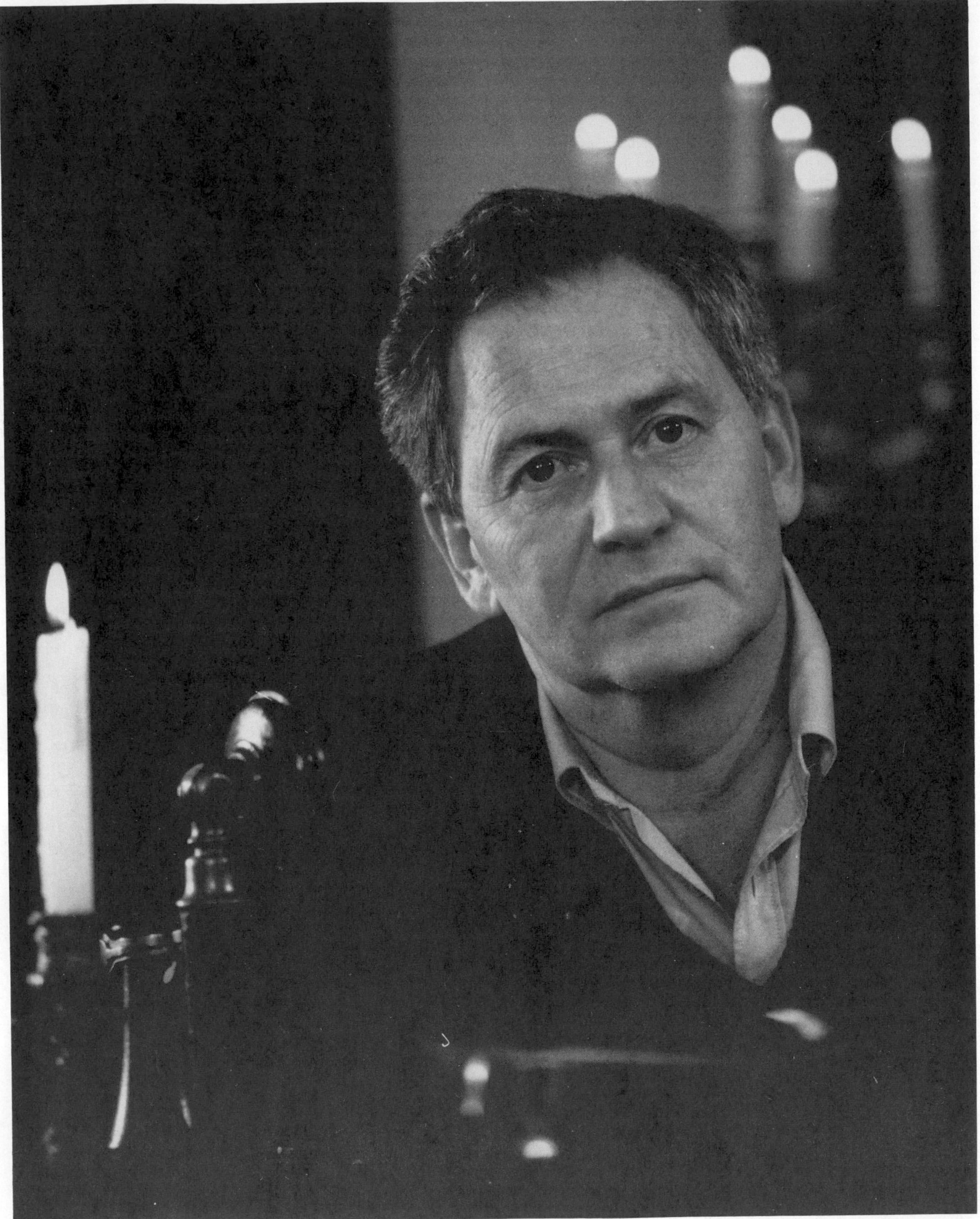

István Szabó

Bohlen, C., "*Meeting Venus* Sings of Politics," in *New York Times,* November 10, 1991.
McCreadie, M., "Istvan Szabo," in *Premiere* (New York), November 1991.
Baron, G., "Harom trilogia," in *Filmkultura* (Budapest), vol. 28, no. 2, 1992.

* * *

István Szabó's films are notable because he works with a rich spectrum of possibilities and decisions, which only when seen in their totality attain the poetic quality that becomes the viewer's primary experience. István Szabó reacts like a sensitive membrane to everything that has happened around him in the past or is just happening. At the same time he builds solely from motives that brand a film reel with the mark of an individual personality. This is true even when he strives for seemingly objective symbols such as, for example, a streetcar—"that constantly recurring, tangibly real and yet poetically long logogram for his individual and very special world." Such were the words of the noted Hungarian historian and film theoretician Josef Marx as he considered the work of director Szabó. They underscore the essential characteristic of Szabó's work: its inventiveness, which in his films takes on general forms in the broadest sense.

Szabó's first feature film, *Álmodozások kora,* together with Gaal's *Sordásban,* was the most expressive confession of an artistic generation and became a model for other artists, while his entire work has built up an unprecedented picture of contemporary life and its activities. In his earliest period Szabó's starting point was his own experience, which he transformed into artistic images. At the same time he carefully absorbed everything that was happening around him. He attempted to discern the essence of modern people, and to come to an understanding of their concerns, endeavors, and aspirations. His films examine young engineers at the start of their careers; the personal ideals of a young man on the threshold of maturity; the changing relationship of two people, framed within a quarter-century of Hungarian history; the dreams and locked-up memories of people living together in an old apartment building; the story of an ordinary city streetcar with an allegorical resemblance to our contemporaries; the love and distrust between a pair of completely different people in a charged wartime atmosphere; and a deep probe into the character of a young actor whose talents are displayed and subordinated by the totalitarian power of nascent German fascism.

All of these films are linked by the setting off of intimate confession against historical reality. The images of Szabó's films are full of poetry and the symbolism of dreamlike conceptions. They capture the small dramas of ordinary people—their disappointments, successes, loves, enthusiasms, moments of anxiety and ardor, joy and pain—as the history of post-war Hungary passes by in contrapuntal detail. István Szabó creates auteur films in which the shaping of the theme and the screenplay are just as important as the direction, so that the resulting works bears a unique stamp. The heroes of his films are not only people, but also cities, streets, houses, parks. In his films, his native Budapest serves as the point of intersection of human fates. Under Szabó's creative eye the city awakens, stirs, arises, wounded after the tumult of the war, and lives with its heroes.

In the early 1980s István Szabó deviated from the rule of auteur films (the model for his film *Mephisto* was a novel by Klaus Mann). This detracted nothing from the importance of the work, which won an Oscar and several other awards. Even in this film the director left his imprint; he managed to develop it into a picture of personal tragedy painted into a fresco of historical events. At the same time, it shows that the creative process is a tireless search for pathways. Only a responsible approach to history and the way it is shaped can help the artist gain a complete understanding of today's world.

"To awaken an interest in the people I want to tell about; to capture their essence so that a viewer can identify with them; to broaden people's understanding and sympathy—and my own as well: That's what I'd like to do," István Szabó once said in an interview. His films are an affirmation of this credo.

—Vacláv Merhaut

TANNER, Alain

Nationality: Swiss. **Born:** Geneva, 6 December 1929. **Education:** Educated in economic sciences, Calvin College, Geneva. **Career:** Shipping clerk, early 1950s; moved to London, worked at British Film Institute, 1955; assistant producer for the BBC, 1958; returned to Switzerland, 1960; co-founder, Association Suisse des Réalisateurs, early 1960s; director for Swiss French TV, 1964-69; began collaboration with writer John Berger on *Une Ville à Chandigarh,* 1966; co-founder, Groupe 5, 1968. **Awards:** Experimental Film Prize, Venice Festival, for *Nice Time,* 1957; Best Screenplay (with Berger), National Society of Film Critics, for *Jonah Who Will Be 25 in the Year 2000,* 1976; Special Jury Prize, Cannes Festival, for *Les Années lumière,* 1981.

Films as Director:

1957 *Nice Time* (short) (co-d)
1959 *Ramuz, passage d'un poète* (short)
1962 *L'Ecole* (sponsored film)
1964 *Les Apprentis* (doc feature)
1966 *Une Ville à Chandigarh*
1969 *Charles, mort ou vif* (*Charles, Dead or Alive*)
1971 *Le Salamandre* (*The Salamander*) 1973; *Le Retour d'Afrique*
1974 *Le Milieu du monde* (*The Middle of the World*)
1976 ***Jonah qui aura 25 ans en l'année 2000*** (*Jonah Who Will Be 25 in the Year 2000*)
1978 *Messidor*
1981 *Les Années lumière* (*Light Years Away*)
1983 *Dans la ville blanche* (*In the White City*)
1985 *No Man's Land*
1986 *François Simon—La présence*
1987 *Flamme dans mon coeur* (*A Flame in My Heart*); *Vallée Fantôme*
1989 *Femme de Rose Hill* (*The Woman of Rose Hill*)
1992 *L'Homme que a perdu son ombre* (+ pr, sc)
1993 *The Diary of Lady M* (+ pr)

Publications

By TANNER: book—

Jonah Who Will Be 25 in the Year 2000, with John Berger, Berkeley, 1983.

By TANNER: articles—

Interview with Michel Delahaye and others, in *Cahiers du Cinéma* (Paris), June 1969.
Interview with L. Bonnard, in *Positif* (Paris), February 1972.
"*Le Milieu du monde,*" an interview with Noel Simsolo and Guy Braucourt, in *Ecran* (Paris), October 1974.
"Irony is a Double-Edged Weapon," an interview with L. Rubinstein, in *Cineaste* (New York), vol. 6, no. 4, 1975.
"Keeping Hope for Radical Change Alive," an interview with L. Rubinstein, in *Cineaste* (New York), Winter 1976/77.
"Alain Tanner: After Jonah," an interview with M. Tarantino, in *Sight and Sound* (London), no.1, 1978/79.
Interview with Jill Forbes, in *Films and Filming* (London), February 1982.
Interview with Martyn Auty, in *Monthly Film Bulletin* (London), November 1983.
Interview with J. Chevallier and Y. Alion, in *Revue du Cinéma* (Paris), September 1985.
Interview with F. Sabouraud and S. Toubiana, in *Cahiers du Cinéma* (Paris), October 1987.
"Tanner in the Year 1991," interview with Bruno Vecchi, in *World Press Review,* December 1991.
"Alain Tanner," interview with M. Buruiana, in *Sequences,* September 1990.

On TANNER: books—

Leach, Jim, *A Possible Cinema: The Films of Alain Tanner,* Metuchen, New Jersey, 1984.
Dimitriu, Christian, *Alain Tanner,* Paris, 1985.

On TANNER: articles—

"Tanner Issue" of *Cinema* (Zurich), vol. 20, no. 1, 1974.
Tarantino, M., "Tanner and Berger: the Voice Off-Screen," in *Film Quarterly* (Berkeley), Winter 1979/80.
Harrild, A. E., "Tanner-Jonah-Ideology," in *Film Directions* (Belfast), vol. 3, no. 11, 1980.
"The Screenwriter as Collaborator," interview of John Berger, in *Cineaste* (New York), Summer 1980.
"*Les Années lumière* Issue" of *Avant-Scène du Cinéma* (Paris), 15 June 1981.
Pulleine, Tim, "Tanner's White City," in *Sight and Sound* (London), Winter 1983/1984.
Buache, Freddy, "Alain Tanner," in *Revue Belge du Cinéma* (Brussels), Winter 1985.
Kinder, M., "'Thelma & Louise' and 'Messidor' as Feminist Road Movies," in *Film Quarterly,* vol. 45, no. 2, 1991/1992.
de Baecque, A., "Entretien avec Alain Tanner," in *Cahiers du Cinéma* (Paris), May 1992.
White, Armond, "Time Zones," in *Film Comment* (New York), May/June 1992.

* * *

Alain Tanner's involvement with film began during his college years. While attending Geneva's Calvin College, he and Claude Goretta formed Geneva's first film society. It was during this time that Tanner developed an admiration for the ethnographic documentaries of Jean Rouch and fellow Swiss Henry Brandt, an influence that continued throughout his career. After a brief stint with the Swiss merchant marine,

Tanner spent a year in London as an apprentice at the BFI, where, with Goretta, he completed an experimental documentary, *Nice Time,* which chronicled the night life of Piccadilly Circus. While in London he participated in the Free Cinema Movement, along with Karel Reisz, Tony Richardson, and Lindsay Anderson. Through Anderson, Tanner made the acquaintance of novelist and art critic John Berger, who would later write the scenarios for *Le Salamandre, Middle of the World, Jonah Who Will Be 25 in the Year 2000,* and *Le Retour d'Afrique.*

Upon returning to Switzerland in 1960, Tanner completed some forty documentaries for television. Among these were: *Les Apprentis,* which concerned the lives of teenagers (and created using the methods of Rouch's direct cinema); *Une Ville à Chandigarh,* on the architecture designed by Le Corbusier for the Punjab capital (the narration for this film was assembled by John Berger); and newsreel coverage of the events of May 1968 in Paris. This last project provided the ammunition for Tanner (once again with Goretta) to form Groupe 5, a collective of Swiss filmmakers. They proposed an idea to Swiss TV for the funding of full-length narrative features to be shot in 16-millimeter and then blown-up to 35-millimeter for release. The plan enabled Tanner to make his first feature, *Charles, Dead or Alive,* which won first prize at Locarno in 1969.

The film tells of a middle-aged industrialist who, on the eve of receiving an award as the foremost business personality of the year, discovers his disaffection for the institution-laden society in which he finds himself. Following an innate sense of anarchism that Tanner posits as universal, he attempts to reject this lifestyle. His retreat into madness is blocked by his family and friends, who compel him, by appealing to his sense of duty, to resume his responsibilities.

All Tanner's films follow a similar scenario: individuals or a group become alienated from society; rejecting it, they try to forge a new society answerable to themselves alone, only to be defeated by the relentless pressures of traditional society's institutions, whose commerce they never cease to require. This theme receives its fullest and most moving expression in *Jonah Who Will Be 25 in the Year 2000.* Here the failure of the collective and the survivors of 1968, who come together at Marguerite's farm outside Geneva, is not viewed as a defeat so much as one generation's attempt to keep the hope of radical social change alive by passing on the fruits of its mistakes, that is, its education or its lore, to the succeeding generation.

Tanner's style is a blend of documentary and fable. He uses techniques such as one scene/one shot, a staple of cinéma-vérité documentary, to portray a fable or folk-story. This tension between fact and fiction, documentary and fable, receives its most exacting treatment in *Le Salamandre.* Rosemonde's indomitable, rebellious vitality repeatedly defeats the efforts of the two journalists to harness it in a pliable narrative form. After *Jonah,* Tanner introduces a darker vision in *Messidor, Light Years Away,* and *Dans la ville blanche.* The possibility of escaping society by returning to nature is explored and shown to be equally provisional. The tyranny of physical need is portrayed as being just as oppressive and compromising as that of the social world.

—Dennis Nastav

TARANTINO, Quentin

Nationality: American. **Born:** Quentin Jerome Tarantino in Knoxville, Tennessee, 27 March 1963; grew up in Los Angeles. **Education:** Studied acting. **Career:** Worked at Video Archives with Roger Avary; did telephone sales for Imperial Entertainment; began writing scripts for Cinetel; formed production company, A Band Apart, with Lawrence Bender. **Awards:** Palme d'Or, Cannes Film Festival, and Academy Award, Best Original Screenplay, for *Pulp Fiction,* 1994. **Address:** A Band Apart Productions, 6525 Sunset Blvd. #G-12, Los Angeles, CA 90028, U.S.A.

Films as Director, Screenwriter, and Actor:

1992 ***Reservoir Dogs***
1994 ***Pulp Fiction***
1995 "Man from Hollywood" episode of *Four Rooms*

Other Films:

1993 *Natural Born Killers* (Stone) (sc); *True Romance* (Tony Scott) (sc); *Eddie Presley* (role as hospital orderly)
1994 *Killing Zoe* (Avary) (sc, exec pr); *Sleep with Me* (role as Sid); *The Coriolis Effect* (short) (role as radio disc jockey); *Somebody to Love* (role as bartender); *Destiny Turns on the Radio* (role as Johnny Destiny)
1995 *Desperado* (Rodriguez) (role as pick-up guy)
1996 *From Dusk till Dawn* (Rodriguez) (sc, co-exec pr, role as Richard Gecko); *Girl 6* (role)

Publications

By TARANTINO: articles—

"A Rare Sorrow," in *Sight and Sound* (London), February 1993.
"Steve Buscemi," in *Bomb* (New York), Winter 1993.

On TARANTINO: articles—

Hoberman, J., "Back on the Wild Side," in *Premiere* (New York), August 1992.
Ciment, M., and H. Niogret, "A chacun sa couleur," in *Positif* (Paris), September 1992.
Pizzello, S., "From Rags to *Reservoir Dogs,*" in *American Cinematographer* (New York), November 1992.
Taubin, A., "The Men's Room," in *Sight and Sound* (London), December 1992.
Ryan, J., "Quentin Tarantino," in *Premiere* (New York), January 1993.
Atkinson, M., "Hype Dreams," in *Movieline* (Escondido, California), March 1993.

* * *

Quentin Tarantino's meteoric rise to fame with the phenomenal critical and popular success of *Pulp Fiction,* his second feature, is not only the result of his considerable talent but of two forces operating within contemporary Hollywood: first, an economic mini-crisis brought on by the box-office and critical failures of many recent high-budget blockbuster productions (*Waterworld* is perhaps the most remarkable example) that has opened the door, as in the past, for young directors who are able to make successful films on small budgets (made for $8 million, *Pulp Fiction* earned almost $64 million at the box office, not counting video sales and rentals); second, the continuing popularity of neo-noir films, a popularity not limited to its most thriving sub-genre, the erotic thriller. If Hollywood's economic hard times have given Tarantino (and others) a chance, it is the director's personal obsessions, so much in tune with what contemporary audiences want to see, that have made him popular.

The widely read and very cineliterate Tarantino has an obvious liking for classic hard-boiled pulp fiction (evidently Jim Thompson

Quentin Tarantino on the set of *Reservoir Dogs*

and W. R. Burnett in particular) and classic film noir (Huston's *Asphalt Jungle* probably served as a model for *Reservoir Dogs*). But like several of the prominent directors of the Hollywood Renaissance in the middle 1970s (especially Martin Scorsese and Paul Schrader), Tarantino also owes a substantial debt to French film noir, especially the work of Jean Pierre Melville and Jean Luc Godard. Godard's modernist refiguration of noir themes and conventions (*Alphaville* is the classic example), however, would hardly please the mass audience Tarantino has in mind. The most substantial contribution of nouvelle vague anti-realism in Tarantino's films can be seen in their creative use of achronicities, disorderings in the storytelling process that make the narratives intriguing puzzles even as they uncover interesting ironies for the spectator, who must take an active role in the deciphering of the plot. The anti-Aristotelianism of this procedure, its disruption of emotional identification with the characters' plight, allows Tarantino to concentrate on thematic elements, especially the role violence plays in American culture.

Like the gang in *Asphalt Jungle,* the crooks in *Reservoir Dogs* assembled to pull a heist (itself never represented) are shown participating in what is simply a "left-handed form of endeavor." If Huston endeavors to demonstrate that criminals too have an ordinary life (households to run, relationships to pursue, bills to pay), Tarantino, in contrast, is more interested in moral dilemmas and conflict, especially as these are brought to life by situations of extraordinary danger and threat. In fact, the central conflicts of *Reservoir Dogs* carry a substantial moral charge and significance, even if, in the end, as the all-knowing spectator alone recognizes, the characters are destroyed no matter if they are sociopaths with a yen for torture or men of good will who stand by their friends even at the cost of their own lives. And yet Tarantino obviously sympathizes with those who despise *mauvaise foi* and make the difficult choices that confront them. A Sartrean and Camusian moralism pervades this film.

Much the same can be said of the similar characters in *Pulp Fiction,* whose existential plights and difficult choices are here examined from a serio-comic perspective. A torpedo working for a drug dealer is given the assignment of looking after the boss's flirtatious wife. He tries to resist her various come-ons, only to be faced with a sudden, more demanding test: she overdoses on heroin, goes into a near-fatal coma from which he can arouse her only by jabbing a harpoon-sized needle into her heart. Amazingly, she recovers, and Tarantino finishes this sequence with a comic leave-taking scene that ends their "date." Once again, in *Pulp Fiction* difficult moral questions are raised. A boxer in the same drug dealer's pay refuses out of personal integrity to throw a fight as ordered. Fleeing town, he meets his boss by accident on a city street. Their confrontation, however, opens unexpectedly onto another moral plane. Both men wind up the prisoners of local sadists, who plan to sodomize, torture, and kill them. The boxer escapes, and, feeling the pang of conscience, goes back to free his erstwhile boss, who forgives the man's earlier betrayal before exacting a terrible vengeance on his torturers, one of whom is a policeman.

With their philosophical dimensions, unremitting representations of venality and depravity among the criminal under and over class, art cinema narrational complexities, and black humor, Tarantino's first two films are strikingly original contributions to an American cinema struggling to rebound from the artistic doldrums of the 1980s. As a screenwriter, he has been no less successful. Written for former video shop co-worker Roger Avary, *Killing Zoe* offers a romantic twist on the themes examined in Tarantino's own directorial efforts. In this case, a somewhat naive and easily swayed young criminal must make a moral stand against his lifelong friend to save the life of a prostitute he has come to care for; the gesture is reciprocated, and the two rescue themselves from a nightmarish world of self-destructive violence and addiction. Similarly, *True Romance* and *Natural Born Killers* offer outlaw couples on the run whose loyalty to each other is rewarded in the end by their escape from a corrupt and disfiguring America that attempts to destroy them.

—R. Barton Palmer

TARKOVSKY, Andrei

Nationality: Soviet Russian. **Born:** Moscow, 4 April 1932. **Education:** Institute of Oriental Languages, graduated 1954; All-Union State Cinematography Institute (VGIK), graduated 1960. **Family:** Married twice (two children by first marriage, one son by second marriage). **Career:** Geological prospector in Siberia, 1954-56; on diploma work *The Steamroller and the Violin,* began collaboration with cameraman Yadim Yusov and Vyacheslav Ovchinnikov, 1960; directed opera *Boris Godunov* at Covent Garden, 1983; made last film, *The Sacrifice,* in Sweden, 1986. **Awards:** Lion of St. Mark for Best Film, Venice Festival, for *Ivan's Childhood,* 1962; International Critics Award, Cannes Festival, for *Andrei Rublev,* 1969; Special Jury Prize, Cannes Festival, for *Solaris,* 1972; Merited Artistic Worker of the RSFSR, 1974; Grand Prix, Cannes Festival, for *The Sacrifice,* 1986. **Died:** Of cancer, in Paris, 29 December 1986.

Films as Director:

1959 *There Will Be No Leave Today* (short)
1960 *Katok i skripka* (*The Steamroller and the Violin*) (+ co-sc)
1962 *Ivanovo detstvo* (*Ivan's Childhood*)
1969 ***Andrei Rublev*** (+ co-sc)
1971 *Solyaris* (*Solaris*) (+ co-sc)
1975 ***Zerkalo*** (*The Mirror*) (+ co-sc)
1979 *Stalker*
1983 *Nostalghia* (*Nostalgia*)
1986 ***Offret*** (*The Sacrifice*)

Publications

By TARKOVSKY: books—

Andrei Rublev, Paris, 1970.
Sculpting in Time: Reflections on the Cinema, London, 1986; revised edition, 1989.

By TARKOVSKY: articles—

Interview with O. Surkova, in *Iskusstvo Kino* (Moscow), July 1977.
"Against Interpretation," an interview with Ian Christie, in *Framework* (Norwich), Spring 1981.
"Tarkovsky in Italy," an interview with T. Mitchell, in *Sight and Sound* (London), Winter 1982/83.
Interview with J. Hoberman, in *American Film* (Washington, D.C.), November 1983.

On TARKOVSKY: books—

Liehm, Mira, and Antonín Liehm, *The Most Important Art: Eastern European Film After 1945,* Berkeley, 1977.
Borin, Fabrizio, *Andrej Tarkovsky,* Venice, 1987.
Jacobsen, Wolfgang, and others, *Andrej Tarkovskij,* Munich, 1987.
Le Fanu, Mark, *The Cinema of Andrei Tarkovsky,* London, 1987.
Gauthier, Guy, *Andrei Tarkovsky,* Paris, 1988.
Turovskaya, Maya, *Tarkovsky: Cinema as Poetry,* London, 1989.

On TARKOVSKY: articles—

Montagu, Ivor, "Man and Experience: Tarkovski's World," in *Sight and Sound* (London), Spring 1973.
Ward, M., "The Idea That Torments and Exhausts," in *Stills* (London), Spring 1981.
Strick, Philip, "Tarkovsky's Translations," in *Sight and Sound* (London), Summer 1981.
Dempsey, M. "Lost Harmony—Tarkovsky's *The Mirror* and *The Stalker,*" in *Film Quarterly* (Berkeley), Fall 1981.
"Tarkovsky Issue" of *Positif* (Paris), October 1981.
Zak, M., in *Iskusstvo Kino* (Moscow), September 1982.
Ratschewa. M., "The Messianic Power of Pictures: The Films of Andrei Tarkovsky," in *Cineaste* (New York), vol. 13, no. 1, 1983.
Mitchell, T., "Andrei Tarkovsky and *Nostalghi,*" in *Film Criticism* (Meadville, Pennysylvania), Spring 1984.
Tarkovsky Section of *Positif* (Paris), October 1984.
Green, P., "The Nostalgia of *The Stalker,*" in *Sight and Sound* (London), Winter 1984/1985.
Tarkovsky Sections of *Positif* (Paris), May and June 1986.
Tarkovsky Section of *Cahiers du Cinéma* (Paris), July/August 1986.
Obituary, in *Variety* (New York), 31 December 1986.
Christie, Ian, "Raising the Shroud," in *Monthly Film Bulletin* (London), February 1987.
Green, Peter, obituary in *Sight and Sound* (London), Spring 1987.
Kennedy, Harlan, "Tarkovsky, a Thought in Nine Parts," in *Film Comment* (New York), May/June 1987.
Leszczylowski, Michal, "A Year with Andrei," in *Sight and Sound* (London), Autumn 1987.
Tarkovsky Section of *Positif* (Paris), February 1988.
Strick, Philip, "Releasing the Balloon, Raising the Bell," in *Monthly Film Bulletin* (London), February 1991.

On TARKOVSKY: film—

Leszczylowski, Michal, *Directed by Andrei Tarkovsky,* 1986.

* * *

"Tarkovsky is the greatest of them all. He moves with such naturalness in the room of dreams. He doesn't explain. What should he explain anyhow?" Thus Ingmar Bergman, in his autobiography *The Magic Lantern,* bows down before the Russian director while also hinting at what makes Tarkovsky's work so awkward to critics: it can verge on the inscrutable. Too opaque to yield concrete meaning, it offers itself as sacral art, demanding a rapt, and even religious, response from its audiences. His 1979 film *Stalker,* for instance, features a place called the Zone where all "desires come true." Rather like the land of Oz, this mysterious outland promises to reveal the secret of things to any intrepid travellers who prospect it to its core. But there are no cowardly lions or tin men to ease the journey, no yellow brick road to follow. The Zone is an austere realm—typical Tarkovsky

Andrei Tarkovsky

territory—of bleak landscapes populated by characters laden with a peculiarly Russian gloom.

Watching Tarkovsky's films, his "sculptures in time," spectators can find themselves on a journey every bit as arduous as that undertaken by the pilgrims who headed toward the Zone. The son of a poet, the director treated film as a medium in which he could express himself in the first person. His six years at the Moscow State Film School, during which he received a thorough grounding in film technique from such Soviet luminaries as Mikhail Romm, did nothing to disabuse him of the notion that cinema was a "high art." He felt he could tap the same vein of poetic intimacy that his father sought in lyric verse. The necessary intrusion of camera crews and actors, and the logistical problems of exhibition and distribution, worried him not a jot. Although all his films are self-reflexive, he does not draw attention to the camera for radical Brechtian reasons. He is not trying to subvert bourgeois narrative codes. He is not even assaulting the tenets of Socialist Realism, a doctrine he found every bit as unappealing as Western mass culture aimed at the "consumer" (although his ex-partner, Konchalovsky, ended up in Hollywood directing Sylvester Stallone vehicles). What his constant use of tracking shots, slow motion, and never-ending pans—indeed his entire visual rhetoric—seems to emphasize is that he is moulding the images. He is a virtuoso, and he wants us to be aware of the fact.

Tarkovsky's first two feature length projects, *Ivan's Childhood* and *Andrei Rublev,* mark a curious collision between the personal and the political. On one level, the former is a propaganda piece, telling yet again the great Soviet story of the defeat of the Nazi scourge during World War II. But Tarkovsky destabilizes the film with dream sequences. The "big questions" that are ostensibly being addressed turn out to be peripheral: the director is more concerned with the poetic rekindling of childhood than with a triumphal narrative of Russian resilience. Similarly, *Rublev,* an epic three-hour biography of a medieval icon painter, is, in spite of the specificity and grandeur of its locations, a rigorous account of the role of the artist in society, as applicable to the 1960s as to the 1300s.

As if to display his versatility, Tarkovsky skipped genres, moving from the distant past to the distant future for his third feature, *Solaris,* a rather ponderous sci-fi movie taken from a novel by the Polish writer Stanislaw Lem. The harsh, Kubrick-like spaceship interiors suit the director far less than his customary wet and muddy landscapes. The musings on love and immortality engaged in by the cosmonauts as they hover above a sea of liquid gas—for a filmmaker with such a flair for images, Tarkovsky resorts to portentous dialogue with surprising frequency—weigh the story down. Still, *Solaris* works on a more intimate level when it explores a man's attempts to come to terms with the death of his wife.

Mirror is quintessential Tarkovsky; ravishing to look at, full of classical music, and so narratively dense as to be almost unfathomable on a first viewing. There are only 200 or so shots in it, and it is a film that fell into shape, almost by accident, late in the editing stage, but it is Tarkovsky's richest and most resonant work. The narrative flits between the present and the past, between the "adult" mentality of the narrator and the memory of his childhood. Moreover, the wide open spaces of the countryside where Tarkovsky spent his earliest years are contrasted with the constricting rooms of city apartments. Poems by the director's father, Arseny, appear on the soundtrack. Complementing these, Tarkovsky is at his most elemental in this film: the wind rustling the trees, fire, and water are constant motifs.

Tarkovsky went to enormous lengths to recreate the landscape of his infancy, planting buckwheat a year before shooting started, and constructing, from memory and old photographs, the bungalow where he had lived. There is a humour and warmth in *Mirror* sometimes absent in his work as a whole. (This may have something to do with the fact that it is his only film to have a woman protagonist. Margarita Terekova, who ranks with Anatoli Solonitzine as Tarkovsky's favourite actor, plays both the narrator's wife and his mother.) Generally, Tarkovsky terrain is desolate, ravaged by war, or threatened with catastrophe, as in *The Sacrifice.* In *Mirror,* however, the forests and rivers and fields are nurturing and colourful. Accused by the authorities of being narratively obscure, Tarkovsky testified that he received many letters from viewers who had seen their own childhoods miraculously crystallize as they watched the film.

Nostalgia was his first film in exile after his defection to the West. Shot in Italy, it showed the Russian pining for his homeland. He wouldn't live to see it again.

The Sacrifice is a typically saturnine final testament from a filmmaker overly aware of his own reputation. Tarkovsky believed that "modern mass culture, aimed at the consumer ... is crippling people's souls." A self-conscious exercise in spiritual plumbing, his last work before his premature death from cancer in 1987 is weighed down by its own gravitas. Shot by Sven Nykvist, who used natural light for the interior scenes, and full of intricate pans, the film has the formal beauty that one has come to associate with the director. But its endless and wordy metaphysical surmising stops it from tugging at memory and emotion in the way of the best of his work, most notably *Mirror.*

—G.C. Macnab

TASHLIN, Frank

Nationality: American. **Born:** Weehawken, New Jersey, 19 February 1913. **Education:** Educated in public school, Astoria, Long Island. **Family:** Married Mary Costa. **Career:** Errand boy for Max Fleischer, 1928; worked on *Aesop's Fables* cartoons at RKO, from 1930, became animator; sold cartoons to magazines under pseudonym "Tish-Tash," until 1936; moved to Hollywood, worked at Vitaphone Corp. on *Merrie Melodies* and *Looney Tunes,* 1933; comic strip *Van Boring* syndicated, 1934-36; gagman at Hal Roach Studios, 1935, then director and scriptwriter for *Looney Tunes*; story director at Disney studios for *Mickey Mouse* and *Donald Duck* series, 1939-40; executive producer, Columbia's Screen Gems Cartoon Studios, 1941; returned to *Merrie Melodies* and *Looney Tunes,* 1942, also directed first *Private Snafu* cartoon for Frank Capra's Army Signal Corps Unit; first non-animated film credit as co-scriptwriter for *Delightfully Dangerous,* 1944; gag writer at Paramount, 1945; writer for Eddie Bracken's CBS radio shows, 1946; took over direction of *The Lemon Drop Kid* at request of Bob Hope, 1950; writer, producer and director for television, from 1952. **Died:** In Hollywood, 5 May 1972.

Films as Director:

1950 *The Lemon Drop Kid* (co-d, uncredited, + co-sc)
1951 *The First Time* (+ co-sc); *Son of Paleface* (+ co-sc)
1953 *Marry Me Again* (+ sc); *Susan Slept Here* (+ co-sc uncredited)
1955 *Artists and Models* (+ co-sc); *The Lieutenant Wore Skirts* (+ co-sc)
1956 *Hollywood or Bust* (+ co-sc uncredited); *The Girl Can't Help It* (+ pr, co-sc)
1957 *Will Success Spoil Rock Hunter?* (+ sc, pr)
1958 *Rock-a-Bye Baby* (+ sc); *The Geisha Boy* (+ sc)
1959 *Say One for Me* (+ co-sc uncredited, pr)
1960 *Cinderfella* (+ sc)
1962 *Bachelor Flat* (+ co-sc)
1963 *It's Only Money* (+ co-sc); *The Man from The Diner's Club*; *Who's Minding the Store?* (+ co-sc)

Frank Tashlin

1964 *The Disorderly Orderly* (+ sc)
1965 *The Alphabet Murders*
1966 *The Glass Bottom Boat*; *Caprice* (+ co-sc)
1968 *The Private Navy of Sergeant O'Farrell* (+ sc)

Other Films:

1944 *Delightfully Dangerous* (Lubin) (sc)
1947 *Variety Girl* (Marshall) (co-sc); *The Paleface* (McLeod) (co-sc); *The Fuller Brush Man* (*That Mad Mr Jones*) (Simon) (co-sc)
1948 *One Touch of Venus* (Seiter) (co-sc); *Love Happy* (Miller) (co-sc)
1949 *Miss Grant Takes Richmond* (*Innocence Is Bliss*) (Bacon) (co-sc); *Kill the Umpire* (Bacon) (sc); *The Good Humor Man* (Bacon) (sc)
1950 *The Fuller Brush Girl* (*The Affairs of Sally*) (Bacon) (sc)
1956 *The Scarlet Hour* (Curtiz) (co-sc)

Publications

By TASHLIN: articles—

"Frank Tashlin—An Interview and an Appreciation," with Peter Bogdanovich, in *Film Culture* (New York), no. 26, 1962.

On TASHLIN: book—

Schneider, Steve, *That's All Folks!: The Art of Warner Bros. Animation*, New York, 1988.

On TASHLIN: articles—

Benayoun, Robert, and others, articles, in *Positif* (Paris), no. 29.
Boussinot, Roger, "Frank Tashlin," in *Cinéma* (Paris), no. 49, 1960.
Cameron, Ian, "Frank Tashlin and the New World," in *Movie* (London), February 1963.
Bogdanovich, Peter, "Tashlin's Cartoons," in *Movie* (London), Winter 1968/69.
Bogdanovich, Peter, "Frank Tashlin," in *The New York Times,* 28 May 1972.
Beylie, Claude, "La Fin d'un amuseur," in *Ecran* (Paris), July/August 1972.
Grisolia, M., "Frank Tashlin ou la poétique de l'objet," in *Cinéma* (Paris), July/August 1972.
Cohen, M.S., "Looney Tunes and Merrie Melodies," in *Velvet Light Trap* (Madison), Autumn 1975.

* * *

Frank Tashlin had achieved recognition as a children's writer when he entered the film industry to work in the animation units at Disney and Warner Bros. Both of these early careers would have decisive import for the major films that Tashlin would direct in the 1950s. This early experience allowed Tashlin to see everyday life as a visually surreal experience, as a kind of cartoon itself, and gave him a faith in the potential for natural experience to resist the increased mechanization of everyday life. Tashlin's films of the 1950s are great displays of cinematic technique, particularly as it developed in a TV-fearing Hollywood. They featured a wide-screen sensibility, radiant color, frenetic editing, and a deliberate recognition of film as film. Tashlin's films often resemble live versions of the Warners cartoons. Jerry Lewis, who acted in many of Tashlin's films, seemed perfect for such a visual universe with his reversions to a primal animality, his deformations of physicality, and his sheer irrationality.

Tashlin's films are also concerned with the ways the modern world is becoming more and more artificial; the films are often filled with icons of the new mass culture (rock and roll, comic books, television, muscle men, Jayne Mansfield, Hollywood) and are quite explicit about the ways such icons are mechanically produced within a consumer society. For example, in *Will Success Spoil Rock Hunter?*, the successful romance of Rita Marlow (Jayne Mansfield) causes other women to engage in dangerous bust-expanding exercises to the point of nervous exhaustion. Yet the very critique of mass culture by an artist working in a commercial industry creates the central contradiction of Tashlin's cinema: if the danger of modern life is its increasing threat of mechanization, then what is the critical potential of an art based on mechanization? Significantly, Tashlin's films can be viewed as a critique of the ostentatious vulgarity of the new plastic age while they simultaneously seem to revel in creating ever better and more spectacular displays of sheer technique to call attention to that age. *The Girl Can't Help It,* for instance, chronicles the making of a non-talent (Jayne Mansfield) into a star, viewing the process with a certain cynicism but at the same time participating in that process. These films are vehicles for Mansfield as Mansfield, and are thus somewhat biographical.

As with Jerry Lewis, serious treatment of Tashlin began in France (especially in the pages of *Positif,* which has always had an attraction to the comic film as an investigator of the Absurd). Anglo-American criticism tended to dismiss Tashlin (for example, Sarris in *American Cinema* called him "vulgar"). In such a context, Claire Johnston and Paul Willemen's *Frank Tashlin* had the force of a breakthrough, providing translations from French journals and analyses of the cinematic and ideological implications of Tashlin's work.

—Dana B. Polan

TATI, Jacques

Nationality: French. **Born:** Jacques Tatischeff in Le Pecq, France, 9 October 1908. **Education:** Attended Lycée de St.-Germain-en-Laye; also attended a college of arts and engineering, 1924. **Family:** Married Micheline Winter, 1944; children: Sophie and Pierre. **Career:** Rugby player with Racing Club de Paris, 1925-30; worked as pantomimist/impressionist, from 1930; recorded one of his stage routines, "Oscar, champion de tennis," on film, 1932; toured European music halls and circuses, from 1935; served in French Army, 1939-45; directed himself in short film, *L'Ecole des facteurs,* 1946; directed and starred in first feature, *Jour de fête,* 1949; offered American television series of 15-minute programs, refused, 1950s; made *Parade* for Swedish television, 1973. **Awards:** Best Scenario, Venice Festival, for *Jour de fête,* 1949; Max Linder Prize (France) for *L'Ecole des facteurs,* 1949; Prix Louis Delluc, for *Les Vacances de M. Hulot,* 1953; Special Prize, Cannes Festival, for *Mon Oncle,* 1958; Grand Prix National des Arts et des Lettres, 1979; Commandeur des Arts et des Lettres. **Died:** 5 November 1982.

Films as Director:

1947 *L'Ecole des facteurs* (+ sc, role)
1949 *Jour de fête* (+ co-sc, role as François the postman)
1953 ***Les Vacances de Monsieur Hulot*** (*Mr. Hulot's Holiday*) (+ co-sc, role as M. Hulot)
1958 *Mon Oncle* (+ co-sc, role as M. Hulot)
1967 ***Playtime*** (+ sc, role as M. Hulot)
1971 *Trafic* (*Traffic*) (+ co-sc, role as M. Hulot)
1973 *Parade* (+ sc, role as M. Loyal)

Other Films:

1932 *Oscar, champion de tennis* (sc, role)
1934 *On demande une brute* (Barrois) (co-sc, role)
1935 *Gai Dimanche* (Berry) (co-sc, role)
1936 *Soigne ton gauche* (Clément) (role)
1938 *Retour à la terre* (pr, sc, role)
1945 *Sylvie et le fant me* (Autant-Lara) (role as ghost)
1946 *Le Diable au corps* (Autant-Lara) (role as soldier)

Publications

By TATI: articles—

"Tati Speaks," with Harold Woodside, in *Take One* (Montreal), no. 6, 1969.
Interview with E. Burcksen, in *Cinématographe* (Paris), May 1977.
Interview with M. Makeieff, in *Cinématographe* (Paris), January 1985.

On TATI: books—

Sadoul, Georges, *The French Film,* London, 1953.
Bazin, André, *Qu'est ce-que le cinéma,* London, 1958.
Carrière, Jean-Claude, *Monsieur Hulot's Holiday,* New York, 1959.
Cauliez, Armand, *Jacques Tati,* Paris, 1968.
Mast, Gerald, *The Comic Mind,* New York, 1973; revised edition, Chicago, 1979.
Kerr, Walter, *The Silent Clowns,* New York, 1975.
Gilliatt, Penelope, *Jacques Tati,* London, 1976.
Maddock, Brent, *The Films of Jacques Tati,* Metuchen, New Jersey, 1977.
Fischer, Lucy, *Jacques Tati: A Guide to References and Resources,* Boston, 1983.
Harding, James, *Jacques Tati: Frame by Frame,* London, 1984.
Chion, Michel, *Jacques Tati,* Paris, 1987.
Dondey, Marc, *Tati,* Paris, 1989.

On TATI: articles—

"Mr. Hulot," in the *New Yorker,* 17 July 1954.
Mayer, A. C., "The Art of Jacques Tati," in *Quarterly of Film, Radio, and Television* (Berkeley), Fall 1955.
Simon, John, "Hulot; or The Common Man as Observer and Critic," in the *Yale French Review* (New Haven, Connecticut), no. 23, 1959.
Houston, Penelope, "Conscience and Comedy," in *Sight and Sound* (London), Summer/Autumn 1959.
Marcabru, Pierre, "Jacques Tati contre l'ironie française," in *Arts* (Paris), 8 March 1961.
Armes Roy, "The Comic Art of Jacques Tati," in *Screen* (London), February 1970.
Dale, R. C., "Playtime and Traffic, Two New Tati's," in *Film Quarterly* (Berkeley), no. 2, 1972-73.
Rosenbaum, Jonathan, "Tati's Democracy," in *Film Comment* (New York), May/June 1973.

Thompson, K., "Parameters of the Open Film: Les Vacances de Monsieur Hulot," in *Wide Angle* (Athens, Ohio), vol. 1, no. 4, 1977.

"Tati Issue" of *Cahiers du Cinéma* (Paris), September 1979.

Schefer, J. L., "Monsieur Tati," in *Cahiers du Cinéma* (Paris), December 1982.

Fischer, Lucy, "*Jour de fête*: Americans in Paris," in *Film Criticism* (Meadville, Pennsylvania), Winter 1983.

"Jacques Tati Issue" of *Cinéma* (Paris), January 1983.

Rosenbaum, Jonathan, "The Death of Hulot," in *Sight and Sound* (London), Spring 1983.

Carriére. J. C. "Comedie à la Française," in *American Film* (New York), December 1985.

Thompson, Kristin, "*Parade,* a Review of an Unreleased Film," in *Velvet Light Trap* (Madison, Wisconsin), no. 22, 1986.

* * *

Jacques Tati's father was disappointed that his son didn't enter the family business, the restoration and framing of old paintings. In Jacques Tati's films, however, the art of framing—of selecting borders and playing on the limits of the image—achieved new expressive heights. Instead of restoring old paintings, Tati restored the art of visual comedy, bringing out a new density and brilliance of detail, a new clarity of composition. He is one of the handful of film artists—the others would include Griffith, Eisenstein, Murnau, Bresson—who can be said to have transformed the medium at its most basic level, to have found a new way of seeing.

After a short career as a rugby player, Tati entered the French music hall circuit of the early 1930s; his act consisted of pantomime parodies of the sports stars of the era. Several of his routines were filmed as shorts in the 1930s (and he appeared as a supporting actor in two films by Claude Autant-Lara), but he did not return to direction until after the war, with the 1947 short *L'Ecole des facteurs.* Two years later, the short was expanded into a feature, *Jour de fête.* Here Tati plays a village postman who, struck by the "modern, efficient" methods he sees in a short film on the American postal system, decides to streamline his own operations. The satiric theme that runs through all of Tati's work—the coldness of modern technology—is already well developed, but more importantly, so is his visual style. Many of the gags in *Jour de fête* depend on the use of framelines and foreground objects to obscure the comic event—not to punch home the gag, but to hide it and purify it, to force the spectator to intuit, and sometimes invent, the joke for himself.

Tati took four years to make his next film, *Les Vacances de Monsieur Hulot (Mr. Hulot's Holiday),* which introduced the character he

Jacques Tati: *Playtime*

was to play for the rest of his career—a gently eccentric Frenchman whose tall, reedy figure was perpetually bent forward as if by the weight of the pipe he always kept clamped in his mouth. The warmth of the characterization, plus the radiant inventiveness of the sight gags, made *Mr. Hulot* an international success, yet the film already suggests Tati's dissatisfaction with the traditional idea of the comic star. Hulot is not a comedian, in the sense of being the source and focus of the humor; he is, rather, an attitude, a signpost, a perspective that reveals the humor in the world around him.

Mon Oncle is a transitional film: though Hulot had abdicated his star status, he is still singled out among the characters—prominent, but strangely marginal. With *Playtime,* released after nine years of expensive, painstaking production, Tati's intentions become clear. Hulot was now merely one figure among many, weaving in and out of the action much like the Mackintosh Man in Joyce's *Ulysses.* And just as Tati the actor refuses to use his character to guide the audience through the film, so does Tati the director refuse to use close-ups, emphatic camera angles, or montage to guide the audience to the humor in the images. *Playtime* is composed almost entirely of long-shot tableaux that leave the viewer free to wander through the frame, picking up the gags that may be occurring in the foreground, the background, or off to one side. The film returns an innocence of vision to the spectator; no value judgements or hierarchies of interest have been made for us. We are given a clear field, left to respond freely to an environment that has not been polluted with prejudices.

Audiences used to being told what to see, however, found the freedom of *Playtime* oppressive. The film (released in several versions, from a 70mm stereo cut that ran over three hours to an absurdly truncated American version of 93 minutes) was a commercial failure. It plunged Tati deep into personal debt.

Tati's last theatrical film, the 1971 *Traffic,* would have seemed a masterpiece from anyone else, but for Tati it was clearly a protective return to a more traditional style. Tati's final project, a 60-minute television film titled *Parade,* has never been shown in America. Five films in 25 years is not an impressive record in a medium where stature is often measured by prolificacy, but *Playtime* alone is a lifetime's achievement—a film that liberates and revitalizes the act of looking at the world.

—Dave Kehr

TAVERNIER, Bertrand

Nationality: French. **Born:** Lyons, 25 April 1941. **Education:** Studied law for one year. **Family:** Married writer Colo O'Hagan (separated), two children. **Career:** Film critic for *Positif* and *Cahiers du Cinema,* Paris, early 1960s; press agent for producer Georges de Beauregard, 1962; freelance press agent, associated with Pierre Rissient, 1965; directed first film, *L'Horloger de St. Paul,* 1974. **Awards:** Prix Louis Delluc, for *L'Horloger de St. Paul,* 1974; Cesar Awards for Best Director and Best Original Screenplay (with Jean Aurenche), for *Que la fête commence,* 1975; European Film Festival Special Prize, for *La Vie et rien d'autre,* 1989.

Films as Director and Co-Scriptwriter:

1964 "Une Chance explosive" episode of *La Chance et l'amour*
1965 "Le Baiser de Judas" episode of *Les Baisers*
1974 *L'Horloger de Saint-Paul* (*The Clockmaker*)
1975 *Que la fête commence* (*Let Joy Reign Supreme*)
1976 *Le Juge et l'assassin* (*The Judge and the Assassin*)
1977 *Des enfants gâtés* (*Spoiled Children*)
1979 *Femmes Fatales*
1980 *La Mort en direct* (*Death Watch*)
1981 *Une Semaine de vacances* (*A Week's Vacation*)
1982 *Coup de torchon* (*Clean Slate*); *Philippe Soupault et le surréalisme*) (doc)
1983 *Mississippi Blues* (*Pays d'Octobre*) (co-d)
1984 *Un Dimanche à la campagne* (*A Sunday in the Country*)
1986 ***Round Midnight*** (*Autour de minuit*)
1987 *Le Passion Béatrice*
1988 *Lyon, le regard intérieur* (doc for TV)
1989 *La Vie et rien d'autre* (*Life and Nothing But*)
1990 *Daddy Nostalgie* (*These Foolish Things*)
1991 *La guerre sans non* (*The Undeclared War*)
1992 *L.627*
1994 *Le fille de D'Artagnan* (*The Daughter of D'Artagnan*); *Anywhere But Here*
1995 *L'appat* (*Fresh Bait*)

Other Films:

1967 *Coplan ouverte le feu à Mexico* (Freda) (sc)
1968 *Capitaine Singrid* (Leduc) (sc)
1977 *Le Question* (Heynemann) (pr)
1979 *Rue du pied de Grue* (Grandjouan) (pr); *Le Mors aux dents* (Heynemann) (pr)
1993 *Des demoiselles ont en 25 ans* (*The Young Girls Turn 25*) (Varda) (appearance); *Francois Truffaut: portraits voles* (*Francois Truffaut: Stolen Portraits*) (Toubiana, Pascal) (appearance)
1994 *Troubles We've Seen: A History of Journalism in Wartime* (pr)
1995 *The World of Jacques Demy* (Varda) (appearance); *American Cinema* (role)

Publications

By TAVERNIER: book—

30 ans de cinéma américaine (30 Years of American Cinema), with Jean-Pierre Coursodon, Paris.
Amis americains: entretiens avec les grands auteurs d'Hollywood, Paris, 1993.

By TAVERNIER: articles—

"Il n'y a pas de genre à proscrire ou à conseiller ...," an interview with D. Rabourdin, in *Cinéma* (Paris), May 1975.
"Les Rapports de la justice avec la folie et l'histoire," in *Avant-Scène du Cinéma* (Paris), June 1976.
"Notes éparses," in *Positif* (Paris), December/January 1977/78.
"Blending the Personal with the Political," an interview with L. Quart and L. Rubinstein, in *Cineaste* (New York), Summer 1978.
"Director of the Year," *International Film Guide* (London, New York), 1980.
"Cleaning the Slate," an interview with I. F. McAsh, in *Films* (London), August 1982.
Interviews in *Films in Review* (New York), March and April 1983.
Interview with Michel Ciment and others, in *Positif* (Paris), May 1984.
Interview with Dan Yakir, in *Film Comment* (New York), September/October 1984.
"*Round Midnight,*" an interview with Jean-Pierre Coursodon, in *Cineaste* (New York), vol. 15, no. 2, 1986.

Bertrand Tavernier (right) directing Michel Piccoli and Christine Pascal in *Des enfants gâtés*

"All the Colors: Bertrand Tavernier Talks about *Round Midnight,*" an interview with Michael Dempsey, in *Film Quarterly* (Berkeley), Spring 1987.

Interview with M. Ruuth, in *Chaplin* (Stockholm), vol. 29, 1987.

Interview, in *Skrien* (Amsterdam), Spring 1987.

Interview, in *Positif* (Paris), September 1989.

Interview by F. Laurendeau, in *Sequences* (Montreal), November 1989.

"La guerre n'est pas finie," an interview with K. Jaehne, in *Cineaste* (New York), vol. 18, no. 1, 1990.

Obituary, of Michael Powell, in *Positif* (Paris), May 1990.

"A la rencontre de Budd Boetticher," in *Positif* (Paris), July/August 1991.

"Journey into light," an interview with Patrick McGilligan, in *Film Comment* (New York), March/April 1992.

Interview by F. Aude and H. Niogret, in *Positif* (Paris), April 1992.

On TAVERNIER: books—

Bion, Danièle, *Bertrand Tavernier: cinéaste de l'émotion,* Renens, 1984.

Mereghetti, Paolo, editor, *Bertrand Tavernier,* Venice, 1986.

Douin, Jean-Luc, *Tavernier,* Paris, 1988.

Mehle, Kerstin, *Blickstrategien im Kino von Bertrand Tavernier,* Frankfurt, 1991.

La vida, la muerte: el cine de Bertrand Tavernier, Valencia, Spain, 1992.

On TAVERNIER: articles—

"*L'Horloger de Saint-Paul* Issue" of *Avant-Scène du Cinéma* (Paris), May 1974.

Auty, M., "Tavernier in Scotland," in *Sight and Sound* (London), Winter 1976/77.

Hennebelle, G., and others, "Le Cinéma de Bertrand Tavernier," in *Ecran* (Paris), September and October 1977.

Magretta, W. R. and J., "Bertrand Tavernier: The Constraints of Convention," in *Film Quarterly* (Berkeley), Summer 1978.

"Bertrand Tavernier Dossier" in *Revue du Cinéma* (Paris), April 1984.

Ciment, Michel, "Sunday in the Country With Bertrand," in *American Film* (Washington, D.C.), October 1984.

Harvey, Stephen, "Focus: *Beatrice,*" in *American Film* (New York), March 1988.

Riding, Alan, "Bertrand Tavernier Films Small Romances Amid Widescale History," in *New York Times,* 11 September 1990.

Seidenberg, Robert, "*Daddy Nostalgia,*" in *American Film* (New York), February 1991.

* * *

It is significant that Bertrand Tavernier's films have been paid little attention by the more important contemporary film critics/theorists:

his work is resolutely "realist," and realism is under attack in critical quarters. Realism has frequently been a cover for the reproduction and reinforcement of dominant ideological assumptions, and to this extent that attack is salutary. Yet Tavernier's cinema demonstrates effectively that the blanket rejection of realism rests on very unstable foundations. Realism has been seen as the bourgeoisie's way of talking to itself. It does not necessarily follow that its only motive for talking to itself is the desire for reassurance; nor need we assume that the only position realist fiction constructs for the reader/viewer is one of helpless passivity (Tavernier's films clearly postulate an alert audience ready to reflect and analyze critically).

Three of Tavernier's films, *Death Watch, Coup de torchon,* and *A Week's Vacation,* while they may not unambiguously answer the attacks on realism, strongly attest to the inadequacy of their formulation. For a start, the films' range of form, tone, and address provides a useful reminder of the potential for variety that the term "classical realist text" tends to obliterate. To place beside the strictly realist *A Week's Vacation* the futurist fantasy of *Death Watch* on the one hand and the scathing, all-encompassing caricatural satire and irony of *Coup de torchon* on the other is to illustrate not merely a range of subject-matter but a range of strategy. Each film constructs for the viewer a quite distinct relationship to the action and to the protagonist, analyzable in terms of varying degrees of identification and detachment which may also shift *within* each film. Nor should the description of *A Week's Vacation* as "strictly realist" be taken to suggest some kind of simulated cinéma-vérité: the film's stylistic poise and lucid articulation, its continual play between looking *with* the protagonist and looking *at* her, consistently encourage an analytical distance.

Through all his films, certainly, the bourgeoisie "talks to itself," but the voice that articulates is never reassuring, and bourgeois institutions and assumptions are everywhere rendered visible and opened to question. Revolutionary positions are allowed a voice and are listened to respectfully. This was clear from Tavernier's first film, *The Clockmaker,* among the screen's most intelligent uses of Simenon. Under Tavernier, the original project is effectively transformed by introducing the political issues that Simenon totally represses, and by changing the crime from a meaningless, quasi-existentialist *acte gratuit* to a gesture of radical protest. But Tavernier's protagonists are always bourgeois: troubled, questioning, caught up in social institutions but not necessarily rendered impotent by them, capable of growth and awareness. The films, while basically committed to a well-left-of-center liberalism, are sufficiently open, intelligent, and disturbed to be readily accessible to more radical positions than they are actually willing to adopt.

Despite the difference in mode of address, the three films share common thematic concerns (most obviously, the fear of conformism and dehumanization, the impulse towards protest and revolt, the difficulties of effectively realizing such a protest in action). They also have in common a desire to engage, more or less explicitly, with interrelated social, political, and aesthetic issues. The caustic analysis of the imperialist mentality and the kind of personal rebellion it provokes (itself corrupt, brutalized, and ultimately futile) in *Coup de torchon* is the most obvious instance of direct political engagement. *Death Watch,* within its science fiction format, is fascinatingly involved with contemporary inquiries into the construction of narrative and the objectification of women. Its protagonist (Harvey Keitel) attempts to create a narrative around an unsuspecting woman (Romy Schneider) by means of the miniature television camera surgically implanted behind his eyes. The implicit feminist concern here becomes the structuring principle of *A Week's Vacation.* Without explicitly raising feminist issues, the film's theme is the focusing of a contemporary bourgeois female consciousness, the consciousness of an intelligent and sensitive woman whose identity is not defined by her relationship with men, who is actively engaged with social problems (she is a schoolteacher), and whose fears (of loneliness, old age, death) are consistently presented in relation to contemporary social realities rather than simplistically defined in terms of "the human condition."

In Tavernier's films through the early 1990s, he has covered a wide variety of moods, styles and settings, with the most representative of these works linked by a common contemplative quality. His concerns are the passage of time and its effect on human relationships and the individual soul. In particular, he is interested in characters who are aged and ill, or have seen too much of the seamier aspects of human behavior. These latter works investigate how they come to terms with loved ones—especially their children.

A Sunday in the Country, set at the turn of the twentieth century, is the story of an elderly painter who resides in the country and is visited one Sunday by his reserved son and daughter-in-law, their three children, and his free-spirited daughter. The film is a pensive, poignant tale of old age and the choices people make in their lives. There is much drama and emotion in *Life and Nothing But,* a thoughtful war film which in fact takes place at a time when there is no fighting and bloodshed. Set after the conclusion of a war, the film concerns a soldier (Tavernier regular Philippe Noiret) who is assigned to chronicle his country's war casualties. Meanwhile, a couple of women have set out in search of their lovers, who are missing in action.

In *Round Midnight,* Tavernier caringly recreates the community of black jazz artists in exile in France. The film is a character study of an aged, alcoholic tenor sax legend, a composite of Bud Powell and Lester Young (and played by Dexter Gordon, himself a jazz great). He settles in Paris in 1959 and plays nightly at a famed jazz club; at the core of the story is his friendship with a young, adoring Frenchman, a dedicated jazz fan. Finally, in *Daddy Nostalgia,* the filmmaker examines the complex alliance between a father (Dirk Bogarde) and daughter (Jane Birkin). He is seriously ill; she visits him for an extended stay and attempts to understand their relationship, and his life.

Interestingly, in Tavernier's most recent films he has abandoned weighty themes for entertaining exercises in genre. *The Daughter of D'Artagnan* is a lightly likable comic swashbuckler, while *L.627* is a gritty police thriller.

We should not celebrate the resurgence of "bourgeois realism" in Tavernier's films (and they do not stand alone) without qualification or misgivings. Certainly, one regrets the failure of contemporary cinema to substantially follow up the radical experimentation with narrative that characterized the most interesting European films of the 1960s and 1970s. Nonetheless, Tavernier's work testifies to the continuing vitality and validity of a tradition many theorists have rejected as moribund.

—Robin Wood, updated by Rob Edelman

TAVIANI, Paolo and Vittorio

Nationality: Italian. **Born:** Paolo born in San Miniato, Pisa, 8 November 1931; Vittorio born in San Miniato, Pisa, 20 September 1929. **Education:** University of Pisa, Paolo in liberal arts, Vittorio in law. **Career:** With Valentino Orsini, ran cine-club at Pisa, 1950; with Cesare Zavattini, directed short on Nazi massacre at San Miniato; together and in collaboration with Orsini, made series of short documentaries, 1954-59; worked with Joris Ivens, Roberto Rossellini, and others, early 1960s; with Orsini, directed first feature, *A Man for Burning,* 1962. **Awards:** Best Film and International Critics Prize, Cannes Festival, for *Padre padrone,* 1977; Special Jury Prize, Cannes Festival, and Best director Award (shared), National Society of Film Critics, for *La notte di San Lorenzo,* 1982.

Films as Directors:

(documentary shorts, sometimes in collaboration with Valentino Orsini)

1954 *San Miniato, luglio '44*
1955 *Voltera, comune medievale*
1955-59 *Curtatone e Montanara*; *Carlo Pisacane*; *Ville della Brianza*; *Lavatori della pietra*; *Pittori in città*; *I Pazzi della domenica*; *Moravia*; *Carbunara*
1960 Episode of *L'Italia non è un paesa povero*

(features)

1962 *Un uomo da bruciare* (*A Man for Burning*) (co-d, co-sc)
1963 *I fuorilegge del matrimonio* (co-d, co-sc)
1967 *Sovversivi* (+ sc, + Vittorio in role)
1969 *Sotto il segno dello scorpione* (*Under the Sign of Scorpio*) (+ sc)
1971 *San Michele aveva un gallo* (+ sc)
1974 *Allonsanfan* (+ sc)
1977 *Padre padrone* (*Father Master*) (+ sc)
1979 *Il prato* (*The Meadow*) (+ sc)
1982 *La notte di San Lorenzo* (+ sc)
1983 *The Night of the Shooting Stars* (+ sc)
1984 ***Kaos***
1986 *Good Morning Babilonia* (*Good Morning Babylon*)
1990 *Il Sole anche di notte* (*Night Sun*) (+ co-sc)
1992 *Fiorile* (+ co-sc)

Publications

By the TAVIANIS: books—

San Michele aveva un gallo/Allonsafan, Cappelli, 1974.
Good Morning Babylon, with Tonino Guerra, London, 1987.

By the TAVIANIS: articles—

Interview with G. Mingrone and others, in *Filmcritica* (Rome), January 1972.
"Très longue rencontre avec Paolo et Vittorio Taviani," with J. A. Gili, in *Ecran* (Paris), July/August 1975.
"The Brothers Taviani," an interview with V. Glaessner, in *Cinema Papers* (Melbourne), January 1978.
Interview with Gary Crowdus, in *Cineaste* (New York), vol. 12, no. 3, 1983.
"Vittorio Taviani: An Interview," with P. Brunette, in *Film Quarterly* (Berkeley), Spring 1983.
Interview with F. Accialini and L. Coluccelli, in *Cineforum* (Bergamo), January 1985.
Interview with Robert Katz, in *American Film* (Washington D.C.), June 1987.
Interview with J.A. Gili, in *Positif* (Paris), June 1987.
Taviani, Paolo and Vittorio, "En promenad vid Villa Pamphili," in *Chaplin* (Stockholm), vol. 30, no. 2/3, 1988.
Interview, in *Cinema* (Paris), June 1990.
Taviani, Paolo and Vittorio, "Fou rire," in *Cahiers du Cinema* (Paris), May 1991 (supplement).
Interview, in *Positif* (Paris), June 1993.
"Your Own Reality: An Interview with Paolo and Vittorio Taviani," with David Ehrenstein, in *Film Quarterly* (Berkeley), Summer 1994.

On the TAVIANIS: books—

Aristarco, Guido, *Sotto il segno dello Scorpione: il cinema dei fratelli Taviani: con un saggio sul film di Valentino Orsini I dannati della terra,* Messina, Florence, 1977.
Camerino, Vincenzo, *Dialettica dell'utopia: il cinema di Paolo e Vittorio Taviani,* Manduria, 1978.
Accialini, Fulvio, *Paolo e Vittorio Taviani,* Florence, 1979.
Ferrucci, Riccardo, editor, *La bottega Taviani: un viaggio nel cinema di San Miniato a Hollywood,* Florence, 1987.
Orto, Nuccio, *La notte dei desideri: il cinema dei fratelli Taviani,* Palermo, 1987.
De Santi, Pier Marco, *I film di Paolo e Vittorio Taviani,* Rome, 1988.

On the TAVIANIS: articles—

Aristarco, Guido, "Dall'utile attraverso il vero verso il bello," in *Cinema Nuovo* (Turin), September/October 1974.
Zambetti, S., editor, "Speciale Taviani," in *Cineforum* (Bergamo), October 1974.
Mitchell, T., "Towards Utopia, By Way of Research, Detachment, and Involvement," in *Sight and Sound* (London), no. 3, 1979.
Ranvaud, Don, "A Tuscan Romance," in *Monthly Film Bulletin* (London), December 1982.
Yakir, Dan, "The Tavianis," in *Film Comment* (New York), March/April 1983.
Quart, Leonard, "A Second Look," in *Cineaste* (New York), vol. 16, no. 1/2, 1987/1988.
Timm, M., article in *Chaplin* (Stockholm), vol. 30, no. 1, 1988.
Romney, Jonathan, "Family Tussles Tuscan-style," *New Statesman & Society,* 24 March 1995.

* * *

Since the early 1960s, when they realized that fiction feature films were going to be their main interest, Paolo and Vittorio Taviani have written scenarios and scripts, designed settings, developed a filmmaking style and philosophy, directed a dozen features, and patiently explained their methods and concepts to many interviewers and audiences in Italy and abroad.

Although influenced to some extent by neorealism—such as the films of Rossellini and De Santis, characterized by on-location settings, natural lighting, authentic environmental sounds, non-professional actors, and an emphasis on "the people" as protagonists—the Tavianis want reviewers to see their films as invented and staged, as interpretations of history rather than as documentaries. They draw upon their early interests and background—as youngsters they saw musicals and concerts but not movies—and use artistic and technical means and methods similar to those utilized in theater and opera. Their films in which music is part of plot and theme reveal an inventory of flutes, accordions, record players, radios, human singing voices, folk tunes, opera, and oratorio (mostly Italian but also German), and even "The Battle Hymn of the Republic."

The photography in their films takes the eye back to the horizon or across a huge field, far along a road or deep into the front of a church or schoolroom. Even casual viewers must realize the frequent alternation of intense close-ups and long shots that never cease to remind one of locale. In addition, thoughts and dreams are often given visual expression: A picture of a girl and her brother studying on a couch follows her interior monologue about missing the long yellow couch in her living room (*La notte di San Lorenzo*); a prisoner in solitary confinement for ten years creates a world of sound and sight expressed on the screen (*San Michele aveva un gallo*).

With theatrical form and technique serving as the framework for their political cinema, and complex, individualistic characters as protagonists, the Tavianis are as concerned with corruption, abuse of power, poverty, and suffering as were the neorealists and their successors. Struck by the autobiography of Gavino Ledda, which became their well-received *Padre Padrone,* they investigate the abuse of power by a father, compelled by tradition and his own need to survive to

Paolo and Vittorio Taviani directing *La notte di San Lorenzo*

keep his son a slave. Amazingly, the illiterate, virtually mute shepherd boy whom a quirk of fate (army service) rescues from lifetime isolation becomes a professor of linguistics through curiosity, will, and energy. In *Un uomo da Bruciare* Salvatore, who wants to help Sicilian peasants break the Mafia's hold, is complex, intellectual, and egotistical.

Other themes and topics in Taviani films include divorce, revolution as an ongoing effort interrupted by interludes of other activity, the changing ways of dealing with power and corruption, resistance in war, fascism, and the necessity of communal action for accomplishment. The Tavianis use the past to illuminate the present, show the suffering of opposing sides, and stress the major role of heritage and environment. Their characters ask questions about their lives that lead to positive solutions (and sometimes to failure). The two directors believe in the possibility of an eventual utopia.

In 1987 the Tavianis made their first English-language film, *Good Morning Babylon,* a poetic, sweetly nostalgic ode to the origins of cinema and the invulnerability of great art. Their scenario chronicles the plight of two Italian-born siblings whose ancestors are craftsmen who for centuries have restored cathedrals. They arrive in America during the 1920s and end up designing sets for D. W. Griffith's *Intolerance.*

This was followed by two works as outstanding as any of their earlier films. *Il Sole anche di notte (Night Sun),* adapted from Tolstoi's "Father Sergius," is the story of a young man who is deeply troubled by the knowledge that he exists in a world of temptation and hypocrisy. He sees that too many of his fellow humans seek sex and status, and then turn to religion only to ease their guilt. All he wishes is to find inner tranquility, so he becomes a monk—and even cuts off his finger rather than give in to his desires and allow himself to be seduced by a temptress. A sensitive man who only wishes to make the world a better place, Father Sergius only can end up disappointed; he becomes an eternal wanderer, forever seeking the true meaning of his life and existence. Ultimately, the Tavianis are able to elicit a special sensitivity toward the human condition in the film.

Fiorile is linked to *Night Sun* as an intricate, sardonic tale of tainted innocence. While on his way from Paris to Tuscany to visit his sick, hermit-like father, whom he hasn't seen in a decade, a man discloses to his two young children the story of their ancestry. He commences by telling them of the nefarious means by which their forefathers became rich during the Napoleonic era—and how this wealth became a family curse for future generations. In *Fiorile,* the Tavianis examine the manner in which ill-gotten affluence will tarnish the soul and only result in misery. While their films are not lacking in political content—they keenly illustrate how greed, cruelty, lust for power, and temptation will wither one's soul—the cinema of Paolo and Vittorio Taviani is one of a simple, but never simplistic, humanism.

—Lillian Schiff, updated by Rob Edelman

TIAN Zhuangzhuang

Nationality: Chinese. **Born:** People's Republic of China, 1952. **Education:** Trained at the Beijing Agricultural Film Studio, 1975; admitted to the Beijing Film Academy, 1978. **Career:** Directed first feature for TV, 1980. **Awards:** Palme d'Or, Cannes Film Festival, for *The Blue Kite*, 1994.

Films as director:

1980 *Our Corner* (for TV)
1982 *The Red Elephant* (co-d with Zhang Jianya)
1984 *September*
1985 *On the Hunting Ground*; ***Daoma Zei*** (*Horse Thief*)
1986 *Travelling Players*
1988 *Rock 'n' Roll Kids*
1990 *Feifa Shengming*
1991 *Li Lianying, the Imperial Eunuch*
1993 ***Lan Fengzheng*** (*The Blue Kite*)

Other Films:

1992 *Family Portrait* (assoc pr)

Publications

On TIAN: books—

Semsel, George, editor, *Chinese Film: The State of the Art in the People's Republic,* New York, 1987.
Berry, Chris, editor, *Perspectives on Chinese Cinema,* London, 1991.
Chow, Rey, *Primitive Passions: Visuality, Sexuality, Ethnography, and Contemporary Chinese Cinema,* New York, 1995.

On TIAN: articles—

Clark, Paul, "Ethnic Minorities in Chinese Films: Cinema and the Exotic," in *East-West Film Journal* (Honolulu, Hawaii), June 1987.
Marchetti, Gina, "Two from China's Fifth Generation: Interviews with Chen Kaige and Tian Zhuangzhuang," in *Continuum* (Ontario), vol. 2, no. 1, 1988/89.
Berry, Chris, "Race: Chinese Film and the Politics of Nationalism," in *Cinema Journal* (Austin, Texas), Winter 1992.
Scofield, Aislinn, "Tibet: Projections and Perceptions," in *East-West Film Journal* (Honolulu, Hawaii), January 1993.
Lopate, Phillip, "Odd Man Out: Tian Zhuangzhuang," in *Film Comment* (New York), July/August 1994.

* * *

Tian Zhuangzhuang: *Lan Fengzheng*

Tian Zhuangzhuang began his career as part of what has become known as the "Fifth Generation" of film directors from the People's Republic of China. He is fairly representative of that group for a number of reasons. Like Chen Kaige, for example, he comes from a family already established in Chinese film circles; Tian's mother, a major film star, headed the Beijing Children's Film Studio for many years, and his father, an actor, headed the Chinese National Film Bureau at one time. Also, like many of his contemporaries who were in their teens or early twenties during the Great Proletarian Cultural Revolution, he joined the army and traveled extensively, visiting remote parts of China few "city kids" with an intellectual family background would have seen without the political and social upheaval of that period. Tian became a photographer at this time, and it is this period in his life that undoubtedly provided the impetus for many of his subsequent film features.

Marked by a politicized youth, Tian and others of his generation began to search for a sense of themselves as artists, as part of a Chinese culture and civilization, as national subjects, as men and women, when they matured in the post-Mao era. Many, including Zhang Yimou, Chen Kaige, the late Zhang Nuanxin, and Tian Zhuangzhuang, looked to those remote areas of China, where questions of identity have historically been perceived as more fluid: the dry, barren, western deserts, the forbidding northern frontier at the edges of the Great Wall, the distinct non-Han (not part of the majority ethnic group of Han Chinese) areas of Mongolia, Tibet, and Manchuria, and the lush jungles and wetlands of the southern border with Thailand and Vietnam. Rather than looking for models of exemplary behavior among a revolutionary elite, these filmmakers searched for Chinese identity among the poor, the illiterate, the unenlightened, the dispossessed of these border regions.

Tian Zhuangzhuang is perhaps the best known of this group for reviving and revitalizing a staple of the Chinese film industry—the "national minority" genre. Made to celebrate the solidarity of the Chinese people under the Communist regime, these films, often made by studios based in the minority areas themselves, showcased the songs, dances, customs, and patriotism of the non-Han community. Stories of liberation, they usually contrast the "backwardness" of traditional life before the Revolution with the benefits of Chinese Communist rule. Tian's *On the Hunting Ground,* made in Inner Mongolia, and *Horse Thief,* set in Tibet, fall within the rough parameters of this genre. However, Tian's work marks a radical break with the aesthetics of earlier generations of Chinese filmmakers. Rather than placing minority peoples within a narrative of liberation accessible to the average Han Chinese viewer, Tian, in *On the Hunting Ground,* for example, emphasizes the relationship between the land and the people. Long shots and long takes dominate; the landscape overpowers any identification with individual characters; dialogue, which is minimal, goes untranslated; rituals and social relationships remain unexplained. The Mongolian steppes—exotic, violent, harsh, and picturesque—become the visual embodiment of an unfathomable part of the Chinese nation, a marker of the limits of an ethnic identity. Clearly, this distance signals that this film may say more about Tian as the eye of the camera, an outsider, an intruder, than about the Mongolians as objects of his observations. These films are not about the plight of a downtrodden "minority" (although the people presented in Tian's films are indeed poor and sometimes desperate), rather these are films about the liminality of Chinese ethnicity and, by implication, political authority, within its own borders. After the Cultural Revolution, a generation became "outsiders" in their own nation, stripped of political certainty and a clear sense of an ethnic, national, and gendered self. (It is not coincidental that *On the Hunting Ground* and *Horse Thief* are peopled principally by non-Han men engaged in "manly," often violent and bloody occupations like hunting, since political, economic, and cultural uncertainties often play themselves out as a search for a more certain sense of gender—a nostalgia for a time or a yearning for a place where "men are men.")

In *Horse Thief,* Tian continues to explore the issues he outlined in *On the Hunting Ground.* However, this film follows a more conventional path, and centers its narrative around the tribulations of Rorbu, the horse thief of the title, who attempts to change his ways after the death of his son. Set before the Chinese annexation of Tibet, the film could be read as a pre-Revolutionary indictment of traditional Tibetan nomads. However, the spectacular images the camera lingers over—from the beauty of the mountains to the grizzly "sky burials," featuring vultures picking the bones of human cadavers, and the other, unexplained Buddhist rites that form the backbone of the film—take attention away from the protagonist and his ethical and economic dilemmas. Rather, like *On the Hunting Ground, Horse Thief* challenges the viewer with an unexplained and unexplainable "otherness" that defies easy recuperation into a Han sense of self. The analogy to the filmmaker's own predicament again becomes clear. Investigating the Tibetan horse thief, an outlaw from a still recalcitrant "minority" nation, takes on the trappings of an investigation of the filmmaker's own sense of self and otherness, rather than of a call for a "free" Tibet or an enlightened, subdued, "revolutionary" Tibet to cure Rorbu's ills. This is an aesthetic search for a new way of depicting China, and a visual call for a reinvention of Chinese cinema.

Ironically, the free experimentation that Tian's earlier work exemplified has been tempered less by government censorship (although Tian has had some problems) and more by the growing pressures on Chinese filmmakers to fit into the new market economy and make films that make money. *Rock 'n' Roll Kids,* for example, exploited interest in rock music among Chinese youth. *Travelling Players,* based on a well-known literary source, followed a more gritty road with its itinerant minstrels; however, *Li Lianying, the Imperial Eunuch* is, in most respects, a conventional costume drama, made on the coattails of films like Bertolucci's *The Last Emperor,* to exploit international interest in pre-Republican palace intrigue and spectacle.

The Blue Kite marks another stage in Tian's career. Almost a companion piece to Zhang Yimou's *To Live, The Blue Kite* takes an epic view of post-Liberation China, primarily focusing on the years of the Cultural Revolution, through the eyes of Tietou, "Iron Head," an innocent who becomes the victim of senseless violence brought on by political turmoil. Although suppressed by the government, *The Blue Kite* still found its way into the international festival circuit and has enjoyed commercial distribution as an "art film" abroad. After its screening at the Cannes Film Festival without official permission, however, Tian was not able to work in the Chinese film industry again until very recently (as an executive producer rather than director). Given that the Chinese government itself is delighted to decry the excesses of the Cultural Revolution publicly in the international press, the controversy generated by the film must spring from an allegorical reading of Tietou as hard-headed China herself, innocent, tough, but ultimately vulnerable and naive. Perhaps Tietou is too much like Tian's generation as a group, victims of and witnesses to a corruption that may or may not be endemic to a system or an era or an identity, and undeniably, like Tietou's family, complicit in that corruption. Like the minority peoples of his earlier films, the child Tietou acts as a mirror of the preoccupations of a generation, and this film functions as a bridge to the more experimental works of Tian's oeuvre.

—Gina Marchetti

TORNATORE, Guiseppe

Nationality: Italian. **Born:** Bagheria, Palermo, Italy, 27 May 1956. **Career:** Directed first film at age sixteen, *Il Carreto,* 1972; directed documentaries and films for Italian television, 1970s-1980s; earned

Giuseppe Tornatore (right) on the set of *L'uomo delle stelle*

international acclaim with *Cinema Paradiso,* 1988. **Awards:** Best Documentary, Salerno Festival, 1982, for *Ethnic Minorities in Sicily;* Academy Award for Best Foreign Language Film, Special Jury Prize at Cannes Festival, and British Academy of Film and Television Arts Awards for Best Original Screenplay and Best Foreign Language Film, all 1988, all for *Cinema Paradiso.* **Address:** via Santamaura 7, Rome, Italy.

Films as Director:

1982 *Ethnic Minorities in Sicily* (doc)
1986 *Il Camorrista* (*The Professor*) (+ sc)
1988 *Nuovo Cinema Paradiso* (*Cinema Paradiso*) (+ sc, story)
1990 *Stanno Tutti Bene* (*Everybody's Fine*) (+ sc)
1991 *La Domenica Specialmente* (*Especially on Sunday*) (segment)
1994 *Una pura formalita* (*A Pure Formality*) (+ sc)
1995 *L'uomo delle stelle* (*The Star Man*) (+ co-sc, ed); *Lo schermo a tre punte* (*The Three-Cornered Screen*) (doc)

Publications

By TORNATORE: article—

Interview in *Cineforum* (Bergamo), May 1989.

On TORNATORE: articles—

Haberman, Clyde, "*Cinema Paradiso* Blows a Kiss to the Movies," *New York Times,* 28 January 1990.
"Oscar on the Shelf and Back to Work," *Variety* (New York), 2 May 1990.

* * *

An overview of the career of Giuseppe Tornatore begins and ends with his delightful, beloved ode to the magic of the cinema, the multi-award-winning *Cinema Paradiso.* That film became an instant classic. Unfortunately, Tornatore has not yet made another film to approach its greatness.

Tornatore began his career as a documentarian and directed for Italian television. His first feature, *Il Camorista,* released as a theatrical film and a five-part television mini-series, is a by-the-numbers account of a famous Neapolitan underworld figure.

There is nothing in *Il Camorista* to hint that Tornatore's next feature would be one of the content and quality of *Cinema Paradiso,* at once an exhilarating comedy-drama and a charming nostalgia piece set during the immediate post-World War II period. Its scenario charts the manner in which Alfredo, a small-town movie projectionist (wonderfully played by Philippe Noiret), comes to affect the life of Salvatore, a precocious little boy (the equally winning Salvatore Cascio). The child becomes enchanted by the local movie house and endeavors to befriend the brusque but ultimately kindly projectionist. Salvatore grows up to become a famous filmmaker, who returns to his town after many years to attend his mentor's funeral. More than anything else *Cinema Paradiso* is a valentine to the art of cinema.

Everybody's Fine, Tornatore's follow-up to *Cinema Paradiso,* proved to be a major letdown. Unlike *Cinema Paradiso,* its nostalgia is far more painful than pleasant. It tells the story of Matteo Scuro (Marcello Mastroianni), an elderly Sicilian who is absorbed in his memories and who travels through Italy to make surprise calls on his five adult children. The point of the story is that the realities of children's lives often are far removed from their parents' dreams and hopes. The son who presents himself as a notable politician actually is a minor cog in a political hierarchy; the successful model-actress daughter really is a lowly underwear model; the son who is not present upon Matteo's arrival later is revealed to have committed suicide. The combination of sentimentality and dramatic power which was so effective in *Cinema Paradiso* here seems strained and manipulative.

Tornatore next directed the first segment of a four-part feature (only the first three of which were released in the United States), *Especially on Sunday.* His short film, about an ornery barber (Philippe Noiret) who is humorously annoyed by a dog, is paper-thin. *A Pure Formality,* despite its potentially powerhouse casting of Gerard Depardieu and Roman Polanski, is simply dreadful—a muddled existential mystery about a murder suspect (Depardieu) being interrogated by a police inspector (Polanski). *The Star Man* is another thin comedy about a hustler who cons unsuspecting Sicilian villagers. In his most recent film, Tornatore returns to his roots as a documentarian in *The Three-Cornered Screen,* a survey of the manner in which his beloved Sicily has been depicted in the movies.

—Rob Edelman

TORRE NILSSON, Leopoldo

Nationality: Argentinian. **Born:** Buenos Aires, 5 May 1924, son of filmmaker Leopoldo Torres Rios. **Family:** Married writer Beatriz Guido. **Career:** Assistant to father, from 1939; with father, directed first feature, 1949; began working with Guido, 1957; founder of production company Producciones Angel, 1959; signed contract with Columbia to make *El ojo de la cerradura,* 1964. **Awards:** International Critics Prize, Cannes Festival, for *Hands in the Trap,* 1961. **Died:** 8 September 1978.

Films as Director:

1947 *El muro* (*The Wall*) (short)
1950 *El crimen de Oribe* (*Oribe's Crime*) (co-d)
1953 *El hijo del crack* (*Son of the "Star"*) (co-d); *La Tigra* (*The Tigress*)

Leopoldo Torre Nilsson: ***La mano en la trampa***

1954 *Días de odio* (*Days of Hate*)
1955 *Para vestir* (*The Spinsters*)
1956 *El protegido* (*The Protégé*); *Graciela*
1957 *La casa del ángel* (*End of Innocence*; *The House of the Angel*) (+ co-sc with Beatriz Guido, based on Guido novel); *Precursores de la pintura argentina* (short) (Guido: sc); *Los arboles de Buenos-Aires* (short) (Guido: sc)
1958 *El secuestrador* (*The Kidnapper*) (+ sc)
1959 *La cáida* (*The Fall*) (+ co-sc with Guido); *Fin de fiesta* (*The Party Is Over*; *The Blood Feast*) (Guido: sc)
1960 *Un guapo del 900* (+ co-pr)
1961 *La mano en la trampa* (*The Hand in the Trap*) (Guido: sc); *Piel de verano* (*Summer Skin*) (+ pr, Guido: sc)
1962 *Setenta veces siete* (*The Female: 70 Times 7*) (Guido: sc); *Homenaje a la hora de la siesta* (*Homage at Siesta Time*) (Guido: sc); *La terraza* (*The Terrace*) (Guido: sc)
1964 *El ojo de la cerradura* (*The Eavesdropper*) (Guido: sc)
1965 *Once Upon a Tractor* (for United Nations) (Guido: sc)
1966 *La chica del lunes* (*Monday's Child*) (Guido: sc); *Los traidores de San Angel* (*The Traitors of San Angel*) (Guido: sc); *Cavar un foso* (*To Dig a Pit*) (Guido: sc)
1968 *Martin Fierro* (Guido: sc)
1969 *El santo de la espada* (*The Knight of the Sword*) (Guido: sc)
1970 *Güemes—La terra en armas* (Guido: sc)
1972 *La maffia* (*The Mafia*) (Guido: sc)
1973 *Los siete locos* (*The Seven Madmen*) (Guido: sc)
1974 *Boquitas pintadas* (*Painted Lips*) (Guido: sc)
1975 *Diario de la guerra del cerdo* (*La guerra del cerdo*; *Diary of the Pig War*) (Guido: sc); *El pibe cabeza* (Guido: sc)
1976 *Piedra libre* (Guido: sc)

Other Films:

1975 *Los gauchos judíos* (*Jewish Gauchos*) (co-pr)

Publications

By TORRE NILSSON: book—

Entre sajones y el arrabal, edited by Jorge Alvarez, Buenos Aires, 1967.

By TORRE NILSSON: articles—

Interview, in *Cuadernos de cine* (Buenos Aires), October 1954.
Interview with Hector Grossi, in *Mundo Argentino* (Buenos Aires), February 1957.
Interview, in *Tiempo de cine* (Buenos Aires), October 1960.
"How to Make a New Wave," in *Films and Filming* (London), November 1962.
Interview with I. León Frías and R. Bedoya, in *Hablemos de Cine* (Lima), April 1979.

On TORRE NILSSON: books—

Martin, Jorge Abel, *Los films de Leopoldo Torre Nilsson,* Buenos Aires, 1980.
Barnard, Tim, *Argentine Cinema,* Toronto, 1986.
King, John, and Nissa Torrents, editors, *Argentine Cinema: The Garden of Forking Paths,* London, 1988.

On TORRE NILSSON: articles—

Trajtenberg, Mario, "Torre-Nilsson and His Double," in *Film Quarterly* (Berkeley), Fall 1961.
Di Nubila, Domingo, "An Argentine Partnership," in *Films and Filming* (London), September 1961.
Botsford, Keith, "Leopoldo Torre-Nilsson: The Underside of the Coin," in *Show* (Hollywood), November 1962.
"Director of the Year," in *International Film Guide 1967,* London, 1966.
Cozarinsky, E., "Torre-Nilsson Remembered," in *Sight and Sound* (London), no. 1, 1978-79.
Mahieu, A., "Revisión Crítica del cine Argentino," in *Cine Cubana* (Havana), vol. 104, 1984.

* * *

Leopoldo Torre Nilsson's international reputation is based on a handful of films made in the late 1950s and at the very beginning of the 1960s, but his career as a director spanned three decades. In addition, through his father, the director Leopoldo Torre Rios, he had direct links with the pioneering days of Argentine cinema. Born in Buenos Aires of part Spanish-Catholic, part Swedish-Protestant ancestry, he began his involvement with cinema at the age of fifteen, when he became his father's assistant. In all, he worked as assistant director on sixteen of his father's films. He also scripted ten features in the 1940s before making his directing debut with a short film, *El Muro,* in 1947. His feature debut, *El Crimen de Oribe,* the first of two films co-directed with his father, already shows some signs of his future concerns: literary adaptation (the film was from a short story by Adolfo Bioy Casares) and stylistic experiment. The same is true of his first solo feature, *Dias de Odio,* adapted from "Emma Zunz," a story by Jorge Luis Borges.

Torre Nilsson himself regarded his first five films as an independent director as apprentice efforts, and certainly they achieved little commercial success in Argentina. He reached maturity as a director and far wider international audiences in 1957, when he began his collaboration with the novelist Beatriz Guido, whom he subsequently married. Complementary personalities, they proved a highly successful team, with Guido creating a claustrophobic world and sets of characters ideally suited to her husband's virtuoso camerawork and concern with symbolic detail. Three highly successful films starring the young Elsa Daniel exemplify the qualities of the pair. *The House of the Angel* provided an acid picture of upper middle-class life in Buenos Aires in the 1920s (a combination of puritanical religion and political corruption) but its central theme is the destruction of virginal innocence, for it features an adolescent heroine bound forever to the man who has half-seduced, half-raped her on the eve of a duel.

The director then evoked with great force and conviction the enclosed, Cocteau-esque world of *The Fall,* which combined the sexual tensions of a young governess with the amorality of the four wild children who become her charges. In 1961 Torre Nilsson adapted two further novels by his wife, both of which depicted a young woman at odds with her elders and caught in a trap of her own devising. In *The Hand in the Trap,* one of the director's most successful works, Elsa Daniel uncovers the secret of her aunt's withdrawal from the world and arranges a confrontation with the man who jilted her. But the cost of this curiosity is high, since she herself falls victim to the same seducer and realizes that she will live out her aunt's story all over again. *Summer Skin,* which shows the director at his brilliant visual best, is a further tale of lost innocence, with Graciela Borges playing a girl who sells herself as "companion" to her dying cousin. The film has an open-air setting of beach and summer resort, but like the previous films it portrays a morally corrupt society.

Even at this period of his greatest acclaim, Torre Nilsson achieved comparatively little success with films outside this narrow range, such as *The Kidnapper,* a study of poverty, or his films on history and politics, *The Party is Over* and *A Tough Guy of 1900.* Torre Nilsson's subsequent attempts to widen the scope of his filmmaking received a mixed reception. Films in which he tried to combine his literary and historical concerns with the requirements of local commercial formulas received little international attention, but his constant struggle to maintain an independent voice made him an important figure within Argentina. He managed to continue working through the difficult years of censorship until two years before his death, when his last feature, *Piedra libre* (1976) was banned. But his reputation rests essentially on the handful of stylish depictions of corruption and loss of innocence which made such an impact on the art cinema and international festival circuits of the years around 1960.

—Roy Armes

TOURNEUR, Jacques

Nationality: American/French. **Born:** Paris, 12 November 1904, son of director Maurice Tourneur; became U.S. citizen, 1919. **Education:** Attended Hollywood High School. **Family:** Married actress Christianne (died). **Career:** Moved to United States with family, 1914; office boy at MGM, 1924, later actor; script clerk for father's last six American films; moved to Paris, edited father's films, 1928; directed first film, in France, 1931; 2nd unit director for MGM, Hollywood, 1935; directed shorts, then B features, from 1939; director for producer Val Lewton at RKO, from 1942; television director, from late 1950s. **Died:** In Bergerac, 19 December 1977.

Films as Director:

1931 *Un vieux garçon*; *Tout ça ne vaut pas l'amour*
1933 *La Fusée*; *Toto*; *Pour être aimée*
1934 *Les Filles de la concierge*
1939 *They All Came Out*; *Nick Carter, Master Detective*
1940 *Phantom Raiders*
1941 *Doctors Don't Tell*
1942 ***Cat People***
1943 *I Walked with a Zombie*; *The Leopard Man*
1944 *Days of Glory*; *Experiment Perilous*
1946 *Canyon Passage*
1947 ***Out of the Past*** (*Build My Gallows High*)
1948 *Berlin Express*
1949 *Easy Living*
1950 *The Flame and the Arrow*; *Stars in My Crown*
1951 *Circle of Danger*; *Anne of the Indies*
1952 *Way of a Gaucho*
1953 *Appointment in Honduras*
1955 *Stranger on Horseback*; *Wichita*
1956 *Great Day in the Morning*
1957 *Nightfall*; *Night of the Demon* (*Curse of the Demon*)
1958 *The Fearmakers*
1959 *Timbuktu*; *La battaglia di Maratona* (*The Battle of Marathon*); *Frontier Rangers* (originally for TV)
1963 *The Comedy of Terrors*
1965 *War Gods of the Deep* (*City Under the Sea*)

Other Films:

1923 *Scaramouche* (Ingram) (role)
1927 *The Fair Co-ed* (Wood) (role); *Love* (Goulding) (role)
1929 *The Trail of '98* (Brown) (role)

Publications

By TOURNEUR: articles—

"Taste without Clichés," in *Films and Filming* (London), November 1956.
Interview with Patrick Brion and Jean-Louis Comolli, in *Cahiers du Cinéma* (Paris), August 1966.
Interview, in *The Celluloid Muse,* edited by Charles Higham and Joel Greenberg, London, 1969.

On TOURNEUR: books—

Siegel, Joel, *Val Lewton: The Reality of Terror,* London, 1972.
Henry, Michel, *Jacques Tourneur, Dossiers du Cinéma,* Paris, 1974.
Selby, Spencer, *Dark City: The Film Noir,* London, 1990.

On TOURNEUR: articles—

Sarris, Andrew, "Esoterica," in *Film Culture* (New York), Spring 1963.
Noames, Jean-Louis, "Trois Tourneur," in *Cahiers du Cinéma* (Paris), May 1964.
Tavernier, Bertrand, "Propos de Tourneur," in *Positif* (Paris), November 1971.
Wood, Robin, "The Shadow Worlds of Jacques Tourneur," in *Film Comment* (New York), Summer 1972.
Henry, M., "Le Jardin aux sentiers qui bifurquent (Sur Jacques Tourneur)," in *Positif* (Paris), April 1973.
McCarty, John, "The Parallel Worlds of Jacques Tourneur," in *Cinefantastique* (Oak Park, Illinois), Summer 1973.
Passek, J.L., "Jacques Tourneur," in *Cinéma* (Paris), February 1978.
Turner, G., "*Out of the Past,*" in *American Cinematographer* (Los Angeles), March 1984.

* * *

The first director Val Lewton hired for his RKO unit was Jacques Tourneur, and the first picture made by that unit was *Cat People,* an original screenplay by DeWitt Bodeen.

When Tourneur's father, Maurice, returned to Paris after a number of years in America, Jacques had gone with him, working as assistant director and editor for his father. In 1933, he made a few directorial solos in the French language and then returned to Hollywood, where he became an assistant director at MGM. It was at this time that he first met Val Lewton, and the two young men worked as special unit directors for Jack Conway on *A Tale of Two Cities*; it was Lewton and Tourneur who staged the storming of the Bastille sequence for that film.

Tourneur remained at MGM, directing over 20 short subjects, and Lewton eventually went on to become David O. Selznick's story editor. When Lewton left Selznick to head his own production unit at RKO, he had already made up his mind that Tourneur would direct his first production. Tourneur came to RKO, where he served as director for Lewton's first three films—*Cat People, I Walked With a Zombie,* and *The Leopard Man.* The front office held his work in such esteem that he was given the "A" treatment—solo direction of a high-budget film called *Days of Glory,* which was Gregory Peck's first starring film. It was not held against him that *Days of Glory* bombed. Tourneur immediately turned to another high budget picture at RKO—*Experiment Perilous,* starring Hedy Lamarr with Paul Lukas and George Brent. Under Tourneur's skillful direction, it became a suspenseful mood period film, certainly one of his and Hedy Lamarr's best.

Tourneur stayed on at RKO to direct Robert Mitchum in one of his finest pictures, *Out of the Past* (aka *Build My Gallows High*), as well as an excellent melodrama, *Berlin Express,* starring Merle Oberon and

Robert Ryan with Paul Lukas. Filmed partially in Berlin, the work was the first Hollywood picture to be made in Germany since the end of the war.

Tourneur then directed three excellent westerns for his friend Joel McCrea—*Stars in My Crown, Stranger on Horseback,* and *Wichita,* which featured McCrea as Wyatt Earp. He also directed *The Flame and the Arrow,* starring Burt Lancaster, and *Great Day in the Morning,* another RKO western with Robert Stack and Virginia Mayo. He then went back to make another horror picture in England, *Night of the Demon,* with Dana Andrews. This film is rated as highly as those he made for Lewton.

Television direction occupied the greater part of Tourneur's time for the next decade, but he retired in 1966 and returned to his native country, where he died in Bergerac on December 19, 1977. The best pictures which he directed were those of suspense and genuine terror, though he also did well with those that had a great deal of action. He wisely resisted scenes with long patches of dialogue. When confronted with such scenes, he typically frowned and said, "It sounds so corny."

—DeWitt Bodeen

TOURNEUR, Maurice

Nationality: French/American. **Born:** Maurice Thomas in Paris, 2 February 1876; became U.S. citizen, 1921. **Education:** Educated at Lycée Condorcet. **Military Service:** Military service in artillery, late 1890s. **Family:** Married Fernande Petit (stage name Van Doren), 1904 (separated 1927), son Jacques Tourneur. **Career:** Illustrator and graphic and interior designer, from 1894; assistant to Auguste Rodin and Puvis de Chavannes; actor, then stage director, from 1900; actor, then director for Eclair films, from 1912; moved to United States, 1914; production head of Paragon studio, 1915; contracted to Jesse Lasky for three Olga Petrova vehicles, 1917; formed own production company, 1918; moved to California, contracted to Paramount, formed Associated Producers Inc. with Thomas Ince and others (failed 1921), 1919; moved to Universal, 1920; quit direction of *The Mysterious Island,* returned to France, 1926; son Jacques edited films, from 1930. **Died:** 1961.

Films as Director:

1912 *Le Friquet* (+ sc); *Jean la poudre* (+ sc); *Le Système du Docteur Goudron et du Professeur Plume*; *Figures de cire*
1913 *Le Dernier Pardon* (+ sc); *Le Puits mitoyen*; *Le Camée*; *Sœurette* (+ sc); *Le Corso rouge*; *Mademoiselle 100 millions*; *Les Gaites de l'escadron* (+ sc); *La Dame de Montsoreau* (+ sc)
1914 *Monsieur Lecocq* (+ sc); *Rouletabille I: Le Mystère de la chambre jaune* (+ sc); *Rouletabille II: La Dernière Incarnation de Larson* (+ sc); *Mother* (+ sc); *The Man of the Hour* (+ sc); *The Wishing Ring* (+ sc); *The Pit*
1915 *Alias Jimmy Valentine* (+ sc); *The Cub*; *Trilby* (+ sc); *The Ivory Snuff Box* (+ sc); *A Butterfly on the Wheel*; *Human Driftwood*
1916 *The Pawn of Fate*; *The Hand of Peril* (+ sc); *The Closed Road* (+ sc); *The Rail Rider*; *The Velvet Paw*
1917 *A Girl's Folly*; *The Whip*; *The Undying Flame*; *Exile*; *The Law of the Land* (+ sc); *The Pride of the Clan*; *The Poor Little Rich Girl*; *Barbary Sheep*; *The Rise of Jennie Cushing*
1918 *Rose of the World*; *A Doll's House*; *The Blue Bird*; *Prunella*; *Woman*; *Sporting Life*
1919 *The White Heather*; *The Life Line*; *Victory*; *The Broken Butterfly* (+ co-sc)
1920 *My Lady's Garter*; *The County Fair*; *Treasure Island*; *The White Circle*; *Deep Waters*; *The Last of the Mohicans*
1921 *The Bait*; *The Foolish Matrons*
1922 *Lorna Doone*
1923 *While Paris Sleeps* (made in 1920); *The Christian*; *The Isle of Lost Ships*; *The Brass Bottle*; *Jealous Husbands*
1924 *Torment* (+ co-sc); *The White Moth*
1925 *Never the Twain Shall Meet*; *Sporting Life* (+ sc) (remake); *Clothes Make the Pirate*
1926 *Aloma of the South Seas*; *Old Loves and New*; *The Mysterious Island* (co-d, sc)
1927 *L'Equipage* (+ co-sc)
1929 *Das Schiff der verlorene Menschen* (*Le Navire des hommes perdus*)
1930 *Accusée, levez-vous*
1931 *Maison de danses*; *Partir ...* (*Partir!*)
1932 *Au nom de la loi*; *Les Gaites de la escadron* (+ co-sc); *L'Idoire* (+ co-sc)
1933 *Les Deux Orphelines* (+ co-sc); *L'Homme mysterieux* (*Obsession*)
1934 *Le Voleur*
1935 *Justin de Marseille*
1936 *Konigsmark*; *Samson*; *Avec le sourire*
1938 *Le Patriote*; *Katia*
1940 *Volpone*
1941 *Péchés de jeunesse*; *Mam'zelle Bonaparte*
1942 *La Main du diable*
1943 *Le Val d'enfer*; *Cecile est morte*
1947 *Après l'amour*
1948 *L'Impasse des deux anges*

Other Films:

1920 *The Great Redeemer* (Brown) (supervisor)

Publications

By TOURNEUR: articles—

"Stylization in Motion Picture Direction," in *Motion Picture* (New York), September 1918.
Interview with M.S. Cheatham, in *Motion Picture Classic* (Brooklyn), February 1920.
Article, in *Film Comment* (New York), July/August 1976, reprinted from *Shadowland,* May 1920.

On TOURNEUR: articles—

Haskins, H., "Work of Maurice Tourneur," in *Motion Picture Classic* (Brooklyn), September 1918.
Geltzer, George, "Maurice Tourneur," in *Films in Review* (New York), April 1961.
Sight and Sound (London), Autumn 1961 (also notes and corrections, Winter 1961).
Beylie, Claude, "Tombeau de Tourneur," in *Cahiers du Cinéma* (Paris), January 1962.
Koszarski, Richard, "Maurice Tourneur: The First of the Visual Stylists," in *Film Comment* (New York), March/April 1973.
Deslandes, J., "Maurice Tourneur—films parlants 1930/1948," in *Avant-Scène du Cinéma* (Paris), 15 June 1977.

Maurice Tourneur

Brownlow, Kevin, letter, in *American Classic Screen* (Shawnee Mission, Kansas), Fall 1979.
Tourneur Section of *Griffithiana* (Pordenone), 1988.

* * *

Maurice Tourneur is one of the greatest pictorialists of the cinema, deriving his aesthetic from his early associations with Rodin and Puvis de Chavannes. Having worked for André Antoine as an actor and producer, he joined the Eclair Film Company in 1912 and travelled to their American Studios at Fort Lee, New Jersey, in 1914. There he directed films based on successful stage plays. In *The Wishing Ring* it is possible to see the charm and visual beauty he brought to his work. His team consisted of John van der Broek, the cameraman who later tragically drowned during one of Tourneur's productions; Ben Carré, the art director; and Clarence Brown, his editor, who would later achieve fame as Garbo's favorite director.

Tourneur was most literate in his pronouncements on the cinema, individualistic and iconoclastic at times. He saw the cinema in perspective and would not concede it a status equal to the other arts. He stated: "To speak of the future development of the art of the cinema is futile. It cannot be. It costs a great deal of money to produce a motion picture. The only way the financial backer can get his money back, to say nothing of a profit, is to appeal to the great masses. And the thing that satisfies millions cannot be good. As Ibsen once wrote, it is the minority which is always right." In practice, however, Tourneur's own work belied this statement. To everything he did he brought a sense of beauty and great responsibility to his audiences.

Tourneur directed Clara Kimball Young in *Trilby,* Mary Pickford in *Pride of the Clan* and *Poor Little Rich Girl,* the latter a very successful film. He made three films with Olga Petrova. In 1918 five memorable films came from his hand: Elsie Ferguson appeared in his *The Doll's House*; two other stage plays, *The Bluebird* by Maeterlinck and *Prunella* by Granville Barker, gave Tourneur full scope for his visual style; *Woman* was a series of episodes that dealt with Adam and Eve, Claudius and Messalina, Heloise and Abelard, a Breton fisherman and a mermaid. and a Civil War story; and *Sporting Life* was significant for its absence of stars and its depiction of a fog-ridden London, anticipating Griffith's *Broken Blossoms* of the following year.

In 1919 Tourneur made Joseph Conrad's *Victory* for Paramount. A year later, he unveiled a delightful *Treasure Island* with Shirley Mason (as Jim Hawkins) and Lon Chaney, who also starred in *While Paris Sleeps.* For Associated Producers he made *The Last of the Mohicans,* which many consider to be his masterpiece, although Clarence Brown took over direction when Tourneur fell ill during production.

Tourneur's remaining Hollywood films included *Lorna Doone, The Christian, The Isle of Lost Ships, The Brass Bottle, The White Moth, Never the Twain Shall Meet,* and *Aloma of The South Seas.* During the production of *The Mysterious Island* for MGM, however, Tourneur grew resentful of a producer's interference. He walked off the set and returned to France. He continued to work in films in Europe, his first being *L'Equipage.* In 1929 he made *Das Schiff der Verlorene* in Germany with Marlene Dietrich. This was his last silent film, but he accepted the coming of sound and, before his death in 1961, he had made over 20 sound films. The most important of these were *Les Deux Orphelines,* the delightful *Katia* with Danielle Darieux, *Volpone* with Harry Baur and Louis Jouvet, *La Main du diable,* made from a story by Gerard de Nerval and featuring Pierre Fresnay, and his last film, *L'Impasse des deux anges.*

Tourneur was a man who had no illusions about working in films. He realized the limitations of Hollywood and the films he was given to direct. However, he brought his considerable talent as a designer to bear on his work, and did not hesitate to experiment. He stylized his sets and was influenced by new movements in the theater, but he also used the effects of nature to heighten his dramas. His awareness of the potentialities of the camera was profound, giving strength to his images.

—Liam O'Leary

TROELL, Jan

Nationality: Swedish. **Born:** Limnhamm, Skane, 23 July 1931. **Career:** Teacher, Sorgenfri primary school, Malmo, for nine years; made short documentaries about life in Malmo, 1960-65; made epic-length chronicles of Swedish history and contemporary life, including *Har har du ditt liv* (*Here Is Your Life*), 1966, and the two-part saga *Utvandrarna* (*The Emigrants*) and *Nybyggarna* (*The New Land*), 1970; later films abroad include *Zandy's Bride* (1974), *Hurricane* (1979) in Bora Bora, and *Ingenjor andrees luftfard* (*The Flight of the Eagle*), 1982; returned to documentary filmmaking with his most ambitious project to date, *Sagolandet* (*The Fairytale Country*), an eighty-hour chronicle of Swedish contemporary life, 1988. **Awards:** State Prize, Swedish Film Institute, for *Johan Ekberg*; Grand Prix, Oberhausen, for *Stopover*; Golden Bear, Berlin Film Festival, for *Who Saw Him Die?*; four Academy Award nominations for *The Emigrants,* and a Best Foreign-Language Film Academy Award nomination for *The Flight of the Eagle.*

Films as Director:

1960 *Stad*
1961 *Baten* (*The Ship*); *Sommartag* (*Summer Train*); *Nyar i Skane* (*New Year's Eve in Skane*)
1962 *Pojken och draken* (*A Boy and His Kite*) (with Bo Widerberg); *Var i Dalby hage* (*Spring in the Pastures of Dalby*)
1964 *De gamla kvarnen* (*The Old Mill*); *Trakom* (*Trachoma*); *Johan Ekberg*
1965 *Portratt av Asa* (*Portrait of Asa*); *Uppehall i myrlandet* (*Stopover in the Marshland*) (episode in *Four by Four*)
1966 *Har har du ditt liv* (*Here Is Your Life*)
1968 *Ole dole doff* (*Who Saw Him Die?*; *Eeny Meeny Miny Moe*)
1970 *Utvandrarna* (*The Emmigrants*); *Nybyggarna* (*The New Land*; *Unto a Good Land*)
1974 *Zandy's Bride*
1977 *Bang!*
1979 *Hurricane*
1982 *Ingenjor andrees luftfard* (*The Flight of the Eagle*)
1988 *Sagolandet* (*The Fairytale Country*)
1991 *Il Capitano*

Other Films:

1963 *Barnvagnen* (*The Baby Carriage*) (Bo Widerberg) (lighting cameraman)

Publications

By TROELL: books—

Jan Troell (portrait and interview), Swedish Film Institute (Stockholm), 1975.

By TROELL: articles—

"John Simon on Jan Troell," interview in *Film Heritage* (New York), Summer 1974.

"Filmmaking in Sweden," in *Interview* (New York), no. 1, n.d.

On TROELL: book—

Cowie, Peter, editor, *Sweden* (Screen Series, Vols. 1 and 2), Stockholm, 1970.

On TROELL: articles—

Landau, Jon, "*The New Land,*" in *Rolling Stone* (New York), 6 December 1973.

Crist, Judith, "A Repast of Things Remembered," *New York,* 27 May 1974.

Steen, Brigitta, "An Interlude with Jan Troell," *Thousand Eyes* (New York), 4 March 1976.

Monaco, James, "Look Back: *Zandy's Bride,*" *Millimeter* (New York), 8 April 1976.

Gilliatt, Penelope, "*Hurricane,*" in *New Yorker,* 23 April 1979.

Chase, Chris, "At the Movies: Jan Troell Calm about Oscar Bid," *New York Times,* 8 April 1983.

Thomas, Kevin, "*Here Is Your Life* Launches UCLA Jan Troell Retrospective," *Los Angeles Times,* 8 January 1990.

Garrett, Robert, "The Journey Outward: The Films of Jan Troell," *Boston Globe,* 16 February 1990.

* * *

"We are the last dinosaurs of Swedish film," lamented Ingmar Bergman to Jan Troell in 1983. At the time neither could yet claim to be an elder statesman—Bergman was sixty-five at the time and Troell was only fifty-two—but both had lived and worked long enough to find themselves somewhat estranged from their own profession. Frequently cited as Sweden's two greatest filmmakers, they have much else in common. Both are fiercely independent artists, trained in film and television, who have made their slow and patient way as chroniclers and critics of the history, myths, and institutions of their native land.

As director, photographer, and editor of his films, Troell has retained an unusual degree of control for most of his career. His films are invariably pictorially beautiful, stylistically conservative, and moderately paced. Excepting an occasional foray into contemporary life, his subjects have been mostly historical in nature.

Troell's first projects drew upon his experiences as a boy and later as a teacher in his native town of Malmo, in the southernmost province of Skane. *Baten* (*The Ship,* 1961) was a documentary about the last journey of the *SS Malmo,* which for many years had carried passengers to Copenhagen. *Sommartag* (*Summer Train,* 1961) was a nostalgic tribute to an Osterlen locomotive. And *Nyar i Skane* (*New Year's Eve in Skane*) recalled the Scanian plains of his childhood.

After winning a state prize for *Johan Ekberg,* a sensitive documentary about a retired railroad worker's coming to terms with old age, and the Oberhausen Grand Prix for *Uppehall i myrlandet* (*Stopover in the Marshland,* 1965), a short film with Max von Sydow as a railroad brakeman, Troell was ready for the most productive phase of his career. Between 1966 and 1979, under the aegis of the Svensk Filmindustry and producer Bengt Forslung, he made eight ambitious features. First came *Har har du ditt liv* (*Here Is Your Life,* 1966), based on Eyvind Johnson's four-volume autobiographical novel. The 167-minute film, the longest Swedish feature made up to that time, was set in the decade after World War I. It is Troell's most picaresque work, a coming-of-age saga of young Olof (Eddie Axberg), who, on the way to becoming a writer, leaves school and survives colorful encounters on the railroad, at a timber camp, in a sawmill, and as a movie projectionist. The serio-comic tone, convoluted editing, and unusual color technique (interspersing black-and-white and color sequences) relates it to the French New Wave, while Troell's characteristic empathy for his characters links him with earlier masters like Sweden's Victor Sjostrom and France's Jean Renoir. Critic Vernon Young admired its sense of the passage of time—a trait to be found in most of Troell's later works. "You don't just *watch* the film, you *live* through it."

Ole dole doff (*Who Saw Him Die?* 1968), by contrast a far more subdued and dark tale of a teacher (Per Oscarsson) alienated from his students, was shot at the Malmo school where Troell himself had taught. Particularly successful, in the opinion of Peter Cowie, was Troell's ability to convey "telling images" of loneliness and despair in the parks, docks, and streets of Malmo.

Troell's best films are concerned with people who measure their dreams and test their characters against the hostilities and vicissitudes of weather and landscape. Perhaps no other director in Swedish film history, save Victor Sjostrom, has as consistently explored this theme. *The Emigrants* and *The New Land* (made in 1970 and released in America three years later), his most famous and most popular films, were based on Vilhelm Moberg's quartet of novels about the emigration of the family of Karl and Kristina Nilsson (Max von Sydow and Liv Ullmann) to America in the mid-nineteenth century. A slow-breathing, deliberately paced story of hardship and survival, it also tracks the changing textures and moods of land and water, from the stony monochrome of the bleak Swedish farmland, to the tossing grey-blue of the pitiless ocean, to the bursting colors of the verdant Minnesota river country. In *Zandy's Bride* (1974) the spectacular vistas of California's Big Sur form the backdrop for the developing relationship between a pioneer rancher, Zandy (Gene Hackman), and his mail-order bride, Hannah (Liv Ullmann). *Hurricane* (1979), shot in Bora Bora, relates the inner turmoil of star-crossed lovers (Mia Farrow and Dayton Ka'ne) to the spectacular elemental fury of a South Seas storm. *The Flight of the Eagle* pits the fool-hardy ambitions of three Swedish explorers, who were bent on reaching the North Pole by balloon, against the implacable hostilities of the frozen wastes.

At first glance, Troell's most recent films might seem to indicate new directions. The ironically titled *Sagolandet* (*The Fairytale Country,* 1988), made for the Swedish Film Institute, is a rather dour, three-hour documentary about contemporary Swedish life. By means of location shooting and numerous interviews—with parliamentary and local politicians, a rural road planner, a plant exterminator, a woodsman, an artist-weaver, etc.—a portrait emerges of a tightly regulated nation where social and technical progress threaten free will and imagination. *Il Capitano* has a much narrower focus, an account of a real-life murder case that attempts to explain how two youths could murder three people in cold blood.

Yet both share Troell's concerns with the alienation of characters from the wellsprings of nature and tradition. There is no breathing room in a world cramped by partitions and conformity; there is no place for the independent and heroic gesture in a society where the machine and a welfare bureaucracy discourage initiative and achievement. Loneliness and isolation are the only rewards.

Troell has not been without his detractors. Many critics have justly complained of the inordinate length and plodding pace of works like *The New Land,* of the unrelieved bleakness of *The Flight of the Eagle,* and of the long intervals of silence in *Zandy's Bride* (indeed, Troell can be the *quietest* of filmmakers). His preoccupation with landscape photography in *Hurricane* aroused Penelope Gilliatt's scorn: "Never has there been so much surf, so much lashing of waves, such a tempest ... and you have never seen so many sunsets or so many pensive wanderings along beaches." Jon Landau characterized too many of his characters as "rigidly humorless and largely unchanging." Other attacks single out Troell's conventional—even old-fashioned—modes of narrative. "He tells a coherent story," defends Peter Cowie, "when

Jan Troell

gritty realism is the cameraman's mode, he persists with poetic imagery. For all this, Jan Troell rides not behind but above his time, resorting to cinema as a means of expressing man's better gifts."

His flaws and obsessions notwithstanding, it seems that the persuasive integrity and earnestness that Troell invests in his subjects has been so consistently maintained that it must eventually earn our respect. "He has the sense of the justice owed to people and the homage owed to nature," writes Pauline Kael. Critic John Simon adds: "You feel you are in the hands of a human being who cares about other human beings, who renders the truths of their lives without rending the veils of their privacy, who has sympathy even for what he deplores."

—John C. Tibbetts

TROTTA, Margarethe von *See* **VON TROTTA, Margarethe**

TRUFFAUT, François

Nationality: French. **Born:** Paris, 6 February 1932. **Education:** Attended Lycée Rollin, Paris. **Military Service:** Enlisted in army, but deserted on eve of departure for Indochina, 1951; later released for "instability of character." **Family:** Married Madeleine Morgenstern, 1957 (divorced), two daughters. **Career:** Founded own cine-club in Paris, lack of funds caused closing, was jailed for inability to pay debts, released with help of André Bazin, 1947; with Godard, Rivette, and Chabrol, member of Ciné-club du Quartier Latin, 1949; briefly employed by the Service Cinématographique of the Ministry of Agriculture, 1953; writer on film for *Cahiers du cinéma,* then *Arts,* from 1953, including seminal article, "Une Certain Tendance du cinéma français," in 1954; with Rivette and Resnais, made short 16mm film, 1955; assistant to Roberto Rossellini, 1956-58; directed first feature, *Les Quatre Cents Coups,* and wrote script for Godard's *A bout de souffle,* 1959; published *Le Cinéma selon Hitchcock,* 1966; instigated shutting down of 1968 Cannes Festival in wake of May uprisings. **Awards:** Best Director, Cannes Festival, for *Les Quatres Cents Coup,* 1959; Prix Louis Delluc, and Best Director, National Society of Film Critics, for *Stolen Kisses,* 1969; Acedemy Award for Best Foreign-Language Film, Best Director, National Society of Film Critics, Best Direction, New York Film Critics, and British Academy Award for Best Direction, for *Day for Night,* 1973. **Died:** Of cancer, in Paris, 21 October 1984.

Films as Director:

1955 *Une Visite* (+ sc, co-ed)
1957 *Les Mistons* (+ co-sc)
1958 *Une Histoire d'eau*

François Truffaut directing *Jules et Jim*

1959 ***Les Quatre Cents Coups*** (*The Four Hundred Blows*) (+ sc)
1960 ***Tirez sur le pianist*** (*Shoot the Piano Player*) (+ co-sc)
1961 ***Jules et Jim*** (*Jules and Jim*) (+ co-sc)
1962 "Antoine et Colette" episode of *L'Amour a vingt ans* (*Love at Twenty*) (+ sc, role)
1964 *La Peau douce* (*The Soft Skin*) (+ co-sc)
1966 *Fahrenheit 451* (+ co-sc)
1967 *La Mariée était en noir* (*The Bride Wore Black*) (+ co-sc)
1968 *Baisers volés* (*Stolen Kisses*) (+ co-sc)
1969 *La Sirène du Mississippi* (*Mississippi Mermaid*) (+ sc); *L'Enfant sauvage* (*The Wild Child*) (+ co-sc, role as Dr. Jean Itard)
1970 *Domicile conjugal* (*Bed and Board*) (+ co-sc)
1971 *Les Deux Anglaises et le continent* (*Two English Girls*) (+ co-sc)
1972 *Une Belle Fille comme moi* (*Such a Gorgeous Kid Like Me*) (+ co-sc)
1973 *La Nuit américaine* (*Day for Night*) (+ co-sc, role as Ferrand)
1975 *L'Histoire d'Adèle H.* (*The Story of Adele H.*) (+ co-sc)
1976 *L'Argent de poche* (*Small Change*) (+ co-sc)
1977 *L'Homme qui aimait les femmes* (*The Man Who Loved Women*) (+ co-sc)
1978 *La Chambre verte* (*The Green Room*) (+ co-sc, role as Julien Davenne)
1979 *L'Amour en fuite* (*Love on the Run*) (+ co-sc)
1980 *Le Dernier Metro* (*The Last Metro*) (+ sc)
1981 *La Femme d'à côté* (*The Woman Next Door*)
1984 *Vivement dimanche!* (*Finally Sunday*)

Other Films:

1977 ***Close Encounters of the Third Kind*** (Spielberg) (role as French scientist)

Publications

By TRUFFAUT: books—

Les Quatre Cent Coups, with Marcel Moussy, Paris, 1959; as *The Four Hundred Blows: A Film by François Truffaut*, New York, 1969.
Le Cinéma selon Hitchcock, Paris, 1967; revised edition published as *Hitchcock*, New York, 1985.
Ce n'est qu'un début, Paris, 1968.
Jules et Jim, New York, 1968.
The Adventures of Antoine Doinel: Four Autobiographical Screenplays, New York, 1971.
La Nuit américaine et le journal de tournage de Farenheit 451, Paris, 1974.

Day for Night, New York, 1975.
Les Films de ma vie, Paris, 1975; published as *The Films in My Life,* New York, 1978.
The Wild Child, New York, 1975.
Small Change, New York, 1976.
The Story of Adele H., New York, 1976.
L'Homme qui aimait les femmes, Paris, 1977.
The Last Metro, New Brunswick, New Jersey, 1985.
Truffaut par Truffaut, edited by Dominique Rabourdin, Paris, 1985; published as *Truffaut on Truffaut,* New York, 1987.
Le Plaisir des yeux, Paris, 1987.
François Truffaut: correspondence, edited by Gilles Jacob and Claude de Givray, Renens, 1988; published as *François Truffaut: Letters,* translated by Gilbert Adair, London, 1990.
La petite voleuse, with Claude de Givray, Paris, 1989.

By TRUFFAUT: articles—

"Une Certain Tendance du cinéma français," in *Cahiers du Cinéma* (Paris), January 1954.
"Renoir in America," with J. Rivette, in *Sight and Sound* (London), July/September 1954.
"La Crise d'ambition du cinéma français," in *Arts* (Paris), 30 March 1955.
Interview of Rossellini, with Maurice Scherer, in *Film Culture* (New York), March/April 1955.
"On the Death of André Bazin," in *Cahiers du Cinéma* (Paris), January 1959.
"On Film: Truffaut Interview," in the *New Yorker,* 20 February 1960.
"*Les Mistons,*" in *Avant-Scéne du Cinéma* (Paris), no. 4, 1961.
"*Histoire d'eau,*" in *Avant-Scéne du Cinéma* (Paris), no. 7, 1961.
"*Jules et Jim,*" in *Avant-Scéne du Cinéma* (Paris), June 1962.
"Sex and Life," in *Films and Filming* (London), July 1962.
"*Vivre sa vie,*" in *Avant-Scène du Cinéma* (Paris), October 1962.
"Sur le cinéma américaine," in *Cahiers du Cinéma* (Paris), December 1963 and January 1964.
"Skeleton Keys," in *Film Culture* (New York), Spring 1964.
"*La Peau douce,*" in *Avant-Scène du Cinéma* (Paris), May 1965.
"*Farenheit 451,*" (working notes by Truffaut), in *Cahiers du Cinéma* (Paris), February/July 1966.
"Jean-Luc Godard," in *Les Lettres Françaises* (Paris), 16 March 1967.
"Georges Sadoul," in *Les Lettres Françaises* (Paris), 18 October 1967.
"Ernst Lubitsch," in *Cahiers du Cinéma* (Paris), February 1968.
"Francoise Dorlèac," in *Cahiers du Cinéma* (Paris), April/May 1968.
"Is Truffaut the Happiest Man on Earth? Yes," in *Esquire* (New York), August 1970.
"*L'Enfant Sauvage,*" in *Avant-Scène du Cinéma* (Paris), October 1970.
"Intensification," an interview with Gordon Gow, in *Films and Filming* (London), July 1972.
"The Lesson of Ingmar Bergman," in *Take One* (Montreal), July 1973.
"A Portrait of Francois Truffaut," an interview with S. Mallow, in *Filmmakers Newsletter* (Ward Hill, Massachusetts), December 1973.
Interview with Charles Higham, in *Action* (Los Angeles), January/February 1974.
"Adèle H.," an interview with Gilbert Adair, in *Sight and Sound* (London), Summer 1975.
"François Truffaut: The Romantic Bachelor," with Melanie Adler, in *Andy Warhol's Inter/View* (New York), March 1976.
"Dialogue on Film: Interview with Truffaut," in *American Film* (Washington, D.C.), May 1976.
"Kid Stuff: François Truffaut on *Small Change,*" with J. McBride and T. McCarthy, in *Film Comment* (New York), September/October 1976.
"Truffaut, Part V," an interview in the *New Yorker,* 18 October 1976.
"François Truffaut: Feminist Filmmaker?," with Annette Insdorf, in *Take One* (Montreal), January 1978.
"Truffaut: Twenty Years After," an interview with D. Allen, in *Sight and Sound* (London), no. 4, 1979.
"My Friend Hitchcock," in *American Film* (Washington, D.C.), March 1979.
Interview with A. Gillain, in *Wide Angle* (Athens, Ohio), vol. 4, no. 4, 1981.
Interview with Marcel Ophuls, in *American Film* (New York), May 1985.

On TRUFFAUT: books—

Petrie, Graham, *The Cinema of François Truffaut,* New York, 1970.
Crisp, C.G., and Michael Walker, *François Truffaut,* New York, 1971.
Fanne, Dominique, *L'Univers de François Truffaut,* Paris, 1972.
Allen, Don, *Finally Truffaut,* London, 1973; revised edition, 1985.
Monaco, James, *The New Wave: Truffaut, Godard, Chabrol, Rohmer, Rivette,* New York, 1976.
Collet, Jean, *Le Cinéma de François Truffaut,* Paris, 1977; revised edition, 1985.
Insdorf, Annette, *François Truffaut,* Boston, 1978.
Walz, Eugene P., *François Truffaut: A Guide to References and Resources,* Boston, 1982.
Winkler, Willi, *Die Film von François Truffaut,* Munich, 1984.
Bergala, Alain, and others, *Le Roman de François Truffaut,* Paris, 1985.
De Fornari, Oreste, *I filme di François Truffaut,* Rome, 1986.
Dalmais, Hervé, *Truffaut,* Paris, 1987.
Ciment, Gilles, and others, *Les 400 Couples de François Truffaut,* Paris, 1988.
Guerif, François, *François Truffaut,* Paris, 1988.
Cahoreau, Gilles, *François Truffaut, 1932-84,* Paris, 1989.
Insdorff, Annette, *François Truffaut: le cinéma est-il magique?,* Paris, 1989.
Merrick, Hélène, *François Truffaut,* Paris, 1989.

On TRUFFAUT: articles—

Sadoul, Georges, "Notes on a New Generation," in *Sight and Sound* (London), October 1959.
Burch, Noël, "Qu'est-ce que la Nouvelle Vague?," in *Film Quarterly* (Berkeley), Winter 1959.
Farber, Manny, "White Elephant Art vs. Termite Art," in *Film Culture* (New York), Winter 1962/63.
Shatnoff, Judith, "François Truffaut—The Anarchist Imagination," in *Film Quarterly* (Berkeley), Spring 1963.
Taylor, Stephen, "After the Nouvelle Vague," in *Film Quarterly* (Berkeley), Spring 1965.
Klein, Michael, "The Literary Sophistication of François Truffaut," in *Film Comment* (New York), Summer 1965.
Braudy, Leo, "Hitchcock, Truffaut, and the Irresponsible Audience," in *Film Quarterly* (Berkeley), Summer 1968.
Wood, Robin, "Chabrol and Truffaut," in *Movie* (London), Winter 1969/70.
Bordwell, David, "A Man Can Serve Two Masters," in *Film Comment* (New York), Spring 1971.
Beylie, Claude, and others, "Le Continent, Truffaut et le deux anglaises," in *Ecran* (Paris), January 1972.
Jebb, Julian, "Truffaut: The Educated Heart," in *Sight and Sound* (London), Summer 1972.
Houston, Beverle, and Marsha Kinder, "Truffaut's Gorgeous Killers," in *Film Quarterly* (Berkeley), Winter 1973/74.
Lefanu, Mark, "The Cinema of Irony: Chabrol, Truffaut in the 1970s," in *Monogram* (London), no. 5, 1974.
Martin, Marcel, "Vingt ans après: une certain constante du cinéma français," in *Ecran* (Paris), January 1974.
Coffey, B., "Art and Film in François Truffaut's *Jules and Jim* and *Two English Girls,*" in *Film Heritage* (New York), Spring 1974.

Hess, J., "La Politique des auteurs: Part 2: Truffaut's Manifesto," in *Jump Cut* (Chicago), July/August 1974.

Thomas, P., "The Sorcerer's Apprentice: Bazin and Truffaut on Renoir," in *Sight and Sound* (London), Winter 1974/75.

Carcassonne, P., "Truffaut le narrateur," in *Cinématographe* (Paris), November 1977.

"*La Chambre vert* Issue" of *Avant-Scène du Cinéma* (Paris), 1 November 1978.

Tintner, A.R., "Truffaut's *La Chambre vert,*" in *Literature/Film Quarterly* (Salisbury, Maryland), vol. 8, no. 2, 1980.

"*Le Dernier Metro* Issue" of *Avant-Scène du Cinéma* (Paris), March 1983.

Turner, D., "Made in USA: The American Child in Truffaut's *400 Blows,*" in *Literature/Film Quarterly* (Salisbury, Maryland), April 1984.

Obituary in *Cahiers du Cinéma* (Paris), November 1984.

"Truffaut Issue" of *Cinéma* (Paris), December 1984.

"Truffaut Issue" of *Cinématographe* (Paris), December 1984.

Truffaut Section of *Wide Angle* (Baltimore), vol. 7, nos. 1/2, 1985.

Jameson, R. T., and others, in *Film Comment* (New York), January/February 1985.

Dixon, W., "François Truffaut: A Life in Film," in *Films in Review* (New York), June/July and August/September 1985.

"*Tirez sur le pianiste* and *Vivement dimanche!* Issue" of *Avant-Scène du Cinéma* (Paris), July/August 1987.

Moullet, Luc, "La balance et le lien," in *Cahiers du Cinéma* (Paris), July/August 1988.

Allen, Don, "Truffaut's *Miller's Tale,*" in *Sight and Sound* (London), Spring 1989.

* * *

François Truffaut was one of five young French film critics, writing for André Bazin's *Cahiers du cinéma* in the early 1950s, who became the leading French filmmakers of their generation. It was Truffaut who first formulated the *politique des auteurs,* a view of film history and film art that defended those directors who were "true men of the cinema"—Renoir, Vigo, and Tati in France; Hawks, Ford, and Welles in America—rather than those more literary, script-oriented film directors and writers associated with the French "tradition of quality." Truffaut's original term and distinctions were subsequently borrowed and translated by later generations of Anglo-American film critics, including Andrew Sarris, Robin Wood, V.F. Perkins, and Dave Kehr. When Truffaut made his first feature in 1959, *Les Quatre Cent Coups,* he put his ideas of cinema spontaneity into practice with the study of an adolescent, Antoine Doinel, who breaks free from the constrictions of French society to face an uncertain but open future. Since that debut, Truffaut's career has been dominated by an exploration of the Doinel character's future (five films) and by the actor (Jean-Pierre Léaud) whom Truffaut discovered to play Antoine. In Truffaut's 25 years of making films, the director, the Doinel character, and Léaud all grew up together.

The rebellious teenager of *Les Quatre Cent Coups* becomes a tentative, shy, sexually clumsy suitor in the "Antoine et Colette" episode of *Love at Twenty.* In *Baisers volés,* Antoine is older but not much wiser at either love or money making. In *Domicile conjugal,* Antoine has married but is still on the run toward something else—the exotic lure of other sexual adventures. And in *L'Amour en fuite,* Antoine is still running (running became the essential metaphor for the Doinel character's existence, beginning with the lengthy running sequence that concludes *Les Quatre Cent Coups*). Although Antoine is now divorced, the novel which he has finally completed has made his literary reputation. That novel, it turns out, is his life itself, the entire Doinel saga as filmed by Truffaut, and Truffaut fills his films with film clips that are both visual and mental recollections of the entire Doinel cycle. Truffaut deliberately collapses the distinction between written fiction and filmed fiction, between the real life of humans and the fictional life of characters. The collapse seems warranted by the personal and professional connections between Truffaut the director, Doinel the character, and Léaud the actor.

Many of Truffaut's non-Doinel films are style pieces that similarly explore the boundaries between art and life, film and fiction. The main character of *Tirez sur le pianist* tries to turn himself into a fictional character, as does Catherine in *Jules et Jim.* Both find it difficult to maintain the consistency of fictional characters when faced with the demanding exigencies of real life. *La Mariée etait en noir* was Truffaut's elegy to Hitchcock, a deliberate style piece in the Hitchcock manner, while *Fahrenheit 451,* his adaption of Ray Bradbury's novel, explores the lack of freedom in a society in which books—especially works of fiction—are burned. Adele H in *L'Histoire d'Adele H* attempts to convert her passion into a book (her diary), but life can neither requite nor equal her passion; instead, it drives her to madness and a total withdrawal from life into the fantasy of her romantic fiction. In *L'Homme qui aimait les femmes,* an incurable womanizer translates his desire into a successful novel, but the existence of that work in no way diffuses, alleviates, or sublimates the desire that vivified it. *The Green Room* is Truffaut's homage to fiction and the novelist's craft—a careful, stylish adaption of a Henry James story.

Given his conscious commitment to film and fiction, it is not surprising that Truffaut devoted one of his films to the subject of filmmaking itself. *La Nuit américaine* is one of the most loving and revealing films about the business of making films, an exuberant illustration of the ways in which films use artifice to capture and convey the illusion of life. This film, in which Truffaut himself plays a film director, is a comically energetic defense of the joys and pains of filmmaking, a deliberate response to the more tortured visions of Fellini's *8½* or Bergman's *Persona.*

Those Truffaut films not concerned with the subject of art are frequently about education. *L'Enfant sauvage* explores the beneficial power and effects of civilization on the savage passions of a child who grew up in the forest, apparently raised by beasts. Truffaut again plays a major role in the film (dedicated to Jean-Pierre Léaud), playing a patient scientist who effects the boy's conversion from savagery to humanity. Like the director he played in *La Nuit américaine,* Truffaut is the wise and dedicated patriarch, responsible for the well-being of a much larger enterprise. *L'Argent de poche* examines the child's life at school and the child's relationships with adults and other children. As opposed to the imprisoning restrictions which confined children in the world of *Les Quarte Cent Coups,* the now adult Truffaut realizes that adults—parents and teachers—treat children with far more care, love, and devotion than the children (like the younger, rebellious Truffaut himself) are able to see.

Unlike his friend and contemporary Jean-Luc Godard, Truffaut remained consistently committed to his highly formal themes of art and life, film and fiction, youth and education, and art and education, rather than venturing into radical political critiques of film forms and film imagery. Truffaut seems to state his position in *Le Dernier Métro,* his most political film, which examines a theater troupe in Nazified Paris. The film director seems to confess that, like those actors in that period, he can only continue to make art the way he knows how, that his commitment to formal artistic excellence will eventually serve the political purposes that powerful art always serves, and that for him to betray his own artistic powers for political, programmatic purposes would perhaps lead to his making bad art and bad political statements. In this rededication to artistic form, Truffaut is probably restating his affinity with the Jean Renoir he wrote about for *Cahiers du cinéma.* Renoir, like Truffaut, progressed from making more rebellious black-and-white films in his youth to more accepting color films in his maturity; Renoir, like Truffaut, played major roles in several of his own films; Renoir, like Truffaut, believed that conflicting human choices could not be condemned according to facile moral or political formulae; and Renoir, like Truffaut, saw the creation of art (and film art) as a genuinely humane and meaningful response to the potentially chaotic disorder of formless reality. Renoir, however, lived much longer than Truffaut, who died of cancer in 1984 at the height of his powers.

—Gerald Mast

ULMER, Edgar

Nationality: Austrian. **Born:** Edgar Georg Ulmer in Vienna, 17 September 1904. **Education:** Studied architecture at Academy of Arts and Sciences, Vienna; studied stage design at Burgteater, Vienna. **Family:** Married Shirley Castle, one daughter. **Career:** Designer for Decla-Bioscope film company, 1918; designer for Max Reinhardt, Vienna, 1919-22; designer for Universal in New York, 1923; returned to Germany as assistant to Murnau, 1924; returned to United States, art director and production assistant at Universal, from 1925; co-directed first film, with Robert Siodmak, 1929; art director at MGM and stage designer for Philadelphia Grand Opera Co., 1930-33; made public health documentaries for minority groups, New York, mid-1930s; director and writer for Producers' Releasing Corporation (PRC), Hollywood, 1942-46; worked in United States, Mexico, Italy, Germany, and Spain, through 1950s. **Died:** In Woodland Hills, California, 30 September 1972.

Films as Director:

(claimed to have directed 128 films; following titles are reported in current filmographies):

1929 *Menschen am Sonntag* (*People on Sunday*) (co-d, co-sc)
1933 *Damaged Lives* (+ co-sc); *Mr. Broadway*
1934 *The Black Cat* (+ co-sc); *Thunder over Texas* (d as "John Warner")
1937 *Green Fields* (co-d)
1938 *Natalka Poltavka* (+ sc, assoc pr); *The Singing Blacksmith* (+ pr); *Zaporosch Sa Dunayem* (*Cossacks in Exile*; *The Cossacks Across the Danube*)
1939 *Die Tlatsche* (*The Light Ahead*) (original title: *Fishe da Krin*) (+ pr); *Moon Over Harlem*; *Americaner Schadchen* (*The Marriage Broker*; *American Matchmaker*); *Let My People Live*
1940 *Cloud in the Sky*
1941 *Another to Conquer*
1942 *Tomorrow We Live*
1943 *My Son, the Hero* (+ co-sc); *Girls in Chains* (+ story); *Isle of Forgotten Sins* (+ story); *Jive Junction*
1944 *Bluebeard*
1945 *Strange Illusion* (*Out of the Night*); *Club Havana*; *Detour*
1946 *The Wife of Monte Cristo* (+ co-sc); *Her Sister's Secret*; *The Strange Woman*
1947 *Carnegie Hall*
1948 *Ruthless*
1949 *I pirati de Capri* (*Pirates of Capri*)
1951 *St. Benny the Dip*; *The Man from Planet X*
1952 *Babes in Bagdad*
1955 *Naked Dawn*; *Murder Is My Beat* (*Dynamite Anchorage*)
1957 *The Daughter of Dr. Jekyll*; *The Perjurer*
1960 *Hannibal*; *The Amazing Transparent Man*; *Beyond the Time Barrier*; *L'Atlantide* (*Antinea, L'amante della città Sepolta*); *Journey Beneath the Desert*) (co-d)
1964 *Sette contro la morte* (*Neunzing Nächte and ein Tag*)
1965 *The Cavern*

Other Films:

1927 ***Sunrise*** (Murnau) (asst prod des)
1934 *Little Man, What Now?* (set design)
1942 *Prisoner of Japan* (story)
1943 *Corregidor* (co-sc); *Danger! Women at Work* (co-story)

Publications

By ULMER: articles—

Interview, in *Cahiers du Cinéma* (Paris), August 1961.
Interview with Peter Bogdanovich, in *Film Culture* (New York), no. 58/60, 1974.

On ULMER: books—

Belton, John, *The Hollywood Professionals Vol. 3,* New York, 1974.
McCarthy, Todd, and Charles Flynn, editors, *Kings of the B's: Working Within the Hollywood System,* New York, 1975.
Belton, John, *Cinema Stylists,* Metuchen, New Jersey, 1983.

On ULMER: articles—

Moullet, Luc, "Edgar G. Ulmer," in *Cahiers du Cinéma* (Paris), April 1956.
Sarris, Andrew, "Esoterica," in *Film Culture* (New York), Spring 1963.
Belton, John, "Prisoners of Paranoia," in *Velvet Light Trap* (Madison, Wisconsin), Summer 1972; reprinted Winter 1977.
Beylie, Claude, "Edgar G. Ulmer, dandy de grand chemin," in *Ecran* (Paris), December 1972.
"*Le Chat Noir* Issue" of *Avant-Scène du Cinéma* (Paris), 1982.
Jenkins, Steve, "Ulmer and PRC: A Detour down Poverty Row," in *Monthly Film Bulletin* (London), July 1982.
Krohn, B., "King of the B's," in *Film Comment* (New York), July/August 1983.
Mandell, P., "Edgar Ulmer and *The Black Cat,*" in *American Cinematographer* (Los Angeles), October 1984.
Prédal, René, "L'usine aux maléfices," in *Avant-Scène du Cinéma* (Paris), March 1985.

* * *

The films of Edgar G. Ulmer have generally been classified as "B" pictures. However, it might be more appropriate to reclassify some of these films as "Z" pictures. On an average, Ulmer's pictures were filmed on a six-day shooting schedule with budgets as small as $20,000. He often worked without a decent script, adequate sets, or convincing actors. But these hardships did not prevent Ulmer from creating an individual style within his films.

Edgar Ulmer: David Manners and Julie Bishop in *The Black Cat*

Part of the look of Ulmer's films was, naturally, a result of their meager budgets. The cast was kept to a minimum., the sets were few and simple, and stock footage helped to keep costs down (even when it did not quite match the rest of the film). The length of the scripts was also kept to a minimum. Most of Ulmer's films ran only 60 to 70 minutes, and it was not uncommon for his pictures to open upon characters who were not formally introduced. Ulmer often plunged his audience into the middle of the action, which would add to their suspense as the story finally did unfold.

Characters in Ulmer's films commonly found themselves in strange and distant surroundings. This plight is especially true for the title character of *The Man from Planet X.* This curious being is stranded on earth (which from his point of view is an alien world) and is at the mercy of the strangers around him. In another example, the Allisons, a young couple on their honeymoon in *The Black Cat,* find themselves trapped in the futuristic home of the bizarre Mr. Poelzig. They are held against their will with all avenues of escape blocked off. Many of Ulmer's characters find that they are prisoners. Some of them are innocent, but many times they live in prisons of their own making.

Another theme that is prevalent in Ulmer's films is fate. His characters rarely have control over their own destiny, an idea verbalized by Al Roberts in *Detour,* who says, "whichever way you turn, Fate sticks out its foot to trip you." In *The Amazing Transparent Man,* a scientist who has been forced to work against his will on experiments with nuclear material explains that he "didn't do anything by choice." The Allisons in *The Black Cat* have no control over their destiny, either—their fate will be determined by the outcome of a game of chess. In most cases the characters in Ulmer's films find themselves swept away in a series of circumstances that they are unable to stop.

The critical recognition of Ulmer's work has been a fairly recent "discovery." Initial reviews of Ulmer's films (and not all of his films received reviews) were far from complimentary. Part of the reason for their dismissal may have been their exploitative nature. Titles like *Girls in Chains* and *Babes in Bagdad* could conceivably have some difficulty finding a respectable niche in the film world. Taken as a whole, however, the work of Edgar Ulmer reveals a personal vision that is, at the very least, different and distinctive from the mainstream of film directors.

—Linda Obalil

VADIM, Roger

Nationality: French. **Born:** Roger Vadim Plemiannikov in Paris, 26 January 1928. **Education:** Educated in political science; studied acting with Charles Dullin. **Family:** Married 1) Brigitte Bardot, 1952 (divorced); 2) Annette Stroyberg, 1958 (divorced), one child; child by Catherine Deneuve; 3) Jane Fonda, 1967 (divorced); 4) Catherine Schneider, 1975 (divorced), one child; 5) Marie-Christine Barrault, 1990. **Career:** Stage actor, 1944-47; assistant to Marc Allégret on

Juliette, 1953, and others; journalist for *Paris-Match,* and TV director, early 1950s; directed first film, *Et ... Dieu créa la femme,* 1956.

Films as Director:

1956 ***Et ... Dieu créa la femme*** (*And ... God Created Woman*) (+ co-sc)
1957 *Sait-on jamais?* (*No Sun in Venice*) (+ sc)
1958 *Les Bijoutiers du clair de lune* (*Heaven Fell That Night*; *The Night That Heaven Fell*) (+ co-sc)
1959 *Les Liaisons dangereuses* (+ co-sc)
1960 *Et mourir de plaisir* (*Blood and Roses*) (+ co-sc)
1961 *La Bride sur le cou* (*Please, Not Now!*) (co-d, uncredited, co-sc)
1962 "L'Orgueil" (Pride) episode of *Les Sept Pechées capitaux* (*Seven Deadly Sins*) (+ co-sc); *Le Repos du guerrier* (*Warrior's Rest*; *Love on a Pillow*) (+ co-sc)
1963 *Le Vice et la vertu* (*Vice and Virtue*) (+ co-sc, pr); *Château en Suede* (*Nutty Naughty Chateau*) (+ co-sc)
1964 *La Ronde* (*Circle of Love*) (+ co-sc, co-adapt)
1966 *La Curée* (*The Game Is Over*) (+ co-sc, pr)
1968 "Metzengerstein" episode of *Histoires extraordinaires* (*Spirits of the Dead*) (+ co-sc); *Barbarella* (+ co-sc)
1971 *Pretty Maids All in a Row*
1972 *Hellé* (+ story)
1973 *Don Juan 1973 ou si Don Juan était une femme* (*Ms. Don Juan*; *Don Juan, or If Don Juan Were a Woman*) (+ co-sc)
1974 *La Jeune Fille assassinée* (*Charlotte*) (+ pr, sc, role)
1976 *Une Femme fidèle* (+ co-sc)
1979 *Night Games*
1980 *The Hot Touch*
1981 *Art of Deceit*
1983 *Surprise Party*
1983 *Come Back*
1987 *Et Dieu créa la femme* (*And God Created Woman*)
1991 *Le Fou amoureaux* (+ sc)

Publications

By VADIM: books—

Les Liaisons dangereuses, with Roger Vailland and Claude Brulé, New York, 1962.
Memoirs of the Devil, New York, 1976.
The Hungry Angel, New York, 1984.
Bardot, Deneuve and Fonda: The Memoirs of Roger Vadim, London, 1986.

Roger Vadim

By VADIM: articles—

"Pretty Maids," in *Playboy* (Chicago), April 1971.
"Meeting the Gallic Svengali," an interview with M. Rosen, in *Millimeter* (New York), October 1975.
"So Who Created Vadim?," an interview with Marc Mancini, in *Film Criticism* (Meadville, Pennsylvania), vol. 24, no. 2, 1988.

On VADIM: books—

Carpozi, George Jr., *The Brigitte Bardot Story,* New York, 1961.
de Beauvoir, Simone, *Brigitte Bardot and the Lolita Syndrome,* London, 1961.
Frydland, Maurice, *Roger Vadim,* Paris, 1963.

On VADIM: articles—

Mardore, Michel, "Roger Vadim," in *Premier Plan* (Lyon), October 1959.
Burch, Noël, "Qu'est-ce que la Nouvelle Vague?," in *Film Quarterly* (Berkeley), Winter 1959.
Billard, G., "Ban on Vadim," in *Films and Filming* (London), November 1959.
Maben, A., "Vadim and Zola," in *Films and Filming* (London), October 1966.

* * *

With *Et ... Dieu créa la femme* Roger Vadim created the commercial climate which made the *nouvelle vague* possible. Despite this, his reputation as director has always lagged behind that as a connoisseur of the beautiful women who inhabit his films. His relationships with Brigitte Bardot, Annette Stroyberg, Catherine Deneuve, Jane Fonda, and others established him, in English-speaking countries at least, as the archetypal "French" director. The American retitling of *Le Repos du guerrier* as *Love on a Pillow,* and *Chateau en Suede* as *Nutty, Naughty Chateau,* glumly emphasizes his raffish image.

Vadim claims in his fanciful autobiography that a prostitute provided by producer Raoul Levy to relieve the tedium of screenwriting furnished him with rationale for Bardot's character in *Et ... Dieu créa la femme*—unselfishness. "If she's not interested in money, people won't think she's a whore." This motive recurs in Vadim's work, where generous, warm-hearted, and sensual women lavish their favors on indifferent, often evil love objects. Fulfillment comes only with death. In *La Jeune Fille assassiné,* Vadim even makes death in the throes of orgasm the sole ambition of his heroine, and his first American film, *Pretty Maids All in a Row,* casts Rock Hudson as an improbable mass-murdering psychiatrist in a girls' college.

For an artist with a single subject, Vadim has proved remarkably imaginative. *Sait-on jamais* exploits Venice with style, the Modern Jazz Quartet's chiming score harmonizing precisely with Vadim's romantic thriller. His lesbian vampire melodrama, *Et mourir de plaisir,* is among the lushest of horror films, enlivened by a clever use of color and a surrealist dream sequence which reminds one that he knew Cocteau and acted in *La Testament d'Orphée.* Jane Fonda never looked more beautiful than in the incest drama *La Curée,* and in *Barbarella* he turned Jean-Claude Forest's comic strip into something between Grand Guignol and an erotic *tableau vivant.* Even his lamentable American re-make of *Et ... Dieu créa la femme* transformed Rebecca de Mornay from rural tart into temptress.

Vadim is at his best in the high style, where the material encourages grand gestures. Bardot in *Le Repos du guerrier* standing like the Winged Victory in a ruined church, face turned into a torrent of wind; Stroyberg in an eighteenth-century white gown gliding through the cypresses of Hadrian's Villa to Jean Prodromides's score of harp and pizzicati strings in *Et mourir de plaisir*—these are images that briefly transcend the novelettish material from which they spring.

—John Baxter

VANDERBEEK, Stan

Nationality: American. **Born:** New York City, 1927. **Education:** Studied painting. **Family:** Married, two children. **Career:** Began making collage-films, early 1960s; built dome-studio ("The Movie-Drome") in Stony Point, New York, mid-1960s; university lecturer and teacher, from mid-1960s; worked at Bell Telephone Laboratory, Murray Hill, New Jersey, on experiments in computer graphics, late 1960s. **Awards:** First Prize in Animation, Bergamo Festival, for *Mankinda,* 1960. **Died:** 19 September 1984.

Films as Director:

1957 *What Who How*; *Mankinda*; *Astral Man*
1957-58 *One and Yet*
1958 *Ala Mode*; *Wheeeeels No.1*; *Visioniii*
1959 *Wheeeeels No. 2*; *Dance of the Looney Spoons*; *Science Friction*; *Achoo Mr. Keroochev*; *Street Meat* (documentary, not completed)
1960 *Skullduggery*; *Blacks and Whites in Days and Nights*
1961 *Snapshots of the City*
1961-62 *Misc. Happenings* (documentaries of Claus Oldenberg happenings); *Summit*
1964 *Breathdeath*; *Phenomenon No.1*
1965 *The Human Face Is a Monument*; *Variations No.5*; *Feedback*
1966 *Poem Field No.2*
1967 *See, Saw, Seems*; *Poem Field No.1*; *Man and His World*; *Panels for the Walls of the World*; *Poem Field No.5*; *Free Fall*; *Spherical Space No.1*; *The History of Motion in Motion*; *T.V. Interview*; *Poem Field No.7*
1968 *Newsreel of Dreams No.1*; *Vanderbeekiana*; *Oh*; *Super-Imposition*; *Will*
1968-70 *Found Film No.1*
1969 *Newsreel of Dreams No.2*
1970 *Film Form No.1*; *Film Form No.2*; *Transforms*
1972 *Symmetricks*; *Videospace*; *Who Ho Ray No.1*; *You Do, I Do, We Do*
1973 *Computer Generation*
1977 *Color Fields*
1978 *Euclidean Illusions*
1980 *Mirrored Reason*; *Plato's Cave Inn*; *Dreaming*
1981 *After Laughter*

Publications

By VANDERBEEK: articles—

"On *Science Friction,*" in *Film Culture* (New York), Summer 1961.
"The Cinema Delimina: Films from the Underground," in *Film Quarterly* (Berkeley), Summer 1961.
"If the Actor is the Audience," in *Film Culture* (New York), Spring 1962.
"Antidotes for Poisoned Movies," in *Film Culture* (New York), Summer 1962.

"Simple Syllogism," in *Film Culture* (New York), no. 29, 1963.
"Interview: Chapter One," in *Film Culture* (New York), no. 35, 1964/65.
"Compound Entendre," in *Film: A Montage of Theories*, edited by Richard MacCann, New York, 1966.
"*Culture: Intercom* and Expanded Cinema," in *Film Culture* (New York), Spring 1966.
"Re: Vision," in *American Scholar* (Washington, D.C.), Spring 1966.
"Disposable Art—Synthetic Media—and Artificial Intelligence," in *Take One* (Montreal), January/February 1969.
"Re Computerized Graphics," in *Film Culture* (New York), no. 48-49, 1970.
"Media (W)rap-around: Or a Man with No Close," in *Filmmakers Newsletter* (Ward Hill, Massachusetts), March 1971.
"Social-Imagistics: What the Future May Hold," in *American Film Institute Report* (Washington, D.C.), May 1973.
"Animation Retrospective," in *Film Comment* (New York), September/October 1977.

On VANDERBEEK: book—

Hanhardt, John, and others, *A History of the American Avant-Garde*, exhibition catalogue, The American Federation of Arts, New York, 1976.

On VANDERBEEK: articles—

Christgau, Robert, "Vanderbeek: Master of Animation," in *Popular Photography* (Boulder, Colorado), September 1965.
Manica, A., and W. Van Dyke, "Four Artists as Filmmakers," in *Art in America* (New York), January 1967.
"New Talent: the Computer," in *Art in America* (New York), January 1970.
Weiss, M.W., "VanDerBeek to Students: Take a High Risk," in *Journal of the University Film Association* (Carbondale), Spring 1982.
"Stan Vanderbeek Obituary," in *Film Comment* (New York), January/February 1985.

* * *

As was typical with a great number of experimental filmmakers, Stan Vanderbeek studied painting before actually beginning his film production. Indeed, his earliest films are animated collage pieces which embody his background in graphics (e.g. *Breathdeath*).

Vanderbeek's career spanned about a third of a century, a period of almost constant creativity with extraordinary amalgamations of media. As such, it is a difficult career to summarize, especially in light of the fact that no definitive list of his truly countless productions seems to exist. Vanderbeek appeared to exude creations at a rate that escaped even his own cataloguing.

Soon after Vanderbeek's early animation work, he focused upon a unique multi-projection apparatus of his own design. This "Movie-Drome" (at Stony Point, New York) provided the presentation of a number of "Vortex-Concerts," prototypes for a satellite-interconnected "Culture Intercom" that might allow better (and quicker) international communication. At the same time, he continued experiments with dance films, paintings, polaroid photography, architecture, 195-degree cinematography, and intermedia events.

Vanderbeek's more recent explorations of computer-generated images and video graphics provide a clear contemporary perspective for his career. In addition, they signalled a technostructural metamorphosis which marks the ongoing evolution of that major genre generally known as the "experimental film." Experimental filmmakers of Vanderbeek's prestige and prominence have, at times, found the fortune of industry support. In the late 1960s, Vanderbeek came to collaborate with such computer specialists as Ken Knowlton of New Jersey's Bell Telephone Laboratories. The result was a number of cathode-ray-tube mosaics called *Poem Fields*. Today these early exercises with computer graphic possibilities still retain aesthetic power as transparent tapestries in electronic metamorphosis. Typically brief, non-narrative and abstract, the various *Poem Fields* often reveal subtle, stunning *mandala* patterns, strikingly similar to classic Asian meditative devices with their symmetrical concentricity.

Vanderbeek's final projects also address electronically constructed imagery. Some of his work (such as *Color Fields*) employs the same interest in abstraction which characterized *Poem Fields*. Others (*Mirrored Reason*, made in video and released in film) are more representational and narrative. Still others (*After Laughter*) recall the rapidly paced irony that marked *Breathdeath* and other examples of Vanderbeek's earliest animation.

This noteworthy quantity, quality, and extraordinary technological diversity of output resulted in exceptional institutional support for Vanderbeek throughout the years. He was artist-in-residence at USC, Colgate, WGBH-TV, and NASA. His work was presented on CBS, ABC, and such CATV showcases as "Night Flight." His performances outside the United States took him to such cities as Berlin, Vienna, Tokyo, Paris, and Toronto; he has been a U.S.I.A. speaker in nations like Israel, Iran, Turkey, Greece, and England. His grants and awards are equally numerous and prestigious, and his academic recognition provided Vanderbeek not only with guest lectures and screenings throughout the United States, but faculty appointments at such schools as Columbia, Washington, and M.I.T.

—Edward S. Small

VAN DYKE, W. S.

Nationality: American. **Born:** Woodbridge Strong Van Dyke II, San Diego, California, 21 March 1889 (known by childhood name, "Woody"). **Military Service:** Mobilized as Marine Corps officer, 1941. **Career:** Debut as child actor, 1892; besides theatrical activities, worked as miner, electrician, music hall performer, and mercenary in Mexico, 1903-15; left theater, became assistant director for Essanay Studios, Chicago, 1915; assistant to D. W. Griffith, 1916; assistant to James Young at Paramount, directed first film, 1917; signed by Thalberg for MGM, 1926. **Died:** 4 February 1943.

Films as Director:

1917 *Her Good Name* (+ sc); *Clouds*; *Mother's Ordeal* (+ sc); *The Land of Long Shadows* (+ sc); *The Range Boss* (+ sc); *The Open Places* (+ sc); *The Men of the Desert* (+ sc); *Our Little Nell* (+ sc); *The Gift o' Gab* (+ sc); *Sadie Goes to Heaven* (+ sc)
1919 *Lady of the Dugouts* (+ co-sc)
1920 *Daredevil Jack* (+ co-sc); *The Hawk's Trail* (+ co-sc)
1921 *Double Adventure* (+ co-sc); *The Fortieth Door* (unfinished); *The Avenging Arrow* (co-d, + co-sc)
1922 *White Eagle* (co-d, + co-sc); *Ruth of the Range* (d of action scenes); *The Milky Way*; *According to Hoyle*; *Forget Me Not*; *The Boss of Camp Four*
1923 *The Girl Next Door* (*You Are in Danger*); *The Destroying Angel*; *The Miracle Makers*; *Half-a-Dollar Bill*
1924 *Loving Lies*; *The Battling Fool*; *The Beautiful Sinner*; *Winner Takes All*; *Gold Heels*
1925 *The Chicago Fire* (*Barriers Burned Away*); *Ranger of the Big Pines*; *The Trail Rider*; *Hearts and Spurs*; *The Timber Wolf*; *The Desert's Prince*

W. S. Van Dyke

1926 *The Gentle Cyclone*; *Eyes of the Totem*; *The Heart of the Yukon* (+ co-sc)

(For Metro-Goldwyn-Mayer):

1926 *War Paint* (*Rider of the Plains*); *Winners of the Wilderness*
1927 *Under the Black Eagle*; *California*; *Foreign Devils*; *The Adventurer* (*The Gallant Gringo*) (completed film); *Spoilers of the West*; *Wyoming* (+ co-sc)
1928 *White Shadows in the South Seas* (co-d)
1929 *The Pagan*
1931 *Trader Horn* (+ co-dialogue); *Guilty Hands*; *Never the Twain Shall Meet*; *The Cuban Love Song* (*Rumba*)
1932 *Tarzan the Ape Man*; *Night Court* (*Justice for Sale*)
1933 *Penthouse*; *The Prizefighter and the Lady* (*Every Woman's Man*) (+ co-pr); *Eskimo* (*Mala the Magnificent*) (+ co-sc)
1934 *Laughing Boy*; *Manhattan Melodrama*; ***The Thin Man***; *Hide Out*; *The Painted Veil* (completed film); *Forsaking All Others*
1935 *Naughty Marietta*; *I Live My Life*; *A Tale of Two Cities* (co-d); *Rose Marie*
1936 *His Brother's Wife* (*Lady of the Tropics*); *San Francisco* (+ co-pr); *The Devil Is a Sissy* (*The Devil Takes the Count*); *Love on the Run*; *After the Thin Man* (*Nick, Gentleman Detective*)
1937 *Personal Property* (*Man in Possession*); *They Gave Him a Gun*; *The Prisoner of Zenda* (d of action scenes); *Rosalie*
1938 *Marie Antoinette*; *Sweethearts*; *Stand Up and Fight*
1939 *It's a Wonderful World*; *Andy Hardy Gets Spring Fever*; *Another Thin Man*; *I Take This Woman*
1940 *I Love You Again*; *Bitter Sweet*
1941 *Rage in Heaven*; *The Feminine Touch*; *Shadow of the Thin Man*; *Dr. Kildare's Victory* (*The Doctor and the Debutante*); *I Married an Angel*; *Cairo*; *Journey for Margaret*
1943 *Dragon Seed* (completed by Jack Conway and Harold Bucquet)

Other Films:

1915 *The Raven* (asst d); *A Daughter of the City* (Windom) (sc)
1916 *The Little Girl Next Door* (Windom) (sc); *The Little Shepherd of Bargain Row* (Berthelet) (sc); *Orphan Joyce* (Berthelet) (sc); *The Chaperon* (Berthelet) (co-sc); *The Discard* (Windom) (sc); *The Return of Eve* (Berthelet) (co-sc); *The Primitive Strain* (Berthelet) (sc); ***Intolerance*** (Griffith) (asst d); *Oliver Twist* (Young) (asst d); *Sins of the Parents* (Nichols) (sc)
1927 *Riders of the Dark* (Grinde) (sc)

Publications

By VAN DYKE: book—

Horning into Africa, Los Angeles, 1931.

By VAN DYKE: articles—

"From Horse Opera to Epic," in *Cue* (New York), 16 March 1935.
"The Motion Picture and the Next War," in *Hollywood Reporter,* 8 June 1936.
"Rx for a Thin Man," in *Stage* (New York), January 1937.

On VAN DYKE: books—

Cannom, Robert, *Van Dyke and the Mythical City of Hollywood,* Culver City, California, 1948.
Crowther, Bosley, *The Lion's Share: The M-G-M Story,* New York, 1957.
Thomas, Bob, *Thalberg, Life and Legend,* New York, 1969.

On VAN DYKE: articles—

Johnston, Alva, "Van Dyke—Lord Fauntleroy in Hollywood," in *New Yorker,* 28 September 1935.
Penfield, Cornelia, "Hollywood Helmsmen: W. S. Van Dyke and Frank Capra," in *Stage* (New York), 13 April 1936.
Riggan, Byron, "Damn the Crocodiles, Keep the Camera Rolling!" in *American Heritage* (New York), June 1968.
Selander, Lesley, "Up from Assistant Director," in *Action* (Los Angeles), January/February 1971.
Dumont, Hervé, "Woody S. Van Dyke et l'age d'or d'Hollywood," in *Travelling* (Lausanne), no. 37, 1973.
Dumont, Hervé, "W. S. Van Dyke (1889-1943)," in *Anthologie du Cinéma* (Paris), July/September 1975.

* * *

The one thing that best characterizes the style of W. S. Van Dyke is exemplified by his famous nickname, "One Take" Van Dyke. Known for the speed and economy such an epithet indicates, Van Dyke was the unofficial "house director" at Metro-Goldwyn-Mayer for most of his career. Because he died before the collapse of the studio system, he did not face the economic constraints many former MGM directors, accustomed to lavish budgets, were forced to deal with during the 1950s. Based on his record for swift and skillful set-ups, and his experience directing series films which involved a recurring set of characters, he presumably would not only have survived the collapse of the studios, but might also have become one of the biggest names in television. As it is, his career stands as a tribute to the studio system and what it could turn out in as as little as three weeks. His films not only pleased those who saw them upon initial release, but they continue to delight new audiences today with their careless charm.

Van Dyke is not an artist. His work is sometimes downright sloppy, with poorly matched cuts and an improvisational quality that is more desperate than deliberate. However, he was a confident craftsman, and his best films are pure fun. Whether he worked with a typical Metro big budget (as in *Marie Antoinette*) or found himself with less money and time (the *Thin Man* films), he stressed story and character, and getting the job done without sacrificing too much of the Metro gloss. He became a favorite with the studio bosses, and directed some of MGM's most successful series films, among them the first Johnny Weismuller/Maureen O'Sullivan Tarzan film, *Tarzan the Ape Man,* and the first Nelson Eddy/Jeanette MacDonald pairing, *Naughty Marietta.* He also directed an Andy Hardy, a Dr. Kildare, and several others in the Eddy/MacDonald series. He is generally given credit for the idea of casting William Powell and Myrna Loy as Nick and Nora Charles in the first *Thin Man* movie, which he directed along with several others in the series.

Van Dyke's first movie (circa 1917) taught him the out-in-the-field improvisational filmmaking of the silent era. When he became a contract director at MGM, he was able to use these skills, as in his 1926 costume film, *Winners of the Wilderness,* one of Joan Crawford's first starring vehicles. It is an effective combination of location shooting, action sequences, and lavish costume drama built around a beautiful female star. Such movies as *White Shadows of the South Seas, Trader Horn,* and *Eskimo* continued his penchant for out-of-doors filming, and for the fresh, open quality such movie-making required.

The interesting thing about Van Dyke's career is that, given the restrictions of working at MGM during the 1930s, he never lost his breezy, off-hand approach to films. Although he seemed willing to assume any assignment, and his overall work does not add up to a personal cinema, he was adept at directing the great female stars that MGM had under contract during those years. He was able to make significant contributions to their personae by seeing in them qualities that were the opposite of those that had originally brought them to stardom. For instance, instead of restricting Myrna Loy to roles as an exotic Oriental beauty, he suggested her for the lead in a modern comedy, helping her to reveal her "good pal" side in order to play the perfect wife of *The Thin Man.* The serious side of Jean Harlow (whose intelligence he respected) and the comic side of Joan Crawford were explored in *Personal Property* and *Love on the Run,* respectively. Norma Shearer's experience as a silent film actress was allowed to flower in the final scenes of *Marie Antoinette,* as he saw her as being more than just a glamorous clothes horse. He also helped turn the unlikely combination of Nelson Eddy and Jeanette MacDonald into one of the most successful screen teams in the history of musical film.

Van Dyke is more or less a forgotten director today. Yet his films are revived regularly, and as Andrew Sarris correctly perceived in *American Cinema,* "he made more good movies than his reputation for carelessness and haste would indicate." Van Dyke made entertainment films, not art, but he is a perfect example of a man who could survive in the studio system.

—Jeanine Basinger

VAN DYKE, Willard

Nationality: American. **Born:** Willard Ames Van Dyke in Denver, Colorado, 5 December 1906. **Education:** University of California. **Family:** Married 1) Mary Gray Barnett, 1938 (divorced 1950), two children; 2) Margaret Barbara Murray Millikin, 1950, two children. **Career:** Photographer on WPA Art Project in San Francisco, 1934; photographer for *Harper's Bazaar,* 1935; cameraman on Pare Lorentz's *The River,* 1936-37; directed first film (with Ralph Steiner), *The City,* 1939; producer for Office of War Information's Motion Picture Bureau, 1941-45; made films for variety of sponsors and for television, 1946-65; director of film department, Museum of Modern Art, New York, 1965-73; vice-president, International Federation of Film Archives. **Died:** In Jackson, Tennessee, 23 January 1986.

Films as Director:

1939 *The City* (co-d, co-pr, co-ph)
1940 *Valley Town* (+ co-sc); *The Children Must Learn* (+ sc); *Sarah Lawrence*; *To Hear Your Banjo Play*; *Tall Tales*
1942 *The Bridge*
1943 *Oswego*; *Steeltown*
1944 *Pacific Northwest* (+ co-ph)
1945 *San Francisco*
1946 *Journey into Medicine*
1947 *The Photographer*
1948 *Terribly Talented*
1949 *This Charming Couple*; *Mount Vernon*
1950 *Years of Change*
1952 *New York University*
1953 *Working and Playing to Health*; *There is a Season*
1954 *Recollections of Boyhood: An Interview with Joseph Welch*; *Cabos Blancos*; *Excursion House*; *Toby and the Tall Corn*
1957 *Life of the Molds*
1958 *Skyscraper* (co-d); *Tiger Hunt in Assam*; *Mountains of the Moon*
1959 *Land of White Alice*; *The Procession*
1960 *Ireland, the Tear and the Smile*; *Sweden*
1962 *So That Men Are Free*; *Search ino Darkness*
1963 *Depressed Area, U.S.A.*
1964 *Rice*; *Frontiers of News*
1965 *Pop Buell, Hoosier Farmer in Laos*; *Taming the Mekong*; *The Farmer: Feast or Famine* (co-d); *Frontline Cameras 1935-1965*
1968 *Shape of Things to Come*

Other Films:

1937 *The River* (Lorentz) (ph)

Publications

By VAN DYKE: articles—

"The Interpretive Camera in Documentary," in *Hollywood Quarterly,* July 1946.

"The American Documentary—Limitations and Possibilities: An Interview with Willard Van Dyke," with Edouard De Laurot and Jonas Mekas, in *Film Culture* (New York), no. 3, 1956.

"Thirty Years of Social Inquiry: An Interview with Willard Van Dyke," with Harrison Engle, in *Film Comment* (New York), Spring 1965.

Interview with B. L. Kevles, in *Film Culture* (New York), Fall 1965.

"The Role of the Museum of Modern Art in Motion Pictures," in *Film Library Quarterly* (New York), Winter 1967-68.

"Willard Van Dyke," in *Documentary Explorations,* edited by G. Roy Levin, Garden City, New York, 1971.

"Glancing Backward ... Without Nostalgia," with Lora Hays, in *Film Library Quarterly* (New York), Summer 1971.

Hitchens, Gordon, "Conversations with Willard Van Dyke," in *Cineaste* (Montreal), vol. 13, no. 1., 1983.

On VAN DYKE: articles—

"Director on Location," in the *Saturday Review* (New York), 10 September 1949.

Zuckerman, Art, "Focus on Willard Van Dyke," in *Popular Photography* (Boulder, Colorado), April 1965.

Obituary, in *Variety* (New York), 29 January 1986.

Lamont, A., Obituary, in *Film Comment* (New York), March/April 1986.

On VAN DYKE: film—

Rothschild, Amalie R., *Conversations with Willard Van Dyke,* 1981.

* * *

During the 1930s and 1940s, an American documentary tradition was established by a group of filmmakers concerned with then-current issues and crises: the Depression-era Dust Bowl (in Pare Lorentz's *The Plow that Broke the Plains*); the destruction of the Mississippi River basin (Lorentz's *The River*); the advantages of electricity in the rural Midwest (Joris Iven's *Power and the Land*); and the construction of oil rigs in the Louisiana swamp (Flaherty's *Louisiana Story*). One of the seminal filmmakers of this period was Willard Van Dyke, who photographed *The River,* and, with Ralph Steiner, made *The City,* a plea for the necessity of city planning.

The City, produced by the American Institute of Planners for screening at the New York World's Fair, is as relevant today as it was in 1939. The focus is on the need for, and development of, model cities

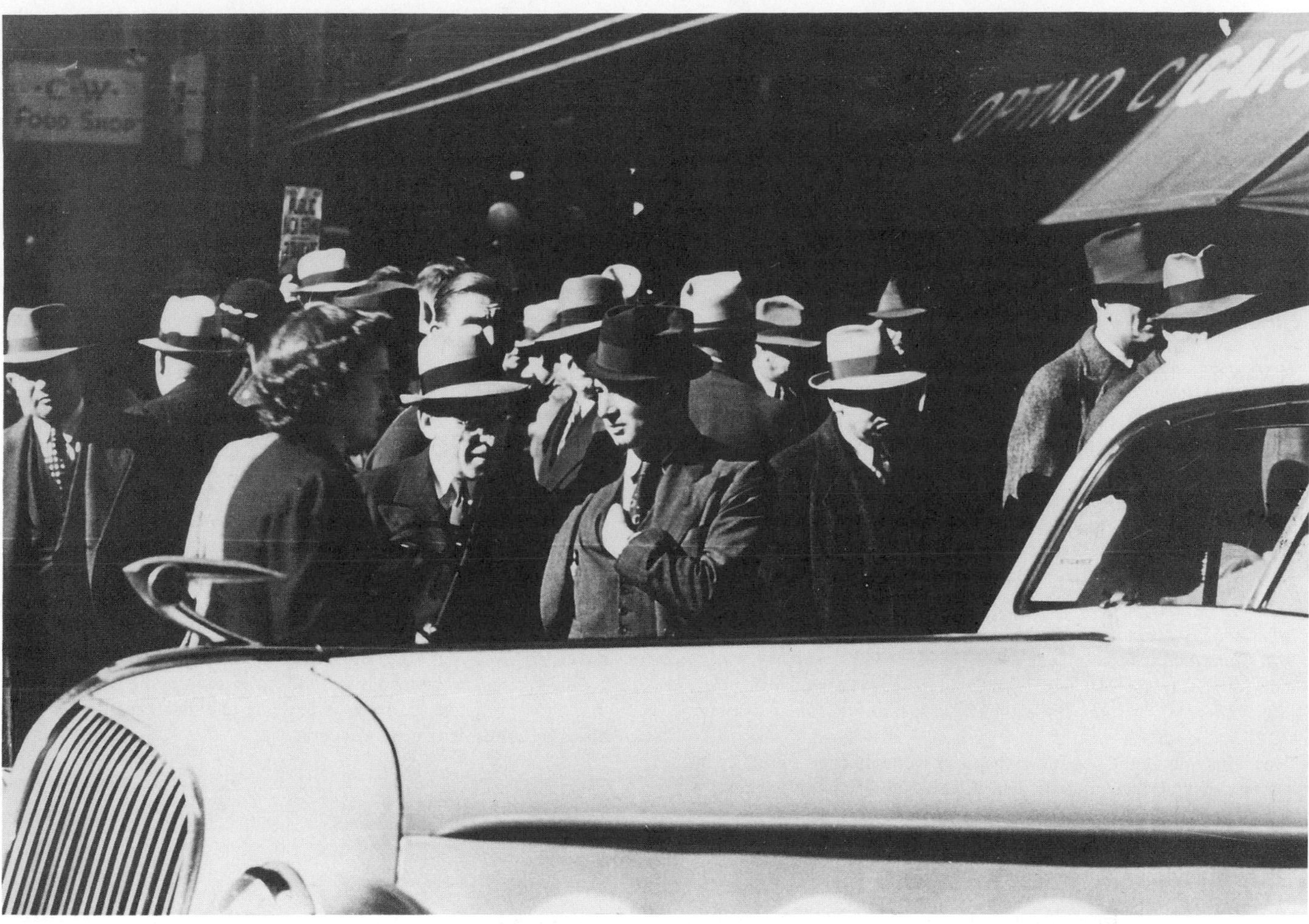

Willard Van Dyke: *The City*

with an emphasis on human and social considerations. Communities must be livable; they must be by, of, and for people. Van Dyke and Steiner trace the development of modern urban America, with an emphasis on the manner in which city planners had erred in judgment. In the film's finale, they present an ideal planned community.

There is a minimum of narration in *The City*: scenes of New York City tenements and subways—and, specifically, a sequence in which a man attempts to cross a street in traffic—are ample proof of the filmmakers' argument. While the film's strength remains its visuals, at the same time the soundtrack music (by Aaron Copland) poignantly expresses emotion. As with Virgil Thomson's score for *The River* and Marc Blitzstein's score for Van Dyke's next documentary, *Valley Town,* the music is as meaningful as the images or words in communicating ideas and feelings. The New York *Herald-Tribune* reported, weeks after the film's premiere, "Already several thousand persons have seen *The City,* many of whom had never before seen a documentary film, and it may be predicted that its cordial reception by critics and public alike will benefit greatly the already widening beginnings of the documentary form in this country."

In *Valley Town,* a stylized examination of the results of automation on the people in a Pennsylvania steel town, Van Dyke had his narrator serve as the town's mayor, who discusses the problems of his municipality. Rarely were any of his later films as trenchant as his first two. He shot documentaries for a variety of sources, including the Office of War Information (during World War II), the U.S. State Department, the Ford Motor Company, the United Church of Christ, and the television shows *Omnibus, High Adventure,* and *Twentieth Century.* Van Dyke's subjects ranged from the folk music of Pete Seeger, Josh White, and Burl Ives (*To Hear Your Banjo Play, Tall Tales*) to the establishment of the United Nations (*San Francisco*). Other topics included recreational therapy in a mental hospital (*Working and Playing to Health*) and life in India (*Tiger Hunt in Assam*), Africa (*Mountains of the Moon*), and Appalachia (*Depressed Area, U.S.A.*).

Willard Van Dyke's most typical subject matter, however, related to the social implications of change, whether again examining the lives of steelworkers (in *Steeltown*), auto workers (*There Is a Season*), farmers in Puerto Rican cooperatives (*Cabos Blancos*), or Protestant clergymen (*The Procession*). All have their roots in *The City* and *Valley Town.*

—Rob Edelman

VAN SANT, Gus

Nationality: American. **Born:** Louisville, Kentucky, 24 July 1952. **Education:** Studied painting, then switched emphasis to film, and graduated from Rhode Island School of Design. **Career:** Made commercials for an advertising agency, New York City; moved to Portland, Oregon, made numerous short films and first independent feature; directed video for rock band Red Hot Chili Peppers. Lives in Portland, Oregon. **Awards:** Best Picture and Best Director, National Society of Film Critics, 1989, for *Drugstore Cowboy.*

Films as Director:

1985 *Mala Noche*
1987 *Five Ways to Kill Yourself* (short); *Ken Death Gets Out of Jail* (short); *My New Friends* (short)
1988 *Junior* (short)
1989 *Drugstore Cowboy*
1991 *My Own Private Idaho*
1994 *Even Cowgirls Get the Blues*
1995 *To Die For*

Publications

By VAN SANT: articles—

Interview with River Phoenix in *Interview,* March 1991.
"Inside Outsider Gus Van Sant," an interview with Adam Block and David Ehrenstein, in *Advocate,* 24 September 1991.
Interview in *Film Threat,* November 1991.
"Gay Film Vagen," an interview with P. Loewe, in *Chaplin,* vol. 33, no. 6, 1991/92.
"Falstaff a Portland," an interview with J. Aghed, in *Positif,* February 1992.
"My Own Private Cinema," an interview with C. Nevers and T. Jousse, in *Cahiers du Cinéma,* December 1992.
"Gus Van Sant," an interview with G. Indiana, in *Bomb,* Fall 1993.
"Mobile Home," an interview with M. Dargis, in *Artforum,* November 1993.
"How Gus Van Sant Cooked Up the Dark Comedy *To Die For,*" an interview with Desmond Ryan, in *Knight-Ridder/Tribune News Service,* 5 October 1995.

On VAN SANT: articles—

Meyer, Thomas J., "Dropping in on the Down and Out," in *New York Times Magazine,* 15 September 1991.
Loud, Lance, "Shakespeare in Black Leather," in *American Film,* September/October 1991.
Lyons, Donald, "Gus Van Sant: Lawless as a Snowflake, Simple as Grass," in *Film Comment,* September/October 1991.
Gallagher, Lawrence J., "Life after *Drugstore,*" in *Esquire,* October 1991.
Handelman, David, "Gus Van Sant's Northwest Passage," in *Rolling Stone,* 31 October 1991.
Signorile, Michelangelo, "Absolutely Queer," in *Advocate,* 19 November 1991.
Ostria, V., "Gus Van Sant, un cineaste de Portland," in *Cahiers du Cinéma,* January 1992.
Roth-Bettoni, D., "*My Own Private Idaho,*" in *Revue du Cinéma,* January 1992.
Reynaud, B., "Gus Van Sant," in *Cahiers du Cinéma,* December 1992.
Block, A., "Perchance to Dream," in *Filmmaker,* vol. 2, no. 1, 1993.
Campbell, V., "The Times of Gus Van Sant," in *Movieline,* October 1993.
Schwager, J., "Back in the Saddle," in *Boxoffice,* February 1994.

* * *

In less than a decade, Gus Van Sant has established himself as one of America's leading and most influential independent filmmakers. His films, often peopled with characters scuffling along on the fringes of American society, explore human feelings and frailties in often understated fashion, and for the most part, Van Sant has proven himself a filmmaker with a deft touch. By the early 1990s, after the success of *Drugstore Cowboy* and *My Own Private Idaho,* some observers were concerned that Van Sant's apparent predilection for exploring the lives of society's outcasts might blunt and ultimately limit his vision. The release of *To Die For* in 1995, however, did much to silence such voices. The wicked black comedy—a skillfully rendered and executed study of a woman obsessed with stardom—indicated that Van Sant's body of work is in no danger of degenerating into formula.

Van Sant's first works, created in the mid-1980s, were a series of short films. Of these, *Mala Noche* (1986) in particular brought him a degree of critical attention, but it was *Drugstore Cowboy* (1989) that established him as one of independent filmmaking's most authoritative new voices. The film's low-key tale of a pack of 1970s-era junkies in perpetual pursuit of drugs won near-unanimous accolades.

Two years later Van Sant released *My Own Private Idaho,* another story of American misfits on the margins of society. The quirky film concerns two male street hustlers, Mike and Scott (played by River Phoenix and Keanu Reeves, respectively), who embark on a journey to find Mike's long-lost mother. Together, Van Sant and Phoenix create a memorable portrait of Mike, a narcoleptic who longs for love. *My Own Private Idaho,* a bold, sometimes dreamlike tale, further cemented Van Sant's reputation.

In 1994, though, Van Sant released *Even Cowgirls Get the Blues,* a film based on Tom Robbins's cult-classic book. *Cowgirls* was a mess in nearly every respect. A poorly executed and disappointing endeavor, it quickly disappeared from the nation's cinema houses. Van Sant recovered nicely, though, with *To Die For* (1995), an adaptation of a novel by Joyce Maynard. Blessed with an inspired performance by Nicole Kidman in the lead role, the film is a withering black comedy that aims venomous barbs at America's television media and star-obsessed culture with deadly accuracy.

—Kevin Hillstrom

VARDA, Agnès

Nationality: Belgian. **Born:** Brussels, 30 May 1928. **Education:** Studied literature and psychology at the Sorbonne, Paris; studied art history at the Ecole du Louvre; studied photography at night school. **Family:** Married director Jacques Demy, one son, one daughter. **Career:** Stage photographer for Theatre Festival of Avignon, then for Theatre National Populaire, Paris, Jean Vilar; directed first film, 1954; accompanied Chris Marker to China as advisor for *Dimanche à Pekin,* 1955; directed two shorts in U.S., 1968; founded production company Ciné-Tamaris, 1977. **Awards:** Prix Méliès for *Cléo de 5 à 7,* 1961; Bronze Lion, Venice Festival, for *Salut les Cubains,* 1964; Prix Louis Delluc, David Selznick Award, and Silver Bear, Berlin Festival, for *Le Bonheur,* 1966; First Prize, Oberhausen, for *Black Panthers,* 1968; Grand Prix, Taormina, for *L'Une chante, l'autre pas,* 1977; Cesar Award, for *Ulysse,* 1984; Golden Lion, Venice Festival, Prix Melies, and Best Foreign Film, Los Angeles Film Critics Association, for *Vagabond,* 1985; Commander des Arts et des Lettres, Chevalier Legion d'honneur. **Address:** c/o Cine-Tamaris, 86 rue Daguerre, 75014 Paris, France.

Films as Director:

1954 *La Pointe courte* (+ pr, sc)
1957 *O saisons, o châteaux* (doc short)
1958 *L'Opéra-Mouffe* (short); *Du côté de la Côte* (short)
1961 ***Cléo de cinq à sept*** (+ sc)
1963 *Salut les Cubains* (*Salute to Cuba*) (+ text) (doc short)

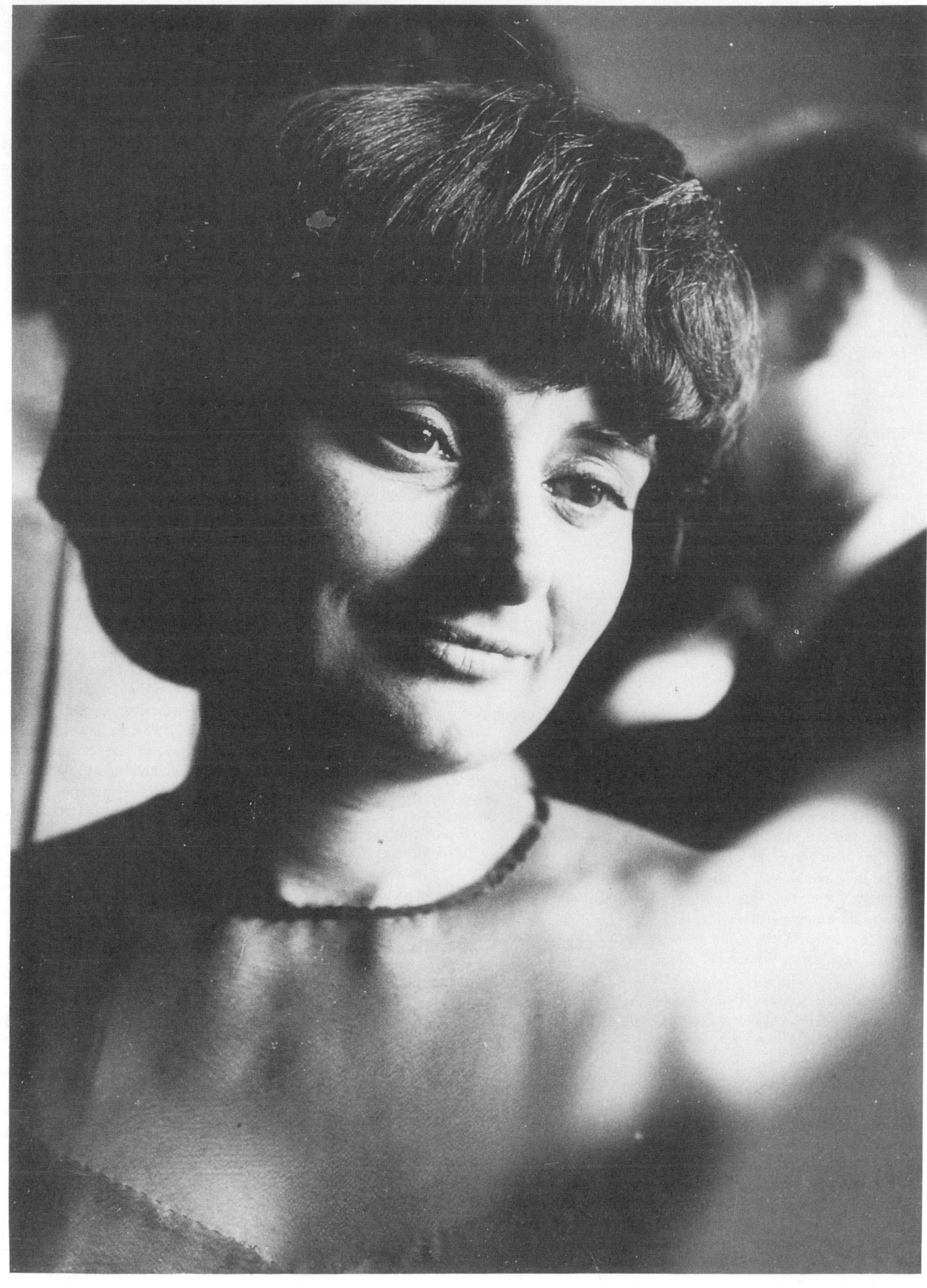

Agnès Varda

1965 *Le Bonheur* (+ sc)
1966 *Les Créatures*
1967 *Uncle Yanco*; episode of *Loin du Vietnam* (*Far from Vietnam*)
1968 *Black Panthers* (*Huey*) (doc)
1969 *Lion's Love* (+ pr)
1970 *Nausicaa* (for TV)
1975 *Daguerrotypes* (+ pr); *Réponses de femmes* (8mm)
1977 *L'Une chante l'autre pas* (*One Sings, the Other Doesn't*)
1980 *Mur Murs* (*Wall Walls*; *Mural Murals*) (+ pr)
1981 *Documenteur: An Emotion Picture* (+ pr)
1983 *Ulysse*
1984 *Les Dites cariatides*; *Sept P., Cuis., S. de B., ... a saisir*
1986 *Vagabonde* (*Sans Toit ni loi,*; *Vagabond*)
1988 *Kung Fu Master* (*Don't Say It*); *Jane B. par Agnès V.* (doc) (appearance)
1991 *Jacquot de Nantes* (+ pr, sc)
1993 *Des demoiselles ont en 25 ans* (*The Young Girls Turn 25*) (doc)
1995 *Les cent et une nuits* (*A Hundred and One Nights*) (+ sc); *L'universe de Jacques Demy* (*The World of Jacques Demy*) (doc)

Other Films:

1971 ***Last Tango in Paris*** (Bertolucci) (co-dialogue)
1978 *Lady Oscar* (Demy) (pr)

Publications

By VARDA: book—

Varda par Agnes, Paris, 1994.

By VARDA: articles—

"*Cleo de cinq à sept*: Script Extract," in *Films and Filming* (London), December 1962.
"Pasolini—Varda—Allio—Sarris—Michelson," in *Film Culture* (New York), Fall 1966.
"*Le Bonheur,*" in *Cinema* (Beverly Hills), December 1966.
"The Underground River," an interview with Gordon Gow, in *Films and Filming* (London), March 1970.
"Mother of the New Wave," an interview with J. Levitin, in *Women and Film* (Santa Monica), vol. 1, no. 5-6, 1974.
"L'Une chante, l'autre pas," an interview with J. Narboni and others, in *Cahiers du Cinéma* (Paris), May 1977.
"One Sings, the Other Doesn't," an interview with R. McCormick, in *Cineaste* (New York), Winter 1977/78.
"Un cinéma plus 'partageable': Agnès Varda," an interview with A. Tournés, in *Jeune Cinéma* (Paris), February 1982.
Interview with J. Sabine, in *Cinema Papers* (Melbourne), October 1982.
"Un jour sous le soleil," in *Monthly Film Bulletin* (London), December 1985.
Interview with Rob Edelman, in *Cineaste* (New York), vol. 15, no. 1, 1986.
Interview with Barbara Quart, in *Film Quarterly* (Berkeley), Winter 1986/1987.
Interview with F. Audé, in *Positif* (Paris), March 1988.
"Vers le visage de Jacques," in *Cahiers du Cinéma* (Paris), December 1990.

On VARDA: books—

Armes, Roy, *French Cinema Since 1946: Vol.2—The Personal Style,* New York, 1966.
Flitterman-Lewis, Sandy, *To Desire Differently: Feminism and the French Cinema,* Urbana, Illinois, 1990.
Acker, Ally, *Reel Women: Pioneers of the Cinema, 1896 to the Present,* New York, 1991.

On VARDA: articles—

Strick, Philip, "Agnès Varda," in *Film* (London), Spring 1963.
Pyros, J., "Notes on Women Directors," in *Take One* (Montreal), November/December 1970.
Roud, Richard, "The Left Bank Revisited," in *Sight and Sound* (London), Summer 1977.
Beylie, Claude, "Les Chardons ardents d'Agnès Varda," in *Ecran* (Paris), 15 April 1979.
Ranvaud, Don, "Travellers Tales," in *Monthly Film Bulletin* (London), May 1986.
Durgnat, Raymond, "Resnais & Co.: Back to the Avant-Garde," in *Monthly Film Bulletin* (London), May 1987.
Prédal, René, "Agnès Varda, une certaine idée de la marginalité," in *Jeune Cinéma* (Paris), October/November 1987.
Forbes, Jill, "Agnès Varda—The Gaze of the Medusa?," in *Sight and Sound* (London), Spring 1989.
Furlan, S., "*Jacques de Nantes,*" in *Ekran* (Paris), vol. 16, no. 4/5, 1991.
Floret, M., and others, "Agnes par Varda," in *Jeune Cinéma* (Paris), April/May 1992.
Kelleher, E., "Director Varda's *Jacquot* Recalls Spouse Demy," in *Film Journal* (New York), May 1993.
Meredyth Talton, Jana, "Agnes Varda: Ahead of the Avant-Garde," in *Ms.* (New York), May/June 1993.

* * *

Agnès Varda's startlingly individualistic films have earned her the title "grandmother of the New Wave" of French filmmaking. Her statement that a filmmaker must exercise as much freedom as a novelist became a mandate for New Wave directors, especially Chris Marker and Alain Resnais. Varda's first film, *La Pointe courte,* edited by Resnais, is regarded, as Georges Sadoul affirms, as "the first film of the French *nouvelle vuage.* Its interplay between conscience, emotions, and the real world make it a direct antecedent of *Hiroshima, mon amour.*"

The use of doubling, and twin story lines; the personification of objects; the artistic determination of cinematic composition, color, texture, form, and time; and the correlation of individual subjectivity to societal objectivity to depict socio-political issues are denominators of Varda's films, which she writes, produces, and directs.

After *La Pointe courte* Varda made three documentaries in 1957-58. The best of these was *L'Opéra-Mouffe,* portraying the Mouffetard district of Paris. Segments of the film are prefaced by handwritten intertitles, a literary element Varda is fond of using. In 1961-62, Varda began but did not complete two film projects: *La Cocotte d'azur* and *Melangite.* Her next film, *Cléo de cinq à sept,* records the time a pop singer waits for results of her exam for cancer. Varda used physical time in *Cleo:* events happening at the same tempo as they would in actual life. The film is divided into chapters, using Tarot cards which symbolize fate. Varda next photographed 4,000 still photos of Castro's revolution-in-progress, resulting in *Salute to Cuba.*

Le Bonheur is considered Varda's most stunning and controversial achievement. Critics were puzzled and pleased. Of her first color film, Varda says it was "essentially a pursuit of the palette.... Psychology takes first place." A young carpenter lives with his wife and children. Then he takes a mistress; when his wife drowns, his mistress takes her place. The film was commended for its superb visual beauties, the use of narrative in *le nouveau roman* literary pattern, and its tonal contrasts and spatial configurations. Critics continue to debate the film's theme.

Elsa is an essay portraying authors Elsa Triolet and her husband Louis Aragon. *Les Créatures* uses a black and white with red color scheme in a fantasy-thriller utilizing an inside-outside plot that mingles real and unreal events. As in *La Pointe courte,* a young couple retreat to a rural locale. The pregnant wife is mute, due to an accident. Her husband is writing a book. He meets a recluse who operates a machine forcing people to behave as his or her subconscious would dictate. The wife gives birth, regaining her speech.

Visiting the United States, Varda and her husband Jacques Demy each made a film. Varda honored her *Uncle Janco* in the film so named. *The Black Panthers* (or *Huey*) followed. Both documentaries were shown at the London Film Festival in 1968. She next directed a segment of the antiwar short *Far from Vietnam.*

Using an American setting and an English-speaking cast, including the co-authors of the musical *Hair,* Varda made *Lions Love* in Hollywood. This jigsaw-puzzle work includes a fake suicide and images of a TV set reporting Robert Kennedy's assassination. G. Roy Levin declared that it was hard to distinguish between the actual and the invented film realities. *Nausicaa* deals with Greeks living in France. Made for television, it was not shown, Varda says, because it was against military-ruled Greece.

In 1971, Varda helped write the script for *Last Tango in Paris.* Varda's involvement in the women's movement began about 1972; a film dealing with feminist issues, *Réponses de femmes,* has yet to be shown. Made for German television, *Daguerreotypes* has no cast. Varda filmed the residents and shops of the Rue Daguerre, a tribute to L. J. M. Daguerre.

In 1977, Varda made *One Sings, the Other Doesn't* and established her own company, Ciné-Tamaris, to finance it. This "family" of workers created the film. Chronicling the friendship of two women over fifteen years, it earned mixed reviews, some referring to it as feminist propaganda or as sentimental syrup. But Varda, narrating the film and writing the song lyrics, does not impose her views. In *One Sings,* she wanted to portray the happiness of being a woman, she says.

Easily Varda's most potent film of the 1980s, and one of the best of her career, is *Vagabond,* an evocative drama about the death and life of a young woman, Mona (Sandrine Bonnaire). She is an ex-secretary who has chosen to become a drifter, and her fate is apparent at the outset. As the film begins, Mona has died. Her frost-bitten corpse is seen in a ditch. Her body is claimed by no one, and she is laid to rest in a potter's field. As *Vagabond* unfolds, Varda explores Mona's identity as she wanders through the rural French countryside hitching rides and begging for the necessities that will sustain her. The scenario also spotlights the manner in which she impacts on those she meets: truck drivers; a gas station owner and his son; a vineyard worker; a professor-researcher; and other, fellow drifters. Varda constructs the film as a series of sequences, some comprised of a single shot lasting several seconds, in which Mona passes through the lives of these people. The result is an eloquent film about one average, ill-fated young woman and the choices she makes, as well as a meditation on chance meetings and missed opportunities. On a much broader level, the film serves as an allegory of the travails a woman must face if she desires to completely liberate herself from the shackles of society.

Varda's most notable recent films have been valentines to her late husband, filmmaker Jacques Demy. *The Young Girls Turn 25* is a nostalgia piece about the filming of Demy's *The Young Girls of Rochefort; The World of Jacques Demy* is an up-close-and-personal documentary-biography consisting of interviews and clips from Demy's films.

A third title, *Jacquot de Nantes,* was the most widely seen. It is an exquisite film: a penetrating, heart-rending account of the measure of a man's life, with Varda moving between sequences of Demy in conversation, filmed in extreme close-up; clips from his films; and a re-creation of his childhood in Nantes and the manner in which he developed a passion for cinema. Varda illustrates how Demy's life and world view impacted on his films; for example, his hatred of violence, which is ever so apparent in his films, was forged by his memories of Nantes being bombed during World War II. But *Jacquot de Nantes* (which was conceived prior to Demy's death) is most effective as a tender love letter from one life partner to another. Varda visually evokes her feeling towards her departed mate in one of the film's opening shots. She pans her camera across a watercolor, whose composition is that of a nude woman and man who are holding hands. With over three decades of filmmaking experience, Varda's reputation as a filmmaker dazzles and endures.

—Louise Heck-Rabi, updated by Rob Edelman

VASILIEV, Sergei and Georgi

Nationality: Soviet. **Born:** Georgi Nikolaievitch Vasiliev born in Vologda, 25 November 1899; Sergei Dmitrievitch Vasiliev born in Moscow, 4 December 1900. (Though not related, they came to be known as the Vasiliev brothers because of a shared surname and because they worked together.) **Education:** Georgi educated at technical institute, Warsaw, and theatre course in Moscow, 1922-23; Sergei educated in filmmaking, Moscow. **Military Service:** Sergei took part in storming of Winter Palace, 1917, then served in Red Army; Georgi served with Red Army, 1918-22. **Career:** Sergei joined Sevzapkino as film editor, 1923; Georgi film editor for Goskino, from 1924; Goskino and Sevzapkino merged, the "brothers" began working together, 1928; Sergei became administrator at Lenfilm Studios, 1944; Sergei directed *The Heroes of Shipka,* 1954; Council of Ministers of the RSFSR created a prize for artistic achievement named for the Vasiliev brothers, 1965. **Awards:** Order of Lenin, 1935; Georgi named Artist of Merit of the RSFSR, 1940; State Prizes for *Chapayev,* 1940, and *The Defense of Tsaritsyn,* 1942; Order of the Red Star for *The Front,* 1944; Sergei named People's Artist of the USSR, 1948, and Best Director, Cannes Festival, for *The Heroes of Shipka,* 1955. **Died:** Georgi Vasiliev died 8 June 1946; Sergei Vasiliev died 16 December 1959.

Films as Directors:

1928 *Podvig vo idach* (*An Exploit on the Ice*; *The Ice-Breaker Krassnin*)
1930 *The Sleeping Beauty* (*The Woman of the Sleeping Forest*) (+ co-sc)
1932 *A Personal Affair* (*A Personal Matter*)
1934 ***Chapayev*** (+ sc)
1937 *Volochayevskiye dni* (*The Days of Volochayev*; *Far East*; *Intervention in the Far East*) (+ sc)
1942 *Oborona Tsaritsina* (*The Defense of Tsaritsyn*) (+ sc)
1943 *Front* (+ sc)
1954 *Geroite na Shipka* (*The Heroes of Shipka*) (Sergei d only)
1958 *Oktiabr' dni* (*October Days*; *The Days of October*) (Sergei d only; co-sc)

Publications

By the VASILIEVS: books—

Chapayev, Moscow, 1936.
Tchapaïev, La Défense de Tsaritsyne, Les Jours de Volotchaïev, in *Scénarios choisis du cinéma soviétique,* vol. 2, Paris, 1951.

On the VASILIEVS: book—

Leyda, Jay, *Kino: A History of the Russian and Soviet Film,* London, 1960.

On the VASILIEVS: articles—

Schmulévitch, Eric, "Les Frères Vasiliev," in *Avant-Scène du Cinéma* (Paris), 1 and 15 January 1977.
Pisarevsky, D., "Brat'ja Vasil'evy: put' i metod," in *Iskusstvo Kino* (Moscow), November 1980.
Shlovsky, Viktor, and others, "*Chapayev*—50," in *Iskusstvo Kino* (Moscow), November 1984.

* * *

The Vasiliev "Brothers" were not related, but met when Goskino and Sevzapkino, where Georgi and Sergei, respectively, were editors, merged. They used the nickname on their first credits and collaborated until Georgi's death. Their evolution faithfully followed the successive stages of Soviet cinema: a documentary compilation, an avant-garde Bolshevik exercise, the patriotic epics of Socialist Realism. But *Chapayev* eclipsed everything, prompting Georgi's rueful reference to an old proverb, "We wet-nursed an elephant and had to feed it all our lives."

The post-Revolutionary scarcity of resources favoured editors, or rather re-editors, who adapted foreign films to Russian tastes and Communist ideology. Shlovski particularly admired an example of Georgi's skill wherein he took the last frame of a man yawning and multiple-printed it to look like an agonised convulsion, with the clinching title, "Death by heart-attack."

The Vasilievs' first feature assembled documentary footage from the Russian expeditions sent to rescue an Italian airship in the Arctic. A scientific documentary (lost, title unknown) on rabbit-rearing charmed spectators by featuring a rabbit as presenter. Their first "artistic" film, *The Sleeping Beauty,* struck a blow for the Bolshevik formalists against "realist" directors surviving from the Tsarist cinema. The film features a Tsarist troupe that performs the "Sleeping Beauty" ballet in a theatre from whose boxes Red Guards hurl pamphlets; the effete and obsolete gestures on stage contrast with virile actions in the auditorium. Perhaps the film failed with audiences, perhaps formalism failed with the bureaucrats, or both, but their next film, *A Personal Affair,* was strenuously realist, subordinating montage to scenario, actors, and "someone to love and someone to hate." Despite alcoholism and sabotage by reactionaries, a man melts a churchbell into a ship's propeller, thus glorifying the tasks of the Reconstruction Era.

Chapayev revisited the Civil War, but to emphasise the continuing struggle and party hegemony over every social sphere. Chapayev (B. Babotchkine, typecast foreverafter) is a dashing, brave, but old-fashioned army commander who becomes increasingly dependent, as he should, on Red Army shells (industrialisation), and on the spiritual and even tactical wisdom of the ever-present Commissar (L. Kmit). As homogenous, even monolithic, as its epic-heroic aspects may seem, it integrated the Vasilievs' hitherto separate aesthetics (and sound, of which the Vasilievs, like Eisenstein, were initially suspicious, accepting its use in "montage" counterpoint to the image but denouncing any "tautology" with the image, lest it lead to "filmed theatre"). The story combined a factual basis, a highly personalised hero, a careful (though not intricate) dramatic structure, and a nimbus of epic and legendary feeling. Monumental graphics, dynamic camera-angles, bold montage, and spare but imaginative sound endowed bodies, huts, fields, and fences with a power and grandeur matching Dovzhenko's. Enormously popular, it conclusively demonstrated the compatibility of formalist, realist, and dramatic qualities, and still repays the closest possible study.

The Vasilievs' subsequent films, though well prized at film festivals, were scantily shown in the West. Vast military frescos with some topical point, they stressed different aspects of leader-mass relationships. The 1937 film *The Days of Volochayev* describes the Civil War campaign against the Japanese, who were then probing Manchuria. It conspicuously lacks any central figure or issue, possibly to encourage general vigilance and suspicion. Stalingrad, besieged through 1942-43, was previously called Tsaritsyn, and in the Vasiliev film *The Defense of Tsaritsyn,* Stalin masterminds its defence in the Civil War. The Vasilievs called *The Front* a "chamber play," based on a theatre piece which criticized Red Army generalship during the first Nazi onslaught (to exculpate Stalin, of course). The 1954 colour film *The Heroes of Shipka* celebrated Russian support for Bulgaria against the Turks in 1877 and 1878, thus exalting the presence of the Red Army throughout Eastern Europe. Friendly critics praised its diversity of precisely-etched character-cameos. *October Days* celebrated the 30th anniversary of the 1917 Army mutinies, taking its cue from the account thereof in John Reed's *Ten Days that Shook the World.* More "chronicle" than "history," it concentrates on the movements of the masses and some vigorously articulated battle-scenes. By the time of the film's creation, Kruschev had denounced "the cult of personality," and continuing uncertainties about de-Stalinisation could explain the relative cloudiness of leader-mass relations (Lenin is everywhere, Stalin fitfully useful). Friendly critics praised its giving life to dry-as-dust historical phrases. The one Vasiliev project to seem not entirely militant was a filmed opera, Tchaikovski's *The Queen of Spades,* begun but soon abandoned in 1943-44.

Sergei's administrative activities included deanship of the Faculty of Cinema at the Unified University of Art Workers. From 1955 he was simultaneously director of Lenfilm Studios and secretary of the Leningrad Branch of the Cineastes' trade union.

—Raymond Durgnat

VERHOEVEN, Paul

Nationality: Dutch. **Born:** Amsterdam, Netherlands, 1938. **Education:** Ph.D. in mathematics and physics, University of Leiden. **Military Service:** Royal Dutch Navy. **Career:** Documentary and feature film writer and director. **Awards:** Best Foreign Language Film, Los Angeles Film Critics Association, for *Soldier of Orange,* 1979; Best Foreign Language Film, Los Angeles Film Critics, International Award, Toronto Film Festival, and Jury Prize, Avoriaz, for *The Fourth Man,* 1979. **Agent:** Marion Rosenberg, 8428 Melrose Place, Los Angeles, CA 90069, U.S.A.

Films as Director:

1960 *A Lizard Too Much* (*Een Hagedis Teveel*)
1963 *Let's Have a Party* (*Feest*)
1966 *The Dutch Marine Corps* (*Hets Korps Mariniers*)
1971 *Business Is Business* (*Wat Zein Ik*)
1973 *Turkish Delight*
1975 *Cathy Tippel* (*Keejte Tippel*)
1979 *The Fourth Man* (*De Vierde Man*); *Soldier of Orange* (+ sc)
1980 *Spetters*
1985 *Flesh and Blood* (+ sc)
1987 *Robocop*
1990 *Total Recall*
1992 *Basic Instinct*
1995 *Showgirls*

Paul Verhoeven on the set of *Total Recall*

Publications

By VERHOEVEN: book—

Showgirls: Portrait of a Film, New Market Press, 1995.

On VERHOEVEN: book—

Cowie, Peter, *Dutch Cinema,* London, 1979.

On VERHOEVEN: articles—

Cronenworth, Brian, "Man of Iron," in *American Film* (Washington, D.C.), October 1987.

Baron, David, "*Total* Director Recalls His Troubles at Home," in *Times-Picayune,* 9 June 1990.

Welkos, Robert W., "Director Trims *Basic Instinct* to Get R Rating," in *Los Angeles Times,* 11 February 1992.

Harrington, Richard, "Director Verhoeven Standing by the Films That Gays Bash," in *Washington Post,* 20 March 1992.

Fleming, Charles, "No Hardcore *Instinct,* Says Verhoeven," in *Variety* (New York), 13 April 1992.

* * *

Paul Verhoeven, a director of international acclaim who has achieved both critical and commercial success, is also one of Hollywood's most controversial. His films, characterized stylistically by his use of deep focus, Christian iconography, and sensuous mise en scene, are perhaps better known for their graphic representations of violence and sexuality.

Verhoeven began his filmmaking career as a director of short subjects and, while serving with the Royal Dutch Navy, documentaries. After returning to civilian life, he continued to work with both fiction and documentary forms, expanding his scope to television. Though his first feature-length motion picture, *Business Is Business* (1971), was a commercial success, Verhoeven did not receive international attention until the release of his second feature, *Turkish Delight* (1973).

Nominated for an Oscar for Best Foreign Language Film by the Academy of Motion Picture Arts and Sciences, *Turkish Delight* not only established Verhoeven as a skilled director, it also began his association with films of explicit sexual content. He continued to receive international critical acclaim with the release of *Soldier of Orange* (1979), which was nominated for a Golden Globe Award and was named Best Foreign Language Film by the Los Angeles Film Critics Association.

Graphic acts of sex and violence were also integral to his two subsequent films: *Spetters* (1980), a film about teenage alienation in Holland; and *The Fourth Man* (1984), winner of the Los Angeles Film Critics Award for Best Foreign Language Film, the Toronto Film Festival's International Award, and the Jury Prize at Avoriaz.

Controversy surrounding Verhoeven's work became more heated with his move to the United States in 1986. His first American feature, *Flesh and Blood,* started a long-running battle between the director and Jack Valenti's Motion Picture Association of America (MPAA) rating authority. *Flesh and Blood*'s brutal depictions of sixteenth-century battles and candid sex scenes began a battle over ratings that would continue through Verhoeven's next three features.

Considered one of the most violent films of 1987, *Robocop,* a post-modernist blend of science fiction, action-adventure, and the Western, is often viewed as a critique of corporate and consumer capitalism. Verhoeven's subsequent film, *Total Recall* (1990), starring Arnold Schwarzenegger, is one of the most expensive feature films ever produced. The negative cost and worldwide marketing budget has been estimated to be over $100 million. Both these films were given the highly restrictive rating of "X"—prohibited to viewers under the age of seventeen—due to what was judged to be excessive violence. The films were then re-edited to meet the requirements of the "R" rating—under seventeen admitted with the accompaniment of an adult.

Perhaps the most controversial film of Verhoeven's career is *Basic Instinct,* released in 1992. The story, with a $3 million script written by Joe Eszterhas, concerned a bi-sexual woman suspected of several murders who engages in a sexual relationship with the male police detective investigating the crimes. The MPAA again found Verhoeven's work problematic on the grounds of both sex and violence. *Basic Instinct* was only the second release from a major studio to receive a rating of "NC-17"—no children under seventeen admitted (the first was *Henry and June,* directed by Philip Kaufman). Like the X, which was abolished in 1990, an NC-17 rating threatens the economic viability of a motion picture at the box office. Many theaters refuse to screen the films, community presses and television stations may reject advertisements, and some video rental outlets will not carry films thus rated. Again, the film was cut to meet the standards of an R rating.

In addition to the ratings controversy, the film was protested by several national gay and lesbian organizations for its stereotypical representations of lesbians and bi-sexuals. The film was criticized because, like many films of the period, it depicted sexual relations outside of the traditional heterosexual marriage as excessive and dangerous, linking homosexuality with violence.

Verhoeven was reunited with the creative team behind the commercially successful *Basic Instinct* in 1995 with the production of *Showgirls.* It was a landmark film, as Verhoeven became the first director in the United States hired by a major motion picture studio to deliver a film without the obligation of achieving an R rating. *Showgirls* was released with an NC-17 rating and generated considerable interest, but generally negative reviews.

—Frances Gateward

VERTOV, Dziga

Nationality: Russian. **Born:** Denis Arkadievitch Kaufman in Byalistok, Poland (then annexed to Russia), 2 January 1896. **Education:** Studeied at the music academy in Byalistok, Poland, 1912-15; also attended medical school in St. Petersburg/Petrograd, 1916-17. **Family:** Married Elizoveta Svilova. **Career:** Set up a lab for the study of sound while student, 1915-17; adopted pseudonym "Dziga Vertov" (translates as "spinning top"), and became editor and writer for newsreel section of Moscow Cinema Committee, 1917; directed first personal film and published Kinoks-Revolution Manifesto, 1919; organized film activities on government agit-steamboats and agit-trains, 1921; began developing theory of "Kino-Glaz" (Kino-Eye), 1922; worked on *Kino-Pravda* and *Goskinokalender* newsreel series, 1922-25; directed newsreel series *Novostidnia,* from 1947. **Died:** 1954.

Films as Director:

1918-19 *Kino-Nedelia* (*Weekly Reels*) series, no. 1-43 (co-d; according to Sadoul, he did not take part in the production of nos. 38-42)

1919 *Godovshchina revoliutsiya* (*Anniversary of the Revolution*) (+ ed); *Protsess Mironova* (*The Trial of Mironov*); *Vskrytie moschei Sergeia Radonezhskogo* (*Exhumation of the Remains of Sergius of Radonezh*)

1920 *Boi pod Tsaritsinom* (*Battle for Tsaritsin*) (+ ed); *Vserusski starets Kalinin* (*All Russian Elder Kalinin*); *Instruktorii Parokhod "Krasnaia Zvezda"* (*Instructional Steamer "Red Star'*)
1921 *Agitpoezd VTsIK* (*The VTIK Train*; *Agit-Train of the Central Committee*)
1922 *Istoriia grazhdenskoi voini* (*History of the Civil War*) (+ ed); *Protsess Eserov* (*Trial of the Social Revolutionaries*); *Univermag* (*Department Store*)
1922-23 ***Kino-Pravda*** (*Cinema-Truth*; *Film-Truth*) series, nos. 1-23
1923-25 *Goskinokalender* series, nos. 1-53; *Sevodiva* (*Today*)
1924 *Sovetskie igrushki* (*Soviet Toys*); *Iumoreski* (*Humoresques*); *Daesh vozkukh* (*Give Us Air*); *Khronika-molniya* (*Newsreel-Lightning*); *Kino-glaz* (*Kino-Eye*)
1925 *Zagranichnii pokhod sudov Baltiiskogo flota kreisere "Aurora" i uchebnogo sudna "Komsomolts," August 8, 1925* (*The Seventh Anniversary of the Red Army*)
1926 *Shagai, Soviet!* (*Stride, Soviet!*); *Shestaya chast' mira* (*A Sixth of the World*)
1928 *Odinnadtsatii* (*The Eleventh Year*)
1929 ***Chelovek s kinoapparatom*** (*The Man with a Movie Camera*)
1931 *Entuziazm: Simfoniia Donbassa* (*Enthusiasm: Symphony of the Don Basin*)
1934 *Tri pensi o Lenine* (*Three Songs of Lenin*)
1937 *Kolibel 'naya* (*Lullaby*) (+ narration); *Pamyati Sergo Ordzhonikidze* (*In Memory of Sergo Ordzhonikidze*); *Sergo Ordzhonikidze* (co-d)
1938 *Slava Sovetskim Geroiniam* (*Famous Soviet Heroes*); *Tri geroini* (*Three Heroines*) (+ co-sc)
1941 *Krov'za krov', smert'za smert': slodeianiya Nemetsko-Fashistkih zakhvatchikov na territorii C.C.C.P. me ne zabudem* (*Blood for Blood, Death for Death*); *Soiuzkinozhurnal No. 77*; *Soiuzkinozhurnal No. 87*
1943 *Tebe, Front: Kazakhstan Front* (*For You at the Front: The Kazakhstan Front*)
1944 *V gorakh Ala-Tau* (*In the Mountains of Ala-Tau*); *Kliatva molodikh* (*Youth's Oath*; *The Oath of Youth*)
1944-54 *Novosti dnia* series (contributed various issues through 1954)

Publications

By VERTOV: books—

Statii, dnevniki, zamysly, edited by S. Drobashenko, Moscow, 1966.
Dsiga Wertow: aus den Tagebüchern, edited by Peter Konlechner and Peter Kubelka, Vienna, 1967.
Articles, Journaux, Projets, edited and translated by Sylviane and Andrée Robel, Paris, 1972.
Kino-Eye: The Writings of Dziga Vertov, edited by Annette Michelson, Berkeley, 1984.

By VERTOV: articles—

"Iz rabochikh tetradei Dziga Vertov," in *Iskusstvo Kino* (Moscow), no. 4, 1957.
"Vespominaiia o s'emkakh V.I. Lenin," in *Iz Istorii Kino* (Moscow), no. 2, 1959.
"Manuscrit sans titre," translated by J. Aumont, in *Cahiers du Cinéma* (Paris), May/June 1970.
"Doklad na pervoi vsesoyuznoi ... ," in *Iz Istorii Kino* (Moscow), no. 8, 1971.
Various articles in *Film Comment* (New York), Spring 1972.
"From the Notebooks of Dziga Vertov," translated by Marco Carynnyk, in *Artforum* (New York), March 1972.
"Dak rodilsja i rasvivalsfa *Kinoglaz,*" in *Iskusstvo Kino* (Moscow), February 1986.

On VERTOV: books—

Bryher, Winnifred, *Film Problems of Soviet Russia,* Terrutent, Switzerland, 1929.
Lozowick, Louis, Joseph Freeman, and Joshua Kunitz, *Voices of October: Art and Literature in Soviet Russia,* New York, 1930.
Marshall, Herbert, *Soviet Cinema,* London, 1945.
Dickinson, Thorold, and Catherine De La Roche, *Soviet Cinema,* London, 1948.
Eisenstein, Sergei, *Film Form,* edited and translated by Jay Leyda, New York, 1949.
Pudovkin, V.I., G. Alexandrov, and I. Piryev, *Soviet Films: Principle Stages of Development,* Bombay, India, 1951.
Babitsky, Paul, and John Rimberg, *The Soviet Film Industry,* New York, 1955.
Abramov, N.P., *Dziga Vertov,* Moscow, 1962; Lyons, 1965.
Borokov, V., *Dziga Vertov,* Moscow, 1967.
Geduld, Harry, editor, *Film Makers on Filmmaking,* Bloomington, Indiana, 1967.
Issari, M. Ali, *Cinéma Vérité,* East Lansing, Michigan, 1971.
Sadoul, Georges, *Dziga Vertov,* Paris, 1971.
Barnouw, Erik, *Documentary: A History of the Non-Fiction Film,* New York, 1974.
Kuleshov, Lev, *Kuleshov on Film,* translated and edited by Ronald Levaco, Berkeley, California, 1974.
Feldman, Seth, *Evolution of Style in the Early Work of Dziga Vertov,* New York, 1977.
Feldman, Seth R., *Dziga Vertov: A Guide to References and Resources,* Boston, 1979.
Marshall, Herbert, *Masters of the Soviet Cinema: Crippled Creative Biographies,* London, 1983.
Waugh, Thomas, editor, *"Show Us Life": Toward a History and Aesthetics of the Committed Documentary,* Metuchen, New Jersey, 1984.
Petric, Vlad, *Constructivism in Film: The Man with the Movie Camera: A Cinematic Analysis,* Cambridge, 1987.

On VERTOV: articles—

Lenauer, Jean, "Vertov, His Work and His Future," in *Close-Up* (London), December 1929.
Hughes, Pennethorne, "Vertov ad Absurdum," in *Close-Up* (London), September 1932.
Koster, Simon, "Dziga Vertov," in *Experimental Cinema* (New York), no. 5, 1934.
Vaughan, Dai, "The Man with the Movie Camera," in *Films and Filming* (London), November 1960.
Sadoul, Georges, "Actualité de Dziga Vertov," in *Cahiers du Cinéma* (Paris), June 1963.
Weinberg, Herman G., "The Man With the Movie Camera," in *Film Comment* (New York), Fall 1966.
Abramov, Nikolai, "Dziga Vertov, Poet and Writer of the Cinema," in *Soviet Film* (Moscow), no. 11, 1968.
Rotha, Paul, and Richard Griffith, in *Documentary Film,* New York, 1968.
Giercke, Christopher, "Dziga Vertov," in *Afterimage* (Rochester), April 1970.
Brik, Osip, "The So-Called 'Formal Method,'" translated by Richard Sherwood, in *Screen* (London), Winter 1971/72.
Bordwell, David, "Dziga Vertov: An Introduction," in *Film Comment* (New York), Spring 1972.
Michelson, Annette, "The Man with the Movie Camera: From Magician to Entomologist," in *Artforum* (New York), March 1972.

Dziga Vertov

Enzensberger, Marsha, "Dziga Vertov," in *Screen* (London), Winter 1972/73.

Feldman, Seth, "Cinema Weekly and Cinema Truth: Dziga Vertov and the Leninist Proportion," in *Sight and Sound* (London), Winter 1973/74.

Brik, Osip, "Mayakovsky and the Literary Movements of 1917-30," translated by Diana Matias, in *Screen* (London), Autumn 1974.

Mayne, J., "Kino-truth and Kino-praxis: Vertov's *Man with a Movie Camera,*" in *Ciné-Tracts* (Montreal), Summer 1977.

Denkin, H., "Linguistic Models in Early Soviet Cinema," in *Cinema Journal* (Evanston), Fall 1977.

Fischer, L., "Enthusiasm: from Kino-eye to Radio-eye," in *Film Quarterly* (Berkeley), Winter 1977/78.

"Dziga Vertov," in *Travelling* (Lausanne), Summer 1979.

Rouch, Jean, "Five Faces of Vertov," in *Framework* (Norwich, England), Autumn 1979.

"Vertov Issue" of *October* (Cambridge, Massachusetts), Winter 1979.

Petric, Vlad, "The Difficult Years of Dziga Vertov: Excerpts from his Diaries," in *Quarterly Review of Film Studies* (New York), Winter 1982.

Tesson, C., "L'homme sans limites," in *Cahiers du Cinéma* (Paris), July-August 1987.

* * *

Dziga Vertov, pioneer Soviet documentarian, was born Denis Arkadievitch Kaufman. He and two younger brothers, Mikhail and Boris, were sons of a librarian in the Polish city of Byalistok, which at the time was within the Tsarist empire. When World War I broke out, the parents took the family to what seemed the comparative safety of Petrograd (St. Petersburg was renamed to expunge the Germanic link). When the Bolshevik revolution began, Denis, who was twenty-one, and Mikhail, who was nineteen, became involved. Denis volunteered to the cinema committee and became a newsreel worker. Soon he was editing footage of revolutionary upheaval and the struggles against American, British, French, and Japanese intervention forces. His hastily assembled reels went out as war reports and morale boosters. He became known as Dziga Vertov, a name that suggested a spinning top and a choice that was perhaps meant to convey perpetual motion. The newsreel, titled *Kino-Nedelia* (*Film Weekly*), continued until the end of the hostilities in 1920. Vertov also used selected footage for the multi-reel *Godovshchina revoliutsiva* (*Anniversary of the Civil War*) and other compilations.

Vertov hoped to launch a more ambitious series of film reports on the building of a new society, but a period of frustration followed. A new economic policy, introduced as a temporary measure, permitted limited private enterprise to stimulate the prostrate economy. Cinemas, which were allowed to import foreign features, were soon filled with old American, German, French, and English films. An outraged Vertov turned into a polemicist, a writer of fiery manifestos. Addressing the film world, he wrote: "'Art' works of pre-revolutionary days surround you like icons and still command your prayerful emotions. Foreign lands abet you in your confusion, sending into the new Russia the living corpses of movie dramas garbed in splendid technological dressing." He tended to look on these films, and even on fiction films in general, as dangerous corrupting influences, another "opium of the people." He urged producers to "come to life."

His vitriol won Vertov enemies in the film world, but he also had support in high places. Early in 1922 Lenin is said to have told his Commissar of Education, Anatoli Lunacharsky, "Of all the arts, for us film is the most important." Lenin emphasized newsreels and proclaimed a "Leninist film-proportion": along with fiction, film programs should include material reflecting "Soviet reality." All this enabled Vertov to launch, in May 1922, the famous *Kino-Pravda* (*Film-Truth*), which continued as an official monthly release until 1925. His wife, Elizoveta Svilova, became film editor. Mikhail Kaufman gave up a planned law career to become his brother's chief cameraman.

The *Kino-Pravda* group scorned prepared scenarios. Vertov outlined ideas, but left wide latitude to Mikhail and other cameramen. Sallying forth with cameras, they caught moments when a Moscow trolley line, long defunct in torn-up streets, was finally put back into action. Army tanks, used as tractors, were seen leveling an area for an airport. They shot footage of the staff of a children's hospital as it tried to save war-starved waifs. A travelling film team was seen arriving in a town, unpacking gear, and preparing an outdoor showing—of *Kino-Pravda.* The reels were always composed of "fragments of actuality," but Vertov also put emphasis on their provocative juxtaposition. Superimpositions, split screens, slowed or speeded motion could play a part in this. If the fragments were "truths," the manipulations were intended to bring out other "truths"—relationships and meanings.

For a time the *Kino-Pravda* releases were virtually the only item in cinema programs that touched the historic movement, and they therefore had a wide impact. Footage was from time to time reused in combination with new footage in feature documentaries. Among the most successful was *Shestaya chast' mira* (*One Sixth of the World*), in which Vertov made impressive use of subtitles. Short, intermittent subtitles formed a continuing apostrophe addressing the people of the Soviet Union. "You in the small villages ... You in the tundra ... You on the ocean." Having established, via footage and words, a vast geographic dispersion, the catalog turned to nationalities, "You Uzbeks ... You Kalmiks." Then it addressed occupations, age groups, sexes. The continuing sentence went on for minutes, then ended with, "You are the owners of one sixth of the world." The incantation style, reminiscent of Walt Whitman—who was much admired by Vertov—continued throughout the film, projecting the destiny foreseen for the "owners." To men and women with only a dim awareness of the scope and resources of their land, the film must indeed have been a prideful pageant.

Vertov's career gradually became clouded, especially in the Stalin years. His aversion to detailed scenarios, which he said were inapplicable to reportage documentaries, marked him as "antiplanning." He agreed to write "analyses" of what he had in mind, but his proposals were often rejected. Articulated social doctrine was increasingly mandatory; experiments in form were decried. Ironically, Vertov remains best known for one of his most experimental films, *Chelovek s kinoapparatom* (*Man with a Movie Camera*). Featuring Mikhail in action, and intended to demonstrate the role of the cameraman in showing "Soviet reality," it also became an anthology of film devices and tricks. Eisenstein, usually a Vertov supporter, criticized it for "unmotivated camera mischief" and even "formalism."

During the following years Vertov and Kaufman worked in the Ukraine studios, apparently a reflection of disfavor in Moscow. But in the Ukraine Vertov created one of the most inventive of early sound films, *Entuziazm: Simfoniia Donbassa* (*Enthusiasm: Symphony of the Don Basin*), a virtuoso exploration of the possibilities of nonsynchronous sound. Another such exploration was the moving *Tri pesni O Lenine* (*Three Songs About Lenin*), which utilized the precious fragments of Lenin footage. But Vertov had lost standing. In his final years he was again a newsreel worker, arriving and leaving the job on schedule, no longer writing manifestos.

Vertov's ideas were, however, echoed in later years in cinéma vérité, the movement of the 1960s named after Vertov's *Kino-Pravda.* The 1960s and 1970s saw an international revival of interest in Vertov. This revival included rehabilitation of his reputation in the Soviet Union, with retrospectives of his films, biographical works, and publication of selections from Vertov's journals, manifestos, and other writings.

—Erik Barnouw

VIDOR, Charles

Nationality: Hungarian/American. **Born:** Budapest, 27 July 1900. **Education:** Attended Universities of Budapest and Berlin. **Military Service:** Infantry lieutenant, World War I. **Family:** Married 1) actress Karen Morley, 1932 (divorced 1943), one son; 2) Mrs. Doris Warner Leroy, 1945, two sons. **Career:** Assistant cutter and assistant director at UFA studios, Berlin, early 1920s; moved to United States, 1924, worked as opera singer and as longshoreman; moved to Hollywood, late 1920s, assistant director, editor and scriptwriter; directed first feature, for MGM, 1932; after dispute with Harry Cohn at Columbia, returned to MGM, 1949; formed Aurora productions, 1956. **Died:** Of heart attack, in Vienna, 4 June 1959.

Films as Director:

1931 *The Bridge* (short)
1932 *The Mask of Fu Manchu* (co-d, uncredited)
1933 *Sensation Hunters*
1934 *Double Door*
1935 *Strangers All*; *The Arizonian*; *His Family Tree*
1936 *Muss 'em Up*
1937 *A Doctor's Diary*; *The Great Gambini*; *She's No Lady*
1939 *Romance of the Redwoods*; *Blind Alley*; *Those High Grey Walls*
1940 *My Son, My Son!*; *The Lady in Question*
1941 *Ladies in Retirement*; *New York Town*
1942 *The Tuttles of Tahiti*
1943 *The Desperadoes*
1944 *Cover Girl*; *Together Again*
1945 *A Song to Remember*; *Over 21*
1946 ***Gilda***
1948 *The Loves of Carmen* (+ pr)
1952 *It's a Big Country* (co-d); *Hans Christian Andersen*
1953 *Thunder in the East*
1954 *Rhapsody*
1955 *Love Me or Leave Me*
1956 *The Swan*
1957 *The Joker Is Wild*
1958 *A Farewell to Arms*
1960 *Song without End* (completed by George Cukor)

Publications

On VIDOR: articles—

Pryor, Thomas, "Vidor Graph," in *The New York Times,* 5 November 1944.

Gray, Martin, "No Swansong for Director Charles Vidor," in *Films and Filming* (London), June 1956.
Obituary, in *The New York Times,* 5 June 1959.
Doane, M.A., "*Gilda*: Epistemology as Striptease," in *Camera Obscura* (Berkeley), Fall 1983.

* * *

Charles Vidor's filmography is as unremarkable as it is varied: an average musical (*Cover Girl*) enhanced by the charm of Gene Kelly, the presence of Rita Hayworth, and the comedy of Phil Silvers and Eve Arden; Grace Kelly's final screen credit (*The Swan*); a cute comedy of a middle-aged man in the military (*Over Twenty-One*); a turgid Alan Ladd adventure (*Thunder in the East*); a fine gothic melodrama (*Ladies in Retirement*); a solid Randolph Scott western (*The Desperadoes*); a campy Boris Karloff vehicle (*The Mask of Fu Manchu,* co-directed with Charles Brabin); a clumsy Hemingway remake (*A Farewell to Arms*); and programmers for various studios during the 1930s.

A majority of Vidor's credits are romances and musicals, and he also specialized in cinematic treatments of the lives of the famous. Vidor's two show-business biographies mix entertainers and mobsters: *The Joker Is Wild,* the life of the nightclub performer Joe E. Lewis, featuring one of Frank Sinatra's better performances; and *Love Me or Leave Me,* a film that included a good Doris Day performance as Ruth Etting and a great James Cagney performance as "The Gimp." He also chronicled the lives of Hans Christian Andersen (in a film of the same name), Fredric Chopin (*A Song to Remember*), and Franz Liszt (*Song without End,* completed by George Cukor on his death). Other Vidor films also have classical settings or origins: *Rhapsody* (wealthy Elizabeth Taylor torn between pianist John Ericson and violinist Vittorio Gassman); *The Loves of Carmen* (again with Hayworth, but without Bizet's music).

Vidor's one fascinating—and very atypical—credit is *Gilda,* which starred Hayworth, his favorite actress. It has an exceptionally erotic quality for 1946, highlighted by Rita's energetic nightclub dance in which she peels off her long white gloves. *Blind Alley* is another noteworthy film, one of Hollywood's initial features which seriously deals with psychology: mobster Chester Morris is analyzed by his hostage, psychiatrist Ralph Bellamy.

Vidor occasionally elicits above-average performances from his stars, and many of his films are enjoyable. But they cannot compare with similar films by other filmmakers, and his actors—with the exception of Hayworth in *Gilda*—give their most characteristic performances elsewhere. *Cover Girl,* by no means a classic musical, is far from Gene Kelly's cinematic zenith. *The Swan* is more of a footnote to Grace Kelly's career. Similarly, *Ladies in Retirement* is no *Wuthering Heights* or *Rebecca. Rhapsody,* next to *Intermezzo,* is hokum. Finally, his classical biographies are not as grotesque as those of Ken Russell, but this is certainly no recommendation. None of his biographies rank with the best in the genre. Charles Vidor is, at best, an entertainer whose films are enhanced by the talents of those in his casts. He cannot truly be considered an artist.

—Rob Edelman

Charles Vidor with Irene Dunne on the set of *Over 21*

VIDOR, King

Nationality: American. **Born:** King Wallis Vidor in Galveston, Texas, 8 February 1894. **Education:** Attended Peacock Military Academy, San Antonio, Texas. **Family:** Married 1) actress Florence Arto, 1915 (divorced 1924), one daughter; 2) actress Eleanor Boardman, 1926 (divorced 1932); 3) Elizabeth Hall, 1932 (died 1973). **Career:** Ticket-taker and part-time projectionist in Galveston's first movie house, 1909-10; amateur newsreel photographer, 1910-15; drove to Hollywood in Model T, financed trip by shooting footage for Ford's advertising newsreel, 1915; worked at various jobs in film industry, then directed first feature, *The Turn in the Road,* 1919; hired by 1st National, built studio called Vidor Village, 1920 (shut down, 1922); director for Goldwyn Studios, 1923, later absorbed by MGM; taught graduate course in cinema, University of California, Los Angeles, 1960s. **Awards:** Best Direction, Venice Festival, for *Wedding Night,* 1935; Special Prize, Edinburgh Festival, 1964; Honorary Academy Award, 1978. **Died:** Of heart failure, in California, 1 November 1982.

Films as Director:

1919 *The Turn in the Road* (+ sc); *Better Times* (+ sc); *The Other Half* (+ sc); *Poor Relations* (+ sc)
1920 *The Jack Knife Man* (+ pr, co-sc); *The Family Honor* (+ co-pr);
1921 *The Sky Pilot*; *Love Never Dies* (+ co-pr)
1922 *Conquering the Woman* (+ pr); *Woman, Wake Up* (+ pr); *The Real Adventure* (+ pr); *Dusk to Dawn* (+ pr)
1923 *Peg-O-My-Heart*; *The Woman of Bronze*; *Three Wise Fools* (+ co-sc)
1924 *Wild Oranges* (+ co-sc); *Happiness*; *Wine of Youth*; *His Hour*
1925 *Wife of the Centaur*; *Proud Flesh*; ***The Big Parade***
1926 *La Bohème* (+ pr); *Bardelys, The Magnificent* (+ pr)
1928 ***The Crowd*** (+ co-sc); *The Patsy*; *Show People*
1929 ***Hallelujah***
1930 *Not So Dumb*; *Billy the Kid*
1931 *Street Scene*; *The Champ*
1932 *Bird of Paradise*; *Cynara*
1933 *Stranger's Return*
1934 *Our Daily Bread* (+ pr, co-sc)
1935 *Wedding Night*; *So Red the Rose*
1936 *The Texas Rangers* (+ pr, co-sc)
1937 *Stella Dallas*
1938 *The Citadel* (+ pr)
1940 *Northwest Passage* (+ pr); *Comrade X* (+ pr)
1941 *H.M. Pulham, Esq.* (+ pr, co-sc)
1944 *American Romance* (+ pr, co-sc)
1946 *Duel in the Sun*
1949 *The Fountainhead*; *Beyond the Forest*
1951 *Lightning Strikes Twice*
1952 *Ruby Gentry* (+ co-pr)
1955 *Man Without a Star*
1956 *War and Peace* (+ co-sc)
1959 *Solomon and Sheba*

King Vidor

Publications

By VIDOR: books—

A Tree is a Tree, New York, 1953; reprinted 1977.
King Vidor on Filmmaking, New York, 1972.
King Vidor, an interview by Nancy Dowd and David Shepard, Metuchen, New Jersey, 1988.

By VIDOR: articles—

"Easy Steps to Success," in *Motion Picture Classic* (New York), August 1919.
"Credo," in *Variety* (New York), January 1920.
Interview with M. Cheatham, in *Motion Picture Classic* (New York), June 1928.
"The Story Conference," in *Films in Review* (New York), June/July 1952.
"Lillian Gish in Opera," in *Films and Filming* (London), January 1955.
"The End of an Era," in *Films and Filming* (London), March 1955.
"Me ... and My Spectacle," in *Films and Filming* (London), October 1959.
Interview with V. F. Perkins and Mark Shivas, in *Movie* (London), July/August 1963.
"King Vidor at N.Y.U.," an interview in *Cineaste* (New York), Spring 1968.
"War, Wheat and Steel," an interview with J. Greenburg, in *Sight and Sound* (London), Autumn 1968.
"King Vidor," an interview with D. Lyons and G. O'Brien, in *Inter/View* (New York), October 1972.
"King Vidor on D.W. Griffith's Influence," an interview with A. Nash, in *Films in Review* (New York), November 1975.

On VIDOR: books—

Brownlow, Kevin, *The Parade's Gone By ...,* New York, 1968.
Higham, Charles, and Joel Greenberg, editors, *The Celluloid Muse: Hollywood Directors Speak,* London, 1969.
Baxter, John, *King Vidor,* New York, 1976.

Comuzio, Ermanno, *King Vidor,* Florence, 1986.
Durgnat, Raymond, and Scott Simmon, *King Vidor—American,* Berkeley, 1988.
Lang, Robert, *American Film Melodrama: Griffith, Vidor, Minnelli,* Princeton, New Jersey, 1989.
Mulvey, Laura, *Visual and Other Pleasures,* London, 1989.

On VIDOR: articles—

Harrington, C., "King Vidor's Hollywood Progress," in *Sight and Sound* (London), April/June 1953.
Brownlow, Kevin, "King Vidor," in *Film* (London), Winter 1962.
Sarris, Andrew, "Second Line," in *Film Culture* (New York), Spring 1963.
"The Directors Choose the Best Films," in *Cinema* (Beverly Hills), August/September 1963.
Mitchell, G.J., "King Vidor," in *Films in Review* (New York), March 1964.
Higham, C., "King Vidor," in *Film Heritage* (Dayton, Ohio), Summer 1966.
"King Vidor at NYU: Discussion," in *Cineaste* (New York), Spring 1968.
Barr, C., "King Vidor," in *Brighton* (London), March 1970.
Luft, H.G., "A Career that Spans Half a Century," in *Film Journal* (New York), Summer 1971.
Higham, C., "Long Live Vidor, A Hollywood King," in *The New York Times,* 3 September 1972.
Durgnat, Raymond, "King Vidor," in two parts, in *Film Comment* (New York), July/August and September/October 1973.
"Vidor Issues" of *Positif* (Paris), September and November 1974.
"*Notre pain quotidien* Issue" of *Avant-Scène du Cinema* (Paris), 1 May 1977.
Dover, B., "Tribute to King Vidor," in *Films in Review* (New York), June/July 1978.
Lang, J., "Hommage à King Vidor," in *Cinéma* (Paris), November 1981.
Carbonner, A., "King Vidor ou l'ambivalence du désir," in *Cinéma* (Paris) December 1982.
Luft, H.G., "King Vidor," in *Films in Review* (New York), December 1982.
Allen, W., "King Vidor and *The Crowd,*" in *Stills* (London), Winter 1982.
Eyman, S., "Remembering King Vidor," in *Films and Filming* (London), January 1983.
Kirkpatrick, S.D., "Hollywood Whodunit," in *American Film* (Washington D.C.), June 1986.
Gillett, John, and Richard Combs, "King Vidor—Worth Overdoing!" in *National Film Theatre Booklet* (London), May 1991.

* * *

King Vidor began work in Hollywood as a company clerk for Universal, submitting original scripts under the pseudonym Charles K. Wallis. (Universal employees weren't allowed to submit original work to the studio.) Vidor eventually confessed his wrongdoing and was fired as a clerk, only to be rehired as a comedy writer. Within days, he lost this job as well when Universal discontinued comedy production.

Vidor next worked as the director of a series of short dramatic films detailing the reform work of Salt Lake City Judge Willis Brown, a Father Flanagan-type. Vidor tried to parlay this experience into a job as a feature director with a major studio but was unsuccessful. He did manage, however, to find financial backing from nine doctors for his first feature, a picture with a Christian Science theme titled *The Turn in the Road.* Vidor spent the next year working on three more features for the newly-christened Brentwood Company, including the comedy *Better Times,* starring his own discovery, Zasu Pitts.

In 1920 Vidor accepted an offer from First National and a check for $75,000. He persuaded his father to sell his business in order that he might build and manage "Vidor Village," a small studio which mirrored similar projects by Chaplin, Sennett, Griffith, Ince, and others. Vidor directed eight pictures at Vidor Village, but was forced to close down in 1922. The following year, he was hired by Louis B. Mayer at Metro to direct aging stage star Laurette Taylor in *Peg-O-My-Heart.* Soon after, he went to work for Samuel Goldywn, attracted by Goldywn's artistic and literary aspirations. In 1924 Vidor returned to Metro as a result of a studio merger that resulted in MGM. He would continue to work there for the next 20 years, initially entrusted with molding the careers of rising stars John Gilbert and Eleanor Boardman, soon to be Vidor's second wife.

The Big Parade changed Vidor's status from contract director to courted screen artist. Produced by Irving Thalberg, the film grew from a minor studio production into one of MGM's two biggest hits of 1926, grossing $18 million. *The Big Parade* satisfied Vidor's desire to make a picture with lasting value and extended exhibition. It was the first of three films he wanted to make on the topics of "wheat, steel, and war." Vidor went on to direct Gilbert and Lillian Gish, a new studio acquisition, in *La Bohème.*

Encouraged by the popularity of German films of the period and their concern with urban life, Vidor made *The Crowd,* "*The Big Parade* of peace." It starred unknown actor James Murray, whose life would end in an alcoholic suicide. (Murray inspired one of Vidor's later projects, an unproduced picture titled *The Actor.*) Like *The Big Parade, The Crowd* presented the reactions of an everyman, this time to the anonymity of the city and the rigors of urban survival. Vidor's silent career then continued with two of Marion Davies' comedies, *The Patsy* and *Show People.* His career extended into "talkies" with a third comedy, *Not So Dumb.* Though only moderately successful, Vidor became a favorite in William Randolph Hearst's entourage.

Vidor was in Europe when the industry announced its conversion to sound. He quickly returned to propose *Hallelujah,* with an all-black cast. Although considered a politically-astute director for Hollywood, the film exposes Vidor's political shortcomings in its paternalistic attitude toward blacks. With similar political naiveté, Vidor's next great film, the pseudo-socialist agricultural drama *Our Daily Bread,* was derived from a *Reader's Digest* article.

By this point in his career, Vidor's thematics were fairly intact. Informing most of his lasting work is the struggle of Man against Destiny and Nature. In his great silent pictures, *The Big Parade* and *The Crowd,* the hero wanders through an anonymous and malevolent environment, war-torn Europe and the American city, respectively. In his later sound films, *The Citadel, Northwest Passage, Duel in the Sun,,* and *The Fountainhead* various forms of industry operate as a vehicle of Man's battle to subdue Nature. Unlike the optimism in the films of Ford and Capra, Vidor's films follow a Job-like pattern in which victory comes, if at all, with a great deal of personal sacrifice. Underlying all of Vidor's great work are the biblical resonances of a Christian Scientist, where Nature is ultimately independent from and disinterested in Man, who always remains subordinate in the struggle against its forces.

Following *Our Daily Bread,* Vidor continued to alternate between films that explored this personal thematic and projects seemingly less suited to his interests. In more than 50 features, Vidor worked for several producers, directing *Wedding Night* and *Stella Dallas* for Samuel Goldwyn; *The Citadel, Northwest Passage,* and *Comrade X* for MGM; *Bird of Paradise,* where he met his third wife Elizabeth Hill, and *Duel in the Sun* for David O. Selznick; *The Fountainhead, Beyond the Forest,* and *Lightning Strikes Twice* for Warner Brothers; and late in his career, *War and Peace* for Dino De Laurentiis. Vidor exercised more control on his films after *Our Daily Bread,* often serving as producer, but his projects continued to fluctuate between intense metaphysical drama and lightweight comedy and romance.

In the 1950s Vidor's only notable film was *Ruby Gentry,* and his filmmaking career ended on a less-than-praiseworthy note with *Solomon and Sheba.* In the 1960s he made two short documentaries,

Truth and Illusion and *Metaphor,* about his friend Andrew Wyeth. Vidor wrote a highly praised autobiography in 1953, *A Tree is a Tree.* In 1979 he received an honorary Oscar (he was nominated as best director five times). In the last years of his life, he was honored in his hometown of Galveston with an annual King Vidor film festival.

—Michael Selig

VIGO, Jean

Nationality: French. **Born:** Paris, 26 April 1905, son of anarchist Miguel Alemreyda (Eugène Bonaventure de Vigo). **Education:** Attended a number of schools, including the Boys School of St. Cloud, until 1917; following death of father, attended boarding school in Nimes, under the name Jean Sales. **Family:** Married Elizabeth Lozinska, 1929, child: Luce. Father found dead under mysterious circumstances in jail cell, 1917; mother confined to a hospital, 1923. **Career:** Experienced health problems, entered clinic in Montpellier, then moved to Nice because of his tuberculosis, 1929; directed first film, *A propos de Nice,* 1930, then returned to live in Paris, 1932; *Zéro de conduite* removed from circulation by censors because of perceived "anti-France" content; became seriously ill with leukemia, 1933. **Died:** 5 October 1934.

Film as Director:

1930 ***À propos de Nice***
1931 *Taris* (*Taris roi de l'eau*; *Jean Taris champion de natation*)
1933 ***Zéro de conduite***
1934 ***L'Atalante***

Publications

By VIGO: books—

The Complete Jean Vigo, London, 1983.
Oeuvres de cinéma: Films, scénarios, projets de films, texts sur le cinéma, edited by Pierre Lherminier, Paris, 1985.

On VIGO: books—

Kyrou, Ado, *Amour, érotisme et cinéma,* Paris, 1957.
Salès-Gomès, P.E., *Jean Vigo,* Paris, 1957; Los Angeles, 1971.
Agel, Henri, *Miroirs de L'insolite dans le cinéma français,* Paris, 1958.
Pornon, Charles, *Le Rêve et le fantastique dans le cinéma français,* Paris, 1959.
Buache, Freddy, and others, editors, *Hommage à Jean Vigo,* Lausanne 1962.
Lherminier, Pierre, *Jean Vigo,* Paria, 1967.
Lovell, Alan, *Anarchist Cinema,* London, 1967.
Martin, Marcel, *Jean Vigo, Anthologie du Cinéma,* vol. 2, Paris, 1967.
Smith, John, *Jean Vigo,* New York, 1971.
Simon, William G., *The Films of Jean Vigo,* Ann Arbor, Michigan, 1981.
Andrew, Dudley, *Film in the Aura of Art,* Princeton, New Jersey, 1984.

On VIGO: articles—

Cavalcanti, Alberto, "Jean Vigo," in *Cinema Quarterly* (Edinburgh), Winter 1935.
Kracauer, Siegfried, "Jean Vigo," in *Hollywood Quarterly,* April 1947.
Weinberg, Herman G., "The Films of Jean Vigo," in *Cinema* (Beverly Hills), July 1947.
Agee, James, "Life and Work of Jean Vigo," in *Nation* (New York), 12 July 1947.
Zilzer, G., "Remembrances of Jean Vigo," in *Hollywood Quarterly,* Winter 1947/48.
"Vigo Issue" of *Ciné-Club* (Paris), February 1949.
"Vigo Issue" of *Positif* (Lyon), no. 7, 1953.
De Laurot, Edouard, and Jonas Mekas, "An Interview with Boris Kaufman," in *Film Culture* (New York), Summer 1955.
Salès-Gomès, P.E., "Le Mort de Jean Vigo," in *Cahiers du Cinéma* (Paris), August/September 1955.
Ashton, D.S., "Portrait of Vigo," in *Film* (London), December 1955.
Tranchant, François, "Dossier Jean Vigo," in *Image et Son* (Paris), October 1958.
"Vigo Issue" of *Premier Plan* (Lyon), no. 19, 1961.
Chevassu, François, "Jean Vigo," in *Image et Son* (Paris), February 1961.
Ellerby, John, "The Anarchism of Jean Vigo," in *Anarchy 6* (London), August 1961.
"Vigo Issue" of *Études Cinématographiques* (Paris), no. 1-52, 1966.
Mills, B., "Anarchy, Surrealism, and Optimism in *Zéro de conduite,*" in *Cinema* (London), no. 8, 1971.
Teush, B., "The Playground of Jean Vigo," in *Film Heritage* (New York), Fall 1973.
Baldwin, D., *L'Atalante* and the Maturing of Jean Vigo," in *Film Quarterly* (Berkeley), Fall 1985.
Wood, Robin, "*L'Atalante*: The Limits of Liberation," in *CineAction!* (Toronto), no. 10, 1987.
Painlevé, J., "Sur un point de détail curieux à l'usage exclusif de vigolâtres érudits," in *Jeune Cinéma* (Paris), October/November 1989.
Thompson, David J., "*L'Atalante,*" in *Sight and Sound* (London), Summer 1990.

* * *

It is difficult to think of another director who made so few films and yet had such a profound influence on other filmmakers. Jean Vigo's *À propos de Nice,* his first film, is his contribution to the French surrealist movement. The film itself is a direct descendant of Vertov's *Man with a Movie Camera.* Certainly, his films make political statements similar to those seen in Vertov's work. Vertov's documentary celebrates a people's revolution, while Vigo's chastises the bourgeois vacationers in a French resort town. Even more importantly, both films revel in the pyrotechnics of the camera and the editing room. They are filled with dizzying movement, fast cutting, and the juxtaposition, from frame to frame, of objects that normally have little relation to each other. In yet another link between the two directors, Vertov's brother photographed *À propos de Nice,* as well as Vigo's other three films.

À propos de Nice provides a look at a reality beyond the prosaic, common variety that so many films give us. The movie attempts nothing less than the restructuring of our perception of the world by presenting it to us not so much through a seamless, logical narrative, but rather through a fast-paced collection of only tangentially related shots.

After *À propos de Nice,* Vigo began combining his brand of surrealism with the poetic realism that would later be so important to a generation of French directors, such as Jean Renoir and Marcel Carné. For his second film, he made another documentary, *Taris,* about France's champion swimmer. Here Vigo takes his camera underwater as Taris clowns at the bottom of a pool and blows at the lens. *Taris* certainly has some striking images, but it is only eleven minutes long. Indeed, if Vigo had died in 1931, after finishing *Taris,* instead of in

Jean Vigo

1934 (and given the constantly precarious state of his health, this would not have been at all unlikely), he would have been remembered, if at all, as a director who had shown great potential, yet who could hardly be considered a major talent.

Vigo's third film, however, secured his place in film history. *Zéro de conduite* stands out as one of the cinema's most influential works. Along with films such as Sagan's *Mädchen in Uniform* and Wyler's *These Three,* it forms one of the more interesting and least studied genres of the 1930s—the children's boarding school film. Although it is Vigo's first fiction film, it continues the work he began with *À propos de Nice.* That first movie good-naturedly condemns the bourgeoisie, showing the rich as absolutely useless, their primary sin being banality rather than greed or cruelty. In *Zéro de conduite,* teachers, and not tourists, are the representatives of the bourgeoisie. But like the Nice vacationers, they are not so much malicious as they are simply inadequate; they instruct their schoolboys in nothing important and prize the school's suffocating regulations above all else. Vigo lets the schoolboys rebel against this sort of mindless monotony. They engage in an apocalyptic pillow fight, and then bombard their teachers with fruit during a stately school ceremony. The film's anarchic spirit led to its being banned in France until 1945. But during the 1950s, it became one of the inspirations for the French New Wave directors. In subject matter, it somewhat resembles Truffaut's *400 Blows.* But it is the film's style—the mixture of classical Hollywood visuals with the dreamlike illogic of slow motion, fast action, and quick cutting—that particularly influenced a new generation of filmmakers.

Vigo's last film, *L'Atalante,* is his masterpiece. It is a love story that takes place on a barge, with Vigo once again combining surrealism with poetic realism. The settings are naturalistic and the characters lower-class, and so bring to mind Renoir's poetic realist films such as *Toni* and *Les Bas-Fonds.* There is also an emphasis on the imagination and on the near-sacredness of banal objects that places the film strongly in the tradition of such surrealist classics as *Un Chien andalou.* After Juliette leaves Jean, the barge captain, Jean jumps into the river and sees his wife's image everywhere around him. The underwater sequence not only makes the viewer think of *Taris,* but also makes us aware that we are sharing Jean's obsession with him. This dreamy visualization of a character's thoughts brings to mind the priority that the surrealists gave to all mental processes. The surrealists prized, too, some of the more mundane aspects of everyday life, and Vigo's film is full of ordinary objects that take on (for Juliette) a magical status. They are only puppets, or fans, or gramophones piled in a heap in the room of Père Jules, Jean's old assistant, but Juliette has spent her entire life in a small town, and for her, these trinkets represent the mysteries of faraway places. They take on a special status, the banal being raised to the level of the exotic.

Despite the movie's links to two film movements, *L'Atalante* defies categorization. It is a masterpiece of mood and characterization, and, along with *Zéro de conduite,* it guarantees Vigo's status as a great director. But he was not granted that status by the critical community until years after his death. Because of the vagaries of film exhibition and censorship, Vigo was little known while he was making films. He received nowhere near the acclaim given to his contemporaries Jean Renoir and René Clair.

—Eric Smoodin

VISCONTI, Luchino

Nationality: Italian. **Born:** Count Don Luchino Visconti di Modrone in Milan, 2 November 1906. **Education:** Educated at private schools in Milan and Como; also attended boarding school of the Calasanzian Order, 1924-36. **Military Service:** Served in Reggimento Savoia Cavalleria, 1926-28. **Career:** Stage actor and set designer, 1928-29; moved to Paris, assistant to Jean Renoir, 1936-37; returned to Italy to assist Renoir on *La Tosca,* 1939; directed first film, *Ossessione,* 1942; directed first play, Cocteau's *Parenti terrible,* Rome, 1945; directed first opera, *La vestale,* Milan, 1954; also ballet director, 1956-57. **Awards:** International Prize, Venice Festival, for *La terra trema,* 1948; 25th Anniversary Award, Cannes Festival, 1971. **Died:** 17 March 1976.

Films as Director:

1942 ***Ossessione*** (+ co-sc)
1947 ***La terra trema*** (+ sc)
1951 *Bellissima* (+ co-sc); *Appunti su un fatto di cronaca* (second in series *Documento mensile*)
1953 "We, the Women" episode of *Siamo donne* (+ co-sc)
1954 *Senso* (+ co-sc)
1957 *Le notti bianche* (*White Nights*) (+ co-sc)
1960 ***Rocco e i suoi fratelli*** (*Rocco and His Brothers*) (+ co-sc)
1962 "Il lavoro (The Job)" episode of *Boccaccio '70* (+ co-sc)
1963 ***Il gattopardo*** (*The Leopard*) (+ co-sc)
1965 *Vaghe stelle dell'orsa* (*Of A Thousand Delights*; *Sandra*) (+ co-sc)

1967 "Le strega bruciata viva" episode of *Le streghe*; *Lo straniero* (*L'Etranger*) (+ co-sc)
1969 ***La caduta degli dei*** (*The Damned*; *Götterdämmerung*) (+ co-sc)
1970 *Alla ricerca di Tadzio*
1971 ***Morte a Venezia*** (*Death in Venice*) (+ pr, co-sc)
1973 *Ludwig* (+ co-sc)
1974 *Gruppo di famiglia in un interno* (+ co-sc)
1976 *L'innocente* (*The Innocent*) (+ co-sc)

Other Films:

1936 *Les Bas-fonds* (Renoir) (asst d)
1937 ***Une Partie de campagne*** (Renoir) (asst d) (released 1946)
1940 *La Tosca* (Renoir) (asst d)
1945 *Giorni di gloria* (De Santis) (asst d)

Publications

By VISCONTI: books—

Senso, Bologna, 1955.
Le notti bianche, Bologna, 1957.
Rocco e i suoi fratelli, Bologna, 1961.
Il gattopardo, Bologna, 1963.
Vaghe stelle dell'orsa (*Sandra*), Bologna, 1965.
Three Screenplays, New York, 1970.
Morte a Venezia, Bologna, 1971.
Il mio teatro, in two volumes, Bologna, 1979.

By VISCONTI: articles—

"Il cinéma antropomorfico," in *Cinema* (Rome), 25 September 1943.
"*La terra trema*," in *Bianco e Nero* (Rome), March 1951.
"*Marcia nuziale*," in *Cinema Nuovo* (Turin), 1 May 1953.
Interview with Jacques Doniol-Valcroze and Jean Domarchi, in *Cahiers du Cinéma* (Paris), March 1959.
"The Miracle That Gave Men Crumbs," in *Films and Filming* (London), January 1961.
"Drama of Non-Existence," in *Cahiers du Cinema in English* (New York), no. 2, 1966.
"Violence et passion," special Visconti issue of *Avant-Scène du Cinéma* (Paris), June 1975.
Interview with Peter Brunette, in *Sight and Sound* (London), Winter 1986/87.

On VISCONTI: books—

Pellizzari, Lorenzo, *Luchino Visconti*, Milan, 1960.
Baldelli, Pio, *I film di Luchino Visconti*, Manduria, Italy, 1965.
Guillaume, Yves, *Visconti*, Paris, 1966.
Nowell-Smith, Geoffrey, *Luchino Visconti*, New York, 1968.
Ferrero, Adelio, editor, *Visconti: il cinema*, Modena, 1977.
Tornabuoni, Lietta, editor, *Album Visconti*, foreward by Michelangelo Antonioni, Milan, 1978.
Stirling, Monica, *A Screen of Time: A Study of Luchino Visconti*, New York, 1979.
Servadio, Gaia, *Luchino Visconti: A Biography*, London, 1981.
Bencivenni, Alessandro, *Luchino Visconti*, Florence, 1982.
Tonetti, Claretta, *Luchino Visconti*, Boston, 1983.
Ishaghpour, Youssef, *Luchino Visconti: Le sens de l'image*, Paris, 1984.
Sanzio, Alain, and Paul-Louis Thirard, *Luchino Visconti: Cinéaste*, Paris, 1984.
De Giusti, Luciano, *I film di Luchino Visconti*, Rome, 1985.
Mancini, Elaine, *Luchino Visconti: A Guide to References and Resources*, Boston, 1986.
Villien, Bruno, *Visconti*, Paris, 1986.
Schifano, Laurence, *Luchino Visconti: Les feux de la passion*, Paris, 1987; published as *Luchino Visconti: The Flames of Passion*, London, 1990.

On VISCONTI: articles—

Renzi, Renzo, "Mitologia e contemplasione in Visconti, Ford e Eisenstein," in *Bianco e Nero* (Rome), February 1949.
Demonsablon, Philippe, "Notes sur Visconti," in *Cahiers du Cinéma* (Paris), March 1954.
Lane, John Francis, "The Hurricane Visconti," in *Films and Filming* (London), December 1954.
Castello, Giulio, "Luchino Visconti," in *Sight and Sound* (London), Spring 1956.
Lane, John Francis, "Visconti—The Last Decadent," in *Films and Filming* (London), July 1956.
Dyer, Peter John, "The Vision of Visconti," in *Film* (London), March/April 1957.
Poggi, Gianfranco, "Luchino Visconti and the Italian Cinema," in *Film Quarterly* (Berkeley), Spring 1960.
"Visconti Issue" of *Premier Plan* (Paris), May 1961.
"Visconti Issue" of *Etudes Cinématographiques* (Paris), no. 26-27, 1963.
Elsaesser, Thomas, "Luchino Visconti," in *Brighton* (London), February 1970.
"Visconti Issue" of *Cinema* (Rome), April 1970.
Aristarco, Guido, "The Earth Still Trembles," in *Films and Filming* (London), January 1971.
Korte, Walter, "Marxism and Formalism in the Films of Luchino Visconti," in *Cinema Journal* (Evanston, Illinois), Fall 1971.
Cabourg, J., "Luchino Visconti, 1906-1976," in *Avant-Scène du Cinéma* (Paris), 1 and 15 March 1977.
Sarris, Andrew, "Luchino Visconti's Legacy," in *The Village Voice* (New York), 15 January 1979.
Rosi, Francesco, "En travaillant avec Visconti: sur le tournage de *La Terra trema*," in *Positif* (Paris), February 1979.
Lyons, D., "Visconti's Magnificient Obsessions," in *Film Comment* (New York), March/April 1979.
Graham, A., "The Phantom Self," in *Film Criticism* (New York), Fall 1984.
Aristarco, Guido, "Luchino Visconti: Critic or Poet of Decadence?," in *Film Criticism* (Meadville, Pennsylvania), Spring 1988.

* * *

The films of Luchino Visconti are among the most stylistically and intellectually influential of postwar Italian cinema. Born a scion of ancient nobility, Visconti integrated the most heterogeneous elements of aristocratic sensibility and taste with a committed Marxist political consciousness, backed by a firm knowledge of Italian class structure. Stylistically, his career follows a trajectory from a uniquely cinematic realism to an operatic theatricalism, from the simple quotidian eloquence of modeled actuality to the heightened effect of lavishly appointed historical melodramas. His career fuses these interests into a mode of expression uniquely Viscontian, prescribing a potent, double-headed realism. Visconti turned out films steadily but rather slowly from 1942 to 1976. His obsessive care with narrative and filmic materials is apparent in the majority of his films.

Whether or not we choose to view the wartime *Ossessione* as a precursor or a determinant of neorealism, or merely as a continuation of elements already present in Fascist period cinema, it is clear that

Luchino Visconti

the film remarkably applies a realist mise-en-scène to the formulaic constraints of the genre film. With major emendations, the film is, following a then-contemporary interest in American fiction of the 1930s, a treatment (the second and best) of James M. Cain's *The Postman Always Rings Twice.* In it the director begins to explore the potential of a long-take style, undoubtedly influenced by Jean Renoir, for whom Visconti had worked as assistant. Having met with the disapproval of the Fascist censors for its depiction of the shabbiness and desperation of Italian provincial life, *Ossessione* was banned from exhibition.

For *La terra trema,* Visconti further developed those documentary-like attributes of story and style generally associated with neorealism. Taken from Verga's late nineteenth-century masterpiece *I malavoglia,* the film was shot entirely on location in Sicily and employed the people of the locale, speaking in their native dialect, as actors. Through them, Visconti explores the problems of class exploitation and the tragedy of family dissolution under economic pressure. Again, a mature long-shot/long-take style is coupled with diverse, extensive camera movements and well-planned actor movements to enhance the sense of a world faithfully captured in the multiplicity of its activities. The extant film was to have become the first episode of a trilogy on peasant life, but the other two parts were never filmed.

Rocco e i suoi fratelli, however, made over a dozen years later, continues the story of this Sicilian family, or at least one very much like it. Newly arrived in Milan from the South, the Parandis must deal with the economic realities of their poverty as well as survive the sexual rivalries threatening the solidarity of their family unit. The film is episodic in nature, affording time to each brother's story (in the original version), but special attention is given to Rocco, the forebearing and protective brother who strives at all costs to keep the group together, and Simone, the physically powerful and crudely brutal one, who is unable to control his personal fears, insecurities, and moral weakness. Unable to find other work, they both drift into prize fighting, viewed here as class exploitation. Jealousy over the prostitute Nadia causes Simone to turn his fists against his brother, then to murder the woman. But Rocco, impelled by strong traditional ties, would still act to save Simone from the police. Finally, the latter is betrayed to the law by Ciro, the fourth youngest and a factory worker who has managed to transfer some of his familial loyalty to a social plane and the labor union. Coming full circle from *La terra trema,* Luca, the youngest, dreams of a day when he will be able to return to the Southern place of his birth. *Rocco* is perhaps Visconti's greatest contribution to modern tragedy, crafted along the lines of Arthur Miller and Tennessee Williams (whose plays he directed in Italy). The Viscontian tragedy is saturated with melodramatic intensity, a stylization incurring more than a suggestion of decadent sexuality and misogyny. There is also, as in other Visconti works, a rather ambiguous intimation of homosexuality (here between Simone and his manager.)

By *Senso* Visconti had achieved the maturity of style that would characterize his subsequent work. With encompassing camera movements—like the opening shot, which moves from the stage of an opera house across the audience, taking in each tier of seats where the protest against the Austrians will soon erupt—and with a melodramatic rendering of historical fact, Visconti begins to mix cinematic realism with compositional elegance and lavish romanticism. Against the colorful background of the Risorgimento, he paints the betrayal by an Austrian lieutenant of his aristocratic Italian mistress who, in order to save him, has compromised the partisans. The love story parallels the approaching betrayal of the revolution by the bourgeois political powers.

Like Gramsci, who often returned to the contradictions of the Risorgimento as a key to the social problems of the modern Italian state, Visconti explores that period once more in *Il gattopardo,* from the Lampedusa novel. An aristocratic Sicilian family undergoes transformation as a result of intermarriage with the middle-class at the same time that the Mezzogiorno is undergoing unification with the North. The bourgeoisie, now ready and able to take over from the dying aristocracy, usurps Garibaldi's revolution; in this period of *transformismo,* the revolutionary process will be assimilated into the dominant political structure and defused.

Still another film that focuses on the family unit as a barometer of history and changing society is *La caduta degli dei.* This treatment of a German munitions industry family (much like Krupp) and its decline into betrayal and murder in the interests of personal gain and the Nazi state intensifies and brings up-to-date an examination of the social questions of the last mentioned films. Here again a meticulous, mobile camera technique sets forth and stylistically typifies a decadent, death-surfeited culture.

Vaghe stelle dell'orsa removes the critique of the family from the social to the psychoanalytic plane. While death or absence of the father and the presence of an uprising surrogate is a thematic consideration in several Visconti films, he here explores it in conjunction with Freudian theory in this deliberate yet entirely transmuted retelling of the Elektra myth. We are never completely aware of the extent of the relationship between Sandra and her brother, and the possibility of past incest remains distinct. Both despise their stepfather Gilardini, whom they accuse of having seduced their mother and having denounced their father, a Jew, to the Fascists. Sandra's love for and sense of solidarity with her brother follows upon a racial solidarity with her father and race, but Gianni's love, on the other hand, is underpinned by a desire for his mother, transferred to Sandra. Nevertheless, dramatic confrontation propels the dialectical investigations of the individual's position with respect to the social even in this, Visconti's most densely psychoanalytic film.

Three films marking a further removal from social themes and observation of the individual, all literary adaptations, are generally felt to be his weakest: *Le notte bianche* from Dostoevski's *White Nights* sets a rather fanciful tale of a lonely man's hopes to win over a despairing woman's love against a decor that refutes, in its obvious, studio-bound staginess, Visconti's concern with realism and material verisimilitude. The clear inadequacy of this Livornian setting, dominated by a footbridge upon which the two meet and the unusually claustrophobic spatiality that results, locate the world of individual romance severed from large social and historical concerns in an inert, artificial perspective that borders on the hallucinatory. He achieves similar results with location shooting in *Lo straniero,* where—despite alterations of the original Camus—he perfectly captures the difficult tensions and tones of individual alienation by utilizing the telephoto lens pervasively. Rather than provide a suitable Viscontian dramatic space rendered in depth, it reduces Mersault to the status of a Kafkaesque insect-man observed under a microscope. Finally, *Morte a Venezia,* based on the fiction of Thomas Mann, while among Visconti's most formally beautiful productions, is one of his least critically successful. The baroque elaboration of mise-en-scène and camera work does not rise above self-pity and self-indulgence, and is cut off from social context irretrievably.

—Joel Kanoff

VON STERNBERG, Josef

Nationality: Austrian. **Born:** Jonas Sternberg in Vienna, 19 May 1894. **Education:** Educated briefly at Jamaica High School, Queens, New York, returned to Vienna to finish education. **Family:** Married 1) Riza Royce, 1926 (divorced 1930); 2) Jeanne Annette McBride, 1943, two children. **Career:** Film patcher for World Film Co. in Fort Lee,

New Jersey, 1911; joined U.S. Army Signal Corps to make training films, 1917; scenarist and assistant for several directors, 1918-24; attached "von" to his name at suggestion of actor Elliot Dexter, 1924; directed first film, *The Salvation Hunters,* then signed eight-picture contract with MGM (terminated after two abortive projects), 1925; directed *The Sea Gull* for Charlie Chaplin (Chaplin did not release it), 1926; director for Paramount, 1926-35; began collaboration with Marlene Dietrich on *Der blaue Engel,* made for UFA in Berlin, 1930; attempted to direct *I, Claudius* for Alexander Korda in England, 1937 (not completed); made documentary *The Town* for U.S. Office of War Information, 1941; taught class in film direction, University of Southern California, 1947. **Awards:** George Eastman House Medal of Honor, 1957; honorary member, Akademie der Künste, Berlin, 1960. **Died:** 22 December 1969.

Films as Director:

1925 *The Salvation Hunters* (+ pr, sc); *The Exquisite Sinner* (+ co-sc) (remade by Phil Rosen); *The Masked Bride* (remade by Christy Cabanne)
1926 *The Sea Gull* (*Woman of the Sea*) (+ sc)
1927 *Children of Divorce* (d add'l scenes only); ***Underworld***
1928 *The Last Command* (+ sc); *The Drag Net*; *The Docks of New York*
1929 *The Case of Lena Smith*; *Thunderbolt*
1930 ***Der blaue Engel*** (*The Blue Angel*); *Morocco*
1931 *Dishonored*; *An American Tragedy*
1932 *Shanghai Express*; *Blonde Venus* (+ co-sc); *I Take This Woman*
1934 ***The Scarlet Empress***
1935 ***The Devil Is a Woman*** (+ co-ph); *Crime and Punishment*
1936 *The King Steps Out*
1939 *Sergeant Madden*; *New York Cinderella* (remade by Frank Borzage and W.S. Van Dyke)
1941 *The Shanghai Gesture* (+ co-sc)
1943-44 *The Town*
1946 *Duel in the Sun* (d several scenes only)
1951 *Macao* (re-shot almost entirely by Nicholas Ray)
1953 *Anatahan* (*The Saga of Anatahan*) (+ sc, ph)
1957 *Jet Pilot* (completed 1950)

Other Films:

(partial list)

1919 *The Mystery of the Yellow Room* (asst d); *By Divine Right* (asst d, sc, ph); *Vanity's Price* (asst d)

Publications

By VON STERNBERG: books—

Daughters of Vienna, free adaptation of stories by Karl Adolph, Vienna, 1922.
Dokumentation, eine Darstellung, Mannheim, Germany, 1966.
Fun in a Chinese Laundry, New York, 1965
The Blue Angel (screenplay), New York, 1968.

By VON STERNBERG: articles—

Interview, in *Motion Picture Classic* (New York), May 1931.
"On Life and Film," in *Films in Review* (New York), October 1952.
"More Light," in *Sight and Sound* (London), Autumn 1955.
"Acting in Film and Theater," in *Film Culture* (New York), Winter 1955.
Interview with D. Freppel and B. Tavernier, in *Cinéma* (Paris), March 1961.
"A Taste for Celluloid," in *Films and Filming* (London), July 1963.
"The von Sternberg Principle," in *Esquire* (New York), October 1963.
"Sternberg at 70," with John Pankake, in *Films in Review* (New York), May 1964.
Interview with Peter Bogdanovich, in *Movie* (London), Summer 1965.
Interview with F. A. Macklin, in *Film Heritage* (Dayton, Ohio), Winter 1965-66.
"*L'Ange bleu,*" in *Avant-Scène du Cinéma* (Paris), March 1966.
Interview with Kevin Brownlow, in *Film* (London), Spring 1966.

On VON STERNBERG: books—

Harrington, Curtis, *An Index to the Films of Josef von Sternberg,* London, 1949.
Sarris, Andrew, *The Films of Josef von Sternberg,* New York, 1966.
Walker, Alexander, *The Celluloid Sacrifice,* New York, 1967.
Weinberg, Herman G., *Josef von Sternberg: A Critical Study,* New York, 1967.
Anthologie du cinéma, Vol. 6, Paris, 1971.
Baxter, John, *The Cinema of Josef von Sternberg,* New York, 1971.
Mérigeau, Pascal, *Josef Von Sternberg,* Paris, 1983.
Studlar, Gaylyn, *In the Realm of Pleasure: Von Sternberg, Dietrich and the Masochistic Aesthetic,* Urbana, Illinois, 1988.
Zucker, Carole, *The Idea of the Image: Josef von Sternberg's Dietrich Films,* Cranbury, New Jersey, 1988.

On VON STERNBERG: articles—

Pringle, Henry, "Profile of Josef von Sternberg," in the *New Yorker,* 28 March 1931.
Harrington, Curtis, "Josef von Sternberg," in *Cahiers du Cinéma* (Paris), October/November 1951.
Labarthe, André, "Un metteur en scène baudelairien," in *Cahiers du Cinéma* (Paris), April 1956.
Weinberg, Herman G., "The Lost Films, Part 1," in *Sight and Sound* (London), August 1962.
Smith, Jack, "A Belated Appreciation of von Sternberg," in *Film Culture* (New York), Winter 1963/64.
Green, O.O., "Six Films of Josef von Sternberg," in *Movie* (London), no. 13, 1965.
Weinberg, Herman G., "Sternberg and Stroheim—Letter," in *Sight and Sound* (London), Winter 1965/66.
Kyrou, Ado, "Sternberg, avant, pendant, après Marlene," in *Positif* (Paris), May 1966.
Camper, Fred, "Essays on Film Style," in *Cinema* (London), no. 8, 1971.
Flinn, T., "Joe, Where Are You?," in *Velvet Light Trap* (Madison, Wisconsin), Fall 1972.
Rheuban, Joyce, "Josef von Sternberg: The Scientist and the Vamp," in *Sight and Sound* (London), Autumn 1973.
Gow, Gordon, "Alchemy: Dietrich and Sternberg," in *Films and Filming* (London), June 1974.
Wood, Robin, "Sternberg's Empress: The Play of Light and Shade," in *Film Comment* (New York), March/April 1975.
Willis, D., "Sternberg: The Context of Passion," in *Sight and Sound* (London), Spring 1978.
Articles from *Ciné-Magazine* reprinted in *Avant-Scène du Ciné* (Paris), 15 March 1980.
Luft, Herbert, "Josef von Sternberg," in *Films in Review* (New York), January 1981.
Magny, Joel, "Josef von Sternberg: la lumière du désir," in *Cinéma* (Paris), December 1982.
Von Sternberg Section of *Skrien* (Amsterdam), April/May 1985.

Josef Von Sternberg

Baxter, Peter, "*Blonde Venus*: Memory, Legend and Desire," and Florence Jacobowitz, "Power and the Masquerade: *The Devil Is a Woman,*" in *CineAction!* (Toronto), no. 8, 1987.

On VON STERNBERG: film:

The Epic That Never Was—"I, Claudius," directed by Bill Duncalf, for BBC-TV, London, 1966.

* * *

There is a sense in which Jonas Sternberg never grew up. In his personality, the twin urges of the disturbed adolescent towards self-advertisement and self-effacement fuse with a brilliant visual imagination to create an artistic vision unparalleled in the cinema. But Sternberg lacked the cultivation of Murnau, the sophistication of his mentor von Stroheim, the humanity of Griffith, or the ruthlessness of Chaplin. His imagination remained immature, and his personality was malicious and obsessive. His films reflect a schoolboy's fascination with sensuality and heroics. That they are sublime visual adventures from an artist who contributed substantially to the sum of cinema technique is one paradox to add to the stock that make up his career.

Much of Sternberg's public utterance, and in particular his autobiography, was calculated to confuse; the disguise of his real Christian name under the diminutive "Jo" is typical. Despite his claims to have done so, he did not "write" all his films, though he did *re*-write the work of some skilled collaborators, notably Jules Furthman and Ben Hecht. While his eye for art and design was highly developed, he never designed sets; he merely "improved" them with props, veils, nets, posters, scribbles, but above all with light. Of this last he was a natural master, the only director of his day to earn membership in the American Society of Cinematographers. Given a set, a face, a camera, and some lights, he could create a mobile portrait of breathtaking beauty.

Marlene Dietrich was his greatest model. He dressed her like a doll, in a variety of costumes that included feathers and sequins, a gorilla suit, a tuxedo, and a succession of gowns by Paramount's master of couture, Travis Banton. She submitted to his every demand with the skill and complaisance of a great courtesan. No other actress provided him with such malleable material. With Betty Compson, Gene Tierney, and Akemi Negishi he fitfully achieved the same "spiritual power," as he called the mood of yearning melancholy which was his ideal, but the effect never equalled that of the seven Dietrich melodramas.

Sternberg was born too early for the movies. The studio system constrained his fractious temperament; the formula picture stifled his urge to primp and polish. He battled with MGM, which offered him a lucrative contract after the success of his von Stroheim-esque expressionist drama *The Salvation Hunters,* fell out with Chaplin, producer of the still-suppressed *Woman of the Sea,* and fought constantly with Paramount until Ernst Lubitsch, acting studio head, "liquidated" him for his intransigence; the later suppression of his last Paramount film, *The Devil Is a Woman,* in a political dispute with Spain merely served to increase Sternberg's alienation.

For the rest of his career, Sternberg wandered from studio to studio and country to country, always lacking the facilities he needed to achieve his best work. Even Korda's lavish *I Claudius,* dogged by disaster and finally terminated in a cost-cutting exercise, shows in its surviving footage only occasional flashes of Sternbergian brilliance. By World War II, he had already achieved his best work, though he lived for another 30 years.

Sternberg alarmed a studio establishment whose executives thought in terms of social and sexual stereotypes, formula plotting, and stock happy endings; their narrative ideal was a *Saturday Evening Post* novelette. No storyteller, Sternberg derided plot; "the best source for a film is an anecdote," he said. From a single coincidence and a handful of characters, edifices of visual poetry could be constructed. His films leap years in the telling to follow a moral decline or growth of an obsession.

The most important film of Sternberg's life was one he never made. After the humiliation of the war years, when he produced only the propaganda short *The Town,* and the nadir of his career, as close-up advisor to King Vidor on *Duel in the Sun,* he wrote *The Seven Bad Years,* a script that would, he said, "demonstrate the adult insistence to follow the pattern inflicted on a child in its first seven helpless years, from which a man could extricate himself were he to realize that an irresponsible child was leading him into trouble." He was never to make this work of self-analysis, nor any film which reflected a mature understanding of his contradictory personality.

Sternberg's theories of cinema were not especially profound, deriving largely from the work of Reinhardt, but they represented a quantum jump in an industry where questions of lighting and design were dealt with by experts who jealously guarded this prerogative. In planning his films not around dialogue but around the performers' "dramatic encounter with light," in insisting that the "dead space" between the camera and subject be filled and enlivened, and above all in seeing every story in terms of "spiritual power" rather than star quality, he established a concept of personal cinema which presaged the *politique des auteurs* and the Movie Brat generation.

In retrospect, Sternberg's contentious personality—manifested in the self-conscious affecting of uniforms and costumes on the set and an epigrammatic style of communicating with performers that drove many of them to frenzy—all reveal themselves as reactions against the banality of his chosen profession. Sternberg was asked late in life if he had a hobby. "Yes. Chinese philately." Why that? "I wanted," he replied in the familiar weary, uninflected voice, "a subject I could not exhaust."

—John Baxter

VON STROHEIM, Erich

Nationality: Austrian. **Born:** Erich Oswald Stroheim in Vienna, 22 September 1885; became U.S. citizen, 1926. **Education:** According to von Stroheim he attended Mariahilfe Military Academy, though several biographers doubt this. **Military Service:** Served briefly in the Austro-Hungarian Army. **Family:** Married 1) Margaret Knox, 1914 (died 1915); 2) May Jones, 1916 (divorced 1918), one son; 3) Valerie Germonprez, 1918 (separated), one son. **Career:** Moved to America and worked as salesman, railroad worker, short story writer, and travel agent, 1909-14; actor, assistant and military adviser for D.W. Griffith, 1914-15; assistant director, military adviser, and set designer for director John Emerson, 1915-17; became known as "The Man You Love to Hate" after role as Prussian officer in *For France,* 1917; directed *Blind Husbands* for Carl Laemmle at Universal, 1918 (terminated contract with Universal, 1922); directed *Greed* for Goldwyn Co., his version cut to ten reels by studio, 1924; moved to France, 1945. **Died:** 12 May 1957.

Films as Director:

1918 *Blind Husbands* (+ sc, art d, role as Lieutenant von Steuben)
1919 *The Devil's Passkey* (+ sc, art d)
1921 ***Foolish Wives*** (+ sc, co-art d, co-costume, role as Count Wladislas Serge Karamazin)
1922 *Merry-Go-Round* (+ sc, co-art d, co-costume) (completed by Rupert Julian)

1924 ***Greed*** (+ sc, co-art d)
1925 *The Merry Widow* (+ sc, co-art d, co-costume)
1927 *The Wedding March* (+ sc, co-art d, co-costume, role as Prince Nicki)
1928 *The Honeymoon* (+ sc, role as Prince Nicki—part two of *The Wedding March* and not released in United States); *Queen Kelly* (+ sc, co-art d) (completed by others)
1933 *Walking Down Broadway* (+ sc) (mostly reshot by Alfred Werker and Edwin Burke and released as *Hello Sister*)

Other Films:

1914 *Captain McLean* (Conway) (role)
1915 *Old Heidelberg* (Emerson) (asst d, military advisor, role as Lutz); *Ghosts* (Emerson) (role); ***The Birth of a Nation*** (Griffith) (role)
1916 ***Intolerance*** (Griffith) (asst d, role as second Pharisee); *The Social Secretary* (Emerson) (asst d, role as a reporter); *Macbeth* (Emerson) (asst d, role); *Less Than the Dust* (Emerson) (asst d, role); *His Picture in the Papers* (Emerson) (asst d, role as the traitor)
1917 *Panthea* (Dwan) (asst d, role as Russian policeman); *Sylvia of the Secret Service* (Fitzmaurice) (asst d, role); *In Again—Out Again* (Emerson) (asst d, art d, role as Russian officer); *For France* (Ruggles) (role as Prussian officer)
1918 *Hearts of the World* (Griffith) (asst d, military advisor, role as German officer); *The Unbeliever* (Crosland) (role as German officer); *The Hun Within* (Cabanne) (role as German officer)
1927 *The Tempest* (sc)
1929 *The Great Gabbo* (Cruze) (role as Gabbo)
1930 *Three Faces East* (del Ruth) (role)
1931 *Friends and Lovers* (Schertzinger) (role)
1932 *The Lost Squadron* (Archimbaud and Sloane) (role); *As You Desire Me* (Fitzmaurice) (role)
1934 *Crimson Romance* (Howard) (military advisor, role as German pilot); *Fugitive Road* (sc/co-sc, military advisor)
1935 *The Crime of Dr. Crespi* (Auer) (role as Dr. Crespi); *Anna Karenina* (Brown) (military advisor)
1936 *Devil Doll* (Browning) (sc/co-sc); *San Francisco* (Van Dyke) (sc/co-sc); *Marthe Richard* (Bernard) (role as German officer)
1937 *Between Two Women* (sc/co-sc); ***La Grande Illusion*** (Renoir) (role as von Rauffenstein); *Mademoiselle Docteur* (Gréville) (role as Col. Mathesius); *L'Alibi* (Chenal) (role as Winkler)
1938 *Les Pirates du rail* (Christian-Jaque) (role as Tschou-Kin); *L'Affaire Lafarge* (Chenal) (role as Denis); *Les Disparus de Saint-Agil* (Christian-Jaque) (role as German professor); *Ultimatum* (Wiene and Siodmak) (role as Général Simovic); *Gibraltar* (role as Marson) (*It Happened in Gibraltar*); *Derrière la façade* (Lacombe) (role as Eric)
1939 *Menaces* (Gréville) (role as Hoffman); *Rappel immédiat* (Mathot) (role as Stanley Wells); *Pièges* (Siodmak) (role as Pears); *Tempète sur Paris* (Bernard-Deschamps) (role as Kohrlick); *La Révolte des vivants* (Pottier) (role as Emile Lasser); *Macao l'enfer* (Delannoy) (role as Knall); *Paris—New York* (Heymann and Mirande) (role)
1940 *I Was an Adventuress* (Ratoff) (role); *So Ends Our Night* (Cromwell) (role)
1943 *Five Graves to Cairo* (Wilder) (role as Field Marshall Rommel); *The North Star* (Milestone) (role as German medic)
1944 *The Lady and the Monster* (Sherman) (role); *Storm over Lisbon* (Sherman) (role)
1945 *The Great Flamarion* (Mann) (role as Flamarion); *Scotland Yard Investigation* (Blair) (role); *The Mask of Dijon* (Landers) (role as Dijon)
1946 *On ne meurt pas comme ça* (Boyer) (role as Eric von Berg)
1947 *La Danse de mort* (Cravenne) (co-adapt, co-dialogue, role as Edgar)
1948 *Le Signal rouge* (Neubach) (role)
1949 *Portrait d'un assassin* (Bernard-Roland) (role)
1950 ***Sunset Boulevard*** (Wilder) (role as Max)
1952 *Minuit, quai de Bercy* (Stengel) (role); *Alraune* (*La Mandragore*) (Rabenalt) (role)
1953 *L'Envers du paradis* (Gréville) (role as O'Hara); *Alerte au sud* (Devaivre) (role)
1954 *Napoléon* (Guitry) (role as Beethoven)
1955 *Série noire* (Foucaud) (role); *La Madone des sleepings* (Diamant-Berger) (role)

Publications

By VON STROHEIM: books—

Paprika, New York, 1935.
Les Feux de la Saint-Jean: Veronica (Part 1), Givors, France, 1951.
Les Feux de la Saint-Jean: Constanzia (Part 2), Givors, France, 1954; reissued 1967.
Poto-Poto, Paris, 1956.
Greed (full screenplay), Cinémathèque Royale de Belgique, Brussels, 1958.

By VON STROHEIM: articles—

Interviews, in *Motion Picture* (New York), August 1920, October 1921, May 1922, September 1923, and April 1927.
"Charges Against Him and His Reply," with C. Belfrage, in *Motion Picture Classic* (Brooklyn), June 1930.
"My Own Story," in *Film Weekly* (London), April/May 1935.
"Stroheim in London," with Karel Reisz, in *Sight and Sound* (London), April/June 1954.
"Erich von Stroheim," in *Interviews with Film Directors*, edited by Andrew Sarris, New York, 1967.
"*Citizen Kane*," in *Positif* (Paris), March 1968 (reprinted from 1941).
"*Les Rapaces (Greed)*," (scenario), in *Avant-Scène du Cinéma* (Paris), September 1968.

On VON STROHEIM: books—

Atasceva, P., and V. Korolevitch, *Erich von Stroheim*, Moscow, 1927.
Drinkwater, John, *The Life and Adventures of Carl Laemmle*, New York, 1931.
Fronval, Georges, *Erich von Stroheim, sa vie, ses films*, Paris, 1939.
Noble, Peter, *Hollywood Scapegoat: The Biography of Erich von Stroheim*, London, 1951.
Bergut, Bob, *Erich von Stroheim*, Paris, 1960.
Barna, Jan, *Erich von Stroheim*, Vienna, 1966.
Gobeil, Charlotte, editor, *Hommage à Erich von Stroheim*, Ottawa, 1966.
Ciment, Michel, *Erich von Stroheim*, Paris, 1967.
Brownlow, Kevin, *The Parade's Gone By ...*, New York, 1968.
Finler, Joel, *Stroheim*, Berkeley, 1968.
Curtiss, Thomas Quinn, *Erich von Stroheim*, Paris, 1969.
Buache, Freddy, *Erich von Stroheim*, Paris, 1972.
Pratt, George C., *Spellbound in Darkness*, Greenwich, Connecticut, 1973.
Weinberg, Herman G., *Stroheim: A Pictorial Record of His Nine Films*, New York, 1975.
Bazin, André, *The Cinema of Cruelty: From Buñuel to Hitchcock*, New York, 1982.

Erich Von Stroheim

Koszarski, Richard, *The Man You Loved to Hate: Erich von Stroheim and Hollywood,* New York, 1983.
Bessy, Maurice, *Erich von Stroheim,* Paris, 1984.

On VON STROHEIM: articles—

Yost, Robert, "Gosh, How They Hate Him!," in *Photoplay* (New York), December 1919.
Weinberg, Herman G., "Erich von Stroheim," in *Film Art* (London), Spring 1937.
"Tribute to Stroheim," in *Film Quarterly* (London), Spring 1947.
"Von Stroheim Issue" of *Ciné-club* (Paris), April 1949.
Schwerin, Jules, "The Resurgence of von Stroheim," in *Films in Review* (New York), April 1950.
Lambert, Gavin, "Stroheim Revisited: The Missing Third in American Cinema," in *Sight and Sound* (London), April/June 1955.
Eisner, Lotte, "Notes sur le style de Stroheim," in *Cahiers du Cinéma* (Paris), January 1957.
"Von Stroheim Issue" of *Cinéma* (Paris), February 1957.
Everson, William K., "The Career of Erich von Stroheim," in *Films in Review* (New York), August/September 1957.
"Von Stroheim Issue" of *Film Culture* (New York), April 1958.
Marion, Denis, "Stroheim, the Legend and the Fact," in *Sight and Sound* (London), Winter 1961/62.
Weinberg, Herman G., "The Legion of Lost Films," in *Sight and Sound* (London), Autumn 1962.
Weinberg, Herman G., "Sternberg and Stroheim," in *Sight and Sound* (London), Winter 1965/66.
"Von Stroheim Issue" of *Etudes Cinématographiques* (Paris), no. 48/50, 1966.
Gilliatt, Penelope, "The Scabrous Poet from the Estate Belonging to No One," in the *New Yorker,* 3 June 1972.
"Von Stroheim Issue" of *Cinema* (Zurich), December 1973.
Rosenbaum, Jonathan, "Second Thoughts on Stroheim," in *Film Comment* (New York), May/June 1974.
Koszarski, Richard, and William K. Everson, "Stroheim's Last 'Lost' Film: The Making and Remaking of *Walking Down Broadway,*" in *Film Comment* (New York), May/June 1975.
Brownlow, Kevin, "The Merry Widow Affair," in *American Film* (Washington, D.C.), July/August 1981.
Wilder, Billy, "Stroheim, l'homme que vous aimerez," in *Positif* (Paris), July/August 1983.
Grindon, Leger, "From Word to Image: Displacement and Meaning in *Greed,*" in *Journal of Film and Video* (Boston), vol. 41, no. 4, 1989.

* * *

Erich von Stroheim had two complementary careers in cinema, that of actor-director, primarily during the silent period, and that of distinguished character actor when his career as a director was frustrated as a result of his inability to bring his genius to terms with the American film industry.

After edging his way into the industry in the humblest capacities, Stroheim's lengthy experience as bit player and assistant to Griffith paid off. His acceptance during the pioneer period of American cinema as Prussian "military adviser," and his bullet-headed physical resemblance to the traditional monocled image of the tight-uniformed Hun officer, enabled him to create a more established acting career and star in his own films. With his first personal film, *Blind Husbands,* he became the prime creator in Hollywood of witty, risqué, European-like sex-triangle comedy-dramas. His initial successes in the early 1920s were characterized by subtle acting touches and a marked sophistication of subject that impressed American audiences of the period as essentially European and fascinatingly decadent. *Blind Husbands* was followed by other films in the same genre, the 12-reel *The Devil's Pass Key* and the critically successful *Foolish Wives.* In all three works, women spectators could easily identify with the common character of the lonely wife, whose seduction by attractively wicked Germanic officers and gentlemen (usually played by Stroheim, now publicized as "the man you love to hate") provided the essential thrill. Stroheim also cunningly included beautiful but excitingly unprincipled women characters in both *The Devil's Pass Key* and *Foolish Wives,* played by Maude George and Mae Busch. Details of bathing, dressing, and the ministration of servants in the preparation of masters or mistresses in boudoir or dressing room were recurrent, and the Stroheim scene always included elaborate banquets, receptions, and social ceremonies.

Stroheim's losing battle with the film industry began in his clashes with Irving Thalberg at Universal. His obsessive perfectionism over points of detail in setting and costume had pushed the budget for *Foolish Wives* to the million dollar mark. Though the publicists boasted of Stroheim's extravagance, the front office preferred hard profits to such self-indulgent expenditures. Thalberg also refused Stroheim's demands that his films should be of any length he determined, and *Foolish Wives* (intended to be in two parts) was finally taken out of his hands and cut from 18-20 to some 12-14 reels. Although a critical success, the film lost money.

Foolish Wives was Stroheim's most discussed film before *Greed.* In it he played a bogus aristocratic officer, in reality a swindler and multi-seducer. His brilliant, sardonic acting "touches" brought a similar psychological verisimilitude to this grimly satiric comedy of manners as Lubitsch was to establish in his *Kammerspielfilme* (intimate films). He also specialized in decor, photographic composition, and lighting. The latticed light and shadow in one sequence, when the seducer in full uniform visits the counterfeiter's underworld den with hope of ravishing the old man's mentally defective daughter, is unforgettable.

Greed, Stroheim's most important film, was based meticulously on Norris's Zolaesque novel, *McTeague.* Stroheim's masterpiece, it was eventually mutilated by the studio because of its unwieldy length; it was reduced over Stroheim's protests from 42 reels to 24 (between 5 and 6 hours), and then finally cut to 10 reels by the studio. Stroheim's emphasis on the ugly and bizarre in human nature emerged in this psychologically naturalistic study of avarice and degradation seen in a mismatched couple—McTeague, the impulsive, primitive (but bird-loving) lower-class dentist, and Trina, the pathologically avaricious spinster member of a German-Swiss immigrant family and winner of a $5,000 lottery. After their marriage, Trina hoards her money as their circumstances decline to the point where the husband becomes drunk and brutal, and the wife mad. After he murders her and becomes a fugitive, McTeague ends up in the isolated wastes of Death Valley, handcuffed to Marcus, his former friend whom he has killed. Using the streets of San Francisco and the house where the actual murder that had inspired Norris had taken place, Stroheim anticipated Rossellini in his use of such locations. But his insistence on achieving an incongruous and stylized realism, which starts with McTeague's courtship of Trina sitting on a sewerpipe and culminates in the macabre sequence in Death Valley, goes beyond that straight neorealism of the future. Joel W. Finler, in his book *Stroheim,* analyzes the wholesale cutting in the 10-reel version, exposing the grave losses that render the action and motivation of the film unclear. But the superb performances of Zasu Pitts and Gibson Gowland compensate, and the grotesque Sieppe family provide a macabre background, enhanced by Stroheim's constant reminder of San Francisco's "mean streets." The film was held to be his masterpiece by many, but also condemned as a "vile epic of the sewer."

Stroheim was to work as director on only five more films: the Ruritanian *Merry Widow* (adapted from the operetta), *The Wedding March* (in two parts, and again severely cut), the erotic *Queen Kelly* (directed for Gloria Swanson, but never completed by Stroheim, though released by Swanson with her own additions), and the sound films

Walking Down Broadway (released as *Hello, Sister*; it was never released in Stroheim's original version), and *The Emperor's Candlesticks,* on which it appears he collaborated only in direction. The silent films portray the same degenerate Imperial Viennese society Stroheim favored. Half-romantic and half-grotesque fantasy, the films once again presented Stroheim's meticulous attention to detail in decor and characterization. *The Wedding March* (in spite of studio intervention) is the high point in Stroheim's career as a director after *Greed.* Subsequently he remained content to star or appear in films made by others, making some 50 appearances between 1929 and 1955. His most notable acting performances during this period were in Renoir's *La Grande Illusion* and Wilder's *Five Graves to Cairo* and *Sunset Boulevard,* in which his past as a director is almost ghoulishly recalled.

—Roger Manvell

VON TROTTA, Margarethe

Nationality: German. **Born:** Berlin, 21 February, 1942. **Education:** Universities of Munich and Paris; studied acting in Munich. **Family:** Married director Volker Schlöndorff. **Career:** Actress in theatres in Dinkelsbül, Stuttgart, and Frankfurt, 1960s; worked only in TV and film, from 1969; directed first film, *Die verlorene Ehre der Katharina Blum,* 1975. **Awards:** Golden Lion, Venice Festival, for *Die Bleierne Zeit,* 1981.

Films as Director:

1975 *Die verlorene Ehre der Katherina Blum* (*The Lost Honor of Katharina Blum*) (co-d, co-sc)
1977 *Das zweite Erwachen der Christa Klages* (*The Second Awakening of Christa Klages*) (+ sc)
1979 *Schwestern oder Die Balance des Glücks* (*Sisters, or The Balance of Happiness*) (+ sc)
1981 ***Die Bleierne Zeit*** (*Leaden Times*; *Marianne and Julianne*; *The German Sisters*) (+ sc)
1983 *Heller Wahn* (*Sheer Madness*) (+ sc)
1986 *Rosa Luxemburg*
1987 episode of *Felix*
1988 *Paura e amore* (*Three Sisters/Love and Fear*)
1990 *Die Rückkehr* (*Return*; *L'Africana*)
1993 *Il lungo silenzio* (*The Long Silence*)
1994 *Das versprechen* (*The Promise*) (+ co-sc)

Other Films:

1968 *Schräge Vögel* (Ehmck) (role)
1969 *Brandstifter* (Lemke) (role); *Götter der Pest* (Fassbinder) (role as Margarethe)
1970 *Baal* (Schlöndorff) (role as Sophie); *Der amerikanische Soldat* (Fassbinder) (role as maid)
1971 *Der plötzliche Reichtum der armen Leute von Kombach* (Schlöndorff) (co-sc, role as Heinrich's woman); *Die Moral der Ruth Halbfass* (Schlöndorff) (role as Doris Vogelsang)
1972 *Strohfeuer* (Schlöndorff) (role as Elisabeth, co-sc)
1973 *Desaster* (Hauff) (role); *Übernachtung in Tirol* (Schlöndorff) (role as Katja)
1974 *Invitation à la chasse* (Chabrol) (for TV) (role as Paulette); *Georgina's Gründe* (Schlöndorff) (for TV) (role as Kate Theory)
1975 *Das andechser Gefühl* (Achternbusch) (role as film actress)
1976 *Der Fangschuss* (Schlöndorff) (co-sc, role as Sophie von Reval)
1984 *Blaubart* (*Bluebeard*) (Zanussi) (role); *Unerreichbare Nahe* (Hirtz) (sc)

Publications

By VON TROTTA: books—

Die Bleierne Zeit, Frankfurt, 1981.
Heller Wahn, Frankfurt, 1983.
Rosa Luxemburg, with Christiane Ensslin, Frankfurt, 1986.

By VON TROTTA: articles—

"*Die verlorene Ehre der Katharina Blum,*" in *Film and Fernsehen* (Berlin), no. 8, 1976.
"Gespräch zwischen Margarethe von Trotta und Christel Buschmann," in *Frauen und Film* (Berlin), June 1976.
"Frauen haben anderes zu sagen ...," an interview with U. Schirmeyer-Klein, in *Film und Fernsehen* (Berlin), no. 4, 1979.
Interview with Sheila Johnston in *Stills* (London), May/June 1986.
Interview with Karen Jaehne and Lenny Rubenstein in *Cineaste* (New York), vol. 15, no. 4, 1987.

On VON TROTTA: books—

Franklin, James, *New German Cinema: From Oberhausen to Hamburg,* Boston, 1983.
Phillips, Klaus, editor, *New German Filmmakers: From Oberhausen through the 1970s,* New York, 1984.
Todd, Janet, editor, *Women and Film: Women and Literature,* New York, 1988.
Elsaesser, Thomas, *New German Cinema: A History,* London, 1989.

On VON TROTTA: articles—

"*Le Coup de grâce* Issue" of *Avant-Scène du Cinéma* (Paris), 1 February 1977.
Elsaesser, Thomas, "Mother Courage and Divided Daughter," in *Monthly Film Bulletin* (London), July 1983.
Dossier on von Trotta, in *Revue du Cinéma* (Paris), November 1983.
Moeller, H.B., "West German Women's Cinema: The case of Margarethe von Trotta," in *Film Criticism* (Meadville, Pennsylvania), Winter 1984/85; reprinted Fall-Winter 1986/87.
Linville, Susan, and Kent Casper, "The Ambiguity of Margarethe von Trotta's *Sheer Madness,*" in *Film Criticism* (Meadville, Pennsylvania), vol. 12, no. 1, 1987.
Donough, Martin, "Margarethe von Trotta: Gynemegoguery and the Dilemmas of a Filmmaker," in *Literature/Film Quarterly* (Salisbury, Maryland), vol. 17, no. 3, 1989.
Kauffman, Stanley, "The Long Silence," in *New Republic,* 30 May 1994.

* * *

An important aspect of Margarethe von Trotta's filmmaking, which affects not only the content but also the representation of that content, is her emphasis on women and the relationships that can develop between them. For example, von Trotta chose as the central theme in two of her films (*Sisters, or The Balance of Happiness* and *Marianne and Juliane*) one of the most intense and complex relationships that can exist between two women, that of sisters. Whether von Trotta is dealing with overtly political themes as in *The Second Awakening of*

Margarethe Von Trotta directing *Das zweite Erwachen der Christa Klages*

Christa Klages (based on the true story of a woman who robs a bank in order to subsidize a daycare center) and *Marianne and Juliane* (based on the experiences of Christine Ensslin and her "terrorist" sister) or with the lives of ordinary women as in *Sisters or the Balance of Happiness* or *Sheer Madness,* von Trotta shows the political nature of relationships between women. By paying close attention to these relationships, von Trotta brings into question the social and political systems which either sustain them or do not allow them to exist.

Although the essence of von Trotta's films is political and critical of the status quo, their structures are quite conventional. Her films are expensively made and highly subsidized by the film production company Bioskop, which was started by her husband Volker Schlöndorff and Reinhard Hauff, both filmmakers. Von Trotta joined the company when she started making her own films. She did not go through the complicated system of incentives and grants available to independent filmmakers in Germany. Rather, she began working for Schlöndorff as an actress and then as a scriptwriter, and finally on her own as a director and co-owner in the production company which subsidizes their films.

Von Trotta has been criticized by some feminists for working too closely within the system and for creating characters and structures which are too conventional to be of any political value. Other critics find that a feminist aesthetic can be found in her choice of themes. For although von Trotta uses conventional women characters, she does not represent them in traditional fashion. Nor does she describe them with stereotyped, sexist clichés; instead, she allows her characters to develop on screen through gestures, glances, and nuances. Great importance is given to the psychological and subconscious delineation of her characters, for von Trotta pays constant attention to dreams, visions, flashbacks, and personal obsessions. In this way, her work can be seen as inspired by the films of Bresson and Bergman, filmmakers who also use the film medium to portray psychological depth.

"The unconscious and subconscious behavior of the characters is more important to me than what they do," says von Trotta. For this reason, von Trotta spends a great deal of time with her actors and actresses to be sure that they really understand the emotions and motivations of the characters which they portray. This aspect of her filmmaking caused her to separate her work from that of her husband, Volker Schlöndorff. During their joint direction of *The Lost Honor of Katharina Blum,* it became apparent that Schlöndorff's manner of directing, which focused on action shots, did not mix with his wife's predilections for exploring the internal motivation of the characters. Her films are often criticized for paying too much attention to the psychological, and thus becoming too personal and inaccessible.

Von Trotta has caused much controversy within the feminist movement and outside of it. Nevertheless, her films have won several awards not only in her native Germany but also internationally, drawing large, diverse audiences. Her importance cannot be minimized. Although she employs the commonly used and accepted structures of popular filmmakers, her message is quite different. Her main characters are women and her films treat them in a serious and innovative fashion. Such treatment of women within a traditional form has in the past been undervalued or ignored. Her presentation of women has opened up possibilities for the development of the image of women on screen and contributed to the development of film itself.

Von Trotta's films have continued to express other concerns that were central to her earlier work as well. These include examinations of German identity and the impact of recent German history on the present; the view of historical events through the perceptions of the individuals those events affect; the personal risks that individuals take when speaking the truth or exposing the hypocrisy of those in power; and, in particular, the strengths of women and the manner in which they relate to each other and evolve as their own individual selves.

Rosa Luxemburg is a highly intelligent, multi-faceted biopic of the idealistic, politically committed, but ill-fated humanist and democratic socialist who had such a high profile on the German political scene near the beginning of the twentieth century. *Love and Fear,* loosely based on Chekhov's *The Three Sisters,* is an absorbing (if sometimes overdone) allegory about how life is forever in transition. It focuses on a trio of sisters, each with a different personality. The senior sibling is a scholarly type who is too cognizant of how quickly time goes by; the middle one lives an aimless life, and is ruled by her feelings; the junior in the group is a fervent, optimistic pre-med student.

The Long Silence is the story of a judge whose life is in danger because of his prosecution of corrupt government officials. After his murder—an unavoidable occurrence, given the circumstances—his gynecologist wife perseveres in continuing his work. *The Promise,* which reflects on the downfall of Communism and the demise of the Berlin Wall, tells of two lovers who are separated in 1961 during a failed attempt to escape from East to West. With the exception of a brief reunion in Prague in 1968, they are held apart until 1989 and the death of Communism in East Germany.

—Gretchen Elsner-Sommer, updated by Rob Edelman

WAJDA, Andrzej

Nationality: Polish. **Born:** Suwałki, Poland, 6 March 1926. **Education:** Fine Arts Academy, Kraków, 1945-48; High School of Cinematography, Lodz, 1950-52. **Military Service:** Served in the A.K. (Home Army) of the Polish government in exile, from 1942. **Family:** Married 1) Beata Tyszkiewicz, 1967 (marriage dissolved), one daughter; 2) Krystyna Zachwatowicz, 1975. **Career:** Assistant to director Aleksandr Ford, 1953, then directed first feature, *Pokolenie,* 1955; directed first play, 1959; made first film outside Poland, *Sibirska Ledi Magbet,* for Avala Films, Belgrade, 1962; directed *Pilatus und andere* for West German TV, 1972; following imposition of martial law, concentrated on theatrical projects in Poland and film productions outside Poland; government dissolved Wajda's Studio X film production group, 1983; managing director, Teatr Powszechny, Warsaw, from 1989; senator, Polish People's Republic, 1989-91. **Awards:** Grand Prix, Moscow Film Festival, for *The Promised Land,* 1975; Palme d'Or, Cannes Festival, for *Man of Iron,* 1981; British Academy Award for services to film, 1982; Officier, Legion d'Honneur, France, 1982.

Films as Director and Scriptwriter:

1950 *Kiedy ty śpisz* (*While You Sleep*); *Zły chłopiec* (*The Bad Boy*)
1951 *Ceramika Iłżecka* (*The Pottery of Ilzecka*)
1955 *Pokolenie* (*A Generation*); *Idę do słońca* (*I Walk to the Sun*)
1957 ***Kanał*** (*They Loved Life*; *Sewer*)
1958 ***Popiół i diament*** (*Ashes and Diamonds*)
1959 *Lotna*
1960 *Niewinni czarodzieje* (*Innocent Sorcerers*)
1961 *Samson*
1972 *Sibirska Ledi Magbet* (*Lady Macbeth of Mtsensk*; *Fury Is a Woman*; *Siberian Lady Macbeth*); "Warszawa" episode of *L'Amour à Vingt Ans*
1965 *Popióły* (*Ashes*)
1967 *Bramy raju* (*Gates to Paradise*; *The Gates of Heaven*; *The Holy Apes*)
1968 *Wszystko na sprzedaż* (*Everything for Sale*); *Przekładaniec* (*Roly-Poly*)
1969 *Polowanie na muchy* (*Hunting Flies*); *Makbet* (*Macbeth*) (for Polish TV)
1970 *Krajobraz po bitwie* (*Landscape after the Battle*); *Brzezina* (*The Birchwood*)
1972 *Pilatus und andere—ein Film für Karfreitag* (*Pilate and Others*); *Wesele* (*The Wedding*)
1974 *Ziemia obiecana* (*Promised Land*) (also as series on Polish TV)
1976 *Smuga cienia* (*The Shadow Line*)
1977 ***Człowiek z marmuru*** (*Man of Marble*); *Bez znieczulenia* (*Without Anesthetic*); *Umarła klasa* (for TV)
1978 *Zaproszenie do wnętrza* (*Invitation to the Inside*) (doc)
1979 *Dyrygent* (*The Conductor*); *Panny z Wilka* (*The Girls from Wilko*)
1981 *Człowiek z żelaza* (*Man of Iron*)
1982 *Danton*
1983 *Eine Liebe in Deutschland* (*Un amour en Allemagne*; *A Love in Germany*)
1985 *Kronika wypadków miłosnych* (*Chronicle of a Love Affair*)
1987 *Les Possédés* (*The Possessed*)
1990 *Korczak*
1993 *The Ring with the Crowned Eagle*
1994 *Natasha*

Publications

By WAJDA: books—

Un Cinéma nommé désir, Paris, 1986.
Double Vision: My Life in Film, New York, 1989; London, 1990.

By WAJDA: articles—

"Destroying the Commonplace," in *Films and Filming* (London), November 1961.
"Andrzej Wajda Speaking," in *Kino* (Warsaw), no. 1, 1968.
"Living in Hope," an interview with Gordon Gow, in *Films and Filming* (London), February 1973.
"Filmer les noces," in *Positif* (Paris), February 1974.
Interview with K. K. Przybylska, in *Literature/Film Quarterly* (Salisbury, Maryland), Winter 1977.
"Between the Permissible and the Impermissible," an interview with D. Bickley and L. Rubinstein, in *Cineaste* (New York), Winter 1980/81.
"Wajda August '81," an interview and article by G. Moszcz, in *Sight and Sound* (London), Winter 1982.
Interview with Gideon Bachmann, in *Film Quarterly* (Berkeley), Winter 1982/83.
Interview with Marcel Ophuls, in *American Film* (Washington, D.C.), October 1983.
Interview with Dan Yakir, in *Film Comment* (New York), November/December 1984.
Interview with K. Farrington and L. Rubenstein, in *Cineaste* (New York), vol. 14, no. 2, 1985.
Interview with W. Wertenstein, in *Sight and Sound* (London), Summer 1985.
Interview with T. Hubelski, in *Kino* (Warsaw), May 1990.
Interview with J. J. Skreiberg, in *Film and Kino* (Oslo), no. 4, 1990.
Interview with P. Dowell, in *Cineaste* (New York), vol. 19, no 4, 1993.

On WAJDA: books—

McArthur, Colin, editor, *Andrzej Wajda: Polish Cinema,* London, 1970.
Michalek, Boleslaw, *The Cinema of Andrzej Wajda,* translated by Edward Rothert, London, 1973.
Douin, Jean-Luc, *Wajda,* Paris, 1981.
Paul, David W., editor, *Politics, Art and Commitment in the Eastern European Cinema,* New York, 1983.
Karpinski, Maciej, *The Theatre of Andrzej Wajda,* Cambridge, 1989.

Andrzej Wajda

On WAJDA: articles—

Szydlowski, Roman, "The Tragedy of a Generation," in *Film* (Poland), no. 46, 1958.
Michalek, Boleslaw, "Polish Notes," in *Sight and Sound* (London), Winter 1958/59.
Higham, Charles, "Grasping the Nettle: The Films of Andrzej Wajda," in *Hudson Review* (Nutley, New Jersey), Autumn 1965.
"Wajda Issue" of *Etudes Cinématographiques* (Paris), no. 69-72, 1968.
Austen, David, "A Wajda Generation," in *Films and Filming* (London), July 1968.
Toeplitz, K., "Wajda Redivivus," in *Film Quarterly* (Berkeley), Winter 1969/70.
Cowie, Peter, "Wajda Redux," in *Sight and Sound* (London), Winter 1979/80.
"Wajda Issue" of *Avant-Scène du Cinéma* (Paris), 1 January 1980.
Aufderheide, Pat, and others, "Solidarity and the Polish Cinema," in *Cineaste* (New York), vol. 13, no. 3, 1984.
Engelberg, S., "Wadja's *Korczak* Sets Loose the Furies," in *New York Times,* 14 April 1991.
Ball, E., "Citizen Wadja," in *Village Voice* (New York), 23 April 1991.

* * *

The history of Polish film is as old as the history of filmmaking in most European countries. For entire decades, however, its range was limited to Polish territory and a Polish audience. Only after the Second World War, at the end of the 1950s, did the phenomenon known as the "Polish school of filmmaking" make itself felt as a part of world cinema. The phenomenon went hand in hand with the appearance of a new generation of film artists who, despite differences in their artistic proclivities, have a number of traits in common. They are approximately the same age, having been born in the 1920s. They spent their early youth in the shadow of the fascist occupation and shared more or less similar postwar experiences. This is also the first generation of cinematically accomplished artists with a complete grasp of both the theoretical and practical sides of filmmaking.

Their debut was conditioned by the social climate, which was characterized by a desire to eliminate the negative aspects of postwar development labelled as the cult of personality. The basic theme of their work was the effort to come to grips with the painful experience of the war, the resistance to the occupation, and the struggle to put a new face on Polish society and the recent past. Temporal distance allowed them to take a sober look at all these experiences without schematic depictions, without illusions, and without pathetic ceremony. They wanted to know the truth about those years, in which the foundations of their contemporary life were formed, and express it in the specific destinies of the individuals who lived, fought, and died in those crucial moments of history. And one of the most important traits uniting all the members of the "school" was the attempt to debunk the myths and legends about those times and the people who shaped them.

The most prominent representative of the Polish school is Andrzej Wajda. In the span of a few short years he made three films, *Pokolenie, Kanał,* and *Popiół i diament,* which form a kind of loose trilogy and can be considered among the points of departure for the emergence of popular Poland. *Pokolenie* tells of a group of young men and women fighting in occupied Warsaw; *Kanał* is a tragic story of the 1944 Warsaw Uprising; *Popiół i diament* takes place at the watershed between war and peace. Crystallized in these three films are the fundamental themes of Wajda's work, themes characteristic of some other adherents of the "school" as well. In these films we also see the formation of Wajda's own artistic stamp, his creative method, which consists of an emotional approach to history, a romantic conception of human fate, a rich visual sense, and dense expression that is elaborate to the point of being baroque. In his debut, *Pokolenie,* he renounces the dramatic aspect of the battle against the occupation and concentrates on the inner world of people for whom discovering the truth about their struggle was the same as discovering the truth about love. In *Kanał* he expresses disagreement with a myth long ago rooted in the consciousness of the Polish people and propounded in portrayals of the Warsaw Uprising—that the greatest meaning of life is death on the barricades. In the film *Popiół i diament* we hear for the first time in clear tones the theme of the Pole at the crossroads of history and the tragedy of his choice. Wajda expresses this theme not in abstract constructions but in a concrete reality with concrete heroes.

Wajda returns to the war experience several times. *Lotna,* in which the historical action precedes the above-mentioned trilogy, takes place in the tragic September of 1939, when Poland was overrun. Here Wajda continues to take a critical view of national tradition. Bitterness and derision toward the romanticization of the Polish struggle are blended here with sober judgment, and also with understanding for the world and for the people playing out the last tragicomic act on the historical stage. In the film *Samson,* the hero, a Jewish youth, throws off his lifelong passivity and by this action steps into the struggle. Finally, there is the 1970 film *Krajobraz po bitwie,* which, however, differs sharply from Wajda's early films. The director himself characterized this difference in the following way: "It's not I who am drawing back [from the war]. It's the war. It and I are growing old together, and therefore it is more and more difficult for me to discover anything in it that was close to me."

Krajobraz po bitwie has become Wajda's farewell to the war for a long time. This does not mean, however, that the fundamental principles of the artistic method found in his early films have disappeared from his work, in spite of the fact that his work has developed in the most diverse directions over the course of forty years. The basic principles remain and, with time, develop, differentiate, and join with other motifs brought by personal and artistic experience. Some of the early motifs can be found in other contexts. Man's dramatic attitude towards history, the Pole at the crossroads of history and his tragic choice—these we can find in the film *Popioły,* in the image of the fate of Poland in the period of the Napoleonic Wars, when a new society was taking shape in the oppressive atmosphere of a defeated country divided up among three victorious powers. People living in a time of great changes are the main heroes of *Ziemia obiecana,* which portrays the precipitous, drastic, and ineluctable course of the transition from feudalism to the capitalist order. A man's situation at dramatic historical moments is also the subject of the films *Człowiek z marmuru, Człowiek z żelaza,* and *Danton,* which have met with more controversy than the preceding works. In *Danton* and similarly in *Les Possédés* another element is present: the description and criticism of destructive revolutionary forces, which lust for power and assert themselves brutally without regard for the rights of others.

Wajda's work reveals many forms and many layers. Over time, historical films alternate with films on contemporary subjects; films with a broad social sweep alternate with films that concentrate on intimate human experiences. Wajda is conscious of these alternations. From history he returns to contemporaneity, so as not to lose contact with the times and with his audience. After a series of war films, he made the picture *Niewinni czarodzieje,* whose young heroes search for meaning in their lives. In the film *Wszystko na sprzedaż,* following the tragic death of his friend, the actor Zbigniew Cybulski, he became absorbed in the traces a person leaves behind in the memories and hearts of friends; at the same time he told of the problems of artistic searching and creation. Wajda's attitudes on these questions are revealed again in the next film, *Polowanie na muchy,* and even more emphatically in *Dyrygent,* where they are linked to the motif of faithfulness to one's work and to oneself, to one's ideals and convictions. The motif links *Dyrygent* with *Popiół i diament.* Another theme of *Dyrygent*—the inseparability of one's personal, private life from one's work life and the mutual influence of the two—is the basic problem treated in *Bez znieczulenia.* In Wajda there are many such examples of the migration of themes and motifs from one film to another. They affirm the unity of his work despite the fact that alongside great and powerful works there are lesser and weaker films. Such, for example, is Wajda's sole attempt in the genre of comedy, *Polowanie na muchy,* or the adaptation of Joseph Conrad's novel *Heart of Darkness,* which underwent a cinematic transformation.

Another unifying element in Wajda's oeuvre is his faithfulness to literary and artistic sources. A significant portion of his films come from literature, while the pictorial aspect finds its inspiration in the romantic artistic tradition. In addition to such broad historical frescoes as *Popióły or Ziemia obiecana,* these include, for example, Stanislaw Wyspianski's drama of 1901, *Wesele,* important for its grasp of Poland at a bleak point in the country's history. Wajda translated it to the screen in all the breadth of its meaning, with an accent on the impossibility of mutual understanding between disparate cultural milieus. The director also selected from the literary heritage works that would allow him to address man's existential questions, attitudes towards life and death. This theme resonates most fully in adaptations of two works by the writer Jaroslaw Iwaszkiewicz, *Brzezina* and *Panny z Wilka,* in which the heroes are found not in history but in life, where they are threatened not by war but by old age, illness, and death, and where they must struggle only with themselves. To address such existential tension Wajda also developed a transcription of Mikhail Bulgakov's prose work *The Master and Margarita,* filmed for television in the German Democratic Republic under the title *Pilatus und andere-ein Film für Karfreitag.*

In the 1980s, after a number of years, Wajda goes back to the subject of war. It is in the nostalgic *Kronika wypadków miłosnych,* which deals with young people into whose loves and disappointments creeps the premonition of a military catastrophe and death. *Eine Liebe in Deutschland* is about the tragic consequences of the love felt by a married German woman for a Polish prisoner. And it is also the subject of *Korczak,* the most important work of Wajda's comeback. The director based *Korczak* on an authentic story, and the hero who gave the film its name is a portrait of a real person. After the arrival of the German occupying forces in Poland, Korczak followed his charges from an orphanage into the Jewish Ghetto, and in the end of his own free will into the extermination concentration camp of Treblinka. With this film about Korczak Wajda closed, for the time being, one of the great subjects of his life and work. He has done this by employing the simplest and therefore the most effective method: black-and-white photography, which renders a sober record of life in a sealed-off ghetto and at the same time pays homage to the unostentatious heroism of a man who, face to face with death, did not forget the moral code of the human race.

Wajda's oeuvre, encompassing artistic triumphs and failures, forms a unified but incomplete whole. The affinity among his films is determined by a choice of themes which enables him to depict great historical syntheses, metaphors, and symbols. He is constantly drawn to those moments in the destinies of individuals and groups that are crossroads of events with tragic consequences. In his films the main motifs of human existence are interwoven—death and life, love, defeat, and the tragic dilemma of having to choose, the impossibility of realizing great aspirations. All these motifs are subordinated to history, even a feeling as subjective as love.

Wajda's films have not been, and are not, uniformly received by audiences or critics. They have always provoked discussions in which enthusiasm has confronted condemnation and agreement has confronted disagreement and even hostility; despite some failures, however, Wajda's films have never been met with indifference.

—Blažena Urgošiková

WALSH, Raoul

Nationality: American. **Born:** New York City, 11 March 1887 (some sources say 1892). **Education:** Attended Public School 93, New York; also attended Seton Hall College. **Family:** Married 1) Miriam Cooper, 1916 (divorced 1927); 2) Mary Edna Simpson, 1941. **Career:** Sailed to Cuba on uncle's trading ship, 1903; horse wrangler in Mexico, 1903-04; worked in variety of jobs in United States, including surgeon's assistant and undertaker, 1904-10; cowboy actor in films for Pathé Studio, New Jersey, then for Biograph, from 1910; actor and assistant to D.W Griffith, then director at Biograph, Hollywood, from 1912; director for William Fox, from 1916; lost eye in auto accident, 1928; introduced John Wayne as feature actor in *The Big Trail,* 1930; director for various studios, then retired to ranch, 1964. **Died:** In California, 31 December 1980.

Films as Director:

1912 *The Life of General Villa* (co-d, role as young Villa); *Outlaw's Revenge*
1913 *The Double Knot* (+ pr, sc, role); *The Mystery of the Hindu Image* (+ pr, sc); *The Gunman* (+ pr, sc; credit contested)
1914 *The Final Verdict* (+ pr, sc, role); *The Bowery*
1915 *The Regeneration* (+ co-sc); *Carmen* (+ pr, sc); *The Death Dice* (+ pr, sc; credit contested); *His Return* (+ pr); *The Greaser* (+ pr, sc, role); *The Fencing Master* (+ pr, sc); *A Man for All That* (+ pr, sc, role); *11:30 P.M.* (+ pr, sc); *The Buried Hand* (+ pr, sc); *The Celestial Code* (+ pr, sc); *A Bad Man and Others* (+ pr, sc); *Home from the Sea*; *The Lone Cowboy* (+ co-sc)
1916 *Blue Blood and Red* (+ pr, sc); *The Serpent* (+ pr, sc); *Pillars of Society*
1917 *The Honor System*; *The Silent Lie*; *The Innocent Sinner* (+ sc); *Betrayed* (+ sc); *The Conqueror* (+ sc); *This Is the Life*
1918 *Pride of New York* (+ sc); *The Woman and the Law* (+ sc); *The Prussian Cur* (+ sc); *On the Jump* (+ sc); *I'll Say So*
1919 *Should a Husband Forgive* (+ sc); *Evangeline* (+ sc); *Every Mother's Son* (+ sc)
1920 *The Strongest* (+ sc); *The Deep Purple*; *From Now On*
1921 *The Oath* (+ pr, sc); *Serenade* (+ pr)
1923 *Lost and Found on a South Sea Island* (*Passions of the Sea*); *Kindred of the Dust* (+ pr, sc)
1924 *The Thief of Bagdad*
1925 *East of Suez* (+ pr); *The Spaniard* (+ co-pr); *The Wanderer* (+ co-pr)
1926 *The Lucky Lady* (+ co-pr); *The Lady of the Harem*; *What Price Glory*
1927 *The Monkey Talks* (+ pr); *The Loves of Carmen* (+ sc)
1928 *Sadie Thompson* (*Rain*) (+ co-sc, role); *The Red Dance*; *Me Gangster* (+ co-sc)
1929 *In Old Arizona* (co-d); *The Cock-eyed World* (+ co-sc); *Hot for Paris* (+ co-sc)
1930 *The Big Trail*
1931 *The Man Who Came Back*; *Women of all Nations*; *The Yellow Ticket*
1932 *Wild Girl*; *Me and My Gal*
1933 *Sailor's Luck*; *The Bowery*; *Going Hollywood*
1935 *Under Pressure*; *Baby Face Harrington*; *Every Night at Night*
1936 *Klondike Annie*; *Big Brown Eyes* (+ co-sc); *Spendthrift*
1937 *O.H.M.S.* (*You're in the Army Now*); *When Thief Meets Thief*; *Artists and Models*; *Hitting a New High*
1938 *College Swing*
1939 *St. Louis Blues*; ***The Roaring Twenties***

Raoul Walsh

1940 *The Dark Command* (+ pr); *They Drive by Night*
1941 ***High Sierra***; *The Strawberry Blonde*; *Manpower*; *They Died With Their Boots On*
1942 *Desperate Journey*; *Gentleman Jim*
1943 *Background to Danger*; *Northern Pursuit*
1944 *Uncertain Glory*; *San Antonio* (uncredited co-d); *Salty O'Rourke*; *The Horn Blows at Midnight*
1946 *The Man I Love*
1947 *Pursued*; *Cheyenne*; *Stallion Road* (uncredited co-d)
1948 *Silver River*; *Fighter Squadron*; *One Sunday Afternoon*
1949 *Colorado Territory*; ***White Heat***
1950 *The Enforcer* (uncredited co-d); *Montana* (uncredited co-d)
1951 *Along the Great Divide*; *Captain Horatio Hornblower*; *Distant Drums*
1952 *The World in His Arms*; *The Lawless Breed*; *Blackbeard the Pirate*
1953 *Sea Devils*; *A Lion in the Streets*; *Gun Fury*
1954 *Saskatchewan*
1955 *Battle Cry*; *The Tall Men*
1956 *The Revolt of Mamie Stover*; *The King and Four Queens*
1957 *Band of Angels*
1958 *The Naked and the Dead*; *The Sheriff of Fractured Jaw*
1959 *A Private's Affair*
1960 *Esther and the King* (+ pr, sc)
1961 *Marines, Let's Go* (+ pr, sc)
1964 *A Distant Trumpet*

Other Films:

1910 *The Banker's Daughter* (Griffith) (role as bank clerk); *A Mother's Love* (role as young man); *Paul Revere's Ride* (Emile Cocteau) (role as Paul Revere)
1915 ***Birth of a Nation*** (Griffith) (role as John Wilkes Booth)

Publications

By WALSH: books—

Each Man in His Time, New York, 1974.
Un Demi-siècle à Hollywood, Paris, 1976.

By WALSH: articles—

Interview with Jean-Louis Noames, in *Cahiers du Cinéma* (Paris), April 1964.
Interview with Guy Braucourt, in *Ecran* (Paris), September/October 1972.
"Can You Ride the Horse?," an interview with J. Childs, in *Sight and Sound* (London), Winter 1972/73.
"Raoul Walsh Talks About D.W. Griffith," with P. Montgomery, in *Film Heritage* (New York), Spring 1975.
"Raoul Walsh Remembers Warners," an interview with P. McGilligan and others, in *Velvet Light Trap* (Madison), Autumn 1975.

On WALSH: books—

Brownlow, Kevin, *The Parade's Gone By ...,* New York, 1968.
Marmin, Michael, *Raoul Walsh,* Paris, 1970.
Canham, Kingsley, *The Hollywood Professionals,* New York, 1973.
Hardy, Phil, editor, *Raoul Walsh,* Edinburgh, 1974.
Comizio, Ermanno, *Raoul Walsh,* Florence, 1982.
Giluiani, Pierre, *Raoul Walsh,* Paris, 1986.

On WALSH: articles—

"Walsh Issue" of *Présence du Cinéma* (Paris), May 1962.
"Walsh Issue" of *Cahiers du Cinéma* (Paris), April 1964.
Dienstfrey, Harris, "Hitch Your Genre to a Star," in *Film Culture* (New York), Fall 1964.
Brownlow, Kevin, "Raoul Walsh," in *Film* (London), Autumn 1967.
Lloyd, R., "Raoul Walsh," in *Brighton* (London), November, December, and January 1970.
Conley, W., "Raoul Walsh—His Silent Films," in *Silent Picture* (London), Winter 1970/71.
Fox, J., "Action All the Way," "Going Hollywood," and "Hollow Victories," in *Films and Filming* (London), June, July, and August 1973.
Farber, Manny, "Raoul Walsh: 'He Used to Be a Big Shot'," in *Sight and Sound* (London), Winter 1974/75.
McNiven, R., "The Western Landscape of Raoul Walsh," in *Velvet Light Trap* (Madison), Autumn 1975.
Cocchi, J., and others, "Raoul Walsh filmographie: l'oeuvre 'parlante' 1929/1961," in *Avant-Scène du Cinéma* (Paris), April 1976.
Halliday, J., "Trying to Remember an Afternoon with Raoul Walsh," in *Framework* (Norwich, England), Spring 1981.
McNiven, R., "Raoul Walsh: 1887-1981," in *Film Comment* (New York), July/August 1981.
Bodeen, De Witt, "Raoul Walsh," in *Films in Review* (New York), April 1982.
Gallagher, John, "Raoul Walsh," in *Films in Review* (New York), October 1987.

* * *

Raoul Walsh's extraordinary career spanned the history of the American motion picture industry from its emergence, through its glory years in the 1930s and 1940s, and into the television era. Like his colleagues Alan Dwan, King Vidor, John Ford, and Henry King, whose careers also covered 50 years, Walsh continuously turned out popular fare, including several extraordinary hits. Movie fans have long appreciated the work of this director's director. But only when auteurists began to closely examine his films was Walsh "discovered," first by the French (in the 1960s), and then by American and British critics (in the 1970s). To these critics Walsh's action films come to represent a unified view, put forth by means of a simple, straightforward technique. Raoul Walsh is now accepted as an example of a master Hollywood craftsman who worked with naive skill and an animal energy, a director who was both frustrated and buoyed by the studio system.

Unfortunately, this view neglects Walsh's important place in the silent cinema. Raoul Walsh began his career with an industry still centered in and around New York City, the director's birthplace. He started as an actor in Pathé westerns filmed in New Jersey, and then journeyed to California to be with D.W. Griffith's Fine Arts production company. Walsh apprenticed with Griffith as an actor, appearing in his most famous role as John Wilkes Booth in *Birth of a Nation.*

Walsh then turned to directing, first for the fledgling Fox Film Company. For the next five years (interrupted by World War I service experience) Walsh would master the craft of filmmaking, absorbing lessons which would serve him for more than forty years. His apprenticeship led to major assignments, and his greatest financial successes came in the 1920s. Douglas Fairbanks's *The Thief of Bagdad* was directed by Walsh at the height of that famous star's career.

Walsh took advantage of this acclaim by moving for a time to the top studio of that era, Paramount, and then signed a lucrative long-term contract with Fox. At that point Fox began expanding into a major studio. Walsh contributed to that success with hits like *What Price Glory?* and *The Cockeyed World.* The introduction of new sound-on-film technology, through its Movietone Newsreels, helped Fox's ascent. Consequently, when Fox was about to convert to all-sound features, corporate chieftains turned to Walsh to direct *In Old Arizona*, in 1929. (It was on location for that film that Walsh lost his eye.) Because of its experience with newsreel shooting, Fox was the only studio at the time that could film and record quality sound on location. Walsh's next film used the 70mm "Grandeur" process on a western, *The Big Trail.* The film did well but could not save the company from succumbing to the Great Depression.

Walsh's career stagnated during the 1930s. He and Fox never achieved the heights of the late 1920s. When Darryl F. Zanuck came aboard with the Twentieth Century merger in 1935, Walsh moved on, freelancing until he signed with Warners in 1939. For slightly more than a decade, Walsh functioned as a contract director at Warners, turning out two or three films a year. Walsh never established the degree of control he had enjoyed over the silent film projects, but he seemed to thrive in the restrictive Warners environment. Walsh's first three films at Warners fit into that studio's mode of crime melodramas: *The Roaring Twenties, They Drive By Night,* and *High Sierra. The Roaring Twenties* was not a classic gangster film, like Warners' *Little Caesar* and *Public Enemy,* but a realistic portrait of the socioeconomic environment in the United States after World War I. *High Sierra* looked ahead to the film noir of the 1940s. In that film the gangster became a sympathetic character trapped by forces he did not understand. During the World War II era Walsh turned to war films with a textbook example of what a war action film ought to be. Walsh continued making crime melodramas and war films in the late 1940s and early 1950s. *Battle Cry, The Naked and the Dead,* and *Marines, Let's Go* proved that he could adapt to changing tastes within familiar genres.

Arguably Walsh's best film of the post-war era was *White Heat,* made for Warners in 1949. The James Cagney character is portrayed against type: we see the gangster hiding and running, trying to escape his past and his social, economic, and psychological background. *White Heat* was the apex of Walsh's work at Warners, for it simultaneously fit into an accepted mode and transcended the formula. *White Heat* has come to symbolize the tough Raoul Walsh action film. Certainly that same sort of style can also be seen in his westerns at Warners, *They Died With Their Boots On, Pursued,* and a remake of *High Sierra* called *Colorado Territory.* But there are other sides of the Walsh oeuvre, usually overlooked by critics, or at most awkwardly positioned among the action films. *The Strawberry Blonde* is a warm, affectionate, turn-of-the-century tale of small town America. *Gentleman Jim* of 1942 also swims in sentimentality. These films indicate that Walsh, though known as an action director, certainly had a soft touch when required. Indeed, when his works are closely examined, it is clear that Walsh had the ability to adapt to many different themes and points of view.

The 1950s seemed to pass Walsh by. Freed from the confines of the rigid studio system, Walsh's output became less interesting. But he was a survivor. He completed his final feature, a cavalry film for Warners called *A Distant Trumpet,* in 1964. By then Raoul Walsh had truly become a Hollywood legend, having reached two career peaks in a more than fifty-year career. To carefully examine the career of Raoul Walsh is to study the history of the American film in toto, for the two are nearly the same length and inexorably intertwined.

—Douglas Gomery

WALTERS, Charles

Nationality: American. **Born:** Pasadena, California, 17 November 1911. **Education:** Attended University of Southern California. **Career:** Broadway debut as actor and dancer in *New Faces,* 1934; began choreographing on Broadway with *Sing Out the News,* 1938; first film appearance, 1942; began as choreographer on *DuBarry Was a Lady,* 1943; shot and staged "Brazilian Boogie" number, in *Broadway Rhythm,* 1944; directed first feature, *Good News,* for Arthur Freed, 1947. **Died:** In Malibu, California, 13 August 1982.

Films as Director:

1942 *Spreadin' the Jam* (short)
1947 *Good News*
1948 *Easter Parade*
1949 *The Barkleys of Broadway*
1950 *Summer Stock* (*If You Feel Like Singing*) (+ choreo)
1951 *Three Guys Named Mike*; *Texas Carnival*
1952 *The Belle of New York*
1953 *Lili* (+ choreo, role); *Dangerous When Wet*; *Torch Song* (+ choreo, role); *Easy to Love*
1955 *The Glass Slipper*; *The Tender Trap*
1956 *Don't Go Near the Water*
1957 *High Society* (+ choreo)
1959 *Ask Any Girl*
1960 *Please Don't Eat the Daisies*
1961 *Two Loves* (*Spinster*)
1962 *Billy Rose's Jumbo*
1964 *The Unsinkable Molly Brown*
1966 *Walk, Don't Run*

Other Films:

1942 *Seven Days Leave* (Whelan) (choreo, role/dancer)
1943 *DuBarry Was a Lady* (Del Ruth) (choreo); *Presenting Lily Mars* (Taurog) (co-choreo, role/dancer); *Best Foot Forward* (Buzzell) (choreo); *Girl Crazy* (Taurog) (choreo, role/dancer)
1944 *Broadway Rhythm* (Del Ruth) (co-choreo); *Three Men in White* (Goldbeck) (choreo); ***Meet Me in St. Louis*** (Minnelli) (choreo)
1945 *Thrill of a Romance* (Thorpe) (choreo); *Her Highness and the Bellboy* (Thorpe) (choreo); *Weekend at the Waldorf* (Leonard) (choreo); *The Harvey Girls* (Sidney) (choreo); *Abbott & Costello in Hollywood* (Simon) (choreo)
1946 *Ziegfeld Follies* (Minnelli and others) (choreo Judy Garland's "An Interview" sequence)
1962 *Summer Holiday* (Yates) (choreo)

Publications

By WALTERS: articles—

"On the Bright Side," an interview with John Cutts, in *Films and Filming* (London), August 1970.
Interview with P. Sauvage, in *Positif* (Paris), November/December 1972.

On WALTERS: books—

Feuer, Jane, *The Hollywood Musical,* London, 1982.
Altman, Rick, *The American Film Musical,* Bloomington, Indiana, 1989.

On WALTERS: articles—

Sarris, Andrew, "Likable but Elusive," in *Film Culture* (New York), Spring 1963.
"Walters Issue" of *Positif* (Paris), November/December 1972.

Charles Walters

McVay, D., "Charles Walters," in *Focus on Film* (London), no. 27, 1977.
Obituary, in *Variety* (New York), 25 August 1982.
Obituary, in *Films and Filming* (London), October 1982.

* * *

Before going to Hollywood Charles Walters spent about eight years on Broadway. For the most part he was a dancer, but in 1938 he choreographed his first show. A few years later Robert Altman introduced him to MGM and he began to stage routines for the screen. He worked with Gene Kelly on a number for *Du Barry Was A Lady,* then began staging musical numbers for some of Metro's leading ladies such as June Allyson, Gloria De Haven, Lucille Ball, and Judy Garland. Garland became a great friend and he worked on a number of her films, sometimes dancing with her. His first effort at directing was Lena Horne's "Brazilian Boogie" number in *Broadway Rhythm.* The following year he directed a short film called *Spreadin' the Jam,* but it was not until 1947 that he made his first feature, *Good News.*

As a dancer, movement was very much on Walters' mind. As a director he moved not only the performers but also the camera, making full use of tracking shots, pans, and crane shots. The studio was impressed with his work and gave him *Easter Parade* with Astaire and Garland. The budget was twice that of his first film, and notable for the "Couple of Swells" number—which Walters danced with her when she did her memorable show at the Palace a few years later. *The Barkleys of Broadway* should have starred Astaire and Garland again, but Garland was ill and Ginger Rogers returned to the screen in her stead.

These first three films were made under Walters' original contract as a choreographer, and at the same fee. But after proving himself with those projects, he was recognized as a director of musicals ready to follow into the footsteps of other MGM stalwarts like Stanley Donen and Vincente Minnelli. *Summer Stock* began with the pleasantly relaxed number "If You Feel Like Singing," as the camera moved through the window into the shower,and followed Garland into the dressing-room. But the rest of the filming was far from relaxed, for Walters had to cope with Garland's nerves and weight problems. The final song, "Get Happy," was staged by Walters after the film was finished because they needed a good number for the climax, and Judy's loss of weight was quite noticeable.

In 1951 Walters directed his first straight picture, *Three Guys Named Mike,* a passable romantic comedy. His least favourite film, *The Belle of New York,* was followed by his favorite, *Lili.* In this light, whimsical piece he drew a charming performance from Leslie Caron and received an Oscar nomination. *Dangerous When Wet* was one of three films he made with Esther Williams. Walters staged the lively opening number with each character taking up the song, and "Ain't Nature Grand," with Charlotte Greenwood showing great vitality in her high kicks. In the dramatic musical *Torch Song* Walters was the first to direct Joan Crawford in a color film. He got to know her well, and put a lot of the real Joan Crawford into the character of Jenny. His careful handling of Frank Sinatra in *The Tender Trap* was most opportune. After a string of dramatic roles, this film confirmed Sinatra's talent as a comedy actor. In 1957 he was reunited with Sinatra for what is arguably his best film, *High Society.* Every number in this film is significant, yet they are all completely different. One of the high spots was Crosby and Sinatra's "Well, Did You Evah," which Walters himself had introduced years before with Betty Grable. It took place in two rooms and was shot without a single cut. In the early 1960s he made *The Unsinkable Molly Brown* and *Billy Rose's Jumbo,* the latter by far the better of the two.

Walters was a sincere director whose musicals had a style of their own. He was equally at home with a field full of dancers as he was with soloist or a group on a bandstand. He not only moved his cameras and his performers, but staged many numbers on moving vehicles—a car, a carriage, a coach, a trolley, a boat, and even a tractor. His use of color and his sudden cuts produced striking effects, and the energy and spirit of his work contributed greatly to the Hollywood musical.

—Colin Williams

WARD, Vincent

Nationality: New Zealander. **Born:** Greytown, New Zealand, 16 February 1956. **Education:** Attended the Ilam School of Art, Christchurch, New Zealand, where he intended to study painting but took up filmmaking instead. **Career:** Directed and co-wrote first films at age twenty-one, 1977-1978; directed first feature, *Vigil,* 1984; came to the United States to work on *Alien3,* 1992; currently is based in Australia and the United States. **Awards:** Silver Hugo Award, Chicago Festival, 1978, for *A State of Siege;* Silver Hugo Award, Chicago Festival, 1980, for *In Spring One Plants Alone;* Grand Prix Award, Prades Festival, Grand Prix Award, Madrid Festival, and Best Film, Imag Fic Festival, all 1984, all for *Vigil;* Australian Film Awards, Best Picture and Best Director, 1988, for *The Navigator: A Medieval Odyssey.* **Agent:** CAA, 9830 Wilshire Blvd., Beverly Hills, CA 90212, U.S.A. **Address:** P.O. Box 423, Kings Cross, NSW 2011, Australia.

Films as Director and Screenwriter:

1977 *Ma Olsen* (short)
1978 *A State of Siege* (short)

1980 *In Spring One Plants Alone* (short)
1984 *Vigil*
1988 *The Navigator: A Medieval Odyssey*
1992 ***Map of the Human Heart*** (+ pr)

Other Films:

1992 *Alien3* (story)

Publications

By WARD: article—

"Ward's Way," interview with Larry Buttrose in *Interview* (New York), March 1989.

On WARD: articles—

Jackson, S., "New Zealand Film Bibliography," in *Filmviews* (Victoria, Australia), Winter 1987.
Nayman, M., "*The Navigator*—Vincent Ward's Past Dreams of the Future," in *Cinema Papers* (Melbourne), May 1988.
Lewis, B., "*The Navigator,*" in *Films & Filming* (London), March 1989.
Griffin, N., "Vincent Ward," in *Premiere* (New York), April 1989.
Insdorf, Annette, "His Vision Charted the Course of *The Navigator,*" in *New York Times,* 16 July 1989.
Wilmington, Michael, "Firestorm and Dry Ice: The Cinema of Vincent Ward," in *Film Comment* (New York), May/June 1993.

* * *

After completing just three feature films, Vincent Ward has established himself as a filmmaker of great individuality, intensity, and creativity. His narrative technique is centered on the fundamental importance of the image; he has a painter's eye for capturing arresting, eye-popping visuals. However, all of his films are united not only by their imagery. While he resists categorizing himself and his work, Ward did admit in an interview with this writer that "I like to make films that say something about people."

Ward's characters are linked in that they consistently are isolated, trapped by the barren, desolate rural environments in which they have come of age. Ward is most interested in examining the manner in which they relate to their surroundings and, even more importantly, how they are touched by the outside world. Clearly, this theme is tied into the filmmaker's own roots in New Zealand, a mostly rural country located at the very bottom of the world.

Vigil is a fine debut feature, the deeply personal story of a young farmgirl, on the cusp of adolescence, who is growing up in an isolated locale in backwoods New Zealand. The outside world comes to her in the person of a hunter, who arrives on the scene upon the death of her father and whose presence impacts on her and her family. Ward man-

Vincent Ward

ages to get inside the mind of this child as he depicts the world around her in all of its realities and contradictions. That world is seen through her perceptions, fantasies, and lack of life experience. There is a raw energy present in *Vigil,* an energy created by a filmmaker who has total admiration for the art of cinema and the power of the moving image.

In Ward's follow-ups, *The Navigator: A Medieval Odyssey* and *Map of the Human Heart,* he expands his characters' horizons in that, near the beginning of each story, he has them leaving their homelands and entering the outside world. *The Navigator* is the stunningly visual account, set in the year 1348, of a group of townspeople in Cumbria who embark on the title journey in order to escape a plague. At the end of their trip, they come upon an ultra-modern, twentieth-century metropolis. Here, the film becomes a view of a contemporary, technological society as seen through the perceptions of medieval man. The special effects in *The Navigator* are especially impressive. Ward cleverly used small-scale cardboard and plywood miniatures to create his "futuristic" city; the film was shot on a modest budget, yet it has the look of a multi-million-dollar Hollywood epic.

Ward's third feature, *Map of the Human Heart,* is a heartrending drama, a thoughtful, emotionally involving film about clashing cultures and the corruption of innocence. Ward tells the story of Avik (Jason Scott Lee), an Eskimo who might easily be described as a child of fate. As a young boy in the early 1930s, Avik's encounter with an Arctic mapmaker (Patrick Bergin) leads him into "civilization," where he meets Albertine (Anne Parillaud), half-Indian and half-French Canadian, who is destined to be his true love. Also key to the story is Avik's becoming a combat pilot, and his participation in World War II. Especially in *The Navigator* and *Map of the Human Heart,* Ward's characters become convinced that by entering the outside world they can alter their lives and their fates. They share a faith in their futures, and it is this very faith that allows them—for better or for worse—to take action by moving out of their native environs and into the world at large.

To date, Ward's sole Hollywood credit is *Alien3,* for which he authored the story upon which the screenplay was based. It is a shame that, entering his forties, this daringly original and always-interesting filmmaker has only three feature films to his credit. "It's easy to get films made that are more generic," Ward states. "I want my films to be accessible, though I also want to do them on my own terms, and to be about my own concerns as a filmmaker."

—Rob Edelman

WARHOL, Andy

Nationality: American. **Born:** Andrew Warhola in McKeesport, Pennsylvania, 6 August 1928. **Education:** Studied at Carnegie Institute of Technology, Pittsburgh, B.F.A., 1949. **Career:** Illustrator for *Glamour Magazine* (New York), 1949-50; commercial artist, New York, 1950-57; independent artist, New York, 1957 until his death in 1987; first silk-screen paintings, 1962; began making films, mainly with Paul Morrissey, a member of his "Factory," 1963; shot by former "Factory" regular Valerie Solanas, 1968; editor, *Inter/View* magazine, New York; made promo video for "Hello Again" by The Cars, 1984. **Awards:** 6th Film Culture Award, New York, 1964; Award, Los Angeles Film Festival, 1964. **Died:** Of cardiac arrest following routine gall bladder operation in New York, 22 February 1987.

Films as Director and Producer:

1963 *Tarzan and Jane Regained ... Sort Of*; *Sleep*; *Kiss*; *Andy Warhol Films Jack Smith Filming Normal Love*; *Dance Movie* (*Roller Skate*); *Salome and Delilah*; *Haircut*; *Blow Job*

1964 *Empire*; *Batman Dracula*; *The End of Dawn*; *Naomi and Rufus Kiss*; *Henry Geldzahler*; *The Lester Persky Story* (*Soap Opera*); *Couch*; *Shoulder*; *Mario Banana*; *Harlot*; *Taylor Mead's Ass*

1965 *Thirteen Most Beautiful Women*; *Thirteen Most Beautiful Boys*; *Fifty Fantastics*; *Fifty Personalities*; *Ivy and John*; *Screen Test I*; *Screen Test II*; *The Life of Juanita Castro*; *Drunk*; *Suicide*; *Horse*; *Vinyl*; *Bitch*; *Poor Little Rich Girl*; *Face*; *Restaurant*; *Afternoon*; *Prison*; *Space*; *Outer and Inner Space*; *Camp*; *Paul Swan*; *Hedy* (*Hedy the Shoplifter or The Fourteen Year Old Girl*); *The Closet*; *Lupe*; *More Milk, Evette*

1966 *Kitchen*; *My Hustler*; *Bufferin* (*Gerard Malanga Reads Poetry*); *Eating Too Fast*; *The Velvet Underground*; ***Chelsea Girls***

1967 ** * * ** (*Four Stars*) [parts of * * * * include *International Velvet*; *Alan and Dickin*; *Imitation of Christ*; *Coutroom*; *Gerard Has His Hair Removed with Nair*; *Katrina Dead*; *Sausalito*; *Alan and Apple*; *Group One*; *Sunset Beach on Long Island*; *High Ashbury*; *Tiger Morse*]; *I, a Man*; *Bike Boy*; *Nude Restaurant*; *The Loves of Ondine*

1968 *Lonesome Cowboys*; *Blue Movie* (*Fuck*); *Flesh* (d Morrissey, pr Warhol)

1970 *Trash* (d Morrissey, pr Warhol)

1972 *Women in Revolt* (co-d with Morrissey); *Heat* (d Morrissey, pr Warhol)

1973 *L'Amour* (co-d, pr, co-sc with Morrissey)

1974 *Andy Warhol's Frankenstein* (d Morrissey, pr Warhol); *Andy Warhol's Dracula* (d Morrissey, pr Warhol)

1977 *Andy Warhol's Bad* (d Morrissey, pr Warhol)

Other Films

1986 *Vamp* (Wenk) (contributing artist)

Publications

By WARHOL: books—

Blue Movie, script, New York, 1970.
The Philosophy of Andy Warhol (From A to B and Back Again), New York, 1975.
The Andy Warhol Diaries, edited by Pat Hackett, New York, 1989.
Andy Warhol: In His Own Words, London, 1991.
Angels, angels, angels, London, 1994.
Cats, cats, cats, London, 1994.

By WARHOL: articles—

Interview with David Ehrenstein, in *Film Culture* (New York), Spring 1966.
"Nothing to Lose," an interview with Gretchen Berg, in *Cahiers du Cinema in English* (New York), May 1967.
Numerous interviews conducted by Warhol, in *Inter/View* (New York).
Interview in *The Film Director as Superstar,* by Joseph Gelmis, Garden City, New York, 1970.
Interview with Tony Rayns, in *Cinema* (London), August 1970.
Interview with Ralph Pomeroy, in *Afterimage* (Rochester), Autumn 1970.

On WARHOL: books—

Coplans, John, *Andy Warhol,* New York, 1970.
Crone, Rainer, *Andy Warhol,* New York, 1970.

Andy Warhol

Gidal, Peter, *Andy Warhol,* New York, 1970.
Wilcox, John, *The Autobiography and Sex Life of Andy Warhol,* New York, 1971.
Koch, Stephen, *Stargazer: Andy Warhol's World and His Films,* New York, 1973; revised edition, 1985.
Smith, Patrick S., *Andy Warhol's Art and Films,* Ann Arbor, Michigan, 1986.
Bourdon, David, *Warhol,* 1989.
Finkelstein, Nat, *Warhol: The Factory Years 1964-67,* London, 1989.
Gidal, Peter, *Materialist Film,* London, 1989.
Guiles, Fred Lawrence, *Loner at the Ball: The Life of Andy Warhol,* New York, 1989.
James, David E., *Allegories of Cinema: American Film in the Sixties,* Princeton, New Jersey, 1989.
O'Pray, Michael, *Andy Warhol: Film Factory,* London, 1989.
Koch, Stephen, *Stargazer: The Life, World, and Films of Andy Warhol,* New York, 1991.
Inboden, Gudrun, *Andy Warhol: White Disaster I, 1963,* Stuttgart, 1992.
Kurtz, Bruce D., ed., *Keith Haring, Andy Warhol, and Walt Disney,* Munich and London, 1992.
Geldzahler, Henry, *Andy Warhol: Portraits of the Seventies and Eighties,* London, 1993.
Katz, Jonathan, *Andy Warhol,* New York, 1993.
Alexander, Paul, *Death and Disaster: The Rise of the Warhol Empire and the Race for Andy's Millions,* New York, 1994.

On WARHOL: articles—

Stoller, James, "Beyond Cinema: Notes on Some Films by Andy Warhol," in *Film Quarterly* (Berkeley), Fall 1966.
Tyler, Parker, "Dragtime and Drugtime: or Film *à la* Warhol," in *Evergreen Review* (New York), April 1967.
"Warhol," in *Film Culture* (New York), Summer 1967.
Lugg, Andrew, "On Andy Warhol," in *Cineaste* (New York), Winter 1967/68 and Spring 1968.
Rayns, Tony, "Andy Warhol's Films Inc.: Communication in Action," in *Cinema* (London), August 1970.
Heflin, Lee, "Notes on Seeing the Films of Andy Warhol," in *Afterimage* (Rochester), Autumn 1970.
Bourdon, David, "Warhol as Filmmaker," in *Art in America* (New York), May/June 1971.
Cipnic, D.J., "Andy Warhol: Iconographer," in *Sight and Sound* (London), Summer 1972.

Larson, R., "A Retrospective Look at the Films of D. W. Griffith and Andy Warhol," in *Film Journal* (New York), Fall/Winter 1972.
James, David E., "The Producer as Author," in *Wide Angle* (Baltimore, Maryland), vol. 7, no. 3, 1985.
Cohn, L., obituary in *Variety* (New York), 25 February 1987.
Babitz, E., "The Soup Can as Big as the Ritz," in *Movieline*, November 1989.
Currie, C., "Andy Warhol: Enigma, Icon, Master," in *Semiotica*, vol. 80, no. 3/4, 1990.
Diana, M., "Blow Cinema," in *Segnocinema*, November/December 1990.
Tully, Judd, "15 Minutes Later: Warhol Now," in *ARTnews*, March 1992.
Byron, Christopher, "Andy's Magic Money Machine," in *New York*, 30 November 1992.
Stevens, Mark, "Saint Andy," in *New York*, 23 May 1994.
Long, Marion, "The Andy Warhol Museum," in *Omni*, June 1994.
Adams, Brooks, "Industrial-Strength Warhol," in *Art in America*, September 1994.
Alexander, Paul, "Murky Image," in *ARTnews*, February 1995.

On WARHOL: films—

American Masters: Superstar—The Life of Andy Warhol, 1990.

* * *

By the time he screened his first films in 1963, Andy Warhol was well on his way to becoming the most famous "pop" artist in the world, and his variations on the theme of Campbell's soup cans had already assumed archetypal significance for art in the age of mechanical reproduction. Given Warhol's penchant for the automatic and mass-produced, his movement from sculpture, canvas, and silk-screen into cinema seemed logical; and his films were as passive, as intentionally "empty," as significant of the artist's absence as his previous work or as the image he projected of himself. One of his earliest films, *Kiss*, was no more nor less than a series of people kissing in closeup, each scene running the three-minute length of a 16mm daylight reel, complete with flash frames at both ends. But it was his 1963 film *Sleep*, a six-hour movie comprised of variously framed shots of a naked sleeping man, which made Warhol a star on the burgeoning New York underground film scene. As though to dispel any doubts that his message was the medium, Warhol followed *Sleep* with *Empire*, an eight-hour stationary view of the Empire State Building, creating a kind of cinematic limit case for the Bazinian integrity of the shot. It was a film of such conceptual significance that if it did not exist it would have to be invented; yet it was a film that was equally unwatchable (even Warhol refused to sit through it).

During the period 1963 to 1967, Warhol made some fifty-five films, ranging in length from four minutes (*Mario Banana*, 1964) to twenty-five hours (* * * *, 1967). All were informed by the passive, mechanical aesthetic of simply turning on the camera to record what was in front of it. Generally, what was recorded were the antics of Warhol's E. 47th Street "Factory" coterie—a host of friends, artists, junkies, transvestites, rock singers, hustlers, fugitives, and hangers-on. Ad-libbing, "camping," being themselves (and often more than themselves) before the unblinking eye of Warhol's camera, they became "superstars"—underground celebrities epitomizing Warhol's consumer-democratic ideal of fifteen minutes' fame for everyone.

Despite Warhol's cultivated image as the "tycoon of passivity," his films display a cool but very dry wit. *Blow Job*, for example, consisted of thirty minutes of a closeup of the expressionless face of a man being fellated outside the frame—a coyly humorous presentation of a forbidden act in an image perversely composed as a denial of pleasure (for the actor and the audience). *Mario Banana* simply presented the spectacle of transvestite Mario Montez eating bananas while in drag. *Harlot*, Warhol's first sound film, featured Mario (again eating bananas) sitting next to a woman in an evening dress, with the entirety of the virtually inaudible dialogue coming from three men positioned off-screen.

In the course of his films, Warhol seemed to be retracing the history of the cinema, from silence to sound to color (*Chelsea Girls*); from a fascination with the camera's "documentary" capabilities (*Empire*) to attempts at narrative by 1965. *Vinyl*, an adaption of Anthony Burgess's *A Clockwork Orange*, involved a single high-angle camera position tightly framing a group of mostly uninvolved factory types, with protagonist Gerard Malanga sitting in a chair, reading his lines off a script on the floor, and being tortured with dripping candle wax and a "popper" overdose. When the camera accidently fell over in the middle of the proceedings, it was quickly returned to its original position without a break in the action. *My Hustler* offered a modicum of story, audible dialogue, and two shots—one of them a repetitive pan from a gay man talking to friends on the deck of a Fire Island beach house to his hired male prostitute sunning himself on the beach. The second shot, which fails to reveal the outcome of a wager made in the first section, shows the hustler and another man taking showers and grooming themselves in a crowded bathroom (a scene which made the pages of *Life* magazine for its brief male nudity).

It was *Chelsea Girls*, however, which resulted in Warhol's breakthrough to national and international exposure. A three-hour film in black-and-white and color, shown on two screens at once, it featured almost all the resident "superstars" in scenes supposedly taking place in various rooms of New York's Chelsea Hotel. After *Chelsea Girls'* financial success, subsequent Warhol films like *I, A Man, Bike Boy, Nude Restaurant*, and *Lonesome Cowboys* became a bit more technically astute and conventionally feature-length. Simultaneously, the scenes taking place in front of the camera in these films, while they maintained their bizarre, directionless, and ad-libbed quality, became more sensational in their presentation of nudity and sex. Warhol's last hurrah, *Lonesome Cowboys*, was actually shot in Arizona. It featured a number of "superstars" dressing in western garb, posing and walking through a nearly non-existent story amongst western movie sets. It was the last film Warhol completed before he was seriously wounded in an assassination attempt by marginal factory character Valerie Solanas.

Warhol's shooting marked the beginning of a period of reclusiveness for the artist. Subsequent "Warhol" films were the product of cohort and collaborator Paul Morrissey, who has been credited with the increasing commercialism of the 1967 films (not to mention the decline of the factory "scene"). While Warhol lay in the hospital recovering from gunshot wounds, Morrissey completed a film on his own entitled *Flesh*—a series of episodes basically recounting a day in the life of Joe Dallesandro (who appears nude more often than not), featuring Warhol-like performances and camera work, but adding a discernible story line and even character motivations.

From 1970 to 1974, Morrissey's films under Warhol's name quickly became not only more commercial, but more technically accomplished and traditionally plotted as well. After *Trash*, a kind of watershed film that featured Joe and Holly Woodlawn in a narrative comedy about some marginal New York junkies and low-lifes, Morrissey even began to tone down the nudity. *Women in Revolt*, which was virtually a full-fledged melodrama, featured three transvestites playing the women of the title. *Heat*, shot in Los Angeles, had Dallesandro and New York cult actress/screen personality Sylvia Miles playing out a sleazy remake of *Sunset Boulevard. L'Amour* took the whole Morrissey coterie to Paris.

Morrissey's big step into mainstream filmmaking came with the 1974 production of *Andy Warhol's Frankenstein*, a preposterously gory, tongue-in-cheek horror film rendered in perfectly seamless, classical Hollywood style, and in a highly accomplished 3-D process. As outrageous as it was in its surrealistically bloody excess, and for all its "high-camp" attitude, the film bore almost no resemblance to the films of Andy Warhol; nor did Morrissey's *Blood for Dracula,* made at the same time, with virtually the same cast, but without 3-D. Since that time, Morrissey has pursued a career apart from Warhol's name as an independent commercial filmmaker.

—Ed Lowry

WATERS, John

Nationality: American. **Born:** Baltimore, Maryland, 1945. **Education:** Attended University of Baltimore, 1965, and New York University, 1966; claims to have been thrown out of film school. **Career:** Made first short film with 8mm camera, 1964; directed first feature, *Mondo Trasho* (financed for $2,000 by father), and began collaboration with Divine, 1969; arrested on eve of premiere of *Mondo Trasho* and charged with "conspiracy to commit indecent exposure"; directed first-ever scratch-and-sniff movie, *Polyester,* 1981; teacher at Baltimore Prison, 1980s.

Films as Director, Producer, and Screenwriter:

1964 *Hag in a Leather Jacket* (short)
1966 *Roman Candles* (3 shorts)
1968 *Eat Your Makeup* (short)
1969 *Mondo Trasho* (+ ed, cin)
1970 *Multiple Maniacs*
1972 *Pink Flamingoes* (+ ed, cin)
1974 *Female Trouble* (+ cin)
1977 *Desperate Living*
1981 *Polyester*
1988 *Hairspray* (co-pr)
1990 *Cry Baby*
1994 *Serial Mom*

Other Films:

1986 *Something Wild* (Demme) (role)
1989 *Homer and Eddie* (Mikhalkov-Konchalovsky) (role)

Publications

By WATERS: books—

Shock Value, New York, 1981.
Crackpot: The Obsessions of John Waters, New York, 1986.
Trash Trio: The Screenplays Pink Flamingoes, Desperate Living, Flamingoes Forever, New York, 1988.

By WATERS: articles—

Interview in *Film Comment* (New York), June 1981.
"John Waters' Guilty Pleasures," in *Film Comment* (New York), July/August 1983.
Interview with Karen Jaehne, in *Stills* (London), November/December 1983.
"Blackboard Jungle," in *American Film* (Washington, D.C.), April 1985.
"How Not to Make a Movie," in *American Film* (Washington, D.C.), July/August 1986.
"Hard Travelling," in *American Film* (Washington, D.C.), November 1986.
Interview in *Interview* (New York), December 1986.
Interview in *A Critical Cinema: Interviews with Independent Filmmakers,* by Scott MacDonald, Berkeley, 1988.
Interview with Jonathan Ross, in *Time Out* (London), 22 June 1988.
"*The National Enquirer,*" in *Time Out* (London), 21 September 1988.
"John Waters: From Sleaze to Tease," an interview with K. Bail, in *Cinema Papers* (Melbourne), November 1988.
"Walgelijk!" an interview with K. Vandemaele, in *Skoop* (Amsterdam), July/August 1990.
Interview with Robert Seidenberg, in *Empire* (London), August 1990.
"Camping Out in Holywood," an interview with David Hockney, in *Interview* (New York), April 1994.
"High Waters Marks," an interview with Kate Meyers, in *Entertainment Weekly* (New York), 29 April 1994.

On WATERS: books—

Hoberman, Jim, and Jonathan Rosenbaum, editors, *Midnight Movies,* New York, 1983.
Ives, John G., *John Waters,* New York, 1992.
McCarty, John, *The Sleaze Merchants: Adventures in Exploitation Filmmaking,* New York, 1995.

On WATERS: articles—

Spratt, M., "John Waters: Good Bad Taste," in *Cinema Papers* (Melbourne), March 1983.
Katsahnias, I., "John Waters," in *Cahiers du Cinéma* (Paris), June 1990.
Thompson, B., "The Filthiest Man in the World," in *New Statesman and Society* (London), 13 July 1990.
Mandelbaum, Paul, "Kink Meister: Filmmaker John Waters Is Living Proof That Nothing Exceeds Like Excess," in *New York Times Magazine,* 7 April 1991.
Clark, John, "Cool Waters," in *Premiere* (New York), April 1994.

* * *

One of the major surprises of *Hairspray* is that, in addition to being quite charmingly benign, it exhibits a technical competence, even flair, totally unsuggested by Waters's earlier works. Between his seventeen-minute home movie *Hag in a Black Leather Jacket* and his semi-overground scratch-and-sniff feature *Polyester,* the Baltimore-based Waters's films improve only insofar as increasing—though still minuscule—budgets allow for such luxuries as colour, synchronised sound, and camera set-ups. His best-known early works, *Pink Flamingoes, Female Trouble,* and *Desperate Living,* manage to combine the conceptually outrageous with all the technical skills of the average home movie or hardcore porno quickie. Financing his first films through shoplifting and surrounding his habitual star—300-pound transvestite Divine—with various comically depraved and/or hideous friends who are at once funnier, grosser, and more extreme than Warhol's factory folk, Waters created in *Mondo Trasho* and *Multiple Maniacs* a self-contained world of the defiantly sick, where beauty and ugliness, good and bad, and restraint and excess are juggled to a surprisingly moral, endearing effect. His scatological obsessions are less Swiftian than pre-adolescent, and he always seems to view his movies as ratty fairy tales in the Saki or Disney manner, often poking fun at the very idea of something being offensive even while going as far as is possible on screen.

Pink Flamingoes is Waters's disposable masterpiece, in which Divine and entourage—including the horrifying Edy Massey—battle with a group of more uptight degenerates—including the talented Mink Stole, who has stuck with Waters throughout his career—for the title of "World's Filthiest Person." Waters simply uses the premise as an excuse for getting as much depravity on screen as possible, winding up with an unforgettable punchline as Divine outgrosses everyone by cheerfully eating dog shit. The rest of the picture matches the tone of this classic moment, with a DIY artificial insemination, a musical rectum, a half-naked egg-sucking grandmother, a touch of hardcore gay sex, a hokey cannibal orgy that satirises *Night of the Living Dead,* plentiful ranting ("filth is my politics, filth is my life," claims Divine), bad-taste Manson jokes, and a sexual act that involves killing chickens to add to the gross-out count. Typical of the film's trashiness and compounding of illegality with the distasteful is the idea of Divine shoplifting a hunk of frozen meat by slipping it into her panties and then serving it to her family for dinner, claiming that it has been "warmed in her own oven." Nevertheless, much of the funniest stuff in the movie is deadpanned, as when Divine's loyal son staunchly reacts to an insult to his mother with "Mama, nobody sends you a turd and expects to live."

Waters has claimed that "I pride myself in the fact that my work has no socially redeeming value," but underneath it all he is an All-American Boy seeing how far he can go before his parents send him up to his room, and his essays—collected in *Shock Value* and *Crackpot*—reveal that he is a witty moralist. At worst, his films are merely tedious, but at best they are life-affirming in the way that Tom Lehrer's gleefully sick songs can be. *Pink Flamingoes,* no matter how difficult it might be to sit through, is a one-of-a-kind movie, disarming and necessary in the way that *Wavelength* and *The Act of Seeing with One's Own Eyes* are, but it proved an almost impossible act to follow. *Female Trouble* and *Desperate Living* are more of the same—with Divine leading a glamorous life of crime in the former and dying beautifully in the electric chair, and Mink Stole running away to join a community of murderous lesbian outcasts in the latter—only not as effectively offensive. Both films have their moments, both of humour (Divine strangling a hare krishna) and sickness (Susan Lowe reversing her sex change by snipping off her new penis with a pair of scissors), but they do not have the demented charm of *Pink Flamingoes. Polyester,* a nervous step towards the mainstream with less overt violence and one name actor (Tab Hunter), is a half-hearted picture, turning its back on sex and violence because Waters justifiably felt that other movies (*Ilsa, She-Wolf of the SS, Thundercrack!, Cafe Flesh, Appointment with Agony*) had gone further than he would care to, but finding little in its leftover soap-opera plot worth guying, although it has a priceless joke about a drive-in cinema advertising "three great Marguerite Duras hits." It was also becoming notable that Waters's mainly amateur casts had never been quite up to the demands of his acid, cleverly turned dialogue, and that Divine—as disastrously revealed in *Lust in the Dust*—was incapable of turning a drag act into an acting performance worth building a film around.

So, after six years of relative inaction—teaching film courses in prisons and writing amusing essays for *Film Comment* and *National Lampoon*—Waters returned with *Hairspray,* a spoof teen movie which retained Divine, albeit in a digestible secondary role, and a fascination with 1960s pop ephemera from the early movies (pirated pop had always been used on Waters's soundtracks, and the plot of *Female Trouble* revolves around cha-cha heels), but which otherwise seems more like the sort of well-observed period picture one might have expected from Baltimore's other resident local auteur, Barry Levinson. Like *Diner* and *Tin Men, Hairspray* is about a specific phenomenon of the place and period, in this case a television dance show. Waters does not take his subject seriously, and enjoys the opportunity to guy more conventional nostalgia movies, but also shows that he has developed a grasp of the needs of real movie-making, including a flair for staging musical numbers that was carried over into *Cry-Baby,* a parody of 1950s juvenile delinquent movies that is very much in the vein of—and, indeed, is slightly overshadowed by—*Hairspray.* The death of Divine forced Waters to cast an actress, Susan Tyrrell, in his role in *Cry-Baby,* with effective results, and his period musicals are further distinguished by his clever and fruitful use of *kitsch* casting—Pia Zadora, Deborah Harry, Troy Donahue, Patty Hearst, Traci Lords, Iggy Pop, Sonny Bono—to replace the bizarro hangers-on who used to populate his movies. *Hairspray* and *Cry-Baby* may be less repulsive than *Pink Flamingoes,* but much of the curiously innocent heart of the earlier film is carried over, along with the major contribution of art director Vincent Periano, as is Waters's love of overheated B-movie melodrama. Currently, he runs the risk of exhausting his musical mode as definitively as he did his filth theme, but he remains an engaging, disarming, and surprising talent.

Waters's most recent work, *Serial Mom,* harkened a semi-return, by the self-billed "Prince of Puke" and self-styled chronicler of his beloved city of Baltimore's high and low life, to the warped world view of his earlier *Female Trouble* and *Polyester,* albeit with a much bigger budget, better production values, and an even more mainstream cast. An occasionally bloody satire on suburban rot, mass murder, and the media's glorification of crime and criminals—familiar Waters obsessions—it starred Kathleen Turner as the title character, an average housewife with a not-so-average predilection for knocking off any and all who pose a threat to her neat and tidy world of domestic bliss. The film never quite jelled, never quite crossed over into Waters's trademark territory of outright lunacy, however. Its twistedness and perversity seemed dulled, its outrageousness muted, as if Waters was pulling his punches in a clear bid for mainstream acceptance. In short, it was too tasteful; either that or the movies had finally caught up with Waters's unique vision, and what once seemed in shocking bad taste had now become all too much the norm.

—Kim Newman, updated by John McCarty

WATKINS, Peter

Nationality: British. **Born:** Norbiton, Surrey, 29 October 1935. **Education:** Christ College, Brecknockshire; studied acting at Royal Academy of Dramatic Art, London. **Military Service:** Served with East Surrey Regiment. **Career:** Assistant producer of TV shorts and commercials for London ad agency, late 1950s; awards for amateur 16mm films led to job as assistant editor, producer, and director of documentaries for the BBC, 1963; *The War Game* banned by BBC, 1965, subsequently shown theatrically; directed first fiction feature, *Privilege,* 1966; moved to Sweden, 1968, then worked in U.S., 1969-71; film biography of August Strindberg, commissioned by Swedish Film Institute, abandoned due to financial disagreements, 1981. **Address:** Šiltadarzio skg. 3-12, Vilnius 2001, Lithuania.

Films as Director:

1956 *The Web* (amateur)
1958 *The Field of Red* (amateur)
1959 *Diary of an Unknown Soldier* (amateur)
1961 *The Forgotten Faces* (amateur)
1962 *Dust Fever* (amateur, unfinished)
1964 *Culloden*
1966 *The War Game*
1967 *Privilege*
1969 *Gladiatorerna* (*The Gladiators*; *The Peace Game*)
1971 *Punishment Park*
1974 *Edvard Munch* (released in U.S. 1976)
1975 *70-Talets Människor* (*The Seventies People*); *Fällen* (*The Trap*)

Peter Watkins directing *The War Game*

1977 *Aftenlandet* (*Evening Land*)
1987 *The Journey* (doc)
1991 *The Media Project*
1994 *The Freethinker*

Publications

By WATKINS: book—

The War Game, New York, 1967.

By WATKINS: articles—

Blue, James, and Michael Gill, "Peter Watkins Discusses His Suppressed Nuclear Film *The War Game,*" in *Film Comment* (New York), Fall 1965.
"Left, Right, Wrong," in *Films and Filming* (London), March 1970.
"Peter Watkins Talks about the Suppression of His Work within Britain," in *Films and Filming* (London), February 1971.
"*Punishment Park* and Dissent in the West," in *Literature/Film Quarterly* (Salisbury, Maryland), no. 4, 1976.
"*Edvard Munch*: A Director's Statement," in *Literature/Film Quarterly* (Salisbury, Maryland), Winter 1977.
Interview with S. MacDonald in *Journal of the University Film Association* (Carbondale, Illinois), Summer 1982.

On WATKINS: books—

Gomez, Joseph A., *Peter Watkins,* Boston, 1979.
Welsh, James M., *Peter Watkins: A Guide to References and Resources,* Boston, 1986.
MacDonald, Scott, *Avant-Garde Film Motion Studies,* Cambridge, 1993.

On WATKINS: articles—

Kawin, B. F., "Peter Watkins: Cameraman at World's End," in *Journal of Popular Film* (Washington, D.C.), Summer 1973.
Gomez, Joseph A., "Peter Watkins's *Edvard Munch,*" in *Film Quarterly* (Berkeley), Winter 1976/77.
Cunningham, Stuart, "Tense, Address, Tendenz: Questions of the Work of Peter Watkins," in *Quarterly Review of Film Studies* (Pleasantville, New York), Fall 1980.
Welsh, James M., "The Dystopian Cinema of Peter Watkins," in *Film Criticism* (Edinboro, Pennsylvania), Fall 1982.
Welsh, James M., "The Modern Apocalypse: *The War Game,*" in *Journal of Popular Film and Television* (Bowling Green, Ohio), Spring 1983.
McDonald, J., and G. Kenny, "Peter Watkins: A Stormy Relationship with Film," in *Filmnews* (Sydney), January/February 1983.
"Peter Watkins Issue" of *Literature/Film Quarterly* (Salisbury, Maryland), October 1983.
Nolley, Ken, "Narrative Innovation in *Edvard Munch,*" in *Literature/Film Quarterly* (Salisbury, Maryland), vol. 15, no. 2, 1987.

Nolley, Ken, "Making *The Journey* with Peter Watkins," in *CineAction!* (Toronto), no. 12, 1988.
"*The Journey:* A Film in the Global Interest," special issue of *Willamette Journal of the Liberal Arts* (Salem, Oregon), supplemental series 5, 1991.

* * *

From his early amateur days to his most recent unfinished projects, Peter Watkins has attempted to make uniquely personal films which delineate disturbing social and political dimensions. Like George Orwell, he is preoccupied with the growth of a repressive world order, the suppression of individual freedoms, and the dangerous spread of a soothing conformity. Beyond these obvious thematic concerns in his work, Watkins has also made significant contributions to the area of film as art. Almost all of his films push beyond the traditions of conventional cinema. Over the years he has developed a particular style of "documentary reconstruction" which often blends realistic and expressionistic structure to the point that his editing techniques have become a stylistic hallmark, and, since *Punishment Park,* he has managed to create sound montages equal in complexity to his visual arrangements. Finally, Watkins, in his films, in various essays, and on numerous worldwide lecture tours, has offered perceptive analysis and stinging criticism of the dangers of the media in today's world.

As early as *The Forgotten Faces,* Watkins subverted the deep-seated cinematic conventions that actors do not see the camera and that the camera always knows what will happen next and therefore is accurately focused and properly framed. On the basis of this amateur film reconstruction of the 1956 Hungarian uprising (which was actually filmed in the back streets of Canterbury), Watkins was hired by the BBC, where he further developed his techniques of reconstruction (the use of amateur actors, extensive cross-cutting, a distinctive interview method, etc.) in *Culloden* and *The War Game.* Part of the impact of the latter film, which chillingly depicts the possible effects of a nuclear attack on Great Britain, derives from what Watkins calls the film's "block structure." This structure juxtaposes the strategies of the present with the supposed "fantasy" of the future, but Watkins cleverly reverses the usual presentation of fantasy and reality. The future in Watkins's films becomes the "reality" and is graphically depicted via newsreel-like techniques. The "fantasy" element of present-day opinions about the aftermath of a nuclear attack is reinforced by the artificiality of the presentation of authority figures and by the use of printed captions and quotations.

Although *The War Game* won an Academy Award for the Best Documentary of 1966, the BBC imposed a worldwide ban on the screening of the film on television. After the suppression of *The War Game,* Watkins resigned from the BBC and, after making *Privilege,* left England because he felt that he could no longer make films there. During this period of exile, which has lasted to the present, he made films in Sweden, Norway, Denmark, and the United States.

The most controversial of these works is *Punishment Park,* a metaphorical depiction in documentary style of the polarization of political attitudes in the U.S. during the war in Vietnam. Through experiments with improvisation and a further development of his interview style in order to elicit direct emotional response from his audience, Watkins hoped to create a film that would serve as a catalyst for the viewer to seek "a new and more meaningful solution to the present human dilemma posed within Western Society."

The intense hostility to this film in the United States has almost been matched by the hostility of Scandinavian critics to *The 70s People* and *Evening Land,* but a majority of film critics on both sides of the Atlantic seem to agree that Watkins's crowning achievement is *Edvard Munch.* This epic yet paradoxically personal work manages to provide a unique balance between the actuality of Munch's statements and the improvisations of non-professional actors expressing their own feelings and concerns. As such, the film functions on multiple levels—it delineates Munch's own fears and anxieties, provides penetrating insight into the nature of his artistic creation, captures accurately the historical nuances of that era in which he lived, and finally allows the viewers to perceive, in this intricate amalgam, problems of contemporary society which touch them directly.

Unfortunately, Peter Watkins still remains very much the outsider whose work is usually either viciously attacked (as "offensive," "hysterical," and "paranoid") or simply ignored. His role in film history, however, is significant, and as Raymond Durgnat rightly notes, "Watkins is as crucial as John Grierson in the development of documentary."

Watkins continued to be marginalized during the 1980s and 1990s. From 1982 until 1987 Watkins worked tirelessly on *The Journey,* originally conceived as an updating of *The War Game* and independently funded by peace groups around the world. This project turned into a thoughtful fourteen-and-one-half-hour documentary keyed to nuclear-related topics (the development of the atom bomb, the Hiroshima memorial, civil defense worldwide, the White Train, for example), Third World poverty, and the failure of media to keep citizens properly informed about global problems.

His next documentary, *The Media Project,* focussed upon the way the Gulf War was covered on television, intending to demonstrate how that coverage was slanted, biased, and altogether too confusing for ordinary citizens to understand. This documentary followed an extended teaching tour Watkins made of New Zealand devoted to media education. The documentary framework is fractured, however, by a dance sequence (called "The Dance of Life") and further complicated by an apparent (though never fully explained) science-fiction narrative framework.

Finally, in 1994 Watkins achieved a long-standing personal goal by completing a four-and-one-half-hour picture about August Strindberg called *The Freethinker,* shot on a modest budget on video at the Bishop's Arno School in Sweden. During the early 1980s Watkins had developed a script for this companion to the *Munch* film and was invited to work with the Swedish Film Institute to complete his biographical film about Strindberg. The initial project collapsed, but Watkins vowed to make the film, completed a dozen years later. The film was shown in Sweden in 1995 and also was scheduled for Britain's National Film Theatre in February of 1996, where Watkins was also invited to discuss *The War Game,* thirty years after it had been banned worldwide by the BBC. This would be his first institutional public appearance in Britain since the late 1960s. Ironically, thirty years after winning an Academy Award for *The War Game,* having worked in both commercial and institutional filmmaking, Watkins had ultimately returned to independent production, his principles and experimental techniques intact.

—Joseph A. Gomez, updated by James M. Welsh

WATT, Harry

Nationality: Scottish. **Born:** Edinburgh, 18 October 1906. **Education:** Attended Edinburgh University. **Career:** Joined Empire Marketing Board (EMB) under John Grierson, 1931 or 1932; joined General Post Office (GPO) film unit after EMB film unit is transferred to GPO, also directed first film, 1934; after outbreak of war, GPO film unit incorporated into newly-formed Ministry of Information, 1939; also worked for Army Film Unit, 1939-42; joined Ealing Studios, 1942; directed films in Australia, 1945-48, and in West Africa, 1951-53; producer for Granada TV, England, 1955; rejoined Ealing Studios, 1956; wrote autobiography, *Don't Look at the Camera,* 1974. **Died:** 2 April 1987.

Harry Watt (left) directing Elisabeth Welch and Sonny Hale in *Fiddlers Three*

Films as Director:

1934 *BBC: Droitwich* (co-d); *6:30 Collection* (co-d)
1936 ***Night Mail*** (co-d); *The Saving of Bill Blewitt* (+ sc)
1937 *Big Money* (co-d)
1938 *North Sea*; *Health in Industry*
1939 *The First Days* (co-d)
1940 *Squadron 992*; *London Can Take It* (co-d); *The Front Line*; *Britain at Bay*
1941 *Target for Tonight* (+ sc); *Christmas Under Fire*
1942 *Dover Revisited*; *21 Miles*
1943 *Nine Men* (+ sc)
1944 *Fiddlers Three* (+ sc)
1946 *The Overlanders* (+ sc)
1949 *Eureka Stockade* (*Massacre Hill*) (+ sc)
1951 *Where No Vultures Fly* (*Ivory Hunter*)
1954 *West of Zanzibar* (+ co-sc)
1958 *People Like Maria*
1959 *The Siege of Pinchgut* (+ co-sc)
1962 *Den Hvide Hingst*
1963 *Messenger of the Mountains*

Other Films:

1937 *Four Barriers* (co-pr)

Publications

By WATT: books—

Don't Look at the Camera, New York, 1974.

On WATT: books—

Lovell, Alan, and Jim Hillier, *Studies in Documentary,* New York, 1972.
Sussex, Elizabeth, *The Rise and Fall of British Documentary: The Story of the Film Movement Founded by John Grierson,* Berkeley, California, 1975.
Vaughan, Dai, *Portrait of an Invisible Man: The Working Life of Stewart McAllister, Film Editor,* London, 1983.
Ellis, Jack C., *The Documentary Idea,* Englewood Cliffs, New Jersey, 1989.
Swann, Paul, *The British Documentary Film Movement 1926-46,* Cambridge, 1989.

On WATT: articles—

Flaherty, Robert, article on *North Sea,* in *Sight and Sound* (London), Summer 1938.
Lacey, Bradner, article on *Where No Vultures Fly,* in *Films in Review* (New York), June/July 1952.
"Personality of the Month," in *Films and Filming* (London), June 1959.

Vaughan, Dai, article on *The Siege of Pinchgut,* in *Films and Filming* (London), October 1959.
Obituary, in *Variety* (New York), 8 April 1987.

* * *

Harry Watt was a member of the Grierson documentary group who, during World War II, moved over into feature film directing, carrying his documentary heritage with him. He was one of the two most talented directors to come out of British documentary of the 1930s (Humphrey Jennings being the other). Whereas Jennings was the poet, Watt was the story teller.

Watt demonstrated his flair for narrative, characterization, and humor early in his career—an ability rare among documentary filmmakers. It first became evident in *Night Mail.* Though the creative origins of that film seem to be genuinely collective, it was unquestionably Watt who drew the engaging performances—the naturalness, the bits of banter and occasional tension—from the cast of mailmen. Next, *The Saving of Bill Blewitt* offered a comic anecdote concocted by Watt about a Cornwall fisherman and the Post Office Savings Bank. In *North Sea,* which followed, Watt's attraction to the dramatic is given full reign. Though a short like the others, the situation—it depicts a disabled fishing trawler awash in high seas, loved ones waiting at home, and efforts to aid the stricken ship—has all of the ingredients for a feature. *Squadron 992* continued to display Watt's feeling for narrative, humor, and excitement into the beginning of the war.

But it was *Target for Tonight* that emerged as Watt's major contribution: it became the prototype for the British wartime semi-documentary feature. This form involved a real situation, though it might be composite and representative rather than actual. In this case the film covered a typical British bombing raid into Germany. The non-actors, here RAF airmen, were given some characterization and dialogue. The exposition, conflict, climax, and denouement follow narrative/dramatic convention. (The bomber on which the film concentrates is hit with flack and the main question becomes whether its crew will return safely.) The semi-documentary was, in other words, half-fact and half-fiction.

As one can infer from his charming autobiography, *Don't Look at the Camera,* Watt had always thought that filmmaking was really the making of fiction feature films for the theaters. Since the semi-documentary form was picked up and developed by the commercial studios as well as by the government Crown Film Unit, however, Watt continued along the semi-documentary lines he had begun when he moved over to Ealing Studios in 1942. Of his features made for Ealing, *The Overlanders* is the most successful, certainly in critical and probably in commercial terms as well. Shot in Australia, it chronicles a cattle drive across the awesome outback occasioned by the fear of Japanese invasion after Japan's entry into World War II. Though actors play the roles, it is a recreation of an actual occurrence. Watt once said of himself as a filmmaker, "I am a dramatic reporter."

—Jack C. Ellis

WEBER, Lois

Nationality: American. **Born:** Allegheny City, Pennsylvania, 1882. **Family:** Married Phillips Smalley, 1906 (divorced 1922). **Career:** Touring concert pianist, then Church Home Missionary in Pittsburgh, 1890s; actress in touring melodrama *Why Girls Leave Home* for company managed by future husband Smalley, 1905; writer and director (then actor) for Gaumont Talking Pictures, from 1908; teamed up with Smalley, moved to Reliance, then Rex, working for Edwin S. Porter; the Smalleys (as they were known) took over Rex, a member of the Universal conglomerate, following Porter's departure, 1912; joined Hobart Bosworth's company, 1914; Universal funded private studio for Weber at 4634 Sunset Boulevard, 1915; founded own studio, 1917; signed contract with Famous Players-Lasky for $50,000 per picture and a percentage of profits, 1920; dropped by company after three unprofitable films, 1921, subsequently lost company, divorced husband, and suffered nervous collapse; briefly resumed directing, late 1920s; script-doctor for Universal, 1930s. **Died:** In Hollywood, 13 November 1939.

Films as Director:

(partial list—directed between 200 and 400 films)

1912 *The Troubadour's Triumph*
1913 *The Eyes of God*; *The Jew's Christmas* (co-d, sc, role); *The Female of the Species* (+ role)
1914 *The Merchant of Venice* (co-d, role as Portia); *Traitor*; *Like Most Wives*; *Hypocrites!* (+ sc); *False Colors* (co-d, co-sc, role); *It's No Laughing Matter* (+ sc); *A Fool and His Money* (+ role); *Behind the Veil* (co-d, sc, role)
1915 *Sunshine Molly* (co-d, role, sc); *Scandal* (co-d, sc, role)
1916 *Discontent* (short); *Hop, the Devil's Brew* (co-d, sc, role); *Where Are My Children?* (co-d, sc); *The French Downstairs*; *Alone in the World* (short); *The People vs. John Doe* (+ role); *The Rock of Riches* (short); *John Needham's Double*; *Saving the Family Name* (co-d, role); *Shoes*; *The Dumb Girl of Portici* (co-d); *The Flirt* (co-d)
1917 *The Hand That Rocks the Cradle* (co-d, pr, role); *Even As You and I*; *The Mysterious Mrs. M*; *The Price of a Good Time*; *The Man Who Dared God*; *There's No Place Like Home*; *For Husbands Only* (+ pr)
1918 *The Doctor and the Woman*; *Borrowed Clothes*
1919 *When a Girl Loves*; *Mary Regan*; *Midnight Romance* (+ sc); *Scandal Mongers*; *Home*; *Forbidden*
1921 *Too Wise Wives* (+ pr, sc); *What's Worth While?* (+ pr); *To Please One Woman* (+ sc); *The Blot* (+ pr, sc); *What Do Men Want?* (+ pr, sc)
1923 *A Chapter in Her Life* (+ co-sc)
1926 *The Marriage Clause* (+ sc)
1927 *Sensation Seekers* (+ sc); *The Angel of Broadway*
1934 *White Heat*

Other Films:

1915 *A Cigarette, That's All* (sc)

Publications

By WEBER: article—

Interview with Aline Carter, in *Motion Picture Magazine* (New York), March 1921.

On WEBER: book—

Heck-Rabi, Louise, *Women Filmmakers: A Critical Reception,* Metuchen, New Jersey, 1984.

On WEBER: articles—

Pyros, J., "Notes on Women Directors," in *Take One* (Montreal), November/December 1970.

Koszarski, Richard, "The Years Have Not Been Kind to Lois Weber," in *Women and the Cinema,* edited by Karyn Kay and Gerald Peary, New York, 1977.

"Lois Weber—Whose Role Is It Anyway?" in *Monthly Film Bulletin* (London), May 1982.

Ostria, V., "Lois Weber, cette inconnue," in *Cahiers du Cinéma* (Paris), April 1985.

"Lois Weber Issue" of *Film History* (Philadelphia), vol. 1, no. 4, 1987.

* * *

Lois Weber was a unique silent film director. Not only was she a woman who was certainly the most important female director the American film industry has known, but unlike many of her colleagues up to the present, her work was regarded in its day as equal to, if not a little better than that of most male directors. She was a committed filmmaker in an era when commitment was virtually unknown, a filmmaker who was not afraid to make features with subject matter in which she devoutly believed, subjects as varied as Christian Science (*Jewel* and *A Chapter in Her Life*) or birth control (*Where Are My Children*). *Hypocrites* was an indictment of hypocrisy and corruption in big business, politics, and religion, while *The People vs. John Doe* opposed capital punishment. At the same time, Lois Weber was quite capable of handling with ease a major spectacular feature such as the historical drama *The Dumb Girl of Portici,* which introduced Anna Pavlova to the screen.

During the 1910s, Lois Weber was under contract to Universal. While at Universal, she appears to have been given total freedom as to the subject matter of her films, all of which where among the studio's biggest moneymakers and highly regarded by the critics of the day. (The Weber films, however, did run into censorship problems, and the director was the subject of a vicious attack in a 1918 issue of *Theatre Magazine* over the "indecent and suggestive" nature of her titles.) Eventually the director felt the urge to move on to independent production, and during 1920 and 1921 she released a series of highly personal intimate dramas dealing with married life and the types of problems which beset ordinary people. None of these films was particularly well received by the critics, who unanimously declared them dull, while the public displayed an equal lack of enthusiasm. Nonetheless, features such as *Too Wise Wives* and *The Blot* demonstrate Weber at her directorial best. In the former she presents a study of two married couples. Not very much happens, but in her characterizations and attention to detail (something for which Weber was always noted), the director is as contemporary as a Robert Altman or an Ingmar Bergman. *The Blot* is concerned with "genteel poverty" and is marked by the underplaying of its principals—Claire Windsor and Louis Calhern—and an enigmatic ending which leaves the viewer uninformed as to the characters' future, an ending unlike any in the entire history

Lois Weber (center)

of the American silent film. These films, as with virtually all of the director's work, were also written by Lois Weber.

Through the end of her independent productions in 1921, Lois Weber worked in association with her husband Phillips Smalley, who usually received credit as associate or advisory director. After the two were divorced, Lois Weber's career went to pieces. She directed one or two minor program features together with one talkie, but none equalled her work from the 1910s and early 1920s. She was a liberated film-maker who seemed lost without the companionship, both at home and in the studio, of a husband. Her career and life were in many ways as enigmatic as the ending of *The Blot.*

—Anthony Slide

WEIR, Peter

Nationality: Australian. **Born:** Peter Lindsay Weir in Sydney, 8 August 1944. **Education:** Arts/Law coursework at University of Sydney. **Family:** Married Wendy Stiles, 1966, two children. **Career:** Worked for family real estate business, then joined television station ATN 7, Sydney, 1967; assistant cameraman and production assistant, Commonwealth Film Unit (now Film Australia), 1969; directed his first internationally distributed feature, *The Cars That Ate Paris,* 1974; had his first international success, *Picnic at Hanging Rock,* 1975; signed multi-film contract with Warner Bros., 1980; directed *Witness,* his first Hollywood film, 1985. **Awards:** Grand Prix, Australian Film Institute, for *Homesdale,* 1971; Academy Award nominations, Best Director for *Witness,* 1985, and *Dead Poets Society,* 1989; Neville Wran Award for excellence in filmmaking, 1988; Academy Award nomination, Best Screenplay, for *Green Card,* 1990.

Films as Director and Scriptwriter:

1967 *Count Vim's Last Exercise* (short)
1968 *The Life and Times of the Reverend Buck Shotte* (short)
1970 "Michael" episode of *Three to Go*
1971 *Homesdale* (short)
1972 *Incredible Floridas* (short)
1973 *Whatever Happened to Green Valley?* (short)
1974 *The Cars That Ate Paris* (*The Cars That Ate People*)
1975 ***Picnic at Hanging Rock*** (d only)
1977 ***The Last Wave***
1978 *The Plumber* (for TV)
1981 *Gallipoli*
1982 *The Year of Living Dangerously*
1985 ***Witness*** (d only)
1986 *The Mosquito Coast* (d only)
1989 *Dead Poets Society*
1990 *Green Card* (+ pr)
1993 *Fearless* (d only)

Publications

By WEIR: articles—

Interview with D. Castell, in *Films Illustrated* (London), November 1976.
Interviews with H. Béhar, in *Image et Son* (Paris), January and February 1978.
Interview with P. Childs, in *Millimeter* (New York), March 1979.
Interview with Brian McFarlane and T. Ryan, in *Cinema Papers* (Melbourne), September/October 1981.
Interview with Michael Dempsey, in *Film Quarterly* (Berkeley), Summer 1982.
Interview with M. Bygrave, in *Stills* (London), May 1985.
"Dialogue on Film: Peter Weir," in *American Film* (Washington, D.C.), March 1986.
Interview with Patrick McGilligan, in *Film Comment* (New York), November/December 1986.
Interview with C. Viviani and others, in *Positif* (Paris), April 1987.
Interview, in *Cinema Papers* (Melbourne), August 1990.
Interview with V. Campbell, in *Movieline,* September 1993.

On WEIR: books—

Tulloch, John, *Australian Cinema: Industry, Narrative, and Meaning,* Sydney, 1982.
Peeters, Theo, *Peter Weir and His Films: A Critical Biography,* Melbourne, 1983.
Mathews, Sue, *35mm Dreams: Conversations with Five Directors About the Australian Film Revival,* Ringwood, Victoria, 1984.
Hall, Sandra, *Critical Business: The New Australian Cinema in Review,* Adelaide, 1985.
Moran, Albert, and Tom O'Regan, editors, *An Australian Film Reader,* Sydney, 1985.
McFarlane, Brian, *Australian Cinema 1970-1985,* London, 1987.

On WEIR: articles—

Nicholls, R., "Peter Weir," in *Lumière* (Melbourne), March 1973.
Brennan, R., "Peter Weir," in *Cinema Papers* (Melbourne), January 1974.
"Director of the Year," *International Film Guide* (London, New York), 1980.
McFarlane, Brian, "The Films of Peter Weir," in *Cinema Papers* (Melbourne), April/May 1980.
Magill, M., "Peter Weir," in *Films in Review* (New York), October 1981.
Poulle, F., "Bienvenu au héros conradien," in *Jeune Cinéma* (Paris), October 1983.
Sesti, M., "Peter Weir e il vuoto della ragione," in *Bianco e Nero* (Rome), October/December 1985.
Griffin, N., "Poetry Man," in *Premiere* (New York), July 1989.
Sesti, M., article, in *Cineforum* (Bergamo), July/August 1989.
Hentzi, G., "Peter Weir and the Cinema of New Age Humanism," in *Film Quarterly* (Berkeley), Winter 1990/91.
Giavarini, L., article, in *Cahiers du Cinema* (Paris), September 1991.
Clark, John, "Peter Weir," in *Premiere* (New York), February 1991.

* * *

If, as Yugoslav director Dusan Makavajev contends, "Australia is Switzerland, but it wants to be Texas," then it's to the Swiss side that Peter Weir belongs. Even his apprentice shorts show an attraction to international concerns and fantasy that is alien to Australia's documentary-based cinema. *Incredible Floridas* is a *hommage* to Rimbaud, *Michael* a vision of a future Australia gripped by revolution, while the macabre *Homesdale* evokes evil in the unlikely setting of an isolated retirement home.

Weir dropped out of university to travel to Europe, an experience that profoundly affected him: "It struck me very strongly that I was a European, that this was where we had come from and where I belonged." An ancient sculpture found on a Tunisian beach prompted *The Last Wave,* and he conceived *The Cars That Ate Paris* when a French autoroute detour triggered the idea of a tiny village where, he

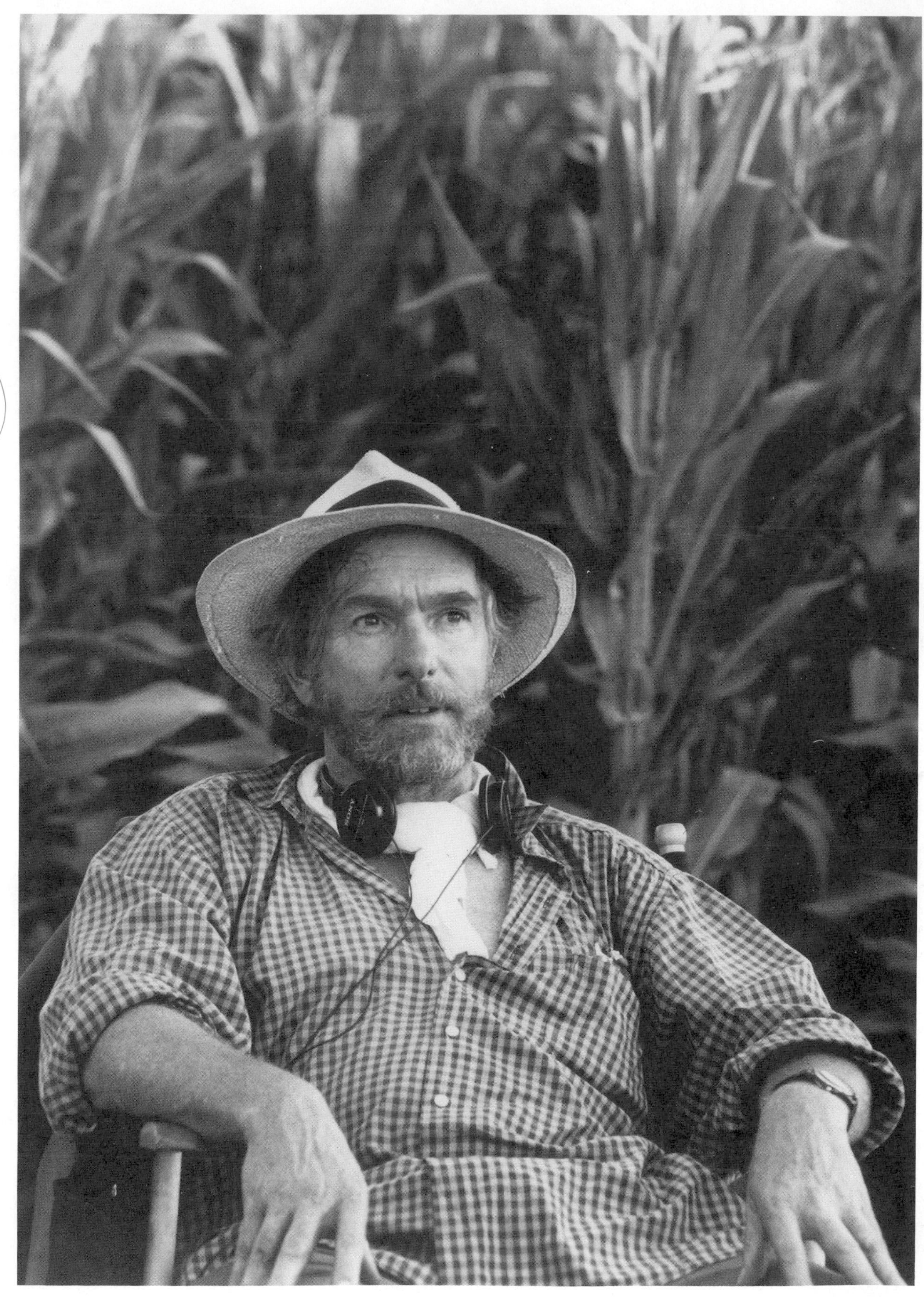

Peter Weir on the set of *Fearless*

surmised, anything might happen—including local hoodlums customising cars into killing machines.

The absurdist vision of *The Cars That Ate Paris* puzzled Australian audiences but interested Hollywood. Roger Corman gave the film a small U.S. release while also borrowing some of its concepts for Bartel's *Death Race 2000.* Universal acclaim, however, greeted *Picnic at Hanging Rock,* a Victorian fantasy with drowsy, cryptic, and sensual qualities. Weir filmed Joan Lindsay's novel with such skill that most audiences believe the feature's tale of the disappearance of three schoolgirls on a rocky monolith on St. Valentine's Day, 1900, to be based on fact.

Weir chose Richard Chamberlain to star in *The Last Wave* as a lawyer who uncovers aboriginal cults which foretell the world's end in a new flood, but Australian audiences greeted the film's obscure theme and American star with suspicion. In reaction, Weir made *The Plumber,* a TV feature recognizable as his work only by its faintly surrealistic premise, in which an unsummoned tradesman invades a baffled housewife's cosy suburban environment.

With *Gallipoli,* which Weir calls his "graduation film," Weir shook off his reputation as an occult specialist and a director of essentially local concerns. Though set against Australia's first military adventure—the disastrous 1916 Dardenelles campaign—its scale, style, and outlook, all broadly international, won *Gallipoli* mass American release, and both director and star Mel Gibson were given Hollywood contracts.

Weir's first fully-funded studio project, *The Year of Living Dangerously,* marked him as an artist capable of handling both big stars and bigger emergencies. When threats of violence from Muslim extremists drove the production out of Manila, he recreated Djakarta in Sydney suburbia. The film turned Mel Gibson into an international romantic lead, and also remade another career when Weir, unsatisfied with the actor playing dwarf Chinese cameraman Billy Kwan, recast the role with Linda Hunt, who delivered an Oscar-winning performance.

When plans to film *The Mosquito Coast* with Jack Nicholson collapsed, Weir stepped up at short notice to direct a thriller that featured Harrison Ford as a city cop finding affinities with the Amish religious fundamentalists who hide him from danger. *Witness,* an unexpected hit, decisively freed Ford from his Indiana Jones image, and the revived *The Mosquito Coast* starred not Nicholson but Ford as Paul Theroux's dizzy technocrat, a man who drags his family to South America in a doomed celebration of American mechanical genius. The film's relative failure in no way harmed Weir's reputation as a director who could change careers and remake images. He went on to direct Robin Williams in *Dead Poets Society,* a film wherein a schoolteacher bucks a version of McCarthyism in the 1950s, Its critical and financial success powered Weir into *Green Card,* his first original screenplay, about an emigre musician marrying an American girl to get a work permit. The story attracted Gérard Depardieu, anxious to penetrate the English-language market. "I have the impression of having discovered a brother," the actor said, "like with Truffaut." Such statements suggest that Weir, while mastering Hollywood, has not lost touch with his early European concerns.

Those same concerns were evidenced yet again in *Fearless,* Weir's most recent feature. *Fearless* is an unusual film for the 1990s: a mainstream project with deeply serious and sobering overtones. Its scenario examines the after-effects of a deadly plane crash. Unlike other Hollywood films dealing with air crashes which might focus on the superficial fireworks involved in the accident—complete with eye-popping special effects—*Fearless* explores the psychological effects the experience has on two of its survivors (played by Jeff Bridges and Rosie Perez). All too often, contemporary movies make no attempt to dramatize the impact of violence on its victims. *Fearless,* though dramatically flawed in its second half, is a refreshing change-of-pace in that it faces up to issues surrounding mortality and spirituality.

—John Baxter, updated by Rob Edelman

WEISS, Jiři

Nationality: Czech. **Born:** Prague, 29 March 1913. **Education:** Educated in law, Charles University, Prague. **Career:** Advertising writer, also made first film, 1935; director for Barrandov Studios, Prague, 1936; following Nazi invasion, escaped to London, 1939; worked with British documentarists for Crown Film Unit, World War II; returned to Prague, 1945; teacher at film school, West Berlin, 1963; at Venice Festival at time of Soviet invasion of Czechoslovakia, sought political asylum in Italy, 1968. **Awards:** Artist of Merit, Czechoslovakia.

Films as Director:

1935 *People in the Sun*
1936 *Give Us Wings*
1937 *Song of a Sad Country*
1938 *Journey from the Shadows*
1939 *The Rape of Czechoslovakia*
1941 *Eternal Prague*
1943 *Before the Raid*
1945 *Věrni zustaneme* (*Interim Balance*) (+ sc)
1947 *Uloupená hranice* (*The Stolen Frontier*) (+ co-sc)
1948 *Dravci* (*Wild Beasts*; *Beast of Prey*) (+ co-sc); *Ves v pohraniči* (*The Village on the Frontier*)
1949 *Píseň o sletu I, II* (*Song of the Meet, I and II*; *High Flies the Hawk, I and II*)
1950 *Vstanou noví bojovníci* (*New Warriors Will Arise*); *Poslední výstřel* (*The Last Shot*)
1953 *Muj přítel Fabián* (*My Friend Fabian*; *My Friend the Gypsy*) (+ co-sc)
1954 *Punt'a a čtyřlístek* (*Punta and the Four-Leaf Clover*; *Doggy and the Four*) (+ co-sc)
1956 *Hra o život* (*Life at Stake*; *Life Was at Stake*) (+ co-sc)
1957 *Vlčí jáma* (*Wolf Trap*) (+ co-sc)
1959 *Taková láska* (*Appassionata*; *That Kind of Love*) (+ co-sc)
1960 *Romeo, Julie a tma* (*Romeo, Juliet and the Darkness*; *Sweet Light in the Dark Window*) (+ co-sc)
1962 *Zbabělec* (*Coward*) (+ co-sc)
1963 *Zlaté kapradí* (*The Golden Fern*) (+ co-sc)
1965 *Třicet jedna ve stínu* (*Ninety in the Shade*) (+ co-sc)
1966 *Vražda po našem* (*Murder Czech Style*) (+ co-sc)
1968 *Prípad pro Selwyn* (*Justice for Selwyn*) (for Czech TV)
1990 *Martha und Ich* (+ sc)

Publications

By WEISS: articles—

"Czech Cinema Has Arrived," in *Films and Filming* (London), March 1959.
"Mixing It," in *Films and Filming* (London), June 1965.
Interview in *Closely Watched Films,* by Antonin Liehm, White Plains, New York, 1974.

On WEISS: books—

Boček, Jaroslav, *Modern Czechoslovak Film,* Prague, 1965.
Pitera, Zbigniew, *Leksykon rezyserow filmowych,* Warsaw, 1978.
Liehm, Mira, and Antonín, *The Most Important Art: East European Film after 1945,* Berkeley, 1977.
Habova, Milada, and Jitka Vysekalova, editors, *Czechoslovak Cinema,* Prague, 1982.

Jiři Weiss

On WEISS: article—

"Martha und ich," in *Kino (Filme der Bundesrepublik Deutschland)*, no. 3, 1990.

* * *

Jiři Weiss is one of the most significant and certainly most interesting Czech directors of the last fifty years. He studied at Jura and had worked as a journalist before making his first film in 1934, a documentary which received a prize at Venice that year. Until the outbreak of war he continued to work on documentaries.

In 1939 Weiss fled the Nazis to England, befriended an English documentarist, and made several films, including *Before the Raid.* Later, as a film specialist, he took part in the battles of the Czech exile army. He returned to his homeland in 1945. His first theatrical film, *Uloupená hranice,* dealt with the Munich accord of 1938, shortly before the fascist occupation of his country. A subsequent film, *Vstanou noví bojovníci,* depicted the establishment of the worker's movement in Czechoslovakia, and brought the director not only official recognition at home but also attention abroad.

Afterward Weiss made films dealing with contemporary problems and people's everyday life. In the 1953 film *My Friend Fabian* he described how the gypsies adjusted, with many difficulties, to a new life in socialist Czechoslovakia. *Hra o život* appeared in 1956, a critical film about the destruction of a bourgeois family in the period of the German occupation. *Taková láska,* a dramatic psychological work, displayed the director's ability to develop richly human characterization.

Vlčí jama impressed further through the deep psychological treatment of the characters and the careful attention to cultural surroundings by which he delineated the *zeitgeist,* the atmosphere and the milieu of the petit bourgeoisie prior to World War I. An honorable mayor of a small city, who feels a devotion for his ageing wife, nevertheless falls in love with a young girl who lives in the same house.

This film revealed the full range of Jiři Weiss's style. It is based in a solid critical realism, rooted in the epic novels of the nineteenth century. This approach sets out fully realized and many-sided human figures within an accurately described milieu. The cinema of Weiss draws on Czech cultural tradition, and at the same time strives toward broader European dimensions. In this way his works attain a certain cosmopolitanism.

On the one hand, Weiss was strongly influenced by neorealism, as were all the other filmmakers of his generation. Although not so pathetically inclined as, for example, Andrzej Wajda, Weiss showed in his masterpiece *Romeo, Julie a tma* the influences of the neorealist aesthetic, especially in the case of the theme, again broadly European, of the tragic fate of two young lovers in Prague in 1942. The Jewish schoolgirl Hanna is hidden by young Pavel, a tender love develops and is cut short by Hanna's death. Weiss had created a tragic and poetic work, without filmic innovation, but nevertheless a serious, noble film.

In the 1960s Weiss made *Zlaté kapradí, Trícet jedna ve stínu,* and *Vražda po našem,* which attained a high standard in terms of craft, but broke no new ground formally or thematically. Living since 1968 in the West, he has made the occasional film for television.

—Maria Racheva

WELLES, Orson

Nationality: American. **Born:** Kenosha, Wisconsin, 6 May 1916. **Education:** Attended Todd School in Woodstock, Illinois, 1926-31. **Family:** Married 1) Virginia Nicholson, 1934 (divorced 1939), one son; 2) Rita Hayworth, 1943 (divorced 1947), one daughter; 3) Paola Mori, 1955, one daughter. **Career:** Actor and director at the Gate Theatre, Dublin, 1931-34; debut on Broadway with Katherine Cornell's road company, also co-directed first film, 1934; collaborated with John Houseman for the Phoenix Theatre Group, 1935, later producer and director for Federal Theater Project; co-founder, with Houseman, Mercury Theatre Group, 1937; moved into radio with "Mercury Theatre on the Air," 1938, including famous dramatization of H. G. Wells's *War of the Worlds,* Halloween, 1938; given contract by RKO, 1939; directed feature debut, *Citizen Kane,* 1941; began documentary *It's All True,* 1942, then Welles and his staff were removed from RKO; directed *The Lady from Shanghai* for Columbia Studios, 1947; directed *Macbeth* for Republic Pictures, 1948; moved to Europe, 1949; completed only one more film in United States, *Touch of Evil,* 1958; appeared in advertisements, and continued to act, from 1960s. **Awards:** 20th Anniversary Tribute, Cannes Festival, 1966; Honorary Academy Award, for "Superlative artistry and versatility in the creation of motion pictures," 1970; Life Achievement Award, American Film Institute, 1975; Fellowship of the British Film Institute, 1983. **Died:** In Hollywood, 10 October 1985.

Films as Director:

1934 *The Hearts of Age* (16mm short) (co-d)
1938 *Too Much Johnson* (+ co-pr, sc) (unedited, not shown publicly, destroyed in 1970 fire)
1941 ***Citizen Kane*** (+ pr, co-sc, role as Charles Foster Kane)
1942 ***The Magnificent Ambersons*** (+ pr, sc); *It's All True* (+ pr, co-sc) (not completed and never shown)
1943 *Journey into Fear* (co-d, uncredited, pr, co-sc, role as Colonel Haki)

1946 *The Stranger* (+ co-sc, uncredited, role as Franz Kindler, alias Professor Charles Rankin)
1948 ***The Lady from Shanghai*** (+ sc, role as Michael O'Hara) (produced in 1946); *Macbeth* (+ pr, sc, co-costumes, role as Macbeth)
1952 *Othello* (+ pr, sc, role as Othello and narration)
1955 *Mr. Arkadin* (*Confidential Report*) (+ sc, art d, costumes, role as Gregory Arkadin and narration); *Don Quixote* (+ co-pr, sc, asst ph, role as himself and narration) (not completed)
1958 ***Touch of Evil*** (+ sc, role as Hank Quinlan)
1962 ***Le Procès*** (*The Trial*) (+ sc, role as Hastler and narration)
1966 ***Chimes at Midnight*** (Falstaff) (+ sc, costumes, role as Sir John Falstaff)
1968 *The Immortal Story* (+ sc, role as Mr. Clay)
1970 *The Deep* (+ sc, role as Russ Brewer)
1972 *The Other Side of the Wind* (+ sc) (filming begun in 1972, uncompleted)
1975 *F for Fake* (+ sc)

Other Films:

1937 ***The Spanish Earth*** (Ivens) (original narration)
1940 *Swiss Family Robinson* (Ludwig) (off-screen narration)
1943 *Jane Eyre* (R. Stevenson) (role as Edward Rochester)
1944 *Follow the Boys* (Sutherland) (revue appearance with Marlene Dietrich)
1945 *Tomorrow is Forever* (Pichel) (role as John McDonald)
1946 *Duel in the Sun* (Vidor) (off-screen narration)
1947 *Black Magic* (Ratoff) (role as Cagliostro)
1948 *Prince of Foxes* (role as Cesare Borgia)
1949 ***The Third Man*** (Reed) (role as Harry Lime)
1950 *The Black Rose* (Hathaway) (role as General Bayan)
1951 *Return to Glennascaul* (Edwards) (role as himself)
1953 *Trent's Last Case* (Wilcox) (role as Sigsbee Manderson); *Si Versailles m'était conté* (Guitry) (role as Benjamin Franklin); *L'uomo, la bestia e la virtu* (Steno) (role as the beast)
1954 *Napoléon* (Guitry) (role as Hudson Lowe); "Lord Mountdrago" segment of *Three Cases of Murder* (O'Ferrall) (role as Lord Mountdrago)
1955 *Trouble in the Glen* (Wilcox) (role as Samin Cejador y Mengues); *Out of Darkness* (documentary) (narrator)
1956 *Moby Dick* (Huston) (role as Father Mapple)
1957 *Pay the Devil* (Arnold) (role as Virgil Renckler); *The Long Hot Summer* (Ritt) (role as Will Varner)
1958 *The Roots of Heaven* (Huston) (role as Cy Sedgwick); *Les Seigneurs de la forêt* (Sielman and Brandt) (off-screen narration); *The Vikings* (Fleischer) (narration)
1959 *David e Golia* (Pottier and Baldi) (role as Saul); *Compulsion* (Fleischer) (role as Jonathan Wilk); *Ferry to Hong Kong* (Gilbert) (role as Captain Hart); *High Journey* (Baylis) (off-screen narration); *South Sea Adventure* (Dudley) (off-screen narration)
1960 *Austerlitz* (Gance) (role as Fulton); *Crack in the Mirror* (Fleischer) (role as Hagolin/Lamorcière); *I tartari* (Thorpe) (role as Barundai)
1961 *Lafayette* (Dréville) (role as Benjamin Franklin); *King of Kings* (Ray) (off-screen narration); *Désordre* (short) (role)
1962 *Der grosse Atlantik* (documentary) (narrator)
1963 *The V.I.P.s* (Asquith) (role as Max Buda); *Rogopag* (Pasolini) (role as the film director)
1964 *L'Echiquier de Dieu* (*La Fabuleuse Aventure de Marco Polo*) (de la Patellière) (role as Ackermann); *The Finest Hours* (Baylis) (narrator)
1965 *The Island of Treasure* (J. Franco) (role); *A King's Story* (Booth) (narrator)
1966 *Is Paris Burning?* (Clément) (role); *A Man for All Seasons* (Zinnemann) (role as Cardinal Wolsey)
1967 *Casino royale* (Huston and others) (role); *The Sailor from Gibralter* (Richardson) (role); *I'll Never Forget Whatshisname* (Winner) (role)
1968 *Oedipus the King* (Saville) (role as Tiresias); *Kampf um Rom* (role as Emperor Justinian); *The Southern Star* (Hayers) (role)
1969 *Tepepa* (role); *Barbed Water* (documentary) (narrator); *Una su 13* (role); *Michael the Brave* (role); *House of Cards* (Guillermin) (role)
1970 *Catch-22* (Nichols) (role as General Dweedle); *Battle of Neretva* (Bulajia) (role); *Start the Revolution Without Me* (Yorkin) (narrator); *The Kremlin Letter* (Huston) (role); *Waterloo* (Bondarchuk) (role as King Louis XVIII)
1971 *Directed by John Ford* (Bogdanovich) (narrator); *Sentinels of Silence* (narrator); *A Safe Place* (Jaglom) (role)
1972 *La Decade prodigieuse* (role); *Malpertius* (role); *I racconti di Canterbury* (Pasolini) (role); *Treasure Island* (Hough) (role as Long John Silver); *Get to Know Your Rabbit* (De Palma) (role)
1973 *Necromancy* (Gordon) (role)
1975 *Bugs Bunny Superstar* (Jones) (narrator)
1976 *Challenge of Greatness* (documentary) (narrator); *Voyage of the Damned* (Rosenberg) (role)
1977 *It Happened One Christmas* (Thomas) (for TV) (role)
1979 *The Late Great Planet Earth* (on-camera narrator); *The Muppet Movie* (Frawley) (role as J. P. Morgan); *Tesla* (role as Yug)
1981 *Butterfly* (Cimber) (role as the judge); *The Man Who Saw Tomorrow* (Guenette) (role)
1984 *Where is Parsifal?* (Helman) (role); *Almonds and Raisins* (Karel) (narrator)
1985 *Genocide* (Schwartzman) (narrator)
1987 *Someone to Love* (Jaglom) (role)

Publications

By WELLES: books—

Everybody's Shakespeare, New York, 1933; revised as *The Mercury Shakespeare,* 1939.
The Trial (script), New York, 1970.
The Films of Orson Welles, by Charles Higham, Berkeley, 1970.
Citizen Kane, script, in *The Citizen Kane Book,* by Pauline Kael, New York, 1971.
This Is Orson Welles, with Peter Bogdanovich, New York, 1972.
Touch of Evil, edited by Terry Comito, New Brunswick, New Jersey, 1985.
The Big Brass Ring: An Original Screenplay, with Oja Kodar, Santa Barbara, California, 1987.
Chimes at Midnight, New Brunswick, New Jersey, 1988.

By WELLES: articles—

Preface to *He That Plays the King,* by Kenneth Tynan, New York, 1950.
Interview with Francis Koval, in *Sight and Sound* (London), December 1950.
"The Third Audience," in *Sight and Sound* (London), January/March 1954.
"For a Universal Cinema," in *Film Culture* (New York), January 1955.
Interviews with André Bazin and Charles Bitsch, in *Cahiers du Cinéma* (Paris), June and September 1958.

"Conversation at Oxford," with Derrick Griggs, in *Sight and Sound* (London), Spring 1960.
"*Citizen Kane,*" in *Avant-Scène du Cinéma* (Paris), January 1962.
"*Le Procès,*" in *Avant-Scène du Cinéma* (Paris), February 1963.
Interview with Everett Sloane, in *Film* (London), no. 37, 1965.
"A Trip to Don Quixoteland: Conversations with Orson Welles," with Juan Cobos and others, in *Cahiers du Cinema in English* (New York), June 1966.
Interview with Kenneth Tynan, in *Playboy* (Chicago), March 1967.
"First Person Singular," with Joseph McBride, in *Sight and Sound* (London), Winter 1971/72.
"Heart of Darkness," in *Film Comment* (New York), November/December 1972.

On WELLES: books—

Fowler, Roy A., *Orson Welles, A First Biography,* London, 1946.
Bazin, André, *Orson Welles,* Paris, 1950.
MacLiammóir, Micheál, *Put Money in Thy Purse,* London, 1952.
Noble, Peter, *The Fabulous Orson Welles,* London, 1956.
Bogdanovich, Peter, *The Cinema of Orson Welles,* New York, 1961.
Cowie, Peter, *The Cinema of Orson Welles,* London, 1965.
Bessy, Maurice, *Orson Welles,* New York, 1971.
Higham, Charles, *The Films of Orson Welles,* Berkeley, 1971.
Kael, Pauline, *The Citizen Kane Book,* New York, 1971.
Houseman, John, *Run Through: A Memoir,* New York, 1972.
McBride, Joseph, *Orson Welles,* London, 1972.
Bazin, André, *Orson Welles: A Critical View,* translated by Jonathan Rosenbaum, New York, 1978.
Naremore, J., *The Magic World of Orson Welles,* New York, 1978.
Valentinetti, Claudio M., *Orson Welles,* Florence, 1981.
Bergala, Alain, and Jean Narboni, editors, *Orson Welles,* Paris, 1982.
Andrew, Dudley, *Film in the Aura of Art,* Princeton, New Jersey, 1984.
Carringer, Robert L., *The Making of Citizen Kane,* Los Angeles, 1985.
Higham, Charles, *Orson Welles: The Rise and Fall of an American Genius,* New York, 1985.
Leaming, Barbara, *Orson Welles: A Biography,* New York, 1985.
Parra, Danièle, and Jacques Zimmer, *Orson Welles,* Paris, 1985.
Taylor, John Russell, *Orson Welles: A Celebration,* London, 1986.
Brady, Frank, *Citizen Welles: A Biography of Orson Welles,* New York, 1989.
Wood, Bret, *Orson Welles: A Bio-Bibliography,* Westport, Connecticut, 1990.
Howard, James, *The Complete Films of Orson Welles,* Secaucus, New Jersey, 1991.
Callow, Simon, *Orson Welles: The Road to Xanadu,* New York, 1995.

On WELLES: articles—

Cocteau, Jean, profile of Welles, in *Cinémonde* (Paris), 6 March 1950.
MacLiammóir, Micheál, "Orson Welles," in *Sight and Sound* (London), July/September 1954.
"L'Oeuvre d'Orson Welles," in *Cahiers du Cinéma* (Paris), September 1958.
Gerasimov, Sergei, "All is Not Welles," in *Films and Filming* (London), September 1959.
Stanbrook, Alan, "The Heroes of Welles," in *Film* (London), no. 28, 1961.
"Welles Issue" of *Image et Son* (Paris), no. 139, 1961.
Weinberg, Herman G., "The Legion of Lost Films," in *Sight and Sound* (London), Autumn 1962.
Tyler, Parker, "Orson Welles and the Big Experimental Film Cult," in *Film Culture* (New York), Summer 1963.
Pechter, William, "Trials," in *Sight and Sound* (London), Winter 1963/64.
Johnson, William, "Orson Welles: Of Time and Loss," in *Film Quarterly* (Berkeley), Fall 1967.
Daney, Serge, "Welles in Power," in *Cahiers du Cinema in English* (New York), September 1967.
"Special Report: Orson Welles," in *Action* (Los Angeles), May/June 1969.
McBride, Joseph, "Welles Before Kane," in *Film Quarterly* (Berkeley), Spring 1970.
Wilson, Richard, "It's Not Quite All True," in *Sight and Sound* (London), Autumn 1970.
Henderson, Brian, "The Long Take," in *Film Comment* (New York), Summer 1971.
Prokosch, Mike, "Orson Welles," in *Film Comment* (New York), Summer 1971.
Goldfarb, Phyllis, "Orson Welles' Use of Sound," in *Take One* (Montreal), July/August 1971.
Coulouris, George, and Bernard Herrmann, "'The *Citizen Kane* Book'," in *Sight and Sound* (London), Spring 1972.
Cohen, H., "The Heart of Darkness in Citizen Kane," in *Cinema Journal* (Evanston), Fall 1972.
Goldfarb, Phyllis, "Heston on Welles," in *Take One* (Montreal), October 1972.
Hale, N., "Welles and the Logic of Death," in *Film Heritage* (New York), Fall 1974.
Gow, Gordon, "A Touch of Orson," in *Films and Filming* (London), December 1974.
"Hollywood Salutes its 'Maverick' Genius Orson Welles," special issue of *American Cinematographer* (Los Angeles), April 1975.
Brady, Frank, "The Lost Film of Orson Welles," in *American Film* (Washington, D.C.), November 1978.
McBride, Joseph, "All's Welles," in *Film Comment* (New York), November/December 1978.
Poague, Lee, "The Great God Orson: Chabrol's 'Ten Days' Wonder," in *Film Criticism* (Edinboro, Pennsylvania), no. 3, 1979.
Neale, Steve, "Re-viewing Welles," in *Screen* (London), May/June 1982.
Houston, Beverle, "Power and Dis-integration in the Films of Orson Welles," in *Film Quarterly* (Berkeley), Summer 1982.
McLean, A. M., "Orson Welles and Shakespeare: History and Consciousness in *Chimes at Midnight,*" in *Literature/Film Quarterly* (Salisbury, Maryland), no. 3, 1983.
Beja, M., "Where You Can't Get at Him: Orson Welles and the Attempt to Escape From Father," in *Literature/Film Quarterly* (Salisbury, Maryland), January 1985.
Strick, Philip, "Orson Welles," in *Films and Filming* (London), July 1985.
McCarthy, Todd, obituary, in *Variety* (London), 16th October 1985.
Kauffmann, Stanley, obituary, in *New Republic* (New York), 11 November 1985.
Stubbs, J. C., "The Evolution of Orson Welles's *Touch of Evil* from Novel to Film," in *Cinema Journal* (Champaign, Illinois), Winter 1985.
Orson Welles Sections of *Cahiers du Cinéma* (Paris), November and December 1985.
Wood, Michael, "The Magnificent Orson," in *American Film* (New York), December 1985.
Maxfield, J., "A Man Like Ourselves," in *Literature/Film Quarterly* (Salisbury, Maryland), no. 3, 1986.
Harper, W. R., "Polanski v Welles on *Macbeth*: Character or Fat?," in *Literature/Film Quarterly* (Salisbury, Maryland), no. 4, 1986.
"Welles Issue" of *Avant-Scène du Cinéma* (Paris), January/February 1986.
Kehr, Dave, obituary, in *Film Comment* (New York), January/February 1986.
Rosenbaum, Jonathan, "The Invisible Orson Welles," in *Sight and Sound* (London), Summer 1986.

Orson Welles on the set of *Citizen Kane*

Bates, Robin, "Fiery Speech in a World of Shadows: Rosebud's Impact on Early Audiences," in *Cinema Journal* (Champaign, Illinois), vol. 26, no. 2, 1987.

Sartre, Jean-Paul, "*Citizen Kane,*" in *Post Script* (Jacksonville, Florida), vol. 7, no. 1, 1987.

Anderegg, Michael, "Every Third Word a Lie: Rhetoric and History in Orson Welles' *Chimes at Midnight,*" in *Film Quarterly* (Berkeley), Spring 1987.

Rodman, Howard A., "The Last Days of Orson Welles," in *American Film* (Washington, D.C.), June 1987.

France, Richard, "Orson Welles' First Film," in *Films in Review* (New York), August/September 1987.

Bywater, William, "The Desire for Embodiment in Orson Welles's *Citizen Kane,*" in *Post Script* (Jacksonville, Florida), vol. 7, no. 2, 1988.

Jewell, Richard B., "Orson Welles, George Schaefer and *It's All True,*" in *Film History* (Philadelphia), vol. 2, no. 4, 1988.

Kalinak, Kathryn, "The Text of Music: A Study of *The Magnificent Ambersons,*" in *Cinema Journal* (Champaign, Illinois), vol. 27, no. 4, 1988.

Perlmutter, Ruth, "Working with Welles: an Interview with Henry Jaglom," in *Film Quarterly* (Berkeley), Spring 1988.

Stainton, A., "*Don Quixote*: Orson Welles' Secret," in *Sight and Sound* (London), Autumn 1988.

White, Armond, "Wishing Welles," in *Film Comment* (New York), October 1988.

"Orson Welles Issue" of *Persistence of Vision* (Maspeth, New York), no. 7, 1989.

Vidal, Gore, "Remembering Orson Welles," in *New York Review of Books,* 1 June 1989.

Bywater, W., "The Visual Pleasure of Patriarchal Cinema: Welles' 'Touch of Evil,'" *Film Criticism,* vol. 14, no. 3, 1990.

Naremore, James, "The Trial: The FBI vs. Orson Welles," in *Film Comment* (New York), January/February 1991.

Hogue, Peter, "The Friends of Kane," in *Film Comment* (New York), November/December 1991.

Jameson, Richard T., "Cries and Whispers," in *Film Comment* (New York), January/February 1992.

Rosenbaum, Jonathan, "The Seven Arkadins," in *Film Comment* (New York), January/February 1992.

Cramer, B., "The Restored 'Othello,'" *Films in Review,* July/August 1992.

McBride, Joseph, "The Last Kingdom of Orson Welles," in *New York Review of Books,* 13 May 1993.

Purtell, Tim, "The Genius Nobody Wanted," in *Entertainment Weekly*, 8 October 1993.
Timm, M., "Orson Welles van ingen martyr!," in *Chaplin*, vol. 35, no. 3, 1993.
Combs, Richard, "Burning Masterworks," in *Film Comment* (New York), January/February 1994.

On WELLES: films

Citizen Kane: The Fiftieth Anniversary, 1991.
Orson Welles: What Went Wrong?, 1992.

* * *

References to Orson Welles as one of America's most influential directors and *Citizen Kane* as one of the great American films have become a simplistic way to encapsulate Welles's unique contribution to cinema. It is a contribution which seems obvious but is difficult to adequately summarize without examining his complex career.

Welles began as an actor in Ireland at Dublin's famous Gate Theater, bluffing his way into the theater's acting troupe by claiming to be well-known on the Broadway stage. He began directing plays in New York, and worked with John Houseman in various theatrical groups. At one point they attempted to stage Marc Blitzstein's leftist, prolabor *The Cradle Will Rock* for the Federal Theatre Project, but government agents blocked the opening night's production. Performers and audience subsequently moved to another theater, and the events surrounding the performance became one of Broadway's most famous episodes. The incident led to Houseman being fired and Welles's resignation from the Project.

Houseman and Welles then formed the Mercury Theatre Group, armed with a manifesto written by Houseman declaring their intention to foster new talent, experiment with new types of plays, and appeal to the same audiences that frequented the Federal Theater plays. Welles's work on the New York stage was generally leftist in its political orientation, and, inspired by the expressionist theater of the 1920s, prefigured the look of his films.

Welles and his Mercury Theater Group expanded into radio as the Mercury Theater on the Air. In contrast to most theater-oriented shows on radio, which consisted merely of plays read aloud, the Mercury group adapted their works in a more natural, personal manner: most of the plays were narrated in the first person. Shrewd imitations of news announcements and technical breakdowns heightened the realism of his 1938 Halloween *War of the Worlds* broadcast to such a degree that the show has become famous for the panic it caused among its American listeners, a number of which thought that New Jersey was actually being invaded by Martians. This event itself has become a pop culture legend, shrouded in exaggeration and half-truths.

RKO studios hired Welles in 1939, hoping he could repeat the success on film for them that he had enjoyed on stage and in radio. Welles, according to most sources, accepted the job because his Mercury Theater needed money to produce an elaborate production called *5 Kings,* an anthology of several of Shakespeare's plays. Whatever the reason, his contract with RKO began an erratic and rocky relationship with the Hollywood industry that would, time and again, end in bitter disappointment for Welles. The situation eventually led him to begin a self-imposed exile in Europe.

The film on which Welles enjoyed the most creative freedom was his first and most famous, *Citizen Kane.* At the time the film created a controversy over both its subject matter and style. Loosely based on the life of newspaper magnate William Randolph Hearst, the film supposedly upset Hearst to such a degree that he attempted to stop the production, and then the distribution and exhibition. In the end, his anger was manifested in the scathing reviews critics gave the film in all his newspapers. The film's innovative structure, which included flashbacks from the differing points-of-view of the various characters, in addition to other formal devices so different from the classic Hollywood cinema, also contributed to *Kane*'s financial failure and commercial downfall, though critics other than those employed at Hearst's papers generally gave the film positive reviews.

Other controversies surrounded the film as well, including one over scriptwriting credit. Originally, Welles claimed solo credit for writing the film, but the Writer's Guild forced him to acknowledge Herman Mankiewicz as co-author. Each writer's *exact* contributions remain unknown, but the controversy was revived during the early 1970s by critic Pauline Kael, who attempted to prove that Mankiewicz was most responsible for the script. Whatever the case, the argument becomes unimportant and even ludicrous given the unique direction which shapes the material, and which is undeniably Welles's.

Due to the failure of *Kane,* Welles was supervised quite closely on his next film, *The Magnificent Ambersons.* After shooting was completed, Welles went to South America to begin work on a documentary, *It's All True,* designed to help dispel Nazi propaganda in Latin America. He took a rough cut of *Ambersons* with him, hoping to coordinate cutting with editor Robert Wise. A sneak preview of Welles's *Ambersons* proved disastrous, however, and the studio cut his 140-minute-plus version to eighty-eight minutes and added a "happy ending." The film was a critical and commercial failure, and the entire Mercury staff was removed from the RKO lot.

Welles spent the remainder of his Hollywood career sparring with various producers or studios over the completed versions of his films and his uncredited direction on films in which he starred. For example, *Journey Into Fear* was begun by Welles but finished by Norman Foster, though Welles claims he made contributions and suggestions throughout. *Jane Eyre,* which made Welles a popular star, was directed by Robert Stevenson, but the gothic overtones, the mise-en-scène, and other stylistic devices suggest a Wellesian contribution. With *The Stranger,* directed for Sam Spiegel, he adhered closely to the script and a preplanned editing schedule, evidently determined to prove that he could turn out a Hollywood product on time and on budget. Welles, though, subsequently referred to *The Stranger* as "the worst of my films," and several Welles scholars agree.

Welles directed one of his best films, *The Lady from Shanghai,* for Harry Cohn of Columbia. The film, a loose, confusing, noirish tale of double-crosses and corrupted innocence, starred Welles's wife at the time, Rita Hayworth. Cohn, who was supposedly already dissatisfied with their marriage because he felt it would reduce Hayworth's box-office value, was furious at Welles for the image she presented in *Shanghai.* The film, shot mostly on location, was made under stressful circumstances, with Welles often re-writing during the shooting. It was edited several times and finally released two years after its completion, but failed commercially and critically. His final Hollywood project, a version of *Macbeth* for Republic Studios, was also considered a commercial flop.

Disenchanted with Hollywood, Welles left for Europe, where he began the practice of acting in other directors' films in order to finance his own projects. His portrayal of Harry Lime in Carol Reed's *The Third Man* is considered his finest work from this period, and Welles continued to create villainous antagonists who are often more interesting, complex, or exciting than the protagonists of the films. In the roles of Col. Haki in *Journey Into Fear,* Will Varner in Martin Ritt's *The Long Hot Summer,* Quinlan in *Touch of Evil,* and in *Mr. Arkadin,* Welles created a sinister persona for which he has become as famous as for his direction of *Citizen Kane.* His last roles were often caricatures of that persona, as in Marlo Thomas's *It Happened One Christmas,* or parodies as in *The Muppet Movie.*

Welles's European ventures include his *Othello,* shot over a period of years between acting assignments, often under chaotic circumstances. The difficulties of the film's production are often described as though they were the madcap adventures of a roguish artist, but in reality it must have been an extreme hardship to assemble and reassemble the cast over the course of the film's shooting. At one point, he "borrowed" equipment under cover of night from the set of Henry King's *The Black Rose* (in which Welles was starring) to quickly shoot a few scenes. Welles later obtained enough financial backing to make *Mr. Arkadin,* a *Kane*-like story of a powerful man who made his fortune as a white slaver, and *Chimes at Midnight.*

Welles returned to America in the late 1950s to direct *Touch of Evil,* starring Charlton Heston. Originally approached only to star in the film, Welles mistakenly thought he was also to direct. Heston intervened and insisted he be allowed to do so. Welles immediately threw out the original script, rewriting it without reading the book, *Badge of Evil,* upon which the script was based. Welles's last works include *The Immortal Story,* a one-hour film made for French television, and *F for Fake,* a strange combination of documentary footage shot by another director, some Welles footage from earlier ventures, and Welles's own narration.

Welles's outsider status in connection with the American film industry is an interesting part of cinema history in itself, but his importance as a director is due to the innovations he introduced through his films and the influence they have had on filmmaking and film theory. Considering the turbulent relationship Welles experienced with Hollywood and the circumstances under which his films were made in Europe, it is surprising there is any thematic and stylistic consistency in his work at all.

The central character in many of his films is often a powerful, egotistical man who lives outside or above the law and society. Kane, Arkadin, and Mr. Clay (*The Immortal Story*) are enabled to do so by their wealth and position; Quinlan (*Touch of Evil*) by his job as a law enforcer, which allows him to commit injustices to suit his own purposes. Even George Minafer (*Ambersons*) becomes an outsider as a modern, industrialized society supersedes his aristocratic, nineteenth-century way of life. These characters are never innocent, but seem to be haunted by an innocence they have lost. *Kane's* "Rosebud," the emblem of childhood that he clings to, is the classic example, but this theme can also be found in *Mr. Arkadin,* where Arkadin is desperate to keep his daughter from discovering his sordid past. Many parallels between the two films have been drawn, including the fact that the title characters are both wealthy and powerful men whose past lives are being investigated by a stranger. Interestingly, just as Kane whispers "rosebud" on his deathbed, Arkadin speaks his daughter's name at the moment of his death. Quinlan, in *Touch of Evil,* is confronted with his memories and his past when he runs into Tanya, now a prostitute in a whorehouse. The ornaments and mementoes in her room (some of them from Welles's personal collection), seem to jog his memory of a time when he was not a corrupt law official. In *Shanghai,* it is interesting to note that Welles does not portray the egotist, Bannister, but instead the "innocent" Michael O'Hara, who is soiled by his dealings with Bannister's wife. That the corrupt antagonist is doomed is often indicated by a prologue or introductory sequence which foreshadows his destruction—the newsreel sequence in *Kane*; the opening montage of *Ambersons,* which condenses eighteen years of George Minafer's life into ten minutes to hint that George will get his "comeuppance" in the end; the opening funeral scene of *Othello*; and the detailing of Mr. Clay's sordid past in *The Immortal Story.* The themes of lost innocence and inescapable fate often shroud Welles's films with a sense of melancholy, which serves to make these characters worthy of sympathy.

Much has been made of Welles's use of deep-focus photography, particularly in *Kane* and *Ambersons.* Though a directorial presence is often suggested in the cinema through the use of editing, with Welles it is through mise-en-scène, particularly in these two films. Many Welles scholars discuss the ambiguous nature of long-shot/deep-focus photography, where the viewer is allowed to sift through the details of a scene and make some of his own choices about what is important to the narrative, plot development, and so on. However, Welles's arrangement of actors in specific patterns; his practice of shooting from unusual angles; and his use of wide-angle lenses, which distort the figures closest to them, are all intended to convey meaning. For example, the exaggerated perspective of the scene where Thatcher gives young Charles Kane a sled makes Thatcher appear to tower over the boy, visually suggesting his unnatural and menacing hold on him (at least from young Kane's point of view).

Welles also employed rather complex sound tracks in *Kane* and *Ambersons,* perhaps a result of his radio experience. The party sequence of *Ambersons,* for example, makes use of overlapping dialogue as the camera tracks along the ballroom, as though one were passing by, catching bits of conversation.

Welles's visual style becomes less outrageous and less concerned with effects as his career continued. There seems to be an increasing concentration on the acting in his latter works, particularly in the Shakespeare films. Welles had a lifelong interest in Shakespeare and his plays, and is well known for his unique handling and interpretations of the material. *Macbeth,* for example, was greatly simplified, with much dialogue omitted and scenes shifted around. A primitive feel is reflected by badly synchronized sound, and much of the impact of the spoken word is lost. *Othello,* shot in Italy and Morocco, makes use of outdoor locations in contrast to the staginess of *Macbeth.* Again, Welles was quite free with interpretation: Iago's motives, for example, are suggested to be the result of sexual impotency. His most successful adaptation of Shakespeare is *Chimes at Midnight,* an interpretation of the Falstaff story with parts taken from *Henry IV,* parts one and two, *Henry V, Merry Wives of Windsor,* and *Richard II.* In *Chimes,* Falstaff, as with many of Welles's central characters, is imprisoned by the past. Like George Minafer, he straddles two ages, one medieval and the other modern. Falstaff is destroyed not only by the aging process but also by the problems of being forced into a new world, as is Minafer (and perhaps Kane). Again Welles is quite individualistic in his presentation of the material, making Falstaff a true friend to the king and an innocent, almost childlike, victim of a new order.

In the years before he died, Welles became known for his appearances in television commercials and on talk shows, playing the part of the celebrity to its maximum. His last role was as a narrator on an innovative episode of the television detective series *Moonlighting,* starring Bruce Willis and Cybill Shepherd. It is unfortunate that his latter-day persona as a *bon vivant* often overshadows his contributions to the cinema.

—Susan Doll

WELLMAN, William

Nationality: American. **Born:** William Augustus Wellman in Brookline, Massachusetts, 29 February 1896. **Education:** Attended Newton High School, Newton Highlands, Massachusetts, 1910-14. **Military Service:** Joined volunteer ambulance corps destined for France, 1917, then joined French Foreign Legion, where he learnt to fly planes; when United States entered World War I, became part of Lafayette Flying Corps, an arm of the Lafayette Escadrille. **Family:** Married 1) Helene Chadwick, 1918 (divorced 1920); three other marriages 1920-33; 5) Dorothy Coonan, 1933, seven children. **Career:** Professional ice hockey player for minor league team, 1914; film actor, United States, from 1919; messenger for Goldwyn Pictures, then directed first film, 1920; director for 20th Century-Fox, 1923; signed by Paramount, 1927. **Awards:** Oscar for *Wings,* 1927; Oscar for Best Writing (Original Story) for *A Star is Born* (shared with Robert Carson), 1937. **Died:** 9 December 1975.

Films as Director:

1920 *The Twins from Suffering Creek*
1923 *The Man Who Won*; *2nd Hand Love*; *Big Dan*; *Cupid's Fireman*
1924 *The Vagabond Trail*; *Not a Drum Was Heard*; *The Circus Cowboy*
1925 *When Husbands Flirt*
1926 *The Boob*; *The Cat's Pajamas*; *You Never Know Women*
1927 *Wings*
1928 *The Legion of the Condemned*; *Ladies of the Mob*; *Beggars of Life*
1929 *Chinatown Nights*; *The Man I Love*; *Woman Trap*
1930 *Dangerous Paradise*; *Young Eagles*; *Maybe It's Love*
1931 *Other Men's Women*; ***The Public Enemy***; *Night Nurse*; *Star Witness*; *Safe in Hell*
1932 *The Hatchet Man*; *So Big*; *Love is a Racket*; *The Purchase Price*; *The Conquerors*
1933 *Frisco Jenny*; *Central Airport*; *Lily Turner*; *Midnight Mary*; *Heroes for Sale*; *Wild Boys of the Road*; *College Coach*
1934 *Looking for Trouble*; *Stingaree*; *The President Vanishes*
1935 *The Call of the Wild*
1936 *The Robin Hood of Eldorado* (+ co-sc); *Small Town Girl*
1937 *A Star is Born* (+ co-sc); *Nothing Sacred*
1938 *Men with Wings* (+ pr)
1939 *Beau Geste* (+ pr); *The Light That Failed* (+ pr)
1941 *Reaching for the Sun* (+ pr)
1942 *Roxie Hart*; *The Great Man's Lady* (+ pr); *Thunder Birds*
1943 *The Ox-Bow Incident*; *The Lady of Burlesque*
1944 *Buffalo Bill*
1945 *This Man's Navy*; *The Story of G.I. Joe*
1946 *Gallant Journey* (+ pr, co-sc)
1947 *Magic Town*
1948 *Iron Curtain*
1949 *Yellow Sky*; *Battleground*
1950 *The Next Voice You Hear*
1951 *Across the Wide Missouri*
1952 *Westward the Women*; *It's a Big Country* (co-d); *My Man and I*
1953 *Island in the Sky*
1954 *The High and the Mighty*; *Track of the Cat*
1955 *Blood Alley*
1958 *Darby's Rangers*; *Lafayette Escadrille* (+ pr, co-sc)

Other Film:

1919 *Knickerbocker Buckaroo* (Parker) (role)

Publications

By WELLMAN: book—

A Short Time for Insanity: An Autobiography, New York, 1974.

By WELLMAN: articles—

"Director's Notebook—Why Teach Cinema?," in *Cinema Progress* (Los Angeles), June/July 1939.
Interview, in *Cinema* (Beverly Hills), July 1966.

On WELLMAN: books—

Brownlow, Kevin, *The Parade's Gone By ...*, New York, 1968.
Thompson, Frank T., *William A. Wellman*, Metuchen, New Jersey, 1983.

On WELLMAN: articles—

Pringle, H.F., "Screwball Bill," in *Collier's* (New York), 26 February 1938.
Griffith, Richard, "Wyler, Wellman, and Huston," in *Films in Review* (New York), February 1950.
Sarris, Andrew, "Fallen Idols," in *Film Culture* (New York), Spring 1963.
Brownlow, Kevin, "William Wellman," in *Film* (London), Winter 1965/66.
Smith, J.M., "The Essential Wellman," in *Brighton* (London), January 1970.
Wellman, William, Jr., "William Wellman: Director Rebel," in *Action* (Los Angeles), March/April 1970.
Brooks, Louise, "On Location with Billy Wellman," in *Film Culture* (New York), Spring 1972.
Fox, J., "A Man's World," in *Films and Filming* (London), March 1973.
Eyman, S., and Allen Eyles, "'Wild Bill' William A. Wellman," in *Focus on Film* (London), no. 29, 1978.
Langlois, Gerard, "William Wellman 1896-1975," in *Avant-Scène du Cinéma* (Paris), 1 March 1978.
Gallagher, John, "William Wellman," in *Films in Review* (New York), May, June/July, and October 1982.

* * *

William Wellman's critical reputation is in many respects still in a state of flux long after re-evaluations and recent screenings of his major films should have established some consensus of opinion regarding his place in the pantheon of film directors. While there is some tentative agreement that he is, if nothing else, a competent journeyman director capable of producing entertaining male-dominated action films, other opinions reflect a wide range of artistic evaluations, ranging from comparisons to D.W. Griffith to outright condemnations of his films as clumsy and uninspired. His own preferred niche, as indicated by his flamboyant personality and his predilection for browbeating and intimidating his performers, would probably be in the same general class as highly masculine filmmakers like Howard Hawks, John Ford, and Raoul Walsh. While those three enjoy a distinct *auteur* status, a similar designation for Wellman is not so easily arrived at since much of his early work for Warner Bros. in the late 1930s is, at first glance, not easily distinguishable from the rest of the studio's output of sociological problem films and exposés of organized crime. In addition, his later films do not compare favorably, in many scholars' opinions, to treatments of similar themes (often employing the same actors and locales) by both Ford and Hawks.

It might be argued, however, that Wellman actually developed what has come to be regarded as the Warner Bros. style to a greater degree than did the studio's other directors. His 1931 *The Public Enemy*, for example, stands above most of the other gangster films of the era in its creative blend of highly vivid images and in the subtle manner in which it created a heightened impression of violence and brutality by giving only hints of it on the screen. Exhibiting similar subtlety, Wellman's depiction of a gangster, beginning with his childhood, graphically alluded to the sociological roots of organized crime. While many of his more typical treatments of men in adversity, like 1927's Academy Award-winning *Wings*, were sometimes artificial, everything worked in *Public Enemy*.

In Wellman's later films like *The Ox-Bow Incident, The Story of G.I. Joe*, and *Battleground*, the interactions of men in various groupings are shaped in such a way as to determine the direction and thematic force of each story. In others, like *Track of the Cat*, the emphasis shifts instead to one individual and his battle with forces of nature beyond his control. Yet in all cases, the issue is one of survival, a concept that manifests itself in some manner in all of Wellman's films. It is overt and recognizable in war dramas like *Battleground* or

William Wellman

in a disaster film like *The High and the Mighty,* but it is reflected at least as much in the psychological tensions of *Public Enemy* as it is in the violence. It becomes even more abstract in a complex picture like *Track of the Cat* when the issue concerns the family unit and the insecurity of its internal relationships. In the more heavy-handed propaganda films such as *The Iron Curtain and Blood Alley,* the theme centers on the threat to democratic forms of government, and finally, in the *Ox-Bow Incident,* the issue is the very fragility of society itself in the hands of a mob.

Wellman's supporters feel that these concerns arise from the latent cynicism of a disappointed romantic but are expressed by an instinctive artist with a keen awareness of the intellectual force of images conveyed with the raw power of many of those in *Public Enemy.* Yet it is the inconsistency of these images and a corresponding lack of inspiration in his work overall that clouds his stature as an *auteur* of the first rank. While, ultimately, it is true that Wellman's films cannot be easily separated from the man behind them, his best works are those that sprang from his emotional and psychological experiences. His lesser ones have been overshadowed by the cult of his personality and are best remembered for the behind-the-scenes fistfights, parties, and wild stunts, all of which detracted from the production. Perhaps he never got the chance to make the one indisputable masterpiece that would thematically support all of the seemingly irreconcilable aspects of his personality and firmly establish him as a director of the first magnitude.

—Stephen L. Hanson

WENDERS, Wim

Nationality: German. **Born:** Wilhelm Wenders in Düsseldorf, 14 August 1945. **Education:** Studied medicine and philosophy; studied at Hochschule für Fernsehen und Film, Munich, 1967-70. **Career:** Film critic in Munich for *Süddeutsche Zeitung* and *Filmkritik,* late 1960s; professional filmmaker, from 1971. **Awards:** Golden Lion, Venice Festival, for *The State of Things,* 1982; Best Director, Cannes Festival, for *Wings of Desire,* 1987. **Agent:** c/o Gary Salt, The Paul Kohner Agency, 9169 Sunset Blvd., Los Angeles, CA 90069, U.S.A.

Films as Director:

1967 *Schauplätze* (*Locations*) (short); *Same Player Shoots Again* (short)
1968 *Silver City* (short); *Victor I* (short)
1969 *Alabama—2,000 Light Years* (short); *Drei amerikanische LPs* (*Three American LPs*) (short)
1970 *Polizeifilm* (*Police Film*) (short); *Summer in the City* (*Dedicated to the Kinks*) (diploma film)
1971 *Die Angst des Tormanns beim Elfmeter* (*The Goalie's Anxiety at the Penalty Kick*)
1972 *Der scharlachrote Buchstabe* (*The Scarlet Letter*)
1973 *Alice in den Städten* (*Alice in the Cities*)
1974 *Aus der Familie der Panzerechsen* (*From the Family of the Crocodilia*) (short, for TV); *Die Insel* (*The Island*) (short, for TV); *Falsche Bewegung* (*Wrong Movement*)
1976 ***Im Lauf der Zeit*** (*Kings of the Road*; *In the Course of Time*)
1977 ***Der amerikanische Freund*** (*The American Friend*)
1981 *Lightning Over Water* (*Nick's Film*)
1982 *Hammett*; *Der Stand der Dinge* (*The State of Things*)
1984 ***Paris, Texas***; *Room 666* (doc)
1985 *Tokyo-Ga* (doc)
1987 *Der Himmel über Berlin* (*Wings of Desire*)
1989 *Aufzeichnungen zu Kleidern und Städten* (*Notebook on Cities and Clothes*) (doc)
1991 *Until the End of the World*
1993 *In weiter Ferne, so nah!* (*Faraway, So Close*)
1995 *Lisbon Story*; *Beyond the Clouds* (co-d with Antonioni)

Other Films:

1985 *I Played it For You* (Blakley) (role)
1987 *Helsinki Napoli: All Night Long* (Mika Kaurismaki); *Yer Demir, Gok Bakir* (Livaneli) (pr)
1990 *Isabelle Eberhardt* (Pringle) (pr)

Publications

By WENDERS: books—

The Film by Wim Wenders: Kings of the Road (In the Course of Time), with Fritz Müller-Scherz, Munich, 1976.
Nick's Film—Lightning over Water, with Chris Sievernich, Frankfurt, 1981.
Paris, Texas, with Sam Shepard, Berlin, 1984.
Written in the West: Photographien aus dem amerikanische Western, Munich, 1987.
Emotion Pictures: Reflections on the Cinema, London, 1989.
The Logic of Images: Essays and Conversations, London, 1992.

By WENDERS: articles—

"*Alice in den Städten,*" an interview with W. E. Bühler and P. B. Kleiser, in *Filmkritik* (Munich), March 1974.
"Wim Wenders über *Im Lauf der Zeit,*" an interview with H. Wiedemann and F. Müller-Scherz, in *Film und Ton* (Munich), May 1976.
"Wenders on *Kings of the Road,*" in *Monthly Film Bulletin* (London), July 1977.
"King of the Road," an interview with Carlos Clarens, in *Film Comment* (New York), September/October 1977.
"Filming Highsmith," an interview with Jan Dawson, in *Sight and Sound* (London), Winter 1977/78.
Interview with P. Lehman and others, in *Wide Angle* (Athens, Ohio), vol. 2, no. 4, 1978.
Interviews with Serge Daney, in *Cahiers du Cinéma* (Paris), December 1980 and June 1982.
Interview with Richard Combs, in *Monthly Film Bulletin* (London), March 1983.
Interview with John Gallagher, in *Films in Review* (New York), June/July 1983.
Interview with Michel Ciment and Hubert Niogret, in *Positif* (Paris), September 1984.
Interview with K. Dieckman, in *Film Quarterly* (Berkeley), Winter 1984/85.
Interview with Coco Fusco, in *Cineaste* (New York), vol. 16, no. 4, 1988.
Interview with Robert Seidenberg, in *American Film* (Washington, D.C.), vol. 13, no. 8, 1988.
Interview with L. Antoccia, in *Films and Filming* (London), August 1988.
Interview with Sean Penn, in *Interview* (New York), January 1992.
"Wenders's Wanderlust," an interview with James Greenberg, in *Connoisseur* (New York), January 1992.
"Wim Wenders's Guilty Pleasures," in *Film Comment* (New York), January/February 1992.

On WENDERS: books—

Dawson, Jan, *Wim Wenders: Cinema as Vision and Desire,* New York, 1976.
Geist, Kathe, *The Cinema of Wim Wenders 1967-77,* Ann Arbor, Michigan, 1981.
Johnston, Sheila, *Wim Wenders,* London, 1981.
Buchka, Peter, *Augen Kann man nicht Kaufen: Wim Wenders und seine Filme,* Munich, 1983.
Franklin, James, *New German Cinema from Oberhausen to Hamburg,* Boston, 1983.
Grob, Norbert, *Die Formen des filmische Blicks: Wenders: Die fruhen Filmwe,* Munich, 1984.
Phillips, Klaus, editor, *New German Filmmakers: From Oberhausen through the 1970s,* New York, 1984.
Devillers, Jean-Pierre, *Berlin, L.A., Berlin: Wim Wenders,* Paris, 1985.
Geist, Kathe, *The Cinema of Wim Wenders: From Paris, France, to Paris, Texas,* Ann Arbor, Michigan, 1988.
Rentschler, Eric, editor, *West German Filmmakers on Film: Visions and Voices,* New York, 1988.
Boujut, Michel, *Wim Wenders: Un Voyage dans ses films,* Paris, 1989.
Elsaesser, Thomas, *New German Cinema: A History,* London, 1989.
Estève, Michel, *Wim Wenders,* Paris, 1989.
Joyce, Paul, *Motion and Emotion: The Films of Wim Wenders,* London, 1989.
Künzel, Uwe, *Wim Wenders: Ein Filmbuch,* 3rd edition, Freiburg, 1989.
Grob, Norbert, *Wenders,* Berlin, 1991.
Kolker, Robert Phillip, and Peter Beiken, *The Films of Wim Wenders,* New York, 1993.

On WENDERS: articles—

Rayns, Tony, "Forms of Address," in *Sight and Sound* (London), Winter 1974/75.
Ghali, N., "Dossier-auteur: Wim Wenders," in *Cinéma* (Paris), December 1976.
Covino, M., "Wim Wenders: A Worldwide Homesickness," in *Film Quarterly* (Berkeley), Winter 1977/78.
Stamelman, P., "Wenders at Warners," in *Sight and Sound* (London), Autumn 1978.
Corrigan, Timothy J., "The Realist Gesture in the Films of Wim Wenders: Hollywood and the New German Cinema," in *Quarterly Review of Film Studies* (Pleasantville, New York), Spring 1980.
"Wenders Issue" of *Caméra/Stylo* (Paris), January 1981.
"*Alice dans les villes* Issue" of *Avant-Scène du Cinéma* (Paris), 1 May 1981.
Bishop, R., and T. Ryan, "Wim Wenders: An American Saga," in *Cinema Papers* (Melbourne), August 1984.
Wim Wenders Section of *Cinéma* (Paris), September 1984.
Wim Wenders Section of *Positif* (Paris), September 1984.
Ranvaud, Don, "*Paris, Texas* to Sydney," and John Pym, "The Road from Wuppertal," in *Sight and Sound* (London), Autumn 1984.
Combs, Richard, "Ich Bin Ein Englander or Show Me the Way to Go Home," in *Monthly Film Bulletin* (London), May 1985.
Corrigan, Timothy, "Cinematic Snuff: German Friends and Narrative Murders," in *Cinema Journal* (Champaign, Illinois), Winter 1985.
Geist, Kathe, "Filmmaking as Research: Wim Wenders's *The State of Things,*" in *Post Script* (Jacksonville, Florida), Winter 1986.
Snyder, Stephen, "Wim Wenders: The Hunger Artist in America," in *Post Script* (Jacksonville, Florida), Winter 1987.
American Friends Section of *Literature/Film Quarterly* (Salisbury, Maryland), vol. 16, no. 3, 1988.
Paneth, Ira, "Wim and His Wings," in *Film Quarterly* (Berkeley), vol. 42, no. 1, 1988.
Green, Peter, "Germans Abroad," in *Sight and Sound* (London), Spring 1988.
Levy, Sean, "Until the End of the World: Wim Wenders's Dance around the Planet," in *American Film* (Washington, D.C.), January/February 1992.

* * *

Of the three young German filmmakers who achieved the greatest international fame in the 1970s as the vanguard of a German New Wave, Wim Wenders had perhaps a less radical though no less distinctive film style than his compatriots R. W. Fassbinder and Werner Herzog. Though critics typically cite American influences upon Wenders's "road trilogy" of the mid-1970s, there is a greater affinity with the modernist tradition of the European "art film" exemplified by the Antonioni of *L'avventura* and *Red Desert*—dramas of alienation in which restless, unrooted individuals wander through haunted, sterile, but bleakly beautiful landscapes within a free-floating narrative structure. (It is most appropriate that Wenders has directed the "frame" sections for some short pieces by the aged Italian master.) True, the *ennui* in these films shades into *angst* and American Beat gestures, and the alienation has strong roots in the spiritual yearning, the love of loneliness and wandering, of German Romanticism. Romanticism seems too to be at the root of Wenders's conception of himself (well articulated in numerous interviews) as an artist: one who evolves spiritually with each work, or reaches dead ends (as he has called *The State of Things*) from which he must break out; and who sees each new work as an adventure, not to be mapped out too much in advance.

A crucial observation about Wenders's art is found in cinematographer Ed Lachman's remark that "light and landscape are actors" in his films. Wenders's characters are typically revealed against urban or rural landscapes, upon which the camera frequently lingers as the actors pass from the frame. Most of the films take place predominantly out-of-doors (the studio sets of *Hammett* making that film all the more of an anomaly), or offer striking views from high-rise windows and moving vehicles. The urban views most often suggest sterility but have a certain grandeur, sharing with his views of desert (*Paris, Texas*) or sea (*The State of Things*) that vastness the Romantics called "sublime." The climactic scene in the peep-show booth in *Paris, Texas* is all the more powerful and inventive in the context of the epic vistas of the rest of the film. And the urban scene finally becomes the central "actor" in *Wings of Desire/Himmel über Berlin,* indeed a "Symphony of a Great City," in which the Wall is no barrier to the gliding camera or the angelic inhabitants.

Wenders's films are dialectical: they structure contrasts not as simple polarities but as rich ongoing dialogue, and the later films seem to be in dialogue with the earlier ones. Among the central concerns from film to film are American versus European culture, the creation of mood versus tight narrative, a sense of "home" versus rootless "freedom," and even black-and-white versus color photography.

Wenders's ambivalent fascination with America has been a favorite topic for critics. None of his films is without interest in this regard, but *Alice in the Cities* is the first to be shot partially in America—a world of boardwalks, motels, neon, and skyscrapers, though still not so different from the urban, industrial Europe of the second half; it is also his first feature to make extensive use of American music, including the Chuck Berry concert in Wuppertal. *The American Friend* is a dizzying vortex of allusiveness, with its gangsters and cowboys, iconographic presences of Nicholas Ray and Dennis Hopper, miniature Statue of Liberty in Paris, Ripley's digs in Hamburg, hints of an allegory of the American film industry in Germany (the pornographers seducing the hapless framemaker), and a narrative derived from a novel by an expatriate American and strongly echoing *Strangers on a Train.* Wenders's "American period" from *Hammett* through *Paris,*

Wim Wenders

Texas is of course of central interest here, with a whimsically mystical and lyrical embracing of humanity and the particulars of physical life that recalls Walt Whitman. Wenders still calls his production company "Road Movies" (in English).

The mid-1970s films may owe much to the American "road movie" of a few years earlier (themselves echoing Kerouac's *On the Road*), but the classical Hollywood cinema is defined by its tight narrative structures, and Wenders can be felt to be wrestling with such a structure in *The American Friend.* He has said of *Paris, Texas,* in a *Film Quarterly* interview, "For once I was making a movie that wasn't meandering all over the place. That's what Sam [Shepard] brought to this movie of mine as an American writer: forward movement, which is very American in a way." Still, *Paris, Texas* is very unlike a classical Hollywood film, though the problematic *Hammett,* ironically enough, *is* like one; and the later *Wings of Desire* is much more a fantasia upon a great city than a classical symphony. (*Tokyo-Ga* too meanders through a great city rather than being a tight documentary on Yasujiro Ozu.)

Also explored dialectically are the concepts of home and homelessness, omni-present concerns in Wenders's films. *Alice in the Cities, Kings of the Road,* and *Until the End of the World* could all have as epigraph a Barbara Stanwyck line from *Clash by Night* quoted by Wenders in a piece on Fritz Lang: "Home is where you get when you run out of places." *The State of Things* is perhaps Wenders's most bleak portrayal of homelessness, while *Paris, Texas* expresses the greatest yearning for home, and *Until the End of the World* portrays home as a trap (both womblike and filled with scientific gadgetry) of obligations to parents—a place the viewers too are trapped for the second half of a long film. *Wings of Desire* features an angel wishing he could "come home like Philip Marlowe and feed the cat;" an acrobat who has always felt "alone" and unattached, but now, in love, can feel "loneliness," which means "I am finally whole;" and a conclusion in which the former angel muses, "I found Home ... instead of forever hovering above"—like Wenders's camera in this film. Obviously the issues of home/homelessness shade into the other prominent Wenders theme of aloneness versus tentative human bonds, explored especially in terms of adult-child friendships, unstable male bondings (see *Faraway, So Close* for its treatments of both of these), and in *Wings,* the angelic/mortal possibilities of adult heterosexual love.

Until the End of the World, Wenders's most ambitious project to date, indeed a would-be magnum opus, is quintessentially Wenders in its fascination with home and the road, memory and dream, the mundane and the sublime; yet it disappoints, despite its fine moments. Its early scenes splendidly evoke a future world through decor, a few striking process shots, and multiple uses of video and computer screens; yet the film is flawed in its vague and inconsistent notions of science in the second half, the amateurish handling of the few action scenes, the implausibility of some of the heroine's motives, and above all in the lack of enough meaningful connections between the "dance around the world" of the first half and the Australian home-as-science-lab second half. The Australian landscapes, and the European ones of the very beginning, are hauntingly resonant, like so many in other Wenders films, though the hopscotch around the continents in the first half seems to turn the beauties of Lisbon and rural Japan into mere postcards, an effect seemingly unintended. Perhaps the film succeeds best in its use of various video or computer-generated images to suggest the working—and inseparability—of dreams, memories, and desires. *Faraway, So Close,* the sequel to *Wings of Desire* in which Damiel's angel partner Cassiel too becomes a mortal but finds it much harder to adjust to a world of time, suffers artistically from an attempt to include too many plot strands, to work farcical gangsters and daring rescue attempts into an otherwise private, meditative film. Wenders seems at his best when his stories are starkly simple, with complexity coming from the textures of the films' environments.

Wenders once claimed, with some relish of paradox, or perhaps recollection of *The Wizard of Oz,* that black-and-white was suited to realism, color to fantasy. Hence those stylized tales of murder *The Goalie's Anxiety* and *The American Friend,* as well as the science-fiction *Until the End of the World,* were in color, and the "road trilogy" not, with *Kings of the Road* immediately declaring itself "a Wim Wenders film in black/white." He further claimed himself to be incapable of making a documentary in color—though he was soon to make more than one. Once again *Wings of Desire* seems a synthesis of previous concerns, if not a downright reversal, with the angels seeing the spiritual essence of things in black-and-white but humans perceiving the particularities of mortal life in color. Such inconsistency—or rather, willingness to change perspective—may be taken as representative of the exploratory nature of Wenders's film work as a whole.

—Joseph Milicia

WHALE, James

Nationality: British. **Born:** Dudley, England, 22 July 1889 (some sources state 1896). **Military Service:** Held in prisoner-of-war camp, World War I. **Career:** Cartoonist for *The Bystander,* from 1910; actor and set designer for Birmingham Repertory Theatre, 1917-25; actor on London stage, from 1925; directed *Journey's End* on London stage, 1929; moved to Hollywood to direct film version, 1930; director for Universal, mostly of horror films, 1931-41; retired from film to pursue painting, 1941; attempted comeback *Hello Out There* failed, 1949; occasional stage director, from 1949. **Died:** 30 May 1957.

Films as Director:

1930 *Journey's End*
1931 *Waterloo Bridge*; ***Frankenstein***
1932 *The Impatient Maiden*; *The Old Dark House*
1933 *The Kiss Before the Mirror*; *The Invisible Man*
1934 *By Candlelight*; *One More River*
1935 ***The Bride of Frankenstein***; *Remember Last Night*
1936 *Showboat*
1937 *The Road Back*; *The Great Garrick*
1938 *The Port of Seven Seas*; *Sinners in Paradise*; *Wives Under Suspicion*
1939 *The Man in the Iron Mask*
1940 *Green Hell*
1941 *They Dare Not Love*

Publications

On WHALE: books—

Clarens, Carlos, *An Illustrated History of the Horror Film,* New York, 1968.
Baxter, John, *Hollywood in the Thirties,* New York, 1970.
Butler, Ivan, *Horror in the Cinema,* 2nd revised edition, New York, 1970.
Anobile, Richard, *James Whale's "Frankenstein,"* New York, 1974.
Everson, William, *Classics of the Horror Film,* Secaucus, New Jersey, 1974.
Tropp, Martin, *Mary Shelley's Monster: The Story of Frankenstein,* Boston, 1976.
Derry, Charles, *Dark Dreams: A Psychological History of the Modern Horror Film,* New York, 1977.

James Whale (right) on the set of *The Impatient Maiden*

Ellis, Reed, *Journey into Darkness: The Art of James Whale's Horror Films,* New York, 1980.
Curtis, James, *James Whale,* Metuchen, New Jersey, 1983.

On WHALE: articles—

Obituary, in the *New York Times,* 30 May 1957.
Edwards, Roy, "Movie Gothick: A Tribute to James Whale," in *Sight and Sound* (London), Autumn 1957.
Durgnat, Raymond, "The Subconscious: From Pleasure Castle to Libido Motel," in *Films and Filming* (London), January 1962.
Fink, Robert, and William Thomaier, "James Whale," in *Films in Review* (New York), May 1962.
Jensen, Paul, "James Whale," in *Film Comment* (New York), Spring 1971.
Milne, Tom, "One Man Crazy: James Whale," in *Sight and Sound* (London), Summer 1973.
Evans, Walter, "Monster Movies: A Sexual Theory," in *Journal of Popular Film* (Bowling Green, Ohio), Fall 1973.
Evans, Walter, "Monster Movies and Rites of Initiation," in *Journal of Popular Film* (Bowling Green, Ohio), Spring 1975.
White, D.L., "The Poetics of Horror: More than Meets the Eye," in *Film Genre: Theory and Criticism,* edited by Barry Grant, Metuchen, New Jersey, 1977.
Clarens, Carlos, and Mary Corliss, "Designed for Film: The Hollywood Art Director," in *Film Comment* (New York), May/June 1978.
Taylor, John Russell, "Tales of the Hollywood Raj," in *Films and Filming* (London), June 1983.
Mank, G., "Mae Clarke Remembers James Whale," in *Films in Review* (New York), May 1985.

* * *

Although he is primarily remembered as the director of the cult horror films *Frankenstein, The Old Dark House, The Invisible Man,* and *The Bride of Frankenstein,* James Whale contributed much more to the cinema. He also handled such stylish and elegant productions as *Waterloo Bridge* and *One More River,* which had little critical impact when they were first released and are, unfortunately, largely unknown today.

A quite, introspective man, James Whale's background was the stage, notably the original London and New York productions of R.C. Sheriff's pacifist play *Journey's End.* Aside from some work assisting Howard Hughes with the direction of *Hell's Angels* (work which is both negligible and best forgotten), James Whale made his directorial debut with *Journey's End,* a film which illustrates many of the qualities which were to mark Whale's later work: close attention to acting and dialogue, a striving for authenticity in settings, and a thoughtful use of camera (here somewhat hampered by the limits imposed on early talkies).

From 1930 through 1937, while Whale was under contract to Universal and under the patronage of studio production head Carl Laemmle Jr., the director was able to turn out a group of literate and accomplished features. Among his varied productions was the First World War melodrama *Waterloo Bridge,* later remade in a gaudy Hollywood fashion by Mervyn LeRoy, but in this version noteworthy for its honest approach to its leading character's prostitution and a stunning performance by Mae Clarke (a favorite Whale actress). Both *The Invisible Man* and *The Bride of Frankenstein* are influenced by the director's earlier *Frankenstein,* but both contain an element of black humor which lifts them above the common horror film genre. *The Kiss Before the Mirror* and *By Candlelight* possess an intangible charm, while *One More River* is simply one of Hollywood's best depictions of upper-class British life, memorable for the ensemble playing of its cast, headed by Diana Wynyard, and the one-liners from Mrs. Patrick Campbell. *Show Boat* demonstrates that Whale could handle a musical as easily as a romantic drama and is, without question, the finest screen version of the Jerome Kern-Oscar Hammerstein hit.

All of Whale's Universal features were well received with the exception of his last, *The Road Back,* based on an Erich Maria Remarque novel and intended as a sequel to *All Quiet on the Western Front. The Road Back* today appears badly constructed, a problem created in part by the studio's interference with the production out of concern that the German government might find the film unacceptable.

Whale's final films after leaving Universal are uniformly without interest, and contemporary response to them was lukewarm at best. The director simply grew tired of the hassles of filmmaking and retired. It has been suggested that Whale's homosexuality may have been unacceptable in Hollywood and helped to end his career, but he was a very private man who kept his personal life to himself, and it seems unlikely that his sexual preference created any problem for him or his employees; certainly Whale's homosexuality is not evident from his films, unless it be in the casting of the delightfully "camp" Ernest Thesiger in *The Old Dark House* and *The Bride of Frankenstein.*

—Anthony Slide

WIENE, Robert

Nationality: German. **Born:** Dresden, 1881. **Career:** Actor, writer, and director, Lessing-Theater, Berlin, until 1913; offered film directing debut by producer Kolowrat, 1913; collaborated with Walter Turszinsky on several comic films, 1915; directed a number of Henny Porten films, 1916; worked in Austria, 1924-26; left Nazi Germany, 1934. **Died:** In Paris, 17 July 1938.

Films as Director:

1912 *Die Waffen der Jugend* (d: Wiene or Friedrich Müller, + sc)
1915 *Frau Eva* (*Arme Eva*) (+ co-sc): *Die Konservanbraut*; *Der springende Hirsch* (*Die Diebe von Günsterburg*) (co-d?)
1916 *Der Sekretär der Königen* (+ sc); *Der Liebesbrief der Königin* (+ sc); *Das wandernde Licht*; *Die Räuberbraut*; *Der Mann Spiegel* (+ sc)
1917 *Der standhafte Benjamin* (+ sc): *Das Leben—ein Traum* (+ co-sc)
1918 *Der Umweg zur Ehe* (d: Wiene or Fritz Freisler, + co-sc); *Die Millionärin*
1919 *Die verführte Heilige* (+ sc); *Ein gefährliche Spiel* (+ sc); *Um das Lächeln einer Frau*
1920 *Die Drei Tänze der Mary Wilford* (+ co-sc); ***Das Kabinett des Dr. Caligari*** (*The Cabinet of Dr. Caligari*); *Genuine*; *Die Nacht der Konigin Isabeau* (+ sc)
1921 *Die Rache einer Frau*; *Das Spiel mit den Feuer* (+ co-sc)
1922 *Die höllische Macht*
1923 *Raskolnikow* (*Schuld und Sühne*) (+ sc); *Der Puppenmacher von Kiang-Ning*; *I.N.R.I.* (*Ein Film der Menschlichkeit*) (+ sc)
1924 *Orlacs Hände*; *Pension Groonen*
1925 *Der Leibgardist* (*Der Gardeoffizier*); *Der Rosenkavalier* (+ co-sc); *Die Königin vom Moulin-Rouge*
1927 *Die Geliebte*; *Die berühmte Frau*; *Le Tombeau sous L'Arc de Triomphe*
1928 *Die Frau auf der Folter*; *Die grosse Abenteuerin*; *Leontines Ehemänner*; *Unfug der Liebe*
1930 *Der Andere* (French version: *Le Procureur Hallers*)

Robert Wiene: *Orlacs Hände*

1931 *Der Liebesexpress* (*Acht Tage Gluck*) (French version: *Huit Jours de bonheur*); *Panik in Chicago*
1933 *Polizeiakte 909* (*Der Fall Tokeramo*) (+ sc)
1934 *Eine Nacht in Venedig* (+ sc)
1938 *Ultimatum* (completed by Robert Siodmak)

Other Films:

1915 *Fräulein Barbier* (Albes) (co-sc); *Arme Marie* (Zeyn and Mack) (sc); *Flucht der Schönheit* (*Seine schöne Mama*) (Rector, i.e. Zeiske) (co-sc); *Die büssende Magdalena* (Albes) (co-sc); *Lottekens Feldzug* (Ziener) (co-sc); *Der Schirm mit dem Schwan* (Froelich) (sc)
1916 *Gelöste Ketten* (Biebrach) (sc)
1917 *Frank Hansens Glück* (Larsen) (sc); *Die Prinzessin von Neutralien* (Biebach) (sc)
1918 *Die Heimkehr des Odysseus* (Biebrach) (sc); *Das Geschlecht derer von Rinwall* (Biebrach) (sc); *Opfer der Gesellschaft* (Grunwald) (sc); *Die Dame, der Teufel und die Probiermamsell* (Biebrach) (sc); *Am Tor des Lebens* (*Am Tor des Todes*) (Conrad Wiene) (sc)
1919 *Satanas* (Murnau) (artistic spvr); *Ihr Sport* (Biebrach) (sc); *Die lebende Tote* (Biebrach) (sc)
1920 *Das Blut der Ahnen* (Gerhardt) (co-sc); *Die Jagd nach dem Tode* (Gerhardt) (co-sc); *Die verbotene Stadt* (Gerhardt) (co-sc); *Die Abenteuer des Dr. Kircheisen* (Biebrach) (sc)
1923 *Die Macht der Finsternis* (Conrad Wiene) (sc)
1924 *Das Wachsfigurenkabinett* (*Waxworks*) (Leni) (artistic spvr)
1928 *Heut Spielt der Strauss* (*Der Walzerkönig*) (Conrad Wiene) (sc)
1936 *The Robber Symphony* (Feher) (artistic spvr)

Publications

By WIENE: book—

The Cabinet of Dr. Caligari, New York, 1972.

On WIENE: books—

Kracauer, Siegfried, *From Caligari to Hitler: A Psychological History of the German Film,* Princeton, New Jersey, 1947.
Eisner, Lotte, *The Haunted Screen,* Berkeley, 1969.
Manvell, Roger, and Heinrich Fraenkel, *The German Cinema,* New York, 1971.
Laqueur, Walter, *Weimar: A Cultural History 1918-1933,* New York, 1974.
Barton, John D., *German Expressionist Film,* Boston, 1982.

On WIENE: article—

Mayer, Carl, "*Le Cabinet du Docteur Caligari,*" in *Avant-Scène du Cinéma* (Paris), July/September 1975.

* * *

Robert Wiene's name will ever be associated with *Das Kabinett des Dr. Caligari (The Cabinet of Dr. Caligari),* his most famous film, although there are critics who would minimize his responsibility for this masterpiece of the cinema. His work is uneven and often blatantly commercial, but in spite of this many of his films show some originality of theme and distinguished performances by actors who worked under him.

Das Kabinett des Dr. Caligari, originally intended for Fritz Lang, put Wiene's name on the map. It is the most important of the expressionist films and today its power seems undiminished and its daring timeless. It ran continuously in Paris for seven years, thereby creating a record, and at the Brussels World's Fair of 1958 it was chosen by 117 film historians from 26 countries as one of the top twelve most important films of all time.

In *Genuine,* Wiene failed to repeat his success in the same genre, although the film was also scripted by the talented Carl Mayer. Three 1923 Wiene films show an interesting range of subject matter. *I.N.R.I.* dealt with the death of Christ and was mounted on a grand scale; it boasted the cream of German acting in the leading roles, and featured settings by the promising young Hungarian designer, Ernö Metzner. *Der Puppenmacher von Kiang-Ning,* a tragic-comedy with a script by Carl Mayer, and *Raskolnikow,* with fantastic sets by the Russian designer Andreiv, completed an interesting trilogy. The latter used emigréé actors in an adaptation of Dostoievsky's *Crime and Punishment.*

From 1924 to 1926 Wiene worked in Austria, where he made other distinguished films. *Orlacs Hände* was a horror film that starred Conrad Viedt as a sensitive musician who has the hands of a murderer grafted on to him. *Der Rosenkavalier,* meanwhile, a film adaptation of the Strauss opera, was co-scripted by Hugo von Hoff-manstahl. It included a special score arranged by the composer, who personally conducted the orchestra when it had its premiere at the Dresden State Opera House and at the Tivoli Cinema in London. The leading roles were taken by the French stars Huguette Duflos and Jacque Catelain.

Wiene returned to Germany, but his later work showed no special qualities and consisted of lightweight comedies with artists like Lily Damita, Dina Gralla, and Maria Jacobini. He also directed Mady Christians and Andre Roanne in a French production, *La Duchesee de Les Folies.* In 1935 he went to England and supervised *The Robber Symphony,* directed by his former actor from *Caligari,* Friedrich Feher. Of his sound films the Johann Strauss operetta *Eine Nacht in Venedig* merits attention.

Wiene died in Paris in 1938 while directing Erich von Stroheim and Dita Parlo in *Ultimatum,* which was completed by Robert Siodmak. While he covered a wide range of material in his films he never developed a personal style. His merit lay in encouraging many diverse talents and his ability to securing often outstanding contributions from them. He controlled his productions, in most cases writing the scripts himself. Wiene lived in a great period of cinema, which he served in his fashion.

—Liam O'Leary

WILDER, Billy

Nationality: Born Samuel Wilder in Sucha, Austria (now part of Poland), 22 June 1906; became U.S. citizen, 1934. **Family:** Married Audrey Young. **Military Service:** Served in U.S. Army as colonel in Psychological Warfare Division of the Occupational Government, Berlin, 1945. **Career:** Journalist in Vienna, then in Berlin, from 1926; collaborated with Robert and Kurt Siodmak, Edgar Ulmer, Fred Zinnemann, and Eugen Schüfftan on *Menschen am Sonntag,* 1929; scriptwriter, mainly for UFA studios, 1929-33; moved to Paris, co-directed *Mauvaise graine,* first directorial effort, then moved to Hollywood, 1933; hired by script department at Columbia, then Twentieth Century-Fox; hired by Paramount, began collaboration with Charles Brackett on *Bluebeard's Eighth Wife,* 1937; directed first American film, *The Major and the Minor,* 1942; began making films as independent producer/director with *The Seven Year Itch,* 1955; began collaboration with writer I. A. L. Diamond on *Love in the Afternoon,* 1957; directed *The Front Page* for Universal, 1974. **Awards:** Oscars for Best Direction and Best Screenplay (with Charles Brackett), and Best Direction Award, New York Film Critics, for *The Lost Weekend,* 1945; Oscar for Best Story and Screenplay (with Charles Brackett), for *Sunset Boulevard,* 1950; Oscars for Best Direction and Best Screenplay (with I. A. L. Diamond), Best Direction Award and Best Writing Award (with Diamond), New York Film Critics, for *The Apartment,* 1960; American Film Institute Lifetime Achievement Award, 1985; Irving G. Thalberg Award, 1988; Kennedy Center Award, 1990; National Medal of Arts, 1993. **Address:** c/o Equitable Investment Corporation, P.O. Box 93877, Hollywood, CA 90093, U.S.A.

Films as Director:

1933 *Mauvaise graine* (co-d)
1942 *The Major and the Minor* (+ co-sc)
1943 *Five Graves to Cairo* (+ co-sc)
1944 ***Double Indemnity*** (+ co-sc)
1945 ***The Lost Weekend*** (+ co-sc)
1948 *The Emperor Waltz* (+ co-sc); *Foreign Affair* (+ co-sc)
1950 ***Sunset Boulevard*** (+ co-sc)
1951 *Ace in the Hole* (*The Big Carnival*) (+ co-pr, co-sc)
1953 *Stalag 17* (+ pr, co-sc)
1954 *Sabrina* (+ pr, co-sc)
1955 *The Seven Year Itch* (+ co-pr, co-sc)
1957 *The Spirit of St. Louis* (+ co-sc); *Love in the Afternoon* (+ co-sc, pr)
1958 *Witness for the Prosecution* (+ co-sc)
1959 ***Some Like It Hot*** (+ co-sc, pr)
1960 ***The Apartment*** (+ co-sc, pr)
1961 *One, Two, Three* (+ co-sc, pr)
1963 *Irma La Douce* (+ co-sc, pr)
1964 *Kiss Me, Stupid* (+ co-sc, pr)
1966 *The Fortune Cookie* (+ co-sc, pr)
1970 *The Private Life of Sherlock Holmes* (+ co-sc, pr)
1972 *Avanti!* (+ co-sc, pr)
1974 *The Front Page* (+ co-sc)
1978 *Fedora* (+ co-pr, co-sc)
1981 *Buddy Buddy* (+ co-sc)

Other Films:

(in Germany)

1929 *Menschen am Sonntag* (*People on Sunday*) (Siodmak) (co-sc); *Der Teufelsreporter* (co-sc)
1930 *Seitensprünge* (story)
1931 *Ihre Hoheit befiehlt* (co-sc); *Der falsche Ehemann* (co-sc); *Emil und die Detektive* (*Emil and the Detectives*) (sc); *Der Mann der seinen Mörder sucht* (*Looking for his Murderer*) (Siodmak) (co-sc)

1932 *Es war einmal ein Walzer* (co-sc); *Ein blonder Traum* (co-sc); *Scampolo, ein Kind der Strasse* (co-sc); *Das Blaue von Himmel* (co-sc)
1933 *Madame wünscht keine Kinder* (co-sc); *Was Frauen träumen* (co-sc)

(in the United States)

1933 *Adorable* (Dieterle) (co-story, based on *Ihre Hoheit befiehlt*)
1934 *Music in the Air* (co-sc); *One Exciting Adventure* (co-story)
1935 *Lottery Lover* (co-sc)
1937 *Champagne Waltz* (Sutherland) (co-story)
1938 *Bluebeard's Eighth Wife* (Lubitsch) (co-sc)
1939 *Midnight* (Leisen) (co-sc); *What a Life* (co-sc); ***Ninotchka*** (Lubitsch) (co-sc)
1940 *Arise My Love* (Leisen) (co-sc)
1941 *Hold Back the Dawn* (Leisen) (co-sc); *Ball of Fire* (Hawks) (co-sc)

Publications

By WILDER: articles—

"Wilder in Paris," with John Gillett, in *Sight and Sound* (London), Winter 1956.
"One Head Is Better than Two," in *Films and Filming* (London), February 1957.
"The Old Dependables," with Colin Young, in *Film Quarterly* (Berkeley), Fall 1959.
Interview with Jean Domarchi and Jean Douchet in *Cahiers du Cinéma* (Paris), August 1962.
"Meet Whiplash Wilder," with Charles Higham, in *Sight and Sound* (London), Winter 1967.
Interview with Robert Mundy and Michael Wallington in *Cinema* (London), October 1969.
"Billy Wilder: Broadcast to Kuala Lampur," with Vanessa Brown, in *Action* (Los Angeles), November/December 1970.
Interview with Michel Ciment in *Positif* (Paris), January 1974.
"In the Picture: *The Front Page,*" with Joseph McBride, in *Sight and Sound* (London), Autumn 1974.
Interview with Gene Phillips in *Film/Literature Quarterly* (Salisbury, Maryland), Winter 1975.
"Wilder Bewildered," an interview with Gilbert Adair, in *Sight and Sound* (London), Winter 1976/77.
"Going for Extra Innings," an interview with J. McBride and T. McCarthy, in *Film Comment* (New York), January/February 1979.
Interview with C. Columbus in *American Film* (Washington D.C.), March 1986.

On WILDER: books—

Madsen, Axel, *Billy Wilder,* Bloomington, Indiana, 1969.
Wood, Tom, *The Bright Side of Billy Wilder, Primarily,* New York, 1970.
Corliss, Richard, *Talking Pictures: Screenwriters in the American Cinema,* New York, 1975.
Seidman, Steve, *The Film Career of Billy Wilder,* Boston, 1977.
Zolotow, Maurice, *Billy Wilder in Hollywood,* New York, 1977.
Dick, Bernard F., *Billy Wilder,* Boston, 1980.
Giannetti, Louis, *Masters of the American Cinema,* Englewood Cliffs, New Jersey, 1981.
Jacob, Jerome, *Billy Wilder,* Paris, 1988.
Seidl, Claudius, *Billy Wilder: Seine Filme, sein Leben,* Munich, 1988.

On WILDER: articles—

Lightman, Herb, "Old Master, New Tricks," in *American Cinematographer* (Los Angeles), September 1950.
McVay, Douglas, "The Eye of the Cynic," in *Films and Filming* (London), January 1960.
Higham, Charles, "Cast a Cold Eye: The Films of Billy Wilder," in *Sight and Sound* (London), Spring 1963.
Sarris, Andrew, "Fallen Idols," in *Film Culture* (New York), Spring 1963.
"The Films of Billy Wilder," in *Film Comment* (New York), Summer 1965.
Mundy, Robert, "Wilder Reappraised," in *Cinema* (London), October 1969.
McBride, Joseph, and Michael Wilmington, "The Private Life of Billy Wilder," in *Film Quarterly* (Berkeley), Summer 1970.
Ciment, Michel, "Sept Réflexions sur Billy Wilder," in *Positif* (Paris), May 1971.
Farber, Stephen, "The Films of Billy Wilder," in *Film Comment* (New York), Winter 1971.
Onosko, Tom, "Billy Wilder," in *Velvet Light Trap* (Madison, Wisconsin), Winter 1971.
"Dialogue on Film: Billy Wilder and I. A. L. Diamond," in *American Film* (Washington, D.C.), July/August 1976.
Sarris, Andrew, "Billy Wilder: Closet Romanticist," in *Film Comment* (New York), July/August 1976.
Fedora Issue of *Avant-Scène du Cinéma* (Paris), 15 November 1978.
Poague, Lee, "Some Versions of Billy Wilder," in *Cinemonkey* (Portland), no. 1, 1979.
Morris, G., "The Private Films of Billy Wilder," in *Film Comment* (New York), January/February 1979.
Allen, T., "Bracketting Wilder," in *Film Comment* (New York), May/June 1982.
Billy Wilder Issue of *Filmcritica* (Florence), November/December 1982.
"Dossier Billy Wilder," in *Positif* (Paris), July/August 1983.
Billy Wilder Section of *Positif* (Paris), September 1983.
Gallagher, Brian, "Sexual Warfare and Homoeroticism in Billy Wilder's *Double Indemnity,*" in *Literature/Film Quarterly* (Salisbury, Maryland), vol. 15, no. 4, 1987.
Willett, R., "Billy Wilder's *A Foreign Affair* (1945-1948): 'the Trials and Tribulations of Berlin'," in *Historical Journal of Film, Radio and Television* (Abingdon, Oxon), March 1987.
Canby, V., "Critic's Notebook: The Wonders of Wilder, the Movies' Master Wit," in *New York Times,* 10 May 1991.
Brown, G., "Something Wilder," in *Village Voice,* 14 May 1991.
Sarris, Andrew, "Why Billy Wilder Belongs in the Pantheon," in *Film Comment,* July/August 1991.
Freeman, David, "*Sunset Boulevard* Revisited: Annals of Hollywood," in *New Yorker,* 21 June 1993.
Sragow, Michael, "The Wilder Bunch," in *Gentleman's Quarterly,* October 1994.

* * *

During the course of his directorial career, Billy Wilder succeeded in offending just about everybody. He offended the public, who shunned several of his movies as decisively as they flocked to others; he offended the press with *Ace in the Hole,* the U.S. Congress with *A Foreign Affair,* the Hollywood establishment with *Sunset Boulevard* ("This Wilder should be horsewhipped!" fumed Louis B. Mayer), and religious leaders with *Kiss Me, Stupid*; he offended the critics, both those who found him too cynical and those who found him not cynical enough. And he himself, in the end, seems to have taken offence at the lukewarm reception of his last two films, and retired into morose silence.

Still, if Wilder gave offence, it was never less than intentional. "Bad taste," the tweaking or flouting of social taboos, is a key tactic throughout his work. His first film as director, *The Major and the Minor,* hints slyly at paedophilia, and several other Wilder movies toy with offbeat sexual permutations: transvestism in *Some Like It Hot,*

Billy Wilder directing Kim Novak in *Kiss Me, Stupid*

spouse-swapping in *Kiss Me, Stupid,* an ageing woman buying herself a young man in *Sunset Boulevard,* the reverse in *Love in the Afternoon.* Even when depicting straightforward romantic love, as in *The Emperor Waltz,* Wilder cannot resist counterpointing it with the eager ruttings of a pair of dogs.

He also relishes emphasising the more squalid of human motives. *Stalag 17* mocks prison-camp mythology by making a mercenary fixer the only hero on offer, and *Double Indemnity* replays *The Postman Always Rings Twice* with greed replacing honest lust. In *The Apartment* Jack Lemmon avidly demeans himself to achieve professional advancement (symbolised by the key to a lavatory door), and virtually everybody in *Ace in the Hole,* perhaps the most acerbic film ever made in Hollywood, furthers personal ends at the expense of a poor dupe dying trapped in an underground crevice. Wilder presents a disillusioned world, one (as Joan Didion put it) "seen at dawn through a hangover, a world of cheap *double entendres* and stale smoke ... the true country of despair."

Themes of impersonation and deception, especially emotional deception, pervade Wilder's work. People disguise themselves as others, or feign passions they do not feel, to gain some ulterior end. Frequently, though—all too frequently, perhaps—the counterfeit turns genuine, masquerade love conveniently developing into the real thing. For all his much-flaunted cynicism, Wilder often seems to lose the courage of his own disenchantment, resorting to unconvincing changes of heart to bring about a slick last-reel resolution. Some critics have seen this as blatant opportunism. "Billy Wilder," Andrew Sarris remarked, "is too cynical to believe even his own cynicism." Others have detected a sentimental undertow, one which surfaces in the unexpectedly mellow, almost benign late films like *Avanti!* and *The Private Life of Sherlock Holmes.*

But although, by comparison with a true moral subversive like Buñuel, Wilder can seem shallow and even facile, the best of his work retains a wit and astringent bite that sets it refreshingly off from the pieties of the Hollywood mainstream. When it comes to black comedy, he ranks at least the equal of his mentor, Lubitsch, whose audacity in wringing laughs out of concentration camps (*To Be or Not To Be*) is matched by Wilder's in pivoting *Some Like It Hot* around the St. Valentine's Day Massacre.

The consistency of Wilder's sardonic vision allows him to operate with assurance across genre boundaries. *Sunset Boulevard*—"full of exactness, cleverness, mastery and pleasure, a gnawing, haunting and ruthless film with a dank smell of corrosive delusion hanging over it," wrote Axel Madsen—has yet to be surpassed among Hollywood-on-Hollywood movies. In its cold fatality, *Double Indemnity* qualifies as archetypal *noir,* yet the same sense of characters trapped helplessly in the rat-runs of their own nature underlies both the erotic farce of *The Seven Year Itch* and the autumnal melancholy of *Sherlock Holmes.* Acclamation, though, falls beyond Wilder's scope: his Lindbergh film, *The Spirit of St. Louis,* is respectful, impersonal, and dull.

By his own admission, Wilder became a director only to protect his scripts, and his shooting style is essentially functional. But though short on intricate camerawork and stunning compositions, his films are by no means visually drab. Several of them contain scenes that lodge indelibly in the mind: Swanson as the deranged Norma Desmond, regally descending her final staircase; Jack Lemmon dwarfed by the monstrous perspectives of a vast open-plan office; Ray Milland (*The Lost Weekend*) trudging the parched length of Third Avenue in search of an open pawn-shop; Lemmon again, tangoing deliriously with Joe E. Brown, in full drag with a rose between his teeth. No filmmaker capable of creating images as potent—and as cinematic—as these can readily be written off.

—Philip Kemp

WISE, Robert

Nationality: American. **Born:** Winchester, Indiana, 19 September 1914. **Education:** Studied journalism at Franklin College. **Family:** Married 1) Patricia Doyle, 1942, one son; 2) Millicent Franklin, 1977. **Career:** Hired as assistant editor at RKO, where brother was employed, 1933; editor, from 1939; took over direction of *The Curse of the Cat People,* 1944; independent producer for Mirisch Corporation, 1959, and for Fox, 1963. **Awards:** Oscar for Best Direction (with Jerome Robbins), for *West Side Story,* 1961; Oscar for Best Direction, and Directors Award, Directors Guild of America, for *The Sound of Music,* 1965; Irving G. Thalberg Memorial Academy Award, 1966.

Films as Director:

1944 *The Curse of the Cat People* (co-d); *Mademoiselle Fifi*
1945 *The Body Snatchers*
1946 *A Game of Death*; *Criminal Court*
1947 *Born to Kill*
1948 *Mystery in Mexico*; *Blood on the Moon*
1949 *The Set-Up*
1950 *Three Secrets*; *Two Flags West*
1951 *The House on Telegraph Hill*; *The Day the Earth Stood Still*
1952 *Destination Gobi*; *Something for the Birds*
1953 *The Desert Rats*; *So Big*
1954 *Executive Suite*
1955 *Helen of Troy*; *Tribute to a Bad Man*
1956 *Somebody Up There Likes Me*
1957 *This Could Be the Night*; *Until They Sail*
1958 *Run Silent, Run Deep*; *I Want to Live*
1959 *Odds against Tomorrow* (+ pr)
1961 ***West Side Story*** (co-d)
1962 *Two for the Seesaw*
1963 *The Haunting* (+ pr)
1965 *The Sound of Music* (+ pr)
1966 *The Sand Pebbles* (+ pr)
1968 *Star!*
1970 *The Andromeda Strain* (+ pr)
1971 *Two People* (+ pr)
1975 *The Hindenburg*
1977 *Audrey Rose*
1979 *Star Trek: The Motion Picture*
1987 *I, Zorba*
1989 *Rooftops*

Other Films:

(partial list)

1940 ***Dance, Girl, Dance*** (Arzner) (ed)
1941 ***Citizen Kane*** (Welles) (ed)
1942 ***The Magnificent Ambersons*** (Welles) (ed)

Publications

By WISE: articles—

Interview in *Directors at Work,* edited by Bernard Kantor and others, New York, 1970.
"Impressions of Russia," in *Action* (Los Angeles), July/August 1971.

Robert Wise directing Shirley MacLaine and Robert Mitchum in *Two for the Seesaw*

"Robert Wise at RKO," an interview with Ruy Nogueira, in *Focus on Film* (London), Winter 1972.

"Robert Wise at Fox," an interview with Ruy Nogueira, in *Focus on Film* (London), Spring 1973.

"Robert Wise Continued," an interview with Ruy Nogueira and Allen Eyles, in *Focus on Film* (London), Autumn 1973.

"Robert Wise to Date," an interview with Ruy Nogueira, in *Focus on Film* (London), Autumn 1974.

"The Production of *The Hindenburg,*" in *American Cinematographer* (Los Angeles), January 1976.

"Robert Wise Talks about 'The New Hollywood'," in *American Cinematographer* (Los Angeles), July 1976.

"*Audrey Rose*: In Search of a Soul," an interview with R. Appelbaum, in *Films and Filming* (London), November 1977.

"Time and Again," an interview in *Monthly Film Bulletin* (London), November 1979.

"An AFI Seminar with Robert Wise and Milton Krasner ASC," in *American Cinematographer* (Los Angeles), March 1980.

"Robert Wise," an interview with L. Vincenzi, in *Millimeter,* March 1989.

On WISE: book—

Grivel, Danièle, and Roland Lacourbe, *Robert Wise,* Paris, 1985.

On WISE: articles—

Stark, Samuel, "Robert Wise," in *Films in Review* (New York), January 1963.

"Wise Issue" of *Dialogue on Film* (Washington, D.C.), vol. 2, no. 1, 1972.

Stamelman, P., "Robert Wise and *The Hindenburg,*" in *Millimeter* (New York), November 1975.

Guérif, F., "Nous avons gagné ce soir," in *Avant-Scène du Cinéma* (Paris), 1 March 1980.

"Robert Wise," in *CinemAction!* (Toronto), January 1992.

* * *

In the early 1940s there were two young men in the editorial department at RKO who worked as editors on Val Lewton pictures: Robert Wise and Mark Robson. The latter was promoted to a full directorship of Lewton's *Seventh Victim,* a moody script by DeWitt Bodeen and Charles O'Neal about a cult of devil worshippers in modern Manhattan.

Meanwhile, Robson's immediate superior in the editorial department, Robert Wise, got his first directorial opportunity when the front office grew displeased with Gunther von Fritsch, who was halfway through *Curse of the Cat People,* and dismissed him because he was behind schedule—a cardinal sin in the days of the studios. It was natural that Robert Wise, being the editor of *Curse of the Cat People,* should take over and complete the film, for only he knew the continuity of what had already been shot. Wise did so admirable a job that Lewton immediately got him assigned to his unit as full director for *Mademoiselle Fifi* with Simone Simon and *The Body Snatcher* with Boris Karloff.

Wise had edited two Orson Welles films for RKO—two that became classics, *Citizen Kane* and *The Magnificent Ambersons.* After now being made a full director, he diligently went into an acting class because he felt that actors had a special knowledge and language of their own; it was the ideal way of seeing film from the actor's point of view. It paid off almost immediately; he got an assignment as director for *The Set-Up,* a realistic picture of the prize ring that made a top star of Robert Ryan and a top director of Wise as well. *The Set-Up* won him the Critics Prize at the Cannes Film Festival.

In 1950 Wise was at Warner Bros., where he directed a distinguished mood film, *Three Secrets,* and went on to direct a remake of Edna Ferber's *So Big* with Jane Wyman, and *The Desert Rats* at Twentieth Century-Fox with Richard Burton. *Executive Suite* at MGM raised his status a notch higher, as did *Tribute to a Bad Man* with James Cagney. *Somebody Up There Likes Me* was an excellent prize-ring picture starring Paul Newman, while *Run Silent, Run Deep* was a splendid submarine thriller for Gable and Lancaster. *I Want to Live* at long last won Susan Hayward an Academy Award as Best Actress for 1958. A couple of years later Wise shared an Academy Award as Best Director with Jerome Robbins for *West Side Story.*

He returned to the mood horror film to make one of the most memorable of all time, *The Haunting,* which he also produced. He was director/producer again for *The Sound of Music,* a top box-office winner which won him once more the Academy's Oscar as Best Director, while *The Sand Pebbles,* with the late Steve McQueen, also earned him admiration. Through the wide range of his work, Wise proved himself to be a highly versatile director.

—DeWitt Bodeen

WISEMAN, Frederick

Nationality: American. **Born:** Boston, 1 January 1930. **Education:** Williams College, B.A., 1951; Yale Law School, L.L.B., 1954; Harvard University. **Family:** Married Zipporah Batshaw, 29 May 1955, two sons. **Military Service:** Served in U.S. Army, 1954-56. **Career:** Practiced law in Paris, and began experimental filmmaking, 1956-58; taught at Boston University Law School, 1958-61; bought rights to *The Cool World* by Warren Miller, and produced documentary version directed by Shirley Clarke; directed first film, *Titicut Follies,* 1966; received foundation grant to do *High School,* 1967; directed three films funded in part by PBS and WNET Channel 13 in New York, 1968-71; contracted to make documentaries for WNET, 1971-81; continued to make films for PBS, through 1980s; also theatre director, late 1980s. **Awards:** Emmy Award, Best Documentary Direction, for *Hospital,* 1970; Peabody Award; Career Achievement Award, International Documentary Association. **Address:** Zipporah Films, Inc., 1 Richdale Avenue, Suite 4, Cambridge, MA 02140, U.S.A.

Films as Director, Producer, and Editor:

1967 *Titicut Follies*
1968 *High School*
1969 *Law and Order*
1970 *Hospital*
1971 *Basic Training*
1972 *Essene*
1973 *Juvenile Court*
1974 *Primate*
1975 *Welfare*; *Meat*
1977 *Canal Zone*
1979 *Sinai Field Mission*
1980 *Manoeuvre*
1981 *Model*
1982 *Seraphita's Diary* (+ sc)
1983 *The Store*
1985 *Racetrack*
1986 *Deaf*; *Blind*; *Multi-Handicapped*; *Adjustment and Work*
1988 *Missile*
1989 *Near Death*
1990 *Central Park*
1991 *Aspen*
1993 *Zoo*
1994 *High School II*
1995 *Ballet*

Other Films:

1964 *The Cool World* (Clarke) (pr)
1968 *The Thomas Crown Affair* (Jewison) (sc, uncredited)

Publications

By WISEMAN: articles—

"The Talk of the Town: New Producer," in *New Yorker,* 14 September 1963.
Interview with Janet Handelman, in *Film Library Quarterly* (New York), Summer 1970.
Interview with Ira Halberstadt, in *Filmmaker's Newsletter* (Ward Hill, Massachusetts), February 1974.
"Vérités et mensonges du cinéma américain," an interview with M. Martin and others, in *Ecran* (Paris), September 1976.
"Wiseman on Polemic," an interview with A. T. Sutherland, in *Sight and Sound* (London), Spring 1978.
"Fictions and Other Realities," an interview with J. Gianvito, in *International Documentary* (Los Angeles), Winter 1990/91.

On WISEMAN: books—

Issari, M. Ali, *Cinema Verité,* Ann Arbor, Michigan, 1971.
Maynard, Richard A., *The Celluloid Curriculum: How to Use Movies in the Classroom,* New York, 1971.
Barsam, Richard, *Nonfiction Film: A Critical History,* New York, 1973.
Atkins, Thomas, editor, *Frederick Wiseman,* New York, 1976.
Ellsworth, Liz, *Frederick Wiseman: A Guide to References and Resources,* Boston, 1979.
Nichols, Bill, *Ideology and the Image: Social Representation in the Cinema and Other Media,* Bloomington, Indiana, 1981.
Benson, Thomas W., and Carolyn Anderson, *Reality Fictions: The Films of Frederick Wiseman,* Carbondale, Illinois, 1989.
Grant, Barry Keith, *Voyages of Discovery: The Cinema of Frederick Wiseman,* Urbana, Illinois, 1992.

On WISEMAN: articles—

Dowd, Nancy, "Popular Conventions," in *Film Quarterly* (Berkeley), Spring 1969.

Frederick Wiseman

Schickel, Richard, "A Verité View of High School," in *Life* (New York), 12 September 1969.
Denby, David, "Documentary America," in *Atlantic Monthly* (Greenwich, Connecticut), March 1970.
Mamber, Stephen, "The New Documentaries of Frederick Wiseman," in *Cinema* (Beverly Hills), Summer 1970.
Williams, Donald, "Frederick Wiseman," in *Film Quarterly* (Berkeley), Fall 1970.
"Frederick Wiseman," in *Documentary Explorations,* edited by G. Roy Levin, New York, 1971.
Atkins, Thomas, "Frederick Wiseman Documents the Dilemmas of Our Institutions," in *Film News* (New York), October 1971.
"Frederick Wiseman," in *Cinema Verité in America: Studies in Uncontrolled Documentary,* by Stephen Mamber, Cambridge, Massachusetts, 1974.
Atkins, Thomas, "American Institutions: The Films of Frederick Wiseman," in *Sight and Sound* (London), Autumn 1974.
Tuch, R., "Frederick Wiseman's Cinema of Alienation," in *Film Library Quarterly* (New York), vol. 11, no. 3, 1978.
Nichols, Bill, "Fred Wiseman's Documentaries: Theory and Structure," in *Film Quarterly* (Berkeley), Spring 1978.
Le Peron, S., "Fred Wiseman," in *Cahiers du Cinéma* (Paris), September 1979.
Armstrong, D., "Wiseman's *Model* and the Documentary Project: Toward a Radical Film Practice," in *Film Quarterly* (Berkeley), Winter 1983/84.
Benson, T. W., and C. Anderson, "The Rhetorical Structure of Frederick Wiseman's *Model,*" in *Journal of Film and Video* (Los Angeles), vol. 36, no. 4, 1984.
Barsam, R. M., "American Direct Cinema: The Re-presentation of Reality," in *Persistence of Vision* (Maspeth, New York), Summer 1986.
"Homage," in *New Yorker,* 20 January 1992.
Pierson, Melissa, "Fly on the Wall," in *Vogue* (New York), June 1993.
Espen, Hal, "The Documentarians," in *New Yorker,* 21 March 1994.

* * *

In the context of their times, Wiseman's classic documentaries of the 1960s and 1970s are comprehensively anti-traditional. They feature no commentary and no music; their soundtracks carry no more than the sounds Wiseman's recorder encounters; they are long, in some cases over three hours; and, until recent years, they were monochrome. Following the Drew/Leacock "direct cinema" filmmakers, Wiseman developed a shooting technique using lightweight equipment and high-speed film to explore worlds previously inaccessible. In direct cinema the aim was to achieve what they considered to be more honest reportage. Wiseman's insight, however, was to recognise that there is no pure documentary, and that all filmmaking is a process of imposing order on the filmed materials.

For this reason he prefers to call his films "reality fictions." Though he shoots in direct cinema fashion (operating the sound system, in his finest achievements in tandem with cameraman William Brayne), the crucial stage is the imposition of structure during editing. As much as forty hours of film may be reduced to one hour of finished product, an activity he has likened to that of a writer structuring a book. This does not mean that Wiseman's films "tell a story" in any conventional sense. The pattern and meaning of Wiseman's movies seem slowly to emerge from events as if somehow contained within them. Only after seeing the film, perhaps more than once, do the pieces fall into place, their significance becoming clear as part of the whole system of relations that forms the movie. Thus, to take a simple example, the opening shots of the school building in *High School* make it look like a factory, yet it is only at the end when the school's principal reads out a letter from a former pupil in Vietnam that the significance of the image becomes clear. The soldier is, he says, "only a body doing a job," and the school a factory for producing just such expendable bodies.

Wiseman is not an open polemicist; his films do not appear didactic. But as we are taken from one social encounter to the next, as we are caught up in the leisurely rhythms of public ritual, we steadily become aware of the theme uniting all the films. In exploring American institutions, at home and abroad, Wiseman shows us social order rendered precarious. As he has put it, he demonstrates that "there is a gap between formal and actual practice, between the rules and the way they are applied." What emerges is a powerful vision of people trapped by the ramifications and unanticipated consequences of their own social institutions.

Some critics, while recognising Wiseman's undoubted skill and intelligence, attack him for lack of passion, for not propagandising more overtly. They argue that when he shows us police violence (*Law and Order*), army indoctrination (*Basic Training*), collapsing welfare services (*Welfare*), or animal experiments (*Primate*) he should be more willing to apportion blame and make his commitments clear. But this is to misunderstand his project. Wiseman avoids the easy taking of sides for he is committed to the view that our institutions over-run us in more complex ways than we might imagine. By forcing us to piece together the jigsaw that he offers, he ensures that we understand more profoundly how it is that our institutions can go so terribly wrong. To do that at all is a remarkable achievement. To do it so uncompromisingly over so many years is quite unique.

In the 1980s he sought to broaden his enterprise somewhat. In 1982, for instance, he turned briefly to "fiction," though *Seraphita's Diary* is hardly orthodox and it is an intelligible extension of his interests. The subsequent documentaries, still produced at regular intervals, have perhaps not had quite the same force as his 1970s work. *Central Park,* for instance, is hypnotic in the rhythms of daily life that it invokes, but lacks the sheer power of the earlier films, which focused on the often ferocious tensions found in the collision between social institutions and people at the end of their tethers. Nevertheless, he has had a huge influence on the shape of modern documentary filmmaking, and, with *Welfare* his most compelling achievement, he remains the most sophisticated and intelligent documentarist of post-war cinema.

—Andrew Tudor

WOO, John

Nationality: Chinese. **Born:** Guangzhou, China, 22 September 1948. **Education:** Matteo Ricci College, Hong Kong, 1967. **Career:** Started making experimental 16mm films in college; joined film industry as production assistant for Cathay Film Company, 1969; joined Shaw Brothers as assistant director to Zhang Che, 1971; made directorial debut with *The Young Dragons,* 1973. **Agent:** Hanson, Jacobson, Keller & Hoberman, 450 N. Roxbury Drive, Beverly Hills, CA 90210, U.S.A.

Films as Director:

1973 *The Young Dragon*
1974 *The Dragon Tamers*
1975 *Princess Chang Ping*; *Hand of Death*
1977 *Money Crazy*; *Follow the Star*
1978 *Last Hurrah for Chivalry*
1979 *From Rags to Riches*
1981 *To Hell with the Devil*; *Laughing Times*
1982 *Plain Jane to the Rescue*
1983 *The Sunset Warrior*
1984 *The Time You Need a Friend*
1985 *Run Tiger Run*
1986 *Heroes Shed No Tears*; *A Better Tomorrow* (+ co-sc)
1987 *A Better Tomorrow II* (+ co-sc); *Just Heroes*
1989 *The Killer* (+ co-sc)
1990 *Bullet in the Head* (+ co-sc, ed)
1991 *Once a Thief* (+ co-sc)
1992 *Hard-Boiled* (+ co-sc, ed, role)
1993 *Hard Target*
1996 *Broken Arrow*

Other Films:

1976 *Countdown in Kung Fu* (sc)
1989 *Starry Is the Night* (role)

John Woo on the set of *Hard Target*

Publications

By WOO: articles—

"John Woo: I Hate Violence," *Interview*, August 1993.
"Things I Felt Were Being Lost: John Woo," *Film Comment*, September-October 1993.

On WOO: articles—

Segers, Frank, "A Trans-Pacific Crossover: Woo at the Helm at U," *Variety*, August 1992.
Uszynski, J., "John Woo: Chopstick Gangster," *Kino*, October 1992.
Wice, Nathaniel, "Wooing Hollywood," *Esquire*, January 1993.
Allen, H., "Guncrazy in the Bayou," *Village Voice*, May 1993.
Corliss, Richard, "John Woo: The First Action Hero," *Time*, August 1993.
Howe, Desson, "Target: America—Director John Woo Brings His Ballets of Bloodletting to the States, with an Unlikely Star," *Washington Post*, August 1993.
Kenny, Glenn, "Master Blaster: John Woo, Cult Favorite," *Entertainment Weekly*, August 1993.
Jonascu, Michael, "Biting the Bullet," *Film Threat*, August 1993.
Wolcott, James, "Blood Test," *New Yorker*, August 1993.
Penner, Jonathan, "Wooing America: China's Premier Action Director, John Woo, Comes to the United States, with a Vengeance," *Harper's Bazaar*, October 1993.

* * *

For sheer visceral excitement and over-the-top graphic violence, few action films made today, either in the United States or abroad, come close to the work of transplanted Hong Kong writer-director John Woo—a twenty-year veteran of Oriental action cinema who began his career making martial arts movies with kung fu superstar Jackie Chan.

With these and several costume epics to his credit, Woo shifted to bloody melodramas about his country's pervasive problems of crime and gangsterism with *A Better Tomorrow* (1986). The film tells the story of an ace counterfeiter gone straight who runs into brutal conflict with his ex-cronies in the mob and his younger brother, an ambitious cop on the Hong Kong police force whose career rise is threatened because of his brother's past reputation and criminal associations.

One of the biggest box-office successes in Hong Kong movie history, *A Better Tomorrow* made a major star out of a charismatic actor in the Cagney/Bogart mold named Chow Yun-Fat, who plays a crippled hit man and confidante of the film's protagonist. John Woo and Chow Yun-Fat quickly became the Robert DeNiro and Martin Scorsese of Hong Kong cinema. They teamed for an equally successful sequel, *A Better Tomorrow II*, in 1987, and have been on an action-filled roll ever since, turning out one gangster film after another—with such titles as *Bullet in the Head* (1990), a grueling saga of revenge and high crime with the Vietnam War serving as a backdrop, *Once a Thief* (1991), and *Hard-Boiled* (1992), a noirish urban melodrama with a thirty-minute finale of gunplay set in a hospital that remains one of the most mesmerizing action sequences in the history of cinema.

The duo's most widely released collaboration Stateside was *The Killer* (1990), the story of a world-weary mob hitman who suffers a crisis of conscience when he accidentally blinds a nightclub singer during a ferocious gangland shoot-out and—in the manner of Bogart's Roy Earle in *High Sierra*—undertakes one last job to pay for an operation to restore her eyesight.

Woo's Hollywood-gangster-film-inspired plots are a mixture of ripe sentimentality and macho romance with a moral grounding in such virtues as friendship, loyalty, and duty to God and country. Like the Italian action specialist Sergio Leone, dean of the "spaghetti Western," Woo treats the cliches of the genre as grand myths. But his most talked-about trademark is his skill at choreographing violent set-pieces (often in slow motion) of a kind not seen on the screen since the passing of Sam Peckinpah, the director Woo seems to have been most influenced by. The climax of Peckinpah's landmark Western *The Wild Bunch* (1969) erupted with what is still one of the most gut-wrenching, pyrotechnical displays of firepower and bloodletting ever put on the screen. Imagine if you will a director who stages all the action sequences in his films—and they are virtually non-stop—in the same in-your-face manner and you have a good idea of what the action films of John Woo are like.

In 1993 Hollywood finally imported Woo to breathe some new "life" into the overexhausted, tired action genre with *Hard Target*, a Woo-style updating of Richard Connell's classic tale of bloodsport, *The Most Dangerous Game*, which marked the Hong Kong action wiz's American film debut. Woo had to do some careful trimming to avoid an NC-17 rating for the film, which *Entertainment Weekly* critic Owen Gleiberman hailed as "an incendiary action orgy, as joyously excessive as the grand finale in a fireworks show." Woo followed *Hard Target* three years later with *Broken Arrow*, a thriller about a terrorist who steals a nuclear missile, starring John Travolta, cast much against type as the bad guy.

Woo has chosen to remain in the United States because he is concerned about what will happen in his native Hong Kong once the communist Chinese government resumes control of the country in 1997. Besides, he says, the opportunities here appear limitless—which indeed they probably are for a filmmaker with his special skills.

—John McCarty

WOOD, Edward D., Jr.

Nationality: American. **Born:** Edward Davis Wood, Poughkeepsie, NY, 10 October 1924. **Education:** Poughkeepsie High School, 1941; Kings School of Dramatic Art, Frank Lloyd Wright Institute, Washington D.C., 1946. **Military Service:** U.S. Marine Corps, 1942-46. **Family:** Married to Kathy O'Hara Everett. **Career:** Wrote, produced, directed and starred in the play *The Casual Company* at the Village Playhouse, Hollywood, 1948; wrote and directed first film, *Crossroads of Laredo*, 1948; wrote, directed, and starred in first Hollywood feature, *Glen or Glenda*, 1953; wrote and directed several short films for the U.S. government, 1960; published first novel, *Black Lace Drag*, 1963. **Died:** 10 December 1978, of a heart attack.

Films as Director and Screenwriter:

1948 *The Streets of Laredo*
1951 *The Sun Was Setting* (+ pr)
1953 *Glen or Glenda*; *Crossroad Avenger: The Adventures of the Tucson Kid*; *Boots*
1954 *Jailbait* (d only, + pr)
1955 *Bride of the Monster* (+ pr)
1956 *Plan Nine from Outer Space* (+ pr)
1957 *Final Curtain* (+ pr); *The Night the Banshee Cried* (+ pr)
1958 *Night of the Ghouls* (+ pr)
1960 *The Sinister Urge* (d only, + story)
1970 *Take It Out in Trade*
1971 *Necromania*; *The Only House*

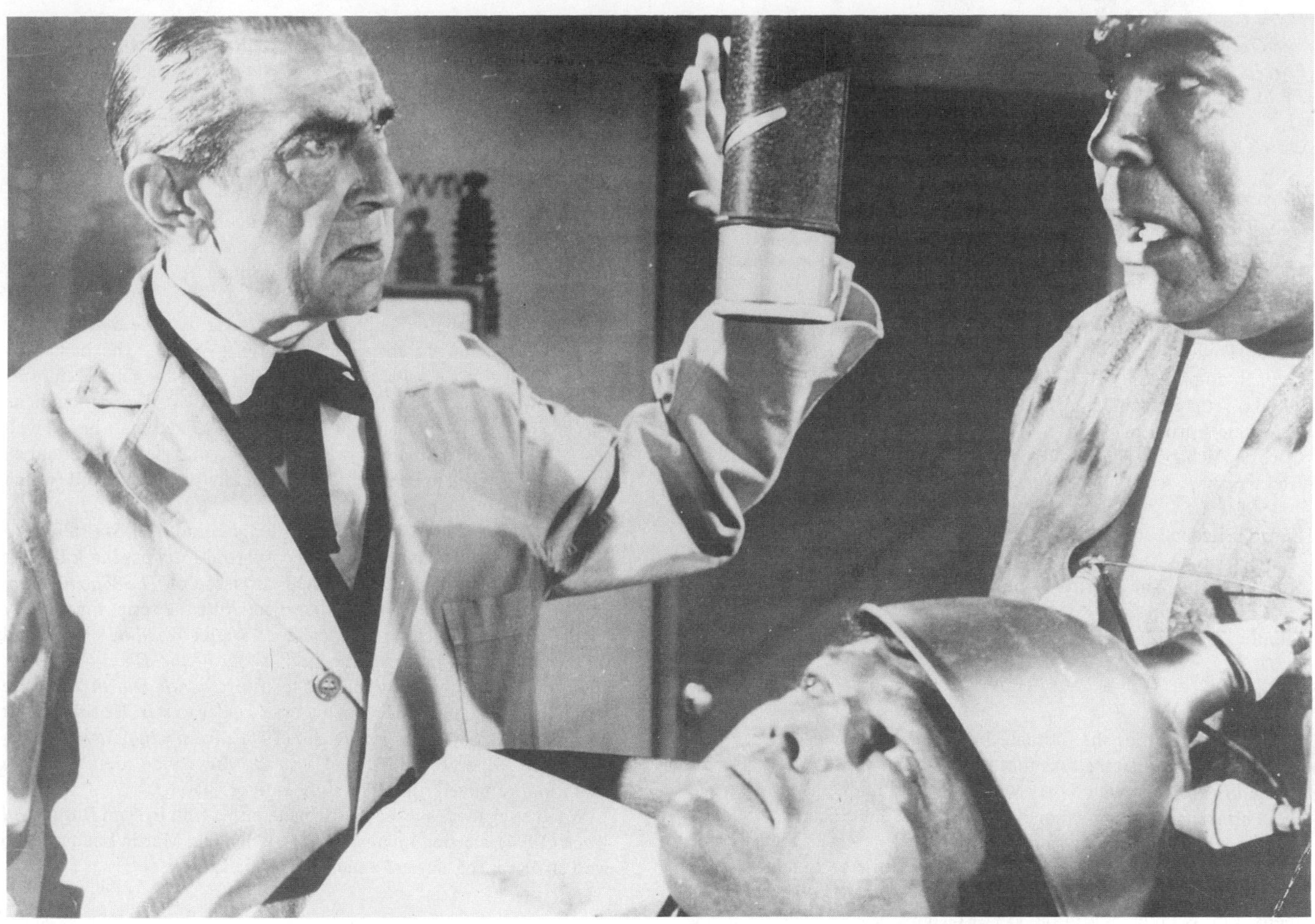

Edward D. Wood, Jr.: *Bride of the Monster*

Films as Screenwriter:

1952 *The Lawless Rider*
1956 *The Violent Years*
1963 *Shotgun Wedding*
1965 *Orgy of the Dead*
1969 *For Love or Money*; *One Million AC/DC*; *Operation Redlight*; *Gun Runners*
1971 *The Undergraduate*
1972 *Class Reunion* (co-sc); *The Cocktail Hostesses* (co-sc); *Dropout Wife* (co-sc)
1974 *Fugitive Girls*
1976 *The Beach Bunnies* (co-sc)

Publications

By WOOD: books—

Black Lace Drag, Raven Books, 1973.
Orgy of the Dead, Greenleaf Classics, 1966.
Parisian Passions, Corinth Publications, 1966.
WATTS—The Difference, Pad Library, 1966.
Side-Show Siren, Sundown Reader, 1966.
Drag Trade, Triumph News, 1967.
Bloodiest Sex Crimes of History, Pad Library, 1967.
Security Risk, Pad Library, 1967.
WATTS...After, Pad Library, 1967.
Devil Girls, Pad Library, 1967.
It Takes One to Know One, Pad Library, 1967.
Death of a Transvestite, Pad Library, 1967.
Suburbia Confidential, Triumph News, 1967.
Night Time Lez, Columbia, 1968.
Bye Bye Broadie, Pendulum Pictorial, 1968.
Raped in the Grass, Pendulum Pictorial, 1968.
The Perverts, Viceroy Books, 1968.
The Gay Underworld, Viceroy Books, 1968.
Sex, Shrouds and Caskets, Viceroy Books, 1968.
The Sexecutives, Private Edition Books, 1968.
Sex Museum, Viceroy Books, 1968.
The Love of the Dead, Viceroy Books, 1968.
One, Two, Three, Viceroy Books, 1968.
Young, Black and Gay, French Line Books, 1968.
Hell Chicks, Private Edition Books, 1968.
Purple Thighs, Private Edition Books, 1968.
Carnival Piece, Private Edition Books, 1969.
Toni: Black Tigress, Private Edition Books, 1969.
Mama's Diary, Toger Books, 1969.
To Make a Homo, Little Library Press, 1971.
A Study of the Sons and Daughters of Erotica, Secs Press, 1971.
Sexual Practices in Witchcraft and Black Magic, Secs Press, 1971.
Black Myth, Secs Press, 1971.
The Sexual Woman, Book Two, Secs Press, 1971.
The Sexual Man, Book Two, Secs Press, 1971.

Mary-Go-Round, Little Library Press, 1972.
The Only House, Little Library Press, 1972.
Forced Entry, Eros Goldstripe, 1974.
TV Lust, Eros Goldstripe, 1974.

On WOOD: books—

Grey, Rudolph, *Nightmare of Ecstasy,* Los Angeles, 1992.
McCarty, John, *The Sleaze Merchants,* New York, 1995.

On WOOD: articles—

Hoberman, J., "Bad Movies," *Film Comment,* July-August 1980.
Lucas, Tim, "*Glen or Glenda,*" *Cinefantastique,* 1982.
Grey, Rudolph, "Hollywood Underground," *Filmfax,* March-April 1987.
Okuda, Ted, "Remembering Ed D. Wood, Jr., a Moviemaker," *Filmfax,* March-April 1987.
Corliss, Richard, "The World's Worst Director," *Time,* January 1992.
Henderson, J. A., "*Plan Nine From Outer Space,*" *Filmfax,* June-July 1992.
Snead, Elizabeth, "Oddball Director Ed Wood Gains Fame, if Not Respect," *USA Today,* July 1993.
Rose, Lloyd, "The World's Worst Filmmaker—and Why We Love Him," *Washington Post,* August 1993.
Gliatto, Tom, "Master Ed," *People Weekly,* October 1994.

* * *

Ed Wood typifies the ultimate in filmmaking independence. His approach to filmmaking was that if no studio would hire him or finance his projects (which they wouldn't and didn't), he would make them himself, scrounging money from any available source. Wood fell in love with the movies at a very young age; he never wanted to be anything but a moviemaker, although he had little or no talent for the job. He began films in 8-millimeter even before he had reached his teens. Following a stint in the U.S. Marine Corps during World War II—where, according to legend, he stormed the beaches at Tarawa wearing ladies' underwear beneath his battle dress—he journeyed to Hollywood to realize his boyhood dream of making it big in the movie business.

His "breakthrough" came in 1953, with the George Weiss-produced exploitation feature on sex-change operations first known as *Behind Locked Doors,* then as *Transvestite,* and finally as *Glen or Glenda.* The film was originally intended to be a documentary on the life of transsexual Christine Jorgensen; ultimately it became a kind of self-portrait of Ed Wood himself, a classic apology for cross-dressing, and an obsessive ode to the delights of wearing angora sweaters.

Wood then made *Jailbait* (1954), which is about a gangster (Timothy Farrell) who undergoes plastic surgery to escape the law. Armed with a broken-down rubber octopus previously seen in a Republic Pictures John Wayne movie called *Wake of the Red Witch* (1948), a leading man (Tom McCoy) who couldn't act (but whose father provided some of the financing), as well as Bela Lugosi, Tor Johnson, and a somewhat better-than-usual script, Wood next created *Bride of the Monster,* an attempt at a horror picture in the style of the classic Universal films Wood had grown up on. What he achieved was closer in spirit to the low-rent series of horror flicks turned out by Monogram in the 1940s.

Wood always cited his masterpiece as *Plan Nine from Outer Space,* the film most closely associated with him. It has earned the reputation over the years as the worst movie ever made, which it isn't, although its shortcomings are enormous. The title (Wood originally wanted to call the film *Grave Robbers from Outer Space*) refers to an alien plot to resurrect the earth's dead. Said aliens arrive in flying saucers made out of Cadillac hubcaps suspended on visible wires. Wood's spaceship interior is a lamely disguised soundstage decked out with a shower curtain and some other "futuristic" touches. These boldly executed shortcomings, however, may be why *Plan Nine* has outlasted many better-made films of the era in the public's mind.

To finance *Plan Nine,* Wood turned to a Baptist minister named J. Edward Reynolds, who saw the film as an opportunity to get into the movie business and use the profits to finance a series of religious films. In return, Wood agreed to have the cast and crew baptized by Reynolds prior to production. Soon he found his alcoholic/cross-dressing personal life under fire. Reynolds used this as a wedge to get control of the finished film, then let it sit on a shelf for three years, unable to find a distributor.

Wood penned the screenplay for *The Bride and the Beast* (1958), about the attraction of a young wife (Charlotte Austin) to her husband's (Lance Fuller) pet gorilla, named "Spanky." But the next feature he directed was *Night of the Ghouls* (1958). Once again, Wood thought he was in Universal's classic monster territory, and once again he fell well shy of his intended mark. Forced to shoot in a severely cramped studio, he hastened to complete the film before the electric bill (which he couldn't pay) came due.

From *Night of the Ghouls* Wood plunged into *The Sinister Urge* (1960), billed as a "smut picture" and "portrait of a psycho killer." It was released as a double feature with a reissue of *The Violent Years* (1956), a film Wood had written. He also wrote the script for a sleazy "white trash" exploitation opus called *Shotgun Wedding* (1963) and for a combination horror-porno flick *Orgy of the Dead* (1965). In 1970, he directed his first "nudie" feature, *Take It Out in Trade,* in which he once again donned an angora sweater to star. He followed it up with the harder-core *Necromania* (1971), from which it was only a small step to porno "loops" and a steady downslide to an untimely death in dire poverty in 1978 at the age of fifty-four.

Wood's saga was subsequently made into a film by Tim Burton, *Ed Wood* (1994), starring Johnny Depp as Wood and Martin Landau (who won an Oscar for his performance) as Bela Lugosi.

—John McCarty

WOOD, Sam

Nationality: American. **Born:** Samuel Grosvenor Wood in Philadelphia, 10 July 1884. **Education:** Attended Stanton School, Philadelphia. **Family:** Married Clara Roush, two daughters. **Career:** Headed west in gold rush, settled in Reno, 1900; real estate broker, Los Angeles, 1904; film acting debut in *A Gentleman of Leisure* for Famous Players Company, 1908; assistant to Cecil B. De Mille, 1914, then director, from 1916; director for Paramount, from 1919; director for newly-formed MGM, 1926-39; directed final scenes of *Gone With the Wind,* 1939; named president of Motion Picture Alliance for the Preservation of American Ideals, 1944; testified before House Un-American Activities Committee, 1947. **Died:** 22 September 1949.

Films as Director:

1920 *Double Speed*; *Excuse My Dust*; *What's Your Hurry?*; *Sick Abed*; *The Dancing Fool*; *City Sparrow*; *Peck's Bad Boy* (+ sc)
1921 *Her First Elopement*; *The Snob*; *Her Beloved Villain*; *The Great Moment*; *Under the Lash*; *Don't Tell Everything*
1922 *Impossible Mrs. Bellew*; *Her Husband's Trademark*; *Beyond the Rocks*
1923 *My American Wife*; *Prodigal Daughters*; *Her Gilded Cage*; *Bluebeard's Eighth Wife*; *His Children's Children*
1924 *Bluff*; *The Female*; *The Next Corner*; *The Mine with the Iron Door*

Sam Wood

1925 *The Re-Creation of Brian Kent*
1926 *Fascinating Youth*; *One Minute to Play*
1927 *The Fair Co-ed*; *Rookies*; *A Racing Romeo*
1928 *Telling the World*; *The Latest from Paris*
1929 *It's a Great Life*; *So This Is College*
1930 *Way for a Sailor*; *The Richest Man in the World*; *Sins of the Children*; *The Girl Said No*; *They Learned About Women* (co-d); *Paid*
1931 *A Tailor Made Man*; *New Adventures of Get-Rich-Quick Wallingford*
1932 *Prosperity*; *Huddle*
1933 *Hold Your Man* (+ pr); *The Barbarian*; *Christopher Bean*
1934 *Stamboul Quest*
1935 ***A Night at the Opera***; *Let 'em Have It*
1936 *Whip Saw*; *The Unguarded Hour*
1937 *Navy Blue and Gold*; *Madame X*; *A Day at the Races* (+ co-pr)
1938 *Stablemates*; *Lord Jeff* (+ co-pr)
1939 *Goodbye, Mr. Chips*
1940 *Raffles*; *Our Town*; *Kitty Royle*; *Rangers of Fortune*
1941 *King's Row*; *The Devil and Miss Jones*
1942 *The Pride of the Yankees*
1943 *For Whom the Bell Tolls* (+ pr)
1944 *Casanova Brown*
1945 *Guest Wife*; *Saratoga Trunk*
1946 *Heartbeat*
1947 *Ivy* (+ co-pr)
1948 *Command Decision*
1949 *The Stratton Story*; *Ambush*

Other Films:

1939 ***Gone with the Wind*** (Fleming: d final scenes)
1944 *Address Unknown* (pr)

Publications

On WOOD: books—

Kaufman, George S., and others, *A Night at the Opera,* New York, 1972.
Pirosh, Robert, and others, *A Day at the Races,* New York, 1972.
Denton, Clive, and others, *The Hollywood Professionals—Vol. 2,* New York, 1974.

On WOOD: articles—

Obituary, in the *New York Times,* 23 September 1949.
"Sam Wood," in *Contracampo* (Madrid), October/November 1980.

* * *

Samuel Grosvenor Wood was one of the more prolific directors in Hollywood history. Working continuously at his craft from 1916 to 1949, he created an average of nearly three films per year. His most noted motion pictures came during the last fifteen years of his career: *A Night at the Opera, A Day at the Races, Goodbye Mr. Chips, Kitty Foyle, King's Row,* and *For Whom the Bell Tolls.* Wood also worked on *Gone With the Wind,* though he was uncredited. Yet in all these films Sam Wood seemed unable to develop an identifiable personal style. He knew the Hollywood system and was able to create clean crisp narratives, but he never transcended the system to create complex films as did his contemporaries, John Ford and Howard Hawks.

In 1908, at age 23, Sam Wood established his career as a Los Angeles real estate agent. But through a chance meeting, he tried acting in motion pictures, and gradually worked his way up to substantial roles for the Famous Players Company. In 1914 he became an assistant to Cecil B. De Mille; in 1916 he was promoted to director. Sam Wood directed films for Famous Players (later Paramount) until 1926. He then signed on with the newly formed Metro-Goldwyn-Mayer Company. He remained with MGM through the studio's salad days of the 1930s. But after his experience with *Gone With the Wind,* Wood struck out on his own. During the 1940s he worked for RKO, Paramount, Warner Bros., MGM, and independent producers Sol Lesser and Sam Goldwyn.

Sam Wood's directorial career seems to be divided into two parts. Until 1935 he was a traditional contract director at two of Hollywood's more important studios: Paramount and MGM. He directed many noted stars (Wallace Reid, Gloria Swanson, Jackie Coogan, Norma Shearer, Robert Montgomery, John Gilbert, Ramon Novarro, Clark Gable, Jean Harlow, and Marie Dressler), and earned a reputation as a solid, dependable director, one who brought films in on time. Sam Wood rose to the top echelon of Hollywood's contract directors through his association with Irving Thalberg and the Marx Brothers. *A Night at the Opera* became one of the major revenue generators of the 1935-36 movie season. From then on Sam Wood was able to pick and choose his projects. By 1939 he was considered a "money director," taking on only those projects with million dollar budgets. From 1939 on his films consistently finished among the top box office draws of the year. He was nominated for the Academy Award for best director in 1939 (*Goodbye Mr. Chips*), 1940 (*Kitty Foyle*), and 1942 (*King's Row*), but never won.

Sam Wood, however, is more often discussed in film history books for his part in organizing an anti-Communist group called the Motion Picture Alliance for the Preservation of American Ideals. Named president in 1944, Wood carried out a campaign to purge the film industry of left-wing sympathizers. Along with Walt Disney, Gary Cooper, King Vidor, and others, Wood used the Alliance to attack proponents of progressive politics. Indeed, on the morning of his fatal heart attack he was quarreling with Columbia Pictures about the necessity of expelling a screenwriter. In his will Wood specified no heir could inherit anything unless he (or she) swore that they "are not now, nor ever have been, a Communist." Sam Wood, a former supporter of Franklin Roosevelt, died amidst front page debate concerning Hollywood's witchhunt. As a result of his involvement, Wood is now remembered more for his right-wing politics than his nearly one hundred films.

—Douglas Gomery

WRIGHT, Basil

Nationality: British. **Born:** Basil Charles Wright in London, 12 June 1907. **Education:** Attended Sherborne School and at Corpus Christi College, Cambridge. **Career:** Joined Empire Marketing Board (EMB) film unit as assistant under John Grierson, 1930; directed first film, 1931; transferred with Grierson to General Post Office (GPO) film unit after EMB film unit dissolved, 1934; formed Realist Film Unit with John Taylor, and joined Film Centre, 1937; began making films for Ministry of Information after its absorption of GPO film unit, 1940; adviser on information technique and policy in Canada, World War II; producer in charge of Crown Film Unit, 1945, later worked at UNESCO under Sir Julian Huxley and John Grierson; formed own production company, International Realist, 1946; lectured on film-making at University of California, 1960s; wrote critical history of film, *The Long View,* 1974. **Died:** In London, 14 October 1987.

Films as Director:

1931 *The Country Comes to Town* (+ co-ph, sc)
1932 *O'er Hill and Dale* (+ ph, sc); *Gibraltar* (+ ph, sc)
1933 *Windmill in Barbados* (+ ph, sc); *Liner Cruising South* (+ ph, sc); *Cargo from Jamaica* (+ ph)
1934 ***Song of Ceylon*** (+ ph, co-sc, ed)
1936 ***Night Mail*** (co-d, co-sc, co-ed)
1937 *Children at School* (+ co-pr)
1938 *The Face of Scotland* (+ sc)
1940 *Harvest Help*
1945 *This Was Japan*
1948 *Bernard Miles on Gun Dogs* (+ pr, sc)
1950 *Waters of Time* (co-d)
1953 *World Without End* (co-d)
1955 *Stained Glass at Fairford* (+ pr)
1958 *The Immortal Land* (+ co-pr)
1959 *Greek Sculpture* (co-d)
1960 *A Place for Gold* (+ pr)

Other Films:

1934 *Pett and Pott* (asst d)
1937 *The Smoke Menace* (asst pr)
1939 *The Londoners* (co-pr)
1945 *A Diary for Timothy* (Jennings) (pr)

Publications

By WRIGHT: books—

The Use of Film, London, 1948.
The Long View, London, 1974.

By WRIGHT: articles—

"The Documentary Dilemma," in *Hollywood Quarterly,* Summer 1951.
Article on *World Without End,* in *Sight and Sound* (London), Summer 1953.
"Basil Wright on the Big Screen," in *Film* (London), December 1955.
"Which Way is Ahead?," in *Film* (London), November/December 1957.
"Basil Wright and *Song of Ceylon,*" an interview with Cecile Starr, in *Filmmakers Newsletter* (Ward Hill, Massachusetts), November 1975.
"Basil Wright on Art, Anthropology and the Documentary," with S. Thomas, in *Quarterly Review of Film Studies* (Pleasantville, New York), Fall 1979.
Interview with P. Mareth and A. Bloom in *Film and History* (Newark, New Jersey), December 1980.

On WRIGHT: books—

Hardy, Forsyth, *Grierson on Documentary,* revised edition, London, 1966.
Levin, G. Roy, *Documentary Explorations,* Garden City, New York, 1972.
Lovell, Alan, and Jim Hillier, *Studies in Documentary,* New York, 1972.
Sussex, Elizabeth, *The Rise and Fall of British Documentary: The Story of the Film Movement Founded by John Grierson,* Berkeley, California, 1975.
Hardy, Forsyth, *John Grierson: A Documentary Biography,* London, 1979.
Ellis, Jack C., *The Documentary Idea,* Englewood Cliffs, New Jersey, 1989.
Swann, Paul, *The British Documentary Film Movement 1926-46,* Cambridge, 1989.

On WRIGHT: articles—

Rotha, Paul, article on *World Without End,* in *Sight and Sound* (London), Summer 1953.
Hardy, Forsyth, article on *World Without End,* in *Sight and Sound* (London), January/March 1954.
Gillett, John, article on *Stained Glass at Fairford,* in *Sight and Sound* (London), Winter 1956/57.
Gay, Ken, article on *The Immortal Land,* in *Films and Filming* (London), December 1958.
Cavender, Kenneth, article on *The Immortal Land,* in *Sight and Sound* (London), Winter 1958/59.
Barrot, O., "Basil Wright," in *Cinéma d'aujourd'hui* (Paris), February/March 1977.
Obituary, in *Variety* (New York), 21 October 1987.
Obituary by Elizabeth Sussex, in *Sight and Sound* (London), Winter 1987/1988.

* * *

Basil Wright was the first of the young men hired by John Grierson at the Empire Marketing Board in the late 1920s, a period that marked the beginning of the development of the British documentary. Wright came from a wealthy liberal family and, like many of the others who joined Grierson, had recently completed his education at Cambridge University. Wright became one of Grierson's most loyal colleagues, remaining involved with him on various projects over many years.

Wright's apprenticeship consisted of editing together bits of stock footage for what were called "poster films." In the first films that he directed, such as *O'er Hill and Dale* and *Cargo from Jamaica,* Wright's special talent for poetic observation became evident. It achieved its fullest expression in *Song of Ceylon,* which is not only Wright's masterpiece but one of the few British documentaries of the 1930s armed with the kind of aesthetic value to keep it in active circulation ever since. *Song of Ceylon* is atypical of early British documentary not only in its extraordinary formal experimentation, but in its subject (an exotic foreign culture) and theme (admiration for the religious spirit of that culture and sadness and perhaps anger at the impact of Western commerce on it). Though a number of people played important roles in its creation (Grierson served as producer, Walter Leigh as composer, Cavalcanti as sound editor), *Song of Ceylon* is very much Wright's film, including most of its marvelous cinematography.

Wright shares directorial credit for *Night Mail* with Harry Watt. The original script seems largely to have been Wright's, and the completed film contains some of the poetic touches one associates with his best work. But the strong narrative line and deft bits of characterization and humor seem much more in keeping with the directorial style that Watt was developing.

In his work which followed, Wright moved into an obvious imitation of the American *March of Times* series, which was greatly admired by Grierson and other British documentarians. *Children at School,* one of a program of shorts sponsored by the British Commercial Gas Association, was an example. Though competent in technique and hard-hitting as exposé, in its impersonality it might have been directed by any number of other documentarians. It represents Wright's deep and genuine social concern arrived at intellectually rather than the emotional core of his being, out of which his most personal and best work came.

In the 1951 *Waters of Time* Wright returned to the poetic; but by then what earlier would have been gentle reflectiveness seems to have become slack. It was made after the Grierson tradition had become diffused. *World Without End,* which had both some poetry and some

Basil Wright

force, was the last of the films with which Wright was involved that are concerned clearly with the Griersonian main line. A big and ambitious film, it was made on behalf of UNESCO in collaboration with Paul Rotha, another veteran of the early Grierson group. Rotha shot in Mexico and Wright in Thailand, with their material being intercut. Ultimately, the film says that the world has grown together and that a low water level in a Mexican lake and a terrible tropical disease are of concern to us all, a very Griersonian idea.

—Jack C. Ellis

WYLER, William

Nationality: American. **Born:** Willy Wyler in Mulhouse (Mülhausen), Alsace-Lorraine, 1 July 1902; became U.S. citizen, 1928. **Family:** Married 1) Margaret Sullavan, 1934 (divorced 1936); 2) Margaret Tallichet, 1938, four children. **Military Service:** U.S. Army Air Corps, 1942-45; major. **Career:** Travelled to America at invitation of cousin Carl Laemmle, 1920; worked in publicity department for Universal in New York, then transferred to Universal City, Hollywood, 1921; assistant director at Universal, from 1924; directed first film, *Crook Buster,* 1925, and first feature, *Lazy Lightning,* 1926; signed contract with Samuel Goldwyn, 1936; helped to found Committee for the First Amendment to counteract Hollywood investigations by House Un-American Activities Committee, 1947; "Hommage à William Wyler" organized by Henri Langlois at the Cinémathèque française, 1966; retired from directing, 1972. **Awards:** Oscar for Best Direction, for *Mrs. Miniver,* 1942; Oscar for Best Direction and New York Film Critics Award for Best Direction, for *The Best Years of Our Lives,* 1946; Oscar for Best Direction, for *Ben Hur,* 1959; Irving G. Thalberg Award, 1965; American Film Institute Lifetime Achievement Award, 1976. **Died:** 29 July 1981.

Films as Director:

1925 *Crook Buster*
1926 *The Gunless Bad Man*; *Ridin' for Love*; *Fire Barrier*; *Don't Shoot*; *The Pinnacle Rider*; *Martin of the Mounted*; *Lazy Lightning*; *Stolen Ranch*
1927 *Two Fister*; *Kelly Gets His Man*; *Tenderfoot Courage*; *The Silent Partner*; *Galloping Justice*; *The Haunted Homestead*; *The Lone Star*; *The Ore Riders*; *The Home Trail*; *Gun Justice*; *Phantom Outlaw*; *Square Shooter*; *The Horse Trader*; *Daze in the West*; *Blazing Days*; *Hard Fists*; *The Border Cavalier*; *Straight Shootin'*; *Desert Dust*
1928 *Thunder Riders*; *Anybody Here Seen Kelly*
1929 *The Shakedown*; *The Love Trap*
1930 *Hell's Heroes*; *The Storm*
1931 *A House Divided*
1932 *Tom Brown of Culver*
1933 *Her First Mate*; *Counselor at Law*
1934 *Glamour*; *The Gay Deception*
1936 *These Three*; *Dodsworth*; *Come and Get It*
1937 *Dead End*
1938 *Jezebel*
1939 *Wuthering Heights*
1940 *The Westerner*; *The Letter*
1941 ***The Little Foxes***
1942 ***Mrs. Miniver***
1944 *Memphis Belle*
1946 ***The Best Years of Our Lives***
1947 *Thunder-Bolt*
1949 *The Heiress*
1951 *Detective Story*
1952 *Carrie*
1953 *Roman Holiday*
1955 *The Desperate Hours*
1956 *Friendly Persuasion*
1958 *The Big Country*
1959 *Ben-Hur*
1962 *The Children's Hour*
1965 *The Collector*
1966 *How to Steal a Million*
1968 *Funny Girl*
1970 *The Liberation of L.B. Jones*

Publications

By WYLER: articles—

"William Wyler: Director with a Passion and a Craft," with Hermine Isaacs, in *Theater Arts* (New York), February 1947.
"Interview at Cannes," in *Cinema* (Beverly Hills), July/August 1965.
Interview with Charles Higham, in *Action* (Los Angeles), September/October 1973.
"Wyler on Wyler," with Alan Cartnel, in *Inter/View* (New York), March 1974.
"Dialogue on Film," in *American Film* (Washington, D.C.), April 1976.
"No Magic Wand," in *Hollywood Directors: 1941-76,* edited by Richard Koszarski, New York, 1977.
Interview with P. Carcassonne and J. Fieschi, in *Cinématographe* (Paris), March/April 1981.
Lecture excerpts in *Films and Filming* (London), October 1981.

On WYLER: books—

Drinkwater, John, *The Life and Adventures of Carl Laemmle,* New York, 1930.
Griffith, Richard, *Samuel Goldwyn: The Producer and His Films,* New York, 1956.
Reisz, Karel, editor, *William Wyler, an Index,* London, 1958.
Madsen, Axel, *William Wyler,* New York, 1973.
Kolodiazhnaia, V., *Uil'iam Uailer,* Moscow, 1975.
Anderegg, Michael A., *William Wyler,* Boston, 1979.
Kern, Sharon, *William Wyler: A Guide to References and Resources,* Boston, 1984.
Fink, Guido, *William Wyler,* Florence, 1989.

On WYLER: articles—

Griffith, Richard, "Wyler, Wellman, and Huston," in *Films in Review* (New York), February 1950.
Reisz, Karel, "The Later Films of William Wyler," in *Sequence* (London), no. 13, 1951.
"Personality of the Month," in *Films and Filming* (London), July 1957.
Heston, Charlton, "The Questions No One Asks About Willy," in *Films and Filming* (London), August 1958.
Reid, John Howard, "A Little Larger Than Life," in *Films and Filming* (London), February 1960.
Reid, John Howard, "A Comparison of Size," in *Films and Filming* (London), March 1960.
Sarris, Andrew, "Fallen Idols," in *Film Culture* (New York), Spring 1963.
Brownlow, Kevin, "The Early Days of William Wyler," in *Film* (London), Autumn 1963.

William Wyler

Heston, Charlton, "Working with William Wyler," in *Action* (Los Angeles), January/February 1967.

Hanson, Curtis, "William Wyler," in *Cinema* (Beverly Hills), Summer 1967.

Carey, Gary, "The Lady and the Director: Bette Davis and William Wyler," in *Film Comment* (New York), Fall 1970.

Doeckel, Ken, "William Wyler," in *Films in Review* (New York), October 1971.

Higham, Charles, "William Wyler," in *Action* (Los Angeles), September/October 1973.

Phillips, Gene, "William Wyler," in *Focus on Film* (London), Spring 1976.

Heston, Charlton, "The *Ben-Hur* Journal," in *American Film* (Washington, D.C.), April 1976.

Swindell, Larry, "A Life in Film," in *American Film* (Washington, D.C.), April 1976.

Renaud, T., "William Wyler: 'L'Homme qui ne fit pas jamais un mauvais film,'" in *Cinéma* (Paris), September 1981.

On WYLER: film—

Directed by William Wyler (Slesin), 1986.

* * *

William Wyler's career is an excellent argument for nepotism. Wyler went to work for "Uncle" Carl Laemmle, the head of Universal, and learned the movie business as assistant director and then director of programmers, mainly westerns. One of his first important features, *A House Divided,* demonstrates many of the qualities that mark his films through the next decades. A transparent imitation of Eugene O'Neill's *Desire under the Elms,* it contains evidence of the staging strategies that identify Wyler's distinctive mise-en-scène. The film's premise holds particular appeal for a director who sees drama in claustrophobic interiors, the actors held in expressive tension by their shifting spatial relationships to each other, the decor, and the camera. In *A House Divided* Wyler extracts that tension from the dynamics implicit in the film's principal set: the downstairs room that confines the crippled father (Walter Huston) and the stairs leading to the landing between the rooms of the son (Kent Douglass) and the young stepmother (Helen Chandler). The stairway configuration is favored by Wyler for the opportunity it gives him to stack the agents of the drama and to fill the frame both vertically and in depth. When he later collaborates with cinematographer Gregg Toland, the potential of that depth and height is enhanced through the use of varying degrees of hard and soft focus. (Many critics, who are certainly unfamiliar with Wyler's early work, have unjustly credited Toland for the depth of staging that characterizes the partnership.)

The implications of focus in Wyler's stylistics go far beyond lighting procedures, lenses, or even staging itself. Focus directs the viewer's attention to varieties of information within the field, whatever its shape or extent. Focus gives simultaneous access to discordant planes, characters, and objects that challenge us to achieve a full, fluctuating reading of phenomena. André Bazin, in his important essay on Wyler in the French edition of *What Is Cinema?,* speaks of the director's "democratic" vision, his way of taking in the wholeness of a field in the unbroken time and space of the "*plan-séquence,*" a shot whose duration and complexity of staging goes far beyond the measure of the conventional shot. Bazin opposes this to the analytic montage of Soviet editing. In doing so he perhaps underestimates the kind of control that Wyler's deep field staging exerts upon the viewer, but he does suggest the richness of the visual text in Wyler's major films.

Counselor At Law is a significant test of Wyler's staging. The Broadway origins of the property are not disguised in the film; instead, they are made into a virtue. The movement through the law firm's outer office, reception room, and private spaces reflects a fluidity that is a function of the camera's mobility and a challenge to the fixed frame of the proscenium. Wyler's *tour de force* rivals that of the film's star, John Barrymore. Director and actor animate the attorney's personal and professional activities in a hectic, ongoing present, sweeping freely through the sharply delineated (and therefore sharply perceived) vectors of the cinematic/theatrical space.

Wyler's meticulousness and Samuel Goldwyn's insistence on quality productions resulted in the series of films, often adaptations of prestigious plays, that most fully represent the director's method. In *Dodsworth,* the erosion of a marriage is captured in the opening of the bedroom door that separates husband and wife; the staircase of *These Three* delimits the public and private spaces of a film about rumor and intimacy; the elaborate street set of *Dead End* is examined from a dizzying variety of camera angles that create a geometry of urban life; the intensity of *The Little Foxes* is sustained through the focal distances that chart the shape of family ties and hatreds.

After the war, the partnership of Wyler and Toland is crowned by *The Best Years of Our Lives,* a film whose subject (the situation of returning servicemen) is particularly pertinent, and whose structure and staging are the most personal in the director's canon.

In his tireless search for the perfect shot, Wyler was known as the scourge of performers, pushing them through countless retakes and repetitions of the same gesture. Since performance in his films is *not* pieced together in the editing room but is developed in complex blockings and shots of long duration, Wyler required a high degree of concentration on the part of the actors. Laurence Olivier, who was disdainful of the medium prior to his work in *Wuthering Heights,* credits Wyler for having revealed to him the possibilities of the movies. But it is Bette Davis who defines the place of the star actor in a Wyler film. The three projects she did with Wyler demonstrate how her particular energies both organize the highly controlled mise-en-scène and are contained within it. For *Jezebel* she won her second Academy Award. In *The Letter,* an exercise in directorial tyranny over the placement of seemingly every element in its highly charged frames, the viewer senses a total correspondence between the focus exercised by director and performer.

During the last decades of Wyler's career, many of the director's gifts, which flourished in contexts of extreme dramatic tension and the exigencies of studio shooting, were dissipated in excessively grandiose properties and "locations." There were, however, exceptions. Wyler's presence is strongly felt in the narrow staircase of *The Heiress* and the dingy station house of *Detective Story.* He even manages to make the final shootout of *The Big Country* adhere to the narrowest of gulches, thereby reducing the dimensions of the title to his familiar focal points. But the epic scope of *Ben Hur* and the ego of Barbra Streisand (in *Funny Girl*) escape the compact economies of the director's boxed-in stackings and plane juxtapositions. Only in *The Collector,* a film that seems to define enclosure (a woman is kept prisoner in a cellar for most of its duration) does Wyler find a congenial property. In it he proves again that the real expanse of cinema is measured by its frames.

—Charles Affron

XIAOXIAN, Hou *See* **HOU Hsiao-Hsien**

XIE Jin

Nationality: Chinese. **Born:** Shaoxing (province of Zhejiang), China, 1923. **Education:** Studied at School of Dramatic Art, Jiang'an, 1946-48; graduated from Political Institute of the People's Revolutionary University, 1953. **Career:** Assistant to directors Wu Renzhi, 1948, and Zheng Xiaoqui, 1949, Datong Film Studio, Shanghai; directed first film, *A Crisis*, 1954; criticized during Cultural Revolution and forced to do manual labor in the countryside, 1966, rehabilitated, c. 1978; vice-chairman of Disabled Persons' Federation, from 1988; member of standing committee, Association for the Promotion of the Peaceful Reunification of China, from 1988; executive vice-chairman of Federation of Literary and Art Circles, from 1988. **Awards:** Veteran Artist Award, First Chinese Film Festival, 1989; five-time winner of Best Film Award, Hundred Flowers Awards Competition. **Address:** c/o Shanghai Film Studio, 595 Caoxi Beilu, Shanghai, People's Republic of China.

Films as Director:

1954 *A Crisis*; *A Wave of Unrest*; *Rendezvous at Orchard Bridge*
1955 *Spring in the Land of Waters*
1957 *Woman Basketball Player Number Five*
1958 episodes of *Small Leaders of the "Big Leap"* and *Small Stories of a Big Storm*; *Huang Baomei*
1960 *The Women's Red Army Detachment*
1962 *Big Li, Young Li, and Old Li*
1964 ***Wutai Jiemei*** (*Two Stage Sisters*)
1972 *The Door*
1975 *Chunmiao*
1976 *The Bay of Rocks*
1977 *Youth*
1980 *Ah, Cradle*
1981 *The Legend of Tianyun Mountain*
1982 *The Herdsman*
1983 *Qiu Jin* (+ sc)
1984 *Garlands at the Foot of the Mountain*
1986 *Fu-Zung Cen*
1987 *Hibiscus Town*
1989 *The Last Aristocrats*

Other Films:

1948 *The Silent Wife* (Wu Renzhi) (asst d)
1949 *The Martyr of the Garden of the Pear Trees* (Zheng Xiaoqiu) (asst d)
1953 *The Feather Letter* (Shi Hui) (asst d)

Publications

On XIE JIN: books—

Leyda, Jay, *Dianying: An Account of Films and the Film Audience in China*, Cambridge, Massachusetts, 1972.
Lösel, Jörg, *Die Politische Funktion des Spielfilms in der Volksrepublic China Zwischen 1949 and 1965*, Munich, 1980.
Rayns, Tony, and Scott Meek, *Electric Shadows: 45 Years of Chinese Cinema*, London, 1980.
Bergeron, Regis, *Le Cinéma chinois 1949-1983*, 3 vols., Paris, 1983-84.
Jenkins, Alan, and Cathy Grant, *A Teaching Guide to the Films of the People's Republic of China*, Oxford, 1984.
Berry, Chris, editor, *Perspectives on Chinese Cinema*, New York, 1985; revised edition, 1991.
Quiquemelle, Marie-Claire, and Jean-Loup Passek, editors, *Le Cinéma chinois*, Paris, 1985.
Armes, Roy, *Third World Filmmaking and the West*, Berkeley, 1987.
Clark, Paul, *Chinese Cinema: Culture and Politics since 1949*, Cambridge, 1987.
Semsel, George Stephen, editor, *Chinese Film: The State of the Art in the People's Republic*, New York, 1987.

On XIE JIN: articles—

Jin Xie Section of *Positif* (Paris), March 1985.
Manceau, J. L., "Portrait de Xie Jin dans le panorama chinois," in *Cinéma* (Paris), 5 March 1986.
Rayns, Tony, "Let a hundred flowers...," in *Monthly Film Bulletin* (London), July 1988.
Kaplan, E. A., "Melodrama/Subjectivity/Ideology: Western Melodrama Theories and Their Relevance to Recent Chinese Cinema," in *East-West Film Journal* (Honolulu, Hawaii), vol. 5, no. 1, 1991.
Luo, J., "One with People: Xie Jin," in *China Screen* (Beijing), no. 1, 1992.
"Xie Jin's Films: A Retrospective," in *China Screen* (Beijing), no. 1, 1992.

* * *

Because of the length of his career, his ability to dramatize popular political sentiments, and his commitment to the melodrama as a vehicle for the expression of his aesthetic vision, Chinese filmmaker Xie Jin has been compared to Douglas Sirk and Frank Capra. Since his career spans over four decades, with contributions to every stage of the development of filmmaking from the earliest days of the post-Revolutionary period, Xie Jin must be counted as one of the most significant filmmaking veterans still making features today in the People's Republic of China. He has not become a mere "fossil" tolerated by an industry grateful for his contributions in the 1950s and early 1960s. Rather, Xie continues to be controversial and exceptionally popular with Chinese audiences both inside and outside of China.

Trained in the theatre, Xie came to the Shanghai studios in the early 1950s and was soon promoted from assistant to full director. His

Xie Jin: poster for *Wutai Jiemei*

name rather rapidly became associated with the political melodramas he is still known for today. His 1957 film *Woman Basketball Player Number Five,* for example, helped to establish his reputation as a "woman's director." Unlike the maligned "woman's film" genre in Hollywood, melodramas featuring strong female leads became the favored vehicle for the dramatic examination of the role the Revolution was playing in reshaping both men's and women's lifestyles and attitudes toward gender in the People's Republic. Blending Soviet socialist realism with the aesthetic directives of Mao and the popularity of classical Hollywood tear-jerkers, Xie was creating a peculiarly Chinese political aesthetic. This aesthetic can still be appreciated today for the ways in which it stretched beyond the modes of representation usually reserved for women at that time in both Asian and Western film cultures.

Before the onset of the Cultural Revolution in the mid-1960s, Xie Jin perfected his revolutionary woman's films in *The Women's Red Army Detachment* and *Two Stage Sisters.* Although *The Women's Red Army Detachment* won the first One Hundred Flowers Award (the PRC equivalent of the Oscar still coveted today), *Two Stage Sisters* was doomed by a storm of criticism unleased by the Cultural Revolution. *Two Stage Sisters* features the story of the relationship between two Shaoxing opera performers from their beginnings as itinerant entertainers in the feudal countryside of 1930s China through success in Shanghai during the Japanese occupation, eventual separation, and reunion during the post-Revolutionary period. Changes in the style of the operas presented in the film (for example, folk opera, Western-influenced critical realist operas, Mao's favored "revolutionary romanticism" in opera form) also parallel broader social and political changes. Although probably the pinnacle of his career and the most complete flowering of his political aesthetic, *Two Stage Sisters* was only fully appreciated after the Cultural Revolution ended.

During the Cultural Revolution, Xie suffered much the same fate as most of his generation. At times under house arrest, he was still enlisted to help direct Jiang Qing's "model opera" films during that period. These films, in fact, are aesthetically and politically at odds with his earlier work.

After the Cultural Revolution, Xie Jin went back to making political melodramas featuring female protagonists. *The Legend of Tianyun Mountain,* in fact, was one of the first films made after the Cultural Revolution to condemn not only its political excesses but also the strains the Anti-Rightist Campaign of the 1950s had placed on Chinese society. He has continued in this socially critical vein with *The Herdsman* and *Hibiscus Town* (both dealing with the Cultural Revolution), while also making patriotic dramas like *Qiu Jin* (based on the life of the well-known Qing Dynasty female revolutionist) and *Garlands at the Foot of the Mountain* (on the recent Sino-Vietnamese war). Xie's *The Last Aristocrats* deals with the lives of four young Chinese women living abroad and was partially shot in the United States.

Ironically, even though Xie Jin has devoted virtually his entire life's work to films about politically active, modern Chinese heroines, he is most often criticized today for his supposed "feudal" depiction of women as "good" wives and mothers. He has also been condemned for his "old-fashioned" style of filmmaking. However, while some younger filmmakers tend to disregard audience tastes, hoping for an art house following in Europe and the United States, Xie Jin, despite his critics, has continued to please Chinese audiences.

In the 1990s, Xie continued to work in the Shanghai film industry, increasingly as a producer rather than director. His influence can be felt as an often unacknowledged, but clearly present indebtedness many younger filmmakers have to his seminal contributions to Chinese film culture. It is difficult, for example, to look at Chen Kaige's critically celebrated *Farewell My Concubine* without seeing *Two Stage Sisters* remade as "Two Stage Brothers," with the same epic sweep and use of Chinese opera to stand as a metaphor for the history of China in the twentieth century. Huang Shuqin's *Woman Demon Human* also covers similar ground, using an opera actress's life on and off the stage as an allegory for China in the post-war era. Although some critics have remarked on the number of recent Chinese films with male-centered narratives, the female-centered melodramas that Xie championed continue to be an important staple of the rapidly changing film culture of the People's Republic.

—Gina Marchetti

YANG, Edward

Nationality: Chinese. **Born:** Yang Dechang, Shanghai, China, 1947; moved to Taiwan with family, 1949. **Education:** Graduated with a degree in engineering, 1969; earned master's degree in computer science, University of Florida, 1972. **Career:** Returned to Taiwan, 1981; worked in television before making his directorial debut, 1982.

Films as Director:

1982 "Expectations" episode in the omnibus film *In Our Time*
1983 *That Day, on the Beach*
1985 *Taipei Story*
1986 *The Terrorizer*
1991 ***Guling Jie Shaonian Sha Ren Shijian*** (*A Brighter Summer Day*)
1994 *A Confucian Confusion*

Publications

On YANG: books—

Berry, Chris, editor, *Perspectives on Chinese Cinema,* London, 1991.
Jameson, Fredric, *The Geopolitical Aesthetic: Cinema and Space in the World System,* Bloomington, Indiana, 1992.
Browne, Nick, Paul G. Pickowicz, Vivian Sobchack, and Esther Yau, editors, *New Chinese Cinemas: Forms, Identities, Politics,* Boston, 1994.

On YANG: articles—

Rayns, Tony, "The Position of Women in New Chinese Cinema," in *East-West Film Journal* (Honolulu, Hawaii), June 1987.
Nornes, Markus, "*The Terrorizer,*" in *Film Quarterly* (Berkeley), Spring 1989.

* * *

Along with Hou Hsiao-hsien and Wan Jen, Edward Yang stands as one of the most recognized of Taiwan's "New Wave" directors. Part of a torrent of talent that flooded international screens with innovative Chinese-language features from Hong Kong, Taiwan, and the People's Republic of China in the 1980s, Yang's work is New Wave in a number of different meanings of that term. Yang's films resemble European New Wave directors' work because of his commitment to formal experimentation within fiction narratives. This is coupled with an interest in the use of film as social commentary and cultural critique. The films Yang directed in the 1980s, in particular, have been favorably compared to the work of Antonio Antonioni because of

Edward Yang: ***Guling Jie Shaonian Sha Ren Shijian***

their "high modernist" exploration of the barren, urban landscape, and the alienation of the individual in contemporary, bourgeois society, as well as their focus on psychologically complex, female protagonists to investigate these themes dramatically.

Also, as was the case with the French New Wave, the Taiwanese New Wave (and, more recently, contemporary Chinese-language cinema generally) benefitted from very fruitful collaborations among a coterie of talented directors, scriptwriters, producers, and actors/actresses. Perhaps the most striking collaboration in Yang's oeuvre, for example, occurred when the noted director Hou Hsiao-hsien took the lead role in *Taipei Story.* Hou's portrayal of Lon, a failed businessman, obsessive baseball fan, and perpetual fiance of the film's female protagonist, embodies many of the uncertainties and contradictions of contemporary Taiwanese society: a nostalgia for a past shaped by Japan and America, an ambivalence toward traditional gender and family roles, and an alienation from the political and economic vicissitudes of urban Taipei. Certainly, film director Hou's reputation for films about rural youth and changes in traditional Chinese culture and society in the postwar, post-Japanese era brings a resonance to the character of Lon that other actors could not hope to convey.

Like members of the European New Wave of the 1960s, Yang has a love/hate relationship with American culture, using it for complex intertextual textures (for example, the use of Elvis Presley as a musical and visual presence in *A Brighter Summer Day*), and aesthetically working against Hollywood through the use of "dead," "negative" space in which "nothing happens" in empty urban landscapes and aggressively long takes. However, despite these similarities, Yang is also a decidedly Taiwanese director, with a commitment to documenting the peculiarities of contemporary Taiwan and situating its society within a global economy and culture. In this respect, Yang's cinema operates as a bridge between Taiwan and the rest of the world. Because of the director's commitment to formal experimentation and interest in finding a niche within a global film culture of festivals and art cinemas, many of his films have done poorly domestically, although they have been lauded internationally. Ironically, as he brings a critical eye to contemporary Taiwan for audiences abroad, that sharp vision has often gone unappreciated at home. Yang's attempt to visualize alienation succeeds all too well and tends to alienate the uninitiated viewer, while winning the praise of intellectuals educated to appreciate a modernist sensibility. Although Yang now has his own production company, several of his earlier, more challenging films were financed by the government-operated Central Motion Picture Corporation, allowing for a freedom of experimentation without the pressing demands of the domestic marketplace.

In most of Yang's oeuvre, women embody the key tensions of modern Taiwan. *That Day, on the Beach* uses an elaborate narrative structure composed of a frustrated, inconclusive murder investigation and a series of flashbacks to paint a portrait of Lin Chia-li, a woman who escaped the pressures of a traditional, patriarchal household only to find herself again trapped by an empty marriage. Although a corpse that may or may not be her husband prompts her interior investigation, the real substance of the film goes beyond a simple critique of

Chinese patriarchy. It looks at contemporary Taiwan, its own uncertain national identity, precarious place in the global economy, and divided political culture through the life of a woman who is both the victim and beneficiary of these monumental social changes.

Taipei Story continues in the same vein. Chin, an unemployed mid-level administrator who has moved into her own apartment against the wishes of her traditional father, must decide whether to marry her fiance, Lon, or move on with her upwardly mobile, female boss, leaving the "old" Taiwan of Lon and her family behind. The final scene, in which Chin is framed against the massive picture window of her boss's new headquarters in an eerily empty office building—a signifier of modernity—as Lon lies bleeding to death in another part of the city, again dramatically portrays the emergence of a new Taiwan in the character of a woman freed by the death of her more traditional lover.

This same theme has an even more bloody enactment in *The Terrorizer.* Chou Yufen, a writer married to a doctor, Li Li-chung, is cured of her writer's block by the anonymous phone calls of a young Eurasian girl, bored during her recovery from a wound sustained during a youth gang street battle, who tells her that her husband is having an affair. Armed with this lie, Chou Yufen writes a story about her plight and leaves her husband. Passed over at the hospital and misunderstood by his estranged wife, Li Li-chung commits suicide (perhaps after killing his new boss and his wife's lover). In New Wave fashion, the details of his death (or even the fact of his death) remain indeterminate. However, as in Yang's earlier films, as the central, male character fades away, the female characters emerge. However, Lin Chia-li, Chin, Chou Yufen, and even the marginal "White Chick," as the Eurasian girl is called, represent a new world tainted by a vacuous modernity, stripped of affect, and literally deadening.

In his work on *The Terrorizer,* Fredric Jameson sees the film as combining a modernist and postmodernist sensibility to explore the interpenetration of traditional, national, multinational, and transnational spaces, and thus the hybrid identity that marks contemporary Taipei. It is debatable whether this film marks a significant break with Yang's earlier, "modernist" work or not. However, it is useful to look at Yang's more recent *A Brighter Summer Day* and *A Confucian Confusion* as moving in a different direction from the director's work in the 1980s. Keeping Yang's characteristically complex and convoluted narrative structure, the former explores youth gangs in postwar Taiwan and the later looks at contemporary "yuppies" in modern Taipei. Unlike his earlier efforts, *A Confucian Confusion* is a comedy (albeit a very dark one). Despite the move away from the serious, woman-centered dramas of the 1980s, however, Yang maintains his commitment to examining carefully Taiwan's experience of modernity, taking Taipei from the margins of the globe and putting it within an international framework that makes local issues poignant for a world audience.

—Gina Marchetti

YOSHIMURA, Kozabura

Nationality: Japanese. **Born:** Shiga Prefecture, 9 September 1911; also known as Kimisaburo Yoshimura. **Education:** Nihon High School, Tokyo, graduated 1929. **Family:** Married Tomoko Oouchi, 1940. **Career:** Assistant director to Yasujiro Shimazu at Shochiku-Kamata Studio, 1929; drafted into military, 1932; after return from service, directed first film, *Sneaking,* 1934; assistant director to Shimazu, Heinosuke Gosho, Dhiro Toyota, and Mikio Naruse, 1934-39; moved to newly established Shochiku-Ofuna studios, 1936; resumed directing, 1939; served in machine gun unit, then as information officer on general staff, 1944; repatriated, spent year in prison and repatriation camp, 1945; began collaboration with scriptwriter Kaneto Shindo, 1947; founded independent production company Kindai Eiga Kyokai (Society of Modern Film), with Shindo, producer Hisao Itoya, director Tengo Yamada, and actor Taiji Tonoyama, 1950; contracted by Daiei Studio, 1956; TV director, 1960. **Awards:** Eiga Seikai-sha New Director's Prize, for *Danryo,* 1939; Kinema Jumpo Number One Film, for *Anjo-ke no bukokai,* 1947; Mainichi Director's Prize, for *Itsureru seiso,* 1951; Shiju-Hosho Decoration, Japanese Government, 1976. **Address:** 4-3-37 Zushi, Zushi City, Kanagawa, Japan.

Films as Directors:

1934 *Nukiashi sashiashi* (*Sneaking*)

1939 *Onna koso ie o momore* (*Women Defend the Home!*; *Women Should Stay at Home*); *Yokina uramachi* (*Cheerful Alley*; *Gay Back Alley*); *Asu no odoriko* (*Dancers of Tomorrow*); *Gonin no kyodai* (*Five Brothers and Sisters*); *Danryu* (*Warm Current*)

1940 *Nishizumi sanshacho den* (*The Story of Tank Commander Nishizumi*)

1941 *Hana* (*Flower*)

1942 *Kancho mada shinazu* (*The Spy Has Not Yet Died*) (+ story); *Minami ni kaze* (*South Wind*); *Zoko minami no kaze* (*South Wind: Sequel*)

1943 *Laisen no zenya* (*The Night before the War Begins*); *Tekki kushu* (*Enemy Air Attack*)

1944 *Kessen* (*A Decisive Battle*)

1947 *Zo o kutta renchu* (*The Fellows Who Ate the Elephant*); *Anjo-ke no butokai* (*The Ball of the Anjo Family*)

1948 *Yuwaku* (*Temptation*; *Seduction*); *Waga shogai no kagayakeru hi* (*The Bright Day of My Life*)

1949 *Shitto* (*Jealousy*); *Mori no Ishimatsu* (*Ishimatsu of the Forest*; *Ishimatsu of Mori*); *Mahiru no enbukyoku* (*Waltz at Noon*)

1950 *Shunsetsu* (*Spring Snow*); *Senka no hate* (*The Height of Battle*; *The End of Battle Fire*)

1951 *Itsuwareru seiso* (*Deceiving Costume*); *Jiyu gakko* (*Free School*); *Genji monogatari* (*A Tale of Genji*)

1952 *Nishijin no shimai* (*Sisters of Nishijin*); *Boryoku* (*Violence*)

1953 *Senba-zuru* (*A Thousand Cranes*); *Yokubo* (*Desire*); *Yoake mae* (*Before the Dawn*)

1954 *Ashizuri misaki* (*Cape Ashizuri*); *Wakai hitotachi* (*Young People*)

1955 "Hanauri musume" (The Flower Girl, The Girl Who Sells Flowers) episode of *Aisureba koso* (*If You Love Me*; *Because I Love*); *Ginza no onna* (*Women of the Ginza*); *Bijo to kairyu* (*The Beauty and the Dragon*)

1956 *Totsugu hi* (*Day of Marriage*; *The Day to Wed*); *Yoru no kawa* (*Night River*; *Undercurrent*); *Yonjuhassai no teiko* (*48-Year-Old Rebel*; *Protest at 48 Years Old*)

1957 *Osaka monogatari* (*An Osaka Story*); *Yoru no cho* (*Night Butterfly*); *Chijo* (*On the Earth*)

1958 *Hitotsubu no mugi* (*One Grain of Barley*); *Yoru no sugao* (*The Naked Face of Night*)

1959 *Denwa wa yugata ni naru* (*Telephone Rings in the Evening*); *Kizoku no kaidan* (*Aristocrat's Stairs*)

1960 "Koi o wasureta onna" (A Woman's Testament, The Woman Who Forgot Love) episode of *Jokei* (*Women's Scroll*); *Onna no saka* (*Woman's Descent*)

1961 *Konki* (*Marriage Time*); *Onna no kunsho* (*Woman's Decoration*)

1962 *Kazoku no jijo* (*A Night to Remember*; *Family's Situation*); *Sono yo wa wasurenai* (*I Won't Forget That Night*)

1963 "Shayo nigo" (Company's Business) episode of *Echizen take ningyo* (*Bamboo Doll of Echizen*)

1966 *Kokoro no sanmyaku* (*The Heart of the Mountains*)

1967 *Daraku suru onna* (*A Fallen Woman*)
1968 *Nemureru bijo* (*Sleeping Beauty*; *The House of the Sleeping Virgins*); *Atsui yoru* (*A Hot Night*)
1971 *Amai himitsu* (*Sweet Secret*)
1973 *Konketsuji Rika* (*Rika, the Mixed-Blood Girl*); *Hamagure no komoriuta* (*Lullaby of Hamagure*)
1974 *Ranru no hata* (*Ragged Flag*)

Publications

By YOSHIMURA: book—

Eiga no gijutsu to mikata [Film Technique and How to Look at Films], 1952.

On YOSHIMURA: books—

Mellen, Joan, *Voices from the Japanese Cinema,* New York, 1975.
Mellen, Joan, *The Waves at Genji's Door,* New York, 1976.
Anderson, Joseph, and Donald Richie, *The Japanese Film,* expanded edition, Princeton, 1982.

* * *

Although Kozaburo Yoshimura's early work followed the drama and comedy conventions of the Shochiku Studio productions of the 1930s, he gradually proved himself an ambitious artist who broke away from these conventions through his varied selections of themes and subjects, and his bold exploration of styles. His technical maturity has been consistent over the years and through all genres, from the melodramatic *Warm Current,* which first brought Yoshimura recognition, through the wartime production *The Story of Tank Commander Nishizumi,* which successfully portrayed the decent, human side of the war hero with exciting action scenes, to the patriotic spy film *The Night before the War Begins,* which stylistically resembles an American suspense film.

The postwar liberation allowed him to employ more freely his favorite American film styles and techniques. Typical of this period is *The Ball of the Anjo Family,* which surprised the Japanese postwar audience not only with its fresh techniques, but also with its striking theme of the contrasts between the falling and emerging social classes of the time.

The challenges of the varied subjects of Yoshimura's subsequent films confirmed his energy and versatility, as in *The Bright Day of My Life,* which illustrated a flamingly passionate love unusual to Japanese films, between a couple who had belonged to opposing political groups before the war. *Ishimatsu of Mori* is regarded as one of the first successful postwar period films. From the familiar legend, Yoshimura made a satirical comedy which alludes critically to the contemporary gangster's mentality. *Deceiving Costume,* a postwar adaption of Mizogushi's prewar masterpiece *Sisters of the Gion,* demonstrated a similar emotional intensity and powerful social criticism through its story of the life of geisha sisters. *The Beauty and the Dragon* is a new adaptation of a popular Kabuki play, made with the assistance of the innovative theater troupe Zenshin-za.

Scenario writer Kaneto Shindo's collaboration with Yoshimura was indispensable to Yoshimura's success, from *The Ball of the Anjo Family* to *The Day to Wed,* during which time they produced twenty-two films together. When in 1950 Shochiku Studio subjected the pair to commercial pressures, they decided to establish an independent production company, Kindai Eiga Kyokai, or Society of Modern Film. It enabled the two to pursue their artistic experimentation and thus produce many masterpieces which attracted critical attention.

Yoshimura became well known for literary adaptations—*A Tale of Genji, A Thousand Cranes, Before the Dawn, Sleeping Beauty,* and *Cape Ashizuri*—as well as for light comedy—*Free School,* about contemporary social life, *Desire, Young People,* and *One Grain of Barley,* among others. Particularly noteworthy is a series of films on the life of contemporary women using many of Daiei Studio's prime actresses, *Night River, Night Butterfly, Naked Face of Night,* and others. He has continued his independent efforts, notably with *Heart of the Mountains* and *Ragged Flag,* which powerfully depicts the life of a pioneering opponent of pollution in Japan in the early years of this century.

Yoshimura has consistently shown excellent story-developing skill, which has won popular support for his films. His best films often contain social criticism, but at the same time do not preach, relying instead on the depiction of heightened emotions among the characters to successfully appeal to the audience.

—Kyoko Hirano

ZANUSSI, Krzysztof

Nationality: Polish. **Born:** Warsaw, 17 June 1939. **Education:** Educated in physics, Warsaw University, 1955-59; faculty of philosophy, University of Cracow, 1959-62; directing course, State Film school, Lodz, graduated 1966. **Career:** Director, from 1966; appointed to faculty of Lodz film school, and named vice-president of Association of Polish Filmmakers, 1973; chosen by Pope John Paul II to make his film biography, *From a Far Country,* 1980; during suppression of Solidarity movement, directed mainly in Western Europe, 1980s; elected president of FERA (Fédération européenne des réalisateurs de l'audiovisuel), 1990. **Awards:** Venice Festival prizewinner for *The Death of a Provincial,* 1966; Best Film, Polish film critics, for *The Structure of Crystals,* 1970; State Award, Polish Minister of Culture and Arts, 1973; Special Prize, VII Polish Film Festival, 1980; Donatello Prize, for *From a Far Country,* 1980; Special Jury Prize, Venice Film Festival, 1982; State Prize 1st Class, 1984; Vittorio De Sica International Film Award, Sorrento, 1990.

Films as Director:

1958 *Droga do nieba* (*The Way to the Skies*) (amateur film in collaboration with Wincenty Ronisz)
1966 *Smierc prowincjala* (*The Death of a Provincial*) (short, diploma film); *Przemysl*; *Maria Dabrowska*
1967 *Komputery* (*Computers*)
1968 *Twarza w twarz* (*Face to Face*) (+ co-sc) (for TV); *Krzysztof Penderecki* (for TV)
1969 *Zaliczenie* (*An Examination, Pass Mark*) (+ co-sc) (for TV); *Struktura krysztalu* (*The Structure of Crystals*) (+ co-sc)
1970 *Gory o zmierzchu* (*Mountains at Dusk*) (for TV); *Zycie rodzinne* (*Family Life*) (+ sc)
1971 *Rola* (*Die Rolle*) (+ sc) (for West German TV); *Za sciana* (*Behind the Wall*) (+ co-sc) (for TV)
1972 *Hipoteza* (*Hypothesis*) (+ sc) (for TV)
1973 *Illuminacja* (*Illumination*) (+ sc)
1974 *The Catamount Killing*
1975 *Milosierdzie platne z gory* (*Nachtdienst*; *Night Duty*) (for TV); *Bilans kwartalny* (*A Woman's Decision*) (+ sc)
1976 *Barwy ochronne* (*Camouflage*) (+ sc)
1977 *Anatomie stunde* (*Lekcja anatomii*; *Anatomy Lesson*) (for TV); *Haus der Frauen* (*House of Women*); *Penderecki, Lutoslawa*; *Brigitte Horney*
1978 *Spirala* (*Spiral*) (+ sc)
1979 *Wagen in der Nacht* (*Ways in the Night*; *Paths into the Night*) (+ sc)
1980 *Constans* (*The Constant Factor*)
1981 *Kontract* (*The Contract*); *From a Far Country*; *Versuchung* (for TV)
1982 *Uerreichbare* (*Imperative*)
1984 *Blaubart* (*Bluebeard*); *Rok spokojnego slonca* (*The Year of the Quiet Sun*)
1985 *Le Pouvoir du mal* (*The Power of Evil*; *Paradigme*)
1987 *Wherever We Are*
1989 *Stan Posiadania* (*Inventory*) (+ sc)
1990 *Dotkniecie* (*Touch*)
1991 *The Last Dance*; *Wittold Lutoslawski* (doc); *Zycie Za Zycie* (*A Life for a Life*)
1992 *The Silent Touch* (+ co-pr)

Other Films:

1978 *Amator* (*Camera Bluff*) (Kieślowski) (role as himself)
1993 *Kolejnosc uczuc* (*Sequence of Feelings*) (Piwowarski) (pr)
1995 "Steps" (Olszewski) and "Pigs and Pearls" (Nikolic), episodes in *Love & Hate* (co-pr)

Publications

By ZANUSSI: articles—

"The Ethics of Being Krzysztof Zanussi," an interview with S. Murray, in *Cinema Papers* (Melbourne), September/October 1976.
"Opcja przekorna: za świadomościa," an interview with T. Krzemień , in *Kino* (Warsaw), February 1977.
"L'Oeuvre de Zanussi: le refus de la compromission," an interview with René Prédal, in *Jeune Cinéma* (Paris), November 1980.
"The Workings of a Pure Heart," an interview with Jiri Weiss, in *Cineaste* (New York), vol. 11, no. 2, 1981.
Interview with P. Pawlikowski, in *Stills* (London), Winter 1982.
Interview, in *La Revue du Cinema* (Paris), April 1983.
Interview, in *Interview* (New York), December 1984.
"Tightrope," an interview with Marcia Pally, in *Film Comment* (New York), January/February 1986.
Interview, in *Etudes Cinematographiques* (Paris), no. 156/158, 1987.
Interview with T. Sobolewski, in *Kino* (Warsaw), June 1988.
"An International Pole," an interview with Ania Witkowska, in *Film* (London), January 1989.
"Applause for a Donkey," an interview with Z. Pietrasik, in *Performing Arts Journal* (New York), vol. 12, no. 2/3, 1990.

On ZANUSSI: books—

D'Agostino, Paolo, *Krzysztof Zanussi,* Florence, 1980.
Pezzali, Giacomo, *Polonia ultimo ciak: l'avventura del film "Da un paese lontano" di Krzysztof Zanussi,* Milan, 1982.
Paul, David W., editor, *Politics, Art and Commitment in the Eastern European Cinema,* New York, 1983.
Estève, Michel, *Krzysztof Zanussi,* Paris, 1987.

On ZANUSSI: articles—

Hopfinger, M., "Zanussiego ćwiczenia z życia," in *Kino* (Warsaw), January 1973.

Krzysztof Zanussi

from 1946; made only acting appearance in Zampa's *Angelina,* 1947; assistant director to Visconti, for films and theatre, from 1947, working on *La Terra trema, Bellissima, Senso*; opera director, from 1953; directed first film, 1957; made *Jesus of Nazareth* for TV, 1977. **Awards:** Academy Award nomination, Best Director, for *Romeo and Juliet,* 1968.

Films as Director:

1957 *Camping* (+ co-sc)
1965 *La Boheme*
1966 *The Taming of the Shrew* (+ co-sc); *Florence—Days of Destruction* (doc)
1968 *Romeo and Juliet* (+ co-sc)
1972 *Fratelli sole sorella luna* (*Brother Sun, Sister Moon*) (+ co-sc)
1977 *Gesu di Nazareth* (*Jesus of Nazareth*) (for TV) (+ co-sc)
1979 *The Champ*
1981 *Endless Love*
1982 *La Traviata* (+ sc); *La Bohème* (for TV)
1983 *Strasphere* (doc)
1986 *Otello* (*Othello*) (+ sc)
1988 *Il Giovane Toscanini* (*Young Toscanini*))
1990 *Hamlet* (+ co-sc)
1992 *Storia di una Capinera* (*The Story of a Blackcap*) (+ sc)
1993 *Sparrow* (+ sc)

Other Films:

1947 *Angelina* (Zampa) (role)
1948 ***La terra trema*** (Visconti) (asst d)
1951 *Bellissima* (Visconti) (asst d)
1954 *Senso* (Visconti) (asst d)
1995 *Placido Domingo: A Musical Life* (role)

Publications

By ZEFFIRELLI: books—

Zeffirelli: The Autobiography of Franco Zeffirelli, London, 1986.

By ZEFFIRELLI: articles—

"Versatility," an interview with Gordon Gow, in *Films and Filming* (London), April 1973.
Interview with B. J. Demby in *Filmmakers Newsletter* (Ward Hill, Massachusetts), September 1973.
"Knowing, Feeling, Understanding, Then Expression," an interview with A. Stuart, in *Films and Filming* (London), August 1979.
"A Dialogue with Franco Zeffirelli," in *American Cinematographer* (Los Angeles), October 1981.
Interview, in *La Revue du Cinema* (Paris), May 1986.
Interview by Jean-Michel Breque, in *L'avant Scene Cinema* (Paris), May 1987.
"Une aventure esaltante mais risquée," an interview with J. M. Brèque, in *Avant-Scène du Cinéma* (Paris), July/August 1988.
Interview with Steve Grant, in *Time Out* (London), 17 April 1991.
"Breaking the Classical Barrier: Franco Zeffirelli Interviewed by John Tibbets," in *Literature-Film Quarterly* (Salisbury, Maryland), April 1994.
"A Beachhead of Anti-politics," an interview with Nathan Gardels, in *Los Angeles Times*, 6 April 1994.
"Anti-politics of the Image," an interview with Nathan Gardels, in *New Perspectives Quarterly* (Los Angeles), Summer 1994.

On ZEFFIRELLI: articles—

Lane, John, "*The Taming of the Shrew,*" in *Films and Filming* (London), October 1966.
Chase, D., "*The Champ*: Round Two," in *American Film* (Washington, D.C.), July/August 1978.
Pursell, M., "Artifice and Authenticity in Zeffirelli's *Romeo and Juliet,*" in *Literature/Film Quarterly* (Salisbury, Maryland), October 1986.
Stivers, Cyndi, "Hamlet Revisited," *Premiere,* February 1991.
"Alas, Poor Mel," in *The Economist* (London), 27 April 1991.
Van Watson, William, "Shakespeare, Zeffirelli, and the Homosexual Gaze," in *Literature-Film Quarterly* (Salisbury, Maryland), October 1992.

* * *

Franco Zeffirelli imbues his theater, opera, and film productions with a dazzling array of baroque imagery, visual pyrotechnics, sumptuous sets and costumes, and overt eroticism. Of his major motion pictures, nearly all are adaptations of classical derivation set in another era. To many viewers, his films are hollow, banal, and superfluous romantic exercises, but Zeffirelli defends his love of the past and tradition by saying: "We have no guarantee for the present or the future. Therefore the only choice is to go back to the past and respect traditions. I have been a pioneer in this line of thinking, and the results have proven me right.... The reason I am box-office everywhere is that I am an enlightened conservative continuing the discourse of our grandfathers and fathers, renovating texts but never betraying them."

After studying architecture at the University of Florence, Zeffirelli took up acting. Luchino Visconti saw him in a production of Jean Cocteau's *Les Parents terribles* and hired him to act in stage productions of two works—*Eurydice,* by Jean Anouilh, and *Crime and Punishment,* by Dostoevsky. Zeffirelli also involved himself in designing sets and costumes for Visconti's stage presentations, and appeared in the film *L'onorevole Angelina,* directed by Luigi Zampa and starring Anna Magnani. As a result of that film, he was offered a seven-year acting contract at RKO-Radio by screenwriter Helen Deutsch. Zeffirelli turned the offer down, however, to become Visconti's assistant on three films—*La terra trema, Bellissima,* and *Senso.*

Zeffirelli's natural talent in the realms of set and costume design and his love of opera provided an obvious segue into staging opera productions. These productions gained a reputation for opulence and for the focusing of attention on the lead female singers. Zeffirelli, who says he "adores fun, fantasy, and women," emphasized these elements in his operas. His most famous and successful association in opera was with the volatile Maria Callas, for whom he staged productions of *La Traviata, Lucia de Lammermoor, Norma,* and *Tosca.*

His lengthy apprenticeship in the various theatrical arts earned Zeffirelli a reputation as a Renaissance man of sorts. He turned to feature film directing in 1967, bringing his romanticized traditionalism to *The Taming of the Shrew,* which starred Elizabeth Taylor and Richard Burton. While unarguably a bowdlerization of Shakespeare, its slapstick and boisterous merriment was engaging.

Romeo and Juliet was another matter entirely. Here the very heart of Shakespeare was replaced with Romeo and Juliet as flower children. It was an unabashed combination of theatricality, nude love scenes, and a Mercutio which Zeffirelli describes as "a self-portrait of Shakespeare himself as a homosexual." The film was tremendously popular with the young movie-going audience and received Academy Awards for cinematography and costume design.

Fratello sole sorella lune (Brother Sun, Sister Moon) was also aimed at the young, this time the "Jesus freaks," members of a fundamentalist religious group, but this outrageous portrait of St. Francis of Assisi was a complete flop.

Boleslaw, M., "The Cinema of Krzysztof Zanussi," in *Film Quarterly* (Berkeley), Spring 1973.

"Krzysztof Zanussi," in *International Film Guide 1976,* London, 1975.

"Director of the Year," *International Film Guide* (London, New York), 1976.

Tassone, A., and others, special Zanussi section of *Positif* (Paris), December 1979.

Martin, Marcel, and others, "Les Constantes de Krzysztof Zanussi," special section of *Image et Son* (Paris), September 1980.

Cowie, Peter, "Made in Poland: The Metaphysical Cinema of Krzysztof Zanussi," in *Film Comment* (New York), September/October 1980.

Paul, David, and S. Glover, "The Difficulty of Moral Choice: Zanussi's *Contract* and *The Constant Factor,*" in *Film Quarterly* (Berkeley), Winter 1983/84.

Josephson, E., article in *Chaplin* (Stockholm), vol. 33, no. 1, 1991.

* * *

The cinema of Krzysztof Zanussi explores a continuum of conflict ranging from the individual and interpersonal to the larger social order. He explores the relationship of the individual's conscience to society's norms of morality. Appearing as himself in Krzysztof Kieslowski's *Camera Buff,* Zanussi says that he feels an obligation to question why the corrupt manipulators are the survivors. His is a provocative, cerebral cinema, objectifying its characters through both attention to detail and cool observation of the stages of conflict. During this process Zanussi demands the intellectual participation of his audience, and ultimately its response. The spectator should attain the level of self-awareness that his protagonists reach.

Zanussi has worked chiefly under a system of government subsidy in his native Poland. He has headed one of the three Polish film units. Yet while West German television has produced many of his recent, non-Polish films, they are still subject to Polish government approval. His films have therefore occupied a space between individual self-expression and government tolerance. Prior self-censorship has been a factor in both his message and the discourse which conveys it. No clear separation exists between the private world of Zanussi the artist-intellectual and the public realm in which he operates.

Three major types of conflicts permeate the films. The first is between determinism and free will (often clouded by chance). He elaborates this as the bridgeable gap between empiricism (rational analysis) and Catholicism (grace) in, for example, *Illumination, The Constant Factor,* and *Imperative.* Zanussi's background in physics and philosophy strongly influences these films. Conflict between the individual and the corruption of (contemporary Polish) society is explored in *Camouflage, The Constant Factor,* and *Contract.* Zanussi masks the conflict in *Ways in the Night,* which presents the dilemma of an intelligent, sensitive young German officer who must uphold the policies of the National Socialists. The third major opposition is between the individual's self-awareness and the invisible (yet pervasive) pressures of the immediate social milieu; this is presented most strongly in *Spiral* and *The Contract.*

From a Far Country, Zanussi's biography of the Polish Pope John Paul II, is an important key to understanding Zanussi's world view. In this film, no separation exists between the actions of the individual and the larger network of social forces in which he moves. The dichotomy of free will and determinism underlies the entire project.

Although Zanussi sets his films in a precise historical context, he does explore some of the issues that have been universally debated by artists and intellectuals for many centuries. What distinguishes him as a filmmaker is his particular deployment of the technology of the cinema as a vehicle for his thematic concerns. His orchestration is meticulous. *Spiral* exemplifies the plight of the solitary individual living disharmoniously with himself and those around him. Zanussi follows the tortured protagonist with a jerky handheld camera through the maze of rooms and characters in a ski resort. In *Family Life* : individual in conflict with his family must resolve his dilemma, whi will otherwise haunt him in his interaction with the larger social ord The director introduces the protagonist through a carefully plot series of zooms, pans, and tilts, contextualizing the different sphe of conflict. In *Contract* Zanussi adds both an aural and a visual dim sion to the conflict between a son and his family. The handheld c era follows his attempt to burn down the family home. Zanussi ir cuts this obsessive behavior with the repetitive sound of bells fr sleigh which carries his family. At the end of *The Constant Fact* stone falls in slow motion from where the protagonist, who has f from occupational grace because of his incorruptibility, is cle windows. It strikes a child playing below; chance plays a han universe beyond the individual's control. Zanussi then cuts majestic, desolate mountains, as if to say there is no rational m for solving the existential dilemma.

In all of Zanussi's films these moments of cinematic sel sciousness alternate with long takes of intellectual debate an tioning. During these probing conversations Zanussi is least ob in the application of cinematic techniques. The irony, how that the ideological imprint of the director is most overt in th tion of these verbal conflicts.

Zanussi's latter films continue to examine human emotions difficulties of human relations as they exist within the co historical events and cultural and political differences. *Inven* subtle, reflective allegory whose characters mirror the do Communism and the resulting political upheaval in Eastern Zanussi tells the story of two women: Julia, an ex-governme who had rebelled against an oppressive system and whose been crushed; and an older woman, a devout Catholic who had played a key role in the resistance against Communist The faith of the latter is tested when her idealistic son fal with Julia.

Other Zanussi films deal with the issues of sacrifice and s they specifically relate to World War II. *The Year of the Q* a poignant drama set immediately after the end of the war abandoned by the Germans and in the process of being r Poland. While one small town begins to be revived, an soldier and Polish refugee fall in love. "This is meant to b gentle emotion," explained the director. "The story I wish love story, whose protagonists don't speak a common lan can understand each other only by gestures, facial expressi ter, and a few isolated words."

A Life for a Life actually is set during the war. In repr escape of a young Silesian from Auschwitz in 1941, the demn ten prisoners to starvation. A Franciscan priest eve fers his life to save that of one of the prisoners, who has Finally, *The Silent Touch* features Max von Sydow as a cla poser who survived the Holocaust. Now in retirement, he to drink in his solitude. The scenario charts how he is in into creativity upon the arrival of a young music student his "guardian angel."

—Howard Feinstein, updated by R

ZEFFIRELLI, Franco

Nationality: Italian. **Born:** Gianfranco Corsi in Florence ary 1923. **Education:** Studied architecture at University and at Accademia di Belle Arti, Florence. **Family:** O daughter. **Career:** Theatre director, from 1945; designe

Franco Zeffirelli

Zeffirelli's 1978 Easter television presentation, *Jesus of Nazareth,* employed a star-studded cast and surprised many serious critics with its sensitivity and restraint. This was not the case, however, with his syrupy diminishing of *The Champ,* a sentimental classic which should never have been updated.

Zeffirelli disavows the explicitly erotic *Endless Love,* a vehicle for Brooke Shields, which, he says, was a beautiful story of the tragedy of two families in its original three-hour-version. He labeled the truncated version "trash" and vowed to stop with his attempts to capture the young audience. Appropriately, his next picture was the opulent and admirably cinematic presentation of *La Traviata.* For his *Hamlet,* however, he courted controversy with his casting of heartthrob Mel Gibson in the title role.

Zeffirelli's *Hamlet* was similar to his earlier *The Taming of the Shrew* in that both attempted to bring Shakespeare to the masses by casting bankable Hollywood names—Mel Gibson, Glenn Close—alongside classically trained Britons—Paul Scofield, Alan Bates, Ian Holm. Zeffirelli defends his extravagant approach to filmmaking by saying, "I am a flag-bearer of the crusade against boredom, bad taste, and stupidity in the theater," but he is still the target of critical barbs such as those from a *Time* magazine reviewer who stated he was "a director in need of a director."

Zeffirelli's other recent film of note is *Sparrow,* a typically ornate but otherwise ponderous account of a young novice nun in 1850s Sicily who is forced out of her convent because of a cholera epidemic. She returns to her hometown and promptly falls in love, but rejects her suitor to return to the nunnery. Once there, she is conflicted by her feelings for her beloved and her religious commitment. Almost driven to insanity, she eventually garners the fortitude to persevere in her religious calling.

In recent years, Zeffirelli primarily has concentrated on directing opera productions in Europe and the United States, including a stint at New York's Metropolitan Opera, where he directed a 1995 production of *La Traviata.*

—Ronald Bowers, updated by Rob Edelman

ZEMECKIS, Robert

Nationality: American. **Born:** Chicago, Illinois, 14 May 1951. **Education:** Attended Northern Illinois University; University of Southern California School of Cinema, graduated 1973. **Family:** Married Mary Ellen Trainor. **Career:** Following graduation, with Bob Gale, asked to develop material for Steven Spielberg and John Milius; also worked as cutter of advertisements, 1970s; directed first feature, *I Wanna Hold Your Hand,* 1978; also writer for TV. **Awards:** Oscar for Best Student Film, for *Field of Honor,* 1973; Oscar for Best Director, for *Forrest Gump,* 1994.

Films as Director:

1973 *Field of Honor* (short) (+ sc)
1978 *I Wanna Hold Your Hand* (+ co-sc)
1980 *Used Cars* (+ co-sc)
1984 *Romancing the Stone*
1985 *Back to the Future* (+ co-sc)
1988 *Who Framed Roger Rabbit?*
1989 *Back to the Future II*
1990 *Back to the Future III*
1992 *Death Becomes Her* (+ co-pr)
1994 ***Forrest Gump***

Other Films:

1979 *1941* (Spielberg) (co-sc)
1992 *Trespass* (Hill) (co-sc, co-exec pr); *The Public Eye* (Franklin) (exec pr)

Publications

By ZEMECKIS: articles—

Interview, in *Filmmakers Newsletter* (Ward Hill, Massachusetts), June 1978.
Interview with A. Crystal, in *Films and Filming* (London), December 1985.
Interview with A. Garel, in *Revue du Cinéma* (Paris), November 1985.
"Back With a Future," an interview with Mark Horowitz in *American Film* (Los Angeles), July/August 1988.
Interview, in *Time Out* (London), 23 November 1988.

On ZEMECKIS: articles—

Richardson, E. A., article in *Extrapolation,* vol. 29, no. 2, 1988.
Ruud, J., "*Back to the Future* as Quintessential Comedy," *Literature Film Quarterly,* vol. 19, no. 2, 1991.
Weinraub, Bernard, "A Director Examines Hollywood's Reshaping," in *New York Times,* 14 July 1992.
Carpenter, T., "Hope I Die Before I Get Old," in *Premiere* (New York), September 1992.
Kehr, Dave, "Who Framed 'Forrest Gump,'" in *Film Comment* (New York), March/April 1995.
Morgenstern, Joe, "Bob Z Can Read Your Mind," in *Playboy* (New York), August 1995.

* * *

Will Robert Zemeckis "out-Spielberg" Spielberg? As it stands now Zemeckis is close to beating his closest mentor at his own game. Still, there has been a catch to all this: Zemeckis's work has been much celebrated for its dazzling technological inventiveness, and then pretty much left at that. While his films, especially recently, are technically impressive, they are also more than that. *Who Framed Roger Rabbit* does indeed blend animation with live action brilliantly, but that observation does not exhaust the film. Zemeckis, in all his work, also displays narratives that work out conflicts arising from a complex dual structure, a fondness for injecting his films with both a serious moral undertone and black comedy, and a carefully controlled kinetic sense that works both to hold these movies together and to keep them extraordinarily dynamic.

All Zemeckis's films present narratives in which different worlds are at odds at each other, starting with his celebrated short *Field of Honor.* Continuing the line, *I Wanna Hold Your Hand* contrasts the frustrating glimpses that the Beatle-crazed protagonists get of the group with the satisfying television representation of them on the Sullivan show. Zemeckis repeatedly returns to this narrative tension as characters' lives interact with highly mediated visions in *Used Cars* (politics clashes with and merges with advertising), *Romancing the Stone* (Kathleen Turner's onscreen adventures contrast with her romance novel ideals), and *Roger Rabbit* (humans interact uneasily with 'toons). In the *Back to the Future* trilogy, the present (1985 suburban California) is contrasted with both the past and the future. Zemeckis's characters generally find the less mediated, more "real" world to be lacking but ultimately acceptable. For instance, in *Romancing the Stone* Michael Douglas does not meet Kathleen Turner's expectations for Jess, her ideal man, but she pines for him anyway, and in the end

Robert Zemeckis (left) with Tom Hanks on the set of *Forrest Gump*

goes to him. Only *Roger Rabbit* suggests that some sort of happy compromise is possible as both types of characters walk off together toward 'Toontown at closure, though a case could be made for *Future III,* which combines the vistas of Ford with the optimism of Hawks.

These films also ponder serious questions in an entertaining way. *Used Cars,* as it explores the commercialization of American politics, itself can be seen as an extended form of the joke often told in reference to Nixon: "Would you buy a used car from this man?" Even more directly, the *Future* films, and to a lesser extent *Roger Rabbit,* overtly address questions concerning the impact that the present has on the future and our responsibilities to history. While bringing up such questions so directly in genre film is fairly rare, the unsystematic treatment such issues get here is not. Christopher Lloyd in the *Future* trilogy illustrates this cavalier treatment well. When faced with a question of how he could risk the space-time continuum so blithely, he responds, "Oh, what the hell." Also, while he repeatedly stresses the risks to the universe occasioned by his inventions, he always fixes his time machine "one last time" and even fashions an entirely new one at the end of *Future III.*

Zemeckis combines this interest in moral questions with an almost Buñuelian sense of humor. His use of black comedy is evident most obviously in *Used Cars,* which, among other things, uses a corpse as a comedy prop. *Romancing the Stone,* meanwhile, contains the following exchange: "Have they found her husband's body yet?" "Just the one piece." Further, the dark vision of 1985 in *Future II* is there at the edges of the other films in the trilogy. The porno theaters and winos that sprout in the middle film are present in the other installments in smaller numbers, often used for comedic effect, as when the same homeless person reappears again and again at different times. Even in *Roger Rabbit* some representations of the victims of World War II can be seen in the Terminal Bar.

Zemeckis makes use of a consistent spatial design to keep these disparate elements together. His spaces often take on readily discernible circular shapes. Chases are almost always chases *around* things: around the New Deal Used Car Lot, around the kitchen during the "Something's Cookin'" segment of *Roger Rabbit,* around the courthouse square in the *Future* films. Fights also usually move around objects: around a broken stick in *Romancing the Stone,* around a cartoon mallet in *Roger Rabbit,* around Biff's speeding car in *Future II.* These broad movements are mirrored by characters and objects in a number of other ways (Roger Rabbit's movements after taking a drink, the looping take-offs of the flying time machines).

On a different level this kinetic concern mirrors the circular narrative elements mentioned above, as the characters explore other worlds and typically settle for the one with which they started. Zemeckis blends these elements to form extremely vital, extremely satisfying wholes.

Since the conclusion of the *Back to the Future* trilogy, Zemeckis's film output has been limited. The overall slightness of *Death Becomes Her,* a black comedy made memorable only by some eye-popping visual effects (and, to a lesser extent, the always watchable Meryl Streep, playing an egocentric actress), makes this film a minor credit on Zemeckis's filmography. This is especially so when contrasted to his follow-up: *Forrest Gump,* which upon its release was christened one of the defining movies of the baby boom generation. The film made "stupid is as stupid does" a national catchphrase, and critics and audiences raved about the film, which went on to win six Academy Awards— including one for Zemeckis as Best Director.

To be sure, *Forrest Gump* is an appealing film. But it also is deeply flawed. Its scenario mirrors the tumultuous events of American history from the 1960s through 1980s as reflected through the experiences of the title character (Tom Hanks). There are the assassinations of John and Robert Kennedy, and the murder of John Lennon; the unwinnable and mismanaged Vietnam War; anti-war protests and the 1960s counterculture; and, finally and tragically, the AIDS plague. The point of the film is that, truly, the baby boom generation is a Lost Generation. Every generation may have its own set of problems: The parents of baby boomers, for instance, contended with the Great Depression and World War II. But for those coming of age during the 1930s and 1940s, problems were clearly defined. There was no debate regarding America's declaration of war against Germany and Japan.

To its credit, *Forrest Gump* does get the Vietnam war right. For too long, Vietnam vets in movies were depicted as stereotypical sadists, drug abusers, and Charles Manson clones, all scapegoats for the folly of Vietnam. However, in such films as *Born on the Fourth of July, Jacknife,* and *Forrest Gump,* Vietnam vets finally were rendered with compassion and thoughtfulness.

But *Forrest Gump* is in many ways a simplistic film. Anti-war activists are depicted as one-dimensional, amoral twits, and many viewers found the film to be reactionary in its political overview. The Vietnam era was a complex time. Surely those millions who came to be against the war deserve far more thoughtful and three-dimensional depictions than may be found in *Forrest Gump.*

—Mark Walker, updated by Rob Edelman

ZETTERLING, Mai

Nationality: Swedish. **Born:** Västeras, 24 May 1925. **Education:** Royal Dramatic Theatre School, Stockholm, 1942-45. **Family:** Married 1) actor Tutte Lemkow (divorced), two children; 2) writer David Hughes (divorced). **Career:** Stage debut and film debut, 1941; in company of Royal Dramatic Theatre, Stockholm, 1945-47; began collaborating on TV documentaries with husband Hughes, 1960s; directed episode of *Mistress of Suspense* for TV, 1990. **Awards:** Golden Lion, Venice Festival, for *The War Game,* 1963. **Died:** March 1994.

Films as Director:

1960 *The Polite Invasion* (short, for BBC TV)
1961 *Lords of Little Egypt* (short, for BBC TV); *The War Game* (short) (+ pr)
1962 *The Prosperity Race* (short, for BBC TV)
1963 *The Do-It-Yourself Democracy* (short, for BBC TV)
1964 *Alskande par* (*Loving Couples*) (co-d with David Hughes)
1966 *Nattlek* (*Night Games*) (co-d with Hughes)
1967 *Doktor Glas* (co-d with Hughes)
1968 *Flickorna* (*The Girls*) (co-d with Hughes)
1971 *Vincent the Dutchman* (co-d with Hughes, pr) (doc)
1973 "The Strongest" episode of *Visions of Eight* (co-d with Hughes)
1976 *We har manje namn* (*We Have Many Names*) (+ ed, role)
1977 *Stockholm* (+ role) (for Canadian TV)
1978 *The Rain's Hat* (+ ed) (for TV)
1982 *Love* (for TV)
1983 *Scrubbers*
1986 *Amorosa* (+ sc, ed)
1990 *Sunday Pursuit*

Other Films:

1941 *Lasse-Maja* (Olsson) (role)
1943 *Jag drapte* (Molander) (role)
1944 *Hets* (*Torment*; *Frenzy*) (Sjöberg) (role); *Prins Gustaf* (Bauman) (role)
1946 *Iris och Lojtnantshjarta* (*Iris and the Lieutenant*) (Sjöberg) (role); *Frieda* (Relph) (role); *Driver dagg faller Regn* (*Sunshine Follows Rain*) (role)
1948 *Musik i morker* (Bergman) (role); *Nu borjar livet* (Molander) (role); *Quartet* (Smart and others) (role); *The Bad Lord Byron* (MacDonald) (role); *Hildegard* (role)
1949 *Portrait from Life* (*The Girl in the Painting*) (Fisher) (role); *The Romantic Age* (Gréville) (role); *The Lost People* (Knowless) (role)
1950 *Blackmailed* (Marc Allégret) (role); *The Ringer* (Hamilton) (role)
1952 *The Tall Headlines* (*The Frightened Bride*) (Young) (role)
1953 *The Desperate Moment* (Bennett) (role); *Knock on Wood* (Frank and Panama) (role)
1954 *Prize of Gold* (Robson) (role); *Dance Little Lady* (Guest) (role)
1956 "Ett dockhem" (A Doll's House) episode of *Giftas* (Henriksson) (role); *Abandon Ship* (*Seven Waves Away*) (Sale) (role)
1957 *The Truth about Women* (Box) (role)
1958 *Lek pa regnbagen* (Kjellgren) (role)
1959 *Jet Storm* (Endfield); *Faces in the Dark* (Eady) (role)
1960 *Piccadilly Third Stop* (Rilla) (role); *Offbeat* (Owen) (role)
1961 *Only Two Can Play* (Gilliat) (role)
1962 *The Main Attraction* (Petrie) (role); *The Man Who Finally Died* (Lawrence) (role)
1963 *The Bay of St. Michel* (Ainsworth) (role)
1965 *The Vine Bridge* (Nykvist) (role)
1988 *Calling the Shots* (doc) (Cole) (appearance)
1989 *The Witches* (Roeg) (role)
1990 ***Hidden Agenda*** (Loach) (role)

Publications

By ZETTERLING: books—

Bird of Passage, New York, 1976.
All Those Tomorrows, London, 1985.

By ZETTERLING: articles—

"Some Notes on Acting," in *Sight and Sound* (London), October/December 1951.
"Mai Zetterling at the Olympic Games," an interview in *American Cinematographer* (Los Angeles), November 1972.
"Mai Zetterling," an interview with A. Jordahl and H. Lahger, in *Chaplin,* vol. 34, no. 3, 1992.

On ZETTERLING: books—

Bjorkman, Stig, *Film in Sweden, the New Directors,* London, 1979.
Heck-Rabi, Louise, *Women Filmmakers: A Critical Reception,* Metuchen, New Jersey, 1984.

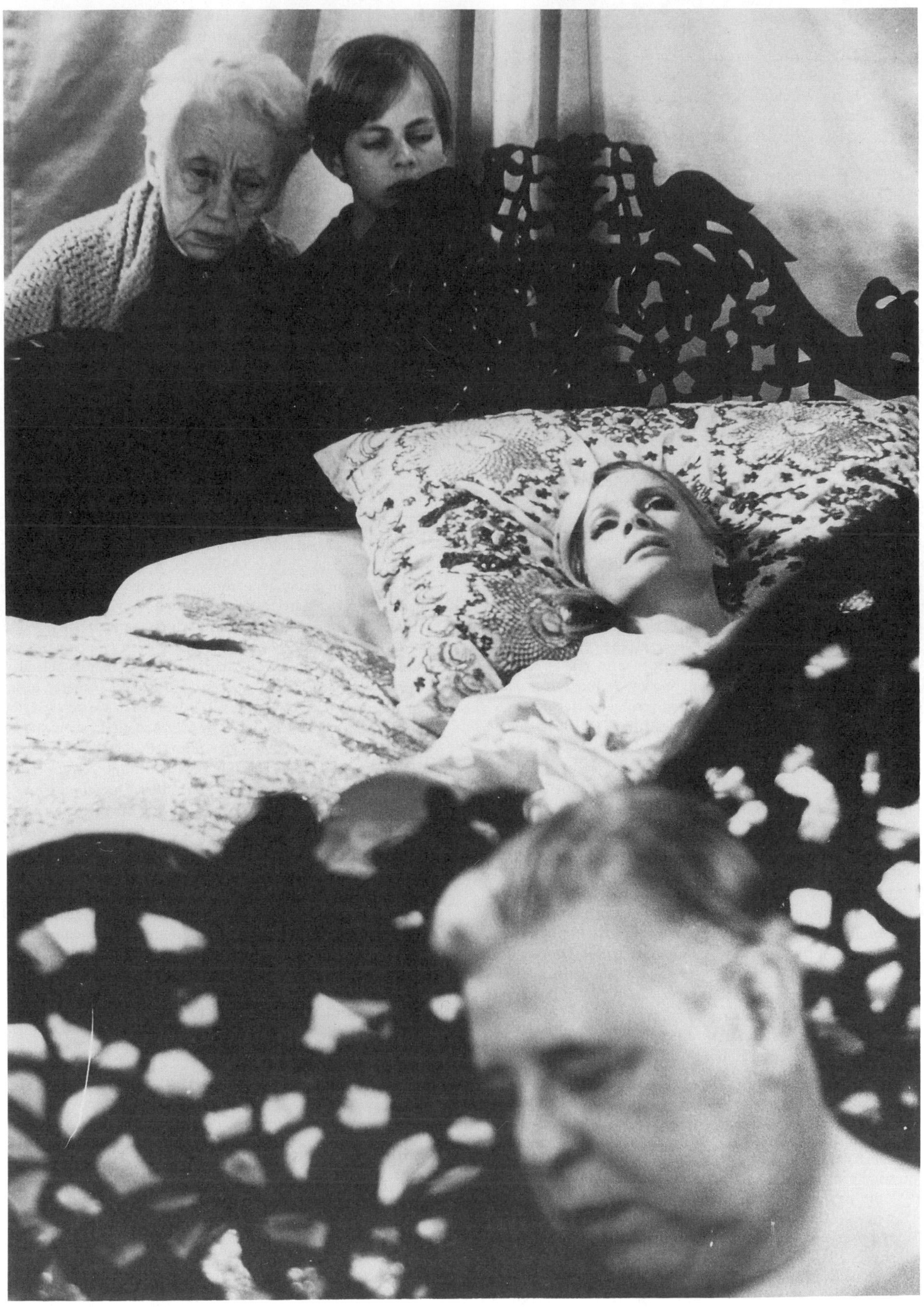

Mai Zetterling: ***Nattlek***

On ZETTERLING: articles—

"Meeting with Mai Zetterling," in *Cahiers du Cinéma in English* (New York), December 1966.
Pyros, J., "Notes on Women Directors," in *Take One* (Montreal), November/December 1970.
McGregor, C., "Mai Is behind the Camera Now," in *New York Times,* 30 April 1972.
Elley, Derek, "Hiding It under a Bushel: Free Fall," in *Films and Filming* (London), April 1974.
Modrzejewska, E. "Wiedzmy," in *Filmowy Serwis Prasowy,* vol. 37, no. 11/12, 1991.

* * *

Mai Zetterling's career as a filmmaker stemmed from her disillusionment with acting. Trained at Stockholm's Royal Dramatic Theater, Zetterling debuted on stage and screen in 1941. She considered the film *Torment* her best acting achievement. She worked in British theatre, enacting roles in Chekhov, Anouilh, and Ibsen plays, and in British films. After one part in a Hollywood film, *Knock on Wood* with Danny Kaye, she spurned contract offers and returned home.

With her husband, David Hughes, she made several documentaries in the 1960s dealing with political issues. Zetterling's feature films depict the social status and psyche of women, reflecting her feminist concerns. The uncompromising honesty of perception and technical virtuosity in her films correspond to the pervasive and dominant themes of loneliness and obsession. Zetterling says: "I want very strongly to do things I believe in. I can't do jobs for the money. I just can't do it."

In 1960, Roger Moorfoot of the BBC financed her idea for a film on the immigration of Swedes to Lapland, *The Polite Invasion.* Three more followed: *The Lords of Little Egypt* depicted the gypsies at Saintes-Maries-de-la-Mer; her view of Swedish affluence in *The Prosperity Race* was not appreciated in Stockholm; and *Do-It-Yourself Democracy* commented on Icelandic society and government. Her first independent effort was the fifteen-minute anti-war film *The War Game,* in which two boys tussle for possession of a toy gun.

Zetterling's first feature film, *Loving Couples,* was based on the fifth volume of Swedish author Agnes von Krusenstjerna's seven-volume novel, *The Misses von Pahlen.* Zetterling wrote the script in one year, with sketches of each shot to indicate camera positions. In it, three expectant mothers in a Stockholm hospital recall their lives in the moment of, and then beyond, the births of their babies. Critic Derek Elley suggests that Zetterling developed her theories and themes of film in *Loving Couples* and rarely deviated from them in later works. She employs elaborate timelines as well as flashbacks, which she uses often and well, intertwining them one within another. Her films peak emotionally in scenes of parties and social gatherings. Her films are cohesive compositions, with a literary base, filmed in the stark contrasts of black to white, with a range of grays intervening. Zetterling's scenes of sexual behavior are integral to her themes of loneliness and obsession. *Loving Couples* exemplifies these characteristics.

Night Games, derived from Zetterling's novel with the same title, was banned from the Venice Film Festival. The critics who saw it were angered by the Marxist and Freudian elements in it; shocked by scenes of vomiting, masturbation, and childbirth. Based on Hjalmar Soderberg's 1905 novel, her next film, *Doktor Glas,* records the haunted love of a young physician for a pastor's wife. Even though the wife does not respond to the physician's erotic overtures, he administers a lethal drug to the pastor. It is Zetterling's grimmest study of loneliness, as Derek Elley observes, and her most pessimistic film, told in one extended flashback, "a far cry from *Night Games.*"

She returned to a strongly feminist story in *Flickorna* and, as in *Loving Couples,* it contains three female roles of equal weight. In *Flickorna* three actresses perform *Lysistrata* on tour, acting out the views of the play in their private lives. Some critics reacted negatively, finding it self-indulgent, a mix of Greek comedy and soap opera, with heavy symbolism and confusing time structures. Other critics liked the various forms of humor effectively employed, and the arresting imagery.

In 1971, Zetterling filmed a documentary in color about Vincent Van Gogh. Titled *Vincent the Dutchman,* it was shown on American and British television. David Wolper then asked her to film any phase of the 1972 Olympics she chose; she filmed the weightlifting sequence, "The Strongest," for *Visions of Eight.*

In the 1970s, Zetterling published three novels, pursuing creative directions other than filmmaking. She also continued making documentaries (one on tennis champion Stan Smith, one dealing with Stockholm, another on marriage customs), along with a seven-hour adaptation for French television of Simone de Beauvoir's *The Second Sex.* Zetterling asserted that whatever she filmed, it would be "something I believe in."

—Louise Heck-Rabi

ZINNEMANN, Fred

Nationality: Austrian/American. **Born:** Vienna, 29 April 1907. **Education:** Educated in law, University of Vienna, degree 1927; studied one year at the Ecole Technique de Photographie et Cinématographie, Paris. **Family:** Married Renée Bartlett, 1936, one son. **Career:** Assistant cameraman in Paris and Berlin, then with Billy Wilder, Eugen Schüfftan, and Robert Siodmak, made *Menschen am Sonntag,* 1928; moved to Hollywood, became assistant cameraman and cutter for Berthold Viertel, 1929; worked with Robert Flaherty on unrealized documentary project, Berlin, 1931; worked in Mexico with Paul Strand on *Los Redes,* 1934-35; hired by MGM to direct short subjects, 1937; directed first feature, 1942; vice-president, Directors Guild of America, 1961-64. **Awards:** Oscars for Best Short Subject, for *That Mothers Might Live,* 1938, and *Benjy,* 1951; Best Direction, New York Film Critics, for *High Noon,* 1952; Oscar for Best Director, and Director Award, Directors Guild of America, for *From Here to Eternity,* 1953; Best Direction, New York Film Critics, for *The Nun's Story,* 1959; Oscar for Best Director, Best Direction, New York Film Critics, and Director Award, Directors Guild of America, for *A Man for All Seasons,* 1966; D. W. Griffith Award, 1971; Order of Arts and Letters, France, 1982; U.S. Congressional Lifetime Achievement Award, 1987; John Huston Award, Artists Rights Foundation, 1994.

Films as Director:

1934/35 ***Los Redes*** (*The Wave*)
1938 *A Friend Indeed* (short for MGM); *The Story of Dr. Carver* (short for MGM); *That Mothers Might Live* (short for MGM); *Tracking the Sleeping Death* (short for MGM); *They Live Again* (short for MGM)
1939 *Weather Wizards* (short for MGM); *While America Sleeps* (short for MGM); *Help Wanted!* (short for MGM); *One Against the World* (short for MGM); *The Ash Can Fleet* (short for MGM); *Forgotten Victory* (short for MGM)
1940 *The Old South* (short for MGM); *Stuffie* (short for MGM); *The Way in the Wilderness* (short for MGM); *The Great Meddler* (short for MGM)
1941 *Forbidden Passage* (short for MGM); *Your Last Act* (short for MGM)

Fred Zinnemann directing Jane Fonda in *Julia*

1942 *The Lady or the Tiger?* (short for MGM); *The Kid Glove Killer*; *Eyes in the Night*
1944 *The Seventh Cross*
1945 *Little Mr. Jim*
1946 *My Brother Talks to Horses*
1947 *The Search*
1948 *Act of Violence*
1950 *The Men*
1951 *Teresa*; *Benjy* (short)
1952 ***High Noon***; *The Member of the Wedding*
1953 ***From Here to Eternity***
1955 *Oklahoma*
1957 *A Hatful of Rain*
1958 *The Nun's Story*
1960 *The Sundowners* (+ pr)
1963 *Behold a Pale Horse* (+ pr)
1966 *A Man for All Seasons* (+ pr)
1973 *The Day of the Jackal* (+ pr)
1977 *Julia* (+ pr)
1982 *Five Days One Summer* (+ pr) (re-edited version released 1988)

Other Films:

1927 *La Marche des machines* (Deslaw) (asst cameraman)
1929 *Ich Küsse Ihre Hand, Madame* (Land) (asst cameraman); *Sprengbagger 1010* (Achaz-Duisberg) (asst cameraman); *Menschen am Sonntag* (*People on Sunday*) (Siodmak) (asst cameraman)
1930 *Man Trouble* (asst d to Berthold Viertel); ***All Quiet on the Western Front*** (Milestone) (bit role)
1931 *The Spy* (asst d to Viertel)
1932 *The Wiser Sex* (asst d to Viertel); *The Man from Yesterday* (asst d to Viertel); *The Kid from Spain* (asst to Busby Berkeley)
1989 *Stand Under the Dark Clock* (doc) (Walker) (role)

Publications

By ZINNEMANN: book—

Fred Zinnemann: My Life in the Movies, New York, 1990.

By ZINNEMANN: articles—

"Different Perspective," in *Sight and Sound* (London), Autumn 1948.
"Choreography of a Gunfight," in *Sight and Sound* (London), July/September 1952.
"The Impact of Television on Motion Pictures," an interview with Gideon Bachmann, in *Film Culture* (New York), no. 2, 1957.
"A Conflict of Conscience," in *Films and Filming* (London), December 1959.
Interview with John Russell Taylor in *Sight and Sound* (London), Winter 1960/61.

"A Discussion: Personal Creation in Hollywood: Can It Be Done?," in *Film Quarterly* (Berkeley), Spring 1962.
"Zinnemann—True or False?," in *Cinema* (Beverly Hills), February/March 1964.
"Revelations," in *Films and Filming* (London), September 1964.
"Zinnemann Talks Back," an interview in *Cinema* (Beverly Hills), October/November 1964.
"Montgomery Clift," in *Sight and Sound* (London), Autumn 1966.
"Some Questions Answered," in *Action* (Los Angeles), May/June 1967.
Interview with Gene D. Phillips in *Focus on Film* (London), Spring 1973.
"Fred Zinnemann and *Julia*," an interview with Cecile Starr, in *Filmmakers Newsletter* (Ward Hill, Massachusetts), November 1977.
"Individualism against Machinery," an interview with Gordon Gow, in *Films and Filming* (London), February 1978.
Interview with M. Buckley in *Films in Review* (New York), January 1983.
"Dialogue on Film: Fred Zinnemann," in *American Film* (Washington D.C.), January/February 1986.
"*From Here to Eternity*," in *Sight and Sound* (London), Winter 1987/1988.

On ZINNEMANN: books—

Griffith, Richard, *Fred Zinnemann*, New York, 1958.
Foreman, Carl, *High Noon*, New York, 1971.
Phillips, Gene D., *The Movie Makers: Artists in an Industry*, Chicago, 1973.

On ZINNEMANN: articles—

Knight, Arthur, "Fred Zinnemann," in *Films in Review* (New York), January 1951.
Hart, Henry, "Zinnemann on the Verge," in *Films in Review* (New York), February 1953.
Schickel, Richard, "Fred Zinnemann: Quiet Man on the Set," in *Show* (Hollywood), August 1964.
Stanbrook, Alan, "A Man for All Movies: The Films of Fred Zinnemann," in *Films and Filming* (London), June 1967.
Adler, D., "Zinnemann's Fate," in *Show* (Hollywood), May 1970.
"*High Noon*," in *Values in Conflict*, edited by Richard Maynard, New York, 1974.
Lueken, V., "Daempfen in aussichtslosen Situationene," in *EPD Film*, September 1992.

* * *

In 1928 Fred Zinnemann worked as assistant to cinematographer Eugene Schüfftan on Robert Siodmak's *Menschen am Sonntag (People on Sunday)*, along with Edgar Ulmer and Billy Wilder, who wrote the scenario for this semi-documentary silent feature made in the tradition of Flaherty and Vertov. Having been strongly influenced by realistic filmmaking, particularly the work of Erich von Stroheim, King Vidor, and Robert Flaherty, Zinnemann immigrated to the United States in 1930 and worked with Berthold Viertel, Flaherty ("probably the greatest single influence on my work as a filmmaker," he later stated), and the New York photographer-documentarist Paul Strand on *Los Redes*, the first of a proposed series intended to document everyday Mexican life. *Los Redes* told the story of the struggle of impoverished fishermen to organize themselves against economic exploitation. The film was shot in Vera Cruz, and Zinnemann was responsible for directing the actors.

Zinnemann's documentary training and background developed his style as a "social realist" in a number of early pictures (several shorts he directed, for example, in MGM's *Crime Does Not Pay* and *The Passing Parade* series) during the years 1937-1942. His medical short *That Mother Might Live* won an Academy Award and enabled Zinnemann to direct feature films. His first feature at MGM was a thriller, *The Kid Glove Killer*, with Van Heflin and Marsha Hunt. *The Seventh Cross* was adapted from Anna Segher's anti-fascist World War II novel. Starring Spencer Tracy, the film was notable for its atmosphere and documentary style. *The Search*, shot on location in Europe in 1948, with Montgomery Clift, gave a realistic portrayal of children who had been displaced by the turmoil of World War II and was a critical as well as a commercial success. *The Men* was the first of a three-picture contract Zinnemann signed with Stanley Kramer and dealt with the problem of paraplegic war veterans, marking Marlon Brando's debut as a film actor. Zinnemann filmed *The Men* on location at the Birmingham Veteran's Hospital and used a number of patients there as actors.

Zinnemann's next film for Kramer, *High Noon*, was significant because of the way Zinnemann's realistic style turned the genre of the Western upside down. It featured Gary Cooper in an Oscar-winning performance as Will Kane, a retired marshal who has taken a Quaker bride (Grace Kelly), but whose marriage is complicated by the anticipated return of paroled desperado Frank Miller, expected on the noon train. Zinnemann treated his "hero" as an ordinary man beset with doubts and fears in an existential struggle to protect himself and the community of Haddleyville, a town that proves to be undeserving of his heroism and bravery. Zinnemann created a tense drama by coordinating screen time to approximate real time, which is extended only when the fateful train arrives, bearing its dangerous passenger. Working against the stylized and mythic traditions that had come to dominate the genre, *High Noon* established the trend of the "psychological" Western and represents one of Zinnemann's finest accomplishments.

Zinnemann's last Kramer picture was *The Member of the Wedding*, a Carson McCullers novel that had been adapted to a popular Broadway production by McCullers herself. The film utilized the same cast that had made the stage production successful (Julie Harris, Brandon de Wilde, and Ethel Waters) but created cinematically an effective atmosphere of entrapment. *Member of the Wedding* is a model of effective theatrical adaption. Zinnemann went on to adapt the 1955 movie version of the Rodgers and Hammerstein classic *Oklahoma!*, removing the exclamation point, as one wit noted, in a spacious and lyrical, but also rather perfunctory, effort.

In 1953 Zinnemann moved to Columbia Pictures to direct the adaption of the popular James Jones novel *From Here to Eternity*, a huge popular success starring Montgomery Clift, Frank Sinatra, and Ernest Borgnine that won Zinnemann an Academy Award for Best Director. Zinnemann's approach effectively utilized newsreel footage of the Japanese attack on Pearl Harbor and his realistic style both tightened and dramatized the narrative. *A Hatful of Rain* applied Zinnemann's documentary approach to the problem of drug addiction in New York. *The Nun's Story* (with Audrey Hepburn and Peter Finch) has been linked to *A Man For All Seasons* in that both reflect conflicts of conscience, a recurring motif in Zinnemann's films. *A Man for All Seasons*, adapted from Robert Bolt's play, won Paul Scofield an Academy Award for his portrayal of St. Thomas More.

Among Zinnemann's political films are *Behold a Pale Horse*, starring Gregory Peck and set during the Spanish Civil War, a picture that also incorporated newsreel authenticity, and *The Day of the Jackal*, a story about an assassin's attempt on the life of Charles de Gaulle, shot on location "like a newsreel." A later and in many ways impressive political film involving a conflict of conscience was Zinnemann's *Julia*, adapted by Alvin Sargent from Lillian Hellman's *Pentimento*, concerning Hellman's love affair with the writer Dashiell Hammett (Jason Robards) and her long-standing friendship with the mysterious Julia (Vanessa Redgrave), the daughter of a wealthy family who becomes a socialist-intellectual politicized by events in Germany under the Nazi regime. *Julia* is a perfect Zinnemann vehicle, impressive in its authenticity and historical reconstruction, and also psychologically tense, particularly in the way Zinnemann films Hellman's suspense-laden journey from Paris to Moscow via Berlin. It demonstrates the director's sense of psychological realism and his apparent determination to make worthwhile pictures that are nevertheless highly entertaining.

—James M. Welsh

ZHUANGZHUANG, Tian *See* **TIAN Zhuangzhuang**

NATIONALITY INDEX

AMERICAN

Robert Aldrich
Woody Allen
Robert Altman
Allison Anders
Kenneth Anger
Gregg Araki
Dorothy Arzner
Hal Ashby
Lloyd Bacon
Bruce Baillie
Robert Benton
Busby Berkeley
J. Stuart Blackton
Budd Boetticher
Peter Bogdanovich
Frank Borzage
Stan Brakhage
Mel Brooks
Richard Brooks
Clarence Brown
Tod Browning
Charles Burnett
Tim Burton
Frank Capra
John Carpenter
John Cassavetes
Michael Cimino
Shirley Clarke
Joel Coen
Bruce Conner
Francis Ford Coppola
Roger Corman
Kevin Costner
Wes Craven
John Cromwell
James Cruze
George Cukor
John Dahl
Jules Dassin
Delmer Daves
Emile De Antonio
Cecil B. De Mille
Jonathan Demme
Brian De Palma
Maya Deren
William Dieterle
Edward Dmytryk
Stanley Donen
Allan Dwan
Clint Eastwood
Blake Edwards
Ed Emshwiller
Abel Ferrara
Robert Flaherty
Richard Fleischer
Victor Fleming
John Ford
Bob Fosse
Jodie Foster
Hollis Frampton
John Frankenheimer
William Friedkin
Samuel Fuller
Tay Garnett
Terry Gilliam
D. W. Griffith
Hal Hartley
Henry Hathaway
Howard Hawks
Todd Haynes
Monte Hellman
George Roy Hill
Walter Hill
William K. Howard
John Huston
Rex Ingram
James Ivory
Jim Jarmusch
Lawrence Kasdan
Philip Kaufman
Elia Kazan
Buster Keaton
Henry King
Barbara Kopple
Stanley Kramer
Stanley Kubrick
Gregory La Cava
Fritz Lang
Spike Lee
Mervyn Leroy
Richard Lester
Barry Levinson
Albert Lewin
Jerry Lewis
Joseph H. Lewis
Richard Linklater
Anatole Litvak
Pare Lorentz
Joseph Losey
Ernst Lubitsch
George Lucas
Sidney Lumet
David Lynch
Terrence Malick
Rouben Mamoulian
Joseph L. Mankiewicz
Anthony Mann
Michael Mann
Gregory Markopoulos
Penny Marshall
Albert Maysles
David Paul Maysles
Paul Mazursky
Leo McCarey
Oscar Micheaux
Lewis Milestone
Vincente Minnelli
Errol Morris
Robert Mulligan
Marshall Neilan
Fred Niblo
Mike Nichols
Marcel Ophuls

Alan J. Pakula
Sam Peckinpah
Arthur Penn
Sydney Pollack
Abraham Polonsky
Edwin S. Porter
Otto Preminger
Bob Rafelson
Yvonne Rainer
Nicholas Ray
Robert Redford
Rob Reiner
Jean Renoir
Martin Ritt
Robert Rodriguez
George A. Romero
Robert Rossen
Alan Rudolph
Victor Saville
John Sayles
Franklin J. Schaffner
Ernest B. Schoedsack
Paul Schrader
Joel Schumacher
Martin Scorsese
Don Siegel
Joan Micklin Silver
Robert Siodmak
Douglas Sirk
Steven Soderbergh
Penelope Spheeris
Steven Spielberg
John M. Stahl
George Stevens
Robert Stevenson
Oliver Stone
John Sturges
Preston Sturges
Quentin Tarantino
Frank Tashlin
Jacques Tourneur
Maurice Tourneur
W. S. Van Dyke
Willard Van Dyke
Gus Van Sant
Stan Vanderbeek
Charles Vidor
King Vidor
Raoul Walsh
Charles Walters
Andy Warhol
John Waters
Lois Weber
Orson Welles
William Wellman
Billy Wilder
Robert Wise
Frederick Wiseman
Edward D. Wood, Jr.
Sam Wood
William Wyler
Robert Zemeckis
Fred Zinnemann

ARGENTINIAN
Hector Babenco
Maria Luisa Bemberg
Fernando Birri
Octavio Getino
Fernando E. Solanas
Leopoldo Torre Nilsson

AUSTRALIAN
Gillian Armstrong
Bruce Beresford
John Duigan
George Miller
Fred Schepisi
Peter Weir

AUSTRIAN
G. W. Pabst
Edgar Ulmer
Josef Von Sternberg
Erich Von Stroheim
Fred Zinnemann

BELGIAN
Chantal Akerman
André Delvaux
Jacques Feyder
Henri Storck
Agnès Varda

BOLIVIAN
Jorge Sanjinés

BRAZILIAN
Alberto Cavalcanti
Carlos Diegues
Humberto Mauro
Nelson Pereira dos Santos
Glauber Rocha

BRITISH
Lindsay Anderson
Anthony Asquith
John Boorman
John Boulting
Roy Boulting
Kenneth Branagh
Charles Chaplin
Jack Clayton
Alex Cox
Charles Crichton
Terence Davies
Basil Dearden
Thorold Dickinson
Terence Fisher
Stephen Frears
Sidney Gilliat
Edmund Goulding

RMAN

GREEK

HUNGARIAN

INDIAN

IRISH

ITALIAN

Peter Greenaway
Robert Hamer
Cecil Hepworth
Alfred Hitchcock
Derek Jarman
Humphrey Jennings
Roland Joffé
Alexander Korda
Frank Launder
Richard Leacock
David Lean
Mike Leigh
Ken Loach
Mike Newell
Alan Parker
George Pearson
Sally Potter
Michael Powell
Emeric Pressburger
Carol Reed
Karel Reisz
Tony Richardson
Nicolas Roeg
Paul Rotha
Ken Russell
Victor Saville
John Schlesinger
Ridley Scott
Robert Stevenson
Peter Watkins
James Whale
Basil Wright

CANADIAN
David Cronenberg
Norman Jewison
Claude Jutra
Jean-Pierre Lefebvre
Pierre Perrault
Mack Sennett
Michael Snow

CHILEAN
Patricio Guzmán
Miguel Littin
Raul Ruiz

CHINESE
Chen Kaige
King Hu
Tian Zhuangzhuang
John Woo
Xie Jin
Edward Yang

CUBAN
Santiago Alvarez
Sara Gómez
Tomás Gutiérrez Alea
Humberto Solas

CZECH
Věra Chytilová
Milos Forman
Martin Frič
Jaromil Jireš
Karel Kachyňa
Jiři Menzel
Jan Nemec
Jiři Weiss
Ján Kadár
Karel Reisz
Evald Schorm

DANISH
Bille August
August Blom
Benjamin Christensen
Carl Theodor Dreyer
Urban Gad
Astrid Henning-Jensen
Bjarne Henning-Jensen
Holger-Madsen
Jørgen Roos

DUTCH
Bert Haanstra
Joris Ivens
Paul Verhoeven

EGYPTIAN
Youssef Chahine

FINNISH
Jörn Donner
Aki Kaurismaki

FRENCH
Alexandre Astruc
Claude Autant-Lara
Jacques Becker
Luc Besson
Bertrand Blier
Robert Bresson
Marcel Carné
Claude Chabrol
René Clair
René Clement
Henri-Georges Clouzot
Jean Cocteau
Constantin Costa-Gavras
Jean Delannoy
Louis Delluc
Jacques Demy
Vittorio De Sica
Germaine Dulac
Marguerite Duras
Julien Duvivier
Jean Epstein
Louis Feuillade
Robert Florey
Georges Franju

Luchino Visconti
Franco Zeffirelli

JAPANESE
Heinosuke Gosho
Susumi Hani
Kon Ichikawa
Tadashi Imai
Shohei Imamura
Juzo Itami
Keisuke Kinoshita
Teinosuke Kinugasa
Masaki Kobayashi
Akira Kurosawa
Kenji Mizoguchi
Mikio Naruse
Nagisa Oshima
Yasujiro Ozu
Kaneto Shindo
Masahiro Shinoda
Kozabura Yoshimura

LITHUANIAN
Jonas Mekas

MAURITANIAN
Med Hondo

MEXICAN
Fernando De Fuentes
Emilio Fernández
Paul Leduc
Arturo Ripstein
Robert Rodriguez

MOZAMBIQUIAN
Ruy Guerra

NEW ZEALANDER
Jane Campion
Peter Jackson
Vincent Ward

POLISH
Agnieszka Holland
Jerzy Kawalerowicz
Krzysztof Kieślowski
Andrzej Munk
Roman Polanski
Jerzy Skolimowski
Andrzej Wajda
Krzysztof Zanussi

PORTUGUESE
Manoel de Oliveira

ROMANIAN
Lupu Pick

RUSSIAN
Boris Barnet
Evgeni Bauer
Maya Deren
Mark Donskoi
Sergei Eisenstein
Josef Heifitz
Grigori Kozintsev
Anatole Litvak
Nikita Mikhalkov
Andrei Mikhalkov-Konchalovsky
Yakov Protazanov
Vsevolod Pudovkin
Mauritz Stiller
Dziga Vertov

SCOTTISH
Bill Forsyth
John Grierson
Alexander Mackendrick
Harry Watt

SENEGALESE
Ousmane Sembene

SERBIAN
Aleksandar Petrovic

SOVIET
Sergei Gerasimov
Lev Kuleshov
Georgi Vasiliev
Sergei Vasiliev

SOVIET GEORGIAN
Otar Ioseliani
Sergei Paradzhanov

SOVIET UKRAINIAN
Esther Shub

SOVIET RUSSIAN
Andrei Tarkovsky

SPANISH
Pedro Almodóvar
Juan Antonio Bardem
Luis Buñuel
Victor Erice
Luis García Berlanga
Carlos Saura

SRI LANKAN
Lester James Peries

SWEDISH
Ingmar Bergman
Lasse Hallstrom
Gustaf Molander
Alf Sjöberg
Victor Sjöström
Mauritz Stiller
Arne Sucksdorff
Jan Troell
Mai Zetterling

FILM TITLE INDEX

The following list of titles cites all films included in the *Directors* volume of this series, including cross-references for alternative or English-language titles. The name(s) in parentheses following the title and date refer the reader to the appropriate entry or entries where full information is given. Titles appearing in bold are covered in the *Films* volume.

Aar Paar, 1954 (Dutt)
Aashik, 1962 (Kapoor)
Aashiyana, 1952 (Kapoor)
Ab Dilli Dur Nahin, 1957 (Kapoor)
Abalone Industry, 1913 (Sennett)
Abandon Ship, 1956 (Zetterling)
Abandonadas, 1944 (Fernández)
Abasheshey, 1962 (Sen)
Abastecimento, nova política, 1968 (Pereira Dos Santos)
Abastecimiento, 1973 (Ruiz)
ABBA—The Movie, 1977 (Hallstrom)
Abbasso la ricchezza!, 1946 (De Sica)
Abbé Constantin, 1925 (Duvivier)
Abbott & Costello in Hollywood, 1945 (Walters)
Abbott and Costello Meet Captain Kidd, 1952 (Aldrich)
ABC do amor, 1966 (Littin)
ABC of Love. *See* ABC do amor, 1966
Abdullah, 1981 (Kapoor)
Abe Gets Even with Father, 1911 (Sennett)
Abe Lincoln in Illinois, 1940 (Cromwell)
Abel Gance—The Charm of Dynamite, 1968 (Anderson)
Abend ... Nacht ... Morgen, 1920 (Murnau)
Abenteuer des Dr. Kircheisen, 1920 (Wiene)
Abenteuer des Prinzen Achmed, 1923-26 (Ruttmann)
Abenteuer des Till Ulenspiegel, 1957 (Ivens)
Abgrund der Seelen, 1920 (Gad)
Abhagin, 1938 (Roy)
Abhijan, 1962 (S. Ray)
Abidjan, port de pêche, 1962 (Rouch)
Abie's Irish Rose, 1929 (Fleming)
Abigail's Party, 1977 (Leigh)
Abismos de pasión, 1953 (Buñuel)
Abominable Snowman. *See* Ostroznie yeti, 1960
Abortion: Desperate Choices, 1993 (Maysles)
About "The White Bus," 1967 (Anderson)
About Argentina. *See* De l'Argentine, 1985
... About Jaroslav Havlíček, 1992 (Jireš)
Above Suspicion, 1943 (Saville)
Abraham Lincoln, 1930 (Griffith)
Abrégeons les formalités!, 1917 (Feyder)
Abril de Giron, 1966 (Alvarez)
Abril de Vietnam en el año del gato, 1975 (Alvarez)
Abroad with Two Yanks, 1944 (Dwan)
Abschied, 1930 (Siodmak)
Abschied von gestern, 1966 (Kluge)
Absence, 1976 (Brakhage)
Absence of Malice, 1981 (Pollack)
Absent-Minded Bootblack, 1903 (Hepworth)
Absent-Minded Professor, 1960 (Stevenson)
Abul Hasan, 1931 (Mehboob)
Abwege, 1928 (Pabst)
Abyss. *See* Afgrunden, 1910
Abyss. *See* Oeuvre au noir, 1988
Ac kurtlar, 1969 (Güney)
Acadie, L'Acadie!, 1970 (Perrault)
Acapulco, 1951 (Fernández)
Accattone, 1961 (Bertolucci, Pasolini)
Acciaio, 1932-33 (Ruttmann)
Accident, 1967 (Losey)
Accident d'auto, 1907 (Feuillade)
Accidental Accidents, 1924 (McCarey)
Accidental Tourist, 1988 (Kasdan)
Accompagnatrice, 1992 (C. Miller)
Accompanist. *See* Accompagnatrice, 1992
Accordfinal, 1939 (Sirk)
According to Hoyle, 1922 (W.S. Van Dyke)
Accroche-coeur, 1938 (Guitry)
Accused, 1948 (Dieterle)
Accused. *See* Obžalovaný, 1964
Accused. *See* Podsudimy, 1985
Accused, 1988 (Foster)
Accusée, levez-vous, 1930 (M. Tourneur)
Ace Eli and Rodger of the Skies, 1973 (Spielberg)
Ace in the Hole, 1951 (Wilder)
Ace of Spades, 1935 (Pearson)
Ace of the Saddle, 1919 (Ford)
Achoo Mr. Keroochev, 1959 (Vanderbeek)
Achraroumès, 1978 (Paradzhanov)
Acht Stunden sind kein Tag, 1972 (Fassbinder)
Acht Tage Gluck. *See* Der Liebesexpress, 1931
Achte Gebot, 1915 (Leni)
Aci, 1971 (Güney)
Aciéries de la marine et d'Homécourt, 1925 (Grémillon)
Acoso, 1964 (Solas)
Acostates første Offer. *See* Krigens Fjende, 1915
Acquittal, 1923 (Brown)
Acquitted. *See* Af Elskovs Naade, 1913
Acres of Alfalfa, 1914 (Sennett)
Across the Alley, 1913 (Sennett)
Across the Araks. *See* Po tu storonu Araksa, 1946
Across the Hall, 1914 (Sennett)
Across the Mexican Line, 1911 (Guy)
Across the Pacific, 1942 (Huston)
Across the River and into the Trees, 1987 (Frankenheimer)
Across the Wide Missouri, 1951 (Wellman)
Act Five, Scene Seven. Fritz Kortner Rehearses Kabale und Liebe. *See* Fünfter Akt, siebte Szene. Fritz Kortner probt Kabale und Liebe, 1965
Act of God, 1981 (Greenaway)
Act of Love, 1954 (Litvak)
Act of Seeing with One's Own Eyes, 1971 (Brakhage)
Act of Violence, 1948 (Zinnemann)
Acta General de Chile, 1986 (Littin)
Actas de Marusia, 1985 (Littin)
Action, 1921 (Ford)
Action B. *See* Akce B, 1951
Action for Slander, 1937 (Saville)
Action in the North Atlantic, 1943 (Bacon)
Action Man. *See* Soleil des voyous, 1967
Action Stations! *See* Branle-Bas de combat, 1943
Acto da primavera, 1963 (Oliveira)
Actor's Revenge. *See* Yukinojo henge, 1963
Actress, 1928 (Lewin)
Actress. *See* Joyu, 1947
Actress. *See* Joyu, 1956
Actress, 1953 (Cukor)
Actress. *See* Eiga Joyu, 1987
Actress and the Cowboys and The Sky Pilot's Intemperance, 1911 (Dwan)
Actress and the Poet. *See* Joyu to shijin, 1935
Acts of Love, 1978 (Kazan)
Acusation, 1965 (Solas)
Adam's Rib, 1923 (De Mille)
Adam's Rib, 1949 (Cukor)
Adams's Apple, 1928 (Launder)
Adauchi, 1964 (Imai)
Addiction, 1995 (Ferrara)
Address Unknown, 1944 (S. Wood)
Adhemar, 1951 (Guitry)
Adieu Bonaparte. *See* Al Wedaa ya Bonaparte, 1984
Adiós Nicanor, 1937 (Fernández)
Adjustment and Work, 1986 (Wiseman)
Admirable Crichton. *See* Male and Female, 1919
Admiral Nakhimov. *See* Amiral Nakhimov, 1946
Adolescents. *See* Veuves de quinze ans, 1964
Adoption. *See* Örökbefogadás, 1975
Adorable, 1933 (Dieterle, Wilder)
Adrienne Lecouvreur, 1938 (L'Herbier)
Adrift. *See* Touha zvaná Anada, 1971
Adua e le compagne, 1960 (Scola)
Adulteress. *See* Thérèse Raquin, 1953
Adulteress. *See* Yoru no tsuzumi, 1958
Adventure, 1925 (Fleming)
Adventure, 1945 (Fleming)

Aru yo no tonosama, 1946 (Kinugasa)
Aruyo futatabi, 1956 (Gosho)
Arvottomat, 1982 (Kaurismaki)
Arzt aus Halberstadt, 1969 (Kluge)
As a Wife, as a Woman. *See* Tsuma toshite onna toshite, 1961
As in a Looking Glass, 1911 (Griffith)
As It Is in Life, 1910 (Griffith)
As pinturas de meu irmão Júlio, 1965 (Oliveira)
As the Bells Rang Out, 1910 (Griffith)
As the Clouds Scatter. *See* Kumo ga chigireru toki, 1961
As You Desire Me, 1932 (Von Stroheim)
As You Like It, 1936 (Lean)
Asa no hamon, 1952 (Gosho)
Asa no namikimichi, 1936 (Naruse)
Asahi wa kagayaku, 1929 (Mizoguchi)
Asani Sanket, 1973 (S. Ray)
Ascending Scale. *See* Arohan, 1982
Ascenseur pour l'échafaud, 1958 (Malle)
Aschenbrödel, 1914 (Gad)
Asemblea General, 1960 (Gutiérrez Alea)
Asfalttilampaat, 1968 (Donner)
Ash Can Fleet, 1939 (Zinnemann)
Ashanti, 1979 (Fleischer)
Ashes and Diamonds. *See* **Popiół i diament**, 1958
Ashes of Desire, 1919 (Borzage)
Ashes of Three, 1913 (Dwan)
Ashes. *See* Popioły, 1965
Ashi ni sawatta koun, 1930 (Ozu)
Ashi ni sawatta onna, 1952 (Ichikawa)
Ashik kerib, 1988 (Paradzhanov)
Ashizuri misaki, 1954 (Yoshimura)
Asi se quiere en Jalisco, 1942 (De Fuentes)
Ask a Policeman, 1939 (Launder)
Ask Any Girl, 1959 (Walters)
Aslan bey, 1968 (Güney)
Aslanlarin dönüsü, 1966 (Güney)
Asleep at the Switch, 1923 (Sennett)
Aspen, 1991 (Wiseman)
Asphalt Jungle, 1950 (Huston)
Asphalt Lambs. *See* Asfalttilampaat, 1968
Assassin a peur la nuit, 1942 (Delannoy)
Assassin habite au vingt-et-un, 1942 (Clouzot)
Assassinat de la rue du Temple, 1904 (Guy)
Assassinat du Courrier de Lyon, 1904 (Guy)
Assassination. *See* Ansatsu, 1964
Assassination Bureau, 1968 (Dearden)
Assassination Game, 1992 (Corman)
Assassination of Trotsky, 1972 (Losey)
Assassino, 1961 (Petri)
Assassins: A Film Concerning Rimbaud, 1985 (Haynes)
Assassins de l'ordre, 1971 (Carné)
Assassins et voleurs, 1957 (Guitry)
Assault on Paradise. *See* Maniac, 1977
Assault on Precinct 13, 1977 (Carpenter)
Assiettes tournantes, 1939 (Lumet)
Assigned to Danger, 1948 (Boetticher)
Assisted Elopement, 1912 (Dwan)
Astonished Heart, 1949 (Fisher)
Astral Man, 1957 (Vanderbeek)
Astray from the Steerage. *See* Away from the Steerage, 1921
Astrologie ou Le Miroir de la vie, 1952 (Grémillon)
Astronautes, 1960 (Marker)
Astronomer's Dream. *See* Lune à un mètre, 1898
Asu no odoriko, 1939 (Yoshimura)
Asu no taiyo, 1959 (Oshima)
Asu o tsukuru hitobito, 1946 (Kurosawa)
Asya, 1977 (Heifitz)
Asya's Happiness. *See* Istoriya Asi Klyachinoi, kotoraya lyubila, da nye vyshla zamuzh, 1967
At avrat silah, 1966 (Güney)
At Coney Island, 1912 (Sennett)
At Dawn We Die. *See* Tomorrow We Live, 1942
At Great Cost. *See* Dorogoi tsenoi, 1957
At hirsizi banus, 1967 (Güney)
At Home Among Strangers. *See* Svoi sriedi chougikh, 1974
At It Again, 1912 (Sennett)
At It Again. *See* Caught in the Rain, 1914
At Land, 1944 (Deren)
At Long Last Love, 1975 (Bogdanovich)
At Play in the Fields of the Lord, 1991 (Babenco)
At the Altar, 1909 (Griffith)
At the Circus, 1938 (LeRoy)
At the Eleventh Hour. *See* Hvem var Forbryderen?, 1912
At the Lörinc Spinnery. *See* A lörinci fonóban, 1971
At the Phone, 1912 (Guy)
At the Risk of My Life. *See* Inochi bo ni furo, 1971
At Twelve O'Clock, 1913 (Sennett)
At War with the Army, 1951 (Jerry Lewis)
Ať žije republika, 1965 (Kachyňa)
Atalante, 1934 (Vigo)
Atalantis, 1991 (Besson)
Atame!, 1990 (Almodóvar)
Ateliers de La Ciotat, 1939 (Lumet)
Atencion prenatal, 1972 (Gómez)
Athens, 1982 (Angelopoulos)
Athlète incomplet, 1932 (Autant-Lara)
Atilla 74, 1975 (Cacoyannis)
Atividades politicas em Sao Paolo, 1950 (Pereira Dos Santos)
Atlantic, 1929 (Dupont)
Atlantic City, 1980 (Malle)
Atlantic Ferry, 1941 (Fisher)
Atlantide, 1921 (Feyder)
Atlantide, 1932 (Pabst)
Atlantik, 1929 (Dupont)
Atlantis, 1913 (Blom, Curtiz)
Atlantis, 1930 (Dupont)
Atlas, 1960 (Corman)
Atom, 1918 (Borzage)
Atomic Kid, 1954 (Edwards)
Atonement of Gösta Berling. *See* **Gösta Berlings saga**, 1923
Atre, 1920 (Gance)
Atsui yoru, 1968 (Yoshimura)
Att Älska, 1964 (Donner)
Att Segla är Nödvändigt, 1937/38 (Fejös)
Atta Boy's Last Race, 1916 (Browning)
Attack!, 1956 (Aldrich)
Attack of the Crab Monsters, 1957 (Corman)
Attack of the Giant Leeches, 1959 (Corman)
Attaque d'un diligence, 1904 (Guy)
Attention Bandits, 1987 (Lelouch)
Atti degli apostoli, 1968 (Rossellini)
Attrait du bouge, 1912 (Feuillade)
Au Bal de Flore, 1900 (Guy)
Au bonheur des dames, 1929 (Duvivier)
Au cabaret, 1899/1900 (Guy)
Au carrefour de la vie, 1949 (Storck)
Au Clair de la lune ou Pierrot malheureux, 1904 (Méliès)
Au coeur de la ville, 1969 (Jutra)
Au cœur de l'Ile de France, 1954 (Grémillon)
Au-delà des grilles, 1948 (Clement)
Au gré des flots, 1913 (Feuillade)
Au hasard Balthazar, 1966 (Bresson, C. Miller)
Au nom de la loi, 1932 (M. Tourneur)
Au patys des jouets, 1908 (Méliès)
Au pays de George Sand, 1926 (Epstein)
Au pays des lions, 1912 (Feuillade)
Au pays des mages noirs, 1947 (Rouch)
Au pays du Roi Lépreux, 1927 (Feyder)
Au pays du scalp, 1931 (Cavalcanti)
Au petit bonheur, 1945 (L'Herbier)
Au Poulailler!, 1905 (Guy)
Au réfectoire, 1897/98 (Guy)

Balloon. *See* Fusen, 1956
Balloon, 1959 (Leacock)
Balloon Explosion. *See* Balloneksplosionen, 1913
Balloonatic, 1923 (Keaton)
Balthazar. *See* Au hasard Balthazar, 1966
Baltic Deputy. *See* Deputat Baltiki, 1936
Baltic Express. *See* Pociag, 1959
Balto, 1995 (Spielberg)
Bambina. *See* Farò da padre ..., 1974
Bambini di Praga, 1993 (Jireš)
Bambini in cittá, 1946 (Comencini)
Bambole, 1964 (Comencini, Risi)
Bamboo Blonde, 1946 (A. Mann)
Bamboo Cross, 1955 (Ford)
Bamboo Doll of Echizen. *See* Echizen take ningyo, 1963
Bamboo Leaf Flute of No Return. *See* Kaeranu sasabue, 1926
Bambuå påldern på Mentawei, 1937/38 (Fejös)
Bana kursun islemez, 1967 (Güney)
Banana Skin/Banana Peel. *See* Peau de banane, 1963
Bananas, 1971 (Allen)
Band of Angels, 1957 (Walsh)
Band of Ninja. *See* Ninja bugeicho, 1967
Band of the Hand, 1986 (M. Mann)
Band Wagon, 1953 (Minnelli)
Bande à part, 1964 (Godard)
Bande des quatre, 1989 (Rivette)
Bande von Hoheneck, 1950 (Staudte)
Bandeau sur les yeux, 1917 (Feuillade)
Bandeirantes, 1940 (Mauro)
Bandera, 1935 (Duvivier)
Banderas del amanecer, 1983 (Sanjinés)
Bandida, 1962 (Fernández)
Bandido, 1956 (Fleischer)
Bandini, 1963 (Roy)
Bandit, 1913 (Sennett)
Bandit Island of Karabei. *See* Return to Treasure Island, 1954
Bandit of Point Loma, 1912 (Dwan)
Bandito, 1946 (Lattuada)
Bandits. *See* Attention Bandits, 1987
Bandits in Rome. *See* Roma coma Chicago, 1969
Bandit's Wager, 1916 (Ford)
Bandit's Waterloo, 1908 (Griffith)
Bang!, 1977 (Troell)
Bangiku, 1954 (Naruse)
Bangville Police, 1913 (Sennett)
Banjo, 1947 (Fleischer)
Banjo on My Knee, 1936 (Cromwell)
Bank, 1915 (Bacon, Chaplin)
Bánk bán, 1914 (Curtiz)
Bank Book. *See* Vildledt Elskov, 1911
Bank Director, Carnival. *See* Karneval, 1908
Bank Holiday, 1938 (Launder, Reed)
Bank of Departure. *See* Ruri no kishi, 1956
Banka, 1957 (Gosho)
Banker's Daughter, 1910 (Walsh, Griffith)
Banner, 1974 (Frampton)
Banquet de Platon, 1989 (Ferreri)
Banquet des fraudeurs, 1951 (Storck)
Banshun, 1949 (Ozu)
Banwara, 1950 (Kapoor)
Banware Nayan, 1950 (Kapoor)
Bara en mor, 1949 (Sjöberg)
Bara gassen, 1949 (Naruse)
Bara ikutabi, 1955 (Kinugasa)
Barabbas, 1953 (Sjöberg)
Barabbas, 1962 (Fleischer)
Barajas, aeropuerto internacional, 1950 (Bardem)
Barbara Frietchie, 1915 (Guy)
Barbarella, 1968 (Vadim)
Barbarian, 1933 (S. Wood)
Barbarian and the Geisha, 1958 (Huston)
Barbarian, Ingomar, 1908 (Griffith)
Barbarian Queen, 1985 (Corman)
Barbaro del Ritmo, 1963 (Alvarez)
Barbarosa, 1981 (Schepisi)
Barbary Coast, 1935 (Hawks)
Barbary Sheep, 1917 (M. Tourneur)
Barbe-Bleue, 1901 (Méliès)
Barbe-Bleue, 1972 (Dmytryk)
Barbed Water, 1969 (Welles)
Barbed Wire, 1927 (Stiller)
Barber Shop, 1933 (Sennett)
Barberousse, 1916 (Gance)
Barber's Daughter, 1929 (Sennett)
Barboni, 1946 (Risi)
Barbora Hlavsová, 1942 (Fric)
Bardelys the Magnificent, 1926 (Florey, K. Vidor)
Bare Fists, 1919 (Ford)
Barefoot Contessa, 1954 (Mankiewicz)
Barefoot in the Park, 1967 (Redford)
Barfly, 1987 (Schroeder)
Bargain Hunt, 1928 (Sennett)
Bariera, 1966 (Skolimowski)
Bariri, 1958 (Olmi)
Barkleys of Broadway, 1949 (Walters)
Barn of the Naked Dead. *See* Terror Circus, 1973
Barndommens gade, 1986 (Henning-Jensen)
Barnet, 1909 (Blom)
Barnet, 1912 (Stiller, Sjöström)
Barnet, 1940 (Christensen)
Barnets Magt, 1914 (Holger-Madsen)
Barney Oldfield's Race for a Life, 1913 (Sennett)
Barnvagnen, 1963 (Troell)
Barnyard Flirtations, 1914 (Sennett)
Baron, 1911 (Sennett)
Baron de l'Ecluse, 1959 (Delannoy)
Baron fantôme, 1942 (Cocteau)
Baron Munchhausen. *See* **Baron Prášil,** 1940
Baron Münchausen's Dream. *See* Hallucinations du Baron Münchausen, 1911
Baron of Arizona, 1950 (Fuller)
Baron Prášil, 1940 (Fric)
Baroque. *See* Barroco, 1989
Baroque Diet, 1992 (Maysles)
Baroud, 1931 (Ingram)
Barque en mer, 1896-97 (Lumet)
Barque sortant du port, 1939 (Lumet)
Barrabas, 1919 (Feuillade)
Barrage contre le Pacifique, 1958 (Clement)
Barravento, 1962 (Pereira Dos Santos, Rocha)
Barren Lives. *See* **Vidas secas**, 1963
Barrier. *See* Bariera, 1966
Barrière, 1915 (Feuillade)
Barriers Burned Away. *See* Chicago Fire, 1925
Barroco, 1989 (Leduc)
Barry Lyndon, 1975 (Kubrick)
Barry MacKenzie Holds His Own, 1974 (Beresford)
Barsaat, 1949 (Kapoor)
Bartered Bride. *See* Die verkaufte Braut, 1932
Bartok, 1964 (Russell)
Bartók Béla: az éjszaka zenéje, 1970 (Gaál)
Barton Fink, 1991 (Coen)
Baruch. *See* Alte Gesetz, 1923
Barwy ochronne, 1976 (Zanussi)
Bas-fonds, 1936 (Becker, Renoir, Visconti)
Bashful Jim, 1925 (Sennett)
Basic Instinct, 1992 (Verhoeven)
Basic Training, 1971 (Wiseman)
Basilisk, 1914 (Hepworth)
Bassae, 1964 (Astruc)
Basta che non si sappia in giro, 1976 (Comencini)
Bastion Promenade 74. *See* Bástyasétány 74, 1974
Bástyasétány 74, 1974 (Schorm)

Bernice Bobs Her Hair, 1976 (Silver)
Bernstein in Israel, 1958 (Leacock)
Bernstein in Moscow, 1959 (Leacock)
Beröringen, 1971 (Bergman)
Berühmte Frau, 1927 (Wiene)
Beruhrte, 1981 (Sanders-Brahms)
Bes svideteley, 1983 (Mikhalkov)
Besame mucho, 1987 (Babenco)
Beside the Bonnie Brier Bush, 1921 (Hitchcock)
Besitzbürgerin, Jahrgang 1908, 1972 (Kluge)
Bespoke Overcoat, 1955 (Clayton)
Bespridannitsa, 1937 (Protazanov)
Best Foot Forward, 1943 (Donen, Walters)
Best Friends, 1982 (Jewison, Levinson)
Best Intentions. *See* Goda Viljan, 1992
Best Man, 1928 (Sennett)
Best Man, 1964 (Ashby, Schaffner)
Best Man Wins, 1912 (Dwan)
Best Man Wins, 1948 (J. Sturges)
Best of Enemies, 1915 (Sennett)
Best Policy, 1912 (Dwan)
Best Things in Life are Free, 1956 (Curtiz)
Best Way of Walking. *See* Meilleure façon de marcher, 1976
Best Woman of My Life. *See* Nejlepší ženská mého života, 1968
Best Years of Our Lives, 1946 (Wyler, Edwards)
Bête humaine, 1938 (Becker, Renoir)
Bête lumineuse, 1982 (Perrault)
Béton dans la ville, 1964-69 (Rohmer)
Betrayal, 1929 (Milestone)
Betrayal, 1948 (Micheaux)
Betrayal of Maggie, 1917 (Sennett)
Betrayed, 1917 (Walsh)
Betrayed, 1988 (Costa-Gavras)
Betrayed by a Hand Print, 1908 (Griffith)
Betrayer. *See* Vanina Vanini, 1961
Bette, 1993 (Chabrol)
Better 'ole, 1918 (Pearson)
Better Chance. *See* Chin shui Lou Tai, 1974
Better Late Than Never, 1916 (Sennett)
Better Times, 1919 (K. Vidor)
Better Tomorrow, 1986 (Woo)
Better Tomorrow II, 1987 (Woo)
Better Way, 1909 (Griffith)
Bettler GmbH, 1918 (Lang)
Betty of Greystone, 1916 (Dwan, Fleming)
Betty to the Rescue, 1917 (De Mille)
Between Calais and Dover. *See* Entre Calais et Douvres, 1897
Between Friends, 1924 (Blackton)
Between Heaven and Earth, 1992 (Delvaux)
Between Heaven and Hell, 1956 (Fleischer)
Between Showers, 1914 (Chaplin, Sennett)
Between the Lines, 1977 (Silver)
Between Three and Five Minutes, 1972 (Nemec)
Between Two Women, 1937 (Von Stroheim)
Between Two Worlds. *See* Delovak Athara, 1966
Between Two Worlds. *See* Der müde Tod: Ein Deutsches Volkslied in Sechs Versen, 1921
Between Wroclaw and Zielona Gora. *See* Miedzy Wrocławiem a Zieloną Górą, 1972
Between Your Hands. *See* Bayn Ideak, 1960
Betwixt Love and Fire, 1913 (Sennett)
Beverly Hillbillies, 1993 (Spheeris)
Beverly Hills Cop III, 1994 (Schroeder)
Bewafa, 1952 (Kapoor)
Beware of a Holy Whore. *See* Warnung vor einer heiligen Nutte, 1970
Beware of the Dog, 1923 (La Cava)
Beware the Boarders, 1918 (Sennett)
Bewitched Inn. *See* Auberge ensorcelée, 1897
Bewitched Trunk. *See* Coffre enchanté, 1904
Beyaz atli adam, 1965 (Güney)
Beyoğlu canavari, 1968 (Güney)
Beyond a Reasonable Doubt, 1956 (Lang)
Beyond Decay. *See* Choraku no kanata, 1924
Beyond JFK: The Question of Conspiracy, 1992 (Kopple)
Beyond Love and Hate. *See* Ai to nikushimi no kanata e, 1951
Beyond Rangoon, 1995 (Boorman)
Beyond the Aegean, 1989 (Kazan)
Beyond the Barricade. *See* Har jeg Ret til at tage mit eget Liv, 1919
Beyond the Clouds, 1995 (Antonioni, Wenders)
Beyond the Forest, 1949 (K. Vidor)
Beyond the Forest. *See* Tam za lesem, 1962
Beyond the River. *See* Bottom of the Bottle, 1956
Beyond the Rocks, 1922 (S. Wood)
Beyond the Square. *See* Tul a Kálvin-téren, 1955
Beyond the Wall. *See* Der müde Tod: Ein Deutsches Volkslied in Sechs Versen, 1921
Beyond Therapy, 1987 (Altman)
Bez końca, 1984 (Kieślowski)
Bez znieczulenia, 1977 (Wajda, Holland)
Bezhin Lug, 1966 (Eisenstein)
Bezhin Meadow. *See* Bezhin Lug, 1966
Bharat Mata, 1957 (Mehboob)
Bharosa, 1963 (Dutt)
Bhowani Junction, 1956 (Cukor)
Bhumika, 1977 (Benegal)
Bhuvan Shome, 1969 (Sen)
Bianca, 1984 (Moretti)
Bianco, rosso e ..., 1971 (Lattuada)
Bibbia, 1965 (Huston)
Bible. *See* Bibbia, 1965
Bible, 1975 (Jarman)
Bible, 1976 (Carné)
Bice skoro propast sveta, 1968 (Petrovic)
Biches, 1968 (Chabrol)
Bicots-nègres, vos voisins, 1973 (Hondo)
Bicycle Flirt, 1928 (Sennett)
Bicycle Thief. *See* **Ladri di biciclette,** 1948
Bid of Roses, 1933 (La Cava)
Bidone, 1955 (Fellini)
Bien amada, 1951 (Fernández)
Bienfaits du cinématographe, 1904 (Guy)
Bienvenido, Mr. Marshall!, 1952 (Bardem, García Berlanga)
Bière, 1924 (Grémillon)
Bièvre, fille perdue, 1939 (Clement)
Bife Titanic, 1980 (Kusturica)
Big, 1988 (Marshall)
Big Bad Mama, 1974 (Corman)
Big Bad Mama II, 1986 (Corman)
Big Bird Cage, 1972 (Corman)
Big Blockade, 1941 (Cavalcanti, Crichton)
Big Blue. *See* Grand bleu, 1988
Big Brother, 1923 (Dwan)
Big Brown Eyes, 1936 (Walsh)
Big Business, 1929 (Stevens)
Big Chill, 1983 (Costner, Kasdan)
Big City, 1928 (Browning)
Big City, 1937 (Borzage)
Big City, 1948 (Donen)
Big City. *See* Mahanagar, 1963
Big City. *See* Grande cidade, 1966
Big Combo, 1954 (Joseph H. Lewis)
Big City Blues, 1932 (LeRoy)
Big Country, 1958 (Ashby, Wyler)
Big Dan, 1923 (Wellman)
Big Day in Bogo, 1958 (Dickinson)
Big Doll House, 1971 (Corman)
Big Dust-up. *See* Der grosse Verhau, 1970
Big Family. *See* Bolshaya semya, 1954
Big Fibber, 1933 (Sennett)
Big Fisherman, 1959 (Borzage)
Big Flame, 1969 (Loach)
Big Gamble, 1931 (Niblo)

Black Moon Rising, 1986 (Carpenter)
Black Narcissus, 1947 (Powell)
Black Oak Conspiracy, 1977 (Corman)
Black on White. *See* Mustaa Valkoisella, 1968
Black Orchid, 1959 (Ritt)
Black Orchids, 1916 (Ingram)
Black Oxfords, 1924 (Sennett)
Black Panthers, 1968 (Varda)
Black Peter. *See* Cerný Petr, 1963
Black Rain. *See* Kuroi Ame, 1988
Black Rain, 1989 (Scott)
Black Rainbow. *See* Fekete szivarvany, 1916
Black River. *See* Kuroi kawa, 1957
Black Robe, 1992 (Beresford)
Black Rose, 1950 (Hathaway, Welles)
Black Roses. *See* Svarta rosor, 1932
Black Sheep, 1912 (Griffith)
Black Sheep, 1935 (Dwan)
Black Sheep, 1995 (Spheeris)
Black Sheep of Whitehall, 1941 (Dearden)
Black Sin. *See* Schwarze Sunde, 1989
Black Stallion, 1979 (Coppola)
Black Stallion Returns, 1983 (Coppola)
Black Sunday, 1976 (Frankenheimer)
Black Swan, 1942 (King)
Black Tide. *See* Kuroi ushio, 1954
Black Vision, 1965 (Brakhage)
Black Watch, 1929 (Ford)
Black Waters, 1929 (Neilan)
Black Widow, 1987 (Rafelson)
Black Windmill, 1974 (Siegel)
Black-Wogs, Your Neighbours. *See* Bicots-nègres, vos voisins, 1973
Blackbeard the Pirate, 1952 (Walsh)
Blackbeard's Ghost, 1968 (Stevenson)
Blackbelt, 1992 (Corman)
Blackboard Jungle, 1955 (Brooks, Mazursky)
Blackened Hills, 1912 (Dwan)
Blackguard, 1925 (Hitchcock)
Blackmail, 1929 (Hitchcock)
Blackmailed, 1950 (Zetterling)
Blackout. *See* Contraband, 1940
Blackout. *See* Murder by Proxy, 1955
Blacks and Whites in Days and Nights, 1960 (Vanderbeek)
Blacksmith, 1922 (Keaton)
Blade af Satans Bog, 1921 (Dreyer)
Blade Runner, 1982 (Scott)
Blaise Pascal, 1975 (Rossellini)
Blame It on the Bellboy, 1992 (Anderson)
Blame It On Rio, 1984 (Donen)
Blame the Woman, 1932 (Niblo)
Blanc et le noir, 1931 (Guitry)
Blanc et le noir, 1932 (Florey)
Blarney, 1926 (Lewin)
Blason, 1915 (Feuillade)
Blaubart, 1984 (Von Trotta, Zanussi)
Blaue Engel, 1930 (Von Sternberg)
Blaue Licht, 1932 (Riefenstahl)
Blaue von Himmel, 1932 (Wilder)
Blazing Days, 1927 (Wyler)
Blazing Saddles, 1974 (Brooks)
Blazing Six Shooters, 1940 (Joseph H. Lewis)
Blázni a devcátka, 1989 (Kachyňa)
Blé en herbe, 1953 (Autant-Lara)
Bleak Moments, 1971 (Leigh)
Blechtrommel, 1979 (Schlöndorff)
Bled, 1929 (Becker, Renoir)
Bleierne Zeit, 1981 (Von Trotta)
Błękitny krzyż, 1955 (Munk)
Bless the Beasts and Children, 1971 (Kramer)
Bless Their Little Hearts, 1983 (Burnett)
Blind, 1986 (Wiseman)
Blind Adventure, 1933 (Schoedsack)
Blind Alley, 1939 (C. Vidor)
Blind Chance. *See* Przypadek, 1981
Blind Date, 1959 (Losey)
Blind Date, 1987 (Edwards)
Blind Desire. *See* Part de l'ombre, 1945
Blind Director. *See* Der Angriff der Gegenwart auf die Ubrige Zeit, 1985
Blind Fate, 1914 (Hepworth)
Blind Fate. *See* Lotteriseddel No. 22152, 1915
Blind Goddess, 1926 (Fleming)
Blind Husbands, 1918 (Von Stroheim)
Blind Justice. *See* Haevnens Nat, 1915
Blind Princess and the Poet, 1911 (Griffith)
Blinde Skaebne. *See* Lotteriseddel No. 22152, 1915
Blindfold. *See* Ojos vendados, 1978
Blindkuh, 1914 (Lubitsch)
Blindness of Devotion, 1915 (Ingram)
Blindness of Fortune, 1918 (Hepworth)
Blinkeyes, 1926 (Pearson)
Bliss, 1967 (Markopoulos)
Blithe Spirit, 1945 (Lean)
Blizna, 1976 (Kieślowski)
Block 15. *See* Blok 15, 1959
Block-notes di un regista, 1969 (Fellini)
Blockade, 1938 (Dieterle)
Blodets röst, 1913 (Sjöström)
Blok 15, 1959 (Schorm)
Blomstertid, 1940 (Sjöberg)
Blond Bombshell. *See* Bombshell, 1933
Blonde from Singapore, 1941 (Dmytryk)
Blonde Inspiration, 1941 (Berkeley)
Blonde Venus, 1932 (Von Sternberg)
Blonder Traum, 1932 (Wilder)
Blonde's Revenge, 1926 (Sennett)
Blondie of the Follies, 1932 (Goulding)
Blood Alley, 1955 (Wellman)
Blood and Roses. *See* Et mourir de plaisir, 1960
Blood and Sand, 1922 (Arzner, Niblo)
Blood and Sand, 1941 (Mamoulian)
Blood and Soul. *See* Chi to rei, 1923
Blood and Water, 1913 (Guy)
Blood Barrier, 1920 (Blackton)
Blood Bath, 1965 (Corman)
Blood Brothers, 1978 (Mulligan)
Blood Feast. *See* Fin de fiesta, 1959
Blood Feud, 1983 (Newell)
Blood for Blood, Death for Death. *See* Krov'za krov', smert'za smert': slodeianiya Nemetsko-Fashistkih zakhvatchikov na territorii C.C.C.P. me ne zabudem, 1941
Blood for Dracula, 1974 (Polanski)
Blood Kin, 1969 (Lumet)
Blood Need Not Be Spilled. *See* Ne nado krovi, 1917
Blood of Minas. *See* Sangue Mineiro, 1929
Blood of Others. *See* Sang des autres, 1983
Blood of the Condor. *See* **Yawar mallku**, 1969
Blood of the Pomegranates. *See* Sayat nova, 1969
Blood on the Balcony. *See* Benito Mussolini, 1961
Blood on the Moon, 1948 (Wise)
Blood Orange, 1953 (Fisher)
Blood Relatives, 1978 (Chabrol)
Blood Simple, 1984 (Coen)
Blood Sisters. *See* Sisters, 1973
Blood Wedding. *See* Bodas de sangre, 1981
Bloodfist, 1989 (Corman)
Bloodfist II, 1990 (Corman, Craven)
Bloodfist 3, 1992 (Corman)
Bloodfist 4, 1992 (Corman)
Bloodhounds of the North, 1913 (Dwan)
Blood's Tone. *See* Three Films, 1965
Bloodstain, 1912 (Guy)
Bloody Kids, 1980 (Fric)

Bond Boy, 1922 (King)
Bond Street, 1948 (Clayton)
Bonds of Hate. *See* Prometheus I-II, 1919
Bonds That Chafe. *See* **Erotikon**, 1920
Bonehead. *See* His Favorite Pastime, 1914
Bonfire of the Vanities, 1990 (De Palma)
Bonheur, 1934 (L'Herbier)
Bonheur, 1965 (Varda)
Bonheur d'être aimée, 1962 (Storck)
Bonheur des autres, 1918 (Dulac)
Bonheur toi-même, 1980 (Goretta)
Bonita of El Cajon, 1911 (Dwan)
Bonjour Mr. Lewis, 1982 (Scorsese)
Bonjour, New York!, 1928 (Florey)
Bonjour sourire, 1956 (Sautet)
Bonjour Tristesse, 1957 (Preminger)
Bonne Absinthe, 1899/1900 (Guy)
Bonne année, 1913 (Feuillade)
Bonne année, 1972 (Lelouch)
Bonne Bergère et la méchante princesse, 1908 (Méliès)
Bonne chance, 1935 (Guitry)
Bonne Farce avec ma tête, 1904 (Méliès)
Bonnes Femmes, 1960 (Chabrol)
Bonnie and Clyde, 1967 (Benton, Penn)
Bonnie, Bonnie Lassie, 1919 (Browning)
Bonnie Brier Bush. *See* Beside the Bonnie Brier Bush, 1921
Boob, 1926 (Wellman)
Boobs and Bricks, 1913 (Dwan)
Boobs in the Woods, 1925 (Capra, Sennett)
Book Bargain, 1935 (Cavalcanti)
Boom, 1963 (De Sica)
Boom!, 1968 (Losey)
Boomerang, 1947 (Kazan)
Boon. *See* Kondura/Anugrahan, 1977
Boot, 1981 (Petersen)
Boot Polish, 1954 (Kapoor)
Boots, 1953 (E. Wood)
Boots Malone, 1952 (Dieterle)
Boquitas pintadas, 1974 (Torre Nilsson)
Border, 1982 (Richardson)
Border Cavalier, 1927 (Wyler)
Border Feud. *See* Gränsfolken, 1913
Border Incident, 1949 (A. Mann)
Border Legion, 1924 (Hathaway, Howard)
Border Radio, 1988 (Anders)
Border Wolves, 1938 (Joseph H. Lewis)
Borets i kloun, 1957 (Barnet)
Borgne, 1981 (Ruiz)
Borinage. *See* Misére au Borinage, 1934
Born for Glory. *See* Brown on Resolution, 1935
Born Lucky, 1932 (Powell)
Born on the Fourth of July, 1989 (Stone)
Born Reckless, 1930 (Ford)
Born to Be Bad, 1950 (N. Ray)
Born to Kill, 1947 (Wise)
Born to Kill. *See* Cockfighter, 1974
Born to Sing, 1941 (Berkeley)
Born Yesterday, 1950 (Cukor)
Boro no kesshitai, 1943 (Imai)
Borom Sarret, 1963 (Sembene)
Borrowed Babies. *See* Kölcsönkért csecsemök, 1914
Borrowed Clothes, 1918 (Weber)
Borrowed Finery, 1914 (Ingram)
Borsós Miklós, 1966 (Mészáros)
Boryoku, 1952 (Yoshimura)
Boss of Camp Four, 1922 (W.S. Van Dyke)
Boss of Hangtown Mesa, 1942 (Joseph H. Lewis)
Bossu, 1944 (Delannoy)
Boston Strangler, 1968 (Fleischer)
Boston Tea Party, 1908 (Porter)
Bostonians, 1984 (Ivory)
Both Ends of the Candle. *See* Helen Morgan Story, 1957
Both You and I. *See* Ore mo omae mo, 1946
Bottle, 1915 (Hepworth)
Bottle Imp, 1917 (Neilan)
Bottom of the Bottle, 1956 (Hathaway)
Boucher, 1970 (Chabrol)
Bouclette, 1917 (L'Herbier)
Boudoir Brothers, 1932 (Sennett)
Boudu sauvé des eaux, 1932 (Becker, Renoir)
Boudu Saved from Drowning. *See* **Boudu sauvé des eaux**, 1932
Boukoki, 1973 (Rouch)
Boulangerie de Monceau, 1963 (Rohmer, Schroeder)
Boulder Blues and Pearls and, 1992 (Brakhage)
Boulevard, 1960 (Duvivier)
Boulevard Slush. *See* Slyakot' bulvarnaya, 1918
Boulevards d'Afrique—bac ou mariage, 1988 (Rouch)
Bound for Glory, 1976 (Ashby)
Bound in Morocco, 1918 (Dwan)
Boundary House, 1918 (Hepworth)
Bounteous Summer. *See* Schedroe leto, 1950
Bourbon Street Blues, 1978 (Fassbinder, Sirk)
Bourgogne, 1936 (Epstein)
Bourreau turc, 1904 (Méliès)
Bourse ou la vie. *See* Piednadze albo zycie, 1961
"Bout-de-Zan" series, 1912/16 (Feuillade)
Bow Wow, 1922 (Sennett)
Bowery, 1914 (Walsh)
Bowery, 1933 (Walsh)
Bowery Boy, 1940 (Fuller)
Bowery Boys, 1914 (Sennett)
Bowling Match, 1913 (Sennett)
Box of Sun. *See* Boîte à soleil, 1988
Boxcar Bertha, 1972 (Corman, Scorsese)
Boxing. *See* Boks, 1961
Boy and His Kite. *See* Pojken och draken, 1962
Boy and the Law, 1914 (Stahl)
Boy and the Pigeon. *See* Malchik i golub, 1961
Boy and the Sea, 1953 (Brakhage)
Boy Friend, 1928 (McCarey)
Boy Friend, 1971 (Russell)
Boy from Oklahoma, 1954 (Curtiz)
Boy in Blue. *See* Der Knabe in Blau, 1919
Boy in the Tree. *See* Pojken i trädet, 1961
Boy Meets Girl, 1938 (Bacon)
Boy of the Revolution, 1911 (Cruze)
Boy of the Sea. *See* Kaikoku danji, 1926
Boy of Two Worlds. *See* Paw, 1959
Boy Who Stole a Million, 1960 (Crichton)
Boy Who Turned Yellow, 1972 (Powell)
Boy with Green Hair, 1949 (Losey)
Boy. *See* **Shonen**, 1969
Boyevoy kinosbornik no. 3, 1941 (Barnet)
Boyevoy kinosbornik no. 10, 1942 (Barnet)
Boyfriends and Girlfriends. *See* Ami de mon amie, 1987
Boys from Brazil, 1978 (Schaffner)
Boys from Fengkuei. *See* Fêng Kuei Lai Tê Jen, 1984
Boys from the West Coast. *See* Vesterhavsdrenge, 1950
Boys in the Band, 1970 (Friedkin)
Boys Next Door, 1985 (Spheeris)
Boys of Paul Street. *See* Pál utcai fiúk, 1968
Boys of the City, 1940 (Joseph H. Lewis)
Boys Will Be Boys, 1932 (Stevens)
Bra flicka reder sig själv, 1914 (Sjöström)
Braconniers, 1903 (Guy)
Brahma Diamond, 1909 (Griffith)
Brahmane et le papillon, 1901 (Méliès)
Brahmin and the Butterfly. *See* Brahmane et le papillon, 1901
Brain Eaters, 1958 (Corman)
Braindead, 1992 (Jackson)
Bram Stoker's Dracula, 1992 (Coppola)
Bramy raju, 1967 (Wajda)

British Family in Peace and War, 1940 (Pearson)
British Sounds, 1969 (Godard)
British Youth, 1941 (Pearson)
Broad-Minded, 1930 (LeRoy)
Broadcast. *See* Ekpombi, 1968
Broadway, 1929 (Fejös)
Broadway after Dark, 1924 (LeRoy)
Broadway Ahead. *See* Sweetheart of the Campus, 1941
Broadway Babies, 1929 (LeRoy)
Broadway Bill, 1934 (Capra)
Broadway Blues, 1929 (Sennett)
Broadway by Light, 1957 (Resnais)
Broadway Daddies. *See* Broadway Babies, 1929
Broadway Danny Rose, 1984 (Allen)
Broadway Gondolier, 1935 (Bacon)
Broadway Melody, 1929 (Goulding)
Broadway Rhythm, 1944 (Walters)
Broadway Rose, 1922 (Goulding)
Broadway Serenade, 1939 (Berkeley)
Bröderna, 1913 (Stiller)
Broke in China, 1927 (Sennett)
Broken Arrow, 1950 (Daves)
Broken Arrow, 1996 (Woo)
Broken Blossoms, 1919 (Griffith)
Broken Butterfly, 1919 (M. Tourneur)
Broken Chains, 1922 (Garnett)
Broken Chains. *See* Yevo prizyv, 1925
Broken Coin, 1915 (Ford)
Broken Commandment. *See* Hakai, 1962
Broken Cross, 1911 (Griffith)
Broken Doll, 1910 (Griffith)
Broken Doll, 1921 (Dwan)
Broken Drum. *See* Yabure daiko, 1949
Broken English, 1979 (Jarman)
Broken Fetters, 1916 (Ingram)
Broken Hearts of Hollywood, 1926 (Bacon)
Broken in the Wars, 1918 (Hepworth)
Broken Lance, 1954 (Dmytryk)
Broken Locket, 1909 (Griffith)
Broken Lullaby. *See* Man I Killed, 1932
Broken Ties, 1912 (Dwan)
Broken Violin. *See* Lulli ou le violon brisé, 1908
Broken Ways, 1913 (Griffith)
Bröllöpsresan, 1935 (Molander)
Bromo and Juliet, 1926 (McCarey)
Bronco Billy, 1980 (Eastwood)
Bronco Buster, 1952 (Boetticher)
Bronco Busting for Flying A Pictures, 1912 (Dwan)
Bronenosets Potemkin, 1925 (Eisenstein)
Bronsteins Kinder, 1991 (Kawalerowicz)
Bronzes, 1978 (Leconte)
Brood, 1978 (Cronenberg)
Brookfield Recreation Center, 1964 (Baillie)
Brother from Another Planet, 1984 (Sayles)
Brother of a Hero. *See* Brat geroya, 1940
Brother Orchid, 1940 (Bacon)
Brother Sun, Sister Moon. *See* Fratelli sole sorella luna, 1972
Brotherhood, 1968 (Ritt)
Brotherhood of the Yakuza. *See* Yakuza, 1975
Brothers, 1912 (Griffith)
Brothers. *See* Bröderna, 1913
Brothers, 1913 (Dwan)
Brothers and Sisters of the Toda Family. *See* Toda-ke no kyodai, 1941
Brothers in Law, 1957 (Boulting, Schlesinger)
Brothers Karamazov, 1958 (Brooks)
Brouillard sur la ville. *See* Gaz mortels, 1916
Brown on Resolution, 1935 (Fisher)
Brown Wallet, 1936 (Powell)
Browning, 1913 (Feuillade)
Browning Version, 1950 (Asquith)
Browning Version, 1994 (Scott)
Brown's Seance, 1912 (Sennett)
Brubaker, 1980 (Rafelson, Redford)
Bruciati da cocente passione, 1976 (Lattuada)
Brunkul, 1941 (Henning-Jensen)
Brussels "Loops," 1958 (Clarke)
Brutalität in Stein, 1960 (Kluge)
Brutality, 1912 (Griffith)
Brutality in Stone. *See* Brutalität in Stein, 1960
Brute. *See* Dùvad, 1959
Brute Force. *See* In Prehistoric Days, 1913
Brute Force, 1947 (Brooks, Dassin)
Bruto, 1952 (Buñuel)
Brutti, sporchi e cattivi, 1976 (Scola)
Bruyère, 1964-69 (Rohmer)
Bryggerens Datter, 1912 (Dreyer)
Brzezina, 1970 (Wajda)
Bu vatanin cocuklari, 1958 (Güney)
Buccaneer, 1938 (De Mille)
Buccaneer, 1958 (De Mille)
Buchanan Rides Alone, 1958 (Boetticher)
Buchhalterin, 1918 (Dupont)
Büchse der Pandora, 1928 (Pabst)
Bucket of Blood, 1959 (Corman)
Bucking Broadway, 1917 (Ford)
Bucking Society, 1916 (Sennett)
Bucklige und die Tanzerin, 1920 (Murnau)
Bucovina-Ukrainian Land. *See* Bukovyna-Zemlya Ukrayinska, 1940
Budapest, amiért szeretem, 1971 (Szabó)
Budapest Tales. *See* Budapesti mesék, 1976
Budapest, Why I Love It. *See* Budapest, amiért szeretem, 1971
Budapesti mesék, 1976 (Szabó)
Buddy Buddy, 1981 (Wilder)
Buenos dias, Buenos Aires, 1960 (Birri)
Buffalo Bill, 1944 (Wellman)
Buffalo Bill and the Indians, or Sitting Bull's History Lesson, 1976 (Altman, Rudolph)
Buffer Zone. *See* Cserepek, 1981
Bufferin, 1966 (Warhol)
Buffet froid, 1979 (Blier)
Bugambilia, 1944 (Fernández)
Bugiarda, 1965 (Comencini)
Bugs Bunny Superstar, 1975 (Welles)
Bugsy, 1991 (Levinson)
Bugsy Malone, 1976 (Foster, Parker)
Build My Gallows High. *See* **Out of the Past**, 1947
Builders, 1954 (Altman)
Building, 1968-73 (Potter)
Building the Great Los Angeles Aqueduct, 1913 (Dwan)
Building the Pyramids, 1973 (Jarman)
Buio in sala, 1950 (Risi)
Bukovyna-Zemlya Ukrayinska, 1940 (Dovzhenko)
Bulbule Baghdad, 1933 (Mehboob)
Bull and Sand, 1924 (Sennett)
Bull Durham, 1988 (Costner)
Bull Fighter, 1927 (Sennett)
Bulldog Drummond's Peril, 1938 (Dmytryk)
Bulldog Jack, 1935 (Launder)
Bulles de savon animées, 1906 (Méliès)
Bullet in the Head, 1990 (Woo)
Bullets Cannot Pierce Me. *See* Bana kursun islemez, 1967
Bullets for O'Hara, 1941 (Howard)
Bullets over Broadway, 1994 (Allen, Reiner)
Bullfight, 1955 (Clarke)
Bullfight at Málaga, 1958 (Leacock)
Bullfighter and the Lady, 1951 (Boetticher)
Bulls and Bears, 1929 (Sennett)
Bull's Eye for Farmer Pietersen. *See* Boer Pietersen schiet in de roos, 1949
Buncoed Stage Johnnie, 1908 (Méliès)
Bungalow Boobs, 1924 (McCarey)
Bungalow Troubles, 1920 (Sennett)
Bungawan Solo, 1951 (Ichikawa)

Bunny Lake Is Missing, 1965 (Preminger)
Buon natale, buon anno, 1989 (Comencini)
buone notizie, 1979 (Petri)
Buongiorno elefante!, 1952 (De Sica)
Buongiorno natura, 1955 (Olmi)
Buono, il brutto, il cattivo, 1966 (Eastwood, Leone)
Buraikan, 1970 (Shinoda)
Burcak tarlasi, 1966 (Güney)
Burden of Life. *See* Jinsei no onimotsu, 1935
Burglar, 1928 (Capra, Sennett)
Burglar on the Roof, 1898 (Blackton)
Burglar's Dilemma, 1912 (Griffith)
Burial Path, 1978 (Brakhage)
Buried Hand, 1915 (Walsh)
Buried Secret. *See* Det unge Blod, 1915
Burlesque Suicide, 1902 (Porter)
Burma Victory, 1945 (Boulting)
Burmese Harp. *See* **Biruma no tategoto**, 1956
Burn! *See* Queimada, 1969
Burned Hand, 1915 (Browning)
Burning, 1967 (Frears)
Burning Season, 1994 (Frankenheimer)
Burning Secret. *See* Brennende Geheimnis, 1933
Burning Soil. *See* Der Brennende Acker, 1922
Burning Stable, 1900 (Hepworth)
Burning the Pyramids. *See* Garden of Luxor, 1972
Burnt by the Sun. *See* **Outomlionnye solntsem**, 1994
Burroughs, 1982 (Jarmusch)
Bus Driver's Tale, 1990 (Baillie)
Bus Riley's Back in Town, 1965 (Hellman)
Bushido: Samurai Saga. *See* Bushido zankoku monogatari, 1963
Bushido zankoku monogatari, 1963 (Imai)
Business Is Business, 1971 (Verhoeven)
Büssende Magdalena, 1915 (Wiene)
Busted Hearts. *See* Those Love Pangs, 1914
Busted Johnny. *See* Making a Living, 1914
Buster Keaton Rides Again, 1965 (Keaton)
Buster Keaton Story, 1956 (De Mille)
Buster se marie, 1930 (Autant-Lara)
Busters verden, 1984 (August)
Busy Day, 1914 (Chaplin, Sennett)
Busybody, 1923 (La Cava)
But the Greatest of These Is Charity, 1912 (Cruze)
Buta to gunkan, 1961 (Imamura)
Butch and Sundance: The Early Days, 1979 (Lester)
Butch Cassidy and the Sundance Kid, 1969 (Redford, G. Hill)
Butcher Boy, 1917 (Keaton)
Butter Fingers, 1925 (Sennett)
Butterfly, 1924 (Brown)
Butterfly, 1981 (Welles)
Butterfly Girl. *See* Ch'iao Ju Ts'ai Tieh Fei Fei Fei, 1981
Butterfly on the Wheel, 1915 (M. Tourneur)
Butterfly Revolution. *See* Summer Camp Nightmare, 1987
Button My Back, 1929 (Sennett)
Buttons, 1915 (Pearson)
Büyük cellatlar, 1967 (Güney)
Bwana Toshi no uta, 1965 (Hani)
By Candlelight, 1934 (Whale)
By Design, 1980 (Jutra)
By Divine Right, 1919 (Von Sternberg)
By Golly, 1920 (Sennett)
By Heck, 1922 (Sennett)
By Hook or By Crook. *See* I Dood It, 1943
By Indian Post, 1919 (Ford)
By Love Possessed, 1961 (J. Sturges)
By Rocket to the Moon. *See* Frau im Mond, 1929
By Stork Delivery, 1916 (Sennett)
By the Deep Blue Sea. *See* U samogo sinego morya, 1935
By the Lake. *See* U ozera, 1969
By the Law. *See* Po zakonu, 1926
By the Light of the Moon, 1911 (Porter)
By the Sea, 1915 (Chaplin)
By ved navn København, 1960 (Roos)
Bye Bye Brasil, 1980 (Diegues)
Bye Bye Braverman, 1968 (Lumet)
Bye Bye Monkey, 1978 (Ferreri)
Bye-Bye Red Riding Hood. *See* Piroska és a farkas, 1988
Byelyi orel, 1928 (Protazanov)
Byłem żołnierzem, 1970 (Kieślowski)
Byn vid den Trivsamma Brunnen, 1937/38 (Fejös)
Bytva za nashu Radyansku Ukrayinu, 1943 (Dovzhenko)

C.I.D., 1956 (Dutt)
C.O.D., 1932 (Powell)
Cab No. 519. *See* Droske 519, 1909
Cabaret, 1972 (Fosse)
Cabareteras, 1980 (Fernández)
Cabbage Fairy. *See* Fée aux choux, 1896
Cabeza de la hidra, 1981 (Leduc)
Cabezas cortadas, 1970 (Rocha)
Cabin Boy, 1994 (Burton)
Cabin in the Cotton, 1932 (Curtiz)
Cabin in the Sky, 1942 (Minnelli)
Cabinet of Dr. Caligari. *See* **Kabinett des Dr. Caligari**, 1920
Cabinet of Dr. Ramirez, 1991 (Lynch)
Cabinets de physique au XVIIIème siècle, 1964-69 (Rohmer)
Cabiria, 1914 (Pastrone)
Cabos Blancos, 1954 (Willard Van Dyke)
Caccia alla volpe, 1938 (Blasetti)
Caccia alla volpe, 1966 (De Sica)
Caccia in brughiera, 1949 (Risi)
Caccia tragica, 1947 (De Santis)
Cactus Land, 1988 (Jarman)
Cactus Nell, 1917 (Sennett)
Cadaveri eccelenti, 1976 (Rosi)
Caddy, 1953 (Jerry Lewis)
Cadena Perpetua, 1978 (Ripstein)
Caduta degli dei, 1969 (Visconti)
Caduta di Troia, 1910 (Pastrone)
Cage of Gold, 1950 (Dearden)
Caged, 1950 (Cromwell)
Caged Heat, 1974 (Corman, Demme)
Cagna. *See* Liza, 1972
Caicara, 1950 (Cavalcanti)
Caida de Sodoma, 1974 (Almodóvar)
Cáida, 1959 (Torre Nilsson)
Cain and Mabel, 1936 (Bacon)
Caine, 1967 (Fuller)
Caine Mutiny, 1954 (Dmytryk, Kramer)
Caine Mutiny Court-Martial, 1988 (Altman)
Cairo, 1942 (Mankiewicz, W.S. Van Dyke)
Cairo as Told by Youssef Chahine, 1991 (Chahine)
Cairo Station. *See* **Bab el Hadid**, 1958
Caissounbouw Rotterdam, 1929 (Ivens)
Cake-Walk de la pendule, 1903 (Guy)
Cake-Walk Infernal, 1903 (Méliès)
Calabuch, 1956 (García Berlanga)
Calais-Douvres, 1931 (Litvak)
Calamitous Elopement, 1908 (Griffith)
Calamity. *See* Kalamita, 1980
Calamity Anne, Detective, 1913 (Dwan)
Calamity Anne Parcel Post, 1913 (Dwan)
Calamity Anne's Beauty, 1913 (Dwan)
Calamity Anne's Inheritance, 1913 (Dwan)
Calamity Anne's Trust, 1913 (Dwan)
Calamity Anne's Vanity, 1913 (Dwan)
Calamity Anne's Ward, 1912 (Dwan)
Calandria, 1933 (De Fuentes)
Calcutta, 1969 (Malle)
Calcutta 71, 1972 (Sen)
Calcutta Cruel City. *See* **Do Bigha Zamin**, 1953
Calcutta, My El Dorado, 1990 (Sen)

Calendar Girl, 1947 (Dwan)
Calendar Girl, 1993 (Marshall)
Calendar of the Year, 1936 (Cavalcanti, Grierson)
Caliente Love, 1933 (Sennett)
California, 1927 (W.S. Van Dyke)
California Dolls. *See* All the Marbles, 1981
California Split, 1974 (Altman, Rudolph)
Calimari Union, 1985 (Kaurismaki)
Call, 1909 (Griffith)
Call a Cop, 1921 (Sennett)
Call a Cop!, 1931 (Stevens)
Call from Space, 1989 (Fleischer)
Call Me Mister, 1951 (Bacon, Berkeley)
Call Northside 777, 1948 (Hathaway)
Call of the Canyon, 1923 (Fleming, LeRoy)
Call of the East, 1917 (Cruze)
Call of the North, 1914 (De Mille)
Call of the Open Range, 1911 (Dwan)
Call of the Wild, 1908 (Griffith)
Call of the Wild, 1935 (Wellman)
Call of Youth, 1920 (Hitchcock)
Call to Arms, 1902 (Hepworth)
Call to Arms, 1910 (Griffith, Sennett)
Call to Arms, 1913 (Dwan)
Callas Text mit Doppel-beleuchtung, 1968 (Schroeter)
Callas Walking Lucia, 1968 (Schroeter)
Calle Mayor, 1956 (Bardem)
Called Back, 1912 (Cruze)
Callejón sin salida, 1964 (Fernández)
Calling Bulldog Drummond, 1951 (Saville)
Calling Hubby's Bluff, 1929 (Sennett)
Calling the Shots, 1988 (Zetterling)
Calling the Tune, 1936 (Dickinson)
Calmos, 1975 (Blier)
Calvaire, 1914 (Feuillade)
Cambrioleur et agent, 1904 (Guy)
Cambrioleurs, 1897/98 (Guy)
Cambrioleurs de Paris, 1904 (Guy)
Came the Dawn, 1928 (McCarey)
Camée, 1913 (M. Tourneur)
Cameo Kirby, 1914 (De Mille)
Cameo Kirby, 1923 (Ford)
Camera Bluff. *See* Amator, 1978
Camera d'Afrique, 1983 (Sembene)
Cameraman, 1928 (Keaton)
Cameriera bella presenza offresi, 1951 (De Sica, Fellini)
Camicie Rosse, 1952 (Rosi)
Camila, 1984 (Bemberg)
Camille, 1927 (Niblo)
Camille, 1937 (Cukor)
Camille ou la Comédie catastrophique, 1971 (C. Miller)
Camille without Camelias. *See* Signora senza camelie, 1953
Camion, 1977 (Duras)
Cammina, cammina, 1983 (Olmi)
Cammino della speranza, 1950 (Fellini, Germi)
Camorrista, 1986 (Tornatore)
Camouflage. *See* Barwy ochronne, 1976
Camp, 1965 (Warhol)
Camp de Thiaroye, 1987 (Sembene)
Campanas tambien pueden doblar mañana, 1983 (Alvarez)
Campi sperimentali, 1957 (Olmi)
Camping, 1957 (Zeffirelli)
Campo dei fiori, 1943 (Fellini)
Campus Carmen, 1928 (Sennett)
Campus Crushes, 1929 (Sennett)
Campus Vamp, 1928 (Sennett)
Canadian Officers in the Making, 1917 (Pearson)
Canal Zone, 1977 (Wiseman)
Canale, 1965/66 (Bertolucci)
Canary Bananas, 1935 (Leacock)
Cançao do berço, 1930 (Cavalcanti)
Cancer, 1968 (Rocha)
Cancion de cuna, 1952 (De Fuentes)
Candid Camera, 1932 (Sennett)
Candidate, 1972 (Redford)
Candidate. *See* Der Kandidat, 1980
Candle and the Moth. *See* Evangeliemandens Liv, 1914
Candle in the Wind. *See* Fuzen no tomoshibi, 1957
Candlelight in Algeria, 1943 (Fisher)
Candleshoe, 1978 (Foster)
Candy, 1968 (Huston)
Candy Mountain, 1987 (Jarmusch)
Candy Stripe Nurses, 1974 (Corman)
Canker of Jealousy, 1915 (Hepworth)
Cannery Row, 1982 (Huston)
Cannibals. *See* Os Canibais, 1988
Cannon Ball, 1915 (Sennett)
Cannon Ball Express, 1924 (Sennett)
Cannonball, 1931 (Sennett)
Cannonball, 1976 (Corman, Scorsese)
Cannot Exist, 1995 (Brakhage)
Cannot Not Exist, 1995 (Brakhage)
Canpazari, 1968 (Güney)
Canta delle marane, 1960 (Pasolini)
Cantata. *See* Oldás és kötés, 1963
Cantata de Chile, 1975 (Solas)
Cantate pour deux généraux, 1990 (Rouch)
Canterbury Tale, 1944 (Powell)
Canterbury Tales. *See* I racconti di Canterbury, 1972
Canterville Ghost, 1944 (Dassin)
Cantiere d'inverno, 1955 (Olmi)
Canyon Dweller, 1912 (Dwan)
Canyon Passage, 1946 (J. Tourneur)
Canzone del sole, 1933 (De Sica)
Cap du sud, 1935 (Storck)
Cap perdu, 1930 (Dupont)
Cape Ashizuri. *See* Ashizuri misaki, 1954
Cape Fear, 1991 (Scorsese, Spielberg)
Cape Forlorn, 1930 (Dupont)
Cape Town Affair, 1953 (Fuller)
Capitaine Fracasse, 1928 (Cavalcanti)
Capitaine Fracasse, 1942 (Gance)
Capitaine Singrid, 1968 (Tavernier)
Capital versus Labor, 1909 (Porter)
Capitano, 1991 (Troell)
Capitu, 1968 (Diegues)
Capkovy povídky, 1947 (Fric)
Capone, 1975 (Corman)
Caporal épinglé, 1962 (Renoir)
Cappotto, 1952 (Ferreri, Lattuada)
Cappriccio all'italiana, 1967 (Pasolini)
Caprice, 1966 (Tashlin)
Caprice de princesse, 1933 (Clouzot)
Capricious Summer. *See* Rozmarné lěto, 1968
Captain Blood, 1935 (Curtiz)
Captain Boycott, 1947 (Launder)
Captain Eddie, 1945 (Bacon)
Captain EO, 1986 (Lucas)
Captain Fly-by-Night, 1922 (Howard)
Captain from Castille, 1947 (King)
Captain Hates the Sea, 1934 (Milestone)
Captain Horatio Hornblower, 1951 (Walsh)
Captain Lightfoot, 1954 (Sirk)
Captain McLean, 1914 (Von Stroheim)
Captain of the Guard, 1930 (Fejös)
Captains Courageous, 1937 (Fleming, Hawks)
Captains of the Clouds, 1942 (Curtiz)
Captive, 1915 (De Mille)
Captive Heart, 1946 (Dearden)
Captive Soul. *See* Rablélek, 1913
Captive Wild Woman, 1943 (Dmytryk)
Captive's Island. *See* Shokei no shima, 1966

Capture, 1950 (J. Sturges)
Capture of the Biddle Brothers, 1902 (Porter)
Capture of Yegg Bank Burglars, 1904 (Porter)
Car Wash, 1976 (Schumacher)
Carabiniere, 1963 (Rossellini)
Carabiniers, 1963 (Godard)
Caravaggio, 1986 (Jarman)
Caravan pour Zagora. *See* Secret des hommes bleus, 1960
Carbunara, 1955-59 (Taviani)
Cardeuse de Matelas, 1906 (Méliès)
Cardinal, 1963 (Huston, Preminger)
Cardinal Richelieu's Ward, 1914 (Cruze)
Cardinal's Conspiracy, 1909 (Griffith)
Cardinal's Visit, 1981 (Baillie)
Care and Affection. *See* Szeretet, 1963
Career of a Chambermaid. *See* Telefoni bianchi, 1975
Career of Dima. *See* Dimy Gorina, 1961
Caretaker, 1963 (Roeg)
Caretaker's Daughter, 1925 (McCarey)
Carey Treatment, 1972 (Edwards)
Cargaison blanche, 1937 (Siodmak)
Cargo from Jamaica, 1933 (Grierson, Wright)
Carillons, 1936 (Storck)
Carl Dreyer, Le Celluloid et la marbre, 1965 (Rohmer)
Carl Nielsen 1865-1931, 1978 (Roos)
Carl Th. Dreyer, 1966 (Roos)
Carlito's Way, 1993 (De Palma, Mazursky)
Carlo Pisacane, 1955-59 (Taviani)
Carlos und Elisabeth—Eine Herrschertragődie, 1924 (Dieterle)
Carlton-Browne of the F.O., 1959 (Boulting)
Carmen, 1900/07 (Guy)
Carmen, 1915 (De Mille, Walsh)
Carmen, 1916 (Chaplin)
Carmen, 1918 (Lubitsch)
Carmen, 1926 (Feyder)
Carmen, 1983 (Saura)
Carmen, 1984 (Rosi)
Carmen Comes Home. *See* Karumen kokyo ni kaeru, 1951
Carmen Jones, 1954 (Preminger)
Carmen nejen podle Bizeta, 1968 (Schorm)
Carmen, Not According to Bizet. *See* Carmen nejen podle Bizeta, 1968
Carmen's Pure Love. *See* Karumen junjo su, 1952
Carnal Knowledge, 1971 (Nichols)
Carnaval, 1953 (Pagnol)
Carnaval des vérités, 1919 (Autant-Lara, L'Herbier)
Carnavals, 1950 (Storck)
Carne, 1991 (Ferreri)
Carnet de bal, 1937 (Duvivier)
Carnet de viaje, 1961 (Ivens)
Carnets du Major Thompson, 1957 (P. Sturges)
Carnival in Flanders. *See* **Kermesse héroïque,** 1935
Carnival Rock, 1957 (Corman)
Carnosaur, 1993 (Corman)
Carnosaur 2, 1995 (Corman)
Carny, 1980 (Foster)
Caro Diario, 1994 (Moretti)
Caro Papa, 1979 (Risi)
Carol, 1970 (Emshwiller)
Carolina, 1934 (King)
Caroline Cherie, 1967 (De Sica)
Carosello Napoletano, 1954 (Rosi)
Carousel, 1956 (King)
Carpetbaggers, 1963 (Dmytryk)
Carquake. *See* Cannonball, 1976
Carriage to Vienna. *See* Kočár do Vídně, 1966
Carrie, 1952 (Wyler)
Carrie, 1976 (De Palma)
Carriere de Suzanne, 1963 (Schroeder)
Carrière de Suzanne, 1963 (Rohmer)
Carrington VC, 1956 (Asquith)
Carro armato dell '8 settembre, 1960 (Pasolini)
Carrosse d'or, 1953 (Renoir)
Carrots and Peas, 1969 (Frampton)
Cars That Ate Paris, 1974 (Weir)
Cars That Ate People. *See* Cars That Ate Paris, 1974
Carta al mundo. *See* Rte.: Nicaragua, 1984
Cartas del parque, 1988 (Gutiérrez Alea)
Carte a Sara, 1956 (Bardem)
Cartes vivants, 1905 (Méliès)
Carthusian. *See* Karthauzi, 1916
Cartographer's Girlfriend, 1987 (Hartley)
Cas de malheur, 1958 (Autant-Lara)
Casa del ángel, 1957 (Torre Nilsson)
Casa del ogro, 1938 (De Fuentes)
Casa del Sorriso, 1991 (Ferreri)
Casablanca, 1942 (Curtiz, Siegel)
Casablanca, 1961 (Solas)
Casanova, 1927 (Delannoy, Litvak)
Casanova, 1976 (Fellini)
Casanova '70, 1964 (Ferreri)
Casanova Brown, 1944 (S. Wood)
Casanova di Federico Fellini. *See* Casanova, 1976
Cascade de Feu, 1904 (Méliès)
Case Is Closed. *See* Kharij, 1982
Case of Jonathan Drew. *See* Story of the London Fog, 1926
Case of Lena Smith, 1929 (Von Sternberg)
Case of the Curious Bride, 1935 (Curtiz)
Casey and His Neighbor's Goat, 1903 (Porter)
Casey's Frightful Dream, 1904 (Porter)
Casey's Shadow, 1978 (Ritt)
Casey's Vendetta, 1914 (Browning)
Cash, 1933 (Crichton)
Casino, 1995 (Scorsese)
Casino de Paris, 1957 (De Sica)
Casino Royale, 1967 (Allen, Huston, Roeg, Welles)
Casket for Living. *See* Tosei tamatebako, 1925
Caso Haller, 1933 (Blasetti)
Caso Mattei, 1972 (Rosi)
Casper, 1995 (Spielberg)
Casque d'Or, 1952 (Becker)
Cassette de l'emigrée, 1912 (Feuillade)
Cassis, 1966 (Mekas)
Cassoto, 1980 (Foster)
Cassowary. *See* Hikuidori, 1926
Cast-Iron. *See* Tudzi, 1964
Castagne sono buone, 1970 (Germi)
Castagnino, diario romano, 1966 (Birri)
Castaway, 1986 (Roeg)
Castel Sant'Angelo, 1946 (Blasetti)
Castelli in aria, 1938 (Castellani, De Sica)
Castillo de la Pureza, 1972 (Ripstein)
Castle Keep, 1969 (Pollack)
Castle of Purity. *See* Castillo de la Pureza, 1972
Castle of the Spider's Web. *See* Kumonosu-jo, 1957
Castle on the Hudson, 1940 (Litvak)
Castle within a Castle. *See* Et Slot I Et Slot, 1954
Castles in the Sky and Rhinestones. *See* Wolkenbau und Flimmerstern, 1919
Castro Street, 1966 (Baillie)
Casualties of War, 1989 (De Palma)
Caswallan Trilogy, 1986 (Brakhage)
Cat and Mouse, 1958 (Rotha)
Cat and Mouse. *See* Chat et la souris, 1975
Cat and the Canary, 1927 (Leni)
Cat and the Fiddle, 1933 (Howard)
Cat Chaser, 1989 (Ferrara)
Cat o' Nine Tails, 1971 (Argento)
Cat of the Night. *See* Yoru no mesuneko, 1929
Cat on a Hot Tin Roof, 1958 (Brooks)
Cat People, 1942 (J. Tourneur)
Cat People, 1981 (Schrader)
Catacombs. *See* Katakomby, 1940
Catalan, 1984 (Jarman)

Chambre blanche, 1969 (Lefebvre)
Chambre en ville, 1982 (Demy)
Chambre obscure. *See* Laughter in the Dark, 1969
Chambre verte, 1978 (Truffaut)
Champ, 1931 (K. Vidor)
Champ, 1979 (Zeffirelli)
Champagne, 1928 (Hitchcock, Launder)
Champagne Charlie, 1944 (Cavalcanti)
Champagne Charlie. *See* Night Out, 1915
Champagne Murders. *See* Scandale, 1967
Champagne Waltz, 1937 (Wilder)
Champion, 1913 (Sennett, Bacon)
Champion, 1915 (Chaplin)
Champion, 1949 (Kramer)
Chance Deception, 1912 (Griffith)
Chance et l'amour, 1964 (Chabrol, Tavernier)
Chance Meeting. *See* Blind Date, 1959
Chance Meeting. *See* Young Lovers, 1954
Chances, 1931 (Dwan)
Chandi Sona, 1977 (Kapoor)
Chang, 1927 (Schoedsack)
Change of Heart, 1909 (Griffith)
Change of Spirit, 1912 (Griffith)
Changes in the Village. *See* Gamperaliya, 1964
Changing Earth. *See* Ont staan en vergaan, 1954
Channel Incident, 1940 (Asquith)
Chanson d'armor, 1934 (Epstein)
Chanson d'une nuit, 1932 (Clouzot, Litvak)
Chanson des peupliers, 1931 (Epstein)
Chanson du souvenir, 1936 (Sirk)
Chant de Styrène, 1958 (Resnais)
Chant of Jimmie Blacksmith, 1978 (Schepisi)
Chanteur inconnu, 1931 (Clouzot)
Chantons sous l'Occupation, 1976 (Rouch)
Chapayev, 1934 (Vasiliev)
Chapayev Is with Us, 1939 (Gerasimov)
Chapeau. *See* Coup de vent, 1905
Chapeau de paille d'Italie, 1927 (Clair)
Chapeaux à transformations, 1939 (Lumet)
Chaperon, 1916 (W.S. Van Dyke)
Chaplin Revue, 1959 (Chaplin)
Chapman Report, 1962 (Cukor)
Chapter in Her Life, 1923 (Weber)
Char Dil Char Rahen, 1959 (Kapoor)
Charade, 1963 (Donen)
Charandas Chor, 1975 (Benegal)
Charandas the Thief. *See* Charandas Chor, 1975
Charcuterie mécanique, 1939 (Lumet)
Charge of the Light Brigade, 1936 (Curtiz)
Charge of the Light Brigade, 1968 (Richardson)
Chariots of Fire, 1981 (Anderson)
Charité du prestidigitateur, 1905 (Guy)
Charlatan, 1901 (Méliès)
Charlatan. *See* Kuruzslo, 1917
Charles Bukowski Tapes, 1985 (Schroeder)
Charles, Dead or Alive. *See* Charles, mort ou vif, 1969
Charles, mort ou vif, 1969 (Tanner)
Charleston Chain Gang, 1902 (Porter)
Charleston-Parade. *See* Sur un air de Charleston, 1927
Charley My Boy, 1926 (McCarey)
Charley Varrick, 1973 (Siegel)
Charlie and the Sausages. *See* Mabel's Busy Day, 1914
Charlie and the Umbrella. *See* Between Showers, 1914
Charlie at the Races. *See* Gentlemen of Nerve, 1914
Charlie at the Studio. *See* Film Johnnie, 1914
Charlie Bubbles, 1967 (Frears)
Charlie Chaplin's Burlesque on Carmen. *See* Carmen, 1916
Charlie on the Ocean. *See* Shanghaied, 1915
Charlie on the Spree. *See* In the Park, 1915
Charlie the Burglar. *See* Police!, 1916
Charlie the Hobo. *See* Tramp, 1915
Charlie the Sailor. *See* Shanghaied, 1915
Charlie's Day Out. *See* By the Sea, 1915
Charlie's Recreation. *See* Tango Tangles, 1914
Charlotte and Her Steak. *See* Présentation ou Charlotte et son steak, 1951
Charlotte et son Jules, 1958 (Cocteau, Godard)
Charlotte et Véronique ou Tous les garçons s'appellent Patrick, 1957 (Godard)
Charlotte Löwenskjöld, 1930 (Molander)
Charlotte Löwensköld. *See* Charlotte Löwenskjöld, 1930
Charlotte. *See* Jeune Fille assassinée, 1974
Charm School, 1920 (Cruze)
Charmant FrouFrou, 1901 (Guy)
Charme discret de la bourgeoisie, 1972 (Buñuel)
Charmes de l'existence, 1949 (Grémillon)
Charming Sinners, 1930 (Arzner)
Charrette fantôme, 1939 (Epstein, Duvivier)
Charro Negro, 1940 (Fernández)
Chartres, 1923 (Grémillon)
Chartres Series, 1994 (Brakhage)
Charulata, 1964 (S. Ray)
Chase, 1913 (Dwan)
Chase, 1966 (Penn, Redford)
Chase. *See* Caza, 1966
Chasing Dreams, 1982 (Costner)
Chasse à l'hippopotame, 1950 (Rouch)
Chasse au cambrioleur, 1903/04 (Guy)
Chasse au lion à l'arc, 1965 (Rouch)
Chasseurs de lions, 1913 (Feuillade)
Chat et la souris, 1975 (Lelouch)
Chateau de la peur, 1912 (Feuillade)
Chateau de rêve, 1933 (Clouzot)
Chateau de verre, 1950 (Clement)
Château en Suede, 1963 (Vadim)
Châteaux de France, 1948 (Resnais)
Chatelaine du Liban, 1933 (Epstein)
Chatollets Hemmelighed, eller Det gamle chatol, 1913 (Dreyer)
Chatte métamorphosée en femme, 1909 (Feuillade)
Chaudhwin ka Chand, 1960 (Dutt)
Chaudron infernal, 1903 (Méliès)
Chaussette, 1906 (Guy)
Che, 1969 (Fleischer)
Che? *See* What?, 1973
Che, Buenos Aires, 1962 (Birri)
Che gioia vivere, 1961 (Clement)
Che ora e, 1990 (Scola)
Che si dice a Roma, 1979 (Scola)
Cheap, 1974 (Corman)
Cheat, 1915 (De Mille)
Cheaters. *See* Tricheurs, 1958
Cheaters. *See* Tricheurs, 1983
Cheating Cheaters, 1919 (Dwan)
Checkmate, 1912 (Dwan)
Checkmate, 1935 (Pearson)
Cheerful Alley. *See* Yokina uramachi, 1939
Cheerful Canary. *See* Vessiolaia kanareika, 1929
Cheerful Wind. *See* Feng Erh T'i T'a Ts'ai, 1980
Cheering Town. *See* Kanko no machi, 1944
Cheers for Miss Bishop, 1941 (Garnett)
Chefs de demain, 1944 (Clement)
Chelovek s kinoapparatom, 1929 (Vertov)
Chelsea Girls, 1966 (Warhol)
Chemin d'Ernoa, 1921 (Delluc)
Chemin de Rio. *See* Cargaison blanche, 1937
Chemines de l'Exile ou Les Dernières Années de Jean-Jacques Rousseau, 1978 (Goretta)
Chemist, 1936 (Keaton)
Cherchez la femme, 1921 (Curtiz)
Chernaya lyubov, 1917 (Kuleshov)
Chess Fever. *See* Shakhmatnaya goryachka, 1925
Chess Players. *See* Shatranj Ke Khilari, 1977
Chesty: A Tribute to a Legend, 1970 (Ford)
Cheval d'Orgueil, 1980 (Chabrol)

Chevalier des neiges, 1912 (Méliès)
Cheyenne, 1947 (Walsh)
Cheyenne Autumn, 1964 (Ford)
Cheyenne Warrior, 1994 (Corman)
Cheyenne's Pal, 1917 (Ford)
Chez le magnétiseur, 1897/98 (Guy)
Chez le Maréchal-Ferrant, 1899/1900 (Guy)
Chez le photographe, 1900 (Guy)
Chi l'ha vistro?, 1942 (Fellini)
Chi to rei, 1923 (Mizoguchi)
Chica del lunes, 1966 (Torre Nilsson)
Chicago, Chicago. *See* Gaily, Gaily, 1969
Chicago Fire, 1925 (W.S. Van Dyke)
Chichi ariki, 1942 (Ozu)
Chicken, 1928 (Sennett)
Chicken Chaser, 1914 (Sennett)
Chicken-Hearted Jim, 1916 (Ford)
Chicos, 1959 (Ferreri)
Chiedo asilo, 1979 (Ferreri)
Chiefs, 1969 (Leacock)
Chief's Daughter, 1911 (Griffith)
Chief's Predicament, 1913 (Sennett)
Chief's Son Is Dead. *See* Hövdingens Son är död, 1937/38
Chien andalou, 1929 (Buñuel)
Chien jouant á la balle, 1905 (Guy)
Chienne, 1931 (Renoir)
Chiens perdus sans collier, 1955 (Delannoy, Guerra)
Chiens savants, 1902 (Guy)
Chiffonier, 1899/1900 (Guy)
Chiheisen, 1984 (Shindo)
Chiisana boken ryoko, 1964 (Oshima)
Chiisana tobosha, 1967 (Kinugasa)
Chijo, 1957 (Yoshimura)
Chikagai nijuyo-jikan, 1947 (Imai)
Chikamatsu monogatari, 1954 (Mizoguchi)
Chikuzan hitori-tabi, 1977 (Shindo)
Child. *See* Barnet, 1912
Child. *See* Barnets Magt, 1914
Child. *See* Dziecko, 1973
Child and the Killer, 1959 (Roeg)
Child Is Born, 1940 (Bacon, Rossen)
Child is Waiting, 1962 (Cassavetes, Kramer)
Child of Calabria. *See* Ragazzo di Calabria, 1987
Child of Divorce, 1947 (Fleischer)
Child of Manhattan, 1933 (P. Sturges)
Child of the Big City. *See* Ditya Bol'shogo Goroda, 1914
Child of the Ghetto, 1910 (Griffith)
Child of the Streets, 1967 (Benegal)
Child Thou Gavest Me, 1920 (Stahl)
Child Went Forth, 1941 (Losey)
Childhood of Gorky. *See* Detstvo Gorkovo, 1938
Childhood of Maxim Gorki. *See* Detstvo Gorkovo, 1938
Children, 1974 (Davies)
Children. *See* Enfants, 1985
Children at School, 1937 (Grierson, Wright)
Children, Books. *See* Gyermekek, könyvek, 1962
Children Galore, 1954 (Fisher)
Children Hand in Hand. *See* Te o tsunagu kora, 1962
Children in the Classroom. *See* Kyoshitsu no kodomotachi, 1954
Children Must Learn, 1940 (Willard Van Dyke)
Children of Angyalfold. *See* Angyalföldi fiatalok, 1955
Children of Bullerby Village, 1986 (Hallstrom)
Children of Change, 1930 (Launder)
Children of Darkness. *See* Kinder der Finsternis, 1922
Children of Divorce, 1927 (Von Sternberg)
Children of Nagasaki. *See* Kono ko o nokoshite, 1983
Children of Paradise. *See* **Enfants du paradis,** 1945
Children of the Age. *See* Deti Veka, 1915
Children of the Atomic Bomb. *See* Genbakuno-ko, 1952
Children of the Dust, 1923 (Borzage)
Children of the Good Earth. *See* Ta Ti Erh Nü, 1964

Children of the Soviet Arctic. *See* Romantiki, 194
Children of the Street. *See* Gatans barn, 1914
Children of This Country. *See* Bu vatanin cocukla
Children Upstairs, 1955 (Anderson)
Children Were Watching, 1961 (Leacock)
Children Who Draw. *See* Eo kaku kodomotachi, 19
Children's Corner, 1939 (L'Herbier)
Children's Friend, 1909 (Griffith)
Children's Hour, 1962 (Ashby, Wyler)
Child's Faith, 1910 (Griffith)
Child's First Adventure. *See* Chiisana boken ryoko,
Child's Garden and the Serious Sea, 1991 (Brakhag
Child's Impulse, 1910 (Griffith)
Child's Love. *See* Barnet, 1909
Child's Play, 1972 (Lumet)
Child's Remorse, 1912 (Griffith)
Child's Sacrifice, 1910 (Guy)
Child's Strategem, 1910 (Griffith)
Chiller, 1985 (Craven)
Chilly Green Lake. *See* Ts'ui Hu Han, 1977
Chilly Scenes of Winter, 1979 (Silver)
Chiltern Country, 1938 (Cavalcanti)
Chimes at Midnight, 1966 (Welles)
Chimmie Fadden, 1915 (De Mille)
Chimmie Fadden Out West, 1915 (De Mille)
Chin shui Lou Tai, 1974 (Hou)
China 9, Liberty 37, 1978 (Hellman, Peckinpah)
China Doll, 1958 (Borzage)
China Gate, 1957 (Fuller)
China Girl, 1942 (Hathaway)
China Girl, 1987 (Ferrara)
China is Near. *See* Cina è vicina, 1967
China Seas, 1935 (Garnett, Lewin)
China Story. *See* Satan Never Sleeps, 1961
China Venture, 1953 (Siegel)
China's Four Hundred Million. *See* Four Hundred Millio
Chinatown, 1974 (Huston, Polanski)
Chinatown Nights, 1929 (Wellman)
Chinese Parrot, 1927 (Leni)
Chinese Roulette. *See* Chinesisches Roulette, 1976
Chinese Roulette, 1977 (Schroeder)
Chinese Shadows. *See* Ombres chinoise, 1982
Chinese Vase. *See* Vasens Hemmelighed, 1913
Chinesisches Roulette, 1976 (Fassbinder)
Ching Lin Foo Outdone, 1900 (Porter)
Chinmoku, 1971 (Shinoda)
Chino. *See* Valdez il mezzosangue, 1973
Chinoise ou plutôt à la chinoise, 1967 (C. Miller, Godard)
Chiny i liudi, 1929 (Protazanov)
Chip Off the Old Block, 1913 (Sennett)
Chips Are Down. *See* Jeux sont faits, 1947
Chiriakhana, 1967 (S. Ray)
Chirurgie fin de siècle, 1900 (Guy)
Chiseler, 1931 (Sennett)
Chithod Vijay, 1947 (Kapoor)
Chiu Shih Liu Liu Tê T'a, 1979 (Hou)
Chlen pravitelstva, 1940 (Heifitz)
Chloe, 1934 (Neilan)
Chloe in the Afternoon. *See* Amour l'après-midi, 1972
Choca, 1973 (Fernández)
Chocolate Girl. *See* Chokoreito garu, 1932
Chocolate Soldier, 1941 (Saville)
Choice. *See* Al Ekhtiar, 1970
Choice Chance Woman Dance, 1971 (Emshwiller)
Choirboys, 1977 (Aldrich)
Chokon yasha, 1928 (Kinugasa)
Chokoreito garu, 1932 (Naruse)
Choose Me, 1984 (Rudolph)
Choose Your Partner. *See* Two Girls on Broadway, 1940
Choosing a Husband, 1909 (Griffith)
Choraku no kanata, 1924 (Kinugasa)

Cita de amor, 1956 (Fernández)
Citadel, 1938 (K. Vidor, Saville)
Citadel of Silence. *See* Citadelle du silence, 1937
Citadelle du silence, 1937 (L'Herbier)
Citizen Kane, 1941 (Welles, Wise)
Citizen Karel Havliček. *See* Občan Karel Havliček, 1966
Citizen's Band, 1977 (Demme)
Città dei traffici, 1949 (Risi)
Città delle donne, 1980 (Fellini)
Città dolente, 1948 (Fellini)
Città si difende, 1951 (Fellini)
City, 1939 (Cavalcanti, Lorentz, Willard Van Dyke)
City Beneath the Sea, 1953 (Boetticher)
City Called Copenhagen. *See* En by ved navn København, 1960
City for Conquest, 1940 (Kazan, Litvak, Siegel)
City Gone Wild, 1927 (Cruze)
City Hall, 1995 (Schrader)
City Hall to Harlem in Fifteen Seconds via the Subway Route, 1904 (Porter)
City Has Your Face. *See* Městomă svou tvář, 1958
City Heat, 1984 (Eastwood)
City Life, 1990 (Kieślowski)
City Lights, 1931 (Chaplin)
City Map. *See* Várostérkép, 1977
City of Desire. *See* Joen no chimata, 1923
City of Hope, 1991 (Sayles)
City of Joy, 1992 (Joffé)
City of Pirates. *See* Ville des pirates, 1983
City of Sadness. *See* Pei Ch'ing Ch'êng Shih, 1989
City of Women. *See* Città delle donne, 1980
City Prepares. *See* First Days, 1939
City Sparrow, 1920 (S. Wood)
City Speaks, 1946 (Rotha)
City Streaming, 1990 (Brakhage)
City Streets, 1931 (Mamoulian)
City That Never Sleeps, 1924 (Cruze)
City Tramp. *See* Der Stadtstreicher, 1965
City Under the Sea. *See* War Gods of the Deep, 1965
Civil Rights: The Struggle Continues, 1989 (Kopple)
Claim Jumpers, 1911 (Dwan)
Clair de femme, 1979 (Costa-Gavras)
Clair de lune sous Richelieu, 1911 (Gance)
Claire's Knee. *See* Genou de Claire, 1970
Clan of the Cave Bear, 1985 (Sayles)
Clan—Tale of the Frogs. *See* Klanni—tarina sammokoitten, 1984
Clancy, 1974 (Brakhage)
Clancy at the Bat, 1929 (Sennett)
Clara's Heart, 1988 (Mulligan)
Claro, 1975 (Rocha)
Clash by Night, 1952 (Lang)
Class Relations. *See* Klassenverhältnisse, 1985
Class Reunion, 1972 (E. Wood)
Classe, 1897/98 (Guy)
Classe operaia va in paradiso, 1971 (Petri)
Classe tous risques, 1960 (Sautet)
Classification des plantes, 1982 (Ruiz)
Claudia, 1943 (Goulding)
Clavigo, 1970 (Ophuls)
Clay Heart. *See* Guldets Gift, eller Lerhjertet, 1916
Clay Pigeon, 1949 (Fleischer)
Clay. *See* Argila, 1940
Clayton & Catherine. *See* China 9, Liberty 37, 1978
Clean Heart, 1924 (Blackton)
Clean Machine, 1987 (G. Miller)
Clean Slate. *See* Coup de torchon, 1982
Clear All Wires, 1933 (Daves)
Cléo de cinq à sept, 1961 (Godard, Varda)
Cleopatra, 1934 (De Mille)
Cleopatra, 1963 (Mankiewicz)
Cléopâtre, 1899 (Méliès)
Clever Dummy, 1917 (Sennett)
Clever Girl Takes Care of Herself. *See* Bra flicka reder sig själv, 1914
Client, 1994 (Schumacher)
Client sérieux, 1932 (Autant-Lara)
Cliff. *See* Shiroi gake, 1960
Climax. *See* Immorale, 1967
Climber, 1917 (King)
Climbing High, 1939 (Reed)
Cloak. *See* Shinel, 1926
Cloak and Dagger, 1946 (Lang)
Cloches de Paques, 1912 (Feuillade)
Clock, 1945 (Minnelli)
Clockers, 1995 (S. Lee, Scorsese)
Clockmaker. *See* Horloger de Saint-Paul, 1974
Clockmaker's Dream. *See* Rêve d'horloger, 1904
Clockwork Orange, 1971 (Kubrick)
Cloister's Touch, 1909 (Griffith)
Close Call, 1911 (Sennett)
Close Encounters of the Third Kind, 1977 (Schrader, Spielberg, Truffaut)
Close Harmony, 1929 (Cromwell)
Close Shave, 1929 (Sennett)
Close to Eden. *See* Urga, 1990
Close to Nature, 1968 (Benegal)
Close-up: The Blood. *See* Közelrölia: a vér, 1965
Closed Road, 1916 (M. Tourneur)
Closely Watched Trains. *See* **Ostře sledované vlaky**, 1966
Closet, 1965 (Warhol)
Clothes Make the Pirate, 1925 (M. Tourneur)
Clouds, 1917 (W.S. Van Dyke)
Clouds at Sunset. *See* Akanegumo, 1967
Clouds at Twilight. *See* Yuyake-gumo, 1956
Clouds Like White Sheep, 1962 (Frampton)
Clouds of Glory, Parts I and II, 1978 (Russell)
Clouds Will Roll Away. *See* Není stále zamrečeno, 1950
Clown and Policeman, 1900 (Hepworth)
Clown and the Alchemist, 1900 (Porter)
Clown en sac, 1904 (Guy)
Clowns, 1902 (Guy)
Clowns. *See* I clowns, 1970
Club, 1981 (Beresford)
Club de femmes, 1936 (Delannoy)
Club Extinction. *See* Docteur M, 1990
Club of the Big Deed. *See* S.V.D., 1927
Clubman and the Tramp, 1908 (Griffith)
Clum perdesi, 1960 (Güney)
Clunked on the Corner, 1929 (Sennett)
Cluny Brown, 1946 (Lubitsch)
Coalface, 1935 (Cavalcanti, Grierson)
Coals of Fire, 1918 (Niblo)
Coast of Folly, 1925 (Dwan)
Coat's Tale, 1914 (Sennett)
Cobbler Stay at Your Bench. *See* Skomakare bliv vid din läst, 1915
Cobra Verde, 1987 (Herzog)
Cobra Woman, 1944 (Brooks, Siodmak)
Cobweb, 1916 (Hepworth)
Cobweb, 1955 (Minnelli)
Coca-Cola Kid, 1985 (Makavejev)
Cocaine Wars, 1986 (Corman)
Cochecito, 1960 (Ferreri)
Cocher de fiacre endormi, 1897/98 (Guy)
Cock Crows Twice. *See* Niwatori wa futatabi naku, 1954
Cock-eyed World, 1929 (Walsh)
Cockfighter, 1974 (Corman, Hellman)
Cocktail, 1937 (Henning-Jensen)
Cocktail Hostesses, 1972 (E. Wood)
Cocktails, 1928 (Launder)
Cocoanuts, 1929 (Florey)
Cocorico, Monsieur Poulet, 1974 (Rouch)
Cocotiers, 1963 (Rouch)
Cocteau dans la plaie, 1962 (Litvak)
Code Name: Trixie. *See* Crazies, 1973
Code of Honor, 1916 (Borzage)
Code of the Sea, 1924 (Fleming)

Code of the West, 1925 (Howard)
Code Seven, Victim Five. *See* Victim Five, 1964
Coeur de Gueux, 1936 (Epstein)
Coeur de Lilas, 1932 (Litvak)
Coeur en Hiver, 1992 (Sautet)
Coeur fidèle, 1923 (Epstein)
Coeurs farouches, 1924 (Duvivier)
Coffee and Cigarettes, 1987 (Jarmusch)
Coffee and Cigarettes (Memphis Version), 1989 (Jarmusch)
Coffee and Cigarettes (Somewhere in California), 1993 (Jarmusch)
Coffee House. *See* Kaffeehaus, 1971
Coffre enchanté, 1904 (Méliès)
Coffret de Tolède, 1914 (Feuillade)
Cohen at Coney Island. *See* Cohen Collects a Debt, 1912
Cohen Collects a Debt, 1912 (Sennett)
Cohen Saves the Flag, 1913 (Sennett)
Cohen's Advertising Scheme, 1904 (Porter)
Cohens and the Kellys, 1927 (Florey)
Cohens and the Kellys in Trouble, 1933 (Stevens)
Cohen's Outing, 1913 (Sennett)
Cold Comfort Farm, 1996 (Schlesinger)
Cold Heaven, 1992 (Roeg)
Cold Showers. *See* Kholodnye Dushi, 1914
Cold Turkey, 1925 (Sennett)
Colette, 1950 (Cocteau)
Colle universelle, 1907 (Méliès)
Collectionneuse, 1967 (Rohmer)
Collector, 1965 (Schroeder, Wyler)
College, 1927 (Keaton)
College Coach, 1933 (Wellman)
College Is a Nice Place. *See* Daigaku yoi toko, 1936
College Kiddo, 1927 (Sennett)
College Rhythm, 1934 (Dmytryk)
College Swing, 1938 (Walsh)
Collège swing, 1946 (Duvivier)
College Vamp, 1931 (Sennett)
Collier de la reine, 1909 (Feuillade)
Collier de perles, 1915 (Feuillade)
Collisions, 1976 (Emshwiller)
Colloque de chiens, 1977 (Ruiz)
Colonel. *See* Az ezredes, 1917
Colonel Bogey, 1948 (Fisher)
Colonel Bontemps, 1913/16 (Feuillade)
Colonel Redl. *See* Redl Ezredes, 1985
Colonia penal, 1971 (Ruiz)
Colonie Sicedison, 1958 (Olmi)
Colony Beneath the Earth. *See* Gyarmat a föld alatt, 1951
Color Fields, 1977 (Vanderbeek)
Color of Money, 1986 (Scorsese)
Color of Pomegranates. *See* Sayat nova, 1969
Color Purple, 1986 (Spielberg)
Colorado Legend and the Ballad of the Colorado Ute, 1961 (Brakhage)
Colorado Territory, 1949 (Walsh)
Colored Girl's Love, 1914 (Sennett)
Colored Villainy, 1915 (Sennett)
Colorful China. *See* Színfoltok Kínaböl, 1957
Colors Are Dreaming. *See* Boje sanjaju, 1958
Colors of China. *See* Színfoltok Kínaböl, 1957
Colors of Vásárhely. *See* Vásárhelyi szinek, 1961
Colosso di Rodi, 1961 (Leone)
Colossus of Rhodes. *See* Colosso di Rodi, 1961
Colpa e la pena, Abbasso lo zio, 1958 (Bellocchio)
Colpo di pistola, 1941 (Castellani)
Colter Craven Story, 1960 (Ford)
Comanche Station, 1960 (Boetticher)
Comancheros, 1962 (Curtiz)
Comandos comunales, 1972 (Guzmán)
Comata, the Sioux, 1909 (Griffith)
Combat naval en Grèce, 1897 (Méliès)
Come and Get It, 1936 (Hawks, Wyler)
Come Back, 1983 (Vadim)
Come Back, Little Shicksa, 1949 (Jerry Lewis)
Come Back to the Five and Dime, Jimmy Dean, Jimmy Dean, 1982 (Altman)
Come Drink with Me. *See* Ta Tsui Hsia, 1965
Come Have Coffee With Us. *See* Venga a prendere il caffe ... da noi, 1970
Come Live with Me, 1941 (Brown)
Come on Marines!, 1934 (Hathaway)
Come On, George!, 1939 (Dearden)
Come On Leathernecks, 1938 (Cruze)
Come See the Paradise, 1990 (Parker)
Come September, 1961 (Mulligan)
Come Sono Buoni I Bianchi, 1987 (Ferreri)
Come to My Place, I'm Living at My Girlfriend's. *See* Viens chez moi, j'habite chez une copine, 1981
Come un bambino, 1990 (Risi)
Comedians. *See* Cómicos, 1954
Comedie du bonheur, 1940 (Cocteau, L'Herbier)
Comédien, 1948 (Guitry)
Comedy of Terrors, 1963 (J. Tourneur)
Comenzo a retumbar el Momtombo, 1981 (Alvarez)
Comes a Horseman, 1978 (Pakula)
Comet Over Broadway, 1938 (Berkeley)
Comfort and Joy, 1984 (Forsyth)
Comfort of Strangers, 1990 (Schrader)
Comic Grimacer, 1901 (Hepworth)
Cómicos, 1954 (Bardem)
Comin' Thro' the Rye, 1916 (Hepworth)
Comin' Thro' the Rye, 1922 (Hepworth)
Coming Home, 1978 (Ashby)
Coming of Angelo, 1913 (Griffith)
Coming of the Dial, 1933 (Grierson)
Coming Out Party, 1965 (Loach)
Comizi d'amore, 1964 (Pasolini)
Command, 1953 (Fuller)
Command Decision, 1948 (S. Wood)
Command Performance, 1937 (Pearson)
Commanding Officer, 1915 (Dwan)
Commandos, 1969 (Argento)
Commare secca, 1962 (Bertolucci, Pasolini)
Comme on fait son lit on se couche, 1903/04 (Guy)
Comme une lettre à la poste, 1938 (Storck)
Comment ça va, 1976 (Godard)
Comment monsieur prend son bain, 1903 (Guy)
Comment on disperse les foules, 1903/04 (Guy)
Comment on dort á Paris!, 1905 (Guy)
Comment savoir, 1966 (Jutra)
Comment Yukong déplaça les montagnes, 1976 (Ivens)
Commissaire est bon enfant, le gendarme est sans pitie, 1935 (Becker)
Commissario, 1962 (Comencini)
Commissario Lo Gatto, 1987 (Risi)
Commissario Pepe, 1968 (Scola)
Commitments, 1991 (Parker)
Common Cause, 1918 (Blackton)
Common Clay, 1930 (Fleming)
Common Ground , 1990 (Newell)
Communal Organization. *See* Comandos comunales, 1972
Commune. *See* Gromada, 1952
Commute, 1995 (Baillie)
Como era gostoso o meu francês, 1971 (Pereira Dos Santos)
Como, por qué y para qué asesina a un general?, 1971 (Alvarez)
Como ves?, 1982 (Leduc)
Compact with Death. *See* Dařbuján a Pandrhola, 1960
Compadre Mendoza, 1933 (De Fuentes)
Compagnia dei matti, 1928 (De Sica)
Compagnie des fous. *See* Compagnia dei matti, 1928
Compagno Don Camillo, 1964 (Comencini)
Compagnons de voyage encombrants, 1903 (Guy)
Compañero Presidente, 1971 (Littin)
Company of Wolves, 1984 (Jordan)
Company She Keeps, 1951 (Cromwell)
Compartiment tueurs, 1966 (Costa-Gavras)

Damned. *See* **Caduta degli dei**, 1969
Damned Holiday. *See* Prokleti praznik, 1958
Dämon des Meeres, 1931 (Curtiz, Dieterle)
Dams and Waterways, 1911 (Dwan)
Damsel in Distress, 1937 (Stevens)
Damy, 1955 (Gerasimov)
Dan the Dandy, 1911 (Griffith)
Dance Chromatic, 1959 (Emshwiller)
Dance Contest in Esira. *See* Danstävlingen i Esira, 1935/36
Dance, Girl, Dance, 1940 (Arzner, Wise)
Dance Hall, 1950 (Crichton)
Dance Hall Marge, 1931 (Sennett)
Dance in the Rain. *See* Ples v dezju, 1961
Dance in the Sun, 1954 (Clarke)
Dance Little Lady, 1954 (Zetterling)
Dance Madness, 1925 (Florey)
Dance Movie, 1963 (Warhol)
Dance of Death. *See* Totentanz, 1919
Dance of Life, 1929 (Cromwell)
Dance of the Damned, 1989 (Corman)
Dance of the Looney Spoons, 1959 (Vanderbeek)
Dance of the Seven Veils, 1970 (Russell)
Dance of the Vampires. *See* Fearless Vampire Killers, 1967
Dance, Pretty Lady, 1931 (Asquith)
Dance Shadows by Danielle Helander. *See* Caswallan Trilogy, 1986
Dance Training. *See* Kyoren no buto, 1924
Dance with a Stranger, 1985 (Newell)
Dance with Death, 1992 (Corman)
Dancer of Izu. *See* Izu no odoriko, 1933
Dancers, 1925 (Goulding)
Dancers of Tomorrow. *See* Asu no odoriko, 1939
Dancer's Revenge. *See* Danserindens Haevn, 1915
Dancer's Strange Dream. *See* Danserindens Kaerlighedsdrøm, 1915
Dances in Japan. *See* Nihon no buyo, 1958
Dances with Wolves, 1990 (Costner)
Dancing Fool, 1920 (S. Wood)
Dancing Girl, 1915 (Dwan)
Dancing Girl. *See* Nautch Girl, 1934
Dancing Girl. *See* Maihime, 1951
Dancing Girl of Butte, 1909 (Griffith, Sennett)
Dancing in a Harem. *See* Danse au sérail, 1897
Dancing Mad. *See* Der Tänzer meiner Frau, 1925
Dancing Mothers, 1926 (Goulding)
Dandelion. *See* **Tampopo**, 1986
Dandy in Aspic, 1968 (A. Mann)
Danger Ahead, 1923 (Howard)
Danger Girl, 1916 (Sennett)
Danger, Love at Work, 1937 (Preminger)
Danger Signal, 1945 (Florey)
Danger Stalks Near. *See* Fuzen no tomoshibi, 1957
Danger! Women at Work, 1943 (Ulmer)
Dangerous Age, 1923 (Stahl)
Dangerous Curves Behind, 1925 (Sennett)
Dangerous Flirt, 1924 (Browning)
Dangerous Game. *See* Snake Eyes, 1993
Dangerous Hours, 1920 (Niblo)
Dangerous Liaisons, 1988 (Frears)
Dangerous Lies, 1921 (Hitchcock)
Dangerous Love, 1988 (Corman)
Dangerous Paradise, 1920 (Goulding)
Dangerous Paradise, 1930 (Wellman)
Dangerous to Know, 1938 (Florey)
Dangerous Toys, 1921 (Goulding)
Dangerous When Wet, 1953 (Walters)
Dangerously They Live, 1941 (Florey)
Dangers de l'acoolisme, 1899/1900 (Guy)
Dangers of a Bride, 1917 (Sennett)
Dani, 1963 (Petrovic)
Daniel, 1983 (Lumet)
Daniel Boone, 1907 (Porter)
Danish Brigade in Sweden. *See* Brigaden i Sverige, 1945
Danish Design, 1960 (Roos)
Danish Island. *See* De danske Sydhavsøer, 1944
Danish Village Church. *See* Landsbykirken, 1947
Danjuro sandai, 1944 (Mizoguchi)
Dann schon lieber Lebertran, 1930 (Ophüls)
Danny Boy. *See* Angel, 1982
Danryu, 1939 (Yoshimura)
Dans la brousse, 1912 (Feuillade)
Dans la vie, 1911 (Feuillade)
Dans la ville blanche, 1983 (Tanner)
Dans les coulisses, 1900 (Guy)
Dans l'ouragan de la vie, 1916 (Dulac)
Dans un miroir, 1985 (Ruiz)
Dans une île perdue, 1930 (Cavalcanti)
Danse au sérail, 1897 (Méliès)
Danse basque, 1901 (Guy)
Danse de l'ivresse, 1900 (Guy)
Danse de mort, 1947 (Von Stroheim)
Danse des Saisons, 1900 (Guy)
Danse du papillon, 1900 (Guy)
Danse du pas des foulards par des almées, 1900 (Guy)
Danse du ventre, 1900/01 (Guy)
Danse fleur de lotus, 1897 (Guy)
Danse mauresque, 1902 (Guy)
Danse serpentine, 1900 (Guy)
Danse serpentine par Mme Bob Walter, 1899/1900 (Guy)
Danserinden. *See* Ballettens Datter, 1913
Danserindehs Haevn, 1915 (Holger-Madsen)
Danserindens Kaerlighedsdrøm, 1915 (Holger-Madsen)
Danses, 1900 (Guy)
Danses espagnoles, 1900 (Lumet)
Dansk politi i Sverige, 1945 (Henning-Jensen)
Danstävlingen i Esira, 1935/36 (Fejös)
Dante Quartet, 1987 (Brakhage)
Dante's Inferno, 1924 (Goulding)
Dante's Inferno, 1967 (Russell)
Danton, 1982 (Wajda, Holland)
Danube—Fishes—Birds. *See* Duna—halak—madarak, 1971
Danulon gyártás, 1961 (Mészáros)
Danulon Production. *See* Danulon gyártás, 1961
Danza delle lancette, 1936 (Lattuada)
Daoma Zei, 1985 (Tian)
Daphne, 1936 (Rossellini)
Daraku suru onna, 1967 (Yoshimura)
Dařbuján a Pandrhola, 1960 (Fric)
Darby O'Gill and the Little People, 1959 (Stevenson)
Darby's Rangers, 1958 (Wellman)
Daredevil. *See* Smelchak, 1919
Dare-Devil, 1923 (Sennett)
Daredevil Jack, 1920 (W.S. Van Dyke)
Dark at Noon, 1992 (Ruiz)
Dark City, 1950 (Dieterle)
Dark Command, 1940 (Walsh)
Dark Corner, 1946 (Hathaway)
Dark Eyes. *See* Oci ciornie, 1987
Dark Half, 1990 (Romero)
Dark Horse, 1932 (LeRoy)
Dark Journey, 1937 (Saville)
Dark Lover's Play, 1915 (Sennett)
Dark Mirror, 1946 (Siodmak)
Dark Night. *See* Noche oscura, 1989
Dark Passage, 1947 (Daves)
Dark Secrets, 1923 (Fleming, Goulding)
Dark Star, 1919 (Dwan)
Dark Star, 1974 (Carpenter)
Dark Tower, 1943 (Fisher)
Dark Town Strutters, 1975 (Corman)
Dark Victory, 1939 (Goulding)
Dark Wind, 1992 (Morris)
Darkest Africa, 1936 (Joseph H. Lewis)
Darkness at Noon. *See* Mahiru no ankoku, 1956

Delayed Proposal, 1911 (Sennett)
Delhi Way, 1964 (Ivory)
Délibábok országa, 1983 (Meszaros)
Delicacies of Molten Horror Synapse, 1991 (Brakhage)
Delicate Balance, 1973 (Richardson)
Delicate Delinquent, 1957 (Jerry Lewis)
Delightfully Dangerous, 1944 (Tashlin)
Delinquent Girl. *See* Furyo shojo, 1949
Delinquents, 1955 (Altman)
Delirium in a Studio. *See* Ali Barbouyou et Ali Bouf à l'huile, 1907
Delitto d'amore, 1974 (Comencini)
Delitto di Giovanni Episcopo, 1947 (Fellini, Lattuada)
Delitto Matteotti, 1973 (De Sica)
Deliverance, 1972 (Boorman)
Deliverance. *See* Sadgati, 1981
Della nube alla resistenza, 1979 (Straub)
Delovak Athara, 1966 (Peries)
Delta Factor, 1970 (Garnett)
Delta Phase I, 1962 (Haanstra)
Demain à Nanguila, 1960 (Ivens)
Demanty noci, 1964 (Nemec)
Déménagement. *See* Moving In, 1993
Déménagement à la cloche de bois, 1897/98 (Guy)
Déménagement à la cloche de bois, 1907 (Guy)
Dément du Lac Jean Jeune, 1947 (Jutra)
Dementia, 1963 (Coppola, Corman)
Demetrius and the Gladiators, 1954 (Daves)
Demi-Paradise, 1943 (Asquith)
Demise of Father Mouret. *See* Faute de l'Abbé Mouret, 1970
Demoiselle du notaire, 1912 (Feuillade)
Demoiselles de Rochefort, 1967 (C. Miller, Demy)
Démolition d'un mur, 1939 (Lumet)
Demon of Fear, 1916 (Borzage)
Demon Pond. *See* Yashagaike, 1979
Demonio y carne. *See* Susana, 1950
Demons, 1986 (Argento)
Demons 2, 1987 (Argento)
Demons of the Swamp. *See* Attack of the Giant Leeches, 1959
Demonstratie van proletarische solidariteit, 1930 (Ivens)
Demonstration of Proletarian Solidarity. *See* Demonstratie van proletarische solidariteit, 1930
Demütige und die Sängerin, 1925 (Dupont)
Den, der sejrer. *See* Syndens Datter, 1915
Den of Beasts. *See* Kedamono no yado, 1951
Den of Thieves, 1905 (Hepworth)
Dengamle Baenk, Left Alone. *See* Under Mindernes Trae, 1913
Denmark Grows Up, 1947 (Henning-Jensen)
Dent récalcitrante, 1902 (Guy)
Dentellière, 1977 (Goretta)
Dentist. *See* Laughing Gas, 1914
Dentist, 1919 (Sennett)
Dentist, 1932 (Sennett)
Denwa wa yugata ni naru, 1959 (Yoshimura)
Départ, 1967 (Skolimowski)
Départ en voiture, 1939 (Lumet)
Départ pour les vacances, 1904 (Guy)
Department Store. *See* Univermag, 1922
Departure of a Grand Old Man. *See* Ukhod velikovo startza, 1912
Deported, 1950 (Siodmak)
Depressed Area, U.S.A., 1963 (Willard Van Dyke)
Deprisa, deprisa, 1980 (Saura)
Deputat Baltiki, 1936 (Heifitz)
Derby, 1919 (Dupont)
Derecho de asilo, 1972 (Fernández)
Derek Jarman: You Know What I Mean, 1988 (Jarman)
Derkovitz Gyula 1894-1934, 1958 (Jancsó)
Dernier Atout, 1942 (Becker)
Dernier Bolchevik, 1993 (Marker)
Dernier Choc, 1932 (Clouzot)
Dernier Combat, 1983 (Besson)
Dernier des six, 1941 (Clouzot)
Dernier Metro, 1980 (Truffaut)
Dernier Milliardaire, 1934 (Clair)
Dernier Moment. *See* Last Moment, 1928
Dernier Pardon, 1913 (M. Tourneur)
Dernier Tango à Paris. *See* **Last Tango in Paris,** 1972
Dernière Femme. *See* Ultima donna, 1976
Dernières Fiançailles, 1973 (Lefebvre)
Derniers Jours de Pompéi, 1948 (L'Herbier)
Derrière la façade, 1938 (Von Stroheim)
Dersu Uzala, 1975 (Kurosawa)
Des demoiselles ont en 25 ans, 1993 (Tavernier, Varda)
Des enfants gâtés, 1977 (Tavernier)
Des Haares und der Liebe Wellen, 1929 (Ruttmann)
Des journées entières dans les arbres, 1976 (Duras)
Des Teufels General, 1955 (Käutner)
Des Verschollene Inka-Gold, 1978 (Staudte)
Desa Nisa, 1972 (Peries)
Desafio, 1979 (Alvarez)
Desafios, 1970 (Erice)
Desaster, 1973 (Von Trotta)
Désastres de la guerre, 1951 (Grémillon)
Descendants of Taro Urashima. *See* Urashima Taro no koei, 1946
Description d'un combat, 1960 (Marker)
Desdemona, 1911 (Blom)
Desert, 1976 (Brakhage)
Desert Dust, 1927 (Wyler)
Desert Flower, 1925 (LeRoy)
Desert Fox, 1951 (Hathaway)
Desert Fury, 1947 (Rossen)
Desert Laughs. *See* Yaban gülü, 1961
Desert Mice, 1959 (Dearden)
Desert Rats, 1953 (Wise)
Desert Song, 1942 (Florey)
Desert Tribesman, 1914 (Cruze)
Desert Victory, 1943 (Boulting)
Desert Wooing, 1918 (Niblo)
Deserted at the Altar, 1922 (Howard)
Deserter. *See* Dezertir, 1933
Deserter, 1971 (Huston)
Déserteuse, 1917 (Feuillade)
Deserto rosso, 1964 (Antonioni)
Desert's Prince, 1925 (W.S. Van Dyke)
Desert's Toll, 1926 (Stevens)
Desiderio, 1943 (De Santis, Rossellini)
Design for Death, 1947 (Fleischer)
Design for Living, 1933 (Lubitsch)
Design of a Human Being. *See* Ningen moyo, 1949
Designing Woman, 1957 (Minnelli)
Desire, 1936 (Borzage, Lubitsch)
Désiré, 1937 (Guitry)
Desire. *See* Yokubo, 1953
Desire. *See* Yoku, 1958
Desire Me, 1947 (Cukor, LeRoy)
Desired Woman, 1927 (Curtiz)
Desistfilm, 1954 (Brakhage)
Desordre, 1951 (Cocteau)
Désordre, 1961 (Welles)
Despair. *See* Reise ins Licht, 1977
Despegue a la 18.00, 1969 (Alvarez)
Desperado, 1995 (Rodriguez, Tarantino)
Desperadoes, 1943 (C. Vidor)
Desperate, 1947 (A. Mann)
Desperate Crime. *See* Histoire d'un crime, 1906
Desperate Hours, 1955 (Wyler)
Desperate Hours, 1990 (Cimino)
Desperate Journey, 1942 (Walsh)
Desperate Living, 1977 (Waters)
Desperate Lover, 1912 (Sennett)
Desperate Moment, 1953 (Zetterling)
Desperate Search, 1952 (Joseph H. Lewis)
Desperate Trails, 1921 (Ford)

D'est, 1993 (Akerman)
Destin fabuleux de Desirée Clary, 1942 (Guitry)
Destination Gobi, 1952 (Wise)
Destination Tokyo, 1944 (Daves)
Destination Unknown, 1933 (Garnett)
Destinées, 1952 (Delannoy)
Destins de Manoel, 1985 (Ruiz)
Destiny. *See* Der müde Tod: Ein Deutsches Volkslied in Sechs Versen, 1921
Destiny Turns on the Radio, 1994 (Tarantino)
Destroy She Said. *See* Détruire, dit-elle, 1969
Destroyer. *See* Wir verbauen 3 x 27 Milliarden Dollar in einen Angriffs-schlachter, 1971
Destroying Angel, 1923 (W.S. Van Dyke)
Det är min modell, 1946 (Molander)
Det bødes der for. *See* Haevnet, 1911
Det brinner en eld, 1943 (Molander, Sjöström)
Det definitive afslag på anmodningen om et kys, 1949 (Roos)
Det er tilladt at vaere åndssvag, 1969 (Roos)
Det første Honorar, 1912 (Blom)
Det gamle Købmandshus, 1911 (Blom)
Det gyldne Smil, 1935 (Fejös)
Det hemmelighedsfulde X, 1913 (Christensen)
Det mørke Punkt, 1911 (Blom)
Det mørke Punkt, 1913 (Holger-Madsen)
Det omringgade huset, 1922 (Sjöström)
Det regnar på vår kärlek, 1946 (Bergman)
Det röda tornet, 1914 (Stiller)
Det sjunde inseglet, 1957 (Bergman)
Det Største i Verden, 1919 (Holger-Madsen)
Det stjaalne Ansigt, 1914 (Holger-Madsen)
Det stora äventyret, 1953 (Sucksdorff)
Det store Fald or Malstrømmen, 1911 (Holger-Madsen)
Det store Hjerte, 1924 (Blom)
Det unge Blod, 1915 (Holger-Madsen)
Det var i Maj, 1914 (Sjöström)
Detective. *See* Father Brown, 1954
Detective, 1985 (Godard)
Detective Clive, Bart. *See* Scotland Yard, 1930
"Détective Dervieux" series, 1912/13 (Feuillade)
Detective Lloyd. *See* Lloyd of the CID, 1931
Detective Story, 1951 (Wyler)
Déterminés à vaincre, 1968 (Ivens)
Deti Veka, 1915 (Bauer)
Détruire, dit-elle, 1969 (Duras)
Detstvo Gorkovo, 1938 (Donskoi)
Deus e o diablo na terra do sol, 1964 (Rocha)
Deus Ex, 1971 (Brakhage)
Deutsche Panzer; Aberglaube, 1940 (Ruttmann)
Deutsche Waffenschmiede, 1940 (Ruttmann)
Deutschland bleiche mutter, 1980 (Sanders-Brahms)
Deutschland im Herbst, 1978 (Fassbinder, Kluge, Schlöndorff)
Deux Anglaises et le continent, 1971 (C. Miller, Truffaut)
Deux coverts, 1935 (Guitry)
Deux fois cinquante ans de cinema Francais, 1995 (Godard)
Deux Françaises, 1915 (Feuillade)
Deux Gamines, 1920 (Clair, Feuillade)
Deux Gosses, 1906 (Feuillade)
Deux hommes dans Manhattan, 1959 (Melville)
Deux Mondes, 1930 (Dupont)
Deux Orphelines, 1933 (M. Tourneur)
Deux ou trois choses que je sais d'elle, 1967 (Godard)
Deux Rivaux, 1903/04 (Guy)
Deux Timides, 1928 (Clair)
Deuxième Souffle, 1966 (Melville)
Devdas, 1935 (Roy)
Devdas, 1954 (Roy)
Development of the Stalk and the Root. *See* A szár és a gyökér fejlődése, 1961
Devi, 1960 (S. Ray)
Devil, 1908 (Griffith)
Devil. *See* Az ördög, 1918
Devil, 1920 (Goulding)
Devil and Daniel Webster. *See* All That Money Can Buy, 1940
Devil and Miss Jones, 1941 (S. Wood)
Devil at Four O'Clock, 1961 (LeRoy)
Devil Commands, 1941 (Dmytryk)
Devil Crag. *See* Seytan kayaliklari, 1970
Devil Dancer, 1927 (Niblo)
Devil Dogs of the Air, 1935 (Bacon)
Devil Doll, 1936 (Browning, Von Stroheim)
Devil Horse, 1926 (Stevens)
Devil in a Blue Dress, 1995 (Demme)
Devil in Evening Dress, 1973 (G. Miller)
Devil in Love. *See* Arcidiavolo, 1966
Devil in the Flesh, 1986 (Bellocchio)
Devil in the Flesh. *See* **Diable au corps,** 1947
Devil Is a Sissy, 1936 (W.S. Van Dyke)
Devil Is a Woman, 1935 (Von Sternberg)
Devil of the Desert. *See* Shaitan el Sahara, 1954
Devil on Horseback, 1936 (Joseph H. Lewis)
Devil Rides Out, 1968 (Fisher)
Devil Stone, 1917 (De Mille)
Devil Strikes at Night. *See* Nachts wann der Teufel kam, 1957
Devil Takes the Count. *See* Devil Is a Sissy, 1936
Devils, 1971 (Jarman, Russell)
Devil's Angels, 1967 (Cassavetes, Corman)
Devils at the Elgin, 1974 (Jarman)
Devil's Bishop, 1988 (Pontecorvo)
Devil's Bride. *See* Devil Rides Out, 1968
Devil's Cargo, 1925 (Fleming)
Devil's Circus, 1926 (Christensen)
Devil's Doorway, 1950 (A. Mann)
Devil's Envoys. *See* Visiteurs du soir, 1942
Devil's Eye. *See* Djävulens öga, 1960
Devil's Holiday, 1930 (Goulding)
Devil's in Love, 1933 (Dieterle)
Devil's Island. *See* Aku Ryoto, 1980
Devil's Pass. *See* Czarci źleb, 1948
Devil's Passkey, 1919 (Von Stroheim)
Devil's Playground, 1976 (Schepisi)
Devil's Protege. *See* Hvide Djaevel, 1915
Devil's Toy. *See* Rouli-Roulant, 1966
Devil's Wanton. *See* Fängelse, 1949
Devil's Wheel. *See* Chyortovo koleso, 1926
Devil-May-Care, 1929 (Lewin)
Devoradora, 1946 (De Fuentes)
Devushka s korobkoi, 1927 (Barnet)
Devushka s Ulitsy. *See* Ditya Bol'shogo Goroda, 1914
Dezertir, 1933 (Gerasimov, Pudovkin)
Dhadram Karam, 1975 (Kapoor)
Dhoon, 1953 (Kapoor)
Di, 1978 (Rocha)
Dia de Noviembre, 1972 (Solas)
Día Paulino, 1963 (Sanjinés)
Diable au coeur, 1927 (Autant-Lara, L'Herbier)
Diable au corps, 1947 (Autant-Lara, Tati)
Diable boiteux, 1949 (Guitry)
Diable dans la ville, 1924 (Dulac)
Diable et les dix commandements, 1962 (Duvivier)
Diable noir, 1905 (Méliès)
Diable probablement, 1977 (Bresson)
Diabolic Tenant. *See* Locataire diabolique, 1910
Diaboliquement vôtre, 1967 (Duvivier)
Diaboliques, 1954 (Clouzot)
Dial M for Murder, 1954 (Hitchcock)
Dialog, 1968 (Skolimowski)
Diálogo de exilados, 1974 (Ruiz)
Dialogue. *See* Dialog, 1968
Dialogue of Exiles. *See* Diálogo de exilados, 1974
Dialogue of Forms, 1986 (Jireš)
Dialogue with Conscience of the Past, 1988 (Jireš)
Diamant du Sénéchal, 1914 (Feuillade)
Diamánt noir, 1939 (Delannoy)

Diamond Cut Diamond, 1932 (Niblo)
Diamond Jim, 1935 (P. Sturges)
Diamond Ship. *See* Brillantenschiff, 1920
Diamond Star, 1910 (Griffith)
Diamonds of the Night. *See* Demanty noci, 1964
Diaries, Notes, and Sketches. *See* Walden, 1968
Diaries of the Peasants. *See* Pamiętniki chłopów, 1952
Diario de la guerra del cerdo, 1975 (Torre Nilsson)
Diario di un Vizio, 1993 (Ferreri)
Diary for My Loves. *See* Napló szerelmeimnek, 1987
Diary for Timothy, 1945 (Jennings, Wright)
Diary For My Children. *See* Napló gyermekeimnek, 1982
Diary For My Father and My Mother. *See* Napló apámnak, anyámnak, 1990
Diary of a Chambermaid, 1946 (Renoir)
Diary of a Country Priest. *See* **Journal d'un curé de campagne,** 1950
Diary of a Lost Girl. *See* **Tagebuch einer Verlorenen**, 1929
Diary of a Maniac. *See* Diario di un Vizio, 1993
Diary of a Nobody, 1964 (Russell)
Diary of a Poor Young Man. *See* Romanzo di un Giovane Povero, 1995
Diary of a Shinjuku Thief. *See* Shinjuku dorobo nikki, 1969
Diary of a Young Man, 1964 (Loach)
Diary of an Unknown Soldier, 1959 (Watkins)
Diary of Anne Frank, 1959 (Ashby, Stevens)
Diary of Forbidden Dreams. *See* What?, 1973
Diary of Lady M, 1993 (Tanner)
Diary of One Who's Disappeared, 1978 (Jireš)
Diary of Sueko. *See* Nianchan, 1959
Diary of the Pig War. *See* Diario de la guerra del cerdo, 1975
Diary of Yunbogi. *See* Yunbogi no nikki, 1965
Dias melhores virao, 1990 (Diegues)
Días de odio, 1954 (Torre Nilsson)
Diavolo innamorato. *See* Arcidiavolo, 1966
Dice of Destiny, 1920 (King)
Dick Whittington and His Cat, 1913 (Guy)
Dictator, 1922 (Cruze)
Dictator, 1935 (Saville)
Did Mother Get Her Wash, 1911 (Sennett)
Diebe, 1928 (Dieterle)
Diebe von Günsterburg. *See* Der springende Hirsch, 1915
Diece minuti di vita, 1943 (De Sica)
Dieric Bouts. *See* Dirk Bouts, 1975
Diese Machine ist mein antihumanistisches Kunstwerk, 1982 (Jarman)
Dieu a besoin des hommes, 1950 (Delannoy)
Dieux du feu, 1961 (Storck)
Difficile morire, 1977 (Jancsó)
Difficult Life. *See* Vita difficile, 1961
Diga sul Pacifico. *See* Barrage contre le Pacifique, 1958
Digi sul ghiaccio, 1953 (Olmi)
Digterkongen. *See* Gudernes Yndling, 1919
Digue, ou Pour sauver la Hollande, 1911 (Gance)
Dijkbouw, 1952 (Haanstra)
Dike Builders. *See* Dijkbouw, 1952
Dil Hi To Hai, 1963 (Kapoor)
Dil Ki Raani, 1947 (Kapoor)
Dilawar, 1931 (Mehboob)
Dillinger and Capone, 1995 (Corman)
Dillinger è morto, 1968 (Ferreri)
Dillinger Is Dead. *See* Dillinger è morto, 1968
Dim Little Island, 1949 (Jennings)
Dimanche à la campagne, 1984 (Tavernier)
Dimanche à Pekin, 1956 (Marker)
Dimanche de la vie, 1965 (C. Miller)
Dimanche Matin. *See* Niedzielny poranek, 1955
Dimboola, 1979 (Duigan)
Dimenticare Palermo, 1990 (Rosi)
Dimy Gorina, 1961 (Gerasimov)
Din tillvaros land, 1940 (Sucksdorff)
Diner, 1982 (Levinson)
Dinner at Eight, 1933 (Cukor)
Dinner Jest, 1926 (Sennett)
Dinner Under Difficulties. *See* Salle à manger fantastique, 1898
Dinty, 1920 (Neilan)
Dionysos, 1984 (Rouch)
Dionysus in '69, 1970 (De Palma)
Diplomacy, 1926 (Neilan)
Diplomaniacs, 1933 (Mankiewicz)
Diplomatic Courier, 1952 (Hathaway)
Diplomatic Pouch. *See* Teka dypkuryera, 1927
Direct au coeur, 1933 (Pagnol)
Directed by John Ford, 1971 (Bogdanovich, Welles)
Direction: Nowa Huta. *See* Kierunek Nowa Huta, 1951
Directors, 1963 (Germi, Godard, Hitchcock, Huston)
Direktørens Datter, 1912 (Blom)
Dirigible, 1931 (Capra)
Dirk Bouts, 1975 (Delvaux)
Dirty Dozen, 1967 (Aldrich, Cassavetes)
Dirty Duck, 1977 (Corman)
Dirty Hands. *See* Innocents aux mains sales, 1975
Dirty Harry, 1971 (Eastwood, Siegel)
Dirty Story, 1984 (Donner)
Dirty Work in a Laundry, 1915 (Sennett)
Dis-moi, 1980 (Akerman)
Disbarred, 1937 (Florey)
Discard, 1916 (W.S. Van Dyke)
Disclosure, 1994 (Levinson)
Discontent, 1916 (Weber)
Discord and Harmony, 1914 (Dwan)
Discreet Charm of the Bourgeoisie. *See* **Charme discret de la bourgeoisie,** 1972
Discussion, 1939 (Lumet)
Discussion de M. Janssen et de M. Lagrange, 1939 (Lumet)
Dishevelled Hair. *See* Midare-gami, 1961
Dishonored, 1931 (Hathaway, Von Sternberg)
Dishonoured Lady, 1947 (Stevenson)
Dislike. *See* Kirai Kirai Kirai, 1960
Dislocations mystérieuses, 1901 (Méliès)
Disorderly Orderly, 1964 (Jerry Lewis, Tashlin)
Dispara!, 1993 (Saura)
Disparus de Saint-Agil, 1938 (Von Stroheim)
Dispatch from Reuter's, 1940 (Dieterle)
Disputed Passage, 1939 (Borzage)
Disque 927, 1928 (Dulac)
Distant Clouds. *See* Toi kumo, 1955
Distant Drums, 1951 (Walsh)
Distant Jamaica. *See* Fernes Jamaica, 1969
Distant Relative, 1912 (Dwan)
Distant Thunder. *See* Asani Sanket, 1973
Distant Trumpet, 1952 (Fisher)
Distant Trumpet, 1964 (Walsh)
Distant Voices, Still Lives, 1988 (Davies)
Distractions, 1960 (Chabrol)
Distress Call, 1938 (Cavalcanti)
Dita Saxová, 1967 (Menzel)
Dites cariatides, 1984 (Varda)
Dites-lui que je l'aime, 1977 (C. Miller)
Ditte: Child of Man. *See* Ditte Menneskebarn, 1946
Ditte Menneskebarn, 1946 (Henning-Jensen)
Ditto, 1937 (Keaton)
Ditya Bol'shogo Goroda, 1914 (Bauer)
Dive Bomber, 1941 (Curtiz)
Divers at Work on the Wreck of the Maine. *See* Visite sous-marine du Maine, 1898
Diverse Reports: We Should Have Won, 1985 (Loach)
Divertimento, 1993 (Rivette)
Divertissement, 1952 (Rivette)
Divide and Conquer, 1943 (Litvak)
Divided Heart, 1954 (Crichton, Schlesinger)
Divided Love. *See* Geteilte liebe, 1988
Divided World. *See* En kluven värld, 1948
Divina, 1989 (Haynes)
Divine, 1935 (Ophüls)
Divine croisière, 1929 (Duvivier)

Doldertal 7, 1971 (Markopoulos)
Dole plotovi, 1962 (Makavejev)
Dolken, 1915 (Stiller)
Doll. *See* Child's Sacrifice, 1910
Dollar, 1937 (Molander)
Dollar-a-Year Man, 1921 (Cruze)
Dollar Did It, 1913 (Sennett)
Dollar Down, 1925 (Browning)
Dollar Mambo, 1993 (Leduc)
Dollars, 1971 (Brooks)
Dollars of Dross, 1916 (Borzage)
Dolls. *See* Bambole, 1964
Doll's House, 1918 (M. Tourneur)
Doll's House, 1973 (Losey)
Dolly macht Karriere, 1930 (Litvak)
Dolorosa, 1934 (Grémillon)
Dom na Trubnoi, 1928 (Barnet)
Dom za vesanje, 1988 (Kusturica)
Domain of the Moment, 1977 (Brakhage)
Domani accadra, 1988 (Moretti)
Domani è troppo tardi, 1950 (De Sica)
Domaren, 1960 (Sjöberg)
Dömen icke, 1914 (Sjöström)
Domenica d'agosto, 1949 (Rosi)
Domenica è sempre domenica, 1958 (De Sica)
Domenica Specialmente, 1991 (Tornatore)
Domicile conjugal, 1970 (C. Miller, Truffaut)
Domingo, 1961 (Diegues)
Dominion, 1974 (Brakhage)
Domino Principle, 1976 (Kramer)
Don Diego and Pelagea. *See* Dondiego i Pelaguya, 1928
Don Giovanni, 1979 (Losey)
Don Giovanni in Sicilia, 1967 (Lattuada)
Don Is Dead, 1973 (Fleischer)
Don Juan. *See* Amór de Don Juan, 1956
Don Juan 68, 1968 (Jireš)
Don Juan 1973 ou si Don Juan était une femme, 1973 (Vadim)
Don Juan DeMarco, 1995 (Coppola)
Don Juan et Faust, 1922 (Autant-Lara, L'Herbier)
Don Juan, or If Don Juan Were a Woman. *See* Don Juan 1973 ou si Don Juan était une femme, 1973
Don Pasquale, 1940 (De Santis)
Don Quichotte, 1933 (Pabst)
Don Quichotte, 1964-69 (Rohmer)
Don Quintin el amargao, 1935 (Buñuel)
Don Quintín el amargao. *See* Hija del engaño, 1951
Don Quixote, 1955 (Welles)
Don Quixote, 1957 (Kozintsev)
Don Winslow of the Coast Guard, 1943 (Brooks)
Doña Barbara, 1943 (De Fuentes)
Dondiego i Pelaguya, 1928 (Protazanov)
Dongo Horendi, 1966 (Rouch)
Dongo Hori, 1973 (Rouch)
Dongo Yenendi, 1966 (Rouch)
Donkey Skin. *See* Szamárbör, 1918
Donkey Skin. *See* Peau d'ane, 1971
Donna che venne del mare, 1957 (De Sica)
Donna d'una notte. *See* Femme d'une nuit, 1930
Donna del fiume, 1954 (Pasolini)
Donna del Montagna, 1943 (Castellani)
Donna della domenica, 1975 (Comencini)
Donna scimmia, 1964 (Ferreri)
Donne e soldati, 1954 (Ferreri)
Donne-moi tes yeux, 1943 (Guitry)
Donne proibite, 1953 (De Santis)
Donovan Affair, 1929 (Capra)
Donovan's Kid, 1931 (Niblo)
Donovan's Reef, 1963 (Ford)
Don's Party, 1975 (Beresford)
Don't Believe in Monuments. *See* Spomenicima ne treba verovati, 1958
Don't Bet on Blonds, 1935 (Florey)
Don't Bet on Women, 1931 (Howard)
Don't Bite Your Dentist, 1930 (Sennett)
Don't Change Your Husband, 1919 (De Mille)
Don't Cry, Pretty Girls. *See* Szép lányok, ne sirjatok, 1970
Don't Drink the Water, 1966 (Allen)
Don't Drink the Water, 1994 (Allen)
Don't Ever Marry, 1920 (Neilan)
Don't Get Jealous, 1929 (Sennett)
Don't Give Up the Ship, 1959 (Jerry Lewis)
Don't Go Near the Water, 1956 (Walters)
Don't Leave Your Husband. *See* Dangerous Toys, 1921
Don't Let It Kill You. *See* Ne faut pas mourir pour ça, 1967
Don't Look Now, 1973 (Roeg)
Don't Make Waves, 1967 (Mackendrick)
Don't Marry for Money, 1923 (Brown)
Don't Park There!, 1924 (Garnett)
Don't Play Bridge with Your Wife, 1933 (Sennett)
Don't Raise the Bridge, Lower the River, 1967 (Jerry Lewis)
Don't Say It. *See* Kung Fu Master, 1988
Don't Shoot, 1926 (Wyler)
Don't Shoot the Composer, 1966 (Russell)
Don't Tell Dad, 1925 (Sennett)
Don't Tell Everything, 1922 (De Mille, S. Wood)
Don't Trust Your Husband, 1948 (Bacon)
Don't Weaken, 1920 (Sennett)
Donto okoze, 1959 (Oshima)
Donzoko, 1957 (Kurosawa)
Dooley Scheme, 1911 (Sennett)
Doom Generation, 1995 (Araki)
Doomed Love. *See* **Amor de perdicão**, 1978
Door, 1972 (Xie)
Doors, 1991 (Stone)
Doorway of Destruction, 1915 (Ford)
Dorado de Pancho Villa, 1967 (Fernández)
Doraku shinan, 1928 (Gosho)
Dornröschen, 1917 (Leni)
Doroga v ad. *See* Tol'ko Raz v Godu, 1914
Dorogoi moi chelovek, 1958 (Heifitz)
Dorogoi tsenoi, 1957 (Donskoi)
Dorothea Angermann, 1959 (Siodmak)
Dorothy Vernon of Haddon Hall, 1924 (Neilan)
Dorothys Bekenntnis, 1921 (Curtiz)
Dos putas, o, Historia de amor que termina en boda, 1974 (Almodóvar)
Dos rostros y una sola imagen, 1984 (Alvarez)
Dotkniecie, 1990 (Zanussi)
Dottie Gets Spanked, 1993 (Haynes)
Dotty World of James Lloyd, 1964 (Russell)
Douaniers et contrebandiers, 1905 (Guy)
Double Adventure, 1921 (W.S. Van Dyke)
Double Amour, 1925 (Epstein)
Double Bed. *See* Lit à deux places, 1965
Double Door, 1934 (C. Vidor)
Double Indemnity, 1944 (Wilder)
Double jeu, 1916 (Feuillade)
Double Knot, 1913 (Walsh)
Double Life, 1947 (Cukor)
Double Life of Véronique. *See* Podwójne życie Weroniky, 1991
Double Man, 1967 (Schaffner)
Double or Nothing, 1937 (Dmytryk)
Double Speed, 1920 (LeRoy, S. Wood)
Double Suicide. *See* Shinju ten no Amijima, 1969
Double tour, 1959 (Chabrol)
Double vie de Véronique. *See* Podwójne życie Weroniky, 1991
Double Wedding, 1913 (Sennett)
Double Wedding, 1937 (Mankiewicz)
Doubling in the Quickies, 1932 (Sennett)
Douce, 1943 (Autant-Lara)
Douche aprés le bain, 1896-97 (Lumet)
Douche d'eau bouillanie, 1907 (Méliès)
Dough and Dynamite, 1914 (Chaplin, Sennett)
Doughboys, 1930 (Keaton)

Doughnut Designer. *See* Dough and Dynamite, 1914
Doulos, 1963 (Melville)
Douro, faina fluvial, 1931 (Oliveira)
Dov'è la libertà, 1953 (Rossellini)
Dove in the Eagle's nest, 1913 (Cruze)
Dover Revisited, 1942 (Watt)
Down among the Sheltering Palms, 1952 (Goulding)
Down and Dirty. *See* Brutti, sporchi e cattivi, 1976
Down and Out in Beverly Hills, 1986 (Mazursky)
Down by Law, 1986 (Jarmusch)
Down Memory Lane, 1949 (Sennett)
Down on the Farm, 1920 (Sennett)
Down to Earth, 1917 (Fleming)
Down to the Sea in Ships, 1949 (Hathaway)
Down to the Sea in Shoes, 1923 (Sennett)
Down with the Fences. *See* Dole plotovi, 1962
Downfall of Osen. *See* Orizuru osen, 1934
Downhill, 1927 (Hitchcock)
Downhill Racer, 1967 (Redford)
Dozen Socks, 1927 (Sennett)
Dracula, 1931 (Browning)
Dracula, 1958 (Fisher)
Dracula cerca sangue di vergine e ... morì di sete!!, Blood for Dracula. *See* Andy Warhol's Dracula, 1974
Dracula—Prince of Darkness, 1965 (Fisher)
Dracula Rising, 1993 (Corman)
Drag Net, 1928 (Von Sternberg)
Dragnet Girl. *See* Hijosen no onna, 1933
Dragon Gate. *See* Lung Men Fêng Yun, 1976
Dragon Gate Inn. *See* Lung Men K'o Chan, 1967
Dragon of Komodo. *See* Draken på Komodo, 1937/38
Dragon Seed, 1943 (W.S. Van Dyke)
Dragon Tamers, 1974 (Woo)
Dragonen, 1925 (Blom)
Dragones de Ha-Long, 1976 (Alvarez)
Dragonfire, 1993 (Corman)
Dragons de Villars, 1900/07 (Guy)
Dragonwyck, 1946 (Mankiewicz)
Dragotsennye zerna, 1948 (Heifitz)
Draken på Komodo, 1937/38 (Fejös)
Drama von Mayerling. *See* Tragödie im Hause Habsburg, 1924
Dramatic School, 1938 (LeRoy)
Drame au Château d'Acre, 1915 (Gance)
Drame au pays basque, 1913 (Feuillade)
Drame de Shanghai, 1938 (Pabst)
Dramma della gelosia—Tutti i particolari in cronaca, 1970 (Scola)
Dranem, 1900/07 (Guy)
Drastic Demise, 1945 (Anger)
Draughtsman's Contract, 1982 (Greenaway)
Dravci, 1948 (Weiss)
Drawing Lesson. *See* Statue animée, 1903
Dream. *See* His Prehistoric Past, 1914
Dream about a House. *See* Alom a házröl, 1971
Dream Flight. *See* Polioty vo sne naiavou, 1983
Dream Girl, 1916 (De Mille)
Dream House, 1932 (Sennett)
Dream Lover, 1986 (Pakula)
Dream Machine, 1983 (Jarman)
Dream, NYC, The Return, The Flower, 1976 (Brakhage)
Dream of a Rarebit Fiend, 1906 (Porter)
Dream of an Opium Fiend. *See* Rêve d'un fumeur d'opium, 1908
Dream of David Gray. *See* **Vampyr,** 1932
Dream of Death. *See* Dødsdrømmen, 1911
Dream of Light. *See* Sol del Membrillo, 1992
Dream of Love, 1928 (Niblo)
Dream of Passion, 1978 (Dassin)
Dream One, 1982 (Boorman)
Dream Path of Youth. *See* Seishun no yumeji, 1923
Dream Street, 1921 (Griffith)
Dream Stuff, 1933 (Sennett)
Dream Valley. *See* Drömda dalen, 1947
Dream Woman, 1914 (Guy)
Dreaming, 1980 (Vanderbeek)
Dreaming Lips, 1937 (Lean)
Dreams. *See* Kvinnodröm, 1955
Dreams, 1990 (Kurosawa, Scorsese)
Dreams of Monte Carlo. *See* Monte Carlo, 1926
Dreams of Youth. *See* Wakodo no yume, 1928
Dreams That Money Can Buy, 1944-47 (Richter)
Drei amerikanische LPs, 1969 (Wenders)
Drei Tänze der Mary Wilford, 1920 (Wiene)
Drei Unteroffiziere, 1950 (Staudte)
Dreigroschenoper, 1931 (Pabst)
Dreigroschenoper, 1963 (Staudte)
Dreiklang, 1938 (Sirk)
Dress Rehearsal. *See* Generalprobe, 1980
Dressed to Kill, 1980 (De Palma)
Dressmaker from Paris, 1925 (Hawks)
Dreyfus Affair. *See* Affaire Dreyfus, 1899
Drifter, 1988 (Corman)
Drifters, 1929 (Grierson)
Drifting, 1923 (Browning)
Drifting Clouds. *See* Wakare-gumo, 1951
Driftwood, 1912 (Dwan)
Driftwood, 1947 (Dwan)
Driller Killer, 1979 (Ferrara)
Drink's Lure, 1912 (Griffith)
Dripping Water, 1968/69 (Snow)
Dritte Generation, 1979 (Fassbinder)
Drive a Crooked Road, 1954 (Edwards)
Drive for Life, 1909 (Griffith)
Drive, He Said, 1972 (Rafelson)
Driven from Home. *See* Austreibung, 1923
Driver, 1978 (W. Hill)
Driver dagg faller Regn, 1946 (Zetterling)
Driving Miss Daisy, 1989 (Beresford)
Droga do nieba, 1958 (Zanussi)
Droit à la vie, 1917 (Gance)
Drôle de drame, 1937 (Carné)
Drömda dalen, 1947 (Sucksdorff)
Drömmen om Amerika, 1976 (Donner)
DROP Squad, 1994 (S. Lee)
Dropout Wife, 1972 (E. Wood)
Droppington's Devilish Dream, 1915 (Sennett)
Droppington's Family Tree, 1915 (Sennett)
Droske 519, 1909 (Blom)
Drowning by Numbers, 1988 (Greenaway)
Drowning Pool, 1975 (W. Hill)
Drug Wars: The Camarena Story, 1990 (M. Mann)
Drug Wars: The Cocaine Cartel, 1992 (M. Mann)
Drugstore Cowboy, 1989 (Van Sant)
Druhá směna, 1940 (Fric)
Druides, 1906 (Guy)
Drum, 1975 (Frampton)
Drum Beat, 1954 (Daves)
Drummer's Vacation, 1912 (Sennett)
Drums along the Mohawk, 1939 (Ford)
Drums of Love, 1928 (Griffith)
Drunk, 1965 (De Antonio, Warhol)
Drunkard. *See* Konyakci, 1965
Drunkard's Reformation, 1909 (Griffith)
Drunken Angel. *See* Yoidore tenshi, 1948
Dry Lake. *See* Kawaita mizuumi, 1960
Dry Rot, 1956 (Clayton)
Du côté de la Côte, 1958 (Varda)
Du fil à l'aiguille, 1924 (Grémillon)
Du haut en bas, 1933 (Pabst)
Du mouron pour les petits oiseaux, 1962 (Carné)
Du Rififi chez les hommes, 1955 (Dassin)
Du sang de la volupté et de la mort, 1947 (Markopoulos)
Du skal elske din Naeste, 1915 (Blom)
Du Skal Aere Din Hustru, 1925 (Dreyer)

Engagement. *See* I fidanzati, 1963
Engelein, 1913 (Gad)
Engeleins Hochzeit, 1914 (Gad)
Engenhos e usinas, 1945-56 (Mauro)
Engineer Prite's Project. *See* Proyekt inzhenera Praita, 1918
English Potter, 1933 (Flaherty)
Englishman and the Girl, 1910 (Griffith, Sennett)
Engrenage, 1919 (Feuillade)
Enhörningen, 1955 (Molander)
Enigma, 1987 (Rouch)
Enigma of Kaspar Hauser. *See* **Jeder für sich und Gott gegen alle**, 1974
Enigme de dix heures, 1916 (Gance)
Enigme, 1919 (Feuillade)
Enjo, 1958 (Ichikawa)
Enlèvement en automobile et mariage précipite, 1903 (Guy)
Enlisted Man's Honor, 1911 (Guy)
Ennemi public, 1937 (Storck)
Enoch Arden, Part I, 1911 (Griffith)
Enoch Arden, Part II, 1911 (Griffith)
Enormous Changes at the Last Minute, 1985 (Sayles)
Enough of It. *See* Et Huskors, 1914
Enough Rope. *See* Meurtrier, 1963
Enrico IV, 1983 (Bellocchio)
Ensayo de un crimen, 1955 (Buñuel)
Ensom Kvinde, 1914 (Blom)
Entanglement. *See* Karami-ai, 1962
Entente cordiale, 1939 (L'Herbier)
Enter Laughing, 1967 (Reiner)
Enterrement du Hogon, 1973 (Rouch)
Entertainer, 1960 (Richardson)
Enthusiasm: Symphony of the Don Basin. *See* Entuziazm: Simfoniia Donbassa, 1931
Entotsu no mieru basho, 1953 (Gosho)
Entr'acte, 1924 (Clair)
Entre Calais et Douvres, 1897 (Méliès)
Entre tinieblas, 1983 (Almodóvar)
Entuziazm: Simfoniia Donbassa, 1931 (Vertov)
Envers du paradis, 1953 (Von Stroheim)
Eo kaku kodomotachi, 1955 (Hani)
Epervier, 1933 (L'Herbier)
Ephemeral Solidity, 1993 (Brakhage)
Epilepsy, 1976 (Benegal)
Epilog, 1950 (Käutner)
Episode in Netherlands. *See* City Life, 1990
Epistemology of Jean Piaget. *See* Jean Piaget, 1977
Epitaph to My Love. *See* Waga koi no tabiji, 1961
Epitome. *See* Shukuzu, 1953
Epoch of Loyalty. *See* Kinno jidai, 1926
Epreuve, 1914 (Feuillade)
E'primavera, 1949 (Castellani)
Equilibriste, 1902 (Guy)
Equine Spy, 1912 (Guy)
Equinox, 1993 (Rudolph)
Equinox Flower. *See* **Higanbana**, 1958
Equipage, 1927 (M. Tourneur)
Equipage, 1935 (Litvak)
Equus, 1977 (Lumet)
Er du grønlaender. *See* Kaláliuvit, 1970
Er i bange, 1971 (Roos)
Era notte a Roma, 1960 (Rossellini)
Eradicating Auntie, 1909 (Griffith)
Eraku nare, 1932 (Naruse)
Eraserhead, 1978 (Lynch)
Erbföster, 1915 (Dieterle)
Erdbebenin Chile, 1974 (Sanders-Brahms)
Eremitten. *See* Syndig Kaerlighed, 1915
Erendira, 1983 (Guerra)
Erh Tzu Tê Ta Wan Ou, 1983 (Hou)
Eroe dei nostri tempi, 1958 (Lattuada)
Erogami no onryo, 1930 (Ozu)
Eroica, 1957 (Munk)
Eroica—Polen 44. *See* **Eroica**, 1957
Eros, O Basileus, 1967 (Markopoulos)
Erosion, 1971 (Greenaway)
Erotic Tales. *See* Cuentos eróticos, 1979
Erotica. *See* Amore difficile, 1960
Erótica, 1978 (Fernández)
Erotikon, 1920 (Stiller)
Erotique. *See* Erotyk, 1960
Erotyk, 1960 (Skolimowski)
Errand Boy, 1961 (Jerry Lewis)
Erreur de poivrot, 1904 (Guy)
Erreur judiciaire, 1899/1900 (Guy)
Erreur tragique, 1913 (Feuillade)
Eruption of Mount Pelée. *See* Eruption volcanique à la Martinique, 1902
Eruption volcanique à la Martinique, 1902 (Méliès)
Es geschah am 20 Juli, 1955 (Pabst)
Es hilft nicht, wo Gewalt herrscht. *See* Nicht versöhnt oder Es hilft nur Gewalt, wo Gewalt herrscht, 1965
Es ist nicht leicht ein Gott zu sein, 1989 (Herzog)
Es leuchtet meine Liebe, 1922 (Dieterle)
Es war einmal ein Walzer, 1932 (Wilder)
Es werde Licht, 1917/18 (Pick)
Es werde Licht, 1918 (Dupont)
Esa pareja feliz, 1951 (Bardem, García Berlanga)
Escalada del chantaje, 1965 (Alvarez)
Escambray, 1961 (Alvarez)
Escamotage d'une dame chez Robert-Houdin, 1896 (Méliès)
Escapade de Filoche, 1915 (Feuillade)
Escapade in Japan, 1957 (Eastwood)
Escapades of Eva. *See* Eva tropí hlouposti, 1939
Escape, 1914 (Griffith)
Escape, 1925 (Florey)
Escape, 1940 (LeRoy)
Escape, 1948 (Mankiewicz)
Escape Artist, 1982 (Coppola)
Escape at Dawn. *See* Akatsuki no dasso, 1950
Escape Episode, 1944 (Anger)
Escape Episode, 1946 (Anger)
Escape from Alcatraz, 1979 (Eastwood, Siegel)
Escape from Dartmoor. *See* Cottage on Dartmoor, 1929
Escape from East Berlin. *See* Tunnel 28, 1962
Escape from Fort Bravo, 1953 (J. Sturges)
Escape from New York, 1981 (Carpenter)
Escape in the Desert, 1944 (Florey)
Escape Me Never, 1935 (Lean)
Escape on the Fog, 1945 (Boetticher)
Escape to Burma, 1955 (Dwan)
Escape to Victory. *See* Victory, 1981
"Escaped the Law, But ...". *See* Største Kaerlighed, 1914
Escapes Home. *See* Útěky domu, 1980
Esconocido. *See* Playa prohibida, 1955
Escopeta nacional, 1978 (García Berlanga)
Escuela de sordomudos, 1967 (Guzmán)
Eskimo, 1933 (W.S. Van Dyke)
Eskimo Village, 1933 (Grierson)
Eskiya celladi, 1967 (Güney)
Esmeralda, 1905 (Guy)
Espagne 1937/España leal en armas!, 1937 (Buñuel)
Especially on Sunday. *See* Domenica Specialmente, 1991
Espion, 1966 (Godard)
Espionage Agent, 1939 (Bacon)
Espions, 1955 (Clouzot)
Espiritu de la colmena, 1973 (Erice)
Esrefpasali, 1966 (Güney)
Essence. *See* Susman, 1986
Essene, 1972 (Wiseman)
Esta tierra nuestra, 1959 (Gutiérrez Alea)
Estampida, 1971 (Alvarez)
Este pueblo no hay ladrones, 1964 (Buñuel)
Esther, 1910 (Feuillade)
Esther and the King, 1960 (Walsh)

Estrella, 1976 (Almodóvar)
Estudios para un retrato, 1978 (Leduc)
Et ... Dieu créa la femme, 1956 (Vadim)
Et år med Henry, 1967 (Roos)
Et Bankrun. *See* Pressens Magt, 1913
Et Budskab til Napoleon paa Elba, 1909 (Blom)
Et crac!, 1969 (Chabrol)
Et Dieu créa la femme, 1987 (Vadim)
Et forfejlet Spring. *See* Højt Spil, 1913
Et Haremseventyr, 1914 (Holger-Madsen)
Et Hjerte af Guld. *See* Hjertets Guld, 1912
Et Huskors, 1914 (Holger-Madsen)
Et la lumière fut, 1989 (Ioseliani)
Et Laereaar, 1914 (Blom)
Et mourir de plaisir, 1960 (Vadim)
Et Skud i Mørket. *See* Truet Lykke, 1915
Et Slot I Et Slot, 1954 (Dreyer)
Et vanskeligt Valg. *See* Guldet og vort Hjerte, 1913
Eta del ferro, 1964 (Rossellini)
Etat de siège, 1973 (Costa-Gavras)
Eternal City, 1915 (Porter)
Eternal Faust, 1985 (Jireš)
Eternal Love, 1929 (Lubitsch)
Eternal Love. *See* Liang Shan-po yü Chu Ying T'ai, 1963
Eternal Mother, 1911 (Griffith)
Eternal Prague, 1941 (Weiss)
Eternal Rainbow. *See* Kono ten no niji, 1958
Eternal Return. *See* Eternel Retour, 1943
Eternal Three, 1923 (Neilan)
Eternally Yours, 1939 (Garnett)
Eternel Retour, 1943 (Cocteau, Delannoy)
Ethel Gets Consent, 1914/15 (Browning)
Ethel's Teacher, 1914 (Browning)
Ethnic Minorities in Sicily, 1982 (Tornatore)
Etirage des ampoules électriques, 1924 (Grémillon)
Etnocidio: notas sobre el Mezquital, 1978 (Leduc)
Etoile disparaît, 1932 (Delannoy)
Etrange Madame X, 1951 (Grémillon)
Etrange Monsieur Victor, 1938 (Grémillon)
Etrange aventure de Lemmy Caution, 1965 (Godard)
Etranger. *See* Lo straniero, 1967
Etsuraku, 1965 (Oshima)
Ett Hemligt giftermaål, 1912 (Sjöström)
Ett horn i norr, 1950 (Sucksdorff)
Ettore Fieramosca, 1938 (Blasetti)
Ettore lo fusto, 1972 (De Sica)
Etude, 1961 (Gaál)
Etude cinégraphique sur une arabesque, 1929 (Dulac)
Etudes de mouvements, 1928 (Ivens)
Etudiante d'aujourd'hui, 1966 (Rohmer)
Euclidean Illusions, 1978 (Vanderbeek)
Eugenie Grandet. *See* Conquering Power, 1921
Eureka, 1982 (Roeg)
Eureka Stockade, 1949 (Watt)
Europa '51, 1952 (Fellini, Rossellini)
Europa di notte, 1959 (Blasetti)
Europa, Europa, 1990 (Holland)
Europa-Postlagernd, 1918 (Dupont)
European Nights. *See* Europa di notte, 1959
European Rest Cure, 1904 (Porter)
Europeans, 1979 (Ivory)
Eva, 1948 (Bergman, Molander)
Eva tropí hlouposti, 1939 (Fric)
Evangeliemandens Liv, 1914 (Holger-Madsen)
Evangeline, 1919 (Walsh)
Evangeline et la tonnerre. *See* Tonnerre, 1921
Evangelium, 1923 (Holger-Madsen)
Evariste Galois, 1965 (Astruc)
Eve, 1962 (Losey)
Eve of St. Mark, 1944 (Edwards, Stahl)
Eveillé du pont de l'Alma, 1985 (Ruiz)
Evelyn Prentice, 1934 (Howard)
Evelyn the Beautiful. *See* Skonne Evelyn, 1916
Even As You and I, 1917 (Weber)
Even Cowgirls Get the Blues, 1994 (Van Sant)
Even Dwarfs Started Small. *See* Auch Zwerge haben klein angefangen, 1970
Evènement le plus important depuis que l'homme a marché sur la lune, 1973 (Demy)
Evening at Abdon's, 1974 (Holland)
Evening Land. *See* Aftenlandet, 1977
Evening Stream. *See* Yoru no nagare, 1960
Evening with the Royal Ballet, 1963 (Asquith)
Evensong, 1934 (Saville)
Eventful Journey. *See* Hitch Hike Lady, 1936
Eventyr paa Fodrejsen, 1911 (Blom)
Ever Since Eve, 1937 (Bacon)
Evergreen, 1934 (Saville)
Every Day Except Christmas, 1957 (Anderson, Reisz)
Every Day's a Holiday, 1964 (Roeg)
Every Man for Himself. *See* Sauve qui peut, 1980
Every Man for Himself and God against All. *See* **Jeder für sich und Gott gegen alle**, 1974
Every Minute Counts. *See* Count the Hours, 1953
Every Mother's Son, 1919 (Walsh)
Every Night at Night, 1935 (Walsh)
Every Night Dreams. *See* Yogoto no yume, 1933
Every Revolution Is a Throw of the Dice. *See* Toute révolution est un coup de dés, 1977
Every Which Way but Loose, 1978 (Eastwood)
Every Woman for Herself and All for Art, 1977 (Jarman)
Every Woman's Man. *See* Prizefighter and the Lady, 1933
Everybody Dance, 1936 (Fisher)
Everybody Does It, 1949 (Goulding)
Everybody Go Home! *See* Tutti a casa, 1960
Everybody Wins, 1989 (Reisz)
Everybody's Acting, 1926 (Neilan)
Everybody's Doing It, 1916 (Browning)
Everybody's Fine. *See* Stanno Tutti Bene, 1990
Everybody's Woman. *See* Jedermanns Frau, 1924
Everyday, 1929 (Eisenstein)
Everyday Stories. *See* Mindennapi történetek, 1955
Everyman, 1962 (Baillie)
Everything Ends Tonight. *See* Dnes večer všechno skonči, 1955
Everything for Sale. *See* Wszystko na sprzedaż, 1968
Everything Revolves. *See* Alles dreht sich, alles bewegt sich, 1928-29
Everything That Lives. *See* Ikitoshi Ikerumono, 1934
Everything Turns. *See* Alles dreht sich, alles bewegt sich, 1928-29
Everything You Always Wanted to Know about Sex but Were Afraid to Ask, 1972 (Allen)
Everywhere, Nowhere Maybe. *See* Partout ou peut-être nulle part, 1969
Everywoman's Man. *See* Prizefighter and the Lady, 1933
Eve's Daughter, 1914 (Ingram)
Evil Angels. *See* Cry in the Dark, 1988
Evil Genius. *See* Truet Lykke, 1915
Evil Inheritance, 1912 (Dwan)
Evil Men Do, 1915 (Ingram)
Evil Roy Slade, 1972 (Marshall)
Ewige Nacht, 1914 (Gad)
Ewigkeit von gestern. *See* Brutalität in Stein, 1960
Ex-Convict, 1904 (Porter)
Ex-lady, 1932 (Florey)
Ex-Sweeties, 1931 (Sennett)
Ex-voto, 1919 (Autant-Lara)
Ex-Voto. *See* Diable au coeur, 1927
Examination Day at School, 1910 (Griffith)
Examination, Pass Mark. *See* Zaliczenie, 1969
Example. *See* Ibret, 1971
Excalibur, 1981 (Boorman)
Excess Baggage, 1928 (Cruze, Daves)
Exchange Is No Robbery, 1898 (Hepworth)
Exciting Courtship, 1914 (Browning)
Excursion a Vueltabajo, 1965 (Gómez)

Excursion House, 1954 (Willard Van Dyke)
Excuse My Dust, 1920 (S. Wood)
Executioner. *See* **Verdugo**, 1963
Executioner. *See* Azrail benim, 1968
Executive Suite, 1954 (Wise)
Exhumation of the Remains of Sergius of Radonezh. *See* Vskrytie moschei Sergeia Radonezhskogo, 1919
Exile, 1917 (M. Tourneur)
Exile, 1931 (Micheaux)
Exile, 1947 (Ophüls)
Exiled. *See* Aeventyrersken, 1914
Exiles. *See* De Landsflyktige, 1921
Existentialist, 1964 (Emshwiller)
Exode, 1910 (Feuillade)
Exodus, 1960 (Preminger)
Exorcist, 1973 (Friedkin)
Exorcist II: The Heretic, 1977 (Boorman)
Expedition. *See* Abhijan, 1962
Experiment, 1943 (Fric)
Experiment in Evil. *See* Testament du Docteur Cordelier, 1959
Experiment in Terror, 1962 (Edwards)
Experiment Perilous, 1944 (J. Tourneur)
Expiated Innocence. *See* Sonad oskuld, 1915
Expiation, 1909 (Griffith)
Expiation, 1915 (Feuillade)
Exploit on the Ice. *See* Podvig vo idach, 1928
Exploits of an Intelligence Agent. *See* Podvig razvedchika, 1947
Explosion of a Motor Car, 1900 (Hepworth)
Exposition de 1900, 1900 (Méliès)
Expostulations, 1960/62 (Romero)
Exposure, 1958 (Dickinson)
Express Train in a Railway Cutting, 1899 (Hepworth)
Expropriación, 1973 (Ruiz)
Expropriation. *See* Expropriación, 1973
Exquisite Sinner, 1924 (Florey, Von Sternberg)
Exquisite Thief, 1919 (Browning)
Exterminating Angel. *See* Ángel exterminador, 1962
Extinguished Cinders. *See* Brasa dormida, 1928
Extra! Extra!, 1922 (Howard)
Extra Girl, 1923 (Sennett)
Extraordinary Adventures of Mr. West in the Land of the Bolsheviks. *See* **Neobychainye priklucheniya Mistera Vesta v stranye bolshevikov**, 1924
Extraordinary Child, 1954 (Brakhage)
Extraordinary Illusions. *See* Dislocations mystérieuses, 1901
Extraordinary Illusions. *See* Illusions funambulesques, 1903
Extraordinary Seaman, 1968 (Frankenheimer)
Extraordinary Years. *See* Neobyčejná léta, 1952
Extreme Prejudice, 1987 (W. Hill)
Eye for an Eye, 1996 (Schlesinger)
Eye Myth, 1972 (Brakhage)
Eye Myth, 1981 (Brakhage)
Eye of the Eagle 3, 1992 (Corman)
Eye of the Vichy. *See* Oeil de Vichy, 1993
Eyes. *See* Pittsburgh Documents, 1971
Eyes. *See* Desa Nisa, 1972
Eyes Do Not Want to Close at All Times or Perhaps One Day Rome Will Permit Herself to Choose in Her Turn, Othon. *See* Othon, 1969
Eyes in the Night, 1942 (Zinnemann)
Eyes of God, 1913 (Weber)
Eyes of Laura Mars, 1978 (Carpenter)
Eyes of Mystery, 1918 (Browning)
Eyes of the Totem, 1926 (W.S. Van Dyke)
Eyes of the World, 1930 (King)
Eyes That Could Not Close, 1913 (Guy)
Eyes That See Not, 1912 (Porter)
Eyes, the Mouth. *See* Gli occhi, la bocca, 1982
Eyes without a Face. *See* **Yeux sans visages**, 1959
Eyewitness. *See* Sudden Terror, 1970

F for Fake, 1975 (Bogdanovich, Welles)
F. Murray Abraham: Man and Actor, 1987 (Jireš)
F.I.S.T., 1978 (Jewison)
Fabbrica del Duomo, 1948 (Risi)
Fábián Bálint találkozása Istennel, 1979 (Fábri)
Fabiola, 1948 (Blasetti)
Fable of the Beautiful Pigeon-Fancier. *See* Fábula de la bella palomera, 1988
Fabrication du ciment artificiel, 1924 (Grémillon)
Fabrication du fil, 1924 (Grémillon)
Fabryka, 1970 (Kieślowski)
Fábula de la bella palomera, 1988 (Guerra)
Face. *See* Ansiktet, 1958
Face, 1965 (Warhol)
Face at the Window, 1910 (Griffith)
Face at the Window, 1912 (Guy)
Face behind the Mask, 1940 (Florey)
Face from the Past. *See* Natsukashi no kao, 1941
Face in the Crowd, 1957 (Kazan, Neilan)
Face of a Murderer. *See* Satsujinsha no kao, 1949
Face of Britain, 1935 (Rotha)
Face of Hope, 1991 (Chytilová)
Face of Scotland, 1938 (Grierson, Wright)
Face of the Enemy. *See* Fashizm budet razbit, 1941
Face Off, 1977 (Emshwiller)
Face on the Barroom Floor, 1908 (Porter)
Face on the Barroom Floor, 1914 (Chaplin, Sennett)
Face on the Barroom Floor, 1923 (Ford)
Face the Music, 1954 (Fisher)
Face to Face. *See* Twarza w twarz, 1968
Face to Face. *See* Ansikte mot ansikte, 1976
Face Value, 1927 (Florey)
Faces, 1968 (Cassavetes, Schroeter)
Faces in the Dark, 1959 (Zetterling)
Faces of America, 1965 (Emshwiller)
Faces of Children. *See* Visages d'enfants, 1925
Faces of Switzerland. *See* Visages Suisse, 1990
Facing the Music, 1933 (Launder)
Facing the Wind. *See* Veter v litso, 1930
Facteur trop ferré, 1907 (Feuillade)
Faction, 1902 (Guy)
Factory Front. *See* Cause commune, 1940
Factory. *See* Fabryka, 1970
Factotum. *See* Portaborse, 1991
Faded Lilies, 1909 (Griffith)
Fader og Søn, 1911 (Blom)
Faderen, 1909 (Blom)
Fadern, 1969 (Sjöberg)
Fado, Majeur et Mineur, 1994 (Ruiz)
Faedrenes Synd, 1914 (Blom)
Fahlstrom, 1980 (Ruiz)
Fahrendes Volk, 1938 (Feyder)
Fahrenheit 451, 1966 (Truffaut)
Faictz ce que vouldras, 1995 (Ferreri)
Fail Safe, 1964 (Lumet)
Failure, 1911 (Griffith)
Failure's Song is Sad. *See* Haizan no uta wa kanashi, 1923
Faim ... L' occasion ... L'herbe tendre, 1904 (Guy)
Faint Heart, 1922 (La Cava)
Fainting Lover, 1931 (Sennett)
Fair Co-ed, 1927 (J. Tourneur, S. Wood)
Fair Exchange, 1909 (Griffith)
Fair Exchange. *See* Getting Acquainted, 1914
Fair Sussex, 1913 (Pearson)
Fairfax Avenue, 1949 (Jerry Lewis)
Fairytale Country. *See* Sagolandet, 1988
Faisons un rêve, 1936 (Guitry)
Faites vos jeux. *See* Feu à volonté, 1964
Faithful, 1910 (Griffith)
Faithful Heart, 1932 (Saville)
Faithful Taxicab, 1913 (Sennett)
Faithful unto Death. *See* Hjertets Guld, 1912
Faits divers, 1923 (Autant-Lara)

Fajr Yum Jadid, 1964 (Chahine)
Fake Girl. *See* Karakuri musume, 1927
Faking with Society. *See* Caught in a Cabaret, 1914
Fakir de Singapoure, 1908 (Méliès)
Fala Brasilia, 1965 (Pereira Dos Santos)
Falbalas, 1945 (Becker)
Falcon and the Snowman, 1985 (Schlesinger)
Falcon in San Francisco, 1945 (Joseph H. Lewis)
Falcon Strikes Back, 1943 (Dmytryk)
Falcons. *See* Magasiskola, 1970
Fall. *See* Cáida, 1959
Fall. *See* Queda, 1978
Fall Molander, 1944 (Pabst)
Fall of Mauryas. *See* Maurya Patan, 1929
Fall of Sodom. *See* Caida de Sodoma, 1974
Fall of the House of Usher, 1960 (Corman)
Fall of the Roman Empire, 1964 (A. Mann)
Fall of the Romanov Dynasty. *See* Padenye dinastii romanovykh, 1927
Fall Rosentopf, 1918 (Lubitsch)
Fall Tokeramo. *See* Polizeiakte 909, 1933
Fällen, 1975 (Watkins)
Fallen Angel, 1945 (Preminger)
Fallen Angels, 1993 (Soderbergh)
Fallen Champ: The Untold Story of Mike Tyson, 1993 (Kopple)
Fallen Hero, 1913 (Browning)
Fallen Idol, 1948 (Reed)
Fallen Star, 1916 (Hepworth)
Fallen Woman. *See* Daraku suru onna, 1967
Falling Down, 1993 (Schumacher)
Falling for You, 1933 (Launder, Stevenson)
Falling Leaves, 1912 (Guy)
Falling Leaves. *See* Listopad, 1966
Falls, 1980 (Greenaway)
Falsche Arzt. *See* Namenlos, 1923
Falsche Bewegung, 1974 (Wenders)
Falsche Ehemann, 1931 (Wilder)
Falschung, 1981 (Schlöndorff, Skolimowski)
False Colors, 1914 (Weber)
False Evidence. *See* For sin Faders Skyld, 1916
False Evidence. *See* Return of Wild Bill, 1940
False Impressions, 1932 (Sennett)
False Road, 1920 (Niblo)
Falsely Accused, 1905 (Hepworth)
Famalicão, 1940 (Oliveira)
Fame, 1980 (Parker)
Fame Is the Spur, 1947 (Boulting)
Famiglia, 1987 (Scola)
Familia Dressel, 1935 (De Fuentes)
Familia provisional, 1955 (García Berlanga)
Familie Schimeck, 1926 (Dieterle)
Familjens hemlighet, 1936 (Molander)
Family. *See* Famiglia, 1987
Family Business, 1984 (Akerman)
Family Business, 1985 (Costa-Gavras)
Family Business, 1989 (Lumet)
Family Entrance, 1925 (McCarey)
Family Focus, 1975 (Emshwiller)
Family Game. *See* Kazoku gemu, 1983
Family Home. *See* His Trysting Place, 1914
Family Honor, 1920 (K. Vidor)
Family Jewels, 1965 (Jerry Lewis)
Family Life. *See* Zycie rodzinne, 1970
Family Life, 1971 (Loach)
Family Mixup, 1912 (Sennett)
Family Plot, 1976 (Hitchcock)
Family Portrait, 1950 (Jennings)
Family Portrait, 1992 (Tian)
Family Relations. *See* Rodnya, 1982
Family Secret. *See* Familjens hemlighet, 1936
Family Ties. *See* Rodnya, 1982
Family Troubles, 1932 (Stevens)
Family Way, 1966 (Boulting)
Family's Honor, 1913 (Ingram)
Family's Situation. *See* Kazoku no jijo, 1962
Famous All Over Town, 1988 (Demme)
Famous Box Trick. *See* Illusions fantasmagoriques, 1898
Famous Ferguson Case, 1932 (Bacon)
Famous Mrs. Fair, 1923 (Niblo)
Famous Soviet Heroes. *See* Slava Sovetskim Geroiniam, 1938
Famous Sword Bijomaru. *See* Meito Bijomaru, 1945
FAMU Newsreel. *See* Zurnál FAMU, 1961
Fan, 1949 (Preminger)
Fandango, 1985 (Costner)
Fandy, ó Fandy, 1982 (Kachyňa)
Fandy, Oh Fandy. *See* Fandy, ó Fandy, 1982
Fanfare, 1958 (Haanstra)
Fanfarron. *See* Aquí llego el valentón, 1938
Fange no. 113, 1916 (Dreyer, Holger-Madsen)
Fange nr. 1, 1935 (Fejös)
Fängelse, 1949 (Bergman)
Fangerfamilie i Thuledistriktet, 1967 (Roos)
Fangschuss, 1976 (Schlöndorff, Von Trotta)
Fanny, 1932 (Pagnol)
Fanny and Alexander. *See* **Fanny och Alexander,** 1982
Fanny by Gaslight, 1944 (Asquith)
Fanny och Alexander, 1982 (Bergman)
Fantasia sottomarina, 1939 (Rossellini)
Fantasma del convento, 1934 (De Fuentes)
Fantasmi a Roma, 1960 (Scola)
Fantasmo d'amore, 1981 (Risi)
Fantassin Guignard, 1905 (Guy)
Fantastic Tale of Naruto. *See* Naruto hicho, 1957
Fantastic Voyage, 1966 (Fleischer)
Fantômas, 1931 (Fejös)
"Fantômas" series, 1913/14 (Feuillade)
Fantôme de la liberté, 1974 (Buñuel)
Fantôme du Moulin Rouge, 1924 (Clair)
Fantômes du chapelier, 1982 (Chabrol)
Far Call, 1929 (Dwan)
Far Country, 1955 (A. Mann)
Far East. *See* Volochayevskiye dni, 1937
Far East, 1982 (Duigan)
Far from the Madding Crowd, 1967 (Roeg, Schlesinger)
Far from Vietnam. *See* Loin du Vietnam, 1967
Faraon, 1965 (Kawalerowicz)
Faraway, So Close. *See* In weiter Ferne, so nah!, 1993
Farces de cuisinière, 1902 (Guy)
Farces de Jocko, 1897/98 (Guy)
Farenheit 451, 1966 (Roeg)
Farewell My Concubine. *See* **Ba Wang Bie Ji,** 1991
Farewell, My Lovely, 1944 (Dmytryk)
Farewell to Arms, 1932 (Borzage)
Farewell to Arms, 1957 (De Sica, Huston, C. Vidor)
Farewell to Childhood, 1950 (Peries)
Farewell to Your Love. *See* Wadaat Hobak, 1957
Fargo, 1996 (Coen)
Farkas, 1916 (Curtiz)
Farlig Forbryder, 1913 (Blom)
Farlig vår, 1940s (Sjöström)
Farlige Alder, 1911 (Blom)
Farmer aux Texas, 1925 (Leni)
Farmer: Feast or Famine, 1965 (Willard Van Dyke)
Farmer Takes a Wife, 1935 (Fleming)
Farmer's Daughter, 1940 (Daves)
Farmers of Fermathe, 1960 (Dickinson)
Farmer's Wife, 1928 (Hitchcock)
Farò da padre ..., 1974 (Lattuada)
Fårö 1979. *See* Fårö-dokument 1979, 1979
Fårö Document. *See* Fårö-dokument, 1969
Fårö-dokument, 1969 (Bergman)
Fårö-dokument 1979, 1979 (Bergman)
Far's Sorg. *See* Smil, 1916

Fascinating Mrs. Frances, 1909 (Griffith)
Fascinating Youth, 1926 (S. Wood)
Fascination, 1922 (Goulding)
Fascism Will Be Destroyed. *See* Fashizm budet razbit, 1941
Fashions for Women, 1927 (Arzner)
Fashions of 1934, 1934 (Berkeley, Dieterle)
Fashizm budet razbit, 1941 (Shub)
Fast and Furious, 1939 (Berkeley)
Fast and Loose, 1930 (P. Sturges)
Fast and the Furious, 1954 (Corman)
Fast, Cheap & Out of Control, 1996 (Morris)
Fast Company, 1929 (Mankiewicz)
Fast Company, 1953 (J. Sturges)
Fast Company, 1978 (Cronenberg)
Fast Freight, 1921 (Cruze)
Fast Workers, 1933 (Browning)
Fasters miljoner, 1934 (Molander)
Fästmö uthyres, 1951 (Molander)
Fastnachtsbeichte, 1960 (Dieterle)
Fat City, 1972 (Huston)
Fat Man and Little Boy, 1989 (Joffé)
Fat Man and the Thin Man. *See* Gros et le maigre, 1961
Fat Wives for Thin, 1929 (Sennett)
Fata Morgana, 1969 (Herzog)
Fatal Chocolate, 1911 (Sennett)
Fatal Flirtation, 1914 (Sennett)
Fatal Glass of Beer. *See* Deadly Glass of Beer, 1916
Fatal Glass of Beer, 1933 (Sennett)
Fatal High, 1914 (Sennett)
Fatal Hour, 1908 (Griffith)
Fatal Hour, 1937 (Pearson)
Fatal Lie. *See* Fru Potifar, 1911
Fatal Mallet, 1914 (Chaplin, Sennett)
Fatal Mirror, 1912 (Dwan)
Fatal Orchids. *See* Black Orchids, 1916
Fatal Passions. *See* **Dr. Mabuse, der Spieler**, 1921/22
Fatal Promise. *See* Chalice of Sorrow, 1916
Fatal Sweet Tooth, 1914 (Sennett)
Fate, 1912 (Griffith)
Fate of a Flirt, 1925 (Lewin)
Fate of Lee Khan. *See* Ying Ch'un Ko Chih Fêng Po, 1973
Fate's Interception, 1912 (Griffith)
Fate's Turning, 1910 (Griffith)
Father. *See* Apa, 1966
Father. *See* Fadern, 1969
Father. *See* Baba, 1971
Father Amine. *See* Baba Amine, 1950
Father and His Son. *See* Oyaji to sono ko, 1929
Father Brown, 1954 (Hamer)
Father Gets in the Game, 1908 (Sennett, Griffith)
Father Master. *See* Padre padrone, 1977
Father of the Bride, 1950 (Minnelli)
Father Panchali. *See* **Pather Panchali**, 1955
Father Sergius. *See* Otets Sergii, 1918
Father Sorrow. *See* Smil, 1916
Father to Be, 1979 (Hallstrom)
Father Was a Fullback, 1949 (Stahl)
Fatherland, 1986 (Loach)
Father's Choice, 1913 (Sennett)
Father's Dilemma. *See* Prima comunione, 1950
Father's Favorite, 1912 (Dwan)
Father's Grief. *See* Faderen, 1909
Father's Little Dividend, 1951 (Minnelli)
Fatty Again, 1914 (Sennett)
Fatty and Mabel Adrift, 1916 (Sennett)
Fatty and Mabel at the San Diego Exposition, 1915 (Sennett)
Fatty and Mabel Viewing the World's Fair at San Francisco, 1915 (Sennett)
Fatty and Minnie-He-Haw, 1914 (Sennett)
Fatty and the Broadway Stars, 1915 (Sennett)
Fatty and the Heiress, 1914 (Sennett)
Fatty at Coney Island, 1917 (Keaton)
Fatty at San Diego, 1913 (Sennett)
Fatty Joins the Force, 1913 (Sennett)
Fatty's Chance Acquaintance, 1915 (Sennett)
Fatty's Day Off, 1913 (Sennett)
Fatty's Debut, 1914 (Sennett)
Fatty's Faithful Fido, 1915 (Sennett)
Fatty's Finish, 1914 (Sennett)
Fatty's Flirtation, 1913 (Sennett)
Fatty's Gift, 1914 (Sennett)
Fatty's Jonah Day, 1914 (Sennett)
Fatty's Magic Pants, 1914 (Sennett)
Fatty's New Role, 1915 (Sennett)
Fatty's Reckless Fling, 1915 (Sennett)
Fatty's Wine Party, 1914 (Sennett)
Faun, 1918 (Korda)
Faunovo prilis pozdni odpoledne, 1983 (Chytilová)
Faust, 1900/07 (Guy)
Faust, 1926 (Murnau)
Faust, 1970 (Syberberg)
Faust 3: Candida Albacore, 1988 (Brakhage)
Faust 4, 1989 (Brakhage)
Faust and Marguerite, 1900 (Porter)
Faust and Marguerite. *See* Damnation du Docteur Faust, 1904
Faust aux enfers, 1903 (Méliès)
Faust des Riesen, 1917 (Dupont)
Faust—Eine Deutsche Volkssage, 1926 (Dieterle)
Faust et Méphistophélès, 1903 (Guy)
FaustFilm: An Opera, 1987 (Brakhage)
Faustrecht der Freiheit, 1974 (Fassbinder)
Faust's Other: An Idyll, 1988 (Brakhage)
Faute d'orthographe, 1919 (Feyder)
Faute de l'Abbé Mouret, 1970 (Franju)
Faut-il les marier?, 1932 (Clouzot)
Favela dos meus amores, 1934 (Mauro)
Favela of My Loves. *See* Favela dos meus amores, 1934
Favoris de la Lune, 1984 (Ioseliani)
Favorite Fool, 1915 (Sennett)
Favorite Wife of the Maharaja II. *See* Maharadjaens Yndlingshustru II, 1918
Fayette, 1961 (De Sica)
Fayette, una spada per due bandiere. *See* Fayette, 1961
Fazil, 1927 (Hawks)
FBI Story, 1959 (LeRoy)
Fear, 1912 (Dwan)
Fear. *See* Angst, 1954
Fear, 1995 (Craven)
Fear and Desire, 1953 (Kubrick, Mazursky)
Fear City, 1984 (Ferrara)
Fear Eats the Soul. *See* **Angst essen Seele auf,** 1973
Fear No Evil, 1990 (Scorsese)
Fear o' God. *See* Mountain Eagle, 1926
Fear of Fear. *See* Angst vor der Angst, 1975
Fear Strikes Out, 1957 (Mulligan, Pakula)
Fearless, 1993 (Weir)
Fearless Fagan, 1952 (Donen)
Fearless Frank, 1967 (Kaufman)
Fearless Vampire Killers, 1967 (Polanski)
Fearmakers, 1958 (J. Tourneur)
Feast. *See* Utage, 1967
Feast at Zhirmunka. *See* Pir v Girmunka, 1941
Feast of St Jorgen. *See* Prazdnik svyatovo Iorgena, 1930
Feather Letter, 1953 (Xie)
Federal Man-Hunt, 1938 (Fuller)
Fedora, 1916 (Korda)
Fedora, 1978 (Wilder)
Fée au printemps, 1906 (Guy)
Fée aux choux, 1896 (Guy)
Fée caraboose ou le Poignard fatal, 1906 (Méliès)
Feedback, 1965 (Vanderbeek)
Feeding Time, 1913 (Sennett)
Feel My Pulse, 1928 (La Cava)
Feest. *See* Let's Have a Party, 1963

Fireworks, 1947 (Anger)
Fireworks over the Sea. *See* Umi no hanabi, 1951
Firm, 1993 (Pollack)
Firm Man, 1974 (Duigan)
Firma Heiratet, 1914 (Lubitsch)
First a Girl, 1935 (Saville)
First and the Last. *See* Twenty-One Days, 1937
First Comes Courage, 1943 (Arzner)
First Days, 1939 (Cavalcanti, Jennings, Watt)
First Gentleman, 1948 (Cavalcanti)
First Hundred Years, 1924 (Capra, Sennett)
First Hymn to the Night-Novalis, 1994 (Brakhage)
First Lad. *See* Pervyi paren, 1958
First Legion, 1951 (Sirk)
First Love. *See* Pervaya Lyubov', 1915
First Love. *See* Hatsukoi, 1926
First Love. *See* Hatsukoi, 1947
First Love. *See* Pierwsza miłość, 1973
First Love. *See* Primo amore, 1978
First Mrs. Fraser, 1932 (Dickinson)
First Name: Carmen. *See* Prenom: Carmen, 1983
First Teacher. *See* Pyervy uchityel, 1965
First Time, 1951 (Tashlin)
First Travelling Saleslady, 1956 (Eastwood)
First Year, 1926 (Borzage)
First Year, 1932 (Howard)
First Year. *See* Primer año, 1970
First Years. *See* Pierwsze lata, 1949
Fischio al naso, 1967 (Ferreri)
Fish Called Wanda, 1988 (Crichton)
Fisher Folks, 1911 (Griffith)
Fisher King, 1991 (Gilliam)
Fishergirl's Folly, 1914 (Pearson)
Fishing Village. *See* Fiskebyn, 1919
Fishy Affair, 1913 (Sennett)
Fiskebyn, 1919 (Stiller)
Fistful of Dollars, 1964 (Eastwood)
Fistful of Dollars. *See* Per un pugno di dollari, 1964
Fists in the Pocket. *See* **I pugni in tasca,** 1965
Fitzcarraldo, 1981 (Herzog)
Five Acres of Land. *See* Akkara Paha, 1969
Five Angles on Murder. *See* Woman in Question, 1950
Five Branded Women. *See* Jovanka e le altre, 1959
Five Brothers and Sisters. *See* Gonin no kyodai, 1939
Five Card Stud, 1968 (Hathaway)
Five Copies. *See* Fem Kopier, 1913
Five Corners, 1988 (Foster)
Five Days in Milan, 1973 (Argento)
Five Days One Summer, 1982 (Zinnemann)
Five Easy Pieces, 1970 (Rafelson)
Five Evenings. *See* Pyat vecheroc, 1979
Five Fingers, 1952 (Mankiewicz)
Five Girls to Cope With. *See* Pět holek na krku, 1966
Five Graves to Cairo, 1943 (Von Stroheim, Wilder)
Five Man Army, 1970 (Argento)
Five Men in the Circus. *See* Sakasu gonin-gumi, 1935
Five Miles to Midnight. *See* Cocteau dans la plaie, 1962
Five Postcards from Capital Cities, 1967 (Greenaway)
Five Star Final, 1930 (LeRoy)
Five-storied Pagoda. *See* Goju-no to, 1944
Five Thousand Fingers of Dr. T, 1953 (Kramer)
Five Ways to Kill Yourself, 1987 (Van Sant)
Fixed Bayonets, 1951 (Fuller)
Fixer, 1968 (Frankenheimer)
Flame and the Arrow, 1950 (J. Tourneur)
Flame and the Flesh, 1954 (Brooks)
Flame in My Heart. *See* Flamme dans mon coeur, 1987
Flame of New Orleans, 1940 (Clair)
Flame Within, 1935 (Goulding)
Flamenco, 1995 (Saura)
Flames of Royal Love. *See* V žáru královské lásky, 1991
Flames over Baku. *See* Ogni Baku, 1950
Flaming Arrow. *See* Wigwam, 1911
Flaming Star, 1960 (Siegel)
Flaming Sword. *See* Verdens Undergang, 1915
Flaming Years. *See* Povest plamennykh let, 1961
Flamingo Road, 1949 (Curtiz)
Flamme, 1923 (Lubitsch)
Flamme dans mon coeur, 1987 (Tanner)
Flamme merveilleuse, 1903 (Méliès)
Flammes sur l'Adriatique, 1968 (Astruc)
Flammesvaerdet. *See* Verdens Undergang, 1915
Flap, 1970 (Reed)
Flash of Light, 1910 (Griffith)
Flashing Spikes, 1962 (Ford)
Flatliners, 1990 (Schumacher)
Flavor of Green Tea over Rice. *See* Ochazuke no aji, 1952
Flaw, 1955 (Fisher)
Fledermaus '55. *See* Oh! Rosalinda, 1955
Fleet That Came to Stay, 1946 (Boetticher)
Flesh, 1931 (Ford)
Flesh, 1932 (Goulding)
Flesh, 1968 (Warhol)
Flesh. *See* Carne, 1991
Flesh and Blood, 1912 (Guy)
Flesh and Blood, 1951 (Clayton)
Flesh and Blood, 1985 (Verhoeven)
Flesh and Fantasy, 1943 (Duvivier)
Flesh and the Devil, 1927 (Brown)
Flesh and Woman. *See* Grand Jeu, 1954
Flesh Is Hot. *See* Buta to gunkan, 1961
Flesh of Morning, 1956 (Brakhage)
Flesh Will Surrender. *See* Delitto di Giovanni Episcopo, 1947
Fleur de l'âge, 1947 (Carné)
Fleur des ruines, 1916 (Gance)
Fleurs sauvages, 1982 (Lefebvre)
Flic, 1972 (Meszaros)
Flicker Fever, 1935 (Sennett)
Flickering Youth, 1924 (Capra, Sennett)
Flickorna, 1968 (Zetterling)
Fliegenden Ärzte von Ostafrika, 1969 (Herzog)
Fliehende Schatten, 1922 (Pick)
Flight, 1929 (Capra)
Flight. *See* Flugten, 1942
Flight, 1974 (Brakhage)
Flight Command, 1941 (Borzage)
Flight Commander, 1927 (Saville)
Flight from Folly, 1944 (Fisher, Goulding)
Flight from Life. *See* Har jeg Ret til at tage mit eget Liv, 1919
Flight from the Millions. *See* Flugten fra millionerne, 1934
Flight Nurse, 1954 (Dwan)
Flight of the Eagle. *See* Ingenjor andrees luftfard, 1982
Flight of the Phoenix, 1966 (Aldrich)
Flight of the Spruce Goose, 1986 (Romero)
Flight over the Swamp. *See* Let nad mocvarom, 1956
Flight to Fury, 1964 (Hellman)
Flights of Fancy. *See* Polioty vo sne naiavou, 1983
Flip Flops, 1923 (Sennett)
Flipping, 1973 (Chabrol)
Flirt, 1916 (Weber)
Flirt, 1995 (Hartley)
Flirtation Walk, 1934 (Borzage, Daves)
Flirting, 1989 (G. Miller)
Flirting, 1990 (Duigan)
Flirting Husband, 1912 (Sennett)
Flirting in the Park, 1933 (Stevens)
Flirts. *See* Between Showers, 1914
Flirt's Mistake, 1914 (Sennett)
Flirty Four-Flushers, 1926 (Sennett)
Flirty Sleepwalker, 1932 (Sennett)
Floating Clouds. *See* Ukigumo, 1955
Floating Vessel. *See* Ukifune, 1957

For Your Love Only. *See* Reifezeugnis, 1982
För att inte tala om alla dessa kvinnor, 1964 (Bergman)
För sin kädleks skull, 1913 (Sjöström, Stiller)
Forbidden, 1919 (Weber)
Forbidden, 1932 (Capra)
Forbidden Fruit, 1921 (De Mille)
Forbidden Games. *See* **Jeux interdits,** 1951
Forbidden Passage, 1941 (Zinnemann)
Forbidden Room, 1914 (Dwan)
Forbidden Songs. *See* Zakazane piosenki, 1947
Forbidden Thing, 1920 (Dwan)
Forbidden Valley, 1920 (Blackton)
Forbidden World, 1982 (Corman)
Forbryders Liv og Levned, eller En Forbryders Memoirer, 1916 (Dreyer)
Forbush and the Penguins, 1971 (Sucksdorff)
Force of Arms, 1951 (Curtiz)
Force of Evil, 1948 (Aldrich, Polonsky)
Forced Bravery, 1913 (Sennett)
Forced Take-Off. *See* Qiangxing Qifei, 1984
Foreclosure, 1912 (Dwan)
Foreign Affair, 1948 (Wilder)
Foreign Correspondent, 1940 (Hitchcock)
Foreign Devils, 1927 (W.S. Van Dyke)
Foreign Skies. *See* Wish You Were There, 1985
Foreman and the Jury, 1913 (Sennett)
Foreman Went to France, 1941 (Cavalcanti, Hamer)
Forest, 1931 (Gerasimov)
Forest on the Hill, 1919 (Hepworth)
Forestalled. *See* Two Fisted Rangers, 1939
Forêt secrète d'Afrique, 1968 (Storck)
Forever Amber, 1947 (Preminger, Stahl)
Forever and a Day, 1943 (Clair, Goulding, Keaton, Saville, Stevenson)
Forever England. *See* Brown on Resolution, 1935
Forever in Love, Body and Soul. *See* Pride of the Marines, 1945
Forever Yours. *See* Hub illal Abad, 1959
Forfaiture, 1937 (L'Herbier)
Forgery. *See* Fälschung, 1981
Forget Me Not, 1922 (W.S. Van Dyke)
Forgotten. *See* **Olvidados,** 1950
Forgotten Faces, 1936 (Dupont)
Forgotten Faces, 1961 (Watkins)
Forgotten Prayer, 1916 (Borzage)
Forgotten Victory, 1939 (Zinnemann)
Forjadores de la paz, 1962 (Alvarez)
Føroyar Faerøerne, 1961 (Roos)
Forraederen, 1910 (Blom)
Forrest Gump, 1994 (Zemeckis)
Forsaking All Others, 1934 (Mankiewicz, W.S. Van Dyke)
Förseglade löppar, 1927 (Molander)
Første Kaerlighed, 1912 (Blom)
Förster-christel, 1926 (Dieterle)
Fort Apache, 1948 (Ford)
Fortieth Door, 1921 (W.S. Van Dyke)
Fortini/Cani, 1976 (Straub)
Fortuna di essere donna, 1955 (Blasetti)
Fortune, 1975 (Nichols)
Fortune Cookie, 1966 (Wilder)
Fortune Hunters, 1913 (Guy)
Fortune Is a Woman, 1956 (Launder)
Fortunella, 1958 (Fellini)
Forty Guns, 1957 (Fuller)
Forty Hearts. *See* Sorok serdets, 1930
Forty Leagues from Paradise, 1970 (Peries)
Forty Little Mothers, 1940 (Berkeley)
Forty Years of Experiment, 1928-29 (Richter)
Forward Flag of Independence. *See* Susume dokuritsuki, 1943
Forward into the Future, 1964 (Peries)
Fossils. *See* Kaseki, 1975
Fou, 1970 (Goretta)
Fou amoureaux, 1991 (Vadim)
Fou de la falaise, 1916 (Gance)
Foul Play, 1976 (Bardem)
Found Film No.1, 1968-70 (Vanderbeek)
Foundations of Progress, 1972 (Benegal)
Foundling, 1915 (Dwan)
Foundling of Fate. *See* Hittebarnet, 1916
Fountain, 1934 (Cromwell)
Fountainhead, 1949 (K. Vidor)
Fountainhead. *See* Izumi, 1956
Fountains of Bakhisarai, 1909 (Protazanov)
Four Adventures of Reinette and Mirabelle. *See* Quatre Aventures de Reinette et Mirabelle, 1987
Four against the Bank. *See* Vier genen die bank, 1976
Four American Composers, 1983 (Greenaway)
Four around a Woman. *See* Kämpfende Herzen, 1920
Four Bags Full. *See* Traversée de Paris, 1956
Four Barriers, 1937 (Cavalcanti, Grierson, Watt)
Four Chimneys. *See* **Entotsu no mieru basho**, 1953
Four Dark Hours. *See* Green Cockatoo, 1937
Four Daughters, 1938 (Curtiz)
Four Days in July, 1985 (Leigh)
Four Devils, 1928 (Murnau)
Four Feathers, 1929 (Schoedsack)
Four Flies on Grey Velvet, 1971 (Argento)
Four Flights to Love. *See* Paradis perdu, 1939
Four for Texas, 1963 (Aldrich)
Four Friends, 1981 (Penn)
Four Frightened People, 1934 (De Mille)
Four Horsemen of the Apocalypse, 1921 (Ingram)
Four Horsemen of the Apocalypse, 1962 (Minnelli)
Four Hundred Blows. *See* **Quatre Cents Coups**, 1959
Four Hundred Million, 1939 (Ivens)
Four Jills in a Jeep, 1944 (Niblo)
Four Love Stories. *See* Yottsu no koi no monogatari, 1947
Four Love Stories, Part II: Even Parting Is Enjoyable. *See* Yottsu no koi no monogatari, II: Wakare mo tanoshi, 1947
Four Masked Men, 1934 (Pearson)
Four Men and a Prayer, 1938 (Ford)
Four Moods. *See* Hsi Nu Ai Le, 1970
Four Musketeers, 1975 (Lester)
Four Nights of a Dreamer. *See* Quatre Nuits d'un rêveur, 1971
Four Orphans, 1923 (La Cava)
Four Poster, 1952 (Kramer)
Four Rooms, 1995 (Anders, Rodriguez, Tarantino)
Four Seasons of Tateshina. *See* Tateshina no shiki, 1966
Four Sided Triangle, 1953 (Fisher)
Four Sons, 1928 (Ford)
Four Stars. *See* **** (Four Stars), 1967
Four Steps in the Clouds. *See* Quattro passi fra le nuvole, 1942
Four Times about Bulgaria. *See* Ctyřikrát o Bulharsku, 1958
Four Troublesome Heads. *See* Homme de tête, 1898
Four Ways Out. *See* Città si difende, 1951
Four Weddings and a Funeral, 1994 (Newell)
Four Wives, 1939 (Curtiz)
Fourberies de Pingouin, 1916 (Feuillade)
Four's a Crowd, 1938 (Curtiz)
Fourteen Hours, 1951 (Cassavetes, Hathaway)
Fourteen's Good, Eighteen's Better, 1980 (Armstrong)
Fourth Estate, 1940 (Rotha)
Fourth Man, 1979 (Verhoeven)
Fourth Marriage of Dame Margaret. *See* Prästänkan, 1920
Fourth Musketeer, 1923 (Howard)
Fourth War, 1989 (Frankenheimer)
Fox. *See* Faustrecht der Freiheit, 1974
Foxes, 1980 (Foster)
Foxes of Harrow, 1947 (Stahl)
Foxfire, 1987 (Schumacher)
Foxfire Childwatch, 1971 (Brakhage)
Foxtrot, 1975 (Ripstein)
Fra Diavolo, 1912 (Guy)
Fra Fyrste til Knejpevaert, 1913 (Holger-Madsen)
Fra Vincenti, 1909 (Feuillade)

Fragment of an Empire. *See* Oblomok imperii, 1929
Fragments of War, 1987 (G. Miller)
Från yttersta skären, 1931 (Molander)
Français vus par ..., 1988 (Lynch)
Française et l'amour, 1960 (Clair, Delannoy)
Frances, 1982 (Costner)
Francesco—giullare di Dio, 1950 (Fellini, Rossellini)
Franches lippées, 1933 (Delannoy)
Francis Bacon. *See* Estudios para un retrato, 1978
Francis in the Navy, 1955 (Eastwood)
Francis of Assisi, 1961 (Curtiz)
Francisca, 1981 (Oliveira)
Franciscain de Bourges, 1967 (Autant-Lara)
Francois Truffaut: portraits voles, 1993 (Astruc, Rohmer, Tavernier)
Francois Truffaut: Stolen Portraits. *See* Francois Truffaut: portraits voles, 1993
François Simon—La présence, 1986 (Tanner)
Frank Hansens Glück, 1917 (Wiene)
Frankenstein, 1931 (Florey, Whale)
Frankenstein and the Monster from Hell, 1973 (Fisher)
Frankenstein Created Woman, 1966 (Fisher)
Frankenstein Must Be Destroyed, 1969 (Fisher)
Frankenstein Unbound, 1989 (Corman)
Frankenweenie, 1982 (Burton)
Franks, 1909 (Griffith)
Frånskild, 1951 (Bergman, Molander)
Frantic. *See* Ascenseur pour l'échafaud, 1958
Frantic, 1988 (Polanski)
Fratelli, 1988 (Lattuada)
Fratelli sole sorella luna, 1972 (Zeffirelli)
Frau auf der Folter, 1928 (Wiene)
Frau Blackburn, Born 5 Jan. 1872, Is Filmed. *See* Frau Blackburn, geb. 5 Jan. 1872, wird gefilmt, 1967
Frau Blackburn, geb. 5 Jan. 1872, wird gefilmt, 1967 (Kluge)
Frau Dorothys Bekenntnis. *See* Dorothys Bekenntnis, 1921
Frau Eva, 1915 (Wiene)
Frau im Mond, 1929 (Lang)
Frau mit dem schlechten Ruf, 1924 (Christensen)
Frau mit den Orchiden, 1919 (Lang)
Frau nach Mass, 1940 (Käutner)
Frau Sorge, 1928 (Dieterle)
Frau über Bord, 1945 (Staudte)
Frau von vierzig Jahren, 1925 (Leni)
Fraud that Failed, 1913 (Dwan)
Frauen in New York, 1977 (Fassbinder)
Frauenopfer, 1922 (Dieterle, Leni)
Fraulein Berlin, 1983 (Jarmusch)
Fräulein Barbier, 1915 (Wiene)
Fräulein Doktor, 1968 (Lattuada)
Fräulein Julie, 1921 (Dieterle)
Fräulein Piccolo, 1914 (Lubitsch)
Fräulein Seifenschaum, 1914 (Lubitsch)
Frayle, 1959 (Olmi)
Freaks, 1932 (Browning)
Freaks of the Deep, 1932 (Sennett)
Freaky Friday, 1976 (Foster)
Freccia nel fianco, 1945 (Lattuada)
Freckles, 1917 (Neilan)
Fred Barry, comédien, 1959 (Jutra)
Fredaines de Pierrette, 1900 (Guy)
Free and Easy, 1930 (De Mille, Keaton, Niblo)
Free Fall, 1967 (Vanderbeek)
Free School. *See* Jiyu gakko, 1951
Free Soul, 1931 (Brown)
Free Woman. *See* Strohfeuer, 1971
Freed 'em and Weep, 1929 (McCarey)
Freedom Committee. *See* Frihedsfonden, 1945
Freedom Radio, 1940 (Asquith)
Freedom Road, 1978 (Kadár)
Freethinker, 1994 (Watkins)
Freeze Out, 1921 (Ford)
Frei bis zum nächsten Mal, 1969 (Fassbinder)
Freight Prepaid. *See* Fast Freight, 1921
Freiheit, 1965-67 (Lucas)
Freiwild, 1928 (Holger-Madsen)
Frelsende Film, 1915 (Holger-Madsen)
Fremde, 1917 (Pick)
Fremde Frau, 1950 (Staudte)
Fremde Vogel, 1911 (Gad)
French. *See* Gaulois, 1988
French Cancan, 1955 (Renoir, Rivette, Straub)
French Communique, 1940 (Hamer)
French Connection, 1971 (Friedkin)
French Connection II, 1975 (Frankenheimer)
French Cops Learning English, 1908 (Méliès)
French Downstairs, 1916 (Weber)
French Dressing, 1927 (Dwan)
French Dressing, 1963 (Russell)
French Duel, 1909 (Griffith)
French Kiss, 1995 (Kasdan)
French Lieutenant's Woman, 1981 (Reisz)
French Line, 1954 (Bacon)
French Mistress, 1960 (Boulting)
French, They Are a Funny Race. *See* Carnets du Major Thompson, 1957
French White Cargo. *See* Cargaison blanche, 1937
French without Tears, 1939 (Asquith, Lean)
Frenzy. *See* Hets, 1944
Frenzy, 1972 (Hitchcock)
Frère de lait, 1916 (Feyder)
Fresa y chocolate, 1993 (Gutiérrez Alea)
Fresh Bait. *See* Appat, 1995
Fresh from the City, 1920 (Sennett)
Freud, 1963 (Huston)
Freud: The Secret Passion. *See* Freud, 1963
Freudlose Gasse, 1925 (Pabst)
Freundschaft siegt. *See* Naprozod mlodziezy, 1952
Fric-Frac, 1939 (Autant-Lara)
Frida. *See* Frida: Naturaleza vita, 1984
Frida: Naturaleza vita, 1984 (Leduc)
Frida's Songs. *See* Fridas visor, 1930
Fridas visor, 1930 (Molander)
Friday the Thirteenth, 1933 (Launder, Saville)
Frieda, 1947 (Dearden, Zetterling)
Friedemann Bach, 1950 (Staudte)
Friedensfahrt. *See* Wyscig pokoju Warszawa-Berlin-Praga, 1952
Friend. *See* Przy Jaciel, 1960
Friend. *See* Arkadas, 1974
Friend Fleeing, 1962 (Baillie)
Friend Husband, 1918 (Sennett)
Friend Indeed, 1938 (Zinnemann)
Friend Next to a Friend. *See* Uz druga je drug, 1955
Friend of the Family, 1909 (Griffith)
Friend of the People. *See* Folkets Ven, 1918
Friendly Enemies, 1942 (Dwan)
Friendly Persuasion, 1956 (Wyler)
Friends, 1912 (Griffith)
Friends and Lovers, 1931 (Von Stroheim)
Friendship Triumphs. *See* Naprozod mlodziezy, 1952
Frieze, an Underground Film, 1973 (G. Miller)
Frightened Bride. *See* Tall Headlines, 1952
Frighteners, 1995 (Jackson)
Frigid Souls. *See* Kholodnye Dushi, 1914
Frihedsfonden, 1945 (Henning-Jensen)
Friluft, 1959 (Roos)
Fringe Dwellers, 1985 (Beresford)
Friquet, 1912 (M. Tourneur)
Frisco Jenny, 1933 (Wellman)
Frisco Kid, 1935 (Bacon)
Frisco Kid, 1979 (Aldrich)
Frisky. *See* Pane, amore e gelosia, 1954
Frissons. *See* Shivers, 1975
Fritz Kortner Recites Faust. *See* Fritz Kortner spricht Faust, 1966
Fritz Kortner Recites Monologues for a Record. *See* Fritz Kortner spricht

Geheimnis der Orplid. *See* Epilog, 1950
Geheimnis des Abbe, 1927 (Dieterle)
Geheimnis des Amerika-Docks, 1917 (Dupont)
Geheimnis des blauen Zimmers, 1950 (Staudte)
Geheimnisvolle Tiefen, 1949 (Pabst)
Geier-Wally, 1921 (Dieterle, Dupont, Leni)
Geierwally. *See* Geier-Wally, 1921
Geisha Boy, 1958 (Jerry Lewis, Tashlin)
Gekka no kyojin, 1926 (Kinugasa)
Gelegenheitsarbeit einer Sklavin, 1973 (Kluge)
Geliebte, 1927 (Wiene)
Gelignite Gang, 1956 (Fisher)
Gelosia, 1953 (Germi)
Gelöste Ketten, 1916 (Wiene)
Gemischte Frauenchor, 1916 (Lubitsch)
Gemma orientale di Papi, 1946 (Blasetti)
GEN—Jiří Anderle, 1993 (Jireš)
GEN—Josef Skvorecký, 1993 (Jireš)
GEN—Miloš Kopecký, 1995 (Jireš)
Genbakuno-ko, 1952 (Shindo)
Genboerne, 1939 (Henning-Jensen)
Gendai no joo, 1924 (Mizoguchi)
Gendarme est sans culotte, 1914 (Feuillade)
Gendarme est sans pitié, 1932 (Autant-Lara)
Gendarmes, 1907 (Guy)
Gendre de Monsieur Poirier, 1934 (Pagnol)
General, 1926 (Keaton)
General Died at Dawn, 1936 (Milestone)
General Idi Amin Dada, 1974 (Schroeder)
General Line. *See* Generalnaia linia, 1929
General Nogi and Kuma-san. *See* Nogi Taisho to Kuma-san, 1926
General Nuisance, 1941 (Keaton)
General Statement on Chile. *See* Acta General de Chile, 1986
Generale della Rovere, 1959 (De Sica, Rossellini)
Generalnaia linia, 1929 (Eisenstein)
Generalprobe, 1980 (Schroeter)
Generation. *See* Pokolenie, 1954
Generosity. *See* Aedel Daad or Den store Flyver, 1911
Genesis, 1986 (Sen)
Genesis: The Creation and the Flood, 1994 (Olmi)
Génie de feu, 1908 (Méliès)
Genii of Fire. *See* Génie de feu, 1908
Genio due compari e un pollo, 1975 (Leone)
Genius, 1970 (Markopoulos)
Genji monogatari, 1951 (Shindo, Yoshimura)
Gennem Kamp til Sejr, 1911 (Gad)
Genocide, 1985 (Welles)
Genopstandelsen. *See* En Opstandelse, 1914
Genou de Claire, 1970 (Rohmer, Schroeder)
Gens d'Abitibi, 1979 (Perrault)
Gens du mil, 1951 (Rouch)
Gens du voyage, 1938 (Feyder)
Gens qui pleurent et gens qui rient, 1900 (Méliès)
Gente del Po, 1947 (Antonioni)
Gentilhomme des bas-fonds, Les Chevaliers de la nuit. *See* Ritter der Nacht, 1928
Gentle Cyclone, 1926 (W.S. Van Dyke)
Gentle Gunman, 1952 (Dearden)
Gentleman Burglar, 1908 (Porter)
Gentleman Burglar, 1914 (Sennett)
Gentleman Jim, 1942 (Walsh)
Gentleman of Leisure, 1915 (De Mille)
Gentleman of Paris, 1931 (Launder)
Gentleman of the Room. *See* Kammarjunkaren, 1913
Gentleman Tramp, 1975 (Bogdanovich)
Gentleman's Agreement, 1935 (Pearson)
Gentleman's Agreement, 1947 (Kazan)
Gentlemen of Nerve, 1914 (Chaplin, Sennett)
Gentlemen Prefer Blondes, 1953 (Hawks)
Genuine, 1920 (Wiene)
Geo le mysterieux, 1916 (Dulac)
Geography Films Series, 1944/49 (Leacock)
Geordie, 1955 (Launder)
George and Margaret, 1940 (Fisher)
George Dumpson's Place, 1964 (Emshwiller)
Georgina's Gründe, 1974 (Schlöndorff, Von Trotta)
Gerald Cranston's Lady, 1924 (Goulding)
Gerald's Film, 1976 (Jarman)
Gerard Has His Hair Removed with Nair, 1967 (Warhol)
Gerechtigkeit, 1925 (Dieterle)
German Sisters. *See* **Bleierne Zeit**, 1981
Germania, anno zero, 1947 (Rossellini)
Germany in Autumn. *See* Deutschland im Herbst, 1978
Germany Nine Zero. *See* Allemagne Neuf Zero, 1991
Germany, Pale Mother. *See* Deutschland bleiche mutter, 1980
Germany, Year Zero. *See* Germania, anno zero, 1947
Germination d'un haricot, 1928 (Dulac)
Geroite na Shipka, 1954 (Vasiliev)
Geronimo: An American Legend, 1993 (W. Hill)
Gershwin, 1992 (Resnais)
Gertrud, 1964 (Dreyer)
Gervais, 1956 (Clement)
Geschichte des kleinen Muck, 1953 (Staudte)
Geschichtsunterricht, 1972 (Straub)
Geschlecht derer von Rinwall, 1918 (Wiene)
Geschlecht in Fesseln—Die Sexualnot der Gefangenen, 1928 (Dieterle)
Gespensterschiff, 1921 (Leni)
Gespensterstunde, 1917 (Gad)
Gestes du silence, 1960 (Storck)
Gesu di Nazareth, 1977 (Zeffirelli)
Gesunkenen, 1925 (Dieterle)
Gesuzza la sposa Garibaldina. *See* 1860, 1934
Get Back, 1991 (Lester)
Get Charlie Tully. *See* Ooh ... You Are Awful, 1972
Get Out Your Handkerchiefs. *See* Preparez vos mouchoirs, 1977
Get Rich Quick, 1913 (Sennett)
Get-Rich-Quick Wallingford, 1915 (Niblo)
Get-Rich-Quick Wallingford, 1921 (Borzage)
Get Shorty, 1995 (Marshall)
Get to Know Your Rabbit, 1972 (De Palma, Welles)
Get Your Man, 1921 (Howard)
Get Your Man, 1927 (Arzner)
Getaway, 1972 (Peckinpah, W. Hill)
Getaway, 1994 (W. Hill)
Geteilte liebe, 1988 (Sanders-Brahms)
Getting Acquainted, 1914 (Chaplin, Sennett)
Getting Even, 1909 (Griffith)
Getting Gertie's Garter, 1927 (Garnett)
Getting Gertie's Garter, 1945 (Dwan)
Getting His Goat. *See* Property Man, 1914
Getting Mary Married, 1919 (Dwan)
Getting of Wisdom, 1977 (Beresford)
Gewalt, 1971 (Sanders-Brahms)
Gewehr über, 1950 (Staudte)
Gezeichneten, 1922 (Dreyer)
Ghare Bahire, 1984 (S. Ray)
Ghost, 1911 (Sennett)
Ghost and Mrs. Muir, 1947 (Mankiewicz)
Ghost Breaker, 1914 (De Mille)
Ghost Breaker, 1922 (LeRoy)
Ghost Flower, 1918 (Borzage)
Ghost Goes West, 1935 (Clair)
Ghost of Folly, 1926 (Sennett)
Ghost of Love. *See* Fantasmo d'amore, 1981
Ghost of the Variety. *See* Spøgelset i Gravkaelderen, 1910
Ghost Parade, 1931 (Sennett)
Ghost Story of Youth. *See* Seishun kaidan, 1955
Ghost Train, 1931 (Launder)
Ghost Train, 1941 (Launder)
Ghosts, 1915 (Von Stroheim)
Ghosts Before Breakfast. *See* Vormittagsspuk, 1927-28
Ghosts Italian Style. *See* Questi fantasmi, 1967

Ghosts of Rome. *See* Fantasmi a Roma, 1960
Giacomo l'idealista, 1942 (Lattuada, Risi)
Giant, 1956 (Stevens)
Giardino dei Finzi Contini, 1970 (De Sica)
Gibraltar, 1932 (Wright)
Gibraltar, 1938 (Von Stroheim)
Gibson Goddess, 1909 (Griffith, Sennett)
Giddy Age, 1932 (Sennett)
Giddy, Gay and Ticklish, 1915 (Sennett)
Gideon of Scotland Yard, 1959 (Ford)
Gideon's Day. *See* Gideon of Scotland Yard, 1959
Gidslet, 1913 (Christensen)
Gielgud: Scenes from Nine Decades, 1994 (Branagh)
Gift, 1973 (Brakhage)
Gift o' Gab, 1917 (W.S. Van Dyke)
Gift of Friendship, 1970s (Newell)
Giftas, 1956 (Zetterling)
Giftpilen, 1915 (Blom)
Gigi, 1958 (Minnelli)
Gigolo, 1926 (Howard)
Gilda, 1946 (C. Vidor)
Gilda Live, 1980 (Nichols)
Gilded Highway, 1926 (Blackton)
Gill-Women of Venus. *See* Voyage to the Planet of the Prehistoric Women, 1966
Gillekop, 1919 (Blom, Dreyer)
Gimme Shelter, 1970 (Maysles)
Gin-Shinju, 1956 (Shindo)
Ginger and Fred, 1986 (Fellini)
Gingham Girl, 1920 (Sennett)
Ginpei from Koina. *See* Toina no Ginpei, 1933
Ginrei no hate, 1947 (Kurosawa)
Ginza Cosmetics. *See* Ginza gesho, 1951
Ginza gesho, 1951 (Naruse)
Ginza no onna, 1955 (Yoshimura)
Ginza no yanagi, 1932 (Gosho)
Ginza Sanshiro, 1950 (Ichikawa)
Giochi di Colonia, 1958 (Olmi)
Gion bayashi, 1953 (Mizoguchi)
Gion Festival Music. *See* Gion bayashi, 1953
Gion Festival. *See* Gion matsuri, 1933
Gion matsuri, 1933 (Mizoguchi)
Gion no shimai, 1936 (Mizoguchi)
Giornata balorda, 1960 (Pasolini)
Giornata particolare, 1977 (Scola)
Giorni d'amore, 1954 (De Santis, Petri)
Giorni di gloria, 1945 (De Santis, Visconti)
Giorno nella vita, 1946 (Blasetti)
Giovane normale, 1969 (Risi)
Giovane Toscanini, 1988 (Zeffirelli)
Giovanna d'Arco al rogo, 1954 (Rossellini)
Giovanni Mariti, 1958 (Pasolini)
Giovedi, 1963 (Risi)
Gioventù perduta, 1947 (Germi)
Gipsy Joe, 1916 (Sennett)
Girl. *See* Eltávozott nap, 1968
Girl 6, 1996 (S. Lee, Tarantino)
Girl and Her Trust, 1912 (Griffith)
Girl and the Bronco Buster, 1911 (Guy)
Girl and the Gun, 1912 (Dwan)
Girl and the Outlaw, 1908 (Griffith)
Girl at Dojo Temple. *See* Musume Dojoji, 1946
Girl at Home, 1917 (Neilan)
Girl Back Home, 1912 (Dwan)
Girl Can't Help It, 1956 (Tashlin)
Girl Crazy, 1929 (Sennett)
Girl Crazy, 1943 (Berkeley, Walters)
Girl Friend. *See* Kanojo, 1926
Girl from Chicago, 1932 (Micheaux)
Girl from Everywhere, 1927 (Sennett)
Girl from Lorraine. *See* Provinciale, 1980
Girl from Maxim's, 1933 (Crichton, Korda)
Girl from the Street. *See* Ditya Bol'shogo Goroda, 1914
Girl From Nowhere, 1928 (Sennett)
Girl Getters. *See* System, 1964
Girl Guardian, 1916 (Sennett)
Girl I Loved. *See* Waga koiseshi otome, 1946
Girl in Black, 1957 (Cacoyannis)
Girl in Every Port, 1928 (Hawks)
Girl in Number 29, 1920 (Ford)
Girl in the Crowd, 1934 (Powell)
Girl in the Moon. *See* Frau im Mond, 1929
Girl in the News, 1940 (Launder, Reed)
Girl in the Painting. *See* Portrait from Life, 1948
Girl in the Red Velvet Swing, 1955 (Fleischer)
Girl in the Rumor. *See* Uwasa no musume, 1935
Girl in the Tonneau, 1932 (Sennett)
Girl in White, 1952 (J. Sturges)
Girl Isn't Allowed to Love. *See* Bara ikutabi, 1955
Girl Missing, 1932 (Florey)
Girl Must Live, 1939 (Launder, Reed)
Girl Named Tamiko, 1962 (J. Sturges)
Girl Next Door, 1923 (W.S. Van Dyke)
Girl of the Golden West, 1915 (De Mille)
Girl of Yesterday, 1915 (Dwan)
Girl on the Canal. *See* Painted Boats, 1945
Girl Said No, 1930 (S. Wood)
Girl Was Young. *See* Young and Innocent, 1937
Girl Who Stayed at Home, 1919 (Griffith)
Girl with Green Eyes, 1964 (Richardson)
Girl with the Green Eyes, 1916 (Guy)
Girl with the Hat Box. *See* Devushka s korobkoi, 1927
Girl Worth While, 1913 (Cruze)
Girlfriends. *See* Amiche, 1955
Girlfriends. *See* Biches, 1968
Girls, 1957 (Cukor)
Girls. *See* Flickorna, 1968
Girls About Town, 1931 (Cukor)
Girls and a Daddy, 1908 (Griffith)
Girl's Folly, 1917 (M. Tourneur)
Girls from Wilko. *See* Panny z Wilka, 1979
Girls Marked Danger. *See* Tratta della bianche, 1952
Girls of Izu. *See* Izu no musumetachi, 1945
Girls on the Beach, 1965 (Corman)
Girls Own Story, 1984 (Campion)
Girls School, 1949 (Dutt)
Girl's Strategem, 1913 (Griffith)
Gishiki, 1971 (Oshima)
Gitanella, 1914 (Feuillade)
Giù la testa, 1972 (Leone)
Giudizio universale, 1961 (De Sica)
Giulietta degli spiriti, 1965 (Fellini)
Giulietta e Romeo, 1954 (Castellani)
Give a Girl a Break, 1953 (Donen, Fosse)
Give My Regards to Broadway, 1948 (Bacon)
Give Us Air. *See* Daesh vozkukh, 1924
Give Us Wings, 1936 (Weiss)
Gives Us This Day, 1949 (Dmytryk)
Glace a trois faces, 1927 (Epstein)
Glad Eye, 1927 (Saville)
Glad Rag Doll, 1929 (Curtiz)
Gladiator, 1986 (Ferrara)
Gladiatorerna, 1969 (Watkins)
Gladiators. *See* Gladiatorerna, 1969
Glaedens Dag, eller Miskendt, 1918 (Dreyer)
Glamour, 1934 (Wyler)
Glas, 1958 (Haanstra)
Glas du Père Césaire, 1909 (Gance)
Glas Wasser, 1960 (Käutner)
Glasberget, 1953 (Molander)
Glass. *See* Glas, 1958
Glass Bottom Boat, 1966 (Tashlin)

Glass Shield, 1994 (Burnett)
Glass Slipper, 1955 (Walters)
Glass Works, 1914/15 (Phalke)
Glassmakers of England, 1933 (Flaherty)
Glaube und Währung, 1980 (Herzog)
Glaze of Cathexis, 1990 (Brakhage)
Gleisdreieck, 1950 (Staudte)
Glen or Glenda, 1953 (E. Wood)
Glenn Miller Story, 1954 (A. Mann)
Gli altri, gli altri e noi, 1967 (De Sica)
Gli attendenti, 1961 (De Sica)
Gli eroi della domenica, 1952 (Risi)
Gli incensurati, 1960 (De Sica)
Gli Intoccabili, 1968 (Cassavetes)
Gli occhi, la bocca, 1982 (Bellocchio)
Gli sbanditi, 1955 (Birri)
Gli ultimi cinque minuti, 1955 (De Sica)
Gli ultimi giorni di Pompeii, 1959 (Leone)
Gli uomini che mascalzoni!, 1932 (De Sica)
Gli uomini non guardano il cielo, 1951 (De Sica)
Gli zitelloni, 1958 (De Sica)
Glimpse of Los Angeles, 1914 (Sennett)
Glimpse of the San Diego Exposition, 1915 (Sennett)
Glimpses of the Moon, 1923 (Dwan)
Glitterbug, 1993 (Jarman)
Glocken aus der Tiefe. *See* Bells from the Deep, 1993
Glomdalsbruden, 1926 (Dreyer)
Gloria, 1977 (Autant-Lara, Frampton)
Gloria, 1980 (Cassavetes)
Glories of Iran, 1971 (Lelouch)
Glorious Adventure, 1922 (Blackton)
Glorious Lady, 1919 (Goulding)
Glorious Sixth of June, 1934 (Jennings)
Glory! Glory!, 1988 (Anderson)
Glory of the Sunset. *See* Yen Shuio Han, 1976
Glory on the Summit: Burning Youth. *See* Yama no sanka: moyuru wakamono-tachi, 1962
Glory to Us, Death to the Enemy. *See* Slava Nam—Smert' Vagram, 1914
Glücklichen Jahre der Thorwalds, 1962 (Staudte)
Glumov's Film Diary. *See* Kinodnevik Glumova, 1923
Glutton's Nightmare, 1901 (Hepworth)
Gnome Mobile, 1967 (Stevenson)
Go and Get It, 1920 (Neilan)
Go-Between, 1970 (Losey)
Go-Getter, 1937 (Berkeley, Daves)
Go into Your Dance, 1935 (Florey, Berkeley)
Go West, 1925 (Keaton)
Go West, Young Man, 1936 (Hathaway)
Goalie's Anxiety at the Penalty Kick. *See* Angst des Tormanns beim Elfmeter, 1971
Goat, 1921 (Keaton)
Gobbo, 1960 (Pasolini)
God Is My Co-Pilot, 1944 (Florey)
God King, 1973 (Peries)
God Needs Men. *See* Dieu a besoin des hommes, 1950
God Runs Backwards. *See* Isten hátrafelé megy, 1990
God Shiva, 1955 (Haanstra)
God Told Me To, 1976 (Corman)
God Within, 1912 (Griffith)
God's Country, 1946 (Keaton)
God's Country, 1985 (Malle)
God's Gift to Women, 1931 (Curtiz)
God's Little Acre, 1958 (A. Mann)
God's Stepchildren, 1938 (Micheaux)
God's Unfortunate, 1912 (Dwan)
Goda Viljan, 1992 (August, Bergman)
Goddag børn. *See* Newborn, 1953
Goddag Dyr!, 1947 (Roos)
Goddess, 1958 (Cromwell)
Goddess. *See* Devi, 1960
Goddess of Sagebrush Gulch, 1912 (Griffith)
Godelureaux, 1961 (Chabrol)
Godfather, 1972 (Coppola)
Godfather, Part II, 1974 (Coppola, Corman)
Godfather, Part III, 1991 (Coppola)
Godless Girl, 1929 (De Mille)
Godovshchina revoliutsiya, 1919 (Vertov)
Gods and the Dead. *See* Os deuses e os mortos, 1970
Gods of the Plague. *See* Götter der Pest, 1969
Gøglerblod, Artists. *See* Troløs, 1913
Gøgleren. *See* Elskovs Magt, 1912
Going and Coming Back. *See* Partir, revenir, 1985
Going Ashore. *See* Strandhugg, 1950
Going Ga-ga, 1928 (McCarey)
Going Gay, 1933 (Dickinson)
Going Gently, 1981 (Fric)
Going Highbrow, 1935 (Florey)
Going Hollywood, 1933 (Walsh)
Going My Way, 1944 (McCarey)
Going Places. *See* Valseuses, 1973
Going Up, 1923 (LeRoy)
Goju-no to, 1944 (Gosho)
Gold and Glitter, 1912 (Griffith)
Gold Digger of Weepah, 1927 (Sennett)
Gold Diggers, 1983 (Potter)
Gold Diggers in Paris, 1938 (Berkeley)
Gold Diggers of 1933, 1933 (Berkeley, LeRoy)
Gold Diggers of 1935, 1935 (Berkeley)
Gold Diggers of 1937, 1936 (Bacon, Berkeley)
Gold Dust Gertie, 1931 (Bacon)
Gold from the Gutter. *See* Alt paa ét Kort, 1912
Gold Ghost, 1934 (Keaton)
Gold Heels, 1924 (W.S. Van Dyke)
Gold is Not All, 1910 (Griffith)
Gold is Where You Find It, 1938 (Curtiz)
Gold Lust, 1911 (Dwan)
Gold of Naples. *See* Oro di Napoli, 1954
Gold Rush, 1925 (Chaplin)
Gold Seekers, 1910 (Griffith)
Golden Bed, 1925 (De Mille)
Golden Boat, 1990 (Jarmusch, Ruiz, Schroeder)
Golden Boy, 1939 (Mamoulian)
Golden Chance, 1915 (De Mille)
Golden Coach. *See* **Carrosse d'or**, 1953
Golden Demon. *See* Konjiki yasha, 1923
Golden Earrings, 1947 (Polonsky)
Golden Eighties. *See* Années 80, 1983
Golden Fern. *See* Zlaté kapradí, 1963
Golden Fortress. *See* Sonar Kella, 1974
Golden Gates. *See* Zolotye vorota, 1969
Golden Girl, 1951 (Bacon)
Golden Gloves, 1940 (Dmytryk)
Golden Ilsy. *See* De gouden Ilsy, 1957
Golden Lake. *See* Der Goldene See, 1919
Golden Louis, 1909 (Griffith)
Golden Pavement, 1915 (Hepworth)
Golden Shovel. *See* Aranyáso, 1914
Golden Smile. *See* Det gyldne Smil, 1935
Golden Supper, 1910 (Griffith)
Golden Vision, 1968 (Loach)
Goldene Schmetterling, 1926 (Curtiz, Leni)
Goldene See, 1919 (Lang)
Goldflakes. *See* Flocons d'or, 1976
Goldflocken. *See* Flocons d'or, 1976
Goldstein, 1964 (Kaufman)
Golem, 1936 (Duvivier)
Golf Nut, 1927 (Sennett)
Golfers, 1929 (Sennett)
Golfos, 1960 (Saura)
Golgotha, 1935 (Duvivier)
Golod ... golod ... golod, 1921 (Pudovkin)
Golpe de estado, 1976 (Guzmán)

Golpeando en la selva, 1967 (Alvarez)
Golu Hadawatha, 1968 (Peries)
Gólyakalifa, 1917 (Korda)
Gone to Earth, 1950 (Powell)
Gone with the Wind, 1939 (Cukor, Fleming, Hawks, S. Wood)
Gonin no kyodai, 1939 (Yoshimura)
Gönül kusu, 1965 (Güney)
Gonza, the Spearman. *See* Yari no Gonza, 1986
Gonzague ou L'Accordeur, 1933 (Grémillon)
Good and the Bad. *See* Bon et les méchants, 1975
Good Bad Man, 1916 (Dwan, Fleming)
Good-bye Kiss, 1928 (Sennett)
Good Companions, 1933 (Pearson, Saville)
Good Day for Fighting. *See* Custer of the West, 1968
Good Die Young, 1954 (Clayton)
Good Earth, 1937 (Fleming, Lewin)
Good Fairy, 1935 (P. Sturges)
Good Fairy. *See* Zemma, 1951
Good Father, 1986 (Newell)
Good-for-Nothing. *See* His New Profession, 1914
Good Glue Sticks. *See* Colle universelle, 1907
Good Humor Man, 1950 (Bacon, Tashlin)
Good Intentions, 1930 (Howard)
Good Land. *See* Nybyggarna, 1970 (Troell)
Good Light. *See* Dobré svetlo, 1985
Good Little Devil, 1913 (Porter)
Good Love and the Bad, 1912 (Dwan)
Good Luck of a Souse. *See* Y a un dieu pour les ivrognes, 1908
Good Man in Africa, 1994 (Beresford)
Good Men, Good Women. *See* Haonan Haonu, 1995
Good Morning Babilonia, 1986 (Taviani)
Good Morning Babylon. *See* Good Morning Babilonia, 1986
Good Morning Boys, 1937 (Launder)
Good Morning, Judge, 1913 (Cruze)
Good Morning, Madam, 1925 (Sennett)
Good Morning, Nurse!, 1925 (Sennett)
Good Morning, Taipei. *See* Tsao an Taipei, 1977
Good Morning, Vietnam, 1987 (Levinson)
Good Mothers. *See* Mødrehjaelpen, 1942
Good News, 1930 (Daves)
Good News, 1947 (Walters)
Good Night, Nurse!, 1918 (Keaton)
Good Provider, 1922 (Borzage)
Good Sam, 1948 (McCarey)
Good Shepherdess and the Evil Princess. *See* Bonne Bergère et la méchante princesse, 1908
Good Taste, 1995 (Jackson)
Good, the Bad, and the Ugly. *See* **Buono, il brutto, il cattivo**, 1966
Good Time Charley, 1927 (Curtiz)
Good Times, 1967 (Friedkin)
Goodbye Again, 1933 (Curtiz)
Goodbye Again. *See* Aimez-vous Brahms?, 1961
Goodbye Charlie, 1964 (Minnelli)
Goodbye, Children. *See* Au Revoir les enfants, 1987
Goodbye, Hello. *See* Sayonara, konnichiwa, 1959
Goodbye Legs, 1929 (Sennett)
Goodbye, Mr. Chips, 1939 (S. Wood, Saville)
Goodbye, Summer, 1914 (Ingram)
GoodFellas, 1990 (Scorsese)
Goole by Numbers, 1976 (Greenaway)
Goonies, 1985 (Spielberg)
Goopy Gyne Bagha Byne, 1969 (S. Ray)
Goose Girl, 1915 (De Mille)
Goose Hangs High, 1925 (Cruze)
Goose Steps Out, 1942 (Dearden)
Goose Woman, 1925 (Brown)
Gooseland, 1926 (Sennett)
Gopichand Jasoos, 1982 (Kapoor)
Gopinath, 1948 (Kapoor)
Gordon Jacob, 1959 (Russell)
Gorgeous Hussy, 1936 (Brown, Mankiewicz)
Gorgon, 1964 (Fisher)
Gorgon, the Space Monster, 1962-70 (Carpenter)
Gorgon versus Godzilla, 1962-70 (Carpenter)
Gorilla, 1939 (Dwan)
Gorilla, 1954/6 (Romero)
Gorilla Bathes at Noon, 1993 (Makavejev)
Gorizont, 1933 (Kuleshov)
Gorizont, 1962 (Heifitz)
Gory o zmierzchu, 1970 (Zanussi)
Goryachie dyenechki, 1935 (Heifitz)
Gosh-Darn Mortgage, 1926 (Sennett)
Goskinokalender, 1923-25 (Vertov)
Gospel According to Saint Matthew. *See* **Vangelo secondo Matteo**, 1964
Gospordaze, 1972 (Kieślowski)
Gosseline, 1923 (Feuillade)
Gossette, 1923 (Dulac)
Gösta Berlings saga, 1923 (Stiller)
Got a Match, 1911 (Sennett)
Gothic, 1986 (Russell)
Götter der Pest, 1969 (Fassbinder, Von Trotta)
Götterdämmerung. *See* **Caduta degli dei**, 1969
Gottesgeisel, 1920 (Curtiz)
Goumbe des jeunes noceurs, 1965 (Rouch)
Goupi Mains rouges, 1943 (Becker)
Goût de la farine, 1976 (Perrault)
Goûter de bébé, 1896-97 (Lumet)
Goutte de sang, 1924 (Epstein)
Governor, 1977 (Brakhage)
Governor's Daughter. *See* Guvernørens Datter, 1912
Governor's Daughters. *See* Lankshövdingens dottrar, 1916
Governor's Lady, 1915 (De Mille)
Gowri, 1943 (Kapoor)
Goyosen, 1926 (Kinugasa)
Gozenchu no jikanwari, 1972 (Hani)
Grønland, 1980 (Roos)
Grønlandske dialektoptagelser og trommedanse fra Thuledistriktet, 1967 (Roos)
Gra, 1968 (Kawalerowicz)
Graa Dame, 1909 (Holger-Madsen)
Graal. *See* Lancelot du Luc, 1974
Grabd Carnaval, 1985 (Besson)
Gracias Santiago, 1984 (Alvarez)
Graciela, 1956 (Torre Nilsson)
Graduate, 1967 (Nichols)
Graf von Charolais, 1922 (Dieterle)
Grafen Pocci—Einige Kapitel zur Geschichte einer Familie, 1967 (Syberberg)
Graffiti Blackboard. *See* Rakugaki kokuban, 1959
Gräfin Donelli, 1924 (Pabst)
Gramo von Balet, 1966 (Schorm)
Gran calavera, 1949 (Buñuel)
Gran Casino, 1947 (Buñuel)
Gran salto al vacio, 1979 (Alvarez)
Gran varietà, 1953 (De Sica)
Grand barrage, 1961 (Olmi)
Grand bleu, 1988 (Besson)
Grand Canyon, 1991 (Kasdan)
Grand Duke's Finances. *See* Finanzen des Grossherzogs, 1924
Grand Hotel, 1932 (Goulding)
Grand Hotel Babylon, 1919 (Dupont)
Grand Illusion. *See* **Grande Illusion**, 1937
Grand Jeu, 1934 (Feyder)
Grand Jeu, 1954 (Siodmak)
Grand Méliès, 1952 (Franju)
Grand Parade, 1930 (Goulding)
Grand Prix, 1966 (Frankenheimer)
Grand Refrain, 1936 (Siodmak)
Grand Rue. *See* Calle Mayor, 1956
Grand Slam, 1933 (Dieterle)
Grand Slam Opera, 1936 (Keaton)
Grand Theft Auto, 1977 (Corman)
Grande abbuffata. *See* **Grande bouffe,** 1973
Grande allure, 1986 (Perrault)

Grande Amour de Beethoven, 1936 (Gance)
Grande attacco, 1977 (Huston)
Grande bouffe, 1973 (Ferreri)
Grande Chartreuse, 1938 (Clement)
Grande cidade, 1966 (Diegues, Rocha)
Grande Epoque, 1959 (Clair)
Grande feira, 1965 (Rocha)
Grande Fille tout simple, 1947 (L'Herbier)
Grande Illusion, 1937 (Becker, Renoir, Von Stroheim)
Grande paese d'Acciaio, 1960 (Olmi)
Grande Passion, 1929 (Delannoy)
Grande Pastorale, 1943 (Clement)
Grande strada azzurra, 1957 (Pontecorvo)
Grande Vie. *See* Kunstseidene Mädchen, 1960
Grandes Manoeuvres, 1955 (Clair)
Grandeur et Decadence d'un Petit Commerce du Cinema, 1986 (Godard)
Grandi magazzini, 1939 (Castellani, De Sica)
Grandma's Girl, 1929 (Sennett)
Grandmother. *See* Nagymama, 1916
Grandmother, 1970 (Lynch)
Grandmother Sabella. *See* Nonna Sabella, 1957
Grandmother's Story. *See* Au patys des jouets, 1908
Grands Moments, 1965 (Lelouch)
Granpa. *See* Dědáček, 1968
Gränsfolken, 1913 (Stiller)
Granton Trawler, 1934 (Cavalcanti, Grierson)
Grapes of Wrath, 1940 (Ford)
Grass, 1925 (Schoedsack)
Grass Is Greener, 1960 (Donen)
Grass Is Singing, 1982 (August)
Grasshopper, 1970 (Marshall)
Gratuités, 1927 (Grémillon)
Grausige Nächte, 1921 (Pick)
Gravy Train, 1974 (Malick)
Gray Dame. *See* Graa Dame, 1909
Greaser, 1915 (Walsh)
Greaser and the Weakling, 1912 (Dwan)
Greaser's Gauntlet, 1908 (Griffith)
Great Adventure, 1918 (Guy)
Great Adventure. *See* Det stora äventyret, 1953
Great Beginning. *See* Chlen pravitelstva, 1940
Great Clown. *See* Muharraj el Kabir, 1951
Great Consoler. *See* Velikii uteshitel, 1933
Great Day, 1920 (Hitchcock)
Great Day in the Morning, 1956 (J. Tourneur)
Great Dictator, 1940 (Chaplin)
Great Ecstasy of the Sculptor Steiner. *See* Grosse Ekstase des Bildschnitzers Steiner, 1974
Great Escape, 1963 (J. Sturges)
Great Expectations, 1946 (Lean)
Great Flamarion, 1945 (A. Mann, Von Stroheim)
Great Gabbo, 1929 (Cruze, Von Stroheim)
Great Gambini, 1937 (C. Vidor)
Great Garrick, 1937 (LeRoy, Whale)
Great Gatsby, 1974 (Clayton, Coppola, Redford)
Great Gay Road, 1931 (Dickinson)
Great Gilbert and Sullivan. *See* Story of Gilbert and Sullivan, 1953
Great Harmony, 1913 (Dwan)
Great Imposter, 1961 (Mulligan)
Great Land, 1944 (Gerasimov)
Great Lie, 1941 (Goulding)
Great Love, 1918 (Griffith)
Great Love, 1925 (Neilan)
Great Man's Lady, 1942 (Wellman)
Great Manhunt. *See* State Secret, 1950
Great McGinty, 1940 (P. Sturges)
Great Meddler, 1940 (Zinnemann)
Great Moment, 1921 (S. Wood)
Great Moment, 1944 (P. Sturges)
Great Northfield Minnesota Raid, 1972 (Kaufman)
Great O'Malley, 1937 (Dieterle)
Great Pearl Tangle, 1916 (Sennett)
Great Pie Mystery, 1931 (Sennett)
Great Problem, 1916 (Ingram)
Great Race, 1965 (Edwards)
Great Redeemer, 1920 (Brown, M. Tourneur)
Great Road. *See* Veliky put', 1927
Great Scott, 1920 (Sennett)
Great Sinner, 1949 (LeRoy, Siodmak)
Great Sioux Uprising, 1953 (Bacon)
Great St. Trinian's Train Robbery, 1966 (Launder)
Great Stone Face, 1970 (Keaton)
Great Temptation. *See* Porte du large, 1936
Great Texas Dynamite Chase. *See* Dynamite Women, 1976
Great Toe Mystery, 1914 (Sennett)
Great Train Robbery, 1903 (Porter)
Great Universal Mystery, 1914 (Dwan)
Great Vacuum Robbery, 1915 (Sennett)
Great Van Robbery, 1959 (Roeg)
Great Waldo Pepper, 1975 (Redford, G. Hill)
Great Waltz. *See* Waltzes from Vienna, 1933
Great Waltz, 1938 (Duvivier, Fleming)
Great White Hope, 1970 (Ritt)
Greater Love, 1913 (Dwan)
Greater Love Hath No Man, 1915 (Guy)
Greater than Love, 1921 (Niblo, Stahl)
Greatest in the World. *See* Det Største i Verden, 1919
Greatest Love. *See* Europa '51, 1952
Greatest Question, 1919 (Griffith)
Greatest Show on Earth, 1952 (De Mille)
Greatest Story Ever Told, 1965 (Ashby, Stevens)
Greatest Thing in Life, 1918 (Griffith)
Greed, 1924 (Ingram, Von Stroheim)
Greek Sculpture, 1959 (Wright)
Greek Testament, 1942 (Cavalcanti, Crichton)
Green and Pleasant Land, 1955 (Anderson)
Green Berets, 1968 (LeRoy)
Green Bird. *See* Der grüne Vogel, 1979
Green Card, 1990 (Weir)
Green Cockatoo, 1937 (Howard)
Green Dolphin Street, 1947 (Saville)
Green Eyed Monster, 1912 (Dwan)
Green Fields, 1937 (Ulmer)
Green Flood. *See* Zöldár, 1965
Green for Danger, 1946 (Launder)
Green, Green Grass of Home. *See* Tsai Nei Ho P'an Ch'ing Ts'ao Ch'ing, 1982
Green Hell, 1940 (Whale)
Green Light, 1937 (Borzage)
Green Man, 1956 (Dearden, Launder)
Green Manuela. *See* Grüne Manuela, 1923
Green Mare. *See* Jument verte, 1959
Green Mountains. *See* Aoi sanmyaku, 1949
Green Mountain Land, 1950 (Flaherty)
Green Ray. *See* Rayon vert, 1986
Green Room. *See* Chambre verte, 1978
Green Years, 1946 (Saville)
Green Years. *See* Zöldár, 1965
Greene Murder Case. *See* Night of Mystery, 1937
Greengage Summer, 1961 (Saville)
Greetings, 1968 (De Palma)
Gregory's Girl, 1980 (Forsyth)
Grekh, 1916 (Protazanov)
Gremlins, 1984 (Spielberg)
Gremlins 2: The New Batch, 1990 (Spielberg)
Grenoble. *See* Treize jours en France, 1968
Gretel, 1973 (Armstrong)
Grève des apaches, 1908 (Feuillade)
Grevinde Hjerteløs, 1915 (Holger-Madsen)
Grevindens Aere, 1918 (Blom, Dreyer)
Grey Gardens, 1975 (Maysles)
Grey Gold. *See* Or gris, 1980

Grezy, 1915 (Bauer)
Gribiche, 1925 (Feyder)
Grido, 1957 (Antonioni)
Grido della città, 1950 (Risi)
Grierson, 1972 (Haanstra, Ivens)
Griff nach den Sternen, 1955 (Käutner)
Grifters, 1990 (Frears, Scorsese)
Grihadaha, 1936 (Roy)
Grihalaxmi, 1934 (Mehboob)
Grim Reaper. *See* Commare secca, 1962
Grimace, 1966 (Blier)
Grin and Bear It, 1933 (Stevens)
Griot Badye, 1977 (Rouch)
Grip of Fear. *See* Experiment in Terror, 1962
Grisbi. *See* Touchez pas au Grisbi, 1954
Grissom Gang, 1971 (Aldrich)
Grocery Clerk's Romance, 1912 (Sennett)
Gromada, 1952 (Kawalerowicz)
Gros et le maigre, 1961 (Polanski)
Gross Fatigue, 1994 (Polanski)
Grosse Abenteuerin, 1928 (Wiene)
Grosse Atlantik, 1962 (Welles)
Grosse Ekstase des Bildschnitzers Steiner, 1974 (Herzog)
Grosse Freiheit Nr. 7, 1944 (Käutner)
Grosse Liebe, 1931 (Preminger)
Grosse Spiel, 1950 (Staudte)
Grosse Sprung, 1927 (Riefenstahl)
Grosse Verhau, 1970 (Kluge)
Grotesk—Burlesk—Pittoresk, 1968 (Schroeter)
Group, 1966 (Lumet)
Group Instruction. *See* Group no shido, 1956
Group no shido, 1956 (Hani)
Group One, 1967 (Warhol)
Group Portrait with Lady. *See* Gruppenbild mit Dame, 1977
Grov Spøg, 1908 (Holger-Madsen)
Growing Up. *See* Takekurabe, 1955
Growing Up. *See* Hsiao Pi Te Ku Shih, 1982
Grown-Ups, 1980 (Leigh)
Growth of a Pea Plant, 1911 (Phalke)
Grubstake Mortgage, 1912 (Dwan)
Grumpy, 1930 (Cukor)
Grüne Manuela, 1923 (Dieterle, Dupont)
Grüne Vogel, 1979 (Szabó)
Gruppenbild mit Dame, 1977 (Petrovic)
Gruppo di famiglia in un interno, 1974 (Visconti)
Gryning, 1945 (Sucksdorff)
Guaglio. *See* Proibito rubare, 1948
Guantanamera, 1995 (Gutiérrez Alea)
Guapo del 900, 1960 (Torre Nilsson)
Guardia del corpo, 1942 (De Sica)
Guardian, 1990 (Friedkin)
Guardsman, 1931 (Lewin)
Gubben Kommer, 1939 (Sjöström)
Gubijinso, 1935 (Mizoguchi)
Gudernes Yndling, 1919 (Holger-Madsen)
Guelwaar, 1992 (Sembene)
Güemes—La terra en armas, 1970 (Torre Nilsson)
Guendalina, 1956 (Lattuada)
Guerilla Fighter. *See* Padatik, 1973
Guérité. *See* Douaniers et contrebandiers, 1905
Guernica, 1950 (Resnais)
Guernica, 1978 (Kusturica)
Guerra del cerdo. *See* Diario de la guerra del cerdo, 1975
Guerra necessaria, 1980 (Alvarez)
Guerra olvidados, 1967 (Alvarez)
Guerre du silence, 1959 (Lelouch)
Guerre est finie, 1966 (Resnais)
Guerre la plus glorieuse, 1988 (Petrovic)
Guerre populaire au Laos, 1969 (Ivens)
Guerre sans non, 1991 (Tavernier)
Guerrilla, 1908 (Griffith)
Guess Who's Coming to Dinner?, 1967 (Kramer)
Guest Wife, 1945 (S. Wood)
Guestless Dinner Party. *See* Store Middag, 1914
Guests of Honour, 1941 (Cavalcanti, Crichton)
Guests of Hotel Astoria, 1989 (Burnett)
Gueule d'amour, 1937 (Grémillon)
Gueule ouverte, 1974 (Pialat)
Guidance to the Indulgent. *See* Doraku shinan, 1928
Guiding Conscience. *See* Lykken, 1916
Guilty as Sin, 1993 (Lumet)
Guilty by Suspicion, 1991 (Polonsky, Scorsese)
Guilty by Suspicion. *See* Cry in the Dark, 1988
Guilty Hands, 1931 (W.S. Van Dyke)
Guinea Pig, 1948 (Boulting)
Guinguette, 1958 (Delannoy)
Guirlande merveilleuse, 1903 (Méliès)
Guitar Craze, 1959 (Russell)
Guldet og vort Hjerte, 1913 (Holger-Madsen)
Guldets Gift, 1915 (Holger-Madsen)
Guldets Gift, eller Lerhjertet, 1916 (Dreyer)
Guldmønten. *See* Alt paa ét Kort, 1912
Guldspindeln, 1914 (Sjöström)
Guling Jie Shaonian Sha Ren Shijian, 1991 (Yang)
Gull! *See* Trut!, 1944
Gumshoe, 1971 (Frears)
Gun Crazy, 1949 (Joseph H. Lewis)
Gun Fightin' Gentleman, 1919 (Ford)
Gun Fury, 1953 (Walsh)
Gun in His Hand, 1945 (Losey)
Gun Justice, 1927 (Wyler)
Gun Law, 1919 (Ford)
Gun Packer, 1919 (Ford)
Gun Pusher. *See* Gun Packer, 1919
Gun Runners, 1958 (Siegel)
Gun Runners, 1969 (E. Wood)
Gun Woman, 1918 (Borzage)
Gundown, 1996 (W. Hill)
Güney ölüm saciyor, 1969 (Güney)
Gunfight at the O.K. Corral, 1957 (J. Sturges)
Gunfighter, 1950 (King)
Gunga Din, 1939 (Hawks, Stevens)
Gunki hatameku shitani, 1972 (Shindo)
Gunless Bad Man, 1926 (Wyler)
Gunman, 1911 (Dwan)
Gunman, 1913 (Walsh)
Gunn, 1967 (Edwards)
Gunnar Hede's Saga, The Old Mansion. *See* Gunnar Hedes saga, 1922
Gunnar Hedes saga, 1922 (Stiller)
Gunpowder Plot, 1900 (Hepworth)
Gunrunner, 1984 (Costner)
Guns. *See* **Fuzis**, 1964
Guns for the Dictator. *See* Arme à gauche, 1965
Guns in the Afternoon. *See* **Ride the High Country**, 1962
Guns of Darkness, 1962 (Asquith)
Guns of the Trees, 1961 (Mekas)
Guns of Wyoming. *See* Cattle King, 1963
Guns, Sin, and Bathtub Gin. *See* Lady in Red, 1979
Guns West, 1954 (Corman)
Gunsaulus Mystery, 1921 (Micheaux)
Gunslinger, 1956 (Corman)
Guru, 1968 (Ivory)
Gusher, 1913 (Sennett)
Gussie Rivals Jonah, 1915 (Sennett)
Gussie Tied to Trouble, 1915 (Sennett)
Gussie's Backward Way, 1915 (Sennett)
Gussie's Day of Rest, 1915 (Sennett)
Gussie's Wayward Path, 1915 (Sennett)
Gussle the Golfer, 1914 (Sennett)
Gutei kenkei, 1931 (Gosho)
Gutter. *See* Dobu, 1954
Guvernørens Datter, 1912 (Blom)

Guy, a Gal and a Pal, 1945 (Boetticher, Edwards)
Guy Could Change, 1946 (Howard)
Guy Named Joe, 1943 (Edwards, Fleming)
Guys and Dolls, 1955 (Mankiewicz)
Guys of the Sea. *See* Umi no yarodomo, 1957
Gwiazdy muszą płonąć, 1954 (Munk)
Gyarmat a föld alatt, 1951 (Fábri)
Gycklarnas afton, 1953 (Bergman)
Gyermekek, könyvek, 1962 (Mészáros)
Gymnasium Jim, 1922 (Sennett)
Gymnasts, 1961 (Baillie)
Gypsies. *See* Cigányok, 1962
Gypsy, 1962 (LeRoy)
Gypsy and the Gentleman, 1958 (Losey)
Gypsy Blood. *See* Zigeunerblut, 1911
Gypsy Cavalier, 1922 (Blackton)
Gypsy Moths, 1969 (Frankenheimer)
Gypsy Queen, 1913 (Sennett)

H is for House, 1973 (Greenaway)
H.M. Pulham, Esq., 1941 (K. Vidor)
H.O., 1966 (Ripstein)
Haar Jeet, 1939 (Roy)
Habanera, 1937 (Sirk)
Habit of Happiness, 1916 (Dwan, Fleming)
Haceldama ou Le Prix du Sang, 1919 (Duvivier)
Hachi-Ko, 1988 (Shindo)
Hachigatsu No Kyohshikyoku, 1991 (Kurosawa)
Hadaka no jukyu-sai, 1970 (Shindo)
Hadaka no shima, 1960 (Shindo)
Hadaka no taiyo, 1958 (Shindo)
Hadota Misreya, 1982 (Chahine)
Haevnens Nat, 1915 (Christensen)
Haevnet, 1911 (Blom)
Hag in a Leather Jacket, 1964 (Waters)
Hagiographia, 1971 (Markopoulos)
Haha, 1963 (Shindo)
Haha o kowazu-ya, 1934 (Ozu)
Haha wa shinazu, 1942 (Naruse)
Haha yo, kimi no na o kegasu nakare, 1928 (Gosho)
Hahayo koishi, 1926 (Gosho)
Hahn im Korb, 1925 (Dieterle)
Haikyo no naka, 1923 (Mizoguchi)
Hail Mary, 1985 (Godard)
Hail the Conquering Hero, 1944 (P. Sturges)
Hail to Freedom. *See* Viva la libertad, 1965
Hair, 1979 (Forman, N. Ray)
Hair Trigger Casey. *See* Immediate Lee, 1916
Hair Trigger Casey, 1922 (Borzage)
Haircut, 1963 (Warhol)
Hairdresser's Husband. *See* Mari de la coiffeuse, 1990
Hairpins, 1920 (Niblo)
Hairspray, 1988 (Waters)
Haizan no uta wa kanashi, 1923 (Mizoguchi)
Haizi Wang, 1987 (Chen)
Hajnal, 1971 (Szabó)
Hakai, 1948 (Kinoshita)
Hakai, 1962 (Ichikawa)
Hakarka ha a dom, 1954 (Dickinson)
Hakoiri musume, 1935 (Ozu)
Hakuchi, 1951 (Kurosawa)
Hakuchu no torima, 1966 (Oshima)
Halálcsengö, 1917 (Curtiz)
Halbblut, 1919 (Lang)
Half a Bride, 1928 (La Cava)
Half a Man, 1925 (Garnett)
Half-Back of Notre Dame, 1924 (Sennett)
Half-Breed, 1916 (Dwan, Fleming)
Half Breed. *See* Halvblod, 1913
Half Caste. *See* Halbblut, 1919
Half Holiday, 1931 (Sennett)
Half Life, 1988 (Corman)
Half Naked Truth, 1932 (La Cava)
Half-a-Dollar Bill, 1923 (W.S. Van Dyke)
Halfway House, 1944 (Cavalcanti, Dearden)
Halhatatlanság, 1959 (Jancsó)
Halil, the Crow-Man. *See* Kargaci Halil, 1968
Halimeden mektup var, 1964 (Güney)
Hall of Lost Steps. *See* Sál ztracených kroku, 1960
Hallelujah, 1929 (K. Vidor)
Hallelujah, I'm a Bum, 1933 (Milestone)
Hallelujah the Hills, 1963 (Emshwiller)
Hallelujah Trail, 1965 (J. Sturges)
Halliday Brand, 1957 (Joseph H. Lewis)
Hallo! Hallo! Hier spricht Berlin. *See* Allo Berlin? Ici Paris!, 1931
Halloween, 1978 (Carpenter)
Halloween II, 1981 (Carpenter)
Halloween III: Season of the Witch, 1983 (Carpenter)
Halls of Anger, 1970 (Reiner)
Halls of Montezuma, 1951 (Milestone)
Hallucination. *See* Lidércnyomás, 1920
Hallucinations du Baron Münchausen, 1911 (Méliès)
Hallucinations pharmaceutiques, 1908 (Méliès)
Halvblod, 1913 (Sjöström)
Ham Artist. *See* Face on the Bar-Room Floor, 1914
Hamagure no komoriuta, 1973 (Yoshimura)
Hamari Baat, 1943 (Kapoor)
Hamburg, 1961 (Roos)
Hamles, 1960 (Skolimowski)
Hamlet, 1910 (Blom)
Hamlet, 1963 (Kozintsev)
Hamlet, 1969 (Dmytryk, Richardson)
Hamlet, 1990 (Zeffirelli)
Hamlet, 1996 (Branagh)
Hamlet Goes Business. *See* Hamlet Liikemaailmassa, 1987
Hamlet Liikemaailmassa, 1987 (Kaurismaki)
Hamlet's Castle. *See* Shakespeare og Kronborg, 1950
Hammett, 1982 (Coppola, Wenders)
Hämnaren, 1915 (Stiller)
Hamnstad, 1948 (Bergman)
Hampi, 1965 (Rouch)
Hamrahi, 1945 (Roy)
Hana, 1941 (Yoshimura)
Hana hiraku, 1948 (Ichikawa)
Hana no nagadosu, 1954 (Kinugasa)
Hanakago no uta, 1937 (Gosho)
Hanamuko no negoto, 1935 (Gosho)
Hanaoko Seishu no tsuma, 1967 (Shindo)
Hanare goze Orin, 1977 (Shinoda)
Hanasake jijii, 1923 (Kinugasa)
Hanasaku minato, 1943 (Kinoshita)
Hanayome no negoto, 1933 (Gosho)
Hanayome san wa sekai-ichi, 1959 (Shindo)
Hand, 1981 (Stone)
Hand in the Trap. *See* Mano en la trampa, 1961
Hand Movie, 1968 (Rainer)
Hand of Death, 1975 (Woo)
Hand of Peril, 1916 (M. Tourneur)
Hand That Rocks the Cradle, 1917 (Weber)
Handful of Rice. *See* En Handfull Ris, 1938
Handfull Ris, 1938 (Fejös)
Handicapped Future. *See* Behinderte Zukunft, 1970
Handle With Care. *See* Citizen's Band, 1977
Händler der vier Jahreszeiten, 1971 (Fassbinder)
Handmaid's Tale, 1990 (Schlöndorff)
Hands over the City. *See* Mani sulla città, 1963
Hands Up!, 1917 (Browning)
Hands Up! *See* Rece do gory, 1967
Hang 'em High, 1967 (Eastwood)
Hanged Man, 1964 (Siegel)
Hanging Out Yonkers, 1973 (Akerman)
Hanging Tree, 1959 (Daves)

Hangman, 1959 (Curtiz)
Hangman's House, 1928 (Ford)
Hangmen Also Die!, 1943 (Lang)
Hangover. *See* Baksmålla, 1973
Hangup, 1974 (Hathaway)
Hangyaboly, 1971 (Fábri)
Hanna K, 1983 (Costa-Gavras)
Hannah and Her Sisters, 1986 (Allen)
Hanneles Himmelfahrt, 1922 (Gad)
Hannibál tonár úr, 1956 (Fábri)
Hanno rapito un uomo, 1937 (De Sica)
Hanoi, martes 13, 1967 (Alvarez)
Hans and Grethe. *See* Hans og Grethe, 1913
Hans bröllopsnatt, 1915 (Stiller)
Hans Christian Andersen, 1952 (C. Vidor)
Hans engelska fru, 1926 (Molander)
Hans første Honorar. *See* Det første Honorar, 1912
Hans gode Genius, 1920 (Blom)
Hans' Good Fortune. *See* Hans im gluck, 1976
Hans hustrus förflutna, 1915 (Stiller)
Hans im gluck, 1976 (Petersen)
Hans nåds testamente, 1919 (Sjöström)
Hans og Grethe, 1913 (Dreyer)
Hans rigtige Kone, 1916 (Dreyer, Holger-Madsen)
Hans Trutz im Schlaraffenland, 1915 (Lubitsch)
Hans vanskeligste Rolle, 1912 (Blom)
Hansel and Gretel, 1909 (Porter)
Hansom Cabman, 1924 (Capra, Sennett)
Hansom Driver, 1913 (Sennett)
Hantise, 1912 (Feuillade)
Hanussen, 1988 (Szabó)
Haonan Haonu, 1995 (Hou)
Hapax Legomena, 1972 (Frampton)
Happening, 1966 (Chabrol)
Happiest Days of Your Life, 1950 (Launder)
Happiness, 1924 (K. Vidor)
Happiness Ahead, 1928 (Goulding)
Happiness Ahead, 1934 (LeRoy)
Happiness of Eternal Night. *See* Schast'e Vechnoi Nochi, 1915
Happy Canary. *See* Vesyolaya kanareika, 1929
Happy-End im siebten Himmel. *See* Der Traum von Lieschen Müller, 1961
Happy Ending, 1931 (Launder)
Happy Ending, 1969 (Brooks)
Happy Ever After, 1932 (Stevenson)
Happy Hooligan, 1900 (Blackton)
Happy Hooligan Surprised, 1901 (Porter)
Happy Hooligan Turns Burglar, 1902 (Porter)
Happy in the Morning, 1938 (Cavalcanti)
Happy Is the Bride, 1957 (Boulting)
Happy Mother's Day, 1963 (Leacock)
Happy New Year. *See* Bonne année, 1972
Happy New Year, 1988 (Lelouch)
Happy Though Married, 1919 (Niblo)
Happy Time, 1952 (Fleischer, Kramer)
Happy Warrior, 1925 (Blackton)
Happy We, 1983 (Hallstrom)
Har har du ditt liv, 1966 (Troell)
Har jeg Ret til at tage mit eget Liv, 1919 (Holger-Madsen)
Här Börjar Äventyret, 1965 (Donner)
Hara-Kiri, 1919 (Lang)
Haracima dokunma, 1965 (Güney)
Harakiri. *See* **Seppuku**, 1962
Harald Sæverud—1 en alder af 88 år, 1985 (Roos)
Harangok Rômába mentek, 1958 (Jancsó)
Harangok városa—Veszprém, 1966 (Mészáros)
Hard Boiled, 1925 (McCarey)
Hard Cash, 1913 (Ingram)
Hard Choices, 1984 (Sayles)
Hard Cider, 1914 (Sennett)
Hard Day's Night, 1964 (Lester)
Hard Fists, 1927 (Wyler)
Hard Is the Life of an Adventurer. *See* Těžký život dobrodruha, 1941
Hard Knocks and Love Taps, 1921 (Sennett)
Hard Labor on the River Douro. *See* Douro, faina fluvial, 1931
Hard Labour, 1972 (Leigh)
Hard Luck, 1921 (Keaton)
Hard Summer. *See* Vizivárosi Nyár, 1965
Hard Target, 1993 (Woo)
Hard Times. *See* Fukeiki jidai, 1930
Hard Times, 1975 (W. Hill)
Hard to Beat, 1909 (Porter)
Hard to Handle, 1933 (LeRoy)
Hard to Handle: Bob Dylan with Tom Petty and the Heartbreakers, 1986 (Armstrong)
Hard Way, 1991 (Marshall)
Hård klang, 1952 (Sjöström)
Hard-Boiled, 1992 (Woo)
Hardcore, 1978 (Schrader)
Hardly Working, 1980 (Jerry Lewis)
Hare Krishna, 1966 (Mekas)
Harem, 1967 (Ferreri)
Harem Knight, 1926 (Sennett)
Hari Hondal Bargadar, 1980 (Benegal)
Harlan County, U.S.A., 1976 (Kopple)
Harlot, 1964 (Warhol)
Harmony Heaven, 1930 (Launder)
Harmony Lane, 1935 (Joseph H. Lewis)
Harold and Maude, 1971 (Ashby)
Harold Teen, 1928 (LeRoy)
Három csillág, 1960 (Jancsó)
Harp of Burma. *See* **Biruma no tategoto**, 1956
Harri! Harri! *See* Hemåt i Natten, 1977
Harrison and Barrison. *See* Harrison és Barrison, 1917
Harrison és Barrison, 1917 (Korda)
Harrowing, 1993 (Brakhage)
Harry and Tonto, 1974 (Mazursky)
Haru koro no hana no en, 1958 (Kinugasa)
Haru no mezame, 1947 (Naruse)
Haru no yume, 1960 (Kinoshita)
Haru wa gofujin kara, 1932 (Ozu)
Harun al Raschid, 1924 (Curtiz)
Harvest Help, 1940 (Wright)
Harvest in the Cooperative "Dosza". *See* Arat az Orosházi Dözsa, 1953
Harvest of My Lai, 1970 (Ophuls)
Harvest of Tears. *See* Pressens Magt, 1913
Harvester, 1936 (Joseph H. Lewis)
Harvey Girls, 1945 (Walters)
Has Anybody Seen My Gal?, 1952 (Sirk)
Hash House Fraud, 1915 (Sennett)
Hash-House Hero. *See* Star Boarder, 1914
Hash House Mashers, 1915 (Sennett)
Hashi no nai kawa, 1969 (Imai)
Hashi no nai kawa II, 1970 (Imai)
Hasta cierto punto, 1983 (Gutiérrez Alea)
Hasta la victoria siempre, 1967 (Alvarez)
Hasta que perdio Jalisco, 1945 (De Fuentes)
Hataraku ikka, 1939 (Naruse)
Hatari!, 1962 (Hawks)
Hatchet Man, 1932 (Wellman)
Haters, 1912 (Dwan)
Hateshinaki jonetsu, 1949 (Ichikawa)
Hateshinaki yokubo, 1958 (Imamura)
Hatful of Rain, 1957 (Zinnemann)
Hatmaker. *See* Fantômes du chapelier, 1982
Hatred. *See* Mollenard, 1938
Hatred. *See* Nenavist, 1978
Hats Off, 1936 (Fuller)
Hatsukoi, 1926 (Gosho)
Hatsukoi, 1947 (Kurosawa)
Hatsuoki jig ok uhen, 1968 (Hani)
Hatta Marri, 1932 (Sennett)
Haunted, 1995 (Coppola)

Haunted and the Hunted. *See* Dementia, 1963
Haunted Bedroom, 1919 (Niblo)
Haunted Castle. *See* Schloss Vogelöd, 1921
Haunted Homestead, 1927 (Wyler)
Haunted Hotel, 1907 (Blackton)
Haunted House, 1921 (Keaton)
Haunted House, 1928 (Christensen)
Haunted Palace, 1963 (Corman)
Haunting, 1963 (Wise)
Haunting Shadows, 1919 (King)
Hauptmann von Köpenick, 1956 (Käutner)
Haus der Frauen, 1977 (Zanussi)
Haus der Lüge, 1925 (Pick)
Haus in Montevideo, 1963 (Käutner)
Haut Bas Fragile, 1995 (Rivette)
Haut les mains!, 1912 (Feuillade)
Haute Lisse, 1956 (Grémillon)
Havana, 1990 (Pollack, Redford)
Have You Thought of Talking to the Director?, 1962 (Baillie)
Havel's Audience with History, 1990 (Menzel)
Havets Djävul, 1935/36 (Fejös)
Having a Go, 1983 (Armstrong)
Having a Wild Weekend. *See* Catch Us If You Can, 1965
Havoc, 1925 (Goulding)
Havsgammar. *See* Rösen på Tistelön, 1916
Hawaii, 1966 (G. Hill)
Hawk, 1935 (Dmytryk)
Hawkins and Watkins, 1932 (Sennett)
Hawks and the Sparrows. *See* Uccellacci e uccellini, 1966
Hawk's Nest, 1928 (Christensen)
Hawk's Trail, 1920 (W.S. Van Dyke)
Hawthorne of the U.S.A., 1919 (Cruze)
Häxan, 1922 (Christensen)
Hayfoot, Strawfoot, 1926 (Sennett)
Hayseed, 1919 (Keaton)
Hayseed Romance, 1935 (Keaton)
Haystacks and Steeples, 1916 (Sennett)
Hazasodik az uram, 1913 (Curtiz)
Hazukashii yume, 1927 (Gosho)
He Called Her In, 1913 (Dwan)
He Comes Up Smiling, 1918 (Dwan)
He Did and He Didn't, 1916 (Sennett)
He Died after the War. *See* Tokyo senso sengo hiwa, 1970
He Is My Brother, 1976 (Dmytryk)
He Laughed Last, 1956 (Edwards)
He Loved Her So. *See* Twenty Minutes of Love, 1914
He Loved the Ladies, 1914 (Sennett)
He Stands in the Desert Counting the Seconds of His Life, 1986 (Anger, Mekas)
He Trumped Her Ace, 1930 (Sennett)
He Walked by Night, 1948 (A. Mann)
He was born, he suffered, he died, 1974 (Brakhage)
He Was Her Man, 1934 (Bacon)
He Was Once, 1989 (Haynes)
He Who Gets Slapped, 1924 (Sjöström)
He Who Gets Smacked, 1925 (Sennett)
He Who Must Die. *See* Celui qui doit mourir, 1958
He Who Rides a Tiger, 1965 (Crichton)
He Would A Hunting Go, 1913 (Sennett)
He Wouldn't Stay Down, 1915 (Sennett)
Head, 1968 (Rafelson)
Head of the House, 1952 (Leacock)
Head On, 1980 (Huston)
Head Over Heels. *See* Chilly Scenes of Winter, 1979
Headline Woman, 1935 (Joseph H. Lewis)
Heads or Tails. *See* Aar Paar, 1954
Health, 1979 (Altman)
Health for the Nation, Forty Million People. *See* Health of a Nation, 1939
Health-Giving Waters of Tisza. *See* Eltetö Tisza-víz, 1954
Health in Industry, 1938 (Watt)
Health of a Nation, 1939 (Cavalcanti)
Healthy Neighborhood, 1913 (Sennett)
Heart. *See* Kokoro, 1955
Heart. *See* O coracão, 1960
Heart. *See* Kokoro, 1973
Heart Beats of Long Ago, 1910 (Griffith)
Heart in Winter. *See* **Coeur en Hiver**, 1992
Heart of a Painted Woman, 1915 (Guy)
Heart of Britain, 1941 (Jennings)
Heart of Darkness, 1993 (Roeg)
Heart of Glass. *See* Herz aus Glas, 1976
Heart of Maryland, 1927 (Bacon)
Heart of New York, 1932 (LeRoy)
Heart of Nora Flynn, 1916 (De Mille)
Heart of Oyama, 1908 (Griffith)
Heart of Princess Mitsari, 1915 (Cruze)
Heart of Scotland, 1961/62 (Grierson)
Heart of Show Business, 1957 (De Mille)
Heart of the Mountains. *See* Kokoro no sanmyaku, 1966
Heart of the Wilds, 1918 (Neilan)
Heart of the Yukon, 1926 (W.S. Van Dyke)
Heartbeat, 1946 (S. Wood)
Heartbeat. *See* Szivdobogás, 1961
Heartbreak Ridge, 1986 (Eastwood)
Heartburn, 1986 (Forman, Nichols)
Hearts Adrift, 1914 (Porter)
Hearts and Dollars, 1924 (Litvak)
Hearts and Flowers, 1919 (Sennett)
Hearts and Horses, 1913 (Dwan)
Hearts and Planets, 1915 (Sennett)
Hearts and Sparks, 1916 (Sennett)
Hearts and Spurs, 1925 (W.S. Van Dyke)
Hearts Are Trumps, 1920 (Ingram)
Hearts Divided, 1936 (Borzage)
Hearts in Exile, 1929 (Curtiz)
Hearts of Age, 1934 (Welles)
Hearts of Oak, 1924 (Ford)
Hearts of the World, 1918 (Griffith, Von Stroheim)
Hearts or Diamonds, 1918 (King)
Heart's Voice. *See* Guldet og vort Hjerte, 1913
Heat, 1972 (Warhol)
Heat, 1995 (M. Mann)
Heat and Dust, 1983 (Ivory)
Heat and Mud. *See* Netsudeichi, 1950
Heat Haze. *See* Kagero, 1969
Heat Lightning, 1934 (LeRoy)
Heaven and Earth, 1993 (Stone)
Heaven and Hell. *See* Tengoku to jigoku, 1963
Heaven Avenges, 1912 (Griffith)
Heaven Can Wait, 1943 (Lubitsch)
Heaven Fell That Night. *See* Bijoutiers du clair de lune, 1958
Heaven Knows, Mr. Allison, 1957 (Huston)
Heaven Linked with Love. *See* Tengoku ni musubu koi, 1932
Heavenly Creatures, 1994 (Jackson)
Heavens Above!, 1963 (Boulting)
Heaven's Gate, 1980 (Cimino)
Heavens! My Husband!, 1932 (Sennett)
Hebi himesama, 1940 (Kinugasa)
Hectic Days. *See* Goryachie dyenechki, 1935
Hedda Gabler, 1919 (Pastrone)
Hedy, 1965 (Warhol)
Heel of Italy. *See* Yellow Caesar, 1940
Heerak Rajar Deshe, 1979 (S. Ray)
Heeren der Meere, 1922 (Korda)
Heidi, 1937 (Dwan)
Heidi, 1952 (Comencini)
Heien, 1929 (Ivens)
Height of Battle. *See* Senka no hate, 1950
Heilige Berg, 1926 (Riefenstahl)
Heilige Flamme, 1931 (Dieterle)
Heilige Lüge, 1927 (Holger-Madsen)
Heilige und ihr Narr, 1928 (Dieterle)

Heritage. *See* Odkaz, 1965
Heritage de la Chouette, 1989 (Marker)
Heritage of the Desert, 1924 (Hathaway)
Heritage of the Desert, 1932 (Hathaway)
Héritier des Montdésir, 1939 (Becker)
Herman Teirlinck, 1953 (Storck)
Hermanos de Hierro, 1961 (Fernández)
Hermanos Muerte, 1964 (Fernández)
Hermit. *See* Syndig Kaerlighed, 1915
Hermit's Gold, 1911 (Dwan)
Hero. *See* Nayak, 1966
Hero, 1992 (Frears)
Hero Ain't Nothin' But a Sandwich, 1977 (Corman)
Hero of Little Italy, 1913 (Griffith)
Hero with a Knife. *See* Kamali zeybek, 1964
Heroes Are Made. *See* Kak zakalyalas stal, 1942
Heroes for Sale, 1933 (Wellman)
Heroes of Shipka. *See* Geroite na Shipka, 1954
Heroes of Telemark, 1965 (A. Mann)
Heroes of the Mine, 1913 (Pearson)
Heroes of the Street, 1922 (Goulding)
Heroes Shed No Tears, 1986 (Woo)
Heroes Stand Alone, 1989 (Corman)
Heroïsme de Paddy, 1916 (Gance)
Herr Arnes pengar, 1919 (Molander, Stiller)
Herr Arnes pengar, 1954 (Molander)
Herr der Liebe, 1919 (Lang)
Herr Doktor, 1917 (Feuillade)
Herr Puntila und sein Knecht Matti, 1955 (Cavalcanti)
Herr Storms første Monocle. *See* Min første Monocle, 1911
Herr über Leben und Tod, 1919 (Pick)
Herren mit der weissen Weste, 1970 (Staudte)
Herrenpartie, 1964 (Staudte)
Herrin der Welt, 1918 (Lang)
Herrin der Welt, 1960 (Dieterle)
Herrin von Atlantis. *See* Atlantide, 1932
Herringbone Clouds. *See* Iwashigumo, 1958
Herrliches Dasein, 1974 (Staudte)
Herz aus Glas, 1976 (Herzog)
Herzogin Satanella, 1920 (Curtiz)
Herztrumpt, 1920 (Dupont)
Hesitating Houses, 1926 (Sennett)
Hessian Renegades, 1909 (Griffith)
Hest på sommerferie, 1959 (Henning-Jensen)
Hesten, 1943 (Henning-Jensen)
Hesten paa Kongens Nytorv, 1941 (Henning-Jensen)
Hester Street, 1974 (Silver)
Het dak van de walvis, 1981 (Ruiz)
Het olieveld, 1954 (Haanstra)
Het Verdriet Van Belgie, 1994 (Goretta)
Heterodyne, 1967 (Frampton)
Hets, 1944 (Bergman, Sjöberg, Zetterling)
Hets Korps Mariniers. *See* Dutch Marine Corps, 1966
Hetty King—Performer, 1970 (Anderson)
Heures, 1909 (Feuillade)
Heureuse Intervention, 1919 (Florey)
Heut Spielt der Strauss, 1928 (Wiene)
Hey! Hey! U.S.A.!, 1938 (Launder)
Hey Rookie, 1944 (Donen)
Hi, Mom!, 1970 (De Palma)
Hi, Nellie!, 1934 (LeRoy)
Hibana, 1922 (Kinugasa)
Hibana, 1956 (Kinugasa)
Hibiscus Town, 1987 (Xie)
Hickey and Boggs, 1972 (W. Hill)
Hickory Hill, 1968 (Leacock)
Hidari uchiwa, 1935 (Gosho)
Hidden Agenda, 1990 (Loach, Zetterling)
Hidden City, 1915 (Ford)
Hidden City. *See* Darkest Africa, 1936
Hidden Fortress. *See* Kakushi toride no san-akunin, 1958
Hidden Pearls, 1918 (Cruze)
Hidden River. *See* Río Escondido, 1947
Hidden Room. *See* Obsession, 1949
Hidden Woman, 1922 (Dwan)
Hide and Seek, 1913 (Sennett)
Hide and Seek Detectives, 1918 (Sennett)
Hide Out, 1934 (W.S. Van Dyke)
Hideko the Bus Conductor. *See* Kideko no shasho-san, 1941
Higanbana, 1958 (Ozu)
Higashi Shinaki, 1968 (Imamura)
Hige no chikara, 1931 (Naruse)
High and Low, 1913 (Dwan)
High and Low. *See* Du haut en bas, 1933
High and Low. *See* Tengoku to jigoku, 1963
High and the Mighty, 1954 (Wellman)
High Anxiety, 1977 (Brooks, Levinson)
High Ashbury, 1967 (Warhol)
High Command, 1937 (Dickinson)
High Flies the Hawk, I and II. *See* Píseň o sletu I, II, 1949
High Gear, 1931 (Stevens)
High Heels. *See* Docteur Popaul, 1972
High Heels. *See* Tacomes lejanos, 1991
High Hopes, 1988 (Leigh)
High Infidelity. *See* Alta infedelta, 1964
High Journey, 1959 (Welles)
High Noon, 1952 (Kramer, Zinnemann)
High Plains Drifter, 1972 (Eastwood)
High Pressure, 1932 (LeRoy)
High School, 1968 (Wiseman)
High School II, 1994 (Wiseman)
High School Big Shot, 1959 (Corman)
High Season, 1987 (Branagh)
High Sierra, 1941 (Huston, Walsh)
High Sign, 1921 (Keaton)
High Society, 1957 (Walters)
High Spirits, 1988 (Jordan)
High Spots on Broadway, 1914 (Sennett)
High Stake. *See* Hjerternes Kamp, 1912
High Tension, 1936 (Dwan)
High Tension. *See* Sånt händer inte här, 1950
High Tide, 1987 (Armstrong)
High Time, 1960 (Edwards)
High Treason, 1951 (Boulting)
High Wall. *See* Vysoká zed, 1964
High, Wide and Handsome, 1937 (Mamoulian)
High Wind in Jamaica, 1965 (Mackendrick)
Highbinders, 1915 (Browning)
Higher Law, 1911 (Cruze)
Highs, 1976 (Brakhage)
Highway Dragnet, 1954 (Corman)
Highway Patrolman, 1991 (Cox)
Hija de Juan Simón, 1935 (Buñuel)
Hija del engaño, 1951 (Buñuel)
Hijo del crack, 1953 (Torre Nilsson)
Hijos de Maria Morales, 1952 (De Fuentes)
Hijosen no onna, 1933 (Ozu)
Hikinige, 1966 (Naruse)
Hikkoshi fufu, 1928 (Ozu)
Hikuidori, 1926 (Kinugasa)
Hilarious Posters. *See* Affiches en goguette, 1906
Hilde Warren and Death. *See* Hilde Warren und der Tod, 1917
Hilde Warren und der Tod, 1917 (Lang)
Hildegard, 1948 (Zetterling)
Hill, 1965 (Lumet)
Hill Twenty-Four Doesn't Answer, 1955 (Dickinson)
Hills Are Calling, 1914 (Hepworth)
Hills Have Eyes, 1977 (Craven)
Hills Have Eyes, Part II, 1983 (Craven)
Himeyuri Lily Tower. *See* Himeyuri no to, 1953
Himeyuri Lily Tower. *See* Himeyuri no to, 1982
Himeyuri no to, 1953 (Imai)

Himeyuri no to, 1982 (Imai)
Himiko, 1974 (Shinoda)
Himlaspelet, 1942 (Sjöberg)
Himmel Hoch, 1968 (Schroeter)
Himmel ohne Sterne, 1955 (Käutner)
Himmel über Berlin, 1987 (Wenders)
Himmelskibet, 1917 (Holger-Madsen)
Himself as Herself, 1967 (Markopoulos)
Hind. *See* Alageyik, 1958
Hindenburg, 1975 (Wise)
Hindle Wakes, 1931 (Saville)
Hindoo Dagger, 1908 (Griffith)
Hindu Tomb. *See* Indische Grabmal, 1959
Hintertreppe, 1921 (Dieterle, Leni)
Hipolito el de Santa, 1949 (De Fuentes)
Hipoteza, 1972 (Zanussi)
Hiroshima mon amour, 1959 (Duras, Resnais)
His Alibi, 1916 (Sennett)
His Auto Ruination, 1916 (Sennett)
His Better Self, 1911 (Guy)
His Bitter Pill, 1916 (Sennett)
His Bread and Butter, 1916 (Sennett)
His Brother's Wife, 1936 (W.S. Van Dyke)
His Busted Trust, 1916 (Sennett)
His Butler's Sister, 1943 (Borzage)
His Call. *See* Yevo prizyv, 1925
His Children's Children, 1923 (S. Wood)
His Chum, the Baron, 1913 (Sennett)
His Country. *See* Ship Comes In, 1928
His Country's Bidding, 1914 (Hepworth)
His Crooked Career, 1913 (Sennett)
His Daredevil Queen. *See* Mabel at the Wheel, 1914
His Daughter, 1911 (Griffith)
His Duty, 1909 (Griffith)
His English Wife. *See* Hans engelska fru, 1926
His Ex Marks the Spot, 1940 (Keaton)
His Excellency. *See* Yevo prevosoditelstvo, 1927
His Excellency, 1951 (Hamer)
His Family Tree, 1935 (C. Vidor)
His Father's Footsteps, 1915 (Sennett)
His Favorite Pastime, 1914 (Chaplin, Sennett)
His First Command, 1930 (La Cava)
His First False Step, 1916 (Sennett)
His First Flame, 1927 (Sennett)
His First Job, 1908 (Méliès)
His First Monocle. *See* Min første Monocle, 1911
His First Patient. *See* Det første Honorar, 1912
His Girl Friday, 1940 (Hawks)
His Glorious Night, 1930 (Feyder)
His Guardian Angel. *See* Hans gode Genius, 1920
His Guardian Auto, 1915 (Cruze)
His Halted Career, 1914 (Sennett)
His Hereafter, 1916 (Sennett)
His Hidden Purpose, 1918 (Sennett)
His Hour, 1924 (K. Vidor)
His Innocent Dupe. *See* Sjaeletyven, 1915
His Last Burglary, 1910 (Griffith)
His Last False Step, 1919 (Sennett)
His Last Haul, 1928 (Neilan)
His Last Laugh, 1916 (Sennett)
His Last Scent, 1916 (Sennett)
His Lesson, 1912 (Griffith)
His Lordship, 1932 (Powell)
His Lordship's White Feather, 1912 (Guy)
His Lost Love, 1909 (Griffith)
His Luckless Love, 1915 (Sennett)
His Lying Heart, 1916 (Sennett)
His Majesty, the American, 1919 (Fleming)
His Marriage Wow, 1925 (Capra, Sennett)
His Most Difficult Part. *See* Hans vanskeligste Rolle, 1912
His Mother's Scarf, 1911 (Griffith)
His Mother's Son, 1913 (Griffith)
His Musical Career, 1914 (Chaplin, Sennett)
His Mysterious Adventure. *See* Seine Frau, die Unbekannte, 1923
His Name is Sukhe-Bator. *See* Yevo zovut Sukhe-Bator, 1942
His Naughty Thought, 1917 (Sennett)
His Neighbor's Wife, 1913 (Porter)
His New Job, 1915 (Chaplin)
His New Mama, 1924 (Capra, Sennett)
His New Profession, 1914 (Chaplin, Sennett)
His New Stenographer, 1928 (Sennett)
His Nibs, 1922 (La Cava)
His Old-Fashioned Mother, 1913 (Dwan)
His Own Fault, 1911 (Sennett)
His Picture in the Papers, 1916 (Fleming, Von Stroheim)
His Precious Life, 1917 (Sennett)
His Prehistoric Past, 1914 (Chaplin, Sennett)
His Pride and Shame, 1916 (Sennett)
His Real Wife. *See* Hans Rigtige Kone, 1917
His Reckless Fling. *See* His Favorite Pastime, 1914
His Regeneration, 1914 (Chaplin)
His Return, 1915 (Walsh)
His Robe of Honor, 1918 (Ingram)
His Royal Shyness, 1932 (Sennett)
His Second Childhood, 1914 (Sennett)
His Sister-in-law, 1910 (Griffith)
His Sister's Kids, 1913 (Sennett)
His Sister's Sweetheart, 1911 (Guy)
His Smothered Love, 1918 (Sennett)
His Taking Ways, 1914 (Sennett)
His Talented Wife, 1914 (Sennett)
His Trust, 1910 (Griffith)
His Trust Fulfilled, 1910 (Griffith)
His Trysting Place, 1914 (Chaplin, Sennett)
His Uncle Dudley, 1917 (Sennett)
His Unlucky Night, 1928 (Sennett)
His Ups and Downs, 1913 (Sennett)
His Ward's Love, 1909 (Griffith)
His Wedded Wife, 1914 (Ingram)
His Wedding Night. *See* Hans bröllopsnatt, 1915
His Wedding Night, 1917 (Keaton)
His Wife's Friend, 1918 (Sennett)
His Wife's Mistake, 1916 (Sennett)
His Wife's Mother, 1909 (Griffith)
His Wife's Past. *See* Hans hustrus förflutna, 1915
His Wife's Visitor, 1909 (Griffith)
His Wild Oats, 1916 (Sennett)
His Winning Punch, 1915 (Sennett)
His Wooden Wedding, 1925 (McCarey)
His Youthful Fancy, 1920 (Sennett)
Hisshoka, 1945 (Mizoguchi)
Histoire de puce, 1909 (Feuillade)
Histoire de rire, 1941 (L'Herbier)
Histoire de vent, 1988 (Ivens)
Histoire d'Adèle H., 1975 (C. Miller, Truffaut)
Histoire d'amour. *See* Tavaszi zápor, 1932
Histoire d'amour, 1933 (Ophüls)
Histoire d'eau, 1958 (Godard, Truffaut)
Histoire du soldat inconnu, 1932 (Storck)
Histoire d'un crime, 1906 (Méliès)
Histoire simple, 1978 (Sautet)
Histoires d'Amérique: Food, Family and Philosophy/American Stories, 1989 (Akerman)
Histoires extraordinaires, 1968 (Fellini, Malle, Vadim)
Histoires insolites, 1974 (Chabrol)
Historias de la revolucion, 1961 (Gutiérrez Alea)
Historias prohibidas de Pulgarcito, 1979 (Leduc)
Historien om en Mand, 1944 (Roos)
Historien om en Moder, 1912 (Blom)
Historien om et slot, J. F. Willumsen, 1951 (Roos)
History Is Made at Night, 1937 (Borzage)
History Lessons. *See* Geschichtsunterricht, 1972

History of Albertfalva. *See* Albertfalvai történet, 1955
History of Motion in Motion, 1967 (Vanderbeek)
History of Postwar Japan as Told by a Bar Hostess. *See* Nippon sengoshi: Madamu Omboro no seikatsu, 1970
History of the Civil War. *See* Istoriia grazhdenskoi voini, 1922
History of the Vatican. *See* Vaticano de Pio XII, 1940
History of the World, Part 1, 1981 (Levinson, Brooks)
Hit, 1984 (Frears)
Hit and Run. *See* Hikinige, 1966
Hit Him Again. *See* Fatal Mallet, 1914
Hit Me Again. *See* Smarty, 1933
Hit-the-Trail Holliday, 1918 (Neilan)
Hitch Hike Lady, 1936 (Joseph H. Lewis)
Hitchin' Posts, 1920 (Ford)
Hitler, a Film from Germany. *See* **Hitler: Ein Film aus Deutschland**, 1977
Hitler Lives?, 1945 (Siegel)
Hitler: Ein Film aus Deutschland, 1977 (Syberberg)
Hitler? Connais pas!, 1963 (Blier)
Hitler's Children, 1943 (Dmytryk)
Hitler's Madman, 1943 (Sirk)
Hito hada Kannon, 1937 (Kinugasa)
Hito no issho, 1928 (Mizoguchi)
Hito no yo no sugata, 1928 (Gosho)
Hitori musuko, 1936 (Ozu)
Hitotsubu no mugi, 1958 (Yoshimura)
Hittebarnet, 1916 (Holger-Madsen)
Hitting a New High, 1937 (Walsh)
Hjärtan som mötas, 1914 (Sjöström)
Hjärtats triumf, 1929 (Molander)
Hjerternes Kamp, 1912 (Blom)
Hjertestorme, 1915 (Blom)
Hjertets Guld, 1912 (Blom)
Hjertetyven, 1943 (Roos)
Hobbs in a Hurry, 1918 (King)
Hoboken to Hollywood, 1926 (Sennett)
Hobson's Choice, 1931 (Launder)
Hobson's Choice, 1954 (Lean)
Hochzeit im Ekzentrik Klub, 1917 (Lang)
Hocus Pocus, 1993 (Marshall)
Hoffmanns Erzählungen, 1915 (Pick)
Hoffmeyer's Legacy, 1912 (Sennett)
Hofintrige, 1912 (Blom)
Hofkonzert, 1936 (Sirk)
Hogan Out West, 1915 (Sennett)
Hogan the Porter, 1915 (Sennett)
Hogan's Annual Spree, 1914 (Sennett)
Hogan's Aristocratic Dream, 1915 (Sennett)
Hogan's Messy Job, 1915 (Sennett)
Hogan's Romance Upset, 1915 (Sennett)
Hogan's Wild Oats, 1914 (Sennett)
Hogaraka ni ayume, 1930 (Ozu)
Högfjällets dotter, 1914 (Sjöström)
Hogs and Warships. *See* Buta to gunkan, 1961
Hohoemu jinsei, 1930 (Gosho)
Højt Spil, 1913 (Blom)
Hokusai manga, 1982 (Shindo)
Hokusai, Ukiyoe Master. *See* Hokusai manga, 1982
Holcroft Covenant, 1985 (Frankenheimer)
Hold 'em Navy, 1937 (Dmytryk)
Hold 'er Sheriff, 1931 (Sennett)
Hold Back the Dawn, 1941 (Wilder)
Hold Back the Night, 1956 (Dwan)
Hold Back the Sea. *See* Lage landen, 1960
Hold that Pose, 1927 (Sennett)
Hold-Up, 1911 (Guy)
Hold Your Man, 1933 (S. Wood)
Hole. *See* Ana, 1957
Hole in the Head, 1959 (Capra)
Hole in the Soul, 1995 (Makavejev)
Hole in the Wall, 1928 (Florey)
Holiday, 1938 (Cukor)
Holiday in Mexico, 1946 (Donen)
Hölle der Liebe—Erlebnisse aus einem Tanzpalais, 1926 (Dieterle)
Höllische Macht, 1922 (Wiene)
Hollywood, 1923 (Cruze, De Mille)
Hollywood Babylon, 1992 (Anger)
Hollywood Boulevard, 1936 (Florey)
Hollywood Boulevard, 1976 (Corman)
Hollywood Boulevard, 1991 (Corman)
Hollywood Canteen, 1944 (Daves)
Hollywood Cavalcade, 1939 (Keaton, Sennett)
Hollywood Double, 1932 (Sennett)
Hollywood Extra Girl, 1935 (De Mille)
Hollywood Handicap, 1938 (Keaton)
Hollywood Happenings, 1931 (Sennett)
Hollywood Hero, 1927 (Sennett)
Hollywood Hotel, 1937 (Berkeley)
Hollywood Kid, 1924 (Sennett)
Hollywood Mavericks, 1990 (Rudolph)
Hollywood on Trial, 1976 (Dmytryk)
Hollywood or Bust, 1956 (Jerry Lewis, Tashlin)
Hollywood Party, 1934 (Dwan, Goulding)
Hollywood Revue, 1929 (Keaton)
Hollywood Star, 1929 (Sennett)
Hollywood Ten, 1950 (Dmytryk)
Hollywood Theme Song, 1930 (Sennett)
Hollywood Vice Squad, 1986 (Spheeris)
Hollywood You Never See, 1935 (De Mille)
Hollywood's Wild Angel, 1979 (Scorsese)
Holt vidék, 1971 (Gaál)
Holy Apes. *See* Bramy raju, 1967
Holy Matrimony, 1943 (Stahl)
Holy Office. *See* Santo Oficio, 1974
Homage. *See* Homenaje, 1975
Homage at Siesta Time. *See* Homenaje a la hora de la siesta, 1962
Hombori, 1948 (Rouch)
Hombre, 1967 (Ritt)
Hombre de exito, 1986 (Solas)
Home, 1919 (Weber)
Home and Refuge. *See* Hemåt i Natten, 1977
Home and the World. *See* Ghare Bahire, 1984
Home before Dark, 1958 (LeRoy)
Home Breakers, 1915 (Sennett)
Home Breaking Hound, 1915 (Sennett)
Home Brew. *See* Fireside Brewer, 1920
Home Folks, 1912 (Griffith)
Home for the Holidays, 1995 (Foster)
Home from Babylon. *See* Hem från Babylon, 1941
Home from the Hill, 1960 (Minnelli)
Home from the Sea, 1915 (Walsh)
Home from the Sea, 1962 (Peries)
Home in Indiana, 1944 (Hathaway)
Home-Made Movies, 1922 (Sennett)
Home Movies, 1979 (De Palma)
Home of the Brave, 1949 (Kramer)
Home, Sweet Home, 1914 (Griffith)
Home Sweet Home, 1982 (Leigh)
Home Sweet Homicide, 1946 (Bacon)
Home Talent, 1921 (Sennett)
Home to Danger, 1951 (Fisher)
Home Town. *See* Furusato, 1930
Home Trail, 1927 (Wyler)
Homecoming, 1948 (LeRoy)
Homenaje, 1975 (Almodóvar)
Homenaje a la hora de la siesta, 1962 (Torre Nilsson)
Homer and Eddie, 1989 (Mikhalkov-Konchalovsky, Waters)
Homesdale, 1971 (Weir)
Homesteader, 1919 (Micheaux)
Hometown. *See* Furusato, 1923
Homeward in the Night. *See* Hemåt i Natten, 1977
Homicidal Impulse, 1992 (Corman)
Homicide: Life on the Street, 1993 (Levinson)

If Winter Comes, 1947 (Saville)
If You Feel Like Singing. *See* Summer Stock, 1950
If You Like It. *See* Sukinareba koso, 1928
If You Love Me. *See* Aisureba koso, 1955
Iguana, 1988 (Hellman)
Igyjöttem, 1964 (Jancsó)
Ihr Sport, 1919 (Wiene)
Ihre Hoheit befiehlt, 1931 (Wilder)
Ik-Film, 1929 (Ivens)
Ikari no machi, 1949 (Naruse)
Ikari no umi, 1944 (Imai)
Ikeru shikabane, 1920 (Kinugasa)
Ikimono no kiroku, 1955 (Kurosawa)
Ikinokata Shinsengumi, 1932 (Kinugasa)
Ikiru, 1952 (Kurosawa)
Ikisi de cesurdu, 1963 (Güney)
Ikite-iru Magoroku, 1943 (Kinoshita)
Ikitoshi Ikerumono, 1934 (Gosho)
Il etait une chaise. *See* Chairy Tale, 1957
Il était une fois la révolution. *See* Giù la testa, 1972
Il y a des Jours ... et des Lunes, 1990 (Lelouch)
Il y a des pieds au plafond, 1912 (Gance)
Il y a un dieu pour les ivrognes, 1908 (Méliès)
Ildprøve, 1915 (Holger-Madsen)
Ile au trésor, 1986 (Ruiz)
Île de Pâques, 1935 (Storck)
Iliac Passion, 1967 (Markopoulos)
I'll Be Seeing You, 1944 (Dieterle, Cukor)
I'll Be Yours, 1947 (P. Sturges)
I'll Buy You. *See* Anata kaimasu, 1956
Ill Met By Moonlight, 1956 (Powell)
I'll Never Forget Whatshisname, 1967 (Welles)
I'll Say So, 1918 (Walsh)
I'll See You in My Dreams, 1952 (Curtiz)
Illegally Yours, 1987 (Bogdanovich)
Illicit Interlude. *See* Sommarlek, 1951
Illuminacja, 1973 (Zanussi)
Illumination. *See* Illuminacja, 1973
Illusioniste renversant, 1903 (Guy)
Illusions fantaisistes, 1910 (Méliès)
Illusions fantasmagoriques, 1898 (Méliès)
Illusions funambulesques, 1903 (Méliès)
Illustre Machefer, 1913/16 (Feuillade)
Illustrious Corpses. *See* Cadaveri eccelenti, 1976
Ils étaient neuf célibataires, 1939 (Guitry)
Ilusión viaja en tranvía, 1953 (Buñuel)
I'm All Right Jack, 1959 (Boulting)
Im Banne der Kralle, 1921 (Pabst)
I'm Coming Home, 1968 (Mikhalkov)
Im Dienste der Menschheit, 1938 (Ruttmann)
Im Lauf der Zeit, 1976 (Wenders)
I'm Mad, 1994 (Spielberg)
I'm Still Alive, 1940 (Niblo)
I'm Wandering Through Moscow. *See* Ya shagayu po Moskve, 1964
Ima hitotabi no, 1947 (Gosho)
Image, 1925 (Feyder)
Image, Flesh and Voice, 1969 (Emshwiller)
Images, 1972 (Altman, Emshwiller)
Images d'Ostende, 1929-30 (Storck)
Images du débat, 1979 (Ruiz)
Images of Debate. *See* Images du débat, 1979
Imagining October, 1984 (Jarman)
Imitation of Christ, 1967 (Warhol)
Imitation of Life, 1934 (P. Sturges, Stahl)
Imitation of Life, 1959 (Sirk)
Immagini Populari Siciliane Profane, 1952 (Birri)
Immagini Populari Siciliane Sacre, 1952 (Birri)
Immature Punter, 1898 (Hepworth)
Immediate Family, 1989 (Kasdan)
Immediate Lee, 1916 (Borzage)
Immigrant, 1917 (Chaplin)
Immigrant Experience: The Long Long Journey, 1972 (Silver)
Immorale, 1967 (Germi)
Immortal Land, 1958 (Wright)
Immortal Love. *See* Eien no hito, 1961
Immortal Sergeant, 1942 (Stahl)
Immortal Sins, 1992 (Corman)
Immortal Story, 1968 (Welles)
Immortal Stupa, 1961 (Roy)
Immortality. *See* Halhatatlanság, 1959
Imoto, 1974 (Itami)
Imoto no shi, 1921 (Kinugasa)
Imp, 1919 (Goulding)
Impasse des deux anges, 1948 (M. Tourneur)
Impatient Maiden, 1932 (Whale)
Imperative. *See* Uerreichbare, 1982
Imperatore di Capri, 1949 (Comencini)
Imperceptible Transformations. *See* Transmutations imperceptibles, 1904
Imperial Grace. *See* Ko-on, 1927
Imperio de la Fortuna, 1985 (Ripstein)
Impiegata di papa, 1934 (Blasetti)
Implacable Destiny. *See* Love Me and the World Is Mine, 1927
Implement, 1910 (Griffith)
Importance of Being Earnest, 1951 (Asquith)
Importancia universal del hueco, 1981 (Alvarez)
Imposibrante, 1968 (Guzmán)
Impossible Marriage. *See* Livets Gøglespil, 1916
Impossible Mrs. Bellew, 1922 (S. Wood)
Impossible Object. *See* Impossible Objet, 1973
Impossible Objet, 1973 (Frankenheimer)
Impossible Voyage. *See* Voyage à travers l'impossible, 1904
Imposter, 1944 (Duvivier)
Impostor, 1936 (Fernández)
Impostor, 1956 (Fernández)
Impotence. *See* **Xala**, 1974
Impressioniste fin de siècle, 1899 (Méliès)
Impressions de L'Ile des Morts, 1986 (Leacock)
Imprevisto, 1961 (Lattuada)
Improper Conduct, 1983 (Schroeder)
Impudent Girl. *See* Effrontée, 1985
Imzam kanla yazilir, 1970 (Güney)
In a Hempen Bag, 1909 (Griffith)
In a Lonely Place, 1950 (N. Ray)
In a Mirror. *See* Dans un miroir, 1985
In a Year with Thirteen Moons. *See* In einem Jahr mit dreizehn Monden, 1978
In Again—Out Again, 1917 (Von Stroheim)
In Another's Nest, 1913 (Dwan)
In Between, 1955 (Brakhage)
In Between, 1978 (Mekas)
In Black and White, 1969 (Loach)
In Caliente, 1935 (Bacon, Berkeley)
In Celebration, 1974 (Anderson)
In Cold Blood, 1967 (Brooks)
In Conference, 1931 (Sennett)
In Consideration of Pompeii, 1994 (Brakhage)
In Country, 1989 (Jewison)
In dem grossen Augenblick, 1911 (Gad)
In der Nacht, 1931 (Ruttmann)
In Dickens Land, 1913 (Pearson)
In einem Jahr mit dreizehn Monden, 1978 (Fassbinder)
In Gefahr und grösster Not bringt der Mittelweg den Tod, 1974 (Kluge)
In Harm's Way, 1964 (Preminger)
In Hollywood with Potash and Perlmutter, 1924 (LeRoy)
In jenen Tagen, 1947 (Käutner)
In Life's Cycle, 1910 (Griffith)
In Little Italy, 1909 (Griffith)
In Memoriam László Mészáros. *See* Mészáros László emlékére, 1968
In Memory of Sergo Ordzhonikidze. *See* Pamyati Sergo Ordzhonikidze, 1937
In Name Only, 1939 (Cromwell)
In nome del popolo italiano, 1972 (Risi)
In nome della legge, 1949 (Fellini, Germi)
In Old Arizona, 1929 (Walsh)

Inge bliver voksen, 1954 (Roos)
Ingeborg Holm, 1913 (Sjöström)
Ingenium Nobis Ipsa Puella Fecit, 1975 (Frampton)
Ingenjor andrees luftfard, 1982 (Troell)
Ingmar Inheritance. *See* Ingmarsarvet, 1925
Ingmarsarvet, 1925 (Molander)
Ingmarsönerna, Parts I and II, 1919 (Sjöström)
Ingorgo, una storia impossibile, 1979 (Comencini)
Ingrate, 1908 (Griffith)
Inherit the Wind, 1960 (Kramer)
Inheritance. *See* Karami-ai, 1962
Inheritance of Fuckoffguysgoodbye, 1993 (Chytilová)
Inheritors. *See* Os herdeiros, 1969
Inhumaine, 1923 (Autant-Lara, Cavalcanti, L'Herbier)
Initiation, 1975 (Rouch)
Initiation, 1978 (Clarke)
Initiation à la danse des Possédés, 1949 (Rouch)
Initiation à la mort. *See* Magiciens, 1975
Inn at Osaka. *See* Osaka no yado, 1954
Inn of Evil. *See* Inochi bo ni furo, 1971
Inn Where No Man Rests. *See* Auberge du bon repos, 1903
Inner Circle, 1912 (Griffith)
Inner Circle, 1991 (Mikhalkov-Konchalovsky)
Inner Eye, 1972 (S. Ray)
Innerspace, 1986 (Spielberg)
Innocence Is Bliss. *See* Miss Grant Takes Richmond, 1949
Innocence Unprotected. *See* Nevinost bez zaśtite, 1968
Innocent. *See* Innocente, 1976
Innocent, 1993 (Schlesinger)
Innocent Affair. *See* Don't Trust Your Husband, 1948
Innocent Blood, 1992 (Argento)
Innocent Grafter, 1912 (Dwan)
Innocent Husbands, 1925 (McCarey)
Innocent Magdalene, 1916 (Dwan, Fleming)
Innocent Maid. *See* Hakoiri musume, 1935
Innocent Sinner, 1917 (Walsh)
Innocent Sorcerers. *See* Niewinni czarodzieje, 1960
Innocent Witch. *See* Osore-zan no onna, 1964
Innocente, 1976 (Visconti)
Innocents, 1961 (Clayton)
Innocents aux mains sales, 1975 (Chabrol)
Innocent's Progress, 1918 (Borzage)
Innocents with Dirty Hands. *See* Innocents aux mains sales, 1975
Inocentes, 1962 (Bardem)
Inochi bo ni furo, 1971 (Kobayashi)
Inondation, 1923 (Delluc, Cavalcanti)
Inquest. *See* Voruntersuchung, 1931
Inquest, 1940 (Boulting)
Inquilab, 1935 (Kapoor)
Insatiable Mrs. Kirsch, 1994 (Russell)
Insect Woman. *See* Nippon konchuki, 1963
Insel, 1974 (Wenders)
Insel der Verschollenen, 1921 (Gad)
Inside Daisy Clover, 1966 (Mulligan, Pakula, Redford)
Inside Edges, 1975 (Emshwiller)
Inside Job, 1946 (Browning)
Inside Moves, 1980 (Levinson)
Inside Rooms—The Bathroom, 1985 (Greenaway)
Inside Story, 1948 (Dwan)
Inside the Gelatin Factory, 1972 (Emshwiller)
Insignificance, 1985 (Roeg)
Inspecteur Lavardin, 1985 (Chabrol)
Inspector Clouseau, 1967 (Edwards)
Inspector Hornleigh Goes To It, 1940 (Launder)
Inspector Hornleigh On Holiday, 1939 (Launder)
Inspector Lo Gatto. *See* Commissario Lo Gatto, 1987
Inspector Maigret. *See* Maigret tend un piège, 1957
Inspiration, 1931 (Brown)
Instant de la paix. *See* Der Augenblick des Friedens, 1965
Instinct. *See* Honno, 1966
Instinct est maître, 1917 (Feyder)
Instructional Steamer 'Red Star'. *See* Instruktorii Parokhod "Krasnaia Zvezda", 1920
Instruktorii Parokhod "Krasnaia Zvezda", 1920 (Vertov)
Insurrección de la burguesia, 1974 (Guzmán)
Insurrection of the Bourgeoisie. *See* Insurrección de la burguesia, 1974
Inta Habibi, 1956 (Chahine)
Intelligence Service. *See* Ill Met By Moonlight, 1956
Intentions of Murder. *See* Akai satsui, 1964
Interim, 1952 (Brakhage)
Interim Balance. *See* Věrni zustaneme, 1945
Interior of a Railway Carriage, 1901 (Hepworth)
Interiors, 1978 (Allen, Schumacher)
Interlude, 1957 (Sirk)
Intermezzo, 1936 (Molander)
International Sneak, 1917 (Sennett)
International Spy. *See* Spy Ring, 1938
International Velvet, 1967 (Warhol)
Interpolations I-V, 1992 (Brakhage)
Interrupted Elopement, 1911 (Sennett)
Interrupted Game, 1911 (Sennett)
Interrupted Picnic, 1898 (Hepworth)
Interrupted Solitude, 1974 (Emshwiller)
Intervals, 1969 (Greenaway)
Intervention in the Far East. *See* Volochayevskiye dni, 1937
Interview, 1971 (Sen)
Interview with the Vampire, 1994 (Jordan)
Interview. *See* Intervista, 1987
Intervista, 1987 (Fellini)
Intimate Stranger, 1956 (Losey)
Into the Dark. *See* Entre tinieblas, 1983
Into the Desert, 1912 (Cruze)
Into the Night, 1985 (Cronenberg, Demme, Mazursky, Siegel)
Into the West, 1992 (Newell, Sheridan)
Intolerance, 1916 (Browning, Griffith, W.S. Van Dyke, Von Stroheim)
Introducing the Dial, 1935 (Grierson)
Introduction to Arnold Schoenberg's Accompaniment for a Cinematographic Scene. *See* Einleitung zu Arnold Schoenberg Begleit Musik zu einer Lichtspielscene, 1969
Introduction to Marriage. *See* Kekkon-gaku nyumon, 1930
Intruder. *See* Invader, 1935
Intruder, 1961 (Corman)
Intruder in the Dust, 1949 (Brown)
Intruse, 1913 (Feuillade)
Intrusion at Lompoc, 1912 (Dwan)
Inundados, 1961 (Birri)
Invader, 1935 (Keaton)
Invaders. *See* 49th Parallel, 1941
Invasion. *See* Tatárjárás, 1917
Invasion of the Body Snatchers, 1956 (Peckinpah, Siegel)
Invasion of the Body Snatchers, 1978 (Kaufman, Siegel)
Invasion of the Body Snatchers, 1993 (Ferrara)
Invasion pacifique. *See* Québec-USA, 1962
Invasore, 1943 (Rossellini)
Inventive Love. *See* Elskovs Opfindsomhed, 1913
Inventor's Secret, 1911 (Sennett)
Inventory. *See* Stan Posiadania, 1989
Investigation of a Citizen above Suspicion. *See* Indagine su un cittadino al di sopra di ogni sospietto, 1970
Invincible, 1943 (Gerasimov)
Invisible Ghost, 1941 (Joseph H. Lewis)
Invisible Man, 1933 (Whale)
Invisible Man. *See* Nevidimi chelovek, 1935
Invisible Power. *See* Washington Merry-Go-Round, 1932
Invisible Stripes, 1940 (Bacon)
Invisible Wall. *See* Osynliga muren, 1944
Invitation, 1973 (Goretta)
Invitation à la chasse, 1974 (Von Trotta)
Invitation au voyage, 1927 (Dulac)
Invitation to a Gunfighter, 1964 (Kramer)
Invitation to Hell, 1984 (Craven)
Invitation to the Inside. *See* Zaproszenie do wnętrza, 1978

Invite Monsieur à dîner, 1932 (Autant-Lara)
Invocation of My Demon Brother, 1969 (Anger)
Io amo, tu ami, 1961 (Blasetti)
Io, io, io ... e gli altri, 1966 (Blasetti, De Sica)
Io la conoscevo bene, 1965 (Scola)
Io non vedo, tu non parli, lui non sente, 1971 (De Sica)
Iola's Promise, 1912 (Griffith)
Iphigenia, 1977 (Cacoyannis)
Ipotesi, 1970 (Petri)
Ippan gatana dohyoiri, 1934 (Kinugasa)
Ippocampo, 1943 (De Sica)
Ippodromi all'Alba, 1950 (Blasetti)
Ire a Santiago, 1964 (Gómez)
Ireland, the Tear and the Smile, 1960 (Willard Van Dyke)
Irene, 1926 (LeRoy)
Iris, 1915 (Hepworth)
Iris and the Lieutenant. *See* Iris och Lojtnantshjarta, 1946
Iris och Lojtnantshjarta, 1946 (Sjöberg, Zetterling)
Irish in Us, 1935 (Bacon)
Irma La Douce, 1963 (Wilder)
Iron Crown. *See* Corona di ferro, 1941
Iron Curtain, 1948 (Wellman)
Iron Duke, 1934 (Saville)
Iron Gate. *See* **Bab el Hadid,** 1958
Iron Horse, 1924 (Ford)
Iron Horsemen, 1994 (Kaurismaki)
Iron Man, 1931 (Browning)
Iron Mask, 1929 (Dwan)
Iron Maze, 1991 (Stone)
Iron Nag, 1925 (Sennett)
Iron Ring. *See* Kanawa, 1972
Ironweed, 1988 (Babenco)
Irresistible. *See* Belle ma povere, 1957
Irrgarten der Leidenschaft. *See* Pleasure Garden, 1926
Is Marriage the Bunk?, 1925 (McCarey)
Is Matrimony a Failure?, 1922 (Cruze)
Is Paris Burning? *See* Paris brûle-t-il?, 1966
Is That All There Is?, 1993 (Anderson)
Isabelle Eberhardt, 1990 (Wenders)
Isadora, 1968 (Reisz)
Isadora Duncan, the Biggest Dancer in the World, 1966 (Russell)
Isen brydes, 1947 (Roos)
Ishimatsu of Mori. *See* Mori no Ishimatsu, 1949
Ishimatsu of the Forest. *See* Mori no Ishimatsu, 1949
Ishinaka sensei gyojoki, 1949 (Naruse)
Isidore a la deveine, 1919 (Florey)
Isidore sur le lac, 1919 (Florey)
Iskindiriah Kaman Oue Kaman, 1990 (Chahine)
Iskindria ... Leh?, 1978 (Chahine)
Isla de la pasión, 1941 (Fernández)
Isla del tesero, 1969 (Gómez)
Island. *See* **Hadaka no shima**, 1960
Island. *See* On, 1966
Island. *See* Insel, 1974
Island at the Top of the World, 1974 (Stevenson)
Island in the Sky, 1953 (Wellman)
Island in the Sun, 1957 (Rossen)
Island of Naked Scandal. *See* Shima to ratai jiken, 1931
Island of Silver Herons. *See* Ostrov stříbrných volavek, 1976
Island of Terror, 1966 (Fisher)
Island of the Burning Damned. *See* Night of the Big Heat, 1967
Island of Treasure, 1965 (Welles)
Islands, 1984 (Maysles)
Islands in the Stream, 1977 (Schaffner)
Islas Marías, 1950 (Fernández)
Isle of Lost Ships, 1923 (M. Tourneur)
Isn't Life Terrible, 1925 (McCarey)
Isn't Love Cuckoo, 1925 (Sennett)
Isola bianca, 1950 (Risi)
Isole, 1993 (Moretti)
Isotopes in Medical Science. *See* Izotöpok a gyögyászatban, 1959
Ispaniya, 1939 (Shub)
Isphahan: Lettre Persanne 1977, 1977 (Rouch)
Ispirazione, 1988 (Jarman)
Isten hátrafelé megy, 1990 (Jancsó)
Isten hozta, örnagy úr!, 1969 (Fábri)
Istoriia grazhdenskoi voini, 1922 (Vertov)
Istoriya Asi Klyachinoi, kotoraya lyubila, da nye vyshla zamuzh, 1967 (Mikhalkov-Konchalovsky)
It Ain't No Sin. *See* Belle of the Nineties, 1934
It Always Rains on Sunday, 1947 (Hamer)
It Began in Spain. *See* Zaczęło się w Hiszpanii, 1950
It Conquered the World, 1956 (Corman)
It Depends on Us Too ... . *See* Rajtunk is mulik, 1960
It Happened at the Inn. *See* Goupi Mains rouges, 1943
It Happened in Gibraltar. *See* Gibraltar, 1938
It Happened in Hollywood, 1937 (Fuller)
It Happened in Hollywood, 1972 (Craven)
It Happened in Rome. *See* Souvenir d'Italie, 1957
It Happened in Tokyo. *See* Kawa no aru shitamachi no hanashi, 1955
It Happened One Christmas, 1977 (Welles)
It Happened One Night, 1934 (Capra)
It Happened Tomorrow, 1943 (Clair)
It Happens Every Spring, 1949 (Bacon)
It Isn't Easy Being God. *See* Es ist nicht leicht ein Gott zu sein, 1989
It Must Be Love, 1926 (LeRoy)
It Pays to Exercise, 1918 (Sennett)
It Pays to Wait, 1912 (Dwan)
It Rains in My Village. *See* Bice skoro propast sveta, 1968
It Rains on Our Love. *See* Det regnar på vår kärlek, 1946
It Should Happen to You, 1954 (Cukor)
It Started in Naples, 1960 (De Sica)
It Started in Paris, 1935 (Huston)
It Was a Wonderful Life, 1993 (Foster)
It Was een April, 1935 (Sirk)
It Was in May. *See* Det var i Maj, 1914
Italia non e un paese povero, 1960 (Ivens, Taviani)
Italian-American, 1974 (Scorsese)
Italian Barber, 1910 (Griffith, Sennett)
Italian Blood, 1911 (Griffith)
Italian Secret Service, 1968 (Comencini)
Italiane e l'amore, 1961 (Ferreri)
Italiani, brava gente, 1964 (De Santis)
Italiano in America, 1967 (De Sica)
Italy Is Not a Poor Country. *See* Italia non e un paese povero, 1960
Itél a Balaton, 1932 (Fejös)
Itinéraire d'un enfant gâté, 1988 (Lelouch)
Itinerary of a Spoiled Child. *See* Itinéraire d'un enfant gâté, 1988
It'll Happen Tomorrow. *See* Domani accadra, 1988
Itoshi no wagako, 1926 (Gosho)
It's a Bear. *See* Just a Bear, 1931
It's a Big Country, 1951 (Brown, J. Sturges, C. Vidor, Wellman)
It's a Boy, 1920 (Sennett)
It's a Great Life, 1929 (S. Wood)
It's a Mad, Mad, Mad, Mad, World, 1963 (Jerry Lewis, Keaton, Kramer)
It's a Wonderful Life, 1946 (Capra)
It's a Wonderful World, 1939 (W.S. Van Dyke)
It's All True, 1942 (Welles)
It's Always Fair Weather, 1955 (Donen)
It's Always Sunday, 1955 (Dwan)
It's Forever Springtime. *See* E'primavera, 1949
It's Impossible to Learn to Plow by Reading Books, 1988 (Linklater)
It's in the Air, 1938 (Dearden)
It's Love Again, 1936 (Saville)
It's Magic. *See* Romance on the High Seas, 1948
It's My Model. *See* Det är min modell, 1946
It's No Laughing Matter, 1914 (Weber)
It's Not Just You, Murray, 1964 (Scorsese)
It's Only Money, 1962 (Jerry Lewis, Tashlin)
It's Trad, Dad, 1962 (Lester)
It's Up to You, 1941 (Kazan)
Itsuwareru seiso, 1951 (Shindo, Yoshimura)

Jennifer, 1964 (De Palma)
Jenny, 1936 (Carné)
Jenny's Pearls, 1913 (Sennett)
Jens Langkniv, 1940 (Henning-Jensen)
Jens Mansson i Amerika, 1947 (De Mille)
Jens Mansson in America. *See* Jens Mansson i Amerika, 1947
Jeopardy, 1953 (J. Sturges)
Jeremiah Johnson, 1972 (Pollack, Redford)
Jericho Mile, 1979 (M. Mann)
Jernbanens Datter, 1911 (Blom)
Jérome Perreau, héro des barricades, 1936 (Gance)
Jess, 1912 (Cruze)
Jesse James, 1939 (King)
Jessye Norman Sings Carmen, 1989 (Maysles)
Jester and the Queen. *See* Sasek a kralovna, 1987
Jestoki romans, 1984 (Mikhalkov)
Jesus Christ Superstar, 1973 (Jewison)
Jesus of Nazareth. *See* Gesu di Nazareth, 1977
Jet Pilot, 1957 (Von Sternberg)
Jet Storm, 1959 (Zetterling)
Jetée, 1964 (Marker)
Jeu de l'oie, 1980 (Ruiz)
Jeudi on chantera comme dimanche, 1966 (Storck)
Jeugd-dag, 1929/30 (Ivens)
Jeune Fille. *See* Young One, 1960
Jeune Fille assassinee, 1974 (Astruc, Vadim)
Jeune Fille un seul amour, Magnificent Sinner. *See* Katya, 1960
Jeune Homme et la mort, 1953 (Anger)
Jeunes filles d'aujourd'hui. *See* Maturareise, 1943
Jeunes Filles en détresse, 1939 (Pabst)
Jeunes Loups, 1967 (Carné)
Jeunesses musicales, 1956 (Jutra)
Jeux, 1979 (Ruiz)
Jeux de l'amour, 1959 (Chabrol)
Jeux de l'été et de la mer, 1936 (Storck)
Jeux interdits, 1951 (Clement)
Jeux sont faits, 1947 (Delannoy)
Jewel Case. *See* Sølvdaasen med Juvelerne, 1910
Jewel Robbery, 1932 (Dieterle)
Jeweller's Terror. *See* Juvelerernes Skrœk, eller Skelethaanden, eller Skelethaandens sidste bedrift, 1915
Jewels of a Sacrifice, 1913 (Dwan)
Jewish Gauchos. *See* Gauchos judíos, 1975
Jew's Christmas, 1913 (Weber)
Jezebel, 1938 (Huston, Wyler)
Jézus Krisztus Horoszkója, 1989 (Jancsó)
JFK, 1991 (Costner, Stone)
Jigoku no kifujin, 1949 (Kurosawa)
Jigokumon, 1953 (Kinugasa)
Jigokuno magarikago, 1959 (Imamura)
Jihi shincho, 1927 (Mizoguchi)
Jilt, 1909 (Griffith)
Jim Bludso, 1917 (Browning)
Jim Jam Janitor, 1928 (Sennett)
Jim Thorpe—All American, 1951 (Curtiz)
Jimmy Hollywood, 1994 (Levinson)
Jimmy the Gent, 1934 (Curtiz)
Jimpu Group. *See* Jimpuren, 1933
Jimpuren, 1933 (Mizoguchi)
Jinete fantasma, 1967 (Fernández)
Jinks Joins the Temperance Club, 1911 (Sennett)
Jinkyo, 1924 (Mizoguchi)
Jinruigaku nyumon, 1966 (Imamura)
Jinsei no onimotsu, 1935 (Gosho)
Jinsei o Mitsumete, 1923 (Kinugasa)
Jinsei tonbo-gaeri, 1946 (Imai)
Jinxed!, 1982 (Siegel)
Jiruba no Tetsu, 1950 (Kurosawa)
Jis Desh Me Ganga Behti Hai, 1960 (Kapoor)
Jitney Elopement, 1915 (Bacon, Chaplin)
Jiyu gakko, 1951 (Yoshimura)
JLG/JLG—Autoportrait de Decembre, 1994 (Godard)
JLG/JLG—Self-Portrait in December. *See* JLG/JLG—Autoportrait de Decembre, 1994
Joan of Arc, 1948 (Fleming)
Joan of Arc at the Stake. *See* Giovanna d'Arco al rogo, 1954
Joan of Paris, 1942 (Stevenson)
Joan the Woman, 1917 (De Mille)
Joanna Francesa, 1973 (Diegues)
Job. *See* **Posto**, 1961
Job. *See* Urząd, 1967
Job in a Million, 1937 (Grierson)
Jocko musicien, 1903 (Guy)
Jocular Winds, 1913 (Dwan)
Joe Debbs, 1917 (Lang)
Joe Kidd, 1972 (Eastwood, J. Sturges)
Joe vs. the Volcano, 1989 (Spielberg)
Joen, 1959 (Kinugasa)
Joen no chimata, 1923 (Mizoguchi)
Joe's Bed-Stuy Barbershop: We Cut Heads, 1982 (S. Lee)
Joey Boy, 1965 (Launder)
Jofroi, 1934 (Pagnol)
Johan, 1920 (Stiller)
Johan, 1964 (Troell)
Johann the Coffin Maker, 1927 (Florey)
Johannas Traum, 1975 (Schroeter)
Johannes Jørgensen i Assisi, 1950 (Roos)
Johannes Jørgensen i Svendborg, 1954 (Roos)
Johannes Larsen, 1957 (Roos)
Johannes V. Jensen, 1947 (Roos)
John Ericsson, 1937 (Sjöström)
John Gilpin's Ride, 1908 (Hepworth)
John Halifax Gentleman, 1915 (Pearson)
John Needham's Double, 1916 (Weber)
John, the Tenant. *See* Arendás zsidó, 1917
John the Younger Brother. *See* Jön az öcsem, 1919
Johnny Apollo, 1940 (Hathaway)
Johnny Come Lately, 1943 (Howard)
Johnny Eager, 1941 (LeRoy)
Johnny Get Your Gun, 1919 (Cruze)
Johnny Guitar, 1954 (N. Ray)
Johnny Handsome, 1989 (W. Hill)
Johnny in the Clouds. *See* Way to the Stars, 1945
Johnny O'Clock, 1947 (Rossen)
Johnny One-Eye, 1949 (Florey)
Johnny Tremain, 1957 (Stevenson)
Johnny Vagabond. *See* Johnny Come Lately, 1943
Joi Baba Felunath, 1978 (S. Ray)
Joie de revivre, 1947 (Storck)
Joiuchi, 1967 (Kobayashi)
Joke. *See* Zert, 1968
Joke on the Joker, 1911 (Sennett)
Jokei, 1960 (Yoshimura)
Joker Is Wild, 1957 (C. Vidor)
Jokyo II: Mono o takaku uritsukeru onna, 1959 (Ichikawa)
Jokyu aishi, 1931 (Gosho)
Joli Mai, 1963 (Marker)
Jolly Bad Fellow, 1963 (Hamer)
Jolly Jilter, 1927 (Sennett)
Jolson Story, 1946 (Joseph H. Lewis)
Jön az öcsem, 1919 (Curtiz)
Jonah Man, 1904 (Hepworth)
Jonah qui aura 25 ans en l'an 2000, 1976 (Tanner)
Jonah Who Will Be 25 in the Year 2000. *See* **Jonah qui aura 25 ans en l'an 2000**, 1976
Jonas in the Desert, 1993 (Anger, Mekas, Scorsese)
Jones and His New Neighbors, 1909 (Griffith)
Jones and the Lady Book Agent, 1909 (Griffith)
Jones Family in Hollywood, 1939 (Keaton)
Jones Family in Quick Millions, 1939 (Keaton)
Jones Have Amateur Theatricals, 1909 (Griffith)
Jordan is a Hard Road, 1915 (Dwan)

Kartiki Purnima Festival, 1914/15 (Phalke)
Karumen junjo su, 1952 (Kinoshita)
Karumen kokyo ni kaeru, 1951 (Kinoshita)
Karussell. *See* Körhinta, 1955
Kasař, 1973 (Jireš)
Kaseki, 1975 (Kobayashi)
Kaseki no mori, 1973 (Shinoda)
Kashima Paradise, 1973 (Marker)
Kasimpasali, 1965 (Güney)
Kasimpasali recep, 1965 (Güney)
Katakomby, 1940 (Fric)
Katapult, 1983 (Jireš)
Katchem Kate, 1911 (Sennett)
Katherine Reed Story, 1965 (Altman)
Kathleen Mavourneen, 1906 (Porter)
Katia, 1938 (M. Tourneur)
Katka, 1950 (Kadár)
Katok i skripka, 1960 (Mikhalkov-Konchalovsky, Tarkovsky)
Katrina Dead, 1967 (Warhol)
Kats Is Kats, 1920 (La Cava)
Katya, 1960 (Siodmak)
Katzelmacher, 1969 (Fassbinder)
Katzensteg, 1915 (Leni)
Kavkazskiye mineralniye vody, 1924 (Kuleshov)
Kawa no aru shitamachi no hanashi, 1955 (Kinugasa)
Kawaita hana, 1963 (Shinoda)
Kawaita mizuumi, 1960 (Shinoda)
Kawanakajima kassen, 1941 (Kinugasa)
Kazabana, 1959 (Kinoshita)
Kazaks—Minorité nationale—Sinking, 1977 (Ivens)
Kaze no naka no mendori, 1948 (Ozu)
Kazoku gemu, 1983 (Itami)
Kazoku no jijo, 1962 (Yoshimura)
Kdo hledá zlaté dno, 1975 (Menzel)
Kdo své nebe neunese, 1959 (Schorm)
Kean, 1910 (Blom)
Kedamono no yado, 1951 (Kurosawa)
Keejte Tippel. *See* Cathy Tippel, 1975
Keep, 1983 (M. Mann)
Keep On Rockin', 1971 (Leacock)
Keep Up Your Right. *See* Soigne ta droite, 1987
Keep Walking. *See* Cammina, cammina, 1983
Keeper of the Bees, 1947 (J. Sturges)
Keeper of the Flame, 1942 (Cukor, Saville)
Keepers. *See* Tête contre les murs, 1958
Keepers of Youth, 1931 (Launder)
Keeping On, 1983 (Kopple)
Kegyelet, 1967 (Szabó)
Keiraku hichu, 1928 (Kinugasa)
Keirin shonin gyojoki, 1964 (Imamura)
Kejsaren av Portugallien, 1944 (Molander, Sjöström)
Kekkon, 1947 (Kinoshita)
Kekkon-gaku nyumon, 1930 (Ozu)
Kekkon koshinkyoku, 1951 (Ichikawa)
Kekkon no seitai, 1941 (Imai)
Kelly from the Emerald Isle, 1913 (Guy)
Kelly Gets His Man, 1927 (Wyler)
Kelly's Heroes, 1970 (Eastwood)
Kelp Industry, 1913 (Sennett)
Ken Death Gets Out of Jail, 1987 (Van Sant)
Ken Russell—A British Picture, 1989 (Russell)
Ken Russell's ABC of British Music, 1988 (Russell)
Ken Russell's View of the Planets, 1983 (Russell)
Kennel Murder Case, 1933 (Curtiz)
Kentish Industries, 1913 (Pearson)
Kentucky Kernels, 1934 (Stevens)
Kentucky Pride, 1925 (Ford)
Kenya, South Africa, 1962 (Leacock)
Képi, 1905 (Guy)
Kept Husbands, 1931 (Bacon)
Keresztelö, 1967 (Gaál)
Kermes. *See* Kirmes, 1960
Kermesse héroïque, 1935 (Feyder)
Kermesse héroïque, 1936 (Feyder)
Kes, 1969 (Loach)
Kessen, 1944 (Yoshimura)
Két Félidö a pokolban, 1961 (Fábri)
Kétszívü férfi, 1916 (Korda)
Ketto Kagiya no tsuji, 1951 (Kurosawa)
Key, 1934 (Curtiz)
Key, 1958 (Reed)
Key. *See* Kagi, 1959
Key Largo, 1948 (Brooks, Huston)
Keyhole, 1933 (Curtiz)
Keys of the Kingdom, 1944 (Mankiewicz, Stahl)
Keys to Happiness. *See* Klyuchi shchastya, 1913
Kezunbe vettuk a béke ugyét, 1950 (Jancsó)
Khaan Dost, 1976 (Kapoor)
Khandahar, 1983 (Sen)
Kharij, 1982 (Sen)
Khartoum, 1966 (Dearden)
Kholodnye Dushi, 1914 (Bauer)
Khronika-molniya, 1924 (Vertov)
Kiáltó, 1964 (Mészáros)
Kick-Off, 1931 (Stevens)
Kid, 1921 (Chaplin)
Kid, 1984 (Hartley)
Kid Auto Race. *See* Kid Auto Races at Venice, 1914
Kid Auto Races at Venice, 1914 (Chaplin, Sennett)
Kid for Two Farthings, 1955 (Reed)
Kid from Spain, 1932 (Berkeley, McCarey, Zinnemann)
Kid Galahad, 1937 (Curtiz)
Kid Glove Killer, 1942 (Zinnemann)
Kiddies in the Ruins, 1918 (Pearson)
Kideko no shasho-san, 1941 (Naruse)
Kidnapped, 1935 (Holger-Madsen)
Kidnapped. *See* Unos, 1952
Kidnapped, 1960 (Stevenson)
Kidnapper. *See* Secuestrador, 1958
Kids Play Russian. *See* Enfants jouent a la Russie, 1995
Kiedy ty śpisz, 1950 (Wajda)
Kieron, 1968 (Angelopoulos)
Kierunek Nowa Huta, 1951 (Munk)
Kiiroi karasu, 1957 (Gosho)
Kika, 1993 (Almodóvar)
Kiki, 1926 (Brown)
Kiku and Isamu. *See* Kiku to Isamu, 1958
Kiku to Isamu, 1958 (Imai)
Kilenc hónap, 1976 (Meszaros)
Kilencvenkilenc, 1918 (Curtiz)
Kill Me Again, 1989 (Dahl)
Kill Me Tomorrow, 1957 (Fisher)
Kill the Umpire, 1950 (Bacon, Tashlin)
Killer! *See* Que la bête meure, 1969
Killer, 1989 (Woo)
Killer Bees, 1974 (Schumacher)
Killer Elite, 1975 (Hellman, Peckinpah)
Killer is Loose, 1955 (Boetticher)
Killer McCoy, 1947 (Donen)
Killer of Sheep, 1977 (Burnett)
Killer Shark, 1950 (Boetticher)
Killers, 1946 (Brooks, Huston, Siodmak)
Killers, 1964 (Cassavetes, Siegel)
Killer's Kiss, 1955 (Kubrick)
Killers on Parade. *See* Yuhi ni akai ore no kao, 1961
Killing, 1956 (Kubrick)
Killing Box, 1993 (Hellman)
Killing Field, 1984 (Joffé)
Killing Hearts, 1914 (Sennett)
Killing of a Chinese Bookie, 1976 (Cassavetes)
Killing of Sister George, 1968 (Aldrich)
Killing Zoe, 1994 (Tarantino)

Kim, 1950 (Saville)
Kim G., 1978 (August)
Kimi to iku michi, 1936 (Naruse)
Kimi to wakarete, 1933 (Naruse)
Kína vendégei voltunk, 1957 (Jancsó)
Kind Hearts and Coronets, 1949 (Hamer)
Kind Lady, 1951 (J. Sturges)
Kind Millionaire. *See* Pytlákova schovanka, 1949
Kind of Loving, 1962 (Schlesinger)
Kind ruft, 1914 (Gad)
Kinder der Finsternis, 1921 (Leni)
Kinder der Finsternis, 1922 (Dupont)
Kinder des Generals, 1912 (Gad)
Kindergarten, 1995 (Baillie)
Kindering, 1987 (Brakhage)
Kindling, 1915 (De Mille)
Kindred of the Dust, 1923 (Walsh)
Kinesiske Vase. *See* Vasens Hemmelighed, 1913
Kinfolk. *See* Rodnya, 1982
King: A Filmed Record ... Montgomery to Memphis, 1970 (Lumet)
King and Country, 1964 (Losey)
King and Four Queens, 1956 (Walsh)
King and the Chorus Girl, 1937 (LeRoy)
King and the Woman. *See* Král a žena, 1967
King Charlie. *See* His Prehistoric Past, 1914
King Creole, 1958 (Curtiz)
King David, 1985 (Beresford)
King Game. *See* Hra na krále, 1967
King in New York, 1957 (Chaplin)
King Kong, 1933 (Schoedsack)
King Lear. *See* **Korol Lir**, 1971
King Lear, 1987 (Allen, Godard)
King Log, 1932 (Grierson)
King of Alcatraz, 1937 (Florey)
King of Boda. *See* Bodakunden, 1920
King of Comedy, 1982 (Jerry Lewis, Scorsese)
King of Kings, 1927 (De Mille)
King of Kings, 1961 (N. Ray, Welles)
King of Kings. *See* Krák Králu, 1963
King of Kings. *See* Kirallar kirali, 1965
King of Marvin Gardens, 1973 (Rafelson)
King of New York, 1990 (Ferrara)
King of Paris. *See* Korol' Parizha, 1917
King of the Children. *See* **Haizi Wang,** 1987
King of the Damned, 1935 (Launder)
King of the Gamblers, 1937 (Florey)
King of the Hill, 1993 (Soderbergh)
King of the Khyber Rifles, 1953 (King)
King of the Night. *See* Rei da noite, 1975
King of the Sumava. *See* Král Sumavy, 1959
King of Thieves. *See* Dolandiricilar, 1961
King, Queen, Knave, 1971 (Skolimowski)
King, Queen, Slave. *See* Sahib, Bibi aur Ghulam, 1962
King Solomon's Mines, 1937 (Stevenson)
King Steps Out, 1936 (Von Sternberg)
Kingdom of Diamonds. *See* Heerak Rajar Deshe, 1979
Kingdom of Naples. *See* Regno di Napoli, 1978
Kingdom of the Fairies. *See* Royaume des Fées, 1903
Kings Go Forth, 1958 (Daves)
Kings of the Road. *See* **Im Lauf der Zeit**, 1976
King's Row, 1941 (S. Wood)
King's Story, 1965 (Welles)
Kinno jidai, 1926 (Kinugasa)
Kino za XX liet, 1940 (Pudovkin, Shub)
Kinodnevik Glumova, 1923 (Eisenstein)
Kino-Eye. *See* Kino-glaz, 1924
Kino-glaz, 1924 (Vertov)
Kino-Nedelia, 1918-19 (Vertov)
Kino-Pravda, 1922-23 (Vertov)
Kinuyo monogatari, 1930 (Gosho)
Kinuyo Story. *See* Kinuyo monogatari, 1930
Kipps, 1941 (Launder, Reed)
Kirai Kirai Kirai, 1960 (Itami)
Kirallar kirali, 1965 (Güney)
Kire no ame, 1924 (Kinugasa)
Kiri no minato, 1923 (Mizoguchi)
Kirinji, 1926 (Kinugasa)
Kirmes, 1960 (Staudte)
Kirpitchiki, 1925 (Pudovkin)
Kisenga, Man of Africa. *See* Men of Two Worlds, 1946
Kishin yuri keiji, 1924 (Kinugasa)
Kismet, 1930 (Dieterle)
Kismet, 1943 (Dieterle)
Kismet, 1955 (Minnelli)
Kiss, 1900 (Hepworth)
Kiss, 1929 (Feyder, Lewin)
Kiss, 1963 (Warhol)
Kiss Before the Mirror, 1933 (Whale)
Kiss for Corliss, 1949 (Aldrich)
Kiss from Stadium. *See* Polibek ze stadionu, 1948
Kiss in the Dark, 1949 (Daves)
Kiss Me Again, 1925 (Lubitsch)
Kiss Me and Die. *See* Lady in Red, 1979
Kiss Me Deadly, 1955 (Aldrich, Saville)
Kiss Me Goodbye. *See* Going Gay, 1933
Kiss Me Goodbye, 1982 (Mulligan)
Kiss Me Kate, 1953 (Fosse)
Kiss Me, Stupid, 1964 (Wilder)
Kiss of Death. *See* Dödskyssen, 1917
Kiss of Death, 1947 (Hathaway)
Kiss of Death, 1976 (Leigh)
Kiss of Death, 1995 (Schroeder)
Kiss of the Spider Woman, 1985 (Babenco)
Kiss, Part III: Women's Ways. *See* Kuchizuke, III: Onna doshi, 1955
Kiss Them For Me, 1957 (Donen)
Kissing Bandit, 1948 (Donen)
Kitchen, 1966 (Warhol)
Kitchen Lady, 1918 (Sennett)
Kitsch, 1919 (Pick)
Kitty, 1929 (Saville)
Kitty. *See* Katka, 1950
Kitty from Killarney, 1927 (Sennett)
Kitty Royle, 1940 (S. Wood)
Kitty und die Weltkonferenz, 1939 (Käutner)
Kizil vazo, 1961 (Güney)
Kizilirmak-Karakoyun, 1967 (Güney)
Kizoku no kaidan, 1959 (Yoshimura)
Kizudarake no sanga, 1964 (Shindo)
Klanni—tarina sammokoitten, 1984 (Kaurismaki)
Klansman, 1974 (Fuller)
Klaps, 1976 (Kieślowski)
Klassenverhältnisse, 1985 (Straub)
Kleider machen Leute, 1940 (Käutner)
Kleine Chaos, 1966 (Fassbinder)
Kleiner Film einer grossen Stadt—Die Stadt Düsseldorf am Rhein, 1935 (Ruttmann)
Kleptomaniac, 1905 (Porter)
Kleptomanin, 1918 (Gad)
Kliatva molodikh, 1944 (Vertov)
Klondike Annie, 1936 (Walsh)
Klondike Fury, 1942 (Howard)
Klosterfriede, 1917 (Gad)
Klostret I Sendomir, 1920 (Sjöström)
Klugen Frauen, 1936 (Feyder)
Klute, 1971 (Pakula)
Kluven värld, 1948 (Sucksdorff)
Klyatva Timura, 1942 (Kuleshov)
Klyuchi shchastya, 1913 (Protazanov)
Knabe in Blau, 1919 (Murnau)
Knack—and How to Get It, 1965 (Lester)
Knave of Hearts. *See* Monsieur Ripois, 1954
Knickerbocker Buckaroo, 1919 (Wellman)

Knife in the Water. *See* **Nóz w wodzie**, 1962
Knight of the Black Art. *See* Tambourin fantastique, 1908
Knight of the Road, 1911 (Griffith)
Knight of the Snows. *See* Chevalier des neiges, 1912
Knight of the Street. *See* Kaido no kishi, 1928
Knight of the Sword. *See* Santo de la espada, 1969
Knight without Armour, 1937 (Feyder)
Knightriders, 1981 (Romero)
Kniplinger. *See* Grevindens Aere, 1918
Knivstikkeren. *See* En farlig Forbryder, 1913
Knock for Knock, 1976 (Leigh)
Knock on Any Door, 1949 (N. Ray)
Knock on Wood, 1953 (Zetterling)
Knockout, 1914 (Chaplin, Sennett)
Knockout Kisses, 1933 (Sennett)
Know Your Ally: Britain, 1944 (Capra)
Know Your Enemy: Germany, 1945 (Capra)
Know Your Enemy: Japan, 1945 (Capra)
Knowing to Learn. *See* Comment savoir, 1966
Knud, 1966 (Roos)
Knud Rasmussens mindeekspedition til Kap Seddon, 1982 (Roos)
Knute Rockne—All American, 1940 (Bacon, Howard)
Kobanzame, 1949 (Kinugasa)
Kobayashi Takiji, 1974 (Imai)
København, Kalundborg og—?, 1934 (Holger-Madsen)
Kocaoğlan, 1964 (Güney)
Kočár do Vídně, 1966 (Kachyňa)
Kocero, Mountain Wolf. *See* Dağlarin kurdu Kocero, 1964
Koga Mansion. *See* Koga yashiki, 1949
Koga yashiki, 1949 (Kinugasa)
Koge, 1964 (Kinoshita)
Kohayagawa-ke no aki, 1961 (Ozu)
Kohlhiesels Töchter, 1920 (Lubitsch)
Koi, 1924 (Kinugasa)
Koi no katamichi kippu, 1960 (Shinoda)
Koi no Tokyo, 1932 (Gosho)
Koi to bushi, 1925 (Kinugasa)
Koibito, 1951 (Ichikawa)
Koko: A Talking Gorilla, 1978 (Schroeder)
Koko ni izumi ari, 1955 (Imai)
Kokoro, 1955 (Ichikawa)
Kokoro, 1973 (Shindo)
Kokoro no sanmyaku, 1966 (Yoshimura)
Kölcsönkért csecsemök, 1914 (Curtiz)
Kolejarskie słowo, 1953 (Munk)
Kolejnosc uczuc, 1993 (Zanussi)
Koli-Koli, 1966 (Rouch)
Kolibel 'naya, 1937 (Vertov)
Kome, 1957 (Imai)
Komedie om Geld, 1936 (Ophüls)
Komödianten, 1912 (Gad)
Komödianten, 1941 (Pabst)
Komödie der Leidenschaften, 1921 (Leni)
Komorní harmonie, 1963 (Schorm)
Komputery, 1967 (Zanussi)
Komsomol—Leader of Electrification. *See* K-SH-E, 1932
Komsomol—The Guide to Electrification. *See* K-SH-E, 1932
Komsomolsk, 1938 (Gerasimov)
Koncert, 1961 (Szabó)
Kondura/Anugrahan, 1977 (Benegal)
Konec jasnovidce, 1958 (Chytilová)
Koneč starych casu, 1989 (Menzel)
Kongen bød, 1938 (Henning-Jensen)
Kongres kombatantów, 1949 (Munk)
Koniec wojny, 1956 (Polanski)
Königin vom Moulin-Rouge, 1925 (Wiene)
Königskinder, 1949 (Käutner)
Konigsmark, 1936 (M. Tourneur)
Konjiki yasha, 1923 (Kinugasa)
Konketsuji Rika, 1973 (Yoshimura)
Konki, 1961 (Yoshimura)
Konkurs, 1963 (Forman)
Kono hiroi sora no dokoka ni, 1954 (Kobayashi)
Kono ko o nokoshite, 1983 (Kinoshita)
Kono ten no niji, 1958 (Kinoshita)
Konrad Albert Pocci, der Fussballgraf vom Ammerland—Das vorläufig letzte Kapitel einer Chronik der Familie Pocci, 1967 (Syberberg)
Konrad Albert Pocci, the Football Count from the Ammerland—Provisionally the Last Chapter of a Chronicle of the Pocci Family. *See* Konrad Albert Pocci, der Fussballgraf vom Ammerland—Das vorläufig letzte Kapitel einer Chronik der Familie Pocci, 1967
Konsequenz, 1977 (Petersen)
Konservanbraut, 1915 (Wiene)
Kontract, 1981 (Zanussi)
Kontsert masterov ukrainskogo iskusstva, 1952 (Barnet)
Konyakci, 1965 (Güney)
Konyaku yubiwa, 1950 (Kinoshita)
Konyets Sankt-Peterburga, 1927 (Pudovkin)
Ko-on, 1927 (Mizoguchi)
Kopytem Sem, Kopytem Tam, 1987 (Chytilová)
Korczak, 1990 (Holland, Wajda)
Korea, 1959 (Ford)
Körhinta, 1955 (Fábri)
Körkarlen, 1921 (Sjöström)
Korkuszlar, 1965 (Güney)
Korn, 1943 (Henning-Jensen)
Korol Lir, 1971 (Kozintsev)
Korol' Parizha, 1917 (Bauer, Kuleshov)
Kort är sommaren, 1962 (Henning-Jensen)
Koshiben gambare, 1931 (Naruse)
Koshikei, 1968 (Oshima)
Kotan no kuchibue, 1959 (Naruse)
Kotoshi no koi, 1962 (Kinoshita)
Koumiko Mystery. *See* Mystère Koumiko, 1965
Kourotchka Riaba, 1994 (Mikhalkov-Konchalovsky)
Kouzelna Praha Rudolfa II, 1982 (Jireš)
Kovboy Ali, 1966 (Güney)
Kozanoğlu, 1967 (Güney)
Közelrölia: a vér, 1965 (Jancsó)
Közös útan, 1953 (Jancsó)
Kraftmeier, 1916 (Lubitsch)
Krajina Shábytkem, 1987 (Schorm)
Krajobraz po bitwie, 1970 (Wajda)
Krák Králu, 1963 (Fric)
Král a žena, 1967 (Schorm)
Král Sumavy, 1959 (Kachyňa)
Kramer vs. Kramer, 1979 (Benton)
Krane's Bakery Shop. *See* Kranes Konditori, 1951
Kranes Konditori, 1951 (Henning-Jensen)
Krasnaya palatka, 1971 (Mikhalkov)
Krazha zreniya, 1934 (Kuleshov)
Kremlin Letter, 1970 (Huston, Welles)
Kreutzer Sonata, 1956 (Godard)
Kreuzer Emden, 1932 (Käutner)
Krieg und Frieden, 1983 (Kluge, Schlöndorff)
Kriemhild's Revenge. *See* Kriemhilds Rache, 1924
Kriemhilds Rache, 1924 (Lang)
Krig og Kaerlighed, 1914 (Holger-Madsen)
Krigens Fjende, 1915 (Holger-Madsen)
Krigs-korrespondenten, 1913 (Dreyer)
Krik, 1963 (Jireš)
Kris, 1946 (Bergman)
Kristián, 1939 (Fric)
Kristina Talking Pictures, 1976 (Rainer)
Kristinus Bergman, 1948 (Henning-Jensen)
Křivé zrcadlo, 1956 (Kachyňa)
Krok do tmy, 1938 (Fric)
Krónika, 1967 (Gaál)
Kronika jubileuszowa or Polska kronika filmowa nr 52 A-B, 1959 (Munk)
Kronika wypadków miłosnych, 1985 (Wajda)
Krótki dzień pracy, 1981 (Kieślowski)
Krótki film o milóści, 1988 (Kieślowski)

Lair of the White Worm, 1988 (Russell)
Laisen no zenya, 1943 (Yoshimura)
Laisse aller, c'est une valse, 1970 (Blier)
Lakharani, 1945 (Dutt)
Laliberté, 1987 (Lefebvre)
Lamb. *See* Lamm, 1964
Lamb, the Woman, the Wolf, 1914 (Dwan)
Lament for a Bandit. *See* Llanto por un bandido, 1964
Lamm, 1964 (Staudte)
Lamuru, 1933 (Gosho)
Lan Fengzheng, 1993 (Tian)
Lancelot du Luc, 1974 (Bresson)
Lancelot of the Lake. *See* Lancelot du Luc, 1974
Lancement d'un navire à La Ciotat, 1939 (Lumet)
Land, 1942 (Flaherty)
Land. *See* Ard, 1969
Land and Freedom, 1941 (Eisenstein)
Land and Freedom, 1995 (Loach)
Land Baron of San Tee, 1912 (Dwan)
Land before Time, 1988 (Lucas, Spielberg)
Land des Schweigens und der Dunkelheit, 1971 (Herzog)
Land in Anguish. *See* Terra em transe, 1967
Land in Trance. *See* Terra em transe, 1967
Land Is Forever Land. *See* Terra sempere terra, 1951
Land o' Lizards, 1916 (Borzage)
Land o' Lizards, 1922 (Borzage)
Land of Death, 1912 (Dwan)
Land of Desire. *See* Skepp till Indialand, 1947
Land of Fate. *See* Praesten i Vejlby, 1920
Land of Long Shadows, 1917 (W.S. Van Dyke)
Land of Mirages. *See* Délibábok országa, 1983
Land of Promise, 1945 (Rotha)
Land of Silence and Darkness. *See* Land des Schweigens und der Dunkelheit, 1971
Land of the Lawless, 1923 (Fejös)
Land of the Pharaohs, 1955 (Hawks)
Land of the Soviets. *See* Strana Sovietov, 1937
Land of Water, 1940 (Pearson)
Land of White Alice, 1959 (Willard Van Dyke)
Land Salesman, 1913 (Sennett)
Land Thieves, 1911 (Dwan)
Land without Bread. *See* Hurdes—Tierra sin pan, 1932
Landlady, 1938 (Boulting)
Landlord, 1970 (Ashby, Jewison)
Landlord's Troubled, 1913 (Sennett)
Landru, 1963 (Chabrol, Melville)
Landsbykirken, 1947 (Dreyer)
Landscape after the Battle. *See* Krajobraz po bitwie, 1970
Landscape in the Mist. *See* Topio stia Omichli, 1988
Landscapes of Southern China. *See* Dél-Kína tájain, 1957
Lane That Had No Turning, 1922 (Fleming)
Långt Borta och Nara, 1976 (Donner)
Lanka Dahan, 1916/17 (Phalke)
Lankshövdingens dottrar, 1916 (Sjöström)
Lantern Under a Full Moon. *See* Meigatsu somato, 1951
Lanterne magique, 1903 (Méliès)
Lanton Mills, 1969 (Malick)
Laos, the Forgotten War. *See* Guerra olvidados, 1967
Laputa, 1986 (Sanders-Brahms)
Larceny, Inc., 1942 (Bacon)
Largest Boat Ever Launched Sidewalks, 1913 (Sennett)
Larks on a String. *See* Skřivánci na niti, 1969
Las Vegas Story, 1952 (Stevenson)
Láska, 1972 (Kachyňa)
Láska mezi kapkami deště, 1979 (Kachyňa)
Lásky jedné plavovlásky, 1965 (Forman)
Lass from the Stormy Croft. *See* Tösen från stormyrtorpet, 1918
Lasse-Maja, 1941 (Zetterling)
Last Adventure of Arsène Lupin. *See* Arsén Lupin utolsó kalandja, 1921
Last Adventure of the Skeleton's Hand. *See* Juvelerernes Skrœk, eller Skelethaanden, eller Skelethaandens sidste bedrift, 1915
Last Aristocrats, 1989 (Xie)
Last Betrothal. *See* Dernières Fiançailles, 1973
Last Bohemian. *See* Az utolsó bohém, 1912
Last Bolshevik. *See* Dernier Bolchevik, 1993
Last Butterfly, 1990 (Kachyňa)
Last Call from Passenger Faber, 1991 (Schlöndorff)
Last Castle. *See* Echoes of a Summer, 1975
Last Command, 1928 (Hathaway, Von Sternberg)
Last Couple Out. *See* Sista paret ut, 1956
Last Coupon, 1932 (Launder)
Last Dance, 1991 (Zanussi)
Last Dance. *See* Daibyonin, 1995
Last Dawn. *See* Az utolsó hajnal, 1917
Last Day of the War. *See* Ultimo dia de la guerra, 1969
Last Days of Chez Nous, 1992 (Armstrong)
Last Days of Gomorrah. *See* Letzten tage von Gomorrah, 1974
Last Days of Pompeii, 1935 (Schoedsack)
Last Days of Pompeii. *See* Derniers Jours de Pompéi, 1948
Last Days of Pompeii. *See* Gli ultimi giorni di Pompeii, 1959
Last Deal, 1909 (Griffith)
Last Detail, 1973 (Ashby)
Last Drink of Whiskey, 1914 (Browning)
Last Drop of Water, 1911 (Griffith, Sennett)
Last Embrace, 1979 (Demme)
Last Emperor, 1987 (Bertolucci)
Last Five Minutes. *See* Gli ultimi cinque minuti, 1955
Last Flight, 1931 (Dieterle)
Last Frontier, 1955 (A. Mann)
Last Gangster. *See* Roger Touhy, Gangster, 1943
Last Goal. *See* Két Félidő a pokolban, 1961
Last Hour, 1930 (Launder)
Last House on the Left, 1973 (Craven)
Last Hunt, 1956 (Brooks)
Last Hurrah, 1958 (Ford)
Last Hurrah for Chivalry, 1978 (Woo)
Last Hustle in Brooklyn, 1977 (S. Lee)
Last Laugh. *See* Der Letzte Mann, 1924
Last Man to Hang?, 1956 (Fisher, Schlesinger)
Last Metro. *See* Dernier Metro, 1980
Last Moment, 1928 (Fejös)
Last Movie, 1971 (Fuller)
Last Movie. *See* Splendor, 1989
Last Notch, 1911 (Dwan)
Last of England, 1987 (Jarman)
Last of Mrs. Cheyney, 1937 (Arzner)
Last of Sheila, 1972 (Schumacher)
Last of the Mobile Hot Shots, 1970 (Lumet)
Last of the Mohicans, 1920 (Brown, M. Tourneur)
Last of the Mohicans, 1992 (M. Mann)
Last Outlaw, 1919 (Ford)
Last Page, 1952 (Fisher)
Last Pair Out. *See* Sista paret ut, 1956
Last Party, 1993 (S. Lee, Stone)
Last Performance, 1929 (Fejös)
Last Picture Show, 1971 (Bogdanovich, Rafelson)
Last Round-Up, 1934 (Hathaway)
Last Run, 1971 (Fleischer, Huston)
Last Safari, 1967 (Hathaway)
Last Seduction, 1994 (Dahl)
Last Shot. *See* Poslední výstřel, 1950
Last Stage. *See* Ostatni etap, 1947
Last Stand, 1938 (Joseph H. Lewis)
Last Sunset, 1961 (Aldrich)
Last Supper. *See* Última cena, 1976
Last Tango in Paris, 1972 (Bertolucci, Varda)
Last Temptation of Christ, 1988 (Schrader, Scorsese)
Last Ten Days. *See* Der Letzte Akt, 1955
Last Time I Saw Paris, 1954 (Brooks)
Last Train from Gun Hill, 1959 (J. Sturges)
Last Tycoon, 1976 (Kazan)
Last Wagon, 1956 (Daves)

Last Waltz, 1978 (Scorsese)
Last Warning, 1929 (Leni)
Last Wave, 1977 (Weir)
Last Will of Dr. Mabuse. *See* **Testament des Dr. Mabuse**, 1933
Last Witness. *See* Der letzte Zeuge, 1960
Last Woman. *See* Ultima donna, 1976
Last Woman on Earth, 1958 (Corman, Hellman)
Last Word, 1979 (Boulting)
Last Words. *See* Letzte Worte, 1968
Last Year at Marienbad. *See* **Année dernière à Marienbad**, 1961
Late Autumn. *See* Akibiyori, 1960
Late Chrysanthemums. *See* Bangiku, 1954
Late George Apley, 1947 (Mankiewicz)
Late Great Planet Earth, 1979 (Welles)
Late Lamented, 1917 (Sennett)
Late Mathias Pascal. *See* **Feu Mathias Pascal**, 1925
Late Season. *See* Utószezon, 1967
Late Show, 1977 (Altman, Benton)
Late Spring. *See* **Banshun**, 1949
Latest from Paris, 1928 (S. Wood)
Latest in Life Saving, 1913 (Sennett)
Latin Lovers, 1953 (LeRoy)
Latino Bar, 1990 (Leduc)
Läufer von Marathon, 1933 (Dupont)
Laugh and Get Rich, 1931 (La Cava)
Laugh and the World Laughs. *See* Habit of Happiness, 1916
Laughing Boy, 1934 (W.S. Van Dyke)
Laughing Gas, 1907 (Porter)
Laughing Gas, 1914 (Chaplin, Sennett)
Laughing Irish Eyes, 1936 (Joseph H. Lewis)
Laughing Saskia. *See* Nevető Szaszkia, 1916
Laughing Times, 1981 (Woo)
Laughter in the Dark, 1969 (Richardson)
Laukaus Tehtaalla, 1973 (Donner)
Laundromat, 1985 (Altman)
Laura, 1944 (Preminger)
Lausbubengeschichten, 1964 (Käutner)
Lauter Lügen, 1950 (Staudte)
Lavatori della pietra, 1955-59 (Taviani)
Lavatory moderne, 1900/01 (Guy)
Lavender Hill Mob, 1951 (Crichton)
Laveuses, 1896-97 (Lumet)
Laviamoci il cervello. *See* RoGoPaG, 1962
Law and Disorder, 1958 (Crichton)
Law and Jake Wade, 1958 (J. Sturges)
Law and Order, 1969 (Wiseman)
Law of Desire. *See* Ley del deseo, 1986
Law of God, 1912 (Dwan)
Law of Smuggling. *See* Hudutlarin kanunu, 1966
Law of the Land, 1917 (M. Tourneur)
Law of the Lawless, 1923 (Fleming)
Lawful Holdup, 1911 (Dwan)
Lawful Larceny, 1923 (Dwan)
Lawine, 1923 (Curtiz)
Lawless, 1950 (Losey)
Lawless Breed, 1952 (Walsh)
Lawless Land, 1987 (Corman)
Lawless Rider, 1952 (E. Wood)
Lawless Street, 1955 (Joseph H. Lewis)
Lawrence of Arabia, 1962 (Lean, Roeg)
Lawyer Man, 1933 (Dieterle)
Laxdale Hall, 1952 (Grierson)
Lay Down Your Arms. *See* Ned med Vaabnene, 1914
Lazy Lightning, 1926 (Wyler)
Lazybones, 1925 (Borzage)
Lazybones, 1935 (Powell)
Lea Lyon. *See* Lyon Lea, 1915
Leaden Times. *See* **Bleierne Zeit**, 1981
Leader, 1964 (Conner)
Leading Lizzie Astray, 1914 (Sennett)
Leading Man, 1911 (Sennett)
League of Gentlemen, 1959 (Dearden)
League of Their Own, 1992 (Marshall)
Leak in the Foreign Office, 1914 (Cruze)
Léanyportre, 1971 (Szabó)
Leap into the Void, 1980 (Bellocchio)
Leap Year, 1922 (Cruze)
Leap Year Cowboy, 1912 (Dwan)
Leapfrog as Seen by the Frog, 1900 (Hepworth)
Learn from Experience, Parts I, II. *See* Kafuku I, II, 1937
Learning Modules for Rural Children, 1974/5 (Benegal)
Leather Gloves, 1948 (Edwards)
Leather Stockings, 1909 (Griffith)
Leave 'em Laughing, 1928 (Stevens)
Leave Her to Heaven, 1946 (Stahl)
Leave It to Me. *See* Nechte to na mně, 1955
Leave It to Smiley, 1914 (Browning)
Leavenworth Case, 1936 (Joseph H. Lewis)
Leaves from Satan's Book. *See* Blade af Satans Bog, 1921
Leben von Adolf Hitler, 1961 (Rotha)
Leben—ein Traum, 1917 (Wiene)
Lebende Buddhas, 1924 (Ruttmann)
Lebende Tote, 1919 (Wiene)
Lebender Schatten. *See* Der Schatten, 1918
Lebenskünstler, 1925 (Holger-Madsen)
Lebenszeichen, 1967 (Herzog)
Leçon de bicyclette, 1896-97 (Lumet)
Leçon de danse, 1897 (Guy)
Leçon de danse, 1900 (Guy)
Leçons de boxe, 1898/99 (Guy)
Lecture quotidienne, 1900/01 (Guy)
Lecumberri, 1976 (Ripstein)
Leda. *See* Double tour, 1959
Ledolom, 1931 (Barnet)
Lefayette Escradille, 1958 (Eastwood)
Left Hand of God, 1955 (Dmytryk)
Left-Handed Gun, 1958 (Penn)
Left, Right and Centre, 1959 (Launder)
Legacy. *See* Dedictvi aneb Kurvahosigutntag, 1992
Legal Eagles, 1986 (Redford)
Legand Hall Bombing, 1978 (Joffé)
Legato, 1977 (Gaál)
Legend, 1985 (Scott)
Legend of a Duel to the Death. *See* Shito no densetsu, 1963
Legend of Lylah Clare, 1968 (Aldrich)
Legend of Provence, 1914 (Cruze)
Legend of the Holy Drinker. *See* Leggenda del santo bevitore, 1988
Legend of the Lost, 1957 (Hathaway)
Legend of the Mountain. *See* Shan Chung Ch'uan Chi, 1978
Legend of the Suram Fortress. *See* Legenda o Suramskoj kreposti, 1985
Legend of Tianyun Mountain, 1981 (Xie)
Legenda o Suramskoj kreposti, 1985 (Paradzhanov)
Legende von Sünde und Strafe. *See* Sodom und Gomorrah: Part 1. Die Sünde, 1922
Legende von Sünde und Strafe. *See* Sodom und Gomorrah: Part II. Die Strafe, 1923
Légende de l'arc-en-ciel, 1909 (Gance)
Légende de la fileuse, 1907 (Feuillade)
Légende de Rip van Winkle, 1905 (Méliès)
Légende de Sainte Ursule, 1948 (Cocteau)
Légende des phares, 1909 (Feuillade)
Legge, 1959 (Dassin)
Leggenda del santo bevitore, 1988 (Olmi)
Legion Condor, 1950 (Staudte)
Legion of Death, 1918 (Browning)
Legion of the Condemned, 1928 (Wellman)
Legion of the Damned, 1969 (Argento)
Lehrer im Wandel, 1963 (Kluge)
Leibgardist, 1925 (Wiene)
Lek pa regnbagen, 1958 (Zetterling)
Lekcja anatomii. *See* Anatomie stunde, 1977
Lekkamraterna, 1914 (Stiller)

Life-Bringing Water. *See* Eltető Tisza-víz, 1954
Life for a Kiss, 1912 (Dwan)
Life for a Life. *See* Zhizn' za Zhizn', 1916
Life for a Life. *See* Zycie Za Zycie, 1991
Life for Ruth, 1962 (Dearden)
Life Goes On. *See* Az élet megy tovább, 1959
Life in Sometown, U.S.A., 1938 (Keaton)
Life in the Balance, 1913 (Sennett)
Life is Rising from the Ruins, 1945 (Kadár)
Life Is a Bed of Roses. *See* Vie est un roman, 1983
Life Is Like a Somersault. *See* Jinsei tonbo-gaeri, 1946
Life Is Sweet, 1990 (Leigh)
Life Line, 1919 (M. Tourneur)
Life Love Death. *See* Vie, l'amour, la mort, 1968
Life of a Communist Writer. *See* Kobayashi Takiji, 1974
Life of a Cowboy, 1906 (Porter)
Life of a Film Director: Record of Kenji Mizoguchi. *See* Aru eiga-kantoku no shogai: Mizoguchi Kenji no kiroku, 1975
Life of a London Shopgirl, 1914 (Goulding)
Life of a Mother. *See* Historien om en Moder, 1912
Life of a Woman, 1953 (Shindo)
Life of Adolf Hitler. *See* Leben von Adolf Hitler, 1961
Life of an American Fireman, 1903 (Porter)
Life of an American Policeman, 1905 (Porter)
Life of an Office Worker. *See* Kaisha-in seikatsu, 1929
Life of Chikuzan. *See* Chikuzan hitori-tabi, 1977
Life of Emile Zola, 1937 (Dieterle)
Life of General Villa, 1912 (Walsh)
Life of Her Own, 1950 (Cukor)
Life of Juanita Castro, 1965 (Warhol)
Life of Lord Roberts VC, 1914 (Pearson)
Life of Luxury. *See* Hidari uchiwa, 1935
Life of Moses, 1909/10 (Blackton)
Life of Oharu. *See* **Saikaku ichidai onna**, 1952
Life of Reilly, 1923 (La Cava)
Life of the Molds, 1957 (Willard Van Dyke)
Life Signs. *See* Eletjel, 1954
Life Size. *See* Tamaño natural, 1973
Life Stinks!, 1991 (Brooks)
Life Story. *See* Życiorys, 1975
Life Was at Stake. *See* Hra o život, 1956
Life with Father, 1947 (Curtiz)
Life with Henry, 1941 (Niblo)
Lifelines, 1960 (Emshwiller)
Lifers Group: World Tour, 1992 (Spheeris)
Life's Harmony, 1916 (Borzage)
Light Ahead. *See* Tlatsche, 1939
Light Fantastic. *See* Love Is Better Than Ever, 1952
Light Fantastic, 1960 (Russell)
Light in the Dark, 1922 (Brown)
Light of Day, 1987 (Schrader)
Light of Western Stars, 1925 (Howard)
Light Sleeper, 1992 (Schrader)
Light Snack, 1975 (Leigh)
Light that Came, 1909 (Griffith)
Light That Failed, 1939 (Wellman)
Light Touch, 1951 (Brooks)
Light Years Away. *See* Années lumière, 1981
Lighter Burden, 1913 (Pearson)
Lighthouse. *See* Yorokobi mo kanashimi mo ikutoshitsuki, 1957
Lighthouse Love, 1932 (Sennett)
Lightnin', 1925 (Ford)
Lightnin', 1930 (King)
Lightning, 1927 (Stevens)
Lightning. *See* Inazuma, 1952
Lightning Over Water, 1981 (Jarmusch, N. Ray, Wenders)
Lightning Strikes Twice, 1951 (K. Vidor)
Lights from Circus Life. *See* Det store Hjerte, 1924
Lights of Night. *See* Nishi Ginza eki mae, 1958
Lightship, 1985 (Skolimowski)
Ligne de démarcation, 1966 (Chabrol)
Like a Bird on a Wire. *See* Wie ein Vogel auf dem Draht, 1974
Like Most Wives, 1914 (Weber)
Likely Stories, Volume 1, 1990 (Reiner)
Li'l Abner, 1940 (Keaton)
Li'l Abner, 1960 (Jerry Lewis)
Lili, 1953 (Walters)
Lili Marleen, 1980 (Fassbinder)
Lilies of the Field, 1930 (Korda)
Liliom, 1919 (Curtiz)
Liliom, 1930 (Borzage)
Liliom, 1934 (Lang)
Lilith, 1964 (Rossen)
Lilith und Ly, 1919 (Lang)
Lille Chauffør, 1914 (Blom)
Lille Cirkus, 1984 (Roos)
Lilliputian Minuet. *See* Menuet lilliputien, 1905
Lily of the Tenements, 1910 (Griffith)
Lily Turner, 1933 (Wellman)
Lily's Lovers, 1911 (Sennett)
Limbo, 1972 (Silver)
Limelight, 1952 (Aldrich, Chaplin, Keaton)
Lina Pod Ekspertizoi ili Buinyi Pokoinik, 1917 (Bauer)
Lina Under Examination. *See* Lina Pod Ekspertizoi ili Buinyi Pokoinik, 1917
Lina's Adventure in Sochi. *See* PriklyuchenieLiny v Sochi, 1916
Lincoln Cycle, 1917 (Stahl)
Line, 1969 (Rainer)
Line Cruising South, 1933 (Grierson)
Line of Demarcation. *See* Ligne de démarcation, 1966
Line of Destiny. *See* Rekava, 1956
Line of Life. *See* Rekava, 1956
Line to Tschierva Hut, 1937 (Cavalcanti, Grierson)
Line-Up, 1958 (Siegel)
Liner Cruising South, 1933 (Wright)
Lines of White on the Sullen Sea, 1909 (Griffith)
Liolà, 1964 (Blasetti)
Lion and the Girl, 1916 (Sennett)
Lion and the House, 1932 (Sennett)
Lion and the Mouse, 1928 (Bacon)
Lion and the Souse, 1924 (Sennett)
Lion des Mogols, 1924 (Epstein)
Lion Has Seven Heads. *See* Der leone have sept cabecas, 1970
Lion Has Wings, 1939 (Powell)
Lion Hunters. *See* Chasse au lion à l'arc, 1965
Lion in the Streets, 1953 (Walsh)
Lion nommé l'Américain, 1968 (Rouch)
Lion savant, 1902 (Guy)
Lion with the White Mane. *See* Lev s bílou hřívou, 1987
Lionheart, 1987 (Schaffner)
Lion's Love, 1969 (Bogdanovich, Clarke, Varda)
Lion's Roar, 1928 (Sennett)
Lion's Whiskers, 1925 (Sennett)
Liqueur du couvent, 1903 (Guy)
Lisant le journal, 1932 (Cavalcanti)
Lisboa Cultural, 1983 (Oliveira)
Lisbon Story, 1995 (Wenders)
Lisetta, 1933 (De Sica)
List of Adrian Messenger, 1963 (Huston)
Listen to Britain, 1942 (Jennings)
Listening In, 1932 (Sennett)
Listopad, 1966 (Ioseliani)
Lisztomania, 1975 (Russell)
Lit à deux places, 1965 (Delannoy)
Little American, 1917 (De Mille)
Little Angels of Luck, 1910 (Griffith)
Little Big Man, 1970 (Penn)
Little Big Shot, 1935 (Curtiz)
Little Billy Triumphs, 1914 (Sennett)
Little Billy's City Cousin, 1914 (Sennett)
Little Billy's Strategy, 1914 (Sennett)
Little Bricks. *See* Kirpitchiki, 1925
Little Brother. *See* Bratichka, 1927

Love and Pledge. *See* Ai to chikai, 1945
Love and Rubbish, 1913 (Sennett)
Love and Salt Water, 1914 (Sennett)
Love and Separation in Sri Lanka. *See* Suri Lanka no ai to wakare, 1976
Love and the Devil, 1929 (Korda)
Love and the Frenchwoman. *See* Française et l'amour, 1960
Love and War. *See* Krig og Kaerlighed, 1914
Love at First Sight, 1928 (Sennett)
Love at Large, 1989 (Rudolph)
Love at Twenty. *See* Amour à vingt ans, 1962
Love Between the Raindrops. *See* Láska mezi kapkami deště, 1979
Love Bug, 1969 (Stevenson)
Love Burglar, 1919 (Cruze)
Love by the Light of the Moon, 1901 (Porter)
Love Cage, 1964 (Clement)
Love Comet, 1916 (Sennett)
Love Film. *See* Szerelmesfilm, 1970
Love Finds a Way, 1908 (Griffith)
Love Flower, 1920 (Griffith)
Love Happy, 1948 (Tashlin)
Love Has Tomorrow. *See* Ai Yu Ming T'ien, 1976
Love, Honor, and Behave, 1920 (Sennett)
Love in a Hammock, 1901 (Porter)
Love in a Police Station, 1927 (Sennett)
Love in an Apartment Hotel, 1912 (Griffith)
Love in Armor, 1915 (Sennett)
Love in Germany. *See* Liebe in Deutschland, 1983
Love in Morocco. *See* Baroud, 1931
Love in Rome. *See* Amore a Roma, 1960
Love in the Afternoon, 1957 (Wilder)
Love in the City. *See* Amore in città, 1953
Love in the Hills, 1911 (Griffith)
Love in the Tropics. *See* Tropisk Kaerlighed, 1911
Love in Tokyo. *See* Koi no Tokyo, 1932
Love is a Racket, 1932 (Wellman)
Love is Blind, 1913 (Dwan)
Love Is a Funny Thing. *See* Homme qui me plaît, 1969
Love Is a Many-Splendored Thing, 1955 (King)
Love Is Better Than Ever, 1952 (Donen)
Love Is Blind, 1909 (Porter)
Love Is Blind. *See* Kaerlighed gør blind, 1912
Love Is Colder than Death. *See* Liebe ist kälter als der Tod, 1969
Love Is My Profession. *See* En Cas de malheur, 1958
Love Is News, 1937 (Garnett)
Love Is Strength. *See* Ai wa chikara da, 1930
Love Letters, 1945 (Dieterle)
Love Letters, 1984 (Corman)
Love Life and Laughter, 1923 (Pearson)
Love, Live and Laugh, 1929 (Howard)
Love Loops the Loop, 1918 (Sennett)
Love, Loot and Crash, 1915 (Sennett)
Love Lottery, 1953 (Crichton)
Love Mask, 1916 (De Mille)
Love Me and the World Is Mine, 1927 (Dupont)
Love Me or Leave Me, 1955 (C. Vidor)
Love Me Tonight, 1932 (Mamoulian)
Love Nest, 1923 (Keaton)
Love Nest on Wheels, 1937 (Keaton)
Love Never Dies, 1921 (K. Vidor)
Love of Jeanne Ney. *See* Liebe der Jeanne Ney, 1927
Love of Sumako the Actress. *See* Joyu Sumako no koi, 1947
Love of the West, 1911 (Dwan)
Love Old and New. *See* Shamisen to otobai, 1961
Love on a Pillow. *See* Repos du guerrier, 1962
Love on Credit. *See* Kaerlighed pa kredit, 1955
Love on Skates, 1916 (Sennett)
Love on the Run, 1936 (Mankiewicz, W.S. Van Dyke)
Love on the Run. *See* Amour en fuite, 1979
Love on Toast, 1937 (Dupont)
Love on Wheels, 1932 (Saville)
Love One Another. *See* Gezeichneten, 1922
Love Parade, 1929 (Lubitsch)
Love Riot, 1916 (Sennett)
Love Ritual. *See* Carne, 1991
Love Root. *See* Mandragola, 1965
Love Route, 1915 (Dwan)
Love Should Be Guarded. *See* Asya, 1977
Love Sickness at Sea, 1913 (Sennett)
Love, Speed, and Thrills, 1915 (Sennett)
Love Storm. *See* Cape Forlorn, 1930
Love Story. *See* Douce, 1943
Love Streams, 1984 (Cassavetes)
Love Stronger Than Hatred. *See* Kärlek starkare än hat, 1914
Love Sublime, 1917 (Browning)
Love Sundae, 1926 (Sennett)
Love Test, 1935 (Powell)
Love That Lives. *See* Det Største i Verden, 1919
Love That Whirls, 1949 (Anger)
Love the Magician. *See* Amor brujo, 1985
Love Thief, 1914 (Sennett)
Love Thy Neighbor, 1984 (Marshall)
Love Trap, 1929 (Wyler)
Love Undefeated: Conversations with Derek Jarman, 1993 (Jarman)
Love Will Conquer, 1916 (Sennett)
Love Will Conquer. *See* Kärleken segrar, 1949
Love Will Find a Way, 1908 (Porter)
Love with the Proper Stranger, 1963 (Mulligan, Pakula)
Loveable Cheat, 1949 (Keaton)
Loved By Two. *See* Akit ketten szeretnek, 1915
Loved One, 1965 (Ashby, Richardson)
Lovely Flute and Drum. *See* Natsukashiki fue ya taiko, 1967
Lovely to Look At, 1952 (LeRoy, Minnelli)
Lovemaker. *See* Calle Mayor, 1956
Lovemaking, 1968 (Brakhage)
Lover. *See* Koibito, 1951
Lover. *See* Ai-jin, 1953
Lover and His Lass, 1975 (Hallstrom)
Lover's Call. *See* Nedaa el Ochak, 1961
Lover's Lost Control, 1915 (Sennett)
Lover's Luck, 1914 (Sennett)
Loverboy, 1990 (Silver)
Lovers?, 1927 (Stahl)
Lovers. *See* Amants, 1958
Lovers' Council. *See* Liebeskonzil, 1982
Lovers, Happy Lovers, 1954 (Clement)
Lovers Must Learn. *See* Rome Adventure, 1962
Lovers' Post Office, 1914 (Sennett)
Love's Berry. *See* Yahidka kokhannya, 1926
Love's Boomerang. *See* Perpetua, 1922
Love's Crucible. *See* Vem dömer, 1922
Love's Devotee. *See* Elskovsleg, 1913
Love's False Faces, 1919 (Sennett)
Love's Intrigue, 1924 (Sennett)
Love's Languid Lure, 1927 (Sennett)
Love's Last Laugh, 1926 (Sennett)
Love's Miracle, 1912 (Cruze)
Loves of a Blonde. *See* **Lásky jedné plavovlásky,** 1965
Loves of a Dictator. *See* Dictator, 1935
Loves of Carmen, 1927 (Walsh)
Loves of Carmen, 1948 (C. Vidor)
Loves of Casanova. *See* Casanova, 1927
Loves of Isadora. *See* Isadora, 1968
Loves of Joanna Godden, 1947 (Hamer)
Loves of Omar Khayyam, 1957 (Dieterle)
Loves of Ondine, 1967 (Warhol)
Loves of Zero, 1927 (Florey)
Love's Option, 1928 (Dickinson, Pearson)
Love's Outcast, 1921 (Sennett)
Love's Sweet Piffle, 1924 (Sennett)
Lovesick, 1983 (Huston)
Lovin' Molly, 1974 (Lumet)
Loving, 1957 (Brakhage)

Loving Couples. *See* Alskande par, 1964
Loving Lies, 1924 (W.S. Van Dyke)
Lower Depths. *See* Bas-Fonds, 1936
Lower Depths. *See* Donzoko, 1957
Lowland. *See* Tiefland, 1944
Loyal 47 Ronin. *See* Chushingura, 1932
Loyal Soldier of Pancho Villa. *See* Dorado de Pancho Villa, 1967
Loyalties, 1933 (Dickinson)
Lu, a kokott, 1918 (Curtiz)
Lu, the Cocotte. *See* Lu, a kokott, 1918
Luanda ya no es de San Pablo, 1976 (Alvarez)
Lucette, 1924 (Feuillade)
Luch smerti, 1925 (Kuleshov, Pudovkin)
Luci del varieta, 1950 (Fellini, Lattuada)
Lucía, 1968 (Solas)
Luciano Serra, pilota, 1938 (Rossellini)
Lucien Leuwen, 1973 (Autant-Lara)
Lucifer Rising, 1974 (Anger)
Lucifer Rising, 1980 (Anger)
Lucille, 1912 (Cruze)
Lucille Love, the Girl of Mystery, 1914 (Ford)
Lúcio Flávio, 1978 (Babenco)
Luck o' the Foolish, 1924 (Capra, Sennett)
Luck of the Irish, 1920 (Dwan)
Lucky Dan, 1922 (Howard)
Lucky Horseshoe, 1911 (Sennett)
Lucky Jim, 1909 (Griffith)
Lucky Jim, 1957 (Boulting)
Lucky Lady, 1926 (Walsh)
Lucky Lady, 1975 (Donen)
Lucky Leap, 1915 (Sennett)
Lucky Legs, 1942 (Edwards)
Lucky Luciano. *See* Proposito Lucky Luciano, 1973
Lucky Man, 1994 (Anderson)
Lucky Number, 1933 (Asquith)
Lucky Partners, 1940 (Milestone)
Lucky Star, 1929 (Borzage)
Lucky Stars, 1925 (Capra, Sennett)
Lucky to Be a Woman. *See* Fortuna di essere donna, 1955
Lucky Toothache, 1910 (Sennett)
Lucky Transfer, 1915 (Browning)
Lucrèce Borgia, 1935 (Gance)
Ludwig, 1973 (Visconti)
Ludwig II—Glanz und Elend eines Königs, 1954 (Käutner)
Ludwig II—Requiem for a Virgin King. *See* Ludwig II—Requiem für einen jungfräulichen König, 1972
Ludwig II—Requiem für einen jungfräulichen König, 1972 (Syberberg)
Ludwig der Zweite, König von Bayern, 1930 (Dieterle)
Ludwig's Cook. *See* Theodor Hierneis oder: Wie man ehem. Hofkoch wird, 1972
Lugar sin Limites, 1977 (Ripstein)
Lui per lei, 1971 (Ferreri)
Lukrezia Borgia, 1922 (Dieterle)
Lullaby. *See* Kolibel 'naya, 1937
Lullaby of Hamagure. *See* Hamagure no komoriuta, 1973
Lulli ou le violon brisé, 1908 (Méliès)
Lulu, 1918 (Curtiz)
Lulu, 1967 (Leacock)
Lulu the Tool. *See* Classe operaia va in paradiso, 1971
Lumber Yard Gang, 1916 (Ford)
Lumiere and Company. *See* Lumiere et compagnie, 1995
Lumiere et compagnie, 1995 (Leconte, Sanders-Brahms)
Lumière d'été, 1943 (Grémillon)
Lumière et l'invention du cinématographe, 1953 (Gance)
Luna, 1979 (Bertolucci)
Luna de miel, 1956 (Powell)
Luna sleva, 1928 (Heifitz)
Lunch, 1899/1900 (Guy)
Lune à un mètre, 1898 (Méliès)
Lune des Lapins, 1950 (Anger)
Lung Men Fêng Yun, 1976 (King)
Lung Men K'o Chan, 1967 (King)
Lunga notte del '43, 1960 (Pasolini)
Lunga strada azzurra. *See* Grande strada azzurra, 1957
Lunga Vita alla Signora, 1987 (Olmi)
Lungo il fiume, 1992 (Olmi)
Lungo silenzio, 1993 (Von Trotta)
Lunkhead, 1929 (Sennett)
Lupa, 1953 (Lattuada)
Lupe, 1965 (Warhol)
Lure, 1914 (Guy)
Lure of the Gown, 1909 (Griffith)
Lure of the Jungle. *See* Paw, 1959
Lured, 1947 (Sirk)
Lust for Evil, 1959 (Clement)
Lust for Life, 1956 (Minnelli)
Lustgården, 1961 (Bergman)
Lustige Ehemann, 1919 (Lubitsch)
Lusty Men, 1952 (N. Ray)
Lutte, 1961 (Jutra)
Luttes en Italie. *See* Lotte in Italia, 1969
Lutteurs américains, 1903 (Guy)
Lyana, 1955 (Barnet)
Lyckonälen, 1915 (Stiller)
Lydia, 1918 (Dreyer, Holger-Madsen)
Lydia, 1941 (Duvivier)
Lydia Gilmore, 1916 (Porter)
Lying Lips, 1939 (Micheaux)
Lykkehjulet, 1926 (Gad)
Lykken, 1916 (Holger-Madsen)
Lynet, 1934 (Holger-Madsen)
Lynmouth, 1913 (Pearson)
Lyon, le regard intérieur, 1988 (Tavernier)
Lyon Lea, 1915 (Korda)
Lyon, place Bellecour, 1939 (Lumet)
Lyon, place des Cordeliers, 1939 (Lumet)
Lys de la Vie, 1920 (Clair)
Lyset i natten, 1953 (Roos)
Lysten styret. *See* Et Huskors, 1914
Lyubit cheloveka, 1972 (Gerasimov)
Lyubov' i nenavist', 1936 (Barnet)
Lyulya Bek, 1914 (Bauer)

M, 1931 (Lang)
M, 1951 (Aldrich, Losey)
M is for Man, Music, Mozart, 1991 (Greenaway)
M, Mörder unter Uns. *See* **M**, 1931
Ma and Pa, 1922 (Sennett)
Ma Cousine de Varsovie, 1931 (Clouzot)
Ma es holnap, 1912 (Curtiz)
Ma femme's appelle reviens, 1982 (Leconte)
Ma no ike, 1923 (Kinugasa)
Ma non è una cosa seria!, 1936 (De Sica)
Ma Nuit chez Maud, 1969 (Rohmer, Schroeder)
Ma Olsen, 1977 (Ward)
Maa, 1952 (Roy)
Maaneprinsessen, 1916 (Holger-Madsen)
Mabel and Fatty's Simple Life, 1915 (Sennett)
Mabel at the Wheel, 1914 (Chaplin, Sennett)
Mabel, Fatty and the Law, 1915 (Sennett)
Mabel Lost and Won, 1915 (Sennett)
Mabel's Adventures, 1912 (Sennett)
Mabel's and Fatty's Wash Day, 1915 (Sennett)
Mabel's Awful Mistake, 1913 (Sennett)
Mabel's Bare Escape, 1914 (Sennett)
Mabel's Blunder, 1914 (Sennett)
Mabel's Busy Day, 1914 (Chaplin, Sennett)
Mabel's Dramatic Career, 1913 (Sennett)
Mabel's Flirtation. *See* Her Friend the Bandit, 1914
Mabel's Heroes, 1913 (Sennett)
Mabel's Latest Prank, 1914 (Sennett)
Mabel's Lovers, 1912 (Sennett)

Mabel's Married Life, 1914 (Chaplin, Sennett)
Mabel's Nerve, 1914 (Sennett)
Mabel's New Hero, 1913 (Sennett)
Mabel's New Job, 1914 (Sennett)
Mabel's Stormy Love Affair, 1914 (Sennett)
Mabel's Strange Predicament, 1914 (Chaplin, Sennett)
Mabel's Strategem, 1912 (Sennett)
Mabel's Wilful Way, 1915 (Sennett)
Macadam, 1946 (Feyder)
Macao, 1943 (Delannoy)
Macao, 1951 (Von Sternberg)
Macao l'enfer, 1939 (Von Stroheim)
Macao, l'enfer du jeu, 1939 (Delannoy)
Macaroni. *See* Maccheroni, 1985
MacArthur's Children. *See* Setouchi Shonen Yakyudan, 1984
Macbeth, 1916 (Fleming, Von Stroheim)
Macbeth, 1948 (Welles)
Macbeth. *See* Makbet, 1969
Macbeth, 1971 (Schroeter)
Macbeth, 1972 (Polanski)
Maccheroni, 1985 (Scola)
Macchina ammazzacattivi, 1947 (Rossellini)
Machi no hitobito, 1926 (Gosho)
Machi to gesui, 1953 (Hani)
Machiboke no onna, 1946 (Shindo)
Machine, 1973 (Sanders-Brahms)
Machine à refaire la vie, 1924 (Duvivier)
Machine Age. *See* Kalyug, 1981
Machine Gun Kelly, 1958 (Corman)
Machine Gun McCain. *See* Gli Intoccabili, 1968
Machine of Eden, 1970 (Brakhage)
Machorka-Muff, 1963 (Straub)
Macht der Finsternis, 1923 (Wiene)
Macht der Gefühle, 1983 (Kluge)
Macht des Goldes, 1912 (Gad)
Maciste, 1915 (Pastrone)
Maciste alpino, 1916 (Pastrone)
Mack at it Again, 1914 (Sennett)
Mackintosh Man, 1973 (Huston, W. Hill)
Maclovia, 1948 (Fernández)
Maçons, 1905 (Guy)
Mad Cap. *See* Premi Pagal, 1933
Mad Doctor of Market Street, 1941 (Joseph H. Lewis)
Mad Dog and Glory, 1990 (Scorsese)
Mad Genius, 1931 (Curtiz)
Mad Little Island. *See* Rockets Galore, 1958
Mad Max, 1979 (G. Miller)
Mad Max II, 1981 (G. Miller)
Mad Max III: Beyond Thunderdome, 1985 (G. Miller)
Mad Sex. *See* Sesso matto, 1973
Mad Wednesday, 1947 (P. Sturges)
Madadayo, 1993 (Kurosawa)
Madame Bovary, 1934 (Becker, Renoir)
Madame Bovary, 1949 (Minnelli)
Madame Bovary, 1991 (Chabrol)
M. Butterfly, 1992/3 (Cronenberg)
Madame Curie, 1944 (LeRoy)
Madame De ..., 1953 (De Sica, Ophüls)
Madame de Thèbes, 1915 (Stiller)
Madame du Barry, 1934 (Dieterle)
Madame Pompadour, 1927 (Dupont)
Madame Q, 1929 (McCarey)
Madame Rex, 1911 (Griffith)
Madame Rosa. *See* Vie devant soi, 1977
Madame Sans Gène, 1909 (Blom)
Madame Satan, 1930 (De Mille)
Madame Sousatzka, 1988 (Schlesinger)
Madame Wants No Children. *See* Madame wünscht keine Kinder, 1926
Madame wünscht keine Kinder, 1926 (Korda)
Madame wünscht keine Kinder, 1933 (Wilder)
Madame X, 1937 (S. Wood)
Madamu to nyobo, 1931 (Gosho)
Madchen vom Moorhof, 1935 (Sirk)
Mädchen aus Flandern, 1956 (Käutner)
Mädchen ohne Vaterland, 1912 (Gad)
Maddalena, 1970 (Kawalerowicz)
Maddelena zero in condotta, 1941 (De Sica)
Made for Each Other, 1939 (Cromwell)
Made in Bangkok, 1991 (Joffé)
Made in Heaven, 1987 (Rudolph)
Made in Italy, 1965 (Scola)
Made in the Kitchen, 1921 (Sennett)
Made in U.S.A., 1966 (Godard)
Made Manifest, 1980 (Brakhage)
Mädel vom Ballett, 1918 (Lubitsch)
Madeleine, 1950 (Lean)
Madeleine und der Legionär, 1958 (Staudte)
Mademoiselle 100 millions, 1913 (M. Tourneur)
Mademoiselle, 1965 (Richardson)
Mademoiselle Docteur, 1936 (Pabst, Von Stroheim)
Mademoiselle Fifi, 1944 (Wise)
Mademoiselle France. *See* Reunion, 1942
Mademoiselle from Armentieres, 1926 (Saville)
Mademoiselle Gobette. *See* Presidentessa, 1952
Madhumati, 1958 (Roy)
Madigan, 1968 (Polonsky, Siegel)
Madman. *See* Fou, 1970
Madman in the Dark. *See* Krok do tmy, 1938
Mado, 1976 (Sautet)
Madol Duwa, 1976 (Peries)
Madone des sleepings, 1955 (Von Stroheim)
Madonna and Child, 1980 (Davies)
Madonna of Avenue A, 1929 (Curtiz)
Madriguera, 1969 (Saura)
Maestro di Vigevano, 1963 (Petri)
Maestro i Margerita, 1972 (Petrovic)
Maffia, 1972 (Torre Nilsson)
Mafia. *See* In nome della legge, 1949
Mafia. *See* Maffia, 1972
Mafioso, 1962 (Ferreri, Lattuada)
Magasiskola, 1970 (Gaál)
Magdalene, 1908 (Holger-Madsen)
Magellan, 1972 (Frampton)
Magellan: At the Gates of Death: Part I: The Red Gate, Part II: The Green Gate, 1976 (Frampton)
Maggie, 1954 (Mackendrick)
Maggie's First False Step, 1917 (Sennett)
Mágia, 1917 (Korda)
Magic. *See* Mágia, 1917
Magic Box, 1951 (Boulting)
Magic Christian, 1969 (Polanski)
Magic Fire, 1956 (Dieterle, Dupont)
Magic Flame, 1927 (Florey, King)
Magic Flute. *See* Trollflöjten, 1975
Magic Fountain Pen, 1909 (Blackton)
Magic Lantern. *See* Lanterne magique, 1903
Magic of the Diamond. *See* Magie du diamant, 1958
Magic Prague of Rudolph II. *See* Kouzelna Praha Rudolfa II, 1982
Magic Town, 1947 (Wellman)
Magic Voyage of Sinbad, 1962 (Coppola)
Magic Voyage of Sinbad, 1962 (Corman)
Magic Waltz. *See* Varázskeringö, 1918
Magic World. *See* Mundo mágico, 1966
Magician, 1926 (Ingram)
Magician. *See* Ansiktet, 1958
Magician. *See* Tarot, 1972
Magicians of the Silver Screen. *See* Báječni muži s klikou, 1979
Magicien, 1898 (Méliès)
Magiciens, 1975 (Chabrol)
Magiciens de Wanzerbé, 1948 (Rouch)
Magie du diamant, 1958 (Roos)
Magie noire, 1904 (Guy)

Magirama, 1956 (Gance)
Mágnás Miska, 1916 (Korda)
Magnet Laboratory, 1959 (Leacock)
Magnificent Ambersons, 1942 (Welles, Wise)
Magnificent Cuckold. *See* Magnifico cornuto, 1964
Magnificent Doll, 1946 (Borzage)
Magnificent Fraud, 1939 (Florey)
Magnificent Matador, 1955 (Boetticher)
Magnificent Obsession, 1935 (Stahl, Sirk)
Magnificent Seven, 1960 (J. Sturges)
Magnificent Showman. *See* Circus World, 1964
Magnificent Yankee, 1950 (J. Sturges)
Magnifico cornuto, 1964 (Scola)
Magnum Force, 1973 (Cimino, Eastwood)
Magokoro, 1939 (Naruse)
Magokoro, 1953 (Kobayashi)
Magot de Joséfa, 1964 (Autant-Lara)
Magpie Strategy. *See* Strategija svrake, 1987
Magyar föld ereje, 1916 (Curtiz)
Magyarok, 1977 (Fábri)
Magzat, 1993 (Meszaros)
Mahanagar, 1963 (S. Ray)
Mahaprithivi, 1992 (Scola)
Maharadjaens Yndlingshustru II, 1918 (Blom)
Mahiru no ankoku, 1956 (Imai)
Mahiru no enbukyoku, 1949 (Yoshimura)
Mahler, 1974 (Russell)
Maid and the Man, 1912 (Dwan)
Maid Mad, 1916 (Sennett)
Maiden and Men, 1912 (Dwan)
Maiden's Trust, 1917 (Sennett)
Maidstone, 1968 (Leacock)
Maigret et l'affaire Saint-Fiacre, 1958 (Delannoy)
Maigret tend un piège, 1957 (Delannoy)
Maihime, 1951 (Naruse)
Maihime, 1989 (Shinoda)
Main Attraction, 1962 (Zetterling)
Main du diable, 1942 (M. Tourneur)
Main du professeur Hamilton ou Le Roi des dollars, 1903 (Guy)
Main Event, 1927 (Howard)
Main Nashe Me Hoon, 1959 (Kapoor)
Main Street to Broadway, 1953 (Garnett)
Mainland. *See* Great Land, 1944
Mains négatives, 1978/79 (Duras)
Mains nettes, 1958 (Jutra)
Mainspring, 1917 (King)
Maison aux images, 1955 (Grémillon)
Maison de danses, 1931 (M. Tourneur)
Maison des bois, 1971 (Pialat)
Maison des lions, 1912 (Feuillade)
Maison sous les arbres, 1971 (Clement)
Maisons de la misère, 1937 (Storck)
Maitre Galip, 1962 (Pialat)
Maître de forges, 1933 (Gance)
Maître du temps, 1970 (Guerra)
Maîtres fous, 1954 (Rouch)
Maitresse, 1975 (Schroeder)
Major and the Minor, 1942 (Wilder)
Major Barbara, 1941 (Lean)
Major Dundee, 1965 (Peckinpah)
Majordome, 1964 (Delannoy)
Majority of One, 1961 (LeRoy)
Makbet, 1969 (Wajda)
Make Mine Laughs, 1949 (Fleischer)
Make Way for Tomorrow, 1937 (McCarey)
Makin' It, 1970 (Hitchcock)
Making a Film for Me Is Living, 1995 (Antonioni)
Making a Living, 1914 (Chaplin)
Making a Splash, 1984 (Greenaway)
Making A Living, 1914 (Sennett)
Making of a Man, 1911 (Griffith)
Making of an Automobile Tire, 1913 (Sennett)
Makioka Sisters. *See* Sasameyuki, 1983
Makkhetes, 1916 (Curtiz)
Maksimenko brigád, 1950 (Jancsó)
Makwayela, 1977 (Rouch)
Mal du siècle, 1953 (Lelouch)
Mala Noche, 1985 (Van Sant)
Mala the Magnificent. *See* Eskimo, 1933
Malá mořská víla, 1976 (Kachyňa)
Malade hydrophobe, 1900 (Méliès)
Malakhov Kurgan, 1944 (Heifitz)
Mälarpirater, 1923 (Molander)
Malchik i golub, 1961 (Mikhalkov-Konchalovsky)
Malcolm X, 1992 (S. Lee, Sayles)
Maldone, 1927 (Grémillon)
Maldoror, 1951/52 (Anger)
Male and Female, 1919 (De Mille)
Mâle du siècle, 1975 (Forman)
Maléfice, 1912 (Feuillade)
Malencontre, 1920 (Dulac)
Maleta, 1960 (Ruiz)
Malfray, 1948 (Resnais)
Malgache Adventure. *See* Aventure Malgache, 1944
Malheur n'arrive jamais seul, 1903 (Méliès)
Malheur qui passe, 1916 (Feuillade)
Malheurs de la guerre, 1962 (Storck)
Malia, 1945 (Castellani)
Malibran, 1944 (Cocteau, Guitry)
Malina, 1991 (Schroeter)
Mallarmé, 1964-69 (Rohmer)
Malombra, 1942 (Castellani)
Malpertius, 1972 (Welles)
Malquerida, 1949 (Fernández)
Maltese Falcon, 1941 (Huston)
Malvados, 1965 (Fernández)
Mam'zelle Bonaparte, 1941 (M. Tourneur)
Mama Behave, 1926 (McCarey)
Mama Loves Papa, 1931 (Stevens)
Mama Turns a Hundred. *See* Mamá cumple cien años, 1979
Mamá cumple cien años, 1979 (Saura)
Maman Colibri, 1929 (Duvivier)
Mambo, 1955 (Rossen)
Mamie Rose. *See* Det mørke Punkt, 1911
Mamma Roma, 1962 (Pasolini)
Mamma'a Affair, 1921 (Fleming)
Mammals. *See* Ssaki, 1962
Mammals of Victoria, 1994 (Brakhage)
Mammame, 1986 (Ruiz)
Mammo Kenkoku no Reimei, 1932 (Mizoguchi)
Mammy, 1930 (Curtiz)
Mammy Water, 1953 (Rouch)
Mammy's Rose, 1916 (Borzage)
Man, 1910 (Griffith)
Man, a Woman, and a Bank, 1979 (Mazursky)
Man and a Woman. *See* Homme et une femme, 1966
Man and a Woman: Twenty Years Later. *See* Homme et une femme: Vingt ans déja, 1986
Man and His World, 1967 (Vanderbeek)
Man and the Stars. *See* O homem das estrelas, 1971
Man and the Woman, 1908 (Griffith)
Man and the Woman, 1917 (Guy)
Man Behind the Mask, 1936 (Powell)
Man Between, 1953 (Reed)
Man Called Back, 1932 (Florey)
Man Called John. *See* ... e venne un uomo, 1965
Man Cannot Be Raped. *See* Manrape, 1978
Man die zijn Haar kort liet knippen. *See* Homme au crane rasé, 1966
Man-Eating Sharks, 1932 (Sennett)
Man for All Seasons, 1966 (Welles, Zinnemann)
Man for All That, 1915 (Walsh)
Man for Burning. *See* Uomo da bruciare, 1962

Marito povero, 1946 (De Sica)
Marius, 1931 (Korda, Pagnol)
Marizza, genannt die Schmuggler-Madonna, 1922 (Murnau)
Marja pieni!, 1972 (Donner)
Mark of the Vampire, 1935 (Browning)
Mark of Zorro, 1920 (Niblo)
Mark of Zorro, 1940 (Mamoulian)
Marked Man, 1917 (Ford)
Marked Men, 1919 (Ford)
Marked Time-table, 1910 (Griffith)
Marked Woman, 1937 (Bacon, Rossen)
Market Place. *See* Mandi, 1983
Markurells I Wadköping, 1931 (Sjöström)
Marmara hasan, 1968 (Güney)
Marnie, 1964 (Hitchcock)
Marooned, 1969 (J. Sturges)
Marquiese of O, 1975 (Schroeder)
Marquise d'O ..., 1976 (Rohmer)
Marquise of O .... *See* Marquise d'O ..., 1976
Marquise Von O, 1989 (Syberberg)
Marquitta, 1927 (Renoir)
Marriage. *See* Kekkon, 1947
Marriage. *See* Mariage, 1974
Marriage Agency. *See* Äktenskapsbrydån, 1913
Marriage Circle, 1924 (Lubitsch)
Marriage Circus, 1925 (Sennett)
Marriage Clause, 1926 (Weber)
Marriage, Italian Style. *See* Matrimonio all'italiana, 1964
Marriage License?, 1926 (Borzage)
Marriage of Convenience. *See* Børnevennerne, 1914
Marriage of Maria Braun. *See* **Ehe der Maria Braun,** 1978
Marriage of William Ashe, 1916 (Hepworth)
Marriage Ring, 1918 (Niblo)
Marriage Time. *See* Konki, 1961
Married for the First Time. *See* Vpervye zamuzhem, 1979
Married in Haste. *See* Jitney Elopement, 1915
Married Lady Borrows Money. *See* Okusama shakuyosho, 1936
Married Life, 1920 (Sennett)
Married Life. *See* Kekkon no seitai, 1941
Married to the Mob, 1988 (Demme)
Marry Me, 1925 (Cruze)
Marry Me, 1932 (Asquith)
Marry Me, 1949 (Fisher)
Marry Me Again, 1953 (Tashlin)
Marrying Kind, 1952 (Cukor)
Marseillaise. *See* Captain of the Guard, 1930
Marseillaise, 1938 (Becker, Renoir)
Marshal of Reno, 1944 (Edwards)
Martha, 1973 (Fassbinder)
Martha und Ich, 1990 (Weiss)
Marthe Richard, 1936 (Von Stroheim)
Martin, 1977 (Romero)
Martin Andersen Nexos sidste rejse, 1954 (Roos)
Martin Fierro, 1968 (Torre Nilsson)
Martin Missil Quarterly Reports, 1957 (Brakhage)
Martin of the Mounted, 1926 (Wyler)
Martin Soldat, 1966 (C. Miller)
Martyr of the Garden of the Pear Trees, 1949 (Xie)
Martyre de l'Obèse, 1932 (L'Herbier)
Martyred Presidents, 1901 (Porter)
Martyrs of Love. *See* Mučedníci lásky, 1967
Marusa no onna, 1987 (Itami)
Marusa no onna II, 1988 (Itami)
Marvellous Wreath. *See* Guirlande merveilleuse, 1903
Mary Ann, 1918 (Korda)
Mary Burns, Fugitive, 1935 (Howard)
Mary find the Gold, 1921 (Pearson)
Mary, Mary, 1963 (LeRoy)
Mary of Scotland, 1936 (Ford)
Mary of the Movies, 1923 (Ingram)
Mary Poppins, 1964 (Stevenson)
Mary Regan, 1919 (Weber)
Mary Shelley's Frankenstein, 1994 (Branagh, Coppola)
Mary, Sir John greift ein! *See* Murder, 1930
Mary Stevens M.D., 1933 (Bacon)
Marya Sklodowska-Curie. Ein Mädchen, das die Welt verändert, 1972 (Staudte)
Maryland, 1940 (King)
Mascot, 1914 (Browning)
Mascot of Troop 'C', 1911 (Guy)
Masculin-féminin, 1966 (Godard)
Masculin féminin: quinze faits précis. *See* Masculin-féminin, 1966
M*A*S*H, 1970 (Altman)
Masher, 1910 (Sennett)
Mask, 1984 (Bogdanovich)
Mask of Dijon, 1945 (Von Stroheim)
Mask of Dust, 1954 (Fisher)
Mask of Fu Manchu, 1932 (C. Vidor)
Maske, 1919 (Dupont)
Maske fällt, 1930 (Dieterle)
Masked Bride, 1925 (Florey, Von Sternberg)
Masked Mamas, 1926 (Sennett)
Masks of the Devil, 1928 (Sjöström)
Masque d'horreur, 1912 (Gance)
Masque of the Red Death, 1964 (Corman, Roeg)
Masque of the Red Death, 1989 (Corman)
Masquerade, 1941 (Gerasimov)
Masquerade, 1964 (Dearden)
Masquerader, 1914 (Chaplin, Sennett)
Masques, 1986 (Chabrol)
Mass for the Dakota Sioux, 1964 (Baillie)
Mass Is Ended. *See* Massa e finita, 1985
Mass Production of Eggs. *See* Nagyüzemi tojástermelés, 1962
Massa e finita, 1985 (Moretti)
Massacre, 1912 (Griffith)
Massacre Hill. *See* Eureka Stockade, 1949
Massnahmen gegen Fanatiker, 1968 (Herzog)
Master. *See* Det röda tornet, 1914
Master and Margaret. *See* Maestro i Margerita, 1972
Master Mind, 1914 (De Mille)
Master of Bankdam, 1947 (Fisher)
Master of Love. *See* Der Herr der Liebe, 1919
Master of the House. *See* Du Skal Aere Din Hustru, 1925
Master of the Vineyard, 1911 (Dwan)
Master Samuel. *See* Mästerman, 1920
Master Zoard. *See* Zoárd Mester, 1917
Mästerman, 1920 (Sjöström)
Masters of the Sea. *See* Heeren der Meere, 1922
Masters of Ukrainian Art in Concert. *See* Kontsert masterov ukrainskogo iskusstva, 1952
Mästertjuven, 1915 (Stiller)
Mastery of the Sea, 1941 (Cavalcanti)
Mastery of the Sea, 1941 (Hamer)
Mat, 1926 (Pudovkin)
Mat, 1956 (Donskoi)
Mata au hi made, 1932 (Ozu)
Mata au hi made, 1950 (Imai)
Matador, 1986 (Almodóvar)
Matatabi, 1973 (Ichikawa)
Match Factory Girl. *See* Tulitikkutehtaan Tytto, 1990
Match Play, 1929 (Sennett)
Matches, 1913 (Dwan)
Matchless, 1966 (Lattuada)
Matchmaker. *See* Yeuh Hsia Lao Jen, 1975
Matchmaking Mamas, 1929 (Sennett)
Mate of the Sally Ann, 1917 (King)
Matelas alcoolique, 1906 (Guy)
Mater Dolorosa, 1910 (Feuillade)
Mater Dolorosa, 1917 (Gance)
Mater Dolorosa, 1932 (Gance)
Materi i docheri, 1974 (Gerasimov)
Matewan, 1987 (Sayles)

Matières nouvelles, 1964 (Storck)
Matinee, 1992 (Sayles)
Matinee Idol, 1928 (Capra)
Mating Call, 1928 (Cruze)
Matins, 1988 (Brakhage)
Matira Manisha, 1967 (Sen)
Matisse, or The Talent for Happiness, 1960 (Ophuls)
Matka Joanna od Aniolów, 1961 (Kawalerowicz)
Matrimaniac, 1916 (Fleming)
Matrimonial Bed, 1930 (Curtiz)
Matrimonial Problem. *See* Matrimonial Bed, 1930
Matrimonio, 1953 (De Sica)
Matrimonio all'italiana, 1964 (Castellani, De Sica)
Mattatore, 1960 (Risi, Scola)
Mattei Affair. *See* Caso Mattei, 1972
Matter of Dignity. *See* Final Lie, 1958
Matter of Life and Death, 1946 (Powell)
Matter of Morals. *See* De Sista Stegen, 1960
Matter of Time, 1976 (Minnelli)
Matthias Kneissl, 1970 (Fassbinder)
Maturareise, 1943 (Feyder)
Maudite soit la guerre, 1910 (Feuillade)
Maudits, 1947 (Clement)
Maudits sauvages, 1971 (Lefebvre)
Maulkorb, 1958 (Staudte)
Mauprat, 1926 (Buñuel, Epstein)
Maurice, 1987 (Ivory)
Maurya Patan, 1929 (Mehboob)
Mauvais coeur puni, 1904 (Guy)
Mauvais Fils, 1980 (Sautet)
Mauvaise graine, 1933 (Wilder)
Mauvaise Soupe, 1899/1900 (Guy)
Mauvaises rencontres, 1955 (Astruc)
Maverick, 1994 (Foster)
Max et les ferrailleurs, 1971 (Sautet)
Max, Mon Amour, 1986 (Oshima)
Maximenko Brigade. *See* Maksimenko brigád, 1950
Maxwell's Demon, 1968 (Frampton)
May 1, 1920 in Moscow. *See* Pervoye maya 1920 v Moskve, 1919
May 1st 1952. *See* 1952 Május 1, 1952
May Blossom, 1915 (Dwan)
May-Fly. *See* Maaneprinsessen, 1916
May Fools. *See* Milou en Mai, 1990
Maya, 1936 (Roy)
Maybe It's Love, 1930 (Wellman)
Mayerling, 1936 (Litvak)
Mayerling, 1957 (Litvak)
Mayerling to Sarajevo. *See* De Mayerling à Sarajevo, 1940
Mayo de las tres banderas, 1980 (Alvarez)
Mayol, 1900/07 (Guy)
Mazazo macizo, 1981 (Alvarez)
Mazurka di papà, 1938 (De Sica)
McCabe and Mrs. Miller, 1971 (Altman)
McQ, 1974 (J. Sturges)
Me alquilo para sonar, 1991 (Guerra)
Me and Marlborough, 1935 (Saville)
Me and My Gal, 1932 (Walsh)
Me and You. *See* Mig og dig, 1969
Me Gangster, 1928 (Walsh)
Me Want You. *See* Moi vouloir toi, 1984
Meadow. *See* Prato, 1979
Mean Machine. *See* Longest Yard, 1974
Mean Streets, 1973 (Scorsese)
Meantime, 1983 (Leigh)
Meat, 1975 (Wiseman)
Mécaniciens de l'armée de l'air, 1959 (Lelouch)
Mechanics of the Brain. *See* Mekhanikha golovnovo mozga, 1926
Med livet som insats, 1940 (Sjöberg)
Med tuld Musik, 1933 (Holger-Madsen)
Medals. *See* Seven Days Leave, 1930
Medan staden sover, 1950 (Bergman)
Medbejlerens Haevn, 1910 (Blom)
Meddlers, 1912 (Dwan)
Medea, 1969 (Pasolini)
Médecines et médecins, 1976 (Rouch)
Media Project, 1991 (Watkins)
Medicine Ball Caravan, 1979 (Scorsese)
Medicine Bottle, 1909 (Griffith)
Medico e lo stregone, 1957 (De Sica)
Medikus, 1916 (Curtiz)
Meditation on Violence, 1948 (Deren)
Mediterranée, 1964 (Schroeder)
Meenakshi, 1942 (Roy)
Meet Boston Blackie, 1940 (Florey)
Meet John Doe, 1941 (Capra)
Meet Marlon Brando, 1965 (Maysles)
Meet Me at Dawn, 1947 (Litvak)
Meet Me at the Fair, 1952 (Sirk)
Meet Me in Moscow. *See* Ya shagayu po Moskve, 1964
Meet Me in St. Louis, 1944 (Walters, Minnelli)
Meet My Girl, 1926 (Sennett)
Meet the Feebles, 1989 (Jackson)
Meet the Pioneers, 1948 (Anderson)
Meeting Hearts. *See* Hjärtan som mötas, 1914
Meeting in July. *See* Setkání v červenci, 1977
Meeting on the Atlantic. *See* Spotkanie na Atlantyku, 1979
Meeting Ships. *See* Skepp som motas, 1916
Meeting Venus, 1990 (Szabó)
Meeting with Maxim, 1941 (Gerasimov)
Még kér a nép, 1972 (Jancsó)
Megano, 1955 (Gutiérrez Alea)
Meigatsu somato, 1951 (Kinugasa)
Meiji haruaki, 1968 (Gosho)
Meilleure façon de marcher, 1976 (C. Miller)
Mein Kind, 1956 (Ivens)
Mein Mann—der Nachtredakteur, 1919 (Gad)
Mein Schulefreund, 1960 (Siodmak)
Mein Vater der Schauspieler, 1956 (Siodmak)
Mein Wille ist Gesetz, 1919 (Pick)
Meine Frau, die Filmschauspielerin; Meyer aus Berlin, 1919 (Lubitsch)
Meito Bijomaru, 1945 (Mizoguchi)
Mekhanikha golovnovo mozga, 1926 (Pudovkin)
Melba, 1953 (Milestone)
Mélo, 1986 (Resnais)
Melodie der Welt, 1929 (Ruttmann)
Melody, 1971 (Parker)
Mélomane, 1903 (Méliès)
Melomaniac. *See* Mélomane, 1903
Meltdown, 1994 (Dahl)
Melvin and Howard, 1980 (Demme)
Melvin's Revenge, 1949 (Jerry Lewis)
Member of the Government. *See* Chlen pravitelstva, 1940
Member of the Wedding, 1952 (Kramer, Zinnemann)
Memento Mori, 1989 (Jireš)
Memoire des apparences, 1987 (Ruiz)
Memoire. *See* Hadota Misreya, 1982
Memoirs of a Criminal. *See* En Forbryders Liv og Levned, eller En Forbryders Memoirer, 1916
Memoirs of an Invisible Man, 1991 (Carpenter)
Memorandum on Ana. *See* Apunte sobre Ana, 1971
Memorias de un reencuentro, 1986 (Alvarez)
Memorias del subdesarrollo, 1968 (Gutiérrez Alea)
Memorias do carcere, 1984 (Pereira Dos Santos)
Memórias e confissoes, 1982 (Oliveira)
Memories. *See* Zwischengleis, 1978
Memories and Confessions. *See* Memórias e confissoes, 1982
Memories of Jail. *See* Memorias do carcere, 1984
Memories of Underdevelopment. *See* **Memorias del subdesarrollo**, 1968
Memories of Young Days. *See* Wakaki hi no kangeki, 1931
Memory Lane, 1926 (Stahl)
Memory of Justice, 1976 (Ophuls)
Memory of Our Day, 1963 (Nemec)

Michael the Brave, 1969 (Welles)
Michel Strogoff, 1935 (Delannoy)
Michelino la B, 1956 (Olmi)
Michemin du ciel, 1929 (Cavalcanti)
Michki protiv Youdenitsa, 1925 (Gerasimov, Kozintsev)
Michurin, 1948 (Dovzhenko)
Mickey, 1918 (Sennett)
Mickey One, 1965 (Penn)
Mickey's Pal, 1912 (Guy)
Micki and Maude, 1984 (Edwards)
Midare-gami, 1961 (Kinugasa)
Midaregumo, 1967 (Naruse)
Midareru, 1964 (Naruse)
Middle of the Road Is a Very Dead End. *See* In Gefahr und grösster Not bringt der Mittelweg den Tod, 1974
Middle of the World. *See* Milieu du monde, 1974
Middle Watch, 1930 (Launder)
Middleman. *See* Jana Aranya, 1975
Midnight, 1939 (Wilder)
Midnight Adventure, 1909 (Griffith)
Midnight at Madame Tussaud's, 1937 (Pearson)
Midnight Cowboy, 1969 (Schlesinger)
Midnight Cupid, 1910 (Griffith)
Midnight Daddies, 1929 (Sennctt)
Midnight Elopement, 1912 (Sennett)
Midnight Express, 1978 (Parker, Stone)
Midnight Mary, 1933 (Wellman)
Midnight Ride of Paul Revere, 1907 (Porter)
Midnight Romance, 1919 (Weber)
Midnight Supper, 1909 (Porter)
Midshipman Easy, 1935 (Dickinson, Reed)
Midsommer. *See* Det gamle Købmandshus, 1911
Midsummer Day's Work, 1939 (Cavalcanti)
Midsummer Night's Dream, 1935 (Dieterle)
Midsummer Night's Sex Comedy, 1982 (Allen)
Midsummer-Time. *See* Det gamle Købmandshus, 1911
Midwinter Trip to Los Angeles, 1912 (Dwan)
Midwinter's Tale. *See* In the Bleak Midwinter, 1995
Miedzy Wrocławiem a Zieloną Górą, 1972 (Kieślowski)
Miesta ei voi raiskata, 1977 (August)
Mig og dig, 1969 (Henning-Jensen)
Mighty, 1929 (Cromwell)
Mighty Aphrodite, 1995 (Allen)
Mighty Joe Young, 1949 (Schoedsack)
Mighty Like a Moose, 1926 (McCarey)
Mignon, 1900/07 (Guy)
Mignon or The Child of Fate, 1912 (Guy)
Migratory Birds Under the Moon. *See* Tsuki no watari-dori, 1951
Mikado, 1939 (Dickinson)
Mike, 1926 (Neilan)
Mikey and Nicky, 1976 (Cassavetes)
Mikkel, 1948 (Roos)
Miklós Borsós. *See* Borsós Miklós, 1966
Mil, 1962 (Rouch)
Mil huit cent quatorze, 1910 (Feuillade)
Milagro Beanfield War, 1988 (Redford)
Milano '83, 1984 (Olmi)
Mildred Pierce, 1945 (Curtiz)
Milieu du monde, 1974 (Tanner)
Militaire et nourrice, 1904 (Guy)
Militant Suffragette, 1912 (Cruze)
Militarismo y tortura, 1969 (Ruiz)
Milk We Drink, 1913 (Sennett)
Milky Way, 1922 (W.S. Van Dyke)
Milky Way, 1935 (McCarey)
Milky Way. *See* Voie lactée, 1969
Mill on the Po. *See* Mulino del Po, 1949
Miller's Crossing, 1990 (Coen)
Millhouse: A White Comedy. *See* Millhouse: A White House Comedy, 1971
Millhouse: A White House Comedy, 1971 (De Antonio)
Million, 1931 (Clair)
Million Bid, 1927 (Curtiz)
Million Dollar Bride, 1914 (Browning)
Million Dollar Infield, 1982 (Reiner)
Million Dollar Job. *See* Film Johnnie, 1914
Million Dollar Legs, 1932 (Dmytryk, Mankiewicz)
Million Dollar Legs, 1939 (Dmytryk)
Million Dollar Mermaid, 1952 (Berkeley, LeRoy)
Million Dollar Mystery, 1914 (Cruze)
Million Dollar Mystery, 1987 (Fleischer)
Million Dollar Robbery, 1914 (Guy)
Million Dollar Trio. *See* Trio: Rubinstein, Heifetz and Piatigorsky, 1952
Million Girls. *See* Hyakumanin no musumetachi, 1963
Millionaerdrengen, 1913 (Holger-Madsen)
Millionairess, 1960 (Asquith, De Sica)
Millionärin, 1918 (Wiene)
Millions de la bonne, 1913/16 (Feuillade)
Millions en fuite. *See* Flugten fra millionerne, 1934
Millions Like Us, 1943 (Launder)
Mills of the Gods, 1909 (Griffith)
Milosierdzie platne z gory, 1975 (Zanussi)
Milou en Mai, 1990 (Malle)
Mimikry, 1992 (Jireš)
Min bedstefar er en stok, 1967 (Henning-Jensen)
Min første Monocle, 1911 (Blom)
Min Ven Levy, 1914 (Holger-Madsen)
Minami ni kaze, 1942 (Yoshimura)
Minas Blood. *See* Sangue Mineiro, 1929
Minbo No Onna, 1991 (Itami)
Minbo, Or the Gentle Art of Japanese Extortion. *See* Minbo No Onna, 1991
Mind Benders, 1963 (Dearden)
Mindennapi történetek, 1955 (Mészáros)
Mine Pilot. *See* Minlotsen, 1915
Mine with the Iron Door, 1924 (S. Wood)
Mineral Waters of the Caucasus. *See* Kavkazskiye mineralniye vody, 1924
Miners' Picnic, 1960 (Russell)
Miner's Wife, 1911 (Dwan)
Minerva traduce el mar, 1962 (Solas)
Ming Green, 1966 (Markopoulos)
Minin i Pozharsky, 1939 (Pudovkin)
Ministry of Fear, 1944 (Lang)
Minlotsen, 1915 (Stiller)
Minnie, 1922 (Neilan)
Minnie and Moskowitz, 1971 (Cassavetes)
Minor Apocalypse. *See* Petite Apocalypse, 1993
Minshu no teki, 1946 (Imai)
Minstrel Man, 1944 (Joseph H. Lewis)
Minuit, quai de Bercy, 1952 (Von Stroheim)
Minute de vérité, 1952 (Delannoy)
Minute Hands, The Street Photographer. *See* Minuteros, 1972
Minuteros, 1972 (Ruiz)
Mio, 1970 (Hani)
Mio Dio, come sono caduta in basso!, 1974 (Comencini)
Mio figlio Nerone, 1956 (De Sica)
Mio Figlio Professore, 1946 (Castellani)
Miquette et sa mère, 1949 (Clouzot)
Miracle. *See* Miracolo, 1947
Miracle, 1991 (Jordan)
Miracle Can Happen, 1946 (Huston)
Miracle in Harlem, 1937 (Micheaux)
Miracle in Milan. *See* **Miracolo a Milano,** 1950
Miracle in Soho, 1957 (Powell)
Miracle Makers, 1923 (W.S. Van Dyke)
Miracle of Morgan's Creek, 1944 (P. Sturges)
Miracle Rider, 1935 (Joseph H. Lewis)
Miracle sous l'inquisition, 1904 (Méliès)
Miracle Under the Inquisition. *See* Miracle sous l'inquisition, 1904
Miracle Woman, 1931 (Capra)
Miracle Worker, 1962 (Penn)
Miracles de Brahmane, 1900 (Méliès)
Miracles for Sale, 1939 (Browning)
Miracles of Brahmin. *See* Miracles de Brahmane, 1900

Muscle-Bound Music, 1926 (Sennett)
Musée Grevin, 1958 (Cocteau, Demy)
Musée vivant, 1965 (Storck)
Musen fusen, 1924 (Mizoguchi)
Museo dei sogni, 1948 (Comencini)
Museo dell'amore, 1935 (Lattuada)
Museumsmysteriet, 1909 (Blom)
Mushibameru haru, 1932 (Naruse)
Music. *See* Muzsika, 1984
Music and Faith, 1992 (Jireš)
Music and Pain, 1993 (Jireš)
Music Box. *See* Fine Mess, 1986
Music Box, 1990 (Costa-Gavras)
Music from Mars. *See* Hudba z Marsu, 1954
Music Hall. *See* Tango Tangles, 1914
Music Hall Star. *See* Lydia, 1916
Music Hath Its Charms, 1915 (Browning)
Music in Darkness. *See* Musik i mörker, 1948
Music in the Air, 1934 (Wilder)
Music Lovers, 1970 (Russell)
Music Master, 1927 (Dwan)
Music Room. *See* Jalsaghar, 1958
Musica, 1966 (Duras)
Musical Tramps. *See* His Musical Career, 1914
Musicians' Girl. *See* Muzikantská Liduška, 1940
Musik i morker, 1948 (Zetterling, Bergman)
Musique et danse des chasseurs Gow, 1965 (Rouch)
Musketeers of Pig Alley, 1912 (Griffith)
Muss 'em Up, 1936 (C. Vidor)
Mustaa Valkoisella, 1968 (Donner)
Musuko no seishun, 1952 (Kobayashi)
Musume, 1926 (Gosho)
Musume Dojoji, 1946 (Ichikawa)
Musume tsuma haha, 1960 (Naruse)
Mute Witness, 1913 (Dwan)
Mutiny, 1952 (Dmytryk)
Mutiny on the Bounty, 1935 (Lewin)
Mutiny on the Bounty, 1962 (Milestone)
Mutter Küsters Fahrt zum Himmel, 1975 (Fassbinder)
Mutter und Kind, 1924 (Dieterle)
Muyder Circle Lives Again. *See* De Muiderkring herleeft, 1948
Muž z neznáma, 1939 (Fric)
Muzikantská Liduška, 1940 (Fric)
Muzsika, 1984 (Jancsó)
Muzzle. *See* Kanonen-Serenade, 1958
My American Wife, 1923 (S. Wood)
My Apprenticeship. *See* Vlyudyakh, 1939
My Asylum. *See* Chiedo asilo, 1979
My Aunt's Millions. *See* Fasters miljoner, 1934
My Baby, 1912 (Griffith)
My Beautiful Laundrette, 1985 (Frears)
My Best Friend's Girl. *See* Femme de mon pote, 1982
My Best Gal, 1944 (Brooks, A. Mann)
My Brilliant Career, 1979 (Armstrong)
My Brother Talks to Horses, 1946 (Zinnemann)
My Brother's Wedding, 1983 (Burnett)
My Buddy, 1944 (Edwards)
My Child. *See* Mein Kind, 1956
My Country. *See* Moya rodina, 1933
My Crazy Life. *See* Mi Vida Loca, 1993
My Darling Clementine, 1946 (Ford)
My Dear Bodyguard. *See* Sevgili muhafizin, 1970
My Dear Fellow. *See* Dorogoi moi chelovek, 1958
My Dear Man. *See* Dorogoi moi chelovek, 1958
My Dinner with Andre, 1981 (Malle)
My Dream is Yours, 1949 (Curtiz)
My Enemy, the Sea. *See* Taiheiyo hitoribotchi, 1963
My Eye. *See* Mon Oeil, 1966
My Face Red in the Sunset. *See* Yuhi ni akai ore no kao, 1961
My Fair Lady, 1964 (Cukor)
My Family, Mi Familia, 1995 (Coppola)
My Fatherland. *See* Moya rodina, 1933
My Fault, New Version. *See* Shin ono ga tsumi, 1926
My Favorite Spy, 1942 (Garnett)
My Favorite Wife, 1940 (McCarey)
My Foolish Heart, 1990 (Babenco)
My Forbidden Past, 1951 (Stevenson)
My Friend Fabian. *See* Muj přítel Fabián, 1953
My Friend Irma, 1949 (Jerry Lewis)
My Friend Irma Goes West, 1950 (Jerry Lewis)
My Friend Levy. *See* Min Ven Levy, 1914
My Friend the Gypsy. *See* Muj přítel Fabián, 1953
My Friend the King, 1931 (Powell)
My Girlfriend's Boyfriend. *See* Ami de mon amie, 1987
My Goodness, 1920 (Sennett)
My Heart Belongs to Daddy, 1942 (Siodmak)
My Heart Is Calling, 1934 (Launder)
My Hero, 1912 (Griffith)
My Home Is Copacabana. *See* Mitt hem är Copacabana, 1965
My Husband Lies. *See* Hazasodik az uram, 1913
My Husband's Other Wife, 1919 (Blackton)
My Hustler, 1966 (Warhol)
My Kingdom for..., 1985 (Boetticher)
My Lady's Garter, 1920 (M. Tourneur)
My Learned Friend, 1943 (Dearden, Hamer)
My Left Foot, 1989 (Sheridan)
My Life as a Dog, 1985 (Hallstrom)
My Life for Zarah Leander, 1986 (Sirk)
My Life Story. *See* Mit livs eventyr, 1955
My Life to Live. *See* **Vivre sa vie**, 1962
My Life with Caroline, 1941 (Milestone)
My Life's Bright Day. *See* Waga shogai no kagayakeru hi, 1948
My Life's in Turnaround, 1993 (Sayles)
My Love Burns. *See* Waga koi wa moenu, 1949
My Love to the Swallows. *See* ... A pozdravuji vlaštovky, 1972
My Loving Child. *See* Itoshi no wagako, 1926
My Madonna, 1915 (Guy)
My Man and I, 1952 (Wellman)
My Man Godfrey, 1936 (La Cava)
My Mountain Song 27, 1969 (Brakhage)
My Name is Julia Ross, 1945 (Joseph H. Lewis)
My Name is Nobody, 1973 (Leone)
My Name Is Joker. *See* Mera Naam Joker, 1970
My Name Is Kerim. *See* Benim adim Kerim, 1967
My New Friends, 1987 (Van Sant)
My Night at Maud's. *See* Ma Nuit chez Maud, 1969
My Own Private Idaho, 1991 (Van Sant)
My Partner Mr. Davis, 1936 (Autant-Lara)
My Praguers Understand Me. *See* Mi Prazane me Rozùmeji, 1991
My s Urala, 1944 (Kuleshov)
My Second Brother. *See* Nianchan, 1959
My Sister Eileen, 1955 (Edwards, Fosse)
My Sister, My Love. *See* Imoto, 1974
My Six Convicts, 1952 (Kramer)
My Son. *See* Shodo satsujin: Musukoyo, 1979
My Son John, 1952 (McCarey)
My Son, My Son!, 1940 (C. Vidor)
My Sons' Youth. *See* Musuko no seishun, 1952
My Stupid Brother. *See* Niisan no baka, 1932
My Sweet Little Village. *See* Vesnicko ma strediskova, 1985
My Universities. *See* Moi universiteti, 1940
My Valet, 1915 (Sennett)
My Way. *See* Waga michi, 1974
My Way Home. *See* Igyjöttem, 1964
My Wife's Relations, 1922 (Keaton)
Mya—la mère, 1970 (Rouch)
Myra Breckenridge, 1970 (Huston)
Myrte and the Demons. *See* Myrte en de demonen, 1949
Myrte en de demonen, 1949 (Haanstra)
Mystère de l'Atelier Quinze, 1957 (Marker, Resnais)
Mystère de la chambre jaune, 1930 (L'Herbier)
Mystère de la Tour Eiffel, 1927 (Duvivier)

Mystère Koumiko, 1965 (Marker)
Mystère Picasso, 1956 (Clouzot)
Mystères d'Angkor. *See* Herrin der Welt, 1960
Mysteries, 1968 (Markopoulos)
Mysterious Box. *See* Boîte à malice, 1903
Mysterious Cafe, 1901 (Porter)
Mysterious Companion. *See* Mystiske Selskabsdame, 1916
Mysterious Island, 1926 (M. Tourneur)
Mysterious Island, 1973 (Bardem)
Mysterious Lady. *See* Maaneprinsessen, 1916
Mysterious Lady, 1928 (Niblo)
Mysterious Lady's Companion. *See* Mystiske Selskabsdame, eller Legationens Gidsel, 1917
Mysterious Mr. Davis. *See* My Partner Mr. Davis, 1936
Mysterious Mrs. M, 1917 (Weber)
Mysterious Portrait. *See* Portrait mystérieux, 1899
Mysterious Retort. *See* Alchimiste Prarafaragamus ou la Cornue infernale, 1906
Mysterious Rose, 1914 (Ford)
Mysterious X. *See* Det hemmelighedsfulde X, 1913
Mysterium, 1978 (Clarke)
Mystery in Mexico, 1948 (Wise)
Mystery of the Bermuda Triangle. *See* Triangulo diabolico de la Bermudas, 1977
Mystery of the Hindu Image, 1913 (Walsh)
Mystery of the Leaping Fish, 1916 (Browning, Fleming)
Mystery of the Museum. *See* Museumsmysteriet, 1909
Mystery of the Wax Museum, 1933 (Curtiz)
Mystery of the Yellow Room, 1919 (Von Sternberg)
Mystery Road, 1921 (Hitchcock)
Mystery Sea Raider, 1940 (Dmytryk)
Mystery Street, 1950 (Brooks, J. Sturges)
Mystery Submarine, 1950 (Sirk)
Mystery Train, 1989 (Jarmusch)
Mystic, 1925 (Browning)
Mystic Swing, 1900 (Porter)
Mystical Flame. *See* Flamme merveilleuse, 1903
Mystical Maid of Jamasha Pass, 1912 (Dwan)
Mystiske Fremmede, 1914 (Holger-Madsen)
Mystiske Selskabsdame, 1916 (Blom, Dreyer)

N.U., 1948 (Antonioni)
N.V.V. Congres, 1929/30 (Ivens)
Na estrada da vida, 1980 (Pereira Dos Santos)
Na krasnom fronte, 1920 (Kuleshov)
Na primavera da vida, 1926 (Mauro)
Na samotě u lesa, 1977 (Menzel)
Na vernom sledu, 1925 (Barnet)
Naadige Frøken, 1911 (Blom)
Naar Fruen gaar paa Eventyr, 1913 (Blom)
Naar Fruen skifter Pige. *See* Husassistenten, 1914
Naar man kun er ung, 1943 (Henning-Jensen)
Nabat, 1917 (Bauer, Kuleshov)
Nacer en Leningrado, 1977 (Solas)
Nach Meinem letzten Umzug, 1970 (Syberberg)
Nachi chempiony. *See* Sportivnaya slava, 1950
Nacht, 1985 (Syberberg)
Nacht der Konigin Isabeau, 1920 (Wiene)
Nachtdienst. *See* Milosierdzie platne z gory, 1975
Nächte des Grauens, 1916 (Pick)
Nachtfalter, 1911 (Gad)
Nachts auf den Strassen, 1951 (Käutner)
Nachts wann der Teufel kam, 1957 (Siodmak)
Nacion Clandestina, 1989 (Sanjinés)
Nada, 1974 (Chabrol)
NADA Gang. *See* Nada, 1974
Nadare, 1937 (Naruse)
Nadare, 1952 (Shindo)
Nadeje, 1963 (Kachyňa)
Nadezhda, 1954 (Gerasimov)
Nadezhda, 1973 (Donskoi)
Nadie dijo nada, 1971 (Ruiz)
Nadine, 1987 (Benton)
Nadja, 1994 (Lynch)
Nadja à Paris, 1964 (Rohmer)
Nagareru, 1956 (Naruse)
Nagaya no shinshi roku, 1947 (Ozu)
Nagurareta kochiyama, 1934 (Kinugasa)
Nagymama, 1916 (Korda)
Nagyüzemi tojástermelés, 1962 (Mészáros)
Nails, 1995 (Kopple)
Näinä Päivinä, 1955 (Donner)
Naïs, 1945 (Pagnol)
Naisenkuvia, 1970 (Donner)
Naissance des cigognes, 1925 (Grémillon)
Najma, 1943 (Mehboob)
Naked, 1993 (Leigh)
Naked and the Dead, 1958 (Walsh)
Naked Angels, 1969 (Corman)
Naked City, 1948 (Brooks, Dassin)
Naked Face of Night. *See* Yoru no sugao, 1958
Naked in New York, 1994 (Scorsese)
Naked Island. *See* **Hadaka no shima**, 1960
Naked Jungle, 1953 (Joseph H. Lewis)
Naked Kiss, 1963 (Fuller)
Naked Lunch, 1991 (Cronenberg)
Naked Night. *See* **Gycklarnas afton,** 1953
Naked Nineteen-year-old. *See* Hadaka no jukyu-sai, 1970
Naked Paradise, 1957 (Corman)
Naked Spur, 1953 (A. Mann)
Naked Sun. *See* Hadaka no taiyo, 1958
Naked Youth, a Story of Cruelty. *See* Seishun zankoku monogatari, 1960
Nalla Thangal, 1935 (Roy)
Name the Man, 1924 (Sjöström)
Namenlos, 1923 (Curtiz)
Namida o shishi no tategami ni, 1962 (Shinoda)
Namus ve silah, 1971 (Güney)
Nan Hai Yü Nü Hai Tê Chan Chêng, 1976 (Hou)
Nan of Music Mountain, 1917 (Cruze, De Mille)
Nana, 1923 (Autant-Lara)
Nana, 1926 (Renoir)
Nana, 1934 (Arzner)
Nanairo yubi wa, 1918 (Kinugasa)
Nanami: Inferno of First Love. *See* Hatsuoki jig ok uhen, 1968
Nancy Keith. *See* Testamentets Hemmelighed, 1916
Nanguila Tomorrow. *See* Demain à Nanguila, 1960
Naniwa ereji, 1936 (Mizoguchi)
Nanook of the North, 1922 (Flaherty)
Nanshin josei, 1939 (Shindo)
Nanto no haru, 1925 (Gosho)
Não ou a Vã Glória de Mandar, 1990 (Oliveira)
Naomi and Rufus Kiss, 1964 (Warhol)
Naples Is a Battlefield, 1944 (Clayton)
Napló apámnak, anyámnak, 1990 (Meszaros)
Napló gyermekeimnek, 1982 (Meszaros)
Napló szerelmeimnek, 1987 (Meszaros)
Napoléon, 1954 (Guitry, Von Stroheim, Welles)
Napoléon a Sainte-Hélène, 1929 (Gance, Pick)
Napoleon and Samantha, 1972 (Foster)
Napoleon auf St. Helena. *See* Napoléon a Sainte-Hélène, 1929
Napoléon Bonaparte, 1934 (Gance)
Napoléon vu par Abel Gance, 1927 (Gance)
Napoleon's Barber, 1928 (Ford)
Napoleon's Lucky Stone, 1913 (Cruze)
Napoli che non muore, 1939 (De Sica)
Napoli d'altri tempi, 1938 (De Sica)
Napoli e le terre d'oltremare, 1940 (Blasetti)
Naponta két vonat, 1977 (Gaál)
Nappali sötétség, 1963 (Fábri)
Napraforgós hölgy, 1918 (Curtiz)
Naprozod mlodziezy, 1952 (Ivens)
Nar karlekan dodar, 1913 (Sjöström, Stiller)

När konstnärer älska, 1914 (Stiller)
När larmhlockan ljuder, 1913 (Stiller)
När svärmor regerar, 1912 (Stiller)
Nära livet, 1958 (Bergman)
Narayama bushi-ko, 1958 (Kinoshita)
Narayama bushi-ko, 1983 (Imamura)
Narrow Margin, 1952 (Fleischer)
Narrow Road, 1912 (Griffith)
Narrow Valley, 1921 (Hepworth)
Naruto hicho, 1957 (Kinugasa)
Nas wal Nil, 1968 (Chahine)
Nasanu naka, 1932 (Naruse)
Nasce un campione, 1954 (Petri)
Naser Salah el Dine, 1963 (Chahine)
Nashville, 1975 (Altman, Rudolph)
Nashville Girl, 1976 (Corman)
Nasreddin in Bukhara. *See* Nasreddin v Bukhare, 1943
Nasreddin v Bukhare, 1943 (Protazanov)
Nata di marzo, 1958 (Scola)
Natale al campo 119, 1947 (De Sica)
Natalka Poltavka, 1938 (Ulmer)
Natasha, 1994 (Wajda)
Nathalie Granger, 1972 (Duras)
National Flag. *See* A Bandeira Nacional, 1988
National Parks ... a Necessity, National Parks in the Netherlands. *See* Nationale Parken ... noodzaak, 1978
National Rifle. *See* Escopeta nacional, 1978
National Velvet, 1944 (Brown)
Nationale Parken ... noodzaak, 1978 (Haanstra)
Native Country. *See* Strana rodnaya, 1942
Native Land. *See* Strana rodnaya, 1946
Natsu no imoto, 1972 (Oshima)
Natsukashi no kao, 1941 (Naruse)
Natsukashiki fue ya taiko, 1967 (Kinoshita)
Natten før Kristians Fødelsdag, 1908 (Holger-Madsen)
Nattens Mysterium, 1916 (Holger-Madsen)
Nattens väv, 1955 (Sjöström)
Nattevandreren, 1916 (Holger-Madsen)
Nattlek, 1966 (Zetterling)
Nattvardsgästerna, 1963 (Bergman)
Natura e chimica, 1959 (Olmi)
Natural, 1984 (Levinson, Redford)
Natural Born Killers, 1994 (Stone, Tarantino)
Nature of the Beast, 1919 (Hepworth)
Naufrago de la Calle de la Providencia, 1970 (Ripstein)
Naufragos, 1994 (Littin)
Naughts, 1994 (Brakhage)
Naughty Baby, 1929 (LeRoy)
Naughty Marietta, 1935 (W.S. Van Dyke)
Naughty Nurses. *See* Tender Loving Care, 1973
Nauka bliżej życia, 1951 (Munk)
Naukri, 1954 (Roy)
Nausicaa, 1970 (Varda)
Nautch Girl, 1934 (Mehboob)
Nave bianca, 1941 (Rossellini)
Navigation marchande, 1954 (Franju)
Navigator, 1924 (Keaton)
Navigator: A Medieval Odyssey, 1988 (Ward)
Navire des hommes perdus. *See* Schiff der verlorene Menschen, 1929
Navire Night, 1978 (Duras, Schroeder)
Návrat domu, 1948 (Fric)
Návrat ztraceného syna, 1966 (Schorm)
Navy Blue and Gold, 1937 (S. Wood)
Navy Blues, 1929 (Brown)
Navy Blues, 1941 (Bacon)
Navy Spy, 1937 (Joseph H. Lewis)
Navy Wife, 1935 (Dwan)
Nayak, 1966 (S. Ray)
Nazarín, 1958 (Buñuel)
Nazi Agent, 1942 (Dassin)
Nazis Strike, 1942 (Litvak)
Nazraana, 1961 (Kapoor)
Ne bougeons plus, 1903 (Guy)
Ne faut pas mourir pour ça, 1967 (Lefebvre)
Ne me demandez pas pourquoi. *See* Testament d'Orphée, 1960
Ne nado krovi, 1917 (Protazanov)
Ne tuez pas Dolly!, 1937 (Delannoy)
Neanderthal Man, 1953 (Dupont)
Neapolitan Diary, 1993 (Rosi)
Neapolitanische Geschwister. *See* Regno di Napoli, 1978
Near and Far Away. *See* Långt Borta och Nara, 1976
Near Death, 1989 (Wiseman)
Near to Earth, 1913 (Griffith)
Near-Tragedy, 1911 (Sennett)
Nearer My God to Thee, 1917 (Hepworth)
Nechte to na mně, 1955 (Forman, Fric)
Necklace, 1909 (Griffith)
Necklace of Ramses, 1914 (Ingram)
Necklace of the Dead. *See* Dø des Halsbaand, 1910
Necromancy, 1973 (Welles)
Necromania, 1971 (E. Wood)
Ned Kelly, 1970 (Richardson)
Ned med Vaabnene, 1914 (Holger-Madsen)
Ned Med Vabnene, 1914 (Dreyer)
Nedaa el Ochak, 1961 (Chahine)
Nederland, 1983 (Haanstra)
Nederlandse beeldhouwkunst tijdens de late Middeleeuwen, 1951 (Haanstra)
Nee kofun shicha iya yo, 1931 (Naruse)
Neel Akasher Neechey, 1959 (Sen)
Neel Kamal, 1947 (Kapoor)
Neglected. *See* Glaedens Dag, eller Miskendt, 1918
Nègre blanc, 1912 (Gance)
Negro Soldier, 1944 (Capra)
Neighbor Trouble, 1932 (Sennett)
Neighbors, 1911 (Sennett)
Neighbors, 1921 (Keaton)
Neighbor's Wife and Mine. *See* Madamu to nyobo, 1931
Neither In Nor Out. *See* Se ki, se be, 1919
Nejlepší ženská mého života, 1968 (Fric)
Nel blu dipinto di blu, 1959 (De Sica)
Nel nome del padre, 1971 (Bellocchio)
Nel segno di Roma, 1958 (Leone)
Nell, 1994 (Foster)
Nell Dale's Men Folks, 1916 (Borzage)
Nell of the Pampas, 1912 (Dwan)
Nella città l'inferno, 1959 (Castellani)
Nelly & Monsieur Arnaud, 1995 (Sautet)
Nelly & Mr. Arnaud. *See* Nelly & Monsieur Arnaud, 1995
Nelly Raintseva, 1916 (Bauer)
Nelson Touch. *See* Corvette K-225, 1943
Nema Kiáltás, 1982 (Meszaros)
Nemesis. *See* Faedrenes Synd, 1914
Nemico di mia moglie, 1959 (De Sica)
Nemureru bijo, 1968 (Yoshimura)
Nenavist, 1978 (Mikhalkov)
Není stále zamrečeno, 1950 (Kachyňa)
Neobyčejná léta, 1952 (Kachyňa)
Neobychainye priklucheniya Mistera Vesta v stranye bolshevikov, 1924 (Barnet, Kuleshov, Pudovkin)
Neokontchennaya piesa dlia mekhanitcheskogo pianino, 1977 (Mikhalkov)
Neon Jungle. *See* Neon taiheiki-keieigaku nyumon, 1967
Neon taiheiki-keieigaku nyumon, 1967 (Imamura)
Nepokorenniye, 1945 (Donskoi)
Nero and the Burning of Rome, 1908 (Porter)
Nerone, 1930 (Blasetti)
Nero's Weekend. *See* Mio figlio Nerone, 1956
Nerze Nachts am Strassenrand, 1973 (Staudte)
Nessa bala Rejal, 1952 (Chahine)
Nessuno o tutti—Matti da slegare, 1974 (Bellocchio)
Nessuno torna indietro, 1943 (Blasetti, De Sica, Germi)
Nest, 1943 (Anger)
Nest of Gentlefolk. *See* Dvoranskoye gnezdo, 1969

Nitwits, 1935 (Stevens)
Niwa no kotori, 1922 (Kinugasa)
Niwatori wa futatabi naku, 1954 (Gosho)
Nixon, 1995 (Stone)
No Brakes. *See* Oh, Yeah!, 1929
No Clouds in the Sky. *See* Sora wa haretari, 1925
No Control, 1927 (Garnett)
No Defense, 1929 (Bacon)
No Down Payment, 1957 (Ritt)
No End. *See* Bez końca, 1984
No Exit No Panic. *See* Beruhrte, 1981
No Father to Guide Him, 1925 (McCarey)
No Greater Glory, 1934 (Borzage)
No-Gun Man, 1924 (Arzner)
No Leave, No Love, 1946 (Donen)
No, Mama, No, 1979 (Joffé)
No Man of Her Own, 1932 (Goulding)
No Man's Land, 1985 (Tanner)
No Man's Law, 1927 (Stevens)
No Mercy No Future. *See* Beruhrte, 1981
No Minor Vices, 1948 (Aldrich, Milestone)
No Money, No Fight. *See* Musen fusen, 1924
No More Ladies, 1933 (Cukor)
No More Women, 1934 (Daves)
No Mother to Guide Him, 1919 (Sennett)
No, No, Lady, 1931 (Sennett)
No Nukes, 1981 (Kopple)
No One to Guide Him, 1916 (Sennett)
No One Will Play with Me. *See* Mit mir will keiner spielen, 1976
No Other Way, 1953/55 (Rotha)
No Parking, 1937 (Reed)
No Place to Go, 1927 (LeRoy)
No Regrets for Our Youth. *See* Waga seishun ni kuinashi, 1946
No Resting Place, 1950 (Rotha)
No Return. *See* Kaeranu sasabue, 1926
No Room for the Groom, 1952 (Sirk)
No Smoking, 1993 (Resnais)
No somos de piedra, 1967 (García Berlanga)
No Sun in Venice. *See* Sait-on jamais?, 1957
No Time for Flowers, 1952 (Siegel)
No Time for Sergeants, 1958 (LeRoy)
No Way Out, 1950 (Mankiewicz)
No Way Out, 1987 (Costner)
No Woman Knows, 1921 (Browning)
Noah's Ark, 1929 (Curtiz)
Nob Hill, 1945 (Hathaway)
Nobi, 1959 (Ichikawa)
Nobody Said Nothing. *See* Nadie dijo nada, 1971
Nobody Shall Be Laughing, 1965 (Menzel)
Nobody's Darling, 1943 (A. Mann)
Nobody's Daughter. *See* Syndens Datter, 1915
Nobody's Fool, 1994 (Benton)
Nobody's Son. *See* Senki fia, 1917
Nobody's Woman. *See* Señora de Nadie, 1982
Noc nevěsty, 1967 (Kachyňa)
Noce au lac Saint-Fargeau, 1905 (Guy)
Noces d'argent, 1915 (Feuillade)
Noces de sable, 1948 (Cocteau)
Noces rouges, 1973 (Chabrol)
Noces siciliennes, 1912 (Feuillade)
Noces vénitiennes. *See* Prima notte, 1958
Noch' v sentyabre, 1939 (Barnet)
Noche oscura, 1989 (Saura)
Noctiluca, 1974 (Frampton)
Nocturne, 1919 (Feuillade)
Nodes, 1981 (Brakhage)
Noël de Francesca, 1912 (Feuillade)
Noël du poilu, 1915 (Feuillade)
Nogent, Eldorado du dimanche, 1929 (Carné)
Nogi Taisho to Kuma-san, 1926 (Mizoguchi)
Nogiku no gotoki kimi nariki, 1955 (Kinoshita)
Noi donne siamo fatte cosi, 1971 (Risi, Scola)
Noi siamo le colonne, 1956 (De Sica)
Noire de..., 1966 (Sembene)
Noise from the Deep, 1913 (Sennett)
Noise of Bombs, 1914 (Sennett)
Noises Off, 1992 (Bogdanovich)
Non c'e pace tra gli ulivi, 1949 (De Santis)
Non me lo dire!, 1940 (Fellini)
Non or the Vain Glory of Command. *See* Não ou a Vã Glória de Mandar, 1990
Non sono superstizioso, ma...!, 1943 (De Sica)
Non-Stop New York, 1937 (Stevenson)
Non ti conosco più, 1936 (De Sica)
Non toccate la donna bianca, 1973 (Ferreri)
Non uccidere. *See* Tu ne tueras point, 1961
Nonna Sabella, 1957 (Risi)
Noon. *See* Polden, 1931
Noon Wine, 1966 (Peckinpah)
Nora Helmer, 1973 (Fassbinder)
Nora inu, 1949 (Kurosawa)
Norma Rae, 1979 (Ritt)
Normal Young Man. *See* Giovane normale, 1969
Norman Jacobson, 1967 (Emshwiller)
Noroît, 1976 (Rivette)
North, 1995 (Reiner)
North Bridge. *See* Pont du Nord, 1981
North by Northwest, 1959 (Hitchcock)
North of 57, 1924 (Sennett)
North of Hudson Bay, 1923 (Ford)
North or Northwest, 1938 (Cavalcanti)
North Sea, 1938 (Cavalcanti, Watt)
North Star, 1943 (Milestone, Von Stroheim)
North to Alaska, 1960 (Hathaway)
North West Mounted Police, 1940 (De Mille)
Northern Pursuit, 1943 (Siegel, Walsh)
Northwest. *See* Noroît, 1976
Northwest Outpost, 1947 (Dwan)
Northwest Passage, 1940 (K. Vidor)
Nos amours, 1983 (Pialat)
Nosferatu. *See* Zwolfte Stunde—Eine Nacht des Grauens, 1930
Nosferatu—Eine Symphonie des Grauens, 1921 (Murnau)
Nosferatu—Phantom der Nacht, 1979 (Herzog)
Nosferatu the Vampire. *See* **Nosferatu—Eine Symphonie des Grauens**, 1921
Nosferatu the Vampire. *See* Zwolfte Stunde—Eine Nacht des Grauens, 1930
Nosferatu, the Vampire. *See* Nosferatu—Phantom der Nacht, 1979
Nostalghia, 1983 (Tarkovsky)
Nostalgia, 1971 (Frampton)
Nostalgia. *See* Nostalghia, 1983
Nostalgie. *See* Frühlingsrauschen, 1929
Nostra guerra, 1945 (Lattuada)
Nostri mariti, 1966 (Risi)
Nostros dos, 1954 (Fernández)
Not a Drum Was Heard, 1924 (Wellman)
Not as a Stranger, 1955 (Kramer)
Not as Wicked as That. *See* Pas si méchant que ça, 1975
Not Blood Relations. *See* Nasanu naka, 1932
Not Enough. *See* Pas assez, 1968
Not Guilty, 1908 (Méliès)
Not of This Earth, 1957 (Corman)
Not On Your Life. *See* **Verdugo**, 1963
Not Reconciled. *See* Nicht versöhnt oder Es hilft nur Gewalt, wo Gewalt herrscht, 1965
Not So Dumb, 1930 (K. Vidor)
Not the First Time, 1976 (Frampton)
Note in the Shoe, 1909 (Griffith)
Notebook on Cities and Clothes. *See* Aufzeichnungen zu Kleidern und Städten, 1989
Notes for an African Oresteia. *See* Appunti per una Orestiade africana, 1969
Notes for Jerome, 1981 (Mekas)
Notes on a Green Revolution, 1972 (Benegal)
Notes on the Circus, 1966 (Mekas)

Nothing but Pleasure, 1940 (Keaton)
Nothing But the Best, 1963 (Roeg)
Nothing Else Matters, 1920 (Pearson)
Nothing Sacred, 1937 (Wellman)
Noto—Mandorli—Vulcano—Stromboli—Carnevale, 1992 (Antonioni)
Notorious, 1946 (Hitchcock)
Notorious Affair, 1930 (Bacon)
Notorious Elinor Lee, 1940 (Micheaux)
Notorious Gentleman. *See* Rake's Progress, 1945
Notorious Landlady, 1962 (Edwards)
Notre Dame, cathédrale de Paris, 1957 (Franju)
Notre-Dame de Paris, 1931 (Epstein)
Notre-Dame de Paris, 1956 (Delannoy)
Notre Histoire, 1984 (Blier)
Notre pauvre cœur, 1916 (Feuillade)
Notte, 1960 (Antonioni)
Notte brava, 1959 (Pasolini)
Notte di San Lorenzo, 1982 (Taviani)
Notte di tempesta, 1945 (Castellani)
Notti bianche, 1957 (Visconti)
Notti di Cabiria, 1956 (Fellini, Pasolini)
Nous aurons toute la mort pour dormir, 1977 (Hondo)
Nous deux, 1979 (Lelouch)
Nous n'irons plus au bois, 1951 (Sautet)
Nous ne ferons jamais de cinéma, 1932 (Cavalcanti)
Nous ne vieillirons pas ensemble, 1972 (Pialat)
Nouveau Journal d'une femme en blanc, 1966 (Autant-Lara)
Nouveau Seigneur du village, 1908 (Méliès)
Nouveau Testament, 1936 (Guitry)
Nouveaux Messieurs, 1928 (Feyder)
Nouvelle mission de Judex, 1917 (Feuillade)
Nouvelle Vague, 1990 (Godard)
Nouvelles Luttes extravagantes, 1900 (Méliès)
Nova domaća zivotinja, 1964 (Makavejev)
Nova igračka, 1964 (Makavejev)
Nova sinfonia, 1982 (Alvarez)
Novecento atto I. *See* **1900 (Novecento),** 1976
Novecento atto II. *See* **1900 (Novecento),** 1976
Novelletta, 1937 (Comencini)
November Days: Voices and Choices, 1990 (Ophuls)
Novgorodtsy, 1943 (Barnet)
Novio a la vista, 1953 (Bardem, García Berlanga)
Novosti dnia, 1944-54 (Vertov)
Novyi Vavilon, 1929 (Gerasimov, Kozintsev, Pudovkin)
Now, 1965 (Alvarez)
Now About These Women. *See* För att inte tala om alla dessa kvinnor, 1964
Now and Forever, 1934 (Hathaway)
Now Don't Get Excited. *See* Nee kofun shicha iya yo, 1931
Now That I Was Born a Woman. *See* Onna to umaretakaranya, 1934
Now We Will Call You Brother. *See* Ahor te vamos a llamar hermano, 1971
Nóz w wodzie, 1962 (Polanski, Skolimowski)
N'te promène donc pas toute nue, 1906 (Feuillade)
Nth Commandment, 1923 (Borzage)
Nu borjar livet, 1948 (Zetterling, Molander)
Nude Restaurant, 1967 (Warhol)
Nueva canción Chileña, 1973 (Ruiz)
Nugget Jim's Pardner, 1916 (Borzage)
Nuit agitée, 1897 (Guy)
Nuit agitée, 1908 (Feuillade)
Nuit américaine, 1973 (C. Miller, Truffaut)
Nuit de la revanche, 1924 (Duvivier)
Nuit de la Saint-Jean. *See* Schweigen im Walde, 1929
Nuit de Varennes, 1982 (Scola)
Nuit du carrefour, 1932 (Becker, Renoir)
Nuit et brouillard, 1955 (Resnais)
Nuit et jour, 1991 (Akerman)
Nuit fantastique, 1942 (L'Herbier)
Nuit noire, Calcutta, 1964 (Duras)
Nuit terrible, 1896 (Méliès)
Nuits de feu, 1936 (L'Herbier)
Nuits de la pleine lune, 1984 (Rohmer)
Nuits de Prince, 1928 (L'Herbier)
Nuits rouges, 1974 (Franju)
Nukiashi sashiashi, 1934 (Yoshimura)
Numazu Hei-gakko, 1939 (Imai)
Numazu Military Academy. *See* Numazu Hei-gakko, 1939
Number, 1979 (Boulting)
Number 111. *See* A 111-es, 1919
Number Seventeen, 1932 (Hitchcock)
Number Thirteen, 1922 (Hitchcock)
Numbered Men, 1930 (LeRoy)
Numéro deux, 1975 (Godard)
Nun. *See* Religieuse, 1966
Nunca pasa nada, 1963 (Bardem)
Nun's Story, 1958 (Zinnemann)
Nuovo Cinema Paradiso, 1988 (Tornatore)
Nuptiae, 1969 (Brakhage)
Nur um tausend Dollars, 1918 (Dupont)
Nur zum Spass—Nur zum Spiel, 1977 (Schlöndorff)
Nuremberg Trials, 1946 (Lorentz)
Nuri the Flea. *See* Pire Nuri, 1968
Nurses. *See* Sestricky, 1983
Nursing a Viper, 1909 (Griffith, Sennett)
Nusumareta koi, 1951 (Ichikawa)
Nusumareta yokujo, 1958 (Imamura)
Nut, 1921 (Chaplin)
Nuts, 1987 (Ritt)
Nuts in May, 1976 (Leigh)
Nutty Naughty Chateau. *See* Château en Suede, 1963
Nutty Professor, 1963 (Jerry Lewis)
Nuuk 250 år, 1979 (Roos)
Nyar i Skane, 1961 (Troell)
Nybyggarna, 1970 (Troell)
Nyobo funshitsu, 1928 (Ozu)
Nyonin aishu, 1937 (Naruse)

O Amuleta de Ogum, 1974 (Pereira Dos Santos)
O Bôca de Ouro, 1962 (Pereira Dos Santos)
O.C. and Stiggs, 1983 (Altman)
O canto da saudade, 1952 (Mauro)
O canto do mar, 1953 (Cavalcanti)
O cavalo de Oxumaire, 1961 (Guerra)
O Circo, 1965 (Diegues)
O coracão, 1960 (Oliveira)
O descobrimento do Brasil, 1937 (Mauro)
O despertar da redentora, 1942 (Mauro)
O dragão da maldade contra o santo querreiro. *See* **Antônio das Mortes**, 1969
O Dreamland, 1953 (Anderson)
O grande momento, 1958 (Pereira Dos Santos)
O. Henry's Full House, 1952 (Hathaway, Hawks, King)
O.H.M.S., 1937 (Walsh)
O homem das estrelas, 1971 (Guerra)
O Lucky Man!, 1973 (Anderson, Frears)
O Megalexandros, 1980 (Angelopoulos)
O Melissokomos, 1986 (Angelopoulos)
O Meu Caso—Repeticoes, 1986 (Oliveira)
O něčem jiném, 1963 (Chytilová)
O pão, 1959 (Oliveira)
O passado e o presente, 1972 (Oliveira)
O patio, 1958 (Rocha)
O pintor e a cidade, 1956 (Oliveira)
O Rio de Machado de Assis, 1964 (Pereira Dos Santos)
O saisons, o châteaux, 1957 (Varda)
O samba, 1988 (Scola)
O Sapato de cetim, 1985 (Oliveira)
O scai, 1951 (Pereira Dos Santos)
O segredo das Asas, 1944 (Mauro)
O slavnosti a hostech, 1966 (Nemec, Schorm)
O Sun. *See* Soleil O, 1969
Oath, 1921 (Walsh)
Oath and the Man, 1910 (Griffith)
Oath of Youth. *See* Kliatva molodikh, 1944

One Hundred Meters with Chaplin. *See* Cien Metros con Charlot, 1967
One Hundred Years of Japanese Cinema, 1995 (Oshima)
One Is Business, the Other Crime, 1912 (Griffith)
One Little Indian, 1973 (Foster)
One-Man Band. *See* Homme orchestre, 1900
One Man Mutiny. *See* Court Martial of Billy Mitchell, 1955
One-Man Trail, 1921 (Howard)
One Mile from Heaven, 1937 (Dwan)
One Million AC/DC, 1969 (E. Wood)
One Million Pound Note. *See* Az egymillió fontos bankó, 1916
One Minute to Play, 1926 (S. Wood)
One Minute to Zero, 1952 (Garnett)
One More Chance, 1931 (Sennett)
One More River, 1934 (Whale)
One More Spring, 1935 (King)
One More Time. *See* Ima hitotabi no, 1947
One More Time, 1970 (Jerry Lewis)
One Mysterious Night, 1944 (Boetticher)
One Night. *See* En natt, 1931
One Night, and Then—, 1909 (Griffith)
One Night at Dinner, 1968 (Argento)
One Night Stand, 1915 (Sennett)
One Night Stand, 1984 (Duigan)
One of Our Aircraft Is Missing, 1942 (Lean, Powell)
One of Our Dinosaurs is Missing, 1975 (Stevenson)
One of the Blood. *See* His Majesty, the American, 1919
One of the Many. *See* En av de många, 1915
One of Us. *See* Einer von uns beiden, 1973
One or the Other. *See* Einer von uns beiden, 1973
One P.M., 1971 (Godard, Leacock)
One Parallel Movie. *See* One P.M., 1971
One-Piece Bathing Suit. *See* Million Dollar Mermaid, 1952
One Plus One, 1968 (Godard)
One Potato, Two Potato .... *See* Eci, pec, pec, 1961
One Rainy Afternoon, 1936 (P. Sturges)
One Round O'Brien, 1911 (Sennett)
One Run Elmer, 1935 (Keaton)
One Second in Montreal, 1968/69 (Snow)
One September Night. *See* Noch' v sentyabre, 1939
One She Loved, 1912 (Griffith)
One Single Night. *See* En enda natt, 1938
One Sings, the Other Doesn't. *See* Chante l'autre pas, 1977
One Spooky Night, 1924 (Sennett)
One Sunday Afternoon, 1948 (Walsh)
One Third of a Nation, 1939 (Lumet)
One Touch of Nature, 1908 (Griffith)
One Touch of Venus, 1948 (Tashlin)
One, Two, Three, 1912 (Dwan)
One, Two, Three, 1961 (Wilder)
One Two Three, 1978 (Clarke)
One Two Three Sun. *See* Un deux trois soleil, 1993
One Way or Another. *See* **De cierta manera**, 1977
One Way Passage, 1931 (Garnett)
One Way Ticket to Love. *See* Koi no katamichi kippu, 1960
One Week, 1920 (Keaton)
One Woman's Story. *See* Passionate Friends, 1949
One Wonderful Sunday. *See* Subarashiki nichiyobi, 1947
One Yard to Go, 1931 (Sennett)
Oni azami, 1926 (Kinugasa)
Onibaba, 1964 (Shindo)
Onkel og Nevø. *See* Fader og Søn, 1911
Only a Messenger Boy, 1915 (Sennett)
Only a Mother. *See* Bara en mor, 1949
Only A Farmer's Daughter, 1915 (Sennett)
Only Angels Have Wings, 1939 (Hawks)
Only for Fun—Only for Play. *See* Nur zum Spass—Nur zum Spiel, 1977
Only Game in Town, 1970 (Stevens)
Only House, 1971 (E. Wood)
Only Once a Year. *See* Tol'ko Raz v Godu, 1914
Only One. *See* Edinstvennaia, 1976
Only Saps Work, 1930 (Dmytryk)
Only Saps Work, 1930 (Mankiewicz)
Only Son, 1914 (De Mille)
Only Son. *See* Hitori musuko, 1936
Only the French Can. *See* French Cancan, 1955
Only the Hours. *See* **Rien que les heures,** 1926
Only Two Can Play, 1961 (Launder, Zetterling)
Only Way. *See* Ek Hi Rasta, 1939
Only Way Out. *See* Jedini izlaz, 1958
Only When I Larf, 1968 (Dearden)
Only Yesterday, 1933 (Stahl)
Only You, 1981 (Jarmusch)
Only You, 1994 (Jewison)
Onna, 1948 (Kinoshita)
Onna ga kaidan o agaru toki, 1960 (Naruse)
Onna koso ie o momore, 1939 (Yoshimura)
Onna no kao, 1949 (Imai)
Onna no kunsho, 1961 (Yoshimura)
Onna no machi, 1940 (Imai)
Onna no misoshiru, 1968 (Gosho)
Onna no naka ni iru tanin, 1966 (Naruse)
Onna no rekishi, 1963 (Naruse)
Onna no saka, 1960 (Yoshimura)
Onna no sono, 1954 (Kinoshita)
Onna no za, 1962 (Naruse)
Onna to umaretakaranya, 1934 (Gosho)
Onna wa tamoto o goyojin, 1932 (Naruse)
Onna-yo ayamaru nakare, 1923 (Kinugasa)
Onna yo, kini no na o kegasu nakare, 1930 (Gosho)
Onorata società, 1961 (De Sica)
Ont staan en vergaan, 1954 (Haanstra)
Onu Allah affetsin, 1970 (Güney)
Onyxkopf, 1917 (Dupont)
Ooh ... You Are Awful, 1972 (Launder)
Ookami, 1955 (Shindo)
Open All Night, 1934 (Pearson)
Open at Night. *See* Yoru hiraku, 1931
Open Gate, 1909 (Griffith)
Open Places, 1917 (W.S. Van Dyke)
Open Road. *See* Uppbrott, 1948
Opening in Moscow, 1959 (Clarke)
Opening Night, 1978 (Bogdanovich, Cassavetes)
Opera, 1988 (Argento)
Opera do Malandro, 1986 (Guerra)
Opera in the Vineyard. *See* Opera ve vinici, 1981
Opera ve vinici, 1981 (Jireš)
Opera Zebracka, 1991 (Menzel)
Opéra-Mouffe, 1958 (Varda)
Operabranden, 1912 (Blom)
Operación abril del Caribe, 1982 (Alvarez)
Operation Mad Ball, 1956 (Edwards)
Operation Ogro. *See* Ogro, 1979
Operation Petticoat, 1959 (Edwards)
Operation Redlight, 1969 (E. Wood)
Operation San Gennaro. *See* Operazione San Gennaro, 1966
Opération Béton, 1954 (Godard)
Operazione San Gennaro, 1966 (Risi)
Opfer der Gesellschaft, 1918 (Wiene)
Opfinders Skaebne, 1911 (Blom)
Ophélia, 1962 (Chabrol)
Opiate '67. *See* I mostri, 1963
Opinion Makers, 1964 (Emshwiller)
Opium Smoker's Dream. *See* Opiumsdrømmen, 1914
Opiumsdrømmen, 1914 (Holger-Madsen)
Opstandelse, 1914 (Holger-Madsen)
Opus I, 1921 (Ruttmann)
Opus 1, 1947 (Roos)
Opus II, III, IV, 1920-23 (Ruttmann)
Opus seis, 1969 (Guzmán)
Opus Six. *See* Opus seis, 1969
Opus V, 1925-26 (Ruttmann)
Or des mers, 1932 (Epstein)

Or du Cristobal, 1939 (Becker)
Or gris, 1980 (Ruiz)
Or Pigs and Pearls. *See* Montenegro, 1981
Ora della veritá. *See* Minute de vérité, 1952
Oracle, 1952 (Grierson)
Oracle de Delphes, 1903 (Méliès)
Oracle of Delphi. *See* Oracle de Delphes, 1903
Oratorio for Prague, 1968 (Nemec)
Oratorium for Prague. *See* Oratorio for Prague, 1968
Orchestra Rehearsal. *See* Prova d'orchestra, 1978
Orchid for the Tiger. *See* Tigre se parfume à la dynamite, 1965
Orchids and Ermines, 1927 (LeRoy)
Ordeal of Rosetta, 1918 (Goulding)
Orders Are Orders, 1953 (Grierson)
Orders Is Orders, 1933 (Launder)
Orders to Kill, 1958 (Asquith)
Ordet, 1943 (Molander, Sjöström)
Ordet, 1955 (Dreyer)
Ordinary Madness of a Daughter of Cham. *See* Folie ordinaire d'une fille de Cham, 1986
Ordinary Matter, 1972 (Frampton)
Ordinary People, 1980 (Redford)
Ordinary Ways. *See* Közös útan, 1953
Ordinateur des pompes funèbres, 1976 (C. Miller)
Ore mo omae mo, 1946 (Naruse)
Ore Riders, 1927 (Wyler)
Oreos with Attitude, 1990 (Haynes)
Orfeo, 1985 (Goretta)
Orfeusz es Eurydike, 1985 (Gaál)
Org, 1979 (Birri)
Orgy of the Dead, 1965 (E. Wood)
Oribe's Crime. *See* Crimen de Oribe, 1950
Orient Express, 1954 (Rossellini)
Oriental Love, 1917 (Sennett)
Origin of Sex. *See* Sei no kigen, 1967
Orizuru osen, 1934 (Mizoguchi)
Orlacs Hände, 1924 (Wiene)
Orlando, 1993 (Potter)
Ormens ägg. *See* Schlangenei, 1977
Ornette, Made in America, 1985 (Clarke)
Oro di Napoli, 1954 (De Sica)
Örökbefogadás, 1975 (Meszaros)
Örökseg, 1980 (Meszaros)
Orologio a cucù, 1938 (Castellani, De Sica)
Oros, 1960 (Guerra)
Orphan Joyce, 1916 (W.S. Van Dyke)
Orphans, 1987 (Pakula)
Orphan's Mine, 1913 (Dwan)
Orphans of the Storm, 1921 (Griffith)
Orphée, 1950 (Cocteau, Melville)
Orphelin de Paris, 1923 (Feuillade)
Orpheline, 1921 (Clair, Feuillade, Florey)
Országutak vándora, 1956 (Mészáros)
Orthodox Churches. *See* Sabori, 1965
Orthopedic Paradise. *See* Paraiso ortopedico, 1969
Os cafajestes, 1962 (Guerra)
Os Canibais, 1988 (Oliveira)
Os deuses e os mortos, 1970 (Guerra)
Os filhos do medo, 1978 (Diegues)
Os herdeiros, 1969 (Diegues)
Os mendigos, 1963 (Guerra)
Osaka Elegy. *See* **Naniwa ereji**, 1936
Osaka monogatari, 1957 (Yoshimura)
Osaka natsu no jin, 1937 (Kinugasa)
Osaka no onna, 1958 (Kinugasa)
Osaka no yado, 1954 (Gosho)
Osaka Story. *See* Osaka monogatari, 1957
Ösbemutató, 1974 (Szabó)
Oscar, champion de tennis, 1932 (Tati)
Oshikiri shinkonki, 1930 (Naruse)
Oslo, 1963 (Roos)
Osman the Wanderer. *See* Piyade Osman, 1970
Osmjeh 61, 1961 (Makavejev)
Osone-ke no asa, 1946 (Kinoshita)
Osore-zan no onna, 1964 (Gosho)
Ososhiki, 1984 (Itami)
Ospedale del delitto, 1948 (Comencini)
Ossessione, 1942 (De Santis, Visconti)
Ossis Tagebuch, 1917 (Lubitsch)
Ostatni etap, 1947 (Kawalerowicz)
Ostende, reine des plages, 1930 (Storck)
Osterman Weekend, 1983 (Peckinpah)
Ostia, 1969 (Pasolini)
Ostia, 1986 (Jarman)
Ostře sledované vlaky, 1966 (Menzel)
Ostrov stříbrných volavek, 1976 (Jireš)
Ostroznie yeti, 1960 (Polanski)
Osvobozhdenie, 1940 (Dovzhenko)
Oswego, 1943 (Willard Van Dyke)
Osynliga muren, 1944 (Molander)
Ösz Badacsonyban, 1954 (Jancsó)
Otac na sluzbenoh putu, 1985 (Kusturica)
Otello, 1986 (Zeffirelli)
Otets Sergii, 1918 (Protazanov)
Othello, 1952 (Welles)
Othello. *See* Otello, 1986
Othello, 1995 (Branagh)
Other, 1972 (Mulligan)
Other, 1980 (Brakhage)
Other. *See* Otro, 1984
Other Half, 1912 (Cruze)
Other Half, 1919 (K. Vidor)
Other Man, 1916 (Sennett)
Other Men's Women, 1931 (Wellman)
Other People's Business, 1914 (Sennett)
Other People's Money, 1991 (Jewison)
Other People's Sins, 1931 (Dickinson)
Other Shore. *See* Chuzoi bereg, 1930
Other Side of the Wind, 1972 (Bogdanovich, Welles)
Other Tomorrow, 1930 (Bacon)
Other Wise Man, 1912 (Dwan)
Other Woman. *See* Tsuma toshite onna toshite, 1961
Otherwise Unexplained Fires, 1976 (Frampton)
Othon, 1969 (Straub)
Otoko no kao wa rirekisho, 1966 (Itami)
Otokogokoro, 1925 (Gosho)
Otome-gokoro sannin shimai, 1935 (Naruse)
Ototo, 1960 (Ichikawa, Itami)
Otra isla, 1968 (Gómez)
Otro, 1984 (Ripstein)
Otto e mezzo, 1963 (Fellini)
Ouigours—Minorité nationale—Sinkiang, 1977 (Ivens)
Our Betters, 1933 (Cukor)
Our Champions. *See* Sportivnaya slava, 1950
Our Children, 1913 (Sennett)
Our Cissy, 1973 (Parker)
Our Corner, 1980 (Tian)
Our Country. *See* Strana rodnaya, 1946
Our Country Cousin, 1914 (Sennett)
Our Daily Bread, 1930 (Murnau)
Our Daily Bread, 1934 (Mankiewicz, K. Vidor)
Our Dare Devil Chief, 1915 (Sennett)
Our Hitler. *See* **Hitler: Ein Film aus Deutschland**, 1977
Our Hospitality, 1923 (Keaton)
Our Husbands. *See* Nostri mariti, 1966
Our Large Birds, 1914 (Sennett)
Our Last Spring, 1959 (Cacoyannis)
Our Little Nell, 1917 (W.S. Van Dyke)
Our Man in Havana, 1960 (Reed)
Our Marriage. *See* Watakushi-tachi no kekkon, 1962
Our Mother's House, 1967 (Clayton)
Our Mr. Sun, 1956 (Capra)

Our Russian Front, 1941 (Ivens, Milestone)
Our Story. *See* Notre Histoire, 1984
Our Teacher. *See* Waga kyokan, 1939
Our Town, 1940 (S. Wood)
Our Visit to China. *See* Kína vendégei voltunk, 1957
Our Wife, 1941 (Stahl)
Our Wonderful Years. *See* Kachan to Juichi-nin no Kodomo, 1966
Ouragan sur la montagne, 1922 (Duvivier)
Out, 1957 (Dickinson)
Out 1: noli me tangere, 1971 (Rivette)
Out 1: ombre, 1974 (Rivette)
Out Again—In Again, 1914 (Browning)
Out and In, 1913 (Sennett)
Out in the World. *See* Vlyudyakh, 1939
Out of a Clear Sky, 1918 (Neilan)
Out of Africa, 1985 (Pollack, Redford)
Out of College. *See* Gakuso o idete, 1925
Out of Darkness, 1955 (Welles)
Out of Darkness, 1990 (Kopple)
Out of Season, 1949 (Anderson)
Out of the Blue. *See* Hsiao Pa Pa Te T'ien K'ung, 1984
Out of the Clouds, 1954 (Dearden)
Out of the Darkness. *See* Teenage Caveman, 1958
Out of the Fog, 1941 (Litvak, Rossen)
Out of the Past, 1947 (J. Tourneur)
Out of the Underworld. *See* Nattevandreren, 1916
Out One, 1972 (Schroeder)
Out West, 1918 (Keaton)
Outbreak, 1995 (Petersen)
Outcast, 1936 (Florey)
Outcast. *See* Hakai, 1962
Outcast Among Outcasts, 1912 (Griffith)
Outcast of the Islands, 1951 (Reed)
Outcasts of Poker Flat, 1919 (Ford)
Outcast's Return. *See* Tugthusfange No. 97, 1914
Outcry. *See* Grido, 1957
Outdoor Pajamas, 1924 (McCarey)
Outer and Inner Space, 1965 (Warhol)
Outlaw, 1941 (Hawks)
Outlaw and His Wife. *See* Berg-Ejvind och hans hustru, 1918
Outlaw Colony, 1912 (Dwan)
Outlaw Josey Wales, 1976 (Eastwood, Kaufman)
Outlaws of the Orient, 1937 (Schoedsack)
Outlaw's Revenge, 1912 (Walsh)
Outlaw's Trail, 1911 (Dwan)
Outomlionnye solntsem, 1994 (Mikhalkov)
Outpost in Morocco, 1948 (Florey)
Outrage, 1915 (Hepworth)
Outrage, 1964 (Ritt)
Outside Chance, 1978 (Corman)
Outside the Law, 1921 (Browning)
Outside the Law, 1930 (Browning)
Outsider. *See* Guinea Pig, 1948
Outsiders. *See* Oka Oorie Katha, 1977
Outsiders, 1983 (Coppola)
Outskirts. *See* Okraina, 1933
Ouvert pour cause d'inventaire, 1946 (Resnais)
Over Again. *See* Punnascha, 1961
Over glas gesproken, 1958 (Haanstra)
Over Here, 1924 (Sennett)
Over Silent Paths, 1910 (Griffith)
Over the Hill, 1931 (King)
Over the Moon, 1937 (Howard)
Over There-Abouts, 1925 (Sennett)
Over Twenty-one, 1945 (C. Vidor)
Overcoat. *See* Cappotto, 1952
Overexposed, 1990 (Corman)
Overlanders, 1946 (Watt)
Overnight Stay in the Tyrol. *See* Übernachtung in Tirol, 1974
Overtaking. *See* Sorpasso, 1962
Overture, 1958 (Dickinson)
Ovoce stromů rajských jíme, 1969 (Chytilová)
Owd Bob, 1938 (Launder, Stevenson)
Ox-Bow Incident, 1943 (Wellman)
Oxford and Cambridge Boat Race, 1898 (Hepworth)
Oyaji to sono ko, 1929 (Gosho)
Oysters, 1965 (Emshwiller)
Oyu-sama, 1951 (Mizoguchi)
Oyuki the Madonna. *See* Maria no Oyuki, 1935
Ozawa, 1986 (Maysles)
Oznamuje se láskam vasim, 1988 (Kachyňa)

P ... respecteuse, 1949 (Astruc)
P-38 Pilot, 1990 (Baillie)
P.I. Private Investigations, 1987 (Dahl)
På livets ödesvägar, 1913 (Sjöström)
På solsidan, 1936 (Molander)
Paa Besøg hos Kong Tingeling, 1947 (Roos)
Paa Livets Skyggeside, 1912 (Holger-Madsen)
Paapi, 1953 (Kapoor)
Pablo Casals Breaks His Journey, 1958 (Dickinson)
Pace That Thrills, 1925 (LeRoy)
Pacific Heights, 1990 (Schlesinger)
Pacific Northwest, 1944 (Willard Van Dyke)
Pacifist. *See* Pacifista, 1970
Pacifista, 1970 (Jancsó)
Padatik, 1973 (Sen)
Paddy, 1969 (Corman)
Padenye dinastii romanovykh, 1927 (Shub)
Padlocked, 1926 (Dwan)
Padre, 1912 (Pastrone)
Padre padrone, 1977 (Taviani)
Padri e figli, 1957 (De Sica)
Paean. *See* Sanka, 1972
Pagan, 1929 (W.S. Van Dyke)
Paganini, 1910 (Gance)
Page Miss Glory, 1935 (Daves, LeRoy)
Page of Madness. *See* Kurutta ippeiji, 1926
Pages d'un catalogue, 1980 (Ruiz)
Pages from a Catalogue. *See* Pages d'un catalogue, 1980
Pages from a Life. *See* Stranitsy zhizni, 1948
Pagode, 1915 (Pick)
Pagode, 1923 (Dieterle)
Pahela Admi, 1950 (Roy)
Paid, 1930 (S. Wood)
Paid in Full, 1912 (Dwan)
Paid in Full, 1948 (Dieterle)
Paid to Love, 1927 (Hawks)
Pain. *See* Aci, 1971
Painel, 1951 (Cavalcanti)
Painless Dentistry, 1901
Paint Your Wagon, 1969 (Eastwood)
Painted Boats, 1945 (Crichton)
Painted Lady, 1912 (Griffith)
Painted Lips. *See* Boquitas pintadas, 1974
Painted Skin. *See* Hua Pi Zhi Yinyang Fawang, 1992
Painted Veil, 1934 (W.S. Van Dyke)
Painter and the Town. *See* O pintor e a cidade, 1956
Painters Painting, 1972 (De Antonio, Emshwiller)
Painter's Revenge, 1908 (Porter)
Paintings by Ed Emshwiller, 1955/58 (Emshwiller)
Pair of Tights, 1928 (McCarey)
Paisa Hi Paisa, 1956 (Mehboob)
Paisà, 1946 (Fellini, Rossellini)
Paisan. *See* **Paisà**, 1946
Pajama Game, 1957 (Donen, Fosse)
Pajama Party, 1964 (Keaton)
Pájaro del faro, 1971 (Alvarez)
Pál utcai fiúk, 1968 (Fábri, Jancsó)
Palace of the Arabian Nights. *See* Palais des mille et une nuits, 1905
Palaces of Peking. *See* Pekingi palotái, 1957
Palais des mille et une nuits, 1905 (Méliès)

a, 1945 (Fernández)
es de la couronne, 1937 (Guitry)
ičky na dně, 1964 (Chytilová, Jireš, Nemec, Schorm)
manent Vacation, 1980 (Jarmusch)
meke, 1985 (Storck)
mette? Rocco Papaleo, 1971 (Scola)
mian Strata, 1969 (Conner)
missive Society, 1975 (Leigh)
petua, 1922 (Hitchcock)
rsiane chiuse, 1951 (Comencini, Fellini)
rsona, 1966 (Bergman)
rsonal Affair, 1932 (Vasiliev)
rsonal Column. *See* Pièges, 1939
rsonal History, Adventures, Experience, and Observations of David Copperfield, the Younger. *See* David Copperfield, 1933
ersonal Matter. *See* Personal Affair, 1932
ersonal Property, 1937 (W.S. Van Dyke)
ersonel, 1975 (Kieślowski)
Personnel. *See* Personel, 1975
Peru—Istituto de Verano, 1956 (Olmi)
Pervaya Lyubov', 1915 (Bauer)
Pervoye maya 1920 v Moskve, 1919 (Kuleshov)
Pervyi paren, 1958 (Paradzhanov)
Pescatorella, 1947 (Risi)
Pesn o Gerojach, 1932 (Ivens)
Pesn o metallye, 1928 (Heifitz)
Pesnya katorzhanina, 1911 (Protazanov)
Pesnya Manshuk, 1971 (Mikhalkov)
Pesnya o shchastye, 1934 (Donskoi)
Pest from the West, 1939 (Keaton)
Pest in Florenz, 1919 (Lang)
Pest of Friends, 1927 (Sennett)
Pět holek na krku, 1966 (Schorm)
Petal on the Current, 1919 (Browning)
Petar Dobrovic, 1957 (Petrovic)
Pete 'n' Tillie, 1972 (Ritt)
Pete Roleum and His Cousins, 1939 (Losey)
Peter and Pavla. *See* Cerný Petr, 1963
Peter Gunn, 1989 (Edwards)
Peter Ibbetson, 1935 (Hathaway)
Peter Voss, der Millionendieb, 1932 (Dupont)
Peter Voss, Who Stole Millions. *See* Peter Voss, der Millionendieb, 1932
Peter's Friends, 1992 (Branagh)
Petersburg Slums. *See* Petersburgskiye trushchobi, 1915
Petersburgskiye trushchobi, 1915 (Protazanov)
Peterville Diamond, 1942 (Fisher)
Petey and Johnny, 1961 (Leacock)
Pětistovka, 1949 (Fric)
Petit à petit, 1971 (Rouch)
Petit Babouin, 1932 (Grémillon)
Petit Chaperon rouge, 1929 (Cavalcanti, Renoir)
Petit Chapiteau. *See* Circo mas pequeño, 1963
Petit Discours de la méthode, 1963 (Jutra)
Petit frèree et petite soeur, 1896-97 (Lumet)
Petit Hamlet. *See* Hamles, 1960
Petit Jour, 1963 (Godard)
Petit Manuel d'histoire de France, 1979 (Ruiz)
Petit monastère en Toscane, 1988 (Ioseliani)
Petit Monde de Don Camillo, 1951 (Duvivier)
Petit Roi, 1933 (Duvivier)
Petit Soldat, 1963 (Godard)
Petit Théâtre de Jean Renoir, 1970 (Renoir)
Petite, 1978 (Malle)
Petite Andalouse, 1914 (Feuillade)
Petite Apocalypse, 1993 (Costa-Gavras)
Petite danseuse, 1913 (Feuillade)
Petite Lise, 1930 (Grémillon)
Petite magicienne, 1900 (Guy)
Petite Marchande d'allumettes, 1928 (Renoir)
Petite Voleuse, 1988 (C. Miller)
Petites apprenties, 1911 (Feuillade)
Petites Filles modèles, 1952 (Rohmer)
Petites marionnettes, 1918 (Feuillade)
Petits Coupeurs de bois vert, 1904 (Guy)
Petrified Forest, 1936 (Daves)
Petrified Forest. *See* Kaseki no mori, 1973
Petronella, 1927 (Dieterle)
Pett and Pott, 1934 (Cavalcanti, Grierson, Jennings, Wright)
Petulia, 1968 (Lester, Roeg)
Peuple est invincible, 1969 (Ivens)
Peuple et ses fusils, 1969 (Ivens)
Peuple ne peut rien sans ses fusils, 1969 (Ivens)
Peuple peut tout, 1969 (Ivens)
Peur des coups, 1932 (Autant-Lara)
Pezzo, capopezzo e capitano. *See* Kanonenserenade, 1958
Pfarrer von Kirchfeld, 1926 (Dieterle)
Phaedra, 1962 (Dassin)
Phantasmes, 1918 (L'Herbier)
Phantom, 1922 (Murnau)
Phantom Chariot. *See* **Körkarlen**, 1921
Phantom India. *See* Inde fantôme, 1969
Phantom Lady, 1944 (Siodmak)
Phantom Light, 1935 (Powell)
Phantom of Liberty. *See* Fantôme de la liberté, 1974
Phantom of Love. *See* Ai no borei, 1978
Phantom of the Opera, 1962 (Fisher)
Phantom of the Paradise, 1974 (De Palma)
Phantom Outlaw, 1927 (Wyler)
Phantom Raiders, 1940 (J. Tourneur)
Phantom Riders, 1918 (Ford)
Phantom Strikes. *See* Gaunt Stranger, 1938
Pharaoh. *See* Faraon, 1965
Pharmaceutical Hallucinations. *See* Hallucinations pharmaceutiques, 1908
Pharmacist, 1933 (Sennett)
Phenomena, 1985 (Argento)
Phenomenon No.1, 1964 (Vanderbeek)
Philadelphia, 1993 (Corman, Cox, Demme)
Philadelphia Experiment, 1984 (Carpenter)
Philadelphia Story, 1940 (Cukor, Mankiewicz)
Philippe Soupault et le surréalisme, 1982 (Tavernier)
Philips-Radio, 1931 (Ivens)
Philosopher's Stone. *See* Parash Pathar, 1957
Phir Subah Hogi, 1958 (Kapoor)
Phobia, 1980 (Huston)
Phoenix. *See* Fujicho, 1947
Phone My Wife. *See* Zadzwoncie do mojej zony, 1958
Phoney University Student. *See* Nise Daigakusei, 1960
Photogénie mécanique, 1924 (Grémillon)
Photograph. *See* Zdjęcie, 1968
Photographe, 1939 (Lumet)
Photographer, 1947 (Willard Van Dyke)
Photographie electrique à distance, 1908 (Méliès)
Phynx, 1970 (Berkeley)
Physical Culture Romance, 1914 (Browning)
Piano, 1993 (Campion)
Piano Movers. *See* His Musical Career, 1914
Pianos mécanicos, 1965 (Bardem)
Pianos méchaniques. *See* Pianos mécanicos, 1965
Pibe cabeza, 1975 (Torre Nilsson)
Picador, 1932 (Dulac)
Piccadilly, 1928 (Dupont)
Piccadilly Third Stop, 1960 (Zetterling)
Piccolo mondo antico, 1941 (Lattuada, Risi)
Piccolo mondo di Don Camillo. *See* Petit Monde de Don Camillo, 1951
Picket Guard, 1913 (Dwan)
Picking Peaches, 1924 (Capra, Sennett)
Pickle, 1993 (Mazursky)
Pickpocket, 1959 (Bresson)
Pickup on South Street, 1953 (Fuller)
Picnic at Hanging Rock, 1975 (Weir)
Picnic at Ray's, 1975 (Jarman)

Palanquin. *See* Dochu sugoruku kago, 1926
Pale Flower. *See* Kawaita hana, 1963
Pale Rider, 1985 (Eastwood)
Paleface, 1922 (Keaton)
Paleface, 1947 (Tashlin)
Paleontologie, 1959 (Haanstra)
Palermo oder Wolfsburg, 1980 (Schroeter)
Palermo or Wolfsburg. *See* Palermo oder Wolfsburg, 1980
Palindrome, 1969 (Frampton)
Palio, 1932 (Blasetti)
Pålivets ödesvåger, 1913 (Stiller)
Pallard the Punter, 1919 (Pearson)
Palle alene i Verden, 1949 (Henning-Jensen)
Palle Alone in the World. *See* Palle alene i Verden, 1949
Palm Beach Story, 1942 (P. Sturges)
Palmier à l'huile, 1963 (Rouch)
Palmy Days, 1931 (Berkeley)
Paloma herida, 1963 (Fernández)
Palombella rossa, 1989 (Moretti)
Palomilla brava, 1973 (Ruiz)
Palomita blanca, 1973 (Ruiz)
Palookah from Paducah, 1935 (Keaton)
Pals, 1912 (Dwan)
Pályamunkások, 1957 (Gaál)
Pam Kuso Kar, 1974 (Rouch)
Pamiętniki chłopów, 1952 (Munk)
Pampa gringa, 1962 (Birri)
Pamyati Sergo Ordzhonikidze, 1937 (Vertov)
Pan, 1920 (Fejös)
Pan Passes, 1982 (Emshwiller)
Pandora and the Flying Dutchman, 1951 (Lewin)
Pandora's Box. *See* **Büchse der Pandora**, 1928
Pane, amore e ..., 1955 (De Sica, Risi)
Pane, amore e Andulasia, 1958 (De Sica)
Pane, amore e fantasia, 1953 (Comencini, De Sica)
Pane, amore e gelosia, 1954 (Comencini, De Sica)
Panel. *See* Painel, 1951
Panels for the Walls of the World, 1967 (Vanderbeek)
Panelstory, 1979 (Chytilová)
Panhandle, 1947 (Edwards)
Panic in the Parlor. *See* Sailor Beware!, 1956
Panic in the Streets, 1950 (Kazan)
Panik in Chicago, 1931 (Wiene)
Panique, 1946 (Duvivier)
Panny z Wilka, 1979 (Wajda)
Panorama from Top of a Moving Train. *See* Panorama pris d'un train en marche, 1898
Panorama of the Esplanade by Night, 1901 (Porter)
Panorama pris d'un train en marche, 1898 (Méliès)
Panta Rhei, 1951 (Haanstra)
Pantalon coupé, 1905 (Guy)
Pantano d'avio, 1956 (Olmi)
Panthea, 1917 (Dwan, Von Stroheim)
Pantomimes, 1956 (Cocteau)
Pants and Pansies, 1911 (Sennett)
Panzergewölbe, 1914 (Leni)
Panzergewölbe, 1926 (Pick)
Papacito lindo, 1939 (De Fuentes)
Paparazzi, 1963 (Godard)
Paper. *See* Papir, 1943
Paper Doll's Whisper of Spring. *See* Kaminingyo haru no sayaki, 1926
Paper Flowers. *See* **Kaagaz Ke Phool**, 1959
Paper Hanger. *See* Work, 1915
Paper Moon, 1973 (Bogdanovich)
Papillon, 1973 (Schaffner)
Papir, 1943 (Henning-Jensen)
Paquebot 'Tenacity', 1933 (Duvivier)
Paques rouges, 1914 (Feuillade)
Paquet embarrassant, 1907 (Feuillade)
Par ou t'est rentre? On t'a pas vu sortir, 1984 (Jerry Lewis)
Para recibir el canto de los pajaros, 1995 (Sanjinés)
Para vestir, 1955 (Torre Nilsson)
Paracelsus, 1943 (Pabst)
Parachute, 1969 (Anderson)
Parada, 1962 (Makavejev)
Parade. *See* Parada, 1962
Parade, 1973 (Tati)
Paradigme. *See* Pouvoir du mal, 1985
Paradine Case, 1947 (Hitchcock)
Paradis de Satan, 1938 (Delannoy)
Paradis perdu, 1939 (Gance)
Paradise for Buster, 1952 (Keaton)
Paradise for Two, 1927 (La Cava)
Paradise Lost, 1911 (Sennett)
Paradise Lost. *See* Bristet Lykke, 1913
Paradise Not Yet Lost, or Oona's Fifth Year, 1980 (Mekas)
Paradistorg, 1976 (Bergman)
Paraiso ortopedico, 1969 (Guzmán)
Parakh, 1960 (Roy)
Parallax View, 1974 (Pakula)
Paralytic, 1912 (Guy)
Paramount on Parade, 1930 (Arzner, Goulding, Lubitsch)
Paranoia Corridor, 1994 (Brakhage)
Parapluie fantastique, 1903 (Méliès)
Parapluies de Cherbourg, 1964 (Demy)
Parash Pathar, 1957 (S. Ray)
Parashuram, 1978 (Sen)
Parasite Murders. *See* Shivers, 1975
Parasol. *See* Ombrellone, 1965
Paratroop Command, 1958 (Corman)
Pardessus de demi-saison, 1917 (Feyder)
Pardners, 1956 (Jerry Lewis)
Pardon Me, But Your Teeth Are in My Neck. *See* Fearless Vampire Killers, 1967
Pardon My Berth Marks, 1940 (Keaton)
Pardon My Past, 1946 (Aldrich)
Parent terribles, 1948 (Cocteau)
Parfum de la dame en noir, 1931 (L'Herbier)
Parfums, 1924 (Grémillon)
Parigi e sempre parigi, 1951 (Rosi)
Parigina a Roma, 1954 (Scola)
Parineeta, 1953 (Roy)
Paris, 1925 (Florey)
Paris, 1926 (Goulding)
Paris 1900, 1947 (Resnais)
Paris à l'automne, 1958 (Resnais)
Paris Belongs to Us. *See* Paris nous appartient, 1961
Paris Blues, 1961 (Ritt)
Paris brûle-t-il?, 1966 (Clement, Coppola, Welles)
Paris-Deauville, 1935 (Delannoy)
Paris Does Strange Things. *See* Elena et les hommes, 1956
Paris Exposition, 1900. *See* Exposition de 1900, 1900
Paris Frills. *See* Falbalas, 1945
Paris Holiday, 1958 (P. Sturges)
Paris in the Spring, 1935 (Milestone)
Paris la nuit ou Exploits d' apaches à Montamartre, 1904 (Guy)
Paris nour appartient, 1960 (Chabrol, Demy, Godard, Rivette)
Paris på to måder, 1949 (Roos)
Paris qui dort, 1923 (Clair)
Paris s'en va, 1981 (Rivette)
Paris, Texas, 1984 (Wenders)
Paris Underworld. *See* Apachen, 1919
Paris vu par ..., 1965 (Chabrol, Godard, Rohmer, Rouch, Schroeder)
Paris vu par ... 20 ans après, 1984 (Akerman)
Paris—New York, 1939 (Von Stroheim)
Parisette, 1921 (Clair, Feuillade)
Parisian Nights, 1924 (Florey)
Parisiskor, 1928 (Molander)
Parivar, 1956 (Roy)
Parivartan, 1949 (Kapoor)
Park Row, 1952 (Fuller)
Parking, 1985 (Demy)

Parlor, Bedroom & Bath, 1931 (Keaton)
Pärlorna, 1922 (Molander)
Parnell, 1937 (Stahl)
Parole Fixer, 1939 (Florey)
Parovoz B-1000, 1929 (Kuleshov)
Parrish, 1961 (Daves)
Parsifal, 1983 (Syberberg)
Parson's Widow. *See* Prästänkan, 1920
Part de l'ombre, 1945 (Delannoy)
Part of a documentary on Karl Gass made in East Germany, 1960 (Pereira Dos Santos)
Part Time Wife, 1930 (McCarey)
Partial Eclipse. *See* Neúplné zatmění, 1982
Partie d'ecarté, 1939 (Lumet)
Partie de campagne, 1946 (Becker, Renoir, Visconti)
Partie de plaisir, 1975 (Chabrol)
Partie de tric-trac, 1939 (Lumet)
Parting Trails, 1911 (Dwan)
Partir ..., 1931 (M. Tourneur)
Partir! *See* Partir ..., 1931
Partir, revenir, 1985 (Lelouch)
Partire, 1938 (De Sica)
Partner, 1968 (Bertolucci)
Partners Again, 1926 (King)
Partners in Crime, 1942 (Launder)
Partners Three, 1919 (Niblo)
Parto psicoprofiláctico, 1969 (Leduc)
Partout ou peut-être nulle part, 1969 (Hondo)
Party, 1964 (Altman)
Party, 1968 (Edwards)
Party, 1970 (Schepisi)
Party and the Guests. *See* O slavnosti a hostech, 1966
Party Girl, 1958 (N. Ray)
Party Is Over. *See* Fin de fiesta, 1959
Parvarish, 1958 (Kapoor)
Pas assez, 1968 (Haanstra)
Pas de la mule, 1930 (Epstein)
Pas de Trois, 1975 (Frampton)
Pas de violence entre nous. *See* Quem e beta, 1972
Pas folle la guêpe, 1972 (Delannoy)
Pas si méchant que ça, 1975 (Goretta)
Pasażerka, 1963 (Munk)
Pascal, 1964-69 (Rohmer)
Paseo sobre una guerra antigua, 1949 (Bardem, García Berlanga)
Pasht, 1965 (Brakhage)
Pass the Dumpling, 1927 (Sennett)
Pass the Gravy, 1928 (McCarey)
Passage Through: A Ritual, 1990 (Brakhage)
Passage to India, 1984 (Lean)
Passage to Marseille, 1944 (Curtiz)
Passager de la pluie, 1969 (Clement)
Passagère. *See* Pasażerka, 1963
Passagierin. *See* Pasażerka, 1963
Passant par la Lorraine, 1950 (Franju)
Passatore, 1947 (Fellini)
Passe ton bac d'abord, 1979 (Pialat)
Passé de Monique, 1917 (Feuillade)
Passe-montagne, 1977 (Schroeder)
Passenger. *See* Pasażerka, 1963
Passenger. *See* **Professione: Reporter,** 1975
Passers-By, 1920 (Blackton)
Passes, 1982 (Emshwiller)
Passing Fancy. *See* Dekigokoro, 1933
Passing of a Soul, 1915 (Hepworth)
Passing of Izzy, 1914 (Sennett)
Passing Through. *See* Good Bad Man, 1916
Passion, 1954 (Dwan)
Passion, 1969 (Bergman)
Passion, 1982 (Godard)
Passion Béatrice, 1987 (Tavernier)
Passion de Bernadette, 1990 (Delannoy)
Passion de Jeanne d'Arc, 1928 (Dreyer)
Passion Fish, 1992 (Sayles)
Passion in the Desert. *See* Baroud, 1931
Passion Island. *See* Isla de la pasión, 1941
Passion of a Woman Teacher. *See* Kyoren no onna shisho, 1926
Passion of Anna. *See* En passion, 1969
Passion of Jesus. *See* Acto da primavera, 1963
Passion without End. *See* Hateshinaki jonetsu, 1949
Passionate Adventure, 1924 (Hitchcock)
Passionate Friends, 1949 (Lean)
Passionate Plumber, 1932 (Keaton)
Passionate Quest, 1926 (Blackton)
Passione d'amore, 1981 (Scola)
Passionless Moments, 1984 (Campion)
Passions of the Sea. *See* Lost and Found on a South Sea Island, 1923
Passions—He Had Three, 1913 (Sennett)
Passport to Shame, 1959 (Roeg)
Past, 1950 (Fric)
Past and Present. *See* O passado e o presente, 1972
Past, Present, and Future. *See* Trikaal, 1985
Pasteur, 1922 (Epstein)
Pasteur, 1935 (Guitry)
Pastor Hall, 1940 (Boulting)
Pastoral, 1976 (Ioseliani)
Pat and Mike, 1952 (Cukor)
Pat Garrett and Billy the Kid, 1973 (Fernández, Hellman, Peckinpah)
Patates, 1969 (Autant-Lara)
Pater, 1910 (Feuillade)
Path of Hope. *See* Cammino della speranza, 1950
Pather Panchali, 1955 (S. Ray)
Paths into the Night. *See* Wagen in der Nacht, 1979
Paths of Glory, 1957 (Kubrick)
Patience, 1920 (Leni)
Pâtissier et ramoneur, 1904 (Guy)
Patricia et Jean-Baptiste, 1966 (Lefebvre)
Patrick Dewaere, 1992 (Blier)
Patrimonio nacional, 1980 (García Berlanga)
Patriot, 1928 (Lubitsch)
Patriot and the Spy, 1915 (Cruze)
Patriote, 1938 (M. Tourneur)
Patriotic Woman. *See* Patriotin, 1979
Patriotin, 1979 (Kluge)
Patriots. *See* Okraina, 1933
Patron est mort, 1938 (Storck)
Patrouille en zone minée, 1964 (C. Miller)
Patrullero. *See* Highway Patrolman, 1991
Pat's Day Off, 1912 (Sennett)
Patsy, 1928 (K. Vidor)
Patsy, 1964 (Jerry Lewis)
Pattern of Supply. *See* Olie op reis, 1957
Pattes blanches, 1949 (Grémillon)
Pattes de mouches, 1936 (Grémillon)
Patton, 1970 (Coppola, Schaffner)
Patton: A Salute to a Rebel. *See* Patton, 1970
Patton—Lust for Glory. *See* Patton, 1970
Pattuglia di passo San Giacomo, 1954 (Olmi)
Patty Hearst, 1988 (Schrader)
Paul Delvaux ou les femmes défendues, 1969-70 (Storck)
Paul Revere's Ride, 1910 (Walsh)
Paul Swan, 1965 (Warhol)
Paula—"je reviens", 1968 (Schroeter)
Pauline à la plage, 1983 (Rohmer)
Pauline at the Beach. *See* Pauline à la plage, 1983
Paura. *See* Angst, 1954
Paura e amore, 1988 (Von Trotta)
Pauvre John ou Les Aventures d'un buveur de whiskey, 1907 (Méliès)
Pauvre pompier, 1906 (Guy)
Pavé, 1905 (Guy)
Pavillonens Hemmelighed, 1916 (Dreyer)
Pavlínka, 1974 (Kachyňa)
Paw, 1959 (Henning-Jensen)

Pawn of Fate, 1916 (M. Tourneur)
Pawnbroker, 1965 (Lumet)
Pawnbroker's Heart, 1917 (Sennett)
Pawnshop, 1916 (Chaplin)
Pax Aeterna, 1916 (Holger-Madsen)
Pay as You Enter, 1928 (Bacon)
Pay Day, 1922 (Chaplin)
Pay Dirt, 1916 (King)
Pay-Off. *See* T-Bird Gang, 1959
Pay the Devil, 1957 (Welles)
Paying the Penalty. *See* **Underworld**, 1927
Payoff, 1935 (Florey)
Pays d'Octobre. *See* Mississippi Blues, 1983
Pays d'où je viens, 1956 (Carné)
Pays de la terre sans arbre, 1979 (Perrault)
Pays sans bon sens, 1970 (Perrault)
Pazza di giola, 1940 (De Sica)
Peace Game. *See* Gladiatorerna, 1969
Peace of Britain, 1936 (Rotha)
Peace Tour. *See* Wyscig pokoju Warszawa-Berlin-Praga, 1952
Peace Will Win. *See* Pokoj zwyciezy swiat, 1951
Peaceable Kingdom, 1971 (Brakhage)
Peach Basket Hat, 1909 (Griffith)
Peaches and Plumbers, 1927 (Sennett)
Peacock Alley, 1921 (Goulding)
Peanuts and Bullets, 1915 (Sennett)
Pearl. *See* Perla, 1945
Pearl Necklace. *See* Zhemchuzhnoe Ozherel'e, 1915
Pearl of the South Pacific, 1955 (Dwan)
Pearls of the Crown. *See* Perles de la couronne, 1937
Pearls of the Deep. *See* Perličky na dně, 1964
Peau d'ane, 1971 (Demy)
Peau de banane, 1963 (Ophuls)
Peau de Torpedo, 1969 (Delannoy)
Peau douce, 1964 (Truffaut)
Pečat, 1955 (Makavejev)
Peccato che sia una canaglia, 1954 (Blasetti, De Sica)
Peccatrice, 1940 (De Sica)
Pêche au hareng, 1930 (Storck)
Pêche aux poissons rouges, 1939 (Lumet)
Péchés de jeunesse, 1941 (M. Tourneur)
Pêcheur dans le torrent, 1897 (Guy)
Pêcheurs du Niger, 1962 (Rouch)
Pechmarie, 1950 (Staudte)
Peck's Bad Boy, 1920 (S. Wood)
Pedagoška bajka, 1961 (Makavejev)
Pedales sobra Cuba, 1965 (Alvarez)
Peddler, 1913 (Sennett)
Pedestrian Subway. *See* Przajście podziemne, 1973
Pedreira de São Diogo, 1962 (Pereira Dos Santos)
Pedro's Dilemma, 1912 (Sennett)
Pee-Wee's Big Adventure, 1985 (Burton)
Peel, 1982 (Campion)
Peep Show, 1958 (Russell)
Peeping Pete, 1913 (Sennett)
Peeping Tom, 1960 (Powell)
Peg-O-My-Heart, 1923 (K. Vidor)
Peg o' the Ring, 1916 (Ford)
Peg Woffington, 1912 (Pearson)
Peggy Sue Got Married, 1986 (Coppola)
Peggy, The Will o' th' Wisp, 1917 (Browning)
Pègre de Paris, 1906 (Guy)
Pei Ch'ing Ch'êng Shih, 1989 (Hou)
Pei Chih Ch'iu, 1977 (Hou)
Peine du talion, 1916 (Feuillade)
Peintre et ivrogne, 1905 (Guy)
Peking Express, 1957 (Dieterle)
Pekingi palotái, 1957 (Jancsó)
Pelea cubana contra los demonios, 1971 (Gutiérrez Alea)
Pelican Brief, 1993 (Pakula)
Pelileo Earthquake, 1944/49 (Leacock)
Pelle erobreren, 1987 (August)
Pelle the Conqueror. *See* Pelle erobreren, 1987
Penal Colony. *See* Colonia penal, 1971
Penalty of Fame. *See* Gudernes Yndling, 1919
Penalty of Fame. *See* Okay America, 1932
Penderecki, Lutoslawa, 1977 (Zanussi)
P'eng P'eng I Ch'uan Hsin, 1980 (Hou)
Penge, 1916 (Dreyer)
Péniche tragique, 1924 (Pick)
Penn and Teller Get Killed, 1989 (Penn)
Penny Journey, 1938 (Jennings)
Penny Paradise, 1938 (Dearden, Reed)
Penny Serenade, 1941 (Stevens)
Penrod, 1922 (Neilan)
Pension Groonen, 1924 (Wiene)
Pension Mimosas, 1935 (Feyder)
Pensioners, 1912 (Dwan)
Pente, 1931 (Autant-Lara)
Penthesilea, 1987 (Syberberg)
Penthouse, 1933 (W.S. Van Dyke)
People. *See* Ceddo, 1977
People Against O'Hara, 1951 (J. Sturges)
People and the Nile. *See* Nas wal Nil, 1968
People and Their Guns. *See* Peuple et ses fusils, 1969
People from the Metro. *See* Lidé z metra, 1974
People in the Sun, 1935 (Weiss)
People Like Maria, 1958 (Watt)
People of France. *See* Vie est à nous, 1936
People of One Heart. *See* Lidé jednoho srdce, 1953
People of the Cumberlands, 1937 (Kazan)
People on a Glacier. *See* Lidé na kře, 1978
People on Sunday. *See* Menschen am Sonntag, 1929
People on Wheels. *See* Lidé z maringotek, 1966
People under the Stairs, 1991 (Craven)
People vs. John Doe, 1916 (Weber)
People Who Are Preparing the Year of the Hohenstaufens. *See* Menschen die Staufer-Austellung vorbereiten, 1977
People Will Talk, 1951 (Mankiewicz)
People's Enemy. *See* Minshu no teki, 1946
Pépé-le-Moko, 1937 (Duvivier)
Pepi, Luci, Bom and Lots of Other Girls. *See* Pepi, Luci, Bom y otras chic de montón, 1980
Pepi, Luci, Bom y otras chicas de montón, 1980 (Almodóvar)
Pepita Jiménez, 1945 (Fernández)
Peppermint frappé, 1967 (Saura)
Per qualche dollaro in più, 1965 (Leone)
Per un pugno di dollari, 1964 (Leone)
Perceval, 1964-69 (Rohmer)
Perceval, 1978 (Schroeder)
Perceval le Gaullois, 1978 (Rohmer)
Perché pagare per essere felici!, 1970 (Ferreri)
Pére de mademoiselle, 1953 (L'Herbier)
Père prématuré, 1933 (Delannoy)
Père tranquille, 1946 (Clement)
Perfect Couple, 1979 (Altman)
Perfect Crime, 1921 (Dwan)
Perfect Furlough, 1959 (Edwards)
Perfect Lady. *See* Woman, 1915
Perfect Love, 1919 (Goulding)
Perfect Marriage. *See* Beau Mariage, 1982
Perfect Specimen, 1937 (Curtiz)
Perfect Strangers, 1945 (Korda)
Perfect Understanding, 1932 (Dickinson)
Perfect World, 1993 (Costner, Eastwood)
Perfidy of Mary, 1913 (Griffith)
Performance, 1970 (Roeg)
Perils of Petersboro, 1926 (Sennett)
Perils of the Park, 1916 (Sennett)
Period of Adjustment, 1962 (G. Hill)
Périscope, 1916 (Gance)
Perkele! Kuvia Suomesta, 1971 (Donner)

Picnic on the Grass. *See* Déjeuner sur l'herbe, 1959
Picture of Dorian Gray, 1945 (Lewin)
Picture of Madame Yuki. *See* Yuki Fujin ezu, 1950
Picture of the Time. *See* Bild der Zeit, 1921/22
Picture Snatcher, 1933 (Bacon)
Pictures at an Exhibition. *See* Egy kiállitás képei, 1954
Pictures of My Brother Julio. *See* As pinturas de meu irmão Júlio, 1965
Pida huivsta kiinnim Tatjana, 1994 (Kaurismaki)
Pie in the Sky, 1934 (Kazan)
Piece of Pleasure. *See* Partie de plaisir, 1975
Pied Piper, 1942 (Preminger)
Pied Piper. *See* Pied Piper of Hamelin, 1972
Pied Piper of Hamelin, 1972 (Demy)
Pied qui etreint, 1916 (Feyder)
Piednadze albo zycie, 1961 (Skolimowski)
Piedra libre, 1976 (Torre Nilsson)
Piedra sobre piedra, 1970 (Alvarez)
Piège à pucelles, 1972 (Chabrol)
Pièges, 1939 (Siodmak, Von Stroheim)
Piel de verano, 1961 (Torre Nilsson)
Piera's Story. *See* Storia di Piera, 1983
Pierre et Paul, 1968 (C. Miller)
Pierre philosophe, 1912 (Gance)
Pierres chantantes d'Ayorou, 1968 (Rouch)
Pierrot assassin, 1903/04 (Guy)
Pierrot des bois, 1956 (Jutra)
Pierrot le fou, 1965 (Fuller, Godard)
Pierrot Pierrette, 1924 (Feuillade)
Pierwsza miłość, 1973 (Kieślowski)
Pierwsze lata, 1949 (Ivens)
Piety. *See* Kegyelet, 1967
Pigpen. *See* Porcile, 1969
Pigsty. *See* Porcile, 1969
Pikoo, 1981 (S. Ray)
Pikovaya dama, 1916 (Protazanov)
Pilate and Others. *See* Pilatus und andere—ein Film für Karfreitag, 1972
Pilatus und andere—ein Film für Karfreitag, 1972 (Wajda)
Pile Driver. *See* Fatal Mallet, 1914
Pile Driving. *See* Heien, 1929
Piles of Perils, 1916 (Sennett)
Pilgrim, 1923 (Chaplin)
Pilgrimage, 1933 (Ford)
Pill Pounder, 1923 (La Cava)
Pillars of Society, 1916 (Walsh)
Pillole di Ercole, 1960 (De Sica)
Pilobolus and Joan, 1974 (Emshwiller)
Pilota ritorna, 1942 (Rossellini)
Pimp. *See* Zegen, 1987
Pinched in the Finish, 1917 (Sennett)
Pine à ongles, 1968 (Forman)
Pinhamy, 1979 (Peries)
Pink Cadillac, 1989 (Eastwood)
Pink Flamingoes, 1972 (Waters)
Pink Floyd—The Wall, 1982 (Parker)
Pink Pajamas, 1929 (Sennett)
Pink Panther, 1964 (Edwards)
Pink Panther Strikes Again, 1976 (Edwards)
Pink String and Sealing Wax, 1945 (Hamer)
Pinky, 1949 (Kazan)
Pinnacle Rider, 1926 (Wyler)
Pinned to the Ground. *See* Auf's kreuz gelegt, 1974
Pinocchio, 1972 (De Sica)
Pioneers in Ingolstadt. *See* Pioniere in Ingolstadt, 1971
Pioniere in Ingolstadt, 1971 (Fassbinder)
Pipes of Pan, 1922 (Hepworth)
Pippa Passes, 1909 (Griffith, Sennett)
Pir v Girmunka, 1941 (Pudovkin)
Pirañas, 1967 (García Berlanga)
Piranha, 1978 (Corman, Sayles)
Pirata sono io!, 1940 (Fellini)
Pirate, 1948 (Minnelli)
Pirate Gold, 1912 (Griffith)
Pirate Tape, 1982 (Jarman)
Pirates, 1985 (Polanski)
Pirates du rail, 1938 (Von Stroheim)
Pirate's Gold, 1908 (Griffith)
Pirates on Lake Mälar. *See* Mälarpirater, 1923
Pire Nuri, 1968 (Güney)
Pirogov, 1947 (Kozintsev)
Piroska és a farkas, 1988 (Meszaros)
Píseň o sletu I, II, 1949 (Weiss)
Pisito, 1958 (Ferreri)
Pit, 1914 (M. Tourneur)
Pit. *See* Ana, 1957
Pit and the Pendulum, 1913 (Guy)
Pit and the Pendulum, 1961 (Corman)
Pit and the Pendulum. *See* Puits et le pendule, 1963
Pit Stop, 1969 (Corman)
Pitfalls of a Big City, 1923 (Sennett)
Pithache Panje, 1914 (Phalke)
Pittori in città, 1955-59 (Taviani)
Pittsburgh Documents, 1971 (Brakhage)
Piú bella serata della mia vita, 1972 (Scola)
Pixote, 1981 (Babenco)
Piyade Osman, 1970 (Güney)
Pizhon, 1929 (Donskoi)
Pizza Triangle: A Drama of Jealousy, and Other Things. *See* Dramma della gelosia—Tutti i particolari in cronaca, 1970
Place for Gold, 1960 (Wright)
Place for Lovers. *See* Amanti, 1968
Place in a Crowd, 1964 (Menzel)
Place in the Sun, 1951 (Stevens)
Place to Go, 1963 (Dearden)
Place without Limits. *See* Lugar sin Limites, 1977
Places in the Heart, 1984 (Benton)
Plácido, 1961 (García Berlanga)
Placido Domingo: A Musical Life, 1995 (Zeffirelli)
Plague in Florence. *See* Pest in Florenz, 1919
Plain and Fancy Girls, 1925 (McCarey)
Plain Clothes, 1925 (Capra, Sennett)
Plain Jane to the Rescue, 1982 (Woo)
Plain People. *See* Prostiye Lyudi, 1945
Plain Song, 1910 (Griffith)
Plain Woman. *See* Okame, 1927
Plainsman, 1937 (De Mille)
Plaisir, 1952 (Ophüls)
Plaisirs défendus, 1933 (Cavalcanti)
Plan Nine from Outer Space, 1956 (E. Wood)
Planet of the Apes, 1968 (Schaffner)
Plannbung, 1977 (Petersen)
Planter's Wife, 1908 (Griffith)
Planton du colonel, 1897 (Guy)
Plastiques, 1963 (Storck)
Plateau, 1905 (Guy)
Platinum Blonde, 1931 (Capra)
Platonische Ehe, 1919 (Leni)
Platoon, 1986 (Stone)
Plato's Cave Inn, 1980 (Vanderbeek)
Play, 1968-73 (Potter)
Play It Again, Sam, 1972 (Allen)
Play It As It Lays, 1972 (Schumacher)
Play Misty for Me, 1971 (Eastwood, Siegel)
Play Murder for Me, 1992 (Corman)
Play Square, 1921 (Howard)
Playa prohibida, 1955 (Bardem)
Player, 1992 (Altman, Pollack, Rudolph)
Playgirls and the Bellboy, 1962 (Coppola)
Playgrounds of the Mammals, 1932 (Sennett)
Playhouse, 1921 (Keaton)
Playing Around, 1930 (LeRoy)
Playmates. *See* Lekkamraterna, 1914
Plays for Britain, 1976 (Leigh)

Popióły, 1965 (Wajda)
Poppy. *See* Gubijinso, 1935
Popular Crafts. *See* Artesania popular, 1966
Popular Power. *See* Poder popular, 1979
Por la puerta falsa, 1950 (De Fuentes)
Por la tierra ajena, 1968 (Littin)
Por primera vez elecciones libres, 1984 (Alvarez)
Porcile, 1969 (Ferreri, Pasolini)
Porgy and Bess, 1959 (Preminger)
Pork Chop Hill, 1959 (Milestone)
Porkala, 1956 (Donner)
Pornographers: Introduction to Anthropology. *See* Jinruigaku nyumon, 1966
Port Chicago Vigil, 1966 (Baillie)
Port of Call. *See* Hamnstad, 1948
Port of Seven Seas, 1938 (P. Sturges, Whale)
Port of Shadows. *See* **Quai des brumes,** 1938
Porta del cielo, 1946 (De Sica)
Portaborse, 1991 (Moretti)
Porte chiuse, 1960 (Risi)
Porte des Lilas, 1957 (Clair)
Porte du large, 1936 (L'Herbier)
Porter. *See* New Janitor, 1914
Portes de la maison, 1954 (Storck)
Portes de la nuit, 1946 (Carné)
Porteuse de pain, 1906 (Feuillade)
Porto Novo—la danse des reines, 1971 (Rouch)
Portrait. *See* Shozo, 1948
Portrait, 1993 (Penn)
Portrait d'Henri Goetz, 1947 (Resnais)
Portrait d'un assassin, 1949 (Von Stroheim)
Portrait de Mireille, 1909 (Gance)
Portrait de Raymond Depardon, 1983 (Rouch)
Portrait from Life, 1948 (Fisher, Zetterling)
Portrait mystérieux, 1899 (Méliès)
Portrait of a Girl. *See* Léanyportre, 1971
Portrait of a Goon, 1959 (Russell)
Portrait of a Lady, 1996 (Campion)
Portrait of a Man. *See* Férfiarckép, 1964
Portrait of a Sinner. *See* Rough and the Smooth, 1959
Portrait of a Soviet Composer, 1961 (Russell)
Portrait of a Woman. *See* Femme disparait, 1942
Portrait of a Young Girl at the End of the 1960s in Brussels, 1994 (Akerman)
Portrait of Asa. *See* Portratt av Asa, 1965
Portrait of Geza Anda, 1964 (Leacock)
Portrait of Jason, 1967 (Clarke)
Portrait of Jennie, 1949 (Dieterle)
Portrait of One Who Proved His Mettle. *See* Porträt einer Bewährung, 1964
Portrait of Paul Burkhard, 1964 (Leacock)
Portrait of the Patriotic Heroes. *See* Chung Lieh T'u, 1974
Portrait of Van Cliburn, 1966 (Leacock)
Portrait spirite, 1903 (Méliès)
Portraits of Women. *See* Naisenkuvia, 1970
Porträt einer Bewährung, 1964 (Kluge)
Portratt av Asa, 1965 (Troell)
Positive Negative Electronic Faces, 1973 (Emshwiller)
Poslední výstřel, 1950 (Weiss)
Possédés, 1987 (Holland, Wajda)
Possessed, 1931 (Brown)
Possessed. *See* Possédés, 1987
Possession de l'enfant, 1909 (Feuillade)
Post Haste, 1934 (Grierson, Jennings, Launder)
Post Office Europe. *See* Europa-Postlagernd, 1918
Postcards from the Edge, 1990 (Nichols, Reiner)
Postman Always Rings Twice, 1946 (Garnett)
Postman Always Rings Twice, 1981 (Rafelson)
Posto, 1961 (Olmi)
Postřižny, 1980 (Menzel)
Pot au Feu, 1965 (Altman)
Pot Bouille, 1957 (Duvivier)
Potage indigeste, 1903 (Guy)
Pote tin kyriaki, 1960 (Dassin)
Potifars Hustru, 1911 (Blom)
Potomok Chingis-khan, 1928 (Barnet, Pudovkin)
Pottery of Ilzecka. *See* Ceramika Iłżecka, 1951
Potterymaker, 1925 (Flaherty)
Pottsville Palooka, 1931 (Sennett)
Poule fantaisiste, 1903 (Guy)
Poulet au vinaigre, 1984 (Chabrol)
Pounding Hearts. *See* P'eng P'eng I Ch'uan Hsin, 1980
Pour être aimée, 1933 (J. Tourneur)
Pour la suite du monde, 1963 (Perrault)
Pour le meilleur et pour le pire, 1975 (Jutra)
Pour le mérite, 1950 (Staudte)
Pour le mistral, 1966 (Ivens)
Pour secourer la salade, 1902 (Guy)
Pour un maillot jaune, 1965 (Lelouch)
Pour un sou d'amour, 1931 (Grémillon)
Pour une nuit d'amour, 1920/23 (Protazanov)
Pour vos beaux yeux, 1929-30 (Storck)
Poussières, 1954 (Franju)
Pouta, 1961 (Kachyňa)
Pouvoir du mal, 1985 (Zanussi)
Povere bimbe, 1923 (Pastrone)
Poveri ma belli, 1956 (Risi)
Poveri milionaire, 1958 (Risi)
Povest plamennykh let, 1961 (Dovzhenko)
Povodeň, 1958 (Fric)
Power, 1928 (Garnett)
Power, 1986 (Lumet)
Power Among Men, 1958 (Dickinson)
Power and Glory. *See* Power and the Glory, 1933
Power and the Glory, 1933 (Howard, P. Sturges)
Power and the Land, 1940 (Ivens)
Power Flash of Death, 1913 (Dwan)
Power of Emotions. *See* Macht der Gefühle, 1983
Power of Evil. *See* Pouvoir du mal, 1985
Power of Love. *See* Kaerlighedens Styrke, 1911
Power of Love, 1912 (Dwan)
Power of the Press, 1928 (Capra)
Power of the Press, 1943 (Fuller)
Power to the People, 1972 (Benegal)
Powers That Prey, 1918 (King)
Pozor vizita!, 1981 (Kachyňa)
Práče, 1960 (Kachyňa)
Practical Joke and a Sad End. *See* En grov Spøg, 1908
Praesidenten, 1919 (Dreyer)
Praesten i Vejlby, 1920 (Blom)
Praesten i Vejlby, 1931 (Holger-Madsen)
Praestens Datter, 1916 (Holger-Madsen)
Prague, 1985 (Menzel)
Prague, the Restless Heart of Europe. *See* Praha, neklidne srace Europy, 1985
Praha, neklidne srace Europy, 1985 (Chytilová)
Prangasiz mahkumlar, 1964 (Güney)
Prästänkan, 1920 (Dreyer)
Prästen, 1914 (Sjöström)
Pratidwandi, 1970 (S. Ray)
Pratinidhi, 1964 (Sen)
Prato, 1979 (Taviani)
Pravda, 1969 (Godard)
Prawdziwy koniec wielkiej wojny, 1957 (Kawalerowicz)
Prazdnik svyatovo Iorgena, 1930 (Protazanov)
Precautions against Fanatics. *See* Massnahmen gegen Fanatiker, 1968
Precious Grain. *See* Dragotsennye zerna, 1948
Precursores de la pintura argentina, 1957 (Torre Nilsson)
Prefab Story. *See* Panelstory, 1979
Prelude à l'apres-midi d'une faune, 1938 (Rossellini)
Prem Patra, 1962 (Roy)
Prem Rog, 1982 (Kapoor)
Premature Burial, 1962 (Coppola, Corman)
Préméditation, 1912 (Feuillade)
Premi Pagal, 1933 (Mehboob)
Premiere. *See* Ösbemutató, 1974

Puits mitoyen, 1913 (M. Tourneur)
Pukkelryggede. *See* Kaerligheds Laengsel, 1915
Pullman Bride, 1917 (Sennett)
Pulp Fiction, 1994 (Tarantino)
Pulsating Giant, 1971 (Benegal)
Pulse of Life, 1917 (Ingram)
Pumpkin. *See* Kabocha, 1928
Pumpkin Eater, 1964 (Clayton)
Punch and Judy. *See* Anarchie chez Guignol, 1906
Punchline, 1988 (Mazursky)
Punishment, 1912 (Griffith)
Punishment Island. *See* Shokei no shima, 1966
Punishment Park, 1971 (Watkins)
Punishment Room. *See* Shokei no heya, 1956
Punition, 1962 (Rouch)
Punnascha, 1961 (Sen)
Punt'a a čtyřlístek, 1954 (Weiss)
Punta and the Four-Leaf Clover. *See* Punt'a a čtyřlístek, 1954
Punter's Mishap, 1900 (Hepworth)
Puntila, 1970 (Syberberg)
Pupils of the Seventh Grade, 1938 (Protazanov)
Puppe, 1919 (Lubitsch)
Puppenmacher von Kiang-Ning, 1923 (Wiene)
Puppetmaster, 1993 (Hou)
Puppets, 1916 (Browning)
Puppies. *See* Stěnata, 1957
Puppy Lovetime, 1926 (Sennett)
Pur Sang, 1931 (Autant-Lara)
Pura formalita, 1994 (Tornatore)
Purchase Price, 1932 (Wellman)
Pure Air. *See* Friluft, 1959
Pure Formality. *See* Pura formalita, 1994
Pure Hell of St. Trinian's, 1960 (Launder)
Pure Love. *See* Junjo, 1930
Purgation, 1910 (Griffith)
Purity and After, 1978 (Brakhage)
Purple Heart, 1944 (Milestone)
Purple Noon. *See* Plein soleil, 1959
Purple Rose of Cairo, 1985 (Allen)
Pursued, 1947 (Walsh)
Pursuit at Dawn. *See* Akatsuki no tsuiseki, 1950
Pursuit of Happiness, 1971 (Mulligan)
Pursuit of the Graf Spee. *See* Battle of the River Plate, 1956
Pusher-in-the-Face, 1928 (Florey)
Pushing Hands, 1991 (A. Lee)
Put Yourself in His Place, 1912 (Cruze)
Putevi, 1958 (Petrovic)
Putting One Over. *See* Masquerader, 1914
Putting Pants on Philip, 1926 (Stevens)
Puu-san, 1953 (Ichikawa)
Pyaar, 1950 (Kapoor)
Pyaasa, 1957 (Dutt)
Pyat vecheroc, 1979 (Mikhalkov)
Pyervy uchityel, 1965 (Mikhalkov-Konchalovsky)
Pyesn o Manshuk, 1969 (Mikhalkov-Konchalovsky)
Pygmalion, 1938 (Asquith, Lean)
Pyramide des Sonnengottes, 1965 (Siodmak)
Pyramide humaine, 1961 (Rouch)
Pyramides bleues, 1988 (Marker)
Pytel blech, 1962 (Chytilová)
Pytlákova schovanka, 1949 (Fric)

Q & A, 1990 (Lumet)
Q-bec My Love. *See* Succès commercial, 1970
Qiangxing Qifei, 1984 (Chen)
Qiu Jin, 1983 (Xie)
Quack Doctor, 1920 (Sennett)
Quadrille, 1938 (Guitry)
Quadrille, 1950 (Godard, Rivette)
Quadrille réaliste, 1902 (Guy)
Quai des brumes, 1938 (Carné)
Quai des Orfèvres, 1947 (Clouzot)
Qualen der Nacht, 1926 (Dieterle)
Quality Street, 1927 (Lewin)
Quality Street, 1937 (Stevens)
Quand le rideau se lève, 1957 (Lelouch)
Quand les feuilles tombent, 1911 (Feuillade)
Quand minuit sonna, 1914 (Feyder)
Quand tu liras cette lettre, 1953 (Melville)
Quando a Carnaval chegar, 1972 (Diegues)
Quarrelsome Anglers, 1898 (Hepworth)
Quarry Mystery, 1914 (Hepworth)
Quarta pagina, 1942 (Fellini)
Quartet, 1948 (Zetterling)
Quartet, 1981 (Ivory)
Quartet That Split Up. *See* Kvartetten som sprängdes, 1950
Quartieri alti, 1944 (Castellani)
Quaternion, 1976 (Frampton)
Quatorze Juillet, 1932 (Clair)
Quatorze Juillet, 1954 (Gance)
Quatre Aventures de Reinette et Mirabelle, 1987 (Rohmer)
Quatre Cents Coups, 1959 (Demy, Truffaut)
Quatre Nuits d'un rêveur, 1971 (Bresson)
Quatres Vagabonds, 1931 (Pick)
Quatres vérités, 1962 (Clair)
Quattro passi fra le nuvole, 1942 (Blasetti)
Quattro verita, 1963 (Blasetti)
Que hacer?, 1970 (Ruiz)
Que la bete meure, 1969 (Pialat, Chabrol)
Que la fête commence, 1975 (Tavernier)
Que Viva Mexico!, 1941 (Eisenstein)
Que Viva Mexico!, 1958 (Eisenstein)
Qué me hecho yo para merecer esto?, 1984 (Almodóvar)
Québec-USA, 1962 (Jutra)
Queda, 1978 (Guerra)
Queen and the Cardinal. *See* Jérome Perreau, héro des barricades, 1936
Queen Christina, 1933 (Mamoulian)
Queen Is Dead, 1986 (Jarman)
Queen Kelly, 1928 (Von Stroheim)
Queen of Apollo, 1970 (Leacock)
Queen of Blood, 1966 (Corman)
Queen of Modern Times. *See* Gendai no joo, 1924
Queen of Spades. *See* Pikovaya dama, 1916
Queen of Spades, 1948 (Clayton, Dickinson)
Queen of the Band, 1915 (Browning)
Queen of the Circus. *See* Kyohubadan no joo, 1925
Queen of the Night, 1994 (Cox, Ripstein)
Queen's Diamonds. *See* Three Musketeers, 1974
Queen's Guards, 1961 (Powell)
Queen's Necklace. *See* Affaire du collier de la Reine, 1946
Queen's Secret. *See* Taina koroloevy, 1919
Queimada, 1969 (Pontecorvo)
Quelle joie de vivre. *See* Che gioia vivere, 1961
Quelle strane occasioni, 1976 (Comencini)
Quelques Jours avec moi, 1988 (Sautet)
Quem e beta, 1972 (Pereira Dos Santos)
Quemando tradiciones, 1971 (Alvarez)
Querelle, 1982 (Fassbinder)
Querelle de jardins, 1982 (Ruiz)
Querelle enfantine, 1939 (Lumet)
Quest of Life, 1916 (Goulding)
Questi fantasmi, 1967 (Castellani)
Questi ragazzi, 1937 (De Sica)
Question, 1977 (Tavernier)
Question in Togoland, 1957 (Dickinson)
Question of Attribution, 1991 (Schlesinger)
Question of Leadership, 1981 (Loach)
Question ordinaire, 1969 (C. Miller)
Questions of Leadership, 1983 (Loach)
Qui commande aux fusils, 1969 (Ivens)
Quick, 1932 (Siodmak)
Quick Billy, 1970 (Baillie)

Quick—König der Clowns. *See* Quick, 1932
Quick, Let's Get Married, Seven Different Ways. *See* Confession, 1965
Quicksands, 1923 (Hawks)
Quién me quiere a mi?, 1936 (Buñuel)
Quiet Affair. *See* En stilla flirt, 1934
Quiet American, 1958 (Mankiewicz)
Quiet Day at the End of the War, 1970 (Mikhalkov)
Quiet Days in Clichy. *See* Jours tranquilles a Clichy, 1990
Quiet Little Wedding, 1913 (Sennett)
Quiet Man, 1952 (Ford)
Quiet Place in the Country. *See* Tranquillo posto di campagna, 1968
Quiet Please, 1933 (Stevens)
Quiet Revolution, 1975 (Benegal)
Quiet Takeover, 1963 (Emshwiller)
Quiet Wedding, 1940 (Asquith)
Quilombo, 1984 (Diegues)
Quince Tree Sun. *See* Sol del Membrillo, 1992
Quintet, 1979 (Altman)
Quixote, 1964/65 (Baillie)
Quiz Show, 1994 (Levinson, Redford, Scorsese)
Quo Vadis, 1951 (Huston, LeRoy)

R, 1980 (Frampton)
Raag Yaman Kalyan, 1972 (Benegal)
Raat Bhore, 1956 (Sen)
Raba lubvi, 1976 (Mikhalkov)
Rabbia, 1963 (Pasolini)
Rabbit Case. *See* Causa králík, 1979
Rabbit's Moon. *See* Lune des Lapins, 1950
Rabbit's Moon, 1971 (Anger)
Rabid, 1976 (Cronenberg)
Rabindranath Tagore, 1961 (S. Ray)
Rablélek, 1913 (Curtiz)
Racconti Romani, 1955 (De Sica, Rosi)
Race, 1914 (Sennett)
Race for a Bride, 1914 (Browning)
Race for Life. *See* Mask of Dust, 1954
Race Gang. *See* Green Cockatoo, 1937
Race Symphony. *See* Rennsymphonie, 1928-29
Racers, 1955 (Hathaway)
Racetrack, 1932 (Cruze)
Racetrack, 1985 (Wiseman)
Rache einer Frau, 1921 (Wiene)
Rache ist mein, 1918 (Lang)
Rachel's Sin, 1911 (Hepworth)
Racing. *See* Rennen, 1961
Racing Romeo, 1927 (S. Wood)
Racket, 1928 (Milestone)
Racket, 1951 (Cromwell)
Racket Busters, 1938 (Rossen)
Racket Cheers, 1929 (Sennett)
Rade, 1927 (Cavalcanti)
Rade, 1953 (Cavalcanti)
Radeau avec baigneurs, 1896-97 (Lumet)
Radio Days, 1987 (Allen)
Radio Kisses, 1930 (Sennett)
Radioens Barndom, 1949 (Dreyer)
Radioland Murders, 1994 (Lucas)
Raduga, 1944 (Donskoi)
Rafael Alberti, un retrato del poeta por Fernando Birri, 1983 (Birri)
Raffles, 1914 (Sennett)
Raffles, 1940 (S. Wood)
Raffles, the Amateur Cracksman, 1905 (Blackton)
Rafle de chiens, 1904 (Guy)
Raga and the Emotions, 1971 (Benegal)
Ragazza del bersagliere, 1967 (Blasetti)
Ragazza di Bube, 1963 (Comencini)
Ragazza di Piazza S. Pietro, 1958 (De Sica)
Ragazza in vetrina, 1961 (Pasolini)
Ragazzo di Calabria, 1987 (Comencini)
Rage. *See* Rabid, 1976
Rage de dents, 1900 (Guy)
Rage in Heaven, 1941 (W.S. Van Dyke)
Rage Net, 1988 (Brakhage)
Ragged Flag. *See* Ranru no hata, 1974
Raging Bull, 1980 (Schrader, Scorsese)
Ragtime, 1981 (Forman)
Raid on Rommel, 1971 (Hathaway)
Raid Paris-Monte Carlo en deux heures, 1905 (Méliès)
Raiders of the Lost Ark, 1981 (Kasdan, Kaufman, Lucas, Spielberg)
Rail Rider, 1916 (M. Tourneur)
Rail-rodder, 1965 (Keaton)
Railroad Man. *See* Ferroviere, 1956
Railroaded, 1947 (A. Mann)
Railwayman's Word. *See* Kolejarskie słowo, 1953
Railwaymen. *See* Zelezničáři, 1963
Rain. *See* Sadie Thompson, 1928
Rain. *See* Regen, 1929
Rain, 1932 (Milestone)
Rain Man, 1988 (Levinson)
Rain or Shine, 1930 (Capra)
Rain People, 1969 (Coppola)
Rainbow. *See* Raduga, 1944
Rainbow, 1989 (Russell)
Rainbow Dance, 1936 (Cavalcanti)
Rainbow Jacket, 1954 (Dearden)
Rainbow of This Sky. *See* Kono ten no niji, 1958
Rainbow Round My Shoulder, 1952 (Edwards)
Raining in the Mountain. *See* K'ung Shan Ling Yü, 1979
Raining Stones, 1993 (Loach)
Rains Came, 1939 (Brown)
Rain's Hat, 1978 (Zetterling)
Raintree County, 1957 (Dmytryk)
Rainy Knight, 1925 (Sennett)
Raise Ravens. *See* **Cria cuervos**, 1976
Raising Arizona, 1987 (Coen)
Raising Cain, 1992 (De Palma)
Raja Harishchandra, 1913 (Phalke)
Raja Harishchandra, 1916 (Phalke)
Rajol fi Hayati, 1961 (Chahine)
Rajtunk is mulik, 1960 (Mészáros)
Rake's Progress, 1945 (Launder)
Rakkii-san, 1952 (Ichikawa)
Rakudai wa shita keredo, 1930 (Ozu)
Rakugaki kokuban, 1959 (Shindo)
Rallare, 1947 (Sjöström)
Rally 'round the Flag, Boys!, 1958 (McCarey)
Rambles Through Hopland, 1913 (Pearson)
Rameau's Nephew by Diderot Thanx to Dennis Young by Wilma Schoen, 1972/74 (Snow)
Ramona, 1936 (King)
Rampage, 1963 (Hathaway)
Rampage, 1992 (Friedkin)
Ramuz, passage d'un poète, 1959 (Tanner)
Ran, 1985 (Kurosawa)
Ran Salu, 1967 (Peries)
Ranch Detective, 1912 (Dwan)
Ranch Girl, 1911 (Dwan)
Ranch Life on the Range, 1912 (Dwan)
Ranchero's Revenge, 1913 (Griffith)
Ranchman's Marathon, 1912 (Dwan)
Ranchman's Nerve, 1911 (Dwan)
Rancho alegre, 1940 (Fernández)
Rancho Notorious, 1952 (Lang)
Random Harvest, 1942 (LeRoy)
Range Boss, 1917 (W.S. Van Dyke)
Ranger of the Big Pines, 1925 (W.S. Van Dyke)
Rangers of Fortune, 1940 (S. Wood)
Rango, 1931 (Schoedsack)
Rank and File, 1971 (Loach)
Ranks and People. *See* Chiny i liudi, 1929
Ranru no hata, 1974 (Yoshimura)

Rimal min Zahab, 1966 (Chahine)
Rincón de las Virgenes, 1972 (Fernández)
Ring, 1927 (Hitchcock)
Ring-a-Ding Rhythm. *See* It's Trad, Dad, 1962
Ring of a Spanish Grandee, 1912 (Cruze)
Ring Seller. *See* Baya el Khawatim, 1965
Ring with the Crowned Eagle, 1993 (Wajda)
Ringer, 1950 (Zetterling)
Rings on Her Fingers, 1942 (Mamoulian)
Rink, 1916 (Bacon, Chaplin)
Rio, 40 Degrees. *See* Rio, quarenta graus, 1955
Rio Bravo, 1959 (Hawks)
Rio das Mortes, 1970 (Fassbinder)
Río Escondido, 1947 (Fernández)
Rio Grande, 1950 (Ford)
Rio Lobo, 1970 (Hawks)
Rio, quarenta graus, 1955 (Pereira Dos Santos)
Rio y la muerte, 1954 (Buñuel)
Rio, zona norte, 1957 (Pereira Dos Santos)
Rio, zone nord. *See* Rio, zona norte, 1957
Rio's Love Songs, 1994 (Diegues)
Riot in Cell Block 11, 1954 (Siegel)
Rip & Stitch, Tailors, 1919 (Sennett)
Ripe Earth, 1938 (Boulting)
Riport egy TSZ-elnökröl, 1960 (Mészáros)
Rip's Dream. *See* Légende de Rip van Winkle, 1905
Riptide, 1934 (Goulding)
Rise and Fall of a Little Film Company. *See* Grandeur et Decadence d'un Petit Commerce du Cinema, 1986
Rise and Fall of Legs Diamond, 1960 (Boetticher)
Rise and Shine, 1941 (Dwan)
Rise of Jennie Cushing, 1917 (M. Tourneur)
Rise of Louis XIV. *See* Prise de pouvoir par Louis XIV, 1966
Rising of the Moon, 1957 (Ford)
Rising Sun, 1993 (Kaufman)
Rising Tide, 1933 (Rotha)
Risk. *See* Suspect, 1960
Riso amaro, 1948 (De Santis)
Rita. *See* Lettere di una novizia, 1960
Rite. *See* Riten, 1969
Riten, 1969 (Bergman)
Rites of Death, 1978 (Schroeder)
Ritorna Za-la-mort. *See* Fumeria d'oppio, 1947
Ritorno di Don Camillo. *See* Retour de Don Camillo, 1953
Ritter der Nacht, 1928 (Dieterle)
Ritual. *See* Riten, 1969
Ritual in Transfigured Time, 1946 (Deren)
Ritz, 1976 (Lester)
Riusciranno i nostri eroi a trovare il loro amico misteriosamente scomparso in Africa?, 1968 (Scola)
Rival Mashers. *See* Those Love Pangs, 1914
Rival Servants. *See* To Tjenestepiger, 1910
Rival Sisters. *See* Zhizn' za Zhizn', 1916
Rival Suitors. *See* Fatal Mallet, 1914
Rival World, 1955 (Haanstra)
Rivals, 1912 (Sennett)
Rive Gauche, 1931 (Korda)
River, 1929 (Borzage)
River, 1937 (Lorentz, Willard Van Dyke)
River, 1951 (Renoir)
River Fuefuki. *See* Fuefuki-gawa, 1960
River of No Return, 1954 (Preminger)
River of Romance, 1929 (Cukor)
River Pirate, 1928 (Howard)
River Runs through It, 1992 (Redford)
River Solo Flows. *See* Bungawan Solo, 1951
River without Bridges. *See* Hashi no nai kawa, 1969
River without Bridges II. *See* Hashi no nai kawa, 1970
River Wolves, 1934 (Pearson)
River's Edge, 1957 (Dwan)
River's End, 1920 (Neilan)
River's End, 1930 (Curtiz)
Road Back, 1937 (Whale)
Road I Travel with You. *See* Kimi to iku michi, 1936
Road of Truth, 1956 (Gerasimov)
Road to Corinth. *See* Route de Corinthe, 1967
Road to Glory, 1926 (Hawks)
Road to Glory, 1936 (Hawks)
Road to God. *See* Kami e no michi, 1928
Road to Happiness. *See* Lykken, 1916
Road to Happiness. *See* Der goldene Schmetterling, 1926
Road to Heaven. *See* Himlaspelet, 1942
Road to Hell. *See* Tol'ko Raz v Godu, 1914
Road to Mandalay, 1926 (Browning)
Road to Peace. *See* Béke ut ja, 1917
Road to Ruin, 1913 (Dwan)
Road to Success, 1913 (Dwan)
Road to the Heart, 1909 (Griffith)
Road to Wellville, 1994 (Parker)
Road to Yesterday, 1925 (De Mille)
Road Warrior. *See* Mad Max II, 1981
Roadhouse Queen, 1933 (Sennett)
Roadie, 1980 (Rudolph)
Roadracers, 1994 (Rodriguez)
Roads Across Britain, 1939 (Rotha)
Roads of Exile. *See* Chemines de l'Exile ou Les Dernières Années de Jean-Jacques Rousseau, 1978
Roadside Inn. *See* Hôtel des voyageurs de commerce, 1906
Roadways, 1937 (Cavalcanti)
Roaring Road, 1919 (Cruze)
Roaring Twenties, 1939 (Rossen, Walsh)
Roaring Years. *See* Anni ruggenti, 1962
Robber Spider. *See* Rovedderkoppen, eller Den røde Enke, 1916
Robber Symphony, 1936 (Wiene)
Robbing Cleopatra's Tomb. *See* Cléopâtre, 1899
Robby the Coward, 1911 (Griffith)
Robert et Robert, 1978 (Lelouch)
Robert Frost: A Lover's Quarrel with the World, 1963 (Clarke)
Robert Macaire et Bertrand, 1904 (Guy)
Robert und Bertram, 1915 (Lubitsch)
Roberte, 1978 (Schroeder)
Robin and Marian, 1976 (Lester)
Robin Hood, 1922 (Dwan, Florey)
Robin Hood of Eldorado, 1936 (Wellman)
Robin Hood: Men in Tights, 1993 (Brooks)
Robin Hood: Prince of Thieves, 1991 (Costner)
Robinson Crusoe, 1910 (Blom)
Robinson Girl. *See* Robinsonka, 1974
Robinsonka, 1974 (Kachyňa)
Robocop, 1987 (Verhoeven)
Robotnicy 71 nic o nas bez nas, 1972 (Kieślowski)
Robust Romeo, 1914 (Sennett)
Rocco and His Brothers. *See* **Rocco e i suoi fratelli**, 1960
Rocco e i suoi fratelli, 1960 (Visconti)
Rocco Papaleo. *See* Permette? Rocco Papaleo, 1971
Rock All Night, 1957 (Corman)
Rock 'n' Roll High School, 1979 (Corman)
Rock 'n' Roll High School Forever, 1991 (Corman)
Rock 'n' Roll Kids, 1988 (Tian)
Rock of Ages, 1902 (Porter)
Rock of Riches, 1916 (Weber)
Rockabye, 1932 (Cukor)
Rock-a-Bye Baby, 1958 (Jerry Lewis, P. Sturges, Tashlin)
Rock-a-bye Cowboy, 1933 (Stevens)
Rock-Cut Temples of Ellora, 1914/15 (Phalke)
Rocket Busters, 1938 (Bacon)
Rocket Man, 1954 (Rudolph)
Rockets Galore, 1958 (Dearden)
Rocky Road, 1909 (Griffith)
Rocky Road to Dublin, 1968 (Huston)
Røde Enke. *See* Rovedderkoppen, 1915
Rodelkavalier, 1918 (Lubitsch)

Rodeo, 1929 (Sennett)
Rodin, 1995 (Jireš)
Rodnya, 1982 (Mikhalkov)
Roei no uta, 1938 (Mizoguchi)
Roger Touhy, Gangster, 1943 (Florey)
Rogopag, 1962 (Godard, Pasolini, Rossellini, Welles)
Rogue Regiment, 1948 (Florey)
Rogues' Gallery, 1913 (Sennett)
Rogues of Paris, 1913 (Guy)
Rogues of Rajasthan. *See* Mewad No Mawali, 1930
Rogue's Tricks. *See* Douche d'eau bouillanie, 1907
Roi de Thulé, 1910 (Feuillade)
Roi des Champs-Elysées, 1934 (Delannoy, Keaton)
Roi des palaces, 1932 (Clouzot)
Roi des parfums, 1910 (Gance)
Roi du maquillage, 1904 (Méliès)
Rok spokojnego slonca, 1984 (Zanussi)
Rola, 1971 (Zanussi)
Role. *See* **Bhumika,** 1977
Rolle. *See* Rola, 1971
Rollerball, 1975 (Jewison)
Rolling Home, 1935 (Launder)
Rolling Thunder, 1977 (Schrader)
Rollover, 1981 (Pakula)
Roly-Poly. *See* Przekładaniec, 1968
Roma, 1972 (Fellini)
Roma '90, 1989 (Antonioni)
Roma, città aperta, 1945 (Fellini, Rossellini)
Roma città libera, 1946 (De Sica)
Roma coma Chicago, 1969 (Cassavetes)
Roma ore undici, 1952 (De Santis, Petri)
Roma—Montevideo, 1948 (Antonioni)
Roman aus den Bergen. *See* Der Geier-Wally, 1921
Roman Candles, 1966 (Waters)
Roman d'amour ... et d'aventures, 1918 (Guitry)
Roman d'un jeune homme pauvre, 1935 (Gance)
Roman d'un tricheur, 1936 (Guitry)
Roman de Sœur Louise, 1908 (Feuillade)
Roman de Werther. *See* Werther, 1938
Roman Holiday, 1953 (Wyler)
Roman Numeral Series, 1981 (Brakhage)
Roman Scandals, 1933 (Berkeley)
Romance, 1913 (Dwan)
Romance, 1930 (Brown)
Romance at the Studio: Guidance to Love. *See* Satsueijo romansu: Renai annai, 1932
Romance of a Horsethief, 1971 (Polonsky)
Romance of a Jewess, 1908 (Griffith)
Romance of a War Nurse, 1908 (Porter)
Romance of a Will. *See* Kaerlighedens Triumf, 1914
Romance of Happy Valley, 1919 (Griffith)
Romance of Lovers. *See* Romans o ul jublennyh, 1974
Romance of the Redwoods, 1917 (De Mille)
Romance of the Redwoods, 1939 (C. Vidor)
Romance of the Western Hills, 1910 (Griffith)
Romance of Yushima. *See* Yushima no shiraume, 1955
Romance on the High Seas, 1948 (Curtiz)
Romance sentimentale, 1930 (Eisenstein)
Romancing the Stone, 1984 (Zemeckis)
Romans o ul jublennyh, 1974 (Mikhalkov-Konchalovsky)
Romantic Age, 1927 (Florey)
Romantic Age, 1949 (Zetterling)
Romantic Englishwoman, 1975 (Losey)
Romantic Prince, 1932 (Mehboob)
Romantica avventura, 1940 (Castellani)
Romantiki, 1941 (Donskoi)
Romany Tragedy, 1911 (Griffith)
Romanze in Moll, 1943 (Käutner)
Romanzo di un Giovane Povero, 1995 (Scola)
Rome 11 O'Clock. *See* Roma ore undici, 1952
Rome Adventure, 1962 (Daves)
Rome Eleven O'Clock. *See* Roma ore undici, 1952
Rome Express, 1932 (Launder)
Rome, Open City. *See* **Roma, città aperta**, 1945
Romeo and Juliet, 1924 (Sennett)
Romeo and Juliet, 1936 (Cukor)
Romeo and Juliet. *See* Giulietta e Romeo, 1954
Romeo and Juliet, 1968 (Zeffirelli)
Romeo, Julie a tma, 1960 (Weiss)
Romeo, Juliet and the Darkness. *See* Romeo, Julie a tma, 1960
Romeo und Julia im Schnee, 1920 (Lubitsch)
Roméo pris au piége, 1905 (Guy)
Romero, 1989 (Duigan)
Rommel—Desert Fox. *See* Desert Fox, 1951
Romola, 1925 (King)
Romona, 1910 (Griffith)
Romy. Anatomie eines Gesichts, 1965 (Syberberg)
Romy. Anatomy of a Face. *See* Romy. Anatomie eines Gesichts, 1965
Ronde, 1950 (Ophüls)
Ronde, 1964 (Vadim)
Ronde enfantine, 1896-97 (Lumet)
Rønnes og Nexøs Genopbygning, 1954 (Dreyer)
Roof. *See* Tetto, 1956
Roof Needs Mowing, 1971 (Armstrong)
Rooftops, 1989 (Wise)
Rooftree. *See* Tvärbalk, 1967
Rookie, 1990 (Eastwood)
Rookie of the Year, 1955 (Ford)
Rookies, 1927 (S. Wood)
Room, 1987 (Altman)
Room 666, 1984 (Wenders)
Room at the Top, 1958 (Clayton)
Room in Town. *See* Chambre en ville, 1982
Room Mates, 1933 (Stevens)
Room to Move, 1987 (Duigan)
Room with a View, 1986 (Ivory)
Rooster, 1981 (Hallstrom)
Root of Evil, 1911 (Griffith)
Roots of Heaven, 1958 (Huston, Welles)
Rope, 1948 (Hitchcock)
Rope of Sand, 1949 (Dieterle)
Roped, 1919 (Ford)
Roping Her Romeo, 1917 (Sennett)
Roquevillard, 1922 (Duvivier)
Rosa, 1992 (Greenaway)
Rosa blanca, 1953 (Fernández)
Rosa de los vientos, 1983 (Guzmán)
Rosa Diamant, 1925 (Dieterle)
Rosa Luxemburg, 1986 (Von Trotta)
Rosalie, 1937 (W.S. Van Dyke)
Rose Bernd, 1957 (Staudte)
Rose blanche, 1913 (Feuillade)
Rose des vents, 1982 (Birri)
Rose et Landry, 1963 (Rouch)
Rose-France, 1918 (L'Herbier)
Rose in the Mud. *See* Warui yatsu hodo yoku nemuru, 1960
Rose King. *See* Der Rosenkönig, 1985
Rose Marie, 1935 (W.S. Van Dyke)
Rose Marie, 1954 (Berkeley, LeRoy)
Rose o' Salem Town, 1910 (Griffith)
Rose o' the Sea, 1922 (Niblo)
Rose of Kentucky, 1911 (Griffith)
Rose of Old Mexico, 1913 (Dwan)
Rose of the Circus, 1911 (Guy)
Rose of the Rancho, 1914 (De Mille)
Rose of the Rancho, 1935 (Florey)
Rose of the Sea. *See* Umi no bara, 1945
Rose of the Winds. *See* Rosa de los vientos, 1983
Rose of the World, 1918 (M. Tourneur)
Rose of Thistle Island. *See* Rösen på Tistelön, 1916
Rose on His Arm. *See* Taiyo to bara, 1956
Rose scarlatte, 1940 (De Sica)

Sedmikrásky, 1966 (Chytilová)
Sedotta e abbandonata, 1964 (Germi)
Seduccion, 1983 (Ripstein)
Seduced and Abandoned. *See* Sedotta e abbandonata, 1964
Seducer. *See* Yuri Nagornyi, 1915
Seduction. *See* Yuwaku, 1948
Seduta spiritica, 1949 (Risi)
See Here, Private Hargrove, 1944 (Edwards, Garnett)
See No Evil, 1971 (Fleischer)
See, Saw, Seems, 1967 (Vanderbeek)
See You at Mao. *See* British Sounds, 1969
See You in the Morning, 1989 (Pakula)
See You Later, 1990 (Snow)
See You Tomorrow. *See* Do Widzenia do Jutra, 1960
See You Tonight, 1933 (Sennett)
Seed, 1931 (Stahl)
Seed of Man. *See* Seme dell'uomo, 1969
Seedling. *See* Ankur, 1974
Seeing Nellie Home, 1924 (McCarey)
Seeing Stars, 1938 (Boulting)
Seelenverkäufer, 1919 (Pick)
Seemabaddha, 1971 (S. Ray)
Segantini, il pittore della montagna, 1948 (Risi)
Segno di Venere, 1955 (De Sica, Risi)
Segodnya, 1930 (Shub)
Segretaria per tutti, 1932 (De Sica)
Segreto del bosco vecchio, 1993 (Olmi)
Segunda Declaracion de la Habana, 1965 (Alvarez)
Sehnsucht, 1920 (Murnau)
Sehnsucht der Veronika Voss, 1982 (Fassbinder)
Sehnsucht nach Afrika, 1939 (Sirk)
Sei no kigen, 1967 (Shindo)
Seigneurs de la forêt, 1957 (Storck, Welles)
Seikatsu to mizu, 1952 (Hani)
Seine a rencontré Paris, 1957 (Ivens)
Seine Frau, die Unbekannte, 1923 (Christensen)
Seine Majestät das Bettelkind, 1920 (Korda)
Seine neue Nase, 1916 (Lubitsch)
Seine schöne Mama. *See* Flucht der Schönheit, 1915
Seishu Hanaoka's Wife. *See* Hanaoko Seishu no tsuma, 1967
Seishun, 1925 (Gosho)
Seishun kaidan, 1955 (Ichikawa)
Seishun no kiryu, 1942 (Kurosawa)
Seishun no yume ima izuko, 1932 (Ozu)
Seishun no yumeji, 1923 (Mizoguchi)
Seishun zankoku monogatari, 1960 (Oshima)
Seishun Zenigata Heiji, 1953 (Ichikawa)
Seitensprünge, 1930 (Wilder)
Seizure, 1974 (Stone)
Sekishun-cho, 1959 (Kinoshita)
Sekretär der Königen, 1916 (Wiene)
Self Portrait, 1990 (Mekas)
Self Trio, 1976 (Emshwiller)
Selinunte, 1951 (Birri)
Selskaya uchitelnitsa, 1947 (Donskoi)
Selskiy vrach, 1951 (Gerasimov)
Seltsame Nacht, 1926 (Holger-Madsen)
Seltsame Nacht der Helga Wansen, 1928 (Holger-Madsen)
Seltsamen Abenteuer des Herrn Fridolin B, 1948 (Staudte)
Selva de fuego, 1945 (De Fuentes)
Semaine de vacances, 1981 (Tavernier)
Seme dell'uomo, 1969 (Ferreri)
Semero smelykh, 1936 (Gerasimov)
Seminole, 1953 (Boetticher)
Semya tarassa. *See* Nepokorenniye, 1945
Senba-zuru, 1953 (Yoshimura)
Send Me No Flowers, 1964 (Jewison)
Sengoku gunto den, 1937 (Kurosawa)
Sengoku guntoden, 1960 (Kurosawa)
Seni kaybederesen, 1961 (Güney)
Senka no hate, 1950 (Yoshimura)
Senki fia, 1917 (Curtiz)
Senor muy viejo con unas alas enormes, 1988 (Birri)
Señora de Nadie, 1982 (Bemberg)
Sens de la mort, 1921 (Clair, Protazanov)
Sensation. *See* Szenzáció, 1922
Sensation Hunters, 1933 (C. Vidor)
Sensation Seekers, 1927 (Weber)
Sense and Sensibility, 1995 (A. Lee)
Sense of History, 1992 (Leigh)
Sense of Loss, 1972 (Ophuls)
Senso, 1954 (Rosi, Visconti, Zeffirelli)
Senso to Seishun, 1991 (Imai)
Sensual Paradise. *See* Together, 1971
Sentence of Death, 1913 (Pearson)
Sentinels of Silence, 1971 (Welles)
Senza pietà, 1948 (Fellini, Lattuada)
Senza sapere niente di lei, 1969 (Comencini)
Seppuku, 1962 (Kobayashi)
Sept fois femmes. *See* Woman Times Seven, 1967
Sept P., Cuis., S. de B.,... a saisir, 1984 (Varda)
Sept Péchés capitaux, 1962 (Chabrol, Demy, Godard, Vadim)
Sept pièces pour cinéma noir et blanc, 1983 (Ioseliani)
September, 1984 (Tian)
September, 1988 (Allen)
September Affair, 1950 (Dieterle)
Sequence of Feelings. *See* Kolejnosc uczuc, 1993
Sera'a fil Mina, 1955 (Chahine)
Sera'a fil Wadi, 1953 (Chahine)
Serafino, 1968 (Germi)
Seraphita's Diary, 1982 (Wiseman)
Serdtse materi, 1966 (Donskoi)
Serenade, 1921 (Walsh)
Serenade, 1956 (A. Mann)
Serenity, 1955-61 (Markopoulos)
Sergeant Deadhead, 1965 (Keaton)
Sergeant Madden, 1939 (Von Sternberg)
Sergeant Rutledge, 1960 (Ford)
Sergeant York, 1941 (Hawks, Huston)
Sergeants Three, 1962 (J. Sturges)
Sergo Ordzhonikidze, 1937 (Vertov)
Serial Mom, 1994 (Waters)
Série noire, 1955 (Von Stroheim)
Serious Sixteen, 1910 (Griffith)
Seriously Ill. *See* Daibyonin, 1995
Serp i molot, 1921 (Pudovkin)
Serpent, 1916 (Walsh)
Serpent and the Rainbow, 1988 (Craven)
Serpent's Egg. *See* Schlangenei, 1977
Serpico, 1973 (Lumet)
Servant, 1963 (Losey)
Service de sauvetage sur la côte belge, 1930 (Storck)
Service for Ladies, 1932 (Korda)
Service précipité, 1903 (Guy)
Sesso e violentieri, 1982 (Risi)
Sesso matto, 1973 (Risi)
Sestricky, 1983 (Kachyňa)
Sestry-Sopernitsy. *See* Zhizn' za Zhizn', 1916
Set Free, 1918 (Browning)
Setenta veces siete, 1962 (Torre Nilsson)
Setkání v červenci, 1977 (Kachyňa)
Setouchi Shonen Yakyudan, 1984 (Itami, Shinoda)
Sette canne e un vestito, 1950 (Antonioni)
Sette contro la morte, 1964 (Ulmer)
Settled at the Seaside, 1915 (Sennett)
Setu Bandhan, 1932 (Phalke)
Set-Up, 1949 (Wise)
Seven Ages, 1905 (Porter)
Seven Brides for Seven Brothers, 1954 (Donen)
Seven Chances, 1925 (Keaton)
Seven Colored Ring. *See* Nanairo yubi wa, 1918
Seven Days in January. *See* 7 Dias de enero, 1979

She Has Lived Her Destiny. *See* Kanojo to unmei, 1924
She Loved a Sailor, 1916 (Sennett)
She Loved Him Plenty, 1918 (Sennett)
She Married an Artist, 1937 (Daves)
She Married Her Boss, 1935 (La Cava)
She Needed a Doctor, 1917 (Sennett)
She Played with Fire. *See* Fortune Is a Woman, 1956
She Sighed by the Seaside, 1921 (Sennett)
She Wore a Yellow Ribbon, 1949 (Ford)
Sheba, 1919 (Hepworth)
Sheepman's Daughter, 1911 (Dwan)
Sheer Madness. *See* Heller Wahn, 1983
She-Gods of Shark Reef, 1957 (Corman)
Sheherazade, 1929 (Litvak)
Shelagh Delaney's Salford, 1960 (Russell)
Sheltering Sky, 1990 (Bertolucci)
Shepherd of the Hills, 1941 (Hathaway)
Sheriff Nell's Tussle, 1918 (Sennett)
Sheriff of Fractured Jaw, 1958 (Walsh)
Sheriff's Baby, 1913 (Griffith)
Sheriff's Sisters, 1911 (Dwan)
Sherlock Holmes, 1932 (Howard)
Sherlock Holmes I, 1908 (Holger-Madsen)
Sherlock Holmes III, 1908 (Holger-Madsen)
Sherlock Holmes and the Deadly Necklace, 1962 (Fisher)
Sherlock Holmes in New York, 1976 (Huston)
Sherlock Holmes Jr., 1911 (Porter)
Sherlock Holmes und der Halsband des Todes, 1962 (Fisher)
Sherlock Jr., 1924 (Keaton)
She's a Sweetheart, 1944 (Edwards)
She's Gotta Have It, 1986 (S. Lee)
She's No Lady, 1937 (C. Vidor)
She's Oil Mine, 1941 (Keaton)
She's the Only One. *See* Hon den enda, 1926
Shestaya chast' mira, 1926 (Vertov)
She-Wolf. *See* Lupa, 1953
Shibaido, 1944 (Naruse)
Shichimencho no yukue, 1924 (Mizoguchi)
Shichinin no samurai, 1954 (Kurosawa)
Shiga Naoya, 1958 (Hani)
Shiiku, 1961 (Oshima)
Shikamo karera wa yuku, 1931 (Mizoguchi)
Shima to ratai jiken, 1931 (Gosho)
Shin Heike monogatari, 1955 (Mizoguchi)
Shin josei kagami, 1929 (Gosho)
Shin ono ga tsumi, 1926 (Mizoguchi)
Shindo, 1936 (Gosho)
Shinel, 1926 (Gerasimov, Kozintsev)
Shining, 1980 (Kubrick)
Shining Hour, 1938 (Borzage, Mankiewicz)
Shining in the Red Sunset. *See* Akai yuhi ni terasarete, 1925
Shining Sun Becomes Clouded. *See* Teru hi kumoru hi, 1926
Shinju ten no Amijima, 1969 (Shinoda)
Shinju yoimachigusa, 1925 (Kinugasa)
Shinjuku dorobo nikki, 1969 (Oshima)
Shinkei gyogun, 1956 (Oshima)
Shinsetsu, 1942 (Gosho)
Ship Bound for India. *See* Skepp till Indialand, 1947
Ship Cafe, 1935 (Florey)
Ship Comes In, 1928 (Howard)
Ship of Fools, 1965 (Kramer)
Ship Safety. *See* Watertight, 1943
Ship That Died of Shame, 1955 (Dearden)
Ship. *See* Baten, 1961
Shipmates, 1931 (Daves)
Shipmates Forever, 1935 (Borzage, Daves)
Shipmates o' Mine, 1936 (Pearson)
Ships with Wings, 1941 (Hamer)
Shipyard, 1933 (Rotha)
Shirasagi, 1957 (Kinugasa)
Shirayuri wa nageku, 1925 (Mizoguchi)
Shirins hochzeit, 1976 (Sanders-Brahms)
Shirin's Wedding. *See* Shirins hochzeit, 1976
Shiro Tokisada from Amakusa. *See* Amakusa shiro tokisada, 1962
Shiroi gake, 1960 (Imai)
Shiroi kiba, 1960 (Gosho)
Shiroi yaju, 1949 (Naruse)
Shito no densetsu, 1963 (Kinoshita)
Shitoyakana kemono, 1963 (Shindo)
Shitto, 1949 (Shindo, Yoshimura)
Shivers, 1975 (Cronenberg)
Shizukanaru ketto, 1949 (Kurosawa)
Shock Corridor, 1963 (Fuller)
Shock Troops. *See* Homme de trop, 1967
Shocker, 1989 (Craven)
Shocking Miss Pilgrim, 1946 (Goulding)
Shockproof, 1949 (Fuller, Sirk)
Shodo satsujin: Musukoyo, 1979 (Kinoshita)
Shoes, 1916 (Weber)
Shoes of the Fisherman, 1968 (De Sica)
Shoes That Danced, 1918 (Borzage)
Shoeshine. *See* **Sciuscia,** 1946
Shohin, 1924 (Kinugasa)
Shojo no shi, 1927 (Gosho)
Shojo nyuyo, 1930 (Gosho)
Shojo yo sayonara, 1933 (Gosho)
Shokei no heya, 1956 (Ichikawa)
Shokei no shima, 1966 (Shinoda)
Shokkaku, 1970 (Shindo)
Shokutaku no nai ie, 1985 (Kobayashi)
Shonen, 1969 (Oshima)
Shonen ki, 1951 (Kinoshita)
Shonnenjidai, 1990 (Shinoda)
Shoot! *See* Dispara!, 1993
Shoot the Moon, 1981 (Parker)
Shoot the Piano Player. *See* **Tirez sur le pianist**, 1960
Shooting, 1965 (Corman, Hellman)
Shooting Stars, 1927 (Asquith)
Shootist, 1976 (Siegel)
Shootout, 1971 (Hathaway)
Shop Around the Corner, 1940 (Lubitsch)
Shop on Main Street. *See* **Obchod na korze**, 1965
Shop on the High Street. *See* **Obchod na korze**, 1965
Shopping with Wife, 1932 (Sennett)
Shopworn Angel, 1928 (Hathaway)
Shopworn Angel, 1938 (Mankiewicz)
Shore Acres, 1920 (Ingram)
Shores of Phos: A Fable, 1972 (Brakhage)
Shori no hi made, 1945 (Naruse)
Short and Curlies, 1987 (Leigh)
Short and Very Short Films, 1976 (Emshwiller)
Short Cut. *See* Postřižny, 1980
Short Cuts, 1993 (Altman)
Short Film about Killing. *See* Krótki film o zabi janiu, 1988
Short Film about Love. *See* Krótki film o miłóści, 1988
Short Films: 1975, 1975 (Brakhage)
Short Films: 1976, 1976 (Brakhage)
Short History of France. *See* Petit Manuel d'histoire de France, 1979
Short Is the Summer. *See* Kort är sommaren, 1962
Short Shave, 1965 (Snow)
Short Working Day. *See* Krótki dzień pracy, 1981
Shot. *See* Skottet, 1914
Shot in the Dark, 1933 (Pearson)
Shot in the Dark, 1964 (Edwards)
Shot in the Excitement, 1914 (Sennett)
Shot in the Factory. *See* Laukaus Tehtaalla, 1973
Shotgun Wedding, 1963 (E. Wood)
Shotguns That Kick, 1914 (Sennett)
Should a Husband Forgive, 1919 (Walsh)
Should a Mother Tell?, 1915 (Ingram)
Should Crooners Marry, 1933 (Stevens)
Should Husbands Be Watched?, 1925 (McCarey)